W9-DDD-573

American Casebook Series
Hornbook Series and Basic Legal Texts
Nutshell Series

of

WEST PUBLISHING COMPANY
P.O. Box 64526
St. Paul, Minnesota 55164–0526

ACCOUNTING

Faris' Accounting and Law in a Nutshell, 377 pages, 1984 (Text)

Fiflis, Kripke and Foster's Teaching Materials on Accounting for Business Lawyers, 3rd Ed., 838 pages, 1984 (Casebook)

Siegel and Siegel's Accounting and Financial Disclosure: A Guide to Basic Concepts, 259 pages, 1983 (Text)

ADMINISTRATIVE LAW

Davis' Cases, Text and Problems on Administrative Law, 6th Ed., 683 pages, 1977 (Casebook)

Davis' Basic Text on Administrative Law, 3rd Ed., 617 pages, 1972 (Text)

Gellhorn and Boyer's Administrative Law and Process in a Nutshell, 2nd Ed., 445 pages, 1981 (Text)

Mashaw and Merrill's Cases and Materials on Administrative Law–The American Public Law System, 2nd Ed., 976 pages, 1985 (Casebook)

Robinson, Gellhorn and Bruff's The Administrative Process, 3rd Ed., 978 pages, 1986 (Casebook)

ADMIRALTY

Healy and Sharpe's Cases and Materials on Admiralty, 2nd Ed., 876 pages, 1986 (Casebook)

Maraist's Admiralty in a Nutshell, 390 pages, 1983 (Text)

Sohn and Gustafson's Law of the Sea in a Nutshell, 264 pages, 1984 (Text)

AGENCY—PARTNERSHIP

Fessler's Alternatives to Incorporation for Persons in Quest of Profit, 2nd Ed., 326 pages, 1986 (Casebook)

AGENCY—PARTNERSHIP—Cont'd

Henn's Cases and Materials on Agency, Partnership and Other Unincorporated Business Enterprises, 2nd Ed., 733 pages, 1985 (Casebook)

Reuschlein and Gregory's Hornbook on the Law of Agency and Partnership, 625 pages, 1979, with 1981 pocket part (Text)

Seavey, Reuschlein and Hall's Cases on Agency and Partnership, 599 pages, 1962 (Casebook)

Selected Corporation and Partnership Statutes and Forms, 555 pages, 1985

Steffen and Kerr's Cases and Materials on Agency-Partnership, 4th Ed., 859 pages, 1980 (Casebook)

Steffen's Agency-Partnership in a Nutshell, 364 pages, 1977 (Text)

AGRICULTURAL LAW

Meyer, Pedersen, Thorson and Davidson's Agricultural Law: Cases and Materials, 931 pages, 1985 (Casebook)

ALTERNATIVE DISPUTE RESOLUTION

Kanowitz' Cases and Materials on Alternative Dispute Resolution, 1024 pages, 1986 (Casebook)

AMERICAN INDIAN LAW

Canby's American Indian Law in a Nutshell, 288 pages, 1981 (Text)

Getches and Wilkinson's Cases on Federal Indian Law, 2nd Ed., approximately 870 pages, 1986 (Casebook)

ANTITRUST LAW

Gellhorn's Antitrust Law and Economics in a Nutshell, 3rd Ed., about 425 pages, 1987 (Text)

List current as of July, 1986

CARNEGIE LIBRARY
LIVINGSTONE COLLEGE
SALISBURY, NC 28144

LAW SCHOOL PUBLICATIONS—Continued

ANTITRUST LAW—Cont'd

Gifford and Raskind's Cases and Materials on Antitrust, 694 pages, 1983 with 1985 Supplement (Casebook)

Hovenkamp's Hornbook on Economics and Federal Antitrust Law, Student Ed., 414 pages, 1985 (Text)

Oppenheim, Weston and McCarthy's Cases and Comments on Federal Antitrust Laws, 4th Ed., 1168 pages, 1981 with 1985 Supplement (Casebook)

Posner and Easterbrook's Cases and Economic Notes on Antitrust, 2nd Ed., 1077 pages, 1981, with 1984-85 Supplement (Casebook)

Sullivan's Hornbook of the Law of Antitrust, 886 pages, 1977 (Text)

See also Regulated Industries, Trade Regulation

ART LAW

DuBoff's Art Law in a Nutshell, 335 pages, 1984 (Text)

BANKING LAW

Lovett's Banking and Financial Institutions in a Nutshell, 409 pages, 1984 (Text)

Symons and White's Teaching Materials on Banking Law, 2nd Ed., 993 pages, 1984 (Casebook)

BUSINESS PLANNING

Painter's Problems and Materials in Business Planning, 2nd Ed., 1008 pages, 1984 (Casebook)

Selected Securities and Business Planning Statutes, Rules and Forms, 470 pages, 1985

CIVIL PROCEDURE

Casad's Res Judicata in a Nutshell, 310 pages, 1976 (text)

Cound, Friedenthal, Miller and Sexton's Cases and Materials on Civil Procedure, 4th Ed., 1202 pages, 1985 with 1985 Supplement (Casebook)

Ehrenzweig, Louisell and Hazard's Jurisdiction in a Nutshell, 4th Ed., 232 pages, 1980 (Text)

Federal Rules of Civil-Appellate Procedure—West Law School Edition, about 550 pages, 1986

Friedenthal, Kane and Miller's Hornbook on Civil Procedure, 876 pages, 1985 (Text)

Kane's Civil Procedure in a Nutshell, 2nd Ed., 306 pages, 1986 (Text)

Koffler and Reppy's Hornbook on Common Law Pleading, 663 pages, 1969 (Text)

Marcus and Sherman's Complex Litigation—Cases and Materials on Advanced Civil Procedure, 846 pages, 1985 (Casebook)

Park's Computer-Aided Exercises on Civil Procedure, 2nd Ed., 167 pages, 1983 (Coursebook)

CIVIL PROCEDURE—Cont'd

Siegel's Hornbook on New York Practice, 1011 pages, 1978 with 1985 Pocket Part (Text)

See also Federal Jurisdiction and Procedure

CIVIL RIGHTS

Abernathy's Cases and Materials on Civil Rights, 660 pages, 1980 (Casebook)

Cohen's Cases on the Law of Deprivation of Liberty: A Study in Social Control, 755 pages, 1980 (Casebook)

Lockhart, Kamisar, Choper and Shiffrin's Cases on Constitutional Rights and Liberties, 6th Ed., about 1300 pages, 1986 with 1986 Supplement (Casebook)—reprint from Lockhart, et al. Cases on Constitutional Law, 6th Ed., 1986

Vieira's Civil Rights in a Nutshell, 279 pages, 1978 (Text)

COMMERCIAL LAW

Bailey's Secured Transactions in a Nutshell, 2nd Ed., 391 pages, 1981 (Text)

Epstein and Martin's Basic Uniform Commercial Code Teaching Materials, 2nd Ed., 667 pages, 1983 (Casebook)

Henson's Hornbook on Secured Transactions Under the U.C.C., 2nd Ed., 504 pages, 1979 with 1979 P.P. (Text)

Murray's Commercial Law, Problems and Materials, 366 pages, 1975 (Coursebook)

Nordstrom and Clovis' Problems and Materials on Commercial Paper, 458 pages, 1972 (Casebook)

Nordstrom, Murray and Clovis' Problems and Materials on Sales, 515 pages, 1982 (Casebook)

Nordstrom, Murray and Clovis' Problems and Materials on Secured Transactions, about 500 pages, 1987 (Casebook)

Selected Commercial Statutes, 1389 pages, 1985

Speidel, Summers and White's Teaching Materials on Commercial and Consumer Law, 3rd Ed., 1490 pages, 1981 (Casebook)

Stockton's Sales in a Nutshell, 2nd Ed., 370 pages, 1981 (Text)

Stone's Uniform Commercial Code in a Nutshell, 2nd Ed., 516 pages, 1984 (Text)

Uniform Commercial Code, Official Text with Comments, 994 pages, 1978

UCC Article 9, Reprint from 1962 Code, 128 pages, 1976

UCC Article 9, 1972 Amendments, 304 pages, 1978

Weber and Speidel's Commercial Paper in a Nutshell, 3rd Ed., 404 pages, 1982 (Text)

White and Summers' Hornbook on the Uniform Commercial Code, 2nd Ed., 1250 pages, 1980 (Text)

COMMUNITY PROPERTY

Mennell's Community Property in a Nutshell, 447 pages, 1982 (Text)

Verrall and Bird's Cases and Materials on California Community Property, 4th Ed., 549 pages, 1983 (Casebook)

COMPARATIVE LAW

Barton, Gibbs, Li and Merryman's Law in Radically Different Cultures, 960 pages, 1983 (Casebook)

Glendon, Gordon and Osakive's Comparative Legal Traditions: Text, Materials and Cases on the Civil Law, Common Law, and Socialist Law Traditions, 1091 pages, 1985 (Casebook)

Glendon, Gordon, and Osakwe's Comparative Legal Traditions in a Nutshell, 402 pages, 1982 (Text)

Langbein's Comparative Criminal Procedure: Germany, 172 pages, 1977 (Casebook)

COMPUTERS AND LAW

Maggs and Sprowl's Computer Applications in the Law, about 300 pages, 1986 (Text)

Mason's An Introduction to the Use of Computers in Law, 223 pages, 1984 (Text)

CONFLICT OF LAWS

Cramton, Currie and Kay's Cases-Comments-Questions on Conflict of Laws, 3rd Ed., 1026 pages, 1981 (Casebook)

Scoles and Hay's Hornbook on Conflict of Laws, Student Ed., 1085 pages, 1982 with 1986 P.P. (Text)

Scoles and Weintraub's Cases and Materials on Conflict of Laws, 2nd Ed., 966 pages, 1972, with 1978 Supplement (Casebook)

Siegel's Conflicts in a Nutshell, 469 pages, 1982 (Text)

CONSTITUTIONAL LAW

Barron and Dienes' Constitutional Law in a Nutshell, about 400 pages, 1986 (Text)

Engdahl's Constitutional Power in a Nutshell: Federal and State, 411 pages, 1974 (Text)

Lockhart, Kamisar, Choper and Shiffrin's Cases-Comments-Questions on Constitutional Law, 6th Ed., 1601 pages, 1986 with 1986 Supplement (Casebook)

Lockhart, Kamisar, Choper and Shiffrin's Cases-Comments-Questions on the American Constitution, 6th Ed., about 1200 pages, 1986 with 1986 Supplement (Casebook)—abridgment of Lockhart, et al. Cases on Constitutional Law, 6th Ed., 1986

Manning's The Law of Church-State Relations in a Nutshell, 305 pages, 1981 (Text)

Miller's Presidential Power in a Nutshell, 328 pages, 1977 (Text)

CONSTITUTIONAL LAW—Cont'd

Nowak, Rotunda and Young's Hornbook on Constitutional Law, 3rd Ed., Student Ed., approximately 1100 pages, 1986 (Text)

Rotunda's Modern Constitutional Law: Cases and Notes, 2nd Ed., 1004 pages, 1985, with 1986 Supplement (Casebook)

Williams' Constitutional Analysis in a Nutshell, 388 pages, 1979 (Text)

See also Civil Rights

CONSUMER LAW

Epstein and Nickles' Consumer Law in a Nutshell, 2nd Ed., 418 pages, 1981 (Text)

McCall's Consumer Protection, Cases, Notes and Materials, 594 pages, 1977, with 1977 Statutory Supplement (Casebook)

Selected Commercial Statutes, 1389 pages, 1985

Spanogle and Rohner's Cases and Materials on Consumer Law, 693 pages, 1979, with 1982 Supplement (Casebook)

See also Commercial Law

CONTRACTS

Calamari & Perillo's Cases and Problems on Contracts, 1061 pages, 1978 (Casebook)

Calamari and Perillo's Hornbook on Contracts, 2nd Ed., 878 pages, 1977 (Text)

Corbin's Text on Contracts, One Volume Student Edition, 1224 pages, 1952 (Text)

Fessler and Loiseaux's Cases and Materials on Contracts, 837 pages, 1982 (Casebook)

Friedman's Contract Remedies in a Nutshell, 323 pages, 1981 (Text)

Fuller and Eisenberg's Cases on Basic Contract Law, 4th Ed., 1203 pages, 1981 (Casebook)

Hamilton, Rau and Weintraub's Cases and Materials on Contracts, 830 pages, 1984 (Casebook)

Jackson and Bollinger's Cases on Contract Law in Modern Society, 2nd Ed., 1329 pages, 1980 (Casebook)

Keyes' Government Contracts in a Nutshell, 423 pages, 1979 (Text)

Schaber and Rohwer's Contracts in a Nutshell, 2nd Ed., 425 pages, 1984 (Text)

COPYRIGHT

See Patent and Copyright Law

CORPORATIONS

Hamilton's Cases on Corporations—Including Partnerships and Limited Partnerships, 3rd Ed., 1213 pages, 1986 with 1986 Statutory Supplement (Casebook)

Hamilton's Law of Corporations in a Nutshell, 379 pages, 1980 (Text)

Henn's Teaching Materials on Corporations, 2nd Ed., about 1200 pages, 1986 (Casebook)

CORPORATIONS—Cont'd

Henn and Alexander's Hornbook on Corporations, 3rd Ed., Student Ed., 1371 pages, 1983 with 1986 P.P. (Text)

Jennings and Buxbaum's Cases and Materials on Corporations, 5th Ed., 1180 pages, 1979 (Casebook)

Selected Corporation and Partnership Statutes, Regulations and Forms, 555 pages, 1985

Solomon, Stevenson and Schwartz' Materials and Problems on Corporations: Law and Policy, 1172 pages, 1982 with 1986 Supplement (Casebook)

CORPORATE FINANCE

Hamilton's Cases and Materials on Corporate Finance, 895 pages, 1984 with 1986 Supplement (Casebook)

CORRECTIONS

Krantz's Cases and Materials on the Law of Corrections and Prisoners' Rights, 3rd Ed., 855 pages, 1986 (Casebook)

Krantz's Law of Corrections and Prisoners' Rights in a Nutshell, 2nd Ed., 386 pages, 1983 (Text)

Popper's Post-Conviction Remedies in a Nutshell, 360 pages, 1978 (Text)

Robbins' Cases and Materials on Post Conviction Remedies, 506 pages, 1982 (Casebook)

CREDITOR'S RIGHTS

Bankruptcy Code, Rules and Forms, Law School and C.L.E. Ed., about 800 pages, 1986

Epstein's Debtor-Creditor Law in a Nutshell, 3rd Ed., 383 pages, 1986 (Text)

Epstein and Landers' Debtors and Creditors: Cases and Materials, 2nd Ed., 689 pages, 1982 (Casebook)

LoPucki's Player's Manual for the Debtor-Creditor Game, 123 pages, 1985 (Coursebook)

Riesenfeld's Cases and Materials on Creditors' Remedies and Debtors' Protection, 4th Ed., about 800 pages, 1987 (Casebook)

White's Bankruptcy and Creditor's Rights: Cases and Materials, 812 pages, 1985 (Casebook)

CRIMINAL LAW AND CRIMINAL PROCEDURE

Abrams', Federal Criminal Law and its Enforcement, 882 pages, 1986 (Casebook)

Carlson's Adjudication of Criminal Justice, Problems and References, about 124 pages, 1986 (Casebook)

Dix and Sharlot's Cases and Materials on Criminal Law, 2nd Ed., 771 pages, 1979 (Casebook)

CRIMINAL LAW AND CRIMINAL PROCEDURE—Cont'd

Federal Rules of Criminal Procedure—West Law School Edition, about 465 pages, 1986

Grano's Problems in Criminal Procedure, 2nd Ed., 176 pages, 1981 (Problem book)

Israel and LaFave's Criminal Procedure in a Nutshell, 3rd Ed., 438 pages, 1980 (Text)

Johnson's Cases, Materials and Text on Criminal Law, 3rd Ed., 783 pages, 1985 (Casebook)

Kamisar, LaFave and Israel's Cases, Comments and Questions on Modern Criminal Procedure, 6th Ed., about 1600 pages, 1986 with 1986 Supplement (Casebook)

Kamisar, LaFave and Israel's Cases, Comments and Questions on Basic Criminal Procedure, 6th Ed., about 800 pages, 1986 with 1986 Supplement (Casebook)—reprint from Kamisar, et al. Modern Criminal Procedure, 6th ed., 1986

LaFave's Modern Criminal Law: Cases, Comments and Questions, 789 pages, 1978 (Casebook)

LaFave and Israel's Hornbook on Criminal Procedure, Student Ed., 1142 pages, 1985 with 1985 P.P. (Text)

LaFave and Scott's Hornbook on Criminal Law, 2nd Ed., Student Ed., about 800 pages, 1986 (Text)

Langbein's Comparative Criminal Procedure: Germany, 172 pages, 1977 (Casebook)

Loewy's Criminal Law in a Nutshell, 302 pages, 1975 (Text)

Saltzburg's American Criminal Procedure, Cases and Commentary, 2nd Ed., 1193 pages, 1985 with 1986 Supplement (Casebook)

Uviller's The Processes of Criminal Justice: Investigation and Adjudication, 2nd Ed., 1384 pages, 1979 with 1979 Statutory Supplement and 1986 Update (Casebook)

Uviller's The Processes of Criminal Justice: Adjudication, 2nd Ed., 730 pages, 1979. Soft-cover reprint from Uviller's The Processes of Criminal Justice: Investigation and Adjudication, 2nd Ed. (Casebook)

Uviller's The Processes of Criminal Justice: Investigation, 2nd Ed., 655 pages, 1979. Soft-cover reprint from Uviller's The Processes of Criminal Justice: Investigation and Adjudication, 2nd Ed. (Casebook)

Vorenberg's Cases on Criminal Law and Procedure, 2nd Ed., 1088 pages, 1981 with 1985 Supplement (Casebook)

See also Corrections, Juvenile Justice

DECEDENTS ESTATES

See Trusts and Estates

LAW SCHOOL PUBLICATIONS—Continued

DOMESTIC RELATIONS

Clark's Cases and Problems on Domestic Relations, 3rd Ed., 1153 pages, 1980 (Casebook)

Clark's Hornbook on Domestic Relations, 754 pages, 1968 (Text)

Krause's Cases and Materials on Family Law, 2nd Ed., 1221 pages, 1983 with 1986 Supplement (Casebook)

Krause's Family Law in a Nutshell, 2nd Ed., 444 pages, 1986 (Text)

Krauskopf's Cases on Property Division at Marriage Dissolution, 250 pages, 1984 (Casebook)

ECONOMICS, LAW AND

Goetz' Cases and Materials on Law and Economics, 547 pages, 1984 (Casebook)

See also Antitrust, Regulated Industries

EDUCATION LAW

Alexander and Alexander's The Law of Schools, Students and Teachers in a Nutshell, 409 pages, 1984 (Text)

Morris' The Constitution and American Education, 2nd Ed., 992 pages, 1980 (Casebook)

EMPLOYMENT DISCRIMINATION

Jones, Murphy and Belton's Cases on Discrimination in Employment, about 930 pages, 1986 (Casebook)

Player's Cases and Materials on Employment Discrimination Law, 2nd Ed., 782 pages, 1984 (Casebook)

Player's Federal Law of Employment Discrimination in a Nutshell, 2nd Ed., 402 pages, 1981 (Text)

See also Women and the Law

ENERGY AND NATURAL RESOURCES LAW

Laitos' Cases and Materials on Natural Resources Law, 938 pages, 1985 (Casebook)

Rodgers' Cases and Materials on Energy and Natural Resources Law, 2nd Ed., 877 pages, 1983 (Casebook)

Selected Environmental Law Statutes, about 850 pages, 1986

Tomain's Energy Law in a Nutshell, 338 pages, 1981 (Text)

See also Environmental Law, Oil and Gas, Water Law

ENVIRONMENTAL LAW

Bonine and McGarity's Cases and Materials on the Law of Environment and Pollution, 1076 pages, 1984 (Casebook)

Findley and Farber's Cases and Materials on Environmental Law, 2nd Ed., 813 pages, 1985 (Casebook)

Findley and Farber's Environmental Law in a Nutshell, 343 pages, 1983 (Text)

ENVIRONMENTAL LAW—Cont'd

Rodgers' Hornbook on Environmental Law, 956 pages, 1977 with 1984 pocket part (Text)

Selected Environmental Law Statutes, about 950 pages, 1986

See also Energy Law, Natural Resources Law, Water Law

EQUITY

See Remedies

ESTATES

See Trusts and Estates

ESTATE PLANNING

Kurtz' Cases, Materials and Problems on Family Estate Planning, 853 pages, 1983 (Casebook)

Lynn's Introduction to Estate Planning, in a Nutshell, 3rd Ed., 370 pages, 1983 (Text)

See also Taxation

EVIDENCE

Broun and Meisenholder's Problems in Evidence, 2nd Ed., 304 pages, 1981 (Problem book)

Cleary and Strong's Cases, Materials and Problems on Evidence, 3rd Ed., 1143 pages, 1981 (Casebook)

Federal Rules of Evidence for United States Courts and Magistrates, 337 pages, 1984

Graham's Federal Rules of Evidence in a Nutshell, 429 pages, 1981 (Text)

Kimball's Programmed Materials on Problems in Evidence, 380 pages, 1978 (Problem book)

Lempert and Saltzburg's A Modern Approach to Evidence: Text, Problems, Transcripts and Cases, 2nd Ed., 1232 pages, 1983 (Casebook)

Lilly's Introduction to the Law of Evidence, 490 pages, 1978 (Text)

McCormick, Elliott and Sutton's Cases and Materials on Evidence, 5th Ed., 1212 pages, 1981 (Casebook)

McCormick's Hornbook on Evidence, 3rd Ed., Student Ed., 1156 pages, 1984 (Text)

Rothstein's Evidence, State and Federal Rules in a Nutshell, 2nd Ed., 514 pages, 1981 (Text)

Saltzburg's Evidence Supplement: Rules, Statutes, Commentary, 245 pages, 1980 (Casebook Supplement)

FEDERAL JURISDICTION AND PROCEDURE

Currie's Cases and Materials on Federal Courts, 3rd Ed., 1042 pages, 1982 with 1985 Supplement (Casebook)

Currie's Federal Jurisdiction in a Nutshell, 2nd Ed., 258 pages, 1981 (Text)

LAW SCHOOL PUBLICATIONS—Continued

FEDERAL JURISDICTION AND PROCEDURE—Cont'd

Federal Rules of Civil-Appellate Procedure—West Law School Edition, about 550 pages, 1986

Forrester and Moye's Cases and Materials on Federal Jurisdiction and Procedure, 3rd Ed., 917 pages, 1977 with 1985 Supplement (Casebook)

Redish's Cases, Comments and Questions on Federal Courts, 878 pages, 1983 with 1986 Supplement (Casebook)

Vetri and Merrill's Federal Courts, Problems and Materials, 2nd Ed., 232 pages, 1984 (Problem Book)

Wright's Hornbook on Federal Courts, 4th Ed., Student Ed., 870 pages, 1983 (Text)

FUTURE INTERESTS

See Trusts and Estates

IMMIGRATION LAW

Aleinikoff and Martin's Immigration Process and Policy, 1042 pages, 1985 (Casebook)

Weissbrodt's Immigration Law and Procedure in a Nutshell, 345 pages, 1984 (Text)

INDIAN LAW

See American Indian Law

INSURANCE

Dobbyn's Insurance Law in a Nutshell, 281 pages, 1981 (Text)

Keeton's Cases on Basic Insurance Law, 2nd Ed., 1086 pages, 1977

Keeton's Basic Text on Insurance Law, 712 pages, 1971 (Text)

Keeton's Case Supplement to Keeton's Basic Text on Insurance Law, 334 pages, 1978 (Casebook)

York and Whelan's Cases, Materials and Problems on Insurance Law, 715 pages, 1982, with 1985 Supplement (Casebook)

INTERNATIONAL LAW

Buergenthal and Maier's Public International Law in a Nutshell, 262 pages, 1985 (Text)

Folsom, Gordon and Spanogle's International Business Transactions – a Problem-Oriented Coursebook, 1160 pages, 1986 (Casebook)

Henkin, Pugh, Schachter and Smit's Cases and Materials on International Law, 2nd Ed., about 1200 pages, 1987 with Documents Supplement (Casebook)

Jackson and Davey's Legal Problems of International Economic Relations, 2nd Ed., about 1250 pages, 1986, with Documents Supplement (Casebook)

Kirgis' International Organizations in Their Legal Setting, 1016 pages, 1977, with 1981 Supplement (Casebook)

INTERNATIONAL LAW—Cont'd

Weston, Falk and D'Amato's International Law and World Order—A Problem Oriented Coursebook, 1195 pages, 1980, with Documents Supplement (Casebook)

Wilson's International Business Transactions in a Nutshell, 2nd Ed., 476 pages, 1984 (Text)

INTERVIEWING AND COUNSELING

Binder and Price's Interviewing and Counseling, 232 pages, 1977 (Text)

Shaffer's Interviewing and Counseling in a Nutshell, 353 pages, 1976 (Text)

INTRODUCTION TO LAW STUDY

Dobbyn's So You Want to go to Law School, Revised First Edition, 206 pages, 1976 (Text)

Hegland's Introduction to the Study and Practice of Law in a Nutshell, 418 pages, 1983 (Text)

Kinyon's Introduction to Law Study and Law Examinations in a Nutshell, 389 pages, 1971 (Text)

See also Legal Method and Legal System

JUDICIAL ADMINISTRATION

Nelson's Cases and Materials on Judicial Administration and the Administration of Justice, 1032 pages, 1974 (Casebook)

JURISPRUDENCE

Christie's Text and Readings on Jurisprudence—The Philosophy of Law, 1056 pages, 1973 (Casebook)

JUVENILE JUSTICE

Fox's Cases and Materials on Modern Juvenile Justice, 2nd Ed., 960 pages, 1981 (Casebook)

Fox's Juvenile Courts in a Nutshell, 3rd Ed., 291 pages, 1984 (Text)

LABOR LAW

Gorman's Basic Text on Labor Law—Unionization and Collective Bargaining, 914 pages, 1976 (Text)

Leslie's Labor Law in a Nutshell, 2nd Ed., 397 pages, 1986 (Text)

Nolan's Labor Arbitration Law and Practice in a Nutshell, 358 pages, 1979 (Text)

Oberer, Hanslowe, Andersen and Heinsz' Cases and Materials on Labor Law—Collective Bargaining in a Free Society, 3rd Ed., about 1200 pages, 1986 with Statutory Supplement (Casebook)

See also Employment Discrimination, Social Legislation

LAND FINANCE

See Real Estate Transactions

LAW SCHOOL PUBLICATIONS—Continued

LAND USE

Callies and Freilich's Cases and Materials on Land Use, 1233 pages, 1986 (Casebook)

Hagman's Cases on Public Planning and Control of Urban and Land Development, 2nd Ed., 1301 pages, 1980 (Casebook)

Hagman and Juergensmeyer's Hornbook on Urban Planning and Land Development Control Law, 2nd Ed., Student Edition, approximately 580 pages, 1986 (Text)

Wright and Gitelman's Cases and Materials on Land Use, 3rd Ed., 1300 pages, 1982 (Casebook)

Wright and Wright's Land Use in a Nutshell, 2nd Ed., 356 pages, 1985 (Text)

LEGAL HISTORY

Presser and Zainaldin's Cases on Law and American History, 855 pages, 1980 (Casebook)

See also Legal Method and Legal System

LEGAL METHOD AND LEGAL SYSTEM

Aldisert's Readings, Materials and Cases in the Judicial Process, 948 pages, 1976 (Casebook)

Berch and Berch's Introduction to Legal Method and Process, 550 pages, 1985 (Casebook)

Bodenheimer, Oakley and Love's Readings and Cases on an Introduction to the Anglo-American Legal System, 161 pages, 1980 (Casebook)

Davies and Lawry's Institutions and Methods of the Law—Introductory Teaching Materials, 547 pages, 1982 (Casebook)

Dvorkin, Himmelstein and Lesnick's Becoming a Lawyer: A Humanistic Perspective on Legal Education and Professionalism, 211 pages, 1981 (Text)

Greenberg's Judicial Process and Social Change, 666 pages, 1977 (Casebook)

Kelso and Kelso's Studying Law: An Introduction, 587 pages, 1984 (Coursebook)

Kempin's Historical Introduction to Anglo-American Law in a Nutshell, 2nd Ed., 280 pages, 1973 (Text)

Kimball's Historical Introduction to the Legal System, 610 pages, 1966 (Casebook)

Murphy's Cases and Materials on Introduction to Law—Legal Process and Procedure, 772 pages, 1977 (Casebook)

Reynolds' Judicial Process in a Nutshell, 292 pages, 1980 (Text)

See also Legal Research and Writing

LEGAL PROFESSION

Aronson, Devine and Fisch's Problems, Cases and Materials on Professional Responsibility, 745 pages, 1985 (Casebook)

Aronson and Weckstein's Professional Responsibility in a Nutshell, 399 pages, 1980 (Text)

LEGAL PROFESSION—Cont'd

Mellinkoff's The Conscience of a Lawyer, 304 pages, 1973 (Text)

Mellinkoff's Lawyers and the System of Justice, 983 pages, 1976 (Casebook)

Pirsig and Kirwin's Cases and Materials on Professional Responsibility, 4th Ed., 603 pages, 1984 (Casebook)

Schwartz and Wydick's Problems in Legal Ethics, 285 pages, 1983 (Casebook)

Selected Statutes, Rules and Standards on the Legal Profession, 276 pages, Revised 1984

Smith's Preventing Legal Malpractice, 142 pages, 1981 (Text)

Wolfram's Hornbook on Modern Legal Ethics, Student Edition, 1120 pages, 1986 (Text)

LEGAL RESEARCH AND WRITING

Cohen's Legal Research in a Nutshell, 4th Ed., 450 pages, 1985 (Text)

Cohen and Berring's How to Find the Law, 8th Ed., 790 pages, 1983. Problem book by Foster, Johnson and Kelly available (Casebook)

Cohen and Berring's Finding the Law, 8th Ed., Abridged Ed., 556 pages, 1984 (Casebook)

Dickerson's Materials on Legal Drafting, 425 pages, 1981 (Casebook)

Felsenfeld and Siegel's Writing Contracts in Plain English, 290 pages, 1981 (Text)

Gopen's Writing From a Legal Perspective, 225 pages, 1981 (Text)

Mellinkoff's Legal Writing—Sense and Nonsense, 242 pages, 1982 (Text)

Rombauer's Legal Problem Solving—Analysis, Research and Writing, 4th Ed., 424 pages, 1983 (Coursebook)

Squires and Rombauer's Legal Writing in a Nutshell, 294 pages, 1982 (Text)

Statsky's Legal Research, Writing and Analysis, 2nd Ed., 167 pages, 1982 (Coursebook)

Statsky and Wernet's Case Analysis and Fundamentals of Legal Writing, 2nd Ed., 441 pages, 1984 (Text)

Teply's Programmed Materials on Legal Research and Citation, 2nd Ed., 358 pages, 1986. Student Library Exercises available (Coursebook)

Weihofen's Legal Writing Style, 2nd Ed., 332 pages, 1980 (Text)

LEGISLATION

Davies' Legislative Law and Process in a Nutshell, 2nd Ed., 346 pages, 1986 (Text)

Nutting and Dickerson's Cases and Materials on Legislation, 5th Ed., 744 pages, 1978 (Casebook)

LAW SCHOOL PUBLICATIONS—Continued

LEGISLATION—Cont'd

Statsky's Legislative Analysis: How to Use Statutes and Regulations, 2nd Ed., 217 pages, 1984 (Text)

LOCAL GOVERNMENT

McCarthy's Local Government Law in a Nutshell, 2nd Ed., 404 pages, 1983 (Text)

Reynolds' Hornbook on Local Government Law, 860 pages, 1982 (Text)

Valente's Cases and Materials on Local Government Law, 2nd Ed., 980 pages, 1980 with 1982 Supplement (Casebook)

MASS COMMUNICATION LAW

Gillmor and Barron's Cases and Comment on Mass Communication Law, 4th Ed., 1076 pages, 1984 (Casebook)

Ginsburg's Regulation of Broadcasting: Law and Policy Towards Radio, Television and Cable Communications, 741 pages, 1979, with 1983 Supplement (Casebook)

Zuckman and Gayne's Mass Communications Law in a Nutshell, 2nd Ed., 473 pages, 1983 (Text)

MEDICINE, LAW AND

King's The Law of Medical Malpractice in a Nutshell, 2nd Ed., 342 pages, 1986 (Text)

Shapiro and Spece's Problems, Cases and Materials on Bioethics and Law, 892 pages, 1981 (Casebook)

Sharpe, Fiscina and Head's Cases on Law and Medicine, 882 pages, 1978 (Casebook)

MILITARY LAW

Shanor and Terrell's Military Law in a Nutshell, 378 pages, 1980 (Text)

MORTGAGES

See Real Estate Transactions

NATURAL RESOURCES LAW

See Energy and Natural Resources Law

NEGOTIATION

Edwards and White's Problems, Readings and Materials on the Lawyer as a Negotiator, 484 pages, 1977 (Casebook)

Williams' Legal Negotiation and Settlement, 207 pages, 1983 (Coursebook)

OFFICE PRACTICE

Hegland's Trial and Practice Skills in a Nutshell, 346 pages, 1978 (Text)

Strong and Clark's Law Office Management, 424 pages, 1974 (Casebook)

See also Computers and Law, Interviewing and Counseling, Negotiation

OIL AND GAS

Hemingway's Hornbook on Oil and Gas, 2nd Ed., Student Ed., 543 pages, 1983 with 1986 P.P. (Text)

OIL AND GAS—Cont'd

Kuntz, Lowe, Anderson and Smith's Cases and Materials on Oil and Gas Law, 857 pages, 1986 (Casebook)

Lowe's Oil and Gas Law in a Nutshell, 443 pages, 1983 (Text)

See also Energy and Natural Resources Law

PARTNERSHIP

See Agency—Partnership

PATENT AND COPYRIGHT LAW

Choate and Francis' Cases and Materials on Patent Law, 2nd Ed., 1110 pages, 1981 (Casebook)

Miller and Davis' Intellectual Property—Patents, Trademarks and Copyright in a Nutshell, 428 pages, 1983 (Text)

Nimmer's Cases on Copyright and Other Aspects of Entertainment Litigation, 3rd Ed., 1025 pages, 1985 (Casebook)

PRODUCTS LIABILITY

Noel and Phillips' Cases on Products Liability, 2nd Ed., 821 pages, 1982 (Casebook)

Noel and Phillips' Products Liability in a Nutshell, 2nd Ed., 341 pages, 1981 (Text)

PROPERTY

Bernhardt's Real Property in a Nutshell, 2nd Ed., 448 pages, 1981 (Text)

Boyer's Survey of the Law of Property, 766 pages, 1981 (Text)

Browder, Cunningham and Smith's Cases on Basic Property Law, 4th Ed., 1431 pages, 1984 (Casebook)

Bruce, Ely and Bostick's Cases and Materials on Modern Property Law, 1004 pages, 1984 (Casebook)

Burke's Personal Property in a Nutshell, 322 pages, 1983 (Text)

Cunningham, Stoebuck and Whitman's Hornbook on the Law of Property, Student Ed., 916 pages, 1984 (Text)

Donahue, Kauper and Martin's Cases on Property, 2nd Ed., 1362 pages, 1983 (Casebook)

Hill's Landlord and Tenant Law in a Nutshell, 2nd Ed., 311 pages, 1986 (Text)

Moynihan's Introduction to Real Property, 254 pages, 1962 (Text)

Uniform Land Transactions Act, Uniform Simplification of Land Transfers Act, Uniform Condominium Act, 1977 Official Text with Comments, 462 pages, 1978

See also Real Estate Transactions, Land Use

PSYCHIATRY, LAW AND

Reisner's Law and the Mental Health System, Civil and Criminal Aspects, 696 pages, 1985 (Casebooks)

LAW SCHOOL PUBLICATIONS—Continued

REAL ESTATE TRANSACTIONS

Bruce's Real Estate Finance in a Nutshell, 2nd Ed., 262 pages, 1985 (Text)

Maxwell, Riesenfeld, Hetland and Warren's Cases on California Security Transactions in Land, 3rd Ed., 728 pages, 1984 (Casebook)

Nelson and Whitman's Cases on Real Estate Transfer, Finance and Development, 2nd Ed., 1114 pages, 1981, with 1986 Supplement (Casebook)

Nelson and Whitman's Hornbook on Real Estate Finance Law, 2nd Ed., Student Ed., 941 pages, 1985 (Text)

Osborne's Cases and Materials on Secured Transactions, 559 pages, 1967 (Casebook)

REGULATED INDUSTRIES

Gellhorn and Pierce's Regulated Industries in a Nutshell, 394 pages, 1982 (Text)

Morgan, Harrison and Verkuil's Cases and Materials on Economic Regulation of Business, 2nd Ed., 666 pages, 1985 (Casebook)

See also Mass Communication Law, Banking Law

REMEDIES

Dobbs' Hornbook on Remedies, 1067 pages, 1973 (Text)

Dobbs' Problems in Remedies, 137 pages, 1974 (Problem book)

Dobbyn's Injunctions in a Nutshell, 264 pages, 1974 (Text)

Friedman's Contract Remedies in a Nutshell, 323 pages, 1981 (Text)

Leavell, Love and Nelson's Cases and Materials on Equitable Remedies and Restitution, 4th Ed., 1111 pages, 1986 (Casebook)

McCormick's Hornbook on Damages, 811 pages, 1935 (Text)

O'Connell's Remedies in a Nutshell, 2nd Ed., 320 pages, 1985 (Text)

York, Bauman and Rendleman's Cases and Materials on Remedies, 4th Ed., 1029 pages, 1985 (Casebook)

REVIEW MATERIALS

Ballantine's Problems

Black Letter Series

Smith's Review Series

West's Review Covering Multistate Subjects

SECURITIES REGULATION

Hazen's Hornbook on The Law of Securities Regulation, Student Ed., 739 pages, 1985 (Text)

Ratner's Securities Regulation: Materials for a Basic Course, 3rd Ed., 1000 pages, 1986 (Casebook)

Ratner's Securities Regulation in a Nutshell, 2nd Ed., 322 pages, 1982 (Text)

SECURITIES REGULATION—Cont'd

Selected Securities and Business Planning Statutes, Rules and Forms, 470 pages, 1985

SOCIAL LEGISLATION

Hood and Hardy's Workers' Compensation and Employee Protection Laws in a Nutshell, 274 pages, 1984 (Text)

LaFrance's Welfare Law: Structure and Entitlement in a Nutshell, 455 pages, 1979 (Text)

Malone, Plant and Little's Cases on Workers' Compensation and Employment Rights, 2nd Ed., 951 pages, 1980 (Casebook)

SPORTS LAW

Schubert, Smith and Trentadue's Sports Law, 395 pages, 1986 (Text)

TAXATION

Dodge's Cases and Materials on Federal Income Taxation, 820 pages, 1985 (Casebook)

Dodge's Federal Taxation of Estates, Trusts and Gifts: Principles and Planning, 771 pages, 1981 with 1982 Supplement (Casebook)

Garbis and Struntz' Cases and Materials on Tax Procedure and Tax Fraud, 829 pages, 1982 with 1984 Supplement (Casebook)

Gelfand and Salsich's State and Local Taxation and Finance in a Nutshell, 309 pages, 1986 (Text)

Gunn's Cases and Materials on Federal Income Taxation of Individuals, 785 pages, 1981 with 1985 Supplement (Casebook)

Hellerstein and Hellerstein's Cases on State and Local Taxation, 4th Ed., 1041 pages, 1978 with 1982 Supplement (Casebook)

Kahn and Gann's Corporate Taxation and Taxation of Partnerships and Partners, 2nd Ed., 1204 pages, 1985 (Casebook)

Kragen and McNulty's Cases and Materials on Federal Income Taxation: Individuals, Corporations, Partnerships, 4th Ed., 1287 pages, 1985 (Casebook)

McNulty's Federal Estate and Gift Taxation in a Nutshell, 3rd Ed., 509 pages, 1983 (Text)

McNulty's Federal Income Taxation of Individuals in a Nutshell, 3rd Ed., 487 pages, 1983 (Text)

Posin's Hornbook on Federal Income Taxation of Individuals, Student Ed., 491 pages, 1983 with 1985 pocket part (Text)

Selected Federal Taxation Statutes and Regulations, about 1400 pages, 1986

Solomon and Hesch's Cases on Federal Income Taxation of Individuals, about 800 pages, 1987 (Casebook)

LAW SCHOOL PUBLICATIONS—Continued

TAXATION—Cont'd

Sobeloff and Weidenbruch's Federal Income Taxation of Corporations and Stockholders in a Nutshell, 362 pages, 1981 (Text)

TORTS

Christie's Cases and Materials on the Law of Torts, 1264 pages, 1983 (Casebook)

Dobbs' Torts and Compensation—Personal Accountability and Social Responsibility for Injury, 955 pages, 1985 (Casebook)

Green, Pedrick, Rahl, Thode, Hawkins, Smith and Treece's Cases and Materials on Torts, 2nd Ed., 1360 pages, 1977 (Casebook)

Green, Pedrick, Rahl, Thode, Hawkins, Smith, and Treece's Advanced Torts: Injuries to Business, Political and Family Interests, 2nd Ed., 544 pages, 1977 (Casebook)—reprint from Green, et al. Cases and Materials on Torts, 2nd Ed., 1977

Keeton, Keeton, Sargentich and Steiner's Cases and Materials on Torts, and Accident Law, 1360 pages, 1983 (Casebook)

Kionka's Torts in a Nutshell: Injuries to Persons and Property, 434 pages, 1977 (Text)

Malone's Torts in a Nutshell: Injuries to Family, Social and Trade Relations, 358 pages, 1979 (Text)

Prosser and Keeton's Hornbook on Torts, 5th Ed., Student Ed., 1286 pages, 1984 (Text)

Shapo's Cases on Tort and Compensation Law, 1244 pages, 1976 (Casebook)

See also Products Liability

TRADE REGULATION

McManis' Unfair Trade Practices in a Nutshell, 444 pages, 1982 (Text)

Oppenheim, Weston, Maggs and Schechter's Cases and Materials on Unfair Trade Practices and Consumer Protection, 4th Ed., 1038 pages, 1983 with 1986 Supplement (Casebook)

See also Antitrust, Regulated Industries

TRIAL AND APPELLATE ADVOCACY

Appellate Advocacy, Handbook of, 2nd Ed., 182 pages, 1986 (Text)

Bergman's Trial Advocacy in a Nutshell, 402 pages, 1979 (Text)

Binder and Bergman's Fact Investigation: From Hypothesis to Proof, 354 pages, 1984 (Coursebook)

Goldberg's The First Trial (Where Do I Sit?, What Do I Say?) in a Nutshell, 396 pages, 1982 (Text)

Haydock, Herr and Stempel's, Fundamentals of Pre-Trial Litigation, 768 pages, 1985 (Casebook)

Hegland's Trial and Practice Skills in a Nutshell, 346 pages, 1978 (Text)

Hornstein's Appellate Advocacy in a Nutshell, 325 pages, 1984 (Text)

TRIAL AND APPELLATE ADVOCACY—Cont'd

Jeans' Handbook on Trial Advocacy, Student Ed., 473 pages, 1975 (Text)

Martineau's Cases and Materials on Appellate Practice and Procedure, about 550 pages, 1987 (Casebook)

McElhaney's Effective Litigation, 457 pages, 1974 (Casebook)

Nolan's Cases and Materials on Trial Practice, 518 pages, 1981 (Casebook)

Parnell and Shellhaas' Cases, Exercises and Problems for Trial Advocacy, 171 pages, 1982 (Coursebook)

Sonsteng, Haydock and Boyd's The Trialbook: A Total System for Preparation and Presentation of a Case, Student Ed., 404 pages, 1984 (Coursebook)

TRUSTS AND ESTATES

Atkinson's Hornbook on Wills, 2nd Ed., 975 pages, 1953 (Text)

Averill's Uniform Probate Code in a Nutshell, 425 pages, 1978 (Text)

Bogert's Hornbook on Trusts, 5th Ed., 726 pages, 1973 (Text)

Clark, Lusky and Murphy's Cases and Materials on Gratuitous Transfers, 3rd Ed., 970 pages, 1985 (Casebook)

Gulliver's Cases and Materials on Future Interests, 624 pages, 1959 (Casebook)

Gulliver's Introduction to the Law of Future Interests, 87 pages, 1959 (Casebook)—reprint from Gulliver's Cases and Materials on Future Interests, 1959

McGovern's Cases and Materials on Wills, Trusts and Future Interests: An Introduction to Estate Planning, 750 pages, 1983 (Casebook)

Mennell's Cases and Materials on California Decedent's Estates, 566 pages, 1973 (Casebook)

Mennell's Wills and Trusts in a Nutshell, 392 pages, 1979 (Text)

Powell's The Law of Future Interests in California, 91 pages, 1980 (Text)

Simes' Hornbook on Future Interests, 2nd Ed., 355 pages, 1966 (Text)

Turano and Radigan's Hornbook on New York Estate Administration, approximately 575 pages, 1986 (Text)

Uniform Probate Code, 5th Ed., Official Text With Comments, 384 pages, 1977

Waggoner's Future Interests in a Nutshell, 361 pages, 1981 (Text)

Waterbury's Materials on Trusts and Estates, 1039 pages, 1986 (Casebook)

WATER LAW

Getches' Water Law in a Nutshell, 439 pages, 1984 (Text)

LAW SCHOOL PUBLICATIONS—Continued

WATER LAW—Cont'd

Sax and Abram's Cases and Materials on Legal Control of Water Resources in the United States, 941 pages, 1986 (Casebook)

Trelease and Gould's Cases and Materials on Water Law, 4th Ed., 816 pages, 1986 (Casebook)

See also Energy and Natural Resources Law, Environmental Law

WILLS

See Trusts and Estates

WOMEN AND THE LAW

Kay's Text, Cases and Materials on Sex-Based Discrimination, 2nd Ed., 1045 pages, 1981, with 1986 Supplement (Casebook)

Thomas' Sex Discrimination in a Nutshell, 399 pages, 1982 (Text)

See also Employment Discrimination

WORKERS' COMPENSATION

See Social Legislation

ADVISORY BOARD
AMERICAN CASEBOOK SERIES
HORNBOOK SERIES AND BASIC LEGAL TEXTS
NUTSHELL SERIES AND BLACK LETTER SERIES

JOHN A. BAUMAN
Professor of Law
University of California, Los Angeles

CURTIS J. BERGER
Professor of Law
Columbia University School of Law

JESSE H. CHOPER
Dean and Professor of Law
University of California, Berkeley

DAVID P. CURRIE
Professor of Law
University of Chicago

DAVID G. EPSTEIN
Dean and Professor of Law
Emory University

YALE KAMISAR
Professor of Law
University of Michigan

MARY KAY KANE
Professor of Law
University of California,
Hastings College of tne Law

WAYNE R. LaFAVE
Professor of Law
University of Illinois

RICHARD C. MAXWELL
Professor of Law
Duke University

ARTHUR R. MILLER
Professor of Law
Harvard University

JAMES J. WHITE
Professor of Law
University of Michigan

CHARLES ALAN WRIGHT
Professor of Law
University of Texas

CONSTITUTIONAL RIGHTS AND LIBERTIES

CASES—COMMENTS—QUESTIONS

Sixth Edition

By

William B. Lockhart

Professor of Law, University of California, Hastings
Dean and Professor of Law Emeritus, University of Minnesota

Yale Kamisar

Henry K. Ransom Professor of Law, University of Michigan

Jesse H. Choper

Dean and Professor of Law, University of California, Berkeley

Steven H. Shiffrin

Professor of Law, University of California, Los Angeles

AMERICAN CASEBOOK SERIES

CARNEGIE LIBRARY
LIVINGSTONE COLLEGE
SALISBURY, NC 28144

WEST PUBLISHING CO.
ST. PAUL, MINN., 1986

123228

COPYRIGHT © 1964, 1967, 1970 By WEST PUBLISHING CO.
COPYRIGHT © 1975, 1981 By LOCKHART, KAMISAR & CHOPER
COPYRIGHT © 1986 By LOCKHART, KAMISAR, CHOPER & SHIFFRIN
All rights reserved
Printed in the United States of America

Library of Congress Cataloging in Publication Data

Constitutional rights and liberties.

(American casebook series)
Includes index.
1. Civil rights—United States—Cases. I. Lockhart,
William B. II. Series.

KF4748.C66 1986 342.73'085 86-13143

ISBN 0-314-98074-1 347.30285

L.K.C. & S.Const.Rights & Liberties 6th Ed. ACB

*For Bill Lockhart, who pulls as
heavy an oar as ever,
on his 80th birthday.*

J.C.
Y.K.
S.S.

*

Preface

Casebooks are teaching tools, and this is no exception. What distinguishes this book is its commitment to the proposition that a student's understanding of constitutional law is greatly enriched by exposure to a variety of competing perspectives drawn from the best of legal scholarship. To that end, we have reproduced many selections from the literature or woven them into the notes and questions that follow almost every main case.

The problem in preparing this edition has been to figure out a way to integrate some six years of new cases and articles without producing an oversized monster. One approach to that problem, of course, is to produce a book with microscopic print. We perhaps went too far in that direction in the last edition. Instead we vowed in this edition that the print would be readable, and the book would be slimmer, yet designed not only to reflect recent doctrine and the modern commentary, but also to give a strong sense of how we got to where we are today. To accomplish all this, we paid heed to the adage that selection is the most important part of editing.

That insight is especially applicable to the materials on freedom of expression and association. The time is long past when effective teaching about the first amendment can be accomplished with materials that produce snippets from every free speech case ever decided by the United States Supreme Court. In the fourth edition, we remarked on the massive character of those materials. By this edition, those materials threatened to engulf the book. We, therefore, decided to add a first amendment specialist to the book. The result has been a complete restructuring and reconceptualization of the free speech materials. Older material has been significantly pruned to make room for the new. The overall strategy has been to pick the great teaching cases and to give them detailed treatment. Material, for example, has been added to principal cases throughout, even to such old standbys as *Beauharnais, Chaplinsky,* and *Gitlow.*

The new organization downplays the issues current in the 1950's (e.g., loyalty oaths) and instead requires the student to consider the speech that is *not* protected before moving on to the difficult questions associated with regulating "protected" speech. Freedom of association has risen from an important theme to a major organizational category. the public forum materials have been reduced to teachable proportions, and the movement of some "public forum" materials to an important new section on government support of speech significantly tightens the organization. Finally, new sections have been added on a range of topics including material addressing the relationship between feminism and pornography, public and private speech, copyright and the first amendment.

The addition of a new co-author has allowed the original authors to devote more attention to their areas of special interest. For example, *Roe v. Wade,* and the debate it stirred over "interpretivist"/"noninterpretivist" constitutional decisionmaking have been the subject of uniquely intensive treatment and the sections on Procedural Due Process and The Death Penalty and Related Problems have been greatly enriched. (We are aware that many other constitutional law casebooks completely exclude the "death penalty" cases, but we are convinced that they belong in a constitutional law casebook. Although nominally "cruel and unusual punishment" material, the "death penalty" cases are striking illustrations of standards and methodology in due process adjudication).

We have been unable to include developments during the 1985–86 Supreme Court Term. These materials will appear in a supplement that will be published in the summer of 1986. Important developments thereafter will appear in annual supplements.

Case and statute citations, as well as footnotes, of the Court and commentators have been omitted without so specifying; other omissions are indicated by asterisks or by brackets. Numbered footnotes are from the original materials; lettered footnotes are ours. The composition of the Court on any date may be obtained by consulting the Table of Justices in the Appendix, prepared by Professor John J. Cound, who has also compiled basic biographical data on all members of the Court.

Over the years of these six editions, we have become indebted to many teachers (and students) of constitutional law for their valuable suggestions and insights. The contributions to the first edition by Carl A. Auerbach, John C. Cound and Terrance Sandalow persist to date. Our thanks, for their criticisms and suggestions, go also to Vincent A. Blasi, Arthur E. Bonfield, Frank I. Goodman, Lino A. Graglia, Kenneth Karst, Michael E. Smith, Laurence H. Tribe, and Jonathan Varat. And we are most appreciative of the excellent student research assistance provided by David Westrup.

WILLIAM B. LOCKHART
YALE KAMISAR
JESSE CHOPER
STEVEN SHIFFRIN

June, 1986

Summary of Contents

*

Table of Contents

Table of Cases

The principal cases are in bold type. Cases cited or discussed are in roman type. References are to Pages.

Table of Authorities

For authorities from which extracts have been taken page numbers appear in bold; page numbers for other authorities appear in roman.

lxxvi   TABLE OF AUTHORITIES

CONSTITUTIONAL RIGHTS AND LIBERTIES

CASES—COMMENTS—QUESTIONS

Sixth Edition

*

Chapter 1

NATURE AND SCOPE OF
JUDICIAL REVIEW

SECTION 1. ORIGINS, EARLY CHALLENGES, AND CONTINUING CONTROVERSY

"Whoever hath an absolute authority to interpret any written or spoken laws, it is he who is truly the lawgiver, to all intents and purposes, and not the person who first spoke or wrote them."

> —Bishop Hoadly's Sermon, preached before the King, 1717.

MARBURY v. MADISON
1 Cranch 137, 2 L.Ed. 60 (1803).

[Thomas Jefferson, an Anti-Federalist (or Republican), who defeated John Adams, a Federalist, in the presidential election of 1800, was to take office on March 4, 1801. On January 20, 1801, Adams, the defeated incumbent, nominated John Marshall, Adams' Secretary of State, as fourth Chief Justice of the United States. Marshall assumed office on February 4 but continued to serve as Secretary of State until the end of the Adams administration. During February, the Federalist Congress passed (1) the Circuit Court Act, which, inter alia, doubled the number of federal judges and (2) the Organic Act which authorized appointment of 42 justices-of-the-peace in the District of Columbia. Senate confirmation of Adams' "midnight" appointees, virtually all Federalists, was completed on March 3. Their commissions were signed by Adams and sealed by Acting Secretary of State Marshall, but due to time pressures, several for the justices-of-the-peace (including that of William Marbury) remained undelivered when Jefferson assumed the presidency the next day. Jefferson ordered his new Secretary of State, James Madison, to withhold delivery.

[Late in 1801, Marbury and several others sought a writ of mandamus in the Supreme Court to compel Madison to deliver the commissions. The Court ordered Madison "to show cause why a mandamus should not issue" and the case was set for argument in the 1802 Term.

[While the case was pending, the new Republican Congress—incensed at Adams' efforts to entrench a Federalist judiciary and at the "Federalist" Court's order against a Republican cabinet officer—moved to repeal the Circuit Court Act. Federalist congressmen argued that repeal would be unconstitutional as

1

violative of Art. III's assurance of judicial tenure "during good behavior" and of the Constitution's plan for separation of powers assuring the independence of the Judiciary. It "was in this debate that for the first time since the initiation of the new Government under the Constitution there occurred a serious challenge of the power of the Judiciary to pass upon the constitutionality of Acts of Congress. Hitherto, [it had been the Republicans] who had sustained this power as a desirable curb on Congressional aggression and encroachment on the rights of the States, and they had been loud in their complaints at the failure of the Court to hold the Alien and Sedition laws unconstitutional. Now, however, in 1802, in order to counteract the Federalist argument that the Repeal Bill was unconstitutional and would be so held by the Court, [Republicans] advanced the proposition that the Court did not possess the power." [a]

[The Repeal Law passed early in 1802. To forestall its constitutional challenge in the Supreme Court until the political power of the new administration had been strengthened, Congress also eliminated the 1802 Supreme Court Term. Thus, the Court did not meet between December, 1801 and February, 1803.]

[On] 24th February, the following opinion of the court was delivered by MR. CHIEF JUSTICE MARSHALL: * * *

No cause has been shown, and the present motion is for a mandamus. The peculiar delicacy of this case, the novelty of some of its circumstances, and the real difficulty attending the points which occur in it require a complete exposition of the principles on which the opinion to be given by the court is founded. * * *

1st. Has the applicant a right to the commission he demands? * * *

Mr. Marbury, [since] his commission was signed by the President and sealed by the Secretary of State, was appointed; and as the law creating the office gave the officer a right to hold for five years, independent of the executive, the appointment was not revocable, but vested in the officer legal rights, which are protected by the laws of his country.

To withhold his commission, therefore, is an act deemed by the court not warranted by law, but violative of a vested legal right. [b] * * *

2dly. If he has a right, and that right has been violated, do the laws of his country afford him a remedy?

The very essence of civil liberty certainly consists in the right of every individual to claim the protection of the laws, whenever he receives an injury. One of the first duties of government is to afford that protection. * * *

The government of the United States has been emphatically termed a government of laws, and not of men. It will certainly cease to deserve this high appellation, if the laws furnish no remedy for the violation of a vested legal right. * * *

[W]here the heads of departments are the political or confidential agents of the executive, merely to execute the will of the president, or rather to act in

a. 1 Warren, *The Supreme Court in United States History* 215 (1922).

b. Consider Van Alstyne, *A Critical Guide to Marbury v. Madison,* 1969 Duke L.J. 1, 8: "[T]here is clearly an 'issue' of sorts which preceded any of those touched upon in the opinion. Specifically, it would appear that Marshall should have recused himself in view of his substantial involvement in the background of this controversy. * * * Proof of the status of Marbury's commission not only involved circumstances within the Chief Justice's personal knowledge, it was furnished in the Supreme Court by Marshall's own younger brother who had been with him in his office when, as Secretary of State, he had made out the commissions."

cases in which the executive possesses a constitutional or legal discretion, nothing can be more perfectly clear than that their acts are only politically examinable. But where a specific duty is assigned by law, and individual rights depend upon the performance of that duty, it seems equally clear that the individual who considers himself injured, has a right to resort to the laws of his country for a remedy.[c] * * *

It remains to be inquired whether,

3dly. He is entitled to the remedy for which he applies? This depends on,

1st. The nature of the writ applied for; and,

2dly. The power of this court.

1st. The nature of the writ. * * *

This writ, if awarded, would be directed to an officer of government, and its mandate to him would be, to use the words of Blackstone, "to do a particular thing therein specified, which appertains to his office and duty, and which the court has previously determined, or at least supposes, to be consonant to right and justice." Or, in the words of Lord Mansfield, the applicant, in this case, has a right to execute an office of public concern, and is kept out of possession of that right.

These circumstances certainly concur in this case.

Still, to render the mandamus a proper remedy, the officer to whom it is to be directed, must be one to whom, on legal principles, such writ may be directed; and the person applying for it must be without any other specific and legal remedy.

1st. With respect to the officer to whom it would be directed. The intimate political relation subsisting between the President of the United States and the heads of departments, necessarily renders any legal investigation of the acts of one of those high officers peculiarly irksome, as well as delicate; and excites some hesitation with respect to the propriety of entering into such investigation. Impressions are often received without much reflection or examination, and it is not wonderful that in such a case as this the assertion, by an individual, of his legal claims in a court of justice, to which claims it is the duty of that court to attend, should at first view be considered by some, as an attempt to intrude into the cabinet, and to intermeddle with the prerogatives of the executive.

It is scarcely necessary for the court to disclaim all pretensions to such a jurisdiction. An extravagance, so absurd and excessive, could not have been entertained for a moment. The province of the court is, solely, to decide on the rights of individuals, not to inquire how the executive, or executive officers, perform duties in which they have a discretion. Questions in their nature political, or which are, by the constitution and laws, submitted to the executive, can never be made in this court.

But [what] is there in the exalted station of the officer, which shall bar a citizen from asserting, in a court of justice, his legal rights, or shall forbid a court to listen to the claim, or to issue a mandamus, directing the performance of a duty, not depending on executive discretion, but on particular acts of congress, and the general principles of law? * * *

c. Consider Redlich, *The Supreme Court— 1833 Term,* 40 N.Y.U.L.Rev. 1, 4 (1965): "[T]he Court could have ruled that, since the President had the power to appoint the judges, he also had the power to deliver the commissions which was in a sense the final act of appointment. Viewed as a component of the act of appointment, the delivery of the commissions could have simply been considered as lying within the discretion of the President."

This, then, is a plain case for a mandamus, either to deliver the commission, or a copy of it from the record; and it only remains to be inquired,

Whether it can issue from this court.

The act to establish the judicial courts of the United States authorizes the supreme court "to issue writs of mandamus, in cases warranted by the principles and usages of law, to any courts appointed, or persons holding office, under the authority of the United States." [d]

The secretary of state, being a person holding an office under the authority of the United States, is precisely within the letter of the description; and if this court is not authorized to issue a writ of mandamus to such an officer, it must be because the law is unconstitutional, and therefore absolutely incapable of conferring the authority, and assigning the duties which its words purport to confer and assign. * * *

In the distribution of [the judicial power of the United States] it is declared that "the supreme court shall have original jurisdiction in all cases affecting ambassadors, other public ministers and consuls, and those in which a state shall be a party. In all other cases, the supreme court shall have appellate jurisdiction."

It has been insisted, at the bar, that as the original grant of jurisdiction, to the supreme and inferior courts, is general, and the clause, assigning original jurisdiction to the supreme court, contains no negative or restrictive words, the power remains to the legislature, to assign original jurisdiction to that court in other cases than those specified in the article which has been recited; provided those cases belong to the judicial power of the United States.

If it had been intended to leave it in the discretion of the legislature to apportion the judicial power between the supreme and inferior courts according to the will of that body, it would certainly have been useless to have proceeded further than to have defined the judicial power, and the tribunals in which it should be vested. The subsequent part of the section is mere surplusage, is

---

d. § 13 of the Judiciary Act of 1789 provided: "That the Supreme Court shall have exclusive jurisdiction of all controversies of a civil nature, where a state is a party, except between a state and its citizens; and except also between a state and citizens of other states, or aliens, in which latter case it shall have original but not exclusive jurisdiction. And shall have exclusively all such jurisdiction of suits or proceedings against ambassadors or other public ministers, or their domestics, or domestic servants, as a court of law can have or exercise consistently with the law of nations; and original, but not exclusive jurisdiction of all suits brought by ambassadors or other public ministers, or in which a consul, or vice consul, shall be a party. And the trial of issues of fact in the Supreme Court in all actions at law against citizens of the United States shall be by jury. The Supreme Court shall also have appellate jurisdiction from the circuit courts and courts of the several states, in the cases hereinafter specially provided for; and shall have power to issue writs of prohibition to the district courts, when proceeding as courts of admiralty and maritime jurisdiction, and writs of mandamus, in cases warranted by the principles and usages of law, to any courts appointed, or persons holding office under the authority of the United States."

Consider Van Alstyne, supra, at 15: "Textually, the provision regarding mandamus says nothing expressly as to whether it is part of original or appellate jurisdiction or both, and the clause itself does not speak at all of 'conferring jurisdiction' on the court. The grant of 'power' to issue the writ, however, is juxtaposed with the section of appellate jurisdiction and, in fact, follows the general description of appellate jurisdiction in the same sentence, being separated only by a semicolon. No textual mangling is required to confine it to appellate jurisdiction. Moreover, no mangling is required even if it attaches both to original and to appellate jurisdiction, not as an enlargement of either, but simply as a specification of power which the Court is authorized to use in cases which are *otherwise* appropriately under consideration. Since this case is not otherwise within the specified type of original jurisdiction (e.g., it is not a case in which a state is a party or a case against an ambassador), it should be dismissed."

entirely without meaning, if such is to be the construction. If congress remains at liberty to give this court appellate jurisdiction, where the constitution has declared their jurisdiction shall be original; and original jurisdiction where the constitution has declared it shall be appellate; the distribution of jurisdiction, made in the constitution, is form without substance.

Affirmative words are often, in their operation, negative of other objects than those affirmed; and in this case, a negative or exclusive sense must be given to them, or they have no operation at all.

It cannot be presumed that any clause in the constitution is intended to be without effect; and, therefore, such a construction is inadmissible, unless the words require it. * * *

The authority, therefore, given to the Supreme Court, by the Act establishing the judicial courts of the United States, to issue writs of mandamus to public officers, appears not to be warranted by the Constitution; [e] and it becomes necessary to inquire whether a jurisdiction so conferred can be exercised.

The question whether an Act repugnant to the Constitution can become the law of the land, is a question deeply interesting to the United States; but, happily, not of an intricacy proportioned to its interest. It seems only necessary to recognize certain principles, supposed to have been long and well established, to decide it.

That the people have an original right to establish, for their future government, such principles as, in their opinion, shall most conduce to their own happiness, is the basis on which the whole American fabric has been erected. The exercise of this original right is a very great exertion; nor can it nor ought it to be frequently repeated. The principles, therefore, so established, are deemed fundamental. And as the authority from which they proceed is supreme, and can seldom act, they are designed to be permanent.

This original and supreme will organizes the government, and assigns to different departments their respective powers. It may either stop here, or establish certain limits not to be transcended by those departments.

The government of the United States is of the latter description. The powers of the legislature are defined and limited; and that those limits may not be mistaken, or forgotten, the constitution is written. To what purpose are powers limited, and to what purpose is that limitation committed to writing, if these limits may, at any time, be passed by those intended to be restrained? The distinction between a government with limited and unlimited powers is abolished, if those limits do not confine the persons on whom they are imposed, and if acts prohibited and acts allowed, are of equal obligation. It is a proposition too plain to be contested, that the constitution controls any legislative act repugnant to it; or, that the legislature may alter the constitution by an ordinary act.

Between these alternatives there is no middle ground. The constitution is either a superior paramount law, unchangeable by ordinary means, or it is on a level with ordinary legislative acts, and, like other acts, is alterable when the legislature shall please to alter it.

If the former part of the alternative be true, then a legislative act contrary to the constitution is not law: if the latter part be true, then written constitutions are absurd attempts, on the part of the people, to limit a power in its own nature illimitable.

e. By Marshall's interpretation of Art. III, may Congress authorize the Court to exercise appellate jurisdiction in cases involving foreign consuls? See *Bors v. Preston*, 111 U.S. 252, 4 S.Ct. 407, 28 L.Ed. 419 (1884).

Certainly all those who have framed written constitutions contemplate them as forming the fundamental and paramount law of the nation, and consequently, the theory of every such government must be, that an act of the legislature, repugnant to the constitution, is void.

This theory is essentially attached to a written constitution, and is, consequently, to be considered, by this court, as one of the fundamental principles of our society. It is not therefore to be lost sight of in the further consideration of this subject.

If an act of the legislature, repugnant to the Constitution, is void, does it, notwithstanding its invalidity, bind the courts, and oblige them to give it effect? Or, in other words, though it be not law, does it constitute a rule as operative as if it was a law? This would be to overthrow in fact what was established in theory; and would seem, at first view, an absurdity too gross to be insisted on. It shall, however, receive a more attentive consideration.

It is emphatically the province and duty of the judicial department to say what the law is. Those who apply the rule to particular cases, must of necessity expound and interpret that rule. If two laws conflict with each other, the courts must decide on the operation of each.

So if a law be in opposition to the constitution; if both the law and the constitution apply to a particular case, so that the court must either decide that case conformably to the law, disregarding the constitution; or conformably to the constitution, disregarding the law; the court must determine which of these conflicting rules governs the case. This is of the very essence of judicial duty.

If, then, the courts are to regard the constitution, and the constitution is superior to any ordinary act of the legislature, the constitution, and not such ordinary act, must govern the case to which they both apply.

Those then who controvert the principle that the constitution is to be considered in court, as a paramount law, are reduced to the necessity of maintaining that courts must close their eyes on the constitution, and see only the law.

This doctrine would subvert the very foundation of all written constitutions. It would declare that an Act which, according to the principles and theory of our government, is entirely void, is yet, in practice, completely obligatory. It would declare that if the legislature shall do what is expressly forbidden, such Act, notwithstanding the express prohibition, is in reality effectual. It would be giving to the legislature a practical and real omnipotence, with the same breath which professes to restrict their powers within narrow limits. It is prescribing limits, and declaring that those limits may be passed at pleasure.

That it thus reduces to nothing what we have deemed the greatest improvement on political institutions, a written constitution, would of itself be sufficient, in America, where written constitutions have been viewed with so much reverence, for rejecting the construction. But the peculiar expressions of the Constitution of the United States furnish additional arguments in favor of its rejection.

The judicial power of the United States is extended to all cases arising under the Constitution.

Could it be the intention of those who gave this power, to say that in using it the Constitution should not be looked into? That a case arising under the Constitution should be decided without examining the instrument under which it arises?

This is too extravagant to be maintained.

In some cases, then, the Constitution must be looked into by the judges. And if they can open it at all, what part of it are they forbidden to read or to obey?

There are many other parts of the Constitution which serve to illustrate this subject.

It is declared that "no tax or duty shall be laid on articles exported from any State." Suppose a duty on the export of cotton, of tobacco, or of flour; and a suit instituted to recover it. Ought judgment to be rendered in such a case? Ought the judges to close their eyes on the Constitution, and only see the law?

The Constitution declares "that no bill of attainder or ex post facto law shall be passed."

If, however, such a bill should be passed, and a person should be prosecuted under it, must the court condemn to death those victims whom the Constitution endeavors to preserve?

"No person," says the Constitution, "shall be convicted of treason unless on the testimony of two witnesses to the same overt act, or on confession in open court."

Here the language of the Constitution is addressed especially to the courts. It prescribes, directly for them, a rule of evidence not to be departed from. If the legislature should change that rule, and declare one witness, or a confession out of court, sufficient for conviction, must the constitutional principle yield to the legislative act?

From these, and many other selections which might be made, it is apparent, that the framers of the constitution contemplated that instrument as a rule for the government of courts, as well as of the legislature.

Why otherwise does it direct the judges to take an oath to support it? This oath certainly applies in an especial manner, to their conduct in their official character. How immoral to impose it on them, if they were to be used as the instruments, and the knowing instruments, for violating what they swear to support!

The oath of office, too, imposed by the legislature, is completely demonstrative of the legislative opinion on this subject. It is in these words: "I do solemnly swear that I will administer justice without respect to persons, and do equal right to the poor and to the rich; and that I will faithfully and impartially discharge all the duties incumbent on me as _____, according to the best of my abilities and understanding agreeably to the constitution and laws of the United States."

Why does a judge swear to discharge his duties agreeably to the constitution of the United States, if that constitution forms no rule for his government? If it is closed upon him, and cannot be inspected by him?

If such be the real state of things, this is worse than solemn mockery. To prescribe, or to take this oath, becomes equally a crime.

It is also not entirely unworthy of observation, that in declaring what shall be the supreme law of the land, the constitution itself is first mentioned; and not the laws of the United States generally, but those only which shall be made in pursuance of the constitution, have that rank.

Thus, the particular phraseology of the Constitution of the United States confirms and strengthens the principle, supposed to be essential to all written constitutions, that a law repugnant to the constitution is void; and that courts, as well as other departments, are bound by that instrument.

The rule must be discharged.[f]

"We are under a Constitution, but the Constitution is what the judges say it is."

—Charles Evans Hughes,
Speech, 1907.

Comments and Questions

Further Historical Context

CHARLES WARREN, 1 *The Supreme Court in United States History*, 232, 242–43 (1922): "Contemporary writings make it very clear that the Republicans attacked the decision, not so much because it sustained the power of the Court to determine the validity of Congressional legislation, as because it enounced the doctrine that the Court might issue mandamus to a Cabinet official who was acting by direction of the President. In other words, Jefferson's antagonism to Marshall and the Court at that time was due more to his resentment at the alleged invasion of his Executive prerogative than to any so-called 'judicial usurpation' of the field of Congressional authority. [It] seems plain [that Marshall might] have construed the language of the section of the Judiciary Act [to escape the necessity] to pass upon its constitutionality. Marshall naturally felt that in view of the recent attacks on judicial power it was important to have the great principle firmly established, and undoubtedly he welcomed the opportunity of fixing the precedent in a case in which his action would necessitate a decision in favor of his political opponents."

MORRIS COHEN, *The Faith of a Liberal* 178–80 (1946) (written in 1938): "The section of [the] Act of 1789 which Marshall declared unconstitutional had been drawn up by Ellsworth, his predecessor as Chief Justice, and by others who a short time before had been the very members of the constitutional convention that had drafted its judicial provisions. It was signed by George Washington who had presided over the deliberations of that Convention. Fourteen years later, John Marshall by implication accused his predecessor on the bench, the members of Congress such as James Madison, the Father of the Constitution, and President Washington, of either not understanding the Constitution (which some of them had drawn up), or else wilfully disregarding it. [To] a secular historian, it is obvious that John Marshall was motivated by the fear of impeachment if he granted the mandamus or dared to declare the Republican Judiciary Repeal Act of 1802 unconstitutional. Having thus refused aid to his fellow Federalists ousted from offices created for them by a 'lame duck' congress, he resorted to a line of sophistical dicta to get even with his political enemy, as indeed he did also in the *Aaron Burr* case. In his letter to his colleague Chase, Marshall offered to abandon judicial supremacy in the interpretation of the Constitution in return for security against impeachment." [g]

---

f. Six days later, the Circuit Court Act Repeal Law was held to be constitutional. *Stuart v. Laird,* 5 U.S. (1 Cranch) 299, 2 L.Ed. 115 (1803). After *Marbury,* the Court did not hold an act of Congress unconstitutional until *Dred Scott v. Sandford,* 60 U.S. (19 How.) 393, 15 L.Ed. 691 (1857).

g. In 1804, the House impeached Justice Chase due, inter alia, to what the Republicans believed to be Chase's partisan Federalist ac-

Text of the Constitution

Is the doctrine of "judicial review," which gives the Court power to declare an act of a coordinate branch of the government unconstitutional, compelled because a contrary rule "would subvert the very foundation of all written constitutions"?

WILLIAM VAN ALSTYNE, *A Critical Guide to Marbury v. Madison,* 1969 Duke L.J. 1, 17: "[E]ven in Marshall's time (and to a great extent today), a number of nations maintained written constitutions and yet gave national legislative acts the full force of positive law without providing any constitutional check to guarantee the compatibility of those acts with their constitutions [e.g.,] France, Switzerland, and Belgium (and to some extent Great Britain where Magna Carta and other written instruments are roughly described as the constitution but where acts of Parliament are not reviewable)." [h]

Does the "judges' oath" provision (Art. VI, cl. 3) furnish the necessary textual support for the doctrine of judicial review?

JUSTICE GIBSON, dissenting in *Eakin v. Raub,* 12 S. & R. 330 (Pa.1825): [i] "The oath to support the Constitution is not peculiar to the judges, but is taken indiscriminately by every officer of the government, and is designed rather as a test of the political principles of the man, than to bind the officer in the discharge of his duty: otherwise, it were difficult to determine, what operation it is to have in the case of a recorder of deeds, for instance, who, in execution of his office, has nothing to do with the Constitution. But granting it to relate to the official conduct of the judge, as well as every other officer, and not to his political principles, still, it must be understood in reference to supporting the Constitution, only as far as that may be involved in his official duty; and consequently, if his official duty does not comprehend an inquiry into the authority of the legislature, neither does his oath. * * *

"But do not the judges do a positive act in violation of the Constitution, when they give effect to an unconstitutional law? Not if the law has been passed according to the forms established in the Constitution. The fallacy of the question is, in supposing that the judiciary adopts the acts of the legislature as its own; whereas, the enactment of a law and the interpretation of it are not concurrent acts, and as the judiciary is not required to concur in the enactment, neither is it in the breach of the constitution which may be the consequence of the enactment; the fault is imputable to the legislature, and on it the responsibility exclusively rests."

tivities and statements both on and off the Bench. After a lengthy trial in the Senate, the constitutional majority to convict was not obtained. It was generally assumed that, if the effort had been successful, Marshall and other Federalist judges would suffer the same fate. See generally 1 Warren, supra, ch. 6. For a further account of *Marbury,* see 3 Beveridge, *The Life of John Marshall* 105–156 (1919).

h. Consider Cohen, supra, at 185: "Nor is it necessary to consider in detail the argument that this power is necessary for a federal system. The Swiss constitution is a perfect example of a federal system without the judiciary having such power. The late Justice Holmes said, 'I do not think the United States would come to an end if we lost our power to declare an Act of Congress void. I do think the Union would be imperiled if we could not make that declaration as to the laws of the several states.' "

For discussion of the modern growth of various forms of judicial review in other countries—Australia, Austria, Canada, Cyprus, Denmark, Germany, India, Italy, Japan, Norway, Sweden, Turkey, Yugoslavia—see Cappelletti, *Judicial Review in Comparative Perspective,* 58 Calif.L.Rev. 1017 (1970).

i. This opinion is widely regarded as the most effective answer of the era to Marshall's reasoning supporting judicial review.

What of Art. III, § 2, cl. 1, extending "the judicial Power" "to *all* cases
* * * arising under this Constitution"? See Bickel, *The Least Dangerous Branch* 5–6 (1962).

What of the supremacy clause (Art. VI, cl. 2)? Compare Wechsler, *Toward Neutral Principles of Constitutional Law,* 73 Harv.L.Rev. 1, 3–5 (1959), with Van Alstyne, supra, at 20–22.[1]

The Court as "Final" Arbiter

THOMAS JEFFERSON, writing in 1804, 8 *The Writings of Thomas Jefferson* 310 (1897): "The Judges, believing the [Sedition Law] constitutional, had a right to pass a sentence of fine and imprisonment; because that power was placed in their hands by the Constitution. But the Executive, believing the law to be unconstitutional, was bound to remit the execution of it; because that power has been confided to him by the Constitution. The instrument meant that its co-ordinate branches should be checks on each other. But the opinion which gives to the Judges the right to decide what laws are constitutional, and what not, not only for themselves in their own sphere of action, but for the Legislative and Executive also in their spheres, would make the Judiciary a despotic branch."

ANDREW JACKSON, veto message in 1832 on act to recharter Bank of United States (the constitutionality of which had earlier been upheld by the Court), 2 Richardson, *Messages and Papers of the Presidents* 576, 581–82 (1900): "It is as much the duty of the House of Representatives, of the Senate, and of the President to decide upon the constitutionality of any bill or resolution which may be presented to them for passage or approval as it is of the supreme judges when it may be brought before them for judicial decision. The opinion of the judges has no more authority over Congress than the opinion of Congress has over the judges, and on that point the President is independent of both. The authority of the Supreme Court must not, therefore, be permitted to control the Congress or the Executive when acting in their legislative capacities, but to have only such influence as the force of their reasoning may deserve."

---

[1]. Much has been written on the matter of "historical original intent" in respect to judicial review—generally examining pre-Convention judicial precedents in England and the colonies, statements of the framers both within and outside the Constitutional Convention (see especially Alexander Hamilton in Nos. 78 and 80 of *The Federalist* (1788)), and debate during the ratification period—arriving at conflicting conclusions. See, e.g., Beard, *The Supreme Court and the Constitution* (1912); Berger, *Congress v. The Supreme Court* (1969); Boudin, *Government by Judiciary* (1932); Corwin, *The Doctrine of Judicial Review* (1914); Crosskey, *Politics and the Constitution in the History of the United States* (1953); Goebel, *History of the Supreme Court of the United States: Antecedents and Beginnings to 1801* (1971); Haines, *The American Doctrine of Judicial Supremacy* (2d ed. 1932); Nelson, *Changing Conceptions of Judicial Review: The*

Evolution of Constitutional Theory in the States, 1790–1860, 120 U.Pa.L.Rev. 1166 (1972). Warren, *Congress, the Constitution, and the Supreme Court* (1925). For brief discussion see Levy, *Judicial Review, History, and Democracy: An Introduction,* in Judicial Review and the Supreme Court 1–12 (1967); Kernochan, *On Constitutionalism and the Antecedents of Judicial Review,* in Dowling & Gunther, Constitutional Law 19–31 (7th ed. 1965). For the view that "strict intentionalism" is not a "tenable approach to constitutional decisionmaking," see Brest, *The Misconceived Quest for the Original Understanding,* 60 B.U.L.Rev. 204 (1980).

For review of the broader historical setting, see Bailyn, *The Ideological Origins of the American Revolution* (1967); Wood, *The Creation of the American Republic, 1776–1787* (1969).

ABRAHAM LINCOLN, inaugural address in 1861, 2 Richardson, supra, at 5, 9–10: "I do not forget the position assumed by some that constitutional questions are to be decided by the Supreme Court, nor do I deny that such decisions must be binding in any case upon the parties to a suit as to the object of that suit, while they are also entitled to very high respect and consideration in all parallel cases by all other departments of the Government. And while it is obviously possible that such decision may be erroneous in any given case, still the evil effect following it, being limited to that particular case, with the chance that it may be overruled and never become a precedent for other cases, can better be borne than could the evils of a different practice. At the same time, the candid citizen must confess that if the policy of the Government upon vital questions affecting the whole people is to be irrevocably fixed by decisions of the Supreme Court, the instant they are made in ordinary litigation between parties in personal actions the people will have ceased to be their own rulers, having to that extent practically resigned their Government into the hands of that eminent tribunal. Nor is there in this view any assault upon the court or the judges. It is a duty from which they may not shrink to decide cases properly brought before them, and it is no fault of theirs if others seek to turn their decisions to political purposes."

Are these views inconsistent with *Marbury?* Does *Marbury* decide anything more than that *"the Court may refuse to give effect to an act of Congress where the act pertains to the judicial power itself"?* Van Alstyne, supra, at 34. Than that the Court claimed the power of judicial review "only in the defensive sense of safeguarding the Court's original jurisdiction from congressional enlargement"? Strong, *Judicial Review: A Tri-Dimensional Concept of Administrative-Constitutional Law,* 69 W.Va.L.Rev. 111, 249 (1967).

LEARNED HAND, *The Bill of Rights* 11–15 (1958): "[L]et us try to imagine what would have been the result if the power [of judicial review] did not exist. There were two alternatives, each prohibitive, I submit. One was that the decision of the first 'Department' before which an issue arose should be conclusive whenever it arose later. That doctrine, coupled with its conceded power over the purse, would have made Congress substantially omnipotent, for by far the greater number of issues that could arise would depend upon its prior action.
* * *

"As Hamilton intimated, every legislator is under constant pressure from groups of constituents whom it does not satisfy to say, 'Although I think what you want is right and that you ought to have it, I cannot bring myself to believe that it is within my constitutional powers.' Such scruples are not convincing to those whose interests are at stake; and the voters at large will not usually care enough about preserving 'the balance of the Constitution' to offset the votes of those whose interests will be disappointed. [But] the second alternative would have been even worse, for under it each 'Department' would have been free to decide constitutional issues as it thought right, regardless of any earlier decision of the others. Thus it would have been the President's privilege, and indeed his duty, to execute only those statutes that seemed to him to be constitutional, regardless even of a decision of the Supreme Court. The courts would have entered such judgments as seemed to them consonant with the Constitution; but neither the President, nor Congress, would have been bound to enforce them if he or it disagreed, and without their help the judgments would have been waste paper.

"For centuries it has been an accepted canon in interpretation of documents to interpolate into the text such provisions, though not expressed, as are essential to prevent the defeat of the venture at hand; and this applies with especial force to the interpretation of constitutions, which, since they are designed to cover a great multitude of necessarily unforeseen occasions, must be cast in general language, unless they are constantly amended. If so, it was altogether in keeping with established practice for the Supreme Court to assume an authority to keep the states, Congress, and the President within their prescribed powers. Otherwise the government could not proceed as planned; and indeed would almost certainly have foundered, as in fact it almost did over that very issue.

"However, since this power is not a logical deduction from the structure of the Constitution but only a practical condition upon its successful operation, it need not be exercised whenever a court sees, or thinks that it sees, an invasion of the Constitution."

May a Congressman vote against a bill because he believes it to be unconstitutional even though the Court has held to the contrary? May the President veto such a bill on this ground? If the Court has upheld the constitutionality of a federal criminal statute, may a subsequent President grant pardons to all persons convicted under it (see Art. II, § 2, cl. 1)?

COOPER v. AARON (1958), set forth more fully, p. 853 infra: "Article VI of the Constitution makes the Constitution the 'supreme Law of the Land.' In 1803, [*Marbury*] declared the basic principle that the federal judiciary is supreme in the exposition of the law of the Constitution, and that principle has ever since been respected by this Court and the Country as a permanent and indispensable feature of our constitutional system. [Every] state legislator and executive and judicial officer is solemnly committed by oath taken pursuant to Art. VI, ¶ 3 'to support this Constitution.' * * * Chief Justice Marshall spoke for a unanimous Court in saying that: 'if the legislatures of the several states may, at will, annul the judgments of the courts of the United States, and destroy the rights acquired under those judgments, the constitution itself becomes a solemn mockery * * *.' *United States v. Peters*, 5 Cranch 115, 136. A Governor who asserts a power to nullify a federal court order is similarly restrained." [m]

Cooper involved the refusal of Arkansas officials to abide by federal court decrees requiring school desegregation. In contrast, if the Court *upholds* the constitutionality of a state law, may that state's supreme court subsequently rule that the state law violates the Constitution? Would the state court's ruling "annul the judgment" of the Supreme Court? See Tribe, *American Constitutional Law* 27–33 (1978).

Comparative Competence and "Expertise"

HART & WECHSLER'S *The Federal Courts and the Federal System* 82 (2d ed. 1973): "Congress and the President can obviously contribute to the sound interpretation of the Constitution. But are they, or can they be, so organized [as] to be able, without aid from the courts, to build up a body of coherent and intelligible constitutional principle, and to carry public conviction that these

---

m. For criticism and defense of this "judicial supremacy" analysis, see Farber, *The Su-* *preme Court and the Rule of Law: Cooper v. Aaron Revisited*, 1982 U.Ill.L.Rev. 387.

principles are being observed? In respect of experience and temperament of personnel? Of procedure for decision? Of means of recording grounds of decision? Of opportunity for close examination of particular questions?"

CLIFTON McCLESKEY, *Judicial Review in a Democracy: A Dissenting Opinion,* 3 Hous.L.Rev. 354, 360–61 (1966): "Can we really be sure that it was Marshall or Taney rather than Clay or Webster who did the better job of articulating values? Which of the Civil War Justices excelled Lincoln in voicing the hopes and goals of the republic? Are we to believe that Woodrow Wilson had a poorer grasp of the principles of American government than the Supreme Court Justices of his era? Which Justice in the 1920's gave better tongue than Norris or LaFollette to the American dream? Which Justice before or after the shift of 1937 was better than Franklin Roosevelt at communicating our ideals? [Further,] it appears reasonably clear that a background of political experience for Supreme Court Justices is the prevalent pattern. This not only casts doubt on the thesis that there is something peculiar to the judicial process that brings out these noble traits, but also suggests that even without judicial review the nation would have had the benefit of the wisdom and insights of these persons."

MARTIN SHAPIRO, *Freedom of Speech: The Supreme Court and Judicial Review* 29–30 (1966): "Congressional statutes [are] the product of a series of marginal adjustments and compromises among various semi-independent groups. It is nearly impossible to interject black and white questions like constitutionality into the early stages of such a process. And when the process has been so nearly completed that a bill reaches the final debate and voting stage, so many commitments have already been made that the interjection of a constitutional issue would not only be futile but in many instances appear to be a traitorous repudiation of pre-established agreements. It is, therefore, highly probable that considerations of constitutionality could only take their place among the multitude of other considerations which acquire various weights at various stages of the negotiations depending on how important they appear to any given legislative power holder."

The Standard of Review

JAMES THAYER, *The Origin and Scope of the American Doctrine of Constitutional Law,* 7 Harv.L.Rev. 129, 143–44 (1893): "[The Court] can only disregard the Act [of the legislature] when those who have the right to make laws have not merely made a mistake, but have made a very clear one,—so clear that it is not open to rational question. That is the standard of duty to which the courts bring legislative Acts; that is the test which they apply,—not merely their own judgment as to constitutionality, but their conclusion as to what judgment is permissible to another department which the constitution has charged with the duty of making it. This rule recognizes that, having regard to the great, complex, ever-unfolding exigencies of government, much which will seem unconstitutional to one man, or body of men, may reasonably not seem so to another; that the constitution often admits of different interpretations; that there is often a range of choice and judgment; that in such cases the constitution does not impose upon the legislature any one specific opinion, but leaves open this range of choice; and that whatever choice is rational is constitutional."

ALEXANDER BICKEL, supra, at 37–41: " 'Taken seriously,' Felix S. Cohen wrote in a later day, 'this conception makes of our courts lunacy commissions sitting in judgment upon the mental capacity of legislators and, occasionally, of judicial brethren.' That is cleverly put, but the principle of the constitutional rationality of legislation is nevertheless meaningful [in respect to certain types of issues]. The rule of the clear mistake aims at accommodation with the theory of representative democracy. It proceeds from the realization, in the words of Mr. Justice Frankfurter, that courts 'are not representative bodies. They are not designed to be a good reflex of a democratic society.' Therefore the rule is meant to limit the area of judicial policymaking, keeping the judicial function distinct from the legislative and thus capable of being justified. It is a conceptual tool for distilling out of a typical public issue one element of principle, as distinguished from a number of allowable choices that may be made on grounds of expediency. But the rule does not lead by indirection to a total abdication of the power of judicial review. * * *

"The relevant distinction [on certain types of questions] is not between rationality and lunacy but between rationality and will, or, perhaps it is meaningful to say, between rationality and uncontrolled emotion. It is not lunatic to take the position that the public service must be kept clear of any taint of disloyalty, and that to exclude from it even possibly innocent persons is to take absolutely no chances. That is a sane and a zealous attitude. But it is not rational; it is not even thoughtful. It is governed by a heightened emotion—anxiety, in this case—and it will not pass the test of a calm judgment resting on allowable inferences drawn from common human experience. Such a judgment will vary with what is known of relevant human experience. It must be an informed judgment, and it may change as it becomes better informed. But it will discriminate between arbitrary guesses and calculations of probability. In any event, this is the Court's independent judgment to make, and unless one takes a cynical view of the human capacity to reason, it is a possible judgment and one that will answer to descriptions of 'correct' or 'erroneous.' "

Whatever the deference owed by the Court to Congress (or the President), is the same deference due federal administrative officials? State legislatures? City councils? Local police officers?

Judicial Review and Democracy

ALEXANDER BICKEL, supra, at 16–20: "The root difficulty is that judicial review is a counter-majoritarian force in our system. [W]hen the Supreme Court declares unconstitutional a legislative act or the action of an elected executive, it thwarts the will of representatives of the actual people of the here and now; it exercises control, not in behalf of the prevailing majority, but against it. That [is] the reason the charge can be made that judicial review is undemocratic.

"Most assuredly, no democracy operates by taking continuous nose counts on the broad range of daily governmental activities. * * * Nevertheless, although democracy does not mean constant reconsideration of decisions once made, it does mean that a representative majority has the power to accomplish a reversal. This power is of the essence, and no less so because it is often merely held in reserve.

"It is true, of course, that the process of reflecting the will of a popular majority in the legislature is deflected by various inequalities of representation and by all sorts of institutional habits and characteristics, which perhaps tend most often in favor of inertia.[p]　Yet, impurities and imperfections, if such they be, in one part of the system are no argument for total departure from the desired norm in another part.　*　*　*

"No doubt ['interest' or 'pressure groups'] operate forcefully on the electoral process, and no doubt they seek and gain access to and an effective share in the legislative and executive decisional process.　Perhaps they constitute also, in some measure, an impurity or imperfection.　But no one has claimed that they have been able to capture the governmental process except by combining in some fashion, and thus capturing or constituting (are not the two verbs synonymous?) a majority.　They often tend themselves to be majoritarian in composition and to be subject to broader majoritarian influences.　And the price of what they sell or buy in the legislature is determined in the biennial or quadrennial electoral marketplace.　*　*　* Judicial review works counter to this characteristic.

"It therefore does not follow from the complex nature of a democratic system that, because admirals and generals and the members, say, of the Federal Reserve Board or of this or that administrative agency are not electorally responsible, judges who exercise the power of judicial review need not be responsible either, and in neither case is there a serious conflict with democratic theory.　For admirals and generals and the like are most often responsible to officials who are themselves elected and through whom the line runs directly to a majority.　What is more significant, the policies they make are or should be interstitial or technical only and are reversible by legislative majorities *　*　*—a fact of great consequence.　Nor will it do to liken judicial review to the general lawmaking function of judges.　In the latter aspect, judges are indeed something like administrative officials, for their decisions are also reversible by any legislative majority—and not infrequently they are reversed.[q]　Judicial review, however, is the power to apply and construe the Constitution in matters of the greatest moment, against the wishes of a legislative majority, which is, in turn, powerless to affect the judicial decision."

JESSE CHOPER, *The Supreme Court and the Political Branches: Democratic Theory and Practice*, 122 U.Pa.L.Rev. 810, 830–32 (1974): "In the main, the effect of judicial review in ruling legislation unconstitutional is to nullify the finished product of the lawmaking process.　It is the very rare Supreme Court decision on constitutionality that affirmatively mandates the undertaking of government action.　To make the point in another way, when the Supreme

---

p. For a forceful position ."that there can be no automatic and blanket equation of Congress or the Executive branch with the voice of the people," see Shapiro, supra, at 17–25. Consider Krislov, *The Supreme Court and Political Freedom* 20 (1968): "If one analyzes the actual rules of behavior in the so-called democratic units of government, we find that they also have mixed aspects, with the possibility— sometimes the actuality—of minority control. The power of the Rules Committee, the filibuster, and the Senate are obvious shortcomings; [the] operational consequences of seniority, and the population base of districts likely to maintain continuity in representation are more veiled aspects." See also Kommers, *Professor Kurland, The Supreme Court, and Political Science,* 15 J.Pub.L. 230 (1966).

q. Compare Bishin, *Judicial Review in Democratic Theory,* 50 So.Cal.L.Rev. 1099, 1110 (1977): "Closer examination suggests [that] not all of the decisions that such officeholders make can, in fact or theory, be reversed by majoritarian action. [It] must be remembered [that] Congress—especially the Senate—is so structured that representatives of only a minority of the people can prevent the passage of legislation which would overturn prior decisions *　*　*. Wherever the position of such a minority coincides with the [judge's or administrative officer's] position, therefore, the Constitution gives the principle of reversibility no effect at all."

Court finds legislative acts unconstitutional it holds invalid only those enactments that have survived the many hurdles fixed between incipient proposals and standing law.

"The significance of this [is] that most of the antimajoritarian elements that have been found in the American legislative process [are] negative ones. They work to *prevent* the translation of popular wishes into governing rules rather than to *produce* laws that are contrary to majority sentiment. [S]enators representing only fifteen percent of the population may hold sway in the upper house; but their real impact (as is obviously the case with the filibuster as well) is to halt ultimate action rather than facilitate it. For the enactment of law also requires the concurrence of the lower [house]. Furthermore, within each legislative chamber, the ability of the committees and their chairmen and minority members—and frequently of the lobbies and other interest groups as well—to circumvent the majority will of the assembly is most saliently manifested in obstructing the process rather than in making laws. The more formidable task usually is not to stall or defeat a proposal but to organize the requisite support among the dispersed powers so as to form a coalition for its passage. * * *

"Thus, although exceptions exist, '[a] distinguishing feature of our system, perhaps impelled by heritage of sectional division and heterogeneity, is that our governmental structure, institutional habits, and political parties with their internal factional divisions, have combined to produce a system in which major programs and major new directions cannot be undertaken unless supported by a fairly broad popular consensus. This normally has been far broader than 51 percent and often bipartisan as well.' [Consequently,] when the Supreme Court, itself without conventional political responsibility, says 'thou shalt not' to acts of Congress, it usually cuts sharply against the grain of majority rule. The relatively few laws that finally overcome the congressional obstacle course generally illustrate the national political branches operating at their majoritarian best while the process of judicial review depicts that element of the Court's work and that exertion of federal authority with the most brittle democratic roots.[59] "

J. SKELLY WRIGHT, *The Role of the Supreme Court in a Democratic Society,* 54 Corn.L.Rev. 1, 11 (1968): "This argument for judicial restraint not only overplays the Court's deviancy but also overstresses its immunity from democratic processes. To begin with, the Justices are appointed by the President, the one elected official whose constituency is the nation as a whole. On the average a new appointment is made every twenty-two months.[40] And, as Justice Frankfurter reminds us, 'Judges are men, not disembodied spirits' who are blind to the political reality among them. Moreover, if the Justices are not themselves sufficiently attuned to the times, Congress can bring reality home to them through its power over the Court's appellate jurisdiction. Indeed, if the Court is too far out of touch with the people, the Congress and the executive can annul its directives simply by refusing to execute them, or the people can do so

---

59. Although no detailed examination of the legislative systems in the states and their political subdivisions has been ventured here, the same conclusion appears to have substantially similar merit in respect to the Court's overturning the laws they produce.

40. See Dahl, *Decision-Making in a Democracy: The Supreme Court as a National Policy Maker,* 6 J.Pub.L. 279, 284–86 (1957).

by constitutional amendment. In sum, although the Court is not politically responsible, it is likely to be politically responsive." [r]

LEONARD LEVY, *Judicial Review, History, and Democracy: An Introduction,* in Judicial Review and the Supreme Court 1, 12 (1967): "Judicial review would never have flourished had the people been opposed to it. They have opposed only its exercise in particular cases, but not the power itself. They have the sovereign power to abolish it outright or hamstring it by constitutional amendment. The President and Congress could bring the Court to heel even by ordinary legislation. The Court's membership, size, funds, staff, rules of procedure, and enforcement agencies are subject to the control of the 'political' branches. Judicial review, in fact, exists by the tacit consent of the governed."

EUGENE ROSTOW, *The Democratic Character of Judicial Review,* 66 Harv. L.Rev. 193, 199–209 (1963): "It is error to insist that no society is democratic unless it has a government of unlimited powers, and that no government is democratic unless its legislature has unlimited powers. Constitutional review by an independent judiciary is a tool of proven use in the American quest for an open society of widely dispersed powers. In a vast country, of mixed population, with widely different regional problems, such an organization of society is the surest base for the hopes of democracy.

"[The] price of judicial independence, [Judge Hand] concludes, is that the judges 'should not have the last word in those basic conflicts of "right and wrong—between whose endless jar justice resides." You may ask what then will become of the fundamental principles of equity and fair play which our constitutions enshrine; and whether I seriously believe that unsupported they will serve merely as counsels of moderation. I do not [know]; but this much I think I do know—that a society so riven that the spirit of moderation is gone, no court *can* save; that a society where that spirit flourishes no court *need* save; that in a society which evades its responsibility by thrusting upon the courts the nurture of that spirit, that spirit in the end will perish.' [s]

"This gloomy and apocalyptic view is a triumph of logic over life. It reflects the dark shadows thrown upon the judiciary by the Court-packing fight of 1937. Judge Hand is preoccupied with a syllogism. The people and the Congress have the naked power to destroy the independence of the courts. Therefore the courts

---

r. See also Deutsch, *Neutrality, Legitimacy, and the Supreme Court: Some Intersections Between Law and Political Science,* 20 Stan.L. Rev. 169 (1968).

s. Hand, *The Contribution of an Independent Judiciary to Civilization,* in The Spirit of Liberty 164 (Dilliard 3d ed. 1960); this chapter originally published in 1942.

Further, consider Thayer, *John Marshall* 106 (1904): "[T]he exercise of [judicial review], even when unavoidable, is always attended with a serious evil, namely, that the correction of legislative mistakes comes from the outside, and the people thus lose the political experience, and the moral education and stimulus that come from fighting the question out in the ordinary way, and correcting their own errors. [The] tendency of a common and easy resort to this great function now lamentably too common, is to dwarf the political capacity of the people, and to deaden its sense of moral responsibility." Compare Franklin Roosevelt, message to Congress in 1935, *4 The Public Papers and Addresses of Franklin D. Roosevelt* 297–98 (1938): "Manifestly, no one is in a position to give assurance that the proposed act will withstand constitutional tests. [But] the situation is so urgent and the benefits of the legislation so evident that all doubts should be resolved in favor of the bill, leaving to the courts, in an orderly fashion, the ultimate question of constitutionality. * * * I hope your committee will not permit doubts as to constitutionality, however reasonable, to block the suggested legislation."

must avoid arousing the sleeping lion by venturing to construe the broad and sweeping clauses of the Constitution which would 'demand the appraisal and balancing of human values which there are no scales to weigh.' Presumably he would include in this catalogue of forbidden issues problems of freedom of speech, the separation of church and state, and the limits, if any, to which 'the capable, the shrewd or the strong' should 'be allowed to exploit their powers.' Are we to read the last phrase as encompassing the right of habeas corpus, the central civil liberty and the most basic of all protections against the authority of the state? Would it deny the possibility of constitutional review by the courts for laws denying the vote to Negroes, for searches and seizures without warrant, for bills of attainder or test oaths?

"In the first place, the judicial decisions which brought on the storm in 1937 were not in this area at all. They concerned the division of power between the states and the nation,[21] and between Congress and the President [22]—issues which Judge Hand regards as inescapably within the province of the courts and not likely in any event to have 'seismic consequences.' Further, it is important to reiterate the obvious but sometimes forgotten fact that the historic conception of the Supreme Court's duties, however challenged in 1937, prevailed in that struggle. * * *

"The possibility of judicial emasculation by way of popular reaction against constitutional review by the courts has not in fact materialized in more than a century and a half of American experience. When the Court has differed from the Congress and the President in its notions of constitutional [law] time has unfailingly cured the conflicts, such as they were. * * *

"It may of course be true that no court can save a society bent on ruin. But American society is not bent on ruin. It is a body deeply committed in its majorities to the principles of the Constitution and both willing and anxious to form its policy and programs in a constitutional way. Americans are, however, profoundly troubled by fears—intense and real fears, raised by unprecedented dangers and by the conduct of perilous tasks unprecedented in the history of the government. It is difficult for legislators confronting the menace of the world communist movement to reject any proposals which purport to attack communism or to protect the community from it. This does not mean, however, that the President and the Congress would refuse to obey the Supreme Court's rulings on the constitutionality of some of the means with which they have [chosen]. Ruin can come to a society not only from the furious resentments of a crisis. It can be brought about in imperceptible stages by gradually accepting, one after another, immoral solutions for particular problems. The 'relocation camps' conducted during World War II [for] Americans of Japanese descent [t] are the precedent for the proposal that concentration camps be established for citizens suspected of believing in revolutionary ideas. * * *

"Nor, more broadly, is it true as a matter of experience that a vigorous lead from the Supreme Court inhibits or weakens popular responsibility in the same area. The process of forming public opinion in the United States is a continuous one with many participants—Congress, the President, the press, political parties, scholars, pressure groups, and so on. The discussion of problems and the declaration of broad principles by the courts is a vital element in the community

21. See, e.g., *United States v. Butler*, 297 U.S. 1, 56 S.Ct. 312, 80 L.Ed. 477 (1936).

22. See, e.g., *A.L.A. Schechter Poultry Corp. v. United States*, 295 U.S. 495, 55 S.Ct. 837, 79 L.Ed. 1570 (1935). See also *Youngs-* *town Sheet & Tube Co. v. Sawyer*, 343 U.S. 579, 72 S.Ct. 863, 96 L.Ed. 1153 (1952).

t. See *Korematsu v. United States*, set forth, p. 816 infra.

experience through which American policy is made. The Supreme Court is, among other things, an educational body, and the Justices are inevitably teachers in a vital national seminar." [u]

ALEXANDER BICKEL, supra, at 24–26, 258: "It is a premise we deduce not merely from the fact of a written constitution but from the history of the race, and ultimately as a moral judgment of the good society, that government should serve not only what we conceive from time to time to be our immediate material needs but also certain enduring values. This in part is what is meant by government under law. * * *

"Men in all walks of public life are able occasionally to perceive this second aspect of public questions. Sometimes they are also able to base their decisions on it; that is one of the things we like to call acting on principle. Often they do not do so, however, particularly when they sit in legislative assemblies. There, when the pressure for immediate results is strong enough and emotions ride high enough, men will ordinarily prefer to act on expediency rather than take the long view. * * * Judges have, or should have, the leisure, the training, and the insulation to follow the ways of the scholar in pursuing the ends of government. This is crucial in sorting out the enduring values of a society * * *. Another advantage that courts have is that questions of principle never carry the same aspect for them as they did for the legislature or the executive. Statutes, after all, deal typically with abstract or dimly foreseen problems. The courts are concerned with the flesh and blood of an actual case. This tends to modify, perhaps to lengthen, everyone's view. [v] * * *

u. See also Bishin, supra, at 1136: "Of course, the courts will often be wrong. But their decisions are not irrevocable; in the meantime, their errors nevertheless contribute to understanding. In a sense, the courts become the focus of the trial and error by which the society determines what balance of individual and majority rule it desires. If judicial review did not exist, perhaps a relatively small number of academicians and moralists would involve themselves in the problem of freedom. But it is unlikely that the society generally would engage itself in the process of solving that problem. If this is so, then it is quite arguable that the trial and error process which detractors of judicial review invoke against the institution is one of the strongest arguments for giving courts the power to adjudicate the constitutionality of majority action."

Compare Levy, supra, at 33–34, 36: "[O]ne may say, paraphrasing Rostow in reverse, that it is true as a matter of experience that a vigorous lead from the Supreme Court inhibits or weakens popular responsibility in the areas of liberty, equality, and justice. Bearing in mind that the Court is an institution of enormous prestige whose declaration of principles teaches and leads the nation in the making of public policy, one cannot doubt the pernicious, highly undemocratic influence of the series of decisions in which the Court crippled and voided most of the comprehensive program for protecting the civil rights of Negroes after the Civil War. These decisions paralyzed or supplanted legislative and community action, created bigotry, and played a crucial role in destroying public opinion that favored meeting the challenge of the Negro problem * * *.

"The historian must take the long view of the matter, recalling that the justices on circuit duty enforced the Sedition Act of 1798; that the Fugitive Slave Acts were sustained but the Missouri Compromise and Personal Liberty Laws were invalidated; that the Fourteenth Amendment was turned into a nightmare of injustice for all but corporations; that Congressional statutes to combat the evils of yellow-dog contracts, child labor, and subminimal wages were held unconstitutional; [that] Debs' conviction was sustained under the Espionage Act of 1917 by a unanimous Court in an opinion by Holmes and that President Harding, of all people, pardoned Debs; and so on, ad nauseum."

v. [But, "in dealing with problems of great magnitude and pervasive ramifications, problems with complex roots and unpredictably multiplying complex offshoots," "the judicial process is"] "too remote from conditions, and deals, case by case, with too narrow a slice of reality. It is not accessible to all the varied interests that are in play in any decision of great consequence. It is, very properly, independent. It is passive. It has difficulty controlling the stages by which it approaches a problem. It rushes forward too fast, or it lags;

"Their insulation and the marvelous mystery of time give courts the capacity to appeal to men's better natures, to call forth their aspirations, which may have been forgotten in the moment's hue and cry. This is what Justice Stone called the opportunity for 'the sober second thought.' * * *

"[After the school desegregation decisions, the] southern leaders understood and acted upon an essential truth, which we do not often have occasion to observe * * *. The Supreme Court's law, the southern leaders realized, could not in our system prevail—not merely in the very long run, but within the decade—if it ran counter to deeply felt popular needs or convictions, or even if it was opposed by a determined and substantial minority and received with indifference by the rest of the country. This, in the end, is how and why judicial review is consistent with the theory and practice of political democracy. This is why the Supreme Court is a court of last resort presumptively only."

CLIFTON McCLESKEY, supra, at 357–59, 365: "It is sometimes said that judicial review is compatible with democracy because it cannot really block popular action. [I]t is argued that eventually the will of the people always prevails in spite of any resistance by the judiciary. * * * We have known at least since David Hume that all governments—even the dictatorial ones—rest 'ultimately' on the consent of the governed, but the democratic theory [denies] the propriety of resorting to such a subterfuge—democracy is an attempt to provide popular control here and now, not ultimately. We must therefore reject this justification of judicial review for the same reasons that we would condemn a proposal to schedule national elections only once every quarter century.

"Some proponents of this view, recognizing that judicially-imposed delay is a fact that cannot be denied, have attempted to convert that liability into an asset. Such frustration of popular will, they argue, is itself advantageous to a democracy, for it allows an appeal to be taken from the people drunk to the people sober. [The] most intriguing implication, however, is that someone somewhere must oversee and protect the people from themselves. Is this not the classic line of anti-democrats from time immemorial? [w] * * *

"Now, it may be entirely proper for the Supreme Court to lecture us on the principles of American government, and to have them make whatever use they can of the 'marvelous mystery of time' to formulate appeals to our better nature, for such is the privilege of college professors and of clergymen as well. There is, however, this crucial difference: The strictures emanating from the lectern are not legally enforceable, whereas judges do have the power to compel that 'sober

---

its pace hardly ever seems just right. For all these reasons, it is, in a vast, complex, changeable society, a most unsuitable instrument for the formation of policy." Bickel, *The Supreme Court and the Idea of Progress* 175 (1970).

Compare Barron, *The Ambiguity of Judicial Review: A Response to Professor Bickel,* 1970 Duke L.J. 591, 595, 604: "The difficulty with this approach is that it enormously decreases the role of the Supreme Court in American life. Bickel is really making a radical request: if the great political cases are incapable of principled resolution, then the Court ought to decline decision of such cases. But it is the great political cases which have made the Supreme Court, historically and now, a

branch of government. [The] judiciary is designed to have occasional political uses. [The] enormous resiliency, the constant possibilities for modest advance and subtle retreat, makes the Court one of the most sensitive sources for social change in the United States."

w. Consider Cohen, supra, at 192: "[I]t is curious to note that it is those Americans who are at heart distrustful of democracy who speak of the courts as standing between us and dictatorship and yet their arguments are precisely those which the adherents of Hitler and Mussolini use against the frailty of democratically representative or elective government."

second thought.' No matter how desirable that may be, it still is not democrat-ic."

————

JESSE CHOPER, supra, at 848–58: "The most encompassing argument to 'democratize' the Court's power as ultimate constitutional arbiter has been that judicial review [has] been institutionally adopted by a continuing consensus of American society as an integral rule of the system; that, thus, judicial review operates by majority will, with the consent of the governed.

"Proper evaluation of [this] contention necessitates review of the efficacy and legitimacy of both the general force of public reaction and the particular controls available to elected and appointed officials in responding to the Court's constitutional pronouncements. * * *

"*Constitutional Amendment*—[This] has been employed but four times in our history to overcome the Court's decisions; [120] such meager utilization evidences the difficulty involved. More importantly, there is no more plainly designated antimajoritarian obstacle in our governmental system [than] the constitutionally prescribed amendment procedures. * * *

"*Political Control Over Composition*—[The] authority to impeach sitting Justices, the gravest aspect of this power, may be readily discredited as a factor that enhances the Court's democratic image. [Because] of its severe conse-quences, prodigious energy is needed to put the impeachment machinery in motion. And the critical fact [is] that the two-thirds Senate vote required for conviction strips it of any majoritarian pretenses.

"The authority to appoint new Justices [depends] upon natural fortuities beyond the reach of even the most indomitable President. It may well take several successive presidential terms—[and] cooperative Senates—to change the judicial philosophy of a majority of the bench. Moreover, it requires a keen executive prediction of appointees' present and future views on known and unknown issues, a clairvoyance that our history, even the most recent, has proven to fall far short of being wholly reliable. * * * Manipulation through use of the appointment power further requires the assumption that the new appointees will disregard precedent, [a] quantity that no President can buy with real assurance. * * *

"[Reversing particular constitutional paths the Court has taken has] often been sought by the political departments through use of the power of increasing the number of Justices, coupled with the making of new appointments. [The] most dramatic example concerned the *Legal Tender Cases*. President Grant, on the day that *Hepburn v. Griswold* [124] was decided, nominated two new Justices following a resignation and an increase in the Court's membership from eight to nine; in just a little more than a year, the *Hepburn* decision was overruled [125] because of the votes of the new appointees.

"This last occasion, over a century ago, appears, however, to be the only clear victory achieved by the political branches in exercising the authority to enlarge. [The technique's] most celebrated day occurred when President Frank-

---

120. U.S.Const. amend. XI, adopted 1795—overruling *Chisholm v. Georgia*, p. 1233 infra. U.S.Const. amend. XIV, § 1, adopted 1868—overruling *Scott v. Sandford;* U.S.Const. amend. XVI, adopted 1913—overruling *Pollock v. Farmers' Loan & Trust Co.*, 157 U.S. 429, 15 S.Ct. 673, 39 L.Ed. 759 (1895); U.S.

Const. amend. XXVI, adopted 1971—overruling *Oregon v. Mitchell*, [Ch. 8, Sec. 2].

124. 75 U.S. (8 Wall.) 603 (1870) (5–3 decision).

125. *Legal Tender Cases*, 79 U.S. (12 Wall.) 457 (1871) (5–4 decision).

lin Roosevelt, just elected by an overwhelming popular majority and possessed of legendary influence over Congress, nonetheless saw his Court-packing plan defeated, despite the extremely disreputable position of the Court for having thwarted both executive *and* legislative efforts to combat a great national crisis. [T]he facts are that, even under this extraordinary combination of auspicious circumstances, the Court's traditional independence of the political will survived, and that during subsequent periods of momentous judicial impact and unpopularity the political departments' power over the Court's composition, far from being seriously considered a consequential weapon, has been effectively discredited.

"Political Curtailment of Appellate Jurisdiction—In the past quarter century, the device most frequently threatened by the political branches for use against the Court has been Congress' power, specified in article three, to make 'Exceptions' to and 'Regulations' of the Court's appellate jurisdiction. [But] the theoretical underpinnings for a wide legislative power [are] hardly as firm as the literal phrasing of article three [suggests.] A variety of interpretations of the delegated authority have been offered by prominent constitutional scholars, none of which results in any consequential political check on judicial review.[x] * * *

"But even if this legislative ability to retaliate against the judiciary rested on a firm theoretical foundation, its pragmatic potential as a majoritarian restraint on judicial review would be severely limited. As Herbert Wechsler has lucidly revealed, since the political branches realize that the use of federal courts is essential to administer federal [law,] Congress cannot, as a practical matter, withdraw all federal jurisdiction, even if it were authorized to do so constitutionally. If Congress instead were to choose only to curtail the Supreme Court's appellate jurisdiction, it could attempt to rest final resolution of all constitutional questions with the eleven federal courts of appeals. Although this may be preferable to leaving it to the highest courts of the fifty states—the result of abolishing *all* federal jurisdiction or of restricting the adjudication of some or all constitutional questions to the state courts—the potential for national inconsistency in constitutional interpretation would still be unbearable. Alternatively, the tradition of stare decisis could lead these other courts to follow the very Supreme Court decisions that sparked the congressional counteraction. 'The jurisdictional withdrawal thus might work to freeze the very doctrines that had prompted its enactment, placing an intolerable moral burden on the lower courts. [The] federal system needs federal courts and the judicial institution needs an organ of supreme authority'.[136]

"This convincing line of argument helps explain why on only one occasion in American history—and that one of questionable significance in effect, and ultimately determined to be incomplete in scope [137]—has hostility prompted the political branches (Congress overriding a presidential veto) to utilize article three to diminish the Court's jurisdiction, though many such efforts have been made. * * *

"Conclusion—[The] most entrenched popular barriers to the rule of the Court are both more discrete and less formalized than those already mentioned. [If] either of the political branches opposes a judicial doctrine that requires

x. But see Black, *Decision According to Law* 17–19, 37–39 (1981); Perry, *The Constitution, the Courts and Human Rights* 128–38 (1982). For full discussion, see Sec. 3 infra.

136. Wechsler, *The Courts and the Constitution*, 65 Colum.L.Rev. 1001, 1006–07 (1965).

137. See *Ex parte Yerger*, 75 U.S. (8 Wall.) 85 (1869) (demonstrating that the act of Congress upheld in *Ex parte McCardle*, 74 U.S. (7 Wall.) 506 (1869), closed only one of the existing avenues of appeal to the Supreme Court) [discussed in Sec. 3 infra].

support for its effectuation—and many do, in varying degrees—the legislative or executive opportunity is clear. The presidential response may range from Abraham Lincoln's outright refusal to obey Chief Justice Taney's order in *Ex parte Merryman*,[141] to Andrew Jackson's alleged edict that he would leave John Marshall to enforce his own decision in the *Cherokee Indian Cases*,[142] to Dwight Eisenhower's seeming ambivalence immediately following *Brown v. Board of Education.* The congressional power of the purse may also be employed to enfeeble the Court's will, as is illustrated by the recent repeated efforts to deny funds for school busing to achieve racial desegregation. [Furthermore], lesser officials (including the judges) at all levels of government, and, ultimately, the people themselves, may move grudgingly and hesitatingly in adhering to the Court's mandate, or they may simply refuse to obey, with varying degrees of blatancy.[y]   *   *   *

"Neither this reasoning nor its supporting data, however, lead to the conclusion that judicial review is compatible with majoritarian democracy as traditionally conceived or practiced. Many eventful and controversial constitutional decisions—especially those involving use of the judicial system itself (as in the field of criminal procedure)—although subject to being undercut by resentful administrative officials and lower courts, do not depend for their complete effectiveness on the cooperation of other public agencies or of the people in general. Further, it must be conceded that it is only those Supreme Court mandates perceived as exceedingly flagrant that are capable of generating the intensity of opposition necessary to prevent enforcement. Nor is popular resistance universal in impact, either geographically or temporally; even if certain rulings eventually fall into disuse because of opposition by the requisite majority will, their force will be felt by a segment of the people for some time and often by many of the people for a long time. And impelling the Court to bend or draw up in developing doctrine falls far short of causing the Court to break or retreat.

"At the surface, the antimajoritarian features of all three federal departments bear a certain similarity. The leeway afforded the political branches by the people and the tenacity of popular feeling needed for radical change through election revolt are not absolutely different from the independence granted the judiciary by the Constitution and the assiduous efforts required to affect the Court and its decisions through the restraints ultimately retained by the citizenry and their elected representatives. But in both democratic theory and practice, the distinction between control of the legislature and executive on one side and control of the judiciary on the other, if not one of kind, is one of substantial degree."

Varying Standards of Review

UNITED STATES v. CAROLENE PRODUCTS CO., 304 U.S. 144, 152, n. 4, 58 S.Ct. 778, 783, 82 L.Ed. 1234, 1241 (1938): "There may be narrower scope for operation of the presumption of constitutionality when legislation appears on its face to be within a specific prohibition of the Constitution, such as those of the first ten amendments, which are deemed equally specific when held to be embraced within the Fourteenth.

---

141. 17 F.Cas. 144 (C.C.D.Md.1861).

142. President Jackson's exact words in response to the decision [were] said to be: "John Marshall has made his decision. Now let him enforce it."

y. For elaboration, see Choper, *Judicial Review and the National Political Process* ch. 3—"The Fragile Character of Judicial Review: The Problems of Popular Noncompliance and Exhaustible Institutional Capital"—(1980).

"It is unnecessary to consider now whether legislation which restricts those political processes which can ordinarily be expected to bring about repeal of undesirable legislation, is to be subjected to more exacting judicial scrutiny under the general prohibitions of the Fourteenth Amendment than are most other types of legislation. * * *

"Nor need we enquire whether similar considerations enter into the review of statutes directed at particular religious, or national, or racial minorities: whether prejudice against discrete and insular minorities may be a special condition, which tends seriously to curtail the operation of those political processes ordinarily to be relied upon to protect minorities, and which may call for a correspondingly more searching judicial inquiry." [z]

JESSE CHOPER, *On the Warren Court and Judicial Review,* 17 Cath.U.L. Rev. 20, 38–41 (1967): "Granting that the Supreme Court is a 'deviant institution in the American democracy,' it must also be recognized that [the] Constitution itself is similarly antimajoritarian or, if you will, antidemocratic, at least in a limited fashion. Its provisions set the boundaries of each federal department's power vis-à-vis that of the others, of federal power vis-à-vis that of the states, of governmental power vis-à-vis that of the individual. The Constitution commands that these powers may not be exceeded by simple majority will. * * *

"The perplexing questions here are: *When* is the Constitution violated? *What body* of government should decide? *Marbury* assigned the task to the Court. [But] by what standard should the Court decide?

"In exploring this ultimately crucial problem, it seems to me that we must distinguish between two different types of constitutional issues. One is whether authority over the subject matter of federal action has been 'delegated' by the Constitution to the national government or whether it has been 'reserved to the States.' * * *

"The other general issue that arises [154] is whether a particular exercise of governmental power, national or state, infringes individual rights guaranteed by the Constitution. [O]ne need only refer, as examples, to the original Constitution's prohibitions of bills of attainder and ex post facto laws, to the first eight amendments (popularly known as the Bill of Rights), to the fourteenth amendment's guarantees of due process and equal protection.

"It seems to me that if the constitutional issue is one only of states' rights, the role of the Supreme Court [should] be severely limited. The justification for *judicial* review in this instance, for the final constitutional word to be spoken by a 'deviant institution' in a democracy, is weak. The states, whose constitutional rights are allegedly being assaulted, are well represented in the councils of national government [and] the political process may generally be depended upon to produce a fair judgment. If a majority of the states' representatives (and I believe this is a wholly accurate description of members of Congress) determine that federal power has not been exceeded, then the Court should overturn the decision, if at all, only if it is so clearly in error as not to be 'open to rational question.' [158]

---

z. The impact of this footnote is further discussed at many points in the materials, especially Chs. 3, 4 and 5.

154. The matter of division of power among the federal departments is beyond the specific scope of the discussion.

158. Some limited degree of judicial supervision in this area may be justified if the confinement of federal power to that specified in the Constitution is seen as having a purpose beyond the protection of "states' rights" * * *.

"But if the issue is one of alleged governmental infringement of individual rights protected by the Constitution, it seems to me that the Court's role should be quite different. These constitutional guarantees—such as the freedoms of speech and religion, the constitutional rights of those accused of crime, the right to be free from certain racial discrimination—are generally rights of 'politically impotent minorities.' By definition, the processes of democracy bode poorly for the security of such rights. [Thus], the task of guarding these constitutionally prescribed liberties sensibly falls upon a body that is not politically responsible, that is not beholden to the grace of excited majoritarianism—[the] Supreme Court. Herein lies the great justification for the power of judicial review, the wisdom of *Marbury*. In this area, the Court, if it is properly to fulfill its place in American democratic society, must act more forcefully—perhaps 'by creating a presumption against the validity of the contested action,' perhaps 'by more closely scrutinizing the methods employed and the objectives to which they lead.' "

———

J. SKELLY WRIGHT, *Professor Bickel, The Scholarly Tradition, and the Supreme Court,* 84 Harv.L.Rev. 769, 787–89 (1971): "Professor Bickel [*The Supreme Court and the Idea of Progress* 37 (1970)] appears to believe that reliance on the political process for protection of most fundamental rights and liberties is somehow inherent in democratic theory. [He contends] that in fact minorities play an important though indirect role in most governmental decisions, may be presumed to consent to them, and have substantial opportunity to defend their interests without the help of the courts. No minority willing to wheel and deal with other minorities, he says, need despair of eventually vindicating its rights. [But his "empirical assertion" is] highly doubtful. Perhaps its basic defect is the fact that power is not distributed equally among the various groups in our society. Bickel explicitly recognizes that the formation of majorities at election time is but one part of our political system. At least equally important is the trading and pressuring that goes on all the rest of the time. The Professor would have us believe that this is just fine: those groups with the most 'intense' interests will be the most active in the process, and it is proper that the more 'intense' interests be more richly rewarded. This is nonsense. The big winners in the pluralistic system are the highly organized, wealthy, and motivated groups skilled in the art of insider politics. They have the resources to trade for other benefits, and the resources that it takes to press their claims successfully. Perhaps the interest of a great corporation in a tax break is more 'intense' than that of a political minority in its first amendment rights—that is, if intensity is defined by how conscious of their interests they are, how articulate and persistent they are in presenting them, and how much political muscle they bring to bear. Intensity, so defined, however, is largely an attribute of the already powerful elite. Unorganized, poor, unskilled minorities

[Consider Henkin, *Voice of a Modern Federalism,* in Felix Frankfurter the Judge 68, 71 (Mendelson ed. 1964): "To Justice Frankfurter, in fact, federalism in the United States has been a guarantee of freedom. Like the horizontal separation of powers, the vertical distribution between state and nation was designed, and has served, to frustrate possible tyrannies of centralization. 'Time has not lessened the concern of the Founders in devising a federal system which would likewise be a safeguard against arbitrary government.' He invokes 'the principle of diffusion of power not as a matter of doctrinaire localism but as a promoter of democracy.' "]

simply do not have the sort of 'intense' interests in their rights which the pluralistic system regularly rewards."

ROBERT BORK, *Neutral Principles and Some First Amendment Problems,* 47 Ind.L.J. 1, 2–3 (1971): "[T]he model of government embodied in the structure of the Constitution [may] for convenience, though perhaps not with total accuracy, [be called] 'Madisonian.'

"A Madisonian system is not completedly democratic, if by 'democratic' we mean completely majoritarian. It assumes that in wide areas of life majorities are entitled to rule for no better reason than that they are majorities. [The] model has also a counter-majoritarian premise, however, for it assumes there are some areas of life a majority should not control. [These] are areas properly left to individual freedom, and coercion by the majority in these aspects of life is tyranny.

" * * * Minority tyranny occurs if the majority is prevented from ruling where its power is legitimate. Yet, quite obviously, neither the majority nor the minority can be trusted to define the freedom of the other. This dilemma is resolved in constitutional theory, and in popular understanding, by the Supreme Court's power to define both majority and minority freedom through the interpretation of the Constitution. Society consents to be ruled undemocratically within defined areas by certain enduring principles believed to be stated in, and placed beyond the reach of majorities by, the Constitution.

"But this resolution of the dilemma imposes severe requirements upon the Court. For it follows that the Court's power is legitimate only if it has, and can demonstrate in reasoned opinions that it has, a valid theory, derived from the Constitution, of the respective spheres of majority and minority freedom. If it does not have such a theory but merely imposes its own value choices, or worse if it pretends to have a theory but actually follows its own predilections, the Court violates the postulates of the Madisonian model that alone justifies its power. It then necessarily abets the tyranny either of the majority or of the minority."

Some Further Observations

LOUIS JAFFE, *Impromptu Remarks,* 76 Harv.L.Rev. 1111–12 (1963): "There is no area in which criticism at its most intense is more appropriate [than] the area of constitutional adjudication. There will be and there should be popular response to the Supreme Court's decision; not just the 'informed' criticism of law professors but the deep-felt, emotion-laden, unsophisticated reaction of the laity. This is so because more than any court in the modern world the Supreme Court 'makes policy,' and is at the same time so little subject to formal democratic control. * * * Violently expressed hostility to a decision may indeed increase the difficulty of enforcing it, [but once] granting that public opinion is intrinsic to a democratic system its operation cannot be cabined, cribbed, and confined to formal legal paths. We are, of course, deeply shocked where it is not the private citizen but the public official under oath to uphold the law who leads in flouting it. But great political decisions such as desegregation and reapportionment *do* involve major confrontations of political power and the form in which such decisions become viable is inevitably a consequence of the whole political process, a process which involves a great variety and gradation of lawmaking phenomena. It is precisely to conserve its power and prestige in those cases in which it cannot do otherwise that the Supreme Court should be made aware that each and every bold policy decision will bring it into the political arena." [c]

CHARLES BLACK, *Structure and Relationship in Constitutional Law* 74–76 (1969): "[T]here is nothing in our entire governmental structure which has a more leak-proof claim to legitimacy than the function of the courts in reviewing state acts for federal constitutionality. [I]t seems to me Congress could have provided for this even without an Article III, simply by creating a court and endowing it with the power to perform this necessary and proper function. Insofar, then, as legitimacy in origin is relevant to judicial or public attitude toward the judicial work, the Court ought to feel no slightest embarrassment about its work of reviewing state acts for their federal constitutionality. It seems very clear, moreover, that all present-day political considerations strongly impel toward the same conclusion. In policing the actions of the states for their conformity to federal constitutional guarantees, the Court represents the whole nation, and therefore the whole nation's interest in seeing those guarantees prevail, in their spirit and in their entirety. The Court is in all practical effect the delegate of Congress to do this work.

"[V]irtually all intense political trouble about the Court's role in the last three decades concerns its functioning in the [role] whose legitimacy is not so much as fairly debatable. [T]he Supreme Court in our times is a dangerously controversial institution charged with the duty of bringing the states into line with national law, and [is] it not plain that what is chiefly objected to is not the Court as such, but the fact of being brought into line?"

MARTIN v. HUNTER'S LESSEE, 14 U.S. (1 Wheat.) 304, 4 L.Ed. 97 (1816), came from the Court of Appeals of Virginia, which had refused to obey the mandate of the U.S. Supreme Court, "requiring the judgment rendered in this very cause [at an earlier term] to be carried into due execution." The Court, per STORY, J. (Marshall, C.J., not sitting), held that the federal appellate power "does extend to cases pending in the state courts; and that the 25th section of the judiciary act, which authorizes the exercise of [the instant] jurisdiction is supported by the letter and spirit of the constitution":

"The third article of the constitution is that which must principally attract our attention. [A]ppellate jurisdiction is given by the constitution to the supreme court, in all cases [within 'the judicial power of the United States'] where it has not original [jurisdiction. What] is there to restrain its exercise over state tribunals, in the enumerated cases? [If] the judicial power extends to the case, it will be in vain to search in the letter of the constitution for any qualification as to the tribunal where it depends. [Suppose,] an indictment for a crime, in a state court, and the defendant should allege in his defence, that the crime was created by an ex post facto act of the state, must not the state court [have] a right to pronounce on the validity and sufficiency of the defence? [It] was foreseen, that in the exercise of their ordinary jurisdiction, state courts would incidentally take cognisance of cases arising under the constitution, the laws and

---

c. See also Wellington, *The Nature of Judicial Review*, 91 Yale L.J. 486, 519 (1982): "[I]ncreased political activity over Supreme Court decisions does not constitute disrespect for law. Our law must be based on consent. It is everyone's obligation to insist that all branches of government, including the courts, remain true to this central understanding. Peaceful resistance is part of the minorities' arsenal of weapons against the majority. It is a standard political weapon of minorities and the majority against the Court."

treaties of the United States. Yet, to all these cases, the judicial power, by the very terms of the constitution, is to extend. It cannot extend, by original jurisdiction, if that was already rightfully and exclusively attached in the state courts, which (as has been already shown) may occur; it must, therefore, extend by appellate jurisdiction, or not at all. It would seem to follow, that the appellate power of the United States must, in such cases, extend to state [tribunals].

"It has been argued, that such an appellate jurisdiction over state courts is inconsistent with the genius of our governments, and the spirit of the constitution. That the latter was never designed to act upon state sovereignties, but only upon the people, and that if the power exists it will materially impair the sovereignty of the states, and the independence of their courts. [But the Constitution] is crowded with provisions which restrain or annul the sovereignty of the states, in some of the highest branches of their prerogatives. The tenth section of the first article contains a long list of disabilities and prohibitions imposed upon the states. * * *

"Nor can such a right be deemed to impair the independence of state judges. It is assuming the very ground in controversy, to assert that they possess an absolute independence of the United States. In respect to the powers granted to the United States, they are not independent; they are expressly bound to obedience, by the letter of the constitution * * *. [A]dmitting that the judges of the state courts are, and always will be, of as much learning, integrity and wisdom, as those of the courts of the United States (which we very cheerfully admit), it does not aid the argument. It is manifest, that the constitution has proceeded upon a theory of its own, and given or withheld powers according to the judgment of the American people, by whom it was adopted. We can only construe its powers, and cannot inquire into the policy or principles which induced the grant of them. The constitution has presumed (whether rightly or wrongly, we do not inquire), that state attachments, state prejudices, state jealousies, and state interests, might sometimes obstruct, or control, or be supposed to obstruct or control, the regular administration of justice. * * *

"This is not all. A motive of another kind, perfectly compatible with the most sincere respect for state tribunals, might induce the grant of appellate power over their decisions. * * * Judges of equal learning and integrity, in different states, might differently interpret the statute, or a treaty of the United States, or even the constitution itself: if there were no revising authority to control these jarring and discordant judgments, and harmonize them into uniformity, the laws, the treaties and the constitution of the United States would be different, in different states, and might, perhaps, never have precisely the same construction, obligation or efficiency, in any two states. The public mischiefs that would attend such a state of things would be truly deplorable."

JOHNSON, J., concurred, observing "that the court disavows all intention to decide on the right to issue compulsory process to the state courts; thus leaving us, in my opinion, where the constitution and laws place us—supreme over persons and cases, so far as our judicial powers extend, but not asserting any compulsory control over the state tribunals. In this view, I acquiesce in their opinion, but not altogether in the reasoning * * *."

Notes and Questions

1. *Was the judgment executed?* Charles Warren reports that the Court "decided to avoid the chance of further friction" with the Virginia Court of

Appeals "and accordingly, instead of issuing a second mandate to that Court, it issued its process directly to the District Court [in] which the suit had been originally instituted," 1 Warren, supra, at 450. See also Dodd, *Chief Justice Marshall and Virginia 1813–21*, 12 Am.Hist.Rev. 776, 779 (1907), claiming that the United States marshal was eventually ordered to execute the judgment of the Supreme Court. But William Crosskey insists that execution of judgment was neither issued nor required. Under the Virginia practice, he contends, the proceeding under which the case was brought "served much the same purpose in settling points of law in dispute in land-title controversies, as does a modern action for a declaratory judgment," 2 Crosskey, supra, at 786. Moreover, he adds, "upon the peculiar facts of the case, execution of the judgment would have been a completely vain proceeding; for Hunter could at once have brought a successful action to recover possession again, based on the compromise. There was not a word in the Supreme Court's decision that forbade it." Id. at 806 n.[d]

2. COHENS v. VIRGINIA, 19 U.S. (6 Wheat.) 264, 5 L.Ed. 257 (1821)— which sustained the Court's appellate jurisdiction under § 25 of the Judiciary Act to review state criminal proceedings, and is generally viewed as reaffirming and "supplementing" *Martin*, see 2 Warren, supra, at 10—has stronger historical links with *McCulloch v. Maryland*, 17 U.S. (4 Wheat.) 316, 4 L.Ed. 579 (1819), see 4 Beveridge, *The Life of John Marshall* 343 (1919).

Appellants were found guilty in a Virginia court of selling lottery tickets in violation of state law. Their defense was that the lottery was organized by the City of Washington, under a congressional statute authorizing the lottery. On appeal to the Supreme Court, they were met with the contentions that the Court had no jurisdiction to review a state criminal case and, in any event, Congress had no power to permit the sale of lottery tickets in a state which prohibited such sale. On the jurisdictional point, Virginia argued that (1) if when the state is a party the Supreme Court has original jurisdiction, this grant excludes appellate jurisdiction; (2) federal courts cannot take original jurisdiction over criminal cases, since that rightfully belongs to the courts of the state whose laws have been violated; (3) consequently, the Supreme Court has no jurisdiction at all. As in *Marbury*, MARSHALL, C.J., used the occasion to express a broad view of the Court's powers, but decided the case on a narrow ground in favor of the Jeffersonians—the federal statute authorizing a lottery had no effect outside the City of Washington.

The case was decided at a time when the state autonomy and states' rights generally were being boldly proclaimed. Two years earlier, most southern and western states had vehemently denounced the decision in *McCulloch v. Maryland*, invalidating a state tax on the Bank of the United States. Indeed, in disregard of *McCulloch* and in defiance of a federal circuit court injunction, the state auditor of Ohio had enforced his state's tax on the Bank by entering its vaults, seizing whatever specie and notes he could find, and conveying them to the state treasurer. See 1 Warren, supra, at 514–30. And only a year before *Cohens*, in the hot debate which finally resulted in the Missouri Compromise, "constant fears were expressed by Southern statesmen lest Marshall's broad

---

d. For post-*Martin* instances of state court resistance to Supreme Court orders and various efforts to secure compliance see Murphy, *Lower Court Checks on Supreme Court Power,* 53 Am.Pol.Sci.Rev. 1017 (1959); Warren, *Federal and State Court Interference,* 43 Harv.L. Rev. 345 (1930); Beatty, *State Court Evasion of United States Supreme Court Mandates During the Last Decade of the Warren Court,* 6 Val.L.Rev. 260 (1972); Notes, 67 Harv.L.Rev. 1251 (1954), 56 Yale L.J. 574 (1947). On the theory of "interposition," see Note, *Interposition vs. Judicial Power—A Study of Ultimate Authority in Constitutional Questions,* 1 Race Rel.L.Rep. 465 (1956).

views of the 'necessary and proper' clause of the Constitution might support Congressional interference with the States on the subject of slavery," 2 Warren, supra, at 2–3. "The final settlement" of the existence and powers of the Bank of the United States and the extension of slavery in the new states "were felt to depend largely upon the future trend of the Supreme Court," id. at 4.

In the course of his "immortal Nationalist address," 4 Beveridge, supra, at 343, Marshall said: "When we consider [the] nature of our constitution; the subordination of the state governments to that constitution; the great purpose for which jurisdiction over all cases arising under the constitution and laws of the United States, is confided to the judicial department; are we at liberty to insert in this general grant, an exception of those cases in which a state may be a party? Will the spirit of the constitution justify this attempt to control its words? We think it will not. We think a case arising under the constitution or laws of the United States, is cognizable in the Courts of the Union, whoever may be the parties to that case. * * *

"In many states, the judges are dependent for office and for salary on the will of the legislature. [When] we observe the importance which that constitution attaches to the independence of judges, we are the less inclined to suppose, that it can have intended to leave these constitutional questions to tribunals where this independence may not exist * * *.

"[A] constitution is framed for ages to come, and is designed to approach immortality, as nearly as human institutions can approach it. Its course cannot always be tranquil. It is exposed to storms and tempests, and its framers must be unwise statesmen indeed, if they have not provided it, so far as its nature will permit, with the means of self-preservation from the perils it may be destined to encounter. No government ought to be so defective in its organization, as not to contain within itself, the means of securing the execution of its own laws against other dangers than those which occur every day. Courts of justice are the means most usually employed; and it is reasonable to expect, that a government should repose on its own courts, rather than on others."

SECTION 2. POLITICAL QUESTIONS

Does the principle of judicial review comprehend the Court's acting as "final arbiter" on *all* constitutional questions presented by a case properly within its jurisdiction? Or are some constitutional issues inappropriate for judicial resolution and thus "nonjusticiable"?

BAKER v. CARR

369 U.S. 186, 82 S.Ct. 691, 7 L.Ed.2d 663 (1962).

MR. JUSTICE BRENNAN delivered the opinion of the Court.

[Appellants sought a federal declaratory judgment that the apportionment of the Tennessee General Assembly violated fourteenth amendment equal protection "by virtue of the debasement of their votes." They alleged that, although the state constitution allocated representation on a population basis, no reapportionment law had passed since 1901. They further sought an injunction against any further elections under the 1901 scheme and] until the General Assembly enacts a valid reapportionment, the District Court should either decree a reapportionment by mathematical application of the Tennessee constitutional formulae to the most recent Federal Census figures, or direct the appellees to conduct legislative elections, primary and general, at large. * * *

[W]e hold today only (a) that the court possessed jurisdiction of the subject matter; (b) that a justiciable cause of action is stated upon which appellants would be entitled to appropriate relief; and (c) [that] the appellants have standing to challenge the Tennessee apportionment statutes. Beyond noting that we have no cause at this stage to doubt the District Court will be able to fashion relief if violations of constitutional rights are found, it is improper now to consider what remedy would be most appropriate if appellants prevail at the trial.

JURISDICTION OF THE SUBJECT MATTER

The District Court was uncertain whether our cases withholding federal judicial relief rested upon a lack of federal jurisdiction or upon the inappropriateness of the subject matter for judicial consideration—what we have designated "nonjusticiability." The distinction between the two grounds is significant. In the instance of nonjusticiability, consideration of the cause is not wholly and immediately foreclosed; rather, the Court's inquiry necessarily proceeds to the point of deciding whether the duty asserted can be judicially identified and its breach judicially determined, and whether protection for the right asserted can be judicially molded. In the instance of lack of jurisdiction the cause either does not "arise under" the Federal Constitution, laws or treaties (or fall within one of the other enumerated categories of Art. III, § 2), or is not a "case or controversy" within the meaning of that section; [a] or the cause is not one described by any jurisdictional statute. Our conclusion that this cause presents no nonjusticiable "political question" settles the only possible doubt that it is a case or controversy. Under the present heading of "Jurisdiction of the Subject Matter" we hold only that the matter set forth in the complaint does arise under the Constitution and is within [a statute conferring federal court jurisdiction].

An unbroken line of our precedents sustains the federal courts' jurisdiction of the subject matter of federal constitutional claims of this nature. [Unlike] many other cases in this field which have assumed without discussion that there was jurisdiction, all three opinions filed in *Colegrove v. Green*, 328 U.S. 549, 66 S.Ct. 1198, 90 L.Ed. 1432 (1946), discussed the question. Two of the opinions expressing the views of four of the Justices, a majority, flatly held that there was jurisdiction of that subject matter.[b] * * *

---

a. This topic is considered in Ch. 13, Sec. 1.

b. *Colegrove* affirmed dismissal of a suit by voters in Illinois congressional districts, that had much larger populations than others, to enjoin the forthcoming election on federal constitutional and statutory grounds. Frankfurter, J., joined by Reed and Burton, JJ., held that the applicable congressional apportionment statute did not require equality of population in districts. He also felt that the case should be "dismissed for want of equity" because the issue was "of a peculiarly political nature and therefore not meet for judicial determination." The result of judicial interference might be elections-at-large—"a mode that defies the direction of Congress for selection by districts * * *. In the exercise of its power to judge the qualifications of its own members, the House may reject a delegation of Representatives-at-large. Article I, § 5, Cl. 1." "[T]his controversy concerns matters that bring courts into immediate and active rela-

tions with party contests. * * * Courts ought not to enter this political thicket." Art. I, § 4 of the Constitution confers "upon Congress exclusive authority to secure fair representation by the States in the popular House." If Congress fails, "the remedy ultimately lies with the people."

Rutledge, J., concurred in the result, believing the issues to be "justiciable" but that the case should be dismissed for want of equity due to "the gravity of the constitutional questions" and "the possibilities for collision [with] the political departments of the Government."

Black, J., joined by Douglas and Murphy, JJ., dissented, believing the apportionment to be unconstitutional: "[I]t is a mere 'play on words' to refer to a controversy such as this as 'political' in the sense that courts have nothing to do with protecting and vindicating the right of a voter to cast an effective ballot."

JUSTICIABILITY

[I]t is argued that apportionment cases, whatever the actual wording of the complaint, can involve no federal constitutional right except one resting on the guaranty of a republican form of government, [Art. IV, § 4,] and that complaints based on that clause have been held to present political questions which are nonjusticiable. [But appellants'] claim that they are being denied equal protection is justiciable, and if "discrimination is sufficiently shown, the right to relief under the equal protection clause is not diminished by the fact that the discrimination relates to political rights." *Snowden v. Hughes,* 321 U.S. 1, 11, 64 S.Ct. 397, 402, 88 L.Ed. 497. [B]ecause there appears to be some uncertainty as to why [Guaranty Clause] cases did present political questions, and specifically as to whether this apportionment case is like those cases, we deem it necessary first to consider the contours of the "political question" doctrine.

[I]n the Guaranty Clause cases and in the other "political question" cases, it is the relationship between the judiciary and the coordinate branches of the Federal Government, and not the federal judiciary's relationship to the States, which gives rise to the "political question."

We have said that "In determining whether a question falls within [the political question] category, the appropriateness under our system of government of attributing finality to the action of the political departments and also the lack of satisfactory criteria for a judicial determination are dominant considerations." *Coleman v. Miller,* 307 U.S. 433, 454–455, 59 S.Ct. 972, 982, 83 L.Ed. 1385. The nonjusticiability of a political question is primarily a function of the separation of powers. Much confusion results from the capacity of the "political question" label to obscure the need for case-by-case inquiry. Deciding whether a matter has in any measure been committed by the Constitution to another branch of government, or whether the action of that branch exceeds whatever authority has been committed, is itself a delicate exercise in constitutional interpretation, and is a responsibility of this Court as ultimate interpreter of the Constitution. To demonstrate this requires no less than to analyze representative cases and to infer from them the analytical threads that make up the political question doctrine. We shall then show that none of those threads catches this case.

Foreign relations: There are sweeping statements to the effect that all questions touching foreign relations are political questions. Not only does resolution of such issues frequently turn on standards that defy judicial application, or involve the exercise of a discretion demonstrably committed to the executive or legislature; but many such questions uniquely demand single-voiced statement of the Government's views. Yet it is error to suppose that every case or controversy which touches foreign relations lies beyond judicial cognizance. Our cases in this field seem invariably to show a discriminating analysis of the particular question posed, in terms of the history of its management by the political branches, of its susceptibility to judicial handling in the light of its nature and posture in the specific case, and of the possible consequences of judicial action.[c] For example, though a court will not ordinarily inquire whether a treaty has been terminated, since on that question "governmental action [must] be regarded as of controlling importance," if there has been no conclusive "governmental action" then a court can construe a treaty and may find it provides the answer. * * *

For *Colegrove's* formal demise, see *Wesberry v. Sanders,* p. 982 infra.

c. See generally Henkin, *Viet-Nam in the Courts of the United States: "Political Questions,"* 63 Am.J.Int'l L. 284 (1969).

Dates of duration of hostilities: [H]ere too analysis reveals isolable reasons for the presence of political questions, underlying this Court's refusal to review the political departments' determination of when or whether a war has ended. Dominant is the need for finality in the political determination, for emergency's nature demands "A prompt and unhesitating obedience," *Martin v. Mott,* 12 Wheat. 19, 30, 6 L.Ed. 537 (calling up of militia). [But] deference rests on reason, not habit. The question in a particular case may not seriously implicate considerations of finality—e.g., a public program of importance (rent control) yet not central to the emergency effort. Further, clearly definable criteria for decision may be available. In such case the political question barrier falls away * * *.

Validity of enactments: [*Coleman*] held that the questions of how long a proposed amendment to the Federal Constitution remained open to ratification, and what effect a prior rejection had on a subsequent ratification, were committed to congressional resolution and involved criteria of decision that necessarily escaped the judicial grasp. Similar considerations apply to the enacting process: "The respect due to coequal and independent departments," and the need for finality and certainty about the status of a statute contribute to judicial reluctance to inquire whether, as passed, it complied with all requisite formalities. *Field v. Clark,* 143 U.S. 649, 672, 676–677, 12 S.Ct. 495, 497, 499, 36 L.Ed. 294. But it is not true that courts will never delve into a legislature's records upon such a quest: If the enrolled statute lacks an effective date, a court will not hesitate to seek it in the legislative journals in order to preserve the enactment. The political question doctrine, a tool for maintenance of governmental order, will not be so applied as to promote only disorder. * * *

It is apparent that several formulations which vary slightly according to the settings in which the questions arise may describe a political question, although each has one or more elements which identify it as essentially a function of the separation of powers. Prominent [is] found a textually demonstrable constitutional commitment of the issue to a coordinate political department; or a lack of judicially discoverable and manageable standards for resolving it; or the impossibility of deciding without an initial policy determination of a kind clearly for nonjudicial discretion; or the impossibility of a court's undertaking independent resolution without expressing lack of the respect due coordinate branches of government; or an unusual need for unquestioning adherence to a political decision already made; or the potentiality of embarrassment from multifarious pronouncements by various departments on one question.

Unless one of these formulations is inextricable from the case at bar, there should be no dismissal for non-justiciability on the ground of a political question's presence. The doctrine of which we treat is one of "political questions," not one of "political cases." The courts cannot reject as "no law suit" a bona fide controversy as to whether some action denominated "political" exceeds constitutional authority. * * *

But it is argued that this case shares the characteristics of decisions that constitute a category not yet considered, cases concerning [Art. IV, § 4]. We shall discover that Guaranty Clause claims involve those elements which define a "political question," and for that reason and no other, they are nonjusticiable. In particular, we shall discover that the nonjusticiability of such claims has nothing to do with their touching upon matters of state governmental organization.

Republican form of government: Luther v. Borden, 7 How. 1, 12 L.Ed. 581, though in form simply an action for damages for trespass was, as Daniel Webster said in opening the argument for the defense, "an unusual case." The defendants, admitting an otherwise tortious breaking and entering, sought to justify their action on the ground that they were agents of the established lawful government of Rhode Island, which State was then under martial law to defend itself from active insurrection; that the plaintiff was engaged in that insurrection; and that they entered under orders to arrest the plaintiff. The case arose "out of the unfortunate political differences which agitated the people of Rhode Island in 1841 and 1842," and which had resulted in a situation wherein two groups laid competing claims to recognition as the lawful government. * * *

Clearly, several factors were thought by the Court in *Luther* to make the question there "political": the commitment to the other branches of the decision as to which is the lawful state government; the unambiguous action by the President, in recognizing the charter government as the lawful authority; the need for finality in the executive's decision; and the lack of criteria by which a court could determine which form of government was republican.

But the only significance that *Luther* could have for our immediate purposes is in its holding that the Guaranty Clause is not a repository of judicially manageable standards which a court could utilize independently in order to identify a State's lawful government. The Court has since refused to resort to the Guaranty Clause—which alone had been invoked for the purpose—as the source of a constitutional standard for invalidating state [or congressional] action. [See] *Pacific States Tel. & T. Co. v. Oregon,* 223 U.S. 118, 32 S.Ct. 224, 56 L.Ed. 377 (claim that initiative and referendum negated republican government held nonjusticiable); *Highland Farms Dairy v. Agnew,* 300 U.S. 608, 57 S.Ct. 549, 81 L.Ed. 835 (claim that delegation to agency of power to control milk prices violated republican government, rejected).

[In] *Georgia v. Stanton,* 6 Wall. 50, 18 L.Ed. 721, the State sought by an original bill to enjoin execution of the Reconstruction Acts, claiming that [the] Acts "Instead of keeping the guaranty against a forcible overthrow of its government by foreign invaders or domestic insurgents [are] destroying that very government by force." Congress had clearly refused to recognize the republican character of the government of the suing State. It seemed to the Court that the only constitutional claim that could be presented was under the Guaranty Clause, and Congress having determined that the effects of the recent hostilities required extraordinary measures to restore governments of a republican form, this Court refused to interfere with Congress' action at the behest of a claimant relying on that very guaranty. * * *

We come, finally, to the ultimate inquiry whether our precedents as to what constitutes a nonjusticiable "political question" bring the case before us under the umbrella of that doctrine. [We find none] of the common characteristics which we have been able to identify * * *. The question here is the consistency of state action with the Federal Constitution. We have no question decided, or to be decided, by a political branch of government coequal with this Court. Nor do we risk embarrassment of our government abroad, or grave disturbance at home if we take issue with Tennessee as to the constitutionality of her action here challenged. Nor need the appellants, in order to succeed in this action, ask the Court to enter upon policy determinations for which judicially manageable standards are lacking. Judicial standards under the Equal Protection Clause are well developed [to determine] that a discrimination reflects *no* policy, but simply arbitrary and capricious action.

This case does, in one sense, involve the allocation of political power within a State, and the appellants might conceivably have added a claim under the Guaranty Clause. [Although it] could not have succeeded it does not follow that appellants may not be heard on the equal protection claim which in fact they tender. * * *

Reversed and remanded. * * *

MR. JUSTICE WHITTAKER did not participate in the decision of this case.

MR. JUSTICE DOUGLAS [who joined the Court's opinion], concurring. * * *

So far as voting rights are concerned, there are large gaps in the Constitution. Yet the right to vote is inherent in the republican form of government * * *.[2] That the States may specify the qualifications for voters is implicit in Article I, Section 2, Clause 1 * * *. It is, however, clear that by reason of the commands of the Constitution there are several qualifications that a State may not require [referring to the fifteenth and nineteenth amendments, as well as equal protection].

It is said that any decision in cases of this kind is beyond the competence of courts. Some make the same point as regards the problem of equal protection in cases involving racial segregation. [The] constitutional guide is often vague, as the decisions under the Due Process and Commerce Clauses show. The problem under the Equal Protection Clause is no more intricate.

There are, of course, some questions beyond judicial competence. Where the performance of a "duty" is left to the discretion and good judgment of an executive officer, the judiciary will not compel the exercise of his discretion one way or the other (*Kentucky v. Dennison*, 24 How. 66, 109, 16 L.Ed. 717), for to do so would be to take over the office.

Where the Constitution assigns a particular function wholly and indivisibly [3] to another department, the federal judiciary does not intervene. None of those cases is relevant here. * * *

MR. JUSTICE CLARK, concurring.

[An] examination of Table I accompanying this opinion conclusively reveals that the apportionment picture in Tennessee is a topsy-turvical of gigantic proportions. This is not to say that some of the disparity cannot be explained, but when the entire table is examined—comparing the voting strength of counties of like population as well as contrasting that of the smaller with the

2. The statements in *Luther* that this guaranty is enforceable only by Congress or the Chief Executive is not maintainable [and are] contrary to [the] modern decisions of the Court that give the full panoply of judicial protection to voting rights. * * *

Moreover, the Court's refusal to examine the legality of the regime of martial law which had been laid upon Rhode Island is indefensible, as Mr. Justice Woodbury maintained in his dissent. * * *

What he wrote was later to become the tradition, as expressed by Chief Justice Hughes in *Sterling v. Constantin,* 287 U.S. 378, 401, 53 S.Ct. 190, 196, 77 L.Ed. 375: "What are the allowable limits of military discretion, and whether or not they have been overstepped in a particular case, are judicial questions."

3. The category of the "political" question is, in my view, narrower than the decided cases indicate. * * *

Georgia v. Stanton involved the application of the Reconstruction Acts to Georgia—laws which destroyed by force the internal regime of that State. [The] question was no more "political" than a host of others we have entertained. See, e.g., *Pennsylvania v. West Virginia,* 262 U.S. 553, 43 S.Ct. 658, 67 L.Ed. 1117; *Youngstown Sheet & Tube Co. v. Sawyer,* 343 U.S. 579, 72 S.Ct. 863, 96 L.Ed. 1153 (1952); *Alabama v. Texas,* 347 U.S. 272, 74 S.Ct. 481, 98 L.Ed. 689.

Today would this Court hold nonjusticiable or "political" a suit to enjoin a Governor who, like Fidel Castro, takes everything into his own hands and suspends all election laws? * * *

larger counties—it leaves but one conclusion, namely that Tennessee's apportionment is a crazy quilt without rational basis. * * *

Although I find the Tennessee apportionment statute offends the Equal Protection Clause,[d] I would not consider intervention by this Court into so delicate a field if there were any other relief available to the people of Tennessee. But the majority of the people of Tennessee have no "practical opportunities for exerting their political weight at the polls" to correct the existing "invidious discrimination." Tennessee has no initiative and referendum. [T]he legislative policy has riveted the present seats in the Assembly to their respective constituencies, and by the votes of their incumbents a reapportionment of any kind is prevented. The people have been rebuffed at the hands of the Assembly; they have tried the constitutional convention route, but since the call must originate in the Assembly, it, too, has been fruitless. They have tried Tennessee courts with the same result,[9] and Governors have fought the tide only to flounder. It is said that there is recourse in Congress and perhaps that may be, but from a practical standpoint this is without substance. To date Congress has never undertaken such a task in any State. * * *

Finally, we must consider if there are any appropriate modes of effective judicial relief. [One] plan might be to start with the existing assembly districts, consolidate some of them, and award the seats thus released to those counties suffering the most egregious discrimination. Other possibilities are present and might be more effective. But the plan here suggested would at least release the stranglehold now on the Assembly and permit it to redistrict itself. * * *

[It] is well for this Court to practice self-restraint and discipline in constitutional adjudication, but never in its history have those principles received sanction where the national rights of so many have been so clearly infringed for so long a time. National respect for the courts is more enhanced through the forthright enforcement of those rights rather than by rendering them nugatory through the interposition of subterfuges. * * *

Mr. Justice Stewart, concurring.

The separate writings of my dissenting and concurring Brothers stray so far from the subject of today's decision as to convey, I think, a distressingly inaccurate impression of what the Court decides. * * * Contrary to the suggestion of my Brother Harlan, the Court does not say or imply that "state legislatures must be so structured as to reflect with approximate equality the voice of every voter" [or] that there is anything in the Federal Constitution "to prevent a State, acting not irrationally, from choosing any electoral legislative structure it thinks best suited to the interests, temper, and customs of its people." * * * My Brother Clark has made a convincing prima facie showing that Tennessee's system of apportionment is in fact utterly arbitrary—without any possible justification in rationality. My Brother Harlan has, with imagination and ingenuity, hypothesized possibly rational bases for Tennessee's system. But the merits of this case are not before us now. * * *

Mr. Justice Frankfurter, whom Mr. Justice Harlan joins, dissenting.

The Court today reverses a uniform course of decision established by a dozen cases [which] reflected the equally uniform course of our political history

---

d. Clark, J., "not being able to muster a court to dispose of the case on the merits," joined the Court's opinion.

9. It is interesting to note that state judges often rest their decisions on the ground that

this Court has precluded adjudication of the federal claim.

regarding the relationship between population and legislative representation—a wholly different matter from denial of the franchise to individuals because of race, color, religion or sex. Such a massive repudiation of the experience of our whole past in asserting destructively novel judicial power demands a detailed analysis of the role of this Court in our constitutional scheme. Disregard of inherent limits in the effective exercise of the Court's "judicial Power" not only presages the futility of judicial intervention in the essentially political conflict of forces by which the relation between population and representation has time out of mind been and now is determined. It may well impair the Court's position as the ultimate organ of "the supreme Law of the Land" in that vast range of legal problems, often strongly entangled in popular feeling, on which this Court must pronounce. The Court's authority—possessed of neither the purse nor the sword—ultimately rests on sustained public confidence in its moral sanction. Such feeling must be nourished by the Court's complete detachment, in fact and in appearance, from political entanglements and by abstention from injecting itself into the clash of political forces in political settlements.

[The claim in this case] is hypothetical and the assumptions [on which it rests] are abstract because the Court does not vouchsafe the lower courts—state and federal—guidelines for formulating specific, definite, wholly unprecedented remedies for the inevitable litigations that today's umbrageous disposition is bound to stimulate in connection with politically motivated reapportionments in so many States. In such a setting, to promulgate jurisdiction in the abstract is meaningless. It is as devoid of reality as "a brooding omnipresence in the sky" for it conveys no intimation what relief, if any, a District Court is capable of affording that would not invite legislatures to play ducks and drakes with the judiciary. [One] of the Court's supporting opinions, as elucidated by commentary, unwittingly affords a disheartening preview of the mathematical quagmire (apart from divers judicially inappropriate and elusive determinants) into which this Court today catapults the lower courts of the country without so much as adumbrating the basis for a legal calculus as a means of extrication. Even assuming the indispensable intellectual disinterestedness on the part of judges in such matters, [t]o charge courts with the task of accommodating the incommensurable factors of policy that underlie these mathematical puzzles is to attribute, however flatteringly, omnicompetence to judges. * * * Considering the gross inequality among legislative electoral units within almost every State, the Court naturally shrinks from asserting that in districting at least substantial equality is a constitutional requirement enforceable by courts [and] implies that geography, economics, urban-rural conflict, and all the other non-legal factors which have throughout our history entered into political districting are to some extent not to be ruled [out]. To some extent—aye, there's the rub. In effect, today's decision empowers the courts of the country to devise what should constitute the proper composition of the legislatures of the fifty States. * * *

We were soothingly told at the bar of this Court that we need not worry about the kind of remedy a court could effectively fashion once the abstract constitutional right to have courts pass on a statewide system of electoral districting is recognized as a matter of judicial rhetoric, because legislatures would heed the Court's admonition. This is not only a euphoric hope. It implies a sorry confession of judicial impotence in place of a frank acknowledgment that there is not under our Constitution a judicial remedy for every political mischief, for every undesirable exercise of legislative power. The Framers carefully and with deliberate forethought refused so to enthrone the judiciary. In this situation, as in others of like nature, appeal for relief does not belong here. Appeal must be to an informed, civically militant electorate. In a democratic society like ours, relief must come through an aroused popular conscience that sears the conscience of the people's representatives. [From] its earliest opinions this Court has consistently recognized a class of controversies which do not lend themselves to judicial standards and judicial remedies. To classify the various instances as "political questions" is rather a form of stating this conclusion * * *.

The Court has been particularly unwilling to intervene in matters concerning the structure and organization of the political institutions of the States. * * *

The cases involving Negro disfranchisement are no exception to the principle of avoiding federal intervention into matters of state government in the absence of an explicit and clear constitutional imperative. For here the controlling command of Supreme Law is plain and unequivocal. * * *

The present case [is], in effect, a Guarantee Clause claim masquerading under a different label. But it cannot make the case more fit for judicial action that appellants invoke the Fourteenth Amendment rather than Art. IV, § 4, where, in fact, the gist of their complaint is the same. * * *

At first blush, this charge of discrimination based on legislative underrepresentation is given the appearance of a more private, less impersonal claim, than the assertion that the frame of government is askew. Appellants appear as representatives of a class that is prejudiced as a class, in contradistinction to the polity in its entirety. However, the discrimination relied on is the deprivation of what appellants conceive to be their proportionate share of political influence. * * * Hardly any distribution of political authority that could be assailed as rendering government nonrepublican would fail similarly to operate to the prejudice of some groups, and to the advantage of others, within the body politic. [T]he real battle over the initiative and referendum, or over a delegation of power to local rather than statewide authority, is the battle between forces whose influence is disparate among the various organs of government to whom power may be given. [What] Tennessee illustrates is an old and still widespread method of representation—representation by local geographical division, only in part respective of population—in preference to others, others, forsooth, more appealing. Appellants contest this choice and seek to make this Court the arbiter of the disagreement. * * * Certainly, "equal protection" is no more secure a foundation for judicial judgment of the permissibility of varying forms of representative government than is "Republican Form." * * *

The notion that representation proportioned to the geographic spread of population is so universally accepted as a necessary element of equality between man and man that it must be taken to be the standard of a political equality preserved by the Fourteenth Amendment—that it is, in appellants' words "the basic principle of representative government"—is, to put it bluntly, not true. However desirable and however desired by some among the great political thinkers and framers of our government, it has never been generally practiced, today or in the past. It was not the English system, it was not the colonial system, it was not the system chosen for the national government by the Constitution, it was not the system exclusively or even predominantly practiced by the States at the time of adoption of the Fourteenth Amendment, it is not predominantly practiced by the States today. Unless judges, the judges of this Court, are to make their private views of political wisdom the measure of the Constitution—views which in all honesty cannot but give the appearance, if not reflect the reality, of involvement with the business of partisan politics so inescapably a part of apportionment controversies—the Fourteenth Amendment [provides] no guide for judicial oversight of the representation problem. * * *

[In] all of the apportionment cases which have come before the Court, a consideration which has been weighty in determining their nonjusticiability has been the difficulty or impossibility of devising effective judicial remedies in this class of case. An injunction restraining a general election unless the legislature reapportions would paralyze the critical centers of a State's political system * * *. A declaration devoid of implied compulsion of injunctive or other relief would be an idle threat. Surely a Federal District Court could not itself remap the State [and] the choice of elections at large as opposed to elections by district, however unequal the districts, is a matter of sweeping political judgment having enormous political implications, the nature and reach of which are certainly beyond the informed understanding of, and capacity for appraisal by, courts.

In Tennessee, moreover, the *McCanless* [case] said, "There is no provision of law for election of our General Assembly by an election at large over the State." 200 Tenn., at 277, 292 S.W.2d, at 42. Thus, a legislature elected at large would not be the legally constituted legislative authority of the State. [A] federal court cannot provide the authority requisite to make a legislature the proper governing body of the State of Tennessee. * * *

Dissenting opinion of MR. JUSTICE HARLAN, whom MR. JUSTICE FRANKFURTER joins.

[I]n my opinion, appellants' allegations [do not] show an infringement by Tennessee of any rights assured by the Fourteenth Amendment. Accordingly, I believe the complaint should have been dismissed for "failure to state a claim upon which relief can be granted." [Thus], we need not reach the issues of "justiciability" or "political question" * * *.

In the last analysis, what lies at the core of this controversy is a difference of opinion as to the function of representative government. It is surely beyond argument that those who have the responsibility for devising a system of representation may permissibly consider that factors other than bare numbers should be taken into account. The existence of the United States Senate is proof enough of that. To consider that we may ignore the Tennessee Legislature's judgment in this instance because that body was the product of an asymmetrical electoral apportionment would in effect be to assume the very conclusion here disputed. Hence we must accept the present form of the Tennessee Legislature as the embodiment of the State's choice, or, more realistically, its compromise, between competing political philosophies. The federal courts have not been empowered by the Equal Protection Clause to judge whether this resolution of the State's internal political conflict is desirable or undesirable, wise or unwise. * * *

The claim that Tennessee's system of apportionment is so unreasonable as to amount to a capricious classification of voting strength stands up no better under dispassionate analysis.[e] * * *

e. In his opinion and in an appendix to it, Harlan, J., challenged Clark, J.'s original formula for determining how many representatives each county presently had. He then demonstrated that no feasible formula "could provide proportionately equal 'total representation' for each of Tennessee's 95 counties," and argued the relevancy and legitimacy of factors other than numbers, e.g., "a proper balance between urban and rural interest," "the size of a county in terms of its total area," "the location within a county of some major industry," "various economic, political, and geographical considerations," and deferring reapportionment "in the interest of stability of government."

The suggestion of my Brother Frankfurter that courts lack standards by which to decide such cases as this, is relevant not only to the question of "justiciability," but also, and perhaps more fundamentally, to the determination whether any cognizable constitutional claim has been asserted in this case. [Those] observers of the Court who see it primarily as the last refuge for the correction of all inequality or injustice, no matter what its nature or source, will no doubt applaud this decision and its break with the past. Those who consider that continuing national respect for the Court's authority depends in large measure upon its wise exercise of self-restraint and discipline in constitutional adjudication, will view the decision with deep concern. * * *[f]

POWELL v. McCORMACK, 395 U.S. 486, 89 S.Ct. 1944, 23 L.Ed.2d 491 (1969): Petitioner was elected to the House of Representatives for the 90th Congress. Although he met the age, citizenship and residence requirements of Art. I, § 2, cl. 2, he was not permitted to take his seat pursuant to a House resolution after a Select Committee "reported that Powell had asserted an unwarranted privilege and immunity from the processes of the courts of New York; that he had wrongfully diverted House funds for the use of others and himself; and that he had made false reports on expenditures of foreign currency to the Committee on House Administration." Powell sought, inter alia, a federal declaration that his exclusion was unconstitutional and that his salary be paid by the Sergeant-at-Arms. The lower courts dismissed the complaint.

The Court, per WARREN, C.J., reversed, (Stewart, J., dissenting on the ground that the case was moot) holding that the claim did not present a political question. It rejected the contention—after lengthy examination of the pre-Constitutional Convention precedents of the English Parliament and American colonial assemblies, the debates at the Constitutional Convention and state conventions, and the early and more recent congressional precedents—that Art. I, § 5, cl. 1 ("Each House shall be the Judge of the * * * Qualifications of its own Members") contained a "textually demonstrable constitutional commitment" to the House of "judicially unreviewable power to set qualifications for membership and to judge whether prospective members meet those qualifications." "In order to determine whether there has been a textual commitment to a co-ordinate department of the Government, we must interpret the Constitution. [Our] examination of the relevant historical materials leads us to the conclusion [that] the Constitution leaves the House without authority to *exclude* any person, duly elected by his constituents, who meets all the requirements for membership expressly prescribed in" Art. I, § 2.[g]

---

f. For detailed consideration of the reapportionment problem, see Ch. 6, Sec. 4, I, A.

g. For a contrary conclusion, see Dionisopoulous, *A Commentary on the Constitutional Issues in the Powell and Related Cases,* 17 J.Pub.L. 103 (1968). Consider Sandalow, in *Symposium,* 17 U.C.L.A.L.Rev. 164, 172–73 (1969): "The most striking feature of the Court's review of history [is] that not until the *Powell* case can one find any suggestion that courts are empowered to sit in judgment on the question whether the House or Senate exceeded their authority in excluding a person elected to membership. [Having] begun by asking the right question, whether there was a 'constitutional commitment of the issue' to the House, the Court proceeded to answer a quite different one, whether the 'qualifications' which Article I, Section 5 authorized the House to 'judge' were only those specified in Article I, Section 2 (and perhaps elsewhere in the Constitution). The opinion reflects, in short, a classic instance of confusion between 'jurisdiction'—the power to decide—and 'the merits'—the correctness of decisions."

Query: Could Congress enact a mandatory retirement age for its members?

"Had the intent of the Framers emerged from these materials with less clarity, we would nevertheless have been compelled to resolve any ambiguity in favor of a narrow construction of the scope of Congress' power to exclude members-elect. A fundamental principle of our representative democracy is, in Hamilton's words, 'that the people should choose whom they please to govern them.' As Madison pointed out at the Convention, this principle is undermined as much by limiting whom the people can select as by limiting the franchise itself. * * * Unquestionably, Congress has an interest in preserving its institutional integrity, but in most cases that interest can be sufficiently safe-guarded by the exercise of its power to punish its members for disorderly behavior and, in extreme cases, to expel a member with the concurrence of two-thirds." The Court expressed no view on what limitations may exist on Congress' power to "expel or otherwise punish" a member, under Art. I, § 5, cl. 2 once he has been seated.

"Respondents' alternate contention is that the case presents a political question because judicial resolution of petitioners' claim would produce a 'poten-tially embarrassing confrontation between coordinate branches' of the Federal Government. But, [our interpretation of Art. I, § 5] falls within the traditional role accorded courts to interpret the law, and does not involve a 'lack of respect due [a] coordinate branch of government,' nor does it involve an 'initial policy determination of a kind clearly for nonjudicial discretion.' *Baker.* Our system of government requires that federal courts on occasion interpret the Constitution in a manner at variance with the construction given the document by another branch. The alleged conflict that such an adjudication may cause cannot justify the courts' avoiding their constitutional responsibility. * * *

"Nor are any of the other formulations of a political question 'inextricable from the case at bar.' *Baker.* Petitioners seek a determination [for] which clearly there are 'judicially manageable standards.' Finally, a judicial resolu-tion of petitioners' claim will not result in 'multifarious pronouncements by various departments on one question.' For, as we noted in *Baker,* it is the responsibility of this Court to act as the ultimate interpreter of the Constitution. * * *

"Petitioners seek additional forms of equitable relief, including mandamus for the release of Petitioner Powell's back pay. The propriety of such remedies, however, is more appropriately considered in the first instance by the courts below." [i]

Notes and Questions

1. *"Judicially manageable standards."* COLEMAN v. MILLER stated: "[T]he question of a reasonable time [for the pendency of a constitutional amendment before the states involves] an appraisal of a great variety of relevant conditions, political, social and economic, which can hardly be said to be within the appropriate range of evidence receivable in a court of justice and as to which it would be an extravagant extension of judicial authority to assert judicial notice. [T]hese conditions are appropriate for the consideration of the political

---

i. Powell was re-elected to the 91st Con-gress. Pursuant to a House resolution, he was seated but fined $25,000 and denied all prior seniority. Would a suit challenging this ac-tion present a "political question"?

Suppose a defeated House candidate brings an action challenging the House's seating of his opponent—who is a 23 year-old alien who has never resided outside of the District of Columbia since coming to the United States?

See generally *Symposium*, 17 U.C.L.A.L.Rev. 1 (1969).

departments of the Government. The questions they involve are essentially political and not justiciable." If the *Coleman* question was "political" for this reason, what of the questions in *Baker* and *Powell?* What of the questions in the *School Segregation Cases,* p. 823 infra? Is this a helpful test by which to determine justiciability?

2. *Foreign relations.* GOLDWATER v. CARTER, 444 U.S. 996, 100 S.Ct. 533, 62 L.Ed.2d 428 (1979), summarily reversed a court of appeals decision that the President had power to terminate a treaty with Taiwan without congressional approval. REHNQUIST, J., joined by Burger, C.J., and Stewart and Stevens, JJ., believed "that the controversy [is] a nonjusticiable political dispute [because] it involves foreign relations—specifically a treaty commitment to use military force in the defense of a foreign government if attacked. [W]e are asked to settle a dispute between coequal branches of our government, each of which has resources available to protect and assert its interests, resources not available to private litigants outside the judicial forum."

POWELL, J., concurred because of "prudential considerations": "[A] dispute between Congress and the President is not ready for judicial review unless and until each branch has taken action asserting its constitutional authority. [Since] Congress has taken no official [action], we do not know whether there ever will be an actual confrontation between the Legislative and Executive Branches."

But "reliance upon the political-question doctrine is inconsistent with our precedents. [First,] the text of the Constitution does not unquestionably commit the power to terminate treaties to the President alone. Second, there is no 'lack of judicially discoverable and manageable [standards.]' Resolution of the question may not be easy, but it only requires us to apply normal principles of interpretation to the constitutional provisions at issue. [This] case 'touches' foreign relations, but the question presented to us concerns only the constitutional division of power between Congress and the President. [Finally,] [i]nterpretation of the Constitution does not imply lack of respect for a coordinate branch. *Powell.* * * *" [a]

BRENNAN, J., who would have affirmed on the merits, dissented: "[T]he political question doctrine restrains courts from reviewing an exercise of foreign policy judgment by the coordinate political branch [but] the doctrine does not pertain when a court is faced with the *antecedent* question whether a particular branch has been constitutionally designated as the repository of political decisionmaking power. Cf. *Powell.* The issue of decisionmaking authority must be resolved as a matter of constitutional law, not political discretion; accordingly, it falls within the competence of the courts." [b]

3. *Controversial nature of subject matter.* Should this be an important criterion for determining "political questions"? If so, was it omitted from the *Baker* "checklist"? Consider Finkelstein, *Judicial Self-Limitation,* 37 Harv.L. Rev. 338, 344 (1924): "There are certain cases which are completely without the sphere of judicial interference. They are called, for historical reasons, 'political questions'. [The term] applies to all those matters of which the court, at a given time, will be of the opinion that it is impolitic or inexpedient to take jurisdiction. Sometimes this idea of expediency will result from the fear of the vastness of the consequences that a decision on the merits might entail." See generally Bickel, *The Least Dangerous Branch* 183–98 (1962). Compare Weston, *Political Ques-*

---

a. Marshall, J., concurred in the result.

b. Blackmun, J., joined by White, J., dissented. They "would set the case for oral

argument and give it the plenary consideration it so obviously deserves."

tions, 38 Harv.L.Rev. 296, 298–99 (1925): "[T]he courts in the obligatory exercise of unquestioned jurisdiction walk every day upon ground still shaken by the conflict of public opinion."

4. *"Textually demonstrable constitutional commitment."* (a) *Amending process.* (i) Concurring in *Coleman v. Miller,* Black, J., joined by Roberts, Frankfurter and Douglas, JJ., stated that Art. V "grants Congress exclusive power [over] the amending process" and that Congress "is under no duty to accept the pronouncements upon that exclusive power by this Court." Does this distinguish *Coleman* from *Baker?* From *Colegrove* (see note 1 after *Wesberry v. Sanders,* p. 983 infra)? From *Powell?* Does the language of Art. V support Black, J.? Suppose Congress submitted a proposed constitutional amendment to the states and provided that no black could participate in the state ratification process? See generally Tribe, *A Constitution We Are Amending: In Defense of a Restrained Judicial Role,* 97 Harv.L.Rev. 433 (1983); Dellinger, *The Legitimacy of Constitutional Change: Rethinking the Amendment Process,* 97 Harv.L.Rev. 386 (1983).

(ii) In *Coleman,* the Court held that "the question of the efficacy of ratifications by state legislatures, in the light of previous rejection or attempted withdrawal, should be regarded as a political question pertaining to the political departments, with the ultimate authority in the Congress in the exercise of its control over the promulgation of the adoption of the Amendment." Does this also apply to the question of whether a state legislature, which has already ratified a proposed amendment, may subsequently rescind that ratification? [c]

(iii) If, pursuant to Art. V, "the legislatures of two-thirds of the several states" apply to Congress to "call a convention for proposing amendments" and Congress ignores the application, is an action for a mandatory injunction "nonjusticiable"? See Bonfield, *The Dirksen Amendment and the Article V Convention Process,* 66 Mich.L.Rev. 949, 976–85 (1968).

(b) *Impeachment.* Does Art. I, § 3, cl. 6—"The Senate shall have the sole power to try all impeachments"—"demonstrably commit" final constitutional decision "to a coordinate political department"? Consider Berger, *Impeachment: The Constitutional Problems* 105–06, 117–18, 120 (1973): "Like the three qualifications of Art. I, § 2(2) [in *Powell*], impeachment, by Art. II, § 4, is limited to three grounds, 'treason, bribery, or other high crimes and misdemeanors,' * * *. Although impeachment was chiefly designed to check Executive abuses and oppressions, there was no thought of delivering either the President or the Judiciary to the unbounded discretion of Congress. This is attested by the Framers' rejection of the unfettered removal by Address [formal request of Congress], by their rejection of 'maladministration' because that was 'so vague' as to leave tenure, 'at the pleasure' of the Senate, and by the substitution of 'high crimes and misdemeanors' with knowledge that it had a 'limited' and 'technical meaning.' * * * 'Limits' on Congress determined by Congress itself would be no limits at all. [I]f it be assumed that the 'sole power to try' conferred insulation from review, it must yield to the subsequent Fifth Amendment ['due process' provision]." See also Rezneck, *Is Judicial Review of Impeachment Coming?* 60 A.B.A.J. 681, 682–83 (1974): "Nothing in the text of the Constitution expressly bars judicial review of an impeachment conviction. On the

c. For varying views on this issue, both as to justiciability and the merits, see Kanowitz & Klinger, *Can a State Rescind Its Equal Rights Amendment Ratification: Who Decides and How?* 28 Hast.L.J. 979 (1977); Comment, *The Equal Rights Amendment and Article V: A Framework for Analysis of the Extension and Rescission Issues,* 127 U.Pa.L.Rev. 494 (1978); Note, *The Process of Constitutional Amendment,* 79 Colum.L.Rev. 109 (1979).

contrary, Art. III provides that the 'judicial Power' of the [federal courts] 'shall extend to all cases, in Law and Equity, arising under this Constitution.' [If, in *Powell*], the constitutional provision that 'Each House shall be the Judge of the Elections, Returns and Qualifications of its own Members' did not commit the final determination of Powell's exclusion to the House of Representatives, why should the language on impeachment be read to commit final decision of all impeachment questions to the Senate? The grant of power to 'judge' is at least as comprehensive as a power to 'try,' but it did not prevent judicial review in *Powell.* [Moreover, the] use of the word 'try' suggests a limited, not absolute, measure of finality for decisions of the Senate in an impeachment proceeding. [The] 'trial,' in which the facts are determined, is different from an 'appeal' or other mode of review in which questions of law are resolved in an appellate court."

Compare Black, *Impeachment: A Handbook* 54–55, 61–62 (1974): "If the Supreme Court [were] to order reinstatement of an impeached and convicted president, there would be, to say the least, a very grave and quite legitimate doubt whether that decree had any title to being obeyed, or whether it was [as] widely outside judicial jurisdiction as would be a judicial order to Congress to increase the penalty for counterfeiting. To cite the most frightening consequence, our military commanders would have to decide for themselves which president they were bound to obey, the reinstated one or his successor. [It] would be most unfortunate if the notion got about that the Senate's verdict were somewhat tentative. [No] senator should be encouraged to think he can shift to any court responsibility for an unpalatable or unpopular decision. [Further,] if a removed president tried [judicial review], and had his case (as would almost surely happen) dismissed for want of jurisdiction, he might be able, though quite wrongly, to persuade a part of the people that he had been denied his rightful day in court."

(c) *Regulating the militia.* In GILLIGAN v. MORGAN, 413 U.S. 1, 93 S.Ct. 2440, 37 L.Ed.2d 407 (1973), students at Kent State University sought various relief against government officials to prevent repetition of events that had occurred on that campus in May 1970. The court of appeals instructed the federal district court to evaluate the "pattern of training, weaponry and orders in the Ohio National Guard" so as to determine whether it made "inevitable the use of fatal force in suppressing civilian disorders." The Court, per BURGER, C.J., reversed, relying heavily on Art. I, § 8, cl. 16—which grants to Congress "the responsibility for organizing, arming and disciplining the Militia (now the National Guard), with certain responsibilities being reserved to the respective States"—and on federal legislation enacted pursuant thereto: "[T]he nature of the questions to be resolved on remand are subjects committed expressly to the political branches of government. [It] would be difficult to think of a clearer example of the type of governmental action that was intended by the Constitution to be left to the political branches [or] of an area of governmental activity in which the courts have less competence. The complex, subtle, and professional decisions as to the composition, training, equipping, and control of a military force are essentially professional military judgments, subject *always* to civilian control of the Legislative and Executive Branches [which] are periodically subject to electoral accountability." [e]

e. Douglas, Brennan, Stewart and Marshall, JJ., dissented because "this case is now moot."

(d) Do *Baker, Powell, Coleman* and *Gilligan* establish that the "political question" doctrine is "a function of the separation of powers"—presently confined exclusively to "the relationship between the judiciary and the coordinate branches of the Federal Government"? That the other *Baker* criteria—including "judicially manageable standards" (note 1 supra) and "effective judicial remedies" (note 5 infra)—are all subsumed within this specific principle? See Jackson, *The Political Question Doctrine: Where Does It Stand After Powell v. McCormack, O'Brien v. Brown and Gilligan v. Morgan,* 44 U.Colo.L.Rev. 477 (1973). If so, and if the political branches specifically authorize the Court to decide the question, may (should) the Court do so? See Choper, *Judicial Review and the National Political Process* 405–15 (1980). See also note 3, after *Poe v. Ullman,* p. 1231 infra.

For the view that the leading political question cases have *not* "involved abstention from judicial review, or other extraordinary deference" to the political branches—i.e., that the Court has *not* held that the other branches' "determinations were binding on the courts 'right or wrong,' constitutional or unconstitutional"—but rather involved the Court's either "accept[ing] decisions by the political branches [as being] within their constitutional authority," or "refus[ing] some (or all) remedies for want of equity," see Henkin, *Is There a Political Question Doctrine?* 85 Yale L.J. 597 (1976). See also Note, *A Dialogue on the Political Question Doctrine,* 1978 Utah L.Rev. 523.

(e) O'BRIEN v. BROWN, 409 U.S. 1, 92 S.Ct. 2718, 34 L.Ed.2d 1 (1972), per curiam, stayed judgments which had adjudicated the merits of challenges to "recommendations of the Credentials Committee of the 1972 Democratic National Convention regarding the seating of certain delegates to the convention that will meet three days hence": "[N]o holding of this Court up to now gives support for judicial intervention in the circumstances presented here, involving as they do, relationships of great delicacy and essentially political in nature. [It] has been understood since our national political parties first came into being as voluntary associations of individuals that the convention itself is the proper forum for determining intra-party disputes as to which delegates shall be seated. [While] the Court is unwilling to undertake final resolution of the important constitutional questions presented without full briefing and argument and adequate opportunity for deliberation, we entertain grave doubts as to the action taken by the Court of Appeals." [f]

Douglas, White and Marshall, JJ., would have denied the stays, Marshall, J., joined by Douglas, J., believing that "the doctrine of 'political questions' was fashioned to deal with a very different problem, which has nothing to do with this case. [T]he full convention of the National Democratic Party [is] most assuredly not a coordinate branch of government to which the federal courts owe deference within the meaning of the separation of powers or the political question doctrine." [g]

5. *Effective judicial remedies.* To what extent should "the difficulty or impossibility of devising effective judicial remedies" influence "justiciability"? [h] How effective (seemly?) were the possible remedies available in *Baker*? What remedies could (should) a court afford in the various situations discussed in the above notes?

---

f. Brennan, J., concurred in the result.

g. Does *O'Brien* suggest a revival of Frankfurter, J.'s view in *Colegrove* and *Baker*?

h. For detail, see p. 986 infra.

6. *"Judicial restraint" and the political process.* Consider Frank, *Political Questions,* in Supreme Court & Supreme Law 36, 46 (Cahn ed. 1954): "[T]he basic objective of a plan of government ought to be to put the responsibility for the decision of questions some place, and [the] political question doctrine is useful when it operates to put responsibility at the best place, and is harmful when it puts the decision no place. [W]hat happens in the redistricting cases is that the responsibility, if not taken by the court, is transferred to a body which has a completely vested interest in the maldistricting." Does this adequately respond to Frankfurter, J.'s "appeal must be to an informed, civically militant electorate" argument? Compare Auerbach, *The Reapportionment Cases: One Person, One Vote—One Vote, One Value,* 1964 Sup.Ct.Rev. 1, 2: "It is paradoxical [for] the advocates of judicial self-limitation to criticize the Court for helping to make majority rule effective, because the case for self-restraint rests on the assumption that the Court is reviewing the legislative acts of representatives who are put in office and can be turned out of office by a majority of the people. Since malapportionment destroys this assumption, judicial intervention to remove this obstacle to majority rule may be less intolerable than the self-perpetuation of minority rule."

7. *Republican form of government.* (a) Do you agree with *Baker* "that Guaranty Clause claims involve those elements which define a 'political question' and for that reason are nonjusticiable"? Consider Emerson, *Malapportionment and Judicial Power,* 72 Yale L.J. 64, 67–68 (1962): "[S]ince Brennan, J., repudiates the notion that 'political questions' are to be determined by blanket categories and makes clear that each case must be determined on its own facts, it would seem that the issue of justiciability under the guaranty clause would likewise turn on whether the essential elements of a 'political question' are present in any particular case." See McCloskey, *The Reapportionment Case,* 76 Harv.L.Rev. 54, 63 (1962): "[I]f the guaranty clause intrinsically raises political questions, this cannot be because it 'is not a repository of judicially manageable standards.' Its standards are not any more nebulous than those of the equal protection clause in this context." See also Bonfield, *Baker v. Carr: New Light on the Constitutional Guarantee of Republican Government,* 50 Calif.L.Rev. 245, 250 (1962): "The clause is neither textually committed to the exclusive enforcement of another department, nor bare of judicially discoverable or manageable standards for resolving questions dependent for their resolution upon it. It is therefore the 'political question' aspects of the issue raised under the guarantee and not the mere invocation of that provision that should determine justiciability." For an attempt to demonstrate the existence of satisfactorily ascertainable standards under the guaranty clause, see Bonfield, *The Guarantee Clause of Article IV, Section 4: A Study in Constitutional Desuetude,* 46 Minn.L.Rev. 513 (1962). See also Scharpf, *Judicial Review and the Political Question: A Functional Analysis,* 75 Yale L.J. 517, 589–96 (1966).

(b) If Congress, legislating under the guaranty clause, permitted a state to establish its government as a monarchy, would a dissenting citizen be barred from Supreme Court review on the ground that this was a "political question"? Is this what Douglas, J., had in mind in his fn. 3? How would Brennan, J., decide this? Frankfurter and Harlan, JJ.? Consider Bonfield, supra, at 564–65: "[J]udicial abstinence would give Congress unlimited power to impose on the states whatever government it deemed republican. Not only would such authority spell the complete end of our federal system, but it would also create an unchecked power capable of destroying rather than guaranteeing republican government."

SECTION 3. CONGRESSIONAL REGULATION OF JUDICIAL POWER

Beginning with the Judiciary Act of 1789, Congress has enacted various statutes defining the Supreme Court's jurisdiction. For example, it was not until 1914 that the Court was authorized to review state court decisions holding state laws violative of the Constitution. The Court's original jurisdiction, which typically comprises only a handful of cases each year (mainly concerning "controversies between two or more states"), is presently governed by 28 U.S.C. § 1251. The most important current provisions respecting the Court's appellate jurisdiction are 28 U.S.C. §§ 1254 (federal courts of appeals) and 1257 (state courts).

---

§ 1254. Cases in the courts of appeals may be reviewed by the Supreme Court by the following methods:

(1) By writ of certiorari granted upon the petition of any party to any civil or criminal case, before or after rendition of judgment or decree;

(2) By appeal by a party relying on a State statute held by a court of appeals to be invalid as repugnant to the Constitution, treaties or laws of the United States, but such appeal shall preclude review by writ of certiorari at the instance of such appellant, and the review on appeal shall be restricted to the Federal questions presented;

(3) By certification at any time by a court of appeals of any question of law in any civil or criminal case as to which instructions are desired, and upon such certification the Supreme Court may give binding instructions or require the entire record to be sent up for decision of the entire matter in controversy.

§ 1257. Final judgments or decrees rendered by the highest court of a State in which a decision could be had, may be reviewed by the Supreme Court as follows:

(1) By appeal, where is drawn in question the validity of a treaty or statute of the United States and the decision is against its validity.

(2) By appeal, where is drawn in question the validity of a statute of any state on the ground of its being repugnant to the Constitution, treaties or laws of the United States, and the decision is in favor of its validity.

(3) By writ of certiorari, where the validity of a treaty or statute of the United States is drawn in question or where the validity of a State statute is drawn in question on the ground of its being repugnant to the Constitution, treaties or laws of the United States, or where any title, right, privilege or immunity is specially set up or claimed under the Constitution, treaties or statutes of, or commission held or authority exercised under, the United States.

*   *   *

EX PARTE McCARDLE

74 U.S. (7 Wall.) 506, 19 L.Ed. 264 (1869).

[On February 5, 1867, Congress empowered federal courts to grant habeas corpus to persons restrained in violation of the Constitution, treaty, or federal law. Appeal could be to the Supreme Court. McCardle—imprisoned by the military government of Mississippi pursuant to the Reconstruction Acts for publishing "incendiary and libelous" articles—"alleging unlawful restraint by military force," sought habeas corpus which was denied by the Circuit Court. He appealed to the Supreme Court, apparently presenting it with the opportunity finally to reach the merits of the Reconstruction laws' constitutionality. However, in 1868, after argument but before decision, Congress (over President Johnson's veto) passed the following act:] "That so much of the act approved February 5, 1867 [as] authorized an appeal from the judgment of the Circuit Court to the Supreme Court of the United States, or the exercise of any such jurisdiction by said Supreme Court, on appeals which have been, or may hereafter be taken, [is] hereby repealed."

* * * Argument was now heard upon the effect of the repealing act.

The CHIEF JUSTICE [CHASE] delivered the opinion of the Court.

[T]he appellate jurisdiction of this Court is not derived from acts of Congress. It is, strictly speaking, conferred by the Constitution. But it is conferred "with such exceptions and under such regulations as Congress shall make."

It is unnecessary to consider whether, if Congress had made no exceptions and no regulations, this court might not have exercised general appellate jurisdiction under rules prescribed by itself. From among the earliest acts of the first Congress [was the Judiciary Act of 1789 which] provided for the organization of this court, and prescribed regulations for the exercise of its jurisdiction.

[In] *Durousseau v. United States* [6 Cranch, 307 (1810)], particularly, the whole matter was carefully examined, and the court held, that [the] judicial act was an exercise of the power given by the Constitution to Congress "of making exceptions to the appellate jurisdiction of the Supreme Court." "They have described affirmatively," said the court, "its jurisdiction, and this affirmative description has been understood to imply a negation of the exercise of such appellate power as is not comprehended within it."

The principle [thus] established, it was an almost necessary consequence that acts of Congress, providing for the exercise of jurisdiction, should come to be spoken of as acts granting jurisdiction and not as acts making exceptions to the constitutional grant of it.

The exception to appellate jurisdiction in the case before us, however, is not an inference from the affirmation of other appellate jurisdiction. It is made in terms. * * *

We are not at liberty to inquire into the motives of the legislature. We can only examine into its power under the Constitution * * *.

What, then, is the effect of the repealing act upon the case before us? * * * Jurisdiction is power to declare the law, and when it ceases to exist the only function remaining to the court is that of announcing the fact and dismissing the cause. And this is not less clear upon authority than upon principle. [J]udicial duty is not less fitly performed by declining ungranted jurisdiction than in exercising firmly that which the Constitution and the laws confer.

Counsel seem to have supposed, if effect be given to the repealing act in question, that the whole appellate power of the court, in cases of habeas corpus, is denied. But this is an error. The act of 1868 does not except from that jurisdiction any cases but appeals from Circuit Courts under the act of 1867. It does not affect the jurisdiction which was previously exercised.

The appeal [must] be dismissed for want of jurisdiction.[a]

Notes and Questions

1. *Extent of the decision.* (a) In *Ex Parte Yerger,* 75 U.S. (8 Wall.) 85, 19 L.Ed. 332 (1869), also challenging the Reconstruction Acts, the Court, upholding its appellate jurisdiction by writ of certiorari in a habeas corpus proceeding based on pre-1867 legislation, said of *McCardle*: "The effect of the Act was to oust the court of its jurisdiction of the particular case then before it on appeal, and it is not to be doubted that such was the effect intended. Nor will it be questioned that legislation of this character is unusual and hardly to be justified except upon some imperious public exigency." More recently, Douglas, J., joined by Black, J., stated: "There is a serious question whether [*McCardle*] could command a majority view today." *Glidden Co. v. Zdanok,* 370 U.S. 530, 605 n. 11, 82 S.Ct. 1459, 1501–02, 8 L.Ed.2d 671, 718–19 (1962).

(b) How great an incursion into the Court's jurisdiction did *McCardle* really permit? Consider Ratner, *Congressional Power Over the Appellate Jurisdiction of the Supreme Court,* 109 U.Pa.L.Rev. 157, 180 (1960): "The statute [did] not deprive the Court of jurisdiction to decide McCardle's case; he could still petition the Supreme Court for [an original] writ of habeas corpus * * *. The legislation did no more than eliminate one procedure for Supreme Court review of decisions denying habeas corpus while leaving another equally efficacious one available."

(c) Does *McCardle* stand for the proposition that Congress may *completely* deprive the Court of power to review certain federal questions? Apart from *McCardle,* does Congress have this power? The power to deprive the Court of *all* appellate jurisdiction? If not, what is the meaning of the "Exceptions" language in Art. III? Is it "that Congress may except certain cases otherwise subject only to the Court's appellate jurisdiction *by adding them to the Court's original jurisdiction*"? Van Alstyne, *A Critical Guide to Marbury v. Madison,* 1969 Duke L.J. 1, 32. It is that the Constitution *itself* only grants appellate jurisdiction in "all the other cases before mentioned" and that Congress may make "Exceptions" to this by adding to the appellate jurisdiction cases that Art. III has assigned to the original jurisdiction? For the position that this clause was intended to permit congressional control of the Court's appellate jurisdiction only as to questions of fact, not questions of law, see Merry, *Scope of the Supreme Court's Appellate Jurisdiction: Historical Basis,* 47 Minn.L.Rev. 53 (1962); Berger, *Congress v. The Supreme Court* 285–86 (1969).[c]

Consider Ratner, supra at 171–72: "It is reasonable to conclude [that the Constitutional] Convention gave Congress authority to specify * * * orderly procedures and to modify the jurisdiction from time to time in response to prevailing social and political requirements, within the limits imposed by the Court's essential constitutional role. It is not reasonable to conclude that the Convention gave Congress the power to destroy that role. Reasonably interpreted the clause means 'With such exceptions and under such regulations as

---

a. For an historical account, see Fairman, *Reconstruction and Reunion, 1864–88, Part One,* c. X (1971).

c. See also *Luckenbach S.S. Co. v. United States,* 272 U.S. 533, 47 S.Ct. 186, 71 L.Ed. 394 (1926) (upholding statute limiting Supreme Court review of Court of Claims decisions to questions of law); *Barry v. Mercein,* 46 U.S. (5 How.) 103, 12 L.Ed. 70 (1847) (Supreme Court review of action based on diversity of citizenship unavailable because action did not involve minimum monetary value required by statute).

Congress may make, not inconsistent with the essential functions of the Supreme Court under this Constitution.' "

What is the Court's "essential constitutional role"? Consider Ratner, *Majoritarian Constraints on Judicial Review: Congressional Control of Supreme Court Jurisdiction*, 27 Vill.L.Rev. 929, 935, 956 (1982): "The supremacy clause of article VI mandates one supreme federal law throughout the land, and article III establishes the Supreme Court as the constitutional instrument for implementing that clause. [As] such, its essential functions under the Constitution are: 1) ultimately to resolve inconsistent or conflicting interpretations of federal law, and particularly of the Constitution, by state and federal courts; 2) to maintain the supremacy of federal law, and particularly the Constitution, when it conflicts with state law or is challenged by state authority." Compare Redish, *Congressional Power to Regulate Supreme Court Appellate Jurisdiction Under the Exceptions Clause: An Internal and External Examination*, 27 Vill.L.Rev. 900, 907 (1982): "I might well agree, as a policy matter, that Congress should not possess the power to tamper with performance of the Supreme Court's role, [but] I can find no constitutional basis for erecting such a limitation." See also Rice, *Congress and the Supreme Court's Jurisdiction*, 27 Vill.L.Rev. 959, 962–81 (1982). Contrast Sager, *Constitutional Limitations on Congress' Authority to Regulate the Jurisdiction of the Federal Courts*, 95 Harv.L.Rev. 17, 57 (1981): "The Court must be available to superintend *state compliance* with federal law unless Congress provides effective review elsewhere within the *federal* judiciary." [d]

2. *Legislative proposals.* From the early nineteenth century, there have been numerous congressional attempts to limit the Supreme Court's appellate jurisdiction over various issues.[e] Since the late 1970s, the most prominent have concerned abortion, school prayer, and busing for school integration. See Baucus & Kay, *The Court Stripping Bills*, 27 Vill.L.Rev. 988 (1982).

Suppose Congress sought to deny Supreme Court appellate jurisdiction in any case brought by a black? Is this distinguishable from the recent proposals? What role do other constitutional provisions play in respect to the "Exceptions and Regulations" clause? See Tribe, *Jurisdictional Gerrymandering: Zoning Disfavored Rights Out of the Federal Courts*, 16 Harv.Civ.Rts.-Civ.Lib.L.Rev. 129, 141–46 (1981); Sager, note 1(c) supra, at 78–80. Compare Bator, *Congressional Power Over the Jurisdiction of the Federal Courts*, 27 Vill.L.Rev. 1030, 1034–37 (1982).

3. *Proposal for a National Court of Appeals.* In 1972, a committee chaired by Professor Paul Freund, appointed by Chief Justice Burger "to study the case load of the Supreme Court," proposed, inter alia: "The establishment [of] a National Court of Appeals, [with] seven judges drawn on a rotating basis from the federal courts of appeals and serving staggered three-year terms. This Court would have the two-fold function of (1) screening all petitions for certiorari and appeals that would at present be filed in the Supreme Court, referring the most review-worthy [to] the Supreme Court [and] denying the rest; and (2) retaining for decision on the merits cases of genuine conflict between circuits (except those of special moment, which would be certified to the Supreme Court)." Federal

d. For a detailed study of the background and debates in the Constitutional Convention and during the ratification process, reaching a similar conclusion, see Clinton, *A Mandatory View of Federal Court Jurisdiction: A Guided Quest for the Original Understanding of Article III*, 132 U.Pa.L.Rev. 741 (1984).

e. See Elliott, *Court-Curbing Proposals in Congress*, 33 Not.D.Law. 597 (1958); Nagel, *Court-Curbing Periods in American History*, 18 Vand.L.Rev. 925 (1965).

Judicial Center Study Group, *Report on the Case Load of the Supreme Court* (1972).

Does this recommendation of the "Freund Report" comport with Art. III? Consider Black, *The National Court of Appeals: An Unwise Proposal,* 83 Yale L.J. 883, 885–86 (1974): "A court that can finally determine, *for the whole nation,* questions over the whole range of federal law, without the possibility of further review, is a 'Supreme Court' in everything but name, and the Constitution provides for *one* Supreme Court, quite as clearly as it provides for one President. This National Court of Appeals * * * would (in its own unreviewable discretion) be a 'Supreme Court,' for the entire nation, *on the full and final merits* of all questions where, in its own view, an intercircuit conflict happened to have arisen." [f] Compare Freund, *Why We Need the National Court of Appeals,* 59 A.B.A.J. 247, 251 (1973): "[T]he appellate jurisdiction of the Supreme Court, from 1789 to the present day, has never extended by law over the full range of cases to which it might extend under Article III. [F]or a long time there was a special jurisdictional amount requirement for review of circuit court decisions, [and] for a century criminal cases could reach the Supreme Court from the circuit courts only on a certificate of division in the circuit court. Review of state court decisions depended on how the state court decided a federal question; thus for a time, when workmen's compensation was held unconstitutional in a state court, there was no possible review in the Supreme Court. Were all these tribunals—the circuit courts and the state courts—the Supreme Court, in violation of Article III?" Contrast Black, supra, at 886: "[These] examples [are] one and all broadly and crucially distinguishable for they excepted from or regulated the exercise of the uniquely 'supreme' appellate review rather than providing an alternative supreme appellate review—just what we cannot do if we are to have 'one Supreme Court.' " [g]

SECTION 4.　DISCRETIONARY REVIEW

If review in the Supreme Court is authorized by "appeal," the Court is obligated to decide the case; but if it is authorized by "writ of certiorari," the Court has discretion whether to grant the petition for review. Because of the Court's increasing difficulty in managing its docket, Congress, as early as 1891, authorized the Court to exercise some discretion in selecting cases to hear and decide. This discretion was greatly enlarged at the behest of the Court itself in the so-called Judges' Bill of 1925, as presently reflected in the statutory provisions set forth in Sec. 3 supra. Prior to 1925, the appellate docket contained about 80% obligatory and 20% discretionary cases. As a result of the Judges' Bill, less than 10% of the present docket consists of appeals. In the words of Vinson, C.J., 69 S.Ct. vi (1949), the Supreme Court is not "primarily concerned with the correction of errors in lower court decisions. In almost all cases within the Court's appellate jurisdiction, the petitioner has already received one appellate review of his [case]. If we took every case in which an interesting legal question is raised, or our prima facie impression is that the decision below is

f. See also Gressman, *The Constitution v. The Freund Report,* 41 Geo.Wash.L.Rev. 951 (1973); Note, *The National Court of Appeals: A Constitutional "inferior* Court"? 72 Mich.L. Rev. 290 (1973).

g. For a proposal "to leave with the present Court final jurisdiction for review of constitutionality, transferring finality [for non-

constitutional] judicial review to one or more separate judicial bodies," see Strong, *The Time Has Come to Talk of Major Curtailment in the Supreme Court's Jurisdiction,* 48 N.C.L. Rev. 1 (1969).

Other proposals of the Freund Report (and others) to reduce the Court's workload are considered in Sec. 4 infra.

erroneous, we could not fulfill the Constitutional and statutory responsibilities placed upon the Court. To remain effective, the Supreme Court must continue to decide only those cases which present questions whose resolution will have immediate importance far beyond the particular facts and parties involved."

UNITED STATES SUPREME COURT RULES

Rule 17. Considerations Governing Review on Certiorari

1. A review on writ of certiorari is not a matter of right, but of judicial discretion, and will be granted only when there are special and important reasons therefor. The following, while neither controlling nor fully measuring the Court's discretion, indicate the character of reasons that will be considered:

(a) When a federal court of appeals has rendered a decision in conflict with the decision of another federal court of appeals on the same matter; or has decided a federal question in a way in conflict with a state court of last resort; or has so far departed from the accepted and usual course of judicial proceedings, or so far sanctioned such a departure by a lower court, as to call for an exercise of this Court's power of supervision.

(b) When a state court of last resort has decided a federal question in a way in conflict with the decision of another state court of last resort or of a federal court of appeals.

(c) When a state court or a federal court of appeals has decided an important question of federal law which has not been, but should be, settled by this Court, or has decided a federal question in a way in conflict with applicable decisions of this Court. * * *

Notes and Questions

1. *Proper judicial discretion.* What considerations beyond those outlined in Rule 17 should be pertinent ("proper," "principled") to the granting of certiorari? Consider Harper & Rosenthal, *What The Supreme Court Did Not Do In The 1949 Term—An Appraisal of Certiorari*, 99 U.Pa.L.Rev. 293, 299, 300 (1950): "[T]he Court, in determining whether the issue involved is of the required importance, may, and indeed perhaps should in some instances, consider whether the time is one for decision of the particular question. [Further], a justice [might] very properly vote for denial because persuaded that if the writ were granted, five or more justices might decide the issue wrongly. It is altogether understandable that a justice who has strong convictions about a case of public importance might prefer to have the decision of an inferior court stand rather than to have it authenticated in affirmance by the highest Court." [b]

b. Compare Henkin *On Drawing Lines*, 82 Harv.L.Rev. 63, 90–91 (1968): "Surely the Court did not consider the question [in *Mora v. McNamara*, 389 U.S. 934, 88 S.Ct. 282, 19 L.Ed.2d 287 (1967), of the constitutionality of United States military activity in Vietnam,] 'unimportant.' Rather, [one] is tempted to guess that the Court recognized that if it heard the case it could not give the relief requested. Even if the Justices privately thought that the President exceeded his constitutional authority in sending Mr. Mora to fight in Vietnam, it would not so declare and presume to restrain the President. Nor would the Court adjudicate claims that acts of the political branches violate international law. If it heard the case, the Court would have to decide that the issues are 'political questions' and not justiciable; or, that even if the war is illegal, Mora is not justified thereby in refusing to serve and therefore the legality of the war is not properly in issue; or that the war is not in fact illegal. Any of these judgments might be less politic than a decision not to hear the case at all, might give the impression that the Court supports the political branches in the Vietnam war, and might make the Court itself a target of the national malaise. Denying certiorari may well have been the better part of valor. [Or the] Justices might

2. *The Court's increased workload.* The past decade and a half has produced a flurry of proposals to reduce the Court's workload.

(a) The "FREUND REPORT" (note 3, Sec. 3 supra), justified its recommending creation of a National Court of Appeals to relieve the Supreme Court of some of its present duties, because "the statistics of the Court's current workload, both in absolute terms and in the mounting trend, are impressive evidence that the conditions essential for the performance of the Court's mission do not exist." The figures revealed that "approximately three times as many cases were filed in the 1971 Term as in the 1951 Term"—"by 1971, 3,643 new cases were filed, an increase of 1,458 in ten years.[f] [The] most dramatic growth has been in the number of cases filed in forma pauperis (ifp) by persons unable to pay the cost of litigation,[g] mostly defendants in criminal cases [resulting] both from a substantive enlargement of defendants' rights in the field of criminal justice and from the greater availability [of] counsel to indigent criminal defendants. [The] regular appellate filings (the non-ifp cases) have also steadily increased" due to the general population growth and because "more subjects are committed to the courts as the fields covered by legislation expand. Civil rights, environmental, safety, consumer, and other social and economic legislation are recent illustrations. And lawyers are now provided to a markedly increasing extent for persons who cannot afford litigation. Changes in constitutional doctrines have also contributed, as the reapportionment and school desegregation cases, as well as the criminal cases, attest." Further, "the percentage of petitions for certiorari granted has sharply dropped as the filings have [increased]. In 1971, 5.8% were granted[h] in contrast to 17.5%, 11.1% and 7.4% in 1941, 1951 and 1961, respectively." Similarly, "the number of cases argued and decided by opinion has not changed significantly despite the rising flood of petitions and appeals. [At] the 1971 Term 143 cases were so disposed of, with 129 opinions of the Court;[i] during the preceding 15 years the average was 120 cases, with 100 opinions."

The report suggested that the decline in the percentage of petitions granted "would seem to reflect, not a lessening of the proportion of cases worthy of

at least like to keep open the possibility of intervention rather than read themselves out 'forever.' " Contrast Hughes, *Civil Disobedience and the Political Question Doctrine,* 43 N.Y.U.L.Rev. 1, 15 (1968): "Those who advocate civil disobedience have, I think, some warrant for saying that a dearth of reasoned opinions on the political question doctrine in its application to issues that surround the war in Vietnam leaves them without a satisfactory response to their challenge. And by a satisfactory response I do not of course mean one that agrees with the petitioner nor one that will enable neat predictions to be made in the future, but only one which presents a reasoned justification for the denial of his claim." See also Rehnquist, J., dissenting from denial of certiorari in *Ratchford v. Gay Lib,* 434 U.S. 1080, 98 S.Ct. 1276, 55 L.Ed.2d 789 (1978): "[T]he existence [of] discretion does not imply that it should be used as a sort of judicial storm cellar to which we may flee to escape from controversial or sensitive cases."

f. In the 1973 to 1978 Terms, the number of new cases filed averaged about 3900. See Casper & Posner, *The Caseload of The Supreme Court: 1975 and 1976 Terms,* 1977 Sup. Ct. 87. For the 1979 to 1984 Terms, the average increased to almost 4200.

g. For a description of in forma pauperis proceedings, see Stern & Gressman, *Supreme Court Practice* ch. 8 (5th ed. 1978).

h. The percentage granted continued to be "around 6%" into the late 1970s, Stern & Gressman, supra, at 260, but fell to an average of below 4.5% in the 1979 to 1984 Terms.

i. These figures remained substantially constant through the late 1970s. See Hellman, *The Business of the Supreme Court Under the Judiciary Act of 1925: The Plenary Docket in the 1970's,* 91 Harv.L.Rev. 1711, 1728 (1978), who also shows a significant increase in the number of opinions by the Burger Court as compared to the Warren and Vinson Courts, id. at 1730–34. In the 1980 to 1984 Terms, the Court disposed of an average of 164 cases by signed opinion.

review, but rather the need to keep the number of cases argued and decided on the merits within manageable limits as the docket increases." Thus, "two consequences can be inferred. Issues that would have been decided on the merits a generation ago are passed over by the Court today; and second, the consideration given to the cases actually decided on the merits is compromised by the pressures of 'processing' the inflated docket of petitions and appeals."

See also Griswold, *Rationing Justice—The Supreme Court's Caseload and What the Court Does Not Do,* 60 Corn.L.Rev. 335, 341-43 (1975): "It is a rather astonishing fact that less than 1% of the cases decided by our courts of appeals are reviewed on the merits by the Supreme Court [and] this had led, I think, to a considerable lack of what I would call institutional responsibility on the part of many court of appeals judges. [In consequence], it is hard to say that there is any national law on many subjects. [If] 10% of the court of appeals cases were reviewed by a court with national authority, the law would soon be clarified and stabilized, and the amount of litigation could be markedly reduced. [Further], I do not think that the public or the bar is fully aware of the extent to which the Supreme Court of the United States has become a civil rights court.ʲ [If] all our Court can do is to handle the most important civil rights cases, and a few others, then we are rationing justice, and should be prepared to do something about it."

(b) Apart from the constitutionality of the Freund Report's National Court of Appeals proposal (see note 3, Sec. 3 supra), is it necessary? Desirable? BICKEL, THE CASELOAD OF THE SUPREME COURT 15–19 (1973) fairly summarizes the "main grounds of objection": ˡ "(1) Contrary to the study group's conclusion, no need for relief has been shown, certainly no imperative need. 'The case for our "overwork" is a myth,' Mr. Justice Douglas [remarked]. The increase in the caseload, he continued, had been largely [filed] by prisoners free of cost and often without benefit of counsel. Most such cases are wholly frivolous and extraordinarily few of them are ever accepted for review. They burden no one. 'We are' said the justice, 'if anything, underworked, not overworked.' The Court disposes of 'vast leisure time.' [19]

"Former Chief Justice Warren declared that the study group's 'facile and unevaluated use of numbers [leaves] the public with a false impression as to the workload of the Court and the ability of the justices to manage that workload.' He also emphasized the large number of in forma pauperis cases and added that more than half of the rest of the docket consisted of cases that 'were equally without certiorari merit and were doubtless denied with a minimum expenditure of the justices' time and effort.' [20] Mr. Justice Brennan stated categorically 'that I spent no more time screening the 3,643 cases of the 1971 term than I did screening half as many in my first term in 1956.' [21] * * *

"(2) Even critics who did not subscribe to Justice Douglas's view that the Court commands 'vast leisure time' doubted that the justices are or need to be very heavily occupied in the task of screening cases. [Judge Friendly suggested] that the justices might find it possible to dispose of petitions for certiorari more speedily, on the basis of one-sentence memoranda from their law clerks or just a

j. In support, see Casper & Posner, *The Workload of the Supreme Court* (1976); Hellman, supra, at 1737–46.

l. Professor Bickel was a member of the Freund committee and supported its report.

19. *Tidewater Oil Co. v. United States,* 409 U.S. 151, 174, 93 S.Ct. 408, 421, 34 L.Ed.2d 375 (1972) (dissenting opinion).

20. Warren, *Attacks Freund Study Group's Composition and Proposal,* 59 A.B.A.J. 721, 724, 726 (1973).

21. Brennan, [*The National Court of Appeals: Another Dissent,* 40 U.Chi.L.Rev. 473, 479 (1973)].

few minutes' talk with them. Or else, he wrote, the justices could pool their clerks, which [a] few of them are [doing], instead of each getting a memorandum on each case from one of his own clerks. Then again, the justices could have more clerks or a small senior staff.[23] * * *

"(3) A common theme among the critics is that the study group's proposal would entail a loss of control, as Chief Justice Warren put it, over 'national priorities in constitutional and legal matters.' [The] flow of petitions for review, it has been argued, enables the Court to keep its finger on the pulse of the legal order. 'Across the screen each Term' wrote Mr. Justice Douglas, 'come the worries and concerns of the American people—high and low—presented in concrete, tangible form.' Chief Justice Warren observed: 'The very flow of those cases through the chambers of the Court serves to inform the justices of what is happening to the system of justice.'

"Occasional dissents by one or more justices from a denial of review, Justice Brennan pointed out, 'often herald the appearance on the horizon of a possible reexamination' of previously settled law. The judges of the new National Court would have and could acquire no sense of such impending changes. Only the justices of the Supreme Court in their own assessment of their own collective thinking can know what changes may be trembling on the brink. [The] judges of the new court, wrote Chief Justice Warren, being necessarily 'trained to follow precedent,' would 'deny review of those decisions that fall into the traditional molds and that seem correctly decided in terms of precedent and settled law.' Former Justice Goldberg thought [m] it doubtful that many of the cases in which the Court in the 1960s reformed various aspects of criminal procedure, [or] even the first legislative apportionment case (*Baker v. Carr*), or indeed *Brown v. Board of Education* would ever have reached the Supreme Court from a new National Court of Appeals. * * *

"(4) The other side of the coin of loss of control by the Court is loss of access to [it]. Chief Justice Warren [said] the Court 'would lose its symbolic but vitally important status as the ultimate tribunal to which all citizens, poor or rich, may submit their claims.'" [n]

(c) Several other plans for relieving the Supreme Court's workload by creating a new federal appellate court inferior to it—but one that would not interfere with the Supreme Court's power to control its own docket—have been proposed. An ABA-developed suggestion would have Congress authorize "the Supreme Court [to] refer classes of cases or individual cases for initial recommendations or initial decision by the new court. The Supreme Court retains its power to accept or to reject any case for hearing," and the final authority to review decisions. Hufstedler, *Courtship and Other Legal Arts*, 60 A.B.A.J. 545, 548 (1974). In 1975, the congressionally established Commission on Revision of the Federal Appellate Court System (chaired by Sen. Roman Hruska) made a similar proposal (see 67 F.R.D. 195).[o]

---

23. Friendly, *Federal Jurisdiction: A General View* 48–51 (1973).

m. Goldberg, *One Supreme Court*, New Republic, Feb. 10, 1973, p. 14.

n. In contrast, several justices, although "not giving immediate and unqualified endorsement of the study group's principal recommendation" solicited its "open-minded consideration." Bickel, supra, at 14. See Burger, *Defends Freund Study Group's Composition and Proposal*, 59 A.B.A.J. 721 (1973); Rehn-

quist, *The Supreme Court: Past and Present*, 59 A.B.A.J. 361 (1973). Compare Black, note 3, Sec. 3 supra; Gressman, fn. e, Sec. 3 supra and authorities cited therein.

o. "Of the active members of the Court (all of whom were polled by the Commission), Justice Rehnquist was perhaps the most emphatic in joining the Commission's criticism of the present system. The Justice stated flatly that the Supreme Court can no longer meet the country's need for thorough and deliberative

(d) One of the Freund Report's recommendations was "the substitution of certiorari for appeal in all cases where appeal is now the prescribed procedure for review in the Supreme Court." In 1979, the Senate passed a bill to eliminate the Court's obligatory appellate jurisdiction in almost all cases. The proposal was drafted by the Justice Department and endorsed by the ABA and all witnesses at the Senate hearings. It was also unanimously supported by the Court which pointed out that "during the 1976 term almost half of the cases decided by this Court on the merits were cases brought here as of right under the Court's mandatory jurisdiction [and] unduly expended the Court's resources on cases better left to other courts." Enactment by the House of Representatives was stalled by an unrelated amendment. See generally Gressman, *Requiem for the Supreme Court's Obligatory Jurisdiction,* 65 A.B.A.J. 1325 (1979). In 1982, a similar bill passed the House (H.R. 6872, 97th Cong. 2d Sess.), but not the Senate.

MARYLAND v. BALTIMORE RADIO SHOW, INC.
338 U.S. 912, 70 S.Ct. 252, 94 L.Ed. 562 (1950).

Opinion of MR. JUSTICE FRANKFURTER respecting the denial of the petition for writ of certiorari. * * *

A variety of considerations underlie denials of the writ, and as to the same petition different reasons may lead different Justices to the same result. This is especially true of petitions for review on writ of certiorari to a State court. Narrowly technical reasons may lead to denials. [For detail, see Sec. 5 infra.] A

decision making on important issues of federal constitutional and statutory law. The Chief Justice and Justices White, Blackmun, and Powell were somewhat more guarded, but they plainly agreed with Justice Rehnquist. [On] the other hand, Justices Douglas, Brennan, Stewart, and Marshall see no present need for the creation of a new court [and former] Justices Fortas and Goldberg are also opposed." Owens, *The Hruska Commission's Proposed National Court of Appeals,* 23 U.C. L.A.L.Rev. 580, 591 & n. 53 (1976). For criticism of the proposal, see id.; Casper & Posner, fn. j supra.

More recently, see the dissenting opinions of Stevens, J., in *Michigan v. Long,* 463 U.S. 1032, 103 S.Ct. 3469, 77 L.Ed.2d 1201 (1983), and *Florida v. Meyers,* 466 U.S. 380, 104 S.Ct. 1852, 80 L.Ed.2d 381 (1984) (joined by Brennan and Marshall, JJ.), complaining of "error" in the Court's "allocation of resources": "I believe that in reviewing the decisions of state courts, the primary role of the Court is to make sure that persons who seek to *vindicate* federal rights have been fairly heard. [Since] the beginning of the 1981 term, the Court has decided in summary fashion 19 [cases] concerning the constitutional rights of persons accused or convicted of crimes. All 19 were decided on the petition of the warden or prosecutor, and in all he was successful in obtaining reversal of a decision upholding a claim of constitutional right. [The] result is a docket swollen with requests by states to reverse judgments that their courts have rendered in favor of their citizens."

See also Choper, in Choper, Kamisar & Tribe, *The Supreme Court: Trends and Developments 1981–82* 260–61 (1983): "[O]f the 24 criminal law-criminal procedure cases [that] the Court has already taken for review for the next Term, 22 involve petitions or appeals either by the state or by the United States. That means that the court below held the challenged criminal procedure rule or criminal law rule unconstitutional. I think at least four members of the Court feel a compulsion to correct that lower Court decision. As I looked over the other constitutional decisions, there were 17 cases involving the constitutionality of federal, state, or local actions. Thirteen involved rulings of unconstitutionality by the courts below. Now, I do not want to take the view that none of these cases is important. But if one perceives the role of the United States Supreme Court (as I do) [as] dominantly concerned with protecting the interests of minorities against the majoritarian political process, it does seem to me [a] somewhat wasteful expenditure of judicial resources to simply take up a large number of cases in which the courts below may have given, in the opinion of four Justices, undue protection to minorities. One way of curing the work load is to let what may be perhaps an overly expansive interpretation of constitutional rights stand for at least awhile."

Legislation to implement the approach of the Hruska Commission continues to be introduced in Congress. See Hellman, *Caseload, Conflicts and Decisional Capacity: Does the Supreme Court Need Help?,* 67 Judic. 28 (1983).

decision may satisfy all these technical requirements and yet may commend itself for review to fewer than four members of the Court. Pertinent considerations of judicial policy here come into play. A case may raise an important question but the record may be cloudy. It may be desirable to have different aspects of an issue further illumined by the lower courts. Wise adjudication has its own time for ripening.

Since there are these conflicting and, to the uninformed, even confusing reasons for denying petitions for certiorari, it has been suggested from time to time that the Court indicate its reasons for denial. Practical considerations preclude. [The] time that would be required is prohibitive, apart from the fact as already indicated that different reasons not infrequently move different members of the Court * * *. It becomes relevant here to note that failure to record a dissent from a denial of a petition for writ of certiorari in nowise implies that only the member of the Court who notes his dissent thought the petition should be granted. * * *

SECTION 5. PREREQUISITES TO FEDERAL JURISDICTION AND JUDICIAL REVIEW: AN INTRODUCTION

Under Art. III, federal judicial power extends only to resolving "cases" and "controversies." Thus, federal courts are precluded from giving "advisory opinions" or deciding "moot" cases. In determining whether there is a "case or controversy" capable of and suitable for resolution by federal courts, parties asserting particular contentions must have "standing"; at a minimum, they must allege "such a personal stake in the outcome of the controversy as to assure that concrete adverseness which sharpens the presentation of issues." [a] Further, claims must be asserted at a time when they are "ripe" for adjudication: "a hypothetical threat is not enough"; [b] "determination of [the] constitutionality of legislation in advance of its immediate adverse effect in the context of a concrete case involves too remote and abstract an inquiry for the proper exercise of the judicial function." [c]

Because all these matters must be resolved before a federal court may consider the merits of a constitutional contention, they could profitably be explored in detail here. But their consideration is often intertwined with and requires understanding of the substantive constitutional provision in issue. Thus, their presentation is deferred to Ch. 9 when students will be better equipped to comprehend and evaluate them.

a. *Baker v. Carr,* Sec. 2 supra.

b. *United Public Workers v. Mitchell,* p. 1221 infra.

c. *International Longshoremen's and Warehousemen's Union v. Boyd,* 347 U.S. 222, 74 S.Ct. 447, 98 L.Ed. 650 (1954).

Chapter 2

SUBSTANTIVE PROTECTION OF ECONOMIC INTERESTS

PREFATORY NOTE

Most of the remaining chapters are concerned with constitutional limitations on governmental power, independent of limitations arising out of the distribution of powers within the federal system. Some of the limitations are identical, or nearly so, whether applied to the state or federal governments, but are based on different sources. The major limitations on the federal government are found in the Bill of Rights and in Art. I, § 9, while those on state government are based largely on the thirteenth, fourteenth, and fifteenth amendments and on Art. I, § 10. But the fourteenth amendment has now been held to impose on the states most of the limitations the Bill of Rights imposes on the federal government.

These materials do not deal with all limitations based on the federal Constitution but only those of major significance and difficulty. State constitutions include additional limitations on state government, some similar to federal limitations though occasionally interpreted differently, and some quite dissimilar in terms and purposes. Study of the federal limitations should provide adequate training and background for handling the state-imposed limitations with professional skill.

SECTION 1. ORIGINS OF SUBSTANTIVE DUE PROCESS AS A LIMITATION ON GOVERNMENTAL POWER

INTRODUCTION

One important concern of this and later chapters is the extent to which the due process clauses of the fifth and fourteenth amendments may be invoked to impose limits on the *substance* of governmental regulations and other activities, as well as to govern the *procedures*—the due process—by which government affects "life, liberty and property." That the due process clauses could be thought to embody any limitation on the substance of state legislation requires some initial explanation, since the clauses appear to related only to "due process."

Professor Edward S. Corwin traced the origin and evolution of due process as a substantive limitation on governmental power in a series of articles[a], later revised in his *Liberty Against Government* (1948). This book, concerned primarily with judicial evolution of concepts designed to limit government regulation of property and economic interests, provides a valuable background for understanding, as well, some of the underpinnings for the later use of the due process clause and first amendment to limit governmental interference with the more basic personal liberties.

Space limits preclude detailed study here of the judicial search for tools by which to limit governmental power, culminating in the "substantive due process" concept. Here we only sketch, by suggestive excerpts, some of the more significant steps.

I. JUDICIAL RESPONSE TO PHILOSOPHICAL LIMITATIONS ON GOVERNMENTAL POWER

CALDER v. BULL, 3 U.S. (3 Dall.) 386, 1 L.Ed. 648 (1798), is not remembered for its ruling, declining to interfere with the state legislature's setting aside a probate court ruling, but for two opinions expressing diametrically opposed views on the nature and source of limitations on governmental power:

"CHASE, JUSTICE. [I] cannot subscribe to the omnipotence of a State legislature, or that it is absolute and without control; although its authority should not be expressly restrained by the constitution, or fundamental law of the state. The people of the United States erected their constitutions, or forms of government, to establish justice, to promote the general welfare, to secure the blessings of liberty, and to protect their persons and property from violence. The purposes for which men enter into society will determine the nature and terms of the social compact; and as they are the foundation of the legislative power, they will decide what are the proper objects of it. The nature and ends of legislative power will limit the exercise of it. This fundamental principle flows from the very nature of our free republican governments, that no man should be compelled to do what the laws do not require; nor to refrain from acts which the laws permit. There are acts which the federal, or state, legislature cannot do, without exceeding their authority. There are certain vital principles in our free republican governments, which will determine and overrule an apparent and flagrant abuse of legislative power; as to authorize manifest injustice by positive law; to take away that security for personal liberty, or private property, for the protection whereof the government was established. An act of the legislature (for I cannot call it a law), contrary to the great first principles of the social compact, cannot be considered a rightful exercise of legislative authority. The obligation of a law in governments established on express compact, and on republican principles, must be determined by the nature of the power on which it is founded. A few instances will suffice to explain what I mean. A law that punished a citizen for an innocent action or, in other words, for an act, which, when done, was in violation of no existing law; a law that destroys, or impairs, the lawful private contracts of citizens; a law that makes a man a judge in his own cause; or a law that takes property from A and gives it to B: It is against all reason and justice, for a people to intrust a legislature with SUCH powers; and therefore, it cannot be presumed that they have done it. The genius, the

a. Corwin, *The Doctrine of Due Process of Law Before the Civil War*, 24 Harv.L.Rev. 366, 460 (1911); Corwin, *The Basic Doctrine of American Constitutional Law*, 12 Mich.L.Rev. 247 (1914); Corwin, *The "Higher Law" Background of American Constitutional Law*, 42 Harv.L.Rev. 149, 365 (1928–1929).

nature, and the spirit, of our State governments, amount to a prohibition of such acts of legislation; and the general principles of law and reason forbid them.[a]

"IREDELL, JUSTICE. "[I]t has been the policy of all the American states, which have, individually, framed their state constitutions, since the revolution, and of the people of the United States, when they framed the federal constitution, to define with precision the objects of the legislative power, and to restrain its exercise within marked and settled boundaries. If any act of Congress, or of the legislature of a state, violates those constitutional provisions, it is unquestionably void. [If], on the other hand, the legislature of the Union, or the legislature of any member of the Union, shall pass a law, within the general scope of their constitutional power, the court cannot pronounce it to be void, merely because it is, in their judgment, contrary to the principles of natural justice. The ideals of natural justice are regulated by no fixed standard: the ablest and the purest men have differed upon the subject; and all that the court could properly say, in such an event, would be that the legislature (possessed of an equal right of opinion) had passed an act which, in the opinion of the judges, was inconsistent with the abstract principles of natural justice. * * *"

Notes and Questions

1. Compare the following by Lord Coke in *Dr. Bonham's Case,* 8 Co. 113b, 118a, 77 Eng.Rep. 646, 652 (1610): "And it appears in our books, that in many cases, the common law will controul Acts of Parliament, and sometimes adjudge them to be utterly void: for when an Act of Parliament is against common right and reason, or repugnant, or impossible to be performed, the common law will controul it, and adjudge such Act to be void." For commentary on the influence of the Coke dictum, see Corwin, *Liberty Against Government* 34–40 (1948).

2. For philosophical origins of the Chase viewpoint, see Corwin, *Liberty Against Government* 10–57 (1948); Corwin, *The "Higher Law" Background of American Constitutional Law,* 42 Harv.L.Rev. 149, 365 (1928–1929). For the extent to which similar viewpoints crept into judicial opinions and decisions between the revolution and 1830, see Corwin, *Liberty Against Government* 58–67 (1948): "The truth is that Iredell's tenet that courts were not to appeal to natural rights and the social compact as furnishing a basis for constitutional decisions was disregarded at one time or another by all of the leading judges and advocates of the initial period of our constitutional history, an era which closes about 1830."

3. *Other early reflections of natural law.* Some early decisions combined the Chase philosophy in *Calder* with broad interpretations of the contract clause, forbidding state legislative impairment of the obligation of contracts, as a means of protecting property rights against state legislative encroachments. Note, e.g., MARSHALL, J.'s, conclusion in FLETCHER v. PECK, 10 U.S. (6 Cranch.) 87, 3 L.Ed. 162 (1810) (contract clause barred law annulling land title bought in good faith from grantee of corruptly secured legislative grant): "It is, then, the unanimous opinion of the court, that, in this case, the estate having passed into the hands of a purchaser for a valuable consideration, without notice, the state of Georgia was restrained, either by general principles which are common to our free institutions, or by the particular provisions of the Constitution of the United States, from passing a law whereby the estate of the plaintiff in the premises so

---

a. Dean Ely interprets Chase, J.'s, opinion as a philosophical, not a constitutional, argument. See Ely, *On Discovering Fundamental Values,* 92 Harv.L.Rev. 5, 26–27 n. 95 (1978).

purchased could be constitutionally and legally impaired and rendered null and void."

JOHNSON, J., concurred in the result: "I do not hesitate to declare that a state does not possess the power of revoking its own grants. But I do it on a general principle, on the reason and nature of things: a principle which will impose laws even on the deity."

Note also STORY, J.'s, similar reasoning in TERRETT v. TAYLOR, 13 U.S. (9 Cranch.) 43, 3 L.Ed. 650 (1815) (barring Virginia from claiming title to church property under a statute authorizing its sale and the use of the proceeds for the poor of the parish: "[We] think ourselves standing upon the principles of natural justice, upon the fundamental laws of every free government, upon the spirit and the letter of the constitution of the United States, and upon the decisions of most respectable judicial tribunals in resisting such a doctrine."

During this same period the state courts were protecting vested property rights against legislative interference through a variety of rationales similar to that in *Calder*. See Corwin, *Liberty Against Government* 65–82 (1948).

II. NARROWING OF FEDERAL CONSTITUTIONAL LIMITS ON STATES

Bill of Rights applicable to states. BARRON v. MAYOR AND CITY COUNCIL, 32 U.S. (7 Pet.) 243, 8 L.Ed. 672 (1833), per MARSHALL, C. J., ruled that the fifth amendment prohibition on taking private property for a public use without compensation applied only to action by the federal government, not to the states or their subdivisions: "Each state established a constitution for itself, and in that constitution, provided such limitations and restrictions on the powers of its particular government as its judgment dictated. The people of the United States framed such a government for the United States as they supposed best adapted to their situation, and best calculated to promote their interests. The powers they conferred on this government were to be exercised by itself; and the limitations on power, if expressed in general terms are naturally, and, we think, necessarily applicable to the government created by the instrument. They are limitations of power granted in the instrument itself; not of distinct governments framed by different persons and for different [purposes].

"[The] great revolution which established the constitution of the United States was not effected without immense opposition. Serious fears were extensively entertained that those powers which the patriot statesmen, who then watched over the interests of our country, deemed essential to union, and to the attainment of those invaluable objects for which union was sought, might be exercised in a manner dangerous to liberty. In almost every convention by which the constitution was adopted, amendments to guard against the abuse of power were recommended. These amendments demanded security against the apprehended encroachments of the general government, not against those of the local governments.

"In compliance with a sentiment thus generally expressed, to quiet fears thus extensively entertained, amendments were proposed by the required majority in Congress, and adopted by the states. These amendments contain no expression indicating an intention to apply them to the state governments. This court cannot so apply them."

Formally the Court has consistently adhered to the *Barron* ruling that the Bill of Rights applies only to the federal government, but during the twentieth century most of its limitations have gradually been made applicable to the states through the fourteenth amendment. See Ch. 7–9 infra.

Shrinking contract clause protection. Four years after *Barron,* the Court also began to narrow the protective scope of the contract clause. *Charles River Bridge v. Warren Bridge* (1837)[a] refused to view a state grant of the right to operate a toll bridge as implying an obligation not to authorize a competing bridge. This was only step one in the Court's growing unwillingness to use the contract clause to block state action needed to protect vital public interests,[b] but the opinion seemed designed to discourage resort to the federal constitution to escape regulation of economic interests: "It is well settled by the decisions of this court, that a state law may be retrospective in its character, and may divest vested rights; and yet not violate the constitution of the United States, unless it also impairs the obligation of a contract." "Thus it *became more and more evident that the doctrine of vested rights must, to survive, find anchorage in some clause or other of the various State constitutions.*" Corwin, *Liberty Against Government* 89 (1948).

III. DEVELOPMENT OF STATE CONSTITUTIONAL BASIS

With federal constitutional grounds not available to protect against most encroachments on economic interests, lawyers and state judges resorted to the "due process" and "law of the land" clauses of state constitutions. These provisions originally referred to proceeding in accordance with the law and accepted legal procedure. Professor Corwin pointed out how the state courts began to evolve out of these clauses a substantive limitation on legislative power, aimed first at special legislation designed to affect the rights of specific individuals, and then applied to general legislation interfering with vested rights. See Corwin, *Liberty Against Government* 89–115 (1948); Corwin, *The Doctrine of Due Process of Law Before the Civil War,* 24 Harv.L.Rev. 366, 460 (1911). He summarized in *Liberty Against Government* 173–74:

"Most State constitutions contained from the outset a paraphrase of chapter 29 of Magna Carta, which declared that no person should be deprived of his 'estate' 'except by the law of the land or a judgment of his peers'; and following the usage of the Fifth Amendment of the United States Constitution, more and more State constitutions came after 1791 to contain a clause which, paraphrasing a statute of Plantagenet times, declared that 'no person shall be deprived of life, liberty or property without due process of law.' By the outbreak of the Civil War a more or less complete transference of the doctrine of vested rights and most of its Kentian corollaries had been effected in the vast majority of the State jurisdictions. One exception was Kent's distinction between the power of 'regulation,' which he conceded the State, and that of 'destruction,' which he denied it unless it was prepared to compensate disadvantaged owners. The division of judicial opinion on this point was signalized in the middle fifties, when the New York Court of Appeals, in the great *Wynehamer* case, stigmatized a State-wide prohibition statute as an act of destruction, in its application to existing stocks of liquor, which was beyond the power of the State legislature to authorize *even by*

---

a. 36 U.S. (11 Pet.) 420, 9 L.Ed. 773, 9 L.Ed. 938 (1837).

b. A few years later *West River Bridge Co. v. Dix,* 47 U.S. (6 How.) 507, 12 L.Ed. 535 (1848) ruled that a state grant of the exclusive privilege to operate a toll bridge did not prevent the state from acquiring it by eminent domain. *Stone v. Mississippi,* 101 U.S. (11 Otto) 814, 25 L.Ed. 1079 (1879) held that for the legislature to ban a lottery business 3 years after giving it a 25 year charter did not violate the contract clause in view of the vital public interest at stake. For more current cases see those discussed in Sec. 5 infra.

the procedures of due process of law. In several other States similar statutes were sustained in the name of the 'police power.' " [a]

WYNEHAMER v. PEOPLE, 13 N.Y. 378 (1856) held by a divided court that a New York prohibition statute violated the state due process clause as applied to the sale of liquor owned at the time of the enactment of the statute. Professor Corwin commented on *Wynehamer* in *Liberty Against Government* 103, 114–15:

"In *Wynehamer,* [the] court was confronted with a frankly penal statute which provided a procedure, for the most part unexceptionable, for its enforcement. That statute was nonetheless overturned under the due 'process of law' clause, which was hereby plainly made to prohibit, regardless of the matter of procedure, a certain kind or degree of exertion of legislative power altogether. The result serves to throw into strong light once more the dependence of the derived notion of due process of law on extra constitutional principles; for it is nothing less *than the elimination of the very phrase under construction from the constitutional clause in which it occurs.* The main proposition of [*Wynehamer*] is that the legislature cannot destroy by any method whatever what by previous law was property. But why not? To all intents and purposes the answer of the court is simply that 'no person shall be *deprived* of life, liberty or *property.*'

* * *

"In less than twenty years from the time of its rendition the crucial ruling in *Wynehamer* was far on the way to being assimilated into the accepted constitutional law of the country.[b] The 'due process' clause, which had been intended originally to consecrate a *mode of procedure,* had become a constitutional test of ever increasing reach of *the substantive content of legislation.* Thus was the doctrine of vested rights brought within the constitutional fold, although without dominating it. For confronting it was the still-expanding concept of the police power."

IV. FOURTEENTH AMENDMENT

Historical background. The history of the Civil War amendments, particularly the fourteenth, insofar as that history relates to the problems considered in this and later chapters, is thoroughly treated elsewhere. See, e.g., Fairman, *Does the Fourteenth Amendment Incorporate the Bill of Rights? The Original Understanding,* 2 Stan.L.Rev. 5 (1949); Bickel, *The Original Understanding and the Segregation Decision,* 69 Harv.L.Rev. 1 (1955); Frank & Munro, *The Original Understanding of "Equal Protection of the Laws"* 1972 Wash.U.L.Q. 421 (where other historical studies are cited).

SLAUGHTER–HOUSE CASES, 83 U.S. (16 Wall.) 36, 21 L.Ed. 394 (1873), per MILLER, J., upheld a legislatively-granted monopoly to operate slaughterhouses in the New Orleans area, subject to letting others use the facilities at state-regulated fees. The Court viewed this as an "appropriate, stringent, and effectual" means to "remove from the more densely populated part of the city, the noxious slaughterhouses and large and offensive collections of animals, [and]

---

a. Extracts from this book reprinted with permission of the publisher, copyright © 1948 Louisiana State University Press.

b. Corwin was referring here to the broad principle exemplified by *Wynehamer*; its actu-al ruling on state liquor prohibition was rejected by all states but one. See id. at 107.

to locate them where the convenience, health and comfort of the people require," [a] but that was not the basis for its rejection of the challenge to the monopoly under the privileges and immunities clause of the fourteenth amendment:

"The first section of the fourteenth article, to which our attention is more specially invited, opens with a definition of citizenship—not only citizenship of the United States, but citizenship of the states. * * * 'All persons born or naturalized in the United States, and subject to the jurisdiction thereof, are citizens of the United States and of the state wherein they reside.' [T]he distinction between citizenship of the United States and citizenship of a state is clearly recognized and established. Not only may a man be a citizen of the United States without being a citizen of a state, but an important element is necessary to convert the former into the latter. He must reside within the state to make him a citizen of it, but it is only necessary that he should be born or naturalized in the United States to be a citizen of the Union. * * *

"The language is, 'No state shall make or enforce any law which shall abridge the privileges or immunities of citizens of the United States.' It is a little remarkable, if this clause was intended as a protection to the citizen of a state against the legislative power of his own state, that the word citizen of the state should be left out when it is so carefully used, and used in contradistinction to citizens of the United States, in the very sentence which precedes it. It is too clear for argument that the change in phraseology was adopted understandingly and with a purpose.

"Of the privileges and immunities of the citizen of the United States, and, of the privileges and immunities of the citizen of the state, and what they respectively are, we will presently consider; but we wish to state here that it is only the former which are placed by this clause under the protection of the federal Constitution, and that the latter, whatever they may be, are not intended to have any additional protection by this paragraph of the amendment."

The opinion distinguished Article IV "privileges and immunities" for which states must give equal treatment to the citizens of other states: "[U]p to the adoption of the recent amendments, no claim or pretence was set up that those rights depended on the federal government for their existence or protection, beyond the very few express limitations which the federal Constitution imposed upon the states—such, for instance, as the prohibition against ex post facto laws, bills of attainder, and laws impairing the obligation of contracts. But with the exception of these and a few other restrictions, the entire domain of the privileges and immunities of citizens of the states [lay] within the constitutional and legislative power of the states, and without that of the federal government. Was it the purpose of the Fourteenth Amendment by the simple declaration that no state should make or enforce any law which shall abridge the privileges and immunities of *Citizens of the United States,* to transfer the security and protection of all the civil rights which we have mentioned, from the states to the federal government? And where it is declared that Congress shall have the power to enforce that article, was it was intended to bring within the power of

---

a. See Hovenkamp, *Technology, Politics and Regulated Monopoly: An American Historical Perspective,* 62 Tex.L.Rev. 1263, 1295–1308 (1984), for a dramatic historical account of the legislative conversion of the fragmented, unhealthful, mislocated New Orleans slaughtering industry into a well-placed, price-regulated public utility monopoly open to every butcher to use, which solved the health problem and drastically reduced the price of beef.

Congress the entire domain of civil rights heretofore belonging exclusively to the states?

"All this and more must follow, if the proposition of the plaintiffs in error be sound. [F]urther, such a construction [would] constitute this court a perpetual censor upon all legislation of the states, on the civil rights of their own citizens, with authority to nullify such as it did not approve as consistent with those rights as they existed at the time of the adoption of this amendment. [When] these consequences are [so] great a departure from the structure and spirit of our institutions; [when] in fact it radically changes the whole theory of the relations of the state and federal governments to each other and of both these governments to the people; the argument has a force that is irresistible, in the absence of language which expresses such a purpose too clearly to admit of doubt.

"We are convinced that no such results were intended by the Congress which proposed these amendments, nor by the legislatures of the states which ratified them.[b]

"The argument has not been much pressed in these cases that the defendant's charter deprives the plaintiffs of their property without due process of law, or that it denies to them the equal protection of the law. The first of these paragraphs has been in the Constitution since the adoption of the Fifth Amendment, as a restraint upon the federal power. It is also to be found in some form of expression in the constitutions of nearly all the states, as a restraint upon the power of the States.

"[U]nder no construction of that provision that we have ever seen, or any that we deem admissible, can the restraint imposed by the state of Louisiana upon the exercise of their trade by the butchers of New Orleans be held to be a deprivation of property within the meaning of that provision.

"[In] the light of the history of these amendments, and the pervading purpose of them, which we have already discussed, it is not difficult to give a meaning to [the equal protection] clause. [We] doubt very much whether any action of a state not directed by way of discrimination against the negroes as a class, or on account of their race, will ever be held to come within the purview of this provision. It is so clearly a provision for that race and that emergency, that a strong case would be necessary for its application to any other."

FIELD, J., dissented.[c] "If this [clause] only refers, as held by the majority of the court in their opinion, to such privileges and immunities as were before its

b. Here the opinion added:

"[L]est it should be said that no such privileges and immunities are to be found if those we have been considering are excluded, we venture to suggest some which owe their existence to the federal government, its national character, its Constitution, or its laws.

"One of these is well described in *Crandall v. Nevada*, 73 U.S. (6 Wall.) 35, 18 L.Ed. 745. It is said to be the right of the citizen of this great country, protected by implied guarantees of its Constitution, 'to come to the seat of government to assert any claim he may have upon that government, to transact any business he may have with it, to seek its protection, to share its offices, to engage in administering its functions.' * * *

"The right to peaceably assemble and petition for redress of grievances, the privilege of the writ of habeas corpus, are rights of the citizen guaranteed by the federal Constitution. The right to use the navigable waters of the United States, however they may penetrate the territory of the several states, all rights secured to our citizens by treaties with foreign nations, are dependent upon citizenship of the United States, and not citizenship of a state. [To] these may be added the rights secured by the thirteenth and fifteenth articles of amendment, and by the other clause of the fourteenth."

c. Chase, C.J., and Swayne and Bradley, J., joined this dissent. Bradley, J., joined by Swayne, J., also dissented, asserting that the statute also violated due process and equal protection.

adoption specially designated in the Constitution or necessarily implied as belonging to citizens of the United States, it was a vain and idle enactment, which accomplished nothing, and most unnecessarily excited Congress and the people on its passage. With privileges and immunities thus designated or implied no State could ever have interfered by its laws, and no new constitutional provision was required to inhibit such interference. The supremacy of the Constitution and the laws of the United States always controlled any State legislation of that character. But if the amendment refers to the natural and inalienable rights which belong to all citizens, the inhibition has a profound significance and consequence. * * *

"The terms, privileges and immunities, are not new in the amendment; they were in the Constitution before the amendment was adopted. They are found in [Art. IV, § 2.] The privileges and immunities designated are those which of right belong to the citizens of all free governments. Clearly among these must be placed the right to pursue a lawful employment in a lawful manner, without other restraint than such as equally affects all persons. In the discussions in Congress upon the passage of the Civil Rights Act repeated reference was made to this language of Mr. Justice Washington. It was cited by Senator Trumbull with the observation that it enumerated the very rights belonging to a citizen of the United States set forth in the first section of the [act].

"The privileges and immunities designated in [Art. IV, § 2] are, then, according to the decision cited, those which of right belong to the citizens of all free governments. [What] the clause in question did for the protection of the citizens of one State against hostile and discriminating legislation of other States, the fourteenth amendment does for the protection of every citizen of the United States against hostile and discriminating legislation against him in favor of others, whether they reside in the same or in different [States].

"This equality of right, with exemption from all disparaging and partial enactments, in the lawful pursuits of life, throughout the whole country, is the distinguishing privilege of citizens of the United States. To them, everywhere, all pursuits, all professions, all avocations are open without other restrictions than such as are imposed equally upon all others of the same age, sex, and condition. The State may prescribe such regulations for every pursuit and calling of life as will promote the public health, secure the good order and advance the general prosperity of society, but when once prescribed, the pursuit or calling must be free to be followed by every citizen who is within the conditions designated, and will conform to the regulations. This is the fundamental idea upon which our institutions rest, and unless adhered to in the legislation of the country our government will be a republic only in name."

Notes and Questions

1. *Objectives of privileges and immunities and citizenship provisions.* An historical study protests that the *Slaughter-House* opinion flies in the face of the congressional purpose for inserting the citizenship sentence. Graham, supra, at 23–26: "Significantly, no one observed that while citizenship was made dual in this first sentence, only the privileges or immunities of 'citizens of the United States' were specifically protected in the second sentence against abridgment by the states. The reason for this apparent oversight is that ever since Birney's day, opponents of slavery had regarded all important 'natural' and constitutional rights as being privileges and immunities of *citizens of the United States*. This had been the cardinal premise of antislavery theory from the beginning, and this

had been the underlying theory and purpose of Section One from the beginning. The real purpose of adding this citizenship definition was to remove any possible or lingering doubt about the freedman's citizenship."

2. *Resulting scope of privileges and immunities.* Professor McGovney paraphrased the clause as interpreted: "No State shall make or enforce any law which shall abridge any privilege or immunity conferred *by this Constitution, the statutes or treaties of the United States* upon any person who is a citizen of the United States." He then commented, "This narrower construction [renders] it an idle provision, in that it only declares a principle already more amply and more simply expressed in the constitution." McGovney, *Privileges or Immunities Clause, Fourteenth Amendment,* 4 Iowa Law Bull. (now Ia.L.Rev.) 219, 220, 221 (1918).

3. *The "idle provision."* The restrictive interpretation given the privileges and immunities clause in *Slaughter-House* has been consistently followed. Except for one quickly-overruled case,[d] the Court has never invalidated state legislation under the fourteenth amendment privileges and immunities clause. On a few occasions a minority of the Court invoked the clause. For details and analysis see Tribe, *American Constitutional Law* 418–26 (1978).

4. *Creative dicta.* Two closely related factors played important roles in the emergence of substantive due process. (1) Lawyers in speeches, treatises, articles and briefs strongly advanced the *laissez faire* concept of government, often urging the due process clause as a constitutional limitation on governmental regulation of business. See the remarkable study of the influence of lawyers in this respect in Twiss, *Lawyers and the Constitution* 18–173 (1942). (2) Supreme Court justices in dissenting opinions, and state courts, strongly reflected these views, until majority opinions sustaining state regulation began also to recognize that the due process clause imposes some limits on the regulatory power of government. See Corwin, *Liberty Against Government* 129–152 (1948).

LOCHNER v. NEW YORK

198 U.S. 45, 25 S.Ct. 539, 49 L.Ed. 937 (1905).

MR. JUSTICE PECKHAM delivered the opinion of the Court.

[The Court held invalid a New York statute forbidding employment in a bakery for more than 60 hours a week or 10 hours a day.]

[It] must, of course, be conceded that there is a limit to the valid exercise of the police power by the state. [Otherwise] the 14th Amendment would have no efficacy and the legislatures of the states would have unbounded power. [In] every case that comes before this court, therefore, where legislation of this character is concerned, and where the protection of the Federal Constitution is sought, the question necessarily arises: Is this a fair, reasonable, and appropriate exercise of the police power of the state, or is it an unreasonable, unnecessary, and arbitrary interference with the right of the individual to his personal liberty, or to enter into those contracts in relation to labor which may seem to him appropriate or necessary for the support of himself and his family? Of course the liberty of contract relating to labor includes both parties to it. The one has as much right to purchase as the other to sell labor.

---

d. *Colgate v. Harvey*, 296 U.S. 404, 56 S.Ct. 252, 80 L.Ed. 299 (1935), overruled by *Madden v. Kentucky*, 309 U.S. 83, 60 S.Ct. 406, 84 L.Ed. 590 (1940).

This is not a question of substituting the judgment of the court for that of the legislature. If the act be within the power of the state it is valid, although the judgment of the court might be totally opposed to the enactment of such a law. But the question would still remain: Is it within the police power of the state? and that question must be answered by the court.

The question whether this act is valid as a labor law, pure and simple, may be dismissed in a few words. There is no reasonable ground for interfering with the liberty of person or the right of free contract, by determining the hours of labor, in the occupation of a baker. There is no contention that bakers as a class are not equal in intelligence and capacity to men in other trades or manual occupations, or that they are not able to assert their rights and care for themselves without the protecting arm of the state. [They] are in no sense wards of the state. Viewed in the light of a purely labor law, with no reference whatever to the question of health, we think that a law like the one before us involves neither the safety, the morals, nor the welfare, of the public, and that the interest of the public is not in the slightest degree affected by such an act. The law must be upheld, if at all, as a law pertaining to the health of the individual engaged in the occupation of a baker. It does not affect any other portion of the public than those who are engaged in that occupation. Clean and wholesome bread does not depend upon whether the baker works but ten hours per day or only sixty hours a week. [There] is, in our judgment, no reasonable foundation for holding this to be necessary or appropriate as a health law to safeguard the public health, or the health of the individuals who are following the trade of a baker.   *   *   *

We think that there can be no fair doubt that the trade of a baker, in and of itself, is not an unhealthy one to that degree which would authorize the legislature to interfere with the right to labor, and with the right of free contract on the part of the individual, either as employer or employee. In looking through statistics regarding all trades and occupations, it may be true that the trade of a baker does not appear to be as healthy as some other trades, and is also vastly more healthy than still others. To the common understanding the trade of a baker has never been regarded as an unhealthy one. [Some] occupations are more healthy than others, but we think there are none which might not come under the power of the legislature to supervise and control the hours of working therein, if the mere fact that the occupation is not absolutely and perfectly healthy is to confer that right upon the legislative department of the government. [It] is unfortunately true that labor, even in any department, may possibly carry with it the seeds of unhealthiness. But are we all, on that account, at the mercy of legislative majorities? A printer, a tinsmith, a locksmith, a carpenter, a cabinet maker, a dry goods clerk, a bank's, a lawyer's, or a physician's clerk, or a clerk in almost any kind of business, would all come under the power of the legislature, on this assumption. No trade, no occupation, no mode of earning one's living, could escape this all-pervading power, and the acts of the legislature in limiting the hours of labor in all employments would be valid, although such limitation might seriously cripple the ability of the laborer to support himself and his family. In our large cities there are many buildings into which the sun penetrates for but a short time in each day, and these buildings are occupied by people carrying on the business of bankers, brokers, lawyers, real estate, and many other kinds of business, aided by many clerks, messengers, and other employees. Upon the assumption of the validity of this act under review, it is not possible to say that an act, prohibiting lawyers' or bank clerks, or others, from contracting to labor for their employers more than eight hours a day would be invalid. * * *

It is also urged, pursuing the same line of argument, that it is to the interest of the state that its population should be strong and robust, and therefore any legislation which may be said to tend to make people healthy must be valid as health laws, enacted under the police power. If this be a valid argument and a justification for this kind of legislation, it follows that the protection of the Federal Constitution from undue interference with liberty of person and freedom of contract is visionary, wherever the law is sought to be justified as a valid exercise of the police power. Scarcely any law but might find shelter under such assumptions. [Not] only the hours of employees, but the hours of employers, could be regulated, and doctors, lawyers, scientists, all professional men, as well as athletes and artisans, could be forbidden to fatigue their brains and bodies by prolonged hours of exercise, lest the fighting strength of the state be impaired. We mention these extreme cases because the contention is extreme. We do not believe in the soundness of the views which uphold this law. [The] act is not, within any fair meaning of the term, a health law, but is an illegal interference with the rights of individuals, both employers and employees, to make contracts regarding labor upon such terms as they may think best, or which they may agree upon with the other parties to such contracts. Statutes of the nature of that under review, limiting the hours in which grown and intelligent men may labor to earn their living, are mere meddlesome interferences with the rights of the individual. * * *

This interference on the part of the legislatures of the several states with the ordinary trades and occupations of the people seems to be on the increase. [It] is impossible for us to shut our eyes to the fact that many of the laws of this character, while passed under what is claimed to be the police power for the purpose of protecting the public health or welfare, are, in reality, passed from other motives. We are justified in saying so when, from the character of the law and the subject upon which it legislates, it is apparent that the public health or welfare bears but the most remote relation to the [law].

It seems to us that the real object and purpose were simply to regulate the hours of labor between the master and his employees (all being men, sui juris), in a private business, not dangerous in any degree to morals, or in any real and substantial degree to the health of the employees. Under such circumstances the freedom of master and employee to contract with each other in relation to their employment [cannot] be prohibited or interfered with, without violating the Federal Constitution. * * *

Mr. Justice Holmes dissenting: * * *

This case is decided upon an economic theory which a large part of the country does not entertain. If it were a question whether I agree with that theory, I should desire to study it further and long before making up my mind. But I do not conceive that to be my duty, because I strongly believe that my agreement or disagreement has nothing to do with the right of a majority to embody their opinions in law. It is settled by various decisions of this court that state constitutions and state laws may regulate life in many ways which we as legislators might think as injudicious, or if you like as tyrannical, as this, and which, equally with this, interfere with the liberty to contract. Sunday laws and usury laws are ancient examples. A more modern one is the prohibition of lotteries. The liberty of the citizen to do as he likes so long as he does not interfere with the liberty of others to do the same, which has been a shibboleth for some well-known writers, is interfered with by school laws, by the Postoffice, by every state or municipal institution which takes his money for purposes thought desirable, whether he likes it or not. The 14th Amendment does not enact Mr. Herbert Spencer's *Social Statics*. [Some] of these laws embody convictions or prejudices which judges are likely to share. Some may not. But a Constitution is not intended to embody a particular economic theory, whether of paternalism and the organic relation of the citizen to the state or of laissez faire. It is made for people of fundamentally differing views, and the accident of our finding certain opinions natural and familiar, or novel, and even shocking, ought not to conclude our judgment upon the question whether statutes embodying them conflict with the Constitution of the United States.

[I] think that the word "liberty," in the 14th Amendment, is perverted when it is held to prevent the natural outcome of a dominant opinion, unless it can be said that a rational and fair man necessarily would admit that the statute proposed would infringe fundamental principles as they have been understood by the traditions of our people and our law. It does not need research to show that no such sweeping condemnation can be passed upon the statute before us. A reasonable man might think it a proper measure on the score of health. Men whom I certainly could not pronounce unreasonable would uphold it as a first instalment of a general regulation of the hours of work. * * *

MR. JUSTICE HARLAN (with whom MR. JUSTICE WHITE and MR. JUSTICE DAY concurred) dissenting:

[Whether] or not this be wise legislation it is not the province of the court to inquire. Under our systems of government the courts are not concerned with the wisdom or policy of legislation.

[The opinion quoted from writers on health problems of workers, pointing out that long hours, night hours, and difficult working conditions, such as excessive heat and exposure to flour dust, were injurious to the health of bakers, who "seldom live over their fiftieth year."]

We judicially know that the question of the number of hours during which a workman should continuously labor has been, for a long period, and is yet, a subject of serious consideration among civilized peoples, and by those having special knowledge of the laws of health. * * *

I do not stop to consider whether any particular view of this economic question presents the sounder theory. [It] is enough for the determination of this case, and it is enough for this court to know, that the question is one about which there is room for debate and for an honest difference of opinion. There are many reasons of a weighty, substantial character, based upon the experience of mankind, in support of the theory that, all things considered, more than ten hours' steady work each day, from week to week, in a bakery or confectionery establishment, may endanger the health and shorten the lives of the workmen, thereby diminishing their physical and mental capacity to serve the state and to provide for those dependent upon them.

If such reasons exist that ought to be the end of this case, for the state is not amenable to the judiciary, in respect of its legislative enactments, unless such enactments are plainly, palpably, beyond all question, inconsistent with the Constitution of the United States. * * *

SECTION 2. THREE DECADES OF CONTROL OVER LEGISLATIVE POLICY

From *Lochner* in 1905 to *Nebbia* in 1934, infra, the Court frequently substituted its judgment for that of Congress and state legislatures on the wisdom of economic regulation interfering with contract and property interests.[a] It relied mainly upon the due process clauses of the fifth and fourteenth amendments, with occasional resort to the equal protection clause. Between 1899 and 1937, after excluding the civil rights cases, 159 Supreme Court decisions held state statutes unconstitutional under the due process and equal protection clauses and 25 more statutes were struck down under the due process clause coupled with some other provision of the Constitution. Wright, *The Growth of American Constitutional Law* 154 (1942).

The Court most freely substituted its judgment for that of the legislature in labor legislation, regulation of prices, and limitations on entry into business. It was most tolerant in the regulation of trade and business practices, such as insurance, financial institutions and competitive practices.[b] A few examples will suffice to show the extent to which the Court interfered with legislative policymaking in economic regulation. With regularity Holmes, J., dissented from this use of the due process clause, joined later by Brandeis and Stone, JJ., and Hughes, C.J.

1. *Control over hours of labor.* We have already seen how the Court barred control over the hours of labor, even in an industry where long hours threatened health. *Lochner* (1905). But in 1908 the Court sustained regulation of work hours for women in *Muller v. Oregon*, 208 U.S. 412, 28 S.Ct. 324, 52 L.Ed. 551 (1908), basing the decision on special considerations relating to women, and in 1917 the Court overruled *Lochner* 5 to 3 in sustaining a regulation of work hours for men in manufacturing establishments. *Bunting v. Oregon*, 243 U.S. 426, 37 S.Ct. 435, 61 L.Ed. 830 (1917). In *Muller* the majority was influenced by the so-called "Brandeis brief," which furnished the Court with overwhelming documentation justifying regulation of hours of labor for women. Felix Frankfurter, Esq., successfully followed the same technique in *Bunting*. See 208 U.S. at 419–20, and 243 U.S. at 433; Bikle, *Judicial Determination of Questions of Fact Affecting the Constitutional Validity of Legislative Action*, 38 Harv.L.Rev. 6, 13 (1924).

2. *Control over anti-union discrimination.* At an early date the Court struck down labor legislation forbidding discrimination by employers for union activity and requiring employees to sign "yellow dog" agreements not to join a union. *Adair v. United States*, 208 U.S. 161, 28 S.Ct. 277, 52 L.Ed. 436 (1908) (5th amendment); *Coppage v. Kansas*, 236 U.S. 1, 35 S.Ct. 240, 59 L.Ed. 441 (1915) (14th amendment).

Adair held that for Congress to forbid an interstate railroad to discharge an employee for union membership denied due process. For the Court, Harlan, J., who had dissented in *Lochner*, relied upon the liberty of contract approach in *Lochner* and equated the right of an employee to quit his employment with "the right of the employer, for whatever reason, to dispense with the services of the employee." McKenna and Holmes, JJ., dissented. *Coppage*, per Pitney, J.,

---

a. See Pound, *Liberty of Contract*, 18 Yale L.J. 454 (1909); Brown, *Due Process of Law, Police Power, and the Supreme Court*, 40 Harv. L.Rev. 943 (1927).

b. See summary of such cases in *Nebbia v. New York*, 291 U.S. 502, 527–529, 54 S.Ct. 505, 511–13, 78 L.Ed. 940, 950–53 (1934), infra.

rejected the claim that the legislature could protect employees from being required to sign yellow dog contracts to obtain or keep needed employment.

These restrictive decisions were distinguished away in *Texas & N.O.R.R. v. Brotherhood of Ry. & S.S. Clerks,* 281 U.S. 548, 50 S.Ct. 427, 74 L.Ed. 1034 (1930) and *NLRB v. Jones & Laughlin Steel Corp.* (1937). They were finally expressly overruled in *Phelps Dodge Corp. v. NLRB,* 313 U.S. 177, 61 S.Ct. 845, 85 L.Ed. 1271 (1941) and *Lincoln Fed. Labor Union v. Northwestern Iron & Met. Co.* (1949), Sec. 3 infra.

3. *Regulation of wages.* Six years after the Court had upheld regulation of hours of labor, it held 5 to 3 that regulation of wages violated due process. *Adkins v. Children's Hosp.,* 261 U.S. 525, 43 S.Ct. 394, 67 L.Ed. 785 (1923) (fifth amendment); *Murphy v. Sardell,* 269 U.S. 530, 46 S.Ct. 22, 70 L.Ed. 396 (1925) (14th amendment); *Morehead v. New York ex rel. Tipaldo,* 298 U.S. 587, 56 S.Ct. 918, 80 L.Ed. 1347 (1936) (same). Not until 1937 were these decisions overruled in *West Coast Hotel Co. v. Parrish,* Sec. 3 infra, where the Court expressly recognized the unequal bargaining position of workers, and that the wisdom of debatable policy is for the legislature.

4. *Regulation of prices.* The Court also held that regulation of prices for commodities and services violated due process except for a limited class labeled "business affected with a public interest."[c] *Tyson & Bro. v. Banton,* 273 U.S. 418, 47 S.Ct. 426, 71 L.Ed. 718 (1927) (theatre tickets); *Ribnik v. McBride,* 277 U.S. 350, 48 S.Ct. 545, 72 L.Ed. 913 (1928) (fees of employment agency); *Williams v. Standard Oil Co.,* 278 U.S. 235, 49 S.Ct. 115, 73 L.Ed. 287 (1929) (gasoline prices); cf. *Wolff Packing Co. v. Industrial Court,* 262 U.S. 522, 43 S.Ct. 630, 67 L.Ed. 1103 (1923) (compulsory arbitration of wages). *Nebbia v. New York* (1934) severely limited these rulings and they were expressly overruled in *Olsen v. Nebraska ex rel. Western Ref. & Bond Ass'n* (1941), both in Sec. 3 infra.

5. *Limitations on entry into business.* The Court also relied on the "liberty of contract" concept to strike down legislation limiting entry into a business, despite strong demonstrations of need for such limitations. *New State Ice Co. v. Liebmann,* 285 U.S. 262, 52 S.Ct. 371, 76 L.Ed. 747 (1932) (invalid to deny entry into ice business without a finding of "necessity" and that existing facilities are not "sufficient to meet the public needs"); *Louis K. Liggett Co. v. Baldridge,* 278 U.S. 105, 49 S.Ct. 57, 73 L.Ed. 204 (1928) (invalid to limit new entrants into pharmacy business to pharmacists; *Adams v. Tanner,* 244 U.S. 590, 37 S.Ct. 662, 61 L.Ed. 1336 (1917) (invalid to ban private employment agencies that charge fees paid by employees).

In 1973, *North Dakota State Board v. Snyder's Drug Stores,* Sec. 3 infra, overruled *Liggett.* While no cases precisely like *Adams* or *New State Ice* have arisen, the Court in 1963 asserted in effect that *Adams* had been overruled when it unanimously sustained a state prohibition on engaging in the debt adjusting business. See *Ferguson v. Skrupa,* Sec. 3 infra.

c. See McAllister, *Lord Hale and Business Affected with a Public Interest,* 43 Harv.L.Rev. 759 (1930); Hamilton, *Affectation with Public Interest,* 39 Yale L.J. 1089 (1930); Finkelstein, *From Munn v. Illinois to Tyson v. Banton: A Study in the Judicial Process,* 27 Colum.L.Rev. 769 (1927).

SECTION 3. DECLINE OF CONTROL OVER LEGISLATIVE POLICY

NEBBIA v. NEW YORK

291 U.S. 502, 54 S.Ct. 505, 78 L.Ed. 940 (1934).

MR. JUSTICE ROBERTS delivered the opinion of the Court.

[The Court upheld New York's regulation of minimum milk prices, aimed at assuring a "reasonable return" to producers and milk dealers, which was adopted after extensive legislative study.]

[T]he guaranty of due process, as has often been held, demands only that the law shall not be unreasonable, arbitrary, or capricious, and that the means selected shall have a real and substantial relation to the object sought to be attained. [A] regulation valid for one sort of business, or in given circumstances, may be invalid for another sort, or for the same business under other circumstances, because the reasonableness of each regulation depends upon the relevant facts.

[The opinion here summarized many different kinds of business and property regulations and controls previously sustained against due process attacks.]

The legislative investigation of 1932 was persuasive of the fact [that] unrestricted competition aggravated existing evils and the normal law of supply and demand was insufficient to correct maladjustments detrimental to the community. The inquiry disclosed destructive and demoralizing competitive conditions and unfair trade practices which resulted in retail price cutting and reduced the income of the farmer below the cost of production. [The Legislature] believed conditions could be improved by preventing destructive price-cutting by stores which, due to the flood of surplus milk, were able to buy at much lower prices than the larger distributors and to sell without incurring the delivery costs of the latter. In the order of which complaint is made the Milk Control Board fixed a price of 10 cents per quart for sales by a distributor to a consumer, and 9 cents by a store to a consumer, thus recognizing the lower costs of the store, and endeavoring to establish a differential which would be just to both. In the light of the facts the order appears not to be unreasonable or arbitrary, or without relation to the purpose to prevent ruthless competition from destroying the wholesale price structure on which the farmer depends for his livelihood, and the community for an assured supply of milk.

But we are told that because the law essays to control prices it denies due process. Notwithstanding the admitted power to correct existing economic ills by appropriate regulation of business, [the] appellant urges that direct fixation of prices is a type of regulation absolutely forbidden. [The] argument runs that the public control of rates or prices is per se unreasonable and unconstitutional, save as applied to businesses affected with a public interest; that a business so affected is one in which property is devoted to an enterprise of a sort which the public itself might appropriately undertake, or one whose owner relies on a public grant or franchise for the right to conduct the business, or in which he is bound to serve all who apply; in short, such as is commonly called a public utility; or a business in its nature a monopoly. The milk industry, it is said, possesses none of these characteristics.

[T]here is no closed class or category of businesses affected with a public interest, and the function of courts in the application of the Fifth and Fourteenth Amendments is to determine in each case whether circumstances vindicate the challenged regulation as a reasonable exertion of governmental authority or condemn it as arbitrary or discriminatory. The phrase "affected with a public interest" can, in the nature of things, mean no more than that an industry, for adequate reason, is subject to control for the public good. [There] can be no doubt that upon proper occasion and by appropriate measures the state may regulate a business in any of its aspects, including the prices to be charged for the products or commodities it sells.

So far as the requirement of due process is concerned, and in the absence of other constitutional restriction, a state is free to adopt whatever economic policy may reasonably be deemed to promote public welfare, and to enforce that policy by legislation adapted to its purpose. The courts are without authority either to declare such policy, or, when it is declared by the legislature, to override it. If the laws passed are seen to have a reasonable relation to a proper legislative purpose, and are neither arbitrary nor discriminatory, the requirements of due process are satisfied. [If] the legislative policy be to curb unrestrained and harmful competition by measures which are not arbitrary or discriminatory it does not lie with the courts to determine that the rule is unwise. With the wisdom of the policy adopted, with the adequacy or practicability of the law enacted to forward it, the courts are both incompetent and unauthorized to deal.
* * *

Separate opinion of MR. JUSTICE MCREYNOLDS.

[P]lainly, I think, this Court must have regard to the wisdom of the enactment. At least, we must inquire concerning its purpose and decide whether the means proposed have reasonable relation to something within legislative power—whether the end is legitimate, and the means appropriate. * * *

The court below [has] not attempted to indicate how higher charges at stores to impoverished customers when the output is excessive and sale prices by producers are unrestrained, can possibly increase receipts at the farm. * * *

Not only does the statute interfere arbitrarily with the rights of the little grocer to conduct his business according to standards long accepted—complete destruction may follow; but it takes away the liberty of 12,000,000 consumers to buy a necessity of life in an open market. It imposes direct and arbitrary burdens upon those already seriously impoverished with the alleged immediate design of affording special benefits to others. * * *[a]

Notes and Questions

1. *The Nebbia rationale.* (a) Did *Nebbia* appear to retain any degree of judicial review over legislative policy in state economic regulation? What standards of judgment did *Nebbia* suggest the Court would apply? May the makeup of the majority explain the standards advanced in the opinion?

(b) *Interests justifying price controls; sources of information.* Do you see any significance in the type of interests the Court found sufficient to justify price controls in *Nebbia?* In the sources relied upon by the Court to establish the factual basis for justifying price regulation?

2. *Control over wages.* WEST COAST HOTEL CO. v. PARRISH, 300 U.S. 379, 57 S.Ct. 578, 81 L.Ed. 703 (1937), sustained 5 to 4 a state regulation of women's wages, overruling earlier decisions. The opinion, per HUGHES, C. J.,

---

a. Van Devanter, Sutherland and Butler,
JJ., concurred in the dissent.

devoted substantial space to the reasons for regulation of women's wages, stressing the special problems of protecting women from "unscrupulous and overreaching employers," and to the need for protecting "workers who are in an unequal position with respect to bargaining power and are thus relatively defenseless against the denial of a living wage." The Court found that the legislative conclusion "cannot be regarded as arbitrary or capricious and that is all we have to decide. Even if the wisdom of the policy be regarded as debatable and its effects uncertain, still the Legislature is entitled to its judgment." Four years later, the Court sustained federal regulation of men's wages over due process objection, citing *Parrish* as authority. *United States v. Darby*, 312 U.S. 100, 125, 61 S.Ct. 451, 462–63, 85 L.Ed. 609, 623 (1941).

3. *Does the Court still review economic policy?* UNITED STATES v. CAROLENE PRODUCTS CO., 304 U.S. 144, 58 S.Ct. 778, 82 L.Ed. 1234 (1938), per STONE, J., sustained against due process challenge a federal statute excluding "filled milk" (non-milk fats added) from interstate commerce: "[R]egulatory legislation affecting ordinary commercial transactions is not to be pronounced unconstitutional unless in the light of the facts made known or generally assumed it is of such a character as to preclude the assumption that it rests upon some rational basis within the knowledge and experience of the legislators."

4. *Renunciation of former due process philosophy.* (a) OLSEN v. NEBRAS-KA, 313 U.S. 236, 61 S.Ct. 862, 85 L.Ed. 1305 (1941), upheld a Nebraska statute fixing maximum fees for employment agencies. DOUGLAS, J.'s, unanimous opinion [a] bluntly rejected the state court's reliance on *Ribnik v. McBride*, 277 U.S. 350, 48 S.Ct. 545, 72 L.Ed. 913 (1928), which had held a similar statute violated due process: "The drift away from *Ribnik* has been so great that it can no longer be deemed a controlling authority. [The Court summarized several cases overruling earlier due process rulings.] These cases represent more than scattered examples of constitutionally permissible price-fixing schemes. They represent in large measure a basic departure from the philosophy and approach of the majority in *Ribnik*. The standard there employed [was] that the constitutional validity of price-fixing legislation, at least in absence of a so-called emergency, was dependent on whether or not the business in question was 'affected with a public interest'. [That] test, labelled by Mr. Justice Holmes in his dissent in [*Tyson*] as 'little more than a fiction', was discarded in *Nebbia*.

"The *Ribnik* case, freed from the test which it employed, can no longer survive. But respondents maintain that the statute here in question is invalid for other reasons. They insist that special circumstances must be shown to support the validity of such drastic legislation as price-fixing, that the executive technical and professional workers which respondents serve have not been shown to be in need of special protection from exploitation, that legislative limitation of maximum fees for employment agencies is certain to react unfavorably upon those members of the community for whom it is most difficult to obtain jobs, that the increasing competition of public employment agencies and of charitable, labor union and employer association employment agencies have curbed excessive fees by private agencies, and [that] there are no conditions which the legislature might reasonably believe would redound to the public injury unless corrected by such legislation.

"We are not concerned, however, with the wisdom, need, or appropriateness of the legislation. Differences of opinion on that score suggest a choice which

---

a. McReynolds, J., the last of the four *Nebbia* and *West Coast Hotel* dissenters, re- tired two days before *Darby* and two months before *Olsen*.

'should be left where [it] was left by the Constitution—to the states and to Congress.' *Ribnik,* dissenting opinion. There is no necessity for the state to demonstrate before us that evils persist despite the competition which attends the bargaining in this field. In final analysis, the only constitutional prohibitions or restraints which respondents have suggested for the invalidation of this legislation are those notions of public policy embedded in earlier decisions of this Court but which, as Mr. Justice Holmes long ago admonished, should not be read into the Constitution. [Since] they do not find expression in the Constitution, we cannot give them continuing vitality as standards by which the constitutionality of the economic and social programs of the states is to be determined."

Is the absence in *Olsen* of any judicial explanation of the need to regulate employment agency rates significant? Were there reasons in 1941 to be less skeptical of the *Olsen* expression of no concern over "the wisdom, the need, or appropriateness of the legislation" than of the similar statement in *Nebbia* in 1934?

(b) After *Olsen* the Court consistently repudiated *Lochner*-type reasoning in rejecting substantive due process challenges to economic regulation.[b]

5. *Social, as distinct from economic, regulation.* WHALEN v. ROE, 429 U.S. 589, 97 S.Ct. 869, 51 L.Ed.2d 64 (1977), per STEVENS, J., upheld a New York law requiring those who fill prescriptions for specified harmful drugs to send copies to the New York Department of Health, where the information, including the patient's name, was to be retained on computers for five years under strict non-disclosure regulations: "There was a time when [the state's inability to demonstrate the need for patient identification] would have provided a basis for invalidating the statute. *Lochner.* [The] holding in *Lochner* has been implicitly rejected many times. State legislation which has some effect on individual liberty or privacy may not be held unconstitutional simply because a court finds

---

b. *Lincoln Fed. Labor Union v. Northwestern Iron & Met. Co.,* 335 U.S. 525, 69 S.Ct. 251, 93 L.Ed. 212 (1949), per Black, J., sustained a state right-to-work law that barred employers' pro-union discrimination: "This Court beginning at least as early as 1934, when [*Nebbia*] was decided, has steadily rejected the due process philosophy enunciated in the *Adair-Coppage* line of cases. [Just] as we have held that the due process clause erects no obstacle to block legislative protection of union members [see Sec. 2, note 2, par. 3 supra], we now hold that legislative protection can be afforded non-union workers.

Day-Brite Lighting, Inc. v. Missouri, 342 U.S. 421, 72 S.Ct. 405, 96 L.Ed. 469 (1952), per Douglas, J., sustained a requirement that employees have four hours off work with full pay in order to vote: "The liberty of contract argument pressed on us is reminiscent of the philosophy of [*Lochner, Coppage, Adkins v. Children's Hospital*] and others of that vintage. Our recent decisions make plain that we do not sit as a super-legislature to weigh the wisdom of legislation nor to decide whether the policy it expresses offends the public welfare. * * * The judgment of the legislature that time out for voting should cost the employee nothing may be a debatable one. [But] if our recent cases mean anything, they leave debatable issues as respects business,

economic and social affairs to legislative decisions." Jackson, J., dissented and Frankfurter, J., concurred in the result without opinion.

Similarly, *Ferguson v. Skrupa,* 372 U.S. 726, 83 S.Ct. 1028, 10 L.Ed.2d 93 (1963), per Black, J., unanimously spurned a due process challenge to a state law that barred all but lawyers from the business of debt adjusting: "Under the system of government created by our Constitution, it is up to the legislatures, not the courts, to decide on the wisdom and utility of legislation. [The] doctrine that prevailed in *Lochner, Coppage, Adkins* and like cases [has] long since been discarded. We have returned to the original constitutional proposition that courts do not substitute their social and economic beliefs for the judgment of legislative bodies, who are elected to pass [laws]. [Arguments that] the business of debt adjusting has social utility [are] properly addressed to the legislature, not to us." Harlan, J., concurred in the judgment on the ground that "[this] measure bears a rational relation to a constitutionally permissible objective."

For similar rulings and opinions see *Williamson v. Lee Optical of Okla.,* 348 U.S. 483, 75 S.Ct. 461, 99 L.Ed. 563 (1955); *North Dakota State Bd. v. Snyders' Store,* 414 U.S. 156, 94 S.Ct. 407, 38 L.Ed.2d 379 (1973).

it unnecessary, in whole or in part. For we have frequently recognized that individual States have broad latitude in experimenting with possible solutions to problems of vital local concern.

"The New York statute challenged in this case represents a considered attempt to deal with such a problem. It is manifestly the product of an orderly and rational legislative decision. It was recommended by a specially appointed commission which held extensive hearings on the proposed legislation, and drew on experience with similar programs in other States. There surely was nothing unreasonable in the assumption that the patient identification requirement might aid in the enforcement of laws designed to minimize the misuse of dangerous drugs. For the requirement could reasonably be expected to have a deterrent effect on potential violators as well as to aid in the detection or investigation of specific instances of apparent abuse. At the very least, it would seem clear that the State's vital interest in controlling the distribution of dangerous drugs would support a decision to experiment with new techniques for control. For if an experiment fails—if in this case experience teaches that the patient identification requirement results in the foolish expenditure of funds to acquire a mountain of useless information—the legislative process remains available to terminate the unwise experiment." [c]

ABSTENTION FOR FIVE DECADES

When faced with substantive due process challenges to economic legislation after 1940, the Court's actual decisions gave full effect to its strong opinions repeatedly asserting that on such matters legislative policy is for the legislature, not the courts. Not since 1937 has the Court struck down economic legislation as violating substantive due process;[a] and only in rare instances have individual justices withheld their approval of opinions renouncing power under the due process clause to review the wisdom, need, or soundness of such legislation.[b]

Referring to the foregoing due process decisions, and to a similar line of equal protection decisions,[c] Professor McCloskey concluded in 1962: "[T]here could be little doubt as to the practical result: no claim of substantive economic rights would now be sustained by the Supreme Court. The judiciary has abdicated the field." [d]

Has the Court "abdicated?" Has it renounced all substantive due process review power over economic legislation? Or has the Court hedged its opinions sufficiently to enable it, without recanting, to reassert substantive due process if it ever concludes that a legislative economic enactment is devoid of any arguable justification? [e]

c. For cases applying stricter scrutiny to legislation impinging on a limited category of "fundamental" personal rights. See Ch. 7, Sec. 2. However, *Whalen* ruled that the New York law did not unduly impinge on the right to privacy. Ch. 3, Sec. 2.

a. The last substantive due process decision invalidating economic legislation was *Thompson v. Consolidated Gas Co.*, 300 U.S. 55, 57 S.Ct. 364, 81 L.Ed. 510 (1937), where the regulation was viewed as taking property for a private purpose.

b. See the Harlan concurrence in *Ferguson v. Skrupa*, and the Jackson dissent and Frankfurter concurrence "in the result" in *Day-Brite Lighting*.

c. For the equal protection cases relating to economic regulation see Ch. 6, Sec. 1.

d. McClosky, *Economic Due Process and the Supreme Court*, 1962 Sup.Ct.Rev. 34, 38.

e. Cf. Wonnell, *Economic Due Process and the Preservation of Competition*, 11 Hast. Const.L.Q. 91 (1983) (a strongly reasoned argument that substantive due process should be extended to protect "free and open competition for society's lawful occupations [as] a constitutional value" that could invalidate legislation enforcing monopoly conditions, absent a sufficiently strong state interest).

With such questions in mind, consider DUKE POWER CO. v. CAROLINA ENV. STUDY GROUP, INC., 438 U.S. 59, 98 S.Ct. 2620, 57 L.Ed.2d 595 (1978). *Duke Power,* per BURGER, C.J., upheld the Price-Anderson Act's limit on the aggregate liability for a single nuclear incident in the atomic energy industry to the amount available through private insurance ($60 million) plus the $500 million indemnification undertaken by the federal government: [f] "[I]t is clear that Congress' purpose was to remove the economic impediments in order to stimulate the private development of electric energy by nuclear power while simultaneously providing the public compensation in the event of a catastrophic nuclear incident. The liability limitation provision thus emerges as a classic example of an economic regulation—a legislative effort to structure and accommodate 'the burdens and benefits of economic life.' *Usery v. Turner Elkhorn Mining Co.,* 428 U.S. 1, 96 S.Ct. 2882, 49 L.Ed.2d 752 (1976). 'It is by now well established that [such] legislative Acts [come] to the Court with a presumption of constitutionality, and that the burden is on one complaining of a due process violation to establish that the legislature has acted in an arbitrary and irrational way.' Ibid. That the accommodation struck may have profound and far-reaching consequences, contrary to appellees' suggestion, provides all the more reason for this Court to defer to the congressional judgment unless it is demonstrably arbitrary or irrational.

"When examined in light of this standard of review, the Price-Anderson Act, in our view, passes constitutional muster. The record before us fully supports the need for the imposition of a statutory limit on liability to encourage private industry participation and hence bears a rational relationship to Congress' concern for stimulating the involvement of private enterprise in the production of electric energy through the use of atomic power; nor do we understand appellees or the District Court to be of a different view. Rather, their challenge is to the alleged arbitrariness of the *particular figure* of $560 million, which is the statutory ceiling on liability. The District Court aptly summarized its position: 'The amount of recovery is not rationally related to the potential losses, [which] could well be many, many times [that] limit.'

"Assuming, arguendo, that the $560 million fund would not insure full recovery in all conceivable circumstances,—and the hard truth is that no one can ever know—it does not by any means follow that the liability limitation is therefore irrational and violative of due process. The legislative history clearly indicates that the $560 million figure was not arrived at on the supposition that it alone would necessarily be sufficient to guarantee full compensation in the event of a nuclear incident. Instead, it was conceived of as a 'starting point' or a working hypothesis. The reasonableness of the statute's assumed ceiling on liability was predicated on two corollary considerations—expert appraisals of the exceedingly small risk of a nuclear incident involving claims in excess of $560 million, and the recognition that in the event of such an incident, Congress would likely enact extraordinary relief provisions to provide additional relief, in accord with prior practice. * * *

"Given our conclusion that in general limiting liability is an acceptable method for Congress to utilize in encouraging the private development of electric energy by atomic power, candor requires acknowledgment that whatever ceiling figure is selected will, of necessity, be arbitrary in the sense that any choice of a figure based on imponderables like those at issue here can always be so

---

f. Stewart, Rehnquist and Stevens, JJ., concurred in the result without reaching the merits.

characterized. This is not, however, the kind of arbitrariness which flaws otherwise constitutional action. When appraised in terms of both the extremely remote possibility of an accident where liability would exceed the limitation and Congress' now statutory commitment to 'take whatever action is deemed necessary and appropriate to protect the public from the consequences of' any such disaster, 42 U.S.C. § 2210(e) (1970 ed. Supp. V), we hold the congressional decision to fix a $560 million ceiling, at this stage in the private development and production of electric energy by nuclear power, to be within permissible limits and not violative of due process."

Notes and Questions

1. *The standard of review.* Was the standard of review that *Turner Elkhorn* and *Duke Power* asserted with no dissenting voices—"demonstrably arbitrary or irrational"—consistent with the opinions from *Olsen* (1941) to *Snyder* (1973)? In forecasting future decisions on such issues, is it significant that *Duke Power* used four pages to explain why Price-Anderson was not "arbitrary or irrational" and hence "passes constitutional muster?"

(b) Did "arbitrary or irrational" mean something different in 1978 than from 1905 (*Lochner*) to 1934 (*Nebbia*)? *North Dakota State Board v. Snyder's Store* (1973), supra, per Douglas, J., in overruling *Liggett Co. v. Baldridge* (1928) [Sec. 2, note 5 supra] to uphold a requirement that pharmacies be owned by pharmacists noted that " 'a pronounced shift in emphasis since [*Liggett*]' had deprived the words 'unreasonable' and 'arbitrary' of the meaning which *Liggett* ascribed to them." Realistically, what appears to be the standard after *Duke Power?*

2. *Substance or style?* Does *Duke Power* portend a difference in the results of due process challenges to economic regulation, or does it reflect only a different pattern of opinion writing?

3. *Protection of "personal" rights.* The Court gives far stricter scrutiny and greater constitutional protection to some *personal* rights, often viewed as "fundamental," than to *economic* or *social welfare* interests. This development is considered primarily in Ch. 3, Sec. 2, and Ch. 6, Sec. 4.

4. *Equal protection.* The rise and fall of judicial protection of economic and social welfare interests under the equal protection clause is similar to that under due process, though equal protection issues involve somewhat different concerns and values. See Ch. 6, Sec. 1.

5. *Substantive due process under state constitutions.* Most state constitutions contain due process clauses identical or similar to that in the fourteenth amendment. Not all state courts, whose interpretations and applications of their own state constitutions are not ordinarily subject to Supreme Court review, have followed the Court's lead in leaving economic policy decisions to the legislature. Several have continued to follow the Court's 1905–1934 approach, invalidating under state due process clauses economic legislation that the Supreme Court would have upheld.[g]

g. The cases to 1958 are found in Paulsen, *The Persistence of Substantive Due Process in the States,* 34 Minn.L.Rev. 91 (1950); Hetherington, *State Economic Regulation and Substantive Due Process of Law,* 53 Nw.U.L.Rev. 13, 226 (1958). A few such decisions continue. See e.g. *Gillette Dairy, Inc. v. Nebraska Dairy Products Bd.,* 192 Neb. 89, 219 N.W.2d 214 (1974) (milk price control).

SECTION 4. "TAKING" OF PROPERTY INTERESTS

INTRODUCTION

The fifth amendment limits the federal government's power of eminent domain: "nor shall private property be taken for a public use without just compensation." Similarly the due process clause has long been held to require a state to compensate the owner when it takes property for a public use,[a] and to forbid taking property for a private use, even with compensation.[b] Space limits do not permit consideration of the extensive body of law relating to eminent domain. Two aspects only are considered here: (1) What are the limits, if any, on the purposes for which property may be taken, even with compensation? (2) Under what circumstances may, or should, a regulation be considered a "taking" that requires compensation?

I. PURPOSE OF "TAKING"

BERMAN v. PARKER, 348 U.S. 26, 75 S.Ct. 98, 99 L.Ed. 27 (1954), per DOUGLAS, J., unanimously upheld the District of Columbia Redevelopment Act, which authorized the Redevelopment Agency to acquire and assemble, by eminent domain or otherwise, real property "for the redevelopment of blighted territory (and) the prevention, reduction, or elimination of blighting factors." The Agency was empowered to transfer such property to public agencies for streets, utilities, recreational facilities and schools; and to lease or sell the remainder, preferably to a private redevelopment company, under terms that required the lessee or purchaser to conform to the redevelopment plan adopted by the National Capital Planning Commission. The Court found no fifth amendment violation in the Agency's taking by eminent domain a well-maintained department store posing no blight or health problem itself, located in a redevelopment area where roughly two-thirds of the dwellings were beyond repair or otherwise blighted:

"The power of Congress over the District of Columbia includes all the legislative powers which a state may exercise over its affairs. We deal, in other words, with what traditionally has been known as the police power. [Subject] to specific constitutional limitations, when the legislature has spoken, the public interest has been declared in terms well-nigh conclusive. In such cases the legislature, not the judiciary, is the main guardian of the public needs to be served by social legislation. [This] principle admits of no exception merely because the power of eminent domain is involved. The role of the judiciary in determining whether that power is being exercised for a public purpose is an extremely narrow one.

"Public safety, public health, morality, peace and quiet, law and order— these are some of the more conspicuous examples of the traditional application of the police power to municipal affairs. Yet they merely illustrate the scope of the power and do not delimit it. Miserable and disreputable housing conditions may do more than spread disease and crime and immorality. They may also suffocate the spirit * * *; make living an almost insufferable burden. They

---

a. See *Chicago, B. & Q.R.R. v. Chicago,* 166 U.S. 226, 241, 17 S.Ct. 581, 586, 41 L.Ed. 979, 986 (1897).

b. *Missouri Pac. Ry. v. Nebraska,* 164 U.S. 403, 17 S.Ct. 130, 41 L.Ed. 489 (1896).

may [be] a blight on the community which robs it of charm, which makes it a place from which men turn. * * *

"We do not sit to determine whether a particular housing project is or is not desirable. The concept of the public welfare is broad and inclusive. The values it represents are spiritual as well as physical, aesthetic as well as monetary. It is within the power of the legislature to determine that the community should be beautiful as well as healthy, spacious as well as clean, well-balanced as well as carefully patrolled. In the present case, the Congress and its authorized agencies have made determinations that take into account a wide variety of values. It is not for us to reappraise them. If those who govern the District of Columbia decide that the Nation's Capital should be beautiful as well as sanitary, there is nothing in the Fifth Amendment that stands in the way.

"Once the object is within the authority of Congress, the right to realize it through the exercise of eminent domain is clear. For the power of eminent domain is merely the means to the end. [Here] one of the means chosen is the use of private enterprise for redevelopment of the area. Appellants argue that this makes the project a taking from one businessman for the benefit of another businessman. But the means of executing the project are for Congress and Congress alone to determine, once the public purpose has been established. [We] cannot say that public ownership is the sole method of promoting the public purposes of community redevelopment projects. * * *

"In the present case, Congress and its authorized agencies attack the problem of the blighted parts of the community on an area rather than on a structure-by-structure basis. [It] was not enough, they believed, to remove existing buildings that were insanitary or unsightly. It was important to redesign the whole area so as to eliminate the conditions that cause slums—the overcrowding of dwellings, the lack of parks, the lack of adequate streets and alleys, the absence of recreational areas, the lack of light and air, the presence of outmoded street patterns. [The] entire area needed redesigning so that a balanced, integrated plan could be developed for the region, including not only new homes but also schools, churches, parks, streets, and shopping centers. [Such] diversification in future use is plainly relevant to the maintenance of the desired housing standards and therefore within congressional power."

Notes and Questions

1. *Historical development.* For a study of the rise and fall of limitations on the exercise of the power of eminent domain see Note, *The Public Use Limitation on Eminent Domain: An Advance Requiem,* 58 Yale L.J. 599 (1949); Dunham, *Griggs v. Allegheny County in Perspective: Thirty Years of Supreme Court Expropriation Law,* 1962 Sup.Ct.Rev. 63, 65.

2. *"Taking" to lessen concentrated land ownership.* HAWAII HOUSING AUTHORITY v. MIDKIFF, 467 U.S. 229, 104 S.Ct. 2321, 81 L.Ed.2d 186 (1984), per O'CONNOR, J., upheld the use of eminent domain to lessen the concentration of fee simple land ownership, inherited from Hawaii's early feudal land tenure system. In the 1960's the Hawaii legislature found that 72 private owners owned 47% of Hawaiian land, and the state and federal government 49%, leaving only 4% for all other private owners. On Oahu, the most urbanized island, 22 landowners owned 72.5% of the fee simple titles. The legislature found, as summarized by the Court, that such concentrated land ownership was "responsible for skewing the State's residential fee simple market, inflating land prices, and injuring public tranquillity and welfare." The resulting Land

Reform Act authorized "eligible tenants" from residential tracts of at least five acres to invoke the Hawaii Housing Authority's (HHA) power to acquire the fee owners "right, title and interest" at a "fair market value" set by negotiation between the lessee and the lessor or by condemnation trial, and then to sell that fee title interest to the tenant-lessee.[a]

[The] Court relied heavily on *Berman* from which it concluded, "The 'public use' requirement is thus coterminus with the scope of a sovereign's police powers. [Where] the exercise of the eminent domain power is rationally related to a conceivable public purpose, the Court has never held a compensated taking to be proscribed by the Public Use Clause.

[The] land oligopoly has, according to the Hawaii Legislature, created artificial deterrents to the normal functioning of the State's residential land market and forced thousands of individual homeowners to lease, rather than buy, the land underneath their homes. Regulating oligopoly and the evils associated with it is a classic exercise of a State's police powers. We cannot disapprove of Hawaii's exercise of this power.

"[When] the legislature's purpose is legitimate and its means are not irrational, our cases make clear that empirical debates over the wisdom of takings—no less than debates over the wisdom of other kinds of socioeconomic legislation—are not to be carried out in the federal courts. Redistribution of fees simple to correct deficiencies in the market determined by the state legislature to be attributable to land oligopoly is a rational exercise of the eminent domain power. Therefore, the Hawaii statute must pass the scrutiny of the Public Use Clause:" [b]

II. "TAKING" THROUGH REGULATION

PENN CENTRAL TRANSP. CO. v. NEW YORK CITY
438 U.S. 104, 98 S.Ct. 2646, 57 L.Ed.2d 631 (1978).

MR. JUSTICE BRENNAN delivered the opinion of the Court.

[Pursuant to New York City's Landmarks Preservation Law, the Preservation Commission designated Grand Central Terminal, owned by Penn Central, as a "landmark."[a] It denied Penn Central a certificate of "appropriateness" to construct a 55 story office building resting on the roof of the Terminal, cantilevered to preserve the existing Terminal facade. The Commission emphasized the harmful effect of the proposed construction on the dramatic view of the Terminal from Park Avenue South.[b] Choosing not to modify its proposal, or to

a. In fn. 1 the opinion listed the requisites for an "eligible tenant" as one who "owns a house on the lot, has a bona fide intent to live on the lot or be a resident of the State, shows proof of ability to pay for a fee interest in it, and does not own residential land elsewhere nearby." The HHA was authorized to proceed under the Act only when 25 such eligible tenants from the tract, or those from half the lots in the tract, whichever is less, filed applications with HHA for the remedy provided by the Act.

b. Marshall, J., did not participate.

a. The Commission's report stated:

"Grand Central Station, one of the great buildings of America, evokes a spirit that is unique in this City. It combines distinguished architecture with a brilliant engineering solution, wedded to one of the most fabulous railroad terminals of our time. Monumental in scale, this great building functions as well today as it did when built. In style, it represents the best of the French Beaux Arts."

b. "[To] balance a 55-story office tower above a flamboyant Beaux-Arts facade seems nothing more than an aesthetic joke. Quite simply, the tower would overwhelm the Terminal by its sheer mass. The 'addition' would be four times as high as the existing structure and would reduce the Landmark itself to the status of a curiosity.

"Landmarks cannot be divorced from their settings—particularly when the setting is a dramatic and integral part of the original use its right under New York laws to transfer its unused landmark site development rights to one or more of its eight nearby lots, Penn Central unsuccessfully challenged in the New York courts the constitutionality of this application of the Landmarks Law. The Court upheld the Law as applied.]

Over the past 50 years, all 50 States and over 500 municipalities have enacted laws to encourage or require the preservation of buildings and areas with historic or aesthetic importance.

[The issue is] whether the restrictions [upon] appellants' exploitation of the Terminal site effect a "taking" of appellants' property for a public use within the meaning of the Fifth Amendment, [made] applicable to the States through the Fourteenth.[25]

A. [W]hat constitutes a "taking" for purposes of the Fifth Amendment has proved to be a problem of considerable difficulty. While this Court has recognized that the "Fifth Amendment's guarantee [is] designed to bar Government from forcing some people alone to bear public burdens which, in all fairness and justice, should be borne by the public as a whole," *Armstrong v. United States,*[c] this Court, quite simply, has been unable to develop any "set formula" for determining when "justice and fairness" require that economic injuries caused by public action be compensated by the government, rather than remain disproportionately concentrated on a few persons. See *Goldblatt v. Hempstead,* 369 U.S. 590, 594, 82 S.Ct. 987, 8 L.Ed.2d 130 (1962). Indeed, we have frequently observed that whether a particular restriction will be rendered invalid by the government's failure to pay for any losses proximately caused by it depends largely "upon the particular circumstances [in that] case." *United States v. Central Eureka Mining Co.,* 357 U.S. 155, 168, 78 S.Ct. 1097, 2 L.Ed.2d 1228 (1958), see *United States v. Caltex, Inc.,* 344 U.S. 149, 156, 73 S.Ct. 200, 97 L.Ed. 157 (1952).

In engaging in these essentially ad hoc, factual inquiries, the Court's decisions have identified several factors that have particular significance. The economic impact of the regulation on the claimant and, particularly, the extent to which the regulation has interfered with distinct investment-backed expectations are, of course, relevant considerations. See *Goldblatt.* So, too, is the character of the governmental action. A "taking" may more readily be found when the interference with property can be characterized as a physical invasion by government, see, e.g., *United States v. Causby,* 328 U.S. 256, 66 S.Ct. 1062, 90 L.Ed. 1206 (1946), than when interference arises from some public program adjusting the benefits and burdens of economic life to promote the common good.

"Government hardly could go on if to some extent values incident to property could not be diminished without paying for every such change in the general law,"[d] *Pennsylvania Coal Co. v. Mahon,* 260 U.S. 393, 413, 43 S.Ct. 158,

concept. The Terminal, in its setting, is a great example of urban design. Such examples are not so plentiful in New York City that we can afford to lose any of the few we have. And we must preserve them in a meaningful way—with alterations and additions of such character, scale, materials and mass as will protect, enhance and perpetuate the original design rather than overwhelm it."

25. As is implicit in our opinion, we do not embrace the proposition that a "taking" can never occur unless government has transferred physical control over a portion of a parcel.

c. 364 U.S. 40, 49, 80 S.Ct. 1563, 4 L.Ed.2d 1554 (1960). *Armstrong* found a "taking" in the destruction of a materialman's lien when, on default of the builder, the government took possession of boats he was building for the United States.

d. When writing this sentence, Holmes, J., was probably tempted to refer to "the petty larceny of the police power," a phrase he had used about six weeks earlier in the original draft of his opinion in *Jackman v. Rosenbaum Co.,* 260 U.S. 22, 43 S.Ct. 9, 67 L.Ed. 107 (1922), but deleted at the urging of "my

67 L.Ed. 322 (1922), and this Court has accordingly recognized, in a wide variety of contexts, that government may execute laws or programs that adversely affect recognized economic values. ＊ ＊ ＊

[I]n instances in which a state tribunal reasonably concluded that "the health, safety, morals, or general welfare" would be promoted by prohibiting particular contemplated uses of land, this Court has upheld land-use regulations that destroyed or adversely affected recognized real property interests. See *Nectow v. Cambridge,* 277 U.S. 183, 188, 48 S.Ct. 447, 72 L.Ed. 842 (1928). Zoning laws are, of course, the classic example, see *Euclid v. Ambler Realty Co.,* 272 U.S. 365, 47 S.Ct. 114, 71 L.Ed. 303 (1926) (prohibition of industrial use); *Gorieb v. Fox,* 274 U.S. 603, 608, 47 S.Ct. 675, 71 L.Ed. 1228 (1927) (requirement that portions of parcels be left unbuilt); *Welch v. Swasey,* 214 U.S. 91, 29 S.Ct. 567, 53 L.Ed. 923 (1909) (height restriction), which have been viewed as permissible governmental action even when prohibiting the most beneficial use of the property. See *Goldblatt.*

Zoning laws generally do not affect existing uses of real property, but "taking" challenges have also been held to be without merit in a wide variety of situations when the challenged governmental actions prohibited a beneficial use to which individual parcels had previously been devoted and thus caused substantial individualized harm. *Miller v. Schoene,* 276 U.S. 272, 48 S.Ct. 246, 72 L.Ed. 568 (1928), is illustrative. In that case, a state entomologist, acting pursuant to a state statute, ordered the claimants to cut down a large number of ornamental red cedar trees because they produced cedar rust fatal to apple trees cultivated nearby. Although the statute provided for recovery of any expense incurred in removing the cedars, and permitted claimants to use the felled trees, it did not provide compensation for the value of the standing trees or for the resulting decrease in market value of the properties as a whole. A unanimous Court held that this latter omission did not render the statute invalid. The Court held that the State might properly make "a choice between the preservation of one class of property and that of the other" and since the apple industry was important in the State involved, concluded that the State had not exceeded "its constitutional powers by deciding upon the destruction of one class of property [without compensation] in order to save another which, in the judgment of the legislature, is of greater value to the public."

Again, *Hadacheck v. Sebastian,* 239 U.S. 394, 36 S.Ct. 143, 60 L.Ed. 348 (1915), upheld a law prohibiting the claimant from continuing his otherwise lawful business of operating a brickyard in a particular physical community on the ground that the legislature had reasonably concluded that the presence of the brickyard was inconsistent with neighboring uses. ＊ ＊ ＊

Goldblatt is a recent example. There, a 1958 city safety ordinance banned any excavations below the water table and effectively prohibited the claimant from continuing a sand and gravel mining business that had been operated on the particular parcel since 1927. The Court upheld the ordinance against a "taking" challenge, although the ordinance prohibited the present and presumably most beneficial use of the property and had, like the regulations in *Miller* and *Hadacheck,* severely affected a particular owner. The Court assumed that the ordinance did not prevent the owner's reasonable use of the property since the owner made no showing of an adverse effect on the value of the land. Because the restriction served a substantial public purpose, the Court thus held

brethern, as usual and as I expected." See 1
Holmes-Laski Letters 456–57 (Howe ed. 1953).

no taking had occurred. It is, of course, implicit in *Goldblatt* that a use restriction on real property may constitute a "taking" if not reasonably necessary to the effectuation of a substantial public purpose, see *Nectow;* or perhaps if it has an unduly harsh impact upon the owner's use of the property.

Pennsylvania Coal is the leading case for the proposition that a state statute that substantially furthers important public policies may so frustrate distinct investment-backed expectations as to amount to a "taking." There the claimant had sold the surface rights to particular parcels of property, but expressly reserved the right to remove the coal thereunder. A Pennsylvania statute, enacted after the transactions, forbade any mining of coal that caused the subsidence of any house, unless the house was the property of the owner of the underlying coal and was more than 150 feet from the improved property of another. Because the statute made it commercially impracticable to mine the coal, and thus had nearly the same effect as the complete destruction of rights claimant had reserved from the owners of the surface land, the Court held that the statute was invalid as effecting a "taking" without just compensation. See also *Armstrong.* (Government's complete destruction of a materialman's lien in certain property held a "taking"). [See] generally Michelman, *Property, Utility, and Fairness: Comments on the Ethical Foundations of "Just Compensation" Law,* 80 Harv.L.Rev. 1165, 1229–1234 (1967).

Finally, government actions that may be characterized as acquisitions of resources to permit or facilitate uniquely public functions have often been held to constitute "takings." *Causby* is illustrative. In holding that direct overflights above the claimant's land, that destroyed the present use of the land as a chicken farm, constituted a "taking," *Causby* emphasized that Government had not "merely destroyed property [but was] using a part of it for the flight of its planes." See also *Griggs v. Allegheny County,* 369 U.S. 84, 82 S.Ct. 531, 7 L.Ed. 2d 585 (1962) (overflights held a taking); *United States v. Cress,* 243 U.S. 316, 37 S.Ct. 380, 61 L.Ed. 746 (1917) (repeated floodings of land caused by water project is taking). See generally Michelman, supra, at 1226–29; Sax, *Takings and the Police Power,* 74 Yale L.J. 36 (1964).

B.   [A]ppellants do not contest that New York City's objective of preserving structures and areas with special historic, architectural, or cultural significance is an entirely permissible governmental goal. [They] do not challenge any of the specific factual premises of the decision below. They accept for present purposes both that the parcel of land occupied by Grand Central Terminal must, in its present state, be regarded as capable of earning a reasonable return, and that the transferable development rights afforded appellants by virtue of the Terminal's designation as a landmark are valuable, even if not as valuable as the rights to construct above the Terminal. In appellants' view none of these factors derogate from their claim that New York City's law has effected a "taking."

[First, they] urge that the Landmarks Law has deprived them of any gainful use of their "air rights" above the Terminal, [entitling] them to "just compensation" measured by the fair market value of these air rights.

[T]he submission that appellants may establish a "taking" simply by showing that they have been denied the ability to exploit a property interest that they heretofore had believed was available for development is quite simply untenable. Were this the rule, this Court would have erred not only in upholding laws restricting the development of air rights, see *Welch,* but also in approving those prohibiting both the subjacent, see *Goldblatt,* and the lateral, see *Gorieb,* development of particular parcels. "Taking" jurisprudence does not divide a single parcel into discrete segments and attempt to determine whether rights in a particular segment have been entirely abrogated. In deciding whether a particular governmental action has effected a taking, this Court focuses rather both on the character of the action and on the nature and extent of the interference with rights in the parcel as a whole—here, the city tax block designated as the "landmark site."

Secondly, appellants [argue that the New York law] effects a "taking" because its operation has significantly diminished the value of the Terminal site. Appellants concede that the decisions sustaining other land use-regulations, which, like the New York City law, are reasonably related to the promotion of the general welfare, uniformly reject the proposition that diminution in property value, standing alone, can establish a "taking," see *Euclid* (75% diminution in value caused by zoning law); *Hadacheck* (87½% diminution in value). [But] appellants argue that New York City's regulation of individual landmarks is fundamentally different from zoning or from historic-district legislation because the controls imposed by New York City's law apply only to individuals who own selected properties.

Stated baldly, appellants' position appears to be that the only means of ensuring that selected owners are not singled out to endure financial hardship for no reason is to hold that any restriction imposed on individual landmarks pursuant to the New York City scheme is a "taking" requiring the payment of "just compensation." Agreement with this argument would, of course, invalidate not just New York City's law, but all comparable landmark legislation in the Nation. We find no merit in it.

It is true [that] both historic-district legislation and zoning laws regulate all properties within given physical communities whereas landmark laws apply only to selected parcels. But, contrary to appellants' suggestions, landmark laws are not like discriminatory, or "reverse spot," zoning: that is, a land-use decision which arbitrarily singles out a particular parcel for different, less favorable treatment than the neighboring ones. See 2 Rathkopf, *The Law of Zoning and Planning* 26–4 and 26–4–26–5, n. 6 (4th ed. 1978). In contrast to discriminatory zoning, which is the antithesis of land-use control as part of some comprehensive plan, the New York City law embodies a comprehensive plan to preserve structures of historic or aesthetic interest wherever they might be found in the city, and as noted, over 400 landmarks and 31 historic districts have been designated pursuant to this plan. * * *

Next, appellants observe that New York City's law differs from zoning laws and historic-district ordinances in that the Landmarks Law does not impose identical or similar restrictions on all structures located in particular physical communities. It follows, they argue, that New York City's law is inherently incapable of producing the fair and equitable distribution of benefits and burdens of governmental action which is characteristic of zoning laws and historic-district legislation and which they maintain is a constitutional requirement if "just compensation" is not to be afforded. It is, of course, true that the Landmarks Law has a more severe impact on some landowners than on others, but that in itself does not mean that the law effects a "taking." Legislation designed to promote the general welfare commonly burdens some more than others. The owners of the brickyard in *Hadacheck,* of the cedar trees in *Miller,* and of the gravel and sand mine in *Goldblatt,* were uniquely burdened by the legislation sustained in those cases.[30] Similarly, zoning laws often affect some

---

30. Appellants attempt to distinguish these cases on the ground that, in each, government was prohibiting a "noxious" use of land and that in the present case, in contrast, property owners more severely than others but have not been held to be invalid on that account. ∗ ∗ ∗

[T]he New York City law applies to vast numbers of structures in the city in addition to the Terminal—all the structures contained in the 31 historic districts and over 400 individual landmarks, many of which are close to the Terminal. Unless we are to reject the judgment of the New York City Council that the preservation of landmarks benefits all New York citizens and all structures, both economically and by improving the quality of life in the city as a whole—which we are unwilling to do—we cannot conclude that the owners of the Terminal have in no sense been benefited by the Landmarks Law. Doubtless appellants believe they are more burdened than benefited by the law, but that must have been true, too, of the property owners in *Miller, Hadacheck, Euclid,* and *Goldblatt.* ∗ ∗ ∗

C. [A]ll we thus far have established is that the [law] is not rendered invalid by its failure to provide "just compensation" whenever a landmark owner is restricted in the exploitation of property interests, such as air rights, to a greater extent than provided for under applicable zoning laws. We now must consider whether the interference with appellants' property is of such a magnitude that "there must be an exercise of eminent domain and compensation to sustain [it]." *Pennsylvania Coal.* That inquiry may be narrowed to the question of the severity of the impact of the law on appellants' parcel, and its resolution in turn requires a careful assessment of the impact of the regulation on the Terminal site.

Unlike the governmental acts in *Goldblatt, Miller, Causby, Griggs,* and *Hadacheck,* the [law] does not interfere in any way with the present uses of the Terminal. Its designation as a landmark not only permits but contemplates that appellants may continue to use the property precisely as it has been used for the past 65 years: as a railroad terminal containing office space and concessions. So the law does not interfere with what must be regarded as Penn Central's primary expectation concerning the use of the parcel. More importantly, on this record, we must regard the [law] as permitting Penn Central not only to profit from the Terminal but also to obtain a "reasonable return" on its investment.

Appellants, moreover, exaggerate the effect of the law on their ability to make use of the air rights above the Terminal in two respects. First, it simply cannot be maintained, on this record, that appellants have been prohibited from occupying *any* portion of the airspace above the Terminal. While the Commission's actions in denying applications to construct an office building in excess of 50 stories above the Terminal may indicate that it will refuse to issue a certificate of appropriateness for any comparably sized structure, nothing the Commission has said or done suggests an intention to prohibit *any* construction above the Terminal. The Commission's report emphasized that whether any construction would be allowed depended upon whether the proposed addition "would harmonize in scale, material and character with [the Terminal]." Since appellants have not sought approval for the construction of a smaller structure,

---

appellants' proposed construction above the Terminal would be beneficial. We observe that the uses in issue in *Hadacheck, Miller,* and *Goldblatt* were perfectly lawful in themselves. They involve no "blameworthiness, [moral] wrongdoing or conscious act of dangerous risk-taking which induce[d society] to shift the cost to a pa[rt]icular individual." Sax, *Takings and the Police Power,* 74 Yale L.J. 36, 50 (1964). These cases are better understood as resting not on any supposed "noxious" quality of the prohibited uses but rather on the ground that the restrictions were reasonably related to the implementation of a policy—not unlike historic preservation—expected to produce a widespread public benefit and applicable to all similarly situated property.

we do not know that appellants will be denied any use of any portion of the airspace above the Terminal.[34] * * *

On this record we conclude that the application of New York City's [law] has not effected a "taking" of appellants' property. The restrictions imposed are substantially related to the promotion of the general welfare and not only permit reasonable beneficial use of the landmark site but afford appellants opportunities further to enhance not only the Terminal site proper but also other properties.[36] * * *

MR. JUSTICE REHNQUIST, with whom The Chief Justice and Mr. Justice Stevens join, dissenting.

[The] question in this case is whether the cost associated with the city of New York's desire to preserve a limited number of "landmarks" within its borders must be borne by all of its taxpayers or whether it can instead be imposed entirely on the owners of the individual properties. * * *

Appellees have thus destroyed—in a literal sense, "taken"—substantial property rights of Penn Central. [Because] "not every destruction or injury to property by governmental action has been held to be a 'taking' in the constitutional sense," however, this does not end our inquiry. But an examination of the two exceptions where the destruction of property does *not* constitute a taking demonstrates that a compensable taking has occurred here.

1. As early as 1887, the Court recognized that the government can prevent a property owner from using his property to injure others without having to compensate the owner for the value of the forbidden use. [Thus], there is no "taking" where a city prohibits the operation of a brickyard within a residential city, see *Hadacheck,* or forbids excavation for sand and gravel below the water line, see *Goldblatt.* Nor is it relevant, where the government is merely prohibiting a noxious use of property, that the government would seem to be singling out a particular property owner. *Hadacheck.*[8] * * * Appellees are not prohibiting a nuisance. [Instead], Penn Central is prevented from further developing its property basically because *too good* a job was done in designing and building [it].

2. Even where the government prohibits a noninjurious use, the Court has ruled that a taking does not take place if the prohibition applies over a broad cross section of land and thereby "secure[s] an average reciprocity of advantage." *Pennsylvania Coal.* It is for this reason that zoning does not constitute a "taking." While zoning at times reduces *individual* property values, the burden is shared relatively evenly and it is reasonable to conclude that on the whole an individual who is harmed by one aspect of the zoning will be benefited by another.

Here, however, a multimillion dollar loss has been imposed on appellants; it is uniquely felt and is not offset by any benefits flowing from the preservation of some 400 other "landmarks" in New York City. Appellees have imposed a substantial cost on less than one one-tenth of one percent of the buildings in

---

34. Counsel for appellants admitted at oral argument that the Commission has not suggested that it would not, for example, approve a 20-story office tower along the lines of that which was part of the original plan for the Terminal.

36. We emphasize that our holding today is on the present record which in turn is based on Penn Central's present ability to use the Terminal for its intended purposes and in a gainful fashion. The city conceded at oral argument that if appellants can demonstrate at some point in the future that circumstances have changed such that the Terminal ceases to be, in the city's counsel's words, "economically viable," appellants may obtain relief.

8. Each of the cases cited by the Court for the proposition that legislation which severely affects some landowners but not others does not effect a "taking" involved noxious uses of property. See *Hadacheck; Miller; Goldblatt.*

New York City for the general benefit of all its people. It is exactly this imposition of general costs on a few individuals at which the "taking" protection is [directed.] *Armstrong.*

As Mr. Justice Holmes pointed out in *Pennsylvania Coal,* "the question at bottom" in an eminent domain case "is upon whom the loss of the changes desired should fall." The benefits that appellees believe will flow from preservation of the Grand Central Terminal will accrue to all the citizens of New York City. There is no reason to believe that appellants will enjoy a substantially greater share of these benefits. If the cost of preserving Grand Central Terminal were spread evenly across the entire population of the city of New York, the burden per person would be in cents per year—a minor cost appellees would surely concede for the benefit accrued. Instead, however, appellees would impose the entire cost of several million dollars per year on Penn Central. But it is precisely this sort of discrimination that the Fifth Amendment prohibits.

Appellees in response would argue that a taking only occurs where a property owner is denied *all* reasonable value of his property. The Court has frequently held that, even where a destruction of property rights would not *otherwise* constitute a taking, the inability of the owner to make a reasonable return on his property requires compensation under the Fifth Amendment. But the converse is not true. A taking does not become a noncompensable exercise of police power simply because the government in its grace allows the owner to make some "reasonable" use of his property. "[I]t is the character of the invasion, not the amount of damage resulting from it, so long as the damage is substantial, that determines the question whether it is a taking." *Cress,*[e] 243 U.S. 316, 328, 37 S.Ct. 380, 61 L.Ed. 746 (1917). *Causby.*[f] * * *[g]

Notes and Questions

1. *The "character of the governmental action."* *Penn Central* recognizes that uncompensated banning of noxious or harmful uses of property, or uncompensated land use zoning that secures an "average reciprocal advantage to all affected land," are not "takings," while government actions that amount to appropriation of private property for "uniquely public functions" or "strictly governmental purposes" are "takings." Absent such "clear cases," does "the character of the governmental action" appear from *Penn Central* to have any

e. Compensation required for damage to property when a federal dam raised water level in tributary stream, causing frequent overflows in one case and loss of water power for mill in the other.

f. The dissenters doubted that the transfer development rights available to Penn Central constituted "just compensation" within the "strict meaning" of the fifth amendment, but would have remanded that issue to the Court of Appeals for determination. At that point the dissent suggested in its fn. 14 other ways to preserve landmarks: "The Court suggests that if appellees are held to have 'taken' property rights of landmark owners, not only the New York City Landmarks Preservation Law, but 'all comparable landmark legislation in the Nation,' must fall. [This] ignores the fact that many States and cities in the Nation have chosen to preserve landmarks by

purchasing or condemning restrictive easements over the facades of the landmarks and are apparently quite satisfied with the results. The British National Trust has effectively used restrictive easements to preserve landmarks since 1937. Other States and cities have found that tax incentives are also an effective means of encouraging the private preservation of landmark sites."

g. On the "taking" issue, see generally—in addition to articles cited in *Penn Central*— Kratovil & Harrison, *Eminent Domain—Policy and Concept,* 42 Calif.L.Rev. 596 (1954); Dunham, *Griggs v. Allegheny County in Perspective: Thirty Years of Supreme Court Expropriation Law,* 1962 Sup.Ct.Rev. 63; Sax, *Takings, Private Property and Public Right,* 81 Yale L.J. 149 (1971); Note, *Zoning,* 91 Harv.L. Rev. 1427, 1462–86 (1978); 92 Harv.L.Rev. 222–32 (1977).

relevance to "taking" issues other than its bearing on whether the challenged action advances a "permissible governmental goal"?

2. *Balancing judgments?* (a) Earlier decisions led thoughtful commentators to conclude that in determining whether a regulation constituted a "taking" the "extent of the diminution of the owner's rights must be weighed against the importance of that diminution to the public," [a] and that "[c]ourts have never been able to develop [a] standard more meaningful than balancing the public need against the private cost." [b] For a helpful critique of such a balancing approach, see Michelman, *Property, Utility, Fairness,* 80 Harv.L.Rev. at 1193–96, 1234–35.

(b) Is such balancing consistent with *Penn Central?* Did *Penn Central* "demonstrat[e] a method by which competing social and individual interests might be weighed"? Did it "balance public necessity and legitimacy of the regulation against the degree of physical invasion and economic harm"? See Note, 11 Conn.L.Rev. 273, 290 (1979). Or did *Penn Central* reflect "a belief that given the validity of the governmental interest asserted, the nature of the interest plays no further role in determining whether a taking has occurred," and that "[a]ny nondiscriminatory enactment reasonably related to a goal within the police power will be subjected only to a test of economic impact"? See 92 Harv.L.Rev. at 229.

(c) What *ought* the standard to be? *Should* the extent of economic harm that can be imposed without compensation depend on the degree of importance of an admittedly valid governmental interest?

3. *Economic impact on claimant.* What factors appear relevant to deciding whether the "economic impact of the regulation on the claimant" suffices to support a judgment of "taking?" Does *Penn Central* mean that, absent the "clear cases" stated in note 1, an economic impact will not suffice if the regulation permits continuation of the property's pre-regulation uses and a "reasonable return" on the investment? What kinds of problems are likely to arise from basing such decisions on factors like "reasonable return on investment, "investment-backed expectations," and "primary expectation concerning use?" Cf. 92 Harv.L.Rev. at 231.

4. *Permanent physical occupation.* LORETTO v. TELEPROMPTER MANHATTAN CATV CORP., 458 U.S. 419, 102 S.Ct. 3164, 73 L.Ed.2d 868 (1982), per MARSHALL, J., found a "taking" in a New York law that, as applied, authorized cable TV installations for tenants of privately-owned apartment houses. The cables, permanently attached to the roofs and outside walls by bolts, screws and other means, were subject to a one-time $1 payment to the landlord:

"[We] have long considered a physical intrusion by government to be a property restriction of an unusually serious character for purposes of the Takings Clause. Our cases further establish that when the physical intrusion reaches the extreme form of a permanent physical occupation, a taking has occurred. In such a case, 'the character of the government action' not only is an important factor in resolving whether the action works a taking but is determinative.

"When faced with a constitutional challenge to a permanent physical occupation of real property, this Court has invariably found a taking.[5] * * *

a. Kratovil & Harrison, fn. g supra, at 609.

b. Dunham, fn. g supra, at 76.

5. Professor Michelman has accurately summarized the case [law]: "[The] modern significance of physical occupation is that courts, while they sometimes do hold nontrespassory injuries compensable, *never* deny compensation for a physical takeover. The

"To the extent that the government permanently occupies physical property it effectively destroys" the rights to possess, use and dispose of it. 'The owner has no right to possess the occupied space himself [or] to exclude the occupier.' It 'denies the owner any power to control the use of the property [or] to dispose of [it] by sale, [since] the purchaser will be unable to make any use of' it.

"Our holding today is very narrow. We affirm the traditional rule that a permanent physical occupation of property is a taking. In such a case, the property owner entertains an historically-rooted expectation of compensation, and the character of the invasion is qualitatively more intrusive than perhaps any other category of property regulation. We do not, however, question the equally substantial authority upholding a State's broad power to impose appropriate restrictions upon an owner's *use* of his property."

BLACKMUN, J., joined by Brennan and White, JJ., dissented: "In a curiously anachronistic decision, the Court today acknowledges its historical disavowal of set formulae in almost the same breath as it constructs a rigid *per se* takings rule. * * *

"The Court's recent Takings Clause decisions teach that *nonphysical* government intrusions on private property, such as zoning ordinances and other land-use restrictions, have become the rule rather than the exception. Modern government regulation exudes intangible 'externalities' that may diminish the value of private property far more than minor physical touchings. * * *

"Precisely because the extent to which the government may injure private interests now depends so little on whether or not it has authorized a 'physical contact,' the Court has avoided per se takings rules resting on outmoded distinctions between physical and nonphysical intrusions. As one commentator has observed, a takings rule based on such a distinction is inherently suspect because 'its capacity to distinguish, even crudely, between significant and insignificant losses is too puny to be taken seriously.' Michelman.

"In sum, history, teaches that takings claims are properly evaluated under a multifactor balancing test. By directing that all 'permanent physical occupations' automatically are compensable, 'without regard to whether the action achieves an important public benefit or has only minimal economic impact on the owner,' the Court does not further equity so much as it encourages litigants to manipulate their factual allegations to gain the benefit of its per se rule. I do not relish the prospect of distinguishing the inevitable flow of certiorari petitions attempting to shoehorn insubstantial takings claims into today's 'set formula.' "

SECTION 5. CONTRACT CLAUSE

ALLIED STRUCTURAL STEEL CO. v. SPANNAUS
438 U.S. 234, 98 S.Ct. 2716, 57 L.Ed.2d 727 (1978).

MR. JUSTICE STEWART delivered the opinion of the Court.

[In 1963, Allied adopted an employer-funded pension plan that provided monthly pensions based on earnings and length of employment. Under the plan, rights to the pension vested, regardless of later termination of employment,

one incontestable case for compensation (short of formal expropriation) seems to occur when the government [or] the public at large, 'regularly' use, or 'permanently' occupy, space or a thing [theretofore] under private ownership." Michelman, *Property, Utility, and Fairness:* *Comments on the Ethical Foundations of "Just Compensation" Law,* 80 Harv.L.Rev. 1165, 1184 (1967) (emphasis original). See also 2 Sackman, *Nichols' Law of Eminent Domain* 6–50—6–51 (rev. 3d ed. 1980); Tribe, *American Constitutional Law* 460 (1978).

when an employee worked to age 65, or worked for 15 years to age 60 or for 20 years to age 55. Those who quit or were terminated before the pension vested acquired no rights. Allied made yearly contributions to the pension trust fund based on actuarial predictions. It retained the right to terminate the plan at any time for any reason, subject to use of the fund's assets to meet its obligations under vested pensions in a specified order of priorities. Pension benefits were payable only from fund assets. Allied informed its employees that the plan implied no assurance against dismissal from employment at any time.

[A 1974 Minnesota Act required Minnesota employers with an employee pension plan, who terminated the plan or went out of business in Minnesota, to provide full pensions for all Minnesota employees who had worked for 10 years, and, if the pension fund was insufficient, to pay a "pension funding charge" in an amount that would purchase deferred annuities that would make up the deficiency. In July 1974, as the first step in closing its 30-employee Minnesota activity, Allied, based in Illinois, terminated 11 Minnesota employees, 9 of whom had worked for Allied more than 10 years but not long enough to acquire vested pension rights under the plan. Under the Minnesota Act, Allied's "pension funding charge" was $185,000. The Court held 5 to 3 that this application of the Act violated the contract clause.]

The Act substantially altered [the company's contractual relationships with its employees] by superimposing pension obligations upon the company conspicuously beyond those that it had voluntarily agreed to undertake. But it does not inexorably follow that the Act, as applied to the company, violates the Contract Clause. * * *

Although it was perhaps the strongest single constitutional check on state legislation during our early years as a Nation, the Contract Clause receded into comparative desuetude [with] the development of the large body of jurisprudence under the Due Process Clause.[12] Nonetheless, the Contract Clause remains part of the Constitution. It is not a dead [letter.]

First of all, [the] Contract Clause does not operate to obliterate the police power of the States. "[It] does not prevent the State from exercising such powers as are vested in it for the promotion of the common weal, or are necessary for the general good of the public, though contracts previously entered into between individuals may thereby be affected. This power, which in its various ramifications is known as the police power, is an exercise of the sovereign right of the Government to protect the lives, health, morals, comfort and general welfare of the people, and is paramount to any rights under contracts between individuals." *Manigault v. Springs,* 199 U.S. 473, 480, 26 S.Ct. 127, 50 L.Ed. 274.[a] As Mr. Justice Holmes succinctly put the matter [in] *Hudson Water Co. v. McCarter,* 209 U.S. 349, 357, 28 S.Ct. 529, 52 L.Ed. 828: "One whose rights, such as they are, are subject to state restriction, cannot remove them from the power of the State by making a contract about them. The contract will carry with it the infirmity of the subject matter."

---

12. Indeed, at least one commentator has suggested that "the results might be the same if the contract clause were dropped out of the Constitution, and the challenged statutes all judged as reasonable or unreasonable deprivations of property." Hale, *The Supreme Court and the Contract Clause,* 57 Harv.L.Rev. 852, 890–91 (1944).

a. *Manigault* held the contract clause did not bar legislation that authorized a riparian owner to dam a creek to facilitate reclamation of lowlands, in violation of his contract with another riparian owner. Cf. *Union Dry Goods Co. v. Georgia Pub. Service Corp.,* 248 U.S. 372, 39 S.Ct. 117, 63 L.Ed. 309 (1919) (contract clause not violated by statute authorizing utility to charge rates fixed by commission higher than pre-existing contract rate).

If the Contract Clause is to retain any meaning at all, however, it must be understood to impose *some* limits upon the power of a State to abridge existing contractual relationships, even in the exercise of its otherwise legitimate police power. The existence and nature of those limits were clearly indicated in a series of cases in this Court arising from the efforts of the States to deal with the unprecedented emergencies brought on by the severe economic depression of the early 1930's.

In *Home Building & Loan Assn. v. Blaisdell*, 290 U.S. 398, 54 S.Ct. 231, 78 L.Ed. 413 (1934), the Court upheld [a] mortgage moratorium law that Minnesota had enacted to provide relief for homeowners threatened with foreclosure. Although the legislation conflicted directly with lenders' contractual foreclosure rights, the Court there acknowledged that, despite the Contract Clause, the States retain residual authority to enact laws "to safeguard the vital interests of [their] people." In upholding the state mortgage moratorium law, the Court found five factors significant. First, the state legislature had declared in the Act itself that an emergency need for the protection of homeowners existed. Second, the state law was enacted to protect a basic societal interest, not a favored group. Third, the relief was appropriately tailored to the emergency that it was designed to meet. Fourth, the imposed conditions were reasonable.[b] And, finally, the legislation was limited to the duration of the emergency.

The *Blaisdell* opinion thus clearly implied that if the Minnesota moratorium legislation had not possessed the characteristics attributed to it by the Court, it would have been invalid under the Contract Clause of the Constitution. These implications were given concrete force in [cases] that followed closely in *Blaisdell's* wake.[c]   *   *   *

The most recent Contract Clause case in this Court was *United States Trust Co. v. New Jersey*.[d] In that case the Court again recognized that although the absolute language of the Clause must leave room for "the 'essential attributes of sovereign power,' necessarily reserved by the States to safeguard the welfare of their citizens," that power has limits when its exercise effects substantial modifications of private contracts. Despite the customary deference courts give to state laws directed to social and economic problems, "[l]egislation adjusting the rights and responsibilities of contracting parties must be upon reasonable conditions and of a character appropriate to the public purpose justifying its adoption." Evaluating with particular scrutiny a modification of a contract to which the State itself was a party, the Court in that case held that legislative alteration of the rights and remedies of Port Authority bondholders violated the Contract Clause because the legislation was neither necessary nor reasonable.

In applying these principles to the present case, the first inquiry must be whether the state law has, in fact, operated as a substantial impairment of a contractual relationship.[16] The severity of the impairment measures the height

b. *Blaisdell* stressed that the law did not impair the mortgage indebtedness, that the ultimate right to foreclosure and a deficiency judgment remained, that interest continued to accrue, and that the mortgagor must pay the rental value to be applied to taxes, insurance, and interest.

c. The Court briefly stated the rulings in three cases of contract clause violations: *W.B. Worthen v. Thomas*, 292 U.S. 426, 54 S.Ct. 816, 78 L.Ed. 1344 (1934); *W.B. Worthen v. Kavanaugh*, 295 U.S. 56, 55 S.Ct. 555, 79 L.Ed. 1298 (1935); *Treigie v. Acme Homestead Assn.*, 297 U.S. 189, 56 S.Ct. 408, 80 L.Ed. 575 (1936).

d. 431 U.S. 1, 97 S.Ct. 1505, 52 L.Ed.2d 92 (1977).

16. [The] narrow view that the Clause forbids only state laws that diminish the duties of a contractual obligor and not laws that increase them, a view arguably suggested by *Satterlee v. Matthewson*, 2 Pet. 380, 7 L.Ed. 458, has since been expressly repudiated. *Detroit United Ry. v. Michigan*, 242 U.S. 238, 37 S.Ct. 87, 61 L.Ed. 268; *Georgia Ry. & Power* of the hurdle the state legislation must clear. Minimal alteration of contractual obligations may end the inquiry at its first stage. Severe impairment, on the other hand, will push the inquiry to a careful examination of the nature and purpose of the state legislation.

The severity of an impairment of contractual obligations can be measured by the factors that reflect the high value the Framers placed on the protection of private contracts. Contracts enable individuals to order their personal and business affairs according to their particular needs and interests. Once arranged, those rights and obligations are binding under the law, and the parties are entitled to rely on them.

Here, the company's contracts of employment with its employees included as a fringe benefit or additional form of compensation, the pension plan. The company's maximum obligation was to set aside each year an amount based on the plan's requirements for vesting. The plan satisfied the current federal income tax code and was subject to no other legislative requirements. [The] company [had] no reason to anticipate that its employees' pension rights could become vested except in accordance with the terms of the plan. It relied heavily, and reasonably, on this legitimate contractual expectation in calculating its annual contributions to the pension fund.

The effect of Minnesota's [Act] on this contractual obligation was severe. The company was required in 1974 to have made its contributions throughout the pre-1974 life of its plan as if employees' pension rights had vested after 10 years, instead of vesting in accord with the terms of the plan. Thus a basic term of the pension contract—one on which the company had relied for 10 years—was substantially modified. The result was that although the company's past contributions were adequate when made, they were not adequate when computed under the 10-year statutory vesting requirement. The Act thus forced a current recalculation of the past 10 years' contributions based on the new, unanticipated 10-year vesting requirement.

Not only did the state law thus retroactively modify the compensation that the company had agreed to pay its employees from 1963 to 1974, but it did so by changing the company's obligations in an area where the element of reliance was vital—the funding of a pension plan.[18] * * *

[The company was] forced to make all the retroactive changes in its contractual obligations at one time. By simply proceeding to close its office in Minnesota, a move that had been planned before the passage of the Act, the company was assessed an immediate pension funding charge of approximately $185,000.

Thus, the [statute] nullifies express terms of the company's contractual obligations and imposes a completely unexpected liability in potentially disabling amounts. [Yet] there is no showing in the record before us that this severe disruption of contractual expectations was necessary to meet an important

Co. v. Decatur, 262 U.S. 432, 43 S.Ct. 613, 67 L.Ed. 1065. Moreover, in any bilateral contract the diminution of duties on one side effectively increases the duties on the other.

The even narrower view that the Clause is limited in its application to state laws relieving debtors of obligations to their creditors is, as the dissent recognizes, completely at odds with this Court's decisions. See generally Hale, 57 Harv.L.Rev. 512, 514–16 (1944).

18. In some situations the element of reliance may cut both ways. Here, the company had relied upon the funding obligation of the pension plan for more than a decade. There was no showing of reliance to the contrary by its employees. Indeed, Minnesota did not act to protect any employee reliance interest demonstrated on the record. Instead, it compelled the employer to exceed bargained-for expectations and nullified an express term of the pension plan.

general social problem. The presumption favoring "legislative judgment as to the necessity and reasonableness of a particular measure," *United States Trust Co.,* simply cannot stand in this case.

[Whether] or not the legislation was aimed largely at a single employer, [which closed one of its Minnesota plants and attempted to terminate its pension plan] [20] it clearly has an extremely narrow focus. It applies only to private employers [who] have established voluntary private pension plans, [and] only when such an employer closes his Minnesota office or terminates his pension plan. Thus, this law can hardly be characterized, like the law at issue in the *Blaisdell* case, as one enacted to protect a broad societal interest rather than a narrow class.[22]

[This] legislation, imposing a sudden, totally unanticipated, and substantial retroactive obligation upon the company to its employees, was not enacted to deal with a situation remotely approaching the broad and desperate emergency economic conditions of the early 1930's—conditions of which the Court in *Blaisdell* took judicial notice.[24] * * *

This Minnesota law simply does not possess the attributes of those state laws that in the past have survived challenge under the Contract Clause of the Constitution. The law was not even purportedly enacted to deal with a broad, generalized economic or social problem. Cf. *Blaisdell.* It did not operate in an area already subject to state regulation at the time the company's contractual obligations were originally undertaken, but invaded an area never before subject to regulation by the State. It did not effect simply a temporary alteration of the contractual relationships of those within its coverage, but worked a severe, permanent, and immediate change in those relationships—irrevocably and retroactively. And its narrow aim was leveled, not at every Minnesota employer, not even at every Minnesota employer who left the State, but only at those who had in the past been sufficiently enlightened as voluntarily to agree to establish pension plans for their employees. * * *

MR. JUSTICE BRENNAN, with whom Mr. Justice White and Mr. Justice Marshall join, dissenting.[e] * * *

[The Minnesota Act] does not abrogate or dilute any obligation due a party to a private contract; rather, like all positive social legislation, the Act imposes new, additional obligations on a particular class of persons. In my view, any constitutional infirmity in the law must therefore derive, not from the Contract Clause, but from the Due Process Clause of the Fourteenth Amendment.

---

20. In *Malone v. White Motor Corp.,* 435 U.S. at 501 n. 5, 98 S.Ct. 1185, 55 L.Ed.2d 443, the Court noted that the White Motor Corp., an employer of more than 1,000 Minnesota employees, had been prohibited from terminating its pension plan until the expiration date of its collective-bargaining agreement, May 1, 1974. On April 9, 1974, the Minnesota Act was passed, to become effective the following day. When White Motor proceeded to terminate its collectively bargained pension plan at the earliest possible date, May 1, 1974, the State assessed a deficiency of more than $19 million, based upon the Act's 10-year vesting requirement. [*Malone* decided only that the Minnesota Act was not preempted by federal legislation until 1975. It left the contract clause issue to the District Court.]

22. In upholding the constitutionality of the Act, the District Court referred to Minnesota's interest in protecting the economic welfare of its older citizens, as well as their surrounding economic communities.

24. This is not to suggest that only an emergency of great magnitude can constitutionally justify a state law impairing the obligations of contracts. See, e.g., *Veix v. Sixth Ward Building & Loan Assn.,* 310 U.S. at 39–40, 60 S.Ct. 792, 84 L.Ed. 1061; *East New York Savings Bank v. Hahn,* 326 U.S. 230, 66 S.Ct. 69, 90 L.Ed. 34; *El Paso v. Simmons.*

e. Blackmun, J., did not participate.

[The Act was] designed to remedy a serious social problem arising from the operation of private pension plans. [Not] only would employers often neglect to furnish their employees with adequate information concerning their rights under the plans, leading to erroneous expectations, but because employers often failed to make contributions to the pension funds large enough adequately to fund their plans, employees often ultimately received only a small amount of those benefits they reasonably anticipated. [Denial] of all pension benefits not because of job related failings but only because the employees are unfortunate enough to be employed at a plant that closes for purely economic reasons is harsh indeed. [The] closing of a plant is a contingency outside the range of normal expectations of both the employer and the employee. [Although] the Court glides over this fact, it should be apparent that the Act will impose only minor economic burdens on employers whose pension plans have been adequately funded. [An] adequate pension plan fund would include contributions on behalf of terminated employees of 10 or more years service whose rights had not vested. Indeed, without the Act, the closing of the plant would create a windfall for the employer, because, due to the resulting surplus in the fund, his future contributions would be reduced. * * *

[The] Act does not relieve either the employer or his employees of any existing contract obligation. Rather, the Act simply creates an additional, supplemental duty of the employer, no different in kind from myriad duties created by a wide variety of legislative measures which defeat settled expectations but which have nonetheless been sustained by this Court. For this reason, the Minnesota Act, in my view, does not implicate the Contract Clause in any way. The basic fallacy of today's decision is its mistaken view that the Contract Clause protects all contract-based expectations, including that of an employer that his obligations to his employees will not be legislatively enlarged beyond those explicitly provided in his pension plan.

A. Historically, [the] Contract Clause was not intended to embody a broad constitutional policy of protecting all reliance interests grounded in private contracts. It was made part of the Constitution to remedy a particular social evil—the state legislative practice of enacting laws to relieve individuals of their obligations under certain contracts—and thus was intended to prohibit States from adopting "as [their] policy the repudiation of debts or the destruction of contracts or the denial of means to enforce them," *Blaisdell.* But the Framers never contemplated that the Clause would limit the legislative power of States to enact laws creating duties that might burden some individuals in order to benefit others.

B. [It] is nothing less than an abuse of the English language to interpret, as does the Court, the term "impairing" as including laws which create new duties. While such laws may be conceptualized as "enlarging" the obligation of a contract when they add to the burdens that had previously been imposed by a private agreement, such laws cannot be prohibited by the Clause because they do not dilute or nullify a duty a person had previously obligated himself to perform.[7] * * *

---

7. In *Georgia Ry. & Power Co. v. Decatur, Detroit United Ry. v. Michigan,* [fn. 16 supra], and in dictum in other cases, this Court embraced, without any careful analysis and without giving any consideration to *Satterlee v. Matthewson,* the contrary view that the impairment of a contract may consist in "adding to its burdens" as well as in diminishing its efficacy. These opinions reflect the then-prevailing philosophy of economic due process which has since been repudiated. See *Ferguson v. Skrupa.* In my view, the reasoning of *Georgia Ry.* and *Detroit United Ry.* is simply wrong.

C. [More] fundamentally, the Court's distortion of the meaning of the Contract Clause [threatens] to undermine the jurisprudence of property rights developed over the last 40 years. The Contract Clause, of course, is but one of several clauses in the Constitution that protect existing economic values from governmental interference. The Fifth Amendment's command that "private property [shall not] be taken for public use, without just compensation" is such a clause. A second is the Due Process Clause, which during the heyday of substantive due process, see *Lochner,* largely supplanted the Contract Clause in importance and operated as a potent limitation on Government's ability to interfere with economic expectations. Decisions over the past 50 years have developed a coherent, unified interpretation of all the constitutional provisions that may protect economic expectations and these decisions have recognized a broad latitude in States to effect even severe interference with existing economic values when reasonably necessary to promote the general welfare. See, *Penn Central; Goldblatt.* At the same time the prohibition of the Contract Clause, consistently with its wording and historic purposes, has been limited in application to state laws that diluted, with utter indifference to the legitimate interests of the beneficiary of a contract duty, the existing contract obligation, *W.B. Worthen Co. v. Kavanaugh*; see *United States Trust Co.*; cf. *El Paso*; *Blaisdell.*

[There] is nothing sancrosanct about expectations rooted in contract that justify according them a constitutional immunity denied other property rights. Laws that interfere with settled expectations created by state property law (and which impose severe economic burdens) are uniformly held constitutional where reasonably related to the promotion of the general welfare. * * *

There is no logical or rational basis for sustaining the duties created by the laws in *Miller* and *Hadacheck,* but invalidating the duty created by the Minnesota Act. Surely, the Act effects no greater interference with reasonable reliance interests than did these other laws. Moreover, the laws operate identically: they all create duties that burden one class of persons and benefit another. The only difference between the present case and *Hadacheck* or *Miller* is that here there was a prior contractual relationship between the members of the benefited and burdened classes. I simply cannot accept that this difference should possess constitutional significance. The only means of avoiding this anomaly is to construe the Contract Clause consistently with its terms [and] hold it is inapplicable to laws which create new duties. * * *

Notes and Questions

1. *Contract vs. other property rights.* (a) In what respects, if any, is there a significant difference in the Court's review of economic legislation when challenged under the contract clause as compared to due process? Consider particularly (1) the professed standard of review, (2) the degree of deference to the legislature or strictness of judicial scrutiny, (3) the Court's willingness to hypothesize state purposes to justify the legislation. Cf. 92 Harv.L.Rev. 94–99 (1978).

(b) Ought the degree of judicial protection from legislative interference differ under the constitution as between preexisting contract interests and preexisting noncontractual property interests?

2. *Legislatively-added burdens.* Did *Allied Steel* soundly interpret the contract clause to protect against "impairment" by legislatively-added burdens that increase those stated in the contract? Would it have made a difference in the law's validity if it added a burden of sounder *funding* of the contractual pension benefits without adding to the *benefits?*

3. *"Incidental effect" of regulation.* EXXON CORP. v. EAGERTON, 462 U.S. 176, 103 S.Ct. 2296, 76 L.Ed.2d 497 (1983), per MARSHALL, J., unanimously held that a ban on oil and gas producers passing a severance tax increase on to consumers did not violate the contract clause even though pre-existing contracts required consumers to reimburse producers for all severance taxes:

"[T]he pass-through prohibition did not prescribe a rule limited in effect to contractual obligations or remedies, but instead imposed a generally applicable rule of conduct designed to advance 'a broad societal interest,' *Allied Steel,* protecting consumers from excessive prices. The prohibition applied to all oil and gas producers, regardless of whether they happened to be parties to sale contracts that contained a provision permitting them to pass tax increases through to their purchasers. The effect of the pass-through prohibition on existing contracts that did contain such a provision was incidental to its main effect of shielding consumers from the burden of the tax increase.

"Because the pass-through prohibition imposed a generally applicable rule of conduct, it is sharply distinguishable from the measures struck down in *United States Trust* and *Allied Steel.* *United States Trust* involved New York and New Jersey statutes whose sole effect was to repeal a covenant that the two States had entered into with the holders of bonds issued by The Port Authority of New York and New Jersey. Similarly, the statute at issue in *Allied Steel* directly 'adjust[ed] the rights and responsibilities of contracting parties,' quoting *United States Trust.* * * *

"Alabama's power to prohibit oil and gas producers from passing the increase in the severance tax on to their purchasers is confirmed by several decisions of this Court rejecting Contract Clause challenges to state rate-setting schemes that displaced any rates previously established by contract. * * * And if the Contract Clause does not prevent a State from dictating the price that sellers may charge their customers, plainly it does not prevent a State from requiring that sellers absorb a tax increase themselves rather than pass it through to their customers."

4. *The law summarized.* For a unanimous summary of the controlling considerations in modern contract clause cases see Blackmun, J.'s, opinion in *Energy Reserves Group, Inc. v. Kansas Power and Light Co.,* 459 U.S. 400, 103 S.Ct. 697, 74 L.Ed.2d 569 (1983).

Chapter 3

PROTECTION OF INDIVIDUAL RIGHTS: DUE PROCESS, THE BILL OF RIGHTS, AND NONTEXTUAL CONSTITUTIONAL RIGHTS

SECTION 1. NATURE AND SCOPE OF FOURTEENTH AMENDMENT DUE PROCESS; APPLICABILITY OF THE BILL OF RIGHTS TO THE STATES

I. THE "ORDERED LIBERTY—FUNDAMENTAL FAIRNESS," "TOTAL INCORPORATION" AND "SELECTIVE INCORPORATION" THEORIES

Twining v. New Jersey, 211 U.S. 78, 29 S.Ct. 14, 53 L.Ed. 97 (1908); *Palko v. Connecticut*, 302 U.S. 319, 58 S.Ct. 149, 82 L.Ed. 2888 (1937); and *Adamson v. California*, 332 U.S. 46, 67 S.Ct. 1672, 91 L.Ed. 1903 (1947), rejected the "total incorporation" view of the history of the fourteenth amendment, the view—which has never commanded a majority—that the fourteenth amendment made all of the provisions of the Bill of Rights fully applicable to the states.[a] But *Twining* recognized that "it is possible that some of the personal rights safeguarded by the first eight Amendments against National action may also be safeguarded against state action, because a denial of them would be a denial of due process" or because "the specific pledge of particular amendments have been found to be implicit in the concept of ordered liberty and thus through the Fourteenth Amendment, become valid as against the states" (*Palko*). And the Court early found among the procedural requirements of fourteenth amendment due process certain rules paralleling provisions of the first eight amendments. For example, *Powell v. Alabama*, 287 U.S. 45, 53 S.Ct. 55, 77 L.Ed. 158 (1932), held that defendants in a capital case were denied due process when a state

a. *Palko*, which held that the fourteenth amendment did not encompass at least certain aspects of the double jeopardy prohibition of the fifth amendment, was overruled in *Benton v. Maryland* (1969), discussed below. The *Twining-Adamson* view that the fifth amendment privilege against self-incrimination is not incorporated in the fourteenth was rejected in *Malloy v. Hogan* (1964), discussed below. *Griffin v. California* (1965), Part IV infra, subsequently applied *Malloy* to overrule the specific holdings of *Twining* and *Adamson*, which had permitted comment on a defendant's failure to take the stand at his criminal trial. These later decisions, however, were still consistent with the rejection of the "total incorporation" interpretation.

refused them the aid of counsel. "The logically critical thing, however," pointed out Harlan, J., years later, "was not that the rights had been found in the Bill of Rights, but that they were deemed * * * fundamental."[b]

Under the "ordered liberty"—"fundamental fairness" test, which procedural safeguards included in the Bill of Rights were applicable to the states and which were not? Consider CARDOZO, J., speaking for the *Palko* Court: "[On reflection and analysis there] emerges the perception of a rationalizing principle which gives to discrete instances a proper order and coherence. The right to trial by jury and the immunity from prosecution except as the result of an indictment [are] not of the very essence of a scheme of ordered liberty. To abolish them is not to violate a 'principle of justice so rooted in the traditions and conscience of our people as to be ranked as fundamental.' [What] is true of jury trials and indictments is true also, as the cases show, of the immunity from compulsory self-incrimination. This too might be lost, and justice still be [done.][c]

"We reach a different plane of social and moral values when we pass [to those provisions of the Bill of Rights] brought within the Fourteenth Amendment by a process of absorption. These in their origin were effective against the federal government alone. If the Fourteenth Amendment has absorbed them, the process of absorption has had its course in the belief that neither liberty nor justice would exist if they were sacrificed. This is true, for illustration, of freedom of thought and speech. Of that freedom one may say that it is the

---

b. *Duncan v. Louisiana* (dissent joined by Stewart, J.), discussed below.

c. As pointed out in fn. a supra, the fifth amendment privilege against self-incrimination was subsequently held to be fully applicable to the states via the fourteenth amendment. So was the sixth amendment right to jury trial in criminal cases. *Duncan v. Louisiana* (1968), discussed below.

The above language in *Palko* and language in *Adamson*, infra, and other cases are susceptible of the interpretation that when the Court held that a particular Bill of Rights guarantee was not "incorporated into," or implicit in, fourteenth amendment due process it was *completely* "out." But such a reading of these cases seems unsound. Typically the Court dealt with state procedures transgressing the "outer edges," rather than the basic concept, of a particular Bill of Rights guarantee. It seems most doubtful that in sustaining such challenged procedures the Court was authorizing the states to abolish completely—or to violate the "hardcore" of—e.g., the protection against double jeopardy, or the privilege against self-incrimination, or the right to trial by jury in criminal cases. Rather the Court probably meant that the state rules did not violate the fourteenth amendment because the Bill of Rights guarantee invoked by defendant did not apply to the states *to the full extent* it applied to the federal government. To hold that a particular provision of the Bill of Rights is not *totally* "incorporated," i.e., not binding on the states *in its entirety*, is not to say it is *completely* "*out*" of the fourteenth amendment. See generally Henkin, *"Selective Incorporation" in the*

Fourteenth Amendment, 73 Yale L.J. 74, 79 & n. 18, 80–81 (1963).

At issue in *Palko* was not whether a state could completely disregard the basic notion against twice putting a person in jeopardy for the same offense, but a Connecticut statute permitting prosecution appeals "upon all questions of law arising [in criminal trials] with the permission of the presiding judge." Thus, elsewhere in the opinion the Court asked: "Is *that kind of double jeopardy* to which the [Connecticut] statute has subjected [appellant] *a hardship so acute and shocking that our polity will not endure it?* [What] the answer would have to be if the state were permitted *after a trial free from error* to try the accused over again or to bring another case against him, we have no occasion to consider." (Emphasis added).

Nor should *Adamson* be read for the proposition that a state could make it a felony for a person to "plead the fifth" or for a defendant to refuse to take the stand. Rather the Court merely sustained a California provision infringing upon the *periphery* of the guarantee by allowing comment upon a defendant's failure to explain or to deny evidence against him.

Nor, as the Court later emphasized in *Duncan,* discussed below, did *Maxwell v. Dow* (1900), discussed below, hold that a state could abolish trial by jury *altogether* in criminal cases; only that fourteenth amendment due process did not prevent a state from trying a noncapital defendant before a jury with fewer than 12 persons.

matrix, the indispensable condition, of nearly every other form of freedom.
* * * Fundamental too in the concept of due process, and so in that of liberty,
is the thought that condemnation shall be rendered only after trial. The
hearing, moreover, must be a real one, not a sham or pretense [discussing *Powell*
which] did not turn upon the fact that the benefit of counsel would have been
guaranteed to the defendants by [the] Sixth Amendment if they had been
prosecuted in a federal court [but on] the fact that in the particular situation laid
before us [the aid of counsel] was essential to the substance of a hearing."

The "total incorporation" position received its strongest support in the
Adamson dissents. In the principal dissent, BLACK, J., joined by Douglas, J.,
observed: "I cannot consider the Bill of Rights to be an outworn 18th Century
'strait jacket' as the *Twining* opinion did. Its provisions may be thought
outdated abstractions by some. And it is true that they were designed to meet
ancient evils. But they are the same kind of human evils that have emerged
from century to century wherever excessive power is sought by the few at the
expense of the many. In my judgment the people of no nation can lose their
liberty so long as a Bill of Rights like ours survives and its basic purposes are
conscientiously interpreted, enforced and respected so as to afford continuous
protection against old, as well as new, devices and practices which might thwart
those purposes. I fear to see the consequences of the Court's practice of
substituting its own concepts of decency and fundamental justice for the language of the Bill of Rights as its point of departure in interpreting and enforcing
that Bill of Rights. If the choice must be between the selective process of the
Palko decision applying some of the Bill of Rights to the States, or the *Twining*
rule applying none of them, I would choose the *Palko* selective process. But
rather than accept either of these choices, I would follow what I believe was the
original purpose of the Fourteenth Amendment—to extend to all the people of
the nation the complete protection of the Bill of Rights. To hold that this Court
can determine what, if any, provisions of the Bill of Rights will be enforced, and
if so to what degree, is to frustrate the great design of a written Constitution.

"Conceding the possibility that this Court is now wise enough to improve on
the Bill of Rights by substituting natural law concepts for the Bill of Rights, I
think the possibility is entirely too speculative to agree to take that course. I
would therefore hold in this case that the full protection of the Fifth Amendment's proscription against compelled testimony must be afforded by California.
This I would do because of reliance upon the original purpose of the Fourteenth
Amendment.

"[T]o pass upon the constitutionality of statutes by looking to the particular
standards enumerated in the Bill of Rights and other parts of the Constitution is
one thing; to invalidate statutes because of application of 'natural law' deemed
to be above and undefined by the Constitution is another. 'In the one instance,
courts proceeding within clearly marked constitutional boundaries seek to execute policies written into the Constitution; in the other they roam at will in the
limitless area of their own beliefs as to reasonableness and actually select
policies, a responsibility which the Constitution entrusts to the legislative
representatives of the people.' " [d]

d. Dissenting separately in *Adamson*, Murphy, J., joined by Rutledge, J., "agree[d] that
the specific guarantees of the Bill of Rights
should be carried over intact into [the fourteenth amendment but was] not prepared to
say that the latter is entirely and necessarily
limited by the Bill of Rights. Occasions may
arise where a proceeding falls so far short of
conforming to fundamental standards of procedure as to warrant constitutional condemnation in terms of a lack of due process despite
the absence of a specific provision of the Bill
of Rights." In this connection, consider fn. e
infra.

Responding, FRANKFURTER, J.'s concurrence in *Adamson* stressed the "independent potency" of the fourteenth amendment due process clause, maintaining that it "neither comprehends the specific provisions by which the founders deemed it appropriate to restrict the federal government nor is confined to them":[e] "Between the incorporation of the Fourteenth Amendment into the Constitution and the beginning of the present membership of the Court—a period of 70 years—the scope of that Amendment was passed upon by 43 judges. Of all these judges only one, who may respectfully be called an eccentric exception, ever indicated the belief that the Fourteenth Amendment was a shorthand summary of the first eight Amendments theretofore limiting only the Federal Government, and that due process incorporated those eight Amendments as restrictions upon the powers of the States. [To] suggest that it is inconsistent with a truly free society to begin prosecutions without an indictment, to try petty civil cases without the paraphernalia of a common law jury, to take into consideration that one who has full opportunity to make a defense remains silent is, in de Tocqueville's phrase, to confound the familiar with the necessary.

"[Those] reading the English language with the meaning which it ordinarily conveys, those conversant with the political and legal history of the concept of due process, those sensitive to the relations of the States to the central government as well as the relation of some of the provisions of the Bill of Rights to the process of justice, would hardly recognize the Fourteenth Amendment as a cover for the various explicit provisions of the first eight Amendments. Some of these are enduring reflections of experience with human nature, while some express the restricted views of Eighteenth-Century England regarding the best methods for the ascertainment of facts. The notion that the Fourteenth Amendment was a covert way of imposing upon the States all the rules which it seemed important to Eighteenth Century statesmen to write into the Federal Amendments, was rejected by judges who were themselves witnesses of the process by which the Fourteenth Amendment became part of the Constitution. [A]t the time of the ratification of the Fourteenth Amendment the constitutions of nearly half of the ratifying States did not have the rigorous requirements of the Fifth Amendment for instituting criminal proceedings through a grand jury. It could hardly have occurred to these States that by ratifying the Amendment they uprooted their established methods for prosecuting crime and fastened upon themselves a new prosecutorial system.

"Indeed, the suggestion that the Fourteenth Amendment incorporates the first eight Amendments as such is not unambiguously urged. [There] is suggested merely a selective incorporation of the first eight Amendments into the Fourteenth Amendment. Some are in and some are out, but we are left in the dark as to which are in and which are out. Nor are we given the calculus for determining which go in and which stay out. If the basis of selection is merely that those provisions of the first eight Amendments are incorporated which commend themselves to individual justices as indispensable to the dignity and

e. See also Friendly, *The Bill of Rights as a Code of Criminal Procedure*, 53 Calif.L.Rev. 929, 937 (1965): "[N]o facile formula will enable the Court to escape its assigned task of deciding just what the Constitution protects from state action, as *Estes v. Texas*, 381 U.S. 532, 85 S.Ct. 1628, 14 L.Ed.2d 543 (1965), where no 'specific' could be invoked, showed [for] procedural due process, and *Griswold v.* *Connecticut* [Sec. 2 infra] demonstrated for substantive due process." Consider, too, *In re Winship*, Part IV infra, holding that "proof beyond a reasonable doubt is among the essentials of due process" over the protest of dissenting Justice Black that nowhere in the Bill of Rights could he find any command that conviction of crime or adjudication of delinquency requires such a high standard of proof.

happiness of a free man, we are thrown back to a merely subjective test. [In] the history of thought 'natural law' has a much longer and much better founded meaning and justification than such subjective selection of the first eight Amendments for incorporation into the Fourteenth. If all that is meant is that due process contains within itself certain minimal standards which are 'of the very essence of a scheme of ordered liberty,' *Palko,* putting upon this Court the duty of applying these standards from time to time, then we have merely arrived at the insight which our predecessors long ago expressed. * * *

"A construction which gives to due process no independent function but turns it into a summary of the specific provisions of the Bill of Rights [would] deprive the States of opportunity for reforms in legal process designed for extending the area of freedom. It would assume that no other abuses would reveal themselves in the course of time than those which had become manifest in 1791. Such a view not only disregards the historic meaning of 'due process.' It leads inevitably to a warped construction of specific provisions of the Bill of Rights to bring within their scope conduct clearly condemned by due process but not easily fitting into the pigeonholes of the specific provisions.

"* * * Judicial review of [the Due Process Clause] of the Fourteenth Amendment inescapably imposes upon this Court an exercise of judgment upon the whole course of the proceedings in order to ascertain whether they offend those canons of decency and fairness which express the notions of justice of English-speaking peoples even toward those charged with the most heinous offenses. These standards of justice are not authoritatively formulated anywhere as though they were prescriptions in a pharmacopoeia. But neither does the application of the Due Process Clause imply that judges are wholly at large. The judicial judgment in applying the Due Process Clause must move within the limits of accepted notions of justice and is not to be based upon the idiosyncracies of a merely personal judgment."

Notes and Questions

1. Are Frankfurter and Black, JJ., each more persuasive in demonstrating why the *other's* test is subjective, ill-defined and unilluminating than in explaining why his own is *not?*

2. *Escape from the "idiosyncrasy of a personal judgment".* If, as Frankfurter, J., insists, the *Palko-Adamson* test is not based upon "the idiosyncrasies of a merely personal judgment," *whose* moral judgments furnish the answer? And *where* and *how* are they discoverable? The opinions of the progenitors and architects of our institutions? The opinions of the policy-making organs of state governments? Of state courts? The opinions of other countries? Of other countries in the Anglo-Saxon tradition? See Kadish, *Methodology and Criteria in Due Process Adjudication—A Survey and Criticism,* 66 Yale L.J. 319, 328–333 (1957). What judgments were relied on in *Palko* and *Adamson?* In *Rochin v. California,* Part III infra?

3. *History.* Historical research has produced ample support—and ample skepticism—for the "incorporation" theory. Compare 2 Crosskey, *Politics and the Constitution,* chs. XXXI, at 1083, XXXII, at 1119 (1953); Flack, *The Adoption of the Fourteenth Amendment* (1908); and Guthrie, *The Fourteenth Article of Amendment to the Constitution of the United States* (1898) with tenBroek, *The Antislavery Origins of the Fourteenth Amendment* (1951); Fairman, *Does the Fourteenth Amendment Incorporate the Bill of Rights? The Original Understanding,* 2 Stan.L.Rev. 5 (1949); Graham, *The "Conspiracy Theory" of the*

Fourteenth Amendment, 47 Yale L.J. 371 (1938). For brief but incisive criticism of both Black, J.'s position and Professor Fairman's attack, see Kelly, *Clio and the Court: An Illicit Love Affair,* 1965 Sup.Ct.Rev. 119, 132–34.

Is further historical search likely to do more than "further obscure the judicial value-choosing inherent in due process adjudication which can proceed with greater expectation of success if pursued openly and deliberately rather than under disguise"? Is due process more a moral command than a jural or historical concept? Ought it be? See Kadish, supra, at 340–41.

———

Although the Court continued to apply the "*Palko* selective process" approach to the Bill of Rights, DUNCAN v. LOUISIANA, 391 U.S. 145, 88 S.Ct. 1444, 20 L.Ed.2d 491 (1968) (holding the sixth amendment right to jury trial applicable to the states via the fourteenth amendment), no longer employed the Cardozo-Frankfurter terminology (e.g., whether a particular guarantee was "implicit in the concept of ordered liberty" or required by "the 'immutable principles of justice' as conceived by a civilized society") but instead inquired whether the procedural safeguard included in the Bill of Rights was "fundamental to the *American scheme of justice*" (emphasis added) or "fundamental *in the context of the criminal processes maintained by the American states*" (emphasis added). As WHITE, J., noted for the *Duncan* majority (fn. 14), the different phraseology is significant:

"Earlier the Court can be seen as having asked, when inquiring into whether some particular procedural safeguard was required of a State, if a civilized system could be imagined that would not accord the particular protection [quoting from *Palko*]. The recent cases, on the other hand, have proceeded upon the valid assumption that state criminal processes are not imaginary and theoretical schemes but actual systems bearing virtually every characteristic of the common-law system that has been developing contemporaneously in England and this country. The question thus is whether given this kind of system a particular procedure is fundamental—whether, that is, a procedure is necessary to an Anglo-American regime of ordered liberty. It is this sort of inquiry that can justify the conclusions that state courts must exclude evidence seized in violation of the Fourth Amendment, *Mapp v. Ohio* [Part IV infra] [and] that state prosecutors may not comment on a defendant's failure to testify, *Griffin v. California* [fn. a supra]. [Of] each of these determinations that a constitutional provision originally written to bind the Federal Government should bind the States as well it might be said that the limitation in question is not necessarily fundamental to fairness in every criminal system that might be imagined but is fundamental in the context of the criminal processes maintained by the American States.

"When the inquiry is approached in this way the question whether the States can impose criminal punishment without granting a jury trial appears quite different from the way it appeared in the older cases opining that States might abolish jury trial. A criminal process which was fair and equitable but used no juries is easy to imagine. It would make use of alternative guarantees and protections which would serve the purposes that the jury serves in the English and American systems. Yet no American State has undertaken to construct such a system. Instead, every American State, including Louisiana, uses the jury extensively, and imposes very serious punishments only after a trial at which the defendant has a right to a jury's verdict. In every State, including Louisiana, the structure and style of the criminal process—the supporting framework and the subsidiary procedures—are of the sort that naturally complement jury trial, and have developed in connection with and in reliance upon jury trial." [f]

Because the *Duncan* Court believed that "trial by jury in criminal cases is fundamental to the American scheme of justice," it held that it was guaranteed by the fourteenth amendment: "The guarantees of jury trial in the Federal and State Constitutions reflect a profound judgment about the way in which law should be enforced and justice administered. A right to jury trial is granted to criminal defendants in order to prevent oppression by the Government. Those who wrote our constitutions knew from history and experience that it was necessary to protect against unfounded criminal charges brought to eliminate enemies and against judges too responsive to the voice of higher authority. The framers of the constitutions strove to create an independent judiciary but insisted upon further protection against arbitrary action. Providing an accused with the right to be tried by a jury of his peers gave him an inestimable safeguard against the corrupt or overzealous prosecutor and against the compliant, biased, or eccentric judge. If the defendant preferred the common-sense judgment of a jury to the more tutored but perhaps less sympathetic reaction of the single judge, he was to have it. Beyond this, the jury trial provisions in the Federal and State Constitutions reflect a fundamental decision about the exercise of official power—a reluctance to entrust plenary powers over the life and liberty of the citizen to one judge or to a group of judges. Fear of unchecked power, so typical of our State and Federal Governments in other respects, found expression in the criminal law in this insistence upon community participation in the determination of guilt or innocence. The deep commitment of the Nation to the right of jury trial in serious criminal cases as a defense against arbitrary law enforcement qualifies for protection under the Due Process Clause of the Fourteenth Amendment, and must therefore be respected by the States."

HARLAN, J., joined by Stewart, J., dissented: "Even if I could agree that the question before us is whether Sixth Amendment jury trial is totally ['incorporated into' the fourteenth amendment] or totally 'out' [see Sec. II infra], I can find in the Court's opinion no real reasons for concluding that it should be 'in.' The basis for distinguishing among clauses in the Bill of Rights cannot be that [only] some are old and much praised, or that only some have played an important role in the development of federal law. These things are true of all. The Court says that some clauses are more 'fundamental' than others, but [uses] this word in a sense that would have astonished Mr. Justice Cardozo and which, in addition, is of no help. The word does not mean 'analytically critical to procedural fairness' for no real analysis of the role of the jury in making procedures fair is even attempted. Instead, the word turns out to mean 'old,' 'much praised,' and 'found in the Bill of Rights.' The definition of 'fundamental' thus turns out to be circular.

---

f. See also Powell, J., concurring in the companion 1972 "jury unanimity" cases of *Johnson v. Louisiana* and *Apodaca v. Oregon,* discussed below: "I agree with Mr. Justice White's analysis in *Duncan* that the departure from earlier decisions was, in large measure, a product of a change in focus in the Court's approach to due process. No longer are questions regarding the constitutionality of particular criminal procedures resolved by focusing alone on the element in question and ascertaining whether a system of criminal justice might be imagined in which a fair trial could be afforded in the absence of that particular element. Rather, the focus is, as it should be, on the fundamentality of that element viewed in the context of the basic Anglo-American jurisprudential system common to the States. That approach to due process readily accounts both for the conclusion that jury trial *is* fundamental and that unanimity *is not.*"

"[Jury trial] is of course not without virtues [but its] principal original virtue—[the limitations it] imposes on a tyrannous judiciary—has largely disappeared. [The] jury system can also be said to have some inherent defects, which are multiplied by the emergence of the criminal law from the relative simplicity that existed when the jury system was devised. It is a cumbersome process, not only imposing great cost in time and money on both the State and the jurors themselves, but also contributing to delay in the machinery of justice. [That] trial by jury is not the only fair way of adjudicating criminal guilt is well attested by the fact that it is not the prevailing way, either in England or in this country.

"[The majority recognizes that not every, or any particular, criminal trial before a judge alone is unfair, or less fair than one held before a jury.] I agree. I therefore see no reason why this Court should reverse the conviction of appellant absent any suggestion that his particular trial was in fact unfair, or compel the State of Louisiana to afford jury trial in an as yet unbounded category of cases that can, without unfairness, be tried to a court.

"[In] sum, there is a wide range of views on the desirability of trial by jury, and on the ways to make it most effective when it is used; there is also considerable variation from State to State in local conditions such as the size of the criminal caseload, the ease or difficulty of summoning jurors, and other trial conditions bearing on fairness. We have before us, therefore, an almost perfect example of a situation in which [the states should serve as laboratories.] [Instead,] the Court has chosen to impose upon every State one means of trying criminal cases; it is a good means, but it is not the only fair means, and it is not demonstrably better than the alternatives States might devise." [g]

Although the Court has remained unwilling to accept the total incorporationists' reading of the fourteenth amendment, in the 1960s it "selectively" "incorporated" or "absorbed" more and more of the specifics of the Bill of Rights into the fourteenth amendment. As WHITE, J., observed in *Duncan*:

"In resolving conflicting claims concerning the meaning of this spacious [fourteenth amendment] language, the Court has looked increasingly to the Bill of Rights for guidance; many of the rights guaranteed by the first eight Amendments to the Constitution have been held to be protected against state action by the Due Process Clause of the Fourteenth Amendment.[h] That clause now protects [the] Fourth Amendment rights to be free from unreasonable searches and seizures and to have excluded from criminal trials any evidence illegally seized; the right guaranteed by the Fifth Amendment to be free of compelled self-incrimination; and the Sixth Amendment rights to counsel, to a

---

g. Cf. *McKeiver v. Pennsylvania*, 403 U.S. 528, 91 S.Ct. 1976, 29 L.Ed.2d 647 (1971), holding that a state may use its juvenile court proceedings to prosecute a juvenile for a criminal act without providing trial by jury because, inter alia, the jury is not "a necessary component of accurate fact-finding" and its "inject[ion] into the juvenile court system as a matter of right" might bring with it "the traditional delay, the formality and the clamor of the adversary system, and, possibly, the public trial."

h. See also Black, J., joined by Douglas, J., concurring in *Duncan*: "[I] believe as strongly as ever that the Fourteenth Amendment was intended to make the Bill of Rights applicable to the States. I have been willing to support the selective incorporation doctrine, however, as an alternative, although perhaps less historically supportable than complete incorporation [because it] keeps judges from roaming at will in their own notions of what policies outside the Bill of Rights are desirable and what are not. And, most importantly for me, the selective incorporation process has the virtue of having already worked to make most of the Bill of Rights' protections applicable to the States."

speedy and public trial [*Klopfer v. North Carolina*, 386 U.S. 213, 87 S.Ct. 988, 18 L.Ed.2d 1 (1967); *In re Oliver*, 330 U.S. 257, 68 S.Ct. 499, 92 L.Ed. 682 (1942)], to confrontation of opposing witnesses [*Pointer v. Texas*, 380 U.S. 400, 85 S.Ct. 1065, 13 L.Ed.2d 923 (1965)] and to compulsory process for obtaining witnesses [*Washington v. Texas*, 388 U.S. 14, 87 S.Ct. 1920, 18 L.Ed.2d 1019 (1967)]." [i]

II. SHOULD THE "SELECTED" PROVISION APPLY TO THE STATES "JOT–FOR–JOT"? "BAG AND BAGGAGE"?

In the 1960s, the Court seemed to be "incorporating" not only the basic notion or general concept of the "selected" provision of the Bill of Rights, but applying the provision to the states *to the same extent* it applied to the federal government. As some justices, especially Harlan, protested, the federal guarantees were being incorporated into the fourteenth "freighted with their entire accompanying body of federal doctrine" (Harlan, J., joined by Clark, J., dissenting in *Malloy v. Hogan*, discussed below); "jot-for-jot and case-for-case" (Harlan, J., joined by Stewart, J., dissenting in *Duncan*); "bag and baggage, however securely or insecurely affixed they may be by law and precedent to federal proceedings" (Fortas, J., concurring in *Duncan*).

Thus, BRENNAN, J., observed for a majority in *Malloy v. Hogan*, 378 U.S. 1, 84 S.Ct. 1489, 12 L.Ed.2d 653 (1964): "We have held that the guarantees of the First Amendment, the prohibition of unreasonable searches and seizures of the Fourth Amendment, *Ker v. California*, 374 U.S. 23, 83 S.Ct. 1623, 10 L.Ed.2d 726 (1965), and the right to counsel guaranteed by the Sixth Amendment, *Gideon v. Wainwright* [Sec. IV infra], are all to be enforced against the States under the Fourteenth Amendment *according to the same standards that protect those personal rights against federal encroachment.* [The] Court thus has rejected the notion that the Fourteenth Amendment applies to the States only a 'watered-down, subjective version of the individual guarantees of the Bill of Rights.'" (Emphasis added.)

And WHITE, J., put it for a majority in *Duncan:* "Because we believe that trial by jury in criminal cases is fundamental to the American scheme of justice, we hold that the Fourteenth Amendment guarantees a right of jury trial in all criminal cases which—*were they to be tried in a federal court*—would come within the Sixth Amendment's guarantee." (Emphasis added.)

Similarly, MARSHALL, J., observed for a majority in *Benton v. Maryland*, 395 U.S. 784, 89 S.Ct. 2056, 23 L.Ed.2d 707 (1969): "Once it is decided that a particular Bill of Rights guarantee is 'fundamental to the American scheme of justice,' the same constitutional standards apply against both the State and Federal Governments. [Like] the right to trial by jury, [the guarantee against double jeopardy] is clearly 'fundamental to the American scheme of justice.' The validity of [the conviction] must be judged, not by the watered-down standard enunciated in *Palko*, but *under this Court's interpretations of the Fifth Amendment double jeopardy provision.*" (Emphasis added.)

HARLAN, J., repeatedly voiced his opposition to the *Malloy-Duncan-Benton* approach to fourteenth amendment due process. "The ultimate result," he protested in his *Malloy* dissent, "is compelled uniformity, which is inconsistent

---

i. In the area of criminal procedure, the Court has come very close to incorporating all of the relevant Bill of Rights guarantees. But still on the books, is a lonely exception. *Hurtado v. California*, 110 U.S. 516, 4 S.Ct. 111, 28 L.Ed. 232 (1884), refusing to apply to the states the fifth amendment requirement that prosecution be initiated by grand jury indictment.

with the purpose of our federal system and which is achieved either by encroachment on the State's sovereign powers or by dilution in federal law enforcement of the specific protections found in the Bill of Rights."

Dissenting in *Duncan*, HARLAN, J., joined by Stewart, J., protested: "Today's Court still remains unwilling to accept the total incorporationists' view of the history of the Fourteenth Amendment. This, if accepted, would afford a cogent reason for applying the Sixth Amendment to the States. The Court is also, apparently, unwilling to face the task of determining whether denial of trial by jury in the situation before us, or in other situations, is fundamentally unfair. Consequently, the Court has compromised on the ease of the incorporationist position, without its internal logic. It has simply assumed that the question before us is whether the Jury Trial Clause of the Sixth Amendment should be incorporated into the Fourteenth, jot-for-jot and case-for-case, or ignored. Then the Court merely declares that the clause in question is 'in' rather than 'out.'

"The Court has justified neither its starting place nor its conclusion. If the problem is to discover and articulate the rules of fundamental fairness in criminal proceedings, there is no reason to assume that the whole body of rules developed in this Court constituting Sixth Amendment jury trial must be regarded as a unit. The requirement of trial by jury in federal criminal cases has given rise to numerous subsidiary questions respecting the exact scope and content of the right. It surely cannot be that every answer the Court has given, or will give, to such a question is attributable to the Founders; or even that every rule announced carries equal conviction of this Court; still less can it be that every such subprinciple is equally fundamental to ordered liberty.

"Examples abound. I should suppose it obviously fundamental to fairness that a 'jury' means an 'impartial jury.' I should think it equally obvious that the rule, imposed long ago in the federal courts, that 'jury' means 'jury of exactly twelve,' is not fundamental to anything: there is no significance except to mystics in the number 12. Again, trial by jury has been held to require a unanimous verdict of jurors in the federal courts, although unanimity has not been found essential to liberty in Britain, where the requirement has been abandoned."

Concurring in *Duncan*, FORTAS, J., too, balked: "Neither logic nor history nor the intent of the draftsmen of the Fourteenth Amendment can possibly be said to require that the Sixth Amendment or its jury trial provision be applied to the States together with the total gloss that this Court's decisions have supplied. The draftsmen of the Fourteenth Amendment intended what they said, not more or less: that no State shall deprive any person of life, liberty, or property without due process of law. It is ultimately the duty of this Court to interpret, to ascribe specific meaning to this phrase. There is no reason whatever for us to conclude that, in so doing, we are bound slavishly to follow not only the Sixth Amendment but all of its bag and baggage, however securely or insecurely affixed they may be by law and precedent to federal proceedings. To take this course, in my judgment, would be not only unnecessary but mischievous because it would inflict a serious blow upon the principle of federalism. The Due Process Clause commands us to apply its great standard to state court proceedings to assure basic fairness. It does not command us rigidly and arbitrarily to impose the exact pattern of federal proceedings upon the 50 States. [Our] Constitution sets up a federal union, not a monolith."

Concurring in *Pointer*, GOLDBERG, J., responded to Justice Harlan's repeated criticism of the "selective" incorporation approach as follows: "[My Brother

Harlan] would have the Fourteenth Amendment apply to the States 'only a "watered-down, subjective version of the individual guarantees of the Bill of Rights."' It would allow the States greater latitude than the Federal Government to abridge concededly fundamental liberties protected by the Constitution. While I quite agree with Mr. Justice Brandeis that '[i]t is one of the happy incidents of the federal system that [a State may] serve as a laboratory; and try novel social economic experiments,' I do not believe that this includes the power to experiment with the fundamental liberties of citizens safeguarded by the Bill of Rights. My Brother Harlan's view would also require this Court to make the extremely subjective and excessively discretionary determination as to whether a practice, forbidden the Federal Government by a fundamental constitutional guarantee, is, as viewed in the factual circumstances surrounding each individual case, sufficiently repugnant to the notion of due process as to be forbidden the States.

"Finally, I do not see that my Brother Harlan's view would further any legitimate interests of federalism. It would require this Court to intervene in the state judicial process with considerable lack of predictability and with a consequent likelihood of considerable friction. [T]o deny to the States the power to impair a fundamental constitutional right is not to increase federal power, but, rather, to limit the power of both federal and state governments in favor of safe-guarding the fundamental rights and liberties of the individual. In my view this promotes rather than undermines the basic policy of avoiding excess concentration of power in government, federal or state, which underlies our concepts of federalism." [a]

In the 1970s matters were brought to a head by the "right to jury trial" cases: *Baldwin v. New York,* 399 U.S. 66, 90 S.Ct. 1914, 26 L.Ed.2d 437 (1970) (no offense can be deemed "petty," thus dispensing with the fourteenth and sixth amendment rights to jury trial, where more than six months incarceration is authorized); *Williams v. Florida,* 399 U.S. 78, 90 S.Ct. 1893, 26 L.Ed.2d 446 (1970) ("that jury at common law was composed of precisely 12 is an historical accident, unnecessary to effect the purposes of the jury system"; thus 6-person jury in criminal cases does not violate sixth amendment, as applied to the states via fourteenth); [b] and the 1972 *Apodaca* and *Johnson* cases, discussed below, dealing with whether unanimous jury verdicts are required in criminal cases.

Dissenting in *Baldwin* and concurring in *Williams,* HARLAN, J., maintained: "[*Williams*] evinces [a] recognition that the 'incorporationist' view of the Due Process Clause of the Fourteenth Amendment, which underlay *Duncan* and is now carried forward into *Baldwin,* must be tempered to allow the States more elbow room in ordering their own criminal systems. With that much I agree. But to accomplish this by diluting constitutional protections within the federal system itself is something to which I cannot possibly subscribe. Tempering the rigor of *Duncan* should be done forthrightly, by facing up to the fact that at least in this area the 'incorporation' doctrine does not fit well with our federal structure, and by the same token that *Duncan* was wrongly decided.

a. To the same effect is the opinion of Black, J., joined by Douglas, J., concurring in *Duncan* and responding to the views of Harlan, J., dissenting and Fortas, J., concurring.

b. But *Ballew v. Georgia,* 435 U.S. 223, 98 S.Ct. 1029, 55 L.Ed.2d 234 (1978), subsequently held that a state trial in a non-petty criminal case to a jury of only five persons did deprive a defendant of the right to trial by jury guaranteed by the sixth and fourteenth amendments.

"[Rather] than bind the States by the hitherto undeviating and unquestioned federal practice of 12-member juries, the Court holds, based on a poll of state practice, that a six-man jury satisfies the guarantee of a trial by jury in a federal criminal system and consequently carries over to the States. This is a constitutional *renvoi*. With all respect, I consider that before today it would have been unthinkable to suggest that the Sixth Amendment's right to a trial by jury is satisfied by a jury of six, or less, as is left open by the Court's opinion in *Williams*, or by less than a unanimous verdict, a question also reserved in today's decision.[c]

"[These decisions] demonstrate that the difference between a 'due process' approach, that considers each particular case on its own bottom to see whether the right alleged is one 'implicit in the concept of ordered liberty,' and 'selective incorporation' is not an abstract one whereby different verbal formulae achieve the same results. The internal logic of the selective incorporation doctrine cannot be respected if the Court is both committed to interpreting faithfully the meaning of the federal Bill of Rights and recognizing the governmental diversity that exists in this country. The 'backlash' in *Williams* exposes the malaise, for there the Court dilutes a federal guarantee in order to reconcile the logic of 'incorporation,' the 'jot-for-jot and case-for-case' application of the federal right to the States, with the reality of federalism. Can one doubt that had Congress tried to undermine the common law right to trial by jury before *Duncan* came on the books the history today recited would have barred such action? Can we expect repeated performances when this Court is called upon to give definition and meaning to other federal guarantees that have been 'incorporated'?

"[I]t is time [for] for this Court to face up to the reality implicit in today's holdings and reconsider the 'incorporation' doctrine before its leveling tendencies further retard development in the field of criminal procedure by stifling flexibility in the States and by discarding the possibility of federal leadership by example."

In the companion cases of *Apodaca v. Oregon*, 406 U.S. 404, 92 S.Ct. 1628, 32 L.Ed.2d 184 (1972) and *Johnson v. Louisiana*, 406 U.S. 356, 92 S.Ct. 1620, 32 L.Ed.2d 152 (1972), upholding the constitutionality of less-than-unanimous jury verdicts in state criminal cases, eight justices adhered to the *Duncan* position that each element of the sixth amendment right to jury trial applies to the states to the same extent it applies to the federal government, but split 4–4 over whether the federal guarantee *did require* jury unanimity in criminal cases. State convictions by less than unanimous votes were sustained only because the ninth member of the Court, newly appointed POWELL, J., read the sixth amendment as requiring jury unanimity, but—taking a Harlan-type approach—concluded that *this feature* of the federal right is not "so fundamental to the essentials of jury trial" as to require unanimity in state criminal cases as a matter of fourteenth amendment due process:[d]

---

c. Cf. Frankfurter, J., for the Court in *Rochin v. California* (1952) (discussed in Part III infra): "Words being symbols do not speak without a gloss. [T]he gloss may be the deposit of history, whereby a term gains technical content. Thus the requirements of the Sixth and Seventh Amendments for trial by jury in the federal courts have a rigid meaning. No changes or chances can alter the content of the verbal symbol of 'jury'—a body of twelve men who must reach a unanimous conclusion if the verdict is to go against the defendant."

d. But *Burch v. Louisiana*, 441 U.S. 130, 99 S.Ct. 1623, 60 L.Ed.2d 96 (1979), subsequently held, without a dissent on this issue, that conviction by a nonunanimous *six-person* jury in a state criminal trial for a nonpetty offense did violate the sixth and fourteenth amendment rights to trial by jury.

"[I]n holding that the Fourteenth Amendment has incorporated 'jot-for-jot and case-for-case' every element of the Sixth Amendment, the Court derogates principles of federalism that are basic to our system. In the name of uniform application of high standards of due process, the Court has embarked upon a course of constitutional interpretation that deprives the States of freedom to experiment with adjudicatory processes different from the federal model. At the same time, the Court's understandable unwillingness to impose requirements that it finds unnecessarily rigid (e.g., *Williams*), has culminated in the dilution of federal rights that were, until these decisions, never seriously questioned. The doubly undesirable consequence of this reasoning process, labeled by Mr. Justice Harlan as 'constitutional schizophrenia,' may well be detrimental both to the state and federal criminal justice systems. Although it is perhaps late in the day for an expression of my views, I [believe] that, at least in defining the elements of the right to jury trial, there is no sound basis for interpreting the Fourteenth Amendment to require blind adherence by the States to all details of the federal Sixth Amendment standards." [e]

BRENNAN, J., joined by Marshall, J., dissented: "Readers of today's opinions may be understandably puzzled why convictions by 11–1 and 10–2 jury votes are affirmed [when] a majority of the Court agrees that the Sixth Amendment requires a unanimous verdict in federal criminal jury trials, and a majority also agrees that the right to jury trial guaranteed by the Sixth Amendment is to be enforced against the States according to the same standards that protect that right against federal encroachment. The reason is that while my Brother Powell agrees that a unanimous verdict is required in federal criminal trials, he does not agree that the Sixth Amendment right to a jury trial is to be applied in the same way to State and Federal Governments. In that circumstance, it is arguable that the affirmance of the convictions [is] not inconsistent with a view that today's decision is a holding that only a unanimous verdict will afford the accused in a state criminal prosecution the jury trial guaranteed him by the Sixth Amendment. In any event, the affirmance must not obscure that the majority of the Court remains of the view that, as in the case of every specific of the Bill of Rights that extends to the States, the Sixth Amendment's jury trial guarantee, however it is to be construed, has identical application against both State and Federal Governments." [f]

e. In his continued resistance to "jot-for-jot" or "bag and baggage" incorporation of a "selected" provision of the Bill of Rights, Powell, J., has gained two allies. See Powell, J., joined by Burger, C.J., and Rehnquist, J., dissenting in *Crist v. Bretz*, 437 U.S. 28, 98 S.Ct. 2156, 57 L.Ed.2d 24 (1978) (holding that federal rule as to when jeopardy "attaches" in jury trials applies to state cases). In *Ballew*, fn. b supra, although he concurred in the judgment, Powell, J., again joined by Burger, C.J., and Rehnquist, J., did not join Blackmun, J.'s opinion because it "assumes full incorporation of the Sixth Amendment, contrary to my view in *Apodaca*."

See also Burger, C.J.'s separate opinion in *Crist v. Bretz* and Rehnquist, J.'s separate opinion in *Buckley v. Valeo*, p. 674 infra, maintaining that "not all of the strictures which the First Amendment imposes upon Congress are carried over against the States by the Fourteenth Amendment, [but] only the 'general principle' of free speech."

f. In a separate dissent, Stewart, J., joined by Brennan and Marshall, JJ., protested that "unless *Duncan* is to be overruled," "the only relevant question here is whether the Sixth Amendment's guarantee of trial by jury embraces a guarantee that the verdict of the jury must be unanimous. The answer to that question is clearly 'yes,' as my Brother Powell has cogently demonstrated."

III. BODILY EXTRACTIONS: ANOTHER LOOK AT THE "DUE PROCESS" AND "SELECTIVE INCORPORATION" APPROACHES

As noted earlier, dissenting in *Baldwin* and concurring in *Williams,* Harlan, J., maintained that "the difference between a 'due process' approach [and] 'selective incorporation' is not an abstract one whereby different formulae achieve the same results." But he made this observation in the context of the applicability to the states of the sixth amendment right to trial by jury, which had, or was thought to have, a relatively rigid meaning. Most language in the Bill of Rights, however, is rather vague and general, at least when specific problems arise under a particular phrase. In such cases, does dwelling on the literal language simply *shift the focus of broad judicial inquiry* from "due process" to e.g., "freedom of speech," "establishment of religion," "unreasonable searches and seizures," "excessive bail," "cruel and unusual punishments," and "the assistance of counsel"? See Friendly, *The Bill of Rights as a Code of Criminal Procedure,* 53 Calif.L.Rev. 929, 937 (1965); Kadish, *Methodology and Criteria in Due Process Adjudication—A Survey and Criticism,* 66 Yale L.J. 319, 337–39 (1957); Wechsler, *Toward Neutral Principles of Constitutional Law,* 73 Harv.L.Rev. 1, 17–18 (1959).

In considering whether the right to counsel "begins" at the time of arrest, preliminary hearing, arraignment, or not until the trial itself, or includes probation and parole revocation hearings or applies to juvenile delinquency proceedings, deportation hearings or civil commitments, or, where the defendant is indigent, includes the right to *assigned* counsel or an assigned psychiatrist at state expense, how helpful is the sixth amendment language entitling an accused to "the assistance of counsel for his defense"? Is the specificity or direction of this language significantly greater than the "due process" clause?

To turn to another cluster of problems—which form the basis for this section—in considering whether, and under what conditions, the police may direct the "pumping" of a person's stomach to uncover incriminating evidence, or the taking of a blood sample from him, without his consent, do the "specific guarantees" in the Bill of Rights against "unreasonable searches and seizures" and against compelling a person to be "a witness against himself" free the Court from the demands of appraising and judging involved in answering these questions by interpreting the "due process" clause?

ROCHIN v. CALIFORNIA, 342 U.S. 165, 72 S.Ct. 205, 96 L.Ed. 183 (1952) arose as follows: Having "some information" that Rochin was selling narcotics, three deputy sheriffs "forced upon the door of [his] room and found him sitting partly dressed on the side of the bed, upon which his wife was lying. On a 'night stand' beside the bed the deputies spied two capsules. When asked 'Whose stuff is this?' Rochin seized the capsules and put them in his mouth. A struggle ensued, in the course of which the three officers 'jumped upon him' and [unsuccessfully] attempted to extract the capsules. [Rochin] was handcuffed and taken to a hospital. At the direction of one of the officers a doctor forced an emetic solution through a tube into Rochin's stomach against his will. This 'stomach pumping' produced vomiting. In the vomited matter were found two capsules which proved to contain morphine. [Rochin was convicted of possessing morphine] and sentenced to sixty days' imprisonment. The chief evidence against him was the two capsules."

The Court, per FRANKFURTER, J., concluded that the officers' conduct violated fourteenth amendment due process: "This is conduct that shocks the conscience. Illegally breaking into the privacy of the petitioner, the struggle to open his mouth and remove what was there, the forcible extraction of his stomach's contents—this course of proceeding by agents of government to obtain evidence is bound to offend even hardened sensibilities. They are methods too close to the rack and the screw to permit of constitutional differentiation.

"It has long since ceased to be true that due process of law is heedless of the means by which otherwise relevant and credible evidence is obtained. [The confession cases are] only instances of the general requirement that States in their prosecutions respect certain decencies of civilized conduct. Due process of law, as a historic and generative principle, precludes defining, and thereby confining, these standards of conduct more precisely than to say that convictions cannot be brought about by methods that offend 'a sense of justice.' It would be a stultification of the responsibility which the course of constitutional history has cast upon this Court to hold that in order to convict a man the police cannot extract by force what is in his mind but can extract what is in his stomach.

"[E]ven though statements contained in them may be independently established as true[,] [c]oerced confessions offend the community's sense of fair play and decency. So here, to sanction the brutal conduct which naturally enough was condemned by the court whose judgment is before us, would be to afford brutality the cloak of law. Nothing would be more calculated to discredit law and thereby to brutalize the temper of a society."

Concurring, BLACK, J., reasoned that the fifth amendment's protection against compelled self-incrimination applied to the states and that "a person is compelled to be a witness against himself not only when he is compelled to testify, but also when as here, incriminating evidence is forcibly taken from him by a contrivance of modern science." He maintained that "faithful adherence to the specific guarantees in the Bill of Rights insures a more permanent protection of individual liberty than that which can be afforded by the nebulous [fourteenth amendment due process] standards stated by the majority."

DOUGLAS, J., concurring, also criticized the majority's approach. He contended that the privilege against self-incrimination applied to the states as well as the federal government and because of the privilege "words taken from [an accused's] lips, capsules taken from his stomach, blood taken from his veins are all inadmissible provided they are taken from him without his consent. [This] is an unequivocal, definite and workable rule of evidence for state and federal courts. But we cannot in fairness free the state courts from the [restraints of the fifth amendment privilege against self-incrimination] and yet excoriate them for flouting the 'decencies of civilized conduct' when they admit the evidence. This is to make the rule turn not on the Constitution but on the idiosyncracies of the judges who sit here." [a]

---

a. *Irvine v. California,* 347 U.S. 128, 74 S.Ct. 381, 98 L.Ed. 561 (1954), limited *Rochin* to situations involving coercion, violence or brutality to the person. In *Irvine* the police made repeated illegal entries into petitioner's home, first to install a secret microphone and then to move it to the bedroom, in order to listen to the conversations of the occupants—for over a month. Jackson, J., who announced the judgment of the Court and wrote the principal opinion, recognized that "few police measures have come to our attention that more flagrantly, deliberately, and persistently violated the fundamental principle declared by the Fourth Amendment as a restriction on the Federal Government," but adhered to the holding in *Wolf v. Colorado* (1949) (Part IV infra) that the exclusionary rule in federal search and seizure cases is not binding on the states. (*Wolf* was overruled in *Mapp v. Ohio*

BREITHAUPT v. ABRAM, 352 U.S. 432, 77 S.Ct. 408, 1 L.Ed.2d 448 (1957), illustrated that under the *Rochin* test state police had considerable leeway even when the body of the accused was "invaded." In *Breithaupt,* the police took a blood sample from an unconscious person who had been involved in a fatal automobile collision. A majority, per CLARK, J., affirmed a manslaughter conviction based on the blood sample (which showed intoxication), stressing that the sample was "taken under the protective eye of a physician" and that "the blood test procedure has become routine in our everyday life." The "interests of society in the scientific determination of intoxication, one of the great causes of the mortal hazards of the road," outweighed "so slight an intrusion" of a person's body.

Dissenting, WARREN, C.J., joined by Black and Douglas, JJ., deemed *Rochin* controlling and argued that police efforts to curb the narcotics traffic, involved in *Rochin,* "is surely a state interest of at least as great magnitude as the interest in highway law enforcement. [Only] personal reaction to the stomach pump and the blood test can distinguish the [two cases]."

DOUGLAS, J., joined by Black, J., dissented, maintaining that "if the decencies of a civilized state are the test, it is repulsive to me for the police to insert needles into an unconscious person in order to get the evidence necessary to convict him, whether they find the person unconscious, give him a pill which puts him to sleep, or use force to subdue him."

Nine years later, even though in the meantime the Court had held in *Mapp v. Ohio,* Part IV infra, that the federal exclusionary rule in search and seizure cases was binding on the states and in *Malloy v. Hogan,* supra, that the fifth amendment's protection against compelled self-incrimination was likewise applicable to the states, the Court still upheld the taking by a physician, at police direction, of a blood sample from an injured person, over his objection. SCHMERBER v. CALIFORNIA, 384 U.S. 757, 86 S.Ct. 1826, 16 L.Ed.2d 908 (1966). In affirming the conviction for operating a vehicle while under the influence of intoxicating liquor, a 5–4 majority, per BRENNAN, J., ruled: (1) that the extraction of blood from petitioner under the aforementioned circumstances "did not offend 'that "sense of justice" ' of which we spoke in *Rochin,*" thus reaffirming *Breithaupt;* (2) that the privilege against self-incrimination, now binding on the states, "protects an accused only from being compelled to testify against himself, or otherwise provide the State with evidence of a testimonial or communicative nature and that the withdrawal of blood and use of the analysis in question did not involve compulsion to these ends"; and (3) that the protection against unreasonable search and seizure, now binding on the states, was satisfied because (a) "there was plainly probable cause" to arrest and charge petitioner and to suggest "the required relevance and likely success of a test of petitioner's blood for alcohol"; (b) the officer "might reasonably have believed that he was confronted with an emergency, in which the delay necessary to obtain a warrant, under the circumstances, threatened 'the destruction of evidence' "; and (c) "the

(1961) (Part IV infra)). Nor did Jackson, J., deem *Rochin* applicable: "However obnoxious are the facts in the case before us, they do not involve coercion, violence or brutality to the person [as did *Rochin*], but rather a trespass to property, plus eavesdropping."

Because of the "aggravating" and "repulsive" police misconduct in *Irvine,* Frankfurter, J., joined by Burton, J., dissenting, maintained that *Rochin* was controlling, not *Wolf.* (He had written the majority opinions in both cases.) Black, J., joined by Douglas, J., dissented separately, arguing that petitioner had been convicted on the basis of evidence "extorted" from him in violation of the self-incrimination clause, which he considered applicable to the states. Douglas, J., dissenting separately, protested against the use in state prosecutions of evidence seized in violation of the fourth amendment.

test chosen to measure petitioner's blood-alcohol level was [reasonable and] performed in a reasonable manner."

Dissenting, BLACK, J., joined by Douglas, J., expressed amazement at the majority's "conclusion that compelling a person to give his blood to help the State to convict him is not equivalent to compelling him to be a witness against himself." "It is a strange hierarchy of values that allows the State to extract a human being's blood to convict him of a crime because of the blood's content but proscribes compelled production of his lifeless papers." [a]

Notes and Questions

1. In light of *Rochin, Breithaupt* and *Schmerber*, when courts decide constitutional questions by "looking to" the Bill of Rights, to what extent do they proceed, as Black, J., said in *Adamson*, "within clearly marked constitutional boundaries"? To what extent does resort to these "particular standards" enable courts to avoid substituting their "own concepts of decency and fundamental justice" for the language of the Constitution?

2. Did *Mapp* and *Malloy*, decided in the interim between *Breithaupt* and *Schmerber*, affect any justice's vote? Did the applicability of the "particular standards" of the fourth and fifth amendments inhibit Black, Douglas or Brennan, JJ., from employing their own concepts of "decency" and "justice" in *Schmerber*? After *Schmerber*, how much force is there in Black, J.'s view, concurring in *Rochin*, that "faithful adherence to the specific guarantees in the Bill of Rights assures a more permanent protection of individual liberty than that which can be afforded by the nebulous standards stated by the majority"?

3. For other recent illustrations of standards and methodology in due process adjudication, see the "death penalty" cases (although nominally "cruel and unusual punishment" cases), Sec. 4 infra. See also the "right of privacy" cases, Sec. 2 infra.

IV. LEADING CRIMINAL PROCEDURE DECISIONS AND THE RETROACTIVE EFFECT OF A HOLDING OF UNCONSTITUTIONALITY

In recent years, the Court has considered the retroactive effect of a holding that a law or practice is unconstitutional primarily in the context of criminal procedure decisions.[a] *Linkletter v. Walker*, 381 U.S. 618, 85 S.Ct. 1731, 14 L.Ed. 2d 601 (1965), took the position that "the Constitution neither prohibits nor requires retrospective effect," [b] and that a determination of the effect of a

a. Warren, C.J., and Douglas, J., dissented in separate opinions, each adhering to his dissenting views in *Breithaupt*. In a third dissent, Fortas, J., maintained that "petitioner's privilege against self-incrimination applies" and, moreover, "under the Due Process Clause, the State, in its role as prosecutor, has no right to extract blood from [anyone] over his protest."

a. In none of these cases, apparently, did the Court seriously consider applying the new constitutional ruling "purely prospectively," i.e., not even giving the litigant in the very case the benefit of the decision. "Pure prospectivity" raises "difficult problems concerning the nature of a court's functions; persuasive arguments can be made that courts are

badly suited for the general determination and proclamation of future rules and, indeed, that for them to do so violates the Constitution's grant to the judiciary only of power over 'cases' and 'controversies.'" 80 Harv.L.Rev. 140 (1966). Another frequently made point, although it may carry less weight in the criminal procedure area, is that "if the Supreme Court begins regularly to announce new rules prospectively only, petitioners, knowing they will be unlikely to benefit personally, will be deterred from pressing for the new rules." Id.

b. "If an unconstitutional statute or practice effectively never existed as a lawful justification for state action [perhaps the dominant view in the era between the Civil War and the Depression—compare *Norton v. Shelby Coun-*

judgment of unconstitutionality would turn on "the prior history of the rule in question, its purpose and effect," "whether retrospective operation of the rule will further or retard its operation" and what adverse impact on the administration of justice retroactivity would be likely to have. Two years later, the Court articulated "the criteria guiding resolution of the [retroactivity] question": "(a) the purpose to be served by the new standards"—e.g., protecting the reliability of the fact-finding process (such as the right to counsel at trial or the ban against coerced confessions) or furthering some other, independent interest, such as individual privacy—"(b) the extent of the reliance by law enforcement authorities on the old standards, and (c) the effect on the administration of justice of a retroactive application of the new standards." [c]

Consider the retroactivity problem in the context of the leading criminal procedure cases of the past two decades:

GIDEON v. WAINWRIGHT, 372 U.S. 335, 83 S.Ct. 792, 9 L.Ed.2d 799 (1963), held that, at least in all felony prosecutions,[d] an indigent defendant must be appointed counsel. Because, as Black, J., maintained, dissenting in the case *Gideon* was to overrule 20 years later,[e] "whether [one] is innocent cannot be determined from a trial [in which] denial of counsel has made it impossible to [tell] that the defendant's case was adequately represented," and because, as Black, J., pointed out for the Court in *Gideon*, "any person haled into court, who is too poor to hire a lawyer, cannot be assured a fair trial unless counsel is provided for him," *Gideon* was given complete retroactive effect.[f]

---

ty, 118 U.S. 425, 6 S.Ct. 1121, 30 L.Ed. 178 (1886) with *Chicot County Drainage Dist. v. Baxter State Bank*, 308 U.S. 371, 60 S.Ct. 317, 84 L.Ed. 329 (1940)], individuals convicted under the statute or in trials which tolerated the practice were convicted unlawfully even if their trials took place before the declaration of unconstitutionality; such a declaration should have a fully retroactive effect, and previously convicted individuals should be able to win their freedom through the writ of habeas corpus. Alternatively, if a judgment of unconstitutionality affects only the case at hand [a view which also had support], the legality of the convictions of individuals previously tried is not affected. In *Linkletter*, the Court rejected both extremes." Tribe, *American Constitutional Law* 25 (1978).

c. *Stovall v. Denno*, 388 U.S. 293, 87 S.Ct. 1967, 18 L.Ed.2d 1199 (1967), concerning the retroactive effect of the lineup decisions, infra.

d. A decade and a half later, *Scott v. Illinois*, 440 U.S. 367, 99 S.Ct. 1158, 59 L.Ed.2d 383 (1979) (per Rehnquist, J.), held that the sixth and fourteenth amendments require that, regardless of whether the offense be classified as a "misdemeanor" or "felony," "no indigent criminal defendant be sentenced to a term of imprisonment unless the State has afforded him the right to assistance of appointed counsel in his defense." But the Court declined to apply the *Gideon* principle to a case where one is charged with an offense for which imprisonment is *authorized*, but *not*

actually imposed. See also *Argersinger v. Hamlin*, 407 U.S. 25, 92 S.Ct. 2006, 32 L.Ed.2d 530 (1972).

e. *Betts v. Brady*, 316 U.S. 455, 62 S.Ct. 1252, 86 L.Ed. 1595 (1942).

f. Other decisions given retroactive effect: *Ivan v. New York*, 407 U.S. 203, 92 S.Ct. 1951, 32 L.Ed.2d 659 (1972) (per curiam), held that "the major purpose" of the constitutional requirement of "proof beyond a reasonable doubt" announced in *In re Winship*, 397 U.S. 358, 90 S.Ct. 1068, 25 L.Ed.2d 368 (1970) "was to overcome an aspect of a criminal trial that substantially impairs the truth-finding function" and thus *Winship* should be given "complete retroactive effect." In *Robinson v. Neil*, 409 U.S. 505, 93 S.Ct. 876, 35 L.Ed.2d 29 (1973), the Court ruled that because *Waller v. Florida*, 397 U.S. 387, 90 S.Ct. 1184, 25 L.Ed. 2d 435 (1970), holding that the double jeopardy clause barred two prosecutions, state and municipal, based on the same act or offense, was "squarely directed to the prevention of the second trial's taking place at all, even though it might have been conducted with a scrupulous regard for [all] constitutional procedural rights," *Waller* "is to be accorded full retroactive effect." In *Brown v. Louisiana*, 447 U.S. 323, 100 S.Ct. 2214, 65 L.Ed.2d 159 (1980), because he viewed *Burch v. Louisiana*, 441 U.S. 130, 99 S.Ct. 1623, 60 L.Ed.2d 96 (1979), holding that conviction of a nonpetty offense by a nonunanimous *six-person* jury violates a defendant's right to trial by jury, as

MAPP v. OHIO, 367 U.S. 643, 81 S.Ct. 1684, 6 L.Ed.2d 1081 (1961), overruling *Wolf v. Colorado,* 338 U.S. 25, 69 S.Ct. 1359, 93 L.Ed. 1782 (1949), held that the federal "exclusionary rule" in search and seizure cases [g] was binding on the

establishing that "the concurrence of six jurors was constitutionally required to preserve the substance of the jury trial and assure the reliability of its verdict," Brennan, J., joined by Stewart, Marshall and Blackmun, JJ., would give *Burch* full retroactive effect. Since Powell, J., joined by Stevens, J., believed that new constitutional rules should apply retroactively in cases still pending on direct review—and Burch's case was pending on direct appeal—they concurred in the reversal of Burch's conviction on this ground.

g. As noted in Oaks, *Studying the Exclusionary Rule in Search and Seizure,* 37 U.Chi. L.Rev. 665–66 (1970), the Court "currently enforces an exclusionary rule in state and federal criminal proceedings as to four major types of violations: searches and seizures that violate the fourth amendment [and wiretapping and electronic eavesdropping that violate the fourth amendment or federal statutory law], confessions obtained in violation of the fifth and sixth amendments, identification testimony obtained in violation of these amendments [see the landmark lineup cases, *United States v. Wade* and *Gilbert v. California,* both briefly discussed infra], and evidence obtained by methods so shocking that its use would violate the due process clause [see *Rochin,* supra]. The exclusionary rule is the Supreme Court's sole technique for enforcing these vital constitutional rights." In addition to being the most frequent occasion for application of the exclusionary rule, one quality that sets search and seizure apart from other areas is that evidence obtained by an illegal search and seizure "is just as reliable as evidence obtained by legal means. This cannot always be said of evidence obtained by improper methods of lineup identification or interrogation." Id. at 666.

The search and seizure exclusionary rule has been subjected to persistent, heavy attack in recent years. Perhaps the most significant post-*Mapp* decision on the scope of the exclusionary rule is *United States v. Calandra,* 414 U.S. 338, 94 S.Ct. 613, 38 L.Ed.2d 561 (1974). In ruling that a grand jury witness may not refuse to answer questions on the ground that they are based on the fruits of an unlawful search, the *Calandra* Court, per Powell, J., called the exclusionary rule "a judicially created remedy designed to safeguard Fourth Amendment rights generally through its deterrent effect, rather than a personal constitutional right of the party aggrieved." Thus, whether grand jury questions based on evidence seized in violation of the Fourth Amendment should be prohibited "present[ed] a question, not of rights, but of remedies"—a question to be answered by weighing the "potential inquiry" to the functions of the grand jury against the "potential benefits" of the exclusionary rule in this context; or more generally, by weighing the "likely 'costs' " of the rule against its "likely 'benefits' " in the particular context.

The exclusionary rule "lost" in *Calandra*—as it usually does when the question is presented this way. See *Stone v. Powell,* 428 U.S. 465, 96 S.Ct. 3037, 49 L.Ed.2d 1067 (1976) (state prisoner may not be granted federal habeas corpus relief on search-and-seizure grounds unless denied opportunity for "full and fair litigation" of claim in state courts); *United States v. Janis,* 428 U.S. 433, 96 S.Ct. 3021, 49 L.Ed.2d 1046 (1976) (rule's deterrent purpose would not be served by excluding from federal civil tax proceedings evidence that was obtained illegally by state police); *United States v. Ceccolini,* 435 U.S. 268, 98 S.Ct. 1054, 55 L.Ed.2d 268 (1978) (exclusionary rule "should be invoked with much greater reluctance" where defense seeks to suppress live-witness testimony rather than an inanimate object); *United States v. Havens,* 446 U.S. 620, 100 S.Ct. 1912, 64 L.Ed.2d 559 (1980) (illegally obtained evidence may impeach not only direct testimony of defendant but also statements first elicited from him on cross-examination, if prosecutor's questions were "reasonably suggested" by the direct testimony); *INS v. Lopez-Mendoza,* ___ U.S. ___, 104 S.Ct. 3479, 82 L.Ed.2d 778 (1984) (because high costs of applying the rule in this setting outweigh the marginal benefits, exclusionary rule inapplicable in a civil deportation hearing).

The most dramatic application to date of the "deterrence" rationale, and its concomitant cost-benefit analysis, is *United States v. Leon,* ___ U.S. ___, 104 S.Ct. 3405, 82 L.Ed.2d 677 (1984), per White, J., where the Court's "evaluation of the costs and benefits of suppressing reliable physical evidence" led it to establish a "good faith" or "reasonable mistake" exception to the fourth amendment exclusionary rule, at least in search warrant cases, so that evidence obtained by police officers pursuant to an invalid search warrant is admissible so long as the police acted in the "reasonable, good-faith belief" that the challenged search or seizure was in accord with the fourth amendment:

Until *Leon,* one could still say that the Court's "deconstitutionalization" of the exclusionary rule—its view that the rule is only a "judicially created" "remedial device" whose application turns on a "pragmatic analysis of [its] usefulness in a particular context" (*Stone v. Powell,* supra)—had only narrowed the thrust of the exclusionary rule in "peripheral" or "collateral" settings, but had not affected the rule in its central application: the prose-states—"all evidence obtained by searches and seizures in violation of the [fourth and fourteenth amendments] is, by the same authority, inadmissible in a state court." *Linkletter v. Walker,* supra, however, declined to apply *Mapp* to state convictions which had become final prior to the overruling of *Wolf:* [h] The "prime purpose" of the "exclusionary rule"—deterring lawless police action—reasoned

cutor's case-in-chief against the direct victim of a fourth amendment violation. Indeed, *Stone* and other cases had suggested that at least in its central application the exclusionary rule would be spared the ordeal of being subjected to "interest-balancing" or "cost-benefit" analysis—that at least in these circumstances it would not have to demonstrate that it can "pay its way." As *Leon* makes plain, however, this is not the case.

Although the "deterrence" rationale has been in the ascendency ever since *Calandra,* it has not escaped forceful criticism on and off the Court. In *Calandra* itself, dissenting Justice Brennan, joined by Douglas and Marshall, JJ., maintained that curtailment of fourth amendment violations was not (nor should it be) the exclusionary rule's *raison d'etre:* the goals "uppermost in the minds of the framers of the rule" were "enabling the judiciary to avoid the taint of partnership in official lawlessness" and "assuring the people [that] the government would not profit from its lawless behavior, thus minimizing the risk of seriously undermining popular trust in government." A decade later, dissenting in *Leon,* Brennan, J., joined by Marshall, J., observed:

"[T]he question whether the exclusion of evidence would deter future police misconduct was never considered a relevant concern in the early [federal search and seizure cases]. In these formative decisions, the Court plainly understood that the exclusion of illegally obtained evidence was compelled not by judicially fashioned remedial purposes, but rather by a direct constitutional command. [The Fourth Amendment] directly contemplates that some reliable and incriminating evidence will be lost to the government; therefore, it is not the exclusionary rule, but the Amendment itself that has imposed this cost.

"In addition, the Court's decisions over the past decade have made plain that the entire enterprise of attempting to assess the benefits and costs of the exclusionary rule in various contexts is a virtually impossible task for the judiciary to perform honestly or accurately. Although the Court's language in those cases suggests that some specific empirical basis may support its analyses, the reality is that the Court's opinions represent inherently unstable compounds of intuition, hunches, and occasional pieces of partial and often inconclusive data. [By] remaining within its redoubt of empiricism and by basing the rule solely on the deterrence rationale, the Court has robbed the rule of legitimacy. A doctrine that is explained as if it were an empirical proposition but for which there is only limited empir-

ical support is both inherently unstable and an easy mark for critics."

There is a vast literature on the "exclusionary rule." The various arguments are analyzed in 1 LaFave, *Search and Seizure: A Treatise on the Fourth Amendment* 3–39 (1978). See also the Kamisar-Wilkey debate, 62 Judic. 66, 214, 337, 351 (1978–79). For criticism of the *Calandra-Stone-Leon* line of cases, see, e.g., Kamisar, *Does (Did) (Should) The Exclusionary Rule Rest on a "Principled Basis" Rather than an "Empirical Proposition"?,* 16 Creighton L.Rev. 565 (1983); LaFave, *"The Seductive Call of Expediency": U.S. v. Leon, Its Rationale and Ramifications,* 1984 U.Ill.L.Rev. 895 (1984); Schrock & Welsh, *Up from Calandra: The Exclusionary Rule as a Constitutional Requirement,* 59 Minn.L.Rev. 251 (1974); Wasserstrom & Mertens, *The Exclusionary Rule on the Scaffold: But Was It A Fair Trial?,* 22 Am.Crim.L.Rev. 85 (1984). For criticism of the Burger Court's cost-benefit approach to judicial decisionmaking generally, see Tribe, *Constitutional Calculus: Equal Justice or Economic Efficiency?,* 98 Harv.L.Rev. 592 (1985).

h. *Mapp,* however, had been applied to state cases still pending on direct appeal at the time it was handed down. But four years later, *Desist v. United States,* 394 U.S. 244, 89 S.Ct. 1030, 22 L.Ed.2d 248 (1969), concluded that another new fourth amendment decision, *Katz v. United States,* 389 U.S. 347, 88 S.Ct. 507, 19 L.Ed.2d 576 (1967), should only be given what the Court called "wholly prospective application," i.e., applied only to *police activity* occurring after the date of the decision. See also the Court's treatment of the 1967 line up decisions, infra.

Katz held that the reach of the fourth amendment "cannot turn upon the presence or absence of a physical intrusion into any given enclosure" and that electronic eavesdropping upon private conversations constituted a search and seizure which must meet fourth amendment requirements. All of the reasons for applying *Katz* prospectively only, observed *Desist,* per Stewart, J., author of the *Katz* opinion, "also undercut any distinction between final convictions and those still pending on review. Both the deterrent purpose of the exclusionary rule and the reliance of law enforcement officers focus upon the time of the search, not any subsequent point in the prosecution as the relevant date." In a long, powerful dissent, Harlan, J., concluded, inter alia, that "*Linkletter* was right in insisting that all 'new' rules of constitutional law must, at minimum, be applied to all those cases the Court, per Clark, J., author of the *Mapp* opinion, would not be furthered by making the rule retroactive. "The misconduct of the police prior to *Mapp* has already occurred and will not be corrected by releasing the prisoners involved. [T]he ruptured privacy of the victim's home and effects cannot be restored. Reparation comes too late."

Moreover, retroactive application of *Mapp* to "finalized" cases "would tax the administration of justice to the utmost. Hearings would have to be held on the excludability of evidence long since destroyed, misplaced or deteriorated. [To] thus legitimate such an extraordinary procedural weapon *that has no bearing on guilt* would seriously disrupt the administration of justice." (Emphasis added.)

The Court recognized that it had given full retroactive effect to cases developing a sophisticated and sensitive approach to the admissibility of "coerced" confessions and to cases establishing an indigent's right to assigned counsel at trial, and his right to be furnished a trial transcript on appeal,[i] but those principles "went to the fairness of the trial—the very integrity of the fact-finding process. Here the fairness of the trial is not under attack."

BLACK, J., joined by Douglas, J., dissented: "Despite the Court's resounding promises throughout the *Mapp* opinion that convictions based on such 'unconstitutional evidence' would 'find no sanction in the judgments of the courts,' Linkletter, convicted in the state court by use of 'unconstitutional evidence,' is today denied relief by the judgment of this Court because his conviction became 'final' before *Mapp* was decided. Linkletter must stay in jail; Miss Mapp, whose offense was committed before Linkletter's, is free. This different treatment of Miss Mapp and Linkletter points up at once the arbitrary and discriminatory nature of the judicial contrivance utilized here to break the promise of *Mapp* by keeping all people in jail who are unfortunate enough to have had their unconstitutional convictions affirmed before [the date of the *Mapp* decision]."

GRIFFIN v. CALIFORNIA, 380 U.S. 609, 85 S.Ct. 1229, 14 L.Ed.2d 106 (1965), held that the fifth amendment privilege against self-incrimination, binding on the states via the fourteenth amendment, prohibits adverse comment by prosecutor or judge on a defendant's failure to take the stand in a criminal case. But a 5–2 majority, per Stewart, J., declined to apply the rule to state cases "finalized" before *Griffin* was decided,[j] observing that "the basic purposes that lie behind the privilege against self-incrimination do not relate to protecting the innocent from conviction, but rather to [effectuating] values reflecting the concern of our society for the right of each individual to be let alone." More-

which are still subject to direct review by this Court at the time the 'new' decision is handed down." Douglas and Fortas, JJ., also filed separate dissents.

More than a decade later, however, relying heavily on Harlan, J.'s dissent in *Desist, United States v. Johnson,* 457 U.S. 537, 102 S.Ct. 2579, 73 L.Ed.2d 202 (1982), per Blackmun, J., applied *Payton v. New York,* 445 U.S. 573, 100 S.Ct. 1371, 63 L.Ed.2d 639 (1980) (holding that police must obtain an arrest warrant when entering a suspect's home to make a routine felony arrest) to cases still pending on direct

appeal at the time *Payton* was decided. The Court pointed out that "*Payton* overturned no long-standing practice approved by a near-unanimous body of lower court authority [and thus] does not fall into that narrow class of decisions whose nonretroactivity is effectively preordained because they unmistakably signal 'a clear break with the past.'"

i. *Griffin v. Illinois,* 351 U.S. 12, 76 S.Ct. 585, 100 L.Ed. 891 (1956).

j. *Tehan v. United States ex rel. Shott,* 382 U.S. 406, 86 S.Ct. 459, 15 L.Ed.2d 453 (1966).

over, "for more than half a century" the states had relied, in good faith on the *Twining* rule [fn. a, Sec. I supra].[k]

MIRANDA v. ARIZONA, 384 U.S. 436, 86 S.Ct. 1602, 16 L.Ed.2d 694 (1966), probably the most famous and controversial Warren Court criminal procedure case, applied the privilege against self-incrimination to the stationhouse and other "custodial surroundings" and required the police to give a suspect the familiar "*Miranda* warnings" and to obtain a waiver of his rights before subjecting him to "custodial interrogation." But a week later, the Court, per WARREN, C.J., author of the *Miranda* opinion, held that the new ruling affected only those cases in which *the trial began* after the date of the landmark decision: [1]

While *Miranda* "guard[s] against the possibility of unreliable statements in every instance of in-custody interrogation, [it] encompass[es] situations in which the danger is not necessarily as great as when the accused is subjected to overt and obvious coercion. At the same time, our case law is available for persons whose trials have already been completed. [They] may invoke [the 'voluntariness' or 'coerced confession' test, based on the 'totality of circumstances' in each case, which] has become increasingly meticulous throughout the years [and] now takes specific account of [although it does not give decisive weight to] the failure to advise the accused of his privilege against self-incrimination or to allow him access to outside assistance. [Thus], although *Miranda* provides important new safeguards against the use of unreliable statements at trial, [its nonretroactivity] will not preclude persons whose trials have already been completed from invoking the same safeguards as part of an involuntariness claim." [m]

Black and Douglas, JJ., dissented, again for substantially the same reasons stated in their *Linkletter* dissent.[n] Three years later, dissenting in another case applying a new decision prospectively only,[o] Douglas, J., called the Court's treatment of *Miranda* "the most notorious example" of its unsatisfactory approach in this area. On the eve of *Miranda*, he recalled, the Court had some 80 cases before it raising the question decided in *Miranda*. "We took [and disposed

---

k. Warren, C.J., and Fortas, J., took no part. Black, J., joined by Douglas, J., dissented for essentially the same reasons in their *Linkletter* dissent.

l. *Johnson v. New Jersey*, 384 U.S. 719, 86 S.Ct. 1772, 16 L.Ed.2d 882 (1966).

A decade and a half later, however, relying heavily on *United States v. Johnson* and Harlan, J.'s reasoning in *Desist*, fn. h, supra, that principled decisionmaking and fairness to similarly situated petitioners requires application of a new rule to all cases pending on direct review, *Shea v. Louisiana*, ___ U.S. ___, 105 S.Ct. 1065, 84 L.Ed.2d 38 (1985), per Blackmun, J., applied *Edwards v. Arizona*, 451 U.S. 477, 101 S.Ct. 1880, 68 L.Ed.2d 378 (1981) (restricting ability of police to obtain waiver of rights when suspect specifically asserts right to counsel) retroactively to all cases in which the process of appeal had not yet been completed when *Edwards* was decided. White, J., joined by Burger, C.J., and Rehnquist and O'Connor, JJ., dissenting, deemed "hollow" the claim that the majority's rule serves fairness:

"[T]he attempt to distinguish between direct and collateral challenges for purposes of retroactivity is misguided. Under the majority's rule, otherwise identically situated defendants may be subject to different constitutional rules, depending on just how long ago now-unconstitutional conduct occurred and how quickly cases proceed through the criminal justice system. The disparity is no different in kind from that which occurs when the benefit of a new constitutional rule is retroactively afforded to the defendant in whose case it is announced but to no others; the Court's new approach equalizes nothing except the numbers of defendants within the disparately treated classes."

m. But see note 2 infra.

n. The four *Miranda* dissenters (Clark, Harlan, Stewart and White, JJ.,) concurred in the opinion of the Court applying *Miranda* prospectively, but noted continued adherence to their dissent in *Miranda*.

o. *Desist v. United States*, fn. h supra.

of four of them], applying the rule retroactively [in those four cases]. But [we denied relief in the rest]. Yet it was sheer coincidence that those precise four were chosen. Any other single case in the group or any other four would have been sufficient for our purposes."

UNITED STATES v. WADE, 388 U.S. 218, 87 S.Ct. 1926, 18 L.Ed.2d 1149 (1967) and GILBERT v. CALIFORNIA, 388 U.S. 263, 87 S.Ct. 1951, 18 L.Ed.2d 1178 (1967) established the right to counsel at certain pre-trial lineups and other identification proceedings.[p] Unlike *Mapp,* which applied to police searches and seizures conducted *before* the date of this decision—so long as the case was still pending on appeal—and unlike *Miranda,* which applied to police questioning conducted *before* the date of this decision—so long as *the trial* began after the date—*Stovall v. Denno,* supra, held that *Wade* and *Gilbert* "affect only those cases [involving] *confrontations for identification purposes* conducted in the absence of counsel *after* [the date of these decisions]" (emphasis added). Thus, the landmark lineup decisions were completely prospective, except that they overturned the convictions of Wade and Gilbert themselves. Selection of *the date of the police* conduct, rather than the date of the trial or some other point in the criminal process indicated that *police reliance* is a major factor in retroactivity disputes.[q]

Notes and Questions

1. Consider Haddad, *"Retroactivity Should Be Rethought": A Call for the End of the Linkletter Doctrine,* 60 J.Crim.L.C. & P. 417, 439 (1969): "The alternative to the prospective-only technique is a more conservative approach to constitutional criminal procedure. Deference to varying state practices would be required. Detailed federal standards such as those laid down in *Miranda* would no longer be possible. Adoption of safeguards, such as the right to counsel at lineups, which not a single state anticipated, would also be impossible. For liberals, the choice is clear." See also F. Allen, *The Judicial Quest for Penal Justice: The Warren Court and the Criminal Cases,* 1975 U.Ill.L.F. 518, 530 (although "at first glance the prospectivity rule appears to be an act of judicial self-abnegation," "in reality [it] encourages the making of new law by reducing some of the social costs").

2. *Miranda. Johnson v. New Jersey,* supra, reasoned that "while [*Miranda*] provide[s] *important new safeguards* against the use of *unreliable* statements" (emphasis added), its nonretroactivity will not prevent defendants "from invoking *the same safeguards* as part of an involuntariness claim." (Emphasis added.) Did *Miranda* indicate dissatisfaction with—and lack of confidence in—the actual operation of the "voluntariness" test, just as *Gideon* manifested dissatisfaction with the overruled *Betts v. Brady* approach? See, e.g., Kamisar, *A Dissent from the Miranda Dissents,* 65 Mich.L.Rev. 59 (1966). If past defendants could be adequately protected by a judicial examination into whether their

---

p. The Court subsequently held that the *Wade-Gilbert* rule did not apply to identification proceedings that took place before the defendant was indicted or otherwise formally charged with a crime, *Kirby v. Illinois,* 406 U.S. 682, 92 S.Ct. 1877, 32 L.Ed.2d 411 (1972), nor to photographic identifications, whether conducted before or after the defendant had been formally charged, *United States v. Ash,* 413 U.S. 300, 93 S.Ct. 2568, 37 L.Ed.2d 619 (1973).

q. Similarly, as discussed in fn. h supra, *Desist* applied *Katz* only to *police conduct* violating reasonable expectations of privacy under the new *Katz* doctrine which occurred after the date of that decision.

confessions were "voluntary," then was *Miranda* wrongly decided? See Johnson, *Retroactivity in Retrospect,* 56 Calif.L.Rev. 1612, 1617 (1968); 80 Harv.L.Rev. 138–39 (1966).

3. To a considerable extent the "retroactivity" cases adopt the analysis of Mishkin, *The High Court, the Great Writ, and the Due Process of Time and Law,* 79 Harv.L.Rev. 56 (1965). But consider H. Schwartz, *Retroactivity, Reliability, and Due Process: A Reply to Professor Mishkin,* 33 U.Chi.L.Rev. 719, 748–49 (1966): "Since newly declared constitutional criminal procedure rights 'are of the very essence [of] "ordered liberty," ' states should not be allowed to continue to deprive persons of their freedom on the basis of proceedings now considered contrary to 'the kind of fair trial which is this country's constitutional goal.' [I]f the accusatorial system and the privilege against self-incrimination are indeed of the essence of our system of criminal justice, was a trial which [violated that system any less a violation] merely because it happened five or even twenty-five years ago? [Has] it not always been wrong to compel a man to incriminate himself, or to allow him, because of ignorance, to waive his rights either in the police station or in court?

"[The truth is] that recent decisions have not discovered or created new rights; rather, they have only granted new federal remedies for old wrongs. These remedies have been granted only recently not because the rights they protect are newly conceived or newly relevant, but rather because concern for considerations of federalism has lessened and perhaps because sensitivity to due process problems has increased. But the newness of the remedy does not eliminate the faults of the condemned proceeding, for just as we cannot tolerate the continued imprisonment of a man whose conviction was based on unreliable evidence, so we cannot tolerate the continued imprisonment of a man whose conviction failed in other respects to meet the fundamental legal standards of the community."

SECTION 2. THE RIGHT OF "PRIVACY" (OR "AUTONOMY" OR "PERSONHOOD")

Introductory Note

"Whether as substantive due process or as Privacy, 'fundamentality' needs elaboration, especially with respect to the weight particular rights are to enjoy in the balance against public good. Justices Stone and Cardozo suggested that the freedoms of speech, press and religion required extraordinary judicial protection against invasions even for the public good, because of their place at the foundations of democracy and because of the unreliability of the political process in regard to them. If other rights—those to be described as within the Rights of Privacy—are also to be specially guarded against the democratic political process, similar or other justifications must be found—if there are any. Perhaps unusual respect for autonomy and idiosyncrasy as regards some 'personal' matters is intuitively felt by all of us, including Justices; that such deference is 'self-evident' is not self-evident."

—Henkin, *Privacy and Autonomy,* 74 Colum.L.Rev. 1410, 1428–29 (1974).

————

As noted in Lupu, *Untangling the Strands of the Fourteenth Amendment,* 77 Mich.L.Rev. 981, 1029–30 (1979), "unlike the all-inclusive theory of the *Lochner* era that held all liberties equally inviolable, and unlike the procedural due process theory that assesses the weight of any protected interest in a refined way for purposes of 'balancing' [Sec. 5 infra], [what might be called] modern substantive due process theory has a distinct all-or-nothing quality to it. Most liberties lacking textual support are of the garden variety—like liberty of contract—and thus their deprivation is constitutional if rationally necessary to the achievement of a public good. [See, e.g., *Williamson v. Lee Optical Co.*, p. 76 supra]. Several select liberties, on the other hand, have attained the status of 'fundamental' or 'preferred,' with the consequence that the Constitution permits a state to abridge them only if it can demonstrate an extraordinary justification." A notable example is *Roe v. Wade*, infra, where the Court held that the "right of privacy" encompassed "a woman's decision whether or not to terminate her pregnancy" and thus certain restrictions on abortion could be justified "only by a 'compelling state interest.'" See also *Shapiro v. Thompson*, p. 1027 infra, which can be viewed as a "right to travel" case, which, in the course of invalidating a one-year durational residence requirement for welfare, rejected the argument that "a mere showing of a rational relationship between the waiting period and [administrative governmental] objectives will suffice [for] in moving from state to state [appellees] were exercising a constitutional right, and any classification which serves to penalize the exercise of that right, unless shown to be necessary to promote a *compelling* governmental interest, is unconstitutional." As Lupu observes, ibid., "[b]ecause the review standard for ordinary liberties is so deferential, and the standard for preferred liberties so rigid, outcomes are ordained by the designation of 'preferred' [or 'fundamental'] or not."

Regulations dealing with "fundamental rights" call for "strict scrutiny" review just as government classifications based upon what have come to be known as "suspect" criteria trigger "strict" equal protection review. "[T]here is a case to be made for a significant degree of judicial deference to legislative and administrative choices in some spheres. Yet the idea of strict scrutiny acknowledges that other political choices—those burdening fundamental rights, or suggesting prejudice against racial or other minorities—must be subjected to close analysis in order to preserve substantive values of equality and liberty. Although strict scrutiny in this form ordinarily appears as a standard for judicial review, it may also be understood as admonishing lawmakers and regulators as well to be particularly cautious of their *own* purposes and premises and of the effects of their choices." Tribe, *American Constitutional Law* 1000 (1978).

Not infrequently, as in *Skinner v. Oklahoma* (discussed immediately below), which is an "equal protection" case in form, and which never mentioned any "right of privacy," but to which "the development of a constitutionally protected 'right of privacy' in sexual matters can be traced," Nowak, Rotunda & Young, *Constitutional Law* 736 (2d ed. 1983), a decision can be viewed as either an "equal protection" or a "fundamental rights" (or "substantive due process") case.

Indeed, observes Lupu, at 983–84, "the tangling [of 'liberty' and 'equality'] is most apparent and most serious when viewed in its relationship to the so-called 'fundamental rights' developments in both equal protection and due process clause interpretation. In the sense used here, fundamental rights include all the claims of individual rights, drawn from sources outside of the first eight amendments, that the Supreme Court has elevated to preferred status (that is, rights which the government may infringe only when it demonstrates extraordinary justification). [Which] new rights properly derive from the liberty strand, and which from the equality strand?[6] Sometimes the Court tells us; other times it

6. Compare *Roe v. Wade* [infra] (due process) with *Eisenstadt v. Baird* [infra] (analo- gous interests protected by the equal protection clause), and *Loving v. Virginia* [p. 832

does not. Often, members of the Court agree upon the preferred status of an interest but disagree about its textual source.[7] On occasion, members of the Court concede that an interest has no textual source, yet battle still over which strand of the fourteenth amendment protects it from state interference."[8]

SKINNER v. OKLAHOMA, 316 U.S. 535, 62 S.Ct. 1110, 86 L.Ed. 1655 (1942), per DOUGLAS, J., held violative of equal protection Oklahoma's Habitual Criminal Sterilization Act, which authorized the sterilization of persons previously convicted and imprisoned two or more times of crimes "amounting to felonies involving moral turpitude" and thereafter convicted of such a felony and sentenced to prison. (Petitioner, previously convicted of "chicken-stealing" and robbery, had again been convicted of robbery.) Expressly exempted were embezzlement, political offenses and revenue act violations. Thus a person convicted three times of larceny could be subjected to sterilization, but the embezzler could not—although "the nature of the two crimes is intrinsically the same" and they are otherwise punishable in the same manner. The Court recognized that "if we had here only a question as to a State's classification of crimes, such as embezzlement or larceny," no substantial federal question would be presented. "But the instant legislation runs afoul of the equal protection clause" because—

"We are dealing here with legislation which involves one of the basic civil rights of man. Marriage and procreation are fundamental to the very existence and survival of the race. [In] evil or reckless hands [the power to sterilize] can cause races or types which are inimical to the dominant group to wither and disappear. There is no redemption for the individual whom the law touches. [He] is forever deprived of a basic liberty.[a] We mention these matters [in] emphasis of our view that strict scrutiny of the classification which a State makes in a sterilization law is essential, lest unwittingly, or otherwise, invidious discriminations are made against groups or types of individuals in violation of the constitutional guaranty of just and equal laws. [When] the law lays an unequal hand on those who have committed intrinsically the same quality of offense and sterilizes one and not the other, it has made as invidious a discrimination, as if it had selected a particular race or nationality for oppressive treatment."[b]

STONE, C.J., concurred in the result: "[I]f we must presume that the legislature knows—what science has been unable to ascertain—that the criminal tendencies of any class of habitual offenders are transmissible regardless of the varying mental characteristics of its individuals, I should suppose that we must

---

infra] (analogous interests protected by the due process clause) (alternative ground).

7. The reference is to *Griswold v. Connecticut* [infra], in which Bill of Rights' penumbras, the ninth amendment, and "pure" substantive due process compete for attention.

8. In *Shapiro v. Thompson*, the majority held that the equal protection clause protected the right to travel, while Justice Harlan in dissent believed that the due process clause was the relevant shield. A similar doctrinal dispute split the Court in *Zablocki v. Redhail* [infra], where the majority held that the equal protection clause protected the right to marry. Justice Powell, in a concurring opinion, felt the right found its source in the due process clause.

a. The Court began its opinion by observing: "This case touches a sensitive and important area of human rights. Oklahoma deprives certain individuals of a right which is basic to the perpetuation of a race—the right to have offspring."

b. As for *Buck v. Bell*, 274 U.S. 200, 47 S.Ct. 584, 71 L.Ed. 1000 (1927), upholding a sterilization law applicable only to mental defectives in state institutions, "it was pointed out that 'so far as the operations enable those who otherwise must be kept confined to be returned to the world, and thus open the asylum to others, the equality aimed at will be more nearly reached.' Here there is no such saving feature."

likewise presume that the legislature, in its wisdom, knows that the criminal tendencies of some classes of offenders are more likely to be transmitted than those of others. And so I think the real question [is] not one of equal protection, but whether the wholesale condemnation of a class to such an invasion of personal liberty, without opportunity to any individual to show that his is not the type of case which would justify resort to it, satisfies the demands of due process.

"There are limits to the extent to which the presumption of constitutionality can be pressed, especially where the liberty of the person is concerned [referring to his famous *Carolene Products* footnote, pp. 23–24 supra] and where the presumption is resorted to only to dispense with a procedure which the ordinary dictates of prudence would seem to demand for the protection of the individual from arbitrary action. Although petitioner here was given a hearing to ascertain whether sterilization would be detrimental to his health, he was given none to discover whether his criminal tendencies are of an inheritable type. * * *

"Science has found and the law has recognized that there are certain types of mental deficiency associated with delinquency which are inheritable. But the State does not contend—nor can there be any pretense—that either common knowledge or experience, or scientific investigation, has given assurance that the criminal tendencies of any class of habitual offenders are universally or even generally inheritable. In such circumstances, inquiry whether such is the fact in the case of any particular individual cannot rightly be dispensed with. [A] law which condemns, without hearing, all the individuals of a class to so harsh a measure as the present because some or even many merit condemnation, is lacking in the first principles of due process." c

Notes and Questions

1. *Did the Skinner Court "abdicate its responsibility"?* Consider Foote, *The Proper Role of the United States Supreme Court in Civil Liberties Cases*, 10 Wayne L.Rev. 457, 471–72 (1964): "*Skinner* presented [a] purely scientific question of heredity and habitual criminality, and the biological evidence was overwhelmingly against the reasonableness of the statute. The [due process question] was squarely posed [and] has not become any riper for decision [since] the Court dodged the question. [A]lthough only one litigant was directly before the Court in *Skinner* and although the Court's equal protection vagary saved him from sterilization, behind him were thousands of institutional inmates in [many states] who were and are subject to sterilization under laws most of which would not be voided by the *Skinner* formulation. As a practical matter, *Skinner* represented their only hope for a constitutional adjudication of their rights. To apply a conceptual theory of the narrowest possible decision-making in the face of such facts seems to me an abdication of the Court's responsibility."

2. *Did the Lochner era haunt the Skinner Court?* Why was *Skinner* "unrestrained in its vigorous protection of a nontextual liberty, yet cautious in its grounds that went no farther than the particular case at hand"? To what extent does *Skinner's* "1942 vintage" explain why the Court preferred "a relatively narrow equal protection ground of decision to a broader preferred liberty theory that would have impugned all involuntary sterilization schemes"?

c. In a separate concurrence, Jackson, J., agreed that the hearings provided are "too limited [to] afford due process" and also agreed with the Court that the classification denies equal protection.

No matter how serious the issue, was the Court unwilling to reinstate "substantive activism" a short five years after its repudiation? See Lupu, supra, at 1019.

3. *To what extent was Skinner colored by the Court's concern that the statute invited prejudiced action against powerless minorities?* Consider Tribe, supra, at 1010–11: "Clearly prominent [in] *Skinner* was [the Court's] concern to protect within the realm of personal autonomy 'one of the basic civil rights of man,' the right to reproduce. Yet the Court's opinion makes evident an even greater preoccupation with the notion that the state's classifications had been promulgated with their harshest effect against a relatively powerless minority, that of lower-class, as opposed to white-collar, criminals. [Although] not willing to characterize the group discriminated against as automatically deserving the protection of special judicial scrutiny, the Court combined allusion to the invidiousness of discrimination against the class with discussion of the fundamental right involved. Indeed, since that right—personal autonomy in reproductive matters—had not previously been held fundamental, it seems likely that *Skinner* was moved to give the right such a status, and thereby to assure the most rigorous scrutiny of future governmental intrusions into the reproductive realm, in large part *because* of fear about the invidiously selective and ultimately genocidal way in which governmental control over that realm might tend to be exercised—a fear illustrated by the facts of *Skinner* itself.

"[*Skinner*] is the leading instance in which a new star appears to have been added to the firmament of preferred freedoms primarily because of concerns about invidious discrimination and majoritarian domination. Such concerns of course move to center stage once we are prepared to treat the classification employed by government as so plainly invidious or prejudiced that, quite without regard to the nature of the choice burdened or the interest unequally distributed, strict scrutiny seems required if any semblance of equal justice under law is to be preserved. The theory of invidious or suspect classification [Ch. 11, Secs. 2–3,] thus takes us beyond *Skinner* to a realm in which, even without finding a fundamental right, our tolerance will be at low ebb."

"[In *Griswold*, Douglas, J.,] skipped through the Bill of Rights like a cheerleader—'Give me a P . . . give me an R . . . an I . . . ,' and so on, and found P–R–I–V–A–C–Y as a derivative or penumbral right."

—Dixon, *The "New" Substantive Due Process and the Democratic Ethic: A Prolegomenon,* 1976 B.Y.U.L.Rev. 43, 84.

GRISWOLD v. CONNECTICUT
381 U.S. 479, 85 S.Ct. 1678, 14 L.Ed.2d 510 (1965).

Mr. Justice Douglas delivered the opinion of the Court.

Appellant Griswold is Executive Director of the Planned Parenthood League of Connecticut. Appellant Buxton [is] Medical Director for the League at its Center in New Haven—a center open [from] November 1 to November 10, 1961, when appellants were arrested.

They gave information, instruction, and medical advice to *married persons* as to the means of preventing conception. * * * Fees were usually charged, although some couples were serviced free.

The statutes whose constitutionality is involved [are] §§ 53–32 and 54–196 of the General Statutes of Connecticut (1958 rev.). The former provides: "Any person who uses any drug, medicinal article or instrument for the purpose of preventing conception shall be fined not less than fifty dollars or imprisoned not less than sixty days nor more than one year or be both fined and imprisoned." Section 54–196 provides: "Any person who assists, abets, counsels, causes, hires or commands another to commit any offense may be prosecuted and punished as if he were the principal offender."

The appellants were found guilty as accessories and fined $100 [each].

Coming to the merits,[a] we are met with a wide range of questions that implicate the Due Process Clause of the Fourteenth Amendment. Overtones of some arguments suggest that *Lochner* should be our guide. But we decline that invitation ∗ ∗ ∗. We do not sit as a super-legislature to determine the wisdom, need, and propriety of laws that touch economic problems, business affairs, or social conditions. This law, however, operates directly on an intimate relation of husband and wife and their physician's role in one aspect of that relation.

The association of people is not mentioned in the Constitution nor in the Bill of Rights. The right to educate a child in a school of the parents' choice— whether public or private or parochial—is also not mentioned. Nor is the right to study any particular subject or any foreign language. Yet the First Amendment has been construed to include certain of those rights. [See] *Pierce v. Society of Sisters,* 268 U.S. 510, 45 S.Ct. 571, 69 L.Ed. 1070 (1925) [and] *Meyer v. Nebraska,* 262 U.S. 390, 43 S.Ct. 625, 67 L.Ed. 1042 (1923).[b]   [T]he State may not,

---

a. For resolution of the issue of standing, see p. 1219 infra.

b. Consider Nowak, Rotunda and Young, *Constitutional Law* 735 (2d ed. 1983): In both *Meyer,* invalidating a state law forbidding all grade schools from teaching subjects in any language other than English, and in *Pierce,* holding a state law requiring students to attend public schools violative of due process, "the majority [per McReynolds, J.] found that the law restricted individual freedom without any relation to a valid public interest. Freedom of choice regarding an individual's personal life was recognized as constitutionally protected. These decisions may only have reflected the attitude of the Court towards government regulation during the apex of 'substantive due process.' While these decisions might today be grounded on the First Amendment, their existence is important to the growth of the right to privacy. If nothing else, they show a historical recognition of a right to private decision making regarding family matters as inherent in the concept of liberty."

Consider, too, Lupu, supra, at 988–89, commenting that although *Meyer* and *Pierce* "can be, and at times have been, rerationalized, as attempts to protect values derived from the first amendment," the most recent reliance on these cases, citing e.g., *Moore v. East Cleveland,* infra, and *Roe v. Wade,* infra, "have stressed their nontextual underpinnings of protected interests in family autonomy. The survival of those two cases in that form suggests that the only durable objection to the *Lochner* era's handiwork is that it generally selected the 'wrong' values for protection."

See also Hutchinson, *Unanimity and Desegregation: Decisionmaking in the Supreme Court, 1948–58,* 68 Geo.L.J. 1, 49–51 (1979) (Frankfurter, J., long an outspoken critic of the McReynolds opinions in *Meyer* and *Pierce,* warned that the method used in these cases could just as easily produce "another *Lochner* "); Posner, *The Uncertain Protection of Privacy by the Supreme Court,* 1979 Sup.Ct. Rev. 173, 195–96 ("under ostensible modern test of substantive due process," *Meyer* was "incorrectly decided"; its citation in "privacy" cases shows "survival of substantive due process despite frequent disclaimers.")

Cf. *Runyon v. McCrary* (1976), p. 1183 infra, per Stewart, J., holding (unanimously on this issue) that a federal statute that "prohibits private schools from excluding qualified children solely because they are Negroes" violates neither "parental rights" nor the "right of privacy": "No challenge is made to the petitioners' right to operate their private schools or the right of parents to send their children to a particular private school rather than a public school. Nor do these cases involve a challenge to the subject matter which is taught at any private school. Thus, the [private schools] remain presumptively free to inculcate whatever values and standards they deem desirable. *Meyer* and its progeny entitle them to no more." Further, "it does not follow that because government is largely or even entirely precluded from regulating the child-bearing decision, it is similarly restricted by the Constitution from regulating the implementation of parental decisions concerning a child's education. [See] *Pierce; Meyer.*"

consistently with the spirit of the First Amendment, contract the spectrum of available knowledge. The right of freedom of speech and press includes not only the right to utter or to print, but the right to distribute, the right to receive, the right to read and freedom of inquiry, freedom of thought, and freedom to teach— indeed the freedom of the entire university community. Without those peripheral rights the specific rights would be less secure. And so we reaffirm the principle of the *Pierce* and the *Meyer* cases.

In *NAACP v. Alabama* [p. 629 infra], we protected the "freedom to associate and privacy in one's associations," noting that freedom of association was a peripheral First Amendment right. [In] other words, the First Amendment has a penumbra where privacy is protected from governmental intrusion. In like context, we have protected forms of "association" that are not political in the customary sense but pertain to the social, legal, and economic benefit of the members. *NAACP v. Button*, 371 U.S. 415, 83 S.Ct. 328, 9 L.Ed.2d 405 (1963). [W]hile [association] is not expressly included in the First Amendment its existence is necessary in making the express guarantees fully meaningful.

The foregoing cases suggest that specific guarantees in the Bill of Rights have penumbras, formed by emanations from those guarantees that help give them life and substance. See *Poe v. Ullman*, 367 U.S. 497, 516–522, 81 S.Ct. 1752, 6 L.Ed.2d 989 (1961) [Douglas, J., dissenting]. Various guarantees create zones of privacy. The right of association contained in the penumbra of the First Amendment is one, as we have seen. The Third Amendment in its prohibition against the quartering of soldiers "in any house" in time of peace without the consent of the owner is another facet of that privacy. The Fourth Amendment [is another]. The Fifth Amendment in its Self-Incrimination Clause enables the citizen to create a zone of privacy which government may not force him to surrender to his detriment. The Ninth Amendment provides: "The enumeration in the Constitution, of certain rights, shall not be construed to deny or disparage others retained by the people."

The Fourth and Fifth Amendments were described in *Boyd v. United States*, 116 U.S. 616, 630, 6 S.Ct. 524, 532, 29 L.Ed. 746 (1886), as protection against all governmental invasions "of the sanctity of a man's home and the privacies of life." We recently referred in *Mapp v. Ohio* to the Fourth Amendment as creating a "right to privacy, no less important than any other right carefully and particularly reserved to the people." See Beaney, *The Constitutional Right to Privacy*, 1962 Sup.Ct.Rev. 212; Griswold, *The Right to be Let Alone*, 55 Nw.U.L. Rev. 216 (1960).

We have had many controversies over these penumbral rights of "privacy and repose." [*Skinner* and other cases] bear witness that the right of privacy which presses for recognition here is a legitimate one.

The present case, then, concerns a relationship lying within the zone of privacy created by several fundamental constitutional guarantees.[c] And it concerns a law which, in forbidding the *use* of contraceptives rather than regulating their manufacture or sale, seeks to achieve its goals by means having a maximum destructive impact upon that relationship. Such a law cannot stand

c. Did the Court omit the free exercise clause of the first amendment? Like religious beliefs, are beliefs in the areas of marriage, procreation and child rearing "often deeply held, involving loyalties fully as powerful as those that bind the citizen to the state"? Will the choice of whom to marry or whether or not to have a child, once taken, "have as strong an impact on the life patterns of the individuals involved [as] any adoption of a religious belief or viewpoint"? See Heymann & Barzelay, *The Forest and the Trees: Roe v. Wade and Its Critics*, 53 B.U.L.Rev. 765, 773–74 (1973).

in light of the familiar principle [that] a "governmental purpose to control or prevent activities constitutionally subject to state regulation may not be achieved by means which sweep unnecessarily broadly and thereby invade the area of protected freedoms." *NAACP v. Alabama*. Would we allow the police to search the sacred precincts of marital bedrooms for telltale signs of the use of contraceptives? The very idea is repulsive to the notions of privacy surrounding the marriage relationship.[d]

We deal with a right of privacy older than the Bill of Rights * * *. Marriage is a coming together for better or for worse, hopefully enduring, and intimate to the degree of being sacred. It is an association that promotes a way of life, not causes; a harmony in living, not political faiths; a bilateral loyalty, not commercial or social projects. Yet it is an association for as noble a purpose as any involved in our prior decisions.

Reversed.

MR. JUSTICE GOLDBERG, whom THE CHIEF JUSTICE and MR. JUSTICE BRENNAN join, concurring.

I [join the Court's opinion]. Although I have not accepted the view that "due process" as used in the Fourteenth Amendment includes all of the first eight Amendments, I do agree that the concept of liberty protects those personal rights that are fundamental, and is not confined to the specific terms of the Bill of Rights. My conclusion [that] it embraces the right of marital privacy though that right is not mentioned explicitly in the Constitution [1] is supported both by numerous decisions [and] by the language and history of the Ninth Amendment [which] reveal that the Framers of the Constitution believed that there are additional fundamental rights, protected from governmental infringement.

[The] Ninth Amendment [was] proffered to quiet expressed fears that a bill of specifically enumerated rights could not be sufficiently broad to cover all essential rights and that the specific mention of certain rights would be interpreted as a denial that others were protected.

[While] this Court has had little occasion to interpret the Ninth Amendment,[6] "[i]t cannot be presumed that any clause in the constitution is intended to be without effect." [To] hold that a right so basic and fundamental and so deep-rooted in our society as the right of privacy in marriage may be infringed because that right is not guaranteed in so many words by the first eight amendments to the Constitution is to ignore the Ninth Amendment and to give it no effect whatsoever. * * * I do not mean to imply that the Ninth

---

d. But consider *Posner,* fn. b supra, at 194: "Such a search would indeed be an invasion of privacy in a conventional sense. But it would be a justifiable invasion if the statute were not otherwise constitutionally objectionable. This case can be seen by imagining that the statute in question forbade not contraception but murder and that the police had probable cause to believe that the suspected murderer had secreted the weapon to his mattress. Furthermore, even if some methods of enforcing the Connecticut statute [violated the Fourth Amendment], that would mean only that the statute was difficult to enforce. [As] the facts of *Griswold* show, the State could enforce the statute without invading anyone's privacy, simply by prosecuting, as accessories, the employees of birth-control clinics."

1. [This Court] has never held that the Bill of Rights or the Fourteenth Amendment protects only those rights that the Constitution specifically mentions by name. See, e.g., *Bolling v. Sharpe* [p. 829 infra]; *Aptheker v. Secretary of State; Kent v. Dulles* [Sec. 3 infra]; *Carrington v. Rash* [p. 1011 infra]; *NAACP v. Alabama; Pierce; Meyer.* * * *

6. [It] has been referred to as "*The Forgotten Ninth Amendment,*" in a book with that title by Bennett B. Patterson (1955). Other commentary [includes] Redlich, *Are There "Certain Rights* * * * *Retained by the People"?* 37 N.Y.U.L.Rev. 787 (1962), and Kelsey, *The Ninth Amendment of the Federal Constitution,* 11 Ind.L.J. 309 (1936). * * *

Amendment is applied against the States by the Fourteenth [nor] to state that the Ninth Amendment constitutes an independent source of rights protected from infringement by either the States or the Federal Government. Rather, the Ninth Amendment shows a belief of the Constitution's authors that fundamental rights exist that are not expressly enumerated in the first eight amendments and an intent that the list of rights included there not be deemed exhaustive.[d] [T]his Court has held, often unanimously, that the Fifth and Fourteenth Amendments protect certain fundamental personal liberties from abridgment by the Federal Government or the States. [I] do not see how this [interpretation of the Ninth Amendment] broadens the authority of the Court; rather it serves to support what this Court has been doing in protecting fundamental rights.

[While] the Ninth Amendment—and indeed the entire Bill of Rights— originally concerned restrictions upon *federal* power, the subsequently enacted Fourteenth Amendment prohibits the States as well from abridging fundamental personal liberties. [In] sum, the Ninth Amendment simply lends strong support to the view that the "liberty" protected by the Fifth and Fourteenth Amendments from infringement by the Federal Government or the States is not restricted to rights specifically mentioned in the first eight amendments.

In determining which rights are fundamental, judges are not left at large to decide cases in light of their personal and private notions. Rather, they must look to the "traditions and [collective] conscience of our people" to determine whether a principle is "so rooted [there] [as] to be ranked as fundamental." * * * "Liberty" also "gains content from the emanations [of] specific [constitutional] guarantees" and "from experience with the requirements of a free society." *Poe* (dissenting opinion of Douglas, J.).

[The] entire fabric of the Constitution and the purposes that clearly underlie its specific guarantees demonstrate that the rights to marital privacy and to marry and raise a family are of similar order and magnitude as the fundamental rights specifically protected.

[Surely] the Government, absent a showing of a compelling subordinating state interest, could not decree that all husbands and wives must be sterilized after two children have been born to them.[e] Yet by [the dissenters'] reasoning such an invasion of marital privacy would not be subject to constitutional challenge because, while it might be "silly," no provision of the Constitution specifically prevents the Government from curtailing the marital right to bear children and raise a family. [I]f upon a showing of a slender basis of rationality, a law outlawing voluntary birth control by married persons is valid, then, by the same reasoning, a law requiring compulsory birth control also would seem to be valid. In my view, however, both types of law would unjustifiably intrude upon rights of marital privacy which are constitutionally protected.

In a long series of cases this Court has held that where fundamental personal liberties are involved, they may not be abridged by the States simply on

---

d. See generally Note, *The Uncertain Renaissance of the Ninth Amendment*, 33 U.Chi.L. Rev. 814 (1966); Paust, *Human Rights and the Ninth Amendment; A New Form of Guarantee*, 60 Corn.L.Rev. 231 (1975).

e. Compare Comment, *Population Control—The Legal Approach to a Biological Imperative*, 1 Ecol.L.Q. 143, 167 (1971): "It is not completely clear [whether] Justice Goldberg's vaguely defined marital and family rights include the right to unlimited procreation. Clearly, one family right which is not protected against legislative control is the right to decide how many spouses to have. By custom Americans have one spouse and many children but there would seem to be little difference between legislative control of the number of spouses and the number of children." See also Note, *Legal Analysis and Population Control: The Problem of Coercion*, 84 Harv.L.Rev. 1856 (1971).

a showing that a regulatory statute has some rational relationship to the effectuation of a proper state purpose. "Where there is a significant encroachment upon personal liberty, the State may prevail only upon showing a subordinating interest which is compelling," *Bates v. Little Rock* [p. 687 infra]. [The] State, at most, argues that there is some rational relation between this statute and what is admittedly a legitimate subject of state concern—the discouraging of extra-marital relations. It says that preventing the use of birth-control devices by married persons helps prevent the indulgence by some in such extra-marital relations. The rationality of this justification is dubious, particularly in light of the admitted widespread availability to all persons [in] Connecticut, unmarried as well as married, of birth-control devices for the prevention of disease, as distinguished from the prevention of conception. But in any event, it is clear that the state interest in safeguarding marital fidelity can be served by a more discriminately tailored statute, which does not, like the present one, sweep unnecessarily broadly, reaching far beyond the evil sought to be dealt with and intruding upon the privacy of all married couples. * * *

Finally, it should be said of the Court's holding today that it in no way interferes with a State's proper regulation of sexual promiscuity or misconduct. As my Brother Harlan so well stated in his dissenting opinion in *Poe:* "Adultery, homosexuality and the like are sexual intimacies which the State forbids [but] the intimacy of husband and wife is necessarily an essential and accepted feature of the institution of marriage, an institution which the State not only must allow, but which always and in every age it has fostered and protected.

* * *

MR. JUSTICE HARLAN, concurring in the judgment.

I [cannot] join the Court's opinion [as] it seems to me to evince an approach [that] the Due Process Clause of the Fourteenth Amendment does not touch this Connecticut statute unless the enactment is found to violate some right assured by the letter or penumbra of the Bill of Rights. [W]hat I find implicit in the Court's opinion is that the "incorporation" doctrine may be used to *restrict* the reach of Fourteenth Amendment Due Process. For me this is just as unacceptable constitutional doctrine as is the use of the "incorporation" approach to *impose* upon the States all the requirements of the Bill of Rights. * * *

[T]he proper constitutional inquiry in this case is whether this Connecticut statute infringes the Due Process Clause of the Fourteenth Amendment because the enactment violates basic values "implicit in the concept of ordered liberty." For reasons stated at length in my dissenting opinion in *Poe v. Ullman* [discussed below], I believe that it does. While the relevant inquiry may be aided by resort to one or more of the provisions of the Bill of Rights, it is not dependent on them or any of their radiations. The Due Process Clause of the Fourteenth Amendment stands, in my opinion, on its own bottom.

[While] I could not more heartily agree that judicial "self restraint" is an indispensable ingredient of sound constitutional adjudication, I do submit that the formula suggested [by the dissenters] for achieving it is more hollow than real. "Specific" provisions of the Constitution, no less than "due process," lend themselves as readily to "personal" interpretations by judges whose constitutional outlook is simply to keep the Constitution in supposed "tune with the times".

[Judicial self-restraint will] be achieved in this area, as in other[s], only by continual insistence upon respect for the teachings of history, solid recognition of the basic values that underlie our society, and wise appreciation of the great roles that the doctrines of federalism and separation of powers have played in establishing and preserving American freedoms. Adherence to these principles will not, of course, obviate all constitutional differences of opinion among judges, nor should it. Their continued recognition will, however, go farther toward keeping most judges from roaming at large in the constitutional field than will the interpolation into the Constitution of an artificial and largely illusory restriction on the content of the Due Process Clause.

[Dissenting in POE v. ULLMAN, 367 U.S. 497, 523, 81 S.Ct. 1752, 6 L.Ed.2d 989 (1961), which failed to reach the merits of the constitutional challenge to the Connecticut anti-birth control statute, Harlan, J., had maintained that the statute, "as construed to apply to these appellants, violates the Fourteenth Amendment" because "a statute making it a criminal offense for *married couples* to use contraceptives is an intolerable and unjustifiable invasion of privacy in the conduct of the most intimate concerns of an individual's personal life." Harlan, J., "would not suggest that adultery, homosexuality, fornication and incest are immune from criminal enquiry, however privately practiced," but "the intimacy of husband and wife is necessarily an essential and accepted feature of the institution of marriage, an institution which the State not only must allow, but which always and every age it has fostered and protected. It is one thing when the State exerts its power either to forbid extra-marital sexuality altogether, or to say who may marry, but it is quite another when, having acknowledged a marriage and the intimacies inherent in it, it undertakes to regulate by means of the criminal law the details of that intimacy."

[Although the state had argued the constitutional permissibility of the moral judgment underlying the challenged statute, Harlan, J., could not find anything that "even remotely suggests a justification for the obnoxiously intrusive means it has chosen to effectuate that policy." He deemed "the utter novelty" of the statute "conclusive." "Although the Federal Government and many States have at one time or another [prohibited or regulated] the distribution of contraceptives, none [has] made the *use* of contraceptives a crime. Indeed, a diligent search has revealed that no nation, including several which quite evidently share Connecticut's moral policy, had seen fit to effectuate that policy by the means presented here." He had to agree with Jackson, J., concurring in *Skinner,* that "there are limits to the extent to which a legislatively represented majority may [experiment] at the expense of the dignity and personality" of the individual and, in this instance, found these limits "reached and passed."

[Because the constitutional challenges to the Connecticut statute "draw their basis from no explicit language of the Constitution, and have yet to find expression in any decision of this Court," Harlan, J., deemed it "desirable at the outset to state the framework of Constitutional principles in which I think the issue must be judged":

["[Were] due process merely a procedural safeguard it would fail to reach those situations where the deprivation of life, liberty or property was accomplished by legislation which by operating in the future could, given even the fairest possible procedure in application to individuals, nevertheless destroy the enjoyment of all three. [I]t is not the particular enumeration of rights in the first eight Amendments which spells out the reach of Fourteenth Amendment due process, but rather [those concepts embracing] rights 'which [are] *fundamental;* which belong [to] the citizens of all free governments.'

["[T]hrough the course of this Court's decisions [due process] has represented the balance which our Nation, built upon postulates of respect for the liberty of the individual, has struck between that liberty and the demands of organized society. [The] balance of which I speak is the balance struck by this country, having regard to what history teaches are the traditions from which it developed as well as the traditions from which it broke. That tradition is a living thing. A decision of this Court which radically departs from it could not long survive, while a decision which builds on what has survived is likely to be sound. No formula could serve as a substitute, in this area, for judgment and restraint.

["It is this outlook which has led the Court continuingly to perceive distinctions in the imperative character of Constitutional provisions, since that character must be discerned from a particular provision's larger context. And inasmuch as this context is one not of words, but of history and purposes, the full scope of the liberty guaranteed by the Due Process Clause cannot be found in or limited by the precise terms of the specific guarantees elsewhere provided in the Constitution. This 'liberty' is not a series of isolated points pricked out in terms of [the] freedom of speech, press, and religion; [the] freedom from unreasonable searches and seizures; and so on. It is a rational continuum which, broadly speaking, includes a freedom from all substantial arbitrary impositions and purposeless restraints [and] which also recognizes, what a reasonable and sensitive judgment must, that certain interests require particularly careful scrutiny of the state needs asserted to justify their abridgment. Cf. *Skinner*.][f]

MR. JUSTICE WHITE, concurring in the judgment.

In my view this Connecticut law as applied to married couples deprives them of "liberty" without [due process] guaranteed by the Fourteenth Amendment against arbitrary or capricious [denials]. Surely the right [to] be free of regulation of the intimacies of the marriage relationship, "come[s] to this Court with a momentum for respect lacking when appeal is made to liberties which derive merely from shifting economic arrangements." *Kovacs v. Cooper* [p. 579 infra] (opinion of Frankfurter, J.).

The Connecticut anti-contraceptive statute deals rather substantially with this relationship. [And] the clear effect of these statutes, as enforced, is to deny disadvantaged citizens of Connecticut, those without either adequate knowledge or resources to obtain private counseling, access to medical assistance and up-to-date information in respect to proper methods of birth control. In my view, a statute with these effects bears a substantial burden of justification when attacked under the Fourteenth Amendment.

An examination of the justification offered, however, cannot be avoided by saying that the Connecticut anti-use statute invades a protected area of privacy and association or that it demeans the marriage relationship. The nature of the right invaded is pertinent, to be sure, for statutes regulating sensitive areas of liberty do, under the cases of this Court, require "strict scrutiny," *Skinner,* and "must be viewed in the light of less drastic means for achieving the same basic purpose." *Shelton v. Tucker* [p. 654 infra]. But such statutes, if reasonably necessary for the effectuation of a legitimate and substantial state interest, and not arbitrary or capricious in application, are not invalid under the Due Process Clause. [There] is no serious contention that Connecticut thinks the use of artificial or external methods of contraception immoral or unwise in itself, or that the anti-use statute is founded upon any policy of promoting population expansion. Rather, the statute is said to serve the State's policy against all forms of promiscuous or illicit sexual relationships, be they premarital or extramarital, concededly a permissible and legitimate legislative goal.

---

f. See also the extracts from this dissent in fn. g of note 8 after *Roe v. Wade*, infra.

Without taking issue with the premise that the fear of conception operates as a deterrent to such relationships in addition to the criminal proscriptions Connecticut has against such conduct, I wholly fail to see how the ban on the use of contraceptives by married couples in any way reinforces the State's ban on illicit sexual relationships. [It] is purely fanciful to believe that the broad proscription on use facilitates discovery of use by persons engaging in a prohibited relationship or for some other reason makes such use more unlikely and thus can be supported by any sort of administrative consideration. Perhaps the theory is that the flat ban on use prevents married people from possessing contraceptives and without the ready availability of such devices for use in the marital relationship, there will be no or less temptation to use them in extra-marital ones. This reasoning rests on the premise that married people will comply with the ban in regard to their marital relationship, notwithstanding total nonenforcement in this context and apparent nonenforcibility, but will not comply with criminal statutes prohibiting extramarital affairs and the anti-use statute in respect to illicit sexual relationships, a premise whose validity has not been demonstrated and whose intrinsic validity is not very evident. At most the broad ban is of marginal utility to the declared objective. A statute limiting its prohibition on use to persons engaging in the prohibited relationship would serve the end posited by Connecticut in the same way, and with the same effectiveness, or ineffectiveness, as the broad anti-use statute under attack in this case. I find nothing in this record justifying the sweeping scope of this [statute].

MR. JUSTICE BLACK, with whom MR. JUSTICE STEWART joins, dissenting.

[There are] guarantees in certain specific constitutional provisions which are designed in part to protect privacy at certain times and places with respect to certain activities. [But] I think it belittles [the Fourth] Amendment to talk about it as though it protects nothing but "privacy." [The] average man would very likely not have his feelings soothed any more by having his property seized openly than by having it seized privately and by stealth. [And] a person can be just as much, if not more, irritated, annoyed and injured by an unceremonious public arrest by a policeman as he is by a seizure in the privacy of his office or home.

One of the most effective ways of diluting or expanding a constitutionally guaranteed right is to substitute for the crucial word or words of a constitutional guarantee another word or words, more or less flexible and more or less restricted in meaning. This fact is well illustrated by the use of the term "right of privacy" as a comprehensive substitute for the Fourth Amendment's guarantee against "unreasonable searches and seizures." * * *[1] I like my privacy as well as the next one, but I am nevertheless compelled to admit that government has a right to invade it unless prohibited by some specific constitutional provision.

[This] brings me to the arguments made by my Brothers Harlan, White and Goldberg * * *. I discuss the due process and Ninth Amendment arguments together because on analysis they turn out to be the same thing—merely using different words to claim for this Court and the federal judiciary power to

---

1. The phrase "right to privacy" appears first to have gained currency from an article written by Messrs. Warren and (later Mr. Justice) Brandeis in 1890 which urged that States should give some form of tort relief to persons whose private affairs were exploited by others. *The Right to Privacy*, 4 Harv.L. Rev. 193. * * * Observing that "the right of privacy presses for recognition here," today this Court, which I did not understand to have power to sit as a court of common law, now appears to be exalting a phrase which Warren and Brandeis use in discussing grounds for tort relief, to the level of a constitutional [rule].

invalidate any legislative act [that] it considers to be arbitrary, capricious, unreasonable, or oppressive, or this Court's belief that a particular state law under scrutiny has no "rational or justifying" purpose, or is offensive to a "sense of fairness and justice." If these formulas based on "natural justice," or others which mean the same thing, are to prevail, they require judges to determine what is or is not constitutional on the basis of their own appraisal of what laws are unwise or unnecessary. [I] readily admit that no legislative body, state or national, should pass laws that can justly be given any of the invidious labels invoked as constitutional excuses to strike down state laws. But perhaps it is not too much to say that no legislative body ever does pass laws without believing that they will accomplish a sane, rational, wise and justifiable purpose. [I] do not believe that we are granted power by the Due Process Clause or any [other] provisions to measure constitutionality by our belief that legislation is arbitrary, capricious or unreasonable, or accomplishes no justifiable purpose, or is offensive to our own notions of "civilized standards of conduct." Such an appraisal of the wisdom of legislation is an attribute of the power to make laws, [a] power which was specifically denied to federal courts by the [Framers].

Of the cases on which my Brothers White and Goldberg rely so heavily, undoubtedly the reasoning of two of them supports their result here—[*Meyer* and *Pierce*]. *Meyer* [relying on *Lochner*,] held unconstitutional, as an "arbitrary" and unreasonable interference with the right of a teacher to carry on his occupation and of parents to hire him, a state law forbidding the teaching of modern foreign languages to young children in the schools.[7] [*Pierce*, per McReynolds, J.] said that a state law requiring that all children attend public schools interfered unconstitutionally with the property rights of private school corporations because it was an "arbitrary, unreasonable, and unlawful interference" which threatened "destruction of their business and property." Without expressing an opinion as to whether either of those cases reached a correct result in light of our later decisions applying the First Amendment to the States through the Fourteenth, I merely point out that the reasoning stated in *Meyer* and *Pierce* was the same natural law due process philosophy which many later opinions repudiated, and which I cannot accept. Brothers White and Goldberg also cite other cases, such as *NAACP v. Button; Shelton v. Tucker;* which held that States [could not] pass unnecessarily broad laws which might indirectly infringe on First Amendment [freedoms.] Brothers White and Goldberg now apparently would start from this requirement [and] extend it limitlessly to require States to justify any law restricting "liberty" as my Brethren define "liberty." This would mean at the very least, I suppose, that every state criminal statute—since it must inevitably curtail "liberty" to some extent— would be suspect, and would have to be justified to this Court.

My Brother Goldberg has adopted the recent discovery [12] that the Ninth Amendment as well as the Due Process Clause can be used by this Court as

7. In *Meyer*, in the very same sentence quoted in part by my Brethren in which he asserted that the Due Process Clause gave an abstract and inviolable right "to marry, establish a home and bring up children," Mr. Justice McReynolds asserted also that the Due Process Clause prevented States from interfering with "the right of the individual to contract."

12. See Patterson, *The Forgotten Ninth Amendment* (1955). Mr. Patterson urges that the Ninth Amendment be used to protect un-

specified "natural and inalienable rights." The Introduction by Roscoe Pound states that "there is a marked revival of natural law ideas throughout the world. Interest in the Ninth Amendment is a symptom of that revival."

In Redlich, *Are There "Certain Rights * * * Retained by the People"?*, 37 N.Y.U.L. Rev. 787, Professor Redlich, in advocating reliance on the Ninth and Tenth Amendments to invalidate the Connecticut law before us, frankly states: "[There] are two possible authority to strike down all state legislation which this Court thinks violates "fundamental principles of liberty and justice," or is contrary to the "traditions and collective conscience of our people." [One] would certainly have to look far beyond the language of the Ninth Amendment to find that the Framers vested in this Court any such awesome veto powers over lawmaking. [The Ninth] Amendment was passed [to] limit the Federal Government to the powers granted expressly or by necessary implication. [This] fact is perhaps responsible for the peculiar phenomenon that for a period of a century and a half no serious suggestion was ever made that [that] Amendment, enacted to protect state powers against federal invasion, could be used as a weapon of federal power to prevent state legislatures from passing laws they consider appropriate to govern local affairs. * * *

I realize that many good and able men have eloquently spoken and written [of] the duty of this Court to keep the Constitution in tune with the times [but I] reject that philosophy. The Constitution makers knew the need for change and provided for it. [The] Due Process Clause with an "arbitrary and capricious" or "shocking to the conscience" formula was liberally used by this Court to strike down economic legislation in the early decades of this century, threatening, many people thought, the tranquility and stability of the Nation. See, e.g., *Lochner.* That formula, based on subjective considerations of "natural justice," is no less dangerous when used to enforce this Court's views about personal rights than those about economic rights. I had thought that we had laid that formula, as a means for striking down state legislation, to [rest]. So far as I am concerned, Connecticut's law as applied here is not forbidden by any provision of the Federal Constitution as that Constitution was written, and I would therefore affirm.

Mr. Justice Stewart, whom Mr. Justice Black joins, dissenting.

[I] think this is an uncommonly silly law. As a practical matter, the law is obviously unenforceable, except in the oblique context of the present case. As a philosophical matter, I believe the use of contraceptives in the relationship of marriage should be left to personal and private [choice]. As a matter of social policy, I think professional counsel about methods of birth control should be available to all, so that each individual's choice can be meaningfully made. But we are not [asked] whether we think this law is unwise, or even asinine. We are asked to hold that it violates the United States Constitution. And that I cannot do.

In the course of its opinion the Court refers to no less than six Amendments [but] does not say which of these Amendments, if any, it thinks is infringed by this Connecticut law. [As] to the First, Third, Fourth, and Fifth Amendments, I can find nothing in any of them to invalidate this Connecticut law, even assuming that all those amendments are fully applicable against the States. [The] Ninth Amendment, like its companion the Tenth [was] simply to make clear that the adoption of the Bill of Rights did not alter the plan that the *Federal* Government was to be a government of express and limited powers, and that all rights and powers not delegated to it were retained by the people and the individual States. Until today no member of this Court has ever suggested that the Ninth Amendment meant anything [else].

[paths]. One is to revert to a frankly flexible due process concept even on matters that do not involve specific constitutional prohibitions. The other is to attempt to evolve a new constitutional framework within which to meet this and similar problems which are likely to arise."

What provision of the Constitution, then, does make this state law invalid? The Court says it is the right of privacy "created by several fundamental constitutional guarantees." [I] can find no such general right of privacy in the Bill of Rights, in any other part of the Constitution, or in any case ever before decided by this Court.[7]

At the oral argument [we] were told that the Connecticut law does not "conform to current community standards." But it is not the function of this Court to decide cases on the basis of community standards. [If], as I should surely hope, the law before us does not reflect the standards of the people of Connecticut, the people of Connecticut can freely exercise their true Ninth and Tenth Amendment rights to persuade their elected representatives to repeal it. That is the constitutional way to take this law off the books.

Notes and Questions

1. *Is Douglas, J.'s argument logical?* Consider Henkin, *Privacy and Autonomy,* 74 Colum.L.Rev. 1410, 1421–22 (1974): "Although it is not wholly clear, Justice Douglas's argument seems to go something like this: since the Constitution, in various 'specifics' of the Bill of Rights and in their penumbra, protects rights which partake of privacy, it protects other aspects of privacy as well, indeed it recognizes a general, complete right of privacy. And since the right emanates from specific fundamental rights, it too is 'fundamental,' its infringement is suspect and calls for strict scrutiny, and it can be justified only by a high level of public good. A logician, I suppose, might have trouble with that argument. A legal draftsman, indeed, might suggest the opposite: when the Constitution sought to protect private rights it specified them; that it explicitly protects some elements of privacy, but not others, suggests that it did not mean to protect those not mentioned."

2. *Did Griswold successfully avoid "renewing the romance" with "substantive due process"?* Griswold, observes Lupu, at 994, "provided the severest test for a Court determined to advance chosen values [without] renewing the romance with the dreaded demon of substantive due process. [Douglas, J.,] drew upon the incorporation legacy, rather than a doctrine of 'naked' substantive due process, and tortured the Bill of Rights into yielding a protected zone of privacy that would not tolerate a law banning contraceptive use by married couples. Justice Goldberg's reliance upon the ninth amendment [was] equally disingenuous in its attempt to avoid the jaws of substantive due process. Only Justices White and Harlan were willing to grapple directly with the fearful creature, and concluded that a law invading marital choice about contraception violated the due process clause itself, independent of links with the Bill of Rights. Shocking though that analysis may have been at the time, subsequent developments seem to have confirmed the White-Harlan view, and not the magical mystery tour of the zones of privacy, as the prevailing doctrine of *Griswold* [referring to *Moore v. East Cleveland* (1977), infra]."

3. *Emanations-and-penumbras theory and "economic" vs. "personal" rights.* Do any of the Justices analytically distinguish between "economic" and "personal" rights? Or is the distinction "only self-imposed"? Consider Kauper, *Penumbras, Peripheries, Emanations, Things Fundamental and Things Forgotten: The Griswold Case,* 64 Mich.L.Rev. 235, 253 (1965).

---

7. [The] Court does not say how far the new constitutional right of privacy announced today extends. I suppose, however, that even after today a State can constitutionally still punish at least some offenses which are not committed in public.

4. *"Privacy" or "equality"*? "Seen in the context of the Warren Court's general jurisprudence," observes M. Shapiro, *Fathers and Sons: The Court, the Commentators, and the Search for Values,* in The Burger Court 218, 228 (V. Blasi ed. 1983), "the fact situation in [*Griswold*] was crucial. The living law of Connecticut was that middle-class women received birth control information and purchased birth control supplies, and the Connecticut statute was enforced only to block the operation of birth control clinics that would bring these services to the poor. *Griswold* was an equality not a privacy decision ∗ ∗ ∗."

5. *Skinner and Griswold taken together.* Consider Tribe, *American Constitutional Law* 923 (1978): "Taken together with *Griswold,* which recognized as equally protected the individual's decision *not* to bear a child, the meaning of *Skinner* is that *whether one person's body shall be the source of another's life must be left to that person and that person alone to decide.* That principle collides in the abortion cases [infra] with a command that seems no less fundamental: *an innocent life may not be taken except to save the life of another."*

Griswold invalidated a ban on the *use* of contraceptives by *married* couples. EISENSTADT v. BAIRD, 405 U.S. 438, 92 S.Ct. 1029, 31 L.Ed.2d 349 (1972), overturned a conviction for violating a Massachusetts law making it a felony to *distribute* contraceptive materials, *except* in the case of registered physicians and pharmacists furnishing the materials to married persons. Baird had given a woman a package of vaginal foam at the end of her lecture on contraception. He was not charged with distributing to an unmarried person. No proof was offered as to the recipient's marital status. The crime charged was that Baird had no license, and thus no authority, to distribute to anyone. The Court, per BRENNAN, J., concluded that, since the statute is riddled with exceptions making contraceptives freely available and since, if protection of health were the rationale, the statute would be both discriminatory and overbroad, "the goals of deterring premarital sex and regulating the distribution of potentially harmful articles cannot reasonably be regarded as legislative aims." "[V]iewed as a prohibition on contraception per se" the statute "violates the rights of single persons under the Equal Protection Clause." For, "whatever the rights of the individual to access to contraceptives may be, the rights must be the same for the married and the unmarried alike":

"If under *Griswold* the distribution of contraceptives to married persons cannot be prohibited, a ban on distribution to unmarried persons would be equally impermissible. It is true that in *Griswold* the right of privacy in question inhered in the marital relationship. Yet the marital couple is not an independent entity with a mind and heart of its own, but an association of two individuals each with a separate intellectual and emotional make-up. If the right of privacy means anything, it is the right of the *individual,* married or single, to be free from unwarranted governmental intrusion into matters so fundamentally affecting a person as the decision whether to bear or beget a child. On the other hand, if *Griswold* is no bar to a prohibition on the distribution of contraceptives, the State could not, consistently with [equal protection,] outlaw distribution to unmarried but not to married persons. In each case the evil, as perceived by the State, would be identical, and the underinclusion would be invidious."

WHITE, J., joined by Blackmun, J., concurred, emphasizing that "the State did [not] convict Baird for distributing to an unmarried person [but because]

Baird had no license and therefore no authority to distribute to anyone." "Given *Griswold,* and absent proof of the possible hazards of using vaginal foam, we could not sustain [Baird's] conviction had it been for selling or giving away foam to a married person. Just as in *Griswold,* where the right of married persons to use contraceptives was 'diluted or adversely affected' by permitting a conviction for giving advice as to its exercise, so here to sanction a medical restriction upon distribution of a contraceptive not proved hazardous to health would impair the exercise of the constitutional right. That Baird could not be convicted for distributing [foam] to a married person disposes of this case. Assuming arguendo that the result would be otherwise had the recipient been unmarried, nothing has been placed in the record to indicate her marital status." [a]

BURGER, C.J., dissented, "see[ing] nothing in the Fourteenth Amendment or any other part of the Constitution that even vaguely suggests that these medicinal forms of contraceptives must be available in the open market. [By] relying on *Griswold* in the present context, the Court has passed beyond the penumbras of the specific guarantees into the uncircumscribed area of personal predilections."

Notes and Questions

1. *Does Eisenstadt offer a new rationale for Griswold?* Did *Eisenstadt* decide one of *Griswold* 's open issues—the constitutionality of a ban on the use or distribution of contraceptive devices that excluded from its reach the married couple—"by assertion, without a pretext of reasoning"? Wellington, *Common Law Rules and Constitutional Double Standards,* 83 Yale L.J. 221, 296 (1973), so charges: "[W]hether the 'different classes' (married, not married) are [as *Eisenstadt* states] 'wholly unrelated to the objective of the statute,' depends on whether, as *Griswold* insists, the marriage relationship is important to that aspect of liberty that the Court calls privacy. How, then, [could the Court write *Eisenstadt* the way it did] without offering a new rationale for *Griswold*[?]" *Cf.* Gerety, *Doing Without Privacy,* 42 Ohio St.L.J. 143–44 (1981).

2. *Griswold "unmasked"?* Consider Posner, *The Uncertain Protection of Privacy by the Supreme Court,* 1979 Sup.Ct.Rev. 173, 198: "*Griswold* had at least attempted to relate the right to use contraceptives to familiar notions of privacy by speculating on the intrusive methods by which a statute banning the use of contraceptives might be enforced. This ground was unavailable in [*Eisenstadt*] because the statute there forbade not the use, but only the distribution, of contraceptives. [*Eisenstadt*] is thus a pure essay in substantive due process. It unmasks *Griswold* as based on the idea of sexual liberty rather than privacy." *Cf.* Perry, *Abortion, the Public Morals, and the Police Power,* 23 U.C.L.A.L.Rev. 689, 705–06 (1976).

3. *Griswold and Eisenstadt extended.* As pointed out in Tribe 922, "the effect of *Eisenstadt v. Baird* was to single out as decisive in *Griswold* the element of reproductive autonomy, something the Court made clear in 1977, when it extended *Griswold* and *Baird* " in CAREY v. POPULATION SERVICES INT'L, 431 U.S. 678, 97 S.Ct. 2010, 52 L.Ed.2d 675 (1977), to invalidate a New York law which allowed only pharmacists to sell non-medical contraceptive devices to persons over 16 and prohibited the sale of such items to those under 16. (The

a. Douglas, J., who joined the Court's opinion, also concurred on free speech grounds.
Powell and Rehnquist, JJ., did not participate.

Court relied in part on the 1973 *Abortion Cases,* infra.) In striking down the restriction on sales to adults, BRENNAN, J., spoke for six justices; in invalidating the ban on sales to those under 16, he spoke for a four-justice plurality.

As for the restriction on distribution to adults, "where a decision as fundamental as that whether to bear or beget a child is involved, regulations imposing a burden on it may be justified only by compelling interests, and must be narrowly drawn to express only those interests"—and the Court found none of the state interests advanced (e.g., protecting health, facilitating enforcement of other laws) to be "compelling." [a] The state argued that *Griswold* dealt only with the *use* of contraceptives, not their manufacture or sale, but read "in light of its progeny, the teaching of *Griswold* is that the Constitution protects individual decisions in matters of childbearing from unjustified intrusion by the State."

As for the ban on sales to those under 16, Brennan, J., joined by Stewart, Marshall, and Blackmun, JJ., applied a test "apparently less rigorous than the 'compelling state interest' test applied to restrictions on the privacy rights of adults"—restrictions inhibiting privacy rights of minors are valid "only if they serve 'any significant state interest [that] is not present in the case of an adult.' *Planned Parenthood v. Danforth,* infra]." The plurality then rejected what it called "the argument [that] minors' sexual activity may be deterred by increasing the hazards attendant on it," pointing out that that argument had already been rejected by the Court in related areas.[b]

POWELL, J., concurred in the judgment, observing that by restricting not only the kinds of retail outlets that may distribute contraceptives, "but even prohibit[ing] distribution by mail to adults"—"thus requiring individuals to buy contraceptives over the counter"—the New York provision "heavily burdens constitutionally protected freedom." He saw "no justification for subjecting restrictions on the sexual activity of the young to heightened judicial review"—"a standard that for all practical purposes approaches the 'compelling interest' standard"—but concurred in the invalidation of the "distribution to minors" restriction on narrow grounds.[c]

---

a. The Court recognized, however, that "other restrictions may well be reasonably related to the objective of quality control," and thus "express[ed] no opinion on, for example, restrictions on the distribution of contraceptives through vending machines."

b. Nor was the restriction on the privacy rights of minors "saved" by another provision authorizing physicians to supply minors with contraceptives. As with limitations on distribution to adults, "less than total restrictions on access to contraceptives that significantly burden the right to decide whether to bear children must also pass constitutional muster. [This provision] delegates the State's authority to disapprove of minors' sexual behavior to physicians, who may exercise it arbitrarily * * *."

c. White, J., concurred in the invalidation of the restriction on minors "primarily because the State has not demonstrated that [the restriction] measurably contributes to the deterrent purposes which the State advances as justification for the restriction."

Stevens, J., too, concurred only in the judgment with respect to the restriction on minors: "[The State's] central argument is that the statute has the important *symbolic* effect of communicating disapproval of sexual activity by minors. In essence, therefore, the statute is defended as a form of propaganda, rather than a regulation of behavior. Although the State may properly perform a teaching function, [an] attempt to persuade by inflicting harm on the listener is an unacceptable means of conveying a message that is otherwise legitimate. The propaganda technique used in this case significantly increases the risk of unwanted pregnancy and venereal disease. It is as though a State decided to dramatize its disapproval of motorcycles by forbidding the use of safety helmets. One need not posit a constitutional right to ride a motorcycle to characterize such a restriction as irrational and perverse."

Rehnquist, J., dissented, observing that if those responsible for the Bill of Rights and Civil War Amendments could have lived to

ORAL ARGUMENTS IN THE ABORTION CASES *

* * *

THE COURT: [I]s it critical to your case that the fetus not be a person under the due process clause? [W]ould you lose your case if the fetus was a person?

SARAH WEDDINGTON [on behalf of appellant Roe]: Then you would have a balancing of interests.

THE COURT: Well you say you have [that] anyway, don't you? * * *

THE COURT: [If] it were established that an unborn fetus is a person, [protected by] the Fourteenth Amendment, you would have almost an impossible case here, would you not?

WEDDINGTON: I would have a very difficult case. * * *

THE COURT: Could Texas constitutionally, in your view, declare [by] statute [that] the fetus is a person, for all constitutional purposes, after the third month of gestation?

WEDDINGTON: I do not believe that the State legislature can determine the meaning of the Federal Constitution. It is up to this Court to make that determination. * * *

ROBERT FLOWERS [on behalf of appellee]: [I]t is the position of the State of Texas that, upon conception, we have a human being; a person, within the concept of the Constitution of the United States, and that of Texas, also.

THE COURT: Now how should that question be decided? Is it a legal question? A constitutional question? A medical question? A philosophical question? Or, a religious question? Or what is it?

FLOWERS: [W]e feel that it could be best decided by a legislature, in view of the fact that they can bring before it the medical testimony * * *.

THE COURT: So then it's basically a medical question?

FLOWERS: From a constitutional standpoint, no, sir. * * *

THE COURT: Of course, if you're right about [the fetus being a person within the meaning of the Constitution], you can sit down, you've won your case. * * * Except insofar as, maybe, the Texas abortion law presently goes too far in allowing abortions.

FLOWERS: Yes, sir. That's exactly right. * * *

THE COURT: Do you think [you have] lost your case, then, if the fetus or the embryo is not a person? Is that it?

FLOWERS: Yes sir, I would say so. * * *

THE COURT: Under State law [there] are some rights given to the fetus?

FLOWERS: Yes, sir.

THE COURT: And you are asserting these rights against the right of the mother. [And] that's wholly aside from whether the fetus is a person under the Federal Constitution. * * *

FLOWERS: Yes, sir. * * *

know what their efforts had wrought "it is not difficult to imagine their reaction." Burger, C.J., dissented without opinion.

* These extracts are taken from 75 *Landmark Briefs and Arguments of the Su-* *preme Court of the United States: Constitutional Law* 807–33 (Kurland & Casper ed.).

THE COURT: I want you to give me [a] medical writing of any kind that says that at the time of conception the fetus is a person. * * *

FLOWERS: [I] find no way [that] any court or any legislature or any doctor anywhere can say that here is the dividing line. Here is not a life; and here is a life, after conception. Perhaps it would be better left to that legislature. * * *

THE COURT: Well, if you're right that an unborn fetus is a person, then you can't leave it to the legislature to play fast and loose dealing with that person. [I]f you're correct, in your basic submission that an unborn fetus is a person, then abortion laws such as that which New York has are grossly unconstitutional, isn't it?

FLOWERS: That's right, yes.

THE COURT: Allowing the killing of people.

FLOWERS: Yes, sir. * * *

[Rebuttal argument of Weddington]

THE COURT: [I] gather your argument is that a state may not protect the life of the fetus or prevent an abortion [at] any time during pregnancy? Right up until the moment of birth? * * *

WEDDINGTON: [T]here is no indication [that] the Constitution would give any protection prior to birth. That is not before the Court. * * *

THE COURT: Well, I don't know whether it is or isn't. * * *

ROE v. WADE

410 U.S. 113, 93 S.Ct. 705, 35 L.Ed.2d 147 (1973).

MR. JUSTICE BLACKMUN delivered the opinion of the Court.

This Texas federal appeal and its Georgia companion, *Doe v. Bolton*, [infra,] present constitutional challenges to state criminal abortion legislation. The Texas statutes [are] typical of those that have been in effect in many States for approximately a century. The Georgia statutes, in contrast, have a modern cast and are a legislative product that, to an extent at least, obviously reflects the influences of recent attitudinal change, of advancing medical knowledge and techniques, and of new [thinking].

The Texas statutes [make procuring an abortion a crime except] "by medical advice for the purpose of saving the life of the mother."

[Jane] Roe alleged that she was unmarried and pregnant [and] that she was unable to get a "legal" abortion in Texas because her life did not appear to be threatened by the continuation of her pregnancy.[a] [The district court held the

a. Who was "Jane Roe"? Her real name was Norma McCorvey. According to Friendly & Elliott, *The Constitution: That Delicate Balance* 202–04 (1984), she had become pregnant through rape, had tried to get an abortion, but had been unable to pay the price ($650) demanded by a doctor she finally found who was willing to perform an abortion. Bobbitt, *Constitutional Fate* 165 (1982), describes "Jane Roe" as follows: "[She] was an unskilled, young white woman. She was also a lesbian."

When pressed by the lawyer who would eventually argue her case in the U.S. Supreme Court, Ms. McCorvey assured her that she would fight the Texas abortion law "all the way." But because she had a young child from a previous marriage and did not want the child subjected to "public ridicule," Ms. McCorvey had one stipulation: she wanted to be anonymous. In June of 1970, a year and a half before her case was first argued in the U.S. Supreme Court, Ms. McCorvey gave birth to a daughter. She never saw the child again

Texas abortion statutes unconstitutional, but denied the injunctive relief requested. Roe appealed.]

[R]estrictive criminal abortion laws [like Texas'] in effect in a majority of States [today] derive from statutory changes effected, for the most part, in the latter half of the 19th century. [The Court then reviewed, in some detail, "ancient attitudes," "the Hippocratic Oath" which forbids abortion, "the common law," "the English statutory law," and "the American law." Subsequently, it described the positions of the American Medical Association, the American Public Health Association, and the American Bar Association. Thus,] at common law, at the time of the adoption of our Constitution, and throughout the major portion of the 19th century, [a] woman enjoyed a substantially broader right to terminate a pregnancy than she does in most States today. * * *

Three reasons have been advanced to explain historically the enactment of criminal abortion laws in the 19th century and to justify their [continuance].

It has been argued occasionally that these laws were the product of a Victorian social concern to discourage illicit sexual conduct. Texas, however, does not advance this justification [and] it appears that no court or commentator has taken the argument seriously.

[A] second reason is [that when] most criminal abortion laws were first enacted, the procedure was a hazardous one for the woman. [But] medical data indicat[es] that abortion in early pregnancy, that is, prior to the end of first trimester, although not without its risk, is now relatively safe.

[The] third reason is the State's interest—some phrase it in terms of duty—in protecting prenatal life. Some of the argument for this justification rests on the theory that a new human life is present from the moment of conception. * * * Only when the life of the pregnant mother herself is at stake, balanced against the life she carries within her, should the interest of the embryo or fetus not prevail. [In] assessing the State's interest, recognition may be given to the less rigid claim that as long as at least *potential* life is involved, the State may assert interests beyond the protection of the pregnant woman alone.

[It] is with these interests, and the weight to be attached to them, that this case is concerned.

The Constitution does not explicitly mention any right of privacy. [But] the Court has recognized that a right of personal privacy, or a guarantee of certain areas or zones of privacy, does exist under the Constitution. In varying contexts the Court or individual Justices have indeed found at least the roots of that right in the First Amendment, *Stanley v. Georgia* [p. 389 infra]; in the Fourth and Fifth Amendments; in the penumbras of the Bill of Rights, *Griswold;* in the Ninth Amendment, id. (Goldberg, J., concurring); or in the concept of liberty guaranteed by the first section of the Fourteenth Amendment, see *Meyer.* These decisions make it clear that only personal rights that can be deemed "fundamental" or "implicit in the concept of ordered liberty," are included in this guarantee of personal privacy. They also make it clear that the right has some extension to activities relating to marriage, *Loving;* procreation, *Skinner;* contraception, *Eisenstadt;* family relationships, *Prince v. Massachusetts* [p. 763 infra]; and child rearing and education, *Pierce.*[b]

after she left the hospital. See Friendly & Elliott, supra.

b. Do these parental rights permit parents to forbid public school teachers from imposing corporal punishment on their children? See *Ingraham v. Wright* (1977), Sec. 5, II infra.

This right of privacy, whether it be founded in the Fourteenth Amendment's concept of personal liberty [as] we feel it is, [or] in the [Ninth Amendment], is broad enough to encompass a woman's decision whether or not to terminate her pregnancy. The detriment that the State would impose upon the pregnant woman by denying this choice altogether is apparent. Specific and direct harm medically diagnosable even in early pregnancy may be [involved]. Psychological harm may be imminent. Mental and physical health may be taxed by child care. There is also the distress, for all concerned, associated with the unwanted child, and there is the problem of bringing a child into a family already unable, psychologically and otherwise, to care for it. In other cases, as in this one, the additional difficulties and continuing stigma of unwed motherhood may be involved. All these are factors the woman and her responsible physician necessarily will consider in consultation.

On the basis of elements such as these, appellants and some amici argue that the woman's right is absolute and that she is entitled to terminate her pregnancy at whatever time, in whatever way, and for whatever reason she alone chooses. With this we do not agree. [The] Court's decisions recognizing a right of privacy also acknowledge that some state regulation in areas protected by that right is appropriate. [A] state may properly assert important interests in safeguarding health, in maintaining medical standards, and in protecting potential life. At some point in pregnancy, these respective interests become sufficiently compelling to sustain regulation of the factors that govern the abortion decision. [In] fact, it is not clear to us that the claim [that] one has an unlimited right to do with one's body as one pleases bears a close relationship to the right of privacy previously articulated in the Court's decisions. The Court has refused to recognize an unlimited right of this kind in the past. *Jacobson v. Massachusetts*, 197 U.S. 11, 25 S.Ct. 358, 49 L.Ed. 643 (1905), (vaccination); *Buck v. Bell* (sterilization).

[Where] certain "fundamental rights" are involved, the Court has held that regulation limiting these rights may be justified only by a "compelling state interest," and that legislative enactments must be narrowly drawn to express only the legitimate state interests at stake.

[The] appellee and certain amici argue that the fetus is a "person" within the language and meaning of the Fourteenth Amendment. [If so,] appellant's case, of course, collapses, for the fetus' right to life is then guaranteed specifically by the Amendment.

[The] Constitution does not define "person" in so many words. [The Court then listed each provision in which the word appears.] But in nearly all these instances, the use of the word is such that it has application only postnatally. None indicates, with any assurance, that it has any possible pre-natal application. All this, together with our observation that throughout the major portion of the 19th century prevailing legal abortion practices were far freer [than] today, persuades us that the word "person," as used in the Fourteenth Amendment, does not include the unborn. [Thus,] we pass on to other considerations.

The pregnant woman cannot be isolated in her privacy. She carries an embryo and, later, a fetus. [The] situation therefore is inherently different from marital intimacy, or bedroom possession of obscene material, or marriage, or procreation, or education, with which *Eisenstadt, Griswold, Stanley, Loving, Skinner, Pierce,* and *Meyer* [were] concerned.

[Texas] urges that, apart from the Fourteenth Amendment, life begins at conception and is present throughout pregnancy, and that, therefore, the State has a compelling interest in protecting that life from and after conception. We need not resolve the difficult question of when life begins. When those trained [in] medicine, philosophy, and theology are unable to arrive at any consensus, the judiciary, at this point in the development of man's knowledge, is not in a position to speculate as to the answer.

[W]e do not agree that, by adopting one theory of life, Texas may override the rights of the pregnant woman that are at stake. We repeat, however, that the State does have an important and legitimate interest in preserving and protecting the health of the pregnant woman [and] that it has still *another* important and legitimate interest in protecting the potentiality of human life. These interests are separate and distinct. Each grows in substantiality as the woman approaches term and, at a point during pregnancy, each becomes "compelling."

With respect to [the] interest in the health of the mother, the "compelling" point, in the light of present medical knowledge, is at approximately the end of the first trimester. This is so because of the now established medical fact that until the end of the first trimester mortality in abortion is less than mortality in normal childbirth. It follows that, from and after this point, a State may regulate the abortion procedure to the extent that the regulation reasonably relates to the preservation and protection of maternal health. Examples of permissible state regulation in this area are requirements as to the qualifications of the person who is to perform the abortion; [as] to the facility in which the procedure is to be performed, [and] the like. This means, on the other hand, that, for the period of pregnancy prior to this "compelling" point, the attending physician, in consultation with his patient, is free to determine, without regulation by the State, that in his medical judgment the patient's pregnancy should be terminated. If that decision is reached, the judgment may be effectuated by an abortion free of interference by the State.

With respect to [the] interest in potential life, the "compelling" point is at viability [which "is usually placed at about seven months (28 weeks) but may occur earlier, even at 24 weeks."] This is so because the fetus then presumably has the capability of meaningful life outside the mother's womb.[c] State regula-

---

c. Earlier in its opinion, 410 U.S. at 160, the Court described the point "at which the fetus becomes 'viable'" as the point that the fetus is "potentially able to live outside the mother's womb, albeit with artificial aid." *Planned Parenthood v. Danforth* (1976) (other aspects of which are discussed infra), per Blackmun, J., upheld a Missouri abortion statute defining "viability" as "that stage of fetal development when the life of the unborn child may be continued indefinitely outside the womb by natural or artificial life-supportive systems." In rejecting contentions that the Missouri statute unduly expanded the *Roe* Court's definition of "viability," failed to contain any reference to a gestational time period, and failed to incorporate and reflect the three stages of pregnancy, the Court observed: "[W]e recognized in *Roe* that viability was a matter of medical judgment, skill, and technical ability, and we preserved the flexibility of the term. [The Missouri statute] does the same. [I]t is not the proper function of the legislature or the courts to place viability,

which essentially is a medical concept, at a specific point in the gestation period. The time when viability is achieved may vary with each pregnancy, and the determination of whether a particular fetus is viable is, and must be, a matter for the judgment of the responsible attending physician. [The statutory definition] merely reflects this fact."

Consider, too, *Colautti v. Franklin,* 439 U.S. 379, 99 S.Ct. 675, 58 L.Ed.2d 596 (1979), per Blackmun, J., striking down on "void for vagueness" grounds a Pennsylvania provision requiring use of a statutorily prescribed technique when the fetus is "viable" or when there is "sufficient reason to believe that the fetus may be viable": "[The provision] subjects the physician to potential criminal liability without regard to fault. [I]t is not unlikely that experts will disagree over whether a particular fetus in the second trimester has advanced to the stage of viability. The prospect of such disagreement, in conjunction with a statute imposing liability for an erroneous de-tion protective of fetal life after viability thus has both logical and biological justifications. If the State is interested in protecting fetal life after viability, it may go as far as to proscribe abortion during that period except when it is necessary to preserve the life or health of the mother.

Measured against these standards, [the Texas statute] sweeps too broadly [and] therefore, cannot survive the constitutional attack made upon it here.

[In] *Doe* [infra], procedural requirements contained in one of the modern abortion statutes are considered. That opinion and this one [are] to be read together.[67]

This holding, we feel, is consistent with the relative weights of the respective interests involved, with the lessons and examples of medical and legal history, with the lenity of the common law, and with the demands of the profound problems of the present day. The decision leaves the State free to place increasing restrictions on abortion as the period of pregnancy lengthens, so long as those restrictions are tailored to the recognized state interests. The decision vindicates the right of the physician to administer medical treatment according to his professional judgment up to the points where important state interests provide compelling justifications for intervention. Up to those points, the abortion decision in all its aspects is inherently, and primarily, a medical decision, and basic responsibility for it must rest with the physician. If an individual practitioner abuses the privilege of exercising proper medical judgment, the usual remedies, judicial and intra-professional, are available. * * *

MR. JUSTICE STEWART, concurring.

termination of viability, could have a profound chilling effect on the willingness of physicians to perform abortions near the point of viability in the manner indicated by their best medical judgment." (White, J., joined by Burger, C.J. and Rehnquist, J., dissented, disagreeing with the Court's interpretation of the statute).

On similar analysis, the *Colautti* majority held "void for vagueness" a provision requiring that "the abortion technique employed shall be that which would provide the best opportunity for the fetus to be aborted alive so long as a different technique would not be necessary to preserve the life or health of the mother."

Colautti reaffirmed that the determination of "viability" is "a matter for medical judgment" and that that point is reached "when, in the judgment of the attending physician on the particular facts of the case before him, there is a reasonable likelihood of the fetus' sustained survival outside the womb, with or without artificial support. Because this point may differ with each pregnancy, neither the legislature nor the courts may proclaim one of the elements entering into the ascertainment of viability—be it weeks of gestation or fetal weight or any other single factor—as the determinant of when the State has a compelling interest in the life or health of the fetus."

Does the *Roe-Danforth-Colautti* approach to viability focus more on the physician's right to practice medicine than on the patient's right of privacy? Do medical advances in extra-

uterine gestation threaten the *practicability* of the woman's right to choose abortion? May the state assert its interest in potential life to whatever extent biotechnological advances enable a fetus to survive outside the womb, *no matter how early in its development*? Should the Court limit the definition of viability to the reasonable likelihood of survival outside the womb *without* technological support, thus designating a period in which a woman's decision to abort would be immune from state intervention? But where would we draw the line? Is an incubator a form of technological support? Should the focus of the abortion inquiry be not on the existing state of medical technology, but on the state of fetal development—the point at which a fetus becomes a "thinking, conscious being" (said to be between 19 and 30 weeks after conception)? See generally Notes, 27 U.C.L.A.L.Rev. 1340 (1980), 29 U.C.L.A.L.Rev. 1194 (1982). See also notes 12 & 13 following *Roe;* Justice O'Connor's dissent in *Akron v. Akron Center for Reproductive Health,* infra; and the notes following *Akron.*

67. Neither in this opinion nor in *Doe* do we discuss the father's rights, if any exist in the constitutional context, in the abortion decision. No paternal right has been asserted in either of the [cases]. North Carolina, for example, requires written permission for the abortion from the husband when the woman is a married minor [and] if the woman is an unmarried minor, written permission from the parents is required. * * *

In 1963, this Court, in *Ferguson v. Skrupa* [p. 76 fn. b supra], purported to sound the death knell for the doctrine of substantive due process, [but] [b]arely two years later, in *Griswold*, the Court held a Connecticut birth control law unconstitutional. In view of what had been so recently said in *Skrupa*, the Court's opinion in *Griswold* understandably did its best to avoid reliance on the Due Process Clause of the Fourteenth Amendment as the ground for decision, [but] it was clear to me then, and it is equally clear to me now, that the *Griswold* decision can be rationally understood only as a holding that the Connecticut statute substantively invaded the "liberty" that is protected by the Due Process Clause of the Fourteenth Amendment. As so understood, *Griswold* stands as one in a long line of pre-*Skrupa* cases decided under the doctrine of substantive due process, and I now accept it as such.

[The] Constitution nowhere mentions a specific right of personal choice in matters of marriage and family life, but the "liberty" protected by the Due Process Clause of the Fourteenth Amendment covers more than those freedoms explicitly named in the Bill of Rights. [As] recently as last Term, in *Eisenstadt*, we recognized "the right of the *individual*, married or single, to be free from unwarranted governmental intrusion into matters so fundamentally affecting a person as the decision whether to bear or beget a child." That right necessarily includes the right of a woman to decide whether or not to terminate her pregnancy. [It] is evident that the Texas abortion statute infringes that right directly. [The] question then becomes whether the state interests advanced to justify this abridgment can survive the "particularly careful scrutiny" that the Fourteenth Amendment here requires.

The asserted state interests are protection of the health and safety of the pregnant woman, and protection of the potential future human life within her. These are legitimate objectives, amply sufficient to permit a State to regulate abortions as it does other surgical procedures, and perhaps sufficient to permit a State to regulate abortions more stringently or even to prohibit them in the late stages of pregnancy. But such legislation is not before us, and I think the Court today has thoroughly demonstrated that these state interests cannot constitutionally support the broad abridgment of personal liberty worked by the existing Texas law. Accordingly, I join the Court's opinion holding that the law is invalid under the Due Process Clause of the Fourteenth Amendment.

MR. JUSTICE DOUGLAS, concurring [in *Doe* as well as in *Roe*].

While I join the opinion of the Court, I add a few words.

The questions presented [involve] the right of privacy. [The] Ninth Amendment obviously does not create federally enforceable rights. [But] a catalogue of [the rights "retained by the people"] includes customary, traditional, and time-honored rights, amenities, privileges, and immunities that come within the sweep of "the Blessings of Liberty" mentioned in the preamble to the Constitution. Many of them in my view come within the meaning of the term "liberty" as used in the Fourteenth Amendment.

First is the autonomous control over the development and expression of one's intellect, interests, tastes, and personality. These are rights protected by the First Amendment and in my view they are absolute * * *.

Second is freedom of choice in the basic decisions of one's life respecting marriage, divorce, procreation, contraception, and the education and upbringing of children. These rights, unlike those protected by the First Amendment, are subject to some control by the police power. [They] are "fundamental" and we have held that in order to support legislative action the statute must be narrowly and precisely drawn and that a "compelling state interest" must be shown in support of the limitation. * * *[4]

[Third] is the freedom to care for one's health and person, freedom from bodily restraint or compulsion, freedom to walk, stroll, or loaf. These rights, though fundamental, are likewise subject to regulation on a showing of "compelling state interest." * * * Elaborate argument is hardly necessary to demonstrate that childbirth may deprive a woman of her preferred life style and force upon her a radically different and undesired future.

[Such reasoning] is, however, only the beginning of the problem. [V]oluntary abortion at any time and place regardless of medical standards would impinge on a rightful concern of society. The woman's health is part of that concern; as is the life of the fetus after quickening. These concerns justify the State in treating the procedure as a medical one.

[T]he Georgia statute outlaws virtually all such operations—even in the earliest stages of pregnancy. In light of modern medical evidence [it] cannot be seriously urged that so comprehensive a ban is aimed at protecting the woman's health. Rather, [this ban] can rest only on a public goal of preserving both embryonic and fetal life.

The present statute has struck the balance between the woman and the State's interests wholly in favor of the latter. [We] held in *Griswold* that the States may not preclude spouses from attempting to avoid the joinder of sperm and egg. [I]t is difficult to perceive any overriding public necessity which might attach precisely at the moment of conception.

* * *

[The] protection of the fetus when it has acquired life is a legitimate concern of the State. Georgia's law makes no rational, discernible decision on that score. For under the Act the developmental stage of the fetus is irrelevant when pregnancy is the result of rape or when the fetus will very likely be born with a permanent defect or when a continuation of the pregnancy will endanger the life of the mother or permanently injure her health. When life is present is a question we do not try to resolve. While basically a question for medical experts, [it is], of course, caught up in matters of religion and morality. * * *

MR. JUSTICE WHITE, with whom MR. JUSTICE REHNQUIST joins, dissenting [in *Doe* as well as in *Roe*].

At the heart of the controversy in these cases are those recurring pregnancies that pose no danger whatsoever to the life or health of the mother but are nevertheless unwanted for any one or more of a variety of reasons— convenience, family planning, economics, dislike of children, the embarrassment of illegitimacy, etc. The common claim before us is that for any one of such reasons, or for no reason at all, and without asserting or claiming any threat to life or health, any woman is entitled to an abortion at her request if she is able to find a medical advisor willing to [perform it].

---

4. My Brother Stewart, writing in the present cases, says that our decision in *Griswold* reintroduced substantive due process that had been rejected in [*Skrupa*]. There is nothing specific in the Bill of Rights that covers [the marital relation]. Nor is there anything in the Bill of Rights that in terms protects the right of association or the privacy in one's association. [Other] peripheral rights are the right to educate one's children as one chooses, and the right to study the German language. These decisions with all respect, have nothing to do with substantive due process. One may think they are not peripheral rights to other rights that are expressed in the Bill of Rights. But that is not enough to bring into play the protection of substantive due process. * * *

The Court for the most part sustains this position [and] simply fashions and announces a new constitutional right [and], with scarcely any reason or authority for its action, invests that right with sufficient substance to override most existing state abortion statutes. The upshot is that the people and the legislatures of the 50 States are constitutionally disentitled to weigh the relative importance of the continued existence and development of the fetus on the one hand against a spectrum of possible impacts on the mother on the other hand. As an exercise of raw judicial power, the Court perhaps has authority [but] in my view its judgment is an improvident and extravagant exercise of the power of judicial review * * *.

MR. JUSTICE REHNQUIST, dissenting. * * *

I have difficulty in concluding [that] the right of "privacy" is involved in this case. [Texas] bars the performance of a medical abortion by a licensed physician on a plaintiff such as Roe. A transaction resulting in an operation such as this is not "private" in the ordinary usage of that word. Nor is the "privacy" which the Court finds here even a distant relative of the freedom from searches and seizures protected by the Fourth Amendment.

[If] the Court means by the term "privacy" no more than that the claim of a person to be free from unwanted state regulation of consensual transactions may be a form of "liberty" * * * I agree [with] Mr. Justice Stewart [that that "liberty"] embraces more than the rights found in the Bill of Rights. But that liberty is not guaranteed absolutely against deprivation, but only against deprivation without due process of law. The test traditionally applied in the area of social and economic legislation is whether or not a law such as that challenged has a rational relation to a valid state objective. [If] the Texas statute were to prohibit an abortion even where the mother's life is in jeopardy, I have little doubt that such a statute would lack a rational relation to a valid state [objective].[d] But the Court's sweeping invalidation of any restrictions on abortion during the first trimester is impossible to justify under that [standard]. As in *Lochner* and similar cases applying substantive due process standards to economic and social welfare legislation, the adoption of the compelling state interest standard will inevitably require this Court to examine the legislative policies and pass on the wisdom of these policies in the very process of deciding whether a particular state interest put forward may or may not be "compelling." The decision here to break the term of pregnancy into three distinct terms and to outline the permissible restrictions the State may impose in each one, for example, partakes more of judicial legislation than it does of a determination of the intent of the drafters of the Fourteenth Amendment.

The fact that a majority of the States, reflecting after all the majority sentiment in those States, have had restrictions on abortions for at least a century seems to me as strong an indication there is that the asserted right to an abortion is not "so rooted in the traditions and conscience of our people as to be ranked as fundamental." Even today, when society's views on abortion are changing, the very existence of the debate is evidence that the "right" to an abortion is not so universally accepted as the appellants would have us believe.

[By] the time of the adoption of the Fourteenth Amendment in 1868 there were at least 36 laws enacted by state or territorial legislatures limiting abortion. [The] only conclusion possible from this history is that the drafters did

---

d. Is it "irrational" or "invalid" for a state to weigh the *possibility* (or even *probability*) that the mother will die without an abortion against the *certainty* that the fetus will not survive with one and then to legislate against abortions in such situations?

not intend to have the Fourteenth Amendment withdraw from the States the power to legislate with respect to this matter.   *   *   *

DOE v. BOLTON, 410 U.S. 179, 93 S.Ct. 739, 35 L.Ed.2d 201 (1973), the companion case to *Roe v. Wade,* sustained, against the contention that it had been rendered unconstitutionally vague by a three-judge district court's interpretation, a Georgia provision that permitted a physician to perform an abortion when "based upon his best clinical judgment that an abortion is necessary." (The district court had struck down the statutorily specified reasons: because continued pregnancy would endanger a pregnant woman's life or injure her health; the fetus would likely be born with a serious defect; or the pregnancy resulted from rape.) "The net result of the District Court's decision," observed the Court, "is that the abortion determination, so far as the physician is concerned, is made in the exercise of his professional, that is, his 'best clinical,' judgment in the light of all the attendant circumstances. He is not now restricted to the three situations originally specified. Instead, [the] medical judgment may be exercised in light of all factors—physical, emotional, psychological, familial, and the woman's age—relevant to the well-being of the patient. All these factors may relate to health. This allows the attending physician the room he needs to make his best medical judgment. And it is room that operates for the benefit, not the disadvantage, of the pregnant woman."

However, despite the fact that the Georgia statute was patterned after the American Law Institute's Model Penal Code (1962), which had served as the model for recent legislation in about one-fourth of the states, the Court, per BLACKMUN, J., invalidated substantial portions of the statute. Struck down were requirements (1) that the abortion be performed in a hospital accredited by the Joint Commission on Accreditation of Hospitals (JCAH); (2) that the procedure be approved by a hospital staff abortion committee; and (3) that the performing physician's judgment be confirmed by independent examinations of the patient by two other physicians.

As for (1): There is no restriction of the performance of nonabortion surgery in a hospital not accredited by the JCAH. "[T]he State must show more than it has in order to prove that only the full resources of a licensed hospital, rather than those of some other appropriately licensed institution, satisfy [appropriate] health interests. [This requirement], because it fails to exclude the first trimester of pregnancy, see *Roe,* is also invalid." As for (2), [we] see no constitutionally justifiable pertinence [for] the advance approval by the abortion committee. With regard to the protection of potential life, the medical judgment is already completed prior to the committee stage, and review by a committee once removed from diagnosis is basically redundant. We are not cited to any other surgical procedure made subject to committee approval as a matter of state criminal law. The woman's right to receive medical care in accordance with the licensed physician's best judgment and the physician's right to administer it are substantially limited by this statutorily imposed overview." As for (3), the two-doctor concurrence, "the statute's emphasis [is] on the attending physician's 'best clinical judgment that an abortion is necessary.' That should be sufficient. [No] other voluntary medical or surgical procedure for which Georgia requires confirmation by two other physicians has been cited to us."

COMMENTARY ON THE *ABORTION CASES:* (A) WHY THE CASES WERE WRONGLY DECIDED; (B) HOW A BETTER OPINION REACHING THE SAME RESULT MIGHT HAVE BEEN WRITTEN; AND (C) WHAT LIGHT THE CASES SHED ON THE NATURE OF THE BURGER COURT'S ACTIVISM

1. *The power of the state to define who is a person.* Consider JOHN NOONAN, *The Root and Branch of Roe v. Wade,* 63 Neb.L.Rev. 668, 672–73 (1984): "Whoever has the power to define [personhood] has a power that can make nonsense of any particular constitutional right. That this power belongs to the state itself is a point of view associated [with] Hans Kelsen. As he [views it], even the apparently natural physical person is a construction of juristic thinking.

"[*Roe*] was profoundly ambivalent—indeed, to speak bluntly, it was schizoid in its approach to the power of the state to determine who was a person. [The] precedents that the Court [relied on] were all cases that treated family rights as having a natural basis superior to the law of the state. The cases included *Meyer* and *Pierce,* recognizing a superior right of parents to educate their children; *Skinner,* recognizing that a man has a natural right to procreate and so cannot be arbitrarily sterilized by the state; *Loving,* where the natural right to marry was invoked in the course of invalidating a miscegenation statute; and *Griswold,* where the rights of the married were also asserted * * *.

"All of these cases rested on the supposition that the family rights being protected were those of persons, and that these persons could not be unmade at will by the state. [At] the same time that it invoked such precedents in *Roe,* the Court, when treating of the unborn, felt free to impose its own notions of reality.

"In one passage the Court spoke of the unborn before viability as 'a theory of life,' as though there were competing views as to whether life in fact existed before viability. The implication could also be found that there was no reality there in the womb but merely theories about what was there. [To] judge from the weight the Court gave the being in the womb—found to be protectible in any degree only in the last two months of pregnancy—the Court itself must have viewed the unborn as pure potentiality or a mere theory before viability. The Court's opinion appeared to rest on the assumption that the biological reality could be subordinated or ignored by the sovereign speaking through the Court." [a]

2. *The impact of Roe on a pluralistic society.* Consider GUIDO CALABRE-SI, *Ideals, Beliefs, Attitudes, and the Law* 95–97 (1985): "The Court, when it said that fetuses are not persons for purposes of due process, said to a large and politically active group: '*Your* metaphysics are not part of *our* constitution.' This is far worse (and more dangerous) in a pluralistic society than the statement the Court sought to avoid making, namely, 'Sorry, but your metaphysics are wrong. A fetus is not alive.' The Court said it does not matter whether a

---

a. But compare Tribe, note 8 infra. Consider, too, Macklin, *Personhood and the Abortion Debate,* in *Abortion: Moral and Legal Perspectives* 80 (Garfield & Hennessey eds. 1984): "That the task of determining the personhood of the fetus has proved as intractable as the abortion question itself seems not to deter those who believe this line of inquiry to be fruitful. [T]hat most discussions of personhood are found within the context of the abortion debate should prompt the recognition that the concept of personhood is not value neutral, so there can be no value-free inquiry into this subject. [A]ppeal to the concept of personhood is entirely unhelpful in any effort to resolve the fundamentals of the abortion controversy. Writers either choose a definition of personhood that comports with the moral view they already hold on the abortion issue; or else they attempt to show that the personhood of the fetus is quite irrelevant to settling moral and legal aspects of abortion."

fetus is alive (whether *your* metaphysics are correct). A fetus still is not protected by *our* Constitution. Such a statement is about as bad as can be made by the Supreme Court [in] the area of conflicting beliefs.

"[When] the Court proclaimed [that] anti-abortion beliefs as to commencement of life, *whether true or not,* are not part of our Constitution [it] made that Constitution unacceptable to the holders of these beliefs. It said to highly defensive groups comprised in significant part of recent immigrants that their highest beliefs [are] not part of *our* law as represented by its most fundamental statement, the Constitution. [It] told them, in as dramatic a way as one can through a legal opinion, that even now, even after all their other assimilations, they could not be true Americans so long as they held to their beliefs. This was catastrophic because it reinforced doubts which the holders of anti-abortion beliefs already had about their full acceptance in American society.

"[The *Roe* opinion] opened wounds one wishes were closed. The decision made it impossible for the opposing views to live with each other, and created a situation in which one side seemed to need to *win* over the other. And, while that may be the side the Court supported, the losers will not quickly forget their exclusion (just as they have not forgotten their treatment as recent immigrants) to the detriment of our pluralistic society."

3. *What if the Court had held that a fetus is a person?* Consider Chemerinsky, *Rationalizing the Abortion Debate: Legal Rhetoric and the Abortion Controversy,* 31 Buffalo L.Rev. 107, 112–13 (1982): "If personhood begins at conception, then the state may not discriminate against persons who are fetuses by offering them less protection than other individuals in society. [If] the fetus is a person there is no basis for discriminating against those conceived during rape or incest. [By] defining life as beginning at conception, the Court would be compelled to require that all abortions be prohibited, unless the mother's life is in danger.[30] Furthermore, once it is assumed that the fetus is a person, then there is no legal basis for punishing abortion differently than homicide."

4. *More on the Meyer-Pierce-Skinner-Griswold-Eisenstadt line of cases.* PHILIP HEYMANN & DOUGLAS BARZELAY, *The Forest and the Trees: Roe v. Wade and its Critics,* 53 B.U.L.Rev. 765, 772–76 (1973) read this line of cases very differently than Professor Noonan:

"[T]aken together, [these cases] clearly delineate a sphere of interests— which the Court now groups and denominates 'privacy'—implicit in the 'liberty' protected by the fourteenth amendment. At the core of this sphere is the right of the individual to make for himself—except where a very good reason exists for placing the decision in society's hands—the fundamental decisions that shape family life: whom to marry; whether and when to have children; and with what values to rear those children. * * *

"Plainly the right of a couple to decide whether or not to prevent the birth of a child by abortion falls within the class of interests involving marriage, procreation and child rearing which the Court has considered 'fundamental' in [the *Meyer-Eisenstadt* line of cases]. The question of constitutionality in the case of abortion statutes is a more difficult one than that involved in *Griswold* and

30. This is precisely what the West German Federal Constitutional Court held [in 1975 when it struck down an act of Parliament permitting abortion by a licensed physician during the first twelve weeks of pregnancy]. The dissenters on the [West German Court] criticized the majority for ignoring principles of judicial review by substituting its judgment for the legislature's. The dissenters maintained that the "question is a matter of legislative responsibility." Gorby & Jonas, *West Germany Abortion Decision: A Contrast to Roe v. Wade,* 9 J.Mar.J.Prac. & Proc. 551 (1976). * * *

Eisenstadt only because the asserted state interest is more important, not because of any difference in the individual interests involved. The couple's right to decide whether to have a family is the very same right as that established and protected in the cases dealing with contraception; considerations identical to those that justify protecting the broader class require careful scrutiny of regulations concerning abortion. The point is made most clearly by considering what a conclusion that abortion did not fall within a category of specially protected interests would have meant. A state, on a slender showing of rationality, could have required abortions—perhaps as incident to limiting a woman to two children—unless of course the fetus' rights were fundamental even though the mother's were not.[b] It could have forced a woman to carry the child of her rapist to term; it could have conditioned the right to an abortion on the payment of a fee or the discretionary approval of a state official.

"Recognizing that abortion falls within the class of fundamental interests of 'privacy' does not mean that statutes prohibiting abortion had to be considered unconstitutional—only that they had to be justified by compelling state interests. The Court might logically have concluded that the state's interest in protecting the unborn was compelling enough to override the parents' rights, without seriously threatening the broad range of individual rights already established under the line of decisions from *Meyer* through *Eisenstadt*. What it could not do, unless it was prepared to discard the principles of those cases, was to avoid evaluating the state's interest to see if it justified taking from the mother all discretion in the matter of abortion. [N]either the difficulty nor the impassioned setting of the decision was a principled ground on which the Court could refuse to make an evaluation it was otherwise called upon to make."

But consider Regan, *Rewriting Roe v. Wade*, 77 Mich.L.Rev. 1569, 1639 (1979): "[The *Meyer-Eisenstadt* line of cases which Heymann & Barzelay say] establish a 'realm of private decision as to matters of marriage, procreation and child rearing' [are] a rag-tag lot. Most of them either claim to be or are best understood as being primarily about something other than 'marriage, procreation and child-rearing.' "[c] Moreover, continues Regan, supra, at 1641–42: "Whether or not the cases from *Meyer* to *Eisenstadt* establish a right of family-related freedom-of-choice, none of these cases involves a state interest remotely like the interest in protecting 'potential' but *already conceived* human life. Accordingly none of those cases establishes or even suggests that the right of family-related freedom-of-choice is weighty enough to overcome the state's interest in forbidding abortion."

Consider, too, Epstein, *Substantive Due Process by Any Other Name: The Abortion Cases*, 1973 Sup.Ct.Rev. 159, 170–72: "If we must hazard an attempt to find the common thread which runs through [the *Meyer-Eisenstadt* line of cases], it might well be the principle of classic liberalism: the state is entitled to restrict the liberty of any individual within its jurisdiction only where necessary to

b. Consider, too, Chemerinsky, note 3 supra, at 117: "[I]f the Court grants the legislatures authority to permit or prohibit abortions, it must also allow the legislatures to enact laws requiring abortions. It is conceivable that a state might someday choose to compel pregnant women to undergo amniocentesis and abort defective children. If the Court may only protect rights stated in the Constitution, leaving all else to the political process, then it would be powerless to halt mandatory abortions." See also Gibbons, *Keynote Address*, 56 N.Y.U. L.Rev. 260, 273–74 (1981) (discussion of hypothetical statute drafting women into armed services and providing that if they become pregnant they shall submit to an abortion or be court martialed).

c. See also Ely, *The Wages of Crying Wolf: A Comment on Roe v. Wade*, 82 Yale L.J. 920, 931–32 n. 79 (1973).

protect other persons from harm. [But] the general principle will have only an empty exception if 'harm to another' does not cover the death of another person. Let it be accepted that the unborn child is a person (or even is to be treated like one), and it is clear beyond all question that abortion cases fall not within the general rule that protects the liberty of each person to do as he pleases but within the exception that governs the infliction of harm to others. And the case, moreover, becomes instantly distinguishable from that posed by the state regulation of contraception, because no one claims that there is a person before conception."

5. *"Privacy" or "autonomy"—or "fundamentality"?* What the Court has been talking about in cases like *Griswold, Eisenstadt* and *Roe,* observes LOUIS HENKIN, *Privacy and Autonomy,* 74 Colum.L.Rev. 1410, 1424–27 (1974), "is not at all what most people mean by privacy. [The] Court has been vindicating not a right to freedom from official intrusion, but to freedom from official regulation (and not regulation that intrudes particularly on 'hard-core privacy'. (I have called freedom from regulation 'autonomy,' although there are, of course, aspects of autonomy in freedom from official intrusion as well). * * *

"Primarily and principally the new Right of Privacy is a zone of prima facie autonomy, of presumptive immunity from regulation, in addition to that established by the first amendment. The zone, Justice Blackmun told us, consists of 'personal rights' that can be deemed 'fundamental,' that are 'implicit in the concept of ordered liberty.' The right has 'some extension' to marriage, sexual relations, contraception, unwanted children, family relations and parental autonomy. But we will know which rights are and which are not within the zone only case by case, with lines drawn and redrawn, in response to individual and societal initiatives and the imaginativeness of lawyers. * * *

"[T]he Right of Privacy aggravates uncertainties in the jurisprudence of individual rights and public goods under the Constitution. We had had two categories of constitutional rights, with those of the first amendment 'fundamental,' 'preferred.' Now we have restored independent importance to 'liberty-autonomy,' with an additional bifurcation of its own. Most aspects of an individual's life are not 'fundamental,' and in these his liberty is subject to the police power of federal and state governments, with presumptions of statutory validity, and a heavy, generally hopeless, burden on a resisting individual to show that a regulation has no conceivable public purpose, or that there is no rational relation between means and ends. Some, fewer, aspects of individual life are 'fundamental,' constitute a zone of prima facie autonomy (called Privacy), are presumed sacrosanct, and will bow only to a compelling public good clearly established. We are not told the basis—in language, history, or whatever else may be relevant to constitutional interpretation—for concluding that 'liberty' includes some individual autonomy that is 'fundamental' and much that is not. We are not told what is the touchstone for determining 'fundamentality.' We are not told why Privacy satisfies that test (unless Privacy is a tautology for fundamentality). [What] is it that makes my right to use contraceptives a right of Privacy, and fundamental, but my right to contract to work 16 hours a day or to pay more for milk than the law fixes, not a right of Privacy and not fundamental? [d] Is it, as some suspect, that the game is being played backwards:

d. Posner, *The Uncertain Protection of Privacy in The Supreme Court,* 1979 Sup.Ct.Rev. 173, 199, maintains that in the sense "privacy" is used in *Eisenstadt* and *Roe* —what is private is "simply what the Court thinks should not be subject to public control"—"the right to follow the occupation of one's choice without hindrance from government could equally well be regarded as an aspect of the right of privacy. The Justices who thought that the private right which intuitively commends itself as valuable in our society in our time, or at least to a majority of our Justices at this time, is called fundamental, and if it cannot fit comfortably into specific constitutional provisions it is included in Privacy?"

6. *Should " 'privacy' semantics" be abandoned in cases such as Roe?* One reason the Court utilizes the "privacy" terminology, observes Perry, *Substantive Due Process Revisited,*[e] 71 Nw.U.L.Rev. 417, 440–41 (1976), is "precisely *because* it obfuscates what is actually going on in a case like *Roe.* Abandoning the privacy approach for the analytical framework set forth herein would require the Court to unmask the methodology and function of substantive due process for all to see, something the Court has been rather shy to do." See also Lupu, *Untangling the Strands of the Fourteenth Amendment,* 77 Mich.L.Rev. 981, 1032–33 (1979): "If the 'naked' substantive due process decisions had to be summed up in a brief capsule, rights of 'familial choice' would be a far more accurate description than rights of 'privacy.' But rights of 'familial choice' stand starkly naked, since no amount of Bill of Rights penumbra-fashioning can responsibly lead to 'family rights' as a protected category."

7. *Variations in the strength of the woman's interest.* Consider ROBERT BENNETT, *Abortion and Judicial Review: Of Burdens and Benefits, Hard Cases and Some Bad Law,* 75 Nw.U.L.Rev. 978, 1008 (1981): "*Roe v. Wade* rests on a judgment that the burdens on pregnant women are unfair because they are very great and, until after viability, the state's interest is not weighty enough to justify the burdens. A major weakness of the Court's opinion, however, is insufficient attention to variations in the strength of the woman's interest.

"The Court was obviously aware that women have varying degrees of interest in obtaining abortions. The Court's opinion permits abortion after viability (despite the presence of a 'compelling' state interest in forbidding it) when the woman's interest is particularly strong because her life or health is in danger. In the earlier periods of pregnancy, however, the Court seems trapped by its privacy rationale into viewing the weight of the interests of all women in obtaining abortions as equivalent. Thus, the Court rotely applied its tripartite scheme in *Wade*'s companion case, *Doe v. Bolton,* although the [American Law Institute-based] Georgia statute involved in *Bolton* allowed abortions when the women's health was seriously jeopardized, when a seriously defective child was in prospect, or when the pregnancy resulted [from] rape. These are clearly the most compelling cases for abortion and might have been thought to require additional explanations of why a statute forbidding abortions in only less urgent cases still imposed unfair burdens."

Consider, too, Freund, *Storms over the Supreme Court,* 69 A.B.A.J. 1474, 1480 (1983): "A law that absolutely made criminal all kinds and forms of abortion could not stand up; it is not a reasonable accommodation of interests. The Court went further. It adopted what might be called the medical point of view—

that the Constitution protected the right of employer and employee to set the terms of employment without government interference simply lacked the wit to justify their belief in the language of privacy." But see Craven, *Personhood: The Right To Be Let Alone,* 1976 Duke L.J. 699, 701–02 ("a right of 'personhood' can be given meaningful protection without awakening the long dormant shade of *Lochner* "; "the term, which originated with Professor Paul Freund, includes elements of the concepts of individuality, autonomy, and privacy, but none of these words is sufficient").

e. See, too, Dixon, *The 'New' Substantive Due Process and the Democratic Elite,* 1976 B.Y.U.L.Rev. 43, 84–85: "[A]lthough the privacy label is tossed about loosely as though it had some intrinsic meaning, [*Griswold* and *Roe* involved] not ['privacy,' but] a particular freedom of action. [B]ecause 'privacy' has no single, generally accepted meaning, the mold remains pure *Lochner.*"

making distinctions that turn on trimesters and on the development of the fetus and its viability. There are other lines that could have been drawn—for instance, the proposal of the American Law Institute to immunize abortions [under certain circumstances, e.g., when the pregnancy is the result of rape or incest, or the fetus is severely abnormal]. That is not so much a medical as an ethical approach. Physicians probably would not be entirely happy with it. If the Court had said that a state must adopt one or another or some similar set of distinctions, [some] of the bitter debate on the issue might have been averted. The animus against the Court might at least have been diverted to the legislative halls." [f]

8. *Was the state's justification for interference with individual decision a "moral" or "philosophical" or "religious" one?* Professor Henkin asks, supra, at 1431–32: "Once, [the] promotion and protection of morals was clearly a proper concern of government; does the Right of Privacy imply that it is no longer? While the rights to use contraceptives, to have an abortion, to read obscene materials, were held not offset by hypothesized, particular public goods, were they not all essentially 'morals legislation'? And does it essentially all come down to the Court's saying [in effect] that these are not 'the law's business'? Does the Constitution, then, permit government to be only utilitarian not 'moral'? Or, if that inference is unwarranted, which morals may society promote, by what means? How much attention may it give in legislation to national history, to ancestral or contemporary religion, to the prevailing morality of the time?"

But compare Cox, *The Role of the Supreme Court* 113–14 (1976): "My criticism of *Roe* is that the Court failed to establish the legitimacy of the decision by not articulating a precept of sufficient abstractness to lift the ruling above the level of a political judgment based upon the evidence currently available from the medical, physical and social sciences. Nor can I articulate such a principle— unless it be that a State cannot interfere with individual decisions relating to sex, procreation, and family with only a moral or philosophical State justification: a principle which I cannot accept or believe will be accepted by the American people.[g] The failure to confront the issue in principled terms leaves

f. See also Ginsburg, *Some Thoughts on Autonomy and Equality in Relation to Roe v. Wade,* 63 N.C.L.Rev. 375, 381–82 (1985) ("*Roe* ventured too far in the change it ordered"; if Court had not adopted a "medical approach" but given states more leeway "the legislative trend might have continued in the direction in which it was headed in the early 1970s"); Sandalow, *Federalism and Social Change,* 43 Law & Contemp.Prob. 35, 36 (1980) (because "a national consensus plainly had not evolved regarding abortion" and the political process was at work, offering the prospect that "the law might come to reflect a tolerable accommodation of competing views, differing from state to state," the Court should not have adopted "an extraordinarily detailed set of restrictions on state power").

g. Consider Harlan, J., dissenting in *Poe v. Ullman:* "[T]he very inclusion of the category of morality among state concerns indicates that society is not limited in its objects only to the physical well-being of the community, but has traditionally concerned itself with the

moral soundness of its people as well. Indeed to attempt a line between public behavior and that which is purely consensual or solitary would be to withdraw from community concern a range of subjects with which every society in civilized times has found it necessary to deal. The laws regarding marriage which provide both when the sexual powers may be used and the legal and societal context in which children are born and brought up, as well as laws forbidding adultery, fornication and homosexual practices which express the negative of the proposition, confining sexuality to lawful marriage, form a pattern so deeply pressed into the substance of our social life that any Constitutional doctrine in this area must be built upon that basis.

"* * * If we had a case before us which required us to decide simply, and in abstraction, whether the moral judgment implicit in the application of the present statute to married couples was a sound one, the very controversial nature of these questions would, I think, require us to hesitate long before con-the opinion to read like a set of hospital rules and regulations, whose validity is good enough this week but will be destroyed with new statistics upon the medical risks of childbirth and abortion or new advances in providing for the separate existence of a foetus."

But consider LAURENCE TRIBE, *Toward a Model of Roles in the Due Process of Life and Law,* 87 Harv.L.Rev. 1 (1973). "Viability," observes Tribe, "marks a point after which a secular state could properly conclude that permitting abortion would be tantamount to permitting murder [on] the secular and quite practical ground that a state wishing to prevent the killing of infants simply has no way to distinguish the deliberate destruction of the latter from what is involved in postviability abortions." But "just as the state is unable to distinguish postviability 'abortions' from infanticide, so it is unable—within the limits of the secular—to treat previability abortions as though they involved the murder of infants." *Until viability,* is the state's justification for interference with individual decision a "moral or philosophical" one, as Professor Cox characterizes it, or a "religious" one? To borrow language from Tribe, supra, at 32, does "the first amendment concern for religious-political disentanglement" provide "a general frame of reference which, in the setting of the contemporary social experience with abortion, indicates that defining and applying the criteria for permissible abortion should not be a governmental function before viability"? Observes Tribe, at 18–22, 24–25:

"If there were general agreement about a developmental stage as of which the fetus should be regarded as a human being with independent moral claims, then the propriety of entrusting its protection to government would follow from the consensus that states must have relatively wide latitude in fulfilling their responsibility to protect existing human lives from destruction.[86]

"But the reality is that the 'general agreement' posited above simply does not exist. [T]he advance of embryology and medicine over the past century and a half rendered untenable any notion that the fetus suddenly 'came to life' in a physiological sense at a definable point during pregnancy. * * *

"As often occurs when the progress of science exposes the complexity beneath events formally conceived in simpler terms, inchoate feelings that could at one time have been clothed in secular trappings were thus forced into the mold of religious affirmations. [T]he only bodies of thought that have purported in this century to locate the crucial line between potential and actual life [of an embryo or fetus] have been those of organized religious doctrine. It is important to recognize that this has not been an accident; for the question when human life truly begins [asks for] a decision as to what characteristics should be regarded as defining a human being. And, at least at this point in the history of industrialized Western civilization, that decision in turn entails not an inference or demonstration from generally shared premises, whether factual or moral, but a statement of religious faith upon which people will invariably differ widely. [So] it was that Justice Blackmun, writing for the Court in *Roe,* had to recognize

cluding that the Constitution precluded Connecticut from choosing as it has among these various views. [But we] are not presented simply with this moral judgment to be passed on as an abstract proposition."

But compare Law, note 12 infra.

86. Even if one starts from the premise that the fetus is fully a human being throughout pregnancy, there remains considerable doubt as to the morality of requiring a woman to carry it to term. [However,] I proceed on the assumption that legislatively resolving such doubt against the woman's choice would not violate the Constitution.

[But see Professor Regan's argument in defense of the Abortion Cases, note 10 infra, an argument that "does not depend on refusing to allow the state to regard the fetus as a person."]

the highly charged and distinctly sectarian religious controversy that the abortion issue had predictably come to stir. * * *

"[T]he theory suggested here would find excessive entanglement only when the involvement of religious groups in the political process surrounding a subject of government control is convincingly traceable, as it is in the case of abortion, to an intrinsic aspect of the subject itself in the intellectual and social history of the period. * * * Forbidding the destruction of living human beings [states] a compelling secular purpose, but [this justification is] not one whose connection with the destruction of fetal 'life' can be established in any wholly secular way. Thus, given the problem of religious entanglement, any justification for a government role in the abortion decision must be grounded in some other compelling secular objective." [h]

Five years later, Professor Tribe revised his position, Tribe, *American Constitutional Law* 928–29 (1978): "Suggestions have been advanced that the interest in fetal life is intrinsically religious, or at least that the inescapable involvement of religious groups in the debate over abortion rendered the subject inappropriate for political resolution and hence proper only for decision by the woman herself [citing his 1973 article]. But, on reflection, that view appears to give too little weight to the value of allowing religious groups freely to express their convictions in the political process, underestimates the power of moral convictions unattached to religious beliefs on this issue, and makes the unrealistic assumption that a constitutional ruling could somehow disentangle religion from future public debate on the question.

"It has also been proposed that restrictions on the woman's decision to terminate a pregnancy are unconstitutional when they reflect merely a moral, as opposed to an instrumental or utilitarian, justification [citing Henkin, supra]. But *all* normative judgments are rooted in moral premises; surely the judgment that it is wrong to kill a two-week old infant is no less 'moral' in inspiration than the judgment, less frequently made but no less strongly felt by many of those who make it, that it is wrong to kill a two-day old fetus. Archibald Cox seems correct, therefore, when he concludes that *Roe* must be wrong if it rests on the premise that a state can never interfere with individual decisions relating to sex or procreation 'with only moral justification.' It is less clear, however, that he is correct when he says that *Roe* must rest on such a premise."

Was Professor Tribe right the first time? Law, *Rethinking Sex and the Constitution*, 132 U.Pa.L.Rev. 955, 1026 n. 249 (1984), finds Tribe's grounds for rejecting his earlier views unpersuasive: "No one challenges the right of religious groups to 'express their convictions in the political process.' The first amendment protects advocacy of racism and the natural subordination of women and fetal rights, and it protects advocacy doubly when the views promoted are religiously based. [There] are undoubtedly people opposed to abortion on

h. Cf. Richards, *Constitutional Privacy, Religious Disestablishment, and the Abortion Decisions,* in *Abortion: Moral and Legal Perspectives* 148, 171–72 (Garfield & Hennessey eds. 1984): "The implicit premises" of the argument that "the fetus is in all stages of pregnancy a moral person on a par with normal persons" "surely are specifically religious or metaphysical assumptions about the fetus at all points having an individual soul: the soul requiring baptism for release from original sin (so that killing prior to birth has disastrous religious consequences for the soul); [and] the

like. [But] an argument which requires specifically religious or other assumptions to bridge the gap [between potential personhood and actual personhood], assumptions not shared by many other religious and nonreligious people * * * is exactly the kind of endorsement of nonneutral values by the state which the religion clauses forbid." See also Emerson, *The Power of Congress to Change Constitutional Decisions of the Supreme Court: The Human Life Bill,* 77 Nw.U.L.Rev. 129, 131 (1982).

grounds of 'moral conviction unattached to religious beliefs.' [But] where moral values are in such sharp conflict, the first amendment requires respect for diversity."

Does Professor Tribe underestimate the difficulty of determining which moral convictions are "attached" to religious beliefs and which are not? Are not people who hold strong religious beliefs likely to call them moral convictions? And to believe sincerely that they are moral convictions? The judgment that it is wrong to kill a two-week old child is universally held in our society, but can the same be said for the judgment that it is wrong to kill a two-day old fetus? If the latter view may properly be called a moral judgment, then what religious conviction, if any, *may not?*

If the view that it is wrong to kill a *two-week old infant* and the view that it is wrong to kill a *two-day old fetus* are *both* "moral judgments," and if the state can interfere with individual decision relating to procreation and family on the basis of a "moral justification," then why does Professor Tribe say, three pages after the passages quoted above, that "serious enforcement of a ban on abortions in the first few days of pregnancy was as unthinkable as enforcement of a ban on contraception itself"? Why can't a state regulate abortion in the first few days of pregnancy as stringently as it can pregnancy in the last trimester—or as stringently as infanticide itself? Why, in 1978, does Tribe make such short shrift of the "excessive religious-government entanglement" argument he utilized in 1973? Does *any* constitutional ruling in the church-state area *ever* disentangle religion from future public debate on the question? If not, does it follow that all the "excessive entanglement" and "political divisiveness" analyses in the church-state cases (see Ch. 5, Sec. 1, III) are unsound? Irrelevant?

9. *Does Roe reflect the same circular reasoning of the earlier substantive due process cases?* Consider JOSEPH GRANO, *Judicial Review and a Written Constitution in a Democratic Society,* 28 Wayne L.Rev. 1, 24 (1981): "*Roe* reflects the same circular reasoning and the same subjectivity that plagued the Court's earlier noninterpretivist efforts [referring to *Allgeyer* and *Lochner*].[i] The right to terminate a pregnancy can be deemed fundamental only if the fetus is not regarded as a form of life entitled to protection. No *a priori* moral principle can resolve the question of the fetus' status. By declaring the woman's right 'fundamental,' however, the Court necessarily rejected the legislative judgment that fetal life deserves protection. At this point, some might object that the Court merely concluded that public opinion was too divided to justify such a restraint on the woman's choice, but this conclusion went to the weight of the state's interest. The Court's test required that it first decide whether a fundamental right was implicated, and it could not do this, any more than it could in *Allgeyer* or *Lochner,* or any more than Justice Harlan could in *Poe v. Ullman,* without making its own moral assessment of the activity in question, an assessment not subject to demonstration by analytic reasoning."

10. *Constitutional values prohibiting abortion: a defense of Roe even assuming that the fetus is a person.* Agreeing with Professor Ely (see p. 169 infra) that "constitutional argument ought to be based on values that can be inferred from the text of the Constitution, the thinking of the Framers, or the structure of our national government," DONALD REGAN, note 4 supra, at 1618–42, maintains that such constitutional argument against laws prohibiting abortion

---

i. For extensive commentary on the "interpretivist"/"noninterpretivist" debate generated by *Roe,* see p. 166 infra.

may be made, based on three constitutional values: "non-subordination, freedom from physical invasion, and equal protection".[j]

"The non-subordination value that is implicit in the bad-samaritan principle of the common law [k] is at the core of the thirteenth amendment [which] speaks not merely of slavery, but of 'involuntary servitude.' * * * Unwilling pregnancy is not slavery in its fullest sense, [but] it certainly involves the disposition and coercion of the (intensely) personal service of one 'man' for another's benefit. The second value, freedom from physical invasion or imposed physical pain or hardship, is embodied in the eighth amendment and also plainly counts among those fundamental values of our society which are traditionally subsumed under fifth and fourteenth amendment due process. [There] is no other case, I believe, in which the law imposes comparable physical invasion and hardship as an obligation of samaritanism. * * *

"[E]ven if those parts of our tradition which forbid subordination or physical invasion have historically included an exception for abortion laws, the exception is impermissible. It creates an inequality that is inconsistent with an even more fundamental part of our tradition, reflected in the equal protection clause and the due process clause of the fifth amendment.

"[To] see the equal protection problem, we must look at abortion in a broader context. Life in society [provides] many opportunities to be a good or bad samaritan. The objection to an anti-abortion statute is that it picks out certain potential samaritans, namely women who want abortions, and treats them in a way that is at odds with the law's treatment of other potential samaritans. Women who want abortions are required to give aid in circumstances where closely analogous potential samaritans are not. And they are required to give aid of a *kind* and an *extent* that is required of no other potential samaritan.

"[I]t is important that the inequality of treatment between pregnant women and other potential samaritans touches on the constitutional values of non-subordination and freedom from physical invasion. A woman who is denied an abortion is compelled to serve the fetus and to suffer physical invasion, pain, and hardship. [That it can plausibly] be argued that the Constitution prohibits this imposition outright, [surely] means that any inequality of treatment we can point to becomes harder to justify. * * *

"Other reasons for the Court to give the abortion problem special attention are related to the suspect classification idea. Only women need abortions. [T]he one potential samaritan who is singled out for specially burdensome treatment is a potential samaritan who must, given human physiology, be female. Why is this important?

j. As Professor Regan acknowledges, his article builds on an argument made in Thomson, *A Defense of Abortion*, 1 Phil. & Pub.Aff. 47 (1971). Space limitations only permit use of a few passages from Professor Regan's 77-page article to sketch the main thrusts of his thesis.

k. At the outset of his article, id. at 1569, Professor Regan contends that "abortion should be viewed as presenting a problem in what we might call 'the law of samaritanism,' that is, the law concerning obligations imposed on certain individuals to give aid to others. It is a deeply rooted principle of American law that an individual is ordinarily not required to volunteer aid to another individual who is in danger or in need of assistance. [I]f we require a pregnant woman to carry the fetus to term and deliver it—if we forbid abortion, in other words—we are compelling her to be a Good Samaritan. [I]f we consider the special nature of the burdens imposed on pregnant women by laws forbidding abortion, we must eventually conclude that the equal protection clause forbids imposition of these burdens on pregnant women." Regan refers to "the established principle that one does not have to volunteer aid" as the "bad-samaritan principle," id. at 1572.

"First, any inequality that flows from an unchosen and unalterable characteristic is likely to be specially resented. It also works against the idea, deeply
rooted in our culture, that people ought to be masters of their own destinies, at
least within the limits of legally acceptable behavior that apply to everyone.
Since pregnancy happens only to women, and since no one has any choice about
whether to be a woman, susceptibility to pregnancy (and to being in the position
of wanting an abortion) is a nonchosen characteristic. (It is not an unalterable
characteristic, since a woman might have herself sterilized, but this method of
altering the characteristic itself involves a significant physical invasion.)

"It might be objected that even if susceptibility to pregnancy is an unchosen
characteristic, pregnancy itself is not, and that laws attaching unpleasant
consequences to pregnancy therefore do not interfere with women's controlling
their own destinies. [But] the only method of avoiding pregnancy with certainty
requires, for many people, extraordinary self-denial [and] does not, to my mind,
eliminate the force of the suggestion that pregnancy is often sufficiently 'unchosen' so that laws specially disadvantaging pregnant women limit women's
control of their lives, are justifiably resented, and deserve more-than-minimal
judicial attention.[1]

"[M]ost legislatures would defend laws against abortion on the ground that
they protect human life (or potential life). [But the] inequality between the
treatment of pregnant women and the treatment of other potential samaritans
who are not required to undertake burdens (often very much smaller burdens) in
order to save life is too great. The inequality trenches on two distinct constitutionally protected interests—the interest in non-subordination and the interest
in freedom from serious physical invasion. In addition, the inequality disadvantages a class that is defined by a non-chosen characteristic (whether sex or
unwanted pregnancy) and that has suffered from a history of discrimination.
This is more than any reasonable American legislature would tolerate. * * *

"Perhaps the greatest advantage of my argument is that it makes it possible
to avoid the question of whether the fetus is, or may be treated by the state as, a
person. Justice Blackmun claims at one point that the Court need not decide
'when life begins'. But his general argument [seems] plainly to assume that the

1. Consider MacKinnon, *Roe v. Wade: A
Study in Male Ideology,* in *Abortion: Moral
and Legal Perspectives* 45, 46–48 (Garfield &
Hennessey eds. 1984): "Feminist investigations suggest [that women do not significantly
control sex]. * * * Feminism has found
that women feel compelled to preserve the
appearance—which, acted upon, becomes the
reality—of male direction of sexual expression, as if it is male initiative itself that we
want: it is that which turns us on. Men
enforce this. It is much of what men want in
a woman. * * *

"Under these conditions, women often do
not use birth control because of its social
meaning, a meaning we did not create. Using
contraception means acknowledging and planning and taking direction of intercourse, accepting one's sexual availability, and appearing nonspontaneous. It means appearing
available to male incursions. A good user of
contraception is a bad girl. She can be presumed sexually available and, among other
consequences, raped with relative impunity.

(If you think this isn't true, you should consider rape cases in which the fact that a woman
had a diaphragm in is taken as an indication
that what happened to her was intercourse,
not rape. 'Why did you have your diaphragm
in?') * * * I wonder if a woman can be
presumed to control access to her sexuality if
she feels unable to interrupt intercourse to
insert a diaphragm; or worse, cannot even
want to, aware that she risks a pregnancy she
knows she does not want. * * * Sex doesn't
look a whole lot like freedom when it appears
normatively less costly for women to risk an
undesired, often painful, traumatic, dangerous, sometimes illegal, and potentially life-
threatening procedure, than it is to protect
oneself in advance. Yet abortion policy has
never been explicitly approached in the context of how women get pregnant; that is, as a
consequence of intercourse under conditions of
gender inequality; that is, as an issue of
forced sex."

See also Law, note 12 infra. Cf. Calabresi,
note 2 supra, at 101.

fetus is *not* a person until the point of viability (at the earliest). Indeed, Blackmun elsewhere suggests that if the fetus were a person within the meaning of the fourteenth amendment, the woman's claim to an abortion would be foreclosed by the Constitution itself.

"On the last point, I think Blackmun is mistaken. [The] people who need the assistance of potential samaritans in ordinary samaritan cases are persons under the fourteenth amendment, and yet the general common law bad-samaritan principle is not unconstitutional. (Similarly, the fact that fourteenth amendment persons are killed does not vitiate the ordinary law of self-defense.)

"[My] argument, unlike Blackmun's, does not depend on refusing to allow the state to regard the fetus as a person. Everything I have said is consistent with the assumption that the fetus is a person. Other persons are allowed to die when potential samaritans are authorized by the bad-samaritan principle to deny aid. The personhood of the fetus, even if it be conceded, is not an adequate reason (indeed it is no reason at all) for treating the pregnant woman differently from other potential samaritans.

"[M]y argument justifies more clearly than the Court's argument the Court's conclusion that abortion may not be forbidden even in the third trimester when the life or health of the mother is at stake. If the problem is ultimately one of balancing, as the Court's opinion suggests, it is not clear why the state's compelling interest (as the Court describes it) in protecting the potential life of a fetus already capable of 'meaningful life outside the mother's womb' (in the Court's phrase) is outweighed even by the woman's life, much less by her health. On my approach, however, the matter is clear. Even the reader who rejects my general conclusions must admit that there is no other case in which we would even consider requiring one individual to sacrifice his life or health to rescue another." [m]

11. *Prohibiting the government from "coercing intimate acts."* The argument that a state may not compel a pregnant woman to be "a Good Samaritan" is questioned by PHILIP BOBBITT, *Constitutional Fate* 163 (1982): "This argument seems to treat the embryonic child as a stranger who merely happens to be inconveniently placed proximate to the mother. There is much law, however, for the proposition that one owes a duty of care to one's child. This puts us back in the position of deciding when a child's life begins, a position the *Roe* Court was doctrinally forced to take in its argument despite its disclaimers and one which sound constitutional decision ought to avoid completely." Professor Bobbitt proposes a somewhat different "ethical argument [that] avoids the necessity for this determination" and one that "would decide *Roe*" (id. at 160–65):

"Government may not coerce intimate acts. Stated generally, does anyone really doubt this? * * * Whatever else may be an intimate act, carrying a child within one's body and giving birth must be a profoundly intimate act. * * * Who was Jane Roe? Perhaps a fuller record would have strengthened the case for the ethical approach I have advocated and would have made the ethical aspects of coercion and intimacy all the more forceful. [She] was an unskilled, young white woman. She was also a lesbian. She had become

m. See also Calabresi, note 2 supra, at 102–06. For criticism of Regan's argument, see Alexander, *Modern Equal Protection Theories: A Metatheoretical Taxonomy and Critique,* 42 Ohio St.L.J. 3, 40–42 n. 114 (1981). See also Bobbitt, note 11 infra; Davis, *Abor-* *tion and Self-Defense,* in *Abortion: Moral and Legal Perspectives* 186 (Garfield & Hennessey eds. 1984) (hereinafter referred to as *"Abortion"*); P. Foot, *Killing and Letting Die,* in *Abortion* 175, 184–85; Michaels, *Abortion and the Claims of Samaritanism,* in *Abortion* 213.

pregnant through rape. By the time of the [Supreme Court] argument, she had already terminated her pregnancy. [N]o fetus was left to protect. It is an extreme claim to hold that the state should have prosecuted her and sent her to prison because she had refused to wholly and forever choose the most intimate of human experiences."

12. *"Privacy" or "sex equality"? The "sex-specific impact" of laws restricting abortion.* "Nothing the Supreme Court has ever done," observes SYLVIA LAW, note 8 supra, at 981, "has been more concretely important for women [than the decision in *Roe*]. Laws denying access to abortion have a sex-specific impact. Although both men and women seek to control reproduction, only women become pregnant. Only women have abortions. Laws restricting access to abortion have a devastating sex-specific impact. Despite the decision's overwhelming importance to women, it was not grounded on the principle of sex equality. The plaintiffs [in *Roe* and *Doe*] had not challenged the abortion restrictions as sex discriminatory." Continues Professor Law (id. at 1020, 1028):

"The rhetoric of privacy, as opposed to equality, blunts our ability to focus on the fact that it is *women* who are oppressed when abortion is denied. [The] rhetoric of privacy also reinforces a public/private dichotomy that is at the heart of the structures that perpetuate the powerlessness of women. [T]he drive to criminalize abortion is animated by an affirmation of the value of a patriarchal society. [But] application of the constitutional ideal of equality to men and women prohibits the state from using its coercive power to enforce patriarchal relations. [The] high place of equality in our constellation of democratic and constitutional values demands that something more compelling than traditionalist moral conviction justify state actions denying women that which is indispensably necessary to their ability to act as moral beings and to participate in civil society. If and when it becomes technologically possible to grow children outside of a woman's body, the moral and constitutional issues we confront in relation to abortion will be categorically different than they are today. But for today, reproductive freedom is, inescapably, the core issue of women's equality and liberty." [n]

13. *In Roe did the woman patient take a back seat to the male physician?* In *Roe*, maintains ANDREA ASARO, *The Judicial Portrayal of the Physician in Abortion and Sterilization Decisions*, 6 Harv. Women's L.J. 51, 53–55 (1983), Justice Blackmun "subsumed the woman's right to privacy within the ambit of the doctor-patient relationship, and ultimately subordinated her interest to the physician's. [For] Blackmun, the key issue was quite simply one of medical discretion, in other words: '[F]or the period of pregnancy prior to the "compelling" point, the attending physician, in consultation with his patient, is free to determine [that], in his medical judgment, the patient's pregnancy should be terminated.' Interestingly, the abortion decision is characterized here neither as primarily the woman's nor as fundamentally or initially a moral or personal one. Blackmun's perspective is clinical, and the woman patient has taken a back seat to the male physician-protagonist. [Concluding] his *Roe* opinion by summarizing the impact of the decision on the state and on the physician [Justice Blackmun states]: '[The] decision vindicates the right of the physician to administer medical treatment according to his professional judgment up to the points where important state interests provide compelling justifications for intervention. Up to these points, *the abortion decision in all its aspects is inherently, and*

---

n. See also Ginsburg, fn. f. supra, at 382–86; Karst, *Foreword: Equal Citizenship Under the Fourteenth Amendment*, 91 Harv.L. Rev. 1, 57–59 (1977).

primarily, a medical decision, and basic responsibility for it must rest with the physician. * * *' ° Blackmun has neglected even to mention the pregnant woman as party to the abortion decision! The state, the physician, and the court have displaced Ms. Roe altogether." P

14. *Protection of the viable fetus.* Did *Roe* assume that the mother's interest in her life or health predominates over the identical interests of the viable fetus? If so, why? Should the interests of mother and viable fetus be weighed equally in resolving conflicts between them? If, for example, continued pregnancy threatens a mother's life or health at a time when her unborn child is viable, should we first consider separating them by a procedure designed to minimize the risks to both? Answering in the affirmative is King, *The Juridical Status of the Fetus: A Proposal for Legal Protection of the Unborn,* 77 Mich.L. Rev. 1647, 1682–89 (1979). She concludes, id. at 1687: "[W]hether the fetus is a 'person' is irrelevant to whether it should have legal protection.q [The] juridical status of developing humans has historically depended upon their capacity for a separate and independent existence. [Revising that traditional understanding in the context of greater scientific knowledge], capacity to have independent existence points to viability instead of birth as the determinative moment in development. [V]iable fetuses merit all protection currently given the newborn infant." r

But consider Comment, 27 U.C.L.A.L.Rev. 1340, 1348 n. 45 (1980): "Professor King's proposal that "the competing interests in the life of the viable fetus and the pregnant [be] balanced on an issue-by-issue basis" "implies that the viable fetus has constitutional rights at least equivalent to those of the pregnant woman. It is in direct conflict with *Roe.* If adopted, the proposal would create a deterrent against carrying a pregnancy to term even to the woman who wants her child as well as to the child's father, because after fetal viability there would be no guarantee that in the case of a contest between the life of the unborn child and the pregnant woman, the woman's life would prevail."

Given *Roe's* acceptance of the state's interest in protecting "potential life," does the constitutional right recognized in *Roe* encompass the right to have the fetus destroyed? Consider Tribe, *Toward a Model of Roles in the Due Process of Life and Law,* 87 Harv.L.Rev. 1, 4 n. 24 (1973): "Since the procedures for removal of a viable fetus typically present the same risks to the woman whether the fetus is saved or destroyed, it seems questionable that the Court actually intended to mandate a choice in favor of the latter. The only situations in which a justification for such a choice could be plausibly advanced would be those involving a troublesome deference to the woman's desire to preserve her mental health by assuring that the unwanted fetus be killed."

o. Emphasis added by Ms. Asaro.

p. See also Law, note 12 supra, at 1020.

q. Cf. *Ely,* fn. c supra, at 926: "[T]he argument that fetuses lack constitutional rights is simply irrelevant. For it has never been held or even asserted that the state interest needed to justify forcing a person to refrain from an activity, *whether or not that activity is constitutionally protected,* must implicate either the life or the constitutional rights of another person. Dogs are not 'persons in the whole sense' nor have they constitutional rights, but that does not mean the state cannot prohibit killing them: It does not even mean the state

cannot prohibit killing them in the exercise of the First Amendment right of political protest. Come to think of it, draft cards aren't persons either [referring to *United States v. O'Brien* (p. 515 infra)]."

What Professor Ely's argument overlooks, maintains Comment, 29 U.C.L.A.L.Rev. 1194, 1205 (1982), "is that if the fetus is not a separate human being, then it is a part of the woman's body. This is not true of [dogs and] draft cards. [A] law that forbids the destruction of draft cards [does] not impinge upon the right of privacy with respect to procreation."

r. See fn. c to the *Roe* opinion.

Are there other plausible reasons for the woman's desire to have the unwanted fetus destroyed? If "mental and physical health may be taxed by child care," may she also wish to avoid the economic burden of sustaining the viable fetus (or is "prematurely born child" the more accurate term?) until other people (or the state) assume this burden? Does *Roe* obligate the state to assume the financial burden at once? In respect to these issues what is the significance of the fact that, although "the project would be expensive, [with] improved techniques and equipment, going beyond the incubator towards the artificial womb, probably the vast majority of fetuses could survive apart from their mother after 12 or 14 weeks of pregnancy"? Note, 7 U.C.Davis L.Rev. 432, 451 (1974).

If the woman's right in *Roe* does not encompass destruction of the viable fetus, may the state require a pregnant woman to submit to blood transfusions where necessary to "save the life" of the viable fetus? See King, supra, at 1683. If it could be demonstrated that the intake of alcohol or drugs during pregnancy is likely to harm the fetus, could the state prohibit a pregnant woman from drinking or taking drugs? See id. at 1682. If the woman's right in *Roe* does not encompass destruction of the viable fetus, to what extent does (should) it oblige the pregnant woman to delay abortion until viability? See Vieira, *Roe and Doe: Substantive Due Process and the Right of Abortion*, 25 Hast.L.J. 867, 875 (1974).

15. *Roe and the Court's attitudes toward federalism.* "[T]he Court's decisions in the sex discrimination cases and those involving childbearing," observes Sandalow, *Federalism and Social Change*, 43 Law & Contemp. Prob. 35, 38 (1980) "offer an important perspective [on] the Court's attitude toward federalism during the past decade. [The] Court's failure to concede any role to the states in mediating the conflicts generated by the most important social change of the decade—indeed, its seeming unawareness that the denial of such a role required justification or even comment—is a remarkable demonstration of the extent to which a unitary system of government has evolved in the United States. The Burger Court is not responsible for that development, but its decisions have confirmed it in much the same way that the actions of the Eisenhower Administration confirmed the New Deal. [T]he Court's response to the most important legal issues arising during the past decade demonstrates how deeply embedded the assumption has become that the nation, not the states, is responsible for responding to important issues of social change."

16. *The "peculiar nature" of the Burger Court's activism.* Unlike the Warren Court, which was "fired by a vision of the equal dignity of man" and whose justices' doctrinal compromises "took place against a background in which the direction of constitutional development was both clear and, to many, inspiring," observes VINCENT BLASI, *The Rootless Activism of the Burger Court*, in *The Burger Court: The Counter-Revolution that Wasn't* 198, 212–13 (V. Blasi ed. 1983), the *Roe* justices "could not plausibly justify their decision as the working out of a theme implicit in several previous decisions, still less as the vindication of values deeply embedded in the nation's constitutional tradition. The Court's opinion in *Roe* is best characterized as an ad hoc comparison of material interests: the woman has an interest in avoiding the physical and psychological burdens of an unwanted pregnancy and childbirth; the state has an interest in protecting the woman's health and the potentiality of life represented by the fetus. Grounded not on principle but on contingent considerations, these interests either grow or diminish during the course of the pregnancy, and in fact change as technological developments alter the capacity to sustain a fetus outside the womb. No effort was made in the *Roe* opinion to relate the woman's

burdens to more general conceptions of choice-making capacity, bodily integrity, nonsubordination to other human beings, or equality of treatment. Similarly, no effort was made to assess the state's claim to regulate in terms of the much mooted dispute over whether government is entitled to enforce moral precepts.

"[T]he peculiar nature of the Burger Court's activism can be seen from the fact that even so fundamental an issue as abortion was treated by this Court as a conflict of particularized, material interests—a conflict that could be resolved by accommodating those interests in the spirit of compromise. Thus, third trimester abortions can be prohibited but earlier abortions cannot. The state cannot prohibit all abortions outright, but can refuse to fund them [see *Maher v. Roe* and *Harris v. McRae,* infra], even while funding the alternative of childbirth and thereby encouraging pregnant women to forgo the abortion option. The woman's husband cannot veto her choice to have an abortion [*Planned Parenthood v. Danforth,* infra] but a minor's parents can do so under certain limited circumstances. These doctrinal lines are not necessarily incoherent. But each has in fact taken on a highly arbitrary character because in grappling with the issues that followed in *Roe*'s wake, the justices were unable to draw upon any sort of theory, or vision, or even framework for determining the contours of the right they had recognized. Each variation on the abortion issue was treated by the Court as an isolated, practical problem."

ROE v. WADE AND THE DEBATE IT STIRRED OVER "INTERPRETIVIST"/"NONINTERPRETIVIST" CONSTITUTIONAL DECISIONMAKING [a]

1. Consider Lupu, *Constitutional Theory and the Search for the Workable Premise,* 8 Dayton L.Rev. 579, 583 (1983): "*Roe* clarified, as had no other case

a. Although the materials in this section inevitably overlap to some extent with the preceding set of Notes & Questions, it seems useful to focus separately on the general constitutional debate generated by the 1973 *Abortion Cases.*

"Interpretivism" indicates that "judges deciding constitutional issues should confine themselves to enforcing norms that are stated or clearly implicit in the written Constitution"; "noninterpretivism" indicates that "courts should go beyond that set of references and enforce norms that cannot be discovered within the four corners of the document." Ely, *Democracy and Distrust* 1 (1980). "What distinguishes interpretivism from its opposite is its insistence that the work of the political branches is to be invalidated only in accord with an inference whose starting point, whose underlying premise, is fairly discoverable in the Constitution. That the complete inference will not be found there—because the situation is not likely to have been foreseen—is general common ground." Id. at 1–2.

"Noninterpretivism," comments Van Alstyne, *Interpretations of the First Amendment* 94 n. 27 (1984), "signals a frank resolve to detach judicial review from the Constitution itself by stipulating it purports not to be interpreting the Constitution. It may say too

much about the current condition of constitutional scholarship that 'noninterpretivism' is willingly adopted as a mode of describing one's own work in constitutional law. If there were not writers who evidently welcome its fit, e.g., Perry, *Noninterpretive Review in Human Rights Cases: A Functional Justification,* 56 N.Y.U.L.Rev. 278 (1981), one might have supposed that its use was limited and purely pejorative * * *." But compare Professor Perry's early writings with his most recent article, *The Authority of Text, Tradition, and Reason: A Theory of Constitutional "Interpretation,"* 58 S.Cal.L.Rev. 551 (1985).

As might be expected, there is disagreement over the appropriate terminology. Dean Bennett prefers the term "originalists" to describe those who "argue that constitutional language, understood in light of the substantive intentions or values behind its enactment, is the sole proper source for constitutional interpretation," because this term "better captures the static pretense of the approach that seems to me to be its principal flaw." Bennett, *Objectivity in Constitutional Law,* 132 U.Pa.L. Rev. 445, 446 & n. 3 (1984). "On the other side of the debate are 'noninterpretivists' or 'nonoriginalists' who believe it is legitimate for judges to look beyond text and original intention in interpreting constitutional lansince World War II, the Supreme Court's willingness to reach results which no defensible interpretivist position could support. Although rhetorically tied to the meaning of 'liberty' in the fourteenth amendment due process clause, and loosely aligned with the penumbral analysis developed in *Griswold, Roe* cut fundamental rights adjudication loose from the constitutional text. [There followed] a vast array of doctrinal, methodological, and theoretical inquiries into the outcome in *Roe.* More or less detached from the case itself, these scholarly efforts offered a variety of justifications for noninterpretive review—natural law underpinings of the 1787 Constitution,[25] transplantation of common law method into constitutional adjudication,[26] the search for enduring or traditional unwritten norms,[27] [and] judicial manifestation of consensus morality." [28]

2. Ely, *Democracy and Distrust* 2–3 (1980), suggests why "interpretivism may be entering a period of comparative popularity": The first is that *Roe,* "the clearest example of noninterpretivist 'reasoning' [in] four decades," "forced all of

guage," but they "are divided on what particular sources should replace or supplement originalist sources and on how to justify their use." Id. at 446.

"There are some legal theorists," observes Fiss, *Objectivity and Interpretation,* 34 Stan.L. Rev. 739, 743 (1982), "who would limit legal interpretation to highly specific constitutional clauses. This school, misleadingly called 'interpretivism,' [should] more properly [be] called 'textual determinism' * * *. For an interpretivist only a specific text can be interpreted. Interpretation is thus confused with execution—the application of a determinate meaning to a situation—and is unproblematic only with regard to clauses like that requiring the president to be at least 35 years old. Most interpretivists, including Justice Black, would recognize the narrowness of such a perspective and want to acknowledge a role for less specific clauses, like freedom of speech; but in truth such provisions are hardly obvious in their meaning and require substantial judicial interpretation to be given their proper effect."

Grey, *Do We Have an Unwritten Constitution?,* 27 Stan.L.Rev. 703 (1975), probably originated the use of the "interpretivist-noninterpretivist" terminology, but he now thinks these labels "distort the debate": "If the current interest in interpretive theory [does] nothing else, at least it shows that the concept of interpretation is broad enough to encompass any plausible mode of constitutional adjudication. We are all interpretivists; the real arguments are not over whether judges should stick to interpreting, but over what they should interpret and what interpretive attitudes they should adopt. Repenting past errors, I will therefore use the less misleading labels 'textualists' and 'supplementers' for, respectively, those who consider the text the sole legitimate source of operative norms in constitutional adjudication, and those who accept supplementary sources of constitutional law [such as 'conventional morality']." Grey, *The Constitution as Scripture,* 37 Stan.L.Rev. 1 (1984).

Professor Grey notes the emergence in recent years of a third group of constitutional theorists, id. at 1–2, those "who reject the very question ('text alone, or text plus supplement?') to which textualists and supplementers propose different answers. According to these 'rejectionists,' judges are always interpreting the constitutional text, but this is not the kind of significant constraint on judicial activism that textualists think it is—the text, if read with an appropriately generous notion of context, provides as lively a Constitution as the most activist judge might need."

See also Sandalow, *Constitutional Interpretation,* 79 Mich.L.Rev. 1033, 1045–46 (1981): "[A]ll the decisions shaping constitutional law to contemporary values [can] be understood as coming within the general intentions of the framers. All that is necessary is to state those intentions at a sufficiently high level of abstraction. [By] wrenching the framers' 'larger purposes' from the particular judgments that revealed them, we incur a loss of perspective, a perspective that might better enable us to see that the particular judgments they made were not imperfect expressions of a larger purpose but a particular accommodation of competing purposes. In freeing ourselves from those judgments we are not serving larger ends determined by the framers but making room for the introduction of contemporary values."

25. See Grey, note 9 infra.

26. See, e.g., Brest, *The Misconceived Quest for the Original Understanding,* 60 B.U.L.Rev. 204 (1980); Michelman, *Constancy to an Ideal Object,* 56 N.Y.U.L.Rev. 406 (1981); Wellington, *Common Law Rules and Constitutional Double Standards,* 83 Yale L.J. 221 (1973).

27. See, e.g., Lupu, note 10 infra.

28. See, e.g., Perry, *Abortion, the Public Morals, and the Police Power,* 23 U.C.L.A.L. Rev. 689 (1976). [But cf. Perry, *The Authority of Text, Tradition, and Reason: A Theory of Constitutional "Interpretation,"* 58 S.Cal.L. Rev. 551 (1985).]

us who work in the area to think about which camp we fall into, with the result that a number of persons would today label themselves interpretivists who had not previously given the choice much notice. The second may be that, *Roe* notwithstanding, the Burger Court is by and large a politically conservative Court—or at least more conservative than its predecessor. This means that observers who might earlier have been content to let the justices enforce their own values (or their rendition of society's values) are now somewhat uneasy about doing so and are more likely to pursue an interpretivist line, casting their lot with the values of the framers."

3. Consider JOSEPH GRANO, *Judicial Review and a Written Constitution in a Democratic Society*, 28 Wayne L.Rev. 1, 25, 59 (1981): [An objection to criticisms of *Roe*] might be that the Court's poor choice of methodology is not a valid argument against noninterpretivism. The truth, however, is that the Court's methodology is basically all there is. Noninterpretivism is a methodology of *fundamental* rights, [for] no one maintains that the judiciary should require "compelling" reasons for all laws, including those that prohibit swindling or murder. Noninterpretivism's first requirement is that the judiciary separate that which is fundamental from that which is not, and it is this very task that requires the judiciary to take normative and moral positions that cannot be demonstrated.

"[*Roe*] is as wrong as the proposed constitutional amendment to protect the fetus, and for the same reason: it seeks to bind succeeding generations to our generation's thinking, or at least to the thinking of a segment of it. Through the Supreme Court, our generation has dictated to future generations that they can prohibit abortions only by mustering the requisite super-majority to amend the Constitution. Again, we have no way of being sure that subsequent generations will not express revulsion at our morality on this issue. *Roe* is just one example of judicial noninterpretivism, a methodology that permits the judiciary to decide the difficult moral issues of our time under the rubric of constitutional law. Whether the issue be abortion, the right of the family or unrelated individuals to share living quarters,[c] [or] the right to a greater share of the wealth, every noninterpretivist decision recognizing one of these claims adds, in effect, a new provision to the written constitution and thereby imposes an additional moral restraint on subsequent generations. Every such decision assumes that if the moral position taken is not the last word, it nevertheless is presumptively correct and should bind our successors unless they can obtain the necessary super-majority to amend the Constitution.[267]"

---

c. See *Moore v. East Cleveland*, discussed at length infra.

267. Noninterpretivism is sometimes defended by positing horribles that only noninterpretivism can correct. Professor Karst, for example, invited us to imagine legislation prohibiting marriage: "All would agree—even Justice Rehnquist, I suppose—that an arbitrary denial by the state of the freedom to marry would violate the Fourteenth Amendment." Karst, *The Freedom of Intimate Association*, 89 Yale L.J. 624, 667 (1980). Thus, extremely confident, Karst concluded, "*Of course* there is a right to marry." Id. [I] am quite certain I do not agree. I cannot conceive of a legislature prohibiting marriage, but the reason is that I cannot foresee the circumstances that would prompt such legislation. Presumably, however, such a decision would occur only after some event convinced a majority or supermajority of the population that marriage should be banned. Assuming such a society (again, one we cannot really conceive), it cannot be obvious that such a ban should be struck down as unconstitutional. "Ah!," you answer, "but suppose the legislature passes such a law without popular support?" Anyone who believes that noninterpretivism or anything else in constitutional law, or in any other law, can safeguard society from such a legislature is welcome to his views, for I have nothing further to say to such a person. Cf. J. Ely, *Democracy and Distrust* 182 (1980) (discussing hypothetical law banning gall bladder operations) * * *.

4. *Are the Abortion Cases "bad constitutional law" or "not constitutional law"?* Consider JOHN ELY, *The Wages of Crying Wolf: A Comment on Roe v. Wade,* 82 Yale L.J. 920, 935–37, 939, 943, 947–49 (1973): "What is unusual about *Roe* is that the liberty involved is accorded [a] protection more stringent [than] that the present Court accords the freedom of the press explicitly guaranteed by the First Amendment. What is frightening about *Roe* is that this super-protected right is not inferable from the language of the Constitution, the framers' thinking respecting the specific problem in issue, any general value derivable from the provisions they included, or the nation's governmental structure. Nor is it explainable in terms of the unusual political impotence of the group judicially protected vis-á-vis the interest that legislatively prevailed over it.[d] And [that] is a charge that can responsibly be leveled at no other decision of the past twenty years. At times the inferences the Court has drawn from the values the Constitution marks for special protection have been controversial, even shaky, but never before has its sense of an obligation to draw one been so obviously lacking.

"[The] problem with *Roe* is not so much that it bungles the question it sets itself, but rather that it sets itself a question the Constitution has not made the Court's business. It *looks* different from *Lochner*—it has the shape if not the substance of a judgment that is very much the Court's business, one vindicating an interest the Constitution marks as special—and it is for that reason perhaps more dangerous. Of course in a sense it is more candid than *Lochner*. But the employment of a higher standard of judicial review, no matter how candid the recognition that it is indeed higher, loses some of its admirability when it is accompanied by neither a coherent account of why such a standard is appropriate nor any indication of why it has not been satisfied.

"[*Roe* is] a very bad decision. Not because it will perceptibly weaken the Court—it won't; and not because it conflicts with either my idea of progress or what the evidence suggests is society's—it doesn't. It is bad because it is bad constitutional law, or rather because it is *not* constitutional law and gives almost no sense of an obligation to try to be. [The] point that often gets lost in the commentary, and obviously got lost in *Roe*, is that *before* the Court can get to the

---

d. Elsewhere in his article, id. at 933–35, Professor Ely argues that Justice Stone's suggestion in his famous *Carolene Products* footnote that the Court provide extraordinary constitutional protection for " 'discrete and insulate minorities' unable to form effective political alliances" does not apply to *Roe*: "Compared with men, very few women sit in our legislatures, [but] *no* fetuses sit [there]. Of course they have their champions, but so have women. The two interests have clashed repeatedly in the political arena, and had continued to do so up to the date of [*Roe*], generating quite a wide variety of accommodations. [Justice Stone's suggestion] was clearly intended and should be reserved for those interests which, as compared with the interests to which they have been subordinated, constitute minorities usually incapable of protecting themselves. Compared with men, women may constitute such a 'minority'; compared with the unborn, they do not."

Professor Ely's challenge of the appropriateness of judicial intervention in *Roe* "is mis-

guided, however," maintains Bennett, *Abortion and Judicial Review,* 75 Nw.U.L.Rev. 978, 995–96 n. 71 (1981), "because it assumes that fetuses are political actors—indeed a political minority—whose 'powerlessness' is relevant to assessing the Court's appropriate role in the abortion controversy. Each political system must define, explicitly or implicitly, the universe of relevant political actors. [But] outside the abortion context there are no indications that fetuses are considered relevant political actors. [E]ven within the context of abortion-related issues, the suggestion that fetuses are a part of the larger political community appears, as in Ely's formulation, only incidentally and as part of the abortion discussion. It is, of course, possible for a legislature to take into account interests outside its own political community. [But] with fetuses, as with other interests outside the relevant universe of political actors, the legislative process can only take them into account insofar as relevant political actors subsume those interests into their own."

'balancing' stage, *before* it can worry about the next case and the case after that (or even about its institutional position) it is under an obligation to trace its premises to the charter from which it derives its authority. A neutral and durable principal may be a thing of beauty and joy forever. But if it lacks connection with any value the Constitution marks as special, it is not a constitutional principle and the Court has no business imposing it."[e]

5. *Is it a question of "inventing" a new right, or of the state having to justify an invasion of liberty?* Consider the remarks of Professor Tribe in Choper, Kamisar & Tribe, *The Supreme Court: Trends and Developments 1982-83* (1984) at 215: "[The *Roe* Court] is said to have invented the right to abortion. [To quote Professor Ely], *Roe* was not just *bad* constitutional law, it was not constitutional law at all. I have never found it easy to understand what that criticism means in this context. Once one concedes that the word 'liberty' has substantive content in its application against the states through the Fourteenth Amendment—and it must, if any substantive provisions of the Bill of Rights are to be enforced against the states through the Fourteenth Amendment—it becomes not a question of inventing a new right, but of asking what the justification is for a state intrusion into what is indisputably an aspect of someone's personal liberty."

6. *"The Constitution" vs. "the original Constitution."* "[H]ow," asks Michelman, *Commentary* (panel discussion), 56 N.Y.U.L.Rev. 525, 532 (1981), "is it arguably an offense or violation of the Constitution for the New York legislature to do what it did in *Lochner* or for a state legislature to criminalize abortion? [M]y answer to that question is: There is no argument that I can see to the effect that those statutes violate the original Constitution. The argument has to be that they violate the Constitution—meaning the original Constitution with all the interpretive precedents that have arisen in the course of the judicial attempt to carry out the office of the Court, which is to decide hard cases under the Constitution when they arise."

7. *Should the legitimacy of Roe be debated in terms of "institutional continuity"?* "It is plausible," maintains ROBERT BENNETT, *Objectivity in Constitutional Law,* 132 U.Pa.L.Rev. 445, 486 (1984), to see prior decisions protecting the interests of adults with regard to procreation and those of parents with regard to children "as opening a future that could accommodate *Roe.* To be sure *Roe* did require a value judgment beyond those captured by prior decisions. In that respect the case was no more unusual than *Yick Wo v. Hopkins* (1886) [p. 1169 infra] [applicability of fourteenth amendment equal protection to discriminatory administration of ordinance against resident Chinese aliens] or hundreds of other constitutional cases, except perhaps that the judgment required was a particularly wrenching one.

"My point is not that *Roe* was rightly decided, but that the debate about whether the Supreme Court could legitimately invalidate laws prohibiting abortion is often misconceived. Viewed as a question of judicial objectivity, the legitimacy of *Roe* turns not on whether there is some authoritative basis on which the Court can substitute its value judgment for that of the legislature but on whether the Court can successfully define its opinion as a natural outgrowth of what it has received. [The legitimacy of *Roe*] should be debated in terms of institutional continuity and of its substantive merits and not by reference to one

e. See also Forrester, *Are We Ready for Truth in Judging?,* 63 A.B.A.J. 1212 (1977); Lusky, *By What Right?* 14, 16–17, 20 (1975); Monaghan, *The Constitution Goes to Harvard,* 13 Harv.Civ.Rts.-Civ.Lib.L.Rev. 116, 131 (1978); Posner, *The Uncertain Protection of Privacy in the Supreme Court,* 1979 Sup.Ct. Rev. 173, 199–200.

or another dubious and inevitably incomplete standard of authoritativeness. In contrast to *Roe,* the state legislative apportionment cases, favorites of Ely, seem much less justifiable in terms of institutional continuity." [f]

8. *Why noninterpretive review is a "necessary postulate" for constitutional adjudication.* Consider ROBERT SEDLER, *The Legitimacy Debate in Constitutional Adjudication,* 44 Ohio St.L.J. 110, 118–19, 122 (1983): "[T]he Court apparently believes that it is acting legitimately as long as it looks to the text or internal inferences of the Constitution as the starting point for its constitutional decisions. The Court likewise apparently believes that it is acting legitimately when, in the process of defining broadly phrased and open-ended limitations on governmental power contained in the Constitution, it goes beyond values purportedly constitutionalized by the framers. It has not looked to these criteria as the sole or even the primary source of meaning for the Constitution or for its application to particular situations at a much later time in the Nation's history. The Court has not viewed interpretive review as a tenable methodology for determining the meaning and application of the Constitution. Rather, it has viewed noninterpretive review as a necessary postulate for constitutional adjudication under the Constitution. The Court, therefore, has engaged in noninterpretive review throughout its history, convinced that its actions were legitimate and consistent with the Court's function under our constitutional system. [The] meaning of a constitutional provision develops incrementally, and that provision's line of growth strongly influences its application in particular cases.[167] The framework within which constitutional decision making has operated, then, is a significant constraint on the results that the Court will reach when it is engaged in that decision making.

"[The] argument that noninterpretive review is fully supportive of constitutional governance established by the Constitution proceeds as follows: (1) The overriding principle in the structure of constitutional governance established by the Constitution is the limitation on governmental power. (2) Many of the limitations on governmental power designed to protect individual rights that are contained in the Constitution are broadly phrased and open ended, and these majestic generalities directed toward the protection of individual rights are a part of our constitutional tradition.[g] (3) Since many of the limitations on

---

f. See also the remarks of Tribe, note 5 supra, at 215–16.

167. * * *[B]y the time the Court decided *Roe,* constitutional protection for reproductive freedom had been firmly established. [I]t would not have been inconsistent with the line of growth of constitutional protection for reproductive freedom for the Court to have held that the asserted governmental interest in protecting potential human life was constitutionally more important than the woman's interest in reproductive freedom. [But] because the Court had previously held that reproductive freedom is entitled to constitutional protection, the holding in *Roe,* extending that protection to the abortion decision, was fully consistent with the line of growth of constitutional protection for reproductive freedom.

g. "But," maintains Monaghan, *Commentary* (panel discussion), 56 N.Y.U.L.Rev. 525, 526 (1981), "the Constitution doesn't contain generalities. The due process clause and the

ninth amendment in my judgment are judge-made and commentator-made generalities. Take the phrase 'due process of law.' If there was ever a phrase that had a fixed, certain meaning when it was introduced in the Constitution and adopted in 1868, it was that phrase. It was the judges who transformed it into a general license to review the substance of legislation. * * * Let's assume that the Constitution contains some generalities like freedom of speech and let's assume that you are going to need a Hercules to interpret such provisions. Even if that Hercules has to rely on some external political theory, which can't be fairly related or thought to underlie the constitutional text, at least the first amendment is a stopping point: it limits the subjects about which judges ought to be concerned. But take the question of abortion. There's nothing in the constitutional text or in its history to 'constitutionalize.' Nor is the theory that would authorize review containable."

governmental power contained in the Constitution are broadly phrased and open ended, these limitations cannot be fully operable in contemporary society as a limitation on governmental power if their meaning is determined solely or even primarily by referring to values purportedly constitutionalized by the framers at an earlier time. (4) Therefore, given items (1) and (3) above, noninterpretive review is not only legitimate, but is also a necessary postulate for constitutional adjudication under our constitutional system."

9. *The "pure interpretive model" of constitutional adjudication vs. adjudication going beyond the norms implicit in text and original history.* Consider THOMAS GREY, *Do We Have an Unwritten Constitution?* 27 Stan.L.Rev. 703 (1975), who rejects the view that constitutional adjudication must rest on values derived by normal process of textual interpretation from the written Constitution—what he calls "the pure interpretive model"—as too narrow to capture the full scope of legitimate judicial review. He maintains, id. at 710–14, that "numerous and important substantive constitutional doctrines" would seem "unjustified under a consistently applied pure interpretive model of judicial review. First and most obvious is virtually the entire body of doctrine developed under the due process clauses of the 5th and 14th amendments. If those clauses can be seen as having any specific normative content attributable to their framers, it is probably only that given to them by Mr. Justice Black. In his view, due process requires only that deprivations of life, liberty or property be authorized by law duly enacted, rather than carried out by arbitrary executive action.

"[W]hat many regard as the core of due process doctrine—its flexible requirement of 'fundamentally fair' procedures in criminal and civil proceedings—cannot be reconciled with the interpretive model. These doctrines are developments of the 'living constitution' concept *par excellence.* [A] striking point often overlooked by contemporary interpretivists [who most often focus their attack on 'substantive due process'] is that the demise of substantive due process must constitutionally free the federal government to engage in explicit racial discrimination. There is no textual warrant for reading into the due process clause of the fifth amendment any of the prohibitions directed against the states by the equal protection clause [see Ch. 11, fn. a to Introductory Note].

"Equally strikingly, the application of the provisions of the Bill of Rights to the states cannot be justified under an interpretive model—unless one strains to accept, as the Court clearly has declined to do, the flimsy historical evidence that the framers of the 14th amendment intended this result. Freedom of speech, freedom of religion, and the requirement of just compensation in the taking of property, as well as the procedural provisions of the fourth, fifth, sixth, and eighth amendments must then no longer be seen as federal constitutional restraints on state power.

"All of the 'fundamental interests' that trigger 'strict scrutiny' under the equal protection clause would have to be discarded, if the interpretive model were to control constitutional adjudication. [If] the values implicit in the equal protection clause are limited only to those that its framers intended at the time of enactment, the clause clearly does not speak to questions of eligibility for the franchise or of legislative apportionment.

"[I]t should be clear that an extraordinarily radical purge of established constitutional doctrine would be required if we candidly and consistently applied the pure interpretive model. Surely that makes out at least a prima facie practical case against the model. Conservatives ought to be cautious about adopting any abstract premise which requires so drastic a change in accepted practice, and liberals presumably will be dismayed by the prospect of any major diminution in the courts' authority to protect basic human rights."

Professor Grey also suggests an "affirmative justification" for judicial review that "goes beyond interpretation" (id. at 715–17): "For the generation that framed the Constitution, the concept of a 'higher law,' protecting 'natural rights,' and taking precedence over ordinary positive law as a matter of political obligation, was widely shared and deeply felt. An essential element of American constitutionalism was the reduction to written form—and hence to positive law—of some of the principles of natural rights. But at the same time, it was generally recognized that written constitutions could not completely codify the higher law. Thus in the framing of the original American constitutions it was widely accepted that there remained unwritten but still binding principles of higher law. The ninth amendment is the textual expression of this idea in the federal Constitution.[h]

"[The] intellectual framework against which [constitutional rights clearly not derived by textual interpretation, such as the right of privacy, the right to vote, and the right to travel,] have developed is different from the natural-rights tradition of the founding fathers—its rhetorical reference points are the Anglo-American tradition and basic American ideals, rather than human nature, the social contract, or the rights of man. But it is the modern offspring, in a direct and traceable line of legitimate descent, of the natural-rights tradition that is so deeply embedded in our constitutional origins."[i]

10. *The "ethical function of judicial review"; "consensus" or "conventional morality"; "deeply embedded" values.* MICHAEL PERRY, *Abortion, the Public Morals, and the Police Power: The Ethical Function of Substantive Due Process,* 23 U.C.L.A.L.Rev. 689, 694 (1976), maintains that "the police power is limited, inherently, to pursuit of the 'public welfare,' and that the restrictive abortion legislation struck down in *Roe* transgressed this limit." Consider id. at 720–21, 726–27, 733–35: "There is little practical difference between giving specific content to a vague, textually based norm by referring to culturally shared ethical ideals, and giving specific content to a textually based, but essentially normless limit, such as 'ordered liberty,' or the 'public welfare,' by referring to culturally shared ideals. Put another way, the difference between the ethical function of judicial review implicit in the notion of textually based but organic norms and the ethical function implicit in the concept of the public welfare limit is less a difference of kind than of degree. And even the difference of degree is slight. Both ethical functions—or more precisely, both variations on the ethical function—involve the transformation of culturally shared ethical ideals and sensibilities into judicially enforceable constitutional constraints.

h. But consider Monaghan, *Our Perfect Constitution,* 56 N.Y.U.L.Rev. 353, 366–67 (1981): "[Like the clause guaranteeing every state 'a Republican Form of Government,' art. IV, § 4], the ninth amendment seems to me entirely empty, supplying no ascertainable direction to the courts. It is, accordingly, far too indefinite to provide any judicial authority for the development of substantive rights against the political process. * * * No relevant evidence [supports] an inference that [the ninth amendment] was intended to have a dynamic character."

i. For sharp disagreement, see Berger, *Government by Judiciary* 388–90, 411–13 (1977). See also Berger, *The Scope of Judicial Review: An Ongoing Debate,* 6 Hast.Con.L.Q. 527 (1979); Lusky, *"Government by Judiciary": What Price Legitimacy?* 6 Hast.Con.L.Q. 403 (1979). Compare Professor Grey's views in the article quoted above with his more recent views, *The Constitution as Scripture* (1984), fn. a supra.

"[In] the Abortion Cases, the real issue decided (albeit impliedly) by the Court was whether conventional moral culture supported placing the criminal sanction behind a moral imperative against most abortions or whether, on the other hand, the legislation involved what is essentially a personal matter outside the scope of the public morals. The Court-as-jury concluded that through the second semester abortion is essentially a personal matter beyond the public morals (except to the extent health problems might be involved after the first trimester). In retrospect, it seems quite clear that the Court's implicit evaluation of conventional moral culture vis à vis restrictive abortion legislation was essentially accurate. [C]onventional moral sensibilities appear to hold that a post-viability abortion is more like infanticide than contraception, that viability marks the line between ending a pregnancy and ending a separate life. The fact that this distinction between pre-and post-viability abortions does not proceed inexorably from textually demonstrable first principles is beside the point; the distinction is drawn by the existing moral culture (at least arguably), and the Court, in assaying conventional moral culture, should be sensitive to such distinctions." [j]

See also Wellington, *Common Law Rules and Constitutional Double Standards; Some Notes on Adjudication,* 83 Yale L.J. 221, 299, 311 (1973): "My claim has been that the plaintiff's interest [in *Roe*] is protected under the Fourteenth Amendment by reference to the people: that the meaning of liberty in that Amendment and its weight in the context of the Texas abortion statute depends, in the first instance, upon its weight in conventional morality. [The] Court's task is to ascertain the weight of the principle in conventional morality and to convert the moral principle into a legal one by connecting it with the body of constitutional law."

Because of the rapidity of social change that renders exceedingly difficult any meaningful conclusions about "conventional morality," does the Perry-Wellington view put the Court "at terrible risk that it will misperceive the near future"? Support in conventional morality may be a *necessary* condition for substantive due process activism on behalf of unenumerated rights, but is it a *sufficient* condition? IRA LUPU, *Untangling the Strands of the Fourteenth Amendment,* 77 Mich.L.Rev. 981, 1037–1041 (1979), thinks not. He contends that proper sources for judicial discovery of fundamental libertarian values outside the constitutional text and structure—but "the only proper sources"—are "those which demonstrate that the values are 'deeply embedded' within American society," id. at 985, *"values treasured by both past and present, values behind which the society and its legal system have unmistakably thrown their weight.* Contemporary consensus, even if discoverable, is not enough, due to the risks canvassed above." Id. at 1040. According to Professor Lupu, if (a) historically, American institutions have recognized the liberty claim as one of "paramount stature" *and* (b) contemporary society values the asserted liberty "at a level of high priority," the Court should preclude any state interference with that liberty, "absent extraordinary justification." Id. at 1040–41. See also Tushnet, *The Newer Property: Suggestions for the Revival of Substantive Due Process,* 1975 Sup.Ct.Rev. 261, 271 ("general agreement on the social importance" of the right

---

j. But cf. Perry, *The Authority of Text, Tradition and Reason: A Theory of Constitutional "Interpretation,"* 58 S.Cal.L.Rev. 551 (1985), abandoning his earlier approach, which sharply contrasted "interpretative" and "noninterpretative" constitutional decision-making. On the basis of Perry's 1985 article, Grey, fn. a supra, at 1–2, calls him a "rejectionist," a constitutional theorist discussed in fn. a.

and "the settled weight of responsible opinion" should govern the establishment of substantive due process rights).

But consider JOHN ELY, *Democracy and Distrust*, 63–64, 67–69 (1980): "The idea that society's 'widely shared values' should give content to the Constitution's open-ended provisions [turns] out to be at the core of most 'fundamental values' positions. * * * Consensus or conventional morality is postulated as something 'out there' that can be discovered. And in theory it is not undemocratic. Quite to the contrary, it is billed by [Dean] Wellington as a 'reference to the people.' [But] there is a growing literature that argues that in fact there is no consensus to be discovered (and to the extent that one may seem to exist, that is likely to reflect only the domination of some groups by others). [Even if we assume that] there *is* a consensus lurking out there that contradicts the judgment of our elected representatives, there would still remain the point, sufficient in itself, that that consensus is not reliably discoverable, at least not by courts.

"[B]y viewing society's values through one's own spectacles [one] can convince oneself that some invocable consensus supports almost any position a civilized person might want to see supported. [But] as between courts and legislatures, it is clear that the latter are better situated to reflect consensus. Sophisticated commentary never tires of reminding us that legislatures are only imperfectly democratic. [B]ut that isn't going to make courts more democratic than legislatures.

"An appeal to consensus [may] make some sense in a 'common law' context, where the court is either filling in the gaps left by the legislature [or,] perhaps, responding to a broad legislative delegation of decision-making authority. [The] problem is that the constitutional context is worlds away: the legislature has spoken, and the question is whether the court is to overrule it in a way that can be undone only by the cumbersome process of constitutional amendment. [To overrule the legislature] on the theory that the legislature does not truly speak for the people's values, but the Court does, is ludicrous.

"[There] are two possible reasons one might look to consensus to give content to the Constitution's open-ended provisions. One *might* say one was seeking to protect the rights of the majority by ensuring that legislation truly reflect popular values. If that were the purpose, however, the legislative process would plainly be better suited to it than the judicial. This leaves the other possible reason for the reference, to protect the rights of individuals and minority groups against the actions of the majority. [But] it makes no sense to employ the value judgments of the majority as the vehicle for protecting minorities from the value judgments of the majority."

Consider, however, Lupu, supra, at 1042–43: "[W]hat is the Constitution itself, if not a collection of '[enduring] *value judgments of the majority*,' interpreted and applied by the courts so as to be 'the vehicle for protecting minorities from the [momentary] value judgments of the majority'? [The] 'value judgments of the majority' are not only a *sensible* source of protection of minorities; these judgments turn out, in the end, to be the *only* source of protection for minorities against the hostile passions of an occasional, transient majority.

"[Ely's] rejection of the 'value judgments of the majority' as a source of rights fails to distinguish among national, statewide, and local majorities. [If] one reads [the last sentence quoted above from *Democracy and Distrust*] his sentence runs 'it simply makes no sense to employ the value judgments of [national] majorities as the vehicle for protecting [local] minorities from the value judgments of the [local] majority.' If *that* is what Professor Ely means, then he thinks that *judicial review under any substantive provision addressed to the states* makes no sense. But we know he doesn't think that at all."

POST-*ROE* ABORTION AND BIRTH CONTROL REGULATION

1. *Spousal and parental consent.* PLANNED PARENTHOOD v. DAN-FORTH, 428 U.S. 52, 96 S.Ct. 2831, 49 L.Ed.2d 788 (1976), per BLACKMUN, J., struck down, inter alia, provisions of a post-*Roe* Missouri abortion statute requiring the spouse's consent to abortion and, in the case of an unmarried woman under 18, parental consent. (These consents were required when a woman sought an abortion during the first trimester unless a physician certified that the abortion was "necessary [to] preserve the life of the mother.")

As for "spousal consent," "the State cannot 'delegate to a spouse a veto power which the state itself is absolutely and totally prohibited from exercising during the first trimester of pregnancy.' [Even] if the State had the ability to delegate to the husband a power it itself could not exercise, [the] obvious fact is that when the wife and the husband disagree on this decision, the view of only one of the two marriage partners can prevail. Since it is the woman who physically bears the child and who is the more directly and immediately affected by the pregnancy, as between the two, the balance weighs in her favor." As for "parental consent," here, too, "the State does not have the constitutional authority to give a third party an absolute, and possibly arbitrary, veto over the decision of the physician and his patient to terminate the patient's pregnancy, regardless of the reason for withholding the consent." The Court emphasized, however, that its holding "does not suggest that every minor, regardless of age or maturity, may give effective consent for termination of her pregnancy."

WHITE, J., joined by Burger, C.J., and Rehnquist, J., dissented, baffled how the Court could find anything in the Constitution or in the 1973 *Abortion Cases* *requiring* a state to "assign a greater value to a mother's decision to cut off a potential human life by abortion than to a father's decision to let it mature into a live child." Nor did he see how it followed from the fact that the mother's interest in seeking an abortion "outweighs the *State's* interest in the potential life of the fetus, that the husband's interest is also outweighed and may not be protected by the State." As for parental consent, a state "is entitled to protect the minor unmarried woman from making the decision [whether or not to obtain an abortion] in a way which is not in her own best interests, and it seeks to achieve this goal by requiring consultation and consent. This is the traditional way by which States have sought to protect children from their own immature and improvident decisions; there is absolutely no reason expressed by the majority why the State may not utilize that method here."

STEVENS, J., joined the Court's invalidation of other provisions, but dissented on parental consent: "[The] Court seems to assume that the capacity to conceive a child and the judgment of the physician are the only constitutionally permissible yardsticks for determining whether a young woman can independently make the abortion decision. I doubt the accuracy of the Court's empirical judgment. Even if it were correct, however, as a matter of constitutional law I think a State has power to conclude otherwise and to select a chronological age as its standard." [a]

Notes and Questions

(a) *If the issue is balancing.* Consider Regan, *Rewriting Roe v. Wade,* 77 Mich.L.Rev. 1569, 1644 (1979): "[I]f the whole issue is one of balancing [as the *Roe* opinion suggests], might it not be that the state's interest, which is less than the interest of the woman or of the woman and her husband together when they are aligned, is greater than the *difference* between the interests of the woman and her husband when they are opposed? Indeed, given the weightiness of the state's interest and the similarity of the woman's interests to her husband's (especially while the Court emphasizes the 'family-planning' aspect rather than the physical burdens of pregnancy), is it not quite likely?" On Regan's approach, however, "the state can no more make the unwilling woman serve the fetus and her husband than it can make her serve the fetus alone."

(b) *Sex discrimination.* Consider Burt, *The Constitution of the Family,* 1979 Sup.Ct.Rev. 329, 394: "[T]he Court's explicit assumption that the father of the fetus is as much a stranger to it as any other community member is not plausible. The Court's apparent position that the mother always has the superior claim and interest, no matter how much the father might show that her burden in childbearing would be less than his burden in losing his child, appears to me an invidious sex discrimination. Whether or not the Court should forbid all other institutions from engaging in such discrimination, it should not indulge in its own."

2. *Parental or judicial consent.* BELLOTTI v. BAIRD (*Bellotti II*), 443 U.S. 622, 99 S.Ct. 3035, 61 L.Ed.2d 797 (1979), struck down a Massachusetts law which (unlike the statute in *Danforth*) required an unmarried pregnant minor to obtain the consent of both parents for an abortion or, if parental consent was not obtained, authorization from a state judge if he concluded that abortion was in her best interest. POWELL, J., joined by Burger, C.J., and Stewart and Rehnquist, JJ.,[a] announced the judgment of the Court, concluding that if the state requires a pregnant minor to obtain one or both parents' consent to an abortion, it also must provide an "alternative procedure" (which need not be a judicial proceeding) for obtaining authorization for the abortion "ensur[ing] that [the parental consent requirement] does not in fact amount to the 'absolute, and possibly arbitrary, veto' that was found impermissible in *Danforth*." In such a proceeding a pregnant minor is entitled to show either: (1) that she is able "to make her abortion decision, in consultation with her physician, independently of her parents' wishes"; or (2) that, even if she is not, "the desired abortion would be in her best interests." Such a proceeding must also be conducted "with anonymity and sufficient expedition to provide an effective opportunity for an abortion to be obtained."

The statute fell short "in two respects: First, it permits judicial authorization for an abortion to be withheld from a minor [the court finds] to be mature

a. Cf. *Parham v. J.R.* (1979) (pp. 207, 290 infra), rejecting the contention that *Danforth* and other cases require that the parents' decision to commit a child to a mental hospital must be subjected to exacting constitutional scrutiny, including a preadmission adversary hearing: "[*Danforth*] involved an absolute parental veto over the child's ability to obtain an abortion," but Georgia parents have no "absolute right to commit their children to state mental hospitals; the statute requires [each regional hospital superintendent] to exercise independent judgment as to the child's need for confinement."

a. Rehnquist, J., joined only until "this Court is willing to reconsider" *Danforth.*

and fully competent to make this decision independently. Second, it requires parental consultation or notification in every instance, without affording the pregnant minor an opportunity to receive an independent judicial determination that she is mature enough to consent or that an abortion would be in her best interests." [b]

STEVENS, J., joined by Brennan, Marshall and Blackmun, JJ., concurred in the judgment, deeming *Danforth* controlling: "It is inherent in the right to make the abortion decision that the right may be exercised without public scrutiny and in defiance of the contrary opinion of the sovereign or other third parties. In Massachusetts, however, every minor who cannot secure the consent of both her parents—which under *Danforth* cannot be an absolute prerequisite to an abortion—is required to secure the consent of the sovereign." Moreover, "the best interest of the minor" standard "provides little real guidance to the judge, and his decision must necessarily reflect personal and societal values and mores whose enforcement upon the minor [is] fundamentally at odds with privacy interests underlying the constitutional protection afforded to her decision." [c]

A Note on Bellotti II and its Aftermath

For an illuminating and extremely readable case study of *Bellotti II,* see Mnookin, *In the Interest of Children* 150–264 (1985). "The result in *Bellotti,*" observes Professor Mnookin, "can perhaps be best understood as a judicially imposed compromise—a compromise of difficult philosophical, political, and policy issues. Nobody won, but nobody quite lost either. [In] essence, Justice Powell rejected the moral claims of both those who argued that a pregnant minor should have the *same* abortion rights as an adult woman and those who argued that parental involvement should be required. On the level of principle, neither parents nor kids get to decide alone. The result can certainly be seen as a political compromise." Id. at 260. Continues Mnookin, id. at 262–63:

"[F]or me, [Justice Powell's plurality opinion] reflects an unwarranted confidence in the ability of judges to make sound decisions on behalf of individual pregnant minors, and to make sound policy for our society as a whole. [I]n essence, it seemed the judge was to act like a parent, with broad discretion to use his personal values to make a decision on behalf of a pregnant woman. Powell's opinion seemed a high water mark of judicial arrogance. Neither legislatures nor families are to be trusted; nor are pregnant minors and their doctors. Only the modern-day secular priest, a judge, is to be trusted with the abortion decision for young women.

"My recent examination of the actual operation of the [post-*Bellotti II* Massachusetts statute] revealed that the new judicial process does not in fact involve a careful individualized assessment, but is instead a rubber-stamp, administrative operation. [Between April 1981, when the statute first went into effect, and February 1983], [n]one of the 1,300 young women who have gone to court have been successfully refused an abortion.[a] [This finding] is perhaps not

---

b. Powell, J., explicated: "If, all things considered, the court determines that an abortion is in the minor's best interests, she is entitled to court authorization without any parental involvement. On the other hand, the court may deny the abortion request of an immature minor in the absence of parental consultation if it concludes that her best interests would be served thereby, or the court may in such a case defer decision until there is

parental consultation in which the court may participate. But this is the full extent to which parental involvement may be required."

c. Only White, J., dissented.

a. Under the new statute, the judge's discretion to deny an abortion is limited. If he decides the young woman is "mature," he allows her to decide for herself. If the judge so surprising. After all, the proceedings before the judges are not contested, and the judge has no independent source of information. More fundamentally, even if the judge decides that the young woman before him is not mature, on what basis (other than moral revulsion to abortion) could he possibly decide that it is not in the best interests of an immature minor to have a first-trimester abortion? [H]ow could the judge determine that it is in the interest of a minor to give birth to a child if she is too immature even to decide to have an abortion? Indeed, if one looks only at the result for pregnant minors who go to court, the process seems an unnecessary and expensive waste of time."

3. *Parental notice.* Distinguishing *Danforth* and *Bellotti v. Baird* (1979) (*Bellotti II*), H.L. v. MATHESON, 450 U.S. 398, 101 S.Ct. 1164, 67 L.Ed.2d 388 (1981), per BURGER, C.J., upheld a Utah statute, as applied to an unemancipated minor living with and dependent upon her parents, that required a physician to "notify, if possible" the parents of a minor upon whom an abortion is to be performed. Although appellant challenged the statute as unconstitutional on its face, contending that it was "overbroad in that it can be construed to apply to all unmarried minor girls, including those who are mature and emancipated," the Court held that since appellant, a 15-year-old living with, and dependent on, her parents, had not shown that she was "mature or emancipated," she lacked standing to bring such a challenge. In a narrow ruling, the Court sustained the law as applied to appellant and members of her class:

"The Utah statute gives neither parents nor judges a veto power over the minor's abortion decision.[17] [As] applied to immature and dependent minors, the statute plainly serves the important considerations of family integrity and protected adolescents [identified] in *Bellotti II.* [Moreover], the statute serves a significant state interest by providing an opportunity for parents to supply essential medical and other information to a physician." The notice requirement may inhibit some minors from seeking abortions, but "the Constitution does not compel a state to fine-tune its statutes so as to encourage or facilitate abortions. To the contrary, state action 'encouraging child-birth except for the most urgent circumstances' is 'rationally related to the legitimate governmental objective of protecting potential life.' *Harris v. McRae* [infra]." [a]

does not find the minor to be "mature," he gets to decide according to her "best interest." In about 90 percent of the cases the Supreme Court simply found the minor to be "mature." In the remaining cases the court found the abortion to be in the minor's best interest in virtually all instances. See id. at 239, 261–62.

Although the requirement of judicial authorization is not leading to the denial of abortion *for those who go to court,* "the business of Massachusetts abortion clinics has significantly declined. It would appear that many girls who formerly would have secured abortions in Massachusetts are now going to other states, particularly New Hampshire." Id. at 242.

17. The main premise of the dissent seems to be that a requirement of notice to the parents is the equivalent of a requirement of parental consent. In *Bellotti II,* however, we expressly declined to equate notice requirements with consent requirements.

a. Powell, J., joined by Stewart, J., concurred, emphasizing that they joined the

Court's opinion "on the understanding that it leaves open the question whether [the Utah statute] unconstitutionally burdens the right of a mature minor or a minor whose best interests would not be served by parental notification." For the reasons set forth in his plurality opinion in *Bellotti II* (dealing with parental *consent*), Powell maintained that "a state may not validly require notice to parents in all cases, without providing an independent decisionmaker to whom a pregnant minor can have recourse if she believes that she is mature enough to make the abortion decision independently or that notification otherwise would not be in her best interests."

Stevens, J., concurring only in the judgment, would reach the question reserved by the Court and uphold the statute as applied to *all* unmarried women who are suffering unwanted pregnancies and desire to terminate them, but may not do so because their physicians insist on complying with state law.

Dissenting JUSTICE MARSHALL, joined by Brennan and Blackmun, JJ., contended that appellant had standing to challenge the statute in its application to all minors. He then found the statute unconstitutional: "Many minor women will encounter interference from their parents after the state-imposed notification. In addition to parental disappointment and disapproval, the minor may confront physical or emotional abuse, withdrawal of financial support, or actual obstruction of the abortion decision. Furthermore, the threat of parental notice may cause some minor women to delay past the first trimester of pregnancy, after which the health risks increase significantly. [Others] may attempt to self-abort or to obtain an illegal abortion rather than risk parental notification. Still others may foresake an abortion and bear an unwanted [child]. And that hardship is not a mere disincentive created by the State [referring to the abortion funding case of *Harris v. McRae*, infra], but is instead an actual state-imposed obstacle to the exercise of the minor woman's free choice. * * * Significantly, the interference sanctioned by the statute does not operate in a neutral fashion. No notice is required for other pregnancy-related medical care, so only the minor women who wish to abort encounter the burden imposed by the notification statute. * * *

"None of the reasons offered by the State justifies [the infringement upon a minor woman's constitutional right to privacy], for the statute is not tailored to serve them. Rather than serving to enhance the physician's judgment, in cases such as appellant's, the statute prevents implementation of the physician's medical recommendation. Rather than promoting the transfer of information held by parents to the minor's physician, the statute neglects to require anything more than a communication from the physician moments before the abortion. Rather than respecting the private realm of family life, the statute invokes the criminal machinery of the State in an attempt to influence the interactions within the family."

4. *Abortion funding.* MAHER v. ROE, 432 U.S. 464, 97 S.Ct. 2376, 53 L.Ed. 2d 484 (1977) (also discussed at p. 1060 infra), per POWELL, J., sustained Connecticut's use of Medicaid funds to reimburse women for the costs of childbirth and "medically necessary" first trimester abortions (defined to include "psychiatric necessity"), but not for the costs of elective or nontherapeutic first trimester abortions.[a]

On "the central question"—"whether the regulation 'impinges upon a fundamental right explicitly or implicitly protected by the Constitution' "—the Court held that *Roe* did not establish "an unqualified 'constitutional right to an abortion,' " but only a "right protect[ing] the woman from unduly burdensome interference with her freedom to decide whether to terminate her pregnancy. It implies no limitation on the authority of a State to make a value judgment favoring childbirth over abortion, and to implement that judgment by the allocation of public funds. [The] State may have made childbirth a more attractive alternative, thereby influencing the woman's decision, but it has imposed no restriction on access to abortions that was not already there. The indigency that may make it difficult—and in some cases, perhaps, impossible—

a. In a companion case, *Beal v. Doe,* 432 U.S. 438, 97 S.Ct. 2366, 53 L.Ed.2d 464 (1977), per Powell, J., held that the Medicaid Act does not require state funding of nontherapeutic first trimester abortions as a condition of participation in the joint federal-state program.

In another companion case, *Poelker v. Doe,* 432 U.S. 519, 97 S.Ct. 2391, 53 L.Ed.2d 528 (1977), per curiam, for the reasons set forth in *Maher,* found "no constitutional violation by the city of St. Louis in electing, as a policy choice, to provide publicly financed hospital services for childbirth without providing corresponding services for nontherapeutic abortions."

for some women to have abortions is neither created nor in any way affected by the [regulation.]

"Our conclusion signals no retreat from *Roe* or the cases applying it. There is a basic difference between direct state interference with a protected activity and state encouragement of an alternative activity consonant with legislative policy. [This] distinction is implicit in [*Meyer* and *Pierce*, fn. b in *Griswold*]. Both cases invalidated substantial restrictions on constitutionally protected liberty interests [but] neither case denied to a State the policy choice of encouraging the preferred course of action. Indeed, in *Meyer* the Court was careful to state that the power of the State 'to prescribe a curriculum' that included English and excluded German in its free public schools 'is not questioned.' Similarly, *Pierce* casts no shadow over a State's power to favor public education by funding [it]. We think it abundantly clear that a State is not required to show a compelling interest for its policy choice to favor normal childbirth any more than a State must so justify its election to fund public but not private education."

The Court then sustained the regulation "under the less demanding test of rationality that applies in the absence of a suspect classification or the impingement of a fundamental right." It had little difficulty finding the distinction drawn between childbirth and nontherapeutic abortion " 'rationally related' to a 'constitutionally permissible' purpose." "*Roe* itself explicitly acknowledged the State's strong interest in protecting the potential life of the fetus. [The] State unquestionably has a 'strong and legitimate interest in encouraging normal childbirth' " and subsidizing the substantial and significantly increasing costs incident to childbirth is "a rational means of encouraging childbirth." [13]

BRENNAN, J., joined by Marshall and Blackmun, JJ., dissented, accusing the majority of "a distressing insensitivity to the plight of impoverished pregnant women." The "disparity in funding [clearly] operates to coerce indigent pregnant women to bear children they would not otherwise choose to have, and just as clearly, this coercion can only operate upon the poor, who are uniquely the victims of this form of financial pressure." *Roe* and its progeny held that "an area of privacy invulnerable to the State's intrusion surrounds the decision of a pregnant woman whether or not to carry her pregnancy to term. The Connecticut scheme clearly infringes upon that area of privacy."

The dissenters maintained that in other abortion cases the Court had rejected the notion that there is a basic difference between direct state interference with a fundamental right and state encouragement of an alternative activity: The spousal consent requirement struck down in *Danforth* was an "absolute obstacle" to abortion "only in the limited sense that a woman who was unable to persuade her spouse to [consent] was prevented from obtaining one. Any woman whose husband [did agree with her] was free to obtain an abortion, and the State never imposed directly any burden of its own." As for the majority's conclusion that the state's interest "in protecting the potential life of the fetus" is sufficient, "[s]ince only the first trimester of pregnancy is involved

---

13. Much of the rhetoric of the three dissenting opinions would be equally applicable if Connecticut had elected not to fund either abortions or childbirth. Yet none of the dissents goes so far as to argue that the Constitution *requires* such assistance for all indigent pregnant women.

[Compare Simson, *Abortion, Poverty and the Equal Protection of the Laws,* 13 Ga.L.Rev.

505, 508 (1979): "[I]f Connecticut funded neither childbirth nor abortion, poverty would not lead indigent women to prefer childbirth to abortion. Rather, since a safe abortion in the early months of pregnancy is materially cheaper than a safe childbirth, financial considerations probably would militate strongly *in favor of* abortion."]

in this case, that justification is totally foreclosed if the Court is not overruling the holding of *Roe* that '[w]ith respect to the State's important and legitimate interest in potential life, the "compelling" point is at viability,' occurring at about the end of the second trimester."

As for *Poelker*, "the fundamental right of a woman freely to choose to terminate her pregnancy has been infringed by the city of St. Louis through a deliberate policy based on opposition to elective abortions on moral grounds by city officials. [The] city policy is a significant, and in some cases insurmountable, obstacle to indigent pregnant women who cannot pay for abortions in [clinics or private hospitals].

In a second dissent, MARSHALL, J., thought it "all too obvious that the governmental actions in these cases, ostensibly taken to 'encourage' women to carry pregnancies to term, are in reality intended to impose a moral viewpoint that no State may constitutionally enforce. Since efforts to overturn [*Roe* and *Doe*] have been unsuccessful, the opponents of abortion have attempted every imaginable means to circumvent the commands of the Constitution and impose their moral choices upon the rest of society. The present cases involve the most vicious attacks yet devised. The impact of the regulations here fall tragically upon those among us least able to help or defend themselves."

In a third dissent, BLACKMUN, J., joined by Brennan and Marshall, JJ., charged that "the Court concedes the existence of a constitutional right but denies the realization and enjoyment of that right on the ground that existence and realization are separate and distinct. [Implicit in today's holdings] is the condescension that [the indigent woman] may go elsewhere for her abortion. I find that disingenuous and alarming, almost reminiscent of: 'Let them eat cake.' "

5. *More on abortion funding; The Hyde Amendment.* Title XIX of the Social Security Act established the Medicaid program to provide federal financial assistance to states choosing to reimburse certain costs of medical treatment for needy persons. Since 1976, various versions of the so-called Hyde Amendment have limited federal funding of abortions under the Medicaid program to those necessary to save the life of the mother and certain other exceptional circumstances.[a] HARRIS v. McRAE, 448 U.S. 297, 100 S.Ct. 2671, 65 L.Ed.2d 784 (1980), per STEWART, J., determined that Title XIX does not obligate a participating state to pay for those medically necessary abortions for which Congress has withheld federal funding and then held—relying heavily on *Maher*—that the Hyde Amendment is constitutionally valid:

"The Hyde Amendment, like [the regulation upheld] in *Maher,* places no governmental obstacle in the path of a woman who chooses to terminate her pregnancy, but rather, by means of unequal subsidization of abortion and other medical services, encourages alternative activity deemed in the public interest. The present case does differ factually from *Maher* insofar as that case involved a failure to fund nontherapeutic abortions, whereas the Hyde Amendment withholds funding of certain medically necessary abortions. [But] regardless of [how] the freedom of a woman to choose to terminate her pregnancy for health reasons [is characterized], it simply does not follow that [this freedom] carries with it a

---

a. The version of the Hyde Amendment applicable for fiscal year 1980 prohibited federal funding of abortions "except where the life of the mother would be endangered if the fetus were carried to term" or except for cases of rape or incest "when such rape or incest has been reported promptly to a law enforcement agency or public health service." But the initial version of the Hyde Amendment, which triggered the instant case, did not include the "rape or incest" exception.

constitutional entitlement to the financial resources to avail herself of the full range of protected choices. The reason why was explained in *Maher:* although government may not place obstacles in the path of a woman's exercise of her freedom of choice, it need not remove those not of its own creation. [T]he Hyde Amendment leaves an indigent woman with at least the same range of choice in deciding whether to obtain a medically necessary abortion as she would have had if Congress had chosen to subsidize no health costs at all.

"[Acceptance of appellees' argument] would mark a drastic change in our understanding of the Constitution. It cannot be that because government may not prohibit the use of contraceptives, *Griswold,* or prevent parents from sending their child to a private school, *Pierce,* government, therefore, has an affirmative constitutional obligation to assure that all persons have the financial resources to obtain contraceptives or send their children to private [schools.]**[b]**

Responding to the arguments of the dissents—especially Stevens, J.'s—WHITE, J. concurring, characterized the constitutional right recognized in *Roe* as "the right to choose to undergo an abortion without coercive interference by the government. [*Roe*] dealt with the circumstances in which the governmental interest in potential life would justify official interference with the abortion choices of pregnant women. There is no such calculus involved here. [The pregnant] woman's choice remains unfettered, the government is not attempting to use its interest in life to justify a coercive restraint, and hence in disbursing its Medicaid funds it is free to implement rationally what *Roe* recognized to be its legitimate interest in a potential life by covering the medical costs of childbirth but denying funds for abortions. Neither *Roe* [nor its progeny] invalidates this legislative preference. We decided as much in *Maher* * * *."

Four justices dissented—Brennan, Marshall and Blackmun, JJ. (the three *Maher* dissenters), and Stevens, J. who had joined the opinion of the Court in *Maher.*

STEVENS, J., maintained that the instant case presented "[a] fundamentally different question" than the one decided in *Maher:* "This case involves the pool of benefits that Congress created by enacting [Title XIX]. Individuals who satisfy two neutral criteria—financial need and medical need—are entitled to equal access to that pool. The question is whether certain persons who satisfy those criteria may be denied access to benefits solely because they must exercise the constitutional right to have an abortion in order to obtain the medical care they need. Our prior cases plainly dictate [the answer].

"Unlike these plaintiffs, [those] in *Maher* did not satisfy the neutral criterion of medical need; they sought a subsidy for nontherapeutic abortions—medical

b. The Court then rejected the contention that the Hyde Amendment violates the Establishment Clause because, as the argument ran, "it incorporates into law the doctrines of the Roman Catholic Church": A statute does not run afoul of the Establishment Clause "because it 'happens to coincide or harmonize with the tenets of some or all religions,' *McGowan v. Maryland* [p. 717 infra]"; the Hyde Amendment "is as much a reflection of 'traditionalist' values toward abortion, as it is an embodiment of the views of any particular religion."

"Again draw[ing] guidance from" *Maher,* the Court also rejected the argument that the Hyde Amendment "violates the equal protec-

tion component of the Fifth Amendment": The Hyde Amendment "is not predicated on a constitutionally suspect classification. [Here,] as in *Maher,* the principal impact of [the] Amendment falls on the indigent. But that fact alone does not itself render the funding restriction constitutionally invalid, for this Court has held repeatedly that poverty, standing alone, is not a suspect classification." See generally Ch. 6, Sec. 3, I and Sec. 4, IV. Thus, the Hyde Amendment need only satisfy the rational-basis standard of review and it does—"by encouraging childbirth except in the most urgent circumstances, [it] is rationally related to the legitimate governmental objective of protecting potential life."

procedures which by definition they did not need. [This case] involves a special exclusion of women who, by definition, are confronted with a choice between two serious harms: serious health damage to themselves on the one hand and abortion on the other. The competing interests are the interest in maternal health and the interest in protecting potential human life. It is now part of our law that the pregnant woman's decision as to which of these conflicting interests shall prevail is entitled to constitutional protection.

"[If] a woman has a constitutional right to place a higher value on avoiding either serious harm to her own health or perhaps an abnormal childbirth [3] than on protecting potential life, the exercise of that right cannot provide the basis for the denial of a benefit to which she would otherwise be entitled. The Court's sterile equal protection analysis evades this critical though simple point. The Court focuses exclusively on the 'legitimate interest in protecting the potential life of the fetus.' [Roe] squarely held that the States may not protect that interest when a conflict with the interest in a pregnant woman's health exists. It is thus perfectly clear that neither the Federal Government nor the States may exclude a woman from medical benefits to which she would otherwise be entitled solely to further an interest in potential life when a physician, 'in appropriate medical judgment,' certifies that an abortion is necessary 'for the preservation of the life or health of the mother.' Roe. The Court totally fails to explain why this reasoning is not dispositive here.[4]

"[Nor] can it be argued that the exclusion of this type of medically necessary treatment of the indigent can be justified on fiscal grounds. [For] the cost of an abortion is only a small fraction of the costs associated with childbirth.[9] Thus, the decision to tolerate harm to indigent persons who need an abortion in order to avoid 'serious and long lasting health damage' is one that is financed by draining money out of the pool that is used to fund all other necessary medical procedures. Unlike most invidious classifications, this discrimination harms not only its direct victims but also the remainder of the class of needy persons that the pool was designed to benefit. * * *

"Having decided to alleviate some of the hardships of poverty by providing necessary medical care, the Government must use neutral criteria in distributing benefits. It may not deny benefits to a financially and medically needy

---

3. The Court relies heavily on the premise [that] the State's legitimate interest in preserving potential life provides a sufficient justification for funding medical services that are necessarily associated with normal childbirth without also funding abortions that are not medically necessary. The *Maher* opinion repeatedly referred to the policy of favoring "normal childbirth." But this case involves a refusal to fund abortions which are medically necessary to avoid abnormal childbirth.

4. [In] responding to my analysis of this case, Mr. Justice White has described the constitutional right recognized in *Roe* as "the right to choose to undergo an abortion without coercive interference by the Government" or a right "only to be free from unreasonable official interference with private choice." No such language is found in the *Roe* opinion itself. Rather, that case squarely held that State interference is unreasonable if it attaches a greater importance to the interest in potential life than to the interest in protecting

the mother's health. One could with equal justification describe the right protected by the First Amendment as the right to make speeches without coercive interference by the Government and then sustain a Government subsidy for all medically needy persons except those who publicly advocate a change of administration.

9. [*Williams v. Zbaraz*, 448 U.S. 358, 100 S.Ct. 2694, 65 L.Ed.2d 831 (1980), a companion case], found that the average cost to the State of Illinois of an abortion was less than $150 as compared with the cost of a childbirth which exceeded $1,350. Indeed, based on an estimated cost of providing support to children of indigent parents together with their estimate of the number of medically necessary abortions that would be funded but for the Hyde Amendment, appellees in *Zbaraz* contend that [in] Illinois alone the effect of the Hyde Amendment is to impose a cost of about $20,000,000 per year on the public fisc. * * *

person simply because he is a Republican, a Catholic, or an Oriental—or because he has spoken against a program the Government has a legitimate interest in furthering. In sum, it may not create exceptions for the sole purpose of furthering a governmental interest that is constitutionally subordinate to the individual interest that the entire program was designed to protect. The Hyde amendments not only exclude financially and medically needy persons from the pool of benefits for a constitutionally insufficient reason; they also require the expenditure of millions of dollars in order to thwart the exercise of a constitutional right, thereby effectively inflicting serious and long lasting harm on impoverished women who want and need abortions for valid medical reasons. [Thus,] these amendments constitute an unjustifiable, and indeed blatant, violation of the sovereign's duty to govern impartially."

The other three dissenters wrote separately, each voicing agreement with Stevens, J.'s analysis. BRENNAN, J., joined by Marshall and Blackmun, JJ., expressed his "continuing disagreement with the Court's mischaracterization of the nature of the fundamental right recognized in *Roe* and its misconception of the manner in which that right is infringed [by] legislation withdrawing all funding for medically necessary abortions":

"The proposition for which [*Roe* and its progeny stand] is not that the State is under an affirmative obligation to ensure access to abortions for all who may desire them; it is that the State must refrain from wielding its enormous power and influence in a manner that might burden the pregnant woman's freedom to choose whether to have an abortion. [By] injecting coercive financial incentives favoring childbirth into a decision that is constitutionally guaranteed to be free from governmental intrusion, the Hyde Amendment deprives the indigent woman of her freedom to choose abortion over maternity, thereby impinging on the due process liberty recognized in *Roe*. [W]hat the Court fails to appreciate is that it is not simply the woman's indigency that interferes with her freedom of choice, but the combination of her own poverty and the government's unequal subsidization of abortion and childbirth."

Although he called this case "perhaps the most dramatic illustration to date of the deficiencies in the Court's obsolete 'two-tiered' approach to the Equal Protection Clause" [see generally Ch. 6, Sec. 3, I], Marshall, J. was "unable to see how even a minimally rational legislature could conclude that the interest in fetal life outweighs the brutal effect of the Hyde Amendment on indigent women."

Notes and Questions

(a) Consider the remarks of Professor Choper in Choper, Kamisar & Tribe, *The Supreme Court: Trends and Developments, 1979–80* (1981) (hereinafter referred to as *Trends and Developments*) at 81–82: "Suppose a state passed the following statute: anyone who has to take time off from work to vote gets reimbursed, except if he votes Republican. My contention is that this is analytically identical to the situation in [*McRae*]. That is, a citizen has a constitutional right to vote Democratic. He has a constitutional right to vote Republican. A woman has a constitutional right to carry her pregnancy to term. She has a constitutional right to an abortion.

"The Court argued that the federal government is not adding any impediment in the way of an abortion that would not have existed if no funding took place at all. The government is funding one and not the other with the express purpose of encouraging the former and not the latter. Could the Court not say the very same thing about my hypothetical Democratic-Republican statute? Could the Court not say that since the state does not have to fund anyone's costs of voting, it therefore can fund it any way it wants to, even though it discriminates against the exercise of a constitutional right in the process[?]"

(b) But compare the remarks of Professor Tribe in *Trends and Developments* 257, 290: "[Unlike the hypothetical situation where the government subsidizes those who vote Democratic but not those who vote Republican], the interest being served in [*McRae*] is *not* illegitimate. Even those who believe *Roe v. Wade* was clearly right could hardly argue that it is illegitimate for the state to encourage and facilitate healthy, normal childbirth as opposed to abortion—even at some medical risk to the mother. Child care clinics, infant care, and the like—all such things encourage healthy childbirth and child rearing and, correspondingly, make abortions, therapeutic as well as elective, less likely. Making childbirth less burdensome and hazardous may indeed be the only thing that justifies such programs; it is not an illegitimate aim.

"If there *is* something wrong in the abortion funding decision, I think it is neither the illegitimacy of what the government was trying to achieve, nor even the fact that there was discrimination between the rich and the poor, with only the latter being subject to such strong "encouragement" (although this feature *may* be seen as constitutionally troublesome). The key may be that the 'right' to have an abortion is arguably meaningless for the very poor unless government pays for it. I think the Court majority realized that and shrunk from it."

"[In *McRae*] Congress is just saying, 'If you don't have abortion, we'll cover you *for the costs of childbirth—not* childbirth costs plus some bonus.' As long as no 'lure' is being offered to deflect women from abortion beyond the 'bait' implicit in knowing that [the bills] will at least be paid if childbirth is chosen, I cannot see why government's policy must be condemned as tilting in a forbidden direction. After all, it is *not* as though Congress has been commanded by the Constitution, even as construed in *Roe v. Wade,* to be neutral on the issue of *how well* childbirth is provided for, or to *care as much* about abortion as about childbirth."

(c) *On looking at the government's purpose.* Perry, *Why the Supreme Court was Plainly Wrong in the Hyde Amendment Case,* 32 Stan.L.Rev. 1113, 1122 (1980), observes that, although *Roe* does not forbid all government actions that might have the effect of making a woman prefer childbirth to abortion (e.g., the government could decide to fund childbirth *solely* in order to increase the size of the labor force), "*Roe* does require that government take no action, including the selective withholding of Medicaid funds, predicated on the view that abortion is per se morally objectionable—just as government has an undisputed obligation (to borrow one of the Court's own examples) not to take action predicated on the view that sending one's children to a private school is morally objectionable. [This means] that the central question in *McRae* ought to have been whether the Hyde Amendment is predicated on the illicit view. [The *McRae* majority] never even addressed that crucial question." After pointing out, inter alia, that Congressman Hyde stated that the purpose of his Amendment was "not to fund abortion because it's the killing of an innocently inconvenient pre-born child," Professor Perry concludes, id. at 1126, that "[i]t strains credulity to the breaking point to suggest that those charged with defending the Hyde Amendment in court could possibly establish that the view that abortion is per se morally objectionable did not play a but-for role in passage of the Amendment."

(d) *On not looking at the government's purpose.* Consider Tribe, *Trends and Developments* 286–87: "Purpose is a treacherous inquiry. It is manipulable. If someone had told Representative Hyde that he had better be careful to talk only about 'encouraging childbirth' and to say nothing nasty about women who choose abortions, I am sure he could have managed to contain himself long enough. In addition, many think it is an affront to a coordinate branch of government to make what is going on inside its head the touchstone for constitutional adjudication. And it may be an affront to the woman to hold that her life, her freedom, depends on Representative Hyde's motivations. [The] reason that the Court began looking to purpose, in cases involving race, is that the central concern of the Equal Protection Clause in the context of suspect classification has been stigma and the subjugation it reinforces. In deciding whether government is singling someone out as a member of a distinct and dominated minority, it is relevant what government *says* and even what it *means,* as well as what it has *done.* But it has never been established doctrine that, when we're talking about fundamental rights as opposed to suspect classes, 'purpose' is the start, or the core, of the inquiry. * * *

"Suppose the government studied the problem and concluded, 'Divorce is a terrible, traumatic thing. We want to discourage divorce. So we're going to give people who are considering divorces bonuses if they go to marriage counselors. We're going to pay them extra money, and we're doing it specifically to *discourage* divorce.' I do not think that somebody who believes that there is a fundamental right to sever a marriage, a right underlying *Boddie v. Connecticut* [p. 1375 infra], should feel that he is in a corner and has to say the government cannot try to discourage divorce through providing such subsidies and thereby helping people stay married. The government's purpose cannot be the touchstone in a case where (a) you can't really find out what it was; (b) they can gimmick up the record to make it look right if you make the result turn on apparent motive; and (c) it doesn't make a damn bit of difference to the individual *what* the government's purpose was. Outside the limited area where purpose is critical because we're talking about symbolism and stigma, a strong case could be made for junking the whole issue of purpose."

(e) *The difference between Maher and McRae.* Much of the criticism of *McRae* also applies to *Maher.* But consider Note, 94 Harv.L.Rev. 96, 101–05 (1980): "The majority would have been correct to follow [*Maher*], had *McRae* involved an attempt to require the government to subsidize an activity solely because it was protected. However, that was not the right at stake. *McRae* dealt with medically necessary abortions, in the context of a program that was designed to cover all medically necessary services. [*Thus,*] whereas *Maher* had sustained a refusal to subsidize that was based on a permissible criterion—medical necessity—*McRae* involved an exception Congress had carved out from the standard of medical need. The right asserted, then, was not to have abortions funded, but to have medically necessary services funded on a nondiscriminatory basis.

"The refusal to fund medically necessary abortions can only be validated if a permissible basis for discriminating between medically necessary services exists. The Court's analysis rested on its view that the classification was premised on a permissible criterion: the state's interest in potential life. [But *Wade,* as made clearer by its progeny,] held that abortion involves the kind of judgment that the Constitution reserves not for institutions, but for the individuals intimately affected. [Thus,] the classification created by the [Hyde Amendment] was an impermissible one. It rested on a choice that is in a protected zone of individual autonomy and therefore beyond the power of the state to make." See also Bennett, *Abortion and Judicial Review,* 75 Nw.U.L.Rev. 978 (1981).

(f) *Abortion as a private privilege, not a public right.* Consider MacKinnon, *Roe v. Wade: A Study in Male Ideology,* in *Abortion: Moral and Legal Perspectives* 45, 52–53 (Garfield & Hennessey eds. 1984): "[*Roe*] presumes that government nonintervention into the private sphere promotes a woman's freedom of choice. When the alternative is jail, there is much to be said for this argument. But the *McRae* result sustains the meaning of privacy in *Roe*: women are guaranteed by the public no more than what they can get in private—that is, what we can extract through our intimate associations with men. Women with privileges get rights.

"So women got abortion as a private privilege, not as a public right. We got control over reproduction that is controlled by "a man or The Man," an individual man or the doctors or the government. Abortion was not decriminalized, it was legalized. ∗ ∗ ∗

"It is not inconsistent, then, that framed as a privacy right a woman's decision to abort would have no claim on public support and would genuinely not be seen as burdened by that deprivation. Privacy conceived as a right from public intervention and disclosure is the opposite of the relief that *McRae* sought for welfare women. State intervention would have provided a choice women did *not* have in private. The women in *McRae*, women whose sexual refusal has counted for particularly little, needed something to make their privacy effective. The logic of the court's response resembles the logic by which women are supposed to consent to sex. Preclude the alternatives, then call the sole remaining option her choice. The point is that the alternatives are precluded *prior* to the reach of the chosen legal doctrine. They are precluded by conditions of sex, race, and class—the very conditions the privacy frame not only leaves tacit, but which it exists to *guarantee*."

JUSTICE O'CONNOR'S BROAD ATTACK ON, BUT THE COURT'S REAFFIRMATION OF, *ROE*'S ANALYSIS

In AKRON v. AKRON CENTER FOR REPRODUCTIVE HEALTH, 462 U.S. 416, 103 S.Ct. 2481, 76 L.Ed.2d 687 (1983), a 6–3 majority, per POWELL, J., struck down five provisions of an ordinance regulating abortions: (1) a requirement that after the first trimester all abortions be "performed in a hospital," thus preventing abortions in outpatient clinics that are not part of an acute-care, full-service hospital; (2) a prohibition of abortions on unmarried minors under 15 without consent of one of her parents or a court order; (3) a "truly informed" consent provision requiring the "attending physician" to inform his patient, inter alia, of the physical and emotional complications that may result from an abortion and the particular risks associated with her pregnancy and the abortion technique to be utilized; (4) a mandatory 24-hour waiting period after the pregnant woman signs a consent form; and (5) a requirement that physicians performing abortions "insure that the remains of the unborn child are disposed of in a humane and sanitary manner."

The Court reaffirmed that "a state's interest in health regulation becomes compelling at approximately the end of the first trimester,[a] but [the] state's

---

a. The Court noted (fn. 11) that "*Roe* identified the end of the first trimester as the compelling point because until that time—according to the medical literature available in 1973—'mortality in abortion may be less than mortality in normal childbirth.'" The Court recognized that "[t]here is substantial evidence that developments in the past decade, particularly the development of a much safer method for performing second-trimester regulation may be upheld only if it is reasonably designed to further that state interest." As for (1) the second-trimester requirement, Akron's defense of it "as a reasonable health regulation [had] strong support at the time of *Roe*, [but since then] the safety of second-trimester abortions has increased dramatically. The principal reason is that the [dilation and evacuation] D & E procedure is now widely and successfully used for the second-trimester abortions.

"[A]n even more significant factor is that experience indicates that D & E may be performed safely on an outpatient basis in appropriate nonhospital facilities. The evidence is strong enough to have convinced the American Public Health Association (APHA) to abandon its prior recommendation of hospitalization for all second-trimester [abortions]. Similarly, the American College of Obstetricians and Gynecologists (ACOG) no longer suggests that all second-trimester abortions be performed in a hospital.

"[These] developments, and the professional commentary supporting them, constitute impressive evidence that—at least during the early weeks of the second trimester—D & E abortions may be performed as safely in an outpatient clinic as in a full-service hospital. [Thus,] 'present medical knowledge' convincingly undercuts Akron's justification for requiring that *all* second-trimester abortions be performed in a hospital.

"[Although] a state abortion regulation is not unconstitutional simply because it does not correspond perfectly in all cases to the asserted state interest, [the] lines drawn in a state regulation must be reasonable, and this cannot be said of [the hospitalization requirement]. By preventing the performance of D & E abortions in an appropriate nonhospital setting, Akron has imposed a heavy, and unnecessary, burden on women's access to a relatively inexpensive, otherwise accessible, and safe abortion procedure. [The hospitalization requirement] unreasonably infringes upon a woman's constitutional right to obtain an abortion."

As for (2) the parental consent requirement, "we do not think the Akron ordinance, as applied to Ohio juvenile proceedings, is reasonably susceptible of being construed to create an 'opportunity for case-by-case evaluations of the maturity of pregnant minors.' *Bellotti II.*"

As for (3) the "informed consent" provision, much of the information required, such as the provisions that the physician inform his patient of the numerous possible physical and psychological complications of abortions and inform her that "the unborn child is a human life from the moment of conception," "is designed not to inform the woman's consent but rather to persuade her to withhold it altogether. [A]n additional, and equally decisive, objection to [this provision] is its intrusion upon the discretion of the pregnant woman's physician. This provision specifies a litany of information that the

abortions, have extended the period in which abortions are safer than childbirth." But it deemed it "prudent [to] retain *Roe's* identification of the beginning of the second trimester as the approximate time at which the State's interest in maternal health becomes sufficiently compelling to justify significant regulation of abortion. We note that the medical evidence suggests that until approximately the end of the first trimester, the State's interest in maternal health would not be served by regulations that restrict the manner in which abortions are performed by a licensed physician. [The] *Roe* trimester standard thus continues to provide a reasonable legal framework for limiting a State's authority to regulate abortions. Where the State adopts a health regulation governing the performance of abortions during the second trimester, the determinative question should be whether there is a reasonable medical basis for the regulation. The comparison between abortion and childbirth mortality rates may be relevant only where the State employs a health rationale as a justification for a complete prohibition on abortions in certain circumstances."

physician must recite to each woman regardless of whether in his judgment the information is relevant to her personal decision. [By] insisting upon recitation of a lengthy and inflexible list of information, Akron unreasonably has placed 'obstacles in the path of the doctor upon whom [the woman is] entitled to rely for advice in connection with her decision.' *Whalen v. Roe.*"

As for (4) the mandatory 24-hour waiting provision, which increases the cost of obtaining an abortion by requiring the woman to make two separate trips to the abortion facility, "Akron has failed to demonstrate that any legitimate state interest is furthered by an arbitrary and inflexible waiting period. [I]f a woman, after appropriate counseling, is prepared to give her written informed consent and proceed with the abortion, a State may not demand that she delay the effectuation of that decision."

As for (5), the provision dealing with the disposal of fetal remains, the phrase "humane and sanitary" suggests, as the court below noted, "a possible intent to 'manifest some sort of "decent burial" of an embryo at the earliest stage of formation.' This level of uncertainty is fatal where criminal liability is imposed."

In the face of a dissenting opinion which, said the Court, "rejects the basic premise of *Roe* and its progeny," the Court stated at the outset: "[A]rguments continue to be made, [that in *Roe*] we erred in interpreting the Constitution. Nonetheless, the doctrine of stare decisis, while perhaps never entirely persuasive on a constitutional question, is a doctrine that demands respect in a society governed by the rule of law.[1] We respect it today, and reaffirm *Roe*."

Before specifically addressing the regulations at issue, O'CONNOR, J., joined by White and Rehnquist, JJ., dissenting, launched a broad attack on the Court's approach and the "trimester framework adopted in *Roe*.": "It is apparent from the Court's opinion that neither sound constitutional theory nor our need to decide cases based on the application of neutral principles can accommodate an analytical framework that varies according to the 'stages' of pregnancy, where those stages, and their concomitant standards of review, differ according to the level of medical technology available when a particular challenge to state regulation occurs. The Court's analysis of the Akron regulations is inconsistent both with the methods of analysis employed in previous cases dealing with abortion, and with the Court's approach to fundamental rights in other areas.

"Our recent cases indicate that a regulation imposed on 'a lawful abortion "is not unconstitutional unless it unduly burdens the right to seek an abortion." '

---

1. There are especially compelling reasons for adhering to stare decisis in applying the principles of *Roe*. That case was considered with special care. [Since then] the Court repeatedly and consistently has accepted and applied the basic principle that a woman has a fundamental right to make the highly personal choice whether or not to terminate her pregnancy.

Today, however, the dissenting opinion rejects the basic premise of *Roe* and its progeny. The dissent stops short of arguing flatly that *Roe* should be overruled. Rather, it adopts reasoning that, for all practical purposes, would accomplish precisely that result. The dissent states that "[e]ven assuming that there is a fundamental right to terminate pregnancy in some situations," the State's compelling interests in maternal health and

potential human life "are present *throughout* pregnancy" (emphasis in original). The existence of these compelling interests turns out to be largely unnecessary, however, for the dissent does not think that even one of the numerous abortion regulations at issue imposes a sufficient burden on the "limited" fundamental right, to require heightened scrutiny.

[I]t appears that the dissent would uphold virtually any abortion regulation under a rational-basis test. It also appears that even where heightened scrutiny is deemed appropriate, the dissent would uphold virtually any abortion-inhibiting regulation because of the State's interest in preserving potential human life. [This] analysis is wholly incompatible with the existence of the fundamental right recognized in *Roe*.

Maher v. Roe (quoting *Bellotti I*). In my view, this 'unduly burdensome' standard should be applied to the challenged regulations throughout the entire pregnancy without reference to the particular 'stage' of pregnancy involved. If the particular regulation does not 'unduly burden[ ]' the fundamental right, then our evaluation of that regulation is limited to our determination that the regulation rationally relates to a legitimate state purpose.

"[D]espite the Court's purported adherence to the trimester approach adopted in *Roe*, the lines drawn in that decision have now been 'blurred' because of what the Court accepts as technological advancement in the safety of abortion procedure. The State may no longer rely on a 'bright line' that separates permissible from impermissible regulation, and it is no longer free to consider the second trimester as a unit and weigh the risks posed by all abortion procedures throughout that trimester. Rather, the State must continuously and conscientiously study contemporary medical and scientific literature in order to determine whether the effect of a particular regulation is to 'depart from accepted medical practice' insofar as particular procedures and particular periods within the trimester are concerned. Assuming that legislative bodies are able to engage in this exacting task, it is difficult to believe that our Constitution *requires* that they do it as a prelude to protecting the health of their citizens. It is even more difficult to believe that this Court, without the resources available to those bodies entrusted with making legislative choices, believes itself competent to make these inquires and to revise these standards every time the ACOG or similar group revises its views about what is and what is not appropriate medical procedure in this area. [As] today's decision indicates, medical technology is changing, and this change will necessitate our continued functioning as the nation's 'ex officio medical board with powers to approve or disapprove medical and operative practices and standards throughout the United States.' *Danforth* (White, J., concurring in part and dissenting in part).

"Just as improvements in medical technology inevitably will move *forward* the point at which the State may regulate for reasons for maternal health, different technological improvements will move *backward* the point of viability at which the State may proscribe abortions except when necessary to preserve the life and health of the mother. * * *

"The *Roe* framework, then, is clearly on a collision course with itself. As the medical risks of various abortion procedures decrease, the point at which the State may regulate for reasons of maternal health is moved further forward to actual childbirth. As medical science becomes better able to provide for the separate existence of the fetus, the point of viability is moved further back toward conception. Moreover, it is clear that the trimester approach violates the fundamental aspiration of judicial decision making through the application of neutral principles 'sufficiently absolute to give them roots throughout the community and continuity over significant periods of time.' Cox, *The Role of the Supreme Court in American Government* 114 (1976). The *Roe* framework is inherently tied to the state of medical technology that exists whenever particular litigation ensues. Although legislatures are better suited to make the necessary factual judgments in this area, the Court's framework forces legislatures, as a matter of constitutional law, to speculate about what constitutes 'accepted medical practice' at any given time. Without the necessary expertise or ability, courts must then pretend to act as science review boards and examine those legislative judgments. [Even] assuming that there is a fundamental right to terminate pregnancy in some situations, there is no justification in law or logic for the trimester framework adopted in *Roe* and employed by the Court today on the basis of stare decisis.

"[I agree with *Roe* that the state has legitimate and important interests in seeing that abortion is 'performed under circumstances that insure maximum safety for the patient' and in 'protecting the potentiability of life'], but in my view, the point at which these interests become compelling does not depend on the trimester of pregnancy. Rather, these interests are present *throughout* pregnancy. [The] fallacy inherent in the *Roe* framework is apparent: just because the State has a compelling interest in ensuring maternal safety once an abortion may be more dangerous [than] childbirth, it simply does not follow that the State has *no* interest before that point that justifies state regulation to ensure that first-trimester abortions are performed as safely as possible.

"The state interest in potential human life is likewise extant throughout pregnancy. In *Roe*, the Court held [that] that interest could not become compelling until the point at which the fetus was viable. The difficulty with this analysis is clear: *potential* life is no less potential in the first weeks of pregnancy than it is at viability or afterward. At any stage in pregnancy, there is the *potential* for human life. Although the Court refused to 'resolve the difficult question of when life begins,' [it] chose the point of viability—when the fetus is *capable* of life independent of its mother—to permit the complete proscription of abortion. The choice of viability as the point at which the state interest in *potential* life becomes compelling is no less arbitrary than choosing any point before viability or any point afterward. Accordingly, I believe that the State's interest in protecting potential human life exists throughout the pregnancy.

" ' * * * *Roe* did not declare an unqualified "constitutional right to an abortion," [but] protects the woman from unduly burdensome interference with her freedom to decide whether to terminate her pregnancy.' *Maher*. The Court and its individual Justices have repeatedly utilized the 'unduly burdensome' standard in abortion cases.

"[The] 'undue burden' required in the abortion cases represents the required threshold inquiry that must be conducted before this Court can require a State to justify its legislative actions under the exacting 'compelling state interest' standard. [In] determining whether the State imposes an 'undue burden,' we must keep in mind that when we are concerned with extremely sensitive issues, such as the one involved here, 'the appropriate forum for their resolution in a democracy is the legislature. * * * ' "

Justice O'Connor then concluded that neither (1) the second-trimester hospitalization requirement nor (2) the parental consent provision nor (3) the "informed consent" provision nor (4) the mandatory 24-hour waiting period "unduly burdened" the abortion decision. As for (5) the disposal of fetal remains, since there is no indication that physicians are required to provide " 'decent burials' for fetuses" and since " 'humane' is no more vague than the term 'sanitary,' the vagueness of which Akron Center does not question," the provision could not be deemed void for vagueness.

———————

A companion case to *Akron*, PLANNED PARENTHOOD v. ASHCROFT, 462 U.S. 476, 103 S.Ct. 2517, 76 L.Ed.2d 733 (1983), invalidated a Missouri second-trimester hospitalization requirement under the *Akron* analysis, but upheld other statutory provisions requiring the presence of a second physician during abortions performed after viability; a pathology report for each abortion performed in clinics as well as in hospitals; and that minors seeking abortion secure parental or judicial consent.

As for the second-physician requirement, POWELL, J., joined by Burger, C.J., reasoned that "[b]y giving medical attention to a fetus that is delivered alive, the second physician will assure that the State's interests are protected more fully than the first physician alone would be able to do. And given the compelling interest that the State has in preserving life, we cannot say that [the second-physician requirement] in those unusual circumstances where Missouri permits a third-trimester abortion is unconstitutional." O'CONNOR, J., joined by White and Rehnquist, JJ., concurred in the result "because the State possesses a compelling interest in protecting and preserving fetal life," but maintained that "this state interest is extant throughout pregnancy."

As for the requirement that minors secure parental consent or consent from the juvenile court for an abortion, POWELL, J., joined by Burger, C.J., concluded that, as interpreted by the Court of Appeals to mean that the juvenile court could not deny a petition "for good cause" unless it first found that the minor was not mature enough to make her own decision, the provision avoided any constitutional infirmities. "Assuming arguendo that the State cannot impose a parental veto on the decision of a minor to undergo an abortion," O'CONNOR, J., joined by White and Rehnquist, JJ., agreed that the parental consent provision was constitutional. "However, I believe that the provision is valid because it imposes no undue burden on any right that a minor may have to undergo an abortion."

BLACKMUN, J., joined by Brennan, Marshall and Stevens, JJ., would strike down all the challenged provisions. As for the second-physician requirement, it imposes an unjustified burden on women because "when a D & E abortion is performed, the second physician can do nothing to further the State's compelling interest in protecting life." As for the pathology-report requirement, it "is not in accord with 'generally accepted medical standards'" and "the State has not 'met its burden of demonstrating that [it] furthers important health-related concerns.' *Akron.*" As for the provision prohibiting the performance of an abortion on an unemancipated minor absent parental consent or a court order, "[u]ntil today, the Court has never upheld 'a requirement of a consent substitute, either parental or judicial.'" Justice Blackmun continued to adhere to the views expressed by four Justices in *Bellotti II* that "any judicial-consent statute would suffer from the same flaw identified in *Danforth:* it would give a third party an absolute veto over the decision of the physician and his patient (opinion of Stevens, J.).[a]

a. Another companion case to *Akron, Simopoulos v. Virginia,* 462 U.S. 506, 103 S.Ct. 2532, 76 L.Ed.2d 755 (1983), per Powell, J., upheld the conviction of a physician for performing an abortion during the second trimester of pregnancy outside of a licensed "hospital." Unlike the hospitalization requirements invalidated in *Akron* and *Ashcroft,* "the Virginia Statute and regulations do not require that second-trimester abortions be performed exclusively in full-service hospitals. [O]utpatient surgical hospitals may qualify for licensing as 'hospitals' [for this purpose]." As the Court interpreted the Virginia regulations, it saw "no reason to doubt that an adequately equipped clinic could, upon proper application, obtain an outpatient hospital license permitting the performance of second-trimester abortions. [The State's] requirement that second-trimester abortions be performed in licensed clinics is not an unreasonable means of furthering the State's compelling interest in 'protecting the woman's own health and safety.' *Roe.* [The requirement] appears to comport with accepted medical practice, and leaves the method and timing of the abortion precisely where they belong— with the physician and the patient." O'Connor, J., joined by White and Rehnquist, JJ., concurred in the judgment, but did "not agree that the constitutional validity of the Virginia mandatory hospitalization requirement is contingent in any way on the trimester in which it is imposed. Rather, I believe

Notes and Questions

1. *"The Court's discomfort before reality" and other criticism of the Akron case.* Consider JOHN NOONAN, *The Root and Branch of Roe v. Wade,* 63 Neb. L.Rev. 668, 677–78 (1984): "[One of the holdings] of *Akron* was that the city could not require that a physician give counselling to the abortion seeker * * *. [This holding was] interestingly inconsistent with the general implication of *Roe* as to the importance of the family physician. In *Roe* the physician was treated as an heroic figure, one on whom the abortion seeker could depend; but when an attempt was made to build upon this deference to the doctor in a way that the Court found restrictive of the abortion liberty, the Court's deference was swallowed up by its desire to extend the liberty as widely as possible.

"Most striking of all, *Akron* held that there could not be a legal requirement that a woman seeking an abortion be informed that the being she wished put to death was a child, that the child was alive, and that the child was human. The Court treated this information as prejudicing the choice of whether to abort or not—as a kind of unfair interference with free choice. [This holding was] the invention of a kind of censorship by the Court itself. [The] facts that would have been provided to a woman under the Akron ordinance are the same kind of facts that would be provided in a modern course in biology.

"[A] final provision of the Akron ordinance was that 'the remains of the unborn child' be 'disposed in a humane and sanitary manner.' [The Sixth Circuit] found the word 'humane' impermissibly vague in a criminal statute. The ordinance could, the court said, mean to 'mandate some sort of "decent burial" of an embryo at the earliest stages of formation.' Justice Powell quoted this analysis and agreed; humane and sanitary burial was beyond the comprehension of a reasonable doctor.

"In this conclusion one can observe in the most concrete way the Court's discomfort before reality. The Court cannot uphold a requirement of humane burial without conceding that the being who is to be buried is human. A mask has been placed over this being. Even death cannot remove this mask."

2. *Should the focus of the abortion inquiry be on the state of fetal development rather than on the existing state of medical technology?* "If the legal system adheres to the reasoning of *Roe*," warns Comment, 29 U.C.L.A.L.Rev. 1194, 1204–05 (1982), "there is no limit to the extent to which advances in technology may diminish a woman's right to an abortion. [I]f, however, the focus is placed upon the degree of fetal development [rather than on viability], the courts can avoid the problems resulting from technological advances. The ultimate question should be at what point does the fetus become a human being." Continues the UCLA Comment (at 1207–11, 1215):

"An appropriate standard for determining the beginning of human life is when the fetal brain is developed to the point where the fetus is a thinking, conscious being. A survey of existing scientific research indicates that a fetus [reaches this stage] between twelve and thirty-two weeks [and primarily between 19 and 30 weeks] after conception.

"[If] the competing interests of the woman and society are balanced by asking at what point the fetus becomes a human being, then advances in

that the requirement in this case is not an undue burden on the decision to undergo an abortion."

technology will not erode the balance that is struck. In fact, [such advances will enable us] to more accurately determine when the fetus becomes a human being.

"[A] standard for determining when human life begins based on brain function [would] provide a workable and religiously neutral resolution of the competing interests of the woman and the fetus [and] also create a symmetry between the legal definitions for the beginning and end of life, thereby giving us a unified legal theory of what constitutes a human being."

3. *Is the "Roe framework," as Justice O'Connor maintains, "on a collision course with itself"?* Consider the remarks of LAURENCE TRIBE in Choper, Kamisar & Tribe, *The Supreme Court: Trends and Developments, 1982–83* (1984) at 257–58: "I think that [Justice O'Connor is] simply confused about one important aspect of the abortion decision. There are two different rationales on which the states purport to regulate abortion. One is to protect the health of the mother. As to that, it's true that medical advances make later and later abortions safe and, thereby, make it more and more difficult for the government to justify regulating even very late abortions. The other and wholly independent rationale, having absolutely nothing to do with a woman's safety or her health, is the protection of the life of the fetus. As to that, the Supreme Court [concluded] that the power of the state to coerce a woman to remain pregnant is inherently linked to the viability of the fetus. That is, it is when the fetus is not yet viable that saving its life requires coercing continued pregnancy.

"Once, of course, the fetus is viable, then a desire to protect it is no longer necessarily coincident with forcing a woman to remain, as it were, an involuntary incubator. If fetal viability is possible earlier in pregnancy as a result of medical advances, it is possible simultaneously to respect the woman's right not to be pregnant involuntarily, and the fetus' right to survive.

"The fact that medical advances may bring about a kind of brave new world of artificial placenta and artificial uteri earlier and earlier in the pregnancy simply means that regulation on the rationale of protecting the fetus, as opposed to the rationale of protecting the woman's health, may justify governmental intervention even in the first trimester to say, 'If you don't want to remain pregnant, fine. Give us the fetus, and we'll take care of it in the hospital.' Some would find that a nightmarish prospect because it would substitute technology for what ought to be a human undertaking. But that really raises an issue of a very different kind from those in the abortion case itself, and I think that Justice O'Connor is simply wrong in assuming that the two kinds of regulations are on a collision course."

THE HUMAN LIFE BILL [a]

Section 5 of the fourteenth amendment gives Congress the authority "to enforce" that amendment by "appropriate legislation." As reported out by the Senate Subcommittee on the Separation of Powers in 1981, the Human Life Bill provides that pursuant to its Section 5 authority Congress "find" that "the life of each human being begins at conception" and "recognize" that for the purpose of enforcing the fourteenth amendment "each human life exists from conception" and that " 'person' includes all human beings."

Defending the constitutionality of the Human Life Bill, STEPHEN GALEBACH, *A Human Life Statute*, Hum.Life Rev., Winter, 1981, reprinted in

a. For a general discussion of Congress's Section 5 power to enforce the fourteenth amendment, see Ch. 8, Sec. 2.

Abortion: Moral and Legal Perspectives 123 (Garfield & Hennessey eds. 1984) argues (id. at 134, 135, 140–41, 146): "To define 'life' and 'person' is only the first and smallest step that must be taken if any branch of the federal government is rationally to determine what scope of human life falls within the protection of the Fourteenth Amendment. * * * Not only is the line between life and nonlife a difficult one, more appropriately drawn by the legislature than by the courts; it is also a line that the *Roe* opinion itself explicitly declared the courts unable to draw.   Under the approach of *Katzenbach v. Morgan* [p. 1156 infra], the Court's prior definition of 'person' in *Roe* poses no greater barrier to congressional enforcement action than [the holding in *Lassiter v. Northampton County Board of Elections,* p. 1491 infra] posed to Congress's nationwide prohibition of literacy tests.   [I]t might be argued that Congress may not decide anything about the beginnings of life because the issue is inherently religious [but] one does not have to hold any religious beliefs in order to be able to examine biological evidence on the development of unborn children—or to look at an aborted child—and conclude that the unborn are likely to be human life. [The] relative competence of the courts and Congress to decide when life begins suggests that Congress not only *can* do this, but *should*.   It is because of the courts' limitations as fact-finders and policy-makers that they have left the nation without any answer to the question of when life begins.   Since Congress does not share these limitations, it is positioned to fill this gap by serving as the proper institution to reflect and express society's answer to this question."

But consider SAMUEL ESTREICHER, *Congressional Power and Constitutional Rights: Reflections on Proposed "Human Life" Legislation,* 68 Va.L.Rev. 333, 340, 351, 358 (1982): "In the abortion area, Congress can have no greater authority than a state legislature to regulate abortions. *Roe* and its progeny define the limits of governmental action in this area, and ordinary legislation cannot undo those limits. * * * Proponents of the 'human life' position hinge much of their argument on the [*Roe* Court's] comment that '[w]hen those trained in the respective disciplines of medicine, philosophy, and theology are unable to arrive at any consensus, the judiciary, at this point in the development of man's knowledge, is not in a position to speculate as to [when life begins].'   This passage, however, must be read in light of the Court's conclusion that 'by adopting one theory of life, Texas may [not] override the rights of the pregnant woman that are at stake.'   Rather than indicating judicial abstention in favor of a legislative judgment, the passage indicates the Court's refusal to hold that a state interest resting on such a speculative, disputable premise can have sufficient force to defeat the claims of reproductive autonomy.   Whatever the caliber of its moral and constitutional theory, *Roe* is a definitive resolution—subject to whatever elasticity inheres in the concept of viability—that a state's interest in protecting the life of a fetus is not compelling until the point of viability.   [T]he *Roe* Court's upholding of a right of reproductive autonomy in the face of admitted uncertainty about the precise point of life's beginning required a value judgment of constitutional dimension that the fetus's potential life did not justify restricting access to abortion.   [W]hat [the Court] constitutionalized in *Roe* was a value judgment, not a variable factual determination." [b]

b. See also Emerson, *The Power of Congress to Change Constitutional Decisions of the Supreme Court: The Human Life Bill,* 77 Nw. U.L.Rev. 129, 136 (1982) ("the Human Life Bill clearly does not 'enforce' the provisions of the fourteenth amendment, but instead drastically alters them, and thereby deprives millions of citizens of rights to which the Supreme Court has held they are entitled"); Gordon, *The Nature and Uses of Congressional Power under Section Five of the Fourteenth Amendment to Overcome Decisions of the Supreme Court,* 72 Nw.U.L.Rev. 656, 690 (1977) ("*Roe* is an absolute rather than a contingent deci-

WHAT IF *ROE* WERE OVERRULED AND THE ABORTION CONTROVERSY MOVED TO THE LEGISLATIVE ARENA?

"Should the abortion controversy ever move from the judicial to the legislative chambers," observes Collins, *Is There "Life" (or "Choice") After Roe?*, 3 Const.Comm. 91 (1986), "the probable scenarios could bring unexpected victories and losses for both sides." Recalling that prior to *Roe* more than a third of the states permitted abortions under circumstances objectionable to the "pro-life" advocates of the 1980s, Collins predicts that "once the abortion right is stripped of its federal constitutional cloak, 'pro-choice' defenders will apply pressure on legislators with all the fervor of a martyr's cause. Just as *Roe* opened the horizon to a 'pro-life' movement, so too could its demise carry the opposition to the zenith of its political power. In such an atmosphere, how likely would it be for lawmakers to ban abortions, say, within the first twelve weeks of pregnancy?"

Lamana, *Social Science and Ethical Issues*, in *Abortion: Understanding Differences*, 1, 4–7 (Callahan & Callahan eds. 1984), points out that, according to the poll data; only 25% support abortion as defined in *Roe*, but even fewer—almost 20%—support the pro-life position. About 55% are in between, approving abortion in some circumstances, but not in others. Similarly, Luker, *Abortion and the Politics of Motherhood* 224 (1984), emphasizes that all the available data indicates that *neither* the pro-life *nor* the pro-choice movement "has ever been 'representative' of how most Americans feel about abortion."

All but a tiny minority of Americans support abortion for "hard" reasons (e.g., when the woman's health is at risk, the pregnancy is the result of rape or incest, or there is a likelihood that the child will be born with substantial handicaps), yet many Americans feel a deep uneasiness about abortions and balk at abortions for "soft" reasons (e.g., the woman is unmarried or a teenager or simply does not want a child). See Lamana, supra, at 4–7; Luker, supra, at 226–30. "If the pro-life movement were able to 'sell' the American public an anti-abortion law that protected abortions for the 'hard' reasons, it is possible that under certain conditions much of the present support for abortion could evaporate," comments Luker (at 234, 239), but if the pro-life movement were to accept a law permitting abortion in e.g., cases of rape or incest, "it would be conceding a great deal of ideological ground."

If the abortion controversy were to move to the legislative chambers, "the best the pro-life movement could hope for," according to Luker (at 242–43), would be "a modern form of the Prohibition experience"—a "situation in which abortions become harder and more expensive to get but still continue to exist in almost the same numbers as before. * * * Pro-choice people, however, can take little comfort from this prospect. Prohibition, after all, was the law of the land for many years, and it took considerable political resources to overturn it."

sion"; the woman's autonomy over the abortion decision before the point of fetal viability "was held to be absolute in the sense that the state could not prohibit the exercise of that right under virtually any circumstances"). Cf. Cherminsky, *Rationalizing the Abortion Debate*, 31 Buffalo L.Rev. 107, 157–58 (1982): If one reads *Roe* as standing for the proposi-tion that "abortion is a private moral judgment, then women have the right to remove fetuses from their bodies even if the fetus is a person and even if removal will kill that person. Thus, even granting Congress authority under section five [to] define 'person' as including a fetus, the Human Life Bill would still be unconstitutional."

FAMILY LIVING ARRANGEMENTS, PARENTAL RIGHTS, AND
THE "RIGHT TO MARRY"

As illustrated by WHALEN v. ROE (1977), p. 76 supra (sustaining a New York law that doctors disclose the names of persons obtaining certain drugs for storage in a central computer file), those attacking legislation can often cast their challenge in terms of an invasion of a constitutionally protected "zone of privacy." But the Court upheld the legislation as "a reasonable exercise of New York's broad police powers," holding that the program did not require extraordinary justification because it "does not, on its face, pose a sufficiently grievous threat" to either the "privacy" interest "in avoiding disclosure of personal matters" [a] or the "privacy" interest "in independence in making certain kinds of important decisions [e.g., abortion, marriage]." The cases discussed below deal with the latter "privacy" interest.

———

1. *Zoning; choice of household companions; "extended family" relationships.* Relying on earlier decisions sustaining local zoning regulations, BELLE TERRE v. BORAAS, 416 U.S. 1, 94 S.Ct. 1536, 39 L.Ed.2d 797 (1974), per DOUGLAS, J., upheld a village ordinance restricting land use to one-family dwellings (defining "family" to mean not more than two unrelated persons living together as a single housekeeping unit, and expressly excluding from the term lodging, boarding, fraternity or multiple-dwelling houses). Appellees, who had leased their houses to six unrelated college students, challenged the ordinance, inter alia, on the ground that it "trenches on the newcomers' rights of privacy." The Court disagreed: "We deal with economic and social legislation where legislatures have historically drawn lines which we respect [if the law] bears 'a rational relationship to a [permissible] state objective.' " "[B]oarding houses, fraternity houses, and the like present urban problems. [The] police power is not confined to elimination of filth, stench, and unhealthy places."

MARSHALL, J., dissented: The ordinance burdened "fundamental rights of association and privacy," and thus required extraordinary justification, not a mere showing that the ordinance "bears a rational relationship to the accomplishment of legitimate governmental objectives." He viewed "the right to 'establish a home' " as an "essential part" of fourteenth amendment liberty and maintained that "the choice of household companions"—which "involves deeply personal considerations as to the kind and quality of intimate relationships within the home"—"surely falls within the right to privacy protected by the Constitution." The state's purposes "could be as effectively achieved by means

a. The Court, however, specifically did *not* decide "any question which might be presented by the unwarranted disclosure of accumulated private data—whether intentional or unintentional—or by a system that did not contain [adequate] security provisions."

See also *Paul v. Davis,* per Rehnquist, J., Sec. 5, I infra, holding that police disclosure of a person's shoplifting arrest did not violate his right of privacy: "His claim is based not upon any challenge to the State's ability to restrict his freedom of action in a sphere contended to be 'private,' but instead on a claim that the State may not publicize a record of an official act such as an arrest. None of our substantive privacy decisions hold this or anything like this and we decline to enlarge them in this manner." Brennan, J., joined by Marshall, J., observed that "a host of state and federal courts, relying on both privacy notions and the presumption of innocence, have begun to develop a line of cases holding that there are substantive limits on the power of the Government to disseminate unresolved arrest records outside the law enforcement [system]. I fear that after today's decision, these nascent doctrines will never have the opportunity for full growth and analysis."

of an ordinance that did not discriminate on the basis of constitutionally protected choices of life style." [b]

Distinguishing *Belle Terre* as involving an ordinance "affect[ing] only *unrelated* individuals," MOORE v. EAST CLEVELAND, 431 U.S. 494, 97 S.Ct. 1932, 52 L.Ed.2d 531 (1977), invalidated a housing ordinance that limited occupancy to single families, but defined "family" so as to forbid appellant from having her two grandsons live with her. (It did not permit living arrangements if, as in this case, the grandchildren were cousins rather than brothers.) [a] POWELL, J., announcing the Court's judgment and joined by Brennan, Marshall, and Blackmun, JJ., struck down the ordinance on substantive due process grounds:

"[O]n its face [the ordinance] selects certain categories of relatives who may live together and declares that others may not. [When] a city undertakes such intrusive regulation of the family [the] usual judicial deference to the legislature is inappropriate. 'This Court has long recognized that freedom of personal choice in matters of marriage and family life is one of the liberties protected by [due process].' Of course the family is not beyond regulation. But when the government intrudes on choices concerning family living arrangements, this Court must examine carefully the importance of the governmental interests advanced and the extent to which they are served by the challenged regulation [referring to Harlan, J.'s dissent in *Poe v. Ullman*]." "[T]hus examined, this ordinance cannot survive." [3] Although the city's goals—preventing overcrowding, minimizing congestion and avoiding financial strain on its school system—were "legitimate," the ordinance served them "marginally at best."

"[T]he history of the *Lochner* [era] counsels caution and restraint [but] it does [not] require what the city urges here: cutting off any family rights at the first convenient, if arbitrary boundary—the boundary of the nuclear family. * * * Appropriate limits on substantive due process come not from drawing arbitrary lines but rather from careful 'respect for the teachings of history [and] solid recognition of the basic values that underlie our society.' *Griswold* (Harlan, J., concurring). Our decisions teach that the Constitution protects the sanctity of the family precisely because the institution of the family is deeply rooted in this Nation's history and tradition. [Ours] is by no means a tradition limited to respect for [the] nuclear family. The tradition of uncles, aunts, cousins, and especially grandparents sharing a household along with parents and children [especially in times of adversity] has roots equally venerable and equally deserving of constitutional recognition. [In *Pierce*, the Constitution prevented a state from] 'standardiz[ing] its children by forcing them to accept instruction from public teachers only.' By the same token the Constitution prevents East Cleveland from standardizing its children—and its adults—by forcing all to live in certain narrowly defined family patterns." [b]

b. Compare Marshall, J.'s views in *Belle Terre* with the Court's discussion of "freedom of intimate association" in *Roberts v. United States Jaycees,* p. 644, infra.

a. The second grandson came to live with his grandmother after the death of his mother.

3. Appellant also claims that the ordinance contravenes the Equal Protection Clause, but it is not necessary for us to reach that contention.

b. Brennan, J., joined by Marshall, J., concurred, characterizing the ordinance as "senseless," "arbitrary" and "eccentric" and

as reflecting "cultural myopia" and "a distressing insensitivity toward the economic and emotional needs of a very large part of our society." He called the "extended family" "virtually a means of survival" for many poor and black families. [The] 'nuclear family' is the pattern so often found in much of white suburbia," but "the Constitution cannot * * * tolerate the imposition by government upon the rest of us of white suburbia's preference in patterns of family living." But see dissenting Justice Stewart's response, infra.

Stevens, J., concurring, thought this "unprecedented ordinance" unconstitutional even

STEWART, J., joined by Rehnquist, J., dissented, rejecting the argument that "the importance of the 'extended family' in American society" renders appellant's "decision to share her residence with her grandsons," like the decisions involved in bearing and raising children, "an aspect of 'family life'" entitled to substantive constitutional protection. To equate appellant's interest in sharing her residence with some of her relatives "with the fundamental decisions to marry and to bear children," he maintained, "is to extend the limited substantive contours of the Due Process Clause beyond recognition." He thought the challenged "family" definition "rationally designed to carry out the legitimate governmental purposes identified in *Belle Terre*." A different line "could hardly be drawn that would not sooner or later become the target of a challenge like the appellant's," such as "the hard case of an orphaned niece or nephew."

Nor could he understand "why it follows that the residents of East Cleveland are constitutionally prevented from following what Justice Brennan calls the 'pattern' of 'white suburbia,' even though that choice may reflect 'cultural myopia.' In point of fact, East Cleveland is a predominantly Negro community, with a Negro City Manager and City Commission." [c]

WHITE, J., dissenting, voiced disbelief "that the interest in residing with more than one set of grandchildren is one that calls for any kind of heightened protection under the Due Process Clause. [The] present claim is hardly one of which it could be said that 'neither liberty nor justice would exist if [it] were sacrificed.' *Palko*."

He maintained that Powell, J.'s approach—construing the Due Process Clause to protect from all but "quite important" state interests any right "that in his estimate is deeply rooted in the country's traditions"—"suggests a far too expansive charter for this Court. [What] the deeply rooted traditions of the country are is arguable; which of them deserve [due process protection] is even more debatable. The suggested view would broaden enormously the horizons of the Clause." [d]

Notes and Questions

(a) *The elusiveness of the search for sources of fundamental rights. Moore v. East Cleveland*, maintains Grano, *Judicial Review and a Written Constitution in a Democratic Society*, 28 Wayne L.Rev. 1, 25–27 (1981), "demonstrates both how elusive the search for sources of fundamental rights can be and how unsatisfying the Court's attempts at demonstration necessarily are. Justice Powell's plurali-

under the "limited standard of review of zoning decisions": "The city has failed totally to explain the need for a rule which would allow a homeowner to have two grandchildren live with her if they are brothers, but not if they are cousins. Since the ordinance has not been shown to have any 'substantial relation to [East Cleveland's] public health, safety, morals or general welfare' [and] since it cuts so deeply into a fundamental right normally associated with the ownership of residential property—that of an owner to decide who may reside on his or her property—it must fall [as] a taking of property without due process and without just compensation."

c. "[I]n assessing [appellant's] claim that the ordinance is 'arbitrary' and 'irrational,'" Stewart, J., considered a provision permitting her to request a variance "particularly per-

suasive evidence to the contrary. [The] variance procedure, a traditional part of American land-use law, bends the straight lines of East Cleveland's ordinance, shaping their contours to respond more flexibly to the hard cases that are the inevitable byproduct of legislative linedrawing."

Burger, C.J., dissented on the ground that appellant should have pursued the "plainly adequate administrative remedy" of seeking a variance, thus finding it "unnecessary to reach the difficult constitutional issue."

d. "[A]n approach grounded in history," replied Justice Powell [fn. 12], "imposes limits on the judiciary that are more meaningful than any based on [White, J.'s] abstract formula taken from *Palko*."

ty opinion concluded that 'the Constitution protects the sanctity of the family precisely because the institution of the family is deeply rooted in the Nation's history and tradition.' Societies do change, however, and cognizant of this, the Court could not have intended to become constitutionally committed to every practice rooted in our history and tradition. In particular, progress toward racial and sexual equality depends upon success in freeing ourselves from the yoke of history and tradition. Moreover, by implication, Justice Powell's opinion suggested that the result would have been different had an unrelated neighbor taken charge of Mrs. Moore's grandson, [but did not explain] why history and tradition would not protect a neighbor's decision to do what Mrs. Moore did. Nor did he explain why, if it would not, history and tradition should be determinative. [Justice White's dissent], while accepting noninterpretivism with caution, rejected Justice Powell's history and tradition test for defining fundamental rights. [T]he issue that prompted [the Powell-White] exchange is intractable: freed from the need to use the written Constitution as a source of judgment, noninterpretivist judges may select any source that is personally appealing." [a]

(b) *Should Moore have been decided on "naked substantive due process grounds"?* *Moore's* choice of rationale, comments Lupu, *Untangling the Strands of the Fourteenth Amendment,* 77 Mich.L.Rev. 981, 1017 (1979), "reversed a pattern that had endured for four decades: it was the first decision since the 1937 revolution to invalidate a statute on naked substantive due process grounds when equal protection grounds seemed readily available. [*Griswold* and *Roe*] had not presented such alternatives; in both cases, the complained-of prohibition swept broadly across the state's entire population, and thus offered no classification readily subject to equal protection attack. In *Moore,* by contrast, the 'family' definition in the ordinance seemed perfect for invalidation as an arbitrary [classification]. The plurality opinion stood at least thirty years of conventional wisdom on its head by adopting a substantive due process theory and proclaiming in a one-sentence footnote that the due process holding rendered it unnecessary for the Court to reach the equal protection claims."

If *Moore* had invalidated the ordinance on equal protection grounds, observes Lupu, at 1019, it might have suggested "the permissibility of other, less arbitrary definitions of 'family.' Instead, *Moore* holds that families, defined by blood and marriage relations, cannot be carved up unless such limitations are critically necessary to achieve substantial zoning objectives." [b]

(c) *Was the purpose of the ordinance quite straightforward?* How significant is it that "East Cleveland is a predominantly Negro community, with a Negro City Manager and City Commissioner"? Consider Burt, *The Constitution of the Family,* 1979 Sup.Ct.Rev. 329, 389: "The plurality viewed the ordinance as directed against [over-crowding, minimizing traffic and the like, but] did not consider that the purpose of the ordinance was quite straightforward: to exclude from a middle-class, predominantly black community, that saw itself as socially and economically upwardly mobile, other black families most characteristic of lower-class ghetto life. Perhaps the Court did not see this purpose or, if it did,

a. But see Sedler, *The Legitimacy Debate in Constitutional Adjudication,* 44 Ohio St. L.J. 93, 111–13 (1983) (neither White, J., who alluded to the legitimacy question in *Moore,* nor any other Justice on the Court "has ever disputed that it was legitimate for the Court to have imputed a substantive meaning to the due process clause").

b. But see Gerety, *Doing Without Privacy,* 42 Ohio St.L.J. 143, 156–59 (1981) (*Moore* demonstrates need for "privacy" rationale and inadequacy of "pure equal protection theory of individual rights").

considered this an 'illegitimate goal,' though in other cases the Court had been exceedingly solicitous of white middle-class communities' attempts to preserve a common social identity—'zones,' as the Court had put the matter three years earlier [in *Belle Terre*]—'where family values, youth values, and the blessings of the quiet seclusion and clean air make the area a sanctuary for people.' [Although Brennan, J., had dissented in *Belle Terre*], I find in his characterization of the East Cleveland ordinance as 'senseless' and 'eccentric,' precisely what he alleges in it: 'a depressing insensitivity toward the economic and emotional needs' of the current majority of residents in East Cleveland."

(d) *Was Moore a dispute about the meaning of "family"?* Which way does it cut that the East Cleveland ordinance was "unusual" or even "eccentric"? Was victory for Mrs. Moore "total defeat" for the other city residents, but victory for them "not total defeat for her, except insofar as she wished to remain in their community while transferring its membership to her taste"? Consider *Burt*, supra, at 391: "[T]he very oddity of the East Cleveland ordinance suggests that Mrs. Moore is not alone in her opposition to it, that the city residents are more the vulnerable, isolated dissenters than she in the broader society, that they more than she deserve special judicial solicitude as a 'discrete and insular minority.' The Court in *Moore* myopically saw the case as a dispute between 'a family' and 'the state' rather than as a dispute among citizens about the meaning of 'family.' "

2. *Adoption and rights of the natural father.* QUILLOIN v. WALCOTT, 434 U.S. 246, 98 S.Ct. 549, 54 L.Ed.2d 511 (1978): Under Georgia law, if the natural father has not "legitimated" his offspring (appellant had not sought to do so during the 11 years between the child's birth and the adoption petition), only the mother's consent is required for the adoption of the illegitimate child. When the child was 11, the mother consented to his adoption by her husband with whom she and her son were living. Appellant attempted to block the adoption, but did not seek custody or object to the child's continuing to live with his mother and stepfather. On the basis of various findings (e.g., appellant had provided support only on an irregular basis, the child himself expressed a desire to be adopted by his stepfather who was found to be fit to adopt the child), the trial court concluded that the adoption would be in the "best interests of the child."

A unanimous Court, per MARSHALL, J., affirmed: "We have recognized on numerous occasions that the relationship between parent and child is constitutionally protected, e.g. *Wisconsin v. Yoder* [p. 770 infra]; *Stanley v. Illinois* [p. 1403 infra] [and] [w]e have little doubt that the Due Process Clause would be offended '[i]f a State were to attempt to force the breakup of a natural family, over the objection of the parents and their children, without some showing of unfitness and for the sole reason that to do so was thought to be in the children's best interests.' *Smith v. Organization of Foster Families*, 431 U.S. 816, 862, 97 S.Ct. 2094, 53 L.Ed.2d 14 (1977) (Stewart, J., concurring). But this is not a case [where] the unwed father had, or sought [custody, or where] the proposed adoption would place the child with a new set of parents with whom the child had never before lived. Rather, the result of the adoption in this case is to give full recognition to a family unit already in existence, a result desired by all concerned, except appellant. [Under these circumstances it suffices that the state found] that the adoption, and denial of legitimation, was in the 'best interests of the child.' "

3. *Right to marry.* ZABLOCKI v. REDHAIL, 434 U.S. 374, 98 S.Ct. 673, 54 L.Ed.2d 618 (1978): A Wisconsin law forbade marriage by any resident with

minor children not in his custody whom he is under court order to support, unless he proves compliance with the support obligation and that the children "are not then and are not likely thereafter to become public charges." Appellee and the woman he desired to marry were expecting a child, but he was denied a marriage license because he had not satisfied his support obligations to his illegitimate child who had been a public charge since birth. In the course of striking down the marriage prohibition under the "fundamental rights" branch of equal protection doctrine (see Ch. 6, Sec. 4)—which Stewart, J., concurring, called, "in a case like [this] no more than substantive due process by another name"—the Court, per MARSHALL, J., had a good deal to say about "the right to marry":

"Since our past decisions make clear that the right to marry is of fundamental importance, and since the classification at issue here significantly interferes with the exercise of that right, we believe that 'critical examination' of the state's interests advanced in support of the classification is required. [Cases] subsequent to *Griswold* and *Loving v. Virginia* (1967) p. 832 infra, invalidating state miscegenation laws] have routinely categorized the decision to marry as among the personal decisions protected by the right of privacy. [It] is not surprising that the decision to marry has been placed on the same level of importance as decisions relating to procreation, childbirth, child rearing, and family relationships [for] it would make little sense to recognize a right of privacy with respect to other matters of family life and not with respect to the decision to enter the relationship that is the foundation of the family in our society. The woman whom appellee desired to marry had a fundamental right to seek an abortion of their expected child or to bring the child into life to suffer [the] disabilities that the status of illegitimacy brings. Surely, a decision to marry and raise the child in a traditional family setting must receive equivalent protection. And, if appellee's right to procreate means anything at all, it must imply some right to enter the only relationship in which [the state] allows sexual relations legally to take place.

"By reaffirming the fundamental character of the right to marry, we do not mean to suggest that every state regulation which relates in any way to the incidents of or prerequisites for marriage must be subjected to rigorous scrutiny. [R]easonable regulations that do not significantly interfere with decisions to enter into the marital relationships may legitimately be imposed. See *Califano v. Jobst*, 434 U.S. 47, 98 S.Ct. 95, 54 L.Ed.2d 228 (1977), n. 12 infra." However, because the statute prevents any Wisconsin resident in the affected class from marrying anywhere without a court order, some in the affected class, like appellee, "are absolutely prevented from ever getting married," for "they either lack the financial means to meet their support obligations or cannot prove that their children will not become public charges"; and because "many others [will] be sufficiently burdened by having to [satisfy the statute's requirements] that they will in effect be coerced into foregoing their right to marry," this statute "clearly does interfere directly and substantially with the right to marry.[12]

12. The directness and substantiality of the interference with the freedom to marry distinguish the instant case from *Jobst*. In *Jobst* [applying the "rationality" standard of review] we upheld sections of the Social Security Act providing, inter alia, for termination of a dependent child's benefits upon marriage to an individual not entitled to benefits under the Act. As the opinion for the Court express- ly noted, the rule terminating benefits upon marriage was not "an attempt to interfere with the individual's freedom to make a decision as important as marriage." The Social Security provisions placed no direct legal obstacle in the path of persons desiring to get married, [and] there was no evidence that the laws significantly discouraged, let alone made "practically impossible," any marriages. In-

"When a statutory classification significantly interferes with the exercise of a fundamental right, it cannot be upheld unless it is supported by sufficiently important state interests and is closely tailored to effectuate only those interests. [Assuming that the state interests said to be served by the statute—furnishing an opportunity to counsel the applicant as to the need to fulfill his prior support obligations, and protecting the welfare of the out-of-custody children—] are legitimate and substantial interests, [since] the means selected by the State for achieving these interests unnecessarily impinge on the right to marry, the statute cannot be sustained.

"[The counseling interest] obviously cannot support the withholding of court permission to marry once counseling is completed. [As for the argument that the statute provides incentive for the applicant to make support payments to his children], with respect to [those] unable to meet the statutory requirements, the statute merely prevents the applicant from getting married, without delivering any money at all into the hands of the [children]. More importantly, [the] State already has numerous other means for exacting compliance with support obligations, means that are at least as effective as the instant statute's and yet do not impinge upon the right to marry [such as wage assignments, civil contempt proceedings and criminal penalties]."

As for the suggestion that the statute protects the ability of marriage applicants to meet prior support obligations by preventing the applicants from incurring new ones, the statute is "grossly underinclusive" since it in no way limits other new financial commitments and "substantially overinclusive as well," for the new spouse may actually improve the applicant's financial situation. "[P]reventing the marriage may only result in [new] children being born out of wedlock, as in fact occurred in appellee's case. Since the support obligation is the same whether the child is born in or out of wedlock, the net result of preventing the marriage is simply more illegitimate children." [a]

STEWART, J., concurred: "I do not agree with the Court that there is a 'right to marry' in the constitutional sense. [A] State may not only 'significantly interfere with decisions to enter into the marriage relationship,' but may in many circumstances absolutely prohibit it. Surely, for example, a State may legitimately say that no one can marry his or her sibling, that no one can marry who is not at least 14 years old, that no one can marry without first passing an examination for venereal disease, or that no one can marry who has a living husband or wife. But, just as surely, in regulating the intimate human relationship of marriage, there is a limit beyond which a State may not constitutionally go.

"[S]ome people simply cannot afford to meet the statute's financial requirements. To deny these people permission to marry penalizes them for failing to do that which they cannot do. Insofar as it applies to indigents, the state law is an irrational means of achieving these objectives of the State. As directed against either the indigent or the delinquent parent, the law is substantially more rational if viewed as a means of assuring the financial viability of future marriages. [But] the State's legitimate concern with the financial soundness of prospective marriages must stop short of telling people they may not marry because they are too poor or because they might persist in their financial irresponsibility. The invasion of constitutionally protected liberty and the

deed, the provisions had not deterred the individual who challenged the statute from getting married, even though he and his wife were both disabled. * * *

a. Burger, C.J., joined the Court's opinion and briefly concurred.

chance of erroneous prediction are simply too great. A legislative judgment so alien to our traditions and so offensive to our shared notions of fairness offends the Due Process Clause of the Fourteenth Amendment.

"[E]qual protection doctrine has become the Court's chief instrument for invalidating state laws. Yet, in a case like this one, the doctrine is no more than substantive due process by another name. [T]he effect of the Court's decision in this case is not to require Wisconsin to draw its legislative classifications with greater precision or to afford similar treatment to similarly situated persons. Rather, the message of the Court's opinion is that Wisconsin may not use its control over marriage to achieve the objectives of the state statute. Such restrictions on basic governmental power are at the heart of substantive due process. The Court is understandably reluctant to rely on substantive due process. But to embrace the essence of that doctrine under the guise of equal protection serves no purpose but obfuscation."

POWELL, J., concurred in the judgment, but wrote separately "because the majority's rationale sweeps too broadly in an area which traditionally has been subject to state regulation": "The Court apparently would subject all state regulation which 'directly and substantially' interferes with the decision to marry in a traditional family setting to 'critical examination' or 'compelling state interest' analysis. Presumably, 'reasonable regulations that do not significantly interfere with decisions to enter into the marital relationship may legitimately be imposed.' The Court does not present, however, any principal means for distinguishing between the two types of regulations. Since state regulation in this area typically takes the form of a prerequisite or barrier to marriage or divorce, the degree of 'direct' interference with the decision to marry or to divorce is unlikely to provide either guidance for state legislatures or a basis for judicial oversight.

"[State] regulation has included bans on incest, bigamy, and homosexuality, as well as various preconditions to marriage, such as blood tests. Likewise, a showing of fault on the part of one of the partners traditionally has been a prerequisite to the dissolution of an unsuccessful union. A 'compelling state purpose' inquiry would cast doubt on the network of restrictions that the States have fashioned to govern marriage and divorce.

"State power over domestic relations is not without constitutional limits. The Due Process Clause requires a showing of justification 'when the government intrudes on choices concerning family living arrangements' in a manner which is contrary to deeply rooted traditions, *Moore v. East Cleveland,* [and it also limits] the extent to which the State may monopolize the process of ordering certain human relationships while excluding the truly indigent from that process. *Boddie v. Connecticut* [p. 1041 infra]. Furthermore, under the Equal Protection Clause, the means chosen by the State in this case must bear 'a fair and substantial relation' to the object of the legislation [citing *Reed v. Reed* and his concurring opinion in *Craig v. Boren,* both in Ch. 7, Sec. 3, IV].

"The Wisconsin measure in this case does not pass muster under either due process or equal protection standards. [As for the state's 'collection device' justification, [t]o the extent this restriction applies to persons who are able to make the required payments but simply wish to shirk their moral and legal obligation, the Constitution interposes no bar to this additional collection mechanism. The vice inheres not in the collection concept, but in the failure to make provision for those without the means to comply with child-support obligations. [As for the state interest in preserving 'the ability of marriage applicants to support their prior issue by preventing them from incurring new obligations'], [the law is] so grossly underinclusive with respect to this objective, given the many ways that additional financial obligations may be incurred by the applicant quite apart from a contemplated marriage, that the classification 'does not bear a fair and substantial relation to the object of the legislation.' *Craig* (Powell, J., concurring)."

STEVENS, J., concurred on the ground that the challenged statute reflected a judgment that "persons who have demonstrated an inability to support their offspring should not be permitted to marry and [to have] additional children" and that "that sort of reasoning cannot justify this deliberate discrimination against the poor": "Under this statute, a person's economic status may determine his eligibility to enter into a lawful marriage. A noncustodial parent whose children are 'public charges' may not marry even if he has met his court-ordered obligations. Thus, within the class of parents who have fulfilled their court-ordered obligations, the rich may marry and the poor may not. This type of statutory discrimination is, I believe, totally unprecedented, as well as inconsistent with our tradition of administering justice equally to the rich and to the [poor.]" [b]

Notes and Questions

(a) Consider Lupu, supra, at 1072: "[If *Zablocki*] had assessed the Wisconsin statute by analogy to the libertarian principles governing free expression, it would have discovered a significant threat to preferred liberty: the delegation to judges of power to authorize the marriage under the highly discretionary standard 'that such children [are] not likely thereafter to become public charges.' Once the liberty to marry is recognized as fundamental, doctrines requiring clear and imminent danger to legitimate state interests and confining the discretion to make that determination should play as critical a role as they traditionally do in speech cases."

(b) In response to the district court's invalidation of the statute at issue in *Zablocki*, Wisconsin enacted a replacement statute limited to *previously married persons* who had incurred support obligations and who now intended to marry, establishing a *rebuttable presumption* that the remarriage of a person with support obligations for children not in custody would substantially affect the children's welfare and, finally, providing that the applicant who submits proof that "for reasonable cause" he was unable to meet support obligations may remarry. Under *Zablocki*, would this replacement statute (subsequently repealed) pass constitutional muster? See Note, 1979 Wis.L.Rev. 682.

(c) *"Significant interference."* Is the key to a clear application of *Zablocki* "the identification of what constitutes a significant interference with the right to marry"? Does the Court's reconciliation of *Zablocki* and *Jobst* provide much guidance on this point? See Note, *The Constitution and the Family*, 93 Harv.L. Rev. 1156, 1251–55 (1980): "[*Zablocki*] explicitly identifies directness as important to the determination of significance. [A] direct interference makes the state an actual participant in the decision to marry, [i.e.], represents a determination by the state that an individual should not be permitted to marry unless he meets some condition prior to marriage. An indirect interference, on the other hand,

b. Rehnquist, J., dissented, "view[ing] this legislative judgment in the light of the traditional presumption of validity [, just as] the traditional standard of review was applied in *Jobst*, despite the claim that the statute there in question burdened [the] right to marry." He concluded that the challenged statute, "despite its imperfections, is sufficiently rational to satisfy the demands of the Fourteenth Amendment."

weighs the choice by imposing certain consequences upon marriage but leaves the ultimate choice with the individual. It is consistent with the concept of a free society to let the individual determine whether he can meet the burdens of marriage rather than, as in [*Zablocki*], to have the state decide whether the burdens of marriage will make it too difficult to manage problems like meeting child support payments."

4. *Civil commitment of children by their parents.* In rejecting the argument that only a formal hearing prior to parents' commitment of their minor children to a mental institution could adequately protect a child's rights, *Parham v. J.R.* (1979), per Burger, C.J. (a case treated more fully in the "procedural due process" section, infra), applied "the traditional presumption that the parents act in the best interests of the child." That some parents may act against the interests of the child some times "is hardly a reason to discard wholesale those pages of human experience that teach that parents generally do act in the child's best interests."

Is *Parham*, like *Planned Parenthood v. Danforth*, p. 176 supra, a situation in which the parents cannot be relied on to speak for the child's interests? Consider Note, 93 Harv.L.Rev. 89, 94 (1979): "[The *Danforth* Court] ruled that parents cannot prevent their daughters from having abortions [, reasoning] that the existence of the pregnancy itself fractured the family unit too severely to suggest that parental authority should be upheld to preserve the family structure. This reasoning is clearly applicable to a situation in which parents seek to remove a child from the family." Cf. Burt, supra, at 336; Garvey, *Children and the Idea of Liberty*, 68 Ky.L.J. 809, 832–33 (1979–80).

SEXUAL CONDUCT, "LIFESTYLES", THE RIGHTS OF THE INVOLUNTARILY COMMITTED MENTALLY RETARDED, AND THE "RIGHT TO DIE"

1. *Consensual adult homosexual conduct.* DOE v. COMMONWEALTH'S ATTORNEY, 425 U.S. 901, 96 S.Ct. 1489, 47 L.Ed.2d 751 (1976), summarily aff'g 403 F.Supp. 1199 (E.D.Va.1975) (three-judge court): Homosexual males unsuccessfully sought federal declaratory relief, contending that Virginia's sodomy statute, as applied to consensual homosexual acts performed in private by adults, violated the right of privacy. A 2–1 majority of the district court quoted dicta in Harlan, J.'s dissent in *Poe v. Ullman* (see *Griswold* and fn. g after *Roe*) that homosexuality could be criminally prohibited even if privately practiced, and maintained that regulation of personal sexual conduct is constitutionally suspect only when it "trespasses upon the privacy of the incidents of marriage [or] the sanctity of the home [or] the nurture of family life." Dissenting, Merhige, J., maintained that *Roe* and *Eisenstadt* (neither of which had been mentioned by the majority) demonstrated that "intimate personal decisions or private matters of substantial importance to the well-being of the individuals involved are protected by [due process and that the] right to select consenting adult sexual partners must be considered within this category." The Supreme Court's summary affirmance (Brennan, Marshall and Stevens, JJ., voting to note probable jurisdiction), however, may have "relatively limited precedential value";[a] in-

---

a. Tribe, *American Constitutional Law* 943 (1978). "There appears to have been no evidence that any of the parties was threatened with prosecution," notes Tribe; "arguably the case thus was no more ripe for adjudication than *Poe v. Ullman* [p. 1227 infra], had been.

[The summary affirmance] demonstrates nothing, since the doctrine of *Poe* is discretionary in character rather than jurisdictional, and an affirmance would have been entirely consistent with the view that the district court reached the right result—denying relief—for deed, a year later, in *Carey v. Population Services Int'l*, supra, the Court itself viewed the issue as unsettled.[b]

Notes and Questions

(a) Professor Gerald Gunther has called the Court's summary affirmance in *Doe* "irresponsible" and "lawless." See N.Y. Times, April 8, 1976, p. 37. Under the circumstances, was the summary affirmance also "cynical"? Is the most plausible explanation for the Court's action that while six justices "sympathized with the result reached below, they would have been hard-pressed to compose a palatable opinion justifying their position"? See Perry, *Substantive Due Process Revisited: Reflections on (and Beyond) Recent Cases*, 71 Nw.U.L.Rev. 417, 443 (1976).

(b) Plaintiffs' contention in *Doe*, observes *Tribe*, supra, at 943–44, "should ultimately prevail in light of [the] crucial fact that the conduct proscribed is central to the personal identities of those singled out by the state's law. [A]lthough it is probably the case that the protection provided by *Griswold* was initially limited to acts occurring within a traditional, state-sanctioned relationship, [it] seems clear that 'the liberties of adult intimacy in our society are [too] fundamental' to be indefinitely limited to conduct implicitly sanctioned by the state's compact with the partners to a marriage. 'Equal protection alone requires a more even-handed dispensation.' " [a]

(c) Wilkinson & White, *Constitutional Protection for Personal Lifestyles*, 62 Corn.L.Rev. 562, 596 (1977), not only describe the question raised by *Doe* as "difficult" but provide concrete evidence of the difficulty—their inability to agree on the answer: "The question [is]: Should the State be constitutionally required to abandon an ancient sanction, when abandonment might in time lead to increasing, although statistically unpredictable, defections from heterosexual behavior and traditional family life? On the answer to this last question the authors have been unable to agree. Mr. Wilkinson would uphold the state's interest in the preservation of the traditional family; Mr. White would desire stronger empirical proof that the state interest is truly put in jeopardy by homosexual practices among consenting adults. Both authors acknowledge the intuitive elements in their judgments."

(d) But Richards, *Homosexuality and the Constitutional Right to Privacy*, 8 N.Y.U.Rev.L. & Soc.Change 311, 314 (1979), does not consider the question raised by *Doe* at all difficult: "There is no principled way to defend the earlier right to

---

the wrong reason." See also Wilkinson & White, *Constitutional Protection for Personal Lifestyles*, 62 Corn.L.Rev. 562, 593 (1977); Note, 1979 U.Ill.L.F. 469, 506.

b. *Carey*, per Brennan, J., noted that "the Court has not definitively answered the difficult question whether and to what extent the Constitution prohibits state statutes regulating [private consensual sexual] behavior among adults" and that "we do not purport to answer that question now," an observation that Rehnquist, J., dissenting, could not "let pass without comment": "While we have not ruled on every conceivable regulation affecting such conduct the facial constitutional validity of criminal statutes prohibiting certain consensual acts, [citing *Doe*], has been 'definitively' established."

a. Both quotations are from Gerety, *Redefining Privacy*, 12 Harv.C.R.–C.L.L.Rev. 233, 279–80 (1979).

For the view that neither the right of privacy nor the first amendment is broad enough in its conception of sexual orientation nor wide-ranging enough in its remedies to offer an adequate legal response to "the problem of gay inequality," but that the courts "should recognize homosexuality as a suspect classification [and] therefore subject laws that discriminate on the basis of sexual preference to heightened scrutiny, beyond the 'rational basis' test currently applied," see Note, 98 Harv. L.Rev. 1285, 1287–88, 1309 (1985). See generally Note, 57 S.Cal.L.Rev. 797 (1984).

privacy cases and not extend the right to homosexuality, other than the circular and question-begging assumption that homosexuality, as such, is intrinsically immoral and unnatural, when, in fact, it is a form of non-procreational sexual conduct, not in principle different from other forms of non-procreational sex, which must be liberated from the indefensible procreational model of sexual conduct. The difference between homosexuality and contraception, pornography in the home, and abortion is not constitutional or moral principle, but *popularity:* namely, that the non-procreational model in the other areas is supported by substantial popular sentiment, whereas homosexuality is still the settled object of widespread social hostility and opprobrium. It is the supreme paradox that the constitutional right to privacy has been applied to areas where there is either majoritarian consensus (contraception) or at least substantial popular support (abortion) and not applied to the protection of an oppressed minority, the settled object of unjustified social hate, that is paramountly entitled to the protection of the countermajoritarian rights of the constitutional design." [b]

(e) Consider, however, Grey, *Eros, Civilization and the Burger Court,* Law & Contemp.Probs., Summer 1980, at 83, 86–87, 90: "[T]he Court has given no support to the notion that the right of privacy protects sexual freedom. Not only has the homosexuals' challenge been summarily rejected, but in addition the Court has bypassed a number of chances to make a first incursion into the fantastic array of American laws that have traditionally forbidden virtually all sexual expression except wedded missionary-position intercourse. For example, the Court has [recently twice upheld] two of the ludicrous 'crime against nature' sodomy statutes against void-for-vagueness attacks. [c]

"[In] another recent case, the Court declined to review a decision upholding the sodomy conviction *of a husband and wife for an act of fellatio with each other.* The charge was evidently brought because photographs of the act taken by a third party had fallen into the hands of the couple's children, and a conviction for the appropriate offense—child abuse—had been reversed on appeal by the state courts.[28] In [still another case] the Court denied certiorari from a decision upholding the discharge of two public library employees for adulterous cohabitation, where the woman had become pregnant and the man had moved in with her before obtaining a divorce from his wife.[29]

"These cases strongly suggest that the Court meant what it said in *Griswold:* that the right of privacy protects only the historically sanctified institutions of marriage and the family, and has no implication for laws regulating sexual expression outside of traditional marriage.

"[Although some commentators thought that *Griswold* marked the first step in the constitutionalization of some contemporary version of John Stuart Mill's principle that the only legitimate reason for state coercion is to prevent harm to others, the failure to carry the principle through] must represent a prudential guess that to place the protection of the Constitution behind what most people

---

b. See also Perry, supra, at 437–38; Regan, *Rewriting Roe v. Wade,* 77 Mich.L.Rev. 1569, 1645 (1979); Richards, *Sexual Autonomy and the Constitutional Right of Privacy,* 30 Hast.L.J. 957 (1979); Rivera, *Our Straight-Laced Judges: The Legal Position of Homosexuality in the United States,* 30 Hast.L.J. 799, 944–47 (1979).

c. *Rose v. Locke,* 423 U.S. 48, 96 S.Ct. 243, 46 L.Ed.2d 185 (1975) (per curiam) (Brennan, Stewart and Marshall, JJ., dissenting); *Wain-*

wright v. Stone, 414 U.S. 21, 94 S.Ct. 190, 38 L.Ed.2d 179 (1973) (per curiam).

28. *Lovisi v. Slayton,* 363 F.Supp. 620 (E.D. Va.1973), affirmed 539 F.2d 349 (4th Cir.1976) (en banc), cert. denied 429 U.S. 977, 97 S.Ct. 485, 50 L.Ed.2d 585 (1976).

29. *Hollenbaugh v. Carnegie Free Library,* 439 U.S. 1052, 99 S.Ct. 734, 58 L.Ed. 713 (1979) (Marshall, J., dissenting from denial of certiorari).

still reject as unnatural sexual practices would too much strain the Court's limited stock of public good will. Such a theory might indeed explain *Doe v. Commonwealth's Attorney.* Perhaps the Court has been surprised by the depth and persistence of the opposition to the abortion decisions, and the swing justices were not ready to risk a foray into the explosive issue of gay rights. But if Mill's principle is in the wings, why have no hints of it appeared in opinions? At least why has the Court not taken some first step, perhaps striking down one of the absurd 'crime against nature' statutes on vagueness grounds—a decision that would invite little public wrath outside the lunatic fringe?"

———

Relying in part on *Doe v. Commonwealth's Attorney*—noting that "the Supreme Court's summary disposition of a case constitutes a vote on the merits; as such, it is binding on lower federal courts"—DRONENBURG v. ZECH, 741 F.2d 1388 (D.C.Cir.1984), per BORK, J., rejected the argument that the U.S. Navy's policy of mandatory discharge for homosexual conduct violated appellant's constitutional rights to privacy and equal protection. Even assuming that *Doe* is a "somewhat ambiguous precedent," the court could "find no constitutional right to engage in homosexual conduct [and], as judges, we have no warrant to create one":

"[T]he suggestion that we apply [the *Griswold-Roe* line of cases] to protect homosexual conduct in the Navy [presents] a peculiar jurisprudential problem. When the Supreme Court decides cases under a specific provision [of] the Constitution it explicates the meaning and suggests the contours of a value already stated in the document or implied by the Constitution's structure and history. The lower court judge finds in the Supreme Court's reasoning about these legal materials, as well as in the materials themselves, guidance for applying the provision [to] a new situation. But when the Court creates new rights [the] lower courts have none of these materials available and can look only to what the Supreme Court has stated to be the principle involved. [In the 'privacy' cases] we do not find any principle articulated even approaching in breadth that which appellant seeks to have us adopt. The Court has listed as illustrative of the right of privacy such matters as activities relating to marriage, procreation, contraception, family relationships, and child rearing and education. It need hardly be said that none of these covers a right to homosexual conduct.

"[In] dealing with a topic like this, in which we are asked to protect from regulation a form of behavior never before protected, and indeed traditionally condemned, we do well to bear in mind the concerns expressed by Justice White, dissenting in *Moore v. East Cleveland* that '[the Judiciary] is the most vulnerable and comes nearest to illegitimacy when it deals with judge-made constitutional law having little or no cognizable roots in the language or even the design of the Constitution. * * *' [If] the revolution in sexual mores that appellant proclaims is in fact ever to arrive, we think it must arrive through the moral choices of the people and their elected representatives, not through the ukase of this court.

"[Appellant] contends that the existence of moral disapproval for certain types of behavior is the very fact that disables government from regulating it. He says [the fact that] the particular choice of partner may be repugnant to the majority argues for its vigilant protection—not its vulnerability to sanction. This theory that majority morality and majority choice is always made presumptively invalid by the Constitution attacks the very predicate of democratic government. When the Constitution does not speak to the contrary, the choices of those put in authority by the electoral process, or those who are accountable to such persons, come before us not as suspect because majoritarian but as conclusively valid for that very reason. We stress [that] this deference to democratic choice does not apply where the Constitution removes the choice from majorities. [It] is to be doubted that very many laws exist whose ultimate justification does not rest upon the society's morality. For these reasons, appellant's arguments will not withstand examination.

"[Thus, we need ask] only whether the Navy's policy is rationally related to a permissible end. We have said that legislation may implement morality. So viewed, this regulation bears a rational relationship to a permissible end. [Assuming that] a naval regulation, unlike the act of a legislature, must be rationally related not to morality for its own sake but to some further end which the Navy is entitled to pursue because of the Navy's assigned function, [the] effects of homosexual conduct within a naval or military unit are almost certain to be harmful to morale and discipline. The Navy is not required to produce social science data or the results of controlled experiments to prove what common sense and common experience demonstrate." [a]

2. *Fornication, cohabitation and adultery.* (a) After examining the state interests which laws forbidding fornication and cohabitation might serve and suggesting that several of these interests are "compelling"—deterring illegitima-

---

a. Dissenting from a denial of rehearing en banc in *Dronenburg,* 746 F.2d 1579 (D.C. Cir.1984), Robinson, C.J., joined by Wald, Mikva and Edwards, JJ., found "completely unconvincing the suggestion that *Doe v. Commonwealth's Attorney* controls this case" and maintained that "the dangers hypothesized by [the three-judge panel] provide patently inadequate justification for a ban on homosexuality in a Navy that includes personnel of both sexes and places no parolled ban on all types of heterosexual conduct."

In a separate statement, Bork, J., joined by Scalia, J., could not "take seriously the dissent's suggestion that the Navy may be constitutionally required to treat heterosexual conduct and homosexual conduct as either morally equivalent or as posing equal dangers to the Navy's mission. Relativism in these matters may or may not be an arguable moral stance, [but] moral relativism is hardly a constitutional command, nor is it, we are certain, the moral stance of a large majority of naval personnel."

Did the *Dronenburg* court fail to follow its own warning on judicial restraint? Consider Note, 63 N.C.L.Rev. 749, 764–66 (1985): "[T]he military setting of [the] case provided the court with an obvious analytic framework that the court relegated to minor importance. [The doctrine that the armed services constitute a 'separate community'] allows lower courts to give greater deference to military restrictions on individual rights. [By] expanding the analysis beyond the military context, the *Dronenburg* decision broadly affects all cases seeking right-of-privacy protection for homosexual persons. The court failed to

follow its own warning on judicial restraint and decided larger issues [that] should have remained separate from the military setting of [the case]. Besides posing a challenge to military regulations, [*Dronenburg* is hardly the best case for determining whether the right of privacy protects consensual homosexual behavior between adults because] the case involves activities occurring on military premises and a relationship between a petty officer [appellant] and a lower ranked enlisted man."

For a broad attack on *Dronenburg,* see Note, 3 Yale L. & Pol.Rev. 245 (1984), concluding, id. at 261–62, that the case "offers a significant example of how some judges rely on traditional misconceptions about homosexuality to justify repression of nonconformist behavior. Also, the manner in which [Judge] Bork's decision confines doctrinally important Supreme Court cases to their facts allows courts, when faced with issues involving unconventional activity, to abandon their obligation to protect fundamental rights against infringement."

For a defense of the result reached in *Dronenburg,* see Note, 26 Wm. & Mary L.Rev. 645 (1985), concluding, id. at 681 that the right to privacy "never was intended to protect sodomy. Because the Supreme Court created the right to privacy by judicial Lochnerization, the right must be defined narrowly. The equal protection attacks on sodomy statutes are inapposite because homosexuals are not a suspect class, because no fundamental right to sodomy exists, and because the sodomy statutes rationally support a legitimate state purpose."

cy, preventing disease, and preserving the family—Note, *Fornication, Cohabitation, and the Constitution,* 77 Mich.L.Rev. 252, 257, 301–05 (1978), concludes that the laws do not actually serve these interests. "[T]he best evidence—the behavior of the states which have enacted but rarely enforced these laws—shows that [they] are hardly necessary to achieve these [governmental] interests."

Can a "right of sexual expression outside marriage" be reconciled with *Doe v. Commonwealth's Attorney,* assuming that that case approves laws prohibiting sodomy? Consider id. at 292–93: "[H]omosexuality can be distinguished from heterosexuality in terms of the very societal traditions which necessitate a right to sexual freedom. [H]omosexuality may fail the 'traditions and collective conscience' test, since, however wrongly, Americans have long regarded (and still do regard) homosexuality with special reprobation. [T]here is a tension between, on one hand, establishing a right to full sexual expression for most members of society on the grounds that they need it to fulfill their individuality, and, on the other hand, barring the rest from any kind of sexual expression which appeals to them [but,] however unjustifiably, homosexuality is still widely regarded as a threat to social stability and to psychological health in a way that every heterosexual conduct is not." See also Note, 1979 U.Ill.L.F. 469, 508–09.

(b) If not sufficient to justify laws against fornication, are state interests strong enough to justify laws against adultery? Consider Tribe, supra, at 946: "Adultery is often not a 'victimless crime'. [When] there is truly a victimized spouse, it would seem that the state may choose to use the sanctions of law to punish the wrong to the marriage partner—and the marriage—inflicted by adultery. It is less clear whether the social interest in protecting and strengthening marriages generally—through deterrence, or through a symbolic expression of social condemnation which may enter into the solemnity with which people view marriage as an institution—can sustain a per se criminal prohibition on extramarital sexual contacts by married persons. Such an outcome seems to assign too much weight to sex acts themselves as a cause of marital disintegration, and to accord too little weight to the importance of other intimacies in the definition of individual human beings." Compare Wilkinson & White, supra, at 599–600.

3. *Personal appearance and lifestyles.* KELLEY v. JOHNSON, 425 U.S. 238, 96 S.Ct. 1440, 47 L.Ed.2d 708 (1976), per REHNQUIST, J., held that regulations directed at the style and length of male police officers' hair, sideburns and mustaches, and prohibiting beards and goatees except for medical reasons, violated no " 'liberty' interest protected by the Fourteenth Amendment": "The 'liberty' interest claimed [here] is distinguishable from [those] protected in *Roe, Eisenstadt* [and] *Griswold,* [which] involved a substantial claim of infringement on the individual's freedom of choice with respect to certain basic matters of procreation, marriage, and family life."

Assuming that "the citizenry at large has some sort of 'liberty' interest within the Fourteenth Amendment in matters of personal appearance," this assumption is insufficient to topple the regulation, for respondent has sought constitutional protection "as an employee of the county and, more particularly, as a policeman. [T]he county has chosen a mode of organization which it undoubtedly deems the most efficient in enabling its police to carry out the duties assigned to them under state and local law. Such a choice necessarily gives weight to the overall need for discipline, esprit de corps, and uniformity.

"The promotion of safety of persons and property is unquestionably at the core of the State's police [power]. Choice of organization, dress and equipment for law enforcement personnel is a decision entitled to the same sort of presumption of legislative validity as are state choices designed to promote other aims within the cognizance of the State's police power. [Thus] the question is not [whether] the State can 'establish' a 'genuine public need' for the specific regulation [but] whether respondent can demonstrate that there is no rational connection between the regulation, based as it is on petitioner's method of organizing its police force, and the promotion of safety of persons and property.

"[The courts are not] in a position to weigh the policy arguments in favor of and against a rule regulating hairstyles as a part of regulations governing a uniformed civilian service. The constitutional issue [is whether the] determination that such regulations should be enacted is so irrational that it may be branded 'arbitrary,' and therefore a deprivation of respondent's 'liberty' interest in freedom to choose his own hairstyle. *Williamson v. Lee Optical Co.* [p. 800 infra]. The overwhelming majority of state and local police of the present day are uniformed. This fact itself testifies to the recognition by those who direct those operations, and by the people of the States and localities who directly or indirectly choose such persons, that similarity in appearance of police officers is desirable. This choice may be based on a desire to make police officers readily recognizable to the members of the public, or a desire for the esprit de corps which such similarity is felt to inculcate within the police force itself. Either one is a sufficiently rational justification for" the regulations.[a]

MARSHALL, J., joined by Brennan, J., dissented: "An individual's personal appearance may reflect, sustain, and nourish his personality and may well be used as a means of expressing his attitude and lifestyle.[2] In taking control over a citizen's personal appearance, the Government forces him to sacrifice substantial elements of his integrity and identity as well. To say that the liberty guarantee of the Fourteenth Amendment does not encompass matters of personal appearance would be fundamentally inconsistent with the values of privacy, self-identity, autonomy, and personal integrity that I have always assumed the Constitution was designed to protect [referring, e.g., to *Roe* and *Griswold*].[b]

"[While] fully accepting the aims of 'identifiability' and maintenance of esprit de corps, I find no rational relationship between the challenged regulation and these goals. As for the first justification offered by the Court, I simply do not see how requiring policemen to maintain hair of under a certain length could rationally be argued to contribute to making them identifiable to the public as policemen. [As] for the Court's second justification, the fact that it is the President of the Patrolmen's Benevolent Association, in his official capacity, who has challenged the regulation here would seem to indicate that the regulation would if anything, decrease rather than increase the police force's esprit de

a. Powell, J., joined the Court's opinion, but underscored that, unlike the dissenters, he found "no negative implications in the opinion with respect to a liberty interest within the Fourteenth Amendment as to matters of personal appearance." See also Tribe, supra, at 964: "[R]egulations which exclude someone from a single public position are far less intrusive, and hence less likely to be invalidated, than those which work an exclusion from an entire profession, or from any public employment [or] from all public education."

2. While the parties did not address any First Amendment issues in any detail in this Court, governmental regulation of a citizen's personal appearance may in some circumstances not only deprive him of liberty under the Fourteenth Amendment but violate his First Amendment rights as well. *Tinker v. Des Moines School District* [p. 522 infra].

b. See also Wilkinson & White, supra, at 605: "Appearance, like speech, is a chief medium of self-expression that involves important choices about how we wish to project ourselves and be perceived by others. To link appearance with privacy and speech values is not, of course, to require similar constitutional treatment. It does imply, however, that we deal with a substantive constitutional liberty."

corps.[6] And even if one accepted the argument that substantial similarity in appearance would increase a force's esprit de corps, I simply do not understand how implementation of this regulation could be expected to create any increment in similarity of appearance among members of a uniformed police force. While the regulation prohibits hair below the ears or the collar and limits the length of sideburns, it allows the maintenance of any type of hair style, other than a pony tail. Thus, as long as their hair does not go below their collars, two police officers, with an 'Afro' hair style and the other with a crew cut could both be in full compliance with the regulation.[7] * * *[8]"

(b) *Student "long hair" cases.* Apart from *Kelley,* what of such cases as KARR v. SCHMIDT, 460 F.2d 609 (5th Cir.1972), (holding that a school board's regulation restricting the length of male students' hair violated no constitutionally protected right)? The board had argued that the regulation served the goals of inhibiting "classroom distraction" and disruption and eliminating potential health and safety hazards and *Karr* had called these "legitimate objectives." Consider Wilkinson & White, supra, at 606: "Long hair on males is intrinsically no less healthy and no more distracting and disruptive of classroom work than long hair on females. Any difference is the result of custom alone; [and] conformity to custom [seems] insufficient to justify the limitation on individual choice. The rationale suggests the untenable: that mere unconventionality of appearance is enough to bring the state's regulatory apparatus into play."

4. *The substantive due process rights of involuntarily-committed mentally retarded persons.* In YOUNGBERG v. ROMEO, 457 U.S. 307, 102 S.Ct. 2452, 73 L.Ed.2d 28 (1982), the Court considered for the first time the substantive due process rights of involuntarily-committed mentally retarded persons. On his mother's petition, Romeo, a profoundly retarded 33-year-old was involuntarily committed to a Pennsylvania state institution (Pennhurst). Subsequently, concerned about injuries Romeo had suffered at Pennhurst, his mother filed a federal action against institution officials claiming that her son had constitutional rights to (1) safe conditions of confinement, (2) freedom from bodily restraint, and (3) "a constitutional right to minimally adequate habilitation," i.e., minimal training and development of needed skills. (In light of his severe retardation, however, respondent conceded that no amount of training would make his release possible.) The Court, per POWELL, J., pointed out that respondent's first two claims "involve liberty interests recognized by prior decisions of this Court, interests that involuntary commitment proceedings do not extinguish," but found respondent's remaining claim "more troubling":

6. Nor, to say the least, is the esprit de corps argument bolstered by the fact that the International Brotherhood of Police Officers, a 25,000 member union representing uniformed police officers, has filed a brief as amicus curiae arguing that the challenged regulation is unconstitutional.

7. The regulation itself eschews what would appear to be a less intrusive means of achieving similarity in the hair length of on-duty officers. According to the regulation, a policeman cannot comply with the hair length requirements by wearing a wig with hair of the proper length while on duty. The regulation prohibits the wearing of wigs or hair pieces "on duty in uniform except for cosmetic reasons to cover natural baldness or physical disfiguration." Thus, while the regulation in terms applies to grooming standards of policemen while on duty, the hair length provision effectively controls both on-duty and off-duty appearance.

[Why did the *Kelley* majority see no need to respond to the dissent's point that simply requiring a police officer to wear an appropriate wig while on duty would serve all of the county's articulated interests? See Tribe, supra, at 962.]

8. Because, to my mind, the challenged regulation fails to pass even a minimal degree of scrutiny, there is no need to determine whether, given the nature of the interests involved and the degree to which they are affected, the application of a more heightened scrutiny would be appropriate.

"On the basis of the record before us, it is quite uncertain whether respondent seeks any 'habilitation' or training unrelated to [his constitutionally protected liberty interest in] safety and freedom from bodily restraints. [If,] as seems the case, respondent seeks only training related to safety and freedom from restraints, this case does not present the difficult question whether a mentally retarded person, involuntarily committed to a state institution, has some general constitutional right to training per se, even when no type or amount of training would lead to freedom. [On the basis of the record], we conclude that respondent's liberty interests require the State to provide minimally adequate or reasonable training to ensure safety and freedom from undue restraint. [W]e need go no further in this case.

"[But the question] is not simply whether a liberty interest has been infringed but whether the extent or nature of the restraint or lack of absolute safety is such as to violate due process. In determining whether a substantive right protected by the Due Process Clause has been violated, it is necessary to balance 'the liberty of the individual' and 'the demands of an organized society.' "

The Court then considered "the proper standard for determining whether a State adequately has protected the rights of the involuntarily-committed mentally retarded." It agreed with the concurring judge below "that 'the Constitution only requires that the courts make certain that professional judgment was in fact exercised. It is not appropriate for the courts to specify which of several professionally acceptable choices should have been made.' Persons who have been involuntarily committed are entitled to more considerate treatment [than] criminals whose conditions of confinement are designed to punish. At the same time, the standard is lower than [a] 'compelling' or 'substantial' necessity [test for justifying restraints] that would place an undue burden on the administration of [state institutions] and also would restrict unnecessarily the exercise of professional judgment as to the needs of residents.

"[In] determining what is 'reasonable'—in this and in any case presenting a claim for training by a state—we emphasize that courts must show deference to the judgment exercised by a qualified professional. [The] decision, if made by a professional, is presumptively valid; liability may be imposed only when the decision by the professional is such a substantial departure from accepted professional judgment, practice or standards as to demonstrate that the person responsible actually did not base the decision on such a judgment.[a] In an action for damages against a professional in his individual capacity, however, the professional will not be liable if he was unable to satisfy his normal professional standards because of budgetary constraints; in such a situation, good-faith immunity would bar liability."

BLACKMUN, J., joined by Brennan and O'Connor, JJ., joined the Court's opinion, but concurred separately to clarify why, because of the uncertainty in the record, "that opinion properly leaves open two difficult and important questions." Unlike Burger, C.J., who considered the issue "frivolous," Blackmun, J., believed that whether Pennsylvania could accept respondent for "care and treatment" and then constitutionally refuse to provide him any "treatment," as that term is defined by state law, would, if properly before the Court, present "a serious issue." As for the second difficult question left open— whether respondent had an "independent constitutional claim [to] that 'habilita-

a. Does this place "a seemingly insurmountable burden" on plaintiff mental patients? See Note, 96 Harv.L.Rev. 77, 85 (1982).

tion' or training necessary to *preserve* those basic self-care skills he possessed when he first entered Pennhurst"—he believed that "it would be consistent with the Court's reasoning today to include within the 'minimally adequate training required by the Constitution' such training as is reasonably necessary to prevent a person's pre-existing self-care skills from *deteriorating* because of his commitment" and he viewed such deterioration "because of the State's unreasonable refusal to provide him training [a] loss of liberty quite distinct from—and as serious as—the loss of safety and freedom from unreasonable restraints."

BURGER, C.J., concurring, agreed with much of the Court's opinion, but "would hold flatly that respondent has no constitutional right to training, or 'habilitation,' per se." He agreed that "some amount of self-care instruction may be necessary to avoid unreasonable infringement of a mentally-retarded person's interests in safety and freedom from restraint"; but he thought it "clear" that "the Constitution does not otherwise place an affirmative duty on the State to provide any particular kind of training or habilitation—even such as might be encompassed under the essentially standardless rubric 'minimally adequate training,' to which the Court refers." Since respondent had asserted "a right to 'minimally adequate' habilitation '[q]uite apart from its relationship to decent care,'" unlike the Court he saw "no way to avoid the issue."

5. *The "right to die."* Although the Supreme Court is yet to decide the question, the highly publicized case of IN RE QUINLAN, 70 N.J. 10, 355 A.2d 647 (1976), assumed that the right of privacy enumerated by the Supreme Court "is broad enough to encompass a patient's decision to decline medical treatment under certain circumstances [even if the decision might lead to the patient's death], in much the same way as it is broad enough to encompass a woman's decision to terminate pregnancy under certain conditions." More recently, the President's Commission for the Study of Ethical Problems in Medicine and Biomedical and Behavioral Research, *Deciding to Forego Life-Sustaining Treatment* 32 (1983) (President's Commission Report) stated that "[r]egardless of how interests are weighed in specific cases, a decision to forego life-sustaining treatment has been firmly established as a constitutionally protected right that can be overcome only by marshalling countervailing considerations of substantial weight."

Assuming this is so, the *Quinlan* case dealt with a person who obviously lacked the capacity to make or express a decision on the subject (she was in a "chronic persistent vegetative state"), and the court dismissed Ms. Quinlan's previous views on the subject as so casual and equivocal as to lack the requisite probative value. The court ruled, nevertheless, that Ms. Quinlan could be taken off her respirator (it was assumed that such removal would cause her death, but it did not) on the approval of her family, subject to agreement by an "ethics committee" that "there is no reasonable possibility of [her] ever emerging from her present comatose condition to a cognitive, sapient state":

"[The] only practical way to prevent destruction of the right [of privacy] is to permit the guardian and family of Karen to render their best judgment [subject to certain safeguards] as to whether she would exercise it in these circumstances. If their conclusion is in the affirmative, this decision should be accepted by a society the overwhelming majority of whose members would, we think, in similar circumstances, exercise such a choice in the same way for themselves or for those closest to them. [Thus,] Karen's right of privacy may be asserted in her behalf, in this respect, by her guardian and family."

Notes and Questions

(a) For the view that *Quinlan* was not a "right of privacy" or "right-to-die" case, although it was almost universally reported and discussed as such, but a "quality of life" case that badly smudged the distinction between the right to choose one's own death and the right to choose someone else's, see Kamisar, *Karen Ann Quinlan and the "Right-to-Die,"* 29 Law Quad Notes 3–4 (Summer, 1985). See also Nowak, Rotunda & Young, *Constitutional Law* 764–65 (2d ed. 1983); Note, 1979 U.Ill.L.F. 469, 517–18.

For close analyses of *Quinlan,* see, e.g., Burt, *Taking Care of Strangers* 144–73 (1979); Grisez & Boyle, *Life and Death with Liberty and Justice* 83–84, 96–98, 283–88 (1979); Ramsey, *Ethics at the Edges of Life* 268–99 (1978); Veatch, *Death, Dying, and the Biological Revolution* 137–44, 152–53, 174–76 (1976); Cantor, *Quinlan, Privacy, and the Handling of Incompetent Patients,* 30 Rutg.L.Rev. 243 (1977). For commentary on *Quinlan* in the context of a general discussion of the "surrogate-choice" approach to constitutional freedoms, see Garvey, *Freedom and Choice in Constitutional Law,* 94 Harv.L.Rev. 1756, 1778–85 (1981). For discussion of euthanasia generally, see President's Commission Report, supra; *Privacy and the Family in Medical Decisions: A Symposium,* 23 J. Family Law 173 (1984–85); Capron, *Euthanasia,* 2 Ency.Crime & Justice 709 (S. Kadish ed. 1983).

(b) Consider Tribe, supra, at 936–37: "The court's belief that Karen's rights were more jeopardized on the facts before it than in a situation where she wished to terminate a still conscious life seems perplexing. Given the supposedly vegetative state that alone justified the court's holding, attributing 'rights' to Karen at all was problematic; more realistically at stake were the desire of her anguished parents to be rid of their torment and the interest of society in freeing medical decision makers from blind adherence to a practice of keeping vegetative persons 'alive' simply out of a fear of prosecution. But to give *those* interests constitutional status even where the state interposes an objection in the interest of the child's life seems most troubling. If, on the other hand, Karen were fully conscious and chose after careful reflection to end her life, the proposition that the state should be empowered to prevent her from carrying out that design, and even to punish her for the attempt, seems hard to square with her dignity and integrity as a person."

(c) *Post-Quinlan cases.* See *Superintendent v. Saikewicz,* 373 Mass. 728, 370 N.E.2d 417 (1977), where physicians obtained judicial authorization to withhold an apparently painful course of chemotherapy for a mentally retarded and institutionalized 67-year-old suffering from leukemia. The case is discussed in Annas, *The Incompetent's Right to Die,* Hastings Center Report 8 (Feb. 1978); Annas, *After Saikewicz: No Fault Death,* Hastings Center Report 8 (June 1978); Burt, supra, at 144–58; Ramsey, supra, at 300–17.

But compare *Quinlan* and *Saikewicz* with *In re Storar,* 52 N.Y.2d 363, 438 N.Y.S.2d 266, 420 N.E.2d 64 (1981): Storar, a profoundly retarded 52-year-old man, suffering from incurable cancer of the bladder, received blood transfusions for several weeks. Then the patient's mother, who was also his legal guardian, refused consent on the ground that the transfusions would only prolong her son's discomfort and would be against his wishes if he were competent. But the court ruled that a state official's request to continue the transfusions should have been granted. Storar "was never competent at any time in his life. [Thus,] it is unrealistic to attempt to determine whether he would want to continue [the] treatment if he were competent. [Even] when the parents' decision to decline necessary treatment is based on constitutional grounds, such as religious beliefs, it must yield to the State's interests [in] protecting the health and welfare of the child. [The] transfusions were analogous to food—they would not cure the cancer, but they could eliminate the risk of death from another treatable cause. [A] court should not in the circumstances of this case allow an incompetent patient to bleed to death because [his family or guardian] feels this is best for one with an incurable disease."

Nine years after its historic decision in the *Quinlan* case, the Supreme Court of New Jersey modified its earlier views, *In re Conroy*, 98 N.J. 321, 486 A.2d 1209 (1985), observing, inter alia: (1) life-sustaining treatment, even artificial feeding, may be withheld or withdrawn from an incompetent person "when it is clear that the particular patient would have refused the treatment under the circumstances involved," because the patient had, e.g., executed a "living will"; (2) absent adequate proof of the incompetent patient's previous wishes, "it is naive to pretend that the right to self-determination serves as the basis for substituted decision-making"; and (3) in the absence of trustworthy evidence that the patient would have declined life-saving treatment, such treatment may still be withheld or withdrawn from a formerly competent person if, but only if, "the net burdens of the patient's life with the treatment should clearly and markedly outweigh the benefits that the patient derives from life," but "[the] unavoidable and severe pain of the patient's life with the treatment should be such that the effect of administering life-sustaining treatment would be inhumane." According to Curran, *Defining Appropriate Medical Care: Providing Nutrients and Hydration for the Dying*, 313 New Eng.J.Med. 940, 942 (1985), "the [*Conroy*] court's position in allowing removal of nutrition and hydration as well as other forms of life support is without precedent in the American courts."

SECTION 3. THE RIGHT TO TRAVEL

Introduction

"The 'right to travel' from state to state has been a favorite of both the Warren and Burger Courts. The Constitution makes no mention of any such right. By now we know that cannot be determinative, but we are entitled to some sort of explanation of why the right is appropriately attributable. In recent years the Court has been almost smug in its refusal to provide one." [a]

—Ely, *Democracy and Distrust* 177 (1980).

Dissenting in *Shapiro v. Thompson* (1969) (discussed at p. 1027 infra), Harlan, J., observed: "Opinions of the Court and of individual Justices have suggested four provisions of the Constitution as possible sources of a right to travel enforceable against the federal or state governments: the Commerce Clause; the Privileges and Immunities Clause of Art. IV, § 2; the Privileges and Immunities Clause of the Fourteenth Amendment; and the Due Process Clause of the Fifth Amendment." (He concluded that "the right to travel interstate is a 'fundamental' right which, for present purposes, should be regarded as having its

---

a. At this point Professor Ely refers to language in *Shapiro v. Thompson* and *United States v. Guest*, both quoted infra. See also Note, 40 U.M.K.C.L.Rev. 66, 77 (1971): "In some situations, the Court has refused to pinpoint the source of the protection it is giving to free travel, in effect saying: 'We know the right to travel is protected by the Constitution and we don't need to say where.'"

source in [the fifth amendment due process clause].") Other possible sources for the constitutional right to travel are the equal protection clause, the "penumbra" of the first amendment, the ninth amendment and "the nature of the federal union." [b] One recent constitutional law text discusses the right to travel in its "equal protection" chapter,[c] another treats the subject primarily in a chapter on "rights of privacy and personhood." [d]

APTHEKER v. SECRETARY OF STATE, 378 U.S. 500, 84 S.Ct. 1659, 12 L.Ed.2d 992 (1964), concerned an attack by top-ranking leaders of the Communist Party on § 6 of the Subversive Activities Control Act of 1950, which denied passports to members of an organization "with knowledge or notice" that it was required to register as "a Communist organization." The Court, per GOLDBERG, J., struck down § 6 as "unconstitutional on its face" because it "too broadly and indiscriminately restricts the right to travel and thereby abridges the liberty guaranteed by the Fifth Amendment." It pointed to the dictum in *Kent v. Dulles,* 357 U.S. 116, 78 S.Ct. 1113, 2 L.Ed.2d 1204 (1958), that "The right to travel is a part of the 'liberty' of which the citizen cannot be deprived without [fifth amendment due process]. Freedom of movement across frontiers in either direction, and inside frontiers as well, was a part of our heritage. Travel abroad, like travel within the country [is] basic in our scheme of values." "Since freedom of association is itself guaranteed in the First Amendment, restrictions imposed upon the right to travel cannot be dismissed by asserting that the right to travel could be fully exercised if the individual would first yield up his membership in a given association." [a]

As for the government's argument that § 6 should be held constitutional as applied to "the top-ranking Party leaders involved here," such a "construction" would require "substantial rewriting" of the statute and would "inject an element of vagueness into the statute's scope," a course neither proper nor desirable "in dealing with a section which so severely curtails personal liberty." Since "freedom of travel is a constitutional liberty closely related to rights of free speech and association, [appellants] should not be required to assume the burden of demonstrating that Congress could not have written a statute constitutionally prohibiting their travel."

DOUGLAS, J., joined the Court's opinion, adding that "the right to move freely from State to State is a privilege and immunity of national citizenship." "Absent war, I see no way to keep a citizen from traveling within or without the country [unless] he has been convicted of a crime [or] there is probable cause for issuing a warrant [to arrest him]. Freedom of movement [is] the very essence of our free society, setting us apart. Like the right of assembly and the right of association, it often makes all other rights meaningful—knowing, studying, arguing, exploring, conversing, observing and even thinking." [b]

---

b. See generally Lupu, *Untangling the Strands of the Fourteenth Amendment,* 77 Mich.L.Rev. 981, 993, 1031, 1060–64 (1979); Notes, 22 U.C.L.A.L.Rev. 1129, 1140–45 (1975); 40 U.M.K.C.L.Rev. 66, 67–77, 93–95 (1971); 55 Neb.L.Rev. 117–22, 132 (1975) and authorities collected therein.

c. Nowak, Rotunda & Young, *Constitutional Law* 802–16 (2d ed.1983).

d. Tribe, *American Constitutional Law* 896–97, 953–58 (1978).

a. *Kent* invalidated State Department regulations denying passports to Communists on the ground they exceeded the congressional grant of authority, thus avoiding the constitutional question.

b. Clark, J., joined by Harlan and White, JJ., dissented, maintaining that the Due Pro-

ZEMEL v. RUSK, 381 U.S. 1, 85 S.Ct. 1271, 14 L.Ed.2d 179 (1965), concerned refusal to issue passports to United States citizens for travel to Cuba "unless specifically endorsed [by] the Secretary of State." Appellant sought a passport "to satisfy my curiosity about the state of affairs in Cuba and to make me a better informed citizen." The Court, per WARREN, C.J., affirmed denial of the request: "The requirements of due process are a function not only of the extent of the governmental restriction imposed, but also of the extent of the necessity for the restriction. [The] United States and other members of the Organization of American States have determined that travel between Cuba and the other countries of the Western Hemisphere is an important element in the spreading of subversion. [In light of this factor and others], the Secretary has justifiably concluded that travel to Cuba by American citizens might involve the Nation in dangerous international incidents, and that the Constitution does not require him to validate passports for such travel.

"The right to travel *within* the United States is of course also constitutionally protected. But that freedom does not mean that areas ravaged by flood, fire or pestilence cannot be quarantined when it can be demonstrated that unlimited travel to the area would directly and materially interfere with the safety and welfare of the area or the Nation as a whole. So it is with international travel. [That the challenged restriction] is supported by the weightiest considerations of national security is perhaps best pointed up by recalling that the Cuban Missile crisis of October 1962 preceded the filing of appellant's complaint by less than two months."

DOUGLAS, J., joined by Goldberg, J., dissented: "[T]here are areas [such as those stricken by pestilence or war] to which Congress can [prohibit] travel. [But] the only so-called danger present here is the Communist regime in Cuba. The world, however, is filled with Communist thought [and] if we are to know them and understand them, we must mingle with [them]. Restrictions on the right to travel in times of peace should be so particularized that a First Amendment right is not precluded unless some clear countervailing national interest stands in the way of its assertion." [a]

HAIG v. AGEE, 453 U.S. 280, 101 S.Ct. 2766, 69 L.Ed.2d 640 (1981) (other aspects of which are discussed at p. 496 infra), arose as follows: Agee, a former

cess Clause does not prohibit "reasonable regulation" of the right to travel abroad and that Congress had "a rational basis" for denying passports to members of the Communist Party.

a. Compare *Zemel* with *Regan v. Wald*, 468 U.S. 222, 104 S.Ct. 3026, 82 L.Ed.2d 171 (1984). In 1982, in order to "reduce Cuba's hard currency earnings from travel by U.S. persons to and from Cuba," a treasury regulation was amended to restrict travel-related economic transactions. Respondents, American citizens who wanted to travel to Cuba, challenged the amendment on both statutory and constitutional grounds. After devoting most of its opinion to a discussion of why the regulation was authorized by Congress, a 5–4 majority, per Rehnquist, J., rejected the constitutional challenge:

"We see no reason to differentiate between the travel restrictions imposed by the Presi-

dent in the present case and the passport restrictions imposed by the Secretary of State in *Zemel*. Both have the practical effect of preventing travel to Cuba by most American citizens, and both are justified by weighty concerns of foreign policy. Respondents apparently feel that only a Cuban missile crisis in the offing will make area restrictions on international travel constitutional. [The] holding in *Zemel*, however, was not tied to the Court's independent foreign policy analysis, [but] merely an example of [our] classical deference to the political branches in matters of foreign policy."

Blackmun, J., joined by Brennan, Marshall and Powell, JJ., dissented, maintaining that the restrictions on travel-related expenditures in Cuba were not authorized by Congress.

CIA employee then residing in West Germany, announced and engaged in a campaign to expose undercover CIA agents stationed abroad and "to drive them out of the countries where they are operating." In carrying out his campaign he travelled in various countries. On several occasions, his public identifications of alleged CIA agents in foreign countries were "followed by episodes of violence against the persons and organizations." Because of Agee's activities, his passport was revoked on the basis of a 1966 regulation authorizing passport revocation when the Secretary of State determines that an American citizen's activities abroad "are causing or likely to cause serious damage to the national security or the foreign policy of the United States." a After holding that the Passport Act of 1926 authorized the revocation of Agee's passport pursuant to the policy announced by the challenged regulation, such policy being " 'sufficiently substantial and consistent' to compel the conclusion that Congress has approved it," b a

a. As a condition for his employment by the CIA, Agee contracted not to make any public statements about Agency matters, either during or after the term of his employment by the Agency, "without specific approval by the Agency." In a separate action brought by the government to enforce Agee's agreement, a federal district court held that "Agee has shown a flagrant disregard for the requirements of the Secrecy Agreement."

b. Relying on Kent v. Dulles, Agee argued that "the only way the Executive can establish implicit congressional approval is by proof of longstanding and consistent enforcement of the claimed power: that is by showing that many passports were revoked on national security and foreign policy grounds." The Court disagreed, pointing out that there were few occasions to call the Secretary's authority into play: "The exercise of a power emerges only in relation to a factual situation, and the continued validity of the power is not diluted simply because there is no need to use it. [Although] a pattern of actual enforcement is one indicator of Executive policy, it suffices that the Executive has 'openly asserted' the power at issue. Kent is not to the contrary. [In that case, the] Court had serious doubts as to whether there was in reality any definite policy in which Congress could have acquiesced."

Relying on language in Kent that "illegal conduct" and problems of allegiance were "the only [grounds] which it could fairly be argued were adopted by Congress in light of prior administrative practice," Agee also contended that "this enumeration was exclusive and is controlling here." Again the Court disagreed: "The Kent Court had no occasion to consider whether the Executive had the power to revoke the passport of an individual whose conduct is damaging the national security and foreign policy of the United States. Kent involved denials of passports solely on the basis of political beliefs entitled to First Amendment protection. [As Aptheker illustrates, the] protections accorded beliefs standing alone is very different from the protection accorded conduct. [But] [b]eliefs and speech

are only part of Agee's 'campaign to fight the United States CIA.' In that sense, this case contrasts markedly with the facts in Kent and Aptheker. No presumptions, rebuttable or otherwise, are involved, for Agee's conduct in foreign countries presents a serious danger to the national security."

Blackmun, J., concurring, "would have preferred to have the Court disavow forthrightly the aspects of Zemel and Kent that may suggest that evidence of a longstanding Executive policy or construction in this area is not probative of the issue of congressional authorization. Nonetheless, believing this is what the Court in effect has done," he joined the Court's opinion.

Brennan, J., joined by Marshall, J., dissenting, read Kent as "stat[ing] that any infringement of [the 'right to travel'] can only 'be pursuant to the lawmaking functions of the Congress,' and that delegations to the Executive Branch that curtail that liberty must be construed narrowly. Because the Passport Act of 1926—the same statute at issue here—did not expressly authorize the denial of passports to alleged Communists, the Court examined cases of actual passport refusals [to] determine whether 'it could be fairly argued' that the category of passport refusals was 'adopted by Congress in light of prior administrative practice.' The Court was unable to find such prior administrative practice, and therefore held that the regulation was unauthorized."

"[C]learly neither Zemel nor Kent holds," protested the dissenters, "that a longstanding Executive policy or construction is sufficient proof that Congress has implicitly authorized the Secretary's action. The cases hold that an administrative practice must be demonstrated; in fact Kent unequivocally states that mere construction by the Executive—no matter how longstanding and consistent—is not sufficient. [Not] only does the Court ignore the Kent-Zemel requirement that Executive discretion be supported by a consistent administrative practice, but it also relies on the very Execu-

7–2 majority, per BURGER, C.J., rejected Agee's contention that the revocation violated, inter alia, his "right to travel," stressing the distinction between interstate and international travel:

"Revocation of a passport undeniably curtails travel, but the freedom to travel abroad with a 'letter of introduction' in the form of a passport issued by the sovereign is subordinate to national security and foreign policy considerations; as such, it is subject to reasonable governmental regulation. The Court has made it plain that the *freedom* to travel outside the United States must be distinguished from the *right* to travel within the United States. This was underscored in *Califano v. Aznavorian*. 439 U.S. 170, 99 S.Ct. 471, 58 L.Ed.2d 435 (1978).[c]

"It is 'obvious and unarguable' that no governmental interest is more compelling than the security of the Nation. Protection of the foreign policy of the United States is a governmental interest of great importance, since foreign policy and national security considerations cannot neatly be compartmentalized. [Not] only has Agee jeopardized the security of the United States, but he has endangered the interests of countries other than the United States—thereby creating serious problems for American foreign relations and foreign policy. Restricting Agee's foreign travel, although perhaps not certain to prevent all of Agee's harmful activities, is the only avenue open to the Government to limit these activities.[60]"

BRENNAN, J., joined by Marshall, J., dissenting, devoted most of his opinion to the argument that the regulation under which Agee's passport had been revoked was "invalid as an unlawful exercise of authority by the Secretary [of State] under the Passport Act of 1926."[d] He then cited *Agee* as "a prime example of the adage that 'bad facts make bad law.'" "Agee is hardly a model representative of our Nation, [but] just as the Constitution protects both popular and unpopular speech, it likewise protects both popular and unpopular travelers."[e]

tive construction and policy deemed irrelevant in *Kent*.

"[The] point that *Kent* and *Zemel* make, and that today's opinion should make, is that the Executive authority to revoke passports touches an area fraught with important constitutional rights, and that the Court should therefore 'construe narrowly all delegated powers that curtail or dilute them.' *Kent*. The presumption is that Congress must expressly delegate authority to the Secretary to deny or revoke passports for foreign policy or national security reasons before he may exercise such authority. To overcome the presumption against an implied delegation, the Government must show 'an administrative practice sufficiently substantial and consistent.' *Zemel*. Only in this way can the Court satisfy itself that Congress has implicitly approved such exercise of authority by the Secretary."

c. In upholding a provision of the Social Security Act denying certain benefits for any month during all of which the recipient is outside the United States, the *Aznovorian* Court, per Stewart, J., rejected the view that international travel, no less than interstate travel, is "a basic constitutional right." In light of the "crucial distinction between the *freedom* to travel internationally and the *right* of interstate travel" (emphasis added), a statute "said to infringe the freedom to travel abroad is not to be judged by the same standard applied to laws that penalize the right of interstate travel, such as durational residency requirements imposed by the States [referring to the cases discussed at pp. 1027–37 infra]." See generally Note, 19 Va.J.Int'l L. 707 (1979).

60. Agee argues that the Government should be limited to an injunction ordering him to comply with his secrecy agreement [see fn. a]. This argument ignores the governmental interests at stake. As Agee concedes, such an injunction would not be enforceable outside of the United States.

d. See fn. b. supra.

e. Although the dissenters did not specifically address Agee's contention that the challenged regulation violated his right to travel, they did comment briefly on "the Court's whirlwind treatment" of Agee's first amendment claims.

Notes and Questions

1. *The shift from Kent to Agee.* Consider Farber, *National Security, The Right to Travel, and the Court,* 1981 Sup.Ct.Rev. 263, 285–87: "[*Agee*] represents a major shift from previous travel cases such as *Kent* [which] laid heavy stress on the importance of the right to travel and took a correspondingly grudging approach to discretionary travel controls. *Agee,* on the other hand, distinguishes the *right* to travel within the United States from the mere *freedom* to travel outside the United States. It takes a correspondingly generous view of executive discretion. For three reasons, the *Kent* approach is preferable, even ignoring the matter of stare decisis.

"First is the importance of the right to travel itself. [One] important aspect of international travel is its relation to freedom of speech. Without the right to travel, criticism of foreign policy is greatly impeded. [Second,] *Kent* 's grudging attitude toward executive discretion is amply supported by history. [The] *Agee* Court seems to have assumed that the discretion to control travel had only been exercised on a principled basis. Too many counterexamples exist to allow reliance on this assumption. The third reason for preferring *Kent* to *Agee* is that *Kent* aligns more closely with congressional intent. Since *Kent,* Congress has strongly supported the principle of freedom of travel. Despite urgent pleas from [President Eisenhower], Congress refused to supply the statutory power held lacking in *Kent.* ∗ ∗ ∗ Twenty years later, Congress abolished the other major elements of the Cold War program of travel control [area restrictions and a penalty for travel without a passport]. In sum, not only the holding but also the underlying policies of *Kent* have received congressional endorsement. This is of critical importance, because both *Kent* and *Agee* proceed from the premise that the President's power flows from Congress. Indeed, even if the President did have some inherent power in the area, that power would be greatly diminished by Congressional disapproval."

2. *The right to travel intrastate.* Is *intrastate* travel entitled to as much protection as travel across state lines? See *King v. New Rochelle Municipal Housing Auth.,* 442 F.2d 646 (2d Cir.1971) (it "would be meaningless to describe the right to travel between states as a fundamental precept of personal liberty and not to acknowledge a correlative constitutional right to travel within a state"). See also Tribe, supra, at 953–54; Note, 22 U.C.L.A.L.Rev. 1129, 1145–46 (1975). But see Comment, 55 Neb.L.Rev. 117, 128–29 (1975) ("intrastate travel is not a fundamental right" and statutes limiting such travel will be upheld on "reasonable basis" test).

3. *Zoning ordinances.* The "one-family dwellings" zoning ordinance upheld in *Belle Terre,* Sec. 2 supra, was challenged, inter alia, on the ground that "it interferes with the right to migrate to and settle within a State." The Court, per Douglas, J., made short shrift of this contention, noting that the ordinance "is not aimed at transients." Professor Tribe, supra, at 956, agrees that "qualitative as opposed to quantitative restraints on how a jurisdiction's land may be developed or used should [be] immune to challenge on right-to-travel grounds so long as they do not discriminate against new residents." At some point, however, "local laws making towns and municipalities homogeneous enclaves might cumulatively lead to a society in which migration from one jurisdiction to another, as a practical matter, becomes extremely difficult. If a showing is made that persons must in effect choose between changing their way of life and staying put, a right-to-travel challenge should succeed. Cf. *Aptheker.*"

Id. at n. 19. See generally Notes, 39 U.Chi.L.Rev. 612 (1972); 12 Harv.J.Leg. 244 (1975); 84 Yale L.J. 1564 (1975).

4. *A rationale for the right to travel.* Consider Ely, *Democracy and Distrust* 178–79 (1980): "The right at issue in the modern cases [is] not simply a right to travel to or through a state but rather a right to move there—the right, if you will, to relocate. [To] a large extent America was founded by persons escaping from environments they found oppressive. Mobility was quite free during the colonial period, and '[a]s a result, most colonials who dissented from their own community's conception of right and justice could move without great difficulty to a more congenial community.' And of course the symbolism, and indeed the reality, of 'the frontier' took much of its sustenance from the notion that a person should have the option of pulling up stakes and starting over elsewhere. [I think this tradition] points us in the right direction, one that associates the right to relocate not with the idea that it is some kind of handmaiden of majoritarian democracy but, quite to the contrary, with the notion that one should have an option of escaping an incompatible majority. [A dissenting member of a community] should have the option of exiting and relocating in a community whose values he or she finds more compatible. [S]ome differences remain [among the states]—relating perhaps most pertinently to the extent to which deviance of various sorts is tolerated or represented by law or enforcement policy, and indeed to the scope of such government services as education and welfare. [I]t's an old idea, dating back at least as far as Rousseau's 'droit d'emigration': it's just that the Court hasn't fixed on it. That is unfortunate, since it provides something the Court hasn't, a rationale for the right to travel it in fact has established."

See also Tribe at 957–58: "[C]lose surveillance and control of travel in both its senses [as an aspect of expression or education and as a means of changing one's residence and starting life anew] has always been a central technique of the totalitarian state, but centuries of experience should suffice to mark as especially suspect any governmental measure designed to prevent the emigration of those dissatisfied with the existing order, or the immigration of those who might alter the status quo. Just as government should be forbidden to expel the citizen who has become a source of unrest, so it cannot be permitted to imprison the citizen who seeks freedom in another land."

SECTION 4. THE DEATH PENALTY AND RELATED PROBLEMS: CRUEL AND UNUSUAL PUNISHMENT

Introduction

"The question of capital punishment has been the subject of endless discussion and will probably never be settled so long as men believe in punishment. [The] reasons why it cannot be settled are plain. There is first of all no agreement as to the objects of punishment. Next there is no way to determine the results of punishment. [Moreover,] questions of this sort, or perhaps of any sort, are not settled by reason; they are settled by prejudices and sentiments or by emotion. When they are settled they do not stay settled, for the emotions change as new stimuli are applied to the machine."

—Clarence Darrow, *Crime, Its Cause and Treatment* 166 (1922).

At the time he made it, Darrow's prediction that the question of capital punishment "will probably never be settled" appeared well-founded. That the issue might ever be settled as a matter of constitutional law seemed almost inconceivable. The Court had already specifically sanctioned death by firing squad and by electrocution. Indeed, 25 years after Darrow's remarks, *Louisiana ex rel. Francis v. Resweber,* 329 U.S. 459, 67 S.Ct. 374, 91 L.Ed. 422 (1947), sustained what the dissenters called the horror of "death by installments." (After a first attempt to electrocute petitioner had failed because of mechanical difficulties, the state strapped him in the electric chair a second time and threw the switch again.) And in the 1950s the Court twice upheld the execution of men whose sanity was in doubt, leaving the question to the judgment of a governor and a warden. See Kamisar, *The Reincarnation of the Death Penalty: Is it Possible?* Student Lawyer, May 1973, pp. 22–23.

In *Trop v. Dulles,* 356 U.S. 86, 78 S.Ct. 590, 2 L.Ed.2d 630 (1958), speaking for four justices, (Brennan, J., had found the "expatriation" provision invalid on other grounds), Warren, C.J., deemed deprivation of a native-born American's citizenship because of wartime desertion from the army—leaving him "stateless"—a "fate forbidden by the principle of civilized treatment guaranteed by the Eighth Amendment," but was quick to add: "[W]hatever the arguments may be against the [death penalty, it] has been employed throughout our history, and, in a day when it is still widely accepted, it cannot be said to violate the constitutional concept of cruelty." As late as 1968, a close student of the problem, observed: "[N]ot a single death penalty statute, not a single statutorily imposed mode of execution, not a single attempted execution has ever been held by any court to be 'cruel and unusual punishment' under any state or federal constitution. Nothing less than a mighty counterthrust would appear to be required to alter the direction of these decisions." Bedau, *The Courts, the Constitution, and Capital Punishment,* 1968 Utah L.Rev. 201.

In the 1960s the NAACP Legal Defense and Educational Fund, Inc. (LDF), led by Professor Anthony Amsterdam, did launch a major constitutional assault on the death penalty. Convinced that "each year the United States went without executions, the more hollow would ring claims that the American people could not do without them" and that "the longer death-row inmates waited, the greater their numbers, the more difficult it would be for the courts to permit the first execution," the LDF developed a "moratorium strategy," creating "a death-row logjam." Meltsner, *Cruel and Unusual: The Supreme Court and Capital Punishment* 107 (1973).

Largely as a result of LDF efforts in blocking all executions on every conceivable legal ground, when the Court handed down *Furman,* infra, in 1972, there had not been a single execution in five years.

Actually, the number of executions had started to decline as early as the 1940s and had dropped dramatically in the 1960s, several years before the LDF had successfully developed its moratorium strategy. After peaking in the 1930s (152 per year during this decade, and reaching an all-time high of 199 executions in 1935), the annual rate of executions averaged 128 in the 1940s and 72 in the 1950s. There were only 21 executions in 1963, 15 in 1964 and a mere seven in 1965. (In the 1930–50 period, executions had averaged more than ten *a month*). See Greenberg, *Capital Punishment as a System,* 91 Yale L.J. 908, 924–25 (1982); Kamisar, supra.

If, as appeared to be the case, the Court was reluctant to enter into the hotly contested capital punishment debate, yet equally hesitant to "legitimate" the punishment, the preferable way to proceed would seem to have been to continue to chip away at the procedural administration of the death penalty rather than launch a more frontal assault as the Court did (or most thought it did at the time) in *Furman*. Thus, LDF lawyers suffered a serious set-back in 1971 when the Court "refused an invitation to abolish capital punishment piecemeal." Meltsner, supra, at 244–45. *McGautha v. California* and *Crampton v. Ohio*, 402 U.S. 183, 91 S.Ct. 1454, 28 L.Ed.2d 711 (1971), rejected (1) petitioners' common claim that permitting the jury to impose the death penalty without any governing standards violated due process and (2) the Ohio petitioner's contention that allowing the jury to impose the death penalty in the same proceeding and verdict which determines the issue of guilt "creates an intolerable tension" between one's constitutional right not to be compelled to be a witness against himself on the issue of guilt and his constitutional right to be heard on the issue of punishment, a tension which can be avoided by a bifurcated trial, such as that required by California and five other states.[a]

In rejecting the contention that the states had to develop and articulate criteria under which convicted felons should be chosen to live and die, a 6–3 majority (including Stewart and White, JJ., whose votes would be pivotal in *Furman*) observed, per Harlan, J.:

"To identify before the fact those characteristics of criminal homicides and their perpetrators which call for the death penalty, and to express those characteristics in language which can be fairly understood and applied by the sentencing authority, appear to be tasks which are beyond present human ability. * * * In light of history, experience, and the present limitations of human knowledge, we find it quite impossible to say that committing to the untrammeled discretion of the jury the power to pronounce life or death in capital cases is offensive to anything in the Constitution. The States are entitled to assume that jurors confronted with the truly awesome responsibility of decreeing death for a fellow human will act with due regard for the consequences of their decision and will consider a variety of factors * * *. For a court to attempt to catalog the appropriate factors in this elusive area could inhibit rather than expand the scope of consideration, for no list of circumstances would ever be really complete." [b]

Consider Weisberg, *Deregulating Death,* 1983 Sup.Ct.Rev. 305, 313: "In the end, Harlan concludes [in *McGautha*] that, morally and intellectually, the Court has nothing to teach the states about capital punishment. One can of course dispute the truth of Harlan's central insight—that we cannot write a law of capital punishment in conventional legal language. Even if one accepts that truth, one can reject Harlan's inference from it—that the Court must leave the issue to the states. Indeed what follows *McGautha* is a struggle over both the truth and the significance of Harlan's assertion."

---

a. To what extent did the Court reject *McGautha* and *Crampton* in subsequent decisions?

b. Brennan, J., joined by Douglas and Marshall, JJ., dissenting, refused to "believe that the legislatures of the 50 states are so devoid of wisdom and the power of rational thought that they are unable to face the problem of capital punishment directly, and to determine for themselves the criteria under which convicted felons should be chosen to live or die." He maintained that such procedures may take a variety of forms, e.g., requiring the decision to rest upon the presence or absence of specific factors, or directing the decision-maker's attention to the basic policy determinations underlying the death penalty statute.

I. IS THE DEATH PENALTY ALWAYS—OR EVER— "CRUEL AND UNUSUAL"?

FURMAN v. GEORGIA, 408 U.S. 238, 92 S.Ct. 2726, 33 L.Ed.2d 346 (1972), considered the death sentence in three cases (all involving black defendants), two dealing with a murderer and rapist in Georgia, the third a rapist in Texas.[c] (Each had been sentenced to death after trial by jury. Under the applicable state statutes, the judge or jury had discretion to impose the death penalty.) Also at stake, however, were the lives of almost 600 condemned persons who had "piled up" in "death rows" throughout the land in recent years. Striking down the laws of 39 states [d] and various federal statutory provisions, a 5–4 majority, per curiam, held that "the imposition and carrying out" of the death penalty under the current arbitrarily and randomly administered system constitutes "cruel and unusual" punishment in violation of the eighth and fourteenth amendments. Each of the justices wrote a separate concurring or dissenting opinion explaining his reasons for invalidating or upholding the death penalty. (The nine opinions totalled 230 pages in the official reports.) *Furman* has been called "not so much a case as a badly orchestrated opera, with nine characters taking turns to offer their own arias." Weisberg, *Deregulating Death*, 1983 Sup. Ct.Rev. 305, 315.

The pivotal opinions of Stewart and White, JJ., left open the question whether *any* system of capital punishment, as opposed to the presently capriciously administered one, would be unconstitutional. A third member of the majority, Douglas, J., also reserved for another day whether a nondiscriminatorily operated mandatory death penalty would be constitutional.

STEWART, J.: "If we were reviewing death sentences imposed under [laws making death the mandatory punishment for every person convicted of engaging in certain designated criminal conduct] we would be faced with the need to decide whether capital punishment is unconstitutional for all crimes and under all circumstances. We would need to decide whether a legislature—state or federal—could constitutionally determine that certain criminal conduct is so atrocious that society's interest in deterrence and retribution wholly outweighs any considerations of reform or rehabilitation of the perpetrator, and that, despite the inconclusive empirical evidence, only the automatic penalty of death will provide maximum deterrence.

"On that score I would say only that I cannot agree that retribution is a constitutionally impermissible ingredient in the imposition of punishment. The instinct for retribution is part of the nature of man, and channeling that instinct in the administration of criminal justice serves an important purpose in promoting the stability of a society governed by law. When people begin to believe that organized society is unwilling or unable to impose upon criminal offenders the punishment they 'deserve,' then there are sown the seeds of anarchy—of self-help, vigilante justice, and lynch law.

"The constitutionality of capital punishment in the abstract is not, however, before us in these cases. For the Georgia and Texas legislatures have not provided that the death penalty shall be imposed upon all those who are found

---

c. Since 1930, murder and rape had accounted for nearly 99% of total executions and murder alone for about 87%. But various jurisdictions also permitted capital punishment for other crimes, e.g., kidnapping, treason, espionage, aircraft piracy.

d. Forty states authorized capital punishment for a variety of crimes, but since Rhode Island's only capital statute, murder by a life term prisoner, carried a mandatory death sentence, it was not invalidated by the instant case.

guilty of forcible rape [or] murder. In a word, neither State has made a legislative determination that forcible rape and murder can be deterred only by imposing the penalty of death upon all who perpetrate those offenses. As [concurring] Justice White so tellingly puts it, the 'legislative will is not frustrated if the penalty is never imposed.'

"Instead, the death sentences now before us are the product of a legal system that brings them, I believe, within the very core of the Eighth Amendment's guarantee against cruel and unusual punishments, a guarantee applicable against the States through the Fourteenth Amendment. In the first place, it is clear that these sentences are 'cruel' in the sense that they excessively go beyond, not in degree but in kind, the punishments that the state legislatures have determined to be necessary. In the second place, it is equally clear that these sentences are 'unusual' in the sense that the penalty of death is infrequently imposed for murder, and that its imposition for rape is extraordinarily rare. But I do not rest my conclusion upon these two propositions alone.

"These death sentences are cruel and unusual in the same way that being struck by lightning is cruel and unusual. For, of all the people convicted of rapes and murders in 1967 and 1968, many just as reprehensible as these, the petitioners are among a capriciously selected random handful upon whom the sentence of death has in fact been imposed. My concurring Brothers have demonstrated that, if any basis can be discerned for the selection of these few to be sentenced to die, it is the constitutionally impermissible basis of race. But racial discrimination has not been proved, and I put it to one side. I simply conclude that the Eighth and Fourteenth Amendments cannot tolerate the inflicting of a sentence of death under legal systems that permit this unique penalty to be so wantonly and so freakishly imposed."

WHITE, J.: "The imposition and execution of the death penalty are obviously cruel in the dictionary sense. But the penalty has not been considered cruel and unusual punishment in the constitutional sense because it was thought justified by the social ends it was deemed to serve. At the moment that it ceases realistically to further these purposes, however, the emerging question is whether its imposition in such circumstances would violate the Eighth Amendment. It is my view that it would, for its imposition would then be the pointless and needless extinction of life with only marginal contributions to any discernible social or public purposes. A penalty with such negligible returns to the State would be patently excessive and cruel and unusual punishment violative of the Eighth Amendment.

"It is also my judgment that this point has been reached with respect to capital punishment as it is presently administered under the statutes involved in these cases. [A]s the statutes before us are now administered, the penalty is so infrequently imposed that the threat of execution is too attenuated to be of substantial service to criminal justice.

" * * * I must arrive at judgment; and I can do no more than state a conclusion based on 10 years of almost daily exposure to the facts and circumstances of hundreds and hundreds of federal and state criminal cases involving crimes for which death is the authorized penalty. [T]he death penalty is exacted with great infrequency even for the most atrocious crimes [and] there is no meaningful basis for distinguishing the few cases in which it is imposed from the many cases in which it is not.[e] The short of it is that the policy of vesting

e. But consider Vance, *The Death Penalty* *after Furman*, 48 Notre Dame Law. 850, 858 (1973): "Actually there is a fairly universal consensus on which cases should receive the sentencing authority primarily in juries—a decision largely motivated by the desire to mitigate the harshness of the law and to bring community judgment to bear on the sentence as well as guilt or innocence—has so effectively achieved its aims that capital punishment within the confines of the statutes now before us has for all practical purposes run its course.

"[P]ast and present legislative judgment with respect to the death penalty loses much of its force when viewed in light of the recurring practice of delegating sentencing authority to the jury and the fact that a jury, in its own discretion and without violating its trust or any statutory policy, may refuse to impose the death penalty no matter what the circumstances of the crime. Legislative 'policy' is thus necessarily defined not by what is legislatively authorized but by what juries and judges do in exercising the discretion so regularly conferred upon them. In my judgment what was done in these cases violated the Eighth Amendment."

DOUGLAS, J.: "The words 'cruel and unusual' certainly include penalties that are barbaric. But the words, at least when read in light of the English proscription against selective and irregular use of penalties, suggest that it is 'cruel and unusual' to apply the death penalty—or any other penalty—selectively to minorities whose numbers are few, who are outcasts of society, and who are unpopular, but whom society is willing to see suffer though it would not countenance general application of the same penalty across the boards. * * *

"A law that stated that anyone making more than $50,000 would be exempt from the death penalty would plainly fall, as would a law that in terms said that Blacks, those who never went beyond the fifth grade in school, or those who made less than $3,000 a year, or those who were unpopular or unstable should be the only people executed. A law which in the overall view reaches that result in practice has no more sanctity than a law which in terms provides the same.

"[T]hese discretionary statutes are unconstitutional in their operation. They are pregnant with discrimination and discrimination is an ingredient not compatible with the idea of equal protection of the laws that is implicit in the ban on 'cruel and unusual' punishments."

Although Stewart and White, JJ., concurring, and the four dissenters all asserted that the remaining members of the majority—Brennan and Marshall, JJ.—had concluded that the eighth amendment prohibits capital punishment for all crimes and under all circumstances, this is not clear from their opinions.

As BRENNAN, J., perceived the question, there are four principles "recognized in our cases and inherent in" the eighth amendment prohibition "sufficient to permit a judicial determination whether a challenged punishment" "does not comport with human dignity" and therefore is "cruel and unusual": (1) "a punishment must not be so severe as to be degrading to the dignity of human beings"; (2) the government "must not arbitrarily inflict a severe punishment"; (3) "a severe punishment must not be unacceptable to contemporary society"; and (4) "a severe punishment must not be excessive," i.e., "unnecessary."

harshest penalties. [It] is only in the bizarre murder, the killing for hire or during another serious crime, and a few other isolated instances that the people of this country want to see the death penalty applied. [Any prosecutor] (as well as any judge or defense attorney) can listen to a set of facts and tell you whether it is a death penalty case. [T]here *should* be very few death penalty sentences. Only a very few cases warrant this extreme measure. It takes two essential [ingredients]: (1) overwhelming proof [of] guilt and (2) an extremely aggravated fact situation. What is so surprising is Justice White's and Justice Stewart's conclusion that there is something highly improper in so few people receiving the death penalty."

Applying the first and "primary" principle, Brennan, J., concluded that capital punishment "involves by its very nature a denial of the executed person's humanity" and, in comparison to all other punishments today, "is uniquely degrading to human dignity." He "would not hesitate to hold, on that ground alone, that death is today a 'cruel and unusual punishment,' *were it not that death is a punishment of longstanding usage and acceptance in this country.*" [Emphasis added.] He then turned to a discussion of the other three principles, in each instance relying heavily upon the fact that today the death sentence is inflicted very rarely and most arbitrarily:

"When the punishment of death is inflicted in a trivial number of the cases in which it is legally available, the conclusion is virtually inescapable that it is being inflicted arbitrarily. Indeed, it smacks of little more than a lottery system. * * *

"When there is a strong probability that an unusually severe and degrading punishment is being inflicted arbitrarily, we may well expect that society will disapprove of its infliction. I turn, therefore, to the third principle. An examination of the history and present operation of the American practice of punishing criminals by death reveals that this punishment has been almost totally rejected by contemporary society.

"* * * When an unusually severe punishment is authorized for wide-scale application but not, because of society's refusal, inflicted save in a few instances, the inference is compelling that there is a deep-seated reluctance to inflict it. Indeed, the likelihood is great that the punishment is tolerated only because of its disuse. The objective indicator of society's view of an unusually severe punishment is what society does with it. And today society will inflict death upon only a small sample of the eligible criminals. Rejection could hardly be more complete without becoming absolute.[f] At the very least, I must conclude that contemporary society views this punishment with substantial doubt.

"[As for the final principle], whatever the speculative validity of the assumption that the threat of death is a superior deterrent, there is no reason to believe that as currently administered the punishment of death is necessary to deter the commission of capital crimes. * * *

"In sum, the punishment of death is inconsistent with all four principles: Death is an unusually severe and degrading punishment; there is a strong probability that it is inflicted arbitrarily; its rejection by contemporary society is virtually total; and there is no reason to believe that it serves any penal purpose more effectively than the less severe punishment of imprisonment. The function of these principles is to enable a court to determine whether a punishment comports with human dignity. Death, quite simply, does not."

MARSHALL, J.'s "historical foray" led to the question "whether American society has reached a point where abolition is not dependent on a successful grass roots movement in particular jurisdictions, but is demanded by the Eighth Amendment."[g] He concluded that the death penalty constitutes "cruel and

---

f. But consider Polsby, *The Death of Capital Punishment?*, 1972 Sup.Ct.Rev. 1, 20: "An entirely valid inference [from the infrequent imposition of the death penalty] would be, not that the society has repudiated the penalty, but that it wishes to reserve its use to a small number of cases. A reluctance to impose a penalty is not necessarily the same as its repudiation. Reluctance may spring from

moral revulsion; but it may just as commonly proceed from a human and heartfelt sorrow."

g. Consider Levy, *Against the Law* 401 (1974): "In effect, the question [Marshall, J.,] asked was this: In view of the fact that the democratic process had failed to achieve abolition, should the Court impose a new public policy upon the country by a novel construction of the cruel-and-unusual punishments unusual" punishment on two independent grounds: (1) "it is excessive and serves no valid legislative purpose," i.e., it is not a more effective deterrent than life imprisonment; (2) "it is abhorrent to currently existing moral values."

As for the first ground: "Punishment for the sake of retribution" is "not permissible under the Eighth Amendment. [At] times a cry is heard that morality requires vengeance to evidence society's abhorrence of the act. But the Eighth Amendment is our insulation from our baser selves. The cruel and unusual language limits the avenues through which vengeance can be channeled.[h] Were this not so, the language would be empty and a return to the rack and other tortures would be possible in a given case." Nor, "in light of the massive amount of evidence before us, [showing no correlation between the rate of murder or other capital crimes and the presence or absence of the death penalty, can capital punishment] be justified on the basis of its deterrent effect. [The] statistical evidence is not convincing beyond all doubt, but, it is persuasive. [The] point has now been reached at which deference to the legislatures is tantamount to abdication of our judicial roles as factfinders, judges and ultimate arbiters of the Constitution. [There] is no rational basis for concluding that capital punishment is not excessive. It therefore violates the Eighth Amendment."

As for the second independent ground: Although recent opinion polls indicate that Americans are about equally divided on the question of capital punishment, "whether or not a punishment is cruel or unusual depends, not on whether its mere mention 'shocks the conscience and sense of justice of the people,' but on whether people who were fully informed as to the purposes of the penalty and its liabilities would find the penalty shocking, unjust and unacceptable." Marshall, J., then concluded that *if* the average citizen possessed "knowledge of all the facts presently available" (for example, that death is no more effective a deterrent than life imprisonment; "convicted murderers are rarely executed"; "no attempt is made in the sentencing process to ferret out likely recidivists for execution"; the punishment "is imposed discriminatorily against certain identifiable classes of people"; "innocent people have been executed";) "the average citizen *would,* in my opinion, find [capital punishment] shocking to

clause?" But cf. Kamisar, supra, at 24: "Because a decision 'legitimating' capital punishment would be interpreted by many as 'approving' it, the result would undoubtedly have been a stifling of the current movement for reform in nonjudicial forums and the lending of the Court's prestige to those forces favoring the continuation of the death penalty. [T]o give the imprimatur of legitimacy to the now broadly challenged death penalty 'would defeat the very reason behind judicial restraint—encouragement of decision by the other branches of government' [Goldberg & Dershowitz, *Declaring the Death Penalty Unconstitutional,* 83 Harv.L.Rev. 1773, 1805 (1970)]."

h. But consider Polsby, fn. f supra, at 37, 39–40: "The confusion between the proposition that the death penalty deters and the proposition that it is appropriate is a fairly stable feature of retentionist argument. [I submit] that the declaration that the death

penalty is a superior deterrent to serious crime, in spite of evidence to the contrary, amounts to nothing more than the expression of a value preference that, whether the penalty is a superior deterrent or not, it ought to be used. A priori, I can find nothing wrong with this value preference. It may be flinty and stern, but it does not seem to me necessarily barbaric, that someone might believe that certain criminals ought to be put to death, the inhuman brutality of their crimes being so great as to outrun all possibility of forgiveness or amends. But if the argument is to rest upon straight moralistic dogma [why] should it dress itself up in the guise of a utilitarian argument instead? [One] answer may be that retentionists would be ashamed to admit to having such values. If so, surely it is relevant to a judgment whether death is a cruel and unusual punishment." Cf. Black, *Capital Punishment: The Inevitability of Caprice and Mistake* 23–28 (1974).

his conscience and sense of justice. [Emphasis added.][i] For this reason alone capital punishment cannot stand."

There were four separate dissenting opinions. BURGER, C.J., warned that "it is essential to our role as a court that we not seize upon the enigmatic character of the [eighth amendment] guarantee as an invitation to enact our personal predilictions into law." As for the argument that the death penalty was "excessive" or "unnecessary," he found "no authority suggesting that the Eighth Amendment was intended to purge the law of its retributive elements" nor any basis for prohibiting "all punishments the States are unable to prove necessary to deter crime."

"Real change," maintained the Chief Justice, "could clearly be brought about [by legislatures responding to today's ruling if they] provided mandatory death sentences in such a way as to deny juries the opportunity to bring in a verdict on a lesser charge; under such a system, the death sentence could only be avoided by a verdict of acquittal. If this is the only alternative that the legislatures can safely pursue under today's ruling, I would have preferred that the Court opt for total abolition.

"It seems remarkable to me that with our basic trust in lay jurors as the keystone in our system of criminal justice, it should now be suggested that we take the most sensitive and important of all decisions away from them. I could more easily be persuaded that mandatory sentences of death, without the intervening and ameliorating impact of lay jurors, are so arbitrary and doctrinaire that they violate the Constitution. The very infrequency of death penalties imposed by jurors attests their cautious and discriminating reservation of that penalty for the most extreme [cases.] I do not see how [the history of American abhorrence of the mandatory death sentence] can be ignored and how it can be suggested that the Eighth Amendment demands the elimination of the most sensitive feature of the sentencing system. * * *

"Quite apart from the limitations of the Eighth Amendment itself, the preference for legislative action is justified by the inability of the courts to participate in the debate at the level where the controversy is focused. The case against capital punishment is not the product of legal dialectic but rests primarily on factual claims, the truth of which cannot be tested by conventional judicial processes."

BLACKMUN, J., filed a separate dissent, "personally rejoicing" at the Court's result, but unable to accept it "as a matter of history, of law, or of constitutional pronouncement."

In a third dissent, POWELL, J., called the Court's ruling "the very sort of judgment that the legislative branch is competent to make and for which the judiciary is ill-equipped." He maintained that "the sweeping judicial action undertaken today reflects a basic lack of faith and confidence in the democratic process."

"[T]he weight of the evidence," he observed, "indicates that the public generally has not accepted either the morality or the social merit of [the abolitionists' views]. But however one may assess the amorphous ebb and flow of public opinion generally on this volatile issue,[j] this type of inquiry lies at the

i. Is this a valid means of ascertaining whether "popular sentiment" or "the average citizen" abhors capital punishment? Or does Marshall, J.'s approach represent excessive speculation or inappropriate "elitism" about moral judgment? Compare Kamisar, supra, at 48, and Polsby, supra, at 23–24 with Radin, *The Jurisprudence of Death*, 126 U.Pa.L.Rev. 989, 1040–42 (1978).

j. "The unpopularity of [*Furman*] is attested by the fact that several months later, acperiphery—not the core—of the judicial process in constitutional cases. The assessment of public opinion is essentially a legislative, not a judicial function."

In a fourth dissent, REHNQUIST, J., concluded that the majority's ruling "significantly lack[ed]" the "humility" and "deference to legislative judgment" with which the task of judging constitutional cases must be approached; indeed, "it is not an act of judgment, but rather an act of will."

Notes and Questions

1. Of *"life" and "limb."* Consider Levy, fn. g supra, at 396: "To argue as a matter of public morality or policy that the state should not take a life as a penalty for crime is an appropriate task for legislation. The responsible [Supreme Court justice] has a different task. In this case the text of the Constitution itself seemed confining, indeed, seemed to erect an insuperable barricade against acceptance of the abolitionist position. The [Eighth Amendment prohibition] appears in the same Bill of Rights that clearly sanctions the death penalty. The Fifth Amendment begins with a guarantee [that] '[n]o person shall be held to answer for a *capital,* or otherwise infamous crime, unless * * *.' The same amendment [also provides]: 'nor shall any person be subject for the same offense to be twice put in jeopardy of *life* or limb' [nor] 'be deprived of *life,* liberty, or property without due process * * *.' In 1868 the Fourteenth Amendment made an identical due-process clause applicable to the [states]. Thus, the Constitution itself in four places recognizes and permits capital punishment, a penalty that was common when the Fifth, Eighth and Fourteenth Amendments were adopted." See also Berger, *Death Penalties: The Supreme Court's Obstacle Course* 43–50 (1982). But cf. Levy, supra, at 402: "[Brennan, J.,] relegated to one of his footnotes a stunning retort to the dissenters who so heavily stressed the fact that the language of the Fifth Amendment authorized the death penalty. One of its clauses prohibited placing any person in double jeopardy of life 'or limb,' [but] Brennan asserted correctly that no one now contends that the reference to jeopardy of limb 'provides a perpetual constitutional sanction for such corporal punishments as branding and earcropping, which were common punishments when the Bill of Rights was adopted' [n. 28]. Not one of the four dissenters took note of the point; it was irrefutable." See also Radin, fn. i supra, at 1031.

2. *McGautha and Furman.* Why didn't Stewart and White JJ., take the route offered a year earlier by *McGautha* rather than the broader avenue presented in *Furman?* Was it because, in *Furman,* they were free of a powerful force which had operated on them the previous year—the restraining influence of that great "judge's judge"—Harlan, J.? Was it because they did not themselves know until the "moment of decision" that they *would* vote to strike down the death penalty? Was it because, after struggling for years to avoid meeting the issue head-on, when they finally had to do so they simply could not bring themselves to authorize "pulling the switch"—even if they had to go off on grounds which seem quite inconsistent with their previous position in *McGautha?*

cording to a Gallup Poll, 57 percent of the Nation favored capital punishment, [a 20-year high and] an increase of 7 percent from the figure at about the time of the decision." Levy, fn. g supra, at 419. Since then, support for the death penalty has risen significantly. A decade after *Furman,* more than 70 percent of the general public and almost the same percentage of college freshmen and ABA member lawyers favored continuation of the death penalty. See Streib, *Executions under the Post-Furman Capital Punishment Statutes,* 15 Rutgers L.J. 443, 483–84 n. 413 (1984); *Special Project: Capital Punishment in 1984,* 69 Corn.L.Rev. 1129, 1131–32 n. 8 (1984).

3. *The "analytic" and "normative" approaches of the Furman majority.*
Daniel Polsby has called "the Douglas-Stewart-White approach to the Eighth
Amendment 'analytic' to distinguish it from the 'normative' approach of Brennan and Marshall." He observes, Polsby, fn. f supra at 24–25: "[The analytic
approach's chief virtue is at the same time its chief vice: it avoids the core
normative question whether the 'evolving standards of decency that mark the
progress of a maturing society' have now risen high enough to wash the death
penalty away. [W]hatever the analytic approach gains in avoiding subjective
and impressionistic sallies into the shadow world of language, it also fails to
meet Mr. Justice Brennan's implicit objection that the Eighth Amendment—
whatever it means—must mean something, and, indeed, must mean something
different from the other provisions of the Constitution. The arguments of
Justices Douglas, Stewart, and White seem rather intent on avoiding, if possible,
that core question. Rather, they prefer to emphasize the use of the Eighth
Amendment as a tool for testing whether the penalty of death is evenhandedly
applied. Why they should have done this is obscure in view of the fact that
existing doctrines of equal protection (which was the emphasis of the Douglas
opinion) or due process of law should have furnished more than adequate ground
for striking down the death penalty, once the factual premises which these three
Justices proffer (relating to the arbitrariness or irrationality of the penalty's use,
or in Douglas's case, to its use on despised or dispossessed minorities) are
accepted.[k] To view the Eighth Amendment in those terms deprives it of a
dimension which is latent in almost all of the previous [decisions]—as an
independently potent moral force which is at the disposal of the least dangerous
branch of government and which may be used to make the most dangerous
branch a little less so."

GREGG v. GEORGIA, 428 U.S. 153, 96 S.Ct. 2909, 49 L.Ed.2d 859 (1976),
upheld the constitutionality of Georgia's post-*Furman* capital-sentencing procedures, rejecting the basic contention that "the punishment of death always,
regardless of the enormity of the offense or the procedure followed in imposing
the sentence, is cruel and unusual punishment in violation of the Constitution."
STEWART, J., who announced the judgment of the Court and an opinion joined by
Powell and Stevens, JJ., concluded that "the concerns expressed in *Furman* that
the penalty of death not be imposed in an arbitrary or capricious manner can be
met by a carefully drafted statute that ensures that the sentencing authority is
given adequate information and guidance. As a general proposition these
concerns are best met by a system [such as Georgia's] that provides for a
bifurcated proceeding at which the sentencing authority is apprised of the
information relevant to the imposition of sentence and provided with standards
to guide its use of the information." [a]

By contrast with the procedures before the Court in *Furman*, the new
Georgia sentencing procedures "focus the jury's attention on the particularized

k. But in *Furman* and companion cases
certiorari was granted limited to the following
question: "Does the imposition and carrying
out of the death penalty in [these cases] constitute cruel and unusual punishment in violation of the Eighth and Fourteenth Amendments?"

a. "We do not intend to suggest," added
Stewart, J., "that only the above-described

procedures would be permissible under
Furman or that any sentencing system constructed along these general lines would inevitably satisfy the concerns of *Furman,* for each
distinct system must be examined on a individual basis."

nature of the crime and the particularized characteristics of the individual defendant. While the jury is permitted to consider any aggravating or mitigating circumstances,[b] it must find and identify at least one [of 10 statutory aggravating circumstances[c] beyond a reasonable doubt] before it may impose a penalty of death. In this way the jury's discretion is channelled. No longer can a jury wantonly and freakishly impose the death sentence; it is always circumscribed by the legislative guidelines. In addition, the review function of the Supreme Court of Georgia [which is required to review every death sentence to determine, inter alia, whether it was imposed under the influence of passion or prejudice and whether it is 'excessive or disproportionate to the penalty imposed in similar cases, considering both the crime and the defendant'] affords additional assurance that the concerns that prompted our decision in *Furman* are not present to any significant degree in the Georgia procedure applied here."

At the guilt stage (or guilt trial) of Georgia's bifurcated procedure, the jury found petitioner guilty of two counts of armed robbery and two counts of murder. At the sentencing stage, which took place before the same jury, the judge instructed the jury that it would not be authorized to consider the death penalty unless it first found beyond a reasonable doubt one of these statutorily defined "aggravating circumstances": (1) that murder was committed while the offender was engaged in the commission of "another capital felony," to-wit armed robbery; (2) the offender committed murder "for the purpose of receiving money"; (3) the murder was "outrageously or wantonly vile [in] that it [involved] depravity of the mind." Finding the first two "aggravating circumstances," the jury returned verdicts of death on each count. The Georgia Supreme Court affirmed the convictions. After reviewing the record and comparing the evidence and sentences in similar cases, the court upheld the death sentences for the murders, but vacated the armed robbery sentences on the ground, inter alia, that the death penalty had rarely been imposed in Georgia for that crime. In rejecting petitioner's claim that his death sentence under the Georgia statute constituted "cruel and unusual" punishment, the plurality observed:

"[A]n assessment of contemporary values concerning the infliction of a challenged sanction is relevant to the application of the Eighth Amendment, [but] our cases also make clear that public perceptions of standards of decency with respect to criminal sanctions are not conclusive. A penalty also must accord with 'the dignity of man,' which is the 'basic concept underlying the Eighth Amendment.' *Trop* (plurality opinion). This means, at least, that the punishment not be 'excessive.' When a form of punishment in the abstract [is challenged], the inquiry into 'excessiveness' has two aspects. First, the punishment must not involve the unnecessary and wanton infliction of pain. Second,

b. The plurality pointed out that the jury is not *required* to find any mitigating circumstance in order to make a recommendation of mercy that is binding on the court, "but it must find a *statutory* aggravating circumstance before recommending a sentence of death."

c. Georgia authorized the death penalty for six categories of crime: murder, kidnapping under certain circumstances, rape, treason and aircraft hijacking. The statutory aggravating circumstances for murder include "a prior record of conviction for a capital offense" or "a substantial history of serious assaultive criminal convictions"; commission of the crime against a police officer or fireman while performing his official duties; commission of the crime while engaged in certain other felonies; or commission of an "outrageously or wantonly vile, horrible or inhuman" murder (§ (b)(7)). *Godfrey v. Georgia*, 446 U.S. 420, 100 S.Ct. 1759, 64 L.Ed.2d 398 (1980), held that the Georgia courts had "adopted such a broad and vague construction" of the § (b)(7) aggravating circumstance as to violate the eighth and fourteenth amendments.

the punishment must not be grossly out of proportion to the severity of the crime.

"[I]n assessing a punishment selected by a democratically elected legislature against the constitutional measure, we presume its validity. We may not require the legislature to select the least severe penalty possible so long as the penalty selected is not cruelly inhumane or disproportionate to the crime involved. And a heavy burden rests on those who would attack the judgment of the representatives of the people.

"This is true in part because the constitutional test is intertwined with an assessment of contemporary standards and the legislative judgment weighs heavily in ascertaining such standards. [The] deference we owe to the decisions of the state legislatures under our federal system is enhanced where the specification of punishments is concerned, for 'these are peculiarly questions of legislative policy.'

"[Petitioners renew the argument made in *Furman* that 'standards of decency' have evolved to the point where capital punishment no longer can be tolerated, a view accepted only by Justices Brennan and Marshall four years ago], but developments [since] *Furman* have undercut substantially the assumptions upon which [this] argument rested. [It] is now evident that a large proportion of American society continues to regard [capital punishment] as an appropriate and necessary criminal sanction.

"The most marked indication of society's endorsement of the death penalty for murder is the legislative response to *Furman*. The legislatures of at least 35 States have enacted new statutes that provide for the death penalty for at least some crimes that result in the death of another person.[d] And the Congress of the United States, in 1974, enacted a statute providing the death penalty for aircraft piracy that results in death.

"[The] jury also is a significant and reliable objective index of contemporary values because it is so directly involved. [It] may be true that evolving standards have influenced juries in recent decades to be more discriminating in imposing the sentence of death. But the relative infrequency of jury verdicts imposing the death sentence does not indicate rejection of capital punishment per se. Rather, [it] may well reflect the humane feeling that this most irrevocable of sanctions should be reserved for a small number of extreme cases.

"[H]owever, the Eighth Amendment demands more than that a challenged punishment be acceptable to contemporary society. The Court also must ask whether is comports with the basic concept of human dignity at the core of the Amendment. *Trop* (plurality opinion). * * *

"The death penalty is said to serve two principal social purposes: retribution and deterrence of capital crimes by prospective offenders.

"In part, capital punishment is an expression of society's moral outrage at particularly offensive conduct. This function [is] essential in an ordered society

---

d. But consider Zimring & Hawkins, *Capital Punishment and the Eighth Amendment: Furman and Gregg in Retrospect*, 18 U.C.Davis L.Rev., 927, 950 (1985): The "legislative extravaganza" of post-*Furman* death penalty statutes "is reminiscent of the 'pouring panic of capital statutes' which was a feature of the history of the criminal law in eighteenth-century England. Whatever the social psychology of that development may have been, the post-*Furman* reaction in America would prob-ably be best characterized as a typical frustration-aggression response. Like parallel incidents in school prayer and pornography, legislative backlash was entirely to be expected by anyone familiar with the history of judicial invalidation in this country."

For a useful summary of the post-*Furman* statutes, see Gillers, *Deciding Who Dies*, 129 U.Pa.L.Rev. 1, 13, 101–10 (1980).

that asks its citizens to rely on legal processes rather than self-help to vindicate their wrongs. 'The instinct for retribution is part of the nature of man, and channeling that instinct in the administration of criminal justice serves an important purpose in promoting the stability of a society governed by law. When people begin to believe that organized society is unwilling or unable to impose upon criminal offenders the punishment they "deserve," then there are sown the seeds of anarchy—of self-help, vigilante justice, and lynch law.' *Furman* (Stewart, J., concurring). 'Retribution is no longer the dominant objective of the criminal law,' but neither is it a forbidden objective nor one inconsistent with our respect for the dignity of men. * * *

"Statistical attempts to evaluate the death penalty as a deterrent [have] occasioned a great deal of debate. The results simply have been inconclusive.

"[The] value of capital punishment as a deterrent of crime is a complex factual issue the resolution of which properly rests with the legislatures, which can evaluate the results of statistical studies in terms of their own local conditions and with a flexibility of approach that is not available to the courts.[e] Indeed, many of the post-*Furman* statutes reflect just such a responsible effort to define those crimes and those criminals for which capital punishment is most probably an effective deterrent.

"In sum, we cannot say that the judgment of the Georgia legislature that capital punishment may be necessary in some cases is clearly wrong. Considerations of federalism, as well as respect for the ability of a legislature to evaluate, in terms of its particular state the moral consensus concerning the death penalty and its social utility as a sanction, require us to conclude, in the absence of more convincing evidence, that the infliction of death as a punishment for murder is not without justification and thus is not unconstitutionally severe.

"[Georgia's] procedures require the jury to consider the circumstances of the crime and the criminal before it recommends sentence. No longer can a Georgia jury do as Furman's jury did: reach a finding of the defendant's guilt and then, without guidance or direction, decide whether he should live or die. Instead, the jury's attention is directed to the specific circumstances of the crime [and its] attention is focused on the characteristics of the person who committed the crime. [Thus], 'the discretion to be exercised is controlled by clear and objective standards so as to produce non-discriminatory application.'

"[Moreover] to guard further against a situation comparable to that presented in *Furman,* the Supreme Court of Georgia compares each death sentence with the sentences imposed on similarly situated defendants to ensure that the sentence of death in a particular case is not disproportionate. On their face these procedures seem to satisfy the concerns of *Furman.*

"[Petitioner] contends, however, that the changes in the Georgia sentencing procedures are only cosmetic, [focusing] on the opportunities for discretionary action that are inherent in the processing of any murder case under Georgia law. He notes that the state prosecutor has unfettered authority to select those persons whom he wishes to prosecute for a capital offense and to plea bargain with them. Further, at the trial the jury may choose to convict a defendant of a lesser included offense rather than find him guilty of a crime punishable by death, even if the evidence would support a capital verdict. And finally, a

---

e. But see Black, *Due Process for Death,* 26 Cath.U.L.Rev. 1, 14 (1976): "Now that is nothing but sheer fiction. * * * The law, to be sure, is full of fictions, but a fiction known to go in the face of fact ought to play no part, not the slightest, in deciding whether the state may rightly take a life."

defendant who is convicted and sentenced to die may have his sentence commuted by the Governor of the State and the Georgia Board of Pardons and Paroles.[f]

"The existence of these discretionary stages is not determinative of the issues before us. [*Furman*] dealt with the decision to impose the death sentence on a specific individual who had been convicted of a capital offense. Nothing in any of our cases suggests that the decision to afford an individual defendant mercy violates the Constitution. *Furman* held only that, in order to minimize the risk that the death penalty would be imposed on a capriciously selected group of offenders, the decision to impose it had to be guided by standards so that the sentencing authority would focus on the particularized circumstances of the crime and the defendant.[50] "

WHITE, J., joined by Burger, C.J., and Rehnquist, J., concurred in the judgment: "Petitioner's argument that there is an unconstitutional amount of discretion in the system which separates those suspects who receive the death penalty from those who receive life imprisonment, a lesser penalty, or are acquitted or never charged, seems to be in final analysis an indictment of our entire system of justice. Petitioner has argued, in effect, that no matter how effective the death penalty may be as a punishment, government, created and run as it must be by humans, is inevitably incompetent to administer it. This cannot be accepted as a proposition of constitutional law. [I] decline to interfere with the manner in which Georgia has chosen to enforce [the death penalty] on what is simply an assertion of lack of faith in the ability of the system of justice to operate in a fundamentally fair manner." [g]

BRENNAN, J., dissented: "In *Furman,* I read 'evolving standards of decency' as requiring focus upon the essence of the death penalty itself and not primarily or solely upon the procedures under which the determination to inflict the penalty upon a particular person was made. [That] continues to be my view."

MARSHALL, J., also dissented: "Since the decision in *Furman,* the legislatures of 35 States have enacted new statutes authorizing the imposition of the death sentence for certain crimes, and Congress has enacted a law providing the death penalty for air piracy resulting in death. I would be less than candid if I did not acknowledge that these developments have a significant bearing on a realistic assessment of the moral acceptability of the death penalty to the American

f. For a forceful statement of the view that the post-*Furman* statutes do not effectively restrict jury discretion by any real standards and that capital sentencing statutes "never will"—"no society is going to kill everybody who meets certain present verbal requirements"—see Black, *Capital Punishment: The Inevitability of Caprice and Mistake* 67–68 (1974).

50. The petitioner's argument is nothing more than a veiled contention that *Furman* indirectly outlawed capital punishment by placing totally unrealistic conditions on its use. In order to repair the alleged defects pointed to by the petitioner, it would be necessary to require that prosecuting authorities charge a capital offense whenever arguably there had been a capital murder and that they refuse to plea bargain with the defendant. If a jury refused to convict even though the evidence supported the charge, its verdict would have to be reversed and a verdict of

guilty entered or a new trial ordered, since the discretionary act of jury nullification would not be permitted. Finally, acts of executive clemency would have to be prohibited. Such a system, of course, would be totally alien to our notions of criminal justice.

Moreover, it would be unconstitutional. Such a system in many respects would have the vices of the mandatory death penalty statutes we hold unconstitutional today in *Woodson* and *Stanislaus Roberts* [infra].

g. For the reasons stated in dissent in *Stanislaus Roberts,* infra, White, J., also disagreed with petitioner's "other basic argument that the death penalty, however imposed and for whatever crime, is cruel and unusual punishment."

Blackmun, J., concurred in the judgment, referring solely to his dissenting opinion in *Furman.*

people. But if the constitutionality of the death penalty turns, as I have urged, on the opinion of an *informed* citizenry, then even the enactment of new death statutes cannot be viewed as conclusive. * * *

"Even assuming however, that the post-*Furman* enactment of statutes authorizing the death penalty renders the prediction of the views of an informed citizenry an uncertain basis for a constitutional decision, the enactment of those statutes has no bearing whatsoever on the conclusion that the death penalty is unconstitutional because it is excessive. An excessive penalty is invalid under the Cruel and Unusual Punishments Clause 'even though popular sentiment may favor' [it.]

"The two purposes that sustain the death penalty as nonexcessive in the Court's view are general deterrence and retribution. [The] evidence I reviewed in *Furman* remains convincing, in my view, that 'capital punishment is not necessary as a deterrent to crime in our society.' The justification for the death penalty must be found elsewhere.

"[The plurality's view of the important purpose served by 'channeling' 'the instinct for retribution' in the administration of criminal justice] is wholly inadequate to justify the death penalty. [It] simply defies belief to suggest that the death penalty is necessary to prevent the American people from taking the law into their own hands.

"[The contention] that the expression of moral outrage through the imposition of the death penalty serves to reinforce basic moral values [also] provides no support for the death penalty. It is inconceivable that any individual concerned about conforming his conduct to what society says is 'right' would fail to realize that murder is 'wrong' if the penalty were simply life imprisonment. * * *

"There remains for consideration, however, what might be termed the purely retributive justification for the death penalty—that the death penalty is appropriate, not because of its beneficial effect on society, but because the taking of the murderer's life is itself morally good. Some of the language of the plurality's opinion appears positively to embrace this notion of retribution for its own sake as a justification for capital punishment.

"[T]hat society's judgment that the murderer 'deserves' death must be respected not simply because the preservation of order requires it, but because it is appropriate that society make the judgment and carry it out [is a notion] fundamentally at odds with the Eighth Amendment. The mere fact that the community demands the murderer's life in return for the evil he has done cannot sustain the death penalty, for as the plurality reminds us, 'the Eighth Amendment demands more than that a challenged punishment be acceptable to contemporary society.' [Under appropriate Eighth Amendment] standards, the taking of life 'because the wrong-doer deserves it' surely must fall, for such a punishment has as its very basis the total denial of the wrong-doer's dignity and worth."

Notes and Questions

1. *The Texas statute upheld in Jurek: predictions of future violence.* In companion cases to *Gregg*, dividing the same way, the Court upheld the constitutionality of two other state capital-sentencing procedures which, it concluded, essentially resembled the Georgia system. *Proffitt v. Florida*, 428 U.S. 242, 96 S.Ct. 2960, 49 L.Ed.2d 913 (1976); *Jurek v. Texas*, 428 U.S. 262, 96 S.Ct. 2950, 49 L.Ed.2d 929 (1976). For forceful criticism of *Jurek* and for the view that the Texas statute is "much worse than either the Georgia or the Florida statutes,

bad as they are," see Black, *Due Process for Death,* 26 Cath.U.L.Rev. 1, 2 (1976). See also 90 Harv.L.Rev. 71–75 (1976).

Under the Texas capital sentencing procedure, the key question a jury must answer in the affirmative for the death penalty to be imposed is "whether there is a probability that the defendant would commit criminal acts of violence that would constitute a continuing threat to society." This, maintains Black, supra, at 4–6, "is a phrase composed of hopelessly vague terms. 'Criminal' as a blow with the fist is criminal? 'Violent' as such a blow is violent? A 'threat' of what? 'To society' in what sense, since the person is to be in prison, under whatever restraints the state finds necessary, and need not be released until the state is satisfied [that] he is not a threat to society?"

Consider Gillers, *The Quality of Mercy: Constitutional Accuracy at the Selection Stage of Capital Sentencing,* 18 U.C.Davis 1037, 1099–1100 (1985): "Surely, our faith in predictive accuracy is not strong enough to rest a death sentence on the anticipated inadequacy of solitary confinement for particular defendants or on conjecture about their powers of escape, at least not without some proof. Yet if social or medical scientists believe that this projection can be made with confidence, they have so far chosen to remain silent. Does the availability of the less harsh, apparently adequate response of solitary confinement exclude incapacitation as a justification for execution? * * * Assuming [that] the answer is no, *Jurek* also failed to discuss whether a death penalty statute must offer the sentencer the less extreme option of greatly restrictive confinement before the sentencer may conclude that incapacitation demands nothing less than execution."

2. *Gregg, Jurek* and *Proffitt* reached the question reserved in *Furman* — "the constitutionality of capital punishment in the abstract"—and upheld it. But consider Black, *Reflections on Opposing the Penalty of Death,* 10 St. Mary's L.J. 1, 7 (1978): "[T]he *only* question that actually confronts us [is] whether it is right to kill such people as are chosen by our system as it stands. [I]t doesn't really make any difference at all what I think about the abstract rightness of capital punishment. There exists no abstract capital punishment." See also Amsterdam, *Capital Punishment,* in Bedau, *The Death Penalty in America* 346, 349–51 (3rd ed. 1982); Black, *The Death Penalty Now,* 51 Tul.L.Rev. 429, 445 (1977).

3. ZANT v. STEPHENS, 462 U.S. 862, 103 S.Ct. 2733, 77 L.Ed.2d 235 (1983), per STEVENS, J., upheld a Georgia death sentence under the following circumstances: In a bifurcated Georgia trial, a jury found defendant guilty of murder and imposed the death penalty. At the sentencing phase, the judge instructed the jury that it could consider all the evidence received during the guilt phase of the trial as well as all circumstances presented in mitigation or aggravation during the sentencing proceeding, and that it must find and designate in writing one or more specified statutory aggravating circumstances in order to impose the death penalty. The jury found three aggravating circumstances: (1) defendant had a prior conviction of a capital felony, (2) the murder was committed by a jail escapee, and (3) defendant had "a substantial history of serious assaultive criminal convictions." While defendant's appeal was pending, the state supreme court, in another case, struck down the third aggravating circumstance as unconstitutionally vague. But it then upheld defendant's death sentence on the ground that the two other aggravating circumstances adequately supported the penalty. The U.S. Supreme Court agreed:

"In Georgia, unlike some other states, the jury is not instructed to give any special weight to any aggravating circumstance, to consider multiple aggravating circumstances any more significant than a single such circumstance, or to balance aggravating against mitigating circumstances pursuant to any special standard. Thus, in Georgia, the finding of an aggravating circumstance does not play any role in guiding the sentencing body in the exercise of its discretion, apart from its function of narrowing the class of persons convicted of murder who are eligible for the death penalty.

"[Defendant] argues that the mandate of *Furman* is violated by a scheme that permits the jury to exercise unbridled discretion in determining whether the death penalty should be imposed after it has found that the defendant is a member of the class made eligible for that penalty by statute. But that argument could not be accepted without overruling our specific holding in *Gregg*.

* * *

"The Georgia scheme provides for categorical narrowing at the definition stage, and for individualized determination and appellate review at the selection stage. We therefore remain convinced, as we were in 1976, that the structure of the statute is constitutional. Moreover, the narrowing function has been properly achieved in this case by the two valid aggravating circumstances upheld by the Georgia Supreme Court * * *. These two findings adequately differentiate this case in an objective, evenhanded, and substantively rational way from the many Georgia murder cases in which the death penalty may not be imposed. Moreover, the Georgia Supreme Court in this case reviewed the death sentence to determine whether it was arbitrary, excessive, or disproportionate. Thus the absence of legislative or court-imposed standards to govern the jury in weighing the significance of either or both of those aggravating circumstances does not render the Georgia capital sentencing statute invalid as applied in this case." [a]

4. *How much "guidance" does the Georgia statute provide?* Consider Weisberg, *Deregulating Death*, 1983 Sup.Ct.Rev. 305, 322, 375: "In the end * * * all the rhetoric about 'guidance' and 'channeling' interwoven through [the *Gregg* plurality's] summary of the statute amounts to little more than judicial sighs of relief over how Georgia has allowed the Court to escape gracefully from the responsibility it posed for itself in *Furman*. One can say little with certainty about *Gregg* except that it makes a great many things constitutionally significant, but makes nothing either constitutionally necessary or clearly constitutionally sufficient. * * * Weighing and balancing legally defined factors may be useful in helping the jury frame the issue, but the penalty decision is ultimately irreducible to legal terms. With enhanced rules of murder liability and aggravating circumstances about the defendant's crime and criminal record, the law perhaps can sensibly screen out those defendants who do not deserve to die. But that leaves no legal theory about which defendants *do* deserve to die." See also Ely, *Democracy and Distrust* 175–76 (1980); Kaplan, *Administering Capital*

---

a. The Court then rejected the contention that the death sentence was impaired because the judge's instructions with regard to the invalid statutory aggravating circumstance may have unduly influenced the jury's deliberations: "[T]he invalid aggravating circumstance found by the jury in this case was struck down [by the state supreme court because] it fail[ed] to provide an adequate basis for distinguishing a murder case in which the death penalty may be imposed from those cases in which [it may not]. The underlying evidence is nevertheless fully admissible at the sentencing phase. [Thus,] any evidence on which the jury may have relied in this case to find that [defendant] had previously been convicted of a substantial number of serious assaultive offenses, as he concedes he had been, was properly adduced at the sentencing hearing and was fully subject to explanation by the defendant."

Punishment, 36 U.Fla.L.Rev. 177, 188–89 (1984). Does the system of capital punishment upheld in *Gregg* even screen out those who do *not* deserve to die? Consider W. White, *Life in the Balance* 30 (1984): Although in theory requiring the sentencer to find an aggravating circumstance potentially reduces the number of capital defendants subject to arbitrary action, "[u]nder most [post-*Furman*] statutes [the] aggravating circumstances taken together are so broad that almost any traditional first-degree murder case could be found to include at least one of them." See also Bentele, *The Death Penalty in Georgia: Still Arbitrary,* 62 Wash.U.L.Q. 573, 581 (1985) (at least one of Georgia's ten statutory aggravating circumstances "occurs in the great majority of murder cases"). See also notes 9 and 10 infra.

5. *Deterrence.* The *Gregg* plurality alludes to the debate occasioned by statistical attempts to evaluate whether the death penalty is a better deterrent than life imprisonment for murder and concludes: "The results simply have been inconclusive." But, as pointed out, in Lempert, *Desert and Deterrence: An Assessment of the Moral Bases for Capital Punishment,* 69 Mich.L.Rev. 1177, 1207 (1981), only *one* empirical study suggesting deterrence is cited in support of this proposition—Isaac Ehrlich's *The Deterrent Effect of Capital Punishment: A Question of Life and Death,* 65 Am.Econ.Rev. 397 (1975), the first purportedly scientific study ever to find that capital punishment does deter homicides more than life imprisonment. Using regression analysis involving an elaborate mathematical model, Ehrlich, a University of Chicago econometrician, reported that abolition of capital punishment may result in the deaths of as many as eight persons for every murderer who is not executed. Does (should) one study "neutralize" the general consensus of the scientific establishment to the contrary?

Ehrlich's study has been severely and widely criticized on various grounds. See the summary and discussion of this body of research in Bedau, *The Death Penalty in America* 94–97 (3d ed. 1982); Amsterdam, note 2 supra; Lempert, supra; Zeisel, *The Deterrent Effect of the Death Penalty: Facts v. Faith,* 1976 Sup.Ct.Rev. 317. Lempert reports that "the body of econometric research overwhelmingly favors the conclusion that executions do not deter" and he concludes, on the basis of his own and other studies, that, although we lack, and can never obtain, absolute proof that capital punishment, as historically administered, does not save life, "when we look at all the evidence, we find proof to a moral certainty." Lempert, supra, at 1222. Amsterdam, Bedau and Zeisel also conclude, on the basis of their own work and the substantial body of research criticizing Ehrlich, that the negative judgment on the deterrent superiority of death penalty over long-term imprisonment is overwhelming. But Ernest van den Haag, probably the nation's leading proponent of capital punishment, maintains that Ehrlich's findings "have stood up sturdily under criticism," which he has "convincingly refuted." Van den Haag & Conrad, *The Death Penalty: A Debate* 298–99 (1983) (hereinafter referred to as Debate). See also Berns, *For Capital Punishment* 97–103 (1979).

6. *Assuming that evidence whether the death penalty is a better deterrent than life imprisonment is "inconclusive," what follows?* Consider Amsterdam, supra, at 355: *"Because* the [Supreme Court deemed the evidence] inconclusive, [it] held that the Constitution did not forbid judgment either way. But if the evidence is inconclusive, is it *your* judgment that we should conclusively kill people on a factual theory that the evidence does not conclusively sustain?" But consider van den Haag, Debate at 69: "[I]f we are not sure [whether the death penalty adds to deterrence], we must choose either to (1) trade the certain death,

by execution, of a convicted murderer for the probable survival of an indefinite number of murder victims whose future murder is less likely (whose survival is more likely)—if the convicted murderer's execution deters prospective murderers, as it might, or to (2) trade the certain survival of the convicted murderer for the probable loss of the lives of future murder victims more likely to be murdered because the convicted murderer's nonexecution might not deter prospective murderers, who could have been deterred by executing the convicted murderer. * * * I'd rather execute a man convicted of having murdered others than to put the lives of innocents at risk. I find it hard to understand the opposite choice." But see Kaplan, *The Problem of Capital Punishment,* 1983 U.Ill.L.Rev. 555, 559–62.

7. *Whatever the answer when the issue is one of legislative policy, once a state enacts a death penalty statute, is it plain who has the "burden of proof"?* The *Gregg* plurality thought so. It "presumed" the "validity" of the challenged statute, put "a heavy burden [on] those who would attack the judgment of the representatives of the people" and framed the issue in terms of whether the Georgia legislature's judgment was "clearly wrong." But see Radin, *The Jurisprudence of Death,* 126 U.Pa.L.Rev. 989, 1029–30, 1064 & n. 280 (1978): "The conjunction of the factors of irrevocability, enormity and fundamental right peculiar to the death penalty demands a searching analysis with no initial presumptions in favor of the past. The death penalty should be subject to strict scrutiny for cruelty. [If] we as a society are seriously divided on whether a fundamental interest may be invaded by the government under certain circumstances, it is morally wrong to behave as if there existed a moral consensus that justified invading that interest. [*Roe v. Wade*] recognized that in a conflict between fundamental rights of individuals and the interests of the state, questions of the validity of a moral theory concerning which there exists no consensus should be resolved against the state."

8. *"Mercy."* Consider Black, note 1 supra, at 12: "[T]he question posed is not whether [as the *Gregg* plurality put it] 'the decision to afford an individual defendant mercy violates the Constitution,' [but] whether a 'legal system' which regularly, and in great numbers, runs the death question through a gauntlet of decisions in no way even formally standard-bound, so that, at the end of the process, no one can say why some were selected and others were not selected for death, rises to due process. That is not a trivial question and it cannot [be] answered by calling it, [as Justice White does, concurring in *Gregg*], 'in final analysis an indictment of our entire system of justice.' If it is that, it is an indictment pleading to which would present some difficulty, for it is hard to find informed persons today who think very well of our entire system' of criminal justice. But death is unique, and the procedures we must use, having no better, in our entire system of justice—and that is really the kindest thing one can say of that system—may still not be good enough for the death choice. The Court has not really focused on and answered that question—in reason, I mean, and not by fiat." See also Radin, note 7 supra, at 1024.

But consider van den Haag, *Refuting Reiman and Nathanson,* 14 Philosophy & Public Affairs 165, 173–74 (1985): "If we grant that some (even all) murderers of blacks,[b] or, some (even all) white and rich murderers, escape the death

---

b. A number of studies indicate that blacks with white victims are most likely to be sentenced to death and that whites with black victims are least likely to be. The race of the victim seems to be a much more significant factor than the race of the defendant. See, e.g., Gross & Mauro, *Patterns of Death,* 37 Stan.L.Rev. 27 (1984), finding discrimination based on the race of the victim in post-*Furman* capital sentencing in each of the penalty, how does that reduce the guilt of murderers of whites, or of black and poor murderers, so that they should be spared execution too? Guilt is personal. No murderer becomes less guilty, or less deserving of punishment, because another murderer was punished leniently, or escaped punishment altogether. We should try our best to bring every murderer to justice. But if one got away with murder wherein is that a reason to let anyone else get away? A group of murderers does not become less deserving of punishment because another equally guilty group is not punished, or punished less. We can punish only a very small proportion of all criminals. Unavoidably they are selected accidentally. We should reduce this accidentality as much as possible but we cannot eliminate it."

9. *An examination of the 85 murder convictions decided by the Georgia Supreme Court of 1981.* After studying the 85 appeals of murder convictions decided by the Georgia Supreme Court in 1981, Bentele, note 4 supra, at 585, finds no "objective and measurable difference between the twenty defendants sentenced to death and the sixty-five who, despite the presence of aggravating circumstances in most cases, received life sentences. Neither detailed and specific comparisons of cases involving similar facts nor broader comparisons of aggravating categories, such as murders during robberies or murders of policemen, explains why some defendants received the ultimate penalty while others received life sentences." Bentele concludes, inter alia, id. at 638, that "the broad, unreviewable discretion of prosecutors, deemed either not significant for eighth amendment purposes or assumed to be exercised properly by the Justices in *Gregg,* contributes immeasurably to the risk of arbitrary or discriminatory imposition of death sentences." Although Bentele's study focuses on the Georgia experience, she maintains that her conclusions have broad application "because the Georgia system is typical of modern American capital punishment schemes." See also Baldus, Pulaski & Woodworth, *Comparative Review of Death Sentences: An Empirical Study of the Georgia Experience,* 74 J.Crim.L. & C. 661, 730 (1983) (authors' data suggest that Georgia death-sentencing system has "continued to impose the type of inconsistent, arbitrary death sentences" condemned in *Furman* and that the state supreme court's sentence review process has "failed to identify and vacate such death sentences").

10. *An examination of the eleven cases which resulted in executions from 1977–83.* Ending a moratorium on executions which lasted for almost ten years, Utah executed Gary Gilmore in January of 1977. In the next seven years ten more persons were executed.[a] After a detailed analysis of these eleven offenders and their crimes, Streib, *Executions under the Post-Furman Capital Punishment Statutes,* 15 Rutgers L.J. 443, 485–86 (1984), observes: "[S]ix of the homicides were fairly ordinary killings that occurred during armed robberies. [Only one-

eight states examined, and suggesting that in a society that remains segregated socially, and in which most jurors are white, jurors are more likely to identify with white victims. See also Baldus, Pulaski & Woodworth, *Comparative Review of Death Sentences: An Empirical Study of the Georgia Experience,* 74 J.Crim.L. & C. 661, 707–10 (1983); Bowers & Pierce, *Arbitrariness and Discrimination under Post-Furman Capital Statutes,* 26 Crime & Delinq. 563 (1980); Foley & Powell, *The Discretion of Prosecutors, Judges, and Juries in Capital Cases,* 7 Crim.Just.J. 16 (1982); Paternoster, *Race of Victim and Location of Crime:*

The Decision to Seek the Death Penalty in South Carolina, 74 J.Crim.L. & C. 754 (1983); Zeisel, *Race Bias in the Administration of the Death Penalty: The Florida Experience,* 95 Harv.L.Rev. 456 (1981).

a. But the pace of executions then increased. In the first seven months of 1984, eleven more executions were carried out, half of the 22 inmates executed since January of 1977. See *Special Project: Capital Punishment in 1984,* 69 Corn.L.Q. 1129, 1130–31 (1984).

fourth of the crimes] could be considered particularly heinous. * * * Comparative analysis of [these eleven cases] with the 3,000 death sentences not resulting in executions or with the many thousands of similar crimes in which the death sentence was not imposed leads to only one conclusion: No particularly distinguishing factors can be identified which would place these eleven cases in a clearly unique category. Caprice may well have played a role in these executions and the rare and random pattern of their occurrence could lead one to conclude that the death penalty is being freakishly imposed and carried out."

11. *Death row "population control."* Consider the observations of the then Director-Counsel of the NAACP Legal Defense Fund, Greenberg, *Capital Punishment as a System,* 91 Yale L.J. 908, 926 (1982): "While sentencing hundreds to death per year, [the present capital punishment] system accomplishes death row population control mainly by judicial review and only rarely by killing. It is a roller coaster system of capital justice, in which large numbers of people are constantly spilling into and out of death row, but virtually no actual executions take place. Yet, if we are to have any legal executions in this country, it must be under this type of system. Such a system has not only proved necessary to assure that innocent people are not executed, that constitutional rights are not violated, and that invidious considerations such as race are not the true motivating forces behind executions; it also accurately reflects, it seems, our civilized society's fundamental unwillingness actually to kill the hundreds of people that the decisions of judges and juries place on death row each year." Does any theoretical penological justification for the death penalty support the system as now administered? See id. at 927.

According to Streib, note 10 supra, at 487, even if the rate of actual executions reaches the all-time high of 1935 (199 executions), if the death sentencing rate continues at about the same pace (approximately 200 per year), "[t]he result will be the continuation of an irreducible five to ten years backlog of condemned prisoners on death row. If the actual execution rate rises to only fifty per year, which is more likely, then *the population on death row will double every decade.*" (Emphasis added.) Can a system that keeps prisoners under a death sentence for many years, even decades, with only a slight probability that they will ever be executed, be squared with the eighth amendment? See id.

II. MANDATORY DEATH SENTENCES

Unlike Georgia, Florida and Texas, whose new capital-sentencing procedures were designed to guide and to channel sentencing authority, 10 states responded to *Furman* by replacing discretionary jury sentencing in capital cases with *mandatory death penalties.* North Carolina did so for a broad range of murders; Louisiana did so for five categories of murder. These mandatory death statutes were invalidated in WOODSON v. NORTH CAROLINA, 428 U.S. 280, 96 S.Ct. 2978, 49 L.Ed.2d 944 (1976) and STANISLAUS ROBERTS v. LOUISIANA,[a] 429 U.S. 325, 96 S.Ct. 3001, 49 L.Ed.2d 974 (1976), both decided the same day as *Gregg.*

STEWART, J., announced the judgment in *Woodson* and an opinion joined by Powell and Stevens, JJ. The history of mandatory death penalty statutes in this country, he observed, reveals that the practice "has been rejected as unduly

---

a. The plurality, per Stewart, J., noted in *Woodson* that "[t]his case does not involve a mandatory death penalty statute limited to an extremely narrow category of murder, such as murder by a prisoner serving a life sentence, defined in large part in terms of the character or record of the offender. We thus express no opinion regarding the constitutionality of such a statute."

harsh and unworkably rigid. The two crucial indicators of evolving standards of decency respecting the imposition of punishment in our society—jury determination and legislative enactments—both point conclusively to the repudiation of automatic death sentences." He dismissed the post-*Furman* enactments as merely "attempts [to] retain the death penalty in a form consistent with the Constitution, rather than a renewed social acceptance of mandatory death sentencing."

"A separate deficiency" of the North Carolina statute was its failure to respond adequately to "*Furman's* rejection of unbridled jury discretion in the imposition of capital sentences." In light of the widespread and persistent jury resistance to mandatory death penalties—and the high probability that many juries, despite their oaths, would exercise discretion in deciding which murderers "shall live and which shall die" under these "mandatory" statutes—North Carolina had not remedied "the problem of unguided and unchecked jury discretion" that was "central to the limited holding in *Furman*," but "simply papered over" it. Not only does North Carolina's mandatory death penalty statute provide "no standards to guide the jury in its inevitable exercise" of discretion, but "there is no way under [state law] for the judiciary to check arbitrary and capricious exercise of that power through a review of death sentences. Instead of rationalizing the sentencing process, a mandatory scheme may well exacerbate the problem identified in *Furman* by resting the penalty determination on the particular jury's willingness to act lawlessly."

"A third constitutional shortcoming of the North Carolina statute is its failure to allow the particularized consideration of relevant aspects of the character and record of each convicted defendant before the imposition upon him of a sentence of death. [D]eath is a punishment different from all other sanctions in kind rather than degree. A process that accords no significance to relevant facets of the character and record of the individual offender or the circumstances of the particular offense excludes from consideration in fixing the ultimate punishment of death the possibility of compassionate or mitigating factors stemming from the diverse frailties of humankind. It treats all persons convicted of a designated offense not as uniquely individual human beings, but as members of a faceless, undifferentiated mass to be subjected to the blind infliction of the penalty of death." [b]

Dissenting, REHNQUIST, J., rejected the view that the 10 post-*Furman* mandatory death statutes merely represented "a wrong-headed reading [of] *Furman*. While those States may be presumed to have preferred their prior systems reposing sentencing discretion in juries or judges, they indisputably preferred mandatory capital punishment to no capital punishment at all. Their willingness to enact statutes providing that penalty is utterly inconsistent with the notion that they regarded mandatory capital sentencing as beyond 'evolving standards of decency.'"

"The Court's insistence on 'standards' to 'guide the jury in its inevitable exercise of the power to decide which murderer shall live and which shall die,' is squarely contrary [to the *McGautha* opinion], authorized by Justice Harlan and subscribed to by five other [justices] only five years ago. So is [the Court's claim] that *Furman* requires 'objective standards to guide, regularize, and make rationally reviewable the process for imposing a sentence of death.'"

---

b. For the reasons stated in their *Gregg* dissents, Brennan and Marshall, JJ., con-curred in both *Woodson* and *Stanislaus Roberts*, infra.

"[What] the plurality opinion has actually done is to import into the Due Process Clause [what] it conceives to be desirable procedural guarantees where the punishment of death, concededly not cruel and unusual for the crime of which the defendant was convicted, is to be imposed. This is squarely contrary to *McGautha,* and unsupported by any other decision of this Court." [c]

Dissenting in *Stanislaus Roberts* (which invalidated a Louisiana mandatory death sentence statute the *Woodson* plurality deemed fatally similar to North Carolina's), WHITE, J., joined by Burger, C.J., and Blackmun and Rehnquist, JJ., maintained: "As the plurality now interprets the Eighth Amendment, the Louisiana and North Carolina statutes are infirm because the jury is deprived of all discretion once it finds the defendant guilty. Yet in the next breath it invalidates these statutes because they are said to invite or allow too much discretion: despite their instructions, when they feel that defendants do not deserve to die, juries will so often and systematically disobey their instructions and find the defendant not guilty or guilty of a noncapital offense that the statute fails to satisfy the standards of *Furman.* If it is truly the case that Louisiana juries will exercise *too much* discretion—and I do not agree that it is— then it seems strange indeed that the statute is also invalidated because it purports to give the jury *too little* discretion by making the death penalty mandatory. Furthermore, if there is danger of freakish and too infrequent imposition of capital punishment under a mandatory system such as Louisiana's, there is very little ground for believing that juries will be any more faithful to their instructions under the Georgia and Florida systems where the opportunity is much, much greater for juries to practice their own brand of unbridled discretion.

"[The Louisiana and North Carolina] legislatures have not deemed mandatory punishment, once the crime is proven, to be unacceptable; nor have their juries rejected it, for the death penalty has been imposed with some regularity. Perhaps we would prefer that these States had adopted a different system, but the issue is not our individual preferences but the constitutionality of the mandatory systems chosen by these two States. I see no warrant under the Eighth Amendment for refusing to uphold these statutes.

"[I]n *Gregg,* [the plurality] lectures us at length about the role and place of the judiciary and then proceeds to ignore its own advice, the net effect being to suggest that observers of this institution should pay more attention to what we do than what we say. The plurality claims that it has not forgotten what the past has taught about the limits of judicial review; but I fear that it has again surrendered to the temptation to make policy for and to attempt to govern the country through a misuse of the powers given this Court under the Constitution." [d]

Notes and Questions

1. *Gregg and the "mandatory death" cases.* Are *Gregg* and *Woodson* and *Roberts,* handed down the same day, reconcilable? The *Woodson* plurality points out that "instead of rationalizing the sentencing process, a mandatory scheme may well exacerbate the problem identified in *Furman* by resting the penalty

c. White, J., joined by Burger, C.J., and Rehnquist, J., also dissented, rejecting the Court's analysis for the reasons stated in his dissent in *Stanislaus Roberts,* infra. Blackmun, J., also dissented in *Woodson* for the reasons stated in his *Furman* dissent. All four *Woodson* dissenters also dissented in *Roberts.*

d. Burger, C.J., and Blackmun, J., also dissented separately for the reasons set forth in their *Furman* dissents.

determination on the particular jury's willingness to act lawlessly." But are not "these lawless juries, whose lawlessness will taint and bend a mandatory system," the very same juries who are supposed "to follow with patient care the intricacies of the Georgia and Florida statutes [upheld the same day in *Gregg* and *Proffitt*], and the unfathomed mysteries of the Texas statute [upheld the same day in *Jurek*], and base these answers on nothing but sound discretion guided by law"? What reason is there to think that juries "will manipulate frankly mandatory statutes, in order to produce a result seen as equitable," but "not manipulate, to the same ends, a scheme relatively sophisticated—but far from being beyond easy comprehension by people fitted to be on juries at all—such as the scheme in [Texas or Georgia] or many other states"? See Black, *Due Process for Death*, 26 Cath.U.L.Rev. 1, 10 (1976); Black, *The Death Penalty Now*, 51 Tul.L.Rev. 429, 441 (1977). See also Bedau, *Are Mandatory Capital Statutes Unconstitutional?*, in *The Courts, the Constitution, and Capital Punishment* 106 (1977).

2.   HARRY ROBERTS v. LOUISIANA, 431 U.S. 633, 97 S.Ct. 1993, 52 L.Ed. 2d 637 (1977) (per curiam) held that the imposition of a mandatory death penalty for the intentional killing of a police officer "engaged in the performance of his lawful duties" constitutes cruel and unusual punishment. Although "the fact that the murder victim was a peace officer may be regarded as an aggravating circumstance," "it is incorrect to suppose that no mitigating circumstances can exist [in such a case]. [T]he youth of the offender, the absence of any prior conviction, [and] the influence of drugs, alcohol or extreme emotional disturbance [are] examples of mitigating facts which might attend the killing of a peace officer and which are considered relevant in other jurisdictions. As we emphasized repeatedly in *Stanislaus Roberts,* [it] is essential that the capital sentencing decision allow for consideration of whatever mitigating circumstances may be relevant to either the particular offender or the particular offense."

REHNQUIST, J., joined by White, J., dissenting, protested that the Court's holding "would have shocked those who drafted the Bill of Rights" and "would commend itself only to the most imaginative observer as being required by today's 'evolving standards of decency'": "I [remain unpersuaded] that a mandatory death sentence for all, let alone for a limited class of persons, who commit premeditated murder constitutes 'cruel and unusual punishment.' [But] even were I now persuaded otherwise [I would still] disagree with today's decision.[1]

"[The Court] has asked the wrong question. The question is not whether mitigating factors might *exist* [in the case of an intentional murder of an officer], but, rather, whether whatever 'mitigating' factors that might exist are of sufficient *force* so as to constitutionally require their consideration as counterweights to the admitted aggravating circumstance. Like Mr. Justice White [dissenting in *Stanislaus Roberts*], I am unable to believe that a State is not entitled to determine that the premeditated murder of a peace officer is so

---

1. In *Woodson,* the plurality noted that a public opinion poll "revealed that a 'substantial majority' of persons opposed mandatory capital punishment." It does not follow, even accepting that poll, that a "substantial majority" oppose mandatory capital punishment for the murderers of police officers. What meager statistics there are indicate that public opinion is at best pretty evenly divided on the subject [referring to various polls and surveys]. With such substantial public support [for mandatory capital punishment for murderers of officers], one would have thought that the determination as to whether a mandatory death penalty should exist was for the legislature, not for the judiciary through some newfound construction of the term "cruel and unusual punishment."
* * *

heinous and intolerable a crime that no combination of mitigating factors can overcome the demonstration 'that the criminal's character is such that he deserves death.'"

III. OTHER CONSTITUTIONAL CHALLENGES: "GROSSLY DISPROPORTIONATE" PUNISHMENT; RESTRICTING CONSIDERATION OF MITIGATING CIRCUMSTANCES; THE NEED FOR "COMPARATIVE PROPORTIONALITY REVIEW"; THE ROLE OF THE JURY IN CAPITAL SENTENCING

COKER v. GEORGIA, 433 U.S. 584, 97 S.Ct. 2861, 53 L.Ed.2d 982 (1977): While serving life terms for murder, rape and kidnapping (all capital felonies) and another sentence for aggravated assault, petitioner escaped and raped and abducted an adult woman (after robbing and tying up her husband). After his conviction for rape and other offenses, petitioner was sentenced to death when the jury found two of the statutory aggravating circumstances present: the rape was (i) by a person with a prior capital felony conviction and (ii) in the course of another capital felony, armed robbery of the husband. (The jury was instructed that even if aggravating circumstances were present, the death penalty need not be imposed if it found they were outweighed by mitigating circumstances.) The Court invalidated the death sentence. The principal opinion was written by WHITE, J., joined by Stewart, Blackmun and Stevens, JJ.,[a] who concluded that death is a "grossly disproportionate and excessive punishment" for raping an adult woman and therefore forbidden by the Eighth Amendment:

"At no time in the last 50 years has a majority of the States authorized death as a punishment for rape [and] none of the [34] States that had not previously authorized death for rape [changed its position after *Furman*]. Of the 16 States in which rape had been a capital offense only three provided for rape of an adult woman in their [post-*Furman*] statutes—Georgia, North Carolina, and Louisiana. In the latter two States, the death penalty was mandatory and those laws were invalidated by *Woodson* and *Stanislaus Roberts*. [Louisiana and North Carolina then] reenacted the death penalty for murder but not for rape. [Thus,] Georgia is the sole [American] jurisdiction [that presently] authorizes a sentence of death when the rape victim is an adult woman.[b] [Moreover, in] the vast majority of [rape] cases, at least nine out of 10, [Georgia juries] have not imposed the death sentence. * * *

"Rape is without doubt deserving of serious punishment; but in terms of moral depravity and of the injury to the person and to the public, it does not compare with murder, which does involve the unjustified taking of human life. [Rape] does not include the death or even the serious injury to [another]. Life is over for the [murder victim]; for the rape victim, life may not be nearly so happy

---

a. Brennan and Marshall, JJ., concurred in the judgment, adhering to their view that the death penalty is in all circumstances cruel and unusual punishment. Powell, J., concurred in the judgment "on the facts of this case, and also in its reasoning supporting the view that ordinarily death is a disproportionate punishment for the crime of raping an adult woman, [i.e., when, as here,] there is no indication that petitioner's offense was committed with excessive brutality or that the victim sustained serious or lasting injury." But he dissented from what he regarded as the plurality's unnecessarily broad holding

that "capital punishment *always*—regardless of the circumstances—is a disproportionate penalty for the crime of rape. [I]t may be that the death penalty is not disproportionate punishment for the crime of aggravated rape."

b. The Court noted that two other jurisdictions, Florida and Mississippi, provide capital punishment when the rape victim is a child. Tennessee had also authorized the death penalty in some circumstances when the victim was a child, but its statute had been invalidated because the death penalty was mandatory.

as it was, but it is not over and normally is not beyond repair. We have the abiding conviction that the death penalty, which 'is unique in its severity and revocability,' is an excessive penalty for the rapist who, as such, does not take human life.

"This does not end the matter; for under Georgia law, death may not be imposed [unless] the jury finds one of the statutory aggravating circumstances and then elects to impose that sentence. [But neither of the aggravating circumstances found in the present case], nor both of them together, change our conclusion that [Coker's sentence] is a disproportionate punishment for rape. [Coker's prior capital felony convictions] do not change the fact that the instant crime being punished is a rape not involving the taking of life."

BURGER, C.J., joined by Rehnquist, J., dissenting, protested that the Court's holding prevents the imposition of "any effective punishment upon Coker for his latest rape" and "bars Georgia from guaranteeing its citizens that they will suffer no further attacks from this habitual rapist.[c] * * *

"Unlike the Court, I would narrow the inquiry in this case to the question actually presented: Does the Eighth Amendment's ban against cruel and unusual punishment prohibit [a state] from executing a person who has, within the space of three years, raped three separate women, killing one and attempting to kill another, who is serving prison terms exceeding his probable lifetime and who has not hesitated to escape confinement at the first available opportunity? Whatever one's view may be as to the State's constitutional power to impose the death penalty upon a rapist who stands before a court convicted for the first time, this case reveals a chronic rapist whose continuing danger to the community is abundantly clear. [T]he Eighth Amendment does not prevent the State from taking an individual's 'well-demonstrated propensity for life-endangering behavior'[d] into account in devising punitive measures which will prevent inflicting further harm upon innocent victims.

"[I]t is myopic to base sweeping constitutional principles upon the narrow experience of the past five years. [L]egislatures were left in serious doubt [by *Furman*] as to whether this Court would sustain *any* statute imposing death as a criminal sanction. Failure of more States to enact statutes imposing death for rape of an adult woman may thus reflect hasty legislative compromise occasioned by time pressures following *Furman*, a desire to wait on the experience of those States which did enact such statutes, or simply an accurate forecast of today's holding.[e] "

Notes and Questions

1. Was the question raised by *Coker* whether the eighth amendment prohibits the death penalty for rape or whether the death penalty is "so irrational as to offend due process, an issue that exists quite independently [of] the eighth amendment"? See Packer, fn. d supra at 1074.

c. In 1971 Coker raped and murdered a young woman. Less than 8 months later, he kidnapped, raped and severely beat a 16-year-old woman, leaving her for dead in a wooded area. In 1974, he escaped from the state prison and promptly raped another 16-year-old, for which the death sentence under review was imposed.

d. At this point, the dissent is quoting from Packer, *Making the Punishment Fit the*

Crime, 77 Harv.L.Rev. 1071, 1080 (1964): "A well-demonstrated propensity for life-endangering behavior is thought to provide a more solid basis for infliction of the most severe measures of incapacitation than does the fortuity of a single homicidal incident."

e. See also Note, 78 Colum.L.Rev. 1714, 1718 (1979).

2. Coker's prior convictions for capital felonies, stated the *Coker* plurality, "do not change the fact that the instant crime being punished is a rape not involving the taking of life." Why not? Realistically, when a prior capital felony conviction is made an aggravating circumstance in the punishment for rape, isn't the offender being punished *in part* for rape and *in part* for the earlier capital felony? If, as a number of states provide, capital punishment may be based on a murder committed *after* a conviction for rape and a murder *in the course of* committing a rape, does barring capital punishment for a rape committed after a conviction for murder "make the acceptable level of punishment turn on fortuities of timing in the commission of offenses"? See Note, 78 Colum.L. Rev. 1714, 1724–25 (1978).

3. After *Coker,* would the Court sustain the death penalty for treason? Would the absence of a death "directly traceable" to the treasonous activity render the death penalty disproportionate to the crime or would treason be viewed as "a crime against masses of people [causing] more aggregate harm than a single murder"? See 91 Harv.L.Rev. 124, 128 (1977). See also Note, 78 Colum. L.Rev. 1714, 1729 (1979) (discussion of death penalty for hijacking).

4. Was it (should it have been) crucial that only three post-*Furman* statutes made rape a capital offense? The Court gave little weight to legislative enactments in *Roe v. Wade,* which invalidated a Texas abortion statute despite the fact that most states had enacted similar laws. Isn't "[a] defendant's right to life [at] least as fundamental as the mother's right of privacy"? See 91 Harv.L.Rev. 124 n. 127 (1977).

5. None of the opinions in *Coker* makes any mention of the "racial factor" in the administration of the death penalty for rape. Should the Court have explicitly discussed this factor? Despite the Court's silence on this matter, to what extent was it nevertheless influenced by it? Bedau, *The Death Penalty in America* 188 (3d ed. 1982), calls rape "the most dramatic type of case in which we can see how the racist heritage of our society made the death penalty fall with disproportionate and unfair frequency on nonwhite offenders. [T]he best explanation for the pattern of death sentences for rape in the South [a] is the race of the (black) offender and of the (white) victim." The mid-1960's constitutional assault on the death penalty "began with a campaign to eliminate the discriminatory application of the death penalty for rape. Between 1930 and the present, of the 455 persons executed for rape, 405 were black and two were members of other minorities. Almost 90% of those executed were black men convicted for the rape of white women." Greenberg, *Capital Punishment as a System,* 91 Yale L.J. 908, 912 (1982). See also Meltsner, *Cruel and Unusual* 75–77 (1973); Wolfgang & Reidel, fn. a supra.

6. *Jurek and Coker compared.* Under the statute upheld in *Jurek v. Texas* (discussed in note 1, p. 239 supra), observes Gillers, *The Quality of Mercy: Constitutional Accuracy at the Selection Stage of Capital Sentencing,* 18 U.C. Davis 1037, 1101 (1985), "[a]n accused may be preventively executed because a sentencer *predicts* he will commit conduct for which he could not be executed if he were actually to commit it. [Under the Texas capital-sentencing procedure, the violence that a death-eligible defendant is prone to commit] need not be homicidal; the prediction may be of robberies or assaults. *Jurek* would allow the sentencer to condemn [a] defendant because of what it foresees he will

a. Since 1930, all of the executions for rape were in southern or border states or the District of Columbia. In ten of these states and the District of Columbia, 137 blacks were executed for rape since 1930, but only five whites. See Wolfgang & Reidel, *Race, Judicial Discretion, and the Death Penalty,* 407 Annals 119 (1973).

probably do, while *Coker* would prohibit execution if the same defendant were spared and subsequently committed that or an even worse crime."

7.   *Enmund v. Florida,* 458 U.S. 782, 102 S.Ct. 3368, 73 L.Ed.2d 1140 (1982): While his codefendants went to a farmhouse to rob an elderly couple, Enmund remained in a nearby parked car, waiting to help the robbers escape. When one of the victims resisted, Enmund's codefendants killed both. This was enough under Florida law to make Enmund a constructive aider and abettor and hence a principal in the murder upon whom the death penalty could be imposed. After looking to "the historical development of the punishment at issue, legislative judgments, international opinion, and the sentencing decisions juries have made," a 5–4 majority, per White, J., concluded that the eighth amendment barred the imposition of the death penalty on "one such as Enmund [who] does not himself kill, attempt to kill, or intend that a killing take place or that lethal force will be employed.   *   *   * As was said of the crime of rape in *Coker,* we have the abiding conviction that the death penalty, which is 'unique in its severity and irrevocability,' is an excessive penalty for the robber who, as such, does not take human life." Dissenting Justice O'Connor, joined by Burger, C.J., and Powell and Rehnquist, JJ., maintained that the Court had failed to show that "contemporary standards" preclude imposition of the death penalty for "accomplice murder." The Court's holding, protested the dissent, "interferes with state criteria for assessing legal guilt by recasting intent as a matter of federal constitutional law."

Under the rubric of "proportionality," did the *Enmund* Court try to use its eighth amendment powers to prod some reform in state homicide law? See Weisberg, *Regulating Death,* 1983 Sup.Ct.Rev. 305, 334. Is it easy to distinguish *Enmund* from a felony-murder case in which a defendant is sentenced to death after *accidentally* killing the victim during the perpetration of a felony? See Weisberg, supra, at 334 n. 119; W. White, *Life in the Balance* 93–95 (1984); Note, 73 J.Crim.L. & C. 1553 (1982).

––––––

LOCKETT v. OHIO, 438 U.S. 586, 98 S.Ct. 2954, 57 L.Ed.2d 973 (1978): Petitioner, a 21-year-old black woman was charged with "aggravated murder," the aggravating circumstances being that the murder (1) was committed to avoid apprehension for aggravated robbery, and (2) occurred in the course of committing aggravated robbery. (Petitioner had been sitting in the "getaway" car when the robbery victim, who had grabbed a robber's gun when the "stickup" was announced, was fatally shot in his store.) Once a verdict of aggravated murder with specifications had been returned, the Ohio death penalty statute required the trial judge to impose the death sentence unless, after "considering the nature and circumstances of the offense" and defendant's "history, character, and condition," he found at least one of the following circumstances: (1) the victim induced or facilitated the offense; (2) it is unlikely the offense would have been committed but for the fact that the offender "was under duress, coercion, or strong provocation," or (3) the offense was primarily the product of the offender's "psychosis or mental deficiency." Finding none of the three narrowly defined mitigating circumstances present, the trial judge sentenced petitioner to death, stating that he had "no alternative."

A 7–1 majority reversed the judgment insofar as it upheld the death penalty. On this issue, there was no opinion of the Court. BURGER, C.J., joined by Stewart, Powell and Stevens, JJ., concluded that "the Eighth and Fourteenth Amendments require that the sentencer, in all but the rarest kind of capital case,[11] not be precluded from considering *as a mitigating factor,* any aspect of a defendant's character or record and any of the circumstances of the offense that the defendant proffers as a basis for a sentence less than death. [The] nonavailability of corrective or modifying mechanisms with respect to an executed capital sentence underscores the need for individualized consideration as a constitutional requirement in imposing the death sentence.

"[Under the Ohio statute, the] absence of direct proof that the defendant intended to cause the death of the victim is relevant for mitigating purposes only if it is determined that it sheds some light on one of the three statutory mitigating factors. Similarly, considerations of a defendant's comparatively minor role in the offense, or age, would generally not be permitted, as such, to affect the sentencing decision. [To] meet constitutional requirements, a death penalty statute must not preclude consideration of relevant mitigating factors." [a]

Dissenting JUSTICE REHNQUIST protested: "If a defendant as a matter of constitutional law is to be permitted to offer as evidence in the sentencing hearing any fact, however bizarre, which he wishes [the] new constitutional doctrine will not eliminate arbitrariness or freakishness in the imposition of sentences, but will codify and institutionalize it. By encouraging defendants in capital cases, and presumably sentencing judges and juries, to take into consideration anything under the sun as a 'mitigating circumstance,' it will not guide sentencing discretion but will totally unleash it."

Notes and Questions

1. *Why was Lockett sentenced to death, but not the "triggerman"?* Lockett declined to accept several offers by the prosecutor to plea bargain, but the "triggerman" did accept a negotiated plea, thus saving his own life, in return for his willingness to testify against Lockett. His testimony was "substantially all the evidence" against her. See Black, *The Death Penalty Now,* 51 Tul.L.Rev. 429, 430 (1977).

Consider Black, supra, at 434–35 (written before the Court's decision): "To all intents and purposes, [Lockett] is going to be killed because she insisted on being tried. [I]t may be inevitable that people who insist on being tried be punished more severely than those who do not, [but] is not death too great a punishment for refusal to enter into this process? Is the state's interest in avoiding trial—which is basically an interest in economy—great enough that we can be willing to execute people for not serving it?"

2. *A return to pre-Furman days?* The majority justices in *Lockett,* observes *Special Project: The Constitutionality of the Death Penalty in New Jersey,* 15 Rutgers L.J. 261, 289 (1984), "walked into the very trap they themselves constructed in *Gregg.* In practice, requiring the sentencer to consider *all* mitigating evidence necessarily makes each sentencing decision as individual and unique as each defendant. Sentences in capital cases which are individual

11. We express no opinion as to whether the need to deter certain kinds of homicide would justify a mandatory death sentence as, for example, when a prisoner—or escapee—under a life sentence is found guilty of murder.

a. White, J., disagreed with the plurality opinion's reasoning (continuing to believe that a mandatory death sentence does not violate the eighth amendment), but concurred in the result on the ground that "it violates the Eighth Amendment to impose the penalty of death without a finding that the defendant possessed a purpose to cause the death of the victim." (See Justice White's opinion for the Court four years later in *Enmund v. Florida,* note 7, supra.) Marshall and Blackmun, JJ., also concurred in the result. Brennan, J., did not participate in the case.

and unique run dangerously close to the 'freakish' and 'arbitrary' sentences deplored as unconstitutional in *Furman* and later cases." Consider Greenberg, *Capital Punishment as a System,* 91 Yale L.J. 908, 924 (1982): "[The *Lockett* Court] held that the sentencer should have had the opportunity to take into account [the defendant's] background and character and the circumstances of the crime, even though the statutory list of mitigating circumstances precluded her doing so. [Dissenting Justice Rehnquist argued that this amounted to] a return to the pre-*Furman* period, when 'similar cases' were treated differently. In a sense he is correct. On the one hand, similar cases should be treated similarly; but on the other, each case is different, if only because every individual is unique. Both the majority and the dissent were right, each according to its own terms. If capital punishment is retained, there is no solution to this dilemma." But cf. Gillers, *Deciding Who Dies,* 129 U.Pa.L.Rev. 1, 34–37 (1980); Kaplan, *Evidence in Capital Cases,* 11 Fla.St.L.Rev. 369, 371–72 (1983).

3. *Eddings v. Oklahoma,* 455 U.S. 104, 102 S.Ct. 869, 71 L.Ed.2d 1 (1982), underscored the Court's commitment to the principle that *all* mitigating evidence must be considered by the sentencer. At the time of the murder, Eddings was 16 years old, but he was tried as an adult. The Oklahoma death penalty statute provides that in a death sentencing proceeding evidence may be presented, inter alia, as to "any mitigating circumstances." But the trial judge refused, as a matter of law, to consider as mitigation the circumstances of Eddings' unhappy upbringing. The state appellate court found the excluded evidence irrelevant because it did not tend to provide a legal excuse from criminal responsibility. A 5–4 majority of the Court, per Powell, J., vacated the death sentence: "[T]he rule in *Lockett* [reflects] the law's effort to develop a system of capital punishment at once consistent and principled but also humane and sensible to the uniqueness of the individual. * * * Just as the State may not by statute preclude the sentencer from considering any mitigating factor, neither may the sentencer refuse to consider, *as a matter of law,* any relevant mitigating evidence. The sentencer, and [the state appellate court] may determine the weight to be given relevant mitigating evidence. But they may not give it no weight by excluding such evidence from their consideration."

But consider *Special Project,* note 2 supra, at 293–94: "[T]he sentencer must consider only mitigating evidence that is *introduced.* [T]here is no federal standard which requires that all possible mitigating evidence be presented at trial. When defense attorneys fail to make meaningful presentations of such evidence, still another variable is introduced into the capital sentencing scheme. Thus, the extent to which individual defendants receive personalized sentencing under [*Lockett* and *Eddings*] is determined largely by the skill and experience of their attorneys. Broad variations in attorney skill, experience, judgment—in short, varying levels of defense attorney competency—can result in 'freakish' and 'arbitrary' results as much as evidentiary rules or jury selection." See generally Goodpaster, *The Trial for Life: Effective Assistance of Counsel in Death Penalty Cases,* 58 N.Y.U. L.Rev. 299 (1983).

———

SOLEM v. HELM, 463 U.S. 277, 103 S.Ct. 3001, 77 L.Ed.2d 637 (1983). From 1964–75 Helm was convicted of six nonviolent felonies.[a] None was a crime against a person and alcohol was a contributing factor in each case. In 1979, he

a. He was convicted of third-degree burglary (three times), obtaining money under false pretenses, grand larceny (which occurs, inter alia, when the value of the property taken exceeds $50) and third-offense driving while intoxicated.

was convicted of a seventh nonviolent felony (apparently alcohol was again a contributing factor), uttering a "no-account" check for $100. Ordinarily this carries a maximum punishment of five years imprisonment, but as a result of his prior criminal record Helm was subject to South Dakota's recidivist statute, which provides that when a defendant has three or more prior convictions in addition to the principal felony "the sentence for the principal felony shall be enhanced to the sentence for a Class 1 felony." The maximum penalty for a "Class 1 felony" was life imprisonment. Moreover, state law explicitly provides that a person sentenced to life imprisonment is not eligible for parole. Immediately after accepting Helm's guilty plea, the court sentenced him to life imprisonment, explaining, inter alia, that Helm's record indicated that he was "beyond rehabilitation." Two years later, the Governor denied Helm's request that his sentence be commuted to a fixed term of years so that he would be eligible for parole when he had served three-fourths of his new sentence. A 5–4 majority, per POWELL, J., held that Helm's sentence "is significantly disproportionate to his crime, and is therefore prohibited by the Eighth Amendment":

"The constitutional principle of proportionality has been recognized in this Court for almost a century. [The Court then referred to *Weems v. United States,* 217 U.S. 349, 30 S.Ct. 544, 54 L.Ed.2d 793 (1910) [b] and to *Robinson v. California,* 370 U.S. 660, 82 S.Ct. 1417, 8 L.Ed.2d 758 (1962), finding, as the Court characterized the case, a 90-day sentence "excessive for the crime of being 'addicted to the use of narcotics.' "] Most recently, the Court has applied the principle of proportionality to hold capital punishment excessive in certain circumstances [referring to *Enmund* and *Coker*].

"It is true that the 'penalty of death differs from all other forms of capital punishment, not in degree, but in kind.' [This] does not mean, however, that proportionality is entirely inapplicable in noncapital cases. [N]o penalty is per se constitutional. As the Court noted in *Robinson,* a single day in prison may be unconstitutional in some circumstances.

"[A] court's proportionality analysis under the Eighth Amendment should be guided by objective criteria, including (i) the gravity of the offense and the harshness of the penalty; (ii) the sentences imposed on other criminals in the same jurisdiction; and (iii) the sentences imposed for commission of the same crime in other jurisdictions. * * *

"Helm's crime was 'one of the most passive felonies a person could commit.' It involved neither violence nor the threat of violence to any person. The $100 face value of Helm's 'no account' check was not trivial, but neither was it a large

---

b. In *Weems,* a public official, working in the Philippine Islands at a time when they were subject to the jurisdiction of the United States, was convicted of falsifying a public record. The sentence imposed, under a provision of the Spanish Penal Code still in force, was the punishment known as "cadena temporal"—a minimum term of 12 years' imprisonment at hard labor while chained at ankle and wrist, together with harsh "accessory" penalties (such as loss of parental and property rights and surveillance for life upon release).

Over the dissent of Holmes and White, JJ., the Court struck down Weems' sentence under the eighth amendment. But consider Packer, *Making the Punishment Fit the Crime,* 77 Harv.L.Rev. 1071, 1075–76 (1964): "It was

plainly not the length of [Weems'] imprisonment alone, considered in relation to the gravity of the offense, that determined [the Court's] result. Rather, it was the combination of an excessive but conventional mode of punishment with a good deal of laid-on unpleasantness offensive for its novelty as well as its severity that supported the characterization of Weems' punishment as cruel and unusual. The case is much closer to the conventional view that cruel and unusual punishment is a matter of mode not proportion than it is usually thought to be. Whether mode or proportion or both, the case is in the eighth amendment tradition. It speaks to the issue of decency, not rationality." See also Meltsner, *Cruel and Unusual* 173–75 (1973).

amount. [A] State is justified in punishing a recidivist more severely than it punishes a first offender. Helm's status, however, cannot be considered in the abstract. His prior offenses, although classified as felonies, were all relatively minor. * * * Helm's sentence is the most severe punishment that the State could have imposed on any criminal for any crime. Only capital punishment, a penalty not authorized in South Dakota when Helm was sentenced, exceeds it.

"Criminals committing [other offenses punishable by life imprisonment in South Dakota, such as murder and kidnapping, and a large group of very serious offenses for which life imprisonment was not authorized] ordinarily would be thought more deserving of punishment than one uttering a 'no account' check— even when the bad-check writer had already committed six minor felonies. Moreover, there is no indication [that] any habitual offender other than Helm has ever been given the maximum sentence on the basis of comparable crimes. * * *

"Finally, we compare the sentences imposed for commission of the same offense in other jurisdictions. The Court of Appeals found that 'Helm could have received a life sentence without parole for his offense in only one other state, Nevada,' [but we] are not advised that any defendant, such as Helm, whose prior offenses were so minor, actually has received the maximum penalty in Nevada. It appears that Helm was treated more severely than he would have been in any other State."

BURGER, C.J., joined by White, Rehnquist and O'Connor, JJ., dissented: "Only two Terms ago, we held in *Rummel v. Estelle*, 445 U.S. 263, 100 S.Ct. 1133, 63 L.Ed.2d 382 (1980),[c] that a life sentence imposed after only a *third* nonviolent felony conviction did not constitute cruel and unusual punishment under the Eighth Amendment. Today, the Court ignores its recent precedent and holds that a life sentence imposed after a *seventh* felony conviction constitutes cruel and unusual punishment under the Eighth Amendment. Moreover, I reject the fiction that all Helm's crimes were innocuous or nonviolent. Among his felonies were three burglaries and a third conviction for drunk driving. By comparison Rummel was a relatively 'model citizen.' * * *

"The *Rummel* Court emphasized, as has every opinion in capital cases in the past decade, that it was possible to draw a 'bright line' between 'the punishment of death and the various other permutations and commutations of punishment short of that ultimate sanction'; similarly, a line could be drawn between the punishment in *Weems* and 'more traditional forms of imprisonment imposed under the Anglo-Saxon system.' However, the *Rummel* Court emphasized that drawing lines between different sentences of imprisonment would thrust the Court inevitably 'into the basic line-drawing process that is preeminently the province of the legislature' and produce judgments that were no more than the visceral reactions of individual Justices. * * *

"By asserting the power to review sentences of imprisonment for excessiveness the Court launches into uncharted and unchartable waters. Today it holds that a sentence of life imprisonment, without the possibility of parole, is

c. When convicted of a third nonviolent property-related felony, Rummel was given a mandatory life sentence pursuant to Texas's recidivist statute. Stressing the "unique nature of the death penalty for purposes of Eighth Amendment analysis" and finding a "reluctance to renew legislatively mandated terms of imprisonment" "implicit" in the Court's previous decisions, a 5–4 majority, per Rehnquist, J., rejected Rummel's contention that his life sentence was so "grossly disproportionate" to the crime he had committed as to constitute cruel and unusual punishment. Powell, joined by Brennan, Marshall and Stevens, JJ., dissented. The *Helm* majority consisted of the four *Rummel* dissenters plus Blackmun, J.

excessive punishment for a seventh allegedly 'nonviolent' felony. How about the eighth 'non-violent' felony? The ninth? The twelfth? Suppose one offense was a simple assault? Or selling liquor to a minor? Or statutory rape? Or price-fixing? The permutations are endless and the Court's opinion is bankrupt of realistic guiding principles."

Notes and Questions

1. In an age when the death penalty is imposed rarely and barbaric punishments rejected, would limiting proportionality review along the lines suggested by the *Helm* dissent have rendered the eighth amendment "nearly obsolete"? See Note, 97 Harv.L.Rev. 127, 135 (1983).

2. Did the *Helm* majority embrace a philosophy discordant with a utilitarian view of punishment? Applied to the concept of "excessive punishment," do retributivist and utilitarian analyses yield conflicting results? See Note, 26 Ariz.L.Rev. 871, 873, 883 (1984).

———

PULLEY v. HARRIS, 465 U.S. 37, 104 S.Ct. 871, 79 L.Ed.2d 29 (1984): Harris contended that the California capital punishment system was invalid because it failed to provide "comparative proportionality review," i.e., failed to require the state supreme court to determine whether, although the death penalty is appropriate in the abstract for murder, it was nonetheless unacceptable in his case because disproportionate to the punishment imposed on similarly situated defendants. A 6–3 majority, per WHITE, J., disagreed: Although most post-*Furman* capital sentencing statutes, such as Georgia's, "require the reviewing court, to some extent at least, to determine whether, considering both the crime and the defendant, the sentence is disproportionate to that imposed in similar cases," there is no basis in the Court's precedents for holding that such review is required "in every case in which the death penalty is imposed and the defendant requests it. Indeed, to so hold would effectively overrule *Jurek v. Texas* [a companion case to *Gregg*] and would substantially depart from the sense of *Gregg* * * *. Assuming that there could be a capital sentencing system so lacking in other checks on arbitrariness that it would not pass constitutional muster without comparative proportionality review, [the] California statute is not of that sort. * * * Any capital sentencing scheme may occasionally produce aberrational outcomes. Such inconsistencies are a far cry from the major systemic defects identified in *Furman*."

BRENNAN, J., joined by Marshall, J., dissented: "Chief among the reasons for [the] unpredictability [of the administration of the death penalty] is the fact that similarly situated defendants, charged and convicted for similar crimes within the same state, often receive vastly different sentences. [The dissent then quotes from Kaplan, *The Problem of Capital Punishment*, 1983 U.Ill.L.F. 555, 576] [This type of error] can only be eliminated after sentencing disparities are identified. And the most logical way to [do that] is for a court of state-wide jurisdiction to conduct comparisons between death sentences imposed by different judges or juries within the State. [S]uch review often serves to identify the most extreme examples of disproportionality among similarly situated defendants. * * * If only to further the limited purpose, therefore, [the] Constitution's prohibition on the irrational imposition of the death penalty requires that this procedural safeguard be provided."

Notes and Questions

1. Consider Goodpaster, *Judicial Review of Death Sentences*, 74 J.Crim.L. & C. 786, 825–86 (1983): "Those who assert that rigorous appellate and proportionality review are not constitutionally required * * * must argue that those capitally convicted felons who now live because a state supreme court determined that their sentences were imposed arbitrarily should have died anyway, and that defendants similarly sentenced in the future should die. If this is what the Constitution permits, there can be no guarantee of principled, consistent and just imposition of death sentences." See also Rodriguez, Perlin & Apicella, *Proportionality Review in New Jersey: An Indispensable Safeguard in the Capital Sentencing Process*, 15 Rutgers L.J. 399 (1984). But see Note, 98 Harv.L.Rev. 97, 104–06 (1984).

2. In arguing for comparative proportionality review, *Special Project: Capital Punishment in 1984*, observes that such review "has led the Georgia Supreme Court to vacate death sentences in at least seven cases since 1974 [and] has produced similar results in other states." But Bentele, *The Death Penalty in Georgia: Still Arbitrary*, 62 Wash.U.L.Q. 573, 638 (1985) concludes that the post-*Furman* Georgia capital punishment system "has failed to bring about fair and evenhanded imposition of death sentences. [E]ven a system as carefully calibrated [as Georgia's] is unequal to the task of selecting murderers for the extreme penalty who can be distinguished in a rational and objective way from other murderers who are either not charged with a capital crime or not sentenced to death." Bentele charges, inter alia, id. at 596, that "[i]nstead of reviewing all similar murder cases to determine whether a particular defendant merits a death sentence, the [Georgia] court appears to see its task as justifying whatever death sentences juries impose, no matter how inconsistent or irrational."

———

SPAZIANO v. FLORIDA, ___ U.S. ___, 104 S.Ct. 3154, 82 L.Ed.2d 340 (1984), per BLACKMUN, J., rejected the contention that allowing a judge to impose the death sentence after the jury has recommended life imprisonment violates the eighth amendment, finding "nothing in the safeguards necessitated by the Court's recognition of the qualitative difference of the death penalty that requires that the sentence be imposed by a jury." Even accepting the premise that "the retributive purpose behind the death penalty is the element that sets the penalty apart, it does not follow that the sentence must be imposed by a jury. [The] community's voice is heard at least as clearly in the legislature when the death penalty is authorized and the particular circumstances in which death is appropriate are defined." The Court recognized that "30 out of 37 jurisdictions with a capital-sentencing statute give the life-or-death decision to the jury, with only 3 of the remaining 7 allowing a judge to override a jury's recommendation of life," but "the fact that a majority of jurisdictions has adopted a different practice * * * does not establish that contemporary standards of decency are offended by the jury override."

Dissenting JUSTICE STEVENS, joined by Brennan and Marshall, JJ., maintained that "because it is the one punishment that cannot be prescribed by a rule of law as judges normally understand such rules, but rather is ultimately understood only as an expression of the community's outrage—its sense that an individual has lost his moral entitlement to life—[the] danger of an excessive response can only be avoided if the decision to impose the death penalty is made by a jury [a representative cross-section of the community] rather than by a single governmental official. * * * Judges simply cannot acceptably mirror [the community's moral] sensibilities—the very notion of a right to trial by jury trial is premised on that realization. Judicial sentencing in capital cases cannot provide the type of community participation in the process upon which its legitimacy depends." If the state cannot persuade a jury of defendant's peers that death is the appropriate punishment for his offense, it cannot be said "with an acceptable degree of assurance that imposition of the death penalty would be consistent with the community's sense of proportionality."

Notes and Questions

1. For a powerful statement of the view that "the collective sentencing decisions of capital juries are a constitutionally necessary indicator of—in fact, define—whether the death penalty in a class of cases or in all cases has ceased to reflect 'the evolving standards of decency that mark the progress of a maturing society'" and that "[t]here is no effective way other than through juries of knowing the status of the 'evolving standards of decency' on the acceptability of the death penalty as a punishment," see Gillers, *Deciding Who Dies*, 129 U.Pa.L. Rev. 1, 40–41, 69 (1980).

2. But consider Note, 98 Harv.L.Rev. 97, 107–08 (1984): "Although sentencing by juries may be more consistent with the retributive goals of capital punishment, the Supreme Court should not impose a particular ordering of values on the states by determining that retribution is a more important goal of capital punishment than is deterrence or incapacitation. Moreover, even if retribution is taken to be the primary goal of capital punishment, the states should not be constitutionally required to further the retributive aims of capital sentencing at the expense of consistency in its application."

3. *Is* judicial sentencing likely to lead to greater consistency in capital cases? Compare Harvard Note, supra, at 103, 107, with Gillers, note 1 supra, at 57–59.

SECTION 5. PROCEDURAL DUE PROCESS IN NON–CRIMINAL CASES [a]

I. DEPRIVATION OF "LIBERTY" AND "PROPERTY" INTERESTS

"When a litigant is adversely affected entirely as a predictable consequence of procedural grossness and not as a consequence of ulterior design by government (or by its agents) to utilize constitutionally impermissible substantive standards, he is in serious difficulty. The essence of his complaint is to the felt unfairness of procedural grossness itself—that it builds in such a large margin of probable mistake as itself to be intolerable in a humane society. [But] *unlike* his freedom [of expression and religion] (sheltered by the first amendment), and *unlike* his entitlement to privacy (sheltered by the fourth and fifth amendments), [the litigant] cannot anchor a claim to freedom from procedural grossness per se in any clause of the Constitution.

   a. The creditors' remedies cases are briefly considered in *Flagg Bros. v. Brooks*, p. 1129 infra.

"He cannot rely upon the equal protection clause, for we are here dealing with situations in which all similarly situated persons are uniformly subject to the same degree of procedural grossness * * *. Nor can one say (as doubtless is one's first impulse) that the individual's entitlement to 'due' process is obviously anchored in the very clauses sheltering due process. The difficulty is that such reasoning (ironically akin to the reasoning that created the right-privilege distinction) must imagine a clause *which in fact is not there*. It imagines that the fourteenth amendment (or the same phrase in the fifth amendment) provides something like this: 'No State [shall] deprive any person of life, liberty, property, or of due process of law, without due process of law * * *.' Alternatively, it imagines that the next clause of the fourteenth amendment provides something like this '[Nor shall any State] deny to any person [either] due process of law or the equal protection of the laws.'

"[But as the amendments] read in fact, due process is not itself a protected entitlement. [It] stands in relation to ['life, liberty, [and] property'] not as an equivalent constitutionally established entitlement, but only as a condition to be observed insofar as the state may move to imperil one of the named [interests]. [P]rocedural due process appears never to be anything more than a kind of 'constitutional condition.' It is evidently not a free standing human interest."

—Van Alstyne, *Cracks in "The New Property": Adjudicative Due Process in the Administrative State*, 62 Corn.L.Rev. 445, 450–52 (1977).[b]

---

b. But Professor Van Alstyne goes on to say, id. at 487, that "it is plausible [to] treat *freedom from arbitrary adjudicative procedures* as a substantive element of one's liberty"—"a freedom whose abridgement government must sustain the burden of justifying, even as it must do when it seeks to subordinate other freedoms, such as those of speech and privacy"—"that the protected essences of personal freedom include a freedom from fundamentally unfair modes of governmental action, an immunity (if you will) from procedural arbitrariness." Simon, *Liberty and Property in the Supreme Court: A Defense of Roth and Perry*, 71 Calif.L.Rev. 146, 186 (1983) is not persuaded: "At bottom, Van Alstyne's position seems to be that procedural protection, like Beauty, 'is its own excuse for being.' * * * Procedures are important, not for themselves and not as symbols of the perfect society, but only as a means of protecting matters of value. These matters of value are not the procedures themselves, but the interests which they protect. If there is no sufficiently valuable right at stake, as the Court determined there was not in [*Board of Regents v. Roth*, infra], procedures by themselves are not valuable." See also Smolla, *The Reemergency of the Right-Privilege Distinction in Constitutional Law*, 35 Stan.L.Rev. 69, 85–86 (1982); Williams, *Liberty and Property: The Problem of Government Benefit*, 12 J.Legal Stud. 3, 17–19 (1983).

Compare Van Alstyne, supra, with Ely, *Democracy and Distrust* 19 (1980), maintaining that the phrase "life, liberty or property" used to be, and ought to be, "read as a unit and given an open-ended, functional interpretation," meaning that the government cannot "*seriously hurt* you without due process of law" (emphasis added). But consider Terrell, *"Property," "Due Process," and the Distinction Between Definition and Theory in Legal Analysis*, 70 Geo.L.J. 861, 899–900 (1982): "[I]f the phrase seriously hurt [has] discoverable substance, then its content necessarily would develop [judicially] in the same manner that the substance of 'life, liberty, or property' has developed. [The] analysis would raise the same sort of questions previously raised about property: what is the definition of 'seriously hurt'? [And] why do we use this phrase rather than one which is more restrictive, such as 'extremely seriously hurt,' or less restrictive, such as 'slightly hurt'? That is, what is the justificatory theory for Ely's substitute phrase?

"This analysis indicates that Ely's objection to the Court's treatment of 'life, liberty, or property' is based on an apparent belief that the Court should not engage in a definitional exercise at all. In effect, he argues that the purpose of the due process clause is to protect citizens from government arbitrariness, and, therefore, that these terms should relate solely to that justification. [Ely] recognizes by his use of the phrase seriously hurt the need for a trigger mechanism that must precede any due process inquiry. Yet if arbitrariness is the evil to avoid, why have any preliminary obstacle to judicial scrutiny, much less the one he has rather casually identified?"

1. According to most commentators, the "procedural due process revolution" began with GOLDBERG v. KELLY, 397 U.S. 254, 90 S.Ct. 1011, 25 L.Ed.2d 287 (1970), holding that due process requires that welfare recipients be afforded an evidentiary hearing *prior* to the termination of benefits. As pointed out in Simon, fn. b supra, at 150, *Goldberg* "did not in fact present the issue of whether welfare benefits were within the 'life, liberty or property' protected by the due process clauses, because [the Social Services Commissioner] conceded that 'the protections of the due process clause apply.' a Nevertheless, [the Court] addressed this issue [suggesting] that whether the right to continue receiving a government benefit was within the protection of the due process clause turned upon the importance of the benefit to the individual." Thus, the Court, per BRENNAN, J., observed:

"[Welfare] benefits are a matter of statutory entitlement for persons qualified to receive them.b Their termination involves state action that adjudicates important rights. The constitutional challenge cannot be answered by an argument that public assistance benefits are 'a "privilege" and not a "right."' Relevant constitutional restraints apply as much to the withdrawal of public assistance benefits as to disqualification for unemployment compensation or to denial of a tax exemption or to discharge from public employment. The extent to which procedural due process must be afforded the recipient is influenced by the extent to which he may be 'condemned to suffer grievous loss,' and depends upon whether the recipient's interest in avoiding the loss outweighs the governmental interest in summary adjudication."

2. As observed in Monaghan, *Of "Liberty" and "Property,"* 62 Corn.L.Rev. 401, 407 (1977), BELL v. BURSON, 402 U.S. 535, 91 S.Ct. 1586, 29 L.Ed.2d 90 (1971), "represented the high-water mark of [the] approach [that] whether an interest deserved due process clause process protection involved a simple pragmatic assessment of its 'importance' to the individual." The Court, per BRENNAN, J., invalidated a Georgia statute providing that the vehicle registration and driver's license of an uninsured motorist involved in an accident shall be suspended unless he posts security to cover the damages claimed by agreed parties in accident reports: "[Although a state could bar] the issuance of licenses to all motorists who did not carry liability insurance [or] post security, [o]nce licenses are issued, as in petitioner's case [a clergyman whose ministry requires him to cover three rural communities by car], their continued possession may become *essential* in the pursuit of a livelihood. Suspension of issued licenses thus involves state action that adjudicates *important interests* of the licensees. In such cases the licenses are not to be taken away without that procedural due process required by the Fourteenth Amendment." (Emphasis added.)

Bell "eschewed a tight, textually-oriented examination of the interests secured by the due process clause. [It] could have said that the license was sufficient to qualify as 'property,' or that a suspension of an individual's freedom

---

a. "[W]hile there were three dissents in *Goldberg* respecting the *fullness* of the procedure that government would be required to observe before terminating an allegedly ineligible welfare recipient, no one (not even the government itself, as Justice Brennan observed) dissented from the proposition that the due process clause was applicable to the case." Van Alstyne 456.

b. At this point, the Court noted [fn. 8] that "[i]t may be more realistic today to re-

gard welfare entitlements as more like 'property' than a 'gratuity,' " citing Reich, *The New Property,* 73 Yale L.J. 733 (1964), and quoting extensively from Reich, *Individual Rights and Social Welfare: The Emerging Social Issues,* 74 Yale L.J. 1245 (1965). In these articles Professor Reich maintained that public employment, welfare assistance, franchises, licenses and other forms of governmental largess should be given the kind of protection afforded traditional property rights.

to drive was a restriction on his 'liberty.' The Court said neither; the importance of the interest alone sufficed, and 'importance' was determined as a matter of federal, not state, law." Monaghan 407–08.

3. But "*Bell's* latitudinarian approach to 'liberty' and 'property,'" Monaghan 408, did not prevail. Stressing that before deciding what form of hearing is required by procedural due process the Court must "determine whether due process requirements apply in the first place," i.e., whether one has been deprived of "liberty" or "property"—and in doing so "we must look not to the 'weight' but to the nature of the interest at stake"—BOARD OF REGENTS v. ROTH, 408 U.S. 564, 92 S.Ct. 2701, 33 L.Ed.2d 548 (1972), per STEWART, J., for the first time, rejected a procedural due process claim because it implicated neither "liberty" nor "property." Hired by Wisconsin State University for a fixed term of one year, and given no tenure rights to continued employment, Roth had been informed that he would not be rehired for the next academic year. The Court rejected his contention that the University's failure to give him any reason for its decision or any opportunity to challenge it at any sort of hearing violated procedural due process: "The requirements of procedural due process apply only to the deprivation of interests encompassed within the Fourteenth Amendment's protection of liberty and property. When protected interests are implicated, the right to some kind of prior hearing is paramount. But the range of interests protected by procedural due process is not infinite.

"[The] State, in declining to rehire [Roth], did not make any charge against him that might seriously damage his standing and associations in his community [e.g., accuse him of dishonesty or immorality,] [a] [nor] impose on him a stigma or other disability that foreclosed his freedom to take advantage of other employment opportunities. [It did not, for example, bar him] from all other public employment in State universities.[b] [O]n the record before us,[c] all that clearly appears is that [Roth] was not rehired for one year at one University. It stretches the concept too far to suggest that [one] is deprived of 'liberty' when he simply is not rehired in one job but remains as free as before to seek another.

"[As for 'property' interests protected by procedural due process, to] have a property interest in a benefit, [one] must have more than a unilateral expectation of it. He must, instead, have a legitimate claim of entitlement to [it]. Property interests, of course, are not created by the Constitution, [but by, and] defined by existing rules or understandings that stem from an independent

a. "Had it done so," noted the Court, "this would be a different case. For '[w]here a person's good name, reputation, honor, or integrity is at stake because of what the government is doing to him, notice and an opportunity to be heard are essential.' *Wisconsin v. Constantineau,* 400 U.S. 433, 91 S.Ct. 507, 27 L.Ed.2d 515 (1971)." *Constantineau* (Burger, C.J., and Black and Blackmun, JJ., dissenting on procedural grounds), invalidated on due process grounds a state law providing that when, by "excessive drinking," one produces certain conditions or exhibits certain traits (e.g., exposing himself or family "to want" or becoming "dangerous to the peace"), designated officials may—without notice or hearing to the person involved—post a notice in all retail liquor stores that sales or gifts of liquor to him are forbidden for one year. But cf. *Paul v. Davis* (1976), infra.

b. "Had it done so," noted the Court, "this, again, would be a different case."

c. Roth had also alleged that non-renewal of his contract was based on his exercise of his right to freedom of speech, but this allegation was not before the Court. *Perry v. Sindermann,* 408 U.S. 593, 92 S.Ct. 2694, 33 L.Ed.2d 570 (1972), a companion case, made clear that the lack of a public employee's "right" to reemployment "is immaterial to his free speech claim." For "even though a person has no 'right' to a valuable governmental benefit and even though the government may deny him the benefit for any number of reasons, there are some reasons upon which the government may not act. It may not deny a benefit to a person on a basis that infringes his constitutionally protected interests—especially, his interest in freedom of speech."

source such as state law—rules or understandings that secure certain benefits and that support claims of entitlement to those benefits. Thus the welfare recipients in *Goldberg* had a claim of entitlement to [payments] grounded in the statute defining eligibility for them. [So, too, Roth's] 'property' interest in employment at the [University] was created and defined by the terms of his employment. [But these terms] specifically provided that [his] employment was to terminate on June 30. They did not provide for contract renewal absent 'sufficient cause.' Indeed, they made no provision for renewal whatsoever.[d] [Thus, although Roth] surely had an abstract concern in being rehired, [he lacked] a *property* interest sufficient to require the University [to] give him a hearing when [declining] to renew his contract of employment." [e]

4. *"The bitter with the sweet."* ARNETT v. KENNEDY, 416 U.S. 134, 94 S.Ct. 1633, 40 L.Ed.2d 15 (1974): Kennedy, a nonprobationary federal civil service employee in a regional OEO office, was removed by the Regional Director for allegedly publicly accusing the Director of bribery "in reckless disregard" of the facts. The relevant statutes provided, inter alia, that, prior to removal the employee had a right to reply to the charges orally and in writing and to submit affidavits to the official authorized to remove him (the Regional Director).[a] Instead of responding to the charges against him in a proceeding to be conducted and decided by the very person he had allegedly slandered, and who had filed the complaint against him, Kennedy instituted a federal suit, asserting that the discharge procedures denied him procedural due process because they failed to provide for a trial-type hearing before an impartial agency official prior to removal. The Court, with no majority opinion, held that the procedures satisfied due process.

The plurality opinion was by REHNQUIST, J., joined by Burger, C.J., and Stewart, J., but (as pointed out by White, J. joined by three other justices, dissenting in *Bishop v. Wood,* infra) the two justices who concurred in *Arnett,* as well as the four who dissented on this issue, rejected the plurality's analysis. As described by Van Alstyne, supra, at 462, according to Rehnquist, J., it was unnecessary to reach step two and "decide whether submitting Mr. Kennedy's fate to the judgment of his accuser was incompatible with [due process] because a close examination of Mr. Kennedy's property interest made it clear that *nothing*

d. But *Sindermann,* fn. c supra, involving another state college teacher serving on a year-to-year basis whose appointment had not been renewed and who had not received a hearing, per Stewart, J., held that a "lack of a contractual or tenure right to re-employment, taken alone," does not defeat one's claim that nonrenewal of his contract violated procedural due process. Sindermann had ten years service and had alleged, but not been permitted to prove, that the college had a de facto tenure program and that he had tenure under that program. He must, ruled the Court, be given an opportunity to prove the legitimacy of his claim of entitlement to continued employment absent "sufficient cause" "in light of 'the policies and practices of the institution.'" (Roth, on the other hand, had failed to establish "anything approaching a 'common law' of re-employment.")

e. Dissenting, Marshall, J., maintained that "every citizen who applies for a govern-

ment job is entitled to it unless the government can establish some reason for denying the employment. This is the 'property' right [that] is protected by the Fourteenth Amendment and that cannot be denied 'without due process of law.' And it is also liberty—liberty to work—which is the 'very essence of the personal freedom and opportunity' secured by the Fourteenth Amendment."

Dissenting, Brennan, J., joined by Douglas, J., agreed with Marshall, J., that Roth had been denied due process when his contract had not been renewed without being informed of the reasons or given a chance to respond. Powell, J., did not participate.

a. The employee may also appeal an adverse decision to a reviewing authority within the agency. Only on appeal is he entitled to an evidentiary trial-type hearing, but if reinstated on appeal he receives full back pay.

was in fact being taken from him to which he had *any* legally recognizable entitlement. In short, he failed at step one." Observed Rehnquist, J.:

"[A]ppellee did have a statutory expectancy that he not be removed other than for 'such cause as will promote the efficiency of the service.' But the very section of the statute [granting him that right] expressly provided also for the procedure by which 'cause' was to be determined, and expressly omitted the procedural guarantees [appellee claims]. Only by bifurcating the very sentence of the [statute conferring] the right not to be removed save for cause could it be said that he had an expectancy of that substantive right without the procedural limitations which Congress attached to it. [An] employee's statutorily defined right is not a guarantee against removal without cause in the abstract, but such a guarantee as enforced by the procedures which Congress has designated for the determination of cause. [W]here the grant of a substantive right is inextricably intertwined with the limitations on the procedures which are to be employed in determining that right, a litigant in the position of appellee must take the bitter with the sweet. [Here] the property interest [in] employment was itself conditioned by procedural limitations [accompanying] the grant of that interest."

As for appellee's contention that the charges on which his dismissal was based "in effect accused [him] of dishonesty, and that therefore a hearing was required before he could be deprived of this element of his 'liberty' ": "Since the purpose of [such a hearing] is to provide the person 'an opportunity to clear his name,' a hearing afforded by administrative appeal procedures after the actual dismissal is a sufficient compliance with [due process requirements]."

POWELL, J., joined by Blackmun, J., concurred in the result, but criticized the plurality's approach: "[The Rehnquist analysis] would lead directly to the conclusion that whatever the nature of [one's] statutorily created property interest, deprivation of that interest could be accomplished without notice or a hearing at any time. This view misconceives the origin of the right to procedural due process. That right is conferred not by legislative grace, but by constitutional guarantee. While the legislature may elect not to confer a property interest in federal employment, it may not constitutionally authorize the deprivation of such an interest, once conferred, without appropriate procedural safeguards." [b]

But after "weighing" the government's interest against the affected employee's,[c] Powell concluded that "a prior evidentiary hearing" was not required before removal. "The Government's interest in being able to act expeditiously to remove an unsatisfactory employee is substantial" and, since he would be reinstated and awarded back pay if he prevailed on the merits, Kennedy's "actual injury" would consist only of "a temporary interruption of his income during the interim." Thus, the challenged statutes and regulations "comport with due process by providing a reasonable accommodation of the competing interests." [d]

b. This passage was quoted with approval by the Court in *Vitek v. Jones* (1980), *Logan v. Zimmerman Brush Co.* (1982), and *Cleveland Board of Education v. Loudermill* (1985), all discussed infra.

c. For a more extensive articulation of Powell, J.'s "balancing process," see his opinion for the Court in *Mathews v. Eldridge,* Part II infra.

d. White, J., concurring in part and dissenting in part, rejected the Rehnquist plural-

ity's analysis and largely agreed with Powell, J.'s constitutional analysis. (Consider his opinion for the Court in *Vitek v. Jones,* infra). Although he found the pretermination procedures involved in *Arnett* generally adequate, White, J., would affirm the lower court's judgment, ordering reinstatement and backpay, "due to the failure to provide an impartial hearing officer at the pretermination hearing"—a right he maintained that the chal-

Notes and Questions

(a) *Was Kennedy's property interest "something similar to Swiss cheese"?* Consider, Terrell, first fn. b supra, at 890–91: As Rehnquist, J., viewed the matter, "[i]nstead of a complete [property] interest, Kennedy obtained something similar to Swiss cheese when he went to work for the government, with the holes corresponding to the rights that the government never extended to Kennedy. When the government terminated his employment without a hearing, it was as if a potential tortfeasor had jabbed at Kennedy's property, his job, and missed because the blow went harmlessly into one of its holes. He had nothing to complain about because there was no property interest at that spot to be infringed. Kennedy argued in effect that the government could not constitutionally provide jobs that looked 'solid' because of the guarantee of no termination without cause, but actually provide something full of procedural holes. Justice Rehnquist determined that the government could do exactly that. These procedural holes were part of the factual, substantive description—the definition—of the job Kennedy had accepted."

(b) *Circumventing Goldberg.* "The only difference" between *Arnett* and *Goldberg*, comments D. Shapiro, *Mr. Justice Rehnquist: A Preliminary View*, 90 Harv.L.Rev. 293, 324 (1976), "is that [in *Goldberg*] the statutes and regulations governing eligibility were not 'inextricably intertwined' with [those] providing for post-termination but not pre-termination hearings. Thus, under Justice Rehnquist's approach all the legislature would have to do to circumvent [*Goldberg*] would be to place the procedural limitations (which presumably could deny *any* opportunity to be heard at any time) in the same statutory section with the substantive provisions on eligibility. Surely, as six members of the Court seemed to agree, the effect would be to turn what looked like a landmark constitutional decision into the flimsiest of trivia."

(c) *Did Powell miss Rehnquist's point?* Consider Van Alstyne at 464–65: In *Arnett*, Powell, J., "fully recognized the devastating effect of the Rehnquist treatment of the new property, [but] seemed to miss Rehnquist's point in his own reply." Recall that Powell, J., stated that the legislature "may not constitutionally authorize the deprivation of [a property interest in employment], *once conferred*, without appropriate safeguards" (emphasis added). Comments Van Alstyne: "But to speak of '[a property] interest, *once conferred*,' plainly begs the question Justice Rehnquist had raised: What 'interest' *was* 'conferred'? Show us a title or a jot of 'interest' actually 'conferred' by the legislature apart from the interest Kennedy held—the interest exactly bounded, as Rehnquist said, by the procedural provisions of the only source giving it any substance at all."

(d) *Must a government employee always "take the bitter with the sweet"?* "It is clear," comments Van Alstyne at 462, that he "need *not* [if] the bitter is a substantive restriction forbidden to government by the Constitution (which applies, of course, even when the government is operating as an employer), whether the bitter requires one to abstain from insisting upon one's first amendment rights or to relinquish one's rights to due process."

5. BISHOP v. WOOD, 426 U.S. 341, 96 S.Ct. 2074, 48 L.Ed.2d 684 (1976), per STEVENS, J., held—over the protest of the dissenters that the majority was

lenged statute, although silent on the matter, should be construed as requiring in this case.

Dissenting, Marshall, J., joined by Douglas and Brennan, JJ., rejected the plurality's analysis on grounds similar to Powell's, but as Marshall "balanced" the interests involved (stressing the long delay in the processing of adverse personnel actions), Kennedy was entitled to "an evidentiary hearing before an impartial decision-maker prior to dismissal."

adopting an analysis rejected by six members of the Court in *Arnett*—that the dismissal of a city policeman implicated neither the "property" or "liberty" interests protected by due process. The City Manager of Marion, North Carolina, terminated petitioner's employment as a policeman without affording him a hearing to determine the sufficiency of the cause for his dismissal. Petitioner brought suit, contending that since he was classified as a "permanent employee" he had a constitutional right to a pretermination hearing.[a] During pretrial discovery he was informed that he had been discharged for insubordination, "causing low morale," and "conduct unsuited to an officer." The Court reasoned: "A property interest in employment can, of course, be created by ordinance, or by an implied contract. In either case, however, the sufficiency of the claim of entitlement must be decided by reference to state law. The [state supreme court] has held that an enforceable expectation of continued [state employment] can exist only if the employer, by statute or contract, has actually granted some form of guarantee. Whether [this is so] can be determined only by an examination of the particular statute or ordinance in question. * * *

"Based on his understanding of state law, [the federal district court] concluded that petitioner 'held his position at the will and pleasure of the city.' [As the ordinance was thus construed], the City Manager's determination of the adequacy of the grounds for discharge is not subject to judicial review; the employee is merely given certain procedural rights which the District Court found not to have been violated in this case. The District Court's reading of the ordinance is tenable; it derives some support from a [state supreme court decision]; and it was accepted by [the] Fourth Circuit. These reasons are sufficient to foreclose our independent examination of the state law issue. Under [this view], petitioner's discharge did not deprive him of a property interest protected by the Fourteenth Amendment.[b]

"Petitioner's claim that he has been deprived of liberty has two components. He contends that the reasons given for his discharge are so serious as to constitute a stigma that may severely damage his reputation in the community; in addition, he claims that those reasons were false.[c] * * *

"In *Roth*, we recognized that the nonretention of an untenured college teacher might make him somewhat less attractive to other employers, but nevertheless concluded that it would stretch the concept too far 'to suggest that a person is deprived of "liberty" when he simply is not retained in one position but remains as free as before to seek another.' This same conclusion applies to the discharge of a public employee whose position is terminable at the will of the employer when [prior to his instituting a law suit] there is no public disclosure of the reasons for the discharge.

---

a. The relevant provision of the city ordinance provided:

"*Dismissal.* A permanent employee whose work is not satisfactory over a period of time' shall be notified in what way his work is deficient and what he must do if his work is to be satisfactory. If a permanent employee fails to perform work up to the standard of the classification held, or continues to be negligent, inefficient, or unfit to perform his duties, he may be dismissed by the City Manager. Any discharged employee shall be given written notice of his discharge setting forth the effective date and reasons for his discharge if he shall request such a notice."

b. In *Kennedy*, noted Stevens, J., "the Court concluded that because the employee could only be discharged for cause, he had a property interest which was entitled to constitutional protection. In this case, a holding that as a matter of state law the employee 'held his position at the will and pleasure of the city' necessarily establishes that he had *no* property interest."

c. Since the District Court granted summary judgment against petitioner, noted the Court, "we [must] assume that his discharge was a mistake and based on incorrect information."

"[Even if the reasons given for petitioner's discharge were false], the reasons stated to him in private had no different impact on his reputation than if they had been true. And the answers to his interrogatories, whether true or false, did not cause the discharge. The truth or falsity of the City Manager's statement determines whether or not his decision to discharge the petitioner was correct or prudent, but neither enhances nor diminishes petitioner's claim that his constitutionally protected interest in liberty has been impaired.[13] A contrary evaluation of his contention would enable every discharged employee to assert a constitutional claim merely by alleging that his former supervisor made a mistake.

"The federal court is not the appropriate forum in which to review the multitude of personnel decisions that are made daily by public agencies.[14] We must accept the harsh fact that numerous individual mistakes are inevitable in the day-to-day administration of our affairs. The United States Constitution cannot feasibly be construed to require federal judicial review for every such error. In the absence of any claim that the public employer was motivated by a desire to curtail or to penalize the exercise of an employee's constitutionally protected rights, we must presume that official action was regular and, if erroneous, can best be corrected in other ways. The Due Process Clause of the Fourteenth Amendment is not a guarantee against incorrect or ill-advised personnel decisions." [d]

BRENNAN, J., joined by Marshall, J., dissented: "Petitioner was discharged as a policeman on the grounds of insubordination, 'causing low morale,' and 'conduct unsuited to an officer.' It is difficult to imagine a greater 'badge of infamy' that could be imposed on one following petitioner's calling; in a profession in which prospective employees are invariably investigated, petitioner's job prospects will be severely constricted by the governmental action in this case. Although our case law would appear to require that petitioner thus be accorded an opportunity 'to clear his name' of this calumny, the Court [holds he] was deprived of no liberty interest thereby. [It holds] that a State may tell an employee that he is being fired for some nonderogatory reason, and then turn around and inform prospective employers that [he] was in fact discharged for a stigmatizing reason that will effectively preclude future employment.

---

13. Indeed, the impact on petitioner's constitutionally protected interest in liberty is no greater even if we assume that the City Manager deliberately lied. Such fact might conceivably provide the basis for a state law claim, the validity of which would be entirely unaffected by our analysis of the federal constitutional question.

14. [U]nless we were to adopt Mr. Justice Brennan's remarkably innovative suggestion that we develop a federal common law of property rights, or his equally far reaching view that almost every discharge implicates a constitutionally protected liberty interest, the ultimate control of state personnel relationships is, and will remain, with the States; they may grant or withhold tenure at their unfettered discretion. In this case, whether we accept or reject the construction of the ordinance adopted by the two lower courts, the power to change or clarify that ordinance will remain in the hands of the City Council of the city of Marion.

[But see Rabin, *Job Security and Due Process: Monitoring Discretion Through a Reasons Requirement*, 44 U.Chi.L.Rev. 60, 72 (1976) "[*Bishop's* reference to] 'Justice Brennan's remarkably innovative suggestion that we develop a federal common law of property' [goes] to the heart of the matter. For if the cases beginning with *Goldberg* were not developing 'a federal common law of property rights' it is impossible to comprehend the decisions. One would have thought that the dialogue sparked by Justice Rehnquist in *Arnett* made that clear."]

d. Smolla, first fn. b supra, 88–89, points to this "profoundly honest passage" as providing "the best insights into the motivations that underlie the Court's adoption of the entitlement doctrine."

"The Court purports to limit its holding to situations in which there is 'no public disclosure of the reasons for the discharge,' but in this case the stigmatizing reasons have been disclosed, and there is no reason to believe that respondents will not convey these actual reasons to petitioner's prospective employers. [The stigma was not imposed until after petitioner brought suit, but] the 'claim' does not arise until the State has officially branded petitioner in some way, and the purpose of the due process hearing is to accord him an opportunity to clear his [name].

"[T]he strained reading of the local ordinance, which the Court deems to be 'tenable,' cannot be dispositive of the existence vel non of petitioner's 'property' interest. There is certainly a federal dimension to the definition of 'property' in the Federal Constitution [and] at least before a state law is definitively construed as not securing a 'property' interest, the relevant inquiry is whether it was objectively reasonable for the employee to believe he could rely on continued employment.[4] [At] a minimum, this would require in this case an analysis of the common practices utilized and the expectations generated by respondents, and the manner in which the local ordinance would reasonably be read by respondents' employees.[5]"

WHITE, J., joined by Brennan, Marshall and Blackmun, JJ., also dissented: "The majority's holding that petitioner had no property interest in his job in spite of the unequivocal language in the city ordinance that he may be dismissed only for certain kinds of cause rests, then, on the fact that state law provides no *procedures* for assuring that the City Manager dismiss him only for cause. The right to his job apparently given by the first two sentences of the ordinance is thus redefined, according to the majority, by the procedures provided for in the third sentence and as redefined is infringed only if the procedures are not followed.

"This is precisely the reasoning which was embraced by only three and expressly rejected by six Members of this Court in [*Kennedy*]. [The] ordinance plainly grants petitioner a right to his job unless there is cause to fire him. Having granted him such a right it is the Federal Constitution,[3] not state law,

---

4. By holding that States have "unfettered discretion" in defining "property" for purposes of the Due Process Clause, [the] Court is, as my Brother White argues, effectively adopting the analysis rejected by a majority of the Court in [*Kennedy*]. More basically, the Court's approach is a resurrection of the discredited rights/privileges distinction, for a State may now avoid all due process safeguards attendant upon the loss of even the necessities of life, cf. *Goldberg*, merely by labeling them as not constituting "property."

5. For example, petitioner was hired for a "probationary" period of six months, after which he became a "permanent" employee. No reason appears on the record for this distinction, other than the logical assumption, confirmed by a reasonable reading of the local ordinance, that after completion of the former period, an employee may only be discharged for "cause." As to respondents' personnel practices, it is important to note that in a department which currently employs 17 persons, petitioner's was the only discharge, for cause or otherwise, during the period of over three years from the time of his hiring until the time of pretrial discovery.

3. The majority intimates in [fn. b] that the views of the three plurality Justices in [*Kennedy*] were rejected because the other six Justices disagreed on the question of how the federal *statute* involved in that case should be construed. This is incorrect. All Justices agreed on the meaning of the statute. [I]t was the constitutional significance of the statute on which the six disagreed with the plurality.

Similarly, here, I do not disagree with the majority or the courts below on the meaning of the state law. If I did, I might be inclined to defer to the judgments of the two lower courts. The state law says that petitioner may be dismissed by the City Manager only for certain kinds of cause and then provides that he will receive notice and an explanation, but no hearing and no review. I agree that as a matter of state law petitioner has no remedy no matter how arbitrarily or erroneously the City Manager has acted. This is what the lower courts say the statute means. I differ with those courts and the majority only with which determines the process to be applied in connection with any state decision to deprive him of it." [e]

Notes and Questions

(a) Consider Van Alstyne at 468–69: "[According to the Court], Bishop, as a 'permanent employee,' had even less fourteenth amendment property than had Roth, probationary employee at Oshkosh, Wisconsin. Roth had the enforceable assurance of at least the one year of assistant professor status (which he had completed) before encountering the hazard of nonrenewal. Although unknown to him, Bishop as a 'permanent employee' literally had no job *even from day to day,* but was dependent upon the non-happening of an event (receipt of notice of dismissal from the City Manager) as a condition precedent to vest affirmatively in him each day's entitlement to his status."

(b) *Bishop,* maintains HENRY MONAGHAN at 440, "is wrongly reasoned, or at least wrongly phrased. The Court erred in thinking that the 'sufficiency of the claim of entitlement must be decided by reference to state law.' The nature and character of the entitlement is surely 'decided by reference to state law,' but not its 'sufficiency' to constitute a 'legitimate' entitlement and therefore 'property' in the constitutional sense. An illustration clarifies this. Suppose that a state motor vehicle statute invested automobiles with all the attributes of property as that term is generally understood, but also provided that no person who bought a car after the statute was passed would be deemed to have a 'right to continued' ownership as against the state. If the state were suddenly to confiscate automobiles for revenue purposes, surely the Supreme Court, upon assessing the state law, would conclude that the owner's interest had sufficient attributes of 'property' at least to implicate the due process clause." See also Rabin, fn. 14, supra, at 72–74.

(c) Professor Monaghan's argument is "unpersuasive," maintains PETER SIMON, first fn. b supra, at 182–83, "not because the hypothetical law he gives us is constitutional, but because *Roth* in fact does leave the courts a role that would allow them, consistent with *Roth,* to decide for themselves whether an interest is protectible 'property' or not. First, *Roth* and its progeny do in fact reserve to the courts the determination of whether interests defined by the state are fourteenth amendment property. [T]he state may define the incidents of a particular expectation, but it is up to the courts to decide whether the expectation is fourteenth amendment property. [Second,] it is implicit in *Roth* that the 'life, liberty or property' interests protected by the due process clauses include not only state-created interests, but also interests 'created' or 'recognized' by the Constitution itself. *Roth* itself provides an example. [Although the Court rejected Roth's claim, it held that if the nonrenewal of his current job] had been based on grounds which implicated his 'good name, reputation, honor, or integrity,' it would have deprived him of 'liberty,' and he would then have been entitled to notice and a hearing to clear his name. [Roth] had a *substantive* interest entitled to protection under the due process clause. That the state had chosen

respect to the constitutional significance of an unambiguous state law. A majority of the Justices in *Arnett* stood on the proposition that the Constitution requires procedures *not* required by state law when the state conditions dismissal on "cause."

e. In a third dissent, Blackmun, J., joined by Brennan, J., maintained that the Marion ordinance "contains a 'for cause' standard for dismissal and [thus] creates a proper expectation of privacy of continued employment so long as [the employee] performs his work satisfactorily. At this point, the Federal Constitution steps in and requires that appropriate procedures be followed before the employee may be deprived of his property interest."

not to protect a particular interest—here, an interest in reputation—did not by itself remove it from due process protection."

Continues Professor Simon, id. at 184: "The Court might conceivably find private ownership of automobiles so important that a statute like [Monaghan's hypothetical law], which does not treat the automobiles as property, is unconstitutional; it might hold that whether or not an individual 'owned,' or had the right to continued use and possession of, a particular car, could not be made to turn on the discretion of an administrator. This question is substantive: whether there is a fourteenth amendment right to private ownership of automobiles. The importance of *Roth* is that it allows the Court to deal openly with such substantive questions. In doing so, the Court will be free to reject the substantive balance struck by the legislature, and it would not by so doing depart from *Roth*'s analytical approach. All that *Roth* requires is that substantive decisions not be disguised as procedural questions." See also Terrell, first fn. b supra, at 896–97.

(d) After noting that "the civil service bureaucracy has great potential for adversely affecting the constitutional rights of the citizen" and that "[a]side from judicial review, civil service tenure helps free lower level bureaucrats from political control," Tushnet, *The Newer Property: Suggestions for the Revival of Substantive Due Process*, 1975 Sup.Ct.Rev. 261, 284, suggests: "The sheer number of governmental employees, when taken in conjunction with these constitutional overtones, supports the idea that civil service tenure ought to be recognized as constitutionally protected."

But cf. Van Alstyne at 482–87: "[E]ven according to the proposed terms of Professor Tushnett's test, the analysis is applicable only insofar as widely prevailing practice provides convincing evidence that a particular status limitation is indefensible. [T]he test would very seldom be met. Enough jurisdictions doubtless keep their public school teachers on annual contracts, for instance, and enough police departments use 'at will' arrangements (as in *Bishop*) that it would require a Court virtually as presumptuous as that which decided *Lochner* itself to declare that such arrangements have *no* rational connection with *any* defensible interest.

"[Moreover], I do not believe it is truly correct (or persuasive) to say that what bothers one in [*Arnett*] is that [respondent] was deprived of his *property* without due process. [What] really bothers one in [*Arnett*] is that [respondent] was not treated *fairly*. And surely there must be a way to carry forward the simplicity of that concern by more direct means, without vindicating property in all its meanness, as was done in *Lochner*.

"The concept of public sector status as property both overstates and understates the problem. It overstates the problem by carrying with it additional notions of personal entitlement and of sinecurism that no constitutional court since *Lochner* should desire to encourage. At the same time, it understates the problem by ignoring a vast number of situations in which it is impossible to describe the relationship as one giving rise to property, but in which the government's procedural grossness is nevertheless profoundly unfair and objectionable." [a]

Consider, too, Tribe *American Constitutional Law* 525–26 (1978): "[T]here is a degree of circularity to [the dissenters'] argument that there may have been 'reasonable expectations' in *Bishop* that justified a finding of a property interest:

a. See also the discussion in first fn. b, supra.

it is questionable whether a person can truly be said to 'justifiably rely' on continued employment where the person's contract or statute expressly indicates either that the employment can be terminated without cause, or that cause is theoretically required but no hearing is to be allowed. This circle can be broken only by an assertion of substantive values or norms in the name of the Constitution—norms as to what an employee, for example, is *entitled* to expect *whatever* the contract or statute may say. Indeed, breaking the circle would require an acceptance of the proposition that due process is not merely a means to the end of implementing the state's own substantive rules and allocations but either a means to some very different and larger purpose, or—as in the intrinsic approach to procedural safeguards—an end in itself."

(e) *Public employment, welfare benefits, and the "government as monopolist" theory.* Consider TIMOTHY TERRELL, first fn. b supra, at 864–65, 902–04, 907–08, "propos[ing] a threshold inquiry for determining whether a particular government entitlement should be considered a protected property interest under the due process clause[,] [the] 'government as monopolist' theory. [W]hen government acts as a 'monopolist' [then] the due process constraint is properly applied to balance the power of government over the individual's life. When the individual is not forced to deal with government, however, but chooses to do so freely and voluntarily, the constitutional protection of due process is misplaced. In this case, the 'market' created by existing alternatives to the government's offer already has established the balance between government and the individual. * * *

"Based on this factor of individual choice, cases involving government employment—such as *Roth, Bishop,* and *Arnett*—and potentially other contractual relations would seem to fall generally into the permissible arbitrariness, not the due process, set. Government is rarely a monopolist in these contractual situations, as either the only available employer or the only supplier or purchaser of a particular item. [O]nce an individual voluntarily accepts a job that has less than full due process protections for termination, then the individual has indeed taken 'the bitter with the sweet' and should not be able to base a cause of action on the inadequacy of these protections. * * * Welfare benefits cases, like professional licenses cases, should fall in the due process set, just as the Court concluded in *Goldberg.* [M]ost welfare recipients would appear to have no viable alternative to which they could turn for subsistence. Consequently, their position is probably best seen as one of forced association automatically attended by some degree of procedural protection.

"[This analysis] confirms the correctness of the majority decision in *Roth* and the plurality opinion in *Arnett* since college professors and non-specialized civil servants have available alternative markets for their skills that do not require them to move out of their respective career fields. [T]he conclusion reached by the *Bishop* majority requires further scrutiny. [S]ome types of government employment might be sufficiently unique to give government the kind of monopoly position it holds over professional licenses. Bishop's job as a policeman is a good example. [A policeman's job] is unique because state law gives a policeman certain immunities from liability that are not available to private individuals making a citizen's arrest. Thus, the loss of a job as a policeman might involve a move out of a relevant career field, notwithstanding the availability of similar private sector employment. If it does, then the majority's conclusion in *Bishop* seems quite wrong: government should *not* be free to attach an arbitrary termination process to these positions such that they fail to rise to the level of 'property.'

"This reasoning, however, ignores a second factor that allows individual choice to operate as a constraint even when government in the aggregate appears to assume a monopoly position in offering equivalent forms of the same item. [Although] a policeman might not find a similar job in the private sector, he still has a wide choice among competing government employers. [Thus,] the element of individual choice survives, despite a government monopoly in the aggregate * * *. Consequently, the *Bishop* majority's implicit conclusion that there should be no *constitutional* impediment to the structuring by a local government of the job of policeman is precisely correct."

6. *Reading "liberty" narrowly.* PAUL v. DAVIS, 424 U.S. 693, 96 S.Ct. 1155, 47 L.Ed.2d 405 (1976), arose as follows: After respondent Davis had been arrested on a shoplifting charge, petitioner police officials circulated a "flyer" to 800 merchants in the Louisville, Ky. area designating him an "active shoplifter." When the shoplifting charge was dismissed, Davis brought a § 1983 action alleging that the police officials' action under color of law had deprived him of his constitutional rights, by inhibiting him from entering business establishments and by impairing his employment opportunities. A 5–3 majority, per REHNQUIST, J., was unimpressed:

"[R]espondent's complaint would appear to state a classical claim for defamation actionable in the courts of virtually every State, [but he] brought his action [not] in the state courts of Kentucky, but in a [federal court]. [He contends that since petitioners are government officials] his action is thereby transmuted into one for deprivation by the State of rights secured under the Fourteenth Amendment. [It] is hard to perceive any logical stopping place to [respondent's] line of reasoning. [His] construction would seem almost necessarily to result in every legally cognizable injury which may have been inflicted by a state official acting under 'color of law' establishing a violation of the Fourteenth Amendment. [While we have] pointed out the frequently drastic effect of the 'stigma' which may result from defamation by the government in a variety of contexts, this line of cases does not establish the proposition that reputation alone, apart from some more tangible interests such as employment, is either 'liberty' or 'property' by itself sufficient to invoke the procedural protection of the Due Process Clause." Thus, no inquiry had to be made as to whether the police officials had followed adequate procedures before issuing the flyers.

The Court distinguished *Constantineau*, fn. c in *Bell v. Burson*, supra, as dependent on the fact that posting the person's name in liquor stores as a chronic drinker "deprived [him] of a right previously held under state law—the right [to] obtain liquor in common with the rest of the citizenry"—and thus "significantly altered his status as a matter of state law. [I]t was that alteration of legal status which, combined with the injury resulting from the defamation, justified the invocation of procedural safeguards." Interests "comprehended within the meaning of either 'liberty' or 'property' as meant in the Due Process Clause attain this constitutional status by virtue of the fact that they have been initially recognized and protected by state law,[5] and we have repeatedly ruled that the procedural guarantees of the Fourteenth Amendment apply whenever the State seeks to remove or significantly alter that status. [But] the interest in reputation alone which respondent seeks to vindicate [is] quite different from the

5. There are other interests, of course, protected not by virtue of their recognition by the law of a particular State, but because they are guaranteed in one of the provisions of the Bill of Rights which has been "incorporated" into the Fourteenth Amendment. Section 1983 makes a deprivation of such rights actionable independently of state law.

'liberty' or 'property' recognized in [such decisions as *Bell v. Burson*]. Kentucky law does not extend to respondent any legal guarantee of present enjoyment of reputation which has been altered as a result of petitioners' actions. [Although the interest in reputation is protected by the state by virtue of its tort law], any harm or injury to that interest, even where as here inflicted by an officer of the State, does not result in a deprivation of any 'liberty' or 'property' recognized by state or federal law, nor has it worked any change of respondent's status as theretofore recognized under the State's laws."

BRENNAN, J., joined by White and Marshall, JJ., dissented: "The Court today holds that public officials, acting in their official capacities as law enforcers, may on their own initiative and without trial constitutionally condemn innocent individuals as criminals and thereby brand them with one of the most stigmatizing and debilitating labels in our society. If there are no constitutional restraints on such oppressive behavior, the safeguards constitutionally accorded an accused in a criminal trial are rendered a sham, and no individual can feel secure that he will not be arbitrarily singled out for similar *ex parte* punishment by those primarily charged with fair enforcement of the law.

"[There] is no attempt by the Court to analyze the question as one of reconciliation of constitutionally protected personal rights and the exigencies of law enforcement. No effort is made to distinguish the 'defamation' that occurs when executive officials arbitrarily and without trial declare a person an 'active criminal.' Rather, the Court by mere fiat and with no analysis wholly excludes personal interest in reputation from the ambit of 'life, liberty, or property' under the Fifth and Fourteenth Amendments, thus rendering due process concerns *never* applicable to the official stigmatization, however arbitrary, of an individual. The logical and disturbing corollary of this holding is that no due process infirmities would inhere in a statute constituting a commission to conduct *ex parte* trials of individuals, so long as the only official judgment pronounced was limited to the public condemnation and branding of a person as a Communist, a traitor, an 'active murderer,' a homosexual, or any other mark that 'merely' carries social approbrium. The potential of today's decision is frightening for a free people."

Despite the majority's efforts to distinguish them, cases such as *Roth, Constantineau* ᵃ and *Goss v. Lopez*,ᵇ maintained Brennan, J., "are cogent authority that a person's interest in his good name and reputation falls within the broad term 'liberty' and clearly require that the government afford procedural protec-

a. For the view that "the heart of the complaint" in *Constantineau* was "defamation, not restriction of access to liquor," see Monaghan at 431. See also id. at 423–24; Mashaw, *Due Process in the Administrative State* 95 (1985); D. Shapiro, *Mr. Justice Rehnquist: A Preliminary View*, 90 Harv.L.Rev. 293, 326 (1976); Smolla, *The Displacement of Federal Due Process Claims by State Tort Remedies*, 1982 U.Ill.L.F. 831, 839–40, 845.

b. GOSS v. LOPEZ, 419 U.S. 565, 95 S.Ct. 729, 42 L.Ed.2d 725 (1975) (also discussed in Part II infra), held that students suspended from public high schools for up to ten days were entitled to procedural protections against unfair suspensions. The *Goss* Court, per WHITE, J., pointed out that state law had established a "property interest" in educational benefits, but also recognized "the liberty interest in reputation" implicated by suspensions: "The Due Process Clause also forbids arbitrary deprivations of liberty. 'Where a person's good name, reputation, honor, or integrity is at stake because of what the government is doing to him,' the minimal requirements of the Clause must be satisfied. *Constantineau.* [If] sustained and recorded, [the charges of misconduct] could seriously damage the students' standing with their fellow pupils and their teachers as well as interfere with later opportunities for higher education and employment. * * * Neither the property interest in educational benefits temporarily denied nor the liberty interest in reputation, which is also implicated, is so insubstantial that suspensions may constitutionally be imposed by any procedure the school chooses, no matter how arbitrary."

tions before infringing that name and reputation by branding a person as a criminal. [It] is inexplicable how the Court can say that a person's status is 'altered' when the State suspends him from school, revokes his driver's license, fires him from a job, or denies him the right to purchase a drink of alcohol, but is in no way 'altered' when it officially pins upon him the brand of a criminal." c

Notes and Questions

(a) *"An unsettling conception of liberty."* Consider HENRY MONAGHAN at 424–27: "Taken at face value, *Paul* would radically reorient thinking about the nature of the 'liberty' protected by the due process clause. The case's rationale would confine the *federal content* of 'liberty' to specific constitutional guarantees and to the *Roe* right of privacy, and, perhaps, to the Framer's understanding of liberty as freedom from personal restraint. Otherwise, interests 'attain this constitutional status [as liberty] by virtue of the fact that they have been initially recognized and protected by state law,' and it is only state conduct 'officially removing the interest from the recognition and protection previously afforded by the State, which [is] sufficient to invoke [due process] procedural guarantees.' This language [in *Paul*] suggests that any state conduct *imposing a new legal disability* on any prior freedom (including a presumably general right to be let alone) would implicate 'liberty' in the constitutional sense. [But] standing alone, defamation does not qualify as such a 'liberty' because the victim of the defendant suffers no additional legal disabilities. The plaintiff in *Paul* could vote, drive his vehicle, and buy liquor—all just as before the defamatory act.

"[I]t is an unsettling conception of 'liberty' that protects an individual against state interference with his access to liquor but not with his reputation in the community. * * * Defamation is a serious assault upon an individual's sense of 'self-identity,' and has from ancient times been viewed as 'psychic mayhem.' Accordingly, the Court's conclusion that such an assault implicates no constitutionally protected interest stands wholly at odds with our ethical, political, and constitutional assumption about the worth of each individual."

(b) *Majority support for a second cornerstone of Justice Rehnquist's approach.* Consider Shapiro, fn. a supra at 324–28: "Two years after [*Arnett*], Justice Rehnquist was able to gain majority support in *Paul* for a second cornerstone of his approach to procedural due process: entitlement theory is the basis for procedural protection not only of interests in government largesse, but of a broad range of interests not usually thought of as deriving from positive law. [Apparently] Davis had not been deprived of constitutionally protected liberty or property because Kentucky's allowance of a cause of action for damage to reputation was not sufficient state recognition and protection to create an entitlement attaining constitutional status.

"Justice Rehnquist noted that there are nonentitlement interests which receive protection because, by virtue of 'incorporation' of provisions of the Bill of Rights, they are 'encompassed within the concept of "liberty" expressed in the Fourteenth Amendment' [n. 5]. The opinion obliquely suggests that only in these areas of incorporation is the state's power to regulate conduct limited. [Outside of these areas], the state's power is limited only by its own decisions as to which interests should be recognized and protected, since it is only deprivation

---

c. Stevens, J., did not participate, but a year later, dissenting in *Ingraham v. Wright,* discussed in fn. d infra, he suggested that *Paul* "may have been correctly decided on an incorrect rationale." See the extract from his opinion in fn. d.

of these interests that must be accompanied by procedural fairness. Justice Rehnquist and those who concurred with him in [*Arnett*] would presumably remove even this constraint, for they would allow the state to attach procedural limitations to state-created rights and thereby avoid any constitutional due process requirements with respect to those rights so long as it acts according to its own specified procedures."

(c) *A defense of the result in, but not the reasoning of, Paul v. Davis.* Consider RODNEY SMOLLA, fn. a supra, at 841–47: "The critics of *Paul* have never explained satisfactorily how a section 1983 action is in any substantive law sense an improvement on the law of libel. [A § 1983] action shifts the substantive focus of the lawsuit away from the two issues that have always been at the core of libel actions: the truth or falsity of the defamatory language, and the conduct of the defendant in publishing it. * * * Substantive law aside, the critics of *Paul* have also failed to build a convincing case for construing the fourteenth amendment as mandating an alternate federal forum for what are essentially defamation actions. [Rehnquist, J.,] might have argued, as he would eventually come to argue, that there is no need to treat deprivations of interests in liberty or property as matters of federal concern as long as the state has an adequate system in place to compensate victims of those deprivations.[d] This

d. Consider JUSTICE REHNQUIST's opinion for the Court in PARRATT v. TAYLOR, 451 U.S. 527, 101 S.Ct. 1908, 68 L.Ed.2d 420 (1981). Although the state had a torts claim procedure which provided a remedy for tortious losses at the hands of the state, respondent, a state prisoner, brought a § 1983 action against prison officials, alleging that they had negligently lost certain hobby materials he had ordered by mail, thus depriving him of property without due process of law. The Court thought it plain that the prison officials had acted under color of state law; the lost materials constituted "property"; and that the alleged loss, although negligently caused, amounted to a "deprivation." But standing alone, "these three elements do not establish a violation of the Fourteenth Amendment. Nothing in that Amendment protects against all deprivations of life, liberty, or property by the State. [The Amendment] protects only against deprivations 'without due process of law.'" The Court then addressed the question whether "the tort remedies which Nebraska provides as a means of redress for property deprivations satisfy the requirements of procedural due process" and concluded that they did:

"There is no contention [that] it was practicable for the State to provide a predeprivation hearing. [The State] has provided respondent with the means by which he can receive redress for the deprivation. [Through its] torts claims procedure the State hears and pays claims of prisoners housed in its penal institutions. This procedure was in existence at the time of the loss here in question but respondent did not use it. [Although] the state remedies may not provide the respondent with all the relief which may have been available if he could have proceeded under § 1983, [they] are

sufficient to satisfy the requirements of due process."

Noting that citation to *Paul* is prominent in *Parratt*, Smolla comments, id. at 843, that "the Supreme Court, in looking back at *Paul*, seems to have revised history to place *Paul* within the post-deprivation due process framework," but that "concept—the idea that state tort remedies were all the process due Mr. Davis—was not the rationale used by Justice Rehnquist [and] the rationale that he did use has evoked an endless chain of muddled conundrums."

Parratt was extended to intentional deprivations of property in *Hudson v. Palmer*, ___ U.S. ___, 104 S.Ct. 3194, 82 L.Ed.2d 393 (1984). Respondent, an inmate in a Virginia prison, brought a § 1983 action against a prison official, alleging that the latter had engaged in an unreasonable "shakedown" search of respondent's locker and cell and that during the search, in violation of respondent's right to due process, had intentionally destroyed some of respondent's noncontraband personal property. The Court, per Burger, C.J., viewed the reasoning of *Parratt* applicable to intentional deprivation of property:

"We can discern no logical distinction between negligent and intentional deprivation of property insofar as the 'practicability' of affording predeprivation process is concerned. The State can no more anticipate and control in advance the random and unauthorized intentional conduct of its employees than it can anticipate similar negligent conduct. [If] negligent deprivations of property do not violate [due process] because predeprivation process is impracticable, it follows that intentional deprivations do not [either] [provided that] adequate state postdeprivation remedies are reasoning would not have denied that reputation was a sufficiently substantial interest to deserve characterization as property or liberty; such a position would merely have held that the interest in reputation was not deprived 'without due process of law' as long as the state courts remain ready, willing and able to provide 'due process' in the form of post-deprivation compensation.

"[In *Constantineau*] the Wisconsin posting statute may very well have pre-empted the normal remedies of the common law by authorizing the very posting procedure used by the police chief against Mrs. Constantineau, in all likelihood immunizing the police chief from the 'common law process' to which the police chiefs in Kentucky were still subject. [The] constitutional fault in Wisconsin's posting statute was thus systemic. It is precisely in cases in which the state enacts a regime that allows the state to visit substantial harm on its citizens without traditional recourse to the courts for compensation that federal constitutional law *should* be activated to override that system and 'superimpose a font of tort law' on the deficient state.

"[Rehnquist, J.,] could have finished off Davis' claim by simply pointing out that Davis continued to enjoy precisely the right and status that he always had under Kentucky law: the right to sue the police chiefs in a common law action for damages. Such a finish would have built upon the truism of modern legal thought that 'reputation' is not a right with Platonic *a priori* existence, but rather a collection of remedial and procedural devices that the state guarantees it will make available to permit one wrongfully deprived of reputation to seek redress. If Kentucky had taken away from Davis his common law tort cause of action, *then* it would have extinguished 'a right or status previously recognized by state law.' But Kentucky did not.

"[As] much as Paul's language and logic were muddled and misleading, [its] result was sound. The result, however, was not justified by the reason Justice Rehnquist gave—that Kentucky law did not extend its protection to Mr. Davis' reputation—but by precisely the opposite fact: because Kentucky law *did* protect Davis, Kentucky did nothing to violate the due process clause." [e]

available." Because Virginia did furnish such an adequate remedy, "even if petitioner intentionally destroyed respondent's personal property during the challenged shakedown search, the destruction did not violate the Fourteenth Amendment."

e. Professor Smolla then turns to INGRAHAM V. WRIGHT, 430 U.S. 651, 97 S.Ct. 1401, 51 L.Ed.2d 711 (1977) (also discussed in Part II infra), a case finding that the "paddling" of students as a means of maintaining discipline in the public schools "implicates a constitutionally protected liberty interest," but concluding that the Due Process Clause does not require notice and hearing prior to imposition of corporal punishment as that practice is authorized and limited by the common law—the state's traditional common-law constraints and remedies "are fully adequate to afford due process." Comments Smolla at 847–48:

"As was true in *Paul*, in *Ingraham* state law had in place a remedial scheme that provided redress for the harm that was alleged to form the basis of the due process violation. The Court in *Ingraham* avoided the confusion of *Paul*, however, by steering clear of the notion

that the existence of state tort law remedies somehow automatically displaced the due process clause. Instead [*Ingraham*] conceded the logical point that *Paul* had irrationally and stubbornly seemed to deny, recognizing that at a threshold level, common law protection and constitutional protection could be duplicative. [U]nlike the reputational interest at issue in *Paul,* an interest without independent federal content, the liberty interest in *Ingraham* was undeniably 'constitutional'—the right to be free of physical restraint and punishment, *Ingraham* thus made it clear that state common law remedies could serve as an adequate surrogate for due process safeguards even when 'hard core' constitutional interests in property or liberty were at stake."

Dissenting in *Ingraham,* Stevens, J. (who did not participate in *Paul*), observed: "When only an invasion of a property interest is involved, there is a greater likelihood that a damage award will make a person completely whole than when an invasion of the individual's interest in freedom from bodily restraint and punishment has occurred. In the property context, therefore, frequently a postdeprivation state remedy may be all the

7. (a) *In some situations, at least, a litigant need not "take the bitter with the sweet."* A Nebraska law, § 83–180(1), provides that if a designated physician finds that a prisoner "suffers from a mental disease or defect" that cannot be properly treated in prison the Director of Correctional Services may transfer a prisoner to a mental hospital.   Jones maintained that a prisoner is entitled to certain procedural protections, including notice, an adversary hearing and provision of counsel, before he is transferred to a state mental hospital for treatment. The Court agreed, VITEK v. JONES, 445 U.S. 480, 100 S.Ct. 1254, 63 L.Ed.2d 552 (1980), per WHITE, J.   The involuntary transfer of a state prisoner to a mental hospital implicates a constitutionally protected "liberty interest" and once a state grants prisoners such an interest "due process protections are necessary 'to insure that the state-created right is not arbitrarily abrogated' "—these protections "being a matter of federal law, they are not diminished by the fact that the State may have specified its own procedures that it may deem adequate for determining the preconditions to adverse official action":

"We have repeatedly held that state statutes may create liberty interests that are entitled to the procedural protections of the Due Process Clause of the Fourteenth Amendment. There is no 'constitutional or inherent right' to parole, *Greenholtz v. Nebraska Penal Inmates,* 442 U.S. 1, 7, 99 S.Ct. 2100, 2103, 60 L.Ed. 2d 668 (1979),[a] but once a State grants a prisoner the conditional liberty properly dependent on the observance of special parole restrictions, due process protections attach to the decision to revoke parole. *Morrissey v. Brewer,* 408 U.S. 471, 92 S.Ct. 2593, 33 L.Ed.2d 484 (1972). The same is true of the revocation of

process that the Fourteenth Amendment requires. It may also be true—although I do not express an opinion on the point—that an adequate state remedy for defamation may satisfy the due process requirement when a State has impaired an individual's interest in his reputation. [Thus,] *Paul* may have been correctly decided on an incorrect rationale. Perhaps the Court will one day agree with Mr. Justice Brennan's appraisal of the importance of the constitutional interest at stake in [*Paul*] and nevertheless conclude that an adequate state remedy may prevent every state inflicted injury to a person's reputation from violating 42 U.S.C. § 1983."

a. The *Greenholtz* Court observed, per Burger, C.J., that "there is no constitutional right of a convicted person to be conditionally released before the expiration of a valid sentence. The natural desire of an individual to be released is indistinguishable from the initial resistance to being confined. But the conviction, with all its procedural safeguards, has extinguished that liberty right: 'Given a valid conviction, the criminal defendant has been constitutionally deprived of his liberty.' " But "[w]e can accept respondents' view that the expectancy of release provided by this statute is entitled to some measure of constitutional protection. However, we emphasize that this statute has unique structure and language and thus whether any other state statute provides a protectible entitlement must be decided on a case-by-case basis." See also Professor Nowak's discussion of *Greenholtz,* p. 294 infra.

Cf. *Connecticut Bd. of Pardons v. Dumschat,* 452 U.S. 458, 101 S.Ct. 2460, 69 L.Ed.2d 158 (1981), per Burger, C.J., rejecting the argument that "the fact that the Connecticut Board of Pardons has granted approximately three-fourths of the applications for commutation of the applications for commutation of life sentences creates a constitutional 'liberty interest' or 'entitlement' in life-term inmates so as to require that Board to explain its reasons for denial of an application for commutation": "In terms of the Due Process Clause, a Connecticut felon's expectation that a lawfully imposed sentence will be commuted or that he will be pardoned is no more substantial than an inmate's expectation, for example, that he will not be transferred to another prison; it is simply a unilateral hope. * * * No matter how frequently a particular form of clemency has been granted, the statistical probabilities standing alone generate no constitutional protections; a contrary conclusion would trivialize the Constitution. [T]he requirement for articulating reasons for denial of parole in *Greenholtz* derived from unique mandates of the Nebraska statutes. [When] Nebraska statutes directed that [those] eligible for parole 'shall' be released 'unless' a certain finding has been made, the statutes created a right. By contrast, the mere existence of a power to commute a lawfully imposed sentence, and the granting of commutations to many petitioners, create no right or 'entitlement.' A state cannot be required to explain its reasons for a decision when it is not required to act on prescribed grounds."

probation. *Gagnon v. Scarpelli,* 411 U.S. 778, 93 S.Ct. 1756, 36 L.Ed.2d 656 (1973). In *Wolff v. McDonnell,* 418 U.S. 539, 94 S.Ct. 2963, 41 L.Ed.2d 935 (1974), we held that a state-created right to good-time credits, which could be forfeited only for serious misbehavior, constituted a liberty interest protected by the Due Process Clause.

"[In] *Meachum v. Fano,* 427 U.S. 215, 96 S.Ct. 2532, 49 L.Ed.2d 451 (1976), and *Montanye v. Haymes,* 427 U.S. 236, 96 S.Ct. 2543, 49 L.Ed.2d 466 (1976), we held that the transfer of a prisoner from one prison to another does not infringe a protected liberty interest. But in those cases transfers were discretionary with the prison authorities, and in neither case did the prisoner possess any right or justifiable expectation that he would not be transferred except for misbehavior or upon the occurrence of other specified events.[b]

"[The] 'objective expectation, firmly fixed in state law and official penal complex practice,' that a prisoner would not be transferred unless he suffered from a mental disease or defect that could not be adequately treated in the prison, gave Jones a liberty interest that entitled him to the benefits of appropriate procedures in connection with determining the conditions that warranted his transfer to a mental hospital. [Appellants] maintain that any state-created liberty interest that Jones had was completely satisfied once a [designated physician] made the findings required by § 83–180(1) and that Jones was not entitled to any procedural protections.[6] But if the State grants a prisoner a right or expectation that adverse action will not be taken against him except upon the occurrence of specified behavior, 'the determination of whether such behavior has occurred becomes critical, and the minimum requirements of procedural due process appropriate for the circumstances must be observed.' *Wolff.* These minimum requirements being a matter of federal law, they are not diminished by the fact that the State may have specified its own procedures that it may deem adequate for determining the preconditions to adverse official action. In *Morrissey, Gagnon,* and *Wolff,* the States had adopted their own

b. The *Meachum* Court, per Rehnquist, J., rejected the contention that "*any* change in the conditions of confinement having a substantial adverse impact on the prisoner involved" invokes due process protections, maintaining instead that the original valid conviction and imprisonment decision "sufficiently extinguished the defendant's liberty interest to empower the State to confine him in *any* of its prisons." *Meachum,* comments Tribe, supra, at 522, "was wary of subjecting to 'judicial review a wide spectrum of discretionary actions that traditionally have been the business of prison administrations rather than of federal courts.' "

See also *Olim v. Wakinekona,* 461 U.S. 238, 103 S.Ct. 1741, 75 L.Ed.2d 813 (1983), per Blackmun, J., ruling that the transfer of a state prisoner from Hawaii to a maximum security facility in California "does not deprive an inmate of any liberty interest protected by the Due Process Clause in and of itself": "Just as an inmate has no justifiable expectation that he will be incarcerated in any particular prison within a state, he has no justifiable expectation that he will be incarcerated in any particular State. [For] any number of reasons, a state may lack prison facilities capable of providing appropriate correctional programs for all offenders." Cf. *Hewitt v. Helms,* 459 U.S. 460, 103 S.Ct. 864, 74 L.Ed.2d 675 (1983) (transfer of inmate from general prison population to administrative segregation implicates no liberty interest "independently protected by the Due Process Clause").

6. A majority of the Justices rejected an indentical position in *Arnett* [referring to the separate opinions of White, Marshall and Powell, JJ., and then quoting extensively from Powell, J.'s concurring opinion].

[But consider Terrell, supra, at 935 n. 378: "[T]he government as monopolist theory explains far more satisfactorily [than the *Vitek* Court did] the Court's reluctance to let a state designate its own procedures in prison situations. In the prison context, a state is obviously in the position of absolute monopolist, whereas it is not such a monopolist concerning employment. Thus, this theory satisfactorily explains both the conclusion reached by the plurality in *Arnett,* permitting the state to narrow the definition of a job, and the conclusion in *Vitek,* limiting the state's ability to transfer prisoners to mental institutions."]

procedures for determining whether conditions warranting revocation of parole, probation, or good-time credits had occurred; yet we held that those procedures were constitutionally inadequate. In like manner, Nebraska's reliance on the opinion of a designated physician [for] determining whether the conditions warranting a transfer exist neither removes the prisoner's interest from due process protection nor answers the question of what process is due under the Constitution."

(b) *Recognizing a protected 'liberty interest' independently of state law.* The *Vitek* Court went on to hold that "independently of § 83–180(1), the transfer of a prisoner from a prison to a mental hospital must be accompanied by appropriate procedural protections":

"[F]or the ordinary citizen, commitment to a mental hospital produces 'a massive curtailment of liberty' [and thus] 'requires due process protection.' The loss of liberty produced by an involuntary commitment is more than a loss of freedom from confinement. It is indisputable that commitment to a mental hospital 'can engender adverse social consequences to the individual' and that '[w]hether we label this phenomena "stigma" [or] something else [it can occur and it] can have a very significant impact on the individual.' * * * Compelled treatment in the form of mandatory behavior modification programs, [to which] Jones was exposed in this case was a proper factor to be weighed * * *.

"Were an ordinary citizen to be subjected involuntarily to these consequences, it is undeniable that protected liberty interests would be unconstitutionally infringed absent compliance with the procedures required by the Due Process Clause. We conclude that a convicted felon also is entitled to the benefit of procedures appropriate in the circumstances before he is found to have a mental disease and transferred to a mental hospital.

"[Appellants] maintain that the transfer of a prisoner to a mental hospital is within the range of confinement justified by imposition of a prison sentence, at least after certification by a qualified person that a prisoner suffers from a mental disease or defect. We cannot agree. None of our decisions holds that conviction for a crime entitles a State not only to confine the convicted person but also to determine that he has a mental illness and to subject him involuntarily to institutional care in a mental hospital. Such consequences visited on the prisoner are qualitatively different from the punishment characteristically suffered by a person convicted of a crime. [A] criminal conviction and sentence of imprisonment extinguish an individual's right to freedom from confinement for the term of his sentence, but they do not authorize the State to classify him as mentally ill and to subject him to involuntary psychiatric treatment without affording him additional due process protections." [c]

8. (a) *A state is not free to employ such procedures as it pleases for adjudicating a claim it need not have created.* In LOGAN v. ZIMMERMAN BRUSH CO., 455 U.S. 422, 102 S.Ct. 1148, 71 L.Ed.2d 265 (1982), appellant filed a charge with the Illinois Employment Practices Commission, alleging that his employment had been lawfully terminated because of his physical handicap. This triggered the Commission's statutory obligation to convene a fact-finding conference within 120 days, but, apparently through inadvertence, the conference was scheduled five days *after* expiration of the statutory period. The state court held that the failure to convene a conference within 120 days deprived the Commission of jurisdiction to consider appellant's claim under the Illinois Fair

---

c. Because they believed the case was not properly before the Court, Burger, C.J., and Stewart, Blackmun and Rehnquist, JJ., dissented without reaching the merits.

Employment Practices Act (FEPA). The Court, per BLACKMUN, J., reversed, deeming appellant's FEPA claim "a species of property" protected by fourteenth amendment due process and holding that the state scheme had deprived appellant of his property right.

The Court pointed out that its recent cases had emphasized that "[t]he hallmark of property [is] an individual entitlement grounded in state law, which cannot be removed except 'for cause.' [And] an FEPA claim, which presumably can be surrendered for value, is at least as substantial as the right to an education labeled as property in *Goss v. Lopez*. Certainly, it would require a remarkable reading of a 'broad and majestic term' to conclude that a horse trainer's license is a protected property interest under the Fourteenth Amendment, while a state-created right to redress discrimination is not."

"Because the entitlement arises from statute, the [state supreme court] reasoned, it was the legislature's prerogative to establish the 'procedures to be followed upon a charge.' [This analysis] misunderstands the nature of the Constitution's due process guarantee. [B]ecause 'minimum [procedural] requirements [are] a matter of federal law, they are not diminished by the fact that the State may have specified its own procedures that it may deem adequate for determining the preconditions to adverse official action.' *Vitek*. Indeed, any other conclusion would allow the State to destroy at will virtually any state-created property interest. The Court has considered and rejected such an approach [quoting from that portion of the *Vitek* opinion quoting with approval from Powell, J.'s concurring opinion in *Arnett*].

"Of course, the State remains free to create substantive defenses or immunities for use in adjudication—or to eliminate its statutorily created causes of action altogether—just as it can amend or terminate its welfare or employment programs [or adjust benefit levels]. [But the 120-day limitation] is a procedural limitation on the claimant's ability to assert his rights, not a substantive element of the FEPA claim."

(b) *Why can't a state "enfeeble" any entitlement it creates?* Consider Easterbrook, *Substance and Due Process*, 1982 Sup.Ct.Rev. 85–86, 109–110, 120: "The process a legislature describes for vindicating the entitlements that it creates is a way of indicating how effective its plan should be. The more process it affords, the more the legislature values the entitlements and thus is willing to sacrifice to avoid mistakes. A court that protects the legislative power to define substantive entitlements ought to give it control of process as well.

"[The] Court's justification for specifying process once the statute has specified substance is that 'any other conclusion would allow the State to destroy at will virtually any state-created property interest.' This would be a good argument if the Court could explain why a state may not destroy the interest it creates, at least prospectively. But the Court has never so argued. Under the Court's decisions legislatures are free to enact precatory statutes, statutes that contain no rules of decision, retroactive statutes, statutes that lack any methods of enforcement, statutes creating absolute immunities, and otherwise to have vacuous 'entitlements.' To use some invented numbers, if states may elect ten percent reliability in enforcement (the amount of adherence to a precatory statute), why can they not elect ninety percent (the amount obtained from rudimentary procedures)? Why, in other words, is the expedient of enfeebling a statutory entitlement by providing 'deficient' procedures out of bounds? The Court's cases contain no answers to this question because they are not consistent. There is no single view that could be respected in the name of stare decisis.

"[Illinois] need not have created any right to be free of discrimination because of handicap or given the right of any particular dimensions. That being so, [Illinois] also should have been allowed to employ such procedure as it pleased for adjudicating (or not adjudicating) Logan's claim.[105] "

(c) *Why wasn't Logan's right to sue the Commission in tort for its negligence in losing his claim sufficient to satisfy due process?* The Zimmerman Brush Company had another argument in support of the Illinois Supreme Court's decision. As described in Smolla, p. 273 fn. a supra, at 860, the Company argued that even if Logan possessed an "entitlement" under Illinois law "no federal due process violation existed, because Logan could sue the Commission for damages under the Illinois Court of Claims Act for having negligently destroyed his 'property'—his [FEPA cause of action]. Logan in effect had an action for 'malpractice' against the Commission, just as he would have had an action against his own attorney if the attorney had negligently caused Logan's claim to lapse. Under the reasoning in *Parratt v. Taylor* [p. 275 fn. d supra], the Company argued, the state had not deprived Logan of property without due process since the state's own tort remedies were adequate to make Logan whole." This argument, responded the Court, "misses *Parratt's* point":

"In *Parratt,* the Court emphasized that it was dealing with 'a tortious loss [of] property as a result of a random and unauthorized act by a state employee [rather than] some established procedure.' Here, in contrast, it is the state system itself that destroys a complainant's property interest, by operation of law, whenever the Commission fails to convene a timely conference—whether the Commission's action is taken through negligence, maliciousness, or otherwise. *Parratt* was not designed to reach such a situation. Unlike the complainant in *Parratt,* Logan is challenging not the Commission's error, but the 'established state procedure' that destroys his entitlement without according him proper procedural safeguards.

"In any event, the Court's decisions suggest that, absent 'the necessity of quick action by the State or the impracticality of providing any predeprivation process,' a post-deprivation hearing here would be constitutionally inadequate. *Parratt.* [That] is particularly true where, as here, the State's only post-termination process comes in the form of an independent tort action.[10] Seeking redress through a tort suit is apt to be a lengthy and speculative process, which in a situation such as this one will never make the complainant entirely whole: the Illinois Court of Claims Act does not provide for reinstatement [and] even a successful suit will not vindicate entirely Logan's right to be free from discriminatory treatment."

(d) *The post-deprivation due process doctrine: reconciling Zimmerman Brush and Parratt.* The relationship between *Zimmerman Brush* and *Parratt,* observes

---

105. [As] the Supreme Court of Illinois saw things, the statute (effectively) allowed Logan's claim to be distinguished for no reason at all. Thus the statute gave Logan no property right. *Bishop.* The Court never told us why it was disregarding the state court's construction of the state's statute.

10. In *Ingraham v. Wright* [p. 276 fn. e supra] the Court concluded that state tort remedies provided adequate process for students subjected to corporal punishment in school, [but it] emphasized that the state scheme "preserved what 'has always been the

law of the land,' " [and] that adding additional safeguards would be unduly burdensome. Here neither of those rationales is available. Terminating potentially meritorious claims in a random manner is hardly a practice in line with our common-law traditions. And the State's abandonment of the challenged practice [after the inception of the present litigation] makes it difficult to argue that requiring a determination on the merits will impose undue burdens on the state administrative process.

Smolla at 861–62, "parallels the relationship that arguably existed between *Constantineau* and *Paul.* Random and unauthorized harm caused by the state, for which the state itself provides a remedy, does not implicate the Constitution. But when the state consciously enacts a system that places its imprimatur on arbitrary conduct, whether it be through a bizarre posting statute or a capricious administrative structure for handling handicap discrimination, federal court intervention under the due process clause is warranted."

9. *"[I]t is settled that the 'bitter with the sweet' approach misconceives the [due process] guarantee."* CLEVELAND BOARD OF EDUCATION v. LOUDERMILL, __ U.S. __, 105 S.Ct. 1487, 84 L.Ed.2d 494 (1985): Under Ohio law, respondents Loudermill and Donnelly were "classified civil servants" who could be discharged only for cause. Loudermill, a security guard, was dismissed because of dishonesty in filling out his employment application. He was not afforded an opportunity to respond to the dishonesty charge or to challenge the dismissal.[a] Donnelly was fired as a bus mechanic because he had failed an eye examination. He appealed to the Civil Service Commission, which ordered him reinstated without pay. "The statute plainly supports the conclusion [that] respondents possessed property rights in continued employment," but petitioners contended that "the property right is defined by, and conditioned on, the legislature's choice of procedures for its deprivation. [Petitioners stress] that in addition to specifying the grounds for termination, the statute sets out procedures by which termination may take place [and that these procedures were followed]. [Therefore,] '[t]o require additional procedures would in effect expand the scope of the property interest itself.'" The Court, per WHITE, J., rejected this approach:

"[Petitioners' argument] has its genesis in the plurality opinion in *Arnett.* [This approach] garnered three votes in *Arnett,* but was specifically rejected by the other six Justices. [I]n light of [*Vitek* and *Zimmerman Brush*], it is settled that the 'bitter with the sweet' approach misconceives the [due process] guarantee. If a clearer holding is needed, we provide it today. The point is straightforward: the Due Process Clause provides that certain substantive rights—life, liberty, and property—cannot be deprived except pursuant to constitutionally adequate procedures. The categories of substance and procedure are distinct. Were the rule otherwise, the Clause would be reduced to a mere tautology. 'Property' cannot be defined by the procedures provided for its deprivation any more than can life or liberty. The right to due process 'is conferred, not by legislative grace, but by constitutional guarantee. While the legislature may elect not to confer a property interest in [public] employment, it may not constitutionally authorize the deprivation of such an interest, once conferred, without appropriate procedural safeguards.' *Arnett* (Powell, J., [concurring opinion]); see id. (White, J., [concurring in part]). [O]nce it is determined that the Due Process Clause applies, 'the question remains what process is due.' The answer is not to be found in the Ohio statute."[b]

---

a. On his 1979 job application, Loudermill stated that he had never been convicted of a felony. Eleven months later it was discovered that he had been convicted of grand larceny in 1968. Loudermill maintained that he had thought his larceny conviction was for a misdemeanor rather than a felony.

b. The Court then held that respondents were not entitled to a "full adversarial hearing prior to adverse governmental action. [A]ll the process that is due is provided by a pretermination opportunity to respond, coupled with [a full post-termination hearing as] provided by the Ohio statute." This aspect of *Loudermill* is treated in Part II infra.

REHNQUIST, J., the sole Justice to dissent on this issue, maintained that the Fourteenth Amendment "does not support the conclusion that Ohio's effort to confer a limited form of tenure upon respondents resulted in the creation of a 'property right' in their employment":

"Here, as in *Arnett,* '[t]he employee's statutorily defined right is not a guarantee against removal without cause in the abstract, but such a guarantee as enforced by the procedures which [the Ohio legislature] has designated for the determination of cause' (opinion of Rehnquist, J.). [We] ought to recognize the totality of the State's definition of the property right in question, and not merely seize upon one of several paragraphs in a unitary statute to proclaim that in that paragraph the State has inexorably conferred upon a civil service employee something which it is powerless to qualify in the next paragraph of the statute. [While] it does not impose a federal definition of property, the Court departs from the full breadth of the holding in *Roth* by its selective choice from among the sentences the Ohio legislature chooses to use in establishing and qualifying a right."

II. WHAT KIND OF HEARING—AND WHEN?

GOLDBERG v. KELLY, 397 U.S. 254, 90 S.Ct. 1011, 25 L.Ed.2d 287 (1970), per BRENNAN, J. (Burger, C.J., and Black and Stewart, JJ., dissenting) held that due process requires an evidentiary hearing prior to termination of welfare benefits, stressing the "crucial factor [that] termination of aid pending resolution of a controversy over eligibility may deprive an *eligible* recipient of the very means by which to live while he waits. Since he lacks independent resources, his situation becomes immediately desperate. His need to concentrate upon [survival], in turn, adversely affects his ability to seek redress from the welfare bureaucracy." The hearing "need not take the form of a judicial or quasi-judicial trial," but a recipient must have "timely and adequate notice detailing the reasons for a proposed termination, and an effective opportunity to defend by confronting any adverse witnesses and by presenting his own arguments and evidence orally." The Court declined to "say that counsel must be provided" but the recipient must be allowed to retain counsel.

Consider JERRY MASHAW, *Due Process in the Administrative State* 35–36 (1985): "[T]he underprotectionist critic may claim that the due process revolution has stopped short of its essential goals: building legal security and democratic control into the administrative state. Legal security for the welfare claimant, for example, would at a minimum require that the hearing right be oriented to the issues that produce erroneous deprivations and that the recipient class has the necessary resources to make use of hearings to protect its interests. Yet neither condition seems to obtain. A careful study of errors suggests that they occur at least as often through misinterpretation of policy as through mistakes on questions of fact. The *Goldberg* decision limits due process hearings to facts. Moreover, welfare recipients generally lack the human or material resources to make use of the hearings *Goldberg* provided. Except for an occasional flurry of political activism expressed through appeals requests, hearings have been utilized about as infrequently after *Goldberg* as before.

"This sort of criticism may be pressed further to suggest that the hearing technique—the demand for individualized and detailed attention through quasi-judicial process—simply misses the point of the welfare state. The problem has become one of mass, not individual, justice. Legal security for the class of welfare claimants lies, not in hearings, but in good management. Unless due process, therefore, comes to terms with administration, becomes systems—rather than case-oriented, it will be irrelevant.

"The underprotectionist case goes further. *Goldberg*'s hearing rights extend only to the protection of what can be termed 'positive entitlements,' substantive interests already enjoying common law or statutory legal significance. Due process hearings are thus only an addition to the legal security of existing rights. They provide no access to the administrative forums in which rights are being created and no opportunity to avoid the application of general rules on the basis of individual circumstances. *Goldberg*'s hearing rights thus leave untouched the contemporary concern with (1) the remoteness of administrative policy making from immediate participation by affected interests and (2) the unfairness and irrationality that seem to attend bureaucratic implementation of general rules." [a]

MATHEWS v. ELDRIDGE, 424 U.S. 319, 96 S.Ct. 893, 47 L.Ed.2d 18 (1976), per POWELL, J., held that although Social Security disability benefits constitute "a statutorily created 'property' interest protected by the Fifth Amendment," due process does not require a *Goldberg*-type hearing prior to their termination on the ground that "the worker is no longer disabled": "In recent years this Court increasingly has had occasion to consider the extent to which due process requires an evidentiary hearing prior to the deprivation of some type of property interest even if such a hearing is provided thereafter. In only one case, *Goldberg*, has the Court held that a hearing closely approximating a judicial trial is necessary. [For example,] *Bell v. Burson* [held] that due process required only that the prerevocation hearing involve a probable-cause determination as to the fault of the licensee, noting that the hearing 'need not take the form of a full adjudication of the question of liability.' [O]ur prior decisions indicate that identification of the specific dictates of due process generally requires consideration of three distinct factors: First, the private interest that will be affected by the official action; second, the risk of an erroneous deprivation of such interest through the procedures used, and the probable value, if any, of additional or substitute procedural safeguards; and finally, the government's interest, includ-

a. At this point, Professor Mashaw turns to O'BANNON V. TOWN COURT NURSING CENTER, 447 U.S. 773, 100 S.Ct. 2467, 65 L.Ed.2d 506 (1980), per STEVENS, J., holding that, because nursing home residents had no government-established entitlement to continued residence at a particular home, they had no right to a hearing before the government decertified the home as provider of services at government expenses under Medicare and Medicaid agreements. Decertification would force the patients to seek care elsewhere and would probably mean that they would be separated from each and might mean that they would have to relocate away from their friends and families. But, responded the Court, Medicaid provisions only give recipients "the right to choose among a range of *qualified* providers, without government interference, [not the right] to enter an unqualified home and demand a hearing to certify it, nor [the right] to continue to receive benefits for care in a home that has been decertified. [A]lthough the regulations do protect patients

by limiting the circumstances under which a *home* may transfer or discharge a Medicaid recipient, they do not purport to limit the Government's right to make a transfer necessary by decertifying a facility. [Whatever rights the patients may have against the nursing home] for failing to maintain its status[,] enforcement by [state and federal agencies] of their valid regulations did not directly affect their legal rights or deprive them of any constitutionally protected interest in life, liberty or property."

Blackmun, J., concurred, but found the Court's analysis "simplistic and unsatisfactory." He did not find the distinction between "direct" and "indirect" losses helpful and, in any event, had "great difficulty concluding that the patients' loss of their home should be characterized as 'indirect and incidental.'" For extensive criticism of *O'Bannon*, see Mashaw, supra, at 36–41; Terrell, supra, at 927–35.

ing the function involved and the fiscal and administrative burdens that the additional or substitute procedural requirement would entail." [a]

First, in contrast to *Goldberg*, "eligibility for disability benefits [is] not based upon financial need." Rather, such benefits are "wholly unrelated to the worker's income or support from many other sources, such as earnings of other family members, workmen's compensation awards, tort claims awards, savings, [insurance, pensions and public assistance.]" Thus, "there is less reason here than in *Goldberg* to depart from the ordinary principle, established by our decisions, that something less than an evidentiary hearing is sufficient prior to adverse administrative action."

Second, "the potential value of an evidentiary hearing, or even oral presentation to the decisionmaker, is substantially less in this context than in *Goldberg*." Here, "a medical assessment of the worker's physical or mental condition is required. This is a more sharply focused and easily documented decision than the typical determination of welfare entitlement [where] a wide variety of information may be deemed relevant, and issues of witness credibility and veracity often are critical to the decision-making process." Further, "the information critical [in the disability case] usually is derived from medical sources, [which are likely] to communicate more effectively through written documents than are welfare recipients or the lay witnesses supporting their cause."

Third, as to the "additional cost in terms of money and administrative burden" if pretermination hearings were required, "at some point the benefit of an additional safeguard to the individual affected by the administrative action and to society in terms of increased assurance that the action is just, may be outweighed by the cost. Significantly, the cost of protecting those whom the preliminary administrative process has identified as likely to be found undeserving may in the end come out of the pockets of the deserving since resources available for any particular program of social welfare are not unlimited."

Finally, "in assessing what process is due in this case, substantial weight must be given to the good-faith judgments of the individuals charged by Congress with the administration of the social welfare system that the procedures they

a. The Court subsequently utilized the factors set forth in *Eldridge* in analyzing *Ingraham v. Wright* (corporal punishment in public schools) and *Parham v. J.R.* (parents' commitment of minor children), both discussed in the notes following this case. The *Eldridge* "balancing approach" was also utilized in, e.g., *Dixon v. Love*, 431 U.S. 105, 97 S.Ct. 1723, 52 L.Ed.2d 172 (1977) (Blackmun, J.) (no prior evidentiary hearing required for driver license revocation pursuant to regulation mandating such revocation if license had been suspended three times within 10 years for conviction of traffic violations); *Memphis Light, Gas & Water Division v. Craft*, 436 U.S. 1, 98 S.Ct. 1554, 56 L.Ed.2d 30 (1978) (Powell, J.) (municipal utility must provide its customers with some administrative procedure for entertaining complaints before cutting off services); *Mackey v. Montrym*, 443 U.S. 1, 99 S.Ct. 2612, 61 L.Ed.2d 321 (1979) (Burger, C.J.) (license of driver lawfully arrested for drunk driving may be suspended for 90 days without prior hearing for refusing to take breath-analysis test so long as immediate post-suspension hearing is available; *Little v. Streater*, 452 U.S. 1, 101 S.Ct. 2202, 68 L.Ed.2d 627 (1981) (Burger, C.J.) (state's refusal to pay cost of blood grouping test for indigent defendant in paternity action, a proceeding with " 'quasi-criminal' overtones," denies him "meaningful opportunity to be heard" and thus violates procedural due process); *Walters v. National Association of Radiation Survivors*, ___ U.S. ___, 105 S.Ct. 3180, 87 L.Ed.2d 220 (1985) (Rehnquist, J.) (federal statute limiting to $10 the fee that may be paid an attorney or agent representing one seeking benefits from Veterans Administration (VA) for service-connected death or disability does not violate procedural due process; since benefits are not granted on basis of need, they are more like social security benefits involved in *Eldridge* than welfare benefits involved in *Goldberg*; elimination of fee limitation "would bid fair to complicate a proceeding which Congress wished to keep as simple as possible").

have provided assure fair consideration of the entitlement claims of individuals." [b]

The *Eldridge* approach, observes Mashaw, *The Supreme Court's Due Process Calculus for Administrative Adjudication in Mathews v. Eldridge*, 44 U.Chi.L. Rev. 28, 39 (1976), "is subjective and impressionistic. [The Court] assumes that disability recipients are less dependent on income support than welfare recipients. This assumption is buttressed only by the notion that welfare is for the needy and disability insurance is for prior taxpayers. [But], any number of circumstances might make a terminated welfare recipient's plight less desperate than that of his disabled SSA counterpart,[42] or vice versa." Mashaw finds several of the *Eldridge* conclusions questionable, especially that it was dealing with an essentially medical determination. Id. at 40. "The *Goldberg* decision's approach to prescribing due process—specification of the attributes of adjudicatory hearings by analogy to judicial trial—makes the Court resemble an administrative engineer with an outdated professional education. It is at once intrusive and ineffectual. Retreating from this stance, [*Eldridge*] relies on the administrator's good faith—an equally troublesome posture in a political system that depends heavily on judicial review for the protection of countermajoritarian values." Id. at 58.

----

1. *"Educational due process" cases.* (a) GOSS v. LOPEZ, 419 U.S. 565, 95 S.Ct. 729, 42 L.Ed.2d 725 (1975) (also discussed at p. 273 fn. b supra), per WHITE, J., held that "as a general rule," before a student is given a temporary suspension (ten days or less) from public school, due process requires "that the student be given oral or written notice of the charges against him and, if he denies them, an explanation of the evidence the authorities have and an opportunity to present his side of the story": "[T]otal exclusion from the educational process for more than a trivial period, and certainly if the suspension is for 10 days, is a serious event in the life of the suspended child. [T]he State is constrained to recognize a student's legitimate entitlement to a public education as a property interest which is protected by the Due Process Clause and which may not be taken away for misconduct without adherence to the minimum procedures required by that clause. [Due process] also forbids arbitrary deprivations of liberty. [Many] charges could seriously damage the students' standing with their fellow pupils and their teachers as well as interfere with later opportunities for higher education and employment."

POWELL, J., joined by Burger, C.J., and Blackmun and Rehnquist, JJ., dissented: "[H]owever, one may define the entitlement to education provided by Ohio law, [a] deprivation of not more than 10 days' suspension from school, imposed as a routine disciplinary measure, does not assume constitutional dimensions." "Whether *any* procedural protections are due" turns on the extent

----

b. Brennan, J., joined by Marshall, J., dissented: "[I]n the present case, it is indicated that because disability benefits were terminated there was a foreclosure upon the Eldridge home and the family's furniture was repossessed, forcing Eldridge, his wife and children to sleep in one bed. [It] is also no argument that a worker, who has been placed in the untenable position of having been denied disability benefits, may still seek other forms of public assistance." Stevens, J., did not participate.

42. The terminated [welfare] recipient may have access to home or general relief depending upon his residence, whereas the disability claimant in a different state or locality may not. The disability claimant may be totally dependent for his livelihood on the disability payments, whereas the welfare recipient who is terminated may have been receiving a small AFDC payment to supplement inadequate family earnings.

to which one will be "condemned to suffer *grievous* loss," [but] the record in this case reflects no educational injury to appellees. Each completed the semester in which the suspension occurred and performed at least as well as he or she had in previous years. [Few] rulings would interfere more extensively in the daily functioning of schools than subjecting routine discipline to the formalities and judicial oversight of due process." [a]

(b) But cf. INGRAHAM v. WRIGHT, 430 U.S. 651, 97 S.Ct. 1401, 51 L.Ed.2d 711 (1977) (also discussed at p. 608 fn. e supra), per POWELL, J., holding that disciplinary corporal punishment in public school "implicates a constitutionally protected liberty interest," but that procedural due process does not require notice and an opportunity to be heard prior to imposition of that punishment as it is authorized and limited by Florida common law: "Were it not for the common-law privilege permitting teachers to inflict reasonable corporal punishment [and] the availability of the traditional remedies for abuse, the case for requiring advance procedural safeguards would be strong indeed. [But the disciplinarian] must exercise prudence and restraint. [And if] the punishment inflicted is later found to have been excessive [the] school authorities inflicting it may be held liable in damages to the child and, if malice is shown, they may be subject to criminal penalties.

"[Moreover,] because paddlings are usually inflicted in response to conduct directly observed by teachers in their presence, the risk that a child will be paddled without cause is typically insignificant. In the ordinary case, a disciplinary paddling neither threatens seriously to violate any substantive rights nor condemns the child 'to suffer grievous loss of any kind.'

"[T]he low incidence of abuse, and the availability of established judicial remedies in the event of abuse, distinguish this case from *Goss*. [The] subsequent [proceedings] available in this case may be viewed as affording substantially greater protection to the child than the informal conference mandated by *Goss*. [E]ven if the need for advance procedural safeguards were clear, the question would remain whether the incremental benefit could justify the [cost.] 'At some point the benefit of an additional safeguard [may] be outweighed by the cost.' *Eldridge*. We think that point has been reached in this case."

WHITE, J., joined by Brennan, Marshall and Stevens, JJ., dissented: "To guard against [the] risk of punishing an innocent child, the Due Process Clause [requires] simply 'an informal give-and-take between student and disciplinarian' which gives the student 'an opportunity to explain his version of the facts.' *Goss*. The Court now holds that [this is] not required if the student is punished with 'appreciable physical pain' rather than with a suspension, even though both punishments deprive the student of a constitutionally protected interest.

"[The common law] tort action is utterly inadequate to protect against erroneous infliction of punishment for two reasons. First, under Florida law

a. Consider Rabin, *Job Security and Due Process: Monitoring Administrative Discretion Through a Reasons Requirement*, 44 U.Chi.L. Rev. 60, 82–83 (1976): "Despite repeated references by the Court to a right to a hearing, it is arguably the absence of an adequate explanation that is central to the controversial holding in *Goss*. [Although] the Court referred to the procedural safeguards it imposed as a form of hearing, the requirements are a far cry from earlier efforts to employ an evidentiary model. [While six of the *Goss* plaintiffs] engaged in disruptive conduct witnessed by the administrator who suspended them, the other three fall into a very different category. [Indeed, no one testified that any one of the three was involved.] What these students were not given, and what I regard as fundamental to the holding, was an explanation of how the administration identified them as troublemakers warranting suspension. The arbitrariness resided in substituting an edict for an explanation."

[the] student has no remedy at all for punishment imposed on the basis of mistaken facts, at least as long as the punishment was reasonable from the point of view of the disciplinarian, uninformed by any prior hearing. [Second], [the] lawsuit occurs after the punishment has been finally imposed. The infliction of physical pain is final and irreparable; it cannot be undone in a subsequent proceeding." [b]

(c) *Criticism of Ingraham.* "Government's interests in punishing guilty students first and asking questions about guilt later," maintain Alexander & Horton, *Ingraham v. Wright: A Primer for Cruel and Unusual Jurisprudence,* 52 S.Cal.L.Rev. 1305, 1384–85 (1979), "surely pale in significance when compared to the interests of innocent students in avoiding punishment.[282] Usually no emergency is averted by instantaneous corporal punishment.[283] The costs—monetary and otherwise—of providing pre-punishment hearings for the guilty are more than justified by the savings to the innocent. Finally, the burden imposed on the innocent in bringing post-deprivation actions is undoubtedly heavier than the burden imposed on government by a requirement of pre-punishment hearings. [In] none of the cases [upholding] a post-deprivation hearing was there both the strong likelihood of irreparable injury and the absence of a compelling justification for prompt action precluding a prior hearing."

"In other cases in which a post-deprivation hearing has been held adequate," emphasizes Rosenberg, *Ingraham v. Wright: The Supreme Court's Whipping Boy,* 78 Colum.L.Rev. 75, 91 (1978), "the interest involved was 'property' rather than 'liberty.' Postponement of the hearing in the property context can often be viewed as compatible with the interest implicated, because the property, if wrongfully taken or withheld, can, at a later date, be fully restored. Where a liberty interest is invoked, the injured person is considerably less likely to be made whole by a belated award of damages. Particularly is this true in the case of corporal punishment, where the liberty interest is freedom from 'infliction of appreciable physical pain.'" Professor Rosenberg continues, id. at 93–94:

"To [the] very real barriers impairing vindication of the child's rights [by bringing a tort action] [c] must be added not only the defense of sovereign immunity available to school boards, and the possible defense of good faith mistake available to teachers, but also the inadequacy of money damages as a means of repairing physical and psychological injury deliberately inflicted on a child. Criminal prosecutions afford even less protection to the child, because they require proof of malice and the exercise of prosecutorial discretion against public school officials.

"[The *Ingraham* Court] suggested that 'the impracticability of formulating a rule of procedural due process that varies with the severity of the particular imposition,' would lead inexorably to a requirement of a hearing in every case of corporal punishment, no matter how 'trivial.' [Thus,] the Court refused to

---

b. Compare *Ingraham* and *Parratt* (p. 275 fn. d supra) with *Zimmerman Brush* (p. 279 supra).

282. [*Ingraham*] is an easy case in this respect, considering that a more reparable student interest (freedom from 10-day suspension) outweighed similar government interests in *Goss.*"

283. In that respect, corporal punishment differs from temporary suspensions, without pre-deprivation hearings, which may avert dangers to persons and property.

c. Rosenberg notes, e.g., that it may prove difficult to secure an attorney willing to accept a case of this sort; completion of state court actions may take years, during which time "the child's memory of the controverted events may dim"; the formality of a jury trial is "considerably less conducive to articulate testimony by the public than an informal pre-punishment hearing would be"; and that a teacher is more likely to be believed than his or her ex-pupil. See id. at 92–93.

attempt to distinguish between trivial and severe corporal punishment, while at the same time invoking [the] existence of common law and statutory restraints against *unreasonable* corporal punishment. In effect, the majority was asking the nation's school teachers to make the sorts of decisions about reasonableness that, if erroneous, could lead to tort liability, while at the same time acknowledging its own inability (or unwillingness) to make such judgments."

(d) *In defense of Ingraham.* "Tort law," observes Smolla, *The Displacement of Federal Due Process Claims by State Tort Remedies,* 1982 U.Ill.L.Rev. 831, 850–51, "has always awarded money for the taking of interests without any objectively discernable value—millions of dollars are awarded for lost reputation, for emotional distress, and for pain and suffering. [A] substantial damage award against a school teacher for excessive corporal punishment is easily conceivable, particularly in communities in which a consensus against such conduct prevails. It is not at all obvious that the threat of such awards is any less a deterrent to misconduct than internal administrative hearings, in which teachers who know the administrative ropes may often be able to prevail in proceedings stacked against students.

"[Professor Rosenberg's point] that the Supreme Court preferred to allow school teachers to make decisions about the reasonableness of discipline that the Court felt unable or unwilling to make is correct, but the Court's reticence is grounds for criticism only if one first assumes that federal court judges are or should be better qualified than school teachers to make such judgments. The Supreme Court's point in *Ingraham* is ultimately that teachers are teachers and judges are judges, and no vast eternal constitutional plan would be upset if the felt need in some states for summarily administered corporal punishment in schools is allowed its free reign. Local school boards can always alter punishment policies and procedures, and they are accountable through the political process if parents or students are displeased. As long as a state keeps its courts open to police abuses there is enough 'due process of law' available to guarantee balance against excess.

"[*Ingraham*] did not totally eliminate federal concern with paddling—a due process violation could still exist if a state were to disable its own courts in their policing of local practices—but it placed federal law in a back-up role. *Ingraham* is in this sense consistent with the Court's general movement in procedural due process cases, toward initial deference to local prerogative in setting procedural norms when the substantive interests at stake are heavily imbued with localized values."

(e) BOARD OF CURATORS v. HOROWITZ, 435 U.S. 78, 98 S.Ct. 948, 55 L.Ed.2d 124 (1978), per REHNQUIST, J., "decline[d] to ignore the historic judgment of educators [and] formalize the academic dismissal process by requiring a hearing." Because of dissatisfaction with her clinical performance and personal hygiene, and after notice from and discussion with the dean of the medical school, a state medical school student was put on probation. After continued dissatisfaction with her work, and pursuant to a faculty-student council recommendation (supported by the dean and the provost), she was dismissed from school in her final year. Assuming but not deciding that there was "a liberty interest" in pursuing a medical career, "respondent has been awarded at least as much due process as the Fourteenth Amendment requires." The Court underscored the distinction between "academic evaluations of a student" and "disciplinary determinations," contrasting the instant case with *Goss,* where "[t]he requirement of a hearing [could] 'provide a meaningful hedge against erroneous action.' The decision to dismiss respondent, by comparison, rested on the academic judgment of school officials," a judgment "by its nature more subjective and evaluative than the typical factual questions presented in the average disciplinary decision."

2. *"Family due process."* (a) Balancing the three factors set forth in *Eldridge,* PARHAM v. J.R., 442 U.S. 584, 99 S.Ct. 2493, 61 L.Ed.2d 101 (1979) (also discussed at p. 177 fn. a and p. 207 supra), per BURGER, C.J., held that a preadmission adversary hearing is not required when parents (or a state agency acting in loco parentis) seek to commit their minor children to a mental institution—so long as the commitment is approved by an "independent medical judgment." The Court "assume[d] that a child has a protectible interest not only in being free of unnecessary bodily restraints but also in not being labelled erroneously" as "mentally ill," but concluded that "our precedents permit the parents to retain a substantial, if not the dominant, role in the decision, absent a finding of neglect or abuse, and that the traditional presumption that the parents act in the best interests of the child should apply. [But the] child's rights and the nature of the commitment decision are such that parents cannot always have absolute and unreviewable discretion [to institutionalize their child]. [They] retain plenary authority [to do so], subject to a physician's independent examination and medical judgment." In the course of a wide-ranging opinion the Court observed:

"That some parents 'may at times be acting against the interests of their children' [is reason] for caution, [but] hardly a reason to discard wholesale those pages of human experience that teach that parents generally do act in the child's best interests. The statist notion that governmental power should supersede parental authority in *all* cases because *some* parents abuse and neglect children is repugnant to American tradition.

"[Appellees] urge that [the] liberty interest of the child and the likelihood of parental abuse require us to hold that the parents' decision to have a child admitted to a mental hospital must be subjected to an exacting constitutional scrutiny, including a formal adversary, pre-admission hearing. [This argument] sweeps too broadly. Simply because the decision of a parent is not agreeable to a child or because it involves risks does not automatically transfer the power to make that decision from the parents to [the] state. The same characterizations can be made for a tonsillectomy, appendectomy, or other medical procedure. Most children, even in adolescence, simply are not able to make sound judgments concerning many decisions, including their need for medical care or treatment. Parents can and must make those judgments.

"[Appellees] place particular reliance on *Planned Parenthood v. Danforth* [Sec. 2 supra], arguing that its holding indicates how little deference to parents is appropriate when the child is exercising a constitutional right. [But that case] involved an absolute parental veto over the child's ability to obtain an abortion. Parents in Georgia in no sense have an absolute right to commit their children to state mental hospitals; the statute requires [each regional hospital superintendent] to exercise independent judgment as to the child's need for confinement.

"[W]hat process is constitutionally due cannot be divorced from the nature of the ultimate decision that is being made. Not every determination by state officers can be made most effectively by use of 'the procedural tools of judicial or administrative decisionmaking.' *Board of Curators v. Horowitz.* [Here,] the questions are essentially medical in character. [W]e recently stated in *Adding-*

ton v. Texas, 439 U.S. 908, 99 S.Ct. 276, 58 L.Ed.2d 254 (1979),[a] that the determination of 'whether a person is mentally ill turns on the *meaning* of the facts which must be interpreted by expert psychiatrists and psychologists.' [We reject] the notion that the shortcomings of specialists can always be avoided by shifting the decision [to] an untrained judge or administrative hearing officer after a judicial-type hearing. Even after a hearing, the nonspecialist decisionmaker must make a medical-psychiatric decision. Common human experience and scholarly opinions suggest that the supposed protections of an adversary proceeding to determine the appropriateness of medical decisions for the commitment and treatment of mental and emotional illness may well be more illusory than real. * * *

" '[P]rocedural due process rules are shaped by the risk of error inherent in the truthfinding process as applied to the generality of cases, not the rare exceptions.' *Eldridge.* In general, we are satisfied that an independent medical decision-making process, [followed] by additional periodic review of a child's condition, will protect children who should not be admitted; we do not believe the risks of error in that process would be significantly reduced by a more formal, judicial-type hearing."

Concurring and dissenting in part, BRENNAN, J., joined by Marshall and Stevens, JJ., agreed that the parent-child relationship "militate[s] in favor of postponement of formal commitment proceedings and against mandatory adversary preconfinement commitment hearings." But "[w]hile the question of the frequency of postadmission review hearings may properly be deferred, the right to at least one post-admission hearing can and should be affirmed now." "This case is governed by the rule of *Danforth.* The right to be free from wrongful incarceration, physical intrusion, and stigmatization has significance for the individual surely as great as the right to an abortion. [Indeed,] *Danforth* involved only a potential dispute between parent and child, whereas here a break in family autonomy has actually resulted in the parents' decision to surrender custody of their child to a state mental institution. [A] child who has been ousted from his family has even greater need for an independent advocate." [b]

(b) *Parental prerogatives and governmental intrusions: Parham and Ingraham compared.* Consider Burt, *The Constitution of the Family,* 1979 Sup.Ct.Rev. 329, 332–33: "The Court spoke in *Parham* as if it were upholding parental prerogatives against governmental intrusions. [The Chief Justice stated that] 'the statist notion that governmental power should supersede parental authority in *all* cases because *some* parents abuse and neglect children is repugnant to American tradition.' This is an odd way to describe the issue at stake in *Parham.* Parents there were not seeking to resist governmental power over their children; they were invoking that power by attempting to confine their children in state psychiatric institutions.

---

a. *Addington* held that one's interest in the outcome of a civil commitment proceeding is so important that due process requires the state to justify confinement by "clear and convincing" evidence, rather than the normal "preponderance of the evidence" standard. Consider Note, 93 Harv.L.Rev. 89, 98 (1979): "It is difficult to reconcile *Parham* with *Addington.* [In] insisting on a strict standard of proof [*Addington*] assumed that an individual could not be confined without an adversary

hearing. In *Parham,* by contrast, the Court allowed minors to be institutionalized with fewer procedural standards than is required for the termination of welfare benefits. The presumption that parents or state agencies will act in a child's best interests is too tenuous a rationale to justify the denial of an adversary hearing."

b. See also Note, 93 Harv.L.Rev. 89, 94 (1979).

"This paean to parental prerogatives would have had greater relevance if state officials had sought to impose behavioral controls on children against their parent's wishes. The Court did consider a case two years earlier that directly implicated that question. School officials had administered corporal punishment to children. [In *Ingraham,* the] Court majority, composed of the same conservative nucleus as in *Parham* [but here joined by Stewart, J., with White, J., dissenting], ruled that school officials were free to disregard parental objections to this form of behavior control of their children. Justice Powell [said this] for the Court: 'Although the early cases viewed the authority of the teacher as deriving from the parents, [this concept] has been replaced by the view [that] the State itself may impose such corporal punishment as is reasonably necessary for the proper education of the child and for the maintenance of group discipline.' So much for the American tradition—paraded in *Parham* as well as 'the early cases'—that 'governmental power should [not] supersede parental authority.'"

(c) *"The subtleties and nuances of psychiatric diagnoses": Parham and Vitek compared.* The *Parham* Court, observes Mashaw, *Due Process in the Administrative State* 111 (1985), did not believe that a minor need be given a hearing prior to commitment to a mental institution, "apparently in substantial part because a hearing could provide little additional protection from error: 'Common human experience and scholarly opinions suggest that the proposed protections of an adversary hearing to determine the appropriateness of [these psychiatric decisions] may well be more illusory than real.' Yet, somehow, when in *Vitek* [p. 277 supra] the question was whether a prisoner should have a hearing prior to being transferred to a mental hospital, the suggestion that psychiatric judgment was involved elicited the following judicial response: 'The medical nature of the [inquiry] does not justify dispensing with due process requirements. *It is precisely the subtleties and nuances of psychiatric diagnoses that justify the requirement of adversary hearings.'"* [Emphasis added by Mashaw.] See also Garvey, *Children and the Idea of Liberty,* 68 Ky.L.J. 809, 826–30 (1979–80).

(d) *Parental status termination proceedings.* LASSITER v. DEPARTMENT OF SOCIAL SERVICES, 452 U.S. 18, 101 S.Ct. 2153, 68 L.Ed.2d 640 (1981), per STEWART, J., rejected the view that due process requires the appointment of counsel in every parental status termination proceeding involving indigent parents and left the appointment of counsel in such proceedings to be determined by the state courts on a case-by-case basis: "The pre-eminent generalization that emerges from this Court's precedents on an indigent's right to appointed counsel is that such a right has been recognized to exist only where the litigant may lose his physical liberty if he loses the litigation. * * * Significantly, as a litigant's interest in personal liberty diminishes, so does his right to appointed counsel. [Thus, *Gagnon v. Scarpelli,* 411 U.S. 778, 93 S.Ct. 1756, 36 L.Ed.2d 656 (1973),] declined to hold that indigent probationers have, per se, a right to counsel at revocation hearings, and instead left the decision whether counsel should be appointed to be made on a case-by-case basis."

The Court then held that in the circumstances of this case the trial judge did not deny Ms. Lassiter due process when he failed to appoint counsel for her: "The record shows that the petition to terminate parental rights contained no allegations of neglect or abuse upon which criminal charges could be based; the department was represented at the hearing by counsel, but no expert witness testified, and the case presented no specially troublesome points of law, either procedural or substantive. While hearsay evidence was no doubt admitted, and while Ms. Lassiter no doubt left incomplete her defense that the Department had not adequately assisted her in rekindling her interest in her son, the weight of the evidence that she had few sparks of such an interest was sufficiently great that the presence of counsel for [her] could not have made a determinative difference." [c]

BLACKMUN, J., joined by Brennan and Marshall, JJ., dissented: "In this case, the State's aim is not simply to influence the parent-child relationship but to *extinguish* it. A termination of parental rights is both total and irrevocable. Unlike other custody proceedings, it leaves the parent with no right to visit or communicate with the child, to participate in, or even to know about, any important decision affecting the child's religious, educational, emotional, or physical development. It is hardly surprising that this forced dissolution of the parent-child relationship has been recognized as a punitive sanction by courts, Congress, and commentators.

"[Faced] with a formal accusatory adjudication, with an adversary—the State—that commands great investigative and prosecutorial resources, with standards that involve ill-defined notions of fault and adequate parenting, and with the inevitable tendency of a court to apply subjective values or to defer to the State's 'expertise,' the defendant parent plainly is outstripped if he or she is without the assistance of 'the guiding hand of counsel.' When the parent is indigent, lacking in education, and easily intimidated by figures of authority, the imbalance may well become insuperable. [W]here as here, the threatened loss of liberty is severe and absolute, the State's role is so clearly adversarial and punitive, and the cost involved is relatively slight, there is no sound basis for refusing to recognize the right to counsel as a requisite of due process in a proceeding initiated by the State to terminate parental rights." [d]

STEVENS, J., also dissented: "[T]he Court appears to treat this case as though it merely involved the deprivation of an interest in property that is less worthy of protection than a person's liberty. The analysis employed in *Eldridge,* in which the Court balanced the costs and benefits of different procedural mechanisms for allocating a finite quality of material resources among competing claimants, is an appropriate method of determining what process is due in property cases. Meeting the Court on its own terms, Justice Blackmun demonstrates that the *Eldridge* analysis requires the appointment of counsel in this type of case. I agree [but] would take one further step.

"In my opinion the reasons supporting the conclusion that [due process] entitle the defendant in a criminal case to representation by counsel apply with equal force to a case of this kind. The issue is one of fundamental fairness, not of weighing the pecuniary costs against the societal benefits. Accordingly, even if the costs to the State were not relatively insignificant but rather were just as great as the costs of providing prosecutors, judges, and defense counsel to ensure the fairness of criminal proceedings, I would reach the same result in this category of cases. For the value of protecting our liberty from deprivation by the State without due process of law is priceless." [e]

c. Burger, C.J., who joined the Court's opinion, also added, in a brief concurrence responding to the dissenters, that the purpose of the parental status termination proceeding "was not 'punitive'" but "*protective* of the child's best interests."

d. The dissent then examined the termination hearing in considerable detail and, "[i]n light of the unpursued avenues of defense, and of the experience petitioner underwent at this hearing," found "virtually incredible" the Court's conclusion that the termination proceeding was fundamentally fair.

e. For varying degrees of lack of enthusiasm for *Lassiter,* see Choper, Kamisar & Tribe, *The Supreme Court: Trends and Developments, 1980–81* 171–78 (1982); Note, 95 Harv.L.Rev. 132 (1981).

Compare *Lassiter* with SANTOSKY v. KRAMER, 455 U.S. 745, 102 S.Ct. 1388, 71 L.Ed.2d 599 (1982). Under New York law, the state may terminate, over parental objection, the rights of parents in their natural child upon a finding that the child is "permanently neglected," a finding that need be supported only by a "fair preponderance of the evidence." Because "the private interest affected is commanding; the risk of error from using a preponderance standard is substantial; and the countervailing government interest favoring that standard is comparatively slight," a 5–4 majority, per BLACKMUN, J., held that a "fair preponderance of the evidence" standard in such proceedings violates due process. Thus, before a state may terminate permanently the rights of parents in their natural child, it must support its allegations by at least "clear and convincing evidence." Such a standard "strikes a fair balance" between the parents' rights and the State's concerns and only such a standard "adequately conveys to the factfinder the level of subjective certainty [about] factual conclusions necessary to satisfy due process. [Unlike] a constitutional requirement of hearings or court-appointed counsel, a stricter standard of proof [than 'preponderance'] would reduce factual error without imposing substantial fiscal burdens upon the State."

Given the flexibility of the due process principle, dissenting JUSTICE REHNQUIST, joined by Burger, C.J., and White and O'Connor, JJ., thought it "obvious that a proper due process inquiry cannot be made by focusing upon one narrow provision of the challenged statutory scheme. [Courts] must examine *all* procedural protections offered by the State, and must assess the *cumulative* effect of such safeguards." The dissent then pointed to the "host of procedural protections" the state had "placed around parental rights and interests." In addition to the basic fairness of the statutory scheme, "the standard of proof chosen by New York clearly reflects a constitutionally permissible balance of the interests at stake in this case. [When] the interests of the child and the State in a stable, nurturing homelife are balanced against the interests of the parents in the rearing of their child, it cannot be said that either set of interests is so clearly paramount as to require that the risk of error be allocated to one side or the other."

3. *"Open analysis of the values at stake."* Consider Nowak, *Foreword—Due Process Methodology in the Postincorporation World,* 70 J.Crim.L. & C. 397, 403 (1979): "Although one may disagree with the results in [cases such as *Parham,* which employed the *Eldridge* 'balancing test,'] the Court's open analysis of the values at stake [and] its attempt to accommodate the competing values of liberty and efficient administrative procedures certainly is preferable to the masking of such decisions through vaguely worded opinions or formalistic interpretations of constitutional provisions. [By contrast], in *Greenholtz v. Nebraska Prison Inmates* (1979) [p. 277 fn. a supra], [holding] that inmates of penal institutions were not entitled to due process protection in decisionmaking processes related to their possible release on parole, a majority of the Justices totally failed to analyze the basic due process question. [*Greenholtz,* per Burger, C.J., found] no liberty interest meriting protection by the due process clause at issue in these proceedings. The four Justices [Brennan, Marshall, Powell and Stevens] who dissented, at least in part, found that the individual prisoners had a liberty interest at stake [and thus] struggled openly with the problem of determining what, if any, procedural safeguards should be given to [them]. Even if one agreed with the majority's conclusion[,] [it is] easier to accept the separate opinion of Justice Powell, [recognizing] that inmates had an interest worthy of protection by the due process clause [but finding] that the need of efficiently

processing inmate files outweighed the interest in freedom preceding the expiration of a properly imposed sentence. [Powell, J.'s] balancing approach is more satisfying than the majority's simple assertion that the possibility of parole is no more than a hope—'a hope which is not protected by due process.' By failing to adopt the Powell approach it was possible to avoid questions of fairness and value identification even in due process decisions."

4. *Separating the "property" or "liberty" issue from that of "what process is due."* While recent cases "fall short of providing the full inventory of procedural safeguards required by *Goldberg,*" observes ROBERT RABIN, *Job Security and Due Process: Monitoring Administrative Discretion Through A Reasons Requirement,* 44 U.Chi.L.Rev. 60, 74–79 (1976), they proceed from the same basic assumption about the relationship between property interests and procedural due process: at a minimum, procedural due process contemplates some kind of a hearing—an opportunity to join issue, through the presentation of evidence to a decision maker who is then obliged to reach a reasoned determination on the basis of the submissions. Underlying this conception is the vital interest in promoting an accurate decision, in assuring that facts have been correctly established and properly characterized in conformity with the applicable legal [standard.]

"By equating procedural due process with a value that seems to require a right to some kind of a hearing, the Court has correspondingly been driven to set too high a threshold when arriving at an initial determination of whether a property interest exists. In theory, of course, the inquiry into whether a form of government largess creates a property interest can, as the Court and commentators [and, in a way, the editors of this casebook] suggest, be neatly separated from the question of 'what process is due.' In practice, however, whether an entitlement is established or not is determined with an eye to the minimum procedural requirements that would follow as a consequence of a decision in favor of the recipient's claim. A threshold perception of security of interest focuses both on the existence of a 'property' interest and the procedural safeguards attendant upon its recognition. [The] result, as *Roth* and *Bishop* illustrate, is that when the state equivocates about job security, a court cognizant of the high costs of a hearing requirement in terms of administrative efficiency is likely to be reluctant to recognize a property interest. The court then ends up affording no procedural protection at all, even though the employee in such a case may be on a tenure track or even in a 'permanent' position.

"In what way is a threshold linked to the right to some kind of hearing too high? First, because preoccupation with a hearing has diverted attention from the fact that a significant measure of respect can be afforded the interest in accuracy with a more modest procedural safeguard that does not have the same consequences for administrative efficiency. Second, because excessive attention to the hearing safeguard has concealed the existence of an independent interest—what I will refer to as the interest in an adequate explanation—which has a compelling claim for protection through a more limited due process safeguard.

"Fundamental to the concept of procedural due process is the right to a reasoned explanation of government conduct that is contrary to the expectations the government has created by conferring a special status upon an individual. [It] is crucial that this value be seen as distinct from the concern about administrative accuracy—the interest in correcting wrong decisions. Obviously, the two are related[, but] I would insist that the respect for individual autonomy that is at the foundation of procedural due process imposes a distinct obligation upon the government to explain fully its adverse status decision. * * *

"Procedural due process can be viewed as a layered approach aimed at accomplishing a fundamental objective—protection against arbitrary conduct by the state. One could view the [various rights][a] as various layers intended to provide increasingly effective insulation from arbitrariness: each layer adds something to the defensive capacity to ward off an arbitrary effort to destroy a status relationship. In some cases—a job security case involving a first amendment claim, for example—the balance struck between the individual values to be protected and the costs of administration weighs so heavily in favor of the individual claimant that a many-layered approach, some form of 'evidentiary hearing,' seems clearly required. But as we respond to less exigent claims by peeling away the layers of protection—indeed as we strip away any semblance of a 'hearing'—it is essential that we retain the core safeguard against arbitrariness, the right to receive a meaningful explanation of what is being done to the individual."

a. For factors—"roughly in order of priority"—that have been considered to be elements of a fair hearing, see Friendly, *"Some Kind of Hearing,"* 123 U.Pa.L.Rev. 1267, 1279–95 (1975): (1) "an unbiased tribunal" (but recall *Arnett v. Kennedy*); (2) "notice of the proposed action and the grounds asserted for it"; (3) "an opportunity to present reasons why the proposed action should not be taken"; (4), (5) and (6) "the right to call witnesses, to know the evidence against one, and to have decision based only on the evidence presented"; (7) "counsel"; (8) and (9), "the making of a record and a statement of reasons"; (10) "public attendance"; and (11) "judicial review."

Chapter 4

FREEDOM OF EXPRESSION AND ASSOCIATION

SECTION 1. WHAT SPEECH SHOULD BE PROTECTED AND HOW MUCH PROTECTION SHOULD IT GET?

The first amendment provides that "Congress shall make no law ∗ ∗ ∗ abridging the freedom of speech, or of the press." Some have stressed that no law means NO LAW. For example, Black, J., dissenting in *Konigsberg v. State Bar,* 366 U.S. 36, 81 S.Ct. 997, 6 L.Ed.2d 105 (1961) argued that the "First Amendment's unequivocal command ∗ ∗ ∗ shows that the men who drafted our Bill of Rights did all the 'balancing' that was to be done in this field."

Laws forbidding speech, however, are commonplace. Laws against perjury, blackmail, and fraud prohibit speech.[a] So does much of the law of contracts. Black, J., himself conceded that speech pursued as an integral part of criminal conduct was beyond first amendment protection. Indeed no one contends that citizens are free to say anything, anywhere, at any time. As Holmes, J., observed, citizens are not free to yell "fire" falsely in a crowded theater.

The spectre of a man crying fire falsely in the theater, however, has plagued first amendment theory. The task is to formulate principles that separate the protected from the unprotected. But speech interacts with too many other values in too many complicated ways to expect that a single formula will prove productive.

Are advocates of illegal action, pornographers selling magazines, or publishers of defamation like that person in the theater or are they engaged in freedom of speech? Do citizens have a right to speak on government property? Which property? Is there a right of access to the print or broadcast media? Can government force private owners to grant access for speakers? Does the first amendment offer protection for the wealthy, powerful corporations, and media conglomerates against government attempts to assure greater equality in the intellectual marketplace? Can government demand information about private political associations or reporters' confidential sources without first amendment limits? Does the first amendment require government to produce information it might otherwise withhold?

---

a. But see fn. b in *Roth v. United States,* p. 377 infra.

The Court has approached questions such as these without much attention to the language or history [b] of the first amendment and without a commitment to any general theory.[c] Rather it has sought to develop principles on a case-by-case basis and has produced a complex and conflicting body of constitutional precedent. Many of the basic principles were developed in a line of cases involving the advocacy of illegal action.[d]

I. ADVOCACY OF ILLEGAL ACTION

A. EMERGING PRINCIPLES

SCHENCK v. UNITED STATES, 249 U.S. 47, 39 S.Ct. 247, 63 L.Ed. 470 (1919): Defendants were convicted of a conspiracy to violate the 1917 Espionage Act by causing and attempting to cause insubordination in the armed forces of the United States, and obstruction of the recruiting and enlistment service of the United States, when at war with Germany, by printing and circulating to men accepted for military service approximately fifteen thousand copies of the document described in the opinion. In affirming, HOLMES, J., said for a unanimous Court:

"The document in question upon its first printed side recited the first section of the Thirteenth Amendment, said that the idea embodied in it was violated by the conscription act and that a conscript is little better than a convict. In impassioned language it intimated that conscription was despotism in its worst form and a monstrous wrong against humanity in the interest of Wall Street's chosen few. It said, 'Do not submit to intimidation,' but in form at least confined itself to peaceful measures such as a petition for the repeal of the act. The other and later printed side of the sheet was headed 'Assert Your Rights.' It stated reasons for alleging that any one violated the Constitution when he refused to recognize 'your right to assert your opposition to the draft,' and went on, 'If you do not assert and support your rights, you are helping to deny or disparage rights which it is the solemn duty of all citizens and residents of the United States to retain.' It described the arguments on the other side as coming from cunning politicians and a mercenary capitalist press, and even silent consent to the conscription law as helping to support an infamous conspiracy. It denied the power to send our citizens away to foreign shores to shoot up the people of other lands, and added that words could not express the condemnation such coldblooded ruthlessness deserves, &c., &c., winding up, 'You must do your

b. See, e.g., Perry, *The Constitution, The Courts, and Human Rights,* 63–64 (1982). For a variety of views about the history surrounding the adoption of the first amendment, compare Levy, *Legacy of Suppression* (1960) with Levy, *Emergence of a Free Press* (1985); Levy, *The Legacy Reexamined,* 37 Stan.L.Rev. 767 (1985); Levy, *On the Origins of the Free Press Clause,* 32 U.C.L.A.L.Rev. 177 (1984) and Anastaplo, *Book Review,* 39 N.Y.U.L.Rev. 735 (1964); Anderson, *The Origins of the Press Clause,* 30 U.C.L.A.L.Rev. 455 (1983); Hamburger, *The Development of the Law of Seditious Libel and the Control of the Press,* 37 Stan.L.Rev. 661 (1985); Mayton, *Seditious Libel and the Lost Guarantee of a Freedom of Expression,* 84 Colum.L.Rev. 91 (1984); Rabban, *The Ahistorical Historian: Leonard Levy on Freedom of Expression in Early American History,* 37 Stan.L.Rev. 795 (1985).

c. On the difficulties involved in developing general theory, see Alexander & Horton, *The Impossibility of a Free Speech Principle,* 78 Nw.U.L.Rev. 1319 (1983); Shiffrin, *The First Amendment and Economic Regulation: Away From a General Theory of the First Amendment,* 78 Nw.U.L.Rev. 1212 (1983); Tribe, *Toward A Metatheory of Free Speech,* 10 Sw.U.L.Rev. 237 (1978).

d. For discussion of the case law preceding *Schenck v. United States,* infra, see Rabban, *The First Amendment in Its Forgotten Years,* 90 Yale L.J. 514 (1981). A general history of free speech and suppression is much needed. For useful commentary see Chafee, *Free Speech in the United States* (1941); Whipple, *The Story of Civil Liberty in the United States* (1927); Kairys, *Freedom of Speech* in The Politics of Law 160 (Kairys ed. 1982).

share to maintain, support and uphold the rights of the people of this country.' Of course the document would not have been sent unless it had been intended to have some effect, and we do not see what effect it could be expected to have upon persons subject to the draft except to influence them to obstruct the carrying of it out. The defendants do not deny that the jury might find against them on this point.

"But it is said, suppose that that was the tendency of this circular, it is protected by the First Amendment to the Constitution. [We] admit that in many places and in ordinary times the defendants in saying all that was said in the circular would have been within their constitutional rights. But the character of every act depends upon the circumstances in which it is done. The most stringent protection of free speech would not protect a man in falsely shouting fire in a theatre and causing a panic. [The] question in every case is whether the words used are used in such circumstances and are of such a nature as to create a clear and present danger that they will bring about the substantive evils that Congress has a right to prevent. It is a question of proximity and degree.[a] When a nation is at war many things that might be said in time of peace are such a hindrance to its effort that their utterance will not be endured so long as men fight and that no Court could regard them as protected by any constitutional right. It seems to be admitted that if an actual obstruction of the recruiting service were proved, liability for words that produced that effect might be enforced. The statute of 1917 punishes conspiracies to obstruct as well as actual obstruction. If the act, (speaking, or circulating a paper), its tendency and the intent with which it is done are the same, we perceive no ground for saying that success alone warrants making the act a crime." [b]

DEBS v. UNITED STATES, 249 U.S. 211, 39 S.Ct. 252, 63 L.Ed. 566 (1919): Defendant was convicted of violating the Espionage Act for obstructing and attempting to obstruct the recruiting service and for causing and attempting to cause insubordination and disloyalty in the armed services. He was given a ten-year prison sentence on each count, to run concurrently. His criminal conduct consisted of giving the anti-war speech described in the opinion at the state convention of the Socialist Party of Ohio, held at a park in Canton, Ohio, on a

---

a. Although Schenck was convicted for violating a conspiracy statute, Holmes appears to have used the occasion to import the law of criminal attempts into the freedom of expression area. "In *Schenck*, 'clear and present danger,' 'a question of proximity and degree' bridged the gap between the defendant's acts of publication and the [prohibited interferences with the war.] This connection was strikingly similar to the Holmesian analysis of the requirement of 'dangerous proximity to success' [quoting from an earlier Holmes opinion] that, in the law of attempts, bridges the gap between the defendant's acts and the completed crime. In either context, innocuous efforts are to be ignored." Rogat, *Mr. Justice Holmes: Some Modern Views—The Judge as Spectator,* 31 U.Chi.L.Rev. 213, 215 (1964). See also Chafee, *Free Speech in the United States* 81–82 (1941); Shapiro, *Freedom of Speech* 55–58 (1966). But see Holmes, J., dissenting in *Abrams* infra, and fn. b below.

b. See also *Frohwerk v. United States,* 249 U.S. 204, 39 S.Ct. 249, 63 L.Ed. 561 (1919), where a unanimous Court, per Holmes, J., sustained a conviction for conspiracy to obstruct recruiting in violation of the Espionage Act, by means of a dozen newspaper articles praising the spirit and strength of the German nation, criticizing the decision to send American troops to France, maintaining that the government was giving false and hypocritical reasons for its course of action and implying that "the guilt of those who voted the unnatural sacrifice" is greater than the wrong of those who seek to escape by resistance: "[Schenck decided] that a person may be convicted of a conspiracy to obstruct recruiting by words of persuasion. [S]o far as the language of the articles goes there is not much to choose between expressions to be found in them and those before us in *Schenck*."

June 16, 1918 Sunday afternoon before a general audience of 1,200 persons. At the time of the speech, defendant was a national political figure.[a] In affirming, HOLMES, J., observed for a unanimous Court:

"The main theme of the speech was socialism, its growth, and a prophecy of its ultimate success. With that we have nothing to do, but if a part or the manifest intent of the more general utterances was to encourage those present to obstruct the recruiting service and if in passages such encouragement was directly given, the immunity of the general theme may not be enough to protect the speech. [Defendant had come to the park directly from a nearby jail, where he had visited three socialists imprisoned for obstructing the recruiting service. He expressed sympathy and admiration for these persons and others convicted of similar offenses, and then] said that the master class has always declared the war and the subject class has always fought the battles—that the subject class has had nothing to gain and all to lose, including their lives; [and that] 'You have your lives to lose; you certainly ought to have the right to declare war if you consider a war necessary.' [He next said of a woman serving a ten-year sentence for obstructing the recruiting service] that she had said no more than the speaker had said that afternoon; that if she was guilty so was [he].

"There followed personal experiences and illustrations of the growth of socialism, a glorification of minorities, and a prophecy of the success of [socialism], with the interjection that 'you need to know that you are fit for something better than slavery and cannon fodder.' [Defendant's] final exhortation [was] 'Don't worry about the charge of treason to your masters; but be concerned about the treason that involves yourselves.' The defendant addressed the jury himself, and while contending that his speech did not warrant the charges said 'I have been accused of obstructing the war. I admit it. Gentlemen, I abhor war. I would oppose the war if I stood alone.' The statement was not necessary to warrant the jury in finding that one purpose of the speech, whether incidental or not does not matter, was to oppose not only war in general but this war, and that the opposition was so expressed that its natural and intended effect would be to obstruct recruiting. If that was intended and if, in all the circumstances, that would be its probable effect, it would not be protected by reason of its being part of a general program and expressions of a general and conscientious belief.

"[Defendant's constitutional objections] based upon the First Amendment [were] disposed of in *Schenck*.

"[T]he admission in evidence of the record of the conviction [of various persons he mentioned in his speech was proper] to show what he was talking about, to explain the true import of his expression of sympathy and to throw light on the intent of the address. [Properly admitted, too, was an 'Anti-war Proclamation and Program' adopted the previous year, coupled with testimony that shortly before his speech defendant had stated that he approved it]. Its first recommendation was, 'continuous, active, and public opposition to the war, through demonstrations, mass petitions, and all other means within our power.' Evidence that the defendant accepted this view and this declaration of his duties at the time that he made his speech is evidence that if in that speech he used words tending to obstruct the recruiting service he meant that they should have

---

a. Debs had run for the Presidency on the Socialist ticket for the fourth time in 1912. At the 1920 election, while in prison, Debs ran again and received over 900,000 votes as the Socialist candidate, a significant portion of all votes cast in that election. Consider Kalven,

Ernst Freund and the First Amendment Tradition, 40 U.Chi.L.Rev. 235, 237 (1973): "To put the case in modern context, it is somewhat as though George McGovern had been sent to prison for his criticism of the [Vietnam] war."

that effect. [T]he jury were most carefully instructed that they could not find the defendant guilty for advocacy of any of his opinions unless the words used had as their natural tendency and reasonably probable effect to obstruct the recruiting service [and] unless the defendant had the specific intent to do so in his mind."

Notes and Questions

1. *Reflections.* (a) Consider Kalven, *Ernst Freund and the First Amendment Tradition,* 40 U.Chi.L.Rev. 235, 236–38 (1973): "It has been customary to lavish care and attention on the *Schenck* case, [but *Debs,* argued well before *Schenck* was handed down and decided just one week later,] represented the first effort by Justice Holmes to apply what he had worked out about freedom of speech in *Schenck.* The start of the law of the first amendment is not *Schenck;* it is *Schenck* and *Debs* read together. [Deb's speech] fell into the genre of bitter criticism of government and government policy, sometimes called seditious libel; freedom of such criticism from government marks, we have come to understand, 'the central meaning of the First Amendment' [*New York Times v. Sullivan,* p. 347 infra]. During the Vietnam War thousands of utterances strictly comparable in bitterness and sharpness of criticism, if not in literacy, were made; it was pretty much taken for granted they were beyond the reach of government.[b] [*Debs*] raises serious questions as to what the first amendment, and more especially, what the clear and present danger formula can possibly have meant at the time. [Holmes] does not comment on the fact difference between [*Schenck* and *Debs*]: the defendant in *Schenck* had sent his leaflets directly to men who awaited draft call whereas [*Debs*] was addressing a general audience at a public meeting. Holmes offers no discussion of the sense in which Debs's speech presented a clear and present danger. [In fact, *Debs*] did not move [Holmes] to discuss free speech at all; his brief opinion is occupied with two points about admissibility of [evidence]. It was for Holmes a routine criminal appeal."

(b) Chafee, *Free Speech in the United States* 85 (1941), observes: "Debs was convicted of an attempt to cause insubordination in the army and obstruct recruiting, yet no provocation to any such definite and particular acts was proved. [Not one word uttered by Debs] was designed for soldiers, not one word urged his hearers to resist the draft, objectionable as he considered it. Undoubtedly he admitted at his trial that he had obstructed the war, [but] the only question before the jury was whether he had tried to obstruct it in the ways made unlawful in the statute. If all verbal or written opposition to the war furnishes a basis for conviction, because it is dangerous under the circumstances and indicates a criminal mind, then none but the most courageous will dare speak out against a future war."

(c) Consider Freund, *The Debs Case and Freedom of Speech,* The New Republic, May 3, 1919, p. 13, reprinted in 40 U.Chi.L.Rev. 239, 240–41 (1973): "[*Debs*] illustrates most clearly the arbitrariness of the whole idea of implied provocation. A violent, if you please, a seditious speech is made; a docile jury finds a design to obstruct recruiting, and the finding is conclusive because the court does not consider it inconsistent with possibility. What are the intrinsic probabilities? An experienced speaker like Debs knows the effect of words. He must have known that while he might keep alive and even create disaffection, his power to create actual obstruction to a compulsory draft was practically nil,

b. Compare *Debs* with *Bond v. Floyd,* p. 338 infra.

and he could hardly have intended what he could not hope to achieve; in fact it is difficult to conceive of a form of obstruction that can be opposed to a compulsory draft.[c] [Yet] Holmes would make us believe that the relation of the speech to obstruction is like that of the shout of Fire! in a crowded theatre to the resulting panic! Surely implied provocation in connection with political offenses is an unsafe doctrine if it has to be made plausible by a parallel so manifestly inappropriate."

2. *"Breathing space" for free speech under the Espionage Act.* Consider Chafee, supra, at 50–51: "[With a few exceptions, notably Judge Learned Hand's opinion in *Masses,* infra, the lower federal courts] allowed conviction [under the Espionage Act] for any words which had an indirect effect to discourage recruiting and the war spirit [so long as] the intention to discourage existed. [Moreover, the] requirement of intention became a mere form since it could be inferred from the existence of the indirect injurious effect. [T]he words of the Espionage Act of 1917 bear slight resemblance to the Sedition Law of 1798, but the judicial construction is much the same, except that under the Sedition Law truth was a defense."

Consider Ernst Freund's criticism of *Debs,* supra at 240–41: "To know what you may do and what you may not do, and how far you may go in criticism, is the first condition of political liberty; to be permitted to agitate at your own peril, subject to a jury's guessing at motive, tendency and possible effect, makes the right of free speech a precarious gift. [For] arbitrary executive, [the Espionage Act] practically substitutes arbitrary, judicial power; since a jury's findings, within the limits of a conceivable psychological nexus between words and deeds, are beyond scrutiny and control; and while the jury may have been a protection against governmental power when the government was a thing apart from the people, its checking function fails where government policies are supported by majority opinion." See also Chafee, supra, at 70: "[As a federal judge] said after much experience in Espionage Act cases: '[I] tried war cases before jurymen [who] under ordinary circumstances would have had the highest respect for my declarations of law, but during that period they looked back into my eyes with the savagery of wild animals, saying by their manner, "Away with the twiddling, let us get at him." Men believed during that period that the only verdict in a war case, which could show loyalty, was a verdict of guilty.' "

Holmes, J.'s response, in private correspondence, see Ginsburg, *Afterword,* 40 U.Chi.L.Rev. 243, 245 (1973), to Professor Freund's objection, in his article on *Debs,* to a jury "guessing at motive, tendency and possible effect" was that this could be said about "pretty much the whole body of the law, which for thirty years I have made my brethren smile by insisting to be everywhere a matter of degree." Holmes recalled the comment he made in a case involving a criminal prosecution under the Sherman Act that "the law is full of instances where a man's fate depends on his estimating rightly, that is, as the jury subsequently estimates it, some matter of degree. If his judgment is wrong, not only may he incur a fine or [prison term, but] the penalty of death."

3. Would a construction of the Espionage Act which punished "direct advocacy" of violations of existing laws or "direct counselling" of others to do so, but protected other antiwar discussion or agitation, be more "workable" than the clear and present danger test of *Schenck* and *Debs*? More consistent with the first amendment? Preferable to the clear and present danger test reiterated

c. See also Nelles, *Espionage Act Cases* 77–80 (1918).

(clarified, revised) in the *Abrams* dissent, infra? Could a jury pass on the *actual nature of the words used* by a speaker much better than it could the "tendency" and "effects" of his words? Moreover, would a standard which focused on the nature of the words not only give the jury something definite to consider but be more easily understood by the opponents of the war? See Chafee, supra, at 42–45, 63, praising the approach taken by "that judge who during the war gave the fullest attention to the meaning of free speech," Learned Hand in *Masses*, set forth below—two years before the Espionage Act reached the Supreme Court. To what extent is Hand's test, which avoids the clear and present danger formula, reflected decades later in *Yates, Scales* and *Noto*, p. 330 infra? In *Brandenburg*, p. 338 infra? In *Bond v. Floyd*, p. 338 infra? In the First Circuit's opinion in the *Spock* case, p. 337 infra?

4. MASSES PUBLISHING CO. v. PATTEN, 244 F. 535 (S.D.N.Y.1917): The Postmaster of New York advised plaintiff that an issue of his monthly revolutionary journal, *The Masses*, would be denied the mails under the Espionage Act since it tended to encourage the enemies of the United States and to hamper the government in its conduct of the war. The Postmaster subsequently specified as objectionable several cartoons entitled, e.g., "Conscription," "Making the World Safe for Capitalism"; several articles admiring the "sacrifice" of conscientious objectors and a poem praising two persons imprisoned for conspiracy to resist the draft. Plaintiff sought a preliminary injunction against the postmaster from excluding its magazine from the mails. LEARNED HAND, D.J., granted relief:

"[The postmaster maintains] that to arouse discontent and disaffection among the people with the prosecution of the war and with the draft tends to promote a mutinous and insubordinate temper among the troops. This [is] true; men who become satisfied that they are engaged in an enterprise dictated by the unconscionable selfishness of the rich, and effectuated by a tyrannous disregard for the will of those who must suffer and die, will be more prone to insubordination than those who have faith in the cause and acquiesce in the means. Yet to interpret the word 'cause' [in the statutory language forbidding one to 'willfully cause' insubordination in the armed forces] so broadly would [necessarily involve] the suppression of all hostile criticism, and of all opinion except what encouraged and supported the existing policies, or which fell within the range of temperate argument. It would contradict the normal assumption of democratic government that the suppression of hostile criticism does not turn upon the justice of its substance or the decency and propriety of its temper. Assuming that the power to repress such opinion may rest in Congress in the throes of a struggle for the very existence of the state, its exercise is so contrary to the use and wont of our people that only the clearest expression of such a power justifies the conclusion that it was intended.

"The defendant's position, therefore, in so far as it involves the suppression of the free utterance of abuse and criticism of the existing law, or of the policies of the war, is not, in my judgment, supported by the language of the statute. Yet there has always been a recognized limit to such expressions, incident indeed to the existence of any compulsive power of the state itself. One may not counsel or advise others to violate the law as it stands. Words are not only the keys of persuasion, but the triggers of action, and those which have no purport but to counsel the violation of law cannot by any latitude of interpretation be a part of that public opinion which is the final source of government in a democratic state. [To] counsel or advise a man to an act is to urge upon him either that it is his interest or his duty to do it. While, of course, this may be accomplished as well by indirection as expressly, since words carry the meaning that they impart, the definition is exhaustive, I think, and I shall use it. Political agitation, by the passions it arouses or the convictions it engenders, may in fact stimulate men to the violation of law. Detestation of existing policies is easily transformed into forcible resistance of the authority which puts them in execution, and it would be folly to disregard the causal relation between the two. Yet to assimilate agitation, legitimate as such, with direct incitement to violent resistance, is to disregard the tolerance of all methods of political agitation which in normal times is a safeguard of free government. The distinction is not a scholastic subterfuge, but a hard-bought acquisition in the fight for freedom, and the purpose to disregard it must be evident when the power exists. If one stops short of urging upon others that it is their duty or their interest to resist the law, it seems to me one should not be held to have attempted to cause its violation. If that be not the test, I can see no escape from the conclusion that under this section every political agitation which can be shown to be apt to create a seditious temper is illegal. I am confident that by such language Congress had no such revolutionary purpose in view.

"It seems to me, however, quite plain that none of the language and none of the cartoons in this paper can be thought directly to counsel or advise insubordination or mutiny, without a violation of their meaning quite beyond any tolerable understanding. I come, therefore to the [provision of the Act forbidding] any one from willfully obstructing [recruiting or enlistment]. I am not prepared to assent to the plaintiff's position that this only refers to acts other than words, nor that the act thus defined must be shown to have been successful. One may obstruct without preventing, and the mere obstruction is an injury to the service; for it throws impediments in its way. Here again, however, since the question is of the expression of opinion, I construe the sentence, so far as it restrains public utterance, [as] limited to the direct advocacy of resistance to the recruiting and enlistment service. If so, the inquiry is narrowed to the question whether any of the challenged matter may be said to advocate resistance to the draft, taking the meaning of the words with the utmost latitude which they can bear.

"As to the cartoons it seems to me quite clear that they do not fall within such a test. [T]he most that can be said [is that they] may breed such animosity to the draft as will promote resistance and strengthen the determination of those disposed to be recalcitrant. There is no intimation that, however, hateful the draft may be, one is in duty bound to resist it, certainly none that such resistance is to one's interest. I cannot, therefore, even with the limitations which surround the power of the court, assent to the assertion that any of the cartoons violate the act.

"[As for the text], it is plain enough that the [magazine] has the fullest sympathy for [those who resist the draft or obstruct recruiting], that it admires their courage, and that it presumptively approves their conduct. [Moreover,] these passages, it must be remembered, occur in a magazine which attacks with the utmost violence the draft and the war. That such comments have a tendency to arouse emulation in others is clear enough, but that they counsel others to follow these examples is not so plain. Literally at least they do not, and while, as I have said, the words are to be taken, not literally, but according to their full import, the literal meaning is the starting point for interpretation. One may admire and approve the course of a hero without feeling any duty to follow him. There is not the least implied intimation in these words that others are under a duty to follow. The most that can be said is that, if others do follow, they will get the same admiration and the same approval. Now, there is surely an appreciable distance between esteem and emulation; and unless there is here some advocacy of such emulation, I cannot see how the passages can be said to fall within the [law.] Surely, if the draft had not excepted Quakers, it would be too strong a doctrine to say that any who openly admire their fortitude or even approved their conduct was willfully obstructing the draft.

"When the question is of a statute constituting a crime, it seems to me that there should be more definite evidence of the act. The question before me is quite the same as what would arise upon a motion to dismiss an indictment at the close of the proof: Could any reasonable man say, not that the indirect result of the language might be to arouse a seditious disposition, for that would not be enough, but that the language directly advocated resistance to the draft? I cannot think that upon such language any verdict would stand." [d]

What result if the Court had applied the *Masses* test in *Schenck* or *Debs*? In *Abrams* or *Gitlow,* infra?

JUSTICE HOLMES—DISSENTING IN ABRAMS v. UNITED STATES

250 U.S. 616, 624, 40 S.Ct. 17, 20, 63 L.Ed. 1173, 1178 (1919).

[In the summer of 1918, the United States sent a small body of marines to Siberia. Although the defendants maintained a strong socialist opposition to "German militarism," they opposed the "capitalist" invasion of Russia, and characterized it as an attempt to crush the Russian Revolution. Shortly thereafter, they printed two leaflets and distributed several thousand copies in New York City. Many of the copies were thrown from a window where one defendant was employed; others were passed around at radical meetings. Both leaflets supported Russia against the United States; one called upon workers to unite in a general strike. There was no evidence that workers responded to the call.

[The Court upheld the defendants' convictions for conspiring to violate two provisions of the 1918 amendments to the Espionage Act. One count prohibited language intended to "incite, provoke and encourage resistance to the United States"; the other punished those who urged curtailment of war production. As the Court interpreted the statute, an intent to interfere with efforts against a *declared* war was a necessary element of both offenses. Since the United States had not declared war upon Russia, "the main task of the government was to establish an [*intention*] to interfere with the war with Germany." Chafee, supra, at 115. The Court found intent on the principle that "Men must be held to have intended, and to be accountable for, the effects which their acts were likely to produce. Even if their primary purpose and intent was to aid the cause of the Russian Revolution, the plan of action which they adopted necessarily involved, before it could be realized, defeat of the war program of the United States * * *."

[HOLMES, J., dissented in an opinion with which Brandeis, J., concurred:]

[I] am aware of course that the word "intent" as vaguely used in ordinary legal discussion means no more than knowledge at the time of the act that the

d. In reversing, 246 Fed. 24 (1917), the Second Circuit observed: "If the natural and probable effect of what is said is to encourage resistance to a law, and the words are used in an endeavor to persuade to resistance, it is immaterial that the duty to resist is not mentioned, or the interest of the person addressed in resistance is not suggested. That one may willfully obstruct the enlistment service, without advising in direct language against enlistments, and without stating that to refrain from enlistment is a duty or in one's interest, seems to us too plain for controversy."

consequences said to be intended will ensue. [But,] when words are used exactly, a deed is not done with intent to produce a consequence unless that consequence is the aim of the deed. It may be obvious, and obvious to the actor, that the consequence will follow, and he may be liable for it even if he regrets it, but he does not do the act with intent to produce it unless the aim to produce it is the proximate motive of the specific act although there may be some deeper motive behind.

It seems to me that this statute must be taken to use its words in a strict and accurate sense. They would be absurd in any other. A patriot might think that we were wasting money on aeroplanes, or making more cannon of a certain kind than we needed, and might advocate curtailment with success, yet even if it turned out that the curtailment hindered and was thought by other minds to have been obviously likely to hinder the United States in the prosecution of the war, no one would hold such conduct a crime.   *   *   *

I never have seen any reason to doubt that the questions of law that alone were before this Court in the cases of *Schenck, Frohwerk* and *Debs* were rightly decided. I do not doubt for a moment that by the same reasoning that would justify punishing persuasion to murder, the United States constitutionally may punish speech that produces or is intended to produce a clear and imminent danger that it will bring about forthwith certain substantive evils that the United States constitutionally may seek to prevent. The power undoubtedly is greater in time of war than in time of peace because war opens dangers that do not exist at other times.

But as against dangers peculiar to war, as against others, the principle of the right to free speech is always the same. It is only the present danger of immediate evil or an intent to bring it about that warrants Congress in setting a limit to the expression of opinion where private rights are not concerned. Congress certainly cannot forbid all effort to change the mind of the country. Now nobody can suppose that the surreptitious publishing of a silly leaflet by an unknown man, without more, would present any immediate danger that its opinions would hinder the success of the government arms or have any appreciable tendency to do so.[a] Publishing those opinions for the very purpose of obstructing, however, might indicate a greater danger and at any rate would have the quality of an attempt.[b]   *   *   *

a. See also Chafee, supra, at 140: "The maximum sentence available against a formidable pro-German plot [20 years] was meted out [for] the silly, futile circulars of five obscure and isolated young aliens, misguided by their loyalty to their endangered country and ideals, who hatched their wild scheme in a garret, and carried it out in a cellar." But cf. Wigmore, *Abrams v. U.S.: Freedom of Speech and Freedom of Thuggery in War-Time and Peace-Time*, 14 Ill.L.Rev. 539, 549–50 (1920): "[The *Abrams* dissent] is dallying with the facts and the law. None know better than judges that what is lawful for one is lawful for a thousand others. If these five men could, without the law's restraint, urge munition workers to a general strike and armed violences then others could lawfully do so; and a thousand disaffected undesirables, aliens and natives alike, were ready and waiting to do so. Though this circular was 'surreptitious,' the next ones need not be so. If such urgings were lawful, every munitions factory in the country could be stopped by them. The relative amount of harm that one criminal act can effect is no measure of its criminality, and no measure of the danger of its criminality. To put forward such a palliation is merely to reveal more clearly the indifference to the whole crisis. [At a time] when the fate of the civilized world hung in the balance, how could the Minority Opinion interpret law and conduct in such a way as to let loose men who were doing their hardest to paralyze the supreme war efforts of our country?"

b. Would it, if, under the circumstances, the defendant had no reasonable prospect of success? If his efforts were utterly ineffectual? Is bad intention or purpose, without more, an attempt? Or even everything done in furtherance of that bad intention? Or is unlawful "intention" or "purpose" merely one factor in determining whether defendant's

I do not see how anyone can find the intent required by the statute in any of the defendants' words. The leaflet advocating a general strike is the only one that affords even a foundation for the charge, and [its only object] is to help Russia and stop American intervention there against the popular government—not to impede the United States in the war that it was carrying on. * * *

In this case sentences of twenty years imprisonment have been imposed for the publishing of two leaflets that I believe the defendants had as much right to publish as the Government has to publish the Constitution of the United States now vainly invoked by them. [E]ven if what I think the necessary intent were shown; the most nominal punishment seems to me all that possibly could be inflicted, unless the defendants are to be made to suffer not for what the indictment alleges but for the creed that they avow—[which,] although made the subject of examination at the trial, no one has a right even to consider in dealing with the charges before the Court.

Persecution for the expression of opinions seems to me perfectly logical. If you have no doubt of your premises or your power and want a certain result with all your heart you naturally express your wishes in law and sweep away all opposition. To allow opposition by speech seems to indicate that you think the speech impotent, as when a man says that he has squared the circle, or that you do not care whole-heartedly for the result, or that you doubt either your power or your premises. But when men have realized that time has upset many fighting faiths, they may come to believe even more than they believe the very foundations of their own conduct that the ultimate good desired is better reached by free trade in ideas—that the best test of truth is the power of the thought to get itself accepted in the competition of the market, and that truth is the only ground upon which their wishes safely can be carried out.[c] That at any rate is the theory of our Constitution. It is an experiment, as all life is an experiment. Every year if not every day we have to wager our salvation upon some prophecy based upon imperfect knowledge. While that experiment is part of our system I

conduct comes dangerously near success or stamps the actor as sufficiently dangerous? Cf. Holmes, *The Common Law* 65–66, 68–69 (1881): "Intent to commit a crime is not itself criminal. [Moreover], the law does not punish every act which is done with the intent to bring about a crime. [We] have seen what amounts to an attempt to burn a haystack [lighting a match with intent to start fire to a haystack]; but it was said in the same case, that, if the defendant had gone no further than to buy a box of matches for the purpose, he would not have been liable. [Relevant considerations are] the nearness of the danger, the greatness of the harm and the degree of apprehension felt." See also Holmes, C.J., in *Commonwealth v. Peaslee*, 177 Mass. 267, 59 N.E. 55 (1901) ("if the preparation comes very near to the accomplishment of the act, the intent to complete it renders the crime so probable" that the conduct will constitute an attempt); Holmes, J., dissenting in *Hyde v. United States*, 255 U.S. 347, 387, 32 S.Ct. 793, 56 L.Ed. 1114 (1912) (preliminary acts become an attempt when "so near to the result [completed crime] that if coupled with an intent to produce that result, the danger is very great"). See generally Chafee, supra, at 46–47; Linde,

"Clear and Present Danger" Reexamined, 22 Stan.L.Rev. 1163, 1168–69, 1183–86 (1970); Shapiro, *Freedom of Speech* 55–58 (1966).

c. But see Wigmore, fn. a supra, at 550–51: "This apotheosis of Truth, however, shows a blindness to the deadly fact that meantime the 'power of the thought' of these circulars might 'get itself accepted in the competition of the market,' by munitions workers, so as to lose the war; in which case, the academic victory which Truth, 'the ultimate good,' might later secure in the market, would be too 'ultimate' to have any practical value for a defeated America. [To] weigh in juxtaposition the dastardly sentiments of these circulars and the great theme of world-justice for which [we were fighting], and then to assume the sacred cause of Truth as equally involved in both, is to misuse high ideals. This [dissenting opinion, if it had commanded a majority], would have ended by our letting soldiers die helpless in France, through our anxiety to protect the distribution of a leaflet whose sole purpose was to cut off the soldiers' munitions and supplies. How would this have advanced the cause of Truth?"

think that we should be eternally vigilant against attempts to check the expression of opinions that we loathe and believe to be fraught with death, unless they so imminently threaten immediate interference with the lawful and pressing purposes of the law that an immediate check is required to save the country. [Only] the emergency that makes it immediately dangerous to leave the correction of evil counsels to time warrants making any exception to the sweeping command, "Congress shall make no law * * * abridging the freedom of speech." Of course I am speaking only of expressions of opinion and exhortations, which were all that were uttered [here].

Notes and Questions

1. *"Marketplace of ideas."* (a) Contrast Holmes' statement of the "marketplace of ideas" argument with John Milton's statement in *Areopagitica:* "And though all the winds of doctrine were let loose to play upon the earth, so Truth be in the field, we do injuriously by licensing and prohibiting to misdoubt her strength. Let her and Falsehood grapple; who ever knew Truth put to the worse, in a free and open encounter?" Holmes claims that the competition of the market is the best test of truth; Milton maintains that truth will emerge in a free and open encounter. How would one verify either hypothesis?

Is the "marketplace of ideas" a "free and open encounter"? Consider Lindblom, *Politics and Markets* 207 (1977): "Early, persuasive, unconscious conditioning—[to] believe in the fundamental politico-economic institutions of one's society is ubiquitous in every society. These institutions come to be taken for granted. Many people grow up to regard them not as institutions to be tested but as standards against which the correctness of new policies and institutions can be tested. When that happens, as is common, processes of critical judgment are short-circuited." Consider also Tribe, *American Constitutional Law* 577 (1978): "Especially when the wealthy have more access to the most potent media of communication than the poor, how sure can we be that 'free trade in ideas' is likely to generate truth?"

For a specific example, see Shiffrin, *The First Amendment and Economic Regulation: Away From A General Theory of the First Amendment,* 78 Nw.U.L. Rev. 1212, 1281 (1983): "Living in a society in which children and adults are daily confronted with multiple communications that ask them to purchase products inevitably places emphasis on materialistic values. The authors of the individual messages may not intend that general emphasis, but the whole is greater than the sum of the parts. [Advertisers] spend some sixty billion dollars per year. [Those] who would oppose the materialist message must combat forces that have a massive economic advantage. Any confidence that we will know what is truth by seeing what emerges from such combat is ill placed."

Do the different market failure considerations offered by Lindblom, Tribe, and Shiffrin add up to a rebuttal of the marketplace argument? Consider *Nimmer on Freedom of Speech* 1–12 (1984): "If acceptance of an idea in the competition of the market is not the 'best test' [what] is the alternative? It can only be acceptance of an idea by some individual or group narrower than that of the public at large. Thus, the alternative to competition in the market must be some form of elitism. It seems hardly necessary to enlarge on the dangers of that path." Is elitism the only alternative to the marketplace perspective? Is elitism always wrong?

(b) Evaluate the following hypothetical commentary: "Liberals have favored government intervention in the economic marketplace but pressed for laissez-faire in the intellectual marketplace. Conservatives have done the reverse. Liberals and conservatives have one thing in common: inconsistent positions."

(c) Does the marketplace argument overvalue truth? Consider Schauer, *Free Speech: A Philosophical Enquiry* 23 (1982). Government may seek to suppress opinions "because their expression is thought to impair the authority of a lawful and effective government, interfere with the administration of justice (such as publication of a defendant's criminal record in advance of a jury trial), cause offence, invade someone's privacy, or cause a decrease in public order. When these are the motives for suppression, the possibility of losing some truth is relevant but hardly dispositive. [In such circumstances] the argument from truth [is] not wholly to the point." Is Holmes persuasive when he maintains that before we can suppress opinion we must wait until "an immediate check is required to save the country"?

(d) Does the marketplace argument threaten first amendment values? Consider Ingber, *The Marketplace of Ideas: A Legitimizing Myth*, 1984 Duke L.J. 1, 4–5 "[C]ourts that invoke the marketplace model of the first amendment justify free expression because of the aggregate benefits to society, and not because an individual speaker receives a particular benefit. Courts that focus their concern on the audience rather than the speaker relegate free expression to an instrumental value, a means toward some other goal, rather than a value unto itself. Once free expression is viewed solely as an instrumental value, however, it is easier to allow government regulation of speech if society as a whole 'benefits' from a regulated system of expression."

(e) Does the marketplace argument slight other important free speech values? Consider Wolff, *The Poverty of Liberalism* 18 (1968) "[I]t is not to assist the advance of knowledge that free debate is needed. Rather, it is in order to guarantee that every legitimate interest shall make itself known and felt in the political [process]. Justice, not truth, is the ideal served by liberty of speech." Compare Chevigny, *Philosophy of Language and Free Expression*, 55 N.Y.U.L. Rev. 157 (1980); Leitner, *Liberalism, Separation and Speech*, 1985 Wis.L.Rev. 79, 89–90 & 103–04. See also Shiffrin, *Liberalism, Radicalism, and Legal Scholarship*, 30 U.C.L.A.L.Rev. 1103, 1197–98 (1983): "Freedom of speech [is] associated with a multiplicity of more general moral rights and interests that are valuable, including, but not limited to, individual self-expression, social communion, political participation, the search for truth and for informed choice, social catharsis, the social affirmation of the rights of equality, dignity, and respect, and the freedom from arbitrary, official aggrandizing or excessively intrusive government regulation." The standard starting place for discussion of free speech values continues to be Emerson, *The System of Freedom of Expression* 6–9 (1970).

(f) For a powerful critique of marketplace models, see Baker, *Scope of the First Amendment Freedom of Speech*, 25 U.C.L.A.L.Rev. 964 (1978). For an analytical defense, albeit heavily qualified, see Schauer, *Language, Truth, and the First Amendment*, 64 Va.L.Rev. 263 (1978).

2. In *Schenck*, did the Court ask whether the particular speech interfered with some specific phase of the war effort or whether a *category* of speech *could* interfere with the war effort? In *Abrams*, what did Holmes, J., dissenting, ask? In *Schenck*, did the Court seek to ascertain the speaker's actual intent as one of the factors surrounding the speech which bear on whether a clear and present danger exists or did it simply infer the intent from the general tendency of the speech? In *Abrams*, what did Holmes, J., dissenting, try to do? See Shapiro, *Freedom of Speech* 48–49 (1966).

3. Why did *Abrams,* but not *Debs,* stir Holmes to speak seriously and eloquently about freedom of speech? One suggestion is that "Holmes was biding his time until the Court should have before it a conviction so clearly wrong as to let him speak out his deepest thoughts about the First Amendment" and that "the opportunity [came] eight months after Debs went to prison, in *Abrams,*" Chafee, supra, at 86. For the view that the criticism of *Debs* in both the Ernst Freund article and in Learned Hand's correspondence with Holmes may have contributed to a marked change in Holmes' thinking about the first amendment between *Debs* and *Abrams,* see Ginsburg, *Afterword,* 40 U.Chi.L.Rev. 243 (1973). The literature on Holmes' first amendment views and their connection to his larger world view is substantial. See, e.g., Rogat & O'Fallon, *Mr. Justice Holmes: A Dissenting Opinion—The Speech Cases,* 36 Stan.L.Rev. 1349 (1984); Rabban, *The Emergence of Modern First Amendment Doctrine,* 50 U.Chi.L.Rev. 1205 (1983). For further analysis of the Holmes-Hand correspondence, see Gunther, *Learned Hand and the Origins of Modern First Amendment Doctrine: Some Fragments of History,* 27 Stan.L.Rev. 719 (1975).

B. STATE SEDITION LAWS

The second main group of cases in the initial development of first amendment doctrine involved state "sedition laws" of two basic types: criminal anarchy laws, typified by the New York statute in *Gitlow,* infra, and criminal syndicalism laws similar to the California statute in *Whitney,* infra. Most states enacted anarchy and syndicalism statutes between 1917 and 1921, in response to World War I and the fear of Bolshevism that developed in its wake, but the first modern sedition law was passed by New York in 1902, soon after the assassination of President McKinley. The law, which prohibited not only actual or attempted assassinations or conspiracies to assassinate, but advocacy of anarchy as well, lay idle for nearly twenty years, until the *Gitlow* prosecution.

GITLOW v. NEW YORK, 268 U.S. 652, 45 S.Ct. 625, 69 L.Ed. 1138 (1925): Defendant was a member of the Left Wing Section of the Socialist Party and a member of its National Council, which adopted a "Left Wing Manifesto," condemning the dominant "moderate Socialism" for its recognition of the necessity of the democratic parliamentary state; advocating the necessity of accomplishing the "Communist Revolution" by a militant and "revolutionary Socialism" based on "the class struggle"; and urging the development of mass political strikes for the destruction of the parliamentary state. Defendant arranged for printing and distributing, through the mails and otherwise, 16,000 copies of the Manifesto in the Left Wing's official organ, The Revolutionary Age. There was no evidence of any effect from the publication and circulation of the Manifesto.

In sustaining a conviction under the New York "criminal anarchy" statutes, prohibiting the "advocacy, advising or teaching the duty, necessity or propriety of overthrowing or overturning organized government by force or violence" and the publication or distribution of such matter, the majority, per SANFORD, J., stated that for present purposes we may and do assume [a] that first amendment freedoms of expression "are among the fundamental personal rights and 'liber-

---

a. Although *Gitlow* is often cited for the proposition that first amendment freedoms apply to restrict state conduct, its language is dictum. Some would say the first case so holding is *Fiske v. Kansas,* 274 U.S. 380, 47 S.Ct. 655, 71 L.Ed. 1108 (1927) (no evidence to support criminal syndicalism conviction) even though no reference to the first amendment appears in the opinion. See Chafee at 352. Perhaps the honor belongs to *Near v. Minnesota* (1931), p. 473 infra.

ties' protected by the due process clause of the Fourteenth Amendment from impairment by the States," but ruled:

"By enacting the present statute the State has determined, through its legislative body, that utterances advocating the overthrow of organized government by force, violence and unlawful means, are so inimical to the general welfare and involve such danger of substantive evil that they may be penalized in the exercise of its police power. That determination must be given great weight. Every presumption is to be indulged in favor of the validity of the statute. And the case is to be considered 'in the light of the principle that the State is primarily the judge of regulations required in the interest of public safety and welfare'; and that its police 'statutes may only be declared unconstitutional where they are arbitrary or unreasonable attempts to exercise authority vested in the State in the public interest.' That utterances inciting to the overthrow of organized government by unlawful means, present a sufficient danger of substantive evil to bring their punishment within the range of legislative discretion, is clear. Such utterances, by their very nature, involve danger to the public peace and to the security of the State. They threaten breaches of the peace and ultimate revolution. And the immediate danger is none the less real and substantial, because the effect of a given utterance cannot be accurately foreseen. The State cannot reasonably be required to measure the danger from every such utterance in the nice balance of a jeweler's scale. A single revolutionary spark may kindle a fire that, smoldering for a time, may burst into a sweeping and destructive conflagration. It cannot be said that the State is acting arbitrarily or unreasonably when in the exercise of its judgment as to the measures necessary to protect the public peace and safety, it seeks to extinguish the spark without waiting until it has enkindled the flame or blazed into the conflagration. It cannot reasonably be required to defer the adoption of measures for its own peace and safety until the revolutionary utterances lead to actual disturbances of the public peace or imminent and immediate danger of its own destruction; but it may, in the exercise of its judgment, suppress the threatened danger in its incipiency.[b]

"[It] is clear that the question in [this case] is entirely different from that involved in those cases where the statute merely prohibits certain acts involving the danger of substantive evil, without any reference to language itself, and it is sought to apply its provisions to language used by the defendant for the purpose of bringing about the prohibited results. There, if it be contended that the statute cannot be applied to the language used by the defendant because of its protection by the freedom of speech or press, it must necessarily be found, as an original question, without any previous determination by the legislative body, whether the specific language used involved such likelihood of bringing about

---

b. See also Bork, *Neutral Principles and Some First Amendment Problems*, 47 Ind.L.J. 1, 33 (1971): "To his point that proof of the effect of speech is inherently unavailable and yet its impact may be real and dangerous, Sanford might have added that the legislature is not confined to consideration of a single instance of speech or a single speaker. It fashions a rule to dampen thousands of instances of forcible overthrow advocacy. Cumulatively these may have enormous influence, and yet it may well be impossible to show any effect from any single example. The 'clear and present danger' requirement [is improper] because it erects a barrier to legislative rule where none should exist. The speech concerned has no political value within a republican system of government. Whether or not it is prudent to ban advocacy of forcible overthrow and law violation is a different [question]. Because the judgment is tactical, implicating the safety of the nation, it resembles very closely the judgment that Congress and the President must make about the expediency of waging war, an issue that the Court has wisely thought not fit for judicial determination."

the substantive evil as to deprive it of the constitutional protection. In such cases it has been held that the general provisions of the statute may be constitutionally applied to the specific utterance of the defendant if its natural tendency and probable effect was to bring about the substantive evil which the legislative body might prevent. *Schenck; Debs.* And the general statement in the *Schenck* case that the 'question in every case is whether the words are used in such circumstances and are of such a nature as to create a clear and present danger that they will bring about the substantive evils,' [was] manifestly intended, as shown by the context, to apply only in cases of this class, and has no application to those like the present, where the legislative body itself has previously determined the danger of substantive evil arising from utterances of a specified character."

HOLMES, J., joined by Brandeis, J., dissented: "The general principle of free speech, it seems to me, must be taken to be included in the Fourteenth Amendment, in view of the scope that has been given to the word 'liberty' as there used, although perhaps it may be accepted with a somewhat larger latitude of interpretation than is allowed to Congress by the sweeping language that governs or ought to govern the laws of the United States. If I am right then I think that the criterion sanctioned by the full Court in *Schenck* applies. [It] is true that in my opinion this criterion was departed from in *Abrams,* but the convictions that I expressed in that case are too deep for it to be possible for me as yet to believe that it [has] settled the law. If what I think the correct test is applied it is manifest that there was no present danger of an attempt to overthrow the government by force on the part of the admittedly small minority who shared the defendant's views. It is said that this manifesto was more than a theory, that it was an incitement. Every idea is an incitement. It offers itself for belief and if believed it is acted on unless some other belief outweighs it or some failure of energy stifles the movement at its birth. The only difference between the expression of an opinion and an incitement in the narrower sense is the speaker's enthusiasm for the result. Eloquence may set fire to reason. But whatever may be thought of the redundant discourse before us it had no chance of starting a present conflagration. If in the long run the beliefs expressed in proletarian dictatorship are destined to be accepted by the dominant forces of the community, the only meaning of free speech is that they should be given their chance and have their way.

"If the publication of this document had been laid as an attempt to induce an uprising against government at once and not at some indefinite time in the future it would have presented a different question. The object would have been one with which the law might deal, subject to the doubt whether there was any danger that the publication could produce any result, or in other words, whether it was not futile and too remote from possible consequences. But the indictment alleges the publication and nothing more."

Notes and Questions

1. *What if in the long run the belief in genocide is destined to be accepted?* Consider Bickel, *The Morality of Consent* 72 (1975): "[Although, in *Gitlow*, he saw no clear and present danger, Holmes] did admit that all ideas carried the seed of future dangers as well as benefits. His answer was this: 'If in the long run the beliefs expressed in proletarian dictatorships are destined to be accepted [, the] only meaning of free speech [—*the only*—] is that they should be given their chance and have their way.' If in the long run the belief, let us say, in

genocide is destined to be accepted [, the] only meaning of free speech is that it should be given its chance and have its way. Do we believe that? Do we accept it?" But consider Wellington, *On Freedom of Expression*, 88 Yale L.J. 1105, 1142 (1979): "The state cannot prevent advocacy [of genocide] on the ground that individuals will come to believe this false doctrine. But when there is a clear and present danger of action, the state must have the power to stop advocacy. [It] remains unfortunately imaginable that genocide could be implemented in a secular democracy: the state—including the courts—could be captured by a coalition of sick and evil minorities. But I do not believe that more restrictive control of expression would prevent such a catastrophe: unlike his cruelty, man's laws do have effective limits."

2. The statute in *Schenck* was not aimed directly at expression, but at conduct, i.e., certain actual or attempted interferences with the war effort. Thus, an analysis in terms of proximity between the words and the conduct prohibited (by a concededly valid law) seemed useful. But in *Gitlow* (and in *Dennis*, p. 319 infra) the statute was directed expressly against *advocacy* of a certain doctrine. Once the legislature *designates the point at which words became unlawful*, how helpful is the clear and present danger test? Is the question still how close words come to achieving certain consequences? In *Gitlow*, did Holmes "evade" the difficulty of applying an unmodified *Schenck* test to a different kind of problem? See Rogat, *Mr. Justice Holmes: Some Modern Views—The Judge as Spectator*, 31 U.Chi.L.Rev. 213, 217 (1964). See also Berns, *Freedom, Virtue and the First Amendment* 63 (Gateway ed. 1965); Linde, *"Clear and Present Danger" Reexamined*, 22 Stan.L.Rev. 1163, 1169–79 (1970).

3. Evaluate the following hypothetical commentary: "*Gitlow*'s abandonment of clear and present danger was insignificant because *Schenck*'s reference to clear and present danger was toothless. *Schenck* made no effort to prove that the defendant's communication presented a genuine danger. Rather the assumption (followed in *Debs* and *Abrams*) was that any communication intended to encourage resistance to a war was unprotected speech. *Gitlow*'s real significance was that it applied a war policy during a time of peace."

4. Consider Linde, supra, at 1171: "Since New York's law itself defined the prohibited speech, the [*Gitlow*] Court could choose among three positions. It could (1) accept this legislative judgment of the harmful potential of the proscribed words, subject to conventional judicial review; (2) independently scrutinize the facts to see whether a 'danger,' as stated in *Schenck*, justified suppression of the particular expression; or (3) hold that by legislating directly against the words rather than the effects, the lawmaker had gone beyond the leeway left to trial and proof by the holding in *Schenck* and had made a law forbidden by the first amendment." Which course did the *Gitlow* majority choose? The dissenters? Which position should the Court have chosen?

Cases such as *Whitney*, infra, raise questions not only about freedom of speech, but also about the right of assembly. In turn, *Whitney* raises the issue of the existence and scope of a right not mentioned in the first amendment: freedom of association. Freedom of association, together with its connections to speech and assembly is explored in Sec. 9 infra. Several of the cases which follow are primarily characterized as speech cases because the assemblies or associations at issue were designed for the purpose of organizing future speech activity.

WHITNEY v. CALIFORNIA

274 U.S. 357, 47 S.Ct. 641, 71 L.Ed. 1095 (1927).

MR. JUSTICE SANFORD delivered the opinion of the Court.

[Charlotte Anita Whitney was convicted of violating the 1919 Criminal Syndicalism Act of California whose pertinent provisions were]:

"Section 1. The term 'criminal syndicalism' as used in this act is hereby defined as any doctrine or precept advocating, teaching or aiding and abetting the commission of crime, sabotage (which word is hereby defined as meaning willful and malicious physical damage or injury to physical property), or unlawful acts of force and violence or unlawful methods of terrorism as a means of accomplishing a change in industrial ownership or control, or effecting any political change.

"Sec. 2. Any person who: * * * 4. Organizes or assists in organizing, or is or knowingly becomes a member of, any organization, society, group or assemblage of persons organized or assembled to advocate, teach or aid and abet criminal syndicalism; * * *

"Is guilty of a felony and punishable by imprisonment."

The first count of the information, on which the conviction was had, charged that on or about November 28, 1919, in Alameda County, the defendant, in violation of the Criminal Syndicalism Act, "did then and there unlawfully, willfully, wrongfully, deliberately and feloniously organize and assist in organizing, and was, is, and knowingly became a member of [a group] organized and assembled to advocate, teach, aid and abet criminal syndicalism." * * *

1. While it is not denied that the evidence warranted the jury in finding that the defendant became a member of and assisted in organizing the Communist Labor Party of California, and that this was organized to advocate, teach, aid or abet criminal syndicalism as defined by the Act, it is urged that the Act, as here construed and applied, deprived the defendant of her liberty without due process of law. [Defendant's] argument is, in effect, that the character of the state organization could not be forecast when she attended the convention; that she had no purpose of helping to create an instrument of terrorism and violence; that she "took part in formulating and presenting to the convention a resolution which, if adopted, would have committed the new organization to a legitimate policy of political reform by the use of the ballot"; that it was not until after the majority of the convention turned out to be "contrary minded, and other less temperate policies prevailed" that the convention could have taken on the character of criminal syndicalism; and that as this was done over her protest, her mere presence in the convention, however violent the opinions expressed therein, could not thereby become a crime. This contention [is in effect] an effort to review the weight of the evidence for the purpose of showing that the defendant did not join and assist in organizing the Communist Labor Party of California with a knowledge of its unlawful character and purpose. This question, which is foreclosed by the verdict of the jury, [is] one of fact merely which is not open to review in this Court, involving as it does no constitutional question whatever. * * *

[That a state] may punish those who abuse [freedom of speech] by utterances inimical to the public welfare, tending to incite to crime, disturb the public peace, or endanger the foundations of organized government and threaten its overthrow by unlawful means, is not open to question. [Gitlow].

The essence of the offense denounced by the Act is the combining with others in an association for the accomplishment of the desired ends through the advocacy and use of criminal and unlawful methods. It partakes of the nature of a criminal conspiracy. That such united and joint action involves even greater danger to the public peace and security than the isolated utterances and acts of individuals is clear. We cannot hold that, as here applied, the Act is an unreasonable or arbitrary exercise of the police power of the State, unwarrantably infringing any right of free speech, assembly or association, or that those persons are protected from punishment by the due process clause who abuse such rights by joining and furthering an organization thus menacing the peace and welfare of the State. * * *

Affirmed.

MR. JUSTICE BRANDEIS (concurring.) * * *

The felony which the statute created is a crime very unlike the old felony of conspiracy or the old misdemeanor of unlawful assembly. The mere act of assisting in forming a society for teaching syndicalism, of becoming a member of it, or assembling with others for that purpose is given the dynamic quality of crime. There is guilt although the society may not contemplate immediate promulgation of the doctrine. Thus the accused is to be punished, not for attempt, incitement or conspiracy, but for a step in preparation, which, if it threatens the public order at all, does so only remotely. The novelty in the prohibition introduced is that the statute aims, not at the practice of criminal syndicalism, nor even directly at the preaching of it, but at association with those who propose to preach it.

Despite arguments to the contrary which had seemed to me persuasive, it is settled that the due process clause of the Fourteenth Amendment applies to matters of substantive law as well as to matters of procedure. Thus all fundamental rights comprised within the term liberty are protected by the federal Constitution from invasion by the states. The right of free speech, the right to teach and the right of assembly are, of course, fundamental rights. These may not be denied or abridged. But, although the rights of free speech and assembly are fundamental, they are not in their nature absolute. Their exercise is subject to restriction, if the particular restriction proposed is required in order to protect the state from destruction or from serious injury, political, economic or moral. That the necessity which is essential to a valid restriction does not exist unless speech would produce, or is intended to produce,[a] a clear and imminent danger of some substantive evil which the state constitutionally may seek to prevent has been settled. See *Schenck.*

[The] Legislature must obviously decide, in the first instance, whether a danger exists which calls for a particular protective measure. But where a statute is valid only in case certain conditions exist, the enactment of the statute cannot alone establish the facts which are essential to its validity. Prohibitory legislation has repeatedly been held invalid, because unnecessary, where the denial of liberty involved was that of engaging in a particular business. The powers of the courts to strike down an offending law are no less when the interests involved are not property rights, but the fundamental personal rights of free speech and assembly.

a. Unless speech would produce, *or* is intended to produce? Unless speech *would produce* a clear and imminent danger, although the harm produced was neither advocated nor intended by the speaker? Unless the speaker *intended* to produce a clear and imminent danger, even under extrinsic conditions of actual harmlessness? Compare *Brandenburg v. Ohio,* p. 338 infra. See generally Linde, supra, at 1168–69, 1181, 1185.

CARNEGIE LIBRARY
LIVINGSTONE COLLEGE
SALISBURY, NC 28144

This Court has not yet fixed the standard by which to determine when a danger shall be deemed clear; how remote the danger may be and yet be deemed present; and what degree of evil shall be deemed sufficiently substantial to justify resort to abridgment of free speech and assembly as the means of protection. To reach sound conclusions on these matters, we must bear in mind why a state is, ordinarily, denied the power to prohibit dissemination of social, economic and political doctrine which a vast majority of its citizens believes to be false and fraught with evil consequence.

Those who won our independence believed that the final end of the state was to make men free to develop their faculties, and that in its government the deliberative forces should prevail over the arbitrary. They valued liberty both as an end and as a means. They believed liberty to be the secret of happiness and courage to be the secret of liberty. They believed that freedom to think as you will and to speak as you think are means indispensable to the discovery and spread of political truth; that without free speech and assembly discussion would be futile; that with them, discussion affords ordinarily adequate protection against the dissemination of noxious doctrine; that the greatest menace to freedom is an inert people; that public discussion is a political duty; and that this should be a fundamental principle of the American government. They recognized the risks to which all human institutions are subject. But they knew that order cannot be secured merely through fear of punishment for its infraction; that it is hazardous to discourage thought, hope and imagination; that fear breeds repression; that repression breeds hate; that hate menaces stable government; that the path of safety lies in the opportunity to discuss freely supposed grievances and proposed remedies; and that the fitting remedy for evil counsels is good ones. Believing in the power of reason as applied through public discussion, they eschewed silence coerced by law—the argument of force in its worst form. Recognizing the occasional tyrannies of governing majorities, they amended the Constitution so that free speech and assembly should be guaranteed.

Fear of serious injury cannot alone justify suppression of free speech and assembly. Men feared witches and burnt women. It is the function of speech to free men from the bondage of irrational fears. To justify suppression of free speech there must be reasonable ground to fear that serious evil will result if free speech is practiced. There must be reasonable ground to believe that the danger apprehended is imminent. There must be reasonable ground to believe that the evil to be prevented is a serious one.[b] Every denunciation of existing law tends in some measure to increase the probability that there will be violation of it. Condonation of a breach enhances the probability. Expressions of approval add to the probability. Propagation of the criminal state of mind by teaching syndicalism increases it. Advocacy of lawbreaking heightens it still further. But even advocacy of violation, however reprehensible morally, is not a justification for denying free speech where the advocacy falls short of incitement and there is nothing to indicate that the advocacy would be immediately acted on. The wide difference between advocacy and incitement, between preparation and attempt, between assembling and conspiracy, must be borne in mind. In order to support a finding of clear and present danger it must be shown either that immediate serious violence was to be expected or was advocated,[c] or that

---

b. Does this suffice, regardless of the intent of the speaker? Regardless of the nature of the words he uses?

c. What if violence is advocated, but the advocacy is utterly ineffectual? What if the speaker neither desires nor advocates vio-

LIVINGSTONE COLLEGE
SALISBURY, NC 28144

the past conduct furnished reason to believe that such advocacy was then contemplated.

Those who won our independence by revolution were not cowards. They did not fear political change. They did not exalt order at the cost of liberty. To courageous, self-reliant men, with confidence in the power of free and fearless reasoning applied through the processes of popular government, no danger flowing from speech can be deemed clear and present, unless the incidence of the evil apprehended is so imminent that it may befall before there is opportunity for full discussion. If there be time to expose through discussion the falsehood and fallacies, to avert the evil by the processes of education, the remedy to be applied is more speech, not enforced silence. Only an emergency can justify repression. Such must be the rule if authority is to be reconciled with freedom. Such, in my opinion, is the command of the Constitution. It is therefore always open to Americans to challenge a law abridging free speech and assembly by showing that there was no emergency justifying it.

Moreover, even imminent danger cannot justify resort to prohibition of these functions essential to effective democracy, unless the evil apprehended is relatively serious. Prohibition of free speech and assembly is a measure so stringent that it would be inappropriate as the means for averting a relatively trivial harm to society. A police measure may be unconstitutional merely because the remedy, although effective as means of protection, is unduly harsh or oppressive. Thus, a state might, in the exercise of its police power, make any trespass upon the land of another a crime, regardless of the results or of the intent or purpose of the trespasser. It might, also, punish an attempt, a conspiracy, or an incitement to commit the trespass. But it is hardly conceivable that this court would hold constitutional a statute which punished as a felony the mere voluntary assembly with a society formed to teach that pedestrians had the moral right to cross uninclosed, unposted, waste lands and to advocate their doing so, even if there was imminent danger that advocacy would lead to a trespass. The fact that speech is likely to result in some violence or in destruction of property is not enough to justify its suppression. There must be the probability of serious injury to the State.[d] Among free men, the deterrents ordinarily to be applied to prevent crime are education and punishment for violations of the law, not abridgement of the rights of free speech and assembly.

* * * Whenever the fundamental rights of free speech and assembly are alleged to have been invaded, it must remain open to a defendant to present the issue whether there actually did exist at the time a clear danger, whether the danger, if any, was imminent, and whether the evil apprehended was one so substantial as to justify the stringent restriction interposed by the Legislature. The legislative declaration, like the fact that the statute was passed and was sustained by the highest court of the State, creates merely a rebuttable presumption that these conditions have been satisfied.

Whether in 1919, when Miss Whitney did the things complained of, there was in California such clear and present danger of serious evil, might have been made the important issue in the case. She might have required that the issue be

lence, but, under the circumstances the speech nevertheless is "expected" to produce violence?

d. But see Bork, *Neutral Principles and Some First Amendment Problems,* 47 Ind.L.J. 1, 34 (1971): "It is difficult to see how a constitutional court could properly draw the distinction proposed. Brandeis offered no analysis to show that advocacy of law violation merited protection by the Court. Worse, the criterion he advanced is the importance, in the judge's eye, of the law whose violation is urged."

determined either by the court or the jury. She claimed below that the statute as applied to her violated the federal Constitution; but she did not claim that it was void because there was no clear and present danger of serious evil, nor did she request that the existence of these conditions of a valid measure thus restricting the rights of free speech and assembly be passed upon by the court or a jury. On the other hand, there was evidence on which the court or jury might have found that such danger existed. I am unable to assent to the suggestion in the opinion of the court that assembling with a political party, formed to advocate the desirability of a proletarian revolution by mass action at some date necessarily far in the future, is not a right within the protection of the Fourteenth Amendment. In the present case, however, there was other testimony which tended to establish the existence of a conspiracy, on the part of members of the International Workers of the World, to commit present serious crimes, and likewise to show that such a conspiracy would be furthered by the activity of the society of which Miss Whitney was a member. Under these circumstances the judgment of the State court cannot be disturbed. * * *

MR. JUSTICE HOLMES joins in this opinion.[e]

Notes and Questions

1. *"They valued liberty both as an end and as a means."* Should recognition of the value of liberty[f] as an end augment the marketplace perspective or replace it? Compare Baker, *Scope of the First Amendment Freedom of Speech,* 25 U.C.L.A.L.Rev. 964 (1978) (liberty theory should replace marketplace theory) with Redish, *The Value of Free Speech,* 130 U.Pa.L.Rev. 591 (1982) (self-realization should be regarded as the first amendment's exclusive value) and Shiffrin, *The First Amendment and Economic Regulation: Away From a General Theory of the First Amendment,* 78 Nw.U.L.Rev. 1212 (1983) (many values including liberty and self-realization underpin the first amendment; single valued orientations are reductionist). But see Schauer, *Must Speech Be Special,* 78 Nw.U.L. Rev. 1284 (1983) (neither liberty nor self-realization should play *any* role in first amendment theory).

2. *Scope of the opinions.* Did Brandeis, J., simply reaffirm the clear and present danger test? Significantly clarify it? Significantly change it? Did Sanford, J., modify the position he had taken in *Gitlow*? Did he at least make it plain in *Whitney* that some state sedition convictions may be set aside under the first and fourteenth amendments? See Chafee, supra, at 351.

3. Ten years after *Whitney, DeJonge v. Oregon,* 299 U.S. 353, 57 S.Ct. 255, 81 L.Ed. 278 (1937) held that mere participation in a meeting called by the Communist party could not be made a crime. The right of peaceable assembly was declared to be "cognate to those of free speech and free press and is equally fundamental."

---

e. For background concerning the views of Brandeis and Holmes, JJ., and the relationship between those views and democratic theory generally, see Cover, *The Left, The Right and the First Amendment: 1919–28,* 40 Md.L. Rev. 349 (1981).

f. For discussion of the value of autonomy and its connection to the problem of advocacy of illegal action, compare Scanlon, *A Theory of Freedom of Expression,* 1 Philosophy & Pub. Aff. 204 (1972) with Scanlon, *Freedom of Expression and Categories of Expression,* 40 U.Pitt.L.Rev. 519 (1979).

C. COMMUNISM AND ILLEGAL ADVOCACY

Kent Greenawalt has well described the pattern of decisions for much of the period between *Whitney* and *Dennis* infra: "[T]he clear and present danger formula emerged as the applicable standard not only for the kinds of issues with respect to which it originated but also for a wide variety of other First Amendment problems. If the Court was not always very clear about the relevance of that formula to those different problems, its use of the test, and its employment of ancillary doctrines, did evince a growing disposition to protect expression." *Speech and Crime,* 1980 Am.B.Found.Res.J. 645, 706. By 1951, however, anti-communist sentiment was a powerful theme in American politics. The Soviet Union had detonated a nuclear weapon; communists had firm control of the Chinese mainland; the Korean War had reached a stalemate; Alger Hiss had been convicted of perjury in congressional testimony concerning alleged spying activities for the Soviet Union while he was a State Department official; and Senator Joseph McCarthy of Wisconsin had created a national sensation by accusations that many "card carrying Communists" held important State Department jobs. In this context, the top leaders of the American Communist Party asked the Court to reverse their criminal conspiracy convictions.

DENNIS v. UNITED STATES
341 U.S. 494, 71 S.Ct. 857, 95 L.Ed. 1137 (1951).

MR. CHIEF JUSTICE VINSON announced the judgment of the Court and an opinion in which MR. JUSTICE REED, MR. JUSTICE BURTON and MR. JUSTICE MINTON join.

Petitioners were indicted in July, 1948, for violation of the conspiracy provisions of the Smith Act during the period of April, 1945, to July, 1948. * * * A verdict of guilty as to all the petitioners was [affirmed by the Second Circuit]. We granted certiorari, limited to the following two questions: (1) Whether either § 2 or § 3 of the Smith Act, inherently or as construed and applied in the instant case, violates the First Amendment and other provisions of the Bill of Rights; (2) whether either § 2 or § 3 of the Act, inherently or as construed and applied in the instant case, violates the First and Fifth Amendments, because of indefiniteness.

Sections 2 and 3 of the Smith Act provide as follows:

"Sec. 2.

"(a) It shall be unlawful for any person—

"(1) to knowingly or willfully advocate, abet, advise, or teach the duty, necessity, desirability, or propriety of overthrowing or destroying any government in the United States by force or violence, or by the assassination of any officer of any such government; * * *

"Sec. 3. It shall be unlawful for any person to attempt to commit, or to conspire to commit, any of the acts prohibited by the provisions [of] this title."

The indictment charged the petitioners with wilfully and knowingly conspiring (1) to organize as the Communist Party of the United States of America a society, group and assembly of persons who teach and advocate the overthrow and destruction of the Government of the United States by force and violence, and (2) knowingly and wilfully to advocate and teach the duty and necessity of overthrowing and destroying the Government of the United States by force and violence. The indictment further alleged that § 2 of the Smith Act proscribes these acts and that any conspiracy to take such action is a violation of § 3 of the Act.

The trial of the case extended over nine months, six of which were devoted to the taking of evidence, resulting in a record of 16,000 pages. Our limited grant of the writ of certiorari has removed from our consideration any question as to the sufficiency of the evidence to support the jury's determination that petitioners are guilty of the offense charged. Whether on this record petitioners did in fact advocate the overthrow of the Government by force and violence is not before us, and we must base any discussion of this point upon the conclusions stated in the opinion of the Court of Appeals, which treated the issue in great detail [and] held that the record supports the following broad conclusions: [that] the Communist Party is a highly disciplined organization, adept at infiltration into strategic positions, use of aliases, and double-meaning language; that the Party is rigidly controlled; that Communists, unlike other political parties, tolerate no dissension from the policy laid down by the guiding [forces]; that the literature of the Party and the statements and activities of its leaders, petitioners here, advocate, and the general goal of the Party was, during the period in question, to achieve a successful overthrow of the existing order by force and violence. * * *

The obvious purpose of the statute is to protect existing Government, not from change by peaceable, lawful and constitutional means, but from change by violence, revolution and terrorism. That it is within the *power* of the Congress to protect the Government of the United States from armed rebellion is a proposition which requires little discussion. Whatever theoretical merit there may be to the argument that there is a "right" to rebellion against dictatorial governments is without force where the existing structure of the government provides for peaceful and orderly change. We reject any principle of governmental helplessness in the face of preparation for revolution, which principle, carried to its logical conclusion, must lead to anarchy. No one could conceive that it is not within the power of Congress to prohibit acts intended to overthrow the Government by force and violence. The question with which we are concerned here is not whether Congress has such *power*, but whether the *means* which it has employed conflict with the First and Fifth Amendments to the Constitution.

One of the bases for the contention that the means which Congress has employed are invalid takes the form of an attack on the face of the statute on the grounds that by its terms it prohibits academic discussion of the merits of Marxism-Leninism, that it stifles ideas and is contrary to all concepts of a free speech and a free press. [This] is a federal statute which we must interpret as well as judge. Herein lies the fallacy of reliance upon the manner in which this Court has treated judgments of state courts. Where the statute as construed by the state court transgressed the First Amendment, we could not but invalidate the judgments of conviction.

The very language of the Smith Act negates the interpretation which petitioners would have us impose on that Act. It is directed at advocacy, not discussion. Thus, the trial judge properly charged the jury that they could not convict if they found that petitioners did "no more than pursue peaceful studies and discussions or teaching and advocacy in the realm of ideas." * * * Congress did not intend to eradicate the free discussion of political theories, to destroy the traditional rights of Americans to discuss and evaluate ideas without fear of governmental sanction. * * *

But although the statute is not directed at the hypothetical cases which petitioners have conjured, its application in this case has resulted in convictions for the teaching and advocacy of the overthrow of the Government by force and violence, which, even though coupled with the intent to accomplish that overthrow, contains an element of speech. For this reason, we must pay special heed to the demands of the First Amendment marking out the boundaries of speech.

[T]he basis of the First Amendment is the hypothesis that speech can rebut speech, propaganda will answer propaganda, free debate of ideas will result in the wisest governmental policies. [An] analysis of the leading cases in this Court which have involved direct limitations on speech, however, will demonstrate that both the majority of the Court and the dissenters in particular cases have recognized that this is not an unlimited, unqualified right, but that the societal value of speech must, on occasion, be subordinated to other values and considerations. * * *

Although no case subsequent to *Whitney* and *Gitlow* has expressly overruled the majority opinions in those cases, there is little doubt that subsequent opinions have inclined toward the Holmes-Brandeis rationale. * * *

In this case we are squarely presented with the application of the "clear and present danger" test, and must decide what that phrase imports. We first note that many of the cases in which this Court has reversed convictions by use of this or similar tests have been based on the fact that the interest which the State was attempting to protect was itself too insubstantial to warrant restriction of speech. * * * Overthrow of the Government by force and violence is certainly a substantial enough interest for the Government to limit speech. Indeed, this is the ultimate value of any society, for if a society cannot protect its very structure from armed internal attack, it must follow that no subordinate value can be protected. If, then, this interest may be protected, the literal problem which is presented is what has been meant by the use of the phrase "clear and present danger" of the utterances bringing about the evil within the power of Congress to punish.

Obviously, the words cannot mean that before the Government may act, it must wait until the putsch is about to be executed, the plans have been laid and the signal is awaited. If Government is aware that a group aiming at its overthrow is attempting to indoctrinate its members and to commit them to a course whereby they will strike when the leaders feel the circumstances permit, action by the Government is required. The argument that there is no need for Government to concern itself, for Government is strong, it possesses ample powers to put down a rebellion, it may defeat the revolution with ease needs no answer. For that is not the question. Certainly an attempt to overthrow the Government by force, even though doomed from the outset because of inadequate numbers or power of the revolutionists, is a sufficient evil for Congress to prevent. The damage which such attempts create both physically and politically to a nation makes it impossible to measure the validity in terms of the probability of success, or the immediacy of a successful attempt. In the instant case the trial judge charged the jury that they could not convict unless they found that petitioners intended to overthrow the Government "as speedily as circumstances would permit." This does not mean, and could not properly mean, that they would not strike until there was certainty of success. What was meant was that the revolutionists would strike when they thought the time was ripe. We must therefore reject the contention that success or probability of success is the criterion.

The situation with which Justices Holmes and Brandeis were concerned in *Gitlow* was a comparatively isolated event, bearing little relation in their minds to any substantial threat to the safety of the community. [They] were not confronted with any situation comparable to the instant one—the development of an apparatus designed and dedicated to the overthrow of the Government, in the context of world crisis after crisis.

Chief Judge Learned Hand, writing for the majority below, interpreted the phrase as follows: "In each case [courts] must ask whether the gravity of the 'evil,' discounted by its improbability, justifies such invasion of free speech as is necessary to avoid the danger." We adopt this statement of the rule. As articulated by Chief Judge Hand, it is as succinct and inclusive as any other we might devise at this time. * * *

Likewise, we are in accord with the court below, which affirmed the trial court's finding that the requisite danger existed. The mere fact that from the period 1945 to 1948 petitioners' activities did not result in an attempt to overthrow the Government by force and violence is of course no answer to the fact that there was a group that was ready to make the attempt. The formation by petitioners of such a highly organized conspiracy, with rigidly disciplined members subject to call when the leaders, these petitioners, felt that the time had come for action, coupled with the inflammable nature of world conditions, similar uprisings in other countries, and the touch-and-go nature of our relations with countries with whom petitioners were in the very least ideologically attuned, convince us that their convictions were justified on this score. And this analysis disposes of the contention that a conspiracy to advocate, as distinguished from the advocacy itself, cannot be constitutionally restrained, because it comprises only the preparation. It is the existence of the conspiracy which creates the danger. * * *

Although we have concluded that the finding that there was a sufficient danger to warrant the application of the statute was justified on the merits, there remains the problem of whether the trial judge's treatment of the issue was correct. He charged the jury, in relevant part, as follows:

"In further construction and interpretation of the statute I charge you that it is not the abstract doctrine of overthrowing or destroying organized government by unlawful means which is denounced by this law, but the teaching and advocacy of action for the accomplishment of that purpose, by language reasonably and ordinarily calculated to incite persons to such action. Accordingly, you cannot find the defendants or any of them guilty of the crime charged unless you are satisfied beyond a reasonable doubt that they conspired to organize a society, group and assembly of persons who teach and advocate the overthrow or destruction of the Government of the United States by force and violence and to advocate and teach the duty and necessity of overthrowing or destroying the Government of the United States by force and violence, with the intent that such teaching and advocacy be of a rule or principle of action and by language reasonably and ordinarily calculated to incite persons to such action, all with the intent to cause the overthrow or destruction of the Government of the United States by force and violence as speedily as circumstances would permit. * * *

"If you are satisfied that the evidence establishes beyond a reasonable doubt that the defendants, or any of them, are guilty of a violation of the statute, as I have interpreted it to you, I find as matter of law that there is sufficient danger of a substantive evil that the Congress has a right to prevent to justify the application of the statute under the First Amendment of the Constitution. This is matter of law about which you have no concern. ＊ ＊ ＊ "

It is thus clear that he reserved the question of the existence of the danger for his own determination, and the question becomes whether the issue is of such a nature that it should have been submitted to the jury.

[When] facts are found that establish the violation of a statute, the protection against conviction afforded by the First Amendment is a matter of law. The doctrine that there must be a clear and present danger of a substantive evil that Congress has a right to prevent is a judicial rule to be applied as a matter of law by the courts. The guilt is established by proof of facts. Whether the First Amendment protects the activity which constitutes the violation of the statute must depend upon a judicial determination of the scope of the First Amendment applied to the circumstances of the case.

[In] *Schenck* this Court itself examined the record to find whether the requisite danger appeared, and the issue was not submitted to a jury. And in every later case in which the Court has measured the validity of a statute by the "clear and present danger" test, that determination has been by the court, the question of the danger not being submitted to the jury. ＊ ＊ ＊ Petitioners intended to overthrow the Government of the United States as speedily as the circumstances would permit. Their conspiracy to organize the Communist Party and to teach and advocate the overthrow of the Government of the United States by force and violence created a "clear and present danger" of an attempt to overthrow the Government by force and violence. They were properly and constitutionally convicted ＊ ＊ ＊.

Affirmed.

MR. JUSTICE CLARK took no part in the consideration or decision of this case.

MR. JUSTICE FRANKFURTER, concurring in affirmance of the judgment.

[The] demands of free speech in a democratic society as well as the interest in national security are better served by candid and informed weighing of the competing interests, within the confines of the judicial process, than by announcing dogmas too inflexible for the non-Euclidian problems to be solved.

But how are competing interests to be assessed? Since they are not subject to quantitative ascertainment, the issue necessarily resolves itself into asking, who is to make the adjustment?—who is to balance the relevant factors and ascertain which interest is in the circumstances to prevail? Full responsibility for the choice cannot be given to the courts. Courts are not representative bodies. They are not designed to be a good reflex of a democratic society. Their judgment is best informed, and therefore most dependable, within narrow limits. Their essential quality is detachment, founded on independence. History teaches that the independence of the judiciary is jeopardized when courts become embroiled in the passions of the day and assume primary responsibility in choosing between competing political, economic and social pressures.

Primary responsibility for adjusting the interests which compete in the situation before us of necessity belongs to the Congress. [We] are to set aside the judgment of those whose duty it is to legislate only if there is no reasonable basis for [it]. Free-speech cases are not an exception to the principle that we are not legislators, that direct policy-making is not our province. How best to reconcile competing interests is the business of legislatures, and the balance they strike is a judgment not to be displaced by ours, but to be respected unless outside the pale of fair judgment. [A] survey of the relevant decisions indicates that the results which we have reached are on the whole those that would ensue from careful weighing of conflicting interests. The complex issues presented by regulation of speech in public places by picketing, and by legislation prohibiting advocacy of crime have been resolved by scrutiny of many factors besides the imminence and gravity of the evil threatened. The matter has been well summarized by a reflective student of the Court's work. "The truth is that the clear-and-present-danger test is an oversimplified judgment unless it takes account also of a number of other factors: the relative seriousness of the danger in comparison with the value of the occasion for speech or political activity; the availability of more moderate controls than those which the state has imposed; and perhaps the specific intent with which the speech or activity is launched. No matter how rapidly we utter the phrase 'clear and present danger,' or how closely we hyphenate the words, they are not a substitute for the weighing of values. They tend to convey a delusion of certitude when what is most certain is the complexity of the strands in the web of freedoms which the judge must disentangle." Freund, *On Understanding the Supreme Court* 27–28 [1949].

* * *

To make validity of legislation depend on judicial reading of events still in the womb of time—a forecast, that is, of the outcome of forces at best appreciated only with knowledge of the topmost secrets of nations—is to charge the judiciary with duties beyond its equipment. * * *

Even when moving strictly within the limits of constitutional adjudication, judges are concerned with issues that may be said to involve vital finalities. The too easy transition from disapproval of what is undesirable to condemnation as unconstitutional, has led some of the wisest judges to question the wisdom of our scheme in lodging such authority in courts. But it is relevant to remind that in sustaining the power of Congress in a case like this nothing irrevocable is done. The democratic process at all events is not impaired or restricted. Power and responsibility remain with the people and immediately with their representation. All the Court says is that Congress was not forbidden by the Constitution to pass this enactment and that a prosecution under it may be brought against a conspiracy such as the one before us. * * *

MR. JUSTICE JACKSON, concurring.

[E]ither by accident or design, the Communist strategem outwits the antianarchist pattern of statute aimed against "overthrow by force and violence" if qualified by the doctrine that only "clear and present danger" of accomplishing that result will sustain the prosecution.

The "clear and present danger" test was an innovation by Mr. Justice Holmes in the *Schenck* case, reiterated and refined by him and Mr. Justice Brandeis in later cases, all arising before the era of World War II revealed the subtlety and efficacy of modernized revolutionary techniques used by totalitarian parties. In those cases, they were faced with convictions under so-called criminal syndicalism statutes aimed at anarchists but which, loosely construed, had been applied to punish socialism, pacifism, and left-wing ideologies, the charges often resting on farfetched inferences which, if true, would establish only technical or trivial violations. They proposed "clear and present danger" as a test for the sufficiency of evidence in particular cases.

I would save it, unmodified, for application as a "rule of reason" in the kind of case for which it was devised. When the issue is criminality of a hotheaded speech on a street corner, or circulation of a few incendiary pamphlets, or parading by some zealots behind a red flag, or refusal of a handful of school children to salute our flag, it is not beyond the capacity of the judicial process to gather, comprehend, and weigh the necessary materials for decision whether it is a clear and present danger of substantive evil or a harmless letting off of steam. It is not a prophecy, for the danger in such cases has matured by the time of trial or it was never present. The test applies and has meaning where a conviction is sought to be based on a speech or writing which does not directly or explicitly advocate a crime but to which such tendency is sought to be attributed by construction or by implication from external circumstances. The formula in such cases favors freedoms that are vital to our society, and, even if sometimes applied too generously, the consequences cannot be grave. But its recent expansion has extended, in particular to Communists, unprecedented immunities. Unless we are to hold our Government captive in a judge-made verbal trap, we must approach the problem of a well-organized, nation-wide conspiracy, such as I have described, as realistically as our predecessors faced the trivialities that were being prosecuted until they were checked with a rule of reason.

I think reason is lacking for applying that test to this case.

If we must decide that this Act and its application are constitutional only if we are convinced that petitioner's conduct creates a "clear and present danger" of violent overthrow, we must appraise imponderables, including international and national phenomena which baffle the best informed foreign offices and our most experienced politicians. We would have to foresee and predict the effectiveness of Communist propaganda, opportunities for infiltration, whether, and when, a time will come that they consider propitious for action, and whether and how fast our existing government will deteriorate. And we would have to speculate as to whether an approaching Communist coup would not be anticipated by a nationalistic fascist movement. No doctrine can be sound whose application requires us to make a prophecy of that sort in the guise of a legal decision. The judicial process simply is not adequate to a trial of such far-flung issues. The answers given would reflect our own political predilections and nothing more.

The authors of the clear and present danger test never applied it to a case like this, nor would I. If applied as it is proposed here, it means that the Communist plotting is protected during its period of incubation; its preliminary stages of organization and preparation are immune from the law; the Government can move only after imminent action is manifest, when it would, of course, be too late.

The highest degree of constitutional protection is due to the individual acting without conspiracy. But even an individual cannot claim that the Constitution protects him in advocating or teaching overthrow of government by force or violence. I should suppose no one would doubt that Congress has power to make such attempted overthrow a crime. But the contention is that one has the constitutional right to work up a public desire and will to do what it is a crime to attempt. I think direct incitement by speech or writing can be made a crime, and I think there can be a conviction without also proving that the odds favored its success by 99 to 1, or some other extremely high ratio. * * *

What really is under review here is a conviction of conspiracy, after a trial for conspiracy, on an indictment charging conspiracy, brought under a statute outlawing conspiracy. With due respect to my colleagues, they seem to me to discuss anything under the sun except the law of conspiracy. * * *

The Constitution does not make conspiracy a civil right. [Although] I consider criminal conspiracy a dragnet device capable of perversion into an instrument of injustice in the hands of a partisan or complacent judiciary, it has an established place in our system of law, and no reason appears for applying it only to concerted action claimed to disturb interstate commerce and withholding it from those claimed to undermine our whole Government. * * *

I do not suggest that Congress could punish conspiracy to advocate something, the doing of which it may not punish. Advocacy or exposition of the doctrine of communal property ownership, or any political philosophy unassociated with advocacy of its imposition by force or seizure of government by unlawful means could not be reached through conspiracy prosecution. But it is not forbidden to put down force or violence, it is not forbidden to punish its teaching or advocacy, and the end being punishable, there is no doubt of the power to punish conspiracy for the purpose. * * *

MR. JUSTICE BLACK, dissenting. * * *

So long as this Court exercises the power of judicial review of legislation, I cannot agree that the First Amendment permits us to sustain laws suppressing freedom of speech and press on the basis of Congress' or our own notions of mere "reasonableness." Such a doctrine waters down the First Amendment so that it amounts to little more than an admonition to Congress. The Amendment as so construed is not likely to protect any but those "safe" or orthodox views which rarely need its protection. I must also express my objection to the holding because, as Mr. Justice Douglas' dissent shows, it sanctions the determination of a crucial issue of fact by the judge rather than by the jury. * * *

Public opinion being what it now is, few will protest the conviction of these Communist petitioners. There is hope, however, that in calmer times, when present pressures, passions and fears subside, this or some later Court will restore the First Amendment liberties to the high preferred place where they belong in a free society.

MR. JUSTICE DOUGLAS, dissenting.

If this were a case where those who claimed protection under the First Amendment were teaching the techniques of sabotage, the assassination of the President, the filching of documents from public files, the planting of bombs, the art of street warfare, and the like, I would have no doubts. The freedom to speak is not absolute; the teaching of methods of terror and other seditious conduct should be beyond the pale along with obscenity and immorality. This case was argued as if those were the facts. The argument imported much seditious conduct into the record. That is easy and it has popular appeal, for the activities of Communists in plotting and scheming against the free world are common knowledge. But the fact is that no such evidence was introduced at the trial. There is a statute which makes a seditious conspiracy unlawful. Petitioners, however, were not charged with a "conspiracy to overthrow" the Government. They were charged with a conspiracy to form a party and groups and assemblies of people who teach and advocate the overthrow of our Government by force or violence and with a conspiracy to advocate and teach its overthrow by force and violence. It may well be that indoctrination in the techniques of terror to destroy the Government would be indictable under either statute. But the teaching which is condemned here is of a different character.

So far as the present record is concerned, what petitioners did was to organize people to teach and themselves teach the Marxist-Leninist doctrine contained chiefly in four books: *Foundations of Leninism* by Stalin (1924); *The Communist Manifesto* by Marx and Engels (1848); *State and Revolution* by Lenin (1917); *History of the Communist Party of the Soviet Union* (B.) (1939).

Those books are to Soviet Communism what *Mein Kampf* was to Nazism. If they are understood, the ugliness of Communism is revealed, its deceit and cunning are exposed, the nature of its activities becomes apparent, and the chances of its success less likely. That is not, of course, the reason why petitioners chose these books for their classrooms. They are fervent Communists to whom these volumes are gospel. They preached the creed with the hope that some day it would be acted upon.

The opinion of the Court does not outlaw these texts nor condemn them to the fire, as the Communists do literature offensive to their creed. But if the books themselves are not outlawed, if they can lawfully remain on library shelves, by what reasoning does their use in a classroom become a crime? It would not be a crime under the Act to introduce these books to a class, though that would be teaching what the creed of violent overthrow of the Government is. The Act, as construed, requires the element of intent—that those who teach the creed believe in it. The crime then depends not on what is taught but on who the teacher is. That is to make freedom of speech turn not on *what is said,* but on the *intent* with which it is said. Once we start down that road we enter territory dangerous to the liberties of every citizen. * * *

The vice of treating speech as the equivalent of overt acts of a treasonable or seditious character is emphasized by a concurring opinion, which by invoking the law of conspiracy makes speech do service for deeds which are dangerous to society. [N]ever until today has anyone seriously thought that the ancient law of conspiracy could constitutionally be used to turn speech into seditious conduct. Yet that is precisely what is suggested. I repeat that we deal here with speech alone, not with speech *plus* acts of sabotage or unlawful conduct. Not a single seditious act is charged in the indictment. To make a lawful speech unlawful because two men conceive it is to raise the law of conspiracy to appalling proportions. * * *

There comes a time when even speech loses its constitutional immunity. Speech innocuous one year may at another time fan such destructive flames that it must be halted in the interests of the safety of the Republic. That is the meaning of the clear and present danger test. When conditions are so critical that there will be no time to avoid the evil that the speech threatens, it is time to call a halt. Otherwise, free speech which is the strength of the Nation will be the cause of its destruction.

Yet free speech is the rule, not the exception. The restraint to be constitutional must be based on more than fear, on more than passionate opposition against the speech, on more than a revolted dislike for its contents. There must be some immediate injury to society that is likely if speech is allowed. * * *

I had assumed that the question of the clear and present danger, being so critical an issue in the case, would be a matter for submission to the jury. [The] Court, I think, errs when it treats the question as one of law.

Yet, whether the question is one for the Court or the jury, there should be evidence of record on the issue. This record, however, contains no evidence whatsoever showing that the acts charged viz., the teaching of the Soviet theory of revolution with the hope that it will be realized, have created any clear and present danger to the Nation. The Court, however, rules to the contrary. [The majority] might as well say that the speech of petitioners is outlawed because Soviet Russia and her Red Army are a threat to world peace.

The nature of Communism as a force on the world scene would, of course, be relevant to the issue of clear and present danger of petitioners' advocacy within the United States. But the primary consideration is the strength and tactical position of petitioners and their converts in this country. On that there is no evidence in the record. If we are to take judicial notice of the threat of Communists within the nation, it should not be difficult to conclude that *as a political party* they are of little consequence. Communists in this country have never made a respectable or serious showing in any election. I would doubt that there is a village, let alone a city or county or state, which the Communists could carry. Communism in the world scene is no bogeyman; but Communism as a political faction or party in this country plainly is. Communism has been so thoroughly exposed in this country that it has been crippled as a political force. Free speech has destroyed it as an effective political party. It is inconceivable that those who went up and down this country preaching the doctrine of revolution which petitioners espouse would have any success. In days of trouble and confusion, when bread lines were long, when the unemployed walked the streets, when people were starving, the advocates of a short-cut by revolution might have a chance to gain adherents. But today there are no such conditions. The country is not in despair; the people know Soviet Communism; the doctrine of Soviet revolution is exposed in all of its ugliness and the American people want none of it.

[Unless] and until extreme and necessitous circumstances are shown our aim should be to keep speech unfettered and to allow the processes of law to be invoked only when the provocateurs among us move from speech to action. * * *[a]

Notes and Questions

1. What was the "substantive evil" in the *Dennis* case, the danger of which was sufficiently "clear and present" to warrant the application of the rule as originally formulated by Holmes and Brandeis? A *successful* revolution? An *attempted* revolution, however futile such an attempt might be? A *conspiracy* to plan the overthrow of the government by force and violence? A "conspiracy *to advocate*" such overthrow? See Gorfinkel & Mack, *Dennis v. United States and the Clear and Present Danger Rule,* 39 Calif.L.Rev. 475, 496–501 (1951); Nathanson, *The Communist Trial and the Clear-and-Present-Danger Test,* 63 Harv.L. Rev. 1167, 1168, 1173–75 (1950). Suppose it were established in *Dennis* that the odds were 99–1 against the Communists attempting an overthrow of the Government until 1961? 1971? Same result?

2. *Suppression of "totalitarian movements".* Consider Auerbach, *The Communist Control Act of 1954,* 23 U.Chi.L.Rev. 173, 188–89 (1956): "[I]n suppressing totalitarian movements a democratic society is not acting to protect the status quo, but the very same interests which freedom of speech itself seeks to secure— the possibility of peaceful progress under freedom. That suppression may sometimes have to be the means of securing and enlarging freedom is a paradox which is not unknown in other areas of the law of modern democratic states.

a. Eighteen years later, concurring in *Brandenburg,* p. 338 infra, Douglas, J., declared: "I see no place in the regime of the First Amendment for any 'clear and present danger' test whether strict and tight as some would make it or free-wheeling as the Court in *Dennis* rephrased it. When one reads the opinions closely and sees when and how the 'clear and present danger' test has been applied, great misgivings are aroused. First, the threats were often loud but always puny and made serious only by judges so wedded to the status quo that critical analysis made them nervous. Second, the test was so twisted and perverted in *Dennis* as to make the trial of those teachers of Marxism an all-out political trial which was part and parcel of the cold war that has eroded substantial parts of the First Amendment."

The basic 'postulate,' therefore, which should 'limit and control' the First Amendment is that it is part of the framework for a constitutional democracy and should, therefore, not be used to curb the power of Congress to exclude from the political struggle those groups which, if victorious, would crush democracy and impose totalitarianism. Whether in any particular case and at any particular time, Congress should suppress a totalitarian movement should be regarded as a matter of wisdom for its sole determination. But a democracy should claim the moral and constitutional right to suppress these movements whenever it deems it advisable to do so." See also Bork, *Neutral Principles and Some First Amendment Problems*, 47 Ind.L.J. 1, 30–33 (1971).

3. *Seditious conspiracy.* Consider Jaffe, *Foreword*, 65 Harv.L.Rev. 107, 111 (1951): "[Douglas, J., views the *Dennis* case] as one in which men are being held guilty for teaching the contents of four books. [Vinson, C.J.'s opinion] plays into the hand of such obfuscation by refusing to face the fact that the statute and the indictment indeed do little more than allege mere advocacy, be it in classroom or elsewhere. But the great questions were first whether it had been proved that the defendants were maintaining an organization thoroughly drilled, alert and ready to convert advocacy into sabotage, espionage and subversion at the first propitious moment; second, whether the proof of such organization could avail to define and limit the fatally wide scope of the pleading and the statute; and finally, whether the statute so defined was constitutional. These questions were neither clearly asked nor answered."

See also Shapiro, *Freedom of Speech* 63–64 (1966): "Brandeis had demanded no restriction while there was still time to call the police. The trouble in [*Dennis*] was that the police had been called but hadn't found any evidence of wrong-doing. The prosecution was instituted under the advocacy provisions because there was not sufficient evidence to meet the normal requirements of the criminal law of sedition. Thus, paradoxically, the defendants were convicted in an area where they were protected by the supposedly rigorous demands of the First Amendment *precisely because* they could not be convicted in an area under the routine protections of criminal law."

4. *Deference to legislative judgment.* Consider Linde, *"Clear and Present Danger" Reexamined*, 22 Stan.L.Rev. 1163, 1176–78 (1970): "The Smith Act in 1940 wrote into federal law almost the exact terms of the New York Criminal Anarchy Act sustained in *Gitlow.* New York had enacted that law in 1902, soon after the assassination of [President McKinley]. Between the occupation of Czechoslovakia and the Ribbentrap-Molotov pact of 1939, the House of Representatives was working on a bill [H.R. 5138] whose provenance was the fear of anarchist agitation in 1900 and the hatred of alien radicalism in 1919. It became law in 1940. * * *

"What was the legislative judgment that would deserve deference for its assessment of the danger from revolutionary speech? [A] member of the 76th Congress presumably might stand up in 1940 and demand to know whether H.R. 5138 [violated the first amendment]. Constitutional law, in its original function antecedent to judicial review, owes him an answer. The Congressman's decision must be constitutionally right or wrong, in that place and at that time—not only a prosecutor's, a jury's, or a judge's decisions at the time of a later trial.

"The answer the Congressman would get in 1940, of course, would be that in 1925 the Supreme Court had held that the New York legislature could reasonably have believed in 1902 that advocacy of violent overthrow of government was too dangerous to be permitted. [That theory] simply accepts a lawmaker's judgment of danger intrinsic in the content of such advocacy, quite independent of any extrinsic conditions. This answer would not pretend to anticipate in 1940 the external dangers in an atomic age that were invoked to sustain the act in 1951, nor would it need to. [I]s the answer Holmes and Brandeis would give the member of the 76th Congress more satisfactory—that it all depended on the circumstances; that the constitutionality of H.R. 5138 could be determined only in the context of future eventualities of clear and present danger which he might now be unable to foresee; that the danger which would justify his law to suppress revolutionary speech and organization might shift from indigenous rampages to foreign military menaces and back again so that the bill presently before him for enactment might well be unconstitutional now but might be constitutional in the light of diverse events in 1945, in 1948, in 1951, in 1957, and in 1961, perhaps not in 1966, but again in 1968?"

In 1954, Senator McCarthy was condemned by the United States Senate for acting contrary to its ethics and impairing its dignity. In 1957, when the convictions of the "second string" communist leaders reached the Supreme Court in *Yates,* McCarthy had died, and so had McCarthyism. Although strong anti-communist sentiment persisted, the political atmosphere in *Yates'* 1957 was profoundly different from that of *Dennis'* 1951.

YATES v. UNITED STATES, 354 U.S. 298, 77 S.Ct. 1064, 1 L.Ed.2d 1356 (1957), reversed the convictions of 14 "second-string" Communist Party officials for conspiring, in violation of §§ 2(a)(1) and (3) of the Smith Act, (1) to advocate and teach the duty and necessity of overthrowing the federal government by force and violence, and (2) to organize, as the Communist Party of the United States, a group who so advocate and teach, all with the intent of causing the overthrow of the government by force and violence as speedily as circumstances would permit.

The trial judge, as the Court described it, "regarded as immaterial, and intended to withdraw from the jury's consideration, any issue as to the character of the advocacy in terms of its capacity to stir listeners to forcible action," by instructing the jury: "The kind of advocacy and teaching which is charged and upon which your verdict must be reached is not merely a desirability but a necessity that the Government of the United States be overthrown and destroyed by force and violence and not merely a propriety but a duty to overthrow [by] force and violence." Both the petitioners and the Government had submitted proposed instructions "which would have required the jury to find that the proscribed advocacy was not of a mere abstract doctrine of forcible overthrow, but of action to that end, by the use of language reasonably and ordinarily calculated to incite persons to such action," but the trial court had rejected these instructions on the basis of *Dennis.*

The Court was "thus faced with the question whether the Smith Act prohibits advocacy and teaching of forcible overthrow, as an abstract principle, divorced from any effort to instigate action to that end, so long as such advocacy or teaching is engaged in with evil intent." In holding that it did not, the Court, per HARLAN, J., avoided resolution of the issue "in terms of constitutional compulsion"[a] and construed the Smith Act—in light of the legislative history showing "beyond all question that Congress was aware of the distinction between the advocacy or teaching of abstract doctrine and the advocacy or teaching of

---

a. But see *Brandenburg*, Part D infra.

action, and that it did not intend to disregard it"—as "aimed at the advocacy and teaching of concrete action for the forcible overthrow of the Government, and not of principles divorced from action":

"The Government's reliance on this Court's decision in *Dennis* is misplaced. The jury instructions which were refused here were given there, and were referred to by this Court as requiring 'the jury to find the facts *essential* to establish the substantive crime.' (Emphasis added). It is true that at one point in the late Chief Justice's opinion it is stated that the Smith Act 'is directed at advocacy, not discussion,' but it is clear that the reference was to advocacy of action, not ideas, for in the very next sentence the opinion emphasizes that the jury was properly instructed that there could be no conviction for 'advocacy in the realm of ideas.' * * *

"In failing to distinguish between advocacy of forcible overthrow as an abstract doctrine and advocacy of action to that end, the District Court appears to have been led astray by the holding in *Dennis* that advocacy of violent action to be taken at some future time was enough. [T]he District Court apparently thought that *Dennis* obliterated the traditional dividing line between advocacy of abstract doctrine and advocacy of action.

"This misconceives the situation confronting the Court in *Dennis* and what was held there. Although the jury's verdict, interpreted in light of the trial court's instructions, did not justify the conclusion that the defendants' advocacy was directed at, or created any danger of, immediate overthrow, it did establish that the advocacy was aimed at building up a seditious group and maintaining it in readiness for action at a propitious time. [The] essence of the *Dennis* holding was that indoctrination of a group in preparation for future violent action, as well as exhortation to immediate action, by advocacy found to be directed to 'action for the accomplishment' of forcible overthrow, to violence as 'a rule or principle of action,' and employing 'language of incitement,' is not constitutionally protected when the group is of sufficient size and cohesiveness, is sufficiently oriented towards action, and other circumstances are such as reasonably to justify apprehension that action will occur. This is quite a different thing from the view of the District Court here that mere doctrinal justification of forcible overthrow, if engaged in with the intent to accomplish overthrow, is punishable per se under the Smith Act. That sort of advocacy, even though uttered with the hope that it may ultimately lead to violent revolution, is too remote from concrete action to be regarded as the kind of indoctrination preparatory to action which was condemned in *Dennis*.

"[*Dennis* was] not concerned with a conspiracy to engage at some future time in seditious advocacy, but rather with a conspiracy to advocate presently the taking of forcible action in the future. It was action, not advocacy, that was to be postponed until 'circumstances' would 'permit.' * * *

"In light of the foregoing we are unable to regard the District Court's charge upon this aspect of the case as adequate. [T]he trial court's statement that the proscribed advocacy must include the 'urging,' 'necessity,' and 'duty' of forcible overthrow, and not merely its 'desirability' and 'propriety,' may not be regarded as a sufficient substitute for charging that the Smith Act reaches only advocacy of action for the overthrow of government by force and violence. The essential distinction is that those to whom the advocacy is addressed must be urged to *do* something, now or in the future, rather than merely to *believe* in something.
* * *

"We recognize that distinctions between advocacy or teaching of abstract doctrines, with evil intent, and that which is directed to stirring people to action, are often subtle and difficult to grasp, for in a broad sense, as Mr. Justice Holmes said in his dissenting opinion in *Gitlow*: 'Every idea is an incitement.' But the very subtlety of these distinctions required the most clear and explicit instructions with reference to them, for they concerned an issue which went to the very heart of the charges against these petitioners. The need for precise and understandable instructions on this issue is further emphasized by the equivocal character of the evidence in this [record]. Instances of speech that could be considered to amount to 'advocacy of action' are so few and far between as to be almost completely overshadowed by the hundreds of instances in the record in which overthrow, if mentioned at all, occurs in the course of doctrinal disputation so remote from action as to be almost wholly lacking in probative value. Vague references to 'revolutionary' or 'militant' action of an unspecified character, which are found in the evidence, might in addition be given too great weight by the jury in the absence of more precise instructions. Particularly in light of this record, we must regard the trial court's charge in this respect as furnishing wholly inadequate guidance to the jury on this central point in the case."

On the basis of its interpretation of the Smith Act, the Court ordered an acquittal of five of the 14 petitioners,[b] finding "no adequate evidence in the record" to sustain their convictions on retrial.[c]

BLACK, J., joined by Douglas, J., dissented in part, maintaining, as they had in *Dennis*, that the Smith Act provisions on which the prosecutions were based violated the first amendment and that therefore acquittal should have been directed for all 14 petitioners.

CLARK, J., dissented: "*Dennis* merely held that a charge was sufficient where it requires a finding that 'the Party advocates the theory that there is a duty and necessity to overthrow the Government by force and violence [as] a program for winning adherents and as a policy to be translated into action' as soon as the circumstances permit [concurring opinion of Frankfurter, J.]." Thus, "the trial judge charged in essence all that was required under the *Dennis* opinion." He also maintained that instead of freeing five of the petitioners "solely on the *facts*"—which he regarded an unprecedented usurpation of the jury's function— the Court should have afforded the Government an opportunity, on remand, to present its evidence against petitioners "under the new theories announced by the Court for Smith Act prosecutions." [d]

Notes and Questions

1. *Dennis and Yates compared.* (a) On what did *Yates* focus: whether a *conspiracy* itself presents a "clear and present" danger or whether the *speech* of the conspirators does? On what did *Dennis* focus? Did *Yates* attach the same significance as did *Dennis* to membership in the Communist Party, as either an indication of intent or proof of membership in a conspiracy? To what extent

b. None of the remaining nine petitioners were ever tried again. Upon remand, the government requested dismissal of the indictments, explaining that a "comprehensive review [establishes] that we cannot satisfy the evidentiary requirements laid down by" the Court in *Yates*. See Mollan, *Smith Act Prosecutions: The Effect of the Dennis and Yates Decisions*, 26 U.Pitt.L.Rev. 705, 732 (1965).

c. The type of evidence which led the Court to order the acquittal of the five petitioners and the kind of evidence which caused it to deny directed acquittals as to the nine others are summarized in *Scales* infra.

d. Brennan and Whittaker, JJ., took no part. Burton, J.'s concurrence is omitted.

does the fact that the *Yates* petitioners were not first-string leaders of the Party account for the result?

(b) Is it understandable that the *Yates* trial judge was "misled" by language in Vinson, C.J.'s *Dennis* opinion into thinking that punishment of the advocacy of abstract doctrine was permissible under the first amendment? Consider Greenawalt, *Speech and Crime*, 1980 Am.B.Found.Res.J. 645, 720 n. 279: "In defense of the trial court's instruction, it might be said that if someone is told he has a duty to participate in the forcible overthrow of the government, that signifies that he should perform illegal actions when the time arises. If all the Supreme Court opinion demanded is an explicit urging that listeners perform illegal actions at some future time, it is hard to distinguish that from what is clearly implied in advocacy of the ' "duty" of forcible overthrow.' But Justice Harlan may have meant that the advocacy must be more closely linked with action, either in the sense of recommending specific action or in the sense of being more positively directed to producing action among listeners." See generally Gellhorn, *American Rights* 79–80 (1960); Pritchett, *Congress vs. The Supreme Court, 1957–1960,* at 63–66 (1961); 71 Harv.L.Rev. 123–25 (1957).

2. *Advocating "doctrine" and advocating "action."* Consider Gellhorn, supra, at 80–81: "[O]ne can recognize a qualitative distinction between a speaker who expresses the opinion before a student audience that all law professors are scoundrels whose students should band together to beat them within an inch of their lives, and a second speaker who, taking up that theme, urges the audience to obtain baseball bats, meet behind the law faculty building at three o'clock next Thursday afternoon, and join him in attacking any professor who can then be found. The first speaker, in [the *Yates*] view, should not be prosecuted; the second has stepped over the line between advocating a belief and advocating an illegal action." Cf. Hand, *The Bill of Rights* 59–60 (1958).

3. *Clear and present danger test.* After *Yates,* was a call for concrete, forcible action even in the unspecified future still "unprotected speech" and participation in a group calling for such action still "unprotected association"? Did the constitutional criteria developed by Harlan, J.'s majority opinions in *Yates* and *Scales* and *Noto,* infra, concern the advocate's intent and the content of his advocacy or the probability of its success? See Linde, *"Clear and Present Danger" Reexamined,* 22 Stan.L.Rev. 1163, 1166 (1970). To what extent is Harlan, J.'s analysis similar to Judge Hand's in *Masses,* p. 303 supra?

Does *Yates* scrap the clear-and-present standard or establish a special category within that standard? When a subversive group is involved, may evidence of the "presentness of its organizational effectiveness" be substituted for the presentness of the danger? See Shapiro, *Freedom of Speech* 66, 71 (1966).

In an effort to avoid the demanding evidentiary requirements of *Yates,* the government began prosecuting communists under the "membership clause" of the Smith Act, 18 U.S.C. § 2385. After *Scales* and *Noto,* infra, the government abandoned Smith Act prosecutions altogether.

SCALES v. UNITED STATES, 367 U.S. 203, 81 S.Ct. 1469, 6 L.Ed.2d 782 (1961) affirmed the conviction of the Chairman of the North and South Carolina Districts of the Communist Party under the "membership clause" of the Smith Act, 18 U.S.C. § 2385, described by the Court, per HARLAN, J., as making a felony "the acquisition or holding of knowing membership in any organization which advocates the overthrow of the [federal] Government by force or violence." [1] The trial judge had instructed the jury that, as the Supreme Court described it, "in order to convict it must find [that] (1) the Communist Party advocated the violent overthrow of the Government, in the sense of 'present advocacy of action' to accomplish that end as soon as circumstances were propitious; and (2) petitioner was an 'active' member of the Party, and not merely 'a nominal, passive * * *' member, with knowledge of the Party's illegal advocacy and a specific intent to bring about violent overthrow 'as speedily as circumstances would permit.' "

The Court held that "the membership clause permissibly bears the construction put upon it below" and as thus construed neither "imputes guilt to an individual merely on the basis of his associations and sympathies" in violation of due process nor infringes First Amendment freedoms:

"It was settled in *Dennis* that the advocacy with which we are here concerned is not constitutionally protected speech, and it was further established that a combination to promote such advocacy, albeit under the aegis of what purports to be a political party, is not such association as is protected by the First Amendment. We can discern no reason why membership, when it constitutes a purposeful form of complicity in a group engaging in this same forbidden advocacy, should receive any greater degree of protection from the guarantees of that Amendment.

"The [membership] clause does not make criminal all association with an organization, which has been shown to engage in illegal advocacy. There must be clear proof that a defendant 'specifically intend[s] to accomplish [the aims of the organization] by resort to violence.' *Noto* [this Part infra]. Thus the member for whom the organization is a vehicle for the advancement of legitimate aims and policies does not fall within the ban of the statute: he lacks the requisite specific intent 'to bring about the overthrow of the government as speedily as circumstances would permit.' Such a person may be foolish, deluded, or perhaps merely optimistic, but he is not by this statute made a criminal."

The Court also rejected the contention "that the evidence was insufficient to establish that the Communist Party was engaged in present advocacy of violent overthrow of the Government in the sense required by the Smith Act": "[T]he evidentiary question here is controlled in large part by *Yates* [which] rested on the view (not articulated in the opinion, though perhaps it should have been) that the Smith Act offenses, involving as they do subtler elements than are present in most other crimes, call for strict standards in assessing the adequacy of the proof needed to make out a case of illegal advocacy. This premise is as applicable to prosecutions under the membership clause of the Smith Act as it is to conspiracy prosecutions under that statute as we had in *Yates*. [*Yates*] indicates what type of evidence is needed to permit a jury to find that (a) there was 'advocacy of action' and (b) the Party was responsible for such advocacy.

"First, *Yates* makes clear what type of evidence is not *in itself* sufficient to show illegal advocacy. This category includes evidence of the following: the

---

1. Section 2385 (whose membership clause we place in italics) reads: "Whoever organizes or helps or attempts to organize any society, group, or assembly of persons who teach, advocate, or encourage the overthrow or destruction of any such government by force or violence; *or becomes or is a member of,* or affiliates with, *any such society, group, or assembly of persons, knowing the purposes thereof—*

"Shall be fined not more than $20,000 or imprisoned not more than twenty years, or both, and shall be ineligible for employment by the United States or any department or agency thereof, for the five years next following his conviction. * * *"

teaching of Marxism-Leninism and the connected use of Marxist 'classics' as textbooks; the official general resolutions and pronouncements of the Party at past conventions; dissemination of the Party's general literature, including the standard outlines on Marxism; the Party's history and organizational structure; the secrecy of meetings and the clandestine nature of the Party generally; statements by officials evidencing sympathy for and alliance with the U.S.S.R. It was the predominance of evidence of this type which led the Court to order the acquittal of several *Yates* [defendants].

"Second, *Yates* also indicates what kind of evidence is sufficient. There the Court pointed to two series of events which justified the denial of directed acquittals as to nine of the *Yates* defendants. The Court noted that with respect to seven of the defendants, meetings in San Francisco might be considered to be 'the systematic teaching and advocacy of illegal action which is condemned by the statute.' In those meetings, a small group of members were not only taught that violent revolution was inevitable, but they were also taught techniques for achieving that end. [T]he Court [also] referred to certain activities in the Los Angeles area 'which might be considered to amount to "advocacy of action" ' and with which two *Yates* defendants were linked. Here again, the participants did not stop with teaching of the inevitability of eventual revolution, but went on to explain techniques, both legal and illegal, to be employed in preparation for or in connection with the revolution. [Viewed] together, these events described in *Yates* indicate at least two patterns of evidence sufficient to show illegal advocacy: (a) the teaching of forceful overthrow, accompanied by directions as to the type of illegal action which must be taken when the time for the revolution is reached; and (b) the teaching of forceful overthrow, accompanied by a contemporary, though legal, course of conduct clearly undertaken for the specific purpose of rendering effective the later illegal activity which is advocated."

After examining the *Scales* record, the Court concluded "this evidence sufficed to make a case for the jury on the issue of illegal Party advocacy. *Dennis* and *Yates* have definitely laid at rest any doubt that present advocacy of *future* action for violent overthrow satisfies statutory and constitutional requirements equally with advocacy of *immediate* action to that end. Hence this record cannot be considered deficient because it contains no evidence of advocacy for immediate overthrow. [T]he evidence amply showed that Party leaders were continuously preaching during the indictment period the inevitability of eventual forcible overthrow [and] the jury, under instructions which fully satisfied the requirements of *Yates*,[27] was entitled to infer from this systematic preaching

---

27. The trial court charged: "Moreover, the teaching in the abstract or teaching objectively, that is, teaching, discussing, explaining, or expounding what is meant by the aim or purpose of any author, group, or society of overthrowing the Government by force and violence is not criminal. * * *

"However, if the Party went further, and with the intention of overthrowing the Government by force and violence, it taught, or advocated a rule or principle of action which both, one, called on its members to take forcible and concrete action at some advantageous time thereafter to overthrow the Government by force and violence, and, two, expressed that call in such written or oral words as would reasonably and ordinarily be calculated to incite its members to take concrete and forcible

action for such overthrow; then, if the Communist Party did that, the Party became such a society or group, as was outlawed by the Smith Act.

"To be criminal the teaching or advocacy, or the call to action just described need not be for immediate action, that is, for action today, tomorrow, next month, or next year. It is criminal, nonetheless, if the action is to be at an unnamed time in the future, to be fixed by the circumstances or on signal from the Party.

"It is criminal if it is a call upon the members to be ready, or to stand in readiness for action, or for a summons to action at a favorable, or opportune time in the future, or as speedily as circumstances will permit, provided always that the urging of such readiness

[that] the doctrine of violent revolution [was] put forward as a guide to future action * * *; in short that 'advocacy of action' was engaged in." And "such advocacy was sufficiently broadly based to permit its attribution to the Party."

DOUGLAS, J., dissented: "When we allow petitioner to be sentenced to prison for six years for being a 'member' of the Communist Party, we make a sharp break with traditional concepts of First Amendment [rights]. Even the Alien and Sedition Laws—shameful reminders of an early chapter in intolerance— never went so far as we go today. They were aimed at conspiracy and advocacy of insurrection and at the publication of 'false, scandalous and malicious' writing against the Government. [There] is here no charge of conspiracy, no charge of any overt act to overthrow the Government by force and violence, no charge of any other criminal act. The charge is being a 'member' of the Communist Party, 'well-knowing' that it advocated the overthrow of the Government by force and violence, 'said defendant intending to bring about such overthrow by force and violence as speedily as circumstances would permit.' That falls far short of a charge of conspiracy. Conspiracy rests not in intention alone but in an agreement with one or more others to promote an unlawful project. * * *

"The case is not saved by showing that petitioner was an active member. None of the activity constitutes a crime. [Scales] recruited new members into the Party, and promoted the advanced education of selected young Party members in the theory of communism to be undertaken at secret schools. He was a director of one such school [at which] students were told (by someone else) that one of the Party's weaknesses was in failing to place people in key industrial positions. One witness told of a meeting arranged by Scales at which the staff of the school urged him to remain in his position in an industrial plant rather than return to college. In Scales' presence, students at the school were once shown how to kill a person with a pencil, a device which, it was said, might come in handy on a picket line. Other evidence showed Scales [at different times to have said or distributed literature which said] that the Party line was that the Negroes in the South and the working classes should be used to foment a violent revolution; that a Communist government could not be voted into power in this country because the Government controlled communication media, newspapers, the military, and the educational system, and that force was the only way to achieve the revolution; [that] the revolution would come within a generation; that it would be easier in the United States than in Russia to effectuate the revolution because of assistance and advice from Russian Communists. * * *

"Not one single illegal act is charged to petitioner. That is why the essence of the crime covered by the indictment is merely belief—belief in the proletarian revolution, belief in Communist creed."

BLACK, J., dissented primarily for the reasons of Douglas and Brennan, JJ. He also maintained that although the Court had suggested in other cases in which it had applied the "balancing test," that it was justified "because no direct abridgment of First Amendment freedoms was involved," in the instant case "petitioner is being sent to jail for the express reason that he has associated with people who have entertained unlawful ideas and said unlawful things, and that

be by words which would reasonably and ordinarily be calculated to spur a person to ready himself for, and to take action towards, the overthrow of the Government. But those to whom the advocacy or urging is addressed must be urged to do something now or in the future, rather than merely to believe in some-thing. In other words, the advocacy must be of concrete action, and not merely a belief in abstract doctrine. However, the immediate concrete action urged should be intended to lead towards the forcible overthrow, and be so understood by those to whom the advocacy is addressed."

of course is a *direct* abridgment of his freedoms of speech and assembly * * *. Nevertheless, [the] Court relies upon its prior decisions to the effect that the Government has power to abridge speech and assembly if its interest in doing so is sufficient to outweigh the interest in protecting these First Amendment freedoms. This, I think, demonstrates the unlimited breadth and danger of the 'balancing test' as it is currently being employed by a majority of this Court." [a]

In another Smith Act "membership clause" case, the same day as *Scales*, NOTO v. UNITED STATES, 367 U.S. 290, 81 S.Ct. 1517, 6 L.Ed.2d 836 (1961), per HARLAN, J., reversed the conviction of a communist worker in upstate New York, finding that the record "bears much of the infirmity that we found in the *Yates* record, and requires us to conclude that the evidence of illegal Party advocacy was insufficient to support this conviction." There was much evidence of "the Party's teaching of abstract doctrine that revolution is an inevitable product of the 'proletarian' effort to achieve communism in a capitalistic society," but testimony of evidence which supported an inference of " 'advocacy of action' to accomplish that end" was "sparse indeed" and "lacked the compelling quality which in *Scales* was supplied by the petitioner's utterances and systematic course of conduct as a high Party official."

Notes and Questions

1. See Shapiro, *Freedom of Speech* 119 (1966) for the view that when Congress had prohibited "membership" in organizations advocating the forcible overthrow of the government, it plainly had *not* meant "active" membership with "specific intent" and "the acrobatic display of statutory interpretation necessary to have made it mean all that simply demonstrated again the paradox of modest Justices who cannot bring themselves to challenge Congress, but yet cannot completely escape the feeling that they owe some independent duty to the Constitution."

2. Could Scales have been convicted under the advocacy or conspiracy to advocate clauses of the Smith Act? Could any really "active" Party member probably be? Without sufficient proof to satisfy *Yates*, can the government prove "membership" of the sort required for conviction in *Scales* and *Noto*? As a practical matter, did the Court eliminate the membership clause of the Smith Act as a separate means of prosecuting Communist Party members? See Shapiro, supra, at 120; 75 Harv.L.Rev. 116–17 (1961).

3. *Spock*. Dr. Spock, Rev. Coffin and others were convicted of conspiring to counsel and abet Selective Service registrants to refuse to have their draft cards in their possession and to disobey other duties imposed by the Selective Service Act of 1967. Spock signed a document entitled "A Call to Resist Illegitimate Authority," which "had 'a double aspect: in part it was a denunciation of governmental policy [in Vietnam] and, in part, it involved a public call to resist the duties imposed by the [Selective Service] Act.' " Several weeks later, Spock attended a demonstration in Washington, D.C., where an unsuccessful attempt was made to present collected draft cards to the Attorney General. *United States v. Spock*, 416 F.2d 165 (1st Cir.1969), per Aldrich, J., ruled that Spock should have been acquitted:

---

a. Brennan, J., joined by Warren, C.J., and Douglas, J., dissented on the ground that sub- sequent legislation had superseded the membership provision of the Smith Act.

"[Spock] was one of the drafters of the Call, but this does not evidence the necessary intent to adhere to its illegal aspects. [H]is speech was limited to condemnation of the war and the draft, and lacked any words or content of counselling. The jury could not find proscribed advocacy from the mere fact [that] he hoped the frequent stating of his views might give young men 'courage to take active steps in draft resistance.' This is a natural consequence of vigorous speech. Similarly, Spock's actions lacked the clear character necessary to imply specific intent under the First Amendment standard. [H]e was at the Washington demonstration, [but took] no part in its planning. [His statements at this demonstration did not extend] beyond the general anti-war, anti-draft remarks he had made before. His attendance is as consistent with a desire to repeat this speech as it is to aid a violation of the law. The dissent would fault us for drawing such distinctions, but it forgets the teaching of [*Bond v. Floyd* [b]] that expressing one's views in broad areas is not foreclosed by knowledge of the consequences, and the important lesson of *Noto, Scales* and *Yates* that one may belong to a group, knowing of its illegal aspects, and still not be found to adhere thereto."

D. A MODERN "RESTATEMENT"

BRANDENBURG v. OHIO

395 U.S. 444, 89 S.Ct. 1827, 23 L.Ed.2d 430 (1969).

PER CURIAM.

The appellant, a leader of a Ku Klux Klan group, was convicted under [a 1919] Ohio Criminal Syndicalism statute of "advocat[ing] the duty, necessity, or propriety of crime, sabotage, violence, or unlawful methods of terrorism as a means of accomplishing industrial or political reform" and of "voluntarily assembl[ing] with any society, group or assemblage of persons formed to teach or advocate the doctrines of criminal syndicalism." He was fined $1,000 and sentenced to one to 10 years' imprisonment. * * *

The record shows that a man, identified at trial as the appellant, telephoned an announcer-reporter on the staff of a Cincinnati television station and invited him to come to a Ku Klux Klan "rally" to be held at a farm in Hamilton County. With the cooperation of the organizers, the reporter and a cameraman attended the meeting and filmed the events. Portions of the films were later broadcast on the local station and on a national network.

The prosecution's case rested on the films and on testimony identifying the appellant as the person who communicated with the reporter and who spoke at the rally. The State also introduced into evidence several articles appearing in the film, including a pistol, a rifle, a shotgun, ammunition, a Bible, and a red hood worn by the speaker in the films.

One film showed 12 hooded figures, some of whom carried firearms. They were gathered around a large wooden cross, which they burned. No one was present other than the participants and the newsmen who made the film. Most of the words uttered during the scene were incomprehensible when the film was projected, but scattered phrases could be understood that were derogatory of Negroes and, in one instance, of Jews. Another scene on the same film showed

b. *Bond v. Floyd*, 385 U.S. 116, 87 S.Ct. 339, 17 L.Ed.2d 235 (1966) found ambiguity in expressions of support for those unwilling to respond to the draft that earlier opinions would have characterized as clear advocacy of illegal action. As Thomas Emerson puts it "the distance traversed [from *Schenck* and *Debs* to *Bond*] is quite apparent." *Freedom of Expression in Wartime*, 116 U.Pa.L.Rev. 975, 988 (1968).

the appellant, in Klan regalia, making a speech. The speech, in full, was as follows:

"This is an organizers' meeting. We have had quite a few members here today which are—we have hundreds, hundreds of members throughout the State of Ohio. I can quote from a newspaper clipping from the Columbus Ohio Dispatch, five weeks ago Sunday morning. The Klan has more members in the State of Ohio than does any other organization. We're not a revengent organization, but if our President, our Congress, our Supreme Court, continues to suppress the white, Caucasian race, it's possible that there might have to be some revengence taken.

"We are marching on Congress July the Fourth, four hundred thousand strong. From there we are dividing into two groups, one group to march on St. Augustine, Florida, the other group to march into Mississippi. Thank you."

The second film showed six hooded figures one of whom, later identified as the appellant, repeated a speech very similar to that recorded on the first film. The reference to the possibility of "revengence" was omitted, and one sentence was added: "Personally, I believe the nigger should be returned to Africa, the Jew returned to Israel." Though some of the figures in the films carried weapons, the speaker did not.

[*Whitney*] sustained the constitutionality of California's Criminal Syndicalism Act, the text of which is quite similar to that of the laws of Ohio. The Court upheld the statute on the ground that, without more, "advocating" violent means to effect political and economic change involves such danger to the security of the State that the State may outlaw it. But *Whitney* has been thoroughly discredited by later decisions [such as *Dennis* which] have fashioned the principle that the constitutional guarantees of free speech and free press do not permit a State to forbid or proscribe advocacy of the use of force or of law violation except where such advocacy is directed to inciting or producing imminent lawless action and is likely to incite or produce such action.[2] As we said in *Noto*, "the mere abstract teaching [of] the moral propriety or even moral necessity for a resort to force and violence, is not the same as preparing a group for violent action and steeling it to such action." See also *Bond v. Floyd*. A statute which fails to draw this distinction impermissibly intrudes upon the freedoms guaranteed by the First and Fourteenth Amendments. It sweeps within its condemnation speech which our Constitution has immunized from governmental control. Cf. *Yates* * * *.

Measured by this test, Ohio's Criminal Syndicalism Act cannot be sustained. The Act punishes persons who "advocate or teach the duty, necessity, or propriety" of violence "as a means of accomplishing industrial or political reform"; or who publish or circulate or display any book or paper containing such advocacy; or who "justify" the commission of violent acts "with intent to exemplify, spread or advocate the propriety of the doctrines of criminal syndicalism"; or [who] "voluntarily assemble" with a group formed "to teach or advocate the doctrines of criminal syndicalism." Neither the indictment nor the trial judge's instructions to the jury in any way refined the statute's bald definition of

2. It was on the theory that the Smith Act embodied such a principle and that it had been applied only in conformity with it that this Court sustained the Act's constitutionality. That this was the basis for *Dennis* was emphasized in *Yates*, in which the Court over-turned convictions for advocacy of the forcible overthrow of the Government under the Smith Act, because the trial judge's instructions had allowed conviction for mere advocacy, unrelated to its tendency to produce forcible action.

the crime in terms of mere advocacy not distinguished from incitement to imminent lawless action.[3]

Accordingly, we are here confronted with a statute which, by its own words and as applied, purports to punish mere advocacy and to forbid, on pain of criminal punishment, assembly with others merely to advocate the described type of action.[4] Such a statute falls within the condemnation of the First and Fourteenth Amendments. The contrary teaching of *Whitney* cannot be supported, and that decision is therefore overruled.

Reversed.

MR. JUSTICE BLACK, concurring.

I agree with the views expressed by Mr. Justice Douglas in his concurring opinion in this case that the "clear and present danger" doctrine should have no place in the interpretation of the First Amendment. I join the Court's opinion, which, as I understand it, simply cites *Dennis*, but does not indicate any agreement on the Court's part with the "clear and present danger" doctrine on which *Dennis* purported to rely.

MR. JUSTICE DOUGLAS, concurring.

While I join the opinion of the Court, I desire to enter a caveat.

[Whether] the war power—the greatest leveler of them all—is adequate to sustain [the "clear and present danger"] doctrine is debatable. The dissents in *Abrams* [and other cases] show how easily "clear and present danger" is manipulated to crush what Brandeis called "the fundamental right of free men to strive for better conditions through new legislation and new institutions" by argument and discourse even in time of war. Though I doubt if the "clear and present danger" test is congenial to the First Amendment in time of a declared war, I am certain it is not reconcilable with the First Amendment in days of peace.

* * *

Mr. Justice Holmes, though never formally abandoning the "clear and present danger" test, moved closer to the First Amendment ideal when he said in dissent in *Gitlow* [quoting the passage beginning, "Every idea is an incitement."] We have never been faithful to the philosophy of that dissent.

"[In *Dennis*, we distorted] the "clear and present danger" test beyond recognition. [I] see no place in the regime of the First Amendment for any "clear and present danger" test whether strict and tight as some would make it or free-wheeling as the Court in *Dennis* rephrased it.

Notes and Questions

1. What pre-*Brandenburg* decisions, if any, "have fashioned the principle" that advocacy may not be prohibited "except [where] directed to inciting or producing *imminent* lawless action *and* * * * *likely* to incite or produce such action"? (Emphasis added.) Did *Dennis, Yates* and *Scales* take pains to *deny* that the unlawful action advocated need be "imminent" or that the advocacy

3. The first count of the indictment charged that appellant "did unlawfully by word of mouth advocate the necessity, or propriety of crime, violence, or unlawful methods of terrorism as a means of accomplishing political reform * * *." The second count charged that appellant "did unlawfully voluntarily assemble with a group or assemblage of persons formed to advocate the doctrines of criminal syndicalism * * *." The trial judge's charge merely followed the language of the indictment. * * *

4. Statutes affecting the right of assembly, like those touching on freedom of speech, must observe the established distinctions between mere advocacy and incitement to lawless action * * *.

must be "likely" to produce the forbidden action? See Linde, *"Clear and Present Danger" Reexamined*, 22 Stan.L.Rev. 1163, 1166–67, 1183–86 (1970).

2. Is "the *Brandenburg* version of the clear and present danger test"—as Professor Emerson calls it (is this a misnomer?)—subject to criticism on the ground that "it permits government interference with expression at too early a stage, allowing officials to cut speech off as soon as it shows signs of being effective"? That it is "an ad hoc test" that does not enable the speaker to "know in advance what the limits will be found to be"? That the test is "excessively vague"? See Emerson, *First Amendment Doctrine and the Burger Court*, 68 Calif.L.Rev. 422, 437–38 (1980).

3. Does *Brandenburg* adopt the *Masses* incitement test as a major part of the required showing? Consider Gunther, *Learned Hand and the Origins of Modern First Amendment Doctrine: Some Fragments of History*," 27 Stan.L.Rev. 719, 754–55 (1975): "An incitement-nonincitement distinction had only fragmentary and ambiguous antecedents in the pre-*Brandenburg* era; it was *Brandenburg* that really 'established' it; and, it was essentially an establishment of the legacy of Learned Hand. [Under] *Brandenburg*, probability of harm is no longer the central criterion for speech limitations. The inciting language of the speaker—the Hand focus on 'objective' words—is the major consideration. And punishment of the harmless inciter is prevented by the *Schenck*–derived requirement of a likelihood of dangerous consequences." (citing *Brandenburg*'s note 4.) But see Shiffrin, *Defamatory Non-Media Speech and First Amendment Methodology*, 25 U.C.L.A.L.Rev. 915, 947 n. 206 (1978): "Several leading commentators assume that *Brandenburg* adopts an incitement requirement. [The] conclusion is apparently based on this line from *Brandenburg*: 'Neither the indictment nor the trial judge's instructions to the jury in any way refined the statute's bald definition of the crime in terms of mere advocacy, not distinguished from incitement to imminent lawless action' [also citing note 4]. The difficulty with attaching significance to this ambiguous statement is that the term 'incitement' is used in the alternative in the Court's statement of its test. Thus, advocacy of imminent lawless action is protected unless it is directed to inciting *or* producing imminent lawless action and is likely to incite *or* produce imminent lawless action. Thus, even assuming that the use of the word incitement refers to express use of language, as opposed to the nature of results (an interpretation which is strained in light of the Court's wording of the test), incitement is not necessary to divorce the speech from first amendment protection. It is enough that the speech is directed to producing imminent lawless action and is likely to produce such action."

If one wants to argue that *Brandenburg* adopted *Masses*, is there anything to be made of the phrase "directed to" in the *Brandenburg* test? Alternatively, did *Yates* adopt the *Masses* test? If so, does its favorable citation in *Brandenburg* constitute an adoption of the *Masses* test?

4. The *Brandenburg* "inciting or producing imminent lawless action" standard was the basis for reversal of a disorderly conduct conviction in HESS v. INDIANA, 414 U.S. 105, 94 S.Ct. 326, 38 L.Ed.2d 303 (1973) (per curiam). After antiwar demonstrators on the Indiana University campus had blocked a public street, police moved them to the curbs on either side. As an officer passed him, appellant stated loudly, "We'll take the fucking street later (or again)," which led to his disorderly conduct conviction. His statement, observed the Court, "was not addressed to any person or group in particular" and "his tone, although loud, was no louder than that of the other people in the area. [At] best, [the] statement could be taken as counsel for present moderation; at worst, it

amounted to nothing more than advocacy of illegal action at some indefinite future time." This was insufficient, under *Brandenburg*, to punish appellant's words, as the State had, on the ground that they had a "tendency to produce violence." It could not be said that appellant "was advocating, in the normal sense, any action" and there was "no evidence" that "his words were intended to produce, and likely to produce, *imminent* disorder."

REHNQUIST, J., joined by Burger, C.J., and Blackmun, J., dissented: "The simple explanation for the result in this case is that the majority has interpreted the evidence differently from the courts below." The dissenters quarrelled with the Court's conclusion that appellant's advocacy "was not directed towards inciting imminent action. [T]here are surely possible constructions of the statement which would encompass more or less immediate and continuing action against the police. They should not be rejected out of hand because of an unexplained preference for other acceptable alternatives." [a]

5. Does *Yates* survive *Brandenburg*'s emphasis on *imminent* lawless action? Is light shed on the question by *Communist Party of Indiana v. Whitcomb*, 414 U.S. 441, 94 S.Ct. 656, 38 L.Ed.2d 635 (1974), invalidating an Indiana statute denying a political party or its candidates access to the ballot unless the party files an affidavit that it "does not advocate the overthrow of local, state or national government by force or violence"? The Court, per Brennan J., maintained that the required oath (which had been interpreted to include advocacy of abstract doctrine) violated the principle of *Brandenburg* and stated that the principle applied not only to attempted denials of public employment, bar licensing, and tax exemption, but also to ballot access denials. The flaw with the state's position was that it furnished access to the ballot "not because the Party urges others 'to *do* something now *or in the future* [but] merely to believe in something,' [*Yates*]" (Second emphasis added).

What happened to the "imminent lawless action" requirement? Does the *Whitcomb* language clarify *Brandenburg*? Modify it? Is the Court simply confused?

6. Does *Brandenburg* apply to the advocacy of trivial crimes? Suppose the advocacy of trespass across a lawn? What result under *Brandenburg*? What result under *Dennis*? Is *Dennis* potentially more speech protective than *Brandenburg*?

7. Does *Brandenburg* apply to solicitation of crime in private or non-ideological contexts? Consider Shiffrin, note 3 supra, at 950: "How different it might be if the factual context were to involve advocacy of murder in a non-socio-political context. One suspects that little rhetoric about the marketplace of ideas or other first amendment values would be employed and that the serious and explicit advocacy of murder in a concrete way would suffice to divorce the

---

a. See also *NAACP v. Claiborne Hardware Co.*, 458 U.S. 886, 102 S.Ct. 3409, 73 L.Ed.2d 1215 (1982). The Court stated that the remarks of Charles Evers "might have been understood" as inviting violence, but stated that when "such appeals do not incite lawless action, they must be regarded as protected speech." If violent action had followed his remarks, a "substantial question" of liability would have been raised. The Court also observed, however, that the defendant might be held criminally liable for the acts of others if the speeches could be taken as evidence that

the defendant gave "other specific instructions to carry out violent acts or threats." Compare *Watts v. United States*, 394 U.S. 705, 89 S.Ct. 1399, 22 L.Ed.2d 664 (1969) (statute prohibiting knowing and wilful threat of bodily harm upon the President is constitutional on its face) (dictum). For commentary on threats and the first amendment, compare Justice Linde's opinion in *State v. Robertson*, 293 Or. 402, 649 P.2d 569 (1982) with Greenawalt, *Criminal Coercion and Freedom of Speech*, 78 Nw.U.L.Rev. 1081 (1984).

speech from first amendment protection even in the absence of a specific showing of likelihood." Would it matter if it were not explicit or not concrete? For trenchant analysis of the issues raised by the shift in context from public to private or in subject matter from ideological to non-ideological, see Greenawalt, *Speech and Crime,* 1980 Am.B.Found.Res.J. 645.

8. Should the line of cases from *Schenck* to *Brandenburg* fuel cynicism about the binding force of legal doctrine and about the willingness or capacity of the judiciary to protect dissent? [b] To what extent does the focus on Supreme Court cases exaggerate the frailty of legal doctrine? [c]

II. REPUTATION AND PRIVACY

In an important article, Harry Kalven coined the phrase "two level theory." Kalven, *The Metaphysics of the Law of Obscenity,* 1960 Sup.Ct.Rev. 1, 11. As he described it, *Beauharnais,* infra, and other cases employed a first amendment methodology that classified speech at two levels. Some speech—libel, obscenity, "fighting words"—was thought to be so bereft of social utility as to be beneath first amendment protection. At the second level, speech of constitutional value was thought to be protected unless it presented a clear and present danger of a substantive evil.

In considering libel and privacy, we will witness the collapse of "two level theory." The purpose is not a detailed examination of libel and privacy law. Our interests include the initial exclusion of defamation from first amendment protection, the themes and methods contributing to the erosion of that exclusion, and the articulation of basic first amendment values having implications and applications beyond defamation and the right to privacy.

A. GROUP LIBEL

BEAUHARNAIS v. ILLINOIS, 343 U.S. 250, 72 S.Ct. 725, 96 L.Ed. 919 (1952), per FRANKFURTER, J., sustained a statute prohibiting exhibition in any public place of any publication portraying "depravity, criminality, unchastity, or lack of virtue of a class of citizens, of any race, color, creed or religion [which exposes such citizens] to contempt, derision or obloquy or which is productive of breach of the peace or riots." The Court affirmed a conviction for organizing the distribution of a leaflet which petitioned the Mayor and City Council of Chicago "to halt the further encroachment, harassment and invasion of white people, their property, neighborhoods and persons by the Negro"; called for "one million self respecting white people in Chicago to unite"; and warned that if "the need to prevent the white race from becoming mongrelized by the Negro will not unite us, then the [aggressions], rapes, robberies, knives, guns, and marijuana of the Negro, surely will.":

"Today every American jurisdiction [punishes] libels directed at individuals. '[There] are certain well-defined and narrowly limited classes of speech, the

b. In fashioning first amendment doctrine, should the overriding objective be at "all times [to] equip the first amendment to do maximum service in those historical periods when intolerance of unorthodox ideas is most prevalent and when governments are most able and most likely to stifle dissent systematically"? Should the first amendment "be targeted for the worst of times"? What impact would such a perspective have on the general development of first amendment doctrine? See Blasi, *The Pathological Perspective and the First Amendment,* 85 Colum.L.Rev. 449 (1985).

c. For a comprehensive review and critical analysis of the problems and policies raised by advocacy of illegal action, see Greenawalt, note 7 supra.

prevention and punishment of which have never been thought to raise any constitutional problem. These include the lewd and obscene, the profane, the libelous, and the insulting or "fighting" words—those which by their very utterance inflict injury or tend to incite to an immediate breach of the peace. It has been well observed that such utterances are no essential part of any exposition of ideas, and are of such slight social value as a step to truth that any benefit that may be derived from them is clearly outweighed by the social interest in order and morality. "Resort to epithets or personal abuse is not in any proper sense communication of information or opinion safeguarded by the Constitution, and its punishment as a criminal act would raise no question under that instrument." *Cantwell v. Connecticut*, [p. 762 infra].' Such were the views of a unanimous Court in *Chaplinsky v. New Hampshire*, 315 U.S. 568, 62 S.Ct. 766, 86 L.Ed. 1031 (1942).[6]

"No one will gainsay that it is libelous falsely to charge another with being a rapist, robber, carrier of knives and guns, and user of marijuana. The [question is whether the fourteenth amendment] prevents a State from punishing such libels—as criminal libel has been defined, limited and constitutionally recognized time out of mind—directed at designated collectivities and flagrantly disseminated. [I]f an utterance directed at an individual may be the object of criminal sanctions, we cannot deny to a State power to punish the same utterance directed at a defined group, unless we can say that this is a wilful and purposeless restriction unrelated to the peace and well-being of the State.

"Illinois did not have to look beyond her own borders to await the tragic experience of the last three decades to conclude that wilful purveyors of falsehood concerning racial and religious groups promote strife and tend powerfully to obstruct the manifold adjustments required for free, orderly life in a metropolitan, polyglot community. From the murder of the abolitionist Lovejoy in 1837 to the Cicero riots of 1951, Illinois has been the scene of exacerbated tension between races, often flaring into violence and destruction. In many of these outbreaks, utterances of the character here in question, so the Illinois legislature could conclude, played a significant [part.]

"In the face of this history and its frequent obligato of extreme racial and religious propaganda, we would deny experience to say that the Illinois legislature was without reason in seeking ways to curb false or malicious defamation of racial and religious groups, made in public places and by means calculated to have a powerful emotional impact on those to whom it was presented. [I]t would be out of bounds for the judiciary to deny the legislature a choice of policy, provided it is not unrelated to the problem and not forbidden by some explicit limitation on the State's power. That the legislative remedy might not in practice mitigate the evil, or might itself raise new problems, would only manifest once more the paradox of reform. It is the price to be paid for the trial-and-error inherent in legislative efforts to deal with obstinate social issues.

"[It would] be arrant dogmatism, quite outside the scope of our authority [for] us to deny that the Illinois Legislature may warrantably believe that a man's job and his educational opportunities and the dignity accorded him may depend as much on the reputation of the racial and religious group to which he willynilly belongs, as on his own merits. This being so, we are precluded from saying that speech concededly punishable when immediately directed at individ-

---

6. In all but five States, the constitutional guarantee of free speech to every person is explicitly qualified by holding him "responsible for the abuse of that right." * * *

uals cannot be outlawed if directed at groups with whose position and esteem in society the affiliated individual may be inextricably involved. * * *[18]

"As to the defense of truth, Illinois in common with many States requires a showing not only that the utterance state the facts, but also that the publication be made 'with good motives and for justifiable ends'. Both elements are necessary if the defense is to prevail. [The] teaching of a century and a half of criminal libel prosecutions in this country would go by the board if we were to hold that Illinois was not within her rights in making this combined requirement. Assuming that defendant's offer of proof directed to a part of the defense was adequate, it did not satisfy the entire requirement which Illinois could exact."

The Court ruled that the trial court properly declined to require the jury to find a "clear and present danger": "Libelous utterances not being within the area of constitutionally protected speech, it is unnecessary, either for us or for the State courts, to consider the issues behind the phrase 'clear and present danger.' Certainly no one would contend that obscene speech, for example, may be punished only upon a showing of such circumstances. Libel, as we have seen, is in the same class."

BLACK, J., joined by Douglas, J., dissented: "[The Court] acts on the bland assumption that the First Amendment is wholly irrelevant. [Today's] case degrades First Amendment freedoms to the 'rational basis' level. [We] are cautioned that state legislatures must be left free to 'experiment' and to make legislative judgments. [State] experimentation in curbing freedom of expression is startling and frightening doctrine in a country dedicated to self-government by its people.

"[As] 'constitutionally recognized,' [criminal libel] has provided for punishment of false, malicious, scurrilous charges against individuals, not against huge groups. This limited scope of the law of criminal libel is of no small importance. It has confined state punishment of speech and expression to the narrowest of areas involving nothing more than private feuds. Every expansion of the law of criminal libel so as to punish discussion of matters of public concern means a corresponding invasion of the area dedicated to free expression by the First Amendment.

"[Whether] the words used in their context here are 'fighting words' in the same sense [as *Chaplinsky*] is doubtful, but whether so or not they are not addressed to or about *individuals*. Moreover, the leaflet used here was also the means adopted by an assembled group to enlist interest in their efforts to have legislation enacted. And the 'fighting' words were but a part of arguments on questions of wide public interest and importance. Freedom of petition, assembly, speech and press could be greatly abridged by a practice of meticulously scrutinizing every editorial, speech, sermon or other printed matter to extract two or three naughty words on which to hang charges of 'group libel.'

"[If] there be minority groups who hail this holding as their victory, they might consider the possible relevancy of this ancient remark: 'Another such victory and I am undone.' "

REED, J., joined by Douglas, J., dissenting, argued that the statute was unconstitutionally vague: "These words—'virtue,' 'derision,' and 'obloquy'—have

---

18. [If] a statute sought to outlaw libels of political parties, quite different problems not now before us would be raised. For one thing, the whole doctrine of fair comment as indispensable to the democratic political process would come into play. Political parties, like public men, are, as it were, public property.

neither general nor special meanings well enough known to apprise those within their reach as to limitations on speech. Philosophers and poets, thinkers of high and low degree from every age and race have sought to expound the meaning of virtue.   *   *   * Are the tests of the Puritan or the Cavalier to be applied, those of the city or the farm, the Christian or non-Christian, the old or the young?"

DOUGLAS, J., dissented: "Hitler and his Nazis showed how evil a conspiracy could be which was aimed at destroying a race by exposing it to contempt, derision, and obloquy. I would be willing to concede that such conduct directed at a race or group in this country could be made an indictable offense. For such a project would be more than the exercise of free speech. [It] would be free speech plus.

"I would also be willing to concede that even without the element of conspiracy there might be times and occasions when the legislative or executive branch might call a halt to inflammatory talk, such as the shouting of 'fire' in a school or a theatre.

"My view is that if in any case other public interests are to override the plain command of the First Amendment, the peril of speech must be clear and present, leaving no room for argument, raising no doubts as to the necessity of curbing speech in order to prevent disaster."

JACKSON, J., dissenting, argued that the fourteenth amendment does not incorporate the first, as such, but permits the states more latitude than the Congress. He concluded, however, that due process required the trier of fact to evaluate the evidence as to the truth and good faith of the speaker and the clarity and presence of the danger. He was unwilling to assume danger from the tendency of the words and felt that the trial court had precluded the defendant's efforts to show truth and good motives.

Notes and Questions

1. *The right to petition.* Should it make a difference that the leaflet was in the form of a petition to the mayor and city council? Does the right of the people "to petition the Government for a redress of grievances" add anything of substance to Beauharnais' other first amendment arguments? Consider Kalven, *The Negro and the First Amendment* 40 (1965): "If it would make a difference whether the petition was genuine and not just a trick of form, can the Court penetrate the form and appraise the true motivation or must it, as it does with congressional committees accept the official motivation?" [a]

2. *Equality and freedom of speech.* Consider the following hypothetical commentary: "Group libel statutes pose uniquely difficult issues for they involve a clash between two constitutional commitments: the principle of equality and the principle of free speech. They force us to decide what we want to express as a nation: Do we want a powerful symbol of our belief in uninhibited debate or do we want to be the kind of nation that will not tolerate the public calumny of religious, ethnic, and racial groups?" Compare Beth, *Group Libel and Free Speech*, 39 Minn.L.Rev. 167, 180–81 (1955).

3. *Tolerance and freedom of speech.* Should the first amendment be a means of institutionalizing a national commitment to the value of tolerance? By tolerating the intolerable, would we carve out one area of social interaction for

---

a. See *McDonald v. Smith*, ___ U.S. ___, 105 S.Ct. 2787, 86 L.Ed.2d 384 (1985) (denying   any special first amendment status for the Petition Clause).

extraordinary self-restraint and thereby develop [b] and demonstrate a vital social capacity? See generally Bollinger, *The Tolerant Society: Freedom of Speech and Extremist Speech in America* (1986); Bollinger, *Free Speech and Intellectual Values,* 92 Yale L.J. 438 (1983); Bollinger, *Book Review,* 80 Mich.L.Rev. 617 (1982).

4. *Civility and freedom of speech.* By allowing prosecutions for group libel in the most "odious cases" or cases "so public and offensive that they cannot be avoided" would we "encourage confidence in the discipline of judging itself" and "encourage others to make judgments as well, not simply on group defamation, but on other matters that raise questions about propriety and decency and the obligations that individuals may have to one another"? See Arkes, *Civility and the Restriction of Speech: Rediscovering the Defamation of Groups,* 1974 Sup.Ct. Rev. 281, 331.

5. *Libel, group libel, and seditious libel.* Consider Kalven, supra, at 15, 16 and 50–51: Seditious libel "is the doctrine that criticism of government officials and policy may be viewed as defamation of government and may be punished as a serious crime. [On] my view, the absence of seditious libel as a crime is the true pragmatic test of freedom of speech. This I would argue is what freedom of speech is about. [The] most revealing aspect of the opinions, and particularly that of Justice Frankfurter, is the absence of any sense of the proximity of the case before them to seditious libel. The case presents almost a perfect instance of that competition among analogies which Edward Levi has emphasized as the essential circumstance of legal reasoning. In the middle we have group libel and Justice Frankfurter's urging its many resemblances to individual libel. [If] the Court's speech theory had been more grounded, as it seems to me it should be, on the relevance of the concept of seditious libel and less on the analogy to the law of attempts found in the slogan 'clear and present danger,' it is difficult to believe that either the debate or the result in *Beauharnais* would have been the same."

B. PUBLIC OFFICIALS AND SEDITIOUS LIBEL

NEW YORK TIMES CO. v. SULLIVAN

376 U.S. 255, 84 S.Ct. 710, 11 L.Ed.2d 686 (1964).

MR. JUSTICE BRENNAN delivered the opinion of the Court.

[Sullivan, the Montgomery, Ala. police commissioner, sued the New York Times and four black Alabama clergymen for alleged libelous statements in a paid, full-page fund-raising advertisement signed by a "Committee to defend Martin Luther King and the struggle for freedom in the South." The advertisement stated that "truckloads of police armed with shotguns and tear-gas ringed Alabama State College Campus" in Montgomery, and that "the Southern violators [have] bombed [Dr. King's] home, assaulted his person [and] arrested him seven times." In several respects the statements were untrue. Several witnesses testified that they understood the statements to refer to Sullivan because he supervised Montgomery police. Sullivan proved he did not participate in the events described. He offered no proof of pecuniary loss.[3] Pursuant to Alabama law, the trial court submitted the libel issue to the jury, giving general and

b. For skepticism about the capacity of courts to achieve any substantial impact in promoting tolerance, see Nagel, *How Useful Is Judicial Review in Free Speech Cases?*, 69 Corn.L.Rev. 302 (1984).

3. Approximately 394 copies of the edition of the Times containing the advertisement were circulated in Alabama. Of these, about 35 copies were distributed in Montgomery punitive damages instructions. It returned a $500,000 verdict for Sullivan against all of the defendants.] We hold that the rule of law applied by the Alabama courts is constitutionally deficient for failure to provide the safeguards for freedom of speech and of the press that are required by the First and Fourteenth Amendments in a libel action brought by a public official against critics of his official conduct.[4] We further hold that under the proper safeguards the evidence presented in this case is constitutionally insufficient to support the judgment for respondent.

I. [The] publication here [communicated] information, expressed opinion, recited grievances, protested claimed abuses, and sought financial support on behalf of a movement whose existence and objectives are matters of the highest public interest and concern. That the Times was paid for publishing the advertisement is as immaterial in this connection as is the fact that newspapers and books are sold. *Smith v. California* [p. 404 infra]. Any other conclusion would discourage newspapers from carrying "editorial advertisements" of this type, and so might shut off an important outlet for the promulgation of information and ideas by persons who do not themselves have access to publishing facilities.

II. Under Alabama law [once] "libel per se" has been established, the defendant has no defense as to stated facts unless he can persuade the jury that they were true in all their particulars. [His] privilege of "fair comment" for expressions of opinion depends on the truth of the facts upon which the comment is based. [Unless] he can discharge the burden of proving truth, general damages are presumed, and may be awarded without proof of pecuniary injury.

[Respondent] relies heavily, as did the Alabama courts, on statements of this Court to the effect that the Constitution does not protect libelous publications. Those statements do not foreclose our inquiry here. None of the cases sustained the use of libel laws to impose sanctions upon expression critical of the official conduct of public officials. [L]ibel can claim no talismanic immunity from constitutional limitations. It must be measured by standards that satisfy the First Amendment.

The First Amendment, said Judge Learned Hand, "presupposes that right conclusions are more likely to be gathered out of a multitude of tongues, than through any kind of authoritative selection. To many this is, and always will be, folly; but we have staked upon it our all." [Thus] we consider this case against the background of a profound national commitment to the principle that debate on public issues should be uninhibited, robust, and wide-open, and that it may well include vehement, caustic, and sometimes unpleasantly sharp attacks on government and public officials. The present advertisement, as an expression of grievance and protest on one of the major public issues of our time, would seem

---

County. The total circulation of the Times for that day was approximately 650,000 copies.

4. [The] Times contends that the assumption of jurisdiction over its corporate person by the Alabama courts overreaches the territorial limits of the Due Process Clause. The latter claim is foreclosed from our review by the ruling of the Alabama courts that the Times entered a general appearance in the action and thus waived its jurisdictional objection. * * *

[Since *New York Times* the Court has upheld expansive personal jurisdiction against media defendants. *Calder v. Jones*, 465 U.S. 783, 104 S.Ct. 1482, 79 L.Ed.2d 804 (1984); *Keeton v. Hustler*, 465 U.S. 770, 104 S.Ct. 1473, 79 L.Ed.2d 790 (1984). *Calder* rejected the suggestion that first amendment concerns enter into jurisdictional analysis. It feared complicating the inquiry and argued that because first amendment concerns are taken into account in limiting the substantive law of defamation, "to reintroduce those concerns at the jurisdictional stage would be a form of double counting."]

clearly to qualify for the constitutional protection. The question is whether it forfeits that protection by the falsity of some of its factual statements and by its alleged defamation of respondent.

Authoritative interpretations of the First Amendment guarantees have consistently refused to recognize an exception for any test of truth—whether administered by judges, juries, or administrative officials—and especially not one that puts the burden of proving truth on the speaker. [E]rroneous statement is inevitable in free debate, and [it] must be protected if the freedoms of expression are to have the "breathing space" that they "need [to] survive."

[Injury] to official reputation affords no more warrant for repressing speech that would otherwise be free than does factual error. Where judicial officers are involved, this Court has held that concern for the dignity and reputation of the courts does not justify the punishment as criminal contempt of criticism of the judge or his decision. This is true even though the utterance contains "half-truths" and "misinformation." Such repression can be justified, if at all, only by a clear and present danger of the obstruction of justice. If judges are to be treated as "men of fortitude, able to thrive in a hardy climate," surely the same must be true of other government officials, such as elected city commissioners. Criticism of their official conduct does not lose its constitutional protection merely because it is effective criticism and hence diminishes their official reputations.

If neither factual error nor defamatory content suffices to remove the constitutional shield from criticism of official conduct, the combination of the two elements is no less inadequate. This is the lesson to be drawn from the great controversy over the Sedition Act of 1798, 1 Stat. 596, which first crystallized a national awareness of the central meaning of the First Amendment. [Although] the Sedition Act was never tested in this Court, the attack upon its validity has carried the day in the court of history. Fines levied in its prosecution were repaid by Act of Congress on the ground that it was unconstitutional. * * * Jefferson, as President, pardoned those who had been convicted and sentenced under the Act and remitted their fines. [Its] invalidity [has] also been assumed by Justices of this Court. [These] views reflect a broad consensus that the Act, because of the restraint it imposed upon criticism of government and public officials, was inconsistent with the First Amendment. * * *

What a State may not constitutionally bring about by means of a criminal statute is likewise beyond the reach of its civil law of libel. The fear of damage awards under a rule such as that invoked by the Alabama courts here may be markedly more inhibiting than the fear of prosecution under a criminal statute. [The] judgment awarded in this case—without the need for any proof of actual pecuniary loss—was one thousand times greater than the maximum fine provided by the Alabama criminal [libel law], and one hundred times greater than that provided by the Sedition Act. And since there is no double-jeopardy limitation applicable to civil lawsuits, this is not the only judgment that may be awarded against petitioners for the same publication.[18] Whether or not a newspaper can survive a succession of such judgments, the pall of fear and timidity imposed upon those who would give voice to public criticism is an atmosphere in which the First Amendment freedoms cannot [survive].

---

18. The Times states that four other libel suits based on the advertisement have been filed against it by [others]; that another $500,000 verdict has been awarded in [one]; and that the damages sought in the other three total $2,000,000.

The state rule of law is not saved by its allowance of the defense of truth. A defense for erroneous statements honestly made is no less essential here than was the requirement of proof of guilty knowledge which, in *Smith v. California*, we held indispensable to a valid conviction of a bookseller for possessing obscene writings for [sale].

A rule compelling the critic of official conduct to guarantee the truth of all his factual assertions—and to do so on pain of libel judgments virtually unlimited in amount—leads to a comparable "self-censorship." Allowance of the defense of truth, with the burden of proving it on the defendant, does not mean that only false speech will be deterred.[19] [Under] such a rule, would-be critics of official conduct may be deterred from voicing their criticism, even though it is believed to be true and even though it is in fact true, because of doubt whether it can be proved in court or fear of the expense of having to do so. They tend to make only statements which "steer far wider of the unlawful zone." The rule thus dampens the vigor and limits the variety of public [debate].

The constitutional guarantees require, we think, a federal rule that prohibits a public official from recovering damages for a defamatory falsehood relating to his official conduct unless he proves that the statement was made with "actual malice"—that is, with knowledge that it was false or with reckless disregard of whether it was false or [not].

Such a privilege for criticism of official conduct is appropriately analogous to the protection accorded a public official when *he* is sued for libel by a private citizen. In *Barr v. Matteo*, 360 U.S. 564, 575, 79 S.Ct. 1335, 1341, 3 L.Ed.2d 1434 (1959), this Court held the utterance of a federal official to be absolutely privileged if made "within the outer perimeter" of his duties. The States accord the same immunity to statements of their highest officers, although some differentiate their lesser officials and qualify the privilege they enjoy. But all hold that all officials are protected unless actual malice can be proved. The reason for the official privilege is said to be that the threat of damage suits would otherwise "inhibit the fearless, vigorous, and effective administration of policies of government" and "dampen the ardor of all but the most resolute, or the most irresponsible, in the unflinching discharge of their duties." *Barr.* Analogous considerations support the privilege for the citizen-critic of government. It is as much his duty to criticize as it is the official's duty to administer. [It] would give public servants an unjustified preference over the public they serve, if critics of official conduct did not have a fair equivalent of the immunity granted to the officials themselves. We conclude that such a privilege is required by the First and Fourteenth Amendments.[23]

III. [W]e consider that the proof presented to show actual malice lacks the convincing clarity [a] which the constitutional standard demands, and hence that

---

19. Even a false statement may be deemed to make a valuable contribution to the public debate, since it brings about "the clearer perception and livelier impression of truth, produced by its collision with error." Mill, *On Liberty* 15 (1947).

23. We have no occasion here to determine how far down into the lower ranks of government employees the "public official" designation would extend for purposes of this rule, or otherwise to specify categories of persons who would or would not be included. [Nor] need we here determine the boundaries of the "official conduct" concept. * * *

a. Compare *Bose Corp. v. Consumers Union*, 466 U.S. 485, 104 S.Ct. 1949, 80 L.Ed. 2d 502 (1984) (appellate courts "must exercise independent judgment and determine whether the record establishes actual malice with convincing clarity."). Should independent appellate judgment be required in all first amendment cases? All constitutional cases? For broadranging commentary, see Monaghan, *Constitutional Fact Review*, 85 Colum.L.Rev. 229 (1985).

it would not constitutionally sustain the judgment for respondent under the proper rule of law. [T]here is evidence that the Times published the advertisement without checking its accuracy against the news stories in the Times' own files. The mere presence of the stories in the files does [not] establish that the Times "knew" the advertisement was false, since the state of mind required for actual malice would have to be brought home to the persons in the Times' organization having responsibility for the publication of the advertisement. With respect to the failure of those persons to make the check, the record shows that they relied upon their knowledge of the good reputation of many [whose] names were listed as sponsors of the advertisement, and upon the letter from A. Philip Randolph, known to them as a responsible individual, certifying that the use of the names was authorized. There was testimony that the persons handling the advertisement saw nothing in it that would render it unacceptable under the Times' policy of rejecting advertisements containing "attacks of a personal character"; their failure to reject it on this ground was not unreasonable. We think the evidence against the Times supports at most a finding of negligence in failing to discover the misstatements, and is constitutionally insufficient to show the recklessness that is required for a finding of actual malice.

[T]he evidence was constitutionally defective in another respect: it was incapable of supporting the jury's finding that the allegedly libelous statements were made "of and concerning" respondent. [On this point, the Supreme Court of Alabama] based its ruling on the proposition that: "[The] average person knows that municipal agents, such as police and firemen, and others, are under the control and direction of the city governing body, and more particularly under the direction and control of a single commissioner. In measuring the performance or deficiencies of such groups, praise or criticism is usually attached to the official in complete control of the body."

This proposition has disquieting implications for criticism of governmental conduct. [It would transmute] criticism of government, however impersonal it may seem on its face, into personal criticism, and hence potential libel, of the officials of whom the government is composed. [Raising] as it does the possibility that a good-faith critic of government will be penalized for his criticism, the proposition relied on by the Alabama courts strikes at the very center of the constitutionally protected area of free expression. We hold that such a proposition may not constitutionally be utilized to establish that an otherwise impersonal attack on governmental operations was a libel of an official responsible for those operations. Since it was relied on exclusively here, and there was no other evidence to connect the statements with respondent, the evidence was constitutionally insufficient to support a finding that the statements referred to respondent. * * *[b]

MR. JUSTICE BLACK, with whom MR. JUSTICE DOUGLAS joins (concurring).

* * * "Malice," even as defined by the Court, is an elusive, abstract concept, hard to prove and hard to disprove. The requirement that malice be proved provides at best an evanescent protection for the right critically to discuss public affairs and certainly does not measure up to the sturdy safeguard embodied in the First Amendment. Unlike the Court, therefore, I vote to reverse exclusively on the ground that the Times and the individual defendants

b. For a similar ruling that impersonal criticism of a government operation cannot be the basis for defamation "of and concerning" the supervisor of the operation, see *Rosenblatt* *v. Baer,* 383 U.S. 75, 86 S.Ct. 669, 15 L.Ed.2d 597 (1966): "[T]antamount to a demand for recovery based on libel of government."

had an absolute, unconditional constitutional right to publish in the Times advertisement their criticisms of the Montgomery agencies and [officials].

The half-million-dollar verdict [gives] dramatic proof [that] state libel laws threaten the very existence of an American press virile enough to publish unpopular views on public affairs and bold enough to criticize the conduct of public officials. [B]riefs before us show that in Alabama there are now pending eleven libel suits by local and state officials against the Times seeking $5,600,000, and five such suits against the Columbia Broadcasting System seeking $1,700,000. Moreover, this technique for harassing and punishing a free press—now that it has been shown to be possible—is by no means limited to cases with racial overtones; it can be used in other fields where public feelings may make local as well as out-of-state newspapers easy prey for libel verdict seekers.

In my opinion the Federal Constitution has dealt with this deadly danger to the press in the only way possible without leaving the press open to destruction—by granting the press an absolute immunity for criticism of the way public officials do their public duty.

[This] Nation, I suspect, can live in peace without libel suits based on public discussions of public affairs and public officials. But I doubt that a country can live in freedom where its people can be made to suffer physically or financially for criticizing their government, its actions, or its officials. * * *[c]

———

Professor Kalven observed that the Court in *New York Times* was moving toward "the theory of free speech that Alexander Meiklejohn has been offering us for some fifteen years now." Kalven, *The New York Times Case: A Note On "The Central Meaning of the First Amendment,"* 1964 Sup.Ct.Rev. 191, 221. Indeed Kalven reported Meiklejohn's view that the case was " 'an occasion for dancing in the streets.' " Id. at 221 n. 125. Consider the following excerpts from Meiklejohn's most significant work and Zechariah Chafee's pointed response.

ALEXANDER MEIKLEJOHN—FREE SPEECH AND ITS RELATION TO SELF–GOVERNMENT

3, 26–27, 93–94, 89–91 (1948), reprinted in Meiklejohn, *Political Freedom* 9, 27–28, 79–80, 75–77 (1960).
Reprinted with permission of the publisher; copyright © 1948, 1960 by Harper & Brothers.

We Americans think of ourselves as politically free. We believe in self-government. If men are to be governed, we say, then that governing must be done, not by others, but by themselves. So far, therefore, as our own affairs are concerned, we refuse to submit to alien control. That refusal, if need be, we will carry to the point of rebellion, of revolution. And if other men, within the jurisdiction of our laws, are denied their right to political freedom, we will, in the same spirit, rise to their defense. Governments, we insist, derive their just powers from the consent of the governed. If that consent be lacking, governments have no just powers.

[The] principle of the freedom of speech springs from the necessities of the program of self-government. It is not a Law of Nature or of Reason in the

---

c. Goldberg, J., joined by Douglas, J., concurring, also asserted for "the citizen and [the] press an absolute unconditional privilege to criticize official conduct," but maintained that the imposition of liability for "[p]urely private defamation" did not abridge the first amendment because it had "little to do with the political ends of a self-governing society."

abstract. It is a deduction from the basic American agreement that public issues shall be decided by universal suffrage.

If, then, on any occasion in the United States it is allowable to say that the Constitution is a good document it is equally allowable, in that situation, to say that the Constitution is a bad document. If a public building may be used in which to say, in time of war, that the war is justified, then the same building may be used in which to say that it is not justified. If it be publicly argued that conscription for armed service is moral and necessary, it may likewise be publicly argued that it is immoral and unnecessary. If it may be said that American political institutions are superior to those of England or Russia or Germany, it may, with equal freedom, be said that those of England or Russia or Germany are superior to ours. These conflicting views may be expressed, must be expressed, not because they are valid, but because they are relevant. If they are responsibly entertained by anyone, we, the voters, need to hear them. When a question of policy is "before the house," free men choose to meet it not with their eyes shut, but with their eyes open. To be afraid of ideas, any idea, is to be unfit for self-government. Any such suppression of ideas about the common good, the First Amendment condemns with its absolute disapproval. The freedom of ideas shall not be abridged. * * *

If, however, as our argument has tried to show, the principle of the freedom of speech is derived, not from some supposed "Natural Right," but from the necessities of self-government by universal suffrage, there follows at once a very large limitation of the scope of the principle. The guarantee given by the First Amendment is not, then, assured to all speaking. It is assured only to speech which bears, directly or indirectly, upon issues with which voters have to deal—only, therefore, to the consideration of matters of public interest. Private speech, or private interest in speech, on the other hand, has no claim whatever to the protection of the First Amendment. If men are engaged, as we so commonly are, in argument, or inquiry, or advocacy, or incitement which is directed toward our private interests, private privileges, private possessions, we are, of course, entitled to "due process" protection of those activities. But the First Amendment has no concern over such protection. * * *

Here, then, are the charges which I would bring against the "clear and present danger" theory. They are all, it is clear, differing forms of the basic accusation that the compact of self-government has been ignored or repudiated.

First, the theory denies or obscures the fact that free citizens have two distinct sets of civil liberties. As the makers of the laws, they have duties and responsibilities which require an absolute freedom. As the subjects of the laws, they have possessions and rights, to which belongs a relative freedom.

Second, the theory fails to keep clear the distinction between the constitutional status of discussions of public policy and the corresponding status of discussions of private policy.

Third, the theory fails to recognize that, under the Constitution, the freedom of advocacy or incitement to action *by the government* may never be abridged. It is only advocacy or incitement to action by individuals or nonpolitical groups which is open to regulation.

Fourth, the theory regards the freedom of speech as a mere device which is to be abandoned when dangers threaten the public welfare. On the contrary, it is the very presence of those dangers which makes it imperative that, in the midst of our fears, we remember and observe a principle upon whose integrity rests the entire structure of government by consent of the governed.

Fifth, the Supreme Court, by adopting a theory which annuls the First Amendment, has struck a disastrous blow at our national education. It has denied the belief that men can, by processes of free public discussion, govern themselves.   *   *   *

The unabridged freedom of public discussion is the rock on which our government stands. With that foundation beneath us, we shall not flinch in the face of any clear and present—or, even, terrific—danger.

ZECHARIAH CHAFEE, JR.—BOOK REVIEW

62 Harv.L.Rev. 891, 894–901 (1949).
Reprinted with permission of the publisher; copyright © 1949, by the
Harvard Law Review Association.

[M]y main objection to Mr. Meiklejohn's book [is that he] places virtually all his argument against current proposals for suppression on a constitutional position which is extremely dubious. Whereas the supporters of these measures are genuinely worried by the dangers of Communism, he refuses to argue that these dangers are actually small. Instead, his constitutional position obliges him to argue that these dangers are irrelevant. No matter how terrible and immediate the dangers may be, he keeps saying, the First Amendment will not let Congress or anybody else in the Government try to deal with Communists who have not yet committed unlawful [acts.]

Mr. Meiklejohn's basic proposition is that there are two distinct kinds of freedom of speech, protected by quite different clauses of the Constitution. Freedom of speech on matters affecting self-government is protected by the First Amendment and is not open to restrictions by the Government. [By] contrast, private discussion is open to restrictions because it is protected by [fifth amendment due process].

The truth is, I think, that the framers had no very clear idea as to what they meant by "the freedom of speech or of the press," but we can say three things with reasonable assurance. First, these politicians, lawyers, scholars, churchgoers and philosophers, scientists, agriculturalists, and wide readers used the phrase to embrace the whole realm of thought. Second, they intended the First Amendment to give all the protection they desired, and had no idea of supplementing it by the Fifth Amendment. Finally, the freedom which Congress was forbidden to abridge was not, for them, some absolute concept which had never existed on earth. It was the freedom which they believed they already had— what they had wanted before the Revolution and had acquired through independence. In thinking about it, they took for granted the limitations which had been customarily applied in the day-to-day work of colonial courts. Now, they were setting up a new federal government of great potential strength, and (as in the rest of Bill of Rights) they were determined to make sure that it would not take away the freedoms which they then enjoyed in their thirteen sovereign states.

Still, the First Amendment has the power of growing to meet new needs. As Marshall said, it is a *Constitution* which we are interpreting. Although in 1791 the Amendment did not mean what Mr. Meiklejohn says, perhaps it ought to mean that now. But the Supreme Court is unlikely to think so in any foreseeable future. The author condemns the clear and present danger test as "a peculiarly inept and unsuccessful attempt to formulate an exception" to the constitutional protection of public discussion, but he does not realize how unworkable his own views would prove when applied in litigation.

In the first place, although it may be possible to draw a fairly bright line between speech which is completely immune and action which may be punished, some speech on public questions is so hateful that the Court would be very reluctant to protect it from statutory penalties. We are not dealing with a philosopher who can write what he pleases, but with at least five men who are asked to block legislators and prosecutors. The history of the Court Plan in 1937 shows how sure judges have to be of their ground to do that. Take a few examples. A newspaper charges the mayor with taking bribes. Ezra Pound broadcasts from an Italian radio station that our participation in the war is an abominable mistake. A speaker during a very bad food shortage tells a hungry mass of voters that the rationing board is so incompetent and corrupt that the best way to avoid starvation is to demand the immediate death of its members, unless they are ready to resign. Plainly few judges can grant constitutional protection to such speeches.

Even the author begins to hedge. Although his main insistence is on immunity for all speech connected with self-government, as my examples surely are, occasionally he concedes that "repressive action by the government is imperative for the sake of the general welfare," e.g., against libelous assertions, slander, words inciting men to crime, sedition, and treason by words. Here he is diving into very deep water. Once you push punishment beyond action into the realm of language, then you have to say pretty plainly how far back the law should go. You must enable future judges and jurymen to know where to stop. That is just what Holmes did when he drew his line at clear and present danger and the author gives us no substitute test for distinguishing between good public speech and bad public speech. He never faces the problem of Mark Anthony's Oration—discussion which is calculated to produce unlawful acts without ever mentioning them.

At times he hints that the line depends on the falsity of the assertions or the bad motives of the speakers. In the mayor's case, it is no answer to say that false charges are outside the Constitution; the issue is whether a jury shall be permitted to find them false even if they are in fact true. Moreover, in such charges a good deal of truth which might be useful to the voters is frequently mixed with some falsehood, so that the possibility of a damage action often keeps genuine information away from voters. And the low character of speakers and writers does not necessarily prevent them from uttering wholesome truths about politics. Witness the Essays of Francis Bacon. Mr. Meiklejohn has a special dislike for paid "lobbyists for special interests." But if discussing public questions with money in sight is outside the First Amendment, how about speeches by aspirants to a $75,000 job in Washington or editorials in newspapers or books on Free Speech? Dr. Johnson declared that any man who writes except for money is a fool. In short, the trouble with the bad-motive test is that courts and juries would apply it only to the exponents of unpopular views. If what is said happens to be our way, the speaker is as welcome as an ex-revolutionist to the Un-American Committee.

The most serious weakness in Mr. Meiklejohn's argument is that it rests on his supposed boundary between public speech and private speech. That line is extremely blurred. Take the novel *Strange Fruit*, which was lately suppressed in Massachusetts. It did not discuss any question then before the voters, but it dealt thoughtfully with many problems of the relations between whites and Negroes, a matter of great national concern. Was this under the First Amendment or the Fifth? [The] truth is that there are public aspects to practically every subject. [The] author recognizes this when he says that the First Amendment is directed against "mutilation of the thinking process of the community." [This] attitude, however, offers such a wide area for the First Amendment that very little is left for his private speech under the Fifth Amendment. For example, if books and plays are public speech, how can they be penalized for gross obscenity or libels?

On the other hand, if private speech does include scholarship (as the author suggests) and also art and literature, it is shocking to deprive these vital matters of the protection of the inspiring words of the First Amendment. The individual interest in freedom of speech, which Socrates voiced when he said that he would rather die than stop talking, is too precious to be left altogether to the vague words of the due process clause. Valuable as self-government is, it is in itself only a small part of our lives. That a philosopher should subordinate all other activities to it is indeed surprising.

[Even] if Holmes had agreed with Mr. Meiklejohn's view of the First Amendment, his insistence on such absolutism would not have persuaded a single colleague, and scores of men would have gone to prison who have been speaking freely for three decades. After all, a judge who is trying to establish a doctrine which the Supreme Court will promulgate as law cannot write like a solitary philosopher. He has to convince at least four men in a specific group and convince them very soon. The true alternative to Holmes' view of the First Amendment was not at all the perfect immunity for public discussion which Mr. Meiklejohn desires. It was no immunity at all in the face of legislation. Any danger, any tendency in speech to produce bad acts, no matter how remote, would suffice to validate a repressive statute, and the only hope for speakers and writers would lie in being tried by liberal jurymen. * * * Holmes worked out a formula which would invalidate a great deal of suppression, and won for it the solid authority of a unanimous Court. Afterwards, again and again, when his test was misapplied by the majority, Holmes restated his position in ringing words which, with the help of Brandeis and Hughes, eventually inspired the whole Court.[a]

Notes and Questions

1. To what extent does *New York Times* incorporate Meiklejohn's perspective?[b] What is the "central meaning" of the first amendment?

a. Compare Berns, *Freedom, Virtue and the First Amendment* 50–56 (Gateway ed. 1965): "The first thing to be remembered [about the clear and present danger test] is that Schenck was sent to jail with it. The second is that Abrams and Gitlow, with Holmes dissenting in ringing clear and present danger language, were jailed despite it. The third is that [the communists in *Dennis*] were sent to jail with it. [Only *Taylor v. Mississippi*, 319 U.S. 583, 63 S.Ct. 1200, 87 L.Ed. 1600 (1943), reversing the conviction of Jehovah's Witnesses, prosecuted under a wartime state sedition law for publicly urging people not to support the war and for advocating and teaching refusal to salute the flag], can illustrate the use of the [Holmes] doctrine to cause the triumph of free speech over national [security]. Thus, [in] the area in which the rule was first enunciated, the clear and present danger test has been of assistance only to a Jehovah's Witness—not to a Socialist

like Debs or a Communist like Gitlow or Dennis, or to anyone else whose opinions are both hated *and* feared. [The test] actually becomes a rationale for avoiding the impossible prohibitions of the First Amendment and for convicting persons for speech that the government has forbidden."

b. For elaboration and modification of Meiklejohn's views, see Meiklejohn, *The First Amendment Is an Absolute,* 1961 Sup.Ct.Rev. 245. For commentary, see Bollinger, *Free Speech and Intellectual Values,* 92 Yale L.J. 438 (1983); Kalven, p. 352 supra. For work proceeding from a politically based interpretation of the first amendment, see Anastaplo, *The Constitutionalist* (1971); BeVier, *The First Amendment and Political Speech: An Inquiry Into the Substance and Limits of Principle,* 30 Stan.L.Rev. 299 (1978); Bloustein, *The First Amendment and Privacy: The Supreme Court Justice and the Philosopher,* 28

2. *New York Times, definitional balancing, and the two-level theory of the first amendment.* By holding that some libel was within the protection of the first amendment, did the Court dismantle its two-level theory? See Kalven, supra, at 217–218. Or did the Court merely rearrange its conception of what was protected and what was not?

Does *Garrison v. Louisiana,* 379 U.S. 64, 85 S.Ct. 209, 13 L.Ed.2d 125 (1964) shed light on the question? The Court stated: "Calculated falsehood falls into that class of utterances '[of] such slight social value as a step to truth that any benefit that may be derived from them is clearly outweighed by the social interest in order and morality.' *Chaplinsky.*"

Could the judicial process here fairly be called *definitional* classification— defining which categories of libel are to be viewed as "speech" within the first amendment, and which are not? Consider Nimmer, *The Right to Speak from Times to Time, First Amendment Theory Applied to Libel and Misapplied to Privacy,* 56 Calif.L.Rev. 935, 942–43 (1968): "[*New York Times*] points the way to the employment of the balancing process on the definitional rather than the litigation or ad hoc level, [that is,] balancing not for the purpose of determining which litigant deserves to prevail in the particular case, but only for the purpose of defining which forms of speech are to be regarded as 'speech' within the meaning of the first amendment. [By] in effect holding that knowingly and recklessly false speech was not 'speech' within the meaning of the first amendment, the Court must have implicitly (since no explicit explanation was offered) referred to certain competing policy considerations. This is surely a kind of balancing, but it is just as surely not ad hoc balancing." [c]

3. *The scope of New York Times.* Professor Kalven argued that given the Court's conception of freedom of speech, its holding could not be confined: "the invitation to follow a dialectic progression from public official to government policy to public policy to matters in the public domain, like art, seems * * * overwhelming." Kalven, supra, at 221.

(a) *Public officials.* New York Times, fn. 23 left open "how far down into the lower ranks of governmental employees" the rule would extend, but later applied the rule in *Rosenblatt v. Baer,* 383 U.S. 75, 86 S.Ct. 669, 15 L.Ed.2d 597 (1966) to the supervisor of a publicly owned ski resort, saying it applies to those

Rutg.L.Rev. 41 (1974); Bork, *Neutral Principles and Some First Amendment Problems,* 47 Ind.L.J. 1 (1971). See also Brennan, *The Supreme Court and the Meiklejohn Interpretation of the First Amendment,* 79 Harv.L.Rev. 1 (1965).

c. The literature about balancing is voluminous. Compare, e.g., Frantz, *The First Amendment in the Balance,* 71 Yale L.J. 1424 (1962); Frantz, *Is the First Amendment Law? —A Reply to Professor Mendelson,* 51 Calif.L. Rev. 729 (1963) with Mendelson, *On the Meaning of the First Amendment: Absolutes in the Balance,* 50 Calif.L.Rev. 821 (1962); Mendelson, *The First Amendment and the Judicial Process: A Reply to Mr. Frantz,* 17 Vand.L. Rev. 479 (1984). For a philosophical attack on cost benefit analysis, see Tribe, *Policy Science: Analysis or Ideology?,* 2 Phil. & Pub.Aff. 66 (1972); Tribe, *Technology Assessment and the Fourth Discontinuity: The Limits of Instrumental Rationality,* 46 So.Cal.L.Rev. 617

(1973). For philosophical defenses of balancing, see Schlag, *An Attack on Categorical Approaches to Freedom of Speech,* 30 U.C.L.A.L. Rev. 671 (1983); Shiffrin, *Liberalism, Radicalism, and Legal Scholarship,* 30 U.C.L.A.L.Rev. 1103 (1983) (both resisting any necessary connection between balancing and instrumentalism or cost-benefit analysis). For more doctrinally focused analysis, compare, e.g., Emerson, *First Amendment Doctrine and the Burger Court,* 68 Calif.L.Rev. 422 (1980); Tribe, *Constitutional Calculus: Equal Justice or Economic Efficiency?,* 98 Harv.L.Rev. 592 (1985) with Schauer, *Categories and the First Amendment: A Play in Three Acts,* 34 Vand.L.Rev. 265 (1981); Shiffrin, *The First Amendment and Economic Regulation: Away From a General Theory of the First Amendment,* 78 Nw. U.L.Rev. 1212 (1983); Van Alstyne, *A Graphic Review of the Free Speech Clause,* 70 Calif.L. Rev. 107 (1982).

who "appear to the public to [have] substantial responsibility for or control over the conduct of government affairs." Should criticism of the official conduct of *very* high ranking government officials (e.g., the President, the Secretary of State, a general commanding troops in war) be given greater protection than that afforded in *New York Times?*

(b) *Private conduct of public officials and candidates.* *Garrison,* extended *New York Times* to "anything which might touch on an official's fitness for office," even if the defamation did not concern official conduct in office. Invoking that standard, *Monitor Patriot Co. v. Roy,* 401 U.S. 265, 91 S.Ct. 621, 28 L.Ed. 2d 35 (1971) applied *New York Times* to a news column describing a candidate for public office as a "former small-time bootlegger."

(c) *Public figures.* In CURTIS PUB. CO. v. BUTTS and ASSOCIATED PRESS v. WALKER, 388 U.S. 130, 87 S.Ct. 1975, 18 L.Ed.2d 1094 (1967), HARLAN, J., contended that because public figures were not subject to the restraints of the political process, any criticism of them was not akin to seditious libel and was, therefore, a step removed from the central meaning of the first amendment. Nonetheless, he argued that public figure actions should not be left entirely to the vagaries of state defamation law and would have required that public figures show "highly unreasonable conduct constituting an extreme departure from the standards of investigation and reporting ordinarily adhered to by responsible publishers" as a prerequisite to recovery. In response, WARREN, C.J., argued that the inapplicability of the restraints of the political process to public figures underscored the importance for uninhibited debate about their activities since "public opinion may be the only instrument by which society can attempt to influence their conduct." He observed that increasingly "the distinctions between governmental and private sectors are blurred," that public figures, like public officials, "often play an influential role in ordering society," and as a class have a ready access to the mass media "both to influence policy and to counter criticism of their views and activities." He accordingly concluded that the *New York Times* rule should be extended to public figures. Four other justices in *Butts* and *Walker* were willing to go at least as far as Warren, C.J., and subsequent cases have settled on the position that public figures must meet the *New York Times* requirements in order to recover in a defamation action. The critical issues are how to define the concept of public figure and how to apply it in practice. See *Gertz, infra.*

(d) *Private plaintiffs and public issues.* Without deciding whether any first amendment protection should extend to matters not of general or public interest, a plurality led by BRENNAN, J., joined by Burger, C.J., and Blackmun, J., argued in ROSENBLOOM v. METROMEDIA, INC., 403 U.S. 29, 91 S.Ct. 1811, 29 L.Ed. 2d 296 (1971), that the *New York Times* rule should be extended to defamatory statements involving matters of public or general interest "without regard to whether the persons involved are famous or anonymous." BLACK, J., would have gone further, opining that the first amendment "does not permit the recovery of libel judgments against the news media even when statements are broadcast with knowledge they are false," and Douglas, J., shared Black, J.'s approach (at least with respect to matters of public interest, although he did not participate in *Rosenbloom.*) WHITE, J., felt that the *New York Times* rule should apply to reporting on the official actions of public servants and to reporting on those involved in or affected by their official action. That principle was broad enough to cover Rosenbloom, a distributor of nudist magazines who had been arrested by the Philadelphia police for distributing obscene materials. The defamatory broadcast wrongly assumed his guilt. Dissenting, Harlan, Stewart and Marshall, JJ., counselled an approach similar to that taken in *Gertz, infra.*

After *Rosenbloom* the lower courts rather uniformly followed the approach taken by the plurality. By 1974, however, the composition of the Court had changed and so had the minds of some of the justices.

C. PRIVATE INDIVIDUALS AND PUBLIC FIGURES

GERTZ v. ROBERT WELCH, INC.

418 U.S. 323, 94 S.Ct. 2997, 41 L.Ed.2d 789 (1974).

MR. JUSTICE POWELL delivered the opinion of the Court.

[Respondent published *American Opinion,* a monthly outlet for the John Birch Society. It published an article falsely stating that Gertz, a lawyer, was the "architect" in a "communist frameup" of a policeman convicted of murdering a youth whose family Gertz represented in resultant civil proceedings, and that Gertz had a "criminal record" and had been an officer in a named "Communist-fronter" organization that advocated violent seizure of our government. In Gertz' libel action there was evidence that *Opinion* 's managing editor did not know the statements were false and had relied on the reputation of the article's author and prior experience with the accuracy of his articles. After a $50,000 verdict for Gertz, the trial court entered judgment n.o.v., concluding that the *New York Times* rule applied to any discussion of a "public issue." The court of appeals affirmed, ruling that the publisher did not have the requisite "awareness of probable falsity." The Court held that *New York Times* did not apply to defamation of private individuals, but remanded for a new trial "because the jury was allowed to impose liability without fault [and] to presume damages without proof of injury."]

II. The principal issue in this case is whether a newspaper or broadcaster that publishes defamatory falsehoods about an individual who is neither a public official nor a public figure may claim a constitutional privilege against liability for the injury inflicted by those statements. * * *

In his opinion for the plurality in *Rosenbloom,* Mr. Justice Brennan took the *Times* privilege one step further [than *Butts* and *Walker*]. He concluded that its protection should extend to defamatory falsehoods relating to private persons if the statements concerned matters of general or public interest. He abjured the suggested distinction between public officials and public figures on the one hand and private individuals on the other. He focused instead on society's interest in learning about certain issues: "If a matter is a subject of public or general interest, it cannot suddenly become less so merely because a private individual is involved or because in some sense the individual did not choose to become involved." Thus, under the plurality opinion, a private citizen involuntarily associated with a matter of general interest has no recourse for injury to his reputation unless he can satisfy the demanding requirements of the *Times* [test].

III. [Under] the First Amendment there is no such thing as a false idea. However pernicious an opinion may seem, we depend for its correction not on the conscience of the judges and juries but on the competition of other ideas. But there is no constitutional value in false statements of fact. Neither the intentional lie nor the careless error materially advances society's interest in "uninhibited, robust, and wide-open" debate on public issues. * * *

Although the erroneous statement of fact is not worthy of constitutional protection, it is nevertheless inevitable in free debate. [P]unishment of error runs the risk of inducing a cautious and restrictive exercise of the constitutionally guaranteed freedoms of speech and press. [The] First Amendment requires that we protect some falsehood in order to protect speech that matters.

The need to avoid self-censorship by the news media is, however, not the only societal value at issue. [The] legitimate state interest underlying the law of libel is the compensation of individuals for the harm inflicted on them by defamatory falsehoods. We would not lightly require the State to abandon this purpose, for, as Mr. Justice Stewart has reminded us, the individual's right to the protection of his own good name "reflects no more than our basic concept of the essential dignity and worth of every human being—a concept at the root of any decent system of ordered liberty. * * *" *Rosenblatt.*

Some tension necessarily exists between the need for a vigorous and uninhibited press and the legitimate interest in redressing wrongful injury. [In] our continuing effort to define the proper accommodation between these competing concerns, we have been especially anxious to assure to the freedoms of speech and press that "breathing space" essential to their fruitful exercise. To that end this Court has extended a measure of strategic protection to defamatory falsehood.

The *New York Times* standard defines the level of constitutional protection appropriate to the context of defamation of [public figures and those who hold governmental office]. Plainly many deserving plaintiffs, including some intentionally subjected to injury, will be unable to surmount the barrier of the *New York Times* test. [For] the reasons stated below, we conclude that the state interest in compensating injury to the reputation of private individuals requires that a different rule should obtain with respect to them.

[W]e have no difficulty in distinguishing among defamation plaintiffs. The first remedy of any victim of defamation is self-help—using available opportunities to contradict the lie or correct the error and thereby to minimize its adverse impact on reputation. Public officials and public figures usually enjoy significantly greater access to the channels of effective communication and hence have a more realistic opportunity to counteract false statements than private individuals normally enjoy.[9] Private individuals are therefore more vulnerable to injury, and the state interest in protecting them is correspondingly greater.

More important than the likelihood that private individuals will lack effective opportunities for rebuttal, there is a compelling normative consideration underlying the distinction between public and private defamation plaintiffs. An individual who decides to seek governmental office must accept certain necessary consequences of that involvement in public affairs. He runs the risk of closer public scrutiny than might otherwise be the case. [Those] classed as public figures stand in a similar [position.]

---

9. Of course, an opportunity for rebuttal seldom suffices to undo harm of defamatory falsehood. Indeed, the law of defamation is rooted in our experience that the truth rarely catches up with a lie. But the fact that the self-help remedy of rebuttal, standing alone, is inadequate to its task does not mean that it is irrelevant to our inquiry. [Consider Shiffrin, *Defamatory Non-Media Speech and First Amendment Methodology,* 25 U.C.L.A.L.Rev. 915, 952–53 (1978): "[F]ootnote nine, has seemingly left the first amendment in a peculiar spot. *Gertz* holds that the first amendment offers some protection for defamatory utterances presumably so that our Constitution can continue 'to preserve an uninhibited marketplace of ideas in which truth will ultimately prevail. * * *' And yet the Court recognizes that 'an opportunity for rebuttal seldom suffices to undo [the] harm of defamatory falsehood,' i.e., truth does not emerge in the marketplace of ideas. Is the Court trapped in an obvious contradiction?"]

Even if the foregoing generalities do not obtain in every instance, the communications media are entitled to act on the assumption that public officials and public figures have voluntarily exposed themselves to increased risk of injury from defamatory falsehoods concerning them. No such assumption is justified with respect to a private individual. He has not accepted public office nor assumed an "influential role in ordering society." *Butts.* He has relinquished no part of his interest in the protection of his own good name, and consequently he has a more compelling call on the courts for redress of injury inflicted by defamatory falsehood. Thus, private individuals are not only more vulnerable to injury than public officials and public figures; they are also more deserving of recovery.

For these reasons we conclude that the States should retain substantial latitude in their efforts to enforce a legal remedy for defamatory falsehood injurious to the reputation of a private individual. The extension of the *Times* test proposed by the *Rosenbloom* plurality would abridge this legitimate state interest to a degree that we find unacceptable. And it would occasion the additional difficulty of forcing state and federal judges to decide on an ad hoc basis which publications address issues of "general or public interest" and which do not—to determine, in the words of Mr. Justice Marshall, "what information is relevant to self-government." *Rosenbloom.* We doubt the wisdom of committing this task to the conscience of judges. [The] "public or general interest" test for determining the applicability of the *Times* standard to private defamation actions inadequately serves both of the competing values at stake. On the one hand, a private individual whose reputation is injured by defamatory falsehood that does concern an issue of public or general interest has no recourse unless he can meet the rigorous requirements of *Times.* This is true despite the factors that distinguish the state interest in compensating private individuals from the analogous interest involved in the context of public persons. On the other hand, a publisher or broadcaster of a defamatory error which a court deems unrelated to an issue of public or general interest may be held liable in damages even if it took every reasonable precaution to ensure the accuracy of its assertions. And liability may far exceed compensation for any actual injury to the plaintiff, for the jury may be permitted to presume damages without proof of loss and even to award punitive damages.

We hold that, so long as they do not impose liability without fault, the States may define for themselves the appropriate standard of liability for a publisher or broadcaster of defamatory falsehood injurious to a private individual. This approach provides a more equitable boundary between the competing concerns involved here. It recognizes the strength of the legitimate state interest in compensating private individuals for wrongful injury to reputation, yet shields the press and broadcast media from the rigors of strict liability for defamation. At least this conclusion obtains where, as here, the substance of the defamatory statement "makes substantial danger to reputation apparent." *Butts.* This phrase places in perspective the conclusion we announce today. Our inquiry would involve considerations somewhat different from those discussed above if a State purported to condition civil liability on a factual misstatement whose content did not warn a reasonably prudent editor or broadcaster of its defamatory potential. Cf. *Time, Inc. v. Hill* [Part D infra]. Such a case is not now before us, and we intimate no view as to its proper resolution.

IV. [T]he strong and legitimate state interest in compensating private individuals for injury to reputation [extends] no further than compensation for actual injury. For the reasons stated below, we hold that the States may not permit recovery of presumed or punitive damages, at least when liability is not based on a showing of knowledge of falsity or reckless disregard for the truth.

The common law of defamation is an oddity of tort [law]. Juries may award substantial sums as compensation for supposed damage to reputation without any proof that such harm actually occurred. [This] unnecessarily compounds the potential of any system of liability for defamatory falsehood to inhibit the vigorous exercise of First Amendment freedoms [and] invites juries to punish unpopular opinion rather than to compensate individuals for injury sustained by the publication of a false fact. More to the point, the States have no substantial interest in securing for plaintiffs such as this petitioner gratuitous awards of money damages far in excess of any actual injury.

We would not, of course, invalidate state law simply because we doubt its wisdom, but here we are attempting to reconcile state law with a competing interest grounded in the constitutional command of the First Amendment. It is therefore appropriate to require that state remedies for defamatory falsehood reach no farther than is necessary to protect the legitimate interest involved. It is necessary to restrict defamation plaintiffs who do not prove knowledge of falsity or reckless disregard for the truth to compensation for actual injury. We need not define "actual injury," as trial courts have wide experience in framing appropriate jury instructions in tort action. Suffice it to say that actual injury is not limited to out-of-pocket loss. Indeed, the more customary types of actual harm inflicted by defamatory falsehood include impairment of reputation and standing in the community, personal humiliation, and mental anguish and suffering. Of course, juries must be limited by appropriate instructions, and all awards must be supported by competent evidence concerning the injury, although there need be no evidence which assigns an actual dollar value to the injury.

We also find no justification for allowing awards of punitive damages against publishers and broadcasters held liable under state-defined standards of liability for defamation. In most jurisdictions jury discretion over the amounts awarded is limited only by the gentle rule that they not be excessive. Consequently, juries assess punitive damages in wholly unpredictable amounts bearing no necessary relation to the actual harm caused. And they remain free to use their discretion selectively to punish expressions of unpopular views. [J]ury discretion to award punitive damages unnecessarily exacerbates the danger of media self-censorship; [punitive] damages are wholly irrelevant to the state interest that justifies a negligence standard for private defamation actions. They are not compensation for injury. Instead, they are private fines levied by civil juries to punish reprehensible conduct and to deter its future occurrence. In short, the private defamation plaintiff who establishes liability under a less demanding standard than that stated by *Times* may recover only such damages as are sufficient to compensate him for actual injury.[a]

V. Notwithstanding our refusal to extend the *New York Times* privilege to defamation of private individuals, respondent contends that we should affirm the judgment below on the ground that petitioner is [a] public figure. [That] designation may rest on either of two alternative bases. In some instances an individual may achieve such pervasive fame or notoriety that he becomes a public figure for all purposes and in all contexts. More commonly, an individual

---

a. On remand, Gertz was awarded $100,000 in compensatory damages and $300,000 in punitive damages. In the prior trial, he had been awarded only $50,000 in damages.

voluntarily injects himself or is drawn into a particular public controversy and thereby becomes a public figure for a limited range of issues. In either case such persons assume special prominence in the resolution of public questions.

Petitioner has long been active in community and professional affairs. He has served as an officer of local civic groups and of various professional organizations, and he has published several books and articles on legal subjects. Although petitioner was consequently well known in some circles, he had achieved no general fame or notoriety in the community. None of the prospective jurors called at the trial had ever heard of petitioner prior to this litigation, and respondent offered no proof that this response was atypical of the local population. We would not lightly assume that a citizen's participation in community and professional affairs rendered him a public figure for all purposes. Absent clear evidence of general fame or notoriety in the community, and pervasive involvement in the affairs of society, an individual should not be deemed a public personality for all aspects of his life. It is preferable to reduce the public-figure question to a more meaningful context by looking to the nature and extent of an individual's participation in the particular controversy giving rise to the defamation.

In this context it is plain that petitioner was not a public figure. He played a minimal role at the coroner's inquest, and his participation related solely to his representation of a private client. He took no part in the criminal prosecution of Officer Nuccio. Moreover, he never discussed either the criminal or civil litigation with the press and was never quoted as having done so. He plainly did not thrust himself into the vortex of this public issue, nor did he engage the public's attention in an attempt to influence its outcome. We are persuaded that the trial court did not err in refusing to characterize petitioner as a public figure for the purpose of this litigation.

We therefore conclude that the *New York Times* standard is inapplicable to this case and that the trial court erred in entering judgment for respondent. Because the jury was allowed to impose liability without fault and was permitted to presume damages without proof of injury, a new trial is necessary.[b]

MR. JUSTICE BRENNAN, dissenting.

[I] adhere to my view expressed in *Rosenbloom* that we strike the proper accommodation between avoidance of media self-censorship and protection of individual reputations only when we require States to apply the *New York Times* knowing-or-reckless-falsity standard in civil libel actions concerning media reports of the involvement of private individuals in events of public or general interest. [Although] acknowledging that First Amendment values are of no less significance when media reports concern private persons' involvement in matters of public concern, the Court refuses to provide, in such cases, the same level

---

b. Blackmun, J., concurred: "[Although I joined Brennan, J.'s plurality opinion in *Rosenbloom*, from which the Court's opinion in the present case departs, I join] the Court's opinion and its judgment for two reasons:

"1. By removing the spectres of presumed and punitive damages in the absence of *Times* malice, the Court eliminates significant and powerful motives for self-censorship that otherwise are present in the traditional libel action. By so doing, the Court leaves what should prove to be sufficient and adequate breathing space for a vigorous press. What the Court has done, I believe, will have little,

if any, practical effect on the functioning of responsible journalism.

"2. The Court was sadly fractionated in *Rosenbloom*. A result of that kind inevitably leads to uncertainty. I feel that it is of profound importance for the Court to come to rest in the defamation area and to have a clearly defined majority position that eliminates the unsureness engendered by *Rosenbloom's* diversity. If my vote were not needed to create a majority, I would adhere to my prior view. A definitive ruling, however, is paramount."

of constitutional protection that has been afforded the media in the context of defamation of public [persons].

While [the Court's] arguments are forcefully and eloquently presented, I cannot accept them for the reasons I stated in *Rosenbloom:* "The *New York Times* standard was applied to libel of a public official or public figure to give effect to the Amendment's function to encourage ventilation of public issues, not because the public official has any less interest in protecting his reputation than an individual in private life. [In] the vast majority of libels involving public officials or public figures, the ability to respond through the media will depend on the same complex factor on which the ability of a private individual depends: the unpredictable event of the media's continuing interest in the story. Thus the unproved, and highly improbable, generalization that an as yet [not fully defined] class of 'public figures' involved in matters of public concern will be better able to respond through the media than private individuals also involved in such matters seems too insubstantial a reed on which to rest a constitutional distinction."

[Adoption], by many States, of a reasonable care standard in cases where private individuals are involved in matters of public interest—the probable result of today's decision—[will] lead to self-censorship since publishers will be required carefully to weigh a myriad of uncertain factors before publication. The reasonable care standard is "elusive," *Time, Inc. v. Hill;* it saddles the press with "the intolerable burden of guessing how a jury might assess the reasonableness of steps taken by it to verify the accuracy of every reference to a name, picture or portrait." Ibid. Under a reasonable care regime, publishers and broadcasters will have to make pre-publication judgments about juror assessment of such diverse considerations as the size, operating procedures, and financial condition of the newsgathering system, as well as the relative costs and benefits of instituting less frequent and more costly reporting at a higher level of accuracy. See 85 Harv.L.Rev. 228 (1971). [And] most hazardous, the flexibility which inheres in the reasonable care standard will create the danger that a jury will convert it into "an instrument for the suppression of those 'vehement, caustic, and sometimes unpleasantly sharp attacks,' [which] must be protected if the guarantees of the First and Fourteenth Amendments are to prevail." *Monitor Patriot Co.*

[A] jury's latitude to impose liability for want of due care poses a far greater threat of suppressing unpopular views than does a possible recovery of presumed or punitive damages. Moreover, the Court's broad-ranging examples of "actual injury" [allow] a jury bent on punishing expression of unpopular views a formidable weapon for doing so. [E]ven a limitation of recovery to "actual injury"—however much it reduces the size or frequency of recoveries—will not provide the necessary elbow room for First Amendment expression. "[The] very possibility of having to engage in litigation, an expensive and protracted process, is threat enough to cause discussion and debate to 'steer far wider of the unlawful zone' thereby keeping protected discussion from public cognizance. * * *" *Rosenbloom.*

[I] reject the argument that my *Rosenbloom* view improperly commits to judges the task of determining what is and what is not an issue of "general or public interest." [3] I noted in *Rosenbloom* that performance of this task would

---

3. The Court, taking a novel step, would not limit application of First Amendment protection to private libels involving issues of general or public interest, but would forbid the States from imposing liability without fault in any case where the substance of the defamatory statement made substantial danger to reputation apparent. As in *Rosen-*

not always be easy.   But surely the courts, the ultimate arbiters of all disputes concerning clashes of constitutional values, would only be performing one of their traditional functions in undertaking this duty.   [The] public interest is necessarily broad; any residual self-censorship that may result from the uncertain contours of the "general or public interest" concept should be of far less concern to publishers and broadcasters than that occasioned by state laws imposing liability for negligent falsehood.   * * * [c]

MR. JUSTICE WHITE, dissenting.

[T]he Court, in a few printed pages, has federalized major aspects of libel law by declaring unconstitutional in important respects the prevailing defamation law in all or most of the 50 States.   * * *

I.   [These] radical changes in the law and severe invasions of the prerogatives of the States [should] at least be shown to be required by the First Amendment or necessitated by our present circumstances.   Neither has been [demonstrated.]

The central meaning of *New York Times,* and for me the First Amendment as it relates to libel laws, is that seditious libel—criticism of government and public officials—falls beyond the police power of the State.   In a democratic society such as ours, the citizen has the privilege of criticizing his government and its officials.   But neither *New York Times* nor its progeny suggest that the First Amendment intended in all circumstances to deprive the private citizen of his historic recourse to redress published falsehoods damaging to reputation or that, contrary to history and precedent, the amendment should now be so interpreted.   Simply put, the First Amendment did not confer a "license to defame the citizen."   Douglas, *The Right of the People* 38 (1958).

[T]he law has heretofore put the risk of falsehood on the publisher where the victim is a private citizen and no grounds of special privilege are invoked.   The Court would now shift this risk to the victim, even though he has done nothing to invite the calumny, is wholly innocent of fault, and is helpless to avoid his injury.   I doubt that jurisprudential resistance to liability without fault is sufficient ground for employing the First Amendment to revolutionize the law of

bloom, I would leave open the question of what constitutional standard, if any, applies when defamatory falsehoods are published or broadcast concerning either a private or public person's activities not within the scope of the general or public interest.

Parenthetically, my Brother White argues that the Court's view and mine will prevent a plaintiff—unable to demonstrate some degree of fault—from vindicating his reputation by securing a judgment that the publication was false.   This argument overlooks the possible enactment of statutes, not requiring proof of fault, which provide for an action for retraction or for publication of a court's determination of falsity if the plaintiff is able to demonstrate that false statements have been published concerning his activities.   Cf. Note, *Vindication of the Reputation of a Public Official,* 80 Harv.L.Rev. 1730, 1739–1747 (1967). Although it may be that questions could be raised concerning the constitutionality of such statutes, certainly nothing I have said today (and, as I read the Court's opinion, nothing said there) should be read to imply that a

private plaintiff, unable to prove fault, must inevitably be denied the opportunity to secure a judgment upon the truth or falsity of statements published about him.

c.   Douglas, J., dissented, objecting to "continued recognition of the possibility of state libel suits for public discussion of public issues" as diluting first amendment protection. He added: "Since this case involves a discussion of public affairs, I need not decide at this point whether the First Amendment prohibits all libel actions.   'An unconditional right to say what one pleases about public affairs is what I consider to be *the minimum guarantee* of the First Amendment.'   *New York Times* (Black, J., concurring) (emphasis added).   But 'public affairs' includes a great deal more than merely political affairs.   Matters of science, economics, business, art, literature, etc., are all matters of interest to the general public.   Indeed, any matter of sufficient general interest to prompt media coverage may be said to be a public affair.   Certainly police killings, 'Communist conspiracies,' and the like qualify."

libel, and in my view, that body of legal rules poses no realistic threat to the press and its service to the public. The press today is vigorous and robust. To me, it is quite incredible to suggest that threats of libel suits from private citizens are causing the press to refrain from publishing the truth. I know of no hard facts to support that proposition, and the Court furnishes none.

[I]f the Court's principal concern is to protect the communications industry from large libel judgments, it would appear that its new requirements with respect to general and punitive damages would be ample protection. Why it also feels compelled to escalate the threshold standard of liability I cannot fathom, particularly when this will eliminate in many instances the plaintiff's possibility of securing a judicial determination that the damaging publication was indeed false, whether or not he is entitled to recover money damages. [I] find it unacceptable to distribute the risk in this manner and force the wholly innocent victim to bear the injury; for, as between the two, the defamer is the only culpable party. It is he who circulated a falsehood that he was not required to publish. * * * [d]

V. [I] fail to see how the quality or quantity of public debate will be promoted by further emasculation of state libel laws for the benefit of the news media.[41] If anything, this trend may provoke a new and radical imbalance in the communications process. Cf. Barron, *Access to the Press—A New First Amendment Right,* 80 Harv.L.Rev. 1641, 1657 (1967). It is not at all inconceivable that virtually unrestrained defamatory remarks about private citizens will discourage them from speaking out and concerning themselves with social problems. This would turn the First Amendment on its head. Note, *The Scope of First Amendment Protection for Good-Faith Defamatory Error,* 75 Yale L.J. 642, 649 (1966). * * * [e]

Notes and Questions

1. *Gertz and Meiklejohn.* By affording some constitutional protection to all media defamatory speech whether or not it relates to public issues, does the Court squarely reject the Meiklejohn theory of the first amendment?[f] Consider Shiffrin, *Defamatory Non-Media Speech and First Amendment Methodology,* 25 U.C.L.A.L.Rev. 915, 929 (1978): "It may be that the Court has refused to adopt the Meiklejohn 'public issues' test not because it believes that private speech (i.e., speech unrelated to public issues) is as important as public speech but

---

d. White, J., also argued strongly against the Court's rulings on actual and punitive damages.

41. Cf. Pedrick, *Freedom of the Press and the Law of Libel: The Modern Revised Translation,* 49 Cornell L.Q. 581, 601–02 (1964): "A great many forces in our society operate to determine the extent to which men are free in fact to express their ideas. Whether there is a privilege for good faith defamatory misstatements on matters of public concern or whether there is strict liability for such statements may not greatly affect the course of public discussion. How different has life been in those states which heretofore followed the majority rule imposing strict liability for misstatements of fact defaming public figures from life in the minority states where the good faith privilege held sway?" See also Emerson, *The System of Freedom of Expres-*

sion 519 (1970): "[O]n the whole the role of libel law in the system of freedom of expression has been relatively minor and essentially erratic."

e. Burger, C.J., also dissented: "I am frank to say I do not know the parameters of a 'negligence' doctrine as applied to the news media. [I] would prefer to allow this area of law to continue to evolve as it has up to now with respect to private citizens rather then embark on a new doctrinal theory which has no jurisprudential ancestry. [I would remand] for reinstatement of the verdict of the jury and the entry of an appropriate judgment on that verdict."

f. For consideration of the distinction between public and private speech and of the media non–media distinction, see *Greenmoss,* p. 465 infra.

rather because it doubts its ability to distinguish unerringly between the two. [B]y placing all defamatory media speech within the scope of the first amendment, the Court may believe it has protected relatively little non-public speech. On the other hand, [putting aside comments about public officials and public figures], the Court may fear that if *Gertz* were extended to non-media speech, the result would be to protect much speech having nothing to do with public issues, while safeguarding relatively little that does." [g]

2. *Public figures.* TIME, INC. v. FIRESTONE, 424 U.S. 448, 96 S.Ct. 958, 47 L.Ed.2d 154 (1976), per REHNQUIST, J., declared that persons who have not assumed a role of especial prominence in the affairs of society are not public figures unless they have " 'thrust themselves to the forefront of particular public controversies in order to influence the resolution of the issues involved.' " It held that a divorce proceeding involving one of America's wealthiest industrial families and containing testimony concerning the extramarital sexual activities of the parties did not involve a "public controversy," "even though the marital difficulties of extremely wealthy individuals may be of interest to some portion of the reading public." Nor was the filing of a divorce suit, or the holding of press conferences ("to satisfy inquiring reporters") thought to be freely publicizing the issues in order to influence their outcome. Recall *Gertz* doubted the wisdom of forcing judges to determine on an ad hoc basis what is and is not of "general or public interest." Is there a basis for distinguishing a public figure test requiring judges to determine on an ad hoc basis what is or is not a "public controversy"?

What does it mean to assume a role of especial prominence in the affairs of society? If Elmer Gertz, a prominent Illinois attorney, does not qualify, does Johnny Carson? Julia Child? Mr. Rogers? If so, is the slide from public officials to television chefs and personalities too precipitous because the latter "have little, if any effect, on questions of politics, public policy, or the organization and determination of societal affairs"? See Schauer, *Public Figures,* 25 Wm. & Mary L.Rev. 905 (1984). For replies, see Ashdown, *Of Public Figures and Public Interest—The Libel Law Conundrum,* Id. at 937; Daniels, *Public Figures Revisited,* Id. at 957. Does a narrow definition of public figures discriminate in favor of orthodox media and discourage attempts "to illuminate previously unexposed aspects of society." Does the negligence concept itself threaten to discriminate "against media or outlets whose philosophies and methods deviate from those of the mainstream"? See generally Anderson, *Libel and Press Self-Censorship,* 53 Tex.L.Rev. 422, 453, 455 (1975).

3. *"There is no constitutional value in false statements of fact."* Consider Shiffrin, supra at 954: "This is dangerous doctrine. It begins with the presumption that false speech is unprotected and looks to determine if other factors are present which necessitate protection nonetheless. This begs the basic first amendment question: When can government perceptions of truth or falsity be

g. For the claim that speech on private matters deserves as much protection as speech on public matters, see id. at 938–42. For discussion of the different meanings of public and private speech, see Schauer, *"Private" Speech and the "Private" Forum: Givhan v. Western Line School District,* 1979 Sup.Ct.Rev. 217. For additional commentary on the question of whether *Gertz* should extend to nonmedia defendants see, e.g., Hill, *Defamation and Privacy Under the First Amendment,* 76 Colum.L.Rev. 1205 (1976); Lange, *The Speech and Press Clauses,* 23 U.C.L.A.L.Rev. 77 (1975); Nimmer, *Is Freedom of the Press a Redundancy: What Does It Add to Freedom of Speech?,* 26 Hast.L.J. 639 (1975); Van Alstyne, Comment: *The Hazards to the Press of Claiming a "Preferred Position,"* 28 Hast.L.J. 761 (1977); Note, *Mediaocracy and Mistrust: Extending New York Times Defamation Protection to Nonmedia Defendants,* 95 Harv.L.Rev. 1876 (1982).

imposed upon the individual? Moreover, it demeans the interests of self-expression and cathartic release. In the final analysis, however, the *Gertz* formulation may make no difference. By recognizing that some false speech must be protected in order to prevent true speech from being driven out of the marketplace, *Gertz* arrives at the same results which would be reached if it were assumed that speech is protected whether true or false unless other important interests predominate. Nonetheless, starting points can influence [decisions]." See also Schauer, *Categories and the First Amendment: A Play in Three Acts,* 34 Vand.L.Rev. 265, 280–81 (1981).

4. *"Under The First Amendment there is no such thing as a false idea." Gertz* has been widely interpreted to protect defamatory "opinions." For commentary on the sagacity of such a reading and on the utility and meaning of the fact/opinion distinction, see Christie, *Defamatory Opinions and the Restatement (Second) of Torts,* 75 Mich.L.Rev. 1621 (1977); Hill, supra; Franklin & Bussel, *The Plaintiff's Burden in Defamation: Awareness and Falsity,* 25 Wm. & Mary L.Rev. 825 (1984); Schauer, *Language, Truth and the First Amendment: An Essay in Memory of Harry Canter,* 64 Va.L.Rev. 263 (1978); Comment, *The Fact-Opinion Distinction in First Amendment Libel Law: The Need For a Bright-Line Rule,* 72 Geo.L.J. 1817 (1984).

5. *The Law in Practice and Pleas for Reform.* For valuable material on how the *Gertz* rules work in practice, see Franklin, *Suing Media for Libel: A Litigation Study,* 1981 Am.B.Found.Res.J. 795; Franklin, *Winners and Losers and Why: A Study of Defamation Litigation,* 1980 Am.B.Found.Res.J. 455. For commentary suggesting reforms, see Lewis, *New York Times v. Sullivan Reconsidered: Time to Return to "The Central Meaning of the First Amendment,"* 83 Colum.L.Rev. 603 (1983); Franklin, *Good Names and Bad Law: A Critique of Libel Law and a Proposal,* 18 U.S.F.L.Rev. 1 (1983); Ingber, *Defamation: A Conflict Between Reason and Decency,* 65 Va.L.Rev. 785 (1979); Smolla, *Let the Author Beware: The Rejuvenation of the American Law of Libel,* 132 U.Pa.L. Rev. 1 (1983).

D. PRIVACY

TIME, INC. v. HILL, 385 U.S. 374, 87 S.Ct. 534, 17 L.Ed.2d 456 (1967), applied the *New York Times* knowing and reckless falsity standard to a right of privacy action for publishing an erroneous but not defamatory report about private individuals involved in an incident of public interest. In 1952 the Hill family was the subject of national news coverage when held hostage in its home for 19 hours by three escaped convicts who treated the family courteously with no violence. This incident formed part of the basis for a novel, later made into a play, which involved violence against the hostage family. In 1955 *Life* published a picture story that showed the play's cast reenacting scenes from the play in the former Hill home. According to *Life,* the play "inspired by the [Hill] family's experience" "is a heartstopping account of how a family arose to heroism in a crisis." Hill secured a $30,000 judgment for compensatory damages against the publisher under the New York Right to Privacy statute, which, as interpreted, made truth a complete defense to actions based on "newsworthy people or events" but gave a right of action to one whose name or picture was the subject of an article containing "material and substantial falsification." The Court, per BRENNAN, J., reversed, holding that "the constitutional protections for speech and press preclude the application of the New York statute to redress false reports of matters of public interest in the absence of proof that the defendant published the report with knowledge of its falsity or in reckless disregard of the truth," and that the instructions did not adequately advise the jury that a verdict for Hill required a finding of knowing or reckless falsity:

"The guarantees for speech and press are not the preserve of political expression or comment upon public affairs, essential as those are to healthy government. One need only pick up any newspaper or magazine to comprehend the vast range of published matter which exposes persons to public view, both private citizens and public officials. Exposure of the self to others in varying degrees is a concomitant of life in a civilized community. The risk of this exposure is an essential incident of life in a society which places a primary value on freedom of speech and press. [We] have no doubt that the subject of the *Life* article, the opening of a new play linked to an actual incident, is a matter of public interest. 'The line between the informing and the entertaining is too elusive for the protection of [freedom of the press.]' Erroneous statement is no less inevitable in such case than in the case of comment upon public affairs, and in both, if innocent or merely negligent, '[it] must be protected if the freedoms of expression are to have the "breathing space" that they "need [to] survive".' [*New York Times*.] We create a grave risk of serious impairment of the indispensable service of a free press in a free society if we saddle the press with the impossible burden of verifying to a certainty the facts associated in news articles with a person's name, picture or portrait, particularly as related to non-defamatory matter. Even negligence would be a most elusive standard, especially when the content of the speech itself affords no warning of prospective harm to another through falsity. A negligence test would place on the press the intolerable burden of guessing how a jury might assess the reasonableness of steps taken by it to verify the accuracy of every reference to a name, picture or [portrait].

"We find applicable here the standard of knowing or reckless falsehood not through blind application of *New York Times*, relating solely to libel actions by public officials, but only upon consideration of the factors which arise in the particular context of the application of the New York statute in cases involving private individuals."

BLACK, J., joined by Douglas, J., concurred in reversal on the grounds stated in the Brennan opinion "in order for the Court to be able at this time to agree on an opinion in this important case based on the prevailing constitutional doctrine expressed in *New York Times*," but reaffirmed their belief that the "malicious," "reckless disregard of the truth" and "knowing and reckless falsity" exceptions were impermissible "abridgments" of freedom of expression. DOUGLAS, J., also filed a separate concurrence, deeming it "irrelevant to talk of any right of privacy in this context. Here a private person is catapulted into the news by events over which he had no control. He and his activities are then in the public domain as fully as the matters at issue in *New York Times*. Such privacy as a person normally has ceases when his life has ceased to be private."

HARLAN, J., concurring in part and dissenting in part, would have made the test of liability negligence, rather than the *New York Times* "reckless falsity": "It would be unreasonable to assume that Mr. Hill could find a forum for making a successful refutation of the *Life* material or that the public's interest in it would be sufficient for the truth to win out by comparison as it might in that area of discussion central to a free society. Thus the state interest in encouraging careful checking and preparation of published material is far stronger than in *Times*. The dangers of unchallengeable untruth are far too well documented to be summarily dismissed.

"Second, there is a vast difference in the state interest in protecting individuals like Mr. Hill from irresponsibly prepared publicity and the state interest in similar protection for a public official. In *Times* we acknowledged public officials to be a breed from whom hardiness to exposure to charges, innuendos, and criticisms might be demanded and who voluntarily assumed the risk of such things by entry into the public arena. But Mr. Hill came to public attention through an unfortunate circumstance not of his making rather than his voluntary actions and he can in no sense be considered to have 'waived' any protection the State might justifiably afford him from irresponsible publicity. Not being inured to the vicissitudes of journalistic scrutiny such an individual is more easily injured and his means of self-defense are more limited. The public is less likely to view with normal skepticism what is written about him because it is not accustomed to seeing his name in the press and expects only a disinterested report.

"The coincidence of these factors in this situation leads me to the view that a State should be free to hold the press to a duty of making a reasonable investigation of the underlying facts and limiting itself to 'fair comment' on the materials so gathered. Theoretically, of course, such a rule might slightly limit press discussion of matters touching individuals like Mr. Hill. But, from a pragmatic standpoint, until now the press, at least in New York, labored under the more exacting handicap of the existing New York privacy law and has certainly remained robust. Other professional activity of great social value is carried on under a duty of reasonable care and there is no reason to suspect the press would be less hardy than medical practitioners or attorneys." [a]

Notes and Questions

1. Does *Hill* survive *Gertz?* Consider the following statement: "In *Hill* and *Gertz* the same class of plaintiffs have to meet different constitutional standards in order to recover. Only the name of the tort has changed. This makes no sense." Is the state interest significantly different in *Gertz* than in *Hill?* Should it matter whether the statement at issue would appear innocuous to a reasonable editor? Offensive? What if a post-*Gertz* plaintiff sues for negligent infliction of emotional distress? Does *Hill* bar recovery without a showing of knowing or reckless falsehood? For commentary on the "quite startling" possibilities for plaintiffs, see Van Alstyne, *First Amendment Limitations on Recovery From the Press—An Extended Comment on "The Anderson Solution,"* 25 Wm. & Mary L.Rev. 793 (1984).

2. *False news.* Is injury to any particular person a prerequisite to state regulation of false publications? Consider *Keeton v. Hustler Magazine, Inc.,* 465 U.S. 770, 104 S.Ct. 1473, 79 L.Ed.2d 790 (1984): "False statements of fact harm both the subject of the falsehood *and* the readers of the statement. New Hampshire may rightly employ its libel laws to discourage the deception of its citizens." Could New Hampshire make it a criminal offense to publish false statements with knowledge of their falsity without any requirement of injury to any particular person?

3. *Truth and privacy.* Should privacy or defamation recoveries depend upon a showing of falsity? Suppose a disgruntled ex-lover posts true notices about the sex life of a person all over a small town? Should it make a difference if embarrassing private facts are published without malice? Compare *Briscoe v.*

---

a. Fortas, J., joined by Warren, C.J., and Clark, J., dissented, because "the jury instruc-   tions, although [not] a textbook model, satisfied [the *New York Times*] standard."

Reader's Digest, 4 Cal.3d 529, 93 Cal.Rptr. 866, 483 P.2d 34 (1971) (truthful reports about suspects of recent crimes protected by first amendment, but otherwise non-newsworthy plaintiff states cause of action for violation of privacy against truthful publication that he had committed and been convicted of a hijacking eleven years previously) with *Cox Broadcasting Corp. v. Cohn,* 420 U.S. 469, 95 S.Ct. 1029, 43 L.Ed.2d 328 (1975) (state cannot impose right of privacy liability for dissemination of the name of a rape victim derived from public court documents; "[A]t the very least, the First and Fourteenth Amendments will not allow exposing the press to liability for truthfully publishing information released to the public in [official records].") [b]

III. OWNERSHIP OF SPEECH

HARPER & ROW v. NATION ENTERPRISES, ___ U.S. ___, 105 S.Ct. 2218, 85 L.Ed.2d 588 (1985): Former President Ford had contracted with Harper & Row and Readers Digest to publish his memoirs and granted them the right to license prepublication excerpts concentrating on his pardon of former President Nixon. Some weeks before a licensed article in Time was to appear, an unknown person presented the editor of The Nation with an unauthorized copy of the 200,000 word Ford manuscript from which the editor wrote a 2,250 word article entitled, "The Ford Memoirs—Behind the Nixon Pardon." The article included 26 verbatim quotations totalling 300 words of Ford's copyrighted expression and was timed to scoop Time. Accordingly, Time cancelled its article and refused to pay the publishers the remaining half of its $25,000 contract price.

In defense against the publishers' copyright claim, The Nation maintained that its publication was protected by the fair use provision of the Copyright Revision Act of 1976, 17 U.S.C. § 107 and by the first amendment. The Court, per O'CONNOR, J., concluded that neither defense was viable and that the fair use provision properly accommodated the relevant first amendment interests: "Article I, § 8, of the Constitution provides that: 'The Congress shall have Power * * * to Promote the Progress of Science and useful Arts, by securing for limited Times to Authors and Inventors the exclusive Right to their respective Writings and Discoveries.' '[This] limited grant is a means by which an important public purpose may be achieved. It is intended to motivate the creative activity of authors and inventors by the provision of a special reward, and to allow the public access to the products of their genius after the limited period of exclusive control has expired.' The monopoly created by copyright thus rewards the individual author in order to benefit the public. This principle applies equally to works of fiction and nonfiction. The book at issue here, for example, was two years in the making, and began with a contract giving the author's copyright to the publishers in exchange for their services in producing and marketing the work. In preparing the book, Mr. Ford drafted essays and word portraits of public figures and participated in hundreds of taped interviews that were later distilled to chronicle his personal viewpoint. It is evident that the

b. For a sampling of the abundant commentary, see Zimmerman, *Requiem for a Heavyweight: A Farewell to Warren and Brandeis's Privacy Tort,* 68 Corn.L.Rev. 291 (1983); Emerson, *The Right of Privacy and Freedom of the Press,* 14 Harv.C.R.–C.L.L.Rev. 329 (1979); Hill, *Defamation and Privacy Un-* *der the First Amendment,* 76 Colum.L.Rev. 1205 (1976); Nimmer, *The Right to Speak from Times to Time: First Amendment Theory Applied to Libel and Misapplied to Privacy,* 56 Calif.L.Rev. 935 (1968); Kalven, *Privacy in Tort Law—Were Warren and Brandeis Wrong?,* 31 Law & Contemp.Prob. 326 (1966).

monopoly granted by copyright actively served its intended purpose of inducing the creation of new material of potential historical value.

"Section 106 of the Copyright Act confers a bundle of exclusive rights to the owner of the copyright. [T]hese rights—to publish, copy, and distribute the author's work—vest in the author of an original work from the time of its creation. In practice, the author commonly sells his rights to publishers who offer royalties in exchange for their services in producing and marketing the author's work. The copyright owner's rights, however, are subject to certain statutory exceptions. Among these is § 107 which codifies the traditional privilege of other authors to make 'fair use' of an earlier writer's work.[2] In addition, no author may copyright facts or ideas. § 102. The copyright is limited to those aspects of the work—termed 'expression'—that display the stamp of the author's originality.

"[T]here is no dispute that the unpublished manuscript of 'A Time to Heal,' as a whole, was protected by § 106 from unauthorized reproduction. Nor do respondents dispute that verbatim copying of excerpts of the manuscript's original form of expression would constitute infringement unless excused as fair use. Yet copyright does not prevent subsequent users from copying from a prior author's work those constituent elements that are not original—for example, quotations borrowed under the rubric of fair use from other copyrighted works, facts, or materials in the public domain—as long as such use does not unfairly appropriate the author's original contributions. Perhaps the controversy between the lower courts in this case over copyrightability is more aptly styled a dispute over whether The Nation's appropriation of unoriginal and uncopyrightable elements encroached on the originality embodied in the work as a whole. Especially in the realm of factual narrative, the law is currently unsettled regarding the ways in which uncopyrightable elements combine with the author's original contributions to form protected expression.

"We need not reach these issues, however, as The Nation has admitted to lifting verbatim quotes of the author's original language [constituting] some 13% of The Nation article. [To thereby] lend authenticity to its account of the forthcoming memoirs, The Nation effectively arrogated to itself the right of first publication, an important marketable subsidiary right. For the reasons set forth below, we find that this use of the copyrighted manuscript, even stripped to the verbatim quotes conceded by The Nation to be copyrightable expression, was not a fair use within the meaning of the Copyright Act.

"[The] nature of the interest at stake is highly relevant to whether a given use is fair. [The] right of first publication implicates a threshold decision by the author whether and in what form to release his work. First publication is inherently different from other § 106 rights in that only one person can be the first publisher; as the contract with Time illustrates, the commercial value of

---

2. Section 107 states: "Notwithstanding the provisions of section 106, the fair use of a copyrighted work [for] purposes such as criticism, comment, news reporting, teaching (including multiple copies for classroom use), scholarship, or research, is not an infringement of copyright. In determining whether the use made of a work in any particular case is a fair use the factors to be considered shall include—

"(1) the purpose and character of the use, including whether such use is of a commercial nature or is for nonprofit educational purposes;

"(2) the nature of the copyrighted work;

"(3) the amount and substantiality of the portion used in relation to the copyrighted work as a whole; and

"(4) the effect of the use upon the potential market for or value of the copyrighted work."

the right lies primarily in exclusivity. [Under] ordinary circumstances, the author's right to control the first public appearance of his undisseminated expression will outweigh a claim of fair use.

"Respondents, however, contend that First Amendment values require a different rule under the circumstances of this case. [Respondents] advance the substantial public import of the subject matter of the Ford memoirs as grounds for excusing a use that would ordinarily not pass muster as a fair use—the piracy of verbatim quotations for the purpose of 'scooping' the authorized first serialization. Respondents explain their copying of Mr. Ford's expression as essential to reporting the news story it claims the book itself represents. In respondents' view, not only the facts contained in Mr. Ford's memoirs, but 'the precise manner in which [he] expressed himself was as newsworthy as what he had to say.' Respondents argue that the public's interest in learning this news as fast as possible outweighs the right of the author to control its first publication.

"The Second Circuit noted, correctly, that copyright's idea/expression dichotomy 'strike[s] a definitional balance between the First Amendment and the Copyright Act by permitting free communication of facts while still protecting an author's expression.' No author may copyright his ideas or the facts he narrates.

"Respondents' theory, however, would expand fair use to effectively destroy any expectation of copyright protection in the work of a public figure. Absent such protection, there would be little incentive to create or profit in financing such memoirs and the public would be denied an important source of significant historical information. The promise of copyright would be an empty one if it could be avoided merely by dubbing the infringement a fair use 'news report' of the book. * * *

"In our haste to disseminate news, it should not be forgotten that the Framers intended copyright itself to be the engine of free expression. By establishing a marketable right to the use of one's expression, copyright supplies the economic incentive to create and disseminate ideas. * * *

"Moreover, freedom of thought and expression 'includes both the right to speak freely and the right to refrain from speaking at all.' We do not suggest this right not to speak would sanction abuse of the copyright owner's monopoly as an instrument to suppress facts. But 'The essential thrust of the First Amendment is to prohibit improper restraints on the *voluntary* public expression of ideas; it shields the man who wants to speak or publish when others wish him to be quiet. There is necessarily, and within suitably defined areas, a concomitant freedom *not* to speak publicly, one which serves the same ultimate end as freedom of speech in its affirmative aspect.' *Estate of Hemingway v. Random House,* 23 N.Y.2d 341, 348, 296 N.Y.2d 771, 776, 244 N.E.2d 250, 255 (1968). * * *

"In view of the First Amendment protections already embodied in the Copyright Act's distinction between copyrightable expression and uncopyrightable facts and ideas, and the latitude for scholarship and comment traditionally afforded by fair use, we see no warrant for expanding the doctrine of fair use to create what amounts to a public figure exception to copyright. Whether verbatim copying from a public figure's manuscript in a given case is or is not fair must be judged according to the traditional equities of fair use."

In assessing the equities, the Court found the purpose of the article to count against fair use, noting that the publication "went beyond simply reporting uncopyrightable information" and made "a 'news event' out of its unauthorized first publication," that the publication was "commercial as opposed to non-profit," that The Nation intended to supplant the "right of first publication," and that it acted in bad faith, for it "knowingly exploited a purloined manuscript." In considering the nature of the copyrighted work, the Court found it significant not only that Ford's work was yet unpublished, but also that The Nation had focused "on the most expressive elements of the work" in a way that exceeded "that necessary to disseminate the facts" and in a "clandestine" fashion that afforded no "opportunity for creative or quality control" by the copyright holder. In evaluating the amount and substantiality of the portion used, the Court cited the district court finding that the " 'Nation took what was essentially the heart of the book' " and pointed to the "expressive value of the excerpts and their key role in the infringing work." Finally, the Court observed that the effect of the use on the market for the copyrighted work was the most important element. It found the Time contract cancellation to be "clear cut evidence of actual damage."

BRENNAN, J., joined by White and Marshall, JJ., dissented: "When The Nation was not quoting Mr. Ford, [its] efforts to convey the historical information in the Ford manuscript did not so closely and substantially track Mr. Ford's language and structure as to constitute an appropriation of literary form.

"[The] Nation is thus liable in copyright only if the quotation of 300 words infringed any of Harper & Row's exclusive rights under § 106 of the Act. [Limiting] the inquiry to the propriety of a subsequent author's use of the copyright owner's literary form is not easy in the case of a work of history. Protection against only substantial appropriation of literary form does not ensure historians a return commensurate with the full value of their labors. The literary form contained in works like 'A Time to Heal' reflects only a part of the labor that goes into the book. It is the labor of collecting, sifting, organizing and reflecting that predominates in the creation of works of history such as this one. The value this labor produces lies primarily in the information and ideas revealed, and not in the particular collocation of words through which the information and ideas are expressed. Copyright thus does not protect that which is often of most value in a work of history and courts must resist the tendency to reject the fair use defense on the basis of their feeling that an author of history has been deprived of the full value of his or her labor. A subsequent author's taking of information and ideas is in no sense piratical because copyright law simply does not create any property interest in information and ideas.

"The urge to compensate for subsequent use of information and ideas is perhaps understandable. An inequity seems to lurk in the idea that much of the fruit of the historian's labor may be used without compensation. This, however, is not some unforeseen by-product of a statutory scheme intended primarily to ensure a return for works of the imagination. Congress made the affirmative choice that the copyright laws should apply in this way: 'Copyright does not preclude others from using the ideas or information revealed by the author's work. It pertains to the literary [form] in which the author expressed intellectual concepts.' This distinction is at the essence of copyright. The copyright laws serve as the 'engine of free expression,' only when the statutory monopoly does not choke off multifarious indirect uses and consequent broad dissemination of information and ideas. To ensure the progress of arts and sciences and the integrity of First Amendment values, ideas and information must not be freighted with claims of proprietary right.[13]

13. This congressional limitation on the scope of copyright does not threaten the pro- duction of history. That this limitation results in significant diminution of economic

"In my judgment, the Court's fair use analysis has fallen to the temptation to find copyright violation based on a minimal use of literary form in order to provide compensation for the appropriation of information from a work of history."

Since news reporting is ordinarily conducted for profit and marked by attempts to "scoop" the opposition and by attempts to create "news events," Brennan, J., found the drawing of any negative implications from these factors to be inconsistent with congressional recognition in § 107 that news reporting is a prime example of fair use. He found reliance on bad faith to be equally unwarranted: "No court has found that The Nation possessed the Ford manuscript illegally or in violation of any common law interest of Harper & Row; all common law causes of action have been abandoned or dismissed in this case. Even if the manuscript had been 'purloined' by someone, nothing in this record imputes culpability to The Nation. On the basis of the record in this case, the most that can be said is that The Nation made use of the contents of the manuscript knowing the copyright owner would not sanction the use.

"[T]he Court purports to rely on [the] factual findings that The Nation had taken 'the heart of the book.' This reliance is misplaced, and would appear to be another result of the Court's failure to distinguish between information and literary form. When the District Court made this finding, it was evaluating not the quoted words at issue here but the 'totality' of the information and reflective commentary in the Ford work. The vast majority of what the District Court considered the heart of the Ford work, therefore, consisted of ideas and information The Nation was free to use. It may well be that, as a qualitative matter, most of the value of the manuscript did lie in the information and ideas the Nation used. But appropriation of the 'heart' of the manuscript in this sense is irrelevant to copyright analysis because copyright does not preclude a second author's use of information and ideas.

"At least with respect to the six particular quotes of Mr. Ford's observations and reflections about President Nixon, I agree with the Court's conclusion that The Nation appropriated some literary form of substantial quality. I do not agree, however, that the substantiality of the expression taken was clearly excessive or inappropriate to The Nation's news reporting purpose.

"Had these quotations been used in the context of a critical book review of the Ford work, there is little question that such a use would be fair use within the meaning of § 107 of the Act. The amount and substantiality of the use—in both quantitative and qualitative terms—would have certainly been appropriate to the purpose of such a use. It is difficult to see how the use of these quoted words in a news report is less appropriate.

"The Nation's publication indisputably precipitated Time's eventual cancellation. But that does not mean that The Nation's use of the 300 quoted words caused this injury to Harper & Row. Wholly apart from these quoted words, The Nation published significant information and ideas from the Ford manuscript. [If] The Nation competed with Time, the competition was not for a share of the market in excerpts of literary form but for a share of the market in the new information in the Ford work. * * *

"Because The Nation was the first to convey the information in this case, it did perhaps take from Harper & Row some of the value that publisher sought to garner for itself through the contractual arrangement with Ford and the license

incentives is far from apparent. In any event noneconomic incentives motivate much historical research and writing. For example, former public officials often have great incentive to "tell their side of the story." And much history is the product of academic scholarship. Perhaps most importantly, the urge to preserve the past is as old as human kind.

to Time. Harper & Row had every right to seek to monopolize revenue from that potential market through contractual arrangements but it has no right to set up copyright [as] a shield from competition in that market because copyright does not protect information. The Nation had every right to seek to be the first to publish that information. * * *

"The Court's exceedingly narrow approach to fair use permits Harper & Row to monopolize information. This holding 'effect[s]' an important extension of property rights and a corresponding curtailment in the free use of knowledge and of ideas.' The Court has perhaps advanced the ability of the historian—or at least the public official who has recently left office—to capture the full economic value of information in his or her possession. But the Court does so only by risking the robust debate of public issues that is the 'essence of self-government.' *Garrison.* The Nation was providing the grist for that robust debate. The Court imposes liability upon The Nation for no other reason than that The Nation succeeded in being the first to provide certain information to the public."

Notes and Questions

1. Compare ZACCHINI v. SCRIPPS–HOWARD BROADCASTING CO., 433 U.S. 562, 97 S.Ct. 2849, 53 L.Ed.2d 965 (1977): Zacchini performed as a "human cannonball," being shot from a cannon into a net some 200 feet away. Without Zacchini's permission to film or broadcast his act, Scripps-Howard obtained and broadcast the tape of his "shot" on the news. The Ohio Supreme Court held the telecast was protected under *Time, Inc. v. Hill* as a newsworthy event. The Court, per WHITE, J., reversed. *Hill* was distinguishable because Zacchini's claim was based not on privacy or reputation but "in protecting the proprietary interest," an interest "closely analogous to the goals of patent and copyright law." Unlike *Hill,* the issue was not whether Zacchini's act would be available to the public: "[T]he only question is who gets to do the publishing." [a]

2. Assume The Nation acquires a "purloined" manuscript of Chief Justice Burger's memoirs. Assume Time is soon to publish exclusive excerpts from his forthcoming book. The editors of The Nation want to run a news story about the book before the Time article appears. They want to know whether they can write a story, whether they can quote from the book, what they should do to reduce the risk in writing the story, and whether their right to quote from the book would be enhanced if they made their story a book review. Advise.

3. Will *Harper & Row* chill freedom of the press? Does it matter? To what extent was the Court influenced by the belief that there was no immediate need for the public to know about the Ford memoirs? Suppose California outlaws broadcast presentations in California of presidential election results (and exit polls or the like) until after the California polls have closed. Constitutional? [b]

4. *Gertz* was reluctant to make ad hoc judgments as to whether statements are or are not of general or public interest.[c] Should the Court be similarly

---

a. Powell, J., joined by Brennan and Marshall, JJ., dissented, observing that there was no showing that the broadcast was a "subterfuge or cover for private or commercial exploitation." Stevens, J., dissented on procedural grounds.

b. For commentary, see Fischer, *Network "Early Calls" of Elections,* 14 Sw.U.L.Rev. 428

(1984); Note, *Exit Polls and the First Amendment,* 98 Harv.L.Rev. 1927 (1985); Comment, *Restricting the Broadcast of Election Day Projections: A Justifiable Protection of the Right to Vote,* 9 U.Dayton L.Rev. 297 (1984).

c. *But see Greenmoss,* p. 465 infra.

reluctant to make ad hoc judgments as to the bona fide news purpose of an article,[d] as to whether expression goes to the "heart of the book," or whether quoted words are "necessary" to communicate the "facts"? Is there an alternative to the making of such judgments?

5. Professor Nimmer has argued that in most cases the idea/expression dichotomy is central to resolving the clash between copyright and the first amendment. *Does Copyright Abridge the First Amendment Guarantees of Free Speech and Press?* 17 U.C.L.A.L.Rev. 1180 (1970). See also Goldstein, *Copyright and the First Amendment,* 70 Colum.L.Rev. 983 (1970). Is the distinction satisfactory? Consider *Cohen v. California,* p. 414 infra, protecting Cohen's use of the phrase "Fuck the Draft": "[W]e cannot indulge the facile assumption that one can forbid particular words without running a substantial risk of suppressing ideas in the process." Cohen's counsel was—Professor Nimmer. Does *Nimmer On Copyright* collide with *Nimmer on Freedom of Speech?* For Nimmer's answer, see id. § 2.05(c), at 72–77; § 3.04, at 28 n.11.

IV. OBSCENITY

A. EVOLUTION TOWARD A STANDARD

Roth v. United States, infra, contains the Court's first extended discussion of the constitutionality of obscenity laws. The Court's opinion was framed by briefs that proceeded from sharply different visions of first amendment law. Roth argued that no speech including obscenity could be prohibited without meeting the clear and present danger test, that a danger of lustful thoughts was not the type of evil with which a legislature could be legitimately concerned, and that no danger of anti-social conduct had been shown. On the other hand, the government urged the Court to adopt a balancing test that prominently featured a consideration of the value of the speech involved. The government tendered an illustrative hierarchy of nineteen speech categories with political, religious, economic, and scientific speech at the top; entertainment, music, and humor in the middle; and libel, obscenity, profanity, and commercial pornography at the bottom.

ROTH v. UNITED STATES

ALBERTS v. CALIFORNIA

354 U.S. 476, 77 S.Ct. 1304, 1 L.Ed.2d 1498 (1957).

MR. JUSTICE BRENNAN delivered the opinion of the Court. [Roth and Alberts were convicted of violating the federal and California obscenity laws respectively. The issues raised were whether the statutes, *"on their faces and in a*

---

d. Compare *Regan v. Time, Inc.,* __ U.S. __, 104 S.Ct. 3262, 82 L.Ed.2d 487 (1984): 18 U.S.C. § 474 makes it a crime to photograph United States currency, but exceptions for articles and books for newsworthy purposes are permitted so long as certain size and color requirements are satisfied. 18 U.S.C. § 504. The Court, per White, J., invalidated the purpose requirement: "A determination concerning the newsworthiness [of] a photograph cannot help but be based on the content of the photograph and the message it delivers. [Regulations] which permit the Government to discriminate on the basis of the content of the message cannot be tolerated under the First Amendment. The purpose requirement of § 504 is therefore constitutionally infirm." Stevens, J., dissenting on this point, observed that if the Court's language were applied literally, the constitutionality of the fair use provision of the Copyright Act would be "highly suspect."

vacuum, violated the freedom of expression and definiteness requirements of the Constitution." [a]]

The dispositive question is whether obscenity is utterance within the area of protected speech and press.[8] Although this is the first time the question has been squarely presented to this Court [expressions] found in numerous opinions indicate that this Court has always assumed that obscenity is not protected by the freedoms of speech and press.

The guaranties of freedom of expression in effect in 10 of the 14 States which by 1792 had ratified the Constitution, gave no absolute protection for every utterance. Thirteen of the 14 States provided for the prosecution of libel, and all of those States made either blasphemy or profanity, or both, statutory crimes. As early as 1712, Massachusetts made it criminal to publish "any filthy, obscene, or profane song, pamphlet, libel or mock sermon" in imitation or mimicking of religious services. * * *

In light of this history, it is apparent that the unconditional phrasing of the First Amendment was not intended to protect every utterance. This phrasing did not prevent this Court from concluding that libelous utterances are not within the area of constitutionally protected speech. *Beauharnais.* At the time of the adoption of the First Amendment, obscenity law was not as fully developed as libel law, but there is sufficiently contemporaneous evidence to show that obscenity, too, was outside the protection intended for speech and press.[b]

The protection given speech and press was fashioned to assure unfettered interchange of ideas for the bringing about of political and social changes desired by the people. [All] ideas having even the slightest redeeming social importance—unorthodox ideas, controversial ideas, even ideas hateful to the prevailing climate of opinion—have the full protection of the guaranties, unless excludable because they encroach upon the limited area of more important interests. But implicit in the history of the First Amendment is the rejection of obscenity as utterly without redeeming social importance. This rejection for that reason is mirrored in the universal judgment that obscenity should be restrained, reflected in the international agreement of over 50 nations, in the obscenity laws of all of the 48 States, and in the 20 obscenity laws enacted by the Congress from 1842 to 1956. This is the same judgment expressed by this Court in *Chaplinsky* [p. 409 infra]: "There are certain well-defined and narrowly limited classes of speech, the prevention and punishment of which have never been thought to raise any Constitutional problem. *These include the lewd and obscene. [It] has been well observed that such utterances are no essential part of any exposition of ideas, and are of such slight social value as a step to truth that any benefit that may be*

---

a. See Lockhart & McClure, *Censorship of Obscenity: The Developing Constitutional Standards,* 45 Minn.L.Rev. 5, 13 (1960).

8. No issue is presented in either case concerning the obscenity of the material involved.

b. The Court here cited three state court decisions (1808 to 1821) recognizing as a common law offense the distribution or display of obscene or indecent materials, and four state statutes aimed at similar conduct (1800 to 1842). For the contention that obscenity is not "speech" within the meaning of the first amendment (let alone, not *protected* speech), see Schauer, *Free Speech: A Philosophical Enquiry* 181–84 (1982) (a sex aid, not speech). See generally Schauer, *Speech and "Speech"—*

Obscenity and "Obscenity": An Exercise in the Interpretation of Constitutional Language, 67 Geo.L.J. 899 (1979). But see Alexander & Horton, *The Impossibility of a Free Speech Principle,* 78 Nw.U.L.Rev. 1319, 1331–34 (1984). Compare Greenawalt, *Criminal Coercion and Freedom of Speech,* 78 Nw.U.L.Rev. 1081 (1983) (discussing the question of whether all ordinary language should be included within the scope of the first amendment, even if much is ultimately unprotected, and contending that some ordinary language should be wholly outside the scope of the first amendment). But see Haiman, *Comments on Kent Greenawalt's Criminal Coercion and Freedom of Speech,* id. at 1125.

derived from them is clearly outweighed by the social interest in order and morality." (Emphasis added [by Court].)

We hold that obscenity is not within the area of constitutionally protected speech or press.

It is strenuously urged that these obscenity statutes offend the constitutional guaranties because they punish incitation to impure sexual *thoughts,* not shown to be related to any overt antisocial conduct which is or may be incited in the persons stimulated to such *thoughts.* [It] is insisted that the constitutional guaranties are violated because convictions may be had without proof either that obscene material will perceptibly create a clear and present danger of antisocial conduct, or will probably induce its recipients to such conduct. But, in light of our holding that obscenity is not protected speech, the complete answer to this argument is in the holding of this Court in *Beauharnais:* "Libelous utterances not being within the area of constitutionally protected speech, it is unnecessary, either for us or for the State courts, to consider the issues behind the phrase 'clear and present danger.' Certainly no one would contend that obscene speech, for example, may be punished only upon a showing of such circumstances. * * *"

However, sex and obscenity are not synonymous. Obscene material is material which deals with sex in a manner appealing to prurient interest.[20] The portrayal of sex, e.g., in art, literature and scientific works, is not itself sufficient reason to deny material the constitutional protection of freedom of speech and press. Sex, a great and mysterious motive force in human life, has indisputably been a subject of absorbing interest to mankind through the ages; it is one of the vital problems of human interest and public [concern].

The fundamental freedoms of speech and press have contributed greatly to the development and well-being of our free society and are indispensable to its continued growth. [It] is therefore vital that the standards for judging obscenity safeguard the protection of freedom of speech and press for material which does not treat sex in a manner appealing to prurient interest.

The early leading standard of obscenity allowed material to be judged merely by the effect of an isolated excerpt upon particularly susceptible persons. *Regina v. Hicklin,* [1868] L.R. 3 Q.B. 360. Some American courts adopted this standard but later decisions have rejected it and substituted this test: whether to the average person, applying contemporary community standards, the dominant theme of the material taken as a whole appeals to prurient interest. The *Hicklin* test, judging obscenity by the effect of isolated passages upon the most susceptible persons, might well encompass material legitimately treating with sex, and so it must be rejected as unconstitutionally restrictive of the freedoms of speech and press. On the other hand, the substituted standard provides safeguards adequate to withstand the charge of constitutional infirmity. Both trial

---

20. I.e., material having a tendency to excite lustful thoughts. *Webster's New International Dictionary* (Unabridged, 2d ed., 1949) defines *prurient,* in pertinent part, as follows:

"Itching; longing; uneasy with desire or longing; of persons, having itching, morbid, or lascivious longings; of desire, curiosity, or propensity, lewd * * *."

We perceive no significant difference between the meaning of obscenity developed in the case law and the definition of the A.L.I., *Model Penal Code,* § 207.10(2) (Tent. Draft No. 6, 1957), viz.: "[A] thing is obscene if, considered as a whole, its predominant appeal is to prurient interest, i.e. a shameful or morbid interest in nudity, sex, or excretion, and if it goes substantially beyond customary limits of candor in description or representation of such [matters]." See Comment, id. at 10, and the discussion at page 29 et seq.

courts below sufficiently followed the proper standard. Both courts used the proper definition of obscenity.[c]

[It] is argued that the statutes do not provide reasonably ascertainable standards of guilt and therefore violate the constitutional requirements of due process. *Winters v. New York*, 333 U.S. 507, 68 S.Ct. 665, 92 L.Ed. 840 (1948). The federal obscenity statute makes punishable the mailing of material that is "obscene, lewd, lascivious, or filthy [or] other publication of an indecent character." The California statute makes punishable, inter alia, the keeping for sale or advertising material that is "obscene or indecent." The thrust of the argument is that these words are not sufficiently precise because they do not mean the same thing to all people, all the time, everywhere. Many decisions have recognized that these terms of obscenity statutes are not precise. This Court, however, has consistently held that lack of precision is not itself offensive to the requirements of due process. "[T]he Constitution does not require impossible standards"; all that is required is that the language "conveys sufficiently definite warning as to the proscribed conduct when measured by common understanding and [practices.]" * * *

In summary, then, we hold that these statutes, applied according to the proper standard for judging obscenity, do not offend constitutional safeguards against convictions based upon protected material, or fail to give men in acting adequate notice of what is prohibited. * * *

Affirmed.

MR. CHIEF JUSTICE WARREN, concurring in the result.

[It] is not the book that is on trial; it is a person. The conduct of the defendant is the central issue, not the obscenity of a book or picture. The nature of the materials is, of course, relevant as an attribute of the defendant's conduct. [The] defendants in both these cases were engaged in the business of purveying textual or graphic matter openly advertised to appeal to the erotic interest of their customers. They were plainly engaged in the commercial exploitation of the morbid and shameful craving for materials with prurient effect. * * *

MR. JUSTICE HARLAN, concurring in the result in [*Alberts*], and dissenting in [*Roth*].

I. [The] Court seems to assume that "obscenity" is a peculiar genus of "speech and press," which is as distinct, recognizable, and classifiable as poison ivy is among other plants. On this basis the *constitutional* question before us simply becomes, as the Court says, whether "obscenity," as an abstraction, is protected by the First and Fourteenth Amendments, and the question whether a *particular* book may be suppressed becomes a mere matter of classification, of "fact," to be entrusted to a fact-finder and insulated from independent constitutional judgment. But surely the problem cannot be solved in such a generalized

---

c. The opinion quoted with apparent approval from the trial court's instruction in *Roth:* "[The] test is not whether it would arouse sexual desires or sexual impure thoughts in those comprising a particular segment of the community, the young, the immature or the highly prudish or would leave another segment, the scientific or highly educated or the so-called worldly-wise and sophisticated indifferent and unmoved. [The] test in each case is the effect of the book, picture or publication considered as a whole, not upon any particular class, but upon all those whom it is likely to reach. In other words, you determine its impact upon the average person in the community. The books, pictures and circulars must be judged as a whole, in their entire context, and you are not to consider detached or separate portions in reaching a conclusion. You judge the circulars, pictures and publications which have been put in evidence by present-day standards of the community. You may ask yourselves does it offend the common conscience of the community by present-day standards."

fashion. Every communication has an individuality and "value" of its own. The suppression of a particular writing or other tangible form of expression is, therefore, an *individual* matter, and in the nature of things every such suppression raises an individual constitutional problem, in which a reviewing court must determine for *itself* whether the attacked expression is suppressable within constitutional [standards].

I do not think that reviewing courts can escape this responsibility by saying that the trier of the facts, be it a jury or a judge, has labeled the questioned matter as "obscene," for, if "obscenity" is to be suppressed, the question whether a particular work is of that character involves not really an issue of fact but a question of constitutional *judgment* of the most sensitive and delicate kind. Many juries might find that Joyce's "Ulysses" or Bocaccio's "Decameron" was obscene, and yet the conviction of a defendant for selling either book would raise, for me, the gravest constitutional problems, for no such verdict could convince me, without more, that these books are "utterly without redeeming social importance." [I] am very much afraid that the broad manner in which the Court has decided these cases will tend to obscure the peculiar responsibilities resting on state and federal courts in this field and encourage them to rely on easy labeling and jury verdicts as a substitute for facing up to the tough individual problems of constitutional judgment involved in every obscenity case.

[In] California the book must have a "tendency to deprave or corrupt its readers"; under the federal statute it must tend "to stir sexual impulses and lead to sexually impure thoughts." [T]he Court compounds confusion when it superimposes on these two statutory definitions a third, drawn from the American Law Institute's *Model Penal Code,* Tentative Draft No. 6: "A thing is obscene if, considered as a whole, its predominant appeal is to prurient interest." The bland assurance that this definition is the same as the ones with which we deal flies in the face of the authors' express rejection of the "deprave and corrupt" and "sexual thoughts" tests.[d] [T]he Court merely assimilates the various tests into one indiscriminate potpourri. * * *

II. I concur in [*Alberts*]. [T]he [California] legislature has made the judgment that printed words *can* "deprave or corrupt" the reader—that words can incite to anti-social or immoral action. [It] is well known, of course, that the validity of this assumption is a matter of dispute among critics, sociologists, psychiatrists, and penologists. [I]t is not our function to decide this question. That function belongs to the state legislature. [I]t is not irrational, in our present state of knowledge, to consider that pornography can induce a type of sexual conduct which a State may deem obnoxious to the moral fabric of [society].

Furthermore, even assuming that pornography cannot be deemed ever to cause, in an immediate sense, criminal sexual conduct, other interests within the

d. The opinion quoted the explanation in the Tentative Draft: "Obscenity [in the Tentative Draft] is defined in terms of material which appeals predominantly to prurient interest in sexual matters and which goes beyond customary freedom of expression in these matters. We reject the prevailing test of tendency to arouse lustful thoughts or desires because it is unrealistically broad for a society that plainly tolerates a great deal of erotic interest in literature, advertising, and art, and because regulation of thought or desire, unconnected with overt misbehavior, raises the most acute constitutional as well as practical difficulties. We likewise reject the common definition of obscene as that which 'tends to corrupt or debase.' If this means anything different from tendency to arouse lustful thought and desire, it suggests that change of character or actual misbehavior follows from contact with obscenity. Evidence of such consequences is lacking. [On] the other hand, 'appeal to prurient interest' refers to qualities of the material itself: the capacity to attract individuals eager for a forbidden look."

proper cognizance of the States may be protected by the prohibition placed on such materials. The State can reasonably draw the inference that over a long period of time the indiscriminate dissemination of materials, the essential character of which is to degrade sex, will have an eroding effect on moral standards. And the State has a legitimate interest in protecting the privacy of the home against invasion of unsolicited obscenity.

[I] concur in the judgment because, upon an independent perusal of the material involved, and in light of the considerations discussed above, I cannot say that its suppression would so interfere with the communication of "ideas" in any proper sense of that term that it would offend the Due Process Clause.[e]

MR. JUSTICE DOUGLAS, with whom MR. JUSTICE BLACK concurs, dissenting.

When we sustain these convictions, we make the legality of a publication turn on the purity of thought which a book or tract instills in the mind of the reader. I do not think we can approve that standard and be faithful to the command of the First Amendment * * *.

The tests by which these convictions were obtained require only the arousing of sexual thoughts. Yet the arousing of sexual thoughts and desires happens every day in normal life in dozens of ways. Nearly 30 years ago a questionnaire sent to college and normal school women graduates asked what things were most stimulating sexually. Of 409 replies, 9 said "music"; 18 said "pictures"; 29 said "dancing"; 40 said "drama"; 95 said "books"; and 218 said "man." Alpert, *Judicial Censorship of Obscene Literature*, 52 Harv.L.Rev. 40, 73 (1938).

The test of obscenity the Court endorses today gives the censor free range over a vast domain. To allow the State to step in and punish mere speech or publication that the judge or the jury thinks has an *undesirable* impact on thoughts but that is not shown to be a part of unlawful action is drastically to curtail the First Amendment. As recently stated by two of our outstanding authorities on obscenity, "The danger of influencing a change in the current moral standards of the community, or of shocking or offending readers, or of stimulating sex thoughts or desires apart from objective conduct, can never justify the losses to society that result from interference with literary freedom." Lockhart & McClure, *Literature, The Law of Obscenity, and the Constitution*, 38 Minn.L.Rev. 295, 387 (1954).

If we were certain that impurity of sexual thoughts impelled to action, we would be on less dangerous ground in punishing the distributors of this sex literature. But it is by no means clear that obscene literature, as so defined, is a significant factor in influencing substantial deviations from the community standards. [The] absence of dependable information on the effect of obscene literature on human conduct should make us wary. It should put us on the side of protecting society's interest in literature, except and unless it can be said that the particular publication has an impact on action that the government can [control.]

Any test that turns on what is offensive to the community's standards is too loose, too capricious, too destructive of freedom of expression to be squared with the First Amendment. Under that test, juries can censor, suppress, and punish what they don't like, provided the matter relates to "sexual impurity" or has a tendency "to excite lustful thoughts." This is community censorship in one of

---

e. Harlan, J., dissented in *Roth*. He would have limited federal power to reach only "what the Government has termed as 'hard-core' pornography." He stressed both the ab- sence of federal "power over sexual morality" and the danger to free expression of a "blanket ban over the Nation" on such books as *Lady Chatterley's Lover*.

its worst forms. It creates a regime where in the battle between the literati and the Philistines, the Philistines are certain to win. If experience in this teaches anything, it is that "censorship of obscenity has almost always been both irrational and indiscriminate." Lockhart & McClure at 371.

[The Court today defines] obscene material as that "which deals with sex in a manner appealing to prurient interest." [T]hat standard does not require any nexus between the literature which is prohibited and action which the legislature can regulate or [prohibit].

I do not think that the problem can be resolved by the Court's statement that "obscenity is not expression protected by the First Amendment." With the exception of *Beauharnais* none of our cases has resolved problems of free speech and free press by placing any form of expression beyond the pale of the absolute prohibition of the First Amendment. Unlike the law of libel, wrongfully relied on in *Beauharnais*, there is no special historical evidence that literature dealing with sex was intended to be treated in a special manner by those who drafted the First Amendment. [I] reject too the implication that problems of freedom of speech and of the press are to be resolved by weighing against the values of free expression, the judgment of the Court that a particular form of that expression has "no redeeming social importance." * * *

I would give the broad sweep of the First Amendment full support. I have the same confidence in the ability of our people to reject noxious literature as I have in their capacity to sort out the true from the false in theology, economics, politics, or any other field.

Notes and Questions

1. *Non-obscene advocacy of "sexual immorality."* Two years after *Roth*, KINGSLEY INT'L PICTURES CORP. v. REGENTS, 360 U.S. 684, 79 S.Ct. 1362, 3 L.Ed.2d 1512 (1959), per STEWART, J., underlined the distinction between obscenity and non-obscene "portrayal of sex" in art and literature. *Kingsley* held invalid New York's denial of a license to exhibit the film *Lady Chatterley's Lover* pursuant to a statute requiring such denial when a film "portrays acts of sexual immorality [as] desirable, acceptable or proper patterns of behavior":

"The Court of Appeals unanimously and explicitly rejected any notion that the film is obscene [but] found that the picture as a whole 'alluringly portrays adultery as proper behavior.' [What] New York has done, [is] to prevent the exhibition of a motion picture because that picture advocates an idea—that adultery under certain circumstances may be proper behavior. Yet the First Amendment's basic guarantee is of freedom to advocate ideas. The State, quite simply, has thus struck at the very heart of constitutionally protected liberty.

"[T]he guarantee is not confined to the expression of ideas that are conventional or shared by a majority. It protects advocacy of the opinion that adultery may sometimes be proper, no less than advocacy of socialism or the single tax. And in the realm of ideas it protects expression which is eloquent no less than that which is unconvincing. Advocacy of conduct proscribed by law is not, as Mr. Justice Brandeis long ago pointed out, 'a justification for denying free speech where the advocacy falls short of incitement and there is nothing to indicate that the advocacy would be immediately acted on.' *Whitney*." [f]

---

f. While joining the opinion, Black and Douglas, JJ., also stated that prior censorship of motion pictures violates the first amendment. See discussion of this issue in Sec. 2, II

infra. Harlan, J., joined by Frankfurter and Whittaker, JJ., concurred in the result. While "granting that abstract public discussion [of] adultery, unaccompanied by obscene

2. *Ideas and the first amendment.* Consider Kalven, *The Metaphysics of the Law of Obscenity,* 1960 Sup.Ct.Rev. 1, 15–16: "The classic defense of John Stuart Mill and the modern defense of Alexander Meiklejohn do not help much when the question is why the novel, the poem, the painting, the drama, or the piece of sculpture falls within the protection of the First Amendment. Nor do the famous opinions of Hand, Holmes, and Brandeis. [The] people do not need novels or dramas or paintings or poems because they will be called upon to vote. Art and belles-lettres do not deal in such ideas—at least not good art or belles-lettres—and it makes little sense here to talk [of] whether there is still time for counter-speech.

[B]eauty has constitutional status too, [and] the life of the imagination is as important to the human adult as the life of the intellect. I do not think that the Court would find it difficult to protect Shakespeare, even though it is hard to enumerate the important ideas in the plays and poems. I am only suggesting that Mr. Justice Brennan might not have found it so easy to dismiss obscenity because it lacked socially useful ideas if he had recognized that as to this point, at least, obscenity is in the same position as all art and literature."

3. *The moral rationale for prohibition.* Consider Clor, *Obscenity and Public Morality* 41–43 (1969): *Roth* "rejected the government's formula for the decision of obscenity cases, a formula which would have involved it in judgments concerning the importance of public morality and the role of government, as well as judgments concerning the effects of obscenity and the relative value of different forms of speech. The Court preferred to decide the case on the narrow and negative grounds that obscenity is without redeeming social importance. [W]hile the idea of redeeming social importance can be valuable as a definition of what should be protected, it cannot serve as a defense of regulation. Justices Harlan and Douglas can be answered only by a course of reasoning which provides some grounds for government activity in the area of morality, showing that the ends are legitimate and important, which provides some justification for the claims of community conscience, and which explores, more thoroughly than does the Court, the character of the 'thoughts' with which the law is here concerned."

The Court does assert that any value of obscenity as a step to truth is "outweighed by the social interest in order and morality.'" But consider Richards, *Free Speech and Obscenity Law: Toward A Moral Theory of the First Amendment,* 123 U.Pa.L.Rev. 45, 81 (1974): "[P]ornography can be seen as the unique medium of a vision of sexuality * * * a view of sensual delight in the erotic celebration of the body, a concept of easy freedom without consequences, a fantasy of timelessly repetitive indulgence. In opposition to the Victorian view that narrowly defines proper sexual function in a rigid way that is analogous to ideas of excremental regularity and moderation, pornography builds a model of plastic variety and joyful excess in sexuality. In opposition to the sorrowing Catholic dismissal of sexuality as an unfortunate and spiritually superficial concomitant of propagation, pornography affords the alternative idea of the independent status of sexuality as a profound and shattering ecstasy."

Even if these characterizations were somewhat overwrought with respect to Roth's publications (e.g., *Wild Passion* and *Wanton By Night*) what of the view that individuals should be able to decide what they want to read and make moral

portrayal or actual incitement [may] not constitutionally be proscribed," they concluded that the New York Court of Appeals had found the film obscene, but on viewing the film they concluded it was not obscene. Clark, J., concurred in the result because the statutory standard was too vague.

decisions for themselves? Consider John Stuart Mill's statement of the harm principle in *On Liberty:* "[T]he only purpose for which power can be rightfully exercised over any member of a civilized community, against his will is to prevent harm to others."

Does the liberal view overestimate human rational capacity and underestimate the importance of the state in promoting a virtuous citizenry? See generally Clor, supra. Do liberals fail to appreciate the morally corrosive effects of obscenity? Consider the following observation: "Obscenity emphasizes the base animality of our nature, reduces the spirituality of humanity to mere bodily functions, and debases civilization by transforming the private into the public." Consider Kristol, *Reflections of a Neoconservative* 45, 47 (1983): "Bearbaiting and cockfighting are prohibited only in part out of compassion for the suffering animals; the main reason they were abolished was because it was felt that they debased and brutalized the citizenry who flocked to witness such spectacles. And the question we face with regard to pornography and obscenity is whether [they] can or will brutalize and debase our citizenry. We are, after all, not dealing with one passing incident—one book, or one play, or one movie. We are dealing with a general tendency that is suffusing our entire culture. [W]hen men and women make love, as we say, they prefer to be alone—because it is only when you are alone that you can make love, as distinct from merely copulating in an animal and casual way. And that, too, is why those who are voyeurs, if they are not irredeemably sick, also feel ashamed at what they are witnessing. When sex is a public spectacle, a human relationship has been debased into a mere animal connection." See also Clor, supra; Berns, *Pornography vs. Democracy: The Case for Censorship,* 22 Pub.Int. 13 (1971).

4. *Feminism and pornography.* Does the Court's cryptic recitation of the interests in order and morality obscure the implications of pornography for women in a male-dominated culture? Consider Brownmiller, *Against Our Will: Men, Women & Rape* 442–43, 444 (1976): Pornography is a "systematized commercially successful propaganda machine" encouraging males to get a "sense of power from viewing females as anonymous, panting playthings, adult toys, dehumanized objects to be used, abused, broken and discarded." See also MacKinnon, *Not a Moral Issue,* 2 Yale L. & Pol.Rev. 321, 327 (1984): "[T]he liberal defense of pornography as human sexual liberation, as de-repression— whether by feminists, lawyers, or neo-Freudians—is a defense not only of force and sexual terrorism, but of the subordination of women. Sexual liberation in the liberal sense frees male sexual aggression in the feminist sense. What in the liberal view looks like love and romance looks a lot like hatred and torture to the feminist. Pleasure and eroticism become violation. Desire appears as lust for dominance and submission."

5. *The impact of obscenity on anti-social conduct.* After citing the conclusion of the U.S. Commission on Obscenity and Pornography that " 'empirical research has found no evidence to date that exposure to explicit sexual materials plays a significant role in the causation of delinquent or criminal behaviour among youth or adults,' " the British Committee on Obscenity and Film Censorship concluded: "It is still possible to say [that] there does not appear to be any strong evidence that exposure to sexually explicit material triggers off anti-social sexual behaviour. [T]his is consistent with what we learned from the clinical experience of those experienced medical witnesses we consulted." Williams, Chair, *Report of the Committee on Obscenity and Film Censorship* § 6.16, at 66 (1979). More recent studies claim to strongly "link exposure to pornographic material among men to an increase in the acceptance of violence against

women." Malamuth & Billings, *Why Pornography? Models of Functions and Effects,* 34 J. of Comm. 117, 129 (1984). For an analysis of much of the recent research (some of it contending that the changes in attitudes and arousal are directly related to aggression against women), see *Pornography & Sexual Aggression* (Malamuth & Donnerstein eds. 1984).

———————

After a majority of the Court agreed on the *Roth* standard for obscenity in 1957 without applying it to particular materials, it was not until *Miller* in 1973 that a majority could again reach agreement upon the key issue—the standard for determining what material is outside the first amendment because "obscene." But during that era a majority of the justices, voting on the basis of differing views as to the appropriate method of dealing with obscenity, produced informal coalitions that reached consistent results. *Memoirs* reflects the divisions within the Court on that key issue during this era.

MEMOIRS v. MASSACHUSETTS, 383 U.S. 413, 86 S.Ct. 975, 16 L.Ed.2d 1 (1966), reversed a ruling that Clelland's *Memoirs of a Woman of Pleasure ("Fanny Hill")* was obscene under Massachusetts law and not entitled to first amendment protection. BRENNAN, J., joined by Warren, C.J., and Fortas, J., delivered the plurality opinion: "[T]he sole question before the state courts was whether *Memoirs* satisfies the test of obscenity established in *Roth* [under whose definition of obscenity], as elaborated in subsequent cases, three elements must coalesce: it must be established that (a) the dominant theme of the material taken as a whole appeals to a prurient interest in sex; (b) the material is patently offensive because it affronts contemporary community standards relating to the description or representation of sexual matters;[a] and (c) the material is utterly without redeeming social value.[b]

"[R]eversal is required because the [Supreme Judicial Court] misinterpreted the social value criterion [thus]: 'It remains to consider whether the book can be said to be "utterly without social importance." We are mindful that there was expert testimony, much of which was strained, [that] *Memoirs* is a structural novel with literary merit; that the book displays a skill in characterization and a gift for comedy; that it plays a part in the history of the development of the English novel; and that it contains a moral, namely, that sex with love is superior to sex in a brothel. But the fact that the testimony may indicate this book has some minimal literary value does not mean it is of any social importance. We do not interpret the "social importance" test as requiring that a book which appeals to prurient interest and is patently offensive must be unqualifiedly worthless before it can be deemed obscene.'

"The Supreme Judicial Court erred in holding that a book need not be 'unqualifiedly worthless before it can be deemed obscene.' A book can not be

---

a. This element crept into the standard for obscenity in an opinion by Harlan, J., joined only by Stewart, J., in *Manual Enterprises, Inc. v. Day,* 370 U.S. 478, 82 S.Ct. 1432, 8 L.Ed. 2d 639 (1962). They concluded that photographs of nude males were not obscene because not "so offensive on their face as to affront community standards of decency." In their view, obscenity required "patent offensiveness" as well as "appeal to the prurient interest." The other justices concurred in the result on grounds that did not reach the obscenity issue.

b. While absence of "social value" was not expressly stated in the standard for obscenity in *Roth,* the opinion gave its absence as a reason for not protecting obscenity. Brennan, J., joined only by Goldberg, J., expressly stated the "utterly without social importance" requirement for the first time in *Jacobellis v. Ohio,* 378 U.S. 184, 84 S.Ct. 1676, 12 L.Ed.2d 793 (1964), where none of the other justices expressed views on that factor.

proscribed unless it is found to be *utterly* without redeeming social value. This is so even though the book is found to possess the requisite prurient appeal and to be patently offensive. Each of the three federal constitutional criteria is to be applied independently; the social value of the book can neither be weighed against nor canceled by its prurient appeal or patent offensiveness. Hence, even on the view of the court below that *Memoirs* possessed only a modicum of social value, its judgment must be reversed as being founded on an erroneous interpretation of a federal constitutional standard.

"It does not necessarily follow from this reversal that a determination that *Memoirs* is obscene in the constitutional sense would be improper under all circumstances. On the premise, which we have no occasion to assess, that *Memoirs* has the requisite prurient appeal and is patently offensive, but has only a minimum of social value, the circumstances of production, sale, and publicity are relevant in determining whether or not the publication or distribution of the book is constitutionally protected. Evidence that the book was commercially exploited for the sake of prurient appeal, to the exclusion of all other values, might justify the conclusion that the book was utterly without redeeming social importance. It is not that in such a setting the social value test is relaxed so as to dispense with the requirement that a book be *utterly* devoid of social value, but rather that [where] the purveyor's sole emphasis is on the sexually provocative aspects of his publications, a court could accept his evaluation at its face value."

Black and Douglas, JJ., each independently concurred in the reversal, restating their views that the first amendment afforded protection for obscene materials. BLACK, J.'s criticism of the social value test maintained that "Whether a particular treatment of a particular subject is with or without social value in this evolving, dynamic society of ours is a question upon which no uniform agreement could possibly be reached among politicians, statesmen, professors, philosophers, scientists, religious groups or any other type of group."

STEWART, J., separately concurred, citing his dissent in *Ginzburg v. United States*, 383 U.S. 463, 86 S.Ct. 942, 16 L.Ed.2d 31 (1966) that only hard core pornography could be constitutionally suppressed. Having said in a prior case that "I cannot define it, but I know it when I see it," he elaborated in *Ginzburg*: "In order to prevent any possible misunderstanding, I have set out in the margin description, borrowed from the Solicitor General's brief, of the kind of thing to which I have reference.[3] See also Lockhart and McClure, [1960] 63–64."

HARLAN, J.'s separate dissent limited the federal government to the regulation of hard core pornography that he would describe "substantially" as does Stewart, J. For state governments, he would require only that it "apply criteria rationally related to the accepted notion of obscenity and that it reach results not wholly out of step with current American standards."

CLARK and WHITE, JJ., each separately dissenting, rejected social value as a "separate and distinct" or "independent test of obscenity" but viewed it as

---

3. "[Such] materials include photographs, both still and motion picture, with no pretense of artistic value, graphically depicting acts of sexual intercourse, including various acts of sodomy and sadism, and sometimes involving several participants in scenes of orgy-like character. They also include strips of drawings in comic-book format grossly depicting similar activities in an exaggerated fashion. There are, in addition, pamphlets and book- lets, sometimes with photographic illustrations, verbally describing such activities in a bizarre manner with no attempt whatsoever to afford portrayals of character or situation and with no pretense to literary value. All of this material [cannot] conceivably be characterized as embodying communication of ideas or artistic values inviolate under the First Amendment."

"relevant." Clark, J., would consider evidence of "social importance [together] with evidence that the material [appeals] to prurient interest and is patently offensive." White, J., viewed "social importance" as "relevant only to determining the predominant prurient interest of the material [based] on the material itself and all the [evidence], expert or otherwise." Each would have upheld the obscenity finding in *Memoirs* and rejected the possibility that "beautiful prose" or "literary style" could protect well-written obscenity.

Notes and Questions

1. *Utterly without redeeming social value.* Should material dealing with sex be entitled to full immunity if it has slight social value, regardless of its prurience and offensiveness? Should courts require *redeeming* social value? Consider Clor, supra, at 78: "Justice Brennan's opinion constitutes a rejection [of] judicial effort to attach some meaning to the first two words in the expression 'redeeming social importance.' Since opposing factors may not be weighed, judges may not consider whether the values ascribed to a work are indeed 'redemptive.' And it would seem that they are also forbidden to consider whether the importance ascribed to a work is really 'social' importance. [Evidently] a work is to be protected though its 'dominant theme, taken as a whole' be both prurient and patently offensive. In this manner the Court goes to the verge of an explicit rejection of the *Roth* rule, while continuing to affirm that that rule governs obscenity cases."

See also Frank, *Obscenity: Some Problems of Values and the Use of Experts,* 41 Wash.L.Rev. 631, 665 (1966): "The practical difference between the Brennan approach and the Clark-White approach is illustrated in *Fanny Hill.* The book is as totally dedicated to the appeal to prurience as anything can be—it has lived for this purpose alone for two hundred years. Certainly no one would choose it very seriously for the sake of the story or for the skill of its expression or as a serious description of 18th century London; * * * Justice Clark makes absolute hash out of its literary pretensions. Yet it is not totally without literary skill in the sense that a dirty postcard might be; it is at least passable writing. If no more is required, then under the Brennan test the book clears; while if the exceedingly low level of literary accomplishment is balanced against other factors, then the book fails."

2. *Variable obscenity.* The plurality's suggestion that the same book may be obscene in some contexts but not in others has been endorsed in several different contexts. *Butler v. Michigan,* 352 U.S. 380, 77 S.Ct. 524, 1 L.Ed.2d 412 (1957) held that the state could not ban sales to the general public of material unsuitable for children: "The State insists that [by] quarantining the general reading public against books not too rugged for grown men and women in order to shield juvenile innocence, it is exercising its power to promote the general welfare. Surely, this is to burn the house to roast the pig. [The] incidence of this enactment is to reduce the adult population of Michigan to reading only what is fit for children." *Ginsberg v. New York,* 390 U.S. 629, 88 S.Ct. 1274, 20 L.Ed.2d 195 (1968), however, held that the state could bar the distribution to children of books that were suitable for adults, the Court recognizing it was adopting a "variable" concept of obscenity.[c]

c. See also *Ginzburg v. United States,* supra ("pandering" method of marketing supports obscenity conviction even though the materials might not otherwise have been considered obscene); *Mishkin v. New York,* 383 U.S. 502, 86 S.Ct. 958, 16 L.Ed.2d 56 (1966) (material designed for and primarily disseminated to deviant sexual group can meet prurient appeal requirement even if the material lacks appeal to an average member of the

The approach had previously been advocated and elaborated by Lockhart and McClure, *Censorship of Obscenity: The Developing Constitutional Standards,* 45 Minn.L.Rev. 5, 77 (1960): "Under variable obscenity, material is judged by its appeal to and effect upon the audience to which the material is primarily directed. In this view, material is never inherently obscene; instead, its obscenity varies with the circumstances of its dissemination. Material may be obscene when directed to one class of persons but not when directed to [another]. Variable obscenity also makes it possible to reach, under obscenity statutes, the panderer who advertises and pushes non-pornographic material as if it were hard-core pornography, seeking out an audience of the sexually immature who bring their 'pornographic intent to something which is not itself pornographic.' "

See also Krislov, *From Ginzburg to Ginsberg: The Unhurried Children's Hour in Obscenity Litigation,* 1968 Sup.Ct.Rev. 153, 196: " 'Variable obscenity' provides an oven to roast the pig—and a precisely fitted one at that. There is no longer need to burn the barn." Compare Schauer, *The Law of Obscenity,* 95 (1976): "[W]hat the idea of variable obscenity adds in terms of realities and flexibility, it may subtract in terms of the best possible notice or warning of what is prohibited. As with any statutory or regulatory scheme, maximum predictability often provides less than optimum 'fairness,' and the converse is equally true."

3. *The law in action.* The Court's failure in *Memoirs* to arrive at a definition of obscenity did not prevent it from reversing obscenity findings in 31 cases between 1967 and 1971,[d] usually by reference to REDRUP v. NEW YORK, 386 U.S. 767, 87 S.Ct. 1414, 18 L.Ed.2d 515 (1967), an opinion which was crafted to transcend the Court's differences. The key language in *Redrup* stated that: "Two members of the Court have consistently adhered to the view that a State is utterly without power to suppress, control, or punish the distribution of any writings or pictures upon the ground of their 'obscenity.' A third has held to the opinion that a State's power in this area is narrowly limited to a distinct and clearly identifiable class of material. Others have subscribed to a not dissimilar standard [quoting the three-factor formula in Brennan, J.'s *Memoirs* opinion.] Another justice has not viewed the 'social value' element as an independent factor in the judgment of obscenity. Whichever of these constitutional views is brought to bear upon the cases before us, it is clear that the judgments cannot stand."

B. THE SEARCH FOR A RATIONALE

STANLEY v. GEORGIA, 394 U.S. 557, 89 S.Ct. 1243, 22 L.Ed.2d 542 (1969), per MARSHALL, J., reversed a conviction for knowing "possession of obscene matter," based on three reels of obscene films found in Stanley's home when police entered under a search warrant for other purposes: "[*Roth*] and the cases following it discerned [an] 'important interest' in the regulation of commercial distribution of obscene material. That holding cannot foreclose an examination of the constitutional implications of a statute forbidding mere private possession

---

general public; appeal is to be tested with reference to the sexual interests of the intended and probable recipient group).

d. In *Huffman v. United States,* 470 F.2d 386, 395–402 (D.C.Cir.1971), Leventhal, J., classified and described the materials involved in each such case. Where the material was textual, all obscenity findings were reversed, including books featuring monotonously re-

peated explicit descriptions of varieties of sexual episodes. Where the materials were pictorial, still or in motion, obscenity findings were reversed where only nudity was shown, including those that focused on male and female genitalia, and where sexual activity was only suggested. But where pictures explicitly depicted sexual activity, the obscenity findings were allowed to stand.

of such material. [The constitutional] right to receive information and ideas, regardless of their social worth [*Winters*] is fundamental to our free society. Moreover, in the context of this case—a prosecution for mere possession of printed or filmed matter in the privacy of a person's own home—that right takes on an added dimension. For also fundamental is the right to be free, except in very limited circumstances, from unwanted governmental intrusions into one's privacy.

" 'The makers of our Constitution undertook to secure conditions favorable to the pursuit of happiness. They recognized the significance of man's spiritual nature, of his feelings and of his intellect. [They] sought to protect Americans in their beliefs, their thoughts, their emotions and their sensations. They conferred, as against the government, the right to be let alone—the most comprehensive of rights and the right most valued by civilized man.' *Olmstead v. United States*, 277 U.S. 438, 48 S.Ct. 564, 72 L.Ed. 944 (1928) (Brandeis, J., dissenting). * * *

"These are the rights that appellant is asserting in the case before us. He is asserting the right to read or observe what he pleases—the right to satisfy his intellectual and emotional needs in the privacy of his own home. He is asserting the right to be free from state inquiry into the contents of his library. Georgia contends that appellant does not have these rights, that there are certain types of materials that the individual may not read or even possess. [W]e think that mere categorization of these films as 'obscene' is insufficient justification for such a drastic invasion of personal liberties guaranteed by the First and Fourteenth Amendments. Whatever may be the justifications for other statutes regulating obscenity, we do not think they reach into the privacy of one's own home. If the First Amendment means anything, it means that a State has no business telling a man, sitting alone in his own house, what books he may read or what films he may watch. Our whole constitutional heritage rebels at the thought of giving government the power to control men's minds.

"[I]n the face of these traditional notions of individual liberty, Georgia asserts the right to protect the individual's mind from the effects of obscenity. We are not certain that this argument amounts to anything more than the assertion that the State has the right to control the moral content of a person's thoughts.[8] To some, this may be a noble purpose, but it is wholly inconsistent with the philosophy of the First Amendment. [*Kingsley Pictures.*] Nor is it relevant that obscenity in general, or the particular films before the Court, are arguably devoid of any ideological content. The line between the transmission of ideas and mere entertainment is much too elusive for this Court to draw, if indeed such a line can be drawn at all. [*Winters*]. Whatever the power of the state to control public dissemination of ideas inimical to the public morality, it cannot constitutionally premise legislation on the desirability of controlling a person's private thoughts.

"[Georgia] asserts that exposure to obscenity may lead to deviant sexual behavior or crimes of sexual violence. There appears to be little empirical basis for that assertion. But more importantly, if the State is only concerned about

---

8. "Communities believe, and act on the belief, that obscenity is immoral, is wrong for the individual, and has no place in a decent society. They believe, too, that adults as well as children are corruptible in morals and character, and that obscenity is a source of corruption that should be eliminated. Obscenity is not suppressed primarily for the protection of others. Much of it is suppressed for the purity of the community and for the salvation and welfare of the 'consumer.' Obscenity, at bottom, is not crime. Obscenity is sin." Henkin, *Morals and the Constitution: The Sin of Obscenity*, 63 Col.L.Rev. 391, 395 (1963).

literature inducing antisocial conduct, we believe that in the context of private consumption of ideas and information we should adhere to the view that '[a]mong free men, the deterrents ordinarily to be applied to prevent crime are education and punishment for violations of the [law].' *Whitney* (Brandeis, J., concurring). See Emerson, *Toward a General Theory of the First Amendment*, 72 Yale L.J. 877, 938 (1963). Given the present state of knowledge, the State may no more prohibit mere possession of obscenity on the ground that it may lead to antisocial conduct than it may prohibit possession of chemistry books on the ground that they may lead to the manufacture of homemade spirits.

"It is true that in *Roth* this Court rejected the necessity of proving that exposure to obscene material would create a clear and present danger of antisocial conduct or would probably induce its recipients to such conduct. But that case dealt with public distribution of obscene materials and such distribution is subject to different objections. For example, there is always the danger that obscene material might fall into the hands of children, see *Ginsberg*, or that it might intrude upon the sensibilities or privacy of the general public. No such dangers are present in this [case.]

"We hold that the First and Fourteenth Amendments prohibit making mere private possession of obscene material a crime. *Roth* and the cases following that decision are not impaired by today's holding. As we have said, the States retain broad power to regulate obscenity; that power simply does not extend to mere possession by the individual in the privacy of his own home." [a]

Notes and Questions

1. *Obscenity and the first amendment.* Is *Stanley* consistent with the constitutional theory of *Roth?* Can the first amendment rationally be viewed as applicable to *private use* but not to *public distribution* of obscenity? Cf. Katz, *Privacy and Pornography,* 1969 Sup.Ct.Rev. 203, 210–11. Might the definitional two-level approach reconcile *Stanley* with *Roth?*

2. *Implications of Stanley.* Could *Stanley*'s recognition of a first amendment right to "receive" and use obscene matter in the home fairly be viewed as implying a right to purchase it from commercial suppliers, or to import it for personal use, or to view it in a theater limited to consenting adults?

PARIS ADULT THEATRE v. SLATON
413 U.S. 49, 93 S.Ct. 2628, 37 L.Ed.2d 446 (1973).

[The entrance to Paris Adult Theatres I & II was conventional and inoffensive without any pictures. Signs read: "Adult Theatre—You must be 21 and able to prove it. If viewing the nude body offends you, Please Do Not Enter." The District Attorney, nonetheless, had brought an action to enjoin the showing of two films that the Georgia Supreme Court described as "hard core pornography" leaving "little to the imagination." The Georgia Supreme Court assumed that the adult theaters in question barred minors and gave a full warning to the general public of the nature of the films involved, but held that the showing of the films was not constitutionally protected.]

MR. CHIEF JUSTICE BURGER delivered the opinion of the Court. * * *

[We] categorically disapprove the theory [that] obscene, pornographic films acquire constitutional immunity from state regulation simply because they are

a. Black, J., concurred separately. Stewart, J., joined by Brennan and White, JJ., concurred in the result on search and seizure grounds.

exhibited for consenting adults only. [Although we have] recognized the high importance of the state interest in regulating the exposure of obscene materials to juveniles and unconsenting adults, this Court has never declared these to be the only legitimate state interests permitting regulation of obscene material.

* * *

[W]e hold that there are legitimate state interests at stake in stemming the tide of commercialized obscenity, even assuming it is feasible to enforce effective safeguards against exposure to juveniles and to the passerby.[7] [These] include the interest of the public in the quality of life and the total community environment, the tone of commerce in the great city centers, and, possibly, the public safety itself. The Hill-Link Minority Report of the Commission on Obscenity and Pornography indicates that there is at least an arguable correlation between obscene material and crime. Quite apart from sex crimes, however, there remains one problem of large proportions aptly described by Professor Bickel: "It concerns the tone of the society, the mode, or to use terms that have perhaps greater currency, the style and quality of life, now and in the future. A man may be entitled to read an obscene book in his room, or expose himself indecently there. [We] should protect his privacy. But if he demands a right to obtain the books and pictures he wants in the market, and to foregather in public places—discreet, if you will, but accessible to all—with others who share his tastes, *then to grant him his right is to affect the world about the rest of us, and to impinge on other privacies.* Even supposing that each of us can, if he wishes, effectively avert the eye and stop the ear (which, in truth, we cannot), what is commonly read and seen and heard and done intrudes upon us all, want it or not." 22 *The Public Interest* 25, 25–26 (Winter, 1971). (Emphasis supplied.) [T]here is a "right of the Nation and of the States to maintain a decent [society]," *Jacobellis* (Warren, C.J., dissenting).

But, it is argued, there is no scientific data which conclusively demonstrates that exposure to obscene materials adversely affects men and women or their society. It is urged [that], absent such a demonstration, any kind of state regulation is "impermissible." We reject this argument. It is not for us to resolve empirical uncertainties underlying state legislation, save in the exceptional case where that legislation plainly impinges upon rights protected by the Constitution itself. [Although] there is no conclusive proof of a connection between antisocial behavior and obscene material, the legislature of Georgia could quite reasonably determine that such a connection does or might exist. In deciding *Roth,* this Court implicitly accepted that a legislature could legitimately act on such a conclusion to protect *"the social interest in order and morality."*

From the beginning of civilized societies, legislators and judges have acted on various unprovable assumptions. Such assumptions underlie much lawful state regulation of commercial and business affairs. See *Ferguson v. Skrupa; Lincoln Fed. Labor Union v. Northwestern Iron & Metal Co.* [p. 76 supra]. The

---

7. It is conceivable that an "adult" theatre can—if it really insists—prevent the exposure of its obscene wares to juveniles. An "adult" bookstore, dealing in obscene books, magazines, and pictures, cannot realistically make this claim. The Hill-Link Minority Report of the Commission on Obscenity and Pornography emphasizes evidence (the Abelson National Survey of Youth and Adults) that, although most pornography may be bought by elders, "the heavy users and most highly exposed people to pornography are adolescent females (among women) and adolescent and young males (among men)." *The Report of the Commission on Obscenity* 401 (1970). The legitimate interest in preventing exposure of juveniles to obscene materials cannot be fully served by simply barring juveniles from the immediate physical premises of "adult" bookstores, when there is a flourishing "outside business" in these materials.

same is true of the federal securities, antitrust laws and a host of other federal regulations. [Likewise], when legislatures and administrators act to protect the physical environment from pollution and to preserve our resources of forests, streams and parks, they must act on such imponderables as the impact of a new highway near or through an existing park or wilderness area. [The] fact that a congressional directive reflects unprovable assumptions about what is good for the people, including imponderable aesthetic assumptions, is not a sufficient reason to find that statute unconstitutional.

If we accept the unprovable assumption that a complete education requires certain books, and the well nigh universal belief that good books, plays, and art lift the spirit, improve the mind, enrich the human personality and develop character, can we then say that a state legislature may not act on the corollary assumption that commerce in obscene books,[a] or public exhibitions focused on obscene conduct, have a tendency to exert a corrupting and debasing impact leading to antisocial behavior? [The] sum of experience, including that of the past two decades, affords an ample basis for legislatures to conclude that a sensitive, key relationship of human existence, central to family life, community welfare, and the development of human personality, can be debased and distorted by crass commercial exploitation of sex. Nothing in the Constitution prohibits a State from reaching such a conclusion and acting on it legislatively simply because there is no conclusive evidence or empirical data.

[Nothing] in this Court's decisions intimates that there is any "fundamental" privacy right "implicit in the concept of ordered liberty" to watch obscene movies in places of public accommodation. [W]e have declined to equate the privacy of the home relied on in *Stanley* with a "zone" of "privacy" that follows a distributor or a consumer of obscene materials wherever he goes.[b]

[W]e reject the claim that Georgia is here attempting to control the minds or thoughts of those who patronize theatres. Preventing unlimited display or distribution of obscene material, which by definition lacks any serious literary, artistic, political, or scientific value as communication, is distinct from a control of reason and the intellect. Cf. Finnis, *"Reason and Passion": The Constitutional Dialectic of Free Speech and Obscenity*, 116 U.Pa.L.Rev. 222, 229–230, 241–243 (1967).

---

a. The only case after *Roth* in which the Court upheld a conviction based upon books was in *Mishkin* and most, if not all, of those books were illustrated. *Kaplan v. California,* 413 U.S. 115, 93 S.Ct. 2680, 37 L.Ed.2d 492 (1973) held that books without pictures can be legally obscene "in the sense of being unprotected by the First Amendment." It observed that books are "passed hand to hand, and we can take note of the tendency of widely circulated books of this category to reach the impressionable young and have a continuing impact. A State could reasonably regard the 'hard core' conduct described by *Suite 69* as capable of encouraging or causing antisocial behavior, especially in its impact on young people." Is *Kaplan*'s explanation in tension with *Butler v. Michigan?* Why should the obscenity standard focus on the average adult if the underlying worry is that books will fall in the hands of children?

b. In a series of cases, the Court limited *Stanley* to its facts. It held that *Stanley* did not protect the mailing of obscene material to consenting adults, *United States v. Reidel,* 402 U.S. 351, 91 S.Ct. 1410, 28 L.Ed.2d 813 (1971) or the transporting or importing of obscene materials for private use, *United States v. Orito,* 413 U.S. 139, 93 S.Ct. 2674, 37 L.Ed.2d 513 (1973) (transporting); *United States v. 12 200 Ft. Reels,* 413 U.S. 123, 93 S.Ct. 2665, 37 L.Ed.2d 500 (1973) (importing). Dissenting in *Reels,* Douglas, J., argued that *Stanley* rights could legally be realized "only if one wrote or designed a tract in his attic and printed or processed it in his basement, so as to be able to read it in his study." Do these decisions take the first amendment out of *Stanley?* Are they justified by the rationale in *Paris Adult Theatre?* For example, does importation for personal use intrude "upon us all"? Affect the total community environment?

[Finally], petitioners argue that conduct which directly involves "consenting adults" only has, for that sole reason, a special claim to constitutional protection. Our Constitution establishes a broad range of conditions on the exercise of power by the States, but for us to say that our Constitution incorporates the proposition that conduct involving consenting adults only is always beyond state regulation,[14] is a step we are unable to take.[15] [The] issue in this context goes beyond whether someone, or even the majority, considers the conduct depicted as "wrong" or "sinful." The States have the power to make a morally neutral judgment that public exhibition of obscene material, or commerce in such material, has a tendency to injure the community as a whole, to endanger the public safety, or to jeopardize, in Mr. Chief Justice Warren's words, the States' "right [to] maintain a decent society." *Jacobellis* (dissenting). * * *

MR. JUSTICE BRENNAN, with whom MR. JUSTICE STEWART and MR. JUSTICE MARSHALL join, dissenting.

[I] am convinced that the approach initiated 15 years ago in *Roth* and culminating in the Court's decision today, cannot bring stability to this area of the law without jeopardizing fundamental First Amendment values, and I have concluded that the time has come to make a significant departure from that [approach.]

[The] decision of the Georgia Supreme Court rested squarely on its conclusion that the State could constitutionally suppress these films even if they were displayed only to persons over the age of 21 who were aware of the nature of their contents and who had consented to viewing them. [I] am convinced of the invalidity of that conclusion [and] would therefore vacate the [judgment]. I have no occasion to consider the extent of State power to regulate the distribution of sexually oriented materials to juveniles or to unconsenting [adults.] [*Stanley*] reflected our emerging view that the state interests in protecting children and in protecting unconsenting adults may stand on a different footing from the other asserted state interests. It may well be, as one commentator has argued, that "exposure to [erotic material] is for some persons an intense emotional experience. A communication of this nature, imposed upon a person contrary to his wishes, has all the characteristics of a physical assault * * *. [And it] constitutes an invasion of his [privacy]."[24] [But] whatever the strength of the state interests in protecting juveniles and unconsenting adults from exposure to sexually oriented materials, those interests cannot be asserted in defense of the holding of the Georgia Supreme Court, [which] assumed for the purposes of its decision that the films in issue were exhibited only to persons over the age of 21 who viewed them willingly and with prior knowledge of the nature of their contents. [The] justification for the suppression must be found, therefore, in some independent interest in regulating the reading and viewing habits of consenting [adults].

In *Stanley* we pointed out that "[t]here appears to be little empirical basis for" the assertion that "exposure to obscene materials may lead to deviant sexual behavior or crimes of sexual violence." In any event, we added that "if the State is only concerned about printed or filmed materials inducing antisocial

14. Cf. Mill, *On Liberty* 13 (1955).

15. The state statute books are replete with constitutionally unchallenged laws against prostitution, suicide, voluntary self-mutilation, brutalizing "bare fist" prize fights, and duels, although these crimes may only directly involve "consenting adults." Statutes making bigamy a crime surely cut into an individual's freedom to associate, but few today seriously claim such statutes violate the First Amendment or any other constitutional provision.

24. Emerson, *The System of Freedom of Expression* 496 (1970).

conduct, we believe that in the context of private consumption of ideas and information we should adhere to the view that '[a]mong free men, the deterrents ordinarily to be applied to prevent crime are education and punishment for violations of the [law].' "

Moreover, in *Stanley* we rejected as "wholly inconsistent with the philosophy of the First Amendment," the notion that there is a legitimate state concern in the "control [of] the moral content of a person's thoughts." [The] traditional description of state police power does embrace the regulation of morals as well as the health, safety, and general welfare of the citizenry. [But] the State's interest in regulating morality by suppressing obscenity, while often asserted, remains essentially unfocused and ill-defined. And, since the attempt to curtail unprotected speech necessarily spills over into the area of protected speech, the effort to serve this speculative interest through the suppression of obscene material must tread heavily on rights protected by the First Amendment. * * *[27]

In short, while I cannot say that the interests of the State—apart from the question of juveniles and unconsenting adults—are trivial or nonexistent, I am compelled to conclude that these interests cannot justify the substantial damage to constitutional rights and to this Nation's judicial machinery that inevitably results from state efforts to bar the distribution even of unprotected material to consenting adults.[c]

MR. JUSTICE DOUGLAS, dissenting. * * *

"Obscenity" at most is the expression of offensive ideas. There are regimes in the world where ideas "offensive" to the majority (or at least to those who control the majority) are suppressed. There life proceeds at a monotonous pace. Most of us would find that world offensive. One of the most offensive experiences in my life was a visit to a nation where bookstalls were filled only with books on mathematics and books on religion.

I am sure I would find offensive most of the books and movies charged with being obscene. But in a life that has not been short, I have yet to be trapped into seeing or reading something that would offend me. I never read or see the materials coming to the Court under charges of "obscenity," because I have thought the First Amendment made it unconstitutional for me to act as a censor. * * *

When man was first in the jungle he took care of himself. When he entered a societal group, controls were necessarily imposed. But our society—unlike most in the world—presupposes that freedom and liberty are in a frame of reference that makes the individual, not government, the keeper of his tastes, beliefs, and ideas. That is the philosophy of the First Amendment; and it is the article of faith that sets us apart from most nations in the world.

C. A REVISED STANDARD

MILLER v. CALIFORNIA

413 U.S. 15, 93 S.Ct. 2607, 37 L.Ed.2d 419 (1973).

MR. CHIEF JUSTICE BURGER delivered the opinion of the Court. [The Court remanded, "for proceedings not inconsistent" with the opinion's obscenity stan-

---

27. See Henkin, *Morals and the Constitution: The Sin of Obscenity,* 63 Col.L.Rev. 391, 395 (1963).

c. For the portion of Brennan, J.'s dissent addressing the difficulties of formulating an acceptable constitutional standard, see *Miller v. California,* infra.

dard, Miller's conviction under California's obscenity law for mass mailing of unsolicited pictorial advertising brochures depicting men and women in a variety of group sexual activities.]

This is one of a group of "obscenity-pornography" cases being reviewed by the Court in a re-examination of standards enunciated in earlier cases involving what Mr. Justice Harlan called "the intractable obscenity problem." [I]n this context [a] [we] are called on to define the standards which must be used to identify obscene material that a State may [regulate].

[E]ven as they repeated the words of *Roth,* the *Memoirs* plurality produced a drastically altered test that called on the prosecution to prove a negative, i.e., that the material was "*utterly* without redeeming social value"—a burden virtually impossible to discharge under our criminal standards of proof. [Apart] from the initial formulation in *Roth,* no majority of the Court has at any given time been able to agree on a standard to determine what constitutes obscene, pornographic material subject to regulation under the States' police power. See, e.g., *Redrup.* [3] This is not remarkable, for in the area of freedom of speech and press the courts must always remain sensitive to any infringement on genuinely serious literary, artistic, political, or scientific expression. ＊ ＊ ＊

II.   This much has been categorically settled by the Court, that obscene material is unprotected by the First Amendment. [We] acknowledge, however, the inherent dangers of undertaking to regulate any form of expression. State statutes designed to regulate obscene materials must be carefully limited. As a result, we now confine the permissible scope of such regulation to works which depict or describe sexual conduct. That conduct must be specifically defined by the applicable state law, as written or authoritatively construed.[6] A state offense must also be limited to works which, taken as a whole, appeal to the prurient interest in sex, which portray sexual conduct in a patently offensive way, and which, taken as a whole, do not have serious literary, artistic, political, or scientific value.

The basic guidelines for the trier of fact must be: (a) whether "the average person, applying contemporary community standards" would find that the work, taken as a whole, appeals to the prurient interest, (b) whether the work depicts or describes, in a patently offensive way, sexual conduct specifically defined by the applicable state law, and (c) whether the work, taken as a whole, lacks serious literary, artistic, political, or scientific value. We do not adopt as a constitutional standard the "*utterly* without redeeming social value" test of *Memoirs;* that concept has never commanded the adherence of more than three

---

a.   The "context" was that in *Miller* "sexually explicit materials have been thrust by aggressive sales action upon unwilling recipients."   But nothing in *Miller* limited the revised standard to that context, and the companion case, *Paris Adult Theatre,* applied the same standard to dissemination limited to consenting adults.

[3].   In the absence of a majority view, this Court was compelled to embark on the practice of summarily reversing convictions for the dissemination of materials that at least five members of the Court, applying their separate tests, found to be protected by the First Amendment. *Redrup.* [Beyond] the necessity of circumstances, however, no justification has

ever been offered in support of the *Redrup* "policy." The *Redrup* procedure has cast us in the role of an unreviewable board of censorship for the 50 States, subjectively judging each piece of material brought before us.

6.   See, e.g., Oregon Laws 1971, c. 743, Art. 29, §§ 255–262, and Hawaii Penal Code, Tit. 37, §§ 1210–1216, 1972 Hawaii Session Laws, pp. 126–129, Act 9, Pt. II, as examples of state laws directed at depiction of defined physical conduct, as opposed to expression. [We] do not hold, as Mr. Justice Brennan intimates, that all States other than Oregon must now enact new obscenity statutes. Other existing state statutes, as construed heretofore or hereafter, may well be adequate.

Justices at one time.[7] If a state law that regulates obscene material is thus limited, as written or construed, the First Amendment values applicable to the States [are] adequately protected by the ultimate power of appellate courts to conduct an independent review of constitutional claims when necessary.

We emphasize that it is not our function to propose regulatory schemes for the States. [It] is possible, however, to give a few plain examples of what a state statute could define for regulation under the second part (b) of the standard announced in this opinion, supra:

(a) Patently offensive representations or descriptions of ultimate sexual acts, normal or perverted, actual or simulated.

(b) Patently offensive representations or descriptions of masturbation, excretory functions, and lewd exhibition of the genitals.[b]

Sex and nudity may not be exploited without limit by films or pictures exhibited or sold in places of public accommodation any more than live sex and nudity can be exhibited or sold without limit in such public places.[8] At a minimum, prurient,[c] patently offensive depiction or description of sexual conduct must have serious literary, artistic, political, or scientific value to merit First Amendment protection. For example, medical books for the education of physicians and related personnel necessarily use graphic illustrations and descriptions of human anatomy. In resolving the inevitably sensitive questions of fact and law, we must continue to rely on the jury system, accompanied by the safeguards

---

7. "[We] also reject, as a constitutional standard, the ambiguous concept of 'social importance'." [*Hamling v. United States*, 418 U.S. 87, 94 S.Ct. 2887, 41 L.Ed.2d 590 (1974) upheld a conviction in which the jury had been instructed to find that the material was "utterly without redeeming social value." Defendant argued that the latter phrase was unconstitutionally vague and cited *Miller*. The Court rejected the vagueness challenge: "[O]ur opinion in *Miller* plainly indicates that we rejected the '[social] value' formulation, not because it was so vague as to deprive criminal defendants of adequate notice, but instead because it represented a departure from [*Roth*], and because in calling on the prosecution to 'prove a negative,' it imposed a '[prosecutorial] burden virtually impossible to discharge' and which was not constitutionally required."]

b. *Jenkins v. Georgia*, 418 U.S. 153, 94 S.Ct. 2750, 41 L.Ed.2d 642 (1974) held the film *Carnal Knowledge* not obscene because it did not "'depict or describe patently offensive "hard core" sexual conduct'" as required by *Miller*: "[While there] are scenes in which sexual conduct including 'ultimate sexual acts' is to be understood as taking place, the camera does not focus on the bodies of the actors at such times. There is no exhibition whatever of the actors' genitals, lewd or otherwise, during these scenes. There are occasional scenes of nudity, but nudity alone is not enough to make material legally obscene under the *Miller* standards." *Ward v. Illinois*, 431 U.S. 767, 97 S.Ct. 2085, 52 L.Ed.2d 738

(1977) held that it was not necessary for the legislature or the courts to provide an "exhaustive list of the sexual conduct [the] description of which may be held obscene." It is enough that a state adopt *Miller*'s explanatory examples. Stevens, J., joined by Brennan, Stewart and Marshall, JJ., dissented: "[I]f the statute need only describe the 'kinds' of proscribed sexual conduct, it adds no protection to what the Constitution itself creates. [The] specificity requirement as described in *Miller* held out the promise of a principled effort to respond to [the vagueness] argument. By abandoning that effort today, the Court withdraws the cornerstone of the *Miller* [structure]."

8. Although we are not presented here with the problem of regulating lewd public conduct itself, the States have greater power to regulate nonverbal, physical conduct than to suppress depictions or descriptions of the same behavior. * * *

c. *Brockett v. Spokane Arcades, Inc.*, ___ U.S. ___, 105 S.Ct. 2794, 86 L.Ed.2d 394 (1985) held that appeals to prurient interest could not be taken to include appeals to "normal" interests in sex. Only appeals to a "shameful or morbid interest in sex" are prurient. Although the Court was resolute in its position that appeals to "good, old fashioned, healthy" interests in sex were constitutionally protected, it did not further specify how "normal" sex was to be distinguished from the "shameful" or "morbid."

that judges, rules of evidence, presumption of innocence and other protective features [provide].

Mr. Justice Brennan [has] abandoned his former positions and now maintains that no formulation of this Court, the Congress, or the States can adequately distinguish obscene material unprotected by the First Amendment from protected expression, *Paris Adult Theatre v. Slaton* (Brennan, J., dissenting). Paradoxically, Mr. Justice Brennan indicates that suppression of unprotected obscene material is permissible to avoid exposure to unconsenting adults, as in this case, and to juveniles, although he gives no indication of how the division between protected and nonprotected materials may be drawn with greater precision for these purposes than for regulation of commercial exposure to consenting adults only. Nor does he indicate where in the Constitution he finds the authority to distinguish between a willing "adult" one month past the state law age of majority and a willing "juvenile" one month younger.

Under the holdings announced today, no one will be subject to prosecution for the sale or exposure of obscene materials unless these materials depict or describe patently offensive "hard core" sexual conduct specifically defined by the regulating state law, as written or construed. We are satisfied that these specific prerequisites will provide fair notice to a dealer in such materials that his public and commercial activities may bring prosecution. If the inability to define regulated materials with ultimate, god-like precision altogether removes the power of the States or the Congress to regulate, then "hard core" pornography may be exposed without limit to the juvenile, the passerby, and the consenting adult alike, as indeed, Mr. Justice Douglas contends.

[N]o amount of "fatigue" should lead us to adopt a convenient "institutional" rationale—an absolutist, "anything goes" view of the First Amendment—because it will lighten our burdens. [Nor] should we remedy "tension between state and federal courts" by arbitrarily depriving the States of a power reserved to them under the Constitution, a power which they have enjoyed and exercised continuously from before the adoption of the First Amendment to this day. See *Roth*. "Our duty admits of no 'substitute for facing up to the tough individual problems of constitutional judgment involved in every obscenity case.'" *Jacobellis* (opinion of Brennan, J.).

III.   Under a national Constitution, fundamental First Amendment limitations on the powers of the States do not vary from community to community, but this does not mean that there are, or should or can be, fixed, uniform national standards of precisely what appeals to the "prurient interest" or is "patently offensive." These are essentially questions of fact, and our nation is simply too big and too diverse for this Court to reasonably expect that such standards could be articulated for all 50 States in a single formulation, even assuming the prerequisite consensus exists. When triers of fact are asked to decide whether "the average person, applying contemporary community standards" would consider certain materials "prurient," it would be unrealistic to require that the answer be based on some abstract formulation. The adversary system, with lay jurors as the usual ultimate factfinders in criminal prosecutions, has historically permitted triers-of-fact to draw on the standards of their community, guided always by limiting instructions on the law. To require a State to structure obscenity proceedings around evidence of a *national* "community standard" would be an exercise in [futility].

We conclude that neither the State's alleged failure to offer evidence of "national standards," nor the trial court's charge that the jury consider state community standards, were constitutional errors. Nothing in the First Amendment requires that a jury must consider hypothetical and unascertainable "national standards" when attempting to determine whether certain materials are obscene as a matter of [fact].

It is neither realistic nor constitutionally sound to read the First Amendment as requiring that the people of Maine or Mississippi accept public depiction of conduct found tolerable in Las Vegas, or New York City. People in different States vary in their tastes and attitudes, and this diversity is not to be strangled by the absolutism of imposed uniformity. As the Court made clear in *Mishkin,* the primary concern with requiring a jury to apply the standard of "the average person, applying contemporary community standards" is to be certain that, so far as material is not aimed at a deviant group, it will be judged by its impact on an average person, rather than a particularly susceptible or sensitive person—or indeed a totally insensitive one.[d] [We] hold the requirement that the jury evaluate the materials with reference to "contemporary standards of the State of California" serves this protective purpose and is constitutionally adequate.[e]

* * *

In sum we (a) reaffirm the *Roth* holding that obscene material is not protected by the First Amendment, (b) hold that such material can be regulated by the States, subject to the specific safeguards enunciated above, without a showing that the material is "*utterly* without redeeming social value," and (c) hold that obscenity is to be determined by applying "contemporary community standards," not "national standards." * * *

MR. JUSTICE DOUGLAS, dissenting. * * *

My contention is that until a civil proceeding has placed a tract beyond the pale, no criminal prosecution should be sustained. For no more vivid illustration of vague and uncertain laws could be designed than those we have fashioned. [If] a specific book [or] motion picture has in a civil proceeding been condemned as obscene and review of that finding has been completed, and thereafter a person publishes [or] displays that particular book or film, then a vague law has been made specific. There would remain the underlying question whether the First Amendment allows an implied exception in the case of obscenity. I do not think it does and my views on the issue have been stated

---

d. *Pinkus v. United States,* 436 U.S. 293, 98 S.Ct. 1808, 56 L.Ed.2d 293 (1978) upheld a jury instruction stating "you are to judge these materials by the standard of the hypothetical average person in the community, but in determining this average standard you must include the *sensitive and the insensitive,* in other words, [everyone] in the community." On the other hand, in the absence of evidence that "children were the intended recipients" or that defendant "had reason to know children were likely to receive the materials," it was considered erroneous to instruct the jury that children were part of the relevant community. *Butler.* When the evidence would support such a charge, the Court stated that prurient appeal to deviant sexual groups could be substituted for appeal to the average person; moreover, the jury was entitled to take pandering into account. *Ginzburg.*

e. *Jenkins,* fn. b supra, stated that a judge may instruct a jury to apply "contemporary community standards" without any further specification. Alternatively, the state may choose "to define the standards in more precise geographic terms, as was done by California in *Miller.*" *Hamling v. United States,* fn. 7 supra, interpreted a federal obscenity statute to make the relevant community the one from which the jury was drawn. The judge's instruction to consider the "community standards of the 'nation as a whole' delineated a wider geographical area than would be warranted by [*Miller*]" or the Court's construction of the statute, but the error was regarded as harmless under the circumstances. After these decisions, what advice should lawyers give to publishers who distribute in national markets?

over and again. But at least a criminal prosecution brought at that juncture would not violate the time-honored void-for-vagueness test.[8]

No such protective procedure has been designed by California in this case. Obscenity—which even we cannot define with precision—is a hodge-podge. To send men to jail for violating standards they cannot understand, construe, and apply is a monstrous thing to do in a Nation dedicated to fair trials and due process. * * *

MR. JUSTICE BRENNAN, with whom MR. JUSTICE STEWART and MR. JUSTICE MARSHALL join, dissenting.

In my dissent in *Paris Adult Theatre,* decided this date, I noted that I had no occasion to consider the extent of state power to regulate the distribution of sexually oriented material to juveniles or the offensive exposure of such material to unconsenting adults. [I] need not now decide whether a statute might be drawn to impose, within the requirements of the First Amendment, criminal penalties for the precise conduct at issue here. For it is clear that under my dissent in *Paris Adult Theatre,* the statute under which the prosecution was brought is unconstitutionally overbroad, and therefore invalid on its face. * * *

[In his *Paris Adult Theatre* dissent, Justice Brennan, joined by Stewart and Marshall, JJ., argued that the state interests in regulating obscenity were not strong enough to justify the degree of vagueness. He criticized not only the Court's standard in *Miller,* but also a range of alternatives:]

II. [The] essence of our problem [is] that we have been unable to provide "sensitive tools" to separate obscenity from other sexually oriented but constitutionally protected speech, so that efforts to suppress the former do not spill over into the suppression of the latter. [The dissent traced the Court's experience with *Roth* and its progeny.]

III. Our experience with the *Roth* approach has certainly taught us that the outright suppression of obscenity cannot be reconciled with the fundamental principles of the First and Fourteenth Amendments. For we have failed to formulate a standard that sharply distinguishes protected from unprotected speech, and out of necessity, we have resorted to the *Redrup* approach, which resolves cases as between the parties, but offers only the most obscure guidance to legislation, adjudication by other courts, and primary conduct. [T]he vagueness problem would be largely of our own creation if it stemmed primarily from our failure to reach a consensus on any one standard. But after 15 years of experimentation and debate I am reluctantly forced to the conclusion that none of the available formulas, including the one announced today, can reduce the vagueness to a tolerable level while at the same time striking an acceptable balance between the protections of the First and Fourteenth Amendments, on the one hand, and on the other the asserted state interest in regulating the dissemination of certain sexually oriented materials. Any effort to draw a constitutionally acceptable boundary on state power must resort to such indefinite concepts as "prurient interest," "patent offensiveness," "serious literary value," and the like. The meaning of these concepts necessarily varies with the experience, outlook, and even idiosyncracies of the person defining them. Although we have assumed that obscenity does exist and that we "know it when [we] see it," *Jacobellis* (Stewart, J., concurring), we are manifestly unable to

8. The Commission on Obscenity and Pornography has advocated such a procedure. [See] *Report of the Commission on Obscenity and Pornography* 70–71 (1970).

describe it in advance except by reference to concepts so elusive that they fail to distinguish clearly between protected and unprotected speech.

[Added to the inherent vagueness of standards] is the further complication that the obscenity of any particular item may depend upon nuances of presentation and the context of its dissemination. See *Ginzburg.* [N]o one definition, no matter how precisely or narrowly drawn, can possibly suffice for all situations, or carve out fully suppressable expression from all media without also creating a substantial risk of encroachment upon the guarantees of the Due Process Clause and the First Amendment.

[The] resulting level of uncertainty is utterly intolerable, not alone because it makes "[b]ookselling [a] hazardous profession," *Ginsberg* (Fortas, J., dissenting), but as well because it invites arbitrary and erratic enforcement of the law. [We] have indicated that "stricter standards of permissible statutory vagueness may be applied to a statute having a potentially inhibiting effect on speech; a man may the less be required to act at his peril here, because the free dissemination of ideas may be the loser." * * *

The problems of fair notice and chilling protected speech are very grave standing alone. But [a] vague statute in this area creates a third [set] of problems. These [concern] the institutional stress that inevitably results where the line separating protected from unprotected speech is excessively vague. [Almost] every obscenity case presents a constitutional question of exceptional difficulty. [As] a result of our failure to define standards with predictable application to any given piece of material, there is no probability of regularity in obscenity decisions by state and lower federal courts. [O]ne cannot say with certainty that material is obscene until at least five members of this Court, applying inevitably obscure standards, have pronounced it [so].

We have managed the burden of deciding scores of obscenity cases by relying on per curiam reversals or denials of certiorari—a practice which conceals the rationale of decision and gives at least the appearance of arbitrary action by this Court. More important, [the] practice effectively censors protected expression by leaving lower court determinations of obscenity intact even though the status of the allegedly obscene material is entirely unsettled until final review here. In addition, the uncertainty of the standards creates a continuing source of tension between state and federal [courts].

The severe problems arising from the lack of fair notice, from the chill on protected expression, and from the stress imposed on the state and federal judicial machinery persuade me that a significant change in direction is urgently required. I turn, therefore, to the alternatives that are now open.

IV. 1. The approach requiring the smallest deviation from our present course would be to draw a new line between protected and unprotected speech, still permitting the States to suppress all material on the unprotected side of the line. In my view, clarity cannot be obtained pursuant to this approach except by drawing a line that resolves all doubts in favor of state power and against the guarantees of the First Amendment. We could hold, for example, that any depiction or description of human sexual organs, irrespective of the manner or purpose of the portrayal, is outside the protection of the First Amendment and therefore open to suppression by the States. That formula would, no doubt, offer much fairer notice [and] give rise to a substantial probability of regularity in most judicial determinations under the standard. But such a standard would be appallingly overbroad, permitting the suppression of a vast range of literary, scientific, and artistic masterpieces. Neither the First Amendment nor any free community could possibly tolerate such a standard.

2. [T]he Court today recognizes that a prohibition against any depiction or description of human sexual organs could not be reconciled with the guarantees of the First Amendment. But the Court [adopts] a restatement of the *Roth-Memoirs* definition of obscenity [that] permits suppression if the government can prove that the materials lack "*serious* literary, artistic, political or scientific value." [In] *Roth* we held that certain expression is obscene, and thus outside the protection of the First Amendment, precisely *because* it lacks even the slightest redeeming social value. [The] Court's approach necessarily assumes that some works will be deemed obscene—even though they clearly have *some* social value—because the State was able to prove that the value, measured by some unspecified standard, was not sufficiently "serious" to warrant constitutional protection. That result [is] nothing less than a rejection of the fundamental First Amendment premises and rationale of the *Roth* opinion and an invitation to widespread suppression of sexually oriented speech. Before today, the protections of the First Amendment have never been thought limited to expressions of *serious* literary or political value. *Gooding v. Wilson; Cohen v. California; Terminiello v. Chicago* [Part V infra].

[T]he Court's approach [can] have no ameliorative impact on the cluster of problems that grow out of the vagueness of our current standards. Indeed, even the Court makes no argument that the reformulation will provide fairer notice to booksellers, theatre owners, and the reading and viewing public. Nor does the Court contend that the approach will provide clearer guidance to law enforcement officials or reduce the chill on protected expression [or] mitigate [the] institutional [problems].

Of course, the Court's restated *Roth* test does limit the definition of obscenity to depictions of physical conduct and explicit sexual acts. And that limitation may seem, at first glance, a welcome and clarifying addition to the *Roth-Memoirs* formula. But just as the agreement in *Roth* on an abstract definition of obscenity gave little hint of the extreme difficulty that was to follow in attempting to apply that definition to specific material, the mere formulation of a "physical conduct" test is no assurance that it can be applied with any greater facility. [The] Court surely demonstrates little sensitivity to our own institutional problems, much less the other vagueness-related difficulties, in establishing a system that requires us to consider whether a description of human genitals is sufficiently "lewd" to deprive it of constitutional protection; whether a sexual act is "ultimate"; whether the conduct depicted in materials before us fits within one of the categories of conduct whose depiction the state or federal governments have attempted to suppress; and a host of equally pointless inquiries. * * *

If the application of the "physical conduct" test to pictorial material is fraught with difficulty, its application to textual material carries the potential for extraordinary abuse. Surely we have passed the point where the mere written description of sexual conduct is deprived of First Amendment protection. Yet the test offers no guidance to us, or anyone else, in determining which written descriptions of sexual conduct are protected, and which are not.

Ultimately, the reformulation must fail because it still leaves in this Court the responsibility of determining in each case whether the materials are protected by the First Amendment. * * *

3. I have also considered the possibility of reducing our own role, and the role of appellate courts generally, in determining whether particular matter is obscene. Thus, [we] might adopt the position that where a lower federal or state court has conscientiously applied the constitutional standard, its finding of obscenity will be no more vulnerable to reversal by this Court than any finding of fact. [E]ven if the Constitution would permit us to refrain from judging for ourselves the alleged obscenity of particular materials, that approach would solve at best only a small part of our problem. For while it would mitigate the institutional stress, [it] would neither offer nor produce any cure for the other vices of vagueness. Far from providing a clearer guide to permissible primary conduct, the approach would inevitably lead to even greater uncertainty and the consequent due process problems of fair notice. And the approach would expose much protected, sexually oriented expression to the vagaries of jury determinations. Plainly, the institutional gain would be more than offset by the unprecedented infringement of First Amendment rights.

4. Finally, I have considered the view, urged so forcefully since 1957 by our Brothers Black and Douglas, that the First Amendment bars the suppression of any sexually oriented expression. That position would effect a sharp reduction, although perhaps not a total elimination, of the uncertainty that surrounds our current approach. Nevertheless, I am convinced that it would achieve that desirable goal only by stripping the States of power to an extent that cannot be justified by the commands of the Constitution, at least so long as there is available an alternative approach that strikes a better balance between the guarantee of free expression and the States' legitimate interests.

[I] f would hold, therefore, that at least in the absence of distribution to juveniles or obtrusive exposure to unconsenting adults, the First and Fourteenth Amendments prohibit the state and federal governments from attempting wholly to suppress sexually oriented materials on the basis of their allegedly "obscene" contents. Nothing in this approach precludes those governments from taking action to serve what may be strong and legitimate interests through regulation of the manner of distribution of sexually oriented material.

VI. [I] do not pretend to have found a complete and infallible [answer]. Difficult questions must still be faced, notably in the areas of distribution to juveniles and offensive exposure to unconsenting adults. Whatever the extent of state power to regulate in those areas,[29] it should be clear that the view I espouse today would introduce a large measure of clarity to this troubled area, would reduce the institutional pressure on this Court and the rest of the State and Federal judiciary, and would guarantee fuller freedom of expression while leaving room for the protection of legitimate governmental interests. * * *

Notes and Questions

1. *Serious value.* Consider Clor, *Obscenity and the First Amendment: Round Three,* 7 Loy.L.A.L.Rev. 207, 210, 218 (1974): "The *Miller* decision abandons the requirement that a censorable work must be '*utterly* without redeeming social value' and substitutes the rule of 'serious value'—literary, artistic, political, or scientific. This is the most important innovation in the law

---

f. For the portion of Brennan, J.'s dissent addressing the strength and legitimacy of the state interests, see *Paris Adult Theatre,* supra.

29. The Court erroneously states, *Miller,* that the author of this opinion "indicates that suppression of unprotected obscene material is permissible to avoid exposure to unconsenting adults [and] to juveniles * * *." I defer expression of my views as to the scope of state power in these areas until cases squarely presenting these questions are before the Court.

of obscenity introduced by these decisions. [Serious] literature is to be protected regardless of majority opinions about prurience and offensiveness. *This* is the national principle which is not subject to variation from community to community. If it is to perform this function, the rule will have to be elaborated and the meaning of 'serious value' articulated in some measure. This is the most important item on the legal agenda."

(a) *An independent factor?* Under *Miller* would material found to have "serious artistic value" be entitled to first amendment protection regardless how offensive or prurient? Must each factor in the *Miller* guidelines be independently satisfied, as in *Memoirs? Should* that be so? Would or should that preclude the degree of offensiveness or prurient appeal from affecting the conclusion on the value factor?

(b) *"Serious."* Do you find any guidance for determining when a first amendment value in material depicting sexual conduct is sufficiently "serious" to preclude finding it obscene? Can the "serious" value requisite be reconciled with the first amendment? May material fairly be viewed as having "serious value" whenever the "intent is to convey a literary, artistic, political or scientific idea or message, or to impart information, or advocate a position" rather than "to 'dress up' or try to 'redeem' otherwise obscene matter?" Cf. Schauer, supra, at 140.

(c) *Scope of protected values.* Could the Court consistent with the first amendment exclude serious educational value from those that preclude a finding of obscenity? Serious entertainment value? Could the guidelines be interpreted to include such values? What might explain their omission?

(d) *Based on "community" standards?* Under *Miller* is the presence of "serious value" to be determined under "contemporary community standards" like the offensiveness and pruriency factors? Would this be consistent with the first amendment? With *Miller's* stress on the Court's duty to face up to "the tough individual problems of constitutional judgment in every obscenity case"? Cf. 87 Harv.L.Rev. 169 (1973).

2. *Vagueness and scienter.* Is the *Miller* test intolerably vague? Are there any alternatives that could mitigate the problem? Consider Lockhart, *Escape from the Chill of Uncertainty: Explicit Sex and the First Amendment,* 9 Ga.L. Rev. 533, 563 (1975): "[E]ither legislative action, or constitutional adjudication, could establish as a defense to a criminal obscenity prosecution that the defendant *reasonably believed* that the material involved was not obscene, that is, was constitutionally protected. [Material] that would support such a court or jury finding is not the kind that requires or justifies quick action by the police and prosecutor. The public interest in preventing distribution of borderline material that can reasonably be believed not obscene is not so pressing as to require immediate criminal sanctions and can adequately be protected by a declaratory judgment or injunction action to establish the obscenity of the material."

Smith v. California, 361 U.S. 147, 80 S.Ct. 215, 4 L.Ed.2d 205 (1959) invalidated an ordinance that dispensed with any requirement that a seller of an obscene book have knowledge of its contents, but did not decide what sort of mental element was needed to prosecute. *Hamling v. United States,* supra, stated that it was constitutionally sufficient to show that a distributor of an advertising collage of pictures of sexual acts "had knowledge of the contents of the materials [and] that he knew the character and nature of the materials." Would it be consistent with *Hamling* to afford constitutional protection to a distributor who reasonably believed the material disseminated was not obscene? See Lockhart, supra, at 568.

D. VAGUENESS AND OVERBREADTH: AN OVERVIEW

In *Paris Adult Theatre*, Brennan, J., dissents on the ground that the obscenity statute is unconstitutionally vague. He envisions the possibility that an obscenity statute might overcome his vagueness objection if it were tailored to combat distribution to unconsenting adults or to children. In *Miller*, the materials were in fact distributed to unconsenting adults. There Brennan, J., does not reach the vagueness question but objects on the ground that the statute is overbroad,—i.e., it is not confined to the protection of unconsenting adults and children, but also prohibits distribution of obscene materials to consenting adults. In Brennan, J.'s view, even if the particular conduct at issue in *Miller* might be constitutionally prohibited by a narrower statute, it cannot be reached under a statute that sweeps so much protected speech within its terms.

The doctrines of "vagueness" and "overbreadth" referred to in Brennan, J.'s dissents are deeply embedded in first amendment jurisprudence. At first glance, the doctrines appear discrete. A statute that prohibits the use of the words "kill" and "President" in the same sentence may not be vague, but it is certainly overbroad even though some sentences using those words may be unprotected. Conversely, a vague statute may not be overbroad; it may not pertain to first amendment freedoms at all, or it may clearly be intended to exclude all protected speech from its prohibition but use vague language to accomplish that purpose.

Ordinarily, however, the problems of "vagueness" and "overbreadth" are closely related; indeed the two concepts often merge. Consider, for example, an actual and a hypothetical "red flag" ban. A statute prohibiting anyone from "publicly display[ing] a red flag [or] device of any color or form whatever [as] a sign, symbol or emblem of opposition to organized government" was held fatally vague in *Stromberg v. California*, 283 U.S. 359, 51 S.Ct. 532, 75 L.Ed. 1117 (1931). The statute purported to be less than a total ban, but how much less was ambiguous and uncertain. The "opposition to organized government" language was vague because it might (or might not) be read as banning constitutionally protected red flag displays, e.g., those flown as an expression of peaceful and orderly opposition to the political party currently in power by members of another political party. But a hypothetical "absolute ban" on red flag displays, for any reason or under any circumstances, although *superficially* clear, would presumably also be struck down—for "overbreadth." The same may be said for a hypothetical statute "absolutely banning" picketing or parades—or the sale of literature containing any description of human sexual organs, regardless of the manner or purpose of the portrayal, the dominant theme of the material, the primary audience to which it is sold, or the social, literary, scientific or artistic value of the work.

The *language* of these hypothetical bans may not be vague, but if the language literally covers a variety of constitutionally protected activities, it *cannot be read literally*. Thus, the clarity of the language "is delusive, since it will have to be recast in order to separate the constitutional from the unconstitutional applications. If it is read as applicable only where constitutionally so, the reading uncovers the vagueness that is latent in its terms" and the problem of an "overbroad" law can emerge as "a special case of the problem of vagueness." See Freund, *The Supreme Court of the United States* 67–68 (1961). In other words, one may regard the aforementioned "overbroad" hypothetical statutes as no less vague and indefinite than laws whose very language forbids the public display of a red flag "except where one is constitutionally entitled to display it" or bans picketing "unless, under the circumstances, such conduct is constitutionally protected" or bars literature containing descriptions of human sexual organs "except where such descriptions do not constitute sufficient cause to deny the material the constitutional protection of freedom of speech and press."

Of course, statutes may be interpreted in ways that will avoid vagueness or overbreadth difficulties. See, e.g., *Scales v. United States,* p. 333 supra. It is established doctrine, for example, that an attack based either upon vagueness or overbreadth will be unsuccessful in federal court if the statute in question is "readily subject to a narrowing construction by the state courts." *Young v. American Mini-Theatres, Inc.; Erznoznik v. Jacksonville,* Part VII, A infra. Moreover, "[f]or the purpose of determining whether a state statute is too vague and indefinite to constitute valid legislation [the Court takes] 'the statute as though it read precisely as the highest court of the State has interpreted it.'" *Wainwright v. Stone,* 414 U.S. 21, 94 S.Ct. 190, 38 L.Ed.2d 179 (1973). Under this policy, a litigant can be prosecuted successfully for violating a statute that by its terms appears vague or overbroad but is interpreted by the state court in the same prosecution to mean something clearer or narrower than its literal language would dictate. *Cox v. New Hampshire,* p. 536 infra. The harshness of this doctrine is mitigated somewhat by the fact that "unexpected" or "unforeseeable" judicial constructions in such contexts violate due process. See *Marks v. United States,* 430 U.S. 188, 97 S.Ct. 990, 51 L.Ed.2d 260 (1977).

Somewhat more complicated is the issue of when general attacks on a statute are permitted. Plainly litigants may argue that statutes are vague as to their own conduct or that their own speech is protected. In other words, litigants are always free to argue that a statute is invalid "as applied" to their own conduct. The dispute concerns when litigants can attack a statute without reference to their own conduct, an attack sometimes called "on its face."

A separate question is: when should such attacks result in partial or total invalidation of a statute? The terminology here has become as confused as the issues. In the past, the Court has frequently referred to facial attacks on statutes in a way that embraces attempts at either partial or total invalidation. In some recent opinions, however, including those quoted below, it uses the term "facial attack" or "on its face" to refer only to arguments seeking total invalidation of a statute.

Terminology aside, one of the recurrent questions has been the extent to which litigants may argue that a statute is unconstitutionally overbroad even though their own conduct would not otherwise be constitutionally protected. This is often characterized as a standing issue. Ordinarily litigants do not have standing to raise the rights of others. See Ch. 9, Sec. 1, II, B. But, it has been argued that "[u]nder 'conventional' standing principles, a litigant has always had the right to be judged in accordance with a constitutionally valid rule of law." Monaghan, *Overbreadth,* 1981 S.Ct.Rev. 1, 3. On this view, if a statute is unconstitutionally overbroad, it is not a valid rule of law, and any defendant prosecuted under the statute has standing to raise the overbreadth issue.[a]

---

a. For more recent elaboration, see Monaghan, *Third Party Standing,* 84 Colum.L. Rev. 277 (1984). See also Sedler, *The Assertion of Constitutional Jus Tertii: A Substantive Approach,* 70 Calif.L.Rev. 1308, 1327 (1982) ("It may be the potential chilling effect upon others' expression that makes the statute invalid, but the litigant has his own right not to be subject to the operation of an invalid statute.").

However the issue may be characterized, White, J., has contended for many years that a litigant whose own conduct is unprotected should not prevail on an overbreadth challenge without a showing that the statute's overbreadth is "real and substantial." After much litigation, White, J., has finally prevailed. The "substantial" overbreadth doctrine now burdens all litigants who argue that a statute should be declared overbroad when their own conduct is unprotected.[b] *Brockett v. Spokane Arcades, Inc.; New York v. Ferber*, p. 426 infra.

Less clear are the circumstances in which a litigant whose conduct *is* protected can go beyond a claim that the statute is unconstitutional "as applied." Again, litigants are always free to argue that their own conduct is protected. Moreover, the Court has stated that "[t]here is no reason to limit challenges to case-by-case 'as applied' challenges when the statute [in] all its applications falls short of constitutional demands." [c] *Maryland v. Joseph H. Munson Co.*, 467 U.S. 947, 104 S.Ct. 2839, 81 L.Ed.2d 786 (1984). How far beyond this the Court will go is unclear. In *Brockett v. Spokane Arcades, Inc.*, p. 397 supra, it referred to the "normal rule that partial, rather than facial invalidation" of statutes is to be preferred and observed that: "[A]n individual whose own speech or expressive conduct may validly be prohibited or sanctioned is permitted to challenge a statute on its face because it also threatens others not before the court—those who desire to engage in legally protected expression but who may refrain from doing so rather than risk prosecution or undertake to have the law declared partially invalid. If the overbreadth is 'substantial,' the law may not be enforced against anyone, including the party before the court, until it is narrowed to reach only unprotected activity, whether by legislative action or by judicial construction or partial invalidation.

"It is otherwise where the parties challenging the statute are those who desire to engage in protected speech that the overbroad statute purports to punish, or who seek to publish both protected and unprotected material. There is then no want of a proper party to challenge the statute, no concern that an attack on the statute will be unduly delayed or protected speech discouraged. The statute may forthwith be declared invalid to the extent that it reaches too far, but otherwise left intact." [d]

Brockett takes the view that it must give standing to the otherwise unprotected to raise an overbreadth challenge, in order to secure the rights of those whose speech should be protected. But it sees no purpose in giving standing to the protected in order to secure rights for those whose speech should not be protected. This position is not without its ironies. In some circumstances, a litigant whose speech is unprotected will be in a better position than one whose

b. For commentary on the concept of "substantial" overbreadth, see Redish, *The Warren Court, The Burger Court and the First Amendment Overbreadth Doctrine*, 78 Nw.U.L.Rev. 1031, 1056–69 (1983).

c. There is a terminological dispute here. Compare *Los Angeles City Council v. Taxpayers For Vincent*, p. 583 infra (such challenges are not overbreadth challenges) with *Munson*, supra (such challenges are properly called overbreadth challenges).

d. After the Court has declared that the statute is invalid to the extent it reaches too far, the remaining portion of the statute will be examined to determine whether that portion is severable. That is, it could well be the intent of the legislature that the statute stands or falls as a single package. To invalidate a part, then, could be to invalidate the whole. Alternatively, the legislature may have intended to salvage whatever it might. The question of severability is regarded as one of legislative intent, but, at least with respect to federal legislation, courts will presume that severability was intended. See, e.g., *Regan v. Time, Inc.*, ___ U.S. ___, 104 S.Ct. 3262, 82 L.Ed.2d 487 (1984). The question of whether a provision of a state statute is severable is one of state law.

speech is protected, at least if the litigant's goal is completely to stop enforcement of a statute. Viewed from a standing perspective, those whose speech is protected have no standing to invoke the substantial overbreadth doctrine. Viewed as a substantive rule of law, the substantial overbreadth challenge is selectively available.

The issues with respect to vagueness challenges are similar. It remains possible, however, that the Court will resolve them in ways different from the approaches it has fashioned in the law of overbreadth. White, J., clearly would pursue a different course. He has suggested that vagueness challenges should be confined to "as applied" attacks unless a statute is vague in all of its applications. Accordingly, if a statute clearly proscribes the conduct of a particular defendant, to allow that defendant to challenge a statute for vagueness is in his view "to confound vagueness and overbreadth." *Kolender v. Lawson*, 461 U.S. 352, 103 S.Ct. 1855, 75 L.Ed.2d 903 (1983) (White, J., dissenting). In response, the Court has stated that a facial attack upon a statute need not depend upon a showing of vagueness in all of a statute's applications: "[W]e permit a facial challenge if a law reaches 'a substantial amount of constitutionally protected conduct,'" *Kolender*, supra. Moreover, the Court has previously allowed litigants to raise the vagueness issue "even though there is no uncertainty about the impact of the ordinances on their own rights." *Young*. But see, e.g., *Broadrick v. Oklahoma*, p. 425 infra, in which White, J., writing for the Court suggests that standing to raise the vagueness argument should not be permitted in this situation.

Much less clear are the circumstances in which litigants whose conduct is *not* clearly covered by a statute can go beyond an "as applied" attack.[e] One approach would be to apply the same rule to all litigants, e.g., allowing total invalidation of statutes upon a showing of a "substantial" vagueness. In *Kolender,* the Court made no determination whether the statute involved was vague as to the defendant's own conduct; arguably, the opinion implied that it made no difference. Another approach would analogize to the approach suggested in *Brockett* for overbreadth challenges. Thus, a court might refrain from total invalidation of a statute and confine itself to striking the vague part insofar as the vague part seems to cover protected speech, leaving the balance of the statute intact. *Kolender* itself recites that the Court has "traditionally regarded vagueness and overbreadth as logically related and similar doctrines," but the Court's attitudes toward vagueness remain unclear. The questions of what standards should govern challenges to statutes that go beyond the facts before the Court, who should be able to raise the challenges, and under what circumstances continue to divide the Court.[f]

---

e. Conceivably, it could make a difference whether the litigants in this class of those "not clearly covered" have engaged in protected or unprotected conduct.

f. For commentary on vagueness and overbreadth, see, e.g., *Nimmer on Freedom of Speech*, 4–147—4–162 (1984); Alexander, *Is There an Overbreadth Doctrine?*, 22 San Diego L.Rev. 541 (1985); Amsterdam, *The Void-For-Vagueness Doctrine in the Supreme Court*, 109 U.Pa.L.Rev. 67 (1960); Bogen, *First Amendment Ancillary Doctrines*, 37 Md.L.Rev. 679, 705–26 (1978); Monaghan, supra; Redish, supra; Note, *The First Amendment Overbreadth Doctrine*, 83 Harv.L.Rev. 844 (1970). On the relationship between the overbreadth doctrine and the less drastic means test, see fn. b in *Central Hudson Gas & Elec. Corp. v. Public Serv. Comm'n*, p. 455 infra.

V. "FIGHTING WORDS," OFFENSIVE WORDS AND HOSTILE AUDIENCES

A. FIGHTING WORDS

CHAPLINSKY v. NEW HAMPSHIRE, 315 U.S. 568, 62 S.Ct. 766, 86 L.Ed. 1031 (1942): In the course of proselytizing on the streets, appellant, a Jehovah's Witness, denounced organized religion. Despite the city marshal's warning to "go slow" because his listeners were upset with his attacks on religion, appellant continued and a disturbance occurred. At this point, a police officer led appellant toward the police station, without arresting him. While enroute, appellant again encountered the city marshal who had previously admonished him. Appellant then said to the marshal (he claimed, but the marshal denied, in response to the marshal's cursing him): "You are a God damned racketeer" and "a damned Fascist and the whole government of Rochester are Fascists or agents of Fascists." He was convicted of violating a state statute forbidding anyone to address "any offensive, derisive or annoying word to any other person who is lawfully in any [public place] [or] call[ing] him by any offensive or derisive name." The Court, per MURPHY, J., upheld the conviction:

"There are certain well-defined and narrowly limited classes of speech, the prevention and punishment of which have never been thought to raise any Constitutional problem.[a] These include the lewd and obscene, the profane, the libelous, and the insulting or 'fighting' words—those which by their very utterance inflict injury or tend to incite an immediate breach of the peace. [S]uch utterances are no essential part of any exposition of ideas, and are of such slight social value as a step to truth that any benefit that may be derived from them is clearly outweighed by the social interest in order and morality. * * *

"On the authority of its earlier decisions, the state court declared that the statute's purpose was to preserve the public peace, no words being 'forbidden except such as have a direct tendency to cause acts of violence by the person to whom, individually, the remark is addressed'. It was further said: 'The word "offensive" is not to be defined in terms of what a particular addressee thinks. [The] test is what men of common intelligence would understand would be words likely to cause an average addressee to fight. [The] English language has a number of words and expressions which by general consent are "fighting words" when said without a disarming smile. [Such] words, as ordinary men know, are likely to cause a fight. So are threatening, profane or obscene revilings. Derisive and annoying words can be taken as coming within the purview of the statute as heretofore interpreted only when they have this characteristic of

a. See Haiman, *How Much of Our Speech is Free?*, The Civ.Lib.Rev., Winter, 1975, pp. 111, 123: "[T]his discrimination between two classes of speech made its first U.S. Supreme Court appearance in *Cantwell v. Connecticut* (1940) [p. 762 infra]." Jehovah's Witnesses had been convicted of religious solicitation without a permit and of breach of the peace. The Court set aside both convictions. It invalidated the permit system for "religious" solicitation, because it permitted the licensing official to determine what causes were "religious," thus allowing a "censorship of religion." In setting aside the breach of peace conviction, because the offense covered much protected conduct and left "too wide a discre-

tion in its application," the Court, per Roberts, J., noted: "One may, however, be guilty of [breach of the peace] if he commits acts or makes statements likely to provoke violence and disturbance of good order. [I]n practically all [such decisions to this effect], the provocative language [held to constitute] a breach of the peace consisted of profane, indecent or abusive remarks directed to the person of the hearer. *Resort to epithets or personal abuse is not in any proper sense communication of information or opinion safeguarded by the Constitution,* and its punishment as a criminal act [under a narrowly drawn statute] would raise no question under that instrument." (Emphasis added).

plainly tending to excite the addressee to a breach of the peace. [The] statute, as construed, does no more than prohibit the face-to-face words plainly likely to cause a breach of the peace by the addressee, words whose speaking constitute a breach of the peace by the speaker—including "classical fighting words", words in current use less "classical" but equally likely to cause violence, and other disorderly words, including profanity, obscenity and threats.'

"[A] statute punishing verbal acts, carefully drawn so as not unduly to impair liberty of expression, is not too vague for a criminal law. * * *[8]

"Nor can we say that the application of the statute to the facts disclosed by the record substantially or unreasonably impinges upon the privilege of free speech. Argument is unnecessary to demonstrate that the appellations 'damn racketeer' and 'damn Fascist' are epithets likely to provoke the average person to retaliation, and thereby cause a breach of the peace.

"The refusal of the state court to admit evidence of provocation and evidence bearing on the truth or falsity of the utterances is open to no Constitutional objection. Whether the facts sought to be proved by such evidence constitute a defense to the charge or may be shown in mitigation are questions for the state court to determine. Our function is fulfilled by a determination that the challenged statute, on its face and as applied, does not contravene the Fourteenth Amendment."

Notes and Questions

1. *Fighting words and free speech values.* (a) *Self realization.* Does speech have to step toward truth to be of first amendment value? Consider Redish, *The Value of Free Speech,* 130 U.Pa.L.Rev. 591, 626 (1982): "Why not view Chaplinsky's comments as a personal catharsis, as a means to vent his frustration at a system he deemed—whether rightly or wrongly—to be oppressive? Is it not a mark of individuality to be able to cry out at a society viewed as crushing the individual? Under this analysis, so-called 'fighting words' represent a significant means of self-realization, whether or not they can be considered a means of attaining some elusive 'truth.'"

(b) *Fighting words and truth.* Are fighting words always false? Should truth be a defense? Always?

(c) *Fighting words and self-government.* Was Chaplinsky's statement *something other than* the expression of an idea? Did he wish to inform the marshal of his opinion of him and did he do so "in a way which was not only unquestionably clear, [but] all too clear"? Loewy, *Punishing Flag Desecrators,* 49 N.C.L.Rev. 48, 82 (1970). How significant is it that Chaplinsky's remarks were not made in the context of a public debate or discussion of political or social issues? Taking into account the events preceding Chaplinsky's remarks, and that the addressee was "an important representative of the Rochester city government," may Chaplinsky's epithets be viewed as "a sharply-expressed form of political protest against indifferent or biased police services in the enforcement of his right to free speech"? Rutzick, *Offensive Language and the Evolution of First Amendment Protection,* 9 Harv.Civ.Rts.—Civ.Lib.L.Rev. 1 (1974). If the speech is directed at a police officer or other official in his representative capacity, is "the

---

8. [Even] if the interpretative gloss placed on the statute by the court below be disregarded, the statute had been previously construed as intended to preserve the public peace by punishing conduct, the direct tendency of which was to provoke the person against whom it was directed to acts of violence.

Appellant need not therefore have been a prophet to understand what the statute condemned.

real target the government"? Is even the most outrageous abuse in this context "an expression of some opinion concerning governmental policies or practices"? See id.

2. *The social interest in order and morality.* What was the social interest in this case? (a) *The likelihood and immediacy of violent retaliation?* Should the Court have considered whether a *law enforcement officer* so reviled would have been provoked to retaliate? Whatever is assumed about the reaction of an average citizen to offensive words, may it be assumed that police are "trained to remain calm in the face of citizen anger such as that expressed by Chaplinsky"? Rutzick, supra, at 10. See also Powell, J., concurring in *Lewis v. New Orleans,* p. 422 infra; Note, 53 B.U.L.Rev. 834, 847 (1973).

(b) *The highly personal nature of the insult, delivered face to face?* Was the marshal "verbally slapped in the face"? May the *Chaplinsky* statute be viewed as "a special type of assault statute"? See Loewy, supra, at 83–84. See also Emerson, *The System of Freedom of Expression* 337–38 (1970). To what extent should the tort of intentional infliction of emotional distress raise constitutional problems? Compare Haiman, *Speech and Law in a Free Society* 148–56 (1981) with Downs, *Skokie Revisited: Hate Group Speech and the First Amendment,* 60 Not.D.Law. 629, 673–85 (1985).

B. HOSTILE AUDIENCES

TERMINIELLO v. CHICAGO, 337 U.S. 1, 69 S.Ct. 894, 93 L.Ed. 1131 (1949): Petitioner "vigorously, if not viciously" criticized various political and racial groups and condemned "a surging, howling mob" gathered in protest outside the auditorium in which he spoke. He called his adversaries "slimy scum," "snakes," "bedbugs," and the like. Those inside the hall could hear those on the outside yell, "Fascists, Hitlers!" The crowd outside tried to tear the clothes off those whose entered. About 28 windows were broken; stink bombs were thrown. But in charging the jury, the trial court defined "breach of the peace" to include speech which "stirs the public to anger, *invites dispute,* [or] brings about a condition of unrest (emphasis added)." A 5–4 majority, per DOUGLAS, J., struck down the breach of peace ordinance as thus construed: "[A] function of free speech under our system of government is to invite dispute. It may indeed best serve its high purpose when it induces a condition of unrest, creates dissatisfaction with conditions as they are, or even stirs people to anger. [That] is why freedom of speech, though not absolute, *Chaplinsky,* is nevertheless protected against censorship or punishment, unless shown likely to produce a clear and present danger of a serious substantive evil that rises far above public inconvenience, annoyance, or unrest."

FEINER v. NEW YORK, 340 U.S. 315, 71 S.Ct. 303, 95 L.Ed. 295 (1951): Petitioner made a speech on a street corner in a predominantly black residential section of Syracuse, N.Y. A crowd of 75 to 80 persons, black and white, gathered around him, and several pedestrians had to go into the highway in order to pass by. A few minutes after he started, two police officers arrived and observed the rest of the meeting. In the course of his speech, publicizing a meeting of the Young Progressives of America to be held that evening in a local hotel and protesting the revocation of a permit to hold the meeting in a public school auditorium, petitioner referred to the President as a "bum," to the American Legion as "a Nazi Gestapo," and to the Mayor of Syracuse as a "champagne-sipping bum" who "does not speak for the Negro people." He also indicated in an excited manner: "The Negroes don't have equal rights; they should rise up in arms and fight for them."

These statements "stirred up a little excitement." One man indicated that if the police did not get that "S . . . O . . . B . . . ." off the stand, he would do so himself. There was not yet a disturbance, but according to police testimony "angry muttering and pushing." In the words of the arresting officer whose testimony was accepted by the trial judge, he "stepped in to prevent it from resulting in a fight." After disregarding two requests to stop speaking, petitioner was arrested and convicted for disorderly conduct. The Court, per VINSON, C.J., affirmed: "The language of *Cantwell* is appropriate here. '[Nobody would] suggest that the principle of freedom of speech sanctions incitement to riot or that religious liberty connotes the privilege to exhort others to physical attack upon those belonging to another sect. When clear and present danger of riot, disorder, interference with traffic upon the public street or other immediate threat to public safety, peace, or order, appears, the power of the State to prevent or punish is obvious.'

"[It] is one thing to say that the police cannot be used as an instrument for the suppression of unpopular views, and another to say that, when as here the speaker passes the bounds of argument or persuasion and undertakes incitement to riot, they are powerless to prevent a breach of the peace. Nor in this case can we condemn the considered judgment of three New York courts approving the means which the police, faced with a crisis, used in the exercise of their power and duty to preserve peace and order."

BLACK, J., dissented: "The Court's opinion apparently rests on this reasoning: The policeman, under the circumstances detailed, could reasonably conclude that serious fighting or even riot was imminent; therefore he could stop petitioner's speech to prevent a breach of peace; accordingly, it was 'disorderly conduct' for petitioner to continue speaking in disobedience of the officer's request. As to the existence of a dangerous situation on the street corner, it seems far-fetched to suggest that the 'facts' show any imminent threat of riot or uncontrollable disorder. It is neither unusual nor unexpected that some people at public street meetings mutter, mill about, push, shove, or disagree, even violently, with the speaker. Indeed, it is rare where controversial topics are discussed that an outdoor crowd does not do some or all of these things. Nor does one isolated threat to assault the speaker forebode disorder. Especially should the danger be discounted where, as here, the person threatening was a man whose wife and two small children accompanied him and who, so far as the record shows, was never close enough to petitioner to carry out the threat.

"Moreover, assuming that the 'facts' did indicate a critical situation, I reject the implication of the Court's opinion that the police had no obligation to protect petitioner's constitutional right to talk. The police of course have power to prevent breaches of the peace. But if, in the name of preserving order, they ever can interfere with a lawful public speaker, they first must make all reasonable efforts to protect him. Here the policemen did not even pretend to try to protect petitioner. According to the officers' testimony, the crowd was restless but there is no showing of any attempt to quiet it; pedestrians were forced to walk into the street, but there was no effort to clear a path on the sidewalk; one person threatened to assault petitioner but the officers did nothing to discourage this when even a word might have sufficed. Their duty was to protect petitioner's right to talk, even to the extent of arresting the man who threatened to interfere. Instead, they shirked that duty and acted only to suppress the right to speak.

"Finally, I cannot agree with the Court's statement that petitioner's disregard of the policeman's unexplained request amounted to such 'deliberate defiance' as would justify an arrest or conviction for disorderly conduct. On the contrary, I think that the policeman's action was a 'deliberate defiance' of ordinary official duty as well as of the constitutional right of free speech. For at least where time allows, courtesy and explanation of commands are basic elements of good official conduct in a democratic society. Here petitioner was 'asked' then 'told' then 'commanded' to stop speaking, but a man making a lawful address is certainly not required to be silent merely because an officer directs it. Petitioner was entitled to know why he should cease doing a lawful act. Not once was he told."

DOUGLAS, J., joined by Minton, J., dissented: "A speaker may not, of course, incite a riot any more than he may incite a breach of the peace by the use of 'fighting words'. But this record shows no such extremes. It shows an unsympathetic audience and the threat of one man to haul the speaker from the stage. It is against that kind of threat that speakers need police protection. If they do not receive it and instead the police throw their weight on the side of those who would break up the meetings, the police become the new censors of speech. Police censorship has all the vices of the censorship from city halls which we have repeatedly struck down."

Notes and Questions

1. What was the subject of disagreement in *Feiner*? (1) The standard for police interruption of a speech when danger of violence exists and the speaker intends to create disorder rather than to communicate ideas? (2) The standard when such danger exists, but the speaker only desires to communicate ideas? (3) Whether the danger of disorder and violence *was* plain and imminent? (4) Whether the speaker *did* intend to create disorder and violence?

May *Feiner* be limited to the proposition that when a speaker "incites to riot"—but only then—police may stop him without bothering to keep his audience in check? Cf. *Sellers v. Johnson*, 163 F.2d 877 (8th Cir.1947), cert. denied, 332 U.S. 851 (1948). See Stewart, *Public Speech and Public Order in Britain and the United States*, 13 Vand.L.Rev. 625, 632–33 (1960).

Should the speech *always* be prohibitable when the speaker intends to create disorder, rather than communicate ideas? Should the speech be prohibitable *only* under these circumstances? Should a speech *ever* be prohibitable because listeners arrive or will arrive, as they would have in *Sellers*, with a preconceived intent to create disturbance? Is the only really difficult problem in this area posed when *neither* the speaker *nor* the audience which gathers intends to create disorder, but the audience becomes *genuinely* aroused, honestly—whether or not justifiably—enraged? Here, should the police protect the speechmaking to the fullest extent possible? If they are firmly told they must before they can arrest the speaker, what is the likelihood that adequate preventive steps will be taken? See Gellhorn, *American Rights* 55–62 (1960); Note, 49 Colum.L.Rev. 1118, 1123–24 (1949).

Granted that it is undesirable for the continuation of a demonstration to turn on a police judgment whether a crowd is uncontrollable and that frequently, at least, the police will be able to handle the crowd if they are determined to do so, will occasions arise when crowd hostility *is* uncontrollable? May the demonstrators argue that "they have an interest in the publicity value of their own bloodshed or in any event that they have a right to determine their own risks"? See Note, 80 Harv.L.Rev. 1773, 1775 (1967). In such a case, does the ensuing violence pose a danger to innocent bystanders and the police as well as the demonstrators themselves? See id. If and when, despite their best efforts, law enforcement officers simply cannot "quell the mob," must they be allowed to "quell the speaker"?

2. *Edwards v. South Carolina,* 372 U.S. 229, 83 S.Ct. 680, 9 L.Ed.2d 697 (1963) reversed a breach of the peace conviction of civil rights demonstrators who refused to disperse within 15 minutes of a police command. The Court maintained that the 200 to 300 onlookers did not threaten violence and that the police protection was ample. It described the situation as a "far cry from [*Feiner*]." Clark, J., dissenting, pointed to the racially charged atmosphere ("200 youthful Negro demonstrators were being aroused to a 'fever pitch' before a crowd of some 300 people who undoubtedly were hostile.") and concluded that city officials in good faith believed that disorder and violence were imminent. Did *Edwards* miss a golden opportunity to clarify *Feiner* ? What if the crowd had been pushing, shoving and pressing more closely around the demonstrators in *Edwards* ? Would the case still be a "far cry" from *Feiner* because the demonstrators had not "passed the bounds of argument or persuasion and undertaken incitement to riot"?

3. In the advocacy of illegal action context, the fear of violence arises from audience cooperation with the speaker. In the hostile audience context, the fear of violence arises from audience conflict with the speaker. How do the elements set out in *Brandenburg* relate to those implied in *Feiner* ? How should they relate? Should the standard for "fighting words" cases be different from the "hostile audience" cases?

4. Should police be able to prosecute or silence disruptive audiences? Heckling audiences? In what contexts? See generally *In re Kay,* 1 Cal.3d 930, 83 Cal.Rptr. 686, 464 P.2d 142 (1970).

C. OFFENSIVE WORDS

COHEN v. CALIFORNIA

403 U.S. 15, 91 S.Ct. 1780, 29 L.Ed.2d 284 (1971).

MR. JUSTICE HARLAN delivered the opinion of the Court.

[Defendant was convicted of violating that part of a general California disturbing-the-peace statute which prohibits "maliciously and willfully disturb[ing] the peace or quiet of any neighborhood or person" by "offensive conduct." He had worn a jacket bearing the plainly visible words "Fuck the Draft" in a Los Angeles courthouse corridor, where women and children were present. He testified that he did so as a means of informing the public of the depth of his feelings against the Vietnam War and the draft. He did not engage in, nor threaten, any violence, nor was anyone who saw him violently aroused. Nor was there any evidence that he uttered any sound prior to his arrest. In affirming, the California Court of Appeal construed "offensive conduct" to mean "behavior which has a tendency to provoke *others* to acts of violence or to in turn disturb the peace" and held that the state had proved this element because it was "reasonably foreseeable" that defendant's conduct "might cause others to rise up to commit a violent act against [him] or attempt to forceably remove his jacket."]

In order to lay hands on the precise issue which this case involves, it is useful first to canvass various matters which this record does *not* present.

The conviction quite clearly rests upon the asserted offensiveness of the *words* Cohen used to convey his message to the public. The only "conduct" which the State sought to punish is the fact of communication. Thus, we deal here with a conviction resting solely upon "speech," not upon any separately identifiable conduct which allegedly was intended by Cohen to be perceived by others as expressive of particular views but which, on its face, does not necessarily convey any message and hence arguably could be regulated without effectively repressing Cohen's ability to express himself. Cf. *United States v. O'Brien* [p. 515 infra]. Further, the State certainly lacks power to punish Cohen for the underlying content of the message the inscription conveyed. At least so long as there is no showing of an intent to incite disobedience to or disruption of the draft, Cohen could not, consistently with the First and Fourteenth Amendments, be punished for asserting the evident position on the inutility or immorality of the draft his jacket reflected. *Yates.*

Appellant's conviction, then, rests squarely upon his exercise [of] "freedom of speech" [and] can be justified, if at all, only as a valid regulation of the manner in which he exercised that freedom, not as a permissible prohibition on the substantive message it conveys. This does not end the inquiry, of course, for the First and Fourteenth Amendments have never been thought to give absolute protection to every individual to speak whenever or wherever he pleases, or to use any form of address in any circumstances that he chooses. In this vein, too, however, we think it important to note that several issues typically associated with such problems are not presented here.

In the first place, Cohen was tried under a statute applicable throughout the entire State. Any attempt to support this conviction on the ground that the statute seeks to preserve an appropriately decorous atmosphere in the courthouse where Cohen was arrested must fail in the absence of any language in the statute that would have put appellant on notice that certain kinds of otherwise permissible speech or conduct would nevertheless, under California law, not be tolerated in certain places. No fair reading of the phrase "offensive conduct" can be said sufficiently to inform the ordinary person that distinctions between certain locations are thereby created.[3]

In the second place, as it comes to us, this case cannot be said to fall within those relatively few categories of instances where prior decisions have established the power of government to deal more comprehensively with certain forms of individual expression simply upon a showing that such a form was employed. This is not, for example, an obscenity case. Whatever else may be necessary to give rise to the States' broader power to prohibit obscene expression, such expression must be, in some significant way, erotic. *Roth.* It cannot plausibly be maintained that this vulgar allusion to the Selective Service System would conjure up such psychic stimulation in anyone likely to be confronted with Cohen's crudely defaced jacket.

This Court has also held that the States are free to ban the simple use, without a demonstration of additional justifying circumstances, of so-called "fighting words," those personally abusive epithets which, when addressed to the ordinary citizen, are, as a matter of common knowledge, inherently likely to provoke violent reaction. *Chaplinsky.* While the four-letter word displayed by

---

3. It is illuminating to note what transpired when Cohen entered a courtroom in the building. He removed his jacket and stood with it folded over his arm. Meanwhile, a policeman sent the presiding judge a note suggesting that Cohen be held in contempt of court. The judge declined to do so and Cohen was arrested by the officer only after he emerged from the courtroom.

Cohen in relation to the draft is not uncommonly employed in a personally provocative fashion, in this instance it was clearly not "directed to the person of the hearer." No individual actually or likely to be present could reasonably have regarded the words on appellant's jacket as a direct personal insult. Nor do we have here an instance of the exercise of the State's police power to prevent a speaker from intentionally provoking a given group to hostile reaction. Cf. *Feiner; Terminiello.* There is, as noted above, no showing that anyone who saw Cohen was in fact violently aroused or that appellant intended such a result.

[T]he mere presumed presence of unwitting listeners or viewers does not serve automatically to justify curtailing all speech capable of giving offense. While this Court has recognized that government may properly act in many situations to prohibit intrusion into the privacy of the home of unwelcome views and ideas which cannot be totally banned from the public dialogue, we have at the same time consistently stressed that "we are often 'captives' outside the sanctuary of the home and subject to objectionable speech." The ability of government, consonant with the Constitution, to shut off discourse solely to protect others from hearing it is, in other words, dependent upon a showing that substantial privacy interests are being invaded in an essentially intolerable manner. Any broader view of this authority would effectively empower a majority to silence dissidents simply as a matter of personal predilections.

[Given] the subtlety and complexity of the factors involved if Cohen's "speech" was otherwise entitled to constitutional protection, we do not think the fact that some unwilling "listeners" in a public building may have been briefly exposed to it can serve to justify this breach of the peace conviction where, as here, there was no evidence that persons powerless to avoid appellant's conduct did in fact object to it, and where [unlike another portion of the same statute barring the use of "vulgar, profane or indecent language within [the] hearing of women or children, in a loud and boisterous manner"], the [challenged statutory provision] evinces no concern [with] the special plight of the captive auditor, but, instead, indiscriminately sweeps within its prohibitions all "offensive conduct" that disturbs "any neighborhood or person."

Against this background, the issue flushed by this case stands out in bold relief. It is whether California can excise, as "offensive conduct," one particular scurrilous epithet from the public discourse, either upon the theory of the court below that its use is inherently likely to cause violent reaction or upon a more general assertion that the States, acting as guardians of public morality, may properly remove this offensive word from the public vocabulary.

The rationale of the California court is plainly untenable. At most it reflects an "undifferentiated fear or apprehension of disturbance [which] is not enough to overcome the right to freedom of expression." *Tinker* [p. 522 infra]. We have been shown no evidence that substantial numbers of citizens are standing ready to strike out physically at whoever may assault their sensibilities with execrations like that uttered by Cohen. There may be some persons about with such lawless and violent proclivities, but that is an insufficient base upon which to erect, consistently with constitutional values, a governmental power to force persons who wish to ventilate their dissident views into avoiding particular forms of expression. The argument amounts to little more than the self-defeating proposition that to avoid physical censorship of one who has not sought to provoke such a response by a hypothetical coterie of the violent and lawless, the States may more appropriately effectuate that censorship themselves.

Admittedly, it is not so obvious that the First and Fourteenth Amendments must be taken to disable the States from punishing public utterance of this unseemly expletive in order to maintain what they regard as a suitable level of discourse within the body politic. We think, however, that examination and reflection will reveal the shortcomings of a contrary viewpoint.

[The] constitutional right of free expression is powerful medicine in a society as diverse and populous as ours. It is designed and intended to remove governmental restraints from the arena of public discussion, putting the decision as to what views shall be voiced largely into the hands of each of us, in the hope that use of such freedom will ultimately produce a more capable citizenry and more perfect polity and in the belief that no other approach would comport with the premise of individual dignity and choice upon which our political system rests.

To many, the immediate consequence of this freedom may often appear to be only verbal tumult, discord, and even offensive utterance. These are, however, within established limits, in truth necessary side effects of the broader enduring values which the process of open debate permits us to achieve. That the air may at times seem filled with verbal cacophony is, in this sense not a sign of weakness but of strength. We cannot lose sight of the fact that, in what otherwise might seem a trifling and annoying instance of individual distasteful abuse of a privilege, these fundamental societal values are truly implicated.
* * *

Against this perception of the constitutional policies involved, we discern certain more particularized considerations that peculiarly call for reversal of this conviction. First, the principle contended for by the State seems inherently boundless. How is one to distinguish this from any other offensive word? Surely the State has no right to cleanse public debate to the point where it is grammatically palatable to the most squeamish among us. Yet no readily ascertainable general principle exists for stopping short of that result were we to affirm the judgment below. For, while the particular four-letter word being litigated here is perhaps more distasteful than most others of its genre, it is nevertheless often true that one man's vulgarity is another's lyric. Indeed, we think it is largely because governmental officials cannot make principled distinctions in this area that the Constitution leaves matters of taste and style so largely to the individual.

Additionally, we cannot overlook the fact, because it is well illustrated by the episode involved here, that much linguistic expression serves a dual communicative function: it conveys not only ideas capable of relatively precise, detached explication, but otherwise inexpressible emotions as well. In fact, words are often chosen as much for their emotive as their cognitive force. We cannot sanction the view that the Constitution, while solicitous of the cognitive content of individual speech, has little or no regard for that emotive function which, practically speaking, may often be the more important element of the overall message sought to be communicated. * * *

Finally, and in the same vein, we cannot indulge the facile assumption that one can forbid particular words without also running a substantial risk of suppressing ideas in the process. Indeed, governments might soon seize upon the censorship of particular words as a convenient guise for banning the expression of unpopular views. We have been able [to] discern little social benefit that might result from running the risk of opening the door to such grave results.

It is, in sum, our judgment that, absent a more particularized and compelling reason for its actions, the State may not, consistently with the First and Fourteenth Amendments, make the simple public display here involved of this single four-letter expletive a criminal offense. Because that is the only arguably sustainable rationale for the conviction here at issue, the judgment below must be

Reversed.

[BLACKMUN, J., joined by Burger, C.J., and Black, J., dissented for two reasons: (1) "Cohen's absurd and immature antic [was] mainly conduct and little speech" and the case falls "well within the sphere of *Chaplinsky*"; (2) although it declined to review the state court of appeals' decision in *Cohen*, the California Supreme Court subsequently narrowly construed the breach-of-the-peace statute in another case and *Cohen* should be remanded to the California Court of Appeal in the light of this subsequent construction. White, J., concurred with the dissent on the latter ground.]

Notes and Questions

1. For criticism of *Cohen*, see Bickel, *The Morality of Consent* 72 (1975) (Cohen's speech "constitutes an assault" and this sort of speech "may create [an] environment [in which] actions that were not possible before become possible"); Cox, *The Role of the Supreme Court in American Government* 47–48 (1976) (state has interest in "level at which public discourse is conducted"; state should not have to "allow exhibitionists and [others] trading upon our lower prurient interests to inflict themselves upon the public consciousness and dull its sensibilities"). For a defense (but what not a few would consider a narrow reading) of *Cohen*, see Farber, *Civilizing Public Discourse: An Essay on Professor Bickel, Justice Harlan, and the Enduring Significance of Cohen v. California*, 1980 Duke L.J. 283. See also Ely, *Democracy and Distrust* 114 (1980); Tribe, *American Constitutional Law* 578, 618–19, 666, 680–81 (1978). For an overview of Harlan, J.'s approach to the first amendment, see Farber & Nowak, *Justice Harlan and the First Amendment*, 2 Const.Comm. 425 (1985).

2. To what extent, if at all, and in what ways, if any, does *Cohen* restrict the "fighting words" doctrine? Consider Arkes, *Civility and the Restriction of Speech: Rediscovering the Defamation of Groups*, 1974 Sup.Ct.Rev. 281, 316: *Cohen* turned "the presumptions in *Chaplinsky* around: instead of presuming that profane or defamatory speech was beneath constitutional protection, he presumed that the speech was protected and that the burden of proof lay with those who would restrict it." If "one man's vulgarity is another's lyric," how are discriminations to be made in the "fighting words" area? See Rutzick, p. 410 supra, at 20; Note, 53 B.U.L.Rev. 834, 842 (1973).

3. Was the flaw in the *Chaplinsky* formulation that "[i]ts paradigm was a debating society, a sedate assembly of speakers who calmly discussed the issues of the day and became ultimately persuaded by the logic of one of the competing positions"? That it viewed "emotion" as never entering the debate, "for emotion had nothing to do with 'truth' "? See Rutzick 18. Once it is conceded that "the offensiveness of language used in a political protest often measures the intensity of interest in the outcome of a governmental decision," does "protection for the use of offensive language [become] not a luxury but a necessity in a democratic society"? See id. at 19.

4. By characterizing the proclivities of those who might react violently as "lawless," did the *Cohen* Court give "new vigor to the proposition advanced by

Justice Black [in his *Feiner* dissent] that the proper method to prevent such a violent response to controversial speech [is] to apply the criminal sanction directly to the reactive conduct rather than [to] the initial speech"? See Rutzick 21.

D. OFFENSIVE LANGUAGE: A STATE CONSTITUTIONAL PERSPECTIVE

STATE v. HARRINGTON
67 Or.App. 608, 680 P.2d 666 (1984).

GILLETTE, PRESIDING JUDGE.

The state appeals a trial court order sustaining defendant's demurrer to a complaint charging racial intimidation. The intimidation statute enhances the penalty [for] harassment when such crimes are motivated by the race, color, religion or national origin of the victim. * * *

The complaint charges: "The defendant [by] reason of race and color and with intent to harass, annoy and alarm John Thomas Ritchey, [did] unlawfully publicly insult John Thomas Ritchey by abusive words in a manner likely to provoke a violent and disorderly response, by repeatedly calling John Thomas Ritchey a 'fucking nigger.' "

ORS 166.065(1)(b) provides, in pertinent part: "A person commits the crime of harassment if, with intent to harass, annoy or alarm another person, the actor: * * * Publicly insults another by abusive or obscene words or gestures in a manner likely to provoke a violent or disorderly [response]."

Article I, section 8, of the Oregon Constitution provides: "No law shall be passed restraining the free expression of opinion, or restricting [the] right to speak, write, or print freely on any subject whatever; but every person shall be responsible for the abuse of this right."

In *State v. Robertson,* 293 Or. 402, 649 P.2d 569 (1982), the Oregon Supreme Court held that "Article I, section 8, [forecloses] the enactment of any law written in terms directed to the substance of any 'opinion' or any 'subject' of communication, unless the scope of the restraint is wholly confined within some historical exception that was well established when the first American guarantees of freedom of expression were adopted and that the guarantees then or in 1859 demonstrably were not intended to [reach]." [*Robertson*] requires answering two questions. The first is whether ORS 166.065(1)(b) is "directed to the substance of any opinion or any subject of communication." *Robertson* explains the constitutionally significant distinction between legislation directed against the pursuit of a forbidden effect and a provision directed against speech itself: "[A]rticle I, section 8, prohibits lawmakers from enacting restrictions that focus on the content of speech or writing, either because that content itself is deemed socially undesirable or offensive, or because it is thought to have adverse consequences. [L]aws must focus on proscribing the pursuit or accomplishment of forbidden results rather than on the suppression of speech or writing either as an end in itself or as a means to some other legislative end."

The state argues that ORS 166.065(1)(b) is directed against an "effect," namely, prevention of violence. Both the language of the statute itself and the legislative commentary indicate otherwise.[3] [The] statute indicates that the

---

3. If the legislature's aim is to prevent fights, the legislature could make it a crime to provoke a fight. *See* Linde, *"Clear and Pres-* *ent Danger" Reexamined: Dissonance in the Brandenburg Concerto,* 22 Stan.L.Rev. 1163, 1179–82 (1970).

statute was intended to *protect the listener* from exposure to abusive or obscene language rather than to protect anyone from physical violence. [We] hold that ORS 166.065(1)(b) is directed at communication.

The second question under *Robertson* is whether the statute falls within some historical exception to Article I, section 8. The state argues that the language "likely to provoke a violent or disorderly response" limits the type of language that may be punished to so-called "fighting words" and that punishment of fighting words is an historical exception to Article I, section 8. The basis of this argument is *Chaplinsky* [where] the Supreme Court stated: "[There] are certain well-defined narrowly limited classes of speech, the prevention and punishment of which have never been thought to raise any Constitutional problem. These include the lewd and obscene, profane, the libelous, and the insulting, or 'fighting words'—those which by their very utterances inflict injury or intend to incite an immediate breach of the peace." On the other hand, more recent Supreme Court opinions have struck down statutes proscribing offensive language as overbroad under the First Amendment. See *Gooding v. Wilson*, 405 U.S. 518, 92 S.Ct. 1103, 31 L.Ed.2d 408 (1972); see also *Lewis v. New Orleans*, 415 U.S. 130, 94 S.Ct. 970, 39 L.Ed.2d 214 (1974).[5] Thus, *Chaplinsky* is not necessarily in point.

Even if we were to determine that ORS 166.065(1)(b) codifies the *Chaplinsky* fighting words exception to the First Amendment, however, that would not end our inquiry. *Chaplinsky* stands for the proposition that the United States Supreme Court may determine that some forms of communication are unprotected because "any benefit that may be derived from them is clearly outweighed by the social interest in order and morality." In other words, the court used a balancing test to determine that some forms of expression are unworthy of constitutional protection.

Article I, section 8, by contrast, forbids legislation "restricting the right to speak freely on *any subject whatever.*" (Emphasis supplied). Article I, section 8, precludes the state legislature or the courts from balancing away the right to free expression. The legislature may only proscribe expression when the scope of the restraint is wholly within an historical exception to Article I, section 8.[6] Examples of such historical exceptions are "perjury, solicitation or verbal assistance in crime, some forms of theft, forgery and fraud and their contemporary variants." *Robertson*. As "examples" we do not consider this list to be—or to have been intended to be—exclusive. [L]egislation directed against obscene or abusive speech was not enacted until sometime after the adoption of the Oregon Constitution in 1859. We therefore determine that obscene or abusive language spoken with intent to annoy or alarm is not an "historical exception that was well established when the first American guarantees of freedom of expression were adopted and that the guarantees then or in 1859 demonstrably were not

---

5. The problems in drafting a constitutional statute have been summarized as follows: "[C]lassifying particularly offensive expressions is difficult. Forms of expression vary so much in their contexts and inflections that one cannot specify particular words or phrases as being always 'fighting.' What is gross insult in one setting is crude humor in another. And what is offensive shifts over time." Greenawalt, *Speech and Crime*, 1980 Am.B. Found.Res.J. 645, 770.

6. Article I, section 8, does not preclude a civil action for abuse of the right to speak

freely. See also Comment, *Defamation and State Constitutions: The Search for a State Law Based Standard After Gertz*, 19 Will.L. Rev. 665 (1983). For example, the victim might bring a tort action for intentional infliction of emotional distress. Cf. *Contreras v. Crown Zellerbach*, 88 Wash.2d 735, 565 P.2d 1173 (1977) (abusive racial slurs may constitute "outrageous" conduct within the meaning of *Restatement (Second) Torts* (1965)); see also *Hall v. The May Dept. Stores*, 292 Or. 131, 637 P.2d 126 (1981) (damages recoverable for intentional infliction of emotional distress).

intended to [reach]." *Robertson.* It follows that the trial court's ruling was correct: the statutory scheme offends Article I, section 8, of the Oregon Constitution.

Affirmed.

Notes and Questions

1. Is the interpretive approach applied by the Oregon court to its constitution superior to that used by the United States Supreme Court in interpreting the first amendment? Would the results have been better for the country if the Oregon approach had been applied to the first amendment? [a]

2. Should (does) the first amendment bar an action for intentional infliction of emotional distress under the facts of this case? Is it enough that the words in question inflict injury or must the victim show that the words were likely to promote a fight? Suppose a crowd of whites gathers to taunt a young black child on the way to a previously all white school? Suppose short of using violence, they do everything they can to harm the child? Is it the case that "no government that would call itself a decent government would fail to intervene [and] disperse the crowd" and that "the rights of the crowd [cannot] really stand on the same plane" as the child on the way to school? See Arkes, *Civility and the Restriction of Speech: Rediscovering the Defamation of Groups,* 1979 Sup.Ct. Rev. 281, 310–11. Should the first amendment bar state criminal or civil actions precisely tailored to punish racial insults? Insults directed against the handicapped? For the case in favor of a tort action against racial insults, see Delgado, *Words That Wound: A Tort Action for Racial Insults, Epithets, and Name-Calling,* 17 Harv.Civ.Rts.-Civ.Lib.L.Rev. 133 (1982). For a spirited exchange, see Heins, *Banning Words: A Comment on "Words that Wound,"* 18 Har.Civ.Rts.-Civ.Lib.L.Rev. 585 (1983) and *Professor Delgado Replies,* Id. at 593.

3. A series of cases in the early 1970s reversed convictions involving abusive language. *Gooding v. Wilson* invalidated a Georgia ordinance primarily because it had been previously applied to "utterances where there was no likelihood that the person addressed would make an immediate violent utterance." *Lewis v. New Orleans* ruled that vulgar or offensive speech was protected under the first amendment. Because the statute punished "opprobrious language," it was deemed by the Court to embrace words that do not " 'by their very utterance inflict injury or tend to invite an immediate breach of the peace.' "

Although *Gooding* seemed to require a danger of immediate violence, *Lewis* recited that infliction of injury was sufficient. Dissenting in both cases, Burger, C.J., and Blackmun and Rehnquist, JJ., complained that the majority invoked vagueness and overbreadth analysis "indiscriminately without regard to the nature of the speech in question, the possible effect the statute or ordinance has upon such speech, the importance of the speech in relation to the exposition of ideas, or the purported or asserted community interest in preventing that speech." The dissenters focused upon the facts of the cases (e.g., Gooding to a

---

a. For assembling of and commentary upon state freedom of speech and press provisions, see Collins, *Bills and Declarations of Rights Digest* in *The American Bench* 2483, 2485, 2502–05 (3d ed. 1985) ("[S]tate free speech and press provisions have more in common with each other than they do with the First Amendment."). For commentary on the relationship between state constitutions and the federal constitution, see Linde, *E Pluribus—Constitutional Theory and State Courts,* 18 Ga.L.Rev. 165 (1984); Collins, *Reliance on State Constitutions: The Montana Disaster,* 63 Tex.L.Rev. 1095 (1985); Simon, *Independent But Inadequate: State Constitutions and Protection of Freedom of Expression,* 33 U.Kan.L.Rev. 305 (1985).

police officer: "White son of a bitch, I'll kill you," "You son of a bitch, I'll choke you to death," and "You son of a bitch, if you ever put your hands on me again, I'll cut you to pieces."). They complained that the majority had relegated the facts to "footnote status, conveniently distant and in less disturbing focus." In *Gooding, Lewis,* and the other cases, Powell, J., insisted upon the importance of context in decisionmaking. Dissenting in *Rosenfeld v. New Jersey,* 408 U.S. 901, 92 S.Ct. 2479, 33 L.Ed.2d 321 (1972), he suggested that *Chaplinsky* be extended to the "wilful use of scurrilous language calculated to offend the sensibilities of an unwilling audience"; concurring in *Lewis,* he maintained that allowing prosecutions for offensive language directed at police officers invited law enforcement abuse. Finally, he suggested in *Rosenfeld* that whatever the scope of the "fighting words" doctrine, overbreadth analysis was inappropriate in such cases. He doubted that such statutes deter others from exercising first amendment rights.[b]

VI. NEW CATEGORIES

Suppose a legislature were to outlaw speech whose dominant theme appeals to a morbid interest in violence, that is patently offensive to contemporary community standards, and that lacks serious literary, artistic, political or scientific value. Constitutional? One approach would be to contend that speech is protected unless it falls into already established categorical exceptions to first amendment protection. Another would be to argue by analogy, e.g., if obscenity is beneath first amendment protection, this speech should (or should not) be beneath such protection. Similarly, one could argue that exceptions to first amendment protection has been fashioned by resort to a balancing methodology and that balancing the relevant interests is the right approach. Alternatively, one could proceed from a particular substantive vision of the first amendment, such as the Meiklejohn view. Which approach has been applied by the Court?[a]

New York v. Ferber, infra, is interesting because it involves a new category.

A. HARM TO CHILDREN AND THE OVERBREADTH DOCTRINE

NEW YORK v. FERBER, 458 U.S. 747, 102 S.Ct. 3348, 73 L.Ed.2d 1113 (1982), per WHITE, J., upheld conviction of a seller of films depicting young boys masturbating, under N.Y.Penal Law § 263.15, for "promoting[a] a sexual performance," defined as "any performance [which] includes sexual conduct[b] by a child" under 16. The Court addressed the "single question": " 'To prevent the abuse of children who are made to engage in sexual conduct for commercial purposes, could the New York State Legislature, consistent with the First Amendment,

b. For commentary on Powell, J.'s approach, see Gunther, *In Search of Judicial Quality on a Changing Court: The Case of Justice Powell,* 24 Stan.L.Rev. 1001, 1029–35 (1972).

a. For commentary on the Court's methodology, see Redish, *Freedom of Expression: A Critical Analysis* (1984); Van Alstyne, *Interpretations of the First Amendment* (1984); Van Alstyne, *A Graphic Review of the Free Speech Clause,* 70 Calif.L.Rev. 107 (1982); Farber, *Content Regulation and the First Amendment: A Revisionist View,* 68 Geo.L.J. 727 (1980); Schauer, *Categories and the First Amendment: A Play in Three Acts,* 34 Vand.L.

Rev. 265 (1981); Schlag, *Rules and Standards,* 33 U.C.L.A.L.Rev. 379 (1985); Shiffrin, *Defamatory Non-Media Speech and First Amendment Methodology,* 25 U.C.L.A.L.Rev. 915 (1978).

a. "Promote" was defined to include all aspects of production, distribution, exhibition and sale.

b. Sec. 263.3 defined "sexual conduct" as "actual or simulated sexual intercourse, deviate sexual intercourse, sexual bestiality, masturbation, sado-masochistic abuse, or lewd exhibition of the genitals."

prohibit the dissemination of material which shows children engaged in sexual conduct, regardless of whether such material is obscene?" [c] * * *

"The *Miller* standard, like its predecessors, was an accommodation between the state's interests in protecting the 'sensibilities of unwilling recipients' from exposure to pornographic material and the dangers of censorship inherent in unabashedly content-based laws. Like obscenity statutes, laws directed at the dissemination of child pornography run the risk of suppressing protected expression by allowing the hand of the censor to become unduly heavy. For the following reasons, however, we are persuaded that the States are entitled to greater leeway in the regulation of pornographic depictions of children.

"First. [The] prevention of sexual exploitation and abuse of children constitutes a government objective of surpassing importance. The legislative findings accompanying passage of the New York laws reflect this concern. * * *

"We shall not second-guess this legislative judgment. Respondent has not intimated that we do so. Suffice it to say that virtually all of the States and the United States have passed legislation proscribing the production of or otherwise combatting 'child pornography.' The legislative judgment, as well as the judgment found in the relevant literature, is that the use of children as subjects of pornographic materials is harmful to the physiological, emotional, and mental health of the child. That judgment, we think, easily passes muster under the First Amendment.

"Second. The distribution of photographs and films depicting sexual activity by juveniles is intrinsically related to the sexual abuse of children in at least two ways. First, the materials produced are a permanent record of the children's participation and the harm to the child is exacerbated by their circulation. Second, the distribution network for child pornography must be closed if the production of material which requires the sexual exploitation of children is to be effectively controlled. Indeed, there is no serious contention that the legislature was unjustified in believing that it is difficult, if not impossible, to halt the exploitation of children by pursuing only those who produce the photographs and movies. While the production of pornographic materials is a low-profile, clandestine industry, the need to market the resulting products requires a visible apparatus of distribution. The most expeditious if not the only practical method of law enforcement may be to dry up the market for this material by imposing severe criminal penalties on persons selling, advertising, or otherwise promoting the product. Thirty-five States and Congress have concluded that restraints on the distribution of pornographic materials are required in order to effectively combat the problem, and there is a body of literature and testimony to support these legislative conclusions.

"[The] *Miller* standard, like all general definitions of what may be banned as obscene, does not reflect the State's particular and more compelling interest in prosecuting those who promote the sexual exploitation of children. Thus, the question under the *Miller* test of whether a work, taken as a whole, appeals to the prurient interest of the average person bears no connection to the issue of

c. The opinion gave the background for such legislation: "In recent years, the exploitive use of children in the production of pornography has become a serious national problem. The federal government and forty-seven States have sought to combat the problem with statutes specifically directed at the production of child pornography. At least half of such statutes do not require that the materials produced be legally obscene. Thirty-five States and the United States Congress have also passed legislation prohibiting the distribution of such materials; twenty States prohibit the distribution of material depicting children engaged in sexual conduct without requiring that the material be legally obscene. New York is one of the twenty."

whether a child has been physically or psychologically harmed in the production of the work. Similarly, a sexual explicit depiction need not be 'patently offensive' in order to have required the sexual exploitation of a child for its production. In addition, a work which, taken on the whole, contains serious literary, artistic, political, or scientific value may nevertheless embody the hardest core of child pornography. 'It is irrelevant to the child [who has been abused] whether or not the material [has] a literary, artistic, political, or social value.' We therefore cannot conclude that the *Miller* standard is a satisfactory solution to the child pornography problem.

"Third. The advertising and selling of child pornography provides an economic motive for and is thus an integral part of the production of such materials, an activity illegal throughout the nation. 'It rarely has been suggested that the constitutional freedom for speech and press extends its immunity to speech or writing used as an integral part of conduct in violation of a valid criminal statute.' * * *

"Fourth. The value of permitting live performances and photographic reproductions of children engaged in lewd sexual conduct is exceedingly modest, if not de minimis. We consider it unlikely that visual depictions of children performing sexual acts or lewdly exhibiting their genitals would often constitute an important and necessary part of a literary performance or scientific or educational work. As the trial court in this case observed, if it were necessary for literary or artistic value, a person over the statutory age who perhaps looked younger could be utilized. * * *

"Fifth. Recognizing and classifying child pornography as a category of material outside the protection of the First Amendment is not incompatible with our earlier decisions. 'The question whether speech is, or is not protected by the First Amendment often depends on the content of the speech.' *Young v. American Mini Theatres, Inc.* [p. 437 infra]. '[I]t is the content of an utterance that determines whether it is a protected epithet or [an] unprotected "fighting comment" '. Leaving aside the special considerations when public officials are the target, *New York Times Co. v. Sullivan,* a libelous publication is not protected by the Constitution. *Beauharnais.* [It] is not rare that a content-based classification of speech has been accepted because it may be appropriately generalized that within the confines of the given classification, the evil to be restricted so overwhelmingly outweighs the expressive interests, if any, at stake, that no process of case-by-case adjudication is required. When a definable class of material, such as that covered by § 263.15, bears so heavily and pervasively on the welfare of children engaged in its production, we think the balance of competing interests is clearly struck and that it is permissible to consider these materials as without the protection of the First Amendment.

"There are, of course, limits on the category of child pornography which, like obscenity, is unprotected by the First Amendment. As with all legislation in this sensitive area, the conduct to be prohibited must be adequately defined by the applicable state law, as written or authoritatively construed. Here the nature of the harm to be combatted requires that the state offense be limited to works that *visually* depict sexual conduct by children below a specified age. The category of 'sexual conduct' proscribed must also be suitably limited and described.

"The test for child pornography is separate from the obscenity standard enunciated in *Miller,* but may be compared to it for purpose of clarity. The *Miller* formulation is adjusted in the following respects: A trier of fact need not find that the material appeals to the prurient interest of the average person; it is not required that sexual conduct portrayed be done so in a patently offensive manner; and the material at issue need not be considered as a whole. We note that the distribution of descriptions or other depictions of sexual conduct, not otherwise obscene, which do not involve live performance or photographic or other visual reproduction of live performances, retains First Amendment protection. As with obscenity laws, criminal responsibility may not be imposed without some element of scienter on the part of the defendant. * * *

"It remains to address the claim that the New York statute is unconstitutionally overbroad because it would forbid the distribution of material with serious literary, scientific, or educational value or material which does not threaten the harms sought to be combated by the State. * * *

"The traditional rule is that a person to whom a statute may constitutionally be applied may not challenge that statute on the ground that it may conceivably be applied unconstitutionally to others in situations not before the Court. *Broadrick v. Oklahoma,* 413 U.S. 601, 93 S.Ct. 2908, 37 L.Ed.2d 830 (1973). In *Broadrick,* we recognized that this rule reflects two cardinal principles of our constitutional order: the personal nature of constitutional rights and prudential limitations on constitutional adjudication.[20] [By] focusing on the factual situation before us, and similar cases necessary for development of a constitutional rule,[21] we face 'flesh-and-blood' legal problems with data 'relevant and adequate to an informed judgment.' This practice also fulfills a valuable institutional purpose: it allows state courts the opportunity to construe a law to avoid constitutional infirmities.

"What has come to be known as the First Amendment overbreadth doctrine is one of the few exceptions to this principle and must be justified by weighty countervailing policies. The doctrine is predicated on the sensitive nature of protected expression: persons whose expression is constitutionally protected may well refrain from exercising their rights for fear of criminal sanctions by a statute susceptible of application to protected expression. * * *

"In *Broadrick,* we explained [that]: '[T]he plain import of our cases is, at the very least, that facial overbreadth adjudication is an exception to our traditional rules of practice and that its function, a limited one at the outset, attenuates as the otherwise unprotected behavior that it forbids the State to sanction moves from "pure speech" toward conduct and that conduct—even if expressive—falls within the scope of otherwise valid criminal laws that reflect legitimate state interests in maintaining comprehensive controls over harmful, constitutionally unprotected conduct. * * *'

"[*Broadrick*] examined a regulation involving restrictions on political campaign activity, an area not considered 'pure speech,' and thus it was unnecessary to consider the proper overbreadth test when a law arguably reaches traditional forms of expression such as books and films. As we intimated in *Broadrick,* the requirement of substantial overbreadth extended 'at the very least' to cases involving conduct plus speech. This case, which poses the question squarely, convinces us that the rationale of *Broadrick* is sound and should be applied in

20. In addition to prudential restraints, the traditional rule is grounded in Art. III limits on the jurisdiction of federal courts to actual cases and controversies. * * *

21. Overbreadth challenges are only one type of facial attack. A person whose activity may be constitutionally regulated nevertheless may argue that the statute under which he is convicted or regulated is invalid on its face. See, e.g., *Terminiello.* See generally Monaghan, *Overbreadth,* 1981 S.Ct.Rev. 1, 10–14.

the present context involving the harmful employment of children to make sexually explicit materials for distribution.

"The premise that a law should not be invalidated for overbreadth unless it reaches a substantial number of impermissible applications is hardly novel. On most occasions involving facial invalidation, the Court has stressed the embracing sweep of the statute over protected expression.[26] Indeed, Justice Brennan observed in his dissenting opinion in *Broadrick*: 'We have never held that a statute should be held invalid on its face merely because it is possible to conceive of a single impermissible application, and in that sense a requirement of substantial overbreadth is already implicit in the doctrine.'

"The requirement of substantial overbreadth is directly derived from the purpose and nature of the doctrine. While a sweeping statute, or one incapable of limitation, has the potential to repeatedly chill the exercise of expressive activity by many individuals, the extent of deterrence of protected speech can be expected to decrease with the declining reach of the regulation. This observation appears equally applicable to the publication of books and films as it is to activities, such as picketing or participation in election campaigns, which have previously been categorized as involving conduct plus speech. We see no appreciable difference between the position of a publisher or bookseller in doubt as to the reach of New York's child pornography law and the situation faced by the Oklahoma state employees with respect to the State's restriction on partisan political activity.[d] * * *

"Applying these principles, we hold that § 263.15 is not substantially overbroad. We consider this the paradigmatic case of a state statute whose legitimate reach dwarfs its arguably impermissible applications. [While] the reach of the statute is directed at the hard core of child pornography, the Court of Appeals was understandably concerned that some protected expression, ranging from medical textbooks to pictorials in the National Geographic would fall prey to the statute. How often, if ever, it may be necessary to employ children to engage in conduct clearly within the reach of § 263.15 in order to produce educational, medical, or artistic works cannot be known with certainty. Yet we seriously doubt, and it has not been suggested, that these arguably impermissible applications of the statute amount to more than a tiny fraction of the materials within the statute's reach."[e]

---

26. In *Gooding v. Wilson*, the Court's invalidation of a Georgia statute making it a misdemeanor to use " 'opprobrious words or abusive language, tending to cause a breach of the peace' " followed from state judicial decisions indicating that "merely to speak words offensive to some who hear them" could constitute a "breach of the peace." * * *

d. *Brockett v. Spokane Arcades, Inc.*, p. 397 supra, stated: "The Court of Appeals erred in holding that the *Broadrick* substantial overbreadth requirement is inapplicable where pure speech rather than conduct is at issue. *Ferber* specifically held to the contrary." For commentary on the overbreadth discussion in *Broadrick* and *Ferber*, see Redish, *The Warren Court, The Burger Court and the First Amendment Overbreadth Doctrine*, 78 Nw.U.L.Rev. 1031, 1056–69 (1983).

e. Brennan, J., joined by Marshall, J., agreed "with much of what is said in the

Court's opinion. [This] special and compelling interest (in protecting the well-being of the State's youth), and the particular vulnerability of children, afford the State the leeway to regulate pornographic material, the promotion of which is harmful to children, even though the State does not have such leeway when it seeks only to protect consenting adults from exposure to such materials. * * * I also agree with the Court that the 'tiny fraction' of material of serious artistic, scientific or educational value that could conceivably fall within the reach of the statute is insufficient to justify striking the statute on grounds of overbreadth." But the concurrence stated that application of the statute to such materials as "do have serious artistic, scientific or medical value would violate the First Amendment."

On that issue O'Connor, J., wrote a short concurrence: "Although I join the Court's

Notes and Questions

1. Consider Schauer, *Codifying the First Amendment: New York v. Ferber,* 1982 Sup.Ct.Rev. 285, 295: The new category created in *Ferber* "bears little resemblance to the category of obscenity delineated by *Miller.* The Court in *Ferber* explicitly held that child pornography need not appeal to the prurient interest, need not be patently offensive, and need not be based on a consideration of the material as a whole. This last aspect is most important, because it means that the presence of some serious literary, artistic, political, or scientific matter will not constitutionally redeem material containing depictions of sexual conduct by children. The Court referred to the foregoing factors in terms of having 'adjusted' the *Miller* test, but that is like saying a butterfly is an adjusted camel." What precisely is the new category created in *Ferber* ?

2. What test or standard of review did the Court use to determine whether the speech should be protected? For general discussion, see Schauer, supra. Did it apply a different test or a standard of review when it formulated its rules in *Gertz* ? Are tests or standards of review needed in these contexts? Desirable? Consider Shiffrin, *The First Amendment and Economic Regulation: Away From a General Theory of the First Amendment,* 78 Nw.U.L.Rev. 1212, 1268 (1983): "The complex set of rules produced in *Gertz,* right or wrong, resulted from an appreciation that the protection of truth was important but that the protection of reputation also was important. The Court wisely avoided discussion of levels of scrutiny because any resort to such abstractions would have constitutionalized reductionism." Is "constitutionalized reductionism" desirable because it protects speech and provides guidance to the lower courts?

B. HARM TO WOMEN: FEMINISM AND PORNOGRAPHY

Catharine MacKinnon and Andrea Dworkin have drafted an anti-pornography ordinance that is being considered by a number of jurisdictions. A modified and less comprehensive version was passed by Indianapolis.

PROPOSED LOS ANGELES COUNTY ANTI–PORNOGRAPHY CIVIL RIGHTS LAW

Section 1. Statement of Policy

Pornography is sex discrimination. It exists in the County of Los Angeles, posing a substantial threat to the health, safety, welfare and equality of citizens

opinion, I write separately to stress that the Court does not hold that New York must except 'material with serious literary, scientific or educational value' from its statute. The Court merely holds that, even if the First Amendment shelters such material, New York's current statute is not sufficiently overbroad to support respondent's facial attack. The compelling interests identified in today's opinion suggest that the Constitution might in fact permit New York to ban knowing distribution of works depicting minors engaged in explicit sexual conduct, regardless of the social value of the depictions. For example, a 12-year-old child photographed while masturbating surely suffers the same psychological harm whether the community labels the photograph 'edifying' or 'tasteless.' The audience's appreciation of the depiction is simply irrelevant to New York's asserted interest in protecting children from psychological, emotional, and mental harm."

Stevens, J., also concurred in the judgment in a short opinion that noted his conclusion that the films in the case were not entitled to first amendment protection, and his view that overbreadth analysis should be avoided by waiting until the hypothetical case actually arises.

Blackmun, J., concurred in the result without opinion.

in the community. Existing state and federal laws are inadequate to solve these problems in the County of Los Angeles.

Section 2. Findings

Pornography is a systematic practice of exploitation and subordination based on sex which differentially harms women. The harm of pornography includes dehumanization, sexual exploitation, forced sex, forced prostitution, physical injury, and social and sexual terrorism and inferiority presented as entertainment. The bigotry and contempt pornography promotes, with the acts of aggression it fosters, diminish opportunities for equality of rights in employment, education, property, public accommodations and public services; create public and private harassment, persecution and denigration; promote injury and degradation such as rape, battery, child sexual abuse, and prostitution and inhibit just enforcement of laws against these acts; contribute significantly to restricting women in particular from full exercise of citizenship and participation in public life, including in neighborhoods; damage relations between the sexes; and undermine women's equal exercise of rights to speech and action guaranteed to all citizens under the Constitutions and laws of the United States, the State of California and the County of Los Angeles.

Section 3. Definitions

1. *Pornography* is the graphic sexually explicit subordination of women through pictures and/or words that also includes one or more of the following: (i) women are presented dehumanized as sexual objects, things or commodities; or (ii) women are presented as sexual objects who enjoy pain or humiliation; or (iii) women are presented as sexual objects who experience sexual pleasure in being raped; or (iv) women are presented as sexual objects tied up or cut up or mutilated or bruised or physically hurt; or (v) women are presented in postures of sexual submission, servility, or display; or (vi) women's body parts—including but not limited to vaginas, breasts, or buttocks—are exhibited such that women are reduced to those parts; or (vii) women are presented as whores by nature; or (viii) women are presented as being penetrated by objects or animals; or (ix) women are presented in scenarios of degradation, injury, torture, shown as filthy or inferior, bleeding, bruised or hurt in a context that makes these conditions sexual.

2. The use of men, children, or transsexuals in the place of women in (1) above is also pornography for purposes of this law.

Section 4. Unlawful Practices

1. *Coercion into pornography*: It shall be sex discrimination to coerce, intimidate, or fraudulently induce (hereafter, "coerce") any person, including transsexual, into performing for pornography, which injury may date from any appearance or sale of any product(s) of such performance(s). The maker(s), seller(s), exhibitor(s) and/or distributor(s) of said pornography may be sued, including for an injunction to eliminate the product(s) of the performance(s) from the public view.

Proof of one or more of the following facts or conditions shall not, without more, negate a finding of coercion:

  (i) that the person is a woman; or

  (ii) that the person is or has been a prostitute; or

  (iii) that the person has attained the age of majority; or

(iv) that the person is connected by blood or marriage to anyone involved in or related to the making of the pornography; or

(v) that the person has previously had, or been thought to have had, sexual relations with anyone, including anyone involved in or related to the making of the pornography; or

(vi) that the person has previously posed for sexually explicit pictures with or for anyone, including anyone involved in or related to the making of the pornography at issue; or

(vii) that anyone else, including a spouse or other relative, has given permission on the person's behalf; or

(viii) that the person actually consented to a use of the performance that is changed into pornography; or

(ix) that the person knew that the purpose of the acts or events in question was to make pornography; or

(x) that the person showed no resistance or appeared to cooperate actively in the photographic sessions or in the events that produced the pornography; or

(xi) that the person signed a contract, or made statements affirming a willingness to cooperate in the production of pornography; or

(xii) that no physical force, threats, or weapons were used in the making of the pornography; or

(xiii) that the person was paid or otherwise compensated.

2. *Trafficking in pornography:* It shall be sex discrimination to produce, sell, exhibit, or distribute pornography, including through private clubs.

(i) City, state, and federally funded public libraries or private and public university and college libraries in which pornography is available for study, including on open shelves but excluding special display presentations, shall not be construed to be trafficking in pornography.

(ii) Isolated passages or isolated parts shall not be actionable under this section.

(iii) Any woman has a claim hereunder as a woman acting against the subordination of women. Any man, child, or transsexual who alleges injury by pornography in the way women are injured by it also has a claim.

3. *Forcing pornography on a person:* It shall be sex discrimination to force pornography on a person, including child or transsexual, in any place of employment, education, home, or public place. Only the perpetrator of the force and/or institution responsible for the force may be sued.

4. *Assault or physical attack due to pornography:* It shall be sex discrimination to assault, physically attack or injure any person, including child or transsexual, in a way that is directly caused by specific pornography. The perpetrator of the assault or attack may be sued. The maker(s), distributor(s), seller(s), and/or exhibitor(s) may also be sued, including for an injunction against the specific pornography's further exhibition, distribution or sale.

Section 5. Defenses

1. It shall not be a defense that the defendant in an action under this law did not know or intend that the materials were pornography or sex discrimination.

2.   No damages or compensation for losses shall be recoverable under Sec. 4(2) or other than against the perpetrator of the assault or attack in Sec. 4(4) unless the defendant knew or had reason to know that the materials were pornography.

3.   In actions under Sec. 4(2) or other than against the perpetrator of the assault or attack in Sec. 4(4), no damages or compensation for losses shall be recoverable against maker(s) for pornography made, against distributor(s) for pornography distributed, against seller(s) for pornography sold, or against exhibitor(s) for pornography exhibited, prior to the effective date of this law.

Section 6. Enforcement

a.   Civil Action: Any person, or their estate, aggrieved by violations of this law may enforce its provisions by means of a civil action. No criminal penalties shall attach for any violation of the provisions of this law. Relief for violations of this law, except as expressly restricted or precluded herein, may include compensatory and punitive damages and reasonable attorney's fees, costs and disbursements.

b.   Injunction: Any person who violates this law may be enjoined except that:

(i) In actions under Sec. 4(2), and other than against the perpetrator of the assault or attack under Sec. 4(4), no temporary or permanent injunction shall issue prior to a final judicial determination that the challenged activities constitute a violation of this law.

(ii) No temporary or permanent injunction shall extend beyond such material(s) that, having been described with reasonable specificity by the injunction, have been determined to be validly proscribed under this law.

Section 7. Severability

Should any part(s) of this law be found legally invalid, the remaining part(s) remain valid. A judicial declaration that any part(s) of this law cannot be applied validly in a particular manner or to a particular case or category of cases shall not affect the validity of that part(s) as otherwise applied, unless such other application would clearly frustrate the intent of the Board of Supervisors in adopting this law.

Section 8. Limitation of Action

Actions under this law must be filed within one year of the alleged discriminatory acts.

Notes and Questions

1. *Relationship between obscenity and pornography.* Consider Andrea Dworkin, *Against the Male Flood: Censorship, Pornography, and Equality,* 8 Harv. Women's L.J. 1, 8–9 (1985): "What is at stake in obscenity law is always erection: under what conditions, in what circumstances, how, by whom, by what materials men want it produced in themselves. Men have made this public policy. Why they want to regulate their own erections through law is a question of endless interest and importance to feminists. * * *

"The insult pornography offers, invariably, to sex is accomplished in the active subordination of women: the creation of a sexual dynamic in which the putting-down of women, the suppression of women, and ultimately the brutalization of women, *is* what sex is taken to be. Obscenity in law, and in what it does socially, is erection. Law recognizes the act in this. Pornography, however, is a broader, more comprehensive act, because it crushes a whole class of people through violence and subjugation: and sex is the vehicle that does the crushing. The penis is not the test, as it is in obscenity. Instead, the status of women is the issue. Erection is implicated in the subordinating, but who it reaches and how are the pressing legal and social questions. Pornography, unlike obscenity, is a discrete, identifiable system of sexual exploitation that hurts women as a class by creating inequality and abuse."

Consider MacKinnon, *Pornography, Civil Rights, and Speech,* 20 Harv.Civ. Rts.-Civ.Lib.L.Rev. 1, 50–52 & 16–17 (1985): "To reach the magnitude of this problem on the scale it exists, our law makes trafficking in pornography— production, sale, exhibition, or distribution—actionable. Under the obscenity rubric, much legal and psychological scholarship has centered on a search for the elusive link between pornography defined as obscenity and harm. They have looked high and low—in the mind of the male consumer, in society or in its 'moral fabric,' in correlations between variations in levels of anti-social acts and liberalization of obscenity laws. The only harm they have found has been one they have attributed to 'the social interests in order and morality.' Until recently, no one looked very persistently for harm to women, particularly harm to women through men. The rather obvious fact that the sexes *relate* has been overlooked in the inquiry into the male consumer and his mind. The pornography doesn't just drop out of the sky, go into his head and stop there. Specifically, men rape, batter, prostitute, molest, and sexually harass women. Under conditions of inequality, they also hire, fire, promote, and grade women, decide how much or whether or not we are worth paying and for what, define and approve and disapprove of women in ways that count, that determine our lives.

"In pornography, there it is, in one place, all of the abuses that women had to struggle so long even to begin to articulate, all the *unspeakable* abuse: the rape, the battery, the sexual harassment, the prostitution, and the sexual abuse of children. Only in the pornography it is called something else: sex, sex, sex, sex, and sex, respectively. Pornography sexualizes rape, battery, sexual harassment, prostitution, and child sexual abuse; it thereby celebrates, promotes, authorizes, and legitimizes them. More generally, it eroticizes the dominance and submission that is the dynamic common to them all. It makes hierarchy sexy and calls that 'the truth about sex' or just a mirror of reality." See generally Dworkin, *Pornography: Men Possessing Women* (1981). For a review of the social science evidence relating to pornography and aggression against women, see *Pornography and Sexual Aggression* (Malamuth & Donnerstein, eds. 1984).

2. *The trafficking section.* Is the trafficking section constitutional under *Miller?* Consider the following hypothetical commentary: "The Dworkin-MacKinnon proposal focuses on a narrower class of material than *Miller* because it excludes erotic materials that do not involve subordination. That class of material upon which it does focus appeals to prurient interest because it is graphic and sexually explicit. Moreover, the eroticization of dominance in the ways specified in the ordinance is so patently offensive to community standards that it can be said as a matter of law that this class of materials lacks *serious* literary, artistic, political, or scientific value as a matter of law." Do you agree?

Is there a good analogy to *Beauharnais?* To *Ferber?* Did more or less harm exist in *Gertz? Miller? Ferber?* Was there more or less of a threat to first amendment values in *Gertz? Miller? Ferber?* Should this be accepted as a new category? Consider, Kaminer, *Pornography and the First Amendment: Prior*

Restraints and Private Action, 239, 245 in *Take Back the Night: Women on Pornography* (Lederer ed. 1980): "The Women's Movement is a civil rights movement, and we should appreciate the importance of individual freedom of choice and the danger of turning popular sentiment into law in areas affecting individual privacy.

"Legislative or judicial control of pornography is simply not possible without breaking down the legal principles and procedures that are essential to our own right to speak and, ultimately, our freedom to control our own lives. We must continue to organize against pornography and the degradation and abuse of women, but we must not ask the government to take up our struggle for us. The power it will assume to do so will be far more dangerous to us all than the 'power' of pornography." [a]

3. *The pornography definition.* Is the proposed definition too vague? Is it more or less vague than the terminology employed in *Miller?* Is there a core of clear meaning? How would you revise it to clarify its meaning? Is the definition overbroad? What revisions, if any, would you suggest to narrow its scope?

Consider Emerson, *Pornography and the First Amendment: A Reply to Professor MacKinnon,* 3 Yale L. & Pol. Rev. 130, 131–32 (1985): "The sweep of the Indianapolis Ordinance is breathtaking. It would subject to governmental ban virtually all depictions of rape, verbal or pictorial, and a substantial proportion of other presentations of sexual encounters. More specifically, it would outlaw such works of literature as the *Arabian Nights,* John Cleland's *Fanny Hill,* Henry Miller's *Tropic of Cancer,* William Faulkner's *Sanctuary,* and Norman Mailer's *Ancient Evenings,* to name but a few. The ban would extend from Greek mythology and Shakespeare to the millions of copies of 'romance novels' now being sold in the supermarkets. It would embrace much of the world's art, from ancient carvings to Picasso, well-known films too numerous to mention, and a large amount of commercial advertising.

"The scope of the Indianapolis Ordinance is not accidental. Nor could it be limited by more precise drafting without defeating the purpose of its authors. As Professor MacKinnon emphasizes, male domination has deep, pervasive and ancient roots in our society, so it is not surprising that our literature, art, entertainment and commerical practices are permeated by attitudes and behavior that create and reflect the inferior status of women. If the answer to the

---

a. Compare Hunter & Law, *Brief Amici Curiae of Feminist Anti-Censorship Taskforce* (on appeal in *Hudnut,* below) 14 & 43–44 (1985): The ordinance conceivably "would require the judiciary to impose its views of correct sexuality on a diverse community. The inevitable result would be to disapprove those images that are least conventional and privilege those that are closest to majoritarian beliefs about proper sexuality. [Moreover] [b]y defining sexually explicit images of women as subordinating and degrading to them, the ordinance reinforces the stereotypical view that 'good' women do not seek and enjoy sex. [Finally], the ordinance perpetuates a stereotype of women as helpless victims, incapable of consent, and in need of protection."

For a variety of feminist perspectives, see *Take Back the Night,* supra. See also Snitow,

Stansell & Thompson, etc., *Powers of Desire* 419–67 (1983). For general discussion of the legal issues, see Bryden, *Between Two Constitutions: Feminism and Pornography,* 2 Const. Comm. 147 (1985); Gershel, *Evaluating a Proposed Civil Rights Approach to Pornography: Legal Analyses as if Women Mattered,* 11 Wm. Mitchell L.Rev. 41 (1985); Hoffman, *Feminism, Pornography, and Law,* 133 U.Pa.L.Rev. 497 (1985); Tigue, *Civil Rights and Censorship—Incompatible Bedfellows,* 11 Wm.Mitchell L.Rev. 81 (1985); Note, *Anti-Pornography Laws and First Amendment Values,* 98 Harv. L.Rev. 460 (1984). See also *American Booksellers Ass'n v. Hudnut,* 771 F.2d 323 (7th Cir.1985) (declaring Indianapolis ordinance unconstitutional).

problem, as Professor MacKinnon describes it, is government suppression of sexual expression that contributes to female subordination, then the net of restraint has to be cast on a nearly limitless scale. Even narrowing the proscribed area to depictions of sexual activities involving violence would outlaw a large segment of the world's literature and art."

Is the proposed ordinance susceptible to a narrower construction than that offered by Professor Emerson?

4. *The coercion into pornography section.* Is this part of the proposed ordinance a straightforward application of *Ferber?* Is the conception of coercion constitutional? What was the conception in *Ferber?* If modifications are needed, what should they be?

5. *The assault provision.* Should the maker of a pornographic work be responsible for assaults prompted by the work? Should the maker of non-pornographic works be responsible for imitative assaults. In *Olivia N. v. NBC,* 126 Cal.App.3d 488, 178 Cal.Rptr. 888 (1981), the victim of a sexual assault allegedly imitating a sexual assault in NBC's "Born Innocent" sued the network. Olivia N. claimed that NBC negligently exposed her to serious risk because it knew or should have known that someone would imitate the act portrayed in the movie. Suppose Olivia N. could show that NBC had been advised that such an assault was likely if the movie were shown? Should a court analogize to cases like *Gertz?* The California court ruled that Olivia N. could not prevail unless she met the *Brandenburg* standard.

C. RACIST SPEECH REVISITED: THE NAZIS

"*What do you want to sell in the marketplace? What idea? The idea of murder?*"

Erna Gans, a concentration camp survivor and active leader in the Skokie B'nai B'rith.[a]

COLLIN v. SMITH, 578 F.2d 1197 (7th Cir.), cert. denied, 439 U.S. 916, 99 S.Ct. 291, 58 L.Ed.2d 264 (1978), per PELL, J., struck down a Village of Skokie *"Racial Slur" Ordinance,* making it a misdemeanor to disseminate any material (defined to include "public display of markings and clothing of symbolic significance") promoting and inciting racial or religious hatred. The Village would apparently apply this ordinance to the display of swastikas and military uniforms by the NSPA, a "Nazi organization" which planned to peacefully demonstrate for some 20–30 minutes in front of the Skokie Village Hall.

Although there was some evidence that some individuals "might have difficulty restraining their reactions to the Nazi demonstration," the Village "does not rely on a fear of responsive violence to justify the ordinance, and does not even suggest that there will be any physical violence if the march is held. This confession takes the case out of the scope of *Brandenburg* and *Feiner.* [It] also eliminates any argument based on the fighting words doctrine of *Chaplinsky,* [which] applied only to words with a direct tendency to cause violence by the persons to whom, individually, the words were addressed."

The court rejected, inter alia, the argument that the Nazi march, with its display of swastikas and uniforms, "will create a substantive evil that it has a right to prohibit: the infliction of psychic trauma on resident holocaust survivors [some 5,000] and other Jewish residents. [The] problem with engrafting an

a. Quoted in Friendly & Elliot, *The Constitution: That Delicate Balance* 83 (1984).

exception on the First Amendment for such situations is that they are indistinguishable in principle from speech that 'invite[s] dispute [or] induces a condition of unrest [or] even stirs people to anger,' *Terminiello.* Yet these are among the 'high purposes' of the First Amendment. [Where,] as here, a crime is made of a silent march, attended only by symbols and not by extrinsic conduct offensive in itself, we think the words of *Street v. New York* [p. 529 infra] are very much on point: '[A]ny shock effect [must] be attributed to the content of the ideas expressed. [P]ublic expression of ideas may not be prohibited merely because the ideas are themselves offensive to some of their hearers.'"

Nor was the court impressed with the argument that the proposed march was "not speech, [but] rather an invasion, intensely menacing no matter how peacefully conducted" (most of Skokie's residents are Jewish): "There *need be* no captive audience, as Village residents may, if they wish, simply avoid the Village Hall for thirty minutes on a Sunday afternoon, which no doubt would be their normal course of conduct on a day when the Village Hall was not open in the regular course of business. Absent such intrusion or captivity, there is no justifiable substantial privacy interest to save [the ordinance], when it attempts, by fiat, to declare the entire Village, at all times, a privacy zone that may be sanitized from the offensiveness of Nazi ideology and symbols." [b]

Notes and Questions

1. Is *Beauharnais,* p. 675 supra, still "good law"?

2. *Justifying the result.* Consider Bollinger, *Book Review*, 80 Mich.L.Rev. 617, 631 (1982) (reviewing Neier, *Defending My Enemy: American Nazis, The Skokie Case, and the Risks of Freedom* (1979)): "The value of any act is dependent upon the reasons behind it, and in free speech, as in any other area, getting the reasons straight is of first importance. One can understand [a] choice to protect the free speech activities of Nazis, but not because people should value their message in the slightest or believe it should be seriously entertained, not because a commitment to self-government or rationality logically demands that such ideas be presented for consideration, not because of a simple hope *qua* conviction that anti-Nazi sentiment will win in the end, not because the anti-Nazi belief will be stimulated by open confrontation and argument with the Nazi belief, not because a line could not be drawn that would exclude this ideology without inevitably encroaching on ideas that one likes—not for any of these reasons nor others related to them that are a part of the traditional baggage of the free speech argumentation; but rather because the danger of intolerance toward ideas is so pervasive an issue in our social lives, the process of mastering a capacity for tolerance so difficult, that it makes sense somewhere in the system to attempt to confront that problem and exercise more self-restraint than may be otherwise required. We should be, in short, more concerned with addressing through the act of tolerance the potential problems of intolerance than with valuing the act of speech itself.

b. See also *Skokie v. National Socialist Party,* 69 Ill.2d 605, 14 Ill.Dec. 890, 373 N.E.2d 21 (1978). For commentary relating the Skokie issue to regulation of pornography, and of commercial speech, for the purpose of asking whether there are general principles of freedom of expression and whether freedom of expression should be category-dependent, see Scanlon, *Freedom of Expression and Catego-* *ries of Expression,* 40 U.Pitt.L.Rev. 519 (1979). For assessment of the complicated connection between Skokie and equality values especially in light of the rest of first amendment law, see Tribe, *Constitutional Choices* 219–20 (1985). Compare Downs, *Skokie Revisited: Hate Group Speech and the First Amendment,* 60 Not.D.Law. 629 (1985).

"On this basis, then, tolerance becomes not merely a futile attempt at shoring up the legal barricades, a response devoid of intrinsic value and meaning, but instead a symbolic act indicating an awareness of the risks and dangers of intolerance and a commitment to developing a certain attitude toward the ideas and beliefs of others. At least a part of this attitude is a willingness to recognize the existence of ideas within society that we might otherwise prefer to ignore, and to see the risks involved in succumbing to the wish to refuse to acknowledge their existence. Self-knowledge may be the best defense available against the ideas that we hate."

For rich elaboration of this perspective, see Bollinger, *The Tolerant Society: Freedom of Speech and Extremist Speech in America* (1986).

VII. IS SOME PROTECTED SPEECH LESS EQUAL THAN OTHER PROTECTED SPEECH?

A. NEAR OBSCENE SPEECH

ERZNOZNIK v. JACKSONVILLE, 422 U.S. 205, 95 S.Ct. 2268, 45 L.Ed.2d 125 (1975), per POWELL, J., held invalid on its face an ordinance that prohibited drive-in theaters from showing films containing nudity ("bare buttocks, * * * female bare breasts, or human bare pubic areas") when visible from a public street or public place: "Appellee concedes that its ordinance sweeps far beyond the permissible restraints on obscenity, and thus applies to films that are protected by the First Amendment. [Its] primary argument is that it may protect its citizens against unwilling exposure to materials that may be offensive. Jacksonville's ordinance, however, does not protect citizens from all movies that might offend; rather it singles out films containing nudity, presumably because the lawmakers considered them especially offensive to passersby. * * *

"The plain, if at times disquieting, truth is that in our pluralistic society, constantly proliferating new and ingenious forms of expression, 'we are inescapably captive audiences for many purposes.' Much that we encounter offends our esthetic, if not our political and moral, sensibilities. Nevertheless, the Constitution does not permit the government to decide which types of otherwise protected speech are sufficiently offensive to require protection for the unwilling listener or viewer. Rather,[6] the burden normally falls upon the viewer to 'avoid further bombardment of [his] sensibilities simply by averting [his] eyes.' *Cohen v. California*. The Jacksonville ordinance discriminates among movies solely on the basis of content.[7] Its effect is to deter drive-in theaters from showing movies

---

6. It has also been suggested that government may proscribe, by a properly framed law, "the willful use of scurrilous language calculated to offend the sensibilities of an unwilling audience." *Rosenfeld* (Powell, J., dissenting). [In] the present case, however, appellant is not trying to reach, much less shock, unwilling viewers. Appellant manages a commercial enterprise which depends for its success on *paying* customers, not on freeloading passersby. Presumably, where economically feasible, the screen of a drive-in theater will be shielded from those who do not pay.

7. Scenes of nudity in a movie, like pictures of nude persons in a book, must be considered as a part of the whole work. In this respect such nudity is distinguishable

from the kind of public nudity traditionally subject to indecent exposure laws.

The Chief Justice's dissent, in response to this point, states that "[u]nlike persons reading books, passersby cannot consider fragments of drive-in movies as a part of the 'whole work' for the simple reason that they see but do not *hear* the [performance]." (emphasis in original). At issue here, however, is not the viewing rights of unwilling viewers but rather the rights of those who operate drive-in theatres and the public that attends these establishments. The effect of the Jacksonville ordinance is to increase the cost of showing films containing nudity. See n. 8, infra. In certain circumstances theatres will avoid showing these movies rather than incur containing any nudity, however innocent or even educational.[8] This discrimination cannot be justified as a means of preventing significant intrusions on privacy. The ordinance seeks only to keep these films from being seen from public streets and places where the offended viewer readily can avert his eyes. In short, the screen of a drive-in theater is not 'so obtrusive as to make it impossible for an unwilling individual to avoid exposure to it.' *Redrup*. Thus, we conclude that the limited privacy interest of persons on the public streets cannot justify this censorship of otherwise protected speech on the basis of its [content].

"In this case, assuming the ordinance is aimed at prohibiting youths from viewing the films, the restriction is broader than permissible. The ordinance is not directed against sexually explicit nudity, nor is it otherwise limited. Rather, [it] would bar a film containing a picture of a baby's buttocks, the nude body of a war victim, or scenes from a culture in which nudity is indigenous. The ordinance also might prohibit newsreel scenes of the opening of an art exhibit as well as shots of bathers on a beach. Clearly all nudity cannot be deemed obscene even as to minors. See *Ginsberg*. Nor can such a broad restriction be justified by any other governmental interest pertaining to minors. Speech that is neither obscene as to youths nor subject to some other legitimate proscription cannot be suppressed solely to protect the young from ideas or images that a legislative body thinks unsuitable for them." [a]

Burger, C.J., joined by Rehnquist, J., dissented: "[T]he conclusion that only a limited interest of persons on the public streets is at stake here can be supported only if one completely ignores the unique visual medium to which the Jacksonville ordinance is directed. Whatever validity the notion that passersby may protect their sensibilities by averting their eyes may have when applied to words printed on an individual's jacket, see *Cohen*, [it] distorts reality to apply that notion to the outsize screen of a drive-in movie [theater].

"[The] screen of a drive-in movie theater is a unique type of eye-catching display that can be highly intrusive and distracting. Public authorities have a legitimate interest in regulating such displays under the police power; for

the additional costs. As a result persons who want to see such films at drive-ins will be unable to do so. It is in this regard that a motion picture must be considered as a whole, and not as isolated fragments or scenes of nudity.

[The Chief Justice's response to fn. 7 also stated: "[T]hose persons who legitimately desire to consider the 'work as a whole' are not foreclosed from doing so. The record shows that the film from which appellant's prosecution arose was exhibited in several indoor theaters in the Jacksonville area. And the owner of a drive-in movie theater is not prevented from exhibiting nonobscene films involving nudity so long as he effectively shields the screen from public view. Thus, regardless of whether the ordinance involved here can be loosely described as regulating the content of a certain type of display, it is not a restriction of any 'message.' The First Amendment interests involved in this case are trivial at best."]

8. Such a deterrent, although it might not result in total suppression of these movies, is a

restraint on free expression. The record does not indicate how much it would cost to block public view of appellant's theater. Such costs generally will vary with circumstances. In one case the expense was estimated at approximately a quarter million dollars. See *Olympic Drive-In Theatre, Inc. v. Pagedale*, 441 S.W.2d 5, 8 (Mo.1969).

a. The Court also rejected the argument that the ordinance was aimed at traffic regulation: "[The] ordinance applies to movie screens visible from public places as well as public streets, thus indicating that it is not a traffic regulation. But even if this were the purpose [it] would be invalid" because "strikingly underinclusive" in "singling out [even] the most fleeting and innocent glimpses of nudity," which violated both the equal protection clause and the first amendment by discriminating on the basis of content without justification, since "other scenes in the customary screen diet, ranging from soap opera to violence, would be [no] less distracting to the passing motorist."

example, even though traffic safety may not have been the only target of the ordinance in issue here, I think it not unreasonable for lawmakers to believe that public nudity on a giant screen, visible at night to hundreds of drivers of automobiles, may have a tendency to divert attention from their task and cause accidents." [b]

YOUNG v. AMERICAN MINI THEATRES, INC.

427 U.S. 50, 96 S.Ct. 2440, 49 L.Ed.2d 310 (1976).

MR. JUSTICE STEVENS delivered the opinion of the Court.[*]

[Detroit "Anti-Skid Row" ordinances prohibited "adult motion picture theaters" and "adult book stores" within 1,000 feet of any two other "regulated uses," which included such theaters and book stores, liquor stores, pool halls, pawnshops, and the like. The ordinances defined "adult motion picture theater" as one "presenting material distinguished or characterized by an emphasis on matter depicting, describing or relating to 'Specified Sexual Activities' [a] or 'Specified Anatomical Areas' " [b] and "adult book store" in substantially the same terms. The Court upheld the ordinances, reversing a decision in a federal declaratory judgment action by two theater owners wishing regularly to exhibit "adult" motion pictures.]

I. [R]espondents claim that the ordinances are too vague [because] they cannot determine how much of the ["specified"] activity may be permissible before the exhibition is "characterized by an emphasis" on such matter. [We] find it unnecessary to consider the validity of [this argument. Both] theaters propose to offer adult fare on a regular basis. [Therefore], the element of vagueness in these ordinances has not affected these respondents. * * *

Because the ordinances affect communication protected by the First Amendment, respondents argue that they may raise the vagueness issue even though there is no uncertainty about the impact of the ordinances on their own rights. On several occasions we have determined that a defendant whose own speech was unprotected had standing to challenge the constitutionality of a statute which purported to prohibit protected speech, or even speech arguably protected. *Broadrick*. The exception is justified by the overriding importance of maintaining a free and open market for the interchange of ideas. Nevertheless, if the statute's deterrent effect of legitimate expression is not "both real and substantial" and if the statute is "readily subject to a narrowing construction by the state courts" the litigant is not permitted to assert the rights of third parties.

We are not persuaded that the Detroit Zoning Ordinances will have a significant deterrent effect on the exhibition of films protected by the First Amendment. [T]he only vagueness in the ordinances relates to the amount of

---

b. White, J., also dissented. Douglas, J., concurred.

[*] Part III of this opinion is joined only by The Chief Justice, Mr. Justice White, and Mr. Justice Rehnquist.

a. "Specified Sexual Activities" were defined thus:

"1. Human Genitals in a state of sexual stimulation or arousal;

"2. Acts of human masturbation, sexual intercourse or sodomy;

"3. Fondling or other erotic touching of human genitals, public region, buttock or female breast."

b. "Specified Anatomical Areas" were defined thus:

"1. Less than completely and opaquely covered: (a) human genitals, pubic region, (b) buttock, and (c) female breast below a point immediately above the top of the areola, and

"2. Human male genitals in a discernibly turgid state, even if completely and opaquely covered."

sexually explicit activity that may be portrayed before the material can be said to be "characterized by an emphasis" on such matter. For most films the question will be readily answerable; to the extent that an area of doubt exists, we see no reason why the statute is not "readily subject to a narrowing construction by the state courts." Since there is surely a less vital interest in the uninhibited exhibition of material that is on the border line between pornography and artistic expression than in the free dissemination of ideas of social and political significance,[c] and since the limited amount of uncertainty in the statute is easily susceptible of a narrowing construction, we think this is an inappropriate case in which to adjudicate the hypothetical claims of persons not before the Court. * * *

II. [T]he ordinances prohibit theaters which are not licensed as "adult motion picture theaters" from exhibiting films which are protected by the First Amendment. Respondents argue that the ordinances are therefore invalid as prior restraints on free speech. The ordinances are not challenged on the ground that they impose a limit on the total number of adult theaters which may operate in the city of Detroit. There is no claim that distributors or exhibitors of adult films are denied access to the market or conversely, that the viewing public is unable to satisfy its appetite for sexually explicit fare. Viewed as an entity, the market for this commodity is essentially unrestrained.

It is true, however, that adult films may only be exhibited commercially in licensed theaters. But that is also true of all motion pictures. The city's general zoning laws require all motion picture theaters to satisfy certain locational as well as other requirements; we have no doubt that the municipality may control the location of theaters as well as the location of other commercial establishments, either by confining them to certain specified commercial zones or by requiring that they be dispersed throughout the city. The mere fact that the commercial exploitation of material protected by the First Amendment is subject to zoning and other licensing requirements is not a sufficient reason for invalidating these ordinances.

Putting to one side for the moment the fact that adult motion picture theaters must satisfy a locational restriction not applicable to other theaters, we are also persuaded that the 1,000-foot restriction does not, in itself, create an impermissible restraint on protected communication. The city's interest in planning and regulating the use of property for commercial purposes is clearly adequate to support that kind of restriction applicable to all theaters within the city limits. In short, apart from the fact that the ordinances treat adult theaters differently from other theaters and the fact that the classification is predicated on the content of material shown in the respective theaters, the regulation of the place where such films may be exhibited does not offend the First Amendment. We turn, therefore, to the question whether the classification is consistent with the Equal Protection Clause.

III. [T]he use of streets and parks for the free expression of views on national affairs may not be conditioned upon the sovereign's agreement with

c. But see Hunter & Law, p. 432 supra, at 28–29: "[S]exual speech is political. One core insight of modern feminism is that the personal is political. The question of who does the dishes and rocks the cradle affects both the nature of the home and the composition of the legislature. The dynamics of intimate relations are likewise political, both to the individuals involved and by their multiplied effects to the wider society. To argue [that] sexually explicit speech is less important than other categories of discourse reinforces the conceptual structures that have identified women's concerns with relationships and intimacy as less significant and valuable precisely because those concerns are falsely regarded as having no bearing on the structure of social and political life."

what a speaker may intend to say. [If] picketing in the vicinity of a school is to be allowed to express the point of view of labor, that means of expression in that place must be allowed for other points of view as well. As we said in [*Chicago Police Dep't v. Mosley*, p. 536 infra], "The central problem with Chicago's ordinance is that it describes permissible picketing in terms of its subject matter. [A]bove all else, the First Amendment means that government has no power to restrict expression because of its message, its ideas, its subject matter, or its content. [Any] restriction on expressive activity because of its content would completely undercut the 'profound national commitment to the principle that debate on public issues should be uninhibited, robust, and wide-open.' [*New York Times*]. Selective exclusions from a public forum may not be based on content alone, and may not be justified by reference to content alone."

This statement, and others to the same effect, read literally and without regard for the facts of the case in which it was made, would absolutely preclude any regulation of expressive activity predicated in whole or in part on the content of the communication. But we learned long ago that broad statements of principle, no matter how correct in the context in which they are made, are sometimes qualified by contrary decisions before the absolute limit of the stated principle is reached. When we review this Court's actual adjudications in the First Amendment area, we find this to have been the case with the stated principle that there may be no restriction whatever on expressive activity because of its content. * * *

The question whether speech is, or is not, protected by the First Amendment often depends on the content of the speech. Thus, the line between permissible advocacy and impermissible incitation to crime or violence depends, not merely on the setting in which the speech occurs, but also on exactly what the speaker had to say. Similarly, it is the content of the utterance that determines whether it is a protected epithet or an unprotected "fighting comment." And in time of war "the publication of the sailing dates of transports or the number and location of troops" may unquestionably be restrained, see *Near v. Minnesota* [p. 473 infra].

Even within the area of protected speech, a difference in content may require a different governmental response. [*New York Times*] held that a public official may not recover damages from a critic of his official conduct without proof of "malice" as specially defined in that opinion. Implicit in the opinion is the assumption that if the content of the newspaper article had been different— that is, if its subject matter had not been a public official—a lesser standard of proof would have been adequate. [We] have recently held that the First Amendment affords some protection to commercial speech. [The] measure of [protection] to commercial speech will surely be governed largely by the content of the communication.[32] * * *

More directly in point are opinions dealing with the question whether the First Amendment prohibits the state and federal governments from wholly suppressing sexually oriented materials on the basis of their "obscene character." In *Ginsberg*, the Court upheld a conviction for selling to a minor magazines which were concededly not "obscene" if shown to adults. Indeed, the Members of the Court who would accord the greatest protection to such materials have repeatedly indicated that the State could prohibit the distribution or

32. As Mr. Justice Stewart pointed out in *Virginia Pharmacy*, [p. 444 infra], the "differences between commercial price and product advertising [and] ideological communication" permits regulation of the former that the First Amendment would not tolerate with respect to the latter (concurring opinion).

exhibition of such materials to juveniles and consenting adults. Surely the First Amendment does not foreclose such a prohibition; yet it is equally clear that any such prohibition must rest squarely on an appraisal of the content of material otherwise within a constitutionally protected area.

Such a line may be drawn on the basis of content without violating the Government's paramount obligation of neutrality in its regulation of protected communication. For the regulation of the places where sexually explicit films may be exhibited is unaffected by whatever social, political, or philosophical message the film may be intended to communicate; whether the motion picture ridicules or characterizes one point of view or another, the effect of the ordinances is exactly the same.

Moreover, even though we recognize that the First Amendment will not tolerate the total suppression of erotic materials that have some arguably artistic value, it is manifest that society's interest in protecting this type of expression is of a wholly different, and lesser, magnitude than the interest in untrammeled political debate that inspired Voltaire's immortal comment.[d] Whether political oratory or philosophical discussion moves us to applaud or to despise what is said, every school-child can understand why our duty to defend the right to speak remains the same. But few of us would march our sons and daughters off to war to preserve the citizen's right to see "Specified Sexual Activities" exhibited in the theaters of our choice. Even though the First Amendment protects communication in this area from total suppression, we hold that the State may legitimately use the content of these materials as the basis for placing them in a different classification from other motion pictures.

The remaining question is whether the line drawn by these ordinances is justified by the city's interest in preserving the character of its neighborhoods. [The] record discloses a factual basis for the Common Council's conclusion that this kind of restriction will have the desired effect.[34] It is not our function to appraise the wisdom of its decision to require adult theaters to be separated rather than concentrated in the same areas. In either event, the city's interest in attempting to preserve the quality of urban life is one that must be accorded high respect. Moreover, the city must be allowed a reasonable opportunity to experiment with solutions to admittedly serious problems.

Since what is ultimately at stake is nothing more than a limitation on the place where adult films may be exhibited,[35] even though the determination of whether a particular film fits that characterization turns on the nature of its content, we conclude that the city's interest in the present and future character of its neighborhoods adequately supports its classification of motion pictures.

* * *

MR. JUSTICE POWELL, concurring in the judgment and portions of the opinion.

d. The opinion had earlier quoted Voltaire: "I disapprove of what you say, but I will defend to the death your right to say it."

34. The City Council's determination was that a concentration of "adult" movie theaters causes the area to deteriorate and become a focus of crime, effects which are not attributable to theaters showing other types of films. It is this secondary effect which this zoning ordinance attempts to avoid, not the dissemination of "offensive" speech. In contrast, in *Erznoznik*, the justifications offered by the city rested primarily on the city's interest in protecting its citizens from exposure to unwanted, "offensive" speech. * * *

35. The situation would be quite different if the ordinance had the effect of suppressing, or greatly restricting access to, lawful speech. Here, however, the District Court specifically found that "[t]he Ordinances do not affect the operation of existing establishments but only the location of new ones. There are myriad locations in the City of Detroit which must be over 1000 feet from existing regulated establishments. This burden on First Amendment rights is slight." * * *

Although I agree with much of what is said in the plurality opinion, and concur in Parts I and II, my approach to the resolution of this case is sufficiently different to prompt me to write separately.[1] I view the case as presenting an example of innovative land-use regulation, implicating First Amendment concerns only incidentally and to a limited extent. * * *

In this case, there is no indication that the application of the Anti-Skid Row Ordinance to adult theaters has the effect of suppressing production of or, to any significant degree, restricting access to adult movies. Nortown concededly will not be able to exhibit adult movies at its present location, and the ordinance limits the potential location of the proposed Pussy Cat. The constraints of the ordinance with respect to location may indeed create economic loss for some who are engaged in this business. But in this respect they are affected no differently than any other commercial enterprise that suffers economic detriment as a result of land-use regulation. The cases are legion that sustained zoning against claims of serious economic damage.

The inquiry for First Amendment purposes is not concerned with economic impact; rather, it looks only to the effect of this ordinance upon freedom of expression. This prompts essentially two inquiries: (i) does the ordinance impose any content limitation on the creators of adult movies or their ability to make them available to whom they desire, and (ii) does it restrict in any significant way the viewing of these movies by those who desire to see them? On the record in this case, these inquiries must be answered in the negative. At most the impact of the ordinance on these interests is incidental and minimal.[2] Detroit has silenced no message, has invoked no censorship, and has imposed no limitation upon those who wish to view them. The ordinance is addressed only to the places at which this type of expression may be presented, a restriction that does not interfere with content. Nor is there any significant overall curtailment of adult movie presentations, or the opportunity for a message to reach an audience. On the basis of the District Court's finding, it appears that if a sufficient market exists to support them the number of adult movie theaters in Detroit will remain approximately the same, free to purvey the same message. To be sure some prospective patrons may be inconvenienced by this dispersal. But other patrons, depending upon where they live or work, may find it more convenient to view an adult movie when adult theaters are not concentrated in a particular section of the city.

In these circumstances, it is appropriate to analyze the permissibility of Detroit's action under the four-part test of *United States v. O'Brien* [p. 515 infra].[e] Under that test, a governmental regulation is sufficiently justified, despite its incidental impact upon First Amendment interests, "if it is within the constitutional power of the Government; if it furthers an important government interest; if the government interest is unrelated to the suppression of free expression; and if the incidental restriction [on] First Amendment freedoms is

---

1. I do not think we need reach, nor am I inclined to agree with, the holding in Part III (and supporting discussion) that nonobscene, erotic materials may be treated differently under First Amendment principles from other forms of protected expression. I do not consider the conclusions in Part I of the opinion to depend on distinctions between protected speech.

2. The communication involved here is not a kind in which the content or effectiveness of the message depends in some measure upon where or how it is conveyed. * * *

e. The *O'Brien* test was announced in a case where a course of conduct (publicly burning a selective service card) combined unprotected nonspeech elements (destroying the card) with protected speech elements (expressing antiwar views).

no greater than is essential to the furtherance of that interest." [Powell, J., concluded that the Detroit ordinance satisfied the *O'Brien* test.]

MR. JUSTICE STEWART, with whom MR. JUSTICE BRENNAN, MR. JUSTICE MARSHALL and MR. JUSTICE BLACKMUN join, dissenting.

[This case involves] the constitutional permissibility of selective interference with protected speech whose content is thought to produce distasteful effects. It is elementary that a prime function of the First Amendment is to guard against just such interference. By refusing to invalidate Detroit's ordinance the Court rides roughshod over cardinal principles of First Amendment law, which require that time, place and manner regulations that affect protected expression be content-neutral except in the limited context of a captive or juvenile audience. In place of these principles the Court invokes a concept wholly alien to the First Amendment. Since "few of us would march our sons and daughters off to war to preserve the citizen's right to see 'Specified Sexual Activities' exhibited in the theaters of our choice," the Court implies that these films are not entitled to the full protection of the Constitution. This stands "Voltaire's immortal comment," on its head. For if the guarantees of the First Amendment were reserved for expression that more than a "few of us" would take up arms to defend, then the right of free expression would be defined and circumscribed by current popular opinion. The guarantees of the Bill of Rights were designed to protect against precisely such majoritarian limitations on individual liberty.

The fact that the "offensive" speech here may not address "important" topics—"ideas of social and political significance," in the Court's terminology—does not mean that it is less worthy of constitutional protection. "Wholly neutral futilities [come] under the protection of free speech as fully as do Keats' poems or Donne's sermons." *Winters* (Frankfurter, J., dissenting), accord, *Cohen v. California.* Moreover, in the absence of a judicial determination of obscenity, it is by no means clear that the speech is not "important" even on the Court's terms [*Roth; Kingsley Pictures*].

I can only interpret today's decision as an aberration. The Court is undoubtedly sympathetic, as am I, to the well-intentioned efforts of Detroit to "clean up" its streets and prevent the proliferation of "skid rows." But it is in those instances where protected speech grates most unpleasantly against the sensibilities that judicial vigilance must be at its [height].

The factual parallels between [*Erznoznik* and this case] are striking. There, as here, the ordinance did not forbid altogether the "distasteful" expression but merely required an alteration in the physical setting of the forum. There, as here, the city's principal asserted interest was in minimizing the "undesirable" effects of speech having a particular content. [And] the particular content of the restricted speech at issue in *Erznoznik* precisely parallels the content restricted in [Detroit's] definition of "Specified Anatomical Areas." * * *

The Court must never forget that the consequences of rigorously enforcing the guarantees of the First Amendment are frequently unpleasant. Much speech that seems to be of little or no value will enter the marketplace of ideas, threatening the quality of our social discourse and, more generally, the serenity of our lives. But that is the price to be paid for constitutional freedom. * * *[f]

---

f. Blackmun, J., joined by the other three dissenters, also filed a dissent that protested the rejection of the vagueness argument, concluding on this issue: "As to the third reason, that 'adult' material is simply entitled to less protection, it certainly explains the lapse in applying settled vagueness principles, as indeed it explains this whole case. In joining Mr. Justice Stewart I have joined his forthright rejection of the notion that First Amend-

Notes and Questions

1. *A hierarchy of protected speech.* Stevens, J., contends that as a matter of law some "protected" speech is less worthy than other protected speech. The dissenters and Powell, J., reject that view. Which approach is more likely to preserve first amendment values? Would treating all protected speech equally invite a dilution of the force of the first amendment with respect to the speech that "really" matters? Is the process of allowing judges to pick and choose between types of protected speech too dangerous? Would it be dangerous to protect political speech more than sexually explicit speech? Is sexually explicit speech non-political? If the plaintiff's approach were accepted, would the Court ultimately "rank speech in all its myriad forms, in order of its perceived importance," with new rankings being "created and old ones rejected depending on the Court's view of the worthiness of the speech at issue"? Goldman, *A Doctrine of Worthier Speech: Young v. American Mini Theatres, Inc.,* 21 St. Louis U.L.J. 281, 300–01 (1977).

2. *The exhibitor's free expression.* Did Powell, J., assume that the "first amendment rights [involved] in *Young* were primarily vested in creator and audience"? Note, 42 Mo.L.Rev. 461, 468 (1977); Note, 28 Case W.Res.L.Rev. 456, 482 (1978). Does the plurality opinion and its fn. 35 reflect similar lack of concern for exhibitor's interests? How would a record be built to distinguish *Young* from a similar ordinance in another city?

3. *Exclusionary zoning. Schad v. Mt. Ephraim,* 452 U.S. 61, 101 S.Ct. 2176, 68 L.Ed.2d 671 (1981) invalidated a Borough ordinance that permitted adult theaters and bookstores, but excluded live entertainment from its commercial zone. Even as applied to nude dancing, the Court found that the ordinance was not narrowly drawn to serve a sufficiently substantial state interest. The Court observed that there was no evidence to show that the entertainment at issue was available in reasonably nearby areas. What if it were? Suppose the Borough banned adult theaters and bookstores, but could show they were available nearby?

4. *Public display of "adult" material.* Suppose a city allows the sale of adult material only in establishments that announce their nature, but does not allow their contents to be seen from the outside. Consider Williams, Chair, *Report of the Committee on Obscenity and Film Censorship* 97 (1979): "The basic point that pornography involves by its nature some violation of lines between public and private is compounded when the pornography not only exists for private consumption, but is publicly displayed. The original violation is then forced on the attention of those who have not even volunteered to be voyeurs." Should cities be able to restrict public display of materials they could not otherwise ban? Should a feminist perspective yield different conclusions than those suggested by the Williams report? Is it sufficient to say that people can avoid bombardment by averting their eyes? Should the government be able to "zone" vulgar words on the airwaves to the late hours of the evening? See *FCC v. Pacifica Foundation,* p. 605 infra. For Ronald Dworkin's commentary on the Williams Report, see *A Matter of Principle* 335–72 (1985).

ment protection is diminished for 'erotic materials' that only a 'few of us' see the need to protect."

B. COMMERCIAL SPEECH

VIRGINIA STATE BOARD OF PHARMACY v.
VIRGINIA CITIZENS CONSUMER COUNCIL

425 U.S. 748, 96 S.Ct. 1817, 48 L.Ed.2d 346 (1976).

MR. JUSTICE BLACKMUN delivered the opinion of the Court.

[The Court held invalid a Virginia statute that made advertising the prices of prescription drugs "unprofessional conduct," subjecting pharmacists to license suspension or revocation. Prescription drug prices strikingly varied within the same locality, in Virginia and nationally, sometimes by several hundred percent. Such drugs were dispensed exclusively by licensed pharmacists but 95% were prepared by manufacturers, not compounded by the pharmacists.]

[Appellants] contend that the advertisement of prescription drug prices is outside the protection of the First Amendment because it is "commercial speech." There can be no question that in past decisions the Court has given some indication that commercial speech is unprotected.[a]

Last Term, in *Bigelow v. Virginia*, 421 U.S. 809, 95 S.Ct. 2222, 44 L.Ed.2d 600 (1975), the notion of unprotected "commercial speech" all but passed from the scene. We reversed a conviction for violation of a Virginia statute that made the circulation of any publication to encourage or promote the processing of an abortion in Virginia a misdemeanor. The defendant had published in his newspaper the availability of abortions in New York. The advertisement in question, in addition to announcing that abortions were legal in New York, offered the services of a referral agency in that State. [We] concluded that "the Virginia courts erred in their assumptions that advertising, as such, was entitled to no First Amendment protection," and we observed that the "relationship of speech to the marketplace of products or of services does not make it valueless in the marketplace of ideas."

Some fragment of hope for the continuing validity of a "commercial speech" exception arguably might have persisted because of the subject matter of the advertisement in *Bigelow*. We noted that in announcing the availability of legal abortions in New York, the advertisement "did more than simply propose a commercial transaction. It contained factual material of clear 'public interest.'" And, of course, the advertisement related to activity with which, at least in some respects, the State could not interfere. See *Roe v. Wade* [p. 142 infra]. Indeed, we observed: "We need not decide in this case the precise extent to which the First Amendment permits regulation of advertising that is related to activities the State may legitimately regulate or even prohibit."[b]

Here, [the] question whether there is a First Amendment exception for "commercial speech" is squarely before us. Our pharmacist does not wish to editorialize on any subject, cultural, philosophical, or political. He does not wish to report any particularly newsworthy fact, or to make generalized observations

---

a. Starting with *Valentine v. Chrestensen*, 316 U.S. 52, 62 S.Ct. 920, 86 L.Ed. 1262 (1942), the opinion summarized the decisions and dicta that gave such "indication." Long after *Chrestensen*, strong arguments against a first amendment exception for commercial speech had appeared. See Redish, *The First Amendment in the Market Place*, 39 Geo.Wash.L.Rev. 420 (1971); Note, 50 Ore.L.Rev. 177 (1971); cf. Note, 78 Harv.L.Rev. 1191 (1965).

b. *Bigelow* continued: "Regardless of the particular label asserted by the State—whether it calls speech 'commercial' or 'commercial advertising' or 'solicitation'—a court may not escape the task of assessing the First Amendment interest at stake and weighing it against the public interest allegedly served by the regulation."

even about commercial matters. The "idea" he wishes to communicate is simply this: "I will sell you the X prescription drug at the Y price." Our question, then, is whether this communication is wholly outside the protection of the First Amendment.

V. [Speech] does not lose its First Amendment protection because money is spent to project it, as in a paid advertisement of one form or another. *New York Times Co. v. Sullivan.* Speech likewise is protected even though it is carried in a form that is "sold" for profit. *Smith v. California.* [Our] question is whether speech which does "no more than propose a commercial transaction," is so removed from any "exposition of ideas," and from "truth, science, morality, and arts in general, in its diffusion of liberal sentiments on the administration of Government", *Roth,* that it lacks all protection. Our answer is that it is not.

Focusing first on the individual parties to the transaction that is proposed in the commercial advertisement, we may assume that the advertiser's interest is a purely economic one. That hardly disqualifies him for protection under the First Amendment. The interests of the contestants in a labor dispute are primarily economic, but it has long been settled that both the employee and the employer are protected by the First Amendment when they express themselves on the merits of the dispute in order to influence its outcome. * * *[17]

As to the particular consumer's interest in the free flow of commercial information, that interest may be as keen, if not keener by far, than his interest in the day's most urgent political debate. Appellees' case in this respect is a convincing one. Those whom the suppression of prescription drug price information hits the hardest are the poor, the sick, and particularly the aged. A disproportionate amount of their income tends to be spent on prescription drugs; yet they are the least able to learn, by shopping from pharmacist to pharmacist, where their scarce dollars are best spent. When drug prices vary as strikingly as they do, information as to who is charging what becomes more than a convenience. It could mean the alleviation of physical pain or the enjoyment of basic necessities.

Generalizing, society also may have a strong interest in the free flow of commercial information. Even an individual advertisement, though entirely "commercial," may be of general public interest. The facts of decided cases furnish illustrations: advertisements stating that referral services for legal abortions are available, *Bigelow;* that a manufacturer of artificial furs promotes his product as an alternative to the extinction by his competitors of fur-bearing mammals, see *Fur Information & Fashion Council, Inc. v. E.F. Timme & Son,* 364 F.Supp. 16 (SDNY 1973); and that a domestic producer advertises his product as an alternative to imports that tend to deprive American residents of their jobs, cf. *Chicago Joint Board v. Chicago Tribune Co.,* 435 F.2d 470 (CA7 1970), cert. denied, 402 U.S. 973 (1971). Obviously, not all commercial messages contain the same or even a very great public interest element. There are few to which such

---

17. The speech of labor disputants, of course, is subject to a number of restrictions. The Court stated in *NLRB v. Gissel Packing Co.,* 395 U.S., at 618, 89 S.Ct., at 1942, 23 L.Ed. 2d, at 581 (1969), for example, that an employer's threats of retaliation for the labor actions of his employees are "without the protection of the First Amendment." The constitutionality of restrictions upon speech in the special context of labor disputes is not before us here. We express no views on that complex subject,

and advert to cases in the labor field only to note that in some circumstances speech of an entirely private and economic character enjoys the protection of the First Amendment.

[For the contention that labor speech receives less protection than commercial speech, see Pope, *The Three-Systems Ladder of First Amendment Values: Two Rungs and a Black Hole,* 11 Hast.Con.L.Q. 189 (1984)].

an element, however, could not be added. Our pharmacist, for example, could cast himself as a commentator on store-to-store disparities in drug prices, giving his own and those of a competitor as proof. We see little point in requiring him to do so, and little difference if he does not.

Moreover, there is another consideration that suggests that no line between publicly "interesting" or "important" commercial advertising and the opposite kind could ever be drawn. Advertising, however tasteless and excessive it sometimes may seem, is nonetheless dissemination of information as to who is producing and selling what product, for what reason, and at what price. So long as we preserve a predominantly free enterprise economy, the allocation of our resources in large measure will be made through numerous private economic decisions. It is a matter of public interest that those decisions, in the aggregate, be intelligent and well informed. To this end, the free flow of commercial information is indispensable. And if it is indispensable to the proper allocation of resources in a free enterprise system, it is also indispensable to the formation of intelligent opinions as to how that system ought to be regulated or altered. Therefore, even if the First Amendment were thought to be primarily an instrument to enlighten public decisionmaking in a democracy, we could not say that the free flow of information does not serve that goal.

Arrayed against these substantial individual and societal interests are a number of justifications for the advertising ban. These have to do principally with maintaining a high degree of professionalism on the part of licensed pharmacists. [Price] advertising, it is argued, will place in jeopardy the pharmacist's expertise and, with it, the customer's health. It is claimed that the aggressive price competition that will result from unlimited advertising will make it impossible for the pharmacist to supply professional services in the compounding, handling, and dispensing of prescription drugs. Such services are time-consuming and expensive; if competitors who economize by eliminating them are permitted to advertise their resulting lower prices, the more painstaking and conscientious pharmacist will be forced either to follow suit or to go out of business. [It] is further claimed that advertising will lead people to shop for their prescription drugs among the various pharmacists who offer the lowest prices, and the loss of stable pharmacist-customer relationships will make individual [attention] impossible. Finally, it is argued that damage will be done to the professional image of the pharmacist. This image, that of a skilled and specialized craftsman, attracts talent to the profession and reinforces the better habits of those who are in [it].

The strength of these proffered justifications is greatly undermined by the fact that high professional standards, to a substantial extent, are guaranteed by the close regulation to which pharmacists in Virginia are subject. [At] the same time, we cannot discount the Board's justifications entirely. The Court regarded justifications of this type sufficient to sustain the advertising bans challenged on due process and equal protection [grounds].[c]

The challenge now made, however, is based on the First Amendment. This casts the Board's justifications in a different light, for on close inspection it is seen that the State's protectiveness of its citizens rests in large measure on the advantages of their being kept in ignorance. The advertising ban does not directly affect professional standards one way or the other. It affects them only

---

c. The Court referred here to cases upholding bans on advertising prices for eyeglass frames and optometrist and dental services.

through the reactions it is assumed people will have to the free flow of drug price information. There is no claim that the advertising ban in any way prevents the cutting of corners by the pharmacist who is so inclined. That pharmacist is likely to cut corners in any event. The only effect the advertising ban has on him is to insulate him from price competition and to open the way for him to make a substantial, and perhaps even excessive, profit in addition to providing an inferior service. The more painstaking pharmacist is also protected but, again, it is a protection based in large part on public ignorance.

It appears to be feared that if the pharmacist who wishes to provide low cost, and assertedly low quality, services is permitted to advertise, he will be taken up on his offer by too many unwitting customers. They will choose the low-cost, low-quality service and drive the "professional" pharmacist out of business. [They] will go from one pharmacist to another, following the discount, and destroy the pharmacist-customer relationship. They will lose respect for the profession because it advertises. All this is not in their best interests, and all this can be avoided if they are not permitted to know who is charging what.

[A]n alternative to this highly paternalistic approach [is] to assume that this information is not in itself harmful, that people will perceive their own best interests if only they are well enough informed, and that the best means to that end is to open the channels of communication rather than to close them. If they are truly open, nothing prevents the "professional" pharmacist from marketing his own assertedly superior product, and contrasting it with that of the low-cost, high-volume prescription drug retailer. But the choice among these alternative approaches is not ours to make or the Virginia General Assembly's. It is precisely this kind of choice, between the dangers of suppressing information, and the dangers of its misuse if it is freely available, that the First Amendment makes for [us].

VI. In concluding that commercial speech, like other varieties, is protected, we of course do not hold that it can never be regulated in any way. Some forms of commercial speech regulation are surely permissible. We mention a few. [There] is no claim, for example, that the prohibition on prescription drug price advertising is a mere time, place, and manner restriction. We have often approved restrictions of that kind provided that they are justified without reference to the content of the regulated speech, that they serve a significant governmental interest, and that in so doing they leave open ample alternative channels for communication of the information. Whatever may be the proper bounds of time, place, and manner restrictions on commercial speech, they are plainly exceeded by this Virginia statute, which singles out speech of a particular content and seeks to prevent its dissemination completely.

Nor is there any claim that prescription drug price advertisements are forbidden because they are false or misleading in any way. Untruthful speech, commercial or otherwise, has never been protected for its own sake. *Gertz.* Obviously much commercial speech is not provably false, or even wholly false, but only deceptive or misleading. We foresee no obstacle to a State's dealing effectively with this problem.[24] The First Amendment, as we construe it today,

---

24. [C]ommonsense differences between speech that does "no more than propose a commercial transaction," *Pittsburgh Press* [p. 483 infra,] and other varieties [suggest] that a different degree of protection is necessary to insure that the flow of truthful and legitimate commercial information is unimpaired. The truth of commercial speech, for example, may be more easily verifiable by its disseminator than, let us say, news reporting or political commentary, in that ordinarily the advertiser seeks to disseminate information about a specific product or service that he himself provides and presumably knows more about than anyone else. Also, commercial speech may be more durable than other kinds. Since adverdoes not prohibit the State from insuring that the stream of commercial information flows cleanly as well as freely.

Also, there is no claim that the transactions proposed in the forbidden advertisements are themselves illegal in any way. Finally, the special problems of the electronic broadcast media are likewise not in this case.

What is at issue is whether a State may completely suppress the dissemination of concededly truthful information about entirely lawful activity, fearful of that information's effect upon its disseminators and its recipients. Reserving other questions,[25] we conclude that the answer to this one is in the negative.

* * *

MR. JUSTICE STEWART, concurring.[d]

[I] write separately to explain why I think today's decision does not preclude [governmental regulation of false or deceptive advertising]. The Court has on several occasions addressed the problems posed by false statements of fact in libel cases. [Factual] errors are inevitable in free debate, and the imposition of liability for [such errors] can "dampe[n] the vigor and limi[t] the variety of public debate" by inducing "self-censorship." [In] contrast to the press, which must often attempt to assemble the true facts from sketchy and sometimes conflicting sources under the pressure of publication deadlines, the commercial advertiser generally knows the product or service he seeks to sell and is in a position to verify the accuracy of his factual representations before he disseminates them. The advertiser's access to the truth about his product and its price substantially eliminates any danger that governmental regulation of false or misleading price or product advertising will chill accurate and nondeceptive commercial [expression].

Since the factual claims contained in commercial price or product advertisements relate to tangible goods or services, they may be tested empirically and corrected to reflect the truth without in any manner jeopardizing the free dissemination of thought. Indeed, the elimination of false and deceptive claims serves to promote the one facet of commercial price and product advertising that warrants First Amendment protection—its contribution to the flow of accurate and reliable information relevant to public and private decisionmaking.

MR. JUSTICE REHNQUIST, dissenting.

[Under] the Court's opinion the way will be open not only for dissemination of price information but for active promotion of prescription drugs, liquor, cigarettes and other products the use of which it has previously been thought desirable to discourage. Now, however, such promotion is protected by the First

---

tising is the sine qua non of commercial profits, there is little likelihood of its being chilled by proper regulation and foregone entirely.

Attributes such as these, the greater objectivity and hardiness of commercial speech, may make it less necessary to tolerate inaccurate statements for fear of silencing the speaker. They may also make it appropriate to require that a commercial message appear in such a form, or include such additional information, warnings and disclaimers, as are necessary to prevent its being deceptive. They may also make inapplicable the prohibition on prior restraints. Compare *New York Times v. United States* [p. 488 infra] with *Donaldson v. Read Magazine*, 333 U.S. 178, 68 S.Ct. 591, 92 L.Ed. 628 (1948).

25. We stress that we have considered in this case the regulation of commercial advertising by pharmacists. Although we express no opinion as to other professions, the distinctions, historical and functional, between professions, may require consideration of quite different factors. Physicians and lawyers, for example, do not dispense standardized products; they render professional *services* of almost infinite variety and nature, with the consequent enhanced possibility for confusion and deception if they were to undertake certain kinds of advertising.

d. Burger, C.J., separately concurring, stressed the reservation in fn. 25 of the opinion with respect to advertising by attorneys and physicians. Stevens, J., took no part.

Amendment so long as it is not misleading or does not promote an illegal product or [enterprise].

The Court speaks of the consumer's interest in the free flow of commercial information. [This] should presumptively be the concern of the Virginia Legislature, which sits to balance [this] and other claims in the process of making laws such as the one here under attack. The Court speaks of the importance in a "predominantly free enterprise economy" of intelligent and well-informed decisions as to allocation of resources. While there is again much to be said for the Court's observation as a matter of desirable public policy, there is certainly nothing in the United States Constitution which requires the Virginia Legislature to hew to the teachings of Adam Smith in its legislative decisions regulating the pharmacy profession. E.g., *Nebbia v. New York; Olsen v. Nebraska* [Ch. 2, Sec. 3].

[There] are undoubted difficulties with an effort to draw a bright line between "commercial speech" on the one hand and "protected speech" on the other, and the Court does better to face up to these difficulties than to attempt to hide them under labels. In this case, however, the Court has unfortunately substituted for the wavering line previously thought to exist between commercial speech and protected speech a no more satisfactory line of its own—that between "truthful" commercial speech, on the one hand, and that which is "false and misleading" on the other. The difficulty with this line is not that it wavers, but on the contrary that it is simply too Procrustean to take into account the congeries of factors which I believe could, quite consistently with the First and Fourteenth Amendments, properly influence a legislative decision with respect to commercial advertising.

[S]uch a line simply makes no allowance whatever for what appears to have been a considered legislative judgment in most States that while prescription drugs are a necessary and vital part of medical care and treatment, there are sufficient dangers attending their widespread use that they simply may not be promoted in the same manner as hair creams, deodorants, and toothpaste. The very real dangers that general advertising for such drugs might create in terms of encouraging, even though not sanctioning, illicit use of them by individuals for whom they have not been prescribed, or by generating patient pressure upon physicians to prescribe them are simply not dealt with in the Court's opinion.

* * *

Notes and Questions

1. As compared to political decisionmaking, is commercial advertising "neither more nor less significant than a host of other market activities that legislatures concededly may regulate."? Is there an "absence of any principled distinction between commercial soliciting and other aspects of economic activity"? Has economic due process been "resurrected, clothed in the ill-fitting garb of the first amendment"? See Jackson & Jeffries, *Commercial Speech: Economic Due Process and the First Amendment*, 65 Va.L.Rev. 1, 18 and 30 (1979). Why may government "be paternalistic regarding the purchase of goods but may not be paternalistic regarding information about those goods"? Alexander, *Speech in the Local Marketplace: Implications of Virginia State Board of Pharmacy v. Virginia Citizens Consumer Council, Inc. for Local Regulatory Power*, 14 San Diego L.Rev. 357, 376 (1977).

2. Footnote 24 suggests that *deceptive* commercial speech may be regulated in ways that would be barred if the speech were political. Sound distinction?

(a) *"Commonsense" differences between commercial speech and other speech.*
(1) *Verifiability.* Consider Farber, *Commercial Speech and First Amendment Theory,* 74 Nw.U.L.Rev. 372, 385–86 (1979): "[C]ommercial speech is not necessarily more verifiable than other speech. There may well be uncertainty about some quality of a product, such as the health effect of eggs * * *. On the other hand, political speech is often quite verifiable by the speaker. A political candidate knows the truth about his own past and his present intentions, yet misrepresentations on these subjects are immune from state regulation."
(2) *Durability.* Consider Redish, *The Value of Free Speech,* 130 U.Pa.L.Rev. 591, 633 (1982): "[I]t is also incorrect to distinguish commercial from political expression on the ground that the former is somehow hardier because of the inherent profit motive. It could just as easily be said that we need not fear that commercial magazines and newspapers will cease publication for fear of governmental regulation, because they are in business for profit. Of course, the proper response to this contention is that our concern is not *whether* they will publish, but *what* they will publish: fear of regulation might deter them from dealing with controversial subjects."

(b) *Commercial speech and self-expression.* Is commercial speech distinguishable from political speech because it is unrelated to self-expression? Consider Baker, *Commercial Speech: A Problem in the Theory of Freedom,* 62 Iowa L.Rev. 1, 17 (1976): In commercial speech, the dissemination of the profit motive "breaks the connection between speech and any vision, or attitude, or value of the individual or group engaged in advocacy. Thus the content and form of commercial speech cannot be attributed to individual value allegiances." For criticism, see, e.g., Schlag, *An Attack on Categorical Approaches to Freedom of Speech,* 30 U.C.L.A.L.Rev. 671, 710–21 (1983); Shiffrin, *The First Amendment and Economic Regulation: Away From A General Theory of the First Amendment,* 78 Nw.U.L.Rev. 1212 (1983).

(c) *Contract approach to commercial speech.* Is commercial advertising distinguishable from other forms of speech because of the state interest in regulating contracts? Consider Farber, supra, at 389: "[C]ommercial speech is [more] akin to conduct than are other forms of speech. The unique aspect of commercial speech is that it is a prelude to, and therefore becomes integrated into, a contract, the essence of which is the presence of a promise. Because a promise is an undertaking to ensure that a certain state of affairs takes place, promises obviously have a closer connection with conduct than with self-expression. Second, this approach focuses on the distinctive and powerful state interests implicated by the process of contract formation. In a fundamentally market economy, the government understandably is given particular deference in its enforcement of contractual expectations. Indeed, the Constitution itself gives special protection to contractual expectations in the contract clause. Finally, this approach connects a rather nebulous area of first amendment law with the commonplaces of contract law of which every lawyer has knowledge. Obviously, the technicalities of contract law, with its doctrines of privity, consideration, and the like, should not be blindly translated into first amendment jurisprudence. The basic doctrines of contract law, however, provide a helpful guide in considering commercial speech problems." For discussion, see Alexander & Farber, *Commercial Speech and First Amendment Theory: A Critical Exchange,* 75 Nw.U.L.Rev. 307 (1980).

3. *Limits on regulation of deceptive advertising. Bates v. State Bar,* 433 U.S. 350, 97 S.Ct. 2691, 53 L.Ed.2d 810 (1977), struck down an Arizona Supreme Court rule against a lawyer "publicizing himself" through advertising. It

rejected the claim that attorney price advertising was inherently misleading, but left open the "peculiar problems" associated with advertising claims regarding the quality of legal services.[e] Could a lawyer truthfully advertise that he or she has (1) tried twice as many personal injury cases as any other lawyer in the country? (2) averaged $10,000 more in recoveries per case than any other lawyer in the county? (3) graduated from Harvard Law School in the upper 10% of the class? (4) received "the best legal education this country offers"? Should an advertisement be protected if it is "sufficiently factual to be subject to verification" even if "implications of quality might be drawn from it"? See Canby and Gellhorn, *Physician Advertising: The First Amendment and the Sherman Act,* 1978 Duke L.J. 543, 560–62. Should the Court have deferred to the judgment of the State Bar of Arizona? If not, should it defer to the SEC when it regulates the advertising of securities? The FTC when it regulates automobile advertising? The Virginia Board of Pharmacy when it regulates quality advertising by pharmacists? For deferential treatment of a state ban on the use of tradenames by optometrists, see *Friedman v. Rogers,* 440 U.S. 1, 99 S.Ct. 887, 59 L.Ed.2d 100 (1979).

4. *Truth and commercial advertising.* Should Mercedes Benz be able to truthfully advertise that Frank Sinatra drives its car without getting Sinatra's permission? See Liebeler, *A Property Rights Approach to Judicial Decision Making,* 4 Cato J. 783, 802–03 (1985); Shiffrin, supra note 2, at 1257–58 n. 275; Treece, *Commercial Exploitation of Names, Likenesses, and Personal Histories,* 51 Tex.L.Rev. 637 (1973). Should the state be able to prevent homeowners from posting "for sale" signs in order to prevent panic selling in order to maintain an integrated neighborhood? See *Linmark Associates, Inc., v. Willingboro,* 431 U.S. 85, 97 S.Ct. 1614, 52 L.Ed.2d 155 (1977). May a state regulate the content of contraceptive advertising in order to minimize its offensive character? Cf. *Carey v. Population Services Int'l.* (1977), p. 139 supra (total ban on contraceptive advertising unconstitutional).

———

OHRALIK v. OHIO STATE BAR ASS'N, 436 U.S. 447, 98 S.Ct. 1912, 56 L.Ed.2d 444 (1978) upheld the indefinite suspension of an attorney for violating the anti-solicitation provisions of the Ohio Code of Professional Responsibility. Those provisions generally do not allow lawyers to recommend themselves to anyone who has not sought "their advice regarding employment of a lawyer." Albert Ohralik had approached two young accident victims to solicit employment—Carol McClintock in a hospital room where she lay in traction and Wanda Lou Holbert on the day she came home from the hospital. He employed a concealed tape recorder with Holbert, apparently to insure he would have evidence of her assent to his representation. The next day, when Holbert's mother informed Ohralik that she and her daughter did not want to have

———

e. *Zauderer v. Office of Disciplinary Counsel,* p. 634 infra, held that a state may not discipline attorneys who solicit legal business through newspaper advertisements containing "truthful and nondeceptive information and advice regarding the legal rights of potential clients" or for the advertising use of "accurate and nondeceptive" illustrations. Zauderer had placed illustrated ads in 36 Ohio newspapers publicizing his availability to represent women who had suffered injuries from use of a contraceptive device known as the Dalkon Shield Intrauterine Device. In the ad Zauderer stated that he had represented other women in Dalkon Shield litigation. The Court observed that accurate statements of fact cannot be proscribed "merely because it is possible that some readers will infer that he has some expertise in those areas." But it continued to "leave open the possibility that States may prevent attorneys from making non-verifiable claims regarding the quality of their services. *Bates.*"

appellant represent them, he insisted that the daughter had entered into a binding agreement. McClintock also discharged Ohralik, and Ohralik sued her for breach of contract. The Court ruled, per POWELL, J., that a state may forbid in-person solicitation of clients by lawyers for pecuniary gain:

"Expression concerning purely commercial transactions has come within the ambit of the Amendment's protection only recently. In rejecting the notion that such speech is wholly outside the protection of the First Amendment, *Virginia Pharmacy,* we were careful not to hold that it is wholly undifferentiable from other forms of speech.

"We have not discarded the common sense distinction between speech proposing a commercial transaction, which occurs in an area traditionally subject to government regulation, and other varieties of speech. To require a parity of constitutional protection for commercial and noncommercial speech alike could invite dilution, simply by a leveling process, of the force of the Amendment's guarantee with respect to the latter kind of speech. Rather than subject the First Amendment to such a devitalization, we instead have afforded commercial speech a limited measure of protection, commensurate with its subordinate position in the scale of First Amendment values, while allowing modes of regulation that might be impermissible in the realm of noncommercial expression.

"Moreover, 'it has never been deemed an abridgment of freedom of speech or press to make a course of conduct illegal merely because the conduct was in part initiated, evidenced, or carried out by means of language, either spoken, written, or printed.' *Giboney v. Empire Storage & Ice Co.,* 336 U.S. 490, 502, 69 S.Ct. 684, 691, 93 L.Ed. 834 (1949). Numerous examples could be cited of communications that are regulated without offending the First Amendment, such as the exchange of information about securities, *SEC v. Texas Gulf Sulphur Co.,* 401 F.2d 833 (CA2 1968), cert. denied, 394 U.S. 976, 89 S.Ct. 1454, 22 L.Ed.2d 756 (1969), corporate proxy statements, *Mills v. Electric Auto-Lite Co.,* 396 U.S. 375, 90 S.Ct. 616, 24 L.Ed.2d 593 (1970), the exchange of price and production information among competitors, *American Column & Lumber Co. v. United States,* 257 U.S. 377, 42 S.Ct. 114, 66 L.Ed. 284 (1921), and employers' threats of retaliation for the labor activities of employees, *NLRB v. Gissel Packing Co.,* 395 U.S. 575, 618, 89 S.Ct. 1918, 1942, 23 L.Ed.2d 547 (1969). Each of these examples illustrates that the State does not lose its power to regulate commercial activity deemed harmful to the public whenever speech is a component of that activity. Neither *Virginia Pharmacy* nor *Bates* purported to cast doubt on the permissibility of these kinds of commercial regulation.

"In-person solicitation by a lawyer of remunerative employment is a business transaction in which speech is an essential but subordinate component. While this does not remove the speech from the protection of the First Amendment, as was held in *Bates* and *Virginia Pharmacy,* it lowers the level of appropriate judicial scrutiny. [A] lawyer's procurement of remunerative employment is a subject only marginally affected with First Amendment concerns. It falls within the State's proper sphere of economic and professional regulation. While entitled to some constitutional protection, appellant's conduct is subject to regulation in furtherance of important state [interests].

" 'The interest of the States in regulating lawyers is especially great since lawyers are essential to the primary function of administering justice and have historically been officers of the courts' [and] act 'as trusted agents of their clients and as assistants to the court in search of a just solution to disputes.'

"[The] substantive evils of solicitation have been stated over the years in sweeping terms: stirring up litigation, assertion of fraudulent claims, debasing the legal profession, and potential harm to the solicited client in the form of overreaching, overcharging, underrepresentation, and misrepresentation." In providing information about the availability and terms of proposed legal services "in-person solicitation serves much the same function as the advertisement at issue in *Bates*. But there are significant differences as well. Unlike a public advertisement, which simply provides information and leaves the recipient free to act upon it or not, in-person solicitation may exert pressure and often demands an immediate response, without providing an opportunity for comparison or reflection. The aim and effect of in-person solicitation may be to provide a one-sided presentation and to encourage speedy and perhaps uninformed decisionmaking; there is no opportunity for intervention or counter-education by agencies of the Bar, supervisory authorities, or persons close to the solicited individual. The admonition that 'the fitting remedy for evil counsels is good ones' is of little value when the circumstances provide no opportunity for any remedy at all. In-person solicitation is as likely as not to discourage persons needing counsel from engaging in a critical comparison of the 'availability, nature, and prices' of legal services; it actually may disserve the individual and societal interest, identified in *Bates*, in facilitating 'informed and reliable decisionmaking.'

"[Appellant's argument that none of the evils of solicitation were found in his case] misconceives the nature of the State's interest. The rules prohibiting solicitation are prophylactic measures whose objective is the prevention of harm before it occurs. The rules were applied in this case to discipline a lawyer for soliciting employment for pecuniary gain under circumstances likely to result in the adverse consequences the State seeks to avert. In such a situation, which is inherently conducive to overreaching and other forms of misconduct, the State has a strong interest in adopting and enforcing rules of conduct designed to protect the public from harmful solicitation by lawyers whom it has [licensed].

"The efficacy of the State's effort to prevent such harm to prospective clients would be substantially diminished if, having proved a solicitation in circumstances like those of this case, the State were required in addition to prove actual injury. Unlike the advertising in *Bates*, in-person solicitation is not visible or otherwise open to public scrutiny. Often there is no witness other than the lawyer and the lay person whom he has solicited, rendering it difficult or impossible to obtain reliable proof of what actually took place. This would be especially true if the lay person were so distressed at the time of the solicitation that he or she could not recall specific details at a later date. If appellant's view were sustained, in-person solicitation would be virtually immune to effective oversight and regulation by the State or by the legal profession, in contravention of the State's strong interest in regulating members of the Bar in an effective, objective, and self-enforcing manner. It therefore is not unreasonable, or violative of the Constitution, for a State to respond with what in effect is a prophylactic rule." [a]

a. Marshall and Rehnquist, JJ., each separately concurred in the judgment. Brennan, J., did not participate.

Notes and Questions

1. *Companion case.* IN RE PRIMUS, 436 U.S. 412, 98 S.Ct. 1893, 56 L.Ed. 2d 417 (1978), per POWELL, J., held that a state could not constitutionally discipline an ACLU "cooperating lawyer" who, after advising a gathering of allegedly illegally sterilized women of their rights, initiated further contact with one of the women by writing her a letter informing her of the ACLU's willingness to provide free legal representation for women in her situation and of the organization's desire to file a lawsuit on her behalf. "South Carolina's action in punishing appellant for soliciting a prospective litigant by mail, on behalf of ACLU, must withstand the 'exacting scrutiny applicable to limitations on core First Amendment rights.' [Where] political expression or association is at issue, this Court has not tolerated the degree of imprecision that often characterizes government regulation of the conduct of commercial affairs. The approach we adopt today in *Ohralik* that the State may proscribe in-person solicitation for pecuniary gain under circumstances likely to result in adverse consequences, cannot be applied to appellant's activity on behalf of the ACLU. Although a showing of potential danger may suffice in the former context, appellant may not be disciplined unless her activity in fact involved the type of misconduct at which South Carolina's broad prohibition is said to be directed. The record does not support appellee's contention that undue influence, overreaching, misrepresentation, or invasion of privacy actually occurred in this case."

2. *A hierarchy of protected speech.* Consider Shiffrin, supra, at 1218 & 1220–21 (1983). In *Virginia Pharmacy*, "the Court never admitted that commercial speech was less valuable than political speech. The 'commonsense differences' had nothing to do with value. [Although] Justice Blackmun labored to defend the asserted equal relationship between commercial speech and political speech for the *Virginia Pharmacy* majority, Justice Powell in *Ohralik* was content to lead the Court to an opposite position without explanation. In so doing, Justice Powell steered the Court to accept a hierarchy of protected speech for the first time, despite his own stated opposition [in *Young*] to creating any such hierarchy." Does the concern that the protection of non-commercial speech would be subject to dilution if it were placed on a par with commercial speech presuppose an unexplained difference between the two types of speech? See id. at 1221 n. 59.

CENTRAL HUDSON GAS & ELEC. CORP. v. PUBLIC SERVICE COMM'N, 447 U.S. 557, 100 S.Ct. 2343, 65 L.Ed.2d 341 (1980), per POWELL, J., invalidated a Commission regulation that, in an effort to conserve power, prohibited promotional advertising by an electric utility except for encouraging shifts of consumption from peak demand times: "The Commission's order restricts only commercial speech, that is, expression related solely to the economic interests of the speaker and its audience. [In] commercial speech cases, [a] four-part analysis has developed. At the outset, we must determine whether the expression is protected by the First Amendment. For commercial speech to come within that provision, it at least must concern lawful activity [a] and not be misleading. Next,

a. *Pittsburgh Press Co. v. Human Relations Comm'n*, p. 483 infra, upheld an order forbidding publication of sex-designated help-wanted columns as a forbidden "aid" to prohibited sex discrimination in employment: "Discrimination in employment is *illegal* commercial activity under the ordinance. We have no doubt that a newspaper constitutionally could be forbidden to publish a want-ad proposing a sale of narcotics or soliciting prostitutes."

we ask whether the asserted governmental interest is substantial. If both inquiries yield positive answers, we must determine whether the regulation directly advances the governmental interest asserted, and whether it is not more extensive than is necessary to serve that interest.[b]

"[T]he State's interest in energy conservation is directly advanced by the Commission order at issue here. There is an immediate connection between advertising and the demand for electricity. [Thus], we find a direct link between the state interest in conservation and the Commission's order.

"[T]he critical inquiry [is] whether the Commission's complete suppression of speech ordinarily protected by the First Amendment is no more extensive than necessary to further the State's interest in energy conservation. The Commission's order reaches all promotional advertising, regardless of the impact of the touted service on overall energy use. But the energy conservation rationale, as important as it is, cannot justify suppressing information about electric devices or services that would cause no net increase in total energy use. In addition, no showing has been made that a more limited restriction on the content of promotional advertising would not serve adequately the State's interests.

"Appellant insists that but for the ban, it would advertise products and services that use energy efficiently. These include the 'heat pump,' which both parties acknowledge to be a major improvement in electric heating, and the use of electric heat as a 'back-up' to solar and other heat sources. Although the Commission has questioned the efficiency of electric heating before this Court, neither the Commission's Policy Statement nor its order denying rehearing made findings on this issue. In the absence of authoritative findings to the contrary, we must credit as within the realm of possibility the claim that electric heat can be an efficient alternative in some circumstances.

"The Commission's order prevents appellant from promoting electric services that would reduce energy use by diverting demand from less efficient sources, or that would consume roughly the same amount of energy as do alternative sources. In neither situation would the utility's advertising endanger conservation or mislead the public. To the extent that the Commission's order suppresses speech that in no way impairs the State's interest in energy conservation, the Commission's order violates the First and Fourteenth Amendments and must be invalidated.

"The Commission also has not demonstrated that its interest in conservation cannot be protected adequately by more limited regulation of appellant's commercial expression. To further its policy of conservation, the Commission could attempt to restrict the format and content of Central Hudson's advertising. It might, for example, require that the advertisements include information about the relative efficiency and expense of the offered service, both under current conditions and for the foreseeable future.[13] In the absence of a showing that

---

b. In an earlier footnote, the Court emphasized that this requirement was "not an application of the 'overbreadth' doctrine. The latter theory permits the invalidation of regulations on First Amendment grounds even when the litigant challenging the regulation has engaged in no constitutionally protected activity. [In] this case, the Commission's prohibition acts directly against the promotional activities of Central Hudson, and to the extent the limitations are unnecessary to serve the state's interest, they are invalid."

For a different perspective on the overbreadth doctrine, see Redish, *The Warren Court, The Burger Court and the First Amendment Overbreadth Doctrine*, 78 Nw.U.L.Rev. 1031 (1983).

13. The Commission also might consider a system of previewing advertising campaigns to insure that they will not defeat conservation policy. It has instituted such a program for approving "informational" advertising under the Policy Statement challenged in this case. We have observed that commercial speech is more limited speech regulation would be ineffective, we cannot approve the complete suppression of Central Hudson's advertising."

BLACKMUN, J., joined by Brennan, J., concurring in the judgment, saw in the Court's "four-part analysis" approval of "an intermediate level of scrutiny" whenever a restraint on commercial speech " 'directly advance[s]' a 'substantial' governmental interest and is 'not more extensive than is necessary to serve that interest.' I agree with the Court that this level of intermediate scrutiny is appropriate for a restraint on commercial speech designed to protect consumers from misleading or coercive speech, or a regulation related to the time, place, or manner of commercial speech. I do not agree, however, that the Court's four-part test is the proper one to be applied when a State seeks to suppress information about a product in order to manipulate a private economic decision that the State cannot or has not regulated or outlawed directly.

"Since the Court, without citing empirical data or other authority, finds a 'direct link' between advertising and energy consumption, it leaves open the possibility that the State may suppress advertising of electricity in order to lessen demand for electricity. I, of course, agree with the Court that, in today's world, energy conservation is a goal of paramount national and local importance. I disagree with the Court, however, when it says that suppression of speech may be a permissible means to achieve that goal. * * *

"The Court recognizes that we have never held that commercial speech may be suppressed in order to further the State's interest in discouraging purchases of the underlying product that is advertised. Permissible restraints on commercial speech have been limited to measures designed to protect consumers from fraudulent, misleading, or coercive sales techniques. Those designed to deprive consumers of information about products or services that are legally offered for sale consistently have been invalidated.

"I seriously doubt whether suppression of information concerning the availability and price of a legally offered product is ever a permissible way for the State to 'dampen' demand for or use of the product. Even though 'commercial' speech is involved, such a regulatory measure strikes at the heart of the First Amendment. This is because it is a covert attempt by the State to manipulate the choices of its citizens, not by persuasion or direct regulation, but by depriving the public of the information needed to make a free choice. As the Court recognizes, the State's policy choices are insulated from the visibility and scrutiny that direct regulation would entail and the conduct of citizens is molded by the information that government chooses to give [them].

"If the First Amendment guarantee means anything, it means that, absent clear and present danger, government has no power to restrict expression because of the effect its message is likely to have on the public. See generally Comment, *First Amendment Protection for Commercial Advertising: The New Constitutional Doctrine*, 44 U.Chi.L.Rev. 205, 243–51 (1976). Our cases indicate that this guarantee applies even to commercial speech."

The opinion quoted from *Virginia Pharmacy, Linmark,* and *Carey,* noting that "*Linmark* resolved beyond all doubt that a strict standard of review applies to suppression of commercial information, where the purpose of the restraint is to influence behavior by depriving citizens of information," and that *Carey* "also

such a sturdy brand of expression that traditional prior restraint doctrine may not apply to it. *Virginia Pharmacy.* And in other areas of speech regulation, such as obscenity, we have recognized that a prescreening arrangement can pass constitutional muster if it includes adequate procedural safeguards.

applied to content-based restraints on commercial speech the same standard of review we have applied to other varieties of speech. * * *

"Our prior references to the 'commonsense differences' between commercial speech and other speech 'suggest that a different degree of protection is necessary to insure that the flow of truthful and legitimate commercial information is unimpaired.' *Linmark*. We have not suggested that the 'commonsense differences' between commercial speech and other speech justify relaxed scrutiny of restraints that suppress truthful, nondeceptive, noncoercive commercial [speech].

"It appears that the Court would permit the State to ban all direct advertising of air conditioning, assuming that a more limited restriction on such advertising would not effectively deter the public from cooling its homes. In my view, our cases do not support this type of suppression. If a governmental unit believes that use or over-use of air conditioning is a serious problem, it must attack that problem directly, by prohibiting air conditioning or regulating thermostat levels."

STEVENS, J., joined by Brennan, J., also concurred: "Because 'commercial speech' is afforded less constitutional protection than other forms of speech, it is important that the commercial speech concept not be defined too broadly lest speech deserving of greater constitutional protection be inadvertently suppressed. The issue in this case is whether New York's prohibition on the promotion of the use of electricity through advertising is a ban on nothing but commercial [speech].

"This case involves a governmental regulation that completely bans promotional advertising by an electric utility. This ban encompasses a great deal more than mere proposals to engage in certain kinds of commercial transactions. It prohibits all advocacy of the immediate or future use of electricity. It curtails expression by an informed and interested group of persons of their point of view on questions relating to the production and consumption of electrical energy— questions frequently discussed and debated by our political leaders. For example, an electric company's advocacy of the use of electric heat for environmental reasons, as opposed to wood-burning stoves, would seem to fall squarely within New York's promotional advertising ban and also within the bounds of maximum First Amendment protection. The breadth of the ban thus exceeds the boundaries of the commercial speech concept, however that concept may be defined.

"The justification for the regulation is nothing more than the expressed fear that the audience may find the utility's message persuasive. Without the aid of any coercion, deception, or misinformation, truthful communication may persuade some citizens to consume more electricity than they otherwise would. I assume that such a consequence would be undesirable and that government may therefore prohibit and punish the unnecessary or excessive use of electricity. But if the perceived harm associated with greater electrical usage is not sufficiently serious to justify direct regulation, surely it does not constitute the kind of clear and present danger that can justify the suppression of speech. * * *

"In sum, I concur in the result because I do not consider this to be a 'commercial speech' case. Accordingly, I see no need to decide whether the Court's four-part analysis adequately protects commercial speech—as properly defined—in the face of a blanket ban of the sort involved in this case."

REHNQUIST, J., dissented in a long opinion, summarized in his introduction: "The Court's analysis in my view is wrong in several respects. Initially, I disagree with the Court's conclusion that the speech of a state-created monopoly, which is the subject of a comprehensive regulatory scheme, is entitled to protection under the First Amendment. I also think that the Court errs here in failing to recognize that the state law is most accurately viewed as an economic regulation and that the speech involved (if it falls within the scope of the First Amendment at all) occupies a significantly more subordinate position in the hierarchy of First Amendment values than the Court gives it today. Finally, the Court in reaching its decision improperly substitutes its own judgment for that of the State in deciding how a proper ban on promotional advertising should be drafted. With regard to this latter point, the Court adopts as its final part of a four-part test a 'no more extensive than necessary' analysis that will unduly impair a state legislature's ability to adopt legislation reasonably designed to promote interests that have always been rightly thought to be of great importance to the State."

In commenting on the Court's four part test, Rehnquist, J., stated: "The [test] elevates the protection accorded commercial speech that falls within the scope of the First Amendment to a level that is virtually indistinguishable from that of noncommercial speech. I think the Court in so doing has effectively accomplished the 'devitalization' of the First Amendment that it counseled against in *Ohralik*. I think it has also by labeling economic regulation of business conduct as a restraint on 'free speech' gone far to resurrect the discredited doctrine of cases such as *Lochner*. New York's order here is in my view more akin to an economic regulation to which virtually complete deference should be accorded by this Court.

"I doubt there would be any question as to the constitutionality of New York's conservation effort if the Public Service Commission had chosen to raise the price of electricity, to condition its sale on specified terms, or to restrict its production. In terms of constitutional values, I think that such controls are virtually indistinguishable from the State's ban on promotional advertising."

Notes and Questions

1. *The four part test.* Is Rehnquist, J., correct in stating that the Court's test "elevates the protection of commercial speech to a level that is virtually indistinguishable from that of noncommercial speech"? Is it possible to state "the" test that has been applied to noncommercial speech?

2. *Paternalism and Central Hudson.* Consider Blasi, *The Pathological Perspective and the First Amendment*, 85 Colum.L.Rev. 449, 487 (1985): "[T]he claim of the regulators in the drug and lawyer advertising cases was that consumers would be influenced by the advertising to act against their own self-interest; in the promotional advertising case, the fear was that consumers would act against the public interest in pursuit of their own short range self-interest. The rationale in the first type of case is more paternalistic because it necessarily assumes that listeners cannot evaluate the message even when they have every incentive to try to do so. The rationale in the promotional advertising case is consistent with respect for the message-screening capacities of listeners; what the rationale doubts is the capacity of listeners to behave as public-spirited citizens when prompted to act selfishly by sophisticated advertising techniques."

3. *Defining commercial speech.* In what sense was the speech in *Central Hudson* solely in the economic interests of speaker and audience? [c] Should the

c. Is this category intended to be larger than the category of proposing a commercial transaction? Consider the question in connection with *Greenmoss*, p. 465 infra.

Court decide on an ad hoc basis which advertisements have political impact and which do not? In addressing this question, *Central Hudson,* noted that any product could be tied to public concerns and that since companies are otherwise free to speak about public issues,[d] "there is no reason for providing similar protection when such statements are made only in the context of commercial transactions." Compare *Bolger v. Youngs Drug Products Corp.,* 463 U.S. 60, 103 S.Ct. 2875, 77 L.Ed.2d 469 (1983) ("advertisers should not be permitted to immunize false or misleading product information from government regulation simply by including references to public issues"). If a cigarette company buys space in the *New York Times* to print a deceptive message about health and cigarettes, under what circumstances would the communication be properly characterized as commercial speech? Consider Tribe, *Constitutional Choices* 218 (1985): "The distinction between commercial and noncommercial speech [exemplifies] a propensity for pigeonholing as a method for deciding First Amendment questions. Such a method masks the essentially political nature of the underlying issues by pretending to cabin judicial discretion within the limits established by the category itself." Does this sort of pigeonholing "pars[e] First Amendment doctrine too fine"? Does it "endange[r] the pigeon?" See id.

C. PRIVATE SPEECH

When District Attorney Connick proposed to transfer Assistant D.A. Myers to a different section of the criminal court, she strongly opposed it. Shortly thereafter, Myers prepared and distributed to the other assistants a questionnaire concerning office transfer policy, office morale, the need for a grievance committee and two questions Connick particularly objected to—the level of confidence in various supervisors and whether employees felt pressured to work in political campaigns. Connick then told Myers that she was being terminated for refusal to accept the transfer and that he considered distribution of the questionnaire an act of insubordination. Myers filed suit under 42 U.S.C. § 1983, contending that she was wrongfully discharged because she had exercised her right of free speech. The district court agreed. It found that the questionnaire was the real reason for Myers' termination, and that the state had not "clearly demonstrated" that the survey "substantially interfered" with the operation of the District Attorney's office. The Fifth Circuit affirmed. But CONNICK v. MYERS, 461 U.S. 138, 103 S.Ct. 1684, 75 L.Ed.2d 708 (1983), per WHITE, J., held that respondent's discharge did not offend the first amendment:

"For most of this century, the unchallenged dogma was that a public employee had no right to object to conditions placed upon the terms of employment—including those which restricted the exercise of constitutional rights. The classic formulation of this position was Justice Holmes', who, when sitting on the Supreme Judicial Court of Massachusetts, observed: 'A policeman may have a constitutional right to talk politics, but he has no constitutional right to be a policeman.' *McAuliffe v. Mayor,* 155 Mass. 216, 220, 29 N.E. 517, 517 (1892). For many years, Holmes' epigram expressed this Court's law. *Adler v. Bd. of Educ.,* 342 U.S. 485, 72 S.Ct. 380, 96 L.Ed. 517 (1952); *Garner v. Bd. of Pub. Works,* 341 U.S. 716, 71 S.Ct. 909, 95 L.Ed. 1317 (1951)."

The Court proceeded, however, to recount a series of cases in which it had subsequently repudiated Holmes' epigram.[a] Indeed, for some two decades it had

---

d. See Sec. 10 infra.

a. Most of the cases involved the right of public employees to associate. See Sec. 9, II infra.

become wholly impermissible to deny freedom of expression "by the denial of or placing of conditions upon a benefit or a privilege." As the Court characterized the public employee cases, they were all rooted in the rights of public employees to participate in public affairs.[b] In particular, the Court focused upon *Pickering v. Bd. of Educ.*, 391 U.S. 563, 88 S.Ct. 1731, 20 L.Ed.2d 811 (1968): "In *Pickering*, we stated that a public employee does not relinquish First Amendment rights to comment on matters of public interest by virtue of government employment. [The] repeated emphasis in *Pickering* on the right of a public employee 'as a citizen, in commenting upon matters of public concern,' was not accidental. This language, reiterated in all of *Pickering's* progeny, reflects both the historical evolvement of the rights of public employees, and the common sense realization that government offices could not function if every employment decision became a constitutional matter.[5] * * *

"*Pickering* [held] impermissible under the First Amendment the dismissal of a high school teacher for openly criticizing the Board of Education on its allocation of school funds between athletics and education and its methods of informing taxpayers about the need for additional revenue. Pickering's subject was a matter of legitimate public concern upon which free and open debate is vital to informed decision-making by the electorate. [Most] recently, in *Givhan v. Western Line Cons. School Dist.*, 439 U.S. 410, 99 S.Ct. 693, 58 L.Ed.2d 619 (1979), we held that First Amendment protection applies when a public employee arranges to communicate privately with his employer rather than to express his views publicly. Although the subject-matter of Mrs. Givhan's statements were not the issue before the Court, it is clear that her statements concerning the school district's allegedly racially discriminatory policies involved a matter of public concern.

"*Pickering*, its antecedents and progeny, lead us to conclude that if Myers' questionnaire cannot be fairly characterized as constituting speech on a matter of public concern, it is unnecessary for us to scrutinize the reasons for her discharge. When employee expression cannot be fairly considered as relating to any matter of political, social, or other concern to the community, government officials should enjoy wide latitude in managing their offices, without intrusive oversight by the judiciary in the name of the First Amendment. * * * We do not suggest, however, that Myers' speech, even if not touching upon a matter of public concern, is totally beyond the protection of the First Amendment. * * * [We] in no sense suggest that speech on private matters falls into one of the narrow and well-defined classes of expression which carries so little social value, such as obscenity, that the state can prohibit and punish such expression by all persons in its jurisdiction. See *Chaplinsky; Roth; Ferber.* For example, an employee's false criticism of his employer on grounds not of public concern may be cause for his discharge but would be entitled to the same protection in a libel action accorded an identical statement made by a man on the street. We hold only that when a public employee speaks not as a citizen upon matters of public concern, but instead as an employee upon matters only of personal interest, absent the most unusual circumstances, a federal court is not the appropriate forum in which to review the wisdom of a personnel decision taken

b. But see *Letter Carriers*, p. 637 infra.

5. The question of whether expression is of a kind that is of legitimate concern to the public is also the standard in determining whether a common-law action for invasion of privacy is present. See Restatement (Second) of Torts, § 652D. See also *Cox Broadcasting Co. v. Cohn* (action for invasion of privacy cannot be maintained when the subject-matter of the publicity is matter of public record); *Time, Inc. v. Hill.*

by a public agency allegedly in reaction to the employee's behavior. Our responsibility is to ensure that citizens are not deprived of fundamental rights by virtue of working for the government; this does not require a grant of immunity for employee grievances not afforded by the First Amendment to those who do not work for the state.

"Whether an employee's speech addresses a matter of public concern must be determined by the content, form, and context of a given statement, as revealed by the whole record. In this case, with but one exception, the questions posed by Myers to her coworkers do not fall under the rubric of matters of 'public concern.' We view the questions pertaining to the confidence and trust that Myers' coworkers possess in various supervisors, the level of office morale, and the need for a grievance committee as mere extensions of Myers' dispute over her transfer to another section of the criminal court. * * * Indeed, the questionnaire, if released to the public, would convey no information at all other than the fact that a single employee is upset with the status quo. [T]he focus of Myers' questions is not to evaluate the performance of the office but rather to gather ammunition for another round of controversy with her superiors. These questions reflect one employee's dissatisfaction with a transfer and an attempt to turn that displeasure into a cause célèbre.[8] * * *

"One question in Myers' questionnaire, however, does touch upon a matter of public concern. Question 11 inquires if assistant district attorneys 'ever feel pressured to work in political campaigns on behalf of office supported candidates.' [This issue] is a matter of interest to the community upon which it is essential that public employees be able to speak out freely without fear of retaliatory dismissal.

"Because one of the questions in Myers' survey touched upon a matter of public concern, and contributed to her discharge we must determine whether Connick was justified in discharging Myers. Here the District Court again erred in imposing an unduly onerous burden on the state to justify Myers' discharge. The District Court viewed the issue of whether Myers' speech was upon a matter of 'public concern' as a threshold inquiry, after which it became the government's burden to 'clearly demonstrate' that the speech involved 'substantially interfered' with official responsibilities. Yet *Pickering* unmistakably states, and respondent agrees, that the state's burden in justifying a particular discharge varies depending upon the nature of the employee's expression. Although such particularized balancing is difficult, the courts must reach the most appropriate possible balance of the competing interests. * * *

"We agree with the District Court that there is no demonstration here that the questionnaire impeded Myers' ability to perform her responsibilities. The District Court was also correct to recognize that 'it is important to the efficient and successful operation of the District Attorney's office for Assistants to maintain close working relationships with their superiors.' Connick's judgment, and apparently also that of his first assistant [who] characterized Myers' actions as causing a 'mini-insurrection', was that Myers' questionnaire was an act of

---

8. This is not a case like *Givhan,* where an employee speaks out as a citizen on a matter of general concern, not tied to a personal employment dispute, but arranges to do so privately. Mrs. Givhan's right to protest racial discrimination—a matter inherently of public concern—is not forfeited by her choice of a private forum. Here, however, a questionnaire not otherwise of public concern does not attain that status because its subject matter could, in different circumstances, have been the topic of a communication to the public that might be of general interest. The dissent's analysis of whether discussions of office morale and discipline could be matters of public concern is beside the point—it does not answer whether *this* questionnaire is such speech.

insubordination which interfered with working relationships. When close working relationships are essential to fulfilling public responsibilities, a wide degree of deference to the employer's judgment is appropriate. Furthermore, we do not see the necessity for an employer to allow events to unfold to the extent that the disruption of the office and the destruction of working relationships is manifest before taking action. We caution that a stronger showing may be necessary if the employee's speech more substantially involved matters of public concern.

*   *   *

"Also relevant is the manner, time, and place in which the questionnaire was distributed. '[When] a government employee personally confronts his immediate superior, the employing agency's institutional efficiency may be threatened not only by the content of the employee's message but also by the manner, time, and place in which it is delivered.' Here the questionnaire was prepared, and distributed at the office; the manner of distribution required not only Myers to leave her work but for others to do the same in order that the questionnaire be completed.[13] Although some latitude in when official work is performed is to be allowed when professional employees are involved, and Myers did not violate announced office policy, the fact that Myers, unlike Pickering, exercised her rights to speech at the office supports Connick's fears that the functioning of his office was endangered.

"Finally, the context in which the dispute arose is also significant. This is not a case where an employee, out of purely academic interest, circulated a questionnaire so as to obtain useful research. Myers acknowledges that it is no coincidence that the questionnaire followed upon the heels of the transfer notice. When employee speech concerning office policy arises from an employment dispute concerning the very application of that policy to the speaker, additional weight must be given to the supervisor's view that the employee has threatened the authority of the employer to run the office. Although we accept the District Court's factual finding that Myers' reluctance to accede to the transfer order was not a sufficient cause in itself for her dismissal, [this] does not render irrelevant the fact that the questionnaire emerged after a persistent dispute between Myers and Connick and his deputies over office transfer policy.

"Myers' questionnaire touched upon matters of public concern in only a most limited sense; her survey, in our view, is most accurately characterized as an employee grievance concerning internal office policy. The limited First Amendment interest involved here does not require that Connick tolerate action which he reasonably believed would disrupt the office, undermine his authority, and destroy close working relationships. Myers' discharge therefore did not offend the First Amendment. *   *   *

"Our holding today is grounded in our long-standing recognition that the First Amendment's primary aim is the full protection of speech upon issues of public concern, as well as the practical realities involved in the administration of a government office. Although today the balance is struck for the government, this is no defeat for the First Amendment. For it would indeed be a Pyrrhic victory for the great principles of free expression if the Amendment's safeguarding of a public employee's right, as a citizen, to participate in discussions concerning public affairs were confused with the attempt to constitutionalize the employee grievance that we see presented here."

13. The record indicates that some, though not all, of the questionnaires were distributed during lunch. Employee speech which transpires entirely on the employee's own time, and in non-work areas of the office, bring different factors into the *Pickering* calculus, and might lead to a different conclusion.

BRENNAN, J., joined by Marshall, Blackmun and Stevens, JJ., dissented: "It is hornbook law [that] speech about 'the manner in which government is operated or should be operated' is an essential part of the communications necessary for self-governance the protection of which was a central purpose of the First Amendment. Because the questionnaire addressed such matters and its distribution did not adversely affect the operations of the District Attorney's Office or interfere with Myers' working relationship with her fellow employees, I dissent. * * *

"The balancing test articulated in *Pickering* comes into play only when a public employee's speech implicates the government's interests as an employer. When public employees engage in expression unrelated to their employment while away from the work place, their First Amendment rights are, of course, no different from those of the general public. Thus, whether a public employee's speech addresses a matter of public concern is relevant to the constitutional inquiry only when the statements at issue—by virtue of their content or the context in which they were made—may have an adverse impact on the government's ability to perform its duties efficiently.

"The Court's decision today is flawed in three respects. First, the Court distorts the balancing analysis required under *Pickering* by suggesting that one factor, the context in which a statement is made, is to be weighed *twice*—first in determining whether an employee's speech addresses a matter of public concern and then in deciding whether the statement adversely affected the government's interest as an employer. Second, in concluding that the effect of respondent's personnel policies on employee morale and the work performance of the District Attorney's Office is not a matter of public concern, the Court impermissibly narrows the class of subjects on which public employees may speak out without fear of retaliatory dismissal. Third, the Court misapplies the *Pickering* balancing test in holding that Myers could constitutionally be dismissed for circulating a questionnaire addressed to at least one subject that *was* 'a matter of interest to the community,' in the absence of evidence that her conduct disrupted the efficient functioning of the District Attorney's Office.

"[Based] on its own narrow conception of which matters are of public concern, the Court implicitly determines that information concerning employee morale at an important government office will not inform public debate. To the contrary, the First Amendment protects the dissemination of such information so that the people, not the courts may evaluate its usefulness. The proper means to ensure that the courts are not swamped with routine employee grievances mischaracterized as First Amendment cases is not to restrict artificially the concept of 'public concern,' but to require that adequate weight be given to the public's important interests in the efficient performance of governmental functions and in preserving employee discipline and harmony sufficient to achieve that end.

"The District Court weighed all of the relevant factors identified by our cases. It found that petitioner failed to establish that Myers violated either a duty of confidentiality or an office policy. Noting that most of the questionnaires were distributed during lunch, it rejected the contention that the distribution of the questionnaire impeded Myers' performance of her duties, and it concluded that 'Connick has not shown *any* evidence to indicate that the plaintiff's work performance was adversely affected by her expression.' (emphasis supplied).

"The Court accepts all of these findings. It concludes, however, that the District Court failed to give adequate weight to the context in which the questionnaires were distributed and to the need to maintain close working relationships in the District Attorney's Office. In particular, the Court suggests the District Court failed to give sufficient weight to the disruptive potential of Question 10, which asked whether the Assistants had confidence in the word of five named supervisors. The District Court, however, explicitly recognized that this was petitioner's 'most forceful argument'; but after hearing the testimony of four of the five supervisors named in the question, it found that the question had no adverse effect on Myers' relationship with her superiors.

"To this the Court responds that an employer need not wait until the destruction of working relationships is manifest before taking action. In the face of the District Court's finding that the circulation of the questionnaire had no disruptive effect, the Court holds that respondent may be dismissed because petitioner 'reasonably believed [the action] would disrupt the office, undermine his authority and destroy close working relationships.' Even though the District Court found that the distribution of the questionnaire did not impair Myers' working relationship with her supervisors, the Court bows to petitioner's judgment because '[w]hen close working relationships are essential to fulfilling public responsibilities, a wide degree of deference to the employer's judgment is appropriate.'

"Such extreme deference to the employer's judgment is not appropriate when public employees voice critical views concerning the operations of the agency for which they work. Although an employer's determination that an employee's statements have undermined essential working relationships must be carefully weighed in the *Pickering* balance, we must bear in mind that 'the threat of dismissal from public employment is [a] potent means of inhibiting speech.' If the employer's judgment is to be controlling, public employees will not speak out when what they have to say is critical of their supervisors. In order to protect public employees' First Amendment right to voice critical views on issues of public importance, the courts must make their own appraisal of the effects of the speech in question.

"[T]he District Court found that 'it cannot be said that the defendant's interest in promoting the efficiency of the public services performed through his employees was either adversely affected or substantially impeded by plaintiff's distribution of the questionnaire.' Based on these findings the District Court concluded that the circulation of the questionnaire was protected by the First Amendment. The District Court applied the proper legal standard and reached an acceptable accommodation between the competing interests. * * *

"The Court's decision today inevitably will deter public employees from making critical statements about the manner in which government agencies are operated for fear that doing so will provoke their dismissal. As a result, the public will be deprived of valuable information with which to evaluate the performance of elected officials. Because protecting the dissemination of such information is an essential function of the First Amendment, I dissent."

Notes and Questions

1. *Holmes' epigram.* Does the Court reject Holmes' epigram with one hand and embrace it with the other? Does it to some extent hold that because there is no right to hold a government job, its retention is a revocable privilege? Consider Tribe, *Constitutional Choices* 208 (1985): "*Connick* resurrects the right-

privilege doctrine for 'private' speech by government employees. By hinging protection on the distinction between public and private speech, the Court has embarked on a difficult definitional course. The stated test, which includes the 'content, form, and context' of the expression, provides little guidance. As Justice Brennan pointed out in dissent, the Court significantly narrowed the concept of a public issue in holding that criticism of governmental officials is not necessarily of public concern, but provided no clear alternative formulation. The mere fact that expression constitutes an employee grievance surely cannot be decisive, since the Court found that pressure upon employees to work on political campaigns was of public concern. Nor can the absence of partisan political concerns be determinative, since an employee grievance criticizing hiring and personnel management policies is of public concern if based upon a claim of racial discrimination. What is clear is that, at least until the precise reach of *Connick* is determined, public employees, who often possess unique information, will be discouraged from adding their voices to the debate on government performance." [c]

2. Is *Connick* inconsistent with *Gertz* because it distinguishes public speech from private on an ad hoc basis? Inconsistent with the position of the five justices in *Young* who rejected a hierarchy of "protected" speech? Is *Connick* a public employees case or does it suggest something more general about first amendment theory? For relevant pre-*Connick* commentary, see Schauer, *"Private" Speech and the "Private" Forum: Givhan v. Western Line School District,* 1981 Sup.Ct.Rev. 217.

Before studying *Dun & Bradstreet,* below, review *Gertz,* p. 359 supra, and the materials on commercial speech.

Dun & Bradstreet, Inc., a credit reporting agency, falsely and negligently reported to five of its subscribers that Greenmoss Builders, Inc. had filed a petition for bankruptcy and also negligently misrepresented Greenmoss' assets and liabilities. In the ensuing defamation action, Greenmoss recovered $50,000 in compensatory damages and $300,000 in punitive damages. Dun & Bradstreet argued that, under *Gertz,* its first amendment rights had been violated because presumed and punitive damages had been imposed without instructions requiring a showing of *New York Times* malice. Greenmoss argued that the *Gertz* protections did not extend to non-media defendants and, in any event, did not extend to commercial speech. DUN & BRADSTREET, INC. v. GREENMOSS BUILDERS, INC., ___ U.S. ___, 105 S.Ct. 2939, 86 L.Ed.2d 593 (1985), rejected Dun & Bradstreet's contention, but there was no opinion of the Court. The common theme of the five justices siding with Greenmoss was that the first amendment places less value on "private" speech than upon "public" speech.

POWELL, J., joined by Rehnquist and O'Connor, JJ., noted that the Vermont Supreme Court below had held "as a matter of federal constitutional law" that "the media protections outlined in *Gertz* are inapplicable to nonmedia defamation actions." In affirming, Powell, J., stated that his reasons were "different from those relied upon by the Vermont Supreme Court": "Like every other case in which this Court has found constitutional limits to state defamation laws, *Gertz* involved expression on a matter of undoubted public concern.   *   *   *

---

c. Much of the literature relevant to the "right-privilege" distinction is cited in Ch. 7, Sec. 5. For recent commentary with substantial attention to first amendment issues, see Kreimer, *Allocational Sanctions: The Problem of Negative Rights in a Positive State,* 132 U.Pa.L.Rev. 1293 (1984).

"We have never considered whether the *Gertz* balance obtains when the defamatory statements involve no issue of public concern. To make this determination, we must employ the approach approved in *Gertz* and balance the State's interest in compensating private individuals for injury to their reputation against the First Amendment interest in protecting this type of expression. This state interest is identical to the one weighed in *Gertz.* * * *

"The First Amendment interest, on the other hand, is less important than the one weighed in *Gertz*. We have long recognized that not all speech is of equal First Amendment importance.[5] It is speech on 'matters of public concern' that is 'at the heart of the First Amendment's protection.' [In] contrast, speech on matters of purely private concern is of less First Amendment concern. As a number of state courts, including the court below, have recognized, the role of the Constitution in regulating state libel law is far more limited when the concerns that activated *New York Times* and *Gertz* are absent.[6] In such a case, '[t]here is no threat to the free and robust debate of public issues; there is no potential interference with a meaningful dialogue of ideas concerning self-government; and there is no threat of liability causing a reaction of self-censorship by the press. The facts of the present case are wholly without the First Amendment concerns with which the Supreme Court of the United States has been struggling.' *Harley-Davidson Motorsports, Inc. v. Markley*, 279 Or. 361, 366, 568 P.2d 1359, 1363 (1977).

"While such speech is not totally unprotected by the First Amendment, see *Connick*, its protections are less stringent. [In] light of the reduced constitutional value of speech involving no matters of public concern, we hold that the state interest adequately supports awards of presumed and punitive damages—even absent a showing of 'actual malice.'[7]

5. This Court on many occasions has recognized that certain kinds of speech are less central to the interests of the First Amendment than others. Obscene speech and "fighting words" long have been accorded no protection. *Roth; Chaplinsky*. In the area of protected speech, the most prominent example of reduced protection for certain kinds of speech concerns commercial speech. Such speech, we have noted, occupies a "subordinate position in the scale of First Amendment values." *Ohralik.* * * *

Other areas of the law provide further examples. In *Ohralik* we noted that there are "[n]umerous examples [of] communications that are regulated without offending the First Amendment, such as the exchange of information about securities, * * * corporate proxy statements, [the] exchange of price and production information among competitors, [and] employers' threats of retaliation for the labor activities of employees." Yet similar regulation of political speech is subject to the most rigorous scrutiny. Likewise, while the power of the State to license lawyers, psychiatrists, and public school teachers—all of whom speak for a living—is unquestioned, this Court has held that a law requiring licensing of union organizers is unconstitutional under the First Amendment. *Thomas v. Collins*, [p. 473 infra]; see also *Rosenbloom v. Metromedia* (opinion of Brennan, J.) ("the determinant whether the First Amendment applies to state libel actions is whether the utterance involved concerns an issue of public or general concern").

6. As one commentator has remarked with respect to "the case of a commercial supplier of credit information that defames a person applying for credit"—the case before us today—"If the first amendment requirements outlined in *Gertz* apply, there is something clearly wrong with the first amendment or with *Gertz*." Shiffrin, *The First Amendment and Economic Regulation: Away From a General Theory of the First Amendment*, 78 Nw.L. Rev. 1212, 1268 (1983).

7. The dissent, purporting to apply the same balancing test that we do today, concludes that even speech on purely private matters is entitled to the protections of *Gertz.* * * *

The dissent's "balance" [would] lead to the protection of all libels—no matter how attenuated their constitutional interest. If the dissent were the law, a woman of impeccable character who was branded a "whore" by a jealous neighbor would have no effective recourse unless she could prove "actual malice" by clear and convincing evidence. This is not malice in the ordinary sense, but in the more demanding sense of *New York Times*. The dissent would, in effect, constitutionalize the entire common law of libel.

"The only remaining issue is whether petitioner's credit report involved a matter of public concern. In a related context, we have held that '[w]hether [speech] addresses a matter of public concern must be determined by [the expression's] content, form, and context [as] revealed by the whole record.' *Connick.* These factors indicate that petitioner's credit report concerns no public issue.[8] It was speech solely in the individual interest of the speaker and its specific business audience. Cf. *Central Hudson.* This particular interest warrants no special protection when—as in this case—the speech is wholly false and clearly damaging to the victim's business reputation. Moreover, since the credit report was made available to only five subscribers, who, under the terms of the subscription agreement, could not disseminate it further, it cannot be said that the report involves any 'strong interest in the free flow of commercial information.' *Virginia Pharmacy.* There is simply no credible argument that this type of credit reporting requires special protection to ensure that 'debate on public issues [will] be uninhibited, robust, and wide-open.' *New York Times.*

"In addition, the speech here, like advertising, is hardy and unlikely to be deterred by incidental state regulation. See *Virginia Pharmacy.* It is solely motivated by the desire for profit, which, we have noted, is a force less likely to be deterred than others. Arguably, the reporting here was also more objectively verifiable than speech deserving of greater protection. In any case, the market provides a powerful incentive to a credit reporting agency to be accurate, since false credit reporting is of no use to creditors. Thus, any incremental 'chilling' effect of libel suits would be of decreased significance.

"We conclude that permitting recovery of presumed and punitive damages in defamation cases absent a showing of 'actual malice' does not violate the First Amendment when the defamatory statements do not involve matters of public concern."

Although expressing the view that *Gertz* should be overruled and that the *New York Times* malice definition should be reconsidered, BURGER, C.J., concurring, stated that: "The single question before the Court today is whether *Gertz* applies to this case. The plurality opinion holds that *Gertz* does not apply because, unlike the challenged expression in *Gertz,* the alleged defamatory expression in this case does not relate to a matter of public concern. I agree that *Gertz* is limited to circumstances in which the alleged defamatory expression concerns a matter of general public importance, and that the expression in question here relates to a matter of essentially private concern. I therefore agree with the plurality opinion to the extent that it holds that *Gertz* is inapplicable in this case for the two reasons indicated. No more is needed to dispose of the present case."

WHITE, J., who had dissented in *Gertz,* was prepared to overrule that case or to limit it, but he disagreed with Powell, J.'s, suggestion that the plurality's resolution of the case was faithful to *Gertz:*

"It is interesting that Justice Powell declines to follow the *Gertz* approach in this case. I had thought that the decision in *Gertz* was intended to reach cases

---

8. The dissent suggests that our holding today leaves all credit reporting subject to reduced First Amendment protection. This is incorrect. The protection to be accorded a particular credit report depends on whether the report's "content, form, and context" indicate that it concerns a public matter. We also do not hold, as the dissent suggests we do, that

the report is subject to reduced constitutional protection because it constitutes economic or commercial speech. We discuss such speech, along with advertising, only to show how many of the same concerns that argue in favor of reduced constitutional protection in those areas apply here as well.

that involve any false statements of fact injurious to reputation, whether the statement is made privately or publicly and whether or not it implicates a matter of public importance. Justice Powell, however, distinguishes *Gertz* as a case that involved a matter of public concern, an element absent here. Wisely, in my view, Justice Powell does not rest his application of a different rule here on a distinction drawn between media and non-media defendants. On that issue, I agree with Justice Brennan that the First Amendment gives no more protection to the press in defamation suits than it does to others exercising their freedom of speech. None of our cases affords such a distinction; to the contrary, the Court has rejected it at every turn. It should be rejected again, particularly in this context, since it makes no sense to give the most protection to those publishers who reach the most readers and therefore pollute the channels of communication with the most misinformation and do the most damage to private reputation. If *Gertz* is to be distinguished from this case, on the ground that it applies only where the allegedly false publication deals with a matter of general or public importance, then where the false publication does not deal with such a matter, the common-law rules would apply whether the defendant is a member of the media or other public disseminator or a non-media individual publishing privately. Although Justice Powell speaks only of the inapplicability of the *Gertz* rule with respect to presumed and punitive damages, it must be that the *Gertz* requirement of some kind of fault on the part of the defendant is also inapplicable in cases such as this. * * *

"The question before us is whether *Gertz* is to be applied in this case. For either of two reasons, I believe that it should not. First, I am unreconciled to the *Gertz* holding and believe that it should be overruled. Second, as Justice Powell indicates, the defamatory publication in this case does not deal with a matter of public importance."

BRENNAN, J., joined by Marshall, Blackmun and Stevens, JJ., dissented:

"This case involves a difficult question of the proper application of *Gertz* to credit reporting—a type of speech at some remove from that which first gave rise to explicit First Amendment restrictions on state defamation law—and has produced a diversity of considered opinions, none of which speaks for the Court. Justice Powell's plurality opinion affirming the judgment below would not apply the *Gertz* limitations on presumed and punitive damages [because] the speech involved a subject of purely private concern and was circulated to an extremely limited audience. * * * Justice White also would affirm; he would not apply *Gertz* to this case on the ground that the subject matter of the publication does not deal with a matter of general or public importance. The Chief Justice apparently agrees with Justice White. The four who join this opinion would reverse the judgment of the Vermont Supreme Court. We believe that, although protection of the type of expression at issue is admittedly not the 'central meaning of the First Amendment,' *Gertz* makes clear that the First Amendment nonetheless requires restraints on presumed and punitive damage awards for this expression. * * *

"[Respondent urged that *Gertz* be restricted] to cases in which the defendant is a 'media' entity. Such a distinction is irreconcilable with the fundamental First Amendment principle that '[t]he inherent worth [of] speech in terms of its capacity for informing the public does not depend upon the identity of its source, whether corporation, association, union, or individual.' *First National Bank v. Bellotti* [p. 686 infra]. First Amendment difficulties lurk in the definitional questions such an approach would generate. And the distinction would likely be born an anachronism.[7] Perhaps most importantly, the argument that *Gertz* should be limited to the media misapprehends our cases. We protect the press to ensure the vitality of First Amendment guarantees. This solicitude implies no endorsement of the principle that speakers other than the press deserve lesser First Amendment protection. * * *

"The free speech guarantee gives each citizen an equal right to self-expression and to participation in self-government. [Accordingly,] at least six Members of this Court (the four who join this opinion and Justice White and The Chief Justice) agree today that, in the context of defamation law, the rights of the institutional media are no greater and no less than those enjoyed by other individuals or organizations engaged in the same activities.[10] * * *

"Purporting to 'employ the approach approved in *Gertz*,' Justice Powell balances the state interest in protecting private reputation against the First Amendment interest in protecting expression on matters not of public concern.[11]

"The five Members of the Court voting to affirm the damage award in this case have provided almost no guidance as to what constitutes a protected 'matter of public concern.' Justice White offers nothing at all, but his opinion does indicate that the distinction turns on solely the subject matter of the expression and not on the extent or conditions of dissemination of that expression. Justice Powell adumbrates a rationale that would appear to focus primarily on subject matter.[12] The opinion relies on the fact that the speech at issue was 'solely in the individual interest of the speaker and its *business* audience.' Analogizing explicitly to advertising, the opinion also states that credit reporting is 'hardy' and 'solely motivated by the desire for profit.' These two strains of analysis suggest that Justice Powell is excluding the subject matter of credit reports from 'matters of public concern' because the speech is predominantly in the realm of matters of economic concern."

Brennan, J., pointed to precedents (particularly labor cases) protecting speech on economic matters and argued that, "the breadth of this protection evinces recognition that freedom of expression is not only essential to check

7. Owing to transformations in the technological and economic structure of the communications industry, there has been an increasing convergence of what might be labeled "media" and "nonmedia."

10. Justice Powell's opinion does not expressly reject the media/nonmedia distinction, but does expressly decline to apply that distinction to resolve this case.

11. One searches *Gertz* in vain for a single word to support the proposition that limits on presumed and punitive damages obtained only when speech involved matters of public concern. *Gertz* could not have been grounded in such a premise. Distrust of placing in the courts the power to decide what speech was of public concern was precisely the rationale *Gertz* offered for rejecting the *Rosenbloom* plurality approach. * * *

12. Justice Powell also appears to rely in part on the fact that communication was limited and confidential. Given that his analysis also relies on the subject matter of the credit report, it is difficult to decipher exactly what role the nature and extent of dissemination plays in Justice Powell's analysis. But because the subject matter of the expression at issue is properly understood as a matter of public concern, it may well be that this element of confidentiality is crucial to the outcome as far as Justice Powell's opinion is concerned. In other words, it may be that Justice Powell thinks this particular expression could not contribute to public welfare because the public generally does not receive it. This factor does not suffice to save the analysis. See n. 18 infra.

[In fn. 18, Brennan, J., indicated that, "Dun & Bradstreet doubtless provides thousands of credit reports to thousands of subscribers who receive the information pursuant to the same strictures imposed on the recipients in this case. As a systemic matter, therefore, today's decision diminishes the free flow of information because Dun & Bradstreet will generally be made more reticent in providing information to all its subscribers."]

tyranny and foster self-government but also intrinsic to individual liberty and dignity and instrumental in society's search for truth."

Moreover, he emphasized the importance of credit reporting: "The credit reporting of Dun & Bradstreet falls within any reasonable definition of 'public concern' consistent with our precedents. Justice Powell's reliance on the fact that Dun & Bradstreet publishes credit reports 'for profit' is wholly unwarranted. Time and again we have made clear that speech loses none of its constitutional protection 'even though it is carried in a form that is "sold" for profit.' *Virginia Pharmacy.* More importantly, an announcement of the bankruptcy of a local company is information of potentially great concern to residents of the community where the company is [located]. And knowledge about solvency and the effect and prevalence of bankruptcy certainly would inform citizen opinions about questions of economic regulation. It is difficult to suggest that a bankruptcy is not a subject matter of public concern when federal law requires invocation of judicial mechanisms to effectuate it and makes the fact of the bankruptcy a matter of public record. * * *

"Even if the subject matter of credit reporting were properly considered—in the terms of Justice White and Justice Powell—as purely a matter of private discourse, this speech would fall well within the range of valuable expression for which the First Amendment demands protection. Much expression that does not directly involve public issues receives significant protection. Our cases do permit some diminution in the degree of protection afforded one category of speech about economic or commercial matters. 'Commercial speech'—defined as advertisements that 'do no more than propose a commercial transaction'—may be more closely regulated than other types of speech. [Credit] reporting is not 'commercial speech' as this Court has defined the term.

"[In] *every* case in which we have permitted more extensive state regulation on the basis of a commercial speech rationale—the speech being regulated was pure advertising—an offer to buy or sell goods and services or encouraging such buying and selling. Credit reports are not commercial advertisements for a good or service or a proposal to buy or sell such a product. We have been extremely chary about extending the 'commercial speech' doctrine beyond this narrowly circumscribed category of advertising because often vitally important speech will be uttered to advance economic interests and because the profit motive making such speech hardy dissipates rapidly when the speech is not advertising." [a]

Finally, Brennan, J., argued that even if credit reports were characterized as commercial speech, "unrestrained" presumed and punitive damages would violate the commercial speech requirement that "the regulatory means chosen be narrowly tailored so as to avoid any unnecessary chilling of protected expression. [Accordingly,] Greenmoss Builders should be permitted to recover for any actual damage it can show resulted from Dun & Bradstreet's negligently false credit report, but should be required to show actual malice to receive presumed or punitive damages."

Notes and Questions

1. Which of the following are "private" according to the opinions of Powell, J., Burger, C.J., and White, J.? (a) a report in the *Wall Street Journal* that

a. Brennan, J., cited *Consolidated Edison,* p. 686 infra, which invalidated a regulation that prohibited a utility company from inserting its views on "controversial issues of public policy" into its monthly electrical bill mailings. The mailing that prompted the regulation advocated nuclear power.

Greenmoss has gone bankrupt; (b) a confidential report by Dun & Bradstreet to a bank that a famous politician has poor credit. Would the answer be different if the subject of the report were an actor? (c) a statement in the campus newspaper or by one student to another that a law professor is an alcoholic. Would it make a difference if the law professor was being considered for a Supreme Court appointment?

Consider the relationship between the public/private focus of the *Greenmoss* decision and the "public controversy" aspect of the public figure definition. If the speech does not relate to a "public" controversy, can it be "public" within the terms of *Greenmoss*? Reconsider *Time, Inc. v. Firestone*, p. 699 supra.[b]

Finally, does it matter why the D & B subscribers received the information about Greenmoss? Suppose, for investment or insurance purposes, the subscribers had asked for reports on all aspects of the construction industry in Vermont? Compare *Lowe v. SEC*, p. 484 infra.

2. Should the focus of the decision have been commercial speech instead of private speech? Would an expansion of the commercial speech definition have been preferable to the promotion of ad hoc decisionmaking about the nature of "private" speech? Consider Shiffrin, *The First Amendment and Economic Regulation: Away From A General Theory of the First Amendment*, 78 Nw.U.L.Rev. 1212, 1269 n. 327 (1983): "[D]rawing lines based on underlying first amendment values is a far cry from sending out the judiciary on a general ad hoc expedition to separate matters of general public interest from matters that are not. A commitment to segregate certain commercial speech from *Gertz* protection is not a commitment to general ad hoc determinations."

3. According to Powell, J., in fn. 5, are the *Ohralik* examples, i.e., exchange of information about securities, corporate proxy statements and the like, examples of protected speech subject to regulation? In what sense, are those examples of communication protected? What is the significance of Powell, J.'s suggestion that they are something other than commercial speech? Where do those examples fit into Brennan, J.'s view of the first amendment? For general discussion, see Shiffrin, note 2 supra.

SECTION 2. PRIOR RESTRAINTS

Prior restraint is a technical term in first amendment law. A criminal statute prohibiting all advocacy of violent action would *restrain* speech and would have been enacted *prior* to any restrained communication. The statute would be overbroad, but it would not be a prior restraint. A prior restraint refers only to closely related, distinctive methods of regulating expression that are said to have in common their own peculiar set of evils and problems, in addition to those that accompany most any governmental interference with free expression. "The issue is not whether the government may impose a particular restriction of substance in an area of public expression, such as forbidding obscenity in newspapers, but whether it may do so by a particular method, such as advance screening of newspaper copy. In other words, restrictions which could be validly imposed when enforced by subsequent punishment are, never-

---

b. For discussion of the different meanings of public and private speech, see Schauer, *"Private" Speech and the "Private" Forum: Givhan v. Western Line School District,* 1979 Sup.Ct.Rev. 217. Compare Perry, *Freedom of Expression: An Essay on Theory and Doctrine,* 78 Nw.U.L.Rev. 1137 (1983) (denying any meaningful distinction between personal and political decisions). See generally Symposium, *The Public/Private Distinction,* 130 U.Pa. L.Rev. 1289 (1982). For commentary on the question of whether Gertz should extend to non-media defendants see e.g. sources cited in note 1 after *Gertz,* p. 366 supra.

theless, forbidden if attempted by prior restraint." Emerson, *The Doctrine of Prior Restraint,* 20 Law and Contemp.Prob. 648 (1955).

The classic prior restraints were the English licensing laws which required a license in advance to print any material or to import or to sell any book. One of the questions raised in this chapter concerns the types of government conduct beyond the classic licensing laws that should be characterized as prior restraints. Another concerns the question of when government licensing of speech, press, or assembly should be countenanced. Perhaps, most important, the Section explores the circumstances in which otherwise protected speech may be restrained on an ad hoc basis.

I. FOUNDATION CASES

A. LICENSING

LOVELL v. GRIFFIN, 303 U.S. 444, 58 S.Ct. 666, 82 L.Ed. 949 (1938), per HUGHES, C.J., invalidated an ordinance prohibiting the distribution of handbooks, advertising or literature within the city of Griffin, Georgia without obtaining written permission of the City Manager: "[T]he ordinance is invalid on its face. Whatever the motive which induced its adoption, its character is such that it strikes at the very foundation of the freedom of the press by subjecting it to license and censorship. The struggle for the freedom of the press was primarily directed against the power of the licensor. It was against that power that John Milton directed his assault by his 'Appeal for the Liberty of Unlicensed Printing.' And the liberty of the press became initially a right to publish '*without* a license what formerly could be published only *with* one.'[1] While this freedom from previous restraint upon publication cannot be regarded as exhausting the guaranty of liberty, the prevention of that restraint was a leading purpose in the adoption of the constitutional provision. Legislation of the type of the ordinance in question would restore the system of license and censorship in its baldest form.

"The liberty of the press is not confined to newspapers and periodicals. It necessarily embraces pamphlets and leaflets. These indeed have been historic weapons in the defense of liberty, as the pamphlets of Thomas Paine and others in our own history abundantly attest. The press in its historic connotation comprehends every sort of publication which affords a vehicle of information and opinion. * * *

"The ordinance cannot be saved because it relates to distribution and not to publication. 'Liberty of circulating is as essential to that freedom as liberty of publishing; indeed, without the circulation, the publication would be of little value.' *Ex parte Jackson,* 96 U.S. (6 Otto) 727, 733, 24 L.Ed. 877 (1877).

"[As] the ordinance is void on its face, it was not necessary for appellant to seek a permit under it. She was entitled to contest its validity in answer to the charge against her.

"[Reversed and] remanded."[a]

Notes and Questions

1. *First amendment procedure.* Notice that Lovell would get the benefit of the prior restraint doctrine even if the material she distributed was obscene or otherwise unprotected. In that respect, the prior restraint doctrine is similar to

---

1. See Wickwar, "The Struggle for the Freedom of the Press," p. 15.

a. Cardozo, J., took no part.

the doctrines of overbreadth and vagueness. For particular concerns that underlie the prior restraint doctrine, consider Emerson, *The System of Freedom of Expression* 506 (1970):

"A system of prior restraint is in many ways more inhibiting than a system of subsequent punishment: It is likely to bring under government scrutiny a far wider range of expression; it shuts off communication before it takes place; suppression by a stroke of the pen is more likely to be applied than suppression through a criminal process; the procedures do not require attention to the safeguards of the criminal process; the system allows less opportunity for public appraisal and criticism; the dynamics of the system drive toward excesses, as the history of all censorship shows."

2. *Scope and character of the doctrine.* What is the vice of the licensing scheme in *Lovell*? Is the concern that like vague statutes it affords undue discretion and potential for abuse? Is the real concern the uncontrolled power of the licensor to deny licenses? Suppose licenses were automatically issued to anyone who applied?

To what extent should the prior restraint doctrine apply to non-press activities? To a licensing ordinance that otherwise forbids soliciting membership in organizations that exact fees of their members? See *Staub v. Baxley,* 355 U.S. 313, 78 S.Ct. 277, 2 L.Ed.2d 302 (1958) (yes). To a licensing ordinance that otherwise prohibits attempts to secure contributions for charitable or religious causes? See *Cantwell v. Connecticut,* 310 U.S. 296, 60 S.Ct. 900, 84 L.Ed. 1213 (1940) (yes).

Suppose, in the above cases, that the authority of the licensor were confined by narrow, objective, and definite standards or that licenses were automatically issued to anyone who applied. *Hynes v. Mayor,* 425 U.S. 610, 96 S.Ct. 1755, 48 L.Ed.2d 243 (1976), per Burger, C.J., stated in dictum that a municipality could regulate house to house soliciting by requiring advance notice to the police department in order to protect its citizens from crime and undue annoyance: "A narrowly drawn ordinance, that does not vest in municipal officials the undefined power to determine what messages residents will hear, may serve these important interests without running afoul of the First Amendment." But cf. *Thomas v. Collins,* 323 U.S. 516, 65 S.Ct. 315, 89 L.Ed. 430 (1945) (registration requirement for paid union organizers invalid prior restraint); *Talley v. California,* 362 U.S. 60, 80 S.Ct. 536, 4 L.Ed.2d 559 (1960) (ban on anonymous handbills "void on its face," noting that the "obnoxious press licensing law of England, which was also enforced on the Colonies was due in part to the knowledge that exposure of the names of printers, writers and distributors would lessen the circulation of literature critical of the government").

B. INJUNCTIONS

NEAR v. MINNESOTA

283 U.S. 697, 51 S.Ct. 625, 75 L.Ed. 1357 (1931).

Mr. Chief Justice Hughes delivered the opinion of the Court.

[The *Saturday Press* published articles charging that through graft and incompetence named public officials failed to expose and punish gangsters responsible for gambling, bootlegging, and racketeering in Minneapolis. It demanded a special grand jury and special prosecutor to deal with the situation and to investigate an alleged attempt to assassinate one of its publishers. Under a statute that authorized abatement of a "malicious, scandalous and defamatory newspaper" the state secured, and its supreme court affirmed, a court order that "abated" the Press and perpetually enjoined the defendants from publishing or circulating "any publication whatsoever which is a malicious, scandalous or defamatory newspaper." The order did not restrain the defendants from operating a newspaper "in harmony with the general welfare."]

The object of the statute is not punishment, in the ordinary sense, but suppression of the offending newspaper. [In] the case of public officers, it is the reiteration of charges of official misconduct, and the fact that the newspaper [is] principally devoted to that purpose, that exposes it to suppression. [T]he operation and effect of the statute [is] that public authorities may bring the owner or publisher of a newspaper or periodical before a judge upon a charge of conducting a business of publishing scandalous and defamatory matter—in particular that the matter consists of charges against public officers of official dereliction—and, unless the owner or publisher is able and disposed to bring competent evidence to satisfy the judge that the charges are true and are published with good motives and for justifiable ends, his newspaper or periodical is suppressed and further publication is made punishable as a contempt. This is of the essence of censorship.

The question is whether a statute authorizing such proceedings [is] consistent with the conception of the liberty of the press as historically conceived and guaranteed. [I]t has been generally, if not universally, considered that it is the chief purpose of the guaranty to prevent previous restraints upon publication. The struggle in England, directed against the legislative power of the licenser, resulted in renunciation of the censorship of the press. The liberty deemed to be established was thus described by Blackstone: "The liberty of the press is indeed essential to the nature of a free state; but this consists in laying no *previous* restraints upon publications, and not in freedom from censure for criminal matter when published. Every freeman has an undoubted right to lay what sentiments he pleases before the public; to forbid this, is to destroy the freedom of the press; but if he publishes what is improper, mischievous or illegal, he must take the consequence of his own temerity." [The] criticism upon Blackstone's statement has not been because immunity from previous restraint upon publication has not been regarded as deserving of special emphasis, but chiefly because that immunity cannot be deemed to exhaust the conception of the liberty guaranteed by State and Federal Constitutions.

[T]he protection even as to previous restraint is not absolutely unlimited. But the limitation has been recognized only in exceptional cases. [N]o one would question but that a government might prevent actual obstruction to its recruiting service or the publication of the sailing dates of transports or the number and location of troops. On similar grounds, the primary requirements of decency may be enforced against obscene publications. The security of the community life may be protected against incitements to acts of violence and the overthrow by force of orderly [government].[a]

The exceptional nature of its limitations places in a strong light the general conception that liberty of the press, historically considered and taken up by the Federal Constitution, has meant, principally although not exclusively, immunity from previous restraints or censorship. The conception of liberty of the press in this country had broadened with the exigencies of the colonial period and with

a. For critical commentary on the concessions in *Near,* see Linde, *Courts and Censorship,* 66 Minn.L.Rev. 171 (1981).

the efforts to secure freedom from oppressive administration. That liberty was especially cherished for the immunity it afforded from previous restraint of the publication of censure of public officers and charges of official [misconduct].

The fact that for approximately one hundred and fifty years there has been almost an entire absence of attempts to impose previous restraints upon publications relating to the malfeasance of public officers is significant of the deep-seated conviction that such restraints would violate constitutional right. Public officers, whose character and conduct remain open to debate and free discussion in the press, find their remedies for false accusations in actions under libel laws providing for redress and punishment, and not in proceedings to restrain the publication of newspapers and periodicals. [The] fact that the liberty of the press may be abused by miscreant purveyors of scandal does not make any the less necessary the immunity of the press from previous restraint in dealing with official misconduct. Subsequent punishment for such abuses as may exist is the appropriate remedy, consistent with constitutional [privilege].

The statute in question cannot be justified by reason of the fact that the publisher is permitted to show, before injunction issues, that the matter published is true and is published with good motives and for justifiable ends. If such a statute, authorizing suppression and injunction on such a basis, is constitutionally valid, it would be equally permissible for the Legislature to provide that at any time the publisher of any newspaper could be brought before a court, or even an administrative officer (as the constitutional protection may not be regarded as resting on mere procedural details), and required to produce proof of the truth of his publication, or of what he intended to publish and of his motives, or stand enjoined. If this can be done, the Legislature may provide machinery for determining in the complete exercise of its discretion what are justifiable ends and restrain publication accordingly. And it would be but a step to a complete system of censorship.

[For] these reasons we hold the statute, so far as it authorized the proceedings in this action, [to] be an infringement of the liberty of the press guaranteed by the Fourteenth Amendment. * * *

MR. JUSTICE BUTLER (dissenting).

[T]he *previous restraints* referred to by [Blackstone] subjected the press to the arbitrary will of an administrative officer. [The] Minnesota statute does not operate as a *previous* restraint on publication within the proper meaning of that phrase. It does not authorize administrative control in advance such as was formerly exercised by the licensers and censors, but prescribes a remedy to be enforced by a suit in equity. In this case [t]he business and publications unquestionably constitute an abuse of the right of free press. [A]s stated by the state Supreme Court [they] threaten morals, peace, and good order. [The] restraint authorized is only in respect of continuing to do what has been duly adjudged to constitute a nuisance. [It] is fanciful to suggest similarity between the granting or enforcement of the decree authorized by this statute to prevent *further* publication of malicious, scandalous, and defamatory articles and the *previous restraint* upon the press by licensers as referred to by Blackstone and described in the history of the times to which he alludes. * * *

It is well known, as found by the state supreme court, that existing libel laws are inadequate effectively to suppress evils resulting from the kind of business and publications that are shown in this case. The doctrine [of this decision] exposes the peace and good order of every community and the business and private affairs of every individual to the constant and protracted false and malicious assaults of any insolvent publisher who may have purpose and sufficient capacity to contrive and put into effect a scheme or program for oppression, blackmail or extortion.   *   *   *

MR. JUSTICE VAN DEVANTER, MR. JUSTICE MCREYNOLDS, and MR. JUSTICE SUTHERLAND concur in this opinion.[b]

Notes and Questions

1. *Near and seditious libel: a misuse of prior restraint?* *Near* was decided three decades before *New York Times v. Sullivan,* p. 347 supra. Should the Court have looked to the substance of the regulation rather than its form? Consider Jeffries, *Rethinking Prior Restraint,* 92 Yale L.J. 409, 416–17 (1983): "In truth, *Near* involved nothing more or less than a repackaged version of the law of seditious libel, and this the majority rightly refused to countenance. Hence, there was pressure, so typical of this doctrine, to cram the law into the disfavored category of prior restraint, even though it in fact functioned very differently from a scheme of official licensing. Here there was no license and no censor, no ex parte determination of what was prohibited, and no suppression of publication based on speculation about what somebody might say. Here the decision to suppress was made by a judge (not a bureaucrat), after adversarial (not ex parte) proceedings, to determine the legal character of what had been (and not what might be) published. The only aspect of prior restraint was the incidental fact that the defendants were commanded not to repeat that which they were proved to have done.

"[I]f *Near* reached the right result, does it really matter that it gave the wrong reason? The answer, I think, is that it does matter, at least that it has come to matter as *Near* has become a prominent feature of the First Amendment landscape—a landmark, as the case is so often called, from which we chart our course to future decisions. [T]he Court has yet to explain (at least in terms that I understand) what it is about an injunction that justifies this independent rule of constitutional disfavor."

Should a court be able to enjoin the continued distribution of material it has finally adjudicated to be unprotected defamation under existing law? Suppose it enjoins the publication of any material that does not comply with the mandates of *New York Times* and *Gertz?*

2. *The collateral bar rule.* Does the collateral bar rule shed light on the relationship between prior restraints and injunctions? That rule insists "that a court order must be obeyed until it is set aside, and that persons subject to the order who disobey it may not defend against the ensuing charge of criminal contempt on the ground that the order was erroneous or even unconstitutional." Barnett, *The Puzzle of Prior Restraint,* 29 Stan.L.Rev. 539, 552 (1977). WALKER v. BIRMINGHAM, 388 U.S. 307, 87 S.Ct. 1824, 18 L.Ed.2d 1210 (1967) upheld the rule against a first amendment challenge in affirming the contempt conviction of defendants for violating an ex parte injunction issued by an Alabama court enjoining them from engaging in street parades without a municipal permit issued pursuant to the city's parade ordinance. The Court, per STEWART, J., (Warren, C.J., Brennan, Douglas, and Fortas, JJ., dissenting) held that because the petitioners neither moved to dissolve the injunction nor sought to comply with the city's parade ordinance, their claim that the injunction and

b. For background on the *Near* case, see Friendly, *Minnesota Rag* (1981); Murphy, *Near v. Minnesota in the Context of Historical Developments,* 66 Minn.L.Rev. 95, 133–60 (1981).

ordinance were unconstitutional[c] did not need to be considered: "This Court cannot hold that the petitioners were constitutionally free to ignore all the procedures of the law and carry their battle to the streets. [R]espect for judicial process is a small price to pay for the civilizing hand of law, which alone can give abiding meaning to constitutional freedom." Although *Walker* suggested that its holding might be different if the court issuing the injunction lacked jurisdiction or if the injunction were "transparently invalid or had only a frivolous pretense to validity," it held that Alabama's invocation of the collateral bar rule was not itself unconstitutional.

Cf. *Poulos v. New Hampshire*, 345 U.S. 395, 73 S.Ct. 760, 97 L.Ed. 1105 (1953) (claim of arbitrary refusal to issue license for open air meeting need not be entertained when a licensing statute is considered to be valid on its face in circumstance where speaker fails to seek direct judicial relief and proceeds without a license).[d] Does *Poulos* pose considerable danger to first amendment interests because the low visibility of the administrative decision permits easy abridgement of free expression? See Monaghan, *First Amendment "Due Process,"* 83 Harv.L.Rev. 518, 543 (1970). Do *Lovell, Walker,* and *Poulos* fit easily together? Consider Blasi, *Prior Restraints on Demonstrations,* 68 Mich.L.Rev. 1482, 1555 (1970): "A refuses to apply for a permit; he undertakes a march that could have been prohibited in the first place; he is prosecuted for parading without a permit under a statute that is defective for overbreadth. B applies for a permit; he is rudely rebuffed by a city official in clear violation of the state permit statute (which is not invalid on its face); he marches anyway in a manner that would be protected by the first amendment, he is prosecuted for parading without a permit. C applies for a permit; he is rudely rebuffed; he notifies city officials that he will march anyway; the officials obtain an injunction against the march; the injunction is overbroad and is also based on a state statute that is overbroad; C marches in a manner ordinarily within his constitutional rights; he is prosecuted for contempt. Under the law as it now stands, A wins, but B and C lose!"

3. *The commentators, injunctions, and prior restraint.* Should the link between prior restraint doctrine and injunctions depend upon the collateral bar rule? Does the analogy between licensing systems and injunctions hold only in that event? See Fiss, *The Civil Rights Injunction* 30, 69–74 (1978); Barnett, note 2 supra, at 553–54. Should the prior restraint doctrine be wholly inapplicable to injunctions so long as "expedited appellate review allows an immediate opportunity to test the validity of an injunction against speech and only so long as that opportunity is genuinely effective to allow timely publication should the injunction ultimately be adjudged invalid"? Jeffries, note 1 supra, at 433.[e] Indeed should the whole concept of prior restraint be abandoned? Consider id. at 433–34: "In the context of administrative preclearance, talking of prior restraint is

---

c. Indeed, the ordinance in question was declared unconstitutional two years later. *Shuttlesworth v. Birmingham,* 394 U.S. 147, 89 S.Ct. 935, 22 L.Ed.2d 162 (1969) (ordinance conferring unbridled discretion to prohibit any parade or demonstration is unconstitutional prior restraint).

d. For consideration of when licensing statutes for assemblies are valid, see *Cox v. New Hampshire,* p. 536 infra.

e. For the argument that regulation by injunction is generally more speech protective

than regulation via subsequent punishment, see Mayton, *Toward A Theory of First Amendment Process: Injunctions of Speech, Subsequent Punishment, and the Costs of the Prior Restraint Doctrine,* 67 Corn.L.Rev. 245 (1982). For the contention that this should count in favor of subsequent punishment in many contexts, see Redish, *The Proper Role of the Prior Restraint Doctrine in First Amendment Theory,* 70 Va.L.Rev. 53, 92–93 (1984).

unhelpful, though not inapt. A more informative frame of reference would be overbreadth, the doctrine that explicitly identifies why preclearance is specially objectionable. In the context of injunctions, however, the traditional doctrine of prior restraint is not merely unhelpful, but positively misleading. It focuses on a constitutionally inconsequential consideration of form and diverts attention away from the critical substantive issues of First Amendment coverage. The result is a two-pronged danger. On the one hand, vindication of First Amendment freedoms in the name of prior restraint may exaggerate the legitimate reach of official competence to suppress by subsequent punishment. On the other hand, insistence on special disfavor for prior restraints outside the realm of substantive protection under the First Amendment may deny to the government an appropriate choice of means to vindicate legitimate interests. In my view, neither risk is justified by any compelling reason to continue prior restraint as a doctrinally independent category of contemporary First Amendment analysis."

For a nuanced argument that the prior restraint doctrine should apply to injunctions even in those jurisdictions that reject the applicability of the collateral bar rule to first amendment arguments, see Blasi, *Toward a Theory of Prior Restraint: The Central Linkage*, 66 Minn.L.Rev. 11 (1981). Except in particular contexts, Professor Blasi does not claim that the chilling effect of injunctions on speech is more severe than those associated with criminal laws and civil liability rules. He does argue that unlike criminal laws and civil liability rules, regulation of speech by licensing and injunctions requires abstract and unduly speculative adjudication, stimulates overuse by regulatory agents, can to some extent distort the way in which audiences perceive the message at issue, and unreasonably implies that the activity of disseminating controversial communications is "a threat to, rather than an integral feature of, the social order." Id. at 85. He argues that many of these factors are aggravated if the collateral bar rule applies and that other undesirable features are added. For example, speakers are forced to reveal planned details about their communication. He concludes that the "concept of prior restraint is coherent at the core." Id. at 93.[f]

II. PRIOR RESTRAINTS, OBSCENITY, AND COMMERCIAL SPEECH

KINGSLEY BOOKS, INC. v. BROWN, 354 U.S. 436, 77 S.Ct. 1325, 1 L.Ed.2d 1469 (1957), per FRANKFURTER, J., upheld a state court decree, issued pursuant to a New York statute, enjoining the publisher from further distribution of 14 booklets the state court found obscene. On appeal to the Supreme Court the publisher challenged only the prior restraint, not the obscenity finding:

"The phrase 'prior restraint' is not a self-wielding sword. Nor can it serve as a talismatic test. The duty of closer analysis and critical judgment in applying the thought behind the phrase has thus been authoritatively put by one who brings weighty learning to his support of constitutionally protected liberties: 'What is needed,' writes Professor Paul A. Freund, 'is a pragmatic assessment of its operation in the particular circumstances. The generalization that prior restraint is particularly obnoxious in civil liberties cases must yield to more particularistic analysis.' *The Supreme Court and Civil Liberties*, 4 Vand.L.Rev. 533, 539.

f. For detailed criticism of Blasi's position, all in defense of a different core, see Redish, fn. e, at 59–75.

"Wherein does § 22–a differ in its effective operation from the type of statute upheld in *Alberts,* [p. 377 supra]. One would be bold to assert that the in terrorem effect of [criminal] statutes less restrains booksellers in the period before the law strikes than does § 22–a. Instead of requiring the bookseller to dread that the offer for sale of a book may, without prior warning, subject him to a criminal prosecution with the hazard of imprisonment, the civil procedure assures him that such consequences cannot follow unless he ignores a court order specifically directed to him for a prompt and carefully circumscribed determination of the issue of obscenity. Until then, he may keep the book for sale and sell it on his own judgment rather than steer 'nervously among the treacherous shoals.' [a]

"Criminal enforcement and the proceeding under § 22–a interfere with a book's solicitation of the public precisely at the same stage. In each situation the law moves after publication; the book need not in either case have yet passed into the hands of the public. [H]ere as a matter of fact copies of the booklets whose distribution was enjoined had been on sale for several weeks when process was served. In each case the bookseller is put on notice by the complaint that sale of the publication charged with obscenity in the period before trial may subject him to penal consequences. In the one case he may suffer fine and imprisonment for violation of the criminal statute, in the other, for disobedience of the temporary injunction. The bookseller may of course stand his ground and confidently believe that in any judicial proceeding the book could not be condemned as obscene, but both modes of procedure provide an effective deterrent against distribution prior to adjudication of the book's content—the threat of subsequent penalization.[2] "

The Court pointed out that in both criminal misdemeanor prosecutions and injunction proceedings a jury could be called as a matter of discretion, but that defendant did not request a jury trial and did not attack the statute for its failure to require a jury.

"Nor are the consequences of a judicial condemnation for obscenity under § 22–a more restrictive of freedom of expression than the result of conviction for a misdemeanor. In *Alberts,* the defendant was fined $500, sentenced to sixty days in prison, and put on probation for two years on condition that he not violate the obscenity statute. Not only was he completely separated from society for two months but he was also seriously restrained from trafficking in all obscene publications for a considerable time. Appellants, on the other hand, were enjoined from displaying for sale or distributing only the particular booklets theretofore published and adjudged to be obscene. Thus, the restraint upon appellants as merchants in obscenity was narrower than that imposed on *Alberts.*

"Section 22–a's provision for the seizure and destruction of the instruments of ascertained wrongdoing expresses resort to a legal remedy sanctioned by the long history of Anglo-American law. See Holmes, *The Common Law,* 24–26.

a. In fact, § 22–a did not require a civil adjudication before criminal prosecution, as intimated by the opinion. The feasibility of such a requirement is considered in Lockhart, *Escape from the Chill of Uncertainty,* 9 Ga.L. Rev. 533, 569–86 (1975).

2. This comparison of remedies takes note of the fact that we do not have before us a case where, although the issue of obscenity is ultimately decided in favor of the bookseller, the State nevertheless attempts to punish him for disobedience of the interim injunction. For all we know, New York may impliedly condition the temporary injunction so as not to subject the bookseller to a charge of contempt if he prevails on the issue of obscenity.

"[It] only remains to say that the difference between *Near* and this case is glaring in fact. The two cases are no less glaringly different when judged by the appropriate criteria of constitutional law. Minnesota empowered its courts to enjoin the dissemination of future issues of a publication because its past issues had been found offensive. In the language of Mr. Chief Justice Hughes, 'This is of the essence of censorship.' As such, it was enough to condemn the statute wholly apart from the fact that the proceeding in *Near* involved not obscenity but matters deemed to be derogatory to a public officer. Unlike *Near*, § 22–a is concerned solely with obscenity and, as authoritatively construed, it studiously withholds restraint upon matters not already published and not yet found to be offensive." [b]

TIMES FILM CORP. v. CHICAGO
365 U.S. 43, 81 S.Ct. 391, 5 L.Ed.2d 403 (1961).

MR. JUSTICE CLARK delivered the opinion of the Court.

Petitioner challenges on constitutional grounds the validity on its face of that portion of § 155–4 [1] of the Municipal Code of the City of Chicago which requires submission of all motion pictures for examination prior to their public exhibition. Petitioner is a New York corporation owning the exclusive right to publicly exhibit in Chicago the film known as "Don Juan." It applied for a permit, as Chicago's ordinance required, and tendered the license fee but refused to submit the film for examination. The appropriate city official refused to issue the permit and his order was made final on appeal to the Mayor. The sole ground for denial was petitioner's refusal to submit the film for examination as required. Petitioner then brought this suit seeking injunctive relief ordering the issuance of the permit without submission of the [film] * * *. Its sole ground is that the provision of the ordinance requiring submission of the film constitutes, on its face, a prior restraint [2] * * * [Admittedly,] the challenged section of the ordinance imposes a previous restraint, and the broad justiciable issue is therefore present as to whether the ambit of constitutional protection includes complete and absolute freedom to exhibit, at least once, any and every kind of motion picture. It is that question alone which we decide.

[T]here is not a word in the record as to the nature and content of "Don Juan." We are left entirely in the dark in this regard, as were the city officials and the other reviewing courts. Petitioner claims that the nature of the film is

b. Warren, C.J., dissented, objecting that the New York law "places the book on trial" without any consideration of its "manner of use." Black and Douglas, JJ., dissented, objecting to a state-wide decree depriving the publisher of separate trials in different communities, and to substituting "punishment by contempt for punishment by jury trial." Brennan, J., dissenting, contended that a jury trial is required to apply properly the *Roth* standard for obscenity.

1. The portion of the section here under attack is as follows: "Such permit shall be granted only after the motion picture film for which said permit is requested has been produced at the office of the commissioner of police for examination or censorship. * * *"

2. That portion of § 155–4 of the Code providing standards is as follows: "If a picture or

series of pictures, for the showing or exhibition of which an application for a permit is made, is immoral or obscene, or portrays, depravity, criminality, or lack of virtue of a class of citizens of any race, color, creed, or religion and exposes them to contempt, derision, or obloquy, or tends to produce a breach of the peace or riots, or purports to represent any hanging, lynching, or burning of a human being, it shall be the duty of the commissioner of police to refuse such permit; otherwise it shall be his duty to grant such permit.

"In case the commissioner of police shall refuse to grant a permit as hereinbefore provided, the applicant for the same may appeal to the mayor. Such appeal shall be presented in the same manner as the original application to the commissioner of police. The action of the mayor on any application for a permit shall be final." * * *

irrelevant, and that even if this film contains the basest type of pornography, or incitement to riot, or forceful overthrow of orderly government, it may nonetheless be shown without prior submission for examination. The challenge here is to the censor's basic authority; it does not go to any statutory standards employed by the censor or procedural requirements as to the submission of the film. * * *

Petitioner would have us hold that the public exhibition of motion pictures must be allowed under any circumstances. The State's sole remedy, it says, is the invocation of criminal process under the Illinois pornography statute and then only after a transgression. But this position [is] founded upon the claim of absolute privilege against prior restraint under the First Amendment—a claim without sanction in our cases. To illustrate its fallacy, we need only point to one of the "exceptional cases" which Chief Justice Hughes enumerated in *Near,* namely, "the primary requirements of decency [that] may be enforced against obscene publications." Moreover, we later held specifically "that obscenity is not within the area of constitutionally protected speech or press." *Roth.* Chicago emphasizes here its duty to protect its people against the dangers of obscenity in the public exhibition of motion pictures. To this argument petitioner's only answer is that regardless of the capacity for, or extent of, such an evil, previous restraint cannot be justified. With this we cannot agree. We recognized in [*Joseph Burstyn, Inc. v. Wilson,* 343 U.S. 495, 72 S.Ct. 777, 96 L.Ed. 1098 (1952)] that "capacity for evil [may] be relevant in determining the permissible scope of community control," and that motion pictures were not "necessarily subject to the precise rules governing any other particular method of expression. Each method," we said, "tends to present its own peculiar problems." [It] is not for this Court to limit the State in its selection of the remedy it deems most effective to cope with such a problem, absent, of course, a showing of unreasonable strictures on individual liberty resulting from its application in particular circumstances. * * *

As to what may be decided when a concrete case involving a specific standard provided by this ordinance is presented, we intimate no opinion. [At] this time we say no more than this—that we are dealing only with motion pictures and, even as to them, only in the context of the broadside attack presented on this record.

Affirmed.

MR. CHIEF JUSTICE WARREN, with whom MR. JUSTICE BLACK, MR. JUSTICE DOUGLAS and MR. JUSTICE BRENNAN join, dissenting.

I cannot agree either with the conclusion reached by the Court or with the reasons advanced for its support. To me, this case clearly presents the question of our approval of unlimited censorship of motion pictures before exhibition through a system of administrative licensing. Moreover, the decision presents a real danger of eventual censorship for every form of communication, be it newspapers, journals, books, magazines, television, radio or public speeches. The Court purports to leave these questions for another day, but I am aware of no constitutional principle which permits us to hold that the communication of ideas through one medium may be censored while other media are immune. Of course each medium presents its own peculiar problems, but they are not of the kind which would authorize the censorship of one form of communication and not others. * * *

I hesitate to disagree with the Court's formulation of the issue before us, but, with all deference, I must insist that the question presented in this case is *not* whether a motion picture exhibitor has a constitutionally protected, "complete and absolute freedom to exhibit, at least once, any and every kind of motion picture." [The] question here presented is whether the City of Chicago—or, for that matter, any city, any State or the Federal Government—may require all motion picture exhibitors to submit all films to a police chief, mayor or other administrative official, for licensing and censorship prior to public exhibition within the jurisdiction.

[In *Near,*] the Court recognized that the First Amendment's rejection of prior censorship through licensing and previous restraint is an inherent and basic principle of freedom of speech and press. Now, the Court strays from that principle; it strikes down that tenet without requiring any demonstration that this is an "exceptional case," whatever that might be, and without any indication that Chicago has sustained the "heavy burden" which was supposed to have been placed upon it. Clearly, this is neither an exceptional case nor has Chicago sustained *any* burden. * * *

The booklets enjoined from distribution in *Kingsley* were concededly obscene. There is no indication that this is true of the moving picture here. This was treated as a particularly crucial distinction. Thus, the Court has suggested that, in times of national emergency, the Government might impose a prior restraint upon "the publication of the sailing dates of transports or the number and location of troops." *Near.* But, surely this is not to suggest that the Government might require that all newspapers be submitted to a censor in order to assist it in preventing such information from reaching print. Yet in this case the Court gives its blessing to the censorship of all motion pictures in order to prevent the exhibition of those it feels to be constitutionally unprotected.

[E]ven if the impact of the motion picture is greater than that of some other media, that fact constitutes no basis for the argument that motion pictures should be subject to greater suppression. This is the traditional argument made in the censor's behalf; this is the argument advanced against newspapers at the time of the invention of the printing press. The argument was ultimately rejected in England, and has consistently been held to be contrary to our Constitution.[a] No compelling reason has been predicated for accepting the contention now. * * *[b]

Notes and Questions

1. Should the producers of *Bambi* be forced to submit their film to show it in a particular city? Should they be forced to pay a license fee? Suppose hundreds of cities adopted the Chicago system? If films must be submitted before exhibition, can a city constitutionally require that books be submitted before distribution? What are the "peculiar problems" associated with films?

2. *Procedural safeguards.* FREEDMAN v. MARYLAND, 380 U.S. 51, 85 S.Ct. 734, 13 L.Ed.2d 649 (1965), per BRENNAN, J., set out procedural safeguards designed to reduce the dangers associated with prior restraints of films. It required that the procedure must "assure a prompt final judicial decision, to minimize the deterrent effect of an interim and possibly erroneous denial of a license," that the censor must promptly institute the proceedings, that the burden of proof to show that the speech in question is unprotected must rest on

a. For the contention that the argument has in fact received a warm reception in the twentieth century, see Lively, *Fear and the Media: A First Amendment Horror Show,* 69 Minn.L.Rev. 1071 (1985).

b. Douglas, J., joined by Warren, C.J., and Black, J., dissenting, elaborated on the evils connected with systems of censorship.

the censor, and that the proceedings be adversarial. The *Freedman* standards have been applied in other contexts. *Blount v. Rizzi*, 400 U.S. 410, 91 S.Ct. 423, 27 L.Ed.2d 498 (1971) (postal stop orders of obscene materials); *United States v. Thirty-Seven Photographs*, 402 U.S. 363, 91 S.Ct. 1400, 28 L.Ed.2d 822 (1971) (customs seizure of obscene materials); *Southeastern Promotions Ltd. v. Conrad*, 420 U.S. 546, 95 S.Ct. 1239, 43 L.Ed.2d 448 (1975) (denial of permit to use municipal theater for the musical, Hair); *Carroll v. President and Commissioners*, 393 U.S. 175, 89 S.Ct. 347, 21 L.Ed.2d 325 (1968) (10 day restraining order against particular rallies or meetings invalid because *ex parte*). Should the collateral bar rule apply to *Carroll* ? Do the *Freedman* standards make the *Times Film* decision palatable? [c] For thorough discussion of the procedural issues, see Monaghan, *First Amendment "Due Process,"* 83 Harv.L.Rev. 518 (1970).

3. *Enjoining habitual use of premises to exhibit obscene films.* Could a state authorize state courts to "abate" the "nuisance" of "habitual use [of premises for] commercial exhibition of obscene" films by enjoining future exhibition of any obscene films at the theater, once a finding of such habitual use is made, based on two or more convictions under the obscenity laws? Cf. *Vance v. Universal Amusement Co.*, 445 U.S. 308, 100 S.Ct. 1156, 63 L.Ed.2d 413 (1980). Would this be consistent with *Freedman?* If such an injunction incorporated the *Miller* obscenity standard, would it intrude on first amendment values any more than a criminal statute forbidding exhibition of obscenity? Cf. *Vance*, White, J., dissenting.

4. *Comparing obscenity and commercial speech.* To combat deception, could commercial advertising be constitutionally subjected to a *Times Film* regime? Would such a scheme be permissible for advertising via some media, but not others? Reconsider fn. 24 in *Virginia Pharmacy*, p. 447 supra. Should the prohibition on prior restraints be inapplicable to injunctions against commercial advertising? Should *Freedman* standards be required? Should injunctions be permitted against a newspaper that carries unprotected advertising in addition to the advertiser? PITTSBURGH PRESS CO. v. HUMAN RELATIONS COMM'N, 413 U.S. 376, 93 S.Ct. 2553, 37 L.Ed.2d 669 (1973), per POWELL, J., upheld an order forbidding Pittsburgh Press to carry sex-designated "help wanted" ads, except for exempt jobs: "As described by Blackstone, the protection against prior restraint at common law barred only a system of administrative censorship. [While] the Court boldly stepped beyond this narrow doctrine in *Near* [it] has never held that all injunctions are impermissible. See *Lorain Journal Co. v. United States*, 342 U.S. 143, 72 S.Ct. 181, 96 L.Ed. 162 (1951).[d] The special vice of a prior restraint is that communication will be suppressed, either directly or by inducing excessive caution in the speaker, before an adequate determination that it is unprotected by the First Amendment.

"The present order does not endanger arguably protected speech. Because the order is based on a continuing course of repetitive conduct, this is not a case in which the Court is asked to speculate as to the effect of publication. Moreover, the order is clear and sweeps no more broadly than necessary. And because no interim relief was granted, the order will not have gone into effect

---

c. For the contention that *Freedman* procedures fail to address the main concern of the prior restraint doctrine, see Redish, *The Proper Role of the Prior Restraint Doctrine in First Amendment Theory*, 70 Va.L.Rev. 53, 75–89 (1984).

d. *Lorain* upheld a Sherman Act injunction restraining a newspaper from seeking to monopolize commerce by refusing to carry advertising from merchants who advertised through a competing radio station.

until it was finally determined that the actions of Pittsburgh Press were unprotected."

STEWART, J., joined by Douglas, J., dissented: Putting to one side "the question of governmental power to prevent publication of information that would clearly imperil the military defense of our Nation," "no government agency can tell a newspaper in advance what it can print and what it cannot." [e]

Does *Pittsburgh Press* indicate the Court will not limit permissible prior restraints to the *Near* "exceptional" areas? Does it mean that when a "continuing course of repetitive conduct" enables a court to make an "adequate determination that [a publication] is unprotected by the First Amendment" the policy against prior restraints does not apply when the restraint will not go "into effect until it [is] finally determined [judicially] that the actions [were] unprotected"? If so, what are the implications for the future of the prior restraint doctrine? Or can *Pittsburgh Press* be narrowly limited as applicable only to repetitive conduct in commercial advertising?

5. *Informal prior restraints.* BANTAM BOOKS, INC. v. SULLIVAN, 372 U.S. 58, 83 S.Ct. 631, 9 L.Ed.2d 584 (1963), per BRENNAN, J., (Harlan, J. dissenting) held unconstitutional the activities of a government commission that would identify "objectionable" books (some admittedly not obscene), notify the distributor in writing, inform the distributor of the Commission's duty to recommend obscenity prosecutions to the Attorney General and that the Commission's list of objectionable books was distributed to local police departments. The Commission thanked distributors in advance for their "cooperation," and a police officer usually visited the distributor to learn what action had been taken. In characterizing these practices as a system of prior administrative restraints, rather than mere legal advice, the Court observed that it did not mean to foreclose private consultation between law enforcement officers and distributors so long as such consultations were "genuinely undertaken with the purpose of aiding the distributor to comply" with the laws and avoid prosecution. What if the Commission circulated its list to distributors, police and prosecutors without mentioning prosecution? What if the prosecutor circulates a list of sixty books he or she regards as obscene and subject to prosecution?

III. LICENSING "PROFESSIONALS": A DICHOTOMY BETWEEN SPEECH AND PRESS?

LOWE v. SEC, ___ U.S. ___, 105 S.Ct. 2557, 83 L.Ed.2d 29 (1985): The Investment Advisors Act of 1940 provides for injunctions and criminal penalties against anyone using the mails in conjunction with the advisory business who is not registered with the SEC or otherwise exempt from registration. An investment advisor includes "any person who, for compensation, engages in the business of advising others, either directly or through publications or writings, as to the value of securities or as to the advisability of investing in, purchasing, or selling securities, or who, for compensation and as part of a regular business, issues or promulgates analyses or reports concerning securities; but does not include [the] publisher of any bona fide newspaper, news magazine or business or financial publication of general and regular [circulation]." The SEC sought an injunction against Lowe and his affiliated businesses primarily alleging that Lowe's registration with the SEC had been properly revoked because of various

e. Blackmun, J., dissented "for substantially the reasons stated by" Stewart, J. Burger, C.J., dissenting, argued that the majority had mischaracterized the character and interim effect of the Commission's order.

fraudulent activities,[a] and that by publishing investment newsletters, Lowe was using the mails as an investment advisor. The SEC did not claim that any information in the newsletters had been false or materially misleading or that Lowe had yet profited from the advice tendered. The SEC did contend that Lowe's prior criminal conduct showed his "total lack of fitness" to remain in an occupation with "numerous opportunities for dishonesty and self-dealing." Lowe admitted that his registration had been properly revoked, but denied that his newsletters were covered by the act and argued that, in any event, they were protected against registration and restraint under the first amendment.

The Court, per STEVENS, J., denied that Lowe's publication of financial newsletters made him an investment advisor under the act. The Court's interpretation was strongly influenced by first amendment considerations. It stated that Congress was "undoubtedly aware of two major First Amendment [cases] decided before the enactment of the Act." Citing *Near* and *Lovell,* the Court pointed to the maxim that "It is always appropriate to assume that our elected representatives, like other citizens, know the law." The doctrine against prior restraints and the notion that freedom of the press includes everything from distributing leaflets to mass circulation of magazines was said to support a "broad reading" of the exclusion for bona fide publishers of regular and general circulation:

"The exclusion itself uses extremely broad language that encompasses any newspaper, business publication, or financial publication provided that two conditions are met. The publication must be 'bona fide,' and it must be 'of regular and general circulation.' Neither of these conditions is defined, but the two qualifications precisely differentiate 'hit and run tipsters' and 'touts' from genuine publishers. Presumably a 'bona fide' publication would be genuine in the sense that it would contain disinterested commentary and analysis as opposed to promotional material disseminated by a 'tout.' Moreover, publications with a 'general and regular' circulation would not include 'people who send out bulletins from time to time on the advisability of buying and selling stocks' or 'hit and run tipsters.' Because the content of petitioners' newsletters was completely disinterested, and because they were offered [b] to the general public on a regular schedule, they are described by the plain language of the exclusion.

* * *

"The dangers of fraud, deception, or overreaching that motivated the enactment of the statute are present in personalized communications but are not replicated in publications that are advertised and sold in an open market.[57] To the extent that the chart service contains factual information about past transactions and market trends, and the newsletters contain commentary on general market conditions, there can be no doubt about the protected character of the communications,[58] a matter that concerned Congress when the exclusion was

a. For example, during the period that he was giving personal investment advice, Lowe had been convicted of misappropriating funds of a client, tampering with evidence to cover up fraud of a client, and stealing from a bank.

b. Lowe's newsletters in fact did not appear according to schedule. White, J., concurring, remarked: "As is evident from the Court's conclusion that petitioner's publications meet the regularity requirement, the Court's construction of the requirement adopts the view of our major law reviews on

the issue of regular publication: good intentions are enough."

57. Cf. *Ohralik.* It is significant that the Commission has not established that petitioners have had authority over the funds of subscribers; that petitioners have been delegated decisionmaking authority to handle subscribers' portfolios or accounts; or that there have been individualized, investment-related interactions between petitioners and subscribers.

58. Moreover, because we have squarely held that the expression of opinion about a drafted. The content of the publications and the audience to which they are directed in this case reveal the specific limits of the exclusion. As long as the communications between petitioners and their subscribers remain entirely impersonal and do not develop into the kind of fiduciary, person-to-person relationships that were discussed at length in the legislative history of the Act and that are characteristic of investment adviser-client relationships, we believe the publications are, at least presumptively, within the exclusion and thus not subject to registration under the Act.[59] " c

WHITE, J., joined by Burger, C.J., and Rehnquist, J., concurring, argued that the Court's statutory interpretation was "improvident" and "based on a thinly disguised conviction" that the Act was unconstitutional as applied to prohibit publication by unregistered advisors: "Indeed the Court tips its hand when it discusses [*Lovell*] and *Near*. [While] purporting not to decide the question, the Court bases its statutory holding in large measure on the assumption that Congress already knew the answer to it when the statute was enacted. The Court thus attributes to the 76th Congress a clairvoyance the Solicitor General and the Second Circuit apparently lack—that is, the ability to predict our constitutional holdings 45 years in advance of our declining to reach them."

Finding it necessary to reach the constitutional question, White, J., argued that an injunction against Lowe's publications would violate the first amendment: "The power of government to regulate the professions is not lost whenever the practice of a profession entails speech. The underlying principle was expressed by the Court in *Giboney v. Empire Storage & Ice Co.*, [336 U.S. 490, 69 S.Ct. 684, 93 L.Ed. 834 (1949)]: 'it has never been deemed an abridgment of freedom of speech or press to make a course of conduct illegal merely because the conduct was in part initiated, evidenced, or carried out by means of language, either spoken, written, or printed.'

"Perhaps the most obvious example of a 'speaking profession' that is subject to governmental licensing is the legal profession. Although a lawyer's work is almost entirely devoted to the sort of communicative acts that, viewed in isolation, fall within the First Amendment's protection, we have never doubted that '[a] State can require high standards of qualification, such as good moral character or proficiency in its law, before it admits an applicant to the [bar].' [To] protect investors, the Government insists, it may require that investment advisers, like lawyers, evince the qualities of truth-speaking, honor, discretion, and fiduciary responsibility.

"But the principle that the government may restrict entry into professions and vocations through licensing schemes has never been extended to encompass the licensing of speech per se or of the press. At some point, a measure is no longer a regulation of a profession but a regulation of speech or of the press; beyond that point, the statute must survive the level of scrutiny demanded by the First Amendment.

commercial product such as a loudspeaker is protected by the First Amendment, *Bose Corp.*, p. 350 supra, it is difficult to see why the expression of an opinion about a marketable security should not also be protected.

59. The Commission suggests that an investment adviser may regularly provide, in newsletterform, advice to several clients based on recent developments, without tailoring the advice to each client's individual needs, and that this is the practice of investment advising. However, the Commission does not suggest that this "practice" is involved here; thus, we have no occasion to address this concern.

c. Powell, J., took no part.

"[It] is for us, then, to find some principle by which to answer the question whether the Investment Advisers Act as applied to petitioner operates as a regulation of speech or of professional conduct.

"This is a problem Justice Jackson wrestled with in his concurring opinion in *Thomas v. Collins*. His words are instructive: '[A] rough distinction always exists, I think, which is more shortly illustrated than explained. A state may forbid one without its license to practice law as a vocation, but I think it could not stop an unlicensed person from making a speech about the rights of man or the rights of labor, or any other kind of right, including recommending that his hearers organize to support his views. Likewise, the state may prohibit the pursuit of medicine as an occupation without its license, but I do not think it could make it a crime publicly or privately to speak urging persons to follow or reject any school of medical thought. So the state to an extent not necessary now to determine may regulate one who makes a business or a livelihood of soliciting funds or memberships for unions. But I do not think it can prohibit one, even if he is a salaried labor leader, from making an address to a public meeting of workmen, telling them their rights as he sees them and urging them to unite in general or to join a specific union.'

"Justice Jackson concluded that the distinguishing factor was whether the speech in any particular case was 'associat[ed] [with] some other factor which the state may regulate so as to bring the whole within its official control.' If 'in a particular case the association or characterization is a proven and valid one,' he concluded, the regulation may stand.

"These ideas help to locate the point where regulation of a profession leaves off and prohibitions on speech begin. One who takes the affairs of a client personally in hand and purports to exercise judgment on behalf of the client in the light of the client's individual needs and circumstances is properly viewed as engaging in the practice of a profession. Just as offer and acceptance are communications incidental to the regulable transaction called a contract, the professional's speech is incidental to the conduct of the profession. [Where] the personal nexus between professional and client does not exist, and a speaker does not purport to be exercising judgment on behalf of any particular individual with whose circumstances he is directly acquainted, government regulation ceases to function as legitimate regulation of professional practice with only incidental impact on speech; it becomes regulation of speaking or publishing as such, subject to the First Amendment's [command].

"I do not believe it is necessary to the resolution of this case to determine whether petitioner's newsletters contain fully protected speech or commercial speech. [E]ven where mere 'commercial speech' is concerned, the First Amendment permits restraints on speech only when they are narrowly tailored to advance a legitimate governmental interest. The interest here is certainly legitimate: the Government wants to prevent investors from falling into the hands of scoundrels and swindlers. The means chosen, however, is extreme. [Our] commercial speech cases have consistently rejected the proposition that such drastic prohibitions on speech may be justified by a mere possibility that the prohibited speech will be fraudulent. See *Zauderer; Bates.* * * *

"I emphasize the narrowness of the constitutional basis on which I would decide this case. I see no infirmity in defining the term 'investment adviser' to include a publisher like petitioner, and I would by no means foreclose the application of, for example, the Act's antifraud or reporting provisions to investment advisers (registered or unregistered) who offer their advice through publications. Nor do I intend to suggest that it is unconstitutional to invoke the Act's provisions for injunctive relief and criminal penalties against unregistered persons who, for compensation, offer personal investment advice to individual clients. I would hold only that the Act may not constitutionally be applied to prevent persons who are unregistered (including persons whose registration has been denied or revoked) from offering impersonal investment advice through publications such as the newsletters published by petitioner."

Notes and Questions

1. Is White, J.'s speech/profession dichotomy persuasive? Should the existence of a "profession" justify prior restraints?

2. Does White, J., suggest an element of special privilege for the press? Consider Shiffrin, *The First Amendment and Economic Regulation: Away From a General Theory of the First Amendment,* 78 Nw.U.L.Rev. 1212, 1276 (1983): "The doctrine of prior restraint may have been designed to put the press on an equal footing. People could speak or write without a license and that ought not to change merely because they used a printing press. Yet we now license a good deal of speech (for example, of lawyers), and those licenses are clearly prior restraints. So we have turned the law upside down. To speak you sometimes need a license; to use the press you almost never do. A doctrine designed to create equality for the press has evolved into one that gives it a special place."

3. If lawyers, psychiatrists, and investment advisors can be licensed, what about fortune tellers? Union organizers? Journalists? [c]

IV. PRIOR RESTRAINTS AND NATIONAL SECURITY

NEW YORK TIMES CO. v. UNITED STATES [THE PENTAGON PAPERS CASE]
403 U.S. 713, 91 S.Ct. 2140, 29 L.Ed.2d 822 (1971).

PER CURIAM.

We granted certiorari in these cases in which the United States seeks to enjoin the *New York Times* and the *Washington Post* from publishing the contents of a classified study entitled "History of U.S. Decision-Making Process on Viet Nam Policy." [a]

"Any system of prior restraints of expression comes to this Court bearing a heavy presumption against its constitutional validity." *Bantam Books;* see also *Near.* The Government "thus carries a heavy burden of showing justification for the enforcement of such a restraint." [The district court in the *Times* case and both lower federal courts] in the *Post* case held that the Government had not met that burden. We agree. [T]he stays entered [by this Court five days previously] are vacated. * * *

Mr. Justice Black, with whom Mr. Justice Douglas joins, concurring.

I adhere to the view that the Government's case against the *Post* should have been dismissed and that the injunction against the *Times* should have been

c. On the question of whether the press clause grants a privileged place for the press, see Sec. 9, IV infra.

a. On June 12–14, 1971 the *New York Times* and on June 18 the *Washington Post* published portions of this "top secret" Pentagon study. Government actions seeking temporary restraining orders and injunctions progressed through two district courts and two courts of appeals between June 15–23. After a June 26 argument, ten Supreme Court opinions were issued on June 30, 1971.

vacated without oral argument when the cases were first presented to this Court. I believe that every moment's continuance of the injunctions against these newspapers amounts to a flagrant, indefensible, and continuing violation of the First Amendment. Furthermore, after oral arguments, I agree [with] the reasons stated by my Brothers Douglas and Brennan. In my view it is unfortunate that some of my Brethren are apparently willing to hold that the publication of news may sometimes be enjoined. Such a holding would make a shambles of the First Amendment.

[F]or the first time in the 182 years since the founding of the Republic, the federal courts are asked to hold that the First Amendment does not mean what it says, but rather means that the Government can halt the publication of current news of vital importance to the people of this country.

[Both] the history and language of the First Amendment support the view that the press must be left free to publish news, whatever the source, without censorship, injunctions, or prior restraints.

In the First Amendment the Founding Fathers gave the free press the protection it must have to fulfill its essential role in our democracy. The press was to serve the governed, not the governors. The Government's power to censor the press was abolished so that the press would remain forever free to censure the Government. The press was protected so that it could bare the secrets of government and inform the people. Only a free and unrestrained press can effectively expose deception in government.   *   *   *

The Government does not even attempt to rely on any act of Congress. Instead it makes the bold and dangerously far-reaching contention that the courts should take it upon themselves to "make" a law abridging freedom of the press in the name of equity, presidential power and national security, even when the representatives of the people in Congress have adhered to the command of the First Amendment and refused to make such a law. To find that the President has "inherent power" to halt the publication of news by resort to the courts would wipe out the First Amendment and destroy the fundamental liberty and security of the very people the Government hopes to make "secure." [The] word "security" is a broad, vague generality whose contours should not be invoked to abrogate the fundamental law embodied in the First Amendment.   *   *   *

MR. JUSTICE DOUGLAS, with whom MR. JUSTICE BLACK joins, concurring.

While I join the opinion of the Court I believe it necessary to express my views more fully.

[The First Amendment leaves] no room for governmental restraint on the press.

There is, moreover, no statute barring the publication by the press of the material which the *Times* and *Post* seek to use.   *   *   *

These disclosures may have a serious impact. But that is no basis for sanctioning a previous restraint on the press   *   *   *.

The dominant purpose of the First Amendment was to prohibit the widespread practice of governmental suppression of embarrassing information. [A] debate of large proportions goes on in the Nation over our posture in Vietnam. That debate antedated the disclosure of the contents of the present documents. The latter are highly relevant to the debate in progress.

Secrecy in government is fundamentally anti-democratic, perpetuating bureaucratic errors. Open debate and discussion of public issues are vital to our national health. * * *

The stays in these cases that have been in effect for more than a week constitute a flouting of the principles of the First Amendment as interpreted in *Near*.

MR. JUSTICE BRENNAN, concurring.

I write separately [to] emphasize what should be apparent: that our judgment in the present cases may not be taken to indicate the propriety, in the future, of issuing temporary stays and restraining orders to block the publication of material sought to be suppressed by the Government. So far as I can determine, never before has the United States sought to enjoin a newspaper from publishing information in its possession. * * *

The entire thrust of the Government's claim throughout these cases has been that publication of the material sought to be enjoined "could," or "might," or "may" prejudice the national interest in various ways. But the First Amendment tolerates absolutely no prior judicial restraints of the press predicated upon surmise or conjecture that untoward consequences may result.* Our cases, it is true, have indicated that there is a single, extremely narrow class of cases in which the First Amendment's ban on prior judicial restraint may be overriden. Our cases have thus far indicated that such cases may arise only when the Nation "is at war," [*Schenck*]. Even if the present world situation were assumed to be tantamount to a time of war, or if the power of presently available armaments would justify even in peacetime the suppression of information that would set in motion a nuclear holocaust, in neither of these actions has the Government presented or even alleged that publication of items from or based upon the material at issue would cause the happening of an event of that nature. [Thus,] only governmental allegation and proof that publication must inevitably, directly and immediately cause the occurrence of an event kindred to imperiling the safety of a transport already at sea can support even the issuance of an interim restraining order. In no event may mere conclusions be sufficient: for if the Executive Branch seeks judicial aid in preventing publication, it must inevitably submit the basis upon which that aid is sought to scrutiny by the judiciary. And therefore, every restraint issued in this case, whatever its form, has violated the First Amendment—and not less so because that restraint was justified as necessary to afford the courts an opportunity to examine the claim more thoroughly. Unless and until the Government has clearly made out its case, the First Amendment commands that no injunction may issue.

MR. JUSTICE STEWART, with whom MR. JUSTICE WHITE joins, concurring.

[I]n the cases before us we are asked neither to construe specific regulations nor to apply specific laws. We are asked, instead, to perform a function that the Constitution gave to the Executive, not the Judiciary. We are asked, quite simply, to prevent the publication by two newspapers of material that the Executive Branch insists should not, in the national interest, be published. I am convinced that the Executive is correct with respect to some of the documents involved. But I cannot say that disclosure of any of them will surely result in

---

* *Freedman* and similar cases regarding temporary restraints of allegedly obscene materials are not in point. For those cases rest upon the proposition that "obscenity is not protected by the freedoms of speech and press." *Roth*. Here there is no question but that the material sought to be suppressed is within the protection of the First Amendment; the only question is whether, notwithstanding that fact, its publication may be enjoined for a time because of the presence of an overwhelming national interest. * * *

direct, immediate, and irreparable damage to our Nation or its people. That being so, there can under the First Amendment be but one judicial resolution of the issues before us. I join the judgments of the Court.

MR. JUSTICE WHITE, with whom MR. JUSTICE STEWART joins, concurring.

I concur in today's judgments, but only because of the concededly extraordinary protection against prior restraints enjoyed by the press under our constitutional system. I do not say that in no circumstances would the First Amendment permit an injunction against publishing information about government plans or operations. Nor, after examining the materials the Government characterizes as the most sensitive and destructive, can I deny that revelation of these documents will do substantial damage to public interests. Indeed, I am confident that their disclosure will have that result. But I nevertheless agree that the United States has not satisfied the very heavy burden which it must meet to warrant an injunction against publication in these cases, at least in the absence of express and appropriately limited congressional authorization for prior restraints in circumstances such as these.

The Government's position is simply stated: The responsibility of the Executive for the conduct of the foreign affairs and for the security of the Nation is so basic that the President is entitled to an injunction against publication of a newspaper story whenever he can convince a court that the information to be revealed threatens "grave and irreparable" injury to the public interest; and the injunction should issue whether or not the material to be published is classified, whether or not publication would be lawful under relevant criminal statutes enacted by Congress and regardless of the circumstances by which the newspaper came into possession of the information.

At least in the absence of legislation by Congress, based on its own investigations and findings, I am quite unable to agree that the inherent powers of the Executive and the courts reach so far as to authorize remedies having such sweeping potential for inhibiting publications by the press. [To] sustain the Government in these cases would start the courts down a long and hazardous road that I am not willing to travel at least without congressional guidance and direction.

* * * Prior restraints require an unusually heavy justification under the First Amendment; but failure by the Government to justify prior restraints does not measure its constitutional entitlement to a conviction for criminal publication. That the Government mistakenly chose to proceed by injunction does not mean that it could not successfully proceed in another way.

* * * Congress has addressed itself to the problems of protecting the security of the country and the national defense from unauthorized disclosure of potentially damaging information. Cf. [Steel Seizure Case, p. 18 supra]. It has not, however, authorized the injunctive remedy against threatened publication. It has apparently been satisfied to rely on criminal sanctions and their deterrent effect on the responsible as well as the irresponsible press. * * *

MR. JUSTICE HARLAN, with whom THE CHIEF JUSTICE and MR. JUSTICE BLACKMUN join, dissenting. * * *

With all respect, I consider that the Court has been almost irresponsibly feverish in dealing with these cases.

Both [the] Second Circuit and [the] District of Columbia Circuit rendered judgment on June 23. [This] Court's order setting a hearing before us on June 26 at 11 a.m., a course which I joined only to avoid the possibility of even more peremptory action by the Court, was issued less than 24 hours before. The record in the *Post* case was filed with the Clerk shortly before 1 p.m. on June 25; the record in the *Times* case did not arrive until 7 or 8 o'clock that same night. The briefs of the parties were received less than two hours before argument on June 26.

This frenzied train of events took place in the name of the presumption against prior restraints created by the First Amendment. Due regard for the extraordinarily important and difficult questions involved in these litigations should have led the Court to shun such a precipitate timetable. In order to decide the merits of these cases properly, some or all of the following questions should have been faced: * * *

2. Whether the First Amendment permits the federal courts to enjoin publication of stories which would present a serious threat to national security. See *Near* (dictum). * * *

4. Whether the unauthorized disclosure of any of these particular documents would seriously impair the national security.

5. What weight should be given to the opinion of high officers in the Executive Branch of the Government with respect to questions 3 and 4. * * *

7. Whether the threatened harm to the national security or the Government's possessory interest in the documents justifies the issuance of an injunction against publication in light of—

a. The strong First Amendment policy against prior restraints on publication; b. The doctrine against enjoining conduct in violation of criminal statutes; and c. The extent to which the materials at issue have apparently already been otherwise disseminated.

These are difficult questions of fact, of law, and of judgment; the potential consequences of erroneous decision are enormous. The time which has been available to us, to the lower courts, and to the parties has been wholly inadequate for giving these cases the kind of consideration they deserve. It is a reflection on the stability of the judicial process that these great issues—as important as any that have arisen during my time on the Court—should have been decided under the pressures engendered by the torrent of publicity that has attended these litigations from their inception.

Forced as I am to reach the merits of these cases, I dissent from the opinion and judgments of the Court. Within the severe limitations imposed by the time constraints under which I have been required to operate, I can only state my reasons in telescoped form, even though in different circumstances I would have felt constrained to deal with the cases in the fuller sweep indicated above.

[It] is plain to me that the scope of the judicial function in passing upon the activities of the Executive Branch of the Government in the field of foreign affairs is very narrowly restricted. This view is, I think, dictated by the concept of separation of powers upon which our constitutional system [rests.] I agree that, in performance of its duty to protect the values of the First Amendment against political pressures, the judiciary must review the initial Executive determination to the point of satisfying itself that the subject matter of the dispute does lie within the proper compass of the President's foreign relations power. Constitutional considerations forbid "a complete abandonment of judicial control." Moreover, the judiciary may properly insist that the determination that disclosure of the subject matter would irreparably impair the national security be made by the head of the Executive Department concerned—here the Secretary of State or the Secretary of Defense—after actual personal consideration by that officer. This safeguard is required in the analogous area of executive claims of privilege for secrets of state.

But in my judgment the judiciary may not properly go beyond these two inquiries and redetermine for itself the probable impact of disclosure on the national security. "[T]he very nature of executive decisions as to foreign policy is political, not judicial. Such decisions are wholly confided by our Constitution to the political departments of the government, Executive and Legislative. They are delicate, complex, and involve large elements of prophecy. They are and should be undertaken only by those directly responsible to the people whose welfare they advance or imperil. They are decisions of a kind for which the judiciary has neither aptitude, facilities nor responsibility and which has long been held to belong in the domain of political power not subject to judicial intrusion or inquiry." *Chicago & S. Air Lines v. Waterman S.S. Corp.* (Jackson, J.), 333 U.S. 103, 68 S.Ct. 431, 92 L.Ed. 568 (1948).

Even if there is some room for the judiciary to override the executive determination, it is plain that the scope of review must be exceedingly narrow. I can see no indication in the opinions of either the District Court or the Court of Appeals in the *Post* litigation that the conclusions of the Executive were given even the deference owing to an administrative agency, much less that owing to a co-equal branch of the Government operating within the field of its constitutional prerogative. * * *

Pending further hearings in each case conducted under the appropriate ground rules, I would continue the restraints on publication. I cannot believe that the doctrine prohibiting prior restraints reaches to the point of preventing courts from maintaining the status quo long enough to act responsibly in matters of such national importance as those involved here.

Mr. Justice Blackmun, dissenting.

[The First Amendment] is only one part of an entire Constitution. Article II of the great document vests in the Executive Branch primary power over the conduct of foreign affairs and places in that branch the responsibility for the Nation's safety. Each provision of the Constitution is important, and I cannot subscribe to a doctrine of unlimited absolutism for the First Amendment at the cost of downgrading other provisions. First Amendment absolutism has never commanded a majority of this Court. What is needed here is a weighing, upon properly developed standards, of the broad right of the press to print and of the very narrow right of the Government to prevent. Such standards are not yet developed. The parties here are in disagreement as to what those standards should be. But even the newspapers concede that there are situations where restraint is in order and is constitutional. Mr. Justice Holmes gave us a suggestion when he said in *Schenck*, "It is a question of proximity and degree. When a nation is at war many things that might be said in time of peace are such a hindrance to its effort that their utterance will not be endured so long as men fight and that no Court could regard them as protected by any constitutional right."

I therefore would remand these cases to be developed expeditiously, of course, but on a schedule permitting the orderly presentation of evidence from both sides [and] with the preparation of briefs, oral argument and court opinions of a quality better than has been seen to this point. [T]hese cases and the issues involved and the courts, including this one, deserve better than has been produced thus far. *   *   *[b]

Notes and Questions

1. *What did the case decide?* Do you agree that "the case [did] not make any law at all, good or bad"? That on the question "whether injunctions against the press are permissible, it is clear that [the case] can supply no precedent?" See Junger, *Down Memory Lane: The Case of the Pentagon Papers,* 23 Case W.Res.L.Rev. 3, 4–5 (1971). Or do you find in several concurring opinions a discernible standard that must be satisfied before a majority of the Court would permit an injunction against the press on national security grounds? Cf. 85 Harv.L.Rev. 199, 205–06 (1971). Do you find guidance as to the outcome if Congress were to authorize an injunction in narrow terms to protect national security? Cf. id. at 204–05. Might it fairly be said that this is a separation of powers decision, like the *Steel Seizure* case, as well as a first amendment decision? See Junger, supra, at 19.

2. *Injunctions against publishing specific material.* Is the special policy against prior restraints, as distinct from use of criminal sanctions, appropriately applied to a specific injunction against publishing identified material? Or should the policy against prior restraints, when applied to court injunctions after a hearing, be limited to broad orders against forbidden types of publications, as in *Near?* To what extent are the evils that underlie the general policy against prior restraints applicable to the specific injunction sought in *Pentagon Papers?* Cf. 85 Harv.L.Rev. at 207–08 (1971).

3. *"De facto" prior restraint.* One difficulty with viewing the prior restraint doctrine as "simply creat[ing] a 'presumption' against the validity of the restraint" (Emerson's characterization of the current approach) rather than as "a prohibition on all restraints subject to certain categorical exceptions," observes Emerson, *First Amendment Doctrine and the Burger Court,* 68 Calif.L.Rev. 422, 457–58 (1980), is that "the requirement of ad hoc scrutiny of prior restraints is itself likely to result in a 'de facto' prior restraint." Pointing to Brennan, J.'s comment in *Pentagon Papers* that "every restraint issued in this case [has] violated the First Amendment—and not less so because that restraint was justified as necessary to afford the courts an opportunity to examine the claim more thoroughly," Emerson notes that "[t]his is exactly what happened when the government sought to enjoin *The Progressive* magazine from publishing an article on the manufacture of the hydrogen bomb. The Supreme Court refused to order an expedited appeal from the [federal district court] injunction against publication [and, although the case was ultimately dismissed by the Seventh Circuit,] *The Progressive* remained under effective prior restraint for nearly seven months."

Compare *Near* and *Pentagon Papers* with UNITED STATES v. PROGRESSIVE, INC., 467 F.Supp. 990 (W.D.Wis.1979) (preliminary injunction issued Mar.

b. Marshall, J., concurring, did not deal with first amendment issues but only with separation of powers—the government's attempt to secure through the Court injunctive relief that Congress had refused to authorize.

Burger, C.J., dissenting, complained that because of "unseemly haste," "we do not know the facts of this case. [W]e literally do not know what we are acting on." He expressed no views on the merits, apart from his joinder in Harlan, J.'s opinion, and a statement that he would have continued the temporary restraints in effect while returning the cases to the lower courts for more thorough exploration of the facts and issues: "I cannot believe that the doctrine prohibiting prior restraints reaches to the point of preventing courts from maintaining the status quo long enough to act responsibly in matters of such national importance as those involved here."

28, 1979), request for writ of mandamus den. sub nom. *Morland v. Sprecher,* 443 U.S. 709, 99 S.Ct. 3086, 61 L.Ed.2d 860 (1979), case dismissed, Nos. 79–1428, 79–1664 (7th Cir. Oct. 1, 1979).[c] *The Progressive* planned to publish an article entitled, "The H-Bomb Secret—How We Got It, Why We're Telling It," maintaining that the article would contribute to informed opinion about nuclear weapons and demonstrate the inadequacies of a system of secrecy and classification. Although the government conceded that at least some of the information contained in the article was "in the public domain" or had been "declassified," it argued that "national security" permitted it to censor information originating in the public domain "if when drawn together, synthesized and collated, such information acquires the character of presenting immediate, direct and irreparable harm to the interests of the United States." The Secretary of State stated that publication would increase thermonuclear proliferation and that this would "irreparably impair the national security of the United States." The Secretary of Defense maintained that dissemination of the Morland article would lead to a substantial increase in the risk of thermonuclear proliferation and to use or threats that would "adversely affect the national security of the United States."

Although recognizing that this constituted "the first instance of prior restraint against a publication in this fashion in the [nation's history]," the district court enjoined defendants, pending final resolution of the litigation, from publishing or otherwise disclosing any information designated by the government as "restricted data" within the meaning of The Atomic Energy Act of 1954: "What is involved here is information dealing with the most destructive weapon in the history of mankind, information of sufficient destructive potential to nullify the right to free speech and to endanger the right to life itself. [Faced] with a stark choice between upholding the right to continued life and the right to freedom of the press, most jurists would have no difficulty in opting for the chance to continue to breathe and function as they work to achieve perfect freedom of expression.

"[A] mistake in ruling against *The Progressive* will seriously infringe cherished First Amendment rights. [A] mistake in ruling against the United States could pave the way for thermonuclear annihilation for us all. In that event, our right to life is extinguished and the right to publish becomes moot.

"[W]ar by foot soldiers has been replaced in large part by machines and bombs. No longer need there be any advance warning or any preparation time before a nuclear war could be commenced. [In light of these factors] publication of the technical information on the hydrogen bomb contained in the article is analogous to publication of troop movements or locations in time of war and falls within the extremely narrow exception to the rule against prior restraint [recognized in *Near*].[d]

"The government has met its burden under § 2274 of The Atomic Energy Act [which authorizes injunctive relief against one who would communicate or disclose restricted data 'with reason to believe such data will be utilized to injure the United States or to secure an advantage to any foreign nation.'] [I]t has also

c. The government's action against *The Progressive* was abandoned after information similar to that it sought to enjoin was published elsewhere.

d. One of the reasons the court gave for finding that the objected-to technical portions of the article fell within the *Near* exception was that it was "unconvinced that suppression of [these portions] would in any plausible fashion impede the defendants in their laudable crusade to stimulate public knowledge of nuclear armament and bring about enlightened debate on national policy questions." Should this have been a factor in the decision to issue the preliminary injunction?

met the test enunciated by two Justices in *Pentagon Papers,* namely grave, direct, immediate and irreparable harm to the United States."

The court distinguished *Pentagon Papers* as follows: "[T]he study involved [there] contained historical data relating to events some three to twenty years previously. Secondly, the Supreme Court agreed with the lower court that no cogent reasons were advanced by the government as to why the article affected national security except that publication might cause some embarrassment to the United States. A final and most vital difference between these two cases is the fact that a specific statute is involved here [§ 2274 of The Atomic Energy Act]."

4. *CIA secrecy agreement.* The Central Intelligence Agency requires employees to sign a "secrecy agreement" as a condition of employment, an agreement committing the employee not to reveal classified information nor to publish any information obtained during the course of employment without prior approval of the Agency. In SNEPP v. UNITED STATES, 444 U.S. 507, 100 S.Ct. 763, 62 L.Ed.2d 704 (1980), Snepp had published a book called *Decent Interval* about certain CIA activities in South Vietnam based on his experiences as an agency employee without seeking prepublication review. At least for purposes of the litigation, the government conceded that Snepp's book divulged no confidential information. The Court, per curiam (Stevens, J., joined by Brennan and Marshall, JJ., dissenting) held that Snepp's failure to submit the book was a breach of trust and the government was entitled to a constructive trust on the proceeds of the book: "[E]ven in the absence of an express agreement, the CIA could have acted to protect substantial government interests by imposing reasonable restrictions on employee activities that in other contexts might be protected by the First Amendment. The Government has a compelling interest in protecting both the secrecy of information important to our national security and the appearance of confidentiality so essential to the effective operation of our foreign intelligence service." [e] When employees or past employees do submit publications for clearance, should *Freedman* standards apply? Can former CIA employees be required to submit all public speeches relating to their former employment for clearance? Are extemporaneous remarks permitted? To what extent can secrecy agreements be required of public employees outside the national security area? [f]

SECTION 3. FAIR ADMINISTRATION OF JUSTICE AND THE FIRST AMENDMENT AS SWORD

This section poses two connected problems. The first implicates familiar themes, albeit in a different context. The government seeks to deter or punish speech it regards as threatening to the fair administration of justice, but the speech at issue falls into no recognized category of unprotected speech. Thus, the courts must consider whether absolute protection is called for, or, alterna-

---

e. Compare *Haig v. Agee,* 453 U.S. 280, 101 S.Ct. 2766, 69 L.Ed.2d 640 (1981), stating that "repeated disclosures of intelligence operations and names of intelligence personnel" for the "purpose of obstructing intelligence operations and the recruiting of intelligence personnel" are "clearly not protected by the Constitution." What if the publisher of the information merely has "reason to believe that such activities would impair or impede the foreign intelligence activities of the United States"? See 50 U.S.C. § 421.

f. For criticism of *Snepp,* see Cheh, *Judicial Supervision of Executive Secrecy,* 69 Cornell L.Rev. 690 (1984); Koffler & Gershman, *The New Seditious Libel,* 69 Corn.L.Rev. 816 (1984); Medow, *The First Amendment and the Secrecy State: Snepp v. United States,* 130 U.Pa.L.Rev. 775 (1982).

tively, whether new categories or ad hoc determinations are appropriate, and whether prior restraints are permissible.

A second problem is unique. Government seeks not to punish speech, but to administer justice in private. It refuses to let the public or press witness its handling of prisoners, or its conduct of trial or pre-trial proceedings. The question is whether the first amendment can serve as a sword allowing citizen-critics to gather information. Assuming it can, what are its limits within the justice system? Does a right of access reach beyond the justice system?

Finally, a recurring issue concerns the role of the press. If the press cannot be prevented from speaking about trials, can prosecutors, defense attorneys, litigants and potential witnesses be prevented from speaking to the press? Is this one problem or many problems? Does the first amendment require that the press be granted access not afforded the public? Does the first amendment permit differential access? If so, what are the limits on how government defines the press?

I. JUSTICE AND THE FIRST AMENDMENT AS SHIELD

In a number of cases, defendants have asserted that their rights to a fair trial have been abridged by newspaper publicity. SHEPPARD v. MAXWELL, 384 U.S. 333, 86 S.Ct. 1507, 16 L.Ed.2d 600 (1966) is probably the most notorious "trial by newspaper" case. The Court, per CLARK, J., (Black, J. dissenting) agreed with the "finding" of the Ohio Supreme Court that the atmosphere of defendant's murder trial was that of a " 'Roman holiday' for the news media." The courtroom was jammed with reporters. And in the corridors outside the courtroom, "a host of photographers and television personnel" photographed witnesses, counsel and jurors as they entered and left the courtroom. Throughout the trial, there was a deluge of publicity, much of which contained information never presented at trial, yet the jurors were not sequestered until the trial was over and they had begun their deliberations.

The Court placed the primary blame on the trial judge. He could "easily" have prevented "the carnival atmosphere of the trial" since "the courtroom and courthouse premises" were subject to his control. For example, he should have provided privacy for the jury, insulated witnesses from the media, instead of allowing them to be interviewed at will, and "made some effort to control the release of leads, information, and gossip to the press by police officers, witnesses, and the counsel for both sides." No one "coming under the jurisdiction of the court should be permitted to frustrate its function."

The Court recognized that "there is nothing that proscribes the press from reporting events that transpire in the courtroom. But where there is a reasonable likelihood that prejudicial news prior to trial will prevent a fair trial, the judge should continue the case until the threat abates, or transfer it to another county not so permeated with publicity. In addition, sequestration of the jury was something the judge should have raised sua sponte with counsel. If publicity during the proceedings threatens the fairness of the trial, a new trial should be ordered. But we must remember that reversals are but palliatives; the cure lies in those remedial measures that will prevent the prejudice at its inception."

The Court, however, reiterated its extreme reluctance "to place any direct limitations on the freedom traditionally exercised by the news media for '[w]hat transpires in the courtroom is public property.' " The press "does not simply publish information about trials but guards against the miscarriage of justice by subjecting the police, prosecutors, and judicial processes to extensive public scrutiny and criticism."

In anticipation of the trial of Simants for a mass murder which had attracted widespread news coverage, the county court prohibited everyone in attendance from, inter alia, releasing or authorizing for publication "any testimony given or evidence adduced." Simants' preliminary hearing (open to the public) was held the same day, subject to the restrictive order. Simants was bound over for trial. Respondent Nebraska state trial judge then entered an order which, as modified by the state supreme court, restrained the press and broadcasting media from reporting any confessions or incriminating statements made by Simants to law enforcement officers or third parties, except members of the press, and from reporting other facts "strongly implicative" of the defendant. The order expired when the jury was impaneled. NEBRASKA PRESS ASS'N v. STUART, 427 U.S. 539, 96 S.Ct. 2791, 49 L.Ed.2d 683 (1976), per BURGER, C.J., struck down the state court order:

"To the extent that the order prohibited the reporting of evidence adduced at the open preliminary hearing, it plainly violated settled principles: 'There is nothing that proscribes the press from reporting events that transpire in the courtroom.' *Sheppard*." [a] To the extent that the order prohibited publication "based on information gained from other sources, [the] heavy burden imposed as a condition to securing a prior restraint was not met." The portion of the order regarding "implicative" information was also "too vague and too broad" to survive scrutiny of restraints on first amendment rights.

"[P]retrial publicity—even pervasive, adverse publicity—does not inevitably lead to an unfair trial. The capacity of the jury eventually impaneled to decide the case fairly is influenced by the tone and extent of the publicity, which is in part, and often in large part, shaped by what attorneys, police and other officials do to precipitate news coverage. [T]he measures a judge takes or fails to take to mitigate the effects of pretrial publicity—the measures described in *Sheppard*—may well determine whether the defendant receives a trial consistent [with] due process.

"[The] Court has interpreted [first amendment] guarantees to afford special protection against orders that prohibit the publication or broadcast of particular information or commentary—orders that impose [a] 'prior' restraint on speech. None of our decided cases on prior restraint involved restrictive orders entered to protect a defendant's right to a fair and impartial jury, but [they] have a common thread relevant to this case. * * *

"The thread running through [*Near* and *Pentagon Papers*], is that prior restraints on speech and publication are the most serious and the least tolerable infringement on First Amendment rights. A criminal penalty or a judgment in a defamation case is subject to the whole panoply of protections afforded by deferring the impact of the judgment until all avenues of appellate review have been exhausted. [But] a prior restraint [has] an immediate and irreversible sanction. If it can be said that a threat of criminal or civil sanctions after publication 'chills' speech, prior restraint 'freezes' it at least for the time.

"[I]f the authors of [the first and sixth amendments], fully aware of the potential conflicts between them, were unwilling or unable to resolve the issue

a. The Court added, however, that the county court "could not know that closure of the preliminary hearing was an alternative open to it until the Nebraska Supreme Court so construed state law."

by assigning to one priority over the other, it is not for us to rewrite the Constitution by undertaking what they declined. [Yet] it is nonetheless clear that the barriers to prior restraint remain high unless we are to abandon what the Court has said for nearly a quarter of our national existence and implied throughout all of [it.]

"We turn now to the record in this case to determine whether, as Learned Hand put it, 'the gravity of the "evil," discounted by its improbability, justifies such invasion of free speech as is necessary to avoid the danger,' *Dennis* [2d Cir.], aff'd. To do so, we must examine the evidence before the trial judge when the order was entered to determine (a) the nature and extent of pretrial news coverage; (b) whether other measures would be likely to mitigate the effects of unrestrained pretrial publicity; (c) how effectively a restraining order would operate to prevent the threatened danger. The precise terms of the restraining order are also important. We must then consider whether the record supports the entry of a prior restraint on publication, one of the most extraordinary remedies known to our jurisprudence."

As to (a), although the trial judge was justified in concluding there would be extensive pretrial publicity concerning this case, he "found only 'a clear and present danger that pretrial publicity *could* impinge upon the defendant's right to a fair trial.' [Emphasis added by the Court]. His conclusion as to the impact of such publicity on prospective jurors was of necessity speculative, dealing as he was with factors unknown and unknowable."

As to (b), "there is no finding that alternative means [e.g., change of venue, postponement of trial to allow public attention to subside, searching questions of prospective jurors] would not have protected Simants' rights, and the Nebraska Supreme Court did no more than imply that such measures might not be adequate. Moreover, the record is lacking in evidence to support such a finding."

As to (c), in view of such practical problems as the limited territorial jurisdiction of the trial court issuing the order, the difficulties of predicting what information "will in fact undermine the impartiality of jurors," the problem of drafting an order that will "effectively keep prejudicial information from prospective jurors," and that the events "took place in a community of only 850 people"—throughout which, "it is reasonable to assume," rumors that "could well be more damaging than reasonably accurate news accounts" would "travel swiftly by word of mouth"—"it is far from clear that prior restraint on publication would have protected Simants' rights."

"[It] is significant that when this Court has reversed a state conviction because of prejudicial publicity, it has carefully noted that some course of action short of prior restraint would have made a critical difference. However difficult it may be, we need not rule out the possibility of showing the kind of threat to fair trial rights that would possess the requisite degree of certainty to justify restraint. [We] reaffirm that the guarantees of freedom of expression are not an absolute prohibition under all circumstances, but the barriers to prior restraint remain high and the presumption against its use continues intact. We hold that, with respect to the order entered in this case [the] heavy burden imposed as a condition to securing a prior restraint was not [met]."

BRENNAN, J., joined by Stewart and Marshall, JJ., concurring, would hold that "resort to prior restraints on the freedom of the press is a constitutionally impermissible method for enforcing [the right to a fair trial by a jury]; judges have at their disposal a broad spectrum of devices for ensuring that fundamental fairness is accorded the accused without necessitating so drastic an incursion on the equally fundamental and salutary constitutional mandate that discussion of public affairs in a free society cannot depend on the preliminary grace of judicial censors": "Commentary and reporting on the criminal justice system is at the core of First Amendment values, for the operation and integrity of that system is of crucial import to citizens concerned with the administration of Government. Secrecy of judicial action can only breed ignorance and distrust of courts and suspicion concerning the competence and impartiality of judges; free and robust reporting, criticism, and debate can contribute to public understanding of the rule of law and to comprehension of the functioning of the entire criminal justice system, as well as improve the quality of that system by subjecting it to the cleansing effects of exposure and public accountability.

"[In] effect, we are now told by respondents that the [first and sixth amendments] can no longer coexist when the press possesses and seeks to publish 'confessions and admissions against interest' and other information 'strongly implicative' of a criminal defendant as the perpetrator of a crime, and that one or the other right must therefore be subordinated. I disagree. Settled case law concerning the impropriety and constitutional invalidity of prior restraints on the press compels the conclusion that there can be no prohibition on the publication by the press of any information pertaining to pending judicial proceedings or the operation of the criminal justice system, no matter how shabby the means by which the information is obtained.[15] This does not imply, however, any subordination of Sixth Amendment rights, for an accused's right to a fair trial may be adequately assured through methods that do not infringe First Amendment values.

"[The narrow national security exception mentioned in *Near* and *Pentagon Papers*] does not mean, as the Nebraska Supreme Court assumed, that prior restraints can be justified on an ad hoc balancing approach that concludes that the 'presumption' must be overcome in light of some perceived 'justification.' Rather, this language refers to the fact that, as a matter of procedural safeguards and burden of proof, prior restraints even within a recognized exception to the rule against prior restraints will be extremely difficult to justify; but as an initial matter, the purpose for which a prior restraint is sought to be imposed 'must fit within one of the narrowly defined exceptions to the prohibition against prior restraints.' Indeed, two Justices in [*Pentagon Papers*] apparently controverted the existence of even a limited 'military security' exception to the rule against prior restraints on the publication of otherwise protected material. (Black, J., concurring); (Douglas, J., concurring). And a majority of the other Justices who expressed their views on the merits made it clear that they would take cognizance only of a 'single, extremely narrow class of cases in which the First Amendment's ban on prior judicial restraint may be overridden.' (Brennan, J., concurring). * * *

"The only exception that has thus far been recognized even in dictum to the blanket prohibition against prior restraints against publication of material which would otherwise be constitutionally shielded was the 'military security' situation addressed in [*Pentagon Papers*]. But unlike the virtually certain, direct, and immediate harm required for such a restraint [the] harm to a fair trial that might otherwise eventuate from publications which are suppressed

---

15. Of course, even if the press cannot be enjoined from reporting certain information, that does not necessarily immunize it from civil liability for libel or invasion of privacy or from criminal liability for transgressions of general criminal laws during the course of obtaining that information.

pursuant to orders such as that under review must inherently remain speculative.

"[O]nce the jury is impaneled, the techniques of sequestration of jurors and control over the courtroom and conduct of trial should prevent prejudicial publicity from infecting the fairness of judicial proceedings. Similarly, judges may stem much of the flow of prejudicial publicity at its source, before it is obtained by representatives of the press. But even if the press nevertheless obtains potentially prejudicial information and decides to publish that information, the Sixth Amendment rights of the accused may still be adequately protected. In particular, the trial judge should employ the voir dire to probe fully into the effect of publicity. [We] have indicated that even in a case involving outrageous publicity and a 'carnival atmosphere' in the courtroom, 'these procedures would have been sufficient to guarantee [the defendant] a fair trial.' [For] this reason, the one thing *Sheppard* did not approve were 'any direct limitations on the freedom traditionally exercised by the news media.' Indeed, the traditional techniques approved in *Sheppard* for ensuring fair trials would have been adequate in every case in which we have found that a new trial was required due to lack of fundamental fairness to the accused. * * *

"There are additional, practical reasons for not starting down the path urged by respondents. The ['military security' exception] involves no judicial weighing of the countervailing public interest in receiving the suppressed information; the direct, immediate, and irreparable harm that would result from disclosure is simply deemed to outweigh the public's interest in knowing, for example, the specific details of troop movements during wartime. [H]owever, any attempt to impose a prior restraint on the reporting of information concerning the operation of the criminal justice system will inevitably involve the courts in an ad hoc evaluation of the need for the public to receive particular information that might nevertheless implicate the accused as the perpetrator of a crime. [T]he press may be arrogant, tyrannical, abusive, and sensationalist, just as it may be incisive, probing, and informative. But at least in the context of prior restraints on publication, the decision of what, when, and how to publish is for editors, not judges. Every restrictive order imposed on the press in this case was accordingly an unconstitutional prior restraint * * *."

Although they joined the Court's opinion, White and Powell, JJ., also filed brief concurrences. WHITE, J., expressed "grave doubts" that these types of restrictive orders "would ever be justifiable." POWELL, J., "emphasize[d] the unique burden" resting upon one who "undertakes to show the necessity for prior restraint on pretrial publicity." In his judgment, a prior restraint "requires a showing that (i) there is a clear threat to the fairness of trial, (ii) such a threat is posed by the actual publicity to be restrained, and (iii) no less restrictive alternatives are available. Notwithstanding such a showing, a restraint may not issue unless it also is shown that previous publicity or publicity from unrestrained sources will not render the restraint inefficacious. [A]ny restraint must comply with the standards of specificity always required in the First Amendment context."

STEVENS, J., concurred in the judgment. For the reasons articulated by Brennan, J., he "agree[d] that the judiciary is capable of protecting the defendant's right to a fair trial without enjoining the press from publishing information in the public domain, and that it may not do so." But he reserved judgment, until further argument, on "[w]hether the same absolute protection would apply no matter how shabby or illegal the means by which the information is obtained, no matter how serious an intrusion on privacy might be involved, no matter how demonstrably false the information might be, no matter how prejudicial it might be to the interests of innocent persons, and no matter how perverse the motivation for publishing it." He indicated that "if ever required to face the issue squarely" he "may well accept [Brennan, J.'s] ultimate conclusion." [b]

Notes and Questions

1. *Why the prior restraint reliance?* Does "the reasoning used by all of the justices premised solely on the traditional aversion to prior restraints, insufficiently" protect the press? Sack, *Principle and Nebraska Press Association v. Stuart,* 29 Stan.L.Rev. 411, 411 (1977). Would the *Nebraska Press* order have been "equally objectionable" if "framed as a statutory sanction punishing publication after it had occurred"? Id. at 415. See also Barnett, *The Puzzle of Prior Restraint,* 29 Stan.L.Rev. 539, 542–44, 560 (1977).

2. *Why the Dennis citation?* Consider Schmidt, *Nebraska Press Association: An Expansion of Freedom and Contraction of Theory,* 29 Stan.L.Rev. 431, 459–60 (1977): Burger, C.J.'s reliance on *Dennis* "is remarkable, almost unbelievable, because that test is both an exceedingly odd means of determining the validity of a prior restraint and a controversial and recently neglected technique of first amendment adjudication. [If] the [*Dennis*] test is the right one for prior restraints, what tests should govern a subsequent punishment case resting on legislation?" See also Barnett, note 1 supra, at 542–44. Burger, C.J.'s citation to *Dennis* should be read in conjunction with dictum in his majority opinion in *Landmark Communications, Inc. v. Virginia,* note 6 infra. There he questioned reliance upon the clear and present danger standard but observed: "Properly applied, the test requires a court to make its own inquiry into the imminence and magnitude of the danger said to flow from the particular utterance and then to balance the character of the evil, as well as its likelihood, against the need for free and unfettered expression. The possibility that other measures will serve the State's interests should also be weighed."

3. *Future press restraints.* Was *Nebraska Press* a strong case for restraint? Is it "difficult to believe that any other case will provide an exception to the rule against prior restraints in fair trial/free press cases"? Goodale, *The Press Ungagged: The Practical Effect on Gag Order Litigation of Nebraska Press Association v. Stuart,* 29 Stan.L.Rev. 497, 504 (1977). If so, does the dispute between the justices over the right standard make a difference? Does the collateral bar rule shed light on that question? See id. at 511–12; Barnett, note 1 supra, at 553–58. Should the collateral bar rule apply in this situation?

4. *Application to non-press defendants.* Should *Nebraska Press* standards apply to court orders preventing prosecutors, witnesses, potential witnesses, jurors, defendants, or defense attorneys from talking to the press about the case? Should different standards apply to each category—e.g., do defendants and defense attorneys deserve as much protection as the press? See Freedman & Starwood, *Prior Restraints on Freedom of Expression by Defendants and Defense Attorneys: Ratio Decidendi v. Obiter Dictum,* 29 Stan.L.Rev. 607 (1977).

5. *Obstructing justice.* A series of cases have held that the first amendment greatly restricts contempt sanctions against persons whose comments on pending cases were alleged to have created a danger of obstruction of the judicial

---

b. For background on *Nebraska Press,* see Friendly & Elliot, *The Constitution: That Delicate Balance* 148–58 (1984).

process. "Such repression can be justified, if at all, only by a clear and present danger of the obstruction of justice." *New York Times Co. v. Sullivan,* p. 347 supra. In *Bridges v. California,* 314 U.S. 252, 62 S.Ct. 190, 86 L.Ed. 192 (1941), union leader Bridges had caused publication or acquiesced in publication of a telegram threatening a strike if an "outrageous" California state decision involving Bridges' dock workers were enforced. The Court reversed Bridges' contempt citation. Consider Tribe, *American Constitutional Law* 624 (1978): "If Bridges' threat to cripple the economy of the entire West Coast did not present danger enough, the lesson of the case must be that almost nothing said outside the courtroom is punishable as contempt." [c]

Would it make a difference if a petit jury were impaneled? Suppose Bridges published an open letter to petit jurors? What if copies were sent by Bridges to each juror? Cf. *Wood v. Georgia,* 370 U.S. 375, 82 S.Ct. 1364, 8 L.Ed.2d 569 (1962) (open letter to press and grand jury—contempt citation reversed). But cf. *Cox v. Louisiana,* p. 873 infra (statute forbidding parades near courthouse with intent to interfere with administration of justice upheld): ("[W]e deal not with the contempt power [but] a statute narrowly drawn to punish" not a pure form of speech but expression mixed with conduct "that infringes a substantial state interest in protecting the judicial process.").

6. *Confidentiality and privacy.* A series of cases has rebuffed state efforts to protect confidentiality or privacy by prohibiting publication. *Cox Broadcasting Corp. v. Cohn,* p. 371 supra (state could not impose liability for public dissemination of the name of rape victim derived from public court documents); *Oklahoma Pub. Co. v. District Court,* 430 U.S. 308, 97 S.Ct. 1045, 51 L.Ed.2d 355 (1977) (pretrial order enjoining press from publishing name or picture of 11-year-old boy accused of murder invalid when reporters had been lawfully present at a prior public hearing and had photographed him en route from the courthouse); *Landmark Communications, Inc. v. Virginia,* 435 U.S. 829, 98 S.Ct. 1535, 56 L.Ed.2d 1 (1978) (statute making it a crime to publish information about particular confidential proceedings invalid as applied to non-participant in the proceedings, at least when the information had been lawfully acquired); *Smith v. Daily Mail Pub. Co.,* 443 U.S. 97, 99 S.Ct. 2667, 61 L.Ed.2d 399 (1979) (statute making it a crime for newspapers (but not broadcasters) to publish the name of any youth charged as a juvenile offender invalid as applied to information lawfully acquired from private sources). But cf. *Seattle Times Co. v. Rhinehart,* 467 U.S. 20, 104 S.Ct. 2199, 81 L.Ed.2d 17 (1984) (order enjoining newspaper from disseminating information acquired as a litigant in pretrial discovery valid so long as order is entered on a showing of good cause and does not restrict the dissemination of the information if gained from other' sources).

II. JUSTICE AND THE FIRST AMENDMENT AS SWORD

By 1978, no Supreme Court holding contradicted Burger, C.J.'s contention for a plurality in *Houchins v. KQED,* 438 U.S. 1, 98 S.Ct. 2588, 57 L.Ed.2d 553 (1978) that, "neither the First Amendment nor the Fourteenth Amendment mandates a right of access to government information or sources of information within the government's control." Or as Stewart, J., put it in an often-quoted statement, "The Constitution itself is neither a Freedom of Information Act nor an Official Secrets Act." *"Or of the Press,"* 26 Hast.L.J. 631, 636 (1975).

---

c. Compare Rieger, *Lawyers' Criticism of Judges: Is Freedom of Speech A Figure of Speech?,* 2 Const.Comm. 69 (1985).

Richmond Newspapers, infra, constitutes the Court's first break with its past denials of first amendment rights to information within governmental control.

RICHMOND NEWSPAPERS, INC. v. VIRGINIA
448 U.S. 555, 100 S.Ct. 2814, 65 L.Ed.2d 973 (1980).

[At the commencement of his fourth trial on a murder charge (his first conviction having been reversed and two subsequent retrials having ended in mistrials), defendant moved, without objection by the prosecutor or two reporters present, that the trial be closed to the public—defense counsel stating that he did not "want any information being shuffled back and forth when we have a recess as [to] who testified to what." The trial judge granted the motion, stating that "the statute gives me that power specifically." He presumably referred to Virginia Code § 19.2–266, providing that in all criminal trials "the court may, in its discretion, exclude [any] persons whose presence would impair the conduct of a fair trial, provided that the [defendant's right] to a public trial shall not be violated." Later the same day the trial court granted appellants' request for a hearing on a motion to vacate the closure order. At the closed hearing, appellants observed that prior to the entry of its closure order the court had failed to make any evidentiary findings or to consider any other, less drastic measures to ensure a fair trial. Defendant stated that he "didn't want information to leak out," be published by the media, perhaps inaccurately, and then be seen by the jurors. Noting inter alia that "having people in the Courtroom is distracting to the jury" and that if "the rights of the defendant are infringed in any way [and if his closure motion] doesn't completely override all rights of everyone else, then I'm inclined to go along with" the defendant, the court denied the motion to vacate the closure order. Defendant was subsequently found not guilty.]

MR. CHIEF JUSTICE BURGER announced the judgment of the Court and delivered an opinion in which MR. JUSTICE WHITE and MR. JUSTICE STEVENS joined.

[T]he precise issue presented here has not previously been before this Court for decision. [*Gannett Co. v. DePasquale,* 443 U.S. 368, 99 S.Ct. 2898, 61 L.Ed.2d 608 (1979)] was not required to decide whether a right of access to *trials,* as distinguished from hearings on *pretrial* motions, was constitutionally guaranteed. The Court held that the Sixth Amendment's guarantee to the accused of a public trial gave neither the public nor the press an enforceable right of access to a *pretrial* suppression hearing. One concurring opinion specifically emphasized that "a hearing on a motion before trial to suppress evidence is not a *trial.*" (Burger, C.J., concurring). Moreover, the Court did not decide whether the First and Fourteenth Amendments guarantee a right of the public to attend trials; nor did the dissenting opinion reach this issue. [H]ere for the first time the Court is asked to decide whether a criminal trial itself may be closed to the public upon the unopposed request of a defendant, without any demonstration that closure is required to protect the defendant's superior right to a fair trial, or that some other overriding consideration requires closure.

[T]he historical evidence demonstrates conclusively that at the time when our organic laws were adopted, criminal trials both here and in England had long been presumptively open [, thus giving] assurance that the proceedings were conducted fairly to all concerned, [and] discourag[ing] perjury, the misconduct of participants, and decisions based on secret bias or partiality. [Moreover, the] early history of open trials in part reflects the widespread acknowledgment [that] public trials had significant therapeutic value. [When] a shocking crime occurs, a community reaction of outrage and public protest often follows. Thereafter the open processes of justice serve an important prophylactic purpose, providing an outlet for community concern, hostility, and emotion.

[The] crucial prophylactic aspects of the administration of justice cannot function in the dark; no community catharsis can occur if justice is "done in a corner [or] in any covert manner." [To] work effectively, it is important that society's criminal process "satisfy the appearance of justice," and the appearance of justice can best be provided by allowing people to observe it.

[From] this unbroken, uncontradicted history, supported by reasons as valid today as in centuries past, we are bound to conclude that a presumption of openness inheres in the very nature of a criminal trial under our system of criminal justice. [Nevertheless,] the State presses its contention that neither the Constitution nor the Bill of Rights contains any provision which by its terms guarantees to the public the right to attend criminal trials. Standing alone, this is correct, but there remains the question whether, absent an explicit provision, the Constitution affords protection against exclusion of the public from criminal trials.

[The] expressly guaranteed [first amendment] freedoms share a common core purpose of assuring freedom of communication on matters relating to the functioning of government. Plainly it would be difficult to single out any aspect of government of higher concern and importance to the people than the manner in which criminal trials are conducted * * *.

The Bill of Rights was enacted against the backdrop of the long history of trials being presumptively open. [In] guaranteeing freedoms such as those of speech and press, the First Amendment can be read as protecting the right of everyone to attend trials so as to give meaning to those explicit guarantees. * * * Free speech carries with it some freedom to listen. "In a variety of contexts this Court has referred to a First Amendment right to 'receive information and ideas.'" *Kleindienst v. Mandel,* 408 U.S. 753, 762, 92 S.Ct. 2576, 2581, 33 L.Ed.2d 683 (1972).[a] What this means in the context of trials is that the First Amendment guarantees of speech and press, standing alone, prohibit government from summarily closing courtroom doors which had long been open to the public at the time that amendment was adopted.

[It] is not crucial whether we describe this right to attend criminal trials to hear, see, and communicate observations concerning them as a "right of access," cf. *Gannett* (Powell, J., concurring); *Saxbe v. Washington Post Co.,* 417 U.S. 843, 94 S.Ct. 2811, 41 L.Ed.2d 514 (1974); *Pell v. Procunier,* 417 U.S. 817, 94 S.Ct. 2800, 41 L.Ed.2d 495 (1974),[11] or a "right to gather information," for we have recognized that "without some protection for seeking out the news, freedom of the press could be eviscerated." *Branzburg v. Hayes,* [p. 655 supra]. The explicit, guaranteed rights to speak and to publish concerning what takes place at a trial would lose much meaning if access to observe the trial could, as it was here, be foreclosed arbitrarily.

a. *Mandel* held that the Executive had plenary power to exclude a Belgium journalist from the country, at least so long as it operated on the basis of a facially legitimate and bona fide reason for exclusion. Although the Court decided ultimately not to balance the government's particular justification against the first amendment interest, it recognized that those who sought personal communication with the excluded alien did have a first amendment interest at stake. The Court apparently assumed that the excluded speaker had no rights at stake, and none were asserted on his behalf.

11. *Procunier* and *Saxbe* are distinguishable in the sense that they were concerned with penal institutions which, by definition, are not "open" or public places. * * * See also *Greer v. Spock* (military bases) [p. 541 infra].

The right of access to places traditionally open to the public, as criminal trials have long been, may be seen as assured by the amalgam of the First Amendment guarantees of speech and press; and their affinity to the right of assembly is not without relevance. From the outset, the right of assembly was regarded not only as an independent right but also as a catalyst to augment the free exercise of the other First Amendment rights with which it was deliberately linked by the draftsmen. * * * Subject to the traditional time, place, and manner restrictions, streets, sidewalks, and parks are places traditionally open, where First Amendment rights may be exercised [see generally Sec. 5 infra]; a trial courtroom also is a public place where the people generally—and representatives of the media—have a right to be present, and where their presence historically has been thought to enhance the integrity and quality of what takes place.

* * * Notwithstanding the appropriate caution against reading into the Constitution rights not explicitly defined, the Court has acknowledged that certain unarticulated rights are implicit in enumerated guarantees [referring, inter alia, to the rights of association and of privacy and the right to travel. See generally Ch. 3, Secs. 2 & 3]. [T]hese important but unarticulated rights [have] been found to share constitutional protection in common with explicit guarantees. The concerns expressed by Madison and others have thus been [resolved].[b]

We hold that the right to attend criminal trials [17] is implicit in the guarantees of the First Amendment; without the freedom to attend such trials, which people have exercised for centuries, important aspects of freedom of speech and "of the press could be eviscerated." *Branzburg.*

[In the present case,] the trial court made no findings to support closure; no inquiry was made as to whether alternative solutions would have met the need to ensure fairness; there was no recognition of any right under the Constitution for the public or press to attend the trial. In contrast to the pretrial proceeding dealt with in *Gannett,* there exist in the context of the trial itself various tested alternatives to satisfy the constitutional demands of fairness. [For example, there was nothing] to indicate that sequestration of the jurors would not have guarded against their being subjected to any improper information.[c] * * * Absent an overriding interest articulated in findings, the trial of a criminal case must be open to the public. * * *

Reversed.[d]

MR. JUSTICE BRENNAN, with whom MR. JUSTICE MARSHALL joins, concurring in the judgment.

[*Gannett*] held that the Sixth Amendment right to a public trial was personal to the accused, conferring no right of access to pretrial proceedings that is separately enforceable by the public or the press. [This case] raises the

b. The Chief Justice noted "the perceived need" of the Constitution's draftsmen "for some sort of constitutional 'saving clause' [which] would serve to foreclose application to the Bill of Rights of the maxim that the affirmation of particular rights implies a negation of those not expressly defined. Madison's efforts, culminating in the Ninth Amendment, served to allay the fears of those who were concerned that expressing certain guarantees could be read as excluding others."

17. Whether the public has a right to attend [civil trials is] not raised by this case, but we note that historically both civil and criminal trials have been presumptively open.

c. Once the jurors are selected, when, if ever, will their sequestration *not* be a satisfactory alternative to closure?

d. Powell, J., took no part. In *Gannett,* he took the position that a first amendment right of access applied to courtroom proceedings, albeit subject to overriding when justice so demanded or when confidentiality was necessary.

question whether the First Amendment, of its own force and as applied to the States through the Fourteenth Amendment, secures the public an independent right of access to trial proceedings. Because I believe that [it does secure] such a public right of access, I agree [that], without more, agreement of the trial judge and the parties cannot constitutionally close a trial to the public.[1]

While freedom of expression is made inviolate by the First Amendment, and with only rare and stringent exceptions, may not be suppressed, the First Amendment has not been viewed by the Court in all settings as providing an equally categorical assurance of the correlative freedom of access to information.[2] Yet the Court has not ruled out a public access component to the First Amendment in every circumstance. Read with care and in context, our decisions must therefore be understood as holding only that any privilege of access to governmental information is subject to a degree of restraint dictated by the nature of the information and countervailing interests in security or confidentiality. [Cases such as *Houchins, Saxbe* and *Pell*] neither comprehensively nor absolutely deny that public access to information may at times be implied by the First Amendment and the principles which animate it.

The Court's approach in right of access cases simply reflects the special nature of a claim of First Amendment right to gather information. Customarily, First Amendment guarantees are interposed to protect communication between speaker and listener. When so employed against prior restraints, free speech protections are almost insurmountable. See generally Brennan, *Address,* 32 Rutg.L.Rev. 173, 176 (1979). But the First Amendment embodies more than a commitment to free expression and communicative interchange for their own sakes; it has a *structural* role to play in securing and fostering our republican system of self-government. Implicit in this structural role is not only "the principle that debate on public issues should be uninhibited, robust, and wide-open," but the antecedent assumption that valuable public debate—as well as other civic behavior—must be informed. The structural model links the First Amendment to that process of communication necessary for a democracy to survive, and thus entails solicitude not only for communication itself, but for the indispensable conditions of meaningful communication.

[A]n assertion of the prerogative to gather information must [be] assayed by considering the information sought and the opposing interests invaded. This judicial task is as much a matter of sensitivity to practical necessities as it is of abstract reasoning. But at least two helpful principles may be sketched. First, the case for a right of access has special force when drawn from an enduring and vital tradition of public entree to particular proceedings or information. Such a tradition commands respect in part because the Constitution carries the gloss of history. More importantly, a tradition of accessibility implies the favorable

---

1. Of course, the Sixth Amendment remains the source of the *accused's* own right to insist upon public judicial proceedings. *Gannett.*

That the Sixth Amendment explicitly establishes a public trial right does not impliedly foreclose the derivation of such a right from other provisions of the Constitution. The Constitution was not framed as a work of carpentry, in which all joints must fit snugly without overlapping. * * *

2. A conceptually separate, yet related, question is whether the media should enjoy

greater access rights than the general public. But no such contention is at stake here. Since the media's right of access is at least equal to that of the general public, this case is resolved by a decision that the state statute unconstitutionally restricts public access to trials. As a practical matter, however, the institutional press is the likely, and fitting, chief beneficiary of a right of access because it serves as the "agent" of interested citizens, and funnels information about trials to a large number of individuals.

judgment of experience. Second, the value of access must be measured in specifics. Analysis is not advanced by rhetorical statements that all information bears upon public issues; what is crucial in individual cases is whether access to a particular government process is important in terms of that very process.

[This Court has] persistently defended the public character of the trial process. *In re Oliver,* 333 U.S. 257, 68 S.Ct. 499, 92 L.Ed. 682 (1948), established that [fourteenth amendment due process] forbids closed criminal trials [and] acknowledged that open trials are indispensable to First Amendment political and religious freedoms.

By the same token, a special solicitude for the public character of judicial proceedings is evident in the Court's rulings upholding the right to report about the administration of justice. While these decisions are impelled by the classic protections afforded by the First Amendment to pure communication, they are also bottomed upon a keen appreciation of the structural interest served in opening the judicial system to public inspection. So, in upholding a privilege for reporting truthful information about judicial misconduct proceedings, *Landmark* emphasized that public scrutiny of the operation of a judicial disciplinary body implicates a major purpose of the First Amendment—"discussion of governmental affairs." Again, *Nebraska Press* noted that the traditional guarantee against prior restraint "should have particular force as applied to reporting of criminal proceedings." And *Cox Broadcasting* instructed that "[w]ith respect to judicial proceedings in particular, the function of the press serves to guarantee the fairness of trials and to bring to bear the beneficial effects of public scrutiny upon the administration of justice."

＊ ＊ ＊ Open trials play a fundamental role in furthering the efforts of our judicial system to assure the criminal defendant a fair and accurate adjudication of guilt or innocence. But, as a feature of our governing system of justice, the trial process serves other, broadly political, interests, and public access advances these objectives as well. To that extent, trial access possesses specific structural significance.

[For] a civilization founded upon principles of ordered liberty to survive and flourish, its members must share the conviction that they are governed equitably. That necessity ＊ ＊ ＊ mandates a system of justice that demonstrates the fairness of the law to our citizens. One major function of the trial is to make that demonstration.

Secrecy is profoundly inimical to this demonstrative [purpose]. Public access is essential, therefore, if trial adjudication is to achieve the objective of maintaining public confidence in the administration of justice. But the trial [also] plays a pivotal role in the entire judicial process, and, by extension, in our form of government. Under our system, judges are not mere umpires, but, in their own sphere, lawmakers—a coordinate branch of *government.* [Thus], so far as the trial is the mechanism for judicial factfinding, as well as the initial forum for legal decisionmaking, it is a genuine governmental proceeding.

[More] importantly, public access to trials acts as an important check, akin in purpose to the other checks and balances that infuse our system of government. "The knowledge that every criminal trial is subject to contemporaneous review in the forum of public opinion is an effective restraint on possible abuse of judicial power," *Oliver*—an abuse that, in many cases, would have ramifications beyond the impact upon the parties before the court. ＊ ＊ ＊

Popular attendance at trials, in sum, substantially furthers the particular public purposes of that critical judicial proceeding.[22] In that sense, public access is an indispensable element of the trial process itself. Trial access, therefore, assumes structural importance in our "government of laws."

As previously noted, resolution of First Amendment public access claims in individual cases must be strongly influenced by the weight of historical practice and by an assessment of the specific structural value of public access in the circumstances. With regard to the case at hand, our ingrained tradition of public trials and the importance of public access to the broader purposes of the trial process, tip the balance strongly toward the rule that trials be open.[23] What countervailing interests might be sufficiently compelling to reverse this presumption of openness need not concern us now,[24] for the statute at stake here authorizes trial closures at the unfettered discretion of the judge and parties.[25] [Thus it] violates the First and Fourteenth Amendments * * *.

MR. JUSTICE STEWART, concurring in the judgment.

Whatever the ultimate answer [may] be with respect to pretrial suppression hearings in criminal cases, the First and Fourteenth Amendments clearly give the press and the public a right of access to trials themselves, civil as well as criminal.[2] * * *

In conspicuous contrast to a military base, *Greer v. Spock*; a jail, *Adderley v. Florida* [p. 541 infra]; or a prison, *Pell*, a trial courtroom is a public place. Even more than city streets, sidewalks, and parks as areas of traditional First Amendment activity, a trial courtroom is a place where representatives of the press and of the public are not only free to be, but where their presence serves to assure the integrity of what goes on.

But this does not mean that the First Amendment right of members of the public and representatives of the press to attend civil and criminal trials is absolute. Just as a legislature may impose reasonable time, place and manner restrictions upon the exercise of First Amendment freedoms, so may a trial judge impose reasonable limitations upon the unrestricted occupation of a courtroom by representatives of the press and members of the public. Moreover, [there] may be occasions when not all who wish to attend a trial may do so.[3] And while there exist many alternative ways to satisfy the constitutional demands of a fair

---

22. In advancing these purposes, the availability of a trial transcript is no substitute for a public presence at the trial itself. As any experienced appellate judge can attest, the "cold" record is a very imperfect reproduction of events that transpire in the courtroom. * * *

23. The presumption of public trials is, of course, not at all incompatible with reasonable restrictions imposed upon courtroom behavior in the interests of decorum. Thus, when engaging in interchanges at the bench, the trial judge is not required to allow public or press intrusion upon the huddle. Nor does this opinion intimate that judges are restricted in their ability to conduct conferences in chambers, inasmuch as such conferences are distinct from trial proceedings.

24. For example, national security concerns about confidentiality may sometimes warrant closures during sensitive portions of trial proceedings, such as testimony about state secrets.

25. Significantly, closing a trial lacks even the justification for barring the door to pretrial hearings: the necessity of preventing dissemination of suppressible prejudicial evidence to the public before the jury pool has become, in a practical sense, finite and subject to sequestration.

2. [The] right to speak implies a freedom to listen, *Kleindienst v. Mandel*. The right to publish implies a freedom to gather information, *Branzburg*. See concurring opinion of Justice Brennan, supra.

3. In such situations, representatives of the press must be assured access, *Houchins* (concurring opinion).

trial, those demands may also sometimes justify limitations upon the unrestricted presence of spectators in the courtroom.[5]

Since in the present case the trial judge appears to have given no recognition to the right [of] the press and [the] public to be present at [the] murder trial over which he was presiding, the judgment under review must be reversed.

* * *

MR. JUSTICE WHITE, concurring.

This case would have been unnecessary had *Gannett* construed the Sixth Amendment to forbid excluding the public from criminal proceedings except in narrowly defined circumstances. But the Court there rejected the submission of four of us to this effect, thus requiring that the First Amendment issue involved here be addressed. On this issue, I concur in the opinion of the Chief Justice.

MR. JUSTICE BLACKMUN, concurring in the judgment.

My opinion and vote in partial dissent [in] *Gannett* compels my vote to reverse the judgment. [It] is gratifying [to] see the Court now looking to and relying upon legal history in determining the fundamental public character of the criminal trial. * * *

The Court's ultimate ruling in *Gannett*, with such clarification as is provided by the opinions in this case today, apparently is now to the effect that there is no *Sixth* Amendment right on the part of the public—or the press—to an open hearing on a motion to suppress. I, of course, continue to believe that *Gannett* was in error, both in its interpretation of the Sixth Amendment generally, and in its application to the suppression hearing, for I remain convinced that the right to a public trial is to be found where the Constitution explicitly placed it— in the Sixth Amendment.

[But] with the Sixth Amendment set to one side in this case, I am driven to conclude, as a secondary position, that the First Amendment must provide some measure of protection for public access to the trial. The opinion in partial dissent in *Gannett* explained that the public has an intense need and a deserved right to know about the administration of justice in general; about the prosecution of local crimes in particular; about the conduct of the judge, the prosecutor, defense counsel, police officers, other public servants, and all the actors in the judicial arena; and about the trial itself. It is clear and obvious to me, on the approach the Court has chosen to take, that, by closing this criminal trial, the trial judge abridged these First Amendment interests of the public. * * *

MR. JUSTICE STEVENS, concurring.

This is a watershed case. Until today the Court has accorded virtually absolute protection to the dissemination of information or ideas, but never before has it squarely held that the acquisition of newsworthy matter is entitled to any constitutional protection whatsoever. An additional word of emphasis is therefore appropriate.

Twice before, the Court has implied that any governmental restriction on access to information, no matter how severe and no matter how unjustified, would be constitutionally acceptable so long as it did not single out the press for special disabilities not applicable to the public at large. In a dissent joined by [Brennan and Marshall, JJ.] in *Saxbe*, Justice Powell unequivocally rejected

---

5. This is not to say that only constitutional considerations can justify such restrictions. The preservation of trade secrets, for example, might justify the exclusion of the public from at least some segments of a civil trial. And the sensibilities of a youthful prosecution witness, for example, might justify similar exclusion in a criminal trial for rape, so long as the defendant's Sixth Amendment right to a public trial were not impaired.

[that conclusion.] And in *Houchins,* I explained at length why [Brennan, Powell, JJ.] and I were convinced that "[a]n official prison policy of concealing ✻ ✻ ✻ knowledge from the public by arbitrarily cutting off the flow of information at its source abridges [first amendment freedoms]." Since [Marshall and Blackmun, JJ.] were unable to participate in that case, a majority of the Court neither accepted nor rejected that conclusion or the contrary conclusion expressed in the prevailing opinions. Today, however, for the first time, the Court unequivocally holds that an arbitrary interference with access to important information is an abridgment of the freedoms of speech and of the press protected by the First Amendment.

It is somewhat ironic that the Court should find more reason to recognize a right of access today than it did in *Houchins.* For *Houchins* involved the plight of a segment of society least able to protect itself, an attack on a longstanding policy of concealment, and an absence of any legitimate justification for abridging public access to information about how government operates. In this case we are protecting the interests of the most powerful voices in the community, we are concerned with an almost unique exception to an established tradition of openness in the conduct of criminal trials, and it is likely that the closure order was motivated by the judge's desire to protect the individual defendant from the burden of a fourth criminal trial.[2]

In any event, for the reasons stated [in] my *Houchins* opinion, as well as those stated by the Chief Justice today, I agree that the First Amendment protects the public and the press from abridgment of their rights of access to information about the operation of their government, including the Judicial Branch; given the total absence of any record justification for the closure order entered in this case, that order violated the First Amendment ✻ ✻ ✻.

MR. JUSTICE REHNQUIST, dissenting.

[For] the reasons stated in my separate concurrence in *Gannett,* I do not believe that [anything in the Constitution] require[s] that a State's reasons for denying public access to a trial, where both [the prosecution and defense] have consented to [a court-approved closure order], are subject to any additional constitutional review at our hands.

[The] issue here is not whether the "right" to freedom of the press ✻ ✻ ✻ overrides the defendant's "right" to a fair trial, [but] whether any provision in the Constitution may fairly be read to prohibit what the [trial court] did in this case. Being unable to find any such prohibition in the First, Sixth, Ninth, or any other Amendments to [the] Constitution, or in the Constitution itself, I dissent.

Notes and Questions

1. *Beyond the justice system.* May (should) "public access to information about how government operates" (to use Stevens, J.'s phrase) be denied, as the Chief Justice suggests, simply on the ground that the place at issue has not been *traditionally* open to the public (recall how the Chief Justice distinguishes penal institutions from criminal trials) or should the government also have to advance,

2. Neither that likely motivation nor facts showing the risk that a fifth trial would have been necessary without closure of the fourth are disclosed in this record, however. The absence of any articulated reason for the closure order is a sufficient basis for distinguishing this case from *Gannett.* The decision to-day is in no way inconsistent with the perfectly unambiguous holding in *Gannett* that the rights guaranteed by the Sixth Amendment are rights that may be asserted by the accused rather than members of the general public. ✻ ✻ ✻

as Stevens, J., suggests, "legitimate justification" for "abridging" public access? Compare the controversy over whether "the right to a public forum" should turn on whether the place at issue has *historically* been dedicated to the exercise of first amendment rights or on whether the manner of expression is *basically incompatible* with the normal activity of the place at a particular time. See generally the materials on "Off Limits" Public Property, Sec. 5, II infra. See also Note, *The First Amendment Right to Gather State-Held Information,* 89 Yale L.J. 923, 933–39 (1979). Consider, too, Blasi, *The Checking Value in First Amendment Theory,* 1977 Am.B.Found.Res.J. 521, 609–10:

"[S]ince, under the checking value [the value that first amendment freedoms can serve in checking the abuse of power by public officials], the dissemination of information about the behavior of government officials is the paradigm First Amendment activity, policies and practices that reduce the amount and quality of information disseminated to the public should not be upheld simply because they serve the convenience, or embody traditional prerogatives, of the government. At a minimum, restrictions on press coverage of official activities should be upheld only if it can be shown that the restrictions substantially promote an important governmental objective that cannot be promoted sufficiently by alternative policies having a less restrictive impact on what interested outsiders can learn about official conduct. For example, under this standard all journalists could not be excluded from a police inspection of the scene of a recent crime if a single pool reporter and/or photographer could be admitted without disrupting the investigation.

"Second, under the checking value, the interest of the press (and ultimately the public) in learning certain information relevant to the abuse of official power would sometimes take precedence over perfectly legitimate and substantial government interests such as efficiency and confidentiality. Thus, the First Amendment may require that journalists have access as a general matter to some records, such as certain financial documents, which anyone investigating common abuses of the public trust would routinely want to inspect, even though the granting of such access would undoubtedly entail some costs and risks. Also, the balance might be tilted even more in the direction of access if a journalist could demonstrate that there are reasonable grounds to believe that certain records contain evidence of misconduct by public officials."

But cf. Kamisar, *Right of Access to Information Generated or Controlled by the Government: Richmond Newspapers Examined and Gannett Revisited* in Choper, Kamisar & Tribe, The Supreme Court: Trends and Developments, 1979–80 145, 166 (1981): "I am sure I am not alone when I say that these law review commentaries go quite far. But *someday* the views they advance may be the law of the land. In the meantime, however, many more battles will have to be fought. *Someday* we may look back on *Richmond Newspapers* as the '*Powell v. Alabama*' of the right of access to government-controlled information—but it was a long, hard road from *Powell* to *Gideon*." [e]

2. *Within the justice system.* How far does (should) *Richmond Newspapers* extend within the justice system? To criminal pre-trial proceedings? How is a trial defined? Should it extend to conferences in chambers or at the bench? To

e. For endorsements of generous access, see Haiman, *Speech and Law in a Free Society* 108–14, 368–97 (1981); Yudof, *When Government Speaks* 246–55 (1983); Emerson, *Legal Foundations of the Right to Know,* 1976 Wash. U.L.Q. 1, 14–17; Lewis, *A Public Right to Know about Public Institutions: The First Amendment as Sword,* 1980 Sup.Ct.Rev. 1. But see BeVier, *An Informed Public, an Informing Press: The Search for a Constitutional Principle,* 68 Calif.L.Rev. 482 (1980).

grand jury hearings? To civil trials? To depositions? To records of any or all of the above? Should it apply outside judicial proceedings? Should wardens be permitted to completely preclude access by the public and press to prisons? To executions? What if the prisoner wants to close the execution? For wide-ranging discussion of these and related questions, see Choper, Kamisar, and Tribe, note 1 supra, at 145–206 (Professor Tribe was winning counsel in *Richmond Newspapers*). See also Fenner & Koley, *Access to Judicial Proceedings: To Richmond Newspapers and Beyond,* 16 Harv.Civ.Rts-Civ.Lib.L.Rev. 415 (1981).

3. *Closing trials.* After *Richmond Newspapers,* what showing should suffice to justify closure of a criminal trial? See *Globe Newspaper Co. v. Superior Court,* 457 U.S. 596, 102 S.Ct. 2613, 73 L.Ed.2d 248 (1982) (routine exclusion of press and public during testimony of minor victim of sex offense unconstitutional); *Press-Enterprise Co. v. Superior Court,* 464 U.S. 501, 104 S.Ct. 819, 78 L.Ed.2d 629 (1984) (extending *Richmond Newspapers* to voir dire examination of jurors). To overcome either the first amendment or the sixth amendment right to a public trial, the Court has required that the party seeking to close the proceedings "must advance an overriding interest that is likely to be prejudiced, the closure must be no broader than necessary to protect that interest, the trial court must consider reasonable alternatives to closing the proceeding, and it must make findings adequate to support the closure." *Waller v. Georgia,* 467 U.S. 39, 104 S.Ct. 2210, 81 L.Ed.2d 31 (1984).

4. *Special access rights for the press.* Is a press section in public trials required when the seating capacity would be exhausted by the public? Is a press section permitted? What limits attach to government determinations of who shall get press passes? See, e.g., *Sherrill v. Knight,* 569 F.2d 124 (D.C.Cir.1977) (denial of White House press pass infringes upon first amendment guarantees in the absence of adequate process); *Borreca v. Fasi,* 369 F.Supp. 906 (D.Haw.1974) (preliminary injunction against denial of access of a reporter to Mayor's press conferences justified when basis for exclusion is allegedly "inaccurate" and "irresponsible" reporting); *Los Angeles Free Press, Inc. v. Los Angeles,* 9 Cal.App. 3d 448, 88 Cal.Rptr. 605 (1970) (exclusion of weekly newspaper from scenes of disaster and police press conferences upheld when newspaper did not report policy and fire events "with some regularity"). When access is required, may the press be prevented from taking notes? Is the right to bring tape recorders into public trials protected under *Richmond Newspapers?* What about "unobtrusive" television cameras? Consider Ares, *Chandler v. Florida: Television, Criminal Trials, and Due Process,* 1981 Sup.Ct.Rev. 157, 174: "Television in the courtroom expands public access to public institutions both qualitatively, because of its immediacy, and quantitatively, because of its reach. It is reported that a majority of Americans acquire their news primarily from television rather than from newspapers. To exclude the most important source of information about the working of courts without some compelling reason cannot be squared with the First Amendment." Cf. *Chandler v. Florida,* 449 U.S. 560, 101 S.Ct. 802, 66 L.Ed.2d 740 (1981) (subject to certain safeguards a state may *permit* electronic media and still photography coverage of public criminal proceedings over the objection of the accused).

Does *Chandler's* holding demean the interest in fair trials? Consider Griswold, *The Standards of the Legal Profession: Canon 35 Should Not Be Surrendered,* 48 A.B.A.J. 615, 617 (1962): "The presence of cameras and television [has] an inhibiting effect on some people, and an exhilarating effect on others. In either event, there would be distortion, and an inevitable interference with the administration of justice. With all the improved techniques in the world, the introduction of radio and television to the courtroom will surely and naturally convert it into a stage for those who can act, and into a place of additional burden for those who cannot." Do these objections apply with the same force to appellate proceedings?[f] Consider Kamisar, *Chandler v. Florida: What Can Be Said for a "Right of Access" to Televise Judicial Proceedings?* in Choper, Kamisar, & Tribe, The Supreme Court: Trends and Developments 1980–81, at 149, 168 (1982): "At the present time, no federal court allows TV coverage. *The place to begin* may well be the place that is likely to be the last holdout—the United States Supreme Court."

SECTION 4. UNCONVENTIONAL FORMS OF COMMUNICATION

Special first amendment questions are often said to arise by regulation of the time, place, and manner of speech as opposed to regulation of its content. But the two types of regulation are not mutually exclusive. It is possible to regulate time, place, manner, and content in the same regulation. For example, in *Linmark,* p. 451 supra, the township outlawed signs (but not leaflets) advertising a house for sale (but not other advertisements or other messages) on front lawns (but not other places).

Further, the terms, manner and content are strongly contested concepts. Indeed, an issue recurring in this section is whether the regulations in question are of manner or content. To the extent this section is about manner regulation, it is not exhaustive—much comes later. This section is confined to unconventional forms of expression. Speakers claim protection for burning draft cards, wearing armbands, mutilating flags, nude dancing, wearing long hair. Fact patterns such as these fix renewed attention on the question of how "speech" should be defined. It may be a nice question as to whether obscenity is not speech within the first amendment lexicon, whether it is such speech but has been balanced into an unprotected state, or whether it is not *freedom* of speech or *the* freedom of speech.[a] But assassinating a public figure, even to send a message, raises no first amendment problem. Robbing a bank does not raise a free speech issue. What does? How do we decide?

The fact patterns in this section also invite scrutiny of other issues that appear in succeeding sections. Should it make a difference if the state's interest in regulating speech is unrelated to what is being said? Suppose the state's concern arises from the non-communicative impact of the speech act—from its manner. Should that distinction make a constitutional difference, and, if so, how much? These questions become more complicated because in context it is often difficult to determine what the state interest is and sometimes difficult to determine whether there is a meaningful distinction between what is said and how it is said.

Finally, in this and succeeding sections the question arises of the extent to which freedom of speech should require special sensitivity to the methods and communications needs of the less powerful.

f. See Ares, supra, at 189–90.   a. See fn. b in *Roth,* p. 378 supra.

UNITED STATES v. O'BRIEN

391 U.S. 367, 88 S.Ct. 1673, 20 L.Ed.2d 672 (1968).

MR. CHIEF JUSTICE WARREN delivered the opinion of the Court.

On the morning of March 31, 1966, David Paul O'Brien and three companions burned their Selective Service registration certificates on the steps of the South Boston Courthouse. A sizable crowd, including several [FBI agents] witnessed the event. Immediately after the burning, members of the crowd began attacking O'Brien [and he was ushered to safety by an FBI agent.] O'Brien stated to FBI agents that he had burned his registration certificate because of his beliefs, knowing that he was violating federal law.

[For this act, O'Brien was convicted in federal court.] He [told] the jury that he burned the certificate publicly to influence others to adopt his antiwar beliefs, as he put it, "so that other people would reevaluate their positions with Selective Service, with the armed forces, and reevaluate their place in the culture of today, to hopefully consider my position."

The indictment upon which he was tried charged that he "wilfully and knowingly did mutilate, destroy, and change by burning [his] Registration Certificate; in violation of [§ 462(b)(3) of the Universal Military Training and Service Act of 1948], amended by Congress in 1965 (adding the words italicized below), so that at the time O'Brien burned his certificate an offense was committed by any person, "who forges, alters, *knowingly destroys, knowingly mutilates,* or in any manner changes any such certificate * * *." (Italics supplied.)

[On appeal, the] First Circuit held the 1965 Amendment unconstitutional as a law abridging freedom of speech. At the time the Amendment was enacted, a regulation of the Selective Service System required registrants to keep their registration certificates in their "personal possession at all times." Wilful violations of regulations promulgated pursuant to the Universal Military Training and Service Act were made criminal by statute. The Court of Appeals, therefore, was of the opinion that conduct punishable under the 1965 Amendment was already punishable under the nonpossession regulation, and consequently that the Amendment served no valid purpose; further, that in light of the prior regulation, the Amendment must have been "directed at public as distinguished from private destruction." On this basis, the Court concluded that the 1965 Amendment ran afoul of the First Amendment by singling out persons engaged in protests for special treatment. * * *

When a male reaches the age of 18, he is required by the Universal Military Training and Service Act to register with a local draft board. He is assigned a Selective Service number, and within five days he is issued a registration certificate. Subsequently, and based on a questionnaire completed by the registrant, he is assigned a classification denoting his eligibility for induction, and "[a]s soon as practicable" thereafter he is issued a Notice of Classification. * * *

Both the registration and classification certificates bear notices that the registrant must notify his local board in writing of every change in address, physical condition, and occupational, marital, family, dependency, and military status, and of any other fact which might change his classification. Both also contain a notice that the registrant's Selective Service number should appear on all communications to his local board.

[The 1965] Amendment does not distinguish between public and private destruction, and it does not punish only destruction engaged in for the purpose of expressing views.[a] A law prohibiting destruction of Selective Service certificates no more abridges free speech on its face than a motor vehicle law prohibiting the destruction of drivers' licenses, or a tax law prohibiting the destruction of books and records.

O'Brien nonetheless argues [first] that the 1965 Amendment is unconstitutional [as] applied to him because his act of burning his registration certificate was protected "symbolic speech" within the First Amendment. [He claims that] the First Amendment guarantees include all modes of "communication of ideas by conduct," and that his conduct is within this definition because he did it in "demonstration against the war and against the draft."

We cannot accept the view that an apparently limitless variety of conduct can be labelled "speech" whenever the person engaging in the conduct intends thereby to express an idea. However, even on the assumption that the alleged communicative element in O'Brien's conduct is sufficient to bring into play the First Amendment, it does not necessarily follow that the destruction of a registration certificate is constitutionally protected activity. This Court has held that when "speech" and "nonspeech" elements are combined in the same course of conduct, a sufficiently important governmental interest in regulating the nonspeech element can justify incidental limitations on First Amendment freedoms. To characterize the quality of the governmental interest which must appear, the Court has employed a variety of descriptive terms: compelling; substantial; subordinating; paramount; cogent; strong. [W]e think it clear that a government regulation is sufficiently justified if it is within the constitutional power of the government; if it furthers an important or substantial governmental interest; if the governmental interest is unrelated to the suppression of free expression;[b] and if the incidental restriction on alleged First Amendment freedom is no greater than is essential to the furtherance of that interest. We find that the 1965 Amendment meets all of these requirements, and consequently that O'Brien can be constitutionally convicted for violating it. [Pursuant to its power to classify and conscript manpower for military service], Congress may establish a system of registration for individuals liable for training and service, and may require such individuals within reason to cooperate in the registration system. The issuance of certificates indicating the registration and eligibility classification of individuals is a legitimate and substantial administrative aid in the functioning of this system. And legislation to insure the continuing availability of issued certificates serves a legitimate and substantial purpose in the system's administration.

[O'Brien] essentially adopts the position that [Selective Service] certificates are so many pieces of paper designed to notify registrants of their registration or classification, to be retained or tossed in the wastebasket according to the

---

a. But compare Chief Judge Aldrich below, 376 F.2d at 541: "We would be closing our eyes in the light of the prior law if we did not see on the face of the amendment that it was precisely directed at public as distinguished from private destruction. [In] singling out persons engaging in protest for special treatment the amendment strikes at the very core of what the First Amendment protects."

b. For the contention that the many tests formulated by the Court are best regarded as

prophylactic rules designed to assure that the forbidden purpose of suppressing ideas does not underlie government acts, see Bogen, *Balancing Freedom of Speech*, 38 Md.L.Rev. 387 (1979); Bogen, *The Supreme Court's Interpretation of the Guarantee of Freedom of Speech*, 35 Md.L.Rev. 555 (1976). See generally Bogen, *Bulwark of Liberty: The Court and the First Amendment* (1984).

convenience or taste of the registrant. Once the registrant has received notification, according to this view, there is no reason for him to retain the certificates. [However, the registration and classification certificates serve] purposes in addition to initial notification. Many of these purposes would be defeated by the certificates' destruction or mutilation. Among these are [simplifying verification of the registration and classification of suspected delinquents, evidence of availability for induction in the event of emergency, ease of communication between registrants and local boards, continually reminding registrants of the need to notify local boards of changes in status].

The many functions performed by Selective Service certificates establish beyond doubt that Congress has a legitimate and substantial interest in preventing their wanton and unrestrained destruction and assuring their continuing availability by punishing people who knowingly and wilfully destroy or mutilate them. And we are unpersuaded that the pre-existence of the nonpossession regulations in any way negates this interest.

In the absence of a question as to multiple punishment, it has never been suggested that there is anything improper in Congress providing alternative statutory avenues of prosecution to assure the effective protection of one and the same interest. Here, the pre-existing avenue of prosecution was not even statutory. Regulations may be modified or revoked from time to time by administrative discretion. Certainly, the Congress may change or supplement a regulation.

[The] gravamen of the offense defined by the statute is the deliberate rendering of certificates unavailable for the various purposes which they may serve. Whether registrants keep their certificates in their personal possession at all times, as required by the regulations, is of no particular concern under the 1965 Amendment, as long as they do not mutilate or destroy the certificates so as to render them unavailable. [The 1965 amendment] is concerned with abuses involving *any* issued Selective Service certificates, not only with the registrant's own certificates. The knowing destruction or mutilation of someone else's certificates would therefore violate the statute but not the nonpossession regulations.

We think it apparent that the continuing availability to each registrant of his Selective Service certificates substantially furthers the smooth and proper functioning of the system that Congress has established to raise armies. * * *

It is equally clear that the 1965 Amendment specifically protects this substantial governmental interest. We perceive no alternative means that would more precisely and narrowly assure the continuing availability of issued Selective Service certificates than a law which prohibits their wilful mutilation or destruction. The 1965 Amendment prohibits such conduct and does nothing more. [The] governmental interest and the scope of the 1965 Amendment are limited to preventing a harm to the smooth and efficient functioning of the Selective Service System. When O'Brien deliberately rendered unavailable his registration certificate, he wilfully frustrated this governmental interest. For this noncommunicative impact of his conduct, and for nothing else, he was convicted.

The case at bar is therefore unlike one where the alleged governmental interest in regulating conduct arises in some measure because the communication allegedly integral to the conduct is itself thought to be harmful [distinguishing *Stromberg*, p. 405 supra].

[B]ecause of the Government's substantial interest in assuring the continuing availability of issued Selective Service certificates, because amended § 462(b) is an appropriately narrow means of protecting this interest and condemns only the independent noncommunicative impact of conduct within its reach, and because the noncommunicative impact of O'Brien's act of burning his registration certificate frustrated the Government's interest, a sufficient governmental interest has been shown to justify O'Brien's conviction.

O'Brien finally argues that the 1965 Amendment is unconstitutional as enacted because what he calls the "purpose" of Congress was "to suppress freedom of speech." We reject this argument because under settled principles the purpose of Congress, as O'Brien uses that term, is not a basis for declaring this legislation unconstitutional.

It is a familiar principle of constitutional law that this Court will not strike down an otherwise constitutional statute on the basis of an alleged illicit legislative motive.[c]

[I]f we were to examine legislative purpose in the instant case, we would be obliged to consider not only [the statements of the three members of Congress who addressed themselves to the amendment, all viewing draft-card burning as a brazen display of unpatriotism] but also the more authoritative reports of the Senate and House Armed Services Committees. [B]oth reports make clear a concern with the "defiant" destruction of so-called "draft cards" and with "open" encouragement to others to destroy their cards, [but they] also indicate that this concern stemmed from an apprehension that unrestrained destruction of cards would disrupt the smooth functioning of the Selective Service System. * * *

Reversed.[d]

MR. JUSTICE HARLAN concurring. * * *

I wish to make explicit my understanding that [the Court's analysis] does not foreclose consideration of First Amendment claims in those rare instances when an "incidental" restriction upon expression, imposed by a regulation which furthers an "important or substantial" governmental interest and satisfies the Court's other criteria, in practice has the effect of entirely preventing a "speaker" from reaching a significant audience with whom he could not otherwise lawfully communicate. This is not such a case, since O'Brien manifestly could have conveyed his message in many ways other than by burning his draft card.

MR. JUSTICE DOUGLAS, dissenting.

[Douglas, J., thought that "the underlying and basic problem in this case" was the constitutionality of a draft "in the absence of a declaration of war" and that the case should be put down for reargument on this question. The following Term, concurring in *Brandenburg*, p. 338 supra, he criticized *O'Brien* on the merits. After recalling that the Court had rejected O'Brien's first amendment argument on the ground that "legislation to insure the continuing availability of issued certificates serves a legitimate and substantial purpose in the [selective service] system's administration," he commented: "But O'Brien was not prosecuted for not having his draft card available when asked for by a federal agent. He was indicted, tried, and convicted for burning the card. And this Court's affirmance [was not] consistent with the First Amendment." He observed, more generally in *Brandenburg*:

["Action is often a method of expression and within the protection of the First Amendment. Suppose one tears up his own copy of the Constitution in

---

c. See generally Ch. 6, Sec. 2, III.   d. Marshall, J., took no part.

eloquent protest to a decision of this Court. May he be indicted? Suppose one rips his own Bible to shreds to celebrate his departure from one 'faith' and his embrace of atheism. May he be indicted? * * *

["The act of praying often involves body posture and movement as well as utterances. It is nonetheless protected by the Free Exercise Clause. Picketing [is] 'free speech plus.' [Therefore], it can be regulated when it comes to the 'plus' or 'action' side of the protest. It can be regulated as to the number of pickets and the place and hours, because traffic and other community problems would otherwise suffer. But none of these considerations are implicated in the symbolic protest of the Vietnam war in the burning of a draft card."]

Notes and Questions

1. *Expression v. action.* What of the Court's rejection of the idea that conduct is speech "whenever the person engaging in the conduct intends thereby to express an idea." Was it right to question whether O'Brien's conduct was speech? What was it about O'Brien's conduct that made the Court doubt that it was speech? What if O'Brien had burned a copy of the Constitution? Consider Emerson, *The System of Freedom of Expression* 80 & 84 (1970): "To some extent expression and action are always mingled; most conduct includes elements of both. Even the clearest manifestations of expression involve some action, as in the case of holding a meeting, publishing a newspaper, or merely talking. At the other extreme, a political assassination includes a substantial mixture of expression. The guiding principle must be to determine which element is predominant in the conduct under consideration. Is expression the major element and the action only secondary? Or is the action the essence and the expression incidental? The answer, to a great extent, must be based on a common-sense reaction, made in light of the functions and operations of a system of freedom of expression. * * *

"The burning of a draft card is, of course, conduct that involves both communication and physical acts. Yet it seems quite clear that the predominant element in such conduct is expression (opposition to the draft) rather than action (destruction of a piece of cardboard). The registrant is not concerned with secret or inadvertent burning of his draft card, involving no communication with other persons. The main feature, for him, is the public nature of the burning, through which he expresses to the community his ideas and feelings about the war and the draft."

Compare Ely, *Flag Desecration: A Case Study in the Roles of Categorization and Balancing in First Amendment Analysis,* 88 Harv.L.Rev. 1482, 1495 (1975): "[B]urning a draft card to express opposition to the draft is an undifferentiated whole, 100% action and 100% expression. It involves no conduct that is not at the same time communication, and no communication that does not result from conduct. Attempts to determine which element 'predominates' will therefore inevitably degenerate into question-begging judgments about whether the activity should be protected.

"The *O'Brien* Court thus quite wisely dropped the 'speech-conduct' distinction as quickly as it had picked it up." [e]

---

e. But, as Dean Ely recognizes, the Court picked it up again in *Cohen,* p. 414 supra: "[W]e deal here with a conviction resting solely upon 'speech', cf. *Stromberg,* not upon any separately identifiable conduct which allegedly was intended by Cohen to be perceived by others as expressive of particular views but which, on its face, does not necessarily convey any message and hence arguably could be regulated without effectively repressing Cohen's ability to express himself. Cf. *O'Brien.*"

Consider, too, Baker, *Scope of the First Amendment Freedom of Speech,* 25 U.C.L.A.L.Rev. 964, 1010–12 (1978): "[S]ince both verbal and nonverbal conduct advances first amendment values, the purpose of the [expression-action] distinction is unclear. Moreover, only an extremely crabbed reading of other clauses of the first amendment will be consistent with implementing an expression-action dichotomy. If religion plays a significant role in one's life, its *free exercise* normally will require doing or abstaining from certain conduct. And people typically assemble and associate to multiply their power in order to do something. Nevertheless, even if his 'expression-action' dichotomy is not very helpful, Emerson consistently makes very perceptive analyses of concrete situations; and these analyses frequently appear to make a different distinction: whether or not the conduct is, or is intended to be, coercive or physically injurious to another. All Emerson's examples of unprotected conduct, 'action,' involve coercion or injury to or physical interference with another or damage to physical property. * * *

"Expressive political protests sometimes involve acts of physical obstruction like lying down in front of troop trains, blocking traffic in a city, or pouring blood over files. Emerson argues that these must be considered 'action,' [but] [n]either the physical activity nor the motives of the actor distinguish these 'action' cases from draft card burning, which Emerson characterizes as expression. Rather, Emerson classifies the first examples of civil disobedience 'action' because the '[c]ivil disobedience attempts to achieve results through a kind of *coercion or pressure* * * *.' However, [draft-card burning], unlike failing to carry a draft card [which presumably 'interferes' or 'obstructs' the working of the selective service system], does not involve coercing or directly injuring or physically obstructing any person or government activity. This fact apparently explains why Emerson concludes that the expression element clearly predominates in draft card burning."[f]

2. *Nature of the state interest and first amendment methodology.* Melville Nimmer, *The Meaning of Symbolic Speech under the First Amendment,* 21 U.C.L.A.L.Rev. 29 (1973), followed by John Hart Ely, note 1 supra, and Laurence Tribe, infra, has proposed that the crucial starting point for first amendment methodology is and should be the nature of the state interest.[g] As Ely puts it, at 1497: "The critical question would therefore seem to be whether the harm that the state is seeking to avert is one that grows out of the fact that the defendant is communicating, and more particularly out of the way people can be expected to react to his message, or rather would arise even if the defendant's conduct had no communicative significance whatever."

For one view of the difference that the distinction makes, see Tribe, *American Constitutional Law* § 12–2, at 582 (1978): "The Supreme Court has evolved two distinct approaches to the resolution of first amendment claims; the two correspond to the two ways in which government may 'abridge' speech. If a government regulation is aimed at the communicative impact of an act, analysis should proceed along what we will call *track one.* On that track, a regulation is unconstitutional unless government shows that the message being suppressed poses a 'clear and present danger,' constitutes a defamatory falsehood, or otherwise falls on the unprotected side of one of the lines the Court has drawn to

---

f. For discussion of Professor Baker's approach and refinement of the expression-action dichotomy, see Emerson, *First Amendment Doctrine and the Burger Court,* 68 Calif. L.Rev. 422, 474–80 (1980).

g. The distinction is a major organizing principle in *Nimmer on Freedom of Speech* (1984).

distinguish those expressive acts privileged by the first amendment from those open to government regulation with only minimal due process scrutiny. If a government regulation is aimed at the noncommunicative impact of an act, its analysis proceeds on what we will call *track two*. On that track, a regulation is constitutional, even as applied to expressive conduct, so long as it does not unduly constrict the flow of information and ideas. On track two, the 'balance' between the values of freedom of expression and the government's regulatory interests is struck on a case-by-case basis, guided by whatever unifying principles may be found in past decisions."

Professor Nimmer, in distinguishing between anti-speech interests (track one) and non-speech interests (track two), would apply definitional balancing (with a presumption in favor of speech) to the former and the *O'Brien* test to the latter. Dean Ely would prevent all regulations on track one except for speech that falls "within a few clearly and narrowly defined catagories." Ely, *Democracy and Distrust* 110 (1980) (emphasis deleted). On track two, Ely insists that balancing is desirable and unavoidable. Ely, note 1 supra, at 1496–1502.

(a) *Normative value of the distinction.* Is balancing unavoidable on either track? How does one decide what the categories should be without balancing? Does the metaphor of balancing wrongly imply that all values are reduced to a single measure and imply non-existent quantitative capacities? Is the distinction between the tracks important enough to require rules on track one, even if ad hoc procedures are allowable on track two? Would this mean that *Pentagon Papers*, p. 488 supra is wrong in suggesting that meeting a "heavy burden" could in some circumstances justify a prior restraint to protect national security? On the other hand, if the *Pentagon Papers* presumption is a "rule," what isn't?

Is the distinction between the two tracks at least strong enough to justify a rebuttable presumption that regulation on track one is invalid, but regulation on track two is not? Consider a regulation governing express warranties in commercial advertising. Is much of contract law on track one? Consider "a nationwide ban on *all* posters (intended to conserve paper)." Isn't that on track two? Do these examples suggest that too much emphasis is being placed on a single factor? See Farber, *Content Regulation and the First Amendment: A Revisionist View*, 68 Geo.U.L.Rev. 727, 746–47 (1980).[h]

(b) *Application to O'Brien.* Consider Ely, note 1 supra, at 1498–99: "The interests upon which the government relied were interests, having mainly to do with the preservation of selective service records, that would have been equally threatened had O'Brien's destruction of his draft card totally lacked communicative significance—had he, for example, used it to start a campfire for a solitary cookout or dropped it in his garbage disposal for a lark. (The law prohibited all knowing destructions, public or private)."

Compare Nimmer, note 2 supra, at 41—contending that the *O'Brien* statute was "overnarrow": "[An overnarrow statute] may be said to create a conclusive presumption that in fact the state interest which the statute serves is an anti- rather than a non-speech interest. If the state interest asserted in *O'Brien* were truly the non-speech interest of assuring availability of draft cards, why did Congress choose not to prohibit any knowing conduct which leads to unavailability, rather than limiting the scope of the statute to those instances in which the proscribed conduct carries with it a speech component hostile to governmental policy? The obvious inference to be drawn is that in fact the Congress was

---

h. See generally Redish, *The Content Distinction in First Amendment Analysis*, 34 Stan.L.Rev. 113 (1981). See notes after *Chicago Police Dept. v. Mosley*, p. 536 infra.

completely indifferent to the 'availability' objective, and was concerned only with an interest which the *O'Brien* opinion states is impermissible—an interest in the suppression of free expression." [i]

(c) *Descriptive value of the distinction.* Does the distinction between the two tracks fully explain the Court's approach in *O'Brien*? Suppose again that an assassin truthfully claims that his or her killing was intended to and did communicate an idea? The assassin's first amendment claim would not prevail, but would it fail because the *O'Brien* test was not met or because no first amendment problem was implicated at all? Is a speech/conduct distinction a necessary prerequisite to the application of the *O'Brien* test? [j]

How different is the *O'Brien* test from the methods used to make decisions on track one? Is the *O'Brien* test as phrased potentially more speech protective than its application in the principal case would suggest? More speech protective than tests sometimes used on track one?

3. *Scope of O'Brien.* Is the *O'Brien* test confined to unconventional forms of communication? Would a distinction of this type be defensible? See Ely, note 1 supra, at 1489: "The distinction is its own objection." See also Alfange, *Free Speech and Symbolic Conduct: The Draft-Card Burning Case,* 1968 Sup.Ct.Rev. 1, 23–24; Velvel, *Freedom of Speech and the Draft Card Burning Cases,* 16 U.Kan. L.Rev. 149, 153 (1968); Henkin, *On Drawing Lines,* 82 Harv.L.Rev. 63, 79 (1968).

TINKER v. DES MOINES SCHOOL DISTRICT
393 U.S. 503, 89 S.Ct. 733, 21 L.Ed.2d 731 (1969).

MR. JUSTICE FORTAS delivered the opinion of the Court.

[Petitioners, two high school students and one junior high student, wore black armbands to school to publicize their objections to the Vietnam conflict and their advocacy of a truce. They refused to remove the armbands when asked to do so. In accordance with a ban on armbands which the city's school principals had adopted two days before in anticipation of such a protest, petitioners were sent home and suspended from school until they would return without the armbands. They sought a federal injunction restraining school officials from disciplining them, but the lower federal courts upheld the constitutionality of the school authorities' action on the ground that it was reasonable in order to prevent a disturbance which might result from the wearing of the armbands.]

[T]he wearing of armbands in the circumstances of this case was entirely divorced from actually or potentially disruptive conduct by those participating in it. It was closely akin to "pure speech" which, we have repeatedly held, is entitled to comprehensive protection under the First Amendment. * * *

First Amendment rights, applied in light of the special characteristics of the school environment, are available to teachers and students. It can hardly be argued that either students or teachers shed their constitutional rights to freedom of speech or expression at the schoolhouse gate. This has been the unmistakable holding of this Court for almost 50 years. In *Meyer v. Nebraska* [1923] [discussed in *Griswold v. Connecticut,* p. 458 supra], this Court [held that

---

i. For consideration of whether the Court's considerations of motive or purpose in *O'Brien* is consistent with its treatment of that issue in freedom of religion, regulation of commerce, and equal protection, see Eisenberg, *Disproportionate Impact and Illicit Motive:* *Theories of Constitutional Adjudication,* 52 N.Y.U.L.Rev. 36 (1977).

j. For commentary on the difficulties in defining speech, see Alexander & Horton, *The Impossibility of a Free Speech Principle,* 78 Nw.U.L.Rev. 1319 (1984).

fourteenth amendment due process] prevents States from forbidding the teaching of a foreign language to young students. Statutes to this effect, the Court held, unconstitutionally interfere with the liberty of teacher, student, and parent.

* * *

The problem presented by the present case does not relate to regulation of the length of skirts or the type of clothing, to hair style or deportment. [It] does not concern aggressive, disruptive action or even group demonstrations. Our problem involves direct, primary First Amendment rights akin to "pure speech."

The school officials banned and sought to punish petitioners for a silent, passive, expression of opinion, unaccompanied by any disorder or disturbance on the part of petitioners. There is here no evidence whatever of petitioners' interference, actual or nascent, with the school's work or of collision with the rights of other students to be secure and to be let alone. Accordingly, this case does not concern speech or action that intrudes upon the work of the school or the rights of other students.

Only a few of the 18,000 students in the school system wore the black armbands. Only five students were suspended for wearing them. There is no indication that the work of the school or any class was disrupted. Outside the classrooms, a few students made hostile remarks to the children wearing armbands, but there were no threats or acts of violence on school premises.

[I]n our system, undifferentiated fear or apprehension of disturbance [the District Court's basis for sustaining the school authorities' action] is not enough to overcome the right to freedom of expression. Any departure from absolute regimentation may cause trouble. Any variation from the majority's opinion may inspire fear. Any words spoken, in class, in the lunchroom or on the campus, that deviates from the views of another person, may start an argument or cause a disturbance. But our Constitution says we must take this risk [and] our history says that it is this sort of hazardous freedom—this kind of openness—that is the basis of our national strength and of the independence and vigor of Americans who grow up and live in this relatively permissive, often disputatious society.

In order for the State in the person of school officials to justify prohibition of a particular expression of opinion, it must be able to show that its action was caused by something more than a mere desire to avoid the discomfort and unpleasantness that always accompany an unpopular viewpoint. Certainly where there is no finding and no showing that the exercise of the forbidden right would "materially and substantially interfere with the requirements of appropriate discipline in the operation of the school," the prohibition cannot be sustained. *Burnside v. Byars.*[a]

In the present case, the District Court made no such finding, and our independent examination of the record fails to yield evidence that the school

---

a. In *Burnside,* 363 F.2d 744 (1966), the Fifth Circuit ordered that high school authorities be enjoined from enforcing a regulation forbidding students to wear "freedom buttons." The Supreme Court deemed it "instructive" [fn. 1] that "in *Blackwell v. Issaquena County Board of Education,* 363 F.2d 749 (1966), the same panel on the same day reached the opposite result on different facts. It declined to enjoin enforcement of such a regulation in another high school where the students wearing freedom buttons harassed students who did not wear them and created much disturbance."

Query: why, in *Issaquena,* didn't the school authorities discipline the small number of button-wearers creating the disturbance rather than strike at the idea of wearing the buttons itself? See *Ferrell v. Dallas Ind. School Dist.,* 392 F.2d 697, 705 & n. 1 (5th Cir.1968) (Tuttle, J., dissenting); Wright, *The Constitution on the Campus,* 22 Vand.L.Rev. 1027, 1054 (1969).

authorities had reason to anticipate that the wearing of the armbands would substantially interfere with the work of the school or impinge upon the rights of other students. Even an official memorandum prepared after the suspension that listed the reasons for the ban on wearing the armbands made no reference to the anticipation of such disruption.[3]

On the contrary, the action of the school authorities appears to have been based upon an urgent wish to avoid the controversy which might result from the expression, even by the silent symbol of armbands, of opposition to this Nation's part in the conflagration in Vietnam. * * *

It is also relevant that the school authorities did not purport to prohibit the wearing of all symbols of political or controversial significance. The record shows that students in some of the schools wore buttons relating to national political campaigns, and some even wore the Iron Cross, traditionally a symbol of nazism. The order prohibiting the wearing of armbands did not extend to these. Instead, a particular symbol—black armbands worn to exhibit opposition to this Nation's involvement in Vietnam—was singled out for prohibition. Clearly, the prohibition of expression of one particular opinion, at least without evidence that it is necessary to avoid material and substantial interference with school work or discipline, is not constitutionally permissible.[b]

In our system, state-operated schools may not be enclaves of totalitarianism. School officials do not possess absolute authority over their students. Students in school as well as out of school are "persons" under our Constitution. They are possessed of fundamental rights which the State must respect, just as they themselves must respect their obligations to the State. In our system, students may not be regarded as closed-circuit recipients of only that which the State chooses to communicate. They may not be confined to the expression of those sentiments that are officially approved. In the absence of a specific showing of constitutionally valid reasons to regulate their speech, students are entitled to freedom of expression of their views.

---

3. The only suggestions of fear of disorder in the report are these: "A former student of one of our high schools was killed in Viet Nam. Some of his friends are still in school and it was felt that if any kind of a demonstration existed, it might evolve into something which would be difficult to control.

"Students at one of the high schools were heard to say they would wear arm bands of other colors if the black bands prevailed."

Moreover, the testimony of school authorities at trial indicates that it was not fear of disruption that motivated the regulation prohibiting the armbands; the regulation was directed against "the principle of the demonstration" itself. School authorities simply felt that "the schools are no place for demonstrations," and if the students "didn't like the way our elected officials were handling things, it should be handled with the ballot box and not in the halls of our public schools."

b. Cf. *Guzick v. Drebus,* 305 F.Supp. 473 (N.D.Ohio 1969), upholding "a long-standing and consistently-applied rule prohibiting the wearing of buttons and other insignia on school grounds during school hours unless these are related to a school-sponsored activity" as "reasonably related to the prevention of the distractions and disruptive and violent conduct" at a racially tense high school; although the button in the instant case did not convey an inflammatory message, the blanket prohibition avoids a situation "in which inflammatory and often insulting buttons would be worn"; a policy permitting certain buttons and excluding others would be "unworkable" in the context of the particular school and "would very likely lead to disruption itself"; a selective policy could not "practically be enforced, for it would require the school authorities to patrol the halls and classes in search of offending buttons"; moreover, such a policy would "necessarily involve the school administration in the controversies" at the school, destroy its "image of complete neutrality," "undermine the structure of discipline" and "materially and substantially affect the educational process"; and any attempt to enforce such a selective policy "would likely entangle the school authorities in the First Amendment prohibition against prior restraints on free speech."

[The principle of prior cases underscoring the importance of diversity and exchange of ideas in the schools,] is not confined to the supervised and ordained discussion which takes place in the classroom. The principal use to which the schools are dedicated is to accommodate students during prescribed hours for the purpose of certain types of activities. Among those activities is personal inter-communication among the students.[6] This is not only an inevitable part of the process of attending school. It is also an important part of the educational process.

A student's rights therefore, do not embrace merely the classroom hours. When he is in the cafeteria, or on the playing field, or on the campus during the authorized hours, he may express his opinions, even on controversial subjects like the conflict in Vietnam, if he does so "[without] materially and substantially interfering [with] appropriate discipline in the operation of the school" and without colliding with the rights of others. *Burnside.* But conduct by the student, in class or out of it, which for any reason—whether it stems from time, place, or type of behavior—materially disrupts classwork or involves substantial disorder or invasion of the rights of others is, of course, not immunized by the [first amendment].

We properly read [the first amendment] to permit reasonable regulation of speech-connected activities in carefully restricted circumstances. But we do not confine the permissible exercise of First Amendment rights to a telephone booth or the four corners of a pamphlet, or to supervised and ordained discussion in a school classroom.[c] * * *

Reversed and remanded.

Mr. Justice Stewart, concurring.

Although I agree with much of what is said in the Court's opinion, and with its judgment in this case, I cannot share the Court's uncritical assumption that, school discipline aside, the First Amendment rights of children are co-extensive with those of adults. Indeed, I had thought the Court decided otherwise just last Term in *Ginsberg v. New York* [p. 388 supra.] I continue to hold the view I expressed in that case: "[A] State may permissibly determine that, at least in some precisely delineated areas, a child—like someone in a captive audience—is not possessed of that full capacity for individual choice which is the presupposition of First Amendment guarantees." (concurring opinion).

Mr. Justice White, concurring.

While I join the Court's opinion, I deem it appropriate to note, first, that the Court continues to recognize a distinction between communicating by words and communicating by acts or conduct which sufficiently impinge on some valid state interest; and, second, that I do not subscribe to everything the Court of Appeals said about free speech in its opinion in *Burnside,* a case relied upon by the Court in the matter now before us.

Mr. Justice Black, dissenting. * * *

---

6. In *Hammond v. South Carolina State College,* 272 F.Supp. 947 (D.C.D.S.C.1967). District Judge Hemphill had before him a case involving a meeting on campus of 300 students to express their views on school practices. He pointed out that a school is not like a hospital or a jail enclosure. It is a public place and its dedication to specific uses does not imply that the constitutional rights of persons entitled to be there are to be gauged as if the premises were purely private property.

c. See also Yudof, *When Governments Speak: Toward a Theory of Government Expression and the First Amendment,* 57 Tex.L. Rev. 863, 884–85 (1979).

Assuming that the Court is correct in holding that the conduct of wearing armbands for the purpose of conveying political ideas is protected by the First Amendment [the] crucial remaining questions are whether students and teachers may use the schools at their whim as a platform for the exercise of free speech—"symbolic" or "pure"—and whether the Courts will allocate to themselves the function of deciding how the pupils' school day will be spent. ＊ ＊ ＊

While the record does not show that any of these armband students shouted, used profane language, or were violent in any manner, detailed testimony by some of them shows their armbands caused comments, warnings by other students, the poking of fun at them, and a warning by an older football player that other, nonprotesting students had better let them alone. There is also evidence that the professor of mathematics had his lesson period practically "wrecked" chiefly by disputes with Beth Tinker, who wore her armband for her "demonstration." Even a casual reading of the record shows that this armband did divert students' minds from their regular lessons, and that talk, comments, etc., made John Tinker "self-conscious" in attending school with his armband. While the absence of obscene or boisterous and loud disorder perhaps justifies the Court's statement that the few armband students did not actually "disrupt" the classwork, I think the record overwhelmingly shows that the armbands did exactly what the elected school officials and principals foresaw it would, that is, took the students' minds off their classwork and diverted them to thoughts about the highly emotional subject of the Vietnam war.

[E]ven if the record were silent as to protests against the Vietnam war distracting students from their assigned class work, members of this Court, like all other citizens, know, without being told, that the disputes over the wisdom of the Vietnam war have disrupted and divided this country as few other issues ever have. Of course students, like other people, cannot concentrate on lesser issues when black armbands are being ostentatiously displayed in their presence to call attention to the wounded and dead of the war, some of the wounded and the dead being their friends and neighbors. It was, of course, to distract the attention of other students that some students insisted up to the very point of their own suspension from school that they were determined to sit in school with their symbolic armbands. ＊ ＊ ＊

Mr. Justice Harlan, dissenting.

I certainly agree that state public school authorities in the discharge of their responsibilities are not wholly exempt from the requirements of the Fourteenth Amendment respecting the freedoms of expression and association. At the same time I am reluctant to believe that there is any disagreement between the majority and myself on the proposition that school officials should be accorded the widest authority in maintaining discipline and good order in their institutions. To translate that proposition into a workable constitutional rule, I would, in cases like this, cast upon those complaining the burden of showing that a particular school measure was motivated by other than legitimate school concerns—for example, a desire to prohibit the expression of an unpopular point of view, while permitting expression of the dominant opinion.

Finding nothing in this record which impugns the good faith of respondents in promulgating the arm band regulation, I would affirm the judgment below.

Notes and Questions

1. By equating the wearing of armbands with "pure speech," did the Court avoid the difficult problem of establishing criteria for determining which vari-

eties of symbolic conduct should be viewed as "speech"? See Denno, *Mary Beth Tinker Takes the Constitution to School,* 38 Ford.L.Rev. 35, 43–44 (1968). Which of the following are "pure speech"? Which are not speech, pure or otherwise? Which should trigger the *O'Brien* test?

(a) *Hair.* See *Freeman v. Flake,* 448 F.2d 258, 260 (10th Cir.1971) (long hair not protected under *Tinker:* "The wearing of long hair is not akin to pure speech. At the most it is symbolic speech indicative of expressions of individuality rather than a contribution to the storehouse of ideas.")

New Rider v. Board of Educ., 414 U.S. 1097, 94 S.Ct. 733, 38 L.Ed.2d 556 (1974), declined to review a tenth circuit decision upholding the indefinite suspension from school of male Pawnee Indians who sought to wear their hair in long braids in violation of an Oklahoma school hair-length regulation forbidding hair reaching the shirt collar or ears. Douglas, J., joined by Marshall, J., dissented from the denial of certiorari: "Petitioners [were] attempting to broadcast a clear and specific message to their fellow students and others—their pride in being Indian. This [should] clearly bring this case within the ambit of *Tinker.* [School officials opined] that allowing petitioners to wear their hair in an Indian manner while restricting the hair length of white students would somehow be 'disruptive' in that an 'integrated school system cannot countenance *different groups* and remain *one* organization.' But as we noted in *Tinker,* this Court long ago recognized that our constitutional system repudiates the idea that a State may conduct its schools 'to foster a homogeneous people.' "

Should hair grown in a particular manner in order to convey a given political or cultural "message" be distinguished from other hair styles? Is the wearing of any given hair style done, at least in part (although perhaps not always consciously) for its "meaning effect"? Compare Note, 84 Harv.L.Rev. 1702, 1707–10 (1971) with Nimmer, note 2 supra, 59–60.

Should school authorities be able to ban an "Afro" or Indian braid, or even "long hair," without a showing that such hair styles are likely to cause substantial disruption of, or material interference with, school activities? Would a non-speech interest such as cleanliness suffice? Would an across-the-board restriction on "long hair" per se be defectively overbroad? See Nimmer, supra.

Does the question of hair, and dress, and appearance of school children generally, involve a significantly less crucial form of expression than "political protest"? Compare Professor Chafee's criticism of the supposed "public"-"private" speech boundary, Sec. 1, II, B supra. Do these questions raise a first amendment question at all or a "right to privacy" issue? See *Kelley v. Johnson,* p. 212 supra, and accompanying discussion. See also the materials on gender discrimination, Ch. 6, Sec. 3, IV infra.

(b) *Nude dancing.* Should nude dancing be excluded from first amendment protection because it is not intended to communicate ideas? Should protection for paintings depend upon whether "ideas" are expressed? See *Schad v. Mt. Ephraim,* p. 443 supra: "[N]ude dancing is not without its First Amendment protections from official regulation." Are hair styles distinguishable from nude dancing on the ground that the latter is a form of expressive entertainment? If so, should video games be afforded first amendment protection? See Note, *The First Amendment Side Effects of Curing Pac-Man Fever,* 84 Colum.L.Rev. 744 (1984). But see Schauer, *Book Review,* 84 Colum.L.Rev. 558, 565 (1984) ("Maybe there is something I am missing, but the first amendment importance of the messages from an automatic teller to the bank's central computer completely escapes me, as does the first amendment importance of the mutual exchange of electronic and visual symbols between me and the Pac-Man machine.")

(c) *Sleeping in the park. Clark v. Community for Creative Non-Violence,* 468 U.S. 288, 104 S.Ct. 3065, 82 L.Ed.2d 221 (1984) assumed but did not decide that overnight sleeping in a public park in connection with a demonstration to call attention to the plight of the homeless "is expressive conduct protected to some extent by the First Amendment." The Court found that a ban against sleeping in the park was a reasonable time, place, and manner restriction and sustainable under the *O'Brien* test. In determining whether conduct ordinarily perceived as non-communicative is communicative in a particular instance, should the courts consider whether there is a nexus between the act and the message? Does such a nexus increase "the likelihood that the act was intended to be communicative, and will be understood to be so"? See Note, *First Amendment Protection of Ambiguous Conduct,* 84 Colum.L.Rev. 467, 493 (1984).

2. Would the school authorities' action have been sustained if they had permitted the wearing of armbands on school property, generally, e.g., in the cafeteria and on the playing fields, and merely required their removal while attending class? Fortas, J., points out that school authorities could not forbid discussion of the Vietnam conflict "anywhere on school property except as part of a prescribed classroom exercise." Is the more relevant inquiry whether discussion of the Vietnam conflict could be *permitted* everywhere on school property *except in prescribed classes*? May a student be prohibited from voicing his opinion of the Vietnam War in the middle of a math class? If so, why can't he be prevented from expressing his views on the same issue in the same class by means of "symbolic speech"? Cf. Nahmod, *Beyond Tinker: The High School as an Educational Public Forum,* 5 Harv.Civ.Rts. & Civ.Lib.L.Rev. 278 (1970).

3. Would the *Tinker* regulation have been sustained if many students, rather than a few, made hostile remarks to the children wearing armbands? If the wearing of armbands had generated acts of violence on school premises? Or the school authorities could reasonably forecast that they would? If so, is such "justification" much more likely to exist when the message is unpopular, or at least controversial? Why should the question whether the wearing of armbands or other forms of protest is to be constitutionally protected turn on whether such protest produces, or is likely to produce, violent reaction by those who would deprive the protestors of the very rights they seek to assert? See generally Sec. 1, V supra.

4. Could school authorities adopt a regulation forbidding *teachers* to wear black armbands in the classroom? Or prohibiting teachers from wearing *all* symbols of political or controversial significance in the classroom or anywhere on school property? Are students a "captive" group? Do the views of a teacher occupying a position of authority carry much more influence with a student than would those of students inter sese? Consider *James v. Bd. of Educ.,* 461 F.2d 566 (2d Cir.1972), holding that school officials violated a high school teacher's constitutional rights by discharging him because he had worn a black armband in class in symbolic protest of the Vietnam War. But the court stressed that "the armband did not disrupt classroom activities [nor] have any influence on any students and did not engender protest from any student, teacher or parent." What if it had? By implication, did the court confirm the potency of the "heckler's veto"? See Note, 39 Brook.L.Rev. 918 (1973). Same result if appellant had been a 3rd grade teacher rather than an 11th grade teacher? See Shiffrin, *Government Speech,* 27 U.C.L.A.L.Rev. 565, 647–53 (1980).

SPENCE v. WASHINGTON, 418 U.S. 405, 94 S.Ct. 2727, 41 L.Ed.2d 842 (1974): On May 10, 1970, a few days after the invasion of Cambodia and the killings at Kent State University, appellant, a college student, hung his United States flag upside down from the window of his apartment, attaching to the front and back a peace symbol (a circle enclosing a trident) made of removable black tape. The flag measured about three by five feet and was plainly visible to passersby. The peace symbol occupied roughly half the surface of the flag. Appellant was charged with violating a statute regulating the ways to display or exhibit the American flag. The statute prohibits any person from placing "any word, figure, mark, picture, design, drawing or advertisement of any nature upon any [United States] flag" or "expos[ing] to public view any such [decorated] flag." It was uncontroverted that appellant's actions were a protest to the invasion of Cambodia and the killings at Kent State and that his purpose was to associate the American flag with peace instead of war and violence: "[I] felt that the flag stood for America and I wanted people to know that I thought America stood for peace." The Court held, per curiam, that his conviction violated the first amendment. Among the factors the Court deemed "important" were that the flag was privately-owned, displayed on private property, involved no risk of breach of the peace—"there is no evidence that anyone other than the three [arresting] officers observed the flag"—and, as the State conceded, the display of the flag and its superimposed peace symbol was "a form of communication." The state's concession "is inevitable on this record." Because "appellant did not choose to articulate his views through printed or spoken words," it was "necessary to determine whether his activity was sufficiently imbued with elements of communication to fall within the scope of the [first amendment]. But the nature of appellant's activity, combined with the factual context and environment in which it was undertaken, lead to the conclusion that he engaged in a form of protected expression."

"Moreover, the context in which a symbol is used for purposes of expression is important, for the context may give meaning to the symbol. See *Tinker*. [A]ppellant's activity was roughly simultaneous with and concededly triggered by the Cambodian incursion and the Kent State tragedy, [like the Vietnam hostilities protested in *Tinker*] issues of great public moment. A flag bearing a peace symbol and displayed upside down by a student might be interpreted as nothing more than bizarre behavior, but it would have been difficult for the great majority of citizens to miss the drift of appellant's point at the time that he made it. [Furthermore], this was not an act of mindless nihilism. Rather, it was a pointed expression of anguish by appellant about the then-current domestic and foreign affairs of his government. An intent to convey a particularized message was present, and in the surrounding circumstances the likelihood was great that the message would be understood by those who viewed it.

"[The] first interest at issue is prevention of breach of the peace. [It] is totally without support in the record.

"We are also unable to affirm the judgment below on the ground that the State may have desired to protect the sensibilities of passersby. 'It is firmly settled that under our Constitution the public expression of ideas may not be prohibited merely because the ideas are themselves offensive to some of their hearers.' *Street v. New York*, [394 U.S. 576, 592, 89 S.Ct. 1354, 1366, 22 L.Ed.2d 572 (1969).] Moreover, appellant did not impose his ideas upon a captive audience. Anyone who might have been offended could easily have avoided the display. See *Cohen.* Nor may appellant be punished for failing to show proper respect for our national emblem.[a]

"We are brought then to the state court's thesis that Washington has an interest in preserving the national flag as an unalloyed symbol of our country. The [state] court did not define this interest; it simply asserted it. The dissenting opinion today adopts essentially the same approach. Presumably, this interest might be seen as an effort to prevent the appropriation of a revered national symbol [where] there was a risk that association of the symbol with a particular product or viewpoint might be taken erroneously as evidence of governmental endorsement.[7] Alternatively, it might be argued that the interest asserted is based on the uniquely universal character of the national flag as a symbol. [If the flag] may be destroyed or permanently disfigured, it could be argued that it will lose its capability of mirroring the sentiments of all who view it.

"But we need not decide in this case whether the interest advanced by the court below is valid.[8] We assume arguendo that it is. The statute is nonetheless unconstitutional as applied to appellant's activity. There was no risk that appellant's acts would mislead viewers into assuming that the Government endorsed his viewpoint. To the contrary, he was plainly and peacefully [10] protesting the fact that it was not. Appellant was not charged under the desecration statute, nor did he permanently disfigure the flag or destroy it. He displayed it as a flag of his country in a way closely analogous to the manner in which flags have always been used to convey ideas. Moreover, his message was direct, likely to be understood, and within the contours of the First Amendment. Given the protected character of his expression and in light of the fact that no interest the State may have in preserving the physical integrity of a privately-owned flag was significantly impaired on these facts, the conviction must be invalidated." [b]

REHNQUIST, J., joined by Burger, C.J., and White, J., dissented: "The statute under which petitioner was convicted is no stranger to this Court, a virtually identical statute having been before the Court in *Halter* [which] held that the

a. *Street* stated that: "We have no doubt that the constitutionally guaranteed 'freedom to be intellectually * * * diverse or even contrary,' and the 'right to differ as to things that touch the heart of the existing order,' encompass the freedom to express publicly one's opinions about our flag, including those opinions which are defiant or contemptuous."

7. Undoubtedly such a concern underlies that portion of the improper use statute forbidding the utilization of representations of the flag in a commercial context. [There] is no occasion in this case to address the application of the challenged statute to commercial behavior. Cf. *Halter v. Nebraska,* 205 U.S. 34, 27 S.Ct. 419, 51 L.Ed. 696 (1907). The dissent places major reliance on *Halter,* despite the fact [it] was decided nearly 20 years before the Court concluded that the First Amendment applies to the States by virtue of the Fourteenth Amendment.

8. If this interest is valid, we note that it is directly related to expression in the context of activity like that undertaken by appellant. For that reason and because no other govern-

mental interest unrelated to expression has been advanced or can be supported on this record, the four-step analysis of *O'Brien* is inapplicable.

10. Appellant's activity occurred at a time of national turmoil over the introduction of United States forces into Cambodia and the deaths at Kent State University. It is difficult now, more than four years later, to recall vividly the depth of emotion that pervaded most colleges and universities at the time, and that was widely shared by young Americans everywhere. A spontaneous outpouring of feeling resulted in widespread action, not all of it rational when viewed in retrospect. This included the closing down of some schools, as well as other disruptions of many centers of education. It was against this highly inflamed background that appellant chose to express his own views in a manner that can fairly be described as gentle and restrained as compared to the actions undertaken by a number of his peers.

b. Douglas, J., wrote a brief concurrence; Blackmun, J., concurred without opinion.

State of Nebraska could enforce its statute to prevent use of a flag representation on beer bottles, stating flatly that 'a State will be wanting in care for the well-being of its people if it ignores the fact that they regard the flag as a symbol of their country's power and prestige. [Such] a use tends to degrade and cheapen the flag in the estimation of the people, as well as to defeat the object of maintaining it as an emblem of National power and National honor.'

"The Court today finds *Halter* irrelevant to the present case, pointing out that it was decided almost 20 years before the First Amendment was applied to the States and further noting that it involved 'commercial behavior,' a form of expression the Court presumably will consider another day. Insofar as *Halter* assesses the State's interest, of course, the Court's argument is simply beside the point. [Yet] if the Court is suggesting that *Halter* would now be decided differently, and that the State's interest in the flag falls before any speech which is 'direct, likely to be understood, and within the contours of the First Amendment,' that view would mean the flag could be auctioned as a background to anyone willing and able to buy or copy one. I find it hard to believe the Court intends to presage that result.

"Turning to the question of the State's interest in the flag, it seems to me that the Court's treatment lacks all substance. The suggestion that the State's interest somehow diminishes when the flag is decorated with *removable* tape trivializes something which is not trivial. [Surely] the Court does not mean to imply that petitioner *could* be prosecuted if he subsequently tore the flag in the process of trying to take the tape off. Unlike flag desecration statutes [the instant statute] seeks to prevent personal *use* of the flag, not simply particular forms of *abuse*. The [state] has chosen to set the flag apart for a special purpose, and has directed that it not be turned into a common background for an endless variety of superimposed messages. The physical condition of the flag itself is irrelevant to that purpose.

"The true nature of the State's interest in this case is not only one of preserving 'the physical integrity of the flag,' but also one of preserving the flag as 'an important symbol of nationhood and unity.' [White, J., concurring in *Smith v. Goguen*, 415 U.S. 566, 94 S.Ct. 1242, 39 L.Ed.2d 605 (1974)] Although the Court treats this important interest with a studied inattention, it is hardly one of recent invention and has previously been accorded considerable respect by this Court. * * *

"There was no question in *Halter* of physical impairment of a flag, since no actual flag was even involved. And it certainly would have made no difference to the Court's discussion of the State's interest if the petitioner in that case had chosen to advertise his product by decorating the flag with beer bottles fashioned from some removable substance. It is the character, not the cloth, of the flag which the State seeks to protect.

"The value of this interest has been emphasized in recent as well as distant times. Mr. Justice Fortas, for example, noted in *Street* that 'the flag is a special kind of personalty,' a form of property 'burdened with peculiar obligations and restrictions.' Mr. Justice White has observed that 'the flag is a national property, and the Nation may regulate those who would make, imitate, sell, possess, or use it.' *Goguen* (concurring opinion).[c] I agree. What petitioner here seeks is simply license to use the flag however he pleases, so long as the activity

---

c. In *Goguen*, White, J., thought it clear that Congress could protect the "physical integrity" or "physical character" of the national flag, just as it could forbid "the mutilation of the Lincoln Memorial [or] prevent overlaying it with words or other objects. The flag is itself a monument, subject to similar protection."

can be tied to a concept of speech, regardless of any state interest in having the flag used only for more limited purposes. I find no reasoning in the Court's opinion which convinces me that the Constitution requires such license to be given.

"The fact that the State has a valid interest in preserving the character of the flag does not mean, of course, that it can employ all conceivable means to enforce it. It certainly could not require all citizens to own the flag or compel citizens to salute one. *Barnette.* It presumably cannot punish criticism of the flag, or the principles for which it stands, any more than it could punish criticism of this country's policies or ideas. But the [instant statute] demands no such allegiance. Its operation does not depend upon whether a particular message is deemed commercial or political; upon whether the use of the flag is respectful or contemptuous; or upon whether any particular segment of the State's citizenry might applaud or oppose the intended message.[7] It simply withdraws a unique national symbol from the roster of materials that may be used as a background for communications." [d]

Notes and Questions

1. *Especially protected speech?* Consider Blasi, *The Checking Value in First Amendment Theory,* 1977 Am.B.Found.Res.J. 521, 640: "[A] proponent of the checking value should be particularly solicitous of conduct that attacks the government's own symbols—for example, the burning or defacing of the American flag—because historically the manipulation of patriotic symbols has been one important way by which tyrannical and abusive governments have overwhelmed their critics."

2. What is the significance of *Spence's* observations that "it would have been difficult for the great majority of citizens to miss the drift of appellant's point"; this "was not an act of mindless nihilism [but] a pointed expression of anguish"; "an intent to convey a particularized message was present"; the message "was direct [and] likely to be understood"? Does the Court mean that flag misuse with less obvious communicative purpose, such as that in *Goguen,* would not be protected under a properly-drawn statute? That in order for symbolic conduct to fall "within the contours of the First Amendment," it must be sufficiently "pointed", "direct" or "likely to be understood"? If so, why? Has any court ever held that the incoherence or obscurity of a *spoken* or *written* message strips it of first amendment protection? See Note, 50 Wash.L.Rev. 169, 183, 187 & n. 104 (1974).

Compare *People v. Cowgill,* 274 Cal.App.2d Supp. 923, 78 Cal.Rptr. 853 (1969), dismissed, 396 U.S. 371, 90 S.Ct. 613, 24 L.Ed.2d 590 (1970) (person who cut up and sewed flag into vest and wore the vest on public streets convicted for violating law making it a misdemeanor to publicly mutilate, deface or defile the American flag). For a first amendment claim to be made, is it necessary that viewers of the vest perceived a message *and* that the wearer of the vest

---

7. It is quite apparent that the Court does have considerable sympathy for at least the *form* of petitioner's message [noting that "appellant chose to express his own views in a manner that can fairly be described as gentle and restrained as compared to the actions undertaken by a number of his peers." One would hope that this last observation does not introduce a doctrine of "comparative" expression, which gives more leeway to certain forms of expression when more destructive methods of expression are being employed by others.

d. Burger, C.J., also wrote a brief dissent, maintaining "it should be left to each state and ultimately the common sense of its people to decide how the flag, as a symbol of national unity, should be protected."

communicated a message? Should the focus instead be on the reasons why the state wanted to punish the actor's conduct? For commentary by Cowgill's counsel, see Nimmer, supra, at 57. Compare Note, *Symbolic Conduct,* 68 Colum. L.Rev. 1091, 1109–17 (1968).

3. *Hypothetical national anthem "misuse" or "desecration" statute.* Does the government have a valid interest in preserving the character of the national anthem as an important symbol of nationhood and unity? Could this symbol be withdrawn from the roster of material that may be used as a background for communication? Could Congress prohibit impairment of the "integrity" of the national anthem by those who would ridicule, degrade, cheapen or cast contempt upon it by punishing all public parodying of the anthem? Could one who expressed opposition to or resentment of national attitudes or governmental policies (e.g., alleged failure to accord blacks or females equal treatment) by changing the words of the Star-Spangled Banner (e.g., "land of the female slaves," "home of the white hypocrites") be successfully prosecuted under such a statute? What would Burger, C.J., Rehnquist, J., and White, J., say?

4. Is the state's interest in preserving the "integrity" of the flag "non-speech" or "anti-speech"? Is a symbol qua symbol essentially a component of speech? Is protection of the flag's "physical integrity" in actuality protection of its *meaning*? Is a flag desecration statute, in effect, "a governmental command that one idea (embodied in the flag symbol) is not to be countered by another idea (embodied in the act of flag desecration)"? When the American flag is the medium of expression, as opposed to parades and demonstrations, is the situation in reality always one of "pure communication"? See Nimmer, supra, at 56–57; 50 Wash.L.Rev., note 2 supra, at 186, 189.

5. How significant is it that the federal government "permits, indeed encourages, people to fly [the flag] as a sign of support for the government"? See Loewy, *Punishing Flag Desecrators: The Ultimate in Flag Desecration,* 49 N.C.L. Rev. 48, 64 (1970), pointing out that 36 U.S.C. § 174(d) urges the flag to be displayed "on all days when the weather permits, especially on," e.g., Inauguration Day, Washington's Birthday, Lincoln's Birthday, Mother's Day, Memorial Day, Independence Day, Navy Day, Veteran's Day, Christmas Day. If the government permits the flag to be used "to credit the country," must it also permit it to be used "to discredit the country"? See Loewy, supra. Cf. *Schacht v. United States,* 398 U.S. 58, 90 S.Ct. 1555, 26 L.Ed.2d 44 (1970) (statute authorizing wearing of U.S. military uniform if the portrayal does not tend to discredit the military violates first amendment).

In considering whether flag burning statutes are "neutral as to content" and whether flag burning is "inherently offensive," how significant is it that 36 U.S.C. § 176(j) provides that "when it is in such condition that it is no longer a fitting emblem for display," the flag "should be destroyed in a dignified way, *preferably by burning*" (emphasis added)? See Loewy, supra, at 79–80.

SECTION 5. GOVERNMENT PROPERTY AND THE PUBLIC FORUM [a]

The case law treating the question of when persons can speak on public property has come to be known as public forum doctrine. But "[t]he public

a. For treatment of the related question whether, and if so under what circumstances, there is a first amendment right of access to privately-owned facilities, such as shopping centers, see *Marsh v. Alabama,* p. 1081 infra; *Hudgens v. NLRB,* p. 1117 infra; *Pruneyard Shopping Center v. Robins,* p. 632 infra.

forum saga began, and very nearly ended," Stone, *Fora Americana: Speech in Public Places*, 1974 Sup.Ct.Rev. 233, 236, with an effort by Holmes, J., then on the Supreme Judicial Court of Massachusetts, "to solve a difficult first amendment problem by simplistic resort to a common-law concept," Blasi, *Prior Restraints on Demonstrations*, 68 Mich.L.Rev. 1482, 1484 (1970). For holding religious meetings on the Boston Common, a preacher was convicted under an ordinance prohibiting "any public address" upon publicly-owned property without a permit from the mayor. In upholding the permit ordinance Holmes, J., observed: "For the legislature absolutely or conditionally to forbid public speaking in a highway or public park is no more an infringement of rights of a member of the public than for the owner of a private house to forbid it in the house." *Davis v. Massachusetts*, 162 Mass. 510, 511 (1895). On appeal, a unanimous Supreme Court adopted the Holmes position, 167 U.S. 43, 17 S.Ct. 731, 42 L.Ed. 71 (1897): "[T]he right to absolutely exclude all right to use [public property], necessarily includes the authority to determine under what circumstances such use may be availed of, as the greater power contains the lesser."

This view survived until *Hague v. CIO*, 307 U.S. 496, 59 S.Ct. 954, 83 L.Ed. 1423 (1939), which rejected Jersey City's claim that its ordinance requiring a permit for an open air meeting was justified by the "plenary power" rationale of *Davis*. In rejecting the implications of the *Davis* dictum, Roberts, J., in a plurality opinion, uttered a famous "counter dictum," which has played a central role in the evolution of public forum theory: "Wherever the title of streets and parks may rest, they have immemorially been held in trust for the use of the public and, time out of mind, have been used for purposes of assembly, communicating thoughts between citizens, and discussing public questions. Such use of the streets and public places has, from ancient times, been a part of the privileges, immunities, rights, and liberties of citizens. [This privilege of a citizen] is not absolute, but relative, and must be exercised in subordination to the general comfort and convenience, and in consonance with peace and good order; but it must not, in the guise of regulation, be abridged or denied." Eight months later, the *Hague* dictum was given impressive content by Roberts, J., for the Court, in *Schneider* infra.

I. FOUNDATION CASES

A. MANDATORY ACCESS

SCHNEIDER v. IRVINGTON, 308 U.S. 147, 60 S.Ct. 146, 84 L.Ed. 155 (1939), per ROBERTS, J., invalidated several ordinances prohibiting leafleting on public streets or other public places: "Municipal authorities, as trustees for the public, have the duty to keep their communities' streets open and available for movement of people and property, the primary purpose to which the streets are dedicated. So long as legislation to this end does not abridge the constitutional liberty of one rightfully upon the street to impart information through speech or the distribution of literature, it may lawfully regulate the conduct of those using the streets. For example, a person could not exercise this liberty by taking his stand in the middle of a crowded street, contrary to traffic regulations, and maintain his position to the stoppage of all traffic; a group of distributors could not insist upon a constitutional right to form a cordon across the street and to allow no pedestrian to pass who did not accept a tendered leaflet; nor does the guarantee of freedom of speech or of the press deprive a municipality of power to enact regulations against throwing literature broadcast in the streets. Prohibition of such conduct would not abridge the constitutional liberty since such activity bears no necessary relationship to the freedom to speak, write, print or distribute information or opinion. * * *

"In *Lovell* [p. 472 supra] this court held void an ordinance which forbade the distribution by hand or otherwise of literature of any kind without written permission from the city manager. [Similarly] in *Hague v. C.I.O.*, an ordinance was held void on its face because it provided for previous administrative censorship of the exercise of the right of speech and assembly in appropriate public places.

"The [ordinances] under review do not purport to license distribution but all of them absolutely prohibit it in the streets and, one of them, in other public places as well.

"The motive of the legislation under attack in Numbers 13, 18 and 29 is held by the courts below to be the prevention of littering of the streets and, although the alleged offenders were not charged with themselves scattering paper in the streets, their convictions were sustained upon the theory that distribution by them encouraged or resulted in such littering. We are of opinion that the purpose to keep the streets clean and of good appearance is insufficient to justify an ordinance which prohibits a person rightfully on a public street from handing literature to one willing to receive it. Any burden imposed upon the city authorities in cleaning and caring for the streets as an indirect consequence of such distribution results from the constitutional protection of the freedom of speech and press. This constitutional protection does not deprive a city of all power to prevent street littering. There are obvious methods of preventing littering. Amongst these is the punishment of those who actually throw papers on the streets.

"It is suggested that [the] ordinances are valid because their operation is limited to streets and alleys and leaves persons free to distribute printed matter in other public places. But, as we have said, the streets are natural and proper places for the dissemination of information and opinion; and one is not to have the exercise of his liberty of expression in appropriate places abridged on the plea that it may be exercised in some other place."

MCREYNOLDS, J., "is of opinion that the judgment in each case should be affirmed."

Notes and Questions

1. *Leaflets and the streets as public forum.* Consider Kalven, *The Concept of the Public Forum: Cox v. Louisiana,* 1965 S.Ct.Rev. 1, 18 & 21: "Leaflet distribution in public places in a city is a method of communication that carries as an inextricable and expected consequence substantial littering of the streets, which the city has an obligation to keep clean. It is also a method of communication of some annoyance to a majority of people so addressed; that its impact on its audience is very high is doubtful. Yet the constitutional balance in *Schneider* was struck emphatically in favor of keeping the public forum open for this mode of communication.

"[The] operative theory of the Court, at least for the leaflet situation, is that, although it is a method of communication that interferes with the public use of the streets, the right to the streets as a public forum is such that leaflet distribution cannot be prohibited and can be regulated only for weighty reasons."

2. *Litter prevention as a substantial interest.* Does the interest in distributing leaflets always outweigh the interest in preventing littering? Suppose helicopters regularly dropped tons of leaflets on the town of Irvington?

3. *Beyond leaflets.* COX v. NEW HAMPSHIRE, 312 U.S. 569, 61 S.Ct. 762, 85 L.Ed. 1049 (1941), per HUGHES, C.J., upheld convictions of sixty-eight Jehovah's Witnesses for parading without a permit. They had marched in four or five groups (with perhaps twenty others) along the sidewalk in single file carrying signs and handing out leaflets: "[T]he state court considered and defined the duty of the licensing authority and the rights of the appellants to a license for their parade, with regard only to consideration of time, place and manner so as to conserve the public convenience." The licensing procedure was said to "afford opportunity for proper policing" and " 'to prevent confusion by overlapping parades, [to] secure convenient use of the streets by other travelers, and to minimize the risk of disorder.' " A municipality "undoubtedly" has "authority to control the use of its public streets for parades or processions." But see Baker, *Unreasoned Reasonableness: Mandatory Parade Permits and Time, Place, and Manner Regulations,* 78 Nw.U.L.Rev. 937, 992 (1984): Approximately 26,000 people walked on the same sidewalks during the same hour the defendants in *Cox* "marched." "This single difference in what [the defendants] did—'marching in formation,' which they did for expressive purposes and which presumably is an 'assembly' that the first amendment protects—turned out to have crucial significance. This sole difference, engaging in first amendment protected conduct, made them guilty of a criminal offense. [Surely] something is wrong with this result."

4. *Charging for use of public forum.* *Cox* said there was nothing "contrary to the Constitution" in the exaction of a fee " 'incident to the administration of the [licensing] Act and to the maintenance of public order in the matter licensed.' " Could leafleters be charged for the costs of cleaning up litter? Controversial speakers for the expense of police protection? See generally Goldberger, *A Reconsideration of Cox v. New Hampshire: Can Demonstrators Be Required to Pay the Costs of Using America's Public Forums?,* 62 Tex.L.Rev. 403 (1983); Blasi, *Demonstrations,* supra at 1527–32.

5. *Reasonable time, place, and manner regulations.* As *Cox* reveals, a right of access to a public forum does not guarantee immunity from reasonable time, place, and manner regulations. In *Heffron v. International Soc. For Krishna Consciousness,* 452 U.S. 640, 101 S.Ct. 2559, 69 L.Ed.2d 298 (1981), for example, the Court, per White, J., upheld a state fair rule prohibiting the distribution of printed material or the solicitation of funds except from a duly licensed booth on the fairgrounds. The Court noted that consideration of a forum's special attributes is relevant to the determination of reasonableness, and the test of reasonableness is whether the restrictions "are justified without reference to the content of the regulated speech, that they serve a significant governmental interest, and that in doing so they leave open ample alternative channels for communication of the information" [a] Is there any difference between the *O'Brien* test and the approach used in *Schneider*? Should there be a difference?

B. EQUAL ACCESS

CHICAGO POLICE DEP'T v. MOSLEY, 408 U.S. 92, 92 S.Ct. 2286, 33 L.Ed. 2d 212 (1972), invalidated an ordinance banning all picketing within 150 feet of a

a. Brennan, J., joined by Marshall and Stevens, JJ., dissented in part as did Blackmun, J., in a separate opinion. Their dispute was not with the Court's test, but its application.

school building while the school is in session and one half-hour before and afterwards, except "the peaceful picketing of any school involved in a labor dispute."

The suit was brought by a federal postal employee who, for seven months prior to enactment of the ordinance, had frequently picketed a high school in Chicago. "During school hours and usually by himself, Mosley would walk the public sidewalk adjoining the school, carrying a sign that read: 'Jones High School practices black discrimination. Jones High School has a black quota.' His lonely crusade was always peaceful, orderly, and [quiet]." The Court, per MARSHALL, J., viewed the ordinance as drawing "an impermissible distinction between labor picketing and other peaceful picketing": "The central problem with Chicago's ordinance is that it describes permissible picketing in terms of its subject matter. Peaceful picketing on the subject of a school's labor-management dispute is permitted, but all other peaceful picketing is prohibited. The operative distinction is the message on a picket sign. But, above all else, the First Amendment means that government has no power to restrict expression because of its message, its ideas, its subject matter, or its content.

"[U]nder the Equal Protection Clause, not to mention the First Amendment itself,[a] government may not grant the use of a forum to people whose views it finds acceptable, but deny use to those wishing to express less favored or more controversial views. And it may not select which issues are worth discussing or debating in public facilities. There is an 'equality of status in the field of ideas,' and government must afford all points of view an equal opportunity to be heard. Once a forum is opened up to assembly or speaking by some groups, government may not prohibit others from assembling or speaking on the basis of what they intend to say. Selective exclusions from a public forum may not be based on content alone, and may not be justified by reference to content alone.

"[Not] all picketing must always be allowed. We have continually recognized that reasonable 'time, place and manner' regulations of picketing may be necessary to further significant governmental interests. Similarly, under an equal protection analysis, there may be sufficient regulatory interests justifying selective exclusions or distinctions among picketers. [But] [b]ecause picketing plainly involves expressive conduct within the protection of the First Amendment, discriminations among picketers must be tailored to serve a substantial governmental interest. In this case, the ordinance itself describes impermissible picketing not in terms of time, place and manner, but in terms of subject matter. The regulation 'thus slip[s] from the neutrality of time, place and circumstance into a concern about content.' This is never permitted. * * *

"Although preventing school disruption is a city's legitimate concern, Chicago itself has determined that peaceful labor picketing during school hours is not an undue interference with school. Therefore, under the Equal Protection clause, Chicago may not maintain that other picketing disrupts the school unless that picketing is clearly more disruptive than the picketing Chicago already permits. If peaceful labor picketing is permitted, there is no justification for prohibiting all nonlabor picketing, both peaceful and nonpeaceful. 'Peaceful' labor picketing, however the term 'peaceful' is defined, is obviously no less

a. *Consolidated Edison Co. v. Public Service Comm'n,* p. 686 infra, abandoned equal protection and cited *Mosley* as a first amendment case: "The First Amendment's hostility to content-based regulation extends not only to restrictions on particular viewpoints, but also to prohibition of public discussion of an entire topic." But see, e.g., *Minnesota State Board v. Knight,* 465 U.S. 271, 104 S.Ct. 1058, 79 L.Ed.2d 299 (1984) (stating that *Mosley* is an equal protection case).

disruptive than 'peaceful' nonlabor picketing. But Chicago's ordinance permits the former and prohibits the latter.

"[We also] reject the city's argument that, although it permits peaceful labor picketing, it may prohibit all nonlabor picketing because, as a class, nonlabor picketing is more prone to produce violence than labor picketing. Predictions about imminent disruption from picketing involve judgments appropriately made on an individualized basis, not by means of broad classifications, especially those based on subject matter. Freedom of expression, and its intersection with the guarantee of equal protection, would rest on a soft foundation indeed if government could distinguish among picketers on such a wholesale and categorical basis. '[I]n our system, undifferentiated fear or apprehension of disturbance is not enough to overcome the right to freedom of expression.' *Tinker.* Some labor picketing is peaceful, some disorderly; the same is true for picketing on other themes. No labor picketing could be more peaceful or less prone to violence than Mosley's solitary vigil. In seeking to restrict nonlabor picketing which is clearly more disruptive than peaceful labor picketing, Chicago may not prohibit all nonlabor picketing at the school forum." [b]

Notes and Questions

1. Consider Karst, *Equality as a Central Principle in the First Amendment,* 43 U.Chi.L.Rev. 20, 28 (1975): "*Mosley* is a landmark first amendment decision. It makes two principal points: (1) the essence of the first amendment is its denial to government of the power to determine which messages shall be heard and which suppressed * * *. (2) Any 'time, place and manner' restriction that selectively excludes speakers from a public forum must survive careful judicial scrutiny to ensure that the exclusion is the minimum necessary to further a significant government interest. Taken together, these statements declare a principle of major importance. The Court has explicitly adopted the principle of equal liberty of expression. [The] principle requires courts to start from the assumption that all speakers and all points of view are entitled to a hearing, and permits deviation from this basic assumption only upon a showing of substantial necessity."

2. What if the *Mosley* ordinance had not excepted labor picketing, but had banned *all* picketing within 150 feet of a school during school hours? Consider Karst 37–38: "The burden of this restriction would fall most heavily on those who have something to communicate to the school [population]. Student picketers presenting a grievance against a principal, or striking custodians with a message growing out of a labor dispute, would be affected more seriously by this ostensibly content-neutral ordinance than would, say the proponents of a candidate for Governor [who could just as effectively carry their message elsewhere]. This differential impact amounts to de facto content discrimination, presumptively invalid under the first amendment equality principle.

"[The city faces] an apparent dilemma. [If it] bars all picketing within a certain area, it will effectively discriminate against those groups that can communicate to their audience only by picketing within that area. But if the city adjusts its ordinance to this differential impact, as by providing a student-picketing or labor-picketing exemption, [it runs] afoul of *Mosley* itself. The city

---

b. Burger, C.J., joined the Court's opinion, but also concurred. Blackmun and Rehnquist, JJ., concurred in the result.

can avoid the dilemma by amending the ordinance to ban not all picketing but only noisy picketing." [c]

3. Does equality fully explain the special concern with content regulation? Consider Stone, *Content Regulation and the First Amendment*, 25 Wm. & Mary L.Rev. 189, 207 (1983): "The problem, quite simply, is that restrictions on expression are rife with 'inequalities,' many of which have nothing whatever to do with content. The ordinance at issue in *Mosley*, for example, restricted picketing near schools, but left unrestricted picketing near hospitals, libraries, courthouses, and private homes. The ordinance at issue in *Erznoznik* restricted drive-in theaters that are visible from a public street, but did not restrict billboards. [Whatever] the effect of these content-neutral inequalities on first amendment analysis, they are not scrutinized in the same way as content-based inequalities. Not all inequalities, in other words, are equal. And although the concern with equality may support the content-based/content-neutral distinction, it does not in itself have much explanatory power."

Is the concern with content discrimination explainable because of concerns about communicative impact, distortion of public debate, or government motivation? See generally Stone, supra. See also sources cited in notes 1 & 2 after *O'Brien*, Sec. 4 supra and Cass, *First Amendment Access to Government Facilities*, 65 Va.L.Rev. 1287, 1323–25 (1979); Stephan, *The First Amendment and Content Discrimination*, 68 Va.L.Rev. 203 (1982); Stone, *Restrictions of Speech Because of its Content: The Peculiar Case of Subject-Matter Restrictions*, 46 U.Chi.L.Rev. 81 (1978).

4. An Illinois statute prohibited picketing residences or dwellings—except when the dwelling is "used as a place of business," or is "a place of employment involved in a labor dispute or the place of holding a meeting [on] premises commonly used to discuss subjects of general public interest," or when a "person is picketing his own [dwelling]. Can a conviction for picketing the Mayor of Chicago's home be upheld? Is *Mosley* distinguishable? See *Carey v. Brown*, 447 U.S. 455, 100 S.Ct. 2286, 65 L.Ed.2d 263 (1980). What if all residential picketing were proscribed?

II. NEW FORUMS

Are first amendment rights on government property confined to streets and parks? "[W]hat about other publicly owned property, ranging from the grounds surrounding a public building, to the inside of a welfare office, publicly run bus, or library, to a legislative gallery?" Stone, *Fora Americana*, supra, at 245. Compare the approaches in *Grayned* and *Greer* infra.

GRAYNED v. ROCKFORD, 408 U.S. 104, 92 S.Ct. 2294, 33 L.Ed.2d 222 (1972): Appellant and some 200 others participated in a demonstration about 100 feet from a high school building, protesting the principal's failure to act on black students' grievances. They were convicted, inter alia, of violating an "anti-noise" ordinance providing: "[N]o person, while on public or private grounds adjacent to any [school] building in which [a class] is in session, shall willfully make or assist in the making of any noise or diversion which disturbs or tends to disturb the peace or good order of such school session." An 8–1 majority, per MARSHALL, J., upheld the ordinance against vagueness and overbreadth objections.

c. As Professor Karst notes, such an ordinance was upheld in *Grayned v. Rockford*, Part II infra, the companion case to *Mosley*.

As for the vagueness claim, it was clear to the Court that "the ordinance as a whole" prohibits "deliberately noisy or diversionary activity which disrupts or is about to disrupt normal school activities." In light of Illinois cases construing similar ordinances, "only actual or imminent interference with the 'peace or good order' of the school" is prohibited. At issue is not "a vague, general 'breach of the peace' ordinance, but a specific statute for the school context, where the prohibited disturbances are easily measured by their impact on the normal activities of the school. Given this 'particular context,' the ordinance gives 'fair notice to whom it is directed.' [Rockford's] anti-noise ordinance does not permit punishment for the expression of an unpopular point of view, and it contains no broad invitation to subjective or discriminatory enforcement."

As for the overbreadth claim: "[G]overnment has no power to restrict [expressive] activity because of its message [but] reasonable 'time, place and manner' regulations may be necessary to further significant governmental interests, and are permitted. For example, two parades cannot march on the same street simultaneously, and government may allow only one. *Cox v. New Hampshire.* A demonstration or parade on a large street during rush hour might put an intolerable burden on the essential flow of traffic, and for that reason could be prohibited. If overamplified loudspeakers assault the citizenry, government may turn them down.

"The nature of a place, 'the pattern of its normal activities, dictates the kinds of regulations of time, place, and manner that are reasonable.' Although a silent vigil may not unduly interfere with a public library, *Brown v. Louisiana,* 383 U.S. 131, 86 S.Ct. 719, 15 L.Ed.2d 637 (1966) [a] making a speech in the reading room almost certainly would. That same speech should be perfectly appropriate in a park. The crucial question is whether the manner of expression is basically incompatible with the normal activity of a particular place at a particular time. Our cases make clear that in assessing the reasonableness of regulation, we must weigh heavily the fact that communication is involved; the regulation must be narrowly tailored to further the State's legitimate interest. 'Access to [the streets, sidewalks, parks, and other similar public places] for the purpose of exercising [First Amendment rights] cannot constitutionally be denied broadly * * *.' Free expression 'must not, in the guise of regulation, be abridged or denied.'

"In light of these general principles, we do not think that Rockford's ordinance is an unconstitutional regulation of activity around a school. [Just] as *Tinker* made clear that school property may not be declared off-limits for expressive activity by students, we think it clear that the public sidewalk adjacent to school grounds may not be declared off-limits for expressive activity by members of the public. But in each case, expressive activity may be prohibited if it 'materially disrupts classwork or involves substantial disorder or invasion of the rights of others.' * * *

"Rockford's anti-noise ordinance goes no further than *Tinker* says a municipality may go to prevent interference with its schools. It is narrowly tailored to further Rockford's compelling interest in having an undisrupted school session

a. In *Brown,* only three justices (Fortas, J., joined by Warren and Douglas, JJ.) held there was a constitutional right to conduct a silent demonstration in the library. Brennan, J., found the statute involved to be overbroad and thus found it unnecessary to decide whether the actual conduct was constitutionally protected. White, J., concluded that the demonstrators had been unconstitutionally punished because of their race. Black, J., dissenting joined by Clark, Harlan, and Stewart, JJ., insisted that the first amendment "does not guarantee to any person the right to use someone else's property, even that owned by government and dedicated to other purposes, as a stage to express dissident ideas."

conducive to the students' learning, and does not unnecessarily interfere with First Amendment rights. Far from having an impermissibly broad prophylactic ordinance, Rockford punishes only conduct which disrupts or is about to disrupt normal school activities. That decision is made, as it should be, on an individualized basis, given the particular fact situation. Peaceful picketing which does not interfere with the ordinary functioning of the school is permitted. And the ordinance gives no license to punish anyone because of what he is saying.

"We recognize that the ordinance prohibits some picketing which is neither violent nor physically obstructive. Noisy demonstrations which disrupt or are incompatible with normal school activities are obviously within the ordinance's reach. Such expressive conduct may be constitutionally protected at other places or other times, but next to a school, while classes are in session, it may be prohibited. The anti-noise ordinance imposes no such restriction on expressive activity before or after the school session, while the student/faculty 'audience' enters and leaves the school.

"In *Cox v. Louisiana*, 379 U.S. 559, 85 S.Ct. 476, 13 L.Ed.2d 487 (1965), this Court indicated that, because of the special nature of the place, persons could be constitutionally prohibited from picketing 'in or near' a courthouse 'with the intent of interfering with, obstructing, or impeding the administration of justice.' [b] [Similarly], Rockford's modest restriction on some peaceful picketing represents a considered and specific legislative judgment that some kinds of expressive activity should be restricted at a particular time and place, here in order to protect the schools. Such a reasonable regulation is not inconsistent with the First and Fourteenth Amendments.[49] The anti-noise ordinance is not invalid on its face." [c]

GREER v. SPOCK, 424 U.S. 828, 96 S.Ct. 1211, 47 L.Ed.2d 505 (1976), per STEWART, J., upheld two regulations of the Fort Dix, N.J., Military Reservation, one banning demonstrations, picketing, protest marches, political speeches and similar activities on the post; the other prohibiting the distribution or posting of any publication without prior written approval of post headquarters: [a] "The Court of Appeals was mistaken, in thinking that * * * [whenever] members of the public are permitted freely to visit a place owned or operated by the

---

b. But cf. *United States v. Grace*, 461 U.S. 171, 103 S.Ct. 1702, 75 L.Ed.2d 736 (1983) (invalidating statute prohibiting all leafleting and picketing on sidewalk adjoining Supreme Court).

49. Cf. *Adderley v. Florida*, 385 U.S. 39, 87 S.Ct. 242, 17 L.Ed.2d 149 (1966). In *Adderley* the Court held that demonstrators could be barred from jailhouse grounds not ordinarily open to the public, at least where the demonstration obstructed the jail driveway and interfered with the functioning of the jail. In *Tinker*, we noted that "a school is not like a hospital or a jail enclosure."

[In *Adderley*, Black J. (over the dissent of Douglas, J., joined by Warren, C.J., Brennan, and Fortas, JJ.), had observed broadly that the state no less than a private property owner had power "to control the use of its own property for its own lawful nondiscriminatory purpose." He opposed the premise that "people who want to propagandize protests or

views have a constitutional right to do so whenever and however and wherever they please."]

c. Blackmun, J., concurred in the result. Douglas, J., dissented, maintaining that there was no violence, or boisterous conduct. "[T]he disruptive force loosened at this school was an issue dealing with race—an issue that is preeminently one for solution by First Amendment means. That is all that was done here; and the entire picketing [was] done in the best First Amendment tradition."

a. Those challenging the Regulations included People's Party and Socialist Workers Party candidates for national political office, who had been denied permission to enter the base for the purpose of distributing campaign literature and discussing election issues with service personnel, and others who had been evicted on several occasions for distributing literature not previously approved and who had been barred from re-entering the post.

Government, then that place becomes a 'public forum' for purposes of the First Amendment.[b] Such a principle of constitutional law has never existed, and does not exist now. The guarantees of the First Amendment have never meant 'that people who want to propagandize protests or views have a constitutional right to do so whenever and however and wherever they please.' *Adderley*. 'The State, no less than a private owner of property, has power to preserve the property under its control for the use to which it is lawfully dedicated.' Id. * * *

"One of the very purposes for which the Constitution was ordained and established was to 'provide for the common defence,' and this Court over the years has on countless occasions recognized the special constitutional function of the military in our national life, a function both explicit and indispensable. In short, it is 'the primary business of armies and navies to fight or be ready to fight wars should the occasion arise.' And it is consequently the business of a military installation like Fort Dix to train soldiers, not to provide a public forum. [The] notion that federal military reservations, like municipal streets and parks, have traditionally served as a place for free public assembly and communication of thoughts by private citizens is thus historically and constitutionally false.[c]

"The respondents, therefore, had no generalized constitutional right to make political speeches or distribute leaflets at Fort Dix, and it follows that [the challenged Regulations] are not constitutionally invalid on their face. These regulations, moreover, were not unconstitutionally applied in the circumstances disclosed by the record in the present case.[10]

"What the record shows [is] a considered Fort Dix policy, objectively and evenhandedly applied, of keeping official military activities there wholly free of entanglement with partisan political campaigns of any kind. Under such a policy members of the Armed Forces stationed at Fort Dix are wholly free as individuals to attend political rallies, out of uniform and off base. But the military as such is insulated from both the reality and the appearance of acting as a handmaiden for partisan political causes or candidates.

"Such a policy is wholly consistent with the American constitutional tradition of a politically neutral military establishment under civilian control. [And]

b. See also *United States v. Albertini*, ___ U.S. ___, 105 S.Ct. 2897, 86 L.Ed.2d 536 (1985) (50,000 people come to military base for open house; suggestion of temporary public forum characterized as "dubious").

c. Is there an unbroken tradition of exclusion? *Flower v. United States*, 407 U.S. 197, 92 S.Ct. 1842, 32 L.Ed.2d 653 (1972) summarily reversed a conviction for distributing peace leaflets on a "public street" at a point within a military post after petitioner had been removed therefrom and ordered not to re-enter. "Whatever power [he] may have to restrict general access to a military facility, here the Fort Commander chose not to exclude the public from the street where petitioner was arrested." Under the circumstances, e.g., no guard stationed at either entrance or along the route and a constant flow of civilian vehicular and pedestrian traffic through the post on this street, "the military has abandoned any claim that it has special interests in who walks, talks, or leaflets on the avenue." The Court in *Greer* distinguished *Flower* saying

that no abandonment had occurred at Fort Dix.

Brennan, J., dissenting, argued that the purported lack of abandonment in *Greer* was difficult to reconcile with a prior "history of unimpeded civilian access" to the military post.

10. The fact that other civilian speakers and entertainers had sometimes been invited to appear at Fort Dix did not of itself serve to convert Fort Dix into a public forum or to confer upon political candidates a First or Fifth Amendment right to conduct their campaigns there. The decision of the military authorities that a civilian lecture on drug abuse, a religious service by a visiting preacher at the base chapel, or a rock musical concert would be supportive of the military mission of Fort Dix surely did not leave the authorities powerless thereafter to prevent any civilian from entering Fort Dix to speak on any subject whatever.

it is a policy that the military authorities at Fort Dix were constitutionally free to pursue." [d]

Burger, C.J., and Powell, J., joined the Court's opinion, but also wrote concurrences. POWELL, J., stated that: "An approach analogous to that which must be employed in this case was described in *Grayned.* The Court is to inquire 'whether the manner of expression is basically incompatible with the normal activity of a particular place at a particular time.' As *Tinker* demonstrates, it is not sufficient that the area in which the right of expression is sought to be exercised be dedicated to some purpose other than use as a 'public forum,' or even that the primary business to be carried on in the area may be disturbed by the unpopular viewpoint expressed. [Some] basic incompatibility must be discerned between the communication and the primary activity of an area. Fort Dix is not only an area of property owned by the Government and dedicated to a public purpose. It is also the enclave of a system that stands apart from and outside of many of the rules that govern ordinary civilian life in our country. [In] this context our inquiry is not limited to claims that the exercise of First Amendment rights is disruptive of base activity. We also must consider their functional and symbolic incompatibility with the 'specialized society separate from civilian society,' that has its home on the base."

Powell, J., concluded that "the public interest in insuring the political neutrality of the military justifies the limited infringement on First Amendments rights imposed by [Fort Dix's ban on political rallies and similar activities within the environs of the base]": "Our national policy has been to preserve a distinction between the role of the soldier and that of the citizen. A reasonable place to draw the line is between political activities on military bases and elsewhere. The military enclave is kept free of partisan influences, but individual servicemen are not isolated from participation as citizens in our democratic process."

BURGER, C.J., concurring, argued that "keeping the military separate from political affairs" is a "200-year tradition" that is a "constitutional corollary to the express provision for civilian control of the military in Art. II, § 2, of the Constitution." He observed that "the hard question for me is whether the Constitution requires a ban on [the distribution on base of all political leaflets]." He concluded though that the decision whether to permit distribution is "one properly committed to the judgment of the military authorities."

BRENNAN, J., joined by Marshall, J., dissented: "The Court's opinion speaks in absolutes, exalting the need for military preparedness and admitting of no careful and solicitous accommodation of First Amendment interests to the competing concerns that all concede are substantial. It parades general propositions useless to precise resolution of the problem at hand. According to the Court, [it is the] 'business of a military installation like Fort Dix to train soldiers, not to provide a public forum.' But the training of soldiers does not as a practical matter require exclusion of those who would publicly express their views from streets and theater parking lots open to the general public. Nor does readiness to fight require such exclusion, unless, of course, the battlefields are the streets and parking lots, or the war is one of ideologies and not men.

* * * [6]

---

d. Stevens, J., did not participate.

6. The concurring opinion of my Brother Powell properly recognizes at least the need for careful inquiry in such cases. But I completely disagree with his characterization of the need to secure the Government's interest in a politically neutral military as an interest protected by prohibiting conduct of "symbolic incompatibility" with a military base. I gather that by this notion of "symbolic incompati-

"[Respondents] carefully and appropriately distinguish between a military base considered as a whole and those portions of a military base open to the public. And not only do respondents not go so far as to contend that open places constitute a 'public forum,' but also they need not go so far. [T]he determination that a locale is a "public forum" has never been erected as an absolute prerequisite to all forms of demonstrative First Amendment activity. [In] *Brown,* for example, the First Amendment protected the use of a public library as a site for a silent and peaceful protest by five young black men against discrimination. There was no finding by the Court that the library was a public forum. Similarly, in *Edwards v. South Carolina,* the First Amendment protected a demonstration on the grounds of a state capitol building. Again, the Court never expressly determined that those grounds constituted a public forum. And in *Tinker,* the First Amendment shielded students' schoolroom antiwar protest, consisting of the wearing of black armbands. Moreover, none of the opinions that have expressly characterized locales as public forums has really gone that far, for a careful reading of those opinions reveals that their characterizations were always qualified, indicating that not every conceivable form of public expression would be protected. *Mosley, Cox v. New Hampshire.*

"Those cases permitting public expression without characterizing the locale involved as a public forum, together with those cases recognizing the existence of a public forum, albeit qualifiedly, evidence the desirability of a flexible approach to determining when public expression should be protected. Realizing that the permissibility of a certain form of public expression at a given locale may differ depending on whether it is asked if the locale is a public forum or if the form of expression is compatible with the activities occurring at the locale, it becomes apparent that there is need for a flexible approach. Otherwise, with the rigid characterization of a given locale as not a public forum, there is the danger that certain forms of public speech at the locale may be suppressed, even though they are basically compatible with the activities otherwise occurring at the locale.

"The Court's final retreat in justifying the prohibitions upheld today is the principle of military neutrality. [I] could not agree more that the military should not become a political faction in this country. [But] it borders on casuistry to contend that by evenhandedly permitting public expression to occur in unrestricted portions of a military installation, the military will be viewed as sanctioning the causes there espoused. If there is any risk of partisan involvement, real or apparent, it derives from the exercise of a choice, in this case, the Fort commander's choice to exclude respondents, while, for example, inviting speakers in furtherance of the Fort's religious program. * * *

"More fundamentally, however, the specter of partiality does not vanish with the severing of all partisan contact. It is naive to believe that any organization, including the military, is value neutral. More than this, where the interests and purpose of an organization are peculiarly affected by national affairs, it becomes highly susceptible of politicization. For this reason, it is

bility," my Brother Powell means only to accord recognition to the interest in neutrality, an interest qualitatively different from the more immediate functional interest in training recruits. I, of course, have no quarrel with recognition of the interest. But that recognition as articulated by my Brother Powell is so devoid of limiting principle as to contravene fundamentals of First Amendment jurisprudence. This Court many times has held protected by the First Amendment conduct which was "symbolically incompatible" with the activity upon which it impacted. *See Spence; West Virginia State Bd. of Educ. v. Barnette* [p. 763 infra]. Indeed, the very symbolisms of many of our institutions have been the subject of criticisms held to be unassailably protected by the First Amendment.

precisely the nature of a military organization to tend toward that end.[16] That tendency is only facilitated by action that serves to isolate the organization's members from the opportunity for exposure to the moderating influence of other ideas, particularly where, as with the military, the organization's activities pervade the lives of its members. For this reason, any unnecessary isolation only erodes neutrality and invites the danger that neutrality seeks to avoid." [e]

Notes and Questions

1. *The right test.* Should one test be applied to all cases including access to government property? *Grayned's* incompatibility test? *Greer's* public forum test? The *O'Brien* test? [f]

2. Why does *Greer* fail to cite *Grayned?* Is *Greer* a military case rather than a case enunciating public forum doctrine? Was *Grayned* silently repudiated?

3. Is *Greer* inconsistent with *Mosley?* Is it content discrimination to permit speakers on drug abuse to address the troops but not presidential candidates? Is the suggestion that discriminating among speakers in terms of subject matter in certain forms is acceptable so long as there is no discrimination in terms of viewpoint? See Tribe, *American Constitutional Law* 691 n.21. Would the military be obligated to afford access to a speaker with a different point of view on drug abuse? Is the point that in non-public forum contexts the government has a free hand in drawing lines according to content? See Stone, *Restrictions of Speech Because of its Content: The Peculiar Case of Subject-Matter Restrictions,* 46 U.Chi.L.Rev. 81, 95–96 (1978). That government's latitude for content discrimination increases when government has an intent to communicate? Is the *Mosley* language "ill-suited for application to schools, to libraries, [and] to military training classrooms"? See Shiffrin, *Government Speech,* 27 U.C.L.A.L. Rev. 565, 579 (1980). See generally Yudof, *When Government Speaks: Politics, Law, and Government Expression in America* (1983); Yudof, *When Governments Speak: Toward a Theory of Government Expression and the First Amendment,* 57 Tex.L.Rev. 863 (1979).

16. The testimony in the District Court of the officer representing the commanding officer of Fort Dix is exemplary:

"Q I see. Well, doesn't the war with Vietnam deal with your mission?

"A Oh, yes.

"Q Well, what I guess I am trying to get at is isn't it true that the content of what a proposed visitor intends to say is the basis for whether he is allowed to come on or not? If, for instance, he says 'I intend to urge the soldiers not to use drugs,' that, from what you have said, would be something that the Base might favorably look on. If he is going to inform them of some management principle that they are not aware of—

"A That would further our mission, yes.

"Q But if they are to speak against the war in Vietnam—

"A That certainly wouldn't forward our mission, would it?

"Q So the content of what they are to say, that is the basis of whether or not they are approved?

"A Yes, to a great extent." * * *

[e.] For support for this view, see Blasi, *The Checking Value in First Amendment Theory,* 1977 Am.B.Found.Res.J. 521, 643–44; Yudof, *When Governments Speak: Toward a Theory of Government Expression and the First Amendment,* 57 Tex.L.Rev. 863, 887 (1979).

[f.] For advocacy of an "openness" test, see Zillman & Imwinkelried, *The Legacy of Greer v. Spock: The Public Forum Doctrine and the Principle of the Military's Political Neutrality,* 65 Geo.L.J. 773 (1977). For criticism of the "public forum" test, see *Nimmer on Freedom of Speech* 4–67 to 4–81 (1984); Tribe, *American Constitutional Law* 688–93 (1978); Karst, *Public Enterprise and the Public Forum: A Comment on Southeastern Promotions, Ltd. v. Conrad,* 37 Ohio St.L.J. 247 (1976); Stone, *Fora Americana,* supra; Note, *The Public Forum: Minimum Access, Equal Access, and the First Amendment,* 28 Stan.L.Rev. 117, 132–48 (1975). See also note 1 after *Perry* infra.

III. LIMITED PUBLIC FORUMS AND NONPUBLIC FORUMS

A collective bargaining agreement between the board of education and Perry Education Association (PEA), the duly elected exclusive bargaining representative of the school district's teachers, granted PEA access to the interschool mail system and teacher mailboxes in the district, access rights not available to any rival union such as Perry Local Educators' Association (PLEA). (Prior to the 1978 collective bargaining agreement, PLEA had had equal access to the school mailboxes and delivery system). PLEA maintained that PEA's exclusive access to these facilities violated the first amendment and equal protection. PERRY EDUC. ASS'N v. PERRY LOCAL EDUCATORS' ASS'N, 460 U.S. 37, 103 S.Ct. 948, 74 L.Ed.2d 794 (1983), per WHITE, J., rejected both contentions: "The existence of a right of access to public property and the standard by which limitations upon such a right must be evaluated differ depending on the character of the property at issue.

"In places which by long tradition or by government fiat have been devoted to assembly and debate, the rights of the state to limit expressive activity are sharply circumscribed. At one end of the spectrum are streets and parks which 'have immemorially been held in trust for the use of the public, and, time out of mind, have been used for purposes of assembly, communicating thoughts between citizens, and discussing public questions.' *Hague.* In these quintessential public forums, the government may not prohibit all communicative activity. For the state to enforce a content-based exclusion it must show that its regulation is necessary to serve a compelling state interest and that it is narrowly drawn to achieve that end. The state may also enforce regulations of the time, place, and manner of expression which are content-neutral, are narrowly tailored to serve a significant government interest, and leave open ample alternative channels of communication. *Grayned; Schneider.*

"A second category consists of public property which the state has opened for use by the public as a place for expressive activity. The Constitution forbids a state to enforce certain exclusions from a forum generally open to the public even if it was not required to create the forum in the first place. * * *[7] Although a state is not required to indefinitely retain the open character of the facility, as long as it does so it is bound by the same standards as apply in a traditional public forum. Reasonable time, place and manner regulations are permissible, and a content-based prohibition must be narrowly drawn to effectuate a compelling state interest.

"Public property which is not by tradition or designation a forum for public communication is governed by different standards. [In] addition to time, place, and manner regulations, the state may reserve the forum for its intended purposes, communicative or otherwise, as long as the regulation on speech is reasonable and not an effort to suppress expression merely because public officials oppose the speaker's view.[a]

"The school mail facilities at issue here fall within this third category. [But PLEA contends] that the school mail facilities have become a 'limited public forum' from which it may not be excluded because of the periodic use of the

---

7. A public forum may be created for a limited purpose such as use by certain groups, e.g., *Widmar v. Vincent* [p. 733 infra] (student groups), or for the discussion of certain subjects, e.g., *City of Madison Joint School District v. Wisconsin Pub. Employ. Relat.*

Comm'n, 429 U.S. 167, 97 S.Ct. 421, 50 L.Ed.2d 376 (1976) (school board business).

a. Can speakers be excluded from the Oval Room of the White House "merely because public officials oppose the speaker's view"?

system by private non-school connected groups, and PLEA's own unrestricted access to the system prior to PEA's certification as exclusive representative.

"Neither of these arguments is persuasive. The use of the internal school mail by groups not affiliated with the schools is no doubt a relevant consideration. If by policy or by practice the Perry School District has opened its mail system for indiscriminate use by the general public, then PLEA could justifiably argue a public forum has been created. This, however, is not the case. As the case comes before us, there is no indication in the record that the school mailboxes and interschool delivery system are open for use by the general public. Permission to use the system to communicate with teachers must be secured from the individual building principal. There is [no evidence] that this permission has been granted as a matter of course to all who seek to distribute material. We can only conclude that the schools do allow some outside organizations such as the YMCA, Cub Scouts, and other civic and church organizations to use the facilities. This type of selective access does not transform government property into a public forum. In *Greer,* the fact that other civilian speaker and entertainers had sometimes been invited to appear at Fort Dix did not convert the military base into a public forum. ＊ ＊ ＊

"Moreover, even if we assume that by granting access to the Cub Scouts, YMCAs, and parochial schools, the school district has created a 'limited' public forum, the constitutional right of access would in any event extend only to other entities of similar character. ＊ ＊ ＊

"[According to the Court of Appeals], the access policy adopted by the Perry schools favors a particular viewpoint, that of the PEA, on labor relations, and consequently must be strictly scrutinized regardless of whether a public forum is involved. There is, however, no indication that the school board intended to discourage one viewpoint and advance another. We believe it is more accurate to characterize the access policy as based on the *status* of the respective unions rather than their views. Implicit in the concept of the nonpublic forum is the right to make distinctions in access on the basis of subject matter and speaker identity. These distinctions may be impermissible in a public forum but are inherent and inescapable in the process of limiting a nonpublic forum to activities compatible with the intended purpose of the property. The touchstone for evaluating these distinctions is whether they are reasonable in light of the purpose which the forum at issue serves.

"The differential access provided PEA and PLEA is reasonable because it is wholly consistent with the district's legitimate interest in 'preserv[ing] the property [for] the use to which it is lawfully dedicated.' Use of school mail facilities enables PEA to perform effectively its obligations as exclusive representative of *all* Perry Township teachers. Conversely, PLEA does not have any official responsibility in connection with the school district and need not be entitled to the same rights of access to school mailboxes. [W]hen government property is not dedicated to open communication the government may—without further justification—restrict use to those who participate in the forum's official business. ＊ ＊ ＊

"Finally, the reasonableness of the limitations on PLEA's access to the school mail system is also supported by the substantial alternative channels that remain open for union-teacher communication to take place. These means range from bulletin boards to meeting facilities to the United States mail. During election periods, PLEA is assured of equal access to all modes of communication. There is no showing here that PLEA's ability to communicate with teachers is seriously impinged by the restricted access to the internal mail system. The variety and type of alternative modes of access present here compare favorably with those in other nonpublic forum cases where we have upheld restrictions on access. See, e.g. *Greer* (servicemen free to attend political rallies off-base).

"The Court of Appeals also held that the differential access provided the rival unions constituted impermissible content discrimination in violation of the Equal Protection Clause of the Fourteenth Amendment. We have rejected this contention when cast as a First Amendment argument, and it fares no better in equal protection garb. [Because] PLEA did not have a First Amendment or other right of access to the interschool mail system [the] decision to grant such privileges to the PEA need not be tested by the strict scrutiny applied when government action impinges upon a fundamental right protected by the Constitution. The school district's policy need only rationally further a legitimate state purpose. That purpose is clearly found in the special responsibilities of an exclusive bargaining representative.

"[PLEA's reliance on *Mosley* and *Carey* is misplaced. [The] key to those decisions [was] the presence of a public forum. In a public forum, by definition, all parties have a constitutional right of access and the state must demonstrate compelling reasons for restricting access to a single class of speakers, a single viewpoint, or a single subject.

"When speakers and subjects are similarly situated, the state may not pick and choose. Conversely on government property that has not been made a public forum, not all speech is equally situated, and the state may draw distinctions which relate to the special purpose for which the property is used. As we have explained above, for a school mail facility, the difference in status between the exclusive bargaining representative and its rival is such a distinction."

BRENNAN, J., joined by Marshall, Powell, and Stevens, JJ., dissented: "Based on a finding that the interschool mail system is not a 'public forum,' the Court states that the respondents have no right of access to the system, and that the school board is free 'to make distinctions in access on the basis of subject matter and speaker identity,' if the distinctions are 'reasonable in light of the purpose which the forum at issue serves.'

"[The] Court fundamentally misperceives the essence of [PLEA's claims]. This case does not involve an 'absolute access' claim. It involves an 'equal access' claim. As such it does not turn on whether the internal school mail system is a 'public forum.' In focusing on the public forum issue, the Court disregards the First Amendment's central proscription against censorship, in the form of viewpoint discrimination, in any forum, public or nonpublic. [Generally], the concept of content neutrality prohibits the government from choosing the subjects that are appropriate for public discussion. The content neutrality cases frequently refer to the prohibition against viewpoint discrimination and both concepts have their roots in the First Amendment's bar against censorship. But unlike the viewpoint discrimination concept, which is used to strike down government restrictions on speech by particular speakers, the content neutrality principle is invoked when the government has imposed restrictions on speech related to an entire subject area. The content neutrality principle can be seen as an outgrowth of the core First Amendment prohibition against viewpoint discrimination. See generally, Stone, *Restrictions of Speech Because of its*

Content: The Peculiar Case of Subject-Matter Restrictions, 46 U.Chi.L.Rev. 81 (1978). * * *

"Once the government permits discussion of certain subject matter, it may not impose restrictions that discriminate among viewpoints on those subjects whether a nonpublic forum is involved or not.[5] This prohibition is implicit in the *Mosley* line of cases, in *Tinker,* and in those cases in which we have approved content-based restrictions on access to government property that is not a public forum.[b]

"[The] Court responds to the allegation of viewpoint discrimination by suggesting that there is no indication that the board intended to discriminate and that the exclusive access policy is based on the parties' status rather than on their views. In this case, for the reasons discussed below, the intent to discriminate can be inferred from the effect of the policy, which is to deny an effective channel of communication to the respondents, and from other facts in the case. In addition, the petitioner's status has nothing to do with whether viewpoint discrimination in fact has occurred. If anything, the petitioner's status is relevant to the question of whether the exclusive access policy can be justified, not to whether the board has discriminated among viewpoints.

"Addressing the question of viewpoint discrimination directly, free of the Court's irrelevant public forum analysis, it is clear that the exclusive access policy discriminates on the basis of viewpoint. The Court of Appeals found that 'the access policy * * * favors a particular viewpoint on labor relations in the Perry schools * * *: the teachers inevitably will receive from [the petitioner] self-laudatory descriptions of its activities on their behalf and will be denied the critical perspective offered by [the respondents].' This assessment of the effect of the policy is eminently reasonable. Moreover, certain other factors strongly suggest that the policy discriminates among viewpoints.

"On a practical level, the only reason for the petitioner to seek an exclusive access policy is to deny its rivals access to an effective channel of communication. No other group is explicitly denied access to the mail system. In fact, as the Court points out, many other groups have been granted access to the system. Apparently, access is denied to the respondents because of the likelihood of their expressing points of view different from the petitioner's on a range of subjects. The very argument the petitioner advances in support of the policy, the need to preserve labor peace, also indicates that the access policy is not viewpoint-neutral. * * *

"The petitioner attempts to justify the exclusive access provision based on its status as the exclusive bargaining representative for the teachers and on the state's interest in efficient communication between collective bargaining representatives and the members of the unit. The petitioner's status and the state's interest in efficient communication are important considerations. They are not sufficient, however, to sustain the exclusive access policy.

"[But] the exclusive access policy is both 'overinclusive and underinclusive' as a means of serving the state's interest in the efficient discharge of the

---

5. This is not to suggest that a government may not close a nonpublic forum altogether or limit access to the forum to those involved in the "official business" of the agency. Restrictions of this type are consistent with the government's right "to preserve the property under its control for the use to which it is lawfully dedicated."

b. Brennan, J., characterized *Greer* as involving an unusual nonpublic forum where the speech had been determined to be incompatible with the forum. He concluded that *Greer* and other cases authorized the exclusion of some subjects from such forums, but argued that the exclusions had been viewpoint neutral.

petitioner's legal duties to the teachers. The policy is overinclusive because it does not strictly limit the petitioner's use of the mail system to performance of its special legal duties and underinclusive because the board permits outside organizations with no special duties to the teachers, or to the students, to use the system. The Court of Appeals also suggested that even if the board had attempted to tailor the policy more carefully by denying outside groups access to the system and by expressly limiting the petitioner's use of the system to messages relating to its official duties, 'the fit would still be questionable, for it might be difficult—both in practice and in principle—effectively to separate "necessary" communications from propaganda.' * * *

"Putting aside the difficulties with the fit between this policy and the asserted interests, the Court of Appeals properly pointed out that the policy is invalid 'because it furthers no discernible state interest.' While the board may have a legitimate interest in granting the petitioner access to the system, it has no legitimate interest in making that access exclusive by denying access to the respondents. * * *

"Although the state's interest in preserving labor peace in the schools in order to prevent disruption is unquestionably substantial, merely articulating the interest is not enough to sustain the exclusive access policy in this case. There must be some showing that the asserted interest is advanced by the policy. In the absence of such a showing, the exclusive access policy must fall.[13]"

Notes and Questions

1. *The first amendment and geography.* Consider Farber & Nowak, *The Misleading Nature of Public Forum Analysis: Content and Context in First Amendment Adjudication,* 70 Va.L.Rev. 1219, 1234–35 (1984): "Classification of public places as various types of forums has only confused judicial opinions by diverting attention from the real first amendment issues involved in the cases. Like the fourth amendment, the first amendment protects people, not places. Constitutional protection should depend not on labeling the speaker's physical location but on the first amendment values and governmental interests involved in the case. Of course, governmental interests are often tied to the nature of the place. [To] this extent, the public forum doctrine is a useful heuristic [device]. But when the heuristic device becomes the exclusive method of analysis, only confusion and mistakes can result."

2. *Footnote 7 forums.* What is the relationship between the Court's second category of property and fn. 7? Is the discretion to create forums limited? Is it necessary to show that restrictions on such forums are necessary to achieve a compelling state interest? If a restriction (to certain speakers or subjects) is challenged, can the restrictions be used to show that that the property is not a public forum of the second category? Is this inadmissible circularity? See Tribe, *Equality as a First Amendment Theme: The "Government—as—Private Actor" Exception* in Choper, Kamisar & Tribe, The Supreme Court: Trends and

---

13. The Court also cites the availability of alternative channels of communication in support of the "reasonableness" of the exclusive access policy. In a detailed discussion, the Court of Appeals properly concluded that the other channels of communication available to the respondents were "not nearly as effective as the internal mail system." In addition, the Court apparently disregards the principle that "one is not to have the exercise of his liberty of expression in appropriate places abridged on the plea that it may be exercised in some other place." *Schneider.* In this case, the existence of inferior alternative channels of communication does not affect the conclusion that the petitioner has failed to justify the viewpoint-discriminatory exclusive access policy.

Developments 1982–1983, at 221, 226 (1984).[c] In any event, does fn. 7 create a fourth category of property without setting guiding standards? Are the *Perry* mailboxes fn. 7 forums?

3. *Alternative channels.* Does consideration of alternative channels of communication violate *Schneider's* observation that "one is not to have the exercise of his liberty of expression in appropriate places abridged on the plea that it may be exercised in some other place?" For discussion emphasizing the importance of considering alternative channels of communications and the methods for doing so, see generally Cass, *First Amendment Access to Government Facilities*, 65 Va.L.Rev. 1287 (1979).

4. For commentary on speaker-based restrictions, see Stone, *Content Regulation and the First Amendment*, 25 Wm. & Mary L.Rev. 189, 244–51 (1983).

SECTION 6. GOVERNMENT SUPPORT OF SPEECH

Public forum doctrine recognizes that government is obligated to permit some of its property to be used for communicative purposes without content discrimination, but public forum doctrine also allows other government property to be restricted to some speakers or for talk about selected subjects. See *Greer*; *Perry*. In short, in some circumstances government can provide resources for some speech while denying support for other speech. Indeed, government is a significant actor in the marketplace of ideas. Sometimes the government speaks as government; sometimes it subsidizes speech without purporting to claim that the resulting message is its own. It supports speech in many ways: official government messages; statements of public officials at publicly subsidized press conferences; artistic, scientific, or political subsidies, even the classroom communications of public school teachers.

If content distinctions are suspect when government acts as censor, they are the norm when government speaks or otherwise subsidizes speech. Government makes editorial judgments; it decides that some content is appropriate for the occasion and other content is not. The public museum curator makes content decisions in selecting exhibits; the librarian in selecting books; the public board in selecting recipients for research grants; the public official in composing press releases.

The line between support for speech and censorship of speech is not always bright, however. In any event, the Constitution limits the choices government may make in supporting speech. For example, government support of religious

c. Compare Blackmun, J., dissenting in *Cornelius v. NAACP Legal Defense and Educational Fund, Inc.,* __ U.S. __, 105 S.Ct. 3439, 87 L.Ed.2d 567 (1985): "If the Government does not create a limited public forum unless it intends to provide an 'open forum' for expressive activity, and if the exclusion of some speakers is evidence that the Government did not intend to create such a forum, no speaker challenging denial of access will ever be able to prove that the forum is a limited public forum. The very fact that the Government denied access to the speaker indicates that the Government did not intend to provide an open forum for expressive activity, and [that] fact alone would demonstrate that the forum is not a limited public forum." In *Cornelius*, a 4–3 majority, per O'Connor, J., determined that "government does not create a public forum by inaction or by permitting limited discourse, but only by intentionally opening a non-traditional forum for public discourse." Observing that the Court will look to the policy and practice of the government, the nature of the property and its compatibility with expressive activity in discerning intent, O'Connor, J., insisted that "we will not find that a public forum has been created in the face of clear evidence of a contrary intent, nor will we infer that the Government intended to create a public forum when the nature of the property is inconsistent with expressive activity."

speech is limited under the establishment clause. See Ch. 9. This section explores the extent to which the speech clause or constitutional conceptions of equality should limit government discretion in supporting speech.

I. SUBSIDIES AND TAX EXPENDITURES

REGAN v. TAXATION WITH REPRESENTATION OF WASHINGTON

461 U.S. 540, 103 S.Ct. 1997, 76 L.Ed.2d 129 (1983).

JUSTICE REHNQUIST delivered the opinion of the Court.

[Section 501(c) of the Internal Revenue Code affords tax exempt status to various nonprofit organizations. Section 501(c)(19) affords a tax exemption to veterans' organizations. Moreover, contributions to veterans' organizations are treated by the IRS as deductible (up to 20% of adjusted gross income) even if the veterans organizations engage in substantial lobbying activity at state or federal levels. Section 501(c)(3) grants exempt status to various groups commonly called "charitable" organizations that are "organized and operated exclusively for religious, charitable, scientific [or] educational purposes * * * no substantial part of the activities of which is carrying on propaganda, or otherwise attempting to influence legislation [and] which does not participate in, or intervene in (including the publishing or distributing of statements), any political campaign on behalf of any candidate for public office." Section 501(c)(4) grants exempt status to groups organized for the purposes identified in 501(c)(3) (and for some other purposes) regardless of the amount of lobbying or political activity. Contributions made to groups meeting 501(c)(3) standards are deductible (up to 50% of adjusted gross income); contributions to 501(c)(4) groups are not deductible.

[Taxpayers for Representation of Washington ("TWR"), a group organized to represent the taxpayer's public interest in Washington was denied 501(c)(3) status because of its lobbying activities. It argued that affording tax deductible contributions to the substantial lobbying activities of veterans while denying such benefits to charitable organizations involved in similar activities was unconstitutional discrimination.[a] The District of Columbia Court of Appeals agreed with TWR:[b] "If veterans' organizations and organizations such as Taxation lobby on different sides of the same questions, Congress has chosen to favor one lobbyist on a particular issue over another. If veterans' organizations and [charitable] organizations lobby on entirely distinct matters, Congress has ensured that greater attention will be devoted to some causes than others."

[It concluded that, "[A] First Amendment concern must inform the equal protection analysis in this case. Courts must scrutinize with special care any act of Congress that facilitates the speech of one speaker over another, even when legislation is enacted in the dry, classification-ridden context of the Internal Revenue Code. By subsidizing the lobbying activities of veterans' organizations while failing to subsidize the lobbying of [TWR] and other charitable groups,

---

a. TWR also argued that although the government had no obligation to grant tax advantages to charities, it could not condition receipt of tax advantages on a surrender of the first amendment right to lobby. The Court denied that the tax code called for any such surrender. It suggested that TWR could separately incorporate a lobbying organization un-

der § 501(c)(4) and a non-lobbying organization under § 501(c)(3) so long as it kept records adequate to show that tax deductible contributions were not used for lobbying.

b. *Taxation With Representation of Washington v. Regan,* 676 F.2d 715, (D.C.Cir.1982).

Congress has violated the equal protection guarantees of the Constitution.
* * *

["The First Amendment occupies a preferred place in our scheme of government. This does not mean, however, that its application in a legal dispute is always simple. The lines will seem clearer when Congress directly prohibits a particular group from speaking in a particular place, and more confused when Congress subsidizes First Amendment expression unevenly through the intricacies of the Internal Revenue Code. Nevertheless, the principle remains the same."

[The Supreme Court reversed:] * * *

Both tax exemptions and tax-deductibility are a form of subsidy[c] that is administered through the tax system. A tax exemption has much the same effect as a cash grant to the organization of the amount of tax it would have to pay on its income. Deductible contributions are similar to cash grants of the amount of a portion of the individual's contributions.[5] The system Congress has enacted provides this kind of subsidy to non profit civic welfare organizations generally, and an additional subsidy to those charitable organizations that do not engage in substantial lobbying. In short, Congress chose not to subsidize lobbying as extensively as it chose to subsidize other activities that non profit organizations undertake to promote the public welfare.

[Congress] has not violated TWR's First Amendment rights by declining to subsidize its First Amendment activities. The case would be different if Congress were to discriminate invidiously in its subsidies in such a way as to " 'aim[ ] at the suppression of dangerous ideas.' " But the veterans' organizations that qualify under § 501(c)(19) are entitled to receive tax-deductible contributions regardless of the content of any speech they may use, including lobbying. We find no indication that the statute was intended to suppress any ideas or any demonstration that it has had that effect. The sections of the Internal Revenue Code here at issue do not employ any suspect classification. The distinction between veterans' organizations and other charitable organizations is not at all like distinctions based on race or national origin.

The Court of Appeals nonetheless held that "strict scrutiny" is required because the statute "*affect[s]* First Amendment rights on a discriminatory basis." Its opinion suggests that strict scrutiny applies whenever Congress subsidizes some speech, but not all speech. This is not the law. Congress could, for example, grant funds to an organization dedicated to combatting teenage drug abuse, but condition the grant by providing that none of the money received from Congress should be used to lobby state legislatures. [S]uch a statute would be valid. Congress might also enact a statute providing public money for an organization dedicated to combatting teenage alcohol abuse, and impose no condition against using funds obtained from Congress for lobbying. The existence of the second statute would not make the first statute subject to strict scrutiny. * * *

c. The IRS accepted "the analogy between tax exemptions and direct government subsidies" for purposes of the case (676 F.2d at 725 n. 19), but the question of what should be characterized as a subsidy is much debated in tax circles. Compare e.g., Bittker & Kaufman, *Taxes and Civil Rights: "Constitutionalizing" the Internal Revenue Code,* 82 Yale L.J. 51, 63–68 (1972) with Surrey & McDaniel, *The Tax Expenditure Concept and the Budget Reform Act of 1974,* 17 B.C. Indust. & Comm.L. Rev. 679 (1976).

5. In stating that exemptions and deductions, on one hand, are like cash subsidies, on the other, we of course do not mean to assert that they are in all respects identical. See, e.g., *Walz v. Tax Commission* [p. 719 infra].

These are scarcely novel principles. We have held [that] a legislature's decision not to subsidize the exercise of a fundamental right does not infringe the right, and thus is not subject to strict scrutiny. *Buckley v. Valeo,* [p. 674 infra] upheld a statute that provides federal funds for candidates for public office who enter primary campaigns, but does not provide funds for candidates who do not run in party primaries. We rejected First Amendment and equal protection challenges to this provision without applying strict scrutiny.[d]

The reasoning [is] simple: "although government may not place obstacles in the path of a [person's] exercise [of] freedom of [speech], it need not remove those not of its own creation." * * * Congress—not TWR or this Court—has the authority to determine whether the advantage the public would receive from additional lobbying by charities is worth the money the public would pay to subsidize that lobbying, and other disadvantages that might accompany that lobbying. It appears that Congress was concerned that exempt organizations might use tax-deductible contributions to lobby to promote the private interests of their members.[e] It is not irrational for Congress to decide that tax exempt charities such as TWR should not further benefit at the expense of taxpayers at large by obtaining a further subsidy for lobbying.

It is also not irrational for Congress to decide that, even though it will not subsidize substantial lobbying by charities generally, it will subsidize lobbying by veterans' organizations. Veterans have "been obliged to drop their own affairs and take up the burdens of the nation," "subjecting themselves to the mental and physical hazards as well as the economic and family detriments which are peculiar to military service and which do not exist in normal civil life." Our country has a long standing policy of compensating veterans for their past contributions by providing them with numerous advantages.[f] This policy has "always been deemed to be legitimate."[g] * * *

Notes and Questions

1. The Court observes that veterans' organizations receive tax benefits "regardless of the content of any speech they may use." Is this disingenuous because the content of veterans' organizations' speech is predictable? Could the Congress give money to Republican party organizations "regardless of the content of any speech they may use." What if Congress said it was benefiting veterans' organizations in part because Congress thought such organizations were delivering a message that deserved to be heard? Does it matter that favorable tax treatment assists veterans' lobbying at local, state, and

d. In *Buckley,* Rehnquist, J., dissenting, complained that the scheme for public funding of Presidential candidates "enshrined the Republican and Democratic Parties in a permanently preferred position, and has established requirements for funding minor-party and independent candidates to which the two major parties are not subject. [B]ecause of the First Amendment overtones of the appellants' Fifth Amendment equal protection claim, something more than a merely rational basis for the difference in treatment must be shown, as the Court apparently recognizes." *Buckley* found the funding scheme to be "in furtherance of *sufficiently important* government interests and has not unfairly or unnecessarily burdened the political opportunity of any party or candidate." (Emphasis added).

e. Does this concern apply equally to veterans' organizations? See Note, *Charitable Lobbying Restraints and Tax Exempt Organizations: Old Problems, New Directions?,* 1984 Utah L.Rev. 337, 357–59 (1984).

f. Is it a sufficient response to note that veterans can be rewarded in many ways that do not tread on first amendment equality values?

g. Blackmun, J., joined by Brennan and Marshall, JJ., joined the opinion, but concurred to emphasize the importance of the tax code being administered in a manner that did not discourage lobbying by TWR or other groups.

federal levels? Could Congress withdraw favorable tax treatment from some veterans' organizations on the ground that their lobbying was not "worth the money"? Could Congress benefit charitable organizations, but not the veterans? Some charitable organizations, but not others? Could Congress give favorable tax treatment to lobbying of the Moral Majority, but no other group? [h]

2. Was TWR the wrong plaintiff? Was its claim weak because it failed to show viewpoint discrimination? Should a group whose primary purpose conflicts with that of veterans' groups be granted relief? See Note, *The Tax Code's Differential Treatment of Lobbying Under Section 501(c)(3): A Proposed First Amendment Analysis*, 66 Va.L.Rev. 1513 (1980).

3. If TWR had prevailed, what would have been the appropriate remedy? Denial of the veterans' benefit? Extension of the veterans' benefit to all charitable organizations?

4. Treasury regulations provide that a charitable organization whose primary purpose is education may retain its § 501(c)(3) status even if it advocates a particular position or viewpoint "so long as it presents a sufficiently full and fair exposition of the pertinent facts as to permit an individual or the public to form an independent opinion or conclusion." Treas.Reg. § 1.501(c)(3)–1(d)(3)(i) (1959). Should tax benefits depend upon IRS determinations of "fairness" and its identification of "pertinent" facts? Compare *Big Mama Rag, Inc. v. United States*, 631 F.2d 1030 (D.C.Cir.1980) with *National Alliance v. United States*, 710 F.2d 868 (D.C.Cir.1983).

5. Suppose that nothing in the tax law bars veterans' organizations from using tax deductible contributions for participation in political campaigns on behalf of candidates for public office. Is this more troublesome than the lobbying benefits? Suppose instead of supporting the political speech of others, government itself enters the political fray. Should a city government be able to buy media time to speak on behalf of candidates? To influence the outcome of initiative campaigns? [i]

II. GOVERNMENT AS EDUCATOR AND EDITOR

BOARD OF EDUCATION v. PICO, 457 U.S. 853, 102 S.Ct. 2799, 73 L.Ed.2d 435 (1982): Several members of the Island Trees Board of Education attended a conference sponsored by Parents of New York United (PONYU), a politically conservative organization. At the conference these board members obtained lists of books they described as "objectionable" and "improper fare for school students." On ascertaining that its school libraries contained eleven of the books,[a] the Board informally directed, over the objection of the school superin-

---

h. For general criticism of the tax code's treatment of charitable organizations, see Clark, *The Limitation on Political Activities: A Discordant Note in the Law of Charities*, 46 Va.L.Rev. 439 (1960); Garrett, *Federal Tax Limitations on Political Activities of Public Interest and Educational Organizations*, 59 Geo.L.J. 561 (1971); Troyer, *Charities, Law-Making, and the Constitution: The Validity of the Restrictions on Influencing Legislation*, 31 N.Y.U.Inst. on Fed. Tax'n 1415 (1973).

i. For a variety of views, see Yudof, *When Government Speaks: Politics, Law, and Government Expression in America* (1983); Emerson, *The Affirmative Side of the First Amendment*, 15 Ga.L.Rev. 795 (1981); Kamenshine,

The First Amendment's Implied Political Establishment Clause, 67 Calif.L.Rev. 1104 (1979); Shiffrin; *Government Speech*, 27 U.C. L.A.L.Rev. 565 (1980); Schauer, *Book Review*, 35 Stan.L.Rev. 373 (1983); Yudof, *When Governments Speak: Toward A Theory of Government Expression and the First Amendment*, 57 Tex.L.Rev. 863 (1979); Ziegler, *Government Speech and the Constitution: The Limits of Official Partisanship*, 21 B.C.L.Rev. 578 (1980); Note, *The Constitutionality of Municipal Advocacy in Statewide Referendum Campaigns*, 93 Harv.L.Rev. 535 (1980).

a. As the plurality opinion noted: "The nine [listed] books in the High School library were: *Slaughter House Five*, by Kurt Vontendent, that the books be delivered to the Board's offices so that Board members could read them. The Board justified its action by characterizing the listed books as "anti-American, anti-Christian, anti-Semitic, and just plain filthy" and concluding that it had a "duty" and a "moral obligation" "to protect the children in our school from this moral danger as surely as from physical and medical dangers." The Board then appointed a parent-teacher "Book Review Committee" to recommend to the board which books should be retained. The Committee recommended that only two books be removed and a third be available to students only with parental approval. But the Board, without giving any reasons, decided that nine books should be removed and that another should be made available subject to parental approval. Respondent students then brought an action for declaratory and injunctive relief under 42 U.S.C. § 1983, contending that the Board's actions had violated their first amendment rights. The district court granted summary judgment for the Board, stating that the Board had "restricted access only to certain books which [it] believed to be, in essence, vulgar." A 2–1 majority of the Second Circuit reversed. One member of the majority concluded that at least at the summary judgment stage, the Board had not offered sufficient justification for its action. A second member of the majority "viewed the case as turning on the contested factual issue of whether [the Board's] removal decision was motivated by a justifiable desire to remove books containing vulgarities and sexual explicitness, or rather by an impermissible desire to suppress ideas." The Supreme Court (5–4) upheld reversal of the summary dismissal of the suit, but there was no opinion of the Court. BRENNAN, J., announced the judgment of the Court in an opinion joined by Marshall and Stevens, JJ., and in part by Blackmun, J.:

"The principal question presented is whether the First Amendment imposes limitations upon the exercise by a local school board of its discretion to remove library books from high school and junior high school libraries.

"[P]ublic schools are vitally important 'in the preparation of individuals for participation as citizens,' and as vehicles for 'inculcating fundamental values necessary to the maintenance of a democratic political system.' We are therefore in full agreement with petitioners that local school boards must be permitted 'to establish and apply their curriculum in such a way as to transmit community values,' and that 'there is a legitimate and substantial community interest in promoting respect for authority and traditional values be they social, moral, or political.'

"At the same time, however, we have necessarily recognized that the discretion of the States and local school boards in matters of education must be exercised in a manner that comports with the transcendent imperatives of the First Amendment. In *West Virginia v. Barnette* [p. 1096 infra] we held that under the First Amendment a student in a public school could not be compelled to salute the flag. We reasoned that 'Boards of Education * * * have, of course, important, delicate, and highly discretionary functions, but none that

negut, Jr.; *The Naked Ape,* by Desmond Morris; *Down These Mean Streets,* by Piri Thomas; *Best Short Stories of Negro Writers,* edited by Langston Hughes; *Go Ask Alice,* of anonymous authorship; *Laughing Boy,* by Oliver LaFarge; *Black Boy,* by Richard Wright; *A Hero Ain't Nothin' But A Sandwich,* by Alice Childress; and *Soul On Ice,* by Eldridge Cleaver. The [listed] book in the Junior High School library was *A Reader for Writers,* ed-

ited by Jerome Archer. Still another listed book, *The Fixer,* by Bernard Malamud, was found to be included in the curriculum of a twelfth grade literature course."

The Board subsequently decided that only *Laughing Boy* should be returned to the library without restriction, and that *Black Boy* should be made available subject to parental approval.

they may not perform within the limits of the Bill of Rights. That they are educating the young for citizenship is reason for scrupulous protection of Constitutional freedoms of the individual, if we are not to strangle the free mind at its source and teach youth to discount important principles of our government as mere platitudes.' * * * [I]n sum, students do not 'shed their rights to freedom of speech or expression at the schoolhouse gate,' * * * *Tinker*.

"[We] think that the First Amendment rights of students may be directly and sharply implicated by the removal of books from the shelves of a school library. * * * [W]e have held that in a variety of contexts 'the Constitution protects the right to receive information and ideas.' *Stanley v. Georgia*. [First,] the right to receive ideas follows ineluctably from the *sender's* First Amendment right to send them * * *.

"More importantly, the right to receive ideas is a necessary predicate to the *recipient's* meaningful exercise of his own rights of speech, press, and political freedom. [Of] course all First Amendment rights accorded to students must be construed 'in light of the special characteristics of the school environment.' *Tinker*. But the special characteristics of the school *library* make that environment especially appropriate for the recognition of the First Amendment rights of students.

"A school library, no less than any other public library, is 'a place dedicated to quiet, to knowledge, and to beauty.' *Brown*. *Keyishian v. Board of Regents* [p. 636 infra] observed that 'students must always remain free to inquire, to study and to evaluate, to gain new maturity and understanding.' The school library is the principal locus of such freedom. [Petitioners] emphasize the inculcative function of secondary education, and argue that they must be allowed *unfettered* discretion to 'transmit community values' through the Island Trees schools. But that sweeping claim overlooks the unique role of the school library. It appears from the record that use of the Island Trees school libraries is completely voluntary on the part of students. Their selection of books from these libraries is entirely a matter of free choice; the libraries afford them an opportunity at self-education and individual enrichment that is wholly optional. Petitioners might well defend their claim of absolute discretion in matters of *curriculum* by reliance upon their duty to inculcate community values. But we think that petitioners' reliance upon that duty is misplaced where, as here, they attempt to extend their claim of absolute discretion beyond the compulsory environment of the classroom, into the school library and the regime of voluntary inquiry that there holds sway.

"In rejecting petitioners' claim of absolute discretion to remove books from their school libraries, we do not deny that local school boards have a substantial legitimate role to play in the determination of school library content. [But] that discretion may not be exercised in a narrowly partisan or political manner. If a Democratic school board, motivated by party affiliation, ordered the removal of all books written by or in favor of Republicans, few would doubt that the order violated the constitutional rights of the students denied access to those books. The same conclusion would surely apply if an all-white school board, motivated by racial animus, decided to remove all books authored by blacks or advocating racial equality and integration. Our Constitution does not permit the official suppression of *ideas*. Thus whether petitioners' removal of books from their school libraries denied respondents their First Amendment rights depends upon the motivation behind petitioners' actions. If petitioners *intended* by their removal decision to deny respondents access to ideas with which petitioners disagreed, and if this intent was the decisive factor in petitioners' decision,[22] then petitioners have exercised their discretion in violation of the Constitution. To permit such intentions to control official actions would be to encourage the precise sort of officially prescribed orthodoxy unequivocally condemned in *Barnette*. On the other hand, respondents implicitly concede that an unconstitutional motivation would *not* be demonstrated if it were shown that petitioners had decided to remove the books at issue because those books were pervasively vulgar. And again, respondents concede that if it were demonstrated that the removal decision was based solely upon the 'educational suitability' of the books in question, then their removal would be 'perfectly permissible.' In other words, in respondents' view such motivations if decisive of petitioners' actions, would not carry the danger of an official suppression of ideas, and thus would not violate respondents' First Amendment rights.

"[N]othing in our decision today affects in any way the discretion of a local school board to choose books to *add* to the libraries of their schools. Because we are concerned in this case with the suppression of ideas, our holding today affects only the discretion to *remove* books. In brief, we hold that local school boards may not remove books from school library shelves simply because they dislike the ideas contained in those books and seek by their removal to 'prescribe what shall be orthodox in politics, nationalism, religion, or other matters of opinion.' *Barnette*. Such purposes stand inescapably condemned by our precedents.

"We now turn to the remaining question presented by this case: Do the evidentiary materials that were before the District Court, when construed most favorably to respondents, raise a genuine issue of material fact whether petitioners exceeded constitutional limitations in exercising their discretion to remove the books from the school libraries? We conclude that the materials do raise such a question, which forecloses summary judgment in favor of petitioners.

"Before the District Court, respondents claimed that petitioners' decision to remove the books 'was based upon [their] personal values, morals and tastes.' Respondents also claimed that petitioners objected to the books in part because excerpts from them were 'anti-American.' The accuracy of these claims was partially conceded by petitioners,[23] and petitioners' own affidavits lent further support to respondents' claims. In addition, the record developed in the District Court shows that when petitioners offered their first public explanation for the removal of the books, they relied in part on the assertion that the removed books were 'anti-American,' and 'offensive [to] Americans in general.' Furthermore, while the Book Review Committee appointed by petitioners was instructed to make its recommendations based upon criteria that appear on their face to be permissible—the books' 'educational suitability,' 'good taste,' 'relevance,' and 'appropriateness to age and grade level'—the Committee's recommendations that five of the books be retained and that only two be removed were essentially rejected by petitioners, without any statement of reasons for doing so. Finally, while petitioners originally defended their removal decision with the explanation that 'these books contain obscenities, blasphemies, and perversion beyond description,' one of the books, *A Reader for Writers*, was removed even though it contained no such language.

22. By "decisive factor" we mean a "substantial factor" in the absence of which the opposite decision would have been reached.

23. Petitioners acknowledged that their "evaluation of the suitability of the books was based on [their] personal values, morals, tastes and concepts of educational suitability." But they did not accept, and thus apparently denied, respondents' assertion that some excerpts were objected to as "anti-American."

"Standing alone, this evidence respecting the substantive motivations behind petitioners' removal decision would not be decisive. This would be a very different case if the record demonstrated that petitioners had employed established, regular, and facially unbiased procedures for the review of controversial materials. But the actual record in the case before us suggests the exact opposite. Petitioners' removal procedures were vigorously challenged below by respondents, and the evidence on this issue sheds further light on the issue of petitioners' motivations. Respondents alleged that in making their removal decision petitioners ignored 'the advice of literary experts,' the views of 'librarians and teachers within the Island Trees School system,' the advice of the superintendent of schools, and the guidance of 'publications that rate books for junior and senior high school students.' Respondents also claimed that petitioners' decision was based solely on the fact that the books were named on the PONYU list [and] that petitioners 'did not undertake an independent review of other books in the [school] libraries.' Evidence before the District Court lends support to these claims. [In] sum, respondents' allegations and some of the evidentiary materials presented below do not rule out the possibility that petitioners' removal procedures were highly irregular and ad hoc—the antithesis of those procedures that might tend to allay suspicions regarding petitioners' motivations.

"Construing these claims, affidavit statements, and other evidentiary materials in a manner favorable to respondents, we cannot conclude that petitioners were 'entitled to a judgment as a matter of law.' The evidence plainly does not foreclose the possibility that petitioners' decision to remove the books rested decisively upon disagreement with constitutionally protected ideas in those books, or upon a desire on petitioners' part to impose upon the students of the Island Trees High School and Junior High School a political orthodoxy to which petitioners and their constituents adhered."

In the view of BLACKMUN, J., concurring, "the principle involved here is both narrower and more basic than 'the right to receive information' identified by the plurality. I do not suggest that the State has any affirmative obligation to provide students with information or ideas, something that may well be associated with a 'right to receive.' And I do not believe, as the plurality suggests, that the right at issue here is somehow associated with the peculiar nature of the school library; if schools may be used to inculcate ideas, surely libraries may play a role in that process.[1] Instead, I suggest that certain forms of state discrimination *between* ideas are improper. In particular, our precedents com-

---

1. As a practical matter, however, it is difficult to see the First Amendment right that I believe is at work here playing a role in a school's choice of curriculum. The school's finite resources—as well as the limited number of hours in the day—require that education officials make sensitive choices between subjects to be offered and competing areas of academic emphasis; subjects generally are excluded simply because school officials have chosen to devote their resources to one rather than to another subject. [In] any event, the Court has recognized that students' First Amendment rights in most cases must give way if they interfere "with the schools' work or [with] the rights of other students to be secure and to be let alone," *Tinker*, and such interference will rise to intolerable levels if public participation in the management of the curriculum becomes commonplace. In contrast, library books on a shelf intrude not at all on the daily operation of a school.

I also have some doubt that there is a theoretical distinction between removal of a book and failure to acquire a book. But as Judge Newman observed, there is a profound practical and evidentiary distinction between the two actions: "removal, more than failure to acquire, is likely to suggest that an impermissible political motivation may be present. There are many reasons why a book is not acquired, the most obvious being limited resources, but there are few legitimate reasons why a book, once acquired, should be removed from a library not filled to capacity."

mand the conclusion that the State may not act to deny access to an idea simply because state officials disapprove of that idea for partisan or political reasons.[2]

* * *

"As I view it, this is a narrow principle. School officials must be able to choose one book over another, without outside interference, when the first book is deemed more relevant to the curriculum, or better written, or when one of a host of other politically neutral reasons is present. These decisions obviously will not implicate First Amendment values. And even absent space or financial limitations, First Amendment principles would allow a school board to refuse to make a book available to students because it contains offensive language, cf. *FCC v. Pacifica Foundation* [p. 605 infra] (Powell, J., concurring), or because it is psychologically or intellectually inappropriate for the age group, or even, perhaps, because the ideas it advances are 'manifestly inimical to the public welfare.' And, of course, school officials may choose one book over another because they believe that one subject is more important, or is more deserving of emphasis.

"[I] believe that tying the First Amendment right to the *purposeful* suppression of ideas makes the concept more manageable than Justice Rehnquist acknowledges. Most people would recognize that refusing to allow discussion of current events in Latin class is a policy designed to 'inculcate' Latin, not to suppress ideas. Similarly, removing a learned treatise criticizing American foreign policy from an elementary school library because the students would not understand it is an action unrelated to the *purpose* of suppressing ideas. In my view, however, removing the same treatise because it is 'anti-American' raises a far more difficult issue.

"It is not a sufficient answer to this problem that a State operates a school in its role as 'educator,' rather than its role as 'sovereign,' (Rehnquist, J., dissenting), for the First Amendment has application to all the State's activities. While the State may act as 'property owner' when it prevents certain types of expressive activity from taking place on public lands, for example, few would suggest that the State may base such restrictions on the content of the speaker's message, or may take its action for the purpose of suppressing access to the ideas involved. *Mosley.* And while it is not clear to me from Justice Rehnquist's discussion whether a State operates its public libraries in its 'role as sovereign,' surely difficult constitutional problems would arise if a State chose to exclude 'anti-Amnerican' books from its public libraries—even if those books remained available at local bookstores.

"[S]chool officials may seek to instill certain values 'by persuasion and example,' or by choice of emphasis. That sort of positive educational action, however, is the converse of an intentional attempt to shield students from certain ideas that officials find politically distasteful. Arguing that the majority in the community rejects the ideas involved, does not refute this principle: 'The very purpose of a Bill of Rights was to withdraw certain subjects from the vicissitudes of political controversy, to place them beyond the reach of majorities and officials * * *.' *Barnette.*"

WHITE, J., who concurred in the judgment, noted that although the District Court found that the books were removed because the school board believed them "to be, in essence, vulgar," both Court of Appeals judges in the majority

2. In effect, my view presents the obverse of the plurality's analysis: while the plurality focuses on the failure to provide information, I find crucial the State's decision to single out an idea for disapproval and then deny access to it.

concluded that there was a material issue of fact that precluded summary judgment for petitioners. As White, J., understood it, "[t]he unresolved factual issue [is] the reason or reasons underlying the school board's removal of the books" and he was "not inclined to disagree with the Court of Appeals on such a fact-bound issue. [The] Court seems compelled to go further and issue a dissertation on the extent to which the First Amendment limits the discretion of the school board to remove books from the school library. I see no necessity for doing so at this point. When findings of fact and conclusions of law are made by the District Court, that may end the case."

BURGER, C.J., joined by Powell, Rehnquist, and O'Connor, JJ., dissented: "The First Amendment, as with other parts of the Constitution, must deal with new problems in a changing world. In an attempt to deal with a problem in an area traditionally left to the states, a plurality of the Court, in a lavish expansion going beyond any prior holding under the First Amendment, expresses its view that a school board's decision concerning what books are to be in the school library is subject to federal court review. Were this to become the law, this Court would come perilously close to becoming a 'super censor' of school board library decisions. Stripped to its essentials, the issue comes down to two important propositions: first, whether local schools are to be administered by elected school boards, or by federal judges and teenage pupils; and second, whether the values of morality, good taste, and relevance to education are valid reasons for school board decisions concerning the contents of a school library. In an attempt to place this case within the protection of the First Amendment, the plurality suggests a new 'right' that, when shorn of the plurality's rhetoric, allows this Court to impose its own views about what books must be made available to students. * * *

"It is true that where there is a willing distributor of materials, the government may not impose unreasonable obstacles to dissemination by the third party. And where the speaker desires to express certain ideas, the government may not impose unreasonable restraints. It does not follow, however, that a school board must affirmatively aid the speaker in its communication with the recipient. In short the plurality suggests today that if a writer has something to say, the government through its schools must be the courier. None of the cases cited by the plurality establish this broad-based proposition.

"[The] plurality concludes that under the Constitution school boards cannot choose to retain or dispense with books if their discretion is exercised in a 'narrowly partisan or political manner.' The plurality concedes that permissible factors are whether the books are 'pervasively vulgar' or educationally unsuitable. 'Educational suitability,' however, is a standardless phrase. This conclusion will undoubtedly be drawn in many—if not most—instances because of the decisionmaker's content-based judgment that the ideas contained in the book or the idea expressed from the author's method of communication are inappropriate for teenage pupils. * * *

"Further, there is no guidance whatsoever as to what constitutes 'political' factors. [V]irtually all educational decisions necessarily involve 'political' determinations.

"What the plurality views as valid reasons for removing a book at their core involve partisan judgments. Ultimately the federal courts will be the judge of whether the motivation for book removal was 'valid' or 'reasonable.' Undoubtedly the validity of many book removals will ultimately turn on a judge's evaluation of the books. Discretion must be used, and the appropriate body to exercise that discretion is the local elected school board, not judges. * * *

"No amount of 'limiting' language could rein in the sweeping 'right' the plurality would create. The plurality distinguishes library books from textbooks because library books 'by their nature are optional rather than required reading.' It is not clear, however, why this distinction requires *greater* scrutiny before 'optional' reading materials may be removed. It would appear that required reading and textbooks have a greater likelihood of imposing a 'pall of orthodoxy' over the educational process than do optional reading. In essence, the plurality's view transforms the availability of this 'optional' reading into a 'right' to have this 'optional' reading maintained at the demand of teenagers.

"The plurality also limits the new right by finding it applicable only to the *removal* of books once acquired. Yet if the First Amendment commands that certain books cannot be *removed,* does it not equally require that the same books be *acquired?* Why does the coincidence of timing become the basis of a constitutional holding? According to the plurality, the evil to be avoided is the 'official suppression of ideas.' It does not follow that the decision to *remove* a book is less 'official suppression' than the decision not to acquire a book desired by someone.[8] Similarly, a decision to eliminate certain material from the curriculum, history for example, would carry an equal—probably greater—prospect of 'official suppression.' Would the decision be subject to our review?"

POWELL, J., also dissented: "The plurality's reasoning is marked by contradiction. It purports to acknowledge the traditional role of school boards and parents [in] 'inculcating fundamental values necessary to the maintenance of a democratic political system.' * * * Yet when a school board, as in this case, takes its responsibilities seriously and seeks to decide what the fundamental values are that should be imparted, the plurality finds a constitutional violation.

"[A] school board's attempt to instill in its students the ideas and values on which a democratic system depends is viewed as an impermissible suppression of other ideas and values on which other systems of government and other societies thrive. Books may not be removed because they are indecent; extoll violence, intolerance and racism; or degrade the dignity of the individual. Human history, not the least of the twentieth century, records the power and political life of these very ideas. But they are not our ideas or values. Although I would leave this educational decision to the duly constituted board, I certainly would not *require* a school board to promote ideas and values repugnant to a democratic society or to teach such values to *children.*

"In different contexts and in different times, the destruction of written materials has been the symbol of despotism and intolerance. But the removal of nine vulgar or racist books from a high school library by a concerned local school board does not raise this specter. For me, today's decision symbolizes a debilitating encroachment upon the institutions of a free people." [b]

---

8. The formless nature of the "right" found by the plurality in this case is exemplified by this purported distinction. Presumably a school district could, for any reason, choose not to purchase a book for its library. Once it purchases that book, however, it is "locked in" to retaining it on the school shelf until it can justify a reason for its removal. This anomolous result of "book tenure" was pointed out by the District Court in this case.

Under the plurality view, if a school board wants to be assured that it maintains control over the education of its students, every page of every book sought to be acquired must be read before a purchase decision is made.

b. Powell, J., appended a summary of excerpts from the books at issue collected in the opinion of Judge Mansfield dissenting below.

REHNQUIST, J., joined by Burger, C.J., and Powell, J., "disagree[d] with Justice Brennan's opinion because it is largely hypothetical in character, failing to take account of the facts as admitted by the parties [and] because it is analytically unsound and internally inconsistent":

"Considering only the respondents' description of the factual aspects of petitioners' motivation, Justice Brennan's apparent concern that the Board's action may have been a sinister political plot 'to suppress ideas' may be laid to rest. The members of the Board, in deciding to remove these books, were undoubtedly influenced by their own 'personal values, morals, and tastes,' just as any member of a school board is apt to be so influenced in making decisions as to whether a book is educationally suitable. Respondents essentially conceded that some excerpts of the removed books 'contained profanities, some were sexually explicit, some were ungrammatical, some were anti-American, and some were offensive to racial, religious, or ethnic groups.'

"Respondents also agreed that, '[a]lthough the books themselves were excluded from use in the schools in any way, [petitioners] have not precluded discussion about the themes of the books or the books themselves.' Justice Brennan's concern with the 'suppression of ideas' thus seems entirely unwarranted on this state of the record, and his creation of constitutional rules to cover such eventualities is entirely gratuitous. [Although] I entirely disagree with Justice Brennan's treatment of the constitutional issue, I also disagree with his opinion for the entirely separate reason that it is not remotely tailored to the facts presented by this [case.]

"I can cheerfully concede [that a Democratic school board could not, for political reasons, remove all books by or in favor of Republicans, and that an all-white school board, motivated by racial animus, could not remove all books authored by blacks or advocating racial equality], but as in so many other cases the extreme examples are seldom the ones that arise in the real world of constitutional litigation. In *this case* the facts taken most favorably to respondents suggest that nothing of this sort happened. The nine books removed undoubtedly did contain 'ideas,' but in the light of the excerpts from them found in the dissenting opinion [in the court below], it is apparent that eight of them contained demonstrable amounts of vulgarity and profanity and the ninth contained nothing that could be considered partisan or political. [R]espondents admitted as much. Petitioners did not, for the reasons stated hereafter, run afoul of the First and Fourteenth Amendments by removing these particular books from the library in the manner in which they did. I would save for another day—feeling quite confident that that day will not arrive—the extreme examples posed in Justice Brennan's opinion.

"Considerable light is shed on the correct resolution of the constitutional question in this case by examining the role played by petitioners. Had petitioners been the members of a town council, I suppose all would agree that, absent a good deal more than is present in this record, they could not have prohibited the sale of these books by private booksellers within the municipality. But we have also recognized that the government may act in other capacities than as sovereign, and when it does the First Amendment may speak with a different voice * * *. By the same token, expressive conduct which may not be prohibited by the State as sovereign may be proscribed by the State as property owner [quoting from *Adderley*, p. 541 supra].

"With these differentiated roles of government in mind, it is helpful to assess the role of government as educator, as compared with the role of government as sovereign. When it acts as an educator, at least at the elementary and secondary school level, the government is engaged in inculcating social values and knowledge in relatively impressionable young people. Obviously there are innumerable decisions to be made as to what courses should be taught, what books should be purchased, or what teachers should be employed. In every one of these areas the members of a school board will act on the basis of their own personal or moral values, will attempt to mirror those of the community, or will abdicate the making of such decisions to so-called 'experts.' [5] [In] the very course of administering the many-faceted operations of a school district, the mere decision to purchase some books will necessarily preclude the possibility of purchasing others. The decision to teach a particular subject may preclude the possibility of teaching another subject. A decision to replace a teacher because of ineffectiveness may by implication be seen as a disparagement of the subject matter taught. In each of these instances, however, the book or the exposure to the subject matter may be acquired elsewhere. The managers of the school district are not proscribing it as to the citizenry in general, but are simply determining that it will not be included in the curriculum or school library. In short, actions by the government as educator do not raise the same First Amendment concerns as actions by the government as sovereign.

"Justice Brennan would hold that the First Amendment gives high school and junior high school students a 'right to receive ideas' in the school. This right is a curious entitlement. It exists only in the library of the school, and only if the idea previously has been acquired by the school in book form. It provides no protection against a school board's decision not to acquire a particular book, even though that decision denies access to ideas as fully as removal of the book from the library, and it prohibits removal of previously acquired books only if the remover 'dislike[s] the ideas contained in those books,' even though removal for any other reason also denies the students access to the books.

"But it is not the limitations which Justice Brennan places on the right with which I disagree; they simply demonstrate his discomfort with the new doctrine which he fashions out of whole cloth. It is the very existence of a right to receive information in the junior high school and high school setting, which I find wholly unsupported by our past decisions and inconsistent with the necessarily selective process of elementary and secondary education. * * *

"There are even greater reasons for rejecting Justice Brennan's analysis [than] the significant fact that we have never adopted it in the past. [The] idea that [public school] students have a right of access, *in the school,* to information other than that thought by their educators to be necessary is contrary to the very nature of an inculcative education.

"Education consists of the selective presentation and explanation of ideas. The effective acquisition of knowledge depends upon an orderly exposure to relevant information. Nowhere is this more true than in elementary and secondary schools, where, unlike the broad-ranging inquiry available to university students, the courses taught are those thought most relevant to the young students' individual development. Of necessity, elementary and secondary educators must separate the relevant from the irrelevant, the appropriate from the inappropriate. Determining what information *not* to present to the students is

5. There are intimations in Justice Brennan's opinion that if petitioners had only consulted literary experts, librarians, and teachers their decision might better withstand First Amendment attack. These observations seem to me wholly fatuous; surely ideas are no more accessible or no less suppressed if the school board merely ratifies the opinion of some other group rather than following its own opinion.

often as important as identifying relevant material. This winnowing process necessarily leaves much information to be discovered by students at another time or in another place, and is fundamentally inconsistent with any constitutionally required eclecticism in public education.

"[Unlike] university or public libraries, elementary and secondary school libraries are not designed for free-wheeling inquiry; they are tailored, as the public school curriculum is tailored, to the teaching of basic skills and ideas. Thus, Justice Brennan cannot rely upon the nature of school libraries to escape the fact that the First Amendment right to receive information simply has no application to the one public institution which, by its very nature, is a place for the selective conveyance of ideas.

"After all else is said, however, the most obvious reason that petitioners' removal of the books did not violate respondents' right to receive information is the ready availability of the books elsewhere. Students are not denied books by their removal from a school library. The books may be borrowed from a public library, read at a university library, purchased at a bookstore, or loaned by a friend. The government as educator does not seek to reach beyond the confines of the school. Indeed, following the removal from the school library of the books at issue in this case, the local public library put all nine books on display for public inspection. Their contents were fully accessible to any inquisitive student.

"[If] Justice Brennan truly has found a 'right to receive ideas,' [his] distinction between acquisition and removal makes little sense. The failure of a library to acquire a book denies access to its contents just as effectively as does the removal of the book from the library's shelf. As a result of either action the book cannot be found in the 'principal locus' of freedom discovered by Justice Brennan. * * *

"The final limitation placed by Justice Brennan upon his newly discovered right is a motive requirement: the First Amendment is violated only '[i]f petitioners *intended* by their removal decision to deny respondents access to ideas with which petitioners disagreed.' (Emphasis in original). But bad motives and good motives alike deny access to the books removed. If Justice Brennan truly recognizes a constitutional right to receive information, it is difficult to see why the reason for the denial makes any difference. Of course Justice Brennan's view is that intent matters because the First Amendment does not tolerate an officially prescribed orthodoxy. But this reasoning mixes First Amendment apples and oranges. The right to receive information differs from the right to be free from an officially prescribed orthodoxy. Not every educational denial of access to information casts a pall of orthodoxy over the classroom.

"It is difficult to tell from Justice Brennan's opinion just what motives he would consider constitutionally impermissible. I had thought that the First Amendment proscribes content-based restrictions on the marketplace of ideas. Justice Brennan concludes, however, that a removal decision based solely upon the 'educational suitability' of a book or upon its perceived vulgarity is 'perfectly permissible.' But such determinations are based as much on the content of the book as determinations that the book espouses pernicious political views.

"Moreover, Justice Brennan's motive test is difficult to square with his distinction between acquisition and removal. If a school board's removal of books might be motivated by a desire to promote favored political or religious views, there is no reason that its acquisition policy might not also be so motivated. And yet the 'pall of orthodoxy' cast by a carefully executed book-acquisition program apparently would not violate the First Amendment under Justice Brennan's view."

"Intertwined as a basis for Justice Brennan's opinion, along with the 'right to receive information,' is the statement that 'our Constitution does not permit the official suppression of *ideas.*' (Emphasis in original). There would be few champions, I suppose, of the idea that our Constitution *does* permit the official suppression of ideas; my difficulty is not with the admittedly appealing catchiness of the phrase, but with my doubt that it is really a useful analytical tool in solving difficult First Amendment problems.

"[In] the case before us the petitioners may in one sense be said to have 'suppressed' the 'ideas' of vulgarity and profanity, but that is hardly an apt description of what was done. They ordered the removal of books containing vulgarity and profanity, but they did not attempt to preclude discussion about the themes of the books or the books themselves. Such a decision, on respondents' version of the facts in this case, is sufficiently related to 'educational suitability' to pass muster under the First Amendment. ✳ ✳ ✳

"Accepting as true respondents' assertion that petitioners acted on the basis of their own 'personal values, morals, and tastes,' I find the actions taken in this case hard to distinguish from the myriad choices made by school boards in the routine supervision of elementary and secondary schools. 'Courts do not and cannot intervene in the resolution of conflicts which arise in the daily operation of school systems and which do not directly and sharply implicate basic constitutional values.' In this case respondents' rights of free speech and expression were not infringed, and by respondents' own admission no ideas were 'suppressed.' I would leave to another day the harder cases."

In a brief separate dissent, O'CONNOR, J., observed: "If the school board can set the curriculum, select teachers, and determine initially what books to purchase for the school library, it surely can decide which books to discontinue or remove from the school library so long as it does not also interfere with the right of students to read the material and to discuss it. As Justice Rehnquist persuasively argues, the plurality's analysis overlooks the fact that in this case the government is acting in its special role as educator.

"I do not personally agree with the board's action with respect to some of the books in question here, but it is not the function of the courts to make the decisions that have been properly relegated to the elected members of school boards. It is the school board that must determine educational suitability, and it has done so in this case. I therefore join the Chief Justice's dissent."

Notes & Question

1. Consider Yudof, *Library Book Selection and Public Schools: The Quest for the Archimedean Point,* 59 Ind.L.J. 527, 530 (1984): The critical questions in *Pico* are "who will control socialization of the young, what are the values to which they will be socialized, and how will cultural grounding and critical reflection be accommodated." On the latter point, see Mendelson, *The Habermas-Gadamer Debate,* New German Critique 18 (1979). See also Unger, *Knowledge and Politics* (1975); Cornell, *Toward a Modern/Postmodern Reconstruction of Ethics,* 133 U.Pa.L.Rev. 291 (1985).[c]

c. For a range of views on the scope and propriety of government promotion of particular values, see sources collected in fn. i after *Regan* supra. See also Dworkin, *A Matter of Principle* 181–204, 221–33 (1985); Tussman, *Government and the Mind* (1977); Diamond,

2. Should librarians have a first amendment right to select and retain books against the objections of a school board? Against a city council in a non-school context? See O'Neil, *Libraries, Librarians and First Amendment Freedoms,* 4 Hum.Rts. 295 (1975); O'Neil, *Libraries, Liberties and the First Amendment,* 42 U.Cin.L.Rev. 209 (1973). Should elementary school teachers have a first amendment right to resist interference with their teaching by "politically" motivated administrators or school boards? At secondary levels? Should student newspapers have a first amendment right to resist ad hoc intervention by administrators? See Canby, *The First Amendment and the State as Editor: Implications for Public Broadcasting,* 52 Tex.L.Rev. 1123 (1974). What of an approach that allows (requires?) administrators to set policies and procedures but prohibits ad hoc intervention?

3. Every Justice recognizes that some content discrimination is permitted in selecting books and making curricular decisions. The line between a public forum and a facility subject to the government's editorial discretion, however, may be hard to draw. SOUTHEASTERN PROMOTIONS, LTD. v. CONRAD, 420 U.S. 546, 95 S.Ct. 1239, 43 L.Ed.2d 448 (1975), reacting to reports that the musical *Hair* included nudity and was obscene, a publicly-appointed board denied *Hair's* producers a permit to use a theater dedicated for "cultural advancement and for clean, healthful, entertainment which will make for the upbuilding of a better citizenship." The Court, per BLACKMUN, J., held that the theater was a public forum "designed for and dedicated to expressive activities" and that the board's procedures amounted to a prior restraint in violation of *Freedman* requirements, p. 482 supra. One of the dissenters, REHNQUIST, J., asked: "May a municipal theater devote an entire season to Shakespeare, or is it required to book any potential producer on a first come, first served basis? [T]he Court's opinion [seems] to give no constitutionally permissible role in the way of selection to the municipal authorities." For commentary, see Karst, *Public Enterprise and the Public Forum: A Comment on Southeastern Promotions, Ltd. v. Conrad,* 37 Ohio St.L.J. 247 (1976); Shiffrin, fn. i after *Regan,* supra, at 581–88; Comment, *Access to State-Owned Communications Media—The Public Forum Doctrine,* 26 U.C.L.A.L.Rev. 1410, 1440–44 (1979).

III. GOVERNMENT INVOLVEMENT WITH SPEECH AND THE CAPTIVE AUDIENCE

PUBLIC UTILITIES COMM'N v. POLLAK, 343 U.S. 451, 72 S.Ct. 813, 96 L.Ed. 1068 (1952): A District of Columbia transit company installed FM receivers in its buses and streetcars. An FM station broadcast special programs—in this case 90% music, 5% news and 5% commercial advertising—to which the bus and streetcar radios were fixed-tuned. Advertisers paid "a dollar a thousand

The First Amendment and Public Schools: The Case Against Judicial Intervention, 59 Tex.L.Rev. 477 (1981); Garvey, *Children and the First Amendment,* 57 Tex.L.Rev. 321 (1979); Goldstein, *The Asserted Constitutional Right of Public School Teachers to Determine What They Teach,* 124 U.Pa.L.Rev. 1293 (1976); Moskowitz, *The Making of the Moral Child: Legal Implications of Values Education,* 6 Pepp.L.Rev. 105 (1978); Nahmod, *Con-* *troversy in the Classroom: The High School Teacher and Freedom of Expression,* 39 Geo. Wash.L.Rev. 1032 (1971); van Geel, *The Search for Constitutional Limits on Governmental Authority to Inculcate Youth,* 62 Tex. L.Rev. 197 (1983); Note, *State Indoctrination and the Protection of Non-State Voices in the Schools: Justifying a Prohibition of School Library Censorship,* 35 Stan.L.Rev. 497 (1983).

people" and were assured, "If they can hear—they can hear your commercial." The station described itself to the trade as "delivering a guaranteed audience."[a]

After a hearing, the PUC concluded that the radio programs were not inconsistent with public convenience, comfort and safety and "tends to improve the conditions under which the public ride." Two protesting passengers appealed. The court of appeals ruled that at least the broadcasting of "commercials" and "announcements" infringed constitutional rights. But the Court per BURTON, J., reversed.[b] Assuming that the action of the federally regulated transit company "amounts to sufficient Federal Government action to make the First and Fifth Amendments applicable," neither amendment was violated:

"Pollak and Martin contend that the radio programs interfere with their freedom of conversation and that of other passengers by making it necessary for them to compete against the programs in order to be heard. The Commission, however, did not find, and the testimony does not compel a finding, that the programs interfered substantially with the conversation of passengers or with rights of communication constitutionally protected in public places. It is suggested also that the First Amendment guarantees a freedom to listen only to such points of view as the listener wishes to hear. There is no substantial claim that the programs have been used for objectionable propaganda. There is no issue of that kind before us.[9] The inclusion in the programs of a few announcements explanatory and commendatory of Capital Transit's own services does not sustain such an objection.

"[The protesting passengers] claim is that no matter how much the [transit company] may wish to use [the radios] as part of its service to its passengers and as a source of income, no matter how much the great majority of its passengers may desire [such radios],[c] and however [favorable the Commission's findings on such use], if one passenger objects to the programs as an invasion of his constitutional right of privacy, the use of radio must be discontinued. This position wrongly assumes that the Fifth Amendment secures to each passenger on a [federally regulated public vehicle] a right of privacy substantially equal to the privacy to which he is entitled in his own home. [But the right of privacy] is substantially limited by the rights of other when its possessor [rides] in a public conveyance."

BLACK, J., concurred "in the Court's holding that this record shows no violation of the Due Process Clause of the Fifth Amendment. I also agree that Capital Transit's musical programs have not violated the First Amendment. I am of the opinion, however, that subjecting Capital Transit's passengers to the broadcasting of news, public speeches, views, or propaganda of any kind and by any means would violate the First Amendment. To the extent, if any, that the Court holds the contrary, I dissent."

DOUGLAS, J., dissenting, dwelt on "the right to be let alone"—"the beginning of all freedom": "The present case involves a form of coercion to make people listen. The listeners are of course in a public place. [But] in a practical sense

---

a. See Black, *He Cannot Choose But Hear: The Plight of the Captive Auditor,* 53 Colum.L. Rev. 960, 961 (1953) (the author was counsel for Pollak).

b. Frankfurter, J., recused himself because "my feelings are so strongly engaged as a victim of the [challenged] practice."

9. The Communications Act of 1934, 48 Stat. 1064 et seq., as amended, 47 U.S.C. § 151 et seq., 47 U.S.C.A. § 151 et seq., has been interpreted by the Federal Communications Commission as imposing upon each licensee the duty of fair presentation of news and controversial issues.

c. A poll considered by the PUC revealed that 76% favored buscasting; 17% didn't know or care; only 6.6% disapproved, of whom about half were firmly opposed.

they are forced to ride, since this mode of transportation is today essential for many thousands. Compulsion which comes from circumstances can be as real as compulsion which comes from a command. [T]he man on the streetcar has no choice but to sit and listen, or perhaps to sit and try *not* to listen. When we force people to listen to another's ideas, we give the propagandist a powerful weapon. [Once] a man is forced to submit to one type of radio program, he can be forced to submit to another. It may be but a short step from a cultural program to a political program."

Notes and Questions

1. Consider Emerson, *The System of Freedom of Expression* 711 (1970): "It should be noted that the *Pollak* case did not present a clear-cut issue of government expression. "State action" was involved, to some degree, because the Public Utilities Commission had power to permit or prohibit the communication. But the government of the District of Columbia was not actually doing the broadcasting. [Had] the Capital Transit Company been a governmentally operated enterprise, however, surely broadcasts to the captive audience would have violated the First Amendment. Government communication of that kind, at least on any substantial scale, would quickly destroy freedom of expression. The resulting system would be closer to that depicted in George Orwell's *1984* than to any envisaged by the First Amendment. It has fortunately not been necessary to define the exact contours of the principle that the government may not engage in expression directed at a captive audience, or otherwise force its citizens to listen. There can be no doubt, however, that the principle is central to any system of freedom of expression."

2. Is it a weakness of the *Pollak* case, as presented by the complainants, that they did not pursue the point that the "captive audience" *was being* "propagandized"? The record shows that after the date had been set for the Commission hearing, but prior to the hearing itself, "buscasts" defending "buscasting" were made. The record also discloses that there were "news" broadcasts. Does not this imply the transmission of "views," absolute impartiality being impossible? See Note, 1 J.Pub.L. 507, 512–13 (1952). Moreover, the transit company "buscast" political advertising limited in length to thirty seconds and clearly identified as paid advertising as well as "capsules" of the Republican and Democratic National Conventions. Id.

3. Do captive audiences of government speech have a first amendment right not to be propagandized? Do children educated in public schools have such a right? If ad hoc methods of separating education from propaganda are unreliable, are any institutional structures or processes required? Should this be a constitutional right without a remedy? Consider also captive audiences of prisoners, soldiers, or workers in public institutions. On government speech and the captive audience, see Yudof, *When Government Speaks,* p. 555 supra, at 169–70, 213–18, 231–33, 296–99.

LEHMAN v. SHAKER HEIGHTS
418 U.S. 298, 94 S.Ct. 2714, 41 L.Ed.2d 770 (1974).

MR. JUSTICE BLACKMUN announced the judgment of the Court and an opinion, in which THE CHIEF JUSTICE, MR. JUSTICE WHITE, and MR. JUSTICE REHNQUIST, join.

[A city operating a public transit system sold commercial and public service advertising space for car cards on its vehicles, but permitted no "political" or "public issue" advertising. When petitioner, a candidate for the office of State

Representative to the Ohio General Assembly, failed in his effort to have advertising promoting his candidacy accepted, he unsuccessfully sought declaratory and injunctive relief in the state courts.]

It is urged that the car cards here constitute a public forum protected by the First Amendment, and that there is a guarantee of nondiscriminatory access to such publicly owned and controlled areas of communication "regardless of the primary purpose for which the area is dedicated." We disagree.

* * * "[T]he truth is that open spaces and public places differ very much in their character, and before you could say whether a certain thing could be done in a public place you would have to know the history of the particular place." Although American constitutional jurisprudence, in the light of the First Amendment, has been jealous to preserve access to public places for purposes of free speech, the nature of the forum and the conflicting interests involved have remained important in determining the degree of protection afforded by the Amendment to the speech in question.

Here, we have no open spaces, no meeting hall, park, street corner, or other public thoroughfare. Instead, the city is engaged in commerce. [The] car card space, although incidental to the provision of public transportation, is a part of the commercial venture. In much the same way that a newspaper or periodical, or even a radio or television station, need not accept every proffer of advertising from the general public, a city transit system has discretion to develop and make reasonable choices concerning the type of advertising that may be displayed in its vehicles. * * *

Because state action exists, however, the policies and practices governing access to the transit system's advertising space must not be arbitrary, capricious, or invidious. Here, the city has decided that "[p]urveyors of goods and services saleable in commerce may purchase advertising space on an equal basis, whether they be house builders or butchers." * * * Revenue earned from long-term commercial advertising could be jeopardized by a requirement that short-term candidacy or issue-oriented advertisements be displayed on car cards. Users would be subjected to the blare of political propaganda. There could be lurking doubts about favoritism, and sticky administrative problems might arise in parceling out limited space to eager politicians. In these circumstances, the managerial decision to limit car card space to innocuous and less controversial commercial and service oriented advertising does not rise to the dignity of a First Amendment violation. [Otherwise], display cases in public hospitals, libraries, office buildings, military compounds, and other public facilities would become Hyde Parks open to every would-be pamphleteer and politician. This the Constitution does not require.

No First Amendment forum is here to be found. The city consciously has limited access to its transit system advertising space in order to minimize chances of abuse, the appearance of favoritism, and the risk of imposing upon a captive audience. These are reasonable legislative objectives advanced by the city in a proprietary capacity.

[A]ffirmed.

MR. JUSTICE DOUGLAS, concurring in the judgment. * * *

If the streetcar or bus were a forum for communication akin to that of streets or public parks, considerable problems would be presented. [But] a streetcar or bus is plainly not a park or sidewalk or other meeting place for discussion any more than is a highway. It is only a way to get to work or back home. The fact that it is owned and operated by the city does not without more make it a forum.

Bus and streetcar placards are in the category of highway billboards, [a] form of communication [that] has been significantly curtailed by state regulation adopted pursuant to the Highway Beautification Act of 1965. [T]he fact that land on which a billboard rests is municipal land does not curtail or enhance such regulatory schemes.

If a bus is a forum it is more akin to a newspaper than to a park. Yet, [as we hold today in *Miami Herald Publishing Co. v. Tornillo*, p. 589 infra] the [newspaper] owner cannot be forced to include in his offerings news or other items which outsiders may desire but which the owner abhors. [And] if we are to turn a bus or streetcar into either a newspaper or a park, we take great liberties with people who because of necessity become commuters and at the same time captive viewers or listeners. [T]he right of the commuters to be free from forced intrusions on their privacy precludes the city from transforming its [public vehicles] into forums for the dissemination of ideas upon this captive audience.

Buses are not recreational vehicles [as a public park might be used on holidays]; they are a practical necessity for millions in our urban centers. I have already stated this view in my [*Pollak*] dissent: "[One] who hears disquieting or unpleasant programs in public places [can] get up and leave. But the man on the streetcar has no choice but to sit and listen, or perhaps to sit and to try *not* to listen." There is no difference when the message is visual, not auricular. In each the viewer or listener is captive. * * *

I do not view the content of the message as relevant either to petitioner's right to express it or to the commuters' right to be free from it. Commercial advertisements may be as offensive and intrusive to captive audiences as any political message. But the validity of the commercial advertising program is not before us since we are not faced with one complaining of an invasion of privacy through forced exposure to commercial ads. Since I do not believe that petitioner has any constitutional right to spread his message before this captive audience, I concur in the Court's judgment.

MR. JUSTICE BRENNAN, with whom MR. JUSTICE STEWART, MR. JUSTICE MARSHALL, and MR. JUSTICE POWELL, join, dissenting.

[T]he city created a forum for the dissemination of information and expression of ideas when it accepted and displayed commercial and public service advertisements on its rapid transit vehicles. Having opened a forum for communication, the city is barred by the First and Fourteenth Amendments from discriminating among forum users solely on the basis of message content.

[The city] attempts to justify its ban against political advertising by arguing that the interior advertising space is an inappropriate forum for political expression and debate. To be sure, there are some public places which are so clearly committed to other purposes that their use as public forums for communication is anomalous. [The] determination of whether a particular type of public property or facility constitutes a "public forum" requires the Court to strike a balance between the competing interests of the government, on the one hand, and the speaker and his audience, on the other. Thus, the Court must assess the importance of the primary use to which the public property or facility is committed and the extent to which that use will be disrupted if access for free expression is permitted. [Compare *Edwards* (state capitol grounds) with *Adderley* (jailhouse curtilage)]. In the circumstances of this case, however, we need not decide whether public transit cars *must* be made available as forums for the exercise of First Amendment rights. By accepting commercial and public service advertising, the city effectively waived any argument that advertising in its transit cars is incompatible with the rapid transit system's primary function of providing transportation. A forum for communication was voluntarily established * * *.

[W]hile it is possible that commercial advertising may be accorded *less* First Amendment protection than [political speech], it is "speech" nonetheless, often communicating information and ideas found by many persons to be controversial. [Once] such messages have been accepted and displayed, the existence of a forum for communication cannot be gainsaid. To hold otherwise, and thus sanction the bland commercialism and noncontroversial public service messages over "uninhibited, robust and wide-open" debate on public issues, would reverse the traditional priorities of the First Amendment.

Once a public forum for communication has been established, both free speech and equal protection principles prohibit discrimination based *solely* upon subject matter or content. *Mosley.* [That] the discrimination is among entire classes of ideas, rather than among points of view within a particular class, does not render it any less odious. Subject matter or content censorship in any form is forbidden.[9]

[Few] examples are required to illustrate the scope of the city's policy and practice. For instance, a commercial advertisement peddling snowmobiles would be accepted, while a counter-advertisement calling upon the public to support legislation controlling the environmental destruction and noise pollution caused by snowmobiles would be rejected. [This,] and other examples,[10] make perfectly clear that the selective exclusion of political advertising is not the product of even-handed application of neutral "time, place, and manner" regulations. Rather, the operative—and constitutionally impermissible—distinction is the message of the sign. That conclusion is not dispelled by any of the city's asserted justifications for selectively excluding political advertising.

[The city's solicitous regard for "captive riders"] has a hollow ring in the present case, where [it] has voluntarily opened its rapid transit system as a forum for communication. In that circumstance, the occasional appearance of provocative speech should be expected. * * *

---

9. The existence of other public forums for the dissemination of political messages is, of course, irrelevant [quoting from *Schneider*].

10. In declaring unconstitutional an advertising policy remarkably similar to the city's policy in the present case, the California Supreme Court detailed "the paradoxical scope of the [transit] district's policy [banning political advertising]" in the following manner: "A cigarette company is permitted to advertise the desirability of smoking its brand, but a cancer society is not entitled to caution by advertisements that cigarette smoking is injurious to health. A theater may advertise a motion picture that portrays sex and violence, but the Legion for Decency has no right to post a message calling for clean films. A lumber company may advertise its wood products, but a conservation group cannot implore citizens to write to the President or Governor about protecting our natural resources. An oil refinery may advertise its products, but a citizens' organization cannot demand enforcement of existing air pollution statutes. An insurance company may announce its available policies, but a senior citizens' club cannot plead for legislation to improve our social security program. The district would accept an advertisement from a television station that is commercially inspired, but would refuse a paid nonsolicitation message from a strictly educational television station. Advertisements for travel, foods, clothing, toiletries, automobiles, legal drugs—all these are acceptable, but the American Legion would not have the right to place a paid advertisement reading, 'Support Our Boys in Viet Nam. Send Holiday Packages,'" 68 Cal.2d at 57, 434 P.2d at 986.

The line between ideological and nonideological speech is impossible to draw with accuracy. By accepting commercial and public service advertisements, the city opened the door to "sometimes controversial or unsettling speech" and determined that such speech does not unduly interfere with the rapid transit system's primary purpose of transporting passengers. In the eyes of many passengers, certain commercial or public service messages [referring, e.g., to church advertising] are as profoundly disturbing as some political advertisements might be to other passengers. There is certainly no evidence in the record of this case indicating that political advertisements, as a class, are so disturbing when displayed that they are more likely than commercial or public service advertisements to impair the rapid transit system's primary function of transportation. In the absence of such evidence, the city's selective exclusion of political advertising constitutes an invidious discrimination on the basis of subject matter, in violation of the First and Fourteenth Amendments.

Moreover, even if it were possible to draw a manageable line between controversial and noncontroversial messages, the city's practice of censorship for the benefit of "captive audiences" still would not be justified. [The accepted advertisements] are not broadcast over loudspeakers in the transit cars. The privacy of the passengers is not, therefore, dependent upon their ability "to sit and try *not* to listen." *Pollak* (Douglas, J., dissenting). Should passengers chance to glance at advertisements they find offensive, they can "effectively avoid further bombardment of their sensibilities simply by averting their eyes." *Cohen.* Surely that minor inconvenience is a small price to pay for the continued preservation of so precious a liberty as free speech.

[E]qually unpersuasive [is the city's argument that acceptance of political advertising would suggest political favoritism or city support of the candidate advertised]. Clearly, such ephemeral concerns do not provide the city with carte blanche authority to exclude an entire category of speech from a public forum. [Moreover,] neutral regulations [can] be narrowly tailored to allay the city's fears. The impression of city endorsement can be dispelled by requiring disclaimers to appear prominently on the face of every advertisement. And [the] appearance of favoritism can be avoided by the even-handed regulation of time, place and manner for all advertising, irrespective of subject matter. * * *

Notes and Questions

1. *Turning freedom of expression "upside down."* Does Blackmun, J.'s view that "the managerial decision to limit car card space to innocuous and less controversial commercial and service oriented advertising does not rise to the dignity of a First Amendment violation" turn freedom of expression "upside down"? How, or why, can "speech of sufficient importance to merit the 'dignity' of First Amendment protection [be] excluded from display on the city's trains, while less important speech is allowed"? See Haiman, *How Much of Our Speech Is Free?*, The Civ.Lib.Rev., Winter 1975, pp. 111, 129–30.

Does either the plurality or Douglas, J., explain why political advertising is more controversial or offensive than public service messages for religious organizations or commercial advertising for certain personal products? See Karst, *Equality as a Central Principle in the First Amendment,* 43 U.Chi.L.Rev. 20, 35 (1976). In any event, can greater restraints on "controversial" speech be reconciled with "the familiar first amendment principle that the value of free speech comprehends unsettling or provocative ideas"? See 88 Harv.L.Rev. 154 (1974). Reconsider *Cohen* and *Terminiello*, Sec. 1, V supra.

2. *Lehman and Mosley.* Consider Karst, note 1 supra, at 36: "What made *Mosley* and *Lehman* easy cases—the outrage of *Lehman* being that it was an easy case, wrongly decided—was that in restricting the use of picketing and bus advertising the cities did not merely regulate the time, place or manner of speech, but imposed discriminatory controls over the content of speech." Does *Perry* lend any conceptual support for *Lehman* ? Where would the car cards fit into *Perry's* classification scheme?

3. Is Blackmun, J.'s point that since all those seeking to purchase advertising space for commercial purposes are treated alike, "whether they be house builders or butchers," and all those seeking public issue or political advertising are also treated alike, the equal protection issue disappears? Does it? Were all labor picketers treated alike, and all non-labor picketers treated alike, in *Mosley* ? Is the key equal protection question whether all those *within* the defined classes are treated equally *or* whether the classification *itself* is permissible? See Stone, *Fora Americana,* at 276.

4. Suppose the city decided that it did not want to promote health problems and refused space for cigarette advertisements? Suppose it wanted to avoid offense and refused space for advertisements of X rated films? Must the city treat all advertisers alike?

5. Would access to the card spaces have turned every government bulletin board into a Hyde park? Consider Shiffrin, *Government Speech,* at 579–80: "If the bus space in *Lehman* had been used for messages about the operation of the bus service, an analogy could have properly been made to display cases in other public facilities. [But] the public facilities in *Lehman* were not being used to convey a government message. By letting out the space to private groups for their own messages, the government had admitted that the space was not needed for government purposes. To grant access for political messages would have reaffirmed *Mosley's* equality principle without implying any right of access to every government bulletin board."

6. *"Captivity."* Does "captivity," in the sense of unavoidable *initial* exposure to communication, exist with respect to virtually all forms of communication? While browsing through a newspaper, may an individual unwittingly come across an offensive article or photograph? While switching on his TV or radio, may he suddenly be confronted with distasteful views? Does the "true measure" of an individual's privacy from unwanted communications consist "not in his total protection from *initial* exposure to unwelcome ideas, but rather in his ability to avoid *continued* exposure to those ideas once he has rejected them"? See Stone, *Fora Americana,* at 267. (Emphasis added.) Does exposure to car cards displayed on the interior of a public vehicle "in any sense directly interfere with the ability of passengers to read, converse, meditate, work or even catch a short nap"? See id. at 270. Do passengers exposed to such car cards constitute a captive audience under the *Cohen* formulation—"the ability of government [to] shut off discourse solely to protect others from hearing it [is] dependent upon a showing that substantial privacy interests are being invaded in an essentially intolerable manner"?

7. *The "fifth vote" in Lehman.* Is the "greatest irony" of *Lehman* that "the fifth vote which made it possible for Justices Burger, Blackmun, Rehnquist, and White to prevail came not from Justice Powell but from Justice Douglas"? See Haiman, note 1 supra, at 131. Is Douglas, J.'s failure to deal with Lehman's equal protection claim anomalous? If a transit system accepted commercial advertising, but refused to provide space on an equal basis to blacks, would

Douglas, J., hold that the passengers' constitutional right of privacy, without more, defeated the blacks' constitutional claims? See 88 Harv.L.Rev., note 1 supra, at 150 n. 15.

SECTION 7. CLOSING PARTICULAR CHANNELS OF COMMUNICATION

This section treats cases in which many themes of prior sections coalesce. Prior sections, confronted everything from the banning of black arm bands to the banning of leaflet distribution on public streets. In this section, many of the Justices focus on the banning of a particular channel of communication as a first amendment category.

Sec. 6, III considered the interest in preventing audiences from being captives of speech supported by the government. A theme which runs through many of the cases in this section is an interest in protecting potential "captive" audiences not necessarily from "propaganda," but from the intrusiveness of noise and visual pollution by communication. What importance to attach to the interest in preventing captivity may depend not only on the source (a government or a private speaker) and the place of captivity (for example, at home or in a public forum), but also upon the content of the communication. *Metromedia,* infra, for example, concerns a billboard ban discriminating in part against commercial speech, thus causing reconsideration of the place of commercial speech among first amendment values and the relationship between content discrimination and discrimination against a particular point of view. Finally, *Vincent,* infra, involves the relationship between public forum doctrine and the more general time, place, and manner doctrine.

METROMEDIA, INC. v. SAN DIEGO, 453 U.S. 490, 101 S.Ct. 2882, 69 L.Ed. 2d 800 (1981): An ordinance banning the use of billboards provided for two types of exceptions. First, it allowed "on-site" signs defined to include those "designating the name of the owner or occupant of the premises upon which such signs are placed, or identifying such premises; or signs advertising goods manufactured or produced or services rendered on the premises upon which such signs are placed."

Second, it provided for special categories of exceptions including government signs; signs at bus stops; commemorative plaques of recognized historical societies and organizations; religious symbols; indoor signs not visible from any point on the boundary of the premises; for sale signs; public service signs limited to the depiction of time, temperature or news; signs of buses and taxicabs; and temporary political campaign signs.

The ordinance was challenged by companies engaged in the "outdoor advertising business," i.e., they owned signs and sold space on them. The parties stipulated that "[v]aluable commercial, political and social information is communicated" via the signs, that alternative forms of communication are "insufficient, inappropriate and prohibitively expensive," and that the ordinance would "eliminate the outdoor advertising business" in San Diego. The California Supreme Court upheld the ordinance. WHITE, J., joined by Stewart, Marshall, and Powell, JJ., announcing the judgment of the Court, reversing and remanding, criticized the ordinance's treatment of non-commercial speech: "The California courts may sustain the ordinance by limiting its reach to commercial speech, assuming the ordinance is susceptible to this treatment." On the latter point, Stevens, J., otherwise dissenting, announced that he joined the commercial speech sections of the plurality opinion.

Preliminarily, White, J., observed: "Each method of communicating ideas is 'a law unto itself' and that law must reflect the 'differing natures, values, abuses and dangers' of each method. We deal here with the law of billboards.

"Billboards are a well-established medium of communication, used to convey a broad range of different kinds of messages. [But] whatever its communicative function, the billboard remains a 'large, immobile, and permanent structure which like other structures is subject [to] regulation.' Moreover, because it is designed to stand out and apart from its surroundings, the billboard creates a unique set of problems for land-use planning and development."

Directing his attention first to the ban on off-site commercial billboards, White, J., concluded that the *Central Hudson* test [p. 454 supra] was satisfied. There can be no "substantial doubt" that "traffic safety and the appearance of the city" are "substantial governmental goals." The only serious question was whether those interests were directly advanced. Despite a "meager record," White, J., found nothing to suggest that the "legislative judgment that billboards are traffic hazards" was "unreasonable." As for aesthetic interests, he found no "impermissible purpose": "It is nevertheless argued that the city denigrates its interest in traffic safety and beauty and defeats its own case by permitting on-site advertising and other specified signs. * * *

"In the first place, whether on-site advertising is permitted or not, the prohibition of off-site advertising is directly related to the stated objectives of traffic safety and esthetics. This is not altered by the fact that the ordinance is underinclusive because it permits on-site advertising. Second, the city may believe that off-site advertising, with its periodically changing content, presents a more acute problem than does on-site advertising. Third, San Diego has obviously chosen to value one kind of commercial speech—on-site advertising— more than another kind of commercial speech—off-site advertising. The ordinance reflects a decision by the city that the former interest, but not the latter, is stronger than the city's interests in traffic safety and esthetics. [We] do not reject that judgment. As we see it, the city could reasonably conclude that a commercial enterprise—as well as the interested public—has a stronger interest in identifying its place of business and advertising the products or services available there than it has in using or leasing its available space for the purpose of advertising commercial enterprises located elsewhere. * * *

"It does not follow, however, that San Diego's general ban on signs carrying noncommercial advertising is also valid under the First and Fourteenth Amendments. [O]ur recent commercial speech cases have consistently accorded noncommercial speech a greater degree of protection than commercial speech. San Diego effectively inverts this judgment, by affording a greater degree of protection to commercial than to noncommercial speech. There is a broad exception for on-site commercial advertisements, but there is no similar exception for noncommercial speech. [The] city does not explain how or why noncommercial billboards located in places where commercial billboards are permitted would be more threatening to safe driving or would detract more from the beauty of the city. Insofar as the city tolerates billboards at all, [it] may not conclude that the communication of commercial information concerning goods and services connected with a particular site is of greater value than the communication of noncommercial messages.

"Furthermore, the ordinance contains exceptions that permit various kinds of noncommercial signs, whether on property where goods and services are offered or not, that would otherwise be within the general ban. A fixed sign may be used to identify any piece of property and its owner. Any piece of property may carry or display religious symbols, commemorative plaques of recognized historical societies and organizations, signs carrying news items or telling the time or temperature, signs erected in discharge of any governmental function, or temporary political campaign signs.[19] No other noncommercial or ideological signs meeting the structural definition are permitted, regardless of their effect on traffic safety or esthetics.

"Although the city may distinguish between the relative value of different categories of commercial speech, the city does not have the same range of choice in the area of noncommercial speech to evaluate the strength of, or distinguish between, various communicative interests. *Carey; Mosley.* [Because] some noncommercial messages may be conveyed on billboards throughout the commercial and industrial zones, San Diego must similarly allow billboards conveying other noncommercial messages throughout those zones.[20] * * *

"Because the San Diego ordinance reaches too far into the realm of protected speech, we conclude that it is unconstitutional on its face."

BRENNAN, J., joined by Blackmun, J., concurring, maintained that the practical effect of the ordinance was a total ban on outdoor advertising that would be permissible only if the city could show a sufficiently substantial government interest directly furthered by the ban, and "that any more narrowly drawn restriction, i.e., anything less than a total ban, would promote less well the achievement of that goal." He found a lack of evidence to support a connection between the ordinance and traffic safety. Moreover, he thought the city had failed to show a substantial interest in aesthetics in the commercial and industrial areas of San Diego: "A billboard is not *necessarily* inconsistent with oil storage tanks, blighted areas, or strip development." He expressed confidence that billboard bans could be defended in a "historical community" such as Williamsburg, Virginia or in an environment like Yellowstone National Park. But he expressed no view whether San Diego or other large cities would ever be able to make the required showing.

In addressing the commercial speech issue, "I cannot agree with the plurality's view that an ordinance totally banning commercial billboards but allowing noncommercial billboards would be constitutional.[13] [Of] course the plurality is correct when it observes that 'our cases have consistently distinguished between the constitutional protection afforded commercial as opposed to noncommercial speech,' but it errs in assuming that a *governmental unit* may be put in the position in the first instance of deciding whether the proposed speech is commercial or noncommercial. In individual cases, this distinction is anything but

19. In this sense, this case presents the opposite situation from that in *Lehman.* In both of those cases a government agency had chosen to prohibit from a certain forum speech relating to political campaigns, while other kinds of speech were permitted. In both cases this Court upheld the prohibition, but both cases turned on unique fact situations involving government-created forums and have no application here.

20. Because a total prohibition of outdoor advertising is not before us, we do not indicate whether such a ban would be consistent with the First Amendment. But see *Schad* [p. 443 supra] on the constitutional problems created by a total prohibition of a particular expres-

sive forum, live entertainment in that case. Despite Justice Stevens' insistence to the contrary, we do not imply that the ordinance is unconstitutional because it "does not abridge enough speech." * * *

13. Of course, as a matter of marketplace economics, such an ordinance may prove the undoing of *all* billboard advertising, both commercial and noncommercial. It may well be that no company would be able to make a profit maintaining billboards used solely for noncommercial messages. [Therefore,] the plurality's prescription may represent a *de facto* ban on both commercial and noncommercial billboards. This is another reason to analyze this case as a "total ban" case.

clear. Because making such determinations would entail a substantial exercise of discretion by city's officials, it presents a real danger of curtailing noncommercial speech in the guise of regulating commercial speech.

"[I] would be unhappy to see city officials dealing with the following series of billboards and deciding which ones to permit: the first billboard contains the message 'Visit Joe's Ice Cream Shoppe'; the second, 'Joe's Ice Cream Shoppe uses only the highest quality dairy products'; the third, 'Because Joe thinks that dairy products are good for you, please shop at Joe's Shoppe'; and the fourth, 'Joe says to support dairy price supports; they mean lower prices for you at his Shoppe.' Or how about some San Diego Padres baseball fans—with no connection to the team—who together rent a billboard and communicate the message 'Support the San Diego Padres, a great baseball team.' May the city decide that a United Automobile Workers billboard with the message 'Be a patriot—do not buy Japanese-manufactured cars' is 'commercial' and therefore forbid it? What if the same sign is placed by Chrysler? [14]

"[I] have no doubt that those who seek to convey commercial messages will engage in the most imaginative of exercises to place themselves within the safe haven of noncommercial speech, while at the same time conveying their commercial message. Encouraging such behavior can only make the job of city officials—who already are inclined to ban billboards—that much more difficult and potentially intrusive upon legitimate noncommercial expression."

STEVENS, J., dissenting, saw the issue as whether the city "may entirely ban one medium of communication." His affirmative answer was not affected by what he described as the "content neutral" exceptions contained in the ordinance. He did not think, however, that plaintiffs should have standing to assert the interests of a hypothetical "public spirited or eccentric businessman" wanting "to use a permanent sign on his commercial property to display a noncommercial message."

On the ban question, Stevens, J., thought the case was unique: "Our cases upholding regulation of the time, place, or manner of communication have been decided on the implicit assumption that the net effect of the regulation on free expression would not be adverse. In this case, however, [t]he parties have stipulated, correctly in my view, that the net effect of the city's ban on billboards will be a reduction in the total quantity of communication in San Diego. If the ban is enforced, some present users of billboards will not be able to communicate in the future as effectively as they do now. This ordinance cannot, therefore, be sustained on the assumption that the remaining channels of communication will be just as effective for all persons as a communications marketplace which includes a thousand or more large billboards available for hire.

"The unequivocal language of the First Amendment prohibits any law 'abridging the freedom of speech.' That language could surely be read to foreclose any law reducing the quantity of communication within a jurisdiction. I am convinced, however, that such a reading would be incorrect. [For example, archeologists] use the term 'graffiti' to describe informal inscriptions on tombs and ancient monuments. The graffito was familiar in the culture of Egypt and Greece, in the Italian decorative art of the 15th-century, and it survives today in some subways and on the walls of public buildings. It is an inexpensive means of communicating political, commercial, and frivolous messages to large numbers

---

14. These are not mere hypotheticals that can never occur. The Oil, Chemical and Atomic Workers Int'l Union, AFL–CIO actually placed a billboard advertisement stating: "Support America's First Environment Strike. Don't Buy Shell!" What if Exxon had placed the advertisement? Could Shell respond in kind?

of people; some creators of graffiti have no effective alternate means of publicly expressing themselves. Nevertheless, I believe a community has the right to decide that its interests in protecting property from damaging trespasses and in securing beautiful surroundings outweigh the countervailing interest in uninhibited expression by means of words and pictures in public places. If the First Amendment categorically protected the marketplace of ideas from any quantitative restraint, a municipality could not outlaw graffiti.

"Our prior decisions are not inconsistent with this proposition. Whether one interprets the Court's decision in *Kovacs v. Cooper,* 336 U.S. 77, 69 S.Ct. 448, 93 L.Ed. 513 (1949), as upholding a total ban on the use of sound trucks, or merely a ban on the 'loud and raucous' use of amplifiers, the case at least stands for the proposition that a municipality may enforce a rule that curtails the effectiveness of a particular means of communication. [*Kovacs,*] I believe, forecloses any claim that a prohibition of billboards must fall simply because it has some limiting effect on the communications market.[23]

"[It] seems to be accepted by all that a zoning regulation excluding billboards from residential neighborhoods is justified by the interest in maintaining pleasant surroundings and enhancing property values. The same interests are at work in commercial and industrial zones. Reasonable men may assign different weights to the conflicting interests, but in constitutional terms I believe the essential inquiry is the same throughout the city. * * *

"If one is persuaded, as I am, that a wholly impartial total ban on billboards would be permissible, it is difficult to understand why the exceptions in San Diego's ordinance present any additional threat to the interests protected by the First Amendment. The plurality suggests that, because the exceptions are based in part on the subject matter of noncommercial speech, the city somehow is choosing the permissible subjects for public debate. While this suggestion is consistent with some of the broad dictum in *Consolidated Edison Co. v. Public Service Commission* [p. 686 infra] it does not withstand analysis in this case.

"The essential concern embodied in the First Amendment is that government not impose its viewpoint on the public or select the topics on which public debate is permissible. The San Diego ordinance simply does not implicate this concern. Although *Consolidated Edison* broadly identified regulations based on the subject matter of speech as impermissible content-based regulations, essential First Amendment concerns were implicated in that case because the government was attempting to limit discussion of controversial topics, and thus was shaping the agenda for public debate. [But except] * * * for the provision allowing signs to be used for political campaign purposes for limited periods, none of the exceptions even arguably relates to any controversial subject matter. As a whole they allow a greater dissemination of information than could occur under a total plan. Moreover, it was surely reasonable for the city to conclude that exceptions for clocks, thermometers, historic plaques, and the like, would have a lesser impact on the appearance of the city than the typical large billboards.

"The exception for political campaign signs presents a different question. For I must assume that these signs may be just as unsightly and hazardous as other off-site billboards. Nevertheless, the fact that the community places a

---

23. Our decisions invalidating ordinances prohibiting or regulating door-to-door solicitation and leafletting are not to the contrary. In those cases, the state interests the ordinances purported to serve—for instance, the prevention of littering or fraud—were only indirectly furthered by the regulation of communicative activity. See, e.g., *Schneider; Martin v. Struthers,* 319 U.S. 141, 147–148, 63 S.Ct. 862, 865, 87 L.Ed. 1313 (1943). * * *

special value on allowing additional communication to occur during political campaigns is surely consistent with the interests the First Amendment was designed to protect. Of course, if there were reason to believe that billboards were especially useful to one political party or candidate, this exception would be suspect. But nothing of that sort is suggested by this record. In the aggregate, therefore, it seems to me that the exceptions in this ordinance cause it to have a less serious effect on the communications market than would a total ban."

BURGER, C.J., dissented: "Today the Court takes an extraordinary—even a bizarre—step by severely limiting the power of a city to act on risks it perceives to traffic safety and the environment posed by large, permanent billboards. Those joining the plurality opinion invalidate a city's effort to minimize these traffic hazards and eyesores simply because, in exercising rational legislative judgment, it has chosen to permit a narrow class of signs that serve special needs.

"Relying on simplistic platitudes about content, subject matter, and the dearth of other means to communicate, the billboard industry attempts to escape the real and growing problems every municipality faces in protecting safety and preserving the environment in an urban area. The Court's disposition of the serious issues involved exhibits insensitivity to the impact of these billboards on those who must live with them and the delicacy of the legislative judgments involved in regulating them. American cities desiring to mitigate the dangers mentioned must, as a matter of *federal constitutional law,* elect between two unsatisfactory options: (a) allowing all 'noncommercial' signs, no matter how many, how dangerous, or how damaging to the environment; or (b) forbidding signs altogether. Indeed, lurking in the recesses of today's opinions is a not-so-veiled threat that the second option, too, may soon be withdrawn. This is the long arm and voracious appetite of federal power—this time judicial power—with a vengeance, reaching and absorbing traditional concepts of local authority."

The Chief Justice argued that it made no difference whether the regulation was "viewed as a regulation regarding time, place, and manner, or as a total prohibition on a medium with some exceptions defined, in part, by content": "Although we must ensure that any regulation of speech 'further[s] a sufficiently substantial government interest,' *Schad,* given a reasonable approach to a perceived problem, this Court's duty is not to make the primary policy decisions but instead is to determine whether the legislative approach is essentially neutral to the messages conveyed and leaves open other adequate means of conveying those messages. This is the essence of both democracy and federalism, and we gravely damage both when we undertake to throttle legislative discretion and judgment at the 'grass roots' of our system." [a]

In his view, the ordinance did not discriminate "among ideas or topics": "The city has not undertaken to determine paternalistically, 'what information

a. In response, the plurality complained that the test employed by Burger, C.J., was drawn almost exclusively from cases involving time, place, and manner restrictions: "[T]his Court has never held that the less strict standard of review applied to time, place, and manner restrictions is appropriately used in every First Amendment case, or that it is the most that the First Amendment requires of government legislation which infringes on protected speech. If this were the case, there would be no need for the detailed inquiry this Court consistently pursues in order to answer the question of whether a challenged restriction is in fact a time, place, and manner restriction—the same standard of review would apply regardless of the outcome of that inquiry. [T]he San Diego ordinance is not such a restriction and there is, therefore, no excuse for applying a lower standard of First Amendment review to that ordinance."

is relevant to self-government.'" *Gertz.* "[Where] the ordinance does differentiate among topics, it simply allows such noncontroversial things as conventional signs identifying a business enterprise, time-and-temperature signs, historical markers, and for-sale signs. It borders—if not trespasses—on the frivolous to suggest that, by allowing such signs but forbidding noncommercial billboards, the city has infringed freedom of speech. This ignores what we recognized in *Mosley,* that 'there may be sufficient regulatory interests justifying selective exclusions or [distinctions].' For each exception, the city is either acknowledging the unique connection between the medium and the message conveyed, or promoting a legitimate public interest in information. Similarly, in each instance, the city reasonably could conclude that the balance between safety and aesthetic concerns on the one hand and the need to communicate on the other has tipped the opposite way. More important, in no instance is the exempted topic controversial; there can be no rational debate over, for example, the time, the temperature, the existence of an offer of sale, or the identity of a business establishment. The danger of San Diego setting the agenda of public discussion is not simply de minimis; it is nonexistent. * * *[7]

"The fatal flaw in the plurality's logic comes when it concludes that San Diego, by exempting on-site commercial signs, thereby has 'afford[ed] a greater degree of protection to commercial than to noncommercial speech.' The 'greater degree of protection' our cases have given noncommercial speech establishes a narrow range of constitutionally permissible regulation. To say noncommercial speech receives a greater degree of *constitutional* protection, however, does not mean that a legislature is forbidden to afford differing degrees of *statutory* protection when the restrictions on each form of speech—commercial and noncommercial—otherwise pass constitutional muster under the standards respectively applicable.

"[By] allowing communication of certain commercial ideas via billboards, but forbidding noncommercial signs altogether, a city does not necessarily place a greater 'value' on commercial speech.[8] In these situations, the city is simply recognizing that it has greater latitude to distinguish among various forms of commercial communication when the same distinctions would be impermissible if undertaken with regard to noncommercial speech. Indeed, when adequate alternative channels of communication are readily available so that the message may be freely conveyed through other means, a city arguably is more faithful to the Constitution by treating all noncommercial speech the same than by attempting to impose the same classifications in noncommercial as it has in commercial areas. To undertake the same kind of balancing and content judgment with noncommercial speech that is permitted with commercial speech is far more likely to run afoul of the First Amendment.[9]

7. As Justice Brennan recognizes, the plurality's treatment of the ordinance may well create this very danger, for the plurality appears willing to allow municipal officials to determine what is and is not noncommercial speech.

8. Indeed, in *Lehman* we upheld a municipal policy allowing commercial but not political advertising on city buses. I cannot agree with the plurality that *Lehman* "ha[s] no application here." Although *Lehman* dealt with limited space leased by the city and this case deals with municipal regulation of privately leased space, the constitutional principle is the same: a city may forgo the "lurking doubts about favoritism" in granting space to some, but necessarily not all, political advertisers. The same constitutional dangers do not arise in allocating space among commercial advertisers.

9. See n. 8, supra. If a city were to permit onsite noncommercial billboards, one can imagine a challenge based on the argument that this favors the views of persons who can afford to own property in commercial districts. I intimate no view on whether I would accept such an argument should that case ever arise.

"Thus, we may, consistent with the First Amendment, hold that a city may—and perhaps must—take an all-or-nothing approach with noncommercial speech yet remain free to adopt selective exceptions for commercial speech, as long as the latter advance legitimate governmental interests."

REHNQUIST, J., dissenting, expressed substantial agreement with the views of Burger, C.J., and Stevens, J.: "Nothing in my experience on the bench has led me to believe that a judge is in any better position than a city or county commission to make decisions in an area such as aesthetics. Therefore, little can be gained in the area of constitutional law, and much lost in the process of democratic decisionmaking, by allowing individual judges in city after city to second-guess such legislative or administrative determinations. [In] a case where city planning commissions and zoning boards must regularly confront constitutional claims of this sort, it is a genuine misfortune to have the Court's treatment of the subject be a virtual Tower of Babel, from which no definitive principles can be clearly [drawn]."

Notes and Questions

1. Is a total ban on billboards realistically possible under the plurality opinion? Would a city really prevent a grocery store from putting up a sign saying "grocery store"? How would a business area operate without such signs? If a city allows a grocery store to identify itself, does it follow that it must permit political signs? Could a city function without government signs? Is the plurality suggesting that if a city allows stop signs, it must allow all other noncommercial signs? If not, what is the plurality saying? How may an ordinance be drafted that would satisfy the plurality?

2. *"We deal here with the law of billboards."* Is that all?

(a) In *Martin v. Struthers,* 319 U.S. 141, 63 S.Ct. 862, 87 L.Ed. 1313 (1943), a city forbade knocking on the door or ringing the doorbell of a resident in order to deliver handbills (in an industrial community where many worked night shifts and slept during the day). In striking down the ordinance, the Court, per Black, J., pointed out that the city's objectives could be achieved by means of a law making it an offense for any person to ring the doorbell of a householder who has "appropriately indicated that he is unwilling to be disturbed. This or any similar regulation leaves the decision as to whether distributors of literature may lawfully call at a home where it belongs—with the homeowner himself." [b] By contrast, *Breard v. Alexandria,* 341 U.S. 622, 71 S.Ct. 920, 95 L.Ed. 1233 (1951) upheld an ordinance forbidding the practice of going door to door to solicit orders for the sale of goods. The commercial element was said to distinguish *Martin.* Does *Breard* survive *Virginia Pharmacy*? (p. 444 supra). Does

---

b. Compare *Lamont v. Postmaster General,* 381 U.S. 301, 85 S.Ct. 1493, 14 L.Ed.2d 398 (1965) (invalidating a federal statute permitting delivery of "communist political propaganda" only if the addressee specifically requested in writing that it be delivered because of the chilling effect on willing recipients) and *Rowan v. Post Office,* 397 U.S. 728, 90 S.Ct. 1484, 25 L.Ed.2d 736 (1970) (upholding statute authorizing Postmaster General to issue enforceable orders directing senders to refrain from future mailings to addressees who have notified Post Office that they believe mailings

to be erotically arousing or sexually provocative) ("the mailer's right to communicate is circumscribed only by an affirmative act of the addressee giving notice that he wishes no further mailings from that mailer"). Is *Rowan* problematic because addressees must not only give notice that they want no further mailings, but also that they deem the material to be erotic? Does this implicate impermissible content discrimination? See Stone, *Restrictions of Speech Because of its Content: The Peculiar Case of Subject-Matter Restrictions,* 46 U.Chi.L.Rev. 81, 84–85 (1978).

(should) *Metromedia* settle the issue? What if, as in *Breard,* the solicitor is selling subscriptions for magazines?

(b) Compare *Schneider,* p. 534 supra (prohibition against leaflet distribution on streets unconstitutional) with *Valentine,* p. 444 supra (prohibition against distribution of commercial leaflets upheld). Does (should) the *holding* of *Valentine* survive *Virginia Pharmacy*? Does *Metromedia* settle the issue? [c]

3. What test should apply when the use of a particular medium of communication is foreclosed? [d] See Schauer, *Codifying the First Amendment: New York v. Ferber,* 1982 S.Ct.Rev. 285, 301–02; Stone, *Content Regulation and the First Amendment,* 25 Wm. & M.L.Rev. 189, 234–36 (1983). Does the test not matter because however phrased we will end up with the law of sound trucks, of billboards, of leaflets, etc.?

Los Angeles prohibits posting signs on public property (e.g., sidewalks, crosswalks, street lamp posts, hydrants, or traffic signs). A group ("Taxpayers") contracted with a company to post cardboard campaign signs ("Roland Vincent— City Council") on the cross-arms supporting utility poles. Taxpayers argued that the ordinance was unconstitutional at least as applied to the placing of signs on the cross-arms of utility poles.[a] LOS ANGELES CITY COUNCIL v. TAXPAYERS FOR VINCENT, 466 U.S. 789, 104 S.Ct. 2118, 80 L.Ed.2d 772 (1984), per STEVENS, J., upheld the ordinance: "[T]he First Amendment forbids the government from regulating speech in ways that favor some viewpoints or ideas at the expense of others. That general rule has no application to this case. For there is not even a hint of bias or censorship in [this] ordinance.

"In *O'Brien,* the Court set forth the appropriate framework for reviewing a viewpoint neutral regulation of this kind: [b] '[A] government regulation is sufficiently justified if it is within the constitutional power of the Government; if it furthers an important or substantial governmental interest; if the governmental interest is unrelated to the suppression of free expression; and if the incidental restriction on alleged First Amendment freedoms is no greater than is essential to the furtherance of that interest.'

c. For relevant commentary on the normative issues, see Baker, *Commercial Speech: A Problem in the Theory of Freedom,* 62 Iowa L.Rev. 1 (1976); Redish, *The First Amendment in the Marketplace: Commercial Speech and the Values of Free Expression,* 39 Geo.Wash.L. Rev. 429 (1971); Redish, *The Value of Free Speech,* 130 U.Pa.L.Rev. 591 (1982); Shiffrin, *The First Amendment and Economic Regulation: Away From a General Theory of the First Amendment,* 78 Nw.U.L.Rev. 1212, 1220, 1276–82 (1983).

d. Consider Anastaplo, *Self-Government and the Mass Media: A Practical Man's Guide* in The Mass Media and Modern Democracy 161, 223–24 (Clor ed. 1974): "I see in the abolition of television no serious First Amendment problem. Rather than abridge the 'freedom of speech' [, the] abolition of television (and hence a radical reform of the mass media) would enlarge freedom of speech among us. Television interferes, I have argued, with serious general education in a country such as ours: it affects the ability to read, and hence the ability to think and the very status of thought among us, playing up as it does to the passions. Thus abolition of television would probably contribute *among us* to the preservation of self-government and hence genuine freedom."

a. Taxpayers also argued that the ordinance was overbroad and should be declared invalid on its face. The Court concluded that Taxpayers had failed to demonstrate "a realistic danger that the ordinance [would] significantly compromise recognized First Amendment protections of individuals not before the Court." It, therefore, refused to entertain an overbreadth challenge.

b. Is the Court suggesting that the *O'Brien* test is the appropriate framework for all viewpoint neutral regulations or just for regulations "of this kind"? What "kind" of ordinance is this? How is it different from other kinds of viewpoint neutral regulations?

"In this case, [Taxpayers does] not dispute that it is within the constitutional power of the City to attempt to improve its appearance, or that this interest is basically unrelated to the suppression of ideas. Therefore the critical inquiries are whether that interest is sufficiently substantial to justify the effect of the ordinance on appellees' expression, and whether that effect is no greater than necessary to accomplish the City's purpose.[c]

"In *Kovacs v. Cooper,* the Court rejected the notion that a city is powerless to protect its citizens from unwanted exposure to certain methods of expression which may legitimately be deemed a public nuisance. In upholding an ordinance that prohibited loud and raucous sound trucks, the Court held that the state had a substantial interest in protecting its citizens from unwelcome noise.[24]

* * *

"*Metromedia* considered the city's interest in avoiding visual clutter, and seven Justices explicitly concluded that this interest was sufficient to justify a prohibition of billboards.[d] [The] problem addressed by this ordinance—the visual assault on the citizens of Los Angeles presented by an accumulation of signs posted on public property—constitutes a significant substantive evil within the City's power to prohibit. * * *

"We turn to the question whether the scope of the restriction on appellees' expressive activity is substantially broader than necessary to protect the City's interest in eliminating visual clutter.[e] The incidental restriction on expression which results from the City's attempt to accomplish such a purpose is considered justified as a reasonable regulation of the time, place, or manner of expression if it is narrowly tailored to serve that interest. [By] banning these signs, the City did no more than eliminate the exact source of the evil it sought to remedy. [The] ordinance curtails no more speech than is necessary to accomplish its purpose.[f]

"The Court of Appeals accepted the argument that a prohibition against the use of unattractive signs cannot be justified on esthetic grounds if it fails to apply to all equally unattractive signs wherever they might be located. A comparable argument was categorically rejected in *Metromedia.* In that case it was argued that the city could not simultaneously permit billboards to be used for on-site advertising and also justify the prohibition against offsite advertising on esthetic grounds, since both types of advertising were equally unattractive. The Court held, however, that the city could reasonably conclude that the esthetic interest was outweighed by the countervailing interest in one kind of advertising even though it was not outweighed by the other. So here, the validity of the esthetic interest in the elimination of signs on public property is not compromised by failing to extend the ban to private property. The private

---

c. Is this the same as the *O'Brien* test?

24. Justice Reed wrote: "The unwilling listener is not like the passer-by who may be offered a pamphlet in the street but may not be made to take it. In his home or on the street he is practically helpless to escape this interference with his privacy by loud speakers except through the protection of the municipality." * * *

d. Compare fn. 20 of the plurality opinion in *Metromedia* supra.

e. Does this depart from the *O'Brien* test?

f. The Court distinguished *Schneider,* p. 534 supra by observing that an anti-littering

statute would have been a less restrictive alternative in that case. Does this trivialize *Schneider*? Consider Stone, *O.T. 1983 and the Era of Aggressive Majoritarianism: A Court in Transition,* 19 Ga.L.Rev. 15, 21 (1984): "The Court understood in *Schneider* that not everyone can afford a newspaper or television campaign. In *Vincent,* the Court gave short shrift to this central first amendment insight." See generally Tribe, *Constitutional Calculus: Equal Justice or Economic Efficiency?,* 98 Harv.L.Rev. 592, 601–03 (1985).

citizen's interest in controlling the use of his own property justifies the disparate treatment. Moreover, by not extending the ban to all locations, a significant opportunity to communicate by means of temporary signs is preserved, and private property owners' esthetic concerns will keep the posting of signs on their property within reasonable bounds. Even if some visual blight remains, a partial, content-neutral ban may nevertheless enhance the City's appearance.

"Furthermore, there is no finding that in any area where appellees seek to place signs, there are already so many signs posted on adjacent private property that the elimination of appellees' signs would have an inconsequential effect on the esthetic values with which the City is concerned. There is simply no predicate in the findings of the District Court for the conclusion that the prohibition against the posting of appellees' signs fails to advance the City's esthetic interest.[g]

"While the First Amendment does not guarantee the right to employ every conceivable method of communication at all times and in all places, a restriction on expressive activity may be invalid if the remaining modes of communication are inadequate.[h] * * * [Notwithstanding] appellees' general assertions in their brief concerning the utility of political posters, nothing in the findings indicates that the posting of political posters on public property is a uniquely valuable or important mode of communication, or that appellees' ability to communicate effectively is threatened by ever-increasing restrictions on expression.[30]

"Appellees suggest that the public property covered by the ordinance is either itself a 'public forum' for First Amendment purposes, or at least should be treated in the same respect as the 'public forum' in which the property is located. [But they] fail to demonstrate the existence of a traditional right of access respecting such items as utility poles for purposes of their communication comparable to that recognized for public streets and parks. * * *

"Lampposts can of course be used as signposts, but the mere fact that government property can be used as a vehicle for communication does not mean that the Constitution requires such uses to be permitted. Public property which is not by tradition or designation a forum for public communication may be reserved by the state 'for its intended purposes, communicative or otherwise, as long as the regulation on speech is reasonable and not an effort to suppress expression merely because public officials oppose the speaker's view.' *Perry.* Given our analysis of the legitimate interest served by the ordinance, its viewpoint neutrality, and the availability of alternative channels of communication, the ordinance is certainly constitutional as applied to appellees under this standard.[32]

g. How much advancement is required under the *O'Brien* test?

h. Does this modify the *O'Brien* test?

30. Although the Court has shown special solicitude for forms of expression that are much less expensive than feasible alternatives and hence may be important to a large segment of the citizenry, see, e.g., *Martin v. Struthers* ("Door to door distribution of circulars is essential to the poorly financed causes of little people."), this solicitude has practical boundaries, see, e.g., *Kovacs v. Cooper* ("That more people may be more easily and cheaply reached by sound trucks [is] not enough to call forth constitutional protection for what those

charged with public welfare reasonably think is a nuisance when easy means of publicity are open."). * * *

32. Just as it is not dispositive to label the posting of signs on public property as a discrete medium of expression, it is also of limited utility in the context of this case to focus on whether the tangible property itself should be deemed a public forum. Generally an analysis of whether property is a public forum provides a workable analytical tool. However, "the analytical line between a regulation of the 'time, place, and manner' in which First Amendment rights may be exercised in a traditional public forum, and the question of

"[We] hold that on this record [the city] interests are sufficiently substantial to justify this content neutral, impartially administered prohibition against the posting of appellees' temporary signs on public property and that such an application of the ordinance does not create an unacceptable threat to the 'profound national commitment to the principle that debate on public issues should be uninhibited, robust, and wide-open.' *New York Times Co. v. Sullivan.*"

BRENNAN, J., joined by Marshall and Blackmun, JJ., dissented because that "Los Angeles' total ban sweeps so broadly and trenches so completely on appellees' use of an important medium of political expression" and because "the Court's lenient approach towards the restriction of speech for reasons of aesthetics threatens seriously to undermine the protections of the First Amendment":

"The Court finds that the City's 'interest is sufficiently substantial to justify the restrictive effect of the ordinance on appellees' expression' and that the effect of the ordinance on speech is 'no greater than necessary to accomplish the City's purpose.' These are the right questions [but] Los Angeles has not shown that its interest in eliminating 'visual clutter' justifies its restriction of appellees' ability to communicate with the local electorate. * * *

"In deciding [the] First Amendment question, the critical importance of the posting of signs as a means of communication must not be overlooked. Use of this medium of communication is particularly valuable in part because it entails a relatively small expense in reaching a wide audience, allows flexibility in accommodating various formats, typographies, and graphics, and conveys its message in a manner that is easily read and understood by its reader or viewer. There may be alternative channels of communication, but the prevalence of a large number of signs in Los Angeles is a strong indication that, for many speakers, those alternatives are far less satisfactory.

"Nevertheless, the City of Los Angeles asserts that ample alternative avenues of communication are available. The City notes that, although the posting of signs on public property is prohibited, the posting of signs on private property and the distribution of handbills are not. But there is no showing that either of these alternatives would serve appellees' needs nearly as well as would the posting of signs on public property. First, there is no proof that a sufficient number of private parties would allow the posting of signs on their property. Indeed, common sense suggests the contrary at least in some instances. * * *

"Similarly, the adequacy of distributing handbills is dubious, despite certain advantages of handbills over signs. Particularly when the message to be carried is best expressed by a few words or a graphic image, a message on a sign will typically reach far more people than one on a handbill. The message on a posted sign remains to be seen by passersby as long as it is posted, while a handbill is typically read by a single reader and discarded. Thus, not only must handbills be printed in large quantity, but many hours must be spent distributing them. The average cost of communicating by handbill is therefore likely to be far higher than the average cost of communicating by poster. For that reason, signs posted on public property are doubtless 'essential to the poorly financed causes of little people,' and their prohibition constitutes a total ban on

whether a particular piece of personal or real property owned or controlled by the government is in fact a 'public forum' may blur at the edges," *United States Postal Service v. Greenburgh Civic Ass'n,* 453 U.S. 114, 132, 101 S.Ct. 2676, 2686, 69 L.Ed.2d 517 (1981), and this is particularly true in cases falling between the paradigms of government property interests essentially mirroring analogous private interests and those clearly held in trust, either by tradition or recent convention, for the use of citizens at large.

an important medium of communication. Cf. Stone, *Fora Americana: Speech in Public Places,* 1974 Sup.Ct.Rev. 233, 257. Because the City has completely banned the use of this particular medium of communication, and because, given the circumstances, there are no equivalent alternative media that provide an adequate substitute, the Court must examine with particular care the justifications that the City proffers for its ban. * * *

"The fundamental problem in this kind of case [is] the unavoidable subjectivity of aesthetic judgments—the fact that 'beauty is in the eye of the beholder.' As a consequence of this subjectivity, laws defended on aesthetic grounds raise problems for judicial review that are not presented by laws defended on more objective grounds—such as national security, public health, or public safety. In practice, therefore, the inherent subjectivity of aesthetic judgments makes it all too easy for the government to fashion its justification for a law in a manner that impairs the ability of a reviewing court meaningfully to make the required inquiries.

"Initially, a reviewing court faces substantial difficulties [because the] asserted interest in aesthetics may be only a facade for content-based suppression. [A] governmental interest in aesthetics cannot be regarded as sufficiently compelling to justify a restriction of speech based on an assertion that the content of the speech is, in itself, aesthetically displeasing. *Cohen v. California.* Because aesthetic judgments are so subjective, however, it is too easy for government to enact restrictions on speech for just such illegitimate reasons and to evade effective judicial review by asserting that the restriction is aimed at some displeasing aspect of the speech that is not solely communicative—for example, its sound, its appearance, or its location. An objective standard for evaluating claimed aesthetic judgments is therefore essential * * *.

"For example, in evaluating the ordinance before us in this case, the City might be pursuing either of two objectives, motivated by two very different judgments. One objective might be the elimination of 'visual clutter.' [A] second objective might simply be the elimination of the messages typically carried by the signs.[5] In that case, the aesthetic judgment would be that the signs' messages are themselves displeasing. The first objective is lawful, of course, but the second is not. Yet the City might easily mask the second objective by asserting the first and declaring that signs constitute visual clutter. In short, we must avoid unquestioned acceptance of the City's bare declaration of an aesthetic objective lest we fail in our duty to prevent unlawful trespasses upon First Amendment protections.

"A total ban on an important medium of communication may be upheld only if the government proves that the ban (1) furthers a substantial government objective, and (2) constitutes the least speech-restrictive means of achieving that objective. Here too, however, meaningful judicial application of these standards is seriously frustrated.

"[The] possibility of interdependence between means and ends in the development of policies to promote aesthetics poses a major obstacle to judicial review of the availability of alternative means that are less restrictive of speech. Indeed, when a court reviews a restriction of speech imposed in order to promote an aesthetic objective, there is a significant possibility that the court will be able to do little more than pay lip service to the First Amendment inquiry into the

---

5. The fact that a ban on temporary signs applies to all signs does not necessarily imply content-neutrality. Because particular media are often used disproportionately for certain types of messages, a restriction that is content-neutral on its face may, in fact, be content-hostile. Cf. Stone, supra.

availability of less restrictive alternatives. The means may fit the ends only because the ends were defined with the means in mind. In this case, for example, the City has expressed an aesthetic judgment that signs on public property constitute visual clutter throughout the City and that its objective is to eliminate visual clutter. We are then asked to determine whether that objective could have been achieved with less restriction of speech. But to ask the question is to highlight the circularity of the inquiry. Since the goal, at least as currently expressed, is essentially to eliminate all signs, the only available means of achieving that goal is to eliminate all signs.

"The ease with which means can be equated with aesthetic ends only confirms the importance of close judicial scrutiny of the substantiality of such ends. In this case, for example, it is essential that the Court assess the City's ban on signs by evaluating whether the City has a substantial interest in eliminating the visual clutter caused by *all* posted signs *throughout* the City—as distinguished from an interest in banning signs in some areas or in preventing densely packed signs. If, in fact, either of the latter two objectives constitute the substantial interest underlying this ordinance, they could be achieved by means far less restrictive of speech than a total ban on signs, and the ban, therefore, would be invalid.

"Regrettably, the Court's analysis is seriously inadequate. Because the Court has failed to develop a reliable means of gauging the nature or depth of the City's commitment to pursuing the goal of eradicating 'visual clutter,' it simply approves the ordinance with only the most cursory degree of judicial oversight. [W]here a total ban is imposed on a particularly valuable method of communication, a court should require the government to provide tangible proof of the legitimacy and substantiality of its aesthetic objective. Justifications for such restrictions articulated by the government should be critically examined to determine whether the government has committed itself to addressing the identified aesthetic problem. * * *

"This does not mean that a government must address all aesthetic problems at one time or that a government should hesitate to pursue aesthetic objectives. What it does mean, however, is that when such an objective is pursued, it may not be pursued solely at the expense of First Amendment freedoms, nor may it be pursued by arbitrarily discriminating against a form of speech that has the same aesthetic characteristics as other forms of speech that are also present in the community.

"Accordingly, in order for Los Angeles to succeed in defending its total ban on the posting of signs, the City would have to demonstrate that it is pursuing its goal of eliminating visual clutter in a serious and comprehensive manner. Most importantly, the City would have to show that it is pursuing its goal through programs other than its ban on signs, that at least some of those programs address the visual clutter problem through means that do not entail the restriction of speech, and that the programs parallel the ban in their stringency, geographical scope, and aesthetic focus. In this case, however, [there] is no indication that the City has addressed its visual clutter problem in any way other than by prohibiting the posting of signs—throughout the City and without regard to the density of their presence."

Notes and Questions

1. Why does the Court turn to the *O'Brien* test rather than the public forum line of cases?[i] Does *Vincent* suggest that *O'Brien* should replace the *Perry* standards? Complement them? To what extent does *Vincent* suggest that the *O'Brien* test should apply to all viewpoint neutral regulations? Is there a general point to be drawn from *Vincent*? Or do we deal here with the law of cross-arms supporting utility poles?

2. The Court states that *O'Brien* supplies the appropriate framework, yet seems to deviate from its literal terms at various points in the opinion. Are those constructive modifications of the *O'Brien* test?

3. In reciting the facts, the Court observes that "among the 1,207 signs removed from public property during that week, 48 were identified as 'Roland Vincent' signs. Most of the other signs identified in that report were apparently commercial in character." Should the Court take the predominance of commercial signs into account? The insubstantial development of the messages involved? Do these factors minimize the force of Professor Stone's suggestion, fn. f, that *Vincent* is insensitive to the equality values at stake? In any event, does *Vincent's* appreciation of aesthetic values outstrip the facts? Is a utility pole more beautiful without a sign? Does it make aesthetic sense to allow signs everywhere on business property except on the utility poles?

SECTION 8.   BROADCAST REGULATION AND ACCESS TO THE MASS MEDIA

The mass media are not invariably the most effective means of communication. For example, the right to place messages on utility poles concerning a lost dog may be more important than access to a radio or a television station. In some circumstances, picketing outside a school or placing leaflets in teachers' mailboxes may be the most effective communications medium. Nonetheless, the law regulating access to the mass media is of vital societal importance. This section considers first cases in which government seeks to force newspapers and broadcasters to grant access; second, in *CBS v. DNC*, infra, a claim that the first amendment requires government to afford access for excluded groups to the broadcast media; third, cases in which government commands broadcasters not to carry particular programming at particular times or not to editorialize. A persistent theme is that broadcasting is "special," but whether it is, why it is, and what difference it should make are matters of considerable debate. Beyond this, attitudes about the most effective channel of communication raise questions about our commitment to and understanding of first amendment principles. If the assumption that broadcasting is special is a masquerade, why the masquerade?

I.   ACCESS TO THE MASS MEDIA

A.   ACCESS BY STATUTE: THE FIRST AMENDMENT AS SHIELD

MIAMI HERALD PUB. CO. v. TORNILLO, 418 U.S. 241, 94 S.Ct. 2831, 41 L.Ed.2d 730 (1974), per BURGER, C.J., unanimously struck down a Florida "right of reply" statute, which required any newspaper that "assails" the personal

i. For commentary on the relationship between the *O'Brien* test and the tests employed in the public forum line of cases, see *Nimmer on Freedom of Speech* 4–67 to 4–81 (1984).

character or official record of a candidate in any election to print, on demand, free of cost, any reply the candidate may make to the charges, in as conspicuous a place and the same kind of type, provided the reply takes up no more space than the charges. The opinion carefully explained the aim of the statute to "ensure that a wide variety of views reach the public" even though "chains of newspapers, national newspapers, national wire and news services, and one-newspaper towns, are the dominant features of a press that has become noncompetitive and enormously powerful and influential in its capacity to manipulate popular opinion and change the course of events," placing "in a few hands the power to inform the American people and shape public opinion." [a] Nonetheless, the Court concluded that to require the printing of a reply violated the first amendment:

"Compelling editors or publishers to publish that which ' "reason" tells them should not be published' is what is at issue in this case. The Florida statute operates as a command in the same sense as a statute or regulation forbidding appellant from publishing specified matter. [The] Florida statute exacts a penalty on the basis of the content of a newspaper. The first phase of the penalty resulting from the compelled printing of a reply is exacted in terms of the cost in printing and composing time and materials and in taking up space that could be devoted to other material the newspaper may have preferred to print. It is correct, as appellee contends, that a newspaper is not subject to the finite technological limitations of time that confront a broadcaster but it is not correct to say that, as an economic reality, a newspaper can proceed to infinite expansion of its column space to accommodate the replies that a government agency determines or a statute commands the readers should have available.

"Faced with the penalties that would accrue to any newspaper that published news or commentary arguably within the reach of the right of access statute, editors might well conclude that the safe course is to avoid controversy and that, under the operation of the Florida statute, political and electoral coverage would be blunted or reduced. Government enforced right of access inescapably 'dampens the vigor and limits the variety of public debate,' *New York Times.*

"Even if a newspaper would face no additional costs to comply with a compulsory access law and would not be forced to forego publication of news or opinion by the inclusion of a reply, the Florida statute fails to clear the barriers of the First Amendment because of its intrusion into the function of editors. A newspaper is more than a passive receptacle or conduit for news, comment, and advertising. The choice of material to go into a newspaper, and the decisions made as to limitations on the size of the paper, and content, and treatment of public issues and public officials—whether fair or unfair—constitutes the exercise of editorial control and judgment. It has yet to be demonstrated how governmental regulation of this crucial process can be exercised consistent with First Amendment guarantees of a free press as they have evolved to this time." [b]

---

a. The opinion developed these views at greater length, citing "generally" Barron, *Access to the Press—A New First Amendment Right,* 80 Harv.L.Rev. 1641 (1967); Lange, *The Role of the Access Doctrine in the Regulation of the Mass Media: A Critical Review and Assessment,* 52 N.C.L.Rev. 1, 8–9 (1973).

b. Brennan, J., joined by Rehnquist, J., joined the Court's opinion in a short state-

ment to express the understanding that the opinion "implies no view upon the constitutionality of 'retraction' statutes affording plaintiffs able to prove defamatory falsehoods a statutory action to require publication of a retraction. See generally Note, *Vindication of the Reputation of a Public Official,* 80 Harv.L.Rev. 1730, 1739–1747 (1967)."

The Federal Communications Commission has long imposed on radio and television broadcasters the "fairness doctrine"—requiring that stations (1) devote a reasonable percentage of broadcast time to discussion of public issues and (2) assure fair coverage for each side.[c] At issue in RED LION BROADCASTING CO. v. FCC, 395 U.S. 367, 89 S.Ct. 1794, 23 L.Ed.2d 371 (1969), were the application of the fairness doctrine to a particular broadcast[d] and two specific access regulations promulgated under the doctrine: (1) the "political editorial" rule, requiring that when a broadcaster, in an editorial, "endorses or opposes" a political candidate, it must notify the candidate opposed, or the rivals of the candidate supported, and afford them a "reasonable opportunity" to respond; (2) the "personal attack" rule, requiring that "when, during the presentation of views on a controversial issue of public importance, an attack is made on the honesty, character [or] integrity [of] an identified person or group," the person or group attacked must be given notice, a transcript of the attack, and an opportunity to respond.[e] "[I]n view of [the] scarcity of broadcast frequencies, the Government's role in allocating those frequencies, and the legitimate claims of those unable without government assistance to gain access to those frequencies for expression of their views," a 7–0 majority, per WHITE, J., upheld both access regulations:[f]

"[The broadcasters] contention is that the First Amendment protects their desire to use their allotted frequencies continuously to broadcast whatever they choose, and to exclude whomever they choose from ever using that frequency. No man may be prevented from saying or publishing what he thinks, or from refusing in his speech or other utterances to give equal weight to the views of his opponents. This right, they say, applies equally to broadcasters.

"Although broadcasting is clearly a medium affected by a First Amendment interest, differences in the characteristics of new media justify differences in the First Amendment standards applied to [them]. Just as the Government may limit the use of sound-amplifying equipment potentially so noisy that it drowns

---

White, J., concurred. After agreeing that "prior compulsion by government in matters going to the very nerve center of a newspaper—the decision as to what copy will or will not be included in any given edition—collides with the First Amendment," he returned to his attack on *Gertz,* decided the same day: "Reaffirming the rule that the press cannot be forced to print an answer to a personal attack made by it [throws] into stark relief the consequences of the new balance forged by the Court in the companion case also announced today. *Gertz* goes far toward eviscerating the effectiveness of the ordinary libel action, which has long been the only potent response available to the private citizen libeled by the press. [To] me it is a near absurdity to so deprecate individual dignity, as the Court does in *Gertz,* and to leave the people at the complete mercy of the press, at least in this stage of our history when the press, as the majority in this case so well documents, is steadily becoming more powerful and much less likely to be deterred by threats of libel suits."

c. For helpful background on the origins, justification and administration of the fairness doctrine, see Barrow, *The Fairness Doctrine: A Double Standard for Electronic and Print Media,* 26 Hast.L.J. 659 (1975); Schmidt, *Freedom of the Press vs. Public Access* 157–98 (1976).

d. *Red Lion* grew out of a series of radio broadcasts by fundamentalist preacher Billy James Hargis, who had attacked Fred J. Cook, author of an article attacking Hargis and "hate clubs of the air." When Cook heard about the broadcast, he demanded that the station give him an opportunity to reply. Cook refused to pay for his "reply time" and the FCC ordered the station to give Cook the opportunity to reply whether or not he would pay for it. The Supreme Court upheld the order of free reply time. See Schmidt, fn. c supra, at 161–63.

e. Excepted were "personal attacks [by] legally qualified candidates [on] other such candidates" and "bona fide newscasts, bona fide news interviews, and on-the-spot coverage of a bona fide news event."

f. Surprisingly, none of the justices joining White, J.'s opinion felt the need to make additional remarks, but Douglas, J., who did not participate in *Red Lion,* expressed his disagreement with it in the *CBS* case, infra.

out civilized private speech, so may the Government limit the use of broadcast equipment. The right of free speech of a broadcaster, the user of a sound truck, or any other individual does not embrace a right to snuff out the free speech of [others].

"Where there are substantially more individuals who want to broadcast than there are frequencies to allocate, it is idle to posit an unabridgeable First Amendment right to broadcast comparable to the right of every individual to speak, write, or publish. [It] would be strange if the First Amendment, aimed at protecting and furthering communications, prevented the Government from making radio communication possible by requiring licenses to broadcast and by limiting the number of licenses so as not to overcrowd the spectrum. * * *

"By the same token, as far as the First Amendment is concerned those who are licensed stand no better than those to whom licenses are refused. A license permits broadcasting, but the licensee has no constitutional right [to] monopolize a radio frequency to the exclusion of his fellow citizens. There is nothing in the First Amendment which prevents the Government from requiring a licensee to share his frequency with others and to conduct himself as a proxy or fiduciary with obligations to present those views and voices which are representative of his community and which would otherwise, by necessity, be barred from the airwaves.

"[The] people as a whole retain their interest in free speech by radio and their collective right to have the medium function consistently with the ends and purposes of the First Amendment. It is the right of the viewers and listeners, not the right of the broadcasters, which is paramount. [It] is the purpose of the First Amendment to preserve an uninhibited marketplace of ideas in which truth will ultimately prevail, rather than to countenance monopolization of that market, whether it be by the Government itself or a private licensee. [It] is the right of the public to receive suitable access to social, political, esthetic, moral, and other ideas and experiences which is crucial [here.]

"In terms of constitutional principle, and as enforced sharing of a scarce resource, the personal attack and political editorial rules are indistinguishable from the equal-time provision of § 315 [of the Communications Act], a specific enactment of Congress requiring [that stations allot equal time to qualified candidates for public office] and to which the fairness doctrine and these constituent regulations are important complements. [Nor] can we say that it is inconsistent with the First Amendment goal of producing an informed public capable of conducting its own affairs to require a broadcaster to permit answers to personal attacks occurring in the course of discussing controversial issues, or to require that the political opponents of those endorsed by the station be given a chance to communicate with the public. Otherwise, station owners and a few networks would have unfettered power to make time available only to the highest bidders, to communicate only their own views on public issues, people and candidates, and to permit on the air only those with whom they agreed. There is no sanctuary in the First Amendment for unlimited private censorship operating in a medium not open to all.

"[It is contended] that if political editorials or personal attacks will trigger an obligation in broadcasters to afford the opportunity for expression to speakers who need not pay for time and whose views are unpalatable to the licensees, then broadcasters will be irresistibly forced to self-censorship and their coverage of controversial public issues will be eliminated or at least rendered wholly ineffective. Such a result would indeed be a serious matter, [but] that possibility is at best speculative. [If these doctrines turn out to have this effect], there will be time enough to reconsider the constitutional implications. The fairness doctrine in the past has had no such overall effect. That this will occur now seems unlikely, however, since if present licensees should suddenly prove timorous, the Commission is not powerless to insist that they give adequate and fair attention to public issues. It does not violate the First Amendment to treat licensees given the privilege of using scarce radio frequencies as proxies for the entire community, obligated to give suitable time and attention to matters of great public concern. To condition the granting or renewal of licenses on a willingness to present representative community views on controversial issues is consistent with the ends and purposes of those constitutional provisions forbidding the abridgment of freedom of speech and freedom of the press." [g]

Notes and Questions

1. *Tension between Miami Herald and Red Lion.* Consider Bollinger, *Freedom of the Press and Public Access: Toward a Theory of Partial Regulation of the Mass Media,* 75 Mich.L.Rev. 1, 4–6, 10–12 (1976): "What seems so remarkable about the unanimous *Miami Herald* opinion is the complete absence of any reference to the Court's unanimous decision five years earlier in *Red Lion* [, upholding] the so-called personal attack rule, [which] is almost identical in substance to the Florida statute declared unconstitutional in *Miami Herald*. That omission, however, is no more surprising than the absence of any discussion in *Red Lion* of the cases in which the Court expressed great concern about the risks attending government regulation of the print media.

"[The] scarcity rationale [articulated in *Red Lion* does not] explain why what appears to be a similar phenomenon of natural monopolization within the newspaper industry does not constitute an equally appropriate occasion for access regulation. A difference in the cause of concentration—the exhaustion of a physical element necessary for communication in broadcasting as contrasted with the economic constraints on the number of possible competitors in the print media—would seem far less relevant from a first amendment standpoint than the fact of concentration itself.

"[Instead] of exploring the relevance for the print media of the new principle developed in broadcasting, the Court merely reiterated the opposing, more traditional, principle that the government cannot tell editors what to publish. It thus created a paradox, leaving the new principle unscathed while preserving tradition."

2. *The absence of balancing in Miami Herald.* Did *Miami Herald* present a confrontation between the rights of speech and press? "Nowhere does [*Miami Herald*] explicitly acknowledge [such a confrontation], but implicit recognition of

---

g. The Court noted that it "need not deal with the argument that even if there is no longer a technological scarcity of frequencies limiting the number of broadcasters, there nevertheless is an economic scarcity in the sense that the Commission could or does limit entry to the broadcasting market on economic grounds and license no more stations than the market will support. Hence, it is said, the fairness doctrine or its equivalent is essential to satisfy the claims of those excluded and of the public generally. A related argument, which we also put side, is that quite apart from scarcity of frequencies, technological or economic, Congress does not abridge freedom of speech or press by legislation directly or indirectly multiplying the voices and views presented to the public through time sharing, fairness doctrines, or other devices which limit or dissipate the power of those who sit astride the channels of communication with the general public." For background and discussion of *Red Lion*, see Friendly, *The Good Guys, The Bad Guys and the First Amendment* (1975).

the speech interest," observes Nimmer, *Is Freedom of the Press a Redundancy? What Does it Add to Freedom of Speech?*, 26 Hast.L.J. 639, 645, 657 (1975), "may be found in the Court's reference to the access advocates' argument that, given the present semimonopolistic posture of the press, speech can be effective and therefore free only if enhanced by devices such as a right of reply statute. The Court in accepting the press clause argument in effect necessarily found it to be superior to any competing speech clause claims. [But] the issue cannot be resolved merely by noting, as did [*Miami Herald*], that a right of reply statute 'constitutes the [state] exercise of editorial control and judgment.' This is but one half of the equation. [*Miami Herald*] ignored the strong conflicting claims of 'speech.' Perhaps on balance the press should still prevail, but those who doubt the efficacy of such a result are hardly persuaded by an approach that apparently fails to recognize that any balancing of speech and press rights is required." [h]

3. *Scope of Miami Herald.* Consider Schmidt, supra, note c, at 233–35: "From the perspective of First Amendment law generally, *Miami Herald* would be a stark and unexplained deviation if one were to read the decision as creating absolute prohibitions on access obligations.[i] [The] fact the Court offers no discussion as to why First Amendment rules respecting access should be absolute, while all other rules emanating from that Amendment are relative, suggests that the principle of *Miami Herald* probably is destined for uncharted qualifications and exceptions." Would a statute requiring nondiscriminatory access to the classified ads section of a newspaper pass muster under *Miami Herald?* A requirement that legal notices be published?

4. *Absolute editorial autonomy—some of the time.* Is it ironic that *Gertz,* p. 359 supra was decided the same day as *Miami Herald?* Which poses a greater threat to editorial autonomy—a negligence standard in defamation cases or the guaranteed access contemplated by the Florida statute? Whose autonomy is important—the editors or the owners? May government protect editors from ad hoc intervention by corporate owners? See generally Baker, *Press Rights and Government Power to Structure the Press,* 34 U.Miami L.Rev. 819 (1980).

5. *Why was the Court so averse to a limited right of access to the print media?* "One possible explanation," suggests Blasi, 1977 Am.B.Found.Res.J. 521, 621–22, and one "consistent with the checking value," is that even "such a narrow right of reply could have the effect of shifting newspaper coverage away from topics that are central to the checking function—discussions of the fitness of candidates, particularly those with records in office—and toward less valued subjects for which the reply right would be inapplicable. A more likely reason is that the Justices perceived the print media as having historically enjoyed an adversary relationship with government which could only be compromised, symbolically as well as materially, if officials could dictate, for whatever reason, what the content of a particular publication must be. It is significant in this respect that the only Justice who elaborated on the concept of journalistic

---

h. Does *Miami Herald* demonstrate, as Professor Nimmer believes, at 644–46, that free speech and press can be distinct, even conflicting interests? Lewis, *A Preferred Position for Journalism?*, 7 Hof.L.Rev. 595, 603 (1979), thinks not: "[T]he vice of the [Florida right of reply] law lay in the compulsion to publish; and I think the result would be no different if the case involved a compulsion to speak. If a state statute required any candidate who spoke falsely about another to make a corrective speech, would it survive challenge under the first amendment?"

i. "Even in the area of 'the central freedom of the First Amendment,' which is criticism of the governmental acts of public officials," recalls Professor Schmidt, fn. c supra, at 232, "there is no absolute protection for expression."

discretion as it relates to newspapers, [concurring] Justice White, stressed the role of the press as a watchdog over government. It is even possible that the Court responded more favorably to the print journalists' claim to be free from access legislation than to the similar claim of broadcast journalists precisely because the Justices viewed the electronic media as fulfilling, historically as well as currently, a somewhat different and less significant role in the checking process. The Court may well have been influenced by the fact that the networks have never really had an I.F. Stone or a Seymour Hersh or a Woodward and Bernstein."

6. *The threat to editorial autonomy in Red Lion.* Consider Schmidt, fn. c supra, at 166: *Red Lion* "left broadcaster autonomy almost entirely at the mercy of the FCC." See also Van Alstyne, *The Möbius Strip of the First Amendment: Perspectives on Red Lion,* 29 S.C.L.Rev. 539, 571 (1978): "Indeed, if one continues to be troubled by *Red Lion,* I think it is not because one takes lightly the difficulty of forum allocation in a society of scarce resources. Rather, it is because one believes that the technique of the fairness doctrine in particular may represent a very trivial egalitarian gain and a major first amendment loss; that a twist has been given to the equal protection idea by a device the principal effect of which is merely to level down the most vivid and versatile forum we have, to flatten it out and to render it a mere commercial mirror of each community. What may have been lost is a willingness to risk the partisanship of licensees as catalysts and as active advocates with a freedom to exhort, a freedom that dares to exclaim 'Fuck the draft,' and not be made to yield by government at once to add, 'but on the other hand there is also the view, held by many.' "

Is the right of reply portion of the fairness doctrine less threatening than general fairness requirements? Consider Blasi, note 5 supra, at 627: "I do not believe that loss of editorial control requested by [narrowly] defined rights of reply is likely to undercut journalistic autonomy to such a degree as to dissipate the ethos that makes news organizations view themselves as guardians of the public welfare. And if one's conception of journalistic autonomy derives from the checking value, the preservation of this ethos is the appropriate measure, not some notion of total control analogous to that which an individual must enjoy within a certain sphere if he is to be truly autonomous." But see Karst, *Equality as a Central Principle in the First Amendment,* 43 U.Chi.L.Rev. 20, 49 (1975): "Even though the right-of-reply portion of the fairness doctrine upheld in *Red Lion* is less threatening than the doctrine's more general insistence on fair coverage of issues, a right of reply will give added encouragement to an editorial blandness already promoted by the broadcasters' commercial advertisers; broadcasters will simply minimize the number of newscasts to which a fairness doctrine obligation will attach." Did similar reasoning lead *Miami Herald* to invalidate the state right-of-reply statute directed at newspapers?

7. *The best of both worlds.* "[T]he critical difference between what the Court was asked to do in *Red Lion* and what it was asked to do in *Miami Herald,*" maintains Professor Bollinger note 1 supra, at 27, "involved choosing between a partial regulatory system and a universal one. Viewed from that perspective, the Court reached the correct result in both cases." Continues Bollinger at 27, 32–33, 36–37: "[T]here are good first amendment reasons for being both receptive to and wary of access regulation. This dual nature of access legislation suggests the need to limit carefully the intrusiveness of the regulation in order safely to enjoy its remedial benefits. Thus, a proper judicial response is one that will permit the legislature to provide the public with access *somewhere*

within the mass media, but not throughout the press. The Court should not, and need not, be forced into an all-or-nothing position on this matter; there is nothing in the first amendment that forbids having the best of both worlds."

8. *Cable television.* Can government require cable operators to grant an access channel for the public, for the government, and for educational institutions? Which is the better analogy: *Red Lion* or *Miami Herald?* See, e.g., Pool, *Technologies of Freedom* 151–88 (1983); Price, *Taming Red Lion: The First Amendment and Structural Approaches to Media Regulation,* 31 Fed.Comm.L.J. 215 (1979); Comment, *Access to Cable Television: A Critique of the Affirmative Duty Theory of the First Amendment,* 70 Calif.L.Rev. 1393 (1982). For discussion of other technologies, see Special Issue, *Videotex,* 36 Fed.Comm.L.J. 119 (1984).

B. ACCESS BY CONSTITUTIONAL RIGHT: THE FIRST AMENDMENT AS SWORD

"Like many equal protection issues," observes Karst, note 6 supra, at 45, "the media-access problem should be approached from two separate constitutional directions. First, what does the Constitution *compel* government to do in the way of equalizing? Second, what does the Constitution *permit* government to do in equalizing by statute?" *Red Lion* and *Miami Herald* presented the second question; the first is raised by COLUMBIA BROADCASTING SYSTEM, INC. v. DEMOCRATIC NAT'L COMMITTEE, 412 U.S. 94, 93 S.Ct. 2080, 36 L.Ed.2d 772 (1973) (*CBS*): The FCC rejected the claims of Business Executives' Move for Vietnam Peace (BEM) and the Democratic National Committee (DNC) that "responsible" individuals and groups are entitled to purchase advertising time to comment on public issues, even though the broadcaster has complied with the fairness doctrine. The District of Columbia Circuit held that "a flat ban on paid public issue announcements" violates the first amendment "at least when other sorts of paid announcements are accepted," [a] and remanded to the FCC to develop "reasonable procedures and regulations determining which and how many 'editorial advertisements' will be put on the air." The Supreme Court, per BURGER, C.J., reversed, holding that neither the "public interest" standard of the Communications Act (which draws heavily from the first amendment) nor the first amendment itself—assuming that refusal to accept such advertising constituted "governmental action" for first amendment purposes[b]—requires broadcasters to accept paid editorial announcements. As pointed out in Blasi, note 5 supra, at 613–14, although the Chief Justice "built to some extent" on *Red Lion,* his opinion "evinced a most important change of emphasis. For whereas Justice White based his argument in *Red Lion* on the premise that broadcasters are mere 'proxies' or 'fiduciaries' for the general public, the Chief Justice's opinion [in *CBS*] invoked a concept of 'journalistic independence' or 'journalistic discretion,' the essence of which is that broadcasters do indeed have special First Amendment interests which have to be considered in the constitutional calculus."

a. Compare the access claim advanced in the city bus advertising context in *Lehman v. Shaker Heights,* p. 569 supra.

b. Burger, C.J., joined by Stewart and Rehnquist, JJ., concluded that a broadcast licensee's refusal to accept an advertisement was not "governmental action" for first amendment purposes. Although White, Blackmun and Powell, JJ., concurred in other parts of the Chief Justice's opinion, they did not decide this question for, *assuming* governmental action, they found that the challenged ban did not violate the first amendment. Douglas, J., who concurred in the result, assumed *no* governmental action. Dissenting, Brennan, J., joined by Marshall, J., found that the challenged ban did constitute "governmental action." See p. 1125 infra.

Observed the Chief Justice: "[From various provisions of the Communications Act of 1934] it seems clear that Congress intended to permit private broadcasting to develop with the widest journalistic freedom consistent with its public obligations. Only when the interests of the public are found to outweigh the private journalistic interests of the broadcasters will government power be asserted within the framework of the Act. License renewal proceedings, in which the listening public can be heard, are a principal means of such regulation.

"[W]ith the advent of radio a half century ago, Congress was faced with a fundamental choice between total Government ownership and control of the new medium—the choice of most other countries—or some other alternative. Long before the impact and potential of the medium was realized, Congress opted for a system of private broadcasters licensed and regulated by Government. The legislative history suggests that this choice was influenced not only by traditional attitudes toward private enterprise, but by a desire to maintain for licensees, so far as consistent with necessary regulation, a traditional journalistic [role.]

"The regulatory scheme evolved slowly, but very early the licensee's role developed in terms of a 'public trustee' charged with the duty of fairly and impartially informing the public audience. In this structure the Commission acts in essence as an 'overseer,' but the initial and primary responsibility for fairness, balance, and objectivity rests with the licensee. This role of the Government as an overseer and ultimate arbiter and guardian of the public interest and the role of the licensee as a journalistic 'free agent' call for a delicate balancing of competing interests. The maintenance of this balance for more than 40 years has called on both the regulators and the licensees to walk a 'tightrope' to preserve the First Amendment values written into the Radio Act and its successor, the Communications Act.

"The tensions inherent in such a regulatory structure emerge more clearly when we compare a private newspaper with a broadcast licensee. The power of a privately owned newspaper to advance its own political, social, and economic views is bounded by only two factors: first, the acceptance of a sufficient number of readers—and hence advertisers—to assure financial success; and, second, the journalistic integrity of its editors and publishers. A broadcast licensee has a large measure of journalistic freedom but not as large as that exercised by a newspaper. A licensee must balance what it might prefer to do as a private entrepreneur with what it is required to do as a 'public trustee.' To perform its statutory duties, the Commission must oversee without censoring. This suggests something of the difficulty and delicacy of administering the Communications Act—a function calling for flexibility and the capacity to adjust and readjust the regulatory mechanism to meet changing problems and needs.

"The licensee policy challenged in this case is intimately related to the journalistic role of a licensee for which it has been given initial and primary responsibility by Congress. The licensee's policy against accepting editorial advertising cannot be examined as an abstract proposition, but must be viewed in the context of its journalistic role. It does not help to press on us the idea that editorial ads are 'like' commercial ads, for the licensee's policy against editorial spot ads is expressly based on a journalistic judgment that 10- to 60-second spot announcements are ill-suited to intelligible and intelligent treatment of public issues; the broadcaster has chosen to provide a balanced treatment of controversial questions in a more comprehensive form. Obviously, the licensee's evaluation is based on its own journalistic judgment of priorities and newsworthiness.

"Moreover, the Commission has not fostered the licensee policy challenged here; it has simply declined to command particular action because it fell within the area of journalistic discretion. [The] Commission's reasoning, consistent with nearly 40 years of precedent, is that so long as a licensee meets its 'public trustee' obligation to provide balanced coverage of issues and events, it has broad discretion to decide how that obligation will be met. We do not reach the question whether the First Amendment or the Act can be read to preclude the Commission from determining that in some situations the public interest requires licensees to re-examine their policies with respect to editorial advertisements.[c] The Commission has not yet made such a determination; it has, for the present at least, found the policy to be within the sphere of journalistic discretion which Congress has left with the licensee.

"[I]t must constantly be kept in mind that the interest of the public is our foremost concern. With broadcasting, where the available means of communication are limited in both space and time, [Meiklejohn's admonition] that '[w]hat is essential is not that everyone shall speak, but that everything worth saying shall be said' is peculiarly appropriate.

"[Congress] has time and again rejected various legislative attempts that would have mandated a variety of forms of individual access. [It] has chosen to leave such questions with the Commission, to which it has given the flexibility to experiment with new ideas as changing conditions require. In this case, the Commission has decided that on balance the undesirable effects of the right of access urged by respondents would outweigh the asserted [benefits.]

"The Commission was justified in concluding that the public interest in providing access to the marketplace of 'ideas and experiences' would scarcely be served by a system so heavily weighted in favor of the financially affluent, or those with access to wealth. Even under a first-come-first-served system [the] views of the affluent could well prevail over those of others, since they would have it within their power to purchase time more frequently. Moreover, there is the substantial danger [that] the time allotted for editorial advertising could be monopolized by those of one political persuasion.

"These problems would not necessarily be solved by applying the Fairness Doctrine, including the *Cullman* doctrine [requiring broadcasters to provide free time for the presentation of opposing views if a paid sponsor is unavailable], to editorial advertising. If broadcasters were required to provide time, free when necessary, for the discussion of the various shades of opinion on the issue discussed in the advertisement, the affluent could still determine in large part the issues to be discussed. Thus, the very premise of the Court of Appeals' holding—that a right of access is necessary to allow individuals and groups the opportunity for self-initiated speech—would have little meaning to those who could not afford to purchase time in the first instance.

"If the Fairness Doctrine were applied to editorial advertising, there is also the substantial danger that the effective operation of that doctrine would be jeopardized. To minimize financial hardship and to comply fully with its public

---

c. *Columbia Broadcasting System, Inc. v. FCC*, 453 U.S. 367, 101 S.Ct. 2813, 69 L.Ed.2d 706 (1981) upheld FCC administration of a statutory provision guaranteeing "reasonable" access to the airwaves for federal election candidates. The Court, per Burger, C.J., observed that "the Court has never approved a *general* right of access to the media. *Miami Herald; CBS v. DNC.* Nor do we do so to-

day." But it found that the limited right of access "properly balances the First Amendment rights of federal candidates, the public, and broadcasters." White, J., joined by Rehnquist and Stevens, JJ., dissented on statutory grounds. For criticism on constitutional grounds, see Polsby, *Candidate Access to the Air: The Uncertain Future of Broadcaster Discretion*, 1981 Sup.Ct.Rev. 223.

responsibilities a broadcaster might well be forced to make regular programming time available to those holding a view different from that expressed in an editorial advertisement. [The] result would be a further erosion of the journalistic discretion of broadcasters in the coverage of public issues, and a transfer of control over the treatment of public issues from the licensees who are accountable for broadcast performance to private individuals who are not. The public interest would no longer be 'paramount' but rather subordinate to private whim especially since, under the Court of Appeals' decision, a broadcaster would be largely precluded from rejecting editorial advertisements that dealt with matters trivial or insignificant or already fairly covered by the broadcaster. If the Fairness Doctrine and the *Cullman* doctrine were suspended to alleviate these problems, as respondents suggest might be appropriate, the question arises whether we would have abandoned more than we have gained. Under such a regime the congressional objective of balanced coverage of public issues would be seriously threatened.

"Nor can we accept the Court of Appeals' view that every potential speaker is 'the best judge' of what the listening public ought to hear or indeed the best judge of the merits of his or her views. All journalistic tradition and experience is to the contrary. For better or worse, editing is what editors are for; and editing is selection and choice of material. That editors—newspaper or broadcast—can and do abuse this power is beyond doubt, but that is not reason to deny the discretion Congress provided. Calculated risks of abuse are taken in order to preserve higher values. The presence of these risks is nothing new; the authors of the Bill of Rights accepted the reality that these risks were evils for which there was no acceptable remedy other than a spirit of moderation and a sense of responsibility—and civility—on the part of those who exercise the guaranteed freedoms of expression.

"It was reasonable for Congress to conclude that the public interest in being informed requires periodic accountability on the part of those who are entrusted with the use of broadcast frequencies, scarce as they are. In the delicate balancing historically followed in the regulation of broadcasting Congress and the Commission could appropriately conclude that the allocation of journalistic priorities should be concentrated in the licensee rather than diffused among many. This policy gives the public some assurance that the broadcaster will be answerable if he fails to meet their legitimate needs. No such accountability attaches to the private individual, whose only qualifications for using the broadcast facility may be abundant funds and a point of view. To agree that debate on public issues should be 'robust, and wide-open' does not mean that we should exchange 'public trustee' broadcasting, with all its limitations, for a system of self-appointed editorial commentators.

"[T]he risk of an enlargement of Government control over the content of broadcast discussion of public issues [is] inherent in the Court of Appeals' remand requiring regulations and procedures to sort out requests to be heard—a process involving the very editing that licensees now perform as to regular programming. [Under] a constitutionally commanded and government supervised right-of-access system urged by respondents and mandated by the Court of Appeals, the Commission would be required to oversee far more of the day-to-day operations of broadcasters' conduct, deciding such questions as whether a particular individual or group has had sufficient opportunity to present its viewpoint and whether a particular viewpoint has already been sufficiently aired. Regimenting broadcasters is too radical a therapy for the ailment respondents complain of.

"Under the Fairness Doctrine the Commission's responsibility is to judge whether a licensee's overall performance indicates a sustained good faith effort to meet the public interest in being fully and fairly informed. The Commission's responsibilities under a right-of-access system would tend to draw it into a continuing case-by-case determination of who should be heard and when. Indeed, the likelihood of Government involvement is so great that it has been suggested that the accepted constitutional principles against control of speech content would need to be relaxed with respect to editorial advertisements. To sacrifice First Amendment protections for so speculative a gain is not warranted, and it was well within the Commission's discretion to construe the Act so as to avoid such a result.

"The Commission is also entitled to take into account the reality that in a very real sense listeners and viewers constitute a 'captive audience.' [It] is no answer to say that because we tolerate pervasive commercial advertisement [we] can also live with its political counterparts.

"The rationale for the Court of Appeals' decision imposing a constitutional right of access on the broadcast media was that the licensee impermissibly discriminates by accepting commercial advertisements while refusing editorial advertisements. The court relied on [lower court cases] holding that state-supported school newspapers and public transit companies were forbidden by the First Amendment from excluding controversial editorial advertisements in favor of commercial advertisements.[d] The court also attempted to analogize this case to some of our decisions holding that States may not constitutionally ban certain protected speech while at the same time permitting other speech in public areas [citing e.g., *Grayned* and *Mosley*, Sec. 5 supra].

"These decisions provide little guidance, however, in resolving the question whether the First Amendment required the Commission to mandate a private right of access to the broadcast media. In none of those cases did the forum sought for expression have an affirmative and independent statutory obligation to provide full and fair coverage of public issues, such as Congress has imposed on all broadcast licensees. In short, there is no 'discrimination' against controversial speech present in this case. The question here is not whether there is to be discussion of controversial issues of public importance on the broadcast media, but rather who shall determine what issues are to be discussed by whom, and when."

DOUGLAS, J., concurred in the result, but "for quite different reasons." Because the Court did not decide whether a broadcast licensee is "a federal agency within the context of this case," he assumed that it was not. He "fail[ed] to see," then "how constitutionally we can treat TV and the radio differently than we treat newspapers"[e]:

"I did not participate in [*Red Lion* and] would not support it. The Fairness Doctrine has no place in our First Amendment regime. It puts the head of the camel inside the tent and enables administration after administration to toy with TV or radio in order to serve its sordid or its benevolent ends. [The uniqueness of radio and TV] is due to engineering and technical problems. But the press in a realistic sense is likewise not available to all. [T]he daily newspapers now established are unique in the sense that it would be virtually impossible for a competitor to enter the field due to the financial exigencies of

d. But see *Lehman v. Shaker Heights.*

e. Cf. *Miami Herald;* Barrow, p. 591 supra, at 683–91.

this era. The result is that in practical terms the newspapers and magazines, like the TV and radio, are available only to a select few. [That] may argue for a redefinition of the responsibilities of the press in First Amendment terms. But I do not think it gives us carte blanche to design systems of supervision and control nor empower [the government to] make 'some' laws 'abridging' freedom of the press.

"[O]ne hard and fast principle which [the First Amendment] announces is that government shall keep its hands off the press. [That means] that TV and radio, as well as the more conventional methods for disseminating news, are all included in the concept of 'press' as used in the First Amendment and therefore are entitled to live under the laissez faire regime which the First Amendment [sanctions].

"Licenses are, of course, restricted in time and while, in my view, Congress has the power to make each license limited to a fixed term and nonreviewable, there is no power to deny renewals for editorial or ideological reasons [for] the First Amendment gives no preference to one school of thought over the others.

"The Court in today's decision by endorsing the Fairness Doctrine sanctions a federal saddle on broadcast licensees that is agreeable to the traditions of nations that never have known freedom of press and that is tolerable in countries that do not have a written constitution containing prohibitions as absolute as those in the First Amendment." [f]

BRENNAN, J., joined by Marshall, J., dissented, viewing "the *absolute* ban on the sale of air time for the discussion of controversial issues" as "governmental action" [g] violating the first amendment: "As a practical matter, the Court's reliance on the Fairness Doctrine as an 'adequate' alternative to editorial advertising seriously overestimates the ability—or willingness—of broadcasters to expose the public to the 'widest possible dissemination of information from diverse and antagonistic sources.' [Indeed,] in light of the strong interest of broadcasters in maximizing their audience, and therefore their profits, it seems almost naive to expect the majority of broadcasters to produce the variety and controversiality of material necessary to reflect a full spectrum of viewpoints. Stated simply, angry customers are not good customers and, in the commercial world of mass communications, it is simply 'bad business' to espouse—or even to allow others to espouse—the heterodox or the controversial. As a result, even under the Fairness Doctrine, broadcasters generally tend to permit only established—or at least moderated—views to enter the broadcast world's 'marketplace of ideas.' [24]

"Moreover, the Court's reliance on the Fairness Doctrine as the *sole* means of informing the public seriously misconceives and underestimates the public's interest in receiving ideas and information directly from the advocates of those ideas without the interposition of journalistic middlemen. Under the Fairness Doctrine, broadcasters decide what issues are 'important,' how 'fully' to cover them, and what format, time and style of coverage are 'appropriate.' The retention of such *absolute* control in the hands of a few government licensees is inimical to the First Amendment, for vigorous, free debate can be attained only when members of the public have at least *some* opportunity to take the initiative and editorial control into their own hands.

f. Noting that his views "closely approach those expressed by Mr. Justice Douglas," Stewart, J., also concurred.

24. [Citing many secondary sources to support this statement.]

g. See fn. b supra and p. 1125 infra.

"[S]tanding alone, [the Fairness Doctrine] simply cannot eliminate the need for a further, complementary airing of controversial views through the limited availability of editorial advertising. Indeed, the availability of at least *some* opportunity for editorial advertising is imperative if we are ever to attain the 'free and general discussion of public matters [that] seems absolutely essential to prepare the people for an intelligent exercise of their rights as citizens.'

"Moreover, a proper balancing of the competing First Amendment interests at stake in this controversy must consider, not only the interests of broadcasters and of the listening and viewing public, but also the independent First Amendment interest of groups and individuals in effective self-expression. [I]n a time of apparently growing anonymity of the individual in our society, it is imperative that we take special care to preserve the vital First Amendment interest in assuring 'self-fulfillment [of expression] for each individual.' For our citizens may now find greater than ever the need to express their own views directly to the public, rather than through a governmentally appointed surrogate, if they are to feel that they can achieve at least some measure of control over their own destinies.

"[F]reedom of speech does not exist in the abstract. [It] can flourish only if it is allowed to operate in an effective forum—whether it be a public park, a schoolroom, a town meeting hall, a soapbox, or a radio and television frequency. For in the absence of an effective means of communication, the right to speak would ring hollow indeed. And, in recognition of these principles, we have consistently held that the First Amendment embodies not only the abstract right to be free from censorship, but also the right of an individual to utilize an appropriate and effective medium for the expression of his views.

"[W]ith the assistance of the Federal Government, the broadcast industry has become what is potentially the most efficient and effective 'marketplace of ideas' ever devised. [Thus], although 'full and free discussion' of ideas may have been a reality in the heyday of political pamphleteering, modern technological developments in the field of communications have made the soapbox orator and the leafleteer virtually obsolete. And, in light of the current dominance of the electronic media as the most effective means of reaching the public, any policy that *absolutely* denies citizens access to the airwaves necessarily renders even the concept of 'full and free discussion' practically meaningless.

"[T]he challenged ban can be upheld only if it is determined that such editorial advertising would unjustifiably impair the broadcaster's assertedly overriding interest in exercising *absolute* control over 'his' frequency. Such an analysis, however, hardly reflects the delicate balancing of interests that this sensitive question demands. Indeed, this 'absolutist' approach wholly disregards the competing First Amendment rights of all 'nonbroadcaster' citizens, ignores the teachings of our recent decision in *Red Lion,* and is not supported by the historical purposes underlying broadcast regulation in this Nation. [T]here is simply no overriding First Amendment interest of broadcasters that can justify the *absolute* exclusion of virtually all of our citizens from the most effective 'marketplace of ideas' ever devised.

"[T]his case deals *only* with the allocation of *advertising* time—airtime that broadcasters regularly relinquish to others without the retention of significant editorial control. Thus, we are concerned here not with the speech of broadcasters themselves but, rather, with their 'right' to decide which *other* individuals will be given an opportunity to speak in a forum that has already been opened to the public.

"Viewed in this context, the *absolute* ban on editorial advertising seems particularly offensive because, although broadcasters refuse to sell any airtime whatever to groups or individuals wishing to speak out on controversial issues of public importance, they make such airtime readily available to those 'commercial' advertisers who seek to peddle their goods and services to the public. [Yet an] individual seeking to discuss war, peace, pollution, or the suffering of the poor is denied this right to speak. Instead, he is compelled to rely on the beneficence of a corporate 'trustee' appointed by the Government to argue his case for him.

"It has been long recognized, however, that although access to public forums may be subjected to reasonable 'time, place, and manner' regulations, '[s]elective exclusions from a public forum, may not be based on *content* alone.' *Mosley* (emphasis added). Here, of course, the differential treatment accorded 'commercial' and 'controversial' speech clearly violates that principle. Moreover, and not without some irony, the favored treatment given 'commercial' speech under the existing scheme clearly reverses traditional First Amendment priorities. For it has generally been understood that 'commercial' speech enjoys *less* First Amendment protection than speech directed at the discussion of controversial issues of public importance." [h]

Notes and Questions

1. *"Elitism" and the CBS case?* Consider Bollinger, *Elitism, The Masses and the Idea of Self-Government,* in Constitutional Government in America 99, 104–05 (Collins ed. 1980): "[CBS] seemed to rely on the problems of administration and the need for journalistic discretion as the primary reasons for its result. It was this latter theory of the case that caused the decision to be hailed by the press [as] representing a substantial shift in the Court's thinking from that found in *Red Lion*. [But], the opinion is deceptive on that score; for the emphasis on journalistic discretion did not arise from a pure belief in the wisdom of journalists but rather from a perceived need to maintain control of the content of broadcasting in the hands of those who live under the aegis of government scrutiny.

"[The] difficulty with the claim of BEM and DNC was that it opened the broadcast doors to people who were not made 'responsible' through the subtle processes of government selection and oversight. And the possibilities of exploitation of mass public opinion on such vital matters as the war effort, through techniques of distortion and emotional appeals, was a more pressing danger than any commercial speech * * *.

"All of this is to suggest that [an] elitist view colored the thinking of the Court in *CBS,* as it has in other areas of broadcast regulation. The phenomenon cannot be explained away as simply the reactionary stance of conservative justices to anti-war speech. Whatever one thinks of the outcome of the *CBS* case, the fear of manipulation as a motivating factor in our thinking is not a distinctive characteristic of any particular ideological group. It also supports the position, advocated by many liberals, that something ought to be done to remove or lessen the amount of violence on television."

2. *Confronting scarcity.* Consider Tribe, *American Constitutional Law* 699 (1978): "*CBS* took a step away from *Red Lion* by its treatment of broadcasters as part of the 'press' with an important editorial function to perform rather than as

h. Cf. Brennan, J.'s dissent in *Lehman v. Shaker Heights.*

analogous to the postal or telephone systems, but *CBS* was firmly in the *Red Lion* tradition when it refused to consider the possibility that either the technologically scarce radio and television channels, or the finite time available on such channels, might be allocated much as economically scarce newspaper opportunities are allocated: by a combination of market mechanisms and chance rather than by government design coupled with broadcaster autonomy."

Suppose the government sold the airwaves to the highest bidder and allowed subsequent exchange according to property and contract law. Consider Note, *Reconciling Red Lion and Tornillo: A Consistent Theory of Media Regulation,* 28 Stan.L.Rev. 563, 583 (1976): "This regulatory strategy would remove the government from direct determination of the particular individuals who are allowed to broadcast, leaving this decision to market forces, and would avoid the need for specific behavioral commands and sanctions now necessary to secure compliance by broadcasters with the various obligations imposed by the public interest standard. [Under] strict scrutiny, then, the existence of this clearly identifiable less restrictive alternative indicates that the Communications Act is unconstitutional."

But see Van Alstyne, p. 595 supra, at 563: "Congress may indeed be free to 'sell off' the airwaves, and it may be wholly feasible to allocate most currently established broadcast signals by competitive bidding that, when done, may well produce private licensees operating truly without subsidy. But only a singularly insensitive observer would believe that this choice is not implicitly also a highly speech-restrictive choice by Congress. It is fully as speech-restrictive as though, in the case of land, government were to withdraw from *all* ownership and all subsidized maintenance of all land, including parks, auditoriums, and streets and to remain in the field exclusively as a policeman to enforce the proprietary decisions of all private landowners."

3. *The "fairness" doctrine.* The Court's assumption that the fairness doctrine works tolerably well has been roasted by the commentators. See, e.g., Rowan, *Broadcast Fairness: Doctrine, Practice, Prospects* (1984); Simmons, *The Fairness Doctrine and the Media* (1978); Johnson & Dystel, *A Day in the Life: The Federal Communications Commission,* 82 Yale L.J. 1575 (1973). Consider Krattenmaker & Powe, *The Fairness Doctrine Today: A Constitutional Curiosity and an Impossible Dream,* 1985 Duke L.J. 151, 175: "If the doctrine is to be taken seriously then suspected violations lurk everywhere and the FCC should undertake continuous oversight of the industry. If the FCC will not—or cannot—do that, then the doctrine must be toothless except for the randomly-selected few who are surprised to feel its bite after the fact." For a vigorous defense of the fairness doctrine, see Ferris & Kirkland, *Fairness—The Broadcaster's Hippocratic Oath,* 34 Cath.U.L.Rev. 605 (1985).

4. *The worst of both worlds.* Evaluate the following hypothetical commentary: "*CBS v. DNC* allows government to grant virtually exclusive control over American's most valuable communication medium to corporations who regard it as their mission to 'deliver' audiences to advertisers. The system gives us the worst of both worlds: the world of profit-seeking—without a free market; the world of regulation—without planning." For discussion of alternatives, see Cass, *Revolution in the Wasteland* (1981); Owen, *Economics and Freedom of Expression: Media Structure and the First Amendment* (1975); Firestone & Jacklin, *Deregulation and the Pursuit of Fairness* in Telecommunications Policy and the Citizen 107 (Haight ed. 1979); Owen, *Structural Approaches to the Problem of Television Network Economic Dominance,* 1979 Duke L.J. 191.

5. *First amendment consequences of finding "governmental action."* Although Stewart, J., found no "governmental action" in *CBS,* he observed: "Were the Government really operating the electronic press, it would, as my Brother Douglas points out, be *prevented* by the First Amendment from selection of broadcast content and the exercise of editorial judgment." In articulating his reasons for refusing to find governmental action, Burger, C.J., suggested a similar position: "Journalistic discretion would in many ways be lost to the rigid limitations that the First Amendment imposes on government."[i] Do these characterizations misconceive the role of the government as editor? See, e.g., Canby, *The First Amendment and the State as Editor,* 52 Tex.L.Rev. 1123, 1124–25 (1974). See also Sec. 6 supra.

II. BROADCASTING AND CONTENT REGULATION: BEYOND THE FAIRNESS DOCTRINE

A. INDECENT SPEECH

FCC v. PACIFICA FOUNDATION

438 U.S. 726, 98 S.Ct. 3026, 57 L.Ed.2d 1073 (1978).

[MR. JUSTICE STEVENS delivered the opinion of the Court (Parts I, II, III, and IV–C) and an opinion in which CHIEF JUSTICE BURGER and MR. JUSTICE REHNQUIST joined (Parts IV–A and IV–B).

[In an early afternoon weekday broadcast in October 1973, respondent's New York radio station aired a 12-minute selection called "Filthy Words," from a comedy album by a satiric humorist, George Carlin. The monologue, which had evoked frequent laughter from a live theater audience before whom it had originally been delivered, began by referring to Carlin's thought about the seven words you can't say on the public airwaves, "the ones you definitely wouldn't say ever." He then listed the words ("shit," "piss," "fuck," "motherfucker," "cocksucker," "cunt," and "tits"), "the ones that will curve your spine, grow hair on your hands and (laughter) maybe, even bring us, God help us, peace without honor (laughter) um, and a bourbon (laughter)," and repeated them over and over in a variety of colloquialisms. The monologue was played as part of the station's regular program, which was devoted that day to contemporary attitudes toward the use of language. Immediately prior to the broadcast of the Carlin monologue, listeners were advised that it included sensitive language which some might regard as offensive. Those who might be offended were advised to change the station and return in fifteen minutes.

[The FCC received a complaint from a man in New York stating that while driving in his car with his young son he had heard the broadcast of the Carlin monologue. In response, the FCC issued a Declaratory Order granting the complaint and holding that Pacifica "could have been the subject of administrative sanctions," but that this order would only be "associated with the station's

---

i. Perhaps the most notable "access to state-owned print media" case is *Avins v. Rutgers,* 385 F.2d 151 (3d Cir.1967). In the course of upholding the refusal of the *Rutgers Law Review* to publish an article by a well-known legal commentator, the Third Circuit observed: "[One] does not have the right [to] commandeer the press and columns of [a state university publication] for the publication of his article, at the expense of [the] subscribers and [state] taxpayers, to the exclusion of other articles deemed by the editors to be more suitable for publication. [T]he acceptance or rejection of articles [by a] law review necessarily involves the exercise of editorial judgment and this is in no wise lessened by the fact that the law review is supported [by] the State." But *Avins* may be read narrowly, for "the medium involved, a law review, is one that traditionally has been selective in accepting articles for publication." Schmidt, *Freedom of the Press vs. Public Access* 106 (1976).

license file, and in the event that subsequent complaints are received, the Commission will then decide whether it should utilize any of the available sanctions it has been granted by Congress."]

The Commission characterized the language used in the Carlin monologue as "patently offensive," though not necessarily obscene, and expressed the opinion that it should be regulated by principles analogous to those found in the law of nuisance where the "law generally speaks to *channeling* behavior more than actually prohibiting it. [T]he concept of 'indecent' is intimately connected with the exposure of children to language that describes, in terms patently offensive as measured by contemporary community standards for the broadcast medium, sexual or excretory activities and organs, at times of the day when there is a reasonable risk that children may be in the audience." [5]

Applying these considerations to the language used in the monologue as broadcast by respondent, the Commission concluded that certain words depicted sexual and excretory activities in a patently offensive manner, noted that they "were broadcast at a time when children were undoubtedly in the audience (i.e., in the early afternoon)," and that the prerecorded language, with these offensive words "repeated over and over," was "deliberately broadcast." In summary, the Commission stated: "We therefore hold that the language as broadcast was indecent and prohibited by 18 U.S.C. 1464 [forbidding the use of "any obscene, indecent or profane language" by means of radio communications.]" [6] [The Commission subsequently clarified its opinion, pointing out] that it "never intended to place an absolute prohibition on the broadcast of this type of language, but rather sought to channel it to times of day when children most likely would not be exposed to it." * * *

I. The general statements in the Commission's memorandum opinion do not change the character of its order. Its action was an adjudication under 5 U.S.C. § 554(e); it did not purport to engage in formal rulemaking or in the promulgation of any regulations. The order "was issued in a special factual context"; questions concerning possible action in other contexts were expressly reserved for the future. The specific holding was carefully confined to the monologue "as broadcast." * * *

II. The relevant statutory questions are whether the Commission's action is forbidden "censorship" within the meaning of 47 U.S.C. § 326 and whether speech that concededly is not obscene may be restricted as "indecent" under the authority of 18 U.S.C. § 1464. [The] prohibition against censorship unequivocally denies the Commission any power to edit proposed broadcasts in advance [but] has never been construed to deny the Commission the power to review the content of completed broadcasts in the performance of its regulatory duties. * * *

5. Thus, the Commission suggested, if an offensive broadcast had literary, artistic, political or scientific value, and were preceded by warnings, it might not be indecent in the late evening, but would be so during the day, when children are in the audience.

6. Chairman Wiley concurred in the result without joining the opinion. Commissioners Reid and Quello filed separate statements expressing the opinion that the language was inappropriate for broadcast at any time. Commissioner Robinson, joined by Commissioner Hooks filed a concurring statement ex-pressing the opinion that "we can regulate offensive speech to the extent it constitutes a public nuisance. [The] governing idea is that 'indecency' is not an inherent attribute of words themselves; it is rather a matter of context and conduct. [If] I am called on to do so, I would find that Carlin's monologue, if it were broadcast at an appropriate hour and accompanied by suitable warning, was distinguished by sufficient literary value to avoid being 'indecent' within the meaning of the statute."

III.   The only other statutory question presented by this case is whether the afternoon broadcast of the "Filthy Words" monologue was indecent within the meaning of § 1464.[13] Even that question is narrowly confined by the arguments of the parties.

 * * * Pacifica's claim that the broadcast was not indecent within the meaning of the statute rests entirely on the absence of prurient appeal.

The plain language of the statute does not support Pacifica's argument. The words "obscene, indecent, or profane" are written in the disjunctive, implying that each has a separate meaning. Prurient appeal is an element of the obscene, but the normal definition of "indecent" merely refers to nonconformance with accepted standards of morality.

Pacifica argues, however, that this Court has construed the term "indecent" in related statutes to mean "obscene," as that term was defined in *Miller* [p. 728 supra]. Pacifica relies most heavily on the construction this Court gave to 18 U.S.C. § 1461 [prohibiting the mailing of "obscene, lewd, lascivious, indecent, filthy or vile" material] in *Hamling v. United States* [p. 397 supra].

Because neither our prior decisions nor the language or history of § 1464 supports the conclusion that prurient appeal is an essential component of indecent language, we reject Pacifica's construction of the statute. When that construction is put to one side, there is no basis for disagreeing with the Commission's conclusion that indecent language was used in this broadcast.

IV.   Pacifica makes two constitutional attacks on the Commission's order. First, it argues that the Commission's construction of the statutory language broadly encompasses so much constitutionally protected speech that reversal is required even if Pacifica's broadcast of the "Filthy Words" monologue is not itself protected by the First Amendment. Second, Pacifica argues that inasmuch as the recording is not obscene, the Constitution forbids any abridgment of the right to broadcast it on the radio.

A.   The first argument fails because our review is limited to the question whether the Commission has the authority to proscribe this particular broadcast. As the Commission itself emphasized, its order was "issued in a specific factual context." That approach is appropriate for courts as well as the Commission when regulation of indecency is at stake, for indecency is largely a function of context—it cannot be adequately judged in the abstract.

The approach is also consistent with *Red Lion*. In that case the Court rejected an argument that the Commission's regulations defining the fairness doctrine were so vague that they would inevitably abridge the broadcasters' freedom of speech. * * *

It is true that the Commission's order may lead some broadcasters to censor themselves. At most, however, the Commission's definition of indecency will deter only the broadcasting of patently offensive references to excretory and sexual organs and activities.[18] While some of these references may be protected, they surely lie at the periphery of First Amendment concern. The danger dismissed so summarily in *Red Lion*, in contrast, was that broadcasters would respond to the vagueness of the regulations by refusing to present programs

---

13. [The] statutes authorizing civil penalties incorporate § 1464, a criminal statute. But the validity of the civil sanctions is not linked to the validity of the criminal penalty. [Thus,] we need not consider any question relating to the possible application of § 1464 as a criminal statute.

18. A requirement that indecent language be avoided will have its primary effect on the form, rather than the content, of serious communication. There are few, if any, thoughts that cannot be expressed by the use of less offensive language.

dealing with important social and political controversies. Invalidating any rule on the basis of its hypothetical application to situations not before the Court is "strong medicine" to be applied "sparingly and only as a last resort." *Broadrick* [p. 425 supra]. We decline to administer that medicine to preserve the vigor of patently offensive sexual and excretory speech.

B. When the issue is narrowed to the facts of this case, the question is whether the First Amendment denies government any power to restrict the public broadcast of indecent language in any circumstances. For if the government has any such power, this was an appropriate occasion for its exercise.

The words of the Carlin monologue are unquestionably "speech" within the meaning of the First Amendment. It is equally clear that the Commission's objections to the broadcast were based in part on its content. The order must therefore fall if, as Pacifica argues, the First Amendment prohibits all governmental regulation that depends on the content of speech. Our past cases demonstrate, however, that no such absolute rule is mandated * * *.

The question in this case is whether a broadcast of patently offensive words dealing with sex and excretion may be regulated because of its content.[20] Obscene materials have been denied the protection of the First Amendment because their content is so offensive to contemporary moral standards. *Roth.* But the fact that society may find speech offensive is not a sufficient reason for suppressing it. Indeed, if it is the speaker's opinion that gives offense, that consequence is a reason for according it constitutional protection. For it is a central tenet of the First Amendment that the government must remain neutral in the marketplace of ideas. If there were any reason to believe that the Commission's characterization of the Carlin monologue as offensive could be traced to its political content—or even to the fact that it satirized contemporary attitudes about four letter words[22]—First Amendment protection might be required. But that is simply not this case. These words offend for the same reasons that obscenity offends. Their place in the hierarchy of First Amendment values was aptly sketched by Mr. Justice Murphy when he said, "such utterances are no essential part of any exposition of ideas, and are of such slight social value as a step to truth that any benefit that may be derived from them is clearly outweighed by the social interest in order and morality." *Chaplinsky.*

Although these words ordinarily lack literary, political, or scientific value, they are not entirely outside the protection of the First Amendment. Some uses of even the most offensive words are unquestionably protected. Indeed, we may assume, arguendo, that this monologue would be protected in other contexts. Nonetheless, the constitutional protection accorded to a communication containing such patently offensive sexual and excretory language need not be the same in every context. It is a characteristic of speech such as this that both its capacity to offend and its "social value," to use Mr. Justice Murphy's term, vary with the circumstances. Words that are commonplace in one setting are

20. Although neither Justice Powell nor Justice Brennan directly confronts this question, both have answered it affirmatively, the latter explicitly, at fn. 3, infra, and the former implicitly by concurring in a judgment that could not otherwise stand.

22. The monologue does present a point of view; it attempts to show that the words it uses are "harmless" and that our attitudes toward them are "essentially silly." The Commission objects, not to this point of view, but to the way in which it is expressed. The belief that these words are harmless does not necessarily confer a First Amendment privilege to use them while proselytizing just as the conviction that obscenity is harmless does not license one to communicate that conviction by the indiscriminate distribution of an obscene leaflet.

shocking in another. To paraphrase Mr. Justice Harlan, one occasion's lyric is another's vulgarity. Cf. *Cohen v. California.*[25]

In this case it is undisputed that the content of Pacifica's broadcast was "vulgar," "offensive," and "shocking." Because content of that character is not entitled to absolute constitutional protection under all circumstances, we must consider its context in order to determine whether the Commission's action was constitutionally permissible.

C. We have long recognized that each medium of expression presents special First Amendment problems. And of all forms of communication, it is broadcasting that has received the most limited First Amendment [protection.]

The reasons for these distinctions are complex, but two have relevance to the present case. First, the broadcast media have established a uniquely pervasive presence in the lives of all Americans. Patently offensive, indecent material presented over the airwaves confronts the citizen, not only in public, but also in the privacy of the home, where the individual's right to be let alone plainly outweighs the First Amendment rights of an intruder. *Rowan.* Because the broadcast audience is constantly tuning in and out, prior warnings cannot completely protect the listener or viewer from unexpected program content. To say that one may avoid further offense by turning off the radio when he hears indecent language is like saying that the remedy for an assault is to run away after the first blow. One may hang up on an indecent phone call, but that option does not give the caller a constitutional immunity or avoid a harm that has already taken place.[27]

Second, broadcasting is uniquely accessible to children, even those too young to read. Although Cohen's written message might have been incomprehensible to a first grader, Pacifica's broadcast could have enlarged a child's vocabulary in an instant. Other forms of offensive expression may be withheld from the young without restricting the expression at its source. Bookstores and motion picture theaters, for example, may be prohibited from making indecent material available to children. We held in *Ginsberg* [p. 388 supra] that the government's interest in the "well being of its youth" and in supporting "parents' claim to authority in their own household" justified the regulation of otherwise protected expression.[28] The ease with which children may obtain access to broadcast

---

25. The importance of context is illustrated by the *Cohen* case. [So] far as the evidence showed no one in the courthouse was offended by [Cohen's jacket.]

In holding that criminal sanctions could not be imposed on Cohen for his political statement in a public place, the Court rejected the argument that his speech would offend unwilling viewers; it noted that "there was no evidence that persons powerless to avoid [his] conduct did in fact object to it." In contrast, in this case the Commission was responding to a listener's strenuous complaint, and Pacifica does not question its determination that this afternoon broadcast was likely to offend listeners. It should be noted that the Commission imposed a far more moderate penalty on Pacifica than the state court imposed on Cohen. Even the strongest civil penalty at the Commission's command does not include criminal prosecution.

27. Outside the home, the balance between the offensive speaker and the unwilling audience may sometimes tip in favor of the speaker, requiring the offended listener to turn away. See *Erznoznik.* ∗ ∗ ∗

28. The Commission's action does not by any means reduce adults to hearing only what is fit for children. Cf. *Butler v. Michigan* [p. 388 supra]. Adults who feel the need may purchase tapes and records or go to theatres and nightclubs to hear these words. In fact, the Commission has not unequivocally closed even broadcasting to speech of this sort; whether broadcast audiences in the late evening contain so few children that playing this monologue would be permissible is an issue neither the Commission nor this Court has decided.

material, coupled with the concerns recognized in *Ginsberg,* amply justify special treatment of indecent broadcasting.

It is appropriate, in conclusion, to emphasize the narrowness of our holding. This case does not involve a two-way radio conversation between a cab driver and a dispatcher, or a telecast of an Elizabethan comedy. We have not decided that an occasional expletive in either setting would justify any sanction or, indeed, that this broadcast would justify a criminal prosecution. The Commission's decision rested entirely on a nuisance rationale under which context is all-important. The concept requires consideration of a host of variables. The time of day was emphasized by the Commission. The content of the program in which the language is used will also affect the composition of the audience, and differences between radio, television, and perhaps closed-circuit transmissions, may also be relevant. As Mr. Justice Sutherland wrote, a "nuisance may be merely a right thing in the wrong place—like a pig in the parlor instead of the barnyard." We simply hold that when the Commission finds that a pig has entered the parlor, the exercise of its regulatory power does not depend on proof that the pig is obscene.

[R]eversed.

MR. JUSTICE POWELL, with whom MR. JUSTICE BLACKMUN joins, concurring.

I join Parts I, II, III, and IV(C) of Justice Stevens' opinion. The Court today reviews only the Commission's holding that Carlin's monologue was indecent "as broadcast" at two o'clock in the afternoon, and not the broad sweep of the Commission's opinion. In addition to being consistent with our settled practice of not deciding constitutional issues unnecessarily, this narrow focus also is conducive to the orderly development of this relatively new and difficult area of law, in the first instance by the Commission, and then by the reviewing courts.

I also agree with much that is said in Part IV of Justice Stevens' opinion, and with its conclusion that the Commission's holding in this case does not violate the First Amendment. Because I do not subscribe to all that is said in Part IV, however, I state my views separately.

[T]he language employed is, to most people, vulgar and offensive. It was chosen specifically for this quality, and it was repeated over and over as a sort of verbal shock treatment. The Commission did not err in characterizing the narrow category of language used here as "patently offensive" to most people regardless of age.

The issue, however, is whether the Commission may impose civil sanctions on a licensee radio station for broadcasting the monologue at two o'clock in the afternoon. The Commission's primary concern was to prevent the broadcast from reaching the ears of unsupervised children who were likely to be in the audience at that hour. In essence, the Commission sought to "channel" the monologue to hours when the fewest unsupervised children would be exposed to it. In my view, this consideration provides strong support for the Commission's holding.

[The] Commission properly held that the speech from which society may attempt to shield its children is not limited to that which appeals to the youthful prurient interest. The language involved in this case is as potentially degrading and harmful to children as representations of many erotic acts.

In most instances, the dissemination of this kind of speech to children may be limited without also limiting willing adults' access to it. Sellers of printed and recorded matter and exhibitors of motion pictures and live performances may be required to shut their doors to children, but such a requirement has no effect on adults' access. See *Ginsberg.* The difficulty is that such a physical separation of the audience cannot be accomplished in the broadcast media. During most of the broadcast hours, both adults and unsupervised children are likely to be in the broadcast audience, and the broadcaster cannot reach willing adults without also reaching children. This, as the Court emphasizes, is one of the distinctions between the broadcast and other media to which we often have adverted as justifying a different treatment of the broadcast media for First Amendment purposes. In my view, the Commission was entitled to give substantial weight to this difference in reaching its decision in this case.

[Another difference] is that broadcasting—unlike most other forms of communication—comes directly into the home, the one place where people ordinarily have the right not to be assaulted by uninvited and offensive sights and sounds. *Erznoznik; Cohen; Rowan.* Although the First Amendment may require unwilling adults to absorb the first blow of offensive but protected speech when they are in public before they turn away, see, e.g., *Erznoznik,* but cf. *Rosenfeld* (Powell, J., dissenting), a different order of values obtains in the home. "That we are often 'captives' outside the sanctuary of the home and subject to objectionable speech and other sound does not mean we must be captives everywhere." *Rowan.* The Commission also was entitled to give this factor appropriate weight in the circumstances of the instant case. This is not to say, however, that the Commission has an unrestricted license to decide what speech, protected in other media, may be banned from the airwaves in order to protect unwilling adults from momentary exposure to it in their homes.[2] * * *

The Commission's holding does not prevent willing adults from purchasing Carlin's record, from attending his performances, or, indeed, from reading the transcript reprinted as an appendix to the Court's opinion. On its face, it does not prevent respondent from broadcasting the monologue during late evening hours when fewer children are likely to be in the audience, nor from broadcasting discussions of the contemporary use of language at any time during the day. The Commission's holding, and certainly the Court's holding today, does not speak to cases involving the isolated use of a potentially offensive word in the course of a radio broadcast, as distinguished from the verbal shock treatment administered by respondent here. In short, I agree that on the facts of this case, the Commission's order did not violate respondent's First Amendment rights.

As the foregoing demonstrates, my views are generally in accord with what is said in Part IV(C) of opinion. I therefore join that portion of his opinion. I do not join Part IV(B), however, because I do not subscribe to the theory that the Justices of this Court are free generally to decide on the basis of its content which speech protected by the First Amendment is most "valuable" and hence deserving of the most protection, and which is less "valuable" and hence deserving of less protection.[3] In my view, the result in this case does not turn on whether Carlin's monologue, viewed as a whole, or the words that comprise it,

---

2. It is true that the radio listener quickly may tune out speech that is offensive to him. In addition, broadcasters may preface potentially offensive programs with warnings. But such warnings do not help the unsuspecting listener who tunes in at the middle of a program. In this respect, too, broadcasting appears to differ from books and records, which may carry warnings on their faces, and from

motion pictures and live performances, which may carry warnings on their marquees.

3. The Court has, however, created a limited exception to this rule in order to bring commercial speech within the protection of the First Amendment. See *Ohralik* [p. 451 supra].

have more or less "value" than a candidate's campaign speech. This is a judgment for each person to make, not one for the judges to impose upon him.[4]

The result turns instead on the unique characteristics of the broadcast media, combined with society's right to protect its children from speech generally agreed to be inappropriate for their years, and with the interest of unwilling adults in not being assaulted by such offensive speech in their homes. Moreover, I doubt whether today's decision will prevent any adult who wishes to receive Carlin's message in Carlin's own words from doing so, and from making for himself a value judgment as to the merit of the message and words. These are the grounds upon which I join the judgment of the Court as to Part IV.

MR. JUSTICE BRENNAN, with whom MR. JUSTICE MARSHALL joins, dissenting.

I agree with Justice Stewart that, under *Hamling*, the word "indecent" in 18 U.S.C. § 1464 must be construed to prohibit only obscene speech. I would, therefore, normally refrain from expressing my views on any constitutional issues implicated in this case. However, I find the Court's misapplication of fundamental First Amendment principles so patent, and its attempt to impose *its* notions of propriety on the whole of the American people so misguided, that I am unable to remain silent.

For the second time in two years, see *Young v. American Mini Theatres* [p. 437], the Court refuses to embrace the notion, completely antithetical to basic First Amendment values, that the degree of protection the First Amendment affords protected speech varies with the social value ascribed to that speech by five Members of this Court. See opinion of Justice Powell. Moreover, [all] Members of the Court agree that [the monologue] does not fall within one of the categories of speech, such as "fighting words," or obscenity, that is totally without First Amendment protection. [Yet] despite the Court's refusal to create a sliding scale of First Amendment protection calibrated to this Court's perception of the worth of a communication's content, and despite our unanimous agreement that the Carlin monologue is protected speech, a majority of the Court[1] nevertheless finds that, on the facts of this case, the FCC is not constitutionally barred from imposing sanctions on Pacifica for its airing of the Carlin monologue. This majority apparently believes that the FCC's disapproval of Pacifica's afternoon broadcast of Carlin's "Dirty Words" recording is a permissible time, place, and manner regulation. [The opinions of both Stevens and Powell, JJ.,] rely principally on two factors in reaching this conclusion: (1) the capacity of a radio broadcast to intrude into the unwilling listener's home, and (2) the presence of children in the listening audience. Dispassionate analysis, removed from individual notions as to what is proper and what is not, starkly reveals that these justifications, whether individually or together, simply do not support even the professedly moderate degree of governmental homogeni-

---

4. For much the same reason, I also do not join Part IV(A). I had not thought that the application vel non of overbreadth analysis should depend on the Court's judgment as to the value of the protected speech that might be deterred. Except in the context of commercial speech, see *Bates* [p. 450 supra], it has not in the past. See, e.g., *Lewis v. New Orleans; Gooding.*

As Justice Stevens points out, however, the Commission's order was limited to the facts of this case; "it did not purport to engage in formal rulemaking or in the promulgation of any regulations." In addition, since the Commission may be expected to proceed cautiously, as it has in the past, I do not foresee an undue "chilling" effect on broadcasters' exercise of their rights. I agree, therefore, that respondent's overbreadth challenge is meritless.

1. Where I refer without differentiation to the actions of "the Court," my reference is to this majority, which consists of my Brothers Powell and Stevens and those Members of the Court joining their separate opinions.

zation of radio communications—if, indeed, such homogenization can ever be moderate given the pre-eminent status of the right of free speech in our constitutional scheme—that the Court today permits.

[In] finding [the privacy interests of an individual in his home] sufficient to justify the content regulation of protected speech, [the] Court commits two errors. First, it misconceives the nature of the privacy interests involved where an individual voluntarily chooses to admit radio communications into his home. Second, it ignores the constitutionally protected interests of both those who wish to transmit and those who desire to receive broadcasts that many—including the FCC and this Court—might find offensive.

[A]n individual's actions in switching on and listening to communications transmitted over the public airways and directed to the public at-large do not implicate fundamental privacy interests, even when engaged in within the home. Instead, because the radio is undeniably a public medium, these actions are more properly viewed as a decision to take part, if only as a listener, in an ongoing public discourse. Although an individual's decision to allow public radio communications into his home undoubtedly does not abrogate all of his privacy interests, the residual privacy interests he retains vis-à-vis the communication he voluntarily admits into his home are surely no greater than those of the people present in the corridor of the Los Angeles courthouse in *Cohen* who bore witness to the words "Fuck the Draft" emblazoned across Cohen's jacket. Their privacy interests were held insufficient to justify punishing Cohen for his offensive communication.

Even if an individual who voluntarily opens his home to radio communications retains privacy interests of sufficient moment to justify a ban on protected speech if those interests are "invaded in an essentially intolerable manner," *Cohen,* the very fact that those interests are threatened only by a radio broadcast precludes any intolerable invasion of privacy; for unlike other intrusive modes of communication, such as sound trucks, "[t]he radio can be turned off"—and with a minimum of effort. As Judge Bazelon aptly observed below, "having elected to receive public airwaves, the scanner who stumbles onto an offensive program is in the same position as the unsuspected passers-by in *Cohen* and *Erznoznik;* he can avert his attention by changing channels or turning off the set." Whatever the minimal discomfort suffered by a listener who inadvertently tunes into a program he finds offensive during the brief interval before he can simply extend his arm and switch stations or flick the "off" button, it is surely worth the candle to preserve the broadcaster's right to send, and the right of those interested to receive, a message entitled to full First Amendment protection. To reach a contrary balance, as does the Court, is clearly, to follow Justice Stevens' reliance on animal metaphors, "to burn the house to roast the pig."

The Court's balance, of necessity, fails to accord proper weight to the interests of listeners who wish to hear broadcasts the FCC deems offensive. It permits majoritarian tastes completely to preclude a protected message from entering the homes of a receptive, unoffended minority. No decision of this Court supports such a result. Where the individuals comprising the offended majority may freely choose to reject the material being offered, we have never found their privacy interests of such moment to warrant the suppression of speech on privacy grounds. [In] *Rowan,* the Court upheld a statute, permitting householders to require that mail advertisers stop sending them lewd or offensive materials and remove their names from mailing lists. Unlike the situation here, householders who wished to receive the sender's communications were not prevented from doing so. Equally important, the determination of offensiveness vel non under the statute involved in *Rowan* was completely within the hands of the individual householder; no governmental evaluation of the worth of the mail's content stood between the mailer and the householder. In contrast, the visage of the censor is all too discernable here.

[Although] the government unquestionably has a special interest in the well-being of children and consequently "can adopt more stringent controls on communicative materials available to youths than on those available to adults," *Erznoznik,* the Court has accounted for this societal interest by adopting a "variable obscenity" standard that permits the prurient appeal of material available to children to be assessed in terms of the sexual interests of minors. *Ginsberg.* [But] we have made it abundantly clear that "under any test of obscenity as to minors [to] be obscene 'such expression must be, in some significant way, erotic.'"

Because the Carlin monologue is obviously not an erotic appeal to the prurient interests of children, the Court, for the first time, allows the government to prevent minors from gaining access to materials that are not obscene, and are therefore protected, as to them.[2] It thus ignores our recent admonition that "[s]peech that is neither obscene as to youths nor subject to some other legitimate proscription cannot be suppressed solely to protect the young from ideas or images that a legislative body thinks unsuitable for them." *Erznoznik.*[3] The Court's refusal to follow its own pronouncements is especially lamentable since it has the anomalous subsidiary effect, at least in the radio context at issue here, of making completely unavailable to adults material which may not constitutionally be kept even from children. This result violates in spades the principle of *Butler v. Michigan.* [Powell, J.'s opinion] acknowledges that there lurks in today's decision a potential for " 'reduc[ing] the adult population [to] [hearing] only what is fit for children,'" but expresses faith that the FCC will vigilantly prevent this potential from ever becoming a reality. I am far less certain than [he] that such faith in the Commission is warranted; and even if I shared it, I could not so easily shirk the responsibility assumed by each Member of this Court jealously to guard against encroachments on First Amendment freedoms.

[T]he opinions of Justices Powell and Stevens both stress the time-honored right of a parent to raise his child as he sees fit—a right this Court has consistently been vigilant to protect. Yet this principle supports a result directly contrary to that reached by the Court. *Yoder* and *Pierce,* [Ch. 9, Sec. 2, I], hold that parents, *not* the government, have the right to make certain decisions regarding the upbringing of their children. As surprising as it may be to individual Members of this Court, some parents may actually find Mr. Carlin's unabashed attitude towards the seven "dirty words" healthy, and deem it

---

2. Even if the monologue appealed to the prurient interest of minors, it would not be obscene as to them unless, as to them, "the work, taken as a whole, lacks serious literary, artistic, political, or scientific value." *Miller.*

3. It may be that a narrowly drawn regulation prohibiting the use of offensive language on broadcasts directed specifically at younger children constitutes one of the "other legitimate proscription[s]" alluded to in *Erznoznik.* This is so both because of the difficulties inherent in adapting the *Miller* formulation to communications received by young children, and because such children are "not possessed

of that full capacity for individual choice which is the presupposition of the First Amendment guarantees." *Ginsberg.* (Stewart, J., concurring). I doubt, as my Brother Stevens suggests, that such a limited regulation amounts to a regulation of speech based on its content, since, by hypothesis, the only persons at whom the regulated communication is directed are incapable of evaluating its content. To the extent that such a regulation is viewed as a regulation based on content, it marks the outermost limits to which content regulation is permissible.

desirable to expose their children to the manner in which Mr. Carlin defuses the taboo surrounding the words. Such parents may constitute a minority of the American public, but the absence of great numbers willing to exercise the right to raise their children in this fashion does not alter the right's nature or its existence. Only the Court's regrettable decision does that.[4]

As demonstrated above, neither of the factors relied on by both [Justices Powell and Stevens]—the intrusive nature of radio and the presence of children in the listening audience—can, when taken on its own terms, support the FCC's disapproval of the Carlin monologue. These two asserted justifications are further plagued by a common failing: the lack of principled limits on their use as a basis for FCC censorship. No such limits come readily to mind, and neither of the opinions comprising the Court serve to clarify the extent to which the FCC may assert the privacy and children-in-the-audience rationales as justification for expunging from the airwaves protected communications the Commission finds offensive. Taken to their logical extreme, these rationales would support the cleansing of public radio of any "four-letter words" whatsoever, regardless of their context. The rationales could justify the banning from radio of a myriad of literary works, novels, poems, and plays by the likes of Shakespeare, Joyce, Hemingway, Ben Jonson, Henry Fielding, Robert Burns, and Chaucer; they could support the suppression of a good deal of political speech, such as the Nixon tapes; and they could even provide the basis for imposing sanctions for the broadcast of certain portions of the Bible.

In order to dispel the spectre of the possibility of so unpalatable a degree of censorship, and to defuse Pacifica's overbreadth challenge, the FCC insists that it desires only the authority to reprimand a broadcaster on facts analogous to those present in this case. [Justices Powell and Stevens] take the FCC at its word, and consequently do no more than permit the Commission to censor the afternoon broadcast of the "sort of verbal shock treatment," opinion of Justice Powell, involved here. To insure that the FCC's regulation of protected speech does not exceed these bounds, my Brother Powell is content to rely upon the judgment of the Commission while my Brother Stevens deems it prudent to rely on this Court's ability accurately to assess the worth of various kinds of speech.[6] For my own part, even accepting that this case is limited to its facts,[7] I would place the responsibility and the right to weed worthless and offensive communications from the public airways where it belongs and where, until today, it resided: in a

---

4. The opinions of my Brothers Powell and Stevens rightly refrain from relying on the notion of "spectrum scarcity" to support their result. As Chief Judge Bazelon noted below, "although scarcity has justified *increasing* the diversity of speakers and speech, it has never been held to justify censorship." See *Red Lion*.

6. Although ultimately dependent upon the outcome of review in this Court, the approach taken by my Brother Stevens would not appear to tolerate the FCC's suppression of any speech, such as political speech, falling within the core area of First Amendment concern. The same, however, cannot be said of the approach taken by my Brother Powell, which, on its face, permits the Commission to censor even political speech if it is sufficiently offensive to community standards. A result more contrary to rudimentary First Amendment principles is difficult to imagine.

7. Having insisted that it seeks to impose sanctions on radio communications only in the limited circumstances present here, I believe that the FCC is estopped from using either this decision or its own orders in this case, as a basis for imposing sanctions on any public radio broadcast other than one aired during the daytime or early evening and containing the relentless repetition, for longer than a brief interval, of "language that describes, in terms patently offensive as measured by contemporary community standards for the broadcast medium, sexual or excretory activities and organs." For surely broadcasters are not now on notice that the Commission desires to regulate any offensive broadcast other than the type of "verbal shock treatment" condemned here, or even this "shock treatment" type of offensive broadcast during the late evening.

public free to choose those communications worthy of its attention from a marketplace unsullied by the censor's hand.

The absence of any hesitancy in the opinions of my Brothers Powell and Stevens to approve the FCC's censorship of the Carlin monologue on the basis of two demonstrably inadequate grounds is a function of their perception that the decision will result in little, if any, curtailment of communicative exchanges protected by the First Amendment. Although the extent to which the Court stands ready to countenance FCC censorship of protected speech is unclear from today's decision, I find the reasoning by which my Brethren conclude that the FCC censorship they approve will not significantly infringe on First Amendment values both disingenuous as to reality and wrong as a matter of law.

My Brother Stevens, in reaching a result apologetically described as narrow, takes comfort in his observation that "[a] requirement that indecent language be avoided will have its primary effect on the form, rather than the content, of serious communication," and finds solace in his conviction that "[t]here are few, if any, thoughts that cannot be expressed by the use of less offensive language." The idea that the content of a message and its potential impact on any who might receive it can be divorced from the words that are the vehicle for its expression is transparently fallacious. A given word may have a unique capacity to capsule an idea, evoke an emotion, or conjure up an image. Indeed, for those of us who place an appropriately high value on our cherished First Amendment rights, the word "censor" is such a word. Mr. Justice Harlan, speaking for the Court, recognized the truism that a speaker's choice of words cannot surgically be separated from the ideas he desires to express when he warned that "we cannot indulge the facile assumption that one can forbid particular words without also running a substantial risk of suppressing ideas in the process." *Cohen.* Moreover, even if an alternative phrasing may communicate a speaker's abstract ideas as effectively as those words he is forbidden to use, it is doubtful that the sterilized message will convey the emotion that is an essential part of so many communications. This, too, was apparent to Mr. Justice Harlan and the Court in *Cohen.*

[Stevens, J.] also finds relevant to his First Amendment analysis the fact that "[a]dults who feel the need may purchase tapes and records or go to theatres and nightclubs to hear [the tabooed] words." [Powell, J.,] agrees. [The] opinions of my Brethren display both a sad insensitivity to the fact that these alternatives involve the expenditure of money, time, and effort that many of those wishing to hear Mr. Carlin's message may not be able to afford, and a naive innocence of the reality that in many cases, the medium may well be the message.

The Court apparently believes that the FCC's actions here can be analogized to the zoning ordinances upheld in *American Mini Theatres.* For two reasons, it is wrong. First, the zoning ordinances found to pass constitutional muster [had] valid goals other than the channeling of protected speech. No such goals are present here. Second, and crucial to the opinions of my Brothers Powell and Stevens in *American Mini Theatres*—opinions, which, as they do in this case, supply the bare five-person majority of the Court—the ordinances did not restrict the access of distributors or exhibitors to the market or impair the viewing public's access to the regulated material. Again, this is not the situation [here.]

It is quite evident that I find the Court's attempt to unstitch the warp and woof of First Amendment law in an effort to reshape its fabric to cover the patently wrong result the Court reaches in this case dangerous as well as lamentable. Yet there runs throughout the opinions of my Brothers Powell and Stevens another vein I find equally disturbing: a depressing inability to appreciate that in our land of cultural pluralism, there are many who think, act, and talk differently from the Members of this Court, and who do not share their fragile sensibilities. It is only an acute ethnocentric myopia that enables the Court to approve the censorship of communications solely because of the words they [contain.]

Today's decision will thus have its greatest impact on broadcasters desiring to reach, and listening audiences comprised of, persons who do not share the Court's view as to which words or expressions are acceptable and who, for a variety of reasons, including a conscious desire to flout majoritarian conventions, express themselves using words that may be regarded as offensive by those from different socio-economic backgrounds.[8] In this context, the Court's decision may be seen for what, in the broader perspective, it really is: another of the dominant culture's inevitable efforts to force those groups who do not share its mores to conform to its way of thinking, acting, and speaking.

Pacifica, in response to an FCC inquiry about its broadcast of Carlin's satire on "the words you couldn't say on the public airwaves," explained that "Carlin is not mouthing obscenities, he is merely using words to satirize as harmless and essentially silly our attitudes towards those words." In confirming Carlin's prescience as a social commentator by the result it reaches today, the Court evinces an attitude towards the "seven dirty words" that many others besides Mr. Carlin and Pacifica might describe as "silly." Whether today's decision will similarly prove "harmless" remains to be seen. One can only hope that it will.

MR. JUSTICE STEWART, with whom MR. JUSTICE BRENNAN, MR. JUSTICE WHITE, and MR. JUSTICE MARSHALL join, dissenting.

[The Court today] disregards [the] need to construe an Act of Congress so as to avoid, if possible, passing upon its constitutionality. It is apparent that the constitutional questions raised by the order of the Commission in this case are substantial. Before deciding them, we should be certain that it is necessary to do so.

[T]he clear holding of *Hamling* is that "indecent" as used in 18 U.S.C. § 1461 [prohibiting the mailing of "obscene, lewd, lascivious, indecent, filthy or vile article[s]"] has the same meaning as "obscene" as that term was defined in the *Miller* case.

Nothing requires the conclusion that the word "indecent" has any meaning in § 1464 other than that ascribed to the same word in § 1461. Indeed, although the legislative history is largely silent, such indications as there are support the view that §§ 1461 and 1464 should be construed similarly. * * *

I would hold, therefore, that Congress intended by using the word "indecent" in § 1464, to prohibit nothing more than obscene speech. Under that reading of the statute, the Commission's order in this case was not authorized, and on that basis I would affirm the judgment [below].

---

8. Under the approach taken by my Brother Powell, the availability of broadcasts *about* groups whose members comprise such audiences might also be affected. Both news broadcasts about activities involving these groups and public affairs broadcasts about their concerns are apt to contain interviews, statements, or remarks by group leaders and members which may contain offensive language to an extent my Brother Powell finds unacceptable.

Notes and Questions

1. *Implications for broadcasting.* Consider Krattenmaker & Powe, *Televised Violence: First Amendment Principles and Social Science Theory,* 64 Va.L. Rev. 1123, 1228 (1978): *Pacifica* "marks the first time any theory other than scarcity has received the official imprimatur of the Court. [S]carcity could not have authorized the result in *Pacifica* because regardless of whether one thinks the incredible abundance of radio stations in the United States (and especially in New York City) is insufficient, scarcity supports adding voices not banning them." What is the significance of the Court's comment that "the broadcast media have established a uniquely pervasive presence in the lives of all Americans"? Consider Brenner, *Censoring the Airwaves: The Supreme Court's Pacifica Decision* in Free But Regulated: Conflicting Traditions in Media Law 175, 177 & 79 (1982): "[N]ewspapers, drive-in movies, direct mail advertisements and imprinted T-shirts are media that have also 'established a uniquely pervasive presence' in our lives, in and out of [home]. Offhand comments about broadcasting enjoying 'the most limited' First Amendment protection—What of comic books? Playing cards? Chinese cookie fortunes?—are not simply harmless baffle; they constitute Delphic pronouncements made at a watershed period in the development of electronic media."

Is the Court suggesting that the broadcast media are uniquely powerful? If so, should that factor cut for or against government regulation? See Powe, *"Or of the [Broadcast] Press,"* 55 Tex.L.Rev. 39, 58–62 (1976). Does the *Pacifica* rationale support regulation of sex and violence on television, of "offensive" commercials, of advertising directed toward children? Does it have implications for the regulation of cable?

2. *Cohen and Pacifica.* Consider Tribe, *American Constitutional Law* 66 n. 51 (1979 Supp.): "In order to make *Cohen* illustrate his theme that context is everything, Justice Stevens reinterprets *Cohen,* casting it in the mold of a 'fighting words' case [referring to fn. 25]. [But in] *Cohen* what was clear to Harlan was that California did not arrest [petitioner] to preserve the peace [but] to cleanse public debate of offensive language, something Harlan was certain the state could not safely be entrusted to do. Justice Stevens cannot reasonably claim that his opinion has been misread if one concludes that his position is essentially California's claim against Cohen, albeit limited to the airwaves."

But Farber, *Civilizing Public Disclosure: An Essay on Professor Bickel, Justice Harlan, and the Enduring Significance of Cohen v. California,* 1980 Duke L.J. 283, 294, maintains that *Cohen* has "little relevance" to *Pacifica*: The FCC's justifications for regulating speech in *Pacifica* "turned on the context of the midafternoon broadcast, whereas Justice Harlan found that none of the possible context-related justifications were properly presented in *Cohen.* Instead, the issue [Harlan] did find to be properly presented—and therefore the only issue he decided—was whether the state, acting as a paternalistic guardian of public morality, could ban the use of certain words in *all* contexts. Because *Pacifica* dealt with context and *Cohen* dealt only with content, *Cohen* contributes little to the issue presented in *Pacifica.*"

3. "Offensive speech," observes 92 Harv.L.Rev. 156 (1978), "is a method of precisely communicating the strength of feeling with which an idea is held. In *Pacifica,* for example, Justice Powell was particularly disturbed that indecent words were used in steady repetition to achieve a verbal shock treatment. Yet,

precisely that sort of treatment could be seen as a necessary part of Carlin's attempt to satirize society's attitudes toward essentially harmless words."

4. "The strangest thing about the Court's decision in *Pacifica,*" comments Tribe, supra, at 64–65, "was that no one could suppose that children were listening to WBAI [the radio station that broadcast the Carlin monologue] that October afternoon in 1973. WBAI is a listener-supported station that carries no ads, does not play 'top forty' records, and directs its programming at a distinctly adult, left-to-radical, upper-middle class audience. [S]tudies show that virtually no children listen to any radio station whatsoever at that hour on a weekday for the reason that most children are then in school. That left at risk the two-, three-, and four-year olds who weren't busy watching Sesame Street or playing with their toys.

"[T]he record showed that only one person complained—an unidentified citizen who, while driving in his car with his son, tuned into WBAI, heard Carlin's monologue, and apparently chose not to turn the dial further."

B. "PUBLIC" BROADCASTERS AND EDITORIALS

FCC v. LEAGUE OF WOMEN VOTERS, ___ U.S. ___, 104 S.Ct. 3106, 82 L.Ed.2d 278 (1984): The Public Broadcasting Act of 1967 (Act), a keystone of Congress' program to sponsor independent sources of broadcast programming as an alternative to commercial broadcasting, established the Corporation for Public Broadcasting (CPB), a nonprofit corporation authorized to disburse federal funds to noncommercial TV and radio stations in support of station operations and educational programming. Section 399 of the Act forbids any noncommercial educational station that receives a grant from the CPB to "engage in editorializing." Appellees (Pacifica Foundation, a nonprofit corporation that owns and operates several stations that receive grants from the CPB; the League of Women Voters of California; and a Congressman who regularly listened to and viewed public broadcasting) challenged the constitutionality of § 399. The federal district court granted summary judgment for appellees. A 5–4 majority, per BRENNAN, J. agreed, concluding that "the specific interests sought to be advanced by § 399's ban on editorializing are either not sufficiently substantial or are not served in a sufficiently limited manner to justify the substantial abridgement of important journalistic freedoms which the First Amendment jealously protects":

"Section 399 plainly operates to restrict the expression of editorial opinion on matters of public importance, and, as we have repeatedly explained, communication of this kind is entitled to the most exacting degree of First Amendment protection. Were a similar ban on editorializing applied to newspapers and magazines, we would not hesitate to strike it down as violative of the First Amendment. But, as the Government correctly notes, because broadcast regulation involves unique considerations, our cases have not followed precisely the same approach that we have applied to other media and have never gone so far as to demand that such regulations serve 'compelling' governmental interests. * * * [11] * * * [13].

11. [The] prevailing rationale for broadcast regulation based on spectrum scarcity has come under increasing criticism in recent years. Critics, including the incumbent Chairman of the FCC, charge that with the advent of cable and satellite television technology, communities now have access to such a wide variety of stations that the scarcity doctrine is obsolete. See, *e.g.,* Fowler & Brenner, *A Marketplace Approach to Broadcast Regulation,* 60 Tex.L.Rev. 207, 221–226 (1982).

13. See note 13 on page 620.

"[A]lthough the broadcasting industry plainly operates under restraints not imposed upon other media, the thrust of these restrictions has generally been to secure the public's First Amendment interest in receiving a balanced presentation of views on diverse matters of public concern. As a result of these restrictions, of course, the absolute freedom to advocate one's own positions without also presenting opposing viewpoints—a freedom enjoyed, for example, by newspaper publishers and soapbox orators—is denied to broadcasters. But, as our cases attest, these restrictions have been upheld only when we were satisfied that the restriction is narrowly tailored to further a substantial governmental interest, such as ensuring adequate and balanced coverage of public issues.

"[Before] assessing the government's proffered justifications for the statute, however, two central features of the ban against editorializing must be examined, since they help to illuminate the importance of the First Amendment interests at stake in this case.

"First, the restriction imposed by § 399 is specifically directed at a form of speech—namely, the expression of editorial opinion—that lies at the heart of First Amendment protection. In construing the reach of the statute, the FCC has explained that 'although the use of noncommercial educational broadcast facilities by licensees, their management or those speaking on their behalf for the propagation of the licensee's own views on public issues is not permitted, such prohibition should not be construed to inhibit any *other* presentations on controversial issues of public importance.' (emphasis added). The Commission's interpretation of § 399 simply highlights the fact that what the statute forecloses is the expression of editorial opinion on 'controversial issues of public importance.' As we recently reiterated in *NAACP v. Claiborne Hardware Co.* [p. 634 infra] 'expression on public issues "has always rested on the highest rung of the hierarchy of First Amendment values." '

"[T]he special place of the editorial in our First Amendment jurisprudence simply reflects the fact that the press, of which the broadcasting industry is indisputably a part, carries out a historic, dual responsibility in our society of reporting information and of bringing critical judgment to bear on public affairs. [Because] § 399 appears to restrict precisely that form of speech which the Framers of the Bill of Rights were most anxious to protect—speech that is 'indispensable to the discovery and spread of political truth'—we must be especially careful in weighing the interests that are asserted in support of this restriction and in assessing the precision with which the ban is crafted.

"Second, the scope of § 399's ban is defined solely on the basis of the content of the suppressed speech. A wide variety of non-editorial speech 'by licensees, their management or those speaking on their behalf,' is plainly not prohibited by

We are not prepared, however, to reconsider our long-standing approach without some signal from Congress or the FCC that technological developments have advanced so far that some revision of the system of broadcast regulation may be required.

13. [*Pacifica*] is consistent with the approach taken in our other broadcast cases. There, the Court focused on certain physical characteristics of broadcasting—specifically, that the medium's uniquely pervasive presence renders impossible any prior warning for those listeners who may be offended by indecent language, and, second, that the case with which children may gain access to the medium, especially during daytime hours, creates a substantial risk that they may be exposed to

such offensive expression without parental supervision. The governmental interest in reduction of those risks through Commission regulation of the timing and character of such "indecent broadcasting" was thought sufficiently substantial to outweigh the broadcaster's First Amendment interest in controlling the presentation of its programming. In this case, by contrast, we are faced not with indecent expression, but rather with expression that is at the core of First Amendment protections, and no claim is made by the Government that the expression of editorial opinion by noncommercial stations will create a substantial "nuisance" of the kind addressed in *Pacifica*.

§ 399. Examples of such permissible forms of speech include daily announcements of the station's program schedule or over-the-air appeals for contributions from listeners. Consequently, in order to determine whether a particular statement by station management constitutes an 'editorial' proscribed by § 399, enforcement authorities must necessarily examine the content of the message that is conveyed to determine whether the views expressed concern 'controversial issues of public importance.'

"[Section 399] singles out noncommercial broadcasters and denies them the right to address their chosen audience on matters of public importance. Thus, in enacting § 399 Congress appears to have sought, in much the same way that the New York Public Service Commission had attempted through the regulation of utility company bill inserts struck down in *Consolidated Edison* [p. 686 infra], to limit discussion of controversial topics and thus to shape the agenda for 'public debate. Since, as we observed in *Consolidated Edison*, '[t]he First Amendment's hostility to content-based regulation extends not only to restrictions on particular viewpoints, but also to prohibition of an entire topic,' we must be particularly wary in assessing § 399 to determine whether it reflects an impermissible attempt 'to allow the government [to] control [the] search for political truth.'

"In seeking to defend the prohibition on editorializing imposed by § 399, the Government urges that the statute was aimed at preventing two principal threats to the overall success of [the Act]. According to this argument, the ban was necessary, first, to protect noncommercial educational broadcasting stations from being coerced, as a result of federal financing, into becoming vehicles for government propagandizing or the objects of governmental influence; and, second, to keep these stations from becoming convenient targets for capture by private interest groups wishing to express their own partisan viewpoints. By seeking to safeguard the public's right to a balanced presentation of public issues through the prevention of either governmental or private bias, these objectives are, of course, broadly consistent with the goals identified in our earlier broadcast regulation cases. But, in sharp contrast to the restrictions upheld in *Red Lion* or in *CBS v. FCC*, which left room for editorial discretion and simply required broadcast editors to grant others access to the microphone, § 399 directly prohibits the broadcaster from speaking out on public issues even in a balanced and fair manner. The Government insists, however, that the hazards posed in the 'special' circumstances of noncommercial educational broadcasting are so great that § 399 is an indispensable means of preserving the public's First Amendment interests. We disagree.

"[A]n examination of both the overall legislative scheme established by the 1967 Act and the character of public broadcasting demonstrates that the interest asserted by the Government is not substantially advanced by § 399. First, to the extent that federal financial support creates a risk that stations will lose their independence through the bewitching power of governmental largesse, the elaborate structure established by the Act already operates to insulate local stations from governmental interference. Congress not only mandated that the new Corporation for Public Broadcasting would have a private, bipartisan structure, but also imposed a variety of important limitations on its powers. The Corporation was prohibited from owning or operating any station, it was required to adhere strictly to a standard of 'objectivity and balance' in disbursing federal funds to local stations, and it was prohibited from contributing to or otherwise supporting any candidate for office.

"The Act also established a second layer of protections which serve to protect the stations from governmental coercion and interference. Thus, in addition to requiring the Corporation to operate so as to 'assure the maximum freedom [of local stations] from interference with or control of program content or other activities,' the Act expressly forbids 'any department, agency, officer, or employee of the United States [from] exercis[ing] any direction, supervision, or control over educational television or radio broadcasting, or over the Corporation or any of its [grantees].' Subsequent amendments to the Act have confirmed Congress' commitment to the principle that because local stations are the 'bedrock of the system,' their independence from governmental interference and control must be fully guaranteed.

"[T]he manifest imprecision of the ban imposed by § 399 reveals that its proscription is not sufficiently tailored to the harms it seeks to prevent to justify its substantial interference with broadcasters' speech. Section 399 includes within its grip a potentially infinite variety of speech, most of which would not be related in any way to governmental affairs, political candidacies or elections. Indeed, the breadth of editorial commentary is as wide as human imagination permits. But the Government never explains how, say, an editorial by local station management urging improvements in a town's parks or museums will so infuriate Congress or other Federal officials that the future of public broadcasting will be imperiled unless such editorials are suppressed. Nor is it explained how the suppression of editorials alone serves to reduce the risk of governmental retaliation and interference when it is clear that station management is fully able to broadcast controversial views so long as such views are not labelled as its own.

"The Government appears to recognize these flaws in § 399, because it focuses instead on the suggestion that the source of governmental influence may well be state and local governments, many of which have established public broadcasting commissions that own and operate local noncommercial educational stations. The ban on editorializing is all the more necessary with respect to these stations, the argument runs, because the management of such stations will be especially likely to broadcast only editorials that are favorable to the state or local authorities that hold the purse strings. The Government's argument, however, proves too much. First, § 399's ban applies to the many private noncommercial community organizations that own and operate stations that are not controlled in any way by state or local government. Second, the legislative history of the Act clearly indicates that Congress was concerned with 'assur[ing] complete freedom from any *Federal Government influence*' (emphasis added). Consistently with this concern, Congress refused to create any federally owned stations and it expressly forbid the CPB to own or operate any television or radio stations. By contrast, although Congress was clearly aware in 1967 that many noncommercial educational stations were owned by state and local governments, it did not hesitate to extend Federal assistance to such stations, it imposed no special requirements to restrict state or local control over these stations, and, indeed, it ensured through the structure of the Act that these stations would be as insulated from Federal interference as the wholly private stations.

"Finally, although the Government certainly has a substantial interest in ensuring that the audiences of noncommercial stations will not be led to think that the broadcaster's editorials reflect the official view of the government, this interest can be fully satisfied by less restrictive means that are readily available. To address this important concern, Congress could simply require public broadcasting stations to broadcast a disclaimer every time they editorialize which would state that the editorial represents only the view of the station's management and does not in any way represent the views of the Federal Government or any of the station's other sources of funding. Such a disclaimer—similar to those often used in commercial and noncommercial programming of a controversial nature—would effectively and directly communicate to the audience that the editorial reflected only the views of the station rather than those of the government. * * *

"In sum, § 399's broad ban on all editorializing by every station that receives CPB funds far exceeds what is necessary to protect against the risk of governmental interference or to prevent the public from assuming that editorials by public broadcasting stations represent the official view of government. The regulation impermissibly sweeps within its prohibition a wide range of speech by wholly private stations on topics that do not take a directly partisan stand or that have nothing whatever to do with federal, state or local government.

"Assuming that the Government's second asserted interest in preventing noncommercial stations from becoming a 'privileged outlet for the political and ideological opinions of station owners and management' is legitimate, the substantiality of this asserted interest is dubious. [If] it is true, as the government contends, that noncommercial stations remain free, despite § 399, to broadcast a wide variety of controversial views through their power to control program selection, to select which persons will be interviewed, and to determine how news reports will be presented, then it seems doubtful that § 399 can fairly be said to advance any genuinely substantial governmental interest in keeping controversial or partisan opinions from being aired by noncommercial stations. Indeed, since the very same opinions that cannot be expressed by the station's management may be aired so long as they are communicated by a commentator or by a guest appearing at the invitation of the station during an interview, § 399 clearly 'provides only ineffective and remote support for the government's purpose.' *Central Hudson.*

"In short, § 399 does not prevent the use of noncommercial stations for the presentation of partisan views on controversial matters; instead, it merely bars a station from specifically communicating such views on its own behalf or on behalf of its management. * * *

"Finally, the public's interest in preventing public broadcasting stations from becoming forums for lopsided presentations of narrow partisan positions is already secured by a variety of other regulatory means that intrude far less drastically upon the 'journalistic freedom' of noncommercial broadcasters. *CBS v. DNC.* The requirements of the FCC's fairness doctrine, for instance, which apply to commercial and noncommercial stations alike, ensure that such editorializing would maintain a reasonably balanced and fair presentation of controversial issues. Thus, even if the management of a non-commercial educational station were inclined to seek to further only its own partisan views when editorializing, it simply could not do so. * * *

"In conclusion, we emphasize that our disposition of this case rests upon a narrow proposition. We do not hold that the Congress or the FCC are without power to regulate the content, timing, or character of speech by noncommercial educational broadcasting stations. Rather, we hold only that the specific interests sought to be advanced by § 399's ban on editorializing are either not sufficiently substantial or are not served in a sufficiently limited manner to justify the substantial abridgement of important journalistic freedoms which the First Amendment jealously protects." [a]

a. The Court also held that § 399 cannot be justified on the basis of Congress' spending power as simply determining that Congress will not subsidize public broadcasting station

REHNQUIST, J., joined by Burger, C.J., and White, J., dissented: "All but three paragraphs of the Court's lengthy opinion in this case are devoted to the development of a scenario in which the government appears as the 'Big Bad Wolf,' and appellee Pacifica as 'Little Red Riding Hood.' In the Court's scenario the Big Bad Wolf cruelly forbids Little Red Riding Hood from taking to her grandmother some of the food that she is carrying in her basket. Only three paragraphs are used to delineate a truer picture of the litigants, wherein it appears that some of the food in the basket was given to Little Red Riding Hood by the Big Bad Wolf himself, and that the Big Bad Wolf had told Little Red Riding Hood in advance that if she accepted his food she would have to abide by his conditions. Congress in enacting § 399 of the Public Broadcasting Act has simply determined that public funds shall not be used to subsidize noncommercial, educational broadcasting stations which engage in 'editorializing' or which support or oppose any political candidate. I do not believe that anything in the First Amendment [prevents] Congress from choosing to spend public monies in that manner. Perhaps a more appropriate analogy than that of Little Red Riding Hood and the Big Bad Wolf is that of Faust and Mephistopheles; Pacifica, well aware of § 399's condition on its receipt of public money, nonetheless accepted the public money and now seeks to avoid the conditions which Congress legitimately has attached to receipt of that funding. * * *

"The Court's three-paragraph discussion of why § 399, repeatedly reexamined and retained by Congress, violates the First Amendment is to me utterly unpersuasive. Congress has rationally determined that the bulk of the taxpayers whose monies provide the funds for grants by the CPB would prefer not to see the management of local educational stations promulgate its own private views on the air at taxpayer expense. Accordingly Congress simply has decided not to subsidize stations which engage in that activity. * * *

"The Court seems to believe that Congress actually subsidizes editorializing only if a station uses federal money specifically to cover the expenses that the Court believes can be isolated as editorializing expenses. But to me the Court's approach ignores economic reality. CPB's unrestricted grants are used for salaries, training, equipment, promotion, etc.—financial expenditures which benefit all aspects of a station's programming, including management's editorials. Given the impossibility of compartmentalizing programming expenses in any meaningful way, it seems clear to me that the only effective means for preventing the use of public monies to subsidize the airing of management's views is for Congress to ban a subsidized station from all on-the-air editorializing. Under the Court's view, if Congress decided to withhold a 100% subsidy from a station which editorializes, that decision would be constitutional under the principle affirmed in our *Taxation With Representation* decision. Surely on these facts, the distinction between the government's power to withhold a 100% subsidy, on the one hand, and the 20–30% subsidy involved here, on the other hand, is simply trivialization.

"This is not to say that the government may attach *any* condition to its largess; it is only to say that when the government is simply exercising its power

editorials. It deemed the government's reliance on *Regan v. Taxation With Representation*, p. 552 supra, misplaced. Here, "unlike the situation faced by the charitable organization in *Taxation With Representation*, a noncommercial educational station that receives only 1% of its overall income from CPB grants is barred absolutely from all editorializing. Therefore, in contrast to the appellee in *Taxation With Representation*, such a station is not able to segregate its activities according to the source of its funding. The station has no way of limiting the use of its Federal funds to all non-editorializing activities, and, more importantly, it is barred from using even wholly private funds to finance its editorial activity."

to allocate its own public funds, we need only find that the condition imposed has a rational relationship to Congress' purpose in providing the subsidy and that it is not primarily 'aimed at the suppression of dangerous ideas.' In this case Congress' prohibition is directly related to its purpose in providing subsidies for public broadcasting, and it is plainly rational for Congress to have determined that taxpayer monies should not be used to subsidize management's views or to pay for management's exercise of partisan politics. Indeed, it is entirely rational for Congress to have wished to avoid the appearance of government sponsorship of a particular view or a particular political candidate. Furthermore, Congress' prohibition is strictly neutral. In no sense can it be said that Congress has prohibited only editorial views of one particular ideological bent. Nor has it prevented public stations from airing programs, documentaries, interviews, etc. dealing with controversial subjects, so long as management itself does not expressly endorse a particular viewpoint. And Congress has not prevented station management from communicating its own views on those subjects through any medium other than subsidized public broadcasting.

" * * * I find this case entirely different from the so-called 'unconstitutional condition' cases, wherein the Court has stated that the government 'may not deny a benefit to a person on a basis that infringes his constitutionally protected interests—especially his interest in freedom of speech.' *Perry v. Sinderman,* 408 U.S. 593, 92 S.Ct. 2694, 33 L.Ed.2d 570 (1972). In those cases the suppressed speech was not content-neutral in the same sense as here, and in those cases, there is at best only a strained argument that the legislative purpose of the condition imposed was to avoid *subsidizing* the prohibited speech. *Speiser v. Randall* [p. 636 infra] is illustrative of the difference. In that case California's decision to deny its property tax exemption to veterans who would not declare that they would not work to overthrow the government was plainly directed at suppressing what California regarded as speech of a dangerous content. And the condition imposed was so unrelated to the benefit to be conferred that it is difficult to argue that California's property tax exemption actually subsidized the dangerous speech.

"Here, in my view, Congress has rationally concluded that the bulk of taxpayers whose monies provide the funds for grants by the CPB would prefer not to see the management of public stations engage in editorializing or the endorsing or opposing of political candidates. Because Congress' decision to enact § 399 is a rational exercise of its spending powers and strictly neutral, I would hold that nothing in the First Amendment makes it unconstitutional." [b]

In a separate dissent, STEVENS, J., protested: "By enacting the statutory provision that the Court invalidates today, a sophisticated group of legislators expressed a concern about the potential impact of government funds on pervasive and powerful organs of mass communication. One need not have heard the raucous voice of Adolph Hitler over Radio Berlin to appreciate the importance of that concern.

"As Justice White correctly notes, the statutory prohibitions against editorializing and candidate endorsements rest on the same foundation. In my opinion that foundation is far stronger than merely 'a rational basis' and it is not weakened by the fact that it is buttressed by other provisions that are also designed to avoid the insidious evils of government propaganda favoring particu-

---

b. In a brief dissenting statement, White, J., observed: "Believing that the editorializing and candidate endorsement proscription stand or fall together and being confident that Con- gress may condition use of its funds on abstaining from political endorsements, I join Justice Rehnquist's dissenting opinion."

lar points of view. The quality of the interest in maintaining government neutrality in the free market of ideas—of avoiding subtle forms of censorship and propaganda—outweigh the impact on expression that results from this statute. Indeed, by simply terminating or reducing funding, Congress could curtail much more expression with no risk whatever of a constitutional transgression.

"[Because] the government subsidizes its broadcasts, a federal statute prohibits Pacifica from broadcasting its views—labeled as such—via the radio stations it operates. That statute [§ 399] now provides: 'No noncommercial educational broadcasting station which receives a grant from the Corporation for Public Broadcasting under subpart C of this part may engage in editorializing. No noncommercial educational broadcasting station may support or oppose any candidate for public office.'

"[In] its analysis of the case, the Court assumes that the ban on political endorsements is severable from the first section and that it may be constitutional.[3] In view of the fact that the major difference between the ban on political endorsements is based on the content of the speech, it is apparent that the entire rationale of the Court's opinion rests on the premise that it may be permissible to predicate a statutory restriction on candidate endorsements on the difference between the content of that kind of speech and the content of other expressions of editorial opinion.

"The Court does not tell us whether speech that endorses political candidates is more or less worthy of protection than other forms of editorializing, but it does iterate and reiterate the point that 'the expression of editorial opinion' is a special kind of communication that 'is entitled to the most exacting degree of First Amendment protection.'

"Neither the fact that the statute regulates only one kind of speech, nor the fact that editorial opinion has traditionally been an important kind of speech, is sufficient to identify the character or the significance of the statute's impact on speech. Three additional points are relevant. First, the statute does not prohibit Pacifica from expressing its opinion through any avenue except the radio stations for which it receives federal financial support. It eliminates the subsidized channel of communication as a forum for Pacifica itself, and thereby deprives Pacifica of an advantage it would otherwise have over other speakers, but it does not exclude Pacifica from the marketplace for ideas. Second, the statute does not curtail the expression of opinion by individual commentators who participate in Pacifica's programs. The only comment that is prohibited is a statement that Pacifica agrees or disagrees with the opinions that others may express on its programs. Third, and of greatest significance for me, the statutory restriction is completely neutral in its operation—it prohibits all editorials without any distinction being drawn concerning the subject matter or the point of view that might be expressed.[5]

---

3. The Court actually raises the wrong severability issue. The serious question in this regard is whether the entire public funding scheme is severable from the prohibition on editorializing and political endorsements. The legislative history of the statute indicates the strength of the congressional aversion to these practices. [The] line between education and indoctrination is a subtle one, and it is one Congress did not want these publicly funded stations to cross. [The] majority may view the congressional concerns—potential governmental censorship, giving louder voices to a privileged few station owners, and the use of taxpayer funds to subsidize expression of viewpoints with which the taxpayers may not agree—as insufficiently weighty to justify the statute, but Congress clearly thought they were weighty enough.

5. Section 399's ban on editorializing is a content based restriction on speech, but not in

"The statute does not violate the fundamental principle that the citizen's right to speak may not be conditioned upon the sovereign's agreement with what the speaker intends to say. On the contrary, the statute was enacted in order to protect that very principle—to avoid the risk that some speakers will be rewarded or penalized for saying things that appeal to—or are offensive to—the sovereign.[7] The interests the statute is designed to protect are interests that underlie the First Amendment itself.

"In my judgment the interest in keeping the Federal Government out of the propaganda arena is of overriding importance. That interest is of special importance in the field of electronic communication, not only because that medium is so powerful and persuasive, but also because it is the one form of communication that is licensed by the Federal Government. When the Government already has great potential power over the electronic media, it is surely legitimate to enact statutory safeguards to make sure that it does not cross the threshold that separates neutral regulation from the subsidy of partisan opinion.

"The Court does not question the validity of the basic interests served by § 399. Instead, it suggests that the statute does not substantially serve those interests because [the Act] operates in many other respects to insulate local stations from governmental interference. In my view, that is an indication of nothing more than the strength of the governmental interest involved here—

the sense that the majority implies. The majority speaks of "editorial opinion" as if it were some sort of special species of opinion, limited to issues of public importance. The majority confuses the typical content of editorials with the meaning of editorial itself. An editorial is, of course, a statement of the *management's* opinion on any topic imaginable. The Court asserts that what the statute "forecloses is the expression of editorial opinion on 'controversial issues of public importance.' " The statute is not so limited. The content which is prohibited is that the station is not permitted to state its opinion with respect to any matter. In short, it may not be an on-the-air advocate if it accepts government funds for its broadcasts. The prohibition on editorializing is not directed at any particular message a station might wish to convey. Unlike the Court, I am not troubled by the fact that the stations are allowed to make "daily announcements of the station's program schedule or over-the-air appeals for contributions from listeners," for it is quite plain that this statute is not directed at curtailing expression of particular points of view on controversial issues; it is designed to assure to the extent possible that the station does not become a vehicle for government propaganda.

Paradoxically, section 399 is later attacked by the majority as essentially being underinclusive because it does not prohibit "controversial" national programming that is often aired with substantial federal funding. Here the Court recognizes that the ban imposed by § 399 "is plainly not directed at the potentially controversial content of such programs" which only demonstrates that it is not directed at the substance of communication at all. Next, § 399's ban on editorializing is attacked

by the majority on overinclusive grounds—because it is content-neutral—since it prohibits a "potentially infinite variety of speech, most of which would not be related in any way to governmental affairs, political candidacies or elections." Hence, while earlier the majority attacked § 399 as being content-based, it is now attacked as being non-content based, applying to expressions of opinion—such as "urging improvements in a town's parks or museums"—which does not pose, in the Court's view at least, a realistic danger of governmental interference because of its content.

7. It is ironic indeed that the majority states that it must be particularly wary in assessing § 399 "to determine whether it reflects an impermissible attempt 'to allow the Government [to] control [the] search for political truth' ", given that the very object of § 399 is to prevent the Government from controlling the search for political truth.

Moreover, the statute will also protect the listener's interest in not having his tax payments used to finance the advocacy of causes he opposes. The majority gives extremely short shrift to the Government's interest in minimizing the use of taxpayer monies to promote private views with which the taxpayers may disagree. The Court briefly observes that the taxpayers do not have a constitutionally protected right to enjoin such expenditures and then leaps to the conclusion that given the fact that the funding scheme itself is not unconstitutional, this interest cannot be used to support the statute at issue here. The conclusion manifestly does not follow from the premise, and this interest is plainly legitimate and significant.

Congress enacted many safeguards because the evil to be avoided was so grave. Organs of official propaganda are antithetical to this nation's heritage and Congress understandably acted with great caution in this area. It is no answer to say that the other statutory provisions 'substantially reduce the risk of government interference with the editorial judgments of the local stations without restricting the stations' ability to speak out on matters of public concern.' The other safeguards protect the stations from interference with judgments that they will necessarily make in selecting programming, but those judgments are relatively amorphous. No safeguard is foolproof; and the fact that funds are dispensed according to largely 'objective' criteria certainly is no guarantee. Individuals must always make judgments in allocating funds, and pressure can be exerted in subtle ways as well as through outright fund-cutoffs.

"Members of Congress, not members of the Judiciary, live in the world of politics. When they conclude that there is a real danger of political considerations influencing the dispensing of this money and that this provision is necessary to insulate grantees from political pressures in addition to the other safeguards, that judgment is entitled to our respect."

Notes and Questions

1. *The public/private distinction.* Is there a justification for permitting editorials by commercial broadcasters—but not by noncommercial broadcasters? Public broadcasters are given dollar grants and free, but restricted use of the airwaves (no commercials); commercial broadcasters are given free use of the airwaves and the right to charge advertisers for access. Which is the greater subsidy? It is wrong to characterize commercial broadcasters as unsubsidized and "private" argues Shiffrin, *Book Review,* 96 Harv.L.Rev. 1745, 1753–54 (1983): Commercial broadcasters "after all, are given an in-kind subsidy (relatively unrestricted use of the governmentally controlled airwaves) that is vastly greater than the puny amounts given to public broadcasters; and they are licensed by the government as trustees to manage public resources. Moreover, the government has substantially influenced the content of messages on the 'private' stations. Television in America was organized by government as an enterprise financed by commercial [advertisers]. The result of such government structuring is a society in which people are taught in their homes, through a government subsidized medium, to be acquisitive consumers. [There] may be a case for considering 'private' broadcasters nongovernmental for purposes of state action doctrine, but probing government participation in the formulation of basic values requires rethinking the public-private distinction."

2. Can Congress prohibit public broadcasters from endorsing candidates? Commercial broadcasters? Organizations receiving tax deductible contributions? See Sec. 6, I (supra).

3. How is the Court's test related to the test in *Central Hudson,* p. 454 supra; in *Vincent,* p. 583 supra? Is the Court's test justified by anything in *Red Lion, CBS,* or *Pacifica*? Is the Court's refusal in fn. 11 to reconsider the scarcity rationale an "abdication of its constitutional responsibility." Consider Note, 98 Harv.L.Rev. 205, 216: "If it chooses to recognize that physical scarcity is now no more than a myth, the Court will find itself in possession of a valuable opportunity to adapt constitutional law to economic reality. The special status of broadcasting might then be seen not as an aberration, but as the foundation of a first amendment theory that addresses the economic phenomenon of a modern

communications industry that excludes most Americans from the public debate on which democracy depends."

SECTION 9. THE RIGHT NOT TO SPEAK, THE RIGHT TO ASSOCIATE, AND THE RIGHT NOT TO ASSOCIATE

NAACP v. Alabama ex rel Patterson, 357 U.S. 449, 78 S.Ct. 1163, 2 L.Ed.2d 1488 (1958), per Harlan, J., held that the first amendment barred Alabama from compelling production of NAACP membership lists. The opinion used the phrase freedom of association repeatedly, "elevat[ing] freedom of association to an independent right, possessing an equal status with the other rights specifically enumerated in the first amendment." Emerson, *Freedom of Association and Freedom of Expression*, 74 Yale L.J. 1, 2 (1964).

From the materials on advocacy of illegal action (Sec. 1, I supra) onward, it has been evident that individuals have rights to join with others for expressive purposes. This section explores other aspects of the freedom to associate and its corollary, the freedom not to associate. First, we explore cases which the Court bases on a right not to speak, but might better be understood as establishing a right not to be associated with particular ideas. Second, we explore aspects of free association in the employment context—in particular the claims of employees not to be associated with a political party, or a union or its policies. Those claims are to some extent derived from the cases establishing a right not to be associated with particular ideas. Third, instead of persons resisting forced membership in a group, we confront a group resisting members.

Finally, freedom of association is used to resist government mandated disclosure. There is no general right not to speak. Every day witnesses are subpoenaed to testify against their will. But the first amendment affords a particularized right not to speak when forced disclosure would jeopardize important associational rights. One of the questions of the final part is whether press relationships with confidential sources are uniquely protected associations. That issue carries beyond the subject of the section and back to the question of whether the Constitution contemplates a special role for the institutional press.

I. THE RIGHT NOT TO BE ASSOCIATED WITH PARTICULAR IDEAS

> *"If there is any fixed star in our constitutional constellation, it is that no official, high or petty, can prescribe what shall be orthodox in politics, nationalism, religion, or other matter of opinion or force citizens to confess by word or act their faith therein."*

West Virginia State Bd. of Educ. v. Barnette, p. 763 infra (Jackson, J.) (upholding right of public school students to refuse to salute flag).

———

New Hampshire required that noncommercial vehicles bear license plates embossed with the state motto, "Live Free or Die." "Refus[ing] to be coerced by the State into advertising a slogan which I find morally, ethically, religiously and politically abhorrent," appellee, a Jehovah's Witness, covered up the motto on his license plate, a misdemeanor under state law. After being convicted several times of violating the misdemeanor statute, appellee sought federal injunctive and declaratory relief. WOOLEY v. MAYNARD, 430 U.S. 705, 97 S.Ct. 1428, 51 L.Ed.2d 752 (1977), per BURGER, C.J., held that requiring appellee to display the motto on his license plates violated his first amendment right to "refrain from speaking":

"[T]he freedom of thought protected by the First Amendment [includes] both the right to speak freely and the right to refrain from speaking at all. See *Barnette.* The right to speak and the right to refrain from speaking are complementary components of the broader concept of 'individual freedom of mind.' This is illustrated [by] *Miami Herald Publishing Co. v. Tornillo* [p. 589 infra], where we held unconstitutional a Florida statute placing an affirmative duty upon newspapers to publish the replies of political candidates whom they had criticized.

" * * * Compelling the affirmative act of a flag salute [the situation in *Barnette*] involved a more serious infringement upon personal liberties than the passive act of carrying the state motto on a license plate, but the difference is essentially one of degree. Here, as in *Barnette,* we are faced with a state measure which forces an individual as part of his daily life—indeed constantly while his automobile is in public view—to be an instrument for fostering public adherence to an ideological point of view he finds unacceptable. In doing so, the State 'invades the sphere of intellect and spirit which it is the purpose of the First Amendment [to] reserve from all official control.' *Barnette.*

"New Hampshire's statute in effect requires that appellees use their private property as a 'mobile billboard' for the State's ideological message—or suffer a penalty, as Maynard already has. [The] fact that most individuals agree with the thrust of [the] motto is not the test; most Americans also find the flag salute acceptable. The First Amendment protects the right of individuals to hold a point of view different from the majority and to refuse to foster, in the way New Hampshire commands, an idea they find morally objectionable."

The Court next considered whether "the State's countervailing interest" was "sufficiently compelling" to justify appellees to display the motto on their license plates. The two interests claimed by the state were (1) facilitating the identification of state license plates from those of similar colors of other states and (2) promoting "appreciation of history, state pride, [and] individualism." As to (1), the record revealed that these state license plates were readily distinguishable from others without reference to the state motto and, in any event, the state's purpose could be achieved by "less drastic means," i.e., by alternative methods less restrictive of first amendment freedoms. As to (2), where the State's interest is to communicate an "official view" as to history and state pride or to disseminate any other "ideology," "such interest cannot outweigh an individual's First Amendment right to avoid becoming the courier for such message."

REHNQUIST, J., joined by Blackmun, J., dissented, not only agreeing with what he called "the Court's implicit recognition that there is no protected 'symbolic speech' in this case," but maintaining that "that conclusion goes far to undermine the Court's ultimate holding that there is an element of protected expression here. The State has not forced appellees to 'say' anything; and it has not forced them to communicate ideas with nonverbal actions reasonably likened to 'speech,' such as wearing a lapel button promoting a political candidate or waving a flag as a symbolic gesture.[a] The State has simply required that *all*

---

a. Does *compelled* expression have to be understood by others to be "speech" or does it suffice that the Maynards *subjectively believed* that they were being forced to make an expression? See note 1 following this case.

noncommercial automobiles bear license tags with the state motto. [Appellees] have not been forced to affirm or reject that motto; they are simply required by the State [to] carry a state auto license tag for identification and registration purposes. [The] issue, unconfronted by the Court, is whether appellees, in displaying, as they are required to do, state license tags, the format of which is known to all as having been prescribed by the State, would be considered to be advocating political or ideological views.

"[H]aving recognized the rather obvious differences between [*Barnette* and this case], the Court does not explain why the same result should obtain. The Court suggests that the test is whether the individual is forced 'to be an instrument for fostering public adherence to an ideological point of view he finds unacceptable,' [but] these are merely conclusory words. [For] example, were New Hampshire to erect a multitude of billboards, each proclaiming 'Live Free or Die,' and tax all citizens for the cost of erection and maintenance, clearly the message would be 'fostered' by the individual citizen-taxpayers and just as clearly those individuals would be 'instruments' in that communication. Certainly, however, that case would not fall within the ambit of *Barnette*. In that case, as in this case, there is no *affirmation* of belief. For First Amendment principles to be implicated, the State must place the citizen in the position of either appearing to, or actually, 'asserting as true' the message. This was the focus of *Barnette*, and clearly distinguishes this case from that one." [b]

Notes and Questions

1. *Compelled expression vs. symbolic speech.* In *Wooley,* the lower court had held that by covering up the state motto on their automobile license plate, appellees were engaging in "symbolic speech," inferring the requisite intent to communicate from the use of reflective red tape to mask the motto—which not only called attention to the obscuring of the motto, but also conveyed disagreement with it. But the Supreme Court found it unnecessary to pass judgment on this issue, finding "more appropriate grounds" to affirm the judgment. It did, however, note that the symbolic speech claim was "substantially undermined" by a request for plates without the motto. Were appellees engaged in symbolic speech? If they were not, was *Wooley* correctly decided? Does the answer turn on whether *the state* was engaging in "speech"? Consider Note, 1977 Utah L.Rev. 797, 805–07: "While an objective approach is perhaps useful in finding 'symbolic speech,' [it] becomes suspect when applied to finding 'compelled expression.' [Utilizing] an objective test to find compelled expression defeats [one of the goals of the first amendment], for it forces an individual to express a view not his own. This situation clearly invades 'the sphere [which] it is the purpose of the First Amendment [to] reserve from all official control.' *Barnette*.

"Care must be exercised, however, to distinguish compelled symbolic expression from compelled acts which have no expressive conduct [e.g., compelling one to place a license plate on his car or number on his house]. To make this distinction, an objective test is correctly applied first to ascertain if the [government] intended to communicate [a] message. If it did, then a subjective test is properly applied to determine if the individual citizen was compelled to communicate that message. '[E]xpression' is a prerequisite of 'compelled expression,' and 'expression,' if symbolic in nature, is properly found by using an objective

---

b. White, J., joined by Blackmun and Rehnquist, JJ., dissented on procedural grounds.

test. Expression that is compelled, however, must be found subjectively if the guarantees of the first amendment are to have any real significance. In [*Wooley*], there can be little doubt that the state intended to communicate a message. [Thus], the majority properly applied a subjective test to find that such expression had been compelled in violation of the Maynards' first amendment rights."

2. *Compelling citizens through taxes.* The *Wooley* majority, notes Tribe, *American Constitutional Law* 590 n. 8 (1978), "silently accepted Justice Rehnquist's assertion that citizens of New Hampshire could be compelled through their taxes to pay for the cost of erecting and maintaining billboards proclaiming 'Live Free or Die.'" Should the majority have done so? Consider Tribe, supra: "Any notion that the very relation of taxpayer to government makes the refund argument inherently inapt seems refuted by positing a hypothetical instance in which, say, half the state budget [is spent] broadcasting 'Live Free or Die' across the countryside. In such a case, even assuming that this allocation of public resources does not itself violate the first and fourteenth amendments, the Supreme Court should probably conclude that the broadcast cannot constitutionally be financed with the involuntary contributions of persons who disagree with the message."

3. *Use of private property as a forum for the speech of others.* Appellees sought to enjoin a shopping center from denying them access to the center's central courtyard in order to solicit signatures from passersby for petitions opposing a U.N. resolution. The California Supreme Court held they were entitled to conduct their activity at the center, construing the state constitution to protect "speech and petitioning, reasonably exercised, in shopping centers, even [when] privately owned." PRUNEYARD SHOPPING CENTER v. ROBINS, 447 U.S. 74, 100 S.Ct. 2035, 64 L.Ed.2d 741 (1980) per REHNQUIST, J., affirmed, rejecting, inter alia, the argument, based on *Wooley,* that "a State may not constitutionally require an individual to participate in the dissemination of an ideological message by displaying it on his private property [so] that it be observed and read by the public":

"[In *Wooley*] the government itself prescribed the message, required it to be displayed openly on appellee's personal property that was used 'as part of his daily life,' and refused to permit him [to] cover up the motto even though the Court found that the display of the motto served no important state interest. Here, by contrast, there are a number of distinguishing factors. Most important, [the center] is not limited to the personal use of appellants, [but is] a business establishment that is open to the public to come and go as they please. The views expressed by members of the public in passing out pamphlets or seeking signatures for a petition thus will not likely be identified with those of the owner. Second, no specific message is dictated by the State to be displayed on appellants' property. There consequently is no danger of government discrimination for or against a particular message. Finally, [it appears] appellants can expressly disavow any connection with the message by simply posting signs in the area where the speakers or handbillers stand."

The Court also found appellants' reliance on *Barnette* and *Tornillo* misplaced: Unlike *Barnette,* appellants "are not [being] compelled to affirm their belief in any governmentally prescribed position or view, and they are free to publicly dissociate themselves from the views of the speakers or handbillers. [*Tornillo*] rests on the principle that the State cannot tell a newspaper what it must print. [There was also a danger in *Tornillo* that the invalidated statute requiring a newspaper to publish a political candidate's reply to previously published criticism would deter] editors from publishing controversial political [statements]. Thus, the statute was found to be an 'intrusion into the function of editors.' These concerns obviously are not present here."

POWELL, J., joined by White, J., concurring in part and in the judgment, agreed that "the owner of this shopping center has failed to establish a cognizable First Amendment claim," but maintained that "state action that transforms privately owned property into a forum for the expression of the public's views could raise serious First Amendment questions": "I do not believe that the result in *Wooley* would have changed had [the state] directed its citizens to place the slogan 'Live Free or Die' in their shop windows rather than on their automobiles. [The *Wooley* principle] on its face protects a person who refuses to allow use of his property as a market place for the ideas of others. [One] who has merely invited the public onto his property for commercial purposes cannot fairly be said to have relinquished his right 'to decline to be an instrument for fostering public adherence to an ideological point of view he finds unacceptable.' *Wooley*.

"[E]ven when [as here] no particular message is mandated by the State, First Amendment interests are affected by state action that forces a property owner to admit third-party speakers. [A] right of access [may be] no less intrusive than speech compelled by the State itself. For example, a law requiring that a newspaper permit others to use its columns imposes an unacceptable burden upon the newspaper's First Amendment right to select material for publication. *Tornillo*.

"[If] a state law mandated public access to the bulletin board of a freestanding store [or] small shopping center [or allowed soliciting or pamphleteering in the entrance area of a store] customers might well conclude that the messages reflect the view of the proprietor. [He] either could permit his customers to receive a mistaken impression [or] disavow the messages. Should he take the first course, he effectively has been compelled to affirm someone else's belief. Should he choose the second, he has been forced to speak when he would prefer to remain silent. In short, he has lost control over his freedom to speak or not to speak on certain issues. The mere fact that he is free to dissociate himself from the views expressed on his property cannot restore his 'right to refrain from speaking at all.' *Wooley*.

"A property owner may also be faced with speakers who wish to use his premises as a platform for views that he finds morally repugnant [, for example, a] minority-owned business confronted with leafleteers from the American Nazi Party or the Ku Klux Klan, [or] a church-operated enterprise asked to host demonstrations in favor of abortion. [The] strong emotions evoked by speech in such situations may virtually compel the proprietor to respond.

"The pressure to respond is particularly apparent [in the above cases, but] an owner who strongly objects to some of the causes to which the state-imposed right of access would extend may oppose ideological activities 'of *any* sort' that are not related to the purposes for which he has invited the public onto his property. See *Abood*. To require the owner to specify the particular ideas he finds objectionable enough to compel a response would force him to relinquish his 'freedom to maintain his own beliefs without public disclosure.' *Abood*. Thus, the right to control one's own speech may be burdened impermissibly even when listeners will not assume that the messages expressed on private property are those of the owner.

"[On this record] I cannot say that customers of this vast center [occupying several city blocks and containing more than 65 shops] would be likely to assume that appellees' limited speech activity expressed the views of [the center]. [Moreover, appellants] have not alleged that they object to [appellees' views, nor asserted] that some groups who reasonably might be expected to speak at [the center] will express views that are so objectionable as to require a response even when listeners will not mistake their source. [Thus,] I join the judgment of the Court, [but] I do not interpret our decision today as a blanket approval for state efforts to transform privately owned commercial property into public forums." [c]

4. *Economic pressure to engage in political activity.* NAACP v. CLAIBORNE HARDWARE CO., 458 U.S. 886, 102 S.Ct. 3409, 73 L.Ed.2d 1215 (1982): The NAACP had organized a consumer boycott whose principal objective was, according to the lower court, "to force the white merchants [to] bring pressure upon [the government] to grant defendants' demands or, in the alternative, to suffer economic ruin." Mississippi characterized the boycott as a tortious and malicious interference with the plaintiffs' businesses. The Court, per STEVENS, J., held that the NAACP boycott was immune from state prohibition: Although labor boycotts organized for economic ends had long been subject to prohibition, "speech to protest racial discrimination" was "essential political speech lying at the core of the First Amendment" and was therefore distinguishable. Is the boycott protected association? Are there association rights on the other side? Does the state have a legitimate interest in protecting merchants from being forced to support political change they would otherwise oppose? Cf. *NLRB v. Retail Store Employees Union,* 447 U.S. 607, 100 S.Ct. 2372, 65 L.Ed.2d 377 (1980) (ban on labor picketing encouraging consumer boycott of neutral employer upheld). Are the white merchants neutral? [d] For commentary, compare Harper, *The Consumer's Emerging Right to Boycott: NAACP v. Claiborne Hardware and Its Implications for American Labor Law,* 93 Yale L.J. 409 (1984) with Schwarzschild & Alexander, *Consumer Boycotts and Freedom of Association: Comment on a Recently Proposed Theory,* 22 San Diego L.Rev. 555 (1985).

5. *Orthodoxy and commercial advertising.* ZAUDERER v. OFFICE OF DISCIPLINARY COUNSEL, __ U.S. __, 105 S.Ct. 2265, 85 L.Ed.2d 652 (1985), per WHITE, J., upheld an Ohio requirement that an attorney advertising availability on a contingency basis must disclose in the ad that the clients would have to pay costs if their lawsuits should prove unsuccessful whenever that is the proposed financial arrangement: "[T]he interests at stake in this case are not of the same order as those discussed in *Wooley, Tornillo,* and *Barnette.* Ohio has not attempted to 'prescribe what shall be orthodox in politics, nationalism, religion, or other matters of opinion or force citizens to confess by word or act their faith therein.' The State has attempted only to prescribe what shall be orthodox in commercial advertising, and its prescription has taken the form of a requirement that appellant include in his advertising purely factual and uncontroversial [e] information about the terms under which his services will be available. Because the extension of First Amendment protection to commercial speech is justified principally by the value to consumers of the information such speech provides, *Virginia Pharmacy,* appellant's constitutionally protected interest in

c. For commentary, see Levinson, *Freedom of Speech and the Right of Access to Private Property Under State Constitutional Law* in Developments in State Constitutional Law 51 (McGraw ed. 1985).

d. Stevens, J., also argued in *Claiborne* that the boycott was protected as a right to

petition the government. Are the white merchants the government?

e. What if the requested disclosures are controverted? Do cigarette companies have first amendment grounds to resist forced disclosures?

not providing any particular factual information in his advertising is minimal.

* * *

"We do not suggest that disclosure requirements do not implicate the advertiser's First Amendment rights at all. We recognize that unjustified or unduly burdensome disclosure requirements might offend the First Amendment by chilling protected commercial speech. But we hold that an advertiser's rights are adequately protected as long as disclosure requirements are reasonably related to the State's interest in preventing deception of consumers."

The Court stated that the first amendment interests "implicated by disclosure requirements are substantially weaker than those at stake when speech is actually suppressed." Accordingly it rejected any requirement that the advertisement in question be shown to be deceptive absent the disclosure or that the state meet a "least restrictive means" analysis.

BRENNAN, J., joined by Marshall, J., dissenting on this issue, conceded that the distinction between disclosure and suppression "supports some differences in analysis," but thought the Court had exaggerated the importance of the distinction: "We have noted in traditional First Amendment cases that an affirmative publication requirement 'operates as a command in the same sense as a statute or regulation forbidding [someone] to publish specified matter,' and that a compulsion to publish that which 'reason tells [one] should not be published' therefore raises substantial first amendment concerns. *Tornillo*." Accordingly, he would have required a demonstration that the advertising was inherently likely to deceive or record evidence that the advertising was in fact deceptive, or a showing that another substantial interest was directly advanced by state action extending only as far as the interest served. Applying this standard, Brennan, J., agreed with the Court that a state may require an advertising attorney to include a costs disclaimer, but concluded that the state had provided Zauderer with inadequate notice of what he was required to include in the advertisement.

II. FREEDOM OF ASSOCIATION AND EMPLOYMENT

ELROD v. BURNS, 427 U.S. 347, 96 S.Ct. 2673, 49 L.Ed.2d 547 (1976), (Stevens, J., not participating) declared unconstitutional the dismissal of nonpolicymaking and nonconfidential state and local government employees solely on the ground that they were not affiliated with or sponsored by a particular political party. (The newly elected Democratic Sheriff of Cook County, Illinois, had sought to replace noncivil-service employees in his office, all Republicans, with members of his own party. The employees who brought suit were process servers and a juvenile court bailiff). BRENNAN, J., announced the judgment and an opinion joined by White and Marshall, JJ.: "The cost of the practice of patronage is the restraint it places on freedoms of belief and association. [The] free functioning of the electoral process also suffers. Conditioning political employment on partisan support prevents support of competing public interests. [As] government employment, state or federal, becomes more pervasive, the greater the dependence on it becomes, and therefore the greater becomes the power to starve political [opposition]. Patronage thus tips the electoral process in favor of the incumbent party.

"[P]olitical belief and association constitute the core of those activities protected by the First Amendment. Regardless of the nature of the inducement, whether it be by the denial of public employment or, as in *Barnette*, by the influence of a teacher over students, '[no government official] can prescribe what shall be orthodox in politics [or] other matters of opinion or force citizens to confess by word or act their faith therein.' Ibid. And, though freedom of belief is central, '[t]he First Amendment protects political association as well as political expression.' *Buckley v. Valeo* [p. 671 infra]. * * *

"The Court recognized in *United Public Workers v. Mitchell,* 330 U.S. 75, 100, 67 S.Ct. 556, 569, 91 L.Ed. 754 (1947), that 'Congress may not "enact a regulation providing that no Republican, Jew or Negro shall be appointed to federal office."' This principle was reaffirmed in *Wieman v. Updegraff,* 344 U.S. 183, 73 S.Ct. 215, 97 L.Ed. 216 (1952), which held that a State could not require its employees to establish their loyalty by extracting an oath denying past affiliation with Communists. And in *Cafeteria Workers v. McElroy,* 367 U.S. 886, 898, 81 S.Ct. 1743, 1750, 6 L.Ed.2d 1230 (1961), the Court recognized again that the government could not deny employment because of previous membership in a particular party.[11]

"Particularly pertinent to the constitutionality of the practice of patronage dismissals are *Keyishian v. Board of Regents,* 385 U.S. 589, 87 S.Ct. 675, 17 L.Ed. 2d 629 (1967), and *Perry v. Sindermann,* 408 U.S. 593, 92 S.Ct. 2694, 33 L.Ed.2d 570 (1972). In *Keyishian,* the Court invalidated New York statutes barring employment merely on the basis of membership in 'subversive' organizations. *Keyishian* squarely held that political association alone could not, consistently with the First Amendment, constitute an adequate ground for denying public employment.[12] In *Perry,* the Court broadly rejected the validity of limitations on First Amendment rights as a condition to the receipt of a governmental benefit, stating that the government 'may not deny a benefit to a person on a basis that infringes his constitutionally protected interests—especially, his interest in freedom of speech. For if the government could deny a benefit to a person because of his constitutionally protected speech or associations, his exercise of those freedoms would in effect be penalized and inhibited. This would allow the government to "produce a result which [it] could not command directly." *Speiser v. Randall.* Such interference with constitutional rights is impermissible.' * * *[13]"

11. Protection of First Amendment interests has not been limited to invalidation of conditions on government employment requiring allegiance to a particular political party. This Court's decisions have prohibited conditions on public benefits, in the form of jobs or otherwise, which dampen the exercise generally of First Amendment rights, however slight the inducement to the individual to forsake those rights.

[T]he First Amendment prohibits limiting the grant of a tax exemption to only those who affirm their loyalty to the State granting the exemption. *Speiser v. Randall,* 357 U.S. 513, 78 S.Ct. 1332, 2 L.Ed.2d 1460 (1958).

12. Thereafter, *United States v. Robel,* 389 U.S. 258, 88 S.Ct. 419, 19 L.Ed.2d 508 (1967), similarly held that mere membership in the Communist Party could not bar a person from employment in private defense establishments important to national security.

13. The increasingly pervasive nature of public employment provides officials with substantial power through conditioning jobs on partisan support, particularly in this time of high unemployment. Since the government however, may not seek to achieve an unlawful end either directly or indirectly, the inducement afforded by placing conditions on a benefit need not be particularly great in order to find that rights have been violated. Rights are infringed both where the government fines a person a penny for being a Republican and where it withholds the grant of a penny for the same reason.

Petitioners contend that even though the government may not provide that public employees may retain their jobs only if they become affiliated with or provide support for the in-party, respondents here have waived any objection to such requirements. The difficulty with this argument is that it completely swallows the rule. Since the qualification may not be constitutionally imposed absent an appropriate justification, to accept the waiver argument is to say that the government may do what it may not do. A finding of waiver in this case, therefore, would be contrary to our view that a partisan job qualification abridges the First Amendment.

If the practice is to survive constitutional challenge, "it must further some vital government end by a means that is least restrictive of freedom of belief and association in achieving that end, and the benefit gained must outweigh the loss of constitutionally protected rights." The plurality then considered and rejected three interests offered in justification of patronage—(1) "the need to insure effective government"; (2) "the need for political loyalty of employees" to assure implementation of the new administration's policies; and (3) "the preservation of the democratic process" and the continued vitality of "party politics":

As to (1), the argument fails, inter alia, "because it is doubtful that the mere difference of political persuasion motivates poor performance; nor do we think it legitimately may be used for imputing such behavior. [At] all events, less drastic means for insuring [this interest] are available"—discharge for good cause, "such as insubordination or poor job performance, when those bases exist."

"[Moreover] the lack of any justification for patronage dismissals as a means of furthering government effectiveness and efficiency distinguishes this case from *CSC v. Letter Carriers*, 413 U.S. 548, 93 S.Ct. 2880, 37 L.Ed.2d 796 (1973), and *Mitchell*. In both of those cases, legislative restraints on political management and campaigning by public employees were upheld despite their encroachment on First Amendment rights because, inter alia, they did serve in a necessary manner to foster and protect efficient and effective government. Interestingly, the activities that were restrained by the legislation involved in those cases are characteristic of patronage practices. As the Court observed in *Mitchell*, 'The conviction that an actively partisan governmental personnel threatens good administration has deepened since [1882]. Congress recognizes danger to the service in that political rather than official effort may earn advancement and to the public in that governmental favor may be channeled through political connections.' "

As for the second interest, the need for political loyalty and implementation of new policies "may be adequately met" by limiting patronage dismissals to "policymaking positions." As for the third interest—one "premised on the centrality of partisan politics in the democratic process"—"we are not persuaded [that] the interdiction of patronage dismissals [will cause] the demise of party politics." Political parties existed prior to active patronage and "they have survived substantial reduction in their patronage power through the establishment of the merit system.

"Patronage dismissals thus are not the least restrictive alternative to achieving the contributions they may make to the democratic process. The process functions as well without the practice, perhaps even better, for patronage dismissals clearly also retard that practice. [U]nlike the gain to representative government provided by the Hatch Act in *Letter Carriers* and *Mitchell*, the gain to representative government provided by [the practice], if any, would be insufficient to justify its sacrifice of First Amendment rights.

"To be sure, *Letter Carriers* and *Mitchell* upheld Hatch Act restraints sacrificing political campaigning and management, activities themselves protected by the First Amendment. But in those cases it was the Court's judgment that congressional subordination of those activities was permissible to safeguard the core interests of individual belief and association. Subordination of some First Amendment activity was permissible to protect other such activity. Today, we hold that subordination of other First Amendment activity, that is, patronage dismissals, not only is permissible, but also is mandated by the First Amendment. And since patronage dismissals fall within the category of political campaigning and management, this conclusion irresistibly flows from *Mitchell* and *Letter Carriers*. For if the First Amendment did not place individual belief and association above political campaigning and management, at least in the setting of public employment, the restraints on those latter activities could not have been judged permissible in *Mitchell* and *Letter Carriers*."

STEWART, J., joined by Blackmun, J., concurred: "This case does not require us to consider the broad contours of the so-called patronage system, with all its variations and permutations. In particular, it does not require us to consider the constitutional validity of a system that confines the hiring of some governmental employees to those of a particular political party, and I would intimate no views whatever on that question.

"The single substantive question involved in this case is whether a nonpolicymaking, nonconfidential government employee can be discharged or threatened with discharge from a job that he is satisfactorily performing upon the sole ground of his political beliefs. I agree with the plurality that he cannot. See *Perry v. Sindermann*."

POWELL, J., joined by Burger, C.J., and Rehnquist, J., dissented: "[Here, we have] complaining employees who apparently accepted patronage jobs knowingly and willingly, while fully familiar with the 'tenure' practices long prevailing in the Sheriff's Office. Such employees have *benefited* from their political beliefs and activities; they have not been penalized for them. In these circumstances, I am inclined to [the view that they] may not be heard to challenge [the patronage system] when it comes their turn to be replaced."

Beyond waiver, he complained that the Court "unnecessarily constitutionalizes another element of American life—an element not without its faults but one which generations have accepted on balance as having merit." Powell, J., stressed the importance of political parties and their dependency upon patronage. "History and long prevailing practice across the country support the view that patronage hiring practices make a sufficiently substantial contribution to the practical functioning of our democratic system to support their relatively modest intrusion on First Amendment interests. ∗ ∗ ∗

"It is difficult to disagree with the view, as an abstract proposition, that government employment ordinarily should not be conditioned upon one's political beliefs or activities. But we deal here with a highly practical and rather fundamental element of our political system, not the theoretical abstraction of a political science seminar. [T]he plurality seriously underestimates the strength of the government interest—especially at the local level—in allowing some patronage hiring practices, and it exaggerates the perceived burden on First Amendment rights. ∗ ∗ ∗

"It is naive to think that [local political activity supporting parties is] motivated [by] some academic interest in 'democracy' or other public service impulse. For the most part, the hope of some reward generates a major portion of [such activity]. It is difficult to overestimate the contributions to our system by the major political parties, fortunately limited in number compared to the fractionalization that has made the continued existence of democratic government doubtful in some other countries. ∗ ∗ ∗

"It is against decades of experience to the contrary, then, that the plurality opinion concludes that patronage hiring practices interfere with the 'free functioning of the electoral process.' This *ad hoc* judicial judgment runs counter to the judgments of the representatives of the people in state and local governments, representatives who have chosen, in most instances, to retain some patronage practices in combination with a merit-oriented civil service. One would think that elected representatives of the people are better equipped than we to weigh the need for some continuation of patronage practices in light of the interests above identified,[9] and particularly in view of local conditions. *Letter Carriers; Mitchell.*"[a]

Notes and Questions

1. BRANTI v. FINKEL, 445 U.S. 507, 100 S.Ct. 1287, 63 L.Ed.2d 574 (1980), per STEVENS, J., applied *Elrod* to "protect an assistant public defender who is satisfactorily performing his job from discharge solely because of his political beliefs."[b] The Court rejected the argument that even if party sponsorship is an unconstitutional condition for retaining low-level public employees it is a permissible requirement for an assistant public defender: "[P]arty affiliation is not necessarily relevant to every policymaking or confidential position. The coach of a state university's football team formulates policy, but no one could seriously claim that Republicans make better coaches than Democrats, or vice versa, no matter which party is in control of the state government. On the other hand, it is equally clear that the governor of a state may appropriately believe that the official duties of various assistants who help him write speeches, explain his views to the press, or communicate with the legislature cannot be performed effectively unless those persons share his political beliefs and party commitments. In sum, the ultimate inquiry is not whether the label 'policymaker' or 'confidential' fits a particular position; rather, the question is whether the hiring authority can demonstrate that party affiliation is an appropriate requirement for the effective performance of the public office involved."

The Court concluded that neither the policymaking of an assistant public defender nor the access of client's confidential information had any bearing on partisan political considerations.

2. Might Communists be treated differently from Republican or Democrats for some confidential employment? Consider White, J., dissenting in *Robel* (cited in Brennan, J.'s opinion fn. 12): "[D]enying the opportunity to be employed in some defense plants in a much smaller deterrent to the exercise of associational rights that [a] criminal penalty attached solely to membership, and the Government's interest in keeping potential spies and saboteurs from defense plants is much greater than its interest [in] committing all Party members to

---

9. The plurality might be taken to concede some promotion of the democratic process by patronage hiring practices but to conclude that in net effect such practices will reduce political debate impermissibly by affecting some employees or potential employees and thereby depriving society of the 'unfettered judgment of each citizen on matters of political concern.' In the past the Court has upheld congressional actions designed to increase the overall level of political discourse but affecting adversely the First Amendment interests of some individuals. In *Letter Carriers* we indicated specifically that the First Amendment freedoms of federal employees could be limited in an effort to further the functioning of the democratic process. I do not believe that local legislative judgments as to what will further the democratic process in

light of local conditions should receive less weight than these congressional judgments. Surely that should be the case until we have a record, if one could be created, showing the fears of the plurality to be justified.

a. Burger, C.J., dissented, contending that the decision "represents a significant intrusion into the area of legislative and policy concerns."

b. The Court noted that in *Elrod*, as in the instant case, "the only practice at issue was the *dismissal* of public employees for partisan reasons" and thus there was "no occasion to address petitioner's argument that there is a compelling governmental interest in maintaining a political sponsorship system for *filling vacancies* in the public defender's office." (Emphasis added.)

prison." Compare Israel, *Elfbrandt v. Russell: The Demise of the Oath?*, 1966 Sup.Ct.Rev. 193, 201–07 and O'Neil, *Unconstitutional Conditions*, 54 Calif.L.Rev. 443 (1966) with Van Alstyne, *The Constitutional Rights of Employees*, 16 U.C. L.A.L.Rev. 751 (1969).

COLE v. RICHARDSON, 405 U.S. 676, 92 S.Ct. 1332, 31 L.Ed.2d 593 (1972), per Burger, C.J. (over the dissents of Douglas, J., and Marshall, J., joined by Brennan, J.), upheld the dismissal of Richardson's employment at a state hospital for refusing to sign a loyalty oath calling in part for an affirmation that "I will oppose the overthrow of the government [by] force, violence, or by any illegal or unconstitutional method": "Since there is no constitutionally protected right to overthrow a government by force, violence, or illegal or unconstitutional means, no constitutional right is infringed by an oath to abide by the constitutional system in the future."[c] Should the first amendment permit requiring public employees to oppose that which they have a right to advocate? Is *Cole* consistent with the cases cited in the plurality opinion? With *Robel?* With *Wooley?*

3. The plurality argues that its conclusion flows irresistibly from *Mitchell* and *Letter Carriers?* Were these cases rightly decided? Is a ban on active participation in political campaigns by government employees necessary (as the Court thought in *Letter Carriers*) to avoid the impression that the government practices "political justice" or to prevent the government work force from becoming a "peaceful, invincible, and perhaps corrupt political machine"? Would prohibitions against coercion (such as those commanded by *Elrod*) be sufficient? If not, is the concern about coercion relevant only to participation on behalf of incumbents? See Blasi, *The Checking Value in First Amendment Theory,* 1977 Am.B.Found.Res.J. 521, 634–35. Is it of major import that the restrictions are "not aimed at particular parties, groups or points of [view]"? *Letter Carriers.* Does an emphasis on this factor, denigrate the liberty and associational interests of government employees? See Redish, *The Content Distinction in First Amendment Analysis,* 34 Stan.L.Rev. 113 (1981). Consider the tension between *Letter Carriers* and the *Pickering-Connick* [Sec. 1, VII, C supra] line of cases. Consider also the relationship between *Pickering, Connick,* and *Elrod.* Suppose a deputy sheriff is discharged for meeting with a political opponent of the incumbent sheriff. Does *Elrod* apply or *Pickering-Connick?* What is the difference? For discussion, see Note, *Politics and the Non-Civil Service Public Employee: A Categorical Approach to First Amendment Protection,* 85 Colum.L.Rev. 558 (1985).

In ABOOD v. DETROIT BD. OF EDUC., 431 U.S. 209, 97 S.Ct. 1782, 52 L.Ed. 2d 261 (1977), a Michigan statute permitted an "agency shop" arrangement, whereby all local governmental employees represented by a union, even though not themselves union members, must, as a condition of employment, pay to the union "service charges" equal in amount to union dues. Alleging that they were unwilling to pay union dues, that (1) they opposed public sector collective bargaining and that (2) the union was engaged in non-collective bargaining political-ideological activities which they disapproved, public school teachers challenged the validity of the agency-shop clause in a collective bargaining agreement between the Board of Education and the union. The Court, per STEWART, J., rejected plaintiffs' first contention, but sustained the second—the union's expenditure of a part of such "service charges" "to contribute to political

c. Powell and Rehnquist, JJ., took no part.

candidates and to express political views unrelated to its duties as exclusive bargaining representative" violates the first amendment rights of non-union employees who oppose such causes.

"To compel employees financially to support their collective-bargaining representative has an impact upon their First Amendment interests. An employee may very well have ideological objections to a wide variety of activities undertaken by the union in its role as exclusive representative. His moral or religious views about the desirability of abortion may not square with the union's policy in negotiating a medical benefits plan. One individual might disagree with a union policy of negotiating limits on the right to strike, believing that to be the road to serfdom for the working class, while another might have economic or political objections to unionism itself. An employee might object to the union's wage policy because it violates guidelines designed to limit inflation, or might object to the union's seeking a clause in the collective-bargaining agreement proscribing racial discrimination. The examples could be multiplied. To be required to help finance the union as a collective-bargaining agent might well be thought, therefore, to interfere in some way with an employee's freedom to associate for the advancement of ideas, or to refrain from doing so, as he sees fit. But the judgment clearly made in [*Railway Employees' Dep't v. Hanson,* 351 U.S. 225, 76 S.Ct. 714, 100 L.Ed. 1112 (1956), upholding against first amendment challenge a union-shop clause, authorized by the Railway Labor Act (RLA), requiring financial support of the union by every member of the bargaining unit, and *International Ass'n of Machinists v. Street,* 367 U.S. 740, 81 S.Ct. 1784, 6 L.Ed.2d 1141 (1961), avoiding serious constitutional issues by construing RLA to prohibit the use of compulsory union dues for political purposes] is that such interference as exists is constitutionally justified by the legislative assessment of the important contribution of the union shop to the system of labor relations established by the Congress. '[As long as the union leadership acts] to promote the cause which justified bringing the group together, the individual cannot withdraw his financial support merely because he disagrees with the group's strategy.' *Street* (Douglas, J., concurring).

"[The] desirability of labor peace is no less important in the public sector, nor is the risk of 'free riders' any smaller. [Thus], insofar as the service charge is used to finance expenditures by the union for the purposes of collective bargaining, contract administration, and grievance adjustment, [*Hanson* and *Street*] appear to require validation of the agency-shop agreement before us."

In agreeing with plaintiffs' contention that they fall within the protection of *Elrod* and other cases guaranteeing the freedom to associate for the purpose of advancing ideas and forbidding the government to require one to relinquish first amendment rights as a condition of public employment "because they have been prohibited not from actively associating, but rather from refusing to associate," and in ruling that plaintiffs could constitutionally prevent the union's spending a part of their required service fees for political and ideological purposes unrelated to collective bargaining, the Court pointed out: "The fact that [plaintiffs] are compelled to make, rather than prohibited from making, contributions for political purposes works no less an infringement of their constitutional rights. For at the heart of the First Amendment is the notion that an individual should be free to believe as he will, and that in a free society one's beliefs should be shaped by his mind and his conscience rather than coerced by the State. See [*Elrod.*]

"These principles prohibit a State from compelling an individual [to] associate with a political party, *Elrod,* as a condition of employment. They are no less applicable to the case at bar, and they thus prohibit the [union] from requiring any [plaintiff] to contribute to the support of an ideological cause he may oppose as a condition of holding a job as a public school teacher.

"We do not hold that a union cannot constitutionally spend funds for the expression of political views, on behalf of political candidates, or towards the advancement of other ideological causes not germane to its duties as collective bargaining representative. Rather, the Constitution requires only that expenditures be financed from [charges] paid by employees who do not object to advancing those ideas and who are not coerced into doing so against their will by the threat of loss of government employment."

The Court remanded to devise an appropriate "way of preventing subsidization of ideological activity by employees who object thereto without restricting the union's ability to require every employee to contribute to the cost of collective-bargaining activities."

POWELL, J., joined by Burger, C.J., and Blackmun, J., agreed that a state cannot constitutionally compel public employees to contribute to union political activities which they oppose and thus joined the Court's judgment remanding the case for further proceedings, but balked at the Court's apparent ruling "that public employees can be compelled by the State to pay full union dues to a union with which they disagree, subject only to a possible rebate or deduction if they are willing to step forward, declare their opposition to the union, and initiate a proceeding to establish that some portion of their dues has been spent on 'ideological activities unrelated to collective bargaining.' Such a sweeping limitation of First Amendment rights by the Court is not only unnecessary on this record; it [is] unsupported by either precedent or reason. * * *

"The Court's extensive reliance on *Hanson* and *Street* requires it to rule that there is no constitutional distinction between what the Government can require of its own employees and what it can permit private employees to do. To me the distinction is fundamental. Under the First Amendment the Government may authorize private parties to enter into voluntary agreements whose terms it could not adopt as its own.

"[The] collective-bargaining agreement to which a public agency is a party is not merely analogous to legislation; it has all of the attributes of legislation for the subjects [e.g., residency requirements for state employees] with which it deals. [The] State in this case has not merely authorized union-shop agreements between willing parties; it has negotiated and adopted such an agreement itself. [It] has undertaken to compel employees to pay full dues [to] a union as a condition of employment. Accordingly, the [Board of Education's] collective-bargaining agreement, like any other enactment of state law, is fully subject to the constraints that the Constitution imposes on coercive governmental regulation.

"[I] would make it more explicit [than has the majority] that compelling a government employee to give financial support to a union in the public sector—regardless of the use to which the union puts the contribution—impinges seriously upon interests in free speech and association protected by the First Amendment.

"In *Buckley* [we held that] limitations on political contributions 'impinge on protected associational freedoms.' [That] *Buckley* dealt with a contribution limitation requirement does not alter its importance for this case. An individual can no more be required to affiliate with a candidate by making a contribution than he can be prohibited from such affiliation. The only question after *Buckley* is whether a union in the public sector is sufficiently distinguishable from a political candidate or committee to remove the withholding of financial contributions from First Amendment protection. In my view no principled distinction exists.

"The ultimate objective of a union in the public sector, like that of a political party, is to influence public decisionmaking in accordance with the views and perceived interests of the membership. [In this sense], the public sector union is indistinguishable from the traditional political party in this country.

"[It] is possible that paramount governmental interests may be found—at least with respect to certain narrowly defined subjects of bargaining—that would support this restriction on First Amendment rights. But 'the burden is on the government to show the existence of such an interest.' *Elrod.* Because this appeal reaches this Court on a motion to dismiss, the record is barren of any demonstration by the State that excluding minority views from the processes by which governmental policy is made is necessary to serve overriding governmental objectives. * * *

"Before today it had been well established that when state law intrudes upon protected speech, the State itself must shoulder the burden of proving that its action is justified by overriding state interests. See *Elrod; Speiser v. Randall.* The Court, for the first time in a First Amendment case, simply reverses this principle. Under today's decision, a nonunion employee who would vindicate his First Amendment rights apparently must initiate a proceeding to prove that the union has allocated some portion of its budget to 'ideological activities unrelated to collective bargaining.' I would adhere to established First Amendment principles and require the State to come forward and demonstrate, as to each union expenditure for which it would exact support from minority employees, that the compelled contribution is necessary to serve overriding governmental objectives."

REHNQUIST, J., concurring, noted that had he joined the *Elrod* plurality, he "would find it virtually impossible to join the Court's opinion in this case." He did not "read the Court's opinion as leaving intact the 'unfettered judgment of each citizen on matters of political concern' [*Elrod*] when it holds that Michigan [may] require an objecting member of a public employees' union to contribute to the funds necessary for the union to carry out its bargaining activities. Nor does the Court's opinion leave such a member free 'to believe as he will and to act and associate according to his beliefs' [*Elrod*]." He was "unable to see a constitutional distinction between a governmentally imposed requirement that a public employee be a Democrat or Republican or else lose his job, and a similar requirement that a public employee contribute to the collective-bargaining expenses of a labor union." [a]

Notes and Questions

1. Reading *Elrod* and *Abood* together, Powell, J., and Burger, C.J., maintain that public employees may be forced to support a political party, but not the union which represents them in collective bargaining. Brennan, J., takes exactly the opposite position, except for support of the non-collective bargaining ideological activities of the union. Blackmun, J., votes against forced support

a. Stevens, J., also filed a brief concurrence: "The Court's opinion does not foreclose the argument that the Union should not be permitted to exact a service fee from nonmembers without first establishing a procedure which will avoid the risk that their funds will be used, even temporarily, to finance ideological activities unrelated to collective bargaining."

across the board. Rehnquist, J., sees no difference between forced support of political parties and union collective bargaining expenses (he permits both), but apparently sees a difference between forced support of the ideological activities of political parties (he would permit it) and forced support of the non-collective bargaining ideological activities of unions (by joining the majority, he would not permit it). Which, if any, of the above positions is defensible?

2. Does *Abood* exaggerate the first amendment interests? If Michigan subsidized unions directly, would dissenting taxpayers have a first amendment claim? Suppose Michigan taxed those most likely to benefit from union activity, i.e., the employees? Are compelled contributions different from government taxation? See Shiffrin, *Government Speech*, 27 U.C.L.A.L.Rev. 565, 594 (1980). Suppose the union contract provided for a direct payment from the employer and that union dues were not required of employees? Would this arrangement affect the rules set out in *Abood*?

3. How should the *Abood* rules apply to forced employee payments for union conventions, union newsletters, union social activities or union organizing? See *Ellis v. Brotherhood of Railway, Airline & Steamship Clerks*, 466 U.S. 435, 104 S.Ct. 1883, 80 L.Ed.2d 428 (1984). For exploration of the issues raised by *Abood*, see Cantor, *Forced Payments to Service Institutions and Constitutional Interests in Ideological Non-Association*, 36 Rut.L.Rev. 3 (1984).

III. INTIMATE ASSOCIATION AND EXPRESSIVE ASSOCIATION: THE RIGHT TO EXCLUDE MEMBERS

ROBERTS v. UNITED STATES JAYCEES, ___ U.S. ___, 104 S.Ct. 3244, 82 L.Ed.2d 462 (1984): Appellee U.S. Jaycees, a nonprofit national membership corporation whose objective is to pursue educational and charitable purposes that promote the growth and development of young men's civic organizations, limits regular membership to young men between the ages of 18 and 35. Associate membership is available to women and older men. An associate member may not vote or hold local or national office. Two local chapters in Minnesota violated appellee's bylaws by admitting women as regular members. When they learned that revocation of their charters was to be considered, members of both chapters filed discrimination charges with the Minnesota Department of Human Rights, alleging that the exclusion of women from full membership violated the Minnesota Human Rights Act (Act), which makes it an "unfair discriminatory practice" to deny anyone "the full and equal enjoyment of goods, services, facilities, privileges, advantages, and accommodations of a place of accommodation" because, inter alia, of sex.

Before a hearing on the state charge took place, appellee brought federal suit, alleging that requiring it to accept women as regular members would violate the male members' constitutional "freedom of association." A state hearing officer decided against appellee and the federal district court certified to the Minnesota Supreme Court the question whether appellee is "a place of public accommodation" within the meaning of the Act. With the record of the administrative hearing before it, the state supreme court answered that question in the affirmative. The U.S. Court of Appeals held that application of the Act to appellee's membership policies would violate its freedom of association.[a]

a. When the state supreme court held that appellee was "a place of public accommodation" within the meaning of the Act, it suggested that, unlike appellee, the Kiwanis Club might be sufficiently "private" to be outside the scope of the Act. Appellee then amended its complaint to allege that the state court's interpretation of the Act rendered it unconstitutionally vague. The Eighth Circuit so held, but the Supreme Court reversed.

In rejecting appellee's claims,[b] the Court, per BRENNAN, J., pointed out that the Constitution protects " 'freedom of association' in two distinct senses," what might be called "freedom of intimate association" and "freedom of expressive association": "In one line of decisions, the Court has concluded that choices to enter into and maintain certain intimate human relationships must be secured against undue intrusion by the State because of the role of such relationships in safeguarding the individual freedom that is central to our constitutional scheme. In this respect, freedom of association receives protection as a fundamental element of personal liberty. In another set of decisions, the Court has recognized a right to associate for the purpose of engaging in those activities protected by the First Amendment—speech, assembly, petition for the redress of grievances, and the exercise of religion. The Constitution guarantees freedom of association of this kind as an indispensable means of preserving other individual liberties."

The freedom of intimate association was deemed important because, "certain kinds of personal bonds have played a critical role in the culture and traditions of the Nation by cultivating and transmitting shared ideals and beliefs; they thereby foster diversity and act as critical buffers between the individual and the power of the State.[c] Moreover, the constitutional shelter afforded such relationships reflects the realization that individuals draw much of their emotional enrichment from close ties with others. Protecting these relationships from unwarranted state interference therefore safeguards the ability independently to define one's identity that is central to any concept of liberty.

"The personal affiliations that exemplify these considerations [are] distinguished by such attributes as relative smallness, a high degree of selectivity in decisions to begin and maintain the affiliation, and seclusion from others in critical aspects of the relationship. As a general matter, only relationships with these sorts of qualities are likely to reflect the considerations that have led to an understanding of freedom of association as an intrinsic element of personal liberty. Conversely, an association lacking these qualities—such as a large business enterprise—seems remote from the concerns giving rise to this constitutional protection. * * *

"Between these poles, of course, lies a broad range of human relationships that may make greater or lesser claims to constitutional protection from particular incursions by the State. [We] need not mark the potentially significant points on this terrain with any precision. We note only that factors that may be relevant include size, purpose, policies, selectivity, congeniality, and other characteristics that in a particular case may be pertinent. In this case, however, several features of the Jaycees clearly place the organization outside of the category of relationships worthy of this kind of constitutional protection.

"The undisputed facts reveal that the local chapters of the Jaycees are large and basically unselective groups. * * * Apart from age and sex, neither the national organization nor the local chapters employs any criteria for judging applicants for membership, and new members are routinely recruited and admitted with no inquiry into their backgrounds. In fact, a local officer testified

---

b. There was no dissent. Rehnquist, J., concurred in the judgment. O'Connor, J., joined part of the Court's opinion and concurred in the judgment. See infra. Burger, C.J., and Blackmun, J., took no part.

c. For commentary on this aspect of association from a variety of perspectives, see Nis-

bet, *The Quest For Community* (1969); McIntyre, *After Virtue* (1981); Unger, *Knowledge and Politics* (1975); Frug, *The City as a Legal Concept*, 93 Harv.L.Rev. 1057 (1980); Karst, *Equality and Community: Lessons From the Civil Rights Era*, 56 Not.D.Law. 183 (1980).

that he could recall no instance in which an applicant had been denied membership on any basis other than age or sex. Furthermore, despite their inability to vote, hold office, or receive certain awards, women affiliated with the Jaycees attend various meetings, participate in selected projects, and engage in many of the organization's social functions. Indeed, numerous non-members of both genders regularly participate in a substantial portion of activities central to the decision of many members to associate with one another, including many of the organization's various community programs, awards ceremonies, and recruitment meetings.

"[Thus], we conclude that the Jaycees chapters lack the distinctive characteristics that might afford constitutional protection to the decision of its members to exclude women. We turn therefore to consider the extent to which application of the Minnesota statute to compel the Jaycees to accept women infringes the group's freedom of expressive association. * * *

"Government actions that may unconstitutionally infringe upon [freedom of expressive association] can take a number of forms. Among other things, government may seek to impose penalties or withhold benefits from individuals because of their membership in a disfavored group; it may attempt to require disclosure of the fact of membership in a group seeking anonymity; and it may try to interfere with the internal organization or affairs of the group. By requiring the Jaycees to admit women as full voting members, the Minnesota Act works an infringement of the last type. There can be no clearer example of an intrusion into the internal structure or affairs of an association than a regulation that forces the group to accept members it does not desire. Such a regulation may impair the ability of the original members to express only those views that brought them together. Freedom of association therefore plainly presupposes a freedom not to associate. See *Abood.*

"The right to associate for expressive purposes is not, however, absolute. Infringements on that right may be justified by regulations adopted to serve compelling state interests, unrelated to the suppression of ideas, that cannot be achieved through means significantly less restrictive of associational freedoms. We are persuaded that Minnesota's compelling interest in eradicating discrimination against its female citizens justifies the impact that application of the statute to the Jaycees may have on the male members' associational freedoms.

"[I]n upholding Title II of the Civil Rights Act of 1964, which forbids race discrimination in public accommodations, we emphasized that its 'fundamental object [was] to vindicate "the deprivation of personal dignity that surely accompanies denials of equal access to public establishments."' *Heart of Atlanta Motel.* That stigmatizing injury, and the denial of equal opportunities that accompanies it, is surely felt as strongly by persons suffering discrimination on the basis of their sex as by those treated differently because of their race.

"Nor is the state interest in assuring equal access limited to the provision of purely tangible goods and services. A State enjoys broad authority to create rights of public access on behalf of its citizens. *Pruneyard.* Like many States and municipalities, Minnesota has adopted a functional definition of public accommodations that reaches various forms of public, quasi-commercial conduct. This expansive definition reflects a recognition of the changing nature of the American economy and of the importance, both to the individual and to society, of removing the barriers to economic advancement and political and social integration that have historically plagued certain disadvantaged groups, including women. * * *

"In applying the Act to the Jaycees, the State has advanced those interests through the least restrictive means of achieving its ends. Indeed, the Jaycees have failed to demonstrate that the Act imposes any serious burdens on the male members' freedom of expressive association. See *Hishon v. King & Spalding*, 467 U.S. 69, 104 S.Ct. 2229, 81 L.Ed.2d 59 (1984) (law firm 'has not shown how its ability to fulfill [protected] function[s] would be inhibited by a requirement that it consider [a woman lawyer] for partnership on her merits'). To be sure, a 'not insubstantial part' of the Jaycees' activities constitutes protected expression on political, economic, cultural, and social affairs. [There] is, however, no basis in the record for concluding that admission of women as full voting members will impede the organization's ability to engage in these protected activities or to disseminate its preferred views. The Act requires no change in the Jaycees' creed of promoting the interests of young men, and it imposes no restrictions on the organization's ability to exclude individuals with ideologies or philosophies different from those of its existing members. Moreover, the Jaycees already invite women to share the group's views and philosophy and to participate in much of its training and community activities. Accordingly, any claim that admission of women as full voting members will impair a symbolic message conveyed by the very fact that women are not permitted to vote is attenuated at best.

"[In] claiming that women might have a different attitude about such issues as the federal budget, school prayer, voting rights, and foreign relations, or that the organization's public positions would have a different effect if the group were not 'a purely young men's association,' the Jaycees rely solely on unsupported generalizations about the relative interests and perspectives of men and women. Although such generalizations may or may not have a statistical basis in fact with respect to particular positions adopted by the Jaycees, we have repeatedly condemned legal decisionmaking that relies uncritically on such assumptions. In the absence of a showing far more substantial than that attempted by the Jaycees, we decline to indulge in the sexual stereotyping that underlies appellee's contention that, by allowing women to vote, application of the Minnesota Act will change the content or impact of the organization's speech.

"In any event, even if enforcement of the Act causes some incidental abridgement of the Jaycees' protected speech, that effect is no greater than is necessary to accomplish the State's legitimate purposes. [A]cts of invidious discrimination in the distribution of publicly available goods, services, and other advantages cause unique evils that government has a compelling interest to prevent—wholly apart from the point of view such conduct may transmit. Accordingly, like violence or other types of potentially expressive activities that produce special harms distinct from their communicative impact, such practices are entitled to no constitutional protection."

O'CONNOR, J., concurring, joined the Court's opinion except for its analysis of freedom of expressive association. She maintained that "the Court has adopted a test that unadvisedly casts doubt on the power of States to pursue the profoundly important goal of ensuring nondiscriminatory access to commercial opportunities" yet "accords insufficient protection to expressive associations and places inappropriate burdens on groups claiming the protection of the First Amendment":

"The Court analyzes Minnesota's attempt to regulate the Jaycees' membership using a test that I find both over-protective of activities undeserving of constitutional shelter and under-protective of important First Amendment concerns. The Court declares that the Jaycees' right of association depends on the organization's making a 'substantial' showing that the admission of unwelcome members 'will change the message communicated by the group's speech.' I am not sure what showing the Court thinks would satisfy its requirement of proof of a membership-message connection, but whatever it means, the focus on such a connection is objectionable.

"Imposing such a requirement, especially in the context of the balancing-of-interests test articulated by the Court, raises the possibility that certain commercial associations, by engaging occasionally in certain kinds of expressive activities, might improperly gain protection for discrimination. The Court's focus raises other problems as well. [W]ould the Court's analysis of this case be different if, for example, the Jaycees membership had a steady history of opposing public issues thought (by the Court) to be favored by women? It might seem easy to conclude, in the latter case, that the admission of women to the Jaycees' ranks would affect the content of the organization's message, but I do not believe that should change the outcome of this case. Whether an association is or is not constitutionally protected in the selection of its membership should not depend on what the association says or why its members say it.

"The Court's readiness to inquire into the connection between membership and message reveals a more fundamental flaw in its analysis. The Court pursues this inquiry as part of its mechanical application of a 'compelling interest' test, under which the Court weighs the interests of the State of Minnesota in ending gender discrimination against the Jaycees' First Amendment right of association. The Court entirely neglects to establish at the threshold that the Jaycees is an association whose activities or purposes should engage the strong protections that the First Amendment extends to expressive associations.

"On the one hand, an association engaged exclusively in protected expression enjoys First Amendment protection of both the content of its message and the choice of its members. Protection of the message itself is judged by the same standards as protection of speech by an individual. Protection of the association's right to define its membership derives from the recognition that the formation of an expressive association is the creation of a voice, and the selection of members is the definition of that voice. [A] ban on specific group voices on public affairs violates the most basic guarantee of the First Amendment—that citizens, not the government, control the content of public discussion.

"On the other hand, there is only minimal constitutional protection of the freedom of *commercial* association. There are, of course, some constitutional protections of commercial speech—speech intended and used to promote a commercial transaction with the speaker. But the State is free to impose any rational regulation on the commercial transaction itself. The Constitution does not guarantee a right to choose employees, customers, suppliers, or those with whom one engages in simple commercial transactions, without restraint from the State. A shopkeeper has no constitutional right to deal only with persons of one sex.

"[A]n association should be characterized as commercial, and therefore subject to rationally related state regulation of its membership and other associational activities, when, and only when, the association's activities are not predominantly of the type protected by the First Amendment. It is only when the association is predominantly engaged in protected expression that state regulation of its membership will necessarily affect, change, dilute, or silence one collective voice that would otherwise be heard. An association must choose its market. Once it enters the marketplace of commerce in any substantial degree it loses the complete control over its membership that it would otherwise enjoy if it confined its affairs to the marketplace of ideas.

"[N]otwithstanding its protected expressive activities, [appellee] is, first and foremost, an organization that, at both the national and local levels, promotes and practices the art of solicitation and management. The organization claims that the training it offers its members gives them an advantage in business, and business firms do indeed sometimes pay the dues of individual memberships for their employees. Jaycees members hone their solicitation and management skills, under the direction and supervision of the organization, primarily through their active recruitment of new members. * * *

"Recruitment and selling are commercial activities, even when conducted for training rather than for profit. The 'not insubstantial' volume of protected Jaycees activity found by the Court of Appeals is simply not enough to preclude state regulation of the Jaycees' commercial activities. The State of Minnesota has a legitimate interest in ensuring nondiscriminatory access to the commercial opportunity presented by membership in the Jaycees. The members of the Jaycees may not claim constitutional immunity from Minnesota's anti-discrimination law by seeking to exercise their First Amendment rights through this commercial organization."

Notes and Questions

1. *Freedom of intimate association.* The reference to the freedom of intimate association is the first in the Court's history, but the notion that the concept should serve as an organizing principle is found in Karst, *Freedom of Intimate Association,* 89 Yale L.J. 624 (1980). To what extent should freedom of intimate association itself be regarded as a first amendment right? Compare Karst with Baker, *Scope of the First Amendment Freedom of Speech,* 25 U.C. L.A.L.Rev. 964 (1978) and Raggi, *An Independent Right to Freedom of Association,* 12 Harv.Civ.Rts.-Civ.Lib.L.Rev. 1 (1977).

Although the freedom of intimate association has limited relevance for the 295,000 member Jaycees, the concept "has important implications for other private associations with discriminatory membership policies." Linder, *Freedom of Association After Roberts v. United States Jaycees,* 82 Mich.L.Rev. 1878, 1885 (1984). What are (should be) the implications for golf and country clubs, fraternal societies, athletic clubs and downtown or city clubs? Consider Comment, *Discrimination in Private Social Clubs: Freedom of Association and Right to Privacy,* 1970 Duke L.J. 1181, 1222: "Whether this society is capable of free evolution to social equality seems irrelevant in light of the influence of the social club in perpetuating general racial and religious economic and social inferiority and in light of the urgent need for reversal of racial polarization. Many private social clubs have become so affected with the public interest that some regulation of their membership practices is not only a proper but also a necessary exercise of legislative power." See generally Burns, *The Exclusion of Women From Influential Men's Clubs: The Inner Sanctum and the Myth of Full Equality,* 18 Harv.Civ.Rts.-Civ.Lib.L.Rev. 321 (1983). How do O'Connor and Brennan, JJ., differ on such questions. For appreciation of O'Connor, J.'s perspective, see Linder, supra. For defense of Brennan, J.'s perspective, see Note, 98 Harv.L.Rev. 195 (1984).

2. *A feminist perspective.* From a feminist perspective, is *Roberts* a victory or a defeat? Note that what *Roberts* guarantees is the right of women to join an

organization dedicated to promoting the interests of young men. What if a state attacked the goal of the organization as itself violative of civil rights? Could the Ku Klux Klan or the Nazis be outlawed by a civil rights statute? Reconsider *Beauharnais*, Sec. 1, II, A supra. Is the distinction between race and sex of any importance in this context? Should a distinction be made between organizations designed to promote the interests of advantaged groups and those designed to promote the interests of disadvantaged groups? Compare Ch. 6, Sec. 2, V and Ch. 10, Sec. 3, IV.

IV. GOVERNMENT MANDATED DISCLOSURES AND FREEDOM OF ASSOCIATION

A. POLITICAL ASSOCIATION

BARENBLATT v. UNITED STATES

360 U.S. 109, 79 S.Ct. 1081, 3 L.Ed.2d 1115 (1959).

MR. JUSTICE HARLAN delivered the opinion of the Court. * * *

Broad as it is, the [congressional power of inquiry] is not, however, without limitations. Since Congress may only investigate into those areas in which it may potentially legislate or appropriate, it cannot inquire into matters which are within the exclusive province of one or the other branch of the Government. [And] the Congress, in common with all branches of the Government, must exercise its powers subject to the limitations placed by the Constitution on governmental action, more particularly in the context of this case the relevant limitations of the Bill of Rights.

[In] the present case congressional efforts to learn the extent of a nation-wide, indeed world-wide, problem have brought one of its investigating committees into the field of education. Of course, broadly viewed, inquiries cannot be made into the teaching that is pursued in any of our educational institutions. When academic teaching-freedom and its corollary learning-freedom, so essential to the well-being of the Nation, are claimed, this Court will always be on the alert against intrusion by Congress into this constitutionally protected domain. But this does not mean that the Congress is precluded from interrogating a witness merely because he is a teacher. An educational institution is not a constitutional sanctuary from inquiry into matters that may otherwise be within the constitutional legislative domain merely for the reason that inquiry is made of someone within its walls. * * *

We here review petitioner's conviction under 2 U.S.C. § 192 for contempt of Congress, arising from his refusal to answer certain questions put to him by a Subcommittee of the House Committee on Un-American Activities during the course of an inquiry concerning alleged Communist infiltration into the field of education. * * *

Pursuant to a subpoena, and accompanied by counsel, petitioner on June 28, 1954, appeared as a witness before this congressional Subcommittee. After answering a few preliminary questions and testifying that he had been a graduate student and teaching fellow at the University of Michigan from 1947 to 1950 and an instructor in psychology at Vassar College from 1950 to shortly before his appearance before the Subcommittee, petitioner objected generally to the right of the Subcommittee to inquire into his "political" and "religious" beliefs or any "other personal and private affairs" or "associational activities," upon grounds set forth in a previously prepared memorandum which he was allowed to file with the Subcommittee.[2] Thereafter petitioner specifically declined to answer [the following questions]:

"Are you now a member of the Communist Party? (Count One.)

"Have you ever been a member of the Communist Party? (Count Two.)

* * *

"Were you ever a member of the Haldane Club of the Communist Party while at the University of Michigan? (Count Four.) * * *"

In each instance the grounds of refusal were those set forth in the prepared statement. Petitioner expressly disclaimed reliance upon "the Fifth Amendment." [Upon conviction under all counts in a federal court, petitioner was sentenced to 6 months imprisonment.]

Undeniably, the First Amendment in some circumstances protects an individual from being compelled to disclose his associational relationships. However, the protections of the First Amendment, unlike a proper claim of the privilege against self-incrimination under the Fifth Amendment, do not afford a witness the right to resist inquiry in all circumstances. Where First Amendment rights are asserted to bar governmental interrogation resolution of the issue always involves a balancing by the courts of the competing private and public interests at stake in the particular circumstances shown. * * *

The first question is whether this investigation was related to a valid legislative purpose, for Congress may not constitutionally require an individual to disclose his political relationships or other private affairs except in relation to such a purpose.

That Congress has wide power to legislate in the field of Communist activity in this Country, and to conduct appropriate investigations in aid thereof, is hardly debatable. The existence of such power has never been questioned by this Court, and it is sufficient to say, without particularization, that Congress has enacted or considered in this field a wide range of legislative measures, not a few of which have stemmed from recommendations of the very Committee whose actions have been drawn in question here. In the last analysis this power rests on the right of self-preservation, "the ultimate value of any society," *Dennis.* Justification for its exercise in turn rests on the long and widely accepted view that the tenets of the Communist Party include the ultimate overthrow of the Government of the United States by force and violence, a view which has been given formal expression by the Congress.

We think that investigatory power in this domain is not to be denied Congress solely because the field of education is involved. [Indeed] we do not understand petitioner here to suggest that Congress in no circumstances may inquire into Communist activity in the field of education. Rather, his position is in effect that this particular investigation was aimed not at the revolutionary aspects but at the theoretical classroom discussion of communism.

In our opinion this position rests on a too constricted view of the nature of the investigatory process, and is not supported by a fair assessment of the record before us. An investigation of advocacy of or preparation for overthrow certainly embraces the right to identify a witness as a member of the Communist Party and to inquire into the various manifestations of the Party's tenets. The strict

---

2. In the words of the panel of the Court of Appeals which first heard the case this memorandum "can best be described as a lengthy legal brief attacking the jurisdiction of the committee to ask appellant any questions or to conduct any inquiry at all, based on the First, Ninth and Tenth Amendments, the prohibition against bills of attainder, and the doctrine of separation of powers."

requirements of a prosecution under the Smith Act are not the measure of the permissible scope of a congressional investigation into "overthrow," for of necessity the investigatory process must proceed step by step. Nor can it fairly be concluded that this investigation was directed at controlling what is being taught at our universities rather than at overthrow. The statement of the Subcommittee Chairman at the opening of the investigation evinces no such intention,[31] and so far as this record reveals nothing thereafter transpired which would justify our holding that the thrust of the investigation later changed. [C]ertainly the conclusion would not be justified that the questioning of petitioner would have exceeded permissible bounds had he not shut off the Subcommittee at the threshold.

Nor can we accept the further contention that this investigation should not be deemed to have been in furtherance of a legislative purpose because the true objective of the Committee and of the Congress was purely "exposure." So long as Congress acts in pursuance of its constitutional power, the judiciary lacks authority to intervene on the basis of the motives which spurred the exercise of that power. [Having] scrutinized this record we cannot say that the unanimous panel of the Court of Appeals which first considered this case was wrong in concluding that "the primary purposes of the inquiry were in aid of legislative processes." * * *

Finally, the record is barren of other factors which in themselves might sometimes lead to the conclusion that the individual interests at stake were not subordinate to those of the state. There is no indication in this record that the Subcommittee was attempting to pillory witnesses. Nor did petitioner's appearance as a witness follow from indiscriminate dragnet procedures, lacking in probable cause for belief that he possessed information which might be helpful to the Subcommittee. And the relevancy of the questions put to him by the Subcommittee is not open to doubt.

We conclude that the balance between the individual and the governmental interests here at stake must be struck in favor of the latter, and that therefore the provisions of the First Amendment have not been offended. * * *

Affirmed.

Mr. Justice Black, with whom The Chief Justice, and Mr. Justice Douglas concur, dissenting. * * *

I do not agree that laws directly abridging First Amendment freedoms can be justified by a congressional or judicial balancing process. There are, of course, cases [such as those involving the right of a city to control its streets] suggesting that a law which primarily regulates conduct but which might also indirectly affect speech can be upheld if the effect on speech is minor in relation

31. The following are excerpts from that statement: "[In] opening this hearing, it is well to make clear to you and others just what the nature of this investigation is.

"From time to time, the committee has investigated Communists and Communist activities within the entertainment, newspaper, and labor fields, and also within the professions and the Government. In no instance has the work of the committee taken on the character of an investigation of entertainment organizations, newspapers, labor unions, the professions, or the Government, as such, and it is not now the purpose of this committee to investigate education or educational institutions, as [such.]

"The Committee is equally concerned with the opportunities that the Communist Party has to wield its influence upon members of the teaching profession and students through Communists who are members of the teaching profession. Therefore, the objective of this investigation is to ascertain the character, extent and objects of Communist Party activities when such activities are carried on by members of the teaching profession who are subject to the directives and discipline of the Communist Party." * * *

to the need for control of the conduct. With these cases I agree. [But they do not] even remotely suggest that a law directly aimed at curtailing speech and political persuasion could be saved through a balancing process. * * *

But even assuming what I cannot assume, that some balancing is proper in this case, I feel that the Court after stating the test ignores it completely. At most it balances the right of the Government to preserve itself, against Barenblatt's right to refrain from revealing Communist affiliations. Such a balance, however, mistakes the factors to be weighed. In the first place, it completely leaves out the real interest in Barenblatt's silence, the interest of the people as a whole in being able to join organizations, advocate causes and make political "mistakes" without later being subjected to governmental penalties for having dared to think for themselves. It is this right, the right to err politically, which keeps us strong as a Nation. [It] is these interests of society, rather than Barenblatt's own right to silence, which I think the Court should put on the balance against the demands of the Government, if any balancing process is to be tolerated. Instead they are not mentioned, while on the other side the demands of the Government are vastly overstated and called "self preservation." [Such an approach] reduces "balancing" to a mere play on words and is completely inconsistent with the rules this Court has previously given for applying a "balancing test," where it is proper. * * *

Finally, I think Barenblatt's conviction violates the Constitution because the chief aim, purpose and practice of the House Un-American Activities Committee, as disclosed by its many reports, is to try witnesses and punish them because they are or have been Communists or because they refuse to admit or deny Communist affiliations. The punishment imposed is generally punishment by humiliation and public shame. [T]he proof that the Un-American Activities Committee is here undertaking a purely judicial function is [overwhelming].

It is the protection from arbitrary punishments through the right to a judicial trial with all these safeguards which over the years has distinguished America from lands where drum-head courts and other similar "tribunals" deprive the weak and the unorthodox of life, liberty and property without due process of law. It is this same right which is denied to Barenblatt, because the Court today fails to see what is here for all to see—that exposure and punishment is the aim of this Committee and the reason for its existence. To deny this aim is to ignore the Committee's own claims and the reports it has issued ever since it was established. * * *

Ultimately all the questions in this case really boil down to one—whether we as a people will try fearfully and futilely to preserve democracy by adopting totalitarian methods, or whether in accordance with our traditions and our Constitution we will have the confidence and courage to be free.

[Brennan, J., dissenting, expressed his "complete agreement with my Brother Black that no purpose for the investigation of Barenblatt is revealed by the record except exposure purely for the sake of exposure. This is not a purpose to which Barenblatt's rights under the First Amendment can validly be subordinated."]

Notes and Questions

1. *Compelling testimony vs. investigating.* Is the power of Congress to *compel testimony* in aid of legislation as broad as its power to *investigate* for this purpose. *Ought* it be? When Congress calls a hostile witness, is it concerned with this person's appraisal of the general problem or his advice? What does it

contribute to legislative insight, how does it aid the consideration of general legislation, to call a witness who wishes to *conceal* some thing about his individual case or that of his friends? To "inventory the Communists in the United States one at a time"? Kalven, *Mr. Alexander Meiklejohn and the Barenblatt Opinion*, 27 U.Chi.L.Rev. 315, 327 (1960).

2. *"Balancing".* (a) In "balancing the interests," did *Barenblatt* adequately consider and weigh the *alternative methods* for achieving the investigative purpose? Did it consider the necessity of gathering the information sought by the Subcommittee in the particular way it attempted to obtain it from Barenblatt: by forcing him to disclose or deny Communist affiliation at a *public* hearing? See Kauper, *Civil Liberties and the Constitution* 121 (1962).

(b) What *are* the "interests" on either side that the Court must "balance"? Whatever they are, on what basis can a judge compare them qualitatively without some independent standard to which they can be referred? Does the "balancing process" make it more—or less—difficult for judges to rest on their predispositions? See Frantz, *The First Amendment in the Balance*, 71 Yale L.J. 1424 (1962).

3. *Fifth vs. first amendments.* *Barenblatt* points out that "the protections of the First Amendment, unlike a proper claim of the privilege against self-incrimination [do] not afford a witness the right to resist inquiry in all circumstances. Where First Amendment rights are asserted [the] issue *always* involves a balancing by the courts of the competing private and public interests at stake." (Emphasis added.) Why, when confronted by the same national danger must the fifth amendment always prevail over the care for national security, but the first amendment give way to it? Should the interest of a citizen, and of the nation, in freedom of speech and association be entitled to less weight than the interest of a private individual in his safety from self-incrimination? See Meiklejohn, *The Balancing of Self-Preservation Against Political Freedom*, 49 Calif.L.Rev. 4, 6–7 (1961).

4. *The "Equality Principle."* Although disclosure cases do not follow a uniform course, the Court has manifested more concern about the impact of disclosure on private associations than is exhibited in *Barenblatt*. It has been especially protective of the NAACP. Consider Karst, *Equality as a Central Principle in the First Amendment*, 43 U.Chi.L.Rev. 20, 42–43 (1975): "In the late 1950s, when the civil rights movement was gathering momentum in the South, public disclosure of one's membership in the NAACP typically was followed by annoyances [and] often by more tangible reprisals like being fired. In a series of cases, the Court held that [government] could not constitutionally insist on such disclosure, either by the NAACP itself [a] or by individual members.[b]

a. GIBSON v. FLORIDA LEG. INVESTIG. COMM., 372 U.S. 539, 83 S.Ct. 889, 9 L.Ed.2d 929 (1963), per GOLDBERG, J., reversed a Florida Supreme Court holding that the custodian of NAACP records could be compelled to bring membership lists to legislative hearings so that he could be forced to refer to them in determining whether individuals suspected as being communists were NAACP members. This could not be required said the Court without a substantial relation between the NAACP and "conduct in which the State may have a compelling regulatory concern." Because no substantial relation was shown, compelling the NAACP to disclose its membership

presented "a question wholly different from compelling the Communist Party to disclose its own membership." HARLAN, J., joined by Clark, Stewart, and White, JJ., dissenting, complained that the Court had required "an investigating agency to prove in advance the very things it is trying to find out."

b. *Shelton v. Tucker*, 364 U.S. 479, 81 S.Ct. 247, 5 L.Ed.2d 231 (1960) held that teachers could not be required as a condition of employment to list all of the organizations they had belonged to or contributed to during the preceding five years. Professor Karst suggests that Barenblatt should have received the

"The governments' demands for information in these cases usually were presented for ostensibly neutral purposes. [The] Court, solemnly going along with the gag, took these asserted justifications at face value but concluded nonetheless that the required disclosures unconstitutionally invaded first amendment rights of political association.

"[The] Court's concern in these cases grows out of the first amendment's equality principle. If all the school teachers in Arkansas were to disclose their respective memberships in organizations, it is a safe bet that most Rotarians and Job's Daughters would not be greeted with heavy breathing when they answered the phone at night. The private harassment that concerned the Court was reserved for those associated with an unpopular challenge to the local orthodoxy. The point here is not simply that first amendment liberties normally matter most to underdogs; it is also that these decisions parallel one type of solution to the 'state action' problem that historically has plagued efforts to use the equal protection clause to protect individuals against private racial discrimination. In the disclosure cases, the state is seen as 'encouraging' private discrimination against those who espouse ideas with a particular content, even though the encouragement is embodied in a formally neutral law."

5. *Election disclosure requirements.* BROWN v. SOCIALIST WORKERS, 459 U.S. 87, 103 S.Ct. 416, 74 L.Ed.2d 250 (1982), per MARSHALL, J., held that an Ohio statute requiring every political party to report the names and addresses of campaign contributors and recipients of campaign disbursements could not be applied to the Socialist Workers Party. Citing *Buckley v. Valeo,* p. 674 infra, the Court held that the " 'evidence offered [by a minor party] need show only a reasonable probability that the compelled disclosure [of] names will subject them to threats, harassment, or reprisals from either Government officials or private parties.' " Consider Stone & Marshall, *Brown v. Socialist Workers: Inequality As A Command of the First Amendment,* 1983 Sup.Ct.Rev. 583, 592: "[I]n *Brown* the Court expressly exempted particular political parties from an otherwise content-neutral regulation for reasons directly related to the content of their expression. [The] constitutionally compelled exemption substitutes a content-based law for one that is content neutral. It stands the presumption in favor of 'content neutrality' on its head." Is the decision, nonetheless, consistent with first amendment values? See Stone & Marshall, supra.

B.   REPORTER'S PRIVILEGE

BRANZBURG v. HAYES

40 U.S. 665, 92 S.Ct. 2646, 33 L.Ed.2d 626 (1972).

MR. JUSTICE WHITE delivered the opinion of the Court.

[Branzburg, a Kentucky reporter, wrote articles describing his observations of local hashish-making and other drug violations. He refused to testify before a grand jury regarding his information. The state courts rejected his claim of a first amendment privilege.

[Pappas, a Massachusetts TV newsman-photographer, was allowed to enter and remain inside a Black Panther headquarters on condition he disclose nothing. When an anticipated police raid did not occur, he wrote no story.

same hospitality. But what standard should govern? Should the Court endorse a general right not to speak? A right not to speak about political associations? Suppose, after a wave of racially motivated bombings, the lead-er of a white racist organization is called before a grand jury and asked to reveal the group's membership. What standard should govern?

Summoned before a local grand jury, he refused to answer any questions about what had occurred inside the Panther headquarters or to identify those he had observed. The state courts denied his claim of a first amendment privilege.

[Caldwell, a N.Y. Times reporter covering the Black Panthers, was summoned to appear before a federal grand jury investigating Panther activities. A federal court issued a protective order providing that although he had to divulge information given him "for publication," he could withhold "confidential" information "developed or maintained by him as a professional journalist." Maintaining that absent a specific need for his testimony he should be excused from attending the grand jury altogether, Caldwell disregarded the order and was held in contempt. The Ninth Circuit reversed, holding that absent "compelling reasons" Caldwell could refuse even to attend the grand jury, because of the potential impact of such an appearance on the flow of news to the public.]

[Petitioners' first amendment claims] may be simply put: that to gather news it is often necessary to agree either not to identify [sources] or to publish only part of the facts revealed, or both; that if the reporter is nevertheless forced to reveal these confidences to a grand jury, the source so identified and other confidential sources of other reporters will be measurably deterred from furnishing publishable information, all to the detriment of the free flow of information protected by the First Amendment. Although petitioners do not claim an absolute privilege [they] assert that the reporter should not be forced either to appear or to testify before a grand jury or at trial until and unless sufficient grounds are shown for believing that the reporter possesses information relevant to a crime the grand jury is investigating, that the information the reporter has is unavailable from other sources, and that the need for the information is sufficiently compelling to override the claimed invasion of First Amendment interests occasioned by the disclosure. [The] heart of the claim is that the burden on news gathering resulting from compelling reporters to disclose confidential information outweighs any public interest in obtaining the information.

[We agree] that news gathering [qualifies] for First Amendment protection; without some protection for seeking out the news, freedom of the press could be eviscerated. But this case involves no intrusions upon speech [and no] command that the press publish what it prefers to withhold. [N]o penalty, civil or criminal, related to the content of published material is at issue here. The use of confidential sources by the press is not forbidden or restricted; reporters remain free to seek news from any source by means within the law. No attempt is made to require the press to publish its sources of information or indiscriminately to disclose them on request.

The sole issue before us is the obligation of reporters to respond to grand jury subpoenas as other citizens do and to answer questions relevant to an investigation into the commission of crime. The claim is, [that] reporters are exempt from [the average citizen's] obligations because if forced to respond to subpoenas and identify their sources or disclose other confidences, their informants will refuse or be reluctant to furnish newsworthy information in the future.

[T]he First Amendment does not guarantee the press a constitutional right of special access to information not available to the public generally. [Although] news gathering may be hampered, the press is regularly excluded from grand jury proceedings, our own conferences, the meetings of other official bodies gathered in executive session, and the meetings of private organizations. Newsmen have no constitutional right of access to the scenes of crime or disaster when the general public is excluded, and they may be prohibited from attending or publishing information about trials if such restrictions are necessary to assure a defendant a fair trial before an impartial tribunal. [It] is thus not surprising that the great weight of authority is that newsmen are not exempt from the normal duty of appearing before a grand jury and answering questions relevant to a criminal investigation.

[Because] its task is to inquire into the existence of possible criminal conduct and to return only well-founded indictments, [the grand jury's] investigative powers are necessarily broad. [T]he long standing principle that "the public has a right to every man's evidence," except for those persons protected by a constitutional, common law, or statutory privilege, is particularly applicable to grand jury proceedings.

A [minority] of States have provided newsmen a statutory privilege of varying breadth, [but] none has been provided by federal statute. [We decline to create one] by interpreting the First Amendment to grant newsmen a testimonial privilege that other citizens do not enjoy. [On] the records now before us, we perceive no basis for holding that the public interest in law enforcement and in ensuring effective grand jury proceedings is insufficient to override the consequential, but uncertain, burden on news gathering which is said to result from insisting that reporters, like other citizens, respond to relevant questions put to them in the course of a valid grand jury investigation or criminal trial.

This conclusion [does not] threaten the vast bulk of confidential relationships between reporters and their sources. Grand juries address themselves to the issues of whether crimes have been committed and who committed them. Only where news sources themselves are implicated in crime or possess information relevant to the grand jury's task need they or the reporter be concerned about grand jury subpoenas. Nothing before us indicates that a large number or percentage of *all* confidential news sources fall into either category and would in any way be deterred by [our holding].

It would be frivolous to assert—and no one does in these cases—that the First Amendment, in the interest of securing news or otherwise, confers a license on either the reporter or his news sources to violate otherwise valid criminal laws. [W]e cannot seriously entertain the notion that the First Amendment protects a newsman's agreement to conceal the criminal conduct of his source, or evidence thereof, on the theory that it is better to write about crime than to do something about [it.]

There remain those situations where a source is not engaged in criminal conduct but has information suggesting illegal conduct by others. [But] we remain unclear how often and to what extent informers are actually deterred from furnishing information when newsmen are forced to testify before a grand jury. The available data indicates that some newsmen rely a great deal on confidential sources and that some informants are particularly sensitive to the threat of exposure and may be silenced if it is held by this Court that, ordinarily, newsmen must testify pursuant to subpoenas, but the evidence fails to demonstrate that [our holding would cause] a significant constriction of the flow of news to the public * * *. Estimates of the inhibiting effect of such subpoenas on the willingness of informants to make disclosures to newsmen are widely divergent and to a great extent speculative. It would be difficult to canvass the views of the informants themselves; surveys of reporters on this topic are chiefly opinions of predicted informant behavior and must be viewed in the light of the professional self-interest of the interviewees.[33]   Reliance by the press on confidential informants does not mean that all such sources will in fact dry up because of the later possible appearance of the newsman before a grand jury. The reporter may never be called and if he objects to testifying, the prosecution may not insist.   Also, the relationship of many informants to the press is a symbiotic one which is unlikely to be greatly inhibited by the threat of subpoena: quite often, such informants are members of a minority political or cultural group which relies heavily on the media to propagate its views, publicize its aims, and magnify its exposure to the public.   *   *   *

Accepting the fact, however, that an undetermined number of informants not themselves implicated in crime will nevertheless, for whatever reason, refuse to talk to newsmen if they fear identification by a reporter in an official investigation, we cannot accept the argument that the public interest in possible future news about crime from undisclosed, unverified sources must take precedence over the public interest in pursuing and prosecuting those crimes reported to the press by informants and in thus deterring the commission of such crimes in the future.

[C]oncealment of crime and agreements to do so are not looked upon with favor.   Such conduct deserves no encomium, and we decline now to afford it First Amendment [protection].

We are admonished that refusal to provide a First Amendment reporter's privilege will undermine the freedom of the press to collect and disseminate news.   But this is not the lesson history teaches us.   [T]he common law recognized no such privilege, and the constitutional argument was not even asserted until 1958.   From the beginning of our country the press has operated without constitutional protection for press informants, and the press has [flourished.]

The argument for [a] constitutional privilege rests heavily on those cases holding that the infringement of protected First Amendment rights must be no broader than necessary to achieve a permissible governmental purpose.   We do not deal, however, with a governmental institution that has abused its proper function, as a legislative committee does when it "expose[s] for the sake of exposure."   [Nor is there any] attempt here by the grand juries to invade protected First Amendment rights by forcing wholesale disclosure of names and organizational affiliations for a purpose which is not germane to the determination of whether crime has been committed, and the characteristic secrecy of grand jury proceedings is a further protection against the undue invasion of such rights.   *   *   *

[The] requirements of those cases which hold that a State's interest must be "compelling" or "paramount" to justify even an indirect burden on First Amendment rights, are also met here.   [If] the test is that the Government "convincingly show a substantial relation between the information sought and a subject of overriding and compelling state interest," *Gibson*, it is quite apparent (1) that the State has the necessary interest in extirpating the traffic in illegal drugs, in

---

33.   In his *Press Subpoenas: An Empirical and Legal Analysis* 6–12 (1971), Prof. Blasi discusses these methodological problems. [His] survey found that slightly more than half of the 975 reporters questioned said that they relied on regular confidential sources for at least 10% of their stories.   Of this group of reporters, only 8% were able to say with some certainty that their professional functioning had been adversely affected by the threat of subpoena; another 11% were not certain whether or not they had been adversely affected. [See also Blasi, *The Newsman's Privilege: An Empirical Study,* 70 Mich.L.Rev. 229 (1971).]

forestalling assassination attempts on the President, and in preventing the community from being disrupted by violent disorders endangering both persons and property; and (2) that, based on the stories Branzburg and Caldwell wrote and Pappas' admitted conduct, the grand jury called these reporters as they would others—because it was likely that they could supply information to help the Government determine whether illegal conduct had occurred and, if it had, whether there was sufficient evidence to return an indictment.

Similar considerations dispose of the reporters' claims that preliminary to requiring their grand jury appearance, the State must show that a crime has been committed and that they possess relevant information not available from other sources, for only the grand jury itself can make this determination. [A] grand jury investigation "is not fully carried out until every available clue has been run down and all witnesses examined in every proper way to find if a crime has been committed." * * *

[The] privilege claimed here is conditional, not absolute; given the suggested preliminary showings and compelling need, the reporter would be required to testify. [If] newsmen's confidential sources are as sensitive as they are claimed to be, the prospect of being unmasked whenever a judge determines the situation justifies it is hardly a satisfactory solution to the problem. For them, it would appear that only an absolute privilege would suffice.

We are unwilling to embark the judiciary on a long and difficult journey to such an uncertain destination. The administration of a constitutional newsman's privilege would present practical and conceptual difficulties of a high order. Sooner or later, it would be necessary to define those categories of newsmen who qualified for the privilege, a questionable procedure in light of the traditional doctrine that liberty of the press is the right of the lonely pamphleteer who uses carbon paper or a mimeograph just as much as of the large metropolitan publisher who utilizes the latest photocomposition methods. [The] informative function asserted by representatives of the organized press in the present cases is also performed by lecturers, political pollsters, novelists, academic researchers, and dramatists. Almost any author may quite accurately assert that he is contributing to the flow of information to the public, that he relies on confidential sources of information, and that these sources will be silenced if he is forced to make disclosures before a grand jury.

In each instance where a reporter is subpoenaed to testify, the courts would also be embroiled in preliminary factual and legal determinations with respect to whether the proper predicate had been laid for the reporters' appearance. [I]n the end, by considering whether enforcement of a particular law served a "compelling" governmental interest, the courts would be inextricably involved in distinguishing between the value of enforcing different criminal laws. By requiring testimony from a reporter in investigations involving some crimes but not in others, they would be making a value judgment which a legislature had declined to [make.]

At the federal level, Congress has freedom to determine whether a statutory newsman's privilege is necessary and desirable and to fashion standards and rules as narrow or broad as deemed necessary [and], equally important, to refashion those rules as experience from time to time may dictate. There is also merit in leaving state legislatures free, within First Amendment limits, to fashion their own standards in light of the conditions and problems with respect to the relations between law enforcement officials and press in their own areas.

* * *

In addition, there is much force in the pragmatic view that the press has at its disposal powerful mechanisms of communication and is far from helpless to protect itself from harassment or substantial harm. Furthermore, if what the newsmen urged in these cases is true—that law enforcement cannot hope to gain and may suffer from subpoenaing newsmen before grand juries—prosecutors will be loath to risk so much for so little. Thus, at the federal level the Attorney General has already fashioned a set of rules for federal officials in connection with subpoenaing members of the press to testify before grand juries or at criminal trials.[a] These rules are a major step in the direction petitioners desire to move. They may prove wholly sufficient to resolve the bulk of disagreements and controversies between press and federal officials.

[G]rand jury investigations if instituted or conducted other than in good faith, would pose wholly different issues for resolution under the First Amendment. Official harassment of the press undertaken not for purposes of law enforcement but to disrupt a reporter's relationship with his news sources would have no justification. Grand juries are subject to judicial control and subpoenas to motions to quash. We do not expect courts will forget that grand juries must operate within the limits of the First Amendment as well as the Fifth.

We turn, therefore, to the disposition of the cases before us. [*Caldwell*] must be reversed. If there is no First Amendment privilege to refuse to answer the relevant and material questions asked during a good-faith grand jury investigation, then it is a fortiori true that there is no privilege to refuse to appear before such a grand jury until the Government demonstrates some "compelling need" for a newsman's testimony. [*Branzburg*] must be affirmed. Here, petitioner refused to answer questions that directly related to criminal conduct which he had observed and written about. [If] what petitioner wrote was true, he had direct information to provide the grand jury concerning the commission of serious crimes. [In *Pappas*, we] affirm [and] hold that petitioner must appear before the grand jury to answer the questions put to him, subject, of course, to the supervision of the presiding judge as to "the propriety, purposes, and scope of the grand jury inquiry and the pertinence of the probable testimony."

MR. JUSTICE POWELL, concurring in the opinion of the Court.

I add this brief statement to emphasize what seems to me to be the limited nature of the Court's holding. The Court does not hold that newsmen, subpoenaed to testify before a grand jury, are without constitutional rights with respect to the gathering of news or in safeguarding their sources. [As] indicated in the concluding portion of the opinion, the Court states that no harassment of newsmen will be tolerated. If a newsman believes that the grand jury investigation is not being conducted in good faith he is not without remedy. Indeed, if the newsman is called upon to give information bearing only a remote and tenuous relationship to the subject of the investigation, or if he has some other reason to believe that his testimony implicates confidential source relationships without a legitimate need of law enforcement, he will have access to the Court on a motion to quash and an appropriate protective order may be entered. The asserted claim to privilege should be judged on its facts by the striking of a proper balance between freedom of the press and the obligation of all citizens to give relevant testimony with respect to criminal conduct. The balance of these vital

---

a. The "Guidelines for Subpoenas to the News Media," noted the Court, recognize that "compulsory process in some circumstances may have a limiting effect on the exercise of First Amendment rights" and provide, inter alia, that that factor "must [be] weight[ed]" in every case against the public interest to be served in administering justice.

constitutional and societal interests on a case-by-case basis accords with the tried and traditional way of adjudicating such questions.*

In short, the courts will be available to newsmen under circumstances where legitimate First Amendment interests require protection.

MR. JUSTICE DOUGLAS, dissenting. * * *

It is my view that there is no "compelling need" that can be shown [by the Government] which qualifies the reporter's immunity from appearing or testifying before a grand jury, unless the reporter himself is implicated in a crime. His immunity in my view is therefore quite complete, for absent his involvement in a crime, the First Amendment protects him against an appearance before a grand jury and if he is involved in a crime, the Fifth Amendment stands as a barrier. Since in my view there is no area of inquiry not protected by a privilege, the reporter need not appear for the futile purpose of invoking one to each [question.]

Two principles which follow from [Alexander Meiklejohn's] understanding of the First Amendment are at stake here. One is that the people, the ultimate governors, must have absolute freedom of and therefore privacy of their individual opinions and beliefs regardless of how suspect or strange they may appear to others. Ancillary to that principle is the conclusion that an individual must also have absolute privacy over whatever information he may generate in the course of testing his opinions and beliefs. In this regard, Caldwell's status as a reporter is less relevant than is his status as a student who affirmatively pursued empirical research to enlarge his own intellectual viewpoint. The second principle is that effective self-government cannot succeed unless the people are immersed in a steady, robust, unimpeded, and uncensored flow of opinion and reporting which are continuously subjected to critique, rebuttal, and re-examination. In this respect, Caldwell's status as a newsgatherer and an integral part of that process becomes critical. * * *

Sooner or later any test which provides less than blanket protection to beliefs and associations will be twisted and relaxed so as to provide virtually no protection at all. [A] compelling interest test may prove as pliable as did the clear and present danger test. Perceptions of the worth of state objectives will change with the composition of the Court and with the intensity of the politics of the [times.]

Today's decision will impede the wide open and robust dissemination of ideas and counterthought which a free press both fosters and protects and which is essential to the success of intelligent self-government. Forcing a reporter before a grand jury [will lead] dissidents to communicate less openly to trusted reporters [and] cause editors and critics to write with more restrained pens. * * *

---

* It is to be remembered that Caldwell asserts a constitutional privilege not even to appear before the grand jury unless a court decides that the government has made a showing that meets the three preconditions specified in [Stewart, J.'s dissent]. To be sure, this would require a "balancing" of interests by the Court, but under circumstances and constraints significantly different from the balancing that will be appropriate under the Court's decision. The newsman witness, like all other witnesses, will have to appear; he will not be in a position to litigate at the threshold the State's very authority to subpoena him. Moreover, absent the constitutional preconditions that [the dissent] would impose as heavy burdens of proof to be carried by the State, the court—when called upon to protect a newsman from improper or prejudicial questioning—would be free to balance the competing interests on their merits in the particular case. The new constitutional rule endorsed by [the dissent] would, as a practical matter, defeat such a fair balancing and the essential societal interest in the detection and prosecution of crime would be heavily subordinated.

MR. JUSTICE STEWART, with whom MR. JUSTICE BRENNAN and MR. JUSTICE MARSHALL join, dissenting.

The Court's crabbed view of the First Amendment reflects a disturbing insensitivity to the critical role of an independent press in our society. [While] Mr. Justice Powell's enigmatic concurring opinion gives some hope of a more flexible view in the future, the Court in these cases holds that a newsman has no First Amendment right to protect his sources when called before a grand jury. The Court thus invites state and federal authorities to undermine the historic independence of the press by attempting to annex the journalistic profession as an investigative arm of government. Not only will this decision impair performance of the press' constitutionally protected functions, but it will, I am convinced, in the long run, harm rather than help the administration of justice.

[As] private and public aggregations of power burgeon in size and the pressures for conformity necessarily mount, there is obviously a continuing need for an independent press to disseminate a robust variety of information and opinion through reportage, investigation and criticism, if we are to preserve our constitutional tradition of maximizing freedom of choice by encouraging diversity of expression. * * *

A corollary of the right to publish must be the right to gather news. [This right] implies, in turn, a right to a confidential relationship between a reporter and his source. This proposition follows as a matter of simple logic once three factual predicates are recognized: (1) newsmen require informants to gather news; (2) confidentiality—the promise or understanding that names or certain aspects of communications will be kept off-the-record—is essential to the creation and maintenance of a news-gathering relationship with informants; and (3) the existence of an unbridled subpoena power—the absence of a constitutional right protecting, in *any* way, a confidential relationship from compulsory process—will either deter sources from divulging information or deter reporters from gathering and publishing information. * * *

After today's decision, the potential informant can never be sure that his identity or off-the-record communications will not subsequently be revealed through the compelled testimony of a newsman. A public spirited person inside government, who is not implicated in any crime, will now be fearful of revealing corruption or other governmental wrong-doing, because he will now know he can subsequently be identified by use of compulsory process. The potential source must, therefore, choose between risking exposure by giving information or avoiding the risk by remaining silent.

The reporter must speculate about whether contact with a controversial source or publication of controversial material will lead to a subpoena. In the event of a subpoena, under today's decision, the newsman will know that he must choose between being punished for contempt if he refuses to testify, or violating his profession's ethics [10] and impairing his resourcefulness as a reporter if he discloses confidential information. * * *

The impairment of the flow of news cannot, of course, be proven with scientific precision, as the Court seems to demand. [But] we have never before demanded that First Amendment rights rest on elaborate empirical studies demonstrating beyond any conceivable doubt that deterrent effects exist; we have never before required proof of the exact number of people potentially

---

10. The American Newspaper Guild has adopted the following rule as part of the newsman's code of ethics: "Newspaper men shall refuse to reveal confidences or disclose sources of confidential information in court or before other judicial or investigative bodies."

affected by governmental action, who would actually be dissuaded from engaging in First Amendment activity.

Rather, on the basis of common sense and available information, we have asked, often implicitly, (1) whether there was a rational connection between the cause (the governmental action) and the effect (the deterrence or impairment of First Amendment activity) and (2) whether the effect would occur with some regularity, i.e., would not be de minimus. And, in making this determination, we have shown a special solicitude towards the "indispensable liberties" protected by the First Amendment, *NAACP v. Alabama,* for "freedoms such as these are protected not only against heavy-handed frontal attack, but also from being stifled by more subtle government interference." Once this threshold inquiry has been satisfied, we have then examined the competing interests in determining whether there is an unconstitutional infringement of First Amendment freedoms. * * *

Surely the analogous claim of deterrence here is as securely grounded in evidence and common sense as the claims in [such cases as *NAACP v. Alabama*], although the Court calls the claim "speculative." [To] require any greater burden of proof is to shirk our duty to protect values securely embedded in the Constitution. We cannot await an unequivocal—and therefore unattainable— imprimatur from empirical studies. We can and must accept the evidence developed in the record, and elsewhere, that overwhelmingly supports the premise that deterrence will occur with regularity in important types of newsgathering relationships. Thus, we cannot escape the conclusion that when neither the reporter nor his source can rely on the shield of confidentiality against unrestrained use of the grand jury's subpoena power, valuable information will not be published and the public dialogue will inevitably be impoverished.

[A]ny exemption from the duty to testify before the grand jury "presupposes a very real interest to be protected." Such an interest must surely be the First Amendment protection of a confidential relationship. [This protection] functions to insure nothing less than democratic decisionmaking through the free flow of information to the public, and it serves, thereby, to honor the "profound national commitment to the principle that debate on public issues should be uninhibited, robust and wideopen." *New York Times v. Sullivan.*

[W]hen an investigation impinges on First Amendment rights, the government must not only show that the inquiry is of "compelling and overriding importance" but it must also "convincingly" demonstrate that the investigation is "substantially related" to the information sought. Governmental officials must, therefore, demonstrate that the information sought is *clearly* relevant to a *precisely* defined subject of governmental inquiry. They must demonstrate that it is reasonable to think the witness in question has that information. And they must show that there is not any means of obtaining the information less destructive of First Amendment liberties. * * *

I believe the safeguards developed in our decisions involving governmental investigations must apply to the grand jury inquiries in these cases. Surely the function of the grand jury to aid in the enforcement of the law is no more important than the function of the legislature, and its committees, to make the law. [T]he vices of vagueness and overbreadth which legislative investigations may manifest are also exhibited by grand jury inquiries, since grand jury investigations are not limited in scope to specific criminal acts.

[Thus,] when a reporter is asked to appear before a grand jury and reveal confidences, I would hold that the government must (1) show that there is probable cause to believe that the newsman has information which is clearly relevant to a specific probable violation of law; (2) demonstrate that the information sought cannot be obtained by alternative means less destructive of First Amendment rights; and (3) demonstrate a compelling and overriding interest in the information. * * *

The crux of the Court's rejection of any newsman's privilege is its observation that only "where news sources themselves are implicated in crime or possess information *relevant* to the grand jury's task need they or the reporter be concerned about grand jury subpoenas." (emphasis supplied). But this is a most misleading construct. [G]iven the grand jury's extraordinarily broad investigative powers and the weak standards of relevance and materiality that apply during such inquiries, reporters, if they have no testimonial privilege, will be called to give information about informants who have neither committed crimes nor have information about crime. It is to avoid deterrence of such sources and thus to prevent needless injury to First Amendment values that I think the government must be required to show probable cause that the newsman has information which is clearly relevant to a specific probable violation of criminal law. * * *

Both the "probable cause" and "alternative means" requirements [would] serve the vital function of mediating between the public interest in the administration of justice and the constitutional protection of the full flow of information. These requirements would avoid a direct conflict between these competing concerns, and they would generally provide adequate protection for newsmen.[35] No doubt the courts would be required to make some delicate judgments in working out this accommodation. But that, after all, is the function of courts of law. Better such judgments, however difficult, than the simplistic and stultifying absolutism adopted by the Court in denying any force to the First Amendment in these cases.[36]

[I]n the name of advancing the administration of justice, the Court's decision, I think, will only impair the achievement of that goal. People entrusted with law enforcement responsibility, no less than private citizens, need general information relating to controversial social problems. [W]hen a grand jury may exercise an unbridled subpoena power, and sources involved in sensitive matters become fearful of disclosing information, the newsman will not only cease to be a useful grand jury witness; he will cease to investigate and publish information about issues of public import.

[In Stewart, J.'s view, the Ninth Circuit correctly ruled that in the circumstances of the case, Caldwell need not divulge confidential information and, moreover, that in this case Caldwell had established that "his very appearance [before] the grand jury would jeopardize his relationship with his sources, leading to a severance of the news gathering relationship and impairment of the flow of news to the public." But because "only in very rare circumstances would a confidential relationship between a reporter and his source be so sensitive [as

35. We need not, therefore, reach the question of whether government's interest in these cases is "overriding and compelling." I do not, however, believe, as the Court does, that *all* grand jury investigations automatically would override the newsman's testimonial privilege.

36. The disclaimers in Mr. Justice Powell's concurring opinion leave room for the hope that in some future case the Court may take a less absolute position in this area.

to preclude] his mere appearance before the grand jury," Stewart, J., would confine "*this* aspect of the *Caldwell* judgment [to] its own facts." Thus, he would affirm in *Caldwell* and remand the other cases for further proceedings not inconsistent with his views.]

Notes and Questions

1. *The role of the press.* Consider Blasi, *The Checking Value in First Amendment Theory,* 1977 Am.B.Found.Res.J. 521, 593: The White, J., opinion "characterized the press as a private-interest group rather than an institution with a central function to perform in the constitutional system of checks and balances [and] labeled the source relationships that the reporters sought to maintain 'a private system of informers operated by the press to report on criminal conduct' [cautioning] that this system would be 'unaccountable to the public' were a reporter's privilege to be recognized." In contrast to White, J.'s perspective, consider the remarks of Stewart, J., in a much-discussed address, "*Or of the Press,*" 26 Hast.L.J. 631, 634 (1975): "In setting up the three branches of the Federal Government, the Founders deliberately created an internally competitive [b] system. [The] primary purpose [c] of [the Free Press Clause] was a similar one: to create a fourth institution outside the Government as an additional check on the three official branches." [d] Proceeding from variations of this fourth estate view of the press, most commentators endorse a reporter's privilege. See, e.g.,[e] Baker, *Press Rights and Government Power to Structure the Press,* 34 U.Miami L.Rev. 819, 858 (1980) (absolute protection). But see Bezanson, *The New Free Press Guarantee,* 63 Va.L.Rev. 731, 759–62 (1977) (press clause prevents special governmental assistance for press). Claims for an independent press-clause, however, need not interpret the press clause along fourth estate lines, see *Nimmer on Freedom of Speech* 2–104—2–129 (1984).

2. Whatever role is assigned to the press, are press relationships with confidential sources not entitled to at least the same protections afforded to civil rights groups and minority parties? Does *Branzburg* exhibit insensitivity to free

b. For commentary on how the "cozy connections" between press and government demonstrate that the relationship is often more cooperative than adversarial, see Soifer, *Freedom of the Press in the United States* in Press Law in Modern Democracies 79, 108–110 (Lahav, ed., 1985).

c. For spirited debate about the historical evidence, compare Anderson, *The Origins of the Press Clause,* 30 U.C.L.A.L.Rev. 455 (1983) with Levy, *On the Origins of the Free Press Clause,* 32 U.C.L.A.L.Rev. 177 (1984). See generally Levy, *Emergence of a Free Press* (1985).

d. For Brennan, J.'s views, see *Address,* 32 Rutg.L.Rev. 173 (1979).

e. For criticism of the notion of an independent press clause, see Lange, *The Speech and Press Clauses,* 23 U.C.L.A.L.Rev. 77 (1975); Lewis, *A Preferred Position for Journalism?,* 7 Hof.L.Rev. 595 (1979); Van Alstyne, *The First Amendment and the Free Press: A Comment on Some New Trends and Some Old Theories,* 9 Hof.L.Rev. 1 (1980); Van Alstyne, *The Hazards to the Press of Claiming a "Preferred Position",* 28 Hast.L.J. 761 (1977).

But see Abrams, *The Press is Different: Reflections on Justice Stewart and the Autonomous Press,* 7 Hof.L.Rev. 563 (1979). For an effort to transcend the issues involved, see generally Sack, *Reflections on the Wrong Question: Special Constitutional Privilege for the Institutional Press,* 7 Hof.L.Rev. 629 (1979). Finally, for commentary on the "tension between journalism as the political, sometimes partisan fourth estate and journalism as a profession" purporting to operate as a "neutral and objective medium," see Lahav, *An Outline for a General Theory of Press Law in Democracy* in Press Law in Modern Democracies 339, 352–54 (Lahav ed. 1985). See also Bollinger, *The Press and the Public Interest: An Essay on the Relationship Between Social Behavior and the Language of First Amendment Theory,* 82 Mich.L.Rev. 1447, 1457 (1984) (commenting generally on the pitfalls connected with justifying a free press by arguing that it serves the public interest: "More than most groups (compare lawyers, for example) the press is in conflict over its relationship to the world on which it regularly reports.").

speech values? Consider Blasi, note 1 supra, at 593: Two of the journalists before the Court "were covering the Black Panther Party, [which] claimed to be the victim of an official nationwide policy of persecution and extermination. Yet the White opinion made no reference to the speech value of news about possible official misbehavior obtained from persons against whom abuses of power may have been directed. Instead, Justice White spoke only of the criminal activities of the sources themselves and their peers, and denigrated the speech value at stake as that in 'possible future news about crime from undisclosed, unverified sources.' "

3. *Evaluating Powell, J.'s concurrence.* Did five justices—or only four— hold that grand juries may pursue their goals by any means short of bad faith? May one conclude that the information sought bears "only a remote and tenuous relationship to the subject of investigation" on grounds falling short of demonstrating "bad faith"? Does Powell, J.'s suggested test—the privilege claim "should be judged on its facts by [balancing the] vital constitutional and societal interests on a case-by-case basis"—resemble Stewart, J.'s dissenting approach more than White, J.'s? Extrajudicially, Stewart, J., has referred to *Branzburg* as a case which rejected claims for a journalist's privilege "by a vote of 5–4, or, considering Mr. Justice Powell's concurring opinion, perhaps by a vote of 4½– 4½." Stewart, *"Or of the Press,"* 26 Hast.L.J. 631, 635 (1975). The majority of courts applying *Branzburg* have concluded that Powell, J.'s opinion read together with the dissents affords the basis for a qualified privilege. Among the issues litigated are whether the privilege should be confined to journalists (or extended e.g. to academics) and the related question of how to define journalists and whether the privilege belongs to the source, the reporter, or both. For an exhaustive survey, see Goodale, Moodhe & Imes, *Reporter's Privilege Cases* in Communications Law 1984, at 339 (1984).

4. *Other contexts.* Does *Branzburg's* emphasis on the grand jury's special role in the American criminal justice system warrant different treatment of the journalist's privilege when a prosecutor seeks disclosure? See Murasky, *The Journalist's Privilege: Branzburg and Its Aftermath*, 52 Tex.L.Rev. 829, 885 (1974). Are the interests of civil litigants in compelling disclosure of a journalist's confidences significantly weaker than those of criminal litigants? Should there be an absolute journalist's privilege in civil discovery proceedings? See id. at 898–903. What if the journalist is a party to the litigation?

5. *State "shield laws" and a criminal defendant's right to compulsory process.* As of 1984, 26 states had enacted "shield" laws. Some protect only journalists' sources; some (including New Jersey) protect undisclosed information obtained in the course of a journalist's professional activities as well as sources. See Goodale, Moodhe & Imes, note 3 supra.

In re Farber, 78 N.J. 259, 394 A.2d 330 (1978), cert. denied, 439 U.S. 997, 99 S.Ct. 598, 58 L.Ed.2d 670 (1978): *New York Times* investigative reporter Myron Farber wrote a series of articles claiming that an unidentified "Doctor X" had caused the death of several patients by poisoning. This led to the indictment and eventual prosecution of Dr. Jascalevich for murder. (He was ultimately acquitted.) In response to the defendant's request, the trial court demanded the disclosure of Farber's sources and the production of his interview notes and other information for his in camera inspection. Relying on the first amendment and the state shield law, Farber refused to comply with the subpoenas. After White, J., and then Marshall, J., had denied stays, each deeming it unlikely that four justices would grant certiorari at this stage of the case, Farber was jailed for civil contempt and the *Times* heavily fined.

The state supreme court (5–2) upheld civil and criminal convictions of the *Times* and Farber. Under the circumstances, it ruled, the first amendment did not protect Farber against disclosure. Nor did the New Jersey shield law, for Farber's statutory rights had to yield to Dr. Jascalevich's sixth amendment right "to have compulsory process for obtaining witnesses in his favor." [e]

ZURCHER v. STANFORD DAILY, 436 U.S. 547, 98 S.Ct. 1970, 56 L.Ed.2d 525 (1978), again declined to afford the press special protection—dividing very much as in *Branzburg*.[a] A student newspaper that had published articles and photographs of a clash between demonstrators and police brought this federal action, claiming that a search of its offices for film and pictures showing events at the scene of the police-demonstrators clash (the newspaper was not involved in the unlawful acts) had violated its first and fourth amendment rights. A 5–3 majority, per WHITE, J., held that the fourth amendment does not prevent the government from issuing a search warrant (based on reasonable cause to believe that the "things" to be searched for are located on the property) simply because the owner or possessor of the place to be searched is not reasonably suspected of criminal involvement. The Court also rejected the argument that "whatever may be true of third-party searches generally, where the third party is a newspaper, there are additional [first amendment factors justifying] a nearly per se rule forbidding the search warrant and permitting only the subpoena duces tecum. The general submission is that searches of newspaper offices for evidence of crime reasonably believed to be on the premises will seriously threaten the ability of the press to gather, analyze, and disseminate news.

"[Although] [a]ware of the long struggle between Crown and press and desiring to curb unjustified official intrusions, [the Framers] did not forbid warrants where the press was involved, did not require special showing that subpoenas would be impractical, and did not insist that the owner of the place to be searched, if connected with the press, must be shown to be implicated in the offense being investigated. Further, the prior cases do no more than insist that the courts apply the warrant requirements with particular exactitude when First Amendment interests would be endangered by the search. [N]o more than this is required where the warrant requested is for the seizure of criminal evidence reasonably believed to be on the premises occupied by a newspaper. Properly administered, the preconditions for a warrant—probable cause, specificity [as to] place [and] things to be seized and overall reasonableness—should afford [the press] sufficient protection * * *.

"[R]espondents and amici have pointed to only a very few instances [since] 1971 involving [newspaper office searches]. This reality hardly suggests abuse, and if abuse occurs, there will be time enough to deal with it. Furthermore, the press [is] not easily intimidated—nor should it be."

e. For an exhaustive analysis of the case, see Note, 32 Rutg.L.Rev. 545 (1979). The case is also discussed at length by *New York Times* columnist Anthony Lewis, *A Preferred Position for Journalism?*, 7 Hof.L.Rev. 595, 610–18 (1979). See also Nowak, Rotunda & Young, *Constitutional Law* 912–13 (2d ed. 1983); Tribe, *American Constitutional Law* 73–74 n. 88 (1979 Supp.)

a. In both cases, White, J., joined by Burger, C.J., Blackmun, Powell and Rehnquist, JJ., delivered the opinion of the Court and in both cases the "fifth vote"—Powell, J.,—also wrote a separate opinion which seemed to meet the concerns of the dissent part way. In both cases Stewart, J., dissented, maintaining that the Court's holding would seriously impair "newsgathering." Stevens, J., who had replaced Douglas, J., also dissented in *Zurcher*, as had Douglas in *Branzburg*. Brennan, J., who had joined Stewart, J.'s dissent in *Branzburg*, did not participate in *Zurcher*.

POWELL, J., concurring, rejected Stewart, J.'s dissenting view that the press is entitled to "a special procedure, not available to others," when the government requires evidence in its possession, but added: "This is not to say [that a warrant] sufficient to support the search of an apartment or an automobile would be reasonable in supporting the search of a newspaper office. [While] there is no justification for the establishment of a separate Fourth Amendment procedure for the press, a magistrate asked to issue a warrant for the search of press offices can and should take cognizance of the independent values protected by the First Amendment—such as those highlighted by [Stewart, J., dissenting]—when he weighs such factors." [b]

STEWART, joined by Marshall, J., dissented: "A search warrant allows police officers to ransack the files of a newspaper, reading each and every document until they have found the one named in the warrant, while a subpoena would permit the newspaper itself to produce only the specific documents requested. A search, unlike a subpoena, will therefore lead to the needless exposure of confidential information completely unrelated to the purpose of the investigation. The knowledge that police officers can make an unannounced raid on a newsroom is thus bound to have a deterrent effect on the availability of confidential news sources. [The result] will be a diminishing flow of potentially important information to the public.

"[Here, unlike *Branzburg,* the newspaper does] not claim that any of the evidence sought was privileged [, but] only that a subpoena would have served equally well to produce that evidence. Thus, we are not concerned with the principle, central to *Branzburg,* that ' "the public [has] a right to everyman's evidence," ' but only with whether any significant social interest would be impaired if the police were generally required to obtain evidence from the press by means of a subpoena rather than a search. * * *

"Perhaps as a matter of abstract policy a newspaper office should receive no more protection from unannounced police searches than, say, the office of a doctor or the office of a bank. But we are here to uphold a Constitution. And our Constitution does not explicitly protect the practice of medicine or the business of banking from all abridgement by government. It does explicitly protect the freedom of the press." [c]

Notes and Questions

1. The distinctions between search and subpoena are underscored in Tribe, *American Constitutional Law* 73–75 (1979 Supp.): "When a subpoena is served on the media, it has the opportunity to assert whatever constitutional and statutory rights [such as 'shield laws,' enacted in many states, protecting reporters from divulging information given them in confidence] the press may invoke to keep confidential the information it has gathered. Such protection is circumvented when officials can proceed *ex parte,* by search warrant. And the risk of abuse may be greatest exactly when the press plays its most vital and creative role in our political system, the role of watchdog on official corruption and abuse. Officials who find themselves the targets [of] media investigation may use *Zurcher* as an excuse for conducting searches aimed at finding out precisely what

b. Powell, J., noted that his *Branzburg* concurrence may "properly be read as supporting the view expressed in the text above, and in the Court's [*Zurcher*] opinion," that under the warrant requirement "the magistrate should consider the values of a free press as well as the societal interest in enforcing the criminal laws."

c. Stevens, J., dissented on the general fourth amendment issue.

various journalists have discovered, to retaliate against [those] who have unearthed and reported official wrongdoing."

2. The difficulty in identifying suspects at the early stages of a criminal investigation, relied on by the *Zurcher* majority, does not, maintains Note, 92 Harv.L.Rev. 206–07 (1978), "require that the court refuse to adopt a special rule for those *classes* of witnesses who are so unlikely to destroy evidence as to deserve special protection from third party searches. [One reasonable approach] would be a narrow rule favoring the use of the subpoena only when the material is sought from neutral observers who possess evidence specifically because of the nature of their work, such as journalists, doctors, lawyers and accountants. Such parties are relatively easy to identify and are extremely unlikely to be either culpable or sympathetic to those who are culpable."

Is the clear message of both *Branzburg* and *Zurcher,* however, that the Court "perceives as peculiarly within the competence of legislative bodies the task of revising ordinary [criminal procedures] to account for communicative values"? See Tribe, supra, at 75.[d]

V. BEYOND ASSOCIATION: THE CONSTITUTIONAL PLACE OF THE PRESS REVISITED [a]

While continuing to exempt periodic publications from its general sales and use tax, Minnesota imposed a "use tax" on the cost of paper and ink products consumed in the production of such publications, but exempted the first $100,000 worth of paper and ink consumed in any calendar year. MINNEAPOLIS STAR & TRIBUNE v. MINNESOTA COMMISSIONER OF REVENUE, 460 U.S. 575, 103 S.Ct. 1365, 75 L.Ed.2d 295 (1983), per O'CONNOR, J., held that, although there is no indication, apart from the structure of the tax itself, of any impermissible or censorial motive on the part of the legislature, the special use tax violates the first amendment because it "singles out the press" and also because the effect of the $100,000 exemption is to "target a small group of newspapers":

"By creating this special use tax, which, to our knowledge, is without parallel in the State's tax scheme, Minnesota has singled out the press for special treatment. We then must determine whether the First Amendment permits such special taxation. A tax that burdens rights protected by the First Amendment cannot stand unless the burden is necessary to achieve an overriding governmental interest. * * *

"There is substantial evidence that differential taxation of the press would have troubled the Framers of the First Amendment. [A] power to tax differentially, as opposed to a power to tax generally, gives a government a powerful weapon against the taxpayer selected. When the State imposes a generally applicable tax, there is little cause for concern. We need not fear that a government will destroy a selected group of taxpayers by burdensome taxation if it must impose the same burden on the rest of its constituency. When the State singles out the press, though, the political constraints that prevent a legislature from passing crippling taxes of general applicability are weakened, and the threat of burdensome taxes becomes acute. That threat can operate as effectively as a censor to check critical comment by the press, undercutting the basic

d. For discussion of executive and legislative response to *Zurcher,* see Goodale, Moodhe, and Imes, note 3 supra after *Branzburg,* at 375–77. In particular, see The Privacy Protection Act of 1980, 42 U.S.C. §§ 2000aa–

2000aa–12 (limiting the impact of *Zurcher* on the media).

a. See note 1 after *Branzburg.*

assumption of our political system that the press will often serve as an important restraint on government. * * *

"Further, differential treatment, unless justified by some special characteristic of the press, suggests that the goal of the regulation is not unrelated to suppression of expression, and such a goal is presumptively unconstitutional. See, e.g., *Mosley.* * * *

"Addressing the concern with differential treatment, Minnesota invites us to look beyond the form of the tax to its substance. The tax is, according to the State, merely a substitute for the sales tax, which, as a generally applicable tax, would be constitutional as applied to the press. There are two fatal flaws in this reasoning. First, the State has offered no explanation of why it chose to use a substitute for the sales tax rather than the sales tax itself. * * *

"Further, even assuming that the legislature did have valid reasons for substituting another tax for the sales tax, we are not persuaded that this tax does serve as a substitute. The State asserts that this scheme actually *favors* the press over other businesses, because the same rate of tax is applied, but, for the press, the rate applies to the cost of components rather than to the sales price. We would be hesitant to fashion a rule that automatically allowed the State to single out the press for a different method of taxation as long as the effective burden was no different from that on other taxpayers or the burden on the press was lighter than that on other businesses. One reason for this reluctance is that the very selection of the press for special treatment threatens the press not only with the current *differential* treatment, but with the possibility of subsequent differentially *more burdensome* treatment. Thus, even without actually imposing an extra burden on the press, the government might be able to achieve censorial effects * * *.[11]

"A second reason to avoid the proposed rule is that courts as institutions are poorly equipped to evaluate with precision the relative burdens of various methods of taxation.[12] The complexities of factual economic proof always present a certain potential for error, and courts have little familiarity with the

---

11. Justice Rehnquist's dissent deprecates this concern, asserting that there is no threat, because this Court will invalidate any differentially more burdensome tax. That assertion would provide more security if we could be certain that courts will always prove able to identify differentially more burdensome taxes, a question we explore further, infra.

12. We have not always avoided evaluating the relative burdens of different methods of taxation in certain cases involving state taxation of the Federal Government and those with whom it does business. [In] spite of the rule against direct taxation of the Federal Government, States remain free to impose the *economic* incidence of a tax on the Federal Government, as long as that tax is not discriminatory. In that situation, then, the valid state interest in requiring federal enterprises to bear their share of the tax burden will often justify the use of differential methods of taxation. The special rule prohibiting direct taxation of the Federal Government but permitting the imposition of an equivalent economic burden on the Government may not only justify the State's use of different methods of taxation, but may also force us, within limits, to compare the burdens of two different taxes. Nothing, however, prevents the State from taxing the press in the same manner that it taxes other enterprises. It can achieve its interest in requiring the press to bear its share of the burden by taxing the press as it taxes others, so differential taxation is not necessary to achieve its goals.

Justice White insists that the Court regularly inquires into the economic effect of taxes, relying on a number of cases arising under the Due Process Clause and the Commerce Clause. [In] these cases, the Court required the taxpayer to show "gross overreaching," recognizing "the vastness of the State's taxing power and the latitude that the exercise of that power must be given before it encounters constitutional restraints." When delicate and cherished First Amendment rights are at stake, however, the constitutional tolerance for error diminishes drastically, and the risk increases that courts will prove unable to apply accurately the more finely tuned standards.

process of evaluating the relative economic burden of taxes. In sum, the possibility of error inherent in the proposed rule poses too great a threat to concerns at the heart of the First Amendment, and we cannot tolerate that possibility. Minnesota, therefore, has offered no adequate justification for the special treatment of newspapers.[14]

"Minnesota's ink and paper tax violates the First Amendment not only because it singles out the press, but also because it targets a small group of newspapers. The effect of the $100,000 exemption enacted in 1974 is that only a handful of publishers pay any tax at all, and even fewer pay any significant amount of tax.[15] The State explains this exemption as part of a policy favoring an 'equitable' tax system, although there are no comparable exemptions for small enterprises outside the press. Again, there is no legislative history supporting the State's view of the purpose of the amendment. Whatever the motive of the legislature in this case, we think that recognizing a power in the State not only to single out the press but also to tailor the tax so that it singles out a few members of the press presents such a potential for abuse that no interest suggested by Minnesota can justify the scheme. It has asserted no interest other than its desire to have an 'equitable' tax system. The current system, it explains, promotes equity because it places the burden on large publications that impose more social costs than do smaller publications and that are more likely to be able to bear the burden of the tax. Even if we were willing to accept the premise that large businesses are more profitable and therefore better able to bear the burden of the tax, the State's commitment to this 'equity' is questionable, for the concern has not led the State to grant benefits to small businesses in general. And when the exemption selects such a narrowly defined group to bear the full burden of the tax, the tax begins to resemble more a penalty for a few of the largest newspapers than an attempt to favor struggling smaller enterprises."[a]

WHITE, J., concurred and dissented in part: "This case is not difficult. The exemption for the first $100,000 of paper and ink limits the burden of the Minnesota tax to only a few papers. This feature alone is sufficient reason to invalidate the Minnesota tax and reverse the judgment of the Minnesota

---

14. Disparaging our concern with the complexities of economic proof, Justice Rehnquist's dissent undertakes to calculate a hypothetical sales tax liability for Star Tribune for the years 1974 and 1975. That undertaking, we think, illustrates some of the problems that inhere in any such inquiry. First, the calculation for 1974 and 1975 for this newspaper tells us nothing about the relative impact of the tax on other newspapers or in other years. Since newspapers receive a substantial portion of their revenues from advertising, it is not necessarily true even for profitable newspapers that the price of the finished product will exceed the cost of inputs. Consequently, it is not necessary that a tax imposed on components is less burdensome than a tax at the same rate imposed on the price of the product. Although the relationship of Star Tribune's revenues from circulation and its revenues from advertising may result in a lower tax burden under the use tax in 1974 and 1975, that relationship need not hold for all newspapers or for all time.

Second, if, as the dissent assumes elsewhere, the sales tax increases the price, that price increase presumably will cause a decrease in demand. The decrease in demand may lead to lower total revenues and, therefore, to a lower total sales tax burden than that calculated by the dissent. The dissent's calculations, then, can only be characterized as hypothetical. Taking the chance that these calculations or others like them are erroneous is a risk that the First Amendment forbids.

15. In 1974, 11 publishers paid the tax. Three paid less than $1,000, and another three paid less than $8,000. Star Tribune, one of only two publishers paying more than $100,000, paid $608,634. In 1975, 13 publishers paid the tax. Again, three paid less than $1,000, and four more paid less than $3,000. For that year, Star Tribune paid $636,113 and was again one of only two publishers incurring a liability greater than $100,000.

a. Blackmun, J., joined the Court's opinion except fn. 12.

Supreme Court. The Court recognizes that Minnesota's tax violates the First Amendment for this reason, and I subscribe to [this part] of the Court's opinion and concur in the judgment.

"Having found fully sufficient grounds for decision, the Court need go no further. The question whether Minnesota or another state may impose a use tax on paper and ink that is not targeted on a small group of newspapers could be left for another day.

"[The] Court submits that 'courts as institutions are poorly equipped to evaluate with precision the relative burdens of various methods of taxation,' except, it seems, in cases involving the sovereign immunity of the United States. Why this is so is not made clear, and I do not agree that the courts are so incompetent to evaluate the burdens of taxation that we must decline the task in this case.

"The Court acknowledges that in cases involving state taxation of the Federal government and those with whom it does business, the Court has compared the burden of two different taxes. It is not apparent to me why we are able to determine whether a state has imposed the economic incidence of a tax in a discriminatory fashion upon the federal government, but incompetent to determine whether a tax imposes discriminatory treatment upon the press. * * *

"Moreover, the Court frequently has examined—without complaint—the actual effect of a tax in determining whether the state has imposed an impermissible burden on interstate commerce or run afoul of the Due Process Clause. In a number of cases concerning railroad taxes, for example, the Court considered the tax burden to decide whether it was the equivalent of a property tax or an invalid tax on interstate commerce. The Court has compared the burden of use taxes on competing products from sister states with that of sales taxes on products sold in-state to decide whether the former constituted discrimination against interstate commerce. * * *

"There may be cases, I recognize, where the Court cannot confidently ascertain whether a differential method of taxation imposes a greater burden upon the press than a generally applicable tax. In these circumstances, I too may be unwilling to entrust freedom of the press to uncertain economic proof. But, as Justice Rehnquist clearly shows, this is not such a case. Since it is plainly evident that Minneapolis Star is not disadvantaged and is almost certainly benefitted by a use tax vis-à-vis a sales tax, I cannot agree that the First Amendment forbids a state from choosing one method of taxation over another."

REHNQUIST, J., dissented: "Today we learn from the Court that a State runs afoul of the First Amendment proscription of laws 'abridging the freedom of speech, or of the press' where the State structures its taxing system to the advantage of newspapers. [While] the Court purports to rely on the intent of the 'Framers of the First Amendment,' I believe it safe to assume that in 1791 'abridge' meant the same thing it means today: to diminish or curtail. Not until the Court's decision in this case, nearly two centuries after adoption of the First Amendment has it been read to prohibit activities which in no way diminish or curtail the freedoms it protects.

"[The] Court recognizes [that] the State of Minnesota could avoid constitutional problems by imposing on newspapers the 4% sales tax that it imposes on other retailers. Rather than impose such a tax, however, the Minnesota legislature decided to provide newspapers with an exemption from the sales tax and impose a 4% use tax on ink and paper; thus, while both taxes are part of one 'system of sales and use taxes,' newspapers are classified differently within that system.* The problem the Court finds too difficult to deal with is whether this difference in treatment results in a significant burden on newspapers.

"[The $1,244,747 in use taxes paid by appellant in 1974 and 1975] is significantly less burdensome than the $3,685,092 that could have been levied by a [4%] sales tax. A fortiori, the Minnesota taxing scheme which singles out newspapers for 'differential treatment' has benefited, not burdened, the 'freedom of speech, [and] of the press.'

"[The] 'differential treatment' standard that the Court has conjured up is unprecedented and unwarranted. [*Mosley*] certainly does not stand for this proposition. In *Mosley* all picketing except 'peaceful picketing' was prohibited within a particular public area. Thus, 'differential treatment' was not the key to the Court's decision; rather the essential fact was that unless a person was considered a 'peaceful picketer' his speech through this form of expression would be totally abridged within the area.

"Of course, all governmentally created classifications must have some 'rational basis.' [The] fact that they have been enacted by a presumptively rational legislature, however, arms them with a presumption of rationality. We have shown the greatest deference to state legislatures in devising their taxing schemes. * * *

"Where the state devises classifications that infringe on the fundamental guaranties protected by the Constitution the Court has demanded more of the State in justifying its action. But there is no *infringement,* and thus the Court has never required more, unless the State's classifications *significantly burden* these specially protected rights. [To] state it in terms of the freedoms at issue here, no First Amendment issue is raised unless First Amendment rights have been infringed; for if there has been no infringement, then there has been no 'abridgement' of those guaranties.

"Today the Court departs from this rule, refusing to look at the record and determine whether the classifications in the Minnesota use and sales tax statutes significantly burden the First Amendment rights of petitioner and its fellow newspapers. * * * Considering the complexity of issues this Court resolves each Term [the Court's] admonition [that courts are poorly equipped to evaluate with precision the relative burdens of various methods of taxation] as a general rule is difficult to understand. Considering the specifics of this case, this confession of inability is incomprehensible.

"Wisely not relying solely on its inability to weigh the burdens of the Minnesota tax scheme, the Court also says that even if the resultant burden on the press is lighter than on others [the very selection of the press for special treatment 'threatens the press [with] the possibility of subsequent differentially *more burdensome* treatment']. Surely the Court does not mean what it seems to say. The Court should be well aware from its discussion of *Grosjean* that this Court is quite capable of dealing with changes in state taxing laws which are intended to penalize newspapers.

"[The] State is required to show that its taxing scheme is rational. But in this case that showing can be made easily. [S]o long as the State can find

* The sales tax exemption and use tax liability are not, strictly speaking, for newspapers alone. The term of art used in the Minnesota taxing scheme is "publications." Publications is defined to include such materials as magazines, advertising supplements, shoppers guides, house organs, trade and professional journals, and serially issued comic books.

another way to collect revenue from the newspapers, imposing a sales tax on newspapers would be to no one's advantage; not the newspaper and its distributors who would have to collect the tax, not the State who would have to enforce collection, and not the consumer who would have to pay for the paper in odd amounts.

"[The] Court finds in very summary fashion that the exemption newspapers receive for the first $100,000 of ink and paper used also violates the First Amendment because the result is that only a few of the newspapers actually pay a use tax. I cannot agree. As explained by the Minnesota Supreme Court, the exemption is in effect a $4,000 credit which benefits all newspapers. Minneapolis Star & Tribune was benefited to the amount of $16,000 in the two years in question; $4,000 each year for its morning paper and $4,000 each year for its evening paper. Absent any improper motive on the part of the Minnesota legislature in drawing the limits of this exemption, it cannot be construed as violating the First Amendment.   *   *   *

"To collect from newspapers their fair share of taxes under the sales and use tax scheme and at the same time avoid abridging the freedoms of speech and press, the Court holds today that Minnesota must subject newspapers to millions of additional dollars in sales tax liability. Certainly this is a hollow victory for the newspapers and I seriously doubt the Court's conclusion that this result would have been intended by the 'Framers of the First Amendment.' "

SECTION 10.   WEALTH AND THE POLITICAL PROCESS: CONCERNS FOR EQUALITY

The idea of equality has loomed large throughout this chapter. Some feel it should be a central concern of the first amendment. See Tribe, *Constitutional Choices* 188–220 (1985); Karst, *Equality as a Central Principle in the First Amendment,* 43 U.Chi.L.Rev. 20 (1975). Equality has been championed by those who seek access to government property and to media facilities. It has been invoked in support of content regulation and against it. This section considers government efforts to prevent the domination of the political process by wealthy individuals and business corporations. In the end, it would be appropriate to reconsider the arguments for and against a marketplace conception of the first amendment, to ask whether the Court's interpretations overall (e.g., taking the public forum materials, the media materials, and the election materials together) have adequately considered the interest in equality, and to inquire generally about the relationship between liberty and equality in the constitutional scheme.

BUCKLEY v. VALEO
424 U.S. 1, 96 S.Ct. 612, 46 L.Ed.2d 659 (1976).

PER CURIAM.

[In this portion of a lengthy opinion dealing with the validity of the Federal Election Campaign Act of 1971, as amended in 1974, the Court considers those parts of the Act limiting *contributions* to a candidate for federal office (all sustained), and those parts limiting *expenditures* in support of such candidacy (all held invalid).[a]]

---

   a. Other aspects of *Buckley* are briefly considered in Sec. 6, I supra (public funding); Sec. 9, IV supra (disclosure).

A. *General Principles.* The Act's contribution and expenditure limitations operate in an area of the most fundamental First Amendment activities. Discussion of public issues and debate on the qualifications of candidates are integral to the operation of the system of government established by our Constitution.

[Appellees] contend that what the Act regulates is conduct, and that its effect on speech and association is incidental at most. Appellants respond that contributions and expenditures are at the very core of political speech, and that the Act's limitations thus constitute restraints on First Amendment liberty that are both gross and [direct.]

We cannot share the view [that] the present Act's contribution and expenditure limitations are comparable to the restrictions on conduct upheld in *O'Brien* [p. 515 supra]. The expenditure of money simply cannot be equated with such conduct as destruction of a draft card. Some forms of communication made possible by the giving and spending of money involve speech alone, some involve conduct primarily, and some involve a combination of the two. Yet this Court has never suggested that the dependence of a communication on the expenditure of money operates itself to introduce a non-speech element or to reduce the exacting scrutiny required by the First Amendment. * * *

Even if the categorization of the expenditure of money as conduct were accepted, the limitations challenged here would not meet the *O'Brien* test because the governmental interests advanced in support of the Act involve "suppressing communication." The interests served by the Act include restricting the voices of people and interest groups who have money to spend and reducing the overall scope of federal election campaigns. [Unlike] *O'Brien*, where [the] interest in the preservation of draft cards was wholly unrelated to their use as a means of communication, it is beyond dispute that the interest in regulating the alleged "conduct" of giving or spending money "arises in some measure because the communication allegedly integral to the conduct is itself thought to be harmful."

Nor can the Act's contribution and expenditure limitations be sustained, as some of the parties suggest, by reference to the constitutional principles reflected in such decisions as *Cox v. Louisiana, Adderley,* and *Kovacs,* [Secs. 6, II and 8 supra]. [The] critical difference between this case and those time, place and manner cases is that the present Act's contribution and expenditure limitations impose direct quantity restrictions on political communication and association by persons, groups, candidates and political parties in addition to any reasonable time, place, and manner regulations otherwise imposed.

A restriction on the amount of money a person or group can spend on political communication during a campaign necessarily reduces the quantity of expression by restricting the number of issues discussed, the depth of their exploration, and the size of the audience reached. This is because virtually every means of communicating ideas in today's mass society requires the expenditure of [money].

The expenditure limitations contained in the Act represent substantial rather than merely theoretical restraints on the quantity and diversity of political speech. The $1,000 ceiling on spending "relative to a clearly identified candidate," 18 U.S.C. § 608(e)(1), would appear to exclude all citizens and groups except candidates, political parties and the institutional press from any significant use of the most effective modes of communication.[20] * * *

20. The record indicates that, as of January 1, 1975, one full-page advertisement in a daily edition of a certain metropolitan newspaper costs $6,971.04—almost seven times the

By contrast with a limitation upon expenditures for political expression, a limitation [on] the amount of money a person may give to a candidate or campaign organization [involves] little direct restraint on his political communication, for it permits the symbolic expression of support evidenced by a contribution but does not in any way infringe the contributor's freedom to discuss candidates and issues. While contributions may result in political expression if spent by a candidate or an association to present views to the voters, the transformation of contributions into political debate involves speech by someone other than the contributor.

[There] is no indication [that] the contribution limitations imposed by the Act would have any dramatic adverse effect on the funding of campaigns and political associations.[23] The overall effect of the Act's contribution ceilings is merely to require candidates and political committees to raise funds from a greater number of persons and to compel people who would otherwise contribute amounts greater than the statutory limits to expend such funds on direct political expression, rather than to reduce the total amount of money potentially available to promote political expression. * * *

In sum, although the Act's contribution and expenditure limitations both implicate fundamental First Amendment interests, its expenditure ceilings impose significantly more severe restrictions on protected freedoms of political expression and association than do its limitations on financial contributions.

B. *Contribution Limitations.* [Section] 608(b) provides, with certain limited exceptions, that "no person shall make contributions to any candidate with respect to any election for Federal office which, in the aggregate, exceeds $1,000."[b] * * *

Appellants contend that the $1,000 contribution ceiling unjustifiably burdens First Amendment freedoms, employs overbroad dollar limits, and discriminates against candidates opposing incumbent officeholders and against minor-party candidates in violation of the Fifth Amendment.

[In] view of the fundamental nature of the right to associate, governmental "action which may have the effect of curtailing the freedom to associate is subject to the closest scrutiny." Yet, it is clear that "[n]either the right to associate nor the right to participate in political activities is absolute." *Letter Carriers* [p. 970 supra]. Even a " 'significant interference' with protected rights of political association" may be sustained if the State demonstrates a sufficiently important interest and employs means closely drawn to avoid unnecessary abridgment of associational freedoms. * * *

It is unnecessary to look beyond the Act's primary purpose—to limit the actuality and appearance of corruption resulting from large individual financial

annual limit on expenditures "relative to" a particular candidate imposed on the vast majority of individual citizens and associations by § 608(e)(1).

23. Statistical findings agreed to by the parties reveal that approximately 5.1% of the $73,483,613 raised by the 1161 candidates for Congress in 1974 was obtained in amounts in excess of $1,000. In 1974, two major-party senatorial candidates, Ramsey Clark and Senator Charles Mathias, Jr., operated large-scale campaigns on contributions raised under a voluntarily imposed $100 contribution limitation.

b. As defined, "person" includes "an individual, partnership, committee, association, corporation or any other organization or group." The limitation applies to: (1) anything of value, such as gifts, loans, advances, and promises to give, (2) contributions made direct to the candidate or to an intermediary, or a committee authorized by the candidate, (3) the aggregate amounts contributed to the candidate for each election, treating primaries, run-off elections and general elections separately and all Presidential primaries within a single calendar year as one election.

contributions—in order to find a constitutionally sufficient justification for the $1,000 contribution limitation. [The] increasing importance of the communications media and sophisticated mass mailing and polling operations to effective campaigning make the raising of large sums of money an ever more essential ingredient of an effective candidacy. To the extent that large contributions are given to secure political quid pro quos from current and potential office holders, the integrity of our system of representative democracy is undermined. Although the scope of such pernicious practices can never be reliably ascertained, the deeply disturbing examples surfacing after the 1972 election demonstrate that the problem is not an illusory one.

Of almost equal concern as the danger of actual quid pro quo arrangements is the impact of the appearance of corruption stemming from public awareness of the opportunities for abuse inherent in a regime of large individual financial contributions. In *Letter Carriers,* the Court found that the danger to "fair and effective government" posed by partisan political conduct on the part of federal employees charged with administering the law was a sufficiently important concern to justify broad restrictions on the employees' right of partisan political association. Here, as there, Congress could legitimately conclude that the avoidance of the appearance of improper influence "is also critical [if] confidence in the system of representative Government is not to be eroded to a disastrous extent." [29]

Appellants contend that the contribution limitations must be invalidated because bribery laws and narrowly-drawn disclosure requirements constitute a less restrictive means of dealing with "proven and suspected quid pro quo arrangements." But laws [against] bribes deal with only the most blatant and specific attempts of those with money to influence governmental action. [And] Congress was surely entitled to conclude that disclosure was only a partial measure, and that contribution ceilings were a necessary legislative concomitant to deal with the reality or appearance of corruption inherent in a system permitting unlimited financial contributions, even when the identities of the contributors and the amounts of their contributions are fully disclosed.

The Act's $1,000 contribution limitation focuses precisely on the problem of large campaign contributions—the narrow aspect of political association where the actuality and potential for corruption have been identified—while leaving persons free to engage in independent political expression, to associate actively through volunteering their services. [The] Act's contribution limitations [do] not undermine to any material degree the potential for robust and effective discussion of candidates and campaign [issues].

We find that, under the rigorous standard of review established by our prior decisions, the weighty interests served by restricting the size of financial contributions to political candidates are sufficient to justify the limited effect upon First Amendment freedoms caused by the $1,000 contribution ceiling.[c]

29. Although the Court in *Letter Carriers* found that this interest was constitutionally sufficient to justify legislation prohibiting federal employees from engaging in certain partisan political activities, it was careful to emphasize that the limitations did not restrict an employee's right to express his views on political issues and candidates.

c. The Court rejected the challenges that the $1,000 limit was overbroad because (1) most large contributors do not seek improper influence over a candidate, and (2) much more than $1,000 would still not be enough to influence improperly a candidate or office holder. With respect to (1), "Congress was justified in concluding that the interest in safeguarding against the appearance of impropriety requires that the opportunity for abuse inherent in the process of raising large monetary contributions be eliminated." With respect to (2), "As the Court of Appeals observed, '[a] court has no scalpel to probe, whether, say, a $2,000

C. *Expenditure Limitations.* [1.] Section 608(e)(1) provides that "[n]o person may make any expenditure [relative] to a clearly identified candidate during a calendar year which, when added to all other expenditures made by such person during the year advocating the election or defeat of such candidate, exceeds $1,000." [Its] plain effect [is] to prohibit all individuals, who are neither candidates nor owners of institutional press facilities, and all groups, except political parties and campaign organizations, from voicing their views "relative to a clearly identified candidate" through means that entail aggregate expenditures of more than $1,000 during a calendar year. The provision, for example, would make it a federal criminal offense for a person or association to place a single one-quarter page advertisement "relative to a clearly identified candidate" in a major metropolitan newspaper.

[Although] "expenditure," "clearly identified," and "candidate" are defined in the Act, there is no definition clarifying what expenditures are "relative to" a candidate. [But the "when" clause in § 608(e)(1)] clearly permits, if indeed it does not require, the phrase "relative to" a candidate to be read to mean "advocating the election or defeat of" a candidate.

But while such a construction of § 608(e)(1) refocuses the vagueness question, [it hardly] eliminates the problem of unconstitutional vagueness altogether. For the distinction between discussion of issues and candidates and advocacy of election or defeat of candidates may often dissolve in practical application. Candidates, especially incumbents, are intimately tied to public issues involving legislative proposals and governmental actions. Not only do candidates campaign on the basis of their positions on various public issues, but campaigns themselves generate issues of public interest.

[Constitutionally deficient uncertainty which "compels the speaker to hedge and trim"] can be avoided only by reading § 608(e)(1) as limited to communications that include explicit words of advocacy of election or defeat of a candidate, much as the definition of "clearly identified" in § 608(e)(2) requires that an explicit and unambiguous reference to the candidate appear as part of the communication. This is the reading of the provision suggested by the nongovernmental appellees in arguing that "[f]unds spent to propagate one's views on issues without expressly calling for a candidate's election or defeat are thus not covered." We agree that in order to preserve the provision against invalidation on vagueness grounds, § 608(e)(1) must be construed to apply only to expenditures for communications that in express terms advocate the election or defeat of a clearly identified candidate for federal office.

We turn then to the basic First Amendment question—whether § 608(e)(1), even as thus narrowly and explicitly construed, impermissibly burdens the constitutional right of free expression. * * *

We find that the governmental interest in preventing corruption and the appearance of corruption is inadequate to justify § 608(e)(1)'s ceiling on indepen-

ceiling might not serve as well as $1,000.' Such distinctions in degree become significant only when they can be said to amount to differences in kind."

The Court also rejected as without support in the record the claims that the contribution limitations worked invidious discrimination between incumbents and challengers to whom the same limitations applied.

The Court then upheld (1) exclusion from the $1,000 limit of the value of unpaid volun-

teer services and of certain expenses paid by the volunteer up to a maximum of $500; (2) the higher limit of $5,000 for contributions to a candidate by established, registered political committees with at least 50 contributing supporters and fielding at least five candidates for federal office; and (3) the $25,000 limit on total contributions to all candidates by one person in one calendar year.

dent expenditures. First, assuming arguendo that large independent expenditures pose the same dangers of actual or apparent quid pro quo arrangements as do large contributions, § 608(e)(1) does not provide an answer that sufficiently relates to the elimination of those dangers. Unlike the contribution limitations' total ban on the giving of large amounts of money to candidates, § 608(e)(1) prevents only some large expenditures. So long as persons and groups eschew expenditures that in express terms advocate the election or defeat of a clearly identified candidate, they are free to spend as much as they want to promote the candidate and his views. The exacting interpretation of the statutory language necessary to avoid unconstitutional vagueness thus undermines the limitation's effectiveness as a loophole-closing provision by facilitating circumvention by those seeking to exert improper influence upon a candidate or office-holder. It would naively underestimate the ingenuity and resourcefulness of persons and groups desiring to buy influence to believe that they would have much difficulty devising expenditures that skirted the restriction on express advocacy of election or defeat but nevertheless benefited the candidate's campaign. * * *

Second, [the] independent advocacy restricted by the provision does not presently appear to pose dangers of real or apparent corruption comparable to those identified with large campaign contributions. The parties defending § 608(e)(1) contend that it is necessary to prevent would-be contributors from avoiding the contribution limitations by the simple expedient of paying directly for media advertisements or for other portions of the candidate's campaign activities. [Section] 608(b)'s contribution ceilings rather than § 608(e)(1)'s independent expenditure limitation prevent attempts to circumvent the Act through prearranged or coordinated expenditures amounting to disguised contributions.[53] By contrast, § 608(e)(1) limits expenditures for express advocacy of candidates made totally independently of the candidate and his campaign. [The] absence of prearrangement and coordination of an expenditure with the candidate or his agent not only undermines the value of the expenditure to the candidate, but also alleviates the danger that expenditures will be given as a quid pro quo for improper commitments from the candidate. Rather than preventing circumvention of the contribution limitations, § 608(e)(1) severely restricts all independent advocacy despite its substantially diminished potential for abuse.

While the independent expenditure ceiling thus fails to serve any substantial governmental interest in stemming the reality or appearance of corruption in the electoral process, it heavily burdens core First Amendment expression. [Advocacy] of the election or defeat of candidates for federal office is no less entitled to protection under the First Amendment than the discussion of political policy generally or advocacy of the passage or defeat of legislation.

It is argued, however, that the ancillary governmental interest in equalizing the relative ability of individuals and groups to influence the outcome of elections serves to justify the limitation on express advocacy of the election or defeat of candidates imposed by § 608(e)(1)'s expenditure ceiling. But the

53. Section 608(e)(1) does not apply to expenditures "on behalf of a candidate within the meaning of" § 608(2)(B). That section provides that expenditures "authorized or requested by the candidate, an authorized committee of the candidate, or an agent of the candidate" are to be treated as expenditures of the candidate and contributions by the person or group making the expenditure. [In] view of [the] legislative history and the purposes of the Act, we find that the "authorized or requested" standard of the Act operates to treat all expenditures placed in cooperation with or with the consent of a candidate, his agents, or an authorized committee of the candidate as contributions subject to the limitations set forth in § 608(b).

concept that government may restrict the speech of some elements of our society in order to enhance the relative voice of others [d] is wholly foreign to the First Amendment, which was designed "to secure 'the widest possible dissemination of information from diverse and antagonistic sources,'" and "'to assure unfettered interchange of ideas for the bringing about of political and social changes desired by the people.'" *New York Times Co. v. Sullivan.* The First Amendment's protection against governmental abridgement of free expression cannot properly be made to depend on a person's financial ability to engage in public discussion.[55]

* * * *Mills v. Alabama,* 384 U.S. 214, 86 S.Ct. 1434, 16 L.Ed.2d 484 (1966), held that legislative restrictions on advocacy of the election or defeat of political candidates are wholly at odds with the guarantees of the First Amendment. [Yet] the prohibition on election day editorials invalidated in *Mills* is clearly a lesser intrusion on constitutional freedom than a $1,000 limitation on the amount of money any person or association can spend *during an entire election year* in advocating the election or defeat of a candidate for public office.

For the reasons stated, we conclude that § 608(e)(1)'s independent expenditure limitation is unconstitutional under the First Amendment.

2. [The] Act also sets limits on expenditures by a candidate "from his personal funds, or the personal funds of his immediate family, in connection with his campaigns during any calendar year." § 608(a)(1).[e]

The ceiling on personal expenditures by candidates on their own behalf [imposes] a substantial restraint on the ability of persons to engage in protected First Amendment expression. The candidate, no less than any other person, has a First Amendment right to engage in the discussion of public issues and vigorously and tirelessly to advocate his own election and the election of other candidates. Indeed, it is of particular importance that candidates have the unfettered opportunity to make their views known so that the electorate may intelligently evaluate the candidates' personal qualities and their positions on vital public issues before choosing among them on election day. [Section] 608(a)'s ceiling on personal expenditures by a candidate in furtherance of his own candidacy thus clearly and directly interferes with constitutionally protected freedoms.

The primary governmental interest served by the Act—the prevention of actual and apparent corruption of the political process—does not support the limitation on the candidate's expenditure of his own personal funds. [Indeed], the use of personal funds reduces the candidate's dependence on outside contributions and thereby counteracts the coercive pressures and attendant risks of abuse to which the Act's contribution limitations are directed.

The ancillary interest in equalizing the relative financial resources of candidates competing for elective office, therefore, provides the sole relevant rationale for Section 608(a)'s expenditure ceiling. That interest is clearly not sufficient to justify the provision's infringement of fundamental First Amend-

d. The lower court characterized the issue somewhat differently. Can "the wealthy few [claim] a constitutional guarantee to a stronger political voice than the unwealthy many because they are able to give and spend more money, and because the amounts they give and spend cannot be limited"? 519 F.2d 821, 841 (D.C.Cir.1975).

55. Neither the voting rights cases [Ch. 10, Sec. 4, I, B] nor the Court's decision upholding the FCC's fairness doctrine [p. 591 supra]

lends support to appellees' position that the First Amendment permits Congress to abridge the rights of some persons to engage in political expression in order to enhance the relative voice of other segments of our society. * * *

e. $50,000 for Presidential or Vice Presidential candidates; $35,000 for Senate candidates; $25,000 for most candidates for the House of Representatives.

ment rights. First, the limitation may fail to promote financial equality among candidates. [Indeed], a candidate's personal wealth may impede his [fundraising efforts]. Second, and more fundamentally, the First Amendment simply cannot tolerate § 608(a)'s restriction upon the freedom of a candidate to speak without legislative limit on behalf of his own candidacy. We therefore hold that § 608(a)'s restrictions on a candidate's personal expenditures is unconstitutional.

3. [Section] 608(c) of the Act places limitations on overall campaign expenditures by candidates [seeking] election to federal office. [For Presidential candidates the ceiling is $10,000,000 in seeking nomination and $20,000,000 in the general election campaign; for House of Representatives candidates it is $70,000 for each campaign—primary and general; for candidates for Senator the ceiling depends on the size of the voting age population.]

No governmental interest that has been suggested is sufficient to justify [these restrictions] on the quantity of political expression. [The] interest in alleviating the corrupting influence of large contributions is served by the Act's contribution limitations and disclosure provisions rather than by § 608(c)'s campaign expenditure ceilings. [There] is no indication that the substantial criminal penalties for violating the contribution ceilings combined with the political repercussion of such violations will be insufficient to police the contribution provisions. Extensive reporting, auditing, and disclosure requirements applicable to both contributions and expenditures by political campaigns are designed to facilitate the detection of illegal contributions. * * *

The interest in equalizing the financial resources of candidates competing for federal office is no more convincing a justification for restricting the scope of federal election campaigns. Given the limitation on the size of outside contributions, the financial resources available to a candidate's campaign, like the number of volunteers recruited, will normally vary with the size and intensity of the candidate's support. There is nothing invidious, improper, or unhealthy in permitting such funds to be spent to carry the candidate's message to the electorate. Moreover, the equalization of permissible campaign expenditures might serve not to equalize the opportunities of all candidates but to handicap a candidate who lacked substantial name recognition or exposure of his views before the start of the campaign.

The campaign expenditure ceilings appear to be designed primarily to serve the governmental interests in reducing the allegedly skyrocketing costs of political campaigns. [But the] First Amendment denies government the power to determine that spending to promote one's political views is wasteful, excessive, or unwise. In the free society ordained by our Constitution it is not the government but the people individually as citizens and candidates and collectively as associations and political committees who must retain control over the quantity and range of debate on public issues in a political campaign.

For these reasons we hold that § 608(c) is constitutionally invalid. * * *

MR. CHIEF JUSTICE BURGER, concurring in part and dissenting in part.

[I] agree fully with that part of the Court's opinion that holds unconstitutional the limitations the Act puts on campaign expenditures. [Yet] when it approves similarly stringent limitations on contributions, the Court ignores the reasons it finds so persuasive in the context of expenditures. For me contributions and expenditures are two sides of the same First Amendment coin.

[Limiting] contributions, as a practical matter, will limit expenditures and will put an effective ceiling on the amount of political activity and debate that the Government will permit to take place.[5]

The Court attempts to separate the two communicative aspects of political contributions—the "moral" support that the gift itself conveys, which the Court suggests is the same whether the gift is of $10 or $10,000,[6] and the fact that money translates into communication. The Court dismisses the effect of the limitations on the second aspect of contributions: "[T]he transformation of contributions into political debate involves speech by someone other than the contributor." On this premise—that contribution limitations restrict only the speech of "someone other than the contributor"—rests the Court's justification for treating contributions differently from expenditures. The premise is demonstrably flawed; the contribution limitations will, in specific instances, limit exactly the same political activity that the expenditure ceilings limit, and at least one of the "expenditure" limitations the Court finds objectionable operates precisely like the "contribution" limitations.[8]

The Court's attempt to distinguish the communication inherent in political *contributions* from the speech aspects of political *expenditures* simply will not wash. We do little but engage in word games unless we recognize that people—candidates and contributors—spend money on political activity because they wish to communicate ideas, and their constitutional interest in doing so is precisely the same whether they or someone else utter the words.

[T]he restrictions are hardly incidental in their effect upon particular campaigns. Judges are ill-equipped to gauge the precise impact of legislation, but a law that impinges upon First Amendment rights requires us to make the attempt. It is not simply speculation to think that the limitations on contributions will foreclose some candidacies.[9] The limitations will also alter the nature of some electoral contests drastically.[10]

[In] striking down the limitations on campaign expenditures, the Court relies in part on its conclusion that other means—namely, disclosure and

---

5. The Court notes that 94.9% of the funds raised by congressional candidates in 1974 came in contributions of less than $1,000, n. 27, and suggests that the effect of the contribution limitations will be minimal. This logic ignores the disproportionate influence large contributions may have when they are made early in a campaign; "seed money" can be essential, and the inability to obtain it may effectively end some candidacies before they begin. Appellants have excerpted from the record data on nine campaigns to which large, initial contributions were critical. Campaigns such as these will be much harder, and perhaps impossible, to mount under the Act.

6. Whatever the effect of the limitation, it is clearly arbitrary—Congress has imposed the same ceiling on contributions to a New York or California senatorial campaign that it has put on House races in Alaska or Wyoming. Both the strength of support conveyed by the gift of $1,000 *and* the gift's potential for corruptly influencing the recipient will vary enormously from place to place. * * *

8. The Court treats the Act's provisions limiting a candidate's spending from his *per-*

sonal resources as *expenditure* limits, as indeed the Act characterizes them, and holds them unconstitutional. As Mr. Justice Marshall points out, infra, by the Court's logic these provisions could as easily be treated as limits on *contributions*, since they limit what the candidate can give to his own campaign.

9. Candidates who must raise large initial contributions in order to appeal for more funds to a broader audience will be handicapped. See n. 5, supra. It is not enough to say that the contribution ceilings "merely require candidates [to] raise funds from a greater number of persons," where the limitations will effectively prevent candidates without substantial personal resources from doing just that.

10. Under the Court's holding, candidates with personal fortunes will be free to contribute to their own campaigns as much as they like, since the Court chooses to view the Act's provisions in this regard as unconstitutional "expenditure" limitations rather than "contribution" limitations. See n. 8, supra.

contribution ceilings—will adequately serve the statute's aim. It is not clear why the same analysis is not also appropriate in weighing the need for contribution ceilings in addition to disclosure requirements. Congress may well be entitled to conclude that disclosure was a "partial measure," but I had not thought until today that Congress could enact its conclusions in the First Amendment area into laws immune from the most searching review by this Court. * * *[f]

MR. JUSTICE WHITE, concurring in part and dissenting in part. * * *

I [agree] with the Court's judgment upholding the limitations on contributions. I dissent [from] the Court's view that the expenditure limitations [violate] the First Amendment. [This] case depends on whether the nonspeech interests of the Federal Government in regulating the use of money in political campaigns are sufficiently urgent to justify the incidental effects that the limitations visit upon the First Amendment interests of candidates and their supporters.

[The Court] accepts the congressional judgment that the evils of unlimited contributions are sufficiently threatening to warrant restriction regardless of the impact of the limits on the contributor's opportunity for effective speech and in turn on the total volume of the candidate's political communications by reason of his inability to accept large sums from those willing to give.

The congressional judgment, which I would also accept, was that other steps must be taken to counter the corrosive effects of money in federal election campaigns. One of these steps is § 608(e), which [limits] what a contributor may independently spend in support or denigration of one running for federal office. Congress was plainly of the view that these expenditures also have corruptive potential; but the Court strikes down the provision, strangely enough claiming more insight as to what may improperly influence candidates than is possessed by the majority of Congress that passed this Bill and the President who signed it. Those supporting the Bill undeniably included many seasoned professionals who have been deeply involved in elective processes and who have viewed them at close range over many years.

It would make little sense to me, and apparently made none to Congress, to limit the amounts an individual may give to a candidate or spend with his approval but fail to limit the amounts that could be spent on his behalf. Yet the Court permits the former while striking down the latter limitation. [I] would take the word of those who know—that limiting independent expenditures is essential to prevent transparent and widespread evasion of the contribution limits. * * *

The Court also rejects Congress' judgment manifested in § 608(c) that the federal interest in limiting total campaign expenditures by individual candidates justifies the incidental effect on their opportunity for effective political speech. I disagree both with the Court's assessment of the impact on speech and with its narrow view of the values the limitations will serve.

[M]oney is not always equivalent to or used for speech, even in the context of political campaigns. [There are] many expensive campaign activities that are not themselves communicative or remotely related to speech. Furthermore, campaigns differ among themselves. Some seem to spend much less money than others and yet communicate as much or more than those supported by enormous

---

f. Blackmun, J., also dissented separately from that part of the Court's opinion upholding the Act's restrictions on campaign contributions, unpersuaded that "a principled constitutional distinction" could be made between the contribution and expenditure limitations involved.

bureaucracies with unlimited financing. The record before us no more supports the conclusion that the communicative efforts of congressional and Presidential candidates will be crippled by the expenditure limitations than it supports the contrary. The judgment of Congress was that reasonably effective campaigns could be conducted within the limits established by the Act and that the communicative efforts of these campaigns would not seriously suffer. In this posture of the case, there is no sound basis for invalidating the expenditure limitations, so long as the purposes they serve are legitimate and sufficiently substantial, which in my view they are.

[E]xpenditure ceilings reinforce the contribution limits and help eradicate the hazard of corruption. [Without] limits on total expenditures, campaign costs will inevitably and endlessly escalate. Pressure to raise funds will constantly build and with it the temptation to resort in "emergencies" to those sources of large sums, who, history shows, are sufficiently confident of not being caught to risk flouting contribution [limits.]

The ceiling on candidate expenditures represents the considered judgment of Congress that elections are to be decided among candidates none of whom has overpowering advantage by reason of a huge campaign war chest. At least so long as the ceiling placed upon the candidates is not plainly too low, elections are not to turn on the difference in the amounts of money that candidates have to spend. This seems an acceptable purpose and the means chosen a common sense way to achieve [it.]

I also disagree with the Court's judgment that § 608(a), which limits the amount of money that a candidate or his family may spend on his campaign, violates the Constitution. Although it is true that this provision does not promote any interest in preventing the corruption of candidates, the provision does, nevertheless, serve salutary purposes related to the integrity of federal campaigns. By limiting the importance of personal wealth, § 608(a) helps to assure that only individuals with a modicum of support from others will be viable candidates. This in turn would tend to discourage any notion that the outcome of elections is primarily a function of money. Similarly, § 608(a) tends to equalize access to the political arena, encouraging the less wealthy, unable to bankroll their own campaigns, to run for political office.[g]

Notes and Questions

1. *Expenditure limitations.* Is it "foreign" to the first amendment to curb the spending of the wealthy in an effort to preserve the integrity of the elections process? Would it have been "foreign" to first amendment doctrine to engage in some type of balancing? Does the Court's expenditure ruling denigrate the interest in equality? See, e.g., Tribe, *Constitutional Choices* 193–94 (1985);

g. Marshall, J., dissented from that part of the Court's opinion invalidating the limitation on the amount a candidate or his family may spend on his campaign. He considered "the interest in promoting the reality and appearance of equal access to the political arena" sufficient to justify the limitation: "[T]he wealthy candidate's immediate access to a substantial personal fortune may give him an initial advantage that his less wealthy opponent can never overcome. [With the option of large contributions removed by § 608(b)], the less wealthy candidate is without the means to match the large initial expenditures of money of which the wealthy candidate is capable. In short, the limitations on contributions put a premium on a candidate's personal wealth. "[Section 608(a) then] emerges not simply as a device to reduce the natural advantage of the wealthy candidate, but as a provision providing some symmetry to a regulatory scheme that otherwise enhances the natural advantage of the wealthy."

For background on the *Buckley* case, see Friendly & Elliot, *The Constitution: That Delicate Balance* 91–107 (1984).

Nicholson, *Buckley v. Valeo: The Constitutionality of the Federal Election Campaign Act Amendments of 1974,* 1977 Wis.L.Rev. 323, 336; Wright, *Money and the Pollution of Politics: Is the First Amendment an Obstacle to Political Equality?,* 82 Colum.L.Rev. 609 (1982). Even if the concept of political equity is a "legitimizing myth," is *Buckley* flawed because it underestimates the necessity of promoting political leadership that is autonomous and independent of pluralistic forces? Is state autonomy necessary for minimally adequate state regulation of the economy? See Blum, *The Divisible First Amendment: A Critical Functionalist Approach to Freedom of Speech and Electoral Campaign Spending,* 58 N.Y. U.L.Rev. 1273, 1369–78 (1983). Alternatively, would it be better to solve the wealth problem by redistribution (and control of corporate power), while holding fast to a strong liberty principle? See Baker, *Realizing Self-Realization: Corporate Political Expenditures and Redish's The Value of Free Speech,* 130 U.Pa.L. Rev. 646, 652 (1982); Baker, *Scope of the First Amendment Freedom of Speech,* 25 U.C.L.A.L.Rev. 964, 983–90 (1978).

2. *Varying scrutiny.* (a) Did *Buckley* apply less exacting scrutiny to impairment of associational freedoms by contribution limits than to impairment of free expression by expenditure limits? Cf. 90 Harv.L.Rev. 178–79 (1976). "Granted that freedom of association is merely ancillary to speech, a means of amplifying and effectuating communication but logically secondary to speech," is this also "true of expenditures of money in aid of speech"? See Polsby, *Buckley v. Valeo: The Special Nature of Political Speech,* 1976 Sup.Ct.Rev. 1, 22. Can a lesser degree of scrutiny be justified for contributions? Or were the differing results based on the Court's perceiving a greater threat to first amendment interests in the expenditure limits and less risk of corruption and undue influence in unlimited independent expenditures? Cf. Nicholson, note 1 supra, at 340–45. Does the opinion indicate why greater deference was paid to congressional judgment on review of the contribution limits than on review of the expenditure limits? Cf. Note, 76 Colum.L.Rev. 852, 862 (1976). For a defense of strict scrutiny across the board, see BeVier, *Money and Politics: A Perspective on the First Amendment and Campaign Finance Reform,* 73 Calif.L. Rev. 1045 (1985).

(b) *The O'Brien analogy.* May the Court's rejection of the less-exacting *O'Brien* standard on the ground that the expenditure of money did not introduce a non-speech element fairly be criticized for asking the wrong question: whether "*pure speech* can be regulated where there is some incidental effect on *money,*" rather than whether "the use of *money* can be regulated, by analogy to such conduct as draft-card burning, where there is an undoubted incidental effect on *speech*"? See Wright, *Politics and the Constitution: Is Money Speech?,* 85 Yale L.J. 1001, 1007 (1976).

3. *Federal funding and expenditure limitations.* A separate section of the *Buckley* opinion seemed to approve expenditure limitations imposed upon candidates who accept federal funding: "[A]cceptance of federal funding entails voluntary acceptance of an expenditure ceiling." The existence of federal funding for a candidate has not, however, served to justify limitations on expenditures by groups who work on behalf of, but independently of, the candidate. FEC v. NATIONAL CONSERVATIVE POLITICAL ACTION COMM., ___ U.S. ___, 105 S.Ct. 1459, 84 L.Ed.2d 455 (1985), per REHNQUIST, J., invalidated a provision making it a political offense for such groups to expend more than $1000 to further the nomination or election of a candidate receiving federal financing. The Court argued that *Buckley* protected the freedom of association of "large numbers of individuals of modest means" to join together

and amplify their voices.[h] The Court stressed that the case involved expenditures, not contributions within the meaning of *Buckley;* that the provision was not directed to the size of the contributions the organizations received, and was not confined to corporations.

In dissent, White, J., noted his continuing objection to the distinction between contributions and expenditures, and Marshall, J., a new convert to that position, separately dissented on the same ground. Even assuming *Buckley* was correctly decided, White, J., argued that contributors to political committees were not engaging in speech to any greater extent than those who contribute directly to political campaigns: only the donee had changed. Moreover, he worried, as had Congress, that candidates would "go around hat in hand, begging for money from Washington-based special interest groups, political action committees whose sole purpose for existing is to seek a quid pro quo. [The] candidate may be forced to please the spenders rather than the voters, and the two groups are not identical."

FIRST NAT'L BANK v. BELLOTTI, 435 U.S. 765, 98 S.Ct. 1407, 55 L.Ed.2d 707 (1978), per POWELL, J., held invalid under the first and fourteenth amendments a Massachusetts criminal statute prohibiting banks or business corporations from making contributions or expenditures to influence "the vote on any question submitted to the voters, other than one materially affecting any of the property, business or assets of the corporation," defined to exclude from the exception questions "concerning the taxation of the income, property or transactions of individuals":

"The speech proposed by appellants is at the heart of the First Amendment's protection. [If] the speakers here were not corporations, no one would suggest that the state could silence their proposed speech. It is the type of speech indispensable to decisionmaking in a democracy, and this is no less true because the speech comes from a corporation rather than an individual. The inherent worth of the speech in terms of its capacity for informing the public does not depend upon the identity of its source, whether corporation, association, union or individual.

"The court below nevertheless held that corporate speech is protected by the First Amendment only when it pertains directly to the corporation's business interests. In deciding whether this novel and restrictive gloss on the First Amendment comports with the Constitution and the precedents of this Court, we need not survey the outer boundaries of the Amendment's protection of corporate speech, or address the abstract question whether corporations have the full measure of rights that individuals enjoy under the First Amendment.[13] The question in this case, simply put, is whether the corporate identity of the speaker

h. One defendant had received an average of $75 from 101,000 people during 1979–80; another, an average of $25 from approximately 100,000 people.

13. Nor is there any occasion to consider in this case whether, under different circumstances, a justification for a restriction on speech that would be inadequate as applied to individuals might suffice to sustain the same restriction as applied to corporations, unions, or like entities.

[*Consolidated Edison Co. v. Public Serv. Comm'n,* 447 U.S. 530, 100 S.Ct. 2326, 65 L.Ed. 2d 319 (1980) held that neither Consolidated Edison's corporate status, nor its status as a government regulated monopoly precluded it from asserting a first amendment right to insert controversial messages in its billing envelopes. Citing *Bellotti,* the Court stressed that the worth of speech does not depend upon its source.]

deprives this proposed speech of what otherwise would be its clear entitlement to protection. We turn now to that question.

"[A]ppellee suggests that First Amendment rights generally have been afforded only to corporations engaged in the communications business or through which individuals express themselves. [But] the Court's decisions involving corporations in the business of communication or entertainment are based not only on the role of the First Amendment in fostering individual self-expression but also on its role in affording the public access to discussion, debate, and the dissemination of information and ideas. See *Red Lion*, [p. 591 supra]; *Stanley v. Georgia*, [p. 389 supra]; *Time, Inc. v. Hill*, [p. 368 supra].

"[We] find no support in the First or Fourteenth Amendments, or in the decisions of this Court, for the proposition that speech that otherwise would be within the protection of the First Amendment loses that protection simply because its source is a corporation that cannot prove, to the satisfaction of a court, a material effect on its business or property. The 'materially affecting' requirement is not an identification of the boundaries of corporate speech etched by the Constitution itself. Rather, it amounts to an impermissible legislative prohibition of speech based on the identity of the interests that spokesmen may represent in public debate over controversial issues and a requirement that the speaker have a sufficiently great interest in the subject to justify communication.

"[In] the realm of protected speech, the legislature is constitutionally disqualified from dictating the subjects about which persons may speak and the speakers who may address a public issue. *Chicago Police Dep't v. Mosley*, [p. 536 supra]. If a legislature may direct business corporations to 'stick to business,' it also may limit other corporations—religious, charitable, or civic—to their respective 'business' when addressing the public. Such power in government to channel the expression of views is unacceptable under the First Amendment. Especially where, as here, the legislature's suppression of speech suggests an attempt to give one side of a debatable public question an advantage in expressing its views to the people, the First Amendment is plainly offended. * * *

"The constitutionality of § 8's prohibition of the 'exposition of ideas' by corporations turns on whether it can survive the exacting scrutiny necessitated by a state-imposed restriction of freedom of speech. Especially where, as here, a prohibition is directed at speech itself,[23] and the speech is intimately related to the process of governing, 'the State may prevail only upon showing a subordinating interest which is compelling.' *Bates v. Little Rock*, 361 U.S. 516, 80 S.Ct. 412, 4 L.Ed.2d 480 (1960).

"Preserving the integrity of the electoral process, preventing corruption, and 'sustain[ing] the active, alert responsibility of the individual citizen in a democracy for the wise conduct of government' are interests of the highest importance. *Buckley*. Preservation of the individual citizen's confidence in government is equally important.

"[Appellee's arguments] that these interests are endangered by corporate participation in discussion of a referendum [issue] hinge upon the assumption that such participation would exert an undue influence on the outcome of a

---

23. It is too late to suggest "that the dependence of a communication on the expenditure of money operates itself to introduce a nonspeech element or to reduce the exacting scrutiny required by the First Amendment." *Buckley.* Furthermore, § 8 is an "attempt directly to control speech [rather than] to protect, from an evil shown to be grave, some interest clearly within the sphere of governmental concern." *Speiser* [p. 636 supra]. Compare *O'Brien.*

referendum vote, and—in the end—destroy the confidence of the people in the democratic process and the integrity of government. According to appellee, corporations are wealthy and powerful and their views may drown out other points of view. If appellee's arguments were supported by record or legislative findings that corporate advocacy threatened imminently to undermine democratic processes, thereby denigrating rather than serving First Amendment interests,[a] these arguments would merit our consideration.[b] Cf. *Red Lion*. But there has been no showing that the relative voice of corporations has been overwhelming or even significant in influencing referenda in Massachusetts, or that there has been any threat to the confidence of the citizenry in government.

"[Referenda] are held on issues, not candidates for public office. The risk of corruption perceived in cases involving candidate elections simply is not present [c] in a popular vote on a public issue.[26] To be sure, corporate advertising may influence the outcome of the vote; this would be its purpose. But the fact that advocacy may persuade the electorate is hardly a reason to suppress [it.] We noted only recently that 'the concept that government may restrict the speech of some elements of our society in order to enhance the relative voice of others is wholly foreign to the First Amendment.' *Buckley*. Moreover, the people in our democracy are entrusted with the responsibility for judging and evaluating the relative merits of conflicting arguments.[31] They may consider, in making their

a. Legislatures wishing to support such findings need not look far. See, e.g., Lowenstein, *Campaign Spending and Ballot Propositions: Recent Experience, Public Choice Theory and the First Amendment*, 29 U.C.L.A. L.Rev. 505 (1982); Schockley, *Direct Democracy, Campaign Finance, and the Courts: Can Corruption, Undue Influence, and Declining Voter Confidence Be Found?*, 39 U.Miami L.Rev. 377 (1985). For additional information and commentary, see Cox, *Constitutional Issues in the Regulation of the Financing of Election Campaigns*, 31 Clev.St.L.Rev. 395 (1982); Symposium, *Political Action Committees and Campaign Finance*, 22 Ariz.L.Rev. 351 (1981); Symposium, *Campaign Finance Reform*, 10 Hast.Con.L.Q. 463 (1983).

b. "[I]f *Tornillo* and *Buckley* slammed the door on excessive power arguments, [*Bellotti*] opened a window. [The] Court did not pause, however, to explain why factors found in *Buckley* and *Tornillo* to be foreign to the first amendment would have 'merited consideration' in *Bellotti*." Shiffrin, *Government Speech*, 27 U.C.L.A. L.Rev. 565, 598–99 (1980).

c. *Citizens Against Rent Control v. Berkeley*, 454 U.S. 290, 102 S.Ct. 434, 70 L.Ed.2d 492 (1981) (White, J., dissenting) struck down a city ordinance placing a $250 limitation on contributions to committees formed to support or oppose ballot measures submitted to popular vote. The Court, per Burger, C.J., observed that the case did not involve an ordinance confined to contributions by corporations and that the case involved ballot measures, not candidate elections. Rehnquist, J., concurring noted the presence of a corporate petitioner, but emphasized that the ordinance was not aimed only at corporations. In

separate concurrences Marshall, J., and Blackmun, J., joined by O'Connor, J., noted that the record did not contain the kind of evidence that would warrant consideration under *Bellotti*. For commentary, see Tribe, Constitutional Choices 195–97 (1985); Lowenstein, fn. a supra, at 584–602; Nicholson, *The Constitutionality of Contribution Limitations in Ballot Measure Elections*, 9 Ecol.L.Q. 683 (1981).

26. [Appellants] do not challenge the constitutionality of laws prohibiting or limiting corporate contributions to political candidates or committees, or other means of influencing candidate elections. About half of these laws, including the Federal Corrupt Practices Act, by their terms do not apply to referendum votes. [The] overriding concern behind the enactment of statutes such as the Federal Corrupt Practices Act was the problem of corruption of elected representatives through the creation of political debts. [The] case before us presents no comparable problem, and our consideration of a corporation's right to speak on issues of general public interest implies no comparable right in the quite different context of participation in a political campaign for election to public office. Congress might well be able to demonstrate the existence of a danger of real or apparent corruption in independent expenditures by corporations to influence candidate elections. Cf. *Buckley*.

31. Government is forbidden to assume the task of ultimate judgment, lest the people lose their ability to govern themselves. The First Amendment rejects the "highly paternalistic" approach of statutes like § 8 which restrict what the people may hear. *Virginia Pharmacy* [p. 444 supra].

judgment, the source and credibility of the advocate. But if there be any danger that the people cannot evaluate the information and arguments advanced by appellants, it is a danger contemplated by the Framers of the First Amendment."

The Court rejected the argument that § 8 was justified by the interest in preventing use of corporate resources to advance views with which some shareholders disagreed. In this respect the statute was under-inclusive in not forbidding "the expenditure of corporate funds on any public issue until it becomes the subject of a referendum, though the displeasure of disapproving shareholders is unlikely to be any less. The fact that a particular kind of ballot question has been singled out for special treatment undermines the likelihood of a genuine state interest in protecting shareholders. It suggests instead that the legislature may have been concerned with silencing corporations on a particular subject. Indeed, appellee has conceded that 'the legislative and judicial history of the statute indicates [that] the second crime was "tailor-made" to prohibit corporate campaign contributions to oppose a graduated income tax amendment.'

"[The] over-inclusiveness of the statute is demonstrated by the fact that § 8 would prohibit a corporation from supporting or opposing a referendum proposal even if its shareholders unanimously authorized the contribution or expenditure. Ultimately shareholders may decide, through the procedures of corporate democracy, whether their corporation should engage in debate on public issues.[34]"

BURGER, C.J., who joined the Court's opinion, concurred: "A disquieting aspect of Massachusetts' position is that it may carry the risk of impinging on the First Amendment rights of those who employ the corporate form—as most do—to carry on the business of mass communications, particularly the large media conglomerates. This is so because of the difficulty, and perhaps impossibility, of distinguishing, either as a matter of fact or constitutional law, media corporations from corporations such as appellants.

"Making traditional use of the corporate form, some media enterprises have amassed vast wealth and power and conduct many activities, some directly related—and some not—to their publishing and broadcasting activities. See *Miami Herald*. Today, a corporation might own the dominant newspaper in one

---

34. [White, J.'s] repeatedly expressed concern for corporate shareholders who may be "coerced" into supporting "causes with which they disagree" apparently is not shared by appellants' shareholders. Not a single shareholder has joined appellee in defending the Massachusetts statute, or so far as the record shows, has interposed any objection to the right asserted by the corporations to make the proscribed expenditures.

The dissent of Mr. Justice White relies heavily on *Abood v. Detroit Bd. of Educ.* and *International Assn. of Machinists v. Street*, [Sec. 9, II supra]. These decisions involved the First Amendment rights of employees in closed or agency shops not to be compelled, as a condition of employment, to support with financial contributions the political activities of other union members with which the dissenters disagreed.

Street and *Abood* are irrelevant to the question presented in this case. In those cases employees were required, either by state law

or by agreement between the employer and the union, to pay dues or a "service fee" to the exclusive bargaining representative. To the extent that these funds were used by the union in furtherance of political goals, unrelated to collective bargaining, they were held to be unconstitutional because they compelled the dissenting union member "to furnish contributions of money for the propagation of opinions which he disbelieves."

The critical distinction here is that no shareholder has been "compelled" to contribute anything. Apart from the fact, noted by the dissent, that compulsion by the State is wholly absent, the [shareholder] invests in a corporation of his own volition and is [free to withdraw his investment at any time and for any reason.] A more relevant analogy, therefore, is to the situation where an employee voluntarily joins a union, or an individual voluntarily joins an association, and later finds himself in disagreement with its stance on a political issue. * * *

or more large metropolitan centers, television and radio stations in those same centers and others, a newspaper chain, news magazines with nationwide circulation, national or worldwide wire news services, and substantial interests in book publishing and distribution enterprises. Corporate ownership may extend, vertically, to pulp mills and pulp timberlands to insure an adequate, continuing supply of newsprint and to trucking and steamship lines for the purpose of transporting the newsprint to the presses. Such activities would be logical economic auxiliaries to a publishing conglomerate. Ownership also may extend beyond to business activities unrelated to the task of publishing newspapers and magazines or broadcasting radio and television programs. Obviously, such far-reaching ownership would not be possible without the state-provided corporate form and its 'special rules relating to such matters as limited liability, perpetual life, and the accumulation, distribution, and taxation of assets'. (White, J., dissenting).

"In terms of 'unfair advantage in the political process' and 'corporate domination of the electoral process,' it could be argued that such media conglomerates as I describe pose a much more realistic threat to valid interests than do appellants and similar entities not regularly concerned with shaping popular opinion on public issues. See *Miami Herald.*

"In terms of Massachusetts' other concern, the interests of minority shareholders, I perceive no basis for saying that the managers and directors of the media conglomerates are more or less sensitive to the views and desires of minority shareholders than are corporate officers generally. Nor can it be said, even if relevant to First Amendment analysis—which it is not—that the former are more virtuous, wise, or restrained in the exercise of corporate power than are the latter. Thus, no factual distinction has been identified as yet that would justify government restraints on the right of appellants to express their views without, at the same time, opening the door to similar restraints on media conglomerates with their vastly greater influence."

WHITE, J., joined by Brennan and Marshall, JJ., dissented, stressing two arguments: (1) The statute was designed to protect first amendment rights by "preventing institutions which have been permitted to amass wealth as a result of special advantages extended by the State for certain economic purposes from using that wealth to acquire an unfair advantage in the political process, especially where, as here, the issue involved has no material connection with the business of the corporation. The State need not permit its own creation to consume it. Massachusetts could permissibly conclude that not to impose limits upon the political activities of corporations would have placed it in a position of departing from neutrality and indirectly assisting the propagation of corporate views because of the advantages its laws give to the corporate acquisition of funds to finance such activities. Such expenditures may be viewed as seriously threatening the role of the First Amendment as a guarantor of a free market-place of ideas.

"[This] Nation has for many years recognized the need for measures designed to prevent corporate domination of the political process. The Corrupt Practices Act, first enacted in 1907, has consistently barred corporate contributions in connection with federal elections. This Court has repeatedly recognized that one of the principal purposes of this prohibition is 'to avoid the deleterious influences on federal elections resulting from the use of money by those who exercise control over large aggregations of capital.' *United States v. United Auto. Workers,* 352 U.S. 567, 585, 77 S.Ct. 529, 538, 1 L.Ed.2d 563 (1957). Although this Court has never adjudicated the constitutionality of the Act, there is no suggestion in its cases construing it that this purpose is in any sense illegitimate or deserving of other than the utmost respect; indeed, the thrust of its opinions, until today, has been to the contrary."

(2) The Massachusetts law advances the "overriding interest [of] assuring that shareholders are not compelled to support and financially further beliefs with which they disagree, where [the issue] does not materially affect the business, property, or other affairs of the corporation.[12] [The law] protects the very freedoms that this Court has held to be guaranteed by the First Amendment. [Last Term, in *Abood*, we] held that, a State may not, even indirectly, require an individual to contribute to the support of an ideological cause he may oppose as a condition of [employment].

"Presumably, unlike [*Street* and *Abood*,] the use of funds invested by shareholders with opposing views by Massachusetts corporations in connection with referenda or elections would not constitute state action and, consequently, not violate the First Amendment. Until now, however, the States have always been free to adopt measures designed to further rights protected by the Constitution even when not compelled to do so."

REHNQUIST, J., dissenting, argued that "the Fourteenth Amendment does not require a State to endow a business corporation with the power of political speech": "A State grants to a business corporation the blessings of potentially perpetual life and limited liability to enhance its efficiency as an economic entity. It might reasonably be concluded that those properties, so beneficial in the economic sphere, pose special dangers in the political sphere. [T]he States might reasonably fear that the corporation would use its economic power to obtain further benefits beyond those already bestowed. I would think that any particular form of organization upon which the State confers special privileges or immunities different from those of natural persons would be subject to like regulation, whether the organization is a labor union, a partnership, a trade association, or a corporation." [d]

Notes and Questions

1. *Protecting the privileged.* Consider Tushnet, *An Essay on Rights,* 62 Tex.L.Rev. 1363, 1387 (1984): "The first amendment has replaced the due process clause as the primary guarantor of the privileged. Indeed, it protects the privileged more perniciously than the due process clause ever did. Even in its heyday the due process clause stood in the way only of specific legislation designed to reduce the benefits of privilege. Today, in contrast, the first amendment stands as a general obstruction to all progressive legislative efforts. To protect their positions of privilege, the wealthy can make prudent investments either in political action or, more conventionally, in factories or stocks. But since the demise of substantive due process, their investments in factories and stocks can be regulated by legislatures. Under *Buckley* and *Bellotti*, however, their investments in politics—or politicians—cannot be regulated significantly. Needless to say, careful investment in politics may prevent effective

12. This, of course, is an interest that was not present in *Buckley*, and would not justify limitations upon the activities of associations, corporate or otherwise, formed for the express purpose of advancing a political or social cause.

d. Rehnquist, J., suggested that when the state creates a corporation such as a newspaper, "it necessarily assumes that the corporation is entitled to the liberty of the press essential to the conduct of its business." But a newspaper has "no greater right than any other corporation" to contribute money to political campaigns although its right to endorse a candidate in its editorial columns would be fully protected.

regulation of traditional investments." See also Tushnet, *Corporations and Free Speech* in The Politics of Law 253 (Kairys ed. 1982).[e]

Compare Levinson, *Book Review,* 83 Mich.L.Rev. 939, 945 (1985): "Overtly, justifying restriction of campaign spending by reference to the idea of fair access to the public forum may seem content neutral. However, it is worth considering to what extent we in fact support such restrictions because of tacit assumptions about the contents of the views held by the rich, who would obviously feel most of the burden of the restrictions. If both political views and the propensity to spend money on politics were distributed randomly among the entire populace, it is hard to see why anyone would be very excited about the whole issue of campaign finance."

2. *Distinguishing media corporations.* Consider Nicholson, *The Constitutionality of the Federal Restrictions on Corporate and Union Campaign Contributions and Expenditures,* 65 Corn.L.Rev. 945, 959 (1980): "A solution may be to focus on the distinction between media activities and other activities. A diversified corporation, partially involved in the media, would be entitled to full first amendment protection for its media-related operations. Under this approach, a newspaper would not lose its first amendment rights because it purchased a pulp mill, but it could not extend these rights to its pulp mill operations. An oil company that purchased a newspaper would not gain first amendment rights for its oil operations, but it would be able to assert these first amendment rights in the operation of its newspaper. The problem is not, to paraphrase Chief Justice Burger, the impracticability of making a distinction, but rather the difficulty of finding a theory that will justify a distinction."

Can self-expression serve as a distinguishing factor? See id. at 959–60. Is there more freedom "to choose and create the content of the delivered speech in the communications industry than in other industries"? Does the communication industry "display less allegiance to the profit motive than other industries"? Does it matter that the communications industry's product is speech? Can a fourth estate theory distinguish the press? On that premise, is there no reason to expand the definition of the press to include business corporations? See generally Baker, *Commercial Speech: A Problem in the Theory of Freedom,* 62 Iowa L.Rev. 1, 25–40 (1976); Baker, *Press Rights and Government Power to Structure the Press,* 34 U.Miami L.Rev. 819, 822–36 (1980).

3. *Protecting shareholders.* After *Bellotti,* could government "authorize management to make some kinds of corporate speech, such as commercial speech, but not others, such as political or noncommercial speech, without the approval or express consent of stockholders"? See generally Brudney, *Business Corporations and Stockholders' Rights Under the First Amendment,* 91 Yale L.J. 235 (1981).

4. *Protecting associational rights.* Should the Court have considered the possibly "stronger argument: corporate political expression should be protected as the speech and associational activity of the individual owners"? Cf. Note, 92 Harv.L.Rev. 163, 165–66 (1978). Does this argument slight the extent to which the state has altered political influence by creating corporations and conferring advantages upon them? See Patton & Bartlett, *Corporate "Persons" and Freedom of Speech: The Political Impact of Legal Mythology,* 1981 Wis.L.Rev. 494. Does the association argument also assume too much about the connection

e. For discussion on a broad range of issues concerning the relationship between speech values and property values in Burger Court decisions, see Dorsen & Gara, *Free Speech, Property, and the Burger Court: Old Values, New Balances,* 1982 Sup.Ct.Rev. 195.

between the owners' views and the corporation's speech? See Baker, *Commercial Speech*, note 2 supra and Brudney note 3 supra.

5. *Protecting listeners.* Is *Bellotti* justifiable because of listeners' rights? See Redish, *Self-Realization, Democracy, and Freedom of Expression: A Reply to Professor Baker*, 130 U.Pa.L.Rev. 678–79 (1982). But see Note, *Statutory Limitations on Corporate Spending in Ballot Measure Campaigns: The Case for Constitutionality*, 36 Hast.L.J. 433 (1985) (legal and market limitations on corporate speech inherently negate its value for listeners). Reconsider the arguments for and against the marketplace of ideas argument, Sec. 1, I supra.

6. *Aftermath of fn. 26.* 2 U.S.C. § 441(b) prohibits corporations or unions from making contributions or expenditures in connection with federal elections, but allows corporations and unions to establish and pay the expenses of segregated funds to be used for political purposes during federal elections. It prohibits corporations from soliciting contributions from persons other than its "stockholders and their families and its executive or administrative personnel and their families." In lieu of shareholders, corporations without capital stock are permitted to solicit contributions for such a fund from their "members." FEC v. NATIONAL RIGHT TO WORK COMM., 459 U.S. 197, 103 S.Ct. 552, 74 L.Ed.2d 364 (1982), per REHNQUIST, J., characterized these provisions as sufficiently tailored to prevent corruption or its appearance and to protect corporate contributors as to negate any judgment that restriction on associational interests was "undue." The National Right to Work Committee is an advocacy group organized as a nonprofit corporation without capital stock. It conceded that it was required to set up a segregated fund under § 441(b) but argued that it was entitled to solicit contributions from anyone that had previously responded to any of its prior mass mailings. The Court unanimously held that this conception of membership would render the statutory corporation "meaningless." Without requiring any evidentiary showing, the Court stated that the interest in avoiding corruption or its appearance justified "treating unions, corporations, and similar organizations differently from individuals."

FEC v. National Conservative Political Action Comm., p. 685 supra, per Rehnquist, J., characterized *National Right to Work Committee* as proceeding from the premise that "in return for the special advantages that the State confers on the corporate form, individuals acting jointly through corporations forgo some of the rights they have as individuals." But, citing *Bellotti's* fn. 26, he suggested that the question of whether a corporation could constitutionally be restricted in making independent expenditures to influence elections for public office was still open. Should advocacy groups organized in corporate form be treated like business corporations?

Chapter 5

FREEDOM OF RELIGION

This chapter concerns the "religion clauses" of the first amendment, commonly known as the "establishment clause" (forbidding laws "respecting an establishment of religion") and the "free exercise clause" (forbidding laws "prohibiting the free exercise thereof"). It is difficult to explore either clause in isolation from the other. The extent to which the clauses interact may be illustrated by the matter of public financial aid to parochial schools, the subject of a number of cases that follow: On the one hand, does such aid violate the establishment clause? On the other hand, does a state's failure to provide such aid violate the free exercise clause? Another example of the potential conflict between the clauses—also considered in the materials below—is whether, on the one hand, a state's exemption of church buildings from property taxes contravenes the establishment clause or whether, on the other hand, a state's taxing these buildings contravenes the free exercise clause.

Despite this interrelationship of the two clauses, Sec. 1 deals almost exclusively with the establishment clause. Sec. 2, I then considers conventional problems under the free exercise clause. Sec. 2, II examines the complex issues of defining "religion" for purposes of the first amendment and determining the bona fides of an asserted "religious" belief—both matters usually presumed in the cases decided by the Supreme Court and the former never specifically addressed by a majority of the justices. Finally, issues under each clause having been explored in some detail, Sec. 3 discusses problems presented by government action that attempts to accommodate the seemingly opposing demands of the two religion clauses.

SECTION 1. ESTABLISHMENT CLAUSE

Prior to 1947, only two decisions concerning the establishment clause produced any significant consideration by the Court. *Bradfield v. Roberts,* 175 U.S. 291, 20 S.Ct. 121, 44 L.Ed. 168 (1899) upheld federal appropriations to a hospital in the District of Columbia, operated by the Catholic Church, for ward construction and care of indigent patients. *Quick Bear v. Leupp,* 210 U.S. 50, 28 S.Ct. 690, 52 L.Ed. 954 (1908) upheld federal disbursement of funds, held in trust for the Sioux Indians, to Catholic schools designated by the Sioux for payment of tuition costs. Since 1947, however, a substantial number of cases have dealt with the meaning of the establishment clause. The major areas of controversy have concerned public financial assistance to church-related institutions (mainly parochial schools) and religious practices in the public schools. Other decisions have involved regulatory laws that "aid" religion and, most recently, government action that publicly acknowledges religion.[a]

EVERSON v. BOARD OF EDUC., 330 U.S. 1, 67 S.Ct. 504, 91 L.Ed. 711 (1947): A New Jersey township reimbursed parents for the cost of sending their children "on regular buses operated by the public transportation system," to and from schools, including nonprofit private and parochial schools. The Court, per BLACK, J., rejected a municipal taxpayer's contention that payment for Catholic parochial school students violated the establishment clause, observing that the religion clauses of the first amendment, "as made applicable to the states by the Fourteenth," "reflected in the minds of early Americans a vivid mental picture of conditions and practices which they fervently wished to stamp out in order to preserve liberty for themselves and for their posterity."

The Court detailed the history of religious persecution in Europe "before and contemporaneous with the colonization of America" and the "repetition of many of the old world practices" in the colonies—emphasizing the compulsion "to pay tithes and taxes to support government-sponsored churches whose ministers preached inflammatory sermons designed to strengthen and consolidate the established faith by generating a burning hatred against dissenters." The abhorrence of these practices "reached its dramatic climax in Virginia in 1785–86" when "Madison wrote his great Memorial and Remonstrance" against renewal of "Virginia's tax levy for support of the established church" and the Virginia Assembly "enacted the famous 'Virginia Bill for Religious Liberty' originally written by Thomas Jefferson. [This] Court has previously recognized that the provisions of the First Amendment, in the drafting and adoption of which Madison and Jefferson played such leading roles, had the same objective and were intended to provide the same protection against governmental intrusion on religious liberty as the Virginia statute. [The] interrelationship of these complementary clauses was well summarized [in] *Watson v. Jones,* 13 Wall. 679, 730, 20 L.Ed. 666: 'The structure of our government has, for the preservation of civil liberty, rescued the temporal institutions from religious interference. On the other hand, it has secured religious liberty from the invasions of the civil authority.'

"The 'establishment of religion' clause of the First Amendment means at least this: Neither a state nor the Federal Government can set up a church. Neither can pass laws which aid one religion, aid all religions, or prefer one religion over another. Neither can force nor influence a person to go to or to remain away from church against his will or force him to profess a belief or disbelief in any religion. No person can be punished for entertaining or professing religious beliefs or disbeliefs, for church attendance or non-attendance. No tax in any amount, large or small can be levied to support any religious activities or institutions, whatever they may be called, or whatever form they may adopt to teach or practice religion. Neither a state nor the Federal Government can, openly or secretly, participate in the affairs of any religious organizations or groups and vice versa. In the words of Jefferson, the clause against establishment of religion by law was intended to erect 'a wall of separation between Church and State.'

---

a. For discussion of the various "articulated justifications for the special constitutional place of religion" since 1937 by members of the Supreme Court, see Smith, *The Special Place of Religion in the Constitution,* 1983 Sup.Ct.Rev. 83.

"We must [not invalidate the New Jersey statute] if it is within the state's constitutional power even though it approaches the verge of that power. New Jersey cannot consistently with the 'establishment of religion' clause of the First Amendment contribute tax-raised funds to the support of an institution which teaches the tenets and faith of any church. On the other hand, other language of the amendment commands that New Jersey cannot hamper its citizens in the free exercise of their own religion. Consequently, it cannot exclude individual Catholics, Lutherans, Mohammedans, Baptists, Jews, Methodists, Non-believers, Presbyterians, or the members of any other faith, *because of their faith, or lack of it,* from receiving the benefits of public welfare legislation. While we do not mean to intimate that a state could not provide transportation only to children attending public schools, we must be careful, in protecting the citizens of New Jersey against state-established churches, to be sure that we do not inadvertently prohibit New Jersey from extending its general State law benefits to all its citizens without regard to their religious belief."

Noting that "the New Jersey legislature has decided that a public purpose will be served" by having children "ride in public buses to and from schools rather than run the risk of traffic and other hazards incident to walking or 'hitchhiking,'" the Court conceded "that children are helped to get to church schools. There is even a possibility that some of the children might not be sent to the church schools if the parents were compelled to pay their children's bus fares out of their own pockets when transportation to a public school would have been paid for by the State. [But] state-paid policemen, detailed to protect children going to and from church schools from the very real hazards of traffic, would serve much the same [purpose]. Similarly, parents might be reluctant to permit their children to attend schools which the state had cut off from such general government services as ordinary police and fire protection, connections for sewage disposal, public highways and sidewalks. Of course, cutting off church schools from these services, so separate and so indisputably marked off from the religious function, would make it far more difficult for the schools to operate. But such is obviously not the purpose of the First Amendment. That Amendment requires the state to be a neutral in its relations with groups of religious believers and non-believers; it does not require the state to be their adversary. State power is no more to be used so as to handicap religions, than it is to favor them.

"This Court had said that parents may, in the discharge of their duty under state compulsory education laws, send their children to a religious rather than a public school if the school meets the secular educational requirements which the state has power to impose. See *Pierce v. Society of Sisters,* [p. 127 supra]. It appears that these parochial schools meet New Jersey's requirements. The State contributes no money to the schools. It does not support them. Its legislation, as applied, does no more than provide a general program to help parents get their children, regardless of their religion, safely and expeditiously to and from accredited schools.

"The First Amendment has erected a wall between church and state. That wall must be kept high and impregnable. We could not approve the slightest breach. New Jersey has not breached it here."

RUTLEDGE, J., joined by Frankfurter, Jackson and Burton, JJ., filed the principal dissent, arguing that the statute aided children "in a substantial way to get the very thing which they are sent to the particular school to secure, namely, religious training and teaching. * * * Commingling the religious with the secular teaching does not divest the whole of its religious permeation and emphasis or make them of minor part, if proportion were material. Indeed, on any other view, the constitutional prohibition always could be brought to naught by adding a modicum of the secular. [Transportation] cost is as much a part of the total expense, except at times in amount, as the cost of textbooks, of school lunches, of athletic equipment, of writing and other [materials]. Payment of transportation is [no] less essential to education, whether religious or secular, than payment for tuitions, for teachers' salaries, for buildings, equipment and necessary materials. [No] rational line can be drawn between payment for such larger, but not more necessary, items and payment for transportation. [Now], as in Madison's time, not the amount but the principle of assessment is wrong.

* * *

"But we are told that the New Jersey statute is valid [because] the appropriation is for a public, not a private purpose, namely, the promotion of education, and the majority accept this idea in the conclusion that all we have here is 'public welfare legislation.' If that is true and the Amendment's force can be thus destroyed, what has been said becomes all the more pertinent. For then there could be no possible objection to more extensive support of religious education by New Jersey.

" * * * Public money devoted to payment of religious costs, educational or other, brings the quest for more. It brings too the struggle of sect against sect for the larger share or for any. Here one by numbers alone will benefit most, there another. That is precisely the history of societies which have had an established religion and dissident groups. It is the very thing Jefferson and Madison experienced and sought to guard against, whether in its blunt or in its more screened forms. The end of such strife cannot be other than to destroy the cherished liberty. The dominating group will achieve the dominant benefit; or all will embroil the state in their dissensions. * * *

"No one conscious of religious values can be unsympathetic toward the burden which our constitutional separation puts on parents who desire religious instruction mixed with secular for their children. They pay taxes for others' children's education, at the same time the added cost of instruction for their own. [But] discrimination in the legal sense does not exist. The child attending the religious school has the same right as any other to attend the public school. But he forgoes exercising it because the same guaranty which assures his freedom forbids the public school or any agency of the state to give or aid him in securing the religious instruction he seeks. * * *

"Nor is the case comparable to one of furnishing fire or police protection, or access to public highways. These things are matters of common right, part of the general need for safety. Certainly the fire department must not stand idly by while the church burns." [b]

b. *Application of the establishment clause to the states.* Both opinions state without extensive discussion that the fourteenth amendment applies the establishment clause to the states. Is nonestablishment as "implicit in the concept of ordered liberty" as the freedoms of speech, press, religious exercise, and assembly? See *Palko v. Connecticut,* p. 99 supra. Is it "fundamental to the American scheme"? See *Duncan v. Louisiana,* p. 104 supra.

Brennan, J., has stated: "It has been suggested, with some support in history, that absorption of the First Amendment's ban against congressional legislation 'respecting an establishment of religion' is conceptually impossible because the Framers meant the Establishment Clause also to foreclose any attempt by Congress to disestablish the existing official state churches. [But] the last of the formal state establishments was dissolved more than three decades before the Fourteenth Amendment was ratified, and thus the problem of protecting official state churches from federal encroachments could hardly have been any concern of those who framed the post-Civil War Amendments. [T]he Fourteenth Amendment created a panoply of new

The Court did not again confront the subject of aid to parochial schools until 1968. These decisions are considered in Part III infra. During the intervening two decades, however, the Court was presented with other problems that enabled it to further develop the establishment clause rationale begun in *Everson.*

I. RELIGION AND PUBLIC SCHOOLS

McCOLLUM v. BOARD OF EDUC., 333 U.S. 203, 68 S.Ct. 461, 92 L.Ed. 649 (1948), per BLACK, J., held that a Champaign, Illinois public school released time program violated the establishment clause. Privately employed religious teachers held weekly classes, on public school premises, in their respective religions, for students whose parents signed request cards, while non-attending students pursued secular studies in other parts of the building. "Here not only are the state's tax-supported public school buildings used for the dissemination of religious doctrines. The State also affords sectarian groups an invaluable aid in that it helps to provide pupils for their religious classes through use of the state's compulsory public school machinery."

FRANKFURTER, J., joined by Jackson, Rutledge, and Burton, JJ., concurred: "Designed to serve as perhaps the most powerful agency for promoting cohesion among the heterogeneous democratic people, the public school must keep scrupulously free from entanglement in the strife of sects." In answer to the defense

federal rights for the protection of citizens of the various States. And among those rights was freedom from such state governmental involvement in the affairs of religion as the Establishment Clause had originally foreclosed on the part of Congress.

"It has also been suggested that the 'liberty' guaranteed by the Fourteenth Amendment logically cannot absorb the Establishment Clause because that clause is not one of the provisions of the Bill of Rights which in terms protects a 'freedom' of the individual. The fallacy in this contention, I think, is that it underestimates the role of the Establishment Clause as a coguarantor, with the Free Exercise Clause, of religious liberty. * * *

"Finally, it has been contended that absorption of the Establishment Clause is precluded by the absence of any intention on the part of the Framers of the Fourteenth Amendment to circumscribe the residual powers of the States to aid religious activities and institutions in ways which fell short of formal establishments. That argument relies in part upon the express terms of the abortive Blaine Amendment—proposed several years after the adoption of the Fourteenth Amendment— which would have added to the First Amendment a provision that '[n]o state shall make any law respecting an establishment of religion.' Such a restriction would have been superfluous, it is said, if the Fourteenth Amendment had already made the Establishment Clause binding upon the States.

"The argument proves too much, for the Fourteenth Amendment's protection of the free exercise of religion can hardly be questioned; yet the Blaine Amendment would also have added an explicit protection against state

laws abridging that liberty." *School Dist. v. Schempp,* Part I infra (concurring opinion).

Consider Howe, *The Constitutional Question,* in Religion and the Free Society 49, 55 (1958): "The Court did not seem to be aware of the fact that some legislative enactments respecting an establishment of religion affect most remotely, if at all, the personal rights of religious liberty. [If the Court] reexamined its own interpretations of history [it might allow] the states to take such action in aid of religion as does not appreciably affect the religious or other constitutional rights of individuals * * *."

Compare Choper, *The Establishment Clause and Aid to Parochial Schools,* 56 Calif.L.Rev. 260, 274–75 (1968): "[Howe] assumes that while the fourteenth amendment prevents infringements of liberty which 'significantly affect' the individual, the first amendment forbids abridgements which do not do so. [A] central design of the establishment clause was that it [prevent] government generally from coercing religious belief and specifically from compulsorily taxing individuals for strictly religious purposes. If nonsecular federal action involves either of these consequences, [it] has 'significantly' affected individual freedom. Thus, if such state action involves either, it has seemingly violated the fourteenth amendment by 'significantly' affecting personal liberty. However, if federal action involves neither consequence, then [the] establishment clause itself—as a matter of constitutional construction—has probably not been breached." See also Note, *Toward a Uniform Valuation of the Religion Guarantees,* 80 Yale L.J. 77 (1970).

that the program was voluntary, he maintained, "That a child is offered an alternative may reduce the constraint; it does not eliminate the operation of influence by the school in matters sacred to conscience and outside the school's domain. The law of imitation operates, and nonconformity is not an outstanding characteristic of children. The result is an obvious pressure upon children to attend."

JACKSON, J., concurred in the result. But on the question of what injury was suffered, he commented that "any cost of this plan to the taxpayers is incalculable and negligible" and "it may be doubted whether the Constitution which, of course, protects the right to dissent, can be construed also to protect one from the embarrassment that always attends nonconformity whether in religion, politics, behavior or dress. Since no legal compulsion is applied to complainant's son himself and no penalty is imposed or threatened from which we may relieve him, we can hardly base jurisdiction on this ground." Reed, J., dissented.

Notes and Questions

1. *Financial benefit.* (a) Is the use of public school classrooms for religious education after school hours distinguishable from *McCollum?* Would it be different because it did not involve the use of "the state's compulsory public school machinery"? What does that phrase mean?

(b) Even if the hypothetical situation is distinguishable from *McCollum,* does it nonetheless provide impermissible financial "aid" to religion? Or is the aid "incalculable and negligible" and therefore de minimis?

Consider Choper, *Religion in the Public Schools: A Proposed Constitutional Standard,* 47 Minn.L.Rev. 329, 352 (1963): "Pfeffer contends [*Church, State, and Freedom* 167–68 (1953)] that the principle of de minimis has no application * * *; 'the right sought to be vindicated is a religious right, not an economic one, and it is therefore inappropriate to measure it in economic terms.' [But] when governmental activity [does] not infringe on religious liberty [the] financial expenditure involved must be subject to measurement by the de minimis standard. Otherwise, the appearance of 'In God We Trust' on our coins would be unconstitutional." Do you agree? If so, is the determination of de minimis to be made by examining the cost to the public or the financial benefit to the church?

2. *Reconciliation of McCollum with Everson.* Which situation produced the greater cost to the public? The greater advantage to religious education? May it be said that the program in *McCollum* was "public welfare legislation"?

___

ZORACH v. CLAUSON, 343 U.S. 306, 72 S.Ct. 679, 96 L.Ed. 954 (1952), per DOUGLAS, J., upheld a New York City released time program in which the religious classes were held in church buildings: "[This] program involves neither religious instruction in public school classrooms nor the expenditure of public funds. All costs, including the application blanks, are paid by the religious organizations. The case is therefore unlike *McCollum.*"

First, "it takes obtuse reasoning to inject any issue of the 'free exercise' of religion into the present case" because "there is no evidence [that] the system involves the use of coercion to get public school students into religious classrooms. [If] it were established that any one or more teachers were using their office to persuade or force students to take the religious instruction, a wholly different case would be presented.[7]"

As to the establishment clause: "[T]he First Amendment reflects the philosophy that Church and State should be separated [and] within the scope of its coverage permits no exception; the prohibition is absolute. The First Amendment, however, does not say that in every and all respects there shall be a separation of Church and State. Rather, it studiously defines the manner, the specific ways, in which there shall be no concert or union or dependency one on the other. That is the common sense of the matter. Otherwise the state and religion would be aliens to each other—hostile, suspicious, and even unfriendly. Churches could not be required to pay even property taxes. Municipalities would not be permitted to render police or fire protection to religious groups. Policemen who helped parishioners into their places of worship would violate the Constitution. Prayers in our legislative halls; the appeals to the Almighty in the messages of the Chief Executive; the proclamations making Thanksgiving Day a holiday; 'so help me God' in our courtroom oaths—these and all other references to the Almighty that run through our laws, our public rituals, our ceremonies would be flouting the First Amendment. A fastidious atheist or agnostic could even object to the supplication with which the Court opens each session: 'God save the United States and this Honorable Court.'

"[The] nullification of this law would have wide and profound effects. A Catholic student applies to his teacher for permission to leave the school during hours on a Holy Day of Obligation to attend a mass. A Jewish student asks his teacher for permission to be excused for Yom Kippur. A Protestant wants the afternoon off for a family baptismal ceremony. In each case the teacher requires parental consent in writing. In each case the teacher, in order to make sure the student is not a truant, goes further and requires a report from the priest, the rabbi, or the minister. The teacher in other words cooperates in a religious program to the extent of making it possible for her students to participate in it. Whether she does it occasionally for a few students, regularly for one, or pursuant to a systematized program designed to further the religious needs of all the students does not alter the character of the act.

"We are a religious people whose institutions presuppose a Supreme Being. We guarantee the freedom to worship as one chooses. * * * We sponsor an attitude on the part of government that shows no partiality to any one group and that lets each flourish according to the zeal of its adherents and the appeal of its dogma. When the state encourages religious instruction or cooperates with religious authorities by adjusting the schedule of public events to sectarian needs, it follows the best of our traditions. For it then respects the religious nature of our people and accommodates the public service to their spiritual needs. To hold that it may not would be to find in the Constitution a requirement that the government show a callous indifference to religious groups. That would be preferring those who believe in no religion over those who do believe. [The] problem, like many problems in constitutional law, is one of degree."

BLACK, J., dissented: "In the New York program, as in that of Illinois, the school authorities release some of the children on the condition that they attend the religious classes, get reports on whether they attend, and hold the other

7. [The] only allegation in the complaint that bears on the issue is that the operation of the program "has resulted and inevitably results in the exercise of pressure and coercion upon parents and children to secure attendance by the children for religious instruction." But this charge does not even implicate the school authorities. * * *

children in the school building until the religious hour is over. As we attempted to make categorically clear, the *McCollum* decision would have been the same if the religious classes had not been held in the school buildings."

JACKSON, J., dissented: "If public education were taking so much of the pupils' time as to injure the public or the students' welfare by encroaching upon their religious opportunity, simply shortening everyone's school day would facilitate voluntary and optional attendance at Church classes. But that suggestion is rejected upon the ground that if they are made free many students will not go to the Church. Hence, they must be deprived of freedom for this period, with Church attendance put to them as one of the two permissible ways of using it.

"The greater effectiveness of this system over voluntary attendance after school hours is due to the truant officer who, if the youngster fails to go to the Church school, dogs him back to the public schoolroom. Here schooling is more or less suspended during the 'released time' so the nonreligious attendants will not forge ahead of the churchgoing absentees. But it serves as a temporary jail for a pupil who will not go to Church. It takes more subtlety of mind than I possess to deny that this is governmental constraint in support of religion." As to "the Court's suggestion that opposition to this plan can only be antireligious, atheistic, or agnostic," "my evangelistic brethren confuse an objection to compulsion with an objection to religion. It is possible to hold a faith with enough confidence to believe that what should be rendered to God does not need to be decided and collected by Caesar. * * *

"[The] distinction attempted between [this case and *McCollum*] is trivial * * *. The wall which the Court was professing to erect between Church and State has become even more warped and twisted than I expected. Today's judgment will be more interesting to students of psychology and of the judicial process than to students of constitutional law." [a]

Notes and Questions

1. *Cost.* Can *Zorach* be reconciled with *McCollum* on the ground that the *McCollum* plan involved a significantly greater cost to the public? Brennan, J., has distinguished the cases "not [because] of the difference in public expenditures involved. True, the *McCollum* program involved the regular use of school facilities, classrooms, heat and light and time from the regular school day—even though the actual incremental cost may have been negligible. [But the] deeper difference was that the *McCollum* program placed the religious instructor in the public school classroom in precisely the position of authority held by the regular teachers of secular subjects, while the *Zorach* program did not. The *McCollum* program, in lending to the support of sectarian instruction all the authority of the governmentally operated public school system, brought government and religion into that proximity which the Establishment Clause forbids." *School Dist. v. Schempp,* infra (concurring opinion).

2. *Coercion.* (a) Do you agree that *Zorach* did not involve "the use of coercion to get public school students into religious classrooms"? Would the *Zorach* plan be inherently coercive, and therefore unconstitutional, if it were shown that most children found religious instruction more appealing than

---

a. Frankfurter, J., who agreed with Jackson, J.'s opinion, also filed a separate dissent.

For a description of the interaction of the justices in fashioning the *Everson, McCollum* and *Zorach* opinions, see Note, *The "Released Time" Cases Revisited: A Study of Group Decisionmaking by the Supreme Court,* 83 Yale L.J. 1202 (1974).

remaining in the public schools? Even if the alternative for those remaining was secular instruction with academic credit? See generally Regan, *The Dilemma of Religious Instruction and the Public Schools,* 10 Catholic Law. 42 (1964). If so, would it be permissible to excuse children from classes to enable them to attend special religious services of their faith? Would the first amendment forbid attendance at parochial schools, as an alternative to public schools, on the ground that this was simply one hundred per cent released time?

Under this analysis, would a program of "dismissed time" (all children released early permitting those who so wish to attend religious schools) be unconstitutional? Would "dismissed time" be nonetheless invalid if it could be shown that the purpose for the early school closing was to facilitate religious education? Or is this merely an accommodation "adjusting the schedule of public events to sectarian needs"?

(b) What of the argument that the *Zorach* program is inherently coercive, and therefore unconstitutional, because "the law of imitation operates" placing "an obvious pressure upon children to attend" religious classes? Under this analysis, what result in the case of excusing students to attend a religious service? In the case of parochial schools? In the case of "dismissed time"? Do you agree with Jackson, J.'s assertion in *McCollum* that "it may be doubted whether the Constitution [protects] one from the embarrassment that always attends nonconformity, whether in religion, politics, behavior or dress"?

3. *Free exercise.* (a) Would a contrary decision in *Zorach* have infringed the right of parents to direct the religious education of their children in violation of the free exercise clause? Any more so than the decision in *McCollum*? Is it relevant that parents may send their children to "full-time" or "late afternoon" religious schools? That in the case of excusing children to attend religious services, if the children are not excused they will have to *completely* forego the religious observance?

(b) If affirmance in *Zorach* would raise establishment problems while reversal would raise free exercise problems, how should this be reconciled? For detailed consideration, see note 4, Sec. 3 infra.

ENGEL v. VITALE, 370 U.S. 421, 82 S.Ct. 1261, 8 L.Ed.2d 601 (1962): The New York Board of Regents composed a prayer [a] that a local school board instructed be said aloud daily by each class. The Court, per BLACK, J.,[b] held that this concededly "religious activity" violated the establishment clause which "must at least mean that in this country it is no part of the business of government to compose official prayers for any group of the American people to recite as a part of a religious program carried on by government." The colonists "knew the anguish, hardship and bitter strife that could come when zealous religious groups struggled with one another to obtain the Government's stamp of approval [upon] one particular kind of prayer or one particular form of religious services."

Neither the fact "that the Regents' prayer was 'non-denominational'" nor that students who so wished might "remain silent or be excused from the room" could "free it from the limitations of the Establishment Clause, as it might from the Free Exercise Clause": "Although these two clauses may in certain instances

a. "Almighty God, we acknowledge our dependence upon Thee, and we beg Thy blessings upon us, our parents, our teachers and our country."

b. Douglas, J., concurred. Frankfurter and White, JJ., did not participate.

overlap, they forbid two quite different kinds of governmental encroachment upon religious freedom. The Establishment Clause, unlike the Free Exercise Clause, does not depend upon any showing of direct governmental compulsion and is violated by the enactment of laws which establish an official religion whether those laws operate directly to coerce nonobserving individuals or not. This is not to say, of course, that laws officially prescribing a particular form of religious worship do not involve coercion of such individuals. When the power, prestige and financial support of government is placed behind a particular religious belief, the indirect coercive pressure upon religious minorities to conform to the prevailing officially approved religion is plain. But the purposes underlying the Establishment Clause go much further than that. Its first and most immediate purpose rested on the belief that a union of government and religion tends to destroy government and to degrade religion. [Another] purpose of the Establishment Clause rested upon an awareness of the historical fact that governmentally established religions and religious persecutions go hand in hand." [c]

STEWART, J., dissented: "What is relevant to the issue here is not the history of an established church in sixteenth century England or in eighteenth century America, but the history of the religious traditions of our people, reflected in countless practices of the institutions and officials of our government." Neither the daily invocation to God in the Supreme Court, prayers in Congress, invocations of God by all our presidents, the third stanza of The Star-Spangled Banner (which has religious language), the pledge of allegiance (which contains the words "under God"), the congressionally directed National Day of Prayer, the words "In God We Trust" on our coins, the Declaration of Independence (which relies on "Divine Providence"), nor the Regents' prayer establish an "official religion."

Notes and Questions

1. *Establishment vs. free exercise.* Consider Kauper, *Prayer, Public Schools and the Supreme Court,* 61 Mich.L.Rev. 1031, 1065–66 (1963): "[I]mmature and impressionable children are susceptible to a pressure to conform and to participate in the expression of religious beliefs that carry the sanction and compulsion of the state's authority. [A] decision resting on the narrower ground of freedom of religion or of conscience, explaining why the considerations advanced in support of the prayer were outweighed by the rights of the objectors, and why under the circumstances the feature of voluntary participation did not sufficiently protect the interests of objectors, would have been much more satisfactory."

To what extent was this the basis for *Engel*? Would it permit the Regents' prayer in an elementary school where every child was willing to participate? In *any* high school? Consider Pollak, *Public Prayers in Public Schools,* 77 Harv.L. Rev. 62, 70 (1963): "[T]o have pitched the decision [on the free exercise clause] would presumably have meant that the prayer programs were constitutionally unobjectionable unless and until challenged, and, therefore, that school boards would have been under no discernible legal obligation, as assuredly they now

---

c. In a footnote, the Court distinguished "the fact that school children and others are officially encouraged to express love for our country by reciting historical documents such as the Declaration of Independence which contain references to the Deity or by singing officially espoused anthems which include the composer's professions of faith in a Supreme Being, or with the fact that there are many manifestations in our public life of belief in God. Such patriotic or ceremonial occasions bear no true resemblance to the unquestioned religious exercise that the State of New York has sponsored in this instance."

are, to suspend ongoing prayer programs on their own initiative. [Indeed,] the hypothetical schoolchild plaintiff, whose free exercise rights would thus be enforced, would have to be a child with the gumption not only to disassociate himself from the prayer program but to prefer litigation to the relatively expeditious exit procedure contemplated by the excusal proviso."

Where do the examples cited by Stewart, J., fall under the Court's analysis? Under the Kauper analysis? Under the Pollak analysis? Are these analyses restricted to concededly religious activities? Or do (should) they apply also to religious aspects of activities that are generally nonreligious?

2. *Compulsion.* Consider Griswold, *Absolute is in the Dark—A Discussion of the Approach of the Supreme Court to Constitutional Questions,* 8 Utah L.Rev. 167, 177, (1963): "When the prayer is recited, if [a] child or his parents feel that he cannot participate, he may stand or sit, in respectful attention, while the other children take part in the ceremony. Or he may leave the room. It is said that this is bad, because it sets him apart from other children. It is even said that there is an element of compulsion in this. [But] is this the way it should be looked at? The child of a nonconforming or minority group is, to be sure, different in his beliefs. That is what it means to be a member of a minority. Is it not desirable, and educational, for him to learn and observe this, in the atmosphere of the school—not so much that he is different, as that other children are different from him? And is it not desirable that, at the same time, he experiences and learns the fact that his difference is tolerated and accepted? No compulsion is put upon him. He need not participate. But he, too, has the opportunity to be tolerant. He allows the majority of the group to follow their own tradition, perhaps coming to understand and to respect what they feel is significant to them." See also Sutherland, *Establishment According to Engel,* 76 Harv.L.Rev. 25 (1962); Kurland, *The Regents' Prayer Case: "Full of Sound and Fury, Signifying * * *,"* 1962 Sup.Ct.Rev. 1.

SCHOOL DISTRICT v. SCHEMPP
374 U.S. 203, 83 S.Ct. 1560, 10 L.Ed.2d 844 (1963).

MR. JUSTICE CLARK delivered the opinion of the Court.

[These cases were brought by parents and their children in public schools— *Schempp,* by Unitarians in Abington Township, Pa.; *Murray* by "professed atheists" in Baltimore, Md.—challenging reading of the Bible (without comment) and recitation of the Lord's Prayer as part of daily opening exercises in the schools. In *Schempp,* various students read passages they selected from any version of the Bible. Mr. Schempp testified that "specific religious doctrines purveyed by a literal reading of the Bible" were contrary to the family's religious beliefs; one expert testified that "portions of the New Testament were offensive to Jewish tradition" and, if "read without explanation, they could [be] psychologically harmful to the child and had caused a divisive force within the social media of the school"; a defense expert testified "that the Bible [was] nonsectarian within the Christian faiths." Mr. Schempp had decided against having his children excused from the exercise (as they could be) because he believed "that the children's relationships with their teachers and classmates would be adversely affected." In *Murray,* the child was excused on request of the parent.]

The wholesome "neutrality" [toward religion] of which this Court's cases speak [stems] from a recognition of the teachings of history that powerful sects or groups might bring about a fusion of governmental and religious functions or a concert or dependency of one upon the other to the end that official support of the State or Federal Government would be placed behind the tenets of one or of all orthodoxies. This the Establishment Clause prohibits. And a further reason for neutrality is found in the Free Exercise Clause, which recognizes the value of religious training, teaching and observance and, more particularly, the right of every person to freely choose his own course with reference thereto, free of any compulsion from the state. This the Free Exercise Clause guarantees. Thus, as we have seen, the two clauses may overlap. [The] test may be stated as follows: what are the purpose and the primary effect of the enactment? If either is the advancement or inhibition of religion then the enactment exceeds the scope of legislative power as circumscribed by the Constitution. That is to say that to withstand the strictures of the Establishment Clause there must be a secular legislative purpose and a primary effect that neither advances nor inhibits religion. *Everson; McGowan v. Maryland*, [Part II infra]. The Free Exercise Clause['s] purpose is to secure religious liberty in the individual by prohibiting any invasions thereof by civil authority. Hence it is necessary in a free exercise case for one to show the coercive effect of the enactment as it operates against him in the practice of his religion. The distinction between the two clauses is apparent—a violation of the Free Exercise Clause is predicated on coercion while the Establishment Clause violation need not be so attended.

Applying the Establishment Clause principles to the cases at bar we find that the States are requiring [these exercises] as part of the curricular activities of students who are required by law to attend school. They are held in the school buildings under the supervision and with the participation of teachers employed in those schools. None of these factors, other than compulsory school attendance, was present in the program upheld in *Zorach*. The trial court in [*Schempp*] has found that such an opening exercise is a religious ceremony and was intended by the State to be so. [But the states contend] that the program is an effort to extend its benefits to all public school children without regard to their religious belief. Included within its secular purposes, it says, are the promotion of moral values, the contradiction to the materialistic trends of our times, the perpetuation of our institutions and the teaching of literature. [But] even if its purpose is not strictly religious, it is sought to be accomplished through readings, without comment, from the Bible. Surely the place of the Bible as an instrument of religion cannot be gainsaid, and the State's recognition of the pervading religious character of the ceremony is evident from the rule's specific permission of the alternative use of the Catholic Douay version as well as the recent amendment permitting nonattendance at the exercises. None of these factors is consistent with the contention that the Bible is here used either as an instrument for nonreligious moral inspiration or as a reference for the teaching of secular subjects.

The conclusion follows that in both cases the laws require religious exercises and such exercises are being conducted in direct violation of the rights of the appellees and petitioners.[9] Nor are these required exercises mitigated by the fact that individual students may absent themselves upon parental request, for

9. [T]he requirements for standing to challenge state action under the Establishment Clause, unlike those relating to the Free Exercise Clause, do not include proof that particular religious freedoms are infringed. *McGowan v. Maryland*, 366 U.S., at 429–430, 81 S.Ct., at 1106–1107, 6 L.Ed.2d 393. The parties here are school children and their parents, who are directly affected by the laws and practices against which their complaints are directed. These interests surely suffice to give the parties standing to complain. Compare *Doremus v. Bd. of Educ.*, [p. 1193 infra], which involved the same substantive issues presented here. The appeal was there dismissed upon the graduation of the school child involved and because of the appellants' failure to establish standing as taxpayers.

that fact furnishes no defense to a claim of unconstitutionality under the Establishment Clause. See *Engel.* Further, it is no defense to urge that the religious practices here may be relatively minor encroachments on the First Amendment. The breach of neutrality that is today a trickling stream may all too soon become a raging torrent * * *.

It is insisted that unless these religious exercises are permitted a "religion of secularism" is established in the schools. * * * We do not agree, however, that this decision in any sense has that effect. In addition, it might well be said that one's education is not complete without a study of comparative religion or the history of religion and its relationship to the advancement of civilization. It certainly may be said that the Bible is worthy of study for its literary and historic qualities. Nothing we have said here indicates that such study of the Bible or of religion, when presented objectively as part of a secular program of education, may not be effected * * *.

Finally, we cannot accept that the concept of neutrality, which does not permit a State to require a religious exercise even with the consent of the majority of those affected, collides with the majority's right to free exercise of religion.[10] While the Free Exercise Clause clearly prohibits the use of state action to deny the rights of free exercise to *anyone,* it has never meant that a majority could use the machinery of the State to practice its beliefs. * * *

MR. JUSTICE BRENNAN, concurring. * * *

I join fully in the opinion and the judgment of the Court. * * *

A too literal quest for the advice of the Founding Fathers upon the issues of these cases seems to me futile and misdirected for several reasons: First, on our precise problem the historical record is at best ambiguous * * *.

Second, the structure of American education has greatly changed since the First Amendment was adopted. * * *

Third, [t]oday the Nation is far more heterogeneous religiously, including as it does substantial minorities not only of Catholics and Jews but as well of those who worship according to no version of the Bible and those who worship no God at all. In the face of such profound changes, practices which may have been objectionable to no one in the time of Jefferson and Madison may today be highly offensive to many persons, the deeply devout and the non-believers alike. [Thus], our use of the history of their time must limit itself to broad purposes, not specific practices. * * *

First, it is argued that however clearly religious may have been the origins and early nature of daily prayer and Bible reading, these practices today serve so clearly secular educational purposes that their religious attributes may be overlooked. [These purposes] fall into two categories—those which depend upon an immediately religious experience shared by the participating children; and those which appear sufficiently divorced from the religious content of the devotional material that they can be served equally by nonreligious materials. With respect to the first objective, much has been written about the moral and spiritual values of infusing some religious influence or instruction into the public school classroom. To the extent that only *religious* materials will serve this purpose, it seems to me that the purpose as well as the means is so plainly religious that the exercise is necessarily forbidden by the Establishment Clause.

---

10. We [do] not pass upon a situation such as military service, where the Government regulates the temporal and geographic environment of individuals to a point that, unless it permits voluntary religious services to be conducted with the use of government facilities, military personnel would be unable to engage in the practice of their faiths.

The fact that purely secular benefits may eventually result [could] no doubt have been claimed for the released time program invalidated in *McCollum.*

The second justification assumes that religious exercises at the start of the school day may directly serve solely secular ends—for example, by fostering harmony and tolerance among the pupils, enhancing the authority of the teacher, and inspiring better discipline. To the extent that such benefits result not from the content of the readings and recitation, but simply from the holding of such a solemn exercise at the opening assembly or the first class of the day, it would seem that less sensitive materials might equally well serve the same purpose. * * *

Second, it is argued that the particular practices involved in the two cases before us are unobjectionable because they prefer no particular sect or sects at the expense of others. [But] any version of the Bible is inherently sectarian * * *.

A third element which is said to absolve the practices [is] the provision to excuse or exempt students who wish not to participate. [T]he short, and to me sufficient, answer is that the availability of excusal or exemption simply has no relevance to the establishment question * * *.

The more difficult question, however, is whether the availability of excusal for the dissenting child serves to refute challenges to these practices under the Free Exercise Clause. [The] answer is [that] by requiring what is tantamount in the eyes of teachers and schoolmates to a profession of disbelief, or at least of nonconformity, the procedure may well deter those children who do not wish to participate for any reason based upon the dictates of conscience from exercising an indisputably constitutional right to be excused. * * *

[What] the Framers meant to foreclose, and what our decisions under the Establishment Clause have forbidden, are those involvements of religious with secular institutions which (a) serve the essentially religious activities of religious institutions; (b) employ the organs of government for essentially religious purposes; or (c) use essentially religious means to serve governmental ends, where secular means would suffice. When the secular and religious institutions become involved in such a manner, there inhere in the relationship precisely those dangers—as much to church as to state—which the Framers feared would subvert religious liberty and the strength of a system of secular government. On the other hand, there may be myriad forms of involvements of government with religion which do not import such dangers * * *. I think a brief survey of certain of these forms of accommodation will reveal that the First Amendment commands not official hostility toward religion, but only a strict neutrality * * *.

A. The Conflict Between Establishment and Free Exercise.—There are certain practices, conceivably violative of the Establishment Clause, the striking down of which might seriously interfere with certain religious liberties also protected by the First Amendment. Provisions for churches and chaplains at military establishments for those in the armed services may afford one such example. The like provision by state and federal governments for chaplains in penal institutions may afford another * * *.

Such activities and practices seem distinguishable from the sponsorship of daily Bible reading and prayer recital. For one thing, there is no element of coercion present * * *; the soldier or convict who declines the opportunities for worship would not ordinarily subject himself to the suspicion or obloquy of his peers. Of special significance to this distinction is the fact that we are here usually dealing with adults, not with impressionable children as in the public schools. Moreover, [the] student's compelled presence in school for five days a week in no way renders the regular religious facilities of the community less accessible to him than they are to [others.] I do not say that government *must* provide chaplains * * *.

C. Non-Devotional Use of the Bible In the Public Schools.—The holding of the Court today plainly does not foreclose teaching *about* the Holy Scriptures or about the differences between religious sects in classes in literature or history. * * * If it should sometime hereafter be shown that in fact religion can play no part in the teaching of a given subject without resurrecting the ghost of the practices we strike down today, it will then be time enough to consider questions we must now defer. * * *

MR. JUSTICE GOLDBERG, with whom MR. JUSTICE HARLAN joins, concurring.

[I] join the opinion and judgment of the Court. [But] untutored devotion to the concept of neutrality can lead to invocation or approval of results which partake not simply of that noninterference and noninvolvement with the religious which the Constitution commands, but of a brooding and pervasive devotion to the secular and a passive, or even active, hostility to the religious. Such results are not only not compelled by the Constitution, but, it seems to me, are prohibited by [it.]

The practices here involved do not fall within any sensible or acceptable concept of compelled or permitted accommodation and involve the state so significantly and directly in the realm of the sectarian as to give rise to those very divisive influences and inhibitions of freedom which both religion clauses of the First Amendment preclude. [The] pervasive religiosity and direct governmental involvement inhering in the prescription of prayer and Bible reading in the public schools, during and as part of the curricular day, involving young impressionable children whose school attendance is statutorily compelled, and utilizing the prestige, power, and influence of school administration, staff, and authority, cannot realistically be termed simply accommodation, and must fall within the interdiction of the First Amendment. I find nothing in the opinion of the Court which says more than this. [The] First Amendment does not prohibit practices which by any realistic measure create none of the dangers which it is designed to prevent and which do not so directly or substantially involve the state in religious exercises or in the favoring of religion as to have meaningful and practical impact. It is of course true that great consequences can grow from small beginnings, but the measure of constitutional adjudication is the ability and willingness to distinguish between real threat and mere shadow.

MR. JUSTICE STEWART, dissenting.

* * * I cannot agree with what seems to me the insensitive definition of the Establishment Clause contained in the Court's opinion, nor with the different but, I think, equally mechanistic definitions contained in the separate opinions which have been filed. * * *

That the central value embodied in the First Amendment—and, more particularly, in the guarantee of "liberty" contained in the Fourteenth—is the safeguarding of an individual's right to free exercise of his religion has been consistently recognized [and] there is involved in these cases a substantial free exercise claim on the part of those who affirmatively desire to have their children's school day open with the reading of passages from the Bible.

[It] might be argued here that parents who wanted their children to be exposed to religious influences in school could, under *Pierce v. Society of Sisters* send their children to private or parochial schools. [But] "Freedom of speech, freedom of the press, freedom of religion are available to all, not merely to those who can pay their own way." *Murdock v. Pennsylvania,* [Sec. 2, I infra].

It might also be argued that parents who want their children exposed to religious influences can adequately fulfill that wish off school property and outside school time. [But] a compulsory state educational system so structures a child's life that if religious exercises are held to be an impermissible activity in schools, religion is placed at an artificial and state-created disadvantage. [A] refusal to permit religious exercises thus is seen, not as the realization of state neutrality, but rather as the establishment of a religion of secularism, or at the least, as government support of the beliefs of those who think that religious exercises should be conducted only in private. * * *

The dangers both to government and to religion inherent in official support of instruction in the tenets of various religious sects are absent in the present cases, which involve only a reading from the Bible unaccompanied by comments which might otherwise constitute instruction. [In] the absence of coercion upon those who do not wish to participate—because they hold less strong beliefs, other beliefs, or no beliefs at all—such provisions cannot, in my view, be held to represent the type of support of religion barred by the Establishment Clause. For the only support which such rules provide for religion is the withholding of state hostility—a simple acknowledgment on the part of secular authorities that the Constitution does not require extirpation of all expression of religious belief.

I have said that these provisions authorizing religious exercises are properly to be regarded as measures making possible the free exercise of religion. But it is important to stress that [the] question presented is not whether exercises such as those at issue here are constitutionally compelled, but rather whether they are constitutionally invalid. And that issue, in my view, turns on the question of coercion.

It is clear that the dangers of coercion involved in the holding of religious exercises in a schoolroom differ qualitatively from those presented by the use of similar exercises or affirmations in ceremonies attended by adults. Even as to children, however, the duty laid upon government in connection with religious exercises in the public schools is that of refraining from so structuring the school environment as to put any kind of pressure on a child to participate in those exercises; it is not that of providing an atmosphere in which children are kept scrupulously insulated from any awareness that some of their fellows may want to open the school day with prayer, or of the fact that there exist in our pluralistic society differences of religious belief. * * *

To be specific, it seems to me clear that certain types of exercises would present situations in which no possibility of coercion on the part of secular officials could be claimed to exist. Thus, if such exercises were held either before or after the official school day, or if the school schedule were such that participation were merely one among a number of desirable alternatives, it could hardly be contended that the exercises did anything more than to provide an opportunity for the voluntary expression of religious belief. On the other hand, a law which provided for religious exercises during the school day and which contained no excusal provision would obviously be unconstitutionally coercive upon those who did not wish to participate. And even under a law containing an excusal provision, if the exercises were held during the school day, and no equally desirable alternative were provided by the school authorities, the likelihood that children might be under at least some psychological compulsion to participate would be great. In a case such as the latter, however, I think we would err if we *assumed* such coercion in the absence of any evidence.

Viewed in this light, it seems to me clear that the records in both of the cases before us are wholly inadequate to support an informed or responsible decision. [No] evidence at all was adduced in the *Murray* case, because it was decided upon a demurrer. [In] the *Schempp* case the record shows no more than a subjective prophecy by a parent of what he thought would happen if a request were made to be excused from participation in the exercises under the amended statute. [It] is conceivable that these school boards, or even all school boards, might eventually find it impossible to administer a system of religious exercises during school hours in such a way as to meet this constitutional standard—in such a way as completely to free from any kind of official coercion those who do not affirmatively want to participate.[8] But I think we must not assume that school boards so lack the qualities of inventiveness and good will as to make impossible the achievement of that goal.

I would remand both cases for further hearings.[a]

Notes and Questions

1. *The Court's test.* Is the Court's "purpose and primary effect" test consistent with prior decisions? Do the factors by which the Court distinguishes *Zorach* relate to "purpose and primary effect"? What was the *primary* effect of the plan in *Everson*? Is this concept meaningful? What result in the examples of Stewart, J., in *Engel*? Consider Johnson, *Concepts and Compromise in First Amendment Religious Doctrine,* 72 Calif.L.Rev. 817, 827 (1984): "[There is great difficulty] making sense out of the crucial distinction between *religious* purpose or effect and *secular* purpose or effect. Governments usually act out of secular motives, even when they are directly aiding a particular religious sect. An atheistic ruler might well create an established church because he thinks it a useful way of raising money, or of ensuring that the clergy do not preach seditious doctrines. In democratic societies, elected officials have an excellent secular reason to accommodate (or at least to avoid offending) groups and individuals who are religious, as well as groups and individuals who are not. They wish to be re-elected, and they do not want important groups to feel that the community does not honor their values."

2. *Coercion.* (a) What significance do the opinions in *Schempp* attribute to the "coercive effect" of religious exercises in public schools? Consider Kauper, *Religion and the Constitution* 72 (1964): "[Clark, J.] did not find it enough to say that here the government was sanctioning a practice directed to religious ends, but went on to emphasize the elements of compulsion in this case. He noted that the prayer was approved by state authorities, was prescribed for daily use in a public school for children required to attend under the compulsory education laws, and was supervised by [a] public school teacher. If strict neutrality were the criterion, then it should have been unnecessary for the court to discuss the elements of compulsion." See generally Schumb, *Church, State and the Public Schools,* 4 Santa Clara Law. 54 (1963).

---

8. For example, if the record in [*Schempp*] contained proof (rather than mere prophecy) that the timing of morning announcements by the school was such as to handicap children who did not want to listen to the Bible reading, or that the excusal provision was so ad- ministered as to carry any overtones of social inferiority, then impermissible coercion would clearly exist.

a. The concurring opinion of Douglas, J., who joined the Court's opinion, is omitted.

(b) For Brennan, J., why does Bible reading create the "danger of subverting religious liberty"? Is it because of the "coercive effect"? If so, why does he say that the issue of "availability of excusal for the dissenting child" is relevant only as to the free exercise clause? Is this consistent with his treatment, *under the establishment clause,* of providing chaplains?

(c) Consider Choper, *Religion in the Public Schools: A Proposed Constitutional Standard,* 47 Minn.L.Rev. 329, 330 (1963): "The [standard is that] the establishment clause [is] violated when the state engages in what may be fairly characterized as *solely religious activity* that is likely to result in (1) *compromising* the student's religious or conscientious beliefs or (2) *influencing* the student's freedom of religious or conscientious choice."

Does this test differ from Stewart, J.'s? What evidence of coercion does he require? That the objectors first ask to be excused from participation and then show that social pressures were brought to bear on them? Would this force an objector to surrender his rights in order to vindicate them? Or would Stewart, J., accept the testimony of social scientists that the program was coercive? Could this be judicially noticed? Cf. *Brown v. Board of Educ.,* p. 823 infra. Or would he require a showing that these particular objectors were coerced? Were likely to be coerced? If so, is this a desirable test?

Consider Brown, *Quis Custodiet Ipsos Custodes?—The School Prayer Cases,* 1963 Sup.Ct.Rev. 1, 30–31: "Submitting the question of coercion to a jury will be objected to because: (1) it will produce non-uniform results; and (2) it will make constitutional rights turn upon what is by definition a sampling of the majority. In the context of these cases, the objections are not overwhelming. If the constitutional 'right' is not regarded in purely abstract and doctrinaire fashion, but is dependent upon the fact of an ascertainable and objectionable degree of coercion, that fact will not be uniform under all circumstances and for all persons. To insist upon uniformity of result is only another way to eliminate the question of standing. Giving a jury an opportunity to intervene on at least one aspect of a problem delicately balanced in its general aspects as well as in its individual impact appears a not inappropriate solution."

3. *Other public school practices.* (a) STONE v. GRAHAM, 449 U.S. 39, 101 S.Ct. 192, 66 L.Ed.2d 199 (1980), per curiam, held that a Kentucky statute— requiring "the posting of a copy of the Ten Commandments, purchased with private contributions, on the wall of each public classroom in the State," with the notation at the bottom that "The secular application of the Ten Commandments is clearly seen in its adoption as the fundamental legal code of Western Civilization and the Common Law of the United States"—had "no secular legislative purpose": "The Ten Commandments is undeniably a sacred text in the Jewish and Christian faiths, and no legislative recitation of a supposed secular purpose can blind us to that [fact]. Posting of religious texts on the wall serves [no] educational function. If the posted copies of the Ten Commandments are to have any effect at all, it will be to induce the school children to read, meditate upon, perhaps to venerate and obey, the Commandments. However desirable this might be as a matter of private devotion, it is not a permissible state objective under the Establishment Clause."

REHNQUIST, J., dissented: "The Court's summary rejection of a secular purpose articulated by the legislature and confirmed by the state court is without precedent in Establishment Clause jurisprudence. [This] Court has recognized that 'religion has been closely identified with our history and government,' *Schempp,* and that 'the history of man is inseparable from the history of religion,' *Engel.* Kentucky has decided to make students aware of this fact by demonstrating the secular impact of the Ten Commandments." [b]

(b) In 1978, Alabama enacted § 16–1–20 authorizing a one-minute period of silence in all public schools "for meditation"; in 1981, it enacted § 16–1–20.1 authorizing a period of silence "for meditation or voluntary prayer." WALLACE v. JAFFREE, __ U.S. __, 105 S.Ct. 2479, 86 L.Ed.2d 29 (1985), per STEVENS, J., held that the 1981 law violated the establishment clause, relying, inter alia, on its sponsor's statements that the law's only purpose was an "effort to return voluntary prayer to our public schools," and the fact that "the State did not present evidence of *any* secular purpose": "[E]ven though a statute that is motivated in part by a religious purpose may satisfy the ["secular legislative purpose" requirement], the First Amendment requires that a statute must be invalidated if it is entirely motivated by a purpose to advance religion. * * *

"The legislative intent to return prayer to public schools is, of course, quite different from merely protecting every student's right to engage in voluntary prayer during an appropriate moment of silence during the school day. The 1978 statute already protected that right, containing nothing that prevented any student from engaging in voluntary prayer during a silent minute of meditation. [The] Legislature enacted § 16–1–20.1 despite the existence of § 16–1–20 for the sole purpose of expressing the State's endorsement of prayer activities. [The] addition of 'or voluntary prayer' indicates that the State intended to characterize prayer as a favored practice. Such an endorsement is not consistent with the established principle that the Government must pursue a course of complete neutrality toward religion."

O'CONNOR, J., concurred in the judgment: "A state sponsored moment of silence in the public schools is different from state sponsored vocal prayer or Bible reading. First, a moment of silence is not inherently religious. Silence, unlike prayer or Bible reading, need not be associated with a religious exercise. Second, a pupil who participates in a moment of silence need not compromise his or her beliefs. During a moment of silence, a student who objects to prayer is left to his or her own thoughts, and is not compelled to listen to the prayers or thoughts of others. [It] is difficult to discern a serious threat to religious liberty from a room of silent, thoughtful schoolchildren.

"[Even] if a statute specifies that a student may choose to pray silently during a quiet moment, the State has not thereby encouraged prayer over other specified alternatives. Nonetheless, it is also possible that a moment of silence statute, either as drafted or as actually implemented, could effectively favor the child who prays over the child who does not. For example, the message of endorsement would seem inescapable if the teacher exhorts children to use the designated time to pray. Similarly, the face of the statute or its legislative history may clearly establish that it seeks to encourage or promote voluntary prayer over other alternatives, rather than merely provide a quiet moment that may be dedicated to prayer by those so inclined. The crucial question is whether the State has conveyed or attempted to convey the message that children should use the moment of silence for prayer. This question cannot be answered in the abstract, but instead requires courts to examine the history, language, and administration of a particular statute to determine whether it operates as an endorsement of religion.

b. Stewart, J., also dissented. Burger, C.J., and Blackmun, J., dissented from not giving the case plenary consideration.

"Some general observations on the proper scope of the inquiry are in order. First, the inquiry into the purpose of the legislature in enacting a moment of silence law should be deferential and limited. In determining whether the government intends a moment of silence statute to convey a message of endorsement or disapproval of religion, a court has no license to psychoanalyze the legislators. If a legislature expresses a plausible secular purpose for a moment of silence statute in either the text or the legislative history, or if the statute disclaims an intent to encourage prayer over alternatives during a moment of silence, then courts should generally defer to that stated intent. [Even] if the text and official history of a statute express no secular purpose, the statute should be held to have an improper purpose only if it is beyond purview that endorsement of religion or a religious belief 'was and is the law's reason for existence.' Since there is arguably a secular pedagogical value to a moment of silence in public schools, courts should find an improper purpose behind such a statute only if the statute on its face, in its official legislative history, or in its interpretation by a responsible administrative agency suggests it has the primary purpose of endorsing prayer.

"Justice Rehnquist suggests that this sort of deferential inquiry into legislative purpose 'means little,' because 'it only requires the legislature to express any secular purpose and omit all sectarian references.' It is not a trivial matter, however, to require that the legislature manifest a secular purpose and omit all sectarian endorsements from its laws. That requirement is precisely tailored to the Establishment Clause's purpose of assuring that Government not intentionally endorse religion or a religious practice. It is of course possible that a legislature will enunciate a sham secular purpose for a statute. I have little doubt that our courts are capable of distinguishing a sham secular purpose from a sincere one, or [that] inquiry into the effect of an enactment would help decide those close cases where the validity of an expressed secular purpose is in doubt. [A] moment of silence law that is clearly drafted and implemented so as to permit prayer, meditation, and reflection within the prescribed period, without endorsing one alternative over the others, should pass this test.

"The analysis above suggests that moment of silence laws in many States should pass Establishment Clause scrutiny because they do not favor the child who chooses to pray during a moment of silence over the child who chooses to meditate or reflect. Alabama Code § 16–1–20.1 does not stand on the same footing. However deferentially one examines its text and legislative history, however objectively one views the message attempted to be conveyed to the public, the conclusion is unavoidable that the purpose of the statute is to endorse prayer in public schools. [Given] this legislative history, it is not surprising that the State of Alabama conceded in the courts below that the purpose of the statute was to make prayer part of daily classroom activity, and that both the District Court and the Court of Appeals concluded that the law's purpose was to encourage religious activity. In light of the legislative history and the findings of the courts below, I agree with the Court that the State intended § 16–1–20.1 to convey a message that prayer was the endorsed activity during the state-prescribed moment of silence.[5]" [c]

---

5. The Chief Justice suggests that one consequence of the Court's emphasis on the difference between § 16–1–20.1 and its predecessor statute might be to render the Pledge of Allegiance unconstitutional because Congress amended it in 1954 to add the words "under God". I disagree. In my view, the words "under God" in the Pledge serve as an acknowledgement of religion with "the legitimate secular purposes of solemnizing public occasions, [and] expressing confidence in the future."

---

c. See note c. on page 714.

BURGER, C.J., dissented: "The statute does not remotely threaten religious liberty; it affirmatively furthers the values of religious freedom and tolerance that the Establishment Clause was designed to protect. Without pressuring those who do not wish to pray, the statute simply creates an opportunity to think, to plan, or to pray if one wishes—as Congress does by providing chaplains and chapels. [The] statute also provides a meaningful opportunity for schoolchildren to appreciate the absolute constitutional right of each individual to worship and believe as the individual wishes. The statute 'endorses' only the view that the religious observances of others should be tolerated and, where possible, accommodated. If the government may not accommodate religious needs when it does so in a wholly neutral and noncoercive manner, the 'benevolent neutrality' that we have long considered the correct constitutional standard will quickly translate into the 'callous indifference' that the Court has consistently held the Establishment Clause does not require. * * *

"The several preceding opinions conclude that the principal difference between § 16–1–20.1 and its predecessor statute proves that the sole purpose behind the inclusion of the phrase 'or voluntary prayer' in § 16–1–20.1 was to endorse and promote prayer. * * * Congress amended the statutory Pledge of Allegiance 31 years ago to add the words 'under God.' Do the several opinions in support of the judgment today render the Pledge unconstitutional?[3] [T]he inclusion of the words 'or voluntary prayer' in § 16–1–20.1 is wholly consistent with the clearly permissible purpose of clarifying that silent, voluntary prayer is not *forbidden* in the public school building."

REHNQUIST, J., dissented, examining the history of the religion clauses at some length—including the debates in the First Congress (where "Madison was undoubtedly the most important architect among the members of the House of the amendments which became the Bill of Rights"), the Thanksgiving proclamations issued by Presidents Washington, Adams and Madison, and 19th century congressional appropriations "in support of sectarian Indian education carried on by religious organizations": "The Framers intended the Establishment Clause to prohibit the designation of any church as a 'national' one. The Clause was also designed to stop the Federal Government from asserting a preference for one religious denomination or sect over others. Given the 'incorporation' of the Establishment Clause as against the States via the Fourteenth Amendment in *Everson,* States are prohibited as well from establishing a religion or discriminating between sects. As its history abundantly shows, however, nothing in the Establishment Clause requires government to be strictly neutral between reli-

c. Powell, J., who was the fifth justice to join the Court's opinion, concurred, agreeing "fully with Justice O'Connor's assertion that some moment-of-silence statutes may be constitutional, a suggestion set forth in the Court's opinion as well. * * * I would vote to uphold the Alabama statute if it also had a clear secular purpose. See *Mueller v. Allen,* [Part III infra] (the Court is 'reluctan[t] to attribute unconstitutional motives to the state, particularly when a plausible secular purpose may be discerned from the face of the statute')."

3. The House Report on the legislation amending the Pledge states that the purpose of the amendment was to affirm the principle that "our people and our Government [are dependent] upon the moral directions of the Creator." If this is simply "acknowledgement," not "endorsement," of religion, (O'Connor, J., concurring in the judgment), the distinction is far too infinitesimal for me to grasp.

[Compare Fordham, *The Implications of the Supreme Court Decisions Dealing with Religious Practices in the Public Schools,* 6 J. of Chur. & St. 44, 56 (1964): "In view of the patriotic element here, one may suggest that the likelihood of indirect compulsion is much greater than in the simple prayer case. Here the individual dissenter is made to stand out as one unwilling to engage in a patriotic act and recital. Does this not overbalance the countervailing consideration that the prime purpose is promotion of patriotism and the religious element is secondary?"]

gion and irreligion, nor does that Clause prohibit Congress or the States from pursuing legitimate secular ends through nondiscriminatory sectarian means.

"[There] is simply no historical foundation for the proposition that the Framers intended to build the 'wall of separation' that was constitutionalized in *Everson.* [In] the 38 years since *Everson* our Establishment Clause cases have been neither principled nor unified. [The "purpose" and "effect" tests] have the same historical deficiencies as the wall concept itself: they are in no way based on either the language or intent of the drafters. * * *

"If a constitutional theory has no basis in the history of the amendment it seeks to interpret, is difficult to apply and yields unprincipled results, I see little use in it. [It] would come as much of a shock to those who drafted the Bill of Rights as it will to a large number of thoughtful Americans today to learn that the Constitution, as construed by the majority, prohibits the Alabama Legislature from 'endorsing' prayer."[d]

4. *Alternative means.* (a) Do you agree with Brennan, J., that the establishment clause should forbid a state from using "religious means to serve secular ends where secular means would suffice"? If so, suppose it could be proven by "experienced educators" that nothing worked *quite as well* as reading the Bible to "inspire better discipline" in students? See generally Van Alstyne, *Constitutional Separation of Church and State: The Quest for a Coherent Position,* 57 Am.Pol.Sci.Rev. 865 (1963); Wormuth & Mirkin, *The Doctrine of the Reasonable Alternative,* 9 Utah L.Rev. 254 (1964).

(b) *Military chaplains.* Under the "alternative means" rationale, might it be that, while free exercise considerations may justify government provision for opportunity to worship, the establishment clause nonetheless bars a government subsidized ministry? "Could the governmental interest be satisfied merely by allowing free time for the serviceman to seek non-military worship or by merely giving the religious orders the right to come into the military environment, at their own expense, to provide the opportunity for worship?" Figinski, *Military Chaplains—A Constitutionally Permissible Accommodation Between Church and State,* 24 Md.L.Rev. 377, 409 (1964). Or might it be "that the Government need not necessarily provide chapels and chaplains to those of its armed personnel who are *not* cut off from civilian church facilities"? Herrmann, *Some Considerations on the Constitutionality of the United States Military Chaplaincy,* 14 Am. U.L.Rev. 24, 34 (1964). Consider Figinski, supra: "To allow merely free-time and off-post worship, even where available, would allow the serviceman seeking worship to be flung far and wide, making emergency re-call to duty more difficult and troublesome. Moreover, this means could conceivably place an unforeseen burden on civilian areas of worship that might be resented by the civilians, and increase the possibility of military-civilian friction. Furthermore, in overseas areas the language barrier to effective worship would be considerable. The alternative means of relying on the religious orders of the United States to provide, at their own expense, chaplains is less easily put aside. Three objections can be made. First, if the orders failed to provide chaplains, the military man would be left without effective opportunity for worship. Second, the availability of services would not be as readily available. One can easily conceive of a death situation where the distance the civilian clergyman would need to travel would render his service all but unattainable. The problems of

d. White, J., also dissented, "for the most part agreeing with the opinion of the Chief Justice," and, noting that in light of Rehnquist, J.'s "explication of the history of the religion clauses, [it] would be quite understandable if we undertook to reassess our cases dealing with these clauses, particularly [the] Establishment Clause."

civilian chaplains would be magnified in areas where hostilities were being carried on. Third, if the chaplain were not an officer, the military would not have control over his non-religious life to the extent that it could assure a suitable (in the sense of a non-debt ridden, or even non-subversive) ministry."

5. *Public school secularism.* Consider Manning, *The Douglas Concept of God in Government,* 39 Wash.L.Rev. 47, 63 (1964): "[I]f we forbid the teaching of recognized religions in our public schools and forbid a prayer which simply acknowledges the existence of God and at the same time permit—as, indeed, we must—the teaching of some code of ethical conduct, some system of value norms, does not the system which the school then sponsors become the system of Secular Humanism or simply secular humanism? Do we not then prefer, in public education, one religion, Secular Humanism, over other religions which are founded upon a belief in the existence of God?" Compare Kauper, *Schempp and Sherbert: Studies in Neutrality and Accommodation,* 1963 Relig. & Pub.Or. 3, 23: "[I]n the interest of neutrality as between theistic and humanistic religions, the public schools must carefully avoid any program of indoctrination in ultimate values." May it be argued in response that, simply because the religion of Secular Humanism "adopts" as its own a moral or ideological tenet that is also a publicly accepted behavioral standard, this does not make it a "religious" tenet under the establishment clause for the purpose of its being taught in the public schools? See note 4, Sec. 2, II infra. May public schools teach the theory of evolution to the exclusion of other theories of human origin? See Note, *Freedom of Religion and Science Instruction in Public Schools,* 87 Yale L.J. 515 (1978). If government requires that public employees be of "good moral character," is this a "religious test" for public office? See Freund, *Public Aid to Parochial Schools,* 82 Harv.L.Rev. 1680, 1690 (1969). Compare *McGowan v. Maryland,* Sec. II infra. See generally Note, *Humanistic Values In The Public School Curriculum: Problems In Defining An Appropriate "Wall Of Separation,"* 61 Nw.U.L.Rev. 795 (1966).

6. *"Political" perspective.* Should the Court have avoided decision on the prayer issue altogether? Consider McCloskey, *Principles, Powers, and Values: The Establishment Clause and the Supreme Court,* 1964 Relig. & Pub.Or. 3, 28: "On the basis of power and value considerations taken together, a strong case could be made for judicial avoidance * * *. The subject seems peculiarly well calculated to generate resistance and backlash and peculiarly ill calculated to enlist adequate countervailing support. Congressmen feel that defending prayer is like defending motherhood: it wins them some votes and costs them almost none. If the evil aimed at by the Court was a great one, this expenditure of judicial power might not be excessive. But the evil in its present manifestations is fairly moderate. Even so, judicial correction of it might be warranted, if there were not other, graver wrongs simultaneously pressing for judicial attention and also taxing the power capacities of the Court. [It] would be unfortunate if the Court, in its zeal to wipe out public pieties, impaired its ability to cope with race discrimination, injustice to accused persons, and inhibitions on free expression, not to speak of other massive self-assigned tasks such as control of legislative apportionment, or of further threats to just government that might appear tomorrow or the next day." Are these "legitimate" considerations for the Court in the exercise of its discretion to decide cases?

II. REGULATION IN AID OF RELIGION

McGOWAN v. MARYLAND, 366 U.S. 420, 81 S.Ct. 1101, 6 L.Ed.2d 393 (1961), per WARREN, C.J., held that the "present purpose and effect" of Maryland's Sunday Closing Laws were not religious and did not violate the establishment clause. Although "the original laws which dealt with Sunday labor were motivated by religious forces," the Court showed that secular emphases in language and interpretation have come about, that recent "legislation was supported by labor groups and trade associations," and that "secular justifications have been advanced for making Sunday a day of rest, a day when people may recover from the labors of the week just passed and may physically and mentally prepare for the week's work to come."

"[T]he 'Establishment' Clause does not ban federal or state regulation of conduct whose reason or effect merely happens to coincide or harmonize with the tenets of some or all religions. In many instances, the Congress or state legislatures conclude that the general welfare of society, wholly apart from any religious considerations, demands such regulation." The Court rejected the contention, "however relevant this argument may be," "that the State has other means at its disposal to accomplish its secular purpose, other courses that would not remotely or incidentally give state aid to religion." A "one-day-in-seven" statute might not serve the purpose of setting "one day apart from all others as a day of rest, repose, recreation, [a] day which all members of the family and community have the opportunity to spend and enjoy together * * *. It would seem unrealistic for enforcement purposes and perhaps detrimental to the general welfare to require a State to choose a common day of rest other than that which most persons would select of their own accord."

"Finally, we [do] not hold that Sunday legislation may not be a violation of the 'Establishment' Clause if it can be demonstrated that its purpose—evidenced either on the face of the legislation, in conjunction with its legislative history, or in its operative effect—is to use the State's coercive power to aid religion." [a]

FRANKFURTER, J., joined by Harlan, J., filed a separate opinion that followed substantially the same lines. It applied also to *Braunfeld v. Brown*, Sec. 2, I infra: "If the primary end achieved by a form of regulation is the affirmation or promotion of religious doctrine—primary, in the sense that all secular ends which it purportedly serves are derivative from, not wholly independent of, the advancement of religion—the regulation is beyond the power of the state. This was the case in *McCollum*. Or if a statute furthers both secular and religious ends by means unnecessary to the effectuation of the secular ends alone—where the same secular ends could equally be attained by means which do not have consequences for promotion of religion—the statute cannot stand."

DOUGLAS, J., dissented, his opinion, applying also to *Braunfeld:* "No matter how much is written, no matter what is said," Sunday is a Christian holiday. "There is an 'establishment' of religion in the constitutional sense if any practice of any religious group has the sanction of law behind it."

———

EPPERSON v. ARKANSAS, 393 U.S. 97, 89 S.Ct. 266, 21 L.Ed.2d 228 (1968), per FORTAS, J., held that an "anti-evolution" statute, forbidding teachers in

a. For use of *McGowan* to invalidate the "religiously motivated" Utah firing squad, see Gardner, *Illicit Legislative Motivation as a Sufficient Condition for Unconstitutionality Under the Establishment Clause,* 1979 Wash. U.L.Q. 435.

public schools "to teach the theory or doctrine that mankind ascended or descended from a lower order of animals," violated "the First Amendment's prohibition of laws respecting an establishment of religion or prohibiting the free exercise thereof." "It is of no moment whether the law is deemed to prohibit mention of Darwin's theory, or to forbid any or all of the infinite varieties of communication embraced within the term 'teaching,'" because "Arkansas' law selects from the body of knowledge a particular segment which it proscribes for the sole reason that it is deemed to conflict with a particular religious doctrine." Government may not "promote one religion or religious theory against another or even against the militant opposite."

Citing newspaper advertisements and letters supporting adoption of the statute in 1928, the Court found it "clear that fundamentalist sectarian conviction was and is the law's reason for existence. Its antecedent, Tennessee's 'monkey law,' candidly stated" a religious purpose. "Perhaps the sensational publicity attendant upon the *Scopes* trial induced Arkansas to adopt less explicit language [but] there is no doubt that the motivation for the law was the same * * *. Arkansas' law cannot be defended as an act of religious neutrality. Arkansas did not seek to excise from the curricula of its schools and universities all discussion of the origin of man."

BLACK, J., concurring on the ground of "vagueness," found the first amendment questions "troublesome": "Since there is no indication that the literal Biblical doctrine of the origin of man is included in the curriculum of Arkansas schools, does not the removal of the subject of evolution leave the State in a neutral position toward these supposedly competing religious and anti-religious doctrines?" "It is plain that a state law prohibiting all teaching of human development or biology is constitutionally quite different from a law that compels a teacher to teach as true only one theory of a given doctrine. It would be difficult to make a First Amendment case out of a state law eliminating the subject of higher mathematics, or astronomy, or biology from its curriculum. [T]here is no reason I can imagine why a State is without power to withdraw from its curriculum any subject deemed too emotional and controversial for its public schools." [b]

Notes and Questions

The Court's test. If the "purpose" of the *Epperson* statute, or of some Sunday Closing Law, is found to be "religious," should that alone be enough to invalidate it under the establishment clause? Would these laws "create the dangers the establishment clause was designed to prevent" (Goldberg, J., in *Schempp*)? Would they "subvert religious liberty" (Brennan, J., in *Schempp*)? Some other kind of "liberty"? Are they distinguishable from a public school "dismissed time" program implemented to facilitate religious education? What result, under *Epperson,* for a law requiring that the Biblical version be taught along with other theories of creation? For discussion of the view that "courts carefully consider the legislative history of a law in order to evaluate claims that religion played an impermissibly central role in the law's passage," see Note, *The Establishment Clause and Religious Influences on Legislation,* 75 Nw.U.L. Rev. 944 (1980). Compare Choper, *The Religion Clauses of the First Amendment: Reconciling the Conflict,* 41 U.Pitt.L.Rev. 673, 686–87 (1980): "[I]t is only when

---

b. Harlan, J., concurred in the Court's "establishment of religion" rationale. Stewart, J., concurred on the ground of vagueness.

religious purpose is coupled with threatened impairment of religious freedom that government action should be held to violate the Establishment Clause. [Conceding] that the [*Epperson*] statute had a solely religious purpose, [there] was no evidence that religious beliefs were either coerced, compromised or influenced. That is, it was not shown, nor do I believe that it could be persuasively argued, that the anti-evolution law either (1) induced children of fundamentalist religions to accept the biblical theory of creation, or (2) conditioned other children for conversion to fundamentalism. [Thus,] the accommodation for religion in [*Epperson*] should have survived the Establishment Clause challenge."

III. FINANCIAL AID TO RELIGION

The issue of aid to parochial schools first arose again after *Everson* in BOARD OF EDUC. v. ALLEN, 392 U.S. 236, 88 S.Ct. 1923, 20 L.Ed.2d 1060 (1968). The Court, per WHITE, J., held that New York's lending state-approved secular textbooks to all secondary school children did not violate the establishment clause. Applying the *Schempp* "test," the New York law, like that in *Everson,* had "a secular legislative purpose and a primary effect that neither advances nor inhibits religion." Its purpose "was stated by the New York Legislature to be furtherance of the educational opportunities available to the young. [T]he financial benefit is to parents and children, not to schools.[6] Perhaps free books make it more likely that some children choose to attend a sectarian school, but that was true of the state-paid bus fares in *Everson* * * *. Absent evidence we cannot assume that school authorities [are] unable to distinguish between secular and religious books or that they will not honestly discharge their duties under the law. [On] the meager record before us in this case, we cannot agree [that] all teaching in a sectarian school is religious or that the processes of secular and religious training are so intertwined that secular textbooks furnished to students by the public are in fact instrumental in the teaching of religion." [a]

The problem of aid to parochial schools received extensive consideration in 1971. In the interim, however, the following opinion greatly influenced the Court's subsequent decisions.

WALZ v. TAX COMM'N, 397 U.S. 664, 90 S.Ct. 1409, 25 L.Ed.2d 697 (1970), per BURGER, C.J., upheld a state tax exemption for "real or personal property used exclusively for religious, educational or charitable purposes": "The general principle deducible from the First Amendment and all that has been said by the Court is this: that we will not tolerate either governmentally established religion or governmental interference with religion. Short of those expressly proscribed governmental acts there is room for play in the joints productive of a benevolent neutrality which will permit religious exercise to exist without sponsorship and without interference. * * *

"The legislative purpose of a property tax exemption is neither the advancement nor the inhibition of religion; it is neither sponsorship nor hostility. New York, in common with the other States, has determined that certain entities that exist in a harmonious relationship to the community at large, and that foster its

---

6. [T]he record contains no evidence that any of the private schools in appellants' districts previously provided textbooks for their students. * * *

a. Black, Douglas and Fortas, JJ., dissented. See also Note, *Sectarian Books, The Supreme Court and the Establishment Clause,* 79 Yale L.J. 111 (1969).

'moral or mental improvement,' should not be inhibited in their activities by property taxation or the hazard of loss of those properties for nonpayment of taxes. It [has] granted exemption to all houses of religious worship within a broad class of property owned by nonprofit, quasi-public corporations which include hospitals, libraries, playgrounds, scientific, professional, historical and patriotic groups. * * *

"We find it unnecessary to justify the tax exemption on the social welfare services or 'good works' that some churches perform for parishioners and others—family counselling, aid to the elderly and the infirm, and to children. [To] give emphasis to so variable an aspect of the work of religious bodies would introduce an element of governmental evaluation and standards as to the worth of particular social welfare programs, thus producing a kind of continuing day-to-day relationship which the policy of neutrality seeks to minimize. * * *

" * * * We must also be sure that the end result—the effect—is not an excessive government entanglement with religion. The test is inescapably one of degree. * * * Elimination of exemption would tend to expand the involvement of government by giving rise to tax valuation of church property, tax liens, tax foreclosures, and the direct confrontations and conflicts that follow in the train of those legal processes.

"Granting tax exemptions to churches necessarily operates to afford an indirect economic benefit and also gives rise to some, but yet a lesser, involvement than taxing [them]. Obviously a direct money subsidy would be a relationship pregnant with involvement and, as with most governmental grant programs, could encompass sustained and detailed administrative relationships for enforcement of statutory or administrative standards, but that is not this case. * * *

"It is obviously correct that no one acquires a vested or protected right in violation of the Constitution by long [use]. Yet an unbroken practice of according the exemption to churches [is] not something to be lightly cast aside."

BRENNAN, J., concurred, finding "two basic secular purposes" for the exemption: "First, these organizations are exempted because they, among a range of other private, nonprofit organizations contribute to the well-being of the community in a variety of nonreligious ways, and thereby bear burdens that would otherwise either have to be met by general taxation, or be left undone * * *.

"Second, government [may] properly include religious institutions among the variety of private, nonprofit groups which receive tax exemptions, for each group contribute to the diversity of association, viewpoint and enterprise essential to a vigorous, pluralistic society. * * *

"Tax exemptions and general subsidies [both] provide economic assistance, [but a] subsidy involves the direct transfer of public monies to the subsidized enterprise and uses resources exacted from taxpayers as a whole. An exemption, on the other hand, involves no such transfer.[a] It assists the exempted enterprise only passively, by relieving a privately funded venture of the burden of paying taxes."[b]

DOUGLAS, J., dissented: "If history be our guide, then tax exemption of church property in this country is indeed highly suspect, as it arose in the early days when the church was an agency of the state. [The] financial support

---

a. What of the fact that exemption for churches augments the tax bills of others? See generally Bittker, *Churches, Taxes and The Constitution*, 78 Yale L.J. 1285 (1969).

b. Harlan, J., also concurred.

rendered here is to the church, the place of worship. A tax exemption is a subsidy."

Notes and Questions

1. *Secular purpose.* (a) Does *Walz* abandon the "secular purpose" prerequisite of the "test" developed in *Schempp* and relied on in *Allen?* Consider Duval, *The Constitutionality of State Aid to Nonpublic Elementary and Secondary Schools,* 1970 U.Ill.L.F. 342, 349: "The emphasis in *Walz* is not on whether legislation is intended to promote and in fact does promote purely secular ends. Rather the question is whether either the purpose or effect is to advance or inhibit religion. Thus under *Walz* but not *Allen* if neither the purpose nor effect is to advance or inhibit religion, it is immaterial whether the legislation serves a secular objective." Thus viewed, is *Walz* a direct descendant of *Zorach?*

(b) Do either (or both) of Brennan, J.'s "two basic secular purposes" satisfy the *Schempp-Allen* test? Does the first justify tax exemption for *all* churches? Does it justify direct subsidies to *some* churches? Does the second justify general subsidies to *all* churches—at least so long as other groups that "contribute to the diversity essential to a vigorous, pluralistic society" are included?

2. *Direct subsidies vs. tax exemption.* Apart from the issue of the economic equivalence of subsidies and exemptions, consider Davidow, *Governmental Aid to Church-Affiliated Colleges,* 43 N.D.L.Rev. 659, 687 (1967): "[B]ecause such aid is less 'direct' than that involved in the granting of funds, the degree of governmental approbation of specific religious practices is less; hence, it is not as likely that those not aided will feel pressures to conform—i.e., to affiliate with some groups which are aided through tax exemption." Would small grants to all religions for religious symbols in houses of worship generate "pressures to conform"?

Consider Van Alstyne, note 4 after *Schempp,* supra, at 881: "To finance expanding government services, [taxes] may gradually divert an increasing fraction of total personal income, necessarily leaving proportionately less money in the private sector to each person to spend according to his individual choice, in support of religion or other undertakings. To the extent that the tax revenues thus collected may not be spent by government to support religious enterprises, but must be used exclusively for secular purposes, the net effect, arguably, is to reduce the relative supply of funds available to religion." Does this warrant tax exemption for "religion"? Does it "warrant the judicial junking of the establishment clause"? Id. Is it "equally arguable that government fiscal activity, far from reducing disposable personal income, actually increases it"? Id. See also Schwartz, *The Nonestablishment Principle: A Reply to Professor Giannella,* 81 Harv.L.Rev. 1465, 1469–70 (1968).

3. *"Excessive government entanglement."* To what extent does *Walz* turn on this element? Precisely what does this notion encompass? Does it concern the peculiar problems that would arise in determining the tax valuation of property used exclusively for religious purposes? If so, may tax exemption be accorded church-owned property that is used for commercial, income-producing purposes? May religious organizations be exempted from paying unemployment compensation tax? In any event, consider Warren, Krattenmaker & Snyder, *Property Tax Exemptions for Charitable, Educational, Religious and Governmental Institutions in Connecticut,* 4 Conn.L.Rev. 181, 209 (1971): "The argument that evaluation of property owned by churches may give rise to secular-sectarian

clashes seems farfetched. Alternative use market values would surely serve as a suitable, ideologically neutral touchstone."

4. *"Entanglement" in ecclesiastical disputes.* (a) In JONES v. WOLF, 443 U.S. 595, 99 S.Ct. 3020, 61 L.Ed.2d 775 (1979), a majority of the Vineville Presbyterian Church of Macon, Ga. voted to separate from the Presbyterian Church in the United States (PCUS). A commission of PCUS, acting pursuant to the PCUS constitution (called the Book of Church Order), declared the Vineville minority to be "the true congregation." The minority sued to establish its right to the local church property. The Supreme Court of Georgia applied "the 'neutral principles of law' method for resolving church property disputes. The court examined the deeds to the properties, the state statutes dealing with implied trusts, and the Book of Church Order, to determine whether there was any basis for a trust in favor of the general church. Finding nothing that would give rise to a trust in any of these documents, the court awarded the property on the basis of legal title, which was in the local church, or in the names of trustees for the local church. [Without] further analysis or elaboration, [it] further decreed that the local congregation was represented by the majority faction, respondents herein."

The Court, per BLACKMUN, J., stated the established principle that "the First Amendment prohibits civil courts from resolving church property disputes on the basis of religious doctrine and practice. *Presbyterian Church v. Hull Church,* 393 U.S. 440, 89 S.Ct. 601, 21 L.Ed.2d 658 (1969). As a corollary to this commandment, the Amendment requires that civil courts defer to the resolution of issues of religious doctrine or polity by the highest court of a hierarchical church organization. *Serbian Orthodox Diocese v. Milivojevich,* 426 U.S. 696, 96 S.Ct. 2372, 49 L.Ed.2d 151 (1976)[a] Subject to these limitations, however, * * * 'a State may adopt *any* of various approaches for settling church property disputes so long as it involves no consideration of doctrinal matters, whether the ritual and liturgy of worship or the tenets of faith.' *Maryland & Va. Eldership v. Sharpsburg Church,* 396 U.S. 367, 90 S.Ct. 499, 24 L.Ed.2d 582 (1970) (Brennan, J., concurring) (emphasis in original).

"[W]e think the 'neutral principles of law' approach is consistent with the foregoing constitutional principles. [It] relies extensively on objective, well-established concepts of trust and property law familiar to lawyers and judges. It thereby promises to free civil courts completely from entanglement in questions of religious doctrine, polity, and practice. Furthermore, the neutral principles analysis [affords] flexibility in ordering private rights and obligations to reflect the intentions of the parties. Through appropriate reversionary clauses and trust provisions, religious societies can specify what is to happen to church property in the event of a particular contingency, or what religious body will

a. *Serbian,* per Brennan, J., reversed a state court decision that the Mother Church's removal of respondent as bishop of the American-Canadian diocese was "procedurally and substantively defective under the internal regulations of the Mother Church and were therefore arbitrary and invalid": "[W]hether or not there is room for 'marginal civil court review' under the narrow rubrics of 'fraud' or 'collusion' when church tribunals act in bad faith for secular purposes, no 'arbitrariness' exception—in the sense of an inquiry whether the decisions of the highest ecclesiastical tribunal of a hierarchical church complied with

church laws and regulations—is consistent with the constitutional mandate that civil courts are bound to accept the decisions of the highest judicatories of a religious organization of hierarchical polity on matters of discipline, faith, internal organization, or ecclesiastical rule, custom or law. [I]t is the essence of religious faith that ecclesiastical decisions are reached and are to be accepted as matters of faith whether or not rational or measurable by objective criteria."

Rehnquist and Stevens, JJ., dissented. See 1977 Utah L.Rev. 138.

determine the ownership in the event of a schism or doctrinal controversy. In this manner, a religious organization can ensure that a dispute over the ownership of church property will be resolved in accord with the desires of the members.

"[The] neutral principles method [does require] a civil court to examine certain religious documents, such as a church constitution, for language of trust in favor of the general church. In undertaking such an examination, a civil court must take special care to scrutinize the document in purely secular terms, and not to rely on religious precepts in determining whether the document indicates that the parties have intended to create a trust. In addition, there may be cases where the deed, the corporate charter, or the constitution of the general church incorporates religious concepts in the provisions relating to the ownership of property. If in such a case the interpretation of the instruments of ownership would require the civil court to resolve a religious controversy, then the court must defer to the resolution of the doctrinal issue by the authoritative ecclesiastical body. *Serbian.*"

The Court vacated the judgment, however, since "the grounds for the decision that respondents represent the Vineville church remain unarticulated": "If in fact Georgia has adopted a presumptive rule of majority representation, defeasible upon a showing that the identity of the local church is to be determined by some other means, we think this would be consistent with [the] First Amendment. Majority rule is generally employed in the governance of religious societies. Furthermore, the majority faction generally can be identified without resolving any question of religious doctrine or polity. [Most] importantly, any rule of majority representation can always be overcome, under the neutral principles approach, either by providing, in the corporate charter or the constitution of the general church, that the identity of the local church is to be established in some other way, or by providing that the church property is held in trust for the general church and those who remain loyal to it. Indeed, the State may adopt any method of overcoming the majoritarian presumption, so long as the use of that method does not impair free exercise rights or entangle the civil courts in matters of religious controversy.

"[But] there are at least some indications that under Georgia law the process of identifying the faction that represents the Vineville church [must] be determined according to terms of the Book of Church Order * * *. Such a determination, however, would appear to require a civil court to pass on questions of religious doctrine, and to usurp the function of the commission appointed by the Presbytery * * *. Therefore, if Georgia law provides that the identity of the Vineville church is to be determined according to the 'laws and regulations' of the PCUS, then the First Amendment requires that the Georgia courts give deference to the presbyterial commission's determination of that church's identity."

POWELL, J., joined by Burger, C.J., and Stewart and White, JJ., dissented, finding that the neutral principles "approach inevitably will increase the involvement of civil courts in church controversies": "Until today, [the] first question presented in a case involving an intrachurch dispute over church property was where within the religious association the rules of polity, accepted by its members before the schism, had placed ultimate authority over the use of the church property. The courts, in answering this question have recognized two broad categories of church government. One is congregational, in which authority over questions of church doctrine, practice, and administration rests entirely in the local congregation or some body within it. In disputes over the control and use of the property of such a church, the civil courts enforce the authoritative resolution of the controversy within the local church itself. *Watson v. Jones*, 80 U.S. 679, 20 L.Ed. 666 (1871). The second is hierarchical, in which the local church is but an integral and subordinate part of a larger church and is under the authority of the general church. Since the decisions of the local congregation are subject to review by the tribunals of the church hierarchy, this Court has held that the civil courts must give effect to the duly made decisions of the highest body within the hierarchy that has considered the dispute. [By] doing so, the [civil] court avoids two equally unacceptable departures from the genuine neutrality mandated by the First Amendment. First, it refrains from direct review and revision of decisions of the church on matters of religious doctrine and practice that underlie the church's determination of intrachurch controversies, including those that relate to control of church property.[b] Equally important, by recognizing the authoritative resolution reached within the religious association, the civil court avoids interfering indirectly with the religious governance of those who have formed the association and submitted themselves to its authority."[c]

(b) *Scope of the decision.* After *Jones v. Wolf,* what results in the following situations: (i) A donor who made a bequest "to the First Methodist Church" seeks return of the money because subsequently a majority of the church's members decided to affiliate with another denomination. Suppose the bequest had been "to the First Methodist Church so long as it does not substantially deviate from existing doctrine"? (ii) A state statute makes it a crime for sellers to falsely represent food to be "kosher." See Note, 71 Mich.L.Rev. 1641 (1973).

(c) *Proposed approach.* "The solution most of the time is to honor internal church agreements, just as a court would honor the internal agreements of a secular organization. Only when doctrinal decisions[d] or the imposition of external policies are involved[e] need a court refrain from deciding a dispute. This approach serves both organizational autonomy and the other interests of the church and its members, while preserving the religious neutrality demanded

---

b. In response, the Court pointed out that, under the dissent's approach, "civil courts would always be required to examine the polity and administration of a church to determine which unit of government has ultimate control over church property. In some cases, this task would not prove to be difficult. But in others, the locus of control would be ambiguous, and 'a careful examination of the constitutions of the general and local church, as well as other relevant documents, [would] be necessary to ascertain the form of governance adopted by the members of the religious association.' In such cases, the suggested rule would appear to require 'a searching and therefore impermissible inquiry into church polity.' *Serbian.* The neutral principles approach, in contrast, obviates entirely the need for an analysis or examination of ecclesiastical polity or doctrine in settling church property disputes."

c. In response, the Court contended that "the neutral principles approach cannot be said to 'inhibit' the free exercise of religion, any more than do other neutral provisions of state law governing the manner in which churches own property, hire employees, or

purchase goods. Under the neutral principles approach, the outcome of a church property dispute is not foreordained. At any time before the dispute erupts, the parties can ensure, if they so desire, that the faction loyal to the hierarchical church will retain the church property" by using reversionary clauses, trust provisions, etc.

d. "Few [cases] present the problem of governmental determination of religious doctrine. [More] common are a second group of cases in which the court is asked to determine which religious doctrine the embattled parties agreed to follow. This kind of question is very different and need not present the first amendment difficulties inherent in the first group of cases." Id. at 1414.

e. "[T]he application of judge-made rules of procedural fairness in associational governance, and the use of charitable trust rules concerning the employment and management of charitable assets [are issues that] present the potential for courts to impose government-created policies on religious organizations [rather than rules seeking to fulfill the parties' intentions]." Id. at 1421.

by the first amendment." Ellman, *Driven from the Tribunal: Judicial Resolution of Internal Church Disputes,* 69 Calif.L.Rev. 1378, 1444 (1981).

LEMON v. KURTZMAN
403 U.S. 602, 91 S.Ct. 2105, 29 L.Ed.2d 745 (1971).

MR. CHIEF JUSTICE BURGER delivered the opinion of the Court. * * *

The Rhode Island Salary Supplement Act was enacted in 1969. It rests on the legislative finding that the quality of education available in nonpublic elementary schools has been jeopardized [by] rapidly rising salaries [and] authorizes state officials to supplement the salaries of teachers of secular subjects in nonpublic elementary schools by paying directly to a teacher an amount not in excess of 15% of his current annual salary. As supplemented, however, a nonpublic school teacher's salary cannot exceed the maximum paid to teachers in the State's public schools, and the recipient must be certified by the state board of education [and] must teach in a nonpublic school at which the average per-pupil expenditure on secular education is less than the average in the State's public schools during a specified period. Appellant state Commissioner of Education also requires eligible schools to submit financial data. If this information indicates a per-pupil expenditure in excess of the statutory limitation, the records of the school in question must be examined in order to assess how much of the expenditure is attributable to secular education and how much to religious activity.

The Act also requires that teachers eligible for salary supplement must teach only those subjects that are offered in the State's public schools. They must use "only teaching materials which are used in the public schools." Finally, any teacher applying for a salary supplement must first agree in writing "not to teach a course in religion [for] such time as he or she receives any salary supplements" * * *.

[Under the 1968] Pennsylvania Nonpublic Elementary and Secondary Education Act, [the] State directly reimburses nonpublic schools solely for their actual expenditures for teachers' salaries, textbooks, and instructional materials. A school seeking reimbursement must maintain prescribed accounting procedures [subject to state audit] that identify the "separate" cost of the "secular educational service." * * * Reimbursement is limited to courses [in] the following "secular" subjects: mathematics, modern foreign languages, physical science, and physical education. Textbooks and instructional materials included in the program must be approved by the state Superintendent of Public Instruction. Finally, the statute prohibits reimbursement for any course that contains "any subject matter expressing religious teaching, or the morals or forms of worship of any sect." * * *

Every analysis in this area must begin with consideration of the cumulative criteria developed by the Court over many years. Three such tests may be gleaned from our cases. First, the statute must have a secular legislative purpose; second, its principal or primary effect must be one that neither advances nor inhibits religion, *Allen;* [a] finally, the statute must not foster "an excessive government entanglement with religion." *Walz.*

---

a. Compare Laycock, *Towards a General Theory of the Religion Clauses: The Case of Church Labor Relations and the Right to Church Autonomy,* 81 Colum.L.Rev. 1373, 1381, 1384 (1981): "The 'inhibits' language is at odds with the constitutional text and with the Court's own statements of the origins and purposes of the [establishment] clause. Government support for religion is an element of every establishment claim, just as a burden or

Inquiry into the legislative purposes of the Pennsylvania and Rhode Island statutes affords no basis for a conclusion that the legislative intent was to advance religion. [They sought] to create statutory restrictions designed to guarantee the separation between secular and religious educational functions and to ensure that State financial aid supports only the former. * * * We need not decide whether these legislative precautions restrict the principal or primary effect of the programs to the point where they do not offend the Religion Clauses, for we conclude that the cumulative impact of the entire relationship arising under the statutes in each State involves excessive entanglement between government and religion.

[T]o determine whether the government entanglement with religion is excessive, we must examine the character and purposes of the institutions which are benefited, the nature of the aid that the State provides, and the resulting relationship between the government and the religious authority. * * *

The District Court made extensive findings on the grave potential for excessive entanglement that inheres in the religious character and purpose of the Roman Catholic elementary schools of Rhode Island, to date the sole beneficiaries of the [Act. It] concluded that the parochial schools constituted "an integral part of the religious mission of the Catholic Church." [The] process of inculcating religious doctrine is, of course, enhanced by the impressionable age of the pupils, in primary schools * * *.

[D]ecisions from *Everson* to *Allen* have permitted the States to provide church-related schools with secular, neutral, or non-ideological services, facilities, or materials. Bus transportation, school lunches, public health services, and secular textbooks supplied in common to all students were not thought to offend the Establishment Clause. * * * We cannot, however, refuse here to recognize that [in] terms of potential for involving some aspect of faith or morals in secular subjects, a textbook's content is ascertainable, but a teacher's handling of a subject is not. [The record shows that with] only two exceptions, school principals are [nuns]. By 1969 lay teachers constituted more than a third of all teachers in the parochial elementary schools, and their number is growing. * * *

Several teachers testified, however, that they did not inject religion into their secular classes. And the District Court found that religious values did not necessarily affect the content of the secular instruction. But what has been recounted suggests the potential if not actual hazards of this form of state aid. The teacher is employed by a religious organization, subject to the direction and discipline of religious authorities, and works in a system dedicated to rearing children in a particular faith. These controls are not lessened by the fact that most of the lay teachers are of the Catholic faith. * * *

We need not and do not assume that teachers in parochial schools will be guilty of bad faith [but] simply recognize that a dedicated religious person, teaching in a school affiliated with his or her faith and operated to inculcate its tenets, will inevitably [find] it hard to make a total separation between secular teaching and religious doctrine. What would appear to some to be essential to good citizenship might well for others border on or constitute instruction in religion. * * *

restriction on religion is an element of every free exercise claim. Regulation that burdens religion, enacted because of the government's general interest in regulation, is simply not establishment."

A comprehensive, discriminating, and continuing state surveillance will inevitably be required to ensure that [the statutory] restrictions are obeyed and the First Amendment otherwise respected. Unlike a book, a teacher cannot be inspected once so as to determine the extent and intent of his or her personal beliefs and subjective acceptance of the limitations imposed by the First Amendment. These prophylactic contacts will involve excessive and enduring entanglement between state and church.

There is another area of entanglement in the Rhode Island program that gives concern. The [state inspection of school records] and evaluation of the religious content of a religious organization [is] pregnant with dangers of excessive government direction of church schools and hence of churches.

* * *

The Pennsylvania [complaint] describes an educational system that is very similar to the one existing in Rhode Island. * * *

The Pennsylvania statute, moreover, has the further defect of providing state financial aid directly to the church-related school. This factor distinguishes both *Everson* and *Allen* * * *. The government cash grants before us now provide no basis for predicting that comprehensive measures of surveillance and controls will not follow. In particular the government's post-audit power to inspect and evaluate a church-related school's financial records and to determine which expenditures are religious and which are secular creates an intimate and continuing relationship between church and state.

A broader base of entanglement of yet a different character is presented by the divisive political potential of these state programs. In a community where such a large number of pupils are served by church-related schools, it can be assumed that state assistance will entail considerable political activity [by partisans and opponents]. Candidates will be forced to declare and voters to choose. It would be unrealistic to ignore the fact that many people confronted with issues of this kind will find their votes aligned with their faith.

Ordinarily political debate and division, however vigorous or even partisan, are normal and healthy manifestations of our democratic system of government, but political division along religious lines was one of the principal evils against which the First Amendment was intended to protect. Freund, *Public Aid to Parochial Schools*, 82 Harv.L.Rev. 1680, 1692 (1969).[b] [It] conflicts with our

b. Compare Schwartz, *No Imposition of Religion: The Establishment Clause Value*, 77 Yale L.J. 692, 711 (1968): "If avoidance of strife were an independent [establishment clause] value, no legislation could be adopted on any subject which aroused strong and divided [religious] feelings." See Choper, *The Establishment Clause and Aid to Parochial Schools*, 56 Calif.L.Rev. 260, 273 (1968): "Nor would a denial of aid to parochial schools largely diminish the extent of religious political activity. In fact, it 'might lead to greater political ruptures caused by the alienation of segments of the religious community.' Those who send their children to parochial schools might intensify opposition to increased governmental aid to public education." See also Nowak, Rotunda & Young, *Constitutional Law* 867–68 (1978). Contrast Valente & Stanmeyer, *Public Aid to Parochial Schools— A Reply to Professor Freund*, 59 Geo.L.J. 59, 70 n. 46 (1970): "[O]ne's assessment of the accuracy of the views of Professors Freund, Schwartz, and Choper as to likely political repercussions is itself a political judgment and not judicial, and [the] weighing of political reactions is a function of legislatures and not of courts." See also Ripple, *The Entanglement Test of the Religion Clauses—A Ten Year Assessment*, 27 U.C.L.A.L.Rev. 1195 (1980). For the view that the historical evidence shows "that it is misguided to interpret the first amendment as prohibiting legislative consideration of an issue affecting religion on the ground that the very act of consideration will spawn impermissible religious division," see Schotten, *The Establishment Clause and Excessive Governmental-Religious Entanglement: The Constitutional Status of Aid to Nonpublic Elementary and Secondary Schools*, 15 Wake For.L.Rev. 207, 225 (1979).

whole history and tradition to permit questions of the Religion Clauses to assume such importance in our legislatures and in our elections that they could divert attention from the myriad issues and problems which confront every level of government. [I]n *Walz* we dealt with a status under state tax laws for the benefit of all religious groups. Here we are confronted with successive and very likely permanent annual appropriations which benefit relatively few religious groups. Political fragmentation and divisiveness on religious lines is thus likely to be intensified [and] aggravated [by] the likelihood of larger and larger demands as costs and populations grow. * * *

[Unlike *Walz,* we] have no long history of state aid to church-related educational institutions comparable to 200 years of tax exemption for churches. [M]odern governmental programs have self-perpetuating and self-expanding propensities. These internal pressures are only enhanced when the schemes involve institutions whose legitimate needs are growing and whose interests have substantial political support. Nor can we fail to see that in constitutional adjudication some steps, which when taken were thought to approach "the verge," have become the platform for yet further steps. [The] dangers are increased by the difficulty of perceiving in advance exactly where the "verge" of the precipice lies. As well as constituting an independent evil against which the Religion Clauses were intended to protect, involvement or entanglement between government and religion serves as a warning signal. * * *[c]

TILTON v. RICHARDSON
403 U.S. 672, 91 S.Ct. 2091, 29 L.Ed.2d 790 (1971).

MR. CHIEF JUSTICE BURGER announced the judgment of the Court and an opinion in which MR. JUSTICE HARLAN, MR. JUSTICE STEWART and MR. JUSTICE BLACKMUN join.

* * * Title I of the Higher Education Facilities Act of 1963, which provides [federal] construction grants for buildings and facilities used exclusively for secular educational purposes [was passed] in response to a strong nationwide demand for the expansion of college and university facilities * * *. The United States retains a 20-year interest in any facility constructed with Title I funds. If, during this period, the recipient violates the statutory conditions, the United States is entitled to recover an amount equal to the proportion of its present value which the federal grant bore to the original cost of the facility. During the 20-year period, the statutory restrictions are enforced by the Office of Education primarily by way of on-site inspections. * * *

The stated legislative purpose [expresses] a legitimate secular objective * * *. The crucial question is not whether some benefit accrues to a religious institution as a consequence of the legislative program, but whether its principal or primary effect advances religion. [T]he record shows that some church-related institutions have been required to disgorge benefits for failure to obey [the Act's restrictions]. [N]one of the four church-related institutions in this case has violated the statutory restrictions. The institutions presented evidence that there had been no religious services or worship in the federally financed facilities, that there are no religious symbols or plaques in or on them, and that they had been used solely for nonreligious purposes. * * *

c. The opinions of Brennan, J., concurring, and White, J., dissenting, appear after *Tilton,* below. The concurring opinion of Douglas, J., joined by Black, J.—both of whom joined the Court's opinion—is omitted. Marshall, J., did not participate in the Pennsylvania case but joined Douglas, J.'s concurrence in respect to the Rhode Island case.

[A]ppellants' position depends on the validity of the proposition that religion so permeates the secular education provided by church-related colleges and universities that their religious and secular educational functions are in fact inseparable. The [record] provides no basis for any such assumption here. Two of the five federally financed buildings involved in this case are libraries. The District Court found that no classes had been conducted in either of these facilities and that no restrictions were imposed by the institutions on the books that they acquired. [The] third building was a language laboratory [used] solely to assist students with their pronunciation in modern foreign languages—a use which would seem peculiarly unrelated and unadaptable to religious indoctrination. Federal grants were also used to build a science building at Fairfield University and a music, drama, and arts building at Annhurst College.

There is no evidence that religion seeps into the use of any of these facilities. Indeed, the parties stipulated [that] courses at these institutions are taught according to the academic requirements intrinsic to the subject matter and the individual teacher's concept of professional standards. * * *

Rather than focus on the four defendant colleges and universities involved in this case, however, appellants seek to shift our attention to a "composite profile" that they have constructed of the "typical sectarian" institution of higher education. * * * We cannot, however, strike down an Act of Congress on the basis of a hypothetical "profile."

Although we reject appellants' broad constitutional arguments we do perceive an aspect in which the statute's enforcement provisions are inadequate to ensure that the impact of the federal aid will not advance religion. [Congress found] that after 20 years "the public benefit accruing to the United States" from the use of the federally financed facility "will equal or exceed in value" the amount of the federal grant. [T]herefore, a recipient institution's obligation not to use the facility for sectarian instruction or religious worship would appear to expire at the end of 20 years. [But it] cannot be assumed that a substantial structure has no value after that period and hence the unrestricted use of a valuable property is in effect a contribution of some value to a religious body. [This] circumstance does not require us to invalidate the entire Act, however. * * *

We next turn to the question of whether excessive entanglements characterize the relationship between government and church under the Act. * * *

There are generally significant differences between the religious aspects of church-related institutions of higher learning and parochial elementary and secondary schools. The "affirmative, if not dominant, policy" of the instruction in pre-college church-schools is "to assure future adherents to a particular faith by having control of their total education at an early age." There is substance to the contention that college students are less impressionable and less susceptible to religious indoctrination. [Further], by their very nature, college and postgraduate courses tend to limit the opportunities for sectarian influence by virtue of their own internal disciplines. Many church-related colleges and universities are characterized by a high degree of academic freedom and seek to evoke free and critical responses from their students.

The record here would not support a conclusion that any of these four institutions departed from this general pattern. All four schools are governed by Catholic religious organizations and the faculties and student bodies at each are predominantly Catholic. Nevertheless, the evidence shows that non-

Catholics were admitted as students and given faculty appointments. Not one of these four institutions requires its students to attend religious services. Although all four schools require their students to take theology courses, the parties stipulated that these courses are taught according to the academic requirements of the subject matter and the teacher's concept of professional standards. [The] schools introduced evidence that they made no attempt to indoctrinate students or to proselytize. [Finally], these four schools subscribe to a well-established set of principles of academic freedom, and nothing in this record shows that these principles are not in fact followed. [This] reduces the risk that government aid will in fact serve to support religious activities. Correspondingly the necessity for intensive government surveillance is diminished and the resulting entanglements between government and religion lessened. Such inspection as may be necessary to ascertain that the facilities are devoted to secular education is minimal and indeed hardly more than the inspections that States impose over all private schools within the reach of compulsory education laws.

The entanglement between church and state is also lessened here [unlike *Lemon*] by the nonideological character of the aid which the government provides. [The] risks of government aid to religion and the corresponding need for surveillance are therefore reduced.

Finally, government entanglements with religion are reduced by the circumstance that, unlike [*Lemon*] the government aid here is a one-time, single-purpose construction grant. There are no continuing financial relationships or dependencies, no annual audits, and no government analysis of an institution's expenditures on secular as distinguished from religious activities. Inspection as to use is a minimal contact.

No one of these three factors standing alone is necessarily controlling; cumulatively all of them shape a narrow and limited relationship with [government].

We think that cumulatively these three factors also substantially lessen the potential for divisive religious fragmentation in the political arena. This conclusion is admittedly difficult to document, but neither have appellants pointed to any continuing religious aggravation on this matter in the political processes. Possibly this can be explained by the character and diversity of the recipient colleges and universities and the absence of any intimate continuing relationship or dependency between government and religiously affiliated institutions. The potential for divisiveness inherent in the essentially local problems of primary and secondary schools is significantly less with respect to a college or university whose student constituency is not local but diverse and widely dispersed.
* * *

MR. JUSTICE WHITE, concurring in part and dissenting in part. * * *

It is enough for me that [Rhode Island and Pennsylvania] are financing a separable secular function of overriding importance in order to sustain the legislation here challenged. That religion and private interests other than education may substantially benefit does not convert these laws into impermissible establishments of religion.[1] [Where] a state program seeks to ensure the proper education of its young, in private as well as public schools, free exercise considerations at least counsel against refusing support for students attending

---

1. I accept the Court's invalidation of the [20 year provision in the federal Act].

parochial schools simply because in that setting they are also being instructed in the tenets of the faith they are constitutionally free to practice. * * *

The Court strikes down the Rhode Island statute on its face [accepting] the model for the Catholic elementary and secondary schools that it rejected for the Catholic universities or colleges in [*Tilton.* It] strikes down this Rhode Island statute based primarily on its own model and its own suppositions and unsupported views of what is likely to happen in Rhode Island parochial school [classrooms].

The Court thus creates an insoluble paradox for the State and the parochial schools. The State cannot finance secular instruction if it permits religion to be taught in the same classroom; but if it exacts a promise that religion not be so taught—a promise the school and its teachers are quite willing and on this record able to give—and enforces it, it is then entangled in the "no entanglement" aspect of the Court's Establishment Clause jurisprudence.

Why the federal program in the *Tilton* case is not embroiled with the same difficulties is never adequately explained. Surely the notion that college students are more mature and resistant to indoctrination is a make-weight, for the Court in *Tilton* is careful to note the federal condition on funding and the enforcement mechanism available. If religious teaching in federally financed buildings was permitted, the powers of resistance of college students would in no way save the federal scheme. Nor can I imagine on what basis the Court finds college clerics more reliable in keeping promises than their counterparts in elementary and secondary schools—particularly those in the Rhode Island case since within five years the majority of teachers in Rhode Island parochial schools will be lay persons, with many of them being non-Catholic.

[The Court seizes on the requirement] to verify the amount of school money spent for secular as distinguished from religious purposes. [But] this is also a slender reed on which to strike down this law, [for] only once since the inception of the program has it been necessary to segregate expenditures in this manner.

[The majority] makes much of the fact that under the federal scheme the grant to a religious institution is a one-time matter. But [it] is apparent that federal interest in any grant will be a continuing one since the conditions attached to the grant must be enforced.[d] More important, the federal grant program is an ongoing one. The same grant will not be repeated, but new ones to the same or different schools will be made year after year. Thus the same potential for recurring political controversy accompanies the federal program. * * *

With respect to [*Lemon*] I do agree, however, that the complaint should not have been dismissed for failure to state a cause of action. [O]ne of the legal theories stated in the complaint was that the Pennsylvania Act "finances and participates in the blending of sectarian and secular instruction." [E]vidence showing such a blend in a course supported by state funds [would] establish financing of religious instruction by the State. * * *[2]

d. See also Giannella, *Lemon and Tilton: The Bitter and the Sweet of Church-State Entanglement,* 1971 Sup.Ct.Rev. 147, 175: "The Court's point is probably well taken that religion is more central to the activities of parochial schools than to those of most church-related colleges. But it is highly questionable to conclude that the risk of sectarian instruction creeping into a parochial school's physical education course is greater than the risk of a similar entry into a college history course."

2. [T]he Court [does not reach] the questions that would be presented if the evidence in any of these cases showed that any of the involved schools restricted entry on racial or religious grounds or required all students gaining admission to receive instruction in the tenets of a particular faith. For myself, if

MR. JUSTICE DOUGLAS, with whom MR. JUSTICE BLACK and MR. JUSTICE MARSHALL concur, dissenting.

[I]t is hardly impressive that rather than giving a smaller amount of money annually over a large period of years, Congress instead gives a large amount all at once. [A] parochial school operates on one budget. Money not spent for one purpose becomes available for other purposes. Thus the fact that there are no religious observances in federally financed facilities is not controlling because required religious observances will take place in other buildings. * * *

MR. JUSTICE BRENNAN.

I agree that the [Rhode Island and Pennsylvania programs are unconstitutional.] I dissent in [*Tilton*]. In my view that Act is unconstitutional insofar as it authorizes grants of federal tax monies to sectarian institutions [and] our remand [should] determine whether the four institutional appellees here are sectarian institutions. * * *

In sharp contrast to the "undeviating acceptance given religious tax exemptions from our earliest days as a Nation," subsidy of sectarian educational institutions became embroiled in bitter controversies very soon after the Nation was formed. [Between 1840 and 1900, 35] States added provisions to their constitutions prohibiting the use of public school funds to aid sectarian schools, and [t]oday fewer than a half-dozen States omit such provisions from their constitutions. [If] this history is not itself compelling, [other] forms of governmental involvement which each of the three statutes requires tips the scales in my view against the validity of each of them. * * *

[A] sectarian university is the equivalent in the realm of higher education of the Catholic elementary schools in Rhode Island; it is an educational institution in which the propagation and advancement of a particular religion is a primary function of the institution. [It] is not that religion "permeates" the secular education that is provided. Rather, it is that the secular education is provided within the environment of religion; the institution is dedicated to two goals, secular education *and* religious instruction. When aid flows directly to the institution, both functions benefit. * * * I do not see any significant difference in the Federal Government telling the sectarian university not to teach any nonsecular subjects in a certain building, and Rhode Island telling the Catholic school teacher not to teach religion. [The] plurality suggests that the facts that college students are less impressionable and that college courses are less susceptible to religious permeation may lessen the need for federal policing. But the record shows that such policing has occurred and occurred in a heavy-handed way. [T]he Federal Government imposes restrictions on every class taught in the federally assisted building. It is therefore not the "non-ideological" building which is policed; rather it is the courses given there and the teachers who teach them. Thus the policing is precisely the same as under the state statutes, and that is what offends the Constitution. * * *

Decisions since *Tilton* have continued to uphold aid to higher education. See *Hunt v. McNair,* 413 U.S. 734, 93 S.Ct. 2868, 37 L.Ed.2d 923 (1973) (proceeds of state-issued tax exempt bonds for construction of projects that could not be used for religious purposes; "burden rests on [challenger] to show the extent to which the College [is] an instrument of religious indoctrination"); [e] *Roemer v.*

such proof were made, the legislation would to that extent be unconstitutional.

[e.] Douglas, Brennan and Marshall, JJ., dissented.

Board of Pub. Works, 426 U.S. 736, 96 S.Ct. 2337, 49 L.Ed.2d 179 (1976) (annual grants, of 15% of student cost in state college system, to colleges that promise not to use funds "for sectarian purposes" and who file annual report "describing and itemizing the use of the funds").[f]

However, as discussed in *Grand Rapids School Dist. v. Ball* and *Aguilar v. Felton,* below, the decisions since *Lemon* on aid to elementary and secondary schools have been more complicated than those concerning colleges. Most such forms of aid were held invalid on the *Lemon* analysis that, despite the existence of a "secular legislative purpose," there is "a primary effect that advances religion" and/or "excessive government entanglement with religion." But some programs were sustained. Indeed, *Committee for Pub. Educ. v. Regan,* 444 U.S. 646, 100 S.Ct. 840, 63 L.Ed.2d 94 (1980), per White, J., observed that the "decisions have tended to avoid categorical imperatives and absolutist approaches at either end of the range of possible outcomes. This course sacrifices clarity and predictability for flexibility * * *." For the view "that application of the Court's three-prong test has generated ad hoc judgments which are incapable of being reconciled on any principled basis," see Choper, note after *Epperson,* Part II supra, at 680–81.

The following decision, although not involving financial assistance to elementary and secondary education, played a significant role in *Mueller v. Allen,* below—one the Court's most recent pronouncements on aid to parochial schools.

———

WIDMAR v. VINCENT, 454 U.S. 263, 102 S.Ct. 269, 70 L.Ed.2d 440 (1981), per POWELL, J., held that through its policy of routinely providing university facilities for the meetings of student organizations, the University of Missouri at Kansas City (UMKC) had "created a forum generally open for use by student groups. Having done so, the University has assumed an obligation to justify the discriminations and exclusions under applicable constitutional norms." Thus UMKC's exclusion of a registered student group that wished to use university facilities for "religious worship and discussion" constituted "a content-based discrimination" which could only be justified if "necessary to serve a compelling state interest" and "narrowly drawn to achieve that end."

UMKC argued that "it cannot offer its facilities to religious groups and speakers on the terms available to other groups without violating the Establishment Clause." The Court responded "that an open-forum policy, including nondiscrimination against religious speech, would have a secular purpose [10] and

f. Brennan, Marshall, Stevens and Stewart, JJ., dissented, the last finding *Tilton* distinguishable because "here [the] compulsory theology courses may be 'devoted to deepening religious experiences in the particular faith * * *.' "

See also the summary affirmances of aid to students in church-related colleges in *Smith v. University of North Carolina,* 434 U.S. 803, 98 S.Ct. 39, 54 L.Ed.2d 65 (1977); *Americans United v. Blanton,* 434 U.S. 803, 98 S.Ct. 39, 54 L.Ed.2d 65 (1977).

10. It is the avowed purpose of UMKC to provide a forum in which students can exchange ideas. The University argues that use of the forum for religious speech would undermine this secular aim. But by creating a forum the University does not thereby endorse or promote any of the particular ideas aired there. Undoubtedly many views are advocated in the forum with which the University desires no association.

Because this case involves a forum already made generally available to student groups, it differs from those cases in which this Court has invalidated statutes permitting school facilities to be used for instruction by religious groups, but *not* by others. See, e.g., *McCollum.* In those cases the school may appear to sponsor the views of the speaker.

[May high schools that permit student groups to use their facilities also permit student-initiated voluntary prayer sessions held before or after the curricular day? See generally Comment, *Widmar v. Vincent and the* would avoid entanglement with religion.[11]" As for "primary effect," "it is possible—perhaps even foreseeable—that religious groups will benefit from access to University facilities. But this Court has explained that a religious organization's enjoyment of merely 'incidental' benefits does not violate the prohibition against 'primary advancement' of religion. *McGowan.* [First], an open forum in a public university does not confer any imprimatur of State approval on religious sects or practices. [Second], the forum is available [to] over 100 recognized student groups at UMKC. The provision of benefits to so broad a spectrum of groups is an important index of secular effect. [At] least in the absence of empirical evidence that religious groups will dominate UMKC's open forum, [the] advancement of religion would not be the forum's 'primary effect.' " [a]

WHITE, J., dissented, arguing that the case involved only the question of whether UMKC must permit use of its facilities for "religious worship"—as distinguished from "communication of religious views to a non-religious, public audience" as in cases like *Heffron,* p. 536 supra: "I know of no precedent holding that simply because a public forum is open to all kinds of speech—including speech about religion—it must be open to regular religious worship services as well."

He thought "plainly wrong" the view that "because religious worship uses speech, it is protected by the Free Speech Clause": "Were it right, 'the Religion Clauses would be emptied of any independent meaning in circumstances in which religious practice took the form of speech.' *Stone v. Graham,* "necessarily presumed that the state could not ignore the religious content of the written message, nor was it permitted to treat that content as it would, or must treat, other—secular—messages under the First Amendment's protection of speech. Similarly, the Court's decisions prohibiting prayer in the public schools rest on a content-based distinction between varieties of speech: as a speech act, apart from its content, a prayer is indistinguishable from a biology lesson. Operation of the Free Exercise Clause is equally dependent, in certain circumstances, on recognition of a content-based distinction between religious and secular speech. Thus, in *Torcaso v. Watkins,* [Sec. 2, II infra], the Court struck down, as violative of the Free Exercise Clause, a state requirement that made a declaration of belief in God a condition of state employment. A declaration is again a speech act, but it was the content of the speech that brought the case within the scope of the Free Exercise Clause." [b]

Public Forum Doctrine: Time to Reconsider Public School Prayer, 1984 Wis.L.Rev. 147.]

11. [T]he University would risk greater "entanglement" by attempting to enforce its exclusion of "religious worship and religious speech." Initially, the University would need to determine which words and activities fall within "religious worship and religious teaching." This alone could prove "an impossible task in an age where many and various beliefs meet the constitutional definition of religion." There would also be a continuing need to monitor group meetings to ensure compliance with the rule.

a. Stevens, J., concurred in the judgment.

After *Widmar,* may elementary or secondary schools permit their facilities to be used for instruction by religious groups if they also permit instruction by outside teachers of art,

music, crafts, dance, etc. (cf. *McCollum*)? May they post the Ten Commandments if they also post the symbols of other civic or charitable groups (cf. *Stone*)?

b. The Court found "at least three difficulties with this distinction."

"First, the dissent fails to establish that the distinction has intelligible content. There is no indication when 'singing hymns, reading scripture, and teaching biblical principles' cease to [be] 'speech,' despite their religious subject matter—and become unprotected 'worship.'

"Second, even if the distinction drew an arguably principled line, it is highly doubtful that it would lie within the judicial competence to administer. Merely to draw the distinction would require [courts] to inquire into the significance of words and practices to dif-

MUELLER v. ALLEN

463 U.S. 388, 103 S.Ct. 3062, 77 L.Ed.2d 721 (1983).

JUSTICE REHNQUIST delivered the opinion of the Court.

Minnesota allows taxpayers, in computing their state income tax, to deduct certain expenses incurred in providing for the education of their children.[1] The United States Court of Appeals for the Eighth Circuit held that the Establishment Clause of the First and Fourteenth Amendments was not offended by this arrangement. [A]bout 820,000 students attended [Minnesota's public] school system in the most recent school year. During the same year, approximately 91,000 elementary and secondary students attended some 500 privately supported schools located in Minnesota, and about 95% of these students attended schools considering themselves to be sectarian. * * *

Today's case is no exception to our oft-repeated statement that the Establishment Clause presents especially difficult questions of interpretation and application. [It] is not at all easy [to] apply this Court's various decisions construing the Clause to governmental programs of financial assistance to sectarian schools and the parents of children attending those schools. Indeed, in many of these decisions "we have expressly or implicitly acknowledged that 'we can only dimly perceive the lines of demarcation in this extraordinarily sensitive area of constitutional law.'" *Lemon.*

One fixed principle in this field is our consistent rejection of the argument that "any program which in some manner aids an institution with a religious affiliation" violates the Establishment Clause. * * *

Notwithstanding the repeated approval given programs such as those in *Allen* and *Everson,* our decisions also have struck down arrangements resembling, in many respects, these forms of assistance. See, e.g., [*Lemon.*] Petitioners place particular reliance on our decision in *Committee for Pub. Educ. v. Nyquist,* 413 U.S. 756, 93 S.Ct. 2955, 37 L.Ed.2d 948 (1973), where we held invalid a New York [statute] granting thinly disguised "tax benefits," actually amounting to tuition grants, to the parents of children attending private schools. As explained below, we conclude that § 290.09(22) bears less resemblance to the arrangement struck down in *Nyquist* than it does to assistance programs upheld in our prior [decisions].

Little time need be spent on the question of whether the Minnesota tax deduction has a secular purpose. Under our prior decisions, governmental

ferent religious faiths, and in varying circumstances by the same faith. Such inquiries would tend inevitably to entangle the State with religion in a manner forbidden by our cases. E.g., *Walz.*

"Finally, the dissent [gives] no reason why the Establishment Clause [would] require different treatment for religious speech designed to win religious converts, see *Heffron,* than for religious worship by persons already converted. It is far from clear that the State gives greater support in the latter case than in the former."

1. Minn.Stat. § 290.09(22) (1982) permits a taxpayer to deduct from his or her computation of gross income the following: "[The] amount he has paid to others, not to exceed $500 for each dependent in grades K to 6 and $700 for each dependent in grades 7 to 12, for tuition, textbooks and transportation of each dependent in attending an elementary or secondary school [wherein] a resident of this state may legally fulfill the state's compulsory attendance laws, which is not operated for profit, and which adheres to the provisions of the Civil Rights Act of 1964 * * *. As used in this subdivision, 'textbooks' shall mean and include books and other instructional materials and equipment used in elementary and secondary schools in teaching only those subjects legally and commonly taught in public elementary and secondary schools in this state and shall not include instructional books and materials used in the teaching of religious tenets, doctrines or worship * * *."

assistance programs have consistently survived this inquiry even when they have run afoul of other aspects of the *Lemon* framework. This reflects, at least in part, our reluctance to attribute unconstitutional motives to the states, particularly when a plausible secular purpose for the state's program may be discerned from the face of the statute.

A state's decision to defray the cost of educational expenses incurred by parents—regardless of the type of schools their children attend—evidences a purpose that is both secular and understandable. An educated populace is essential to the political and economic health of any community, and a state's efforts to assist parents in meeting the rising cost of educational expenses plainly serves this secular purpose of ensuring that the state's citizenry is well-educated. Similarly, Minnesota, like other states, could conclude that there is a strong public interest in assuring the continued financial health of private schools, both sectarian and non-sectarian. By educating a substantial number of students such schools relieve public schools of a correspondingly great burden—to the benefit of all taxpayers. In addition, private schools may serve as a benchmark for public schools * * *.

We turn therefore to the more difficult but related question whether the Minnesota statute has "the primary effect of advancing the sectarian aims of the non-public schools." In concluding that it does not, we find several features of the Minnesota tax deduction particularly significant. First, an essential feature of Minnesota's arrangement is the fact that § 290.09(22) is only one among many deductions—such as those for medical expenses and charitable contributions [a]— available under the Minnesota tax laws.[5] Our decisions consistently have recognized that [the] legislature's judgment that a deduction for educational expenses fairly equalizes the tax burden of its citizens and encourages desirable expenditures for educational purposes is entitled to substantial deference.[6]

a. Compare Choper, *Public Financial Assistance to Church-Related Schools,* in Choper, Kamisar & Tribe, *The Supreme Court: Trends and Developments 1982–83,* 48 (1984): "[This is] like saying that an appropriation to build a new church for the First Presbyterian congregation in Washington, D.C. is only one of many appropriations. The reasoning is that since Congress appropriates money for the University of the District of Columbia and for all kinds of other things, this appropriation to build a church should be treated just like one of many appropriations."

5. Deductions for charitable contributions, allowed by Minnesota law, include contributions to religious institutions, and exemptions from property tax for property used for charitable purposes under Minnesota law include property used for wholly religious purposes. In each case, it may be that religious institutions benefit very substantially from the allowance of such deductions. The Court's holding in *Walz* indicates, however, that this does not require the conclusion that such provisions of a state's tax law violate the Establishment Clause.

6. Our decision in *Nyquist* is not to the contrary on this point. We expressed considerable doubt there that the "tax benefits" provided by New York law properly could be regarded as parts of a genuine system of tax laws. Plainly, the outright grants to low-income parents ["of $50 to $100 per child (but no more than 50% of tuition actually paid)"] did not take the form of ordinary tax benefits. As to the benefits provided to middle-income parents, the Court said: "The amount of the deduction is unrelated to the amount of money actually expended by any parent on tuition, but is calculated on the basis of a formula contained in the statute. The formula is apparently the product of a legislative attempt to assure that each family would receive a carefully estimated net benefit, and that the tax benefit would be comparable to, and compatible with, the tuition grant for lower income families." Indeed, the question whether a program having the elements of a "genuine tax deduction" would be constitutionally acceptable was expressly reserved in *Nyquist.* While the economic consequences of the program in *Nyquist* and that in this case may be difficult to distinguish, we have recognized on other occasions that "the form of the [state's assistance to parochial schools must be examined] for the light that it casts on the substance." The fact that the Minnesota plan embodies a "genuine tax deduction" is thus of some relevance, especially given the traditional rule of deference accorded legislative classifications in tax statutes.

Other characteristics of § 290.09(22) argue equally strongly for the provision's constitutionality. Most importantly, the deduction is available for educational expenses incurred by *all* parents, including those whose children attend public schools and those whose children attend non-sectarian private schools or sectarian private schools. Just as in *Widmar*, [so] here: "the provision of benefits to so broad a spectrum of groups is an important index of secular effect."

In this respect, as well as others, this case is vitally different from the scheme struck down in *Nyquist*. There, public assistance amounting to tuition grants, was provided only to parents of children in *nonpublic* schools. This fact had considerable bearing on our decision striking down the New York statute at issue; we explicitly distinguished both *Allen* and *Everson* on the grounds that "In both cases the class of beneficiaries included *all* schoolchildren, those in public as well as those in private schools." Moreover, we intimated that "public assistance (e.g., scholarships) made available generally without regard to the sectarian-nonsectarian or public-nonpublic nature of the institution benefited," might not offend the Establishment Clause. We think the tax deduction adopted by Minnesota is more similar to this latter type of program than it is to the arrangement struck down in *Nyquist*. Unlike the assistance at issue in *Nyquist*, § 290.09(22) permits *all* parents—whether their children attend public school or private—to deduct their children's educational expenses. As *Widmar* and our other decisions indicate, a program, like § 290.09(22), that neutrally provides state assistance to a broad spectrum of citizens is not readily subject to challenge under the Establishment Clause.

We also agree with the Court of Appeals that, by channeling whatever assistance it may provide to parochial schools through individual parents, Minnesota has reduced the Establishment Clause objections to which its action is subject. It is true, of course, that financial assistance provided to parents ultimately has an economic effect comparable to that of aid given directly to the schools attended by their children. It is also true, however, that under Minnesota's arrangement public funds become available only as a result of numerous, private choices of individual parents of school-age children. [It] is noteworthy that all but one of our recent cases invalidating state aid to parochial schools have involved the direct transmission of assistance from the state to the schools themselves. The exception, of course, was *Nyquist*, which, as discussed previously is distinguishable from this case on other grounds. Where, as here, aid to parochial schools is available only as a result of decisions of individual parents no "imprimatur of State approval," *Widmar*, can be deemed to have been conferred on any particular religion, or on religion generally.

[The] Establishment Clause of course extends beyond prohibition of a state church or payment of state funds to one or more churches. We do not think, however, that its prohibition extends to the type of tax deduction established by Minnesota. The historic purposes of the clause simply do not encompass the sort of attenuated financial benefit, ultimately controlled by the private choices of individual parents, that eventually flows to parochial schools from the neutrally available tax benefit at issue in this case.

Petitioners argue that, notwithstanding the facial neutrality of § 290.09(22), [most] parents of public school children incur no tuition expenses, and that other expenses deductible under § 290.09(22) are negligible in value; moreover, they claim that 96% of the children in private schools in 1978–1979 attended religiously-affiliated institutions. Because of all this, they reason, the bulk of deductions taken under § 290.09(22) will be claimed by parents of children in sectarian schools. Respondents reply that petitioners have failed to consider the impact of deductions for items such as transportation, summer school tuition, tuition paid by parents whose children attended schools outside the school districts in which they resided, rental or purchase costs for a variety of equipment, and tuition for certain types of instruction not ordinarily provided in public schools.

We need not consider these contentions in detail. We would be loath to adopt a rule grounding the constitutionality of a facially neutral law on annual reports reciting the extent to which various classes of private citizens claimed benefits under the law. Such an approach would scarcely provide the certainty that this field stands in need of, nor can we perceive principled standards by which such statistical evidence might be evaluated. Moreover, the fact that private persons fail in a particular year to claim the tax relief to which they are entitled—under a facially neutral statute—should be of little importance in determining the constitutionality of the statute permitting such relief.

Finally, [if] parents of children in private schools choose to take especial advantage of the relief provided by § 290.09(22), it is no doubt due to the fact that they bear a particularly great financial burden in educating their children. More fundamentally, whatever unequal effect may be attributed to the statutory classification can fairly be regarded as a rough return for the benefits, discussed above, provided to the state and all taxpayers by parents sending their children to parochial schools. In the light of all this, we believe it wiser to decline to engage in the type of empirical inquiry into those persons benefited by state law which petitioners urge. * * *

Turning to the third part of the *Lemon* inquiry, we have no difficulty in concluding that the Minnesota statute does not "excessively entangle" the state in religion. [T]hat state officials must determine whether particular textbooks qualify for a deduction [does] not differ substantially from making the types of decisions approved in [*Allen*].[11]

Affirmed.

JUSTICE MARSHALL, with whom JUSTICE BRENNAN, JUSTICE BLACKMUN and JUSTICE STEVENS join, dissenting.

[The] Minnesota tax statute violates the Establishment Clause for precisely the same reason as the statute struck down in *Nyquist:* it has a direct and immediate effect of advancing religion. [Although it] allows a deduction for the tuition expenses of children attending public schools, Minnesota public schools [may] assess tuition charges only for students accepted from outside the district. In the 1978–1979 school year, only 79 public school students fell into this category. * * *

---

11. No party to this litigation has urged that the Minnesota plan is invalid because it runs afoul of the rather elusive inquiry, subsumed under the third part of the *Lemon* test, whether the Minnesota statute partakes of the "divisive political potential" condemned in *Lemon*. [Since] this aspect of the "entanglement" inquiry originated with *Lemon*, and the Court's opinion there took pains to distinguish both *Everson* and *Allen*, the Court in *Lemon* must have been referring to a phenomenon which, although present in that case, would have been absent in the two cases it distinguished.

The Court's language in *Lemon* respecting political divisiveness was made in the context of Pennsylvania and Rhode Island statutes which provided for either direct payments of, or reimbursement of, a proportion of teachers' salaries in parochial schools. We think, in the light of the treatment of the point in later cases discussed above, the language must be regarded as confined to cases where direct financial subsidies are paid to parochial schools or to teachers in parochial schools.

As we recognized in *Nyquist,* direct government subsidization of parochial school tuition is impermissible because "the effect of the aid is unmistakably to provide desired financial support for nonpublic, sectarian institutions." "[A]id to the educational function of [parochial schools] necessarily results in aid to the sectarian enterprise as a whole" because "[t]he very purpose of those schools is to provide an integrated secular and religious education." * * *

Indirect assistance in the form of financial aid to parents for tuition payments is similarly impermissible because it is not "subject [to] restrictions" which "guarantee the separation between secular and religious educational functions [and] ensure that State financial aid supports only the former." *Lemon.* [As] was true of the law struck down in *Nyquist,* "it is precisely the function of [Minnesota's] law to provide assistance to private schools, the great majority of which are sectarian. By reimbursing parents for a portion of their tuition bill, the State seeks to relieve their financial burdens sufficiently to assure that they continue to have the option to send their children to religion-oriented schools. And while the other purposes for that aid—to perpetuate a pluralistic educational environment and to protect the fiscal integrity of overburdened public schools—are certainly unexceptional, the effect of the aid is unmistakably to provide desired financial support for nonpublic, sectarian institutions."

That parents receive a reduction of their tax liability, rather than a direct reimbursement, is of no greater significance here than it was in *Nyquist.* "[F]or purposes of determining whether such aid has the effect of advancing religion," it makes no difference whether the qualifying "parent receives an actual cash payment [or] is allowed to reduce [the] sum he would otherwise be obliged to pay over to the State." It is equally irrelevant whether a reduction in taxes takes the form of a tax "credit," a tax "modification," or a tax "deduction." What is of controlling significance is not the form but the "substantive impact" of the financial aid. * * *

The majority first attempts to distinguish *Nyquist* on the ground that Minnesota makes all parents eligible to deduct up to $500 or $700 for each dependent, whereas the New York law allowed a deduction only for parents whose children attended nonpublic schools. Although Minnesota taxpayers who send their children to local public schools may not deduct tuition expenses because they incur none, they may deduct other expenses, such as the cost of gym clothes, pencils, and notebooks, which are shared by all parents of school-age children. * * *

That the Minnesota statute makes some small benefit available to all parents cannot alter the fact that the most substantial benefit provided by the statute is available only to those parents who send their children to schools that charge tuition.[2] Of the total number of taxpayers who are eligible for the tuition deduction, approximately 96% send their children to religious schools. [In] *Nyquist* we unequivocally rejected any suggestion that, in determining the effect of a tax statute, this Court should look exclusively to what the statute on its face purports to do and ignore the actual operation of the challenged

---

2. Even if the Minnesota statute allowed parents of public school students to deduct expenses that were likely to be equivalent to the tuition expenses of private school students, it would still be unconstitutional. Insofar as the Minnesota statute provides a deduction for parochial school tuition, it provides a benefit to parochial schools that furthers the religious mission of those schools. *Nyquist* makes clear that the State may not provide any financial assistance to parochial schools unless that assistance is limited to secular uses.

provision. In determining the effect of the New York statute, we emphasized [that] "tax reductions authorized by this law flow primarily to the parents of children attending sectarian, nonpublic schools." Similarly, in *Sloan v. Lemon,* 413 U.S. 825, 93 S.Ct. 2982, 37 L.Ed.2d 939 (1973), we considered important to our "consider[ation of] the new law's effect [that] 'more than 90% of the children attending nonpublic schools in the Commonwealth of Pennsylvania are enrolled in schools that are controlled by religious institutions or that have the purpose of propagating and promoting religious faith.'" * * *

The majority also asserts that the Minnesota statute is distinguishable from the statute struck down in *Nyquist* in another respect: [Under] the New York law, the amount of deduction was not dependent upon the amount actually paid for tuition but was a predetermined amount which depended on the tax bracket of each taxpayer. The deduction was designed to yield roughly the same amount of tax "forgiveness" for each taxpayer.

This is a distinction without a difference. [As the majority] concedes, the "economic consequence" of these programs is the same, n. 6, for in each case the "financial assistance provided to parents ultimately has an economic effect comparable to that of aid given directly to the schools." It was precisely the substantive impact of the financial support, and not its particular form, that rendered the programs in *Nyquist* and *Sloan* unconstitutional.

* * * Financial assistance for tuition payments has a consequence that "is quite unlike the sort of 'indirect' and 'incidental' benefits that flowed to sectarian schools from programs aiding *all* parents by supplying bus transportation and secular textbooks for their children. *Such benefits were carefully restricted to the purely secular side of church-affiliated institutions* and provided no special aid for those who had chosen to support religious schools. Yet such aid approached the 'verge' of the constitutionally impermissible." *Sloan* (emphasis added in part). As previously noted, the Minnesota tuition tax deduction is not available to *all* parents, but only to parents whose children attend schools that charge tuition, which are comprised almost entirely of sectarian schools. More importantly, the assistance that flows to parochial schools as a result of the tax benefit is not restricted, and cannot be restricted, to the secular functions of those schools.

In my view, Minnesota's tax deduction for the cost of textbooks and other instructional materials is also constitutionally infirm. * * *

The instructional materials which are subsidized by the Minnesota tax deduction plainly may be used to inculcate religious values and belief. In *Meek v. Pittenger,* 421 U.S. 349, 95 S.Ct. 1753, 44 L.Ed.2d 217 (1975), we held that even the use of "wholly neutral, secular instructional material and equipment" by church-related schools contributes to religious instruction because " '[t]he secular education those schools provide goes hand in hand with the religious mission that is the only reason for the schools' existence.'" In *Wolman v. Walter,* 433 U.S. 229, 97 S.Ct. 2593, 53 L.Ed.2d 714 (1977), we concluded that precisely the same impermissible effect results when the instructional materials are loaned to the pupil or his parent, rather than directly to the schools. We stated that "it would exalt form over substance if this distinction were found to justify a result different from that in *Meek*." It follows that a tax deduction to offset the cost of purchasing instructional materials for use in sectarian schools, like a loan of such materials to parents, "necessarily results in aid to the sectarian school enterprise as a whole" and is therefore a "substantial advancement of religious activity" that "constitutes an impermissible establishment of religion."

There is no reason to treat Minnesota's tax deduction for textbooks any differently. Secular textbooks, like other secular instructional materials, contribute to the religious mission of the parochial schools that use those books. [D]istinguishing secular instructional materials and secular textbooks is simply untenable, and is inconsistent with many of our more recent decisions concerning state aid to parochial schools. * * *[6]

[For] the first time, the Court has upheld financial support for religious schools without any reason at all to assume that the support will be restricted to the secular functions of those schools and will not be used to support religious instruction. This result is flatly at odds with the fundamental principle that [the] Court stated in *Everson* and has often repeated, see, e.g., *Meek; Nyquist,* "No tax in any amount, large or small, can be levied to support any religious activities or institutions, whatever they may be called, or whatever form they may adopt to teach or practice religion."

GRAND RAPIDS SCHOOL DIST. v. BALL
___ U.S. ___, 105 S.Ct. 3216, 87 L.Ed.2d 267 (1985).

JUSTICE BRENNAN delivered the opinion of the Court.

[In 1976, the school district adopted two publicly financed programs held on parochial school premises. Under the Shared Time Program, "remedial" and "enrichment" courses in mathematics and reading, and courses in art, music and physical education were taught during the regular school day by public school teachers; supplies, material and equipment were provided at public expense. Under the Community Education Program, classes for children and adults—in subjects such as "Arts and Crafts, Home Economics, Spanish, Gymnastics, Yearbook Production, Christmas Arts and Crafts, Drama, Newspaper, Humanities, Chess, Model Building, and Nature Appreciation"—were taught at the end of the regular school day. Both programs were conducted in parochial school classrooms which were "leased" by the school district and which had to be free of any religious symbols; during the programs, a posted sign stated that it was a "public school classroom." No attempt was made in either program "to monitor [the] courses for religious content."]

Since *Everson,* [we] have often grappled with the problem of state aid to nonpublic, religious schools. In all of these cases, our goal has been to give meaning to the sparse language and broad purposes of the [Establishment] Clause, while not unduly infringing on the ability of the States to provide for [the] education of schoolchildren [which] is surely a praiseworthy purpose. But our cases have consistently recognized that even such a praiseworthy, secular purpose cannot validate government aid to parochial schools when the aid has the effect of promoting a single religion or religion generally or when the aid unduly entangles the government in matters religious. [T]he three-part test first articulated in [*Lemon*] "must not be viewed as setting the precise limits to the necessary constitutional inquiry, but serve[s] only as guidelines with which to identify instances in which the objectives of the Establishment Clause have been impaired." We have particularly relied on *Lemon* in every case involving

---

6. For similar reasons, I would hold that the deduction for transportation expenses is constitutional only insofar as it relates to the costs of traveling between home and school. See *Wolman* (reimbursement of nonpublic schools for field trip transportation impermis-sibly fosters religion because the nonpublic schools control the timing, frequency, and destination of the trips, which, for sectarian schools, are an integral part of the sectarian education). * * *

the sensitive relationship between government and religion in the education of our children. * * *

As has often been true in school aid cases, there is no dispute [that] the purpose of the Community Education and Shared Time programs was "manifestly secular." We [go] on to consider whether the primary or principal effect of the challenged programs is to advance or inhibit religion.

Our inquiry must begin with a consideration of the nature of the institutions in which the programs operate. Of the 41 private schools where these "part-time public schools" have operated, 40 are identifiably religious schools. It is true that each school may not share all of the characteristics of religious schools as articulated, for example, in the complaint in *Lemon.* The District Court found, however, "[that] the religious institutions receiving instructional services from the public schools are sectarian in the sense that a substantial portion of their functions are subsumed in the religious mission." [6] [Thus, the programs] may impermissibly advance religion in three different ways. * * *

(1) [In] *Meek,* the Court invalidated a statute providing for the loan of state-paid professional staff—including teachers—to nonpublic schools to provide remedial and accelerated instruction, guidance counseling and testing, and other services on the premises of the nonpublic schools. Such a program, if not subjected to a "comprehensive, discriminating, and continuing state surveillance," *Lemon,* would entail an unacceptable risk that the the state-sponsored instructional personnel would "advance the religious mission of the church-related schools in which they serve." Even though the teachers were paid by the State, "[t]he potential for impermissible fostering of religion under these circumstances, although somewhat reduced, is nonetheless present." * * *

The programs before us today share the defect that we identified in *Meek.* With respect to the Community Education Program, the District Court found that "virtually every Community Education course conducted on facilities leased from nonpublic schools has an instructor otherwise employed full time by the same nonpublic school." These instructors, many of whom no doubt teach in the religious schools precisely because they are adherents of the controlling denomination and want to serve their religious community zealously, are expected during the regular school day to inculcate their students with the tenets and beliefs of their particular religious faiths. Yet the premise of the program is that those instructors can put aside their religious convictions and engage in entirely secular Community Education instruction as soon as the school day is over. [T]here is a substantial risk that, overtly or subtly, the religious message they are expected to convey during the regular school day will infuse the supposedly secular classes they teach after school. The danger arises "not because the public employee [is] likely deliberately to subvert his task to the service of religion, but rather because the pressures of the environment might alter his behavior from its normal course." *Wolman.* * * *

The Shared Time program [poses] a substantial risk of state-sponsored indoctrination. The most important difference between the programs is that most of the instructors in the Shared Time program are full-time teachers hired by the public schools [although] "[a] significant portion" of the Shared Time

---

6. [Many] of the schools in this case include prayer and attendance at religious services as a part of their curriculum, are run by churches or other organizations whose members must subscribe to particular religious tenets, have faculties and student bodies composed largely of adherents of the particular denomination, and give preference in attendance to children belonging to the denomination.

instructors previously worked in the religious schools.[7] [They] are teaching academic subjects in religious schools in courses virtually indistinguishable from the other courses offered during the regular religious-school day [and] may well subtly (or overtly) conform their instruction to the environment in which they teach, while students will perceive the instruction provided in the context of the dominantly religious message of the institution, thus reinforcing the indoctrinating effect. [Unlike] types of aid that the Court has upheld, such as state-created standardized tests, *Regan,* or diagnostic services, *Wolman,* there is a "substantial risk" that programs operating in this environment would "be used for religious educational purposes."

[T]hat respondents adduced no evidence of specific incidents of religious indoctrination in this case [is] not dispositive. When conducting a supposedly secular class in the pervasively sectarian environment of a religious school, a teacher may knowingly or unwillingly tailor the content of the course to fit the school's announced goals. If so, there is no reason to believe that this kind of ideological influence would be detected or [reported]. After spending the balance of their school day in classes heavily influenced by a religious perspective, [the students] would have little motivation or ability to discern improper ideological content that may creep into a Shared Time or Community Education course. Neither their parents nor the parochial schools would have cause to complain if the effect of the publicly-supported instruction were to advance the schools' sectarian mission. And the public school system itself has no incentive to detect or report any specific incidents of improper state-sponsored indoctrination. * * *

(2) Our cases have recognized that the Establishment Clause guards against more than direct, state-funded efforts to indoctrinate youngsters in specific religious beliefs. [A]n important concern of the effects test is whether the symbolic union of church and state effected by the challenged governmental action is sufficiently likely to be perceived by adherents of the controlling denominations as an endorsement, and by the nonadherents as a disapproval, of their individual religious choices. The [symbolism] of a union between church and state is most likely to influence children of tender years, whose experience is limited and whose beliefs consequently are the function of environment as much as of free and voluntary choice.[10] Consequently, even the student who notices the "public school" sign temporarily posted would have before him a powerful symbol of state endorsement and encouragement of the religious beliefs taught in the same class at some other time during the day. * * *

(3) [With] but one exception, our [cases] have struck down attempts by States to make payments out of public tax dollars directly to primary or secondary religious educational institutions. See, e.g., *Nyquist* (reimbursement for maintenance and repair expenses); *Levitt v. Committee for Pub. Educ.,* 413 U.S. 472, 93 S.Ct. 2814, 37 L.Ed.2d 736 (1973) (reimbursement for teacher-prepared tests); *Lemon.* But see *Regan* (permitting public subsidy for certain routinized recordkeeping and testing services performed by nonpublic schools but required by state law).

---

7. Approximately 10 percent of the Shared Time instructors were previously employed by the religious schools, and many of these were reassigned back to the school at which they had previously taught.

10. Compare *Meek* (invalidating program providing for state-funded remedial services on religious-school premises) with *Wolman* (upholding program providing for similar services at neutral sites off the premises of the religious school).

Aside from cash payments, the Court has distinguished between two categories of programs in which public funds are used to finance secular activities that religious schools would otherwise fund from their own resources. In the first category, the Court has noted ["that] not every law that confers an 'indirect,' 'remote,' or 'incidental' benefit upon religious institutions is, for that reason alone, constitutionally invalid." In such "indirect" aid cases, the government has used primarily secular means to accomplish a primarily secular end, and no "primary effect" of advancing religion has thus been found. On this rationale, the Court has upheld programs providing for loans of secular textbooks to nonpublic school students, *Allen;* see also *Wolman; Meek,* and programs providing bus transportation for nonpublic school children, *Everson.*

In the second category of cases, the Court has relied on the Establishment Clause prohibition of forms of aid that provide "direct and substantial advancement of the sectarian enterprise." In such "direct aid" cases, the government, although acting for a secular purpose, has done so by directly supporting a religious institution. Under this rationale, the Court has struck down state schemes providing for tuition grants and tax benefits for parents whose children attend religious school, see *Sloan; Nyquist,* and programs providing for "loan" of instructional materials to be used in religious schools, see *Wolman; Meek.* In *Sloan* and *Nyquist,* the aid was formally given to parents and not directly to the religious schools, while in *Wolman* and *Meek,* the aid was in-kind assistance rather than the direct contribution of public funds. Nonetheless, these differences in form were insufficient to save programs whose effect was indistinguishable from that of a direct subsidy to the religious school.

Thus, the Court has never accepted the mere possibility of subsidization, as the above cases demonstrate, as sufficient to invalidate an aid program. On the other hand, this effect is not wholly unimportant for Establishment Clause purposes. If it were, the public schools could gradually take on themselves the entire responsibility for teaching secular subjects on religious school premises. The question in each case must be whether the effect of the proffered aid is "direct and substantial," or indirect and incidental. "The problem, like many problems in constitutional law, is one of degree." *Zorach.* Cf. *Wolman* (upholding provision of diagnostic services, which were "general welfare services for children that may be provided by the State regardless of the incidental benefit that accrues to church-related schools.") * * *

Petitioners claim that the aid here, like the textbooks in *Allen,* flows primarily to the students, not to the religious schools.[13] Of course, all aid to religious schools ultimately "flows to" the students, and petitioners' argument if accepted would validate all forms of nonideological aid to religious schools, including those explicitly rejected in our prior cases. Yet in *Meek,* we held unconstitutional the loan of instructional materials to religious schools and in *Wolman,* we rejected the fiction that a similar program could be saved by masking it as aid to individual students. It follows a fortiori that the aid here, which includes not only instructional materials but also the provision of instructional services by teachers in the parochial school building, "inescapably [has] the primary effect of providing a direct and substantial advancement of the sectarian enterprise." * * *

Petitioners also argue that this "subsidy" effect is not significant in this case, because the Community Education and Shared Time programs supplement-

---

13. [Unlike] *Mueller,* the aid provided here is unmediated by the tax code and the "nu-   merous, private choices of individual parents of school-age children."

ed the curriculum with courses not previously offered in the religious schools and not required by school rule or state regulation. [But first,] there is no way of knowing whether the religious schools would have offered some or all of these courses if the public school system had not offered them first. The distinction between courses that "supplement" and those that "supplant" the regular curriculum is therefore not nearly as clear as petitioners allege. Second, although the precise courses offered in these programs may have been new to the participating religious schools, their general subject matter—reading, math, etc.—was surely a part of the curriculum in the past, and the concerns of the Establishment Clause may thus be triggered despite the "supplemental" nature of the courses. Third, and most important, petitioners' argument would permit the public schools gradually to take over the entire secular curriculum of the religious school, for the latter could surely discontinue existing courses so that they might be replaced a year or two later by a Community Education or Shared Time course with the same content. The average religious school student, for instance, now spends 10 percent of the school day in Shared Time classes. But there is no principled basis on which this Court can impose a limit on the percentage of the religious-school day that can be subsidized by the public school. To let the genie out of the bottle in this case would be to permit ever larger segments of the religious school curriculum to be turned over to the public school system, thus violating the cardinal principle that the State may not in effect become the prime supporter of the religious school system. * * *

[AGUILAR v. FELTON, ___ U.S. ___, 105 S.Ct. 3232, 87 L.Ed.2d 290 (1985), a companion case, involved Title I of a federal plan—for "educationally deprived children from low-income families"—similar to the *Grand Rapids* Shared Time Program. Since 1966, New York City paid federal funds to public employees (teachers, guidance counselors, psychologists and social workers) for "remedial" courses and "guidance" services provided in parochial school classrooms (the "vast majority" of which were Catholic)[8] which had to be "clear [of] all religious symbols." Unlike Grand Rapids, New York "adopted a system for monitoring the religious content" of the classes. The Court, per BRENNAN, J., relying on the "administrative surveillance" aspect of *Lemon,* held that "the supervisory system * * * inevitably results in the excessive entanglement of church and state, an Establishment Clause concern distinct from that addressed by the effects doctrine."]

JUSTICE POWELL concurring [in] the Court's opinions * * *.

I agree with the Court that [the] Establishment Clause is violated because there is too great a risk of government entanglement in the administration of the religious schools [and] is compounded by the additional risk of political divisiveness stemming from the aid to religion at issue here. I do not suggest that at this point in our history [the] plans could result in the establishment of a state religion. There likewise is small chance that these programs would result in significant religious or denominational control over our democratic processes. Nonetheless, there remains a considerable risk of continuing political strife over

---

8. Appellants suggest that the degree of sectarianism differs from school to school. This has little bearing on our analysis. As Judge Friendly, writing for the court below, noted: "It may well be that the degree of sectarianism in Catholic schools in, for example, black neighborhoods, with considerable proportions of non-Catholic pupils and teachers, is relatively low; by the same token, in other schools it may be relatively high. [Yet] enforcement of the Establishment Clause does not rest on means or medians. [It] would be simply incredible [that] all, or almost all, New York City's parochial schools receiving Title I aid [have] abandoned 'the religious mission that is the only reason for the schools' existence."

the propriety of direct aid to religious schools and the proper allocation of limited governmental resources. * * *

I recognize the difficult dilemma in which governments are placed by the interaction of the "effects" and entanglement prongs of the *Lemon* test. Our decisions require governments extending aid to parochial schools to tread an extremely narrow line between being certain that the "principal or primary effect" of the aid is not to advance religion, and avoiding excessive entanglement. Nonetheless, the Court has never foreclosed the possibility that some types of aid to parochial schools could be valid under the Establishment Clause [citing *Mueller, Allen* and *Everson*, where] the assistance programs made funds available equally to public and nonpublic schools without entanglement. [If,] for example, Congress could fashion a program of evenhanded financial assistance to both public and private schools that could be administered, without governmental supervision in the private schools, so as to prevent the diversion of the aid from secular purposes, we would be presented with a different question. * * *

CHIEF JUSTICE BURGER, concurring [and] dissenting in part [in *Grand Rapids* and] dissenting [in *Aguilar*].

I agree with the Court that, [under] *Lemon,* the Grand Rapids Community Education Program violates the Establishment Clause. As to the Shared Time Program, I dissent for the reasons stated [hereafter in my dissent in *Aguilar*]. The Court today fails to demonstrate how that interaction occasioned by the program at issue presents any threat to the values underlying the Establishment Clause.

I cannot join in striking down a program that, in the words of the Court of Appeals, "has done so much good and little, if any, detectable harm." The notion that denying these ["desperately needed remedial teaching] services to students in religious schools is a neutral act to protect us from an Established Church has no support in logic, experience, or history. Rather than showing the neutrality the Court boasts of, it exhibits nothing less than hostility toward religion and the children who attend church-sponsored schools.

JUSTICE O'CONNOR, concurring [and] dissenting in part [in *Grand Rapids* and], with whom JUSTICE REHNQUIST joins as to Parts II and III, dissenting [in *Aguilar*].

For the reasons stated [in respect to New York's program, below,] I dissent from the Court's holding that the Grand Rapids Shared Time Program impermissibly advances religion. [But] Community Education courses in the parochial schools are overwhelmingly taught by instructors who are current full-time employees of the parochial school. [In] addition, the supervisors of the Community Education program in the parochial schools are by and large the principals of the very schools where the classes are offered. When full-time parochial school teachers receive public funds to teach secular courses to their parochial school students under parochial school supervision, I agree that the program has the perceived and actual effect of advancing the religious aims of the church-related schools. * * *

I. [By contrast, in New York], in 19 years there has never been a single incident in which a Title I instructor "subtly or overtly" attempted to "indoctrinate the students in particular religious tenets at public expense."

Common sense suggests a plausible explanation for this unblemished record. New York City's public Title I instructors are professional educators who can and do follow instructions not to inculcate religion in their classes. They are unlikely to be influenced by the sectarian nature of the parochial schools where they teach, not only because they are carefully supervised by public officials, but also because the vast majority of them visit several different schools each week and are not of the same religion as their parochial students. In light of the ample record, an objective observer of the implementation of the Title I program in New York would hardly view it as endorsing the tenets of the participating parochial schools. * * *

The only type of impermissible effect that arguably could carry over from the *Grand Rapids* decision to this litigation, then, is the effect of subsidizing "the religious functions of the parochial schools by taking over a substantial portion of their responsibility for teaching secular subjects." That effect is tenuous, however, in light of the statutory directive that Title I funds may be used only to provide services that otherwise would not be available to the participating students. * * *

Even if we were to assume that Title I remedial classes in New York may have duplicated to some extent instruction parochial schools would have offered in the absence of Title I, the Court's delineation of this third type of effect proscribed by the Establishment Clause would be seriously flawed. Our Establishment Clause decisions have not barred remedial assistance to parochial school children, but rather remedial assistance *on the premises of the parochial school.* Under *Wolman,* the New York City classes prohibited by the Court today would have survived Establishment Clause scrutiny if they had been offered in a neutral setting off the property of the private school. Yet it is difficult to understand why a remedial reading class offered on parochial school premises is any more likely to supplant the secular course offerings of the parochial school than the same class offered in a portable classroom next door to the school. * * *

II. Recognizing the weakness of any claim of an improper purpose or effect, the Court today relies entirely on the entanglement prong of *Lemon* to invalidate the New York City Title I program [which] I acknowledge, finds support in some of this Court's precedents. * * *

I would accord these decisions the appropriate deference commanded by the doctrine of stare decisis if I could discern logical support for their analysis. But experience has demonstrated that the analysis [is] flawed. [It] is not intuitively obvious that a dedicated public school teacher will tend to disobey instructions and commence proselytizing students at public expense merely because the classroom is within a parochial school. [Given] that not a single incident of religious indoctrination has been identified as occurring in the thousands of classes offered in Grand Rapids and New York over the past two decades, it is time to acknowledge that the risk [is] greatly exaggerated.

Just as the risk that public schoolteachers in parochial classrooms will inculcate religion has been exaggerated, so has the degree of supervision required to manage that risk. In [New York, public] officials have prepared careful instructions warning public schoolteachers of their exclusively secular mission, and have required Title I teachers to study and observe them. Under the rules, Title I teachers are not accountable to parochial or private school officials; they have sole responsibility for selecting the students who participate in their class, must administer their own tests for determining eligibility, cannot engage in team teaching or cooperative activities with parochial school teachers, must make sure that all materials and equipment they use are not otherwise used by the parochial school, and must not participate in religious activities in the schools or introduce any religious matter into their teaching. To ensure compliance with the rules, a field supervisor and a program coordinator, who are full-time public school employees, make unannounced visits to each teacher's classroom at least once a month. [This] does not differ significantly from the supervision any public schoolteacher receives, regardless of the location of the classroom. Justice Powell suggests that the required supervision is extensive because the State must be *certain* that public schoolteachers do not inculcate religion. That reasoning would require us to close our public schools, for there is always some chance that a public schoolteacher will bring religion into the classroom, regardless of its location. Even if I remained confident of the usefulness of entanglement as an Establishment Clause test, I would conclude that New York's efforts [have] been adequate and have not caused excessive institutional entanglement of church and state.

The Court's reliance on the potential for political divisiveness as evidence of undue entanglement is also unpersuasive. There is little record support for the proposition that New York's admirable Title I program has ignited any controversy other than this litigation. [M]any of the inconsistencies in our Establishment Clause decisions can be ascribed to our insistence that parochial aid programs with a valid purpose and effect may still be invalid by virtue of undue entanglement. For example, we permit a State to pay for bus transportation to a parochial school, *Everson,* but preclude States from providing buses for parochial school field trips, on the theory such trips involve excessive state supervision of the parochial officials who lead them. *Wolman.* To a great extent, the anomalous results in our Establishment Clause cases are "attributable to [the] 'entanglement' prong." Choper, *The Religion Clauses of the First Amendment: Reconciling the Conflict,* 41 U.Pitt.L.Rev. 673, 681 (1980).

[S]tate efforts to ensure that public resources are used only for nonsectarian ends should not in themselves serve to invalidate an otherwise valid statute. The State requires sectarian organizations to cooperate on a whole range of matters without thereby advancing religion or giving the impression that the government endorses religion. *Wallace v. Jaffree* (dissenting opinion of Rehnquist, J.) (noting that State educational agencies impose myriad curriculum, attendance, certificance, fire, and safety regulations on sectarian schools). If a statute lacks a purpose or effect of advancing or endorsing religion, I would not invalidate it merely because it requires some ongoing cooperation between church and state or some state supervision to ensure that state funds do not advance religion.

III. Today's ruling does not spell the end of the Title I program of remedial education for disadvantaged children. [The] only disadvantaged children who lose under the Court's holding are those in cities where it is not economically and logistically feasible to provide public facilities for remedial education adjacent to the parochial school. But [this] includes more than 20,000 New York City schoolchildren and uncounted others elsewhere in the country.

For these children, the Court's decision is tragic. The Court deprives them of a program that offers a meaningful chance at success in life, and it does so on the untenable theory that public schoolteachers (most of whom are of different faiths than their students) are likely to start teaching religion merely because they have walked across the threshold of a parochial school. * * * [a]

---

a. The opinions of White, J., dissenting in *Grand Rapids* and *Aguilar* on the basis of his views in *Lemon,* and of Rehnquist, J., dissenting on the basis of his dissent in *Wallace v. Jaffree,* Part I supra, are omitted.

Notes and Questions

1. *Primary effect.* If "religion pervades" parochial schools, which "operate on one budget" and "money not spent for one purpose becomes available for other purposes," does bus transportation or secular textbooks for parochial school students "have a primary effect that advances religion"? If so, would this forbid stationing traffic police near parochial schools? Having the fire department put out fires in them? Furnishing sidewalks in front of them? If the public did not provide parochial schools with sidewalks and police and fire protection, would the schools have to include these items in their budgets? If so, does the public's supplying them "release" funds? May a public library lend books to parochial school students in which readings have been assigned by their teacher? Suppose it were shown that these books were "in fact instrumental in the teaching of religion"?

Consider Tribe, *American Constitutional Law* 844 (1978): "[T]he provision of such secular services is not offensive because no one perceives police or fire protection as part of the educational enterprise. Such aid goes to institutions not as schools but as parts of the general public. Similarly, aid for secular programs in all colleges, including those with church affiliation, is generally perceived as assistance to non-religious activities. But the moment aid is sent to a parochial school as such, it is widely seen as aid to religion. The number of dollars released for religious purposes may be identical; the symbolism, and hence the constitutional result, is not."

2. *Broad spectrum of beneficiary groups.* (a) After *Mueller*, would an "education voucher" plan pass muster if the vouchers were given to *all* parents for use in *any* school? Consider Sugarman, *Family Choice: The Next Step in the Quest for Equal Educational Opportunity?* 38 Law & Contemp.Probs. 513, 527–28 (1974): "Perhaps we are left [with] a sliding scale which depends upon both the nature and specificity of the program itself and the identity of the beneficiaries. Hence, if the government builds structures for voluntary membership associations, it may not build halls of worship for church groups simply because it builds most of its buildings for non-church groups. This is so because the item which the government provides itself is religious. On the other hand, the state would be able to build a hospital for a church group as part of a general program of building hospitals, even though this means that the church could now afford to build a chapel, and even though undeniably religious activities occur in the hospital along with health care. Since hospitals do in the main serve secular functions, and since the program in fact includes a substantial number of beneficiaries which are not religion-associated, further judicial scrutiny into whether the state is in fact getting full secular value for money may not be needed to protect the concerns underlying the establishment clause. * * * Viewing the voucher plan scenario under this approach to the 'primary effect' test, the argument would be that while the plan does assist religious schools, since the beneficiaries are only in part religious school users, and since schooling is in the main secular, the assistance to religious schools [is] only incidental." See also Nowak, *The Supreme Court, The Religion Clauses and the Nationalization of Education,* 70 Nw.U.L.Rev. 883 (1976).

Compare Choper, fn. a in *Mueller,* at 53–55: "[*Mueller*] opens up a whole new ball game for aid to parochial schools [which] has now become just a matter of form. For example, what New York should have done in *Nyquist* [is] take the statute that had been struck down and amend it to also give the tax credit to parents who send their children to public schools. It would cost New York virtually nothing because there will be virtually no deductions by such parents. [However, in] *Mueller,* the Court said there's a difference between giving tax deductions and giving actual grants. [T]he real practical difference is [if] you can only rely on a tax deduction for the tuition that you pay to a parochial school, the only way you can get the benefit of it is if you have sufficient income to be subject to a tax liability. But if you're a low income person, you are not going to be able to get the benefit of this unless the state can give you an outright grant. [I]f the Court is serious about a tax deduction being different from a grant, then the vouchers may still be invalid."

In light of the position of each justice in *Grand Rapids* and *Aguilar,* would a voucher plan be constitutional?

(b) *Political divisiveness.* To what extent does a "broad spectrum" of beneficiary groups affect this criterion? Consider Note, *The Constitutionality of Tax Relief for Parents of Children Attending Public and Nonpublic Schools,* 67 Minn.L.Rev. 793, 820–21 (1983): "Legislation that primarily aids sectarian education disrupts political equality and promotes rivalry among religious sects by favoring those groups that emphasize private primary and secondary education. [In] contrast, aid which broadly benefits secular as well as sectarian groups is less likely to generate interfaith rivalries or imbalances of power. Even if only some sects receive aid directly, members of other faiths will probably benefit as members of the broader legislative class. Because particular religious groups will not be perceived as the primary beneficiaries of state aid, competition among sects for government funds will also be reduced." For further consideration of "political divisiveness," see *Lynch v. Donnelly,* Part IV infra.

3. *Delegation of government power.* LARKIN v. GRENDEL'S DEN, INC., 454 U.S. 116, 103 S.Ct. 505, 74 L.Ed.2d 297 (1982), per BURGER, C.J., held that a Massachusetts law (§ 16C), giving churches and schools the power "to veto applications for liquor licenses within a five hundred foot radius of the church or school, violates the Establishment Clause": "[T]here can be little doubt about the power of a state to regulate the environment in the vicinity of schools, churches, hospitals and the like by exercise of reasonable zoning laws. [But] § 16C is not simply a legislative exercise of zoning power [because it] delegates * * * discretionary governmental powers [to] religious bodies.[b]

"[The] valid secular objectives [of protecting] spiritual, cultural, and educational centers from the 'hurly-burly' associated with liquor outlets [can] be readily accomplished by other means—either through an absolute legislative ban on liquor outlets within reasonable prescribed distances from churches, schools, hospitals and like institutions, or by ensuring a hearing for the views of affected institutions at licensing proceedings * * *. [But the] churches' power under the statute is standardless [and] may therefore be used by churches [for] explicitly religious goals, for example, favoring liquor licenses for members of that congregation or adherents of that faith. [In] addition, the mere appearance of a joint exercise of legislative authority by Church and State provides a significant symbolic benefit to religion in the minds of some by reason of the power conferred. It does not strain our prior holdings to say that the statute can be seen as having a 'primary' and 'principal' effect of advancing religion. [Finally, § 16C] enmeshes churches in the processes of government and creates the danger of 'political fragmentation and divisiveness along religious lines.'"

b. Does the "delegation" to church-related schools of the authority to satisfy state re- quirements for elementary and secondary education violate the establishment clause?

REHNQUIST, J., dissented: A "flat ban [on] the grant of an alcoholic beverages license to any establishment located within 500 feet of a church or a [school], which the majority concedes is valid, is more protective of churches and more restrictive of liquor sales than the present § 16C. * * * Nothing in the Court's opinion persuades me why the more rigid prohibition would be constitutional, but the more flexible not. [It] does not sponsor or subsidize any religious group or activity. It does not encourage, much less compel, anyone to participate in religious activities or to support religious institutions. To say that it 'advances' religion is to strain at the meaning of the word. [If] a church were to seek to advance the interests of its members [by favoring them for licenses], there would be an occasion to determine whether it had violated any right of an unsuccessful applicant for a liquor license. But our ability to discern a risk of such abuse does not render § 16C violative of the Establishment Clause."

4. *"Excessive entanglement."* (a) Does this forbid application of the National Labor Relations Act's collective bargaining requirements to lay teachers employed by parochial schools? See *NLRB v. Catholic Bishop,* 440 U.S. 490, 99 S.Ct. 1313, 59 L.Ed.2d 533 (1979) (constitutional issue avoided by statutory construction).

(b) Even if classroom surveillance in church-related colleges is not needed to assure a primary secular effect, does the *Tilton* focus on each college's profile itself fail the "entanglement" test? Consider Kauper, *Public Aid for Parochial Schools and Church Colleges: The Lemon, Di Censo and Tilton Cases,* 13 Ariz.L. Rev. 567, 593 (1971): "The question of how sectarian a college may become and still fall within the *Tilton* rationale will be a matter of ad hoc adjudication with respect to individual colleges, and ultimately [the government] faces the unenviable task of measuring a college's sectarianism. [I]t is perhaps ironic that to avoid entanglements the Court has proposed criteria which will require a federal administrative agency to become embroiled and entangled in the issue of sectarianism." Does this type of "entanglement" also invalidate *Zorach* -type programs which authorize released time only for "religious instruction or devotional exercises"? For further consideration, see note 2, Sec. 2, II infra.

5. *Burden of proof.* Of what significance is the question of who—state or recipient—has the burden of proof in respect to each of the establishment clause criteria articulated in the decisions? In fact, to whom was the burden of proof assigned? Is the constitutionality of the programs invalidated still open on a showing that religion no more "permeates the secular education" in primary and secondary parochial schools than it does in church-related colleges?

6. *"Shared time."* Would a state "dual enrollment" plan, allowing parochial school students to take selected courses in the public schools, pass muster? Consider 85 Harv.L.Rev. 178 (1971): "[The] plan would have no impermissible effect, for public school teachers in public school buildings are unlikely to advance religion. However, the legislative purpose behind such a plan would be suspect: the obvious motive for releasing students for part of the day is to preserve the ability of their parents to give them religion-tinged instruction. In addition, such a plan might produce considerable conflict between public and parochial school authorities. If parochial school pupils were educated together with full-time public school pupils, accommodation of the scheduling needs of both systems could be quite difficult. Moreover, parochial school authorities might try to influence the content of the public school [courses]. Finally, since parochial schools would be the only beneficiaries of such legislation any modification of it would precipitate political controversy along religious lines." But

see Haskell, *The Prospects for Public Aid to Parochial Schools,* 56 Minn.L.Rev. 159 (1971).

7. *Other approaches.* Many commentators have proposed various "tests" to measure the validity of public aid to church-related schools. In evaluating those that follow, what results would they produce in the decided cases?

(a) Consider Gordon, *The Unconstitutionality of Public Aid to Parochial Schools,* in The Wall Between Church and State 73, 92 (Oaks ed. 1963): "The [test] is whether it is the church (or church institution) or the state that performs or controls the performance of the services paid for by the state. [It] is reasonable to assume that services performed or controlled by a religious institution could and would be used to further the religious objectives of that institution, whereas services performed or controlled by a public body would be secular in purpose and form." What result in *Everson* if the buses were rented by the parochial school? What about lunches preceded by prayers in the parochial school cafeteria?

(b) Consider Choper, fn. a in *Lemon,* at 265–66: "[G]overnmental financial aid may be extended directly or indirectly to support parochial schools [so] long as such aid does not exceed the value of the secular educational service rendered by the school." [c] Would such aid have "a secular legislative purpose and a primary effect that neither advances nor inhibits religion"? Compare Hammett, *The Homogenized Wall,* 53 A.B.A.J. 929, 932–33 (1967): "[T]he enactment must contain a state secular purpose paramount over any religious purpose which the church attaches to the conduct regulated or promoted by the state. Labeling the religious purpose 'incidental' could be misleading; the purpose, though incidentally religious from the secular state's viewpoint, may have overwhelming religious significance from the church's viewpoint. [If] the net effect of the financial aid is to increase proportionally the influence of both the church and the state, so that their influence relative to each other remains at the same original ratio, the 'primary' effect on religion has been neutral." [d] Contrast Sugarman, *New Perspectives on "Aid" to Private School Users,* in Nonpublic School Aid 64, 66 (West ed. 1976): "Even if the [effect] principle were limited to cases in which there was (or the legislature knew there would be) a *large* beneficial impact on religion, it would intolerably inhibit secular government action. For example, perhaps building roads and running public transportation on Sunday may be shown to have large beneficial impacts on religion. [For] me the concerns underlying the Establishment clause could be satisfied with an affirmative answer to this hypothetical question: Would the legislature have acted as it did were there no interdependency with religion involved? If so, then I think it would be fair to say that there is no subsidy of religion, that the religious benefits are constitutionally permitted side effects."

(c) Consider Dep't of HEW, *Memorandum on the Impact of the First Amendment to the Constitution Upon Federal Aid to Education,* 50 Geo.L.J. 351, 371 (1961): "*What alternative means are available to accomplish the legislative objective without resulting in the religious benefits ordinarily proscribed?* [Within] this category, where the constitutional significance of incidental religious assistance is discounted in part by necessity, one could include many of the

c. See also West, *An Economic Analysis of the Law and Politics of Nonpublic School "Aid",* in Nonpublic School Aid 1 (West ed. 1976).

d. See also Valente, *Aid to Church Related Education—New Directions Without Dogma,*

55 Va.L.Rev. 579 (1969); Legal Dep't, NCWC, *The Constitutionality of the Inclusion of Church-Related Schools in Federal Aid to Education,* 50 Geo.L.J. 397 (1961).

traditional 'benefits' received by church organizations; for example, police protection, fire protection, and sewage disposal * * *. The point is that protection of health and safety within the community cannot reasonably be accomplished without including religious institutions within the class of beneficiaries." e

IV. OFFICIAL ACKNOWLEDGMENT OF RELIGION

MARSH v. CHAMBERS, 463 U.S. 783, 103 S.Ct. 3330, 77 L.Ed.2d 1019 (1983), per BURGER, C.J., upheld the practice of opening each day of the Nebraska legislature with a prayer by a chaplain (since 1965, a Presbyterian minister) paid by the state ($319.75 per month when the legislature is in session) as being "deeply embedded in the history and tradition of this country." The Court pointed, inter alia, to the practice in the colonies (including Virginia after adopting its Declaration of Rights which has been "considered the precursor of both the Free Exercise and Establishment Clauses"), to the opening invocations in federal courts (including the Supreme Court), and to the Continental Congress and First Congress: "Clearly the men who wrote the First Amendment Religion Clause did not view paid legislative chaplains and opening prayers as a violation of that Amendment, for the practice of opening sessions with prayer has continued without interruption ever since that early session of Congress. It has also been followed consistently in most of the states." Although "standing alone, historical patterns cannot justify contemporary violations of constitutional guarantees, [i]n this context, historical evidence sheds light not only on what the draftsmen intended the Establishment Clause to mean, but also on how they thought that Clause applied to the practice authorized by the First Congress— their actions reveal their intent." a

The Court noted that "here, the individual claiming injury by the practice is an adult, presumably not readily susceptible to 'religious indoctrination,' see Tilton, or peer pressure, compare Schempp (Brennan, J., concurring). In light of the unambiguous and unbroken history of more than 200 years, there can be no doubt that the practice of opening legislative sessions with prayer has become part of the fabric of our society. To invoke Divine guidance on a public body entrusted with making the laws [is] simply a tolerable acknowledgment of beliefs widely held among the people of this country. As Justice Douglas observed, 'we are a religious people whose institutions presuppose a Supreme Being.' Zorach."

BRENNAN, J., joined by Marshall, J.—noting that "the Court makes no pretense of subjecting Nebraska's practice of legislative prayer to any of the formal 'tests' that have traditionally structured our inquiry under the Establishment Clause"—dissented: "I have no doubt that, if any group of law students were asked to apply the principles of Lemon to the question of legislative prayer, they would nearly unanimously find the practice to be unconstitutional.

"[That] the 'purpose' of legislative prayer is preeminently religious rather than secular seems to me to be self-evident. [The] 'primary effect' of legislative prayer is also clearly religious. [I]nvocations in Nebraska's legislative halls explicitly link religious belief and observance to the power and prestige of the State. [Finally,] there can be no doubt that the practice of legislative prayer

e. Problems under the free exercise clause raised by the exclusion of parochial schools from public aid programs are considered in note 4 after *Sherbert v. Verner*, Sec. 2, I infra.

a. Of what relevance is it that, subsequently, "Madison acknowledged that he had been quite mistaken in approving—as a member of the House, in 1789—bills for the payment of congressional chaplains"? Van Alstyne, *Trends in the Supreme Court: Mr. Jefferson's Crumbling Wall*, 1984 Duke L.J. 770, 776.

leads to excessive 'entanglement' between the State and religion. [T]he process of choosing a 'suitable' chaplain, whether on a permanent or rotating basis, and insuring that the chaplain limits himself or herself to 'suitable' prayers, involves precisely the sort of supervision that agencies of government should if at all possible avoid." As for "divisive political potential," the "controversy between Senator Chambers and his colleagues [has] split the Nebraska Legislature precisely on issues of religion and religious conformity. [And] in general, the history of legislative prayer has been far more eventful—and divisive—than a hasty reading of the Court's opinion might indicate. ＊ ＊ ＊

"Legislative prayer clearly violates [the] fundamental message of *Engel* and *Schempp*. It intrudes on the right to conscience by forcing some legislators either to participate in a 'prayer opportunity,' with which they are in basic disagreement, or to make their disagreement a matter of public comment by declining to participate. It forces all residents of the State to support a religious exercise that may be contrary to their own beliefs. It requires the State to commit itself on fundamental theological issues. It has the potential for degrading religion by allowing a religious call to worship to be intermeshed with a secular call to order. [This is not] a case in which a State is accommodating individual religious interests. We are not faced here with the right of the legislature to allow its members to offer prayers during the course of general legislative debate. We are certainly not faced with the right of legislators to form voluntary groups for prayer or worship. We are not even faced with the right of the state to employ members of the clergy to minister to the private religious needs of individual legislators. Rather, we are faced here with the regularized practice of conducting official prayers, on behalf of the entire legislature, as part of the order of business constituting the formal opening of every single session of the legislative term. If this is Free Exercise, the Establishment Clause has no meaning whatsoever.

"[S]pecific historical practice should not in this case override [the] clear constitutional imperative.[30] [M]ost importantly, the argument tendered by the Court is misguided because the Constitution is not a static document whose meaning on every detail is fixed for all time by the life experience of the Framers."

STEVENS, J., also filed a brief dissent: "[D]esignation of a member of one religious faith to serve as the sole official chaplain of a state legislature for a period of 16 years constitutes the preference of one faith over another in violation of the Establishment Clause."

LYNCH v. DONNELLY

465 U.S. 668, 104 S.Ct. 1355, 79 L.Ed.2d 604 (1984).

THE CHIEF JUSTICE delivered the opinion of the Court. ＊ ＊ ＊

Each year, [the] City of Pawtucket, Rhode Island, erects a Christmas display as part of its observance of the Christmas holiday season. The display [includes] a Santa Claus house, reindeer pulling Santa's sleigh, candy-striped poles, a Christmas tree, carolers, cutout figures representing such characters as a clown,

---

30. Indeed, the sort of historical argument made by the Court should be advanced with some hesitation in light of certain other skeletons in the congressional closet. See, e.g., An Act for the Punishment of certain Crimes against the United States (1790) (enacted by the First Congress and requiring that persons convicted of certain theft offenses "be publicly whipped, not exceeding thirty-nine stripes"); Act of July 23, 1866 (reaffirming the racial segregation of the public schools in the District of Columbia; enacted exactly one week after Congress proposed Fourteenth Amendment to the States).

an elephant, and a teddy bear, hundreds of colored lights, a large banner that reads "SEASONS GREETINGS," and the crèche at issue here [which] consists of the traditional figures, including the Infant Jesus, Mary and Joseph, angels, shepherds, kings, and animals, all ranging in height from 5" to 5'. In 1973, when the present crèche was acquired, it cost the City $1365; it now is valued at $200. The erection and dismantling of the crèche costs the City about $20 per year; nominal expenses are incurred in lighting the crèche. No money has been expended on its maintenance for the past 10 years. [The] District Court held that the City's inclusion of the crèche in the display violates the Establishment Clause [and] the Court of Appeals for the First Circuit affirmed. * * *

There is an unbroken history of official acknowledgment by all three branches of government of the role of religion in American life from at least 1789. [L]ong before Independence, a day of Thanksgiving was celebrated at a religious holiday to give thanks for the bounties of Nature as gifts from God. President Washington and his successors proclaimed Thanksgiving, with all its religious overtones, a day of national celebration and Congress made it a National Holiday more than a century ago. That holiday has not lost its theme of expressing thanks for Divine aid any more than has Christmas lost its religious significance.

Executive Orders and other official announcements of Presidents and of the Congress have proclaimed both Christmas and Thanksgiving National Holidays in religious terms [and] it has long been the practice that federal employees are released from duties on these National Holidays, while being paid from the same public revenues that provide the compensation of the Chaplains of the Senate and the House and the military services. Thus, it is clear that Government has long recognized—indeed it has subsidized—holidays with religious significance.

Other examples of reference to our religious heritage are found in the statutorily prescribed national motto "In God We Trust," [and] in the language "One nation under God," as part of the Pledge of Allegiance * * *.

Art galleries supported by public revenues display religious paintings of the 15th and 16th centuries, predominantly inspired by one religious faith. The National Gallery in Washington, maintained with Government support, for example, has long exhibited masterpieces with religious messages, notably the Last Supper, and paintings depicting the Birth of Christ, the Crucifixion, and the Resurrection, among many others with explicit Christian themes and messages. The very chamber in which oral arguments on this case were heard is decorated with a notable and permanent—not seasonal—symbol of religion: Moses with Ten Commandments. Congress has long provided chapels in the Capitol for religious worship and meditation [and] has directed the President to proclaim a National Day of Prayer each [year]. Presidential Proclamations and messages have also issued to commemorate Jewish Heritage Week and the Jewish High Holy Days. One cannot look at even this brief resume without finding that our history is pervaded by expressions of religious beliefs * * *.

This history may help explain why the Court consistently has declined to take a rigid, absolutist view of the Establishment Clause. [In] the line-drawing process we have often found it useful to inquire whether the challenged law or conduct has a secular purpose, whether its principal or primary effect is to advance or inhibit religion, and whether it creates an excessive entanglement of government with religion. But, we have repeatedly emphasized our unwillingness to be confined to any single test or criterion in this sensitive area. * * *
We did not, for example, consider that analysis relevant in *Marsh*. * * *

In this case, the focus of our inquiry must be on the crèche in the context of the Christmas season. [F]or example, [*Schempp*] specifically noted that nothing in the Court's holding was intended to "indicat[e] that such study of the Bible or of religion, when presented objectively as part of a secular program of education, may not be effected consistently with the First Amendment." Focus exclusively on the religious component of any activity would inevitably lead to its invalidation under the Establishment Clause.

The Court has invalidated legislation or governmental action on the ground that a secular purpose was lacking, but only when it has concluded there was no question that the statute or activity was motivated wholly by religious considerations. See, e.g., *Stone; Epperson; Schempp; Engel.* Even where the benefits to religion were substantial, as in *Everson; Allen; Walz; Tilton,* we saw a secular purpose and no conflict with the Establishment Clause.

[When] viewed in the proper context of the Christmas Holiday season, it is apparent that, on this record, there is insufficient evidence to establish that the inclusion of the crèche is a purposeful or surreptitious effort to express some kind of subtle governmental advocacy of a particular religious message. In a pluralistic society a variety of motives and purposes are implicated. The City, like the Congresses and Presidents, however, has principally taken note of a significant historical religious event long celebrated in the Western World. The crèche in the display depicts the historical origins of this traditional event long recognized as a National Holiday. [These] are legitimate secular purposes.[6] The District Court's inference, drawn from the religious nature of the crèche, that the City has no secular purpose was, on this record, clearly erroneous.[7]

The District Court found that the primary effect of including the crèche is to confer a substantial and impermissible benefit on religion in general and on the Christian faith in particular. Comparisons of the relative benefits to religion of different forms of governmental support are elusive and difficult to make. But to conclude that the primary effect of including the crèche is to advance religion in violation of the Establishment Clause would require that we view it as more beneficial to and more an endorsement of religion, for example, than [that upheld in *Allen; Everson; Tilton; Roemer; Walz; McGowan; Zorach;* and *Marsh*]. What was said about the legislative prayers in *Marsh,* and implied about the Sunday Closing Laws in *McGowan* is true of the City's inclusion of the crèche: its "reason or effect merely happens to coincide or harmonize with the tenets of [some] religions." [W]hatever benefit to one faith or religion or to all religions, is indirect, remote and incidental; display of the crèche is no more an advancement or endorsement of religion that the Congressional and Executive recognition of the origins of the Holiday itself as "Christ's Mass," or the exhibition of literally hundreds of religious paintings in governmentally supported museums. * * *

Entanglement is a question of kind and degree. In this case, however, there is no reason to disturb the District Court's finding on the absence of administrative entanglement. There is no evidence of contact with church authorities

6. The City contends that the purposes of the display are "exclusively secular." We hold only that Pawtucket has a secular purpose for its display, which is all that *Lemon* requires. Were the test that the government must have "exclusively secular" objectives, much of the conduct and legislation this Court has approved in the past would have been invalidated.

7. Justice Brennan argues that the City's objectives could have been achieved without including the crèche in the display. True or not, that is irrelevant. The question is whether the display of the crèche violates the Establishment Clause.

concerning the content or design of the exhibit prior to or since Pawtucket's purchase of the crèche. No expenditures for maintenance of the crèche have been necessary; and since the City owns the crèche, now valued at $200, the tangible material it contributes is de minimis. In many respects the display requires far less ongoing, day-to-day interaction between church and state than religious paintings in public galleries. * * *

The Court of Appeals correctly observed that this Court has not held that political divisiveness alone can serve to invalidate otherwise permissible conduct. And we decline to so hold today. This case does not involve a direct subsidy to church-sponsored schools or colleges, or other religious institutions, and hence no inquiry into potential political divisiveness is even called for, *Mueller,* n. 11. In any event, apart from this litigation there is no evidence of political friction or divisiveness over the crèche in the 40-year history of Pawtucket's Christmas celebration. [A] litigant cannot, by the very act of commencing a lawsuit, however, create the appearance of divisiveness and then exploit it as evidence of entanglement. * * *

Of course the crèche is identified with one religious faith but no more so than the examples we have set out from prior cases in which we found no conflict with the Establishment Clause. See, e.g., *McGowan; Marsh.* It would be ironic, however, if the inclusion of a single symbol of a particular historic religious event, as part of a celebration acknowledged in the Western World for 20 centuries, and in this country by the people, by the Executive Branch, by the Congress, and the courts for two centuries, would so "taint" the City's exhibit as to render it violative of the Establishment Clause. To forbid the use of this one passive symbol—the crèche—at the very time people are taking note of the season with Christmas hymns and carols in public schools and other public places, and while the Congress and Legislatures open sessions with prayers by paid chaplains would be a stilted over-reaction contrary to our history and to our holdings. If the presence of the crèche in this display violates the Establishment Clause, a host of other forms of taking official note of Christmas, and of our religious heritage, are equally offensive to the Constitution.

The Court has acknowledged that the "fears and political problems" that gave rise to the Religion Clauses in the 18th century are of far less concern today. We are unable to perceive the Archbishop of Canterbury, the Vicar of Rome, or other powerful religious leaders behind every public acknowledgment of the religious heritage long officially recognized by the three constitutional branches of government. Any notion that these symbols pose a real danger of establishment of a state church is far-fetched indeed.

[R]eversed.

JUSTICE O'CONNOR, concurring.

I concur in the opinion of the Court. I write separately to suggest a clarification of our Establishment Clause doctrine. * * *

The Establishment Clause prohibits government from making adherence to a religion relevant in any way to a person's standing in the political community. Government can run afoul of that prohibition in two principal ways. One is excessive entanglement with religious institutions, which may interfere with the independence of the institutions, give the institutions access to government or governmental powers not fully shared by nonadherents of the religion, and foster the creation of political constituencies defined along religious lines. E.g., *Grendel's Den.* The second and more direct infringement is government endorsement or disapproval of religion. Endorsement sends a message to nonadherents that they are outsiders, not full members of the political community, and an accompanying message to adherents that they are insiders, favored members of the political community. Disapproval sends the opposite message. See generally *Schempp.*

In this case, as even the District Court found, there is no institutional entanglement. [In] my view, political divisiveness along religious lines should not be an independent test of constitutionality. * * *

The central issue in this case is whether Pawtucket has endorsed Christianity by its display of the crèche. [The] purpose prong of the *Lemon* test asks whether government's actual purpose is to endorse or disapprove of religion. The effect prong asks whether, irrespective of government's actual purpose, the practice under review in fact conveys a message of endorsement or disapproval. An affirmative answer to either question should render the challenged practice invalid.

* * * I would find that Pawtucket did not intend to convey any message of endorsement of Christianity or disapproval of nonChristian religions. The evident purpose of including the crèche in the larger display [was] celebration of the public holiday through its traditional symbols. [This] is a legitimate secular purpose. * * *

Pawtucket's display of its crèche, I believe, does not communicate a message that the government intends to endorse the Christian beliefs represented by the crèche. [T]he overall holiday setting changes what viewers may fairly understand to be the purpose of the display—as a typical museum setting, though not neutralizing the religious content of a religious painting, negates any message of endorsement of that content. The display celebrates a public holiday [with] very strong secular components and traditions. Government celebration of the holiday, which is extremely common, generally is not understood to endorse the religious content of the holiday, just as government celebration of Thanksgiving is not so understood. The crèche is a traditional symbol of the holiday that is very commonly displayed along with purely secular symbols, as it was in Pawtucket.

These features combine to make the government's display of the crèche in this particular physical setting no more an endorsement of religion than such governmental "acknowledgments" of religion as legislative prayers of the type approved in *Marsh,* government declaration of Thanksgiving as a public holiday, printing of "In God We Trust" on coins, and opening court sessions with "God save the United States and this honorable court." Those government acknowledgments of religion serve, in the only ways reasonably possible in our culture, the legitimate secular purposes of solemnizing public occasions, expressing confidence in the future, and encouraging the recognition of what is worthy of appreciation in society. For that reason, and because of their history and ubiquity, those practices are not understood as conveying government approval of particular religious beliefs. * * *

JUSTICE BRENNAN, with whom JUSTICE MARSHALL, JUSTICE BLACKMUN and JUSTICE STEVENS join, dissenting.

[The] Court's decision implicitly leaves open questions concerning the constitutionality of the public display on public property of a crèche standing alone, or the public display of other distinctively religious symbols such as a cross. Despite the narrow contours of the Court's opinion, [n]othing in the history of such practices or the setting in which the City's crèche is presented obscures or diminishes the plain fact that Pawtucket's action amounts to an impermissible governmental endorsement of a particular faith.

[T]he City claims that its purposes were exclusively secular [—] to participate in the celebration of a national holiday and to attract people to the downtown area in order to promote pre-Christmas retail sales and to help engender the spirit of goodwill and neighborliness commonly associated with the Christmas season. [But] all of Pawtucket's "valid secular objectives can be readily accomplished by other means." Plainly, the City's interest in celebrating the holiday and in promoting both retail sales and goodwill are fully served by the elaborate display of Santa Claus, reindeer, and wishing wells that are already a part of Pawtucket's annual Christmas display. More importantly, the nativity scene, unlike every other element of the Hodgson Park display, reflects a sectarian exclusivity that the avowed purposes of celebrating the holiday season and promoting retail commerce simply do not encompass. [Plainly,] the City and its leaders understood that the inclusion of the crèche in its display would serve the wholly religious purpose of "keep[ing] 'Christ in Christmas.'" From this record, therefore, it is impossible to say with the kind of confidence that was possible in *McGowan* that a wholly secular goal predominates.

The "primary effect" [is] to place the government's imprimatur of approval on the particular religious beliefs exemplified by the crèche. Those who believe in the message of the nativity receive the unique and exclusive benefit of public recognition and approval of their views. [The] effect on minority religious groups, as well as on those who may reject all religion, is to convey the message that their views are not similarly worthy of public recognition nor entitled to public support. * * *

Finally, it is evident that [the] display does pose a significant threat of fostering "excessive entanglement." [A]fter today's decision, administrative entanglements may well develop. Jews and other non-Christian groups, prompted perhaps by the Mayor's remark that he will include a Menorah in future displays, can be expected to press government for inclusion of their symbols, and faced with such requests, government will have to become involved in accommodating the various demands. More importantly, although no political divisiveness was apparent in Pawtucket prior to the filing of respondents' lawsuit, [that] does not immediately suggest the absence of any division on the point [for] the quiescence of those opposed to the crèche may have reflected nothing more than their sense of futility in opposing the majority.[9]

[The] Court apparently believes that once it finds that the designation of Christmas as a public holiday is constitutionally acceptable, it is then free to conclude that virtually every form of governmental association with the celebration of the holiday is also constitutional. The vice of this dangerously superficial argument is that it overlooks the fact that the Christmas holiday in our national

9. The suggestion in *Mueller,* n. 11, relied upon by the Court today, that inquiry into potential political divisiveness is unnecessary absent direct subsidies to church-sponsored schools or colleges, derives from a distorted reading of our prior cases. Simply because the Court in *Lemon*—a case involving such subsidies—inquired into potential divisiveness while distinguishing *Everson* and *Allen*—cases not involving such subsidies—does not provide any authority for the proposition that the Court in *Lemon* meant to confine the divisive-ness inquiry only to cases factually identical to *Lemon* itself. Indeed, in *Walz,* the Court considered the question of divisiveness in the context of state tax exemptions to all religious institutions. I agree, however, with Justice O'Connor's helpful suggestion that while political divisiveness is "an evil addressed by the Establishment Clause," the ultimate inquiry must always focus on "the character of the government activity that might cause such divisiveness."

culture contains both secular and sectarian elements. To say that government may recognize the holiday's traditional, secular elements of giftgiving, public festivities and community spirit, does not mean that government may indiscriminately embrace the distinctively sectarian aspects of the holiday. Indeed, in its eagerness to approve the crèche, the Court has advanced a rationale so simplistic that it would appear to allow the Mayor of Pawtucket to participate in the celebration of a Christmas mass, since this would be just another unobjectionable way for the City to "celebrate the holiday." * * *

When government decides to recognize Christmas day as a public holiday, it does no more than accommodate the calendar of public activities to the plain fact that many Americans will expect on that day to spend time visiting with their families, attending religious services, and perhaps enjoying some respite from preholiday activities. The Free Exercise Clause, of course, does not necessarily compel the government to provide this accommodation, but neither is the Establishment Clause offended by such a step. Cf. *Zorach.* [If] public officials go further and participate in the *secular* celebration of Christmas—by, for example, decorating public places with such secular images as wreaths, garlands or Santa Claus figures—they move closer to the limits of their constitutional power but nevertheless remain within the boundaries set by the Establishment Clause. But when those officials participate in or appear to endorse the distinctively religious elements of this otherwise secular event, they encroach upon First Amendment freedoms. For it is at that point that the government brings to the forefront the theological content of the holiday, and places the prestige, power and financial support of a civil authority in the service of a particular faith.

[T]he crèche is far from a mere representation of a "particular historic religious event." It is, instead, best understood as a mystical re-creation of an event that lies at the heart of Christian faith. To suggest, as the Court does, that such a symbol is merely "traditional" and therefore no different from Santa's house or reindeer is not only offensive to those for whom the crèche has profound significance, but insulting to those who insist for religious or personal reasons that the story of Christ is in no sense a part of "history" nor an unavoidable element of our national "heritage."

[The] Court seems to assume that forbidding Pawtucket from displaying a crèche would be tantamount to forbidding a state college from including the Bible or Milton's Paradise Lost in a course on English literature. But in those cases the religiously-inspired materials are being considered solely as literature. The purpose is plainly not to single out the particular religious beliefs that may have inspired the authors, but to see in these writings the outlines of a larger imaginative universe shared with other forms of literary expression. The same may be said of a course devoted to the study of art; when the course turns to Gothic architecture, the emphasis is not on the religious beliefs which the cathedrals exalt, but rather upon the "aesthetic consequences of [such religious] thought."

In this case, by contrast, the crèche plays no comparable secular role. Unlike the poetry of Paradise Lost which students in a literature course will seek to appreciate primarily for aesthetic or historical reasons, the angels, shepherds, Magi and infant of Pawtucket's nativity scene can only be viewed as symbols of a particular set of religious beliefs. It would be another matter if the crèche were displayed in a museum setting, in the company of other religiously-inspired artifacts, as an example, among many, of the symbolic representation of religious myths. In that setting, we would have objective guarantees that the crèche could not suggest that a particular faith had been singled out for public favor and recognition. The effect of Pawtucket's crèche, however, is not confined by any of these limiting attributes. In the absence of any other religious symbols or of any neutral disclaimer, the inescapable effect of the crèche will be to remind the average observer of the religious roots of the celebration he is witnessing and to call to mind the scriptural message that the nativity symbolizes. The fact that Pawtucket has gone to the trouble of making such an elaborate public celebration and of including a crèche in that otherwise secular setting inevitably serves to reinforce the sense that the City means to express solidarity with the Christian message of the crèche and to dismiss other faiths as unworthy of similar attention and support. * * *

Intuition tells us that some official "acknowledgment" is inevitable in a religious society if government is not to adopt a stilted indifference to the religious life of the people. It is equally true, however, that if government is to remain scrupulously neutral in matters of religious conscience, as our Constitution requires, then it must avoid those overly broad acknowledgments of religious practices that may imply governmental favoritism toward one set of religious beliefs. * * *

[T]he Court has never comprehensively addressed the extent to which government may acknowledge religion by, for example, incorporating religious references into public ceremonies and proclamations, and I do not presume to offer a comprehensive approach. Nevertheless, it appears from our prior decisions that at least three principles [may] be identified. First, although the government may not be compelled to do so by the Free Exercise Clause, it may, consistently with the Establishment Clause, act to accommodate to some extent the opportunities of individuals to practice their religion. See [*Zorach.* This] would justify government's decision to declare December 25th a public holiday.

Second, our cases recognize that while a particular governmental practice may have derived from religious motivations and retain certain religious connotations, it is nonetheless permissible for the government to pursue the practice when it is continued today solely for secular reasons. [*McGowan.*] Thanksgiving Day, in my view, fits easily within this principle, for despite its religious antecedents, the current practice of celebrating Thanksgiving is unquestionably secular and patriotic. We all may gather with our families on that day to give thanks both for personal and national good fortune, but we are free, given the secular character of the holiday, to address that gratitude either to a divine beneficence or to such mundane sources as good luck or the country's abundant natural wealth.

Finally, we have noted that government cannot be completely prohibited from recognizing in its public actions the religious beliefs and practices of the American people as an aspect of our national history and culture. See *Engel,* n. 21. While I remain uncertain about these questions, I would suggest that such practices as the designation of "In God We Trust" as our national motto, or the references to God contained in the Pledge of Allegiance can best be understood [as] a form of "ceremonial deism," protected from Establishment Clause scrutiny chiefly because they have lost through rote repetition any significant religious content. Moreover, these references are uniquely suited to serve such wholly secular purposes as solemnizing public occasions, or inspiring commitment to meet some national challenge in a manner that simply could not be fully served in our culture if government were limited to purely non-religious phrases. The practices by which the government has long acknowledged religion are therefore probably necessary to serve certain secular functions, and that necessity, coupled with their long history, gives those practices an essentially secular meaning.

The crèche fits none of these categories. Inclusion of the crèche is not necessary to accommodate individual religious expression. [Nor] is the inclusion of the crèche necessary to serve wholly secular goals; it is clear that the City's secular purposes of celebrating the Christmas holiday and promoting retail commerce can be fully served without the crèche. And the crèche, because of its unique association with Christianity, is clearly more sectarian than those references to God that we accept in ceremonial phrases or in other contexts that assure neutrality. * * *

The American historical experience concerning the public celebration of Christmas, if carefully examined, provides no support for the Court's decision. [T]here is no evidence whatsoever that the Framers would have expressly approved a Federal celebration of the Christmas holiday including public displays of a nativity scene; accordingly, the Court's repeated invocation of the decision in *Marsh,* is not only baffling, it is utterly irrelevant. Nor is there any suggestion that publicly financed and supported displays of Christmas crèche are supported by a record of widespread, undeviating acceptance that extends throughout our history. Therefore, our prior decisions which relied upon concrete, specific historical evidence to support a particular practice simply have no bearing on the question presented in this case. Contrary to today's careless decision, those prior cases have all recognized that the "illumination" provided by history must always be focused on the particular practice at issue in a given case. Without that guiding principle and the intellectual discipline it imposes, the Court is at sea, free to select random elements of America's varied history solely to suit the views of five Members of this Court. * * *[a]

SECTION 2. FREE EXERCISE CLAUSE AND RELATED PROBLEMS

I. CONFLICT WITH STATE REGULATION

The most common problem respecting free exercise of religion arises when a government regulation, whose purpose is nonreligious, either makes illegal (or otherwise burdens) conduct that is dictated by some religious belief, or requires (or otherwise encourages) conduct that is forbidden by some religious belief. Thus, REYNOLDS v. UNITED STATES, 98 U.S. 145, 25 L.Ed. 244 (1879), the first major decision on the free exercise clause, upheld application of a federal law making polygamy illegal to a Mormon whose religious duty was to practice polygamy: "Congress was deprived of all legislative power over mere opinion, but was left free to reach actions which were in violation of social duties or subversive of good order." CANTWELL v. CONNECTICUT, 310 U.S. 296, 60 S.Ct. 900, 84 L.Ed. 1213 (1940), reemphasized this distinction between religious opinion or belief, on the one hand, and action taken because of religion, on the other, although the Court spoke somewhat more solicitously about the latter: "The [Constitution] forestalls compulsion by law of the acceptance of any creed or the practice of any form of worship. Freedom of conscience and freedom to adhere to such religious organization or form of worship as the individual may

a. The brief dissenting opinion of Blackmun, J., joined by Stevens, J., is omitted.

After *Lynch* and *Widmar v. Vincent,* may a city that permits use of its park for a wide variety of displays and activities—including religious services and singing Christmas carols— deny its use for a privately financed nativity scene during the Christmas season? See *McCreary v. Stone,* 739 F.2d 716 (2d Cir.1984) (denial invalid), affirmed by an equally divided Court, ___ U.S. ___, 105 S.Ct. 1859, 85 L.Ed.2d 63 (1985) (Powell, J., not participating).

choose cannot be restricted by law. [Free exercise] embraces two concepts,—freedom to believe and freedom to act. The first is absolute but, in the nature of things, the second cannot be. [The] freedom to act must have appropriate definition to preserve the enforcement of that protection [although] the power to regulate must be so exercised as not, in attaining a permissible end, unduly to infringe the protected freedom."

Even before *Cantwell*—which first held that the fourteenth amendment made the free exercise guarantee applicable to the states—several decisions invalidating state laws as unreasonably interfering with the "liberty" secured by the fourteenth amendment due process clause (see, e.g., *Pierce v. Society of Sisters,* Sec. 1 supra), carried significant overtones for religious freedom. By contrast, *Hamilton v. Regents,* 293 U.S. 245, 55 S.Ct. 197, 79 L.Ed. 343 (1934), held that a state statute—requiring all male students at the state university to take a course in military training—was not a deprivation of "liberty" without due process of members of the Methodist Episcopal Church whose conscientious beliefs forbade military training.

Beginning with *Cantwell,* a number of cases invalidated application of state laws to conduct undertaken pursuant to religious beliefs. Like *Cantwell,* these decisions, set forth in Ch. 8,[a] rested in whole or in part on the freedom of expression provisions of the first and fourteenth amendments. Similarly, WEST VIRGINIA STATE BD. OF EDUC. v. BARNETTE, 319 U.S. 624, 63 S.Ct. 1178, 87 L.Ed. 1628 (1943),[b] held that compelling a flag salute by public school children whose religious scruples forbade it violated the first amendment: "The test of legislation which collides with the Fourteenth Amendment, because it also collides with the principles of the First, is much more definite than the test when only the Fourteenth is involved. [The] right of a state to regulate, for example, a public utility may well include, so far as the due process test is concerned, power to impose all of the restrictions which a legislature may have a 'rational basis' for adopting. But freedoms of speech and of press, of assembly, and of worship may not be infringed on such slender grounds. They are susceptible of restriction only to prevent grave and immediate danger to interests which the state may lawfully protect. [If] there is any fixed star in our constitutional constellation, it is that no official, high or petty, can prescribe what shall be orthodox in politics, nationalism or other matters of opinion or force citizens to confess by word or act their faith therein."

Other decisions dealt exclusively with the free exercise clause. PRINCE v. MASSACHUSETTS, 321 U.S. 158, 64 S.Ct. 438, 88 L.Ed. 645 (1944), upheld a state law making it a crime for children to sell merchandise in public places as applied to a child who was distributing religious literature with her guardian, emphasizing the state's interest in "the healthy, well-rounded growth of young people" and "the crippling effects of child employment, more especially in public places, and the possible harms arising from other activities subject to all the diverse influences of the street."

BRAUNFELD v. BROWN, 366 U.S. 599, 81 S.Ct. 1144, 6 L.Ed.2d 563 (1961), upheld application of Pennsylvania's Sunday Closing Law (whose nonreligious

a. E.g., *Schneider v. Irvington,* p. 534 supra; *Lovell v. Griffin,* p. 472 supra; *Martin v. Struthers,* p. 579 supra; compare *Cox v. New Hampshire,* p. 536 supra; *Poulos v. New Hampshire,* p. 477 supra. See also *Marsh v. Alabama,* p. 1081 infra.

b. Overruling *Minersville School Dist. v. Gobitis,* 310 U.S. 586, 60 S.Ct. 1010, 84 L.Ed. 1375 (1940).

purpose was sustained in a companion case, *McGowan v. Maryland*, Sec. 1, II supra), to Orthodox Jews whose ability "to earn a livelihood" would be impaired by Sunday closing because their religion forbade work on Saturday. The plurality opinion was by WARREN, C.J., joined by Black, Clark and Whittaker, JJ.: "[L]egislative power over mere opinion is forbidden but it may reach people's actions when they are found to be in violation of important social duties or subversive of good order, even when the actions are demanded by one's religion. [*Barnette*] was careful to point out that 'The freedom asserted by these appellees does not bring them into collision with rights asserted by any other individual. It is such conflicts which most frequently require intervention of the State to determine where the rights of one end and those of another begin. [T]he compulsory flag salute and pledge requires *affirmation of a belief* and an *attitude of mind.*'

"[In *Reynolds* and *Prince*], the religious practices themselves conflicted with the public interest. In such cases, to make accommodation between the religious action and an exercise of state authority is a particularly delicate task because resolution in favor of the State results in the choice to the individual of either abandoning his religious principle or facing criminal prosecution.

"[But] the statute at bar does not make unlawful any religious practices of appellants; the Sunday law simply regulates a secular activity and, as applied to appellants, operates so as to make the practice of their religious beliefs more expensive. [R]ecognizing that the alternatives open to appellants and others similarly situated—retaining their present occupations and incurring economic disadvantage or engaging in some other commercial activity which does not call for either Saturday or Sunday labor—may well result in some financial sacrifice in order to observe their religious beliefs, still the option is wholly different than when the legislation attempts to make a religious practice itself unlawful.

"To strike down, without the most critical scrutiny, legislation which imposes only an indirect burden on the exercise of religion, i.e., legislation which does not make unlawful the religious practice itself, would radically restrict the operating latitude of the legislature. Statutes which tax income and limit the amount which may be deducted for religious contributions impose an indirect economic burden on the observance of the religion of the citizen whose religion requires him to donate a greater amount to his church; statutes which require the courts to be closed on Saturday and Sunday impose a similar indirect burden on the observance of the religion of the trial lawyer whose religion requires him to rest on a weekday. The list of legislation of this nature is nearly limitless.

*   *   *

"Of course, to hold unassailable all legislation regulating conduct which imposes solely an indirect burden on the observance of religion would be a gross oversimplification. If the purpose or effect of a law is to impede the observance of one or all religions or is to discriminate invidiously between religions, that law is constitutionally invalid even though the burden may be characterized as being only indirect. But if the State regulates conduct by enacting a general law within its power, the purpose and effect of which is to advance the State's secular goals, the statute is valid despite its indirect burden on religious observance unless the State may accomplish its purpose by means which do not impose such a burden. See *Cantwell*.[4]

4. Thus in cases like *Murdock v. Pennsylvania*, 319 U.S. 105, 63 S.Ct. 870, 87 L.Ed. 1292 (1943), and *Follett v. McCormick*, 321 U.S. 573, 64 S.Ct. 717, 88 L.Ed. 938 (1944) [overruling *Jones v. Opelika*, 316 U.S. 584, 62 S.Ct. 1231, 86 L.Ed. 1691 (1942)], this Court struck down municipal ordinances which, in application, required religious colporteurs [Je-

"As we pointed out in *McGowan*, we cannot find a State without power to provide a weekly respite from all labor and, at the same time, to set one day of the week apart from the others as a day of rest, repose, recreation and tranquility * * *. [To permit an exemption for Sabbatarians] might well undermine the State's goal of providing a day that, as best possible, eliminates the atmosphere of commercial noise and activity. Although not dispositive of the issue, enforcement problems would be more difficult since there would be two or more days to police rather than one and it would be more difficult to observe whether violations were occurring.

"Additional problems might also be presented by a regulation of this sort. To allow only people who rest on a day other than Sunday to keep their businesses open on that day might well provide these people with an economic advantage over their competitors who must remain closed on that day; this might cause the Sunday-observers to complain that their religions are being discriminated against [and] there could well be the temptation for some, in order to keep their businesses open on Sunday, to assert that they have religious convictions which compel them to close their businesses on what had formerly been their least profitable day. This might make necessary a state-conducted inquiry into the sincerity of the individual's religious beliefs, a practice which a State might believe would itself run afoul of the spirit of constitutionally protected religious guarantees. Finally, in order to keep the disruption of the day at a minimum, exempted employers would probably have to hire employees who themselves qualified for the exemption because of their own religious beliefs, a practice which a State might feel to be opposed to its general policy prohibiting religious discrimination in hiring." c

BRENNAN, J., dissented because the law's "effect is that appellants may not simultaneously practice their religion and their trade, without being hampered by a substantial competitive disadvantage." He relied on *Barnette* for the "appropriate standard of constitutional adjudication in cases in which a statute is assertedly in conflict with the First Amendment":

"What, then, is the compelling state interest which impels Pennsylvania to impede appellants' freedom of worship? What overbalancing need is so weighty in the constitutional scale that it justifies this substantial, though indirect, limitation of appellants' freedom? It is not the desire to stamp out a practice deeply abhorred by society, such as polygamy, as in *Reynolds* [nor] is it the State's traditional protection of children, as in *Prince* * * *. It is not even the interest in seeing that everyone rests one day a week, for appellants' religion requires that they take such a rest. It is the mere convenience of having everyone rest on the same day. * * *

"It is true, I suppose, that [granting an exemption for Sabbatarians] would make Sundays a little noisier, and the task of police and prosecutor a little more difficult. It is also true that a majority [of] States which have general Sunday regulations have exemptions of this kind. We are not told that those States are significantly noisier or that their police are significantly more burdened, than Pennsylvania's. * * * Non-Sunday observers might get an unfair advantage,

hovah's Witnesses] to pay a license tax as a condition to the pursuit of their activities [of spreading religious doctrine by distributing religious pamphlets] because the State's interest, the obtaining of revenue, could be easily satisfied by imposing this tax on nonreligious sources.

c. Frankfurter and Harlan, JJ., rejected the free exercise claim in a separate opinion. Douglas, J., dissented. For extracts from both opinions, see *McGowan*, Sec. 1, II supra.

it is said. [However] widespread the complaint, it is legally baseless, and the State's reliance upon it cannot withstand a First Amendment claim. We are told that an official inquiry into the good faith with which religious beliefs are held might be itself unconstitutional. But this Court indicated otherwise in *United States v. Ballard,* [Sec. II infra]. [Finally], I find the Court's mention of a problem under state anti-discrimination statutes almost chimerical. Most such statutes provide that hiring may be made on a religious basis if religion is a bona fide occupational qualification."

STEWART, J., also dissented: "Pennsylvania has passed a law which compels an Orthodox Jew to choose between his religious faith and his economic survival. That is a cruel choice [and] is not something that can be swept under the rug and forgotten in the interest of enforced Sunday togetherness."

––––––––

In SHERBERT v. VERNER, 374 U.S. 398, 83 S.Ct. 1790, 10 L.Ed.2d 965 (1963), a Seventh-day Adventist, discharged by her employer "because she would not work on Saturday, the Sabbath Day of her faith," was denied unemployment compensation by South Carolina on the ground that she refused to accept "suitable work" due to her religious restriction on Saturday labor. The Court, per BRENNAN, J., held that the "burden on the free exercise of appellant's religion" must be justified by a "compelling state interest": "[T]he consequences of such a disqualification to religious principles and practices may be only an indirect result of welfare legislation within the State's general competence to enact; it is true that no criminal sanctions directly compel appellant to work a six-day week. But this is only the beginning, not the end of our inquiry. [T]o condition the availability of benefits upon this appellant's willingness to violate a cardinal principle of her religious faith effectively penalizes the free exercise of her constitutional liberties.

"Significantly South Carolina expressly saves the Sunday worshipper from having to make the kind of choice which we here hold infringes the Sabbatarian's religious liberty. When in times of 'national emergency' the textile plants are authorized by the State Commissioner of Labor to operate on Sunday, 'if any employee should refuse to work on Sunday on account of [conscience] he or she shall not jeopardize his or her seniority by such refusal or be discriminated against in any other manner.' S.C.Code, § 64–4. [The] unconstitutionality of the disqualification of the Sabbatarian is thus compounded by the religious discrimination which South Carolina's general statutory scheme necessarily effects.

"[A]ppellees suggest no more than a possibility that the filing of fraudulent claims by unscrupulous claimants feigning religious objections to Saturday work [might] dilute the unemployment compensation fund [but] there is no proof whatever to warrant such fears of malingering or deceit [and] it is highly doubtful whether such evidence would be sufficient to warrant a substantial infringement of religious liberties. For [it] would plainly be incumbent upon the appellees to demonstrate that no alternative forms of regulation would combat such abuses without infringing First Amendment rights.

"[T]he state interest asserted in the present case is wholly dissimilar to the interests which were found to justify the less direct burden upon religious practices in *Braunfeld.* [T]he statute [was] saved by a countervailing factor which finds no equivalent in the instant case—a strong state interest in providing one uniform day of rest for all workers. That secular objective could be achieved, the Court found, only by declaring Sunday to be that day of rest.

Requiring exemptions for Sabbatarians, while theoretically possible, appeared to present an administrative problem of such magnitude, or afford the exempted class so great a competitive advantage that such a requirement would have rendered the entire statutory scheme unworkable. In the present case no such justifications underlie the determination of the [state].

"In holding as we do, plainly we are not fostering the 'establishment' of the Seventh-day Adventist religion in South Carolina, for the extension of unemployment benefits to Sabbatarians in common with Sunday worshippers reflects nothing more than the governmental obligation of neutrality in the face of religious differences, and does not represent that involvement of religious with secular institutions which it is the object of the Establishment Clause to forestall. [Nor] do we, by our decision today, declare the existence of a constitutional right to unemployment benefits on the part of all persons whose religious convictions are the cause of their unemployment. This is not a case in which an employee's religious convictions serve to make him a nonproductive member of society." Douglas, J., filed a separate concurrence.

STEWART, J., concurred in the result but, pointing particularly to the school prayer decisions in *Engel* and *Schempp,* argued that the result in *Sherbert* is "clearly to require the State to violate the Establishment Clause as construed by this Court. This poses no problem for me, because I think the Court's mechanistic concept of the Establishment Clause is historically unsound and constitutionally wrong." [d]

Further, "I cannot agree that today's decision can stand consistently with *Braunfeld.* [The] impact upon the appellant's religious freedom in the present case is considerably less onerous. [Even] upon the unlikely assumption that the appellant could not find suitable non-Saturday employment, the appellant at the worst would be denied a maximum of 22 weeks compensation payments" whereas the "undisputed effect" of the criminal statute in *Braunfeld,* "as pointed out by Mr. Justice Brennan in his dissenting opinion in that case, was that 'Plaintiff [will] be unable to continue in his business if he may not stay open on Sunday and he will thereby lose his capital investment.'"

HARLAN, J., joined by White, J., dissented, also maintaining that "the decision necessarily overrules *Braunfeld.*" Further, "in no proper sense can it be said that the State discriminated against the appellant on the basis of her religious beliefs or that she was denied benefits *because* she was a Seventh-day Adventist. She was denied benefits just as any other claimant would be denied benefits who was not 'available for work' for personal reasons. [Thus, the] meaning of today's holding [is] that the [state] must *single out* for financial assistance those whose behavior is religiously motivated, even though it denied such assistance to others whose identical behavior (in this case, inability to work on Saturdays) is not religiously motivated.[2]

"It has been suggested that such singling out of religious conduct for special treatment may violate the constitutional limitations on state action. See Kurland, *Of Church and State and The Supreme Court,* 29 U. of Chi.L.Rev. 1. My own view, however, is that at least under the circumstances of this case it would

---

d. The conflict between the establishment and free exercise clauses is considered in note 4, Sec. 3 infra.

2. The Court does suggest, in a rather startling disclaimer, that its holding is limited in applicability to those whose religious convictions do not make them "non-productive"

members of society [but it cannot] be suggesting that it will make a value judgment in each case as to whether a particular individual's religious convictions prevent him from being "productive." I can think of no more inappropriate function for this Court to perform.

be a permissible accommodation of religion for the State, if it *chose* to do so, to create an exception to its eligibility requirements for persons like the appellant. [Those] situations in which the Constitution may require special treatment on account of religion are, in my view, few and far between * * *. Such compulsion in the present case is particularly inappropriate in light of the indirect, remote, and insubstantial effect of the decision below on the exercise of appellant's religion and in light of the direct financial assistance to religion that today's decision requires." [e]

Notes and Questions

1. *Braunfeld and Sherbert.* Consider 32 Geo.Wash.L.Rev. 392 (1963): "[W]hile Braunfeld's customers might shop elsewhere if he closed the store both Saturday and Sunday, they were not compelled to do so. The economic hardship which confronted him was [not inevitable]. Whether or not he opened his store on Saturday was of no legal significance. On the other hand, Sherbert's refusal to work on Saturday *was* of legal significance. In the eyes of the law, she was 'unavailable for work' * * *. Furthermore, the economic hardship she suffered was not caused by the capricious shopping habits of the consumer or some other non-governmental activity. She was denied directly and positively the economic benefits of public welfare legislation by the state itself." Is the state "responsible" only for the "inevitable" consequences of its action or also for those that are likely?

Consider Note, *A Braunfeld v. Brown Test for Indirect Burdens on the Free Exercise of Religion,* 48 Minn.L.Rev. 1165, 1177–78 (1964): "The state's goals of providing subsistence to the state's unemployed would not be advanced by denying relief to the appellant unless allowing religious claims would so burden the state's program as to necessitate abandonment of all unemployment relief. The state made no showing that such a burden existed. Further, any slight burden of establishing the validity of religious claims would be offset by the more successful satisfaction of the state's goal of providing relief in all appropriate cases of hardship. [In] *Braunfeld* a significant part of the secular goal was to provide a uniform day of rest, which could be accomplished only by allowing no exceptions; on the other hand, in *Sherbert* the goal of relieving the onus of unemployment is more successful when the benefits are not denied." Under this analysis, may a state deny worker's compensation to the widow of an employee who, after being injured at work, died because of his refusal on religious grounds to accept a blood transfusion?

2. *Hamilton and Barnette.* Is *Hamilton v. Regents,* supra, consistent with *Braunfeld* in that it "simply made the practice of religious beliefs more expensive"? Is it consistent with *Sherbert?* What state purpose would be frustrated by exempting these students? Of what significance is it that these students were exempt from the draft because of their religious belief? May the state's purpose be satisfied by alternative means? See Note, 48 Minn.L.Rev. at 1174–75.

Did the law in *Barnette* impose a direct or indirect burden? Is *Barnette* distinguishable from *Hamilton* because college attendance is voluntary, while if the children refused to salute the flag, they would be expelled from school and their parents prosecuted for causing delinquency? If the children could attend a

e. In *Thomas v. Review Bd.* (1981), Part II infra, petitioner, a Jehovah's Witness, quit his job when he was transferred to weapons production because this was contrary "to his religious convictions." The Court, per Burger, C.J., relying on *Sherbert,* held that Indiana's denial of employment compensation, on the ground that petitioner did not quit for "good cause in connection with the work," violated free exercise.

private school where the flag salute was not required, would the case be distinguishable from *Hamilton?* Suppose the children could not afford to attend a private school? Or is *Hamilton* distinguishable because the state has a greater interest in compelling military training than it does in compelling a flag salute? Is this judgment more properly made by a court or a legislature?

Did the freedom asserted by the students in *Hamilton* "collide with the rights of others" any more than in *Barnette?* Is this a meaningful point? Or is it merely another way of examining the substantiality of the state's purpose?

3. *Taxes and religion.* (a) After *Sherbert*—and *Murdock* and *Follett* (fn. 4 in *Braunfeld*)—does the free exercise clause forbid a real property tax on church buildings? Cf. *Walz.* A personal property tax on a church's Communion wine, missals and rosaries? May sellers of merchandise of all kinds constitutionally be made to pay their way by being subject to nondiscriminatory license fees that compensate state and local governments for the cost of registration and protection of the public from fraudulent solicitations? Cf. *Cox v. New Hampshire,* p. 536 supra.

(b) Was the financial burden on religious exercise in *Murdock* more serious than that in *Braunfeld* and *Sherbert* because in *Murdock* the money taken in taxes would have been devoted to the support of the religious movement? If so, is tax exemption required for all commercial enterprises operated by churches? Suppose the enterprise provides the religion's sole source of financial support? May a state impose an income tax on a clergyman's salary? On funds obtained from the collection plate in church?

(c) Do you agree with *Braunfeld's* distinction of *Murdock* and *Follett*—that the municipality "could easily satisfy its revenue needs from other sources"? Was this "alternative means" basis the distinction between *Sherbert* and *Braunfeld?* Under *Sherbert,* suppose a Sabbatarian is dismissed from a job in the post office for refusal to work on Saturday because to grant an exemption would require paying overtime to another employee? [f]

4. *Aid to parochial schools.* (a) Is the Court's conclusion, that denial of financial benefits to parochial schools does not infringe the free exercise rights of attending children, consistent with *Sherbert?* After *Everson,* could a student bus transportation program exclude children who attend parochial schools? See *Luetkemeyer v. Kaufmann,* 419 U.S. 888, 95 S.Ct. 167, 42 L.Ed.2d 134 (1974). If some religions impose a duty on parents to send children to religious schools, may these parents argue that, since they must pay public school taxes, the state's failure to support parochial as well as public schools and thus defray their parochial school tuition costs imposes a serious financial burden on their exercise of religion? That "if the state gives financial assistance only to the school where education is deliberately divorced from religion [this is] preferential treatment of irreligion"? See Drinan, *The Constitutionality of Public Aid to Parochial Schools,* in The Wall Between Church and State 55, 68 (Oaks ed. 1963). That, under *Sherbert,* "conditioning the availability of benefits upon their willingness to violate a cardinal principle of their religious faith effectively penalizes the free exercise of their constitutional liberties"; that there is no "compelling state interest to justify the substantial infringement of their First Amendment rights"? May these parents further argue that their position is stronger than *Sherbert* because the purpose of granting an exemption in that

f. See also *TWA v. Hardison,* 432 U.S. 63, 97 S.Ct. 2264, 53 L.Ed.2d 113 (1977), interpreting the Civil Rights Act prohibition against religious discrimination in employment as permitting dismissal of a Sabbatarian if accommodating his work schedule would require "more than a de minimis cost" by the employer. Brennan and Marshall, JJ., dissented.

case was *solely* to aid religion whereas there is a wholly nonreligious purpose in giving aid to all nonpublic schools—improving the quality of the secular education?

Consider Kauper, *Religion and the Constitution* 36–37 (1964): "If the public policy of the state is to limit the use of educational funds to schools under public control, this involves no discrimination except the distinction between schools under public and those under private control—a distinction well recognized in our law. But if public funds are made available for all educational institutions whether public or private except those that are under the control of a religious body, it is indeed hard to avoid the conclusion that the religious factor is being used as a ground for disqualification from public benefits." Compare 25 U.Pitt. L.Rev. 713 (1964): "If the state in *Sherbert could not deny* compensation to one refusing work for religious reasons how could the state in *Everson* deny transportation reimbursement to students who choose for religious reasons to attend a parochial rather than public school? Suppose that the statute in *Everson* had dictated that all those attending nonpublic schools should not obtain free transportation, except that those students who attended religious schools because of the dictates of their religion also should qualify for fare reimbursement. It is submitted that under the rationale of *Sherbert* such a statute would be constitutional." But see the dictum in *Sloan v. Lemon,* fn. k, Sec. 1, III supra: "[V]alid aid to nonpublic, nonsectarian schools would provide no lever for aid to their sectarian counterparts."

(b) If a state fluoridates drinking water, must it supply nonfluoridated water to persons whose religion forbids such "medicinal aids"? If a state gives financial support to various voluntary and eleemosynary institutions, does *Sherbert* require it to give such support to churches?

WISCONSIN v. YODER

406 U.S. 205, 92 S.Ct. 1526, 32 L.Ed.2d 15 (1972).

MR. CHIEF JUSTICE BURGER delivered the opinion of the Court.

[Respondents, members of the Amish Church who declined to send their children to public school after completing the eighth grade, were convicted for violating a law compelling attendance to age 16 and fined $5 each.] They believed that by sending their children to high school, they [would] endanger their own salvation and that of their children. The State stipulated that respondents' religious beliefs were sincere.

* * * Amish beliefs require members of the community to make their living by farming or closely related activities. [They object to] higher education generally because [it] tends to emphasize intellectual and scientific accomplishments, self-distinction, competitiveness, worldly success, and social life with other students. Amish society emphasizes informal learning-through-doing, a life of "goodness," rather than a life of intellect, wisdom, rather than technical knowledge, community welfare rather than competition, and separation, rather than integration with contemporary worldly society. * * *

The Amish do not object to elementary education [because] they agree that their children must have basic skills in the "three R's" in order to read the Bible, to be good farmers and citizens and to be able to deal with non-Amish people [and] because it does not significantly expose their children to worldly values or interfere with their development in the Amish community during the crucial adolescent period. [An "expert on Amish society"] testified that compulsory high school attendance could not only result in great psychological harm to

Amish children, because of the conflicts it would produce, but would, in his opinion, ultimately result in the destruction of the Old Order Amish church community ∗ ∗ ∗.

[Under *Pierce v. Society of Sisters*], a State's interest in universal education, however highly we rank it, is not totally free from a balancing process when it impinges on other fundamental rights and interests, such as those specifically protected by the Free Exercise Clause [and] the traditional interest of parents with respect to the religious upbringing of their children so long as they, in the words of *Pierce*, "prepare [them] for additional obligations." [O]nly those interests of the highest order and those not otherwise served can overbalance legitimate claims to the free exercise of religion. ∗ ∗ ∗

We come then to the quality of the claims of [respondents]. A way of life, however virtuous and admirable, may not be interposed as a barrier to reasonable state regulation of education if it is based on purely secular considerations; to have the protection of the Religion Clauses, the claims must be rooted in religious belief. Although a determination of what is a "religious" belief or practice entitled to constitutional protection may present a most delicate question, the very concept of ordered liberty precludes allowing every person to make his own standards on matters of conduct in which society as a whole has important interests. Thus, if the Amish asserted their claims because of their subjective evaluation and rejection of the contemporary secular values accepted by the majority, much as Thoreau rejected the social values of his time and isolated himself at Walden Pond, their claim would not rest on a religious basis. Thoreau's choice was philosophical and personal rather than religious, and such belief does not rise to the demands of the Religion Clauses.

Giving no weight to such secular considerations, however, we see that the record in this case abundantly supports the claim that the traditional way of life of the Amish is not merely a matter of personal preference, but one of deep religious conviction, shared by an organized group, and intimately related to daily living. [This] is shown by the fact that it is in response to their literal interpretation of the Biblical injunction from the Epistle of Paul to the Romans, "Be not conformed to this world ∗ ∗ ∗." This command is fundamental to the Amish faith. Moreover, for the Old Order Amish, religion is not simply a matter of theocratic belief. As the expert witnesses explained, the Old Order Amish religion pervades and determines virtually their entire way of life, regulating it with the detail of the Talmudic diet through the strictly enforced rules of the church community. ∗ ∗ ∗

The impact of the compulsory attendance law on respondents' practice of the Amish religion is not only severe, but inescapable, for the Wisconsin law affirmatively compels them, under threat of criminal sanction, to perform acts undeniably at odds with fundamental tenets of their religious beliefs. See *Braunfeld*. [It poses] a very real threat of undermining the Amish community and religious practice as it exists today; they must either abandon belief and be assimilated into society at large, or be forced to migrate to some other and more tolerant region.[9] ∗ ∗ ∗

---

9. Some States have developed working arrangements with the Amish regarding high school attendance. However, the danger to the continued existence of an ancient religious faith cannot be ignored simply because of the assumption that its adherents will continue to be able, at considerable sacrifice, to relocate in some more tolerant State or country or work out accommodations under threat of criminal prosecution. Forced migration of religious minorities was an evil which lay at the heart of the Religion Clauses.

[The] Court must not ignore the danger that an exception from a general obligation of citizenship on religious grounds may run afoul of the Establishment Clause, but that danger cannot be allowed to prevent any exception no matter how vital it may be to the protection of values promoted by the right of free exercise. * * *

The State [argues] that some degree of education is necessary to prepare citizens to participate effectively and intelligently in our open political system [and] to be self-reliant and self-sufficient participants in society. * * *

However, the evidence adduced by the Amish in this case is persuasively to the effect that an additional one or two years of formal high school for Amish children in place of their long established program of informal vocational education would do little to serve those interests. [It] is one thing to say that compulsory education for a year or two beyond the eighth grade may be necessary when its goal is the preparation of the child for life in modern society as the majority live, but it is quite another if the goal of education be viewed as the preparation of the child for life in the separated agrarian community that is the keystone of the Amish faith.

The State attacks respondents' position as one fostering "ignorance" from which the child must be protected by the State. [But] this record strongly shows that the Amish community has been a highly successful social unit within our society even if apart from the conventional "mainstream." Its members are productive and very law-abiding members of society; they reject public welfare in any of its usual modern forms. The Congress itself recognized their self-sufficiency by authorizing exemption of such groups as the Amish from the obligation to pay social security taxes.

It is neither fair nor correct to suggest that the Amish are opposed to education beyond the eighth grade level. ["An expert witness on education"] testified that their system of learning-by-doing was an "ideal system" of education in terms of preparing Amish children for life as adults in the Amish community * * *. A way of life that is odd or even erratic but interferes with no rights or interests of others is not to be condemned because it is different.

The State, however, supports its interest [because] of the possibility that some such children will choose to leave the Amish community, and that if this occurs they will be ill-equipped for life. [But there] is no specific evidence of the loss of Amish adherents by attrition, nor is there any showing that upon leaving the Amish community Amish children, with their practical agricultural training and habits of industry and self-reliance, would become burdens on society because of educational shortcomings. [The] independence and successful social functioning of the Amish community for a period approaching almost three centuries [is] strong evidence that there is at best a speculative gain, in terms of meeting the duties of citizenship, from an additional one or two years of compulsory formal education. Against this background it would require a more particularized showing from the State on this point to justify the severe interference with religious freedom * * *.

We should also note [that there] is no intimation that the Amish employment of their children on family farms is in any way deleterious to their health or that Amish parents exploit children at tender years. * * *

Finally, the State, on authority of *Prince v. Massachusetts,* argues that a decision exempting Amish children from the State's requirement fails to recognize the substantive right of the Amish child to a secondary education * * *. The State has at no point tried this case on the theory that respondents were preventing their children from attending school against their expressed desires, and indeed the record is to the contrary.[21] * * *

Our holding in no way determines the proper resolution of possible competing interests of parents, children, and the State in an appropriate state court proceeding in which the power of the State is asserted on the theory that Amish parents are preventing their minor children from attending high school despite their expressed desires to the contrary. * * *

The State's argument [appears] to rest on the potential that exemption of Amish parents [might] allow some parents to act contrary to the best interests of their children by foreclosing their opportunity to make an intelligent choice between the Amish way of life and that of the outside world. The same argument could, of course, be made with respect to all church schools short of college. There is nothing in the record or in the ordinary course of human experience to suggest that non-Amish parents generally consult with children up to ages 14–16 if they are placed in a church school of the parents' faith.

Indeed it seems clear that if the State is empowered, as parens patriae, to "save" a child from himself or his Amish parents by requiring an additional two years of compulsory formal high school education, the State will in large measure influence, if not determine, the religious future of the child. [But] *Pierce* stands as a charter of the rights of parents to direct the religious upbringing of their children. And, when the interests of parenthood are combined with a free exercise claim of the nature revealed by this record, more than merely a "reasonable relation to some purpose within the competency of the state" is required to sustain the validity of the State's requirement under the First Amendment. To be sure, the power of the parent, even when linked to a free exercise claim, may be subject to limitation under *Prince* if it appears that parental decisions will jeopardize the health or safety of the child, or have a potential for significant social burdens. But in this case, the Amish have introduced persuasive evidence undermining the arguments the State has advanced to support its claims in terms of the welfare of the child and society as a whole. * * *[22] [C]ourts must move with great circumspection in performing the sensitive and delicate task of weighing a State's legitimate social concern when faced with religious claims for exemption from generally applicable educational requirements. It cannot be overemphasized that we are not dealing with a way of life and mode of education by a group claiming to have recently discovered some "progressive" or more enlightened process for rearing children for modern life.

[Respondents have carried the] difficult burden of demonstrating the adequacy of their alternative mode of continuing informal vocational education in terms of precisely those overall interests that the State advances in support of its program of compulsory high school education. In light of this convincing showing, one which probably few other religious groups or sects could make, and

---

21. The only relevant testimony in the record is to the effect that the wishes of the one child who testified corresponded with those of her parents. * * *

[Stewart and Brennan, JJ., who joined the Court's opinion, filed a short concurrence emphasizing this point.]

22. What we have said should meet the suggestion that [an exemption for respondents constitutes] an impermissible establishment of religion. * * * Accommodating the reli-

gious beliefs of the Amish can hardly be characterized as sponsorship or active involvement. The purpose and effect of such an exemption are not to support, favor, advance, or assist the Amish, but to allow their centuries-old religious society, here long before the advent of any compulsory education, to survive free from the heavy impediment compliance with the Wisconsin compulsory education law would impose. * * *

weighing the minimal difference between what the State would require and what the Amish already accept, it was incumbent on the State to show with more particularity how its admittedly strong interest in compulsory education would be adversely affected by granting an exemption to the Amish. *Sherbert.* * * *[23]

Affirmed.

MR. JUSTICE POWELL and MR. JUSTICE REHNQUIST took no part in the consideration or decision of this case.

MR. JUSTICE WHITE, with whom MR. JUSTICE BRENNAN and MR. JUSTICE STEWART join, concurring.

[There] is evidence in the record that many children desert the Amish faith when they come of age. A State has a legitimate interest not only in seeking to develop the latent talents of its children but in seeking to prepare them for the life style which they may later choose or at least to provide them with an option other than the life they have led in the past. In the circumstances of this case, although the question is close, I am unable to say that the State has demonstrated that Amish children who leave school in the eighth grade will be intellectually stultified or unable to acquire new academic skills later. * * *

Decision in cases such as [this] will inevitably involve the kind of close and perhaps repeated scrutiny of religious practices, as exemplified in today's opinion, which the Court has heretofore been anxious to avoid. But such entanglement does not create a forbidden establishment of religion where it is essential to implement free exercise values threatened by an otherwise neutral program instituted to foster some permissible, nonreligious state objective. I join the Court because the sincerity of the Amish religious policy here is uncontested, because the potential adverse impact of the state requirement is great and because the State's valid interest in education has already been largely satisfied by the eight years the children have already spent in school.

MR. JUSTICE DOUGLAS, dissenting in part.

[If] the parents in this case are allowed a religious exemption, the inevitable effect is to impose the parents' notions of religious duty upon their children. Where the child is mature enough to express potentially conflicting desires, it would be an invasion of the child's rights to permit such an imposition without canvassing his views.[a] * * * I therefore join the judgment of the Court as to respondent [whose child testified. But] I must dissent [as to the others]. Our opinions are full of talk about the power of the parents over the child's education. * * * Recent cases, however, have clearly held that the children themselves have constitutionally protectible interests [citing, inter alia, *In re Gault*, 387 U.S. 1, 87 S.Ct. 1428, 18 L.Ed.2d 527 (1967), and *Tinker v. Des Moines School Dist.*, p. 522 supra]. * * *

I think the emphasis of the Court on the "law and order" record of this Amish group of people is quite irrelevant. A religion is a religion irrespective of what the misdemeanor or felony records of its members might be. I am not at

23. Several States have now adopted plans to accommodate Amish religious beliefs through the establishment of an "Amish vocational school." These are not schools in the traditional sense of the word. [There] is no basis to assume that Wisconsin will be unable to reach a satisfactory accommodation with the Amish in light of what we now hold, so as to serve its interests without impinging on respondents' protected free exercise of their religion.

a. Knudsen, *The Education of the Amish Child*, 62 Calif.L.Rev. 1506 (1974); Note, *Adjudicating What Yoder Left Unresolved: Religious Rights for Minor Children After Danforth and Carey*, 126 U.Pa.L.Rev. 1135 (1978).

all sure how the Catholics, Episcopalians, the Baptists, Jehovah's Witnesses, the Unitarians, and my own Presbyterians would make out if we were subjected to such a test. It is, of course, true that if a group or society was organized to perpetuate crime and if that is its motif, we would have rather startling problems akin to those that were raised when some years back a particular sect was challenged here as operating on a fraudulent basis. *United States v. Ballard.* But no such factors are present here, and the Amish, whether with a high or low criminal record, certainly qualify by all historic standards as a religion within the meaning of the First Amendment. * * *

In another way, however, the Court retreats when in reference to Henry Thoreau it says his "choice was philosophical and personal rather than religious, and such belief does not rise to the demands of the Religion Clause." That is contrary to what we held in *United States v. Seeger* [b] * * *.

UNITED STATES v. LEE, 455 U.S. 252, 102 S.Ct. 1051, 71 L.Ed.2d 127 (1982), per BURGER, C.J., held that the free exercise clause does not require an exemption for members of the Old Order Amish from payment of social security taxes even though the Court accepted their contention "that both payment and receipt of social security benefits is forbidden by the Amish faith": "The state may justify a limitation on religious liberty by showing that it is essential to accomplish an overriding governmental interest [and] mandatory participation is indispensable to the fiscal vitality of the social security system. [To] maintain an organized society that guarantees religious freedom to a great variety of faiths requires that some religious practices yield to the common good. [The] tax system could not function if denominations were allowed to challenge the tax system because tax payments were spent in a manner that violates their religious belief. * * * [12]"

STEVENS, J., concurred in the judgment: "In my opinion, it is the objector who must shoulder the burden of demonstrating that there is a unique reason for allowing him a special exemption from a valid law of general applicability. [As] a matter of fiscal policy, an enlarged exemption probably would benefit the social security system because the nonpayment of these taxes by the Amish would be more than offset by the elimination of their right to collect benefits.[c] * * * Nonetheless, I agree with the Court's conclusion that the difficulties associated with processing other claims to tax exemption on religious grounds justify a rejection of this claim.[2]"

------

b. The *Ballard* and *Seeger* cases and the question of what constitutes "religion" are discussed in Part II infra.

12. We note that here the statute compels contributions to the system by way of taxes; it does not compel anyone to accept benefits. Indeed, it would be possible for an Amish member, upon qualifying for social security benefits, to receive and pass them along to an Amish fund having parallel objectives. It is not for us to speculate whether this would ease or mitigate the perceived sin of participation.

c. Stevens, J., found the distinction between this case and *Yoder* "unconvincing because precisely the same religious interest is implicated in both cases and Wisconsin's interest in requiring its children to attend school until they reach the age of 16 is surely not inferior to the federal interest in collecting these social security taxes."

2. In my opinion, the principal reason for adopting a strong presumption against such claims is not a matter of administrative convenience. It is the overriding interest in keeping the government—whether it be the legislature or the courts—out of the business of evaluating the relative merits of differing religious claims. The risk that governmental approval of some and disapproval of others will be perceived as favoring one religion over another is an important risk the Establishment Clause was designed to preclude.

GILLETTE v. UNITED STATES, 401 U.S. 437, 91 S.Ct. 828, 28 L.Ed.2d 168 (1971), per MARSHALL, J., held that the free exercise clause does not forbid Congress from "conscripting persons who oppose a particular war on grounds of conscience and religion. * * *[23]": "The conscription laws [are] not designed to interfere with any religious ritual or practice, and do not work a penalty against any theological position. The incidental burdens felt by persons in petitioners' position are strictly justified by substantial governmental interests that relate directly to the very impacts questioned. And more broadly, of course, there is the Government's interest in procuring the manpower necessary for military purposes * * *."

DOUGLAS, J., dissented: "The question, can a conscientious objector, whether his objection be rooted in 'religion' or in moral values, be required to kill? has never been answered by the court.

"[M]y choice is the dicta of Chief Justice Hughes who, dissenting in *Macintosh,* spoke for Holmes, Brandeis, and Stone: '[Among] the most eminent statesmen here and abroad have been those who condemned the action of their country in entering into wars they thought to be unjustified. [If] the mere holding of religious or conscientious scruples against all wars should not disqualify a citizen from holding office in this country, or an applicant otherwise qualified from being admitted to citizenship, there would seem to be no reason why a reservation of religious or conscientious objection to participation in wars believed to be unjust should constitute such a disqualification.'

"[It] is true that the First Amendment speaks of the free exercise of religion not of the free exercise of conscience or belief. Yet conscience and belief are [the] bedrock of free speech as well as religion. The implied First Amendment right of 'conscience' is certainly as high as the 'right of association' * * *."[d]

BOB JONES UNIV. v. UNITED STATES, 461 U.S. 574, 103 S.Ct. 2017, 76 L.Ed.2d 157 (1983), per BURGER, C.J., held that IRS denial of tax exempt status to private schools that practice racial discrimination on the basis of sincerely held religious beliefs does not violate the free exercise clause: "[T]he Government has a fundamental, overriding interest in eradicating racial discrimination in education [which] substantially outweighs whatever burden denial of tax benefits places on petitioners' exercise of their religious beliefs. The interests asserted by petitioners cannot be accommodated with that compelling governmental interest, see *Lee*; and no 'less restrictive means' are available to achieve the governmental interest."[e] Rehnquist, J., agreeing with the Court's free exercise

---

23. We are not faced with the question whether the Free Exercise Clause itself would require exemption of any class other than objectors to particular wars. * * * We note that the Court has previously suggested that relief for conscientious objectors is not mandated by the Constitution. See *Hamilton v. Regents; United States v. Macintosh,* 283 U.S. at 623–24, 51 S.Ct. at 574–75, 75 L.Ed. 1302 (1931).

d. Did *Gillette* discard the "alternative means" approach of *Sherbert* and *Yoder.* Consider 85 Harv.L.Rev. 184–85 (1971): "Even though the option of a volunteer army might have seemed too expensive a departure to force on Congress or even inconsistent with conscription's purpose of spreading the burden

of military service throughout the society, the Court might have considered alternatives such as an extended conscientious objector term— for example, four years instead of the present two." Or is such "evaluation of alternatives" a task that "inevitably involves judgments about costs and policy objectives that are customarily left to legislatures"? Id.

See generally Macgill, *Selective Conscientious Objection: Divine Will and Legislative Grace,* 54 Va.L.Rev. 1355 (1968); Hochstadt, *The Right to Exemption from Military Service of a Conscientious Objector to a Particular War,* 3 Harv.Civ.Rts.-Civ.Lib.L.Rev. 1 (1967).

e. For a contrary view, see Laycock, *Tax Exemptions for Racially Discriminatory Reli-*

analysis, dissented on the ground that Congress had not authorized the IRS denial of tax exemption.

In JOHNSON v. ROBISON, 415 U.S. 361, 94 S.Ct. 1160, 39 L.Ed.2d 391 (1974), a federal statute granted educational benefits for veterans who served on active duty but disqualified conscientious objectors who performed alternate civilian service. The Court, per BRENNAN, J., found a "rational basis" for the classification and thus no violation of equal protection: The "disruption caused by military service is quantitatively greater" because "the military veteran remains subject to [a Reserve] obligation after release from active duty" whereas a conscientious objector is only "obligated to work for two years." The disruptions are also "qualitatively different. Military veterans suffer a far greater loss of personal freedom during their service careers." The "classification also bears a rational relationship" to the objective of "enhancing and making more attractive" military service.

Further, the statute "involves only an incidental burden upon appellee's free exercise of religion—if, indeed, any burden exists at all.[19] [T]he Government's substantial interest in raising and supporting armies is of 'a kind and weight' clearly sufficient to sustain the challenged legislation, for the burden upon appellee's free exercise [is] not nearly of the same order or magnitude as" in *Gillette.*

DOUGLAS, J., dissented: "Full benefits are available to occupants of safe desk jobs and the thousands of veterans who performed civilian type duties at home and for whom the 'rigors' of the war were far from 'totally disruptive' * * *. Where Government places a price on the Free Exercise of one's religious scruples it crosses the forbidden line." Unlike *Gillette,* this classification is not "religiously neutral" but "excludes only those [with] religious-based objections to war"—and "the only government interest here is the financial one of denying these appellees educational benefits."

McDANIEL v. PATY, 435 U.S. 618, 98 S.Ct. 1322, 55 L.Ed.2d 593 (1978)—an unusual case because it involved a law that singled out religion [f]—invalidated Tennessee provisions disqualifying clergy from being legislators. BURGER, C. J., joined by Powell, Rehnquist and Stevens, JJ., characterized the disqualification as "directed primarily at status, acts and conduct" rather than at "belief." Thus, "the Free Exercise Clause's absolute prohibition of infringements on the 'freedom to believe' is inapposite here." Rather, relying on the "delicate balancing" required by *Sherbert* and *Yoder,* they found the restriction violative

---

gious Schools, 60 Tex.L.Rev. 259 (1982); Freed & Polsby, *Race, Religion, and Public Policy: Bob Jones University v. United States,* 1983 Sup.Ct.Rev. 1, 20–30.

Most recently, four justices rejected the claim, that Nebraska's denial of a driver's license to a person whose sincerely held religious beliefs—pursuant to the Second Commandment prohibition of "graven images"—forbade her to be photographed, violated the free exercise clause. *Quaring v. Peterson,* 728 F.2d 1121 (8th Cir.1984) (free exercise violation), affirmed by an equally divided Court, ___ U.S. ___, 105 S.Ct. 3492, 86 L.Ed.2d 383 (1985) (Powell, J., not participating.)

19. * * * Congress has bestowed relative benefits upon conscientious objectors by permitting them to perform their alternate service obligation as civilians. Thus, Congress' decision to grant educational benefits to military servicemen might arguably be viewed as an attempt to equalize the burdens of military service and civilian alternate service, rather than an effort [to] place a relative burden upon a conscientious objector's free exercise of religion.

f. See also *Torcaso v. Watkins,* Part II infra.

of free exercise: "The essence of the rationale underlying the Tennessee restriction on ministers is that if elected to public office they will necessarily exercise their powers and influence to promote the interests of one sect or thwart the interests of another thus pitting one against the others, contrary to the antiestablishment principle with its command of neutrality. [But] American experience provides no persuasive support for the fear that clergymen in public office will be less careful of antiestablishment interests or less faithful to their oaths of civil office than their unordained counterparts." [g]

BRENNAN, J., joined by Marshall, J., concurred: "The characterization of the exclusion as one burdening appellant's 'career or calling' and not religious belief cannot withstand analysis. [T]o bar from political office persons regarded as deeply committed to religious participation because of that participation—participation itself not regarded as harmful by the State and which therefore must be conceded to be protected"—is "absolutely prohibited" by the free exercise clause.[h]

Further, "the State's goal of preventing sectarian bickering and strife may not be accomplished by regulating religious speech and political association." The "exclusion manifests patent hostility toward, not nonneutrality in respect of, religion, forces or influences a minister or priest to abandon his ministry as the price of public office, and in sum, has a primary effect which inhibits religion." Thus, it also violates the establishment clause.[i]

Notes and Questions

1. *Action vs. inaction.* Does *Prince* survive *Yoder?* Of what significance is it that *Yoder* (and *Sherbert*) involved religious refusal to engage in conduct required by government rather than religiously dictated action forbidden by the state? What results in respect to the religiously mandated *inaction* in the following: (a) Citing for contempt person who refuses to serve on jury. See *In re Jenison,* 265 Minn. 96, 120 N.W.2d 515, vacated 375 U.S. 14, 84 S.Ct. 63, 11 L.Ed. 2d 39, reversed 267 Minn. 136, 125 N.W.2d 588 (1963); (b) Statute requiring smallpox vaccination applied to person whose religion forbids medicinal aids. See *Jacobson v. Massachusetts,* 197 U.S. 11, 25 S.Ct. 358, 49 L.Ed. 643 (1905); (c) Court order of blood transfusion, to save life of pregnant mother and child, for woman of Jehovah's Witness faith which obligates adherents to "abstain from blood." Suppose the woman were not pregnant but had infant children? See *Application of Georgetown College, Inc.,* 331 F.2d 1000, cert. denied, 377 U.S. 978 (1964). Suppose the woman were neither pregnant nor had any children? Suppose there were only a slight chance that the transfusion would save the life? That the woman is a brilliant scientist whose work is vital to national security? Suppose the transfusion is thought necessary not to preserve life but to bring back to good health?

2. *The willingness of others.* In the case of *action* due to religious beliefs, should a distinction be drawn between action that is requested by the people

---

g. Compare Marty, *Of Darters and Schools and Clergymen: The Religion Clauses Worse Confounded,* 1978 Sup.Ct.Rev. 171, 183: "[I]n issues having to do with everything from homosexuality to the Equal Rights Amendment to abortion to pornography, lay and especially clerical leadership in many denominations has been more aggressive, always with an eye to having one's own sect prevail in the legislative and judicial arenas."

h. Stewart, J., concurred separately, essentially on this ground.

i. White, J., concurred, on equal protection grounds, pointing to cases (Ch. 6, Sec. 4, I, C infra) requiring "States to provide substantial justification for any requirement that prevents a class of citizens from gaining ballot access." Blackmun, J., did not participate.

affected and action that is imposed on others? Should the conviction of a religious Spiritualist for fortune telling be sustained despite the fact that fortunes were told only upon request? If not, how do you distinguish the polygamy cases? Should a church member employed by her church be permitted to question its employment practices (such as sex discrimination) as being contrary to statute? See Note, *Title VII and the Appointment of Women Clergy: A Statutory and Constitutional Quagmire*, 13 Colum.J.L. & Soc.Probs. 257 (1977).[j]

II. UNUSUAL RELIGIOUS BELIEFS AND PRACTICES

1. In UNITED STATES v. BALLARD, 322 U.S. 78, 64 S.Ct. 882, 88 L.Ed. 1148 (1944), defendant was indicted for mail fraud. He had solicited funds for the "I Am" movement, asserting, inter alia, that he had been selected as a divine messenger, had the divine power of healing incurable diseases, and had talked with Jesus and would transmit these conversations to mankind. The Court, per DOUGLAS, J., held that the first amendment barred submitting to the jury the question of whether these religious beliefs were true: "Men may believe what they cannot prove. * * * Religious experiences which are as real as life to some may be incomprehensible to others. [The] miracles of the New Testament, the Divinity of Christ, life after death, the power of prayer are deep in the religious convictions of many. If one could be sent to jail because a jury in a hostile environment found those teachings false, little indeed would be left of religious freedom."

(a) Should the prosecution be permitted to prove that, irrespective of whether the incidents described by defendant happened, he did not honestly believe that they had? If so, may the prosecution introduce evidence that the incidents did not in fact happen and that therefore defendant could not honestly believe that they did? Should this line of proof be permitted in the prosecution of an official of the Catholic church for soliciting funds to construct a shrine commemorating the Miracle of Fatima in 1930?

(b) Is it relevant that in *Ballard* the alleged divine revelation was made to defendant himself? Would it be material if the experiences had allegedly occurred at a definite time and place? Many Biblical happenings are so identified. Could the prosecution introduce evidence that Ballard was not physically present at the alleged place at the alleged time? If a Protestant, Catholic or Jewish clergyman were prosecuted and there was overwhelming scientific evidence disputing the Biblical doctrine, what would the jury be likely to find as to the honesty of the beliefs? Should the first amendment permit people to obtain money in the name of religion by knowingly making false statements? See Tribe, *American Constitutional Law* 859–62 (1978).

(c) Should the prosecution be able to prove that defendant had stated on many occasions that he believed none of his representations but that by saying that he did he was amassing great wealth? Suppose it can be shown that a priest or rabbi is *somewhat* skeptical as to the truth of certain Biblical occurrences? Could Ballard be convicted on the ground that fraudulent procurement

j. For general reviews of the cases and refined "balancing" approaches, see Dodge, *The Free Exercise of Religion: A Sociological Approach*, 67 Mich.L.Rev. 679 (1969); Giannella, *Religious Liberty, Nonestablishment, and Doctrinal Development—Part I. The Religious Liberty Guarantee*, 80 Harv.L.Rev. 1381–1423 (1967); Rodes, *Sub Deo et Lege: A Study of Free Exercise*, 4 Relig. & Pub.Or. 3 (1968);   Clark, *Guidelines for the Free Exercise Clause*, 83 Harv.L.Rev. 327 (1969); Marcus, *The Forum of Conscience: Applying Standards Under the Free Exercise Clause*, 1973 Duke L.J. 1217. For the conflict between free exercise and the exigencies of prison discipline, see *Cruz v. Beto*, 405 U.S. 319, 92 S.Ct. 1079, 31 L.Ed.2d 263 (1972); Note, *The Religious Rights of the Incarcerated*, 125 U.Pa.L.Rev. 812 (1977).

of money, just like polygamy, is conduct which may be constitutionally prohibited even if done in the name of religion?

2. *What is "religion."* May the Court determine that asserted religious beliefs and practices do not constitute a valid religion? Consider Weiss, *Privilege, Posture and Protection—"Religion" in the Law,* 73 Yale L.J. 593, 604 (1964): "[T]o define the limits of religious expression may be impossible if philosophically desirable. Moreover, any definition of religion would seem to violate religious freedom in that it would dictate to religions, present and future, what they must [be]. Furthermore, an attempt to define religion, even for purposes of increasing freedom for religions, would run afoul of the 'establishment' clause as excluding some religions, or even as establishing a notion respecting religion."

Is it relevant that the beliefs of a group do not include the existence of God? TORCASO v. WATKINS, per BLACK, J., 367 U.S. 488, 81 S.Ct. 1680, 6 L.Ed.2d 982 (1961), invalidating a Maryland provision requiring a declaration of belief in the existence of God as a test for public office, stated: "Neither [a state nor the federal government can] impose requirements which aid all religions as against nonbelievers, and neither can aid those religions based on a belief in the existence of God as against those religions founded on different beliefs." The Court noted that "among religions in this country which do not teach what would generally be considered a belief in the existence of God are Buddhism, Taoism, Ethical Culture, Secular Humanism and others."

What if the Communist Party claimed religious status? Consider Kauper, *Religion and the Constitution* 31 (1964): "What makes secular humanism a religion? Is it because it is an ideology or system of belief that attempts to furnish a rationale of life? But if any ideology, creed, or philosophy respecting man and society is a religion, then must not democracy, fascism, and communism also qualify as religions? It is not uncommon to refer to these as secular or quasi religions, for some find in these systems an adequate explanation of the meaning and purpose of life and the source of values that command faith and devotion. Certainly in the case of communism, with its discipline, its cultus, its sense of community, and its obligation to duties owing to the system, the resemblance to religion in the conventional sense is [clear]."

May a single person establish his own religion? Consider Konvitz, *Religious Liberty and Conscience* 84 (1968): "[Many religions] had their origin in a 'private and personal' religious experience. Mohammed did not take over an on-going, established religion; the history of Islam records the names of his first three converts. John Wesley is given credit as the founder of Methodism. Mrs. Mary Baker Eddy was the founder of the Christian Science church. Menno Simons organized a division of Anabaptists that in due course became the sect known as the Mennonites. Jacob Ammon broke away from the Mennonites and founded the sect known as the Amish."

How important is it that the group has regular weekly services? Designated leaders who conduct these services? Ceremonies for naming, marrying and burying members? Are any of these factors dispositive? Does the first amendment extend only to those groups that conform to the "conventional" concept of religion? Consider Cox (Harvard Divinity School), N.Y.Times 25 (Feb. 16, 1977): "[C]ourts [often] turn to some vague 'man-in-the-street' idea of what 'religion' should be. [But] a man-in-the-street approach would surely have ruled out early Christianity, which seemed both subversive and atheistic to the religious Romans of the day. The truth is that one man's 'bizarre cult' is another's true path to salvation, and the Bill of Rights was designed to safeguard minorities from the man-on-the-street's uncertain capacity for tolerance. The new challenge to our pluralism often comes from Oriental religious movements, because their views of religion differ so fundamentally from ours." To what extent should a group's "brainwashing," mental coercion techniques affect its constitutional status as a "religion"? Compare Delgado, *Religious Totalism: Gentle and Ungentle Persuasion Under the First Amendment*, 51 So.Cal.L.Rev. 1 (1977) with Note, *Conservatorship and Religious Cults: Divining A Theory of Free Exercise*, 53 N.Y.U.L.Rev. 1247 (1978).

Suppose that a group has certain characteristics of "traditional" religions, such as a holy book, ministers, houses of worship, prescribed prayers, a strict moral code, a belief in the hereafter and an appeal to faith, but also has announced social and economic tenets such as racial segregation? (Methodism developed originally out of social concerns.) Consider Note, *Toward a Constitutional Definition of Religion*, 91 Harv.L.Rev. 1056, 1069 (1978): "Gustavo Gutierrez, a spokesman for the new 'liberation theology' within Catholicism, argues that true religion is to be found in liberation 'as the creation of a new social consciousness and as a social appropriation not only of the means of production, but also of the political processes.' The church, he says, seeks 'the abolition of the exploitation of man by man.' The views of these and other significant Christian theologians coalesce around one important theme: the Christian church will find itself only by discarding what until now has been perceived to be religious and by immersing itself in the secular world." Does the first amendment encompass any philosophical, moral or social doctrine espoused by some group in the name of religion?

UNITED STATES v. SEEGER, 380 U.S. 163, 85 S.Ct. 850, 13 L.Ed.2d 733 (1965), interpreted § 6(j) of the Universal Military Training and Service Act, which exempted from combat any person "who, by reason of religious training and belief, is conscientiously opposed to participation in war in any form. Religious training and belief in this connection means an individual's belief in a relation to a Supreme Being involving duties superior to those arising from any human relation, but does not include essentially political, sociological or philosophical views or a merely personal moral code." [a] The Court, per CLARK, J., avoided constitutional questions and upheld the claims for exemption of three conscientious objectors. Seeger declared "that he preferred to leave the question as to his belief in a Supreme Being open, [and] that his was a 'belief in and devotion to goodness and virtue for their own sakes, and a religious faith in a purely ethical creed.'" Jakobson "believed in a 'Supreme Being' [and] that his religious and social thinking had developed after much meditation and thought. He had concluded that man must be 'partly spiritual' [and] that his 'most important religious law' was that 'no man ought ever to wilfully sacrifice another man's life as a means to any other end.'" Peter said "that he felt it a violation of his moral code to take human life and that he considered this belief superior to his obligation to the state. As to whether his conviction was religious, he quoted with approval Reverend John Haynes Holmes' definition of religion as 'the consciousness of some power manifest in nature which helps man in the ordering of his life in harmony with its demands * * *; it is man thinking his highest, feeling his deepest, and living his best.' The source of his conviction he attributed to reading and meditation 'in our democratic American culture, with its values derived from the western religious and philosophical

---

a. The statute was subsequently amended to omit the "belief in a Supreme Being" element.

tradition.' As to his belief in a Supreme Being, Peter stated that he supposed 'you could call that a belief in the Supreme Being or God. These just do not happen to be the words I use.' "

The Court "concluded that Congress, in using the expression 'Supreme Being' rather than the designation 'God,' was merely clarifying the meaning of religious training and belief so as to embrace all religions and to exclude essentially political, sociological, or philosophical views [and that] the test of belief 'in a relation to a Supreme Being' is whether a given belief that is sincere and meaningful occupies a place in the life of its possessor parallel to that filled by the orthodox belief in God of one who clearly qualifies for the exemption.[b] [No] party claims to be an atheist * * *. We do not deal with or intimate any decision on that situation in these cases. [The] use by Congress of the words 'merely personal' seems to us to restrict the exception to a moral code which is not only personal but which is the sole basis for the registrant's belief and is in no way related to a Supreme Being. [Congress did] not distinguish between externally and internally derived beliefs. Such a determination [would] prove impossible as a practical matter."

In WELSH v. UNITED STATES, 398 U.S. 333, 90 S.Ct. 1792, 26 L.Ed.2d 308 (1970), petitioner, in his application for exemption, "struck the word 'religious' entirely and later characterized his beliefs as having been formed 'by reading in the fields of history and sociology.' " BLACK, J., joined by Douglas, Brennan and Marshall, JJ., held that, under *Seeger,* "if an individual deeply and sincerely holds beliefs which are purely ethical or moral in source and content but that nevertheless impose upon him a duty of conscience to refrain from participating in any war at any time, those beliefs certainly occupy in the life of that individual 'a place parallel to that filled [by] God' in traditionally religious persons." "Although [Welsh] originally characterized his beliefs as nonreligious, he later upon reflection wrote a long and thoughtful letter to his Appeal Board in which he declared that his beliefs were 'certainly religious in the ethical sense of that word.' * * * § 6(j)'s exclusion of those persons with 'essentially political, sociological, or philosophical views or a merely personal moral code' should [not] be read to exclude those who hold strong beliefs about our domestic and foreign affairs or even those whose conscientious objection to participation in all wars is founded to a substantial extent upon considerations of public policy. The two groups of registrants which obviously do fall within these exclusions from the exemption are those whose beliefs are not deeply held and those whose objection to war does not rest at all upon moral, ethical, or religious principle but instead rests solely upon considerations of policy, pragmatism, or expediency." [c]

---

b. Consider Note, 91 Harv.L.Rev. at 1065 n. 37: "[*Seeger*] left several important questions unanswered: What does it mean to say that a principle occupies a place parallel to that of a traditional deity? Must that principle explain the existence of the cosmos, of humankind? Need it be the source of moral precepts, punishing infractions in this life or the next?"

c. In separate opinions, Harlan, J., and White, J., (joined by Burger, C. J., and Stewart, J.) dissented on the issue of statutory construction. For their views on the constitutional issue, see note 4(b), Sec. 3 infra.

See generally Note, *Defining Religion,* 32 U.Chi.L.Rev. 533 (1965); Boyan, *Defining Religion in Operational and Institutional Terms,* 116 U.Pa.L.Rev. 479 (1968); Hollingsworth, *Constitutional Religious Protection: Antiquated Oddity or Vital Reality?* 34 Ohio St.L.J. 15 (1973); Note, *The Sacred and the Profane: A First Amendment Definition of Religion,* 61 Tex.L.Rev. 139 (1982). For criticism of "sincerity," see Comment, *The Legal Relationship of Conscience to Religion: Refusals to Bear Arms,* 38 U.Chi.L.Rev. 583 (1971).

3. *What is "religious belief"?*   (a) Of what significance is it that the practice is an "age-old form" of religious conduct (see *Murdock*)? Is a "cardinal principle" of the asserted religious faith (see *Sherbert*)? Consider Laycock, fn. a in *Lemon*, at 1390–91: "Many activities that obviously are exercises of religion are not required by conscience or doctrine. Singing in the church choir and saying the Roman Catholic rosary are two common examples. Any activity engaged in by a church as a body is an exercise of religion. [Indeed,] many would say that an emphasis on rules and obligations misconceives the essential nature of some religions." Compare Giannella, fn. j, Sec. I supra, at 1427–28: "[Use of hallucinogenics] should be denied the status of religious claims [because] denial [does] not create problems for the individual's conscience similar to those created by traditionally religious claims to freedom of worship. Personal alienation from one's Maker, frustration of one's ultimate mission in life, and violation of the religious person's integrity are all at stake when the right to worship is threatened. Although the seeker of new psychological worlds may feel equally frustrated when deprived of his gropings for a higher reality, there is not the same sense of acute loss—the loss of the Be-all and End-all of life. [A] different problem presents itself when an individual who does not believe in a supernatural or personal God asserts conscientious objection to certain conduct because of its injurious effects on his fellow man. [T]his ethical belief may be held with such a degree of intensity that its violation occasions the same interior revulsion and anguish as does violation of the law of God to the pious." Under this approach, on what evidence should these factual questions be determined? Suppose a drug-use defendant claims "that its use was essential to attain a unique level of spiritual consciousness [and] compared the effect of depriving him of marihuana with that of forbidding a Catholic to celebrate the Mass"? Finer, *Psychedelics and Religious Freedom*, 19 Hastings L.J. 667, 692 (1968).

For the view that "belief [in] 'extratemporal consequences'—whether the effects of actions taken pursuant or contrary to the dictates of a person's beliefs extend in some meaningful way beyond his lifetime—is a sensible and desirable criterion (albeit plainly far short of ideal) for determining when the free exercise clause should trigger judicial consideration of whether an exemption from general government regulations of conduct is constitutionally required," see Choper, *Defining "Religion" in the First Amendment*, 1982 U.Ill.L.Rev. 579, 599, 603–04: [d] "It may be persuasively argued that *all* beliefs that invoke a transcendent reality—and especially those that provide their adherents with glimpses of meaning and truth that make them so important and so uncompromisable—should be encompassed by the special constitutional protection granted 'religion' by the free exercise clause. [In] many ways, however, transcendental explanations of worldly realities are essentially no different [than] conventional exegeses for temporal outcomes that are based on such 'rational' disciplines as economics, political science, sociology, or psychology, or even such 'hard' sciences [as] physics. When justifying competing government policies on such varied matters as social welfare, the economy, and military and foreign affairs, there is at bedrock only a gossamer line between 'rational' and 'supernatural' causation—the former really being little more capable of 'scientific proof' than the latter. [Therefore, government's] plenary authority to regulate the worldly affairs of society [should] not be restricted because of the nature of the causes, which are all basically unverifiable, that different groups believe will produce consequences that the state seeks to achieve."

d. For criticism of this view, see Note, *Religion and Morality Legislation: A Reexami-* *nation of Establishment Clause Analysis*, 59 N.Y.U.L.Rev. 301, 346–52 (1984).

For the view that this approach "does not promise to yield sound results for many free exercise cases," see Greenawalt, *Religion as a Concept in Constitutional Law,* 72 Calif.L.Rev. 753, 763, 815 (1984): "No specification of essential conditions will capture all and only the beliefs, practices, and organizations that are regarded as religious in modern culture and should be treated as such under the Constitution. [Rather, determining] whether questionable beliefs, practices, and organizations are religious by seeing how closely they resemble what is undeniably religious is a method that has been implicitly used by courts in difficult borderline cases [and] is consonant with Supreme Court decisions." See also Freeman, *The Misguided Search for the Constitutional Definition of "Religion,"* 71 Geo.L.J. 1519 (1983).

(b) *Judicial role.* In THOMAS v. REVIEW BD., fn. e in *Sherbert,* petitioner testified that, although his religious convictions forebade him to manufacture weapons, "he could, in good conscience, engage indirectly in the production of materials that might be used ultimately to fabricate arms—for example, as an employee of a raw material supplier or of a roll foundry." The Indiana Supreme Court, viewing petitioner's positions as inconsistent, ruled that "Thomas had made a merely 'personal philosophical choice rather than a religious choice.'"

The Court, per BURGER, C.J. reversed: "The determination of what is a 'religious' belief or practice is more often than not a difficult and delicate task, as the division in the Indiana Supreme Court attests. However, the resolution of that question is not to turn upon a judicial perception of the particular belief or practice in question; religious beliefs need not be acceptable, logical, consistent, or comprehensible to others in order to merit First Amendment protection.

" * * * Thomas' statements reveal no more than that he found work in the roll foundry sufficiently insulated from producing weapons of war. We see, therefore, that Thomas drew a line and it is not for us to say that the line he drew was an unreasonable one. Courts should not undertake to dissect religious beliefs because the believer admits that he is 'struggling' with his position or because his beliefs are not articulated with the clarity and precision that a more sophisticated person might employ.

"The Indiana court also appears to have given significant weight to the fact that another Jehovah's Witness had no scruples about working on tank turrets; for that other Witness, at least, such work was 'scripturally' acceptable. Intrafaith differences of that kind are not uncommon among followers of a particular creed, and the judicial process is singularly ill equipped to resolve such differences in relation to the Religion Clauses. One can, of course, imagine an asserted claim so bizarre, so clearly nonreligious in motivation, as not to be entitled to protection under the Free Exercise Clause; but that is not the case here, and the guarantee of free exercise is not limited to beliefs which are shared by all of the members of a religious sect. Particularly in this sensitive area, it is not within the judicial function and judicial competence to inquire whether the petitioner or his fellow worker more correctly perceived the commands of their common faith. Courts are not arbiters of scriptural interpretation.

"The narrow function of a reviewing court in this context is to determine whether there was an appropriate finding that petitioner terminated his work because of an honest conviction that such work was forbidden by his religion."

4. *Variable definition.* (a) May "religion" be defined differently for purposes of the establishment clause than the free exercise clause? Consider Galanter, *Religious Freedom in the United States: A Turning Point?* 1966 Wis. L.Rev. 217, 266–67: "[For purposes of the establishment clause, the] effect and

purpose of government action are not to be assessed by the religious sensibilities of the person who is complaining of the alleged establishment. It must be essentially religious in some widely shared public understanding. [But, for the free exercise clause, the] claimants' view of religion controls the characterization of their objection as a religious one." See also Tribe, supra, at 827–28. Does this analysis solve the dilemma of Manning, note 5, after *Schempp*, supra, at 66: "If religion need not be predicated on a belief in God or even in a god and if it may not be tested by the common consensus of what reasonable men would reasonably call religion, if it is so private that—so long as it does not inflict injury on society—it is immured from governmental interference and from judicial inquiry, [might] not a group of gymnasts proclaiming on their trampolines that physical culture is their religion be engaged in a religious exercise? And if Congress, in a particular Olympic year, appropriated funds to subsidize their calisthenics would this not [be] an establishment of religion?" See generally Note, *Transcendental Meditation and the Meaning of Religion Under the Establishment Clause,* 62 Minn.L.Rev. 887 (1978).

(b) May a group be considered a religion for the purpose of prosecution for fraudulent solicitation but not a religion for the purposes of statutory tax exemption or draft exemption? May government test the sincerity of asserted religious beliefs in one instance but not the other? See Nowak, Rotunda & Young, *Constitutional Law* 1071 (2d ed. 1983).

SECTION 3. PREFERENCE FOR AND AMONG RELIGIONS

LARSON v. VALENTE
456 U.S. 228, 102 S.Ct. 1673, 72 L.Ed.2d 33 (1982).

JUSTICE BRENNAN delivered the opinion of the Court.

[T]he Minnesota Charitable Solicitation Act [provides] for a system of registration and disclosure respecting charitable organizations, and is designed to protect the contributing public and charitable beneficiaries against fraudulent practices. [U]ntil 1978, all "religious organizations" were exempted [but in] 1978, the Minnesota Legislature [provided] that only those religious organizations that received more than half of their total contributions from members of affiliated organizations would remain exempt. [Appellees, members of the Unification Church, contended that the] fifty per cent rule violated the Establishment Clause. ＊ ＊ ＊

The clearest command of the Establishment Clause is that one religious denomination cannot be officially preferred over another. [*Everson.*]

This constitutional prohibition of denominational preferences is inextricably connected with the continuing vitality of the Free Exercise Clause [which] can be guaranteed only when legislators—and voters—are required to accord to their own religions the very same treatment given to small, new, or unpopular denominations. [W]hen we are presented with a state law granting a denominational preference, our precedents demand that we treat the law as suspect and that we apply strict scrutiny in adjudging its constitutionality.

The fifty per cent rule of § 309.515–1(b) clearly grants denominational preferences of the sort consistently and firmly deprecated in our precedents.[23]

---

23. Appellants urge that § 309.515–1(b) does not grant such preferences, but is merely   "a law based upon secular criteria which may not identically affect all religious organiza-

Consequently, that rule must be invalidated unless it is justified by a compelling governmental interest, and unless it is closely fitted to further that interest.
* * *

[W]e acknowledge, that the State of Minnesota has a significant interest in protecting its citizens from abusive practices in the solicitation of funds for charity, and that this interest retains importance when the solicitation is conducted by a religious organization. We thus agree with the Court of Appeals that the Act, "viewed as a whole, has a valid secular purpose," and we will therefore assume arguendo that the Act generally is addressed to a sufficiently "compelling" governmental interest. But [a]ppellants must demonstrate that the challenged fifty per cent rule is closely fitted to further the interest that it assertedly serves.

* * * Appellants' argument is based on three distinct premises: that members of a religious organization can and will exercise supervision and control over the organization's solicitation activities when membership contributions exceed fifty per cent; that membership control, assuming its existence, is an adequate safeguard against abusive solicitations of the public by the organization; and that the need for public disclosure rises in proportion with the *percentage* of non-member contributions. Acceptance of all three of these premises is necessary to appellants' conclusion, but we find no substantial support for any of them in the record. * * *

In *Lemon,* we announced three "tests" that a statute must pass in order to avoid the prohibition of the Establishment Clause. [These] "tests" are intended to apply to laws affording a uniform benefit to *all* religions, and not to provisions, like § 309.515–1(b)'s fifty per cent rule, that discriminate *among* religions. Although application of the *Lemon* tests is not necessary to the disposition of the case before us, those tests do reflect the same concerns that warranted the application of strict scrutiny to § 309.515–1(b)'s fifty per cent rule. The Court of Appeals found that rule to be invalid under the first two *Lemon* tests. We view the third of those tests as most directly implicated in the present case. * * *

tions." They accordingly cite *McGowan* and cases following *Everson* for the proposition that a statute's "disparate impact among religious organizations is constitutionally permissible when such distinctions result from application of secular criteria." We reject the argument. Section 309.515–1(b) is not simply a facially neutral statute, the provisions of which happen to have a "disparate impact" upon different religious organizations. On the contrary, § 309.515–1(b) makes explicit and deliberate distinctions between different religious organizations. We agree with the Court of Appeals' observation that the provision effectively distinguishes between "well-established churches" that have "achieved strong but not total financial support from their members," on the one hand, and "churches which are new and lacking in a constituency, or which, as a matter of policy, may favor public solicitation over general reliance on financial support from members," on the other hand. * * *

Appellants also argue that reversal of the Court of Appeals is required by *Gillette v.*

United States, [Sec. 2, I supra]. In that case we rejected an Establishment Clause attack upon § 6(j) of the Military Selective Service Act of 1967, which afforded "conscientious objector" status to any person who, "by reason of religious training and belief," was "conscientiously opposed to participation in war in any form." *Gillette* is readily distinguishable from the present case. Section 6(j) "focused on individual conscientious belief, not on sectarian affiliation." Under § 6(j), conscientious objector status was available on an equal basis to both the Quaker and the Roman Catholic, despite the distinction drawn by the latter's church between "just" and "unjust" wars. As we noted in *Gillette,* the "critical weakness of petitioners' establishment claim" arose "from the fact that § 6(j), on its face, simply [did] not discriminate on the basis of religious affiliation." In contrast, the statute challenged in the case before us focuses precisely and solely upon religious organizations.

It [is] plain that, as the Court of Appeals noted, "[T]he burden of compliance with the Act is certainly not de minimis." We do not suggest that the burdens of compliance with the Act would be intrinsically impermissible if they were imposed evenhandedly. But this statute [effects] the *selective* legislative imposition of burdens and advantages upon particular denominations. The "risk of politicizing religion" that inheres in such legislation is obvious, and indeed is confirmed by the provision's legislative history [which] demonstrates that the provision was drafted with the explicit intention of including particular religious denominations and excluding others. For example, [the] legislative history discloses that the legislators perceived that [proposed] language would bring a Roman Catholic archdiocese within the Act, that the legislators did not want the amendment to have that effect, and that an amendment deleting the [proposed] clause was passed in committee for the sole purpose of exempting the archdiocese from the provisions of the Act. On the other hand, there were certain religious organizations that the legislators did not want to exempt from the Act. One state senator explained that the fifty per cent rule was "an attempt to deal with the religious organizations which are soliciting on the street and soliciting by direct mail, but who are not substantial religious institutions [in] our state." Another senator said, "what you're trying to get at here is the people that are running around airports and running around streets and soliciting people and you're trying to remove them from the exemption that normally applies to religious organizations." Still another senator, who apparently had mixed feelings about the proposed provision, stated, "I'm not sure why we're so hot to regulate the Moonies anyway."   *   *   *[a]

JUSTICE WHITE, with whom JUSTICE REHNQUIST joins, dissenting.

[The] premise for the Court's [legal] standard is that the challenged provision is a deliberate and explicit legislative preference for some religious denominations over others. [The] rule itself, however, names no churches or denominations that are entitled to or denied the exemption. It neither qualifies nor disqualifies a church based on the kind or variety of its religious belief. Some religions will qualify and some will not, but this depends on the source of their contributions, not on their brand of religion.

[The Court's conclusion] that the limitation might burden the less well-organized denominations [is] contrary to what the state insists is readily evident from a list of those charitable organizations that have registered under the Act and of those that are exempt. It is claimed that both categories include not only well-established, but also not so well-established organizations. The Court appears to concede that the Minnesota law at issue does not constitute an establishment of religion merely because it has a disparate impact. An intentional preference must be expressed. To find that intention on the face of the provision at issue here seems to me to be patently wrong.[b]

[I] cannot join the Court's easy rejection of the state's submission that a valid secular purpose justifies basing the exemption on the percentage of external funding. [The] state has the same interest in requiring registration by organizations soliciting most of their funds from the public as it would have in requiring any charitable organization to register, including a religious organization, if it wants to solicit funds. And if the state determines that its interest in preventing fraud does not extend to those who do not raise a majority of their

---

a. The brief concurring opinion of Stevens, J., which did not discuss the merits, is omitted.

b. *Gillette* held that there was no religious "gerrymander" if there was "a neutral, secular basis for the lines government has drawn."

funds from the public, its interest in imposing the requirement on others is not thereby reduced in the least. Furthermore, as the state suggests, the legislature thought it made good sense, and the courts, including this one, should not so readily disagree.

[F]inally, the Court agrees with the Court of Appeals [that] the exemption must be extended to all religious organizations. The Court of Appeals noted that the exemption provision, so construed, could be said to prefer religious organizations over non-religious organizations and hence amount to an establishment of religion. Nevertheless, the Court of Appeals did not further address the question, and the Court says nothing of it now. Arguably, however, there is a more evident secular reason for exempting religious organizations who rely on their members to a great extent than there is to exempt all religious organizations, including those who raise all or nearly all of their funds from the public.

* * *[c]

Notes and Questions

1. *The Gillette rationale.* (a) Should the existence of a "neutral, secular justification" suffice to permit government preference—de jure or de facto— among religions? Consider Greenawalt, *All or Nothing at All: The Defeat of Selective Conscientious Objection,* 1971 Sup.Ct.Rev. 31, 71: "If a sociological survey indicated that Protestants generally work harder than Catholics, the government might simplify its hiring problems by interviewing only Protestants. If the doctors of Catholic hospitals were determined to be on the average more qualified than those at Lutheran hospitals, aid might be limited to the Catholic hospitals. It is, of course, inconceivable that such legislation would be passed and its unconstitutionality is [apparent]." How significant was the Court's observation that the *Gillette* law "attempts to accommodate free exercise values"?

(b) Was the Draft Act of 1917, which exempted only conscientious objectors affiliated with some "well-recognized religious sect" whose principles forbade participation in war, also valid under the *Gillette* rationale? Consider 48 Minn. L.Rev. 776–77 (1964): "Since pacifism often arises from religious beliefs, a workable method for ascertaining sincerity may have to be couched in terms of those beliefs. Such a test should be permissible, even though it may theoretically 'prefer' some sincere conscientious objectors over others, if it reasonably advances the [statute's] purpose by aiding local draft boards in administering the act. For example, since membership in an organized pacifist sect may be better evidence of sincerity than the mere assertion of pacificist beliefs, a requirement to that effect should be permissible." See also Comment, 64 Colum.L.Rev. 938 (1964).

2. *The Larson rationale.* Consider Choper, *The Free Exercise Clause,* in Choper, Kamisar & Tribe, *The Supreme Court: Trends and Developments 1982– 83,* 79–84 (1984): "*Larson* is really a free exercise clause decision parading in an establishment clause disguise. [The Court's holding] that discrimination among religions must survive strict scrutiny [is] classic free exercise clause analysis. [The] major disagreement between the majority and the dissent was over whether this law discriminated among religions or was simply a neutral law with a disparate impact on different religious groups. [But] even if the Minnesota statute does not explicitly distinguish among religious sects or churches,

---

c. Rehnquist, J., joined by Burger, C. J. and White and O'Connor, JJ., also dissented on the ground that the Unification Church had no standing.

nonetheless, isn't it bad enough that it expressly deals with the subject of religion and ends up favoring some and disfavoring others? Shouldn't it be as vulnerable as a general, neutral law that says nothing about religion but that happens to have an adverse impact on some religions—like the Wisconsin compulsory education to age 16 law? [The] problem is that when the Court has used the establishment clause, it has applied a much more lenient test for laws that expressly deal with religion and subject some religions to discriminatory treatment, than it has applied under the free exercise clause for general, neutral laws that come into conflict with religious beliefs. [*Gillette*] ruled that under the establishment clause, as long as there is some secular basis for the law, that is enough to validate it. [If] all that was required in [*Larson*] was *some* secular basis, there'd be no problem at all in sustaining the statute. [In] reality, I believe that the federal statute in *Gillette* survived strict scrutiny [because of the] strong government interest in raising an army and the difficulties in administering a draft exemption based on 'just war' beliefs. [I] think the *Gillette* doctrine has now effectively been abandoned, and I suggest rightly so. I think discrimination among religions—a preference of one religion over another— [should] be treated under the free exercise clause. I think *Larson,* although it certainly doesn't say it's using the free exercise clause, explicitly has a rationale that leads to that conclusion."

3. *Preference for "religious" objectors.* Is Congress' limitation of draft exemption to "religious" conscientious objectors valid? Consider Mansfield, *Conscientious Objection—1964 Term,* 1965 Relig. & Pub.Or. 3, 76: "[T]here are really no convincing reasons why the religious objector should be exempt and not the non-religious conscientious objector. [T]he religious objector's opposition rests on somewhat more fundamental grounds [and] makes reference to realities that can more easily be described as spiritual. But the non-religious conscientious objector's opposition does rest on basic propositions about the nature of reality and the significance of human existence; this is what distinguishes it from objection that is not even conscientious. Even if the non-religious conscientious objector does not subscribe to the answers nor perceive the vision of the religious objector, he does at least address himself to questions that are nearly as fundamental, and it is in respect to the dialogue within this general area of fundamental issues that government should take care not to prefer one answer over another." See Cohen & Greenspan, *Conscientious Objection, Democratic Theory, and the Constitution,* 29 U.Pitt.L.Rev. 389, 403 (1968): "Nothing is more repugnant to a sense of fairness than the rejection of the claim of a conscientious objector because he does not believe in a transcendent reality. If his belief were coupled with a belief that the sun controlled man's destiny, communicating it through sun-spots, his exemption would be immediately granted. This places a premium upon madness and is a celebration of cranks and utopians. The concerned citizen, whose belief is intelligible and commends itself more to our understanding is turned away because he did not indulge in fantastic flights of imagination." Does the "religious" exemption result in more or less government "entanglement" with religion than an exemption for *all* conscientious objectors?

4. *The establishment-free exercise "dilemma."* (a) Do the decisions in *Sherbert* and *Yoder* violate the establishment clause because if "government must sanction otherwise prohibited conduct merely because of its religious orientation and if the same activity is forbidden to nonreligionists, is this not a preferential establishment"? Donnici, *Governmental Encouragement of Religious Ideology: A Study of the Current Conscientious Objector Exemption from Military Service,* 13 J.Pub.L. 16, 43 (1964). Consider Kurland, *Religion and the Law* 112 (1962):

"The [free exercise and establishment] clauses should be read as stating a single precept: that government cannot utilize religion as a standard for action or inaction because these clauses, read together as they should be, prohibit classification in terms of religion either to confer a benefit or to impose a burden." [a] Similarly, for the view that the free exercise clause should generally only guarantee "equality of treatment for those who act out of sincere religious belief" and should afford special protection only for acts of "worship," as defined, see Fernandez, *The Free Exercise of Religion*, 36 So.Calif.L.Rev. 546 (1963). For the view that free exercise claims should be treated "no differently than free expression claims," see Marshall, *Solving the Free Exercise Dilemma: Free Exercise as Expression*, 67 Minn.L.Rev. 545 (1983).

Do these approaches falter because they fail to recognize "that both clauses are designed to maximize religious freedoms and that in particular the uniquely American establishment clause is largely designed to implement the free exercise clause"; thus, that "at least some governmental accommodations to religion which are designed to protect the free exercise of religion should be permissible under the establishment clause"? Moore, *The Supreme Court and the Relationship Between the "Establishment" and "Free Exercise" Clauses*, 42 Tex.L.Rev. 142, 196 (1963).

(b) Did the statute in *Gillette*, exempting only "religious" conscientious objectors, impermissibly prefer religion over nonreligion? In WELSH v. UNITED STATES, Sec. 2, II supra, four justices addressed the issue. WHITE, J., joined by Burger, C. J., and Stewart, J., found it valid: "First, § 6(j) may represent a purely practical judgment that religious objectors, however admirable, would be of no more use in combat than many others unqualified for military service. [On] this basis, the exemption has neither the primary purpose nor the effect of furthering religion. * * *

"Second, Congress may have [believed that] to deny the exemption would violate the Free Exercise Clause or at least raise grave problems in this respect. True, this Court has more than once stated its unwillingness to construe the First Amendment, standing alone, as requiring draft exemptions for religious believers. [But] just as in *Katzenbach v. Morgan*, [p. 1156 infra], where we accepted the judgment of Congress as to what legislation was appropriate to enforce the Equal Protection Clause of the Fourteenth Amendment, here we should respect congressional judgment accommodating the Free Exercise Clause and the power to raise armies. This involves no surrender of the Court's function as ultimate arbiter in disputes over interpretation of the Constitution. But it was enough in *Katzenbach* 'to perceive a basis upon which the Congress might resolve the conflict as it did' * * *.

"[If] it is 'favoritism' and not 'neutrality' to exempt religious believers from the draft, is it 'neutrality' and not 'inhibition' of religion to compel religious believers to fight * * *? It cannot be ignored that the First Amendment itself contains a religious classification [and the free exercise clause] protects conduct as well as religious belief and speech. [It] was not suggested [in *Braunfeld*] that the Sunday closing laws in 21 States exempting Sabbatarians and others violated the Establishment Clause because no provision was made for others who claimed nonreligious reasons for not working on some particular day of the week. Nor

---

a. For thoughtful comment, see Kauper, *Book Review*, 41 Texas L.Rev. 467 (1963); Pfeffer, *Religion-Blind Government*, 15 Stan.L. Rev. 389 (1963); Mansfield, *Book Review*, 52 Calif.L.Rev. 212 (1964). See generally Note, *The Conscientious Objector and the First Amendment*, 34 U.Chi.L.Rev. 79 (1966); Kauper, *Government and Religion: The Search for Absolutes*, 11 Mich.Q.Rev., No. 3 (1972).

was it intimated in *Zorach* that the no-establishment holding might be infirm because only those pursuing religious studies for designated periods were released from the public school routine; neither was it hinted that a public school's refusal to institute a released time program would violate the Free Exercise Clause. The Court in *Sherbert* construed the Free Exercise Clause to require special treatment for Sabbatarians under the State's unemployment compensation law. But the State could deal specially with Sabbatarians whether the Free Exercise Clause required it or not * * *.

"The Establishment Clause [is] not wholly auxiliary to the Free Exercise Clause. It bans some involvements of the State with religion which otherwise might be consistent with the Free Exercise Clause. But when in the rationally based judgment of Congress free exercise of religion calls for shielding religious objectors from compulsory combat duty, I am reluctant to frustrate the legislative will by striking down the statutory exemption because it does not also reach those to whom the Free Exercise Clause offers no protection whatsoever."

HARLAN, J., disagreed, believing that Congress could "eliminate *all* exemptions for conscientious objectors. Such a course would be wholly 'neutral' * * *. However, having chosen to exempt, it cannot draw the line between theistic or nontheistic religious beliefs on the one hand and secular beliefs on the other. [I]t must encompass the class of individuals it purports to exclude, those whose beliefs emanate from a purely moral, ethical, or philosophical source.[9] The common denominator must be the intensity of moral conviction with which a belief is [held]. *Everson,* the *Sunday Closing Law Cases* and *Allen,* all sustained legislation on the premise that it was neutral in its application and thus did not constitute an establishment, notwithstanding the fact that it may have assisted religious groups by giving them the same benefits accorded to nonreligious groups.[12] To the extent that *Zorach* and *Sherbert* stand for the proposition that the Government may (*Zorach*), or must (*Sherbert*), shape its secular programs to accommodate the beliefs and tenets of religious groups, I think these cases unsound.[13]"

  (c) In THOMAS v. REVIEW BD., fn. e in *Sherbert,* REHNQUIST, J., dissented, finding the result "inconsistent with many of our prior Establishment Clause cases"[2]: "If Indiana were to legislate what the Court today requires—an

9. * * * I suggested [in *Sherbert*] that a State could constitutionally create exceptions to its program to accommodate religious scruples. [But] any such exception in order to satisfy the Establishment Clause [would] have to be sufficiently broad so as to be religiously neutral. This would require creating an exception for anyone who, as a matter of conscience, could not comply with the statute. * * *

12. [I] fail to see how [§ 6(j)] has "any substantial legislative purpose" apart from honoring the conscience of individuals who oppose war on only religious grounds. * * *

13. [At] the very least the Constitution requires that the State not excuse students early for the purpose of receiving religious instruction when it does not offer to nonreligious students the opportunity to use school hours for spiritual or ethical instruction of a nonreligious nature. Moreover, whether a released-time program cast in terms of improving "con-

science" to the exclusion of artistic or cultural pursuits, would be "neutral" and consistent with the requirement of "voluntarism," is by no means an easy question. * * *

2. To the extent *Sherbert* was correctly decided, it might be argued that cases such as *McCollum, Engel, Schempp, Lemon,* and *Nyquist* were wrongly decided. The "aid" rendered to religion in these latter cases may not be significantly different, in kind or degree, than the "aid" afforded Mrs. Sherbert or Thomas. For example, if the State in *Sherbert* could not deny compensation to one refusing work for religious reasons, it might be argued that a State may not deny reimbursement to students who choose for religious reasons to attend parochial schools. The argument would be that although a State need not allocate any funds to education, once it has done so, it may not require any person to sacrifice his religious beliefs in order to obtain an equal education. There can be little doubt that to the extent secular education provides

unemployment compensation law which permitted benefits to be granted to those persons who quit their jobs for religious reasons—the statute would 'plainly' violate the Establishment Clause as interpreted in such cases as *Lemon* and *Nyquist*. First, [the] proviso would clearly serve only a religious purpose. It would grant financial benefits for the sole purpose of accommodating religious beliefs. Second, there can be little doubt that the primary effect of the proviso would be to 'advance' religion by facilitating the exercise of religious belief. Third, any statute including such a proviso would surely 'entangle' the State in religion far more than the mere grant of tax exemptions, as in *Walz,* or the award of tuition grants and tax credits, as in *Nyquist*. By granting financial benefits to persons solely on the basis of their religious beliefs, the State must necessarily inquire whether the claimant's belief is 'religious' and whether it is sincerely held. [Just] as I think that Justice Harlan in *Sherbert* correctly stated the proper approach to free exercise questions, I believe that Justice Stewart, dissenting in *Schempp,* accurately stated the reach of the Establishment Clause. He explained that the Establishment Clause is limited to 'government support of proselytizing activities of religious sects by throwing the weight of secular authorities behind the dissemination of religious tenets.' See *McCollum* (Reed, J., dissenting) (impermissible aid is only 'purposeful assistance directly to the church itself or to some religious [group] performing ecclesiastical functions'). Conversely, governmental assistance which does not have the effect of 'inducing' religious belief, but instead merely 'accommodates' or implements an independent religious choice does not impermissibly involve the government in religious choices and therefore does not violate the Establishment [Clause]. I would think that in this case, as in *Sherbert,* had the state voluntarily chosen to pay unemployment compensation benefits to persons who left their jobs for religious reasons, such aid would be constitutionally permissible because it redounds directly to the benefit of the individual."

See also Schwartz, *No Imposition of Religion: The Establishment Clause Value,* 77 Yale L.J. 692, 693, 723, 728 (1968): "[T]he dilemma results from an unnecessarily broad reading of the establishment clause; that clause should be read to prohibit only aid which has as its motive or substantial effect the imposition of religious belief or practice * * *. Conversely, aid which does not have the effect of inducing religious belief, but merely accommodates or implements an individual religious choice, does not increase the danger of religion and [does] not violate the no-imposition standard. * * * Exemption of Mrs. Sherbert [represents] a judgment that the exercise of Seventh-day Adventism is more worthy than bowling on Saturdays, but the exemption has no significant effect and arguably no effect at all upon whether someone becomes a Seventh-day Adventist. Similarly, the Sabbatarian exemption from Sunday closing laws does not induce one to become a Jew; draft exemption to conscientious objectors does not normally induce one to become a Quaker; closing the public schools on all religious holidays or on every Wednesday at 2 P.M. does not induce the adoption of religion; and compulsory Sunday closing, while implementing an independent desire to attend church services, has no substantial effect upon the creation of such desire. The availability of preferential aid to religious exercise may, to be sure, induce false claims of religious belief, but the establishment clause is not

answers to important moral questions without reference to religion or teaches that there are no answers, a person in one sense sacrifices his religious belief by attending secular schools. And even if such "aid" were not constitutionally compelled by the Free Exercise Clause, Justice Harlan may well be right in *Sherbert* when he finds sufficient flexibility in the Establishment Clause to permit the States to voluntarily choose to grant such benefits to individuals.

concerned with false claims of belief, only with induced belief." Does this distinguish *Engel* from *Sherbert?* Do you agree with all of the *factual* assumptions made? Under this analysis, what result in *Epperson?* What of a small governmental payment to all persons who would lose salary because they have to be absent from their jobs in order to attend religious services?

Compare Choper, note after *Epperson* supra, at 691, 697–700: "My proposal for resolving the conflict between the two Religion Clauses seeks to implement their historically and contemporarily acknowledged common goal: to safeguard religious liberty. [I]t is only when an accommodation would jeopardize religious liberty—when it would coerce, compromise, or influence religious choice—that it would fail. [For example, in *Yoder*, unless] it could be shown that relieving the Amish [would] tend to coerce, compromise, or influence religious choice—and it is extremely doubtful that it could—the exemption was permissible under the Establishment Clause. In contrast, in *Sherbert*, [the] exemption results in impairment of religious liberty because compulsorily raised tax funds must be used to subsidize Mrs. Sherbert's exercise of religion. [In the draft exemption cases], professing a personal 'religion' (as opposed to 'essentially political, sociological or philosophical considerations') was enough to gain the enormous advantage of avoiding combat duty. [D]raftees seeking exemption would have to formulate a statement of personal doctrine that would pass muster. This endeavor would involve deep and careful thought, and perhaps reading in philosophy and religion. Some undoubtedly would be persuaded by what they read. Moreover, the theory of 'cognitive dissonance'—which posits that to avoid madness we tend to become what we hold ourselves to be and what others believe us to be—also suggests that some initially fraudulent claims of belief in a personal religion would develop into true belief. Thus, a draft exemption for religious objectors threatens values of religious freedom by encouraging the adoption of religious beliefs by those who seek to qualify for the benefit."

(d) Was the "aid" rendered religion by the programs in *McCollum, Engel* and *Schempp* any different, in kind or degree, than the "aid" afforded religion by statutory exemptions from Sunday Closing Laws for Sabbatarians, by draft exemptions for religious conscientious objectors, by government provision of military chaplains? May it be said of any of these that its purpose is "secular" or "nonreligious"? Consider Katz, *Note on the Constitutionality of Shared Time,* 1964 Relig. & Pub.Or. 85, 88: "It is no violation of neutrality for the government to express its concern for religious freedom by measures which merely neutralize what would otherwise be restrictive effects of government action. Provision for voluntary worship in the armed forces is constitutional, not because government policy may properly favor religion, but because the government is not required to exercise its military powers in a manner restrictive of religious freedom. Affirmative government action to maintain religious freedom in these instances serves the secular purpose of promoting a constitutional right, the free exercise of religion."

(e) THORNTON v. CALDOR, INC., __ U.S. __, 105 S.Ct. 2914, 86 L.Ed.2d 557 (1985), per BURGER, C.J., held that a Connecticut law—which provided "that those who observe a Sabbath any day of the week as a matter of religious conviction must be relieved of the duty to work on that day, no matter what burden or inconvenience this imposes on the employer or fellow workers"—"has a primary effect that impermissibly advances a particular religious practice" and thus violates the establishment clause: "The statute arms Sabbath observers with an absolute and unqualified right not to work on whatever day they designate as their Sabbath [and thus] goes beyond having an incidental or remote effect of advancing religion." [b]

O'CONNOR, J., joined by Marshall, J., concurred, distinguishing "the religious accommodation provisions of Title VII of the Civil Rights Act [which] require private employers to reasonably accommodate the religious practices of employees unless to do so would cause undue hardship to the employer's business": "In my view, a statute outlawing employment discrimination based on race, color, religion, sex or national origin has the valid secular purpose of assuring employment opportunity to all groups in our pluralistic society. Since Title VII calls for reasonable rather than absolute accommodation and extends that requirement to all religious beliefs and practices rather than protecting only the Sabbath observance, I believe an objective observer would perceive it as an anti-discrimination law rather than an endorsement of religion or a particular religious practice." [c]

Was the purpose or effect of the *Thornton* statute any different than that of the Court's decisions in *Sherbert, Thomas* and *Yoder?* For purposes of the establishment clause, of what significance, if any, is the fact that the *Thornton* statute grants "an absolute and unqualified right not to work" rather than a Title VII-like exemption? Consider Moore, supra, at 196–97: "[L]aws which protect the *free exercise* of religion should be distinguished from those which merely promote the *exercise* of a particular religion or religious belief. Almost any law favoring religion would fall into this latter [category]. For example, in *Engel* the use of the officially written Regent's prayer in the public schools promotes the exercise of a particular religious belief. The use of the prayer, though, does not protect the free exercise of religion. In fact, strong arguments can be made that such use indirectly threatens free exercise. Because of this distinction, admittedly one of degree, the *Engel* decision under the establishment clause is in no way in conflict with the free exercise clause." If the Regents' prayer "does not protect the *free exercise* of religion," does exempting Mrs. Sherbert do so? Does the state's failure to "favor religion" in each case simply "make the practice of religious beliefs more expensive"?

Does the *Thornton* statute "promote" and "endorse" a particular "religion" or "religious belief" or "religious practice" any moreso than the Court's decisions in *Sherbert, Thomas* and *Yoder,* or than the statutory exemptions from the draft or Sunday Closing Laws? Do all these exemptions simply "accommodate" religion? See Choper, supra.

Consider also O'Connor, J., concurring in *Wallace v. Jaffree,* Sec. 1, I supra, "[A] rigid application of the *Lemon* test would invalidate legislation exempting religious observers from generally applicable government obligations. By definition, such legislation has a religious purpose and effect in promoting the free exercise of religion. On the other hand, judicial deference to all legislation that purports to facilitate the free exercise of religion would completely vitiate the Establishment Clause. Any statute pertaining to religion can be viewed as an 'accommodation' of free exercise rights. Indeed, the statute at issue in *Lemon* [can] be viewed as an accommodation of the religious beliefs of parents who choose to send their children to religious schools.

"It [is] difficult to square any notion of 'complete neutrality' with the mandate of the Free Exercise Clause that government must sometimes exempt a religious observer from an otherwise generally applicable obligation. A government that confers a benefit on an explicitly religious basis is not neutral toward religion. See *Welsh* (White, J., dissenting).

b. Rehnquist, J., dissented without opinion.

c. See also O'Connor, J.'s concurrence in *Wallace v. Jaffree,* below.

"The solution to the conflict between the religion clauses lies not in 'neutrality,' but rather in identifying workable limits to the Government's license to promote the free exercise of religion. [O]ne can plausibly assert that government pursues free exercise clause values when it lifts a government-imposed burden on the free exercise of religion. If a statute falls within this category, then the standard Establishment Clause test should be modified accordingly. [T]he Court should simply acknowledge that the religious purpose of such a statute is legitimated by the Free Exercise Clause. I would also go further. In assessing the effect of such a statute—that is, in determining whether the statute conveys the message of endorsement of religion or a particular religious belief—courts should assume that the 'objective observer,' is acquainted with the Free Exercise Clause and the values it promotes. Thus individual perceptions, or resentment that a religious observer is exempted from a particular government requirement, would be entitled to little weight if the Free Exercise Clause strongly supported the exemption.

"While this 'accommodation' analysis would help reconcile our Free Exercise and Establishment Clause standards, it would not save Alabama's moment of silence law. If we assume that the religious activity that Alabama seeks to protect is silent prayer, then it is difficult to discern any state-imposed burden on that activity that is lifted by Alabama Code § 16–1–20.1. No law prevents a student who is so inclined from praying silently in public schools. [Of] course, the State might argue that § 16–1–20.1 protects not silent prayer, but rather group silent prayer under State sponsorship. Phrased in these terms, the burden lifted by the statute is not one imposed by the State of Alabama, but by the Establishment Clause as interpreted in *Engel* and *Schempp*. In my view, it is beyond the authority of the State of Alabama to remove burdens imposed by the Constitution itself."

Assuming the validity of the distinction between *McCollum, Engel,* and *Schempp,* on the one hand, and the programs such as exemption from the draft etc. on the other, are the above approaches nonetheless undesirable because they result not merely in protection of free exercise (or neutrality or accommodation) but in relieving persons with certain religious beliefs of significant burdens from which many other persons strongly desire to be exempted? That, in this sense, there is "preference" for minority religions and "discrimination" against the other persons because of their religion or lack of it? Should free exercise exemptions "be allowed only if the petitioner agrees to the imposition of some alternative duty or burden"? Note, 91 Harv.L.Rev. at 1082. Consider Galanter, note 4, Sec. 2, II supra, at 290–91: "[In *Sherbert*] it was clear that the state was already solicitous of the scruples of Sunday worshippers, though not of Saturday ones. In such a case, it is easy to appreciate that the exception [required by the decision] is restorative or equalizing. It puts the minority in the same position that the majority enjoys. [But] can it be said that the kind of disparity found in *Sherbert* between the treatment of majority and minority is a unique or unusual thing? Whatever seriously interferes with majority religious beliefs and practices is unlikely to become a legal requirement—for example, work on Sunday or Christmas. And whatever the majority considers necessary for its religious practice is quite unlikely to be prohibited by law. And whatever the majority finds religiously objectionable is unlikely to become a legal requirement—for example, medical practices which substantial groups find abhorrent, like contraception, sterilization, euthanasia, or abortion. Exceptions then, give to minorities what majorities have by virtue of suffrage and representative government. The question is not whether the state may prefer these minorities, but whether it may counterbalance the natural advantages of majorities."

Chapter 6

EQUAL PROTECTION

Virtually no legislation applies universally and treats all persons equally; all laws classify (or "discriminate") by imposing special burdens (or granting exemptions from such burdens) or by conferring special benefits on some people and not others. Under what circumstances do such laws violate the fourteenth amendment's command that no state shall "deny to any person within its jurisdiction the equal protection of the laws"? [a]

Despite the fact that the language of the equal protection clause is not confined to racial discrimination, the *Slaughter-House Cases,* p. 63 supra (the first decision interpreting the Civil War amendments), "doubt[ed] very much whether any action of a state not directed by way of discrimination against the negroes as a class, or on account of their race, will ever be held to come within the purview of this provision." Sec. 2 will concern the "strict scrutiny" given to racial (and ethnic) classifications which the Court has deemed to be "suspect." Sec. 3 will consider the extension of a nondeferential standard of review to government action that disadvantages several other discrete groups. At least as early as 1897, however, the Court invoked the equal protection clause to invalidate a commonplace economic regulation that obligated railroad defendants (but not others) to pay the attorneys' fees of successful plaintiffs. The Court acknowledged that "as a general proposition, [it] is undeniably true [that] it is not within the scope of the Fourteenth Amendment to withhold from States the power of classification." But "it must appear" that a classification is "based upon some reasonable ground—some difference which bears a just and proper

---

a. By its terms, the equal protection clause does not apply to the federal government. A series of decisions, however, has held that the fifth amendment's due process clause—although not containing the language of equal protection—forbids "unjustifiable" discrimination (*Bolling v. Sharpe,* Sec. 2, II infra) and that—except under special circumstances (see Sec. 3, II infra: "Alienage")—the "approach to Fifth Amendment equal protection claims has always been precisely the same as to equal protection claims under the Fourteenth Amendment" (*Weinberger v. Wiesenfeld,* Sec. 3, IV infra).

In 1976, *Hampton v. Wong,* Sec. 3, II infra, advanced a different approach. It stated that "when a federal rule is applicable to only a limited territory, such as the District of Columbia, or an insular possession, and when there is no special national interest involved, the Due Process Clause has been construed as having the same significance as the Equal Protection Clause," but suggested a different standard for "a federal rule having a nation-wide impact." Subsequent decisions, however, have continued to treat equal protection claims against the federal government under the fifth amendment in the same way as equal protection claims against the states under the fourteenth amendment, even though the challenged federal rule had "nationwide impact." See generally Karst, *The Fifth Amendment's Guarantee of Equal Protection,* 55 N.C.L.Rev. 541 (1977).

relation to the attempted classification—and is not a mere arbitrary selection." *Gulf, C. & S. F. Ry. v. Ellis,* 165 U.S. 150, 17 S.Ct. 255, 41 L.Ed. 666 (1897).[b]

Sec. 1 deals with this "traditional approach" under the equal protection clause to general economic and social welfare regulations, as distinguished from either "suspect" or "quasi-suspect" classifications (Secs. 2–3) or laws that affect what have come to be known as "fundamental rights" (Sec. 4).

SECTION 1. TRADITIONAL APPROACH

As observed in Ch. 6, Sec. 2, the due process clause was the usual provision used by the Court in the first third of this century to overturn a great many economic and social welfare regulations. But despite Holmes, J.'s reference during this period to the equal protection clause as "the usual last resort of constitutional arguments," [a] the Court held that approximately twenty such state and local laws violated equal protection.[b] In doing so, the Court employed the deferential standard of judicial review called for by the "traditional approach" which granted a state "a broad discretion in classification in the exercise of its power of regulation" and interposed the "constitutional guaranty of equal protection" only "against discriminations that are entirely arbitrary." [c]

But fuller articulations of the standard of review often appeared to vary significantly. For example, LINDSLEY v. NATURAL CARBONIC GAS CO., 220 U.S. 61, 31 S.Ct. 337, 55 L.Ed. 369 (1911), illustrates an extremely deferential formulation: "1. The equal protection clause [does] not take from the state the power to classify in the adoption of police laws, but admits of the exercise of a wide scope of discretion in that regard, and avoids what is done only when it is without any reasonable basis and therefore is purely arbitrary. 2. A classification having some reasonable basis does not offend against that clause merely because it is not made with mathematical nicety, or because in practice it results in some inequality. 3. When the classification in such a law is called in question, if any state of facts reasonably can be conceived that would sustain it, the existence of that state of facts at the time the law was enacted must be assumed. 4. One who assails the classification in such a law must carry the burden of showing that it does not rest upon any reasonable basis, but is essentially arbitrary." [d] In contrast, ROYSTER GUANO CO. v. VIRGINIA, 253 U.S. 412, 40 S.Ct. 560, 64 L.Ed. 989 (1920), suggests a more active judicial role: "[T]he classification must be reasonable, not arbitrary, and must rest upon some ground of difference having a fair and substantial relation to the object of the legislation, so that all persons similarly circumstanced shall be treated alike."

The materials that follow concern the Court's use of the "traditional approach" under equal protection to economic and social welfare regulations since the late 1930s when it abandoned active substantive due process review of such legislation.

---

b. For an even earlier invocation of the equal protection clause to invalidate a classification of transportation rates, see *Reagan v. Farmer's Loan & Trust Co.,* 154 U.S. 362, 14 S.Ct. 1047, 38 L.Ed. 1014 (1894). For an informative review of the Court's earliest use of the equal protection clause, see 2 Dorsen, Bender, Neuborne & Law, *Political and Civil Rights in the United States* 57–58 (Law School ed., 4th ed. 1979).

a. *Buck v. Bell,* 274 U.S. 200, 47 S.Ct. 584, 71 L.Ed. 1000 (1927).

b. 2 Dorsen et al., supra, at 336.

c. *Smith v. Cahoon,* 283 U.S. 553, 51 S.Ct. 582, 75 L.Ed. 1264 (1931).

d. For more recent reliance on this language, see *McGowan v. Maryland,* 366 U.S. 420, 81 S.Ct. 1101, 6 L.Ed.2d 393 (1961), per Warren, C.J., unanimously rejecting an equal protection challenge to state laws requiring stores to be closed on Sunday but containing numerous exemptions.

RAILWAY EXPRESS AGENCY v. NEW YORK

336 U.S. 106, 69 S.Ct. 463, 93 L.Ed. 533 (1949).

MR. JUSTICE DOUGLAS delivered the opinion of the Court.

[T]he Traffic Regulations of the City of New York [provide]: "No person shall operate [on] any street an advertising vehicle; [except for] business notices upon business delivery vehicles, so long as such vehicles are engaged in the usual business [of] the owner and not used merely or mainly for advertising."

Appellant [operates] about 1,900 trucks in New York City and sells the space on the exterior sides of these trucks for advertising [for] the most part unconnected with its own business. It was convicted * * *.

The court [below] concluded that advertising on [vehicles] constitutes a distraction to vehicle drivers and to pedestrians alike and therefore affects the safety of the public in the use of the streets. We do not sit to weigh evidence on the due process issue in order to determine whether the regulation is sound or appropriate; nor is it our function to pass judgment on its wisdom. See *Olsen v. Nebraska* [p. 399 supra]. * * *

The question of equal protection of the laws is pressed more strenuously on us. [It] is said, for example, that one of appellant's trucks carrying the advertisement of a commercial house would not cause any greater distraction of pedestrians and vehicle drivers than if the commercial house carried the same advertisement on its own truck. Yet the regulation allows the latter to do what the former is forbidden from doing. It is therefore contended that the classification which the regulation makes has no relation to the traffic problem since a violation turns not on what kind of advertisements are carried on trucks but on whose trucks they are carried.

That, however, is a superficial way of analyzing the [problem]. The local authorities may well have concluded that those who advertised their own wares on their trucks do not present the same traffic problem in view of the nature or extent of the advertising which they use. * * *

We cannot say that that judgment is not an allowable one. Yet if it is, the classification has relation to the purpose for which it is made and does not contain the kind of discrimination against which the Equal Protection Clause affords protection. It is by such practical considerations based on experience rather than by theoretical inconsistencies that the question of equal protection is to be answered. And the fact that New York City sees fit to eliminate from traffic this kind of distraction but does not touch what may be even greater ones in a different category, such as the vivid displays on Times Square, is immaterial. It is no requirement of equal protection that all evils of the same genus be eradicated or none at all. * * *

Affirmed.

MR. JUSTICE RUTLEDGE acquiesces in the Court's opinion and judgment, dubitante on the question of equal protection of the laws.

MR. JUSTICE JACKSON, concurring. * * *

The burden should rest heavily upon one who would persuade us to use the due process clause to strike down a substantive [law]. Even its provident use against municipal regulations frequently disables all government—state, municipal and federal—from dealing with the conduct in question because the requirement of due process is also applicable to State and Federal Governments. * * *

Invocation of the equal protection clause, on the other hand, does not disable any governmental body from dealing with the subject at hand. It merely means that the prohibition or regulation must have a broader impact. I regard it as a salutary doctrine that cities, states and the Federal Government must exercise their powers so as not to discriminate between their inhabitants except upon some reasonable differentiation fairly related to the object of regulation. [T]here is no more effective practical guaranty against arbitrary and unreasonable government than to require that the principles of law which officials would impose upon a minority must be imposed generally. Conversely, nothing opens the door to arbitrary action so effectively as to allow those officials to pick and choose only a few to whom they will apply legislation and thus to escape the political retribution that might be visited upon them if larger numbers were affected. Courts can take no better measure to assure that laws will be just than to require that laws be equal in operation. * * *

In this case, if the City of New York should assume that display of any advertising on vehicles tends and intends to distract the attention of persons using the highways and to increase the dangers of its traffic, I should think it fully within its constitutional powers to forbid it all. [Instead], however, the City seeks to reduce the hazard only by saying that while some may, others may not exhibit such appeals. The same display, for example, advertising cigarettes, which this appellant is forbidden to carry on its trucks, may be carried on the trucks of a cigarette dealer. [The] courts of New York have declared that the sole nature and purpose of the regulation before us is to reduce traffic hazards. There is not even a pretense here that the traffic hazard created by the advertising which is forbidden is in any manner or degree more hazardous than that which is permitted. * * *

* * * I do not think differences of treatment under law should be approved on classification because of differences unrelated to the legislative purpose. The equal protection clause ceases to assure either equality or protection if it is avoided by any conceivable difference that can be pointed out between those bound and those left free. This Court has often announced the principle that the differentiation must have an appropriate relation to the object of the [legislation].

The question in my mind comes to this. Where individuals contribute to an evil or danger in the same way and to the same degree, may those who do so for hire be prohibited, while those who do so for their own commercial ends but not for hire be allowed to continue? I think the answer has to be that the hireling may be put in a class by himself and may be dealt with differently than those who act on their own. But this is not merely because such a discrimination will enable the lawmaker to diminish the evil. That might be done by many classifications, which I should think wholly unsustainable. It is rather because there is a real difference between doing in self-interest and doing for hire, so that it is one thing to tolerate action from those who act on their own and it is another thing to permit the same action to be promoted for a price. [I]n view of the control I would concede to cities to protect citizens in quiet and orderly use for their proper purposes of the highways and public places, I think the judgment below must be affirmed.

NEW ORLEANS v. DUKES

427 U.S. 297, 96 S.Ct. 2513, 49 L.Ed.2d 511 (1976).

Per Curiam.

[A 1972 New Orleans ordinance banned all pushcart food vendors in the French Quarter ("Vieux Carre") except those who had continuously operated there for eight or more years. Two vendors had done so for twenty or more years and qualified under the "grandfather clause." Appellee, who had operated a pushcart for only two years, attacked the ordinance.]

* * * Stating expressly [that] *Morey v. Doud,* 354 U.S. 457, 77 S.Ct. 1344, 1 L.Ed.2d 1485 (1957),ᵃ was "our chief guide in resolving this case," the Court of Appeals focused on the "exclusionary character" of the ordinance and its concomitant "creation of a protected monopoly for the favored class member." [Thus,] the ordinance was declared violative of [equal protection].

When local economic regulation is challenged solely as violating the Equal Protection Clause, this Court consistently defers to legislative determinations as to the desirability of particular statutory discriminations. Unless a classification trammels fundamental personal rights or is drawn upon inherently suspect distinctions such as race, religion, or alienage, our decisions presume the constitutionality of the statutory discriminations and require only that the classification challenged be rationally related to a legitimate state interest. States are accorded wide latitude in the regulation of their local economies under their police powers, and rational distinctions may be made with substantially less than mathematical exactitude. Legislatures may implement their program step by step in such economic areas, adopting regulations that only partially ameliorate a perceived evil and deferring complete elimination of the evil to future regulations. See, e.g., *Williamson v. Lee Optical Co.*ᵇ In short, the judiciary may not sit as a superlegislature to judge the wisdom or desirability of legislative policy determinations made in areas that neither affect fundamental rights nor proceed along suspect lines; in the local economic sphere, it is only the invidious discrimination, the wholly arbitrary act, which cannot stand consistently with the Fourteenth Amendment. See, e.g., *Ferguson v. Skrupa.*[5]

[New Orleans'] classification rationally furthers the purpose which [the] city had identified as its objective in enacting the provision, that is, as a means "to preserve the appearance and custom valued by the Quarter's residents and attractive to tourists." The legitimacy of that objective is obvious. The City Council plainly could further that objective by making the reasoned judgment that street peddlers and hawkers tend to interfere with the charm and beauty of

---

a. *Morey* held that an Illinois statute that comprehensively regulated companies that sold money orders, but exempted American Express Co. by name, violated equal protection.

b. In *Lee Optical,* p. 76 supra, the statute generally prohibiting the fitting of eyeglasses without a prescription exempted businesses that sold ready-to-wear glasses. The Court found no violation of equal protection: "Evils in the same field may be of different dimensions and proportions, requiring different remedies. Or so the legislature may think. Or the reform may take one step at a time, addressing itself to the phase of the problem which seems most acute to the legislative mind. The legislature may select one phase of one field and apply a remedy there, neglecting the others. [For] all this record shows, the ready-to-wear branch of this business may not loom large in Oklahoma or may present problems of regulation distinct from the other branch."

5. *Ferguson* [p. 76 supra] presented an analogous situation. There, a Kansas statute excepted lawyers from the prohibition of a statute making it a misdemeanor for any person to engage in the business of debt adjusting. We held that the exception of lawyers was not a denial of [equal protection].

an historic area [and] that to ensure the economic vitality of that area, such businesses should be substantially curtailed in the Vieux Carre, if not totally banned.

It is suggested that the "grandfather provision" [was] a totally arbitrary and irrational method of achieving the city's purpose. But rather than proceeding by the immediate and absolute abolition of all pushcart food vendors, the city could rationally [decide] that newer businesses were less likely to have built up substantial reliance interests in continued operation in the Vieux Carre and that the two vendors who qualified under the "grandfather clause" [had] themselves become part of the distinctive character and charm that distinguishes the Vieux Carre. We cannot say that these judgments so lack rationality that they constitute a constitutionally impermissible denial of equal protection.

Nevertheless, [the] Court of Appeals held that even though the exemption of the two vendors was rationally related to legitimate city interests on the basis of facts extant when the ordinance was amended, the "grandfather clause" still could not stand because "the hypothesis that a present eight year veteran of the pushcart hot dog market in the Vieux Carre will continue to operate in a manner more consistent with the traditions of the Quarter than would any other operator is without foundation." Actually, the reliance on the statute's potential irrationality in *Morey*, as the dissenters in that case correctly pointed out, (Frankfurter, J., joined by Harlan, J., dissenting), was a needlessly intrusive judicial infringement on the State's legislative powers, and we have concluded that the equal protection analysis employed in that opinion should no longer be followed. *Morey* was the only case in the last half century to invalidate a wholly economic regulation solely on equal protection grounds, and we are now satisfied that the decision was erroneous. * * *

Reversed.

MR. JUSTICE MARSHALL concurs in the judgment.

MR. JUSTICE STEVENS took no part in [the] case.

Notes and Questions

1. *Legislative purpose.* Of what relevance in *Railway Express* was it that the state courts "declared that the sole purpose" of the law "is to reduce traffic hazards"? Would it be more accurate (and realistic) to describe the purpose as being "to promote public safety slightly by reducing the number of distractions on the sides of moving vehicles to the extent this is feasible without jeopardizing the economic well-being of those merchants who advertise on their own trucks," Note, *Legislative Purpose, Rationality and Equal Protection,* 82 Yale L.J. 123, 144 (1972)—a purpose to which the classification unquestionably was "rationally related"? Is it not true that many government programs "involve goals that reflect an accommodation of various purposes which are determined by subtle or blatant policy trade-offs"? Id. That often "the legislature is simply a 'market-like arena' in which individuals and special interest groups trade with each other through representatives to further their own private ends"? Bice, *Rationality Analysis in Constitutional Law,* 65 Minn.L.Rev. 1, 19 (1980).

Are such legislative purposes (or goals) "legitimate"? "Constitutionally permissible"? Consider Tussman & tenBroek, *The Equal Protection of the Laws,* 37 Calif.L.Rev. 341, 350 (1949): "[T]he requirement that laws be equal rests upon a theory of legislation quite distinct from that of pressure groups—a theory which puts forward some conception of a 'general good' as the 'legitimate public purpose' at which legislation must aim, and according to which the triumph of

private or group pressure marks the corruption of the legislative process."
Compare Posner, *The DeFunis Case and the Constitutionality of Preferential
Treatment of Racial Minorities*, 1974 Sup.Ct.Rev. 1, 27: "[A] vast part of the
output of the governmental process would be seen to consist of discrimination, in
the sense of an effort to redistribute wealth (in one form or another) from one
group in the community to another, founded on the superior ability of one group
to manipulate the political process rather than on any principle of justice or
efficiency. Yet it would be odd, indeed, to condemn as unconstitutional the most
characteristic product of a democratic (perhaps of any) political system."

The legislative history of state and local legislation is often unrecorded and
not readily available. Should the Court "assess the rationality of the [classifica-
tion] in terms of the *state's* purposes, rather than hypothesizing conceivable
justifications on its own initiative"? Gunther, *In Search of Evolving Doctrine on
a Changing Court: A Model for a Newer Equal Protection*, 86 Harv.L.Rev. 1, 46
(1972). Consider id. at 44–46: "If the Court were to require an articulation of
purpose from an authoritative state source"—"a state court's or attorney general's office description of purpose should be acceptable"—"rather than hypothesizing one on its own, there would at least be indirect pressure on the legislature to
state its own reasons for selecting particular means and classifications [and thus]
improve the quality of the political process [by] encouraging a fuller airing in the
political arena of the grounds for legislative action." Is such improvement of the
political process a proper function of the judiciary? Compare Tribe, *Toward a
Model of Roles in the Due Process of Life and Law*, 87 Harv.L.Rev. 1, 6 n. 28
(1973): "A mismatch between means and ends, when the only ends examined are
those argued in a law's defense by an executive officer, may indicate no more
than that the officer did not advance the right ends in the law's defense. That
his oversight or deliberate choice should be allowed thereby to frustrate the past
efforts of his jurisdiction's legislature seems strange." See also Greenawalt, *The
Unresolved Problems of Reverse Discrimination*, 67 Calif.L.Rev. 87, 107 (1979):
"If it is enough that a lawyer defending the classification state a purpose, then,
since lawyers can be almost as imaginative as judges and are likely to suggest
many purposes in complex and controversial cases, the requirement of articulated purpose is unlikely often to be crucial." See generally Ely, *Democracy and
Distrust* 125–31 (1980).

2. *"One step at a time."* (a) Does the Court's permitting legislatures to
"implement their program step by step" immunize "pressure group" lawmaking
from equal protection attack? Should it? Consider Note, *Equal Protection*, 82
Harv.L.Rev. 1065, 1085 (1969): "To require that the state remedy all aspects of a
particular mischief or none at all might preclude a state from undertaking any
program of correction until its resources were adequate to deal with the entire
problem. Second, in some instances, the state may not be convinced that a
particular policy is a wise one, or it may prove impossible to marshal a
legislative majority in favor of extending the policy's coverage any further.
Thus, to demand application of the policy to all whom it might logically
encompass, would severely restrict the state's opportunities to experiment."[a]

(b) Does the Court's "step by step" approach, combined with its "minimum
rationality" requirement for legislative classifications as reflected in *Railway*

---

a. If the legislature's "step by step" justification is based on (i) "presently inadequate
resources" or (ii) a "desire to experiment,"
should the Court uphold the classification "only for the specific period that corresponds to
the nature of the legislature's timebound objective"? Note, *Reforming the One Step at a
Time Justification in Equal Protection Cases*,
90 Yale L.J. 1777, 1784 (1981).

Express and *Dukes,* mean that "unless a classification trammels fundamental personal rights or is drawn upon inherently suspect distinctions," it will never be held to violate equal protection? May a law that was rationally related to the purpose that caused its enactment subsequently become irrational because of a change of factual circumstances? If so, suppose a present purpose (not even conceivable by the enacting legislature) now rationally supports the law? See generally Linde, *Due Process of Lawmaking,* 55 Neb.L.Rev. 197, 215–22 (1976); Bice, note 1 supra, at 33–45.

3. *Underinclusion.* (a) Does the "step by step" approach, which permits "underinclusive" legislation [b]—allowing "officials to pick and choose only a few to whom they will apply legislation and thus to escape the political retribution that might be visited upon them if larger numbers were affected"—promote "arbitrary and unreasonable government"? Is it inconsistent with the *Carolene Products* concern, Ch. 1, Sec. 1, for "prejudice against discrete and insular minorities"? When "politically disadvantaged minorities are affected," should "the legislative judgment [be] more critically regarded, for such disadvantaged groups wield less influence in legislative councils than their proportion in the population would seem to warrant" and thus "it might be argued that the legislative decisions do not represent a proper majoritarian choice"? Note, 82 Harv.L.Rev. at 1125.

Consider Choper, *Judicial Review and the National Political Process* 75–77 (1980): "Majoritarians should have scant difficulty [with] the Court's assistance of persons who are not represented in the political process *at all*—best illustrated by aliens [or] minority racial groups who were illegally disenfranchised in certain parts of the nation. But the matter becomes painfully more complicated [when] the judicially favored minority is one that, although fully enfranchised in accordance with its numbers, is nonetheless characterized as being 'politically impotent,' 'not adequately represented,' 'discrete and insular,' or the like. The initial complexity arises because almost all, if not all, groups and interests in the American political process are 'minorities.' Thus, each time any group loses any political battle in which it has an interest—and some group always does—it may lay claim to the label of 'political weakness' or 'submerged and beaten minority.' [It] is true that some minorities, because of their sophistication and combined arithmetical and financial strength, are more influential than others on most political issues; and that some groups with modest numbers may win powerful surrogates who give them forceful representation. Similarly, there are some minorities who are less effective than others on most legislative matters because of their geographic isolation, the general inexcitability or unpopularity of their ideas, their relative inarticulateness, their lack of numbers and resources, or because they are viewed with such resentment, distaste, or hatred that they can neither join working coalitions nor prevent hostile action. But there are many disparate groups who may legitimately claim to meet some or all of these varied criteria for judicial solicitude. Thus, the Court may have to be as sympathetic to the pleas of apartment dwellers in Iowa, tobacco farmers in Massachusetts, debt adjustors in Kansas, oil well producers in New York, and cedar tree owners in Virginia as it is to the complaints of Jehovah's Witnesses in Rhode Island, communists in New Hampshire, progressives in Ohio, Asian-Americans in California, and blacks in Mississippi—all these illustrations assuming a given temporal span, presumably also to be determined by the Court." See also REHNQUIST,

b. For the classic discussion of various types of legislative classifications, see Tussman & tenBroek, note 1 supra.

J., dissenting in *Sugarman v. Dougall* and *In re Griffiths*, Sec. 3, II infra, which held state discriminations against aliens subject to "strict scrutiny": "Our society, consisting of over 200 million individuals of multitudinous origins, customs, tongues, beliefs, and cultures is, to say the least, diverse. It would hardly take extraordinary ingenuity for a lawyer to find 'insular and discrete' minorities at every turn of the road. Yet, unless the Court can precisely define and constitutionally justify both the terms and analysis it uses, [the] Court can choose a 'minority' it 'feels' deserves 'solicitude' and thereafter prohibit the States from classifying that 'minority' differently from the 'majority.' I cannot find [any] constitutional authority for such a 'ward of the Court' approach to equal protection." See also Sandalow, *The Distrust of Politics*, 56 N.Y.U.L.Rev. 446, 466–67 (1981): "Corporations also do not vote, but those who argue that aliens should be accorded [special protection] do not frequently complain that corporations should also receive that protection because they lack political influence. Any attempt to appraise the inner workings of the political process must, as the illustration of the corporation suggests, examine the entire process to ascertain the extent of a group's influence. [But] what measure have we, other than an evaluation of outcomes [—i.e., the desirability of the substantive policies enacted by the legislature]?"

(b) To what extent is the objection to underinclusive classifications limited to laws that impose burdens (e.g., *Railway Express*) rather than confer benefits (e.g., *Dukes*)? Consider Note, 82 Harv.L.Rev. at 1086 n. 47: "[W]hen a benefit is extended to one group but refused to another, the excluded group may be seen as suffering a relative burden. Therefore, from their point of view, the situation is one in which a burden has been imposed underinclusively." Were the "burdened" groups in the cases discussed in this Sec.—*Railway Express, Dukes, Morey, Lee Optical, Ferguson*—"politically disadvantaged minorities"? Compare *New York City Transit Auth. v. Beazer*, infra (burden on methadone users).

4. *Overinclusion.* Many laws, based on a plausible (often persuasive) judgment that many or most persons within the classification pose the problem sought to be remedied, subject the entire class to the regulation even though not every person within the class may pose the problem. For example, in *Ferguson*, the law was not only underinclusive in permitting only lawyers to be debt adjusters, but was also overinclusive in that there were surely *some* nonlawyers who would not engage in abusive debt adjusting. A common justification for overinclusive laws is avoidance of the administrative cost and chance of error in making individualized determinations for each person within the class.

Should the Court be more deferential to overinclusiveness because it "poses less danger than underinclusiveness, at least from the viewpoint of political accountability, for overinclusiveness does not exempt potentially powerful opponents from a law's reach"? Tribe, *American Constitutional Law* 999 (1978). Or is overinclusion "less tolerable than underinclusion, for while the latter fails to impose the burden on some who should logically bear it, the former actually does impose the burden on some who do not belong in the class"? Note, 82 Harv.L. Rev. at 1086.[c]

---

c. For the view that the Court should use a "legitimacy principle" in determining equal protection claims—which "requires simply that in enacting classifications legislators must: (1) avoid palpably inaccurate factual judgments; (2) not act discriminatorily, classifying persons, for example, in ways that offend the individualist ethic; and (3) be sensitive to the need for some proportion between the advantages of avoiding individualized determinations and the costs of abridging certain important interests"—see Perry, *Consti-*

The post 1930s cases considered to this point almost all invoke the extremely deferential "minimum rationality" standard of review. This approach has been used often in recent years in rejecting equal protection challenges to economic and social welfare legislation.[d] Several such decisions, in which the challengers unsuccessfully sought to have the classifications characterized as being "suspect" or involving "fundamental rights" (and thus subject to "strict scrutiny"), are considered in Sec. 4 infra. In some situations, however, although employing the traditional "rational basis" standard, the Court has held laws violative of equal protection.[e]

Furthermore, the Court has periodically articulated the "traditional" standard in a way that suggests a more active judicial examination of the challenged classification. For example, JOHNSON v. ROBISON, p. 777 supra, per BRENNAN, J., upheld a federal statute granting educational benefits to military veterans but not to conscientious objectors who performed alternate civilian service under the "rational basis" standard, but stated the *Royster Guano* formulation that the classification "must rest upon some ground of difference having a fair and substantial relation to the object of the legislation," and then devoted several pages to considering the justification.[f]

NEW YORK CITY TRANSIT AUTH. v. BEAZER, 440 U.S. 568, 99 S.Ct. 1355, 59 L.Ed.2d 587 (1979), per STEVENS, J., upheld the exclusion of all methadone users from any Transit Authority (TA) employment. It reversed the federal district court's conclusion that, because about 75% of "patients who have been on methadone maintenance for at least a year are free from illicit drug use" and because the exclusion applied to non-safety sensitive jobs, it had "no rational relation to the demands of the job to be performed": "[A]ny special rule short of total exclusion that TA might adopt is likely to be less precise—and will assuredly be more costly—than the one that it currently enforces. If eligibility is marked at any intermediate point—whether after one year of treatment or later—the classification will inevitably discriminate between employees or applicants equally or almost equally apt to achieve full recovery. [By] contrast, the 'no drugs' policy now enforced by TA is supported by the legitimate inference that as long as a treatment program (or other drug use) continues, a degree of uncertainty persists. Accordingly, [the TA policy] is rational. It is neither unprincipled nor invidious in the sense that it implies disrespect for the excluded subclass.

"[T]he District Court's conclusion was that TA's rule is broader than necessary to exclude those methadone users who are not actually qualified to work for TA. We may assume [that] it is probably unwise for a large employer like TA to rely on a general rule instead of individualized consideration of every job applicant. But these assumptions concern matters of personnel policy that do not implicate the principle safeguarded by the Equal Protection Clause. As the District Court recognized, the special classification created by TA's rule serves the general objectives of safety and efficiency. Moreover, the exclusionary line challenged by respondents [does] not circumscribe a class of persons character-

tutional *"Fairness": Notes on Equal Protection and Due Process*, 63 Va.L.Rev. 383 (1977).

d. For citations, see Nowak, Rotunda & Young, *Constitutional Law* 596–97 (2d ed. 1983).

e. See, e.g., *Eisenstadt v. Baird* (1972), p. 138 supra; *United States Dep't of Agriculture v. Moreno* (1973), Sec. 4, IV infra; *Baxtrom v.*

Herold, 383 U.S. 107, 86 S.Ct. 760, 15 L.Ed.2d 620 (1966) (extensive procedural rights prior to civil commitment except for persons who are ending a prison term); *Logan v. Zimmerman Brush Co.*, infra.

f. See also *Reed v. Reed* (1971), Sec. 3, IV infra, per Burger, C.J., using this formulation in holding a law that discriminated against women violative of equal protection.

ized by some unpopular trait or affiliation, it does not create or reflect any special likelihood of bias on the part of the ruling majority. Under these circumstances, it is of no constitutional significance that the degree of rationality is not as great with respect to certain ill-defined subparts of the classification as it is with respect to the classification as a whole." [a]

POWELL, J., concurred in the Court's opinion as "to employees or applicants who are currently on methadone" but interpreted TA's policy as also excluding "persons currently free of methadone use but who had been on the drug within the previous five years": "[T]here is no rational basis for an absolute bar against the employment of persons who have completed successfully a methadone maintenance program."

WHITE, J., joined by Marshall, J., dissented: Both courts below "found that those who have been maintained on methadone for at least a year and who are free from the use of illicit drugs and alcohol can easily be identified through normal personnel procedures and, for a great many jobs, are as employable as and present no more risk than applicants from the general population. [On] the facts as found [one] can reach the Court's result only if [equal protection] imposes no real constraint at all in this situation. * * *

"Petitioners [presented] nothing to negative the employability of successfully maintained methadone users as distinguished from those who were unsuccessful. * * *

"Of course, the District Court's order permitting total exclusion of all methadone users maintained for less than one year, whether successfully or not, would still exclude some employables and would to this extent be overinclusive. [But although] many of those who have not been successfully maintained for a year are employable, as a class they, unlike the protected group, are not as employable as the general population. Thus, even assuming the bad risks could be identified, serving the end of employability would require unusual efforts to determine those more likely to revert. But that legitimate secondary goal is not fulfilled by excluding the protected [class]. Accordingly, the rule's classification of successfully maintained persons as dispositively different from the general population is left without any justification and, with its irrationality and invidiousness thus uncovered, must fall before the Equal Protection Clause.[15]" [b]

---

a. See also *Vance v. Bradley* (1979), Sec. 3, I infra, per White, J., (sustaining mandatory retirement at age 60 for federal Foreign Service personnel), conceding that the classification was "to some extent both under-and over-inclusive" but holding that "perfection is by no means required. [In] an equal protection case of this type, [those] challenging the legislative judgment must convince the court that the legislative facts on which the classification is apparently based could not reasonably be conceived to be true by the governmental decisionmaker."

Minnesota v. Clover Leaf Creamery Co., 449 U.S. 456, 101 S.Ct. 715, 66 L.Ed.2d 659 (1981), per Brennan, J., relied on this language in unanimously rejecting an equal protection challenge to economic legislation.

15. I have difficulty also with the Court's easy conclusion that the challenged rule was "[q]uite plainly" not motivated "by any special animus against a specific group of persons." Heroin addiction is a special problem of the poor, and the addict population is composed largely of racial minorities that the Court has previously recognized as politically powerless and historical subjects of majoritarian neglect. Persons on methadone maintenance have few interests in common with members of the majority, and thus are unlikely to have their interests protected, or even considered, in governmental decisionmaking. Indeed, petitioners stipulated that "[o]ne of the reasons for [the] drug policy is the fact that [petitioners] feel[ ] an adverse public reaction would result if it were generally known that [petitioners] employed persons with a prior history of drug abuse, including persons participating in methadone maintenance programs." It is hard for me to reconcile that stipulation of animus against former addicts with our past holdings that "a bare [desire] to harm a politically unpopular group cannot constitute a *legitimate* governmental interest." *U.S. Dept.*

---

b. See note b on page 807.

UNITED STATES R.R. RETIREMENT BD. v. FRITZ

449 U.S. 166, 101 S.Ct. 453, 66 L.Ed.2d 368 (1980).

JUSTICE REHNQUIST delivered the opinion of the Court.

The United States District Court [held violative of the "equal protection component of the Fifth Amendment" § 231b(h)] of the Railroad Retirement Act of 1974. [Under the] Act's predecessor statute, a person who worked for both railroad and nonrailroad employers and who qualified for railroad retirement benefits and social security benefits received retirement benefits under both systems and an accompanying "windfall" benefit. [Congress] determined to place the system on a "sound financial basis" by eliminating future accruals of those benefits. Congress also enacted various transitional provisions [which] expressly preserved windfall benefits for some classes of employees.

* * * First, those employees who lacked the requisite 10 years of railroad employment to qualify for railroad retirement benefits as of January 1, 1975, the changeover date, would have their retirement benefits computed under the new system and would not receive any windfall benefit. Second, those individuals already retired and already receiving dual benefits [would] continue to receive a windfall benefit. Third, those employees who had qualified for both railroad and social security benefits as of the changeover date, but who had not yet retired as of that date (and thus were not yet receiving dual benefits), were entitled to windfall benefits if they had (1) performed some railroad service in 1974 or (2) had a "current connection" with the railroad industry as of December 31, 1974,[6] or (3) completed 25 years of railroad service as of December 31, 1974. * * *

Thus, an individual who, as of the changeover date, was unretired and had 11 years of railroad employment and sufficient nonrailroad employment to qualify for social security benefits is eligible for the full windfall amount if he worked for the railroad in 1974 or had a current connection with the railroad as of December 31, 1974, or his later retirement date. But an unretired individual with 24 years of railroad service and sufficient nonrailroad service to qualify for social security benefits is not eligible for a full windfall amount unless he worked for the railroad in 1974, or had a current connection with the railroad as of December 31, 1974 or his later retirement date. * * *

The District Court agreed with appellees that a differentiation based solely on whether an employee was "active" in the railroad business as of 1974 was not "rationally related" to the congressional purposes of insuring the solvency of the railroad retirement system and protecting vested benefits. We disagree and reverse.

---

of Agriculture v. Moreno. On the other hand, the afflictions to which petitioners are more sympathetic, such as alcoholism and mental illness, are shared by both white and black, rich and poor.

Some weight should also be given to the history of the rule. Petitioners admit that it was not the result of a reasoned policy decision and stipulated that they had never studied the ability of those on methadone maintenance to perform petitioners' jobs. Petitioners are not directly accountable to the public, are not the type of official body that normally makes legislative judgments of fact such as those relied upon by the majority today, and are by nature more concerned with

business efficiency than with other public policies for which they have no direct responsibility. Both the State and City of New York, which do exhibit those democratic characteristics, hire persons in methadone programs for similar jobs.

These factors together strongly point to a conclusion of invidious discrimination. * * *

b. White, J., joined by Brennan, J., also dissented on statutory grounds.

6. The term "current connection" is defined [to] mean, in general, employment in the railroad industry in 12 of the preceding 30 calendar months.

The initial issue [is] the appropriate standard of judicial review to be applied when social and economic legislation enacted by Congress is challenged as being violative of the Fifth Amendment * * *. There is no claim here that Congress has taken property in violation of the Fifth Amendment, since railroad benefits, like social security benefits, are not contractual and may be altered or even eliminated at any time. And because the distinctions drawn in § 231b(h) do not burden fundamental constitutional rights or create "suspect" classifications, such as race or national origin, we may put cases involving judicial review of such claims to one side.

Despite the narrowness of the issue, this Court in earlier cases has not been altogether consistent in its pronouncements in this area [contrasting the language in *National Carbonic* and *Royster Guano,* set forth supra].

In more recent years, however, the Court in cases involving social and economic benefits has consistently refused to invalidate on equal protection grounds legislation which it simply deemed unwise or unartfully drawn.

Thus in *Dandridge v. Williams,* [Sec. 4, IV infra], the Court rejected a claim that Maryland welfare legislation violated [equal protection]: "In the area of economic and social welfare, a State does not violate the Equal Protection Clause merely because the classifications made by its law are imperfect. If the classification has some 'reasonable basis', it does not offend the Constitution simply because the classification 'is not made with mathematical nicety or because in practice it results in some inequality.' *National Carbonic Gas.* 'The problems of government are practical ones and may justify, if they do not require, rough accommodations—illogical, it may be, and unscientific.' [The rational basis standard] is true to the principle that the Fourteenth Amendment gives the federal courts no power to impose upon the States their views of what constitutes wise economic or social policy."

Of like tenor are *Vance v. Bradley* and *New Orleans v. Dukes.* * * *

Applying those principles to this case, the plain language of § 231b(h) marks the beginning and end of our inquiry.[10] There Congress determined that some of those who in the past received full windfall benefits would not continue to do so. Because Congress could have eliminated windfall benefits for all classes of employees, it is not constitutionally impermissible for Congress to have drawn lines between groups of employees for the purpose of phasing out those benefits. *Dukes.*

The only remaining question is whether Congress achieved its purpose in a patently arbitrary or irrational way. [Congress] could properly conclude that persons who had actually acquired statutory entitlement to windfall benefits while still employed in the railroad industry had a greater equitable claim to those benefits than the members of appellees' class who were no longer in

---

10. This opinion and Justice Brennan's dissent cite a number of equal protection [cases]. The most arrogant legal scholar would not claim that all of these cases applied a uniform or consistent test under the Equal Protection Clause. And realistically speaking, we can be no more certain that this opinion will remain undisturbed than were those who joined the opinion in *National Carbonic Gas, Royster Guano,* or any of the other cases referred to in this opinion and in the dissenting opinion. But like our predecessors and our successors, we are obliged to apply the equal protection component of the Fifth Amendment as we believe the Constitution requires and in so doing we have no hesitation in asserting, contrary to the dissent, that where social or economic regulations are involved *Dandridge* [and] this case, state the proper application of the test. The comments in the dissenting opinion about the proper cases for which to look for the correct statement of the equal protection rational basis standard, and about which cases limit earlier cases, are just that: comments in a dissenting opinion.

railroad employment when they became eligible for dual benefits. Furthermore, the "current connection" test is not a patently arbitrary means for determining which employees are "career railroaders" * * *. Congress could assume that those who had a current connection with the railroad industry when the Act was passed in 1974, or who returned to the industry before their retirement, were more likely than those who had left the industry prior to 1974 and who never returned, to be among the class of persons who pursue careers in the railroad industry, the class for whom the Railroad Retirement Act was designed.

Where, as here, there are plausible reasons for Congress' action, our inquiry is at an end. It is, of course, "constitutionally irrelevant whether this reasoning in fact underlay the legislative decision," because this Court has never insisted that a legislative body articulate its reasons for enacting a statute. This is particularly true where the legislature must necessarily engage in a process of line drawing. The "task of classifying persons for [benefits] inevitably requires that some persons who have an almost equally strong claim to favorite treatment be placed on different sides of the line," *Mathews v. Diaz,* [Sec. 3, II infra], and the fact the line might have been drawn differently at some points is a matter for legislative, rather than judicial consideration.

Finally, we disagree with the District Court's conclusion that Congress was unaware of what it accomplished or that it was misled by the groups that appeared before it. If this test were applied literally to every member of any legislature that ever voted on a law, there would be very few laws which would survive it. The language of the statute is clear, and we have historically assumed that Congress intended what it enacted. To be sure, appellees lost a political battle in which they had a strong interest, but this is neither the first nor the last time that such a result will occur in the legislative forum.[12]

JUSTICE STEVENS, concurring in the judgment.

In my opinion Justice Brennan's criticism of the Court's approach to this case merits a more thoughtful response than that contained in footnote 10. [When] Congress deprives a small class of persons of vested [rights,] I believe the Constitution requires something more than merely a "conceivable" or a "plausible" explanation for the unequal treatment.

I do not, however, share Justice Brennan's conclusion that every statutory classification must further an objective that can be confidently identified as the "actual purpose" of the legislature. Actual purpose is sometimes unknown. Moreover, undue emphasis on actual motivation may result in identically worded statutes being held valid in one State and invalid in a neighboring State. I therefore believe that we must discover a correlation between the classification and either the actual purpose of the statute or a legitimate purpose that we may reasonably presume to have motivated an impartial legislature. If the adverse impact on the disfavored class is an apparent aim of the legislature, its impartiality would be suspect. If, however, the adverse impact may reasonably be viewed as an acceptable cost of achieving a larger goal, an impartial lawmaker could rationally decide that that cost should be incurred.

In this case, however, we need not look beyond the actual purpose of the legislature. As is often true, this legislation is the product of multiple and somewhat inconsistent purposes that led to certain compromises. One purpose

---

12. As we have recently stated, "The Constitution presumes that, absent some reason to infer antipathy, even improvident decision will eventually be rectified by the democratic processes and that judicial intervention is generally unwarranted no matter how unwisely we may think a political branch has acted." *Vance v. Bradley.*

was to eliminate in the future the benefit that is described by the Court as a "windfall benefit" and by Justice Brennan as an "earned dual benefit." That aim was incident to the broader objective of protecting the solvency of the entire railroad retirement program. Two purposes that conflicted somewhat with this broad objective were the purposes of preserving those benefits that had already vested and of increasing the level of payments to beneficiaries whose rights were not otherwise to be changed. As Justice Brennan emphasizes, Congress originally intended to protect *all* vested benefits, but it ultimately sacrificed some benefits in the interest of achieving other objectives.

Given these conflicting purposes, I believe the decisive questions are (1) whether Congress can rationally reduce the vested benefits of some employees to improve the solvency of the entire program while simultaneously increasing the benefits of others; and (2) whether, in deciding which vested benefits to reduce, Congress may favor annuitants whose railroad service was more recent than that of disfavored annuitants who had an equal or greater quantum of employment.

My answer to both questions is in the affirmative. The congressional purpose to eliminate dual benefits is unquestionably legitimate; that legitimacy is not undermined by the adjustment in the level of remaining benefits in response to inflation in the economy. As for the second question, some hardship—in the form of frustrated long-term expectations—must inevitably result from any reduction in vested benefits. Arguably, therefore, Congress had a duty—and surely it had the right to decide—to eliminate no more vested benefits than necessary to achieve its fiscal purpose. Having made that decision, any distinction it chose within the class of vested beneficiaries would involve a difference of degree rather than a difference in entitlement. I am satisfied that a distinction based upon currency of railroad employment represents an impartial method of identifying that sort of difference. Because retirement plans frequently provide greater benefits for recent retirees than for those who retired years ago—and thus give a greater reward for recent service than for past service of equal duration—the basis for the statutory discrimination is supported by relevant precedent. It follows, in my judgment, that the timing of the employees' railroad service is a "reasonable basis" for the classification as that term is used in *National Carbonic Gas* and *Dandridge,* as well as a "ground of difference having a fair and substantial relation to the object of the legislation," as those words are used in *Royster Guano.* * * *

JUSTICE BRENNAN, with whom JUSTICE MARSHALL joins, dissenting.

[T]he legal standard applicable to this case is the "rational basis" test. [The] Court today purports to apply this standard, but [fails] to scrutinize the challenged classification in the manner established by our governing precedents. I suggest that the mode of analysis employed by the Court in this case virtually immunizes social and economic legislative classifications from judicial review.

[Perhaps] the clearest statement of this Court's present approach to "rational basis" scrutiny may be found in *Johnson v. Robison,* [where] eight Members of this Court agreed [to the *Royster Guano* formulation]. The enactments of Congress are entitled to a presumption of constitutionality, and the burden rests on those challenging a legislative classification to demonstrate that it does not bear the "fair and substantial relation to the object of the legislation" required under the Constitution.

Nonetheless, the rational basis standard "is not a toothless one," *Mathews v. Lucas,* [Sec. 3, III infra], and will not be satisfied by flimsy or implausible justifications for the legislative classification, proffered after the fact by Government attorneys. See, e.g., *U.S. Dept. of Agriculture v. Moreno.* When faced with a challenge to a legislative classification under the rational basis test, the court should ask, first, what the purposes of the statute are, and second, whether the classification is rationally related to achievement of those purposes.

The purposes of the Railroad Retirement Act of 1974 are clear, because Congress has commendably stated them in the House and Senate reports accompanying the Act. A section of the reports is entitled "Principal Purpose of the Bill." It notes generally that "[t]he bill provides for a complete restructuring of the Railroad Retirement Act of 1937, and will place it on a sound financial basis," and then states: "Persons who already have vested rights under both the Railroad Retirement and the Social Security systems will in the future be permitted to receive benefits computed under both systems just as is true under existing law." [3] Moreover, Congress explained that this purpose was based on considerations of fairness and the legitimate expectations of the retirees * * *.

Thus, a "principal purpose" [was] to preserve the vested earned benefits of retirees who had already qualified for them. The classification at issue here, which deprives some retirees of vested dual benefits that they had earned prior to 1974, directly conflicts with Congress' stated purpose. As such, the classification is not only rationally unrelated to the congressional purpose; it is inimical to it.

The Court today avoids the conclusion that § 231b(h) must be invalidated by deviating in three ways from traditional rational basis analysis. * * *

A. The Court states that "the plain language of § 231b(h) marks the beginning and end of our inquiry." [Since] § 231b(h) of the Act deprives appellees of their vested earned dual benefits, the Court apparently assumes that Congress must have *intended* that result. But by presuming purpose from result, the Court reduces analysis to tautology. It may always be said that Congress intended to do what it in fact did. If that were the extent of our analysis, we would find every statute, no matter how arbitrary or irrational, perfectly tailored to achieve its purpose. But equal protection scrutiny under the rational basis test requires the courts first to deduce the independent objectives of the statute, usually from statements of purpose and other evidence in the statute and legislative history, and second to analyze whether the challenged classification rationally furthers achievement of those objectives. The Court's tautological approach will not suffice.

B. The Court analyzes the rationality of § 231b(h) in terms of a justification suggested by Government attorneys, but never adopted by Congress. [But] this Court has frequently recognized that the actual purposes of Congress, rather than the post hoc justifications offered by Government attorneys, must be the primary basis for analysis under the rational basis test. [For example], in *San Antonio Independent School District v. Rodriguez* [Sec. 4, IV infra], this Court stated that a challenged classification will pass muster under "rational basis" scrutiny only if it "rationally furthers some legitimate, *articulated* state purpose," (emphasis added), and in *Massachusetts Board of Retirement v. Murgia* [Sec. 3, I infra], we stated that such a classification will be sustained only if it

---

3. Several pages later, the reports again make clear that persons with vested rights to earned dual benefits would retain [them].

Only in technical discussions and in the section-by-section analyses do the reports re-flect the actual consequences of the Act on the appellee class. * * *

"rationally furthers the purpose *identified by the State.*" (Emphasis added.)
* * *

The Court argues that Congress chose to discriminate against appellees for reasons of equity, [but, as] I have shown, Congress expressed the view that it would be inequitable to deprive any retirees of any portion of the benefits they had been promised and that they had earned under prior law. The Court is unable to cite even one statement in the legislative history by a Representative or Senator that makes the equitable judgment it imputes to Congress. In the entire legislative history of the Act, the only persons to state that the equities justified eliminating appellees' earned dual benefits were representatives of railroad management and labor, whose self-serving interest in bringing about this result destroys any basis for attaching weight to their statements. [They] were not appointed by public officials, nor did they represent the interests of the appellee class, who were no longer active railroaders or union members.

[L]abor representatives demanded that benefits be increased for their current members, the cost to be offset by divesting the appellee class of a portion of the benefits they had earned under prior law. [In] fact, the [management and labor representatives] and Railroad Retirement Board members who testified at congressional hearings perpetuated the inaccurate impression that all retirees with earned vested dual benefits under prior law would retain their benefits unchanged. * * *

Of course, a misstatement or several misstatements by witnesses before Congress would not ordinarily lead us to conclude that Congress misapprehended what it was doing. In this instance, however, where complex legislation was drafted by outside parties and Congress relied on them to explain it, where the misstatements are frequent and unrebutted, and where no Member of Congress can be found to have stated the effect of the classification correctly, we are entitled to suspect that Congress may have been misled. As the District Court found: "At no time during the hearings did Congress even give a hint that it understood that the bill by its language eliminated an earned benefit of plaintiff's class."

Therefore, I do not think that this classification was rationally related to an *actual* governmental purpose.

C. The third way in which the Court has deviated from the principles of rational basis scrutiny is its failure to analyze whether the challenged classification is genuinely related to the purpose identified by the Court. Having suggested that "equitable considerations" underlay the challenged classification—in direct contradiction to Congress' evaluation of those considerations, and in the face of evidence that the classification was the product of private negotiation by interested parties, inadequately examined and understood by Congress—the Court proceeds to accept that suggestion without further analysis.

An unadorned claim of "equitable" considerations is, of course, difficult to assess. It seems to me that before a court may accept a litigant's assertion of "equity," it must inquire what principles of equity or fairness might genuinely support such a judgment. * * *

In my view, the following considerations are of greatest relevance to the equities of this case: (1) contribution to the system; (2) reasonable expectation and reliance; (3) need; and (4) character of service to the railroad industry. With respect to each of these considerations, I would conclude that appellees have as great an equitable claim to their earned dual benefits as do their more favored coworkers, who remain entitled to their earned dual benefits under § 231b(h).

[Because] the Court is willing to accept a tautological analysis of congressional purpose, an assertion of "equitable" considerations contrary to the expressed judgment of Congress, and a classification patently unrelated to achievement of the identified purpose, it succeeds in effectuating neither equity nor congressional intent. ✻ ✻ ✻

Notes and Questions

1. *"Actual purpose."* Does *Fritz* put to rest—at least for a majority of the Court—the issue of "actual" vs. "hypothetically conceivable" legislative purpose? Within three months after *Fritz,* SCHWEIKER v. WILSON, 450 U.S. 221, 101 S.Ct. 1074, 67 L.Ed.2d 186 (1981), per BLACKMUN, J., upheld Congress' denial of SSI "comfort allowances" to needy aged, blind and disabled persons confined in public institutions unless the institutions received federal Medicaid funds: "[T]he pertinent inquiry is whether the [classification] advances legitimate legislative goals in a rational fashion. The Court has said that, although this rational basis standard is 'not a toothless one,' *Mathews v. Lucas,* it does not allow us to substitute our personal notions of good public [policy].[a] We believe that the decision to incorporate the Medicaid eligibility standards into the SSI scheme must be considered Congress' deliberate, considered choice." It "is rationally related to the legitimate legislative desire to avoid spending federal resources on behalf of individuals whose care and treatment are being fully provided for by state and local government units" and "may be said to implement a congressional policy choice to provide supplemental financial assistance for only those residents of public institutions who already receive significant federal support in the form of Medicaid coverage."

POWELL, J., joined by Brennan, Marshall and Stevens, JJ., dissented: "In my view, the Court should receive with some skepticism post hoc hypotheses about legislative purpose, unsupported by the legislative history. When no indication of legislative purpose appears other than the current position of the Secretary, the Court should require that the classification bear a 'fair and substantial relation' to the asserted purpose. See *Royster Guano.* This marginally more demanding scrutiny indirectly would test the plausibility of the tendered purpose, and preserve equal protection review as something more than 'a mere tautological recognition of the fact that Congress did what it intended to do.' *Fritz* (Stevens, J., concurring). ✻ ✻ ✻ I conclude that Congress had no rational reason for refusing to pay a comfort allowance to appellee, while paying it to numerous otherwise identically situated disabled indigents. This unexplained difference in treatment must have been a legislative oversight."[b]

2. *"Means/end fit."* To what extent should the Court employ a "strengthened 'rational' scrutiny" by requiring "that legislative means must substantially further legislative ends"? Gunther, note 1 after *Dukes,* supra. Consider id.: "Examination of means in light of asserted state purposes would directly promote public consideration of the benefits assertedly sought by the proposed legislation; indirectly, it would stimulate fuller political examination, in relation

---

a. See also *Schweiker v. Hogan,* 457 U.S. 569, 102 S.Ct. 2597, 73 L.Ed.2d 227 (1982) (unanimous opinion, per Stevens, J., applying "rationality" test to Medicaid benefits discrimination despite the fact that it "may be inequitable or unwise").

b. For the view that if "rationality is to be a meaningful standard of review, the court must conceive of its task as identifying the legislature's *probable* goals based on the available evidence," see Bice, note 1 after *Dukes,* at 30.

to those benefits, of the costs that would be incurred if the proposed means were adopted."

Compare REHNQUIST, J., dissenting in *Trimble v. Gordon*, Sec. 3, III infra, which held that an Illinois statute, forbidding illegitimate children to inherit from their fathers by intestate succession, violated equal protection: "[Judicial review of means/end fit] requires a conscious second-guessing of legislative judgment in an area where this Court has no special expertise whatever. [In] most cases, [the] 'fit' will involve a greater or lesser degree of imperfection. Then the Court asks itself how much 'imperfection' between means and ends is permissible? In making this judgment it must throw into the judicial hopper the whole range of factors which were first thrown into the legislative hopper. What alternatives were reasonably available? What reasons are there for the legislature to accomplish this 'purpose' in the way it did? What obstacles stood in the way of other solutions?

"[Without] any antecedent constitutional mandate, we have created on the premises of the Equal Protection Clause a school for legislators, whereby opinions of this Court are written to instruct them in a better understanding of how to accomplish their ordinary legislative tasks. [Since] Illinois' distinction is not mindless and patently irrational, I would [affirm]."

For recent expressions of the Court on this issue, see fn. a in *Beazer,* supra.[c]

3. *"Irrationality."* In LOGAN v. ZIMMERMAN BRUSH CO. (1982), p. 279 supra, for the first time in 25 years, a majority of the justices employed "the lowest level of permissible equal protection scrutiny" and found a violation of equal protection. Appellant filed an employment discrimination complaint before an Illinois Commission which inadvertently scheduled the hearing at a date after the statutory time period expired. The state court held that this deprived the Commission of jurisdiction and terminated appellant's claim. BLACKMUN, J., joined by Brennan, Marshall and O'Connor, JJ., found this "patently irrational in light of [the law's] stated purpose": "I cannot agree that terminating a claim that the State itself has misscheduled is a rational way of expediting the resolution of disputes. [The] state's rationale must be something more than the exercise of a strained imagination; while the connection between means and ends need not be precise, it, at the least, must have some objective basis. That is not so here."

POWELL, J., joined by Rehnquist, J., concurred as to "this unusual classification": "As appellants possessed no power to convene hearings, it is unfair and irrational to punish them for the Commission's failure to do so." [d]

4. *Legislative role.* Is the "traditional"—"rational basis"—"minimum rationality" approach premised "on the propriety of unelected federal judges' displacing the judgments of elected state officials, or upon the competence of federal courts to prescribe workable standards of state conduct and devise measures to enforce them"? See Sager, *Fair Measure: The Legal Status of Underenforced Constitutional Norms,* 91 Harv.L.Rev. 1212, 1217 (1978). If so, of what relevance is the "traditional" approach to state and local legislators?

c. For the view that the "rationality" requirement does—and should—function as a balance of costs, benefits, and alternatives as well as the legitimacy of legislative purpose and the closeness of fit between means and ends, see Bennett, *"Mere" Rationality in Constitutional Law: Judicial Review and Democratic Theory,* 67 Calif.L.Rev. 1049 (1979). But

see Barrett, *The Rational Basis Standard for Equal Protection Review of Ordinary Legislative Classifications,* 68 Ky.L.J. 845 (1980).

d. See also *G.D. Searle & Co. v. Cohn,* 455 U.S. 404, 102 S.Ct. 1137, 71 L.Ed.2d 250 (1982), for a dissent by Stevens, J., finding no "rational basis" for a statutory classification.

State judges? Congress? Consider id. at 1218–21: "Institutional rather than analytical reasons appear to have prompted the broad exclusion of state tax and regulatory measures from the reach of the equal protection construct fashioned by the federal judiciary. This is what creates the disparity between this construct and a true conception of equal protection, and thus substantiates the claim that equal protection is an underenforced constitutional norm. [C]onstitutional norms which are underenforced by the federal judiciary should be understood to be legally valid to their full conceptual limits, and federal judicial decisions which stop short of these limits should be understood as delineating only the boundaries of the federal courts' role in enforcing the norm: By 'legally valid,' I mean that the unenforced margins of underenforced norms should have the full status of positive law which we generally accord to the norms of our Constitution, save only that the federal judiciary will not enforce these margins. Thus, the legal powers or legal obligations of government officials which are subtended in the unenforced margins of underenforced constitutional norms are to be understood to remain in full force." For further consideration, see *Katzenbach v. Morgan,* p. 1156 infra, and notes thereafter.[e]

SECTION 2. RACE AND ETHNIC ANCESTRY

I. DISCRIMINATION AGAINST RACIAL AND ETHNIC MINORITIES

The "evil to be remedied" by the equal protection clause, declared the *Slaughter-House Cases,* was "the existence of laws in the States where the newly emancipated negroes resided, which discriminated with gross injustice and hardship against them as a class." STRAUDER v. WEST VIRGINIA, 100 U.S. 303, 25 L.Ed. 664 (1880)—the first post-Civil War racial discrimination case to reach the Court—per STRONG, J., invalidating the state murder conviction of a black on the ground that state law forbade blacks from serving on grand or petit juries,[a] observed that "the true spirit and meaning" of the Civil War amendments was "securing to a race recently emancipated [the] enjoyment of all the civil rights that under the law are enjoyed by [whites]. What is [equal protection but] that all persons, whether colored or white, shall stand equal before the laws of the States, and, in regard to the colored race, for whose protection the amendment was primarily designed, that no discrimination shall be made against them by law because of their color? The words of the amendment [contain] a positive immunity or right, most valuable to the colored race,—the right to exemption from unfriendly legislation against them distinctively as colored,—exemption from legal discriminations, implying inferiority in civil

---

e. For the view that the Court should defer to a *state court's* "factual conclusions" that a state law's classification "was not rationally related to a legitimate state purpose," see Stevens, J., dissenting in *Minnesota v. Clover Leaf Creamery Co.*

a. The Court emphasized that the question was *not* whether a black defendant "has a right to a grand or a petit jury composed in whole or in part of persons of his own race or color, but [whether] all persons of his race or color may be excluded by law solely because of their race or color."

The Court has adhered to *Strauder's* requirement of systematic exclusion. See note 1

following *Yick Wo v. Hopkins,* Sec. III infra. But it has permitted criminal defendants who are not themselves members of the excluded group to challenge the jury's composition on the ground that it violates the defendant's sixth amendment right to a jury "selected from a fair cross section of the community." See, e.g., *Peters v. Kiff,* 407 U.S. 493, 92 S.Ct. 2163, 33 L.Ed.2d 83 (1972) (white challenging exclusion of blacks); *Duren v. Missouri,* 439 U.S. 357, 99 S.Ct. 664, 58 L.Ed.2d 579 (1979) (man challenging exclusion of women).

society, lessening the security of their enjoyment of the rights which others enjoy, and discriminations which are steps towards reducing them to the condition of a subject race.

"That the West Virginia statute respecting juries [is] such a discrimination ought not to be doubted. [And if] in those States where the colored people constitute a majority of the entire population a law should be enacted excluding all white men from jury service, [we] apprehend no one would be heard to claim that it would not be a denial to white men of the equal protection of the laws.[b] Nor if a law should be passed excluding all naturalized Celtic Irishmen, would there be any doubt of its inconsistency with the spirit of the amendment.

* * *

"We do not say that within the limits from which it is not excluded by the amendment a State may not prescribe the qualifications of its jurors, and in so doing make discriminations. It may confine the selection to males, to freeholders, to citizens, to persons within certain ages, or to persons having educational qualifications. We do not believe the Fourteenth Amendment was ever intended to prohibit this. Looking at its history, it is clear it had no such purpose. Its aim was against discrimination because of race or color."

Thus, as stated in *Brown v. Board of Education,* Part II infra, "in the first cases in this Court construing the Fourteenth Amendment, decided shortly after its adoption, the Court interpreted it as proscribing all state-imposed discriminations against the Negro race." Subsequent decisions extended this proscription to state discrimination against persons because of their national origin, such as those of Chinese or Mexican ancestry.[c]

KOREMATSU v. UNITED STATES
323 U.S. 214, 65 S.Ct. 193, 89 L.Ed. 194 (1944).

MR. JUSTICE BLACK delivered the opinion of the Court.

The petitioner, an American citizen of Japanese descent, was convicted in a federal district court for remaining in San Leandro, California, a "Military Area," contrary to Civilian Exclusion Order No. 34 of the Commanding General of the Western Command, U.S. Army, which directed that after May 9, 1942, all persons of Japanese ancestry should be excluded from that area. No question was raised as to petitioner's loyalty to the United States. * * *

[A]ll legal restrictions which curtail the civil rights of a single racial group are immediately suspect. That is not to say that all such restrictions are unconstitutional. It is to say that courts must subject them to the most rigid scrutiny. Pressing public necessity may sometimes justify the existence of such restrictions; racial antagonism never can. * * *

Exclusion Order No. 34 [was] one of a number of military orders [and a] curfew order, [also] promulgated pursuant to Executive Order 9066, subjected all persons of Japanese ancestry in prescribed West Coast military areas to remain in their residences from 8 p.m. to 6 a.m. [In] *Hirabayashi v. United States,* 320 U.S. 81, 63 S.Ct. 1365, 87 L.Ed. 1774 (1943), we sustained a conviction [for] violation of the curfew order [as] an exercise of the power [to] take steps

---

b. The issue of discrimination against the majority race—that of "favorable," "reverse," or "benign" discrimination—is considered in Part V infra.

c. *Yick Wo v. Hopkins* (1886), Sec. III infra; *Hernandez v. Texas,* 347 U.S. 475, 74 S.Ct. 667, 98 L.Ed. 866 (1954).

necessary to prevent espionage and sabotage in an area threatened by Japanese attack.

In the light of the principles we announced in the *Hirabayashi* case, we are unable to conclude that it was beyond the war power of Congress and the Executive to exclude those of Japanese ancestry from the West Coast war area at the time they [did]. Nothing short of apprehension by the proper military authorities of the gravest imminent danger to the public safety can constitutionally justify either. But exclusion from a threatened area, no less than curfew, has a definite and close relationship to the prevention of espionage and sabotage. The military authorities, charged with the primary responsibility of defending our shores, concluded that curfew provided inadequate protection and ordered exclusion [in] accordance with Congressional authority * * *.

Here, as in *Hirabayashi,* "we cannot reject as unfounded the judgment of the military authorities and of Congress that there were disloyal members of that population, whose number and strength could not be precisely and quickly ascertained. We cannot say that the war-making branches of the Government did not have ground for believing that in a critical hour such persons could not readily be isolated and separately dealt with, and constituted a menace to the national defense and safety, which demanded that prompt and adequate measures be taken to guard against it."

[This] answers the contention that the exclusion was in the nature of group punishment based on antagonism to those of Japanese origin. That there were members of the group who retained loyalties to Japan has been confirmed by investigations made subsequent to the exclusion. Approximately five thousand American citizens of Japanese ancestry refused to swear unqualified allegiance to the United States [and] several thousand evacuees requested repatriation to Japan.

[H]ardships are part of war, and war is an aggregation of hardships. [E]xclusion of large groups of citizens from their homes, except under circumstances of direst emergency and peril, is inconsistent with our basic governmental institutions. But when under conditions of modern warfare our shores are threatened by hostile forces, the power to protect must be commensurate with the threatened danger. * * *

It is said that we are dealing here with the case of imprisonment of a citizen in a concentration camp solely because of his ancestry, without evidence or inquiry concerning his loyalty and good disposition towards the United States. [But] we are dealing specifically with nothing but an exclusion order. To cast this case into outlines of racial prejudice, without reference to the real military dangers which were presented, merely confuses the issue. Korematsu was not excluded from the Military Area because of hostility to him or his race. He was excluded because we are at war with the Japanese Empire, because the properly constituted military authorities feared an invasion of our West Coast and felt constrained to take proper security measures, because they decided that the military urgency of the situation demanded that all citizens of Japanese ancestry be segregated from the West Coast temporarily, and finally, because Congress, reposing its confidence in this time of war in our military leaders—as inevitably it must—determined that they should have the power to do just this. There was evidence of disloyalty on the part of some, the military authorities considered that the need for action was great, and time was short. We cannot—by availing ourselves of the calm perspective of hindsight—now say that at that time these actions were unjustified.[a]

Affirmed.

MR. JUSTICE FRANKFURTER [who joined the Court's opinion], concurring.

[To] find that the Constitution does not forbid the military measures now complained of does not carry with it approval of that which Congress and the Executive did. That is their business, not ours.

MR. JUSTICE MURPHY, dissenting.

[In] adjudging the military action taken in light of the then apparent dangers, [it] is necessary only that the action have some reasonable relation to the removal of the dangers of invasion, sabotage and espionage. But the exclusion, either temporarily or permanently, of all persons with Japanese blood in their veins [must] rely for its reasonableness upon the assumption that *all* persons of Japanese ancestry may have a dangerous tendency to commit sabotage and espionage and [it] is difficult to believe that reason, logic or experience could be marshalled in support of such an assumption. [The] reasons appear, instead, to be largely an accumulation of much of the misinformation, half-truths and insinuations that for years have been directed against Japanese Americans by people with racial and economic prejudices—the same people who have been among the foremost advocates of the evacuation. A military judgment based upon such racial and sociological considerations is not entitled to the great weight ordinarily given the judgments based upon strictly military considerations. Especially is this so when every charge relative to race, religion, culture, geographical location, and legal and economic status has been substantially discredited by independent studies made by experts in these matters.

* * *

Moreover, there was no adequate proof that the FBI and the military and naval intelligence services did not have the espionage and sabotage situation well in hand during this long period. Nor is there any denial of the fact that not one person of Japanese ancestry was accused or convicted of espionage or sabotage after Pearl Harbor while they were still free, a fact which is some evidence of the loyalty of the vast majority of these individuals and of the effectiveness of the established methods of combatting these evils. It seems incredible that under these circumstances it would have been impossible to hold loyalty hearings for the mere 112,000 persons involved—or at least for the 70,000 American citizens—especially when a large part of this number represented children and elderly men and women. Any inconvenience that may have accompanied an attempt to conform to procedural due process cannot be said to justify violations of constitutional [rights].

MR. JUSTICE JACKSON, dissenting.

Korematsu was born on our soil, of parents born in Japan. [Had] Korematsu been one of four—the others being, say, a German alien enemy, an Italian alien enemy, and a citizen of American-born ancestors, convicted of treason but out on parole—only Korematsu's presence would have violated the order. The difference between their innocence and his crime would result, not from any-

---

a. Consider, Simon, *Racially Prejudiced Governmental Actions: A Motivation Theory of the Constitutional Ban Against Racial Discrimination*, 15 San Diego L.Rev. 1041, 1074 (1978): "The Japanese exclusion cases [are] most troubling not because the Court found that the challenged rules would have been promulgated even apart from prejudice, but because it refused seriously to consider whether maintaining the exclusionary system and continuing its enforcement as of the time the cases reached the Court could be explained on grounds other than racial prejudice."

thing he did, said, or thought, different than they, but only in that he was born of different racial stock.

Now, if any fundamental assumption underlies our system, it is that guilt is personal and not inheritable. [If] Congress in peace-time legislation should enact such a criminal law, I should suppose this Court would refuse to enforce it.

But [it] would be impracticable and dangerous idealism to expect or insist that each specific military command in an area of probable operations will conform to conventional tests of constitutionality. When an area is so beset that it must be put under military control at all, the paramount consideration is that its measures be successful, rather than legal. * * * I cannot say, from any evidence before me, that the orders of General DeWitt were not reasonably expedient military precautions, nor could I say that they were. But even if they were permissible military procedures, I deny that it follows that they are constitutional. If, as the Court holds, it does follow, then we may as well say that any military order will be constitutional and have done with it.[b]

The limitation under which courts always will labor in examining the necessity for a military order are illustrated by this case. How does the Court know that these orders have a reasonable basis in necessity? No evidence whatever on that subject has been taken by this or any other court. There is sharp controversy as to the credibility of the DeWitt report. So the Court, having no real evidence before it, has no choice but to accept General DeWitt's own unsworn, self-serving statement, untested by any cross-examination, that what he did was reasonable. And thus it will always be when courts try to look into the reasonableness of a military order. * * *

[A] judicial construction of the due process clause that will sustain this order is a far more subtle blow to liberty than the promulgation of the order itself. A military order, however unconstitutional, is not apt to last longer than the military emergency. [But] once a judicial opinion rationalizes [the] Constitution to show that the Constitution sanctions such an order, the Court for all time has validated the principle of racial discrimination in criminal procedure and of transplanting American citizens. The principle then lies about like a loaded weapon ready for the hand of any authority that can bring forward a plausible claim of an urgent need. * * *

My duties as a justice as I see them do not require me to make a military judgment as to whether General DeWitt's evacuation and detention program was a reasonable military necessity. I do not suggest that the courts should have attempted to interfere with the Army in carrying out its task. But I do not think they may be asked to execute a military expedient that has no place in law under the Constitution. I would reverse the judgment and discharge the prisoner.[c]

---

b. Compare Warren, C.J., *The Bill of Rights and the Military,* 37 N.Y.U.L.Rev. 181, 192–93 (1962): "[*Hirabayashi* and *Korematsu*] demonstrate dramatically that there are some circumstances in which the Court will, in effect, conclude that it is simply not in a position to reject descriptions by the Executive of the degree of military necessity. Thus, in a case like *Hirabayashi,* only the Executive is qualified to determine whether, for example, an invasion is imminent. In such a situation, where time is of the essence, if the Court is to deny the asserted right of the military authorities, it must be on the theory that the

claimed justification, though factually unassailable, is insufficient. [S]uch cases would be extraordinary indeed. [To] put it another way, the fact that the Court rules in a case like *Hirabayashi* that a given program is constitutional, does not necessarily answer the question whether, in a broader sense, it actually is."

c. The dissenting opinion of Roberts, J., is omitted. The Japanese evacuation and *Korematsu* have been the subject of extensive criticism. See, e.g., Girdner & Loftis, *The Great Betrayal* (1969); Grodzins, *Americans Betrayed*

Notes and Questions

1. *Standard of review.* *Hirabayashi* and *Korematsu* have been the last instances in which the Court has failed to invalidate intentional (or "de jure") government discrimination against a racial or ethnic minority.[d] In 1967, the Court observed that laws imposing "invidious racial discriminations" bear a "very heavy burden of justification" and "if they are ever to be upheld, they must be shown to be necessary to the accomplishment of some permissible state objective"; they are unlike statutes "involving no racial discrimination" where "the Court has merely asked whether there is any rational foundation for the discriminations, and has deferred to the wisdom of the state legislatures."[e]

2. *"Rigid scrutiny" and "special traits."* (a) Should state discrimination against a racial minority ever be upheld? Consider Douglas, J., *We the Judges* 399 (1956): "Experience shows that liquor has a devastating effect on the North American Indian and Eskimo. It is, therefore, commonly provided [that] no liquor should be sold to those races. Other regulations based on race may likewise be justified by reason of the special traits of those races [and] what at first blush may seem to be an invidious discrimination may on analysis be found to have plausible grounds justifying it."[f]

May a state require that all blacks undergo a blood test for sickle cell anemia? Suppose that "studies have indicated that seven to nine percent of the American Black population carries the sickle cell trait, while 0.3 percent suffer from the disease" and that "the incidence of sickle cell anemia in the White population is negligible"? Note, *Constitutional and Practical Considerations in Mandatory Sickle Cell Anemia Testing*, 7 U.C.D.L.Rev. 509, 519 (1974). Should it make a difference if the state, rather than the individual, pays for the blood test? May "overinclusive" racial laws be distinguished on the basis of the severity of the burden imposed? Compare *Hirabayashi, Korematsu* and *Endo.*

(b) Is a law providing "that anyone whose skin is darker than a certain shade (either attached as an exhibit or defined in terms of albedo or reflecting power) is negligent for walking on a road at night without wearing some light-colored item of clothing" distinguishable from the other situations referred to above? See Kaplan, *Equal Justice in an Unequal World: Equality for the Negro—The Problem of Special Treatment*, 61 Nw.U.L.Rev. 363, 383 (1966).

(c) May the federal government consider racial (religious) differences in assigning personnel to official American posts in foreign countries?

II. SEGREGATION AND OTHER CLASSIFICATIONS

Sec. I involved laws that imposed burdens on racial and ethnic minorities. This section concerns laws that segregate or otherwise classify on a racial basis

(1949); Rostow, *The Japanese American Cases—A Disaster*, in The Sovereign Prerogative 193 (1962); Dembitz, *Racial Discrimination and the Military Judgment*, 45 Colum.L. Rev. 175 (1945); Freeman, *Genesis, Exodus and Leviticus—Genealogy, Evacuation, and Law*, 28 Corn.L.Q. 414 (1943).

d. On the same day as *Korematsu, Ex parte Endo*, 323 U.S. 283, 65 S.Ct. 208, 89 L.Ed. 243 (1944), per Douglas, J., held that Executive Order 9066 did not authorize the continued detention of concededly loyal persons of Japanese ancestry: "This Court [has] favored

that interpretation of legislation which gives it the greater chance of surviving the test of constitutionality."

e. *Loving v. Virginia*, Part II infra. For discussion of "refinements" of the "test," see note 1 after *Loving.*

f. For discussion of federal laws that specially classify members of American Indian tribes, see Tribe, *American Constitutional Law* 1013–19 (1978); Johnson & Crystal, *Indians and Equal Protection*, 54 Wash.L.Rev. 587 (1979).

but, at least in a literal sense, treat all races identically. The principal question is whether (and, if so, why) such laws should be subject to the same "rigid" standard of review.

PLESSY v. FERGUSON

163 U.S. 537, 16 S.Ct. 1138, 41 L.Ed. 256 (1896).

MR. JUSTICE BROWN delivered the opinion of the Court.

[An 1890 Louisiana law required that railway passenger cars have "equal but separate accommodations for the white, and colored races." Plessy, alleging that he "was seven-eights Caucasian and one-eighth African blood; that the mixture of colored blood was not discernible in him; and that he was entitled to every right [of] the white race," was arrested for refusing to vacate a seat in a coach for whites.]

That it does not conflict with the thirteenth amendment [is] too clear for argument. Slavery implies involuntary servitude,—a state of bondage * * *. This amendment [was] regarded by the statesmen of that day as insufficient to protect the colored race from certain laws [imposing] onerous disabilities and burdens, and curtailing their rights in the pursuit of life, liberty, and property to such an extent that their freedom was of little value; [and] the fourteenth amendment was devised to meet this exigency. * * *

The object of the amendment was undoubtedly to enforce the absolute equality of the two races before the law, but, in the nature of things, it could not have been intended to abolish distinctions based upon color, or to enforce social, as distinguished from political, equality, or a commingling of the two races upon terms unsatisfactory to either. [Laws] requiring their separation, in places where they are liable to be brought into contact [have] been generally, if not universally, recognized as within the competency of the state legislatures in the exercise of their police power. The most common instance of this is connected with the establishment of separate schools for white and colored children, which have been [upheld] even by courts of states where the political rights of the colored race have been longest and most earnestly enforced [citing cases from Mass., Ohio, Mo., Cal., La., N.Y., Ind. and Ky.].

Laws forbidding the intermarriage of the two races may be said in a technical sense to interfere with the freedom of contract, and yet have been universally recognized as within the police power of the state. [S]tatutes for the separation of the two races upon public conveyances were held to be constitutional in [federal decisions and cases from Pa., Mich., Ill., Tenn. and N.Y. It is suggested] that the same argument that will justify the state legislature in requiring railways to provide separate accommodations for the two races will also authorize them to require separate cars to be provided for people whose hair is of a certain color, or who are aliens, or who belong to certain nationalities, or to enact laws requiring colored people to walk upon one side of the street, and white people upon the other, or requiring white men's houses to be painted white, and colored men's black, or their vehicles or business signs to be of different colors, upon the theory that one side of the street is as good as the other, or that a house or vehicle of one color is as good as one of another color. The reply to all this is that every exercise of the police power must be reasonable, and extend only to such laws as are enacted in good faith for the promotion of the public good, and not for the annoyance or oppression of a particular class. [In] determining the question of reasonableness, [the state] is at liberty to act with reference to the established usages, customs, and traditions of the people, and with a view to the promotion of their comfort, and the preservation of the public peace and good order. Gauged by this standard, we cannot say [this law] is unreasonable, or more obnoxious to the fourteenth amendment than the [acts] requiring separate schools for colored children in the District of Columbia, the constitutionality of which does not seem to have been questioned or the corresponding acts of state legislatures.[a]

We consider the underlying fallacy of the plaintiff's argument to consist in the assumption that the enforced separation of the two races stamps the colored race with a badge of inferiority. If this be so, it is not by reason of anything found in the act, but solely because the colored race chooses to put that construction upon it. [The] argument also assumes that social prejudices may be overcome by legislation, and that equal rights cannot be secured to the negro except by an enforced commingling of the two races. We cannot accept this proposition. If the two races are to meet upon terms of social equality, it must be the result [of] voluntary consent of individuals. * * * Legislation is powerless to eradicate racial instincts, or to abolish distinctions based upon physical differences, and the attempt to do so can only result in accentuating the difficulties of the present situation. * * *

Affirmed.

MR. JUSTICE BREWER did [not] participate in the decision of this case.

MR. JUSTICE HARLAN dissenting.

[No] legislative body or judicial tribunal may have regard to the race of citizens when the civil rights of those citizens are involved. * * *

It was said in argument that the statute of Louisiana does not discriminate against either race, but prescribes a rule applicable alike to white and colored citizens. But [e]very one knows that [it] had its origin in the purpose, not so much to exclude white persons from railroad cars occupied by blacks, as to exclude colored people from coaches occupied by or assigned to white persons. [The] fundamental objection, therefore, to the statute, is that it interferes with the personal freedom of citizens.[b] * * *

The white race deems itself to be the dominant race in this country. And so it is, in prestige, in achievements, in education, in wealth, and in power. So, I doubt not, it will continue to be for all time, if it remains true to its great heritage, and holds fast to the principles of constitutional liberty. But in view of the constitution, in the eye of the law, there is in this country no superior, dominant, ruling class of citizens. There is no caste here. Our constitution is color-blind * * *.

a. Compare Harris, *The Constitution, Education, and Segregation,* 29 Temp.L.Q. 409, 413 (1956): "[T]he dictum [that] reasonableness is to be construed with reference to established usages, customs and traditions of the people [wholly] ignores the fact that it was to prevent these customs and traditions from being enacted into law that the fourteenth amendment was adopted."

b. See Frank & Munro, *The Original Understanding of "Equal Protection of the Laws,"* 1972 Wash.U.L.Q. 421, 455: "We believe that the equal protection clause, in the eyes of its contemporaries, froze into constitutional law the existing common law obligation of transportation companies to take all comers and to eliminate any possibility of their segregation. Congress decided so often in this period that color classifications were not permissible for purposes of transportation that it is difficult to understand how equal protection could possibly be given another meaning." For a discussion of "civil" rights in the fourteenth amendment's history, see Bickel, *The Original Understanding and the Segregation Decision,* 69 Harv.L.Rev. 1 (1955). Compare Berger, *Government By Judiciary: The Transformation of the Fourteenth Amendment* (1977).

In my opinion, the judgment this day rendered will, in time, prove to be quite as pernicious as the decision made by this tribunal in the *Dred Scott Case* [that] the descendants of Africans who were imported into this country, and sold as slaves, were not included nor intended to be included under the word "citizens" in the constitution; [that,] at the time of the adoption of the constitution, they were "considered as a subordinate and inferior class of beings, who had been subjugated by the dominant race, and, whether emancipated or not, yet remained subject to their authority, and had no rights or privileges but such as those who held the power and the government might choose to grant them." 19 How. 393, 404. The recent amendments of the constitution, it was supposed, had eradicated these principles from our institutions. [What] can more certainly arouse race hate, what more certainly create and perpetuate a feeling of distrust between these races, than state enactments which, in fact, proceed on the ground that colored citizens are so inferior and degraded that they cannot be allowed to sit in public coaches occupied by white citizens? [The] thin disguise of "equal" accommodations for passengers in railroad coaches will not mislead any one, nor atone for the wrong this day done. * * *

I do not deem it necessary to review the decisions of state courts to which reference was made in argument. Some [are] inapplicable, because rendered prior to the adoption of the last amendments of the [constitution]. Others were made at a time [when] race prejudice was, practically, the supreme law of the land. Those decisions cannot be guides in the era introduced by the recent amendments of the supreme law, which established universal civil freedom * * *.[c]

BROWN v. BOARD OF EDUCATION

347 U.S. 483, 74 S.Ct. 686, 98 L.Ed. 873 (1954).

Mr. Chief Justice Warren delivered the opinion of the Court.

These cases come to us from the States of Kansas, South Carolina, Virginia, and Delaware. * * *

In each of the cases, minors of the Negro race [seek] the aid of the courts in obtaining admission to the public schools of their community on a nonsegregated basis. [In] each of the cases other than the Delaware case, a three-judge federal district court denied relief to the plaintiffs on the so-called "separate but equal" doctrine announced by this Court in [*Plessy*]. In the Delaware case, the Supreme Court of Delaware adhered to that doctrine, but ordered that the plaintiffs be admitted to the white schools because of their superiority to the Negro schools.

* * * Argument was heard in the 1952 Term, and reargument was heard this Term on certain questions propounded by the Court.

Reargument was largely devoted to the circumstances surrounding the adoption of the Fourteenth Amendment in 1868. It covered exhaustively consideration of the Amendment in Congress, ratification by the states, then existing practices in racial segregation, and the views of proponents and opponents of the Amendment. This discussion and our own investigation convince us that, although these sources cast some light, it is not enough to resolve the problem with which we are faced. At best, they are inconclusive. The most avid proponents of the post-War Amendments undoubtedly intended them to remove

c. For discussion of *Plessy* and its background, see Oberst, *The Strange Career of Plessy v. Ferguson*, 15 Ariz.L.Rev. 389 (1973).

all legal distinctions among "all persons born or naturalized in the United States." Their opponents, just as certainly, were antagonistic to both the letter and the spirit of the Amendments and wished them to have the most limited effect. What others in Congress and the state legislatures had in mind cannot be determined with any degree of certainty.

An additional reason for the inconclusive nature of the Amendment's history, with respect to segregated schools, is the status of public education at that time. In the South, the movement toward free common schools, supported by general taxation, had not yet taken hold. Education of white children was largely in the hands of private groups. Education of Negroes was almost nonexistent, and practically all of the race were illiterate. In fact, any education of Negroes was forbidden by law in some states. Today, in contrast, many Negroes have achieved outstanding success in the arts and sciences as well as in the business and professional world. It is true that public school education at the time of the Amendment had advanced further in the North, but the effect of the Amendment on Northern States was generally ignored in the congressional debates. Even in the North, the conditions of public education did not approximate those existing today. The curriculum was usually rudimentary; ungraded schools were common in rural areas; the school term was but three months a year in many states; and compulsory school attendance was virtually unknown. As a consequence, it is not surprising that there should be so little in the history of the Fourteenth Amendment relating to its intended effect on public education.

In the first cases in this Court construing the Fourteenth Amendment, decided shortly after its adoption, the Court interpreted it as proscribing all state-imposed discriminations against the Negro race.[5] The doctrine of "separate but equal" did not make its appearance in this Court until 1896 in *Plessy*, involving not education but transportation. [In] this Court, there have been six cases involving the "separate but equal" doctrine in the field of public education. In *Cumming v. Board of Education*, 175 U.S. 528, 20 S.Ct. 197, 44 L.Ed. 262, and *Gong Lum v. Rice*, 275 U.S. 78, 48 S.Ct. 91, 72 L.Ed. 172, the validity of the doctrine itself was not challenged.[8] In more recent cases, all on the graduate school level, inequality was found in that specific benefits enjoyed by white students were denied to Negro students of the same educational qualifications. *Missouri ex rel. Gaines v. Canada*, 305 U.S. 337, 59 S.Ct. 232, 83 L.Ed. 208 [a]; *Sipuel v. Oklahoma*, 332 U.S. 631, 68 S.Ct. 299, 92 L.Ed. 247; *Sweatt v. Painter*, 339 U.S. 629, 70 S.Ct. 848, 94 L.Ed. 1114 [b]; *McLaurin v. Oklahoma State Regents*,

---

5. *Slaughter-House Cases; Strauder* * * *. See also *Virginia v. Rives*, 1879, 100 U.S. 313, 318, 25 L.Ed. 667; *Ex parte Virginia*, 1879, 100 U.S. 339, 344–345, 25 L.Ed. 676. [See generally Brief for the Committee of Law Teachers Against Segregation in Legal Education, *Segregation and the Equal Protection Clause*, 34 Minn.L.Rev. 289 (1950).]

8. In *Cumming*, Negro taxpayers sought an injunction requiring the defendant school board to discontinue the operation of a high school for white children until the board resumed operation of a high school for Negro children. Similarly, in *Gong Lum*, the plaintiff, a child of Chinese descent, contended only that state authorities had misapplied the doctrine by classifying him with Negro children and requiring him to attend a Negro school.

a. *Gaines*, in 1938, invalidated the refusal to admit blacks to the University of Missouri School of Law, despite the state's offer to pay petitioner's tuition at an out-of-state law school pending establishment of a state law school for blacks.

b. *Sweatt*, in 1950, required admission of blacks to the University of Texas Law School despite the recent establishment of a state law school for blacks: "In terms of number of the faculty, variety of courses and opportunity for specialization, size of the student body, scope of the library, availability of law review and similar activities, the University of Texas Law School is superior. What is more important, the University of Texas Law School possesses to a far greater degree those qualities which are incapable of objective measurement but

339 U.S. 637, 70 S.Ct. 851, 94 L.Ed. 1149.[c] In none of these cases was it necessary to re-examine the doctrine to grant relief to the Negro plaintiff. And in *Sweatt,* the Court expressly reserved decision on the question whether *Plessy* should be held inapplicable to public education.

In the instant cases, that question is directly presented. [T]here are findings below that the Negro and white schools involved have been equalized, or are being equalized, with respect to buildings, curricula, qualifications and salaries of teachers, and other "tangible" factors. Our decision, therefore, cannot turn on merely a comparison of these tangible factors in the Negro and white schools involved in each of the cases. We must look instead to the effect of segregation itself on public education.

In approaching this problem, we cannot turn the clock back to 1868 when the Amendment was adopted, or even to 1896 when *Plessy* was written. We must consider public education in the light of its full development and its present place in American life throughout the Nation. Only in this way can it be determined if segregation in public schools deprives these plaintiffs of the equal protection of the laws.

Today, education is perhaps the most important function of state and local governments. Compulsory school attendance laws and the great expenditures for education both demonstrate our recognition of the importance of education to our democratic society. It is required in the performance of our most basic public responsibilities, even service in the armed forces. It is the very foundation of good citizenship. Today it is a principal instrument in awakening the child to cultural values, in preparing him for later professional training, and in helping him to adjust normally to his environment. In these days, it is doubtful that any child may reasonably be expected to succeed in life if he is denied the opportunity of an education. Such an opportunity, where the state has undertaken to provide it, is a right which must be made available to all on equal terms.

We come then to the question presented: Does segregation of children in public schools solely on the basis of race, even though the physical facilities and other "tangible" factors may be equal, deprive the children of the minority group of equal educational opportunities? We believe that it does.

In *Sweatt,* in finding that a segregated law school for Negroes could not provide them equal educational opportunities, this Court relied in large part on "those qualities which are incapable of objective measurement but which make for greatness in a law school." In *McLaurin,* the Court, in requiring that a Negro admitted to a white graduate school be treated like all other students, again resorted to intangible considerations: "[his] ability to study, to engage in

which make for greatness in a law school. Such qualities, to name but a few, include reputation of the faculty, experience of the administration, position and influence of the alumni, standing in the community, traditions and prestige. [Moreover, the law school] cannot be effective in isolation from the individuals and institutions with which the law interacts. Few students and no one who has practiced law would choose to study in an academic vacuum, removed from the interplay of ideas and the exchange of views with which the law is concerned. The law school to which Texas is willing to admit petitioner excludes from its student body members of the racial groups which number 85% of the population of the State and include most of the lawyers, witnesses, jurors, judges and other officials with whom petitioner will inevitably be dealing when he becomes a member of the Texas Bar."

c. *McLaurin,* in 1950, held violative of equal protection requirements that black graduate students at the University of Oklahoma sit at separate desks adjoining the classrooms and separate tables outside the library reading room, and eat at separate times in the school cafeteria.

discussions and exchange views with other students, and in general, to learn his profession." Such considerations apply with added force to children in grade and high schools. To separate them from others of similar age and qualifications solely because of their race generates a feeling of inferiority as to their status in the community that may affect their hearts and minds in a way unlikely ever to be undone. The effect of this separation on their educational opportunities was well stated by a finding in the Kansas case by a court which nevertheless felt compelled to rule against the Negro plaintiffs: "Segregation of white and colored children in public schools has a detrimental effect upon the colored children. The impact is greater when it has the sanction of the law; for the policy of separating the races is usually interpreted as denoting the inferiority of the Negro group. A sense of inferiority affects the motivation of a child to learn. Segregation with the sanction of law, therefore, has a tendency to [retard] the educational and mental development of Negro children and to deprive them of some of the benefits they would receive in a racial[ly] integrated school system." [10] Whatever may have been the extent of psychological knowledge at the time of *Plessy,* this finding is amply supported by modern authority.[11] Any language in *Plessy* contrary to this finding is rejected.

We conclude that in the field of public education the doctrine of "separate but equal" has no place. Separate educational facilities are inherently unequal. Therefore, we hold that the plaintiffs and others similarly situated for whom the actions have been brought are, by reason of the segregation complained of, deprived of [equal protection].

Because these are class actions, because of the wide applicability of this decision, and because of the great variety of local conditions, the formulation of decrees in these cases presents problems of considerable complexity. On reargument, the consideration of appropriate relief was necessarily subordinated to the primary question—the constitutionality of segregation in public education. We have now announced that such segregation is a denial of the equal protection of the laws. In order that we may have the full assistance of the parties in formulating decrees, the cases will be restored to the docket, and the parties are requested to present further argument on Questions 4 and 5 previously propounded by the Court for the reargument this Term.[13] The Attorney General of the United States is again invited to participate. The Attorney General of the

---

10. A similar finding was made in the Delaware case: "I conclude from the testimony that in our Delaware society, State-imposed segregation in education itself results in the Negro children, as a class, receiving educational opportunities which are substantially inferior to those available to white children otherwise similarly situated."

11. Clark, *Effect of Prejudice and Discrimination on Personality Development* (Midcentury White House Conference on Children and Youth, 1950); Witmer and Kotinsky, *Personality in the Making* (1952), c. VI; Deutscher and Chein, *The Psychological Effects of Enforced Segregation: A Survey of Social Science Opinion,* 26 J.Psychol. 259 (1948); Chein, *What are the Psychological Effects of Segregation Under Conditions of Equal Facilities?,* 3 Int.J. Opinion and Attitude Res. 229 (1949); Brameld, *Educational Costs in Discrimination and National Welfare* (MacIver, ed., 1949), 44–48; Frazier, *The Negro in the United States* (1949),

674–681. And, see generally Myrdal, *An American Dilemma* (1944).

13. "4. Assuming it is decided that segregation in public schools violates the Fourteenth Amendment

"(a) would a decree necessarily follow providing that, within the limits set by normal geographic school districting, Negro children should forthwith be admitted to schools of their choice, or

"(b) may this Court, in the exercise of its equity powers, permit an effective gradual adjustment to be brought about from existing segregated systems to a system not based on color distinctions?

"5. On the assumption on which questions 4(a) and (b) are based, and assuming further that this Court will exercise its equity powers to the end described in question 4(b),

"(a) should this Court formulate detailed decrees in these cases;

states requiring or permitting segregation in public education will also be permitted to appear * * *.

Notes and Questions

1. *The Court's rationale.* What was the specific basis for the decision?

(a) *Social science materials.* At trial in several of the cases, psychiatrists and social scientists testified as to the harmful effects of state-imposed segregation on black children. On appeal, appellants filed a statement to this effect by 32 sociologists, anthropologists, psychologists, and psychiatrists who worked in the area of American race relations—reprinted in 37 Minn.L.Rev. 427 (1953).

Was the decision based on this information? Is this desirable? Should *Brown* be modified or overruled if new social science data reaches different conclusions?[d] Consider Cahn, *Jurisprudence,* 30 N.Y.U.L.Rev. 150, 157–58, 167 (1955): "[S]ince the behavioral sciences are so very young, imprecise, and changeful, their findings have an uncertain expectancy of life. Today's sanguine asseveration may be cancelled by tomorrow's new revelation—or new technical fad. It is one thing to use the current scientific findings, however ephemeral they may be, in order to ascertain whether the legislature has acted reasonably in adopting some scheme of social or economic regulation; deference here is shown not so much to the findings as to the legislature. It would be quite another thing to have our fundamental rights rise, fall, or change along with the latest fashions of psychological literature."

(b) Does *Brown* rest on a finding that "in terms of the most familiar and universally accepted standards of right and wrong [racial] segregation under government auspices inevitably inflicts humiliation, [and] official humiliation of innocent, law-abiding citizens is psychologically injurious and morally evil"? Cahn, supra, at 159. If so, where are such "universally accepted standards" found? See Dworkin, *Social Sciences and Constitutional Rights—The Consequences of Uncertainty,* 6 J.L. & Ed. 3 (1977).

(c) *Historical considerations.* (i) Would it have been better for the Court to rely upon the original purpose of the fourteenth amendment as stated in *Strauder:* to grant blacks "the right to exemption from unfriendly legislation against them as distinctively colored"? If so, how should *Plessy* have been treated? Was the *Brown* Court in 1954 a better judge of fourteenth amendment intent than the *Plessy* Court in 1896? Than the *Strauder* Court in 1879?

(ii) Apart from the specific intentions of the framers and ratifiers of the fourteenth amendment in respect to school segregation,[e] of what significance is

"(b) if so, what specific issues should the decrees reach;

"(c) should this Court appoint a special master to hear evidence with a view to recommending specific terms for such decrees;

"(d) should this Court remand to the courts of first instance with directions to frame decrees in these cases, and if so what general directions should the decrees of this Court include and what procedures should the courts of first instance follow in arriving at the specific terms of more detailed decrees?"

d. For extensive discussion and comprehensive listing of the substantial and controversial research and literature on the subject, see Symposia, *School Desegregation: Lessons*

of the First Twenty-Five Years, 42 Law & Contemp.Prob., nos. 3–4 (1978). In particular, see Yudof, *School Desegregation: Legal Realism, Reasoned Elaboration, and Social Science Research in the Supreme Court,* 42 Law & Contemp.Prob. 57, 61 nn. 26–27 (no. 4, 1978). See also Goodman, *De Facto School Segregation: A Constitutional and Empirical Analysis,* 60 Calif.L.Rev. 275 (1972).

e. For the view that the framers did not intend to prohibit it, see Berger, *Government by Judiciary* 117–33 (1977); Perry, *The Constitution, the Courts, and Human Rights* 66–69 (1982). Compare Dimond, *Strict Construction and Judicial Review of Racial Discrimination Under the Equal Protection Clause,* 80 Mich.L.

the fact that "every one of the twenty-six states that had any substantial racial differences among its people either approved the operation of segregated schools already in existence or subsequently established such schools by action of the same law-making body which considered the Fourteenth Amendment"? *Declaration of Constitutional Principles Issued by 19 Senators and 77 Representatives of the Congress*, N.Y. Times, p. 19, col. 2, March 12, 1956. What justified the Court's consideration of "public education in the light of its full development and its present place in American life throughout the Nation"? Consider Bickel, *The Original Understanding and the Segregation Decision*, 69 Harv.L.Rev. 1, 59 (1955): "If the fourteenth amendment were a statute, a court might very well hold [that] it was foreclosed from applying it to segregation in public schools. [But] we are dealing with a constitutional amendment, not a statute. The tradition of a broadly worded organic law not frequently or lightly amended was well-established by 1866, and [it] cannot be assumed that [anyone] expected or wished the future role of the Constitution in the scheme of American government to differ from the past. Should not the search for congressional purpose therefore, properly be twofold? One inquiry should be directed at the congressional understanding of the immediate effect of the enactment on conditions then present. Another should aim to discover what if any thought was given to the long-range effect, under future circumstances, of provisions necessarily intended for permanence."

2. *"Neutral principles."* Consider Wechsler, *Toward Neutral Principles of Constitutional Law*, 73 Harv.L.Rev. 1, 34 (1959): "[A]ssuming equal facilities, the question posed by state-enforced segregation is not one of discrimination at all. Its human and its constitutional dimensions lie [in] the denial by the state of freedom to associate, a denial that impinges in the same way on any groups or races that may be involved. [But] if the freedom of association is denied by segregation, integration forces an association upon those for whom it is unpleasant or repugnant. [W]here the state must practically choose between denying the association to those individuals who wish it or imposing it on those who would avoid it, is there a basis in neutral principles for holding that the Constitution demands that the claims for association should prevail?"

In reply, consider the following from a "draft opinion" of *Brown* by Pollak, *Racial Discrimination and Judicial Integrity: A Reply to Professor Wechsler*, 108 U.Pa.L.Rev. 1, 27, 29–30 (1959): "[W]e start from the base point that in the United States 'all legal restrictions which curtail the civil rights of a single racial group are immediately suspect.' *Korematsu*. [T]here is special need for 'a searching judicial inquiry into the legislative judgment in situations where prejudice against discrete and insular minorities may tend to curtail the operation of those political processes ordinarily to be relied on to protect minorities.' See *United States v. Carolene Products*, n. 4 [p. 23 supra]. We could not, therefore, sustain the reasonableness of these racial distinctions and the absence of harm said to flow from them, unless we were prepared to say that no factual case can be made the other way. [To] the extent that implementation of this decision forces racial mingling on school children against their will, [this] consequence follows because the community through its political processes has [chosen] compulsory education. [The resulting] coerced association [cannot] be said to emanate from this Court or from the Constitution. In any event, parents sufficiently disturbed at the prospect of having their children educated in

Rev. 462 (1982); Grano, *Judicial Review and a Written Constitution in a Democratic Society,* 28 Wayne L.Rev. 1, 67–72 (1981).

democratic fashion in company with their peers are presumably entitled to fulfill their educational responsibilities in other ways."

See also Black, *The Lawfulness of the Segregation Decisions,* 69 Yale L.J. 421, 429 (1960): "The fourteenth amendment [forbids] disadvantaging the Negro race by law. It was surely anticipated that the following of this directive would entail some disagreeableness for some white southerners. [When] the directive of equality cannot be followed without displeasing the white, then something that can be called a 'freedom' of the white must be impaired. If the fourteenth amendment commands equality, and if segregation violates equality, then the status of the reciprocal 'freedom' is automatically settled." [f]

3. *Extent of the decision.* (a) Did *Brown* bar all forms of state-imposed racial segregation? Or did it apply only to public schools? For comment immediately after *Brown,* consider Kauper, *Segregation in Public Education,* 52 Mich.L.Rev. 1137, 1154–55 (1954): "[*Brown*] placed emphasis upon the intangible factors that make the *Plessy* doctrine inapplicable to public schools. Education is an experience and not simply an enjoyment of physical facilities. But with respect to common carrier and public recreational facilities, the emphasis is upon the enjoyment of the physical facilities and services so that it is more nearly possible to speak of equality of enjoyment within the pattern of segregation." Compare McKay, *Segregation and Public Recreation,* 40 Va.L.Rev. 697, 724 (1954): "[T]here appears to be no reason to believe that the sense of inferiority engendered by segregation in recreation is any less than in education." See Pollak, supra, at 29: "[W]here facilities are voluntary the community's asserted need to ordain segregation seems even less weighty [for] those for whom racial mingling is obnoxious are under no obligation to attend."

(b) After *Brown,* the Court, by means of rather summary per curiam decisions, citing *Brown,* consistently held invalid state imposed racial segregation in other public facilities. [g]

4. *Segregation by the federal government.* (a) BOLLING v. SHARPE, 347 U.S. 497, 74 S.Ct. 693, 98 L.Ed. 884 (1954), per WARREN, C.J., held—on the same day as *Brown*—that public school segregation in the District of Columbia "constitutes an arbitrary deprivation [of] liberty in violation of the Due Process Clause" of the fifth amendment: "The Fifth Amendment [does] not contain an equal protection clause as does the Fourteenth Amendment which applies only to the states. But the concepts of equal protection and due process, both stemming from our American ideal of fairness, are not mutually exclusive. The 'equal protection of the laws' is a more explicit safeguard of prohibited unfairness than 'due process of law,' and, therefore, we do not imply that the two are always interchangeable phrases. But, as this Court has recognized, discrimination may be so unjustifiable as to be violative of due process.

"Classifications based solely upon race must be scrutinized with particular care, since they are contrary to our traditions and hence constitutionally suspect. ["Liberty"] extends to the full range of conduct which the individual is free to pursue, and it cannot be restricted except for a proper governmental objective.

f. For the view that "the decision in *Brown* to break with the Court's long-held position on [segregation] cannot be understood without some consideration of the decision's value to whites [in] policymaking positions able to see the economic and political advances at home and abroad that would follow abandonment of segregation," see Bell, *Brown v. Board of Edu-* *cation and the Interest-Convergence Dilemma,* 93 Harv.L.Rev. 518 (1980).

g. For a detailed listing of these and lower court decisions, see Lockhart, Kamisar & Choper, *Constitutional Law: Cases—Comments—Questions* 1206 (3d ed. 1970).

Segregation in public education is not reasonably related to any proper governmental objective * * *.

"In view of our decision that the Constitution prohibits the states from
maintaining racially segregated public schools, it would be unthinkable that the
same Constitution would impose a lesser duty on the Federal Government."

(b) Does every racial classification violative of equal protection also violate
due process? Irrespective of the substance of what is being denied? Suppose
Congress passed a law for the District of Columbia requiring courtroom spectators to be racially segregated? Cf. *Johnson v. Virginia,* 373 U.S. 61, 83 S.Ct.
1053, 10 L.Ed.2d 195 (1963). Suppose a black witness was held in contempt by a
federal judge when she refused to testify unless she was addressed by her last
name, as are whites? Cf. *Hamilton v. Alabama,* 376 U.S. 650, 11 L.Ed.2d 979, 84
S.Ct. 982 (1964). Would it "be unthinkable [to] impose a lesser duty on the
Federal Government"? See fn. a, p. 796 supra.

BROWN v. BOARD OF EDUCATION
349 U.S. 294, 75 S.Ct. 753, 99 L.Ed. 1083 (1955).

MR. CHIEF JUSTICE WARREN delivered the opinion of the Court.

These cases were decided on May 17, 1954. [There] remains for consideration the manner in which relief is to be accorded. * * *

Full implementation of these constitutional principles may require solution
of varied local school problems. School authorities have the primary responsibility for elucidating, assessing, and solving [them]; courts will have to consider
whether the action of school authorities constitutes good faith implementation of
the governing constitutional principles. Because of their proximity to local
conditions and the possible need for further hearings, the courts which originally
heard these cases can best perform this judicial appraisal. Accordingly, we
believe it appropriate to remand the cases to those courts.

In fashioning and effectuating the decrees, the courts will be guided by
equitable principles. Traditionally, equity has been characterized by a practical
flexibility in shaping its remedies and by a facility for adjusting and reconciling
public and private needs. [A]t stake is the personal interest of the plaintiffs in
admission to public schools as soon as practicable on a nondiscriminatory basis.
To effectuate this interest may call for elimination of a variety of obstacles in
making the transition to school systems operated in accordance with the constitutional principles set forth in our May 17, 1954, decision. Courts of equity may
properly take into account the public interest in the elimination of such
obstacles in a systematic and effective manner. But it should go without saying
that the vitality of these constitutional principles cannot be allowed to yield
simply because of disagreement with them.

While giving weight to these public and private considerations, the courts
will require that the defendants make a prompt and reasonable start toward full
compliance with our May 17, 1954, ruling. Once such a start has been made, the
courts may find that additional time is necessary to carry out the ruling in an
effective manner. The burden rests upon the defendants to establish that such
time is necessary in the public interest and is consistent with good faith
compliance at the earliest practicable date. To that end, the courts may
consider problems related to administration, arising from the physical condition
of the school plant, the school transportation system, personnel, revision of
school districts and attendance areas into compact units to achieve a system of
determining admission to the public schools on a nonracial basis, and revision of

local laws and regulations which may be necessary in solving the foregoing problems. They will also consider the adequacy of any plans the defendants may propose to meet these problems and to effectuate a transition to a racially nondiscriminatory school system. During this period of transition, the courts will retain jurisdiction of these cases.

The [cases are remanded] to take such proceedings and enter such orders and decrees consistent with this opinion as are necessary and proper to admit to public schools on a racially nondiscriminatory basis with all deliberate speed the parties to these cases.   *   *   *

Notes and Questions

1. *"Individual" vs. "race" rights.* Was the decree consistent with *Brown I*? Since plaintiffs had only a limited number of years of school remaining, did postponement of relief partially or totally destroy the very rights the decree was intended to enforce? Does the "deliberate speed" formula assume that "Negroes (unlike whites) possess rights as a race rather than as individuals, so that a particular Negro can rightly be delayed in the enjoyment of his established rights if progress is being made in improving the legal status of Negroes generally"? Lusky, *The Stereotype: Hard Core of Racism*, 13 Buf.L.Rev. 450, 457 (1963). See also Carter, *The Warren Court and Desegregation*, 67 Mich.L.Rev. 237, 243 (1968). To what extent may the "deliberate speed" decree "have served the interests of blacks even while it accommodated the opposition of whites"? Gewirtz, *Remedies and Resistance*, 92 Yale L.J. 585, 609–28 (1983).

2. *"Deliberate speed" and the slow pace of desegregation.* What of Black, J.'s view that this formula "delayed the process of outlawing segregation" and that it would have been preferable to treat *Brown* "as an ordinary law suit and force that judgment on the counties it affected that minute"? Transcript, *Justice Black and the Bill of Rights*, CBS News Special, Dec. 3, 1968. Should the Court have relied on social science data that "prompt, decisive action on the part of recognized authorities usually results in less anxiety and less resistance in cases where the public is opposed to the action than does a more hesitant and gradual procedure"? Clark, *Introduction to Argument: The Complete Oral Argument in Brown, 1952–55*, xxxiii (Friedman ed. 1969). Compare Graglia, *The Brown Cases Revisited: Where Are They Now?*, 1 Benchmark 23, 27 (Mar.–Apr. 1984): "There can be little doubt that if the Court had ordered the end of segregation in 1954 or 1955 the result would have been the closing of public schools in much of the South, about which the Court could have done nothing. The principal impact would have been on poor blacks, and *Brown* could have come to be seen as a blunder and symbol of judicial impotence." [a]

3. *Responsibility of local officials.* Was it wise to give *local* school authorities and *local* federal judges "primary responsibility" for effectuating desegregation? To permit "practical flexibility"? Were local school officials "most prone to resent and resist the changes ordered by the Court, and to look upon the newly enunciated constitutional doctrine as a personal repudiation"? Carter, supra, at 245. Were the district courts the sector of the federal judiciary most exposed to community pressures and least willing and able to challenge local mores? See Lusky, *Racial Discrimination and the Federal Law: A Problem in*

a. See also Bickel, *The Decade of School Desegregation: Progress and Prospects*, 64 Colum.L.Rev. 193, 201–02 (1964); Kaplan, *Comment on School Desegregation*, 64 Colum. L.Rev. 223, 224–26 (1964).

Nullification, 63 Colum.L.Rev. 1163 (1963). Was it wise to have the lower federal courts judge compliance under such broad standards as "good faith" and "public interest"? See Carter, *Equal Educational Opportunities for Negroes— Abstraction or Reality,* 1968 U.Ill.L.F. 160, 177–80.[b]

LOVING v. VIRGINIA
388 U.S. 1, 87 S.Ct. 1817, 18 L.Ed.2d 1010 (1967).

MR. CHIEF JUSTICE WARREN delivered the opinion of the Court.

This case presents a constitutional question never addressed by this Court: whether a statutory scheme adopted by Virginia to prevent marriages between persons solely on the basis of racial classifications violates [the] Fourteenth Amendment. [Appellants, a black woman and white man, were married in the District of Columbia, returned to reside in Virginia, and were convicted under the state antimiscegenation statute.]

Virginia is now one of 16 States which prohibit and punish marriages on the basis of racial classifications.[5] * * *

In upholding the constitutionality of these provisions [the] state court concluded that the State's legitimate purposes were "to preserve the racial integrity of its citizens," and to prevent "the corruption of blood," "a mongrel breed of citizens," and "the obliteration of racial pride," obviously an endorsement of the doctrine of White Supremacy. [T]he State [argues] that the meaning of the Equal Protection Clause, as illuminated by the statements of the Framers, is only that state penal laws containing an interracial element as part of the definition of the offense must apply equally to whites and Negroes in the sense that members of each race are punished to the same degree. * * *

Because we reject the notion that the mere "equal application" of a statute containing racial classifications is enough to remove the classifications from the Fourteenth Amendment's proscription of all invidious racial discriminations, we do not accept the State's contention that these statutes should be upheld if there is any possible basis for concluding that they serve a rational purpose. [Here], we deal with statutes containing racial classifications, and the fact of equal application does not immunize the statute from the very heavy burden of justification which the Fourteenth Amendment has traditionally required of state statutes drawn according to race.

The State argues that statements in the Thirty-ninth Congress about the time of the passage of the Fourteenth Amendment indicate that the Framers did not intend the Amendment to make unconstitutional state miscegenation laws. Many of the statements [have] some relevance to the intention of Congress in submitting the Fourteenth Amendment, [but] it must be understood that they pertained to the passage of specific statutes and not to the broader, organic purpose of a constitutional amendment. As for the various statements directly concerning the Fourteenth Amendment, we have said in connection with a related problem, that although these historical sources "cast some light" they are not sufficient to resolve the problem; "[a]t best, they are inconclusive." *Brown.* We have rejected the proposition that the debates in the Thirty-ninth Congress or in the state legislatures which ratified the Fourteenth Amendment supported the theory [that equal protection] is satisfied by penal laws defining

---

b. The developments in implementing *Brown* are considered in Part IV, A infra.

For a fascinating description of the Court's internal decisionmaking process in the segregation cases, see Hutchinson, *Unanimity and*

Desegregation: Decisionmaking in the Supreme Court, 1948–1958, 68 Geo.L.J. 1 (1979).

5. [Over] the past 15 years, 14 States have repealed laws outlawing interracial marriages * * *.

offenses based on racial classifications so long as white and Negro participants in the offense were similarly punished. *McLaughlin v. Florida,* 379 U.S. 184, 85 S.Ct. 283, 13 L.Ed.2d 222 (1964).[a]

The State finds support for its "equal application" theory [in] *Pace v. Alabama,* 106 U.S. 583, 1 S.Ct. 637, 27 L.Ed. 207 (1883). In that case, the Court upheld a conviction under an Alabama statute forbidding adultery or fornication between a white person and a Negro which imposed a greater penalty than that of a statute proscribing similar conduct by members of the same race. The Court reasoned that the statute could not be said to discriminate against Negroes because the punishment for each participant in the offense was the same. However, as recently as the 1964 Term, in rejecting the reasoning of that case, we stated "*Pace* represents a limited view of the Equal Protection Clause which has not withstood analysis in the subsequent decisions of this Court." *McLaughlin.* [The] clear and central purpose of the Fourteenth Amendment was to eliminate all official state sources of invidious racial discrimination in the States. [At] the very least, the Equal Protection Clause demands that racial classifications, especially suspect in criminal statutes, be subjected to the "most rigid scrutiny," and, if they are ever to be upheld, they must be shown to be necessary to the accomplishment of some permissible state objective, independent of the racial discrimination which it was the object of the Fourteenth Amendment to eliminate.[b] Indeed, two [justices] have already stated that they "cannot conceive of a valid legislative purpose [which] makes the color of a person's skin the test of whether his conduct is a criminal offense." *McLaughlin* (Stewart, J., joined by Douglas, J., concurring).

There is patently no legitimate overriding purpose independent of invidious racial discrimination which justifies this classification. The fact that Virginia only prohibits interracial marriages involving white persons demonstrates that the racial classifications must stand on their own justification, as measures designed to maintain White Supremacy.[11] We have consistently denied the constitutionality of measures which restrict the rights of citizens on account of race. There can be no doubt that restricting the freedom to marry solely because of racial classifications violates the central meaning of the Equal Protection Clause.

These statutes also deprive the Lovings of liberty without [due process].

Marriage is one of the "basic civil rights of man," fundamental to our very existence and survival. *Skinner v. Oklahoma* [p. 124 supra]. To deny this fundamental freedom on so unsupportable a basis as the racial classifications embodied in these statutes [surely denies due process].

Reversed.

---

a. *McLaughlin* invalidated a statute making interracial cohabitation a crime.

b. *McLaughlin* also stated that racial classifications were " 'in most circumstances irrelevant' to any constitutionally acceptable legislative purpose." Harlan, J., concurring, added that "necessity, not mere reasonable relationship, is the proper test"; this "test which developed to protect free speech against state infringement should be equally applicable in a case involving state racial discrimination—prohibition of which lies at the very heart of the Fourteenth Amendment."

11. [While] Virginia prohibits whites from marrying any nonwhite (subject to the exception for the descendants of Pocahontas), Negroes, Orientals and any other racial class may intermarry without statutory interference. Appellants contend that this distinction renders Virginia's miscegenation statutes arbitrary and unreasonable even assuming the constitutional validity of an official purpose to preserve "racial integrity." We need not reach this contention because we find the racial classifications in these statutes repugnant to the Fourteenth Amendment, even assuming an evenhanded state purpose to protect the "integrity" of all races.

Mr. Justice Stewart, concurring.

I have previously expressed the belief that "it is simply not possible for a state law to be valid under our Constitution which makes the criminality of an act depend upon the race of the actor." *McLaughlin* (concurring opinion). Because I adhere to that belief, I concur in the judgment of the Court.

Notes and Questions

1. *Standard of review.* Is the constitutional test for laws that *classify* by race or ethnicity different from that for laws that *discriminate* against racial or ethnic minorities? Does *Loving* require only that the state purpose be "permissible" in contrast to *Korematsu's* requirement of "pressing public necessity"? Is *Loving's* seemingly more deferential test attributable to the fact that the antimiscegenation law "punished members of each race to the same degree"? See 2 Dorsen, Bender, Neuborne & Law, *Political and Civil Rights in the United States* 82–85 (Law School ed., 4th ed. 1979). Compare *In re Griffiths*, Sec. 3, II infra: "In order to justify the use of a suspect classification, a State must show that its purpose or interest is both constitutionally permissible [8] and substantial,[9] and that its use of the classification is 'necessary to the accomplishment' of its purpose or the safeguarding of its interest."

2. *Racial information.* ANDERSON v. MARTIN, 375 U.S. 399, 84 S.Ct. 454, 11 L.Ed.2d 430 (1964), held violative of equal protection a statute requiring that the race of candidates for elective office be on the ballot: "The vice lies [in] the placing of the power of the State behind a racial classification that induces racial prejudice at the polls." Should the result turn on whether a black candidate is likely to receive more or less votes because of race being designated? On whether the statute contributes to a more informed electorate? See Comments, 15 Stan.L.Rev. 339 (1963); 111 U.Pa.L.Rev. 827 (1963). May a state collect racial statistics within school districts to effectuate a policy of integration? May a national census include racial information? May a state, for statistical purposes, require designation of the parties' race on every divorce decree? See *Tancil v. Woolls*, 379 U.S. 19, 85 S.Ct. 157, 13 L.Ed.2d 91 (1964).

3. *Family issues.* PALMORE v. SIDOTI, 466 U.S. 429, 104 S.Ct. 1879, 80 L.Ed.2d 421 (1984), per Burger, C.J., held that Florida's denial of child custody to a white mother because her new husband was black violated equal protection: "There is a risk that a child living with a step-parent of a different race may be subject to a variety of pressures and stresses not present if the child were living with parents of the same racial or ethnic origin. [But the] effects of racial prejudice, however real, cannot justify a racial classification removing an infant child from the custody of its natural mother found to be an appropriate person to have such custody."

4. *Law enforcement issues.* May a police department assign all black officers to black residential areas and all white officers to white residential areas? May it *ever* consider race in determining assignment? May prison officials take racial tensions among prisoners into account in maintaining

8. Discrimination or segregation for its own sake is not, of course, a constitutionally permissible purpose.

9. The state interest required has been characterized as "overriding," *Loving,* "compelling," *Graham v. Richardson* [Sec. 3, II infra], "important," *Dunn v. Blumstein,* [Sec. 4, II infra], or "substantial," ibid. We attribute no particular significance to these variations in diction.

security, discipline, or good order? Cf. *Lee v. Washington,* 390 U.S. 333, 88 S.Ct. 994, 19 L.Ed.2d 1212 (1968).

III. DE JURE VS. DE FACTO DISCRIMINATION

Part I involved laws that explicitly discriminated against racial and ethnic minorities. But intentional (or "de jure") discrimination may exist even though the law in question is racially "neutral" on its face: the law may be deliberately administered in a discriminatory way; or a law, although neutral in its language and applied in accordance with its terms, may have been enacted with a purpose (or motive) to disadvantage a "suspect" class. This section concerns these additional types of "de jure" discrimination as well as government action that is racially neutral in its terms, administration, and purpose but which has a discriminatory effect or impact ("de facto" discrimination).

YICK WO v. HOPKINS

118 U.S. 356, 6 S.Ct. 1064, 30 L.Ed. 220 (1886).

Mr. Justice Matthews delivered the opinion of the Court.

[A San Francisco ordinance made it unlawful to operate a laundry without the consent of the board of supervisors except in a brick or stone building. Yick Wo, a Chinese alien who had operated a laundry for 22 years, had certificates from the health and fire authorities, but was refused consent by the board. For violating the ordinance, he was fined $10 and jailed for nonpayment. It was admitted that "there were about 320 laundries in the city [and] about 240 were owned [by] subjects of China, and of the whole number, viz., 320, about 310 were constructed of wood"; that "petitioner, and more than 150 of his countrymen, have been arrested" for violating the ordinance "while those who are not subjects of China, and who are conducting 80 odd laundries under similar conditions, are left unmolested."]

[T]he facts shown establish an administration directed so exclusively against a particular class of persons as to warrant and require the conclusion that, whatever may have been the intent of the ordinances as adopted, they are applied [with] a mind so unequal and oppressive as to amount to a practical denial by the State of [equal protection]. Though the law itself be fair on its face and impartial in appearance, yet, if it is applied and administered by public authority with an evil eye and an unequal hand, so as practically to make unjust and illegal discriminations between persons in similar circumstances, material to their rights, the denial of equal justice is still within the prohibition of the Constitution. * * *

The present cases [are] within this class. It appears [that] petitioners have complied with every requisite deemed by the law, or by the public officers charged with its administration, necessary for the protection of neighboring property from fire, or as a precaution against injury to the public health. No reason whatever, except the will of the supervisors, is assigned why they should not be permitted to carry [on] their harmless and useful occupation, on which they depend for a livelihood; and while this consent of the supervisors is withheld from them, and from 200 others who have also petitioned, all of whom happen to be Chinese subjects, 80 others, not Chinese subjects, are permitted to carry on the same business under similar conditions. The fact of this discrimination is admitted. No reason for it is shown, and the conclusion cannot be resisted that no reason for it exists except hostility to the race and nationality to which the petitioners [belong]. The discrimination is therefore [a] denial of [equal protection].

Notes and Questions

1. *Proving intentional discrimination.* (a) *Jury selection.* In CAS-TANEDA v. PARTIDA, 430 U.S. 482, 97 S.Ct. 1272, 51 L.Ed.2d 498 (1977), respondent challenged the grand jury that indicted him in 1972. He showed that, although 79% of the county's population had Spanish surnames, the average percentage of Spanish-surnamed grand jurors between 1962-72 was 39%. In 1972, 52.5% of persons on the grand jury list had Spanish surnames as did 50% of those on respondent's grand jury list. The Court, per BLACKMUN, J., held that respondent had established a prima facie case of discrimination against Mexican-Americans: [a]

"While the earlier cases involved absolute exclusion of an identifiable group, later cases established the principle that substantial underrepresentation of the group constitutes a constitutional violation as well, if it results from purposeful discrimination. [T]he degree of underrepresentation must be proved, by comparing the proportion of the group in the total population to the proportion called to serve as grand jurors, over a significant period of time.[13] [A] selection procedure that is susceptible of abuse or is not racially neutral supports the presumption of discrimination raised by the statistical showing.[b] Once the defendant has shown substantial underrepresentation of his group, he has made out a prima facie case of discriminatory purpose, and the burden then shifts to the State to rebut that case."

Should the state's proof that a majority of the jury commissioners were Mexican-American rebut the prima facie case? A majority of elected officials in the county? See *Castaneda.* Should jury commissioners be at least required to be composed with proportional racial representation? See Douglas, J., dissenting in *Carter v. Jury Comm'n,* 396 U.S. 320, 90 S.Ct. 518, 24 L.Ed.2d 549 (1970).[c]

(b) *Executive appointments.* In MAYOR OF PHILA. v. EDUCATIONAL EQUALITY LEAGUE, 415 U.S. 605, 94 S.Ct. 1323, 39 L.Ed.2d 630 (1974), respondents contended that in 1971 the mayor had racially discriminated in appointments to the city's Nominating Panel which nominated school board members. Under the city charter, the Panel had thirteen persons—four appointed from the citizenry at large and the others being the highest-ranking officers of nine city-wide organizations (e.g., labor union council, commerce group, parent-teacher association, etc.). Approximately "34% of the population of Philadelphia and approximately 60% of the students attending the city's various schools were Negroes" but "the 1971 Panel had 11 whites and two Negroes."

---

a. Burger, C.J., and Stewart, Powell and Rehnquist, JJ., dissented.

13. [If] a disparity is sufficiently large, then it is unlikely that it is due solely to chance or accident, and, in the absence of evidence to the contrary, one must conclude that racial or other class-related factors entered into the selection process.

b. The Court observed that, "as in *Alexander v. Louisiana,* 405 U.S. 625, 92 S.Ct. 1221, 31 L.Ed.2d 536 (1972), the selection procedure [here] is not racially neutral with respect to Mexican-Americans; Spanish surnames are just as easily identifiable as race was from the questionnaires in *Alexander* or the notations and card colors in *Whitus v. Georgia,* 385 U.S. 545, 87 S.Ct. 643, 17 L.Ed.2d 599 (1967)."

c. See generally Finkelstein, *The Application of Statistical Decision Theory to the Jury Discrimination Cases,* 80 Harv.L.Rev. 338 (1966); Comment, *The Civil Petitioner's Right to Representative Grand Juries and a Statistical Method of Showing Discrimination in Jury Selection Cases Generally,* 20 U.C.L.A.L.Rev. 581 (1973).

The Court, per POWELL, J., held the proof "too fragmentary and speculative" to establish "a prima facie case of racial discrimination." The statistics were "simplistic percentage comparisons [in] the context of this case"; because of the designated qualifications for Panel members, it could not "be assumed that all citizens are fungible for purposes of determining whether members of a particular class have been unlawfully excluded." [d]

2. *Criminal enforcement.* (a) May a black prosecuted for violating a gambling ordinance defend on the ground that the law is enforced only against blacks? May the police justify their conduct on the ground that, since *most* gambling was believed to be taking place in black residential areas, *all* the "gambling squad" was assigned there? Is this different from a state justifying its exclusion of *all* blacks from jury service because *most* did not possess adequate educational qualifications? See generally Johnson, *Race and the Decision to Detain a Suspect,* 93 Yale L.J. 214 (1983).

(b) Is *Yick Wo* distinguishable from the gambling hypothetical because, in *Yick Wo,* "*no* reason for [the discrimination was] shown" and "*no* reason for it exists except hostility to the race"? Is *Yick Wo* distinguishable because defendant operated a lawful business while, in the gambling situation, upholding the equal protection defense permits a "criminal" to go free? [e]

3. *Peremptory challenge.* SWAIN v. ALABAMA, 380 U.S. 202, 85 S.Ct. 824, 13 L.Ed.2d 759 (1965), per WHITE, J., held that it was not violative of equal protection for a prosecutor to use peremptory challenges to strike all blacks from the jury in a particular case. The peremptory was said to be "an arbitrary and capricious right, and it must be exercised with full freedom, or it fails of its full purpose" to permit "rejection for a real or imagined partiality that is less easily designated or demonstrable. [To] subject the prosecutor's challenge in any particular case to the demands and traditional standards of the Equal Protection Clause would entail a radical change in [its] nature and operation." [f]

"But when the prosecutor in a county in case after case whatever the circumstances, whatever the crime and whoever the defendant or the victim may be, is responsible for the removal of Negroes [with] the result that no Negroes ever serve on petit juries, [it] would appear that the purposes of the peremptory challenge are being perverted."

The Court held, however, that the instant record did not present a prima facie case because "it does [not] show when, how often, and under what circumstances the prosecutor alone has been responsible for striking those Negroes who have appeared on petit jury panels. [The] fact remains, of course, that there has not been a Negro on a jury in Talladega County since about 1950. But [p]etitioner has the burden of proof and he has failed to carry it." [g]

---

d. White, J., joined by Douglas, Brennan and Marshall, JJ., dissented.

e. See generally Tieger, *Police Discretion and Discriminatory Enforcement,* 1971 Duke L.J. 717; Givelber, *The Application of Equal Protection Principles to Selective Enforcement of the Criminal Law,* 1971 U.Ill.L.F. 88.

f. Compare Kuhn, *Jury Discrimination: The Next Phase,* 41 So.Cal.L.Rev. 235, 287 (1968): "The peremptory [permits] the lawyer to eliminate heterogeneity in pursuit of the friendliest, i.e., most partial, jury. Since both sides are permitted to play this game, their efforts in some circumstances may cancel each other and produce a reasonably heterogeneous set of jurors whose counteracting biases produce overall impartiality, or may eliminate extremes of partiality and produce a more nearly neutral body of jurors. But where there is a basic community division between a dominant majority and a disfavored minority, [the] majority can altogether eliminate the minority from the jury, while the minority lacks this power over the majority because the latter's number exceeds the peremptories available."

g. Black, J., concurred in the result. Goldberg, J., joined by Warren, C.J., and Douglas, J., dissented.

WASHINGTON v. DAVIS

426 U.S. 229, 96 S.Ct. 2040, 48 L.Ed.2d 597 (1976).

MR. JUSTICE WHITE delivered the opinion of the Court.

This case involves the validity of a qualifying test administered to applicants for positions as police officers in the District of Columbia. [T]he police recruit was required to satisfy certain physical and character standards, to be a high school graduate or its equivalent and to receive a grade of at least 40 out of 80 on "Test 21," which is "an examination that is used generally throughout the federal service," which "was developed by the Civil Service Commission, not the Police Department," and which was "designed to test verbal ability, vocabulary, reading and comprehension."

[Respondents'] evidence, the District Court said, warranted three conclusions: "(a) The number of black police officers, while substantial, is not proportionate to the population mix of the city. (b) A higher percentage of blacks fail the Test than whites. (c) The Test has not been validated to establish its reliability for measuring subsequent job performance." This showing was deemed sufficient to shift the burden of proof to the defendants [but] the court nevertheless concluded that on the undisputed facts [plaintiffs] were not entitled to relief. The District Court relied on several factors. Since August 1969, 44% of new police force recruits had been black; that figure also represented the proportion of blacks on the total force and was roughly equivalent to 20–29-year-old blacks in the 50-mile radius in which the recruiting efforts of the Police Department had been concentrated. It was undisputed that the Department had systematically and affirmatively sought to enroll black officers many of whom passed the test but failed to report for duty. The District Court rejected the assertion that Test 21 was culturally slanted to favor whites and was "satisfied that the undisputable facts prove the test to be reasonably and directly related to the requirements of the police recruit training program and that it is neither so designed nor operates to discriminate against otherwise qualified blacks." [The Court of Appeals held] that lack of discriminatory intent in designing and administering Test 21 was irrelevant; the critical fact was rather [that] four times as many [blacks] failed the test than did whites. This disproportionate impact [was] held sufficient to establish a constitutional violation, absent proof by petitioners that the test was an adequate measure of job performance in addition to being an indicator of probable success in the training program, a burden which the court ruled petitioners had failed to discharge. * * *

The central purpose of the Equal Protection Clause [is] the prevention of official conduct discriminating on the basis of race. [But] our cases have not embraced the proposition that a law or other official act, without regard to whether it reflects a racially discriminatory purpose, is unconstitutional *solely* because it has a racially disproportionate impact.

Almost 100 years ago, *Strauder* established that the exclusion of Negroes from grand and petit juries in criminal proceedings violated the Equal Protection Clause, but the fact that a particular jury or a series of juries does not statistically reflect the racial composition of the community does not in itself make out an invidious discrimination forbidden by the Clause. "A purpose to

---

For the views of Brennan, Marshall, Blackmun, Powell and Stevens, JJ., that *Swain* should be reconsidered, see *McCray v. New York,* 461 U.S. 961, 103 S.Ct. 2438, 77 L.Ed.2d 1322 (1983). See also *Thompson v. United States,* ___ U.S. ___, 105 S.Ct. 443, 83 L.Ed.2d 369 (1984).

discriminate must be present which may be proven by systematic exclusion of eligible jurymen of the prescribed race or by an unequal application of the law to such an extent as to show intentional discrimination." * * *

The school desegregation cases have also adhered to the basic equal protection principle that the invidious quality of a law claimed to be racially discriminatory must ultimately be traced to a racially discriminatory purpose. That there are both predominantly black and predominantly white schools in a community is not alone violative of the Equal Protection Clause. The essential element ["differentiating] between de jure segregation and so-called de facto segregation [is] *purpose* or *intent* to segregate." *Keyes v. School Dist.*, [Part IV infra]. The Court has also recently rejected allegations of racial discrimination based solely on the statistically disproportionate racial impact of various provisions of the Social Security Act because "[t]he acceptance of appellants' constitutional theory would render suspect each difference in treatment among the grant classes, however lacking in racial motivation and however otherwise rational the treatment might be." *Jefferson v. Hackney,* 406 U.S. 535, 548, 92 S.Ct. 1724, 1732, 32 L.Ed.2d 285, 297 (1972).[a]

This is not to say that the necessary discriminatory racial purpose must be express or appear on the face of the statute, or that a law's disproportionate impact is irrelevant. [A] statute, otherwise neutral on its face, must not be applied so as invidiously to discriminate on the basis of race. *Yick Wo.* It is also clear from the cases dealing with racial discrimination in the selection of juries that [a] prima facie case of discriminatory purpose may be proved [by] the absence of Negroes on a particular jury combined with the failure of the jury commissioners to be informed of eligible Negro jurors in a community, or with racially non-neutral selection procedures. With a prima facie case made out, "the burden of proof shifts to the State to rebut the presumption of unconstitutional action by showing that permissible racially neutral selection criteria and procedures have produced the monochromatic result."

Necessarily, an invidious discriminatory purpose may often be inferred from the totality of the relevant facts, including [that] the law bears more heavily on one race than another. It is also not infrequently true that the discriminatory impact—in the jury cases for example, the total or seriously disproportionate exclusion of Negroes from jury venires—may for all practical purposes demonstrate unconstitutionality because in various circumstances the discrimination is very difficult to explain on nonracial grounds. Nevertheless, we have not held that a law, neutral on its face and serving ends otherwise within the power of government to pursue, is invalid under the Equal Protection Clause simply because it may affect a greater proportion of one race than of another. Disproportionate impact [s]tanding alone [does] not trigger the rule that racial classifications are to be subjected to the strictest scrutiny and are justifiable only by the weightiest of considerations.

There are some indications to the contrary in our cases. In *Palmer v. Thompson,* 403 U.S. 217, 91 S.Ct. 1940, 29 L.Ed.2d 438 (1971), the city of Jackson, Miss., following a court decree to this effect, desegregated all of its public facilities save five swimming pools which [were] closed by ordinance pursuant to a determination by the city council that closure was necessary to preserve peace

a. *Jefferson* rejected the contention that Texas' system—of granting a lower percentage of need to AFDC welfare recipients than to other groups of welfare recipients—violated "equal protection because the proportion of AFDC recipients who are Black or Mexican-American is higher than the proportion of the aged, blind or disabled welfare recipients who fall within these minority groups."

and order and that integrated pools could not be economically operated. [T]his Court rejected the argument that [the] otherwise seemingly permissible ends served by the ordinance could be impeached by demonstrating that racially invidious motivations had prompted the city council's action. [The] opinion warned against grounding decision on legislative purpose or motivation, thereby lending support for the proposition that the operative effect of the law rather than its purpose is the paramount factor. But [w]hatever dicta the opinion may contain, the decision did not involve, much less invalidate, a statute or ordinance having neutral purposes but disproportionate racial consequences.[11]

Both before and after *Palmer,* however, various Courts of Appeals have held in several contexts, including public employment, that the substantially disproportionate racial impact of a statute or official practice standing alone and without regard to discriminatory purpose, suffices to prove racial discrimination violating the Equal Protection Clause absent some justification going substantially beyond what would be necessary to validate most other legislative classifications. [T]o the extent that those cases rested on or expressed the view that proof of discriminatory racial purpose is unnecessary in making out an equal protection violation, we are in disagreement.

[Test 21] seeks to ascertain whether those who take it have acquired a particular level of verbal skill; and it is untenable that the Constitution prevents the government from seeking modestly to upgrade the communicative abilities of its employees rather than to be satisfied with some lower level of competence, particularly where the job requires special ability to communicate orally and in writing. Respondents, as Negroes, could no more successfully claim that the test denied them equal protection than could white applicants who also failed. The conclusion would not be different in the face of proof that more Negroes than whites had been disqualified by Test 21. * * *

Nor on the facts of the case before us would the disproportionate impact of Test 21 warrant the conclusion that it is a purposeful device to discriminate against Negroes * * *. [T]he test is neutral on its face and rationally may be said to serve a purpose the government is constitutionally empowered to pursue. Even agreeing with the District Court that the differential racial effect of Test 21 called for further inquiry, we think the District Court correctly held that the affirmative efforts of the Metropolitan Police Department to recruit black officers, the changing racial composition of the recruit classes and of the force in general, and the relationship of the test to the training program negated any inference that the Department discriminated on the basis of race * * *.

Under Title VII [of the Civil Rights Act of 1964], Congress provided that when hiring and promotion practices disqualifying substantially disproportionate numbers of blacks are challenged, discriminatory purpose need not be proved, and that it is an insufficient response to demonstrate some rational basis for the challenged practices. It is necessary, in addition, that they be "validated" in terms of job performance * * *. However this process proceeds, it involves a more probing judicial review of, and less deference to, the seemingly reasonable acts of administrators and executives than is appropriate under the Constitution where special racial impact, without discriminatory purpose, is claimed. We are

---

11. To the extent that *Palmer* suggests a generally applicable proposition that legislative purpose is irrelevant in constitutional adjudication, our prior cases—as indicated in the text—are to the contrary; and very shortly after *Palmer,* all Members of the Court majority in that case [joined] *Lemon v. Kurtzman,* [p. 725 supra], [that] the validity of public aid to church-related schools includes close inquiry into the purpose of the challenged statute.

not disposed to adopt this more rigorous standard for the purposes of applying the Fifth and the Fourteenth Amendments in cases such as this.[b]

A rule that a statute designed to serve neutral ends is nevertheless invalid, absent compelling justification, if in practice it benefits or burdens one race more than another would be far-reaching and would raise serious questions about, and perhaps invalidate, a whole range of tax, welfare, public service, regulatory, and licensing statutes that may be more burdensome to the poor and to the average black than to the more affluent white.[14]

Given that rule, such consequences would perhaps be likely to follow. However, in our view, extension of the rule beyond those areas where it is already applicable by reason of statute, such as in the field of public employment, should await legislative prescription. * * *[c]

MR. JUSTICE STEVENS [who joined the Court's opinion] concurring. * * *

The requirement of purposeful discrimination is a common thread running through the cases summarized [by the Court. But] in each of these contexts, the burden of proving a prima facie case may well involve differing evidentiary considerations. The extent of deference that one pays to the trial court's determination of the factual issue, and indeed, the extent to which one characterizes the intent issue as a question of fact or a question of law, will vary in different contexts.

Frequently the most probative evidence of intent will be objective evidence of what actually happened rather than evidence describing the subjective state of mind of the actor. For normally the actor is presumed to have intended the natural consequences of his deeds. This is particularly true in the case of governmental action which is frequently the product of compromise, of collective decisionmaking, and of mixed motivation. It is unrealistic, on the one hand, to require the victim of alleged discrimination to uncover the actual subjective intent of the decisionmaker or conversely, to invalidate otherwise legitimate action simply because an improper motive affected the deliberation of a participant in the decisional process. A law conscripting clerics should not be invalidated because an atheist voted for it.

My point [is] to suggest that the line between discriminatory purpose and discriminatory impact is not nearly as bright, and perhaps not quite as critical, as the reader of the Court's opinion might assume. I agree [that] a constitutional issue does not arise every time some disproportionate impact is shown. On

b. For materials on the different types of claims that may arise under Title VII and other statutes and the techniques of proof to show a prima facie violation, see Abernathy, *Civil Rights—Cases & Materials* (1980); Eisenberg, *Civil Rights Legislation* (1981).

14. Goodman, *De Facto School Segregation: A Constitutional and Empirical Analysis,* 60 Calif.L.Rev. 275, 300 (1972), suggests that disproportionate-impact analysis might invalidate "tests and qualifications for voting, draft deferment, public employment, jury service, and other government-conferred [benefits]; [s]ales taxes, bail schedules, utility rates, bridge tolls, license fees, and other state-imposed charges." It has also been argued that minimum wage and usury laws as well as professional licensing requirements would require major modifications in light of the une-

qual-impact rule. Silverman, *Equal Protection, Economic Legislation, and Racial Discrimination,* 25 Vand.L.Rev. 1183 (1972). * * *

c. The Court also found no violation of the relevant statutory provisions. Stewart, J., joined only the constitutional aspects of the Court's opinion. Brennan, J., joined by Marshall, J., did not address the constitutional questions but dissented on statutory grounds.

For detailed criticism of this decision, as well as many others, for enshrining the "perpetrator perspective" of racial discrimination and ignoring the "victim perspective," see Freeman, *Legitimizing Racial Discrimination Through Antidiscrimination Law: A Critical Review of Supreme Court Doctrine,* 62 Minn.L. Rev. 1049 (1978).

the other hand, when the disproportion is as dramatic as in *Gomillion v. Lightfoot*, 364 U.S. 339, 81 S.Ct. 125, 5 L.Ed.2d 110 (1960) [d] or *Yick Wo*, it really does not matter whether the standard is phrased in terms of purpose or effect. Therefore, although I accept the statement of the general rule in the Court's opinion, I am not yet prepared to indicate how that standard should be applied in the many cases which have formulated the governing standard in different language.

My agreement with [the] Court's opinion rests on a ground narrower than the Court describes. I do not rely at all on the evidence of good-faith efforts to recruit black police officers. In my judgment, neither those efforts nor the subjective good faith of the District administration, would save Test 21 if it were otherwise invalid.

There are two reasons why I am convinced that the challenge to Test 21 is insufficient. First, the test serves the neutral and legitimate purpose of requiring all applicants to meet a uniform minimum standard of literacy. Reading ability is manifestly relevant to the police function, there is no evidence that the required passing grade was set at an arbitrarily high level, and there is sufficient disparity among high schools and high school graduates to justify the use of a separate uniform test. Second, the same test is used throughout the federal service. The applicants for employment in the District of Columbia Police Department represent such a small fraction of the total number of persons who have taken the test that their experience is of minimal probative value in assessing the neutrality of the test itself. That evidence, without more, is not sufficient to overcome the presumption that a test which is this widely used by the Federal Government is in fact neutral in its effect as well as its "purpose" as that term is used in constitutional adjudication. * * *

———

ARLINGTON HEIGHTS v. METROPOLITAN HOUSING DEV. CORP., 429 U.S. 252, 97 S.Ct. 555, 50 L.Ed.2d 450 (1977), per POWELL, J.—holding that petitioner Village's refusal to rezone land from single-family (R–3) to multiple-family (R–5), so as to permit respondent MHDC's construction of racially integrated housing, did not violate equal protection—amplified *Davis:*

"*Davis* does not require a plaintiff to prove that the challenged action rested solely on racially discriminatory purposes. Rarely can it be said that a legislature or administrative body operating under a broad mandate made a decision motivated solely by a single concern, or even that a particular purpose was the 'dominant' or 'primary' one. In fact, it is because legislators and administrators are properly concerned with balancing numerous competing considerations that courts refrain from reviewing the merits of their decisions, absent a showing of arbitrariness or irrationality. But racial discrimination is not just another competing consideration. When there is proof that a discriminatory purpose has

———

d. In *Gomillion,* an Alabama statute changed the Tuskegee city boundaries from a square to a 28 sided figure, allegedly removing "all save only four or five of its 400 Negro voters while not removing a single white voter or resident." The Court held that the complaint "amply alleges a claim of racial discrimination" in violation of the fifteenth amendment. "If these allegations upon a trial remained uncontradicted or unqualified, the conclusion would be irresistible, tantamount for all practical purposes to a mathematical demonstration, that the legislation is solely concerned with segregating white and colored voters by fencing Negro citizens out of town so as to deprive them of their pre-existing municipal vote."

been a motivating factor in the decision, this judicial deference is no longer justified.[12]

"Determining whether invidious discriminatory purpose was a motivating factor demands a sensitive inquiry into such circumstantial and direct evidence of intent as may be available. The impact of the official action [may] provide an important starting point. Sometimes a clear pattern, unexplainable on grounds other than race, emerges from the effect of the state action even when the governing legislation appears neutral on its face. *Yick Wo; Guinn v. United States,* 238 U.S. 347, 35 S.Ct. 926, 59 L.Ed. 1340 (1915); *Lane v. Wilson,* 307 U.S. 268, 59 S.Ct. 872, 83 L.Ed. 1281 (1939);[a] *Gomillion.* The evidentiary inquiry is then relatively easy.[13] But such cases are rare. Absent a pattern as stark as that in *Gomillion* or *Yick Wo,* impact alone is not determinative,[14] and the Court must look to other evidence.[15]

"The historical background of the decision is one evidentiary source, particularly if it reveals a series of official actions taken for invidious purposes. See *Lane.* The specific sequence of events leading up to the challenged decision also may shed some light on the decision-maker's purposes. *Reitman v. Mulkey,* [p. 1440 infra]. For example, if the property involved here always had been zoned R–5 but suddenly was changed to R–3 when the town learned of MHDC's plans to erect integrated housing, we would have a far different case. Departures from the normal procedural sequence also might afford evidence that improper purposes are playing a role. Substantive departures too may be relevant, particularly if the factors usually considered important by the decisionmaker strongly favor a decision contrary to the one reached.

"The legislative or administrative history may be highly relevant, especially where there are contemporary statements by members of the decisionmaking body, minutes of its meetings, or reports. In some extraordinary instances the members might be called to the stand at trial to testify concerning the purpose of the official action, although even then such testimony frequently will be barred by privilege. See *Tenney v. Brandhove,* 341 U.S. 367, 71 S.Ct. 783, 95 L.Ed. 1019 (1951); *United States v. Nixon,* 418 U.S. 683, 94 S.Ct. 3090, 41 L.Ed.2d 1039 (1974).[18]

"[This] summary identifies, without purporting to be exhaustive, subjects of proper inquiry in determining whether racially discriminatory intent existed."

12. For a scholarly discussion of legislative motivation, see Brest, *Palmer v. Thompson: An Approach to The Problem of Unconstitutional Motive,* 1971 Sup.Ct. 95, 116–118. [Compare Ely, *Legislative and Administrative Motivation in Constitutional Law,* 79 Yale L.J. 1205 (1970).]

a. *Guinn* held that Oklahoma's literacy test for voting violated the fifteenth amendment because its "grandfather clause" effectively exempted whites. Oklahoma then immediately enacted a new law providing that all persons who previously voted were qualified for life but that all others must register within a twelve day period or be permanently disenfranchised. *Lane* held that this new law violated the fifteenth amendment.

13. Several of our jury selection cases fall into this category. Because of the nature of the jury selection task, however, we have permitted a finding of constitutional violation even when the statistical pattern does not approach the extremes of *Yick Wo* or *Gomillion.*

14. This is not to say that a consistent pattern of official racial discrimination is a necessary predicate to a violation of [equal protection]. A single invidiously discriminatory governmental act—in the exercise of the zoning power as elsewhere—would not necessarily be immunized by the absence of such discrimination in the making of other comparable decisions.

15. In many instances, to recognize the limited probative value of disproportionate impact is merely to acknowledge the "heterogeneity" of the nation's population.

18. This Court has recognized, ever since *Fletcher v. Peck* [p. 60 supra], that judicial inquiries into legislative or executive motivation represent a substantial intrusion into the workings of other branches of government. Placing a decisionmaker on the stand is therefore "usually to be avoided."

Both courts below found that the rezoning denial was not racially motivated.

"We also have reviewed the evidence. The impact of the Village's decision does arguably bear more heavily on racial minorities. [But] there is little about the sequence of events leading up to the decision that would spark suspicion. The area [has] been zoned R–3 since 1959, the year when Arlington Heights first adopted a zoning map. Single-family homes surround the 80-acre site, and the Village is undeniably committed to single-family homes as its dominant residential land use. The rezoning request progressed according to the usual procedures. * * *

"The statements by the Plan Commission and Village Board members, as reflected in the official minutes, focused almost exclusively on the zoning aspects of the MHDC petition, and the zoning factors on which they relied are not novel criteria in the Village's rezoning decisions. There is no reason to doubt that there has been reliance by some neighboring property owners on the maintenance of single-family zoning in the vicinity. The Village originally adopted its buffer policy long before MHDC entered the picture and has applied the policy too consistently for us to infer discriminatory purpose from its application in this case. Finally, MHDC called one member of the Village Board to the stand at trial. Nothing in her testimony supports an inference of invidious purpose.

"In sum, [r]espondents simply failed to carry their burden of proving that discriminatory purpose was a motivating factor in the Village's decision.[21] This conclusion ends the constitutional inquiry." [c]

PERSONNEL ADMINISTRATOR v. FEENEY, 442 U.S. 256, 99 S.Ct. 2282, 60 L.Ed.2d 870 (1979), per STEWART, J.,—relying on *Davis* and *Arlington Heights*—upheld Massachusetts' "absolute lifetime preference to veterans" for state civil service positions, even though "the preference operates overwhelmingly to the advantage of males" [a]: "When a statute gender-neutral on its face is challenged on the ground that its effects upon women are disproportionably adverse, a two-fold inquiry [is] appropriate. The first question is whether the statutory classification is indeed neutral * * *. If the classification itself, covert or overt, is not based upon gender, the second question is whether the adverse effect reflects invidious gender-based discrimination. In this second inquiry, impact provides an 'important starting point,' *Arlington Heights,* but purposeful discrimination is 'the condition that offends the Constitution.' "

21. Proof that the decision by the Village was motivated in part by a racially discriminatory purpose would not necessarily have required invalidation of the challenged decision. Such proof would, however, have shifted to the Village the burden of establishing that the same decision would have resulted even had the impermissible purpose not been considered. If this were established, the complaining party in a case of this kind no longer fairly could attribute the injury complained of to improper consideration of a discriminatory purpose.

c. The Court remanded for further consideration of respondents' claims under the Fair Housing Act. Marshall, J., joined by Brennan, J., concurred in the Court's substantive discussion but, along with White, J., would

have remanded "this entire case [for] further proceedings consistent with *Davis.*" Stevens, J., did not participate.

On remand, the court of appeals held that proof of a discriminatory purpose was not required to find a violation of the Fair Housing Act. 558 F.2d 1283 (7th Cir.1977), cert. denied, 434 U.S. 1025 (1978).

a. Sex discrimination is considered in Sec. 3, IV infra. Although such discrimination has not been held to be "suspect," it has been held to be subject to special judicial scrutiny and the Court's approach to the "purpose" vs. "impact" issue has been similar to cases involving discrimination against racial or ethnic minorities.

As to the first question, "The District Court [found] first, that ch. 31 serves legitimate and worthy purposes; second, that the absolute preference was not established for the purpose of discriminating against women. [Thus,] the distinction between veterans and nonveterans drawn by ch. 31 is not a pretext for gender discrimination. * * *

"If the impact of this statute could not be plausibly explained on a neutral ground, impact itself would signal that the real classification made by the law was in fact not neutral. But there can be but one answer to the question whether this veteran preference excludes significant numbers of women from preferred state jobs because they are women or because they are nonveterans. [T]his is not a law that can plausibly be explained only as a gender-based classification. Indeed, it is not a law that can rationally be explained on that ground. Veteran status is not uniquely male. Although few women benefit from the preference, the nonveteran class is not substantially all-female. To the contrary, significant numbers of nonveterans are men, and all nonveterans—male as well as female—are placed at a disadvantage. Too many men are affected by ch. 31 to permit the inference that the statute is but a pretext for preferring men over women. * * *

"The dispositive question, then, is whether the appellee has shown that a gender-based discriminatory purpose has, at least in some measure, shaped [ch. 31. Her] contention that this veterans' preference is 'inherently non-neutral' or 'gender-biased' presumes that the State, by favoring veterans, intentionally incorporated into its public employment policies the panoply of sex-based and assertedly discriminatory federal laws that have prevented all but a handful of women from becoming veterans. There are two serious difficulties with this argument. First, it is wholly at odds with the District Court's central finding that Massachusetts has not offered a preference to veterans for the purpose of discriminating against women. Second, it cannot be reconciled with the assumption made by both the appellee and the District Court that a more limited hiring preference for veterans could be sustained. Taken together, these difficulties are fatal.

"To the extent that the status of veteran is one that few women have been enabled to achieve, every hiring preference for veterans, however modest or extreme, is inherently gender-biased. If Massachusetts by offering such a preference can be said intentionally to have incorporated into its state employment policies the historical gender-based federal military personnel practices, the degree of the preference would or should make no constitutional difference. Invidious discrimination does not become less so because the discrimination accomplished is of a lesser magnitude.[23] Discriminatory intent is simply not amenable to calibration. It either is a factor that has influenced the legislative choice or it is not. The District Court's conclusion that the absolute veterans' preference was not originally enacted or subsequently reaffirmed for the purpose of giving an advantage to males as such necessarily compels the conclusion that the State intended nothing more than to prefer 'veterans.' Given this finding, simple logic suggests that an intent to exclude women from significant public jobs was not at work in this law. * * *

"To be sure, this case is unusual in that it involves a law that by design is not neutral. [As] opposed to the written test at issue in *Davis,* it does not

---

23. This is not to say that the degree of impact is irrelevant to the question of intent. But it is to say that a more modest preference, while it might well lessen impact and, as the State argues, might lessen the effectiveness of the statute in helping veterans, would not be any more or less "neutral" in the constitutional sense.

purport to define a job related characteristic. To the contrary, it confers upon a specifically described group—perceived to be particularly deserving—a competitive head start. But the District Court found, and the appellee has not disputed, that this legislative choice was legitimate. [Thus, it] must be analyzed as is any other neutral law that casts a greater burden upon women as a group than upon men as a group. The enlistment policies of the armed services may well have discriminated on the basis of sex. But the history of discrimination against women in the military is not on trial in this case.

"The appellee's ultimate argument rests upon the presumption, common to the criminal and civil law, that a person intends the natural and foreseeable consequences of his voluntary actions. * * *

" 'Discriminatory purpose,' however, implies more than intent as volition or intent as awareness of consequences. It implies that the decisionmaker, in this case a state legislature, selected or reaffirmed a particular course of action at least in part 'because of,' not merely 'in spite of,' its adverse effects upon an identifiable group.[25] Yet nothing in the record demonstrates that this preference for veterans was originally devised or subsequently re-enacted because it would accomplish the collateral goal of keeping women in a stereotypic and predefined place in the Massachusetts Civil Service."

STEVENS, J., joined by White, J., concurred in the Court's opinion, adding: "If a classification is not overtly based on gender, I am inclined to believe the question whether it is covertly gender-based is the same as the question whether its adverse effects reflect invidious gender-based discrimination. However the question is phrased, for me the answer is largely provided by the fact that the number of males disadvantaged by Massachusetts' Veterans Preference (1,867,000) is sufficiently large—and sufficiently close to the number of disadvantaged females (2,954,000)—to refute the claim that the rule was intended to benefit males as a class over females as a class."

MARSHALL, J., joined by Brennan, J., dissented: "In my judgment, [ch. 31] evinces purposeful gender-based discrimination. * * *

"That a legislature seeks to advantage one group does not, as a matter of logic or of common sense, exclude the possibility that it also intends to disadvantage another. Individuals in general and lawmakers in particular frequently act for a variety of reasons. [S]ince reliable evidence of subjective intentions is seldom obtainable, resort to inference based on objective factors is generally unavoidable. To discern the purposes underlying facially neutral policies, this Court has therefore considered the degree, inevitability, and foreseeability of any disproportionate impact as well as the alternatives reasonably available.

"[T]he impact of the Massachusetts statute on women is undisputed. Any veteran with a passing grade on the civil service exam must be placed ahead of a nonveteran, regardless of their respective scores. [Because] less than 2% of the women in Massachusetts are veterans, the absolute preference formula has rendered desirable state civil service employment an almost exclusively male

---

25. This is not to say that the inevitability or foreseeability of consequences of a neutral rule has no bearing upon the existence of discriminatory intent. Certainly, when the adverse consequences of a law upon an identifiable group are as inevitable as the gender-based consequences of ch. 31, a strong inference that the adverse effects were desired can reasonably be drawn. But in this inquiry— made as it is under the Constitution—an inference is a working tool, not a synonym for proof. When as here, the impact is essentially an unavoidable consequence of a legislative policy that has in itself always been deemed to be legitimate, and when, as here, the statutory history and all of the available evidence affirmatively demonstrate the opposite, the inference simply fails to ripen into proof.

prerogative. [Where] the foreseeable impact of a facially neutral policy is so disproportionate, the burden should rest on the State to establish that sex-based considerations played no part in the choice of the particular legislative scheme.

"Clearly, that burden was not sustained here. The legislative history of the statute reflects the Commonwealth's patent appreciation of the impact the preference system would have on women, and an equally evident desire to mitigate that impact only with respect to certain traditionally female occupations. Until 1971, the statute [and] regulations exempted from operation of the preference any job requisitions 'especially calling for women.' In practice, this exemption, coupled with the absolute preference for veterans, has created a gender-based civil service hierarchy, with women occupying low grade clerical and secretarial jobs and men holding more responsible and remunerative positions.

"[Such] a statutory scheme both reflects and perpetuates precisely the kind of archaic assumptions about women's roles which we have previously held invalid [citing cases in Sec. 3, IV infra]. Particularly when viewed against the range of less discriminatory alternatives available to assist veterans,[2] Massachusetts's choice of a formula that so severely restricts public employment opportunities for women cannot reasonably be thought gender-neutral. The Court's conclusion to the contrary—that 'nothing in the record' evinces a 'collateral goal of keeping women in a stereotypic and predefined place in the Massachusetts Civil Service'—displays a singularly myopic view of the facts established below.[3] "

MOBILE v. BOLDEN, Sec. 4, I, A infra, involved the question of whether a fifteenth amendment violation requires "discriminatory purpose." STEWART, J., joined by Burger, C.J., and Powell and Rehnquist, JJ., relying on *Guinn, Lane* and *Gomillion,* found that it did. WHITE, J., appeared to avoid explicitly addressing the question, finding that the election scheme at issue had a discriminatory purpose. BLACKMUN, J., "assuming that proof of intent is a prerequisite," agreed with White, J.'s finding. STEVENS, J., did not directly address the question, but disagreed with Stewart, J.'s "reach[ing] out to decide [it]."

MARSHALL, J., dissented: "*Davis* required a showing of discriminatory purpose to support racial discrimination claims largely because it feared that a standard based solely on disproportionate impact would unduly interfere with the far-ranging governmental distribution of constitutional gratuities [citing *Davis'* text at fn. 14]. Underlying the Court's decision was a determination that, since the Constitution does not entitle any person to such governmental benefits, courts should accord discretion to those officials who decide how the government shall allocate its scarce resources. If the plaintiff proved only that governmental distribution of constitutional gratuities had a disproportionate effect on a racial minority, the Court was willing to presume that the officials who approved the allocation scheme either had made an honest error or had foreseen that the

---

2. Only four States afford a preference comparable in [scope]. Other States and the Federal Government grant point or tie-breaking preferences that do not foreclose opportunities for women.

3. Although it is relevant that the preference statute also disadvantages a substantial group of men, it is equally pertinent that 47% of Massachusetts men over 18 are veterans, as compared to 0.8% of Massachusetts women. Given this disparity, and the indicia of intent noted supra, the absolute number of men denied preference cannot be dispositive, especially since they have not faced the barriers to achieving veteran status confronted by women.

decision would have a discriminatory impact and had found persuasive, legitimate reasons for imposing it nonetheless. * * *

"Such judicial deference to official decisionmaking has no place under the Fifteenth Amendment. Section 1 of that Amendment differs from the Fourteenth Amendment's prohibition on racial discrimination in two crucial respects: it explicitly recognizes the right to vote free of hindrances related to race, and it sweeps no further. In my view, these distinctions justify the conclusion that proof of racially discriminatory impact should be sufficient to support a claim under the Fifteenth Amendment. The right to vote is of such fundamental importance in the constitutional scheme that the Fifteenth Amendment's command that it shall not be 'abridged' on account of race must be interpreted as providing that the votes of citizens of all races shall be of substantially equal weight. Furthermore, a disproportionate-impact test under the Fifteenth Amendment would not lead to constant judicial intrusion into the process of official decisionmaking. Rather, the standard would reach only those decisions having a discriminatory effect upon the minority's vote. The Fifteenth Amendment cannot tolerate that kind of decision, even if made in good faith, because the Amendment grants racial minorities the full enjoyment of the right to vote, not simply protection against the unfairness of intentional vote dilution along racial lines.[32]

"In addition, it is beyond dispute that a standard based solely upon the motives of official decisionmakers creates significant problems of proof [and] creates the risk that officials will be able to adopt policies that are the products of discriminatory intent so long as they sufficiently mask their motives through the use of subtlety and illusion. [That] risk becomes intolerable [when] the precious right to vote protected by the Fifteenth Amendment is concerned."

In a brief opinion, BRENNAN, J., agreed with Marshall, J.'s conclusion.[a]

In MEMPHIS v. GREENE, 451 U.S. 100, 101 S.Ct. 1584, 67 L.Ed.2d 769 (1981), the city—at the behest of citizens of Hein Park, a white residential community within Memphis—closed a street, West Drive, that traversed Hein Park and was used mainly by blacks who lived in an adjacent area. The Court, per STEVENS, J., agreeing that "the adverse impact on blacks was greater than on whites," found no violation of 42 U.S.C. § 1982 [p. 1138 infra] or the thirteenth amendment: "[T]he critical facts established by the record are these: The city's decision to close West Drive was motivated by its interest in protecting the safety and tranquility of a residential neighborhood. The procedures followed in making the decision were fair and were not affected by any racial or other impermissible factors. The city has conferred a benefit on certain white property owners but there is no reason to believe that it would refuse to confer a comparable benefit on black property owners. The closing has not affected the value of property owned by black citizens, but it has caused some slight inconvenience to black motorists."

32. Even if a municipal policy is shown to dilute the right to vote, however, the policy will not be struck down if the city shows that it serves highly important local interests and is closely tailored to effectuate only those interests.

a. For an opinion of the Court per White, J.—joined by Burger, C.J., and Brennan, Marshall, Blackmun and O'Connor, JJ.—even more strongly suggesting that a fifteenth amendment violation requires a "discriminatory purpose," see Rogers v. Lodge, Sec. 4, I, A infra.

As for § 1982, "the injury to respondents established by the record is the requirement that one public street rather than another must be used for certain trips within the city. We need not assess the magnitude of that injury to conclude that it does not involve any impairment to the kind of property interests that we have identified as being within the reach of § 1982." [a]

As for the thirteenth amendment, the Court "left open the question of whether § 1 of the Amendment by its own terms did anything more than abolish slavery [because] the record discloses no racially discriminatory motive on the part of the City Council [and] a review of the justification for the official action challenged in this case demonstrates that its disparate impact on black citizens could not [be] fairly characterized as a badge or incident of slavery.

"[To] decide the narrow constitutional question presented by this record we need not speculate about the sort of impact on a racial group that might be prohibited by the Amendment itself. We merely hold that the impact of the closing of West Drive on nonresidents of Hein Park [does] not reflect a violation of the Thirteenth Amendment."

MARSHALL, J., joined by Brennan and Blackmun, JJ., dissented on the ground that "a proper reading of the record demonstrates" (1) "that respondents produced at trial precisely the kind of evidence of intent that we deemed probative in *Arlington Heights,*" and (2) "substantial harm to respondent's property rights." Thus, "I would hold that because the closing of West Drive is forbidden on these facts by § 1982, it is a fortiori a violation of the Thirteenth Amendment as well. * * *

"I [do] not mean to imply that all municipal decisions that affect Negroes adversely and benefit whites are prohibited by the Thirteenth Amendment. I would, however, insist that the government carry a heavy burden of justification before I would sustain against Thirteenth Amendment challenge conduct as egregious as erection of a barrier to prevent predominantly-Negro traffic from entering a historically all-white neighborhood. [I] do not believe that the city has discharged that burden in this case, and for that reason I would hold that the erection of the barrier at the end of West Drive amounts to a badge or incident of slavery forbidden by the Thirteenth Amendment."

Notes and Questions

1. *The "discriminatory purpose" requirement.* (a) Should "racially disproportionate impact" alone trigger special judicial scrutiny? Consider Note, 81 Harv.L.Rev. 1511, 1522 (1968): "The close scrutiny traditionally accorded to statutes which single out individuals for differential treatment on the basis of race [can] be attributed to a judicial suspicion that such statutes are the product of a legislature which is not pursuing permissible ends at all, but acting from a desire to make a discriminatory classification for its own sake. [G]overnment action which adversely affects [blacks] may well stem from decisions [which,] although not racially prejudiced, are nevertheless unresponsive to [their needs. Thus,] judges should not be reluctant to intervene." Compare Bennett, *"Mere" Rationality in Constitutional Law: Judicial Review and Democratic Theory,* 67 Calif.L.Rev. 1049, 1076 (1979): "If members of racial minorities statistically obtain benefits and suffer detriments as one or another piece of legislation is

---

a. White, J., concurred in the result on the ground "that a violation of § 1982 requires some showing of racial animus or an intent to discriminate on the basis of race." No other Justice reached this issue. But *General Bldg.*

Contractors Ass'n v. Pennsylvania, 458 U.S. 375, 102 S.Ct. 3141, 73 L.Ed.2d 835 (1982) held (Marshall and Brennan, JJ., dissenting) that 42 U.S.C. § 1981 "can be violated only by purposeful discrimination."

passed without attention to its racial impact, they are obtaining, not being deprived of, equal protection of the laws. To forbid all legislation that disadvantages them would give them the gains from political bargaining without the losses. This would be so regardless of the degree of the racially disproportionate impact or the importance of the interest affected."

Contrast Perry, *The Disproportionate Impact Theory of Racial Discrimination*, 125 U.Pa.L.Rev. 540, 559–60 (1977): "Laws employing a racial criterion of selection are inherently more dangerous than laws involving no racial criterion. The former, unlike the latter, directly encourage racialism [and] are usually difficult if not impossible to justify on legitimate grounds. By contrast, laws having a disproportionate racial impact are quite easy to explain on legitimate grounds because such laws serve a legitimate function in addition to the function of racial selection. Accordingly, the standard of review [should be] more rigorous than that required by the rational relationship test but less rigorous than that required by the strict scrutiny test. [In] determining whether a disproportionate disadvantage is justified, a court would weigh several factors: (1) the degree of disproportion in the impact; (2) the private interest disadvantaged; (3) the efficiency of the challenged law in achieving its objective and the availability of alternative means having a less disproportionate impact; and (4) the government objective sought to be advanced." [a]

Is there a "discriminatory purpose" if it is determined that the challenged law would not have been passed "if its racial impact had been reversed, i.e., if the disparate impact had been on whites rather than on blacks"? Schnapper, *Two Categories of Discriminatory Intent,* 17 Harv.Civ.Rts.—Civ.Lib.L.Rev. 31, 51 (1982). Consider id. at 55–56: "The central issue [in *Feeney*] is whether Massachusetts would have adopted in 1896 a veterans' preference [that would have excluded 98% of all male applicants] or would have amended its statutes successively in 1919, 1943, 1949, and 1968 to assure such preferential treatment for new generations of predominantly female veterans. The all too familiar history of discrimination on the basis of sex in this country renders implausible the suggestion * * *."

(b) *First amendment freedoms.* In cases holding "neutral" laws that had an adverse impact on speech, association or religion to violate the first amendment—such as *In re Primus* (p. 454 supra) and *Wisconsin v. Yoder* (p. 770 supra)—in which the Court required a "compelling state interest" or "more than merely a 'reasonable relation to some purpose within the competency of the state,'" did the Court find that the challenged state programs had a "discriminatory purpose"? If not, how is the disproportionate racial impact situation distinguishable? See Silard, *Toward Nationwide School Desegregation: A "Compelling State Interest" Test of Racial Concentration in Public Education,* 51 N.C.L.Rev. 675 (1973). Consider Perry, supra, at 556: "The first amendment protects values and interests believed indispensable to the democratic functioning of the political process. Government is charged with the duty, under the first amendment, of safeguarding those values and interests [by] acting solicitously toward them as well as by refraining from deliberately abridging them.

a. For a similar "balancing approach," see Eisenberg, *Disproportionate Impact and Illicit Motive: Theories of Constitutional Adjudication,* 52 N.Y.U.L.Rev. 36 (1977). See also Schwemm, *From Washington to Arlington Heights and Beyond: Discriminatory Purpose in Equal Protection Litigation,* 1977 U.Ill.L.F. 961.

For the view that "serious scrutiny is preferable to ad hoc balancing," see Binion, *Intent and Equal Protection: A Reconsideration,* 1983 Sup.Ct.Rev. 397—comprehensively criticizing the "discriminatory purpose" requirement as developed and applied in the cases.

The equal protection clause serves principally as a brake on the lamentable tendency of the majority race wilfully to oppress or exploit racial minorities, and in this regard it prohibits, absent compelling justification, the use of race as a criterion of selection. Traditionally, however, it has not been thought wrong—unfortunate, perhaps, but not wrong—that an individual or group is incidentally burdened by a law serving the public good. [Thus], with respect to racial discrimination equal protection doctrine has focused almost exclusively on *wilful* oppression or exploitation of minorities by the majority. This focus is especially understandable in light of what historically has been this society's severest moral affliction, racial animus." Compare Eisenberg, fn. a supra, at 165–66: "In comparing the relative need for an impact test in race and religion cases, it is unquestionable that those suffering adverse impact because of race lack the modification or abandonment options that are at least physically possible for those suffering because of religious belief. Second, the establishment clause imposes a limitation on official concessions to religious belief that has no direct parallel in the race [area.] Third, consider the relative historical treatment of race and religion. [I] doubt that any religious group could make out a plausible case that it has been subjected in this country to the same degree of mistreatment. In short, the Court's failure to search for an alternative to motive in race cases borders on the irrational when contrasted with its willingness to use impact in religious belief cases." [b]

(c) *Burden of proof.* Who does (should) have the burden of proving a "discriminatory purpose"? What does (should) a challenger have to prove to shift the burden to the state "to rebut the presumption of unconstitutional action"? Consider Simon, fn. a in *Korematsu*, at 1111: "[A] showing of significant disproportionate disadvantage to a racial minority group, *without more,* gives rise to an inference that the action may have been taken or at least maintained or continued with knowledge that such groups would be relatively disadvantaged. [I]t raises a possibility sufficient to oblige the government to come forward with a credible explanation showing that the action was (or would have been) taken quite apart from prejudice. Depending upon the type of governmental action at issue, discharging this burden will often be easy for the government, but sometimes it will be difficult or impossible. In all cases, however, the government should be required to show more than that the action has some racially innocent 'conceivable basis in fact' because, as anyone familiar with this standard is aware, it can result in the validation of actions on the basis of explanations that are virtually incredible." Compare Karst, *The Costs of Motive-Centered Inquiry,* 15 San Diego L.Rev. 1163, 1165 (1978): "Because an individual's behavior results from the interaction of a multitude of motives, and because racial attitudes often operate at the margin of consciousness, in any given case there almost certainly will be an opportunity for a government official to argue that his action was prompted by racially neutral considerations. When that argument is made, should we not expect the judge to give the official the benefit of the moral doubt? When the governmental action is the product of a group decision, will not that tendency toward generosity be heightened? The first objection to a motive-centered doctrine of racial discrimination, then, is that it places a 'very heavy burden' of persuasion on the wrong side of the dispute, to the severe detriment of the constitutional protection of racial equality." See generally Blumstein, *Defining and Proving Race Discrimination: Perspectives on*

b. As to whether "discriminatory purpose" is required in respect to laws that allegedly violate equal protection because they affect "fundamental rights," see *Mobile v. Bolden,* Sec. 4, I, A infra.

the Purpose vs. Results Approach from the Voting Rights Act, 69 Va.L.Rev. 633 (1983).

2. *Prior state discrimination.* (a) Should there be special judicial scrutiny if the disproportionate racial impact of a law, whose purpose is racially neutral, is produced (influenced) by prior intentional state discrimination? See *Lane v. Wilson,* fn. a in *Arlington Heights.* Suppose a state requires that all applicants furnish recommendations from alumni and that there are no black alumni because the university admitted no blacks in the past? Suppose a state hires teachers wholly on the basis of merit and racial segregation in schools has rendered the quality of education of black teachers inferior to that of whites? Would (should) there have been special judicial scrutiny in *Feeney* if the disproportionate impact had been produced (influenced) by prior intentional discrimination by Massachusetts rather than military personnel practices of the federal government? If so, why should Massachusetts' "incorporation" of intentional discrimination by another government agency make a "constitutional difference"?

(b) Does the "prior discrimination" factor provide a limiting principle that ameliorates *Davis'* concern about the "far-reaching" consequences of "disproportionate-impact analysis"? Consider Perry, supra, at 557–58: "When disadvantage is suffered not merely as a consequence of a law, but [also] *as a consequence of prior governmental action that was constitutionally (and ethically) offensive,* it cannot be maintained that the disadvantage is ethically inoffensive. The disadvantage, in such a circumstance, is the fruit of prior government misdeeds and, accordingly, should bear a heavier burden of justification than that required of a truly neutral disadvantage. [The] failure of American society to outlaw racial discrimination—at least those instances of discrimination (in schooling, housing, and employment) most destructive to the social position of blacks—was hardly better, as a moral matter, than the discrimination itself. In terms of moral responsibility this failure, which endured for too long, amounted to complicity. Laws having a disproportionate racial impact burden blacks *because* of their especially disadvantaged position in American society. A failure to require government to take account of that especially disadvantaged social position by selecting and fine-tuning laws to avoid the unnecessary or thoughtless aggravation of the situation would effectively ignore American society's responsibility for that social position. Furthermore, the failure would compound the responsibility."

Compare Fiss, *Groups and the Equal Protection Clause,* 5 Phil. & Pub.Afrs. 107, 145 (1976): "A true inquiry into past discrimination [requires] the courts to construct causal connections that span significant periods of time, periods greater than those permitted under any general statute of limitations (a common device used to prevent the judiciary from undertaking inquiries where the evidence is likely to be stale, fragmentary, and generally unreliable). The difficulties of these backward-looking inquiries are compounded because the court must invariably deal with aggregate behavior, not just a single transaction; it must determine the causal explanation for the residential patterns of an entire community, or the skill levels of all the black applicants." See also Schnapper, *Perpetuation of Past Discrimination,* 96 Harv.L.Rev. 828 (1983); Brest, *In Defense of the Antidiscrimination Principle,* 90 Harv.L.Rev. 1, 42 (1976).

3. *Consequences of "discriminatory purpose."* If it is found that a law "was motivated by a racially discriminatory purpose," should the state be permitted to prove "that the same decision would have resulted had the impermissible purpose not been considered"? *Arlington Heights,* fn. 21. Or should the Court

invalidate the law and "remand to the legislature for a reconsideration [on] the basis of purely legitimate factors"? Schwemm, fn. a supra, at 1020. Would the latter course be futile "because the legislature could immediately pass an identical statute for valid reasons"? Eisenberg, supra, at 116. Consider id.: "[I]t is absurd to assume that all legislators would completely ignore a court holding that the legislature used constitutionally impermissible criteria in initially passing a statute. Some legislators, after being informed that they initially acted unconstitutionally, may refuse to vote for reenactment. Furthermore, if a statute is invalidated on judicial review, the legislature often will decline or fail to consider a new law. In many situations, therefore, judicial action on the basis of motive results in an effective, not a futile, invalidation." If there is a remand and the law is reenacted, should there be a presumption "that the decisionmaker continues to entertain the motives that led to the original decision (and to its invalidation)"? Brest, fn. 12 in *Arlington Heights,* at 125–26.

IV. REMEDYING SEGREGATION

Although there was prompt compliance with *Brown* in the District of Columbia and some of the border states, the initial response in the deep south was one of "massive resistance"—exemplified by the Governor's use of the Arkansas national guard in 1957 to prevent desegregation in Little Rock and Virginia's 1956 legislation closing any racially mixed public schools. See generally McKay, *"With All Deliberate Speed": Legislative Reaction and Judicial Development 1956–1957,* 43 Va.L.Rev. 1205 (1957).

COOPER v. AARON, 358 U.S. 1, 78 S.Ct. 1401, 3 L.Ed.2d 5 (1958), the first decision to follow the remands in *Brown,* involved the Little Rock school board's request to stay an integration plan that had been in operation at Central High School during the 1957–58 school year, but only after federal troops had been sent by the President to protect black students from "extreme public hostility" engendered largely by the Governor's and Legislature's opposition. The opinion, unprecedented in that it was signed by all nine justices (including those appointed since *Brown),* "unanimously reaffirmed" *Brown.* The Court agreed that "the educational progress of all the students [will] continue to suffer if the conditions which prevailed last year are permitted to continue," but denied the request for delay: "The constitutional rights of [black children] are not to be sacrificed or yielded to the violence and disorder which have followed upon the actions of the Governor and Legislature." The difficulties, created by state action, "can also be brought under control by state action." *Brown* "can neither be nullified openly and directly by state legislators or state executive or judicial officers, nor nullified indirectly by them through evasive schemes." [a]

GRIFFIN v. COUNTY SCHOOL BD., 377 U.S. 218, 84 S.Ct. 1226, 12 L.Ed.2d 256 (1964): In 1959, Prince Edward County, Va. closed its public schools rather than comply with a desegregation order. Private schools, supported by state and local tuition grants and tax credits, were operated for white children. The Court, per BLACK, J., held the closing to deny blacks equal protection: States

---

a. Who determines whether public hostility may "be brought under control by state action"? May it ever be found that the hostility is so great that it is uncontrollable? Of what relevance is the financial cost to the state? Suppose the state, although *able,* is *unwilling* to quiet the hostility? See generally Gewirtz, *Remedies and Resistance,* 92 Yale L.J. 585 (1983).

have "wide discretion in deciding whether laws shall operate statewide or shall operate only in certain counties [but] Prince Edward's public schools were closed and private schools operated in their place with state and county assistance, for one reason [only]. Whatever nonracial grounds might support a State's allowing a county to abandon public schools, the object must be a constitutional one, and grounds of race and opposition to desegregation do not qualify as constitutional." [b]

In the late 1950s, some states sought to comply with *Brown* by simply permitting students to apply for transfer to another school. Procedures were complex and time-consuming; standards were vague, making it difficult to show that denials were due to race. See Note, *The Federal Courts and Integration of Southern Schools: Troubled Status of the Pupil Placement Act*, 62 Colum.L.Rev. 1448 (1962). By the early 1960s, most federal courts refused to accept these "tokenism" plans. See Bickel, *The Decade of School Desegregation: Progress and Prospects*, 64 Colum.L.Rev. 193 (1964). *Goss v. Bd. of Educ.*, 373 U.S. 683, 83 S.Ct. 1405, 10 L.Ed.2d 632 (1963), invalidated a provision permitting students, assigned to school zones on a neutral basis, to transfer if the student was in a racial minority: "It is readily apparent that the transfer system proposed lends itself to perpetuation of segregation." Similarly, by 1961, most federal courts rejected "grade-a-year" desegregation plans. See 64 Mich.L.Rev. 341 (1965). *Rogers v. Paul*, 382 U.S. 198, 86 S.Ct. 358, 15 L.Ed.2d 265 (1965), ordered "immediate transfer" of petitioning students who still attended segregated schools because, under the grade-a-year plan, their grade had not been covered. Finally, *Alexander v. Holmes Cty. Bd. of Educ.*, 396 U.S. 19, 90 S.Ct. 29, 24 L.Ed. 2d 19 (1969), ordered denial of "all motions for additional time" and made clear that "the obligation of every school district is to terminate dual school systems at once and to operate now and hereafter only unitary schools."

GREEN v. COUNTY SCHOOL BD., 391 U.S. 430, 88 S.Ct. 1689, 20 L.Ed.2d 716 (1968): The population of New Kent County in rural Virginia was about half black. Although there was no residential segregation, its two combined elementary and high schools, previously segregated by law, remained wholly segregated in fact until 1964. In 1965, the board adopted a "freedom-of-choice" plan to remain eligible for federal financial aid under federal guidelines.[c] After three

b. The Court affirmed the district court's order enjoining public financial aid to the private schools and held (Clark and Harlan, JJ. disagreeing) that "the District Court [may] require the Supervisors to exercise the power that is theirs to levy taxes to raise funds adequate to reopen, operate, and maintain without racial discrimination a public school system [like] that operated in other counties in Virginia."

Griffin was subsequently distinguished in *Palmer v. Thompson* (1971)—involving the closing of swimming pools—discussed in *Washington v. Davis*, Part III supra.

c. The Civil Rights Act of 1964 bars federal financial assistance for any program administered in a racially discriminatory manner. Pursuant thereto, the Dep't of Health, Education and Welfare conditioned eligibility for

federal aid to local school districts either on compliance with existing court desegregation orders or, in the absence of such an order, on submission of a desegregation plan consistent with HEW "guidelines." See generally Dunn, *Title VI, The Guidelines and School Desegregation in the South*, 53 Va.L.Rev. 42 (1967); Note, *The Courts, HEW, and Southern School Desegregation*, 77 Yale L.J. 321 (1967).

In the 1964–65 school year, before implementation of the guidelines, only 2.14% of black students in the eleven "southern states" attended schools in which they were not the racial majority. In 1968, the figure was reported at 20.3%. By the 1972–73 school year, it was 46.3%. Statistical Abstract of the United States 124 (1974). The comparable figure for 1972–73 in the six "border states and the District of Columbia" was 31.8%; for years, no white child chose to go to the black school which 85% of the black children continued to attend. School buses traveled "overlapping routes throughout the county to transport pupils to and from the two schools."

A unanimous Court, per BRENNAN, J., held "it is against this background that 13 years after *Brown II* commanded the abolition of dual systems we must measure the effectiveness of [respondent's] 'freedom-of-choice' plan to achieve that end. The School Board contends that it has fully discharged its obligation by adopting a plan by which every student, regardless of race, may 'freely' choose the school he will attend [and which] may be faulted only by reading the Fourteenth Amendment as universally requiring 'compulsory integration.' [But] what is involved here is the question whether the Board has achieved the 'racially nondiscriminatory school system' *Brown II* held must be [effectuated]. School boards [then] operating state-compelled dual systems [were] clearly charged with the affirmative duty to take whatever steps might be necessary to convert to a unitary system in which racial discrimination would be eliminated root and branch. [It] is incumbent upon the school board to establish that its proposed plan promises meaningful and immediate progress toward disestablishing state-imposed segregation. [Where] more promising courses of action are open to the board, that may indicate a lack of good faith; and at the least it places a heavy burden upon the board to explain its preference for an apparently less effective method. [The instant] plan has operated simply to burden children and their parents with a responsibility which *Brown II* placed squarely on the School Board. The Board must be required to formulate a new plan and, in light of other courses which appear open to the Board, such as zoning, [or consolidating the two schools, one serving grades 1–7, the other, grades 8–12,] fashion steps which promise realistically to convert promptly to a system without a 'white' school and a 'Negro' school, but just schools." [d]

SWANN v. CHARLOTTE–MECKLENBURG
BD. OF EDUC.

402 U.S. 1, 91 S.Ct. 1267, 28 L.Ed.2d 554 (1971).

MR. CHIEF JUSTICE BURGER delivered the opinion of the Court.

[This case concerned desegregation of the Charlotte, N.C. metropolitan area school district, which had had a statutorily mandated dual system.[a] The history included the district court's rejection in 1969 of three plans submitted by respondent board of education; its acceptance of a plan prepared at its request by "an expert in education administration"; modification of the district court decree by the court of appeals; and the district court's subsequent rejection of a plan prepared by HEW and its conclusion that either the education expert's plan or a new plan submitted by a minority of the school board was "reasonable and acceptable."]

The problems encountered by the [lower federal courts] make plain that we should now try to amplify guidelines, however incomplete and imperfect, for the assistance of school authorities and courts. [Elimination of dual school systems] has been rendered more difficult by changes since 1954 in the structure and

---

the 32 "northern and western states" it was 28.3%. Id.

d. See also *Monroe v. Bd. of Comm'rs*, 391 U.S. 450, 88 S.Ct. 1700, 20 L.Ed.2d 733 (1968) (school board's rezoning to create racially mixed schools, but permitting "free-transfer"

which resulted in "resegregation" when whites and blacks returned to their "old" schools, did not satisfy board's burden to eliminate dual system).

a. A companion case involved Mobile, Ala.

patterns of communities, the growth of student population, movement of families, and other changes, some of which had marked impact on school planning, sometimes neutralizing or negating remedial action before it was fully implemented. Rural areas accustomed for half a century to the consolidated school systems implemented by bus transportation could make adjustments more readily than metropolitan areas with dense and shifting population, numerous schools, congested and complex traffic patterns. * * *

If school authorities fail in their affirmative obligations ["to eliminate from the public schools all vestiges of state-imposed segregation"] judicial authority may be invoked. Once a right and a violation have been shown, the scope of a district court's equitable powers to remedy past wrongs is broad, for breadth and flexibility are inherent in equitable remedies. [The] task is to correct, by a balancing of the individual and collective interests, the condition that offends the Constitution. [But] it is important to remember that judicial powers may be exercised only on the basis of a constitutional violation. * * *

School authorities are traditionally charged with broad power to formulate and implement educational policy and might well conclude, for example, that in order to prepare students to live in a pluralistic society each school should have a prescribed ratio of Negro to white students reflecting the proportion for the district as a whole. To do this as an educational policy is within the broad discretionary powers of school authorities; absent a finding of a constitutional violation, however, that would not be within the authority of a federal court. * * *

The school authorities argue that the equity powers of federal district courts have been limited by Title IV of the Civil Rights Act of 1964, 42 U.S.C.A. [§ 2000c(b) which states]: " 'Desegregation' means the assignment of students to public schools and within such schools without regard to their race, color, religion, or national origin, but 'desegregation' shall not mean the assignment of students to public schools in order to overcome racial imbalance."

Section 2000c–6, authorizing the Attorney General to institute federal suits, contains the following proviso: "nothing herein shall empower any official or court of the United States to issue any order seeking to achieve a racial balance in any school by requiring the transportation of pupils [or] otherwise enlarge the existing power of the court to insure compliance with constitutional standards."

* * * § 2000c–6 is in terms designed to foreclose any interpretation of the Act as expanding the *existing* powers of federal courts to enforce the Equal Protection Clause. There is no suggestion of an intention to restrict those powers or withdraw from courts their historic equitable remedial powers. The legislative history of Title IV indicates that Congress was concerned that the Act might be read as creating a right of action under the Fourteenth Amendment in the situation of so-called "de facto segregation," where racial imbalance exists in the schools but with no showing that this was brought about by discriminatory action of state authorities. In short, there is nothing in the Act which provides us material assistance in answering the question of remedy for state-imposed segregation in violation of *Brown I*.[b] * * *

* * * Independent of student assignment, where it is possible to identify a "white school" or a "Negro school" simply by reference to the racial composition

---

b. For a similar disposition in respect to Education Amendments Act of 1972 § 803—providing for stays of any district court orders "which require [the] transportation of any student [for] the purposes of achieving a balance among students with respect to race"—see *Drummond v. Acree*, 409 U.S. 1228, 93 S.Ct. 18, 34 L.Ed.2d 33 (1972) (opinion of Powell, J., as Circuit Justice).

of teachers and staff, the quality of school buildings and equipment, or the organization of sports activities, a prima facie case of violation of substantive constitutional rights under the Equal Protection Clause is shown.

When a system has been dual in these respects, the first remedial responsibility of school authorities is to eliminate invidious racial distinctions. With respect to such matters as transportation, supporting personnel, and extracurricular activities, no more than this may be necessary. Similar corrective action must be taken with regard to the maintenance of buildings and the distribution of equipment. In these areas, normal administrative practice should produce schools of like quality, facilities, and staffs. Something more must be said, however, as to faculty assignment and new school construction.

In the companion *Mobile* case, the Mobile school board has argued that the Constitution requires that teachers be assigned on a "color blind" basis. It also argues that the Constitution prohibits district courts from using their equity power to order assignment of teachers to achieve a particular degree of faculty desegregation. We reject that contention.[c] * * *

The construction of new schools and the closing of old [ones,] when combined with one technique or another of student assignment, will determine the racial composition of the student body in each school in the [system.] People gravitate toward school facilities, just as schools are located in response to the needs of people. The location of schools may thus influence the patterns of residential development of a metropolitan area and have important impact on composition of inner city neighborhoods. [In] devising remedies where legally imposed segregation has been established, it is the responsibility of local authorities and district courts to see to it that future school construction and abandonment is not used and does not serve to perpetuate or re-establish the dual system.

* * *

The central issue in this case is that of student assignment, and there are essentially four problem areas: * * *

(1) *Racial Balances or Racial Quotas.* [I]t is urged that the District Court has imposed a racial balance requirement of 71%–29% on individual schools, [reflecting] the pupil constituency of the system. If we were to read the holding of the District Court to require, as a matter of substantive constitutional right, any particular degree of racial balance or mixing, that approach would be disapproved [for the] constitutional command to desegregate schools does not mean that every school in every community must always reflect the racial composition of the school system as a whole.

[But] the use made of mathematical ratios was no more than a starting point in the process of shaping a [remedy]. As we said in *Green,* a school authority's remedial plan or a district court's remedial decree is to be judged by its effectiveness. Awareness of the racial composition of the whole school system is likely to be a useful starting point in shaping a remedy to correct past constitutional violations. In sum, the very limited use made of mathematical ratios was within the equitable remedial discretion of the District Court.[d]

c. See *Bradley v. School Bd.,* 382 U.S. 103, 86 S.Ct. 224, 15 L.Ed.2d 187 (1965); Lieberman, *Teachers and the Fourteenth Amendment—The Role of the Faculty in the Desegregation Process,* 46 N.C.L.Rev. 313 (1968).

d. Cf. Rehnquist, J., joined by Burger, C.J., and Powell, J., dissenting from denial of certi-orari in *Cleveland Bd. of Educ. v. Reed,* 445 U.S. 935, 100 S.Ct. 1329, 63 L.Ed.2d 770 (1980), in which the district court's remedy required that "every grade in every school [have] a ratio of black and white students in approximate proportion to the systemwide ratio."

(2) *One-Race Schools.* The record in this case reveals the familiar phenomenon that in metropolitan areas minority groups are often found concentrated in one part of the city. In some circumstances certain schools may remain all or largely of one race until new schools can be provided or neighborhood patterns change. [T]he existence of some small number of one-race, or virtually one-race schools within a district is not in and of itself the mark of a system which still practices segregation by law. [But] the burden upon the school authorities will be to satisfy the court that their racial composition is not the result of present or past discriminatory action on their part.

An optional majority-to-minority transfer provision [is] an indispensable remedy for those students willing to transfer to other schools in order to lessen the impact on them of the state-imposed stigma of segregation. [S]uch a transfer arrangement must grant the transferring student free transportation and space must be made available in the school to which he desires to move. * * *

(3) *Remedial Altering of Attendance Zones.* [O]ne of the principal tools employed by school planners and by courts to break up the dual school system has been a frank—and sometimes drastic—gerrymandering of school districts and attendance zones. An additional step was pairing, "clustering," or "grouping" of schools with attendance assignments made deliberately to accomplish the transfer of Negro students out of formerly segregated Negro schools and transfer of white students to formerly all-Negro schools. More often than not, these zones are neither compact nor contiguous; indeed they may be on opposite ends of the city. As an interim corrective measure, this cannot be said to be beyond the broad remedial powers of a court.

Absent a constitutional violation there would be no basis for judicially ordering assignment of students on a racial basis. All things being equal, with no history of discrimination, it might well be desirable to assign pupils to schools nearest their homes. But all things are not equal in a system that has been deliberately constructed and maintained to enforce racial segregation. The remedy for such segregation may be administratively awkward, inconvenient and even bizarre in some situations and may impose burdens on some; but [this] cannot be avoided in the interim period when remedial adjustments are being made to eliminate the dual school systems.

No fixed or even substantially fixed guidelines can be established as to how far a court can go, but it must be recognized that there are limits. The objective is to dismantle the dual school system. "Racially neutral" assignment plans [may] fail to counteract the continuing effects of past school segregation resulting from discriminatory location of school sites or distortion of school size in order to achieve or maintain an artificial racial separation. When school authorities present a district court with a "loaded game board," affirmative action in the form of remedial altering of attendance zones is proper to achieve truly non-discriminatory assignments. [W]e must of necessity rely to a large extent, as this Court has for more than 16 years, on the informed judgment of the district courts in the first instance and on courts of appeals. * * *

(4) *Transportation of Students.* [No] rigid guidelines as to student transportation can be given for application to the infinite variety of problems presented in thousands of situations. Bus transportation has been an integral part of the public education system for [years]. Eighteen million of the nation's public school children, approximately 39%, were transported to their schools by bus in 1969–1970 in all parts of the country.

The importance of bus transportation as a normal and accepted tool of educational policy is readily discernible in this and the companion case.[11] * * *

The decree provided that [trips] for elementary school pupils average about seven miles and the District Court found that they would take "not over 35 minutes at the most."[12] This system compares favorably with the transportation plan previously operated in Charlotte under which each day 23,600 students on all grade levels were transported an average of 15 miles one way for an average trip requiring over an hour. In these circumstances, we find no basis for holding that the local school authorities may not be required to employ bus transportation as one tool of school desegregation. Desegregation plans cannot be limited to the walk-in school.

An objection to transportation of students may have validity when the time or distance of travel is so great as to risk either the health of the children or significantly impinge on the educational process. District courts must weigh the soundness of any transportation plan in light of what is said in subdivisions (1), (2), and (3) above. [L]imits on time of travel will vary with many factors, but probably with none more than the age of the students. The reconciliation of competing values in a desegregation case is, of course, a difficult task with many sensitive facets but fundamentally no more so than remedial measures courts of equity have traditionally employed. * * *

At some point, these school authorities and others like them should have achieved full compliance with this Court's decision in *Brown I*. * * *

It does not follow that the communities served by such systems will remain demographically stable, for in a growing, mobile society, few will do so. Neither school authorities nor district courts are constitutionally required to make year-by-year adjustments of the racial composition of student bodies once the affirmative duty to desegregate has been accomplished and racial discrimination through official action is eliminated from the system. This does not mean that federal courts are without power to deal with future problems; but in the absence of a showing that either the school authorities or some other agency of the State has deliberately attempted to fix or alter demographic patterns to affect the racial composition of the schools, further intervention by a district court should not be necessary. * * *[e]

Notes and Questions

1. *Scope of duty.* (a) May a school district that had a statutorily mandated dual system be relieved of its remedial duty if it proves that continued racial imbalance in its schools is not attributable to its earlier school segregation law?

11. During 1967–1968, for example, the Mobile board used 207 buses to transport 22,094 students daily for an average round trip of 31 miles. During 1966–1967, 7,116 students in the metropolitan area were bused daily. In Charlotte-Mecklenburg [m]ore elementary school children than high school children were to be bused, and four- and five-year-olds travel the longest routes in the system.

12. The District Court found that the school system would have to employ 138 more buses than it had previously operated. But 105 of those buses were already available and the others could easily be obtained. Addition-

ally, it should be noted that North Carolina requires provision of transportation for all students who are assigned to schools more than one and one-half miles from their homes.

e. In a companion case, *North Carolina State Bd. of Educ. v. Swann*, 402 U.S. 43, 91 S.Ct. 1284, 28 L.Ed.2d 586 (1971), the Court held that an Anti-Busing Law, enacted during the instant litigation—barring (1) pupil assignment on the basis of race or to create a racial balance or ratio in the schools, and (2) busing for such purposes—contravened the doctrine "that all reasonable methods be available to formulate an effective remedy."

Or do *Green* and *Swann* effectively create an "irrebuttable presumption" that "yesterday's intentionally segregative laws [have] influenced family residential choices and contributed to the formation of today's one-race neighborhoods [and] today's one-race neighborhood schools"? Goodman, *The Desegregation Dilemma: A Vote for Voluntarism,* 1979 Wash.U.L.Q. 407, 409. See generally Fiss, *School Desegregation: The Uncertain Path of the Law,* 4 Phil. & Pub.Afrs. 3, 18–21 (1974). Compare Yudof, *Equal Educational Opportunity and the Courts,* 51 Tex. L.Rev. 411, 452 (1973): "There is no evidence that segregated schools materially influenced racial isolation by neighborhood in Southern communities. Where the whole structure of society reflects the inferior status assigned to blacks, it is difficult to say that any particular practice or institution caused segregated neighborhoods. [S]egregated housing is far more prevalent in the North where officially sanctioned school segregation was relatively rare."

(b) Do *Green* and *Swann* require school boards that had de jure segregated systems to take "*whatever* steps might be necessary" for "meaningful and immediate progress toward disestablishing state-imposed segregation" (*Green*)? Or need they only adopt plans that are "reasonable, *feasible* and workable" (*Swann*)? Who determines what is "feasible"? Consider Goodman, *Racial Imbalance in the Oakland Public Schools: A Legal Analysis* 69 (1966): "Whether a particular course of action is 'feasible' depends largely upon which elements of the situation are assumed to be fixed and unalterable and which are regarded as freely variable. If, for example, one accepts as a 'given' the basic validity of the neighborhood school concept and the existing facilities and financial resources of the school district, the range of 'feasible' desegregation measures is apt to be rather limited. Drop these assumptions and the range of feasibilities becomes broader. Assume, finally, that money is no obstacle, and that proximity to schools can be dismissed as a mere matter of 'convenience,' and nearly *everything* becomes feasible. [Black] children could be bused to predominantly white schools without regard to space limitations, and those schools placed on double sessions pending the construction of new facilities." Compare Kaplan, *Segregation Litigation and the Schools—Part II: The General Northern Problem,* 58 Nw. U.L.Rev. 157, 183 (1963): "How can the courts weigh the value of a 30 per cent increase in integration against a requirement that students cross a dangerous traffic artery or walk five extra blocks? How could the courts weigh the achievement of integration through busing children against the greater cost and a somewhat larger class size?" Do courts often make judgments of this nature in constitutional litigation? See Fiss, *The Charlotte-Mecklenburg Case—Its Significance for Northern School Desegregation,* 38 U.Chi.L.Rev. 697, 702 (1971): "[Under *Swann*,] if there is a conflict between integration and other values, integration will generally prevail. [In the *Mobile* case, the] Court rejected a desegregation plan that allowed some all-black schools to remain [whose elimination] required assigning students across a major highway that divided the metropolitan area. [The] Court remanded because 'inadequate consideration was given to the possible use of bus transportation and split zoning.' "

2. *Legislation.* In response to *Swann,* legislation to drastically limit busing was introduced in Congress. The result was the Education Amendments Act of 1972, see fn. b supra. The Education Amendments Act of 1974, however, requires (§ 214) that federal courts and agencies give priority to nonbusing remedies and provides (§ 215) that "no court, department or agency of the United States shall" (a) "order the implementation of a plan that would require the transportation of any student to a school other than the school closest or next closest to his place of residence which provides the appropriate grade level

and type of education for such student," or (b) "require directly or indirectly the transportation of any student if such transportation poses a risk to the health of such student or constitutes a significant impingement on the educational process with respect to such student." But this is prefaced by § 203(b)'s statement "that the provisions of this title are not intended to modify or diminish the authority of the courts of the United States to enforce fully the fifth and fourteenth amendments." Since then, several annual appropriations acts in the 1970s have prohibited the use of federal funds to require busing "to a school other than the school which is nearest the students' home, and which offers the courses of study pursued by such student" in order to comply with the desegregation provisions of the Civil Rights Act of 1964.[f]

3. *Resegregation.* (a) In PASADENA BD. OF EDUC. v. SPANGLER, 427 U.S. 424, 96 S.Ct. 2697, 49 L.Ed.2d 599 (1976), a court ordered plan to remedy de jure segregation resulted in no racially imbalanced schools in 1970. But this lasted only one year; by 1974, five of the district's 32 schools were over half black. The Court, per REHNQUIST, J., reversed the district judge's order "to require annual readjustment of attendance zones so that there would not be a majority of any minority in any Pasadena public school": "[The] quite normal pattern of human migration resulted in some changes in the demographics of Pasadena's residential patterns, with resultant shifts in the racial makeup of some of the schools. [But] these shifts were not attributed to any segregative actions on the part of the defendants. [H]aving once implemented a racially neutral attendance pattern in order to remedy the perceived constitutional violations on the part of the defendants, the District Court had fully performed its function of providing the appropriate remedy for previous racially discriminatory attendance patterns." [g]

(b) When the "duty to desegregate has been accomplished" by rezoning etc., may students be assigned to classrooms within the schools (or reassigned among schools) on the basis of "standardized ability and achievement tests" if this tends to result in resegregation? See generally Kirp, *Schools as Sorters: The Constitutional and Policy Implications of Student Classification*, 121 U.Pa.L.Rev. 706 (1973).

––––––––––

KEYES v. SCHOOL DIST., 413 U.S. 189, 93 S.Ct. 2686, 37 L.Ed.2d 548 (1973), was the first case of segregation that had never been statutorily mandated. The district court found that the Denver school board—by school construction, gerrymandering attendance zones, and excessive use of mobile classroom units—"had engaged over almost a decade after 1960 in an unconstitutional policy of deliberate racial segregation with respect to the Park Hill schools," and ordered their desegregation. However, although the "core city schools" were also segregated in fact, the district court found that the school board had no segregative policy as to them and declined to order their desegregation.

The Court, per BRENNAN, J., reversed, first holding that since, in the southwest, Negroes and Hispanos "suffer identical discrimination in treatment

f. For consideration of the constitutionality of such legislation, see note 6(e) p. 1164 infra (§ 5 of the fourteenth amendment).

g. The Court thought "it important to note [that] this case does not involve [a] plan embodying specific revisions of the attendance zones for particular schools, as well as provi-

sions for later appraisal of whether such discrete individual modifications had achieved the 'unitary system' required by *Brown I.*"

Marshall, J., joined by Brennan, J., dissented on the ground that a "unitary system" had not been established. Stevens, J., did not participate.

when compared with the treatment afforded Anglo[s,] schools with a combined predominance of Negroes and Hispanos [should be] included in the category of 'segregated' schools." It then held that "where plaintiffs prove that the school authorities have carried out a systematic program of segregation affecting a substantial portion of the students, schools, teachers and facilities [it] is only common sense to conclude that there exists a predicate for a finding of the existence of a dual school system" because "racially inspired school board actions have an impact beyond the particular schools that are the subjects of those actions. This is not to say, of course, that there can never be a case in which the geographical structure of or the natural boundaries within a school district may have the effect of dividing the district into separate, identifiable and unrelated units. Such a determination is essentially a question of fact to be resolved by the trial court [but] such cases must be rare."

Finally, emphasizing "that the differentiating factor between de jure segregation and so-called de facto segregation [is] *purpose* or *intent* to segregate," it held "that a finding of intentionally segregative school board actions in a meaningful portion of a school system [creates] a prima facie case of unlawful segregative design on the part of school authorities, and shifts to those authorities the burden of proving that other segregated schools within the system are not also the result of intentionally segregative actions. This is true even if it is determined that different areas of the school district should be viewed independently of each [other].[a] In discharging that burden, it is not enough, of course, that the school authorities rely upon some allegedly logical, racially neutral explanation for their actions. Their burden is to adduce proof sufficient to support a finding that segregative intent was not among the factors that motivated their actions." Further, "if the actions of school authorities were to any degree motivated by segregative intent and the segregation resulting from those actions continues to exist, the fact of remoteness in time certainly does not make those actions any less 'intentional.'

"This is not to say, however, that the prima facie case may not be met by evidence supporting a finding that a lesser degree of segregated schooling in the core city area would not have resulted even if the Board had not acted as it [did]. Intentional school segregation in the past may have been a factor in creating a natural environment for the growth of further segregation. Thus, if respondent School Board cannot disprove segregative intent, it can rebut the prima facie case only by showing that its past segregative acts did not create or contribute to the current segregated condition of the core city schools."

Respondent invoked "its 'neighborhood school policy' as explaining racial and ethnic concentrations within the core city schools. [But] the mere assertion of such a policy is not dispositive where, as in this case, the school authorities have been found to have practiced de jure segregation * * *."[b]

---

a. What constitutes a "substantial" or "meaningful portion" of a school system? Consider Comment, *Unlocking the Northern Schoolhouse Doors*, 9 Harv.Civ.Rts.—Civ.Lib. L.Rev. 124, 150 (1974): "Park Hill is a neighborhood of eight schools educating less than thirty-eight percent of Denver's black students and less than ten percent of all pupils in the district. [Thus], a decree compelling extensive desegregation will almost invariably flow from a finding of localized de jure practices." Does

"a finding of intentionally segregative school board actions" for all elementary schools "create a prima facie case of unlawful segregative design" for all secondary schools?

b. Burger, C.J., concurred in the result. Douglas, J., joined the Court's opinion but stated "that there [is] no difference between de facto and de jure segregation." White, J., did not participate.

POWELL, J., filed a lengthy separate opinion, believing that "the facts deemed necessary to establish de jure discrimination present problems of subjective intent which the courts cannot fairly resolve." "In my view we should abandon [the de jure-de facto distinction] and formulate constitutional principles of national rather than merely regional application. [In] imposing on metropolitan southern school districts an affirmative duty, entailing large-scale transportation of pupils, to eliminate segregation in the schools, the Court required these districts to alleviate conditions which in large part did *not* result from historic, state-imposed de jure segregation. Rather, the familiar root cause of segregated schools in *all* the biracial metropolitan areas of our country is essentially the same: one of segregated residential and migratory patterns the impact of which on the racial composition of the schools was often perpetuated and rarely ameliorated by action of public school authorities. This is a national, not a southern phenomenon. And it is largely unrelated to whether a particular State had or did not have segregative school laws. * * * [c]

"I would hold [that] where segregated public schools exist within a school district to a substantial degree, there is a prima facie case that the duly constituted public authorities [are] sufficiently responsible to impose upon them a nationally applicable burden to demonstrate they nevertheless are operating a genuinely integrated school system. [A] system would be integrated in accord with constitutional standards if the responsible authorities had taken appropriate steps to (i) integrate faculties and administration; (ii) scrupulously assure equality of facilities, instruction and curricula opportunities throughout the district; (iii) utilize their authority to draw attendance zones to promote integration; and (iv) locate new schools, close old ones, and determine the size and grade categories with this same objective in mind. Where school authorities decide to undertake the transportation of students, this also must be with integrative opportunities in mind. [An] integrated school system does not mean—and indeed could not mean in view of the residential patterns of most of our major metropolitan areas—that *every school* must in fact be an integrated unit." [d]

c. Powell, J., quoted from Goodman, *De Facto School Segregation: A Constitutional and Empirical Analysis*, 60 Calif.L.Rev. 275, 297 (1972): "Ohio discarded [legally mandated segregation] in 1887, Indiana in 1949, [New York in 1938, New Mexico and Wyoming in 1954 (85 Harv.L.Rev. 85 n. 72 (1971))]. [T]here is no reason to suppose that 1954 is a universally appropriate dividing line between de jure segregation that may safely be assumed to have spent itself and that which may not. For many remedial purposes, adoption of an arbitrary but easily administrable cutoff point might not be objectionable. But in a situation such as school desegregation, where both the rights asserted and the remedial burdens imposed are of such magnitude, and where the resulting sectional discrimination is passionately resented, it is surely questionable whether such arbitrariness is either politically or morally acceptable."

Consider also Karst, *Not One Law at Rome and Another at Athens: The Fourteenth Amendment in Nationwide Application,* 1972 Wash.U.L.Q. 383, 388–89: "If the decisions of a southern school board concerning school location and school sizes can be said to have contributed to racial segregation among residential areas, then with far greater force it can be argued that official state action in northern and western cities has produced residential segregation. Until 1948, racially restrictive covenants in deeds were regularly enforced by state courts; governmental action has often located public housing [as] to intensify residential segregation; and, in a variety of ways, the federal government's programs of subsidy and loan guarantees have explicitly encouraged racial segregation in private housing."

d. Powell, J., further argued that "transportation orders should be applied with special caution to any proposal as disruptive of family life and interests—and ultimately of education itself—as extensive transportation of elementary age children solely for desegregation purposes. As a minimum, this Court should not require school boards to engage in the unnecessary transportation away from their neighborhoods of elementary age children."

Compare 85 Harv.L.Rev. 80 (1971): "[The] critical stages in children's social and educa-

REHNQUIST, J., dissented: "[I]t would be a quite unprecedented application of principles of equitable relief to determine that if the gerrymandering of one attendance zone were proven, particular racial mixtures could be required by a federal district court for every school in the district. [U]nless the Equal Protection Clause [be] held to embody a principle of 'taint,' [such] a result can only be described as the product of judicial fiat. * * *

"The drastic extension of *Brown* which *Green* represented was barely, if at all, explicated in the latter opinion. To require that a genuinely 'dual' system be disestablished, in the sense that the assignment to a child of a particular school is not made to depend on his race, is one thing. To require that school boards affirmatively undertake to achieve racial mixing in schools where such mixing is not achieved in sufficient degree by neutrally drawn boundary lines is quite obviously something else. [Whatever] may be the soundness of that decision in the context of a genuinely 'dual' school system, where segregation [had] once been mandated by law, I can see no constitutional justification for it in a situation such as that which the record shows to have obtained in Denver."

COLUMBUS BOARD OF EDUC. v. PENICK
443 U.S. 449, 99 S.Ct. 2941, 61 L.Ed.2d 666 (1979).

MR. JUSTICE WHITE delivered the opinion of the Court.

The public schools of Columbus, Ohio, are highly segregated by race. In 1976, over 32% of the 96,000 students in the system were black. About 70% of all students attended schools that were at least 80% black or 80% white. Half of the 172 schools were 90% black or 90% white. * * *

We have discovered no reason [to] disturb the judgment of the Court of Appeals, based on the findings and conclusions of the District Court, that the Board's conduct at the time of trial [in 1975] and before not only was animated by an unconstitutional, segregative purpose, but also had current, segregative impact that was sufficiently systemwide to warrant the [systemwide] remedy ordered by the District Court. * * *

First, [t]he Board insists that, since segregated schooling was not commanded by state law ["at least since 1888,"] and since not all schools were wholly black or wholly white in 1954, the District Court was not warranted in finding a dual system. But the District Court found that the "Columbus Public Schools were *officially* segregated by race in 1954"; [6] and in any event, there is no reason to question the finding that as the "direct result of cognitive acts or omissions" the Board maintained "an enclave of separate, black schools on the near east side of Columbus." Proof of purposeful and effective maintenance of a body of separate black schools in a substantial part of the system itself is prima facie proof of a dual school system and supports a finding to this effect absent sufficient contrary proof by the Board, which was not forthcoming in this case. *Keyes.*

tional development are the earliest elementary school years, and if segregation does indeed do educational or social damage, early segregation may do harm that later integration cannot heal."

6. The dissenters [claim] a better grasp of the historical and ultimate facts than the two courts below had. But on the issue of whether there was a dual school system [in] 1954, on the record before us we are much more impressed by the views of the judges who have lived with the case over the years. Also, our dissenting Brothers' suggestion that this Court should play a special oversight role in reviewing the factual determinations of the lower courts in school desegregation cases, asserts an omnipotence and omniscience that we do not have and should not claim.

Second, both courts below declared that since the decision in *Brown II,* the Columbus Board has been under a continuous constitutional obligation to disestablish its dual school system. [Each] failure or refusal to fulfill this affirmative duty continues the violation of the Fourteenth Amendment. *Wright v. Emporia,* 407 U.S. 451, 460, 92 S.Ct. 2196, 2202, 33 L.Ed.2d 51 (1972); [a] *United States v. Scotland Neck Bd. of Educ.,* 407 U.S. 484, 92 S.Ct. 2214, 33 L.Ed.2d 75 (1972) (creation of a new school district in a city that had operated a dual school system but was not yet the subject of court-ordered desegregation).[b] * * *

The Board [has] pointed to nothing in the record persuading us that at the time of trial the dual school system and its effects had been disestablished. The Board does not appear to challenge the finding [that] at the time of trial most blacks were still going to black schools and most whites to white schools. Whatever the Board's current purpose with respect to racially separate education might be, it knowingly continued its failure to eliminate the consequences of its past intentionally segregative policies. * * *

Third, the District Court [also] found that in the intervening years there had been a series of Board actions and practices that could not "reasonably be explained without reference to racial concerns," and that "intentionally aggravated, rather than alleviated," racial separation in the schools. These matters included the general practice of assigning black teachers only to those schools with substantial black student populations, a practice that was terminated only in 1974[;] the intentionally segregative use of optional attendance zones,[8] discontiguous attendance areas,[9] and boundary changes;[10] and the selection of sites for new school construction that had the foreseeable and anticipated effect of maintaining the racial separation of the schools.[11] The court generally noted that "[s]ince the 1954 *Brown* decision, the Columbus defendants or their predecessors were adequately put on notice of the fact that action was required to

a. *Emporia,* per Stewart, J., upheld a district court injunction against "carving out a new school district from an existing district that has not yet completed the process of dismantling" its dual system because the "effect"—wholly apart from the "purpose or motivation"—"hinders [the] process of school desegregation." Burger, C.J., joined by Blackmun, Powell and Rehnquist, JJ., dissented. Cf. Education Amendments Act of 1974 § 216: "In the formulation of remedies [the] lines drawn by a State, subdividing its territory into separate school districts, shall not be ignored or altered except where it is established that the lines were drawn for the purpose, and had the effect, of segregating children among public schools on the basis of race, color, sex, or national origin."

b. In *Scotland Neck,* the school officials defended their action as "necessary to avoid 'white flight' [but this cannot] be accepted as a reason for achieving anything less than complete uprooting" of the dual system. For critical analysis, see Note, *White Flight as a Factor in Desegregation Analysis: A Judicial Recognition of Reality,* 66 Va.L.Rev. 961 (1980). For the view that the Court's "rejection of the white flight argument should not be understood as an absolute principle," see Gewirtz, *Remedies and Resistance,* 92 Yale L.J. 585, 628–65 (1983).

8. Despite petitioners' avowedly strong preference for neighborhood schools, in times of residential racial transition the Board created optional attendance zones to allow white students to avoid predominantly black schools, which were often closer to the homes of the white pupils. * * *

9. This technique was applied when neighborhood schools would have tended to desegregate the involved schools. In the 1960s, a group of white students were bused past their neighborhood school to a "whiter" school. The District Court could "discern no other explanation than a racial one for the existence of the Moler discontiguous attendance area for the period 1963 through 1969." * * *

10. Gerrymandering of boundary lines also continued after 1954. * * *

11. The District Court found that, of the 103 schools built by the Board between 1950 and 1975, 87 opened with racially identifiable student bodies and 71 remained that way at the time of trial. This result was reasonably foreseeable under the circumstances in light of the sites selected, and the Board was often specifically warned that it was, without apparent justification, choosing sites that would maintain or further segregation. * * *

correct and to prevent the increase in" segregation, yet failed to heed their duty to alleviate racial separation in the schools.[12]

[It] is urged that the courts below failed to heed the requirements of *Keyes, Washington v. Davis,* and *Arlington Heights,* that a plaintiff seeking to make out an equal protection violation on the basis of racial discrimination must show purpose. [But] the District Court correctly noted that actions having foreseeable and anticipated disparate impact are relevant evidence to prove the ultimate fact, forbidden purpose. Those cases do not forbid "the foreseeable effects standard from being utilized as one of the several kinds of proofs from which an inference of segregative intent may be properly drawn." * * *

It is also urged that the District Court and the Court of Appeals failed to observe the requirements [of] *Dayton Bd. of Educ. v. Brinkman (Dayton I),* 433 U.S. 406, 97 S.Ct. 2766, 53 L.Ed.2d 851 (1977), which reiterated the accepted rule that the remedy imposed by a court of equity should be commensurate with the violation ascertained, and held that the remedy for the violations that had then been established in that case should be aimed at rectifying the "incremental segregative effect" of the discriminatory acts identified.[13] In *Dayton I,* only a few apparently isolated discriminatory practices had been found; yet a systemwide remedy had been imposed without proof of a systemwide impact.[c] Here, however, the District Court [and the Court of Appeals] repeatedly emphasized that it had found purposefully segregative practices with current, systemwide impact.[15] * * *

Affirmed.[d]

MR. JUSTICE REHNQUIST, with whom MR. JUSTICE POWELL joins, dissenting.

The school desegregation remedy imposed [is] as complete and dramatic a displacement of local authority by the federal judiciary as is possible in our federal system [—] 42,000 of the system's 96,000 students are reassigned to new schools. There are like reassignment of teachers, staff, and administrators,

---

12. [F]or example, the University Commission in 1968 made certain recommendations that it thought not only would assist desegregation of the schools but would encourage integrated residential patterns. The Board['s] response was "minimal." Additionally, the Board refused to create a site selection advisory group to assist in avoiding sites with a segregative effect, refused to ask state education officials to present plans for desegregating the Columbus public schools, and refused to apply for federal desegregation-assistance funds. * * *

13. Petitioners have indicated that a few of the recent violations specifically discussed by the District Court involved so few students and lasted for such a short time that they are unlikely to have any current impact. But that contention says little or nothing about the incremental impact of systemwide practices extending over many years. Petitioners also argue that because many of the involved schools were in areas that had become predominantly black residential areas by the time of trial the racial separation in the schools would have occurred even without the unlawful conduct of petitioners. But, as the District Court found, petitioners' evidence in this respect was insufficient to counter respon-

dents' proof. And the phenomenon described by petitioners seems only to confirm, not disprove, the evidence accepted by the District Court that school segregation is a contributing cause of housing segregation. See *Keyes; Swann.*

c. *Dayton I,* per Rehnquist, J., also observed: "The finding [that many Dayton] schools are either predominantly white or predominantly black"—"standing by itself, is not a violation of the Fourteenth Amendment in the absence of a showing that this condition resulted from intentionally segregative actions on the part of the Board. *Davis.*"

15. Mr. Justice Rehnquist's dissent erroneously states that we have "reliev[ed] school desegregation plaintiffs from any showing of a causal nexus between intentional segregative actions and the conditions they seek to remedy." [But both courts below] found that the Board's purposefully discriminatory conduct and policies had current, systemwide impact— an essential predicate, as both courts recognized, for a systemwide remedy. * * *

d. The concurring opinions of Burger, C.J., and Stewart, J., and the dissenting opinion of Powell, J., appear after *Dayton II,* infra.

reorganization of the grade structure of virtually every elementary school in the system, the closing of 33 schools, and the additional transportation of 37,000 students. * * *

Today the Court affirms [this case] and *Dayton II* in opinions so Delphic that lower courts will be hard pressed to fathom their implications for school desegregation litigation. I can only offer two suggestions. The first is that the Court, possibly chastened by the complexity and emotion that accompanies school desegregation cases, wishes to relegate the determination of a violation of [equal protection] in any plan of pupil assignment, and the formulation of a remedy for its violation, to the judgment of a single District Judge. That judgment should be subject to review under the "clearly erroneous" standard by the appropriate Court of Appeals, in much the same way that actions for an accounting between private partners in a retail shoe business [are] handled. "Discriminatory purpose" and "systemwide violation" are to be treated as talismanic phrases which once invoked, warrant only the most superficial scrutiny by appellate courts.

Such an [approach] disparages both this Court's oft-expressed concern for the important role of local autonomy in educational matters and the significance of the constitutional rights involved. It also holds out the disturbing prospect of very different remedies being imposed on similar school systems because of the predilections of individual judges and their good faith but incongruent efforts to make sense of this Court's confused pronouncements today. * * *

[Alternatively, the] Court suggests a radical new approach to desegregation cases in systems without a history of statutorily mandated separation of the races: if a district court concludes—employing what in honesty must be characterized as an irrebuttable presumption—that there was a "dual" school system at the time of *Brown I,* it must find post-1954 constitutional violations in a school board's failure to take every affirmative step to integrate the system. Put differently, *racial imbalance* at the time the complaint is filed is sufficient to support a systemwide, racial balance school busing remedy if the district court can find *some* evidence of discriminatory purpose prior to 1954, without any inquiry into the causal relationship between those pre-1954 violations and current segregation in the school system.

[As] a matter of history, case law, or logic, there is nothing to support the novel proposition that the primary inquiry in school desegregation cases involving systems without a history of statutorily mandated racial assignment is what happened in those systems before 1954. As a matter of history, 1954 makes no more sense as a benchmark—indeed it makes *less* sense—than 1968, 1971 or 1973. Perhaps the latter year has the most to commend it, if one insists on a benchmark, because in *Keyes* this Court first confronted the problem of school segregation in the context of systems without a history of statutorily mandated separation of the races.

As a matter of logic, the majority's decision to turn the year 1954 into a constitutional Rubicon also fails. [It] is sophistry to suggest that a school board in Columbus in 1954 could have read *Brown* and gleaned from it a constitutional duty "to diffuse black students throughout the system" or take whatever other action the Court today thinks it should have taken. And not only was the school board to anticipate the state of the law 20 years hence, but also to have a full appreciation for discrete acts or omissions of school boards 20 to 50 years earlier.[9] * * *

---

9. [I]ncidents relied on by the District Court occurred anywhere from 1909 to 1943.

Causality plays a central role in *Keyes* [which] held that before the burden of production shifts to the school board, the plaintiffs must prove "that the school authorities have carried out a systematic program of segregation *affecting a substantial portion of the students, schools, teachers and facilities within the school system.*" The Court recognized that a trial court might find "that [at] some point in time the relationship between past segregative acts and present segregation may become so attenuated as to be incapable of supporting a finding of de jure segregation warranting judicial intervention." The relevance of past acts of the school board was to depend on whether "segregation resulting from those actions continues to exist." That inquiry is not central under the approach approved by the Court today. Henceforth, the question is apparently whether pre-1954 acts contributed in some unspecified manner to segregated conditions that existed in 1954. If the answer is yes, then the only question is whether the school board has exploited all integrative opportunities that presented themselves in the subsequent 25 years. If not, a systemwide remedy is in order, despite the plaintiff's failure to demonstrate a link between those past acts and current racial imbalance.

The Court's use of the term "affirmative duty" implies that integration be the pre-eminent—indeed, the controlling—educational consideration in school board decisionmaking. It takes precedence over other legitimate educational objectives subject to some vague feasibility limitation. That implication is dramatically demonstrated in this case. Both lower courts necessarily gave special significance to the Columbus School Board's post-1954 school construction and siting policies as supporting the systemwide remedy in this case. They did not find—in fact, could not have found—that the siting and construction of schools were racially motivated. As the District Court observed: "In 1950, [the] Bureau of Educational Research at The Ohio State University began a comprehensive, scientific and objective analysis of the school plant needs of the school system [and] a number of general and specific recommendations were made [which] included the size and location of new school sites as well as additions to existing sites. The recommendations were conceived to accommodate the so-called 'community or neighborhood school concept.' [The] Board of Education adopted [the] Bureau's recommendations in [proposing] bond issues in 1951, 1953, 1956, 1959 and 1964. * * *" Thus the Columbus Board of Education employed the most objective criteria possible in the placement of new schools.

Nevertheless the District Court and Court of Appeals found that conformity with these recommendations was a violation of the Equal Protection Clause because "in some instances the need for school facilities could have been met in a manner having an integrative rather than a segregative effect."[12] By endorsing this logic, the Court, as a result of its finding of an affirmative duty, employs remedy standards to determine the existence of post-1954 violations in school construction and ignores the previously pivotal role of discriminatory purpose.

This unprecedented "affirmative duty" superstructure sits atop a weak foundation—the existence of a "dual" school system in 1954. This finding was predicated on the presence of four predominantly black elementary schools and one predominantly black junior high school on the "near east side of Columbus," a then and now black residential area. The Columbus School Board at that time employed, as it does now, a neighborhood school policy. The specific Board actions that the District Court cited were racial assignment of teachers and

12. [T]he District Court made specific findings only with respect to two of the 103 schools constructed between 1950 and 1975. [The] sites for both schools followed recommendations by the Bureau * * *.

gerrymandering along part of the border between two school districts. The Court concludes that these violations involved a substantial part of the Columbus school system in 1954, and invokes *Keyes* for the proposition that the finding of a dual school system follows "absent sufficient contrary proof by the Board, which was not forthcoming in this case."

There are two major difficulties with this use of *Keyes*. First, without any explanation the Court for the first time applies it to define the character of a school system remote in time—here 25 or more years ago—without any examination of the justifications for the *Keyes* burden-shifting principles when those principles are used in this fashion.[15] Here violations with respect to five schools, only three of which exist today, occurring over 30 years ago are the key premise for a systemwide racial balance remedy involving 172 schools—most of which did not exist in 1950.

[Second, the] departure from established doctrines of causation and discriminatory purpose [is] also evident in [the] post-1954 violations * * *. [T]he Court of Appeals observed, I think correctly, that these post-1954 incidents "can properly be classified as isolated in the sense that they do not form any systemwide pattern." All the incidents cited, let alone those that can meet a properly applied segregative intent standard, could not serve as the basis for a systemwide racial balance remedy.

[O]bjective evidence [of segregative intent] must be carefully analyzed for it may otherwise reduce the "discriminatory purpose" requirement to a "discriminatory impact" test by another name. [In] a school system with racially imbalanced schools, *every* school board action regarding construction, pupil assignment, transportation, annexation and temporary facilities will promote integration, aggravate segregation or maintain segregation. Foreseeability follows from the obviousness of that proposition. Such a tight noose on school board decisionmaking will invariably move government of a school system [to] the courthouse.

The District Court [held] that it was bound by the standard for segregative intent articulated by [the] Court of Appeals in *Oliver v. Michigan Bd. of Educ.* [I]n *Dayton II*, n. 9, the Court expressly rejects the *Oliver* test, and in its opinion in this case, indicates that the District Court treated foreseeable effects as only another bit of evidence. [But as] far as gauging the purpose underlying specific actions is concerned, it is quite clear [that] the District Court looked for foreseeability per se.

As such, the District Court's treatment of specific post-1954 conduct reflects the same cavalier approach to causality and purpose that underlies the 1954 affirmative duty. [The] court found violations with respect to three optional attendance zones. [One, as to which the District Court found "discriminatory purpose," had been dismantled by 1975], and the District Court clearly suggests that it does not have any current effect on the Columbus school system. [As for

15. [There] is a policy judgment sometimes made [that] the facts on a particular issue are so peculiarly within the knowledge of a certain party that the burden of proof on that issue should be allocated to him. Whatever the merits of the burden-shift to the school board where contemporaneous board decisions are at issue, they do not commend a burden-shift regarding conduct 25 or more years ago.

The Court charges that in questioning the propriety of employing the *Keyes* burden-shift

in this case, we "claim a better grasp of the historical and ultimate facts than the two courts below had." n. 6. But the *Keyes* burden-shift is not an ultimate finding of fact at all. It is a creature of this Court, brought into play by the making of only a prima facie showing, and applied in this case in a completely novel way. * * *

another,] the District Court made no findings as to the current effect of the past violation [and] was clearly of the opinion that no such inquiry was necessary.

The final optional attendance zone demonstrates the influence of the "affirmative duty"—whether the 1954 variety or that which follows from *Oliver*. This optional zone [gave] some students within Highland's boundaries the option of attending the neighboring West Mound Street Elementary School. Again, the District Court found, this permitted transfer to a "whiter" school. But the District Court also found that there was a legitimate educational objective for creation of the zone: Highland was overcrowded and West Mound was under capacity. The District Court, however, concluded that the School Board's actions were objectionable because [other] optional attendance zones could have been drawn which would have had "an integrative effect on West Mound." This again suggests a duty on the School Board to select the most integrative alternative.

The second set of post-1954 actions faulted by the District Court [were] situations where students [were] assigned to a school in a zone not contiguous with their neighborhood. One zone was established in 1963 and involved about 70 students. [The] District Court indicates that this violative condition existed until 1969, presumably because after that date the discontiguous area had a substantial black population and an integrative effect on the Moler Elementary School. Since the discontiguous area now has an integrative effect, one might ask what is its current segregative effect on the school system? [The] District Court made no findings as to the current effect of the [second discontiguous zone which existed between 1957 and 1963].[22]

Thus it is clear that with respect to a number of the post-1954 actions that the District Court found to be independent violations, foreseeability was not one kind of evidence, but the whole ball game * * *. Those findings that could be supported by the concept of discriminatory purpose propounded in *Davis* and *Arlington Heights* were not accompanied by any effort to link those violations with current conditions of segregation in the school system. [I]n any event, the small number of students involved in these instances could not independently support the sweeping racial balance remedy imposed by the District Court. Cf. *Dayton I.* * * *

Once a showing is made that the District Court believes satisfies the *Keyes* requirement of purposeful discrimination in a substantial part of the school system, the school board will almost invariably rely on its neighborhood school policy and residential segregation to show that it is not responsible for the existence of certain predominantly black and white schools in other parts of the school system. Under the District Court's reasoning, [not] only is that evidence not probative on the Board's lack of responsibility, it itself supports an inference of a constitutional violation. In addition, the District Court relied on a general proposition that "there is often a substantial reciprocal effect between the color of the school and the color of the neighborhood it serves" to block any inquiry into whether racially identifiable schools were the product of racially identifiable neighborhoods or whether past discriminatory acts bore a "but for" relationship to current segregative conditions. [But] as the District Court recognized, other factors play an important role in determining segregated residential patterns.

---

22. There is substantial discussion in the District Court's opinion about various groups that gave the Columbus School Board notice that certain decisions would have a segregative rather than integrative impact. But notice in and of itself only goes so far as to establish foreseeability, and foreseeability itself is not the ultimate fact in issue if we continue to adhere to *Davis* and *Arlington Heights*.

[Yet] today the School Board is called to task for all the forces beyond their control that shaped residential segregation in Columbus. There is thus no room for *Keyes* or *Swann* rebuttal either with respect to the school system today or that of 30 years ago.

* * * I do not question that there were constitutional violations on the part of the Columbus School Board in the past, but there are no deterrence or retribution components of the rationale for a school desegregation remedy. The fundamental mission of such remedies is to restore those integrated educational opportunities that would now exist but for purposefully discriminatory school board conduct. Because critically important questions were neither asked nor answered by the lower courts, the record before us simply cannot inform as to whether so sweeping a remedy as that imposed is justified. * * *

DAYTON BOARD OF EDUC. v. BRINKMAN
(DAYTON II)
443 U.S. 526, 99 S.Ct. 2971, 61 L.Ed.2d 720 (1979).

MR. JUSTICE WHITE delivered the opinion of the Court.

[The] public schools of Dayton are highly segregated. [In 1972, when] the complaint was filed, 43% of the students in the Dayton system were black, but 51 of the 69 schools in the system were virtually all-white or all-black. * * *

The District Court's judgment that the Board had violated the Fourteenth Amendment was affirmed by the Court of Appeals; but after twice being reversed on the ground that the prescribed remedy was inadequate to eliminate all vestiges of state-imposed segregation, the District Court ordered the Board [to] assure that each school in the system would roughly reflect the systemwide ratio of black and white students. The Court of Appeals then affirmed.

We reversed [in *Dayton I*, and the District Court then dismissed] the complaint [because] plaintiffs had failed to prove that acts of intentional segregation over 20 years old had any current incremental segregative effects [6] [and that] plaintiffs had failed to show either discriminatory purpose or segregative effect, or both, with respect to the challenged practices and policies of the [Board].[7]

---

6. The District Court observed that "[m]any of these practices, if they existed today, would violate the Equal Protection Clause." The court identified certain Board policies as being "among" such practices: until at least 1934, black elementary students were kept separate from white students; until approximately 1950 high school athletics were deliberately segregated [and] black students at one high school were ordered or induced to sit at the rear of classrooms and suffered other indignities.

7. Reviewing the faculty assignment and hiring practices, the District Court found that until at least 1951 the Board's policies had been intentionally segregative. But in that year the Board instituted a policy of "dynamic gradualism" and "by 1969 all traces of segregation were virtually eliminated." [T]he court ruled that plaintiffs had not established that past discrimination in faculty assignments had an incremental segregative effect.

Similarly, the court ruled that the plaintiff children had not shown that the Board's use of attendance zones and transfers denied equal protection. In certain instances, segregative intent had not been satisfactorily demonstrated. [In] other instances, current segregative effect had not been proved. Though another high school, Dunbar, had been created and maintained until 1962 as a citywide black high school, the District Court found that because of the increasing black population in that area Dunbar would have been virtually all black by 1960 anyway. And though until the early 1950's black orphans had been bused past nearby white schools to all-black schools, this "arguably" discriminatory conduct had not been shown by "objective proof" to have any continued segregative effect.

The court also looked to school construction and siting practices. Although 22 of 24 new schools, 78 of 95 additions, and 26 of 26 porta-

The Court of Appeals reversed [and] held that, "at the time of *Brown I,* defendants were intentionally operating a dual school [system]" and that the "finding of the District Court to the contrary is clearly erroneous." On the record before us, we perceive no basis for petitioners' challenge to this holding of the Court of Appeals.[8]

Concededly, in the early 1950's, "77.6 percent of all students attended schools in which one race accounted for 90 percent or more of the students and 54.3 percent of the black students were assigned to four schools that were 100 percent black." One of these schools was Dunbar High School, which [had] been established as a districtwide black high school [and] remained so at the time of *Brown I* and up until 1962. The District Court also found that "among" the early and relatively undisputed acts of purposeful segregation was the establishment of Garfield as a black elementary school. The Court of Appeals found that two other elementary schools were, through a similar process of optional attendance zones and the creation and maintenance of all-black faculties, intentionally designated and operated as all-black schools in the 1930's [and] at the time of *Brown I.* Additionally, the District Court had specifically found that in 1950 the faculty at 100% black schools was 100% black and that the faculty at all other schools was 100% white.

These facts, the Court of Appeals held, made clear that the Board was purposefully operating segregated schools in a substantial part of the district [at the time of *Brown I*], which warranted an inference and a finding that segregation in other parts of the system was also purposeful absent evidence [as required by *Keyes.*[9]] Based on its review of the entire record, the Court of

ble schools built or utilized by the Board between 1950 and 1972 opened virtually all black or all white, and though many of the accompanying decisions appeared to be so without any rationale as to be "haphazard," the District Court found that the plaintiffs had not shown purposeful segregation. The court also refused to investigate whether the Board had any legitimate grounds for the failure to close some schools and consolidate others when enrollment declined in recent years. Though such a course would have decreased racial separation and saved money, the court found no evidence of discriminatory purpose in those facts. Nor did the court see any hint of impermissible purpose in the Board's decisions in the 1940's to supply school services for legally segregated housing projects and to rent elementary school space in such projects.

Finally, the court held that the Board's rescission of its earlier resolutions ["recognizing its responsibility to eradicate racial separation in the public schools"] was not violative of the Fourteenth Amendment since, in light of the court's finding that the current segregation had no unconstitutional origin, the Board had no constitutional obligation to adopt the resolutions in the first place.

8. We have no quarrel with our Brother Stewart's general conclusion that there is great value in appellate courts showing deference to the fact-finding of local trial judges. The clearly erroneous standard serves that

purpose well. [The] Court of Appeals performed its unavoidable duty in this case and concluded that the District Court had erred. [W]e see no reason on the record before us to upset the judgment of the Court of Appeals in this respect.

9. We do not deprecate the relevance of segregated faculty assignments as one of the factors in proving the existence of a school system that is dual for teachers *and* students; but to the extent that the Court of Appeals understood *Swann* as holding that faculty segregation makes out a prima facie case [of] purposeful racial assignment of students, this is an overreading of *Swann.*

The Court of Appeals also held that the District Court had not given proper weight to *Oliver v. Michigan Bd. of Educ.,* 508 F.2d 178, 182 (CA6 1974), cert. denied, 421 U.S. 963 (1975), where the Court of Appeals had held that "[a] presumption of segregative purpose arises when plaintiffs establish that the natural, probable, and foreseeable result of public officials' action or inaction was an increase or perpetuation of public school segregation" * * *. We have never held that as a general proposition the foreseeability of segregative consequences makes out a prima facie case of purposeful racial discrimination and shifts the burden of producing evidence to the defendants * * *. Of course, as we hold in *Columbus* today, proof of foreseeable consequences is one type of quite relevant evidence of racially discriminatory purpose, and it may

Appeals concluded that the Board had not responded with sufficient evidence to counter the inference that a dual system was in existence in Dayton in 1954.

* * *

Given intentionally segregated schools in 1954, [the] Court of Appeals was quite right in holding that the Board was thereafter under a continuing duty to eradicate the effects of that system, and that the systemwide nature of the violation furnished prima facie proof that current segregation in the Dayton schools was caused at least in part by prior intentionally segregative official acts. Thus, judgment for the plaintiffs was authorized and required absent sufficient countervailing evidence by the defendant school officials. *Keyes.* At the time of trial, Dunbar High School and the three black elementary schools, or the schools that succeeded them, remained black schools; and most of the schools in Dayton were virtually one-race schools, as were 80% of the classrooms. [Against] this background, the Court of Appeals held [that] defendants had failed to come forward with evidence to deny "that the current racial composition of the school population reflects the systemwide impact" of the Board's prior discriminatory conduct.

Part of the affirmative duty imposed by our cases [is] the obligation not to take any action that would impede the process of disestablishing the dual system and its effects. [T]he measure of the post-*Brown* conduct of a school board under an unsatisfied duty to liquidate a dual system is the effectiveness, not the purpose, of the actions in decreasing or increasing the segregation caused by the dual system. *Emporia.* As was clearly established in *Keyes* and *Swann*, the Board had to do more than abandon its prior discriminatory purpose. The Board has had an affirmative responsibility to see that pupil assignment policies and school construction and abandonment practices "are not used and do not serve to perpetuate or re-establish the dual school system," *Columbus,* and the Board has a " 'heavy burden' " of showing that actions that increased or continued the effects of the dual system serve important and legitimate ends.

[Though] the Board was often put on notice of the effects of its acts or omissions, the District Court found that "with one [counterproductive] exception [no] attempt was made to alter the racial characteristics of any of the schools." The Court of Appeals held that far from performing its constitutional duty, the Board had engaged in "post-1954 actions which actually have exacerbated the racial separation existing at the time of *Brown I.*" The court reversed as clearly erroneous the District Court's finding that intentional faculty segregation had ended in 1951; the Court of Appeals found that it had effectively continued into the 1970's.[11] This was a systemwide practice and strong evidence that the Board was continuing its efforts to segregate students. [Furthermore,] the Court of

itself show a failure to fulfill the duty to eradicate the consequences of prior purposefully discriminatory conduct.

[For criticism of the Court's "subjective intent" approach and a supporting rationale for *Oliver's* "institutional segregative intent" test, see Note, *Reading the Mind of the School Board: Segregative Intent and the De Facto/ De Jure Distinction,* 86 Yale L.J. 317 (1976).]

11. Under the policy of "dynamic gradualism" instituted in 1951, see n. 7, black teachers were assigned to white or mixed schools when the surrounding communities were ready to accept black teachers, and white teachers who agreed were assigned to black

schools. By 1969 each school in the system had at least one black teacher. The District Court apparently did not think the post-1951 policy was purposeful discrimination. We think the Court of Appeals was completely justified in finding that conclusion to be clearly erroneous on the undisputed facts. As late as the 1968–1969 school year, the Board assigned 72% of all black teachers to schools that were 90% or more black, and only 9% of white teachers to such schools. And faculty segregation disappeared completely only after efforts of the Department of HEW under Title VI of the Civil Rights Act of 1964.

Appeals held that since 1954 the Board had used some "optional attendance zones for racially discriminatory [purposes]." The District Court's finding to the contrary was clearly erroneous. At the very least, the use of such zones amounted to a perpetuation of the existing dual school system. Likewise, the Board failed in its duty [by] its pattern of school construction and site selection, recited by the District Court, see n. 7 * * *. We see no reason to disturb these factual determinations, which conclusively show the breach of duty found by the Court of Appeals.

[The] Court of Appeals was also quite justified in utilizing the Board's total failure to fulfill its affirmative duty—and indeed its conduct resulting in increased segregation—to trace the current, systemwide segregation back to the purposefully dual system of the 1950's and to the subsequent acts of intentional discrimination. * * *

Affirmed.

MR. JUSTICE STEWART, with whom THE CHIEF JUSTICE joins, concurring in the result in [Columbus] and dissenting in [Dayton II]. * * *

Whether actions that produce racial separation are intentional [present] very difficult and subtle factual questions. Similarly intricate may be factual inquiries into the breadth of any constitutional violation, and hence of any permissible remedy. [I] suspect that it is impossible for a reviewing court factually to know a case from a 6,600 page printed record as well as the trial judge knew it. [T]herefore, I think appellate courts should accept even more readily than in most cases the factual findings of the courts of first instance.

[W]hen the factual issues are as elusive as these, who bears the burden of proof can easily determine who prevails in the litigation. [The] prejudices of the school boards of 1954 (and earlier) cannot realistically be assumed to haunt the school boards of today. [It] is unrealistic to assume that the hand of 1954 plays any major part in shaping the current school systems in [Columbus or Dayton]. For these reasons, I simply cannot accept the shift in the litigative burden of proof adopted by the Court. [Just] as I would defer to the findings of fact made by the District Court in the Dayton case, I would accept the trial court's findings in [the Columbus case].

MR. JUSTICE REHNQUIST, with whom MR. JUSTICE POWELL joins, dissenting [in Dayton II].

* * * Little would be gained by another "blow-by-blow" recitation in dissent of how the Court's cascade of presumptions in this case sweeps away the distinction between de facto and de jure segregation.

[The] District Judge in Dayton did not employ a post-1954 "affirmative duty" test. Violations he did identify were found not to have any causal relationship to existing conditions of segregation in the Dayton school system. He did not employ a foreseeability test for intent, hold the school system responsible for residential segregation, or impugn the neighborhood school policy, as an explanation for some existing one race schools. In short, the Dayton and Columbus district judges had completely different ideas of what the law required.[e] [And] I

---

e. For a detailed review of the Keyes litigation, criticizing the district judge's findings of deliberate segregation and concluding that "perhaps nothing emerges more clearly [than] the fact of the almost totally unrestrained freedom of choice district judges possess in 'desegregation' litigation," see Graglia, Disaster By Decree 162–99 (1976): "If this one judge had found—as he should have and as the federal judges in New Jersey did find in Spencer v. Kugler, 404 U.S. 1027, 92 S.Ct. 707, 30 L.Ed.2d 723 (1972)—that the racial imbalance in the schools was not the result of racial discrimination by school officials, the travail of Denver would have been at an end. Never in our history has the fate of so many people have no doubt that the Court of Appeals' heavy-handed approach in this case is to some degree explained by the perceived inequity of imposing a systemwide racial-balance remedy on Columbus while finding no violation in Dayton. The simple meting out of equal remedies, however, is [not] "equal justice under law."

MR. JUSTICE POWELL, dissenting in [*Columbus*] and [*Dayton II*]. * * *

There are unintegrated schools in every major urban area in the country that contains a substantial minority population. This condition results primarily from familiar segregated housing patterns, which—in turn—are caused by social, economic, and demographic forces for which no school board is responsible. * * *

Holding the school boards of these two cities responsible for *all* of the segregation in the Dayton and Columbus systems and prescribing fixed racial ratios in every school as the constitutionally required remedy necessarily implies a belief that the same school boards—under court supervision—will be capable of bringing about and maintaining the desired racial balance in each of these schools. The experience in city after city demonstrates that this is an illusion. The process of resegregation, stimulated by resentment against judicial coercion and concern as to the effect of court supervision of education, will follow today's decisions as surely as it has in other cities subjected to similar sweeping decrees. * * *

MR. CHIEF JUSTICE BURGER, concurring in the judgment [in *Columbus*].

* * * I agree [with] Mr. Justice Rehnquist's opinion that criticizes the Court's reliance on the finding that both Columbus and Dayton operated "dual school systems" at the time of *Brown I* as a basis for holding that these school boards have labored under an unknown and unforeseeable affirmative duty to desegregate their schools for the past 25 years. Nothing in reason or our previous decisions provides foundation for this novel legal standard.

I also agree with many of the concerns expressed by Mr. Justice Powell [whether] massive public transportation really accomplishes the desirable objectives sought. Nonetheless our prior decisions have sanctioned its use when a constitutional violation of sufficient magnitude has been found. We cannot retry these sensitive and difficult issues in this Court; we can only set the general legal standards and, within the limits of appellate review, see that they are followed.

Notes and Questions

1. *Scope of the decisions.* (a) Do *Keyes*, *Columbus* and *Dayton II* "sweep away the distinction between de facto and de jure segregation"? In a district that presently has substantial racial imbalance in its schools, but that had no statutorily mandated segregation in 1954, if plaintiffs fail to prove "intentionally segregative school board actions in a meaningful portion of the school system" (*Keyes*), does the school board have an "affirmative duty" to desegregate? Do "*Columbus* and *Dayton II* leave open the possibility that if a school board operated a dual system prior to 1954, but abandoned its segregative policies before *Brown I* was decided, it might not be subject to an affirmative duty to desegregate"? 93 Harv.L.Rev. 126 n. 58 (1979). In these circumstances, must the school board prove that the segregation that existed in 1954 (or that exists today) was not "caused" by its earlier intentionally segregative actions? If so, is the presumption of causality "irrebuttable" (Rehnquist, J.)? Is the task of

so importantly depended on the whim of a
single, unelected, lifetime official."

overcoming the presumption "virtually impossible"? "Extraordinarily diffi-cult"? See Choper, Kamisar & Tribe, *The Supreme Court: Trends and Develop-ments, 1978–1979,* 253–54 (1979). What is the relevance of *Pasadena?* Consider Kitch, *The Return of Color-Consciousness to the Constitution: Weber, Dayton, and Columbus,* 1979 Sup.Ct.Rev. 1, 14: "The emphasis in *Columbus* and *Dayton II* on the 'continuing constitutional duty' to desegregate, if taken literally, would mean that the school systems must be perpetually operated in a way that eliminates identifiable black schools each school year. [*Pasadena*] can be distinguished on the ground that the district court had not found that the school system operated a dual school system in 1954, and hence was not under what the Court calls the continuing constitutional duty to desegregate."

(b) In *Keyes,* if plaintiffs make out "a prima facie case of unlawful segrega-tive design on the part of school authorities," is the scope of the burden imposed on the school board "of proving that other segregated schools within the system are not also the result of intentionally segregative actions" consistent with the approach of *Arlington Heights* fn. 21? See Choper, Kamisar & Tribe, supra, at 241. Is the subject of intentional school segregation distinguishable from other forms of intentional racial discrimination?

(c) If, apart from school location and assignment policies, many "other factors play an important role in determining segregated residential patterns" (Rehnquist, J.), do *Keyes, Columbus* and *Dayton II* answer a question left open in *Swann:* if plaintiffs prove "that school segregation is a consequence of other types of state action [see Karst, fn. c. in *Keyes*], without any discriminatory action by the school authorities, is there a constitutional violation requiring remedial action"? See generally Comment, *School Desegregation After Swann: A Theory of Government Responsibility,* 39 U.Chi.L.Rev. 421 (1972).

2. *"De facto" school segregation.* (a) Contrary to *Dayton I,* in the absence of any "intentionally segregative actions" on the part of any state agency, *should* the fact that many schools in a district "are either predominantly white or predominantly black" "standing by itself" violate equal protection? For an early view, see Fiss, *Racial Imbalance in the Public Schools: The Constitutional Concepts,* 78 Harv.L.Rev. 564 (1965).

(b) *Effect on students.* Consider Note, *Racial Imbalance in the Public Schools: Constitutional Dimensions and Judicial Response,* 18 Vand.L.Rev. 1290, 1295–96 (1965): "Fiss points out 'that students in such schools are also deprived of the intellectual stimulation that comes from the exchange of ideas and the development of personal relationships in a racially and socially heterogeneous context.' [Because *Brown*] found that 'to separate [blacks] from others of similar age and qualifications solely because of their race generates a feeling of inferiori-ty,' proponents of racial balance in the schools argue analogously that racial imbalance also breeds inferiority. [A] more damaging aspect of racial imbalance relates to [a] corollary goal of education [which is] 'to induct the young person systematically into the culture and society to which he is an heir and in which he should be a partner.' The Supreme Court recognized [this] in *Brown.* [It] seems clear that regardless of the cause of the separation of the races the isolation of a minority race will prevent the achievement of this educational goal." Compare Yudof, note 1(a) after *Swann,* at 436: "One study of the psychological impact of segregation on black children has found that the black child's self-concept is inversely related to the proportion of white students in the school; the whiter his school the lower the black child rated himself. Other studies have reached the opposite conclusion. Studies of the relationship be-tween personality development and segregation are similarly conflicting. [Moreover,] available studies are inconclusive as to whether integration in fact accelerates academic achievement. Further complicating the evidence are the many additional variables that may alter the effect of integration or segregation: the degree of interracial hostility, the percentage of black students in relation to the school population, the socio-economic makeup of the student body, the existence of ability grouping, and the attitudes of parents, teachers, and administrators." See also Goodman, fn. c. in *Keyes*, at 400–435 for an intensive review of various studies, concluding that "the influence of biracial schooling upon the achievement of black students is highly *uncertain*." Contrast Kaplan, note 1(b) after *Swann*, at 174: "[V]irtually every bit of the sociological evidence of harm presented [in *Brown*] involved compulsory segregation based overtly on race in the social setting of the South where school segregation was merely one facet of the general exclusion of the Negro from the dominant life of the community. It is by no means obvious that harm will automatically follow where the segregation is of the de facto variety, occurring in the Northern setting, and is not purposively based on race."

(c) *Constitutional "values" and judicial interpretation.* Consider Goodman, note 1(b) after *Swann*, at 21–23: "[T]here is a *moral* difference of the first importance between a law which discriminates against citizens solely on the ground of race and one which, though based on racially neutral criteria, operates to the detriment of a minority group.[g] [A] second important difference between legislation requiring, and legislation merely resulting in, racial segregation is the absence in the former case of any legitimate State interest which might countervail the harm inflicted on Negro children. [The] only rationale for segregation which has even a semblance of plausibility is that it helps to avoid needless friction between the races and thus preserves tranquility both in the classroom and in the larger society. In the long run, however, by creating barriers to normal intergroup relations and arousing the resentment and frustration of the minority group, segregation probably does more to defeat than to promote racial peace. And even were this not so, it still could not be said that segregation is a necessary means to that end, for there are many other ways of dealing with the problem of racial conflict. [This] is not the case with de facto segregation. Here the psychological injury suffered by Negro children results from the use of otherwise legitimate means (geographical districting criteria) to accomplish an otherwise legitimate end (the neighborhood school) which could not be accomplished in any other way."

Even if de jure and de facto segregation are distinguishable, is "the cause of racial integration entitled to a 'preferred position' in the hierarchy of constitutional values"? Dorsen, *Northern School Segregation*, 10 How.L.J. 127, 129 (1964). Should de facto segregation be permitted "only if adequate justification exists for its continuation," i.e., "a compelling state interest that cannot be satisfied by any less onerous alternative"? Dimond, *School Segregation in the North: There Is But One Constitution*, 7 Harv.Civ.Rts.—Civ.Lib.L.Rev. 1, 32 (1972). Should the school board at least be required "to take reasonable steps— as opposed to all possible steps [as with de jure segregation]—to eliminate" de

---

g. Compare Goodman, note (b) supra, at 319: "Is there really a decisive moral difference between the state of mind that produces de facto segregation and that which produced de jure segregation? Those who advocate the neighborhood school may not want segregation, but they well know their policy begets it; either they see no harm or they deem the harm an acceptable cost. On the other hand, if de facto segregation is rarely inadvertent, de jure segregation is not always malevolent. Many an avowed segregationist genuinely believes his policy benefits all, black and white alike, offering them a classroom free from racial friction."

facto segregation? Fiss, note 1(b) after *Swann,* at 706. Consider Kaplan, note b supra, at 180: "It is hard [to] argue that the cause of mixing Negro and white children, taken as it must be from the vague words of the equal protection clause, deserves the same standing as the right of free expression which not only is founded in the explicit wording of the first amendment, but also is at the very basis of any free [society]. Integration may be an important value [but] it is hard to argue that it is more fundamental than the right of the state to provide for the health, safety, and education of its children."

Does *Washington v. Davis* plainly reject the view that "other values" should be disregarded in "the cause of racial integration"? Consider Goodman, note b supra, at 306: "[If] it is true that de facto, like de jure segregation, generates feelings of racial inferiority in black school children, the injury is one they incur distinctively as blacks, solely on account of their race. A white child similarly situated would not be similarly affected. In that sense, the neighborhood school policy can be said to inflict a 'racially specific' harm, a harm differing in kind from that inflicted by [the] examples of state action [in fn. 14 of *Davis*] that hurt more blacks than whites, but hurt the individual black no more than his white counterpart."

At the least, contrary to fn. 9 in *Dayton II,* should "the foreseeability of segregative consequences" make out "a prima facie case of purposeful racial discrimination" on the part of the school board and shift the burden to it to prove nonsegregative intent? [h]

3. *Interdistrict remedies.* (a) *Schools.* In MILLIKEN v. BRADLEY, 418 U.S. 717, 94 S.Ct. 3112, 41 L.Ed.2d 1069 (1974), the district court found that various actions of the Detroit Board of Education, the State Board of Education and the Michigan legislature (e.g., barring use of state funds for busing), produced de jure segregation in Detroit; that, because of the city's racial composition, desegregation plans limited to Detroit "would accentuate the racial identifiability of the district as a Black school system, and would not accomplish desegregation." Thus, the district judge ordered a plan encompassing 53 neighboring suburban school districts (in Oakland and Macomb counties). The Court, per BURGER, C.J.,—emphasizing that, apart from one "isolated instance affecting two of the school districts," the record "contains evidence of de jure segregated conditions only in" Detroit—reversed, stating the issue as "whether a federal court may impose a multidistrict [remedy] absent any finding that the other included school districts have failed to operate unitary school systems within their districts, [that] the boundary lines of any affected school district were established with the purpose of fostering racial segregation [, that] the included districts committed acts which effected segregation within the other districts, and absent a meaningful opportunity for the included neighboring school districts to [be] heard on the propriety of a multidistrict remedy or on the question of constitutional violations by those neighboring districts":

"The controlling principle [is] that the scope of the remedy is determined by the nature and extent of the constitutional violation. *Swann.* [Before] imposing a cross-district remedy, it must first be shown that there has been a constitutional violation within one district that produces a significant segregative effect in [another] [a]. The constitutional right of the Negro respondents residing in

---

h. The constitutional issues presented when school boards *voluntarily* undertake to remedy de facto segregation are considered in notes after *Regents of Univ. of California v. Bakke,* Part V infra.

a. Is this allocation of the burden of proof consistent with *Keyes?* Are there reasons for a presumption of segregative intent or effect in a *Keyes*-type situation but not in a *Milliken*-type one?

Detroit is to attend a unitary school system in that district.[b] Unless petitioners drew the district lines in a discriminatory fashion, or arranged for White students residing in the Detroit district to attend schools in Oakland and Macomb Counties, they were under no constitutional duty to make provisions for Negro students to do [so.] [22]"

The courts below assumed "that the Detroit schools could not be truly desegregated—in their view of what constituted desegregation—unless the racial composition of the student body of each school substantially reflected the racial composition of the population of the metropolitan area as a whole. [But this is contrary to] the clear import of" *Swann.*[c]

"No single tradition in public education is more deeply rooted than local [control. Here,] consolidation would give rise to an array [of] problems [such as]: What would be the status and authority of the present popularly elected school boards? [What] board or boards would levy taxes for school operations in these 54 districts constituting the consolidated metropolitan area? [Would] the validity of long-term bonds be jeopardized unless approved by all of the component districts as well as the State? [Who] would establish attendance zones, purchase school equipment, locate and construct new schools, and indeed attend to all the myriad day-to-day decisions that are necessary to school [operations]? [A]bsent a complete restructuring of the laws of Michigan relating to school districts the District Court will become first, a de facto 'legislative authority' to resolve these

---

For a listing of subsequent cases imposing interdistrict remedies, see Note, *Interdistrict Remedies for Segregated Schools,* 79 Colum.L. Rev. 1168 n. 5 (1979). See generally Note, *State Court Desegregation Orders: Multi-District Busing, Supreme Court Review, and the Los Angeles School Case,* 26 U.C.L.A.L.Rev. 1183 (1979); Sedler, *Metropolitan Desegregation in the Wake of Milliken—On Losing Big Battles and Winning Small Wars: The View Largely from Within,* 1975 Wash.U.L.Q. 535; Note, *Interdistrict Desegregation: The Remaining Options,* 28 Stan.L.Rev. 521 (1976).

b. For the view that this states an improperly narrow perception of the constitutional right at issue, see Amaker, *Milliken v. Bradley: The Meaning of the Constitution in School Desegregation Cases,* 2 Hast.Con.L.Q. 349 (1975); Lawrence, *Segregation "Misunderstood": The Milliken Decision Revisited,* 12 U.S.F.L.Rev. 15 (1977).

22. The suggestion in the dissent of Mr. Justice Marshall that schools which have a majority of Negro students are not "desegregated," whatever the racial makeup of the school district's population and however neutrally the district lines have been drawn and administered, finds no support in our prior cases. In *Green,* for example, this Court approved a desegregation plan which would have resulted in each of the schools within the district having a racial composition of 57% Negro and 43% White. In *Emporia,* the optimal desegregation plan would have resulted in the schools being 66% Negro and 34% White, substantially the same percentages as could be obtained under one of the plans involved in this case. * * *

The dissents also seem to attach importance to the metropolitan character of Detroit and neighboring school districts. But the constitutional principles [cannot] vary in accordance with the size or population dispersal of the particular city, county, or school district as compared with neighboring areas.

[What sort of plan should the district court now accept (require) for Detroit—one that results in most (or all) schools having *some* racial mix (predominantly black), or one that leaves most schools virtually all black so as to maintain "true integration" in the few others?]

c. Cf. Rehnquist, J., joined by Stewart and Powell, JJ., dissenting from denial of certiorari in *Delaware State Bd. of Educ. v. Evans,* 446 U.S. 923, 100 S.Ct. 1862, 64 L.Ed.2d 278 (1980), in which the district court found an interdistrict violation and ordered that (1) the county's eleven school boards be replaced by a single board to be court-appointed for five years, and (2) all pupils be reassigned to accomplish a racial balance reflecting the racial composition of the total area involved. The district court acknowledged that the remedy was "formulated without exacting consideration of whether [it] returned [the] county schools to the precise position they would have assumed 'but for' the found constitutional violations."

Burger, C.J. would have granted certiorari if a full Court had been available to consider the case. Stevens, J., did not participate. See also fn. d in *Swann.*

complex questions, and then the 'school superintendent' for the entire area. This [would] deprive the people of control of schools through their elected representatives." [d]

WHITE, J., joined by Douglas, Brennan and Marshall, JJ., dissented: "[The] most promising [proposed "Detroit-only" remedy] would 'leave many of its schools 75 to 90 per cent Black.' Transportation on a 'vast scale' would be required [and] the plan 'would change a school system which is now Black and White to one that would be perceived as Black, thereby increasing the flight of [Whites].' [In] proceeding to design its [interdistrict plan, the district] court's express finding was [that] 'desegregation within the area described is physically easier and more practicable and feasible, than desegregation efforts limited [to] Detroit.' The Court of Appeals [concluded] that an interdistrict remedy 'is supported by the status of school districts under Michigan law and by the historical control exercised over local school districts by the legislature of Michigan and by State agencies and officials.' Obviously, whatever difficulties there might be, they are surmountable; for the Court itself concedes that had there been sufficient evidence of an interdistrict violation, the District Court could have fashioned a single remedy for the districts implicated * * *.

"I am even more mystified how the Court can ignore the legal reality that the constitutional violations, even if occurring locally, were committed by governmental entities for which the State is responsible and that it is the State that must respond to the command of the Fourteenth Amendment. [T]here is no acceptable reason for permitting the party responsible for the constitutional violation to contain the remedial powers of the federal court within administrative boundaries over which the transgressor itself has plenary power.

"[In *Emporia* and *Scotland Neck*], the Court specifically rejected the claim that a new school district, which admittedly would operate a unitary school system within its borders, was beyond the reach of a court-ordered desegregation plan for other school [districts]. Until now the Court has [only] looked to practical considerations in effectuating a desegregation decree, such as excessive distance, transportation time and hazards to the safety of the school [children].

"[The] majority's suggestion that judges should not attempt to grapple with the administrative problems attendant on a reorganization of school attendance patterns is wholly without foundation. It is precisely this sort of task which the district courts have been properly exercising to vindicate the constitutional rights of Negro students since [*Brown I*]. Intradistrict revisions of attendance zones, and pairing and grouping of schools, are techniques unanimously approved in *Swann* which entail the same sensitivity to the interest of parents in the education their children receive as would an interdistrict plan which is likely to employ the very same methods."

MARSHALL, J., joined by Douglas, Brennan, and White, JJ., dissented: "Ironically purporting to base its result on the principle that the scope of the remedy [should] be determined by the nature and the extent of the constitutional

---

d. Stewart, J., who joined the Court's opinion, concurred "in view of some of the extravagant language of the [dissents.] [S]egregative acts within the city alone cannot be presumed to have produced [an] increase in the number of Negro students *in the city as a whole.* It is this essential fact of a predominantly Negro school population in Detroit—caused by unknown and perhaps unknowable factors such as in-migration, birth rates, economic changes, or cumulative acts of private racial fears— that accounts for the 'growing core of Negro schools,' a 'core' that has grown to include virtually the entire city. The Constitution simply does not allow federal courts to attempt to change that situation unless [it] is shown that the State, or its political subdivisions, have contributed to cause the situation to exist[—e.g., "by purposeful racially discriminatory use of state housing or zoning laws."]"

violation, the Court's answer is to provide no remedy at all [thus] guaranteeing that Negro children in Detroit will receive the same separate and inherently unequal education in the future as they have been unconstitutionally afforded in the past. * * *

"The State's creation, through de jure acts of segregation, of a growing core of all-Negro schools inevitably acted as a magnet to attract Negroes to the areas served by such schools [and] helped drive whites to other areas of the city or to the suburbs. [Having] created a system where whites and Negroes were intentionally kept apart so that they could not become accustomed to learning together, the State is responsible for the fact that many whites will react to the dismantling of that segregated system by attempting to flee to the suburbs.[e]

"The State's duty should be no different here than in cases where it is shown that certain of a State's voting districts are malapportioned in violation of the Fourteenth Amendment. See *Reynolds v. Sims,* [Sec. 4, I, A infra]. Over-represented electoral districts are required to participate in reapportionment, although their only 'participation' in the violation was to do nothing about it. Similarly, electoral districts which themselves meet representation standards must frequently be redrawn as part of a remedy for other over- and under-inclusive districts. No finding of fault on the part of each electoral district and no finding of a discriminatory effect on each district is a prerequisite to its involvement in the constitutionally required remedy. * * *

"Today's holding, I fear, is more a reflection of a perceived public mood that we have gone far enough in enforcing the Constitution's guarantee of equal justice than it is the product of neutral principles of law. In the short run, it may seem to be the easier course to allow our great metropolitan areas to be divided up each into two cities—one white, the other black—but it is a course, I predict, our people will ultimately regret."[f]

(b) *Housing.* In HILLS v. GAUTREAUX, 425 U.S. 284, 96 S.Ct. 1538, 47 L.Ed.2d 792 (1976), the district court found that the federal Dep't of Housing (HUD) and the Chicago Housing Authority (CHA) had racially segregated public housing projects in Chicago. The Court, per STEWART, J., held that "nothing in [*Milliken*] suggests a per se rule that federal courts lack authority to order parties found to have violated the Constitution to undertake remedial efforts beyond the municipal boundaries of the city where the violation occurred. [The] proposed remedy in *Milliken* was impermissible because of the limits on the federal judicial power to interfere with the operation of state political entities that were not implicated in unconstitutional conduct. Here, [a] judicial order directing relief beyond the boundary lines of Chicago will not necessarily entail coercion of uninvolved governmental units, because [both] CHA and HUD have the authority to operate outside the Chicago city limits.[14]

"[In] contrast to the desegregation order in [*Milliken*], a metropolitan relief order directed to HUD would not consolidate or in any way restructure local governmental units. The remedial decree would neither force suburban governments to submit public housing proposals to HUD nor displace the rights and

---

e. For evidence that it is doubtful whether metropolitan school desegregation remedies will produce integration without a permanent "ongoing system of student-quota reassignment," see Wolf, *Northern School Desegregation and Residential Choice,* 1977 Sup.Ct.Rev. 63.

f. Douglas, J., also filed a brief dissent.

14. [Although] the state officials in *Milliken* had the authority to operate across school district lines, the exercise of that authority [would] have eliminated numerous independent school districts or at least have displaced important powers granted those uninvolved governmental entities under state law.

powers accorded local government entities under federal or state housing statutes or existing land use laws. The order would have the same effect on the suburban governments as a discretionary decision by HUD to use its statutory powers to provide the respondents with alternatives to the racially segregated Chicago public housing system created by CHA and HUD." [a]

(c) *Other remedies.* In MILLIKEN v. BRADLEY (MILLIKEN II), 433 U.S. 267, 97 S.Ct. 2749, 53 L.Ed.2d 745 (1977), the district court, on remand, fashioned a new decree which required (in addition to a pupil assignment plan for the Detroit school system) a number of "educational components"—including remedial reading and revised testing and counseling programs for pupils, and a training program for teachers. The state, which was ordered to pay for part of these programs, appealed. The Court, per BURGER, C.J., affirmed: "[T]he prerogatives of the Detroit School Board have [not] been abrogated [since it] proposed incorporation of these programs in the first place. [Where] a constitutional violation has been found, the remedy does not 'exceed' the violation if the remedy is tailored to cure the '*condition* that offends the Constitution.' *Milliken I.* [T]he District Court found that [the] educational components [were] necessary to restore the victims of discriminatory conduct to the position they would have enjoyed in terms of education had these four components been provided in a nondiscriminatory manner in a school system free from pervasive de jure racial segregation. [D]iscriminatory student assignment policies can themselves manifest and breed other inequalities built into a dual system founded on racial discrimination." [b]

V. AFFIRMATIVE ACTION AND "BENIGN" DISCRIMINATION

Swann ruled that state officials may—and, in some circumstances, seemingly must—use racial criteria to remedy unconstitutional segregation. This section concerns voluntary government action that employs racial/ethnic criteria or favors members of racial/ethnic minorities in order to remedy (a) unlawful discrimination other than segregation, or (b) racial/ethnic inequality that occurs in the absence of a judicial finding of illegal discrimination.

UNITED JEWISH ORGANIZATIONS v. CAREY, 430 U.S. 144, 97 S.Ct. 996, 51 L.Ed.2d 229 (1977): Three New York City counties became subject to § 5 of the Voting Rights Act (p. 1479 infra) because in 1968 they had used a literacy test for voting and less than 50% of the eligible residents had voted. To comply with the Act's requirement that the Attorney General conclude that any new reapportionment have neither "the purpose [nor] the effect [of] abridging the right to vote on account of race or color," the New York legislature produced a

a. Marshall, J., joined by Brennan and White, JJ., joined the Court's opinion "except insofar as it appears to reaffirm [*Milliken*]."

Is *Gautreaux* faithful to the principle that "the scope of the remedy is determined by the nature and extent of the constitutional violation"? See Kanner, *From Denver to Dayton: The Development of a Theory of Equal Protection Remedies,* 72 Nw.U.L.Rev. 382 (1977); 90 Harv.L.Rev. 223 (1976).

b. For the view that "providing unequal and inadequate school resources and exclud-

ing black parents from meaningful participation in school policymaking are at least as damaging to black children as enforced separation," see Bell, *Serving Two Masters: Integration Ideals and Client Interests in School Desegregation Litigation,* 85 Yale L.J. 470 (1976).

For decisions concerning the validity of state aid to private schools that racially discriminate, see *Norwood v. Harrison* and *Gilmore v. Montgomery,* pp. 1089, 1090 infra.

plan that "deliberately increased the nonwhite majorities in certain districts in order to enhance the opportunity for election of nonwhite representatives from those districts." Petitioners sued on behalf of an Hasidic Jewish community which had been in one district with a white majority but was now split into two districts with nonwhite majorities. They alleged "that they were assigned to electoral districts solely on the basis of race [which] diluted their voting power in violation of the" fourteenth and fifteenth amendments. Although there was no opinion for the Court, it upheld the plan.

WHITE, J., joined by Brennan, Blackmun and Stevens, JJ., held that "the Constitution does not prevent a State subject to the Voting Rights Act from deliberately creating or preserving black majorities in particular districts in order to ensure that its reapportionment plan complies with § 5. [The] permissible use of racial criteria is not confined to eliminating the effects of past discriminatory districting or apportionment."

WHITE, J., joined by Rehnquist and Stevens, JJ., also upheld the plan wholly apart from the requirements of the Voting Rights Act. Although the plan "deliberately used race," it "represented no racial slur or stigma with respect to whites or any other race [and] did not minimize or unfairly cancel out white voting strength. [It] left white majorities in approximately 70% of the [districts] which had a county-wide population that was 65% white. Thus, even if voting in the county occurred strictly according to race, whites would not be under-represented relative to their share of the population. * * *[24]"

STEWART, J., joined by Powell, J., concurred, relying on *Washington v. Davis:* "The clear purpose with which the New York Legislature acted—in response to the position of the United States Department of Justice under the Voting Rights Act—forecloses any finding that it acted with the invidious purpose of discriminating against white voters."

BRENNAN, J., concurred exclusively on the basis of the Voting Rights Act, "content to leave [to] another day [the] thorny question [of] the general propriety of so-called benign discrimination [because] of the objections frequently raised to the use of overt preferential race assignment practices." First, "courts might face considerable difficulty in ascertaining whether a given race classification truly furthers benign rather than illicit objectives. An effort to achieve proportional representation, for example, might be aimed at aiding a group's participation in the political processes by guaranteeing safe political offices, or, on the other hand, might be a 'contrivance to segregate' the group, thereby frustrating its potentially successful efforts at coalition building across racial lines. Compare, e.g., the positions of the black plaintiffs in [*Wright v. Rockefeller,* 376 U.S. 52, 84 S.Ct. 603, 11 L.Ed.2d 512 (1964)], with the black intervenors, id. (Douglas, J., dissenting). * * *

"Second, [an] explicit policy of assignment by race may serve to stimulate our society's latent race consciousness, suggesting the utility and propriety of basing decisions on a factor that ideally bears no relationship to an individual's worth or [needs.]

24. [T]he white voter who as a result of [the] plan is in a district more likely to return a nonwhite representative will be represented, to the extent that voting continues to follow racial lines, by legislators elected from majority white districts. The effect of the reapportionment on whites in districts where nonwhite majorities have been increased is thus mitigated by the preservation of white majority districts in the rest of the county. See Note, 25 Stan.L.Rev. 84, 87 (1972). Of course, if voting does not follow racial lines, the white voter has little reason to complain that the percentage of nonwhites in his district has been increased.

"Third, [we] cannot well ignore the social reality that even a benign policy of assignment by race is viewed as unjust by many in our society [and] may be heightened by the natural consequence of our governing processes that the most "discrete and insular" of whites often will be called upon to bear the immediate, direct costs of benign discrimination. [T]here are indications that [the] mandated 65% rule could have been attained through redistricting strategies that did not slice the Hasidic community in half. State authorities, however, chose to localize the burdens of race reassignment upon the petitioners rather than to redistribute a more varied and diffused range of whites into predominantly nonwhite districts.[1]

"In my view, if and when a decisionmaker embarks on a policy of benign racial sorting, he must weigh the concerns that I have discussed against the need for effective social policies promoting racial justice in a society beset by deep-rooted racial inequities. But I believe that Congress here adequately struck that balance in enacting the carefully conceived remedial scheme embodied in the Voting Rights Act."

BURGER, C.J., dissented: "While petitioners certainly have no constitutional right to remain unified within a single political district, they do have, in my view, the constitutional right not to be carved up so as to create a voting bloc composed of some other ethnic or racial group through the kind of racial gerrymandering the Court condemned in *Gomillion v. Lightfoot.* * * *

"The assumption that 'whites' and 'nonwhites' in the County form homogeneous entities for voting purposes is entirely without foundation. The 'whites' category consists of a veritable galaxy of national origins, ethnic backgrounds, and religious denominations. [T]hose described as 'nonwhites' include, in addition to Negroes, a substantial portion of Puerto Ricans [who have] expressly disavowed any identity of interest with the Negroes, and, in fact, objected to the [plan] because it did not establish a Puerto Rican controlled district within the county. * * *

"The result reached [today] suggests to the voter that only a candidate of the same race, religion or ethnic origins can properly represent that voter's interests, and that such candidate can be elected only from a district with a sufficient minority concentration. The [plan] moves us one step farther away from a truly homogeneous society."

Marshall, J., did not participate.

REGENTS OF UNIV. OF CALIFORNIA v. BAKKE
438 U.S. 265, 98 S.Ct. 2733, 57 L.Ed.2d 750 (1978).

MR. JUSTICE POWELL announced the judgment of the Court.

This case presents a challenge to the special admissions program of the petitioner, the Medical School of the University of California at Davis * * *.

For the reasons stated in the following opinion, I believe that so much of the judgment of the California court as holds petitioner's special admissions program unlawful and directs that respondent be admitted to the Medical School must be affirmed. For the reasons expressed in a separate opinion, my Brothers The

---

1. [While] voting may differ from other activities or entitlements in that one group of voters often derives benefits indirectly from a legislator serving a different constituency— and to that extent I agree that the adverse effects of a racial division are "mitigated," I am not satisfied that this vicarious benefit fully answers the Hasidim's complaint of injustice. * * *

Chief Justice, Mr. Justice Stewart, Mr. Justice Rehnquist, and Mr. Justice Stevens concur in this judgment.

I also conclude [that] the portion of the court's judgment enjoining petitioner from according any consideration to race in its admissions process must be reversed. For reasons expressed in separate opinions, my Brothers Mr. Justice Brennan, Mr. Justice White, Mr. Justice Marshall, and Mr. Justice Blackmun concur in this judgment. * * *

I.† The Medical School * * * [opened] in 1968 with an entering class of 50 students. In 1971, the size of the entering class was increased to 100 students, a level at which it remains. [T]he first class contained three Asians but no Blacks, no Mexican-Americans, and no American Indians. Over the next two years, the faculty devised a special admissions program * * *.

Under the regular admissions procedure, [c]andidates whose overall undergraduate grade point averages fell below 2.5 on a scale of 4.0 were summarily rejected. About one out of six applicants was invited for a personal interview [and] each candidate was rated on a scale of 1 to 100 * * *. The rating embraced the interviewers' summaries, the candidate's overall grade point average, grade point average in science courses, and scores on the Medical College Admissions Test (MCAT), letters of recommendation, extracurricular activities, and other biographical data. The ratings were added together to arrive at each candidate's "benchmark" score. Since five committee members rated each candidate in 1973, a perfect score was 500; in 1974, six members rated each candidate, so that a perfect score was 600. The full committee then reviewed the file and scores of each applicant and made offers of [admission]. The chairman was responsible for placing names on the waiting list. They were not placed in strict numerical order; instead, the chairman had discretion to include persons with "special skills."

The special admissions program operated with a separate committee, a majority of whom were members of minority groups. On the 1973 application form, candidates were asked to indicate whether they wished to be considered as "economically and/or educationally disadvantaged" applicants; on the 1974 form the question was whether they wished to be considered as members of a "minority group," which the medical school apparently viewed as "Blacks," "Chicanos," "Asians," and "American Indians." [No] formal definition of "disadvantage" was ever produced, but the chairman of the special committee screened each application to see whether it reflected economic or educational deprivation.[4] [T]he applications then were rated by the special committee in a fashion similar to that used by the general admissions committee, except that special candidates did not have to meet the 2.5 grade point average [cut-off]. About one-fifth of the total number of special applicants were invited for interviews in 1973 and 1974 [and] the special committee assigned each [a] benchmark score [and] presented its top choices to the general admissions committee. The latter did not rate or compare the special candidates against the general applicants, but could reject recommended special candidates for failure to meet course requirements or other specific deficiencies. The special committee continued to recommend special

† Mr. Justice Brennan, Mr. Justice White, Mr. Justice Marshall, and Mr. Justice Blackmun join Parts I and V–C of this opinion. Mr. Justice White also joins Part III–A of this opinion.

4. The chairman normally checked to see if, among other things, the applicant had been granted a waiver [of] application fee, which required a means test; whether the applicant had worked during college or interrupted his education to support himself or his family; and whether the applicant was a member of a minority group.

applicants until a number prescribed by faculty vote were admitted. [I]n 1973 and 1974, when the class size had doubled to 100, the prescribed number of special admissions also doubled, to 16.

From the year of the increase in class size—1971—through 1974, the special program resulted in the admission of 21 black students, 30 Mexican-Americans, and 12 Asians, [and] the regular admissions program produced one black, six Mexican-Americans, and 37 Asians * * *. Although disadvantaged whites applied to the special program in large numbers, none received an offer of admission through that process. Indeed, in 1974, at least, the special committee explicitly considered only "disadvantaged" special applicants who were members of one of the designated minority groups.

Allan Bakke is a white male who applied [in] 1973 and 1974. In [1973, despite] a strong benchmark score of 468 out of 500, Bakke was rejected. [In 1974, his] faculty interviewer [was] Dr. Lowrey to whom he had written in protest of the special admissions program. Dr. Lowrey found Bakke "rather limited in his approach" to the problems of the medical profession and found disturbing Bakke's "very definite opinions which were based more on his personal viewpoints than upon a study of the total problem." Dr. Lowrey gave Bakke the lowest of his six ratings, an 86; his total was 549 out of 600. Again, Bakke's application was rejected. In neither year did the chairman of the admissions committee, Dr. Lowrey, exercise his discretion to place Bakke on the waiting list. In both years, applicants were admitted under the special program with grade point averages, MCAT scores, and benchmark scores significantly lower than Bakke's.[7] * * *

II. [Powell, J., found that Title VI of the Civil Rights Act of 1964—which provides that "No person in the United States shall, on the ground of race, color, or national origin, be excluded from participation in, be denied the benefits of, or be subjected to, discrimination under any program or activity receiving Federal financial assistance"—proscribes "only those racial classifications that would violate the Equal Protection Clause or the Fifth Amendment."]

III. A. [T]he parties fight a sharp preliminary action over the proper characterization of the special admissions program. Petitioner prefers to view it

---

7. The following table compares Bakke's science grade point average, overall grade point average, and MCAT Scores with the average scores of regular admittees and of special admittees in both 1973 and 1974:

Class Entering in 1973

| | SGPA | OGPA | MCAT (Percentiles) | | | |
			Verbal	Quanti- tative	Science	Gen. Infor.
Bakke	3.44	3.51	96	94	97	72
Average of Regular Admittees	3.51	3.49	81	76	83	69
Average of Special Admittees	2.62	2.88	46	24	35	33

Class Entering in 1974

| | SGPA | OGPA | MCAT (Percentiles) | | | |
			Verbal	Quanti- tative	Science	Gen. Infor.
Bakke	3.44	3.51	96	94	97	72
Average of Regular Admittees	3.36	3.29	69	67	82	72
Average of Special Admittees	2.42	2.62	34	30	37	18

Applicants admitted under the special program also had benchmark scores significantly lower than many students, including Bakke, rejected under the general admissions program, even though the special rating system apparently gave credit for overcoming "disadvantage."

as establishing a "goal" of minority representation in the medical school. Respondent, echoing the courts below, labels it a racial quota.[26]

This semantic distinction is beside the [point]. To the extent that there existed a pool of at least minimally qualified minority applicants to fill the 16 special admissions seats, white applicants could compete only for 84 seats in the entering class, rather than the 100 open to minority applicants. Whether this limitation is described as a quota or a goal, it is a line drawn on the basis of race and ethnic status.

[P]etitioner argues that the court below erred in applying strict scrutiny to the special admissions programs because white males, such as respondent, are not a "discrete and insular minority" requiring extraordinary protection from the majoritarian political process. *Carolene Products Co.,* n. 4, [p. 23 supra. These] characteristics may be relevant in deciding whether or not to add new types of classifications to the list of "suspect" categories or whether a particular classification survives close examination. Racial and ethnic classifications, however, are subject to stringent examination without regard to these additional characteristics. [*Hirabayashi; Korematsu*]

B. This perception of racial and ethnic distinctions is rooted in our Nation's constitutional and demographic history. The Court's initial view of the Fourteenth Amendment was that its "one pervading purpose" was "the freedom of the slave race * * *." *Slaughter-House Cases.* The Equal Protection Clause, however, was "[v]irtually strangled in its infancy by post-civil-war judicial reactionism." [It] was only as the era of substantive due process came to a close [in the mid 1930s] that the Equal Protection Clause began to attain a genuine measure of vitality.

By that time it was no longer possible to peg the guarantees of the Fourteenth Amendment to the struggle for equality of one racial minority. During the dormancy of the Equal Protection Clause, the United States had become a nation of minorities. Each had to struggle—and to some extent struggles still [32]—to overcome the prejudices not of a monolithic majority, but of a "majority" composed of various minority groups of whom it was said—perhaps unfairly in many cases—that a shared characteristic was a willingness to disadvantage other groups. As the Nation filled with the stock of many lands, the reach of the Clause was gradually extended to all ethnic groups seeking protection from official discrimination. See *Strauder* (Celtic Irishmen) (dictum); *Yick Wo* (Chinese); *Truax v. Raich,* 239 U.S. 33, 36 S.Ct. 7, 60 L.Ed. 131 (1915) (Austrian resident aliens); *Korematsu* (Japanese); *Hernandez v. Texas* (Mexican-Americans). * * *

Although many of the Framers of the Fourteenth Amendment conceived of its primary function as bridging the vast distance between members of the Negro race and the white "majority," the Amendment itself was framed in universal terms, without reference to color, ethnic origin, or condition of prior [servitude.]

---

26. Petitioner defines "quota" as a requirement which must be met but can never be exceeded, regardless of the quality of the minority applicants. Petitioner declares that there is no "floor" under the total number of minority students admitted; completely unqualified students will not be admitted simply to meet a "quota." Neither is there a "ceiling," since an unlimited number could be admitted through the general admissions process. On this basis the special admissions program does not meet petitioner's definition of a quota. * * *

32. "Members of various religious and ethnic groups, primarily but not exclusively of eastern, and middle and southern European ancestry, such as Jews, Catholics, Italians, Greeks and Slavic groups [continue] to be excluded from executive, middle-management and other job levels because [of] their religion and/or national origin." 41 CFR § 60–50.1(b) (1977).

Over the past 30 years, this Court has embarked upon the crucial mission of interpreting the Equal Protection Clause with the view of assuring to all persons "the protection of equal laws" in a Nation confronting a legacy of slavery and racial discrimination. * * *

Petitioner urges us to adopt for the first time a more restrictive view [and] hold that discrimination against members of the white "majority" cannot be suspect if its purpose can be characterized as "benign." [34] [But it] is far too late to argue that the guarantee of equal protection to *all* persons permits the recognition of special wards entitled to a degree of protection greater than that accorded others. * * *

Once the artificial line of a "two-class theory" of the Fourteenth Amendment is put aside, the difficulties entailed in varying the level of judicial review according to a perceived "preferred" status of a particular racial or ethnic minority are intractable. The concepts of "majority" and "minority" necessarily reflect temporary arrangements and political judgments. As observed above, the white "majority" itself is composed of various minority groups, most of which can lay claim to a history of prior discrimination at the hands of the state and private individuals. Not all of these groups can receive preferential treatment and corresponding judicial tolerance of distinctions drawn in terms of race and nationality, for then the only "majority" left would be a new minority of White Anglo-Saxon Protestants. There is no principled basis for deciding which groups would merit "heightened judicial solicitude" and which would not.[36] Courts would be asked to evaluate the extent of the prejudice and consequent harm

34. In the view of Mr. Justice Brennan, Mr. Justice White, Mr. Justice Marshall, and Mr. Justice Blackmun, the pliable notion of "stigma" is the crucial element in analyzing racial classifications. The Equal Protection Clause is not framed in terms of "stigma." Certainly the word has no clearly defined constitutional meaning. It reflects a subjective judgment that is standardless. *All* state-imposed classifications that rearrange burdens and benefits on the basis of race are likely to be viewed with deep resentment by the individuals burdened. The denial to innocent persons of equal rights and opportunities may outrage those so deprived and therefore may be perceived as invidious. These individuals are likely to find little comfort in the notion that the deprivation they are asked to endure is merely the price of membership in the dominant majority and that its imposition is inspired by the supposedly benign purpose of aiding others. One should not lightly dismiss the inherent unfairness of, and the perception of mistreatment that accompanies, a system of allocating benefits and privileges on the basis of skin color and ethnic origin. Moreover, Mr. Justice Brennan, Mr. Justice White, Mr. Justice Marshall, and Mr. Justice Blackmun offer no principle for deciding whether preferential classifications reflect a benign remedial purpose or a malevolent stigmatic classification, since they are willing in this case to accept mere post hoc declarations by an isolated state entity—a medical school faculty—unadorned by particularized findings of past discrimination, to establish such a remedial purpose.

36. [M]y Brothers Brennan, White, Marshall, and Blackmun [would] require as a justification for a program such as petitioner's, only two findings: (i) that there has been some form of discrimination against the preferred minority groups "by society at large" (it being conceded that petitioner had no history of discrimination), and (ii) that "there is reason to believe" that the disparate impact sought to be rectified by the program is the "product" of such discrimination * * *.

The breadth of this hypothesis is unprecedented in our constitutional system. The first step is easily taken. No one denies the regrettable fact that there has been societal discrimination in this country against various racial and ethnic groups. The second step, however, involves a speculative leap: but for this discrimination by society at large, Bakke "would have failed to qualify for admission" because Negro applicants—nothing is said about Asians—would have made better scores. Not one word in the record supports this conclusion, and the plurality offers no standard for courts to use in applying such a presumption of causation to other racial or ethnic classifications. This failure is a grave one, since if it may be concluded *on this record* that each of the minority groups preferred by the petitioner's special program is entitled to the benefit of the presumption, it would seem difficult to determine that any of the dozens of minority groups that have suffered "societal discrimination" cannot also claim it, in any area of social intercourse. See Part IV–B, infra.

suffered by various minority groups. Those whose societal injury is thought to exceed some arbitrary level of tolerability then would be entitled to preferential classifications at the expense of individuals belonging to other groups. Those classifications would be free from exacting judicial scrutiny. As these preferences began to have their desired effect, and the consequences of past discrimination were undone, new judicial rankings would be necessary. The kind of variable sociological and political analysis necessary to produce such rankings simply does not lie within the judicial competence—even if they otherwise were politically feasible and socially desirable.[37]

Moreover, there are serious problems of justice connected with the idea of preference itself. First, it may not always be clear that a so-called preference is in fact benign. Courts may be asked to validate burdens imposed upon individual members of particular groups in order to advance the group's general interest. Nothing in the Constitution supports the notion that individuals may be asked to suffer otherwise impermissible burdens in order to enhance the societal standing of their ethnic groups. Second, preferential programs may only reinforce common stereotypes holding that certain groups are unable to achieve success without special protection based on a factor having no relationship to individual worth. Third, there is a measure of inequity in forcing innocent persons in respondent's position to bear the burdens of redressing grievances not of their making.

By hitching the meaning of the Equal Protection Clause to these transitory considerations, we would be holding [that] judicial scrutiny of classifications touching on racial and ethnic background may vary with the ebb and flow of political forces. Disparate constitutional tolerance of such classifications well may serve to exacerbate racial and ethnic antagonisms. [Also,] the mutability of a constitutional principle, based upon shifting political and social judgments, undermines the chances for consistent application of the Constitution from one generation to the next, a critical feature of its coherent interpretation. * * *

If it is the individual who is entitled to judicial protection against classifications based upon his racial or ethnic background because such distinctions impinge upon personal rights, rather than the individual only because of his membership in a particular group, then constitutional standards may be applied consistently. Political judgments regarding the necessity for the particular classification may be weighed in the constitutional balance, *Korematsu,* but the standard of justification will remain constant. This is as it should be, since those political judgments are the product of rough compromise struck by contending groups within the democratic process. When they touch upon an individual's race or ethnic background, he is entitled to a judicial determination that the burden he is asked to bear on that basis is precisely tailored to serve a compelling governmental interest. * * *

---

37. Mr. Justice Douglas has noted the problems associated with such inquiries [in] *DeFunis v. Odegaard,* 416 U.S. 312, 94 S.Ct. 1704, 40 L.Ed.2d 164 (1974) [involving the University of Washington Law School's special admissions program for Blacks, Chicanos, American Indians and Filipinos. The Court held the case moot—see p. 1190 infra. Only Douglas, J., addressed the merits: "[T]hat the state school employed a racial classification in selecting its students subjects it to the strictest scrutiny [and] is in my view 'invidious.' [The] key to the problem is the consideration of each application *in a racially neutral way."* This may include "cultural backgrounds, [an] applicant's prior achievements in light of the barriers that he had to overcome [and] the likelihood that a particular candidate will more likely employ his legal skills to serve communities that are not now adequately represented than will competing candidates." "Such a policy would not be limited to Blacks, or Chicanos or Filipinos or American Indians, although undoubtedly groups such as they may in practice be the principal beneficiaries of it."]

C. Petitioner contends that on several occasions this Court has approved preferential classifications without applying the most exacting scrutiny. * * *

The school desegregation cases are inapposite. Each involved remedies for clearly determined constitutional violations.[39] [Here,] there was no judicial determination of constitutional violation as a predicate for [a] remedial classification.

The employment discrimination cases also do not advance petitioner's cause. For example, in *Franks v. Bowman Transportation Co.*, 424 U.S. 747, 96 S.Ct. 1251, 47 L.Ed.2d 444 (1975), we approved a retroactive award of seniority to a class of Negro truck drivers who had been the victims of discrimination—not just by society at large, but by the respondent in that case. While this relief imposed some burdens on other employees, it was held necessary " 'to make [the victims] whole for injuries suffered on account of unlawful employment discrimination.' " The courts of appeals have fashioned various types of racial preferences as remedies for constitutional or statutory violations resulting in identified, race-based injuries to individuals held entitled to the preference. E.g., *Bridgeport Guardians, Inc. v. Civil Serv. Comm'n*, 482 F.2d 1333 (CA2 1973); *Carter v. Gallagher*, 452 F.2d 327 (CA8 1972). Such preferences also have been upheld where a legislative or administrative body charged with the responsibility made determinations of past discrimination by the industries affected, and fashioned remedies deemed appropriate to rectify the discrimination. E.g., *Contractors Ass'n v. Secretary of Labor*, 442 F.2d 159 (CA3), cert. denied, 404 U.S. 954 (1971);[40] *Associated Gen. Contractors v. Altschuler*, 490 F.2d 9 (CA1 1973), cert. denied, 416 U.S. 957 (1974). But we have never approved preferential classifications in the absence of proven constitutional or statutory violations.[41]

Nor is petitioner's view as to the applicable standard supported by the fact that gender-based classifications are not subjected to this level of scrutiny [citing cases in Sec. 3, IV infra]. [With] respect to gender there are only two possible classifications. The incidence of the burdens imposed by preferential classifications is clear. There are no rival groups who can claim that they, too, are entitled to preferential treatment. Classwide questions as to the group suffering previous injury and groups which fairly can be burdened are relatively managea-

39. [In] *Offermann v. Nitkowski*, 378 F.2d 22 (CA2 1967) [and] *Springfield School Committee v. Barksdale*, 348 F.2d 261 (CA1 1965) [courts] did approve voluntary districting designed to eliminate discriminatory attendance patterns. In neither, however, was there any showing that the school board planned extensive pupil transportation that might threaten liberty or privacy interests. Nor were white students deprived of an equal opportunity for education.

Respondent's position is wholly dissimilar to that of a pupil bused from his neighborhood school to a comparable school in another neighborhood in compliance with a desegregation decree. Petitioner did not arrange for respondent to attend a different medical school in order to desegregate Davis Medical School; instead, it denied him admission and may have deprived him altogether of a medical education.

40. Every decision upholding the requirement of preferential hiring under the authority of Executive Order 11246 has emphasized the existence of previous discrimination as a predicate for the imposition of a preferential remedy.

41. This case does not call into question congressionally authorized administrative actions, such as consent decrees under Title VII or approval of reapportionment plans under § 5 of the Voting Rights Act of 1965. In such cases, there has been detailed legislative consideration of the various indicia of previous constitutional or statutory violations, e.g., *South Carolina v. Katzenbach*, [p. 1144 infra], and particular administrative bodies have been charged with monitoring various activities in order to detect such violations and formulate appropriate remedies.

Furthermore, we are not here presented with an occasion to review legislation by Congress pursuant to its powers under § 2 of the Thirteenth Amendment and § 5 of the Fourteenth Amendment to remedy the effects of prior discrimination. *Katzenbach v. Morgan; Jones v. Alfred H. Mayer Co.*, [p. 1180 infra].

ble for reviewing courts. * * * More importantly, the perception of racial classifications as inherently odious stems from a lengthy and tragic history that gender-based classifications do not share. In sum, the Court has never viewed such classification as inherently suspect or as comparable to racial or ethnic classifications for the purpose of equal-protection analysis.

[P]etitioner contends that our recent decision in *United Jewish Orgs.* [approves] racial classifications designed to benefit certain minorities, without denominating the classifications as "suspect." [42] [*UJO*] properly is viewed as a case in which the remedy for an administrative finding of discrimination encompassed measures to improve the previously disadvantaged group's ability to participate, without excluding individuals belonging to any other group from enjoyment of the relevant opportunity—meaningful participation in the electoral process.

In this case, [there] has been no determination by the legislature or a responsible administrative agency that the University engaged in a discriminatory practice requiring remedial efforts. Moreover, the operation of petitioner's special admissions [program] prefers the designated minority groups at the expense of other individuals who are totally foreclosed from competition for the 16 special admissions seats in every medical school class. [When] a classification denies an individual opportunities or benefits enjoyed by others solely because of his race or ethnic background, it must be regarded as suspect.

IV. [The] special admissions program purports to serve the purposes of: (i) "reducing the historic deficit of traditionally disfavored minorities in medical schools and the medical profession," (ii) countering the effects of societal discrimination; [43] (iii) increasing the number of physicians who will practice in communities currently underserved; and (iv) obtaining the educational benefits that flow from an ethnically diverse student body. It is necessary to decide which, if

---

42. Petitioner also cites our decision in *Morton v. Mancari,* 417 U.S. 535, 94 S.Ct. 2474, 41 L.Ed.2d 290 (1974), [which] approved a hiring preference for qualified Indians in the Bureau of Indian Affairs of the Department of the Interior (BIA). We observed in that case, however, that the legal status of BIA is sui generis. Indeed, we found that the preference was not racial at all, but "an employment criterion reasonably designed to further the cause of Indian self-government and to make the BIA more responsive to the needs of its constituent groups[,] whose lives are governed by the BIA in a unique fashion."

[See fn. f after *Korematsu.*]

43. A number of distinct sub-goals have been advanced as falling under the rubric of "compensation for past discrimination." For example, it is said that preferences for Negro applicants [serve] as a form of reparation by the "majority" to a victimized group as a whole. Bittker, *The Case for Black Reparations* (1973). That justification for racial or ethnic preference has been subjected to much criticism. Finally, it has been argued that ethnic preferences "compensate" the group by providing examples of success whom other members of the group will emulate, thereby advancing the group's interest and society's

interest in encouraging new generations to overcome the barriers and frustrations of the past. Redish, *Preferential Law School Admissions and the Equal Protection Clause: An Analysis of the Competing Arguments,* 22 U.C. L.A.L.Rev. 343, 391 (1974). For purposes of analysis these sub-goals need not be considered separately.

Racial classifications in admissions conceivably could serve a fifth purpose, one which petitioner does not articulate: fair appraisal of each individual's academic promise in the light of some cultural bias in grading or testing procedures. To the extent that race and ethnic background were considered only to [cure] established inaccuracies in predicting academic performance, it might be argued that there is no "preference" at all. Nothing in this record, however, suggests either that any of the quantitative factors considered by the Medical School were culturally biased or that petitioner's special admissions program was formulated to correct for any such biases. Furthermore, if race or ethnic background were used solely to arrive at an unbiased prediction of academic success, the reservation of fixed numbers of seats would be inexplicable.

any, of these purposes is substantial enough to support the use of a suspect classification.

A.   If petitioner's purpose is to assure within its student body some specified percentage of a particular group merely because of its race or ethnic origin, such a preferential purpose must be rejected not as insubstantial but as facially invalid.   Preferring members of any one group for no reason other than race or ethnic origin is discrimination for its own sake.   This the Constitution forbids. E.g., *Loving.*

B.   The State certainly has a legitimate and substantial interest in ameliorating, or eliminating where feasible, the disabling effects of identified discrimination.   [That] goal [is] far more focused than the remedying of the effects of "societal discrimination," an amorphous concept of injury that may be ageless in its reach into the past.

We have never approved a classification that aids persons perceived as members of relatively victimized groups at the expense of other innocent individuals in the absence of judicial, legislative, or administrative findings of constitutional or statutory violations.   After such findings[,] the governmental interest in preferring members of the injured groups at the expense of others is substantial, since the legal rights of the victims must be vindicated.   In such a case, the extent of the injury and the consequent remedy will have been judicially, legislatively, or administratively defined.   Also, the remedial action usually remains subject to continuing oversight to assure that it will work the least harm possible to other innocent persons competing for the benefit.   Without such findings of constitutional or statutory violations,[44] it cannot be said that the government has any greater interest in helping one individual than in refraining from harming another.   Thus, the government has no compelling justification for inflicting such harm.

Petitioner does not purport to have made, and is in no position to make, such findings.   Its broad mission is education, not the formulation of any legislative policy or the adjudication of particular claims of illegality.   For reasons similar to those stated in Part III of this opinion, isolated segments of our vast governmental structures are not competent to make those decisions, at

---

44. Mr. Justice Brennan, Mr. Justice White, Mr. Justice Marshall, and Mr. Justice Blackmun misconceive the scope of this Court's holdings under Title VII when they suggest that "disparate impact" alone is sufficient to establish a violation of that statute and, by analogy, other civil rights measures. [This] was made quite clear in the seminal decision in this area, *Griggs v. Duke Power Co.,* 401 U.S. 424, 91 S.Ct. 849, 28 L.Ed.2d 158 (1971): "*Discriminatory preference for any group, minority or majority, is precisely and only what Congress has proscribed.   What is required by Congress is the removal of artificial, arbitrary, and unnecessary barriers* to employment when the barriers operate invidiously to discriminate on the basis of racial or other impermissible classification." Thus, disparate impact is a basis for relief under Title VII only if the practice in question is not founded on "business necessity," or lacks "a manifest relationship to the employment in question." Nothing *in this record*—as opposed to some of the general literature cited by Mr.

Justice Brennan, Mr. Justice White, Mr. Justice Marshall, and Mr. Justice Blackmun—even remotely suggests that the disparate impact of the general admissions program at Davis Medical School, resulting primarily from the sort of disparate test scores and grades set forth in footnote 7, supra, is without educational justification.

Moreover, the presumption in *Griggs*—that disparate impact without any showing of business justification established the existence of discrimination in violation of the statute—was based on legislative determinations, wholly absent here, that past discrimination had handicapped various minority groups to such an extent that disparate impact could be traced to identifiable instances of past discrimination * * *.   Thus, Title VII principles support the proposition that findings of identified discrimination must precede the fashioning of remedial measures embodying racial classifications.

least in the absence of legislative mandates and legislatively determined criteria.[45] Cf. *Hampton v. Wong* [Sec. 3, II infra]. Compare n. 41, supra. Before relying upon these sorts of findings in establishing a racial classification, a governmental body must have the authority and capability to establish, in the record, that the classification is responsive to identified discrimination. See, e.g., *Califano v. Webster; Califano v. Goldfarb* [Sec. 3, IV infra]. Lacking this capability, petitioner has not carried its burden of justification on this issue.

Hence, the purpose of helping certain groups whom the faculty of the Davis Medical School perceived as victims of "societal discrimination" does not justify a classification that imposes disadvantages upon persons like respondent, who bear no responsibility for whatever harm the beneficiaries of the special admissions program are thought to have suffered. To hold otherwise would be to convert a remedy heretofore reserved for violations of legal rights into a privilege that all institutions throughout the Nation could grant at their pleasure to whatever groups are perceived as victims of societal discrimination. That is a step we have never approved. Cf. *Pasadena Bd. of Ed. v. Spangler.*

C. Petitioner identifies, as another purpose of its program, improving the delivery of health care services to communities currently underserved. It may be assumed that in some situations a State's interest in facilitating the health care of its citizens is sufficiently compelling to support the use of a suspect classification. But there is virtually no evidence in the record indicating that petitioner's special admissions program is either needed or geared to promote that goal. The court below addressed this failure of proof: "The University concedes it cannot assure that minority doctors who entered under the program, all of whom express an 'interest' in participating in a disadvantaged community, will actually do so. It may be correct to assume that some of them will carry out this intention, and that it is more likely they will practice in minority communities than the average white doctor. Nevertheless, there are more precise and reliable [ways]. An applicant of whatever race who has demonstrated his concern for disadvantaged minorities in the past and who declares that practice in such a community is his primary professional goal would be more likely to contribute to alleviation of the medical shortage than one who is chosen entirely on the basis of race and disadvantage. *   *   *"[a]   *   *   *

D. The fourth goal asserted by petitioner is the attainment of a diverse student body. *   *   * Academic freedom, though not a specifically enumerated

---

45. For example, the University is unable to explain its selection of only the four favored groups—Negroes, Mexican-Americans, American Indians, and Asians—for [preference]. The inclusion of the last group is especially curious in light of the substantial numbers of Asians admitted through the regular admissions process.

a. Consider Graglia, *Racially Discriminatory Admission to Public Institutions of Higher Education,* in Constitutional Government in America 255, 259–60 (Collins ed. 1980): "It [is] said that some members of nonwhite groups would prefer to be served by professionals of the same group. [This is a preference] that we can accept in the interest of honoring individual choice, even the choice to racially discriminate, but not one that we should encourage or take extraordinary steps to satisfy. [T]he law should take the position

that the individual's race is irrelevant, in the hope that the educative effect of law will help make this so even where it is not so already. [If] we are concerned [with] increasing the availability of professional services to the poor, that concern can be met simply, directly, and appropriately by subsidizing such services by payments to the poor or to those who serve them." Compare Sandalow, *Minority Preferences in Law School Admissions,* in id. 277, 282: "The ability to 'speak the language' of the client, to understand his perception of his problem, and to deal with others in the community on his behalf are qualities essential to being a 'good lawyer.' These qualifications are more likely to be found among lawyers who share the client's racial or ethnic identity, at least to the extent that the client's life is bound up in a community defined in these terms."

constitutional right, long has been viewed as a special concern of the First Amendment. [Thus,] in arguing that its universities must be accorded the right to select those students who will contribute the most to the "robust exchange of ideas," petitioner invokes a countervailing constitutional interest, [and] must be viewed as seeking to achieve a goal that is of paramount importance in the fulfillment of its mission.

＊ ＊ ＊ Physicians serve a heterogeneous population. An otherwise qualified medical student with a particular background—whether it be ethnic, geographic, culturally advantaged or disadvantaged—may bring to a professional school of medicine experiences, outlooks and ideas that enrich the training of its student body and better equip its graduates to render with understanding their vital service to humanity.

Ethnic diversity, however, is only one element in a range of factors a university properly may consider in attaining the goal of a heterogeneous student body. Although a university must have wide discretion in making the sensitive judgments as to who should be admitted, constitutional limitations protecting individual rights may not be disregarded. [As] the interest of diversity is compelling in the context of a university's admissions program,[b] the question remains whether the program's racial classification is necessary to promote this interest.

V. A. [P]etitioner's argument that this is the only effective means of serving the interest of diversity is seriously flawed. [The] diversity that furthers a compelling state interest encompasses a far broader array of qualifications and characteristics of which racial or ethnic origin is but a single though important element. Petitioner's special admissions program, focused *solely* on ethnic diversity, would hinder rather than further attainment of genuine diversity.

Nor would the state interest in genuine diversity be served by expanding petitioner's two-track system into a multitrack program with a prescribed number of seats set aside for each identifiable category of applicants. Indeed, it is inconceivable that a university would thus pursue the logic of petitioner's two-

---

b. Consider McCormack, *Race and Politics in the Supreme Court: Bakke to Basics,* 1979 Utah L.Rev. 491, 530: "Most educators would agree that some element of diversity in a student body is healthy, but few would assert that this factor is the primary motivation behind minority preferences. [Thus], one problem with this approach is that it is simply not the most honest statement of the objective of the programs. [Further,] it is hard to believe that racial classifications disfavoring racial or ethnic minorities could be justified by a school's claim of academic freedom. This justification would be considered ludicrous if advanced as a basis for preferring members of the white majority. These considerations rob the principle of the very neutrality that Justice Powell was seeking elsewhere in the opinion and suggest the instability of the rationale." See also Van Alstyne, *A Preliminary Report on the Bakke Case,* 64 AAUP Bull. 286, 294 (1978): "[Suspect] classifications [must] survive 'the most exacting judicial scrutiny.' [Yet], in the dispensation the Powell opinion provides to higher education, the purpose to be served, as important as educators may deem it to be, is at best a purpose to furnish a better learning environment for all of the students—a purpose not exactly overwhelming or even nationally compelling."

Was the use of race in connection with peremptory challenges—upheld in *Swain v. Alabama,* Part III supra—justified by a "compelling" interest? See Vieira, *Racial Imbalance, Black Separatism, and Permissible Classification by Race,* 67 Mich.L.Rev. 1553, 1590 (1969).

Does Powell, J.'s point lead to the further conclusion "that there is a strong societal interest in [the] equal participation of blacks [whenever] a 'black [can] bring something that a white person cannot offer,'" and that this extends to *all* "institutions of government, the 'power professions' [such] as law and medicine, [and] the economic system"? Sedler, *Racial Preference and the Constitution: The Societal Interest in the Equal Participation Objective,* 26 Wayne L.Rev. 1227 (1980).

track program to the illogical end of insulating each category of applicants with certain desired qualifications from competition with all other applicants.

The experience of other university admissions programs, which take race into account in achieving the educational diversity valued by the First Amendment, demonstrates that the assignment of a fixed number of places to a minority group is not a necessary means toward that end. An illuminating example is found in the Harvard College program:

"In recent years Harvard College has expanded the concept of diversity to include students from disadvantaged economic, racial and ethnic groups. [When] the Committee on Admissions reviews the large middle group of applicants who are 'admissible' and deemed capable of doing good work in their courses, the race of an applicant may tip the balance in his favor just as geographic origin or a life spent on a farm may tip the balance in other candidates' cases. * * *

"In Harvard College admissions the Committee has not set target-quotas for the number of blacks, or of musicians, football players, physicists or Californians to be admitted in a given year [c] [but that awareness of the necessity of including more than a token number of black students means] that in choosing among thousands of applicants who are not only 'admissible' academically but have other strong qualities, the Committee, with a number of criteria in mind, pays some attention to distribution among many types and categories of students." Brief for Columbia University, Harvard University, Stanford University, and the University of Pennsylvania, as amici curiae.

In such an admissions program, race or ethnic background may be deemed a "plus" in a particular applicant's file,[d] yet it does not insulate the individual from comparison with all [others]. The file of a particular black applicant may be examined for his potential contribution to diversity without the factor of race being decisive when compared, for example, with that of an applicant identified

c. The portion of this paragraph of the Harvard program—omitted by Powell, J., in his opinion but reprinted in full in an appendix to the opinion—is as follows: "At the same time the Committee is aware that if Harvard College is to provide a truly heterogeneous environment that reflects the rich diversity of the United States, it cannot be provided without some attention to numbers. It would not make sense, for example, to have 10 or 20 students out of 1,100 whose homes are west of the Mississippi. Comparably, 10 or 20 black students could not begin to bring to their classmates and to each other the variety of points of view, backgrounds and experiences of blacks in the United States. Their small numbers might also create a sense of isolation [and] thus make it more difficult for them to develop and achieve their potential. Consequently, when making its decisions, the Committee on Admissions is aware that there is some relationship between numbers and achieving the benefits to be derived from a diverse student body, and between numbers and providing a reasonable environment for those students admitted."

d. See Posner, The De Funis Case and the Constitutionality of Preferential Treatment of Racial Minorities, 1974 Sup.Ct.Rev. 1, 12–13:

"The applicant cannot be relied upon to classify himself correctly. [Thus] admissions officials confront the problem both of determining what constitutes membership in a racial group and of requiring appropriate evidence that an applicant belongs to it. In the case of blacks, it is necessary to determine what percentage of Negro ancestry should be required. [If] the president of Mexico marries an American woman and they have a child who is brought up in the United States, is the child a Chicano? Or is the term meant to imply some connection with life in a barrio? [T]he possession (or lack) of a Spanish surname is not decisive evidence since Puerto Ricans, Spaniards, and Latin Americans other than Mexicans also have Spanish surnames, and since a Chicano might be the product of the union of a Chicano woman and a non-Chicano man. [Many] people have some Indian blood without being recognizable as Indian or having a characteristically Indian name. This problem could be avoided by limiting preferential treatment to Indians on reservations, but such a limitation would be difficult to justify to Indians who have recently (or not so recently) left the reservation and may have encountered substantial difficulties in adjusting to life on the outside."

as an Italian-American if the latter is thought to exhibit qualities more likely to promote beneficial educational pluralism. Such qualities could include exceptional personal talents, unique work or service experience, leadership potential, maturity, demonstrated compassion, a history of overcoming disadvantage, ability to communicate with the poor, or other qualifications deemed important. In short, an admissions program operated in this way is flexible enough to consider all pertinent elements of diversity in light of the particular qualifications of each applicant, and to place them on the same footing for consideration, although not necessarily according them the same weight. Indeed, the weight attributed to a particular quality may vary from year to year depending upon the "mix" both of the student body and the applicants for the incoming class.

This kind of program treats each applicant as an individual in the admissions process. The applicant who loses out [to] another candidate receiving a "plus" on the basis of ethnic background will not have been foreclosed from all consideration [simply] because he was not the right color or had the wrong surname. It would mean only that his combined qualifications, which may have included similar nonobjective factors, did not outweigh those of the other applicant. His qualifications would have been weighed fairly and competitively, and he would have no basis to complain of unequal treatment under the Fourteenth Amendment.

It has been suggested that an admissions program which considers race only as one factor is simply a subtle and more sophisticated—but no less effective—means of according racial preference than the Davis program. A facial intent to discriminate, however, is evident [in] this case. No such facial infirmity exists in an admissions program where race or ethnic background is simply one element— to be weighed fairly against other elements—in the selection process. "A boundary line," as Mr. Justice Frankfurter remarked in another connection, "is none the worse for being narrow." And a Court would not assume that a university, professing to employ a facially nondiscriminatory admissions policy, would operate it as a cover for the functional equivalent of a quota system. In short, good faith would be presumed in the absence of a showing to the contrary in the manner permitted by our cases. See, e.g., *Arlington Heights; Washington v. Davis; Swain.*[53]

B. [W]hen a State's distribution of benefits or imposition of burdens hinges on the color of a person's skin or ancestry, that individual is entitled to a

---

53. Universities, like the prosecutor in *Swain,* may make individualized decisions, in which ethnic background plays a part, under a presumption of legality and legitimate educational purpose. So long as the university proceeds on an individualized, case-by-case basis, there is no warrant for judicial interference in the academic process. If an applicant can establish that the institution does not adhere to a policy of individual comparisons, or can show that a systematic exclusion of certain groups results, the presumption of legality might be overcome, creating the necessity of proving legitimate educational purpose.

[Compare Calabresi, *Ideals, Beliefs, Attitudes, and the Law* 90 (1985): "A university admissions committee since it represents hardly anyone—except perhaps the university administration—is a very dangerous group to which to give the power of hidden, subterfuge-based decisions. Indeed, it was just such committees that in the past used diversity for clearly malignant, discriminatory purposes."]

There also are strong policy reasons that correspond to the constitutional distinction between petitioner's preference program and one that assures a measure of competition among all applicants. Petitioner's program will be viewed as inherently unfair by the public generally as well as by [applicants]. Fairness in individual competition for opportunities, especially those provided by the State, is a widely cherished American ethic. Indeed, in a broader sense, an underlying assumption of the rule of law is the worthiness of a system of justice based on fairness to the individual. As Mr. Justice Frankfurter declared in another connection, "[j]ustice must satisfy the appearance of justice."

demonstration that the challenged classification is necessary to promote a substantial state interest. Petitioner has failed to carry this burden. For this reason, that portion of the California court's judgment holding petitioner's special admissions program invalid under the Fourteenth Amendment must be affirmed.

C. In enjoining petitioner from ever considering the race of any applicant, however, the courts below failed to recognize that the State has a substantial interest that legitimately may be served by a properly devised admissions program involving the competitive consideration of race and ethnic origin. For this reason, so much of the California court's judgment as enjoins petitioner from any consideration of the race of any applicant must be reversed.

VI. With respect to respondent's entitlement to an injunction directing his admission to the Medical School, petitioner has conceded that it could not carry its burden of proving that, but for the existence of its unlawful special admissions program, respondent still would not have been admitted. Hence, respondent is entitled to the injunction, and that portion of the judgment must be affirmed.

Opinion of MR. JUSTICE BRENNAN, MR. JUSTICE WHITE, MR. JUSTICE MARSHALL, and MR. JUSTICE BLACKMUN, concurring in the judgment in part and dissenting.

[The] difficulty of this issue [has] resulted in many opinions, no single one speaking for the Court. But [this] must not mask the central meaning of today's opinions: Government may take race into account when it acts not to demean or insult any racial group, but to remedy disadvantages cast on minorities by past racial prejudice, at least when appropriate findings have been made by judicial, legislative, or administrative bodies with competence to act in this area. * * *

We agree with Mr. Justice Powell that, as applied to the case before us, Title VI goes no further in prohibiting the use of race than the Equal Protection [Clause].[e] Since we conclude that the [Davis program] is constitutional, we would reverse the judgment below in all respects. Mr. Justice Powell agrees that some uses of race in university admissions are permissible and, therefore, he joins with us to make five votes reversing the judgment below insofar as it prohibits the University from establishing race-conscious programs in the future.[1]

I. [E]ven today officially sanctioned discrimination is not a thing of the past. Against this background, claims that law must be "color-blind" or that the datum of race is no longer relevant to public policy must be seen as aspiration rather than as description of reality. This is not to denigrate aspiration; for reality rebukes us that race has too often been used by those who would stigmatize and oppress minorities. Yet we cannot [let] color blindness become myopia which masks the reality that many "created equal" have been treated within our lifetimes as inferior both by the law and by their fellow citizens. * * *

III. A. [Our] cases have always implied that an "overriding statutory purpose," *McLaughlin v. Florida,* could be found that would justify racial classifications. See, e.g., *Loving; Korematsu.* [W]e turn [to] articulating what our role should be in reviewing state action that expressly classifies by race.

---

e. The separate opinion of White, J.—that Title VI does not provide for a private cause of action—is omitted.

1. We also agree [that] a plan like the "Harvard" plan is constitutional [at] least so long as the use of race to achieve an integrated student body is necessitated by the lingering effects of past discrimination.

B.   [A] government practice or statute which restricts "fundamental rights" or which contains "suspect classifications" is to be subjected to "strict scrutiny" * * *. But no fundamental right is involved here. See *San Antonio Ind. School Dist. v. Rodriguez,* [Sec. 4, IV infra]. Nor do whites as a class have any of the "traditional indicia of suspectness: the class is not saddled with such disabilities, or subjected to such a history of purposeful unequal treatment, or relegated to such a position of political powerlessness as to command extraordinary protection from the majoritarian political process." Id.

Moreover, [this] is not a case where racial classifications are "irrelevant and therefore prohibited." *Hirabayashi.* Nor has anyone suggested that the University's purposes contravene the cardinal principle that racial classifications that stigmatize—because they are drawn on the presumption that one race is inferior to another or because they put the weight of government behind racial hatred and separatism—are invalid without more. See *Yick Wo.* * * *

On the other hand, the fact that this case does not fit neatly into our prior analytic framework for race cases does not mean that it should be analyzed by applying the very loose rational-basis [standard]. "[T]he mere recitation of a benign, compensatory purpose is not an automatic shield which protects against any inquiry into the actual purposes underlying a statutory scheme." *Califano v. Webster.* Instead, a number of considerations—developed in gender discrimination cases but which carry even more force when applied to racial classifications—lead us to conclude that racial classifications designed to further remedial purposes "must serve important governmental objectives and must be substantially related to achievement of those objectives." *Craig v. Boren,* [Sec. 3, IV infra].[35]

35.   We disagree with our Brother Powell's suggestion, that the presence of "rival groups who can claim that they, too, are entitled to preferential treatment," distinguishes the gender cases or is relevant to the question of scope of judicial review of race classifications.

[W]ere we asked to decide whether any given rival group—German-Americans for example—must constitutionally be accorded preferential treatment, we do have a "principled basis" for deciding this question, one that is well-established in our cases: The Davis program expressly sets out four classes which receive preferred status. The program clearly distinguishes whites, but one cannot reason from this to a conclusion that German-Americans, as a national group, are singled out for invidious treatment. And even if the Davis program had a differential impact on German-Americans, they would have no constitutional claim unless they could prove that Davis intended invidiously to discriminate against German-Americans. See *Arlington Heights; Davis.* If this could not be shown, then [the] only question is whether it was rational for Davis to conclude that the groups it preferred had a greater claim to compensation than the groups it excluded. *Rodriguez* (applying *Katzenbach v. Morgan* test to state action intended to remove discrimination in educational opportunity). Thus, claims of rival groups, although they may create thorny political

problems, create relatively simple problems for the courts.

[Consider Greenawalt, *Judicial Scrutiny of "Benign" Racial Preference in Law School Admissions,* 75 Colum.L.Rev. 559, 597 (1975): "Under the rational basis standard, a law school would be left free to divide much of the 'pie' of places in the student body by preferences for a multiplicity of minority groups. In many parts of the country, a number of minorities make up the majority of the population. If each minority group were assured 'proportional representation,' the result would be much closer to a maximum quota for presently overrepresented groups than any existing preferential policies. The rational basis approach would leave an applicant from an overrepresented group almost defenseless against this result." Would Brennan, J., permit "proportional representation" for minority groups? See his Part IV–C, infra. Would Powell, J.'s "diversity" justification permit it?

[Consider Van Alstyne, *Rites of Passage: Race, the Supreme Court, and the Constitution,* 46 U.Chi.L.Rev. 775, 809 (1979): "The basic question [is] whether the Constitution shall again be 'adjusted' to accommodate a new generation of racial spoils. There [is] very little agreement in measuring racial eligibility for those spoils. [A]nd the Constitution itself providing no articulate basis for the Court simply to 'declare' the proper eligibility,

First, race, like, "gender-based classifications too often [has] been inexcusably utilized to stereotype and stigmatize politically powerless segments of society." While a carefully tailored statute designed to remedy past discrimination could avoid these vices, see *Califano v. Webster*, we nonetheless have recognized that the line between honest and thoughtful appraisal of the effects of past discrimination and paternalistic stereotyping is not so clear and that a statute based on the latter is patently capable of stigmatizing all women with a badge of inferiority. State programs designed ostensibly to ameliorate the effects of past racial discrimination obviously create the same hazard of stigma, since they may promote racial separatism and reinforce the views of those who believe that members of racial minorities are inherently incapable of succeeding on their own.

Second, race, like gender and illegitimacy, is an immutable characteristic which its possessors are powerless to escape or set aside. While a classification is not per se invalid because [of this], it is nevertheless true that such divisions are contrary to our deep belief that "legal burdens should bear some relationship to individual responsibility or wrongdoing," and that advancement sanctioned, sponsored, or approved by the State should ideally be based on individual merit or achievement, or at the least on factors within the control of an individual.[f]

Because this principle is so deeply rooted it might be supposed that it would be considered in the legislative process and weighed against the benefits of programs preferring individuals because of their race. But [t]he "natural consequence of our governing processes [may well be] that the most 'discrete and insular' of whites [will] be called upon to bear the immediate, direct costs of benign discrimination." *UJO* (concurring opinion). [Thus] our review under the Fourteenth Amendment should be strict—not " 'strict' in theory and fatal in fact," because it is stigma that causes fatality—but strict and searching nonetheless.

IV. Davis' articulated purpose of remedying the effects of past societal discrimination is, under our cases, sufficiently important to justify the use of race-conscious admissions programs where there is a sound basis for concluding that minority underrepresentation is substantial and chronic, and that the handicap of past discrimination is impeding access of minorities to the medical school.

the natural expectation is that that racial eligibility will simply be the product of racial competition in the political process. [We] shall not now see racism disappear by employing its own ways of classifying people and of measuring their rights. Rather, one gets beyond racism by getting beyond it now: by a complete, resolute, and credible commitment *never* to tolerate [the] differential treatment of other human beings by race."]

f. Consider Karst & Horowitz, *Affirmative Action and Equal Protection*, 60 Va.L.Rev. 955, 962 (1974): "Whether 'merit' be defined in terms of demonstrated [or] potential achievement, it includes a large and hard-to-isolate ingredient of native talents. These talents resemble race in that they are beyond the control of the individual whose 'merit' is being evaluated. If racial classifications are 'suspect' partly for this reason, then it may be appropriate to insist that public rewards for native talents be justified by a showing of compelling necessity." See also Nagel, *Equal Treatment and Compensatory Discrimination*, 2 Phil. & Pub.Afrs. 348, 357 (1973): "The greatest injustice in this society [is] neither racial nor sexual but intellectual. [Society] provides on the average much larger rewards for tasks that require superior intelligence than for those that do not. This is simply the way things work out in a technologically advanced society with a market economy. It does not reflect a social judgment that smart people *deserve* the opportunity to make more [money]. They may deserve richer educational opportunity, but they do not therefore deserve the material wealth that goes with it. Similar things could be said about society's differential reward of achievements facilitated by other talents or gifts, like beauty, athletic ability, musicality, etc. But intelligence and its development by education provide a particularly significant and pervasive example."

A. At least since *Green v. County School Bd.*, [a] public body which has itself been adjudged to have engaged in racial discrimination cannot bring itself into compliance with the Equal Protection Clause simply by ending its unlawful acts and adopting a neutral stance. Three years later, *Swann* [held] that courts could enter desegregation orders which assigned students and faculty by reference to race, and that local school boards could *voluntarily* adopt desegregation plans which made express reference to race if this was necessary to remedy the effects of past discrimination. Moreover, we stated that school boards, even in the absence of a judicial finding of past discrimination, could voluntarily adopt plans which assigned students with the end of creating racial pluralism by establishing fixed ratios of black and white students in each school. *Swann.*

* * *

Finally, the conclusion that state educational institutions may constitutionally adopt admissions programs designed to avoid exclusion of historically disadvantaged minorities, even when such programs explicitly take race into account, finds direct support in our cases construing congressional legislation designed to overcome the present effects of past discrimination. Congress can and has outlawed actions which have a disproportionately adverse and unjustified impact upon members of racial minorities and has required or authorized race-conscious action to put individuals disadvantaged by such impact in the position they otherwise might have enjoyed. See *Franks v. Bowman; Teamsters v. United States,* 431 U.S. 324, 97 S.Ct. 1843, 52 L.Ed.2d 396 (1977). Such relief does not require as a predicate proof that recipients of preferential advancement have been individually discriminated against; it is enough that each recipient is within a general class of persons likely to have been the victims of discrimination. See id. Nor is it an objection to such relief that preference for minorities will upset the settled expectations of nonminorities. See *Franks.* In addition, we have held that Congress, to remove barriers to equal opportunity, can and has required employers to use test criteria that fairly reflect the qualifications of minority applicants vis-à-vis nonminority applicants, even if this means interpreting the qualifications of an applicant in light of his race. See *Albemarle v. Moody,* 422 U.S. 405, 435, 95 S.Ct. 2362, 45 L.Ed.2d 280 (1975).[37]

These cases cannot be distinguished simply by the presence of judicial findings of discrimination, for race-conscious remedies have been approved where such findings have not been made. *UJO.* Indeed, the requirement of a judicial determination of a constitutional or statutory violation as a predicate for

---

37. In *Albemarle,* we approved "differential validation" of employment tests. That procedure requires that an employer must ensure that a test score of, for example, 50 for a minority job applicant means the same thing as a score of 50 for a nonminority applicant. By implication, were it determined that [a] 50 for a minority corresponded in "potential for employment" to a 60 for whites, the test could not be used consistent with Title VII unless the employer hired minorities with scores of 50 even though he might not hire nonminority applicants with scores above 50 but below 60. Thus, it is clear that employers, to ensure equal opportunity, may have to adopt race-conscious hiring practices.

[Are racial preferences more justifiable in some contexts than others? Consider Neuborne, *Observations on Weber,* 54 N.Y.U.L.

Rev. 546, 547 (1979): "In most settings, [we] do not allocate goods on the basis of an open-ended search for excellence. Rather, we seek a guarantee of a respectable level of competence, and, once that guarantee is present, we use criteria unrelated to competence—such as seniority, first-come first-served, personality, appearance, acquaintanceship, or hunch—to break ties. [But] where desirable positions are allocated on the basis of an open-ended search for excellence, race should never be permitted to effect the substitution of a less qualified candidate for the most qualified candidate. Such a substitution [would] frustrate legitimate expectations which are generally the result of strenuous individual preparation. Moreover, the societal loss [would] be substantial." Under this rationale, what result in *Bakke?*]

race-conscious remedial actions would be self-defeating.   Such a requirement would severely undermine efforts to achieve voluntary compliance with the requirements of law.   And, our society and jurisprudence have always stressed the value of voluntary efforts to further the objectives of the law.   Judicial intervention is a last resort to achieve cessation of illegal conduct or the remedying of its effects rather than a prerequisite to action.

Nor can our cases be distinguished on the ground that the entity using explicit racial classifications had itself violated § 1 of the Fourteenth Amendment or an antidiscrimination regulation, for again race-conscious remedies have been approved where this is not the case.   See *UJO* (opinion of White, Blackmun, Rehnquist, and Stevens, JJ.); id. (opinion of White, Rehnquist, and Stevens, JJ.). Moreover, [the] claims of those burdened by the race-conscious actions of a university or employer who has never been adjudged in violation of an antidiscrimination law are not any more or less entitled to deference than the claims of the burdened nonminority workers in *Franks,* in which the employer had violated Title VII, for in each case the employees are innocent of past discrimination.   And, although it might be argued that, where an employer has violated an antidiscrimination law, the expectations of nonminority workers are themselves products of discrimination and hence "tainted," and therefore more easily upset, the same argument can be made with respect to respondent.   If it was reasonable to conclude—as we hold that it was—that the failure of minorities to qualify for admission at Davis under regular procedures was due principally to the effects of past discrimination, then there is a reasonable likelihood that, but for pervasive racial discrimination, respondent would have failed to qualify for admission even in the absence of Davis' special admissions program.[41]

Thus, our cases under Title VII [have] held that, in order to achieve minority participation in previously segregated areas of public life, Congress may require or authorize preferential treatment for those likely disadvantaged by societal racial discrimination.   Such legislation has been sustained even without a requirement of findings of intentional racial discrimination by those required or authorized to accord preferential treatment,[g] or a case-by-case determination

---

41. Our cases cannot be distinguished by suggesting, as our Brother Powell does, that in none of them was anyone deprived of "the relevant benefit."   Our school cases have deprived whites of the neighborhood school of their choice; our Title VII cases have deprived nondiscriminating employees of their settled seniority expectations; and *UJO* deprived the Hassidim of bloc voting strength.   Each of these injuries was constitutionally cognizable as is respondent's here.

[Consider Fiss, *The Fate of An Idea Whose Time Has Come: Antidiscrimination Law in the Second Decade After Brown v. Board of Education,* 41 U.Chi.L.Rev. 742, 770 (1974): "[T]he causal connection between past discrimination and present results may be significantly more tenuous than what the courts declare it to be.   There is a heavy reliance on presumptions—[e.g.], the dual school system might have played a role in causing the segregated residential pattern of a community or the poor performance of Blacks on voter qualification or employment tests; but the evidence compels none of these connections.   Difficult as it is for the alleged victims to prove

any of these connections, it is equally as difficult for the alleged discriminators to prove the opposite.   [Further], courts do not limit the remedy in these cases to eliminating the portion of the undesired result that they can in all fairness attribute to past discrimination.   A judicial conclusion that there is some causal connection between the past discrimination and a portion of the undesired result is used as a triggering mechanism—the predicate for an order eliminating the entire undesired result."

[For empirical criticism of "this staggering notion [that] discrimination must be the decisive explanation of intergroup differences," see Sowell, *Weber and Bakke, and the Presuppositions of "Affirmative Action,"* 26 Wayne L.Rev. 1309 (1980).]

g. See O'Neil, *Racial Preference and Higher Education: The Larger Context,* 60 Va. L.Rev. 925, 930 (1974): "If previous discrimination were essential to the remedial use of race, only those states that once maintained dual higher educational systems would today be allowed to adopt preferential programs.

that those to be benefited suffered from racial discrimination. These decisions compel the conclusion that States also may adopt race-conscious programs designed to overcome substantial, chronic minority underrepresentation where there is reason to believe that the evil addressed is a product of past racial discrimination.[42]

Title VII was enacted pursuant to Congress' power under the Commerce Clause and § 5 of the Fourteenth Amendment. To the extent that Congress acted under the Commerce Clause power, it was restricted in the use of race in governmental decisionmaking by the equal protection component of the Due Process Clause of the Fifth Amendment precisely to the same extent as are the States by § 1 of the Fourteenth Amendment. Therefore, to the extent that Title VII rests on the Commerce Clause power, our decisions such as *Franks* and *Teamsters* implicitly recognize that the affirmative use of race is consistent with the equal protection component of the Fifth Amendment and therefore of the Fourteenth Amendment. To the extent that Congress acted pursuant to § 5 of the Fourteenth Amendment, those cases impliedly recognize that Congress was empowered under that provision to accord preferential treatment to victims of past discrimination in order to overcome the effects of segregation, and we see no reason to conclude that the States cannot voluntarily accomplish under § 1 of the Fourteenth Amendment what Congress under § 5 of the Fourteenth Amendment validly may authorize or compel either the States or private persons to do. A contrary position would conflict with the traditional understanding recognizing the competence of the States to initiate measures consistent with federal policy in the absence of congressional pre-emption of the subject matter. Nothing whatever in the legislative history of either the Fourteenth Amendment or the Civil Rights Acts even remotely suggests that the States are foreclosed from furthering the fundamental purpose of equal opportunity to which the Amendment and those Acts are addressed. [We] therefore conclude that Davis' goal of

[At] its limits, such an argument would distinguish within states between institutions that once discriminated and those that never did so. Thus the University of Texas at Austin, where racially exclusionary admission policies were once held unconstitutional, could now admit preferentially, while the newer campuses [could] not do so."

42. We do not understand Mr. Justice Powell to disagree that providing a remedy for past racial prejudice can constitute a compelling purpose sufficient to meet strict scrutiny. Yet, because petitioner is a university, he would not allow it to exercise such power in the absence of "judicial, legislative, or administrative findings of constitutional or statutory violations." While we agree that reversal in this case would follow a fortiori had Davis been guilty of invidious racial discrimination or if a federal statute mandated that universities refrain from applying any admissions policy that had a disparate and unjustified racial impact, we do not think it of constitutional significance that Davis has not been so adjudged.

Generally, the manner in which a State chooses to delegate governmental functions is for it to decide. California, by constitutional provision, has chosen to place authority over the operation of the University of California in the Board of Regents [who] have been vested with full legislative (including policymaking), administrative, and adjudicative powers. [W]e, unlike our Brother Powell, find nothing in the Equal Protection Clause that requires us to depart from established principle by limiting the scope of power the Regents may exercise more narrowly than the powers that may constitutionally be wielded by the Assembly.

Because the Regents can exercise plenary legislative and administrative power, it elevates form over substance to insist that Davis could not use race-conscious remedial programs until it had been adjudged in violation of the Constitution or an antidiscrimination statute. For, if the Equal Protection Clause required such a violation as a predicate, the Regents could simply have promulgated a regulation prohibiting disparate treatment not justified by the need to admit only qualified students, and could have declared Davis to have been in violation of such a regulation on the basis of the exclusionary effect of the admissions policy applied during the first two years of its operation.

admitting minority students disadvantaged by the effects of past discrimination is sufficiently important to justify use of race-conscious admissions criteria.

B. * * * Davis had a sound basis for believing that the problem of underrepresentation of minorities was substantial and chronic and that the problem was attributable to handicaps imposed on minority applicants by past and present racial discrimination. Until at least 1973, the practice of medicine in this country [was] largely the prerogative of whites. In 1950, for example, while Negroes comprised 10% of the total population, Negro physicians constituted only 2.2% of the total number of physicians. The overwhelming majority of these, moreover, were educated in two predominantly Negro medical schools, Howard and Meharry. By 1970, [the] number of Negroes employed in medicine remained frozen at 2.2% while the Negro population had increased to 11.1%. The number of Negro admittees to predominantly white medical schools, moreover, had declined in absolute numbers during the years 1955 to 1964.

Moreover, Davis had very good reason to believe that the national pattern of underrepresentation of minorities in medicine would be perpetuated if it retained a single admissions standard. For example, the entering classes in 1968 and 1969, [when] such a standard was used, included only one Chicano and two Negroes out of 100 admittees. Nor is there any relief from this pattern of underrepresentation in the statistics for the regular admissions program in later years.

Davis clearly could conclude that the serious and persistent underrepresentation [is] the result of handicaps under which minority applicants labor as a consequence of a background of deliberate, purposeful discrimination against minorities in education and in society generally, as well as in the medical profession. From the inception of our national life, Negroes have been subjected to unique legal [disabilities]. Under slavery, penal sanctions were imposed upon anyone attempting to educate Negroes. After [the] Fourteenth Amendment the States continued to deny Negroes equal educational opportunity, enforcing a strict policy of segregation that itself stamped Negroes as inferior, which relegated minorities to inferior educational institutions, and which denied them intercourse in the mainstream of professional life necessary to advancement. Segregation was not limited to public facilities. [A]s late as 1908, this Court enforced a state criminal conviction against a private college for teaching Negroes together with whites.

Green v. County School Bd. gave explicit recognition to the fact that the habit of discrimination and the cultural tradition of race prejudice [were] not immediately dissipated [by *Brown I*]. Rather, massive official and private resistance prevented, and to a lesser extent still prevents, attainment of equal opportunity in education at all levels and in the professions. The generation of minority students applying to Davis Medical School since it opened in 1968— most of whom were born before or about the time *Brown I* was decided—clearly have been victims of this discrimination. Judicial decrees recognizing discrimination in public education in California testify to the fact of widespread discrimination suffered by California-born minority applicants; many minority group members living in California, moreover, were born and reared in school districts in southern States segregated by law. [T]he conclusion is inescapable that applicants to medical school must be few indeed who endured the effects of de jure segregation, the resistance to *Brown I,* or the equally debilitating pervasive private discrimination fostered by our long history of official discrimination, cf. *Reitman v. Mulkey,* [p. 1106 infra], and yet come to the starting line with an education equal to whites.

Moreover, [HEW], the expert agency charged by Congress [with] enforcing Title VI, [has concluded] that race may be taken into account in situations where a failure to do so would limit participation by minorities in federally funded programs, and regulations promulgated by the Department expressly contemplate that appropriate race-conscious programs may be adopted by universities to remedy unequal access to university programs caused by their own or by past societal discrimination. [A]lthough an amendment to an appropriations bill was introduced just last year [to prevent HEW] from mandating race-conscious programs in university admissions, proponents of this measure, significantly, did not question the validity of voluntary implementation of race-conscious admissions criteria. In these circumstances, the conclusion implicit in the regulations—that the lingering effects of past discrimination continue to make race-conscious remedial programs appropriate means for ensuring equal educational opportunity in universities—deserves considerable judicial deference. See, e.g., *Katzenbach v. Morgan.*

C. The second prong of our test—whether the Davis program stigmatizes any discrete group or individual and whether race is reasonably used in light of the program's objectives—is clearly satisfied by the Davis program.

It is not even claimed that Davis' program in any way operates to stigmatize or single out any discrete and insular, or even any identifiable, nonminority group. Nor will harm comparable to that imposed upon racial minorities by exclusion or separation on grounds of race be the likely result of the program. It does not, for example, establish an exclusive preserve for minority [students]. Rather, its purpose is to overcome the effects of segregation by bringing the races together. True, whites are excluded from participation in the special admissions program, but this fact only operates to reduce the number of whites to be admitted in the regular admissions program in order to permit admission of a reasonable percentage—less than their proportion of the California population [57]—of otherwise underrepresented qualified minority applicants.[58]

Nor was Bakke in any sense stamped as inferior by [rejection]. Indeed, it is conceded by all that he satisfied those criteria regarded by the School as generally relevant to academic performance better than most of the minority members who were admitted. Moreover, there is absolutely no basis for concluding that Bakke's rejection as a result of Davis' use of racial preference will affect him throughout his life in the same way as the segregation of the Negro school children in [*Brown I*]. Unlike discrimination against racial minorities, the use of racial preferences for remedial purposes does not inflict a pervasive injury upon individual whites in the sense that wherever they go or whatever they do there is a significant likelihood that they will be treated as second-class citizens

---

57. Negroes and Chicanos alone [comprise] 22% of California's population.

58. The constitutionality of [the] program is buttressed by its restriction to only 16% of the positions in the Medical School, a percentage less than that of the minority population in California, and to those minority applicants deemed qualified for admission and deemed likely to contribute to the medical school and the medical profession. This is consistent with the goal of putting minority applicants in the position they would have been in if not for the evil of racial discrimination. Accordingly, this case does not raise the question whether even a remedial use of race would be unconsti-

tutional if it admitted unqualified minority applicants in preference to qualified applicants or admitted, as a result of preferential consideration, racial minorities in numbers significantly in excess of their proportional representation in the relevant population. Such programs might well be inadequately justified by the legitimate remedial objectives. Our allusion to the proportional percentage of minorities in the population of the State administering the program is not intended to establish either that figure or that population universe as a constitutional benchmark.

*   *   *

because of their color. This distinction does not mean that the exclusion of a white resulting from the preferential use of race is not sufficiently serious to require justification; but it does mean that the injury inflicted by such a policy is not distinguishable from disadvantages caused by a wide range of government actions, none of which has ever been thought impermissible for that reason alone.

In addition, there is simply no evidence that the Davis program discriminates intentionally or unintentionally against any minority group which it purports to benefit. The program does not establish a quota in the invidious sense of a ceiling on the number of minority applicants to be admitted. Nor can the program reasonably be regarded as stigmatizing the program's beneficiaries or their race as inferior. The Davis program does not simply advance less qualified applicants; rather, it compensates applicants, whom it is uncontested are fully qualified to study medicine, for educational disadvantage which it was reasonable to conclude was a product of state-fostered discrimination. Once admitted, these students must satisfy the same degree [requirements]; they are taught by the same faculty in the same classes; and their performance is evaluated by the same standards by which regularly admitted students are judged. Under these circumstances, their performance and degrees must be regarded equally with the regularly admitted students with whom they compete for standing. Since minority graduates cannot justifiably be regarded as less well qualified than nonminority graduates by virtue of the special admissions program, there is no reasonable basis to conclude that [they] would be stigmatized as inferior by the existence of such programs.[h]

D. We disagree with the lower courts' conclusion that the Davis program's use of race was unreasonable in light of its objectives. First, as petitioner argues, there are no practical means by which it could achieve its ends in the foreseeable future without the use of race-conscious measures. With respect to any factor (such as poverty or family educational background) that may be used as a substitute for race as an indicator of past discrimination, whites greatly outnumber racial minorities simply because whites make up a far larger percentage of the total population and therefore far outnumber minorities in absolute terms at every socio-economic level. For example, of a class of recent medical school applicants from families with less than $10,000 income, at least 71% were white. Of all 1970 families headed by a person *not* a high school graduate which included related children under 18, 80% were white and 20% were racial minorities. Moreover, while race is positively correlated with differences in GPA and MCAT scores, economic disadvantage is not. Thus, it appears that economically disadvantaged whites do not score less well than economically advantaged whites, while economically advantaged blacks score less well than do disadvantaged whites. * * *

h. But see Nagel, fn. f supra, at 362: "Not only does [a racially preferential policy] inevitably produce resentment in the better qualified who are passed over [but] it also allows those in the discriminated-against group who would in fact have failed to gain a desired position in any case on the basis of their qualifications to feel that they may have lost out to someone less [qualified]. Similarly, such a practice cannot do much for the self-esteem of those who know they have benefited from it, and it may threaten the self-esteem of those in the favored group who would in fact have gained their positions even in the absence of the discriminatory policy, but who cannot be sure that they are not among its beneficiaries." Compare O'Neil, fn. g supra, at 941: [I]t would be perverse if a court were to strike down on this ground a program which had been sought and extensively utilized by minority applicants themselves. Such a judgment would imply a dangerously gratuitous concern about the welfare of minority groups."

Second, [the] program does not simply equate minority status with disadvantage. Rather, Davis considers [each] applicant's personal history to determine whether he or she has likely been disadvantaged by racial discrimination. The record makes clear that only minority applicants likely to have been isolated from the mainstream of American life are considered in the special [program]. True, the procedure by which disadvantage is detected is informal, but we have never insisted that educators conduct their affairs through adjudicatory [proceedings]. A case-by-case inquiry into the extent to which each individual applicant has been affected, either directly or indirectly, by racial discrimination, would seem to be, as a practical matter, virtually impossible, despite the fact that there are excellent reasons for concluding that such effects generally exist.[i] When individual measurement is impossible or extremely impractical, there is nothing to prevent a State from using categorical means to achieve its ends, at least where the category is closely related to the goal. Cf. *Katzenbach v. Morgan*. And it is clear from our cases that specific proof that a person has been victimized by discrimination is not a necessary predicate to offering him relief where the probability of victimization is great. See *Teamsters*.

E. Finally, Davis' special admissions program cannot be said to violate the Constitution simply because it has set aside a predetermined number of places for qualified minority applicants rather than using minority status as a positive factor to be considered in evaluating the applications of disadvantaged minority applicants. For purposes of constitutional adjudication, there is no difference between the two approaches. In any admissions program which accords special consideration to disadvantaged racial minorities, a determination of the degree of preference to be given is unavoidable, and any given preference that results in the exclusion of a white candidate is no more or less constitutionally acceptable than a program such as that at Davis. Furthermore, the extent of the preference inevitably depends on how many minority applicants the particular school is seeking to admit in any particular year so long as the number of qualified minority applicants exceeds that number. There is no sensible, and certainly no constitutional, distinction between, for example, adding a set number of points to the admissions rating of disadvantaged minority applicants as an expression of the preference with the expectation that this will result in the admission of an approximately determined number of qualified minority applicants and setting a fixed number of places for such applicants as was done here.[63]

[That] the Harvard approach does not also make public the extent of the preference and the precise workings of the system while the Davis program employs a specific, openly stated number, does not condemn the [latter]. It may be that the Harvard plan is more acceptable to the public than is the Davis "quota." If it is, any State [is] free to adopt it in preference to a less acceptable alternative, just as it is generally free [to] abjure granting any racial preferences in its admissions program. But there is no basis for preferring a particular

---

i. See Morris, *Equal Protection, Affirmative Action and Racial Preferences in Law Admissions*, 49 Wash.L.Rev. 1, 29–30 (1973): "One need not determine that any specific person has been subjected to racial or ethnic discrimination before the State can administer a corrective preference based on race or ethnicity; even those few minority group members who have 'made it' in American society would probably be much further along the ladder of success if it were not for the racial practices of the dominant white society.

Three hundred years of immorality has taken its toll ∗ ∗ ∗."

63. The excluded white applicant, despite Mr. Justice Powell's contention to the contrary, receives no more or less "individualized consideration" under our approach than under his. [For the view that "public choice theory" "directly supports" this position, see Spitzer, *Multicriteria Choice Processes: An Application of Public Choice Theory to Bakke, the FCC, and the Courts*, 88 Yale L.J. 717 (1979).]

preference program simply because in achieving the same goals that [Davis] is pursuing, it proceeds in a manner that is not immediately apparent to the public.[j] * * *

MR. JUSTICE MARSHALL.

[I]t must be remembered that, during most of the past 200 years, the Constitution as interpreted by this Court did not prohibit the most ingenious and pervasive forms of discrimination against the Negro. Now, when a State acts to remedy the effects of that legacy of discrimination, I cannot believe that this same Constitution stands as a barrier. * * *

The position of the Negro today in America is the tragic but inevitable consequence of centuries of unequal treatment. Measured by any benchmark of comfort or achievement, meaningful equality remains a distant dream for the Negro [—comparing Negro and white statistics on life expectancy, infant mortality, median income, poverty, unemployment, and percentages in professions].

In light of the sorry history of discrimination and its devastating impact on the lives of Negroes, bringing the Negro into the mainstream of American life should be a state interest of the highest order. To fail to do so is to ensure that America will forever remain a divided society. * * *

Since the Congress that considered and rejected the objections to the 1866 Freedmen's Bureau Act concerning special relief to Negroes also proposed the Fourteenth Amendment, it is inconceivable that the Fourteenth Amendment was intended to prohibit all race-conscious relief measures.[k] [T]o hold that it barred state action to remedy the effects [of] discrimination [would] pervert the intent of the framers by substituting abstract equality for the genuine equality the amendment was intended to achieve. * * *

---

j. Consider Perry, *Modern Equal Protection: A Conceptualization and Appraisal,* 79 Colum.L.Rev. 1023, 1048 (1979): "One reason for subjecting any preferential program disadvantaging white persons [to] a heavier burden of justification is that such a program inevitably foments racial resentment and thereby strains the effort to gain wider acceptance for the principle of the moral equality of the races. Therefore, it makes sense to insist, as Powell did, that any preferential program be designed to accomplish its objective in a manner that causes as little resentment as possible." See also Mishkin, *The Uses of Ambivalence: Reflections on the Supreme Court and the Constitutionality of Affirmative Action,* 131 U.Pa.L.Rev. 907, 928 (1983): "The description of race as simply 'another factor' among a lot of others considered in seeking diversity tends to minimize the sense that minority students are separate and different and the recipients of special dispensations. [These] perceptions [can] facilitate or hamper the development of relationships among individuals and groups; they can advance or retard the educational process for all—including, particularly, minority students whose self-image is most crucially involved." Compare Blasi, *Bakke as Precedent: Does Mr. Justice Powell Have a Theory?* 67 Calif.L.Rev. 21, 60 (1979): "[I]t is almost always a bad thing for constitutional standards to be based on the purported perceptions of the populace regarding what is fair or rational rather than on well-considered and explicitly defended arguments respecting fairness and rationality. It is too easy to manufacture a 'general belief' or a 'widespread feeling.' [Second], if admissions programs are to be evaluated not on the basis of what they really entail but instead in terms of how they are generally perceived, educational institutions can only regard the constitutional standard as a legitimation of subterfuge and hypocrisy."

For emphasis on the basic similarity between the opinions of Powell and Brennan, JJ., see Karst & Horowitz, *The Bakke Opinions and Equal Protection Doctrine,* 14 Harv. Civ.Rts.—Civ.Lib.L.Rev. 7 (1979).

k. Consider Pollak, *"Mr. Chief Justice; May It Please the Court:",* in Constitutional Government in America 247, 252 (Collins ed. 1980): "[T]he Freedmen's Bureau [authorized] a large remedial apparatus for the education and economic advancement [of] the freedmen. What could more clearly show that the fourteenth amendment, far from precluding remedial programs particularly designed to assist those groups battered by American history, was expected to be implemented in just such ways?" Compare Graglia, fn. a supra, at 263: "[T]his argument proves too much. It is equally clear that the fourteenth amendment was not intended to prohibit school segregation either."

While I applaud the judgment of the Court that a university may consider race in its admissions process, it is more than a little ironic that, after several hundred years of class-based discrimination against Negroes, the Court is unwilling to hold that a class-based remedy for that discrimination is permissible. [It] is unnecessary in 20th century America to have individual Negroes demonstrate that they have been victims of racial discrimination; the racism of our society has been so pervasive that none, regardless of wealth or position, has managed to escape its impact. The experience of Negroes in America has been different in kind, not just in degree, from that of other ethnic groups. It is not merely the history of slavery alone but also that a whole people were marked as inferior by the law. And that mark has endured. The dream of America as the great melting pot has not been realized for the Negro; because of his skin color he never even made it into the pot.[1]

[H]ad the Court [held in *Plessy*] that the Equal Protection Clause forbids differences in treatment based on race, we would not be faced with this dilemma in 1978. We must remember, however, that the principle that the "Constitution is color-blind" appeared only in the opinion of the lone dissenter. [F]or the next 60 years, from *Plessy* to *Brown*, ours was a Nation where, *by law*, an individual could be given "special" treatment based on the color of his skin.

It is because of a legacy of unequal treatment that we now must permit the institutions of this society to give consideration to race in making decisions about who will hold the positions of influence, affluence and prestige in America.

* * *

I fear that we have come full circle. After the Civil War our government started several "affirmative action" programs. This Court in the *Civil Rights Cases,* [p. 1076 infra], and *Plessy* destroyed the movement toward complete equality. For almost a century no action was taken, and this nonaction was with the tacit approval of the courts. Then we had *Brown* and the Civil Rights Acts of Congress, followed by numerous affirmative action programs. *Now,* we have this Court again stepping in, this time to stop affirmative action programs of the type used by the University of California.

MR. JUSTICE BLACKMUN. * * *

I yield to no one in my earnest hope that the time will come when an "affirmative action" program is unnecessary and is, in truth, only a relic of the past. I would hope that we could reach this stage within a decade at the most. But the story of *Brown,* decided almost a quarter of a century ago, suggests that that hope is a slim one. At some time, however, beyond any period of what some would claim is only transitional inequality, the United States must and will reach a stage of maturity where action along this line is no longer necessary. Then persons will be regarded as persons, and discrimination of the type we address today will be an ugly feature of history that is instructive but that is behind us. * * *

It is somewhat ironic to have us so deeply disturbed over a program where race is an element of consciousness, and yet to be aware of the fact, as we are, that institutions of higher learning, albeit more on the undergraduate than the graduate level, have given conceded preferences up to a point to those possessed of athletic skills, to the children of alumni, to the affluent who may bestow their

1. Consider Calabresi, *Bakke as Pseudo-Tragedy,* 28 Cath.U.L.Rev. 427, 432 (1979): "[I]f benign quotas are limited to blacks and perhaps to American Indians, so long as those groups—however society chooses to define them—remain sufficiently disadvantaged *as groups* so that membership in them can by itself constitute disadvantage without more, no major rejection of the basic universalist, meritocratic ideal would be entailed."

largess on the institutions, and to those having connections with celebrities, the famous, and the powerful. * * *

[That] the Fourteenth Amendment has expanded beyond its original 1868 conception [does] not mean for me, however, that the Fourteenth Amendment has broken away from its moorings and its original intended purposes. Those original aims persist. And that, in a distinct sense, is what "affirmative action," in the face of proper facts, is all about. If this conflicts with idealistic equality, that tension is original Fourteenth Amendment tension [and] it is part of the Amendment's very nature until complete equality is achieved in the area. In this sense, constitutional equal protection is a shield. * * *

I suspect that it would be impossible to arrange an affirmative action program in a racially neutral way and have it successful. To ask that this be so is to demand the impossible. In order to get beyond racism, we must first take account of race. There is no other way. And in order to treat some persons equally, we must treat them differently. We cannot—we dare not—let the Equal Protection Clause perpetrate racial supremacy.

* * * Today, again, we are expounding a *Constitution.* The same principles that governed McCulloch's case in 1819 govern Bakke's case in 1978. There can be no other answer.

MR. JUSTICE STEVENS, with whom THE CHIEF JUSTICE, MR. JUSTICE STEWART, and MR. JUSTICE REHNQUIST join, concurring in the judgment in part and dissenting in part.[l]

[Bakke] challenged petitioner's special admissions program [and the] California Supreme Court upheld his challenge and ordered him admitted. If the state court was correct in its view that the University's special program was illegal, and that Bakke was therefore unlawfully excluded from the medical school because of his race, we should affirm its judgment, regardless of our views about the legality of admissions programs that are not now before the Court.

[Stevens, J., then construed the state court opinion as containing no "outstanding injunction forbidding any consideration of racial criteria in processing applications." m] It is therefore perfectly clear that the question whether race can ever be used as a factor in an admissions decision is not an issue in this case, and that discussion of that issue is inappropriate.

[Stevens, J., then interpreted Title VI as prohibiting "the exclusion of *any* individual from a federally funded program 'on the ground of race.'"] It is therefore our duty to affirm the judgment ordering Bakke admitted * * *.

Notes and Questions

1. *Composition of decisionmaking body.* (a) Of what relevance should it be that those disadvantaged by a racially preferential program are not a "discrete and insular minority requiring extraordinary protection from the majoritarian political process"? Consider Ely, *The Constitutionality of Reverse Racial Discrimination,* 41 U.Chi.L.Rev. 723, 735 (1974): "[T]he reasons for being unusually suspicious, and, consequently, employing a stringent brand of review, are lacking. A White majority is unlikely to disadvantage itself for reasons of racial prejudice; nor is it likely to be tempted either to underestimate the needs and

l. Four Members of the Court have undertaken to announce the legal and constitutional effect of this Court's judgment. See opinion of Justices Brennan, White, Marshall, and Blackmun. [But] only a majority can speak for the Court or determine what is the "central meaning" of any judgment of the Court.

m. For support of this conclusion, see Morris, *The Bakke Decision: One Holding or Two?* 58 Ore.L.Rev. 311, 326–32 (1979).

deserts of Whites relative to those of others, or to overestimate the costs of devising an alternative classification that would extend to certain Whites the advantages generally extended to Blacks." Under this rationale, may a city with a black majority enact an affirmative action program in hiring for public jobs? May a city with a white majority provide that every qualified black voter shall have two votes for all city officers? See Kurland, *Egalitarianism and the Warren Court,* 68 Mich.L.Rev. 629 (1970).

May a school district that has never been racially segregated permit members of racial minorities to elect to confine certain schools to members of their race? (Cf. *Green,* Sec. IV supra). See Note, *Alternative Schools for Minority Students: The Constitution, The Civil Rights Act and the Berkeley Experiment,* 61 Calif.L.Rev. 858 (1973). May this be done so long as any minority student may elect not to go to these schools? Does this assume a "free choice" unrealistic in fact? See Kirp, *Community Control, Public Policy and the Limits of Law,* 68 Mich.L.Rev. 1355 (1970). Suppose the minority in the community that wants the separate schools is white? See Canby, *"Northern" School Segregation: Minority Rights to Integrate and Segregate,* 1971 L. & Soc.Ord. 489. May a state college permit black students to live in all-black dormitories? If so, may it deny white students all-white dormitories? See Jones, *Do Separate Facilities for Black Students Provide Equal Protection, Upside Down?* 1975 U.Ill. L.F. 73.

(b) Consider Sandalow, *Racial Preferences in Higher Education: Political Responsibility and the Judicial Role,* 42 U.Chi.L.Rev. 653, 694–99 (1975): "Ely's analysis [is] troublesome on several grounds. First, in American politics majorities [typically] are coalitions of minorities which have varying [interests]. Resolution of the dispute depends upon which of the minorities is more successful in forging an alliance with those groups which are less immediately affected. The issue whether state schools ought to adopt preferential admissions policies is no exception. The immediate beneficiaries of these policies are the minorities which receive preferential treatment. But there is no reason to suppose that the costs of such policies are borne equally by sub-groups within the white population. To the extent that they are not, the discrimination—though nominally against a majority—is in reality against those sub-groups. * * * Universities have adopted preferential admissions policies without legislative sanction. The precise issue [is] not whether such policies are valid when adopted by a broadly representative, politically responsible legislature, but whether they are valid when adopted by a university [and] whether in determining the validity of state action that trenches upon constitutional values, the courts ought to consider whether the judgment under review is that of the legislature or of an agency that is less representative of the public and lacking direct political responsibility. [O]nly by ignoring all that we know about legislative behavior could it be supposed that a legislature's failure to limit the power of such bodies is equivalent to affirmative legislative approval of their decisions." See also Greenawalt, fn. 35 in *Bakke,* at 573–74: "We may safely suppose that the faculty of most state law schools is almost entirely white, but we may not assume that most faculty members will identify more with marginal white applicants than with black applicants. As most law teachers have done very well academically [they] may have trouble identifying themselves with marginal applicants. [M]any intellectuals may actually find it easier to identify with the plight of the 'oppressed' than the problems of the 'Philistine' middle and lower middle classes, from whom many marginal white applicants may come. Furthermore, two things that are in the obvious and immediate interest of faculty members and administrators are campus peace and a minimum of administrative burdens. Without doubt, some university programs for blacks [have] been adopted after considerable pressure that threatened or actually resulted in disruption. And a straight preferential policy applicable to all members of a minority group is likely to demand much less faculty or administrative time than careful examination of individual applications. Thus, it would be a mistake for judges to suppose that since most law school teachers and educational administrators are white they will not employ preferential policies ill-advisedly."

2. *Remedying constitutional and statutory violations.* (a) Is it clear that at least five justices—Brennan, White, Marshall, Blackmun *and* Powell, JJ.,— would have upheld the Davis plan against constitutional challenge if there had been "judicial, legislative, or administrative findings of constitutional or statutory violations [by] a government body [with] the authority and capability to establish, in the record, that the classification is responsive to identified discrimination" (Powell, J.)? Is it clear that these criteria would be satisfied by findings of Congress? [a] The California legislature? The Board of Regents—at least if it had a "legislative mandate and legislatively determined criteria" (Powell, J.)? Compare Van Alstyne, fn. b supra, at 289–90; O'Neil, *Bakke in Balance: Some Preliminary Thoughts,* 67 Calif.L.Rev. 143, 153–58 (1979), with Choper, *The Constitutionality of Affirmative Action: Views From the Supreme Court,* 70 Ky. L.J. 1, 9–12 (1981–82); Posner, *The Bakke Case and the Future of "Affirmative Action,"* 67 Calif.L.Rev. 171, 178–80 (1979). Would at least five justices have upheld the Davis plan against constitutional challenge if the California legislature—or the Regents—had found "that the disparate impact of Davis' general admissions program resulted primarily from test scores and grades which were without educational justification" (Powell, J., fn. 44)?

Must the legislatively/administratively identified constitutional or statutory violations have been by the Davis Medical School? Or is it enough that the findings trace the illegality to some other government unit? See Powell, J., at fn. 40; Sedler, *Beyond Bakke: The Constitution and Redressing the Social History of Racism,* 14 Harv.Civ.Rights—Civ.Lib.L.Rev. 133, 151–55 (1979). Could the Davis plan be "responsive" to "identified past discrimination" by public elementary, secondary and undergraduate schools—both in and out of California? See Brennan, J.'s Part IV–B. Consider Greenawalt, *The Unresolved Problems of Reverse Discrimination,* 67 Calif.L.Rev. 87, 127 (1979): "[G]iven the lingering effects of discrimination against earlier generations, given people's inevitable advancement through stages of life, and given the tremendous geographic mobility in the United States, people whose opportunities are unequal because of earlier discrimination will typically not have been affected by any discrimination by the organization from which they now seek a job or other benefit. It is not sensible to demand as a matter of constitutional law that that organization itself have discriminated before racial preferences are permissible."

Could a Davis-like plan—in education, employment, or otherwise—be "responsive" to legislatively/administratively "identified" *private* discrimination that is illegal under statutes such as Title VII (which do not require that the discrimination be intentional)—or that would have been illegal if such statutes had been in effect at the time the private discrimination occurred? If so, will any racial preference plan promulgated by a "competent" legislative/administrative body ever be held to violate equal protection?

---

a. See *Fullilove v. Klutznick,* infra.

(b) To what extent must the legislative/administrative findings of "proven constitutional or statutory violations" (Powell, J.) be "in the record," or be factually "documented" rather than "conclusory," etc.? See Choper, supra, at 12–14. Consider Sedler, supra, at 167–68: "[I]n general it is the function of legislative bodies to make determinations of policy rather than to make adjudicatory findings of fact. Whenever a legislative body makes findings of constitutional or statutory violations in the context of racial discrimination, the findings are likely to be generalized rather than based on particular instances of violations. A legislative finding of 'societal discrimination' should therefore be no more objectionable under Justice Powell's analysis than would be any other legislative finding of racial discrimination. The former would reflect 'constitutional or statutory violations' to the same extent [that] any such findings rest on particular violations. If a finding of societal discrimination is acceptable when made by a legislature, then it cannot be that there is an inherently 'amorphous' and 'ageless' quality about the concept which prevents the government from having a valid and substantial interest in redressing the effects of societal discrimination." See also notes 1–3, pp. 1161–62 infra. Consider *Fullilove*, infra.

(c) To what extent is the analysis in notes (a) and (b) above applicable to "judicial findings of constitutional or statutory violations"? Cf. Fiss, fn. 41 in *Bakke*. Are limits imposed by the doctrine of *Washington v. Davis*? See note 2 after *Davis*.

3. *"Burdens" on "innocent individuals."* (a) Are any justices in *Bakke* of the view that the nature of the burden imposed on innocent persons to remedy constitutional or statutory violations is of no consequence? Of what relevance is the availability of remedial measures that spread the burden more widely (equitably)? Compare *Fullilove v. Klutznick*, infra. Consider McCormack, fn. b in *Bakke*, at 536: "Traditional tort theories assume that as between two innocent persons, a loss should stay where it has fallen unless there is some reason to shift its burden to another. In employment contexts, compensation can be made by requiring the employer to pay both innocents, but education operates with limited resources—seats in a class—and often results in a zero sum game." See also Comment, *Beyond Strict Scrutiny: The Limits of Congressional Power to Use Racial Classifications*, 74 Nw.U.L.Rev. 617, 633 (1979): "[In *Milliken II*,] the court-ordered expenditure of public funds to assist black students in overcoming the effects of past discrimination clearly had the effect of reducing the funds available for general educational purposes. Therefore, white students, who were not themselves responsible for the historic discrimination, were saddled with the burden of the program, since there was a reduction in funds available for general use."

(b) UNITED STEEL WORKERS v. WEBER, 443 U.S. 193, 99 S.Ct. 2721, 61 L.Ed.2d 480 (1979), per BRENNAN, J., held that "an affirmative action plan—collectively bargained by an employer and a union—that reserves for black employees 50% of the openings in an inplant craft training program until the percentage of black craft workers in the plant is commensurate with the percentage of blacks in the local labor force," did not violate Title VII of the Civil Rights Act of 1964—which, inter alia, makes it "unlawful [for] any employer, labor organization, or joint labor-management committee [to] discriminate against any individual because of his race, color, religion, sex, or national origin in admission [to] any program established to provide apprenticeship or other training." [b] "It would be ironic indeed if a law triggered by a Nation's concern over centuries of racial injustice [constituted] the first legislative prohibition of all voluntary, private, race-conscious efforts to abolish traditional patterns of racial segregation and hierarchy.

"Our conclusion [is] reinforced by [the] language and legislative history of § 703(j) of Title VII. [It] provides that nothing contained in Title VII 'shall be interpreted to *require* any employer [to] grant preferential treatment [to] any group because of the race [of such] group on account of' a de facto racial imbalance in the employer's work force. The section does *not* state that 'nothing in Title VII shall be interpreted to *permit*' voluntary affirmative efforts to correct racial imbalances. The natural inference is that Congress chose not to forbid all voluntary race-conscious affirmative action.[6]

"We need not today define in detail the line of demarcation between permissible and impermissible affirmative action plans. It suffices to hold that the challenged [plan] falls on the permissible side of the line. The purposes [were] designed to break down old patterns of racial segregation and hierarchy. [At] the same time the plan does not unnecessarily trammel the interests of the white employees. The plan does not require the discharge of white workers and their replacement with new black hires. Cf. *McDonald v. Santa Fe Trail Trans. Co.*, 427 U.S. 273, 96 S.Ct. 2574, 49 L.Ed.2d 493 (1976).[c] Nor does the plan create an absolute bar to the advancement of white employees; half of those trained in the program will be white. Moreover, the plan is a temporary measure; it is not intended to maintain racial balance, but simply to eliminate a manifest racial imbalance. Preferential selection of craft trainees at the Gramercy plant will end as soon as the percentage of black skilled craft workers in the Gramercy plant approximates the percentage of blacks in the local labor force." [d]

(c) In FIREFIGHTERS v. STOTTS, 467 U.S. 561, 104 S.Ct. 2576, 81 L.Ed.2d 483 (1984), blacks in the Memphis fire department had entered into a consent decree with the city (which did not admit past intentional discrimination) to increase black employment. A budget shortage subsequently required reduction of personnel. Although the city's layoff proposal "was not adopted with [the] intent to discriminate," it had an adverse proportionate impact on blacks. The Court, per WHITE, J., held that Title VII precludes a federal district court from modifying the consent decree so as to displace "a non-minority employee with seniority under the contractually established seniority system absent either a

b. The Court emphasized that since the plan "does not involve state action, this case does not present an alleged violation of the Equal Protection Clause."

6. Title VI of the Civil Rights Act of 1964, considered in *Bakke*, contains no provision comparable to § 703(j). This is because Title VI was an exercise of federal power over a matter in which the Federal Government was already directly involved: [—] "program[s] or activit[ies] receiving Federal financial assistance." Congress was legislating to assure federal funds would not be used in an improper manner. Title VII, by contrast, was enacted pursuant to the Commerce power to regulate purely private decisionmaking and was not intended to incorporate and particularize the commands of the Fifth and Fourteenth Amendments. Title VII and Title VI, therefore, cannot be read in pari materia.

c. *McDonald*, emphasizing that it was not considering an affirmative action program, held that an employer violated Title VII (and 42 U.S.C.A. § 1981—pp. 1138, 1183 infra) by discharging white, but not black, employees for theft of company property.

d. Blackmun, J., although sharing "some of the misgivings expressed" in Rehnquist, J.'s dissent, joined the Court's opinion and wrote a separate concurrence. Powell and Stevens, JJ., did not participate. Rehnquist, J., joined by Burger, C.J., dissented, finding that "the legislative history of Title VII is as clear as the language [and] irrefutably demonstrates [that] *no* racial discrimination in employment is permissible under Title VII, not even preferential treatment of minorities to correct racial imbalance." Burger, C.J., also wrote a separate dissent.

finding that the seniority system was adopted with discriminatory intent or a determination that such a remedy was necessary to make whole a proven victim of discrimination": "Title VII protects bona fide seniority systems, and it is inappropriate to deny an innocent employee the benefits of his seniority in order to provide a remedy in [a] suit such as this." Stevens, J., concurred on narrower grounds. Blackmun, J., joined by Brennan and Marshall, JJ., dissented.

4. *Remedying de facto segregation.* In addition to *Swann's* dictum—that "school authorities might well conclude that in order to prepare students to live in a pluralistic society each school should have a prescribed ratio of Negro to white students reflecting the proportion for the district as a whole"—do Powell, J.'s fn. 39 and Brennan, J.'s fn. 41 settle the issue that school officials may voluntarily act on a racial basis to alleviate de facto school segregation? May a school board, to cure racial imbalance, permit only minority students to transfer?

5. *Repealing remedies for de facto segregation.* (a) In WASHINGTON v. SEATTLE SCHOOL DIST., 458 U.S. 457, 102 S.Ct. 3187, 73 L.Ed.2d 896 (1982), shortly after appellee implemented a mandatory busing plan to reduce de facto school segregation, the Washington electorate adopted Initiative 350, providing— with a number of broad exceptions—that "no school board [shall] directly or indirectly require any student to attend a school other than the school which is geographically nearest or next nearest the student's place of residence." The Court, per BLACKMUN, J.—relying on *Hunter v. Erickson,* 393 U.S. 385, 89 S.Ct. 557, 21 L.Ed.2d 616 (1969) [a]—held this violated equal protection: "[T]he political majority may generally restructure the political process to place obstacles in the path of everyone seeking to secure the benefits of governmental action. But a different analysis is required when the State allocates governmental power non-neutrally, by explicitly using the *racial* nature of a decision to determine the decisionmaking process. State action of this kind, [*Hunter*] said, 'places *special* burdens on racial minorities within the governmental process,' (emphasis added), thereby 'making it *more* difficult for certain racial and religious minorities [than for other members of the community] to achieve legislation that is in their interest.' (emphasis added) (Harlan, J., concurring). * * *

"[D]espite its facial neutrality there is little doubt that the initiative was effectively drawn for racial purposes. [T]he District Court found that the text [was] carefully tailored to interfere only with desegregative busing.[b] [It] in fact allows school districts to bus their students 'for most, if not all,' of the non-integrative purposes required by their educational policies.[6] [It] is true [that] the proponents of mandatory integration cannot be classified by race: Negroes and whites may be counted among both the supporters and the opponents of Initiative 350. And it should be equally clear that white as well as Negro children benefit from exposure to 'ethnic and racial diversity in the classroom.' [But]

---

a. In *Hunter,* after the Akron, Ohio city council enacted a fair housing ordinance, the voters amended the city charter to prevent "any ordinance dealing with racial, religious, or ancestral discrimination without the approval of a majority of the voters." The Court, per White, J., held this "explicitly racial classification" whose "impact falls on the minority" violative of equal protection. Black, J., dissented.

b. "The initiative envisioned busing for racial purposes in only one circumstance: it did

not purport to 'prevent any court of competent jurisdiction from adjudicating constitutional issues relating to the public schools.' "

6. At the beginning of the 1978–1979 academic year, approximately 300,000 of the 769,040 students enrolled in Washington's public schools were bused to school. Ninety-five percent of these students were transported for reasons unrelated to race.

desegregation of the public schools, like the Akron open housing ordinance, at bottom inures primarily to the benefit of the minority, and is designed for that purpose. [Given] the racial focus of Initiative 350, this suffices to trigger application of the *Hunter* doctrine.

"We are also satisfied that the practical effect of Initiative 350 is to work a reallocation of power of the kind condemned in *Hunter.* The initiative removes the authority to address a racial problem—and only a racial problem—from the existing decisionmaking body, in such a way as to burden minority interests. Those favoring the elimination of de facto school segregation now must seek relief from the state legislature, or from the statewide electorate. Yet authority over all other student assignment decisions, as well as over most other areas of educational policy, remains vested in the local school board. [As] in *Hunter,* then, the community's political mechanisms are modified to place effective decisionmaking authority over a racial issue at a different level of government.[17] [By] placing power over desegregative busing at the state level, then, Initiative 350 plainly 'differentiates between the treatment of problems involving racial matters and that afforded other problems in the same area.'[23] * * *

"To be sure, 'the simple repeal or modification of desegregation or anti-discrimination laws, without more, never has been viewed as embodying a presumptively invalid racial classification.' *Crawford v. Los Angeles Bd. of Educ.* [infra].

"Initiative 350, however, works something more than the 'mere repeal' of a desegregation law by the political entity that created it. It burdens all future attempts to integrate Washington schools [by] lodging decisionmaking authority over the question at a new and remote level of government. Indeed, the initiative, like the charter amendment at issue in *Hunter,* has its most pernicious effect on integration programs that do '*not* arouse extraordinary controversy.' In such situations the initiative makes the enactment of racially beneficial legislation difficult, though the particular program involved might not have inspired opposition had it been promulgated through the usual legislative processes used for comparable legislation.[27] [And] when the State's allocation of power places unusual burdens on the ability of racial groups to enact legislation

---

17. [While] Justice Powell [finds] it crucial that the proponents of integrated schools remain free to use Washington's initiative system to further their ends, that was true in *Hunter* as well: proponents of open housing were not barred from invoking Akron's initiative procedures to repeal the charter amendment, or to enact fair housing [legislation]. Indeed, *Hunter* would have been virtually identical to this case had the Akron charter amendment simply barred the city council from passing any fair housing ordinance, as Initiative 350 forbids the use of virtually all mandatory desegregation strategies. Surely, however, *Hunter* would not have come out the other way had the charter amendment made *no* provision for the passage of fair housing legislation, instead of subjecting such legislation to ratification by referendum. * * *

23. [W]hat we find objectionable about Initiative 350 is the comparative burden it imposes on minority participation in the political process—that is, the racial nature of the way in which it structures the *process* of decision-

making. It is evident, then, that the horribles paraded by the dissent, n. 14—which have nothing to do with the ability of minorities to participate in the process of self-government—are entirely unrelated to this case. It is equally clear [that] the State remains free to vest all decisionmaking power in state officials, or to remove authority from local school boards in a race-neutral manner.

27. That phenomenon is graphically demonstrated by the circumstances of this litigation. The long-standing desegregation programs in Pasco and Tacoma, as well as the Seattle middle school integration plan, have functioned for years without creating undue controversy. Yet they have been swept away [by] Initiative 350. As a practical matter, it seems most unlikely that proponents of desegregative busing in smaller communities such as Tacoma or Pasco will be able to obtain the statewide support now needed to permit them to desegregate the schools in their communities.

specifically designed to overcome the 'special condition' of prejudice, the governmental action seriously 'curtail[s] the operation of those political processes ordinarily to be relied upon to protect minorities.' *Carolene Products*, n. 4. In a most direct sense, this implicates the judiciary's special role in safeguarding the interests of those groups that are 'relegated to such a position of political powerlessness as to command extraordinary protection from the majoritarian political process.' *Rodriguez*."

POWELL, J., joined by Burger, C.J., and Rehnquist and O'Connor, JJ., dissented: "[I]n the absence of a prior constitutional violation, the States are under no constitutional duty to adopt integration programs in their schools, and certainly [not] to establish a regime of mandatory busing.[6] Nor does the Federal Constitution require that particular decisions concerning the schools or any other matter be made on the local as opposed to the State level. * * *

"The issue here arises only because the Seattle School District [chose] to adopt race specific school assignments with extensive busing. It is not questioned that the District itself, at any time thereafter, could [have] cancelled its integration program without violating the Federal Constitution. Yet this Court holds that neither the legislature nor the people [of] Washington could alter what the District had decided. [It] is a strange notion [that] local governmental bodies can forever preempt the ability of a State—the sovereign power—to address a matter of compelling concern to the State. * * *

"This is certainly not a case where a State [has] established a racially discriminatory requirement. Initiative 350 [is] neutral on its face, and racially neutral as public policy. Children of all races benefit from neighborhood [schools].[9] * * *

"Nothing in *Hunter* supports the Court's extraordinary invasion into the State's distribution of authority. [Initiative 350] simply does not place unique political obstacles in the way of racial minorities. In this case, unlike in *Hunter*, the political system has *not* been redrawn or altered. The authority of the State over the public school system, acting through Initiative or the legislature, is plenary. Thus, the State's political system is not altered when it adopts for the first time a policy, concededly within the area of its authority, for the regulation of local school districts. And certainly racial minorities are not uniquely or

6. [Indeed], in the absence of a finding of segregation by the School District, mandatory busing on the basis of race raises constitutional difficulties of its own. Extensive pupil transportation may threaten liberty or privacy interests. See *Bakke* (opinion of Powell, J.) * * *.

9. [The] people of the State legitimately could decide that unlimited mandatory busing places too great a burden on the liberty and privacy interests of families and students of all races. It might decide that the reassignment of students to distant schools, on the basis of race, was too great a departure from the ideal of racial neutrality in State action. And, in light of the experience with mandatory busing in other cities, the State might conclude that such a program ultimately would lead to greater racial imbalance in the schools.

[See also Sunstein, *Public Values, Private Interests, and the Equal Protection Clause*, 1982 Sup.Ct.Rev. 127, 149, 157–58: "A classification [that] singles out a racial problem for special and disadvantageous treatment is peculiarly likely to be supported by invidious justifications. Like the heightened scrutiny applied to facial racial classifications, heightened scrutiny in *Hunter* is justified by a suspicion that improper justifications are at work. [A]rguments against busing are less likely to be animated by racial bias than are arguments against legislation preventing discrimination in housing. *Seattle* might therefore have been treated differently from *Hunter* on the ground that invidious motives may well not have been at work."]

comparatively burdened by the State's adoption of a policy that would be lawful if adopted by any School District in the State.[12] * * *[13]."

(b) In CRAWFORD v. LOS ANGELES BD. OF EDUC., 458 U.S. 527, 102 S.Ct. 3211, 73 L.Ed.2d 948 (1982), after the state courts had ordered substantial busing to remedy de facto school segregation which the state courts had found violative of the state constitution, the California electorate amended the state constitution by adopting Proposition I, providing that "state courts shall not order mandatory pupil assignment or transportation unless a federal court would do so to remedy a violation of the Equal Protection Clause." The Court, per POWELL, J., found no violation of equal protection, "rejecting the contention that once a State chooses to do 'more' than the Fourteenth Amendment requires, it may never recede. [E]ven after Proposition I, the California Constitution still imposes a greater duty of desegregation than does the Federal Constitution. The state courts of California continue to have an obligation under state law to order segregated school districts to use voluntary desegregation techniques, whether or not there has been a finding of intentional segregation. The school districts themselves retain a state law obligation to take reasonably feasible steps to desegregate, and they remain free to adopt reassignment and busing plans to effectuate desegregation.[14]

"* * * Proposition I does not embody a racial classification. It neither says nor implies that persons are to be treated differently on account of their race. [The] benefit it seeks to confer—neighborhood schooling—is made available regardless of race in the discretion of school boards. Indeed, even if Proposition I had a racially discriminatory effect, in view of the demographic mix of the District it is not clear which race or races would be affected the most or in what way.[16] * * *[18] * * *

12. The Court repeatedly states that the effect of Initiative 350 is "to redraw decision-making authority over racial matters—*and only over racial matters*—in such a way as to place *comparative* burdens on minorities." But the decision by the State to exercise its authority over the schools and over racial matters in the schools does not place a comparative burden on racial minorities. In [*Hunter,*] "fair housing legislation *alone* was subject to an automatic referendum requirement." By contrast, Initiative 350 merely places mandatory busing among the much larger group of matters—covering race relations, administration of the schools, and a variety of other matters—addressed at the State level. Racial minorities, if indeed they are burdened by Initiative 350, are not *comparatively* burdened. In this respect, they are in the same position as any other group of persons who are disadvantaged by regulations drawn at the State level.

13. The Court's decision intrudes deeply into normal State decisionmaking. Under its holding the people [apparently] are forever barred from developing a different policy on mandatory busing where a School District previously has adopted one of its own. This principle would not seem limited to the question of mandatory busing. Thus, if the admissions committee of a State law school devel-

oped an affirmative action plan that came under fire, the Court apparently would find it unconstitutional for any higher authority to intervene unless that authority traditionally dictated admissions policies. As a constitutional matter, the Dean of the Law School, the faculty of the University as a whole, the University President, the Chancellor of the University System, and the Board of Regents might be powerless to intervene despite their greater authority under State law.

After today's decision it is unclear whether the State may set policy in any area of race relations where a local governmental body arguably has done "more" than the Fourteenth Amendment requires. If local employment or benefits are distributed on a racial basis to the benefit of racial minorities, the State apparently may not thereafter ever intervene. Indeed, under the Court's theory one must wonder whether [even] the Federal Government could assert its superior authority to regulate in these areas.

14. In this respect this case differs from the situation presented in *Seattle*.

16. In the Los Angeles school district, white students are now the racial minority. [I]n Los Angeles County, racial minorities, in-

18. See note 18 on page 918.

"Were we to hold that the mere repeal of race related legislation is unconstitutional, we would limit seriously the authority of States to deal with the problems of our heterogeneous population. States would be committed irrevocably to legislation that has proven unsuccessful or even harmful in practice. And certainly the purposes of the Fourteenth Amendment would not be advanced by an interpretation that discouraged the States from providing greater protection to racial minorities. [Moreover], we would not interpret the Fourteenth Amendment to require the people of a State to adhere to a judicial construction of their State Constitution when that Constitution itself vests final authority in the people. * * *

"*Hunter* involved more than a 'mere repeal' of the fair housing ordinance: persons seeking anti-discrimination housing laws—presumptively racial minorities—were 'singled out for mandatory referendums while no other [group] face[d] that obstacle.' By contrast, [Proposition I] is less than a 'repeal' of the California Equal Protection Clause. As noted above, after Proposition I, the State Constitution still places upon school boards a greater duty to desegregate than does the Fourteenth Amendment.

"Nor can it be said that Proposition I distorts the political process for racial reasons or that it allocates governmental or judicial power on the basis of a discriminatory principle. [The] remedies available for violation of the antitrust laws, for example, are different than those available for violation of the Civil Rights Acts. Yet a 'dual court system'—one for the racial majority and one for the racial minority—is not established simply because civil rights remedies are different from those available in other areas.[27] * * *[28]

"[H]aving gone beyond the requirements of the Federal Constitution, the State was free to return in part to the standard prevailing generally throughout the United States. It could have conformed its law to the Federal Constitution in every respect. That it chose to pull back only in part, and by preserving a greater right to desegregation than exists under the Federal Constitution, most assuredly does not render the Proposition unconstitutional on its face.

"The California Court of Appeal also rejected petitioners' claim that Proposition I, if facially valid, was nonetheless unconstitutional because enacted with a discriminatory purpose. The court reasoned that the purposes of the Proposition were well stated in the Proposition itself. Voters may have been motivated by any of these purposes, chief among them the educational benefits of neighborhood schooling. [It] characterized petitioners' claim of discriminatory intent on

---

cluding those of Spanish origin, constitute the majority of the population.

18. Proposition I is not limited to busing for the purpose of racial desegregation. It applies neutrally to "pupil school assignment or pupil transportation" in general. [For a possibly different interpretation of Proposition I, see Choper, *The Repeal of Remedies for De Facto School Segregation,* in Choper, Kamisar & Tribe, *The Supreme Court: Trends and Developments 1981–82* 43–44 (1983).] Even so, it is clear that court ordered busing in *excess* of that required by the Fourteenth Amendment, as one means of desegregating schools, prompted the initiation and probably the adoption of Proposition I.

27. Petitioners contend that Proposition I only restricts busing for the purpose of racial

discrimination. The Proposition is neutral on its face, however, and respondents [take] issue with petitioners' interpretation of the provision.

28. Similarly, a "dual constitution" is not established when the State chooses to go beyond the requirements of the Federal Constitution in some areas but not others. Nor is a "dual executive branch" created when an agency is given enforcement powers in one area but not in another. Cf. *Brown v. Califano,* 627 F.2d 1221 (D.C.Cir.1980) (upholding federal legislation prohibiting a federal executive agency, but not local school officials or federal courts, from requiring busing).

[Compare Note, *The Constitutionality of Excluding Desegregation from the Legal Services Program,* 84 Colum.L.Rev. 1630 (1984).]

the part of millions of voters as but 'pure speculation.' [Here, as in *Reitman v. Mulkey,*] involving the circumstances of passage and the potential impact of a Proposition adopted at a state-wide election, we see no reason to differ with the conclusions of the state appellate court."

BLACKMUN, J., joined by Brennan, J., although joining the Court's opinion, concurred "to address [the] critical distinctions between this case [and] *Seattle*": "State courts do not create the rights they enforce; those rights originate elsewhere—in the state legislature, in the State's political subdivisions, or in the state constitution itself. When one of those rights is repealed, and therefore is rendered unenforceable in the courts, that action hardly can be said to restructure the State's decisionmaking mechanism. While the California electorate may have made it more difficult to achieve desegregation when it enacted Proposition I, [it] did so not by working a structural change in the political *process* so much as by simply repealing the right to invoke a judicial busing remedy. Indeed, ruling for petitioners on a *Hunter* theory seemingly would mean that statutory affirmative action or antidiscrimination programs never could be repealed, for a repeal of the enactment would mean that enforcement authority previously lodged in the state courts was being removed by another political entity.

"In short, the people of California—the same 'entity' that put in place the state constitution, and created the enforceable obligation to desegregate—have made the desegregation obligation judicially unenforceable. The 'political process or the decisionmaking mechanism used to *address* racially conscious legislation' has not been 'singled out for peculiar and disadvantageous treatment,' *Seattle,* for those political mechanisms that create and repeal the rights ultimately enforced by the courts were left entirely unaffected by Proposition I."

MARSHALL, J., dissented: "I fail to see how a fundamental redefinition of the governmental decisionmaking structure with respect to the same racial issue can be unconstitutional when the state seeks to remove the authority from local school boards, yet constitutional when the state attempts to achieve the same result by limiting the power of its [courts]. Despite Proposition I's apparent neutrality, it is 'beyond reasonable dispute,' *Seattle,* and the majority today concedes, that 'court ordered busing in *excess* of that required by [equal protection] prompted the initiation and probably the adoption of Proposition I.' * * *

"Nor can there be any doubt that Proposition I works a substantial reallocation of state power. [After its adoption], the only method of enforcing against a recalcitrant school board the state constitutional duty to eliminate racial isolation is to petition either the state legislature or the electorate as a whole. Clearly, the rules of the game have been significantly changed for those attempting to vindicate this state constitutional right.[3] [It] is equally clear [that] Proposition I is not a 'mere repeal.' [I]n *Seattle, Hunter,* and *Reitman,* the three times that this Court has explicitly rejected the argument that a proposed change constituted a 'mere repeal' of an existing policy, the alleged rescission

---

3. There can be no question that the practical effect of Proposition I will be to deprive state courts of "the sole and exclusive means of eliminating racial segregation from the schools." As we have often noted "bus transportation has long been an integral part of all public educational systems, and it is unlikely that a truly effective remedy could be devised without continued reliance upon it." More-over, Proposition I prevents a state court from ordering school officials to take any action respecting *pupil school assignment,* as well as pupil transportation. Presumably, state courts could not design a remedy involving the "pairing" or "clustering" of schools, even if such a remedy did not involve *any* "busing." * * *

was accomplished by a governmental entity other than the entity that had taken the initial action, and resulted in a drastic alteration of the substantive effect of existing policy. This case falls squarely within this latter category.

" * * * Proposition I has placed an enormous barrier between minority children and the effective enjoyment of their constitutional rights, a barrier that is not placed in the path of those who seek to vindicate other rights granted by state law. [Certainly], *Hunter* and *Seattle* cannot be distinguished on the ground that they concerned the reallocation of legislative power, whereas Proposition I redistributes the inherent power of a court to tailor the remedy to the violation. [Indeed], Proposition I, by denying full access to the only branch of government that has been willing to address this issue meaningfully, is far worse for those seeking to vindicate the plainly unpopular cause of racial integration in the public schools than a simple reallocation of an often unavailable and unresponsive legislative process.[c] * * *

"[Petitioners] assert that the disproportionate impact of Proposition I, combined with the circumstances surrounding its adoption and the history of opposition to integration cited above, clearly indicate the presence of discriminatory intent. Yet despite the fact that *no inquiry* has been conducted into these allegations by either the trial or the appellate court, this Court, in its haste to uphold the banner of 'neighborhood schools,' affirms a factual determination that was never made. Such blind allegiance to the conclusory statements of a lower court is plainly forbidden by our prior decisions."

6. *"Benign quotas."* May jury commissioners purposefully select that number of blacks on each jury panel that is proportionate to the number of eligible blacks in the jurisdiction? Cf. *Cassell v. Texas*, 339 U.S. 282, 287, 70 S.Ct. 629, 631–32, 94 L.Ed. 839, 847 (1950). If the ideal is a jury composed of a community cross-section, how can racial considerations be avoided? May the commissioners assure *at least* a "reasonable" number? A fixed *minimum* percentage?

Suppose that state law limited the number of blacks in a public housing project to that percentage—say 35%—which, if exceeded, would likely cause white persons to leave, thus frustrating integration? Is this valid because its purpose is to *avoid* segregation? If so, how about "public subsidies such as bonuses to landlords whose apartments enjoy a mixed occupancy, grants to Negroes to enable them to rent apartments or purchase homes in residential areas that would otherwise be beyond their means, or payments to induce white families to move or to stay in integrated neighborhoods"? Bittker, *The Case of the Checker-Board Ordinance: An Experiment in Race Relations*, 71 Yale L.J. 1387, 1411 (1962). Of what significance is the fact that some blacks—those denied entrance because the quota is already filled—are being "discriminated" against because of their race? See generally Ackerman, *Integration for Subsidized Housing and the Question of Racial Occupancy Controls*, 26 Stand.L.Rev. 245 (1974); Note, *Benign Steering and Benign Quotas: The Validity of Race-*

---

c. See also Choper, fn. 18 supra, at 44: "It seems to me that, if anything, it was harder for the people of California to achieve a busing remedy after Proposition I than it was for the people of Washington after Initiative 350. That is to say—and I believe our current history demonstrates the validity of this—the easiest place to get busing to remedy de facto school segregation, certainly in California, was in the courts. Proposition I removed the courts' ability to do that. It is true that the California school districts still had this power. But I think that people who want to get a busing remedy for de facto school segregation are probably better off in Washington, even though they must go to the legislature, than they are in California, where they must go to the Los Angeles Board of Education."

Conscious Government Policies to Promote Residential Integration, 93 Harv.L. Rev. 938 (1980).

Consider Rice, *The Legality of De Facto Segregation,* 10 Cath.Law. 309, 320 (1964): "[The benign quota] implies that the presence of [whites] automatically raises the quality of a [housing area] and that a preponderance of [blacks] automatically lowers [it]. [T]his is as much a denial of the Negro's equality under the law as are the indefensible but less sophisticated racial barriers in the South." Compare Gegan, *De Jure Integration in Education,* 11 Cath.Law. 4, 14 (1965): "Legislation designed to integrate racial minorities into the mainstream of society carries no connotation of inferiority not also present in any legislation enacted to assist a socially or economically disadvantaged class. And I know of no responsible person who would argue today that welfare or other anti-poverty legislation bespeaks a judgment that the recipient is an inferior being."

FULLILOVE v. KLUTZNICK, 448 U.S. 448, 100 S.Ct. 2758, 65 L.Ed.2d 902 (1980), rejected "a facial constitutional challenge" to the Public Works Employment Act of 1977 (appropriating $4 billion to state and local governments for public works projects). Section 103(f)(2), the "minority business enterprise" or "MBE" provision, required that: "Except to the extent that the Secretary determines otherwise, no grant shall be made under this Act for any local public works project unless the applicant gives satisfactory assurance to the Secretary that at least 10 per centum of the amount of each grant shall be expended for minority business enterprises. [T]he term 'minority business enterprise' means a business at least 50 per centum of which is owned by minority group members or, in case of a publicly owned business, at least 51 per centum of the stock of which is owned by minority group members. For the purposes of the preceding sentence, minority group members are citizens of the United States who are Negroes, Spanish-speaking, Orientals, Indians, Eskimos, and Aleuts."

BURGER, C.J., announced the judgment and an opinion joined by White and Powell, JJ.: "The origin of the provision was an amendment [on] the floor of the House [which was changed to make clear] that the federal administrator would have discretion to waive the 10% requirement where its application was not feasible. [The] device of a 10% MBE participation requirement, subject to administrative waiver, was thought to be required to assure minority business participation; otherwise it was thought that repetition of the prior experience could be expected, with participation by minority business accounting for an inordinately small percentage of government contracting. The causes of this disparity were perceived as involving the longstanding existence and maintenance of barriers impairing access by minority enterprises to public contracting opportunities, or sometimes as involving more direct discrimination, but not relating to lack ['of] capable and qualified minority [enterprises.']

"The legislative objectives of the MBE provision must be considered against the background of ongoing efforts directed toward deliverance of the century-old promise of equality of economic opportunity. [As] Congress began consideration of the Public Works Employment Act of 1977, the House Committee on Small Business issued a lengthy report [which] summarized a 1975 committee report [prepared] by the House Subcommittee on SBA Oversight and Minority Enterprise [which] took 'full notice [as] evidence for its consideration' of reports submitted to the Congress by the General Accounting Office and by the U.S. Commission on Civil Rights. [The] Civil Rights Commission report discussed at some length the barriers encountered by minority businesses in gaining access to government contracting opportunities at the federal, state and local levels. Among the major difficulties [were] deficiencies in working capital, inability to meet bonding requirements, disabilities caused by an inadequate 'track record,' lack of awareness of bidding opportunities, unfamiliarity with bidding procedures, preselection before the formal advertising process, and the exercise of discretion by government procurement officers to disfavor minority businesses.

*   *   *

"Against this backdrop, [it] is inconceivable that Members of both Houses were not fully aware of the objectives of the MBE [provision].

"[T]he Secretary of Commerce promulgated regulations [and the Economic Development Administration (EDA) published guidelines that make] clear the administrative understanding that a waiver or partial waiver is justified (and will be granted) to avoid subcontracting with a minority business enterprise at an 'unreasonable' price, i.e., a price above competitive levels which cannot be attributed to the minority firm's attempt to cover costs inflated by the present effects of disadvantage or discrimination.

"This administrative approach is consistent with the legislative intention. [I]n the report of the House Subcommittee on SBA Oversight and Minority Enterprise the subcommittee took special care to note that when using the term 'minority' it intended to include 'only such minority individuals as [are] economically or socially disadvantaged.' The subcommittee also was cognizant of existing administrative regulations designed to ensure that firms maintained on the lists of bona fide minority business enterprises be those whose competitive position is impaired by the effects of disadvantage and discrimination. [The] sponsors of the MBE provision, in their reliance on prior administrative practice, intended that the term 'minority business enterprise' would be given that same limited application; this even found expression in the legislative [debates].

"The EDA technical bulletin *   *   * clarifies the definition of 'minority group members.' [a] It [also] outlines a procedure for the processing of complaints of 'unjust participation by an enterprise or individuals in the MBE program,' or of improper administration of the MBE requirement.[b]

a. The definitions, set out in an Appendix to Burger, C.J.'s opinion, are:

"a) Negro—An individual of the black race of African origin.

"b) Spanish-speaking—An individual of a Spanish-speaking culture and origin or parentage.

"c) Oriental—An individual of a culture, origin or parentage traceable to the areas south of the Soviet Union, East of Iran, inclusive of islands adjacent thereto, and out to the Pacific including but not limited to Indonesia, Indochina, Malaysia, Hawaii and the Philippines.

"d) Indian—An individual having origins in any of the original people of North America and who is recognized as an Indian by either a tribe, tribal organization or a suitable authority in the community. (A suitable authority in the community may be: educational institutions, religious organizations, or state agencies.)

"e) Eskimo—An individual having origins in any of the original peoples of Alaska.

"f) Aleut—An individual having origins in any of the original peoples of the Aleutian Islands."

b. The procedure, set out in the Appendix, is:

"Any person [with] information indicating unjust participation by an enterprise or individuals in the MBE program or who believes that the MBE participation requirement is being improperly applied should contact the appropriate EDA [grantee].

"Upon receipt of a complaint, the grantee should attempt to resolve the issues in dispute. [If] the grantee requires assistance in reaching a determination, the grantee should contact the Civil Rights Specialist in the appropriate Regional Office.

"If the complainant believes that the grantee has not satisfactorily resolved the issues raised in his complaint, he may personally contact the EDA Regional Office."

"[The] program was designed to ensure [that] grantees who elect to participate would not employ procurement practices that Congress had decided might
result in perpetuation of the effects of prior discrimination which had impaired
or foreclosed access by minority businesses to public contracting opportunities.
The MBE program does not mandate the allocation of federal funds according to
inflexible percentages solely based on race or ethnicity.

"Our analysis proceeds in two steps. At the outset, we must inquire
whether the *objectives* of this legislation are within the power of Congress.
* * *

"A. In enacting the MBE provision, it is clear that Congress employed an
amalgam of its specifically delegated powers. The [Act,] by its very nature, is
primarily an exercise of the Spending Power [whose reach] is at least as broad as
the regulatory powers of Congress. If, pursuant to its regulatory powers,
Congress could have achieved the objectives of the MBE program, then it may do
so under the Spending Power. [The] legislative history of the MBE provision
shows that there was a rational basis for Congress to conclude that the subcontracting practices of prime contractors could perpetuate the prevailing impaired
access by minority businesses to public contracting opportunities, and that this
inequity has an effect on interstate commerce. [Insofar] as the MBE program
pertains to the actions of private prime contractors, the Congress could have
achieved its objectives under the Commerce Clause. We conclude that in this
respect the objectives of the MBE provision are within the scope of the Spending
Power.

[W]e look to § 5 of the Fourteenth Amendment for the power to regulate the
procurement practices of state and local [government] grantees of federal funds.
[I]n *Oregon v. Mitchell,* [p. 1500 infra], we upheld [a] nationwide prohibition on
the use of various voter-qualification tests and devices in federal, state and local
elections. The Court was unanimous [in] concluding [that] Congress could
reasonably determine that its legislation was an appropriate method of attacking
the perpetuation of prior purposeful discrimination, even though the use of these
tests or devices might have discriminatory effects only. See *Rome v. United
States,* [p. 1512 infra]. Our cases reviewing the parallel power of Congress to
enforce the provisions of the Fifteenth Amendment confirm that congressional
authority extends beyond the prohibition of purposeful discrimination to encompass state action that has discriminatory impact perpetuating the effects of past
discrimination. *South Carolina v. Katzenbach.*

"With respect to the MBE provision, Congress had abundant evidence from
which it could conclude that minority businesses have been denied effective
participation in public contracting opportunities by procurement practices that
perpetuated the effects of prior discrimination. Congress, of course, may legislate without compiling the kind of 'record' appropriate with respect to judicial or
administrative proceedings. Congress had before it, among other data, evidence
of a long history of marked disparity in the percentage of public contracts
awarded to minority business enterprises. This disparity was considered to
result not from any lack of capable and qualified minority businesses, but from
the existence and maintenance of barriers to competitive access which had their
roots in racial and ethnic discrimination, and which continue today, even absent
any intentional discrimination or other unlawful conduct. Although much of
this history related to the experience of minority businesses in the area of
federal procurement, there was direct evidence before the Congress that this
pattern of disadvantage and discrimination existed with respect to state and
local construction contracting as well. In relation to the MBE provision,

Congress acted within its competence to determine that the problem was national in scope.

"Although the Act recites no preambulary 'findings' on the subject, we are satisfied that Congress had abundant historical basis from which it could conclude that traditional procurement practices, when applied to minority businesses, could perpetuate the effects of prior discrimination. Accordingly, Congress reasonably determined that the prospective elimination of these barriers to minority firm access to public contracting opportunities generated by the 1977 Act was appropriate to ensure that those businesses were not denied equal opportunity to participate in federal grants to state and local governments, which is one aspect of the equal protection of the laws. Insofar as the MBE program pertains to the actions of state and local grantees, Congress could have achieved its objectives by use of its power under § 5 of the Fourteenth Amendment. We conclude that in this respect the objectives of the MBE provision are within the scope of the Spending Power. * * *

"B. We now turn to the question whether, as a *means* to accomplish these plainly constitutional objectives, Congress may use racial and ethnic criteria, in this limited [way. We] are not dealing with a remedial decree of a court but with the legislative authority of Congress. Furthermore, petitioners have challenged the constitutionality of the MBE provision on its face; they have not sought damages or other specific relief for injury allegedly flowing from specific applications of the program; nor have they attempted to show that as applied in identified situations the MBE provision violated the constitutional or statutory rights of any party to this case.[71] * * *

"Our review of the regulations and guidelines [reveals] that Congress enacted the program as a strictly remedial measure; moreover, it is a remedy that functions prospectively, in the manner of an injunctive decree. * * *

"As a threshold matter, we reject the contention that in the remedial context the Congress must act in a wholly 'color-blind' fashion. [*Swann.* In the] school desegregation cases we dealt with the authority of a federal court to formulate a remedy for unconstitutional racial discrimination. However, the authority of a court to incorporate racial criteria into a remedial decree also extends to statutory [violations.] *Franks v. Bowman;* see *Teamsters v. United States; Albemarle v. Moody.* In another setting, we have held that a state may employ racial criteria that are reasonably necessary to assure compliance with federal voting rights legislation, even though the state action does not entail the remedy of a constitutional violation. *UJO.* * * *

"Here we deal [not] with the limited remedial powers of a federal court, [but] with the broad remedial powers of Congress. It is fundamental that in no organ of government, state or federal, does there repose a more comprehensive remedial power than in the Congress, expressly charged by the Constitution with competence and authority to enforce equal protection guarantees. Congress not only may induce voluntary action to assure compliance with existing federal statutory or constitutional antidiscrimination provisions, but also, where Congress has authority to declare certain conduct unlawful, it may, as here, authorize and induce state action to avoid such conduct. * * *

---

71. In their complaint, in order to establish standing to challenge the validity of the program, petitioners alleged as "[s]pecific examples" of economic injury three instances where one of their number assertedly would have been awarded a public works contract but for enforcement of the MBE provision. Petitioners requested only declaratory and injunctive relief against continued enforcement of the MBE provision; they did not seek any remedy for these specific instances * * *.

"It is not a constitutional defect in this program that it may disappoint the expectations of nonminority firms. When effectuating a limited and properly tailored remedy to cure the effects of prior discrimination, such 'a sharing of the burden' by innocent parties is not impermissible. *Franks;* see *Albemarle.* The actual 'burden' shouldered by nonminority firms is relatively light in this connection when we consider the scope of this public works program as compared with overall construction contracting opportunities.[72] Moreover, although we may assume that the complaining parties are innocent of any discriminatory conduct, it was within congressional power to act on the assumption that in the past some nonminority businesses may have reaped competitive benefit over the years from the virtual exclusion of minority firms from these contracting opportunities.

"Another challenge to the validity of the MBE program is the assertion that it is underinclusive—that it limits its benefit to specified minority groups rather than extending its remedial objectives to all businesses whose access to government contracting is impaired by the effects of disadvantage or discrimination. [But there] has been no showing in this case that Congress has inadvertently effected an invidious discrimination by excluding from coverage an identifiable minority group that has been the victim of a degree of disadvantage and discrimination equal to or greater than that suffered by the groups encompassed by the MBE program. It is not inconceivable that on very special facts a case might be made to challenge the congressional decision to limit MBE eligibility to the particular minority groups identified in the Act. * * *

"It is also contended that the MBE program is overinclusive—that it bestows a benefit on businesses identified by racial or ethnic criteria which cannot be justified on the basis of competitive criteria or as a remedy for the present effects of identified prior discrimination. It is conceivable that a particular application of the program may have this effect; however, the peculiarities of specific applications are not before [us. But even] in the context of a facial challenge such as is presented in this case, the MBE provision cannot pass muster unless, with due account for its administrative program, it provides a reasonable assurance that application of racial or ethnic criteria will be limited to accomplishing the remedial objectives of Congress and that misapplications of the program will be promptly and adequately remedied administratively. * * *

"The administrative program contains measures to effectuate the congressional objective of assuring legitimate participation by disadvantaged MBE's. Administrative definition has tightened some less definite aspects of the statutory identification of the minority groups encompassed by the program.[73] There is

72. The Court of Appeals [found] that the $4.2 billion in federal grants conditioned upon compliance with the MBE provision amounted to about 2.5% of the total of nearly $170 billion spent on construction in the United States during 1977. Thus, the 10% minimum minority business participation contemplated by this program would account for only 0.25% of the annual expenditure for construction work in the United States.

73. * * * Minority group members are defined as "citizens of the United States who are Negroes, Spanish-speaking, Orientals, Indians, Eskimos and Aleuts." The administrative definitions are set out in [fn. a]. These categories also are classified as minorities in the regulations implementing the nondiscrimination requirements of the Railroad Revitalization and Regulatory Reform Act of 1976, on which Congress relied as precedent for the MBE provision. The House Subcommittee on SBA Oversight and Minority Enterprise [also] recognized that these categories were included within the Federal Government's definition of "minority business enterprise." The specific inclusion of these groups in the MBE provision demonstrates that Congress concluded they were victims of discrimination. Petitioners did not press any challenge to Congress' classification categories in the Court of Appeals; there is no reason for this Court to pass upon the issue at this time.

administrative scrutiny to identify and eliminate from participation in the program MBE's who are not 'bona-fide' [;] for example, spurious minority-front entities can be exposed. A significant aspect of this surveillance is the complaint procedure available for reporting 'unjust participation by an enterprise or individuals in the MBE program.' And even as to specific contract awards, waiver is available to avoid dealing with an MBE who is attempting to exploit the remedial aspects of the program by charging an unreasonable price, i.e., a price not attributable to the present effects of past discrimination. We must assume that Congress intended close scrutiny of false claims and prompt action on them.

"Grantees are given the opportunity to demonstrate that their best efforts will not succeed or have not succeeded in achieving the statutory 10% target for minority firm [participation]. In these circumstances a waiver or partial waiver is available once compliance has been demonstrated. * * *

"That the use of racial and ethnic criteria is premised on assumptions rebuttable in the administrative process gives reasonable assurance that application of the MBE program will be limited to accomplishing the remedial objectives contemplated by Congress and that misapplications of the racial and ethnic criteria can be remedied. In dealing with this facial challenge to the statute, doubts must be resolved in support of the congressional judgment that this limited program is a necessary step to effectuate the constitutional mandate for equality of economic opportunity. The MBE provision may be viewed as a pilot project, appropriately limited in extent and duration, and subject to reassessment [by] Congress prior to any extension or re-enactment. Miscarriages of administration could have only a transitory economic impact on businesses not encompassed by the program, and would not be irremediable. * * *

"Any preference based on racial or ethnic criteria must necessarily receive a most searching examination. [This] opinion does not adopt, either expressly or implicitly, the formulas of analysis articulated in such cases as *Bakke.* However, our analysis demonstrates that the MBE provision would survive judicial review under either 'test' articulated in the several *Bakke* opinions."

POWELL, J., concurring "separately to apply the analysis set forth in my opinion in *Bakke*," found that § 103(f)(2) "serves the compelling government interest in eradicating the continuing effects of past discrimination identified by Congress": "Because the distinction between permissible remedial action and impermissible racial preference rests on the existence of a constitutional or statutory violation, [a] race-conscious remedy is not compelling unless an appropriate governmental authority has found that such a violation has occurred.

"[Unlike] the Regents of the University of California, Congress properly may—and indeed must—address directly the problems of discrimination in our society [relying, inter alia, on *Katzenbach v. Morgan, South Carolina v. Katzenbach* and *Oregon v. Mitchell.*] It is beyond question [that] Congress has the authority to identify unlawful discriminatory practices, to prohibit those practices, and to prescribe remedies to eradicate their continuing effects. The next inquiry is whether Congress has made findings adequate to support its determination that minority contractors have suffered extensive discrimination.

"The petitioners contend that [this] Court should treat the debates on § 103(f)(2) as the complete 'record' of congressional decisionmaking. [But] creation of national rules for the governance of our society simply does not entail the same concept of record-making that is appropriate to a judicial or administrative proceeding. Congress['s] special attribute as a legislative body lies in its broader mission to investigate and consider all facts and opinions that may be [relevant]. One appropriate source is the information and expertise that Congress acquires in the consideration and enactment of earlier legislation. ＊ ＊ ＊

"In my view, the legislative [history] demonstrates that Congress reasonably concluded that private and governmental discrimination had contributed to the negligible percentage of public contracts awarded minority contractors.[4] [I] believe that a court must accept [the] conclusion that purposeful discrimination contributed significantly to the small percentage of federal contracting funds that minority business enterprises have received. Refusals to subcontract work to minority contractors may, depending upon the identity of the discriminating party, violate Title VI of the Civil Rights Act of 1964 or the Fourteenth Amendment. Although the discriminatory activities were not identified with the exactitude expected in judicial or administrative adjudication, it must be remembered that 'Congress may paint with a much broader brush than may this Court.' *Oregon v. Mitchell* (Stewart, J., concurring and dissenting in part).

"[This conclusion] leads to the inquiry whether use of a 10% set-aside is a constitutionally appropriate means. [We] have recognized that the choice of remedies to redress racial discrimination is a 'balancing process left, within appropriate constitutional or statutory limits, to the sound discretion of the trial court.' *Franks v. Bowman* (Powell, J., concurring and dissenting in part). I believe that the enforcement clauses of the Thirteenth and Fourteenth Amendments give Congress a similar measure of discretion. [But the] Judicial Branch has the special responsibility to make a searching inquiry into the justification for employing a race-conscious remedy. Courts must be sensitive to the possibility that less intrusive means might serve the compelling state interest equally as well. I believe that Congress' choice of a remedy should be upheld, however, if the means selected are equitable and reasonably necessary to the redress of identified discrimination. Such a test allows the Congress to exercise necessary discretion but preserves the essential safeguard of judicial review of racial classifications. ＊ ＊ ＊

"[The] set-aside is not a permanent part of federal contracting requirements. As soon as the PWEA program concludes, this set-aside program ends. The temporary nature of this remedy ensures that a race-conscious program will not last longer than the discriminatory effects it is designed to eliminate. ＊ ＊ ＊

"The percentage chosen for the set-aside is within the scope of congressional discretion. [10%] falls roughly halfway between the present percentage of minority contractors and the percentage of minority group members in the Nation.

"Although the set-aside is pegged at a reasonable figure, its effect might be unfair if it were applied rigidly in areas of the country where minority group members constitute a small percentage of the population. To meet this concern, Congress enacted a waiver [provision]. The factors governing issuance of a

---

4. I cannot accept the suggestion [that] § 103(f)(2) must be viewed as serving a compelling state interest if the reviewing court can "perceive a basis" for legislative action, quoting *Katzenbach v. Morgan.* The "perceive a basis" standard refers to congressional authority to act, not to the distinct question whether that action violates the Due Process Clause of the Fifth Amendment.

In my view, a court should uphold a reasonable congressional finding of discrimination.

A more stringent standard of review would impinge upon Congress' ability to address problems of discrimination; a standard requiring a court to "perceive a basis" is essentially meaningless in this context. Such a test might allow a court to justify legislative action even in the absence of affirmative evidence of congressional findings.

waiver include the availability of qualified minority contractors in a particular geographic area, the size of the locale's minority population, and the efforts made to find minority contractors. We have been told that 1261 waivers had been granted by September 9, 1979. * * *

"Consideration of these factors [and others discussed by Burger, C.J.,] persuades me that the set-aside is a reasonably necessary means of furthering the compelling governmental interest in redressing the discrimination. [As my *Bakke*] opinion made clear, I believe that the use of racial classifications [cannot] be imposed simply to serve transient social or political goals, however worthy they may be. [But] Congress has been given a unique constitutional role in the enforcement of the post-Civil War Amendments." [c]

MARSHALL, J., joined by Brennan and Blackmun, JJ., concurred in the judgment: "[T]he racial classifications employed [are] substantially related to the achievement of the important and congressionally articulated goal of remedying the present effects of past racial discrimination. The provision, therefore, passes muster under the equal protection standard I adopted in *Bakke*."

STEWART, J., joined by Rehnquist, J., dissented: "[T]oday's decision is wrong for the same reason that *Plessy* was wrong. [O]ur cases have made clear that the Constitution is wholly neutral in [forbidding] racial discrimination, whatever the race may be of those who are its victims [discussing *Anderson v. Martin, Loving* and *McLaughlin*].[3]

"This history contains one clear lesson. Under our Constitution, the government may never act to the detriment of a person solely because of that person's race.[4] The color of a person's skin and the country of his origin are immutable facts that bear no relation to ability, disadvantage, moral culpability, or any other characteristics of constitutionally permissible interest to government. [From] the perspective of a person detrimentally affected by a racially discriminatory law, the arbitrariness and unfairness is entirely the same, whatever his skin color and whatever the law's purpose, be it purportedly 'for the promotion of the public good' or otherwise. [If] a law is unconstitutional, it is no less unconstitutional just because it is a product of the Congress * * *.

"The Court's attempt to characterize the law as a proper remedial measure [is] remarkably unconvincing. The Legislative Branch of government is not a court of equity. It has neither the dispassionate objectivity nor the flexibility that are needed to mold a race-conscious remedy around the single objective of eliminating the effects of past or present discrimination.

---

c. For the view that the opinions of Burger, C.J., and Powell, J., were "extraordinarily qualified" and that "it would seem fair to postulate that the road ahead for many race-conscious programs will not be an easy one," see Choper, note 2(a) supra, at 8–22.

3. *Bakke* and *UJO* do not suggest a different rule. The Court in *Bakke* invalidated the racially preferential [program]. In *UJO*, [no person] was deprived of his electoral franchise.

[D]uring the Second World War, this Court did find constitutional a governmental program imposing injury on the basis of race. See *Korematsu; Hirabayashi*. Significantly, those cases were decided not only in time of war, but in an era before the Court had held

that the Due Process Clause of the Fifth Amendment imposes the same equal protection standard upon the Federal Government that the Fourteenth Amendment imposes upon the States.

4. A court of equity may, of course, take race into account in devising a remedial decree to undo a violation of a law prohibiting discrimination on the basis of race. See *Teamsters; Franks; Swann*. But such a judicial decree, following litigation in which a violation of law has been determined, is wholly different from generalized legislation that awards benefits and imposes detriments dependent upon the race of the recipients. See text infra.

"But even assuming that Congress has the power, under § 5 of the Fourteenth Amendment or some other constitutional provision, to remedy previous illegal racial discrimination, there is no evidence that Congress has in the past engaged in racial discrimination in its disbursement of federal contracting funds. The MBE provision thus pushes the limits of any such justification far beyond the equal protection standard of the Constitution. Certainly, nothing in the Constitution gives Congress any greater authority to impose detriments on the basis of race than is afforded the Judicial Branch. And a judicial decree that imposes burdens on the basis of race can be upheld only where its sole purpose is to eradicate the actual effects of illegal race discrimination. See *Pasadena Bd. of Educ. v. Spangler.*

"The provision at issue here does not satisfy this condition. Its legislative history suggests that it had at least two other objectives in addition to that of counteracting the effects of past or present racial discrimination in the public works construction industry. One such purpose appears to have been to assure to minority contractors a certain percentage of federally funded public works contracts. But, [since] equal protection immunizes from capricious governmental treatment 'persons'—not 'races,' it can never countenance laws that seek racial balance as a goal in [itself.] Second, there are indications that the MBE provision may have been enacted to compensate for the effects of social, educational, and economic 'disadvantage.' No race, however, has a monopoly on social, educational, or economic disadvantage,[11] and any law that indulges in such a presumption clearly violates the constitutional guarantee of equal protection.[12]

"[Because] of the Court's decision today, our statute books will once again have to contain laws that reflect the odious practice of delineating the qualities that make one person a Negro and make another white. Moreover, racial discrimination, even 'good faith' racial discrimination, is inevitably a two-edged sword. '[P]referential programs may only reinforce common stereotypes holding that certain groups are unable to achieve success without special protection based on a factor having no relationship to individual worth.' *Bakke* (opinion of Powell, J.). Most importantly, by making race a relevant criterion once again in its own affairs, the Government implicitly teaches the public that the apportionment of rewards and penalties can legitimately be made according to race— rather than according to merit or ability—and that people can, and perhaps should, view themselves and others in terms of their racial characteristics.

---

11. For instance, in 1978, 83.4% of persons over the age of 25 who had not completed high school were "white," and in 1977, 79.0% of households with annual incomes of less than $5,000 were "white."

12. Moreover, [even] assuming that the MBE provision was intended solely as a remedy for past and present racial discrimination, it sweeps far too broadly. [No] waiver is provided for any governmental entity that can prove a history free of racial discrimination. Nor is any exemption permitted for nonminority contractors that are able to demonstrate that they have not engaged in racially discriminatory behavior. Finally, the statute makes no attempt to direct the aid it provides solely toward those minority contracting firms that arguably still suffer from the effects of past or present discrimination.

These are not the characteristics of [a] decree that is closely tailored to the evil to be corrected. In today's society, it constitutes far too gross an oversimplification to assume that every single Negro, Spanish-speaking citizen, Oriental, Indian, Eskimo, and Aleut potentially interested in construction contracting currently suffers from the effects of past or present racial discrimination. Since the MBE setaside must be viewed as resting upon such an assumption, it necessarily paints with too broad a brush. Except to make whole the identified victims of racial discrimination, the guarantee of equal protection prohibits the government from taking detrimental action against innocent people on the basis of the sins of others of their own race.

Notions of 'racial entitlement' will be fostered, and private discrimination will necessarily be encouraged. See Van Alstyne, *Rites of Passage: Race, the Supreme Court, and the Constitution,* 46 U.Chi.L.Rev. 775 (1979)." d

STEVENS, J., dissented: "Because racial characteristics so seldom provide a relevant basis for disparate treatment, and because classifications based on race are potentially so harmful to the entire body politic,[5] it is especially important that the reasons for any such classification be clearly identified and unquestionably legitimate.

"The statutory definition of the preferred class includes 'citizens of the United States who are Negroes, Spanish-speaking, Orientals, Indians, Eskimos, and Aleuts.' All aliens and all nonmembers of the racial class are excluded. No economic, social, geographical or historical criteria are relevant for exclusion or inclusion. There is not one word in the remainder of the Act or in the legislative history that explains why any Congressman or Senator favored this particular definition over any other or that identifies the common characteristics that every member of the preferred class was believed to share.[6] Nor does the Act or its history explain why 10% of the total appropriation was the proper amount to set aside for investors in each of the six racial subclasses.[7]

"Four different, though somewhat interrelated, justifications for the racial classification in this Act have been advanced: first, that the 10% set aside is a form of reparation for past injuries to the entire membership of the class; second, that it is an appropriate remedy for past discrimination against minority business enterprises that have been denied access to public contracts; third, that

d. See also *Minnick v. California Dep't of Corrections,* 452 U.S. 105, 101 S.Ct. 2211, 68 L.Ed.2d 706 (1981), involving a challenge to respondent's affirmative action program for hiring and promoting minorities and women. The Court dismissed for want of a "final judgment," but Stewart, J., reached the merits, relying on his views in *Fullilove* and adding: "[I]t is wholly irrelevant whether the State gives a 'plus' or 'minus' value to a person's race, whether the discrimination occurs in a decision to hire or fire or promote, or whether the discrimination is called 'affirmative action' or by some less euphemistic term. * * * California's policy of racial discrimination was sought to be justified as an antidote for previous discrimination in favor of white people. But, even in this context, two wrongs do not make a right. Two wrongs simply make two wrongs." Rehnquist, J., agreed with the Court that there was no "final judgment," but would otherwise "join the dissenting opinion of Justice Stewart."

5. Indeed, the very attempt to define with precision a beneficiary's qualifying racial characteristics is repugnant to our constitutional ideals. The so-called guidelines [fn. a], are so general as to be fairly innocuous; as a consequence they are too vague to be useful. [If] the National Government is to make a serious effort to define racial classes by criteria that can be administered objectively, it must study precedents such as the First Regulation to the Reichs Citizenship Law of November 14, 1935 [defining "Jews."]

6. In 1968, almost 10 years before the Act was passed, the Small Business Administration had developed a program to assist small business concerns owned or controlled by "socially or economically disadvantaged persons." The Agency's description of persons eligible [stated] that such "persons include, but are not limited to, black Americans, American Indians, Spanish-Americans, oriental Americans, Eskimos and Aleuts." [But] the SBA's class of socially or economically disadvantaged persons neither included all persons in the racial class nor excluded all nonmembers of the racial class. Race was used as no more than a factor in identifying the class of the disadvantaged. The difference between the statutory quota involved in this case and the SBA's 1968 description [is] thus at least as great as the difference between the University of California's racial quota and the Harvard admissions system that Mr. Justice Powell regarded as critical in *Bakke.*

7. [The] 10% figure bears no special relationship to the relative size of the entire racial class, to any of the six subclasses, or to the population of the subclasses in the areas where they primarily reside. The Aleuts and the Eskimos, for example, respectively represent less than 1% and 7% of the population of Alaska, while Spanish-speaking or Negro citizens represent a majority or almost a majority in a large number of urban areas.

the members of the favored class have a special entitlement to 'a piece of the action' when government is distributing benefits; and, fourth, that the program is an appropriate method of fostering greater minority participation in a competitive economy. * * *

"I. [In] his eloquent separate opinion in *Bakke,* Mr. Justice Marshall recounted the tragic class-based discrimination against Negroes that is an indelible part of America's history. I assume that the wrong committed against the Negro class is both so serious and so pervasive that it would constitutionally justify an appropriate classwide recovery measured by a sum certain for every member of the injured class. [But] the history of discrimination against black citizens in America cannot justify a grant of privileges to Eskimos or Indians.

"Even if we assume that each of the six racial subclasses has suffered its own special injury at some time in our history, surely it does not necessarily follow that each of those subclasses suffered harm of identical magnitude. Although 'the Negro was dragged to this country in chains to be sold in slavery,' the 'Spanish-speaking' subclass came voluntarily, frequently without invitation, and the Indians, the Eskimos and the Aleuts had an opportunity to exploit America's resources before most American citizens arrived. * * *

"At best, the statutory preference is a somewhat perverse form of reparation for the members of the injured classes. For those who are the most disadvantaged within each class are the least likely to receive any benefit from the special privilege even though they are the persons most likely still to be suffering the consequences of the past wrong. * * *

"[We] can never either erase or ignore the history that Mr. Justice Marshall has recounted. But if that history can justify such a random distribution of benefits on racial lines, [it] will serve [as] a permanent source of justification for grants of special privileges. For if there is no duty to attempt either to measure the recovery by the wrong or to distribute that recovery within the injured class in an evenhanded way, our history will adequately support a legislative preference for almost any ethnic, religious, or racial group with the political strength to negotiate 'a piece of the action' for its members. * * *

"II. [T]he statute grants the special preference to a class that includes (1) those minority owned firms that have successfully obtained business in the past on a free competitive basis and undoubtedly are capable of doing so in the future as well; (2) firms that have never attempted to obtain any public business in the past; (3) firms that were initially formed after the Act was passed, including those that may have been organized simply to take advantage of its provisions; (4) firms that have tried to obtain public business but were unsuccessful for reasons that are unrelated to the racial characteristics of their stockholders; and (5) those firms that have been victimized by racial discrimination.

"Since there is no reason to believe that any of the firms in the first four categories had been wrongfully excluded from the market for public contracts, the statutory preference for those firms cannot be justified as a remedial measure. And since a judicial remedy was already available [under Title VI] for the firms in the fifth category, it seems inappropriate to regard the preference as a remedy designed to redress any specific wrongs.[13] In any event, since it is

---

13. I recognize that the EDA has issued a technical bulletin, relied on heavily by The Chief Justice, which distinguishes between higher bids quoted by minority subcontractors which are attributable to the effects of disadvantage or discrimination and those which are not. [But] even assuming that the technical bulletin accurately reflects Congress' intent in enacting the set-aside, it is not easy to envision how one could realistically demonstrate with any degree of precision, if at all, the extent to which a bid has been inflated by the highly unlikely that the composition of the fifth category is at all representative of the entire class of firms to which the statute grants a valuable preference, it is ill-fitting to characterize this as a 'narrowly tailored' remedial measure.

"III. [In] the short run our political processes might benefit from [the] ability of representatives of minority groups to disseminate patronage to their political backers. [But this] is, in my opinion, a plainly impermissible justification for this racial classification.

"IV. The interest in [facilitating] minority business enterprises in the economy is unquestionably legitimate. [This] statute, however, is not designed to remove any barriers to entry. Nor does its sparse legislative history detail any insuperable or even significant obstacles to entry into the competitive market. * * *

"It [is] true that irrational racial prejudice [continues] to obstruct minority participation in a variety of economic pursuits, presumably including the construction industry. But there are two reasons why this legislation will not [even] tend to eliminate such prejudice. First, prejudice is less likely to be a significant factor in the public sector of the economy than in the private sector because both federal and state laws have prohibited discrimination in the award of public contracts for many years. Second, and of greater importance, an absolute preference that is unrelated to a minority firm's ability to perform a contract inevitably will engender resentment on the part of competitors excluded from the market for a purely racial reason and skepticism on the part of customers and suppliers aware of the statutory classification. * * *

"The argument that our history of discrimination has left the entire membership of each of the six racial classes identified in the Act less able to compete in a free market [is] more easily stated than proved. The reduction in prejudice that has occurred during the last generation has accomplished much less than was anticipated; it nevertheless remains true that increased opportunities have produced an ever increasing number of demonstrations that members of disadvantaged races are entirely capable not merely of competing on an equal basis, but also of excelling in the most demanding professions. But, even though it is not the actual predicate for this legislation, a statute of this kind inevitably is perceived by many as resting on an assumption that those who are granted this special preference are less [qualified]. Because that perception—especially when fostered by [Congress]—can only exacerbate rather than reduce racial prejudice, it will delay the time when race will become a truly irrelevant, or at least insignificant, factor. Unless Congress clearly articulates the need and basis for a racial classification, and also tailors the classification to its justification, the Court should not uphold this kind of statute. * * *

"The ultimate goal must be to eliminate entirely from governmental decisionmaking such irrelevant factors as a human being's race. The removal of barriers to access to political and economic processes serves that goal. But the creation of new barriers can only frustrate true progress.

"[I] am not convinced that the [Due Process] Clause contains an absolute prohibition against any statutory classification based on race. I am nonetheless persuaded that it does impose a special obligation to scrutinize any governmental decisionmaking process that draws nationwide distinctions between citizens on the basis of their race and incidentally also discriminates against noncitizens in the preferred racial classes. [T]hat Congress for the first time in the Nation's

effects of disadvantage or past discrimination. Consequently, while The Chief Justice de-

scribes the set-aside as a remedial measure, it plainly operates as a flat quota.

history has created a broad legislative classification for entitlement to benefits based solely on racial characteristics identifies a dramatic difference between this Act and the thousands of statutes that preceded it. This dramatic point of departure is not even mentioned in the statement of purpose of the Act or in the reports of either the House or the Senate Committee that processed the legislation,[25] and was not the subject of any testimony or inquiry. * * *

"Whenever Congress creates a classification that would be subject to strict scrutiny under the Equal Protection Clause [if] it had been fashioned by a state legislature, it seems to me that judicial review should include a consideration of the procedural character of the decisionmaking process. A holding that the classification was not adequately preceded by a consideration of less drastic alternatives or adequately explained by a statement of legislative purpose would be far less intrusive than a final determination that the substance of the decision is not 'narrowly tailored to the achievement of that goal.' [It] is up to Congress to demonstrate that its unique statutory preference is justified by a relevant characteristic that is shared by the members of the preferred class. In my opinion, because it has failed to make that demonstration, it has also failed to discharge its duty to govern impartially embodied in the Fifth [Amendment]."

SECTION 3. SPECIAL SCRUTINY FOR OTHER CLASSIFICATIONS

I. IN GENERAL

In view of the history and announced purposes of the equal protection clause (see *Slaughter-House Cases,* Sec. 1 supra and *Strauder,* Sec. 2, I supra), are there any classes other than racial and ethnic minorities against whom discrimination should be held "suspect"—or at least subject to judicial scrutiny greater than the "minimum rationality" requirement of the "traditional approach"? Consider Bickel, *The Original Understanding and the Segregation Decision,* 69 Harv.L. Rev. 1, 60 (1955): "[T]he fourteenth amendment, on its face, deals not only with racial discrimination * * *. This cannot have been accidental, since the alternative considered [did] apply only to racial discrimination. Everyone's immediate preoccupation in the 39th Congress [was], of course, with hardships being visited on the colored race. Yet the fact that the proposed constitutional amendment was couched in more general terms could not have escaped those who voted for it."

If there are other classifications that should be subject to special scrutiny, by what criteria should they be identified?

1. *"Unalterable traits."* (a) How significant should it be that legislation discriminates on the basis of "congenital and unalterable traits over which an

---

25. [The] Court quotes three paragraphs from a lengthy report issued by the House Committee on small business in 1977, implying that the contents of that report were considered by Congress when it enacted the 10% minority set-aside. But that report was not mentioned by anyone during the very brief discussion of the set-aside amendment. When one considers the vast quantity of written material turned out by the dozens of congressional committees and subcommittees these days, it is unrealistic to assume that a significant number of legislators read, or even were

aware of, that report. Even if they did, the report does not contain an explanation of this 10% set-aside for six racial subclasses.

Indeed, the broad racial classification in this Act is totally unexplained. Although the legislative history discussed by The Chief Justice and by Mr. Justice Powell explains why Negro citizens are included within the preferred class, there is absolutely no discussion of why Spanish-speaking, Orientals, Indians, Eskimos, and Aleuts were also included. See n. 6, supra.

individual has no control and for which he should receive neither blame nor reward"? Note, *Equal Protection,* 82 Harv.L.Rev. 1065, 1126–27 (1969). Should equal protection be presumptively violated by laws that discriminate against persons who are physically handicapped? Overweight? Illiterate in English? See Note, *The Constitutional Right of Bilingual Children to an Equal Educational Opportunity,* 47 So.Cal.L.Rev. 943, 979–985 (1974). Lacking in certain intellectual or educational qualifications? See *Fay v. New York,* 332 U.S. 261, 67 S.Ct. 1613, 91 L.Ed. 2043 (1947); Note, *Equal Protection and Intelligence Classifications,* 26 Stan.L.Rev. 647 (1974). Homosexuals? See p. 207 supra. May a state classify on the basis of family ancestry? See *Kotch v. Bd. of River Port Pilot Comm'rs,* 330 U.S. 552, 67 S.Ct. 910, 91 L.Ed. 1093 (1947).

Consider Ely, *The Constitutionality of Reverse Racial Discrimination,* 41 U.Chi.L.Rev. 723, 730 n. 36 (1974): "[M]any characteristics that are theoretically changeable are not practically so; distinctions of constitutional magnitude should not partake of the pretense that any poor working man can significantly change his lot in life, or that any optician can become an optometrist, if he will only shape up. Most important, proponents of this view make no attempt [to] build a logical bridge from the immutability of the classifying characteristic to the conclusion that we should be suspicious of the classification." Must a trait be "congenital" in order to be "unalterable"? If not, is discrimination against a person because of a trait over which he "has no control" especially "invidious"?

Or is the "touch-stone" in respect to unalterable traits the fact that such classifications "will usually be perceived as a stigma of inferiority and a badge of opprobrium"? Note, 82 Harv.L.Rev. at 1127. That many (most) such classifications "bear no relation to one's ability to perform or contribute to society"? Id. at 1173. That often (usually) they involve "a traditionally disfavored class in our society [which] is more likely to be used without pausing to consider its justification"; that "habit, rather than analysis, makes it seem acceptable and natural [b]ut that sort of stereotyped reaction may have no rational relationship—other than pure prejudicial discrimination—to the stated purpose for which the classification is made"? Stevens, J., joined by Brennan and Marshall, JJ., dissenting in *Mathews v. Lucas,* Part III infra (concerning discrimination against illegitimate children). Of what significance is it that the unalterable trait, like race, is one of "high visibility"? [a]

(b) *Age.* MASSACHUSETTS BD. OF RETIREMENT v. MURGIA, 427 U.S. 307, 96 S.Ct. 2562, 49 L.Ed.2d 520 (1976), per curiam, upheld—"under the rational basis standard"—a law requiring uniformed state police officers to retire at age 50. After first rejecting the contention "that a right of governmental employment per se is fundamental" so as to make the legislative classification subject to "strict scrutiny" (see Sec. 4, IV infra), the Court continued: "While the treatment of the aged in this Nation has not been wholly free of discrimination, such persons, unlike, say, those who have been discriminated against on the basis of race or national origin, have not experienced a 'history of purposeful unequal treatment' or been subjected to unique disabilities on the basis of stereotyped characteristics not truly indicative of their abilities. The [Massachusetts statute] cannot be said to discriminate only against the elderly. Rather, it draws the line at a certain age in middle life. But even old age does

---

a. For the view that "the doctrine of suspect classifications is a roundabout way of uncovering official attempts to inflict inequality for its own sake—to treat a group worse not in the service of some overriding social goal but largely for the sake of simply disadvantaging its members," see Ely, *Democracy and Distrust* 145–57 (1980). See also Loewy, *A Different and More Viable Theory of Equal Protection,* 57 N.C.L.Rev. 1 (1978).

not define a 'discrete and insular' group, *Carolene Products Co.*, n. 4, in need of 'extraordinary protection from the majoritarian political process.' Instead, it marks a stage that each of us will reach if we live out our normal span. Even if the statute could be said to impose a penalty upon a class defined as the aged, it would not impose a distinction sufficiently akin to those classifications that we have found suspect to call for strict judicial scrutiny." [b]

MARSHALL, J., dissented from "the rigid two-tier model [that] still holds sway as the Court's articulated description of the equal protection test," urging the "flexible equal protection standard" developed in his earlier opinions in *Dandridge v. Williams* and *San Antonio Ind. School Dist. v. Rodriguez*, Sec. 4, IV infra—which would focus "upon the character of the classification in question, the relative importance to individuals in the class discriminated against of the governmental benefits that they do not receive, and the state interests asserted in the support of the classification": "[T]he Court is quite right in suggesting that distinctions exist between the elderly and traditional suspect classes such as [blacks]. The elderly are protected not only by certain antidiscrimination legislation, but by legislation that provides them with positive benefits not enjoyed by the public at large. Moreover, the elderly are not isolated in society, and discrimination against them is not pervasive but is centered primarily in employment. The advantage of a flexible equal protection standard, however, is that it can readily accommodate such variables. The elderly are undoubtedly discriminated against, and when legislation denies them an important benefit— employment—I conclude that to sustain the legislation the Commonwealth must show a reasonably substantial interest and a scheme reasonably closely tailored to achieving that interest." [c]

2. *"Political impotence."* (a) How significant should it be that legislation discriminates against a "discrete and insular" minority? How are such groups to be identified? [d] See note 3(a) after *New Orleans v. Dukes*, Sec. 1 supra. Consider Goodman, *De Facto School Segregation: A Constitutional and Empirical Analysis*, 60 Cal.L.Rev. 275, 313 (1972): "[If] there are groups that have no voice or visibility [it] is by no means clear that the urban black is among them. Numerically, blacks approach a majority in many large cities and are an increasingly formidable voting bloc in most. Numbers aside, they speak with a voice ever more audible [through] civil rights organizations and ad hoc community [groups]. Seldom have their demands been totally ignored."

(b) Consider Ely, note 1(a) supra, at 732–33: "Racial classifications that disadvantage minorities are rooted in 'we-they' generalizations and balances as opposed to 'they-they' generalizations and balances. Few legislators are opticians; but few are optometrists either. [e] Thus, although a decision to distinguish opticians from optometrists incorporates a stereotypical comparison of two classes of people, it is a comparison of two 'they' stereotypes, viz., '*They* [opticians] generally differ from *them* [optometrists] in certain respects that we find sufficient on balance to justify the decision to classify on this basis.'

---

b. See also *Vance v. Bradley*, 440 U.S. 93, 99 S.Ct. 939, 59 L.Ed.2d 171 (1979), upholding mandatory retirement at age 60 for federal Foreign Service personnel.

c. See generally Note, *Constitutional Attacks on Mandatory Retirement: A Reconsideration*, 23 U.C.L.A.L.Rev. 549 (1976).

On discriminations against children, see Tribe, *American Constitutional Law* 1077–82 (1978).

d. Are nonresidents the paradigm example? For further consideration of nonresidency and equal protection, see Sec. 4, II infra.

e. The reference is to *Williamson v. Lee Optical Co.*, fn. b in *New Orleans v. Dukes*, Sec. 1 supra.

Legislators, however, have traditionally not only not been Black; they have been White. A decision to distinguish Blacks from Whites therefore has its roots in a comparison between a 'we' stereotype and a 'they' stereotype * * *.

"The choice between classifying on the basis of a comparative generalization and attempting to come up with a more discriminating formula always involves balancing the increase in fairness that greater individualization will produce against the added costs it will entail. But in we-they situations two dangers inherent in this balancing process are significantly intensified. The first is that legislators will overestimate the costs of bringing 'them' into a position of equality with 'us.' [The second is] an undervaluation of the countervailing interest in fairness. [By] seizing upon the positive myths about our own class and the negative myths about theirs, or for that matter the realities respecting some or most members of the two classes, legislators may too readily assume that not many of 'them' will be unfairly deprived, nor many of 'us' unfairly benefitted, by the proposed classification.[43] " [f]

Compare Sandalow, *The Distrust of Politics,* 56 N.Y.U.L.Rev. 446, 464 (1981): "[T]he wealthy—of if you prefer the very wealthy—are surely a minority in our legislatures and are the victims of widespread prejudice that denies them the empathetic understanding of legislators. How many legislators appreciate the costs imposed upon the wealthy by progressive income and estate taxation? Significantly, our statute books contain far more legislation that discriminates on the basis of wealth and income than legislation that employs racial classifications. Why, then, are blacks but not the wealthy entitled to the benefit of special judicial protection?" See also Posner, *The De Funis Case and the Constitutionality of Preferential Treatment of Racial Minorities,* 1974 Sup.Ct. Rev. 1, 21: "Ely accepts the legitimacy of comparing the costs of discriminating against the members of a racial or ethnic minority with the benefits from thereby avoiding the need to make individual distinctions. He only wants assurance that the balance will be accurately struck. [His] suspicion only warrants that the reviewing court satisfy itself that the legislature has in fact assessed the costs and benefits of the discrimination accurately. Suppose the Post Office were able to demonstrate convincingly that blacks had, on average, inferior aptitudes to whites for supervisory positions, that the costs to the postal system of inadequate supervisors were very great, and that the costs of conducting the inquiries necessary to ascertain whether an individual black had the requisite aptitudes were also great in relation to the probability of discovering qualified blacks. It would seem to follow from Ely's analysis that the Post Office could adopt a rule barring blacks from supervisory positions. By condemning only inefficient discriminations, Ely reduces the scope of the Equal Protection Clause to triviality * * *."

---

43. The analysis suggested in the text probably should be limited to situations where most of the "we"s have always been, and expect to remain "we"s, and will therefore have difficulty being objective about precisely what the difference entails. Classifications based on youth or age should therefore be excluded from the suspicious category. * * *

f. Might the optician-optometrist case be characterized as a "we" (consumers)—"they" (optical suppliers) generalization? Is this par-

ticularly true when *all* sellers of a particular product are subjected to legislative regulation? Is a legislatively (judicially) promulgated lawyer-client privilege "suspect" because most legislators (judges) are lawyers? Cf. *Ferguson v. Skrupa,* fn. 5 in *New Orleans v. Dukes,* Sec. 1 supra. A salary raise for legislators? What about discriminations against "conscientious objectors"? See *Johnson v. Robison,* 415 U.S. 361, 375 n. 14, 94 S.Ct. 1160, 39 L.Ed.2d 301 (1974).

3. *Poverty.* (a) Although the Warren Court had *stated* on several occasions that "lines drawn on the basis of wealth or property" "render a classification highly suspect," [a] the Burger Court observed in 1973 that the Court had "never held that wealth discrimination alone provides an adequate basis for invoking strict scrutiny," [b] and, in 1980, *Harris v. McRae,* p. 182 supra, said that "this Court has held repeatedly that poverty, standing alone, is not a suspect classification. See, e.g. *James v. Valtierra* [infra]." In fact, explicit (or "de jure") government discriminations against poor people are rare. The more common problems concerning poverty and equal protection (considered in Sec. 4, III infra) arise from "de facto" discriminations—e.g., when the state requires payment for certain privileges or benefits (such as a poll tax for voting or a charge for a trial transcript needed to appeal a criminal conviction).[c]

(b) JAMES v. VALTIERRA, 402 U.S. 137, 91 S.Ct. 1331, 28 L.Ed.2d 678 (1971), per BLACK, J., upheld Art. 34 of the California constitution that no low-income public housing project could be developed unless approved by referendum in the locality: "Provisions for referendums demonstrate devotion to democracy, not to bias, discrimination, or prejudice." "California law reveals that persons advocating low-income housing have not been singled out for mandatory referendums [which] are required for approval of state constitutional amendments, for the issuance of general obligation long-term bonds by local governments, and for certain municipal territorial annexations." [d]

MARSHALL, J., joined by Brennan and Blackmun, JJ., dissented,[e] noting that under California law, "publicly assisted housing developments designed to accommodate the aged, veterans, state employees, persons of moderate income, or any class of citizens other than the poor, need not be approved by prior referenda. [Art. 34 is] an explicit classification on the basis of poverty—a suspect classification which demands exacting judicial scrutiny."

(c) Should explicit discriminations against poor people be held "suspect"? Consider Michelman, *On Protecting the Poor Through the Fourteenth Amendment,* 83 Harv.L.Rev. 7, 21 (1969): "[I]f money is power, then a class deliberately defined so as to include everyone who has less wealth or income than any person outside it may certainly be deemed [to] be especially susceptible to abuse by majoritarian process; and classification of 'the poor' as such, may, like classification of racial minorities as such, be popularly understood as a badge of inferiority. Especially is this so in light of the extreme difficulty of imagining proper governmental objectives which require for their achievement the explicit carving out, for relatively disadvantageous treatment, of a class defined by relative paucity of wealth or income." [f] Compare Winter, *Poverty, Economic Equality, and the Equal Protection Clause,* 1972 Sup.Ct.Rev. 41, 97–98: "Race is [the] basis of a stereotype which served as a systematic vehicle of governmental discrimination. Moreover, it is not a stereotype with a pretense at being related to

---

a. *Harper v. Virginia Bd. of Elections* and *McDonald v. Board of Elec. Comm'rs,* Sec. 4, I, B infra.

b. *San Antonio Ind. School Dist. v. Rodriguez,* Sec. 4, IV infra.

c. Such requirements do not automatically exclude poor people (as would a de jure provision that no poor person may vote or appeal a conviction) but their effect seriously disadvantages people with limited funds.

d. If a statute forbade all minors, teachers, lawyers and blacks from serving on juries,

would the statute explicitly discriminate against blacks and thus be "suspect"? See *Hunter v. Erickson,* Sec. 2, V supra.

e. Douglas, J., did not participate.

f. What result if the state were to make it a crime for a person without visible means of support to refuse employment? Bar welfare recipients from public housing because of the risk of rental nonpayment? May the state require welfare recipients to accept "suitable employment"? Job training? To disclose certain intimate personal details?

individual merit, even though it [is] unalterable by the individual. [But] poverty is not absolutely unalterable for all those afflicted by it. The history of this nation is a history of virtually all of its people bettering themselves [economically].[g] Beyond that, [t]here simply has not been any legislation invoking a poverty classification even remotely resembling the widespread, official, racial segregation of schools and other facilities. To the contrary, there is an enormous amount of legislation [to] help the poor. [Finally], to the extent low income is related to low productivity—and it is to a large extent—poverty is not entirely unrelated to individual merit. One need not adopt productivity as the sole criterion of merit to say that poverty resulting from low productivity is far different from legal exclusion from public facilities because of one's race."

II. ALIENAGE

Up to the late 1940s, the Court found a "special public interest"[a] in rejecting almost all challenges to state discriminations against aliens respecting such activities as land ownership, *Terrace v. Thompson,* 263 U.S. 197, 44 S.Ct. 15, 68 L.Ed. 255 (1923); killing wild game, *Patsone v. Pennsylvania,* 232 U.S. 138, 34 S.Ct. 281, 58 L.Ed. 539 (1914); operating poolhalls, *Clarke v. Deckebach,* 274 U.S. 392, 47 S.Ct. 630, 71 L.Ed. 1115 (1927); and working on public construction projects, *Crane v. New York,* 239 U.S. 195, 36 S.Ct. 85, 60 L.Ed. 218 (1915).[b] But *Takahashi v. Fish & Game Comm'n,* 334 U.S. 410, 68 S.Ct. 1138, 92 L.Ed. 1478 (1948), relying on both Congress' "broad constitutional powers in determining what aliens shall be admitted to the United States" and the fourteenth amendment's "general policy" of "equality," invalidated California's denial of licenses for commercial fishing in coastal waters to aliens lawfully residing in the state.[c] Finally, *Graham v. Richardson,* 403 U.S. 365, 91 S.Ct. 1848, 29 L.Ed.2d 534 (1971), reasoning that "aliens as a class are a prime example of a 'discrete and insular minority'" and ruling that "classifications based on alienage [are] inherently suspect and subject to close judicial scrutiny," held that state laws denying welfare benefits to aliens violate equal protection.

g. See also 85 Harv.L.Rev. 129 (1972): "The poor seem to be a less cohesive and less readily identifiable group than are racial minorities. Because the class of 'poor' is constantly in flux, the reinforced sense of stigma which characterizes de jure racial classifications is probably mitigated even where explicit wealth classifications are concerned."

Compare Clune, *The Supreme Court's Treatment of Wealth Discriminations Under the Fourteenth Amendment,* 1975 Sup.Ct.Rev. 289, 329–30: "[Poverty] is one of the most startlingly stable social phenomena (the strata of personal income have remained in uncannily stable ratios to each other for decades); it seems totally immune to political attack or even war; the disabilities and abilities associated with wealth are pervasive and among the most highly important on our scale of values.

[Whether] or not some individuals escape is insignificant compared to those who do not. If the non-escapees are vulnerable and weak economically, socially, and politically, their situation is identical to another class whose individual members are less able to escape."

a. *Truax v. Raich,* 239 U.S. 33, 36 S.Ct. 7, 60 L.Ed. 131 (1915).

b. *Truax,* however, invalidated Arizona's forbidding employers of five or more persons from hiring over 20% aliens.

c. See also *Oyama v. California,* 332 U.S. 633, 68 S.Ct. 269, 92 L.Ed. 249 (1948) (statutory presumption—that land conveyed to citizen, but paid for by alien ineligible to own land, was held for the benefit of the alien—violates equal protection).

BERNAL v. FAINTER

467 U.S. 216, 104 S.Ct. 2312, 81 L.Ed.2d 175 (1984).

JUSTICE MARSHALL delivered the opinion of the Court. * * *

Petitioner, a native of Mexico, is a resident alien who has lived in the United States since 1961. He works as a paralegal for Texas Rural Legal Aid, Inc., helping migrant farm workers on employment and civil rights matters. In order to administer oaths to these workers and to notarize their statements for use in civil litigation, petitioner applied in 1978 to become a notary public. [The] Texas Secretary of State denied petitioner's application because he failed to satisfy the statutory requirement that a notary public be a citizen of the United States. Tex.Civ.Stat.Ann., Art. 5949(2). * * *

As a general matter, a State law that discriminates on the basis of alienage [must] advance a compelling State interest by the least restrictive means available. Applying this principle, we have invalidated an array of State statutes that denied aliens the right to pursue various occupations. In *Sugarman v. Dougall*, 413 U.S. 634, 93 S.Ct. 2842, 37 L.Ed.2d 853 (1973), we struck down a State statute barring aliens from employment in permanent positions in the competitive class of the State civil service. In *In re Griffiths*, 413 U.S. 717, 93 S.Ct. 2851, 37 L.Ed.2d 910 (1973), we nullified a State law excluding aliens from eligibility for membership in the State bar. And in *Examining Bd. v. de Otero*, 426 U.S. 572, 96 S.Ct. 2264, 49 L.Ed.2d 65 (1976), we voided a State law that excluded aliens from the practice of civil engineering.[a]

We have, however, developed a narrow exception to the rule that discrimination based on alienage triggers strict scrutiny. This exception has been labelled the "political function" exception and applies [the "rational basis" standard] to laws that exclude aliens from positions intimately related to the process of democratic self-government. [In] *Foley v. Connelie*, 435 U.S. 291, 98 S.Ct. 1067, 55 L.Ed.2d 287 (1978), we held that a State may require police to be citizens because, in performing a fundamental obligation of government, police "are clothed with authority to exercise an almost infinite variety of discretionary powers" often involving the most sensitive areas of daily life.[b] In *Ambach v. Norwick*, 441 U.S. 68, 99 S.Ct. 1589, 60 L.Ed.2d 49 (1979), we held that a State may bar aliens who have not declared their intent to become citizens from teaching in the public schools because teachers, like police, possess a high degree of responsibility and discretion in the fulfillment of a basic governmental obligation. They have direct, day-to-day contact with students, exercise unsupervised discretion over them, act as role models and influence their students about the government and the political process.[c] Finally, in *Cabell v. Chavez-*

---

a. *Nyquist v. Mauclet*, 432 U.S. 1, 97 S.Ct. 2120, 53 L.Ed.2d 63 (1977), invalidated a state law that denied aliens state financial aid for higher education. Burger, C.J., one of the four dissenters (see note 1 infra), argued that "the prior cases [invalidated] statutes which prohibited aliens from engaging in certain occupations or professions, thereby impairing their ability to earn a livelihood. [The] only other case striking down a classification on the basis of alienage, *Graham*, involved the denial of *welfare* benefits essential to sustain [life.] In] my view, [w]here a fundamental personal interest is not at stake—and higher education is hardly that—the State must be free to exercise its largesse in any reasonable manner."

b. Marshall, J., joined by Brennan and Stevens, JJ., dissented.

c. Blackmun, J., joined by Brennan, Marshall and Stevens, JJ., dissented. They found it "impossible to differentiate" *Griffiths;* and pointed out that both litigants (from England and Finland) had been in the United States more than twelve years, graduated from American colleges, were married to U.S. citizens, and were willing to swear to support the U.S. and state constitutions.

Salido, 454 U.S. 432, 102 S.Ct. 735, 70 L.Ed.2d 677 (1982), we held that a State may bar aliens from positions as probation officers because they, like police and teachers, routinely exercise discretionary power, involving a basic governmental function, that places them in a position of direct authority over other individuals.[d]

The rationale behind the political function exception is that within broad boundaries a State may establish its own form of government and limit the right to govern to those who are full-fledged members of the political community.[e]

* * *

To determine whether a restriction based on alienage fits within the narrow political function exception, we devised in *Cabell* a two-part test. "First, [a] classification that is substantially overinclusive or underinclusive tends to undercut the governmental claim that the classification serves legitimate political [ends.] Second, even if the classification is sufficiently tailored, it may be applied in the particular case only to 'persons holding state elective or important nonelective executive, legislative, and judicial positions,' those officers who 'participate directly in the formulation, execution, or review of broad public policy' and hence 'perform functions that go right to the heart of representative government.'"[7] [Unlike] the statute invalidated in *Sugarman,* Article 5949(2) does not indiscriminately sweep within its ambit a wide range of offices and [occupations]. Less clear is whether Article 5942(2) is fatally underinclusive. Texas does not require court reporters to be United States citizens even though they perform some of the same services as notaries. Nor does Texas require that its Secretary of State be a citizen, even though he holds the highest appointive position in the State and performs many important functions, including supervision of the licensing of all notaries public. We need not decide this issue, however, because of our decision with respect to the second prong of the *Cabell* test. * * *

The State maintains that [the] duties of Texas notaries entail the performance of functions sufficiently consequential to be deemed "political." The Court of Appeals ably articulated this argument: "With the power to acknowledge instruments such as wills and deeds and leases and mortgages; to take out-of-court depositions; to administer oaths; and the discretion to refuse to perform any of the foregoing acts, notaries public in Texas are involved in countless matters of importance to the day-to-day functioning of state government. [Land] titles and property succession depend upon the care and integrity of the notary public, as well as the familiarity of the notary with the community, to verify the authenticity of the execution of the documents." [But] a notary's duties, important as they are, hardly implicate responsibilities that go to the heart of representative government. Rather, these duties are essentially clerical and ministerial. [To] be sure, considerable damage could result from the negligent or dishonest performance of a notary's duties. But the same could be said for the duties performed by cashiers, building inspectors, the janitors who clean up the offices of public officials, and numerous other categories of personnel upon whom

---

d. Blackmun, J., joined by Brennan, Marshall and Stevens, JJ., dissented.

e. See also *Skafte v. Rorex,* 191 Colo. 399, 553 P.2d 830 (1976), appeal dismissed 430 U.S. 961, 97 S.Ct. 1638, 52 L.Ed.2d 352 (1977) (denial of vote to aliens); *Perkins v. Smith,* 370 F.Supp. 134 (D.Md.1974), affirmed 426 U.S. 913, 96 S.Ct. 2616, 49 L.Ed.2d 368 (1976) (exclusion of aliens from juries).

7. We emphasize, as we have in the past, that the political-function exception must be narrowly construed; otherwise the exception will swallow the rule and depreciate the significance that should attach to the designation of a group as a "discrete and insular" minority for whom heightened judicial solicitude is appropriate.

we depend for careful, honest service. What distinguishes such personnel from those to which the political function exception is properly applied is that the latter are either invested with policy-making responsibility or broad discretion in the execution of public policy that requires the routine exercise of authority over individuals. Neither of these characteristics pertain to the functions performed by Texas notaries.

[If] it is improper to apply the political function exception to a citizenship requirement governing eligibility for membership in a State bar, [*Griffiths,*] it would be anomalous to apply the exception to the citizenship requirement that governs eligibility to become a Texas notary. We conclude, then, that the "political function" exception is inapplicable to Article 5949(2) and that the statute is therefore subject to strict judicial scrutiny [and violates equal protection].

JUSTICE REHNQUIST, dissenting.

I dissent for the reasons stated in my dissenting opinion in *Sugarman* [see note 1 infra].

Notes and Questions

1. *Alienage as a "suspect" classification.* Compare REHNQUIST, J., dissenting in *Sugarman* and *Griffiths:* "[T]here is no language [in the fourteenth amendment] nor any historical evidence as to the intent of the Framers, which would suggest to the slightest degree that it was intended to render alienage a 'suspect' classification, that it was designed in any way to protect 'discrete and insular minorities' other than racial minorities * * *.[f]

"Not only do the numerous classifications on the basis of citizenship that are set forth in the Constitution curb against [these] cases; the very Amendment which the Court reads to prohibit classifications based on citizenship establishes [in § 1] the very distinction which the Court now condemns as 'suspect.' [Decisions] holding that an alien is a 'person' within the meaning of the Equal Protection Clause [are] irrelevant to the question of whether [the] Amendment prohibits legislative classifications based upon this particular status. Since that Amendment by its own terms first defined those who had the status as a lesser included class of all 'persons,' the Court's failure to articulate why such classifications under the same Amendment are now forbidden serves only to illuminate the absence of any constitutional foundation for [these] decisions."

In *Mauclet,* the statute (as in *Ambach*) applied only to aliens who declined to affirm their intent to apply for citizenship when eligible. REHNQUIST, J., joined by Burger, C.J., dissented: "[I]t is no doubt true that all aliens are, at some time, members of a discrete and insular minority in that they are identified by a status which they are powerless to change until eligible to become citizens of this country. [Since the statute] does *not* create a discrete and insular minority by placing an inevitable disability based on status, the Court's heightened judicial scrutiny is unwarranted."[g] The Court, per BLACKMUN, J., responded: "By the logic of the dissenting opinion, the suspect class for alienage would be defined to include at most only those who have resided in this country for less than five years, since after that time, if not before, resident aliens are generally

---

f. See also Rehnquist, J.'s views re "discrete and insular minorities" in note 3(a) after *New Orleans v. Dukes,* Sec. 1 supra.

g. Powell, J., joined by Burger, C.J., and Stewart, J., also dissented, "for the reasons set forth in Mr. Justice Rehnquist's dissent, that New York's scheme of financial assistance in higher education does not discriminate against a suspect class."

eligible to become citizens. 8 U.S.C. § 1427(a). The Court has never suggested, however, that the suspect class is to be defined so narrowly."

2. *The role of the supremacy clause. Graham* also held that "an additional reason why the state statutes [in] these cases do not withstand constitutional scrutiny emerges from the area of federal-state relations. [State] laws that restrict the eligibility of aliens for [welfare] conflict [with] overriding national policies in an area constitutionally entrusted to the Federal Government. [In] *Takahashi* it was said that the States 'can neither add to nor take from the conditions lawfully imposed by Congress upon admission, naturalization and residence of aliens in the United States or the several states.'"

TOLL v. MORENO, 458 U.S. 1, 102 S.Ct. 2977, 73 L.Ed.2d 563 (1982), per BRENNAN, J., held that a University of Maryland rule—flatly denying "in-state" tuition to nonimmigrant aliens with G–4 visas (issued to employees of certain international organizations and their immediate families)—violates the supremacy clause. The Court observed that "commentators have noted [that] many of the Court's decisions concerning alienage classifications, such as *Takahashi,* are better explained in preemption than equal protection terms. See, e.g., Perry, *Modern Equal Protection: A Conceptualization and Appraisal,* 79 Colum.L.Rev. 1023, 1060–65 (1979). [Read] together, *Takahashi* and *Graham* stand for the broad principle [17] that 'state regulation not congressionally sanctioned that discriminates against aliens lawfully admitted to the country is impermissible if it imposes additional burdens not contemplated by Congress.' To be sure, when Congress has done nothing more than permit a class of aliens to enter the country temporarily, the proper application of the principle is likely to be a matter of some dispute. But [in] light of Congress' explicit decision not to bar G–4 aliens from acquiring domicile, [the Maryland rule] surely amounts to an ancillary 'burden not contemplated by Congress.' [Further, as] a result of an array of treaties, international agreements, and federal statutes, G–4 visa holders employed by [various international organizations] are relieved of federal, and in many instances, state and local taxes, on the salaries paid by the organizations. [The Maryland rule] frustrates these federal policies." [h]

REHNQUIST, J., joined by Burger, C.J., dissented: "[T]hat a state statute can be said to discriminate against aliens does not, standing alone, demonstrate that the statute is preempted. [A] state law is invalid only if there is 'such actual conflict between the two schemes of regulation that both cannot stand in the same area,' or if Congress has in some other way unambiguously declared its intention to foreclose the state law in question. [The] Court offers no evidence that Congress' intent in permitting respondents to establish 'domicile in the United States' has any bearing at all on the tuition available to them at state universities." As for tax relief, "First, the Federal Government has not barred the States from collecting taxes from many, if not most, G–4 visa holders. Second, as to those G–4 nonimmigrants who *are* immune from state income taxes by treaty, Maryland's tuition policy cannot fairly be said to conflict with those treaties in a manner requiring its preemption." [i]

---

17. Our cases do recognize, however, that a State, in the course of defining its political community, may, in appropriate circumstances, limit the participation of noncitizens in the States' political and governmental functions. See, e.g., *Cabell; Ambach; Foley; Sugarman.*

h. Blackmun, J., who joined the Court's opinion, concurred, vehemently denying the suggestion in Rehnquist, J.'s dissent that "decisions holding resident aliens to be a 'suspect class' no longer are good law."

i. O'Connor, J., concurred in part and dissented in part: "I conclude that the Supremacy Clause does not prohibit the University from charging out-of-state tuition to those G–4 aliens who are exempted by federal law from federal taxes only." See Choper, *Discrimina-*

3. *"Political function" exception.* Is the Court's principle—that distinguishes excluding aliens from "the process of self-government" and discriminating against aliens generally—persuasive? Is the Court's application of this principle in the cases persuasive? Consider Note, *A Dual Standard for State Discrimination Against Aliens,* 92 Harv.L.Rev. 1516, 1531–33 (1979): "Some dual standard [appears] fundamentally consistent with general equal protection doctrine interpreted in light of distinctions the Constitution makes on the basis of citizenship. [But despite *Foley's*] attempt to draw an analogy to exclusion of aliens from voting and holding high office, the existence of those exclusions only underscores the need for close review of other measures disadvantaging aliens. [Since] aliens are politically powerless because of their disenfranchisement and disqualification from high office, [the] political decision to bar aliens from the police should be stringently scrutinized." Compare Rosberg, *Aliens and Equal Protection: Why Not the Right to Vote?* 75 Mich.L.Rev. 1092, 1106 (1977): "[E]xcluding [aliens] from the political process clearly requires the strictest review of all, for it is the very fact of exclusion that made the classification suspect and necessitated strict scrutiny in the first place. Put another way, the invalidation of a statute that excludes the members of a suspect class from participation in the political process is itself a way of eliminating [the] need for strict scrutiny. [Over] time the members of the class will develop the ability to protect their own interests in the legislative process, and the need for extraordinary judicial protection will then disappear."

4. *Federal discrimination.* (a) It has long been held that the national government has power "to exclude aliens altogether from the United States, or to prescribe the terms and conditions upon which they may come to this country." *Sing v. United States,* 158 U.S. 538, 15 S.Ct. 967, 39 L.Ed. 1082 (1895). Thus, MATHEWS v. DIAZ, 426 U.S. 67, 96 S.Ct. 1883, 48 L.Ed.2d 478 (1976), per STEVENS, J., upheld a federal statute denying Medicare benefits to aliens unless they have (1) been admitted for permanent residence and (2) resided for at least five years in the United States: Although "aliens and citizens alike, are protected by the Due Process Clause, [i]n the exercise of its broad power over naturalization and immigration, Congress regularly makes rules that would be unacceptable if applied to citizens.

"[T]he responsibility for regulating the relationship between the United States and [aliens] has been committed to the political branches of the Federal Government. Since decisions in these matters may implicate our relations with foreign powers, and since a wide variety of classifications must be defined in the light of changing political and economic circumstances, such decisions are frequently of a character more appropriate to either the Legislature or the Executive than to the Judiciary. [The] reasons that preclude judicial review of political questions also dictate a narrow standard of review of decisions made by the Congress or the President in the area of immigration and naturalization.

"Since it is obvious that Congress has no constitutional duty to provide *all aliens* with the welfare benefits provided to citizens, the party challenging the constitutionality of the particular line Congress has drawn"—"allowing benefits to some aliens but not to others"—"has the burden of advancing principled

tion *Against Aliens,* in Choper, Kamisar & Tribe, *The Supreme Court: Trends and Developments 1981–82* 14–21 (1983) for the view that (1) *Toll's* use of the supremacy clause was a "salutory development," but that (2) "the Court's major difficulty resulted from its going beyond its 'broad principle' and getting into

the gory details of whether the Maryland regulation actually came into some direct conflict with congressional policy"; "Rehnquist, J.'s argument was fairly strong once you accept *his* premise" of what is required for preemption.

reasoning that will at once invalidate that line and yet tolerate a different line separating some aliens from others. [Since neither of the two requirements] is wholly irrational, this case essentially involves nothing more than a claim that it would have been more reasonable for Congress to select somewhat different requirements of the same kind. [But] it remains true that some line is essential, that any line must produce some harsh and apparently arbitrary consequences, and, of greatest importance, that those who qualify under the test Congress has chosen may reasonably be presumed to have a greater affinity to the United States than those who do not."

Consider Rosberg, *The Protection of Aliens From Discriminatory Treatment By the National Government*, 1977 Sup.Ct.Rev. 275, 336–38: "[*Diaz*] refused to acknowledge the tension between two basic facts: first, the reasons for treating alienage as a suspect classification apply as forcefully to the federal government as to the states, and second, the power to determine the standards for admission of aliens must inevitably give rise to some power to regulate what aliens can and cannot do in this country. [A] condition subsequent on entry is very different from a condition precedent precisely because its impact is felt by residents of the United States, to whom the government has an obligation of fair dealing [in] compliance with the standards of the Constitution. [The Court's] repeated insistence that Congress has plenary power to act against aliens in any way it wants must be seen as an invitation to Congress to act capriciously and without significant concern for the legitimate interests of resident aliens."

(b) HAMPTON v. WONG, 426 U.S. 88, 96 S.Ct. 1895, 48 L.Ed.2d 495 (1976), per STEVENS, J., held that a federal Civil Service Commission regulation, generally barring resident aliens from civil service employment, denied "liberty without due process of law": "[T]he federal power over aliens is [not] so plenary that any agent of the National Government may arbitrarily subject all resident aliens to different substantive rules than those applied to citizens. * * *

"The rule [has] its impact on an identifiable class of persons who [are] already subject to disadvantages not shared by the remainder of the community. [The] added disadvantage resulting [from] ineligibility for employment in a major sector of the economy [is] of sufficient significance to be characterized as a deprivation of an interest in liberty. [It] follows that some judicial scrutiny of the deprivation is mandated by the Constitution. * * *

"When the Federal Government asserts an overriding national interest as justification for a discriminatory rule which would violate the Equal Protection Clause if adopted by a State, due process requires that there be a legitimate basis for presuming that the rule was actually intended to serve that interest.[a] If the agency which promulgates the rule has direct responsibility for fostering or protecting that interest, it may reasonably be presumed that the asserted interest was the actual predicate for the rule. [Or], if the rule were expressly mandated by the Congress or the President, we might presume that any interest which might rationally be served by the rule did in fact give rise to its adoption.

"[We] may assume [that] if the Congress or the President had expressly imposed the citizenship requirement, it would be justified by the national interest in providing an incentive for aliens to become naturalized, or possibly even as providing the President with an expendable token for treaty negotiating purposes; but we are not willing to presume that the Chairman of [CSC] was deliberately fostering an interest so far removed from his normal responsibilities."

a. See fn. a, p. 796 supra.

The Court reviewed the history of the regulation dating to 1884, concluding that it "cannot fairly be construed to evidence either congressional [or presidential] approval or disapproval of the [rule].[46] [Thus,] our inquiry is whether the national interests which the Government identifies as justifications for the Commission rule are interests on which that agency may properly rely in making a decision implicating the constitutional and social values at stake in this litigation. * * *

"The only concern of [the] Commission is the promotion of an efficient federal service. In general it is fair to assume that its goal would be best served by removing unnecessary restrictions on the eligibility of qualified applicants for employment. With only one exception, the interests [put] forth as supporting the Commission regulation at issue in this case are not matters which are properly the business of the Commission. That one exception is the administrative desirability of having one simple rule excluding all noncitizens when it is manifest that citizenship is an appropriate and legitimate requirement for some important and sensitive positions. Arguably, therefore, administrative convenience may provide a rational basis for the general rule.

"[But there] is nothing [to] indicate that the Commission actually made any considered evaluation of the relative desirability of a simple exclusionary rule on the one hand, or the value to the service of enlarging the pool of eligible employees on the other. [Of] greater significance, however, is the quality of the interest at stake. Any fair balancing of the public interest in avoiding the wholesale deprivation of employment opportunities caused by the Commission's indiscriminate policy, as opposed to what may be nothing more than a hypothetical justification, requires rejection of the argument of administrative convenience in this case." [b]

REHNQUIST, J., joined by Burger, C.J., and White and Blackmun, JJ., dissented: "The Court's opinion enunciates a novel conception of the procedural due process guaranteed by the Fifth Amendment, and from this concept proceeds to evolve a doctrine of delegation of legislative authority which seems to me to be quite contrary to the doctrine established by a long [line of] decisions. * * *

"[T]he exclusive power of Congress to prescribe the terms and conditions of entry includes the power to regulate aliens in various ways once they are here. [This] broad congressional power is in some respects subject to procedural limitations imposed by the Due Process Clause of the Fifth Amendment. If an alien * * * lawfully obtains tenured government employment, and is thereby protected against discharge except for cause, he is entitled to a hearing before being discharged. *Arnett v. Kennedy,* [p. 263 supra]. But neither an alien nor a citizen has any protected liberty interests in obtaining federal employment.

"[U]nder the traditional standards governing the delegation of authority the CSC was fully empowered to act in the manner in which it did in this case. [Once] it is determined that [CSC] was properly delegated the power by Congress to make decisions regarding citizenship of prospective civil servants, then the

46. Even if this conclusion were doubtful, in view of the consequences of the rule it would be appropriate to require a much more explicit directive from either Congress or the President * * *.

b. Brennan, J., joined by Marshall, J., joined the Court's opinion "understanding that there are reserved the equal protection questions that would be raised by congression-

al or Presidential enactment of a bar on employment of aliens by the Federal Government."

President Ford subsequently issued such an executive order. Valid? See *Vergara v. Hampton,* 581 F.2d 1281 (7th Cir.1978), cert. denied, 441 U.S. 905 (1979); *Jalil v. Campbell,* 590 F.2d 1120 (D.C.Cir.1978).

reasons for which that power was exercised are as foreclosed from judicial scrutiny as if Congress had made the decision itself. The fact that Congress has delegated a power does not provide a back door through which to attack a policy which would otherwise have been immune from attack."

III. ILLEGITIMACY

MATHEWS v. LUCAS

427 U.S. 495, 96 S.Ct. 2755, 49 L.Ed.2d 651 (1976).

Mr. Justice Blackmun delivered the opinion of the Court.

[The Social Security Act provides survivor's benefits to children who are "dependent" on the deceased parent at time of death; legitimate children and some classes of illegitimate children are statutorily presumed to be dependent; other illegitimate children must prove "that the deceased wage earner was the claimant child's parent and at the time of his death, was living with the child or was contributing to his support." Appellees, illegitimate children, proved that the deceased was their father but "failed to demonstrate their dependency by proof that [he] either lived with them or was contributing to their support at the time of his death, or by any of the statutory presumptions of dependency." Appellees "urged that denial of benefits in this case, where paternity was clear, violated the Fifth Amendment's Due Process Clause, as that provision comprehends the principle of equal protection of the laws, because other children, including all legitimate children, are statutorily entitled, as the Lucas children are not, to survivorship benefits regardless of actual dependency."]

[T]he District Court concluded [that] legislation treating legitimate and illegitimate offspring differently is constitutionally suspect * * *. We disagree.

It is true, of course, that the legal status of illegitimacy, however defined, is, like race or national origin, a characteristic determined by causes not within the control of the illegitimate individual, and it bears no relation to the individual's ability to participate in and contribute to society. The Court recognized in *Weber v. Aetna Casualty & Surety Co.*, 406 U.S. 164, 92 S.Ct. 1400, 31 L.Ed.2d 768 (1972), that visiting condemnation upon the child in order to express society's disapproval of the parents' liaisons "is illogical and unjust. Moreover, imposing disabilities on the illegitimate child is contrary to the basic concept of our system that legal burdens should bear some relationship to individual responsibility or wrongdoing. Obviously, no child is responsible for his birth and penalizing the illegitimate child is an ineffectual—as well as an unjust—way of deterring the parent." But where the law is arbitrary in such a way, we have had no difficulty in finding the discrimination impermissible on less demanding standards than those advocated here. *Levy v. Louisiana,* 391 U.S. 68, 88 S.Ct. 1509, 20 L.Ed.2d 436 (1968).[a] And such irrationality in some classifications does not in itself demonstrate that other, possibly rational, distinctions made in part on the basis of legitimacy are inherently untenable. Moreover, while the law has long placed the illegitimate child in an inferior position relative to the legitimate in certain circumstances, particularly in regard to obligations of support or other aspects of family law, see generally, e.g., Krause, *Illegitimacy: Law and Social*

---

a. *Levy,* per Douglas, J., involved a statute denying illegitimate children the right to recover for the wrongful death of their mother: "[The test] is whether the line drawn is a rational one [but] we have been extremely sensitive when it comes to basic civil rights and have not hesitated to strike down an invidious classification even though it had history and tradition on its side." Harlan, joined by Black and Stewart, JJ., dissented.

Policy 21–42 (1971); Gray & Rudovsky, *The Court Acknowledges the Illegitimate*, 118 U.Pa.L.Rev. 1, 19–38 (1969), perhaps in part because the roots of the discrimination rest in the conduct of the parents rather than the child, and perhaps in part because illegitimacy does not carry an obvious badge, as race or sex do, this discrimination against illegitimates has never approached the severity or pervasiveness of the historic legal and political discrimination against women and Negroes.

We therefore adhere to our earlier view, see *Labine v. Vincent*, 401 U.S. 532, 91 S.Ct. 1017, 28 L.Ed.2d 288 (1971),[b] that the Act's discrimination between individuals on the basis of their legitimacy does not "command extraordinary protection from the majoritarian political process," which our most exacting scrutiny would entail.

Relying on *Weber*,[c] the Court, in *Gomez v. Perez*, 409 U.S. 535, 538, 93 S.Ct. 872, 875, 35 L.Ed.2d 56 (1973), held that "once a State posits a judicially enforceable right on behalf of children to needed support from their natural fathers there is no constitutionally sufficient justification for denying such an essential right to a child simply because its natural father has not married its mother." [d]   The same principle, which we adhere to now, applies when the judicially enforceable right to needed support lies against the Government rather than a natural father. See *New Jersey Welfare Rights Org. v. Cahill*, 411 U.S. 619, 93 S.Ct. 1700, 36 L.Ed.2d 543 (1973).[e] *   *   *

Congress' purpose in adopting [the] presumptions of dependency was obviously to serve administrative convenience. While Congress was unwilling to assume that every child of a deceased insured was dependent at the time of death, by presuming dependency on the basis of relatively readily documented facts, such as legitimate birth, or existence of a support order or paternity decree, which could be relied upon to indicate the likelihood of continued actual dependency, Congress was able to avoid the burden and expense of specific case-by-case determination in the large number of cases where dependency is objectively probable. Such presumptions in aid of administrative functions, though they may approximate, rather than precisely mirror, the results that case-by-case adjudication would show, are permissible under the Fifth Amendment, so long as that lack of precise equivalence does not exceed the bounds of substantiality tolerated by the applicable level of scrutiny.

In cases of strictest scrutiny, such approximations must be supported at least by a showing that the Government's dollar "lost" to overincluded benefit recipients is returned by a dollar "saved" in administrative expense avoided. Under the standard of review appropriate here, however, the materiality of the relation between the statutory classifications and the likelihood of dependency

---

b. *Labine*, per Black, J., upheld a law denying an illegitimate child the same rights as a legitimate child in inheriting from its father who dies intestate even though the father had publicly acknowledged the illegitimate child. Brennan, J., joined by Douglas, White and Marshall, JJ., dissented, finding "no rational basis" for the law.

c. *Weber*, per Powell, J., invalidated a law denying dependent, unacknowledged, illegitimate children recovery of workmen's compensation for the death of their father—finding the discrimination "justified by no legitimate state interest, compelling or otherwise." Blackmun, J., concurred on the ground that,

unlike *Labine*, the decedent in *Weber* was unable, under state law, to qualify the child for benefits. Rehnquist, J., dissented on the ground that equal protection "requires neither that state enactments be 'logical' [nor] 'just' in the common meaning of those terms. It requires only that there be some conceivable set of facts which may justify the classification."

d. Stewart and Rehnquist, JJ., dissented on procedural grounds.

e. *Cahill* invalidated a law denying welfare to households with illegitimate children. Rehnquist, J., dissented.

they assertedly reflect need not be "scientifically substantiated." Nor, in any case, do we believe that Congress is required in this realm of less than strictest scrutiny to weigh the burdens of administrative inquiry solely in terms of dollars ultimately "spent," ignoring the relative amounts devoted to administrative rather than welfare uses. Finally, while the scrutiny by which their showing is to be judged is not a toothless one, the burden remains upon the appellees to demonstrate the insubstantiality of that relation.

Applying these principles, we think that the statutory classifications challenged here are justified as reasonable empirical judgments that are consistent with a design to qualify entitlement to benefits upon a child's dependency at the time of the parent's death. [It] could not have been fairly argued, with respect to any of the statutes struck down in [*Cahill, Gomez, Weber* and *Levy*], that the legitimacy of the child was simply taken as an indication of dependency, or of some other valid ground of qualification. Under all but one of the statutes, not only was the legitimate child automatically entitled to benefits, but an illegitimate child was denied benefits solely and finally on the basis of illegitimacy, and regardless of any demonstration of dependency or other legitimate factor. In *Weber,* the sole partial exception, the statutory scheme provided for a child's equal recovery under a workmen's compensation plan in the event of the death of the father, not only if the child was dependent, but *also* only if the dependent child was legitimate. *Jimenez v. Weinberger,* 417 U.S. 628, 94 S.Ct. 2496, 41 L.Ed.2d 363 (1974), invalidating discrimination among afterborn illegitimate children as to entitlement to a child's disability benefits under the Social Security Act, is similarly distinguishable. Under the somewhat related statutory matrix considered there, [some illegitimate] afterborn children were conclusively denied any benefits, regardless of any showing of dependency. [T]his conclusiveness [is] absent here, for, as we have noted, any otherwise eligible child may qualify for survivorship benefits by showing contribution to support or cohabitation, at the time of death. [Here], the statute does not broadly discriminate between legitimates and illegitimates without more, but is carefully tuned to alternative considerations.[f] The presumption of dependency is withheld only in the absence of any significant indication of the likelihood of actual dependency. * * *

To be sure, none of [the] statutory criteria compels the extension of a presumption of dependency. But the constitutional question is not whether such a presumption is required, but whether it is permitted. [These] matters of practical judgment and empirical calculation are for Congress. [Our] role is simply to determine whether Congress' assumptions are so inconsistent or insubstantial as not to be reasonably supportive of its conclusions that individualized factual inquiry [is] unwarranted as an administrative exercise. [We]

---

f. Compare *Califano v. Boles,* 443 U.S. 282, 99 S.Ct. 2767, 61 L.Ed.2d 541 (1979), per Rehnquist, J., upholding a provision of the Social Security Act granting "mother's benefits" to a deceased's widow or divorced wife (but not to the mother of his illegitimate child). The Court, noting that the illegitimate child received child's benefits, reasoned that the "mother's benefits" program "was not designed [for] child-care subsidies. Instead Congress sought to limit the category of beneficiaries to those who actually suffer economic dislocation upon the death of a wage earner and are likely to be confronted at that junc-

ture with the choice between employment or the assumption of full-time child-care responsibilities. In this [light,] Congress could reasonably conclude that a woman who has never been married to the wage earner is far less likely to be dependent upon the wage earner at the time of his death."

Marshall, J., joined by Brennan, White and Blackmun, JJ., dissented, finding that the program, "both in purpose and effect, is a form of assistance to children," and that its discrimination against illegitimates violates equal protection.

cannot say that these exceptions are unfounded, or so indiscriminate as to render the statute's classifications baseless. * * *

Reversed.

MR. JUSTICE STEVENS, with whom MR. JUSTICE BRENNAN and MR. JUSTICE MARSHALL join, dissenting.

* * * I believe an admittedly illogical and unjust result should not be accepted without both a better explanation and also something more than a "possibly rational" basis. * * *

In this statute, one or another of the criteria giving rise to a "presumption of dependency" exists to make almost all children of deceased wage earners eligible. If a child is legitimate, he qualifies. If the child is illegitimate only because of a nonobvious defect in his parents' marriage, he qualifies. If a court has declared his father to be in fact his father, or has issued an order of support against his father, or if the father has acknowledged the child in writing, he qualifies. Apart from any of these qualifications, if the child is lucky enough to live in a State which allows him to inherit from his intestate father on a par with other children, he also qualifies. And in none of these situations need he allege, much less prove, actual dependency. Indeed, if the contrary fact is undisputed, he is nevertheless qualified. [The presumptions] make eligible many children who are no more likely to be "dependent" than are the children in appellees' situation. Yet in the name of "administrative convenience" the Court allows these survivors' benefits to be allocated on grounds which have only the most tenuous connection to the supposedly controlling factor—the child's dependency on his father.

I am persuaded that the classification [is] more probably the product of a tradition of thinking of illegitimates as less deserving persons than legitimates.[g] The sovereign should firmly reject that tradition. The fact that illegitimacy is not as apparent to the observer as sex or race does not make this governmental classification any less odious. It cannot be denied that it is a source of social opprobrium, even if wholly unmerited, or that it is a circumstance for which the individual has no responsibility whatsoever.[h] * * *

LALLI v. LALLI, 439 U.S. 259, 99 S.Ct. 518, 58 L.Ed.2d 503 (1978), upheld a law forbidding illegitimate children to inherit from their fathers by intestate succession—even though there is "convincing proof of paternity"—unless there was a judicial finding of paternity during the father's lifetime. POWELL, J., joined by Burger, C.J., and Stewart, J., found that the law was "substantially related to the important state interests" of providing "for the just and orderly disposition of property at death" in light of "the peculiar problems of proof implicated in paternal inheritance by illegitimate children": "We do not ques-

---

g. See Stevens, J.'s amplification of this idea in note 1(a), Part I supra.

h. What of a law that bars parents from recovering for the wrongful death of their illegitimate child? Compare *Glona v. American Guar. & Liab. Ins. Co.*, 391 U.S. 73, 88 S.Ct. 1515, 20 L.Ed.2d 441 (1968) (no "rational basis for assuming that if mother is allowed recovery the cause of illegitimacy will be served"; "farfetched to assume that women have illegitimate children so that they can be compensated in damages for their death"),

with *Parham v. Hughes*, Part IV infra (upholding law denying father right to sue unless he had legitimated the child; since he "was responsible for fostering an illegitimate child and for failing to change its status," the law was "neither illogical nor unjust").

For the view that discrimination against unmarried parents should receive the same heightened level of scrutiny as for discriminations against illegitimate children, see Note, *Equal Protection for Unmarried Parents*, 65 Ia.L.Rev. 679 (1980).

tion that there will be some illegitimate children who would be able to establish their relationship to their deceased fathers without serious disruption of the administration of estates and that, as applied to such individuals, § 4–1.2 appears to operate unfairly. But [our inquiry] does not focus on the abstract 'fairness' of a state law, but on whether the statute's relation to the state interests it is intended to promote is so tenuous that it lacks the rationality contemplated by the Fourteenth Amendment. The Illinois statute in *Trimble v. Gordon*, 430 U.S. 762, 97 S.Ct. 1459, 52 L.Ed.2d 31 (1977), was constitutionally unacceptable because it effected a total statutory disinheritance of children born out of wedlock who were not legitimated by the subsequent marriage of their parents. The reach of the statute was far in excess of its justifiable purposes.[a] Section 4–1.2 does not share this defect."

Rehnquist, J., concurred in the judgment "for the reasons stated in his dissent in *Trimble*." [b] Blackmun, J., concurred in the judgment, but was

---

a. *Trimble*, per Powell, J., applying *Lucas'* "not-toothless-scrutiny" approach, observed that "difficulties of proving paternity in some situations do not justify the total statutory disinheritance of illegitimate children whose fathers die intestate. The facts of this case"— in which the deceased had been earlier found to be the father in a state court paternity action—"graphically illustrate the constitutional defect." Although *Labine* was not specifically overruled, "it is difficult to place in the pattern of this Court's equal protection decisions, and subsequent cases [such as *Weber*] have limited its force as a precedent." Burger, C.J., and Stewart, Blackmun and Rehnquist, JJ., dissented.

b. In the course of his long *Trimble* dissent (see note 1 after *N.Y.C. Transit Auth. v. Beazer*, Sec. 1 supra), Rehnquist, J., argued: "The essential problem of the Equal Protection Clause [is] determining where the courts are to look for guidance in defining ["equal"]. Since the Amendment grew out of the Civil War [the] core prohibition was early held to be aimed at the protection of blacks. If race was an invalid sorting tool where blacks were concerned, it followed logically that it should not be valid where other races were concerned either. A logical, though not inexorable, next step, was the extension of the protection to prohibit classifications resting on national origin.

"[W]hen the Court has been required to adjudicate equal protection claims not based on race or national origin, it has faced a much more difficult task. In cases involving alienage, for example, it has concluded that such classifications are 'suspect' because, though not necessarily involving race or national origin, they are enough like the latter to warrant similar treatment. While there may be individual disagreement as to how such classes are to be singled out and as to whether specific classes are sufficiently close to the core area of race and national origin to warrant such treatment, one cannot say that the inquiry is not germane to the meaning of the Clause."

"Illegitimacy [has] never been held by the Court to be a 'suspect classification.' Nonetheless, in several opinions of the Court, statements are found which suggest [that], laws which treat them differently from those born in wedlock will receive a more far-reaching scrutiny under the Equal Protection Clause than will other laws regulating economic and social conditions. The Court's opinion today contains language to that effect [which] is a source of confusion, since the unanswered question remains as to the precise sort of scrutiny to which classifications based on illegitimacy will be subject."

Compare *Mills v. Habluetzel*, 456 U.S. 91, 102 S.Ct. 1549, 71 L.Ed.2d 770 (1982), per Rehnquist, J., holding that a Texas statute— which then provided that, in order to obtain support, a paternity suit must be brought before the child is one year old—violated equal protection: "[I]n support suits by illegitimate children, more than in support suits by legitimate children, the State has an interest in preventing the prosecution of stale or fraudulent claims, and may impose greater restrictions on the former than it imposes on the latter. Such restrictions will survive equal protection scrutiny to the extent they are substantially related to a legitimate state interest. [First], the period for obtaining support granted by Texas to illegitimate children must be sufficiently long in duration to present a reasonable opportunity for those with an interest in such children to assert claims on their behalf. Second, any time limitation placed on that opportunity must be substantially related to the State's interest in avoiding the litigation of stale or fraudulent claims." O'Connor, J., joined by Burger, C.J., and Brennan and Blackmun, JJ.,—and by Powell, J., in his own brief opinion—wrote "separately because I fear that the [Court's] opinion may be misinterpreted as approving the four-year statute of limitations now used in Texas."

A unanimous Court reached the same result for Tennessee's two-year statute of limitations.

unconvinced by "the plurality's valiant struggle to distinguish, rather than overrule, *Trimble*," which he would.

BRENNAN, J., joined by White, Marshall and Stevens, JJ., dissented: "New York has available less drastic means of screening out fraudulent claims of paternity. [In] any event, the fear that unknown illegitimates might assert belated claims hardly justifies cutting off the rights of known illegitimates such as Robert Lalli. [T]he state interest in the speedy and efficient determination of paternity 'is completely served by public acknowledgment of parentage and simply does not apply to the case of acknowledged illegitimate children.'

"I see no reason to retreat [from] *Trimble*. The New York [statute] discriminates against illegitimates through means not substantially related to the legitimate interests that the statute purports to promote." [c]

Notes and Questions

Federal immigration power. (a) FIALLO v. BELL, 430 U.S. 787, 97 S.Ct. 1473, 52 L.Ed.2d 50 (1977), per POWELL, J., upheld a federal law granting immigration preference to "children" and "parents" of citizens—except to (1) an illegitimate child of a citizen who is its natural father and (2) the natural father of a citizen who is his illegitimate child. The Court, emphasizing that Congress' "power over aliens is of a political character and therefore subject only to narrow judicial review," rejected the claim for "more searching judicial scrutiny." "Congress obviously has determined that preferential status is not warranted for illegitimate children and their natural fathers, perhaps because of a perceived absence in most cases of close family ties as well as a concern with the serious problems of proof that usually lurk in paternity determinations."

MARSHALL, J., joined by Brennan, J.—and "substantially" by White, J.—dissented: "The review the majority purports to require turns out to be completely 'toothless.' [Such] abdication [is] particularly inappropriate in this case [which] directly involves the rights of citizens, not aliens [and thus] cannot escape traditional constitutional scrutiny simply because it is set in immigration [legislation]. One can hardly imagine a more vulnerable statute. The class of citizens denied the special privilege of reunification in this country is defined on the basis of two traditionally disfavored classifications—gender and legitimacy. In addition the statute interferes with the fundamental 'freedom of personal choice in matters of marriage and family life.'"

(b) May Congress exclude aliens on the basis of race or ethnicity? Cf. Marshall, J., joined by Brennan, J., dissenting in *Jean v. Nelson*, ___ U.S. ___, 105 S.Ct. 2992, 86 L.Ed.2d 664 (1985) (discrimination on the basis of race or national origin, on whether to parole unadmitted aliens pending determination of their admissibility, is invalid absent "reasons clearly related to immigration concerns").

IV. GENDER

Prior to 1971, the Court used the deferential "traditional approach" (see Sec. 1 supra) for classifications based on gender. The earliest case, *Bradwell v. Illinois*, 83 U.S. 130, 21 L.Ed. 442 (1873), upheld a law denying women the right

---

Pickett v. Brown, 462 U.S. 1, 103 S.Ct. 2199, 76 L.Ed.2d 372 (1983).

c. See generally Maltz, *Illegitimacy and Equal Protection*, 1980 Ariz.St.L.J. 831, contending that "the case law from *Levy* to *Lalli*

yields no obvious unifying principles," and analyzing the decisions "to determine whether the challenged classification appears to be based upon prejudice against illegitimates or upon some extrinsic justification."

to practice law—Bradley, J., concurring with Swayne and Field, JJ., explained that "the natural and proper timidity and delicacy which belongs to the female sex evidently unfits it for many of the occupations of civil life. [The] paramount destiny and mission of woman are to fulfill the noble and benign offices of wife and mother. This is the law of the Creator." *Muller v. Oregon,* 208 U.S. 412, 28 S.Ct. 324, 52 L.Ed. 551 (1908), per Brewer, J., upheld a law barring factory work by women for more than ten hours a day, reasoning that "as healthy mothers are essential to vigorous offspring, the physical well-being of a woman becomes an object of public interest and care." [a] *Goesaert v. Cleary,* 335 U.S. 464, 69 S.Ct. 198, 93 L.Ed. 163 (1948), per Frankfurter, J., upheld a law denying bartender's licenses to most women, reasoning that "the fact that women may now have achieved the virtues that men have long claimed as their prerogatives and now indulge in vices that men have long practiced, does not preclude the States from drawing a sharp line between the sexes, certainly in such matters as the regulation of the liquor traffic." Finally, *Hoyt v. Florida,* 368 U.S. 57, 82 S.Ct. 159, 7 L.Ed.2d 118 (1961), per Harlan, J., sustained a law placing women on the jury list only if they made special request, stating that "woman is still regarded as the center of home and family life." [b]

The first decision holding sex discrimination violative of equal protection, REED v. REED, 404 U.S. 71, 92 S.Ct. 251, 30 L.Ed.2d 225 (1971), per BURGER, C.J., involved a law preferring males to females when two persons were otherwise equally entitled to be the administrator of an estate: "A classification 'must be reasonable, not arbitrary, and must rest upon some ground of difference having a fair and substantial relation to the object of the [law].' *Royster Guano,* [Sec. 1 supra]. The question" is whether the classification "bears a rational relationship to a state objective that is sought to be advanced by the [law]." It was contended that the law had the reasonable "objective of reducing the workload on probate courts by eliminating one class of contests" and that the legislature might reasonably have "concluded that in general men are better qualified to act as an administrator than are women." But "to give a mandatory preference to members of either sex over members of the other, merely to accomplish the elimination of hearings on the merits, is to make the very kind of arbitrary legislative choice forbidden by [equal protection]."

This was followed by FRONTIERO v. RICHARDSON, 411 U.S. 677, 93 S.Ct. 1764, 36 L.Ed.2d 583 (1973), which held violative of equal protection a federal statute permitting males in the armed services an automatic dependency allowance for their wives but requiring servicewomen to prove that their husbands were dependent. BRENNAN, J., joined by Douglas, White and Marshall, JJ., argued that "classifications based upon sex [are] inherently suspect and must therefore be subjected to close judicial scrutiny," finding "at least implicit support for such an approach in [*Reed's*] departure from 'traditional' rationa!

a. But see *Adkins v. Children's Hospital,* 261 U.S. 525, 43 S.Ct. 394, 67 L.Ed. 785 (1923) (minimum wages for women violates due process), overruled, *West Coast Hotel Co. v. Parrish,* p. 74 supra.

b. *Hoyt* was effectively overruled in *Taylor v. Louisiana,* 419 U.S. 522, 95 S.Ct. 692, 42 L.Ed.2d 690 (1975), holding that a similar statute, operating largely to exclude women from jury service, deprived a criminal defendant of the sixth and fourteenth amendment right to an impartial jury drawn from a fair cross section of the community: "It is untenable to suggest these days that it would be a special hardship for each and every woman to perform jury service or that society cannot spare *any* women from their present duties."

basis analysis": [c] "[O]ur Nation has had a long and unfortunate history of sex discrimination. Traditionally, such discrimination was rationalized by an attitude of 'romantic paternalism' which, in practical effect, put women not on a pedestal, but in a cage. * * *

"As a result of notions such as these, [statutes] became laden with gross, stereotypical distinctions between the sexes and, indeed, throughout much of the 19th century the position of women in our society was, in many respects, comparable to that of blacks under the pre-Civil War slave codes. Neither slaves nor women could hold office, serve on juries, or bring suit in their own names, and married women traditionally were denied the legal capacity to hold or convey property or to serve as legal guardians of their own children.[d] And although blacks were guaranteed the right to vote in 1870, women were denied even [that] until adoption of the Nineteenth Amendment half a century later.

"It is true, of course, that the position of women in America has improved markedly in recent decades. [But] in part because of the high visibility of the sex characteristic, women still face pervasive, although at times more subtle, discrimination in our educational institutions, on the job market and, perhaps most conspicuously, in the political arena.[17]

c. For discussion of *Reed's* use of "a disguised balancing test," see Note, *Legislative Purpose, Rationality, and Equal Protection*, 82 Yale L.J. 123, 150–51 (1972).

d. See Note, *Sex Discrimination and Equal Protection: Do We Need a Constitutional Amendment?* 84 Harv.L.Rev. 1499, 1507 (1971): "Arguments justifying different treatment for the sexes on the grounds of female inferiority, need for male protection, and happiness in their assigned roles bear a striking resemblance to the half-truths surrounding the myth of the 'happy slave.'" For discussion of the dissimilarities between race and gender for these purposes, see Wasserstrom, *Racism, Sexism, and Preferential Treatment: An Approach to the Topics*, 24 U.C.L.A.L.Rev. 581 (1977); Rutherglen, *Sexual Equality in Fringe-Benefit Plans*, 65 Va.L.Rev. 199, 205–12 (1979).

17. It is true [that] when viewed in the abstract, women do not constitute a small and powerless minority. Nevertheless, in part because of past discrimination, women are vastly underrepresented in this Nation's decision-making councils. * * *

[See also Note, 84 Harv.L.Rev. at 1505 n. 48: "Political power is a difficult concept [to] define. Furthermore, many [women] are not aware of or do not care about the inequalities based on sex in the legal structure. Others may have decided that, on balance, they are benefited rather than burdened by current laws distinguishing the sexes, and thus they may oppose the principle that no such distinctions should be allowed. These considerations weaken the argument that women can protect their interests through their political power, however defined. Even if women could use their political power to protect their interests, but do not choose to do so, the minority who feel they are discriminated against still should have a right to constitutional protection."

[Compare Ely, *Democracy and Distrust* 166–69 (1980): "[I]n assessing suspiciousness it cannot be enough simply to note that a group does not function as a political bloc. [We must] see if there are systemic bars [to] access. On that score it seems important that today discussion about the appropriate 'place' of women is common among both women and men, and between the sexes as well. The very stereotypes that gave rise to laws 'protecting' women by barring them from various activities are under daily and publicized attack, and are the subject of equally spirited defense. [Given] such open discussion [the] claim that the numerical majority is being 'dominated' [is] one it has become impossible to maintain except at the most inflated rhetorical level. It also renders the broader argument self-contradictory, since to make such a claim in the context of the current debate one must at least implicitly grant the validity of the stereotype, that women are in effect mental infants who will believe anything men tell them to believe. [But] most laws classifying by sex [probably pre-date woman suffrage]: they should be invalidated. [To] put on the group affected the burden of using its recently unblocked access to get the offending laws repealed would be to place in their path an additional hurdle that the rest of us do not have to contend with in order to protect ourselves—hardly an appropriate response to the realization that they have been unfairly blocked in the past. In fact I may be wrong in supposing that because women now are in a position to protect themselves they will, that we are thus unlikely to see in the future the sort of official gender discrimination that has marked our past. But if women don't protect

"Moreover, since sex, like race and national origin, is an immutable characteristic [the] imposition of special disabilities [would] seem to violate 'the basic concept of our system that legal burdens should bear some relationship to individual responsibility.' *Weber.* And what differentiates sex from such non-suspect statuses as intelligence or physical disability [is] that the sex characteristic frequently bears no relation to ability to perform or contribute to society. As a result, statutory distinctions between the sexes often have the effect of invidiously relegating the entire class of females to inferior legal status without regard to the actual capabilities of its individual members.

"[The] Government [maintains] that, as an empirical matter, wives in our society frequently are dependent upon their husbands, while husbands rarely are dependent upon their wives. Thus, the Government argues that Congress might reasonably have concluded that it would be both cheaper and easier simply conclusively to presume that wives of male members are financially dependent upon their husbands, while burdening female members with the task of establishing dependency in fact.

"The Government offers no concrete evidence, however, tending to support its view that such differential treatment in fact saves the Government any money. [And any] statutory scheme which draws a sharp line between the sexes, *solely* [for] administrative convenience [violates equal protection]."

POWELL, J., joined by Burger, C.J., and Blackmun, J., concurring, would rely "on the authority of *Reed* and reserve for the future any expansion of its rationale" because of the "Equal Rights Amendment, which if adopted will resolve [the] question." Stewart, J., concurred, "agreeing that the [statutes] work an invidious discrimination [*Reed.*]" Rehnquist, J., dissented.[e]

Two decisions during this period upheld gender classifications. KAHN v. SHEVIN, 416 U.S. 351, 94 S.Ct. 1734, 40 L.Ed.2d 189 (1974), per DOUGLAS, J., involved a property tax exemption for widows (but not widowers). Unlike *Reed,* the law is "reasonably designed to further the state policy of cushioning the financial impact of spousal loss upon the sex for whom that loss imposes a disproportionately heavy burden." Unlike *Frontiero,* the classification here is not "*solely* for administrative convenience," nor were the statutes there "in any sense designed to rectify the effects of past discrimination against women."[f]

themselves from sex discrimination in the future, it [will be] because for one reason or another—substantive disagreement or more likely the assignment of a low priority to the issue—they don't choose to."]

e. See also *Stanton v. Stanton,* 421 U.S. 7, 95 S.Ct. 1373, 43 L.Ed.2d 688 (1975), per Blackmun, J., relying on *Reed,* holding that a statute requiring child support for males to age 21 but for females only to age 18 violated equal protection: To distinguish "the boy in order to assure him parental support while he attains his education and training, [is] to be self-serving: if the female is not to be supported so long as the male, she hardly can be expected to attend school as long as he does, and bringing her education to an end earlier coincides with the role-typing society has long imposed." Rehnquist, J., dissented on procedural grounds.

f. Brennan, J., joined by Marshall, J., dissented: "[I]n providing special benefits for a needy segment of society long the victim of purposeful discrimination and neglect, the statute serves the compelling state interest of achieving equality for such groups." But it "is plainly overinclusive [because] the State could readily narrow the class of beneficiaries to those widows for whom the effects of past economic discrimination against women have been a practical reality."

White, J., also dissented: "It may be administratively inconvenient to make individual determinations [to] extend the exemption to needy men as well as needy women, but administrative efficiency is not an adequate justification for discriminations based purely on sex. *Frontiero; Reed.*"

SCHLESINGER v. BALLARD, 419 U.S. 498, 95 S.Ct. 572, 42 L.Ed.2d 610 (1975), per STEWART, J., upheld a federal statute providing for the discharge of naval "line" officers who had not been promoted for nine years (males) or thirteen years (females): In "*Reed* and *Frontiero* the challenged classifications [were] premised on overbroad generalizations" and were sought to be justified solely on "administrative convenience." Here, because of navy restrictions on combat and sea duty for women, "Congress [may] quite rationally have believed that women line officers had less opportunity for promotion than did their male counterparts, and that a longer period of tenure for women officers would, therefore, be consistent with the goal to provide women officers with 'fair and equitable career advancement programs.' Cf. *Kahn*." [g]

WEINBERGER v. WIESENFELD, 420 U.S. 636, 95 S.Ct. 1225, 43 L.Ed.2d 514 (1975), per BRENNAN, J., held that Social Security Act § 402(g)'s payment of benefits to the wife—but not to the husband—of a deceased wage earner with minor children violated equal protection because it "unjustifiably discriminated against women wage-earners": [h] As in *Frontiero*, an "'archaic and overbroad' generalization [underlies] the distinction drawn by § 402(g), namely, that male [but not female] workers' earnings are vital to the support of their families." Unlike *Kahn*, "it is apparent both from the statutory scheme itself and from the legislative history of § 402(g) that Congress' purpose [was] not to provide an income to women who were, because of economic discrimination, unable to provide for themselves. Rather, § 402(g), linked as it is directly to responsibility for minor children, was intended to permit women to elect not to work and to devote themselves to the care of children. Since this purpose in no way is premised upon any special disadvantages of women, [the] gender-based distinction of § 402(g) is entirely irrational." [i]

CALIFANO v. GOLDFARB, 430 U.S. 199, 97 S.Ct. 1021, 51 L.Ed.2d 270 (1977), held that Social Security Act § 402(f)'s payment of benefits to a widow of a covered employee, but not to a widower unless he proves dependency on his deceased wife-employee, violated equal protection. BRENNAN, J., joined by White, Marshall and Powell, JJ., found *Wiesenfeld* "dispositive."

STEVENS, J., concurred, noting his agreement with the dissent's contentions that "the relevant discrimination in this case is against surviving male spouses, rather than against deceased female wage earners" and that "a classification

g. Brennan, J., joined by Douglas and Marshall, JJ.—and "for the most part" by White, J.—dissented: "I find quite troublesome the notion that a gender-based difference in treatment can be justified by another, broader, gender-based difference in treatment imposed directly and currently by the Navy itself." See also Kanowitz, *"Benign" Sex Discrimination: Its Troubles and Their Cure,* 31 Hast.L.J. 1379, 1407 (1980): "Nor did *Ballard* take into account another detrimental impact of the policy upon women: the easing of pressure on their superiors to promote them precisely because women officers could stay in the service two years longer than men without being promoted."

h. Against which sex did the provision discriminate? Was the discrimination in *Fron-*

tiero against servicewomen or their male spouses? What about *Kahn?*

i. Powell, J., joined by Burger, C.J., "concur[red] generally in the opinion of the Court." Rehnquist, J., disclaiming reliance on *Frontiero*, concurred in the result because § 402(g) "does not rationally serve any valid legislative purpose, including that for which § 402(g) was obviously designed. This is so because it is irrational to distinguish between mothers and fathers when the sole question is whether a child of a deceased contributing worker should have the opportunity to receive the full-time attention of the only parent remaining to it." Douglas, J., did not participate. See generally Note, *Sex Classifications in the Social Security Benefit Structure,* 49 Ind.L.J. 181 (1973).

which treats certain aged widows more favorably than their male counterparts is not 'invidious.' " Nonetheless, since "the history of the statute is entirely consistent with the view that Congress simply assumed that all widows should be regarded as 'dependents' in some general sense," he was "persuaded that this discrimination against a group of males is merely the accidental by-product of a traditional way of thinking about females." [j]

REHNQUIST, J., joined by Burger, C.J., and Stewart and Blackmun, JJ., dissented: "[C]ases requiring heightened levels of scrutiny for particular classifications [which] have originated [outside] the field of social insurance legislation [should] not be uncritically carried over into that field. [I]n a legislative system which distributes benefit payments among literally millions of people there are at least two characteristics which are not found in many other types of statutes. The first is that the statutory scheme will typically have been expanded by amendment over a period of years so that it is virtually impossible to say that a particular amendment fits with mathematical nicety into a carefully conceived overall plan for payment of benefits. The second is [that] 'administrative convenience' will in this area of the law bear a much more vital relation to the overall legislative plan because of congressional concern for certainty in determination of entitlement and promptness in payment of benefits." Unlike *Wiesenfeld,* "the section under attack in the instant case does not totally foreclose widowers, but simply requires from them a proof of dependency" as in *Mathews v. Lucas.*[k] Further, favoring aged widows "is scarcely an invidious discrimination. [It] in no way perpetuates the economic discrimination which has been the basis for heightened scrutiny of gender-based classifications, and is, in fact, explainable as a measure to ameliorate the characteristically depressed condition of aged widows. *Kahn.*"[l]

CRAIG v. BOREN, 429 U.S. 190, 97 S.Ct. 451, 50 L.Ed.2d 397 (1976), per BRENNAN, J., involving a law forbidding sale of 3.2% beer to males under age 21 and to females under 18, was the first decision (a) to hold an unambiguous discrimination against males violative of equal protection, and (b) to articulate a formal standard of review: "[P]revious cases establish that classifications by gender must serve important governmental objectives and must be substantially related to achievement of those objectives. * * * Decisions following *Reed* [have] rejected administrative ease and convenience as sufficiently important objectives to justify gender-based classifications. * * *

"*Reed* has also provided the underpinning for decisions that have invalidated statutes employing gender as an inaccurate proxy for other, more germane

---

j. Stevens, J., also strongly suggested that he disagreed with *Kahn.*

k. Do the different results in *Lucas* and *Goldfarb* mean "that while both sex and illegitimacy classifications are subject to 'middle tier' scrutiny, sex classifications are viewed as more invidious [and] thus require a more substantial means-end fit"? 91 Harv.L.Rev. 186 (1977).

l. *Wengler v. Druggists Mut. Ins. Co.,* 446 U.S. 142, 100 S.Ct. 1540, 64 L.Ed.2d 107 (1980), per White, J., held that a virtually identical state workers' compensation law discriminated against women (relying on *Goldfarb, Wiesenfeld* and *Frontiero*)—and against men (re-

lying on Stevens, J.'s concurrence in *Goldfarb*)—and thus violated equal protection. Stevens, J., concurred on the basis of his *Goldfarb* concurrence. Only Rehnquist, J., dissented.

See also *Califano v. Westcott,* 443 U.S. 76, 99 S.Ct. 2655, 61 L.Ed.2d 382 (1979), relying on *Goldfarb* and *Wiesenfeld* to unanimously hold violative of equal protection Social Security Act § 407—which "provides benefits to families whose dependent children have been deprived of parental support because of the unemployment of the father, but does not provide such benefits when the mother becomes unemployed."

bases of classification. Hence, 'archaic and overbroad' generalizations concerning the financial position of servicewomen, *Frontiero*, and working women, *Wiesenfeld*, could not justify use of a gender line in determining eligibility for certain governmental entitlements. Similarly increasingly outdated misconceptions concerning the role of females in the home rather than in the 'marketplace and world of ideas' were rejected as loose-fitting characterizations incapable of supporting state statutory schemes that were premised upon their accuracy. *Stanton*. In light of the weak congruence between gender and the characteristic or trait that gender purported to represent, it was necessary that the legislatures choose either to realign their substantive laws in a gender-neutral fashion, or to adopt procedures for identifying those instances where the sex-centered generalization actually comported to fact."

The Court reviewed in detail the state's "statistical evidence" concerning "age-sex differentials" in respect to "drinking and driving" and found that it "cannot support the conclusion that the gender-based distinction closely serves to achieve" the "important" objective of "enhancement of traffic safety [23]": [m]

POWELL, J., joined the Court's opinion, but with "reservations as to some of the discussion concerning the appropriate standard for equal protection analysis.[*]" Relying on *Reed,* he found that "this gender-based classification does not bear a fair and substantial relation to the object of the legislation."

STEVENS, J., who joined the Court's opinion, concurred: "I am inclined to believe that what has become known as the two-tiered analysis of equal protection claims [is] a method the Court has employed to explain decisions that actually apply a single standard in a reasonably consistent fashion. * * *

"In this case, the classification [is] objectionable because it is based on an accident of birth, because it is a mere remnant of the now almost universally rejected tradition of discriminating against males in this age bracket, and because, to the extent it reflects any physical difference between males and females, it is actually perverse.[4] * * *

"The classification is not totally irrational. For the evidence does indicate that there are more males than females in this age bracket who drive and also more who drink. Nevertheless, [i]t is difficult to believe that the statute was actually intended to cope with the problem of traffic safety, since it has only a minimal effect on access to a not-very-intoxicating beverage and does not prohibit its consumption. Moreover, [the] legislation imposes a restraint on one hundred percent of the males in the class allegedly because about 2% of them have probably violated one or more laws relating to the consumption of alcoholic beverages. It is unlikely that this law will have a significant deterrent effect either on that 2% or on the law-abiding 98%. But even assuming some such slight benefit, it does not seem to me that an insult to all of the young men of the State can be justified by visiting the sins of the 2% on the 98%."

REHNQUIST, J.—with whom Burger, C.J., was "in general agreement"—dissented: The Court's "elevated or 'intermediate' level scrutiny, like that

---

23. Insofar as *Goesaert v. Cleary* may be inconsistent, that decision is disapproved. * * *

m. Stewart, J., concurred, relying on *Reed.*

[*] [As] has been true of *Reed* and its progeny, our decision today will be viewed by some as a "middle-tier" approach. While I would not endorse that characterization[,] candor compels the recognition that the relatively defer-

ential "rational basis" standard of review normally applied takes on a sharper focus when we address a gender-based classification. * * *

4. Because males are generally heavier than females, they have a greater capacity to consume alcohol without impairing their driving ability than do females.

invoked in cases dealing with discrimination against females, raises the question of why the statute here should be treated any differently than countless legislative classifications unrelated to sex which have been upheld under a minimum rationality standard. [There] is no suggestion [that] males in this age group are in any way peculiarly disadvantaged, subject to systematic discriminatory treatment, or otherwise in need of special solicitude from the courts. [T]here being no plausible argument that this is a discrimination against females,[2] the Court's reliance on our previous sex-discrimination cases is ill-founded. * * *

"The Court's [standard of review] comes out of thin air. * * * I would think we have had enough difficulty with the two standards of review which our cases have recognized—the norm of 'rational basis,' and the 'compelling state interest' required where a 'suspect classification' is involved—so as to counsel weightily against the insertion of still another 'standard' between those two. How is this Court to divine what objectives are important? How is it to determine whether a particular law is 'substantially' related to the achievement of such objective, rather than related in some other way to its achievement? Both of the phrases used are so diaphanous and elastic as to invite subjective judicial preferences or prejudices relating to particular types of legislation, masquerading as judgments whether such legislation is directed at 'important' objectives or, whether the relationship to those objectives is 'substantial' enough.

"[I]f stereotypes are as pervasive as the Court suggests, they may in turn influence the conduct of the men and women in question, and cause the young men to conform to the wild and reckless image which is their stereotype. * * * Notwithstanding the Court's critique of the statistical evidence, that evidence suggests clear differences between the drinking and driving habits of young men and women. Those differences are grounds enough for the State reasonably to conclude that young males pose by far the greater drunk driving hazard, both in terms of sheer numbers and in terms of hazard on a per-driver basis. The gender-based difference in treatment in this case is therefore not irrational."

CALIFANO v. WEBSTER
430 U.S. 313, 97 S.Ct. 1192, 51 L.Ed.2d 360 (1977).

PER CURIAM.

[Social Security Act § 215(b)(3)'s formula—which has since been amended—afforded the chance of higher old-age benefits to female wage earners than to similarly situated males.]

To withstand scrutiny under [equal protection], "classifications by gender must serve important governmental objectives and must be substantially related to achievement of those objectives." *Craig.* Reduction of the disparity in economic condition between men and women caused by the long history of discrimination against women has been recognized as such an important govern-

---

2. I am not unaware of the argument [that] all discriminations between the sexes ultimately redound to the detriment of females, because they tend to reinforce "old notions" restricting the roles and opportunities of women. As a general proposition applying equally to all sex categorizations, I believe that this argument was implicitly found to carry little weight in our decisions upholding gender-based differences. See *Ballard; Kahn.* Seeing no assertion that it has special applicability [here], I believe it can be dismissed as an insubstantial consideration.

[See generally Sherry, *Selective Judicial Activism in the Equal Protection Context,* 73 Geo. L.J. 89 (1984).]

mental objective. *Ballard; Kahn.* But "the mere recitation of a benign, compensatory purpose is not an automatic shield which protects against any inquiry into the actual purposes underlying a statutory scheme." *Wiesenfeld.* Accordingly, we have rejected attempts to justify gender classifications as compensation for past discrimination against women when the classifications in fact penalized women wage earners, *Goldfarb; Wiesenfeld,* or when the statutory structure and its legislative history revealed that the classification was not enacted as compensation for past discrimination. *Goldfarb; Wiesenfeld.*

[This statute] is more analogous to those upheld in *Kahn* and *Ballard* than to those struck down in *Wiesenfeld* and *Goldfarb.* The more favorable treatment of the female wage earner enacted here was not a result of "archaic and overbroad generalizations" about women, or of "the role-typing society has long imposed" upon women such as casual assumptions that women are "the weaker sex" or are more likely to be child-rearers or dependents. Rather, "the only discernible purpose of [§ 215's more favorable treatment is] the permissible one of redressing our society's longstanding disparate treatment of women." *Goldfarb.*

The challenged statute operated directly to compensate women for past economic discrimination. Retirement benefits [are] based on past earnings. But as we have recognized, "[w]hether from overt discrimination or from the socialization process of a male-dominated culture, the job market is inhospitable to the woman seeking any but the lowest paid jobs." *Kahn.* Thus, allowing women, who as such have been unfairly hindered from earning as much as men, to eliminate additional low-earning years from the calculation of their retirement benefits works directly to remedy some part of the effect of past discrimination.[5]

[T]he legislative history is clear that the differing treatment of men and women in former § 215(b)(3) was not "the accidental byproduct of a traditional way of thinking about females," *Goldfarb* (Stevens, J., concurring in the result), but rather was deliberately enacted to compensate for particular economic disabilities suffered by women.[a]

That Congress changed its mind in 1972 and equalized the treatment of men and women does [not] constitute an admission by Congress that its previous policy was invidiously discriminatory. Congress has in recent years legislated directly upon the subject of unequal treatment of women in the job market. Congress may well have decided that "[t]hese congressional reforms [have] lessened the economic justification for the more favorable benefit computation formula in § 215(b)(3)." Moreover, elimination of the more favorable benefit computation for women wage earners, even in the remedial context, is wholly consistent with those reforms, which require equal treatment of men and women in preference to the attitudes of "romantic paternalism" that have contributed to the "long and unfortunate history of sex discrimination." *Frontiero.* * * *

Reversed.

MR. CHIEF JUSTICE BURGER, with whom MR. JUSTICE STEWART, MR. JUSTICE BLACKMUN, and MR. JUSTICE REHNQUIST join, concurring in the judgment.

---

5. Even with the advantage[,] women on the average received lower retirement benefits than men. "As of December 1972, the average monthly retirement insurance benefit for males was $179.60 and for females, $140.50."

unanimously upholding a "temporary revival" of the classification invalidated in *Goldfarb* "in order to protect the expectations of persons, both men and women, who had planned their retirements based on" it.

a. See also *Heckler v. Mathews,* 465 U.S. 728, 104 S.Ct. 1387, 79 L.Ed.2d 646 (1984),

* * * I find it somewhat difficult to distinguish [*Goldfarb*]. I question whether certainty in the law is promoted by hinging the validity of important statutory schemes on whether five Justices view them to be more akin to the "offensive" provisions struck down in *Wiesenfeld* and *Frontiero,* or more like the "benign" provisions upheld in *Ballard* and *Kahn.* I therefore concur in the judgment [for] reasons stated by Mr. Justice Rehnquist in his dissenting opinion in *Goldfarb,* in which Mr. Justice Stewart, Mr. Justice Blackmun, and I joined.

Notes and Questions

1. *"Benign"—"compensatory"—"remedial" discrimination.* Did the laws in *Kahn, Ballard* and *Webster* fit this description? Consider 88 Harv.L.Rev. 137–38 (1974): "Unlike other forms of invidious discrimination, sex discrimination has been characterized more by paternalistic overprotection than by callous deprivation. Employment opportunities have been closed to women not simply because they have been considered inferior, but also because of the assumption that a woman's place is in the home. Gender-specific classifications are frequently based on such stereotypical thinking, and although many are difficult to characterize as overtly prejudicial to women, even clear 'favors' are part of a pattern of legal and social double standards which, in defining sexual roles, limit a woman's opportunities for individual fulfillment.[58]" See also Johnston, *Sex Discrimination and the Supreme Court—1971–1974,* 49 N.Y.U.L.Rev. 617, 670 (1974): "[*Kahn*] merely repeated stereotyped conclusions from factual generalizations regarding some aspects of the well-known disparity between men and women. [If] these statistics were sufficient, then *Reed* could have been differently decided upon introduction of evidence that, on the average, men have more business education and experience than women [and] *Frontiero* could have been upheld on the basis of evidence showing that more wives are in fact dependent for support on their husbands than vice versa."

Does a "benign," "compensatory" or "remedial" purpose justify discrimination against men? Consider Kanowitz, fn. g supra, at 1394–96: "[A] casual glance at the treatment males have received at the hands of the law solely because they are males suggests that they have paid an awesome price for other advantages they have presumably enjoyed over females in our society. Whether one talks of the male's unique obligation of compulsory military service, his primary duty for spousal and child support, his lack of the same kinds of protective labor legislation that have traditionally been enjoyed by women, or the statutory or judicial preference in child custody disputes that has long been accorded to mothers vis-à-vis fathers of minor children, sex discrimination against males in statutes and judicial decisions has been widespread and severe. * * * How many males, for example, [unable] to benefit from state laws that limited women's working hours and lifting requirements, and prescribed minimum wages for women only, had their health impaired by being forced by their employers to work excessively long hours, lift excessively heavy weights, under excessively onerous conditions, at whatever wage their employer was willing to pay? * * * How many men [were] crushed both emotionally and physically by their striving to meet their exclusive legal obligation to provide for their wives' and children's financial needs?"

58. Although the [*Kahn*] tax exemption standing alone might be of minimal influence on a husband and wife in [their] choices of economic roles, cumulation of such legal "fa- vors" could have the effect of reinforcing the desirability of the man working and the woman staying at home.

2. *Other discriminations against women.* After the decided cases, may wives be denied actions for loss of consortium? May a harsher sentence be mandated for women than for men for the same offense? May women prison guards be excluded from duty in "contact positions" in all-male prisons? See *Dothard v. Rawlinson,* 433 U.S. 321, 97 S.Ct. 2720, 53 L.Ed.2d 786 (1977) (no violation of Title VII). In "high-rape" areas, may female students be subjected to an earlier curfew than males? May women employees, because women live longer, be required to make larger contributions than men to the state pension fund? See *Los Angeles Dep't of Water & Power v. Manhart,* 435 U.S. 702, 98 S.Ct. 1370, 55 L.Ed.2d 657 (1978) (violation of Title VII). May only women be required to wear tops while swimming? May a married woman be required to use her husband's surname to obtain a driver's license? See Comment, 38 Ohio St.L.J. 157 (1977). May a woman be required to designate her marital status to register to vote? See Karst, *"A Discrimination So Trivial": A Note on Law and the Symbolism of Women's Dependency,* 35 Ohio St.L.J. 546 (1974).

3. *Sex-specific traits.* GEDULDIG v. AIELLO, 417 U.S. 484, 94 S.Ct. 2485, 41 L.Ed.2d 256 (1974), per STEWART, J., held that exclusion of "disability that accompanies normal pregnancy and childbirth" from California's disability insurance system "does not exclude [anyone] because of gender * * *. While it is true that only women can become pregnant, it does not follow that every legislative classification concerning pregnancy is [sex-based]. Absent a showing that distinctions involving pregnancy are mere pretexts designed to effect an invidious discrimination against the members of one sex or the other, lawmakers are constitutionally free to include or exclude pregnancy from the coverage of legislation such as this on any reasonable basis, just as with respect to any other physical condition. [The] program divides potential recipients into two groups— pregnant women and nonpregnant persons. While the first group is exclusively female, the second includes members of both sexes. The fiscal and actuarial benefits of the program thus accrue to members of both sexes.[a] [There] is no risk from which men are protected and women are not. Likewise, there is no risk from which women are protected and men are not.[21]" [b]

a. Query: Consider the following description of a law that forbids blacks from unaccredited law schools from becoming lawyers: "The law divides all persons who wish to become lawyers into two groups—blacks from unaccredited schools and all others. While the first group is exclusively black, the second includes members of both races."

What result under *Geduldig* if the disability program excluded only sickle-cell anemia?

How does the rule of *Washington v. Davis* bear on these questions?

21. Indeed, the [data indicated] that both the annual claim rate and the annual claim cost are greater for women than for [men.]

b. *General Electric Co. v. Gilbert,* 429 U.S. 125, 97 S.Ct. 401, 50 L.Ed.2d 343 (1976), held that Title VII's prohibition of sex discrimination did not prevent companies from excluding pregnancy from their disability plans. (But see *Nashville Gas Co. v. Satty,* 434 U.S. 136, 98 S.Ct. 347, 54 L.Ed.2d 356 (1977) (denial of accumulated seniority to persons who take mandatory pregnancy leave violates Title VII).) In response, Congress enacted the Pregnancy Discrimination Act, 42 U.S.C. § 2000e(k) (1978), which defined sex discrimination to include pregnancy discrimination. Some states have given maternity leave rights that go beyond that afforded to non-pregnant employees who are unable to work. Is this sex discrimination? Does a doctrine that ignores the biological differences between men and women regarding abortion, reproduction, and creation of another human being mean that "women can claim equality only insofar as they are like men"? Law, *Rethinking Sex and the Constitution,* 132 U.Pa.L.Rev. 955, 1007 (1984). See also Kay, *Models of Equality,* 1985 U.Ill.L.Rev. 39; Kay, *Equality and Difference: The Case of Pregnancy,* 1 Berkeley Women's L.J. 1 (1985). More generally, should a law be considered discriminatory whenever it "participates in the systematic social deprivation of one sex because of sex"? Are steps that empower a group "whose depowering is the problem" the antithesis of sex discrimination? See generally MacKinnon, *Sexual Harassment of Working Women,* 101– 41 (1979). Alternatively, is an approach based

BRENNAN, J., joined by Douglas and Marshall, JJ., dissented, finding "sex discrimination" in the state's "singling out for less favorable treatment a gender-linked disability peculiar to women [while] men receive full compensation for all disabilities suffered, including those that affect only or primarily their sex, such as prostatectomies, circumcision, hemophilia and gout." [c]

4. *Similar (?) classifications.* Do the gender cases extend to discrimination against homosexuals? See p. 207 supra. Against married persons?

MISSISSIPPI UNIV. FOR WOMEN v. HOGAN
458 U.S. 718, 102 S.Ct. 3331, 73 L.Ed.2d 1090 (1982).

JUSTICE O'CONNOR delivered the opinion of the Court.

[MUW, "the oldest state-supported all-female college in the United States," denied Hogan admission to its School of Nursing solely because of his sex.[a]]

* * * That this statute discriminates against males rather than against females does not exempt it from scrutiny or reduce the standard of review.[8] Our decisions also establish that the party seeking to uphold a statute that classifies individuals on the basis of their gender must carry the burden of showing an "exceedingly persuasive justification" for the classification. *Kirchberg v. Feenstra*, 450 U.S. 455, 461, 101 S.Ct. 1195, 1199, 67 L.Ed.2d 428 (1981).[b] The burden is met only by showing at least that the classification serves "important governmental objectives and that the discriminatory means employed" are "substantially related to the achievement of those objectives." [9]

Although the test [is] straightforward, it must be applied free of fixed notions concerning the roles and abilities of males and females. [Thus,] if the statutory objective is to exclude or "protect" members of one gender because they are presumed to suffer from an inherent handicap or to be innately inferior, the objective itself is illegitimate. See *Frontiero.*

If the State's objective is legitimate and important, we next determine whether the requisite direct, substantial relationship between objective and means is present. The purpose of requiring that close relationship is to assure that the validity of a classification is determined through reasoned analysis rather than through the mechanical application of traditional, often inaccurate, assumptions about the proper roles of men and women. The need for the

upon "special treatment" for women a "double-edged sword"? Williams, *The Equality Crisis: Some Reflections on Culture, Courts and Feminism,* 7 Women's Rts.L.Rptr. 175, 196 (1982) ("if we can't have it both ways, we need to think carefully about which way we want to have it"). Does the phrase "special treatment" presuppose a male perspective?

c. Is it sex discrimination to give a prison sentence to a man but probation to a woman (because she is pregnant) for the identical offense?

For invalidation of a disability for pregnant women, on constitutional grounds other than equal protection, see *Cleveland State Bd. of Educ. v. La Fleur,* Sec. 5 infra.

a. The Court declined "to address the question of whether MUW's admissions policy, as applied to males seeking admission to schools other than the School of Nursing, violates the Fourteenth Amendment."

8. Without question, MUW's admissions policy worked to Hogan's disadvantage. [Hogan] could have attended [one] of Mississippi's state-supported coeducational nursing programs [only] by driving a considerable distance from his home. * * *

b. *Kirchberg* per Marshall, J., held that a Louisiana statute giving a husband exclusive control over disposition of community property was not "substantially related to the achievement of an important governmental objective." Stewart, J., joined by Rehnquist, J., concurred in the result "since men and women were similarly situated for all relevant purposes with respect to the management and disposition of community property."

9. [Because] we conclude that the challenged statutory classification is not substantially related to an important objective, we need not decide whether classifications based upon gender are inherently suspect.

requirement is amply revealed by reference to the broad range of statutes already invalidated by this Court, statutes that relied upon the simplistic, outdated assumption that gender could be used as a "proxy for other, more germane bases of classification," *Craig,* to establish a link between objective and classification. * * *

The State's primary justification for maintaining the single-sex admissions policy of MUW's School of Nursing is that it compensates for discrimination against women and, therefore, constitutes educational affirmative action. [A] state can evoke a compensatory purpose to justify an otherwise discriminatory classification only if members of the gender benefited by the classification actually suffer a disadvantage related to the classification. We considered such a situation in *Webster* [and *Ballard*].

In sharp contrast, Mississippi has made no showing that women lacked opportunities to obtain training in the field of nursing or to attain positions of leadership in that field when the MUW School of Nursing opened its door or that women currently are deprived of such opportunities. In fact, in 1970, the year before the School of Nursing's first class enrolled, women earned 94 percent of the nursing baccalaureate degrees conferred in Mississippi and 98.6 percent of the degrees earned nationwide.[14]

Rather than compensate for discriminatory barriers faced by women, MUW's [policy] tends to perpetuate the stereotyped view of nursing as an exclusively woman's job.[15] By assuring that Mississippi allots more openings in its state-supported nursing schools to women than it does to men, MUW's admissions policy lends credibility to the old view that women, not men, should become nurses, and makes the assumption that nursing is a field for women a self-fulfilling prophecy. Thus, we conclude that, although the State recited a "benign, compensatory purpose," it failed to establish that the alleged objective is the actual purpose underlying the discriminatory classification.[16]

The policy is invalid also because [the] State has made no showing that the gender-based classification is substantially and directly related to its proposed compensatory objective. To the contrary, MUW's policy of permitting men to attend classes as auditors fatally undermines its claim that women, at least those in the School of Nursing, are adversely affected by the presence of men.[17]

Affirmed[c]

CHIEF JUSTICE BURGER, dissenting.

14. Relatively little change has taken place during the past 10 years. In 1980, women received more than 94 percent of the baccalaureate degrees conferred nationwide and constituted 96.5 percent of the registered nurses in the labor force.

15. Officials of the American Nurses Association have suggested that excluding men from the field has depressed nurses' wages. To the extent the exclusion of men has that effect, MUW's admissions policy actually penalizes the very class the State purports to benefit. Cf. *Wiesenfeld.*

16. Even were we to assume that discrimination against women affects their opportunity to obtain an education or to obtain leadership roles in nursing, the challenged policy nonetheless would be invalid, for the State has failed to establish that the legislature intend-

ed the single-sex policy to compensate for any perceived discrimination. * * *

17. Justice Powell's dissent suggests that a second objective is served by the gender-based classification in that Mississippi has elected to provide women a choice of educational environments. Since any gender-based classification provides one class a benefit or choice not available to the other class, however, that argument begs the question. The issue is not whether the benefited class profits from the classification, but whether the State's decision to confer a benefit only upon one class by means of a discriminatory classification is substantially related to achieving a legitimate and substantial goal.

c. The state's contention that Congress had authorized the MUW policy is considered at p. 1164 infra.

I agree generally with Justice Powell's dissenting opinion. I write separately, however, to emphasize that [s]ince the Court's opinion relies heavily on its finding that women have traditionally dominated the nursing profession, it suggests that a State might well be justified in maintaining, for example, the option of an all-women's business school or liberal arts program.

JUSTICE POWELL, with whom JUSTICE REHNQUIST joins, dissenting.

The Court's opinion bows deeply to conformity. Left without honor—indeed, held unconstitutional—is an element of diversity that has characterized much of American education and enriched much of American life. The Court in effect holds today that no State now may provide even a single institution of higher learning open only to women students. [The] only groups with any personal acquaintance with MUW to file amicus briefs are female students and alumnae of MUW. And they have emphatically rejected respondent's arguments. [T]he Court errs seriously by assuming [that] the equal protection standard generally applicable to sex discrimination is appropriate here. That standard was designed to free women from "archaic and overbroad generalizations." *Ballard.* In no previous case have we applied it to invalidate state efforts to *expand* women's choices. Nor are there prior sex discrimination decisions by this Court in which a male plaintiff, as in this case, had the choice of an equal benefit. * * *

By applying heightened equal protection analysis to this case,[9] the Court frustrates the liberating spirit of the Equal Protection Clause. It forbids the States from providing women with an opportunity to choose the type of university they prefer. And yet it is these women whom the Court regards as the *victims* of an illegal, stereotyped perception of the role of women in our society. The Court reasons this way in a case in which no woman has complained, and the only complainant is a man who advances no claims on behalf of anyone else. His claim [is] not that he is being denied a substantive educational opportunity, or even the right to attend an all-male or a coeducational college. It is *only* that the colleges open to him are located at inconvenient distances.

* * * I would sustain Mississippi's right to continue MUW on a rational basis analysis. But I need not apply this "lowest tier" of scrutiny. [More] than 2,000 women presently evidence their preference for MUW by having enrolled [there.] Generations of our finest minds, both among educators and students, have believed that single-sex, college-level institutions afford distinctive benefits. There are many persons, of course, who have different views. But simply because there are these differences is no reason—certainly none of constitutional dimension—to conclude that no substantial state interest is served when such a choice is made available.[17][d]

---

9. Even the Court does not argue that the appropriate standard here is "strict scrutiny"—a standard that none of our "sex discrimination" cases ever has adopted. Sexual segregation in education differs from the tradition [of] "separate but equal" *racial* segregation. It was characteristic of racial segregation that segregated facilities were offered, not as alternatives to increase the choices available to blacks, but as the *sole* alternative. MUW stands in sharp contrast. Of Mississippi's eight public universities and 16 public junior colleges, only MUW considers sex as a criterion for admission. Women consequently are free to select a coeducational education environment for themselves if they so desire;

their attendance of MUW is not a matter of coercion.

17. [It] is understandable that MUW might believe that it could allow men to audit courses without materially affecting its environment. MUW charges tuition but gives no academic credit for auditing. The University evidently is correct in believing that few men will choose to audit under such circumstances. This deviation from a perfect relationship between means and ends is insubstantial.

d. Blackmun, J.'s brief dissenting opinion—agreeing essentially with Powell, J.—is omitted.

Notes and Questions

1. *Segregation.* In *Hogan,* the Court stated that it was "not faced with the question of whether States can provide 'separate but equal' undergraduate institutions for males and females. Cf. *Vorchheimer v. School Dist. of Philadelphia,* 532 F.2d 880 (3d Cir.1976), aff'd by an equally divided Court, 430 U.S. 703 (1977) (Rehnquist, J., not participating; upholding "separate but equal" public schools for boys and girls"). May public schools have separate athletic programs for boys and girls? In all sports? See Stroud, *Sex Discrimination in High School Athletics,* 6 Ind.L.Rev. 661 (1973). May state prisons be sexually segregated? See Note, *The Sexual Segregation of American Prisons,* 82 Yale L.J. 1229 (1973). May state buildings have separate bathrooms for men and women? Of what significance is the constitutional "right of privacy"? See Ch. 7, Sec. 2. Are there reasons to distinguish between race and sex segregation in the above situations? In some, but not all? See generally Wasserstrom, fn. d supra.

2. *The poverty of means-end scrutiny.* Consider Freedman, *Sex Equality, Sex Differences, and the Supreme Court,* 92 Yale L.J. 913, 952–53 (1983): "[When] means-end rationality becomes the dominant element in the opinions, [the] most powerful message the opinions convey is that sex discrimination is irrational as a means to promote the legislature's own goals. [The emphasis] on means-ends rationality runs into difficulty [in] what Professor Wendy Williams has appropriately termed the 'hard' sex discrimination cases [including *Hogan, Michael M.* and *Rostker,* infra]: those in which the Court, and society more generally, is seriously split over whether perceived sex differences are indeed based on 'outmoded' sex stereotypes, or whether the stereotypes are accurate and desirable." See also Karst, *Woman's Constitution,* 1984 Duke L.J. 447, 449: "Any search for the 'true' nature of women will be hindered by the imprint of the stereotype of woman on the mind of the person who is searching, whether that person be male or female. The prevailing construct of woman is largely a male product, for it is men who have held the power to define roles and institutions in our society. And the male stereotype of woman is crucially influenced by men's need to define woman in order to define themselves as men." See generally MacKinnon, *Feminism, Marxism, Method, and the State: Toward Feminist Jurisprudence,* 8 Signs 635, at 635 (1983) ("male and female are created through the erotization of dominance and submission. The man/woman difference and the dominance/submission dynamic define each other"); MacKinnon, *Feminism, Marxism, Method, and the State: An Agenda for Theory,* 7 Signs 515 (1982); On gender roles, see also De Beauvoir, *The Second Sex* (1971); Spender, *Man Made Language* (2d ed. 1985); Olsen, *The Family and the Market: A Study of Ideology and Legal Reform,* 96 Harv.L.Rev. 1497 (1983). On means-end scrutiny in gender cases, see Tribe, *Constitutional Choices* 238–45 (1985); Note, *Toward a Redefinition of Equality,* 95 Harv.L.Rev. 487 (1981).

3. *Other discriminations against men.* (a) *Alimony.* ORR v. ORR, 440 U.S. 268, 99 S.Ct. 1102, 59 L.Ed.2d 306 (1979), considered "two legislative objectives" for an Alabama statute providing that only husbands may be required to pay alimony—(1) to "provide help for needy spouses, using sex as a proxy for need," and (2) to "compensate women for past discrimination during marriage, which assertedly has left them unprepared to fend for themselves." The Court, per BRENNAN, J., held this failed the *Craig* standard: "Under the statute, individualized hearings at which the parties' relative financial circumstances are considered *already* occur. There is no reason, therefore, to use sex as a proxy for need. Needy males could be helped along with needy females with little if any

additional burden on the [state.] Similarly, since individualized hearings can determine which women were in fact discriminated against vis à vis their husbands, as well as which family units defied the stereotype and left the husband dependent on the wife, Alabama's alleged compensatory purpose may be effectuated without placing burdens solely on husbands." e

(b) *Adoption.* CABAN v. MOHAMMED, 441 U.S. 380, 99 S.Ct. 1760, 60 L.Ed.2d 297 (1979), per POWELL, J., held violative of equal protection a New York statute granting the mother (but not the father) of an illegitimate child the right to veto the child's adoption: "Even if the special difficulties attendant upon locating and identifying unwed fathers at birth would justify a legislative distinction between mothers and fathers of newborns, these difficulties need not persist past infancy. When the adoption of an older child is sought, the State's interest in proceeding with adoption cases can be protected by means that do not draw such an inflexible gender-based distinction as that made in § 111. In those cases where the father never has come forward to participate in the rearing of his child, nothing in the Equal Protection Clause precludes the State from withholding from him the privilege of vetoing the adoption of that child. [But] in cases such as this, where the father has established a substantial relationship with the child and admitted his paternity, a State should have no difficulty in identifying [him.] Section 111 both excludes some loving fathers from full participation in the decision whether their children will be adopted and, at the same time, enables some alienated mothers arbitrarily to cut off the paternal rights of fathers. We conclude that this undifferentiated distinction [does] not bear a substantial relationship to the State's asserted interests."

STEVENS, J., joined by Burger, C.J., and Rehnquist, J., dissented: "[I]n the more common adoption situations, the mother [of an illegitimate child] will be the more, and often the only, responsible parent, and [a] paternal consent requirement will constitute a hindrance to the adoption process. Because this general rule is amply justified in its normal application, I would therefore require the party challenging its constitutionality to make some demonstration of unfairness in a significant number of situations before concluding that it violates [equal protection]. That the Court has found a violation without requiring such a showing can only be attributed to its own 'stereotyped reaction' to what is unquestionably, but in this case justifiably, a gender-based distinction." f

(c) *Wrongful death.* PARHAM v. HUGHES, 441 U.S. 347, 99 S.Ct. 1742, 60 L.Ed.2d 269 (1979), upheld a law denying the father (but not the mother) of an illegitimate child the right to sue for the child's wrongful death unless he had

---

e. Blackmun, J., concurred. Burger, C.J., and Powell and Rehnquist, JJ., dissented on procedural grounds to which Stevens, J.'s concurrence responded.

f. Stevens, J., also explained why the Court's holding was "quite narrow": "The procedure to be followed in cases involving infants who are in the custody of their mothers—whether solely or jointly with the father—or of agencies with authority to consent to adoption, is entirely unaffected by the Court's holding or by its reasoning. In fact, as I read the Court's opinion, the statutes now in effect may be enforced as usual unless 'the adoption of older children is sought' and 'the father has established a substantial relation-

ship with the child and admit[s] his paternity.'" Stewart, J., also dissented.

Compare *Lehr v. Robertson,* 463 U.S. 248, 103 S.Ct. 2985, 77 L.Ed.2d 614 (1983), per Stevens, J., upholding (6–3) a New York provision that denies a father, who never had any significant relationship with his illegitimate child, notice and opportunity to be heard before the child may be adopted.

For other decisions dealing with paternal rights in respect to adoption and custody of illegitimate children, see *Stanley v. Illinois,* Sec. 5 infra, and *Quilloin v. Walcott,* p. 202 supra.

legitimated the child. STEWART, J., joined by Burger, C.J., and Rehnquist and Stevens, JJ., found it "clear that the Georgia statute does not invidiously discriminate against the appellant simply because he is of the male sex. The fact is that mothers and fathers of illegitimate children are not similarly situated. Under Georgia law, only a father can by voluntary unilateral action make an illegitimate child legitimate. Unlike the mother of an illegitimate [child,] the identity of the father will frequently be unknown. *Lalli.* [Georgia] has chosen to deal with this problem by allowing only fathers who have established their paternity by legitimating their children to sue for wrongful death, and we cannot say that this solution is an irrational one. [Thus] it is constitutionally irrelevant that the appellant may be able to prove paternity in another manner.

"[Since] fathers who do legitimate their children can sue for wrongful death in precisely the same circumstances as married fathers whose children were legitimate ab initio, the statutory classification does not discriminate against fathers as a class but instead distinguishes between fathers who have legitimated their children and those who have not.[9] Such a classification is quite unlike those condemned in the *Reed, Frontiero,* and *Stanton* cases which were premised upon overbroad generalizations and excluded all members of one sex even though they were similarly situated with members of the other sex."

POWELL, J., concurred because "the gender-based distinction [is] substantially related to achievement of the important state objective of avoiding difficult problems in proving paternity after the death of an illegitimate child."

WHITE, J., joined by Brennan, Marshall and Blackmun, JJ., dissented, finding a "startling circularity" in the plurality's argument: "The issue [is] whether Georgia may require unmarried fathers, but not unmarried mothers, to have pursued the statutory legitimization [procedure]. Seemingly, it is irrelevant that as a matter of state law mothers may not legitimate their children, for they are not required to do so in order to maintain a wrongful death action. That only fathers *may* resort to the legitimization process cannot dissolve the sex discrimination in *requiring* them to.[2] Under the plurality's bootstrap rationale, a State could require that women, but not men, pass a course in order to receive a taxi license, simply by limiting admission to the course to women.[3]"

(d) *Statutory rape.* MICHAEL M. v. SUPERIOR COURT, 450 U.S. 464, 101 S.Ct. 1200, 67 L.Ed.2d 437 (1981), upheld a "statutory rape" law which punished the male, but not the female, party to intercourse when the female was under 18 and not the male's wife. REHNQUIST, J., joined by Burger, C.J., and Stewart and Powell, JJ., observed "that the traditional minimum rationality test takes on a somewhat 'sharper focus' when gender-based classifications are challenged. See *Craig* (Powell, J., concurring). [But] this court has consistently upheld statutes where the gender classification is not invidious, but rather realistically reflects the fact that the sexes are not similarly situated in certain circumstances.

---

9. The ability of a father to make his child legitimate under Georgia law distinguishes this case from *Caban* [where] the father could neither change his children's status nor his own for purposes of the New York adoption statute.

2. The plurality not only fails to examine whether required resort by fathers to the legitimization procedure bears more than a rational relationship to any state interest, but also fails even to address the constitutionality of the sex discrimination in allowing fathers but not mothers to legitimate their children. It is anomalous, at least, to assert that sex discrimination in one statute is constitutionally invisible because it is tied to sex discrimination in another statute, without subjecting *either* [to] an appropriate level of scrutiny.

3. Men and women would therefore not be "similarly situated." Yet requiring a course for women but not for men is quite obviously a classification on the basis of sex.

Parham; Webster; Ballard; Kahn. As the Court has stated, a legislature may 'provide for the special problems of women.' *Wiesenfeld.*   *   *   *

"We are satisfied not only that the prevention of illegitimate [teenage] pregnancy is at least one of the 'purposes' of the statute, but that the State has a strong interest in preventing such pregnancy.[7]

"Because virtually all of the significant harmful and inescapably identifiable consequences of teenage pregnancy fall on the young female, a legislature acts well within its authority when it elects to punish only the participant who, by nature, suffers few of the consequences of his conduct. It is hardly unreasonable for a legislature acting to protect minor females to exclude them from punishment. Moreover, the risk of pregnancy itself constitutes a substantial deterrence to young females. [A] criminal sanction imposed solely on males thus serves to roughly 'equalize' the deterrents on the sexes.

"[The] State persuasively contends that a gender-neutral statute would frustrate its interest in effective enforcement. Its view is that a female is surely less likely to report violations of the statute if she herself would be subject to criminal prosecution. In an area already fraught with prosecutorial difficulties, we decline to hold that the Equal Protection Clause requires a legislature to enact a statute so broad that it may well be incapable of enforcement.

"[Finally], the statute places a burden on males [not] shared by females. But we find nothing to suggest that men, because of past discrimination or peculiar disadvantages, are in need of the special solicitude of the courts.[g] Nor is this a case where the gender classification is made 'solely [for] administrative convenience,' as in *Frontiero,* or rests on 'the baggage of sexual stereotypes' as in *Orr.*"[h]

BRENNAN, J., joined by White and Marshall, JJ., dissented: "None of the three opinions upholding the California statute fairly applies the equal protection analysis this Court has so carefully developed since *Craig.* [The] plurality assumes that a gender-neutral statute would be less effective [in] deterring sexual activity because a gender-neutral statute would create significant enforce-

---

7. Although petitioner concedes that the State has a "compelling" interest in preventing teenage pregnancy, he contends that the "true" purpose [is] to protect the virtue and chastity of young women. As such, the statute is unjustifiable because it rests on archaic stereotypes. [Even] if the preservation of female chastity were one of the motives of the statute, and even if that motive be impermissible, petitioner's argument must fail because "[this] court will not strike down an otherwise constitutional statute on the basis of an alleged illicit legislative motive." *United States v. O'Brien,* [p. 515 supra].

g. Does the statute also discriminate against females? Consider Law, *Rethinking Sex and the Constitution,* 132 U.Pa.L.Rev. 955, 1001 (1984): "[U]nder the California law a young man is free to be sexual as long as he chooses a partner who is older than eighteen, while a young woman may not legally have sex with anyone, except her husband if she is married. [The decision] accepts and reinforces the sex-based stereotype that young men may legitimately engage in sexual activity and young women may not."

h. Blackmun, J., concurred in the judgment on the test "exemplified by" *Reed* and *Craig* "and by *Ballard, Wiesenfeld,* and *Kahn.*"

Stewart, J., concurred, noting "that the statutory discrimination, when viewed as part of the wider scheme of California law, is not as clearcut as might at first appear. Females are not freed from criminal liability in California for engaging in sexual activity that may be harmful. It is unlawful, for example, for any person, of either sex, [to] contribute to the delinquency of anyone under 18 years of age. All persons are prohibited [from] consensual intercourse with a child under 14. [Finally,] females may be brought within the proscription of § 261.5 itself, since a female may be charged with aiding and abetting its violation. [A]pproximately 14% of the juveniles arrested for participation in acts made unlawful by § 261.5 between 1975 and 1979 were females. Moreover, an underage female who is as culpable as her male partner, or more culpable, may be prosecuted as a juvenile delinquent."

ment problems. [But] a State's bare assertion [is] not enough to meet its burden of proof under *Craig.* Rather, the State must produce evidence that will persuade the Court that its assertion is true [and the] State has [not].

"The second flaw in the State's assertion is that even assuming that a gender-neutral statute would be more difficult to enforce, the State has still not shown that those enforcement problems would make such a statute less effective than a gender-based statute in deterring minor females from engaging in sexual intercourse. Common sense, however, suggests that a gender-neutral statutory rape law is potentially a *greater* deterrent of sexual activity than a gender-based law, for the simple reason that a gender-neutral law subjects both men and women to criminal sanctions and thus arguably has a deterrent effect on twice as many potential violators. Even if fewer persons were prosecuted under the gender-neutral law, as the State suggests, it would still be true that twice as many persons would be *subject* to arrest."

STEVENS, J., also dissented: "[T]hat a female confronts a greater risk of harm than a male is a reason for applying the prohibition to her—not a reason for granting her a license to use her own judgment on whether or not to assume the risk. Surely, if we examine the problem from the point of view of society's interest in preventing the risk-creating conduct from occurring at all, it is irrational to exempt 50% of the potential violators. * * *

"Finally, even if my logic is faulty and there actually is some speculative basis for treating equally guilty males and females differently, I still believe that any such speculative justification would be outweighed by the paramount interest in even-handed enforcement of the law. A rule that authorizes punishment of only one of two equally guilty wrongdoers violates the essence of the constitutional requirement that the sovereign must govern impartially."[i]

(e) *Draft registration.* ROSTKER v. GOLDBERG, 453 U.S. 57, 101 S.Ct. 2646, 69 L.Ed.2d 478 (1981), per REHNQUIST, J., upheld a Military Selective Service Act (MSSA) provision "authorizing the President to require the registration of males and not females": "The case arises in the context of Congress' authority over national defense and military affairs, and perhaps in no other area has the Court accorded Congress greater deference. * * *

"Not only is the scope of Congress' constitutional power in this area broad, but the lack of competence on the part of the courts is marked. * * *

"None of this is to say that Congress is free to disregard the Constitution when it acts in the area of military affairs. [B]ut the tests and limitations to be applied may differ because of the military context. We of course do not abdicate our ultimate responsibility to decide the constitutional question, but simply recognize that the Constitution itself requires such deference to congressional choice. In deciding the question before us we must be particularly careful not to substitute our judgment of what is desirable for that of Congress, or our own evaluation of evidence for a reasonable evaluation by [Congress].

"No one could deny that under the test of *Craig,* the Government's interest in raising and supporting armies is an 'important governmental interest.' Congress and its committees carefully considered and debated two alternative means

---

i. Consider Olsen, *Statutory Rape: A Feminist Critique of Rights Analysis,* 63 Tex.L.Rev. 391, ___ (1984): "[The statute] protects minor females from exploitative intercourse with anyone, but does not protect minor males from exploitative intercourse with females who are above the age of consent. [In the dissenters' view,] 'neutrality' would be achieved by placing blame and criminal liability on the woman, not by treating young men as equally in need of state protection or as equally vulnerable to sexual objectification by the state."

of furthering that interest: the first was to register only males for potential conscription, and the other was to register both sexes. Congress chose the former alternative. When that decision is challenged on equal protection grounds, the question a court must decide is not which alternative it would have chosen, [but] whether that chosen by Congress denies equal protection of the laws. * * *

"This case is quite different from several of the gender-based discrimination cases we have considered in [that] Congress did not act 'unthinkingly' or 'reflexively and not for any considered reason.' The question of registering women for the draft not only received considerable national attention and was the subject of wide-ranging public debate, but also was extensively considered by Congress in hearings, floor debate, and in committee. [This] clearly establishes that the decision to exempt women from registration was not the 'accidental byproduct of a traditional way of thinking about women.' *Webster.* * * *

"Congress determined that any future draft, which would be facilitated by the registration scheme, would be characterized by a need for combat troops. [Since] women are [statutorily] excluded from combat, Congress concluded that they would not be needed in the event of a draft, and therefore decided not to register them. [The] exemption of women from registration is not only sufficiently but closely related to Congress' purpose in authorizing registration. See *Michael M.; Craig; Reed.* [As] was the case in *Ballard,* 'the gender classification is not invidious, but rather realistically reflects the fact that the sexes are not similarly situated' in this case. *Michael M.* The Constitution requires that Congress treat similarly situated persons similarly, not that it engage in gestures of superficial equality.

"In holding the MSSA constitutionally invalid the District Court relied heavily on the President's decision to seek authority to register women and the testimony of members of the Executive Branch and the military in support of that decision. As stated by the Administration's witnesses before Congress, however, the President's 'decision to ask for authority to register women is based on equity.' * * * Congress was certainly entitled, in the exercise of its constitutional powers to raise and regulate armies and navies, to focus on the question of military need rather than 'equity.' * * *

"Although the military experts who testified in favor of registering women uniformly opposed the actual drafting of women, there was testimony that in the event of a draft of 650,000 the military could absorb some 80,000 female inductees [to] fill noncombat positions, freeing men to go to the front. In relying on this testimony, [the] District Court palpably exceeded its authority when it ignored Congress' considered response to this line of reasoning.

"In the first place, assuming that a small number of women could be drafted for noncombat roles, Congress simply did not consider it worth the added burdens of including women in draft and registration plans. * * *

"Congress also concluded that whatever the need for women for noncombat roles during mobilization, [it] could be met by volunteers.

"Most significantly, Congress determined that staffing noncombat positions with women during a mobilization would be positively detrimental to the important goal of military flexibility. [The] District Court was quite wrong in undertaking an independent evaluation of this evidence, rather than adopting an appropriately deferential examination of *Congress'* evaluation of that evidence."

WHITE, J., joined by Brennan, J., dissented: "I assume what has not been challenged in this case—that excluding women from combat positions does not offend the Constitution. Granting that, it is self evident that if during mobilization for war, all noncombat military positions must be filled by combat-qualified personnel available to be moved into combat positions, there would be no occasion whatsoever to have any women in the Army, whether as volunteers or inductees. The Court appears to say that Congress concluded as much and that we should accept that judgment even though the serious view of the Executive Branch, including the responsible military services, is to the contrary. * * * I perceive little, if any, indication that Congress itself concluded that every position in the military, no matter how far removed from combat, must be filled with combat-ready men. Common sense and experience in recent wars, where women volunteers were employed in substantial numbers, belie this view of reality. * * *

"I would also have little difficulty agreeing to a reversal if all the women who could serve in wartime without adversely affecting combat readiness could predictably be obtained through volunteers. In that event, [equal protection] would not require the United States to go through, and a large segment of the population to be burdened with, the expensive and essentially useless procedure of registering women. But again I cannot agree with the Court that Congress concluded or that the legislative record indicates that each of the services could rely on women volunteers to fill all the positions for which they might be eligible in the event of mobilization. On the contrary, the [record] supports the District Court's finding that the services would have to conscript at least 80,000 persons to fill positions for which combat-ready men would not be required. * * *

"The Court also submits that because the primary purpose of registration and conscription is to supply combat troops and because the great majority of noncombat positions must be filled by combat-trained men ready to be rotated into combat, the absolute number of positions for which women would be eligible is so small as to be de minimis and of no moment for equal protection purposes, especially in light of the administrative burdens involved in registering all women of suitable age. There is some sense to this; but at least on the record before us, the number of women who could be used in the military without sacrificing combat-readiness is not at all small or insubstantial, and administrative convenience has not been sufficient justification for the kind of outright gender-based discrimination involved [here]."

MARSHALL, J., joined by Brennan, J., dissented: "The Court today places its imprimatur on one of the most potent remaining public expressions of 'ancient canards about the proper role of women.' [W]e are not called upon to decide whether either men or women can be drafted at all, whether they must be drafted in equal numbers, in what order they should be drafted, or once inducted, how they are to be trained for their respective functions. In addition, this case does not involve a challenge to the statutes or policies that prohibit female members of the Armed Forces from serving in combat. It is with this understanding that I turn to the task at hand. [In] my judgment, there simply is no basis for concluding in this case that excluding women from registration is substantially related to the achievement of a concededly important governmental interest in maintaining an effective defense. * * *

"The Government does not defend the exclusion of women from registration on the ground that preventing women from serving in the military is substantially related to the effectiveness of the Armed Forces. Indeed, the successful experience of women serving in all branches of the Armed Services would belie any such claim. * * *

"The most authoritative discussion of Congress' reasons [is] contained in the report prepared by the Senate Armed Services Committee on the Fiscal Year 1981 Defense Authorization Bill. S.Rep. No. 96–826. * * *

"According to the Senate Report, '[t]he policy precluding the use of women in combat is [the] most important reason for not including women in a registration system.' [T]he Report declared: 'Registering women for assignment to combat [would] leave the actual performance of sexually mixed units as an experiment to be conducted in war with unknown risk—a risk that the committee finds militarily unwarranted and dangerous. Moreover, the committee feels that any attempt to assign women to combat positions could affect the national resolve at the time of mobilization, a time of great strain on all aspects of the Nation's resources.' [The] Court then reasons that since women are not eligible for assignment to combat, Congress' decision to exclude them from registration is not unconstitutional discrimination inasmuch as '[m]en and women, because of the combat restrictions on women, are simply not similarly situated for purposes of a draft or registration for a draft.' There is a certain logic to this reasoning, but the Court's approach is fundamentally flawed.

"In the first place, although the Court purports to apply the *Craig* test, the 'similarly situated' analysis the Court employs is in fact significantly different from the *Craig* approach. Compare *Kirchberg* (employing *Craig* test) with id. (Stewart, J., concurring) (employing 'similarly situated' analysis). The Court essentially reasons that the gender classification employed by the MSSA is constitutionally permissible because nondiscrimination is not necessary to achieve the purpose of registration to prepare for a draft of combat troops. In other words, the majority concludes that women may be excluded from registration because they will not be needed in the event of a draft.

"This analysis, however, focuses on the wrong question. The relevant inquiry under the *Craig* test is not whether a *gender-neutral* classification would substantially advance important governmental interests. Rather, the question is whether the gender-based classification is itself substantially related to the achievement of the asserted governmental interest. Thus, the Government's task in this case is to demonstrate that excluding women from registration substantially furthers the goal of preparing for a draft of combat troops. Or to put it another way, the Government must show that registering women would substantially impede its efforts to prepare for such a draft. Under our precedents, the Government cannot meet this burden without showing that a gender neutral statute would be a less effective means of attaining this end. [In] this case, the Government makes no claim that preparing for a draft of combat troops cannot be accomplished just as effectively by *registering* both men and women but *drafting* only men if only men turn out to be needed.[11] Nor can the Government argue that this alternative entails the additional cost and administrative inconvenience of registering women. This Court has repeatedly stated that [administrative convenience] is not an adequate constitutional justification under the *Craig* test.

"The fact that registering women in no way obstructs the governmental interest in preparing for a draft of combat troops points up a second flaw in the Court's analysis. The Court essentially reduces the question of the constitution-

---

11. Alternatively, the Government could employ a classification that is related to the statutory objective but is not based on gender, for example, combat eligibility. Under the current scheme, large subgroups of the male population who are ineligible for combat because of physical handicaps or conscientious objector status are nonetheless required to register.

ality of male-only *registration* to the validity of a hypothetical program for *conscripting* only men. [If] it could indeed be guaranteed in advance that conscription would be reimposed by Congress only in circumstances where, and in a form under which, all conscripts would have to be trained for and assigned to combat or combat rotation positions from which women are categorically excluded, then it could be argued that registration of women would be pointless.

"But of course, no such guarantee is possible. Certainly, nothing about the MSSA limits Congress to reinstituting the draft only in such circumstances. For example, Congress may decide that the All-Volunteer Armed Forces are inadequate to meet the Nation's defense needs even in times of peace and reinstitute peacetime conscription. In that event, the hypothetical draft the Court relied [on] would presumably be of little relevance * * *. The fact that registration is a first step in the conscription process does not mean that a registration law expressly discriminating between men and women may be justified by a valid conscription program which would, in retrospect, make the current discrimination appear functionally related to the program that emerged.

"But even addressing the Court's reasoning on its own terms, its analysis is flawed because the entire argument rests on a premise that is demonstrably false. As noted, the majority simply assumes that registration prepares for a draft in which *every* draftee must be available for assignment to combat. But [this] finds no support in either the testimony before Congress, or more importantly, in the findings of the Senate Report. * * * Testimony about personnel requirements in the event of a draft established that women could fill at least 80,000 of the 650,000 positions for which conscripts would be inducted. Thus, [the] statutes and policies barring women from combat do not provide a reason for distinguishing between male and female potential conscripts; the two groups are, in the majority's parlance, 'similarly situated.' As such, the combat restrictions cannot by themselves supply the constitutionally required justification for the MSSA's gender-based classification. [T]he Court asserts that 'Congress determined that staffing noncombat positions with women during a mobilization would be positively detrimental to the important goal of military flexibility.' [But] to justify the exclusion of women from registration and the draft on this ground, there must be a further showing that staffing even a limited number of noncombat positions with women would impede military flexibility. I find nothing in the Senate Report to provide any basis for the Court's representation that Congress believed this to be the case.

"The Senate Report concluded [that] drafting *'very large numbers* of women' would hinder military flexibility. [But the] testimony on this issue at the congressional hearings was that drafting a limited number of women is quite compatible with the military's need for flexibility. In concluding that the Armed Services could usefully employ at least 80,000 women conscripts out of a total of 650,000 draftees that would be needed in the event of a major European war, the Defense Department took into account both the need for rotation of combat personnel and the possibility that some support personnel might have to be sent into combat. [The] combat restrictions that would prevent a female draftee from serving in a combat or combat rotation position also apply to the 150,000–250,000 women volunteers in the Armed Services. If the presence of increasing but controlled numbers of female volunteers has not unacceptably 'divide[d] the military into two groups,' it is difficult to see how the induction of a similarly limited additional number of women could accomplish this result. [T]he Senate Report establishes that induction of a large number of men but only a limited number of women [would] be substantially related to important governmental interests. But the discussion and findings in the Senate Report do not enable the Government to carry its burden of demonstrating that *completely* excluding women from the draft by excluding them from registration substantially furthers important governmental objectives."[j]

4. *Equal Rights Amendment.* This proposed amendment—that "equality of rights under the law shall not be denied or abridged by the United States or by an State on account of sex"—was approved by 35 states (three less than required for ratification) at its expiration in 1982.

How would this affect the issues considered in this section? See generally Brown, Emerson, Falk & Freedman, *The Equal Rights Amendment: A Constitutional Basis for Equal Rights for Women*, 80 Yale L.J. 871 (1971); *Equal Rights for Women: A Symposium on the Proposed Constitutional Amendment*, 6 Harv. Civ.Rts.-Civ.Lib.L.Rev. 125 (1971).

V. MENTAL RETARDATION

CLEBURNE v. CLEBURNE LIVING CENTER, INC.

—— U.S. ——, 105 S.Ct. 3249, 87 L.Ed.2d 313 (1985).

JUSTICE WHITE delivered the opinion of the Court.

A Texas city denied a special permit for the operation of a group home for the mentally retarded. [Permits under the zoning ordinance must be renewed annually and applicants must "obtain the signatures of the property owners within 200 feet of the property to be used."] It was anticipated that the [Featherston] home would house 13 retarded men and women, who would be under the constant supervision of CLC staff members. * * *

[The] general rule [under the Equal Protection Clause] is that legislation is presumed to be valid and will be sustained if the classification drawn by the statute is rationally related to a legitimate state interest. *Schweiker v. Wilson; United States R.R. Retirement Bd. v. Fritz; Vance v. Bradley; New Orleans v. Dukes*, [Sec. 1 supra]. When social or economic legislation is at issue, the Equal Protection Clause allows the states wide latitude, and the Constitution presumes that even improvident decisions will eventually be rectified by the democratic processes.

---

j. Consider Williams, fn. b, p. 962 supra, at 189–90: "As for *Rostker*, the conflicts among feminists were overtly expressed. Some of us felt it essential that we support the notion that a single-sex draft was unconstitutional; others felt that feminists should not take such a position. These latter groups explicitly contrasted the female ethic of nurturance and life-giving with a male ethic of aggression and militarism and asserted that if we argued to the Court that single-sex registration is unconstitutional we would be betraying ourselves and supporting what we find least acceptable about the male world.

"To me, this latter argument quite overtly taps qualities that the culture has ascribed to woman-as-childrearer and converts them to a normative value statement, one with which it is easy for us to sympathize. This is one of the circumstances in which the feeling that 'I want what he's got but I don't want to be what he's had to be in order to get it' comes quickly to the surface. But I also believe that the reflexive response based on these deeper cultural senses leads us to untenable positions. [To] me, *Rostker* never posed the question of whether women should be forced as men now are to fight wars, but whether we, like them, must take the responsibility for deciding whether or not to fight, whether or not to bear the cost of risking our lives, on the one hand, or resisting in the name of peace, on the other. And do we not, by insisting upon our differences at these crucial junctures, promote and reinforce the us-them dichotomy that permits the Rehnquists and the Stewarts to resolve matters of great importance and complexity by the simplistic, reflexive assertion that men and women 'are simply not similarly situated?'"

The general rule gives way, however, when a statute classifies by race, alienage or national origin. These factors are so seldom relevant to the achievement of any legitimate state interest that laws grounded in such considerations are deemed to reflect prejudice and antipathy—a view that those in the burdened class are not as worthy or deserving as others. For these reasons and because such discrimination is unlikely to be soon rectified by legislative means, these laws are subjected to strict scrutiny * * *.

Legislative classifications based on gender also call for a heightened standard of review. [Rather] than resting on meaningful considerations, statutes distributing benefits and burdens between the sexes in different ways very likely reflect outmoded notions of the relative capabilities of men and women. A gender classification fails unless it is substantially related to a sufficiently important governmental interest. Because illegitimacy is beyond the individual's control and bears "no relation to the individual's ability to participate in and contribute to society," official discriminations resting on that characteristic are also subject to somewhat heightened review. Those restrictions "will survive equal protection scrutiny to the extent they are substantially related to a legitimate state interest." *Mills v. Habluetzel,* [Part III supra].

We have declined, however, to extend heightened review to differential treatment based on [age]. The lesson of *Murgia,* [Part I supra], is that where individuals in the group affected by a law have distinguishing characteristics relevant to interests the state has the authority to implement, the courts have been very reluctant, as they should be in our federal system and with our respect for the separation of powers, to closely scrutinize legislative choices as to whether, how and to what extent those interests should be pursued. In such cases, the Equal Protection Clause requires only a rational means to serve a legitimate end.

Against this background, we conclude [that] the Court of Appeals erred in holding mental retardation a quasi-suspect classification. [First, those] who are mentally retarded have a reduced ability to cope with and function in the everyday world. [T]hey range from those whose disability is not immediately evident to those who must be constantly cared for. They are thus different, immutably so, in relevant respects, and the states' interest in dealing with and providing for them is plainly a legitimate one. How this large and diversified group is to be treated under the law is a difficult and often a technical matter, very much a task for legislators guided by qualified professionals and not by the perhaps ill-informed opinions of the judiciary. Heightened scrutiny inevitably involves substantive judgments about legislative decisions, and we doubt that the predicate for such judicial oversight is present where the classification deals with mental retardation.

Second, the distinctive legislative response, both national and state, to the plight of those who are mentally retarded demonstrates not only that they have unique problems, but also that the lawmakers have been addressing their difficulties in a manner that belies a continuing antipathy or prejudice and a corresponding need for more intrusive oversight by the judiciary. Thus, the federal government has not only outlawed discrimination against the mentally retarded in federally funded programs, see § 504 of the Rehabilitation Act of 1973, 29 U.S.C. § 794, but it has also provided the retarded with the right to receive "appropriate treatment, services, and habilitation" in a setting that is "least restrictive of [their] personal liberty." Developmental Disabilities Assistance and Bill of Rights Act, 42 U.S.C. §§ 6010(1), (2). * * * Texas has similarly enacted legislation that acknowledges the special status of the mentally retarded by conferring certain rights upon them, such as "the right to live in the least restrictive setting appropriate to [their] individual needs and abilities," * * *.[11] [It] may be, as CLC contends, that legislation designed to benefit, rather than disadvantage, the retarded would generally withstand examination under a test of heightened scrutiny. The relevant inquiry, however, is whether heightened scrutiny is constitutionally mandated in the first instance. Even assuming that many of these laws could be shown to be substantially related to an important governmental purpose, merely requiring the legislature to justify its efforts in these terms may lead it to refrain from acting at all. Much recent legislation intended to benefit the retarded also assumes the need for measures that might be perceived to disadvantage them. The Education of the Handicapped Act, for example, requires an "appropriate" education, not one that is equal in all respects to the education of non-retarded children; clearly, admission to a class that exceeded the abilities of a retarded child would not be appropriate. Similarly, the Developmental Disabilities Assistance Act and the Texas act give the retarded the right to live only in the "least restrictive setting" appropriate to their abilities, implicitly assuming the need for at least some restrictions that would not be imposed on others. Especially given the wide variation in the abilities and needs of the retarded themselves, governmental bodies must have a certain amount of flexibility and freedom from judicial oversight in shaping and limiting their remedial efforts.

Third, the legislative response, which could hardly have occurred and survived without public support, negates any claim that the mentally retarded are politically powerless in the sense that they have no ability to attract the attention of the lawmakers. Any minority can be said to be powerless to assert direct control over the legislature, but if that were a criterion for higher level scrutiny by the courts, much economic and social legislation would now be suspect.

Fourth, if the large and amorphous class of the mentally retarded were deemed quasi-suspect, [it] would be difficult to find a principled way to distinguish a variety of other groups who have perhaps immutable disabilities setting them off from others, who cannot themselves mandate the desired legislative responses, and who can claim some degree of prejudice from at least part of the public at large. One need mention in this respect only the aging, the disabled, the mentally ill, and the infirm. We are reluctant to set out on that course, and we decline to do so.

Doubtless, there have been and there will continue to be instances of discrimination against the retarded that are in fact invidious, and that are properly subject to judicial correction under constitutional norms. But the appropriate method of reaching such instances is [to] look to the likelihood that governmental action premised on a particular classification is valid as a general matter, not merely to the specifics of the case before us. Because mental retardation is a characteristic that the government may legitimately take into account in a wide range of decisions, and because both state and federal governments have recently committed themselves to assisting the retarded, we will not presume that any given legislative action, even one that disadvantages retarded individuals, is rooted in considerations that the Constitution will not tolerate.

11. [A] number of states have [laws] prohibiting zoning that excludes the retarded.

Our refusal to recognize the retarded as a quasi-suspect class does not leave them entirely unprotected from invidious discrimination. To withstand equal protection review, legislation that distinguishes between the mentally retarded and others must be rationally related to a legitimate governmental purpose. This standard, we believe, affords government the latitude necessary both to pursue policies designed to assist the retarded in realizing their full potential, and to freely and efficiently engage in activities that burden the retarded in what is essentially an incidental manner. The State may not rely on a classification whose relationship to an asserted goal is so attenuated as to render the distinction arbitrary or irrational. See *Zobel v. Williams,* [Sec. 4, II infra]; *U.S. Dep't of Agriculture v. Moreno,* [Sec. 4, II infra]. Furthermore, some objectives—such as "a bare * * * desire to harm a politically unpopular group," *Moreno* —are not legitimate state interests. Beyond that, the mentally retarded, like others, have and retain their substantive constitutional rights in addition to the right to be treated equally by the law. * * *

The constitutional issue is clearly posed. The City does not require a special use permit in an R–3 zone for apartment houses, multiple dwellings, boarding and lodging houses, fraternity or sorority houses, dormitories, apartment hotels, hospitals, sanitariums, nursing homes for convalescents or the aged (other than for the insane or feeble-minded or alcoholics or drug addicts), private clubs or fraternal orders, and other specified uses. [I]n our view the record does not reveal any rational basis for believing that the Featherston home would pose any special threat to the city's legitimate interests * * *.

The District Court found that the City Council's insistence on the permit rested on several factors. First, the Council was concerned with the negative attitude of the majority of property owners located within 200 feet of the Featherston facility, as well as with the fears of elderly residents of the neighborhood. But mere negative attitudes, or fear, unsubstantiated by factors which are properly cognizable in a zoning proceeding, are not permissible bases for treating a home for the mentally retarded differently from apartment houses, multiple dwellings, and the like. * * *

Second, the Council [was] concerned that the facility was across the street from a junior high school, and it feared that the students might harass the occupants of the Featherston home. But the school itself is attended by about 30 mentally retarded students, and denying a permit based on such vague, undifferentiated fears is again permitting some portion of the community to validate what would otherwise be an equal protection violation. The other objection to the home's location was that it was located on "a five hundred year flood plain." This concern with the possibility of a flood, however, can hardly be based on a distinction between the Featherston home and, for example, nursing homes, homes for convalescents or the aged, or sanitariums or hospitals, any of which could be located on the Featherston site without obtaining a special use permit. The same may be said of another concern of the Council—doubts about the legal responsibility for actions which the mentally retarded might take. If there is no concern about legal responsibility with respect to other uses that would be permitted in the area, such as boarding and fraternity houses, it is difficult to believe that the groups of mildly or moderately mentally retarded individuals who would live at 201 Featherston would present any different or special hazard.

Fourth, the Council was concerned with the size of the home and the number of people that would occupy it. [But] there would be no restrictions on the number of people who could occupy this home as a boarding house, nursing home, family dwelling, fraternity house, or dormitory. [At] least this record does not clarify how, in this connection, the characteristics of the intended occupants of the Featherston home rationally justify denying to those occupants what would be permitted to groups occupying the same site for different purposes. Those who would live in the Featherston home are the type of individuals who, with supporting staff, satisfy federal and state standards for group housing in the community; and there is no dispute that the home would meet the federal square-footage-per-resident requirement for facilities of this type. See 42 CFR § 442.447 (1984). * * *

In the courts below the city also urged that the ordinance is aimed at avoiding concentration of population and at lessening congestion of the streets. These concerns obviously fail to explain why apartment houses, fraternity and sorority houses, hospitals and the like, may freely locate in the area without a permit. So, too, the expressed worry about fire hazards, the serenity of the neighborhood, and the avoidance of danger to other residents fail rationally to justify singling out a home such as 201 Featherston for the special use permit, yet imposing no such restrictions on the many other uses freely permitted in the neighborhood.

The short of it is that requiring the permit in this case appears to us to rest on an irrational prejudice against the mentally retarded. [Thus, the] judgment of the Court of Appeals is affirmed insofar as it invalidates the zoning ordinance as applied to the Featherston home. * * *

JUSTICE STEVENS, with whom THE CHIEF JUSTICE joins, concurring.

[O]ur cases reflect a continuum of judgmental responses to differing classifications which have been explained in opinions by terms ranging from "strict scrutiny" at one extreme to "rational basis" at the other. I have never been persuaded that these so called "standards" adequately explain the decisional process. Cases involving classifications based on alienage, illegal residency, illegitimacy, gender, age, or—as in this case—mental retardation, do not fit well into sharply defined classifications.

[It] would be utterly irrational to limit the franchise on the basis of height or weight; it is equally invalid to limit it on the basis of skin color. None of these attributes has any bearing at all on the citizen's willingness or ability to exercise that civil right. We do not need to apply a special standard, or to apply "strict scrutiny," or even "heightened scrutiny," to decide such cases.

In every equal protection case, we have to ask certain basic questions. What class is harmed by the legislation, and has it been subjected to a "tradition of disfavor" by our laws? What is the public purpose that is being served by the law? What is the characteristic of the disadvantaged class that justifies the disparate treatment? In most cases the answer to these questions will tell us whether the statute has a "rational basis." The answers will result in the virtually automatic invalidation of racial classifications and in the validation of most economic classifications, but they will provide differing results in cases involving classifications based on alienage, gender, or illegitimacy. But that is not because we apply an "intermediate standard of review" in these cases; rather it is because the characteristics of these groups are sometimes relevant and sometimes irrelevant to a valid public purpose, or, more specifically, to the purpose that the challenged laws purportedly intended to serve.

Every law that places the mentally retarded in a special class is not presumptively irrational. The differences between mentally retarded persons and those with greater mental capacity are obviously relevant to certain legislative decisions. * * *

Even so, the Court of Appeals correctly observed that through ignorance and prejudice the mentally retarded "have been subjected to a history of unfair and often grotesque mistreatment." The [record in this case] convinces me that this permit was required because of the irrational fears of neighboring property owners, rather than for the protection of the mentally retarded persons who would reside in respondent's home. * * *

Accordingly, I join the opinion of the Court.

JUSTICE MARSHALL, with whom JUSTICE BRENNAN and JUSTICE BLACKMUN join, concurring in the judgment in part and dissenting in part.

The Court holds [the] ordinance invalid on rational basis grounds and disclaims that anything special, in the form of heightened scrutiny, is taking place. Yet Cleburne's ordinance surely would be valid under the traditional rational basis test applicable to economic and commercial regulation. In my view, it is important to articulate, as the Court does not, the facts and principles that justify subjecting this zoning ordinance to the searching review—the heightened scrutiny—that actually leads to its invalidation. * * *

The Court, for example, concludes that legitimate concerns for fire hazards or the serenity of the neighborhood do not justify singling out respondents to bear the burdens of these concerns, for analogous permitted uses appear to pose similar threats. Yet under the traditional and most minimal version of the rational basis test, "reform may take one step at a time, addressing itself to the phase of the problem which seems most acute to the legislative mind." The "record" is said not to support the ordinance's classifications, but under the traditional standard we do not sift through the record to determine whether policy decisions are squarely supported by a firm factual foundation.

Finally, the Court further finds it "difficult to believe" that the retarded present different or special hazards than other groups. In normal circumstances, the burden is not on the legislature to convince the Court that the lines it has drawn are sensible; legislation is presumptively constitutional, and a State "is not required to resort to close distinctions or to maintain a precise, scientific uniformity with reference" to its goals. [The] same imprecision in a similar ordinance that required opticians but not optometrists to be licensed to practice, see *Williamson v. Lee Optical Co.,* [Sec. 1 supra], or that excluded new but not old businesses from parts of a community, see *Dukes,* [Sec. 1 supra], would hardly be fatal to the statutory scheme.

The refusal to acknowledge that something more than minimum rationality review is at work here is, in my view, unfortunate in at least two respects.[4] The suggestion that the traditional rational basis test allows this sort of searching inquiry creates precedent for this Court and lower courts to subject economic and commercial classifications to similar and searching "ordinary" rational basis review—a small and regrettable step back toward the days of *Lochner v. New York* [p. 67 supra]. Moreover, by failing to articulate the factors that justify today's "second order" rational basis review, the Court provides no principled foundation for determining when more searching inquiry is to be invoked. Lower courts are thus left in the dark on this important question, and this Court

4. The two cases the Court cites in its rational basis discussion, *Zobel* and *Moreno,* expose the special nature of the rational basis test employed today. As two of only a handful of modern equal protection cases striking down legislation under what purports to be a rational basis standard, these cases must be and generally have been viewed as intermediate review decisions masquerading in rational basis language. See, e.g., Tribe, *American Constitutional Law* 1090, n. 10 (1978). (discussing *Moreno*); see also *Moreno* (Douglas, J., concurring); *Zobel* (Brennan, J., concurring).

remains unaccountable for its decisions employing, or refusing to employ, particularly searching scrutiny. * * *

I have long believed the level of scrutiny employed in an equal protection case should vary with "the constitutional and societal importance of the interest adversely affected and the recognized invidiousness of the basis upon which the particular classification is drawn." *Rodriguez* (Marshall, J., dissenting). See also *Dandridge* (Marshall, J., dissenting). When a zoning ordinance works to exclude the retarded from all residential districts in a community, these two considerations require that the ordinance be convincingly justified as substantially furthering legitimate and important purposes.

First, the interest [in] establishing group homes is substantial, [for] as deinstitutionalization has progressed, group homes have become the primary means by which retarded adults can enter life in the community. * * *

Second, the mentally retarded have been subject to a "lengthy and tragic history" of segregation and discrimination that can only be called grotesque. [The] searching scrutiny I would give to restrictions on the ability of the retarded to establish community group homes leads me to conclude that Cleburne's vague generalizations for classifying the "feeble minded" with drug addicts, alcoholics, and the insane, and excluding them where the elderly, the ill, the boarder, and the transient are allowed, are not substantial or important enough to overcome the suspicion that the ordinance rests on impermissible assumptions or outmoded and perhaps invidious stereotypes. * * *

The Court downplays the lengthy "history of purposeful unequal treatment" of the retarded by pointing to recent legislative action that is said to "beli[e] a continuing antipathy or prejudice." Building on this point, the Court similarly concludes that the retarded are not "politically powerless" and deserve no greater judicial protection than "any minority" that wins some political battles and loses others. The import of these conclusions, it seems, is that the only discrimination courts may remedy is the discrimination they alone are perspicacious enough to see. [B]ut history makes clear that constitutional principles of equality, like constitutional principles of liberty, property, and due process, evolve over [time].

It is natural that evolving standards of equality come to be embodied in legislation. When that occurs, courts should look to the fact of such change as a source of guidance on evolving principles of equality [as when the Court] extended heightened scrutiny to gender classifications and drew on parallel legislative developments to support that extension [*Frontiero*].

Moreover, even when judicial action *has* catalyzed legislative change, that change certainly does not eviscerate the underlying constitutional principle. The Court, for example, has never suggested that race-based classifications became any less suspect once extensive legislation had been enacted on the subject.

For the retarded, just as for Negroes and women, much has changed in recent years, but much remains the same; outdated statutes are still on the books, and irrational fears or ignorance, traceable to the prolonged social and cultural isolation of the retarded, continue to stymie recognition of the dignity and individuality of retarded people. * * *

The Court also offers a more general view of heightened [scrutiny]. First, heightened scrutiny is said to be inapplicable where *individuals* in a group have distinguishing characteristics that legislatures properly may take into account in some circumstances. Heightened scrutiny is also purportedly inappropriate when many legislative classifications affecting the *group* are likely to be [valid.]

If the Court's first principle were sound, heightened scrutiny would have to await a day when people could be cut from a cookie mold. Women are hardly alike in all their characteristics, but heightened scrutiny applies to them because legislatures can rarely use gender itself as a proxy for these other characteristics. [Similarly,] that some retarded people have reduced capacities in some areas does not justify using retardation as a proxy for reduced capacity in areas where relevant individual variations in capacity do exist.

The Court's second assertion—that the standard of review must be fixed with reference to the number of classifications to which a characteristic would validly be relevant—is similarly flawed. [Our] heightened scrutiny precedents belie the claim that a characteristic must virtually always be irrelevant to warrant heightened scrutiny. * * * Heightened but not strict scrutiny is considered appropriate in areas such as gender, illegitimacy, or alienage because the Court views the trait as relevant under some circumstances but not others. [An] inquiry into constitutional principle, not mathematics, determines whether heightened scrutiny is appropriate. Whenever evolving principles of equality, rooted in the Equal Protection Clause, require that certain classifications be viewed as *potentially* discriminatory, and when history reveals systemic unequal treatment, more searching judicial inquiry than minimum rationality becomes relevant.

Potentially discriminatory classifications exist only where some constitutional basis can be found for presuming that equal rights are required. [With] regard to economic and commercial matters, no basis for such a conclusion exists, for [t]he structure of economic and commercial life is a matter of political compromise, not constitutional principle, and no norm of equality requires that there be as many opticians as optometrists, see *Lee Optical,* or new businesses as old, see *Dukes.* * * *[24]

---

24. No single talisman can define those groups likely to be the target of classifications offensive to the Fourteenth Amendment and therefore warranting heightened or strict scrutiny; experience, not abstract logic, must be the primary guide. The "political powerlessness" of a group may be relevant, but that factor is neither necessary, as the gender cases demonstrate, nor sufficient, as the example of minors illustrates. [W]e see few statutes reflecting prejudice or indifference to minors, and I am not aware of any suggestion that legislation affecting them be viewed with the suspicion of heightened scrutiny. Similarly, immutability of the trait at issue may be relevant, but many immutable characteristics, such as height or blindness, are valid bases of governmental action and classifications under a variety of circumstances.

The political powerlessness of a group and the immutability of its defining trait are relevant insofar as they point to a social and cultural isolation that gives the majority little reason to respect or be concerned with that group's interests and needs. Statutes discriminating against the young have not been common nor need be feared because those who do

vote and legislate were once themselves young, typically have children of their own, and certainly interact regularly with minors. Their social integration means that minors, unlike discrete and insular minorities, tend to be treated in legislative arenas with full concern and respect, despite their formal and complete exclusion from the electoral process.

The discreteness and insularity warranting a "more searching judicial inquiry" must therefore be viewed from a social and cultural perspective as well as a political one. To this task judges are well suited, for the lessons of history and experience are surely the best guide as to when, and with respect to what interests, society is likely to stigmatize individuals as members of an inferior caste or view them as not belonging to the community. Because prejudice spawns prejudice, and stereotypes produce limitations that confirm the stereotype on which they are based, a history of unequal treatment requires sensitivity to the prospect that its vestiges endure. In separating those groups that are discrete and insular from those that are not, as in many important legal distinctions, "a page of history is worth a volume of logic."

In light of the scrutiny that should be applied here, Cleburne's ordinance sweeps too broadly to dispel the suspicion that it rests on a bare desire to treat the retarded as outsiders, pariahs who do not belong in the community. The Court, while disclaiming that special scrutiny is necessary or warranted, reaches the same conclusion. Rather than striking the ordinance down, however, the Court invalidates it merely as applied to respondents. I must dissent from the novel proposition that "the preferred course of adjudication" is to leave standing a legislative act resting on "irrational prejudice," thereby forcing individuals in the group discriminated against to continue to run the act's gauntlet. * * *

SECTION 4. "FUNDAMENTAL RIGHTS"

I. DISCRIMINATION IN RESPECT TO VOTING

A. "DILUTION" OF THE RIGHT: APPORTIONMENT

The Court's initial hesitancy to consider malapportioned legislatures—largely the product of districts drawn when the nation's rural/urban population ratio was vastly different than in mid 20th century—and its subsequent assertion of jurisdiction are presented in BAKER v. CARR, p. 30 supra.

The first full post-*Baker* opinion on the problem was GRAY v. SANDERS, 372 U.S. 368, 83 S.Ct. 801, 9 L.Ed.2d 821 (1963), invalidating the "county unit system" employed in Georgia primaries for statewide officers. The candidate receiving the highest number of votes in each county obtained "two votes for each representative to which the county is entitled in the lower House of the General Assembly," and the winner was determined on the basis of the county unit vote. Because counties were not represented in the state legislature in accordance with their population, "combination of the units from the counties having the smallest population gives counties having population of one-third of the total in the state a clear majority of county units." The Court, per DOUGLAS, J., emphasizing that the case did not involve legislative districting, held that equal protection requires that "once the geographical unit for which a representative is to be chosen is designated, all who participate in the election are to have an equal vote. [The] conception of political equality from the Declaration of Independence, to Lincoln's Gettysburg Address, to the Fifteenth, Seventeenth, and Nineteenth Amendments can mean only one thing—one person, one vote." [a]

WESBERRY v. SANDERS, 376 U.S. 1, 84 S.Ct. 526, 11 L.Ed.2d 481 (1964), per BLACK, J., struck down the Georgia congressional districting statute which accorded some districts more than twice the population of others: "[T]he command of Art. I, § 2, that Representatives be chosen 'by the People of the several States' means that as nearly as is practicable one man's vote in a congressional election is to be worth as much as another's." [b]

a. Harlan, J., dissented. Is there a distinction between the issue in *Gray* and legislative apportionment? See 77 Harv.L.Rev. 131 (1963).

Is a state primary for selecting delegates to the national political parties' presidential nominating conventions, which awards all of the state's delegates to the candidate with the highest number of votes, valid after *Gray*?

See Blumstein, *Party Reform, the Winner-Take-All Primary, and the California Delegate Challenge: The Gold Rush Revisited,* 25 Vand.L.Rev. 975 (1972).

b. Clark, J., would have remanded for consideration "against the requirements of the Equal Protection Clause." Harlan, J., would have adhered to *Colegrove* and, on the merits (joined by Stewart, J.,) dissented, finding the

Notes and Questions

1. *Commitment to Congress.* Has Art. I—as argued by Harlan, J., in *Wesberry*—"conferred upon Congress exclusive authority to secure fair representation by the States" in the House of Representatives? Consider Lewis, *Legislative Apportionment and the Federal Courts*, 71 Harv.L.Rev. 1057, 1074 (1958): "[That Art. I] casts the right to equal representation in the House in terms of affirmative congressional power should not preclude judicial enforcement of the right in the absence of legislation. Such judicial action is commonplace in other areas, [e.g.,] the commerce clause, which is phrased in the most general language and entirely in terms of congressional power." Is *Wesberry* premised, sub silentio, on the commerce clause analogy? May Congress "overrule" *Wesberry* as it may a commerce clause decision? See *Clark Distilling Co. v. Western Md. Ry.*, 242 U.S. 311, 37 S.Ct. 180, 61 L.Ed. 326 (1917).

2. *Equal representation.* What does *Wesberry* portend for the effective power of some congressional committees to "pigeon-hole" legislation? The Senate filibuster? Are these practices consistent with the principle that "one man's vote in a congressional election is to be worth as much as another's"?

REYNOLDS v. SIMS

377 U.S. 533, 84 S.Ct. 1362, 12 L.Ed.2d 506 (1964).

MR. CHIEF JUSTICE WARREN delivered the opinion of the Court.

[Although the Alabama constitution required the legislature to reapportion decennially on the basis of population, none had taken place since 1901. The federal district court held the existing malapportionment violative of equal protection. Under] 1960 census figures, only 25.1% of the State's total population resided in districts represented by a majority of the members of the Senate, and only 25.7% lived in counties which could elect a majority of the members of the House of Representatives. Population-variance ratios of up to about 41-to-1 existed in the Senate, and up to about 16-to-1 in the House. * * *

Gray and *Wesberry* are of course not dispositive [of] these cases involving state legislative [apportionment]. But neither are they wholly inapposite. [*Gray*] established the basic principle of equality among voters within a State, [and] *Wesberry* clearly established that the fundamental principle of representative government in this country is one of equal representation for equal numbers of people, without regard to race, sex, economic status, or place of residence within a State. Our problem, then, is to ascertain [whether] there are any constitutionally cognizable principles which would justify departures from the basic standard of equality among voters in the apportionment of seats in state legislatures.

A predominant consideration in determining whether a State's legislative apportionment scheme constitutes an invidious discrimination [is] that the rights allegedly impaired are individual and personal in nature. [Since] the right of suffrage is a fundamental matter in a free and democratic society [and] is preservative of other basic civil and political rights, any alleged infringement [must] be carefully and meticulously scrutinized. * * *

Legislators represent people, not trees or acres. Legislators are elected by voters, not farms or cities or economic interests. As long as ours is a representative form of government, [the] right to elect legislators in a free and unimpaired

Court's theory "demonstrably unsound historically."

fashion is a bedrock of our political system. [It] is inconceivable that a state law to the effect that, in counting votes for legislators, the votes of citizens in one part of the State would be multiplied by two, five, or 10, while the votes of persons in another area would be counted only at face value, could be [constitutional]. Of course, the effect of state legislative districting schemes which give the same number of representatives to unequal numbers of constituents is identical. * * *

Logically, in a society ostensibly grounded on representative government, it would seem reasonable that a majority of the people of a State could elect a majority of that State's legislators. [T]o sanction minority control of state legislative bodies would appear to deny majority rights in a way that far surpasses any possible denial of minority rights that might otherwise be thought to result. [T]he concept of equal protection has been traditionally viewed as requiring the uniform treatment of persons standing in the same relation to the governmental action questioned or challenged. With respect to the allocation of legislative representation, all voters, as citizens of a State, stand in the same relation regardless of where they live. Any suggested criteria for the differentiation of citizens are insufficient to justify any discrimination, as to the weight of their votes, unless relevant to the permissible purposes of legislative apportionment. Since the achieving of fair and effective representation for all citizens is concededly the basic aim of legislative apportionment, we conclude that the Equal Protection Clause guarantees the opportunity for equal participation by all voters in the election of state legislators. Diluting the weight of votes because of place of residence impairs basic constitutional rights under the Fourteenth Amendment just as much as invidious discriminations based upon factors such as race, or economic status. Our constitutional system amply provides for the protection of minorities by means other than giving them majority control of state legislatures. * * *

We are told that the matter of apportioning representation in a state legislature is a complex and many-faceted one. We are advised that States can rationally consider factors other than [population]. We are admonished not to restrict the power of the States to impose differing views as to political philosophy on their citizens. We are cautioned about the dangers of entering into political thickets and mathematical quagmires. Our answer is this: a denial of constitutionally protected rights demands judicial protection; our oath and our office require no less of us. [To] the extent that a citizen's right to vote is debased, he is that much less a citizen. [A] nation once primarily rural in character becomes predominantly urban. Representation schemes once fair and equitable become archaic and outdated. But the basic principle of representative government [remains]—the weight of a citizen's vote cannot be made to depend on where he lives. Population is, of necessity, [the] controlling criterion for judgment in legislative [apportionment]. This is the clear and strong command of our Constitution's Equal Protection Clause. This is an essential part of the concept of a government of laws and not men. This is at the heart of Lincoln's vision of "government of the people, by the people, [and] for the people." * * *

We hold that, as a basic constitutional standard, the Equal Protection Clause requires that the seats in both houses of a bicameral state legislature must be apportioned on a population basis. [We] find the federal analogy inapposite and irrelevant to state legislative districting schemes. [T]he Founding Fathers clearly had no intention of establishing a pattern or model for the apportionment of seats in state legislatures when the system of representation in the

Federal Congress was adopted. Demonstrative of this is the fact that the Northwest Ordinance, adopted in the same year, 1787, as the Federal Constitution, provided for the apportionment of seats in territorial legislatures solely on the basis of population.

The system of representation in the two Houses of the Federal Congress [is] based on the consideration that in establishing our type of federalism a group of formerly independent States bound themselves together under one national government. [A] compromise between the larger and smaller States on this matter averted a deadlock in the constitutional convention * * *.

Political subdivisions of States [never] have been considered as sovereign entities. Rather, they have been traditionally regarded as subordinate governmental instrumentalities created by the State. * * *

[The] right of a citizen to equal representation and to have his vote weighted equally with those of all other citizens in the election of members of one house of a bicameral state legislature would amount to little if States could effectively submerge the equal-population principle in the apportionment of seats in the other house. * * * Deadlock between the two bodies might result in compromise and concession on some issues. But in all too many cases the more probable result would be frustration of the majority will through minority veto in the house not apportioned on a population [basis].

We do not believe that the concept of bicameralism is rendered anachronistic and meaningless when the predominant basis of representation in the two state legislative bodies is required to be the same—population. A prime reason for bicameralism, modernly considered, is to insure mature and deliberate consideration of, and to prevent precipitate action on, proposed legislative measures. Simply because the controlling criterion for apportioning representation is required to be the same in both houses does not mean that there will be no differences in the composition and complexion of the two bodies. [The] numerical size of the two bodies could be made to differ, even significantly, and the geographical size of districts from which legislators are elected could also be made to differ. [T]he Equal Protection Clause requires that a State make an honest and good faith effort to construct districts, in both houses of its legislature, as nearly of equal population as is practicable. We realize that it is a practical impossibility to arrange legislative districts so that each one has an identical number of residents, or citizens, or voters. Mathematical exactness or precision is hardly a workable constitutional requirement.

[So] long as the divergences from a strict population standard are based on legitimate considerations incident to the effectuation of a rational state policy, some deviations from the equal-population principle are constitutionally permissible, [b]ut neither history alone, nor economic or other sorts of group interests, are permissible factors in attempting to justify disparities from population-based representation. Citizens, not history or economic interests, cast votes. Considerations of area alone provide an insufficient justification for deviations from the equal-population principle. Again, people, not land or trees or pastures, vote. Modern developments and improvements in transportation and communications make rather hollow, in the mid-1960's, most claims [for] allowing such deviations in order to insure effective representation for sparsely settled areas and to prevent legislative districts from becoming so large that the availability of access of citizens to their representatives is impaired. * * *

A consideration that appears to be of more substance [is] according political subdivisions some independent representation in at least one body of the state legislature, as long as the basic standard of equality of population among districts is maintained. [In] many States much of the legislature's activity involves the enactment of so-called local legislation, directed only to the concerns of particular political subdivisions. And a State may legitimately desire to construct districts along political subdivision lines to deter the possibilities of gerrymandering. However, permitting deviations from population-based representation does not mean that each local governmental unit or political subdivision can be given separate representation, regardless of [population].

* * * Decennial reapportionment appears to be a rational approach to readjustment of legislative representation in order to take into account population shifts and growth [and] if reapportionment were accomplished with less frequency, it would assuredly be constitutionally suspect. * * *

[T]he court below acted with proper judicial restraint, after the Alabama Legislature had failed to act effectively in remedying the constitutional deficiencies in the State's legislative apportionment scheme, in ordering its own temporary reapportionment plan into effect, at a time sufficiently early to permit the holding of elections pursuant to that plan without great difficulty, and in prescribing a plan admittedly provisional in purpose so as not to usurp the primary responsibility for reapportionment which rests with the legislature.[a]

LUCAS v. FORTY–FOURTH GEN. ASSEMBLY, 377 U.S. 713, 84 S.Ct. 1459, 12 L.Ed.2d 632 (1964): In a 1962 referendum, "the Colorado electorate adopted proposed Amendment No. 7 by a vote of 305,700 to 172,725, and defeated proposed Amendment No. 8 by a vote of 311,749 to 149,822." No. 8 provided that "both houses of [the] Legislature would [be] apportioned on a population basis." No. 7, approved by a majority of the voters in every county, "provided for the apportionment of the House of Representatives on the basis of population, but essentially maintained the existing apportionment in the Senate, which was based on a combination of population and various other factors." A three-judge federal court upheld No. 7. The Court, per WARREN, C.J., reversed. Although "the initiative device provides a practicable political remedy to obtain relief against alleged legislative malapportionment," "an individual's constitutionally protected right to cast an equally weighted vote cannot be denied even by a vote of a majority of a State's electorate, if the apportionment scheme adopted by the voters fails to measure up to the requirements of the Equal Protection Clause. [A] citizen's constitutional rights can hardly be infringed simply because a majority of the people choose that it be."[b]

---

a. Clark and Stewart, JJ., each concurred in the result. Harlan, J., dissented from all the 1964 apportionment decisions. His opinion appears at the end of the summaries of the other cases, infra. Further on remedies, *Scott v. Germano,* 381 U.S. 407, 85 S.Ct. 1525, 14 L.Ed.2d 477 (1965), held that federal courts should stay reapportionment proceedings if the state courts are actively concerned with the problem. *Travia v. Lomenzo,* 381 U.S. 431, 85 S.Ct. 1582, 14 L.Ed.2d 480 (1965), refused to stay a district court's order that New York hold a special legislative election—thus shortening the terms of legislators elected under an invalid apportionment—under a reapportionment plan enacted by the legislature but held invalid by the state court because it

provided for more legislators than permitted under the state constitution.

May a court order that a convention be called to amend the state constitution apportionment provisions? Require that all plans be submitted to it for approval? Cf. *Burns v. Richardson,* 384 U.S. 73, 86 S.Ct. 1286, 16 L.Ed.2d 376 (1966). Require changing the size of the legislature? See *67th Minnesota State Senate v. Beens,* 406 U.S. 187, 92 S.Ct. 1477, 32 L.Ed.2d 1 (1972). Order that a malapportioned legislature meet only for limited purposes? See *Fortson v. Toombs,* 379 U.S. 621, 85 S.Ct. 598, 13 L.Ed.2d 527 (1965).

b. Clark, J., dissented: "[I]f one house is fairly apportioned by population [then] the

STEWART, J., joined by Clark, J., dissented in *Lucas* and *WMCA, Inc. v. Lomenzo,* 377 U.S. 633, 84 S.Ct. 1418, 12 L.Ed.2d 568 (1964), which invalidated New York's apportionment: "First, says the Court, it is 'established that the fundamental principle of representative government in this country is one of equal representation for equal numbers of [people].' [But] this 'was not the colonial system, it was not the system chosen for the national government by the Constitution, it was not the system exclusively or even predominantly practiced by the States at the time of adoption of the Fourteenth Amendment, it is not predominantly practiced by the States today.' [c] Secondly, says the Court, unless legislative districts are equal in population, voters in the more populous districts will suffer a 'debasement' amounting to a constitutional injury. [I] find it impossible to understand how or why a voter in California, for instance, either feels or is less a citizen than a voter in Nevada, simply because, despite their population disparities, each of those States is represented by two United States Senators.

"[My] own understanding of the various theories of representative government is that no one theory has ever commanded unanimous [assent]. But even if it were thought that the rule announced today by the Court is, as a matter of political theory, the most desirable, [I] could not join in the fabrication of a constitutional mandate which imports and forever freezes one theory of political thought into our Constitution, and forever denies to every State any opportunity for enlightened and progressive innovation * * *.

"Representative government is a process of accommodating group interests through democratic institutional arrangements. * * * Appropriate legislative apportionment, therefore, should ideally be designed to insure effective representation in the State's legislature, in cooperation with other organs of political power, of the various groups and interests making up the electorate. In practice, of course, this ideal is approximated in the particular apportionment system of any State by a realistic accommodation of the diverse and often conflicting political forces operating within the State.

"[The] fact of geographic districting, the constitutional validity of which the Court does not question, carries with it an acceptance of the idea of legislative representation of regional needs and interests. Yet if geographical residence is irrelevant, as the Court suggests, and the goal is solely that of equally 'weighted' votes, I do not understand why the Court's constitutional rule does not require the abolition of districts and the holding of all elections at large.[12]

---

people should have some latitude in providing on a rational basis, for representation in the other house."

c. See also Bickel, *The Supreme Court and Reapportionment,* in Reapportionment in the 1970's, 57, 58–59 (Polsby ed. 1971): "[A] rigorous majoritarianism is not what our institutions rest [on]. American government [includes] a Supreme Court which wields political power and [is] not elected at all. Our government includes a Senate [in] which each state, regardless of population, has an equal vote that not even a duly enacted and ratified constitutional amendment can, without its own consent, deprive it of. Our government includes a House of Representatives in which each state has at least one vote, even though the whole state may be (as some are) consider-

ably smaller in population than the average congressional district."

12. Even with legislative districts of exactly equal voter population, 26% of the electorate (a bare majority of the voters in a bare majority of the districts) can, [by] the kind of theoretical mathematics embraced by the Court, elect a majority of the legislature under our simple majority electoral system. Thus, the Court's constitutional rule permits minority rule.

Students of the mechanics of voting systems tell us that if all that matters is that votes count equally, the best vote-counting electoral system is proportional representation in statewide elections. [B]ecause electoral systems are intended to serve functions other than satisfying mathematical theories, [however,]

"The fact is, of course, that population factors must often to some degree be subordinated in devising a legislative apportionment plan which is to achieve the important goal of ensuring a fair, effective, and balanced representation of the regional, social, and economic interests within a State. And the further fact is that throughout our history the apportionments of State Legislatures have reflected the strongly felt American tradition that the public interest is composed of many diverse interests, and that in the long run it can better be expressed by a medley of component voices than by the majority's monolithic command. [I] think the cases should be decided by application of accepted principles of constitutional adjudication under the Equal Protection Clause [and that] demands but two basic attributes of any plan of state legislative apportionment. First, it demands that, in the light of the State's own characteristics and needs, the plan must be a rational one. Secondly, it demands that the plan must be such as not to permit the systematic frustration of the will of a majority of the electorate of the State. * * *

"*Colorado.* [In] the Colorado House, the majority unquestionably [rules]. It is true that, as a matter of theoretical arithmetic, a minority of 36% of the voters could elect a majority of the Senate, but this percentage has no real meaning in terms of the legislative process. [N]o possible combination of Colorado senators from rural districts, even assuming arguendo that they would vote as a bloc, could control the Senate. To arrive at the 36% figure, one must include [a] substantial number of urban [districts].

"[T]he people living in each of [the state's] four regions have interests unifying themselves and differentiating them from those in other regions. Given these underlying facts, certainly it was not irrational to conclude [that] planned departures from a strict per capita standard of representation were a desirable way of assuring [that] districts should be small enough in area, in a mountainous State like Colorado, where accessibility is affected by configuration as well as compactness of districts, to enable each senator to have firsthand knowledge of his entire district and to maintain close contact with his constituents * * *.

"[I]f per capita representation were the rule in both houses of the Colorado Legislature, counties having small populations would have to be merged with larger counties having totally dissimilar interests. Their representatives would not only be unfamiliar with the problems of the smaller county, but the interests of the smaller counties might well be totally submerged to the interests of the larger counties with which they are joined. * * * * [d]

proportional representation has not been widely adopted.

[Compare Auerbach, *The Reapportionment Cases: One Person, One Vote—One Vote, One Value,* 1964 Sup.Ct.Rev. 1, 31–34 who demonstrates, historically and statistically, that "the theoretical possibility of minority rule to which Justice Stewart alludes [is] not very real," and concludes: "The Court's figures emphasize the point that territorial constituencies of unequal population enhance the likelihood that the existing system of election and representation will not be consistent with majority rule. For with constituencies of unequal population, the theoretical minimum percentage electing a majority can be considerably less than 26%."]

[d.] Under *Reynolds,* could Colorado still give such counties "effective representation" by permitting them each to have a representative in the legislature, but granting that legislator only a fractional vote determined on a population basis (or granting him a full vote but giving legislators from larger counties a more heavily weighted vote)? Consider Dixon, *Reapportionment Perspectives: What is Fair Representation?,* 51 A.B.A.J. 319, 322 (1965): "[W]eighted voting may be nullified for several reasons. One of the most important reasons would be the consideration that one man casting nineteen votes is not as effective in terms of representation as nineteen separate voices (or lobbyists). Another would be that nineteen men separately elected would pro-

"The present apportionment, adopted overwhelmingly by the people [is] entirely rational, [and] the majority has consciously chosen to protect the minority's interests, and under the liberal initiative provisions of the Colorado Constitution, it retains the power to reverse its decision to do so. Therefore, there can be no question of frustration of the basic principle of majority rule.

"*New York.* [The] apportionment [is] rational, it is applied systematically, and it is kept reasonably current. The formula [provides] that each county shall have at least one representative in the Assembly, that the smaller counties shall have somewhat greater representation in the legislature than representation based solely on numbers would accord, and that some limits be placed on the representation of the largest counties in order to prevent one megalopolis from completely dominating * * *. The rationality of individual county representation becomes particularly apparent in States where legislative action applicable only to one or more particular counties is the permissible tradition.

"[T]he 10 most populous counties in the State control both houses of the legislature under the existing apportionment system. Each of these counties is heavily urban; each is in a metropolitan area. [Thus], the existing system of apportionment clearly guarantees effective majority representation and [control].

"But this is not the whole story. New York City, with [a] budget larger than that of the State, has, by virtue of its concentration of population, homogeneity of interest,[e] and political cohesiveness, acquired [influence] of its own hardly measurable simply by counting the number of its representatives in the legislature. [Surely] it is not irrational for the State [to] be justifiably concerned about balancing such a concentration of political [power]. What the State has done is to adopt a [plan] designed in a rational way to ensure that minority voices may be heard, but that the will of the majority shall prevail."[f]

vide more opportunity for expression of divergent views. [B]oth of these arguments involve going beyond the simple mathematical tenor of the Supreme Court's 'one-man, one-vote' decisions. They involve putting reapportionment in the context of the actual complexities of representation—and the difficulties in determining what is fair and effective representation." Does this objection go similarly to fractional voting? If not, should fractional voting also extend to committee voting? Assignment to committee? Compensation? What else? See generally Banzhaf, *One Man, ? Votes: Mathematical Analysis of Voting Power and Effective Representation,* 36 Geo. Wash.L.Rev. 808 (1968); Note, *Equal Representation and the Weighted Voting Alternatives,* 79 Yale L.J. 311 (1969).

What about a system of cumulative voting? Consider Note, *Apportionment Problems in Local Government,* 49 Not.D.Law. 671, 683–84 (1974): "[E]ach elector has as many votes as there are representatives to be elected from the area at large, and he may cast his votes in any combination for the candidates on the slate. If there are three candidates to be elected, the voter may cast all three votes for one candidate, or give one candidate two votes and give another candidate one vote, or give one vote to each of three candidates. The three candidates with the highest number of votes are the winners. [Where] there are sev-

eral positions to be filled minority groups can easily achieve a voice by running only a few candidates (or only one) and then voting in blocs. In this manner cumulative voting becomes very much like proportional representation."

e. Do all New York City's people have "homogeneity of interest"? Who represents the "interest" of the following New York City resident: a white Republican, whose annual income is $50,000, derived half from his salary as a labor organizer and half from interest and dividends on $300,000 inherited securities, etc., etc.? Must a Negro of Puerto Rican origin be content with the fact that "non-whites" are represented despite his contention that his interests are distinct from those of other blacks? Must an Irish-Catholic be content with representation by an Italian-Catholic? See *United Jewish Orgs. v. Carey,* Sec. 2, V supra.

f. Consider Irwin, *Representation and Election: The Reapportionment Cases in Retrospect,* 67 Mich.L.Rev. 729, 748–49 (1969): "For the Court to have made any attempt whatever to insure the accommodation of any interest—geographical, economic, ethnic, partisan, or 'historical'—in the legislative process would have catapulted [it] into the continuing political questions, not simply of whether, but also of *which* groups are to receive political advan-

MR. JUSTICE HARLAN, dissenting [in all the cases decided that day.][g]

The Court's constitutional discussion [is] remarkable [for] its failure to address itself at all to the Fourteenth Amendment as a whole or to the legislative history of the Amendment pertinent to the matter at hand. [I] am unable to understand the Court's utter disregard of [§ 2 of the fourteenth amendment], which expressly recognizes the States' power to deny "or in any way" abridge the right of their inhabitants to vote for "the members of the [State] Legislature," and its express provision of a remedy for such denial or abridgement. The comprehensive scope of the second section and its particular reference to the state legislatures precludes the suggestion that the first section was intended to have the result reached by the [Court].

The history of the adoption of the Fourteenth Amendment provides conclusive evidence that neither those who proposed nor those who ratified the Amendment believed that the Equal Protection Clause limited the power of the States to apportion their legislatures as they saw fit. Moreover, the history demonstrates that the intention to leave this power undisturbed was deliberate and was widely believed to be essential to the adoption of the Amendment.[h] [N]ote should [also] be taken of the Fifteenth and Nineteenth Amendments. [If] constitutional amendment was the only means by which all men and, later, women, could be guaranteed the right to vote at all, even for *federal* officers, how can it be that the far less obvious right to a particular kind of apportionment of *state* legislatures—a right to which is opposed a far more plausible conflicting

tages in the legislative process. Such [questions] entice the Court into the very political morass which virtually everyone agreed in principle that it should avoid." See also Ely, *Democracy and Distrust* 124–25 (1980): "Everyone without a strong personal stake in the status quo granted that [refusal by the Court to enter the area] was no more compatible with the underlying theory of our Constitution than taking away some people's votes altogether. So the Court entered, and *precisely because of considerations of administrability,* soon found itself with no perceived alternative but to move to a one person, one vote standard. Actually this move was characteristic of the Warren Court, which on several occasions adopted what seemed on the surface the more intrusive rule on the theory that it would be less intrusive in practice. Part of the theory behind *Gideon v. Wainwright,* requiring appointed counsel in all felony cases, was that the previously prevailing 'special circumstances rule,' though requiring counsel on fewer occasions, in fact had repeatedly resulted [in] friction-generating factual inquiries into every case. [Sometimes] more is less." Compare Dixon, *Democratic Representation: Reapportionment in Law and Politics* 19–20 (1968): "All apportionment being fully political, any order made by a court has a significant political impact. Therefore the only relevant question is whether the concededly 'political' judicial order is good or bad, fair or unfair, equitable or inequitable. Such ascertainment is not advanced by putting on blinders and excluding certain kinds of relevant evidence, or even certain kinds of relevant,

albeit politically embarrassing questions, on the ground that to consider [them] would be to 'wallow' in the political thicket."

g. In addition to *Reynolds, Lucas,* and *WMCA,* the Court invalidated apportionments in Maryland, *Maryland Comm. for Fair Rep. v. Tawes,* 377 U.S. 656, 84 S.Ct. 1442, 12 L.Ed. 2d 595; Virginia, *Davis v. Mann,* 377 U.S. 678, 84 S.Ct. 1453, 12 L.Ed.2d 609; Delaware, *Roman v. Sincock,* 377 U.S. 695, 84 S.Ct. 1462, 12 L.Ed.2d 620.

h. For refutation of Harlan, J.'s lengthy historical argument, see Van Alstyne, *The Fourteenth Amendment, The "Right" to Vote, and the Understanding of the Thirty-Ninth Congress,* 1965 Sup.Ct.Rev. 33; Goldberg, *Mr. Justice Harlan, The Uses of History, and the Congressional Globe,* 15 J.Pub.L. 181 (1966).

Consider Auerbach, fn. 12 supra, at 77–78: "To accept Mr. Justice Harlan's view would lead to the astonishing result that—apart from the complicated and never-used remedy provided by the second section of the Fourteenth Amendment—neither the federal courts, nor Congress under the fifth section, could act to prevent a state from denying the right to vote in a state or local election to a class of citizens, otherwise qualified to vote by state law, for reasons which have nothing to do with race, color, or previous condition of servitude, but which nevertheless result in an arbitrary classification, e.g., because the citizens disfranchised are residents of a particular county or because they migrated into the state from outside the state."

interest of the State than the interest which opposes the general right to vote—can be conferred by judicial construction of the Fourteenth Amendment?

[The] consequence of today's decision is that in all but the handful of States which may already satisfy the new requirements the [courts] are given blanket authority and the constitutional duty to supervise apportionment of the State Legislatures. It is difficult to imagine a more intolerable and inappropriate interference by the judiciary with the independent legislatures of the States. [No] set of standards can guide a court which has to decide how many legislative districts a State shall have, or what the shape of the districts shall be, [or] whether a State should have single-member districts or multi-member districts or some combination of both. No such standard can control the balance between keeping up with population shifts and having stable districts. In all these respects, the courts will be called upon to make particular decisions with respect to which a principle of equally populated districts will be of no assistance whatsoever.[i] * * *

Although the Court—necessarily, as I believe—provides only generalities in elaboration of its main thesis, its opinion nevertheless fully demonstrates how far removed these problems are from fields of judicial competence. Recognizing that "indiscriminate districting" is an invitation to "partisan gerrymandering," the Court nevertheless excludes virtually every basis for the formation of electoral districts other than "indiscriminate districting." In one or another of today's opinions, the Court declares it unconstitutional for a State to give effective consideration to any of the following in establishing legislative districts: (1) history; (2) "economic or other sorts of group interests"; (3) area; (4) geographical considerations; (5) a desire "to insure effective representation for sparsely settled areas"; (6) "availability of access of citizens to their representatives"; (7) theories of bicameralism (except those approved by the Court); (8) occupation; (9) "an attempt to balance urban and rural power"; (10) the

---

i. See also Dixon, *Apportionment Standards and Judicial Power,* 38 Notre Dame Law. 367, 387 (1963): "[I]nteresting possibilities exist in the process of apportionment even when existing county lines are used. [A]ssume that County A has 25,000 voters and one seat in the legislature, which Party Y captures because it has a 20,000 to 5,000 edge over Party X in that county. Let us assume that County B has 100,000 voters and also has one seat in the legislature, which Party X captures because it has a 55,000 to 45,000 edge over Party Y in that county. As between the two counties, the 100,000 voters in County B seem underrepresented by a four to one ratio because they have only one seat and County A's 25,000 voters also have one seat. But looking at the political parties in this two-county area we see substantial equality. Party X has a combined total of 60,000 votes in the two counties and gets one seat; Party Y a combined total of 65,000 votes and one seat. If we now reapportion [by] raising County B to four seats we achieve exact numerical equality. But the resultant impact on political party representation will be that Party X with 60,000 votes in this two-county area now has four seats, and Party Y with 65,000 votes has only one seat."

And see Dixon, *The Court, The People, and "One Man, One Vote,"* in Reapportionment in the 1970's 7, 13 (Polsby ed. 1971): "[U]sing new single-member districts, the Democrats in California in 1966 elected majorities of 21–19 and 42–38 in the state senate and house, respectively, even though they polled fewer statewide legislative votes than the Republicans. In the same election the Democrats gained a 21–17 edge in congressional seats, again with a minority of the statewide congressional vote. In New Jersey in 1966 the Democrats gained a 9–6 edge in congressional seats, despite a Republican plurality in the popular vote. By contrast, for the state legislature in New Jersey, using a mixture of new single- and multi-member districts, a comfortable but not overwhelming Republican plurality in popular votes in 1967 produced a sweep of two-thirds of the seats in each house."

See Lucas, *Legislative Apportionment and Representative Government: The Meaning of Baker v. Carr,* 61 Mich.L.Rev. 711, 764–73 (1963); Dixon, *Reapportionment in the Supreme Court and Congress: Constitutional Struggle for Fair Representation,* 63 Mich.L. Rev. 209 (1964) for the further view that equal population districts in no way assure "fair representation."

preference of a majority of voters in the State. So far as presently appears, the *only* factor which a State may consider, apart from numbers, is political subdivisions. But even "a clearly rational state policy" recognizing this factor is unconstitutional if "population is submerged as the controlling consideration * * *."

I know of no principle of logic or practical or theoretical politics, still less any constitutional principle, which establishes all or any of these exclusions. [L]egislators can represent their electors only by speaking for their interests—economic, social, political—many of which do reflect the place where the electors live. The Court does not establish, or indeed even attempt to make a case for the proposition that conflicting interests within a State can only be adjusted by disregarding them when voters are grouped for purposes of representation. * * *

[The] Constitution is not a panacea for every blot upon the public welfare, nor [does] this Court [serve] its high purpose when it exceeds its authority, even to satisfy justified impatience with the slow workings of the political [process.][j]

Notes and Questions

1. *Results.* By mid-1968, "congressional district lines were redrawn in thirty-seven states"; "only nine states had any district with a population deviation in excess of ten per cent from the state average, while twenty-four states had no deviation as large as five per cent from the state norm"; every state legislature "had made some adjustment, and it seemed probable that more than thirty of the state legislatures satisfied any reasonable interpretation of the equal-population principle." McKay, *Reapportionment: Success Story of the Warren Court,* 67 Mich.L.Rev. 223, 229 (1968). A number of studies—as to the impact of reapportionment on state policy and the extent to which reapportioned legislatures are more likely than malapportioned ones to expend funds, be responsive to urban needs and have a competitive political system—have arrived at conflicting conclusions. For a collection and appraisal, see Bicker, *The Effects of Malapportionment in the States—A Mistrial,* in Reapportionment in the 1970's 151 (Polsby ed. 1971); Choper, *Consequences of Supreme Court Decisions Upholding Individual Constitutional Rights,* 83 Mich.L.Rev. 1, 90–94 (1984).

2. *High vote requirements.* (a) GORDON v. LANCE, 403 U.S. 1, 91 S.Ct. 1889, 29 L.Ed.2d 273 (1971), per BURGER, C.J., upheld a West Virginia rule that forbade political subdivisions from incurring bonded indebtedness or increasing tax rates beyond designated limits without 60% approval in a referendum: "The defect [in *Gray v. Sanders* and *Cipriano v. Houma,* Part B infra] lay in the denial or dilution of voting power because of group characteristics—geographic location and property ownership—that bore no valid relation to the interest of those groups in the subject matter of the [election]. In contrast we can discern no independently identifiable group or category that favors bonded indebtedness over other forms of financing. Consequently no sector of the population may be said to be 'fenced out' from the franchise because of the way they will vote. [T]here is nothing in the language of the Constitution, our history or our cases that requires that a majority always prevail on every issue. [The] Constitution itself provides that a simple majority vote is insufficient on some issues [and] the

---

j. A week later, the Court invalidated apportionments in nine additional states. The opinions begin at 378 U.S. 553, 84 S.Ct. 1904, 12 L.Ed.2d 1033. For thoughtful pre-*Reynolds* commentaries on apportionment standards, see Lockhart, Kamisar & Choper, *Constitutional Law: Cases—Comments—Questions* 1318 (3d. ed. 1970).

Bill of Rights removes entire areas of legislation from the concept of majoritarian supremacy. * * * [6] " [a]

(b) Do you agree that in *Lance* "no independently identifiable group" was "fenced out"? See Wilkinson, *The Supreme Court, the Equal Protection Clause, and the Three Faces of Constitutional Equality*, 61 Va.L.Rev. 945, 972–75 (1975). After *Lance*, may a state require a 60% *legislative* vote to establish any public transit system? To enact laws affecting designated counties? Does *Lance* logically (constitutionally) extend to the situations in its fn. 6? May a state require a 60% vote to unseat any incumbent?

(c) LOCKPORT v. CITIZENS FOR COMMUNITY ACTION, 430 U.S. 259, 97 S.Ct. 1047, 51 L.Ed.2d 313 (1977), per STEWART, J., upheld New York laws "that a new county charter will go into effect only if [approved] by separate majorities of the voters who live in the cities [and] outside the cities": "The equal protection principles applicable in gauging the fairness of an election involving the choice of legislative representatives are of limited relevance [in] analyzing the propriety of recognizing distinctive voter interests in a 'single-shot' referendum. [I]nstead of sending legislators off to the state capitol to vote on a multitude of issues, the referendum puts one discrete issue to the voters. That issue is capable [of] being analyzed to determine whether [it] will have a disproportionate impact on an identifiable group of voters. * * *

"The ultimate question then is whether, given the differing interests of city and noncity voters in the adoption of a new county charter in New York, those differences are sufficient under the Equal Protection Clause to justify the classifications made by New York law. If that question were posed in the context of annexation proceedings, the fact that the residents of the annexing city and the residents of the area to be annexed formed sufficiently different constituencies with sufficiently different interests could be readily perceived.[b] [Similarly] a proposal that several school districts join to form a consolidated unit could surely be subject to voter approval in each constituent school district.

"[T]he structural decision to annex or consolidate is similar in impact to the decision to restructure county government in New York. In each case, separate voter approval requirements are based on the perception that the real and long-term impact of a restructuring of local government is felt quite differently by the different county constituent [units].[18] " Burger, C.J. concurred in the judgment.[c]

(d) Are *Lance* and *Lockport* compatible with *Reynolds?* Consider Israel, *Nonpopulation Factors Relevant to an Acceptable Standard of Apportionment*, 38 Not.D.Law. 499, 512 (1963): "[I]f a state can reasonably demand that some legislative action be based on a broader consensus than a bare majority, why could it not insist upon a broader consensus for all legislative action? [If] so,

---

6. We intimate no view on the constitutionality of a provision requiring unanimity or giving a veto power to a very small group. Nor do we decide whether a State [may] require extraordinary majorities for the election of public officers.

a. Harlan, J., concurred in the result. Brennan and Marshall, JJ., dissented.

b. See generally Note, *The Right to Vote in Municipal Annexations*, 88 Harv.L.Rev. 1571, 1588–93 (1975).

18. There is no indication that the classifications created by New York law work to favor city to town voter, or town to city voter.

In some New York counties, city voters outnumber town voters; in other counties, the reverse is true. * * *

The constitutional and statutory provisions in this case also do not appear to be the sustained product of either an entrenched minority or a willful majority. Instead they have been subject historically to fairly frequent revision. * * *

c. For criticism, see Martin, *The Requirement of Concurrent Majorities in a Charter Referendum: The Supreme Court's Retreat from Voting Equity*, 16 Duq.L.Rev. 167 (1978).

then why not achieve the same minority security by allocating approximately one-half of the legislative seats to regional minority groups which represent one-third of the population?" Compare Auerbach, fn. 12 supra, at 48: "The analogy between the rules for choosing legislative representatives and the rules for deciding issues in legislative assemblies [ignores] the difference between the power to take action and the power to block it. Even those who deny that 'effective minority rule' exists simply because a qualified majority is required to take action agree that it exists if a simple majority is required to block action proposed by a minority. [But] this is precisely the consequence of malapportionment. Let us take an [example]—40 per cent of the population lives in legislative (single-member) districts which, theoretically, could elect 67 members of a legislative body of 100 members and 60 per cent live in districts which, theoretically, could elect 33 members. If the legislative body were required to take action by a two-thirds vote, but the 100 districts contained equal numbers of people, members representing 60 per cent of the people could not take any action without the concurrence of at least 7 of the members representing the minority of the population. But then, neither could the 40 members representing the minority take any action unless they obtained the concurrence of at least 27 members of the majority. In the example given, however, members representing 60 per cent of the people are unable to take any action, even under a simple majority rule, while members representing 40 per cent of the people have the power to take any action they please, even under a two-thirds rule. Effective minority rule, theoretically, exists." How clear is the distinction, in respect to "effective minority rule," between "the power to take action and the power to block it"? [c]

(e) Is a ⅔ requirement to amend the state constitution valid? Would it be if *Lance* and *Lockport* had been decided otherwise? What about a provision requiring a ⅔ vote in *each* county? Suppose the counties have substantially equal population?

3. *"Popularly" mandated malapportionment.* Do you agree that malapportionment violates equal protection even if adopted "by a vote of a majority of a State's electorate" (*Lucas*)? What would such a "majority" likely consist of? A combination of (1) almost all those that would be overrepresented plus (2) a minority of those that would be underrepresented? Should such a "majority" mandated malapportionment be insulated from the constitutional challenge of the "minority" that is underrepresented?

Suppose that the "majority" included a majority of those that would be underrepresented? Would this nonetheless be invalid because "a citizen's constitutional rights can hardly be infringed simply because a majority of the people choose that it be"? Would a plan for racially segregated education, supported in a referendum by a majority of both racial groups, be immune from attack under equal protection? Is the "right to cast an equally weighted vote" an "individual" right in the same sense as the right to be free of state imposed racial segregation? Does the relief sought in the segregation situation demand more than that the individual plaintiffs be accorded their constitutional rights? In the apportionment situation? See generally Neal, *Baker v. Carr, Politics in Search of Law,* 1962 Sup.Ct.Rev. 252, 271–74.

---

c. See also Ratner, *Reapportionment and the Constitution,* 38 So.Cal.L.Rev. 540 (1965); Rudolph, *The Reapportionment Cases: A Conservative Defense of Individual Rights,* 43 Neb.L.Rev. 854 (1964).

Even if the right sought to be vindicated in the apportionment situation is different than in the segregation case, may it be defeated by a majority of those affected? Could a state constitutionally make an appropriation to construct a Methodist church building if it had the approval of a majority of the non-Methodist voters? If not, could those non-Methodist voters who wished to contribute do so personally? May those voters who wish to have their own votes "diluted" make personal arrangements to accomplish this? See generally Choper, *On the Warren Court and Judicial Review,* 17 Cath.U.L.Rev. 20, 31–32 (1967).

4. *Permissible population deviation.* (a) MAHAN v. HOWELL, 410 U.S. 315, 93 S.Ct. 979, 35 L.Ed.2d 320 (1973), per REHNQUIST, J., upheld Virginia's state legislative apportionment, which had a maximum percentage deviation from the ideal of "16.4%—[one] district being overrepresented by 6.8% and [another] being underrepresented by 9.6%. [T]he minimum population necessary to elect a majority of the House of Delegates was 49.29%":

"In *Kirkpatrick v. Preisler,* 394 U.S. 526, 89 S.Ct. 1225, 22 L.Ed.2d 519 (1969) and *Wells v. Rockefeller,* 394 U.S. 542, 89 S.Ct. 1234, 22 L.Ed.2d 535 (1969), this Court invalidated state reapportionment statutes for federal congressional districts having maximum percentage deviations of 5.97% and 13.1% respectively. [I]t was concluded that [*Wesberry's*] command 'permits only the limited population variances which are unavoidable despite a good-faith effort to achieve absolute equality, or for which justification is shown.'

"[*Reynolds* suggested] more flexibility was constitutionally permissible with respect to state legislative reapportionment than in congressional redistricting. Consideration was given to the fact [that] there is a significantly larger number of seats in state legislative bodies to be distributed within a State than Congressional seats, and that therefore it may be feasible for a State to use political subdivision lines to a greater [extent].[a] [But] *Wesberry* recognized no excuse [other] than the practical impossibility of drawing equal districts with mathematical precision. * * *[b]

"[Under] Virginia's Constitution, the General Assembly is given extensive power to enact special legislation [regarding] counties, cities, towns and other

a. See also Hobbs, *Book Review,* 16 U.C. L.A.L.Rev. 659, 682 (1969): "[C]ongressmen are assumed to represent the state as a whole as well as their district; state legislators, on the other hand, are expected to be more parochial. Therefore, there is arguably a better case on the state [level] for allowing deviation based on local communities of interest. In addition, on the state level population variations in one house can be compensated for in the other. This [is] impossible in congressional districting."

b. *Kirkpatrick,* per Brennan, J., rejected a "de minimis approach" because there was "no nonarbitrary way to pick a cutoff point" and it "would encourage legislators to strive for that range" rather than for "precise mathematical equality." Even minimizing "opportunities for partisan gerrymandering" could not constitute a satisfactory justification. Opportunities "for gerrymandering are greatest when there is freedom to construct unequally populated districts." Harlan, Stewart and White, JJ., dissented.

See 83 Harv.L.Rev. 103 (1969): "Political subdivision boundaries, natural or historical demarcations, and the goal of district geographical compactness give a political body some sort of guidelines for the task of districting. To require that such guidelines not be used is to take away one of the tools that citizens and members of legislatures use to measure the fairness of districting plans. [When] fragmentation of political subdivisions and bizarrely shaped districts can be explained by politicians as necessary to comply with the 'as nearly as practicable' standard, critics of such districting must launch their attack deprived of any popularly accepted test for the existence of gerrymandering." See generally Dixon, *The Warren Court Crusade for the Holy Grail of "One Man-One Vote,"* 1969 Sup.Ct.Rev. 219; Baker, *Gerrymandering: Privileged Sanctuary or Next Judicial Target?,* in Reapportionment in the 1970's 121 (Polsby ed. 1971).

political subdivisions. The statute redistricting the House of Delegates consistently sought to avoid the fragmentation of such subdivisions, assertedly to afford them a voice in Richmond to seek such local legislation. * * *

"We are not prepared to say that [this] is irrational. [But] a State's policy urged in justification of disparity in district population, however, rational, cannot constitutionally be permitted to emasculate the goal of substantial equality. * * *

"Neither courts nor legislatures are furnished any specialized calipers which enable them to extract from the general language of the Equal Protection Clause [the] mathematical formula which establishes what range of percentage deviations are permissible, and what are not. [While] this percentage may well approach tolerable limits, we do not believe it exceeds them." [c]

BRENNAN, J., joined by Marshall and Douglas, JJ., dissented: "While the State may have a broader range of interests to which it can point in attempting to justify a failure to achieve precise equality in the context of legislative apportionment [than in the context of congressional districting], it by no means follows that the State is subject to a lighter burden of proof or that the controlling constitutional standard is in any sense distinguishable. [Swann v. Adams, 385 U.S. 440, 87 S.Ct. 569, 17 L.Ed.2d 501 (1967)] decisively refutes any suggestion that unequal representation will be upheld so long as some rational basis for the discrimination can be found. A showing of necessity, not rationality is [what] Swann requires. * * *

"[I]n asserting its interest in preserving the integrity of county boundaries, the Commonwealth offers [only] vague references to 'local legislation,' without describing such legislation with precision, without indicating whether such legislation amounts to a significant proportion of the legislature's business, and without demonstrating that the District Court's plan would materially affect the treatment of such legislation." Powell, J., did not participate.

(b) *"Per se" rule for state legislative districts.* GAFFNEY v. CUMMINGS, 412 U.S. 735, 93 S.Ct. 2321, 37 L.Ed.2d 298 (1973), per WHITE, J., held that a Connecticut apportionment, with a maximum deviation from the ideal totaling 7.83%, "failed to make out a prima facie violation" of equal protection "whether those deviations are considered alone or in combination with the additional fact that another plan could be conceived with lower deviations." The "insignificant population variations" required no "justification by the State." "The 'population' of a legislative district is just not that knowable to be used for such refined judgments" because "district populations are constantly changing, often at different rates, up or down" and "if it is the weight of a person's vote that matters, total population—even if stable and accurately taken—may not actually reflect that body of voters whose votes must be counted and weighed for the purposes of reapportionment, because 'census persons' are not voters." [d]

c. Compare *Chapman v. Meier,* 420 U.S. 1, 95 S.Ct. 751, 42 L.Ed.2d 766 (1975), reversing a federal court plan that permitted a 20% deviation: "A court-ordered plan [must] be held to higher standards than a State's own plan. [A]ny deviation from approximate population equality must be supported by enunciation of historically significant state policy or unique features."

Connor v. Finch, 431 U.S. 407, 97 S.Ct. 1828, 52 L.Ed.2d 465 (1977), held that the federal district court had failed to identify "such

'unique features' of the Mississippi political structure as to permit a judicial protection of county boundaries in the teeth of the judicial duty to 'achieve the goal of population equality with little more than de minimis variation.' "

d. *Burns v. Richardson,* 384 U.S. 73, 86 S.Ct. 1286, 16 L.Ed.2d 376 (1966), per Brennan, J., upheld a Hawaii plan that used *registered voters* as the population base, which, "probably because of uneven distribution of military residents—largely unregistered," pro-

BRENNAN, J., joined by Douglas and Marshall, JJ., dissented: "[T]he Court['s] wide margin of tolerable error [is] likely to jeopardize the very substantial gains that have been made during the last four years." [e]

(c) *Congressional districts.* KARCHER v. DAGGETT, 462 U.S. 725, 103 S.Ct. 2653, 77 L.Ed.2d 133 (1983), per BRENNAN, J., reaffirmed *Kirkpatrick's* "population equality as nearly as is practicable" standard—rejecting a maximum percentage deviation of only .7%: "Any number of consistently applied legislative policies might justify some ['minor population deviations'], including, for instance, making districts compact, respecting municipal boundaries, preserving the cores of prior districts, [preserving voting strength of racial minorities], and avoiding contests between incumbent Representatives.[f] [The] State must, however, show with some specificity that a particular objective required the specific deviations in its plan, rather than simply relying on general assertions [as here.]" [g]

WHITE, J., joined by Burger, C.J., and Powell and Rehnquist, JJ., dissented "from the Court's unreasonable insistence on an unattainable perfection. * * * I would not entertain judicial challenges, absent extraordinary circum-

duced results significantly different than if total population figures had been used: States are not "required to include aliens, transients, short-term or temporary residents, or persons denied the vote for conviction of crime in the apportionment [base]. The decision to include or exclude any such group involves choices about the nature of representation with which we have been shown no constitutionally founded reason to interfere. [But use] of a registered voter or actual voter basis [is] susceptible to improper influences by which those in political power might be able to perpetuate underrepresentation of groups constitutionally entitled to participate in the electoral [process]. [W]e hold that the present apportionment satisfies the Equal Protection Clause only because on this record it was found to have produced a distribution of legislators not substantially different from that which would have resulted from the use of [state citizen population, which is] a permissible population base."

e. *White v. Regester,* 412 U.S. 755, 93 S.Ct. 2332, 37 L.Ed.2d 314 (1973) (similarly divided), used the same analysis to uphold a Texas apportionment in which "the total variation between largest and smallest district" was 9.9%—although "very likely larger differences would not be tolerable without qualification."

Most recently, *Brown v. Thompson,* 462 U.S. 835, 103 S.Ct. 2690, 77 L.Ed.2d 214 (1983), per Powell, J., upheld Wyoming's allocation of one seat in its House of Representatives to its least populous county, resulting in a maximum deviation of 89%. The Court emphasized that "appellants deliberately have limited their challenge to the alleged dilution of their voting power resulting from the one representative given to Niobrara County" rather than "the state apportionment plan as a whole."

O'Connor, J., joined by Stevens, J., expressed "the gravest doubts that a statewide legislative plan with an 85% maximum deviation would survive constitutional scrutiny despite the presence of the State's strong interest in preserving county boundaries. I join the Court's opinion on the understanding that nothing in it suggests that this Court would uphold such a scheme."

Brennan, J., joined by White, Marshall and Blackmun, JJ.,—although "stressing how extraordinarily narrow [the decision] is, and how empty of likely precedential value"—dissented.

f. *White v. Weiser,* 412 U.S. 783, 93 S.Ct. 2348, 37 L.Ed.2d 335 (1973), per White, J., *suggested* the validity of a state "policy frankly aimed at maintaining existing relationships between incumbent congressmen and their constituents and preserving the seniority the members of the State's delegation have achieved in [the] House of Representatives."

But see Casper, *Apportionment and the Right to Vote: Standards of Judicial Scrutiny,* 1973 Sup.Ct.Rev. 1, 12: "[A] 'state policy' favoring incumbents often is no more than an euphemism [for] perpetuating themselves as a power elite unaccountable to the voters because of skewed districting. Put differently, 'rotten' legislators can render the right to vote quite as ineffective as 'rotten' boroughs."

g. Stevens, J., who joined the Court's opinion, concurred, relying on the equal protection clause (rather than Art. I, § 2), and contending that it should be held to bar apportionments that egregiously curtail the strength of any defined political group (see his opinion in *Mobile v. Bolden,* infra). Powell, J., dissented, but essentially agreed with Stevens, J., in respect to "partisan gerrymandering."

stances, where the maximum deviation is less than 5%. Somewhat greater deviations, if rationally related to an important state interest may also be permissible." [h]

FORTSON v. MORRIS, 385 U.S. 231, 87 S.Ct. 446, 17 L.Ed.2d 330 (1966): In the 1966 Georgia gubernatorial election, no candidate received a majority of the popular vote. Georgia provided that in such case the Georgia legislature shall elect the governor from the two candidates receiving the highest popular vote. The Court, per BLACK, J., upheld the election: There is no federal constitutional provision "which either expressly or impliedly dictates the method a State must use to select its Governor. A method which would be valid if initially employed is equally valid when employed as an alternative."

DOUGLAS, J., joined by Warren, C.J., and Brennan and Fortas, JJ., dissented, viewing "the legislative choice" as "only a part of the popular election machinery. [A] candidate who received a minority of the popular vote might receive a clear majority of the votes cast in the legislature," thus "contrary to the principle of 'one person, one vote.'"

Scope of the decision. May a state provide that a popularly elected governor shall appoint the entire legislature? Appoint the legislator from any district in which no candidate received a majority ($2/3$) ($3/4$) of the popular vote? That all local officials shall be appointed by the legislature or some part thereof? What provision(s) of the Constitution are most germane in considering these issues? See generally Ely, *Democracy and Distrust* 116–25 (1980); Levinson, *Judicial Review and the Problem of the Comprehensible Constitution,* 59 Tex.L.Rev. 395, 413–15 (1981). [i]

LOCAL GOVERNMENT UNITS

AVERY v. MIDLAND COUNTY, 390 U.S. 474, 88 S.Ct. 1114, 20 L.Ed.2d 45 (1968): The Midland County (Tex.) Commissioners Court was elected from single-member districts of unequal population—414; 828; 852; and 67,906 (the city of Midland, the county's only urban center). The Court, per WHITE, J., finding that the Commissioners Court had "general responsibility and power for local affairs," held that when a state "delegates lawmaking power to local government and provides for the election of local officials from districts [those] qualified to vote [must] have the right to an equally effective voice in the election process.[6]

"Were the Commissioners Court a special purpose unit of government assigned the performance of functions affecting definable groups of constituents more than other constituents, we would have to confront the question whether such bodies may be apportioned in ways which give greater influence to the citizens most affected by the organization's functions."

---

h. See generally Note, *Reapportionment: A Call for a Consistent Quantitative Standard,* 70 Ia.L.Rev. 663 (1985).

i. *Rodriguez v. Popular Democratic Party,* 457 U.S. 1, 102 S.Ct. 2194, 72 L.Ed.2d 628 (1982), per Burger, C.J., relied on *Fortson* to uphold a Puerto Rico statute providing that vacancies in the Puerto Rico legislature caused by death, resignation or removal may be filled—until the next regularly scheduled election—by the political party with which the previous incumbent was affiliated: Puerto Rico "could reasonably conclude that [this] would more fairly reflect the will of the voters than appointment by the Governor or some other elected official."

6. Inequitable apportionment of local governing bodies offends the Constitution even if adopted by a properly apportioned legislature [*Lucas*].

Sailors v. Board of Educ., 387 U.S. 105, 87 S.Ct. 1549, 18 L.Ed.2d 650 (1967) [a] and *Dusch v. Davis,* 387 U.S. 112, 87 S.Ct. 1554, 18 L.Ed.2d 656 (1967) [b] "demonstrate that the Constitution and this Court are not roadblocks in the path of innovation, experiment, and development among units of local government."

HARLAN, J., dissented: "[L]ocal governments [are] often specialized in function. Application of the *Reynolds* rule to such local governments [may] result in a denial of equal treatment to those upon whom the exercise of the special powers has unequal impact.[c] [An] oft-proposed solution to [urban area] problems has been the institution of an integrated government encompassing the entire metropolitan area. [T]he suburbanites often will be reluctant to join the metropolitan government unless they receive a share in the government proportional to the benefits they bring with them and not merely to their numbers. The city dwellers may be ready to concede this much, in return for the ability to tax the suburbs. Under the majority's pronouncements, however, this rational compromise would be forbidden: the metropolitan government must be apportioned solely on the basis of population if it is a 'general' government." [d]

HADLEY v. JUNIOR COLLEGE DIST., 397 U.S. 50, 90 S.Ct. 791, 25 L.Ed.2d 45 (1970): Pursuant to Missouri law, a consolidated junior college district was created by referendum in eight school districts. The Kansas City School District, containing about 60% of the consolidated "school population," was apportioned only three of the six trustees who were empowered to tax, issue bonds, condemn property, and generally manage the junior college.

The Court, per BLACK, J., found "that these powers, while not [as] broad [as] the Midland County Commissioners," "show that the trustees perform important governmental functions": "[A]s a general rule, whenever a state or local government decides to select persons by popular election to perform governmental functions," equal protection requires that if these persons "are chosen from separate districts, each district must be established on [an equal population basis]." To distinguish "between elections for 'legislative' officials and those for 'administrative' officers" would be "unmanageable." Because of available techniques such as those upheld in *Sailors* and *Dusch,* "we do not feel that the States will be inhibited in finding ways to insure that legitimate political goals of representation are achieved."

HARLAN, J., joined by Burger, C.J., and Stewart, J., dissented: First, "if, as the Court speculates, other means will prove as effective as apportionment in the adaptation of local agencies to meet specific needs, presumably those other means will also enable the States just as effectively to accomplish whatever evils

---

a. *Sailors,* noted 81 Harv.L.Rev. 151 (1967), "upheld a procedure for choosing a school board that placed the selection with school boards of component districts even though the component boards had equal votes and served unequal populations." The Court could "find no constitutional reason why state or local officers of the non-legislative character involved here may not be chosen by the governor, by the legislature, or by some other appointive means." "We need not decide [whether] a State may constitute a local legislative body through the appointive rather than the elective process."

b. *Dusch* permitted a city "to choose its legislative body by a scheme that included at-large voting for candidates, some of whom had to be residents of particular districts, even though [the] districts varied widely in population." The scheme followed a city-county consolidation and reflected "a detente between urban and rural communities."

c. Stewart and Fortas, JJ., each dissented stressing this point. Marshall, J., did not participate.

d. See generally Weinstein, *The Effect of the Federal Reapportionment Decisions on Counties and Other Forms of Municipal Government,* 65 Colum.L.Rev. 21, 37 (1965).

the Court thinks it is preventing by today's decision." Second, the 1961 Missouri statute was "sensibly designed to facilitate creation of new educational bodies while guaranteeing to small school districts that they will not be entirely swallowed up by a large partner." Third, just as *Reynolds* "catalogued a number of considerations indicating that 'somewhat more flexibility' might be permissible in state legislative apportionment than in congressional districting, [as] we proceed down the spectrum [to] the single-purpose local entity," a rule should be fashioned to allow "much more play in the joints." [e]

Notes and Questions

1. *Permissible population deviation.* (a) ABATE v. MUNDT, 403 U.S. 182, 91 S.Ct. 1904, 29 L.Ed.2d 399 (1971), per MARSHALL, J., upheld the apportionment of Rockland County, N.Y.'s governing board. Each of the five constituent towns comprised one district and each had at least one representative. The most "underrepresented" district was by 7.1% and the most "overrepresented" by 4.8%—"a total deviation from population equality of 11.9%": "[V]iable local governments may need considerable flexibility [to] meet changing societal needs [and] a desire to preserve the integrity of political subdivisions may justify an apportionment plan which departs from numerical equality. *Reynolds.* [T]hat local legislative bodies frequently have fewer representatives than do their state and national counterparts and that some local legislative districts may have a much smaller population than do congressional and state legislative districts, lend support to the argument that slightly greater percentage deviations may be tolerable for local government [apportionment]." [f]

(b) Would (should) the deviation permitted in *Abate* be equally precedential for Los Angeles (Cal.) County with 7,000,000 residents as for Hamilton (N.Y.) County with 4,700 residents? Consider Note, *Reapportionment—Nine Years into the "Revolution" and Still Struggling,* 70 Mich.L.Rev. 586, 612 (1972): "A 10% deviation affects 700,000 people in Los Angeles. Unless sufficient reason is shown why the district lines could not be redrawn to correct the disparity [without] detracting from the goal of fair and effective representation, the California legislative scheme should be invalidated. However, the same percentage deviation would involve fewer than 500 Hamilton County residents. Redrawing district lines [might] be an enormously difficult task. Therefore, if the other elements of the county's districting scheme fulfill the good-faith and other *Reynolds* requirements, it should pass constitutional muster."

2. *Appointment vs. election.* Under *Sailors,* could the members of the *Avery* Commissioners Court be appointed by the state legislature rather than elected? Consider Weinstein, fn. d supra, at 23: "So long as this system were applied uniformly and state officials were properly elected, there would be no violation of [equal protection]. Although an argument could be made that such an arrangement would violate the clause of the federal constitution guaranteeing a republican form of government, the fact that there would be popular control of the appointing state government and the traditional reluctance of courts to rely upon the guarantee clause combine to minimize any danger [of] unconstitutionality." If so, could the legislature provide for (or follow the practice of) appointing one member of the Commissioners Court from each of the four previously existing districts? If so, suppose state law provided that the

---

e. Burger, C.J., also dissented separately.

f. Harlan and Stewart, JJ., concurred.
Brennan, J., joined by Douglas, J., dissented.

members of the Commissioners Court be appointed by four officials, elected one each from the four previously existing districts?

Is there any local government unit that cannot be constituted through the appointive process? If so, how (where) should the line be drawn? See generally Nahmod, *Reflections on Appointive Local Government Bodies and a Right to an Election,* 11 Duq.L.Rev. 119 (1972).

3. *Residence requirements.* (a) Under *Dusch,* could the members of the Commissioners Court be elected at-large in Midland County, but one member required to be a resident of each of the previously existing districts? Does such a plan comport with *Avery's* (and *Hadley's*) mandate that "those qualified to vote have the right to an equally effective voice in the elective process"? See *Dallas Cty. v. Reese,* 421 U.S. 477, 95 S.Ct. 1706, 44 L.Ed.2d 312 (1975). Consider 81 Harv.L.Rev. 154–55 (1967): "[A] councilman who fails to satisfy his [entire] constituency can only be replaced with another, possibly equally provincial resident of the same [district]. It is clear then that voters in the larger [districts] would probably be forced to elect councilmen they might not otherwise elect absent the residence requirement." See also McKay, *Reapportionment and Local Government,* 36 Geo.Wash.L.Rev. 713, 738 (1968).

(b) MOORE v. OGILVIE, 394 U.S. 814, 89 S.Ct. 1493, 23 L.Ed.2d 1 (1969), per DOUGLAS, J., invalidated a statute requiring that a petition to nominate independent candidates for a state-wide election be signed by at least 25,000 voters, including 200 from each of at least 50 of the state's 102 counties: "Under this Illinois law the electorate in 49 of the counties which contain 93.4% of the registered voters may not form a new political party and place its candidates on the ballot. Yet 25,000 of the remaining 6.6% of registered voters properly distributed among the 53 remaining counties [may]. This law thus discriminates against the residents of the populous counties [in] favor of rural sections." [g]

4. *Exceptions to the "general rule."* (a) Are there *any* "special purpose" units whose decisions do not "affect *all* citizens" in some way? How about a "lawyers' discipline and disbarment board"? By what apportionment scheme may it be elected? (This problem will be considered further in Part B infra in respect to total denial of the vote to some persons within the political unit.)

(b) *Judges.* WELLS v. EDWARDS, 409 U.S. 1095, 93 S.Ct. 904, 34 L.Ed.2d 679 (1973), summarily affirmed Louisiana provisions for election of state supreme court judges from districts established without regard to population. WHITE, J., joined by Douglas and Marshall, JJ., dissented, noting that the lower court—relying on *Hadley*—had "seized upon the phrase 'persons [to] perform governmental functions,' and concluded that such persons were limited to 'officials who performed legislative or executive type duties.' [But judges are] elected (or appointed) to carry out the state government's judicial functions. As such, they most certainly 'perform governmental functions.' [The] judgment of the District Court is questionable [and] at least warrants plenary review here." [h]

g. Stewart, J., joined by Harlan, J., dissented, relying on *Dusch.*

h. Consider Note, 47 Notre Dame Law. 316, 326–27 (1971): "Some would argue [that] the entire rationale [of] 'one man, one vote' is to achieve maximum institutional responsiveness and that by common agreement judges need not be responsive to the popular will or whim and therefore the rule has no applicabil- ity to them. [But this would] overlook the more basic concept of political equality which underlies [*Reynolds*], namely, that irrespective of the elective office involved, full and effective citizenship requires that each man's vote count the same. It should also be noted that a requirement of equal judicial districts in no way implies that the judges elected from those districts need be responsive."

MOBILE v. BOLDEN

446 U.S. 55, 100 S.Ct. 1490, 64 L.Ed.2d 47 (1980).

MR. JUSTICE STEWART announced the judgment of the Court and delivered an opinion in which THE CHIEF JUSTICE, MR. JUSTICE POWELL, and MR. JUSTICE REHNQUIST join.

The City of Mobile, Ala., has since 1911 been governed by a City Commission consisting of three members elected by the voters of the city at-large. [This] is the same basic electoral system that is followed by literally thousands of municipalities and other local governmental units throughout the Nation.
* * *

[The] constitutional objection to multimember districts is not and cannot be that, as such, they depart from apportionment on a population basis in violation of *Reynolds* and its progeny. Rather the focus in such cases has been on the lack of representation multimember districts afford various elements of the voting population in a system of representative legislative democracy. "Criticism [of multimember districts] is rooted in their winner-take-all aspects, their tendency to submerge minorities, [a] general preference for legislatures reflecting community interests as closely as possible and disenchantment with political parties and elections as devices to settle policy differences between contending interests." *Whitcomb v. Chavis*, 403 U.S. 124, 91 S.Ct. 1858, 29 L.Ed.2d 363 (1971).[a]

Despite repeated constitutional attacks upon multimember legislative districts, the Court has consistently held that they are not unconstitutional per se, e.g., *White v. Regester; Whitcomb; Burns v. Richardson; Fortson v. Dorsey*, 379 U.S. 433, 85 S.Ct. 498, 13 L.Ed.2d 401 (1965).[12] We have recognized, however, that such legislative apportionments could violate the Fourteenth Amendment if their purpose were invidiously to minimize or cancel out the voting potential of racial or ethnic minorities. To prove such a purpose it is not enough to show that the group allegedly discriminated against has not elected representatives in proportion to its numbers. A plaintiff must prove that the disputed plan was "conceived or operated as [a] purposeful device[ ] to further racial discrimination." *Whitcomb*.

This burden of proof is simply one aspect of the basic principle that only if there is purposeful discrimination can there be a violation of [equal protection]. See *Washington v. Davis; Arlington Heights; Personnel Adm'r v. Feeney*, [Sec. 2, III supra]. Although dicta may be drawn from a few of the Court's earlier opinions suggesting that disproportionate effects alone may establish a claim of unconstitutional racial vote dilution, the fact is that such a view is not supported by any decision of this Court.[13] More importantly, such a view is not consistent

a. On the issue generally, see Banzhaf, *Multi-Member Electoral Districts—Do They Violate the "One Man, One Vote" Principle*, 75 Yale L.J. 1309 (1966); Carpeneti, *Legislative Apportionment: Multi-member Districts and Fair Representation*, 120 U.Pa.L.Rev. 666 (1972); Tribe, *American Constitutional Law* 750 (1978).

12. We have made clear, however, that a court in formulating an apportionment [plan] should, as a general rule, not permit multimember legislative districts. * * * *Connor v. Finch*. [See *Wise v. Lipscomb*, 437 U.S. 535, 98 S.Ct. 2493, 57 L.Ed.2d 411 (1978), on wheth-

er a reapportionment plan was "court-devised" or "legislatively enacted."]

13. The dissenting opinion of Mr. Justice Marshall reads the Court's opinion in *Dorsey* to say that a claim of vote dilution under the Equal Protection Clause could rest on either discriminatory purpose or effect. [Although] the Court recognized that "designedly or otherwise," multimember districting schemes might, under the circumstances of a particular case, minimize the voting strength of a racial group, an issue as to the constitutionality of such an arrangement "[w]as not [presented]."

with the meaning of the Equal Protection Clause as it has been understood in a variety of other contexts involving alleged racial discrimination. *Davis* (employment); *Arlington Heights* (zoning); *Keyes,* [Sec. 2, IV supra] (public schools); *Akins v. Texas,* 325 U.S. 398, 65 S.Ct. 1276, 89 L.Ed. 1692 (1945) (jury selection).

In only one case has the Court sustained a claim that multimember legislative districts unconstitutionally diluted the voting strength of a discrete group. [*Regester*] upheld a constitutional challenge by Negroes and Mexican-Americans to parts of a legislative reapportionment plan adopted by the State of Texas. [T]he Court held that the plaintiffs had been able to "produce evidence to support the finding that the political processes leading to nomination and election were not equally open to participation by the group[s] in question." In so holding, the Court relied upon evidence in the record that included a long history of official discrimination against minorities as well as indifference to their needs and interests on the part of white elected officials. * * *

Regester is thus consistent with "the basic equal protection principle that the invidious quality of a law claimed to be racially discriminatory must ultimately be traced to a racially discriminatory purpose." [But] where the character of a law is readily explainable on grounds apart from race, as would nearly always be true where, as here, an entire system of local governance is brought into question, disproportionate impact alone cannot be decisive, and courts must look to other evidence to support a finding of discriminatory purpose. [I]t is clear that the evidence in the present case fell far short of showing that the appellants "conceived or operated [a] purposeful device[ ] to further racial discrimination." *Whitcomb.*

[T]he District Court [affirmed by the Court of Appeals] based its conclusion of unconstitutionality primarily on the fact that no Negro had ever been elected to the City Commission, apparently because of the pervasiveness of racially polarized voting in Mobile. The trial court also found that city officials had not been as responsive to the interests of Negroes as to those of white persons. On the basis of these findings, the court concluded that the political processes in Mobile were not equally open to Negroes, despite its seemingly inconsistent findings that there were no inhibitions against Negroes becoming candidates, and that in fact Negroes had registered and voted without hindrance. * * *

First, [i]t may be that Negro candidates have been defeated, but that fact alone does not work a constitutional deprivation.

Second, [evidence] of discrimination by white officials in Mobile is relevant only as the most tenuous and circumstantial evidence of the constitutional invalidity of the electoral system under which they attained their offices.

Third, the District Court and the Court of Appeals supported their conclusion by drawing upon the substantial history of official racial discrimination in Alabama. But past discrimination cannot, in the manner of original sin, condemn governmental action that is not itself unlawful. The ultimate question remains whether a discriminatory intent has been proved in a given [case].

Finally, the District Court and the Court of Appeals pointed to the mechanics of the at-large electoral system itself as proof that the votes of Negroes were being invidiously canceled out. But those features of that electoral system, such as the majority vote requirement, tend naturally to disadvantage any voting

The phrase "designedly or otherwise" [was] repeated, also in dictum, in *Burns.* But the constitutional challenge to the multimember constituencies failed in that case because the plaintiffs demonstrated neither discriminatory purpose nor effect.

minority [and] are far from proof that the at-large electoral scheme represents purposeful discrimination against Negro voters.

We turn finally [to] Justice Marshall's dissenting opinion. The theory [appears] to be that every "political group," or at least every such group that is in the minority, has a federal constitutional right to elect candidates in proportion to its numbers.[22] Moreover, a political group's "right" to have its candidates elected is said to be a "fundamental interest," the infringement of which may be established without proof that a State has acted with the purpose of impairing anybody's access to the political process. This dissenting opinion finds the "right" infringed [because] no Negro has been elected to the Mobile City Commission.

Whatever appeal the dissenting opinion's view may have as a matter of political theory, it is not the law. The Equal Protection Clause [does] not require proportional representation as an imperative of political organization. * * *

It is of course true that a law that impinges upon a fundamental right explicitly or implicitly secured by the Constitution is presumptively unconstitutional. See *Shapiro v. Thompson,* [Part II infra]. See also *San Antonio Ind. School Dist. v. Rodriguez,* [Part IV infra]. But plainly "[i]t is not the province of this Court to create substantive constitutional rights in the name of guaranteeing equal protection of the laws," id. [In] *Whitcomb,* the trial court had found that a multimember state legislative district had invidiously deprived Negroes and poor persons of rights guaranteed them by the Constitution, notwithstanding the absence of any evidence whatever of discrimination against them. Reversing the trial court, this Court said: "The District Court's holding, although on the facts of this case limited to guaranteeing one racial group representation, is not easily contained. It is expressive of the more general proposition that any group with distinctive interests must be represented in legislative halls if it is numerous enough to command at least one seat and represents a majority living in an area sufficiently compact to constitute a single-member district. This approach would make it difficult to reject claims of Democrats, Republicans, or members of any political [organization]. There are also union oriented workers, the university community, religious or ethnic groups occupying identifiable areas of our heterogeneous cities and urban areas. Indeed, it would be difficult for a great many, if not most, multi-member districts to survive analysis under the District Court's view unless combined with some voting arrangement such as proportional representation or cumulative voting aimed at providing representation for minority parties or interests. At the very least, affirmance [would] spawn endless litigation concerning the multi-member district systems now widely employed in this country." * * *

MR. JUSTICE BLACKMUN, concurring in the result.

Assuming that proof of intent is a prerequisite to appellees' prevailing on their constitutional claim of vote dilution, I am inclined to agree with Mr. Justice White that, in this case, "the findings of the District Court amply support

---

22. The dissenting opinion seeks to disclaim this description of its theory by suggesting that a claim of vote dilution may require, in addition to proof of electoral defeat, some evidence of "historical and social factors" indicating that the group in question is without political influence. Putting to the side the evident fact that these gauzy sociological considerations have no constitutional basis, it remains far from certain that they could, in any principled manner, exclude the claims of any discrete political group that happens, for whatever reason, to elect fewer of its candidates than arithmetic indicates it might. Indeed, the putative limits are bound to prove illusory if the express purpose informing their application would be, as the dissent assumes, to redress the "inequitable distribution of political influence."

an inference of purposeful discrimination." I concur in the Court's judgment of reversal, however, because I believe that the relief afforded appellees by the District Court [ordering a new form of government "of a Mayor and a City Council with members elected from single-member districts"] was not commensurate with the sound exercise of judicial discretion. * * *

MR. JUSTICE STEVENS, concurring in the judgment.

[While] I agree with Mr. Justice Stewart that no violation of respondents' constitutional rights has been demonstrated, my analysis of the issue proceeds along somewhat different lines.

[T]his case draws into question a political structure that treats all individuals as equals but adversely affects the political strength of a racially identifiable group. Although I am satisfied that such a structure may be challenged under the Fifteenth Amendment as well as under the Equal Protection Clause of the Fourteenth Amendment, I believe that under either provision it must be judged by a standard that allows the political process to function effectively. * * *

[No] case decided by this Court establishes a constitutional right to proportional representation for racial minorities. What *Gomillion* [Sec. 2, III supra] holds is that a sufficiently "uncouth" or irrational racial gerrymander violates the Fifteenth Amendment. [The] fact that the "gerrymander" condemned in *Gomillion* was equally vulnerable under both Amendments indicates that the essential holding of that case is applicable, not merely to gerrymanders directed against racial minorities, but to those aimed at religious, ethnic, economic and political groups as well.[7]

My conclusion that the same standard should be applied to racial groups as is applied to other groups leads me also to conclude that the standard cannot condemn every adverse impact on one or more political groups without spawning more dilution litigation than the judiciary can manage. [N]othing comparable to the mathematical yardstick used in apportionment cases is available to identify the difference between permissible and impermissible adverse impacts on the voting strength of political groups. * * *

In my view, the proper standard is suggested by three characteristics of the gerrymander condemned in *Gomillion:* (1) the 28-sided configuration [was] manifestly not the product of a routine or a traditional political decision; (2) it had a significant adverse impact on a minority group; and (3) it was unsupported by any neutral justification and thus was either totally irrational or entirely motivated by a desire to curtail the political strength of the minority. These characteristics suggest that a proper test should focus on the objective effects of the political decision rather than the subjective motivation of the decisionmaker. In this case, if the commission form of government in Mobile were extraordinary, or if it were nothing more than a vestige of history, with no greater justification than the grotesque figure in *Gomillion*, it would surely violate the Constitution. That conclusion would follow simply from its adverse impact on black voters plus

---

7. [See], e.g., *Whitcomb* (districts that are "conceived or operated as purposeful devices to further racial *or economic* discrimination" are prohibited by the Fourteenth Amendment) (emphasis supplied); *Dorsey* (an apportionment scheme would be invalid [if] it "operate[d] to minimize or cancel out the voting strength of racial *or political* elements of the voting population") (emphasis supplied).

[For the view that the right to "effective political representation" should be limited to racial groups under the fifteenth amendment and thus "avoid an uncontrolled expansion of the effectiveness principle to countless interest groups," see Note, *United Jewish Organizations v. Carey and the Need to Recognize Aggregate Voting Rights*, 87 Yale L.J. 571 (1978).]

the absence of any legitimate justification for the system, without reference to the subjective intent of the political body that has refused to alter it.

Conversely, I am also persuaded that a political decision that affects group voting rights may be valid even if it can be proved that irrational or invidious factors have played some part in its enactment or retention. The standard for testing the acceptability of such a decision must take into account the fact that the responsibility for drawing political boundaries is generally committed to the legislative process and that the process inevitably involves a series of compromises among different group interests. If the process is to work, it must reflect an awareness of group interests and it must tolerate some attempts to advantage or to disadvantage particular segments of the voting populace. [Accordingly], a political decision that is supported by valid and articulable justifications cannot be invalid simply because some participants in the decisionmaking process were motivated by a purpose to disadvantage a minority group.

The decision to retain the commission form of government in Mobile, Ala., is such a decision. [The] fact that these at-large systems characteristically place one or more minority groups at a significant disadvantage in the struggle for political power cannot invalidate all such systems. See *Whitcomb*. Nor can it be the law that such systems are valid when there is no evidence that they were instituted or maintained for discriminatory reasons, but that they may be selectively condemned on the basis of the subjective motivation of some of their supporters. A contrary view "would spawn endless litigation concerning the multimember districts now widely employed in this Country," and would entangle the judiciary in a voracious political thicket.

MR. JUSTICE BRENNAN, dissenting.

I dissent because I agree with Mr. Justice Marshall that proof of discriminatory impact is sufficient in these cases. I also dissent because, even accepting the plurality's premise that discriminatory purpose must be shown, I agree with [Marshall and White, JJ.,] that the appellees have clearly met that burden.

MR. JUSTICE WHITE, dissenting.

[Both] the District Court and the Court of Appeals properly found that an invidious discriminatory purpose could be inferred from the totality of facts in this case. The Court's cryptic rejection of their conclusions ignores the principles that an invidious discriminatory purpose can be inferred from objective factors of the kind relied on in *Regester* and that the trial courts are in a special position to make such intensely local appraisals.

[T]he plurality today rejects the inference of purposeful discrimination apparently because each of the factors relied upon by the courts below is alone insufficient to support the inference. [By] viewing each of the factors relied upon below in isolation, and ignoring the fact that racial bloc voting at the polls makes it impossible to elect a black commissioner under the at-large system, the plurality rejects the "totality of the circumstances" approach we endorsed in *Regester, Davis,* and *Arlington Heights* * * *.

MR. JUSTICE MARSHALL, dissenting. * * *

The Court does not dispute the proposition that multimember districting can have the effect of submerging electoral minorities. [Further], we decided a series of vote-dilution cases under the Fourteenth Amendment that were designed to protect electoral minorities from precisely the combination of electoral laws and historical and social factors found in the present cases.[4] [Although] we have held that multimember districts are not unconstitutional per se, there is simply no basis for the plurality's conclusion that under our prior cases proof of discriminatory intent is a necessary condition for the invalidation of multimember districting.

[Under] this line of cases, an electoral districting plan is invalid if it has the effect of affording an electoral minority "less opportunity [than] other residents in the district to participate in the political processes and to elect legislators of their choice," *Regester*. It is also apparent that the Court in *Regester* considered equal access to the political process as meaning more than merely allowing the minority the opportunity to vote. *Regester* stands for the proposition that an electoral system may not relegate an electoral minority to political impotence by diminishing the importance of its [vote].

The plurality fails to apply the discriminatory effect standard of *Regester* because that approach conflicts with what the plurality takes to be an elementary principle of law. "[O]nly if there is purposeful discrimination," announces the plurality, "can there be a violation of [equal protection]." That proposition [fails] to distinguish between two distinct lines of equal protection decisions: those involving suspect classifications, and those involving fundamental rights.

* * *

Under the Equal Protection Clause, if a classification "impinges upon a fundamental right explicitly or implicitly protected by the [Constitution], strict judicial scrutiny" is required, *Rodriguez*, regardless of whether the infringement was intentional. As I will explain, our cases recognize a fundamental right to equal electoral participation that encompasses protection against vote dilution. Proof of discriminatory purpose is, therefore, not required to support a claim of vote dilution.[10] The plurality's erroneous conclusion to the contrary is the result of a failure to recognize the central distinction between *Regester* and *Davis*: the former involved an infringement of a constitutionally protected right, while the latter dealt with a claim of racially discriminatory distribution of an interest to which no citizen has a constitutional entitlement.[11] * * *

---

4. [T]hough municipalities must be accorded some discretion in arranging their affairs, see *Abate*, there is all the more reason to scrutinize assertions that municipal, rather than State, multi-member districting dilutes the vote of an electoral minority: "In statewide elections, it is possible that a large minority group in one multi-member district will be unable to elect any legislators, while in another multi-member district where the same group is a slight majority, they will elect the entire slate of legislators. [In] at-large elections, [t]here is no way to balance out the discrimination against a particular minority group because the entire city is one huge election district. The minority's loss is absolute." Berry & Dye, *The Discriminatory Effects of At-Large Elections,* 7 Fla.St.U.L.Rev. 85, 87 (1979). * * *

10. [Although] the right to vote is distinguishable for present purposes from the other fundamental rights our cases have recognized, surely the plurality would not require proof of discriminatory purpose in those cases. The

plurality fails to articulate why the right to vote should receive such singular treatment. Furthermore, the plurality refuses to recognize the disutility of requiring proof of discriminatory purpose in fundamental rights cases. For example, it would make no sense to require such a showing when the question is whether a state statute regulating abortion violates the right of personal choice recognized in *Roe v. Wade,* [p. 142 supra]. The only logical inquiry is whether, regardless of the legislature's motive, the statute has the effect of infringing that right. See, e.g., *Planned Parenthood v. Danforth,* [p. 176 supra].

11. [See] also Comment, *Proof of Racially Discriminatory Purpose Under the Equal Protection Clause,* 12 Harv.C.R.–C.L.L.Rev. 725, 758, n. 175 (1977); Note, *Racial Vote Dilution in Multimember Districts: The Constitutional Standard After Washington v. Davis,* 76 Mich. L.Rev. 694, 722–26 (1978); Comment, *Constitutional Challenges to Gerrymanders,* 45 U.Chi. L.Rev. 845, 869–77 (1978). * * *

Reynolds and its progeny focused solely on the discriminatory *effects* of malapportionment. [In] the present cases, the alleged vote dilution, though caused by the combined effects of the electoral structure and social and historical factors rather than by unequal population distribution, is analytically the same concept: the unjustified abridgement of a fundamental right. It follows, then, that a showing of discriminatory intent is just as unnecessary under the vote-dilution approach adopted in *Dorsey* and applied in *Regester,* as it is under our reapportionment cases. * * *

The plurality's response is that my approach amounts to nothing less than a constitutional requirement of proportional representation for groups. That assertion amounts to nothing more than a red herring.[b] [Appellees] proved that no Negro had ever been elected to the Mobile City Commission, despite the fact that Negroes constitute about one-third of the electorate, and that the persistence of severe racial bloc voting made it highly unlikely that any Negro could be elected at-large in the foreseeable future. Contrary to the plurality's contention, however, I do not find unconstitutional vote dilution in this case simply because of that showing. The plaintiffs convinced the District Court that Mobile Negroes were unable to use alternative avenues of political influence. They showed that Mobile Negroes still suffered pervasive present effects of massive historical official and private discrimination, and that the city commission had been quite unresponsive to the needs of the minority community. Mobile has been guilty of such pervasive racial discrimination in hiring employees that extensive intervention by the Federal District Court has been required. Negroes are grossly underrepresented on city boards and committees. The city's distribution of public services is racially discriminatory. City officials and police were largely unmoved by Negro complaints about police brutality and "mock lynchings." The District Court concluded that "[t]his sluggish and timid response is another manifestation of the low priority given to the needs of the black citizens and of the [commissioners'] political fear of a white backlash vote when black citizens' needs are at stake."

[T]he protection against vote dilution recognized by our prior cases serves as a minimally intrusive guarantee of political survival for a discrete political minority that is effectively locked out of governmental decisionmaking processes. So understood, the doctrine hardly " 'create[s] substantive constitutional rights in the name of guaranteeing equal protection of the laws,' " [but] is a simple reflection of the basic principle that the Equal Protection Clause protects "[t]he right of a citizen to equal representation and to have his vote weighted equally with those of all other citizens." *Reynolds.*

[The] plurality's requirement of proof of *intentional discrimination* [may] represent an attempt to bury the legitimate concerns of the minority beneath the soil of a doctrine almost as impermeable as it is specious. If so, the superficial tranquility created by such measures can be but short-lived. If this Court refuses to honor our long-recognized principle that the Constitution "nullifies sophisticated as well as simple-minded modes of discrimination," it cannot expect the victims of discrimination to respect political channels of seeking redress. I dissent.

---

b. For the view that "PR is the only electoral system that can give equal representation to all groups," see Note, *The Constitutional* *Imperative of Proportional Representation,* 94 Yale L.J. 163 (1984).

ROGERS v. LODGE, 458 U.S. 613, 102 S.Ct. 3272, 73 L.Ed.2d 1012 (1982), per WHITE, J., affirmed a decision that the at-large election system for a Georgia county Board of Commissioners violated equal protection: "The District Court [demonstrated] its understanding of the controlling standard by observing that a determination of discriminatory intent is 'a requisite to a finding of unconstitutional vote dilution' [and] concluded that the [system] 'although racially neutral when adopted, is being *maintained* for invidious purposes.' [For] the most part, the District Court dealt with the evidence in terms of the factors [that had been used by the district court in *Mobile*], but as the Court of Appeals stated: 'Judge Alaimo [did] not treat [those factors] as absolute, but rather considered them only to the extent that they were relevant to the question of discriminatory intent.' Although a tenable argument can be made to the contrary, we are not inclined to disagree with the Court of Appeals' conclusion that the District Court applied the proper legal standard. * * *

"The Court of Appeals [stated that the] District Court correctly anticipated *Mobile* and required appellees to prove that the at-large voting system was maintained for a discriminatory purpose. The Court of Appeals also held that the District Court's findings not only were not clearly erroneous, but its conclusion that the at-large system was maintained for invidious purposes was 'virtually mandated by the overwhelming proof.' [This Court has] noted that issues of intent are commonly treated as factual matters [and] has frequently noted its reluctance to disturb findings of fact concurred in by two lower courts."

POWELL, J., joined by Rehnquist, J., dissented: "[T]he Court's opinion cannot be reconciled persuasively with [*Mobile*]. There are some variances in the largely sociological evidence presented in the two cases. But *Mobile* held that this *kind* of evidence was not enough. * * *

"The Court's decision today relies heavily on the capacity of the federal district courts—essentially free from any standards prepounded by this Court—to determine whether at-large voting systems are 'being maintained for the invidious purpose of diluting the voting strength of the black population.' Federal courts thus are invited to engage in deeply subjective inquiries into the motivations of local officials in structuring local governments. Inquiries of this kind not only can be 'unseemly,' they intrude the federal courts—with only the vaguest constitutional direction—into an area of intensely local and political concern.

"Emphasizing these considerations, Justice Stevens argues forcefully [that] subjective intent is irrelevant to the establishment of a case of racial vote [dilution].[a] I agree with much of what he says [but] would not accept this view. 'The central purpose of the Equal Protection Clause [is] the prevention of official conduct discriminating on the basis of race.' *Davis*. Because I am unwilling to abandon this central principle in cases of this kind, I cannot join Justice Stevens's opinion. [But] in the absence of proof of discrimination by reliance on the kind of objective factors identified by Justice Stevens, I would hold that the factors cited by the Court of Appeals are too attenuated as a matter of law to support an inference of discriminatory intent."[b]

---

a. Stevens, J.'s long dissent expanded his views expressed in *Mobile*.

b. For subsequent congressional action relevant to the problem, p. 1179 infra.

Notes and Questions

Gerrymandering.[a] (a) Has the Court made clear that equal protection bars apportionment gerrymanders that deny "full and effective participation in the political processes"? For alleged racial gerrymanders, see *Connor v. Johnson,* 265 F.Supp. 492 (S.D.Miss.1966), aff'd 386 U.S. 483 (1967); *Ferrell v. Hall,* 339 F.Supp. 73 (W.D.Okl.), aff'd 406 U.S. 939 (1972); compare *United Jewish Orgs. v. Carey,* Sec. 2, V supra. For alleged political gerrymanders, see *Gaffney v. Cummings,* infra. Consider Auerbach, fn. 12 in *Reynolds,* at 65: "[I]t would not be desirable for the Court to attack the partisan gerrymander as a constitutional problem. The 'One Vote, One Value' principle will make gerrymandering more difficult and even more obvious. Inequities in apportionment should not be justified simply because inequities in districting cannot be eliminated at the same time. The great mobility of the American people, the accelerating pace of socioeconomic change and the increasing uncertainties in the futures of both major parties, may be expected to combine with constitutional apportionment to make partisan districting an increasingly risky enterprise." [b] Do you agree? Even if "there are computer techniques for districting which preclude gerrymandering and produce contiguous, compact districts nearly equal in population without breaking up population centers"? Id. For the view that the Court should adjudicate the matter, see Clinton, *Further Explorations in the Political Thicket: The Gerrymander and the Constitution,* 59 Ia.L.Rev. 1 (1973). See fn. g in *Karcher.*

(b) How are gerrymanders to be identified? If districting departs substantially from natural geographic or political boundaries, should a "rational" state policy insulate it from a charge of gerrymandering? Consider Note, *Apportionment and the Courts—A Synopsis and Prognosis: Herein of Gerrymanders and Other Dragons,* 59 Nw.U.L.Rev. 500, 531 (1964): "A legislature might reasonably conclude [that] a minority interest bloc should be concentrated so as to assure that at least one representative will be dedicated to protecting the bloc from submergence. On the other hand, a legislature might reasonably conclude that the election of representatives committed to the general welfare is best accomplished by forming districts that proportionately reflect the composition of the state as a whole." [c] Is gerrymandering on the basis of political party, economic status, or social position "rational"? Constitutional?

a. See Tyler, *Court Versus Legislature,* 27 Law & Contemp.Prob. 390, 400–01 (1962): "[A]n urban majority is converted into a legislative minority by the time-polished techniques of 'cracking [and] stacking' districts. The 'cracked' district is the huge metropolitan center, torn apart into separate pieces, each of which is attached to and outvoted by a surrounding rural hinterland. [The] 'stacked' district is the child of the gerrymander, a delicately carved creature, resembling nothing more than the partisan and rapacious soul of his political creator." For a broader definition of gerrymander to include any intentional manipulation of districts for partisan advantage, see Baker, fn. b in *Mahan,* supra.

b. For the contention that gerrymandering has been encouraged by the reapportionment cases, see Elliot, *Prometheus, Proteus, Pandora, and Procrustes Unbound: The Political Consequences of Reapportionment,* 37 U.Chi.L.

Rev. 474 (1970). See also Dixon, fn. d in *Lucas* supra, at 378, 462; Sickels, *Dragons, Bacon Strips and Dumbbells—Who's Afraid of Reapportionment?* 75 Yale L.J. 1300 (1966).

c. "Rational arguments can be presented on either side of this question. In the more homogeneous district the legislator has better opportunities to gauge the viewpoints of constituents, and fewer constituents are unrepresented by a legislator sensitive to their views. Elections are likely to be more one-sided, with the result that a larger proportion of legislators develop seniority and become skilled in their profession. In the less homogeneous district the legislator is less likely to become the spokesman for a few narrow interests. There is likely to be closer competition between the parties and consequently a better chance for the voters to remove a legislator who is not performing satisfactorily. [If] a court sought to review legislation establishing district lines,

(c) Apart from racial groups or political parties, what other groups (or "interests") may be the object of a gerrymander? How are they to be identified? What about "independent voters"? In GAFFNEY v. CUMMINGS, note 4(b) after *Reynolds,* supra, the Court noted "the reality [that] districting inevitably [is] intended to have substantial political consequences." Thus, the fact "that virtually every Senate and House district line was drawn with the conscious intent to create a districting plan that would achieve a rough approximation of the statewide political strengths of the Democratic and Republican Parties, the only two parties in the State large enough to elect legislators from discernible geographic areas," did not invalidate the plan.

(d) How should a court determine whether a given districting scheme is based on "rational," rather than constitutionally impermissible, considerations? Consider Note, *The Apportionment Case: An Expanded Concept of Equal Protection,* 1965 Wis.L.Rev. 606, 649: "The ultimate issue in the gerrymander [cases]— legislative purpose—is unquestionably difficult to prove. In most cases, one attacking a legislative apportionment scheme has no access bearing directly upon the issue of legislative purpose if the formal documents constituting the legislative history do not contain the relevant information. If either party would be able to come forward with such proof, it would most likely be the supporter of the scheme, who in most cases is part of the official governmental apparatus." And see Dixon, fn. d in *Lucas* supra, at 322: "One guideline [would] be to view a district system as suspect—and perhaps shift the burden of [proof]— whenever it is shown that the system consistently magnifies the legislative strength of one party far beyond its actual state-wide voter strength." See also Engstrom, *The Supreme Court and Equipopulous Gerrymandering: A Remaining Obstacle in the Quest for Fair and Effective Representation,* 1976 Ariz.St.L.J. 277.[d]

B. DENIAL OR QUALIFICATION OF THE RIGHT

CARRINGTON v. RASH, 380 U.S. 89, 85 S.Ct. 775, 13 L.Ed.2d 675 (1965), per STEWART, J., held a Texas provision, barring members of the military who moved to Texas from voting in state elections so long as they remained in the military, "an invidious discrimination": "We deal here with matters close to the core of our constitutional system." Only "where military personnel are involved has Texas been unwilling to develop more precise tests to determine the bona fides of an individual claiming to have actually made his home in the State long enough to vote." " 'Fencing out' from the franchise a sector of the population because of the way they may vote is constitutionally impermissible." [a]

---

it would be forced to determine these questions of policy, at least implicitly." Jewell, *Minority Representation: A Political or Judicial Question,* 53 Ky.L.J. 267, 273 (1965).

d. The burden of proof is placed on the state in respect to changes in districting that are subject to the Voting Rights Act of 1965. See fn. a, p. 1145 infra. See generally Halpin & Engstrom, *Racial Gerrymandering and Southern State Legislative Districting: Attorney General Determinations Under the Voting Rights Act,* 22 J.Pub.L. 37 (1973).

a. Harlan, J., dissented: The classification was "rational" in treating such persons as

"transients for voting purposes" because the "vast majority" will leave "when the military compulsion ends." Finally, Texas "could rationally decide to protect local politics against the influences of military voting strength." Warren, C.J., did not participate.

May a state single out certain groups (students) for a presumption of nonresidency (in the district in which they attend college)? See generally Note, *Student Voting and the Constitution,* 72 Colum.L.Rev. 162 (1972).

HARPER v. VIRGINIA BD. OF ELEC., 383 U.S. 663, 86 S.Ct. 1079, 16 L.Ed. 2d 169 (1966), per DOUGLAS, J., overruling *Breedlove v. Suttles,* 302 U.S. 277, 58 S.Ct. 205, 82 L.Ed. 252 (1937), held that Virginia's $1.50 poll tax as "a prerequisite of voting" was "an 'invidious' discrimination": "[T]he right to vote in state elections is nowhere expressly mentioned" in the Constitution, but "once the franchise is [granted] lines may not be drawn which [violate equal protection].[3]"

"Long ago in *Yick Wo,* [Sec. 2, III supra], the Court referred to 'the political franchise of voting' as a 'fundamental political right, because preservative of all rights.' * * * Wealth, like race, creed, or color, is not germane to one's ability to participate intelligently in the electoral process. Lines drawn on the basis of wealth or property, like those of race, are traditionally disfavored. See *Edwards v. California,* 314 U.S. 160, 62 S.Ct. 164, 86 L.Ed. 119 (1941) (Jackson, J., concurring); *Griffin v. Illinois; Douglas v. California,* [Part III infra]. To introduce wealth or payment of a fee as a measure of a voter's qualifications is to introduce a capricious or irrelevant factor. * * *

"In determining what lines are unconstitutionally discriminatory, we have never been confined to historic notions of equality" and "notions of what constitutes equal treatment for purposes of the Equal Protection Clause *do* change [citing *Plessy* and *Brown,* Sec. 2, II supra]. Our conclusion, like that in *Reynolds,* is founded not on what we think governmental policy should be, but on what the Equal Protection Clause requires.

"We have long been mindful that where fundamental rights and liberties are asserted under the Equal Protection Clause, classifications which might invade or restrain them must be closely scrutinized and carefully confined. See, e.g., *Reynolds; Carrington.*"

BLACK, J., dissented: "[U]nder a proper interpretation of the Equal Protection Clause States are to have the broadest kind of leeway in areas where they have a general constitutional competence to act. [P]oll tax legislation can 'reasonably,' 'rationally' and without an 'invidious' or evil purpose to injure anyone be found to rest on a number of state policies including (1) the State's desire to collect its revenue, and (2) its belief that voters who pay a poll tax will be interested in furthering the State's welfare when they vote. [And] history is on the side of 'rationality' of the State's poll tax policy. Property qualifications existed in the Colonies and were continued by many States after the Constitution was adopted. [The Court] seems to be using the old 'natural-law-due-process formula' to justify striking down state laws as violations of [equal protection]."

HARLAN, J., joined by Stewart, J., dissented: "The [equal protection] test evolved by this Court [is whether] a classification can be deemed to be founded on some rational and otherwise constitutionally permissible state [policy].[3] *Reynolds* [also] marked a departure from these traditional and wise principles. [I]t was probably accepted as sound political theory by a large percentage of Americans through most of our history, that people with some property have a deeper stake in community affairs, and are consequently more responsible, more educated, more knowledgeable, more worthy of [confidence. It] is all wrong, in my view, for the Court to adopt the political doctrines popularly accepted at a

---

3. [While] the "Virginia poll tax was born of a desire to disenfranchise the Negro," we do not stop to determine whether [the] Virginia tax in its modern setting serves the same end.

3. I think the somewhat different application of the Equal Protection Clause to racial discrimination cases finds justification in the fact that insofar as that clause may embody a particular value in addition to rationality, the historical origins of the Civil War Amendments might attribute to racial equality this special status. * * *

particular moment of our history and to declare all others to be irrational and invidious * * *."

KRAMER v. UNION FREE SCHOOL DISTRICT

395 U.S. 621, 89 S.Ct. 1886, 23 L.Ed.2d 583 (1969).

MR. CHIEF JUSTICE WARREN delivered the opinion of the Court.

[§ 2012 of the New York Education Law] provides that in certain New York school districts residents [may] vote in the school district election only if they [or their spouse] (1) own (or lease) taxable real property within the district, or (2) are parents (or have custody of) children enrolled in the local public schools. Appellant, a bachelor who neither owns nor leases taxable real property, [claimed] § 2012 denied him equal protection * * *.

[I]t is important to note what is *not* at issue in this case. The requirements of § 2012 that school district voters must (1) be citizens of the United States, (2) be bona fide residents of the school district, and (3) be at least 21 years of age are not challenged. * * *

[S]tatutes distributing the franchise constitute the foundation of our representative society. Any unjustified discrimination in determining who may participate in political affairs or in the selection of public officials undermines the legitimacy of representative government. [Therefore,] if a [statute] grants the right to vote to some bona fide residents of requisite age and citizenship and denies the franchise to others, the Court must determine whether the exclusions are necessary to promote a compelling state interest. See *Carrington.*

[The] presumption of constitutionality and the approval given "rational" classifications in other types of enactments are based on an assumption that the institutions of state government are structured so as to represent fairly all the people. However, when the challenge to the statute is in effect a challenge of this basic assumption, the assumption can no longer serve as the basis for presuming constitutionality. And, the assumption is no less under attack because the legislature which decides who may participate at the various levels of political choice is fairly elected. * * * [10]

The need for exacting judicial scrutiny of statutes distributing the franchise is undiminished simply because, under a different statutory scheme, the offices subject to election might have been filled through appointment [11] [since] "once the franchise is granted to the electorate, lines may not be drawn which are inconsistent with [equal protection]." *Harper.*

Nor is the need for close judicial examination affected because the district [and] the school board do not have "general" legislative powers. Our exacting examination is necessitated not by the subject of the election [but] because some resident citizens are permitted to participate and some are not. * * *

Besides appellant and others who similarly live in their parents' homes, the statute also disenfranchises the following persons (unless they are parents or guardians of children enrolled in the district public school): senior citizens and others living with children or relatives; clergy, military personnel and others who live on tax-exempt property; boarders and lodgers; parents who neither own nor lease qualifying property and whose children are too young to attend school [or] attend private schools.

---

10. [See] *Avery v. Midland County.*

11. Similarly, no less a showing of a compelling justification for disenfranchising resi-

dents is required merely because the questions scheduled for the election need not have been submitted to the voters.

[A]ppellees argue that the State has a legitimate interest in limiting the franchise in school district elections [to] those "primarily interested in such elections" [and] that the State may reasonably and permissibly conclude that "property taxpayers" (including lessees of taxable property who share the tax burden through rent payments) and parents of the children enrolled in the district's schools are those "primarily interested" in school affairs. * * *

[A]ssuming, arguendo, that New York legitimately might limit the franchise in these school district elections to those "primarily interested in school affairs," close scrutiny of the § 2012 classifications demonstrates that they do not accomplish this purpose with sufficient precision to justify denying appellant the franchise.

[T]he classifications must be tailored so that the exclusion of appellant and members of his class is necessary to achieve the articulated state goal.[14] Section 2012 does not meet the exacting standard of precision [because it permits] inclusion of many persons who have, at best, a remote and indirect interest in school affairs and on the other hand, exclude[s] others who have a distinct and direct interest in the school meeting decisions.[15] * * *

MR. JUSTICE STEWART, with whom MR. JUSTICE BLACK and MR. JUSTICE HARLAN join, dissenting. * * *

Clearly a State may reasonably assume that its residents have a greater stake in the outcome of elections held within its boundaries than do other persons [and] that residents, being generally better informed regarding state affairs than are nonresidents, will be more likely [to] vote responsibly. And the same may be said of legislative assumptions regarding the electoral competence of adults and literate persons on the one hand, and of minors and illiterates on the other. It is clear, of course, that lines thus drawn cannot infallibly perform their intended legislative function. Just as "[i]lliterate people may be intelligent voters," nonresidents or minors might also in some instances be interested, informed, and intelligent participants in the electoral process. Persons who commute across a state line to work may well have a great stake in the affairs of the State in which they are employed; some college students under 21 may be both better informed and more passionately interested in political affairs than many adults. But such discrepancies are the inevitable concomitant of the line-drawing that is essential to lawmaking.[a] So long as the classification is rationally related to a permissible legislative end, therefore—as are residence, literacy, and age requirements imposed with respect to voting—there is no denial of equal protection.

Thus judged, the statutory classification involved here seems to me clearly to be valid [and] the Court does not really argue the contrary. Instead, it [asserts] that the traditional equal protection standard is [inapt]. But the asserted justification for applying [a stricter] standard cannot withstand analysis. [The] voting qualifications at issue have been promulgated not by Union Free School District, but by the New York State Legislature, and the appellant is of course fully able to participate in the election of representatives in that body.

14. Of course, if the exclusions are necessary to promote the articulated state interest, we must then determine whether the interest promoted by limiting the franchise constitutes a compelling state interest. We do not reach that issue in this case.

15. For example, appellant resides with his parents in the school district, pays state and federal taxes and is interested in and affected by school board decisions [but] an uninterested unemployed young man who pays no state or federal taxes, but who rents an apartment in the district, can [vote].

a. See Lee, *Mr. Herbert Spencer and the Bachelor Stockbroker*, 15 Ariz.L.Rev. 457 (1973).

There is simply no claim whatever here that the state government is not "structured so as to represent fairly all the people," including the appellant.

[§ 2012] does not involve racial classifications [and] is not one that impinges upon a constitutionally protected right, and that consequently can be justified only by a "compelling" state interest. For "the Constitution of the United States does not confer the right of suffrage upon any one."

In any event, it seems to me that under *any* equal protection standard, short of a doctrinaire insistence that universal suffrage is somehow mandated by the Constitution, the appellant's claim must be rejected. * * *

PHOENIX v. KOLODZIEJSKI, 399 U.S. 204, 90 S.Ct. 1990, 26 L.Ed.2d 523 (1970), per WHITE, J., relying on *Kramer* and *Cipriano v. Houma,* 395 U.S. 701, 89 S.Ct. 1897, 23 L.Ed.2d 647 (1969),[b] held violative of equal protection a statute permitting only real property taxpayers to vote on "general obligation bonds," issued to finance various municipal improvements, and to be serviced partly by property taxes: "[P]roperty owners and nonproperty owners alike, have a substantial interest in the public facilities and the services available in the city and will be substantially affected by the ultimate outcome of the bond election." Even if *only* property tax revenues were used to service the bonds, "the justification would be insufficient. Property taxes may be paid initially by property owners, but a significant part of the ultimate burden of each year's tax on rental property will very likely be borne by the [tenant]. Moreover, property taxes on commercial property [will] normally be reflected in the prices of goods and services [purchased]." [c]

Notes and Questions

1. *Other laws "distributing the franchise."* (a) After *Kramer,* what of the validity of age, residency and literacy requirements for voting? Consider 83 Harv.L.Rev. 81 (1969): "[T]he danger of an impermissible selection is much less when the goal of a voting test is to select competent voters than when interest differences are involved. The Court refused to assume that some voters have no interest whatsoever, but it must acknowledge that some citizens, like two-year olds and the insane, are not competent. Since such cases of permissible exclusion can be conceived of, a competency classification cannot be termed impermis-

b. *Cipriano* held violative of equal protection a statute giving "only 'property taxpayers' the right to vote in elections [for] issuance of revenue bonds by a municipal utility," pointing out that "the benefits and burdens of the bond issue fall indiscriminately on property owner and nonproperty owner alike." Black and Stewart, JJ., concurred in the result, finding the classification " 'wholly irrelevant to achievement' of the State's objective." Harlan, J., feeling bound by prior decisions, concurred in the result.

c. Stewart, J., joined by Burger, C.J., and Harlan, J., dissented: Since "the weight of repaying [general obligation] bonds will legally fall" on real property owners, this is "an entirely rational public policy."

See also *Evans v. Cornman,* 398 U.S. 419, 90 S.Ct. 1752, 26 L.Ed.2d 370 (1970), unanimously relying on *Kramer* and *Cipriano* to hold viola-

tive of equal protection Maryland's refusal to permit voting in state elections by persons living on the grounds of the National Institutes of Mental Health (a federal enclave within the state); *Hill v. Stone,* 421 U.S. 289, 95 S.Ct. 1637, 44 L.Ed.2d 172 (1975), invalidating Texas provisions limiting the vote in city bond elections to persons who have "rendered" their real or personal property (even though of nominal worth) for taxation.

Does *Phoenix* apply to a law that permits only real property owners to vote in a special assessment election which concerns bonds to finance improvements to the property and which makes each piece of property the sole security for the bonds? See Gaines, *The Right of Non-Property Owners to Participate in a Special Assessment Majority Protest,* 20 U.C. L.A.L.Rev. 201 (1972).

sible in its general purpose." Does this "interest-competency" distinction adequately respond to Stewart, J.'s objections? If *all* 2-year-olds are incompetent, are *all* 17-year-olds? If not, would an 18-year-old voting qualification "meet the exacting standard of precision required of statutes which selectively distribute the franchise"? See *Oregon v. Mitchell,* p. 1166 infra; Notes, *Student Voting and Apportionment: The "Rotten Boroughs" of Academia,* 81 Yale L.J. 35 (1971); *Applying Equal Protection to Bona Fide Residence Requirements,* 59 Ia.L.Rev. 671 (1974). Assuming the continued validity of literacy tests, what of an *English* literacy requirement? Compare the opinions of Douglas and Harlan, JJ., in *Cardona v. Power,* 384 U.S. 672, 86 S.Ct. 1728, 16 L.Ed.2d 848 (1966).

(b) *Felons.* RICHARDSON v. RAMIREZ, 418 U.S. 24, 94 S.Ct. 2655, 41 L.Ed. 2d 551 (1974), per REHNQUIST, J.,—relying on § 2 of the fourteenth amendment— held California's disenfranchising felons not violative of equal protection: "[T]he express language of § 2 [and] the historical and judicial interpretation of the Amendment's applicability to state laws disenfranchising felons, is of controlling significance in distinguishing such laws from those other state limitations on the franchise which have been held [invalid. We] rest on the demonstrably sound proposition that § 1, in dealing with voting rights as it does, could not have been meant to bar outright a form of disenfranchisement which was expressly exempted from the less drastic sanction of reduced representation which § 2 imposed for other forms of disenfranchisement." [a]

(c) *Special purpose units.* (i) SALYER LAND CO. v. TULARE LAKE BASIN WATER STORAGE DIST., 410 U.S. 719, 93 S.Ct. 1224, 35 L.Ed.2d 659 (1973), per REHNQUIST, J., upheld California statutes permitting only landowners to vote in "water storage districts" elections and apportioning votes according to the assessed valuation of the land within the districts. These districts planned projects for water acquisition, conservation and distribution; they were empowered to fix charges for use of water in proportion to services rendered; project costs were assessed against land in accordance with benefits accruing to each tract. Appellee district had a population of 77 (including 18 children), most employed by one of four corporations that farmed 85% of the land; there were also about 200 other small landowners; one of the corporations (Boswell Co.) held a majority of the votes.

"[Appellee], although vested with some typical governmental powers,[7] has relatively limited authority." Apart from water,[8] "it [does] not exercise what might be thought of as 'normal governmental' authority, [and] its actions disproportionately affect landowners" because of the method of allocating project costs and service charges. "In short, there is no way that the economic burdens of district operations can fall on residents qua residents, and the operations of the districts primarily affect the land within their boundaries." Thus, relying on the language of *Avery* and *Hadley* that some elections might not come within

---

a. Marshall, J., joined by Brennan, J., dissented, arguing that "§ 2 was not intended [to] be a limitation on the other sections of the Fourteenth Amendment" and that, under the "compelling state interest test," "the blanket disenfranchisement of ex-felons cannot stand." Douglas, J., dissented on procedural grounds.

Consider Tribe, *American Constitutional Law* 771 (1978): "[§ 2] provides no warrant for circumscribing the reach of the equal protection clause [which] is not bound to the political theories of a particular era but draws

much of its substance from changing social norms and evolving conceptions of equality."

7. The board [can] condemn private property [and] cooperate (including contract) with other agencies, state and federal. Both general obligations bonds and interest-bearing warrants may be authorized.

8. Appellants strongly urge that districts [engage] in flood control activities [but these] are incident to the exercise of the district's primary functions of water storage and distribution.

the doctrine in *Reynolds* and *Kramer,* "we conclude that [appellee], by reason of its special limited purpose and of the disproportionate effect of its activities on landowners as a group, is the sort of exception to the [rule] contemplated."

Thus, the franchise restriction is valid unless " 'wholly irrelevant to achievement of the regulation's objectives.' No doubt residents within the district may be affected by its activities. But [California] could quite reasonably have concluded that the number of landowners and owners of sufficient amounts of acreage whose consent was necessary to organize the district would not have subjected their land to the lien of its possibly very substantial assessments unless they had a dominant voice in its control." [b] As to appellants' "reliance on the various decisions of this Court holding that wealth has no relation to resident-voter qualifications," because "the benefits and burdens to each landowner in the District are in proportion to the assessed value of the land," "we cannot say that the California legislative decision to permit voting in the same proportion is not rationally based." [c]

DOUGLAS, J., joined by Brennan and Marshall, JJ., dissented: In the past, floods were averted by storing water in Buena Vista Lake. "But that was not done in the great 1969 flood" because the board—"dominated [by] Boswell Co.— voted 6–4 to table the motion" because it had an "agricultural lease in the Buena Vista Lake Basin and flooding it would have interfered" with its crops. As a result, the residence of one of the non-landowner appellants "was 15½ feet below the water level of the crest of the flood." "Measured by the *Hadley* test," the district "surely performs 'important governmental functions' which 'have sufficient impact throughout the district' to justify the application of the *Avery* principle. [The] result [here] is a corporate political kingdom undreamed of [by] our Constitution."

(ii) BALL v. JAMES, 451 U.S. 355, 101 S.Ct. 1811, 68 L.Ed.2d 150 (1981), per STEWART, J., applied *Salyer* to an Arizona water district which limited voting to landowners on a "one acre, one vote" basis. Although the district was formed for "storage, delivery, and conservation of water," it had become "a major generator and supplier of hydroelectric power in the State, [and] roughly 40% of the water it delivers goes to urban areas for nonagricultural uses." Although "the District has $290 million of general obligation bonds outstanding that are secured by a lien on lands owned by the voting members, [the] bonds have so far been serviced out of the District's electricity revenues, [and] all capital improvements have been financed by revenue bonds":

"[A]ppellees claim [that] the sheer size of the power operations and the great number of people they affect serve to transform the District into an entity of general governmental power. But no matter how great the number of nonvoting residents buying electricity from the District, the relationship between them and the District's power operations is essentially that between consumers and a

b. Compare Note, 72 Mich.L.Rev. 868, 893–94 (1974): "[W]hether a unit provides an unusual or specialized service should not be determinative. [The] critical question is, rather, whether the impact on the citizens is so uniform that each citizen should participate equally in political decision-making. [*Salyer*] posed the choice as between a unit with specialized powers and disproportionate effects and a unit with general powers and equalized effects and ignored the possibility of a unit with specialized powers but equalized effects."

c. Compare 87 Harv.L.Rev. 100–01 (1973): "[*Salyer*] merely found that landowners were disproportionately affected 'as a group' and made no claim that some landowners were disproportionately affected relative to other landowners. It is unlikely that disproportionate effects on those within the landowner group could be found, since a large landowner, although assessed more on an absolute basis than a small landowner, receives proportionately larger benefits from district activities."

business enterprise from which they buy. Nothing in the *Avery, Hadley,* or *Salyer* cases suggests that the volume of business or the breadth of economic effect of a venture undertaken by a government entity as an incident of its narrow and primary governmental public function can, of its own weight, subject the entity to the one-person-one-vote requirements of the *Reynolds* case.

"[The] voting landowners are the only residents [subject] to the acreage-based taxing power of the District, [and] the only residents who have ever committed capital to the District through stock assessments charged by the Association.[19] The *Salyer* opinion did not say that the selected class of voters for a special public entity must be the only parties at all affected by the operations of the entity, [but rather] whether the effect of the entity's operations on them was disproportionately greater than the effect on those seeking the vote.[20]"

WHITE, J., joined by Brennan, Marshall and Blackmun, JJ., dissented: The district's "power to set its own rates and other conditions of service"—"not subject to control by another state agency"—"constitutes important attributes of sovereignty. When combined with a consideration of the District's wide-ranging operations, [it] is clear that the District exercises broad governmental power. [Here] the landowners could not themselves afford to finance their own project and turned to a public agency [which] now subsidizes the storage and delivery of irrigation water for agricultural purposes by selling electricity to the public at prices that neither the voters nor any representative public agency has any right to control. Unlike the situation in *Salyer,* the financial burden of supplying irrigation water has been shifted from the landowners to the consumers of electricity. [T]he burdens placed upon the lands within the District are so minimal that they cannot possibly serve as a basis for limiting the franchise to property owners. * * *[11]"[d]

(d) *Nonresidents.* HOLT CIVIC CLUB v. TUSCALOOSA, 439 U.S. 60, 99 S.Ct. 383, 58 L.Ed.2d 292 (1978), per REHNQUIST, J., upheld the Alabama "police jurisdiction" statute, which extended a city's police and sanitary regulations and its business-licensing powers (at ½ the fees for city businesses) to residents of adjacent unincorporated communities, but did not permit them to vote in city elections: "[O]ur cases have uniformly recognized that a government unit may legitimately restrict the right to participate in its political processes to those who

---

19. The Court of Appeals found it significant that 98% of the District's revenues come from sales of electricity, and only 2% from charges assessed for water deliveries. This fact in no way affects the constitutionality of the voting scheme. When the consumers of electricity supply those power revenues, they are simply buying electricity; they are neither committing capital to the District nor committing any of their property as security for the credit of the District.

20. The appellees, of course, are qualified voters in Arizona and so remain equal participants in the election of the state legislators who created and have the power to change the District.

[Powell, J., who joined the Court's opinion, emphasized "the importance [of] the Arizona Legislature's control over voting requirements for the [District. It] is large enough and the resources it manages are basic enough that the people will act through their elected legislature when further changes in the govern-

ance of the District are warranted. [For] this Court to dictate how the Board of the District must be elected would detract from the democratic process we profess to protect."]

11. [In] most situations involving a state agency or even a city, the state legislature and ultimately the people could exercise control since any municipal corporation is a creature of the State. The Fourteenth Amendment requires a far more direct sense of democratic participation in elective schemes which is not satisfied by the indirect and imprecise voter control suggested by the Court [in fn. 20] and by Justice Powell.

d. For a careful analysis distinguishing *Ball* from *Salyer* on the ground that the system in *Salyer* (but not in *Ball*) distributed benefits and burdens in a way comporting with the way in which the vote was distributed, see Durchslag, *Salyer, Ball and Holt: Reappraising the Right to Vote in Terms of Political "Interest" and Vote Dilution,* 33 Case W.Res.L.Rev. 1 (1982).

reside within its borders. See, e.g., *Dunn v. Blumstein,* [Part II infra]; *Kramer; Carrington.*[a] [A] city's decisions inescapably affect individuals living immediately outside its borders. The granting of building permits for highrise apartments, industrial plants, and the like on the city's fringe unavoidably contributes to problems of traffic congestion, school districting, and law enforcement immediately outside the city. A rate change in the city's sales or ad valorem tax could well have a significant impact on retailers and property values in areas bordering the city. The condemnation of real property on the city's edge for construction of a municipal [dump] would have obvious implications for neighboring nonresidents. [Yet] no one would suggest that nonresidents likely to be affected [have] a constitutional right to participate in the political processes bringing it about. * * *

"Thus stripped of its voting rights attire, the equal protection issue [is] whether the Alabama statutes [bear] some rational relationship to a legitimate state [purpose].[8]"

STEVENS, J., who joined the Court's opinion, added: "The powers of extraterritorial jurisdiction granted by the challenged statutes are limited. [Nor] is there any claim [that] residents of the police jurisdictions have been charged unreasonable costs for the services they receive."

BRENNAN, J., joined by White and Marshall, JJ., dissented: "[S]tate law characterizations of residency are not controlling for purposes of the Fourteenth Amendment. See, e.g., *Evans; Carrington.* [The] touchstone for determining whether a residency requirement is 'appropriately defined' derives from the purpose of such requirements, which, as stated in *Dunn,* is 'to preserve the basic conception of a political community.' * * *

"The residents of Tuscaloosa's police jurisdiction are vastly more affected by Tuscaloosa's decisionmaking processes than were the plaintiffs in either *Kramer* or *Cipriano* affected by the decisionmaking processes from which they had been unconstitutionally excluded. [The] Court today does [not] provide any standards for determining when those subjected to extraterritorial municipal legislation will have been 'governed enough' to trigger the protections of the Equal Protection Clause.[b]

"[There] is a crystal distinction between those who reside in Tuscaloosa's police jurisdiction, and who are therefore subject to that city's police and sanitary ordinances, licensing fees, and the jurisdiction of its recorders' courts, and those who reside in neither the city nor its police jurisdiction, and who are thus merely affected by the indirect impact of the city's decisions. This distinc-

---

a. Consider 93 Harv.L.Rev. 146–47 (1979): "There are severe constitutional restraints on extraterritorial exercises of direct governmental powers by states [that] ensure that individuals who do not reside in a state will not be forced to submit to its authority in important ways. As a result, nonresidents have little claim to a voice in a state's affairs. There are no comparable restraints on the extraterritorial exercise of municipal powers."

8. [We] do not have before us, of course, a situation in which a city has annexed outlying territory in all but name, and is exercising precisely the same governmental powers over residents of surrounding unincorporated territory as it does over those residing within its corporate limits. * * *

b. Consider Note, 68 Calif.L.Rev. 126, 145–46 (1980): "[Brennan, J.'s] call for full enfranchisement [is] fraught with constitutional difficulties. Holt residents had absolutely no cognizable interest in numerous functions conducted by the City of Tuscaloosa. The grant of an equal voice to extraterritorials, regardless of laudable motives, would necessarily dilute the vote of Tuscaloosa's residents in important matters. [Thus,] a court should look for solutions that will enfranchise extraterritorials *only* to the extent of their interest in the city's affairs." See also Note, *Dilution of Residents' Votes by Extension of the Franchise to Certain Nonresidents,* 64 Ia.L.Rev. 722 (1979). See further note 2 infra.

tion [is] consistent with, if not mandated by, the very conception of a political community underlying constitutional recognition of bona fide residency requirements."

(e) *Annexations.* Must an election on whether a city should annex an adjacent area include the citizens of both the city and the adjacent area? May it exclude persons who reside just outside both areas but who will be "affected"? See Notes, *Annexation Elections and the Right to Vote,* 20 U.C.L.A.L.Rev. 1093 (1973); *The Right to Vote in Municipal Annexations,* 88 Harv.L.Rev. 1571 (1975).

(f) *Time requirements for voting in primaries.* (i) ROSARIO v. ROCKEFEL-LER, 410 U.S. 752, 93 S.Ct. 1245, 36 L.Ed.2d 1 (1973), concerned New York Election Law § 186, requiring voters to enroll in the party of their choice at least 30 days before the November general election in order to vote in the next party primary. This cutoff date "occurs approximately eight months prior to a presidential primary [and] 11 months prior to a nonpresidential primary." The Court, per STEWART, J., rejected the contention that § 186 denied petitioners "their right to vote in [the] primary and abridged their freedom to associate with the political party of their choice" under *Williams v. Rhodes,* Part C infra. The law "did not absolutely disenfranchise" petitioners; rather, their "plight [was caused] by their own failure to take timely steps to effect their enrollment."

The "important state goal" served by § 186's "lengthy" time period "is to inhibit party 'raiding,' whereby voters in sympathy with one party designate themselves as voters of another party so as to influence or determine the results of the other party's primary." "Allowing enrollment any time after the general election would [not] put the voter in the unseemly position of asking to be enrolled in one party while at the same time intending to vote immediately for another." The "time limitation for enrollment is thus tied to a particularized legitimate purpose, and is in no sense invidious or arbitrary."

POWELL, J., joined by Douglas, Brennan and Marshall, JJ., dissented: "Deferment of a right [can] be tantamount to its denial. [The] majority does not identify the standard of scrutiny it applies" but its "formulation, though the terminology is somewhat stronger, resembles the traditional equal protection 'rational basis' test [rejected in *Kramer*]. The state interest here is hardly substantial enough to sustain the presumption, upon which the statute appears to be based, that most persons who change or declare party affiliation nearer than eight to 11 months to a party primary do so with intent to raid that primary. [Citizens] customarily choose a party and vote in its primary simply because it presents candidates and issues more responsive to their immediate concerns and aspirations. Such candidates or issues often are not apparent eight to 11 months before a primary."

(ii) KUSPER v. PONTIKES, 414 U.S. 51, 94 S.Ct. 303, 38 L.Ed.2d 260 (1973), per STEWART, J., invalidated an Illinois statute prohibiting a person "from voting in the primary election of a political party if he has voted in the primary of any other party within the preceding 23 months": "The Illinois law, unlike that [in *Rosario,*] 'locks' voters into a preexisting party affiliation from one primary to the next, and the only way to break the 'lock' is to forego voting in *any* primary for a period of almost two years. [Far] from supporting the validity of the Illinois legislation, [*Rosario*] suggests that the asserted state interest [in preventing "raiding"] can be attained by less drastic means, which do not unnecessarily burden the exercise of constitutionally protected activity." Burger, C.J., concurred in the result. Blackmun and Rehnquist, JJ., dissented.

(g) *Absentee ballots.* (i) McDONALD v. BOARD OF ELEC., 394 U.S. 802, 89 S.Ct. 1404, 22 L.Ed.2d 739 (1969), per WARREN, C.J., upheld an Illinois statute granting absentee ballots to designated classes but not to "unsentenced inmates awaiting trial." The Court applied "the more traditional standards [for] equal protection claims [because it is] not the right to vote that is at stake here but a claimed right to receive absentee ballots." [6] "Indeed, appellants' challenge seems to disclose not an arbitrary scheme or plan but [a] consistent and laudable state policy of adding, over a 50-year period, groups to the absentee [coverage]. That Illinois has not gone still further [should] not render void its remedial legislation, which need [not] 'strike at all evils at the same time.' "

(ii) O'BRIEN v. SKINNER, 414 U.S. 524, 94 S.Ct. 740, 38 L.Ed.2d 702 (1974), per BURGER, C.J., held "wholly arbitrary" and thus violative of equal protection New York's denial of absentee ballots to persons being held for trial and to convicted misdemeanants. Since state law permitted absentee ballots to persons absent from their home county, those held in jail in a county other than their residence could vote, "yet persons confined for the same reason in the county of their residence are completely denied the ballot." [b] BLACKMUN, J., joined by Rehnquist, J., dissented, relying on *McDonald:* Since the state "need not have provided for *any* absentee registration or absentee voting," the "legislature traditionally has been allowed to take reform 'one step at a [time].' " [c]

2. *"Remedial" or "reform" legislation "extending" the franchise.* (a) In KATZENBACH v. MORGAN, p. 1156 infra, Congress suspended state English literacy tests for voting for citizens "educated in American-flag schools (schools located within United States jurisdiction)." The Court held this was not "an invidious discrimination" against other foreign-language citizens. Because the statute "does not restrict or deny the franchise but in effect extends" it, "the principle that calls for the closest scrutiny of distinctions in laws *denying* fundamental rights is inapplicable; for the distinction challenged [is] presented only as a limitation on a reform measure aimed at eliminating an existing barrier to the exercise of the franchise. Rather, in deciding the constitutional propriety of the limitations in such a reform measure we are guided by the familiar principles that a 'statute is not invalid under the Constitution because it might have gone further than it did,' [and] that 'reform may take one step at a time, addressing itself to the phase of the problem which seems most acute to the legislative mind.' " [d]

(b) Does this add any perspective to *McDonald*? By what test does (should) the Court determine whether legislation "distributing the franchise" "restricts or denies" it rather than "extends" it? Is it that if the group given the vote had been excluded by the state, the exclusion would be held "necessary to promote a compelling state interest"? Or is the matter more complex? Did the *Morgan*

---

6. [T]he record is barren of any indication that the State might not, for instance, possibly furnish the jails with special polling booths or facilities on election day, or provide guarded transportation to the polls themselves for certain inmates, or entertain motions for temporary reductions in bail to allow some inmates to get to the polls on their own.

b. Marshall, J., joined by Douglas and Brennan, JJ., joined the Court's opinion, but would have invalidated the discrimination under the "compelling state interest test." See 59 Corn.L.Rev. 1139 (1974).

c. May a state, after *Kramer,* deny absentee voting to persons unable to vote otherwise? What constitutes "inability" to vote? See generally Note, *The Submerged Constitutional Right to an Absentee Ballot,* 72 Mich.L. Rev. 157 (1973).

d. Douglas, J., reserved judgment on the question.

See also *Schilb v. Kuebel,* 404 U.S. 357, 92 S.Ct. 479, 30 L.Ed.2d 502 (1971) (bail reform law).

statute "grant the right to vote to some bona fide residents of requisite age and citizenship and deny the franchise to others"?

Does "extension" of the right to vote "dilute" the voting rights of others? If so, should extensions be justified only by a "compelling state interest"? May a city extend the vote in local elections to all nonresidents who own property in the city? If so, under what standard should its refusal to extend it also to nonresidents who work in the city be judged? Should the "traditional" equal protection standard be applicable because use of the "stricter" standard would invalidate most classifications and the state might well then eliminate extensions altogether? Was such a choice realistically (constitutionally) available to the state after *Reynolds*? *Avery*? *Carrington*? *Harper*? *Kramer* and *Phoenix*? *Salyer*? *Holt*? In some of these, but not all?

C. RESTRICTIONS ON PARTIES AND CANDIDATES

WILLIAMS v. RHODES, 393 U.S. 23, 89 S.Ct. 5, 21 L.Ed.2d 69 (1968): To gain a place on the presidential election ballot, Ohio required new political parties to have an elaborate party structure, hold "a primary election conforming to detailed and rigorous standards," "obtain petitions signed by qualified electors totaling 15% of the number of ballots cast in the last preceding gubernatorial election," and file by Feb. 7 of the election year. Parties on previous ballots remained "simply by obtaining 10% of the votes in the last gubernatorial election."

The Court, per BLACK, J., held that "the totality of" these laws violated equal protection, placing "burdens on two different, although overlapping, kinds of rights—the right of individuals to associate for the advancement of political beliefs, and the right of qualified voters, regardless of their political persuasion, to cast their votes effectively. Both of [these] rank among our most precious freedoms. [In] determining whether the State has power to place such unequal burdens on minority groups where rights of this kind are at [stake,] 'only a compelling state interest in the regulation of a subject within the State's constitutional power to regulate can justify limiting First Amendment freedoms.' *NAACP v. Button*, 371 U.S. 415, 83 S.Ct. 328, [9 L.Ed.2d 405 (1963).

Ohio "does not merely favor a 'two-party system'" to "encourage compromise and political stability," but tends to give the Republicans and Democrats "a complete monopoly." Nor could the state interest in avoiding a "plurality winner" "justify the very severe restrictions." The "very early" filing requirement frustrated the state's interest in promoting cohesiveness of "disaffected" groups. In light of the "experience in many other States" where "a very low number of signatures, such as 1% of the electorate is required," Ohio's concern for voter confusion due to many parties on the ballot was too "remote." [a]

AMERICAN PARTY OF TEXAS v. WHITE, 415 U.S. 767, 94 S.Ct. 1296, 39 L.Ed.2d 744 (1974), per WHITE, J., upheld a method for candidates of "minority political parties" to get on the general election ballot. Candidates of "major" parties (those whose gubernatorial candidate polled more than 200,000 votes in the last general election) could obtain ballot position by being nominated in a primary election. But parties with less than 2% of the total gubernatorial vote

---

a. Harlan, J., concurred in the result. Stewart and White, JJ., dissented. Warren, C.J., dissented without reaching the merits. See generally Barton, *The General-Election Ballot: More Nominees or More Representative Nominees,* 22 Stan.L.Rev. 165 (1970).

in the preceding general election (or new parties) had to hold precinct, county and state nominating conventions and obtain signatures equaling at least 1% of persons voting in the last gubernatorial election (about 22,000 in 1972). Signatories could be persons participating in the precinct convention (required to be held on the same day as the major party primaries) or signing a petition within 55 days thereafter (ending 120 days before the general election). Each had to execute a notarized oath that he had not participated in any other party's primary or nomination process. These requirements "depend upon whether they are necessary to further compelling state interests," but "whether considered alone or in combination," they "are constitutionally valid measures, reasonably taken in pursuit of vital state objectives that cannot be served equally well in significantly less burdensome ways. ＊ ＊ ＊ Texas 'in no way freezes the status quo,' [but] affords minority political parties a real and essentially equal opportunity for ballot qualification." Douglas, J., dissented.

———

ANDERSON v. CELEBREZZE, 460 U.S. 780, 103 S.Ct. 1564, 75 L.Ed.2d 547 (1983), per STEVENS, J., held that Ohio's "early filing deadline"—requiring an independent candidate for President to file more than seven months before the November general election—violates the first and fourteenth amendment rights of voters and candidates:[7] "Although these rights of voters are fundamental, [the] state's important regulatory interests are generally sufficient to justify reasonable, nondiscriminatory restrictions.[9]

"Constitutional challenges to specific provisions of a State's election laws therefore cannot be resolved by any 'litmus-paper' test. [Instead], a court [must] first consider the character and magnitude of the asserted injury to the rights protected [and] then must identify and evaluate the precise interests put forward by the State as justifications for the burden imposed by its rule. In passing judgment, the Court must not only determine the legitimacy and strength of each of these interests; it also must consider the extent to which those interests make it necessary to burden the plaintiff's rights.[b]

---

7. In this case, we [do] not engage in a separate Equal Protection Clause analysis. We rely, however, on the analysis in a number of our prior election cases [which,] applying the "fundamental rights" strand of equal protection analysis, have identified the First and Fourteenth Amendment rights implicated by restrictions on the eligibility of voters and candidates, and have considered the degree to which the State's restrictions further legitimate state interests. See, e.g., *Williams*.

9. We have upheld generally-applicable and evenhanded restrictions that protect the integrity and reliability of the electoral process itself. The State has the undoubted right to require candidates to make a preliminary showing of substantial support in order to qualify for a place on the ballot, because it is both wasteful and confusing to encumber the ballot with the names of frivolous candidates. *Jenness v. Fortson*, 403 U.S. 431, 91 S.Ct. 1970, 29 L.Ed.2d 554 (1971); *American Texas Party*.

＊ ＊ ＊

b. Does *Anderson* employ the same standard of equal protection review as *Williams* and *American Texas Party*? Do the latter

cases use the same standard? *Illinois Bd. of Elections v. Socialist Workers Party*, 440 U.S. 173, 99 S.Ct. 983, 59 L.Ed.2d 230 (1979), per Marshall, J., held a law—that "produced the incongruous result" of requiring new parties to get "substantially more signatures to gain access to the ballot" for an election in Chicago than for a statewide election—violative of equal protection because the classification was not "necessary to serve a compelling interest."

Blackmun, J., joined the opinion but expressed "my unrelieved discomfort with [using] as tests such easy phrases as 'compelling state interest' and 'least drastic [or restrictive] means.' I have never been able fully to appreciate just what a 'compelling state interest' is. If it means 'convincingly controlling,' or 'incapable of being overcome' upon any balancing process, then, of course, the test merely announces an inevitable result, and the test is no test at all. And, for me, 'least drastic means' is a slippery slope and also the signal of the result the Court has chosen to reach. A judge would be unimaginative indeed if he could not come up with something a little less 'drastic' or a little less 'restrictive' in almost any situa-

"[Unlike *Storer v. Brown*, 415 U.S. 724, 94 S.Ct. 1274, 39 L.Ed.2d 714 (1974), per White, J.,—which found a "compelling" interest for a California law barring independent candidates in general elections if they "had a registered affiliation with a qualified political party at any time within one year prior to the immediately preceding primary election" [c]—Ohio's] ballot access rule for presidential elections "has an impact beyond its own borders. Similarly, the State has a less important interest in regulating Presidential elections than statewide or local elections, because the outcome of the former will be largely determined by voters beyond the State's boundaries."

Ohio's rule "prevents persons who wish to be independent candidates from entering the significant political arena established in the State by a Presidential election campaign—and creating new political coalitions of Ohio voters—at any time after mid-to-late March. At this point developments in campaigns for the major-party nominations have only begun, and the major parties will not adopt their nominees and platforms for another five months. Candidates and supporters within the major parties thus have the political advantage of continued flexibility." As for the state's interest in "political stability"—e.g., preventing "a candidate's decision to abandon efforts to win the party primary and to run as an independent"—Ohio's law "is both too broad and too narrow. It is true that [petitioner John Anderson] had previously competed in party primaries [in other states] and then sought to run as an independent [in Ohio]. But the early deadline applies broadly to independent candidates who have not been affiliated in the recent past with any political party. On the other hand, as long as the decision to run is made before the March deadline, Ohio does not prohibit independent candidacies by persons formerly affiliated with a political party, or currently participating in intraparty competition in other States—regardless of the effect on the political party structure."

REHNQUIST, J., joined by White, Powell and O'Connor, JJ., dissented, believing the case governed by *Storer* and finding no support for the Court's conclusion that Ohio's law had a "substantial impact on nonparty candidates and their supporters": "The record shows that in 1980 five independent candidates submitted nominating petitions with the necessary 5,000 signatures by the March 20 deadline and thus qualified for the general election ballot in Ohio. [T]he Constitution does not require that a State allow any particular Presidential candidate to be on its ballot, and so long as the Ohio ballot access laws are rational and allow nonparty candidates reasonable access to the general election ballot, this Court should not interfere with Ohio's exercise of its Article II, § 1, cl. 2 power."

LUBIN v. PANISH, 415 U.S. 709, 94 S.Ct. 1315, 39 L.Ed.2d 702 (1974), per BURGER, C.J., held that California's requirement of a filing fee to get on a primary election ballot or to be a write-in candidate—in this case, 2% of the

tion, and thereby enable himself to vote to strike legislation down."

Burger, C.J., concurred in the judgment. Rehnquist and Stevens, JJ., each also concurred in the judgment because the law bore no "rational" relationship to any state interest.

c. "The State's general policy is to have contending forces within the party employ the primary [to] finally settle their differences.

The general election ballot is reserved for major struggles; it is not a forum for continuing intraparty feuds." Brennan, Douglas and Marshall, JJ., dissented.

What of a law forbidding a person to be a candidate of a political party if he was the candidate (or voted in the primary) of a different political party within the *four* preceding years? See *Lippitt v. Cipollone*, 404 U.S. 1032, 92 S.Ct. 729, 30 L.Ed.2d 725 (1972).

annual salary for the state office sought ($701.60)—as applied to indigents, violated "equal protection [and] rights of expression and association": "[T]he State's interest in keeping its ballots within manageable, understandable limits is of the highest order [but it] must be achieved by a means that does not unfairly or unnecessarily burden either a minority party's or an individual candidate's equally important interest in the continued availability of political opportunity. [V]oters can assert their preferences only through candidates or parties or both and it is this broad interest that must be weighed in the balance. [A] voter [cannot] be assured that a candidate to his liking will be on the ballot, but the process of qualifying candidates [may] not constitutionally be measured solely in dollars."

[The Court relied on *Bullock v. Carter,* 405 U.S. 134, 92 S.Ct. 849, 31 L.Ed.2d 92 (1972), per Burger, C.J., invalidating a Texas statute requiring candidates to pay $50 plus their pro rata share of the costs of the election in order to get on the primary ballot, resulting in fees as high as $8,900: "Because the Texas [scheme] has a real and appreciable impact on the exercise of the franchise, and because this impact is related to the resources of the voters supporting a particular candidate, we conclude, as in *Harper,* that the laws must be 'closely scrutinized' and found reasonably necessary to the accomplishment of legitimate state [objectives]."] [d]

"[A] wealthy candidate with not the remotest chance of election may secure a place on the ballot by writing a check [but, due to filing fees], impecunious but serious candidates may be prevented from running. [W]e hold that in the absence of reasonable alternative means of ballot access, a State may [not] require from an indigent candidate filing fees he cannot pay."

As reasonable alternatives, states may "impose on minor political parties the precondition of demonstrating the existence of some reasonable quantum of voter [support]. See *American Party of Texas.* Similarly, a candidate who establishes that he cannot pay the [fee] may be required to demonstrate the 'seriousness' of his candidacy by persuading a substantial number of voters to sign a petition in his behalf." [e] But "the intimation that a write-in provision without the filing fee required by [California] would constitute 'an acceptable alternative' appears dubious at best." [f]

---

d. In *Bullock,* the Court rejected "the theory that since the candidates are availing themselves of the primary machinery, it is appropriate that they pay that share of the cost which they have occasioned. [A] primary system designed to give the voters some influence at the nominating stage should spread the cost among all of the voters in an attempt to distribute the influence without regard to wealth. Viewing the myriad governmental functions supported from general revenues, it is difficult to single out any of a higher order than the conduct of elections at all levels to bring forth those persons desired by their fellow citizens to govern. Without making light of the State's interest in husbanding its revenues, we fail to see such an element of necessity in the State's present means of financing primaries as to justify the resulting incursion on the prerogatives of voters."

What standard of equal protection review is employed in these opinions by Burger, C.J.?

e. May a state require that *only* those who cannot pay a filing fee demonstrate the "seriousness" of their candidacy? See Note, *The Constitutionality of Candidate Filing Fees,* 70 Mich.L.Rev. 558 (1972).

f. Douglas, J., joined the Court's opinion, adding: "Since classifications based on wealth are 'traditionally disfavored,' *Harper,* the State's inability to show a compelling interest in conditioning the right to run for office on payment of fees cannot stand."

Blackmun, J., joined by Rehnquist, J., concurred in part: "I would regard a write-in procedure, free of fee, as an acceptable alternative" because it "provides the indigent [with] as much ease of access to the ballot as the alternative of obtaining a large number of petition signatures in a relatively short time. See *Storer.*"

CLEMENTS v. FASHING, 457 U.S. 957, 102 S.Ct. 2836, 73 L.Ed. 508 (1982), held that Texas provisions, restricting a public official's ability to run for another office, do not violate equal protection. REHNQUIST, J., joined by Burger, C.J., and Powell and O'Connor, JJ., reasoned: "Far from recognizing candidacy as a 'fundamental right,' we have held that the existence of barriers to a candidate's access to the ballot 'does not of itself compel close scrutiny.' *Bullock*. [Our] ballot access cases, however, do focus on the degree to which the challenged restrictions operate as a mechanism to exclude certain classes of candidates from the electoral process. * * *

"One line of ballot access cases involves classifications based on wealth. In invalidating candidate filing-fee provisions, for example, we have departed from traditional equal protection analysis because such a 'system falls with unequal weight on voters, as well as candidates, according to their economic status.' *Bullock*. * * *

"The second line of ballot access cases involves classification schemes that impose burdens on new or small political parties or independent candidates. [T]he State may not act to maintain the 'status quo' by making it virtually impossible for any but the two major parties to achieve ballot positions for their candidates. See *Williams*. * * *

"It does not automatically follow, of course, that we must apply traditional equal protection principles in examining § 19 and § 65 merely because these restrictions on candidacy do not fall into the two patterns just described. But this fact does counsel against discarding traditional principles without first examining the nature of the interests that are affected and the extent of the burden these provisions place on candidacy. [§ 19] simply requires Baca to complete his four-year term as Justice of the Peace before he may be eligible for the Legislature. At most, therefore, Baca must wait two years—one election cycle—before he may run as a candidate for the legislature. [Unlike] filing fees or the level-of-support requirements, § 19 in no way burdens access to the political process by those who are outside the 'mainstream' of political life. * * *

"A 'waiting period' is hardly a significant barrier to candidacy. [See *Storer*.] We conclude that this sort of insignificant interference with access to the ballot need only rest on a rational predicate in order to survive a challenge under the Equal Protection Clause. * * *

"Finally, it is no argument that § 19 is invalid because it burdens only those officeholders who desire to run for the Legislature. [The] Equal Protection Clause allows the State to regulate 'one step at a time, addressing itself to the phase of the problem which seems most acute.' *Williamson v. Lee Optical Co.*"

STEVENS, J., concurred in the judgment: "I see no reason why a State may not provide that certain offices will be filled on a part-time basis and that others will be filled by persons who may not seek other office until they have fulfilled their duties in the first. There may be no explanation for these classifications that a federal judge would find to be 'rational.' But they do not violate the Equal Protection Clause because there is no federal requirement that a State fit the emoluments or the burdens of different elective state offices into any particular pattern."

BRENNAN, J., joined by White, Marshall and Blackmun, JJ., dissented: "Putting to one side the question of the proper level of equal protection scrutiny to be applied to these restrictions on candidacy for public office,[2] [neither] the State nor the plurality offers any justification for *differential* treatment of various classes of officeholders, and the search for such justification makes clear that the classifications embodied in these provisions lack any meaningful relationship to the State's asserted or supposed interests [and cannot] survive even minimal equal protection scrutiny.[7] "

II. DISCRIMINATION IN RESPECT TO TRAVEL

SHAPIRO v. THOMPSON

394 U.S. 618, 89 S.Ct. 1322, 22 L.Ed.2d 600 (1969).

MR. JUSTICE BRENNAN delivered the opinion of the Court.

These three appeals [are from federal courts] holding unconstitutional [Conn., Pa. and D.C. statutes denying welfare] to residents [who] have not resided within their jurisdictions for at least one [year].

There is no dispute that the effect of the waiting-period requirement [is] to create two classes of needy resident families indistinguishable from each other except that one is composed of residents who have resided a year or more, and the second of residents who have resided less than a year, in the jurisdiction. [T]he second class is denied welfare aid upon which may depend the ability of the families to obtain the very means to subsist—food, shelter, and other necessities of life. [We] agree [that the statutes deny equal protection]. The interests which appellants assert are promoted by the classification either may not constitutionally be promoted by government or are not compelling governmental interests.

Primarily, appellants justify the waiting-period requirement as a protective device to preserve the fiscal integrity of state public assistance programs. It is asserted that people who require welfare assistance during their first year of residence in a State are likely to become continuing burdens on state welfare programs. Therefore, the argument runs, if such people can be deterred from entering the jurisdiction by denying them welfare benefits during the first year, state programs to assist long-time residents will not be impaired. [But] the

2. [Although] we have never defined candidacy as a fundamental right, we have clearly recognized that restrictions on candidacy impinge on First Amendment rights of candidates and voters. See, e.g., *Illinois Elections Bd.; Lubin; American Texas Party; Bullock; Williams.* With this consideration in mind, we have applied strict scrutiny in reviewing most restrictions on ballot access [because] of their impact on the First Amendment *rights* of candidates and voters, not because the *class* of candidates or voters that was burdened was somehow suspect. The plurality offers no explanation as to why the restrictions at issue here, which completely bar some candidates from running and require other candidates to give up their present employment, are less "substantial" in their impact on candidates and their supporters than, for example, the $700 filing fee at issue in *Lubin.*

[May a state require a minimum age for candidates? See 71 Mich.L.Rev. 854 (1973).

May a state limit the number of terms an elected official may serve? May it place major party candidates (or incumbents) at the top of the ballot? See 63 Minn.L.Rev. 517 (1979). Is there a constitutional right to be a candidate? See Tribe, *American Constitutional Law* 775 (1978).]

7. * * * I agree with Justice Stevens that the State may define *many* of the "benefits and burdens of different elective state offices," in a dissimilar manner without offering an explanation for the classifications that a federal judge will find to be rational, so long as such classifications do not mask any racial or ˉotherwise impermissible discrimination. But where the differential treatment concerns a restriction on the right to seek public office—a right protected by the First Amendment—that Amendment supplies the federal interest in equality that may be lacking where the State is simply determining salary, hours, or working conditions of its own employees.

purpose of inhibiting migration by needy persons into the State is constitutionally impermissible.

This Court long ago recognized that the nature of our Federal Union and our constitutional concepts of personal liberty unite to require that all citizens be free to travel throughout the length and breadth of our land uninhibited by statutes, rules, or regulations which unreasonably burden or restrict this movement. [See *United States v. Guest,* p. 1148 infra.

Alternatively, appellants argue that even if it is impermissible for a State to attempt to deter the entry of all indigents, the challenged classification may be justified as a permissible state attempt to discourage those indigents who would enter the State solely to obtain larger benefits. [But] a State may no more try to fence out those indigents who seek higher welfare benefits than it may try to fence out indigents generally. [W]e do not perceive why a mother who is seeking to make a new life for herself and her children should be regarded as less deserving because she considers, among other factors, the level of a State's public assistance. Surely such a mother is no less deserving than a mother who moves into a particular State in order to take advantage of its better educational facilities.

Appellants argue further that the challenged classification may be sustained as an attempt to distinguish between new and old residents on the basis of the contribution they have made to the community through the payment of taxes. [But this] would logically permit the State to bar new residents from schools, parks, and libraries or deprive them of police and fire protection. Indeed it would permit the State to apportion all benefits and services according to the past tax contributions of its citizens. The Equal Protection Clause prohibits such an apportionment of state services.[10]

We recognize that a State [may] legitimately attempt to limit its expenditures, whether for public assistance, public education, or any other program. But a State may not accomplish such a purpose by invidious distinctions between classes of its citizens. It could not, for example, reduce expenditures for education by barring indigent children from its schools. [Thus], appellants must do more than show that denying welfare benefits to new residents saves [money.]

Appellants next advance as justification [four] administrative and related governmental objectives allegedly served by the waiting-period requirement.
* * *

At the outset, we reject appellants' argument that a mere showing of a rational relationship between the waiting period and these four admittedly permissible state objectives will suffice, [for] in moving from State to State or to the District of Columbia appellees were exercising a constitutional right, and any classification which serves to penalize the exercise of that right, unless shown to be necessary to promote a *compelling* governmental interest, is unconstitutional. Cf. *Skinner v. Oklahoma,* [p. 124 supra]; *Korematsu,* [Sec. 2, I supra]; *Sherbert v. Verner,* [p. 766 supra].

The argument that the waiting-period requirement facilitates budget predictability is wholly unfounded. The records in all three cases are utterly devoid of evidence [of use of] the one-year requirement as a means to predict the number of people who will require assistance in the budget year. * * *

The argument that the waiting period serves as an administratively efficient rule of thumb for determining residency similarly will not withstand scrutiny.

---

10. We are not dealing here with state insurance programs which may legitimately tie the amount of benefits to the individual's contributions.

[Before] granting an application, the welfare authorities investigate the applicant [and] in the course of the inquiry necessarily learn the facts upon which to determine whether the applicant is a resident.

Similarly, there is no need for a State to use the one-year waiting period as a safeguard against fraudulent receipt of benefits; for less drastic means are available, and are employed * * *.

Pennsylvania suggests that the one-year waiting period is justified as a means of encouraging new residents to join the labor force promptly. But this logic would also require a similar waiting period for long-term [residents.]

We conclude therefore that appellants [have] no need to use the one-year requirement for the governmental purposes suggested. Thus, even under traditional equal protection tests [the classification] would seem irrational and unconstitutional. But [s]ince the classification here touches on the fundamental right of interstate movement, its constitutionality must be judged by the stricter standard of whether it promotes a *compelling* state interest. Under this standard, the waiting period requirement clearly violates the Equal Protection Clause.[21]

[The Court rejected the contention that Social Security Act § 402(b) approved imposition of one-year residence requirements. But] even if it could be argued that the constitutionality of § 402(b) is [in issue,] Congress may not authorize the States to violate the Equal Protection Clause. * * *

Affirmed.[a]

MR. CHIEF JUSTICE WARREN with whom MR. JUSTICE BLACK joins, dissenting.

[§ 402(b)] intended to authorize state residence requirements of up to one [year.] Congress, pursuant to its commerce power, has enacted a variety of restrictions upon interstate travel. It has taxed air and rail fares and [gasoline]. Many of the federal safety regulations of common carriers which cross state lines burden the right to travel. And Congress has prohibited by criminal statute interstate travel for certain purposes. * * *

The Court's right-to-travel cases lend little support to the view that congressional action is invalid merely because it burdens the right to travel. Most of our cases fall into two categories: those in which *state* imposed restrictions were involved, see e.g., *Edwards v. California,* and those concerning congressional decisions to remove impediments to interstate movement, see, e.g., [*Guest*]. *Aptheker v. Secretary of State,* [p. 219 supra], is the only case in which this Court invalidated on a constitutional basis a congressionally imposed restriction. *Aptheker* also involved [a] claim that the congressional restriction compelled a potential traveler to choose between his right to travel and his First Amendment right of freedom of association. [*Aptheker*] thus contains two characteristics distinguishing it from the [instant case]: a combined infringement of two constitutionally protected rights and a flat prohibition upon travel. [Here], travel itself is not prohibited. Any burden inheres solely in the fact that a potential welfare recipient might take into consideration the loss of welfare benefits for a limited period of time if he changes his residence. Not only is this

---

21. We imply no view of the validity of waiting period *or* residence requirements determining eligibility to vote, [for] tuition-free education, to obtain a license to practice a profession, to hunt or fish, [etc. These] may promote compelling state interests on the one hand, or, on the other, may not be penalties upon the exercise of the constitutional right of interstate travel.

a. Stewart, J., joined the Court's opinion, emphasizing that "the Court simply recognizes" that the statutes impinge upon "the constitutional right of interstate travel."

burden of uncertain degree,[5] but appellees themselves assert there is evidence that few welfare recipients have in fact been deterred by residence requirements.

The insubstantiality of the restriction imposed by residence requirements must then be evaluated in light of the possible congressional reasons for such requirements. [Given] the apprehensions of many States that an increase in benefits without minimal residence requirements would result in an inability to provide an adequate welfare system, Congress deliberately adopted the intermediate course of a cooperative program. [Our] cases require only that Congress have a rational basis for finding that a chosen regulatory scheme is necessary to the furtherance of interstate commerce. See, e.g., *Katzenbach v. McClung,* 379 U.S. 294, 85 S.Ct. 377, 13 L.Ed.2d 290 (1964). I conclude that residence requirements can be imposed by Congress as an exercise of its power to control interstate commerce consistent with the constitutionally guaranteed right to travel. * * *[b]

MR. JUSTICE HARLAN, dissenting. * * *

In upholding the equal protection argument, the Court has applied an equal protection doctrine of relatively recent vintage [—the] "compelling interest" doctrine [which constitutes] an increasingly significant exception to the long-established rule that a statute does not deny equal protection if it is rationally related to a legitimate governmental objective. The "compelling interest" doctrine has two branches. [The] "suspect" criteria [branch today] apparently has been further enlarged to include classifications based upon recent interstate movement, and perhaps those based upon the exercise of *any* constitutional [right].

I think that this branch of the "compelling interest" doctrine is sound when applied to racial classifications, for historically the Equal Protection Clause was largely a product of the desire to eradicate legal distinctions founded upon race. However, I believe that the more recent extensions have been unwise. [When] a classification is based upon the exercise of rights guaranteed against state infringement by the federal Constitution, then there is no need for any resort to the Equal Protection Clause; in such instances, this Court may properly and straightforwardly invalidate any undue burden upon those rights under the Fourteenth Amendment's Due Process Clause.

The second branch of the "compelling interest" principle is even more troublesome. For it has been held that a statutory classification is subject to the "compelling interest" test if the result of the classification may be to affect a "fundamental right," regardless of the basis of the classification. This rule was foreshadowed in *Skinner* [and] re-emerged in *Reynolds v. Sims,* [again] in *Carrington v. Rash* [and] was also an alternate ground in *Harper* and apparently was a basis of the holding in *Williams v. Rhodes.* It has reappeared today in the Court's cryptic suggestion that the "compelling interest" test is applicable merely because the result of the classification may be to deny the appellees "food, shelter, and other necessities of life," as well as in the Court's statement that "[s]ince the classification here touches on the fundamental right of interstate movement, its constitutionality must be judged by the stricter standard of whether it promotes a *compelling* state interest."

I think this branch [is] unfortunate because it creates an exception which threatens to swallow the standard equal protection rule. Virtually every state

---

5. [I]ndigents who are disqualified from categorical assistance by residence requirements are not left wholly without assistance. Each of the appellees in these cases found alternative sources of assistance * * *.

b. As to whether the "federalistic dimension" of the right to travel should limit Congress' power to affect it, see Karst, *The Fifth Amendment's Guarantee of Equal Protection,* 55 N.C.L.Rev. 541, 558–60 (1977).

statute affects important rights. This Court has repeatedly held, for example, that the traditional equal protection standard is applicable to statutory classifications affecting such fundamental matters as the right to pursue a particular occupation, the right to receive greater or smaller wages or to work more or less hours, and the right to inherit property. Rights such as these are in principle indistinguishable from those involved here, and to extend the "compelling interest" rule to all cases in which such rights are affected would go far toward making this Court a "super-legislature." This branch of the doctrine is also unnecessary. When the right affected is one assured by the federal Constitution, any infringement can be dealt with under the Due Process Clause. But when a statute affects only matters not mentioned in the federal Constitution and is not arbitrary or irrational, I must reiterate that I know of nothing which entitles this Court to pick out particular human activities, characterize them as "fundamental," and give them added protection under an unusually stringent equal protection test. * * *

For reasons hereafter set forth, a legislature might rationally find that the imposition of a welfare residence requirement would aid in the accomplishment of at least four valid governmental objectives. It might also find that residence requirements have advantages not shared by other methods of achieving the same goals. [Thus], it cannot be said that the requirements are "arbitrary" or "lacking in rational justification." Hence, I can find no objection to these residence requirements under [equal protection].

The next issue [is] whether a one-year welfare residence requirement amounts to an undue burden upon the right of interstate travel [which I conclude] is a "fundamental" right [that] should be regarded as having its source in the Due Process Clause of the Fifth Amendment.

[In] my view, a number of considerations militate in favor of constitutionality. First, as just shown, four separate, legitimate governmental interests are furthered by residence requirements. Second, the impact of the requirements upon the freedom of individuals to travel interstate is indirect and, according to evidence put forward by the appellees themselves, insubstantial. Third, these are [cases] in which the States have acted within the terms of a limited authorization by the national government, and in which Congress itself has laid down a like rule for the District of Columbia. Fourth, the legislatures which enacted these statutes have been fully exposed to the arguments of the appellees as to why these residence requirements are unwise, and have rejected them. This is not, therefore, an instance in which legislatures have acted without mature deliberation.

Fifth, [the] field of welfare assistance is one in which there is a widely recognized need for fresh solutions and consequently for experimentation. Invalidation of welfare residence requirements might have the unfortunate consequence of discouraging the Federal and State Governments from establishing unusually generous welfare programs in particular areas on an experimental basis, because of fears that the program would cause an influx of persons seeking higher welfare payments. Sixth, [the] statutes come to us clothed with the authority of Congress and attended by a correspondingly heavy presumption of constitutionality. * * *

Notes and Questions

1. *Equal protection vs. due process.* If a state simply eliminated welfare, or granted lower payments than other states, would this "touch on the fundamental

right of interstate movement" just as harshly as the programs in *Shapiro*? "Fence out indigents" at least as much? Would it be invalid under *Shapiro* "unless shown to be necessary to promote a *compelling* governmental interest"? See generally Harvith, *The Constitutionality of Residence Tests for General and Categorical Assistance Programs*, 54 Calif.L.Rev. 567, 593–95 (1966). Or does *Shapiro* deal only with "invidious distinctions between classes of citizens"? Does Harlan, J.'s contention—that "when the right affected is one assured by the Constitution, any infringement can be dealt with under the Due Process Clause"—render the *Shapiro* approach superfluous?[a] Or does *Shapiro's* equal protection analysis add another dimension to the problem by distinguishing between the state interest needed to justify (a) reducing expenditures generally, and (b) reducing expenditures by denying benefits to recent travellers? See *Chicago Police Dep't. v. Mosley*, p. 536 supra. See generally Reinstein, *The Welfare Cases: Fundamental Rights, The Poor, and the Burden of Proof in Constitutional Litigation*, 44 Temp.L.Q. 1, 36–40 (1970); Choper, Kamisar & Tribe, *The Supreme Court: Trends and Developments 1978–1979*, 263–64, 311–12 (1979).

2. *Residence requirements.* (a) After *Shapiro*, may a state deny welfare assistance to transients who have no intention of remaining permanently in the state? Did *Shapiro* not really involve "the interest in freedom of travel" but rather "only the narrower interest in freedom of interstate migration"—i.e., to "resettle, find a new job, and start a new life"? See Barrett, *Judicial Supervision of Legislative Classifications—A More Modest Role for Equal Protection*, 1976 B.Y.U.L.Rev. 89, 117. See also *Memorial Hosp. v. Maricopa Cty.*, note 3(b) infra. Consider Note, *Durational Residence Requirements from Shapiro Through Sosna*, 50 N.Y.U.L.Rev. 622, 675 (1975): "A classification scheme based [on] residency does not penalize exercise of the right to travel because it results in no denial of benefits or privileges: transient nonresidents remain eligible for benefits in the state in which they are residents." See also McCoy, *Recent Equal Protection Decisions—Fundamental Right to Travel or "Newcomers" as a Suspect Class?* 28 Vand.L.Rev. 987, 1016–23 (1975).

(b) DOE v. BOLTON, p. 150 supra, invalidated the residency requirement of the Georgia abortion law: "Just as the Privileges and Immunities Clause, Art. IV, § 2, protects persons who enter other States to ply their trade, so must it protect persons who enter Georgia seeking the medical services that are available there. A contrary holding would mean that a State could limit to its own residents the general medical care available within its borders." Is *Doe* consistent with the analysis in note (a) supra? Compare *Carrington v. Rash*, Part I, B supra. On Art. IV, § 2, see generally Ch. 4, Sec. 1, VII.

(c) What of a residency requirement that affects both freedom of travel and freedom of interstate migration? McCARTHY v. PHILADELPHIA CIVIL SERVICE COMM'N, 424 U.S. 645, 96 S.Ct. 1154, 47 L.Ed.2d 366 (1976), per curiam—involving a Philadelphia fireman who was terminated when he moved to New Jersey—held that "a municipal regulation requiring employees of the city [to] be residents of the city" did not impair the "right to travel interstate as defined in *Shapiro*," which questioned neither "the validity of a condition placed upon municipal employment that a person be a resident *at the time* of his applica-

---

a. For support of this view, see Loewy, *A Different and More Viable Theory of Equal Protection*, 57 N.C.L.Rev. 1 (1978); Perry, *Modern Equal Protection: A Conceptualization and Appraisal*, 79 Colum.L.Rev. 1023 (1979).

tion," [6] nor "the validity of appropriately defined and uniformly applied bona fide residence requirements." [b] Is *McCarthy* consistent with *Shapiro* and *Doe?*

(d) MARTINEZ v. BYNUM, 461 U.S. 321, 103 S.Ct. 1838, 75 L.Ed.2d 879 (1983), per POWELL, J., upheld Texas' denial of free public education to children who, apart from their parents or guardians, reside in the school district "for the sole purpose of attending" the public schools: "A bona fide residence requirement [with] respect to attendance in public free schools does not violate the Equal Protection Clause [7] [nor does it] burden or penalize the constitutional right of interstate travel, for any person is free to move to a State and to establish residence there. [A]t the very least, a school district generally would be justified in requiring school-age children or their parents to satisfy the traditional, basic residence criteria—i.e., to live in the district with a bona fide intention of remaining there—before it treated them as residents." Marshall, J., dissented, mainly on the ground that an "intention of remaining" is not a proper criterion for a bona fide residence requirement. Is *Martinez* consistent with *Shapiro* and *Doe?*

(e) May a state deny welfare to a person who has permanently left the state but who cannot obtain welfare elsewhere? CALIFANO v. TORRES, 435 U.S. 1, 98 S.Ct. 906, 55 L.Ed.2d 65 (1978), per curiam, upheld Social Security Act provisions, which made benefits available in the fifty states but not in Puerto Rico, as applied to U.S. residents who lost benefits when they moved to Puerto Rico. The lower court had "held that the Constitution requires that a person who travels to Puerto Rico must be given benefits superior to those enjoyed by other residents of Puerto Rico if the newcomer enjoyed those benefits in the State from which he came. This Court has never held that the constitutional right to travel embraces any such doctrine [which] would bid fair to destroy the independent power of each State [to] enact laws uniformly applicable to all of its residents." [c]

(f) After *Shapiro,* may a state adopt a "one-year-waiting-period" in which the newcomer receives no more welfare than in the state from which he came?

3. *Other waiting-period requirements.* (a) *Voting.* DUNN v. BLUMSTEIN, 405 U.S. 331, 92 S.Ct. 995, 31 L.Ed.2d 274 (1972), per MARSHALL, J., held that Tennessee's voting registration requirements—of residence in the state for one year and in the county for three months—violate equal protection. Although "States have the power to require that voters be bona fide residents of the relevant political subdivision," it is the "additional *durational* residence requirement which appellee challenges. [Here], whether we look to the benefit withheld by the classification (the opportunity to vote) or the basis for the classification (recent interstate travel)," the classification must be "*necessary* to promote a *compelling* governmental interest. [In] pursuing that important interest, the State cannot choose means which unnecessarily burden or restrict constitutionally protected activity."

6. Nor did [it] involve a public agency's relationship with its own employees which, of course, may justify greater control than over the citizenry at large. Cf. *Pickering v. Board of Educ.* [p. 460 supra]; *Broadrick v. Oklahoma,* [p. 425 supra].

b. Burger, C.J., and Brennan and Blackmun, JJ., would set the case for argument.

7. A bona fide residence requirement implicates no "suspect" classification, and therefore is not subject to strict scrutiny. Indeed,

there is nothing invidiously discriminatory about a bona fide residence requirement if it is uniformly applied. Thus the question is simply whether there is a rational basis for it.

This view assumes, of course, that the "service" that the State would deny to nonresidents is not a fundamental right protected by the Constitution. * * *

c. Brennan, J., dissented. Marshall, J., would have set the case for full argument.

First, as for the state's interest in "preventing fraud [by] keeping nonresidents from voting, [the] record is totally devoid of any evidence that durational residence requirements are in fact necessary to identify bona fide residents." Second, "the State cannot seriously maintain that it is 'necessary' to reside for a year in the State and three months in the county in order to be minimally knowledgeable about congressional, state or even purely local elections. [T]he conclusive presumptions of durational residence requirements are much too crude." [a]

BURGER, C.J., dissented: "It is no more a denial of Equal Protection for a State to require newcomers to be exposed to state and local problems for a reasonable period such as one year before voting, than it is to require children to wait 18 years before [voting.] Some lines must be drawn. To challenge such lines by the 'compelling state interest' standard is to condemn them all." [b]

(b) *Medical care.* MEMORIAL HOSPITAL v. MARICOPA COUNTY, 415 U.S. 250, 94 S.Ct. 1076, 39 L.Ed.2d 306 (1974), per MARSHALL, J., held an Arizona statute—requiring one year's residence in the county for indigents to receive nonemergency hospitalization or medical care at county expense—violative of equal protection: "Although any durational residence requirement impinges to some extent on the right to travel," *Shapiro* "did not declare such requirements to be per se unconstitutional." It is only a state classification that "operates to *penalize* [indigents] for exercising their right to migrate to and settle in that state" which "must be justified by a compelling state interest. [*Dunn*] found that the denial of the franchise, 'a fundamental political right,' was a penalty [and *Shapiro*] found denial of the basic 'necessities of life' to be a penalty. Nonetheless, the Court has declined to strike down state statutes requiring one year of residence as a condition to lower tuition at state institutions of higher education.[12] Whatever the ultimate parameters of the *Shapiro* penalty analysis, it is at least clear that medical care is as much 'a basic necessity of life' to an indigent as welfare assistance." For reasons similar to those in *Shapiro*, the state has not met its "heavy burden of justification." [c]

REHNQUIST, J., dissented: "[F]ees for use of transportation facilities such as taxes on airport users,[12] have been upheld [against] attacks based upon the right to travel. [T]he line to be derived from our prior cases is that some financial impositions on interstate travelers have such indirect or inconsequential impact on travel that they simply do not constitute the type of direct purposeful barriers struck down" in *Shapiro*. "The solicitude which the Court has shown in cases involving the right to vote, and the virtual denial of entry inherent in denial of

a. Blackmun, J., concurred in the result. Powell and Rehnquist, JJ., did not participate.

b. *Marston v. Lewis,* 410 U.S. 679, 93 S.Ct. 1211, 35 L.Ed.2d 627 (1973), per curiam, upheld Arizona's 50-day durational residency requirement for state and local elections as "necessary to permit preparation of accurate voter lists." *Burns v. Fortson,* 410 U.S. 686, 93 S.Ct. 1209, 35 L.Ed.2d 633 (1973), upheld a similar Georgia provision, noting that "the 50-day registration period approaches the outer constitutional limits in this area" (Blackmun, J., concurring only in the result because of objection to this statement).

Marshall, J., joined by Douglas and Brennan, JJ., dissented, observing that *Dunn* "held that a 30-day residency requirement provided

the State with '[ample time to] complete whatever administrative tasks are necessary to prevent fraud' in the process of voter registration."

Compare *Rosario v. Rockefeller,* Part I, B supra.

12. See *Vlandis v. Kline* [Sec. 5 infra].

c. Burger, C.J., and Blackmun, J., concurred in the result. Douglas, J., filed a separate opinion: "So far as interstate travel per se is considered, I share the doubts of my Brother Rehnquist. [Here,] invidious discrimination against the poor [is] the critical issue."

12. See *Evansville-Vanderburgh Airport Auth. Dist. v. Delta Airlines,* 405 U.S. 707, 92 S.Ct. 1349, 31 L.Ed.2d 620 (1972).

welfare benefits—'the very means by which to live'—ought not be so casually extended to the alleged deprivation here. Rather the Court should examine, as it has done in the past, whether the challenged requirement erects a real and purposeful barrier to movement, [or] whether the effects on travel, viewed realistically, are merely incidental and remote."

(c) *Divorce.* SOSNA v. IOWA, 419 U.S. 393, 95 S.Ct. 553, 42 L.Ed.2d 532 (1975), per REHNQUIST, J., upheld a one-year residency requirement to file for divorce: The laws in *Shapiro* and *Maricopa* "were justified on the basis of budgetary or record-keeping considerations which were held insufficient to outweigh the constitutional claims of the individuals. But Iowa's divorce residency requirement is of a different stripe. [A] decree of divorce [will] affect [both spouses'] marital status and very likely their property rights. Where a married couple has minor children, a decree of divorce would usually include provisions for their custody and support. With consequences of such moment riding on a divorce decree issued by its courts, Iowa may insist that one seeking to initiate such a proceeding have the modicum of attachment to the State required here. Such a requirement additionally furthers the State's parallel interests in both avoiding officious intermeddling in matters in which another State has a paramount interest, and in minimizing the susceptibility of its own divorce decrees to collateral attack." [d]

MARSHALL, J., joined by Brennan, J., dissented, relying on *Boddie v. Connecticut,* Part III infra: The right to divorce "is of such fundamental importance" that the law "penalizes interstate travel within the meaning of *Shapiro, Dunn,* and *Maricopa.* [The] Court has not only declined to apply the 'compelling interest' test to this case, it has conjured up possible justifications for the State's restriction in a manner much more akin to the lenient standard" of equal protection review. A "simple requirement of domicile—physical presence plus intent to remain—[would] remove the rigid one-year barrier while permitting the State to restrict the availability of its divorce process to citizens who are genuinely its own." [e]

(d) *The decisions' rationale.* Do the cases explain how the Court determines whether a "waiting-period" requirement "operates to *penalize* " the right to travel? In both *Dunn* and *Maricopa* the Court conceded "that there is no evidence in the record before us that anyone was actually deterred from traveling by the challenged restriction [but] *Shapiro* did not rest upon a finding that denial of welfare actually deterred travel. Nor have other 'right to travel' [cases] always relied on the presence of actual deterrence." Consider 88 Harv.L. Rev. 117–18 (1974): "[T]he Court should consider the deterrent effect [rather] than attempt, as does Justice Marshall's 'penalty' analysis, to assess the importance of various state benefits to immigrants. Insofar as the validity of a given requirement depends upon the latter, what is being protected is not the right to travel, but the right to the withheld benefit."

Does the Court *presume* that withholding of certain benefits (but not others) deters travel? Would this explain the "basic necessity of life" emphasis in *Shapiro* and *Maricopa*? Does it account for the result in *Sosna*? In *Dunn*? Are *Shapiro* and *Maricopa* distinguishable from *Dunn* and *Sosna* because only the

d. White, J., dissented on procedural grounds.

e. For the view that "durational residency requirements for state benefits and services are permissible only to the extent they re-

spond to a reasonable concern for proof of domiciliary intent," see Cohen, *Equal Treatment for Newcomers: The Core Meaning of National and State Citizenship,* 1 Const.Comment. 9 (1984).

former tend to "fence out indigents" (*Shapiro;* cf. Douglas, J., in *Maricopa*)?[f] See Part III infra. Is *Dunn* explicable on other grounds? See Part I, B supra.

(e) *Other problems.* What of the validity of waiting-period requirements to be eligible for public housing? To be a candidate for elective office? See Note, *Durational Residency Requirements for Candidates,* 40 U.Chi.L.Rev. 357 (1973). To be admitted to the bar? To obtain public employment? See Note, 67 Calif.L. Rev. 386 (1979).

4. *Length of residence requirements.* ZOBEL v. WILLIAMS, 457 U.S. 55, 102 S.Ct. 2309, 72 L.Ed.2d 672 (1982), per BURGER, C.J., held that Alaska's scheme of distributing its revenue from state-owned oil reserves to its citizens "in varying amounts, based on the length of each citizen's residence, violates the equal protection rights of newer state citizens." The Court held that two of Alaska's stated objectives—"creating a financial incentive for individuals to establish and maintain Alaska residence, and assuring prudent management of the [oil revenues] and the State's natural and mineral resources"—were "not rationally related to the distinctions Alaska seeks to draw." And, under *Shapiro,* the objective of rewarding "contributions of various kinds, both tangible and intangible, which residents have made during their years of residence," was "not a legitimate state purpose. [Such] reasoning could open the door to state apportionment of other rights, benefits and services according to length of residency. It would permit the states to divide citizens into expanding numbers of permanent classes. Such a result would be clearly impermissible."

BRENNAN, J., joined by Marshall, Blackmun and Powell, JJ., joined the Court's opinion, adding that "the Citizenship Clause of the Fourteenth Amendment [bars] degrees of citizenship based on length of residence. And the Equal Protection Clause would not tolerate such distinctions. In short, as much as the right to travel, equality of citizenship is of the essence in our republic. [Thus], discrimination on the basis of residence must be supported by a valid state interest independent of the discrimination itself. [L]ength of residence may, for example, be used to test the bona fides of citizenship—and allegiance and attachment may bear some rational relationship to a very limited number of legitimate state purposes. Cf. *Chimento v. Stark,* 353 F.Supp. 1211 (D.N.H.), affirmed, 414 U.S. 802, 94 S.Ct. 125, 38 L.Ed.2d 39 (1973) (seven year citizenship requirement to run for governor); U.S. Const., art. I, § 2, cl. 2, § 3, cl. 3; art. II, § 1, cl. 4. But those instances in which length of residence could provide a legitimate basis for distinguishing one citizen from another are rare."

O'CONNOR, J., concurred: "A desire to compensate citizens for their prior contributions is neither inherently invidious nor irrational. Under some circumstances, the objective may be wholly reasonable.[1] Even a generalized desire to reward citizens for past endurance, particularly in a State where years of

---

f. For the view that *Sosna* may be distinguished from *Shapiro* and *Maricopa* because of the absence of impermissible state "motivation," see Loewy, fn. a after *Shapiro,* at 38–39; Clark, *Legislative Motivation and Fundamental Rights in Constitutional Law,* 15 San Diego L.Rev. 953, 984–90 (1978).

1. A State, for example, might choose to divide its largesse among all persons who previously have contributed their time to volunteer community organizations. If the State graded its dividends according to the number of years devoted to prior community service, it could be said that the State intended "to re-

ward citizens for past contributions." Alternatively, a State might enact a tax credit for citizens who contribute to the State's ecology by building alternative fuel sources or establishing recycling plants. If the State made this credit retroactive, to benefit those citizens who launched these improvements before they became fashionable, the State once again would be rewarding past contributions. The Court's opinion would dismiss these objectives as wholly illegitimate. I would recognize them as valid goals and inquire only whether their implementation infringed any constitutionally protected interest.

hardship only recently have produced prosperity, is not innately improper. The difficulty is that plans enacted to further this objective necessarily treat new residents of a State less favorably than the longer-term residents who have past contributions to 'reward.' * * * Stripped to its essentials, the plan denies non-Alaskans settling in the State the same privileges afforded longer-term residents. The Privileges and Immunities Clause of Article IV [addresses] just this type of discrimination.

" * * * I believe [that] application of the Privileges and Immunities Clause to controversies involving the 'right to travel' would at least begin the task of reuniting this elusive right with the constitutional principles it embodies. [I] conclude that Alaska's disbursement scheme violates [the] Privileges and Immunities Clause" because there is nothing "to indicate that noncitizens constitute a peculiar source of the evil at which the statute is aimed" and no " 'substantial relationship' between the evil and the discrimination practiced against the noncitizens. *Hicklin v. Orbeck,* 437 U.S. 518, 98 S.Ct. 2482, 57 L.Ed.2d 397 (1978)."

REHNQUIST, J., dissented: "[T]he illegitimacy of a State's recognizing past contributions of its citizens has been established by the Court only in certain cases considering an infringement of the right to travel, and the majority itself rightly declines to apply the strict scrutiny analysis of those right-to-travel cases. The distribution scheme at issue in this case impedes no person's right to travel to and settle in Alaska; if anything, the prospect of receiving annual cash dividends would encourage immigration to Alaska."[g]

III. DISCRIMINATORY IMPACT ON THE POOR IN THE LITIGATION PROCESS

Several Warren Court decisions (in addition to *Harper v. Virginia Bd. of Elec.,* Part I, B supra) held that state laws or practices that operated to the disadvantage of poor people—in contrast to "de jure" discrimination against the poor (Sec. 3, 1 supra)—violated equal protection (and/or due process). Most of these rulings, as well as those of the Burger Court following this path, concern the question of whether states must waive fees (or provide certain services without charge) to poor people who could not otherwise effectively participate in criminal or civil litigation. These decisions are the subject of this section. Other kinds of laws that have a disproportionate impact on the poor are considered in the section that follows.

GRIFFIN v. ILLINOIS, 351 U.S. 12, 76 S.Ct. 585, 100 L.Ed. 891 (1956), held that a state must furnish an indigent criminal defendant with a free trial transcript (or its equivalent) if it were necessary for "adequate and effective appellate review" of the conviction. BLACK, J., joined by Warren, C.J., and Douglas and Clark, JJ., found that "both equal protection and due process emphasize [that in] criminal trials a State can no more discriminate on account

g. See also *Hooper v. Bernalillo County Assessor,* ___ U.S. ___, 105 S.Ct. 2862, 86 L.Ed. 2d 487 (1985), per Burger, C.J., holding that a New Mexico property tax exemption for only those Vietnam veterans who were state residents before May 1976 "is not rationally related to the State's asserted legislative goal[s]," and thus "suffers the same constitutional flaw [as] *Zobel*": "[T]he Equal Protection Clause [forbids] the State to prefer established resi-dent veterans over newcomers in [the] apportionment of an economic benefit."

Stevens, J., joined by Rehnquist and O'Connor, JJ., dissented: The classification "rationally furthers a legitimate state purpose. [The] need to budget for the future is itself a valid reason for [a limit] on the size of potential beneficiaries."

of poverty than on account of religion, race, or color. Plainly the ability to pay costs in advance bears no rational relationship to a defendant's guilt or innocence and could not be used as an excuse to deprive a defendant of a fair trial. [It] is true that a State is not required by the federal constitution to provide appellate [review]. See, e.g., *McKane v. Durston,* 153 U.S. 684, 687–88, 14 S.Ct. 913, 914–15, 38 L.Ed. 687 (1894). But that is not to say that a State that does grant appellate review can do so in a way that discriminates against some convicted defendants on account of their poverty. * * *

"All of the States now provide some method of appeal from criminal convictions, recognizing the importance of appellate review to a correct adjudication of guilt or innocence. [Thus] to deny adequate review to the poor means that many of them may lose their life, liberty or property because of unjust convictions which appellate courts would set aside. [There] can be no equal justice where the kind of trial a man gets depends on the amount of money he has." [a]

DOUGLAS v. CALIFORNIA, 372 U.S. 353, 83 S.Ct. 814, 9 L.Ed.2d 811 (1963), per DOUGLAS, J., relying on *Griffin,* held that a state must appoint counsel for an indigent for "the first appeal, granted as a matter of [statutory right] from a criminal conviction." It disapproved California's system of appointing counsel only when the appellate court made "an independent investigation of the record and determine[d] it would be of advantage to the defendant or helpful to [the] court": "[A] state can, consistently with the Fourteenth Amendment, provide for differences so long as the result does not amount to a denial of due process or an 'invidious discrimination.' Absolute equality is not [required]. But where the merits of the one and only appeal an indigent has as of right are decided without benefit of counsel, we think an unconstitutional line has been drawn between rich and poor.

"When an indigent is forced to run this gantlet of a preliminary showing of merit, the right to appeal does not comport with fair procedure. [There] is lacking that equality demanded by the Fourteenth Amendment where the rich man, who appeals as of right, enjoys the benefit of counsel's examination into the record, research of the law, and marshalling of arguments on his behalf, while the indigent, already burdened by a preliminary determination that his case is without merit, is forced to shift for himself. The indigent, where the record is unclear or the errors are hidden, has only the right to a meaningless ritual, while the rich man has a meaningful appeal."

HARLAN, J., joined by Stewart, J., dissented from the Court's reliance, as in *Griffin,* "on a blend of the Equal Protection and Due Process Clauses," believing that "this case should be judged solely under the Due Process Clause": "States, of course, are prohibited by the Equal Protection Clause from discriminating between 'rich' and 'poor' *as such* in the formulation and application of their laws. But it is a far different thing to suggest that this provision prevents the State from adopting a law of general applicability that may affect the poor more

---

a. Frankfurter, J., concurred in the result. Burton, Minton, Reed and Harlan, JJ., dissented.

For subsequent application of *Griffin,* see e.g., *Burns v. Ohio,* 360 U.S. 252, 79 S.Ct. 1164, 3 L.Ed.2d 1209 (1959) (indigent criminal defendant cannot be required to pay filing fee for appeal); *Long v. District Court,* 385 U.S. 192,

87 S.Ct. 362, 17 L.Ed.2d 290 (1966) (indigent must be furnished free transcript of state habeas corpus hearing for use on appeal from denial of habeas, although transcript not a sine qua non to access to appellate court). Cf. *Britt v. North Carolina,* 404 U.S. 226, 92 S.Ct. 431, 30 L.Ed.2d 400 (1971) (adequate alternative to transcript existed).

harshly than it does the rich, or, on the other hand, from making some effort to redress economic imbalances while not eliminating them entirely.

"Every financial exaction which the State imposes on a uniform basis is more easily satisfied by the well-to-do than by the indigent. Yet I take it that no one would dispute the constitutional power of the State to levy a uniform sales tax, to charge tuition at a state university, to fix rates for the purchase of water from a municipal corporation, to impose a standard fine for criminal violations, or to establish minimum bail for various categories of offenses. Nor could it be contended that the State may not classify as crimes acts which the poor are more likely to commit than are the rich. And surely, there would be no basis for attacking a state law which provided benefits for the needy simply because those benefits fell short of the goods or services that others could purchase for themselves.

"Laws such as these do not deny equal protection to the less fortunate for one essential reason: the Equal Protection Clause does not impose on the States 'an affirmative duty to lift the handicaps flowing from differences in economic circumstances.' To so construe it would be to read into the Constitution a philosophy of leveling that would be foreign to many of our basic concepts of the proper relations between government and society. [N]o matter how far the state rule might go in providing counsel for indigents, it could never be expected to satisfy an affirmative duty—if one existed—to place the poor on the same level as those who can afford the best legal talent available."

As for due process, "we have today held [that] there is an absolute right to the services of counsel at trial. *Gideon v. Wainwright,* [p. 116 supra]. But [a]ppellate review is in itself not required by the Fourteenth Amendment, [and] thus the question presented is the narrow one whether the State's rules with respect to the appointment of counsel are so arbitrary or unreasonable, *in the context of the particular appellate procedure that it has established,* as to require their invalidation." Clark, J., also dissented.[b]

ROSS v. MOFFIT, 417 U.S. 600, 94 S.Ct. 2437, 41 L.Ed.2d 341 (1974), per REHNQUIST, J., held that *Douglas* does not require counsel for discretionary state appeals or for applications for review in the Supreme Court: As for due process, "it is clear that the State need not provide any appeal at all. The fact that an appeal *has* been provided does not automatically mean that a State then acts unfairly by refusing to provide counsel to indigent defendants at every stage of the way. Unfairness results only if indigents are singled out by the State and denied meaningful access to that system because of their poverty. That question is more profitably considered under an equal protection analysis [which] 'does not require absolute equality or precisely equal advantages,' [but] does require that the state appellate system be 'free of unreasoned distinctions' and that indigents have an adequate opportunity to present their claims fairly within the adversarial system.

"[P]rior to his seeking discretionary review in the State Supreme Court, [respondent's] claims 'had once been presented by a lawyer and passed upon by an [intermediate] appellate court.' *Douglas.* We do not believe that it can be said, therefore, that [respondent] is denied meaningful access to the North Carolina Supreme Court simply because the State does not appoint counsel to aid

b. For exploration of the implications of *Griffin* and *Douglas,* see Kamisar & Choper, *The Right to Counsel in Minnesota: Some* *Field Findings and Legal-Policy Observations,* 48 Minn.L.Rev. 1, 7–14 (1963).

him in seeking review in that court. At that stage he will have, at the very least, [a record] of trial proceedings, a brief on his behalf in the Court of Appeals setting forth his claims of error, and in many cases an opinion by the Court of Appeals disposing of his case. These materials, supplemented by whatever submission respondent may make pro se, would appear to provide the Supreme Court of North Carolina with an adequate basis on which to base its decision to grant or deny [review].

"This is not to say, of course, that a skilled lawyer [would] not prove helpful to any litigant able to employ him. An indigent defendant seeking review in the Supreme Court of North Carolina is therefore somewhat handicapped in comparison with a wealthy [defendant]. But both the opportunity to have counsel prepare an initial brief in the Court of Appeals and the nature of discretionary review in the Supreme Court of North Carolina make this relative handicap far less than the handicap borne by the indigent defendant denied counsel on his initial appeal as of right in *Douglas*. [The] duty of the State under our cases is not to duplicate the legal arsenal that may be privately retained by a criminal defendant, [but] only to assure the indigent defendant an adequate opportunity to present his claims fairly in the context of the State's appellate [process]."

DOUGLAS, J., joined by Brennan and Marshall, JJ., dissented: "The right to discretionary review is a substantial one, and one where a lawyer can be of significant assistance to an indigent defendant. It was correctly perceived below that the 'same concepts of fairness and equality, which require counsel in a first appeal of right, require counsel in other and subsequent discretionary appeals.' " c

---

TATE v. SHORT, 401 U.S. 395, 91 S.Ct. 668, 28 L.Ed.2d 130 (1971): An indigent accumulated $425 in fines for traffic offenses. Texas law provided only for fines but required that those unable to pay be incarcerated to satisfy their fines at the rate of $5 per day. The Court, per BRENNAN, J., reversed: Equal protection " 'requires that the statutory ceiling placed on imprisonment for any substantive offense be the same for all defendants irrespective of their economic status.' *Williams v. Illinois*, 399 U.S. 235, 90 S.Ct. 2018, 26 L.Ed.2d 586 (1970). [Thus, Texas cannot] limit the punishment to payment of the fine if one is able to pay it, yet convert the fine into a prison term for an [indigent]. Imprisonment in such a case is not imposed to further any penal objective of the State. ＊ ＊ ＊

"There are, however, other alternatives [such as procedures for paying fines in installments] to which the State may constitutionally resort to serve its concededly valid interest in enforcing payment of fines. [O]ur decision [should not] be understood as precluding imprisonment as an enforcement method when alternative means are unsuccessful despite the defendant's reasonable efforts to satisfy the fines by those means; the determination of the constitutionality of [that] must await the presentation of a concrete case." Black, J., concurred in the result.a

---

c. See also *United States v. MacCollom*, 426 U.S. 317, 96 S.Ct. 2086, 48 L.Ed.2d 666 (1976) (5–4), relying on *Ross* to uphold provision of a free trial transcript for use in a collateral attack on a federal conviction only if a federal judge certifies that the claim is "not frivolous" and that the transcript is "needed to decide the issue."

See also *Lassiter v. Department of Social Servs.*, p. 292 supra (due process does not *always* require appointment of counsel for indigent parents in state suit to terminate parental status).

a. Harlan, J., concurred on the basis of his concurrence in *Williams* where he "dissociated" himself from the Court's "equal protection

BEARDEN v. GEORGIA, 461 U.S. 660, 103 S.Ct. 2064, 76 L.Ed.2d 221 (1983), per O'CONNOR, J.,—noting that "due process and equal protection principles converge in these cases"—held that "it is fundamentally unfair" to "revoke a defendant's probation for failure to pay the imposed fine and restitution, absent evidence and findings that the defendant was somehow responsible for the failure or that alternative forms of punishment were inadequate": Probation "reflects a determination by the sentencing court that the State's penological interests do not require imprisonment. A probationer's failure to make reasonable efforts to repay his debt to society may indicate that this original determination needs reevaluation, [but 'only if alternate measures' such as 'extend[ing] the time for making payments, or reduc[ing] the fine, or direct[ing] that the probationer perform some form of labor or public service in lieu of the fine'] are not adequate to meet the State's interests in punishment and deterrence may the court imprison a probationer who has made sufficient bona fide efforts to pay." [b]

———

BODDIE v. CONNECTICUT, 401 U.S. 371, 91 S.Ct. 780, 28 L.Ed.2d 113 (1971), per HARLAN, J., sustained indigents' challenge to the state's requiring court fees and costs (averaging $60) in order to sue for divorce: "[M]arriage involves interests of basic importance in our society. [Without] a prior judicial imprimatur, individuals may freely enter into and rescind commercial contracts, for example, but we are unaware of any jurisdiction where private citizens may covenant for or dissolve marriages without state approval. [Thus], although they assert here due process rights as would-be plaintiffs, we think appellants' plight [is] akin to that of defendants faced with exclusion from the only forum effectively empowered to settle their disputes. [D]ue process requires, at a minimum, that absent a countervailing state interest of overriding significance, persons forced to settle their claims of right and duty through the judicial process must be given a meaningful opportunity to be heard." [d]

———

UNITED STATES v. KRAS, 409 U.S. 434, 93 S.Ct. 631, 34 L.Ed.2d 626 (1973), per BLACKMUN, J., held that the Bankruptcy Act's conditioning the right to discharge on payment of $50 fees does not violate fifth amendment due process, including "equal protection": "[A] debtor, in theory, and often in actuality, may adjust his debts by negotiated agreement with his creditors. [Thus,] *Boddie's* emphasis on [judicial] exclusivity finds no counterpart in the bankrupt's situation." Moreover, unlike free speech or marriage, bankruptcy is not a "fundamental" right demanding "the lofty requirement of a compelling

rationale" which, if "fully realized," "would require that the consequence of punishment be the same for all individuals."

Compare Clune, *The Supreme Court's Treatment of Wealth Discriminations Under the Fourteenth Amendment*, 1975 Sup.Ct.Rev. 289, 306: "The Court could require a schedule of fines fairly and thoughtfully designed to produce equal disutility on the average. One possibility would be a fine of an equal percentage of [earnings]. Such a system would go most of the way toward curing the wrong but would not represent a great interference with the states' systems of criminal justice."

b. White, J., joined by Burger, C.J., and Powell and Rehnquist, JJ., concurred on the

ground that the sentencing judge had "automatically" imposed a "long prison term" rather than making "a good-faith effort to impose a jail sentence that in terms of the state's sentencing objectives will be roughly equivalent to the fine and restitution that the defendant failed to pay."

May an indigent accused be denied pretrial release if he is incapable of posting required bail? See *Bandy v. United States*, 81 S.Ct. 197, 5 L.Ed.2d 218 (1960) (Douglas, J., as Circuit Justice).

d. Douglas, J., and Brennan, J., concurred, but relied on the equal protection rationale of *Griffin*. Black, J., dissented.

governmental interest before [it] may be significantly regulated." Bankruptcy legislation "is in the area of economics and social welfare. See *Dandridge v. Williams* [Part IV infra]." Thus, the standard is "rational justification"—and "the rational basis for the fee requirement is readily apparent": Congress' desire "to make the system self-sustaining and paid for by those who use [it]."

STEWART, J., joined by Douglas, Brennan and Marshall, JJ., dissented: "The bankrupt is bankrupt precisely for the reason that the State stands ready to exact all of his debts through garnishment, attachment, and the panoply of other creditor remedies. [I]n the unique situation of the indigent bankrupt the government provides the only effective means of his ever being free of these government imposed obligations. [While] the creditors of a bankrupt with assets might well desire to reach a compromise settlement, that possibility is foreclosed to the truly indigent bankrupt. [The] Court today holds that Congress may say that some of the poor are too poor even to go bankrupt." [e]

———

LITTLE v. STREATER, 452 U.S. 1, 101 S.Ct. 2202, 68 L.Ed.2d 627 (1981), per BURGER, C.J., held violative of due process Connecticut's refusal to pay the cost of blood grouping tests for indigent defendants in paternity actions. The Court stressed "the unique quality of blood grouping tests as a source of exculpatory evidence, the State's prominent role in the litigation,"—since the child was receiving welfare state law required the mother to institute the paternity action—"the 'quasi-criminal' overtones" of paternity proceedings, and the fact that state law made the defendant's testimony alone "insufficient to overcome the plaintiff's prima facie case": "Because appellant has no choice of an alternative forum and his interests, as well as those of the child, are constitutionally significant, this case is comparable to *Boddie* rather than to *Kras* and *Ortwein*."

Notes and Questions

1. *Access to courts in civil proceedings.* (a) *Defendants.* Do the decisions (especially *Boddie*) establish that persons made defendants in civil suits cannot be denied the opportunity to defend—whether as a matter of due process or equal protection—because of their inability to pay a state imposed fee? See Comment, *The Heirs of Boddie: Court Access for Indigents After Kras and Ortwein,* 8 Harv.Civ.Rts.—Civ.Lib.L.Rev. 571 (1973).

(b) *Plaintiffs.* To what extent do the decisions invalidate court access fees for indigent plaintiffs? Does *Boddie* forbid such fees in *all* situations where state law makes courts "the only forum effectively empowered to settle the dispute"? Consider 85 Harv.L.Rev. 107 (1971): "Judicial approval is required to formalize legal relationships in [matters other than divorce]: adoption and custody of children, naturalization, change of a name, settlement of a decedent's estate, adjudication of incompetency, and awards of title to property in rem." Or do *Kras* (and *Ortwein*) also require that the right sought to be vindicated be "fundamental"? "Constitutional"? How do the cases line up in respect to these categories? Is the right to seek recovery for injury to person or property "fundamental"? See Part IV infra. For the view that access to courts generally

e. Douglas, J., joined by Brennan, J., as well as Marshall, J., also dissented.

See also *Ortwein v. Schwab,* 410 U.S. 656, 93 S.Ct. 1172, 35 L.Ed.2d 572 (1973), upholding a requirement that indigents appealing an ad-

verse decision in a welfare hearing pay a $25 state appellate court filing fee. (For further discussion of indigents and appeals, see *Lindsey v. Normet,* Part IV infra.)

may be a right derived from the first amendment, see Note, *A First Amendment Right to Access to the Courts for Indigents*, 82 Yale L.J. 1055 (1973); or a right analogous to voting, see Michelman, *The Supreme Court and Litigation Access Fees: The Right to Protect One's Rights—Part II*, 1974 Duke L.J. 527.

Is the "judicial exclusivity" factor—that for bankruptcy but not for divorce "effective alternatives for the adjustment of differences remain"—meaningful? Desirable as a constitutional principle?   Consider 85 Harv.L.Rev. 108 (1971): "Much of the incentive for parties to agree to private resolution of a dispute is supplied by the threat that either may resort to the judicial process.   Moreover, an agreement is of small value to a party unable to enforce its terms in court. Thus, although a tort claimant does have power to resolve his dispute with the tortfeasor while a divorce plaintiff does not, the likelihood of a settlement for a tort claimant too poor to get into court seems no greater than the possibility that the *Boddie* plaintiffs will obtain the funds necessary to obtain judicial relief." See also Goodpaster, *The Integration of Equal Protection, Due Process Standards, and the Indigent's Right of Free Access to the Courts*, 56 Ia.L.Rev. 223 (1970); Michelman, *supra—Part I*, 1973 Duke L.J. 1153, 1178–85.

2. *Other "payment requirements."* (a) May a state require indigents to pay a marriage license fee (n.b. the constitutional right of privacy)? A driver's license fee or interstate highway tolls or gasoline taxes (n.b. the constitutional right to travel)?   May a state revoke the driver's license of an uninsured indigent who cannot post a security deposit after an accident?   See Note, *Financial Responsibility Laws in Constitutional Perspective*, 61 Calif.L.Rev. 1072 (1973).   Require a "court access fee" of an indigent plaintiff who seeks to enjoin an ordinance allegedly in violation of his first amendment rights?   Require license fees from indigents to engage in certain occupations?

(b) May a public hospital deny abortions to indigents who cannot pay the established service charge? Cf. *Maher v. Roe*, Part IV infra. May a state charge a fee to all those who use public streets or parks for "free speech" purposes to defray costs of cleaning up, etc.? See *Cox v. New Hampshire*, p. 536 supra. Are these situations distinguishable from *Harper* because they do not simply condition the right on payment of a tax but reimburse the state for costs? Compare *Griffin*, *Douglas* and *Lubin v. Panish* (Part I, C supra).

(c) For further consideration, see note 1 after *Rodriguez*, Part IV infra. See generally Brudno, *Poverty, Inequality, and the Law* (1976).

IV. CONFINEMENT OF "FUNDAMENTAL RIGHTS"

DANDRIDGE v. WILLIAMS, 397 U.S. 471, 90 S.Ct. 1153, 25 L.Ed.2d 491 (1970): Maryland's Aid to Families with Dependent Children program gave most eligible families their computed "standard of need," but imposed a "maximum limitation" on the total amount any family could receive. The Court, per STEWART, J., held this did not violate equal protection: "[H]ere we deal with state regulation in the social and economic field, not affecting freedoms guaranteed by the Bill of Rights, and claimed to violate the Fourteenth Amendment only because the regulation results in some disparity in grants of welfare payments to the largest AFDC families.[16] In [this area] a State does not violate [equal protection] merely because the classifications made by its laws are imperfect." "It is enough that the State's action be rationally based and free from invidious discrimination."

16. Cf. *Shapiro*, where, by contrast, the Court found state interference with the consti- tutionally protected freedom of interstate travel.

"To be sure, [many cases] enunciating this [standard] have in the main involved state regulation of business or industry. The administration of public welfare assistance, by contrast, involves the most basic economic needs of impoverished human beings, [but] we can find no basis for applying a different constitutional standard. [By] combining a limit on the recipient's grant with permission to retain money earned, without reduction in the amount of the grant, Maryland provides an incentive to seek gainful employment. And by keeping the maximum family AFDC grants to the minimum wage a steadily employed head of a household receives, the State maintains some semblance of an equitable balance between families on welfare and those supported by an employed breadwinner.

"It is true that in some AFDC families there may be no person who is employable. It is also true that with respect to AFDC families whose determined standard of need is below the regulatory maximum, [the] employment incentive is absent. But the Equal Protection Clause does not require that a State must choose between attacking every aspect of a problem or not attacking the problem at all. [T]he intractable economic, social, and even philosophical problems presented by public welfare assistance programs are not the business of this Court."

MARSHALL, J., joined by Brennan, J., dissented: [a] "[T]he only distinction between those children with respect to whom assistance is granted and those [denied] is the size of the family into which the child permits himself to be born. [This] is grossly underinclusive in terms of the class which the AFDC program was designed to assist, namely *all* needy dependent children, [and requires] a persuasive justification * * *.

"The Court never undertakes to inquire for such a justification; rather it avoids the task by focusing upon the abstract dichotomy between two different approaches to equal protection problems which have been utilized by this Court.

"[The] cases relied on by the Court, in which a 'mere rationality' test was actually used, e.g., *Williamson v. Lee Optical Co.* [Sec. 1 supra], [involve] regulation of business interests. The extremes to which the Court has gone in dreaming up rational bases for state regulation in that area may in many instances be ascribed to a healthy revulsion from the Court's earlier excesses in using the Constitution to protect interests which have more than enough power to protect themselves in the legislative halls.[b] This case, involving the literally vital interests of a powerless minority—poor families without breadwinners—is far removed from the area of business regulation, as the Court concedes.[c]

* * *

a. Douglas, J., dissented on the ground (agreed to also by Marshall and Brennan, JJ.) that the Maryland law was inconsistent with the Social Security Act.

b. Compare Wilkinson, *The Supreme Court, the Equal Protection Clause, and the Three Faces of Constitutional Equality*, 61 Va. L.Rev. 945, 1008–09 (1975): "*Lochner* and cases like it arose precisely because business was not getting its way, because what were then thought traditional employer prerogatives were succumbing to a rising tide of social and regulatory legislation. Conversely, [the] legislative trend ever since the New Deal has been running more and more toward social welfare programs, [whose] stated purpose is to

help the poor and less well off. Indiscriminate application of [Marshall, J.'s] position, therefore, would invite the thought that the major change since *Lochner* is that the Court has switched political sides."

c. Compare Winter, *Poverty, Economic Equality, and the Equal Protection Clause*, 1972 Sup.Ct.Rev. 41, 100–01: "All economic regulation involves the allocation of scarce resources and the distribution of income. One may prefer one kind [over] another kind, but the judgment must be based on personal [values. In] constitutional principle the issues are indivisible. Consider a state minimum wage law. Invalidation of such a law by the Court would surely be considered an illegitimate ex-

"In my view, equal protection analysis of this case is not appreciably advanced by the a priori definition of a 'right,' fundamental [and thus invoking the "compelling" test] or otherwise.[14] Rather, concentration must be placed upon the character of the classification in question, the relative importance to individuals in the class discriminated against of the governmental benefits which they do not receive, and the asserted state interests in support of the classification. * * *

"It is the individual interests here [that] most clearly distinguish this case from the 'business regulation' [cases]. AFDC support to needy dependent children provides the stuff which sustains those children's lives: food, clothing, shelter. And this Court has already recognized [that] when a benefit, even a 'gratuitous' benefit, is necessary to sustain life, stricter constitutional standards, both procedural [17] and substantive,[18] are applied to the deprivation of that benefit.

"Nor is the distinction upon which the deprivation is here based—the distinction between large and small families—one which readily commends [itself]. Indeed, governmental discrimination between children on the basis of a factor over which they have no control [bears] some resemblance to the classification between legitimate and illegitimate children which we condemned [in Sec. 3, III supra]."

On examination, the asserted state interests were either "arbitrary," impermissible, of "minimum rationality," "drastically overinclusive," or "grossly underinclusive." "The existence of [other] alternatives [to satisfy asserted state interests] does not, of course, conclusively establish the invalidity of the maximum grant regulation. It is certainly relevant, however, in appraising the overall interest of the State in the maintenance of the regulation [against] a fundamental constitutional challenge." [d]

---

ercise of substantive due process because what is involved is labeled the '[r]egulation of business or industry.' Many believe such laws help the poor. Most economists [disagree]. Spelling out a 'suspect classification'/'fundamental interest' argument to invalidate such a law would be child's play to a judge whose policy preferences impel him in that direction."

14. Appellees do argue that their "fundamental rights" are infringed [and cite] *Skinner* for the proposition that the "right of procreation" is fundamental. [B]ut the effect of the maximum grant regulation upon the right of procreation is marginal and indirect at best, totally unlike the compulsory sterilization law [in] *Skinner.*

[T]he Court's insistence that equal protection analysis turns on the basis of a closed category of "fundamental rights" involves a curious value judgment. It is certainly difficult to believe that a person whose very survival is at stake would be comforted by the knowledge that his "fundamental" rights are preserved intact. * * *

17. See *Goldberg v. Kelly* [p. 261 supra].

18. [See] *Kirk v. Board of Regents,* 273 Cal. App.2d 430, 440–441, 78 Cal.Rptr. 260, 266–267 (1969), appeal dismissed, 396 U.S. 554

(1970), upholding a one-year residency requirement for tuition-free graduate education at state university, and distinguishing *Shapiro* on the ground that it "involved the immediate and pressing need for preservation of life and health of persons unable to live without public assistance, and their dependent children."

These cases and those cited n. 17, supra, suggest that whether or not there is a constitutional "right" to subsistence (as to which see n. 14, supra), deprivations of benefits necessary for subsistence will receive closer constitutional scrutiny, under both the Due Process and Equal Protection Clauses, than will deprivation of less essential forms of governmental entitlements.

d. See also *Richardson v. Belcher,* 404 U.S. 78, 92 S.Ct. 254, 30 L.Ed.2d 231 (1971), per Stewart, J., upholding a provision of the Social Security Act reducing disability benefits for those who receive state worker's compensation—but not for those who receive compensation from private insurance or from tort claim awards—as "rationally based." Douglas, J., and Marshall, J., joined by Brennan, J., dissented.

See generally Krislov, *The OEO Lawyers Fail to Constitutionalize a Right to Welfare:*

LINDSEY v. NORMET, 405 U.S. 56, 92 S.Ct. 862, 31 L.Ed.2d 36 (1972), per WHITE, J., employing the "traditional" equal protection standard, upheld an Oregon statute permitting a landlord to bring an expedited action for possession under certain circumstances. The Court rejected the contention "that the 'need for decent shelter' and the 'right to retain peaceful possession of one's home' are fundamental interests which are particularly important to the poor and which may be trenched upon only after the State demonstrates some superior interest": "We do not denigrate the importance of decent, safe and sanitary housing. But the Constitution does not provide judicial remedies for every social and economic ill. We are unable to perceive in that document any constitutional guarantee of access to dwellings of a particular quality or any recognition of the right of a tenant to occupy the real property of his landlord beyond the term of his [lease]. Absent constitutional mandate, the assurance of adequate housing and the definition of landlord-tenant relationships are legislative not judicial functions." Douglas, J., dissented on due process grounds; Brennan, J., dissented on procedural grounds; Powell and Rehnquist, JJ., did not participate.

The statute also required tenants who lost at trial to obtain special security for payment to the landlord, if he won on appeal. The Court found this "arbitrary and irrational" discrimination violative of equal protection: "The claim that the double-bond requirement operates to screen out frivolous appeals [not] only bars nonfrivolous appeals by those who are unable to post the bond but also allows meritless appeals by others who can afford the bond." [e] Douglas, J., agreed, but on the theory that housing was "fundamental" and thus the special statutory treatment must be justified by a "compelling interest."

SAN ANTONIO IND. SCHOOL DIST. v. RODRIGUEZ
411 U.S. 1, 93 S.Ct. 1278, 36 L.Ed.2d 16 (1973).

MR. JUSTICE POWELL delivered the opinion of the Court.

This suit attacking the Texas system of financing public education was initiated by Mexican-American parents [as] a class action on behalf of school children throughout the State who are members of minority groups or who are poor and reside in school districts having a low property tax base. * * *

Recognizing the need for increased state funding to help offset disparities in local spending [because of sizable differences in the value of assessable property between local school districts,] the state legislature [established the] Minimum Foundation School Program [which] accounts for approximately half of the total educational expenditures in Texas. [It] calls for state and local contributions to a fund earmarked specifically for teacher salaries, operating expenses, and transportation costs. The State [finances] approximately [80%]. The districts' share, known as the Local Fund Assignment, is apportioned among the school districts under a formula designed to reflect each district's relative taxpaying ability. * * *

The school district in which appellees reside, [Edgewood,] has been compared throughout this litigation with the Alamo Heights [District. Edgewood] is situated in the core-city sector of San Antonio in a residential neighborhood that

---

A Study in the Uses and Limits of the Judicial Process, 58 Minn.L.Rev. 211 (1973).

e. Consider Note, 58 Va.L.Rev. 930, 941 (1972): "[T]hat the state's screening device for frivolous appeals is overinclusive and underinclusive does not in itself render the classifica-

tion 'wholly irrelevant' to the goal of deterring frivolous appeals. [The] Court's analysis of the double-bond provision is essentially a balancing approach disguised in traditional 'rational relationship' terminology."

has little commercial or industrial property. [A]pproximately 90% of the student population is Mexican-American and over 6% is Negro. The average assessed property value per pupil is $5,960—the lowest in the metropolitan area—and the median family income ($4,686) is also the lowest. At an equalized tax rate of $1.05 per $100 of assessed property—the highest in the metropolitan area—the district contributed $26 to the education of each child for the 1967–1968 school year above its Local Fund Assignment for the Minimum Foundation Program. The Foundation Program contributed $222 per pupil for a state-local total of $248. Federal funds added another $108 for a total of $356 per pupil.

Alamo Heights is the most affluent school district in San Antonio. [Its] school population [has] only 18% Mexican-Americans and less than 1% Negroes. The assessed property value per pupil exceeds $49,000 and the median family income is $8,001. In 1967–1968 the local tax rate of $.85 per $100 of valuation yielded $333 per pupil over and above its contribution to the Foundation Program. Coupled with the $225 provided from that Program, the district was able to supply $558 per student. Supplemented by a $36 per pupil grant from federal sources, Alamo Heights spent $594 per pupil.

[M]ore recent partial statistics indicate that [the] trend of increasing state aid has been significant. For the 1970–1971 school year, the Foundation School Program allotment for Edgewood was $356 per [pupil and] Alamo Heights [received] $491 per [pupil].[35] These recent figures also reveal the extent to which these two districts' allotments were funded from their own required contributions to the Local Fund Assignment. Alamo Heights, because of its relative wealth, was required to contribute out of its local property tax collections approximately $100 per pupil, or about 20% of its Foundation grant. Edgewood, on the other hand, paid only $8.46 per pupil, which is about 2.4% of its grant. [Finding] that wealth is a "suspect" classification and that education is a "fundamental" interest, the District Court held that the Texas system could be sustained only if the State could show that it was premised upon some compelling state interest. * * *

II. [The] wealth discrimination discovered [is] quite unlike any of the forms of wealth discrimination heretofore reviewed by this Court. [The] individuals who constituted the class discriminated against in our prior cases shared two distinguishing characteristics: because of their impecunity they were completely unable to pay for some desired benefit, and as a consequence, they sustained an absolute deprivation of a meaningful opportunity to enjoy that benefit [discussing *Griffin v. Illinois* and *Bullock v. Carter*]. *Douglas v. California* [provides] no relief for those on whom the burdens of paying for a criminal defense are, relatively speaking, great but not insurmountable. Nor does it deal with relative differences in the quality of counsel acquired by the less wealthy. [And] *Williams* and *Tate* [do] not touch on the question whether equal protection is

35. [I]t is apparent that Alamo Heights has enjoyed a larger gain [due] to the emphasis in the State's allocation formula on the guaranteed minimum salaries for teachers. Higher salaries are guaranteed to teachers having more years of experience and possessing more advanced degrees. Therefore, Alamo Heights, which has a greater percentage of experienced personnel with advanced degrees, receives more State support. * * * Because more dollars have been given to districts that al- ready spend more per pupil, such Foundation formulas have been described as "anti-equalizing." The formula, however, is anti-equalizing only if viewed in absolute terms. The percentage disparity between the two Texas districts is diminished substantially by State aid. Alamo Heights derived in 1967–1968 almost 13 times as much money from local taxes as Edgewood did. The State aid grants to each district in 1970–1971 lowered the ratio to approximately two to [one].

denied to persons with relatively less money on whom designated fines impose heavier burdens. * * *

[Even] a cursory examination however, demonstrates that neither of the two distinguishing characteristics of wealth classifications can be found here. First, [there] is reason to believe that the poorest families are not necessarily clustered in the poorest property districts. A [recent] Connecticut study found, not surprisingly, that the poor were clustered around commercial and industrial areas—those same areas that provide the most attractive sources of property tax income for school districts. Whether a similar pattern would be discovered in Texas is not known, but there is no basis on the record [for] assuming [otherwise].

Second, [lack] of personal resources has not occasioned an absolute deprivation of the desired benefit. The argument here is not that the children [are] receiving no public education; rather, it is that they are receiving a poorer quality education [than] children in districts having more assessable wealth. [A] sufficient answer to appellees' argument is that at least where wealth is involved the Equal Protection Clause does not require absolute equality or precisely equal advantages. Nor indeed, in view of the infinite variables affecting the educational process, can any system assure equal quality of education except in the most relative sense. Texas asserts that the Minimum Foundation Program provides an "adequate" education for all children in the State. [No] proof was offered at trial persuasively discrediting or refuting the State's assertion. * * *[60]

[Appellees] sought to prove that a direct correlation exists between the wealth of families within each district and the expenditures therein for education. [But] appellees' proof [fails].

This brings us [to] the third way in which the classification scheme might be defined—*district* wealth discrimination. Since the only correlation indicated by the evidence is between district property wealth and expenditures, it may be argued that discrimination might be found without regard to the individual income characteristics of district residents. * * *

However described, it is clear that appellees' suit asks this Court to extend its most exacting scrutiny to review a system that allegedly discriminates against a large, diverse, and amorphous class, unified only by the common factor of residence in districts that happen to have less taxable wealth than other districts. The system of alleged discrimination and the class it defines have none of the traditional indicia of suspectness: the class is not saddled with such disabilities, or subjected to such a history of purposeful unequal treatment, or relegated to such a position of political powerlessness as to command extraordinary protection from the majoritarian political process.

We thus conclude that the Texas system does not operate to the peculiar disadvantage of any suspect class. But [recognizing] that this Court has never heretofore held that wealth discrimination alone provides an adequate basis for

---

60. [If] elementary and secondary education were made available by the State only to those able to pay a tuition assessed against each pupil, there would be a clearly defined class of "poor" people—definable in terms of their inability to pay the prescribed sum—who would be absolutely precluded from receiving an education. That case would present a far more compelling set of circumstances for judicial assistance than [this one].

[Does this extend to higher education as well? See Strickman, *The Tuition-Poor, the Public University, and Equal Protection*, 29 U.Fla.L.Rev. 595 (1977). For the view that "*Dandridge* and its *progeny*" do not apply to situations involving "a total cut-off of welfare that approaches denial of subsistence," see Note, *Intermediate Equal Protection Scrutiny of Welfare Laws that Deny Subsistence*, 132 U.Pa.L.Rev. 1547 (1984).]

invoking strict scrutiny, appellees [also] assert that the State's system impermissibly interferes with the exercise of a "fundamental" right [requiring] the strict standard of judicial review. * * *

Nothing this Court holds today in any way detracts from our historic dedication to public education. [But] the importance of a service performed by the State does not determine whether it must be regarded as fundamental for purposes of examination under the Equal Protection Clause. [In *Shapiro,* the] right to interstate travel had long been recognized as a right of constitutional significance, and the Court's decision therefore did not require an ad hoc determination as to the social or economic importance of that right. *Lindsey* [as well as *Dandridge*] firmly reiterates that social importance is not the critical determinant for subjecting state legislation to strict scrutiny. * * *

The lesson of these cases [is that it] is not the province of this Court to create substantive constitutional rights in the name of guaranteeing equal protection of the laws. Thus the key to discovering whether education is "fundamental" is not to be found in comparisons of the relative societal significance of education as opposed to subsistence or housing [or] by weighing whether education is as important as the right to travel. Rather, the answer lies in assessing whether there is a right to education explicitly or implicitly guaranteed by the Constitution. *Dunn;*[74] *Skinner.*[76]

Education, of course, is not among the rights afforded explicit protection under [the] Constitution. Nor do we find any basis for saying it is implicitly so protected.[a] [But] appellees [contend] that education is distinguishable from other services and benefits provided by the State because it bears a peculiarly close relationship to other rights and liberties accorded protection under the Constitution [in that] it is essential to the effective exercise of First Amendment freedoms and to intelligent utilization of the right to vote. In asserting a nexus between speech and education, appellees urge that the right to speak is meaningless unless the speaker is capable of articulating his thoughts intelligently and persuasively. [A] similar line of reasoning is pursued with respect to the right to [vote]: a voter cannot cast his ballot intelligently unless his reading skills and thought processes have been adequately developed.

We need not dispute any of these propositions. [Yet] we have never presumed to possess either the ability or the authority to guarantee to the citizenry the most *effective* speech or the most *informed* electoral choice. That these may be desirable goals [is] not to be doubted. [But] they are not values to be implemented by judicial intrusion into otherwise legitimate state activities.

74. *Dunn* fully canvasses this Court's voting rights cases and explains that "this Court has made clear that a citizen has a *constitutionally protected right* to participate in elections on an equal basis with other citizens in the jurisdiction." (emphasis supplied). The constitutional underpinnings of [this right] can no longer be doubted even though, as the Court noted in *Harper,* "the right to vote in state elections is nowhere expressly mentioned."

76. *Skinner* applied the standard of close scrutiny to a state law permitting forced sterilization of "habitual criminals." Implicit in the Court's opinion is the recognition that the right of procreation is among the rights of personal privacy protected under the Constitution. See *Roe v. Wade.*

a. For the view that education *is* "fundamental," see Coons, Clune & Sugarman, *Educational Opportunity: A Workable Constitutional Test for State Financial Structures,* 57 Calif.L.Rev. 305 (1969). As to housing, see Sager, *Tight Little Islands: Exclusionary Zoning, Equal Protection, and the Indigent,* 21 Stan.L.Rev. 767 (1969). As to various municipal services, see Ratner, *Inter-Neighborhood Denials of Equal Protection in the Provision of Municipal Services,* 4 Harv.Civ.Rts.—Civ.Lib. L.Rev. 1 (1968); Abascal, *Municipal Services and Equal Protection: Variations on a Theme by Griffin v. Illinois,* 20 Hast.L.J. 1367 (1969).

Massachusetts Bd. of Retirement v. Murgia (1976), Sec. 3, I supra, held that a "right of governmental employment" is *not* fundamental.

Even if it were conceded that some identifiable quantum of education is a constitutionally protected prerequisite to the meaningful exercise of either right, we have no indication that the [present] system fails to provide each child with an opportunity to acquire the basic minimal skills [necessary]. Furthermore, the logical limitations on appellees' nexus theory are difficult * * *. Empirical examination might well buttress an assumption that the ill-fed, ill-clothed, and ill-housed are among the most ineffective participants in the political process and that they derive the least enjoyment from the benefits of the First Amendment. * * *

[The] present case, in another basic sense, is significantly different from any of the cases in which the Court has applied strict scrutiny [to] legislation touching upon constitutionally protected rights. [These] involved legislation which "deprived," "infringed," or "interfered" with the free exercise of some such fundamental personal right or liberty. [Every] step leading to the establishment of the system Texas utilizes today [was] implemented in an effort to *extend* public education and to improve its quality. Of course, every reform that benefits some more than others may be criticized for what it fails to accomplish. But we think it plain that, in substance, the thrust of the Texas system is affirmative and reformatory and, therefore, should be scrutinized under judicial principles sensitive to the nature of the State's efforts and to the rights reserved to the States under the Constitution.

[A] century of Supreme Court adjudication under the Equal Protection Clause affirmatively supports the application of the traditional standard of review, which requires only that the State's system be shown to bear some rational relationship to legitimate state purposes. This case represents [a] direct attack on the way in which Texas has chosen to raise and disburse state and local tax revenues. [This] Court has often admonished against such interferences with the State's fiscal policies under the Equal Protection Clause [and] we continue to acknowledge that the Justices of this Court lack both the expertise and the familiarity with local problems so necessary to the making of wise decisions with respect to the raising and disposition of public revenues. Yet we are urged to direct the States either to alter drastically the present system or to throw out the property tax altogether in favor of some other form of taxation. No scheme of taxation [has] yet been devised which is free of all discriminatory impact. In such a complex arena in which no perfect alternatives exist, the Court does well not to impose too rigorous a standard of scrutiny lest all local fiscal schemes become subjects of criticism under the Equal Protection Clause.

[T]his case also involves the most persistent and difficult questions of educational policy, another area in which this Court's lack of specialized knowledge and experience counsels against premature interference with the informed judgments made at the state and local levels. [On] even the most basic questions in this area the scholars and educational experts are divided. Indeed, one of the hottest sources of controversy concerns the extent to which there is a demonstrable correlation between educational expenditures and the quality of education— an assumed correlation underlying virtually every legal conclusion drawn by the District [Court].

It must be remembered also that every claim arising under the Equal Protection Clause has implications for the relationship between national and state power under our federal system. [I]t would be difficult to imagine a case having a greater potential impact on our federal system than the one now before us, in which we are urged to abrogate systems of financing public education presently in existence in virtually every State. * * *

III. [The] State's contribution, under the Minimum Foundation Program, was designed to provide an adequate minimum educational offering in every school in the State. [T]o fulfill its local Fund Assignment, every district must impose an ad valorem tax on property located within its borders. The Fund Assignment was designed to remain sufficiently low to assure that each district would have some ability to provide a more enriched educational program. [In] large measure, these additional local revenues are devoted to paying higher salaries to more teachers. Therefore, the primary distinguishing attributes of schools in property-affluent districts are lower pupil-teacher ratios and higher salary schedules.[101] [In] part, local control [means] freedom to devote more money to the education of one's children. Equally important, however, is the opportunity it offers for participation in the decision-making process that determines how those local tax dollars will be spent. [No] area of social concern stands to profit more from a multiplicity of viewpoints and from a diversity of approaches than does public education.

[While] it is no doubt true that reliance on local property taxation for school revenues provides less freedom of choice with respect to expenditures for some districts than for others,[107] the existence of "some inequality" in the manner in which the State's rationale is achieved is not alone a sufficient basis for striking down the entire system. [Nor] must the financing system fail because, as appellees suggest, other methods of satisfying the State's interest, which occasion "less drastic" disparities in expenditures, might be conceived. Only where state action impinges on the exercise of fundamental constitutional rights or liberties must it be found to have chosen the least restrictive alternative. It is also well to remember that even those districts that have reduced ability to make free decisions with respect to how much they spend on education still retain under the present system a large measure of authority as to how available funds will be allocated. They further enjoy the power to make numerous other decisions with respect to the operation of the schools.[108] The people of Texas may be justified in believing [that] along with increased control of the purse strings at the state level will go increased control over local policies.

[A]ny scheme of local taxation—indeed the very existence of identifiable local governmental units—requires the establishment of jurisdictional boundaries that are inevitably arbitrary. It is equally inevitable that some localities are going to be blessed with more taxable assets than others. Nor is local wealth

101. [As] previously noted, the extent to which the quality of education varies with expenditure per pupil is debated inconclusively by the most thoughtful students of public education. While all would agree that there is a correlation up to the point of providing the recognized essentials, [the] issues of greatest disagreement include the effect on the quality of education of pupil-teacher ratios and of higher teacher [salaries].

107. Mr. Justice White suggests in his dissent that the Texas system violates [equal protection] because the means it has selected to effectuate its interest in local autonomy fail to guarantee complete freedom of choice to every district. He places special emphasis on the statutory provision that establishes a maximum rate of $1.50 per $100 valuation at which a local school district may tax for school maintenance. The maintenance rate in Edgewood when this case was litigated

[was] $.55 per $100, barely one-third of the allowable rate. (The tax rate of $1.05 per $100 is the equalized rate for maintenance and for the retirement of bonds.) Appellees do not claim that the ceiling presently bars desired tax increases in Edgewood or in any other Texas district. Therefore, the constitutionality of that statutory provision is not before [us].

108. Mr. Justice Marshall['s] assertion, that genuine local control does not exist in Texas, simply cannot be supported. It is abundantly refuted by the elaborate statutory division of responsibilities set out in the Texas Education Code. Although policy decision-making and supervision in certain areas are reserved to the State, the day-to-day authority over the "management and control" of all public elementary and secondary schools is squarely placed on the local school boards [listing a number of their specific powers].

a static quantity. Changes [may] result from any number of events, some of which local residents can and do influence. For instance, commercial and industrial enterprises may be encouraged to locate within a district by various actions—public and private.

Moreover, if local taxation for local expenditure is an unconstitutional method of providing for education then it may be an equally impermissible means of providing other necessary services customarily financed largely from local property taxes, including local police and fire protection, public health and hospitals, and public utility facilities of various kinds. [It has] never been within the constitutional prerogative of this Court to nullify statewide measures for financing public services merely because the burdens or benefits thereof fall unevenly depending upon the relative wealth of the political subdivisions in which citizens live.

[In] its essential characteristics the Texas plan for financing public education reflects what many educators for a half century have thought was an enlightened approach to a problem for which there is no perfect solution. We are unwilling to assume for ourselves a level of wisdom superior to that of legislators, scholars, and educational authorities in 49 States, especially where the alternatives proposed are only recently conceived and nowhere yet tested.

* * *

IV. [T]his Court's action today is not to be viewed as placing its judicial imprimatur on the status quo. The need is apparent for reform in tax systems which may well have relied too long and too heavily on the local property tax. And certainly innovative new thinking as to public education, its methods and its funding, is necessary to assure both a higher level of quality and greater uniformity of opportunity. These matters merit the continued attention of the scholars who already have contributed much by their challenges. But the ultimate solutions must come from the lawmakers and from the democratic pressures of those who elect them.

Reversed.[b]

MR. JUSTICE BRENNAN, dissenting.

Although I agree with my Brother White that the Texas statutory scheme is devoid of any rational basis, [I] also record my disagreement with the Court's rather distressing assertion that a right may be deemed "fundamental" for the purposes of equal protection analysis only if it is "explicitly or implicitly guaranteed by the Constitution." As my Brother Marshall convincingly demonstrates our prior cases stand for the proposition that "fundamentality" is, in large measure, a function of the right's importance in terms of the effectuation of those rights which are in fact constitutionally guaranteed. * * *

MR. JUSTICE WHITE, with whom MR. JUSTICE DOUGLAS and MR. JUSTICE BRENNAN join, dissenting.

[T]his case would be quite different if it were true that the Texas system, while insuring minimum educational expenditures in every district through state funding, extends a meaningful option to all local districts to increase their per-pupil [expenditures. But for] districts with a low per-pupil real estate tax base [the] Texas system utterly fails to extend a realistic choice to parents, because the property tax, which is the only revenue-raising mechanism extended to school districts, is practically and legally unavailable. * * *

---

b. The concurring opinion of Stewart, J., who joined the Court's opinion, is omitted.

In order to equal the highest yield in any other Bexar County district, Alamo Heights would be required to tax at the rate of 68¢ per $100 of assessed valuation. Edgewood would be required to tax at the prohibitive rate of $5.76 per $100. But state law places a $1.50 per $100 ceiling on the maintenance tax [rate]. Requiring the State to establish only that unequal treatment is in furtherance of a permissible goal, without also requiring the State to show that the means chosen to effectuate that goal are rationally related to its achievement, makes equal protection analysis no more than an empty gesture. * * *

MR. JUSTICE MARSHALL, with whom MR. JUSTICE DOUGLAS, concurs, dissenting.

[T]he majority's holding can only be seen as a retreat from our historic commitment to equality of educational opportunity. [The issue] is not whether Texas is doing its best to ameliorate the worst features of a discriminatory scheme, but rather whether the scheme itself is in fact unconstitutionally discriminatory.[35] Authorities concerned with educational quality no doubt disagree as to the significance of variations in per pupil spending. [But it] is an inescapable fact that if one district has more funds available per pupil than another district, the former will have greater choice in educational [planning].

At the very least, in view of the substantial interdistrict disparities in funding, [the] burden of proving that these disparities do not in fact affect the quality of children's education must fall upon the appellants. Yet [they] have argued no more than that the relationship is ambiguous. * * *

Nor can I accept the appellants' apparent suggestion [that equal protection] cannot be offended by substantially unequal state treatment of persons who are similarly situated so long as the State provides everyone with some unspecified amount of education which evidently is "enough." [The] Equal Protection Clause is not addressed to the minimal sufficiency but rather to the unjustifiable inequalities of state action. [Even] if the Equal Protection Clause encompassed some theory of constitutional adequacy, discrimination in the provision of educational opportunity would certainly seem to be a poor candidate for its application. Neither the majority nor appellants informs us how judicially manageable standards are to be derived for determining how much education is "enough" to excuse constitutional discrimination. [In] light of the data introduced before the District Court, the conclusion that the school children of property poor districts constitute a sufficient class for our purposes seems indisputable to me. [Whether] this discrimination, against [them] is violative of the Equal Protection Clause is the question to which we must now turn.

[The] Court apparently seeks to establish [that] equal protection cases fall into one of two neat categories which dictate the appropriate standard of review—strict scrutiny or mere rationality. But [a] principled reading of what this Court has done reveals that it has applied a spectrum of standards [which] clearly comprehends variations in the degree of care with which the Court will scrutinize particular classifications, depending [on] the constitutional and societal importance of the interest adversely affected and the recognized invidiousness of the basis upon which the particular classification is drawn.[c] * * *

---

35. * * * Texas' financing scheme is hardly remedial legislation of the type for which we have previously shown substantial tolerance. Such legislation may in fact extend the vote to "persons who otherwise would be denied it by state law," *Katzenbach v. Morgan,* or it may eliminate the evils of the private bail bondsman, *Schilb v. Kuebel* [Part I, B supra]. But those are instances in which a legislative body has sought to remedy problems for which it cannot be said to have been directly responsible. By contrast, [it] is the State's own scheme which has caused the funding problem, and, thus viewed, that scheme can hardly be deemed remedial.

c. In *Vlandis v. Kline,* Sec. 5 infra,—decided after *Rodriquez*—White, J., stated that he,

I therefore cannot accept the majority's labored efforts to demonstrate that fundamental interests, which call for strict scrutiny of the challenged classification, encompass only established rights which we are somehow bound to recognize from the text of the Constitution itself. * * * [59]

I would like to know where the Constitution guarantees the right to procreate, *Skinner,* or the right to vote in state elections, e.g., *Reynolds v. Sims,*[60] or the right to an appeal from a criminal conviction, e.g., *Griffin.* [61] These are instances in which, due to the importance of the interests at stake, the Court has displayed a strong concern with the existence of discriminatory state treatment. But the Court has [never] indicated that these are interests which independently enjoy full-blown constitutional protection. * * *

The majority is, of course, correct when it suggests that the process of determining which interests are fundamental is a difficult one. But I do not think the problem is insurmountable. [The task] should be to determine the extent to which constitutionally guaranteed rights are dependent on interests not mentioned in the Constitution. As the nexus between the specific constitutional guarantee and the nonconstitutional interest draws closer, the nonconstitutional interest becomes more fundamental and the degree of judicial scrutiny applied when the interest is infringed on a discriminatory basis must be adjusted accordingly. * * * Procreation is now understood to be important because of its interaction with the established constitutional right of privacy. The exercise of the state franchise is closely tied to basic civil and political rights inherent in the First Amendment. And access to criminal appellate processes enhances the integrity of the range of rights implicit in the Fourteenth Amendment guarantee of due process of law. Only if we closely protect the related interests from state discrimination do we ultimately ensure the integrity of the constitutional guarantee itself. This is the real lesson that must be taken from our previous decisions involving interests deemed to be fundamental.

The effect of the interaction of individual interests with established constitutional guarantees upon the degree of care exercised by this Court in reviewing state discrimination affecting such interests is amply illustrated [by] *Eisenstadt v. Baird,* [p. 138 supra]. [The] Court purported to test the statute under its traditional standard [but] clearly did not adhere to these highly tolerant standards of traditional rational review. [Yet] I think the Court's action was entirely appropriate for access to and use of contraceptives bears a close relationship to the individual's constitutional right of privacy.

too, agreed that this has been the Court's approach in applying the equal protection clause. See also the dissent of Marshall, J., joined by Brennan and Blackmun, JJ., in *Cleburne v. Cleburne Living Center, Inc.,* Sec. 3, V supra.

59. Indeed, the Court's theory would render the established concept of fundamental interests in the context of equal protection analysis superfluous, for the substantive constitutional right itself requires that this Court strictly scrutinize any asserted state interest for restricting or denying access to any particular guaranteed right.

60. It is interesting that in its effort to reconcile the state voting rights cases with its theory of fundamentality the majority can muster nothing more than the contention that "[t]he constitutional underpinnings of the right to equal treatment in the voting process can no longer be doubted." If, by this, the Court intends to recognize a substantive constitutional "right to equal treatment in the voting process" independent of the Equal Protection Clause, the source of such a right is certainly a mystery to me.

61. It is true that *Griffin* and *Douglas* also involved discrimination against [indigents]. But, as the majority points out, the Court has never deemed wealth discrimination alone to be sufficient to require strict judicial scrutiny; rather, such review of wealth classifications has been applied only where the discrimination affects an important individual interest, see, e.g., *Harper.* Thus, I believe *Griffin* and *Douglas* can only be understood as premised on a recognition of the fundamental importance of the criminal appellate process.

A similar process of analysis with respect to the invidiousness of the basis on which a particular classification is drawn has also influenced the Court as to the appropriate degree of scrutiny to be accorded any particular case. [It] may be that all of [the] considerations, which make for particular judicial solicitude in the face of discrimination on the basis of race, nationality, or alienage, do not coalesce—or at least not to the same degree—in other forms of discrimination. Nevertheless, these considerations have undoubtedly influenced the care with which the Court has scrutinized other forms of discrimination. [Thus], in *Reed v. Reed*, [Sec. 3, IV supra], the Court [resorted] to a more stringent standard of equal protection review than that employed in cases involving commercial matters. [T]he particularly invidious character of the classification caused the Court to pause and scrutinize with more than traditional care the rationality of state discrimination. Discrimination on the basis [of] sex posed for the Court the spectre of forms of discrimination which it implicitly recognized to have deep social and legal roots without necessarily having any basis in actual differences. Still, the Court's sensitivity to the invidiousness of the basis for discrimination is perhaps most apparent in its decisions protecting the interests of children born out of wedlock from discriminatory state action. [Sec. 3, III supra].

[In] the context of economic interests, we find that discriminatory state action is almost always sustained for such interests are generally far removed from constitutional guarantees. [But] the situation differs markedly when discrimination against important individual interests with constitutional implications and against particularly disadvantaged or powerless classes is involved.[d] The majority suggests, however, that a variable standard of review would give this Court the appearance of a "superlegislature." I cannot agree. Such an approach seems to me a part of the guarantees of our Constitution and of the historic experiences with oppression of and discrimination against discrete, powerless minorities which underlie that Document. In truth, the Court itself will be open to the criticism raised by the majority so long as it continues on its present course of effectively selecting in private which cases will be afforded special consideration without acknowledging the true basis of its action. [Such] obfuscated action may be appropriate to a political body such as a legislature, but it is not appropriate to this Court. Open debate of the bases for the Court's action is essential to the rationality and consistency of our decisionmaking process. * * *

[It] is true that this Court has never deemed the provision of free public education to be required by the Constitution. [But] the fundamental importance of education is amply indicated by the prior decisions of this Court, by the unique status accorded public education by our society, and by the close relationship between education and some of our most basic constitutional [values].

Education directly affects the ability of a child to exercise his First Amendment interests both as a source and as a receiver of information and [ideas]. Indeed, it has frequently been suggested that education is the dominant factor affecting political consciousness and participation.[72] * * * *[74] [T]he issue is

---

d. In *Massachusetts Bd. of Retirement v. Murgia*, Marshall, J., further explained his approach: "[T]here remain rights, not now classified as 'fundamental,' that remain vital to the flourishing of a free society, and classes, not now classified as 'suspect,' that are unfairly burdened by invidious discrimination unrelated to the individual worth of their members. Whatever we call these rights and classes, we simply cannot forgo all judicial protection against discriminatory legislation bearing upon them, but for the rare instances when the legislative choice can be termed 'wholly irrelevant' to the legislative goal."

72. [I]t should be obvious that the political process, like most other aspects of social inter-

74. See note 74 on page 1056.

neither provision of the most *effective* speech nor of the most *informed* vote. Appellees do not now seek the best education Texas might provide [but] an end to state [discrimination].[75]

[We] are told that in every prior case involving a wealth classification, the members of the disadvantaged class have "shared two distinguishing characteristics: because of their impecunity they were completely unable to pay for some desired benefit, and as a consequence, they sustained an absolute deprivation of a meaningful opportunity to enjoy that benefit." I cannot agree. * * *

In *Harper,* the Court struck down [a] poll tax in toto; it did not order merely that those too poor to pay the tax be exempted; complete impecunity clearly was not determinative. [In] *Griffin* and *Douglas* [t]he right of appeal itself was not absolutely denied to those too poor to pay; but because of the cost of a transcript and of counsel, the appeal was a substantially less meaningful right for the poor than for the rich. [This] clearly encompassed degrees of discrimination on the basis of wealth which do not amount to outright denial of the affected right or interest.[77]

This is not to say that the form of wealth classification in this case does not differ significantly from those recognized [in] previous [decisions. Here], the children of the disadvantaged Texas school districts are being discriminated against not necessarily because of [the] wealth of their families, but because of the taxable property wealth of the residents of the district in which they happen to live. The appropriate question, then, is whether the same degree of judicial solicitude and scrutiny that has previously been afforded wealth classifications is warranted here.

[That] wealth classifications alone have not necessarily been considered to bear the same high degree of suspectness as have classifications based on, for instance, race or alienage may be explainable on a number of grounds. The "poor" may not be seen as politically powerless as certain discrete and insular minority groups. Personal poverty may entail much the same social stigma as historically attached to certain racial or ethnic groups [but it] is not a permanent disability; its shackles may be escaped. Perhaps, most importantly, though,

course, is to some degree competitive. It is thus of little benefit to an individual from a property poor district to have "enough" education if those around him have more than "enough."

74. [Whatever] the severity of the impact of insufficient food or inadequate housing on a person's life, they have never been considered to bear the same direct and immediate relationship to constitutional concerns for free speech and for our political processes as education has long been recognized to bear. Perhaps, the best evidence of this fact is the unique status which has been accorded public education as the single public service nearly unanimously guaranteed in the constitutions of our States. Education, in terms of constitutional values, is much more analogous in my judgment, to the right to vote in state elections than to public welfare or public housing. [Indeed,] we have long recognized education as an essential step in providing the disadvantaged with the tools necessary to achieve economic self-sufficiency.

75. The majority's reliance on this Court's traditional deference to legislative bodies in matters of taxation falls wide of the mark [for] in this case we are presented with a claim [that] the revenue producing mechanism directly discriminates against the interests of some of the intended beneficiaries; and in contrast to the taxpayer suits, the interest adversely affected is of substantial constitutional and societal importance. * * *

77. Even putting aside its misreading of *Griffin* and *Douglas,* the Court fails to offer any reasoned constitutional basis for restricting cases involving wealth discrimination to instances in which there is an absolute deprivation of the interest affected. [Equal protection] guarantees equality of treatment of those persons who are similarly situated; it does not merely bar some form of excessive discrimination between such persons. Outside the context of wealth discrimination, the Court's reapportionment decisions clearly indicate that relative discrimination is within the purview of the Equal Protection Clause. * * *

personal wealth may not necessarily share the general irrelevance as a basis for legislative action that race or nationality is recognized to have. While the "poor" have frequently been a legally disadvantaged group, it cannot be ignored that social legislation must frequently take cognizance of the economic status of our citizens. Thus, we have generally gauged the invidiousness of wealth classifications with an awareness of the importance of the interests being affected and the relevance of personal wealth to those interests.

When evaluated with these considerations in mind, it seems to me that discrimination on the basis of group wealth in this case likewise calls for careful judicial scrutiny. First, [it] bears no relationship whatsoever to the interest of Texas school children in the educational opportunity afforded them [by] Texas. Given the importance of that interest, we must be particularly sensitive to the invidious characteristics of any form of discrimination that is not clearly intended to serve it, as opposed to some other distinct state interest. Discrimination on the basis of group wealth may not, to be sure, reflect the social stigma frequently attached to personal poverty. Nevertheless, insofar as group wealth discrimination involves wealth over which the disadvantaged individual has no significant control,[83] it represents in fact a more serious basis of discrimination than does personal wealth. For such discrimination is no reflection of the individual's characteristics or his abilities. And thus—particularly in the context of a disadvantaged class composed of children—we have previously treated discrimination on a basis which the individual cannot control as constitutionally disfavored. Cf. *Weber; Levy,* [Sec. 3, III supra].

The disability of the disadvantaged class in this case extends as well into the political processes upon which we ordinarily rely as adequate for the protection and promotion of all interests. Here legislative reallocation of the State's property wealth must be sought in the face of inevitable opposition from significantly advantaged districts that have a strong vested interest in the preservation of the status [quo]. *Griffin, Douglas, Williams, Tate,* and our other prior cases have dealt with discrimination on the basis of indigency which was attributable to the operation of the private sector. But we have no such simple de facto wealth discrimination here. The means for financing public education in Texas are selected and specified by the State. [At] the same time, governmentally imposed land use controls have undoubtedly encouraged and rigidified natural trends in the allocation of particular areas for residential or commercial use, and thus determined each district's amount of taxable property wealth. In short, this case, in contrast to the Court's previous wealth discrimination decisions, can only be seen as "unusual in the extent to which governmental action *is* the cause of the wealth classifications."

[Here] both the nature of the interest and the classification dictate close judicial [scrutiny. I] do not question that local control of public education, as an abstract matter, constitutes a very substantial state interest. [But] on this record, it is apparent that the State's purported concern with local control is offered primarily as an excuse rather than as a justification for interdistrict inequality.

In Texas statewide laws regulate [the] most minute details of local public education. For example, the State prescribes required courses. All textbooks must be submitted for state [approval]. The State has established the qualifica-

---

83. True, a family may move to escape a property poor school district, assuming it has the means to do so. But such a view would itself raise a serious constitutional question concerning an impermissible burdening of the right to travel, or, more precisely, the concomitant right to remain where one is.

tions necessary for teaching in Texas public schools and the procedures for obtaining certification. The State has even legislated on the length of the school [day.]

Moreover, even if we accept Texas' general dedication to local control in educational matters, [i]f Texas had a system truly dedicated to local fiscal control one would expect the quality of the educational opportunity provided in each district to vary with the decision of the voters in that district as to the level of sacrifice they wish to make for public education. [But local] districts cannot choose to have the best education [by] imposing the highest tax rate. Instead, the quality of the educational opportunity offered by any particular district is largely determined by the amount of taxable property located in the district—a factor over which local voters can exercise no control.

The study introduced in the District Court showed a direct inverse relationship between equalized taxable district property wealth and district tax effort with the result that the property poor districts making the highest tax effort obtained the lowest per pupil yield. * * *

In my judgment, any substantial degree of scrutiny of the operation of the Texas financing scheme reveals that the State has selected means wholly inappropriate to secure its purported interest in assuring its school districts local fiscal control.[96] At the same time, appellees have pointed out a variety of alternative financing schemes which may serve the State's purported interest in local control as well as, if not better than, the present scheme without the current impairment of the educational opportunity of vast numbers of Texas schoolchildren.[98] * * *

Notes and Questions

1. *Wealth classifications.* (a) Does *Rodriguez* hold that de facto discriminations against poor people are subject to "strict scrutiny" only if the classification involves a right "explicitly or implicitly guaranteed by the Constitution"? May *all* the prior "wealth discrimination" cases be explained on this basis? Or does the Court's fn. 60 suggest that a state payment requirement resulting in "an

---

96. [Although] my Brother White purports to reach this result by application of that lenient standard of mere rationality, [it] seems to be that the care with which he scrutinizes the practical effectiveness of the present local property tax as a device for affording local fiscal control reflects the application of a more stringent standard of [review].

98. * * * Central financing would leave in local hands the entire gamut of local educational policy-making—teachers, curriculum, school sites, the whole process of allocating resources among alternative educational objectives.

A second possibility is the much discussed theory of district power equalization put forth by Professors Coons, Clune, and Sugarman in their seminal work, *Private Wealth and Public Education* 201–242 (1970). Such a scheme would truly reflect a dedication to local fiscal control. Under their system, each school district would receive a fixed amount of revenue per pupil for any particular level of tax effort

regardless of the level of local property tax base. * * *

District wealth reapportionment is yet another alternative * * *.

A fourth possibility would be to remove commercial, industrial, and mineral property from local tax rolls, to tax this property on a state-wide basis, and to return the resulting revenues to the local districts in a fashion that would compensate for remaining variations in the local tax bases.

None of these particular alternatives are necessarily constitutionally compelled; rather, they indicate the breadth of choice which remains to the State if the present interdistrict disparities were eliminated.

[For a collection of further commentaries, emphasizing the varying complexities of school finance in constitutional adjudication, see Lockhart, Kamisar & Choper, *Constitutional Law: Cases—Comments—Questions* 1552–53 (4th ed. 1975).]

absolute deprivation" of an "important" (albeit not "fundamental") right requires "strict scrutiny"? If so, what are other "important" rights?

Is education unique because it is compulsory—i.e., is the state barred from requiring it and at the same time imposing a "user-fee" even on those who can't pay? May the public schools impose a charge for all textbooks, even against indigents? May any of the broad range of municipal services—fire and police, parks and recreation, etc.—be conditioned on a "user-fee"? How about water?

(b) *Affirmative obligation.* Suppose a state simply shut its public schools and left the task to private entrepreneurs? In what way is this different than the situation posited in fn. 60? Suppose a state simply shut off all relief and welfare assistance? Is this state action subject to "strict scrutiny" under equal protection? Or does this beg the "state action" issue?

May a state bar impoverished citizens from public housing? If not, may it charge rentals for all public housing that the impoverished can't afford? If not, may it simply not construct public housing, leaving the impoverished to fend for themselves? Or does government have the affirmative obligation to afford at least "minimum protection" (if not "equal protection") to all citizens in respect to those services that are "of such fundamental importance" that "severe deprivation" would otherwise result? See generally Michelman, *On Protecting the Poor Through the Fourteenth Amendment,* 83 Harv.L.Rev. 7 (1969). For the view that it is improper for the judiciary to decide issues of economic allocation, see Wilkinson, fn. b in *Dandridge;* Winter, fn. c in *Dandridge.* Compare generally Rawls, *A Theory of Justice* (1971) with Nozick, *Anarchy, State and Utopia* (1974).

Consider Bendich, *Privacy, Poverty, and the Constitution,* 54 Calif.L.Rev. 407, 420–21 (1966): "It would be perverse to say that one has a fundamental right to be assisted by a lawyer when charged with crime, but that he has no right to such food or medicine as might be required to keep him reasonably healthy and attentive during the process of his trial. [But] if a person charged with crime has a right to such assistance, on what principle is one innocent of such a charge to be denied equal access to assistance? [What] constitutional guarantees other than those which are bound up with the criminal law are denied to persons because of their poverty? Does the fourth amendment's guarantee of the right to be secure in one's person, papers, house, and effects presuppose housing for the people of America? If it does, then clearly the condition of being unable to pay rent can deprive one of this aspect of the right to privacy as effectively as the inability to pay counsel fees [deprives] one of the right to counsel." Are there *any* "constitutional guarantees" that can be effectively exercised without "minimally adequate" food, clothing and shelter? Without "minimally adequate" education and medical assistance? Is the state constitutionally obligated to provide its impoverished citizens "minimally adequate" political campaign expenses? "Minimally adequate" funds to travel throughout the country and abroad? How are the terms "minimally adequate" and "impoverished" to be defined? By whom? Of what relevance does the "cost-to-the-state" factor bear on the "compelling" justification inquiry?

May the state bar indigents from public parks? Golf courses? Opera houses? If not, may it charge a "user-fee"? May it decline to engage in such activities without subsidizing those persons who can't pay their own way? See generally Note, *Discrimination Against the Poor and the Fourteenth Amendment,* 81 Harv.L.Rev. 435 (1967).

(c) *Discrimination against fundamental rights.* MAHER v. ROE, p. 180 supra, per POWELL, J., held that Connecticut's refusal to give medicaid for nontherapeutic abortions, even though it gives medicaid for childbirth, does not violate equal protection: "The Constitution imposes no obligation on the States to pay the pregnancy-related medical expenses of indigent women, or indeed to pay any of the medical expenses of indigents.[5] But when a State decides to alleviate some of the hardships of poverty by providing medical care, the manner in which it dispenses benefits is subject to constitutional limitations. * * *

"This case involves no discrimination against a suspect class. An indigent woman desiring an abortion does not come within the limited category of disadvantaged classes so recognized by our cases. Nor does the fact that the impact of the regulation falls upon those who cannot pay lead to a different conclusion. In a sense, every denial of welfare to an indigent creates a wealth classification as compared to nonindigents who are able to pay for the desired goods or services. But this Court has never held that financial need alone identifies a suspect [class]. See *Rodriguez; Dandridge.*[6] Accordingly, the central question in this case is whether the regulation 'impinges upon a fundamental right explicitly or implicitly protected by the Constitution.' "

In reasoning that "the Connecticut regulation places no obstacles—absolute or otherwise—in the pregnant woman's path to an abortion" the Court also found that "appellees' reliance on the penalty analysis of *Shapiro* and *Maricopa* is misplaced.[8]"

In rejecting the Court's distinction between a state's direct interference with a fundamental right and encouraging an alternative activity, BRENNAN, J., joined by Marshall and Blackmun, JJ., dissenting, added that "First Amendment decisions have consistently held [that] the compelling state interest test is applicable not only to outright denials but also to restraints that make exercise of those rights more difficult. See, e.g., *Sherbert.* [The] compelling state interest test has been applied in voting cases, even where only relatively small infringements upon voting power, such as dilution of voting strength caused by malapportionment, have been involved. [The] Connecticut scheme cannot be distin-

---

5. [Because] Connecticut has made no attempt to monopolize the means for terminating pregnancies through abortion the present case is easily distinguished from *Boddie.* [Does this similarly distinguish *Harper* and *Lubin v. Panish*?]

6. [*Griffin* and *Douglas*] are grounded in the criminal justice system, a governmental monopoly in which participation is compelled. Cf. n. 5, supra. Our subsequent decisions have made it clear that the principles underlying *Griffin* and *Douglas* do not extend to legislative classifications generally.

[For incisive comparison of *Maher* with *Griffin* and *Douglas* —and with *Shapiro* (see fn. 8 infra)—see Brudno, *Wealth Discrimination in the Supreme Court: Equal Protection for the Poor from Griffin to Maher,* in Constitutional Government in America 229 (Collins ed. 1980).]

8. * * * Penalties are most familiar to the criminal law, where criminal sanctions are imposed as a consequence of proscribed conduct. *Shapiro* and *Maricopa* recognized that denial of welfare to one who had recently exercised the right to travel across state lines was sufficiently analogous to a criminal fine to justify strict judicial scrutiny.

If Connecticut denied general welfare benefits to all women who had obtained abortions and who were otherwise entitled to the benefits, we would have a close analogy to the facts in *Shapiro,* and strict scrutiny might be [appropriate]. But the claim here is that the State "penalizes" the woman's decision to have an abortion by refusing to pay for it. *Shapiro* and *Maricopa* did not hold that States would penalize the right to travel interstate by refusing to pay the bus fares of the indigent travelers. We find no support in the right to travel cases for the view that Connecticut must show a compelling interest for its decision not to fund elective abortions.

Sherbert v. Verner, [p. 766 supra], similarly is inapplicable here. In addition, that case was decided in the significantly different context of a constitutionally imposed "governmental obligation of neutrality" originating in [the] Religion Clauses of the First Amendment.

guished from other grants and withholdings of financial benefits that we have held unconstitutionally burdened a fundamental right.[a] [The] governing principle is the same [as in *Sherbert*], for Connecticut grants and withholds financial benefits in a manner that discourages significantly the exercise of a fundamental constitutional right. Indeed, the case for application of the principle actually is stronger than in *Sherbert* since appellees are all indigents and therefore even more vulnerable to the financial pressures imposed by the Connecticut regulations."

MARSHALL, J., dissented: "[*Rodriguez*] stated a test for analyzing discrimination on the basis of wealth that would, if fairly applied here, strike down the regulations. The Court there held that a wealth discrimination claim is made out by persons ['who] because of their impecunity [are] completely unable to pay for some desired benefit, and as a consequence [sustain] an absolute deprivation of a meaningful opportunity to enjoy that benefit.' Medicaid recipients are, almost by definition, 'completely unable to pay for' abortions, and are thereby completely denied 'a meaningful opportunity' to obtain them.[6]"

(d) Whatever the scope of "strict scrutiny" for de facto discriminations against (or among) poor people, does *Rodriguez* restrict the analysis to state action that imposes "payment requirements"? See *Jefferson v. Hackney* (1972), fn. a in *Washington v. Davis*, Sec. 2, III supra.

2. *"Implicitly guaranteed" rights.* (a) Apart from any issue of wealth discrimination, does *Rodriguez* suggest that there may be a "constitutional right" to a *minimum* education? E.g., must a state provide *some* meaningful education to mentally retarded children? To non-English speaking children?

a. Does the Connecticut regulation "discriminate against," rather than simply "burden," a fundamental right? Is there a constitutional difference? See note 1 after *Shapiro*, Part II supra. Consider 91 Harv.L.Rev. 144 (1977): "It can hardly be [that] the state could provide a free forum for indigents' speech only on the condition that no unpopular views be espoused, even though this policy would deny only the specific costs of exercising disfavored speech rights. Similarly, it is difficult to imagine that the Court would uphold a policy of providing free justices of the peace for intraracial but not racially mixed marriages, thereby declining to pay the specific costs of a disfavored but constitutionally protected union, notwithstanding that the state has merely made intraracial marriage a more attractive alternative without creating an obstacle to private marriage opportunities."

See also Brennan, J., dissenting in *Harris v. McRae* (1980), p. 182 supra (which relied on *Maher* to sustain denial of medicaid even for "medically necessary" abortions): "Whether the State withholds only the special costs of a disfavored option or penalizes the individual more broadly for the manner in which she exercises her choice, it cannot interfere with a constitutionally protected decision through the coercive use of governmental largess."

Did *Dandridge* uphold a policy of providing welfare to indigent parents only for sustaining four children and no more? If so, is the law in *Maher* distinguishable?

6. Application of the flexible equal protection standard [urged in Marshall, J.'s *Rodriguez* dissent] would allow the Court to strike down the regulations in these cases without calling into question laws funding public education or English language teaching in public schools. [See the majority's discussion of this point at p. 183 supra.] By permitting a court to weigh all relevant factors, the flexible standard does not logically require acceptance of any equal protection claim that is "identical in principle" under the traditional approach to those advanced here.

[Is there any way other than use of a "flexible equal protection standard" to distinguish *Maher* from the problems raised by the majority in respect to *Meyer* and *Pierce*? Consider Perry, *The Abortion Funding Cases: A Comment on the Supreme Court's Role in American Government*, 66 Geo.L.J. 1191, 1199–1200 (1978): "One need not disapprove of private schools to acknowledge the wisdom of providing free, public education. [But the state's decision in *Maher*] is recognizable solely as a disapproval of and an effort to discourage abortion." See also Perry, *Why the Supreme Court Was Plainly Wrong in the Hyde Amendment Case: A Brief Comment on Harris v. McRae*, 32 Stan.L.Rev. 1113 (1980). Tribe, *American Constitutional Law* 933 n. 77 (1978). Compare Fahy, *The Abortion Funding Cases: A Response to Professor Perry*, 67 Geo.L.J. 1205 (1979).]

See Note, *The Constitutional Right of Bilingual Children to an Equal Educational Opportunity,* 47 So.Cal.L.Rev. 943 (1974).

(b) PLYLER v. DOE, 457 U.S. 202, 102 S.Ct. 2382, 72 L.Ed.2d 786 (1982), per BRENNAN, J., held that a Texas statute (§ 21.031) denying free public education to illegal alien children violated equal protection: "Persuasive arguments support the view that a State may withhold its beneficience from those whose very presence within the United States is the product of their own unlawful conduct. [But the children] in these cases 'can affect neither their parents' conduct nor their own status.' *Trimble v. Gordon,* [Sec. 3, III supra]. Even if the State found it expedient to control the conduct of adults by acting against their children, legislation directing the onus of a parent's misconduct against his children does not comport with fundamental conceptions of justice. * * * *Weber v. Aetna Casualty & Surety Co.* [Sec. 3, III supra].

"We reject the claim that 'illegal aliens' are a 'suspect class.' [U]ndocumented status is not irrelevant to any proper legislative goal. Nor is [it] an absolutely immutable characteristic since it is the product of conscious, indeed unlawful, action. But § 21.031 [imposes] its discriminatory burden on the basis of a legal characteristic over which children can have little control. It is thus difficult to conceive of a rational justification for penalizing these children for their presence within the United States. * * *

"Public education is not a 'right' granted to individuals by the Constitution. *Rodriguez.* But neither is it merely some governmental 'benefit' indistinguishable from other forms of social welfare legislation. Both the importance of education in maintaining our basic institutions, and the lasting impact of its deprivation on the life of the child, mark the distinction. [We] cannot ignore the significant social costs borne by our Nation when select groups are denied the means to absorb the values and skills upon which our social order rests.[20] [Thus], the discrimination contained in § 21.031 can hardly be considered rational unless it furthers some substantial goal of the State.

" * * * Faced with an equal protection challenge respecting the treatment of aliens, we agree that the courts must be attentive to congressional policy; the exercise of congressional power might well affect the State's prerogatives to afford differential treatment to a particular class of aliens. [But] there is no indication that the disability imposed by § 21.031 corresponds to any identifiable congressional policy. The State does not claim that the conservation of state educational resources was ever a congressional concern in restricting immigration. More importantly, the classification reflected in § 21.031 does not operate harmoniously within the federal program. [In] light of the discretionary federal power to grant relief from deportation, a State cannot realistically determine that any particular undocumented child will in fact be deported until after deportation proceedings have been completed. It would of course be most difficult for the State to justify a denial of education to a child enjoying an inchoate federal permission to remain.

"We are reluctant to impute to Congress the intention to withhold from these children, for so long as they are present in this country through no fault of their own, access to a basic education. In other contexts, undocumented status, coupled with some articulable federal policy, might enhance State authority with respect to the treatment of undocumented aliens. But in the area of special

---

20. * * * Whatever the current status of these children, the courts below concluded that many will remain here permanently and that some indeterminate number will eventually become citizens. * * *

constitutional sensitivity presented by this case, and in the absence of any contrary indication fairly discernible in the present legislative record, we perceive no national policy that supports the State in denying these children an elementary education.[a] [We] therefore turn to the state objectives that are said to support § 21.031. * * *

"First, appellants appear to suggest that the State may seek to protect the State from an influx of illegal immigrants. While a State might have an interest in mitigating the potentially harsh economic effects of sudden shifts in population, [t]here is no evidence in the record suggesting that illegal entrants impose any significant burden on the State's economy. To the contrary, the available evidence suggests that illegal aliens underutilize public services, while contributing their labor to the local economy and tax money to the State fisc. The dominant incentive for illegal entry [into] Texas is the availability of employment; few if any illegal immigrants come to this country [to] avail themselves of a free education. * * *

"Second, [appellants] suggest that undocumented children are appropriately singled out for exclusion because of the special burdens they impose on the State's ability to provide high quality public education. But the record in no way supports the claim [and], even if improvement in the quality of education were a likely result of barring some *number* of children from the schools of the State, the State must support its selection of *this* group as the appropriate target for exclusion. In terms of educational cost and need, however, undocumented children are 'basically indistinguishable' from legally resident alien children.

"Finally, appellants suggest that undocumented children are appropriately singled out because their unlawful presence within the United States renders them less likely than other children to remain within the boundaries of the State, and to put their education to productive social or political use within the State. Even assuming that such an interest is legitimate, it is an interest that is most difficult to quantify. The State has no assurance that any child, citizen or not, will employ the education provided by the State within the confines of the State's borders. In any event, the record is clear that many of the undocumented children disabled by this classification will remain in this country indefinitely, and that some will become lawful residents or citizens of the United States. It is difficult to understand precisely what the State hopes to achieve by promoting the creation and perpetuation of a subclass of illiterates within our boundaries, surely adding to the problems and costs of unemployment, welfare, and crime. It is thus clear that whatever savings might be achieved [are] wholly insubstantial in light of the costs involved to these children, the State, and the Nation."[b]

BLACKMUN, J., who joined the Court's opinion, concurred: "I joined [the] Court in *Rodriguez,* and I continue to believe that it provides the appropriate model for resolving most equal protection disputes. [But] I believe the Court's experience has demonstrated that the *Rodriguez* formulation does not settle every issue of 'fundamental rights' arising under the Equal Protection Clause.

a. For the view that "the Court should have followed the lead of *Toll v. Moreno,* [Sec. 3, II supra], and used the Supremacy Clause" to hold the *Plyler* statute invalid because it was neither "sanctioned nor contemplated by Congress," see Choper, fn. i, Sec. 3, II supra, at 21–32. See also 96 Harv.L.Rev. 130 (1982). Compare Gerety, *Children in the Labyrinth:*

The Complexities of Plyler v. Doe, 44 U.Pitt.L. Rev. 379, 380–87 (1983).

b. Marshall, J., joined the Court's opinion but emphasized "that the facts of these cases demonstrate the wisdom of rejecting a rigidified approach to equal protection analysis, and of employing" his suggested approach in *Dandridge* and *Rodriguez.*

Only a pedant would insist that there are *no* meaningful distinctions among the multitude of social and political interests regulated by the States * * *. Children denied an education are placed at a permanent and insurmountable competitive [disadvantage]. And when those children are members of an identifiable group, that group—through the State's action—will have been converted into a discrete underclass. Other benefits provided by the State, such as housing and public assistance, are of course important: to an individual in immediate need, they may be more desirable than the right to be educated. But classifications involving the complete denial of education are in a sense unique, for they strike at the heart of equal protection values by involving the State in the creation of permanent class distinctions. Cf. *Rodriguez* (Marshall, J., dissenting). In a sense, then, denial of an education is the analogue of denial of the right to vote: the former relegates the individual to second-class social status; the latter places him at a permanent political disadvantage.

"This conclusion is fully consistent with *Rodriguez*. The Court there reserved judgment on the constitutionality of a state system that 'occasioned an absolute denial of educational opportunities to any of its children,' noting that 'no charge fairly could be made that the system [at issue in *Rodriguez*] fails to provide each child with an opportunity to acquire * * * basic minimal skills.' [In] such circumstances, the voting decisions suggest that the State must offer something more than a rational basis for its classification."

POWELL, J., who joined the Court's opinion, concurred "to emphasize the unique character of the case": "Although the analogy is not perfect, our holding today does find support in decisions of this Court with respect to the status of illegitimates. [Thus,] review in a case such as this is properly heightened. [These children] have been singled out for a lifelong penalty and stigma. A legislative classification that threatens the creation of an underclass of future citizens and residents cannot be reconciled with one of the fundamental purposes of the Fourteenth Amendment. In these unique circumstances, the Court properly may require that the State's interests be substantial and that the means bear a 'fair and substantial relation' to these interests.[3]"

BURGER, C.J., joined by White, Rehnquist and O'Connor, JJ., dissented: "[B]y patching together bits and pieces of what might be termed quasi-suspect-class and quasi-fundamental-rights analysis, the Court spins out a theory custom-tailored to the facts [and its] opinion rests on such a unique confluence of theories and rationales that it will likely stand for little beyond the results in these particular [cases].[c]

"[I]n some circumstances persons generally, and children in particular, may have little control over or responsibility for such things as their ill health, need for public assistance, or place of residence. Yet a state legislature is not barred from considering, for example, relevant differences between the mentally-healthy and the mentally-ill, or between the residents of different counties,[5]

---

3. [I]n *Rodriguez* no group of children was singled out by the State and then penalized because of their parents' status. [Nor] was any group of children totally deprived of all education as in this case. If the resident children of illegal aliens were denied welfare assistance, made available by government to all other children who qualify, this also—in my opinion—would be an impermissible penalizing of children because of their parents' status.

c. See generally Hutchinson, *More Substantive Equal Protection? A Note on Plyler v. Doe,* 1982 Sup.Ct.Rev. 167.

5. Appellees "lack control" over their illegal residence in this country in the same sense as lawfully resident children lack control over the school district in which their parents reside. Yet in *Rodriguez,* [t]here was no suggestion [that] a child's "lack of responsibility" for his residence in a particular school simply because these may be factors unrelated to individual choice or to any 'wrongdoing.' The Equal Protection Clause protects against arbitrary and irrational classifications, and against invidious discrimination stemming from prejudice and hostility; it is not an all-encompassing 'equalizer' designed to eradicate every distinction for which persons are not 'responsible.' * * *[d]

"The Court's analogy to cases involving discrimination against illegitimate children is grossly misleading. The State has not thrust any disabilities upon appellees due to their 'status of birth.' Cf. *Weber*. Rather, appellees' status is predicated upon the circumstances of their concededly illegal presence in this [country].

"The central question in these cases, as in every equal protection case not involving truly fundamental rights 'explicitly or implicitly guaranteed by the Constitution,' *Rodriguez*, is whether there is some legitimate basis for a legislative distinction between different classes of persons. The fact that the distinction is drawn in legislation affecting access to public education—as opposed to legislation allocating other important governmental benefits, such as public assistance, health care, or housing—cannot make a difference in the level of scrutiny applied.

"Once it is conceded—as the Court does—that illegal aliens are not a suspect class, and that education is not a fundamental right, our inquiry should focus on and be limited to whether the legislative classification at issue bears a rational relationship to a legitimate state purpose. [I]t simply is not 'irrational' for a State to conclude that it does not have the same responsibility to provide benefits for persons whose very presence in the State and this country is illegal as it does to provide for persons lawfully present. * * *

"It is significant that the federal government has seen fit to exclude illegal aliens from numerous social welfare [programs]. Although these exclusions do not conclusively demonstrate the constitutionality of the State's use of the same classification for comparable purposes, at the very least they tend to support the rationality of excluding illegal alien residents of a State from such programs so as to preserve the State's finite revenues for the benefit of lawful residents. * * *

"Denying a free education to illegal alien children is not a choice I would make were I a legislator. Apart from compassionate considerations, the long-range costs of excluding any children from the public schools may well outweigh the costs of educating them. But [the] fact that there are sound *policy* arguments against the Texas legislature's choice does not render that choice an unconstitutional one. [While] the 'specter of a permanent caste' of illegal Mexican residents of the United States is indeed a disturbing one, it is but one segment of a larger problem, which is for the political branches to solve."

3. *Classifications affecting "constitutional" rights.* Are the following statutory classifications subject to "strict scrutiny":

(a) *Travel.* Denying driver's licenses to "drug addicts" but not "alcoholics"? Limiting state scholarships to students who graduate from the state's own high

district had any relevance to the proper standard of review of his [claims.]

d. Compare Choper, supra, at 29: "Although it is true that the children in *Rodriguez* had no effective choice as to where they lived, the statute in *Plyler* [is] much more stigmatizing. It [says] to a class of children that they are no good; that even though what is wrong with them is something over which they have no control, the state is going to penalize them nonetheless. I think [this] provided an effective doctrinal hook on which the Court could have more explicitly hung its decision."

schools? Providing highways, streets and public transport facilities of differing quality throughout the state?

(b) *Privacy.* Forbidding private use of certain euphoric substances but not others (marijuana but not liquor)? Denying state financial aid to "caretakers" of needy children if the caretaker lives with his or her spouse?

(c) *Criminal justice.* Granting a preliminary hearing to defendants charged by information but not to those indicted by a grand jury? Granting a jury trial for petty offenses only in certain counties or for certain offenses? Requiring a unanimous jury verdict to convict only in capital cases? See *Johnson v. Louisiana,* 406 U.S. 356, 92 S.Ct. 1620, 32 L.Ed.2d 152 (1972). Commuting the death sentences of persons tried under a statute held unconstitutional but subjecting persons not yet tried to the newly enacted capital offense statute? See *Dobbert v. Florida,* 432 U.S. 282, 97 S.Ct. 2290, 53 L.Ed.2d 344 (1977). Granting appeal as of right only for some misdemeanors? Dismissing appeals of convicted felons who escape while their appeals are pending and who do not voluntarily surrender within ten days of the escape? See *Estelle v. Dorrough,* 420 U.S. 534, 95 S.Ct. 1173, 43 L.Ed.2d 377 (1975). Affording extensive procedures prior to civil commitments only for some classes of persons—e.g., not for those who are ending a prison term (see *Baxstrom v. Herold,* 383 U.S. 107, 86 S.Ct. 760, 15 L.Ed.2d 620 (1966)); or for those who have just been found not guilty because of insanity (see Note, 1974 Wis.L.Rev. 1203); or for those found incompetent to stand trial (see *Jackson v. Indiana,* 406 U.S. 715, 92 S.Ct. 1845, 32 L.Ed.2d 435 (1972))? Denying persons "good-time credit" toward parole eligibility for imprisonment between conviction and sentence? See *McGinnis v. Royster,* 410 U.S. 263, 93 S.Ct. 1055, 35 L.Ed.2d 282 (1973).

4. *Standards of equal protection review.* (a) Do *Plyler* and Marshall, J.'s *Rodriguez* dissent demonstrate that the Court "has applied a spectrum of standards" as to "the degree of care with which it will scrutinize particular classifications"? See also fns. e and f following *New Orleans v. Dukes,* Sec. 1 supra; *Cleburne,* Sec. 3, V supra.[a]

(b) UNITED STATES DEP'T OF AGRICULTURE v. MORENO, 413 U.S. 528, 93 S.Ct. 2821, 37 L.Ed.2d 782 (1973), per BRENNAN, J., applying " 'traditional' equal protection analysis," held that a provision of the Food Stamp Act—excluding "any household containing an individual who is unrelated to any other member of the household"—was "wholly without any rational basis": It "is clearly irrelevant to the stated purposes of the Act [which are to] raise levels of nutrition among low-income households. [Thus], the challenged classification must rationally further some legitimate governmental interest other than those specifically stated in the congressional 'declaration of policy.'

"[The] little legislative history [that] does exist" indicates that the provision "was intended to [prevent] 'hippie communes' from participating in the food

a. For analysis urging that the Court use three levels of equal protection review and "should validate a statute [that "limits the exercise of a fundamental right by a class of persons"] only if the means used bear a factually demonstrable relationship to a state interest capable of withstanding analysis," see Nowak, *Realigning the Standard of Review Under the Equal Protection Guarantee—Prohibited, Neutral, and Permissive Classifications,* 62 Geo.L.J. 1071 (1974): "The Court will scrutinize the factual support for the legisla-

tion to determine whether its ends are capable of withstanding analysis and whether its means are rationally related to that end."

For analysis urging that the Court weigh the "*nature* of the affected interest" and the "*magnitude* of disadvantage" against the "*nature* of the state's interest" and the "relationship between *means and ends,*" see Simson, *A Method for Analyzing Discriminatory Effects Under the Equal Protection Clause,* 29 Stan.L. Rev. 663 (1977).

stamp program. [But equal protection] at the very least mean[s] that a bare congressional desire to harm a politically unpopular group cannot constitute a *legitimate* governmental interest." Nor does the classification "operate so as rationally to further the prevention of fraud" because, under the Act, "two *unrelated* persons living together" may "avoid the 'unrelated person' exclusion simply by altering their living arrangements so as [to] create two separate 'households,' both of which are eligible for assistance. [Thus], in practical operation, the [provision] excludes from participation [not] those persons who are 'likely to abuse the program' but, rather, only those persons who are so desperately in need of aid that they cannot even afford to alter their living arrangements so as to retain their eligibility."

DOUGLAS, J., concurred: "I could not say that [this] provision has no 'rational' relation to control of fraud. We deal here, however, with the right of association, protected by the First Amendment." Thus, the classification "can be sustained only on a showing of a 'compelling' governmental interest."

REHNQUIST, J., joined by Burger, C.J., dissented: "Congress attacked the problem with a rather blunt instrument, [b]ut I do not think it is unreasonable for Congress to conclude that the basic unit which it was willing to support [with] food stamps is some variation on the family as we know it—a household consisting of related individuals. This unit provides a guarantee which is not provided by households containing unrelated individuals that the household exists for some purpose other than to collect federal food stamps.

"Admittedly, [the] limitation will make ineligible many households which have not been formed for the purpose of collecting federal food stamps, and will [not] wholly deny food stamps to those households which may have been formed in large part to take advantage of the program. But, as the Court concedes, 'traditional' equal protection analysis does not require that every classification be drawn with precise mathematical nicety." [b]

(c) MATHEWS v. de CASTRO, 429 U.S. 181, 97 S.Ct. 431, 50 L.Ed.2d 389 (1976), per STEWART, J., relying on *Dandridge,* upheld a provision of the Social Security Act, granting benefits for a minor or dependent child in her care, to the wife (but not to the divorced former wife) of a man who is retired or disabled: "To be sure, the standard by which legislation ["providing for governmental payments of monetary benefits"] must be judged 'is not a toothless one,' *Mathews v. Lucas,* [Sec. 3, III supra]. But the challenged statute is entitled to a strong presumption of constitutionality. * * * Congress could have rationally assumed that divorced husbands and wives depend less on each other for financial and other support than do couples who stay married." Marshall, J., concurred in the judgment.

---

b. See also 87 Harv.L.Rev. 130–33 (1973): "Congress could reasonably believe that many unrelated households are comprised of ostensibly low-income students and 'voluntary poor' who actually have alternative sources of food money. [Further], Congress could rationally find that either letting the abuse continue or trying to keep truly needy unrelated households in the program would draw too much money away from other needy persons who are not in the class containing the large number of abusers. [Thus], the Court's unacknowledged application of a stricter rationality test suggests that *Moreno* marks a significant if hardly definitive break with the tradition of deference toward welfare and other socioeconomic legislation."

For invalidation of another Food Stamp Act provision, but on a different constitutional theory, see *United States Dep't of Agriculture v. Murry,* Sec. 5 infra.

SECTION 5. IRREBUTTABLE PRESUMPTIONS

A series of decisions in the early 1970s held that "permanent irrebuttable presumptions," which "have long been disfavored under the Due Process Clause," violated "procedural due process," *Vlandis,* infra. But, as the materials indicate, since the analysis of these cases is strikingly similar to the "fundamental rights" branch of equal protection, they are usefully studied here.

VLANDIS v. KLINE, 412 U.S. 441, 93 S.Ct. 2230, 37 L.Ed.2d 63 (1973): Connecticut imposed higher state university tuition on nonresidents. The Court, per STEWART, J., invalidated the statutory conclusive presumption that because the legal address of a student, if married, was outside the state at the time of application or, if unmarried, was outside the state at any point during the preceding year, he remains a nonresident for this purpose during the entire period of attendance at the university:

"*Bell v. Burson,* 402 U.S. 535, 91 S.Ct. 1586, 29 L.Ed.2d 90 (1971), involved a Georgia statute which provided that if an uninsured motorist was involved in an accident and could not post security for the amount of damages claimed, his driver's license must be suspended * * *. The Court held that since the State purported to be concerned with fault in suspending a driver's license, it could not, consistent with procedural due process, conclusively presume fault from the fact that the uninsured motorist was involved in an accident, and could not, therefore, suspend his driver's license without a hearing on that crucial factor.

"Likewise, in *Stanley v. Illinois,* 405 U.S. 645, 92 S.Ct. 1208, 31 L.Ed.2d 551 (1972), the Court [struck] Illinois' irrebuttable statutory presumption that all unmarried fathers are unqualified to raise their children. [T]he statute required the State, upon the death of the mother, to take custody of all such illegitimate [children]. It may be, the Court said, 'that most unmarried fathers are unsuitable and neglectful parents. [But] all unmarried fathers are not in this category; some are wholly suited to have custody of their children.' Hence, [the state] was required by the Due Process Clause to provide a hearing on that [issue].

"The same considerations obtain here. [S]ince Connecticut purports to be concerned with residency [it] is forbidden by the Due Process Clause to deny an individual the resident rates on the basis of a permanent and irrebuttable presumption of nonresidence, when that presumption is not necessarily or universally true in [fact]. Rather, standards of due process require that the State allow such an individual the opportunity to present evidence showing that he is a bona fide resident entitled to the in-state rates. [Our] holding today should in no wise [be] construed to deny a State the right to impose on a student, as one element in demonstrating bona fide residence, a reasonable durational residency requirement, which can be met while in student status.[9]" [a]

---

9. In *Starns v. Malkerson,* 326 F.Supp. 234 (D.Minn.1970), the District Court upheld a regulation of the University of Minnesota providing that no student could qualify as a resident for tuition purposes unless he had been a bona fide domiciliary of the State for at least a year immediately prior thereto. This Court affirmed summarily. [In] *Starns,* a student who applied to the University from out of State could rebut the presumption of nonresidency, after having lived in the State for one

year, by presenting sufficient other evidence to show bona fide domicile within Minnesota. * * *

[Marshall, J., joined by Brennan, J., joined the *Vlandis* opinion, except for "serious question as to the validity of [*Starns*] in light of" *Dunn* and *Shapiro,* Sec. 4, II supra].

a. White, J., concurred in the judgment on the ground that "this bizarre pattern of discrimination [is] invidious and violates" equal

BURGER, C.J., joined by Rehnquist, J., dissented: "[T]he Court applies 'strict scrutiny' [without] explaining why the statute impairs a genuine constitutional interest. [A]t least [*Stanley*] essayed to explain that the rights of fatherhood and family were regarded as 'essential' and 'basic civil rights of man.' [*Burson*] noted that revocation of a driver's license might impair the pursuit of a livelihood, thereby infringing 'important interests of the licensees.' [L]iterally thousands of state statutes create classifications permanent in duration, which are less than perfect, as all legislative classifications are, and might be improved on by individualized determinations so as to avoid the untoward results produced here due to the very unusual facts of this case. [F]or example, a State provides that a person may not be licensed to practice medicine or law unless he or she is a graduate of an accredited professional graduate school; a perfectly capable practitioner may as a consequence be barred 'permanently and irrebuttably' from pursuing his calling, without ever having an opportunity to prove his personal skills. [T]oday the Court makes an unchartered drift toward complications for the Due Process Clause comparable in scope and seriousness with those we are encountering in the equal protection area." [a]

UNITED STATES DEP'T OF AGRICULTURE v. MURRY, 413 U.S. 508, 93 S.Ct. 2832, 37 L.Ed.2d 767 (1974), per DOUGLAS, J., invalidated a federal statute that "any household which includes a member who has reached his eighteenth birthday and who is claimed as a dependent child for federal income tax purposes by a taxpayer who is not a member of an eligible household, shall be ineligible to participate in any food stamp program [during] the tax period such dependency is claimed and for a period of one year after the expiration of such tax period." The provision, a product of congressional concern about non-needy households participating in the food stamp program—and particularly about abuses of the program by "college students; children of wealthy parents"— created "an irrebuttable presumption often contrary to fact. It therefore lacks critical ingredients of due process found wanting in *Vlandis, Stanley,* and *Burson.*" [b]

CLEVELAND BD. OF EDUC. v. LaFLEUR, 414 U.S. 632, 94 S.Ct. 791, 39 L.Ed.2d 52 (1974), per STEWART, J., invalidated school board rules requiring pregnant teachers to take leave without pay at least five months—or, in a companion case from Virginia, four months—before the expected date of birth: "This Court has long recognized that freedom of personal choice in matters of marriage and family life is one of the liberties protected by [due process. The] provisions amount to a conclusive presumption that every pregnant teacher who reaches the fifth or sixth month of pregnancy is physically incapable of continuing. There is no individualized determination by the teacher's doctor—or the

protection: "[A]s the Court's assessment of the weight and value of the individual interest escalates, the less likely it is that mere administrative convenience and avoidance of hearings or investigations will be sufficient to justify what otherwise would appear to be irrational discriminations."

a. Rehnquist, J., joined by Burger, C.J., and Douglas, J., also dissented.

Compare Burger, C.J.'s opinion for the Court in *Jimenez v. Weinberger* —discussed in

Mathews v. Lucas, Sec. 3, III supra—using an irrebuttable presumption-like rationale to hold a discrimination against some classes of illegitimate children violative of equal protection. Rehnquist, J., dissented.

b. Stewart and Marshall, JJ., joined the Court's opinion, but also concurred separately. Rehnquist, J., joined by Burger, C.J., and Powell, J., dissented; Blackmun, J., also dissented.

school board's—as to any particular teacher's ability to continue at her job. [Because] the conclusive presumption [like] that in *Vlandis* [and *Stanley*], is neither 'necessarily nor universally true,' [it] is violative of the Due Process Clause [13] [which] requires the school boards to employ alternative administrative means, which do not so broadly infringe upon basic constitutional liberty, in support of their legitimate goals." [c]

REHNQUIST, J., joined by Burger, C.J., dissented from Stewart, J.'s enlisting "the Court in another quixotic engagement in his apparently unending war on irrebuttable presumptions. [All] legislation involves the drawing of lines, and the drawing of lines necessarily results in particular individuals who are disadvantaged by the line drawn being virtually indistinguishable for many purposes from those individuals who benefit from the legislative classification. The Court's disenchantment with 'irrebutable presumptions,' and its preference for 'individualized determination,' is in the last analysis nothing less than an attack upon the very notion of lawmaking itself."

Notes and Questions

1. *"Type" of due process.* (a) Is the "irrebuttable presumption" doctrine grounded in *procedural* or *substantive* due process? Consider Note, *The Conclusive Presumption Doctrine: Equal Process or Due Protection?*, 72 Mich.L.Rev. 800, 824 (1974): "The [cases] appear to be purely substantive in nature. First, the appellees admitted that the relevant statutory provisions had been properly applied [and], in effect, challenged the legislative fact-finding and demanded that new issues be made relevant. In essence, the Court required that the states extend benefits to those in the appellees' class; in procedural cases the Court does not expand the class of people entitled to receive the benefit but only deals with what procedures are necessary when affecting that interest." [d]

(b) Are the "irrebuttable presumption" cases limited to securing rights that are "explicitly or implicitly guaranteed by the Constitution" (*Rodriguez* Sec. 4, IV supra)—e.g., travel (*Vlandis*), procreation (*Stanley, LaFleur*), association (*Murry*)? Consider Bezanson, *Some Thoughts on the Emerging Irrebuttable Presumption Doctrine,* 7 Ind.L.Rev. 644, 652 (1974): "[The] doctrine seems to have substantive underpinnings, since it seems to be selectively applied to certain types of cases involving important, yet nonfundamental rights. *LaFleur* raised the difficult issue of whether sex-based discrimination is constitutionally suspect. *Vlandis* and *Murry* involved arguably new extensions of the right to travel, a matter which the Court may have preferred to leave untouched. *Stanley* was susceptible to analysis in terms of sex discrimination or the

---

13. [We] are not dealing in these cases with maternity leave regulations requiring a termination of employment at some firm date during the last few weeks of pregnancy. We therefore have no occasion to decide whether such regulations might be justified by considerations not presented in these records—for example, widespread medical consensus about the "disabling" effect of pregnancy on a teacher's job performance during these latter days, or evidence showing that such firm cutoffs were the only reasonable method of avoiding the possibility of labor beginning while some teacher was in the classroom, or proof that adequate substitutes could not be procured without at least some minimal lead [time].

c. Powell, J., concurred in the result because "these regulations are invalid under rational basis standards of equal protection review." Douglas, J., concurred in the result.

d. In any event, is it clear that procedural due process is not at issue because neither *Vlandis* nor *Murry* concerned "property interests"—i.e., "interests that a person has already acquired in specific benefits," or interests to which a person has a "legitimate claim of entitlement" (*Board of Regents v. Roth,* p. 594 supra)? See Note, 72 Mich.L.Rev. at 816–21.

fundamental rights of procreation, privacy, or the like. But selective application of the doctrine to these 'quasi-fundamental' rights or interests can only be gleaned from what the Court has decided in fact, since the Court has made little effort to distinguish or identify in principle the scope of the doctrine's application. Indeed, the value of the doctrine seems to lie in the fact that it permits the Court to avoid the difficult policy issues raised in the cases." [e]

2. *Similarity to equal protection.* To what extent is the "irrebuttable presumption" doctrine no more than a substitute for equal protection analysis? Consider Note, *The Irrebuttable Presumption Doctrine in the Supreme Court,* 87 Harv.L.Rev. 1534, 1552 (1974): "When an equal protection decision requires that persons previously excluded from a benefit must now be included, an additional cost is of course incurred. But this is a cost inherent in the state's decision to award a certain benefit to a group of individuals. [But] when the Court requires that a hearing be given, [the] cost does not represent only benefits supplied to a group of individuals, but also includes a transaction cost in determining who is to receive benefits. [It] may impose substantial costs which a legislature never contemplated and would never have been willing to bear. The choice of classification by a legislature represents a judgment—one that could hardly be called irrational—that the increased accuracy of adjudication is not worth the increased expenditure of time and money." Compare Note, 46 U.Colo.L.Rev. 79, 102 (1974): "[T]he consequence of [the irrebuttable presumption] analysis is not as harsh as invalidating a classification under the usual equal protection analysis, since [t]he state is still left with a rebuttable presumption that it can use to shift the burden to an individual to come forward to refute the presumption in his case. The Court does not have to make the difficult decision to abolish the classification by making the statute operate either on everyone or on no one." See also Bartlett, *Pregnancy and the Constitution: The Uniqueness Trap,* 62 Calif.L.Rev. 1532, 1545–47 (1974): "The irrebuttable presumption model does not give an individual as much protection [as] under the strict scrutiny test of the equal protection and substantive due process models. An individual may be left with the burden of showing what others need not show. [U]nder this model, a statute like that in *Frontiero,* [Sec. 3, III supra,] [might] have been upheld, even though servicemen received [the] benefits without proving spousal dependency. [Moreover,] this opportunity to prove that one should not be restricted in a certain way does not mean that the factor which gave rise to the challenged presumption such as pregnancy, may not be weighed heavily in determining whether that individual belongs in the restricted group. [The] Court did not insist that pregnant teachers be treated the same as teachers with other temporary disabilities. They could be forced to prove their fitness to teach in order to remain in the classroom, even though other potentially unfit or disabled teachers need not do so."

3. *Limits on the doctrine.* (a) *Marshall v. United States,* 414 U.S. 417, 94 S.Ct. 700, 38 L.Ed.2d 618 (1974), per Burger, C.J., held that the Narcotic Rehabilitation Act—which authorizes judges to order treatment in lieu of imprisonment for addicts convicted of a federal offense, but excludes persons with two or more prior felony convictions—was "rational" and not violative of equal protection. *Usery v. Turner Elkhorn Mining Co.,* 428 U.S. 1, 96 S.Ct. 2882, 49

e. For efforts to limit the "irrebuttable presumption" approach to special types of situations, see Marshall, J., fn. b supra; Tribe, *American Constitutional Law* 1092–97 (1978); Gordon & Tenenbaum, *Conclusive Presump-* *tion Analysis: The Principle of Individual Opportunity,* 71 Nw.U.L.Rev. 579 (1977); Chase, *The Premature Demise of Irrebuttable Presumptions,* 47 U.Colo.L.Rev. 653 (1976).

L.Ed.2d 752 (1976), per Marshall, J., held that the Federal Coal Mine Health and Safety Act—which presumes that a miner with pneumoconiosis is totally disabled and, if he dies, that his death was caused by this disease—was not "arbitrary and irrational" and thus not violative of due process. Both cases rejected irrebuttable presumption challenges. See also *N.Y.C. Transit Auth. v. Beazer,* Sec. 1 supra, finding "no merit" in such a challenge.

(b) To what extent does the doctrine survive *Salfi,* infra?

WEINBERGER v. SALFI
422 U.S. 749, 95 S.Ct. 2457, 45 L.Ed.2d 522 (1975).

MR. JUSTICE REHNQUIST delivered the opinion of the Court.

[Within a month of appellee's marriage, her husband, who was allegedly "in apparent good health at the time of the marriage," suffered a heart attack and died five months later. Appellee filed] for mother's insurance benefits for herself and child's insurance benefits for her daughter by a previous marriage [which] were denied [on] the basis of the duration-of-relationship requirements of [the Act which] exclude surviving wives and stepchildren who had their respective relationships to a deceased wage earner for less than nine months prior to his death. * * *

The standard for testing the validity of Congress' Social Security classification was clearly stated in *Flemming v. Nestor,* 363 U.S. 603, 611, 80 S.Ct. 1367, 1373, 4 L.Ed.2d 1435 (1960): "Particularly when we deal with a withholding of a noncontractual benefit under a social welfare [program], we must recognize that the Due Process Clause can be thought to interpose a bar only if the statute manifests a patently arbitrary classification, utterly lacking in rational justification." [The Court cited similar language from *Dandridge,* Sec. 4, IV supra.]

We hold that [*Stanley,* which "referred to the fact that the 'rights to conceive and to raise one's children have been deemed "essential,"'" *Vlandis,* and *LaFleur,* which stated "that freedom of personal choice in matters of marriage and family life is one of the liberties protected" by due process] are not controlling on the issue before us now. Unlike the claims involved in *Stanley* and *LaFleur,* a noncontractual claim to receive funds from the public treasury enjoys no constitutionally protected status,[a] *Dandridge,* though of course Congress may not invidiously discriminate among such claimants on the basis of a "bare congressional desire to harm a politically unpopular group," *U.S. Dep't of Agriculture v. Moreno,* [Sec. 4, IV supra], or on the basis of criteria which bear no rational relation to a legitimate legislative goal. *Jimenez; Murry.* Unlike the statutory scheme in *Vlandis,* the Social Security Act does not purport to speak in terms of the bona fides of the parties to a marriage, but then make plainly relevant evidence of such bona fides inadmissible. As in *Starns,* [appellants] are completely free to present evidence that they meet the specified requirements; failing in this effort, their only constitutional claim is that the test they cannot meet is not so rationally related to a legitimate legislative objective that it can be used to deprive them of benefits available to those who do satisfy that test.

---

a. Consider Tribe, fn. e supra, at 1096: "*Salfi,* of course, did not involve the liberty interest in deciding whether, when, and whom to marry, because any claim that the duration-of-relationship rule in fact affected a particular marriage decision would in effect con- cede to the government the only issue to be addressed at any individualized hearing—i.e., whether the particular marriage was in fact entered into for purposes of obtaining social security benefits."

We think that the District Court's extension of the holdings of *Stanley, Vlandis* and *LaFleur* to the eligibility requirement in issue here would turn the doctrine of those cases into a virtual engine of destruction for countless legislative judgments which have heretofore been thought wholly consistent with [due process]. For example, the very section [which] authorizes an action such as this, [requires] that a claim be filed within 60 days after administrative remedies are exhausted. It is indisputable that this requirement places people who file their claims more than 60 days after exhaustion in a different "class" than people who file their claims within the time limit. If we were to follow the District Court's analysis, we would first try to ascertain the congressional "purpose" behind the provision, and probably would conclude that it was to prevent stale claims from being asserted in court. We would then turn to the question of whether such a flat cutoff provision was necessary to protect the Secretary from stale claims, whether it would be possible to make individualized determinations as to any prejudice suffered by the Secretary as the result of an untimely filing, and whether or not an individualized hearing on that issue should be required in each case. This would represent a degree of judicial involvement in the legislative function which we have eschewed except in the most unusual circumstances * * *.

In *Williamson v. Lee Optical Co.,* [Sec. 1 supra, the] Court said: "The problem of legislative classification is a perennial one, admitting of no doctrinaire definition. Evils in the same field may be of different dimensions and proportions, requiring different remedies. Or so the legislature may think."
* * *

If the Fifth and Fourteenth Amendments permit this latitude to legislative decisions regulating the private sector of the economy, they surely allow no less latitude in prescribing the conditions upon which funds shall be dispensed from the public treasury. *Dandridge* * * *.

Under those standards, the question raised is not whether a statutory provision precisely filters out those, and only those, who are in the factual position which generated the congressional concern reflected in the statute. Such a rule would ban all prophylactic [provisions]. Nor is the question whether the provision filters out a substantial part of the class which caused congressional concern, or whether it filters out more members of the class than nonmembers. The question is whether Congress, its concern having been reasonably aroused by the possibility of an abuse, [could] rationally have concluded both that a particular limitation or qualification would protect against its occurrence, and that the expense and other difficulties of individual determinations justified the inherent imprecision of a prophylactic rule. We conclude that the duration-of-relationship test meets this constitutional standard.

The danger of persons entering a marriage relationship not to enjoy its traditional benefits, but instead to enable one spouse to claim benefits upon the anticipated early death of the wage earner, has been recognized from the very beginning of the Social Security program. [The statute] undoubtedly excludes some surviving wives who married with no anticipation of shortly becoming widows, and it may be that appellee Salfi is among them. It likewise may be true that the requirement does not filter out every such claimant, if a wage earner lingers longer than anticipated, or in the case of illnesses which can be recognized as terminal more than nine months prior to death. But neither of these facts necessarily renders the statutory scheme unconstitutional.

While it is possible to debate the wisdom of excluding legitimate claimants in order to discourage sham relationships, and of relying on a rule which may not exclude some obviously sham arrangements, we think it clear that Congress could rationally choose to adopt such a course. Large numbers of people are eligible for these programs and are potentially subject to inquiry as to the validity of their relationships to wage earners. [Not] only does the prophylactic approach thus obviate the necessity for large number of individualized determinations, but it also protects large numbers of claimants who satisfy the rule from the uncertainties and delays of administrative inquiry into the circumstances of their marriages. Nor is it at all clear that individual determinations could effectively filter out sham arrangements, since neither marital intent, life expectancy nor knowledge of terminal illness has been shown by appellees to be reliably determinable. Finally, the very possibility of prevailing at a hearing could reasonably be expected to encourage sham relationships.

The administrative difficulties of individual eligibility determinations are without doubt matters which Congress may [consider]. In this sense, the duration-of-relationship requirement represents not merely a substantive policy determination that benefits should be awarded only on the basis of genuine marital relationships, but also a substantive policy determination that limited resources would not be well spent in making individual determinations. * * *

Reversed.

MR. JUSTICE BRENNAN, with whom MR. JUSTICE MARSHALL joins, dissenting.

[The] Court today distinguishes *Stanley* and *LaFleur* [because] both dealt with protected rights, while this case deals with "a noncontractual claim to receive funds from the public treasury [which] enjoys no constitutionally protected status." But *Vlandis* also dealt with a government benefit program. [The Court] attempts to wish away *Vlandis* by noting that "where Connecticut purported to be concerned with residency, it might not at the same time deny to one seeking to meet its test of residency the opportunity to show factors clearly bearing on the issue." [b]

Yet, the Connecticut statute in *Vlandis* did not set "residency," undefined, as the criteria of eligibility; it *defined* residency in certain ways. The definitions of "resident" were precisely parallel to the statute here, which defines "widow" and "child" in part by the number of months of marriage.

Similarly, *Murry* and *Jimenez* both dealt with conclusive presumptions contained in statutes setting out criteria for eligibility for government benefits. The Court distinguishes them as cases in which "the criteria bear no rational relation to a legitimate legislative goal." But if the assumptions in *Murry* and *Jimenez* were irrational, the presumption in this case is even more irrational. We have been presented with no evidence at all that the problem of collusive marriages is one which exists at all. Indeed, the very fact that Congress has continually moved back the amount of time required to avoid the irrebuttable presumption suggests that it found, for each time period set, that it was depriving deserving people of benefits without alleviating any real problem of

---

b. *Elkins v. Moreno*, 435 U.S. 647, 98 S.Ct. 1338, 55 L.Ed.2d 614 (1978), per Brennan, J.— involving "in-state" status for tuition at the University of Maryland—avoided "a decision on the continuing vitality of *Vlandis*." But *Turner v. Department of Employment Security*, 423 U.S. 44, 96 S.Ct. 249, 46 L.Ed.2d 181 (1975), per curiam, relied on *LaFleur* to invalidate a Utah law making "pregnant women ineligible for unemployment benefits for a period extending from 12 weeks before the expected date of childbirth until a date six weeks after childbirth." Burger, C.J., and Blackmun, J., would not have summarily disposed of the case. Rehnquist, J., dissented.

collusion. There is no reason to believe that the nine-month period is any more likely to discard a high proportion of collusive marriages than the five-year, three-year, or one-year periods employed earlier.

The Court says: "The administrative difficulties of individual eligibility determinations are without doubt matters which Congress may [consider]." But, as we said in *Stanley:* "[T]he Constitution recognizes higher values than speed and efficiency. * * *"

This is not to say [that] *all* statutory provisions based on assumptions about underlying facts are per se unconstitutional unless individual hearings are provided. But in this case, as in the others in which we have stricken down conclusive presumptions, it *is* possible to specify those factors which, if proven in a hearing, would disprove a rebuttable presumption. See, e.g., *Vlandis.* For example, persuasive evidence of good health at the time of marriage would be sufficient, I should think, to disprove that the marriage was collusive. Also, in this case, as in *Stanley* and *LaFleur,* the presumption, insofar as it precludes people as to whom the presumed fact is untrue from so proving, runs counter to the general legislative policy—here, providing true widows and children with survivors' benefits. And finally, the presumption here, like that in *Vlandis, Murry,* and *Jimenez,* involves a measure of social opprobrium; the assumption is that the individual has purposely undertaken to evade legitimate requirements. When these factors are present, I believe that the Government's interests in efficiency must be surrendered to the individual's interest in proving that the facts presumed are not true as to him. * * *[c]

　c.　The dissent of Douglas, J., is omitted.

Chapter 7

THE CONCEPT OF STATE ACTION

SECTION 1. INTRODUCTION

The "state action" doctrine has long established that, due to their language or history, most provisions of the Constitution that protect individual liberty—including those set forth in Art. 1, §§ 9 and 10, the Bill of Rights, and the fourteenth and fifteenth amendments—impose restrictions or obligations only on government. The subject received its first extensive treatment in the CIVIL RIGHTS CASES, 109 U.S. 3, 3 S.Ct. 18, 27 L.Ed. 835 (1883), which held, per BRADLEY, J., that neither the thirteenth nor fourteenth amendments empowered Congress to pass the Civil Rights Act of 1875, making racial discrimination unlawful in public accommodations (inns, public conveyances, places of public amusement, etc.)—"and no other ground of authority for its passage being suggested, it must necessarily be declared void." Although the issue presented did not simply concern the authority granted the *Court* under § 1 of the thirteenth and fourteenth amendments, but rather involved the scope of *Congress'* power under the final sections of these amendments to enforce their substantive provisions "by appropriate legislation" (a topic to be considered in detail in Ch. 12), the Court's discussion of "state action" remains the classic exposition of the doctrine.

The Court held that, under the fourteenth amendment, "it is state action of a particular character that is prohibited. Individual invasion of individual rights is not the subject-matter of the amendment. [It] nullifies and makes void all state legislation, and state action of every kind, which impairs the privileges and immunities of citizens of the United States, or which injures them in life, liberty, or property without due process of law, or which denies to any of them the equal protection of the laws. [T]he last section of the amendment invests congress with power [to] adopt appropriate legislation for correcting the effects of such prohibited state law and state acts, and thus to render them effectually null, void, and innocuous. [It] does not authorize congress to create a code of municipal law for the regulation of private rights; but to provide modes of redress against the operation of state laws, and the action of state officers, executive or judicial, when these are subversive of the fundamental rights specified in the amendment. * * *

"An inspection of the law shows that [it] proceeds ex directo to declare that certain acts committed by individuals shall be deemed offenses, and shall be prosecuted [by] the United States. It does not profess to be corrective of any

1076

constitutional wrong committed by the states; [it] applies equally to cases arising in states which have the justest laws respecting the personal rights of citizens, and whose authorities are ever ready to enforce such laws as to those which arise in states that may have violated the prohibition of the amendment. In other words, it steps into the domain of local jurisprudence, and lays down rules for the conduct of individuals in society towards each other * * *. [C]ivil rights, such as are guarantied by the constitution against state aggression, cannot be impaired by the wrongful acts of individuals, unsupported by state authority in the shape of laws, customs, or judicial or executive proceedings. The wrongful act of an individual, unsupported by any such authority, is simply a private wrong, or a crime of that individual * * *. An individual cannot deprive a man of his right to vote, to hold property, to buy and to sell, to sue in the courts, or to be a witness or a juror; he may, by force or fraud, interfere with the enjoyment of the right in a particular case; [but] unless protected in these wrongful acts by some shield of state law or state authority, he cannot destroy or injure the right; he will only render himself amenable to satisfaction or punishment; and amenable therefor to the laws of the state where the wrongful acts are committed. [The] abrogation and denial of rights, for which the states alone were or could be responsible, was the great seminal and fundamental wrong which was intended to be remedied."

The Court recognized that the thirteenth amendment "is not a mere prohibition of state laws establishing or upholding slavery, but an absolute declaration that slavery or involuntary servitude shall not exist in any part of the United States [and] that the power vested in congress to enforce the article by appropriate legislation, clothes congress with power to pass all laws necessary and proper for abolishing all badges and incidents of slavery, in the United States * * *. [T]he civil rights bill of 1866, passed in view of the thirteenth amendment, before the fourteenth was adopted, undertook to wipe out these burdens and disabilities, * * * namely, the same right to make and enforce contracts, to sue, be parties, give evidence, and to inherit, purchase, lease, sell, and convey property, as is enjoyed by white citizens. Whether this legislation was fully authorized by the thirteenth amendment alone, without the support which it afterwards received from the fourteenth amendment, after the adoption of which it was re-enacted with some additions, it is not necessary to inquire. It is referred to for the purpose of showing that at that time (in 1866) congress did not assume, under the authority given by the thirteenth amendment, to adjust what may be called the social rights of men and races in the community; but only to declare and vindicate those fundamental rights which appertain to the essence of citizenship, and the enjoyment or deprivation of which constitutes the essential distinction between freedom and slavery.

"[It] would be running the slavery argument into the ground to make it apply to every act of discrimination which a person may see fit to make as to the guests he will entertain, or as to the people he will take into his coach or cab or car, or admit to his concert or theater, or deal with in other matters of intercourse or business. Innkeepers and public carriers, by the laws of all the states, so far as we are aware, are bound, to the extent of their facilities, to furnish proper accommodation to all unobjectionable persons who in good faith apply for them. If the laws themselves make any unjust discrimination, amenable to the prohibitions of the fourteenth amendment, congress has full power to afford a remedy under that amendment and in accordance with it." [a]

a. In *Bell v. Maryland*, 378 U.S. 226, 84 S.Ct. 1814, 12 L.Ed.2d 822 (1964), Goldberg, J., joined by Warren, C.J., and Douglas, J., examining the "historical evidence" in detail, con-

HARLAN, J., dissented: "Was it the purpose of the nation [by the thirteenth amendment] simply to destroy the institution [of slavery], and remit the race, theretofore held in bondage, to the several states for such protection, in their civil rights, necessarily growing out of freedom, as those states, in their discretion, choose to provide? [S]ince slavery [was] the moving or principal cause of the adoption of that amendment, and since that institution rested wholly upon the inferiority, as a race, of those held in bondage, their freedom necessarily involved immunity from, and protection against, all discrimination against them, because of their race, in respect of such civil rights as belong to freemen of other races. Congress, therefore, under its express power to enforce that amendment, by appropriate legislation, may enact laws of a direct and primary character, operating upon states, their officers and agents, and also upon, at least, such individuals and corporations as exercise public functions and wield power and authority under the state. * * *

"It remains now to inquire what are the legal rights of colored persons in respect of the accommodations * * *.

"1. As to public conveyances on land and water. [In] *Olcott v. Sup'rs,* 16 Wall. 694, it was ruled that railroads [are] none the less public highways because controlled and owned by private corporations; that it is a part of the function of government to make and maintain highways for the conveyance of the public; that no matter who is the agent, and what is the agency, the function performed is *that of the state * * *.*

"Such being the relations these corporations hold to the public, it would seem that the right of a colored person to use an improved public highway, upon the terms accorded to freemen of other races, is as fundamental in the state of freedom, established in this country, as are any of the rights which my brethren concede to be so far fundamental as to be deemed the essence of civil freedom.

"2. As to inns. [The] authorities are sufficient to show that a keeper of an inn is in the exercise of a quasi public employment. The law gives him special privileges, and he is charged with certain duties and responsibilities to the public. The public nature of his employment forbids him from discriminating against any person asking admission as a guest on account of the race or color of that person.

"3. As to places of public amusement. [W]ithin the meaning of the act of 1875, [they] are such as are established and maintained under direct license of the law. [The] local government granting the license represents [the colored race] as well as all other races within its jurisdiction. A license from the public to establish a place of public amusement, imports, in law, equality of right, at such places, among all the members of that public.[b]"

cluded that the *Civil Rights Cases* were based on the assumption of the framers of the fourteenth amendment that "under state law, when the Negro's disability as a citizen was removed, he would be assured the same public civil rights that the law had guaranteed white persons," and that "the duties of the proprietors of places of public accommodation would remain as they had long been and that the States would now be affirmatively obligated to insure that these rights ran to Negro as well as white citizens." Black, J., joined by Harlan and White, JJ., disagreed. Cf. Tribe, *American Constitutional Law* 1152 n. 14 (1978). See generally Frank & Munro, *The Original Un-*

derstanding of "Equal Protection of the Laws," 1972 Wash.U.L.Q. 421, 468–72.

b. The position that such businesses cannot constitutionally discriminate has found modern support with Douglas, J., concurring in *Garner v. Louisiana,* 368 U.S. 157, 183–85, 82 S.Ct. 248, 261–63, 7 L.Ed.2d 207, 225–26 (1961) and *Lombard v. Louisiana,* 373 U.S. 267, 281–83, 83 S.Ct. 1122, 1129–30, 10 L.Ed.2d 338, 347–48 (1963). Compare *Moose Lodge v. Irvis,* Sec. 4 infra.

For general support of Harlan, J.'s thirteenth amendment view, see Kinoy, *The Constitutional Right of Negro Freedom,* 21 Rutg.L.

Turning to the fourteenth amendment, "the first clause of the first section— 'all persons born or naturalized in the United States, and subject to the jurisdiction thereof, are citizens of the United States, and of the state wherein they reside'—is of a distinctly affirmative character. In its application to the colored race, previously liberated, it created and granted, as well citizenship of the United States, as citizenship of the state in which they respectively resided. [Further], they were brought, by this supreme act of the nation, within the direct operation of that provision of the constitution which declares that 'the citizens of each state shall be entitled to all privileges and immunities of citizens in the several states.' Article IV, § 2.

"The citizenship thus acquired [may be protected] by congressional legislation of a primary direct character; this, because the power of congress is not restricted to the enforcement of prohibitions upon state laws or state action. It is, in terms distinct and positive, to enforce 'the *provisions of this article*' of amendment * * * *all* of the provisions,—affirmative and prohibitive * * *.

"But what was secured to colored citizens of the United States—as between them and their respective states—by the grant to them of state citizenship? With what rights, privileges, or immunities did this grant from the nation invest them? There is one, if there be no others—exemption from race discrimination in respect of any civil right belonging to citizens of the white race in the same state [by] the state, or its officers, or by individuals, or corporations exercising public functions or authority * * *. It was perfectly well known that the great danger to the equal enjoyment by citizens of their rights, as citizens, was to be apprehended, not altogether from unfriendly state legislation, but from the hostile action of corporations and individuals in the states. * * *

"But if it were conceded that the power of congress could not be brought into activity until the rights specified in the act of 1875 had been abridged or denied by some state law or state action, I maintain that the decision of the court is erroneous. [In] every material sense applicable to the practical enforcement of the fourteenth amendment, railroad corporations, keepers of inns, and managers of places of public amusement are agents of the state, because amenable, in respect of their public duties and functions, to public regulation. * * * I agree that if one citizen chooses not to hold social intercourse with another, he is not and cannot be made amenable to the law for his conduct in that regard; for no legal right of a citizen is violated by the refusal of others to maintain merely social relations with him, even upon grounds of race. [The] rights which congress, by the act of 1875, endeavored to secure and protect are legal, not social, rights. The right, for instance, of a colored citizen to use the accommodations of a public highway upon the same terms as are permitted to white citizens is no more a social right than his right, under the law, to use the public streets of a city, or a town, or a turnpike road, or a public market, or a post-office, or his right to sit in a public building with others, of whatever race, for the purpose of hearing the political questions of the day discussed."

The basic doctrine of the *Civil Rights Cases* —that it is "state action" that is prohibited by the fourteenth amendment—has remained undisturbed. But the

Rev. 387 (1967). Although the Court has since ruled that the thirteenth amendment grants broad enforcement power to *Congress* (see p. 1514 infra), the Court has confined its use of the amendment, absent congressional legislation, to holding state peonage laws invalid.

See *Memphis v. Greene*, p. 848 supra. For discussion of cases on what constitutes "slavery," "involuntary servitude," or "peonage" under the thirteenth amendment and federal enforcement statutes, see Shapiro, *Involuntary Servitude*, 19 Rutg.L.Rev. 65 (1964).

question of what constitutes "state action" has generated significant controversy. It is settled that the term comprehends statutes enacted by national, state and local legislative bodies and the official actions of all government officers. The more difficult problems arise when the conduct of private individuals or groups is challenged as being unconstitutional. Although—as will be pointed out in the materials that follow (see, e.g., note 7 after *Shelley v. Kraemer*, Sec. 3 infra)—it has often been argued that the inquiries are misperceived, the questions that the Court has asked are whether the private actor (a) is performing a "government function," or (b) is sufficiently "involved with" or "encouraged by" the state so as to be held to the state's constitutional obligations. These subjects will be developed in the next two sections of this chapter.

Until quite recently, most of the cases have involved racial discrimination (or, occasionally, denial of free speech). But, as will be detailed in Ch. 12, the enactment and strengthening of federal (and state) civil rights statutes in the past two decades has largely mooted the problem of private racial discrimination. Further, with the growth under the equal protection clause of the number of "suspect" and "quasi-suspect" classifications (see Ch. 6, Sec. 3) and the expansion under the due process clause of the procedural rights that the state must afford persons before depriving them of liberty or property (see Ch. 3, Sec. 5), an increasing number of cases (as will be seen in the final section of this chapter) have involved attempts to require "private" adherence to these constitutional responsibilities.

SECTION 2. "GOVERNMENT FUNCTION"

SMITH v. ALLWRIGHT, 321 U.S. 649, 64 S.Ct. 757, 88 L.Ed. 987 (1944), held the fifteenth amendment forebade exclusion of blacks from primary elections conducted by the Democratic Party of Texas, pursuant to party resolution. The Court, per REED, J., relied heavily on a case from Louisiana, *United States v. Classic* (1941), p. 1141 infra, which held "that Section 4 of Article I of the Constitution authorized Congress to regulate primary as well as general elections, 'where the primary is by law made an integral part of the election machinery.'" *Classic* "makes clear that state delegation to a party of the power to fix the qualifications of primary elections is delegation of a state function that may make the party's action the action of the state." The Court added that the extensive statutory control of primary elections in Texas "makes the party which is required to follow these legislative directions an agency of the state in so far as it determines the participants in a primary election." The Court concluded that the "right to participate in the choice of elected officials without restriction by any state because of race [is] not to be nullified by a state through casting its electoral process in a form which permits a private organization to practice racial discrimination in the election." Frankfurter, J., concurred in the result. Roberts, J., dissented.

TERRY v. ADAMS, 345 U.S. 461, 73 S.Ct. 809, 97 L.Ed. 1152 (1953), involved the exclusion of blacks from the "pre-primary" elections of the Jaybird Democratic Association, an organization of all the white voters in a Texas county that was run like a regular political party and whose candidates since 1889 had nearly always run unopposed and won in the regular Democratic primary and the general election. The record showed "complete absence of any compliance with the state law or practice, or cooperation by or with the State." Although there was no majority opinion, the Court held the election subject to the fifteenth amendment.

BLACK, J., joined by Douglas and Burton, JJ., found that "the admitted party purpose" was "to escape the Fifteenth Amendment's command." The "Amendment excludes social or business clubs" but "no election machinery could be sustained if its purpose or effect was to deny Negroes on account of their race an effective voice in the governmental affairs." "The only election that has counted in this Texas county for more than fifty years has been that held by the Jaybirds." "For a state to permit such a duplication of its election processes is to permit a flagrant abuse [of] the Fifteenth Amendment."

FRANKFURTER, J., stated that the "vital requirement is State responsibility" and found it as follows: "As a matter of practical politics," "we may assume" "those charged by State law with the duty of assuring all eligible voters an opportunity to participate in the selection of candidates at the primary—the county election officials who are normally leaders in their communities—participate by voting in the Jaybird primary" "and condone" "a wholly successful effort to withdraw significance from the State-prescribed primary, to subvert the operation of what is formally the law of the State for primaries in this county."

CLARK, J., joined by Vinson, C.J., and Reed and Jackson, JJ., described the Jaybirds as not merely a "private club" "organized to influence public candidacies or political action," but rather a "part and parcel of the Democratic Party, an organization existing under the auspices of Texas law. [W]hen a state structures its electoral apparatus in a form which devolves upon a political organization the uncontested choice of public officials, that organization itself, in whatever disguise, takes on those attributes of government which draw the Constitution's safeguards into play."

Only MINTON, J., dissented: The Jaybird's activity "seems to differ very little from situations common in many other places [where] a candidate must obtain the approval of a religious group. [It] must be recognized that elections and other public business are influenced by all sorts of pressures from carefully organized groups. [Far] from the activities of these groups being properly labeled as state action, [they] are to be considered as attempts to influence or obtain state action." [a]

MARSH v. ALABAMA, 326 U.S. 501, 66 S.Ct. 276, 90 L.Ed. 265 (1946), held that "a State, consistently with the First and Fourteenth Amendments," cannot "impose criminal punishment on a person who undertakes to distribute religious literature on the premises of a company-owned town contrary to the wishes of the town's management." The town, owned by a shipbuilding company, had "all the characteristics of any other American town." Appellant, a Jehovah's Witness, was warned that she could not distribute the literature and when she refused to leave the sidewalk of the town's "business block," a deputy sheriff, who was paid by the company to serve as the town's policeman, arrested her and she was convicted of trespass.

The Court, per BLACK, J., reversed: Under *Lovell v. Griffin*, p. 472 supra, an ordinary municipality could not have barred appellant's activities, and the fact that "a single company had legal title to all the town" may not result in

a. Are these examples distinguishable because "the only election that has counted in this Texas county for more than fifty years has been that held by the Jaybirds"? If not, are they distinguishable because the fifteenth amendment outlawed discrimination *on the basis of race or color* with respect to the right to vote?

impairing "channels of communication" of its inhabitants or those persons passing through. "Ownership does not always mean absolute dominion. The more an owner, for his advantage, opens up his property for use by the public in general, the more do his rights become circumscribed by the statutory and constitutional rights of those who use it. Thus, the owners of privately held bridges, ferries, turnpikes and railroads may not operate them as freely as a farmer does his farm. Since these facilities are built and operated primarily to benefit the public and since their operation is essentially a public function, it is subject to state regulation." In balancing property rights against freedom of press and religion, "the latter occupy a preferred position" and the former do not "justify the State's permitting a corporation to govern a community of citizens so as to restrict their fundamental liberties and the enforcement of such restraint by the application of a State statute."

Frankfurter, J., concurred and Jackson, J., did not participate. REED, J., joined by Vinson, C.J., and Burton, J., dissented, noting that "there was [no] objection to appellant's use of the nearby public highway and under our decisions she could rightfully have continued her activities [thirty feet parallel] from the spot she insisted upon using." [b]

EVANS v. NEWTON, 382 U.S. 296, 86 S.Ct. 486, 15 L.Ed.2d 373 (1966): In 1911, Senator A.O. Bacon devised land to Macon, Ga., to be used as a park for whites only. After *Pennsylvania v. Board of Trusts*, 353 U.S. 230, 77 S.Ct. 806, 1 L.Ed.2d 792 (1957)—holding that there is "state action" when public officials act as trustees under a private will requiring racial discrimination—the city permitted blacks to use the park. When Bacon's heirs sued to remove the city as trustee, the Georgia courts accepted the city's resignation and appointed private individuals as trustees so that the trust's purpose would not fail.

The Court, per DOUGLAS, J., reversed. Although "when private individuals or groups are endowed by the State with powers or functions governmental in nature, they become agencies or instrumentalities of the State," nonetheless, "the range of government activities is broad and varied, and the fact that government has engaged in a particular activity does not necessarily mean that an individual entrepreneur or manager of the same kind of undertaking suffers the same constitutional inhibitions. While a State may not segregate public schools so as to exclude one or more religious groups, those sects may maintain their own parochial educational systems. *Pierce v. Society of Sisters*, [p. 127 supra]."

"If a testator wanted to leave a school or center for the use of one race only and in no way implicated the State in the supervision, control, or management of that facility, we assume arguendo that no constitutional difficulty would be encountered. This park, however, is in a different posture" because "for years it was an integral part" of the city's activities, assumedly "granted tax exemption" and "swept, manicured, watered, patrolled, and maintained by the city." "The momentum it acquired as a public facility is certainly not dissipated ipso facto by the appointment of 'private' trustees. So far as this record shows, there has been no change in municipal maintenance and concern over this facility. [If] the

---

b. The *Marsh* rationale was extended to a privately owned shopping center in *Food Employees v. Logan Valley Plaza* (1968). *Logan Valley* was subsequently limited in *Lloyd Corp. v. Tanner* (1972) and then overruled in *Hudgens v. NLRB* (1976), set forth in Sec. 4 infra.

municipality remains entwined in the management or control of the park, it remains subject to the restraints of the Fourteenth Amendment."

"This conclusion is buttressed by the" fact that "the service rendered even by a private park of this character is municipal in nature," "more like a fire department or police department" than like "golf clubs, social centers, luncheon clubs, schools such as Tuskegee was at least in origin, and other like organizations in the private sector." "Mass recreation through the use of parks is plainly in the public domain and state courts that aid private parties to perform that public function on a segregated basis implicate the State in conduct proscribed by the Fourteenth Amendment. Like the streets of the company town in *Marsh*, the elective process of *Terry v. Adams*, and the transit system of *Public Utilities Comm'n v. Pollak*,[c] the predominant character and purpose of this park are municipal."

WHITE, J., concurred on a separate ground. He found that a 1905 Georgia statute specifically permitted racial restrictions in charitable trusts but forebade all other private discrimination. Thus, the statute had departed "from a policy of strict neutrality [by] enlisting the State's assistance only in aid of racial discrimination," and so involved "the State in the private choice as to convert the infected private discrimination into state action."[d]

HARLAN, J., joined by Stewart, J., dissented: The majority's "real holding" is not based on any state involvement in the park, but "because a privately operated park whose only criterion for exclusion is racial is within the 'public domain.'" Precedent does "not support this novel state action theory." In *Pollak*, "state action was explicitly premised on the close legal regulation of the company by the public utilities commission and the commission's approval of the particular action under attack. The conclusion might alternatively have rested on the near-exclusive legal monopoly enjoyed by the company, but in all events nothing was rested on any 'public function' theory." In *Terry*, "none of the three prevailing opinions garnered a majority, and some commentators have simply concluded that the state action requirement was read out of the Fifteenth Amendment on that occasion."[e] *Marsh* is the "only Fourteenth Amendment case finding state action in the 'public function' performed by a technically private institution."

The failing of the majority's theory "can be shown by comparing [the] 'public function' of privately established schools with that of privately owned parks. Like parks, the purpose schools serve is important to the public. Like parks, private control exists, but there is also a very strong tradition of public control in this field. Like parks, schools may be available to almost anyone of one race or religion but to no others. Like parks, there are normally alternatives for those shut out but there may also be inconveniences and disadvantages caused by the

c. In *Pollak*, 343 U.S. 451, 72 S.Ct. 813, 96 L.Ed. 1068 (1952), a city transit company subject to public regulation was considered in "sufficiently close relation" with the government as to cause the Court to determine whether the company's playing of radio programs on buses violated due process.

d. The issue of state action due to state "encouragement" of private conduct is considered in note 2 after *Reitman v. Mulkey*, Sec. 3 infra and in *Flagg Bros. v. Brooks*, Sec. 4 infra.

e. Harlan, J., cited Lewis, *The Meaning of State Action*, 60 Colum.L.Rev. 1083, 1094

(1960), who argues that "voting is a purely governmental function. No private organization can decree that a majority vote shall entitle a candidate to public office, while most of the functions involved in [other] cases are those traditionally performed by private organizations or at least within their performance capabilities." See also Note, *The Strange Career of State Action Under the Fifteenth Amendment*, 74 Yale L.J. 1448, 1456–59 (1965).

restriction. Like parks, the extent of school intimacy varies greatly depending on the size and character of the institution." f

"While this process of analogy might be spun out to reach privately owned orphanages, libraries, garbage collection companies, detective agencies, and a host of other functions commonly regarded as nongovernmental though paralleling fields of governmental activity, the example of schools is, I think, sufficient to indicate the pervasive potentialities of this 'public function' theory of state action. It substitutes for the comparatively clear and concrete tests of state action a catch-phrase approach as vague and amorphous as it is far-reaching. [And] it carries the seeds of transferring to federal authority vast areas of concerns whose regulation has wisely been left by the Constitution to the States." g

Notes and Questions

1. *Scope of the decisions.* (a) How "pervasive" are the "potentialities of this 'public function' theory of state action"? Do the decisions logically extend to *all* private activities for which there is "parallel government activity"? Or is their reach limited to those activities—such as conducting elections for public office or operating a town—that are traditionally performed only (almost only) by government?

(b) *Parks.* Into which of the above categories do parks fall? Is there a "strong tradition" of private as well as public operation of parks in cities? Is it likely that, if Senator Bacon had not provided the park in *Evans,* the city would have provided its own? Is this approach too "vague and amorphous" to serve as a constitutional standard?

(c) In *Marsh,* could the shipbuilding company discriminate against blacks in hiring production workers? In hiring peace officers or street cleaners for the town? In *Smith v. Allwright,* could the Democratic Party refuse to hire Jewish secretaries? In *Terry,* could the Jaybirds refuse to hire black secretaries? May "private organizations" that perform "government functions" be subject to some constitutional limitations but not others?

(d) The "government function" issue is considered further in Sec. 4 infra.

2. *Statutory bargaining agents.* Suppose a labor union, acting as exclusive bargaining agent for all employees by authority of federal statute, does not bargain as strenuously for black employees? See generally Hale, *Force and the State: A Comparison of Political and Economic Compulsion,* 35 Colum.L.Rev. 149, 192–98 (1935). Consider Murphy, J. concurring in *Steele v. Louisville & N.R.R.,* 323 U.S. 192, 208, 65 S.Ct. 226, 234, 89 L.Ed. 173, 186 (1944): "While such a union is essentially a private organization, its power to represent and bind all members of a class or craft is derived solely from Congress. [I]t cannot be assumed that Congress meant to authorize the representative to act so to ignore the rights guaranteed by the Constitution. Otherwise the Act would bear the stigma of unconstitutionality under the Fifth Amendment." May such a union, although bargaining fairly for black employees, bar them from union membership?

f. For further consideration of "private schools," see note 4 after *Burton v. Wilmington Parking Auth.,* Sec. 3 infra.

g. Black, J., believing that "the Georgia courts decided no federal constitutional question," agreed with the position also stated by

Harlan, J.'s opinion that "the writ of certiorari should have been dismissed as improvidently granted."

For subsequent litigation in respect to this park, see *Evans v. Abney,* Sec. 3 infra.

3. *"Private" function.* (a) If the activities of private persons or groups may rise to the performance of a "government function," may certain official activities of government ever be considered the performance of a "private function"? Such as acting as trustee under a private will? Is the nature of the trust property relevant? In any case, does the state's official "entwinement" end the matter?

(b) If a privately owned amusement park contracts with a state deputy sheriff, who is regularly employed by the park, to enforce its racial segregation policy, may the state convict blacks, whom the deputy arrests when they refuse to leave the premises, for trespass? See *Griffin v. Maryland,* 378 U.S. 130, 84 S.Ct. 1770, 12 L.Ed.2d 754 (1964).

(c) *State university scholarship funds.* May a state university constitutionally award scholarships which the donor has designated for whites only? For persons of a particular religion only? If the donor personally selects the scholarship recipients each year and racially discriminates, may the university constitutionally admit those selected? Is there a "difference of substance" between these two situations? May a state university constitutionally solicit scholarships to be awarded on racial bases? See generally Note, *Constitutionality of Restricted Scholarships,* 33 N.Y.U.L.Rev. 604 (1958).

SECTION 3. STATE "INVOLVEMENT" OR "ENCOURAGEMENT"

BURTON v. WILMINGTON PARKING AUTHORITY

365 U.S. 715, 81 S.Ct. 856, 6 L.Ed.2d 45 (1961).

MR. JUSTICE CLARK delivered the opinion of the Court.

In this action for declaratory and injunctive relief it is admitted that the Eagle Coffee Shoppe, Inc., a restaurant located within an off-street automobile parking building in Wilmington, Delaware, has refused to serve appellant food or drink solely because he is a Negro. The parking building is owned and operated by the Wilmington Parking Authority, an agency of the State of Delaware, and the restaurant is the Authority's lessee. [The] Supreme Court of Delaware has held that Eagle was acting in "a purely private capacity" under its lease; that its action was not that of the Authority and was not, therefore, state action * * *. It also held that under 24 Del.Code § 1501,[1] Eagle was a restaurant, not an inn, and that as such it "is not required [under Delaware law] to serve any and all persons entering its place of business." * * *

The Authority['s] statutory purpose is to provide adequate parking facilities for the convenience of the public and [the] first project undertaken by the Authority was the erection of a parking facility * * *. [T]he Authority was advised by its retained experts that the anticipated revenue from the parking of cars and proceeds from sale of its bonds would not be sufficient to finance the construction costs of the facility. [To] secure additional capital [the] Authority decided it was necessary to enter long-term leases with responsible tenants for commercial use of some of the space available in the projected "garage building." The public was invited to bid for these leases.

---

1. The statute provides that: "No keeper of an inn, tavern, hotel, or restaurant, or other place of public entertainment or refreshment of travelers, guests, or customers shall be obliged, by law, to furnish entertainment or refreshment to persons whose reception or entertainment by him would be offensive to the major part of his customers, and would injure his business. * * *"

In April 1957 such a private lease, for 20 years [was] made with Eagle Coffee Shoppe, Inc., for use as a "restaurant, dining room, banquet hall, cocktail lounge and bar * * *." [The] lease, however, contains no requirement that its restaurant services be made available to the general public on a nondiscriminatory basis, in spite of the fact that the Authority has power to adopt rules and regulations respecting the use of its facilities * * *.

Other portions of the structure were leased to other tenants, including a bookstore, a retail jeweler, and a food store. Upon completion of the building, the Authority located at appropriate places thereon official signs indicating the public character of the building, and flew from mastheads on the roof both the state and national flags.

[It] is clear, as it always has been since the *Civil Rights Cases,* [that] private conduct abridging individual rights does no violence to the Equal Protection Clause unless to some significant extent the State in any of its manifestations has been found to have become involved in it. Because the virtue of the right to equal protection of the laws could lie only in the breadth of its application, its constitutional assurance was reserved in terms whose imprecision was necessary if the right were to be enjoyed in the variety of individual-state relationships which the Amendment was designed to embrace. For the same reason, to fashion and apply a precise formula for recognition of state responsibility under the Equal Protection Clause is an "impossible task" which "This Court has never attempted." Only by sifting facts and weighing circumstances can the nonobvious involvement of the State in private conduct be attributed its true significance.

[T]he Delaware Supreme Court seems to have placed controlling emphasis on its conclusion, as to the accuracy of which there is doubt, that only some 15% of the total cost of the facility was "advanced" from public funds; that the cost of the entire facility was allocated three-fifths to the space for commercial leasing and two-fifths to parking space; that anticipated revenue from parking was only some 30.5% of the total income, the balance of which was expected to be earned by the leasing; that the Authority had no original intent to place a restaurant in the building, it being only a happenstance resulting from the bidding; that Eagle expended considerable moneys on furnishings; that the restaurant's main and marked public entrance is on Ninth Street without any public entrance direct from the parking area; and that "the only connection Eagle has with the public facility [is] the furnishing [of] rent which is used by the Authority to defray a portion of the operating expense of an otherwise unprofitable enterprise." While these factual considerations are indeed validly accountable aspects[,] we cannot say that they lead inescapably to the conclusion that state action is not present. Their persuasiveness is diminished when evaluated in the context of other factors which must be acknowledged.

The land and building were publicly owned. As an entity, the building was dedicated to "public uses" in performance of the Authority's "essential governmental functions." The costs of land acquisition, construction, and maintenance are defrayed entirely from donations by the City of Wilmington, from loans and revenue bonds and from the proceeds of rentals and parking services out of which the loans and bonds were payable. Assuming that the distinction would be significant, cf. *Derrington v. Plummer,* 5 Cir., 240 F.2d 922, 925, the commercially leased areas were not surplus state property, but constituted a physically and financially integral and, indeed, indispensable part of the State's plan to operate its project as a self-sustaining unit. Upkeep and maintenance of the building, including necessary repairs, were responsibilities of the Authority and were payable out of public funds. * * * Guests of the restaurant are afforded a convenient place to park their automobiles, even if they cannot enter the restaurant directly from the parking area. Similarly, its convenience for diners may well provide additional demand for the Authority's parking facilities. Should any improvements effected in the leasehold by Eagle become part of the realty, there is no possibility of increased taxes being passed on to it since the fee is held by a tax-exempt government agency. Neither can it be ignored, especially in view of Eagle's affirmative allegation that for it to serve Negroes would injure its business, that profits earned by discrimination not only contribute to, but also are indispensable elements in, the financial success of a governmental agency.

Addition of all these activities, obligations and responsibilities of the Authority, the benefits mutually conferred, together with the obvious fact that the restaurant is operated as an integral part of a public building devoted to a public parking service, indicates that degree of state participation and involvement in discriminatory action which it was the design of the Fourteenth Amendment to condemn. It is irony amounting to grave injustice that in one part of a single building, erected and maintained with public funds by an agency of the State to serve a public purpose, all persons have equal rights, while in another portion, also serving the public, a Negro is a second-class citizen [but] at the same time fully enjoys equal access to nearby restaurants in wholly privately owned buildings. [I]n its lease with Eagle the Authority could have affirmatively required Eagle to discharge the responsibilities under the Fourteenth Amendment imposed upon the private enterprise as a consequence of state participation. But no State may effectively abdicate its responsibilities by either ignoring them or by merely failing to discharge them whatever the motive may be. It is of no consolation to an individual denied the equal protection of the laws that it was done in good faith. [By] its inaction, the Authority, and through it the State, has not only made itself a party to the refusal of service, but has elected to place its power, property and prestige behind the admitted discrimination. The State has so far insinuated itself into a position of interdependence with Eagle that it must be recognized as a joint participant in the challenged activity, which, on that account, cannot be considered to have been so "purely private" as to fall without the scope of the Fourteenth Amendment.

Because readily applicable formulae may not be fashioned, the conclusions drawn from the facts and circumstances of this record are by no means declared as universal truths on the basis of which every state leasing agreement is to be tested. Owing to the very "largeness" of government, a multitude of relationships might appear to some to fall within the Amendment's embrace, but that, it must be remembered, can be determined only in the framework of the peculiar facts or circumstances present. * * * Specifically defining the limits of our inquiry, what we hold today is that when a State leases public property in the manner and for the purpose shown to have been the case here, the proscriptions of the Fourteenth Amendment must be complied with by the lessee * * *.

Reversed and remanded.

[STEWART, J., concurred, believing that, by relying on § 1501, the Delaware court "construed this legislative enactment as authorizing discriminatory classification based exclusively on color. Such a law seems to me clearly violative of the Fourteenth Amendment."

[HARLAN, J., joined by Whittaker, J., dissented: "The Court's opinion, by a process of first undiscriminatingly throwing together various factual bits and pieces and then undermining the resulting structure by an equally vague disclaimer, seems to me to leave completely at sea just what it is in this record that satisfies the requirement of 'state action.'" Rather than pass on that question, "the case should first be sent back to the state court for clarification" in respect to how it construed § 1501.[a] If Stewart, J., was correct, Harlan, J., would agree with his conclusion, but the state court could have "meant no more than that under the statute, as at common law, Eagle was free to serve only those whom it pleased."[b]

Notes and Questions

1. *The basis for the decision.* Was there any single factor which persuaded, or should have persuaded, the Court to find state action? See generally Lewis, *Burton v. Wilmington Parking Authority—A Case Without Precedent*, 61 Colum. L.Rev. 1458 (1961).

(a) *Publicly owned property.* What is the significance of the fact that "the land and building were publicly owned"? If the space had been leased to a law firm, could it constitutionally discriminate among its clients?

(i) *"Public function."* In *Derrington v. Plummer*, 240 F.2d 922 (5th Cir.1956), cert. denied, 353 U.S. 924 (1957), a cafeteria in a courthouse was leased to a private party who refused to serve blacks. The conduct of the lessee was held to be state action. The lessee was found to be performing a public function because "the express purpose of the lease was to furnish cafeteria service for the benefit of persons having occasion to be in the County Courthouse." If the county has immunity from tort liability, is the lessee liable for a customer's food poisoning? Under *Derrington*, what result for racial discrimination by Eagle?

May Eagle be found to be performing a "public function" because it "constituted a financially integral and indispensable part of the State's plan to operate its project"? If so, may the other tenants racially discriminate? If Wilmington, instead of including rental space in the parking building, had relied on rental income from other of its properties located throughout the city to help finance the parking facility, could lessees of these properties refuse to do business with blacks?

(ii) *The "motive" test.* Would *Burton* have been an easier case if "the real purpose of the lease" was to permit Eagle to exclude blacks. Is this a logical or desirable point to draw the line? Is either the state's involvement or the effect of discrimination any less if the state's purpose is not discriminatory?

In *Muir v. Louisville Park Theatrical Ass'n*, 347 U.S. 971, 98 L.Ed. 1112, 74 S.Ct. 783 (1954), a city leased its amphitheater for the summer to a private party who denied admission to blacks. No discriminatory purpose on the city's part was shown. The Court vacated a lower court decision denying relief to the blacks. Is *Muir* distinguishable from *Burton* on the ground that construction of an amphitheater is traditionally a "public undertaking" while construction of a restaurant is not? Suppose the city leased the amphitheater for one week to a social organization which excluded blacks from membership and attendance at its meetings?

---

a. Frankfurter, J., agreeing with this point, also dissented.

b. What result if "a state passed a statute which provided that individuals shall have the legal right to engage in racial discrimination in their own homes"? Williams, *The Twilight of State Action*, 41 Texas L.Rev. 347, 384 (1963). See note 2 after *Reitman v. Mulkey*, infra.

(b) What is the significance of the fact that the location of the restaurant in the parking facility "confers mutual benefits"? Suppose Eagle were located in a private building immediately adjacent to the public parking building?

(c) What is the significance of the fact that the city is "profiting from the discrimination" because if it forbade it, Eagle would not pay as high a rental? If the state sells surplus property without requiring its nondiscriminatory use because such a requirement would bring the city a lower price, may the purchaser constitutionally discriminate? If such a requirement were financially irrelevant but the state neglected to include it, may the buyer discriminate?

(d) What is the significance of the facts that the Authority was responsible for "maintenance of the building" and that the property was tax-exempt? Are these factors simply paid for by Eagle in higher rental?

(e) What is the significance of the fact that the Authority "insinuated itself into a position of [financial] interdependence with Eagle"? Consider 75 Harv.L. Rev. 146 (1961): "Thus analyzed, the decision might justify the application of the equal protection clause to the private contractor who built the garage, or to the businessmen who trade extensively with a government agency." Would it extend also to the contractor's or businessmen's suppliers?

(f) What is the significance of the fact that discrimination exists because of the Authority's "inaction"? Does *Burton* stand for the proposition that anytime the state could prevent discrimination, failure to do so is state action?

2. *Extent of the decision.* May Eagle racially discriminate in hiring employees? In buying from suppliers? May Eagle refuse to rent its banquet room to one political party if it rents it to others. May its conduct constitute state action for purposes of the equal protection clause but not for the first amendment?

3. *Sales of public property.* Would the result in *Burton* have been different if Eagle had been sold a fee in the property? Suppose a city sells its swimming pool on condition that the buyer continue to so operate it; if not, reverter to the city. What result if the buyer racially segregates?

4. *Private schools.* (a) NORWOOD v. HARRISON, 413 U.S. 455, 93 S.Ct. 2804, 37 L.Ed.2d 723 (1973), per BURGER, C.J., enjoined Mississippi's lending of textbooks to all students in public and private schools as applied to racially segregated private schools: "[T]hat the Constitution may compel toleration of private discrimination in some circumstances does not mean that it requires state support for such discrimination."

The textbook program, "enacted first in 1940, long before [there] was any occasion to have a policy or reason to foster the development of racially segregated private academies," may have been "motivated by [a] sincere interest in the educational welfare of all Mississippi children. But good intentions as to one valid objective do not serve to negate the State's involvement in violation of a constitutional duty. 'The existence of a permissible purpose cannot sustain an action that has an impermissible effect.' *Wright v. Emporia* [p. 865 supra]." The lower court had found "that the textbook loans did not interfere with or impede the State's acknowledged duty to establish a unitary school system" since "the State's public schools are now fully unitary." The Court, although casting doubt on the finding, held it "irrelevant": "A State's constitutional obligation requires it to steer clear, not only of operating the old dual system of racially segregated schools, but also of giving significant aid to institutions that practice racial or other invidious discrimination."

Plaintiffs had failed to show that "any child enrolled in private school, if deprived of free textbooks, would withdraw from private school and subsequently enroll in the public schools." But "the Constitution does not permit the State to aid discrimination even when there is no precise causal relationship between state financial aid to a private school and the continued well-being of that school. A State may not grant the type of tangible financial aid here involved if that aid has a significant tendency to facilitate, reinforce, and support private discrimination."

"We do not suggest that a State violates its constitutional duty merely because it has provided *any* form of state service that benefits private schools said to be racially discriminatory. Textbooks are a basic educational tool and, like tuition grants, they are provided only in connection with schools; they are to be distinguished from generalized services government might provide to schools in common with others. Moreover, the textbooks provided to private school students by the State in this case are a form of assistance readily available from sources entirely independent of the State—unlike, for example, 'such necessities of life as electricity, water, and police and fire protection.' "

Under *Board of Educ. v. Allen*, [p. 719 supra], states *may* lend textbooks to students in parochial schools "because assistance properly confined to the secular functions of sectarian schools does not substantially promote the readily identifiable religious mission of those schools [but] in the context of this case the legitimate educational function cannot be isolated from discriminatory practices. [In contrast to *Allen*], although the Constitution does not proscribe private bias, it places no value on discrimination as it does on the values inherent in the Free Exercise Clause." Douglas and Brennan, JJ., concurred in the result.

(b) In GILMORE v. MONTGOMERY, 417 U.S. 556, 94 S.Ct. 2416, 41 L.Ed.2d 304 (1974), a federal court enjoined the city's "permitting the use of public park recreational facilities by private segregated school groups and by other non-school groups that racially discriminate in their membership." The Court, per BLACKMUN, J., modified the decree in part: It "was wholly proper for the city to be enjoined from permitting *exclusive* access to public recreational facilities by segregated private schools" (emphasis added), which had been "formed in reaction against" the federal court's school desegregation order. "[T]his assistance significantly tended to undermine the federal court order mandating [a] unitary school system in Montgomery."

But, "upon this record, we are unable to draw a conclusion as to whether the use of zoos, museums, parks, and other recreational facilities by private school groups *in common with others,* and by private nonschool organizations, involves government so directly in the actions of those users as to warrant" intervention (emphasis added). "It is possible that certain uses of city facilities will be judged to be in contravention of the parks [or school] desegregation order, [or] in some way to constitute impermissible 'state action' ascribing to the city the discriminatory actions of the groups."

The latter issue concerns "whether there is significant state involvement in the private discrimination alleged. * * * Traditional state monopolies, such as electricity, water, and police and fire protection—all generalized governmental services—do not by their mere provision constitute a showing of state involvement in invidious discrimination. *Norwood.* The same is true of a broad spectrum of municipal recreational facilities * * *.

"If, however, the city or other governmental entity rations otherwise freely accessible recreational facilities, the case for state action will naturally be stronger than if the facilities are simply available to all comers without condition or reservation. Here, for example, petitioners allege that the city engages in scheduling softball games for an all-white church league and provides balls, equipment, fields, and lighting. The city's role in that situation would be dangerously close to what was found to exist in *Burton* * * *." [a]

WHITE, J., joined by Douglas, J., concurred: "[T]he question is not whether there is state action, but whether the conceded action by the city, and hence by the State, is such that the State must be deemed to have denied the equal protection of the laws. In other words, by permitting a segregated school or group to use city-owned facilities, has the State furnished such aid to the group's segregated policies or become so involved in them that the State itself may fairly be said to have denied equal protection? Under *Burton*, it is perfectly clear that to violate the Equal Protection Clause the State itself need not make, advise, or authorize the private decision to discriminate that involves the State in the practice of segregation or would appear to do so in the minds of ordinary citizens." [b]

(c) *Significance of remedy.* In contrast to *Burton* (where plaintiff sought an injunction against Eagle Coffee Shoppe), since the only remedy sought in *Norwood* and *Gilmore* was against the state or city itself, did these cases really present any "state action" issue at all? Consider Brown, *State Action Analysis of Tax Expenditures,* 11 Harv.Civ.Rts.-Civ.Lib.L. 97, 115–19 (1976): "[T]wo kinds of 'state action' cases should [be] distinguished: only in suits in which relief is sought against a private actor should the private actor's interests be taken into account. [Thus,] it is quite possible that a plaintiff proceeding under a state action theory might prevail in enjoining the government's action but fail in his efforts to enjoin the private activity." Compare McCoy, *Current State Action Theories, the Jackson Nexus Requirement, and Employee Discharges by Semi-Public and State-Aided Institutions,* 31 Vand.L.Rev. 785, 802 (1978): "Although this theoretical distinction has considerable superficial appeal, primarily because it is formulated in terms of balancing competing constitutional interests, closer inspection reveals no significant difference between the cases. [E]ither kind of suit presents the private actor with precisely the same basic option—either modify the private action to conform to fourteenth amendment standards or do without the state aid. In other words, the two kinds of suits are indistinguishable in terms of the private interest interfered with, and therefore they should not present significantly different standards for the level of state aid required." Contrast Brown, supra, at 119 n. 102: "It is of course true that the removal of the government aid will have a coercive effect on the private actor. In some cases the pressure to conform private behavior to constitutional standards generated by the loss of assistance will be as coercive as an injunction. In such a case, however, the fact that withdrawing the aid had a strong influence on private behavior would imply a high level of significance of government involvement with the private actor. In that case it would be appropriate to impose relief on the private actor as well as on the government, so the remedy distinction would not apply."

In any event, since the practices in *Norwood* and *Gilmore* were not shown to be "motivated" to perpetuate racial discrimination, can these decisions be

---

a. Brennan, J., concurred in part but would enjoin *any* "school-sponsored or directed uses of the city recreational facilities that enable private segregated schools to duplicate public school operations at public expense."

b. Marshall, J., generally agreed with White, J.

squared with *Washington v. Davis*, p. 838 supra?   Given the doctrines that (1) public financial aid to parochial schools violates the establishment clause if either the *purpose or effect* advances religion (Ch. 9, Sec. 1, III), whereas (2) a racially discriminatory *purpose* must exist for violation of the equal protection clause (Ch. 10, Sec. 2, III), can *Norwood* be squared with *Board of Educ. v. Allen?* See Choper, *Thoughts on State Action: The "Government Function" and "Power Theory" Approaches,* 1979 Wash.U.L.Q. 757, 765–69.

(d) What results in *Norwood* and *Gilmore* if the remedy sought had been to compel the private schools to desegregate?   Should some or all private schools be held to the requirements of the equal protection clause? [c]

(i) *Financial aid.*   If private schools receive extensive financial aid from the state, does it result in state action only in respect to a specific activity being funded?   Consider Comment, *Tax Incentives as State Action,* 122 U.Pa.L.Rev. 414, 436 (1973): "This [theory] incorrectly assumes that government involvement that bears directly upon a specific activity of an entity can be meaningfully distinguished from government involvement that serves more generally to perpetuate that entity as a whole.   It is an inescapable fact that general government assistance which perpetuates an entity operates indirectly to perpetuate the specific activities of that entity."   May a person whose sole source of income is public relief constitutionally refuse to sell his home to blacks?

(ii) *Public control.*   Suppose the private schools' curriculum and admission policy are subject to state regulation?   If a state statute regulates election procedures of all voluntary organizations, is a social club barred from racially discriminating?   If the state provides private schools with extensive financial aid and strict regulation, are the schools "state functions"?   If the state licenses all barber schools and requires that all barbers attend such schools, are the schools "state functions"?

(iii) *"Government function."*   Even without state aid or regulation, does "the spirit of [the segregation decisions] support the argument that education is a matter of such vital public concern that any action taken in regard to it must be subject to the prohibitions of the fourteenth amendment"?   56 Colum.L.Rev. 285, 287 (1956).   Consider Abernathy, *Expansion of the State Action Concept Under the Fourteenth Amendment,* 43 Corn.L.Q. 375, 407 (1958): "[T]he only purely privately operated functions which properly should be considered as governmental are those which are indispensable to the maintenance of democratic government.   [S]uch a definition does not go so far as to cover operations which are merely useful or desirable as aids to a more efficient or intelligently controlled government.   If these are to be included, then we are no better off than if we equate governmental action with operations affected with a public interest. Education is desirable and useful in a democratic system but it is not indispensable [in] the sense that access to the ballot and the processes of selecting public officials is."   If the state closed all of its public schools, would that make private schools "indispensable to the maintenance of democratic government"?   If so, would some (all) private schools be barred from racially (sexually, religiously) discriminating? [d]

---

c. See *Runyon v. McCrary*, p. 1183 infra, holding that a federal statute prohibits private schools from refusing to accept black students.

d. See generally Note, *The Wall of Racial Separation: The Role of Private and Parochial Schools in Racial Integration*, 43 N.Y.U.L.Rev.

514 (1968); Note, *Segregation Academies and State Action*, 82 Yale L.J. 1436 (1973); O'Neil, *Private Universities and Public Law*, 19 Buf.L. Rev. 155 (1970).

For further consideration of this issue, see note 2(b) after *Flagg Bros. v. Brooks*, Sec. 4 infra.

5. *Tax exempt organizations.* May government give tax exemptions (or permit tax deductions for donations) to private schools, fraternal groups and charitable foundations that fail to adhere to fourteenth amendment requirements? See generally Bittker & Kaufman, *Taxes and Civil Rights: "Constitutionalizing" the Internal Revenue Code,* 82 Yale L.J. 51 (1972). Consider Note, *State Action and the United States Junior Chamber of Commerce,* 43 Geo.Wash. L.Rev. 1407, 1423–24 (1975): "As the legislative history indicates, the Internal Revenue Code's tax exemptions for charitable organizations are based upon the theory that the Government is compensated for the loss of revenue by being relieved of the financial burden that would otherwise have to be met by appropriations of government funds. [Where] the private entity is thus acting as a surrogate for the government, any discrimination connected with the performance of public services, even if not affirmatively approved by the government, subjects the victims to discrimination that would not have occurred had the government performed the services directly. The government cannot avoid these constitutional limitations by delegating its functions to private entities, even if the delegation is well-intentioned." See also Parker, *Evans v. Newton and the Racially Restricted Charitable Trust,* 13 How.L.J. 223 (1967). Reconsider note 4(c) supra.

6. *Private organizations.* Is the state sufficiently "involved" with the following organizations to find their action subject to the fourteenth amendment: An association of white policemen that holds itself out as "the police" and is represented at official meetings where police policy is made. See *Adams v. Miami Police Benev. Ass'n.,* 454 F.2d 1315 (5th Cir.), cert. denied, 409 U.S. 843 (1972). An association of white d entists whose nominees for official state dental boards are always selected. See *Hawkins v. North Carolina Dental Soc'y,* 355 F.2d 718 (4th Cir.1966). An association of black public school teachers that holds its meetings in the school auditorium. See *Auerbach v. African American Teachers Ass'n,* 356 F.Supp. 1046 (E.D.N.Y.1973). An association of over 700 colleges (half of which are public) that governs intercollegiate athletic activities of its members and sponsors virtually all regional and national competitions. See *Howard Univ. v. NCAA,* 510 F.2d 213 (D.C.Cir.1975). An association, federally incorporated, of all males who have served honorably in the armed forces. See *Stearns v. VFW,* 394 F.Supp. 138 (D.D.C.1975). A privately formed organization of broker-dealers whose creation was authorized by statute to enforce the securities laws. See Note, *Governmental Action and the National Association of Securities Dealers,* 47 Ford.L.Rev. 585 (1979). A volunteer fire department that contracts with the city to fight fires. See *Janusaitis v. Middlebury Volunteer Fire Dep't,* 607 F.2d 17 (2d Cir.1979). A privately incorporated "community action agency" that receives substantial public funding and whose policies are regulated by federal law. See *Hines v. Cenla Community Action Committee,* 474 F.2d 1052 (5th Cir.1973).

7. *Redevelopment housing.* Are major urban redevelopment housing projects, undertaken pursuant to statutory authority with benefit of public condemnation power and tax exemption, constitutionally barred from racially discriminating? If so, what about ordinary private housing projects that receive public "aid" in the form of water and sewage disposal, police and fire protection? See generally Comment, *Application of the Fourteenth Amendment to Builders of Private Housing,* 12 Kan.L.Rev. 426 (1964); Note, *Nondiscrimination Implications of Federal Involvement in Housing,* 19 Vand.L.Rev. 865 (1966); 17 J.Pub.L. 175 (1968). Is urban redevelopment distinguishable from a small private housing project because the former has the effect of racial zoning? Is this a

restatement of the "government function" theory? Is the issue of "state action" affected if the claim is that the housing project evicted a tenant without affording procedural due process?

SHELLEY v. KRAEMER
334 U.S. 1, 68 S.Ct. 836, 92 L.Ed. 1161 (1948).

Mr. Chief Justice Vinson delivered the opinion of the Court.

[In two cases from Missouri and Michigan, petitioners were blacks who had purchased houses from whites despite the fact that the properties were subject to restrictive covenants, signed by most property owners in the block, providing that for a specified time (in one case fifty years from 1911) the property would be sold only to Caucasians. Respondents, owners of other property subject to the covenants, sued to enjoin the blacks from taking possession and to divest them of title. The state courts granted the relief.]

Whether the equal protection clause * * * inhibits judicial enforcement by state courts of restrictive covenants based on race or color is a question which this Court has not heretofore been called upon to consider. * * *

It cannot be doubted that among the civil rights intended to be protected from discriminatory state action by the Fourteenth Amendment are the rights to acquire, enjoy, own and dispose of property. Equality in the enjoyment of property rights was regarded by the framers of that Amendment as an essential pre-condition to the realization of other basic civil rights and liberties which the Amendment was intended to guarantee.[7] Thus, § 1978 of the Revised Statutes, derived from § 1 of the Civil Rights Act of 1866 which was enacted by Congress while the Fourteenth Amendment was also under consideration, provides:

"All citizens of the United States shall have the same right, in every State and Territory, as is enjoyed by white citizens thereof to inherit, purchase, lease, sell, hold, and convey real and personal property." * * *

It is likewise clear that restrictions on the right of occupancy of the sort sought to be created by the private agreements in these cases could not be squared with the requirements of the Fourteenth Amendment if imposed by state statute or local ordinance. * * *

But the present cases [do] not involve action by state legislatures or city councils. Here the particular patterns of discrimination and the areas in which the restrictions are to operate, are determined, in the first instance, by the terms of agreements among private individuals. Participation of the State consists in the enforcement of the restrictions so defined. * * *

Since the decision of this Court in the *Civil Rights Cases,* the principle has become firmly embedded in our constitutional law that the action inhibited by the first section of the Fourteenth Amendment is only such action as may fairly be said to be that of the States. That Amendment erects no shield against merely private conduct, however discriminatory or wrongful.

We conclude, therefore, that the restrictive agreements standing alone cannot be regarded as a violation of any rights guaranteed to petitioners by the Fourteenth Amendment. So long as the purposes of those agreements are effectuated by voluntary adherence to their terms, it would appear clear that

---

7. *Slaughter-House Cases* [p. 63 supra].
See Flack, *The Adoption of the Fourteenth Amendment.*

there has been no action by the State and the provisions of the Amendment have not been violated.

But here there was more. These are cases in which the purposes of the agreements were secured only by judicial enforcement by state courts of the restrictive terms of the agreements. The respondents urge that judicial enforcement of private agreements does not amount to state action; or, in any event, the participation of the State is so attenuated in character as not to amount to state action within the meaning of the Fourteenth Amendment. Finally, it is suggested, even if the States in these cases may be deemed to have acted in the constitutional sense, their action did not deprive petitioners of rights guaranteed by the Fourteenth Amendment. * * *

That the action of state courts and of judicial officers in their official capacities is to be regarded as action of the State within the meaning of the Fourteenth Amendment, is a proposition which has long been established * * *. Thus, in *Virginia v. Rives,* 1880, 100 U.S. 313, 318, 25 L.Ed. 667, this Court stated: "It is doubtless true that a State may act through different agencies,—either by its legislative, its executive, or its judicial authorities; and the prohibitions of the amendment extend to all action of the State denying equal protection of the laws, whether it be action by one of these agencies or by another." [In] the *Civil Rights Cases,* this Court pointed out that the Amendment makes void "state action of every kind" which is inconsistent with the guaranties therein contained, and extends to manifestations of "state authority in the shape of laws, customs, or judicial or executive proceedings." * * *

One of the earliest applications of the prohibitions contained in the Fourteenth Amendment to action of state judicial officials occurred in cases in which Negroes had been excluded from jury service * * *. These cases demonstrate, also, the early recognition by this Court that state action in violation of the Amendment's provisions is equally repugnant to the constitutional commands whether directed by state statute or taken by a judicial official in the absence of statute. * * *

The action of state courts in imposing penalties or depriving parties of other substantive rights without providing adequate notice and opportunity to defend, has, of course, long been regarded as a denial of the due process of law guaranteed by the Fourteenth Amendment.

In numerous cases, this Court has reversed criminal convictions in state courts for failure of those courts to provide the essential ingredients of a fair hearing. Thus it has been held that convictions obtained in state courts under the domination of a mob are void. Convictions obtained by coerced confessions, by the use of perjured testimony known by the prosecution to be such, or without the effective assistance of counsel, have also been held to be exertions of state authority in conflict with the fundamental rights protected by the Fourteenth Amendment.

But the examples of state judicial action which have been held by this Court to violate the Amendment's commands are not restricted to situations in which the judicial proceedings were found in some manner to be procedurally unfair. It has been recognized that the action of state courts in enforcing a substantive common-law rule formulated by those courts, may result in the denial of rights guaranteed by the Fourteenth Amendment * * *. Thus, in *AFL v. Swing,* 1941, 312 U.S. 321, 61 S.Ct. 568, 85 L.Ed. 855, enforcement by state courts of the common-law policy of the State, which resulted in the restraining of peaceful picketing, was held to be state action of the sort prohibited by the Amendment's guaranties of freedom of discussion. In *Cantwell v. Connecticut*, 1940, 310 U.S. 296, 60 S.Ct. 900, 84 L.Ed. 1213, a conviction in a state court of the common-law crime of breach of the peace was, under the circumstances of the case, found to be a violation of the Amendment's commands relating to freedom of religion. In *Bridges v. California*, 1941, 314 U.S. 252, 62 S.Ct. 190, 86 L.Ed. 192, enforcement of the state's common-law rule relating to contempts by publication was held to be state action inconsistent with the prohibitions of the Fourteenth Amendment. * * *

We have no doubt that there has been state action in these cases in the full and complete sense of the phrase. The undisputed facts disclose that petitioners were willing purchasers of properties upon which they desired to establish homes. The owners of the properties were willing sellers; and contracts of sale were accordingly consummated. It is clear that but for the active intervention of the state courts, supported by the full panoply of state power, petitioners would have been free to occupy the properties in question without restraint.

These are not cases, as has been suggested, in which the States have merely abstained from action, leaving private individuals free to impose such discriminations as they see fit. Rather, these are cases in which the States have made available to such individuals the full coercive power of government to deny to petitioners, on the grounds of race or color, the enjoyment of property rights in premises which petitioners are willing and financially able to acquire and which the grantors are willing to sell. * * *

The enforcement of the restrictive agreements by the state courts in these cases was directed pursuant to the common-law policy of the States as formulated by those courts in earlier decisions. [The] judicial action in each case bears the clear and unmistakable imprimatur of the State. We have noted that previous decisions of this Court have established the proposition that judicial action is not immunized from the operation of the Fourteenth Amendment simply because it is taken pursuant to the state's common-law policy. Nor is the Amendment ineffective simply because the particular pattern of discrimination, which the State has enforced, was defined initially by the terms of a private agreement. State action, as that phrase is understood for the purposes of the Fourteenth Amendment, refers to exertions of state power in all forms. * * * We have noted that freedom from discrimination by the States in the enjoyment of property rights was among the basic objectives sought to be effectuated by the framers of the Fourteenth Amendment. That such discrimination has occurred in these cases is clear. * * *

Respondents urge, however, that since the state courts stand ready to enforce restrictive covenants excluding white persons[,] enforcement of covenants excluding colored persons may not be deemed a denial of equal protection of the laws to the colored persons who are thereby affected. This contention does not bear scrutiny. [The] rights created by the first section of the Fourteenth Amendment are, by its terms, guaranteed to the individual. The rights established are personal rights. It is, therefore, no answer to these petitioners to say that the courts may also be induced to deny white persons rights of ownership and occupancy on grounds of race or color. Equal protection of the laws is not achieved through indiscriminate imposition of inequalities. * * *

Reversed.

MR. JUSTICE REED, MR. JUSTICE JACKSON, and MR. JUSTICE RUTLEDGE took no part in the consideration or decision of these cases.[a]

---

a. For a history of the battle against restrictive covenants, see Vose, *NAACP Strategy* *in the Covenant Cases*, 6 W.Res.L.Rev. 101 (1955).

Notes and Questions

1. *Authority of prior decisions.* Do the cases holding that "judicial action is state action" call for the result in *Shelley*? Consider Comment, *The Impact of Shelley v. Kraemer on the State Action Concept*, 44 Calif.L.Rev. 718, 724 (1956): "In the cases exemplifying 'orthodox' judicial violation the prohibited activity [e.g., barring blacks from juries] was practiced by the judge himself. [But in *Shelley*] the discrimination originated with private persons." May this be said about "convictions obtained under the domination of a mob"?

As to those cases (*Swing, Cantwell, Bridges*) involving "the action of state courts in enforcing a substantive common-law rule," consider Comment, 45 Mich. L.Rev. 733, 742–43 (1947): "The difficulty of attributing the discrimination effected by the covenants to the enforcing tribunal is not to be escaped by pretending that it forms an element of the common law from which the right to enforcement is derived. The common law is simply the policy of the state in certain of its aspects, [and] that policy as seen in respect to these facts looks no further than to the protection of property and contract rights." Did the state policy in *Cantwell* look any further than to the protection of public tranquility? Did it, in *Bridges*, look any further than to the protection of the integrity of the court? For careful analysis, see Van Alstyne, *Mr. Justice Black, Constitutional Review, and the Talisman of State Action*, 1965 Duke L.J. 219.

Are the considerations in *Shelley* different from all of these cases because it involves equal protection rather than due process? Because these other cases involve the right of free speech? Should there be a distinction between civil suits and criminal prosecutions? Consider Comment, 45 Mich.L.Rev. 733, 746 (1947): "The theory of civil remedies is that the interest of the state in the protection of property and contract rights is ordinarily secondary to that of the individual citizen, that the extent to which the protection of the law is obtained for them is largely discretionary with him. [A] criminal statute is an expression of state policy of a much higher order. In theory, the state pursues purposes of its own in criminal legislation."

2. Is *Shelley* supportable because "so long as it is unconstitutional for a state to require racial segregation by zoning statutes [it] is equally unconstitutional for the state to bring it about by any other form of state action"? McGovney, *Racial Residential Segregation by State Court Enforcement of Restrictive Agreements, Covenants or Conditions in Deeds is Unconstitutional*, 33 Calif. L.Rev. 5, 30 (1945). Is the source of the discrimination the same in both instances? Or is this a variation of the "government function" approach? Consider Groner & Helfeld, *Race Discrimination in Housing*, 57 Yale L.J. 426, 454 (1948): "Where covenants do not presently cover entire areas, experience shows that, if encouraged by court enforcement, covenants do in time cover all of the area available for desirable residences." See also Ming, *Racial Restrictions and the Fourteenth Amendment: The Restrictive Covenant Cases*, 16 U.Chi.L.Rev. 203 (1949).

3. BARROWS v. JACKSON, 346 U.S. 249, 73 S.Ct. 1031, 97 L.Ed. 1586 (1953), held that an action by a co-covenantor to recover damages from a property owner who sold to a black was barred by equal protection. Would this suit, like the one in *Shelley*, involve "the full coercive power of government to deny [on] grounds of race [the] enjoyment of property rights"? Would the suit in *Barrows* have the same effect as a suit to enjoin a white property owner from

breaching the covenant? See *Hurd v. Hodge,* 334 U.S. 24, 68 S.Ct. 847, 92 L.Ed. 1187 (1948).

4. *Other devices.* After *Shelley* and *Barrows,* consider the validity of:

(a) A deed conveying property on condition that if sold to a black it automatically reverts to the original grantor.

(i) Suppose the grantor sues to evict the purchasing black? Suppose the grantor retakes possession and the purchasing black sues to evict? Might a court deny relief in the latter situation on the ground that it had "merely abstained from action, leaving private individuals free to impose such discrimination as they see fit"?

(ii) Suppose a suit for declaratory judgment as to the validity of the reverter? If the reverter were declared invalid, could it be said "that the restrictive agreements standing alone cannot be regarded as a violation of [the] Fourteenth Amendment"? If it were declared valid, could a court deny the original grantor's suit to enjoin the black purchaser's taking possession? See generally Miller, *Racial Discrimination and Private Schools,* 41 Minn.L.Rev. 245, 276–80 (1957).

(b) A will devising property on condition that if the beneficiary marry a person "not born in the Hebrew faith" the property be paid over to someone else. Suppose the beneficiary marries a Catholic and the remainderman sues for the property?

(c) A child custody decree directing the father to pay private school tuition. Suppose the father refuses to pay because the school racially discriminates (cf. *Norwood v. Harrison*) and the mother sues to enforce the decree.

5. *The limits of Shelley.* (a) Consider Comment, 44 Calif.L.Rev. 718, 733 (1956): "If obtaining court aid to carry out 'private' activity 'converts' such private action into 'state' action, then there could never be any private action in any practical sense. So entwined are our lives with the law that the logical result would be that almost *all* action, to be effective, must result in state action. Thus all private activity would be required to 'conform' with the standards of conduct imposed on the states by the fourteenth amendment."

(b) Evaluate the following analyses of *Shelley:*

(i) "[S]ince one's property rights in land are only powers delegated by higher state agencies [and] are legally effective only by virtue of authority granted by the state, then looking only to the face of the Fourteenth Amendment, it applies to all property [rights] used in a prohibited manner." Lathrop, *The Racial Covenant Cases,* 1948 Wis.L.Rev. 508, 515.

(ii) "[T]he *law* of contracts is not a matter of private agreement. The *agreements* entered may be classified as *private* affairs. However, when resort is had to a state court seeking enforcement for breach of such an agreement, it is the *law* of contracts which then must be invoked." Scanlan, *Racial Restriction in Real Estate—Property Values Versus Human Values,* 24 Not.D.Law. 157, 172–73 (1949).

(iii) "Professor Louis Pollak [*Racial Discrimination and Judicial Integrity,* 108 U.Pa.L.Rev. 1, 13 (1959)] would apply *Shelley* to prevent the state from enforcing a discrimination by one who does not wish to discriminate; [b] but he would allow the state to give its support to willing discrimination * * *. [H]is

---

b. See *Moose Lodge v. Irvis,* Sec. 4 infra, for this application of *Shelley*—in the only opinion of the Court (apart from *Barrows v.* *Jackson*) that has relied on *Shelley* to find state action. Cf. also fn. 10 in *Flagg Bros. v. Brooks,* Sec. 4 infra, and note 1 thereafter.

proposal requires important limitation of *Shelley,* and raises a number of possible objections. One may argue, for instance, that while the fourteenth amendment may perhaps protect an individual's 'liberty' to refuse to discriminate as it may protect another's liberty to discriminate, that hardly seems to be the focus of the equal protection clause. That clause seems to be designed to protect the victim against discrimination, not to protect an unwilling 'actor' against being compelled to discriminate. It would seem also an eccentric constitutional provision which protected the aggrieved against involuntary discrimination by private persons but not against voluntary private discrimination. Moreover, the distinction is offered as a definition of 'state action.' But whether the judgment of a court enforces a voluntary discrimination or compels a no-longer-voluntary discrimination, the discrimination is private in origin; in both cases it requires a court judgment to make the discrimination effective. * * * Finally, in *Shelley* itself, is it acceptable to think of the case as one in which the state was compelling discrimination by a grantor of property who no longer wished to discriminate? In essence, the state was enforcing discrimination by the other parties to the covenant." Henkin, *Shelley v. Kraemer: Notes for a Revised Opinion,* 110 U.Pa.L.Rev. 473, 477–78 & n. 10 (1962).

Compare Horowitz, *The Misleading Search for "State Action" Under the Fourteenth Amendment,* 30 So.Cal.L.Rev. 208, 213 (1957): "There is involved here a question of the degree of effect of different forms of state action on a prospective Negro buyer's opportunity to purchase and use land * * *. The state does not substantially deny the Negro that opportunity by *permitting* a private person to refuse to deal with him because of his race. This would be the situation where there was 'voluntary adherence' to the restrictive covenant by the landowner. But the state does to a far greater degree deny the Negro the opportunity to acquire land, because of his race, if it *compels* a landowner not to deal with the Negro. This is the situation where the state enforces the restrictive covenant after a landowner has decided not to adhere to it."

(iv) Since restraints on alienation of property are presumptively void, being valid generally only if the court finds the restraint a reasonable one and consistent with public policy, Restatement, *Property* § 406 (1944), was there state action in *Shelley* because the court placed its imprimatur on a racially discriminatory restraint? Might it be argued that, due to this, the source of discrimination was public rather than private? See Choper, *Thoughts on State Action,* 1979 Wash.U.L.Q. 757, 769–71.

(c) Consider Comment, 44 Calif.L.Rev. 718, 735 (1956): "It is submitted that the doctrine of judicial enforcement as interpreted by *Shelley* is applicable only when the court action abets private discrimination which in the absence of such judicial aid would be ineffective. * * * Where the private activity, admitted in *Shelley* to be valid in itself, is already effective, it is not to be said that the court, recognizing or failing to abolish the activity, is itself an arm of the discrimination; the situation has remained the same, court action or no. It is only where the proponents of discrimination, unable to further their ends privately, seek court aid is the state itself causing discrimination under *Shelley.*"

(i) Suppose plaintiff is denied relief in a breach of contract suit against a cemetery for refusing to bury a black because the burial lot purchase contract was restricted to Caucasians? Compare *Rice v. Sioux City Mem'l Park Cem.,* 349 U.S. 70, 75 S.Ct. 614, 99 L.Ed. 897 (1955) with *Spencer v. Flint Mem'l Park Ass'n,* 4 Mich.App. 157, 144 N.W.2d 622 (1966). What result under *Shelley*? Under the above theory? Would denial of plaintiff's cause of action make the discrimination "effective"? If the body had already been interred, could the cemetery obtain the court's aid in removing it?

(ii) Suppose a collective bargaining agreement authorizes discharge of employees for "just cause" and an employee is so discharged because he is black. What result in the employee's suit for reinstatement? See *Black v. Cutter Lab.,* 351 U.S. 292, 301–03, 76 S.Ct. 824, 828, 100 L.Ed. 1188, 1197 (1956) (dissenting opinion). What result in the employer's suit to restrain the employee from continuing to appear on the job?

(iii) Suppose a landlord seeks the court's aid to evict a tenant whose defense is that the eviction is solely on the grounds of race (or religion, or speech)? Suppose the tenant seeks to restrain the landlord from recovering possession of the leased premises? If the tenant refuses to give up possession and is forcibly evicted by the landlord, what result in the tenant's suit for assault? Would a desirable rule produce different results in the above situations?

(iv) What result in a suit by the state real estate board to revoke a broker's license for having sold property to a black contrary to the owner's instructions? In a suit by a citizen to force the state real estate board to revoke a broker's license for having refused to show property to blacks pursuant to the owner's instructions?

(v) At common law, no person who offered his property for sale could be enjoined from arbitrarily refusing to sell to another. Suppose an owner refuses to sell solely because of the buyer's race. Consider Huber, *Revolution in Private Law?* 6 S.C.L.Q. 8, 26 (1953): "It would seem, under *Shelley,* that he could bring suit alleging denial of equal protection of the laws. Even if the court wished to dismiss the suit as not stating a cause of action [it] would seem that the court could not do so without supporting the discrimination."

6. *Reconsideration of prior problems in light of Shelley.* (a) *Evans v. Newton.* (i) When the state court accepted the city's resignation and appointed private trustees to carry out the testator's discriminatory intent, was this state action that abetted otherwise private discrimination? If the city had not resigned and the state court had granted the relief sought to remove the city as trustee, would this be enforcing discrimination by one who did not wish to discriminate in violation of the *Shelley* rule?

If Senator Bacon had designated a private trustee who was unwilling or unable to act, a new trustee would be appointed by the court. 4 Scott, *Trusts* § 388 (2d ed. 1956). Would discrimination by such an appointee be state action? In most states, charitable trusts are enforced by the attorney general. Id. § 391. If Bacon's will had designated a private trustee who refused to discriminate, would an action by the attorney general to force the trustee to comply with terms of the trust violate equal protection? [c] If the private trustee, in compliance with the terms, discriminates from the outset, would the attorney general's

---

c. Consider Burke & Reber, *State Action, Congressional Power and Creditors' Rights: An Essay on the Fourteenth Amendment,* 46 So.Cal.L.Rev. 1003, 1090–91 (1973): "[By judicial enforcement in *Shelley*], all sellers would be compelled to exercise their choice in favor of discrimination because of the hazard and uncertainty that would accompany any effort to break the racially restrictive deed restrictions. The state judicial action would thus have effectively sealed the deed restrictions and molded them into a racially restrictive ordinance ∗ ∗ ∗. [But] an injunction to force a trustee to comply with the trustor's discriminatory wishes would not be state action since [the state is simply] acknowledging the trustor's decision to discriminate and is not coercing it in any way." Is there "less" state action when a court compels discrimination by a trustee who *never* wished to discriminate than when it compels discrimination by a seller who *earlier* exercised a choice to discriminate?

failure to seek to end the discrimination violate equal protection? What would be the effect of a court approving the trustee's accounts?

(ii) On remand, after *Evans,* the Georgia courts interpreted Senator Bacon's will and held that "because the park's segregated, whites-only character was an essential and inseparable part of the testator's plan," the "cy pres doctrine to amend the terms of the will by striking the racial restrictions" was inapplicable; that, therefore, the trust failed and the trust property "by operation of law reverted to the heirs of Senator Bacon." EVANS v. ABNEY, 396 U.S. 435, 90 S.Ct. 628, 24 L.Ed.2d 634 (1970), per BLACK, J., affirmed, finding that "the Georgia court had no alternative under its relevant trust laws, which are long standing and neutral with regard to race, but to end the Baconsfield trust": "[T]he Constitution imposes no requirement upon the Georgia court to approach Bacon's will any differently than it would approach any will creating any charitable trust of any kind. [T]here is not the slightest indication that any of the Georgia judges involved were motivated by racial animus or discriminatory intent of any sort in construing and enforcing Senator Bacon's will. Nor is there any indication that Senator Bacon in drawing up his will was persuaded or induced to include racial restrictions by the fact that such restrictions were permitted by the Georgia trust statutes." *Shelley* was "easily distinguishable" because here "the termination of the park was a loss shared equally by the white and Negro citizens of Macon."

BRENNAN, J., dissented: "For almost half a century Baconsfield has been a public park." When "a public facility would remain open but for the constitutional command that it be operated on a nonsegregated basis, the closing of that facility conveys an unambiguous message of community involvement in racial discrimination. [But] the Court finds that in this case it is not the State or city but 'a private party which is injecting the racially discriminatory motivation.'" Nonetheless, "this discriminatory closing is permeated with state action": "First, there is state action whenever a State enters into an arrangement which creates a private right to compel or enforce the reversion of a public facility" and, here, "in accepting title to the park," city officials agreed to that "if the city should ever incur a constitutional obligation to desegregate the park. [The] decision whether or not a public facility shall be operated in compliance with the Constitution is an essential *governmental* decision." Second, "nothing in the record suggests that after our decision in *Evans v. Newton* the City of Macon retracted its previous willingness to manage Baconsfield on a nonsegregated basis, or that the white beneficiaries of Senator Bacon's generosity were unwilling to share it with Negroes, rather than have the park revert to his heirs." Thus, contrary to *Shelley,* "this is a case of a state court's enforcement of a racial restriction to prevent willing parties from dealing with one another." [d]

DOUGLAS, J., dissented: "Bacon's will did not leave any remainder or reversion in 'Baconsfield' to his heirs." Thus, giving them the property does "as much violence to Bacon's purpose as would conversion of an 'all-white' park into an 'all-Negro' park. [The] purpose of the will was to dedicate the land for some municipal use. * * * Letting both races share the facility is closer to a realization of Bacon's desire than a complete destruction of the will." Marshall, J., did not participate.

d. Brennan, J., also pointed to White, J.'s opinion in *Evans v. Newton,* contending that the will's racial restriction was so "encouraged" by the 1905 Georgia statute as to make the state "significantly involved" in the discrimination—citing *Burton* and *Reitman v. Mulkey,* infra. See note 2 after *Reitman,* infra.

(iii) Was the Georgia courts' action "a judicial choice between two incompatible terms of his will"—"(1) to keep Negroes out of the park; and (2) to keep Baconsfield a park forever"—thus, state action placing its imprimatur on racial discrimination (see note 5(b)(iv) supra)? Comment, 14 Kan.L.Rev. 613, 625 (1966).

(b) *De facto school segregation.* Consider Comment, 31 Mo.L.Rev. 391, 397 (1966): "[*Shelley*] stands for the proposition that the state may not give discriminatory acts of private persons the force of law. Does not the local school board violate that proposition when [it] assures private persons that if they are able to keep their neighborhoods segregated their schools will be segregated also." Does the school board thus also encourage private housing discrimination?

(c) *Labor unions.* Consider Weiss, *Federal Remedies for Racial Discrimination by Labor Unions,* 50 Geo.L.J. 457, 474–75 (1962): "[*Shelley*] would seem to deny a union access to the courts for enforcement of a racially discriminatory scheme. [Upon] such analysis it becomes clear that the NLRB is without power to certify a labor union which engages in racial discrimination or to provide such a union with the protection normally furnished to exclusive bargaining representatives under the National Labor Relations Act. In other words, the NLRB cannot do *anything* which will further the exercise of power by a discriminating union." May the NLRB or the courts protect such a union from an unfair labor practice? If not, may a covenantor in *Shelley* sue for damage to his property caused by another person?

7. *The balancing approach.* Is the ultimate solution in *Shelley,* and other cases, a balancing of *all* of the particular interests involved? Consider Van Alstyne & Karst, *State Action,* 14 Stan.L.Rev. 3, 44–45 (1961): "[There has been] an attempt to discover or invent the *kind* of state connection which will satisfy the state action requirement. It is suggested, for example, that the state acts in the sense of the amendment when it coerces private discrimination, but not when it simply lends its aid to such racial discrimination as private individuals may choose to practice. [This analysis] perpetuates the untenable distinction between the state action requirement on the one hand and the balance of 'substantive' constitutional interests on the other. This way of looking at the problem [is] even more dangerous than the suggestion's other unfortunate aspect: its assumption that every private discrimination is invalid once the right formal state connection has been found." See also Williams, *Mulkey v. Reitman and State Action,* 14 U.C.L.A.L.Rev. 26 (1966).

Compare Henkin, note 5(b)(iii) supra at 496: "Generally, the equal protection clause precludes state enforcement of private discrimination. There is, however, a small area of liberty favored by the Constitution even over claims to equality. Rights of liberty and property, of privacy and voluntary association, must be balanced, in close cases, against the right not to have the state enforce discrimination against the victim. In the few instances in which the right to discriminate is protected or preferred by the Constitution, the state may enforce it." [e] Is it the contention that the inquiry is not whether state action is present but whether the state policy preference, expressed through its laws, between conflicting claims of individuals, denies equal protection?

Contrast Gilbert, *Theories of State Action as Applied to the "Sit-In" Cases,* 17 Ark.L.Rev. 147, 161 (1963): "The primary weakness in Henkin's approach

e. For support, see Douglas, J., concurring in *Lombard v. Louisiana,* fn. h infra. See also Black, *"State Action," Equal Protection, and California's Proposition 14,* 81 Harv.L.Rev. 69, 83–109 (1967); Sengstock & Sengstock, *Discrimination: A Constitutional Dilemma,* 9 Wm. & M.L.Rev. 59 (1967).

would seem to be that the responsibility of the state arises from its *power* to act in a given situation. It would seem much sounder to impute responsibility where there is a *duty* on the part of the state to act. Thus, where traditional state functions, such as running elections or operating a town, are involved, the state would seem to have a duty to see that these activities are conducted in a constitutional manner. Beyond the area of state functions being performed by private enterprises, the state might have a duty to insure nondiscrimination by enterprises which occupy important positions of public interest. For example, if all the milk producers in an area refused to sell to Negroes, it would seem that the state would have a duty to insure that Negroes could purchase milk on equal terms with whites. In the case of the small corner diner, especially in an area which offers other sources of similar meals to the Negro, it would seem that the state has no duty to insure the Negro a meal there, even though the state would clearly have the power to do so. Here again, an ad hoc approach would be required."

See Horowitz, *Fourteenth Amendment Aspects of Racial Discrimination in "Private" Housing,* 52 Calif.L.Rev. 1, 12–20 (1964): "The determination of the constitutionality under the fourteenth amendment of state law permitting a private person to discriminate, on racial grounds, against another private person in a specific fact situation requires consideration of various interdependent factors: the nature and degree of injury to the person discriminated against, the interest of the discriminator in being permitted to discriminate, and the interest of the discriminatee in having opportunity of access equal to that of other persons to the benefits of governmental assistance to the discriminator * * *. If there is extensive state participation and involvement related to the activities of the discriminator, it is more likely that those activities will be public in nature, with consequent public indignity and humiliation suffered by the person discriminated against, and more likely that denial of access to those activities will be of some significance to the discriminatee. [When] there is governmental assistance to the discriminator in carrying on his activities, and the assistance is being provided to further the purposes of a governmental program designed to provide benefits for the public or a permissible segment of the public, the effect of the discrimination is to deny to the discriminatee the opportunity to have equal opportunity of access to the benefits of the governmental program."[f]

Compare Choper, *Thoughts on State Action,* 1979 Wash.U.L.Q. 757, 762: "[The balancing approaches] contradict a central feature of the fourteenth amendment. Although its major purpose was to augment the authority of the national government to secure certain constitutional rights, its primary thrust was to accomplish this goal by outlawing deprivations of these rights by state governments and their legal structures rather than by the impact of private choice. By effectively obliterating the distinction between state action and private action, these theories eviscerate the fourteenth amendment's restriction on the authority of the national government vis-à-vis the states regarding the regulation of the myriad relationships that occur between one individual and another. [A]t the initiative of any litigant who is offended by another person's behavior, these theories would subject to the scrutiny of federal judges, under

f. For other discussions of a balancing approach, see Glennon & Nowak, *A Functional Analysis of the Fourteenth Amendment "State Action" Requirement,* 1976 Sup.Ct.Rev. 221; Quinn, *State Action: A Pathology and a Proposed Cure,* 64 Calif.L.Rev. 146 (1976); Thompson, *Piercing the Veil of State Action: The Revisionist Theory and a Mythical Application to Self-Help Repossession.* 1977 Wis.L.Rev. 1; Morris & Powe, *Constitutional & Statutory Rights to Open Housing,* 44 Wash.L.Rev. 1–56 (1968).

substantive constitutional standards customarily developed for measuring the actions of government, all sorts of private conduct that because of political constraints and collective good sense would probably never be mandated by law. Further, by permitting private actors to violate constitutional norms when they have a constitutionally protected liberty interest to do so, these theories would delegate to federal judges the power to implement the vague mandate of the due process clause in speaking the final word about the validity of virtually all transactions between individuals. In doing so, the national judiciary would be required to determine whether private conduct was constitutionally immune from government control even though, because of general political sensitivity to individual autonomy, such private conduct probably would never be regulated by the state." See also Lewis, *The Role of Law in Regulating Discrimination in Places of Public Accommodation,* 13 Buf.L.Rev. 402, 416–18 (1964).

Consider also Haber, *Notes on the Limits of Shelley v. Kraemer,* 18 Rutgers L.Rev. 811, 813, 824–25 (1964): "[I]t is dangerous to let any constitutional guarantee rest on an ad hoc balancing test. [I]t is extremely difficult to weigh liberty against equality; the outcome depends entirely on the views of the particular judges. While to some extent this must always be true in constitutional adjudications, it is nevertheless incumbent upon lawyers to develop a principle that will put some restraint even on the membership of the Supreme Court. * * *

"[T]he state can prohibit all racial discrimination. There is no liberty to discriminate. Whatever other incidents of property may be protected by the due process clause, the property and liberty protected by it occurring in the same amendment which guarantees the equal protection of the laws, does not include the right to treat people differently on the basis of their race and color."

Professor Haber would limit *Shelley* as follows: "the principle of state action as applied to judicial and police aid to private discrimination permits such aid only in the following instances: (1) Where the suit is by the victim and he seeks a new remedy based entirely on the discrimination, the state may deny the remedy. (2) Though this is doubtful, conceivably [the] state may also deny the remedy based on a contract voluntarily entered into with the discriminator by the victim of the discrimination or his privy, where the discriminator defends on the basis of a discriminatory provision in the contract. (3) The state may protect all property and personal rights of the discriminator other than the act of discrimination. (4) The state may even protect the act of discrimination provided it has offered the victim an adequate alternative remedy."

8. *"Sit-in" cases.*[g] (a) In PETERSON v. GREENVILLE, 373 U.S. 244, 83 S.Ct. 1119, 10 L.Ed.2d 323 (1963), an ordinance forebade restaurants to seat whites and blacks together. The Court, per WARREN, C.J., reversed trespass convictions of black youths who, when refused service at a lunch counter, refused to leave: "[T]hese convictions cannot stand, even assuming [that] the manager would have acted as he did independently of the existence of the ordinance. [When] a state agency passes a law compelling persons to discriminate [such] a palpable violation of the Fourteenth Amendment cannot be saved by attempting to separate the mental urges of the discriminators."[h] DOUGLAS, J., concurred,

g. In the early 1960s, the Court—employing a variety of doctrines, but never relying on *Shelley*—reversed a long series of trespass convictions of "sit-in" demonstrators who were protesting racial discrimination by restaurants and other businesses. The Civil Rights Act of 1964 largely mooted the constitutional problem of equal rights in public accommodations.

h. See also *Lombard v. Louisiana,* 373 U.S. 267, 83 S.Ct. 1122, 10 L.Ed.2d 338 (1963) finding state action under *Shelley* because "Louisiana has interceded with its judiciary to put criminal sanctions behind racial discrimination in public places."[i] HARLAN, J., noting "a clash of competing constitutional claims of a high order: liberty and equality," would have "the issue of state action" turn on the "question of fact" whether the restaurant "might have preferred for reasons entirely of its own not to serve meals to Negroes along with whites, [or] whether the ordinance played some part in [the] decision to segregate."[j]

(b) In BELL v. MARYLAND, 378 U.S. 226, 84 S.Ct. 1814, 12 L.Ed.2d 822 (1964), GOLDBERG, J., joined by Warren, C.J., and Douglas, J., relying on the historical view in Sec. 1, fn. a, cited *Marsh, Shelley, Terry* and *Barrows* for the view that "a State, obligated under the Fourteenth Amendment to maintain a system of law in which Negroes are not denied protection in their claim to be treated as equal members of the community, may not use its criminal trespass laws to frustrate the constitutionally granted right. Nor, it should be added, may a State frustrate this right by legitimating a proprietor's attempt at self-help."

BLACK, J., joined by Harlan and White, JJ., dissented: Reliance on *Shelley* was "misplaced" because it established only these propositions: "(1) When an owner of property is willing to sell and a would-be purchaser is willing to buy, then the Civil Rights Act of 1866, which gives all persons the same right to 'inherit, lease, sell, hold, and convey' property, prohibits a State, whether through its legislature, executive, or judiciary, from preventing the sale on the grounds of the race or color of one of the parties. * * * (2) Once a person has become a property owner, then he [may] sell his property to whom he pleases and admit to that property whom he will; so long as *both* parties are willing parties, then the principles stated in *Buchanan v. Warley*, 245 U.S. 60, 38 S.Ct. 16, 62 L.Ed. 149 (1917) and *Shelley* protect this right. But equally, when one party is unwilling, as when the property owner chooses *not* to sell to a particular person or *not* to admit that person, [then] he is entitled to rely on the guarantee of due process of law [to] protect his free use and enjoyment of property and to

(statements by city officials that sit-ins "would not be permitted" had "as much coercive effect as an ordinance"); *Robinson v. Florida*, 378 U.S. 153, 84 S.Ct. 1693, 12 L.Ed.2d 771 (1964) (state health regulations, requiring racially separate toilets in restaurants, impose "burdens bound to discourage the serving of the two races together").

If a statute requires private colleges to enact regulations for maintenance of order on campus, must such a college's procedures for dismissal of students comport with procedural due process?

i. See also Douglas, J.'s view that "state policy may be as effectively expressed in *customs* as in formal legislative, executive, or judicial action," *Garner v. Louisiana*, 368 U.S. 157, 82 S.Ct. 248, 7 L.Ed.2d 207 (1961) (concurring opinion) (cf. Karst & Van Alstyne, *Sit-Ins and State Action—Mr. Justice Douglas Concurring*, 14 Stan.L.Rev. 762 (1962)); and Brennan, J.'s view that *Peterson, Lombard*, and *Robinson* "together hold that a state policy of discouraging privately chosen integration or encouraging privately chosen segregation, even though the policy is expressed in a form nondiscriminatory on its face, is unconstitu-

tional and taints the privately chosen segregation it seeks to bring about," *Adickes v. S.H. Kress & Co.*, 398 U.S. 144, 90 S.Ct. 1598, 26 L.Ed.2d 142, (1970) (separate opinion). See further, note 2 after *Reitman v. Mulkey*, infra.

j. Consider Lewis, *The Sit-In Cases: Great Expectations*, 1963 Sup.Ct.Rev. 101, 110: "The Court [was] concerned with persons unknown and unknowable who might be affected by the cumulative pressure of such laws on a variety of proprietors in a variety of environments. [When] only the proprietor can know what his 'mental urges' are, and when even he might find difficulty in separating them, judicial review will be more effective for the mass of cases [if] the Court by the announcement of its rule makes it as certain as it can that proprietors and officials alike appreciate the precise status of segregation laws."

If federal law requires airlines to search passengers for weapons, should the issue of whether such a search by an airline employee is "state action" under the fourth and fourteenth amendments turn on whether the airlines would have conducted the searches regardless of the federal legislation?

know that only by valid legislation, passed pursuant to some constitutional grant of power, can anyone disturb this free use."

REITMAN v. MULKEY
387 U.S. 369, 87 S.Ct. 1627, 18 L.Ed.2d 830 (1967).

MR. JUSTICE WHITE delivered the opinion of the Court.

[Section 26 of the California constitution], an initiated measure submitted to the people [in] a statewide ballot in 1964, provides in part as follows: "Neither the State nor any subdivision or agency thereof shall deny, limit or abridge, directly or indirectly, the right of any person, who is willing or desires to sell, lease or rent any part or all of his real property, to decline to sell, lease or rent such property to such person or persons as he, in his absolute discretion, chooses." The real property covered by § 26 is limited to residential property and contains an exception for state-owned real estate.

[Respondents] sued under § 51 and § 52 of the California Civil Code [forbidding racial discrimination "in all business establishments"] alleging that petitioners had refused to rent them an apartment solely on account of their race. An injunction and damages were demanded. Petitioners moved for summary judgment on the ground that §§ 51 and 52, insofar as they were the basis for the Mulkeys' action, had been rendered null and void by the adoption of [§ 26] after the filing of the complaint. The trial court granted the motion [but the California Supreme Court held that § 26] was invalid as denying [equal protection].

We affirm the judgment [which] quite properly undertook to examine the constitutionality of § 26 in terms of its "immediate objective," its "ultimate impact" and its "historical context and the conditions existing prior to its enactment." Judgments such as these we have frequently undertaken ourselves. *Yick Wo v. Hopkins; Lombard v. Louisiana; Anderson v. Martin.* But here the California Supreme Court has addressed itself to these matters and we should give careful consideration to its views because they concern the purpose, scope, and operative effect of a provision of the California Constitution.

First, the court considered whether § 26 was concerned at all with private discriminations in residential housing. This involved a review of past efforts by the California Legislature to regulate such discriminations. The Unruh Act, on which respondents based their cases, was passed in 1959. [I]n 1963, came the Rumford Fair Housing Act * * * prohibiting racial discriminations in the sale or rental of any private dwelling containing more than four units. * * *

It was against this background that [§ 26] was enacted. Its immediate design and intent, the California court said, was "to overturn state laws that bore on the right of private sellers and lessors to discriminate," the Unruh and Rumford Acts, and "to forestall future state action that might circumscribe this right." * * *

Second, the court conceded that the State was permitted a neutral position with respect to private racial discriminations and that the State was not bound by the Federal Constitution to forbid them. But [the] court deemed it necessary to determine whether [§ 26] invalidly involved the State in racial discriminations in the housing market. Its conclusion was that it did.

To reach this result, the state court examined certain prior decisions in this Court in which discriminatory state action was identified. Based on these cases, it concluded that a prohibited state involvement could be found "even where the state can be charged with only encouraging," rather than commanding discrimination. Also of particular interest to the court was Mr. Justice Stewart's concurrence in *Burton,* where it was said that the Delaware courts had construed an existing Delaware statute as "authorizing" racial discrimination in restaurants and that the statute was therefore invalid. To the California court "[t]he instant case presents an undeniably analogous situation" wherein the State had taken affirmative action designed to make private discriminations legally possible. Section 26 was said to have changed the situation from one in which discriminatory practices were restricted "to one wherein it is encouraged, within the meaning of the cited decisions"; § 26 was legislative action "which authorized private discrimination" and made the State "at least a partner in the instant act of discrimination * * *." The court could "conceive of no other purpose for an application of section 26 aside from authorizing the perpetration of a purported private discrimination * * *." * * *

There is no sound reason for rejecting this judgment. [It] did not read either our cases or the Fourteenth Amendment as establishing an automatic constitutional barrier to the repeal of an existing law prohibiting racial discriminations in housing; nor did the court rule that a State may never put in statutory form an existing policy of neutrality with respect to private discriminations. [It] dealt with § 26 as though it expressly authorized and constitutionalized the private right to discriminate [and] the court assessed the ultimate impact of § 26 in the California environment and concluded that the section would encourage and significantly involve the State in private racial discrimination contrary to the Fourteenth Amendment.

The California court could very reasonably conclude that § 26 would and did have wider impact than a mere repeal of existing statutes. * * * Private discriminations in housing were now not only free from Rumford and Unruh but they also enjoyed a far different status than was true before the passage of those statutes. The right to discriminate, including the right to discriminate on racial grounds, was now embodied in the State's basic charter, immune from legislative, executive, or judicial regulation at any level of the state government. Those practicing racial discriminations need no longer rely solely on their personal choice. They could now invoke express constitutional authority, free from censure or interference of any kind from official sources. * * *

This Court has never attempted the "impossible task" of formulating an infallible test for determining whether the State "in any of its manifestations" has become significantly involved in private discriminations. [Here] the California court, armed as it was with the knowledge of the facts and circumstances concerning the passage and potential impact of § 26, and familiar with the milieu in which that provision would operate, has determined that the provision would involve the State in private racial discriminations to an unconstitutional degree. We accept this holding of the California court.

The assessment of § 26 by the California court is similar to what this Court has done in appraising state statutes or other official actions in other contexts. [I]n *Nixon v. Condon,* 286 U.S. 73, 52 S.Ct. 484, 76 L.Ed. 984, the Court was faced with a statute empowering the executive committee of a political party to prescribe the qualifications of its members [which] was used by the committee to bar Negroes from voting in primary elections. Reposing this power in the executive committee was said to insinuate the State into the self-regulatory, decision-making scheme of the voluntary association; the exercise of the power was viewed as an expression of state authority contrary to the Fourteenth Amendment.

In *Burton,* [the] State neither commanded nor expressly authorized or encouraged the discriminations * * *. [The Court also discussed *Lombard, Peterson v. Greenville* and *Robinson v. Florida,* observing that there was no "proof required that the restaurant owner had actually been influenced by the state statute or regulation."]

None of these cases squarely controls the case we now have before us. But they [do] exemplify the necessity for a court to assess the potential impact of official action in determining whether the State has significantly involved itself with invidious discriminations. * * * Section 26 was intended to authorize, and does authorize, racial discrimination in the housing market. The right to discriminate is now one of the basic policies of the State. The California Supreme Court believes that the section will significantly encourage and involve the State in private discriminations. We have been presented with no persuasive considerations indicating that this judgment should be overturned.

Affirmed.

MR. JUSTICE DOUGLAS, concurring.

While I join the opinion of the Court, I add a word to indicate the dimensions of our problem.

[We] deal here with a problem in the realm of zoning, similar to the one we had in *Shelley* [and § 26] in the setting of our modern housing problem is only another device of the same character.

Real estate brokers [who are licensed in California] and mortgage lenders are largely dedicated to the maintenance of segregated communities. [The] builders join in the same scheme * * *.

[Section 26] is a form of sophisticated discrimination whereby the people of California harness the energies of private groups to do indirectly what they cannot under our decisions allow their government to do. * * *

Zoning is a state and municipal function. When the State leaves that function to private agencies or institutions who are [state licensees], it suffers a governmental function to be performed under private auspices in a way the State itself may not act. The present case is therefore kin to *Terry v. Adams* * * *.

If we were in a domain exclusively private, we would have different problems. But urban housing is in the public domain [and] is clearly marked with the public interest. * * *

MR. JUSTICE HARLAN, whom MR. JUSTICE BLACK, MR. JUSTICE CLARK, and MR. JUSTICE STEWART join, dissenting.

[California] has decided to remain "neutral" in the realm of private discrimination affecting the sale or rental of private residential property * * *. In short, all that has happened is that California has effected a pro tanto repeal of its prior statutes forbidding private discrimination. This runs no more afoul of the Fourteenth Amendment than would have California's failure to pass any such antidiscrimination statutes in the first instance. The fact that such repeal was also accompanied by a constitutional prohibition against future enactment of such laws by the California Legislature cannot well be thought to affect, from a federal constitutional standpoint, the validity of what California has done. * * *

The Court attempts to fit § 26 within the coverage of the Equal Protection Clause by characterizing it as in effect an affirmative call to residents of California to discriminate. [But § 26] is neutral on its face, and it is only by in effect asserting that this requirement of passive official neutrality is camouflage that the Court is able to reach its conclusion. In depicting the provision as tantamount to active state encouragement of discrimination the Court essentially relies on the fact that the California Supreme Court so concluded. * * * I agree, of course, that *findings of fact* by a state court should be given great weight, but this familiar proposition hardly aids the Court's holding in this case.

There is no disagreement whatever but that § 26 was meant to nullify California's fair-housing legislation and thus to remove from private residential property transactions the state-created impediment upon freedom of choice. There were no disputed issues of fact at all * * *. There was no finding, for example, that the defendants' actions were anything but the product of their own private choice. [There] were no findings as to the general effect of § 26. The Court declares that the California court "held the purpose and intent of § 26 was to authorize private racial discriminations in the housing market," but there is no supporting fact in the record for this characterization. * * *

A state enactment, particularly one that is simply permissive of private decision-making rather than coercive[,] should not be struck down [without] persuasive evidence of an invidious purpose or effect. The only "factual" matter relied on by the majority of the California Supreme Court was the context in which [§ 26] was adopted, namely, that several strong antidiscrimination acts had been passed by the legislature and opposed by many of those who successfully led the movement for adoption of [§ 26]. These circumstances, and these alone, the California court held, made § 26 unlawful under this Court's cases interpreting the Equal Protection Clause. This, of course, is nothing but a legal conclusion as to federal constitutional law * * *. I cannot see that its conclusion is entitled to any special weight in the discharge of our own responsibilities. * * *

[The] core of the Court's opinion is that § 26 is offensive to the Fourteenth Amendment because it effectively *encourages* private discrimination. By focusing on "encouragement" the Court, I fear, is forging a slippery and unfortunate criterion by which to measure the constitutionality of a statute simply permissive in purpose and effect, and inoffensive on its face.

It is true that standards in this area have not been definitely formulated, and that acts of discrimination have been included within the compass of the Equal Protection Clause not merely when they were compelled by a state statute or other governmental pressures, but also when they were said to be "induced" or "authorized" by the State. Most of these cases, however, can be approached in terms of the impact and extent of affirmative state governmental activities, e.g., the action of a sheriff, *Lombard;* the official supervision over a park, *Evans v. Newton;* a joint venture with a lessee in a municipally owned building, *Burton.*[2] In situations such as these the focus has been on positive state cooperation or partnership in affirmatively promoted activities, an involvement that could have been avoided. Here, in contrast, we have only the straightforward adoption of a neutral provision restoring to the sphere of free choice, left untouched by the Fourteenth Amendment, private behavior within a limited area of the racial problem. The denial of equal protection emerges only from the conclusion reached by the Court that the implementation of a new policy of governmental neutrality [has] the effect of lending encouragement to those who wish to discriminate. In the context of the actual facts of the case, this

---

2. [There is no] force in the Court's reliance on *Nixon v. Condon,* a voting case decided under the Fifteenth as well as the Fourteenth Amendment.

conclusion appears to me to state only a truism: people who want to discriminate but were previously forbidden to do so by state law are now left free because the State has chosen to have no law on the subject at all. Obviously whenever there is a change in the law it will have resulted from the concerted activity of those who desire the change, and its enactment will allow those supporting the legislation to pursue their private goals.

A moment of thought will reveal the far-reaching possibilities of the Court's new doctrine, which I am sure the Court does not intend. Every act of private discrimination is either forbidden by state law or permitted by it. There can be little doubt that such permissiveness—whether by express constitutional or statutory provision, or implicit in the common law—to some extent "encourages" those who wish to discriminate to do so. Under this theory "state action" in the form of laws that do nothing more than passively permit private discrimination could be said to tinge *all* private discrimination with the taint of unconstitutional state encouragement. * * *

I think that this decision is not only constitutionally unsound, but in its practical potentialities short-sighted. Opponents of state antidiscrimination statutes are now in a position to argue that such legislation should be defeated because, if enacted, it may be unrepealable. More fundamentally, the doctrine underlying this decision may hamper, if not preclude, attempts to deal with the delicate and troublesome problems of race relations through the legislative process. * * *

Notes and Questions

1. *Court's rationale.* (a) What was the specific basis for § 26's invalidity? Was it that it "constitutionalized the private right to discriminate" in housing, making it "immune from legislative, executive, or judicial regulation at any level of state government"—thus making it much more difficult for minorities to get governmental antidiscrimination help? Would this call for the same result even if California had never enacted the Unruh or Rumford Acts? Suppose a state provides that *all* legislation requires approval by ⅔ of the voters? All legislation having *anything* to do with the sale and purchase of real and personal property? Was § 26 a less "neutral provision"? Sufficiently "nonneutral"? Was *this* the thrust of the opinion? If so, does *Reitman* hold that racial discrimination in housing by private individuals in California is "state action"?

(b) Or did the Court rest on the finding (whose finding?) that § 26, given "the milieu in which that provision would operate," "would involve the State in private racial discriminations to an unconstitutional degree"? If so, could "mere repeal of existing statutes" so operate? Failure to enact a proposed antidiscrimination law? The mere absence of an antidiscrimination law? Consider Cox, *The Warren Court* 45 (1968): "The truth would seem to be that the absence of legal restraints gives encouragement of a sort to anyone minded to engage in discrimination, and any defeat of proposed restraints after strong public debate will give moral support to some persons who might not otherwise have been ready to discriminate. The degree of support that is given seems likely to depend upon a congeries of factors far more diffuse and subtle than the differences between repeal of a statute and amendment of a constitution." Compare 42 Wash.L.Rev. 285 (1966). See generally Black, *"State Action," Equal Protection, and California's Proposition 14,* 81 Harv.L.Rev. 69 (1967); Kurland, *Egalitarianism and the Warren Court,* 68 Mich. 629, 668–70 (1970).

Suppose a school board rescinds a resolution of its predecessor that recognized the boards' responsibility for segregation and called for—but did not enact—any remedial action? See *Dayton Bd. of Educ. v. Brinkman,* 433 U.S. 406, 413–14, 97 S.Ct. 2766, 2772, 53 L.Ed.2d 851, 859 (1977).

(c) Did the Court simply "nod in the direction of federalism" and "permit a state court to make the ultimate determinations," with the result "that one state law, impartial on its face but which, in the context of California politics, authorized and encouraged racial discrimination, was held contrary to the fourteenth amendment"—thus leaving open all questions raised above? Horan, *Law and Social Change: The Dynamics of the "State Action" Doctrine,* 17 J.Pub. L. 258, 281 (1968). Consider Karst & Horowitz, *Reitman v. Mulkey: A Telophase of Substantive Equal Protection,* 1967 Sup.Ct.Rev. 39, 48–49: "The Constitution is both a body of national law and a symbol of national unity. The Supreme Court's final responsibility for the law and for the symbol cannot lightly be passed to other bodies. [When] the critical issue decided by the state court depends on the way in which the Supreme Court's own precedents should be interpreted, deference to a purported local assessment of the constitutional balance is both circular in logic and empty of the ingredients of factfinding and value preference that should be indispensable to the making of constitutional law."

2. *State "encouragement" or "authorization."* (a) To what extent does *Reitman* establish the principle that state law which *encourages* (or *authorizes*) private conduct results in "state action"? Is this the basis for White, J.'s approach in *Evans v. Newton*? For Stewart, J.'s concurrence in *Burton*? For Brennan, J.'s view in *Adickes*? Consider Burke & Reber, fn. c after *Shelley*, at 1105–09 (1973): "[The] basic principle limiting the scope of the fourteenth amendment would be destroyed by equating state action with action authorized or encouraged by state law. [California] statutory law authorizes [the] use of force in self-defense; the disposition of real and personal property; [the] creation of a contractual relationship; [the] execution of a will; the formation of a corporation [etc.]. If state authority or encouragement is a valid state action test, then all of the above forms of private conduct would present fourteenth amendment equal protection and due process problems. [The] fallacy in the thesis [is] most readily apparent when one considers the impact of judicial law. It is almost impossible to consider any form of activity that is not somehow authorized by state decisional law. [As] long as the law is permissive in nature and leaves the initial decision to take the action entirely within the realm of private choice, neither the state nor the individual should be held constitutionally responsible under the fourteenth amendment. [Further], constitutional significance should not attach to such extraneous considerations as whether the law restates a long-standing law, clarifies an existing law, changes the law, creates entirely new law or repeals existing law. [First], the effect of a statute as a form of state law authorizing private conduct is precisely the same regardless of the statute's longevity * * *. Second, untoward consequences would follow from a holding that the statute is unconstitutional because of its newness or because it repeals an existing law considered more socially desirable by the Court. Such a holding would constitutionally freeze into state law every form of social legislation or decisional or administrative law deemed constitutionally proper by the Court and would thereby discourage states from experimenting in this regard. It would also produce anomalous and illogical results since the identical private conduct authorized and encouraged by the identical statutory or judicial law

would be valid in some states under the fourteenth amendment but invalid in others solely because of the age of the state law in each jurisdiction."

Compare Note, *State Action: Theories for Applying Constitutional Restrictions to Private Activity,* 74 Colum.L.Rev. 656, 665–66 (1974): "Statutes enlarging common law rights clearly amount to an increase of private powers, while mere statutory codification of common law rights does not amount to authorization [and the] argument that such 'authorizing' statutes involve government by increasing private powers implies that an increase in powers through expansion of common law rights effected by the courts will constitute a government grant of power. Since any particular decision expanding the previously existing common law would thus constitute 'authorization,' the question arises as against when present common law rights are to be measured. The most reasonable starting point for 'state action' cases arising under the fourteenth amendment would seem to be the common law as of adoption of that amendment." See also Horowitz & Karst, *The California Supreme Court and State Action Under the Fourteenth Amendment: The Leader Beclouds the Issue,* 21 U.C.L.A.L.Rev. 1421 (1974).

(b) Is there a distinction for purposes of state action between state law that authorizes racial restrictions in charitable trusts (cf. *Evans* and *Burton*) and state law that authorizes *any* restrictions (cf. *Adickes*)?

(c) The "state 'encouragement' or 'authorization'" issue is considered further in *Flagg Bros. v. Brooks,* Sec. 4 infra.

3. *Repeal of discriminatory legislation.* Recall *Lombard, Peterson* and *Robinson.* Suppose all official pronouncements *requiring* discrimination are repealed or retracted? Is subsequent "private" discrimination in respect to matters previously covered by official pronouncements "state action"? Is the state "significantly involved" because its repeals have now made "private discriminations legally possible"? Have they "authorized" and "encouraged" discrimination? Or is this "mere repeal of existing statutes"? Is discrimination more "authorized and encouraged" by repeal of laws requiring discrimination or by repeal of laws forbidding it?

SECTION 4. RECENT DEVELOPMENTS

MOOSE LODGE v. IRVIS
407 U.S. 163, 92 S.Ct. 1965, 32 L.Ed.2d 627 (1972).

MR. JUSTICE REHNQUIST delivered the opinion of the Court.

Appellee Irvis, a Negro, [who] was refused service [as the guest of a member] by appellant Moose Lodge, [claimed] that because the Pennsylvania liquor board had issued appellant Moose Lodge a private club license that authorized the sale of alcoholic beverages on its premises, the refusal of service to him was "state action" * * *.

A three-judge district court [entered] a decree declaring invalid the liquor license issued to Moose Lodge "as long as it follows a policy of racial discrimination in its membership or operating policies or practices." * * *

Moose Lodge is a private club in the ordinary meaning of that term. [It] conducts all of its activities in a building that is owned by it. It is not publicly funded. Only members and guests are permitted in any lodge of the order; one may become a guest only by invitation * * *.

The Court has never held, of course, that discrimination by an otherwise private entity would be violative of the Equal Protection Clause if the private entity receives any sort of benefit or service at all from the State, or if it is subject to state regulation in any degree whatever. Since state-furnished services include such necessities of life as electricity, water, and police and fire protection, such a holding would utterly emasculate the distinction between private as distinguished from State conduct set forth in *The Civil Rights Cases* and adhered to in subsequent decisions. Our holdings indicate that where the impetus for the discrimination is private, the State must have "significantly involved itself with invidious discriminations," *Reitman,* in order for the discriminatory action to fall within the ambit of the constitutional prohibition.

Our prior decisions dealing with discriminatory refusal of service in public eating places are significantly different factually from the case now before us. [With] one exception, which is discussed infra, there is no suggestion in this record that the Pennsylvania statutes and regulations governing the sale of liquor are intended either overtly or covertly to encourage discrimination. * * *

Here there is nothing approaching the symbiotic relationship between lessor and lessee that was present in *Burton* * * *. Far from apparently holding itself out as a place of public accommodation Moose Lodge quite ostentatiously proclaims the fact that it is not open to the public at large. Nor is it located and operated in such surroundings that although private in name, it discharges a function or performs a service that would otherwise in all likelihood be performed by the State. In short, while Eagle was a public restaurant in a public building, Moose Lodge is a private social club in a private building.

With the exception hereafter noted, the Pennsylvania Liquor Control Board plays absolutely no part in establishing or enforcing the membership or guest policies of the club which it licenses to serve liquor.[3] [The] only effect that the state licensing of Moose Lodge to serve liquor can be said to have on the right of any other Pennsylvanian to buy or be served liquor on premises other than those of Moose Lodge is that for some purposes club licenses are counted in the maximum number of licenses which may be issued in a given municipality. Basically each municipality has a quota of one retail license for each 1,500 inhabitants. Licenses issued to hotels, municipal golf courses and airport restaurants are not counted in this quota, nor are club licenses until the maximum number of retail licenses is reached. Beyond that point, neither additional retail licenses nor additional club licenses may be issued so long as the number of issued and outstanding retail licenses remains above the statutory maximum.

The District Court was at pains to [note that] an applicant for a club license must make such physical alterations in its premises as the board may require, must file a list of the names and addresses of its members and employees, and must keep extensive financial records. The board is granted the right to inspect the licensed premises at any time * * *.

However detailed this type of regulation may be in some particulars, it cannot be said to in any way foster or encourage racial discrimination. Nor can it be said to make the State in any realistic sense a partner or even a joint venturer in the club's enterprise. The limited effect of the prohibition against

---

3. Unlike the situation in *Public Utilities Comm'n v. Pollak,* where the regulatory agency had affirmatively approved the practice of the regulated entity after full investigation * * *.

obtaining additional club licenses when the maximum number of retail licenses allotted to a municipality has been issued, when considered together with the availability of liquor from hotel, restaurant, and retail licensees falls far short of conferring upon club licensees a monopoly in the dispensing of liquor * * *. We therefore hold that, with the exception hereafter noted, the operation of the regulatory scheme enforced by the Pennsylvania Liquor Control Board does not sufficiently implicate the State in the discriminatory guest policies of Moose Lodge * * *.

The District Court found that [Regulations § 113.09] of the Liquor Control Board adopted pursuant to statute affirmatively require that "every club licensee shall adhere to all the provisions of its constitution and by-laws." Appellant argues that the purpose of this provision "is purely and simply and plainly the prevention of subterfuge" * * *. There can be no doubt that the label "private club" can and has been used to evade both regulations of State and local liquor authorities, and statutes requiring places of public accommodation to serve all persons without regard to race, color, religion, or national origin. * * *

[The Moose constitution and by-laws limit membership and guest privileges to male Caucasians.]

Even though the Liquor Control Board regulation in question is neutral in its terms, the result of its application in a case where the constitution and by-laws of a club required racial discrimination would be to invoke the sanctions of the State to enforce a concededly discriminatory private rule. * * * *Shelley v. Kraemer* makes it clear that the application of state sanctions to enforce such a rule would violate the Fourteenth Amendment. * * *

Appellee was entitled to a decree enjoining the enforcement of § 113.09 [but] no more. The judgment of the District Court is reversed * * *.

MR. JUSTICE DOUGLAS, with whom MR. JUSTICE MARSHALL joins, dissenting.

My view of the First Amendment and the related guarantees of the Bill of Rights is that they create a zone of privacy which precludes government from interfering with private clubs or groups.[1] The associational rights which our system honors permits all white, all black, all brown, and all yellow clubs to be formed. [So] the fact that the Moose Lodge allows only Caucasians to join or come as guests is constitutionally irrelevant * * *. And the fact that a private club gets some kind of permit from the State or municipality does not make it ipso facto a public enterprise or undertaking, any more than the grant to a householder of a permit to operate an incinerator puts the householder in the public domain. We must therefore examine whether there are special circumstances involved in the Pennsylvania scheme which differentiate the liquor license possessed by Moose Lodge from the incinerator permit.

[The opinion then agrees with the Court's disposition of Regulations § 113.09]. But there is another flaw in the scheme not so easily cured. Liquor licenses in Pennsylvania [are] not freely available to those who meet racially neutral qualifications. There is a complex quota system, which the majority accurately describes. What the majority neglects to say is that the Harrisburg quota, where Moose Lodge No. 107 is located, has been full for many years. No more club licenses may be issued in that city.

1. [There] was no occasion [below] to consider the question whether perhaps because of a role as a center of community activity, Moose Lodge No. 107 was in fact "private" for equal protection purposes. The decision today, therefore, leaves this question open.

This state-enforced scarcity of licenses restricts the ability of blacks to obtain liquor, for liquor is commercially available *only* at private clubs for a significant portion of each week.[3] [A] group desiring to form a nondiscriminatory club which would serve blacks must purchase a license held by an existing club, which can exact a monopoly price for the transfer. The availability of such a license is speculative at best, however, for, as Moose Lodge itself concedes, without a liquor license a fraternal organization would be hard-pressed to survive.

Thus, the State of Pennsylvania is putting the weight of its liquor license, concededly a valued and important adjunct to a private club, behind racial discrimination. * * *

MR. JUSTICE BRENNAN, with whom MR. JUSTICE MARSHALL joins, dissenting.

When Moose Lodge obtained its liquor license, the State of Pennsylvania became an active participant in the operation of the Lodge bar. Liquor licensing laws [are] primarily pervasive regulatory schemes under which the State dictates and continually supervises virtually every detail of the operation of the licensee's business. Very few, if any, other licensed businesses experience such complete state involvement. [The] opinion of the [court below] most persuasively demonstrates the "state action" present in this case: * * *

"[After describing the regulations, mentioned in the majority opinion, the court below continued:] It is only on compliance with these and numerous other requirements and if the Board is satisfied that the applicant is 'a person of good repute' and that the license will not be 'detrimental to the welfare, health, peace and morals of the inhabitants of the neighborhood,' that the license may issue.

"Once a license has been issued the licensee must comply with many detailed requirements or risk its suspension or revocation. He must in any event have it renewed periodically. Liquor licenses have been employed in Pennsylvania to regulate a wide variety of moral conduct, such as the presence and activities of homosexuals, performance by a topless dancer, lewd dancing, swearing, being noisy or disorderly. So broad is the state's power that the courts of Pennsylvania have upheld its restriction of freedom of expression of a licensee on the ground that in doing so it merely exercises its plenary power to attach conditions to the privilege of dispensing liquor which a licensee holds at the sufferance of the state. * * *" * * *[a]

Notes and Questions

1. *Issue before the Court.* Was the issue in *Moose Lodge* whether the club's refusal to serve Irvis constituted "state action"? Or was it whether Pennsylvania could grant a liquor license to a club that practiced racial discrimination? Are these constitutional issues the same? See note 4(c) after *Burton.*

2. *Court's rationale.* Does *Moose Lodge* rest ultimately on a "balancing approach"? See Note, *State Action and the Burger Court,* 60 Va.L.Rev. 840 (1974). If so, consider Note, *Developing Legal Vistas for the Discouragement of*

---

3. Hotels and restaurants may serve liquor between 7:00 a.m. and 2:00 a.m. the next day, Monday through Saturday. On Sunday, such licensees are restricted to sales between 12:00 a.m. and 2:00 a.m., and between 1:00 p.m. and 10:00 p.m. * * * Club licensees, however, are permitted to sell liquor to members and guests from 7:00 a.m. to 3:00 a.m. the next day, seven-days-a-week. * * *

a. Irvis also complained to the Pennsylvania Human Rights Commission. *Commonwealth v. Loyal Order of Moose,* 448 Pa. 451, 294 A.2d 594, appeal dismissed, 409 U.S. 1052 (1972), upheld the Commission's ruling that the Harrisburg Moose Lodge was a "public accommodation" under state law and could not bar guests on the basis of race.

Private Club Discrimination, 58 Ia.L.Rev. 108, 139 (1972): "[In cases of] large, nationwide fraternal orders which are segregated pursuant to national constitutions, [there] is evidence that these clubs serve substantially economic interests. Furthermore, a glance at the membership requirement and size of these clubs indicates they are not closely knit clubs involving a high quotient of intimacy. They are certainly not primarily religious or political in nature. Hence, under the balancing approach, the associational rights asserted by these clubs would not seem strong."

3. *The "Moral Exemplar Model."* Consider Stone, *Corporate Vices and Corporate Virtues: Do Public/Private Distinctions Matter?*, 130 U.Pa.L.Rev. 1441, 1449–1501 (1982): "[W]e should be readier to deem an actor 'public' when [it is 'symbolically public' and] when the preponderant costs of doing so will be imposed on the benefitting public at-large. * * * There are several ways to interpret the contrasting results in *Burton* and *Moose Lodge.* One way is to contrast the symbolic elements of the situation: after all, the parking authority building flew, quite literally, the flags of government. [Second,] in *Burton,* the government stood to capture essentially all the economic benefits of the discrimination, assuming perfect competition among bidders for the lease. Hence, the Court's decision prohibiting the arrangement eliminated from public revenues essentially the full measure of the ill-gotten gains. [T]he preponderant costs of setting a morally correct example will be borne by the public, which is exactly where they ought to lie. Note that the same consequence, the apportionment of essentially all 'fairness' costs on general revenues, would not result from a plaintiff's victory when the government is insuring mortgages, or guaranteeing loans, or is a regulatory licensor, as in *Moose Lodge.* [In] those situations, extending state action would concentrate costs on a distinct sub-group, a result that courts have been reluctant to decree."

SHOPPING CENTER CASES

AMALGAMATED FOOD EMPLOYEES UNION v. LOGAN VALLEY PLAZA, 391 U.S. 308, 88 S.Ct. 1601, 20 L.Ed.2d 603 (1968), per MARSHALL, J.,— reasoning that a large privately owned shopping center was the "functional equivalent of the business district [involved] in *Marsh*"—held that it could not enjoin peaceful union picketing on its property against a store located in the shopping center. Black and White, JJ., dissented; Harlan, J., did not reach the merits.

Four years later, LLOYD CORP. v. TANNER, 407 U.S. 551, 92 S.Ct. 2219, 33 L.Ed.2d 131 (1972), per POWELL, J., held that a shopping center's refusal to permit antiwar handbilling on its premises was not state action violative of the first and fourteenth amendments. *Logan Valley* was distinguished on the grounds that the picketing there had been specifically directed to a store in the shopping center and the pickets had no other reasonable opportunity to reach their intended audience. *Marsh* was said to have "involved the assumption by a private enterprise of semi-official municipal functions as a delegate of the State. In effect, the owner of the company town was performing the full spectrum of municipal powers and stood in the shoes of the State. In the instant case there is no comparable assumption or exercise of municipal functions or power." [a]

---

a. *Lloyd* also stated: "Although accommodations between the values protected by [the first amendment, the due process clause, and the fifth amendment just compensation clause] are sometimes necessary, and the courts properly have shown a special solicitude for the guarantees of the First Amendment, this Court has never held that a trespasser or an uninvited guest may exercise general rights of free speech on property pri-

Marshall, J., joined by Douglas, Brennan and Stewart, JJ., dissented, finding "no valid distinction" from *Logan Valley*.

Finally, HUDGENS v. NLRB, 424 U.S. 507, 96 S.Ct. 1029, 47 L.Ed.2d 196 (1976), per STEWART, J.,—involving picketing of a store in a shopping center by a union with a grievance against the store's warehouse (located elsewhere)— overruled *Logan Valley* on the ground that *"Lloyd* amounted to [its] total rejection."[b]

MARSHALL, J., joined by Brennan, J., dissented: "*Logan Valley* [recognized] that the owner of the modern shopping center complex, by dedicating his property to public use as a business district, to some extent displaces the 'State' from control of historical First Amendment forums, and may acquire a virtual monopoly of places suitable for effective communication. The roadways, parking lots, and walkways of the modern shopping center may be as essential for effective speech as the streets and sidewalks in the municipal or company-owned town.[c] [No] one would seriously question the legitimacy of the values of privacy and individual autonomy traditionally associated with privately owned property. [But] when a property owner opens his property to public use the force of those values diminishes." [d]

Notes and Questions

1. *Migrant labor camps.* A company that has a large commercial farm owns a "residential community" adjacent to it that is several miles from the nearest municipality. The "community" has duplex homes and apartments for about half of the 300 farmworkers (and their families) who work on the farm

vately owned and used nondiscriminatorily for private purposes only. Even where public property is involved, the Court has recognized that it is not necessarily available for speaking, picketing, or other communicative activities [*Adderley v. Florida*, p. 541 supra]." "It is true that facilities at the Center are used for certain meetings and for various promotional activities. The obvious purpose [is] to bring potential shoppers to the Center, to create a favorable impression, and to generate goodwill. There is no open-ended invitation to the public to use the Center for any and all purposes, however incompatible with the interests of both the stores and the shoppers whom they serve."

b. White, J., concurred in the result, finding that *Logan Valley* "does not cover the facts of this case. The pickets of the Butler Shoe Co. store [were] not purporting to convey information about the 'manner in which that particular [store] was being operated' but rather about the operation of a warehouse not located on the center's premises. The picketing was thus not 'directly related in its purpose to the use to which the shopping center property was being put.'" Powell, J., joined by Burger, C.J., agreed that "the present case can be distinguished narrowly from *Logan Valley.*" Nevertheless, they joined the Court's opinion, agreeing with Black, J.'s dissent in *Logan Valley* that that case and *Marsh* "cannot be harmonized in a principled way." Stevens, J., did not participate.

c. *Logan Valley* noted: "It has been estimated that by the end of 1966 there were between 10,000 and 11,000 shopping centers in the United States and Canada, accounting for approximately 37% of the total retail sales in those two countries. These figures illustrate the substantial consequences for workers seeking to challenge substandard working conditions, consumers protesting shoddy or overpriced merchandise, and minority groups seeking nondiscriminatory hiring policies that a contrary decision here would have. Business enterprises located in downtown areas would be subject to on-the-spot public criticism for their practices, but businesses situated in the suburbs could largely immunize themselves from similar criticism by creating a *cordon sanitaire* of parking lots around their stores. Neither precedent nor policy compels a result so at variance with [the] First Amendment."

d. For a decision that the free speech and petition provisions of the California constitution require that "shopping center owners permit expressive activity on their property," see *Robins v. Pruneyard Shopping Center*, 23 Cal. 3d 899, 153 Cal.Rptr. 854, 592 P.2d 341 (1979). For consideration under the National Labor Relations Act of the statutory right of unions to engage in communicative activity on the employer's premises, see *Eastex, Inc. v. NLRB*, 437 U.S. 556, 98 S.Ct. 2505, 57 L.Ed.2d 428 (1978); *Scott Hudgens*, 230 N.L.R.B. 414 (1977).

either seasonally or year-round. It also has a store that sells food, a cafeteria, and a recreation center. Does *Marsh* or *Hudgens* govern the question of whether the company may exclude union organizers from the "residential community"? See Note, *First Amendment and the Problem of Access to Migrant Labor Camps,* 67 Corn.L.Rev. 560 (1976).

2. *Residential communities.* A company owns a "residential community, covering 129 acres and housing 12,000 family units made up of some 35,000 people, in 171 adjoining and 'interrelated' apartment houses." Does *Marsh* or *Hudgens* govern the question of whether the company may refuse to rent to blacks? May refuse to permit nonresidents to distribute political pamphlets in the apartment houses? On the privately owned "sidewalks" within the community? See *Watchtower Bible & Tract Society v. Metropolitan Life Ins. Co.,* 297 N.Y. 339, 79 N.E.2d 433 (1948), cert. denied, 335 U.S. 886 (1949).

JACKSON v. METROPOLITAN EDISON CO.

419 U.S. 345, 95 S.Ct. 449, 42 L.Ed.2d 477 (1974).

MR. JUSTICE REHNQUIST delivered the opinion of the Court.

Respondent [holds] a certificate of public convenience issued by the Pennsylvania Public Utility Commission empowering it to deliver electricity [and] is subject to extensive regulation by the Commission. Under a provision of its general tariff filed with the Commission, it has the right to discontinue service to any customer on reasonable notice of nonpayment of bills.

Petitioner [sued] Metropolitan [under] 42 U.S.C. § 1983, seeking damages for the termination and an injunction requiring Metropolitan to continue providing power to her residence until she had been afforded notice, a hearing, and an opportunity to pay any amounts found due. She urged that under state law she had an entitlement to reasonably continuous electrical service to her home and that Metropolitan's termination [was] "state action" depriving her of property in violation of the Fourteenth Amendment's guarantee of due process of law.

The District Court [and] Court of Appeals [found] an absence of state action.

* * *

[The] mere fact that a business is subject to state regulation does not by itself convert its action into that of the State for purposes of the Fourteenth Amendment. Nor does the fact that the regulation is extensive and detailed, as in the case of most public utilities, do so. *Pollak.* It may well be that acts of a heavily regulated utility with at least something of a governmentally protected monopoly will more readily be found to be "state" acts than will the acts of an entity lacking these characteristics. But the inquiry must be whether there is a sufficiently close nexus between the State and the challenged action of the regulated entity so that the action of the latter may be fairly treated as that of the State itself. * * *

Petitioner first argues that "state action" is present because of the monopoly status allegedly conferred upon Metropolitan by the State of Pennsylvania. As a factual matter, it may well be doubted that the State ever granted or guaranteed Metropolitan a monopoly.[8] But assuming that it had, this fact is not determina-

---

8. [In] fact Metropolitan does face competition within portions of its service area from another private utility company and from municipal utility companies. Metropolitan was organized in 1874, 39 years before Pennsylvania's adoption of its first utility regulatory scheme in 1913. There is no indication that it faced any greater competition in 1912 than today. As petitioner admits, such public utility companies are natural monopolies created by the economic forces of high threshold capital requirements and virtually unlimited

tive ✳ ✳ ✳. In *Pollak,* where the Court dealt with the activities of the District of Columbia Transit Co., a congressionally established monopoly, we expressly disclaimed reliance on the monopoly status of the transit authority. Similarly, although certain monopoly aspects were presented in *Moose Lodge,* we found that the Lodge's action was not subject to the provisions of the Fourteenth Amendment. In each of those cases, there was insufficient relationship between the challenged actions of the entities involved and their monopoly status. There is no indication of any greater connection here.

Petitioner next urges that state action is present because respondent provides an essential public service [and] hence performs a "public function." We have, of course, found state action present in the exercise by a private entity of powers traditionally exclusively reserved to the State. See, e.g., *Terry v. Adams* (election); *Marsh* (company town); *Evans v. Newton* (municipal park). If we were dealing with the exercise by Metropolitan of some power delegated to it by the State which is traditionally associated with sovereignty, such as eminent domain, our case would be quite a different one. But while the Pennsylvania statute imposes an obligation to furnish service on regulated utilities, it imposes no such obligation on the State. ✳ ✳ ✳

Perhaps in recognition of the fact that the supplying of utility service is not traditionally the exclusive prerogative of the State, petitioner invites the expansion of the doctrine of this limited line of cases into a broad principle that all businesses "affected with the public interest" are state actors in all their actions.

We decline the invitation for reasons stated long ago in *Nebbia v. New York,* [p. 73 supra], in the course of rejecting a substantive due process attack on state legislation: "It is clear that there is no closed class or category of businesses affected with a public interest ✳ ✳ ✳. The phrase 'affected with a public interest' can, in the nature of things, mean no more than that an industry, for adequate reason is subject to control for the public good. ✳ ✳ ✳"

Doctors, optometrists, lawyers, Metropolitan, and Nebbia's upstate New York grocery selling a quart of milk are all in regulated businesses, providing arguably essential goods and services, "affected with a public interest." We do not believe that such a status converts their every action, absent more, into that of the State.

We also reject the notion that Metropolitan's termination is state action because the State "has specifically authorized and approved" the termination practice. In the instant case, Metropolitan filed with the Public Utility Commission a general tariff—a provision of which states Metropolitan's right to terminate service for nonpayment. This provision has appeared in Metropolitan's previously filed tariffs for many years and has never been the subject of a hearing or other scrutiny by the Commission.[11] Although the Commission did hold hearings on portions of Metropolitan's general tariff relating to a general rate increase, it never even considered the reinsertion of this provision in the newly filed general tariff. ✳ ✳ ✳

As a threshold matter, it is less than clear under state law that Metropolitan was even required to file this provision as part of its tariff or that the Commission would have had the power to disapprove it. ✳ ✳ ✳

economy of scale. Regulation was superimposed on such natural monopolies as a substitute for competition and not to eliminate it ✳ ✳ ✳.

11. Petitioner does not contest the fact that Metropolitan had this right at common law before the advent of regulation.

The case most heavily relied on by petitioner is *Pollak*. There the Court dealt with the contention that Capital Transit's installation of a piped music system on its buses violated the First Amendment rights of the bus riders. [The] District of Columbia Public Utilities Commission, on its own motion, commenced an investigation of the effects of the piped music, and after a full hearing concluded [that] the practice "in fact, through the creation of better will among passengers, [tends] to improve the conditions under which the public ride." Here, on the other hand, there was no such imprimatur placed on the practice of Metropolitan about which petitioner complains. The nature of governmental regulation of private utilities is such that a utility may frequently be required by the state regulatory scheme to obtain approval for practices a business regulated in less detail would be free to institute without any approval from a regulatory body. Approval by a state utility commission of such a request from a regulated utility, where the commission has not put its own weight on the side of the proposed practice by ordering it, does not transmute a practice initiated by the utility and approved by the commission into "state action." At most, the Commission's failure to overturn this practice amounted to no more than a determination that a Pennsylvania utility was authorized to employ such a practice if it so desired. * * *

We also find absent in the instant case the symbiotic relationship presented in *Burton*.

Metropolitan is a privately owned corporation, and it does not lease its facilities from the State of Pennsylvania. It alone is responsible for the provision of power to its customers. [I]t is subject to a form of extensive regulation by the State in a way that most other business enterprises are not. But this was likewise true of the appellant club in *Moose Lodge*, where we said: "However detailed this type of regulation may be in some particulars, it cannot be said to in any way foster or encourage racial discrimination. Nor can it be said to make the State in any realistic sense a partner or even a joint venturer in the club's enterprise." * * *

Affirmed.

MR. JUSTICE DOUGLAS, dissenting.

[As] *Burton* made clear, [it] is not enough to examine seriatim each of the factors upon which a claimant relies and to dismiss each individually as being insufficient to support a finding of state action. It is the aggregate that is controlling.

* * * I agree that doctors, lawyers, and grocers are not transformed into state actors simply because they provide arguably essential goods and services and are regulated by the State. In the present case, however, respondent is not just one person among many; it is the only public utility furnishing electric power to the city. When power is denied a householder, the home, under modern conditions, is likely to become unlivable.

Respondent's procedures for termination of service may never have been subjected to the same degree of state scrutiny and approval, whether explicit or implicit, that was present in *Pollak*. [Yet] Pennsylvania has undertaken to regulate numerous aspects of respondent's operations in some detail, and a "hands-off" attitude of permissiveness or neutrality toward the operations in this case is at war with the state agency's functions of supervision over respondent's conduct in the area of servicing householders, particularly where (as here) the State would presumably lend its weight and authority to facilitate the enforcement of respondent's published procedures. Cf. *Reitman v. Mulkey; Shelley v. Kraemer.* * * *

MR. JUSTICE MARSHALL, dissenting. * * *

Our state-action cases have repeatedly relied on several factors clearly presented by this case: a state-sanctioned monopoly; an extensive pattern of cooperation between the "private" entity and the State; and a service uniquely public in nature. Today the Court takes a major step in repudiating this line of authority * * *.

A. [Even] when the Court has not found state action based solely on the State's conferral of a monopoly, it has suggested that the monopoly factor weighs heavily in determining whether constitutional obligations can be imposed on formally private entities. See *Steele v. Louisville & Nashville R. Co.* Indeed, in *Moose Lodge,* the Court was careful to point out that the Pennsylvania liquor-licensing scheme "falls far short of conferring upon club licensees a monopoly in the dispensing of liquor in any given municipality or in the State as a whole."

The majority distinguishes this line of cases with a cryptic assertion that public utility companies are "natural monopolies." * * * Initially, it is far from obvious that an electric company would not be subject to competition if the market were unimpeded by governmental restrictions. Certainly the "start-up" costs of initiating electric service are substantial, but the rewards available in a relatively inelastic market might well be sufficient under the right circumstances to attract competitive investment. Instead, the State has chosen to forbid the high profit margins that might invite private competition or increase pressure for state ownership and operation of electric power facilities.

[To] invite inquiry into whether a particular state-sanctioned monopoly might have survived without the State's express approval grounds the analysis in hopeless speculation. Worse, this approach ignores important implications of the State's policy of utilizing private monopolies to provide electric service. Encompassed within this policy is the State's determination not to permit governmental competition with the selected private company, but to cooperate with and regulate the company in a multitude of ways to ensure that the company's service will be the functional equivalent of service provided by the State.

B. The pattern of cooperation between Metropolitan Edison and the State has led to significant state involvement in virtually every phase of the company's business. * * *

I disagree with the majority's position on three separate grounds. First, the suggestion that the State would have to "put its own weight on the side of the proposed practice by ordering it" seems to me to mark a sharp departure from our previous state-action cases. * * *[2]

Second, I question the wisdom [of] focusing solely on the extent of state support for the particular activity under challenge. In cases where the State's only significant involvement is through financial support or limited regulation of

---

2. In the *Civil Rights Cases,* the Court suggested that state action might be found if the conduct in question were "sanctioned in some way by the state," [and] in *Reitman,* the Court based its "state action" ruling on the fact that the California constitutional provision "was intended to authorize, and does authorize, racial discrimination in the housing market." Even in *Moose Lodge* the Court suggested that if the State's regulation had in any way fostered or encouraged racial discrimination, a state-action finding might have been justified. Certainly this is a less rigid standard than the Court's requirement in this case that the Public Utility Commission be shown to have ordered the challenged conduct, not merely to have approved it.

the private entity, it may be well to inquire whether the State's involvement suggests state approval of the objectionable conduct. But where the State has so thoroughly insinuated itself into the operations of the enterprise, it should not be fatal if the State has not affirmatively sanctioned the particular practice in question.

Finally, it seems to me in any event that the State *has* given its approval to Metropolitan Edison's termination procedures. [That] it was not seriously questioned before approval does not mean that it was not approved. It suggests, instead, that the Commission was satisfied to permit the company to proceed in the termination area as it had done in the past. * * * Apparently, authorization and approval would require the kind of hearing that was held in *Pollak* * * *. I am afraid that the majority has in effect restricted *Pollak* to its facts if it has not discarded it altogether.

C. The fact that the Metropolitan Edison Co. supplies an essential public service that is in many communities supplied by the government weighs more heavily for me than for the majority. The Court * * * reads the "public function" argument too narrowly. [In] my view, utility service is traditionally identified with the State through universal public regulation or ownership to a degree sufficient to render it a "public function."

I agree with the majority that it requires more than a finding that a particular business is "affected with the public interest" before constitutional burdens can be imposed on that business. But when the activity in question is of such public importance that the State invariably either provides the service itself or permits private companies to act as state surrogates in providing it, much more is involved than just a matter of public interest. In those cases, the State has determined that if private companies wish to enter the field, they will have to surrender many of the prerogatives normally associated with private enterprise and behave in many ways like a governmental body. And when the State's regulatory scheme has gone that far, it seems entirely consistent to impose on the public utility the constitutional burdens normally reserved for the State.

Private parties performing functions affecting the public interest can often make a persuasive claim to be free of the constitutional requirements applicable to governmental institutions because of the value of preserving a private sector in which the opportunity for individual choice is maximized. See *Evans v. Newton*. Maintaining the private status of parochial schools * * * advances just this value. In the due process area, a similar value of diversity may often be furthered by allowing various private institutions the flexibility to select procedures that fit their particular needs. But it is hard to imagine any such interests that are furthered by protecting privately owned public utility companies from meeting the constitutional standards that would apply if the companies were state owned. The values of pluralism and diversity are simply not relevant when the private company is the only electric company in town. * * *

What is perhaps most troubling about the Court's opinion is that it would appear to apply to a broad range of claimed constitutional violations by the company. The Court has not adopted the notion, accepted elsewhere, that different standards should apply to state action analysis when different constitutional claims are presented. See *Adickes v. S.H. Kress & Co.* (Brennan, J., concurring and dissenting).[a] Thus, the majority's analysis would seemingly apply as well to a company that refused to extend service to Negroes, welfare recipients, or any other group that the company preferred, for its own reasons, not to serve. I cannot believe that this Court would hold that the State's involvement with the utility company was not sufficient to impose upon the company an obligation to meet the constitutional mandate of nondiscrimination. Yet nothing in the analysis of the majority opinion suggests otherwise.[b]

Notes and Questions

1. *The "power" theory.* (a) Of what significance should it be that Metropolitan was "the only public utility furnishing electricity to the city"? Might it be argued that the "power" held by certain organizations today was conceived by the framers of the fourteenth amendment to be only within the possession of government? That, under a "living Constitution," such "power" creates such a threat to individual freedom that it should fall within the purview of state action? See Note, *State Action: Theories for Applying Constitutional Restrictions to Private Activity,* 74 Colum.L.Rev. 656 (1974).

Does this approach help explain other state action decisions? Consider Nerkin, *A New Deal for the Protection of Fourteenth Amendment Rights: Challenging the Doctrinal Bases of the Civil Rights Cases and State Action Theory,* 12 Harv.Civ.Rts.-Civ.Lib.L.Rev. 297, 364–65 (1977): "For example, the seller in *Shelley* who was being bound to a rule that he could not sell to blacks was not simply a property owner, but rather an owner who had involved his property in a network of power relations through covenants. Thus the Court's concern in *Shelley* was not simply in the two contracting parties before the court [but] the larger social organism which the covenantors represented. Similarly, [we] might end the futile discussion of whether or not shopping malls are a 'public function' by recognizing that, because malls have become centers of commercial activity, the mall which seeks to expel a political protester has the power to guarantee that a large part of the community will have no other opportunity to benefit from such exercise of rights."

Is the "power theory" approach beyond the permissible bounds of constitutional interpretation? Does it extend to holding the only ice skating rink in town to the state's constitutional responsibilities? Or is it limited to an activity that "is of such public importance that the State invariably either provides the service itself or permits private companies to act as state surrogates in providing it"? Does this invoke the "public function"—or "government function"—approach (to be considered further in note 2 after *Flagg Bros. v. Brooks,* infra)? In any event, does *Jackson* preclude this line of analysis?

(b) Does (should) the "power theory" depend on state participation in conferring the status?

(i) *Corporations.* Consider Berle, *Constitutional Limitations on Corporate Activity—Protection of Personal Rights From Invasion Through Economic Power,* 100 U.Pa.L.Rev. 933, 942–43 (1952): "[A corporation should be] as subject to constitutional limitations which limit action as is the state itself. [The] precon-

---

a. See note 2 after *Burton;* note 1(c) after *Evans v. Newton.*

b. Brennan, J., dissented on procedural grounds.

For a decision finding state action under the California constitution when a privately owned utility discriminates in hiring, see *Gay Law Students Ass'n v. Pacific Telephone & Telegraph Co.,* 24 Cal.3d 458, 156 Cal.Rptr. 14, 595 P.2d 592 (1979).

ditions of application are two: the undeniable fact that the corporation was created by the state and the existence of sufficient economic power concentrated in this vehicle to invade the constitutional right of an individual to a material degree. [The] principle is logical because [the] modern state has set up, and come to rely on, the corporate system to carry out functions for which in modern life by community demand the government is held ultimately responsible. * * * Instead of nationalizing the enterprise, this doctrine 'constitutionalizes' the operation." See also St. Antoine, *Color Blindness But Not Myopia: A New Look at State Action, Equal Protection, and "Private" Racial Discrimination,* 59 Mich.L.Rev. 993 (1961); Miller, *The Constitutional Law of the "Security State,"* 10 Stan.L.Rev. 620, 661–66 (1958). Does this rationale apply to *all* corporations? Should it be restricted to entities "created by the state"?

(ii) *Labor organizations.* Suppose a large powerful union, without statutory authority or assistance, becomes the exclusive bargaining agent in a particular industry. May it constitutionally discriminate against blacks? See generally Wellington, *The Constitution, The Labor Union, and "Governmental Action,"* 70 Yale L.J. 345, 346–50 (1961). If not, must such a union afford a member "due process" before expelling him? May such a union refuse to hire black secretaries?

(c) Does the "power theory" aid in analyzing the last series of questions? Might it be argued, for example, that a particular industrial labor union has sufficient "power" in respect to job opportunities in the industry as to be constitutionally forbidden from racially discriminating among its members but insufficient power over general job opportunities as to be constitutionally barred from using a religious test for its office employees? That the "state's duty to take preventive action [or the "state action" issue] varies with the magnitude of the discrimination and the consequent problem it creates"? Friendly, *The Dartmouth College Case and the Public-Private Penumbra* 22 (1969). See generally Choper, *Thoughts on State Action,* 1979 Wash.U.L.Q. 757; compare Leedes, *State Action Limitations on Courts and Congressional Power,* 60 N.C.L.Rev. 747, 757–61 (1981).

2. *Constitutional rights of "power holders."* (a) In COLUMBIA BROADCASTING SYSTEM v. DEMOCRATIC NAT'L COMM., p. 596 supra—in which the FCC had ruled that a broadcaster is not required to accept editorial advertisements—some justices addressed the question of whether the action of the broadcast licensee was "governmental action" for purposes of the first amendment. BURGER, C.J., joined by Stewart and Rehnquist, JJ., concluded that it was not: "The historic aversion to censorship led Congress [to] explicitly [prohibit] the Commission from interfering with the exercise of free speech over the broadcast frequencies * * *. [T]he Commission acts in essence as an 'overseer,' but the initial and primary responsibility for fairness, balance and objectivity rests with the licensee. * * * Moreover, the Commission has not fostered the licensee policy challenged here; it has simply declined to command particular action because it fell within the area of journalistic discretion. * * *

"Thus, it cannot be said that the government is a 'partner' to the action of the broadcast licensee complained of here, nor is it engaged in a 'symbiotic relationship' with the licensee, profiting from the invidious discrimination of its proxy. [In *Pollak*], Congress had expressly authorized the agency to undertake plenary intervention into the affairs of the carrier and it was pursuant to that authorization that the agency investigated the challenged policy and approved it * * *. A more basic distinction, [is] that *Pollak* was concerned with a transportation utility that itself derives no protection from the First Amendment.

"Were we to read the First Amendment to spell out governmental action in the circumstances presented here, few licensee decisions on the content of broadcasts or the processes of editorial evaluation would escape constitutional scrutiny. In this sensitive area so sweeping a concept of governmental action would go far in practical effect to undermine nearly a half century of unmistakable congressional purpose to maintain—no matter how difficult the task— essentially private broadcast journalism held only broadly accountable to public interest standards."

BRENNAN, J., joined by Marshall, J., disagreed: "[T]he public nature of the airwaves, the governmentally created preferred status of broadcast licensees, the pervasive federal regulation of broadcast programming, and the Commission's specific approval of the challenged broadcaster policy combine in this case to bring the promulgation and enforcement of that policy within the orbit of constitutional imperatives. [Here], as in *Pollak,* the broadcast licensees operate 'under the regulatory supervision of [an] agency authorized by Congress.' And, again as in *Pollak,* that agency received 'protests' against the challenged policy and, after formal consideration, 'dismissed' the complaints on the ground that the 'public interest, convenience, and necessity' were not 'impaired' by that policy. Indeed, the argument for finding 'governmental action' here is even stronger than in *Pollak,* for this case concerns not an incidental activity of a bus company but, rather, the primary activity of the regulated entities—communication. * * * [12] "

(b) *Newspapers.* Is the conduct of the only newspaper in a metropolitan area "state action"? May it offer free "society news" space to whites only? May it refuse to hire black employees? After the *CBS* case, may a licensed broadcaster engage in such actions?

RENDELL–BAKER v. KOHN

457 U.S. 830, 102 S.Ct. 2764, 73 L.Ed.2d 418 (1982).

CHIEF JUSTICE BURGER delivered the opinion of the Court.

[New Perspectives is a private school that] specializes in dealing with students who have experienced difficulty completing public high [schools]. In recent years, nearly all of the students at the school have been referred to it by the Brookline or Boston school committees, or by the Drug Rehabilitation Division of the Massachusetts Department of Mental Health. The school issues high school diplomas certified by the Brookline School Committee.[1] In recent

---

12. In his separate concurring opinion, my Brother Stewart suggests [that] a finding of governmental involvement in this case "would simply strip broadcasters of their own First Amendment rights." [W]here, as here, the Government has implicated itself in the actions of an otherwise private individual, that individual must exercise his own rights with due regard for the First Amendment rights of others. In other words, an accommodation of competing rights is required, and "balancing," not the "absolutist" approach suggested by my Brother Stewart, is the result. * * *

I might also note that, contrary to the suggestion of my Brother Stewart, a finding of

governmental involvement in this case does not in any sense command a similar conclusion with respect to newspapers. [The] decision as to who shall operate newspapers is made in the free market, not by Government fiat. The newspaper industry is not extensively regulated and, indeed, in light of the differences between the electronic and printed media, such regulation would violate the First Amendment with respect to newspapers. * * *

1. Chapter 766, Mass.G.L., requires school committees to identify students with special needs and to develop suitable educational programs for such students. Mass.G.L. c. 71B, years, public funds have accounted for at least 90%, and in one year 99%, of respondent's operating budget. There were approximately 50 students at the school in those years and none paid tuition.[2]

To be eligible for tuition funding under Chapter 766, the school must comply with a variety [of] detailed regulations concerning matters ranging from record-keeping to student-teacher ratios. Concerning personnel policies, [the] regulations require the school to maintain written job descriptions [and] statements describing personnel standards and procedures, but they impose few specific requirements.

[By] its contract with the Boston School Committee, [the] school must agree to carry out the individualized plan developed for each student referred to the school by the Committee. [The] school also has a contract with the State Drug Rehabilitation Division. [It] provides for reimbursement for services provided for students referred to the school [and] includes requirements concerning the services to be provided. Except for general requirements, such as an equal employment opportunity requirement, the agreement does not cover personnel policies.

[Petitioners were discharged by the school for, inter alia, supporting student criticisms against various school policies and sued under 42 U.S.C. § 1983.]

While five of the six petitioners were teachers at the school, petitioner Rendell-Baker was a vocational counselor hired under a grant from the federal Law Enforcement Assistance Administration, whose funds are distributed in Massachusetts through the State Committee on Criminal Justice. As a condition of the grant, the Committee on Criminal Justice must approve the school's initial hiring decisions. The purpose of this requirement is to insure that the school hires vocational counselors who meet the qualifications described in the school's grant proposal to the Committee; the Committee does not interview applicants for counselor positions.

Rendell-Baker * * * demanded reinstatement or a hearing. The school agreed to apply a new policy, calling for appointment of a grievance committee, to consider her claims. Rendell-Baker also complained to the State Committee on Criminal Justice, which asked the school to provide a written explanation for her discharge. After the school complied, the Committee responded that it was satisfied with the explanation, but notified the school that it would not pay any back pay or other damage award Rendell-Baker might obtain from it as a result of her discharge. The Committee told Rendell-Baker that it had no authority to order a hearing, although it would refuse to approve the hiring of another counselor if the school disregarded its agreement to apply its new grievance procedure in her case. [The] core issue presented [is] not whether petitioners were discharged because of their speech or without adequate procedural protec-

§ 4 provides that school committees may "enter into an agreement with any public or private school, agency, or institution to provide the necessary special education" for these students. A student identified [may] remain in public school, if his parents object to a placement in a particular private school, unless he is especially disruptive or dangerous. Parents who object to placement in a particular private school may also elect to place their child in a private school of their choice; in such cases, they must pay the tuition.

2. Amicus curiae Massachusetts Association of 766 Approved Private Schools, Inc., of which the New Perspectives School is a member, informs the Court that many of its members have a student population which is more or less evenly divided between students referred and paid for by the State and students referred and paid for by their parents or guardians.

tions, but whether the school's action in discharging them can fairly be seen as state action. * * *

In *Blum v. Yaretsky*, 457 U.S. 991, 102 S.Ct. 2777, 43 L.Ed.2d 534 (1982), [t]he Court considered whether certain nursing homes were state actors for the purpose of determining whether decisions regarding transfers of patients could be fairly attributed to the state, and hence be subjected to Fourteenth Amendment due process requirements. The challenged transfers primarily involved decisions, made by physicians and nursing home administrators, to move patients from "skilled nursing facilities" to less expensive "health related facilities." Like the New Perspectives School, the nursing homes were privately owned and operated. [T]he Court held that, "[A] State normally can be held responsible for a private decision only when it has exercised coercive power or has provided such significant encouragement, either overt or covert, that the choice must in law be deemed to be that of the State." In determining that the transfer decisions were not actions of the state, the Court considered each of the factors alleged by petitioners here to make the discharge decisions of the New Perspective School fairly attributable to the state.

First, the nursing homes, like the school, depended on the State for funds; the State subsidized the operating and capital costs of the nursing homes, and paid the medical expenses of more than 90% of the patients. * * *

The school, like the nursing homes, is not fundamentally different from many private corporations whose business depends primarily on contracts to build roads, bridges, dams, ships, or submarines for the government. Acts of such private contractors do not become acts of the government by reason of their significant or even total engagement in performing public contracts.

The school is also analogous to the public defender found not to be a state actor in *Polk County v. Dodson,* [p. 1482 infra]. There we concluded that, although the State paid the public defender, her relationship with her client was "identical to that existing between any other lawyer and client." Here the relationship between the school and its teachers and counselors is not changed because the State pays the tuition of the students.

A second factor considered in *Blum* was the extensive regulation of the nursing homes by the State. There the State was indirectly involved in the transfer decisions challenged in that case because a primary goal of the State in regulating nursing homes was to keep costs down by transferring patients from intensive treatment centers to less expensive facilities when possible.[a] Both state and federal regulations encouraged the nursing homes to transfer patients to less expensive facilities when appropriate. The nursing homes were extensively regulated in many other ways as well. The Court relied on *Jackson,* where we held that state regulation, even if "extensive and detailed," did not make a utility's actions state action.

Here the decisions to discharge the petitioners were not compelled or even influenced by any state regulation. Indeed, in contrast to the extensive regulation of the school generally, the various regulators showed relatively little interest in the school's personnel matters. The most intrusive personnel regula-

a. Brennan, J., joined by Marshall, J., dissented in *Blum:* "[A]n accurate and realistic appraisal of the procedures actually employed in the State of New York leaves no doubt that not only has the State established the system of treatment levels and utilization review in order to further its own fiscal goals, but that the State prescribes with as much precision as is possible the standards by which individual determinations are to be made. [The] Court thus fails to perceive the decisive involvement of the State in the private conduct challenged by the respondents."

tion promulgated by the various government agencies was the requirement that the Committee on Criminal Justice had the power to approve persons hired as vocational counselors. Such a regulation is not sufficient to make a decision to discharge, made by private management, state action.[6]

The third factor asserted to show that the school is a state actor is that it performs a "public function." However, our holdings have made clear that the relevant question [is] whether the function performed has been "traditionally the *exclusive* prerogative of the State." There can be no doubt that the education of maladjusted high school students is a public function, but that is only the beginning of the inquiry. Chapter 766 [demonstrates] that the State intends to provide services for such students at public expense. That legislative policy choice in no way makes these services the exclusive province of the State. Indeed, [until] recently the State had not undertaken to provide education for students who could not be served by traditional public schools. That a private entity performs a function which serves the public does not make its acts state action.[7]

Fourth, petitioners argue that there is a "symbiotic relationship" [as] in *Burton*. Such a claim was rejected in *Blum*, and we reject it here. In *Burton*, [i]n response to the argument that the restaurant's profits, and hence the State's financial position, would suffer if it did not discriminate, the Court concluded that this showed that the State profited from the restaurant's discriminatory conduct. [Here] the school's fiscal relationship with the State is not different from that of many contractors performing services for the government.[b] * * *

Affirmed.[c]

JUSTICE MARSHALL, with whom JUSTICE BRENNAN joins, dissenting.

[I]t is difficult to imagine a closer relationship between a government and a private enterprise. [The] school's very survival depends on the State. If the State chooses, it may exercise complete control over the school's operations simply by threatening to withdraw financial support if the school takes action that it considers objectionable. [Almost] every decision the school makes is substantially affected in some way by the State's regulations.[1]

The fact that the school is providing a substitute for public education is also an important indicium of state action. [Under Ch. 766], the State is *required* to provide a free education to all children, including those with special needs. Clearly, if the State had decided to provide the service itself, its conduct would be measured against constitutional standards. The State should not be permitted

---

6. [The] Committee had no power to hire or discharge a counselor who had the qualifications specified in the school's grant application. Moreover, the Committee did not take any part in discharging Rendell-Baker; on the contrary, it attempted to use leverage to aid her. [T]here is no evidence that the Committee had any authority to take even those steps.

7. There is no evidence that the State has attempted to avoid its constitutional duties by a sham arrangement which attempts to disguise provision of public services as acts of private parties. Cf. *Evans v. Newton.*

[Compare Brennan, J., joined by Marshall, J., dissenting in *Blum:* "For many, the totality of their social network is the nursing home community. Within that environment, the nursing home operator is the immediate authority, the provider of food, clothing, shelter, and health care, and, in every significant respect, the functional equivalent of a State. Cf. *Marsh.*"]

b. Does this adopt the "moral exemplar model" in note 3 after *Moose Lodge?*

c. White, J., concurred in the judgment (and in *Blum*): "For me, the critical factor is the absence of any allegation that the employment decision was itself based upon some rule of conduct or policy put forth by the State."

1. [By] analyzing the various indicia of state action separately, without considering their cumulative impact, the majority commits a fundamental error.

to avoid constitutional requirements simply by delegating its statutory duty to a private entity. * * *

* * * Petitioners claim that they were discharged because they supported student demands for increased responsibilities in school affairs. [If true,] the school has adopted a specific view of the sort of education that should be provided under the statute, and refuses to tolerate departures from that view. The State, by refusing to intervene, has effectively endorsed that view of its duties under Chapter 766. In short, because petitioners' criticism was directly addressed to the State's responsibilities under Chapter 766, a finding of state action is justified.

The majority repeatedly compares the school to a private contractor * * *. Although shipbuilders and dambuilders, like the school, may be dependent on government funds, they are not so closely supervised by the government. And unlike most private contractors, the school is performing a statutory duty of the State.

The majority [would] apparently concede that actions directly affecting the students could be treated as under color of state law, since the school is fulfilling the State's obligations to those children under Chapter 766. [But] the personnel decisions challenged here are related to the provision of Chapter 766 education. In any event, since the school is funded almost entirely by the State, is closely supervised by the State, and exists solely to perform the State's statutory duty to educate children with special needs—since the school is really just an arm of the State—its personnel decisions may appropriately be considered state action.

* * *

FLAGG BROS., INC. v. BROOKS

436 U.S. 149, 98 S.Ct. 1729, 56 L.Ed.2d 185 (1978).

MR. JUSTICE REHNQUIST delivered the opinion of the Court.

The question presented [is] whether a warehouseman's proposed sale of goods entrusted to him for storage, as permitted by New York Uniform Commercial Code § 7–210, is an action properly attributable to the State * * *.

[R]espondent Shirley Brooks and her family were evicted from their apartment in Mount Vernon, N.Y., on June 13, 1973. The city marshal arranged for Brooks' possessions to be stored by petitioner Flagg Brothers, Inc., in its warehouse. Brooks was informed of the cost of moving and storage, and she instructed the workmen to proceed, although she found the price too high. On August 25, 1973, after a series of disputes over the validity of the charges being claimed by petitioner Flagg Brothers, Brooks received a letter demanding that her account be brought up to date within 10 days "or your furniture will be sold." A series of subsequent letters from respondent and her attorneys produced no satisfaction.

Brooks thereupon initiated this class action in the District Court under 42 U.S.C. § 1983, seeking damages, an injunction against the threatened sale of her belongings, and the declaration that such a sale pursuant to § 7–210 would violate [due process]. She was later joined in her action by [Jones,] whose goods had been stored by Flagg Brothers following her eviction. [T]he District Court * * * dismissed the complaint [and] the Court of Appeals reversed. * * *

It must be noted that respondents have named no public officials as defendants in this action. The city marshal, who supervised their evictions, was dismissed from the case by the consent of all the parties. This total absence of overt official involvement plainly distinguishes this case from earlier decisions imposing procedural restrictions on creditors' remedies such as *North Georgia Finishing, Inc., v. Di-Chem, Inc.,* 419 U.S. 601, 95 S.Ct. 719, 42 L.Ed.2d 751 (1975); *Fuentes v. Shevin,* 407 U.S. 67, 92 S.Ct. 1983, 32 L.Ed.2d 556 (1972); *Sniadach v. Family Finance Corp.,* 395 U.S. 337, 89 S.Ct. 1820, 23 L.Ed.2d 349 (1969).[a] [While] as a factual matter any person with sufficient physical power may deprive a person of his property, only a State or a private person whose action "may be fairly treated as that of the State itself," *Jackson,* may deprive him of "an interest encompassed within the Fourteenth Amendment's protection," *Fuentes* * * *.

Respondents' primary contention is that New York has delegated to Flagg Brothers a power "traditionally exclusively reserved to the State." *Jackson.* They argue that the resolution of private disputes is a traditional function of civil government, and that the State in § 7–210 has delegated this function to Flagg Brothers. Respondents, however, have read too much into the language of our previous cases. While many functions have been traditionally performed by governments, very few have been "exclusively reserved to the State."

One such area has been elections. * * * *Terry v. Adams; Smith v. Allwright.* Although the rationale of these cases may be subject to some dispute, their scope is carefully defined. The doctrine does not reach to all forms of private political activity, but encompasses only state-regulated elections or elections conducted by organizations which in practice produce "the uncontested choice of public officials." *Terry* (Clark, J., concurring). * * *

A second line of cases under the public-function doctrine originated with *Marsh.* Just as the Texas Democratic Party in *Smith* and the Jaybird Democratic Association in *Terry* effectively performed the entire public function of selecting public officials, so too the Gulf Shipbuilding Corp. performed all the necessary municipal functions in the town of Chickasaw, Ala., which it owned. * * *

These two branches of the public-function doctrine have in common the feature of exclusivity.[8] Although the elections held by the Democratic Party and

---

a. *Sniadach* held that a statute—authorizing a creditor to get a summons from a court clerk and thereby obtain prejudgment garnishment of a debtor's wages—violated due process because the statute did not provide the debtor with prior notice and opportunity for a hearing.

Fuentes held that a statute—authorizing a seller of goods under a conditional sales contract to get a writ from a court clerk and thereby obtain prejudgment repossession with the sheriff's help—violated due process because the statute did not provide the buyer with prior notice and opportunity for a hearing.

North Georgia Finishing held violative of due process a statute authorizing a creditor to obtain prejudgment garnishment of a debtor's assets by filing an affidavit with a court clerk stating reasons to fear that the property would otherwise be lost. The Court distinguished *Mitchell v. W.T. Grant Co.,* 416 U.S. 600, 94 S.Ct. 1895, 40 L.Ed.2d 406 (1974), which had upheld a statute that, without requiring prior notice to a buyer-debtor, permit-

ted a seller-creditor holding a vendor's lien to secure a writ of sequestration and, having filed a bond, to cause the sheriff to take possession of the property at issue. *North Georgia Finishing* emphasized that under the sequestration statute in *Mitchell,* unlike the garnishment statute at bar, the writ "was issuable only by a judge upon the filing of an affidavit going beyond mere conclusory allegations and clearly setting out the facts entitling the creditor to sequestration" and that the *Mitchell* statute "expressly entitled the debtor to an immediate hearing after seizure and to dissolution of the writ absent proof by the creditor of the grounds on which the writ was issued."

For general discussion of these cases, see Scott, *Constitutional Regulation of Provisional Creditor Remedies: The Cost of Procedural Due Process,* 61 Va.L.Rev. 807 (1975); Silberman, *Shaffer v. Heitner: The End of an Era,* 53 N.Y.U.L.Rev. 33, 53–62 (1978).

8. Respondents also contend that *Evans v. Newton* establishes that the operation of a park for recreational purposes is an exclusive-its affiliates were the only meaningful elections in Texas, and the streets owned by the Gulf Shipbuilding Corp. were the only streets in Chickasaw, the proposed sale by Flagg Brothers under § 7–210 is not the only means of resolving this purely private dispute. Respondent Brooks has never alleged that state law barred her from seeking a waiver of Flagg Brothers' right to sell her goods at the time she authorized their storage. Presumably, respondent Jones, who alleges that she never authorized the storage of her goods, could have sought to replevy her goods at any time under state law. The challenged statute itself provides a damages remedy against the warehouseman for violations of its provisions. This system of rights and remedies, recognizing the traditional place of private arrangements in ordering relationships in the commercial world,[9] can hardly be said to have delegated to Flagg Brothers an exclusive prerogative of the sovereign.[10]

Whatever the particular remedies available under New York law, we do not consider a more detailed description of them necessary to our conclusion that the settlement of disputes between debtors and creditors is not traditionally an exclusive public function.[11] Creditors and debtors have had available to them

ly public function. We doubt that *Newton* intended to establish any such broad doctrine in the teeth of the experience of several American entrepreneurs who amassed great fortunes by operating parks for recreational purposes. We think *Newton* rests on a finding of ordinary state action under extraordinary circumstances. The Court's opinion emphasizes that the record showed "no change in the municipal maintenance and concern over this facility" after the transfer of title to private trustees. That transfer had not been shown to have eliminated the actual involvement of the city in the daily maintenance and care of the park.

9. Unlike the parade of horribles suggested by our Brother Stevens in dissent, this case does not involve state authorization of private breach of the peace.

10. [It] would intolerably broaden, beyond the scope of any of our previous cases, the notion of state action [to] hold that the mere existence of a body of property law in a State, whether decisional or statutory, itself amounted to "state action" even though no state process or state officials were ever involved in enforcing that body of law.

This situation is clearly distinguishable from cases such as *North Georgia Finishing; Fuentes;* and *Sniadach.* In each of those cases a government official participated in the physical deprivation of what had concededly been the constitutional plaintiff's property under state law before the deprivation occurred. The constitutional protection attaches not because, as in *North Georgia Finishing,* a clerk issued a ministerial writ out of the court, but because as a result of that writ the property of the debtor was seized and impounded by the affirmative command of the law of Georgia. The creditor in *North Georgia Finishing* had not simply sought to pursue the collection of his debt by private means permissible under

Georgia law; he had invoked the authority of the Georgia court, which in turn had ordered the garnishee not to pay over money which previously had been the property of the debtor. See *Virginia v. Rives; Shelley v. Kraemer.*

* * *

11. It may well be, as my Brother Stevens' dissent contends, that "[t]he power to order legally binding surrenders of property and the constitutional restrictions on that power are necessary correlatives in our system." But here New York, unlike Florida in *Fuentes,* Georgia in *North Georgia Finishing,* and Wisconsin in *Sniadach,* has not ordered respondents to surrender any property whatever. It has merely enacted a statute which provides that a warehouseman conforming to the provisions of the statute may convert his traditional lien into good title. There is no reason whatever to believe that either Flagg Brothers or respondents could not, if they wished, seek resort to the New York courts in order to either compel or prevent the "surrenders of property" to which that dissent refers, and that the compliance of Flagg Brothers with applicable New York property law would be reviewed after customary notice and hearing in such a proceeding.

The fact that such a judicial review of a self-help remedy is seldom encountered bears witness to the important part that such remedies have played in our system of property rights. This is particularly true of the warehouseman's lien, which is the source of this provision in the Uniform Commercial Code which is the law in 49 States and the District of Columbia. The lien in this case, particularly because it is burdened by procedural constraints and provides for a compensatory remedy and judicial relief against abuse, is not atypical of creditors' liens historically, whether created by statute or legislatively enacted. The conduct of private actors in relying on the historically a far wider number of choices than has one who would be an elected public official, or a member of Jehovah's Witnesses who wished to distribute literature in Chickasaw, Ala. * * * [12] This is true whether these commercial rights and remedies are created by statute or decisional law. To rely upon the historical antecedents of a particular practice would result in the constitutional condemnation in one State of a remedy found perfectly permissible in another.

[W]e would be remiss if we did not note that there are a number of state and municipal functions not covered by our election cases or governed by the reasoning of *Marsh* which have been administered with a greater degree of exclusivity by States and municipalities than has the function of so-called "dispute resolution." Among these are such functions as education, fire and police protection, and tax collection. We express no view as to the extent, if any, to which a city or State might be free to delegate to private parties the performance of such functions and thereby avoid the strictures of the Fourteenth Amendment. * * *

Respondents further urge that Flagg Brothers' proposed action is properly attributable to the State because the State has authorized and encouraged it in enacting § 7–210. Our cases state "that a State is responsible for [the] act of a private party when the State, by its law, has compelled the act." This Court, however, has never held that a State's mere acquiescence in a private action converts that action into that of the State. The Court rejected a similar argument in *Jackson* * * *. The clearest demonstration of this distinction appears in *Moose Lodge,* which held that the Commonwealth of Pennsylvania, although not responsible for racial discrimination voluntarily practiced by a private club, could not by law require the club to comply with its own discriminatory rules. These cases clearly rejected the notion that our prior cases permitted the imposition of Fourteenth Amendment restraints on private action by the simple device of characterizing the State's inaction as "authorization" or "encouragement."

It is quite immaterial that the State has embodied its decision not to act in statutory form. If New York had no commercial statutes at all, its courts would still be faced with the decision whether to prohibit or to permit the sort of sale threatened here the first time an aggrieved bailor came before them for relief. A judicial decision to deny relief would be no less an "authorization" or "encouragement" of that sale than the legislature's decision embodied in this statute. [If] the mere denial of judicial relief is considered sufficient encouragement to make the State responsible for those private acts, all private deprivations of property would be converted into public acts whenever the State, for whatever reason, denies relief sought by the putative property owner. * * *

Here, the State of New York has not compelled the sale of a bailor's goods, but has merely announced the circumstances under which its courts will not interfere with a private sale. Indeed, the crux of respondents' complaint is not

___

rights established under these liens to resort to self-help remedies does not permit their conduct to be ascribed to the State.

12. This is not to say that dispute resolution between creditors and debtors involves a category of human affairs that is never subject to constitutional constraints. We merely address the public-function doctrine as respondents would apply it to this case.

Self-help of the type involved in this case is not significantly different from creditor reme- dies generally, whether created by common law or enacted by legislatures. New York's statute has done nothing more than authorize (and indeed limit)—without participation by any public official—what Flagg Brothers would tend to do, even in the absence of such authorization, i.e., dispose of respondents' property in order to free up its valuable storage space. The proposed sale pursuant to the lien in this case is not a significant departure from traditional private arrangements.

that the State *has* acted, but that it has *refused* to act. This statutory refusal to act is no different in principle from an ordinary statute of limitations whereby the State declines to provide a remedy for private deprivations of property after the passage of a given period of time. * * *

Reversed.

MR. JUSTICE STEVENS, with whom MR. JUSTICE WHITE and MR. JUSTICE MARSHALL join, dissenting.

[The] question is whether a state statute which authorizes a private party to deprive a person of his property without his consent must meet the requirements of the Due Process Clause of the Fourteenth Amendment. This question must be answered in the affirmative unless the State has virtually unlimited power to transfer interests in private property without any procedural protections.

[Under the Court's] approach a State could enact laws authorizing private citizens to use self-help in countless situations without any possibility of federal challenge. A state statute could authorize the warehouseman to retain all proceeds of the lien sale, even if they far exceeded the amount of the alleged debt; it could authorize finance companies to enter private homes to repossess merchandise; or indeed, it could authorize "any person with sufficient physical power" to acquire and sell the property of his weaker neighbor. An attempt to challenge the validity of any such outrageous statute would be defeated by the reasoning the Court uses today: The Court's rationale would characterize action pursuant to such a statute as purely private action, which the State permits but does not compel, in an area not exclusively reserved to the State.

As these examples suggest, the distinctions between "permission" and "compulsion" on the one hand, and "exclusive" and "non-exclusive," on the other, cannot be determinative factors in state-action analysis. There is no great chasm between "permission" and "compulsion" requiring particular state action to fall within one or the other definitional camp. Even *Moose Lodge*, * * * recognizes that there are many intervening levels of state involvement in private conduct that may support a finding of state action. In this case, the State of New York, by enacting § 7–210 of the Uniform Commercial Code, has acted in the most effective and unambiguous way a State can act. This section specifically authorizes petitioner Flagg Brothers to sell respondents' possessions; it details the procedures that petitioner must follow; and it grants petitioner the power to convey good title to goods that are now owned by respondents to a third party.

While Members of this Court have suggested that statutory authorization alone may be sufficient to establish state action,[6] it is not necessary to rely on those suggestions in this case because New York has authorized the warehouseman to perform what is clearly a state function. [P]etitioners have attempted to argue that the nonconsensual transfer of property rights is not a traditional function of the sovereign. The overwhelming historical evidence is to the contrary, however,[7] and the Court wisely does not adopt this position. Instead,

---

6. See, e.g., *Burton* (Stewart, J., concurring); (Frankfurter, J., dissenting); and (Harlan, J., dissenting).

7. The New York State courts have recognized that the execution of a lien is a traditional function of the State. See also 3 W. Blackstone, *Commentaries* §§ 7–11, pp. * 3–6, which notes that the right of self-help at common law was severely limited.

I fully agree with the Court that the decision of whether or not a statute is subject to

due process scrutiny should not depend on " 'whether a particular class of creditor did or did not enjoy the same freedom to act in Elizabethan or Georgian England.' " Nonetheless some reference to history and well-settled practice is necessary to determine whether a particular action is a "traditional state function." * * *

the Court reasons that state action cannot be found because the State has not delegated to the warehouseman an *exclusive* sovereign function.[8] This distinction, however, is not consistent with our prior decisions on state action; is not even adhered to by the Court in this case;[10] and, most importantly, is inconsistent with the line of cases beginning with *Sniadach.*

Since *Sniadach* this Court has scrutinized various state statutes regulating the debtor-creditor relationship for compliance with the Due Process Clause. In each of these cases a finding of state action was a prerequisite to the Court's decision. The Court today seeks to explain these findings on the ground that in each case there was some element of "overt official involvement." [But] until today, this Court had never held that purely ministerial acts of "minor governmental functionaries" were sufficient to establish state action. The suggestion that this was the basis for due process review in *Sniadach, Fuentes,* and *North Georgia Finishing* marks a major and, in my judgment, unwise expansion of the state-action doctrine. The number of private actions in which a governmental functionary plays some ministerial role is legion;[12] to base due process review on the fortuity of such governmental intervention would demean the majestic purposes of the Due Process Clause.

Instead, cases such as *North Georgia Finishing* must be viewed as reflecting this Court's recognition of the significance of the State's role in defining *and controlling* the debtor-creditor relationship. [In *Fuentes,* the] statutes placed the state power to repossess property in the hands of an interested private party, just as the state statute in this case places the state power to conduct judicially binding sales in satisfaction of a lien in the hands of the warehouseman. "Private parties, serving their own private advantage, may unilaterally invoke state power to replevy goods from another. No state official participates in the decision to seek a writ; no state official reviews the basis for the claim to repossession; and no state official evaluates the need for immediate seizure. There is not even a requirement that the plaintiff provide any information to the court on these matters." Ibid. [Yet] the very defect that made the statutes in *Fuentes* and *North Georgia Finishing* unconstitutional—lack of state control—is, under today's decision, the factor that precludes constitutional review of the state statute. The Due Process Clause cannot command such incongruous

8. As I understand the Court's notion of "exclusivity," the sovereign function here is not exclusive because there may be other state remedies, under different statutes or common-law theories, available to respondents. Even if I were to accept the notion that sovereign functions must be "exclusive," the Court's description of exclusivity is incomprehensible. The question is whether a particular action is a uniquely sovereign function, not whether state law forecloses any possibility of recovering for damages for such activity. For instance, it is clear that the maintenance of a police force is a unique sovereign function, and the delegation of police power to a private party will entail state action. Under the Court's analysis, however, there would be no state action if the State provided a remedy, such as an action for wrongful imprisonment, for the individual injured by the "private" policeman. This analysis is not based on "exclusivity," but on some vague, and highly inappropriate, notion that respondents should

not complain about this state statute if the State offers them a glimmer of hope of redeeming their possessions, or at least the value of the goods, through some other state action. Of course, the availability of other state remedies may be relevant in determining whether the statute provides sufficient procedural protections under the Due Process Clause, but it is not relevant to the state-action issue.

10. As the Court is forced to recognize, its notion of exclusivity simply cannot be squared with the wide range of functions that are typically considered sovereign functions, such as "education, fire and police protection, and tax collection."

12. For instance, state officials often perform ministerial acts in the transferring of ownership in motor vehicles or real estate. It is difficult to believe that the Court would hold that all car sales are invested with state action.

results. If it is unconstitutional for a State to allow a private party to exercise a traditional state power because the state supervision of that power is purely mechanical, the State surely cannot immunize its actions from constitutional *scrutiny* by removing even the mechanical supervision.

Not only has the State removed its nominal supervision in this case, it has also authorized a private party to exercise a governmental power that is at least as significant as the power exercised in *Fuentes* or *North Georgia Finishing.* In *Fuentes,* the Florida statute allowed the debtor's property to be seized and held pending the outcome of the creditor's action for repossession. The property would not be finally disposed of until there was an adjudication of the underlying claim. Similarly, in *North Georgia Finishing,* the state statute provided for a garnishment procedure which deprived the debtor of the use of property in the garnishee's hands pending the outcome of litigation. The warehouseman's power under § 7–210 is far broader * * *.

Whether termed "traditional," "exclusive," or "significant," the state power to order binding, nonconsensual resolution of a conflict between debtor and creditor is exactly the sort of power with which the Due Process Clause is concerned. And the State's delegation of that power to a private party is, accordingly, subject to due process scrutiny. This, at the very least, is the teaching of *Sniadach, Fuentes,* and *North Georgia Finishing.*

It is important to emphasize that, contrary to the Court's apparent fears, this conclusion does not even remotely suggest that "all private deprivations of property [will] be converted into public acts whenever the State, for whatever reason, denies relief sought by the putative property owner." The focus is not on the private deprivation but on the state authorization. [The] State's conduct in this case takes the concrete form of a statutory enactment, and it is that statute that may be challenged.

[It] is only what the State itself has enacted that [respondents] may ask the federal court to review in a § 1983 case. If there should be a deviation from the state statute—such as a failure to give the notice required by the state law—the defect could be remedied by a state court and there would be no occasion for § 1983 relief. [Under] this approach, the federal courts do not have jurisdiction to review every foreclosure proceeding in which the debtor claims that there has been a procedural defect constituting a denial of due process of law. Rather, the federal district court's jurisdiction under § 1983 is limited to challenges to the constitutionality of the state procedure itself * * *.

Finally, it is obviously true that the overwhelming majority of disputes in our society are resolved in the private sphere. But it is no longer possible, if it ever was, to believe that a sharp line can be drawn between private and public actions. The Court['s] description of what is state action does not even attempt to reflect the concerns of the Due Process Clause, for the state-action doctrine is, after all, merely one aspect of this broad constitutional protection.

In the broadest sense, we expect government "to provide a reasonable and fair framework of rules which facilitate commercial transactions." This "framework of rules" is premised on the assumption that the State will control nonconsensual deprivations of property and that the State's control will, in turn, be subject to the restrictions of the Due Process Clause. * * * [b]

---

b. The separate dissent of Marshall, J., is omitted. Brennan, J., did not participate.

Notes and Questions

1. *Authority of prior decisions.* (a) Does the Court's use of *Shelley v. Kraemer* (in fn. 10) refute the dissent's objection that the Court's handling of the prior debtor-creditor decisions establishes the principle that "purely ministerial acts of minor governmental functionaries" constitute state action? If so, then would the Court have found state action in *Flagg Bros.* if the state courts had to be used to enforce the warehouseman's lien? Would this read *Shelley* for all it is worth? Does fn. 10 so read *Shelley*? In any event, is the dissent correct in complaining that "the very defect that made the statutes in *Fuentes* and *North Georgia Finishing* unconstitutional—lack of state control—is, under *Flagg Bros.*, the factor that precludes constitutional review of the state statute"?

(b) LUGAR v. EDMONDSON OIL CO., 457 U.S. 922, 102 S.Ct. 2744, 73 L.Ed. 2d 482 (1982), per WHITE, J.,—involving a statute that authorized a creditor to file a petition with a court clerk and thus obtain a prejudgment attachment of a debtor's property which was executed by the sheriff—relied on all the debtor-creditor decisions as establishing the doctrine "that a private party's joint participation with state officials in the seizure of disputed property is sufficient to characterize that party as a 'state actor' for purposes of the Fourteenth Amendment." POWELL, J., joined by REHNQUIST and O'CONNOR, JJ., dissented: "It is unclear why a private party engages in state action when filing papers seeking an attachment of property, but not [when] summoning police to investigate a suspected crime." BURGER, C.J., also dissented.

2. *"Governmental function."* (a) *Dispute resolution.* Do you agree that the authority exercised by the warehouseman under the New York statute was not a "governmental function"? Consider 92 Harv.L.Rev. 128 (1978): "The exclusivity of the function's exercise may shed some light on this inquiry, but it does not give a final answer to the basic question. Regardless of the fact that there are many ways to go about resolving a private dispute, the ability to conclude unresolved disputes by making authoritative determinations of rights in property is central to our conception of government's role in society. If a state chose to assign part of its judicial function to private tribunals, giving them all the authority of trial courts, there would be little doubt that a vital attribute of sovereignty was involved."

What result in *Flagg Bros.* if the warehouseman's lien had not been "burdened by procedural constraints" and had not provided "for a compensatory remedy and judicial relief against abuse"?

(b) *Education.* Would (should) the Court hold that private schools perform a "government function"? If so, under what circumstances? Consider Choper, *Thoughts on State Action*, 1979 Wash.U.L.Q. 757, 778: "[I]t is clear that the operation of elementary and secondary schools is not an enterprise that is 'traditionally *exclusively* reserved to the State.' But a comprehensive survey of school districts in the United States would surely show that virtually all maintained at least one public elementary and secondary school unless, because of some peculiar development, the educational needs of the community's children were historically always met by a privately funded school. Such a school—or at least one of such schools if there are several in the hypothetical community (and which one is *the* one may present a nice question)—is, in effect, serving as a substitute for the conventional public school that the school district would otherwise provide. In this sense, it is performing a function 'traditionally *exclusively* reserved to the State.'"

3. *The limits (or lack of limits) of the state action concept.* Do you agree that "an ordinary statute of limitations whereby the State declines to provide a remedy for private deprivations of property after the passage of a given period of time" is *not* state action? If it *is* state action, then is New York's rule—that "its courts will not interfere with a private sale" pursuant to a warehouseman's lien—also state action? If so, is it not true that "all private deprivations of property would be converted into public acts whenever the State, for whatever reason, denies relief sought by the putative property owner"? Of what relevance is it that "the State's conduct in *Flagg Bros.* takes the concrete form of a statutory enactment"? May a "state procedure" providing a "framework of rules which facilitate commercial transactions" be promulgated by common law as well as by statute? See generally Brest, *State Action and Liberal Theory: A Casenote on Flagg Brothers v. Brooks,* 130 U.Pa.L.Rev. 1296 (1982).

Chapter 8

CONGRESSIONAL ENFORCEMENT OF CIVIL RIGHTS

The exercise of congressional authority under the commerce and spending powers to protect civil rights was examined in detail in Ch. 2, Secs. 2, V and 3. But the potentially most pervasive sources of federal legislative power to enforce personal liberty are found in the final sections of the thirteenth, fourteenth, and fifteenth amendments which grant Congress power to enforce the substantive provisions of these amendments "by appropriate legislation." Some exertions of this power have already been referred to, see, e.g., pp. 856, 923 supra. Here, detailed consideration is undertaken.

SECTION 1. HISTORICAL FRAMEWORK

I. LEGISLATION

The Civil Rights Act of 1866, enacted pursuant to the thirteenth amendment, was the first Reconstruction Act seeking "to protect all persons in the United States in their civil rights." (See "Historical Background," p. 63 supra.) Its current provisions are:

42 U.S.C. § 1981. *"Equal rights under the law.* All persons within the jurisdiction of the United States shall have the same right in every State and Territory to make and enforce contracts, to sue, be parties, give evidence, and to the full and equal benefit of all laws and proceedings for the security of persons and property as is enjoyed by white citizens, and shall be subject to like punishment, pains, penalties, taxes, licenses, and exactions of every kind, and to no other."

42 U.S.C. § 1982. *"Property rights of citizens.* All citizens of the United States shall have the same right, in every State and Territory, as is enjoyed by white citizens thereof to inherit, purchase, lease, sell, hold, and convey real and personal property."

The 1866 Act then provided criminal penalties against any person denying such rights under color of law. With certain changes (the most important being addition of the word "willfully" in 1909, 35 Stat. 1092, and the substantial increase of penalties in 1968, 82 Stat. 75), this has survived as a significant federal criminal statute enforcing civil rights:

18 U.S.C. § 242. *"Deprivation of rights under color of law.* Whoever, under color of any law, statute, ordinance, regulation, or custom, willfully subjects any inhabitant of any State, Territory, or District to the deprivation of any rights, privileges, or immunities secured or protected by the Constitution or laws of the United States, or to different punishments, pains or penalties, on account of such inhabitant being an alien, or by reason of his color, or race, than are prescribed for the punishment of citizens, shall be fined not more than $1,000 or imprisoned not more than one year, or both; and if death results shall be subject to imprisonment for any term of years or for life."

———

Doubt as to the adequacy of the thirteenth amendment to support the 1866 Act was a significant force leading to adoption of the fourteenth amendment. After ratification of the fifteenth amendment, Congress passed the Act of May 31, 1870, 16 Stat. 140, principally to enforce the right to vote guaranteed by the amendment.[a] One section, barring private conspiracies, evolved as an important existing protection:

18 U.S.C. § 241. *"Conspiracy against rights of citizens.* If two or more persons conspire to injure, oppress, threaten, or intimidate any citizen in the free exercise or enjoyment of any right or privilege secured to him by the Constitution or laws of the United States, or because of his having exercised the same; or

"If two or more persons go on the highway, or on the premises of another, with intent to prevent or hinder his free exercise or enjoyment of any right or privilege so secured—

"They shall be fined not more than $10,000 or imprisoned not more than ten years, or both; and if death results, they shall be subject to imprisonment for any term of years or for life."

———

Next came the Ku Klux Klan Act of 1871, 17 Stat. 13, which made criminal private conspiracies against the operations of government officials or courts, or to deprive persons of equal protection of the laws.[b] The Act also established civil liabilities that have evolved to be important existing provisions. One is the civil counterpart of 18 U.S.C. § 242:

42 U.S.C. § 1983. *"Civil action for deprivation of rights.* Every person who, under color of any statute, ordinance, regulation, custom, or usage, of any State or Territory, subjects, or causes to be subjected, any citizen of the United States or other persons within the jurisdiction thereof to the deprivation of any rights, privileges or immunities secured by the Constitution and laws, shall be liable to the person injured in an action of law, suit in equity, or other proper proceedings for redress."

a. Few of the protections afforded the right to vote survived. *United States v. Reese,* 92 U.S. 214, 23 L.Ed. 563 (1876), held two sections unconstitutional, as not supported by the fifteenth amendment, because the offenses they created for interfering with voting were not limited to denial on the basis of race. Other sections were repealed by the anti-Reconstruction Congress in 1894, 28 Stat. 36–37.

b. The latter proviso was held unconstitutional, as not supported by the fourteenth amendment, in *United States v. Harris,* 106 U.S. 629, 1 S.Ct. 601, 27 L.Ed. 290 (1882), because "directed exclusively against the action of private persons, without reference to the laws of the State or their administration by her officers." The entire part was repealed in 1909, 35 Stat. 1153–54.

Another is roughly the civil counterpart of 18 U.S.C. § 241:

42 U.S.C. § 1985. *"Conspiracy to interfere with civil rights.* * * * (c) If two or more persons in any State or Territory conspire or go in disguise on the highway or on the premises of another, for the purpose of depriving, either directly or indirectly, any person or class of persons of the equal protection of the laws, or of equal privileges and immunities under the laws; or for the purpose of preventing or hindering the constituted authorities of any State or Territory from giving or securing to all persons within such State or Territory the equal protection of the laws; [the] party so injured or deprived may have an action for the recovery of damages, occasioned by such injury or deprivation, against any one or more of the conspirators." [c]

The final Reconstruction enactment in this area was the Civil Rights Act of 1875, dealing with racial discrimination in public accommodations, held invalid in the *Civil Rights Cases,* p. 1076 supra.[d]

No significant congressional action to enforce civil rights took place between 1875 and the Civil Rights Act of 1957. The principal thrust of the 1957 Act and of the Civil Rights Act of 1960 was against racial discrimination in voting.[e] The Civil Rights Act of 1964, although principally concerned with matters already considered, also dealt with voting. But the most comprehensive federal legislation in aid of the franchise is the Voting Rights Act of 1965, 42 U.S.C. § 1973 (examined in detail in *South Carolina v. Katzenbach* and *Katzenbach v. Morgan,* Sec. 2 infra) and its 1970 Amendments (discussed in *Oregon v. Mitchell,* Sec. 2 infra).[f] Finally, the Civil Rights Act of 1968 provides protection against interference with designated "federally protected activities," 18 U.S.C. § 245, and against discrimination in housing, 42 U.S.C. §§ 3601–31—both considered at several points infra. It also deals extensively with "Constitutional Rights of Indians," 25 U.S.C. §§ 1301–41, and imposes criminal penalties for various activities in connection with "civil disorders," 18 U.S.C. §§ 2102–02, 231–33.

II. JUDICIAL DECISIONS

1. *Necessity of "state action" for violation of constitutional rights.* (a) *In general.* Shortly after enactment of the Reconstruction civil rights laws, the Court, in a series of decisions culminating in the *Civil Rights Cases* in 1883 significantly limited their impact by interpreting the fourteenth (and fifteenth) amendments as barring only "state action," thus precluding congressional legis-

----

c. Another potential weapon in the civil rights arsenal derived from the Reconstruction legislation is 28 U.S.C. § 1443(1). It provides for removal by defendant, from state to federal court, of civil or criminal actions "against any person who is denied or cannot enforce in the courts of such State a right under any law providing for the equal civil rights of citizens of the United States, or of all persons within the jurisdiction thereof." For recent, continued narrow construction, see *Johnson v. Mississippi,* 421 U.S. 213, 95 S.Ct. 1591, 44 L.Ed.2d 121 (1975). See generally Redish, *Revitalizing Civil Rights Removal Jurisdiction,* 64 Minn.L.Rev. 523 (1980).

d. For general discussion and evolution of the Reconstruction civil rights legislation, see Gressman, *The Unhappy History of Civil Rights Legislation,* 50 Mich.L.Rev. 1323 (1952); Maslow & Robison, *Civil Rights Legislation and the Fight for Equality, 1862–1952,* 20 U.Chi.L.Rev. 363 (1953); U.S. Comm'n on Civil Rights, *Enforcement* 103–40 (1965).

e. For federal statutory protection of voting to 1961, see 1 U.S. Comm'n on Civil Rights, *Voting* 73–78 (1961).

f. For background and litigation thereunder, see Derfner, *Racial Discrimination and Voting,* 26 Vand.L.Rev. 523 (1973).

lation against "private individuals" for violating rights of persons created by these amendments.[a]

(b) *Sec. 241 exceptions.* But the Court has long recognized that there is a limited category of constitutional rights, protected by § 241, that, as stated in UNITED STATES v. WILLIAMS, 341 U.S. 70, 71 S.Ct. 581, 95 L.Ed. 758 (1951), "Congress can beyond doubt constitutionally secure against interference by private individuals. [T]his category includes rights which arise from the relationship of the individual and the Federal Government. The right of citizens to vote in congressional elections, for instance, may obviously be protected by Congress from individual as well as from State interference. *Ex parte Yarbrough,* 110 U.S. 651, 4 S.Ct. 152, 28 L.Ed. 274."[b] The Court has also included, as "attributes of national citizenship," "the right of the people peaceably to assemble for the purpose of petitioning Congress for a redress of grievances"[c] and the "constitutional right to travel from one State to another."[d]

In addition, *Williams* recognized a number of federal *statutory* rights that fell within § 241's protection against interference by private persons: "In *United States v. Waddell,* 112 U.S. 76, 5 S.Ct. 35, 28 L.Ed. 673, interference with the right to establish a claim under the Homestead Acts brought the offender within § 241. The right did not pertain to United States citizenship; but since it was 'wholly dependent upon the act of Congress,' obstructing its exercise came 'within the purview of the statute and of the constitutional power of Congress to make such statute.' Similarly, the Court has held that assault upon a citizen in the custody of a United States marshal is a violation of the statute, *Logan v. United States,* 144 U.S. 263, 12 S.Ct. 617, 36 L.Ed. 429. And so, a citizen may not be denied the right to inform on violation of federal laws. *In re Quarles,* 158 U.S. 532, 15 S.Ct. 959, 39 L.Ed. 1080 * * *."[e]

2. *Sec. 242.* SCREWS v. UNITED STATES, 325 U.S. 91, 65 S.Ct. 1031, 89 L.Ed. 1495 (1945): Defendants were Georgia police who, after arresting a black,

a. "[*United States v. Cruikshank,* 92 U.S. 542, 23 L.Ed. 588 (1876),] announced that the first section of the Fourteenth Amendment consisted exclusively of restrictions upon the States and that it does not 'add anything to the rights which one citizen has under the Constitution against another.' The only obligation resting upon the United States, said the Court, was to see that the states did not deny their citizens the enjoyment of an equality of rights. '[The] power of the national government is limited to the enforcement of this guaranty.' [*Virginia v. Rives,* 100 U.S. 313, 25 L.Ed. 667 (1879)] restated the proposition. 'The provisions of the Fourteenth Amendment of the Constitution [all] have reference to state action exclusively, and not to any action of private individuals.'" Gressman, fn. d supra, at 1339. See also fn. b supra.

b. *United States v. Classic,* 313 U.S. 299, 61 S.Ct. 1031, 85 L.Ed. 1368 (1941), included within this category the right to vote in the Louisiana congressional primary: "Interference with [this right is] an interference with the effective choice of the voters at the only stage of the election procedure when their choice is of significance, since it is at the only stage when such interference could have any

practical effect on the ultimate result * * *."

c. *United States v. Cruikshank,* fn. a supra (dictum). For potential expansion, see Feuerstein, *Civil Rights Crimes and the Federal Power to Punish Private Individuals for Interference With Federally Secured Rights,* 19 Vand.L.Rev. 641, 654–59 (1966).

d. *United States v. Guest,* Sec. 2 infra.

e. The Civil Rights Act of 1968, 18 U.S. C.A. § 245(b)(1), imposes criminal penalties, in some cases as harsh as life imprisonment (see note 3(b) after *United States v. Guest,* Sec. 2 infra), on whoever "whether or not acting under color of law, by force or threat of force willfully injures, intimidates or interferes with" any person because he is "(B) participating in or enjoying any benefit, service, privilege, program, facility, or activity provided or administered by the United States; (C) applying for or enjoying employment, or any perquisite thereof, by any agency of the United States; (D) serving, or attending upon any court in connection with possible service, as a grand or petit juror in any court of the United States; (E) participating in or enjoying the benefits of any program or activity receiving Federal financial assistance."

knocked him unconscious when he allegedly reached for a gun and beat him to death. There was evidence that defendant Screws held a personal grudge against him. Defendants were convicted under § 242 for violating the prisoner's right to due process which gave one charged with a crime "the right to be tried by a jury and sentenced by a court."

(a) *Color of law.* First, defendants argued that they had not acted "under color of any law" per § 242 because their action was in violation of state law. Six justices rejected the contention. DOUGLAS, J., joined by Stone, C.J., and Black and Reed, JJ., said: " 'Misuse of power, possessed by virtue of state law and made possible only because the wrongdoer is clothed with the authority of state law, is action taken "under color of" state law.' [Here] the state officers [acted] without authority only in the sense that they used excessive force in making the arrest effective. It is clear that under 'color' of law means under 'pretense' of law. Thus acts of officers in the ambit of their personal pursuits are plainly excluded. Acts of officers who undertake to perform their official duties are included whether they hew to the line of their authority or overstep it." Rutledge and Murphy, JJ., agreed in separate opinions. Roberts, J., joined by Frankfurter and Jackson, JJ., dissented.[f]

(b) *Vagueness.* Second, defendants argued that "there is no ascertainable standard of guilt" because the Court has given "broad and fluid definitions of due process." The DOUGLAS opinion construed "willfully" in § 242 "as connoting a purpose to deprive a person of a specific constitutional right. [W]here the punishment imposed is only for an act knowingly done with the purpose of doing that which the statute prohibits, the accused cannot be said to suffer from lack of warning or knowledge that the act which he does is a violation of law. [Take] the case of a local officer who persists in enforcing a type of ordinance which the Court has held invalid as violative of the guarantees of free speech or freedom of worship. Or a local official continues to select juries in a manner which flies in the teeth of decisions of the Court. If those acts are done willfully, how can the officer possibly claim that he had no fair warning that his acts were prohibited by the statute? He violates the statute not merely because he has a bad purpose but because he acts in defiance of announced rules of law. [T]hat the defendants may not have been thinking in constitutional terms is not material where their aim was not to enforce local law but to deprive a citizen of a right and that right was protected by the Constitution. When they so act they at least act in reckless disregard of constitutional prohibitions or guarantees. [Those] who decide to take the law into their own hands and act as prosecutor, jury, judge, and executioner plainly act to deprive a prisoner of the trial which due process of law guarantees him. And such a purpose need not be expressed; it may at times be reasonably inferred from all the circumstances attendant on the act.

"The difficulty here is that this question of intent was not submitted to the jury with the proper instructions."[g]

Dissenting, the ROBERTS opinion contended that "to base federal prosecutions on the shifting and indeterminate decisions of courts is to sanction prosecutions

---

f. Consider Williams, *The Twilight of State Action,* 41 Texas L.Rev. 347, 365 (1963): "If violation of state law excuses a state officer from engaging in state action, most constitutional cases involving individual liberty would go by the board because such actions are or can be made violations of state law." See generally id. at 352–55. For the view that the issue should turn on whether the aggrieved person has an *effective* remedy under state law, see Van Alstyne & Karst, *State Action,* 14 Stan.L.Rev. 3, 9–22 (1961).

g. Rutledge, J., concurred in reversing and remanding for further proceedings so that five justices might make similar disposition of the cause. But he agreed with Murphy, J., that there was no real issue of vagueness in this case, the jury instructions were adequate, and the conviction should be affirmed.

for crimes based on definitions made by courts. This is tantamount to creating a new body of federal criminal common law." [h]

3. *Sec. 1983.* (a) *Damages.* MONROE v. PAPE, 365 U.S. 167, 81 S.Ct. 473, 5 L.Ed.2d 492 (1961), was an action for damages under § 1983 against Chicago police officers for unlawful invasion of plaintiff's home and illegal search, seizure, and detention. The Court, per DOUGLAS, J., relying on *Screws,* held that the complaint alleged a deprivation of a "right secured by the Constitution" (the fourth amendment's guarantee against unreasonable searches and seizures made applicable to the states by the fourteenth amendment) by persons acting "under color of" state law. Further, since § 1983, unlike § 242, establishes a *civil* remedy and does not contain the word "willfully," plaintiff need not prove the "specific intent" required in *Screws*: § 1983 "should be read against the background of tort liability that makes a man responsible for the natural consequences of his actions." [i]

(b) *Specificity of constitutional right.* PAUL v. DAVIS, p. 272 per REHNQUIST, J., held that § 1983 did not afford respondent a cause of action for his having been defamed by government officials: Unlike *Monroe,* "respondent [has] pointed to no specific constitutional guarantee safeguarding the interest he asserts has been invaded. [If] respondent's view is to prevail, [it] would seem almost necessarily to result in every legally cognizable injury which may have been inflicted by a state official acting under 'color of law' establishing a violation of the Fourteenth Amendment. [S]uch a reading would make of the Fourteenth Amendment a font of tort law to be superimposed upon whatever systems may already be administered by the States." [j]

(c) *"Custom or usage."* ADICKES v. S.H. KRESS & CO., 398 U.S. 144, 90 S.Ct. 1598, 26 L.Ed.2d 142 (1970), involved a damages action against a restaurant for having deprived plaintiff of equal protection—alleging that defendant acted

h. On retrial, defendants in *Screws* were acquitted. Proof of the elements of the offense required by *Screws* "is a difficult burden to satisfy and permits the defense attorney to make the persuasive argument to the jury that only a constitutional lawyer would know enough to be able to harbor the requisite intent." Heyman, *Federal Remedies for Voteless Negroes,* 48 Calif.L.Rev. 190, 200 (1960). See generally 5 U.S. Comm'n on Civil Rights, *Justice* 45–52 (1961). But see *Williams v. United States,* 341 U.S. 97, 71 S.Ct. 576, 95 L.Ed. 774 (1951) in which a post-*Screws* conviction was affirmed.

i. As to the measure of damages under § 1983, see *Carey v. Piphus,* 435 U.S. 247, 98 S.Ct. 1042, 55 L.Ed.2d 252 (1978), holding that common-law tort rules of damages should be adapted to provide "fair compensation for injuries caused by the deprivation of a constitutional right," and that damages should not be *presumed* to flow from every deprivation. See generally Love, *Damages: A Remedy for the Violation of Constitutional Rights,* 67 Calif.L. Rev. 1242 (1979).

As to punitive damages, see *Smith v. Wade,* 461 U.S. 30, 103 S.Ct. 1625, 75 L.Ed.2d 632 (1983), holding that they may be recovered for "malicious" and for "recklessly or callously indifferent" deprivation of rights protected by § 1983. See also *Newport v. Fact Concerts, Inc.,* 453 U.S. 247, 101 S.Ct. 2748, 69 L.Ed.2d

616 (1981), holding that although state officials may be subject to punitive damages under § 1983 "in appropriate circumstances," municipalities may not be so held liable even when its officials have acted in bad faith.

Although no federal statute expressly provides civil remedies for a *federal* officer's violation of a person's constitutional rights, *Bivens v. Six Unknown Agents,* 403 U.S. 388, 91 S.Ct. 1999, 29 L.Ed.2d 619 (1971), held that the federal courts could award money damages ("where federally protected rights have been invaded, it has been the rule from the beginning that courts will be alert to adjust their remedies so as to grant the necessary relief"). See also *Davis v. Passman,* 439 U.S. 1113, 99 S.Ct. 1014, 59 L.Ed.2d 71 (1979) ("unless such rights are to become merely precatory, the class of those litigants who allege that their own constitutional rights have been violated, and who at the same time have no effective means other than the judiciary to enforce these rights, must be able to invoke the existing jurisdiction of the courts for the protection of their justiciable constitutional rights"); *Carlson v. Green,* 446 U.S. 14, 100 S.Ct. 1468, 64 L.Ed.2d 15 (1980), upholding the remedy despite existence of a cause of action against the United States under Federal Tort Claims Act.

j. For the dissenting views of Brennan, White and Marshall, JJ., see p. 273 supra.

"under color [of] custom, or usage, of any State." The Court (Douglas and Brennan, JJ., dissenting; Marshall, J., not participating) held "that a 'custom or usage' for purposes of § 1983 requires state involvement and is not simply a practice which reflects long-standing social habits, generally observed by the people in a locality"; it "must have the force of law by virtue of the persistent practices of state officials." [k]

SECTION 2. MODERN DEVELOPMENTS

SOUTH CAROLINA v. KATZENBACH, 383 U.S. 301, 86 S.Ct. 803, 15 L.Ed. 2d 769 (1966): South Carolina challenged the Voting Rights Act of 1965 (enacted pursuant to § 2 of the fifteenth amendment)—"the heart of [which] is a complex scheme of stringent remedies aimed at areas where voting discrimination has been most flagrant." The Court, per WARREN, C.J., referred to "the voluminous legislative history" that showed, inter alia, "unremitting and ingenious defiance of the Constitution," the enactment of literacy tests in Alabama, Georgia, Louisiana, Mississippi, North Carolina, South Carolina, and Virginia, still in use, which, because of their various qualifications, "were specifically designed to prevent Negroes from voting." It pointed out that "discriminatory application of voting tests" "pursuant to a widespread 'pattern or practice'" "is now the principal method used to bar Negroes from the polls," and gave a number of illustrations; that "case-by-case litigation against voting discrimination" under federal statutes of 1957, 1960 and 1964 has "done little to cure the problem."

"As against the reserved powers of the States, Congress may use any rational means to effectuate the constitutional prohibition of racial discrimination in voting. * * *

"The basic test to be applied in a case involving § 2 of the Fifteenth Amendment is the same as in all cases concerning the express powers of Congress with relation to the reserved powers of the [states.] 'Let the end be legitimate, let it be within the scope of the constitution, and all means which are appropriate, which are plainly adapted to that end, which are not prohibited, but consist with the letter and spirit of the constitution, are constitutional.' *McCulloch v. Maryland* [p. 78 supra].

"We therefore reject South Carolina's argument that Congress may appropriately do no more than to forbid violations of the Fifteenth Amendment in general terms—that the task of fashioning specific remedies or of applying them to particular localities must necessarily be left entirely to the courts. [In] the oft-repeated words of Chief Justice Marshall, referring to another specific legislative authorization in the Constitution, 'This power, like all others vested in Congress, is complete in itself, may be exercised to its utmost extent, and acknowledges no limitations, other than are prescribed in the constitution.' *Gibbons v. Ogden*, 22 U.S. (9 Wheat.) 1, 6 L.Ed. 23 (1824).

The Court first held that the prescription of "remedies for voting discrimination which go into effect without any need for prior adjudication" "was clearly a legitimate response to the problem."

---

k. For general analysis and discussion of litigation under § 1983 and its predecessors, and of immunities for states (but not municipalities) and various government officials that have been established by statutory interpretation, see McCormack, *Federalism and Section* *1983: Limitations on Judicial Enforcement of Constitutional Protections,* 60 Va.L.Rev. 1, 250 (1974); Whitman, *Constitutional Torts,* 79 Mich.L.Rev. 5 (1980); Note, *Section 1983 and Federalism,* 90 Harv.L.Rev. 1133 (1977).

The "coverage formula" of the Act applied "to any State, or to any separate political subdivision [for] which two findings have been made: (1) the Attorney General has determined that on November 1, 1964, it maintained a 'test or device,' and (2) the Director of the Census has determined that less than 50% of its voting-age residents were registered on November 1, 1964, or voted in the presidential election of November 1964. These findings are not reviewable * * *. § 4(b). [T]he phrase 'test or device' means any requirement that a registrant or voter must '(1) demonstrate the ability to read, write, understand, or interpret any matter, (2) demonstrate any educational achievement or his knowledge of any particular subject, (3) possess good moral character, or (4) prove his qualifications by the voucher of registered voters or members of any other class.' § 4(c)." Statutory coverage was terminated by a so-called "bail out" provision—if the area obtained a judgment from a three-judge federal court in the District of Columbia "that tests and devices have not been used during the preceding five years to abridge the franchise on racial grounds." "In acceptable legislative fashion, Congress chose to limit its attention to the geographic areas where immediate action seemed necessary."

The areas covered, "for which there was evidence of actual voting discrimination,"—Alabama, Louisiana, Mississippi, Georgia, South Carolina and much of North Carolina—shared the "two characteristics incorporated by Congress into the coverage formula." "It was therefore permissible to impose the new remedies on the few remaining States and political subdivisions covered by the formula, at least in the absence of proof that they have been free of substantial voting discrimination in recent years." That there are excluded areas "for which there is evidence of voting discrimination by other means" is irrelevant: "Congress strengthened existing remedies for voting discrimination in other areas of the country. Legislation need not deal with all phases of a problem in the same way, so long as the distinctions drawn have some basis in political experience." "There are no States or political subdivisions exempted from coverage under § 4(b) in which the record reveals recent racial discrimination involving tests and devices. This fact confirms the rationality of the formula." The findings "which trigger application of the coverage formula" "consist of objective statistical determinations" and the termination procedure "serves as a partial substitute for direct judicial review."

In areas covered, § 4(a) suspended "literacy tests and similar voting qualifications for a period of five years from the last occurrence of substantial voting discrimination," and § 5 suspended "all new voting regulations pending review by [the Attorney General or a three-judge court in the District of Columbia] to determine whether their use would perpetuate voting discrimination." [a] Both were upheld as a "legitimate response to the problem," the Court recounting the evidence Congress had before it of prior discriminatory administration of old tests and use of new tests to evade court decrees. "Congress knew that continuance of the tests and devices in use at the present time, no matter how fairly administered in the future, would freeze the effect of past discrimination in favor of unqualified white registrants. Congress permissibly rejected the alternatives of requiring a complete re-registration of all voters, believing that this would be too harsh on many whites who had enjoyed the franchise for their entire adult lives."

---

a. For examples of the Court's subsequent broad interpretation of "voting regulations" that are subject to the suspension provision of section 5, see *United Jewish Orgs. v. Carey*, p. 882 supra (new or revised reapportionment plan); *Rome v. United States*, infra (election of officials "at large" rather than by district; annexation of adjacent area thus increasing number of eligible voters).

Finally, §§ 6(b), 7, 9, and 13(a) provided that "the Civil Service Commission shall appoint voting examiners whenever the Attorney General certifies either of the following facts: (1) that he has received meritorious written complaints from at least 20 residents alleging that they have been disenfranchised under color of law because of their race, or (2) that the appointment of examiners is otherwise necessary to effectuate the guarantees of the Fifteenth Amendment." These examiners were empowered to list as "eligible voters" "any person who meets the voting requirements of state law." Termination was provided for "(1) if the Attorney General informs the Civil Service Commission that all persons listed by examiners have been placed on the official voting rolls, and that there is no longer reasonable cause to fear abridgement of the franchise on racial grounds, or (2) if the political subdivision has obtained a declaratory judgment from the District Court for the District of Columbia, ascertaining the same facts which govern termination by the Attorney General, and the Director of the Census has determined that more than 50% of the non-white residents of voting age are registered to vote." This, too, was upheld: "In many of the political subdivisions covered by § 4(b) of the Act, voting officials have persistently employed a variety of procedural tactics to deny Negroes the franchise, often in direct defiance or evasion of federal court decrees. Congress realized that merely to suspend voting rules which have been misused or are subject to misuse might leave this localized evil undisturbed." [b]

ROME v. UNITED STATES, 446 U.S. 156, 100 S.Ct. 1548, 64 L.Ed.2d 119 (1980), per MARSHALL, J., held that for states within the "coverage formula," the Act's "bail out" procedure—satisfaction of which would avoid preclearance of new voting regulations by the Attorney General or the three-judge federal court—could only be used by the state itself and not by separate political units within the state. POWELL, J., dissented: "The Court's interpretation [renders the Act] unconstitutional as applied to the city of Rome. The preclearance requirement both intrudes on the prerogatives of state and local governments and abridges the voting rights of all citizens in States covered under the Act. [In] view of the District Court finding that Rome has not denied or abridged the voting rights of blacks, the Fifteenth Amendment provides no authority for continuing those deprivations until the entire State of Georgia satisfies the bailout standards." Rehnquist, J., joined by Stewart, J., dissented on broader grounds—see note 4 after *Oregon v. Mitchell, infra.*

Notes and Questions

Enforcement provisions. Section 11(b) (with criminal penalties) provides that "no person, whether acting under color of law or otherwise, shall intimidate, threaten, or coerce [any] person for voting or attempting to vote, [or] for urging or aiding any person to vote or attempt to vote, or intimidate, threaten, or coerce any [federal official] for exercising any powers or duties under" the Act. Section 12(c) punishes "whoever conspires" to interfere with rights secured by the Act and § 12(d) authorizes injunctions against "any person" who engages

---

b. Black, J., agreed "with substantially all of the Court's opinion" but dissented in respect to § 5: "[I]f all the provisions of our Constitution which limit the power of the Federal Government and reserve other power to the States are to mean anything, they mean at least that the States have power to pass laws [without] first sending their officials hundreds of miles away to beg federal authorities to approve them."

See also Powell, J.'s "reservations as to the constitutionality of the Act['s] selective coverage of certain States only and to the intrusive preclearance procedure," *United States v. Board of Comm'rs,* 435 U.S. 110, 98 S.Ct. 965, 55 L.Ed.2d 148 (1978) (concurring opinion).

or is about to engage in practices prohibited by the Act.[c] Constitutional? See generally McCarty & Stevenson, *The Voting Rights Act of 1965: An Evaluation,* 3 Harv.Civ.Rts.-Civ.Lib.L.Rev. 357 (1968).

UNITED STATES v. PRICE, 383 U.S. 787, 86 S.Ct. 1152, 16 L.Ed.2d 267 (1966), involved "appeals from the dismissal in part of two indictments," for conspiracy and substantive violations under §§ 241 and 242, against three Mississippi police officials and fifteen "nonofficial persons," for having willfully killed three civil rights workers—the police officials first jailing the victims, then releasing them and intercepting them and, then, all 18 defendants "punishing" the victims by shooting them—thus depriving "the victims due process of law."

The Court, treating the case as raising issues "of construction, not of constitutional power," held that, as to the conspiracy count against the "private persons" under § 242, " '[I]t is immaterial to the conspiracy that these private individuals were not acting under color of law' because the count charges that they were conspiring with persons who were so acting. See *United States v. Rabinowich,* 238 U.S. 78, 87, 35 S.Ct. 682, 684, 59 L.Ed. 1211." As to the substantive counts against the "private persons" under § 242, the Court, stating that the statutory language "under color of law" has "consistently been treated as the same thing as the 'state action' required by the Fourteenth Amendment," held that "private persons, jointly engaged with state officials in the prohibited action, are acting 'under color' of law for purposes of the statute. To act 'under color' of law does not require that the accused be an officer of the State. It is enough that he is a wilful participant in joint activity with the State or its agents," citing *Burton v. Wilmington Parking Auth.,* p. 1419 supra. "[A]ccording to the indictment, the brutal joint adventure was made possible by state detention and calculated release of the prisoners by an officer of the State." "Those who took advantage of participation by state officers in accomplishment of the foul purpose alleged must suffer the consequences of that participation." Finally, the Court held that § 241's "language includes rights or privileges protected by the Fourteenth Amendment; that whatever the ultimate coverage of the section may be, it extends to conspiracies otherwise within the scope of the section participated in by officials alone or in collaboration with private persons." Relying on the requirement in *Screws* "that specific intent be proved," the Court rejected the argument "that the constitutionality of § 241 may be affected by undue vagueness of coverage."

Notes and Questions

1. *"Participation" of private persons with state officers.* In *Price,* the "official" and "nonofficial" defendants all appeared to be actively and equally participating in the venture. Could a private person be constitutionally convicted under § 242 if he were a "passive" participant with state officers? Suppose the private person were the "active" participant while the state officers were merely "passive"? See Klitgaard, *The Civil Rights Act and Mr. Monroe,* 49 Calif.L.Rev. 145, 168–69 (1961). Could the private person be convicted if all the state officers are acquitted?

2. Consider the constitutionality of the following prosecutions under § 242:

---

c. The Civil Rights Act of 1968, 18 U.S.C.A. § 245(b)(1), penalizes all persons who interfere, etc. (see fn. e, Sec. 1, II supra) with "(A) voting or qualifying to vote, qualifying or campaigning as a candidate for elective office, or qualifying or acting as a poll watcher or any legally authorized election official, in any primary, special, or general election."

(a) Defendant sheriff beats prisoner to death because prisoner cursed the sheriff. Suppose the sheriff encounters a personal enemy on the street and beats him to death? Suppose this personal enemy declined to resist because he feared the consequences of a victory over a police officer? Suppose the sheriff first tells the personal enemy that he is under arrest?

(b) Defendant private citizen secretly enters a jail and beats a prisoner to death. Suppose the citizen joined the sheriff in beating the prisoner to death in order to obtain a confession?

(c) Defendant sheriff stands by while a private citizen beats to death the sheriff's prisoner, who is the citizen's personal enemy.

(d) Defendant private citizen is part of a mob that so intimidates parents of school children as to cause them to keep the children away from the school with the result that the school is closed.

(e) Defendant bus driver racially segregates passengers because he is commanded by state statute to do so.

(f) Defendant private citizen makes a "citizen's arrest" without probable cause. Suppose the citizen masqueraded as a policeman and made an arrest without probable cause? Suppose this citizen, dressed as a policeman, killed a personal enemy? Suppose the citizen, making an arrest without probable cause, were a private detective who became a "special police officer" by local law? See *Williams v. United States,* 341 U.S. 97, 71 S.Ct. 576, 95 L.Ed. 774 (1951).

(g) Defendant court-appointed trustee embezzles the funds.

(h) Defendant attorney, an "officer of the court," makes false statements in a sanity proceeding which result in the commitment of another person. Suppose defendant is court-appointed? See *Polk County v. Dodson,* 454 U.S. 312, 102 S.Ct. 445, 70 L.Ed.2d 509 (1981) (public defender does not act under color of law when performing traditional adversarial functions as appointed counsel).

UNITED STATES v. GUEST
383 U.S. 745, 86 S.Ct. 1170, 16 L.Ed.2d 239 (1966).

MR. JUSTICE STEWART delivered the opinion of the Court.

[Defendants were indicted] for criminal conspiracy in violation of § 241 [to] deprive Negro citizens of the free exercise and enjoyment of several specified rights secured by the Constitution and laws of the United States. The defendants [successfully] moved to dismiss the indictment on the ground that it did not charge an offense under the laws of the United States. [As] in *Price,* decided today, we deal here with issues of statutory construction, not with issues of constitutional power. * * *

II. The second numbered paragraph of the indictment alleged that the defendants conspired to injure, oppress, threaten, and intimidate Negro citizens of the United States in the free exercise of enjoyment of: "The right to the equal utilization, without discrimination upon the basis of race, of public facilities in the vicinity of Athens, Georgia, owned, operated, or managed by [the State]."

Correctly characterizing this paragraph as embracing rights protected by the Equal Protection Clause [the] District Court held as a matter of statutory construction that § 241 does not encompass any Fourteenth Amendment [rights. This] was in error, as [*Price*] makes abundantly clear. * * *

Moreover, inclusion of Fourteenth Amendment rights within the compass of § 241 does not render the statute unconstitutionally vague. Since the gravamen of the offense is conspiracy, the requirement that the offender must act with a specific intent to interfere with the federal rights in question is satisfied.

Screws. And the rights under the Equal Protection Clause described by this paragraph of the indictment have been so firmly and precisely established by a consistent line of decisions in this Court, that the lack of specification of these rights in the language of § 241 itself can raise no serious constitutional question on the ground of vagueness or indefiniteness.

Unlike the indictment in *Price,* however, the indictment in the present case names no person alleged to have acted in any way under the color of state law. [The] Equal Protection Clause speaks to the State or to those acting under the color of its authority.

In this connection, we emphasize that § 241 by its clear language incorporates no more than the Equal Protection Clause itself; the statute does not purport to give substantive, as opposed to remedial, implementation to any rights secured by that Clause. Since we therefore deal here only with the bare terms of the Equal Protection Clause itself, nothing said in this opinion goes to the question of what kinds of other and broader legislation Congress might constitutionally enact under § 5 of the Fourteenth Amendment to implement that Clause or any other provision of the Amendment.

It is a commonplace that rights under the Equal Protection Clause itself arise only where there has been involvement of the State or of one acting under the color of its authority. * * *

This is not to say, however, that the involvement of the State need be either exclusive or direct. In a variety of situations the Court has found state action of a nature sufficient to create rights under the Equal Protection Clause even though the participation of the State was peripheral, or its action was only one of several cooperative [forces].

This case, however, requires no determination of the threshold level that state action must attain in order to create rights under the Equal Protection Clause [because] the indictment in fact contains an express allegation of state involvement sufficient at least to require the denial of a motion to dismiss. One of the means of accomplishing the object of the conspiracy, according to the indictment, was "By causing the arrest of Negroes by means of false reports that such Negroes had committed criminal acts." [The] allegation of the extent of official involvement in the present case is not clear. [But it] is broad enough to cover a charge of active connivance by agents of the State in the making of the "false reports," or other conduct amounting to official discrimination clearly sufficient to constitute denial of rights protected by the Equal Protection Clause. Although it is possible [that] the proof if the case goes trial, would disclose no cooperative action of that kind by officials of the State, the allegation is enough to prevent dismissal of this branch of the indictment.

III. The fourth numbered paragraph of the indictment alleged that the defendants conspired to injure, oppress, threaten, and intimidate Negro citizens of the United States in the free exercise and enjoyment of: "The right to travel freely to and from the State of [Georgia]."

The District Court was in error in dismissing the indictment as to this paragraph. The constitutional right to travel from one State to another, and necessarily to use the highways and other instrumentalities of interstate commerce in doing so, occupies a position fundamental to the concept of our Federal Union. [See the Court's discussion, Ch. 3, Sec. 3.]

This does not mean, of course, that every criminal conspiracy affecting an individual's right of free interstate passage is within the sanction of § 241. A specific intent to interfere with the federal right must be [proved]. Thus, for example, a conspiracy to rob an interstate traveler would not, of itself, violate

§ 241. But if the predominant purpose of the conspiracy is to impede or prevent the exercise of the right of interstate travel, or to oppress a person because of his exercise of that right, then, whether or not motivated by racial discrimination, the conspiracy becomes a proper object of the federal law under which the indictment in this case was brought. * * *

Reversed and remanded.

MR. JUSTICE CLARK, with whom MR. JUSTICE BLACK and MR. JUSTICE FORTAS join, concurring.

I join the opinion of the Court in this case but believe it worthwhile to comment on [Part II]. The Court's interpretation of the indictment clearly avoids the question whether Congress, by appropriate legislation, has the power to punish private conspiracies that interfere with Fourteenth Amendment rights, such as the right to utilize public facilities. My Brother Brennan, however, [suggests] that the Court indicates sub silentio that Congress does not have the power to outlaw such conspiracies. Although the Court specifically rejects any such connotation, it is, I believe, both appropriate and necessary under the circumstances here to say that there now can be no doubt that the specific language of § 5 empowers the Congress to enact laws punishing all conspiracies—with or without state action—that interfere with Fourteenth Amendment rights.

MR. JUSTICE HARLAN, concurring in part and dissenting in part.

I join [Part] II of the Court's opinion, but I cannot subscribe to Part III in its full sweep. To the extent that it is there held that § 241 reaches conspiracies, embracing only the action of private persons, [to] interfere with the right of citizens freely to engage in interstate travel, I am constrained to dissent. On the other hand, I agree that § 241 does embrace state interference with such interstate travel, and I therefore consider that this aspect of the indictment is sustainable on the reasoning of Part II of the Court's opinion.

This right to travel must be found in the Constitution itself. This is so because [no] "right to travel" can be found in § 241 or in any other law of the United States. [While] past cases do indeed establish that there is a constitutional "right to travel" between States free from unreasonable *governmental* interference, today's decision is the first to hold that such movement is also protected against *private* interference * * *.

[Harlan, J., first reviewed the cases stating "that the right is a privilege and immunity of national citizenship" and concluded] that those cases all dealt with the right of travel simply as affected by oppressive *state* action. * * *

A second possible constitutional basis for the right [is] the Commerce Clause. [Yet] this approach to the right to travel, like that found in the privileges and immunities cases, is concerned with the interrelation of state and federal power, not [with] private interference. * * *

One other possible source for the right to travel should be mentioned [—due process, which] would clearly make it inapplicable to the present case, for due process speaks only to governmental action. * * *

As a general proposition it seems to me very dubious that the Constitution was intended to create certain rights of private individuals as against other private individuals. The Constitutional Convention was called to establish a nation, not to reform the common law. Even the Bill of Rights, designed to protect personal liberties, was directed at rights against governmental authority, not other individuals. It is true that there are a very narrow range of rights against individuals which have been read into the Constitution [referring to cases discussed in note 1(b), Sec. 1, II supra, but these] are narrow, and are essentially concerned with the vindication of important relationships with the Federal Government—voting in federal elections, involvement in federal law enforcement, communicating with the Federal Government. The present case stands on a considerably different footing.

It is arguable that the same considerations which led the Court on numerous occasions to find a right of free movement against oppressive state action now justifies a similar result with respect to private impediments. *Crandall v. Nevada* spoke of the need to travel to the capital, to serve and consult with the offices of government. A basic reason for the formation of this Nation was to facilitate commercial intercourse; intellectual, cultural, scientific, social, and political interests are likewise served by free movement. Surely these interests can be impeded by private vigilantes as well as by state action. Although this argument is not without force, [t]here is a difference in power between States and private groups so great that analogies between the two tend to be misleading. If the State obstructs free intercourse of goods, people, or ideas, the bonds of the union are threatened; if a private group effectively stops such communication, there is at most a temporary breakdown of law and order, to be remedied by the exercise of state authority or by appropriate federal legislation.

[As] to interstate commerce [b]ecause Congress has wide authority to legislate in this area, it seems unnecessary [to] strain to find a dubious constitutional right.[a]

[T]he immunities and commerce provisions of the Constitution leave the way open for the finding of this "private" constitutional right, since they do not speak solely in terms of governmental action. [But to] do so subjects § 241 to serious challenge on the score of vagueness and serves in effect to place this Court in the position of making criminal law under the name of constitutional interpretation. * * *

Mr. Justice Brennan, with whom The Chief Justice and Mr. Justice Douglas join, concurring in part and dissenting in part.

I [reach] the same result as the Court on that branch of the indictment discussed in Part III of its opinion but for other reasons. See footnote 3, infra. And I agree with so much of Part II as construes § 241 to encompass conspiracies to injure, oppress, threaten or intimidate citizens in the free exercise or enjoyment of Fourteenth Amendment rights and holds that, as so construed, § 241 is not void for indefiniteness. I do not agree, however, with the remainder of Part II, which holds, as I read the opinion, that a conspiracy to interfere with the exercise of the right to equal utilization of state facilities is not within the meaning of § 241 [unless] discriminatory conduct by state officers is involved in the alleged conspiracy.

* * * I believe that § 241 reaches such a private conspiracy, not because the Fourteenth Amendment of its own force prohibits such a conspiracy, but because § 241, as an exercise of congressional power under § 5 of that Amendment, prohibits *all* conspiracies to interfere with the exercise of a "right * * * secured [by] the Constitution" and because the right to equal utilization of state

---

a. The Civil Rights Act of 1968, 18 U.S. C.A. § 245(b), penalizes all persons who interfere etc. (see fn. e, Sec. 1, II supra) with "(2) any person because of his race, color, religion or national origin and because he is or has been * * * (E) traveling in or using any facility of interstate commerce, or using any vehicle, terminal, or facility of any common carrier by motor, rail, water, or air."

facilities is a "right * * * secured [by] the Constitution" within the meaning of that phrase as used in § 241.[3]

My difference with the Court stems from its construction of the term "secured" as used in § 241 * * *. The Court tacitly construes the term "secured" so as to restrict the coverage of § 241 to those rights that are "fully protected" by the Constitution or another federal law. Unless private interferences with the exercise of the right in question are prohibited by the Constitution itself or another federal law, the right cannot, in the Court's view, be deemed "secured [by] the Constitution or laws of the United States" so as to make § 241 applicable to a private conspiracy to interfere with the exercise of that right. The Court then premises that neither the Fourteenth Amendment nor any other federal law prohibits private interferences with the exercise of the right to equal utilization of state facilities.

In my view, however, a right can be deemed "secured [by] the Constitution or laws of the United States," within the meaning of § 241, even though only governmental interferences with the exercise of the right are prohibited by the Constitution itself (or another federal law). The term "secured" means "created by, arising under, or dependent upon," rather than "fully protected." A right is "secured [by] the Constitution" within the meaning of § 241 if it emanates from the Constitution, if it finds its source in the Constitution. Section 241 must thus be viewed, in this context, as an exercise of congressional power to amplify prohibitions of the Constitution addressed, as is invariably the case, to government officers; contrary to the view of the Court, I think we are dealing here with a statute that seeks to implement the Constitution, not with the "bare terms" of the Constitution. [Many] of the rights that have been held to be encompassed within § 241 are not additionally the subject of protection of specific federal legislation or of any provision of the Constitution addressed to private individuals [referring to cases discussed in note 1(b), Sec. 1, II supra]. The full import of our decision in *Price* regarding § 241 is to treat the rights purportedly arising from the Fourteenth Amendment in parity with those rights just enumerated, arising from other constitutional provisions. * * *

For me, the right to use state facilities without discrimination on the basis of race is, within the meaning of § 241, a right created by, arising under and dependent upon the Fourteenth Amendment and hence is a right "secured" by that Amendment. It finds its source in that Amendment. [The] Fourteenth Amendment commands the State to provide the members of all races with equal access to the public facilities it owns or manages, and the right of a citizen to use those facilities without discrimination on the basis of race is a basic corollary of this command. Whatever may be the status of the right to equal utilization of *privately owned facilities*, it must be emphasized that we are here concerned with the right to equal utilization of *public facilities owned or operated by or on behalf of the State.* To deny the existence of this right or its constitutional stature is to deny the history of the last decade, or to ignore the role of federal power, predicated on the Fourteenth Amendment, in obtaining nondiscriminatory access to such facilities. * * *

In reversing the District Court's dismissal of the second numbered paragraph, I would therefore hold that proof at the trial of the conspiracy charged to

3. Similarly, I believe that § 241 reaches a private conspiracy to interfere with the right to travel from State to State. I therefore need not reach the question whether the Constitution of its own force prohibits private interferences with that right; for I construe § 241 to prohibit such interferences, and as so construed I am of the opinion that § 241 is a valid exercise of congressional power.

the defendants in that paragraph will establish a violation of § 241 without regard to whether there is also proof that state law enforcement officers actively connived in causing the arrests of Negroes by means of false reports.

My view as to the scope of § 241 requires that I reach the question [of] whether § 241 or legislation indubitably designed to punish entirely private conspiracies to interfere with the exercise of Fourteenth Amendment rights constitutes a permissible exercise of the power granted to Congress by § 5 * * *.

A majority of the members of the Court [6] express the view today that § 5 empowers Congress to enact laws punishing *all* conspiracies to interfere with the exercise of Fourteenth Amendment rights, whether or not state officers or others acting under the color of state law are implicated in the conspiracy. * * * § 5 authorizes Congress to make laws that it concludes are reasonably necessary to protect a right created by and arising under that Amendment; and Congress is thus fully empowered to determine that punishment of private conspiracies interfering with the exercise of such a right is necessary to its full protection. * * *

I acknowledge that some of the decisions of this Court, most notably an aspect of the *Civil Rights Cases,* have declared that Congress' power under § 5 is confined to the adoption of "appropriate legislation for correcting the effects [of] prohibited state law and state [acts]." I do not accept—and a majority of the Court today rejects—this interpretation of § 5. It reduces the legislative power to enforce the provisions of the Amendment to that of the judiciary; [7] and it attributes a far too limited objective to the Amendment's sponsors.[8] Moreover, the language of § 5 of the Fourteenth Amendment and § 2 of the Fifteenth Amendment are virtually the same, and we recently held in *South Carolina v. Katzenbach* that "[t]he basic test to be applied in a case involving § 2 of the Fifteenth Amendment is the same as in all cases concerning the express powers of Congress with relation to the reserved powers of the States." The classic formulation of that test by Chief Justice Marshall in *McCulloch v. Maryland,* was there adopted * * *. Indeed, *South Carolina v. Katzenbach* approvingly refers to *Ex parte Virginia,* 100 U.S. 339, 25 L.Ed. 676 (1879), a case involving the exercise of the congressional power under [§ 5], as adopting the *McCulloch* formulation for "each of the Civil War Amendments."

Viewed in its proper perspective, § 5 appears as a positive grant of legislative power, authorizing Congress to exercise its discretion in fashioning remedies to achieve civil and political equality for all citizens. No one would deny [that]

---

6. The majority consists of the Justices joining my Brother Clark's opinion and the Justices joining this opinion. * * *

7. Congress, not the judiciary, was viewed as the more likely agency to implement fully the guarantees of equality, and thus it could be presumed the primary purpose of the Amendments was to augment the power of Congress, not the judiciary. See James, *The Framing of the Fourteenth Amendment,* 184 (1956); Harris, *The Quest for Equality,* 53–54 (1960); Frantz, *Congressional Power to Enforce the Fourteenth Amendment Against Private Acts,* 73 Yale L.J. 1353, 1356 (1964).

8. As the first Mr. Justice Harlan said in dissent in the *Civil Rights Cases:* "It was perfectly well known that the great danger to

equal enjoyment by citizens of their rights, as citizens, was to be apprehended, not altogether from unfriendly state legislation, but from the hostile action of corporations and individuals in the states. And it is to be presumed that it was intended, by [§ 5], to clothe congress with power and authority to meet that danger."

[For the view that the fourteenth amendment's "Privileges or Immunities Clause (coupled with the § 5 Enforcement Clause)" was intended "as an authorization of Federal legislation to prohibit private racial discrimination if the states did not," see Lusky, *By What Right?* 181–203 (1975). See also Frantz, fn. 7 supra.]

Congress has the power to punish state officers who, in excess of their authority and in violation of state law, conspire to threaten, harass and murder Negroes for attempting to use [state] facilities. And I can find no principle of federalism nor word of the Constitution that denies Congress power to determine that in order adequately to protect the right to equal utilization of state facilities, it is also appropriate to punish other individuals—neither state officers nor acting in concert with state officers—who engage in the same brutal conduct for the same misguided purpose.

Section 241 is certainly not model legislation for punishing private conspiracies to interfere with the exercise of the right of equal utilization of state facilities. It deals in only general language [which] brings § 241 close to the danger line of being void for vagueness.

But, as the Court holds, a stringent scienter requirement saves § 241 from condemnation * * *.

Notes and Questions

1. *Interference with fourteenth (and fifteenth) amendment rights.* Are private persons, who intimidate state officials in an attempt to thwart their racial integration of schools, subject to prosecution under § 241? Private persons who intimidate black school children or their parents in an attempt to stop them from going to integrated schools? Who lynch a prisoner, thus preventing his fair trial by the state? Who intimidate blacks in an effort to prevent them from voting? Cf. note after *South Carolina v. Katzenbach.* Who detain a judge in an effort to prevent him from setting bail?

2. *Scope of congressional power under § 5.* (a) Do you agree with "a majority of the members of the Court" in *Guest* that "§ 5 empowers Congress to enact laws punishing *all* conspiracies to interfere with the exercise of Fourteenth Amendment rights, whether or not state officers or others acting under color of state law are implicated in the conspiracy"? Consider Feuerstein, fn. c, Sec. 1, II supra, at 674–75: "[They] start with the proposition that there is a right to use state facilities without discrimination based upon race, when actually they are saying that there is a right to use state facilities without racial discrimination from any quarter—state or private. The traditional view of the equal protection clause is that it creates a right to be free of discrimination by the state. So defined, the right can only be infringed by state action, and legislation under § 5 must be directed at that infringement. Unfortunately, neither the Brennan nor the Clark opinion directly confronts this traditional approach." [b] Is the majority's rationale limited to "conspiracies" or is Congress empowered, beyond § 241, to penalize individual private acts? Does Brennan, J.'s rationale extend to "the right to equal utilization of *privately owned facilities*"?

(b) *Civil Rights Act of 1968.* 18 U.S.C.A. § 245(b): "Whoever, whether or not acting under color of law, by force or threat of force willfully injures,

b. Compare Stevens, J., concurring in *Great American Fed. S. & L. Ass'n v. Novotny,* 442 U.S. 366, 99 S.Ct. 2345, 60 L.Ed.2d 957 (1979): "[I]f private persons take conspiratorial action that prevents or hinders the constituted authorities of any State from giving or securing equal treatment, the private persons would cause those authorities to violate the Fourteenth Amendment; [but if] private persons engage in purely private acts of discrimination, [they] do not violate the Equal Protection Clause of the Fourteenth Amendment. The rights secured by the Equal Protection and Due Process Clauses of the Fourteenth Amendment are rights to protection against unequal or unfair treatment by the State, not by private parties."

intimidates or interferes with, or attempts to injure, intimidate or interfere with—* * *

"(2) any person because of his race, color, religion or national origin and because he is or has been—

"(A) enrolling in or attending any public school or public college;

"(B) participating in or enjoying any benefit, service, privilege, program, facility or activity provided or administered by any State or subdivision thereof;

"(C) applying for or enjoying employment, or any perquisite thereof, by any private employer or any agency of any State or subdivision thereof, or joining or using the services or advantages of any labor organization, hiring hall, or employment agency;

"(D) serving, or attending upon any court of any State in connection with possible service, as a grand or petit juror; * * *

"(F) enjoying the goods, services, facilities, privileges, advantages, or accommodations of any inn, hotel, motel, or other establishment which provides lodging to transient guests, or of any restaurant, cafeteria, lunchroom, lunch counter, soda fountain, or other facility which serves the public and which is principally engaged in selling food or beverages for consumption on the premises, or of any gasoline station, or of any motion picture house, theater, concert hall, sports arena, stadium, or any other place of exhibition or entertainment which serves the public, or of any other establishment which serves the public and (i) which is located within the premises of any of the aforesaid establishments or within the premises of which is physically located any of the aforesaid establishments, and (ii) which holds itself out as serving patrons of such establishments; or * * *

"(5) any citizen because he is or has been, or in order to intimidate such citizen or any other citizen from lawfully aiding or encouraging other persons to participate, without discrimination on account of race, color, religion or national origin, in any of the benefits or activities described [or] participating lawfully in speech or peaceful assembly opposing any denial of the opportunity to so participate—

"shall be fined not more than $1,000, or imprisoned not more than one year, or both; and if bodily injury results shall be fined not more than $10,000, or imprisoned not more than ten years, or both; and if death results shall be subject to imprisonment for any term of years or for life. * * * Nothing in subparagraph (2)(F) * * * of this subsection shall apply to the proprietor of any establishment which provides lodging to transient guests, or to any employee acting on behalf of such proprietor, with respect to the enjoyment of the goods, services, facilities, privileges, advantages, or accommodations of such establishment if such establishment is located within a building which contains not more than five rooms for rent or hire and which is actually occupied by the proprietor as his residence."

(c) Suppose a private individual murders a black. It is clear that the *effect* (irrespective of the murderer's *intent*) is to prevent the victim's equal use of state facilities; that it prevents his right to vote, etc. These facts would be equally true if the victim were white. May the murderer be punished under § 241? Under a more narrowly drawn federal criminal statute? Consider Cox, *Constitutional Adjudication and the Promotion of Human Rights,* 80 Harv.L.Rev. 91, 116 (1966): "It seems unlikely that much constitutional significance will attach to distinctions in terms of intent. The differences between purpose, awareness that a consequence must follow, conscious indifference, and responsibility for the natural and probable consequences of an act are far too elusive to measure the scope of congressional power. Furthermore, if violence and intimidation are actually interfering with the right to vote or to enjoy state facilities, there is scant practical relevance in the wrongdoers' motivation. The suggestion was once made that the power of Congress to regulate local activities under the commerce clause depended upon the intent with which the activities were conducted, but the idea was shortly abandoned in favor of legislative or administrative determination of the practical effects on commerce."

Does congressional power fail in the above instance because "its authority is confined to instances in which there is a special relationship between the person injured and the state"? Because there is "an utter lack of proportion between the federal punishment [and] the federal interest in safeguarding enjoyment of the constitutional right"? Or is "the responsibility for the federal system" left to Congress: "possession of congressional power should not be confused with its exercise"? Id. at 116–17, 119.

KATZENBACH v. MORGAN
384 U.S. 641, 86 S.Ct. 1717, 16 L.Ed.2d 828 (1966).

MR. JUSTICE BRENNAN delivered the opinion of the Court.

[Section] 4(e) of the Voting Rights Act of 1965 [provides] that no person who has successfully completed the sixth primary grade in a [school] accredited by the Commonwealth of Puerto Rico in which the language of instruction was other than English shall be denied the right to vote in any election because of his inability to read or write English. Appellees, registered voters in New York City, brought this suit to challenge the constitutionality of § 4(e) insofar as it pro tanto prohibits the enforcement of the election laws of New York requiring an ability to read and write English * * *.

Under the distribution of powers effected by the Constitution, [the] qualifications established by the States for voting for members of the most numerous branch of the state legislature also determine who may vote for United States Representatives and Senators, Art. I, § 2; Seventeenth Amendment. But, of course, the States have no power to grant or withhold the franchise on conditions that are forbidden by the Fourteenth Amendment * * *.

The Attorney General of New York argues that an exercise of congressional power under § 5 of the Fourteenth Amendment that prohibits the enforcement of a state [law] cannot be sustained as appropriate legislation to enforce the Equal Protection Clause unless the judiciary decides—even with the guidance of a congressional judgment—that the application of the English literacy requirement prohibited by § 4(e) is forbidden by the Equal Protection Clause itself. We disagree. Neither the language nor history of § 5 supports such a construction.[7] [A] construction of § 5 that would require a judicial determination that the enforcement of the state law precluded by Congress violated the Amendment, as a condition of sustaining the congressional enactment [would] confine the legislative power in this context to the insignificant role of abrogating only those state laws that the judicial branch was prepared to adjudge unconstitutional, or of merely informing the judgment of the judiciary by particularizing the "majestic

7. For the historical evidence suggesting that the sponsors and supporters of the Amendment were primarily interested in augmenting the power of Congress, rather than the judiciary, see generally tenBroek, *The An-* *tislavery Origins of the Fourteenth Amendment* 187–217 (1951). [But see Burt, *Miranda and Title II: A Morganatic Marriage,* 1969 Sup.Ct.Rev. 81–100.]

generalities" of [§ 1]. Accordingly, our decision in *Lassiter v. Northampton Cty. Bd. of Elec.*, 360 U.S. 45, 79 S.Ct. 985, 3 L.Ed.2d 1072 (1959), sustaining the North Carolina English literacy requirement as not in all circumstances prohibited by the first sections of the Fourteenth and Fifteenth Amendments, [did] not present the question before us here: Without regard to whether the judiciary would find that the Equal Protection Clause itself nullifies New York's English literacy requirement as so applied, could Congress prohibit the enforcement of the state law by legislating under § 5? In answering this question, our task is limited to determining whether such legislation is, as required by § 5, appropriate legislation to enforce the Equal Protection Clause.

By including § 5 the draftsmen sought to grant to Congress [the] same broad powers expressed in the Necessary and Proper Clause.[9] The classic formulation of the reach of those powers was established by Chief Justice Marshall in *McCulloch v. Maryland* * * *. *Ex parte Virginia*, decided 12 years after the adoption of the Fourteenth Amendment, held that congressional power under § 5 had this same broad scope * * *. Section 2 of the Fifteenth Amendment grants Congress a similar power [and] we recently held in *South Carolina v. Katzenbach* that [the test was] the one formulated in *McCulloch*. * * * Correctly viewed, § 5 is a positive grant of legislative power authorizing Congress to exercise its discretion in determining whether and what legislation is needed to secure the guarantees of the Fourteenth Amendment. * * *[10]

There can be no doubt that § 4(e) may be regarded as an enactment to enforce the Equal Protection Clause. [S]pecifically, § 4(e) may be viewed as a measure to secure for the Puerto Rican community residing in New York nondiscriminatory treatment by government—both in the imposition of voting qualifications and the provision or administration of governmental services, such as public schools, public housing and law enforcement.

Section 4(e) may be readily seen as "plainly adapted" to furthering these aims of the Equal Protection Clause. The practical effect of § 4(e) is to prohibit New York from denying the right to vote to large segments of its Puerto Rican community [—the] right that is "preservative of all rights." This enhanced political power will be helpful in gaining nondiscriminatory treatment in public services for the entire Puerto Rican community.[11] Section 4(e) thereby enables the Puerto Rican minority better to obtain "perfect equality of civil rights and equal protection of the laws." [It] was for Congress, as the branch that made

9. In fact, earlier drafts of the proposed Amendment employed the "necessary and proper" terminology to describe the scope of congressional power under the Amendment. The substitution of the "appropriate legislation" formula was never thought to have the effect of diminishing the scope of this congressional power. See, e.g., Cong. Globe, 42d Cong., 1st Sess., App. 83 * * *. [But see Note, *Theories of Federalism and Civil Rights*, 75 Yale L.J. 1007, 1046 n. 200 (1966). Compare discussion in *Argument: The Oral Argument Before the Supreme Court in Brown v. Board of Education of Topeka, 1952–55*, 93–94 (Friedman ed. 1969).]

10. Contrary to the suggestion of the dissent, § 5 does not grant Congress power to exercise discretion in the other direction and to enact "statutes so as in effect to dilute equal protection and due process decisions of this Court." We emphasize that Congress' power under § 5 is limited to adopting measures to enforce the guarantees of the Amendment; § 5 grants Congress no power to restrict, abrogate, or dilute these guarantees. Thus, for example, an enactment authorizing the States to establish racially segregated systems of education would not be—as required by § 5—a measure "to enforce" the Equal Protection Clause since that clause of its own force prohibits such state laws.

11. Cf. * * * *United States v. Darby*, 312 U.S. 100, 61 S.Ct. 451, 85 L.Ed. 609 (1941), that the power of Congress to regulate interstate commerce "extends to those activities intrastate which so affect interstate commerce or the exercise of the power of Congress over it as to make regulation of them appropriate means to the attainment of a legitimate end * * *."

this judgment, to assess and weigh the various conflicting considerations—the risk or pervasiveness of the discrimination in governmental services, the effectiveness of eliminating the state restriction on the right to vote as a means of dealing with the evil, the adequacy or availability of alternative remedies, and the nature and significance of the state interests that would be affected by the nullification of the English literacy requirement * * *. It is not for us to review the congressional resolution of these factors. It is enough that we be able to perceive a basis upon which the Congress might resolve the conflict as it did. There plainly was such a [basis]. Any contrary conclusion would require us to be blind to the realities familiar to the legislators.[12]

The result is no different if we confine our inquiry to the question whether § 4(e) was merely legislation aimed at the elimination of an invidious discrimination in establishing voter qualifications. We are told that New York's English literacy requirement originated in the desire to provide an incentive for non-English speaking immigrants to learn the English language and in order to assure the intelligent exercise of the franchise. Yet Congress might well have questioned, in light of the many exemptions provided,[13] and some evidence suggesting that prejudice played a prominent role in the enactment of the requirement,[14] whether these were actually the interests being served. Congress might have also questioned whether denial of a right deemed so precious and fundamental in our society was a necessary or appropriate means of encouraging persons to learn English, or of furthering the goal of an intelligent exercise of the franchise.[15] Finally, Congress might well have concluded that as a means of furthering the intelligent exercise of the franchise, an ability to read or understand Spanish is as effective as ability to read English for those to whom Spanish-language newspapers and Spanish-language radio and television programs are available to inform them of election issues and governmental affairs.[16] Since Congress undertook to legislate so as to preclude the enforcement of the state law, and did so in the context of a general appraisal of literacy requirements for voting, see *South Carolina v. Katzenbach,* to which it brought a

---

12. See, e.g., 111 Cong.Rec. 10676, 10680 (May 20, 1965), 15671 (July 9, 1965); *Literacy Tests and Voter Requirements in Federal and State Elections,* Senate Hearings 507–508.

13. The principal exemption complained of is that for persons who had been eligible to vote before January 1, 1922.

14. This evidence consists in part of statements made in the Constitutional Convention first considering the English literacy requirement * * *. Congress was aware of this evidence. See, e.g., *Literacy Tests and Voter Requirements in Federal and State Elections,* Senate Hearings 507–513; *Voting Rights,* House Hearings 508–513.

15. Other States have found ways of assuring an intelligent exercise of the franchise short of total disenfranchisement of persons not literate in English. For example, in Hawaii, where literacy in either English or Hawaiian suffices, candidates' names may be printed in both languages; New York itself already provides assistance for those exempt from the literacy requirement and are literate in no language; and, of course, the problem of assuring the intelligent exercise of the fran-

chise has been met by those States, more than 30 in number, that have no literacy requirement at all. Section 4(e) does not preclude resort to these alternative methods of assuring the intelligent exercise of the franchise. True, the statute precludes, for a certain class, disenfranchisement and thus limits the States' choice of means of satisfying a purported state interest. But our cases have held that the States can be required to tailor carefully the means of satisfying a legitimate state interest when fundamental liberties and rights are threatened, see, e.g., *Carrington v. Rash; Harper v. Virginia Board of Elections* [pp. 1011–12 supra]; *United States v. Carolene Products Co.* [p. 23 supra]; and Congress is free to apply the same principle in the exercise of its powers.

16. See, e.g., 111 Cong.Rec. 10675 (May 20, 1965), 15102 (July 6, 1965), 15666 (July 9, 1965). The record in this case includes affidavits describing the nature of New York's two major Spanish-language newspapers [and] its three full-time Spanish-language radio stations and affidavits from those who have campaigned in Spanish speaking areas.

specially informed legislative competence,[17] it was Congress' prerogative to weigh these competing considerations. Here again, it is enough that we perceive a basis upon which Congress might predicate a judgment that the application of New York's English literacy requirement * * * constituted an invidious discrimination in violation of the Equal Protection Clause.

[The Court rejected the contention that the "American-flag schools" limitation itself violates "the letter and spirit of the Constitution," see p. 1021 supra].

Reversed.

MR. JUSTICE HARLAN, whom MR. JUSTICE STEWART joins, dissenting.

[Harlan, J., first argued that the New York law was not forbidden by the equal protection clause itself.] I believe the Court has confused the issue of how much enforcement power Congress possesses under § 5 with the distinct issue of what questions are appropriate for congressional determination and what questions are essentially judicial in nature.

When recognized state violations of federal constitutional standards have occurred, Congress is of course empowered by § 5 to take appropriate remedial [measures]. But it is a judicial question whether the condition with which Congress has thus sought to deal is in truth an infringement of the Constitution, something that is the necessary prerequisite to bringing the § 5 power into play at all. Thus, in *Ex parte Virginia,* involving a federal statute making it a federal crime to disqualify anyone from jury service because of race, the Court first held as a matter of constitutional law that "the Fourteenth Amendment secures [an] impartial jury trial, by jurors indifferently selected or chosen without discrimination against such jurors because of their color." Only then did the Court hold that to enforce this prohibition upon state discrimination, Congress could enact a criminal statute of the type under consideration. [In] *South Carolina v. Katzenbach,* [we] reviewed first the "voluminous legislative history" as well as judicial precedents supporting the basic congressional finding that the clear commands of the Fifteenth Amendment had been infringed by various state subterfuges. Given the existence of the evil, we held the remedial steps taken by the legislature under the Enforcement Clause of the Fifteenth Amendment to be a justifiable exercise of congressional initiative.

[The] question here is not whether the statute is appropriate remedial legislation to cure an established violation of a constitutional command, but whether there has in fact been an infringement of that constitutional command, that is, whether a particular state practice or, as here, a statute is so arbitrary or irrational as to offend the command of [equal protection]. That question is one for the judicial branch ultimately to determine. [In] view of [*Lassiter*], I do not think it is open to Congress to limit the effect of that decision as it has undertaken to do by § 4(e). In effect the Court reads § 5 of the Fourteenth Amendment as giving Congress the power to define the *substantive* scope of the Amendment. If that indeed be the true reach of § 5, then I do not see why Congress should not be able as well to exercise its § 5 "discretion" by enacting statutes so as in effect to dilute equal protection and due process decisions of this Court. In all such cases there is room for reasonable men to differ as to whether or not a denial of equal protection or due process has occurred, and the final decision is one of judgment. Until today this judgment has always been one for the judiciary to resolve.

---

17. See, e.g., 111 Cong.Rec. 10676 (Senator Long of Louisiana and Senator Young), 10678 (Senator Holland) (May 20, 1965), drawing on their experience with voters literate in a language other than English. * * *

I do not mean to suggest in what has been said that a legislative judgment of the type incorporated in § 4(e) is without any force whatsoever. Decisions on questions of equal protection and due process are based not on abstract logic, but on empirical foundations. To the extent "legislative facts" are relevant to a judicial determination, Congress is well equipped to investigate them, and such determinations are of course entitled to due respect.[a] In *South Carolina v. Katzenbach,* such legislative findings were made to show that racial discrimination in voting was actually occurring. Similarly, in *Heart of Atlanta Motel, Inc. v. United States,* and *Katzenbach v. McClung,* 379 U.S. 241, 85 S.Ct. 348, 13 L.Ed.2d 258 (1964), the congressional determination that racial discrimination in a clearly defined group of public accommodations did effectively impede interstate commerce was based on "voluminous testimony" which had been put before the Congress and in the context of which it passed remedial legislation.

But no such factual data provide a legislative record supporting § 4(e)[9] by way of showing that Spanish-speaking citizens are fully as capable of making informed decisions in a New York election as are English-speaking citizens. Nor was there any showing whatever to support the Court's alternative argument that § 4(e) should be viewed as but a remedial measure designed to cure or assure against unconstitutional discrimination of other varieties, e.g., in "public schools, public housing and law enforcement" * * *.

Thus, we have [here] what can at most be called a legislative announcement that Congress believes a state law to entail an unconstitutional deprivation of equal protection. Although this kind of declaration is of course entitled to the most respectful consideration, coming as it does from a concurrent branch and one that is knowledgeable in matters of popular political participation, I do not believe it lessens our responsibility to decide the fundamental issue of whether in fact the state enactment violates federal constitutional rights.

In assessing the deference we should give to this kind of congressional expression of policy, it is relevant that the judiciary has always given to congressional enactments a presumption of validity. However, it is also a canon of judicial review that state statutes are given a similar presumption, [and] although it has been suggested that this Court should give somewhat more deference to Congress than to a State Legislature,[10] such a simple weighing of presumptions is hardly a satisfying way of resolving a matter that touches the distribution of state and federal power in an area so sensitive as that of the regulation of the franchise. Rather it should be recognized that while the Fourteenth Amendment is a "brooding omnipresence" over all state legislation, the substantive matters which it touches are all within the primary legislative competence of the States. Federal authority, legislative no less than judicial, does not intrude unless there has been a denial by state action of Fourteenth Amendment [limitations]. At least in the area of primary state concern a state statute that passes constitutional muster under the judicial standard of rationali-

---

a. For the view that "Congress cannot alter the *normative component* of a judicial decision" but that "the *empirical component* [is] the province of Congress," see Gordon, *The Nature and Uses of Congressional Power Under Section Five of the Fourteenth Amendment to Overcome Decisions of the Supreme Court,* 72 Nw.U.L.Rev. 656 (1977). See note 6(b) infra.

9. There were no committee hearings or reports referring to this section, which was introduced from the floor during debate on the full Voting Rights Act.

10. See Thayer, *The Origin and Scope of the American Doctrine of Constitutional Law,* 7 Harv.L.Rev. 129, 154–155 (1893).

ty should not be permitted to be set at naught by a mere contrary congressional pronouncement unsupported by a legislative record justifying that conclusion.

[To] hold, on this record, that § 4(e) overrides the New York literacy requirement seems to me tantamount to allowing the Fourteenth Amendment to swallow the State's constitutionally ordained primary authority in this field. For if Congress by what, as here, amounts to mere ipse dixit can set that otherwise permissible requirement partially at naught I see no reason why it could not also substitute its judgment for that of the States in other fields of their exclusive primary competence as well. * * *

Notes and Questions

1. *Congress and equal protection.* After *Morgan,* may Congress enact legislation prohibiting *all* state discrimination on the basis of alienage, illegitimacy and gender? Cf. Ch. 6, Sec. 3. Forbidding state discrimination against pushcart food vendors, opticians, debt adjustors and methadone users? Cf. Ch. 6, Sec. 1. For the view that, since the Court "underenforces" the provisions of § 1 of the fourteenth amendment because of "institutional" reasons "based upon questions of propriety or capacity," Congress has "the authority to enact legislation which fills in that body's conception" of those provisions, see Sager, *Fair Measure: The Legal Status of Underenforced Constitutional Norms,* 91 Harv.L. Rev. 1212 (1978).

After *Morgan,* may Congress outlaw *all* age and residence requirements for voting? Consider Bickel, *The Voting Rights Cases,* 1966 Sup.Ct.Rev. 79, 100: "[S]uppose Congress decided that aliens or eighteen-year-olds or residents of New Jersey are being discriminated against in New York. The decision would be as plausible as the one concerning Spanish-speaking Puerto Ricans. Could Congress give these groups the vote? If Congress may freely bestow the vote as a means of curing other discriminations, which it fears may be practiced against groups deprived of the vote, essentially because of this deprivation and on the basis of no other evidence, then there is nothing left of state autonomy in setting qualifications for voting."

2. *Analogy to commerce power.* On the scope of Congress' power under the commerce clause, is Congress' discretion limited to determining what are "appropriate means" for regulating intrastate commerce that affects commerce in more than one state, or does it extend to determining *whether* intrastate commerce affects commerce in more than one state? See Comment, 20 Rutg.L.Rev. 826 (1966). Is the *Morgan* standard of judicial review of Congress' power under § 5 the same as the standard for reviewing Congress' power under the commerce clause? Consider Cox note 2(c) after *Guest* at 104: "Conclusory but qualifying phrases like 'reasonable relation' and 'rational' are notably absent from the opinion, in contrast to the public accommodations and voting rights cases where [the opinions] were limited by the need to use terms acceptable to a unanimous bench. It is sufficient that the law 'may be viewed' as a measure for securing equal protection and that the Court can 'perceive a basis' upon which Congress might predicate its judgment. The choice of words cannot have been casual. Evidently, the Court intends to validate any legislation under section 5—at least any legislation dealing with state action—without judging the substantiality of its relation to a permissible federal objective."

3. *Need for a "legislative record."* What of Harlan, J.'s suggestion that other broad exertions of congressional power have been sustained only on the

basis of "factual data" or "voluminous testimony"? Consider Cox, supra, at 105: "[His view] is at odds with the presumption of constitutionality and with a long line of precedents holding that a statute must be judged constitutional if any set of facts which can reasonably be conceived would sustain it. No case has ever held that a record is constitutionally required. The majority's view is also supported by the cases upholding congressional legislation under the commerce clause prior to the 1930s, much of which apparently rested upon factual conclusions for which no legislative record could be cited. The principle is not merely one of deference to Congress or the states. It rests upon appreciation of the fact that the fundamental basis for legislative action is the knowledge, experience, and judgment of the people's representatives only a small part, or even none, of which may come from the hearings and reports of committees or debates upon the floor."

4. *Congress and due process.* After *Morgan,* may Congress impose the federal rules of civil and criminal procedure on the states on the ground that the fourteenth amendment requires that due process be accorded all litigants and that in "its discretion" the federal rules are "needed to secure the guarantees of the Fourteenth Amendment"? Apart from "specific" constitutional prohibitions, under *Morgan,* what are the limits of congressional power? See generally Note, *Congressional Power to Enforce Due Process Rights,* 80 Colum.L.Rev. 1265 (1980).

5. *Congress and state action.* If *Morgan* gives Congress "the power to define the *substantive* scope" of equal protection (and due process), does it similarly permit Congress to determine the question of what constitutes "state action"? For example, might Congress, in "exercise of its discretion," determine that any judicial enforcement of racial discrimination shall be prohibited? That racial discrimination in the sale and rental of housing exists because of the failure of the states to make such discrimination illegal, and that this state "inaction" is state action under the fourteenth amendment that should "appropriately" be "remedied" by federal fair housing legislation? See fn. 8 in Brennan, J.'s opinion in *Guest.*

(a) For another post-*Morgan* approach re federal housing legislation, consider Cox, supra, at 120: "So long as Negroes are confined to racial ghettos, there will be actual or dangerously potential state discrimination in the quantity or quality of public services. First, the isolation of unpopular minorities in poverty-stricken, socially and economically isolated neighborhoods, lacking political influence, invites a lower quality of state services just as withholding the vote from many citizens in Puerto Rican neighborhoods made it less likely that they would receive equal services. Second, the very existence of the ghetto renders it more difficult [for] a state to provide equal services. Children in black ghettos, with an inferior cultural and economic background, lack the environment and associations essential to truly equal educational opportunity. [*Morgan* held that] Congress might legislate to remove an obstacle to the state's performance of its constitutional duty not to discriminate in providing public services, even though the immediate subject matter of the legislation—there the requirement of English literacy—was not itself a violation of the fourteenth amendment. It follows that Congress may likewise legislate to eliminate racial ghettos as obstacles to the states' performance of that same constitutional duty, even though the immediate subject matter of this legislation—the practices that result in ghettos—do not themselves involve violations of the fourteenth amendment. The only important difference is that in *Morgan* the obstacle was itself a state law whereas discrimination in housing has a private origin. [But] that difference in the source of the threat to performance of the state's obligation is irrelevant." [b]

(b) *Civil Rights Act of 1968, Title VIII: Fair Housing.* After declaring "the policy of the United States to provide, within constitutional limitations, for fair housing throughout the United States" (42 U.S.C.A. § 3601), the Act makes unlawful various discriminations "because of race, color, religion, or national origin" (§ 3604) "in the sale or rental of housing" that is "owned or operated by the Federal Government," or financed or supported by various federal programs (§ 3603(a)). It is also applicable "to all other dwellings" *except* "any single family house" when its owner then "does not own" nor have "any interest in" "more than three such," *and* the private owner does not use a real estate broker, or advertising that states a discriminatory preference (§ 3603(b)(1)). § 3603(b)(2) further exempts "rooms or units in dwellings containing living quarters occupied or intended to be occupied by no more than four families living independently of each other, if the owner actually maintains and occupies one of such living quarters as his residence." § 3607 permits certain sales and rentals by "religious" groups to be limited "to persons of the same religion" "unless membership in such religion is restricted on account of race, color, or national origin" and permits "a private club" that "provides lodgings" to limit them "to its members." Constitutional?

6. *Congressional dilution of fourteenth amendment rights.* (a) After *Morgan*, does Congress have power "to dilute equal protection and due process decisions" of the Court? Consider Cox, supra, at 106 n. 86: "According to the conventional theory [enunciated in fn. 10 of *Morgan*], the Court has invalidated state statutes under the due process and equal protection clauses only when no state of facts which can reasonably be conceived would sustain them. Where that is true, a congressional effort to withdraw the protection granted by the clause would lack the foundation of a reasonably conceivable set of facts and would therefore be just as invalid as the state legislation. But while that is true in the realm of economic regulation, the Court has often substituted its own evaluation of actual conditions in reviewing legislation dealing with 'preferred rights.' It is hard to see how the Court can consistently give weight to the congressional judgment in expanding the definition of equal protection in the area of human rights but refuse to give it weight in narrowing the definition where the definition depends upon appraisal of the facts." Does the "answer" lie in a theory that justifies judicial review principally on the need to afford protection to certain minority "rights" from the majority will? Consider Cohen, *Congressional Power to Interpret Due Process and Equal Protection,* 27 Stan.L. Rev. 603, 614 (1975): "[A] theory that distinguishes between congressional competence to make 'liberty' and 'federalism' judgments resolves the dilemma. A congressional judgment rejecting a judicial interpretation of the due process or equal protection clauses—an interpretation that had given the individual procedural or substantive protection from state and federal government alike—is entitled to no more deference than the identical decision of a state legislature.[c]

b. See also Notes, *Toward Limits on Congressional Enforcement Power Under the Civil War Amendments,* 34 Stan.L.Rev. 453 (1982); *Congressional Power Under Section Five of the Fourteenth Amendment,* 25 Stan.L.Rev. 885 (1973).

c. For the view that equal protection challenges to congressional action should be judged by a more lenient (but not "toothless") standard of review than state action, see Bohrer, *Bakke, Weber and Fullilove: Benign Discrimination and Congressional Power to Enforce the Fourteenth Amendment,* 56 Ind. L.J. 473 (1981).

Congress is no more immune to momentary passions of the majority than are the state legislatures. But a congressional judgment resolving at the national level an issue that could—without constitutional objection—be decided in the same way at the state level, ought normally to be binding on the courts, since Congress presumably reflects a balance between both national and state interests and hence is better able to adjust such conflicts." See also Choper, *Judicial Review and the National Political Process* 198–200 (1980).

In MISSISSIPPI UNIV. FOR WOMEN v. HOGAN, p. 962 supra, "the State contended that Congress, in enacting [the] Education Amendments of 1972, expressly had authorized MUW to continue its single-sex admissions policy by exempting public undergraduate institutions that traditionally have used single-sex admissions policies from the gender discrimination prohibition of Title IX. Through that provision, the State argued, Congress limited the reach of the Fourteenth Amendment by exercising its power under § 5 of the Amendment." The Court, relying on fn. 10 of *Morgan,* responded: "Although we give deference to congressional decisions and classifications, neither Congress nor a State can validate a law that denies the rights guaranteed by the Fourteenth Amendment." The four dissenting justices did not address the issue.

(b) *Competence as to "facts."* Does *Miranda v. Arizona,* 384 U.S. 436, 86 S.Ct. 1602, 16 L.Ed.2d 694 (1966), rest on the *factual* assumption that there is "compulsion inherent in custodial surroundings" and thus "no statement obtained from the defendant can truly be the product of his free choice"? Does *Mapp v. Ohio,* p. 117 supra, rest on the *factual* assumption that the exclusionary rule is a "deterrent safeguard without insistence upon which the Fourth Amendment would have been reduced to 'a form of words' "? Does *Gideon v. Wainwright,* 372 U.S. 335, 83 S.Ct. 792, 9 L.Ed.2d 799 (1963), rest on the *factual* assumption that a person "who is too poor to hire a lawyer, cannot be assured a fair trial unless counsel is provided for him"? Does *Brown v. Board of Education,* p. 823 supra, rest on the *factual* assumption that racially "separate educational facilities are inherently unequal"? If so, may Congress, pursuant to § 5, find the *facts* to be otherwise and legislate a contrary rule? See S.Rep. No. 1097, 90th Cong., 2d Sess. 59–63 (1968).

(c) *Line-drawing.* What deference is owed congressional action, pursuant to § 5, that precisely defines (i) how long a delay constitutes denial of the "right to a speedy trial," see *Barker v. Wingo,* 407 U.S. 514, 92 S.Ct. 2182, 33 L.Ed.2d 101 (1972); (ii) how great a deviation from absolute population equality among legislative districts constitutes a violation of the "one person-one vote" requirement, see Ch. 6, Sec. 4, I, A?

(d) *Conflicting constitutional provisions.* May de facto racial segregation in the schools arguably violate equal protection; may use of racial criteria to alleviate de facto segregation arguably violate equal protection (see Ch. 6, Secs. 2, IV–V)? May failure to exempt persons with certain religious beliefs from the burden of some government regulations arguably violate the free exercise clause; may exemption of these persons arguably violate the establishment clause (see Ch. 5, Sec. 2, III)? If so, what deference is owed congressional action, pursuant to § 5, dealing with these matters? See opinion of White, J., in *Welsh v. United States,* p. 790 supra.

(e) *Rights vs. remedies.* May Congress, pursuant to § 5, withdraw (or replace) the "exclusionary rule" of *Mapp v. Ohio* on the ground that this does not "dilute" any substantive constitutional right but merely modifies a remedy for its violation? See fn. g, p. 117 supra. On similar analysis, may Congress forbid busing (or substitute alternatives) to remedy school segregation? See note 2, p. 860 supra. Consider Note, *The Nixon Busing Bills and Constitutional Power*, 81 Yale L.J. 1542, 1570–71 (1972): "Because busing is one remedy among many, Bork [*Constitutionality of the President's Busing Proposals* 21–22 (1972)] argues [that the anti-busing bill] leaves intact the duty *Brown* imposed upon formerly segregated school districts. Such an argument creates an artificial distinction between rights and remedies; the right which cannot be vindicated is not a right at all, and the most that can be said for the distinction is that it may be useful where a right can be vindicated in several ways. [If] busing is in some cases—as it was in *Swann*—the only remedy that would produce desegregation in any real sense, then Bork's argument falls. The real question about the constitutionality of the busing bills is the question that Bork hesitates to answer directly: to what extent does the Equal Protection Clause require that once segregated schools achieve a racial balance? *Swann,* of course, had a simple and direct answer: to the greatest extent possible." See also Rotunda, *Congressional Power to Restrict the Jurisdiction of the Lower Federal Courts and the Problem of School Busing,* 64 Geo.L.J. 839 (1976).

For the view that many judicial decisions implementing constitutional rights are not "true constitutional interpretations" but rather only "constitutional common law" rules that may be modified by Congress, see Monaghan, *Constitutional Common Law,* 89 Harv.L.Rev. 1 (1975). Compare Schrock & Welsh, *Reconsidering the Constitutional Common Law,* 91 Harv.L.Rev. 1117 (1978).

(f) *Definition of "dilution."* If Congress believed that more wrongdoers would be convicted and crime deterred by changing the *Miranda* rule, would such legislation "dilute" the due process rights of the accused, or "secure" the rights of the public generally not to be denied life or property without due process of law? Who should *ultimately* determine these issues?

(g) *"Human Life Bill."* What of the constitutionality of the following proposed statute, S. 158 and H.R. 900, 97th Cong., 1st Sess. (1981):

"Sec. 1. The Congress finds that present day scientific evidence indicates a significant likelihood that actual human life exists from conception.

"The Congress further finds that the fourteenth amendment to the Constitution of the United States was intended to protect all human beings.

"Upon the basis of these findings, and in the exercise of the powers of the Congress, including its power under section 5 of the fourteenth amendment to the Constitution of the United States, the Congress hereby declares that for the purpose of enforcing the obligation of the States under the fourteenth amendment not to deprive persons of life without due process of law, human life shall be deemed to exist from conception, without regard to race, sex, age, health, defect, or condition of dependency; and for this purpose 'person' shall include all human life as defined herein. ＊ ＊ ＊" [d]

(i) *Questions of "fact."* Do the issues of when "human life" begins and what is a "person" involve questions of fact? Consider Tribe, *Prepared Statement,* Hearings on S. 158 at 251: "Such questions [call] at bottom for normative judgments no less profound than those involved in defining 'liberty' or 'equality.' [They] entail 'question[s] to which science can provide no answer,' as the

---

d. For argument in favor of its validity, see Galebach, *A Human Life Statute,* 7 Human Life Rev. 3 (1981), reprinted in Hearings on S. 158, before the Subcomm. on Separation of Powers of the Senate Comm. on the Judiciary, 97th Cong., 1st Sess. 205 (1981); Nagel, *Prepared Statement,* id. 321. For exhaustive consideration, see Estreicher, *Congressional Power and Constitutional Rights: Reflections on Proposed "Human Life" Legislation,* 68 Va.L.Rev. 333 (1982).

National Academy of Sciences itself acknowledged * * *. Congress cannot transform an issue of religion, morality, and law into one of fact by waving the magic wand of Section 5 [which] no more authorizes Congress to transmute a matter of values into a matter of scientific observation than it authorizes Congress to announce a mathematical formula for human freedom." See also Cox, *Prepared Statement,* id. at 340–41.

(ii) *"Dilution" vs. "expansion."* Does the Bill dilute the right to an abortion? Consider Noonan, *Prepared Statement,* id. at 266–67: "In recognizing the unborn as persons, [the] Act treats no one unequally but gives equal protection to one class of humanity now unequally treated. * * * Necessarily, the expression of the rights of one class of human beings has an impact on the rights of others. The elimination of literacy tests in this way 'diluted' the voting rights of the literate. It is inescapable that congressional expression of the right to life will have an impact on the abortion right; but in the eyes of Congress, [there] will be a net gain for Fourteenth Amendment rights by the expansion and the attendant diminution."

OREGON v. MITCHELL

400 U.S. 112, 91 S.Ct. 260, 27 L.Ed.2d 272 (1970).

[In original jurisdiction suits, brought by Oregon and Texas against the Attorney General and by the United States against Arizona and Idaho, the states challenged Congress' power to enact Titles II and III of the Voting Rights Act Amendments of 1970. (1) Section 302 forbade states to deny any citizen, otherwise qualified to vote, the right to vote in any federal, state or local election "on account of age if such citizen is eighteen years of age or older." Black, Douglas, Brennan, White and Marshall, JJ., voted to uphold this provision as to federal elections; Burger, C.J., and Black, Harlan, Stewart and Blackmun, JJ., voted to hold it unconstitutional as to state and local elections. (2) Section 201 extended the Voting Rights Act of 1965 for an additional five years (to 1975) and also extended nationwide § 4(a)'s prohibition of "any test or device" (including literacy tests) "as a prerequisite for voting or registration." This was upheld unanimously.[a] (3) Sec. 202 abolished any state "durational residency requirement as a precondition to voting for President and Vice President"; it required the registration "of all duly qualified residents of such State who apply, not later than thirty days immediately prior to any presidential election," and the provision of "absentee ballots" to those "who may be absent [on] the day such election is held and who have applied therefor not later than seven days immediately prior to such election"; an "otherwise qualified" voter who changes state residency within thirty days of such election must be permitted to vote either "in person" or "by absentee ballot" "in the State or political subdivision in which he resided immediately prior to his removal." Only Harlan, J., voted to hold this provision invalid.]

MR. JUSTICE BLACK, announcing the judgments of the Court in an opinion expressing his own view of the cases.

---

a. In 1975, the Act was amended to extend for an additional seven years, to make § 4(a)'s suspension of "any test or device" indefinite, and to greatly expand the geographic coverage (including, inter alia, areas with at least 5% language minorities) of the requirement that new voting regulations be reviewed by the Attorney General or a federal court. See generally Hunter, *The 1975 Voting Rights Act and Language Minorities,* 25 Cath.U.L.Rev. 250 (1976). The seven year extension was upheld in *Rome v. United States,* note 4 infra. In 1982, the Act's preclearance mechanism was extended for 25 years.

[T]he responsibility of the States for setting the qualifications of voters in congressional elections [in Art. I, § 2] was made subject to the power of Congress to make or alter such regulations [in Art. I, § 4].

Moreover, the power of Congress to make election regulations in national elections is augmented by the Necessary and Proper Clause. [In] *Colegrove v. Green* [p. 36 supra], no Justice of this Court doubted Congress' power to rearrange the congressional districts according to population * * *.

Surely no voter *qualification* was more important to the Framers than the *geographical qualification* embodied in the concept of congressional districts. [There] can be no doubt that the power to alter congressional district lines is vastly more significant in its effect than the power to permit 18-year-old citizens to go to the polls and vote in all federal elections.[b]

* * * Similarly, it is the prerogative of Congress to oversee the conduct of presidential and vice presidential elections and to set the qualifications for voters for electors for those offices. It cannot be seriously contended that Congress has less power over the conduct of presidential elections than it has over congressional elections.[7]

On the other hand, [n]o function is more essential to the separate and independent existence of the States [than] the power to determine within the limits of the Constitution the qualifications of their own voters for state, county, and municipal [offices]. Amendments Fourteen, Fifteen, Nineteen, and Twenty-Four, each of which has assumed that the States had general supervisory power over state elections, are examples of express limitations on the power of the States to govern themselves. [My] Brother Brennan's opinion, if carried to its logical conclusion, would, under the guise of insuring equal protection, blot out all state power, leaving the 50 States little more than impotent figureheads.
* * *

Of course, we have upheld congressional legislation under the Enforcement Clauses in some cases where Congress has interfered with state regulation of the local electoral process [*Morgan; South Carolina v. Katzenbach*]. But division of power between state and national governments, like every provision of the Constitution, was expressly qualified by the Civil War Amendments' ban on racial discrimination. * * *

In enacting the 18-year-old vote provisions of the Act now before the Court, Congress made no legislative findings that 21-year-old vote requirements were used by the States to disenfranchise voters on account of race. I seriously doubt that such a finding, if made, could be supported by substantial evidence. Since Congress has attempted to invade an area preserved to the States by the Constitution without a foundation for enforcing the Civil War Amendments' ban on racial discrimination, I would hold that Congress has exceeded its powers in

---

b. Could the substance of the 24th amendment, barring payment of a poll tax as a condition to vote in federal elections, have been enacted simply by a federal statute?

7. With reference to the selection of the President and Vice President, Art. II, § 1 provides: "Each State shall appoint, in such Manner as the Legislature thereof may direct, a Number of Electors, equal to the whole Number of Senators and Representatives to which the State may be entitled in the Congress * * *." But this Court in *Burroughs v. United States,* 290 U.S. 534, 54 S.Ct. 287, 78

L.Ed. 484 (1934), [rejected] a construction of Art. II, § 1, that would have curtailed the power of Congress to regulate such elections. Finally, and most important, inherent in the very concept of a supreme national government with national officers is a residual power in Congress to insure that those officers represent their national constituency as responsively as possible. This power arises from the nature of our constitutional system of government and from the Necessary and Proper Clause.

attempting to lower the voting age in state and local elections. On the other hand, [i]n enacting the literacy test ban of Title II Congress had before it a long history of the discriminatory use of literacy tests to disfranchise voters on account of their race. [A]s to the Nation as a whole, Congress had before it statistics which demonstrate that voter registration and voter participation are consistently greater in States without literacy tests.

Congress also had before it this country's history of discriminatory educational opportunities in both the North and the South. [There] is substantial, if not overwhelming, evidence from which Congress could have concluded that it is a denial of equal protection to condition the political participation of children educated in a dual school system upon their educational achievement. [Finally in enacting the residency and absentee voting] regulations for national elections Congress was attempting to insure a fully effective voice to all citizens in national elections. What I said [about Congress' power to regulate federal elections] applies with equal force here. * * *

MR. JUSTICE DOUGLAS. * * *

The grant of the franchise to 18-year-olds by Congress is in my view valid across the board.

I suppose that in 1920, when the Nineteenth Amendment was passed giving women the right to vote, it was assumed [that] there was no relief by way of the Equal Protection Clause [but in 1962] discrimination against voters on grounds *other than race* was struck down [in] *Baker v. Carr* [p. 30 supra]. Whatever distinction may have been made, following the Civil War, between "civil" and "political" rights, has passed into history. [Hence] the history of the Fourteenth Amendment tendered by my Brother Harlan is irrelevant to the present problem.

Since the right is civil and not "political," it is protected by the Equal Protection Clause of the Fourteenth Amendment which in turn by § 5 of that Amendment can be "enforced" by Congress. [The] manner of enforcement involves discretion; but that discretion is largely entrusted to [Congress].

I likewise find the objections [to] the literacy and residence requirements of the 1970 Act to be insubstantial.

Literacy. [We] traveled most of the distance needed to sustain this [in *Morgan*].

Residence. [The] right to vote for national officers is a privilege and immunity of national citizenship [and "under § 5" "Congress can determine that it is necessary and proper to abolish" residency requirements "in national elections to effectuate and further the purpose of § 1 as it has been declared by this Court."]

MR. JUSTICE BRENNAN, MR. JUSTICE WHITE, and MR. JUSTICE MARSHALL dissent from the judgment insofar as it declares § 302 unconstitutional as applied to state and local elections * * *.

[Literacy: Arizona] urges that to the extent that any citizens of Arizona have been denied the right to vote because of illiteracy resulting from discriminatory governmental practices, the unlawful discrimination has been by governments other than [Arizona. But] congressional power to remedy the evils resulting from state-sponsored racial discrimination does not end when the subject of that discrimination removes himself from the jurisdiction in which the injury occurred. * * *

[Residency:] Whether or not the Constitution vests Congress with particular power to set qualifications for voting in strictly federal elections, we believe there is an adequate constitutional basis for § 202 in § 5 of the Fourteenth Amendment. [A] durational residence requirement operates to penalize those persons, and only those persons, who have exercised their constitutional right of interstate migration. [I]n such a case, governmental action may withstand constitutional scrutiny only upon a clear showing that the burden imposed is necessary to protect a compelling and substantial governmental interest. *Shapiro v. Thompson* [p. 1361 supra]. [W]e find ample justification for the congressional conclusion that § 202 is a reasonable means for eliminating an unnecessary burden on the right of interstate migration. *Guest.*

[Age:] We believe there is serious question whether a statute [denying] the franchise to citizens [between] the ages of 18 and 21 could, in any event, withstand present scrutiny under the Equal Protection Clause. Regardless of the answer to this question, however, it is clear to us that proper regard for the special function of Congress in making determinations of legislative fact compels this Court to respect those determinations unless they are contradicted by evidence far stronger than anything that has been adduced in these cases.

* * *

A. [W]hen exclusions from the franchise are challenged as violating [equal protection] "the Court must determine whether the exclusions are necessary to promote a compelling state interest."

In the present cases, the States justify exclusion of 18- to 21-year-olds from the voting rolls solely on the basis of the States' interests in promoting intelligent and responsible exercise of the franchise. [But each] of the 50 States has provided special mechanisms for dealing with persons who are deemed insufficiently mature and intelligent to understand, and to conform their behavior to, the criminal laws of the State. Forty-nine of the States have concluded that, in this regard, 18-year-olds are invariably to be dealt with according to precisely the same standards prescribed for their elders. This at the very least is evidence of a nearly unanimous legislative judgment on the part of the States themselves that differences in maturity and intelligence between 18-year-olds and persons over the age of 21 are too trivial to warrant specialized treatment for *any* of the former class in the critically important matter of criminal responsibility. Similarly, every State permits 18-year-olds to marry, and 39 States do not require parental consent for such persons of one or both sexes. [No] State in the Union requires attendance at school beyond the age of 18. [T]hat 18-year-olds as a class may be less educated than some of their elders cannot justify restriction of the franchise for the States themselves have determined that this incremental education is irrelevant to voting qualifications. And finally, we have been cited to no material whatsoever that would support the proposition that intelligence, as opposed to educational attainment, increases between the ages of 18 and 21.

[No] State seeking to uphold its denial of the franchise to 18-year-olds has adduced anything beyond the mere difference in age. [But] perhaps more important is the uniform experience of those States—Georgia since 1943, and Kentucky since 1955—that have permitted 18-year-olds to vote. [E]very person who spoke to the issue in either the House or Senate was agreed that 18-year-olds in both States were at least as interested, able, and responsible in voting as were their [elders].

B. [When] a state legislative classification is subjected to judicial challenge as violating the Equal Protection Clause, it comes before the courts cloaked by the presumption that the legislature has, as it should, acted within constitutional limitations. [But] this limitation on judicial review of state legislative classifications is a limitation stemming not from the Fourteenth Amendment itself, but from the nature of [the] judicial process [which] makes it an inappropriate forum for the determination of complex factual questions of the kind so often involved in constitutional adjudication. [Should Congress, however, pursuant to § 5] undertake an investigation in order to determine whether the factual basis necessary to support a state legislative discrimination actually exists, it need not stop once it determines that some reasonable men could believe the factual basis exists. Section 5 empowers Congress to make its own determination on the matter. See *Morgan.* It should hardly be necessary to add that if the asserted factual basis necessary to support a given state discrimination does not exist, § 5 of the Fourteenth Amendment vests Congress with power to remove the discrimination by appropriate means.

The scope of our review in such matters has been established by a long line of consistent decisions. * * * "[W]here we find that the legislators, in light of the facts and testimony before them, have a rational basis for finding a chosen regulatory scheme necessary [our] investigation is at an end." *Katzenbach v. McClung; Morgan.*[32]

[The] core of dispute [here] is a conflict between state and federal legislative determinations of the factual issues upon which depends decision of a federal constitutional question—the legitimacy, under [equal protection], of state discrimination against persons between the ages of 18 and 21. Our cases have repeatedly emphasized that, when state and federal claims come into conflict, the primacy of federal power requires that the federal finding of fact control. See *England v. Louisiana State Board* [p. 1587 infra]. The Supremacy Clause requires an identical result when the conflict is one of legislative, not judicial, findings.

Finally, it is no answer to say that Title III intrudes upon a domain reserved to the States—the power to set qualifications for voting. It is no longer open to question that the Fourteenth Amendment applies to this, as to all other, exercises of state power. * * *

C. [T]he language of the Fourteenth Amendment [applies] on its face to all assertions of state power, however made. More than 40 years ago, this Court faced for the first time the question whether a State could deny Negroes the right to vote in primary elections. Writing for a unanimous Court, Mr. Justice Holmes observed tartly that "[w]e find it unnecessary to consider the Fifteenth Amendment, because it seems to us hard to imagine a more direct and obvious infringement of the Fourteenth." *Nixon v. Herndon*, 273 U.S. 536, 540–541, 47 S.Ct. 446, 71 L.Ed. 759 (1927). * * *

In any event, it seems to us, the historical record will not bear the weight our Brother Harlan has placed upon it. [Our] reading of the historical background [results] in a somewhat imperfect picture of an era of constitutional confusion, confusion which the Amendment did little to resolve. [The opinion examines in some detail the historical setting, the "politics of the day," the

---

32. As we emphasized in *Morgan*, "§ 5 does not grant Congress power [to] enact 'statutes so as in effect to dilute equal protection and due process decisions of this Court.'" As indicated above, a decision of this Court striking down a state statute expresses, among other things, our conclusion that the legisla-tive findings upon which the statute is based are so far wrong as to be unreasonable. Unless Congress were to unearth new evidence in its investigation, its identical findings on the identical issue would be no more reasonable than those of the state legislature.

changes in language of the proposed Amendment made in the Joint Congressional Committee on Reconstruction, and the "obscure" and sometimes "incongruous" statements made in congressional debates, campaign speeches and the press. It] suggests an alternative hypothesis: that the Amendment was framed by men who possessed differing views on the great question of the suffrage and [who] papered over their differences with the broad, elastic language of § 1 and left to future interpreters of their Amendment the task of resolving in accordance with future vision and future needs the issues which they left unresolved. [Those] who submitted the Fifteenth Amendment [could] well have desired that any prohibition against racial discrimination in voting stand upon a firmer foundation than mere legislative action capable of repeal or the vagaries of judicial decision. [At] least some of the supporters of the Nineteenth Amendment believed that sex discrimination in voting was itself proscribed by the Fourteenth Amendment [and] the Twenty-fourth Amendment was not proposed to the States until this Court had held [that] state laws requiring payment of a poll tax as a prerequisite to voting did not ipso facto violate [equal protection]. Accordingly, we see no reason that the mere enactment of these amendments can be thought to imply that their proponents believed the Fourteenth Amendment did not apply to state allocations of political power. * * *

Nor do we find persuasive our Brother Harlan's argument that § 2 of the Fourteenth Amendment was intended as an exclusive remedy for state restrictions on the franchise * * *. [I]t is at least equally plausible that congressional legislation pursuant to §§ 1 and 5 was thought by the framers of the Amendment to be another potential remedy. Section 2, in such a scheme, is hardly superfluous: it was of critical importance in assuring that, should the Southern States deny the franchise to Negroes, the Congress called upon to remedy that discrimination would not be controlled by the beneficiaries of discrimination themselves. * * *

In sum, Congress had ample evidence upon which it could have based the conclusion [under § 5] that exclusion of citizens 18 to 21 years of age from the franchise is wholly unnecessary to promote any legitimate interest the States may have in assuring intelligent and responsible voting. * * *

MR. JUSTICE HARLAN, concurring in part and dissenting in part.

[Similar to his dissent in *Reynolds v. Sims*, [p. 990 supra], Harlan, J., argued at length "that the history of the Fourteenth Amendment makes it clear beyond any reasonable doubt" that § 1 was never intended to "reach discriminatory voting qualifications," again emphasizing § 2—providing for reduced congressional representation for states denying 21-year old male citizens the right to vote.[c] [That] constitutional amendments were deemed necessary to bring about federal abolition of state restrictions on voting by reason of race (Amend. XV), sex (Amend. XIX), and, even with respect to federal elections, the failure to pay state poll taxes (Amend. XXIV), is itself forceful evidence of the common understanding in 1869, 1919, and 1962, respectively, that the Fourteenth Amendment did not empower Congress to legislate in these respects.

c. "To be sure, one might argue that § 2 is simply a rhetorical flourish, and that the qualifications listed there are merely the ones which the Framers deemed to be consistent with the alleged prohibition of § 1. This argument is not only unreasonable on its face and untenable in light of the historical record; it is fatal to the validity of the reduction of the voting age [before] us.

"The only sensible explanation of § 2, therefore, is that the racial voter qualifications it was designed to penalize were understood to be permitted by § 1 * * *."

It must be recognized, of course, that [the] judiciary has long been entrusted with the task of applying the Constitution in changing circumstances, and as conditions change the Constitution in a sense changes as well. But when the [Court] disregards the express intent and understanding of the Framers, it has invaded the realm of the political process to which the amending power was committed * * *.

[Although] Congress' expression of the view that it does have power to alter state suffrage qualifications is entitled to the most respectful consideration by the judiciary, [this] cannot displace the duty of this Court to make an independent determination whether Congress has exceeded its powers. The reason for this goes beyond Marshall's assertion that "It is emphatically the province and duty of the judicial department to say what the law is." *Marbury*.[86] It inheres in the structure of the constitutional system itself. Congress is subject to none of the institutional restraints imposed on judicial decisionmaking; it is controlled only by the political process. In Article V, the Framers expressed the view that the political restraints on Congress alone were an insufficient control over the process of constitution-making. The concurrence of two-thirds of each House and of three-fourths of the States was needed for the political check to be adequate. [Nor] is that structure adequately protected by a requirement that the judiciary be able to perceive a basis for the congressional interpretation, the only restriction laid down in *Morgan*.

It is suggested that the proper basis for the doctrine enunciated in *Morgan* lies in the relative fact-finding competence of Court, Congress, and state legislatures. * * *

When my Brothers refer to "complex factual questions," they call to mind disputes about primary, objective facts dealing with such issues as the number of persons between the ages of 18 and 21, the extent of their education, and so forth. [But the] disagreement in these cases revolves around the evaluation [of] largely uncontested factual material. On the assumption that maturity and experience are relevant to intelligent and responsible exercise of the elective franchise, are the immaturity and inexperience of the average 18-, 19-, or 20-year-old sufficiently serious to justify denying such a person a direct voice in decisions affecting his or her life? Whether or not this judgment is characterized as "factual," it calls for striking a balance between incommensurate interests. Where the balance is to be struck depends ultimately on the values and the perspective of the decisionmaker. It is a matter as to which men of good will can and do reasonably differ.

I fully agree that judgments of the sort involved here are beyond the institutional competence and constitutional authority of the judiciary. [But judicial] deference is based, not on relative fact-finding competence, but on due regard for the decision of the body constitutionally appointed to decide. Establishment of voting qualifications is a matter for state legislatures. Assuming any authority at all, only when the Court can say with some confidence that the legislature has demonstrably erred in adjusting the competing interests is it justified in striking down the legislative judgment. * * *

The same considerations apply, and with almost equal force, to Congress' displacement of state decisions with its own ideas of wise policy. The sole distinction between Congress and the Court in this regard is that Congress, being

---

86. In fact, however, I do not understand how the doctrine of deference to rational constitutional interpretation by Congress, espoused by the majority in *Morgan*, is consistent with this statement of Chief Justice Marshall or with our reaffirmation of it in *Cooper v. Aaron* [p. 12 supra] * * *.

an elective body, presumptively has popular authority for the value judgment it makes. But since the state legislature has a like authority, this distinction between Congress and the judiciary falls short of justifying a congressional veto on the state judgment. The perspectives and values of national legislators on the issue of voting qualifications are likely to differ from those of state legislators, but I see no reason a priori to prefer those of the national figures, whose collective decision, applying nationwide, is necessarily less able to take account of peculiar local conditions. Whether one agrees with this judgment or not, it is the one expressed by the Framers in leaving voter qualifications to the States. The Supremacy Clause does not, as my colleagues seem to argue, represent a judgment that federal decisions are superior to those of the States whenever the two may differ.

To be sure, my colleagues do not expressly say that Congress or this Court is empowered by the Constitution to substitute its own judgment for those of the States. However, before sustaining a state judgment they require a "clear showing that the burden imposed is necessary to protect a compelling and substantial governmental interest." [88] I should think that [if] my colleagues or a majority of Congress deem a given voting qualification undesirable as a matter of policy, they must consider that the state interests involved are not "compelling" or "substantial" or that they can be adequately protected in other ways. It follows that my colleagues must be prepared to hold invalid as a matter of federal constitutional law all state voting qualifications which they deem unwise, as well as all such qualifications which Congress reasonably deems unwise. For this reason, I find their argument subject to the same objection as if it explicitly acknowledged such a conclusion.

It seems to me that the notion of deference to congressional interpretation of the Constitution, which the Court promulgated in *Morgan*, is directly related to this higher standard of constitutionality which the Court [brought] to fruition in *Kramer v. Union Free School Dist.*, p. 1013 supra. When the scope of federal review of state determinations became so broad as to be judicially unmanageable, it was natural for the Court to seek assistance from the national legislature. [In] this area, to rely on Congress would make that body a judge in its own cause. The role of final arbiter belongs to this Court.

[Beyond] the Fourteenth Amendment [i]t is difficult to see how [the words of Art. I, §§ 2 and 4] could be clearer in stating what Congress can control and what it cannot control. Surely nothing in these provisions lends itself to the view that voting qualifications in federal elections are to be set by Congress.

*   *   *

Even the power to control the "Manner" of holding elections, given with respect to congressional elections by Article I, § 4, is absent with respect to the selection of presidential electors.[89] [Any] shadow of a justification for congres-

---

88. It might well be asked why this standard is not equally applicable to the congressional expansion of the franchise before us. Lowering of voter qualifications dilutes the voting power of those who could meet the higher standard, and it has been held that "the right of suffrage can be denied by a debasement or dilution of the weight of a citizen's vote just as effectively as by wholly prohibiting the free exercise of the franchise." *Reynolds v. Sims.* *   *   *

89. Although Mr. Justice Black rests his decision in part on the assumption that the selection of presidential electors is a "federal" election, the Court held in *In re Green*, 134 U.S. 377, 379, 10 S.Ct. 586, 587, 33 L.Ed. 951 (1890), and repeated in *Ray v. Blair*, 343 U.S. 214, 224–225, 72 S.Ct. 654, 659–660, 96 L.Ed. 894 (1952), that the presidential electors act by authority of the States and are not federal officials.

sional power with respect to congressional elections therefore disappears utterly in presidential elections.

With these major contentions resolved, it is convenient to consider the three sections of the Act [to] determine whether they can be supported by any other basis of congressional power.

A. Voting Age. [For] the reasons already given, it cannot be said that the statutory provision is valid as declaratory of the meaning of [equal protection]. Its validity therefore must rest on congressional power to lower the voting age as a means of preventing invidious discrimination that is within the purview of that clause. [T]he suggestion that members of the age group between 18 and 21 are threatened with unconstitutional discrimination, or that any hypothetical discrimination is likely to be affected by lowering the voting age, is little short of fanciful. [A]ll the evidence indicates that Congress—led on by recent decisions of this Court—thought simply that 18-year-olds were fairly entitled to the vote and that Congress could give it to them by legislation. * * *

B. Residency. For reasons already stated, neither the power to regulate voting qualifications in presidential elections, asserted by my Brother Black, nor the power to declare the meaning of § 1 of the Fourteenth Amendment, relied on by my Brother Douglas, can support [§ 202]. With no specific clause of the Constitution empowering Congress to enact § 202, I fail to see how that nebulous judicial construct, the right to travel, can do so [as urged by the remaining justices].

C. Literacy. [Despite] the lack of evidence of specific instances of discriminatory application or effect, Congress could have determined that racial prejudice is prevalent throughout the Nation, and that literacy tests unduly lend themselves to discriminatory application, either conscious or unconscious. This danger of violation of § 1 of the Fifteenth Amendment was sufficient to authorize the exercise of congressional power under § 2. [While] a less sweeping approach in this delicate area might well have been appropriate, the choice which Congress made was within the range of the reasonable. * * *

MR. JUSTICE STEWART, with whom THE CHIEF JUSTICE and MR. JUSTICE BLACKMUN join, concurring in part and dissenting in part. * * *

[Literacy:] Because the justification for extending the ban on literacy tests to the entire Nation need not turn on whether literacy tests unfairly discriminate against Negroes in every State in the Union, Congress was not required to make state-by-state findings * * *. In the interests of uniformity, Congress may paint with a much broader brush than may this Court, which must confine itself to the judicial function of deciding individual cases and controversies upon individual records. * * * Experience gained under the 1965 Act has now led Congress to conclude that it should go the whole distance. This approach to the problem is a rational one; consequently it is within [the] power of Congress under § 2 of the Fifteenth Amendment.

[Residency:] Freedom to travel from State to State [is] a privilege of United States citizenship. [T]his Court has sustained the power of Congress to protect and facilitate the exercise of privileges of United States citizenship [under] the Necessary and Proper Clause. * * * Congress could rationally conclude that the imposition of durational residency requirements unreasonably burdens and sanctions the privilege of taking up residence in another State. * * *

But even though general constitutional power clearly exists, Congress may not overstep the letter or spirit of any constitutional restriction in the exercise of that power. For example, Congress clearly has power to regulate interstate commerce, but it may not, in the exercise of that power, impinge upon the guarantees of the Bill of Rights. * * *

The Constitution withholds from Congress any general authority to change by legislation the qualifications for voters in federal elections. * * * Article I, § 2, and the Seventeenth Amendment prescribe [as] the federal standard the standard which each State has chosen for itself. * * *

Contrary to the submission of my Brother Black, Article I, § 4 does not create in the federal legislature the power to alter the constitutionally established qualifications to vote in congressional elections. [The] "manner" of holding elections can hardly be read to mean the *qualifications* for voters, when it is remembered that § 2 of the same Article I explicitly speaks of the "qualifications" for voters in elections to choose Representatives. It is plain, in short, that when the Framers meant qualifications they said "qualifications." That word does not appear in Article I, § 4. Moreover, § 4 does not give Congress the power to do anything that a State might not have done [and] the States are not free to prescribe qualifications for voters in federal elections which differ from those prescribed for the most numerous branch of the state legislature. * * *

Different provisions of the Constitution govern the selection of the President and the Vice President. [T]he qualifications which voters must have when the selection of Electors is by popular election [is] left to the States in the exercise of their power to "direct" the manner of choosing Presidential Electors. When Electors are chosen by popular election, the Federal Government has the power to assure that such elections are orderly and free from corruption. *Burroughs v. United States.* But [*Burroughs*] quoted with approval the following passage from *Ex parte Yarbrough:* "[T]he importance to the general government of having the actual election—the voting for those members—free from force and fraud is not diminished by the circumstance that the qualification of the voter is determined by the law of the state where he votes." * * *

[I] am persuaded that the constitutional provisions discussed above are not sufficient to prevent Congress from protecting a person who exercises his constitutional right to enter and abide in any State in the Union from losing his opportunity to vote, when Congress may protect the right of interstate travel from other less fundamental disabilities. The power of the States with regard to the franchise is subject to the power of the Federal Government to vindicate the unconditional personal rights secured to the citizen by the Federal Constitution. The power which Congress has exercised in enacting § 202 is not a general power to prescribe qualifications for voters in either federal or state elections. It is confined to federal action against a particular problem clearly within the purview of congressional authority. Finally, [w]e should strive to avoid an interpretation of the Constitution that would withhold from Congress the power to legislate for the protection of those constitutional rights which the States are unable effectively to secure. * * *

[Age:] Mr. Justice Black is surely correct when he writes, "[T]he whole Constitution reserves to the States the power to set voter qualifications in state and local elections, except to the limited extent that the people through constitutional amendments have specifically narrowed the powers of the States." [I]t is equally plain to me that the Constitution just as completely withholds from Congress the power to alter by legislation qualifications for voters in federal elections, in view of the explicit provisions of Article I, Article II, and the Seventeenth Amendment.

To be sure, recent decisions have established that state action regulating suffrage is not immune from the impact of the Equal Protection Clause. But we have been careful in those decisions to note the undoubted power of a State to establish a qualification for voting based on age. See, e.g., *Kramer*. Indeed, none of the opinions filed today suggest that the States have anything but a constitutionally unimpeachable interest in establishing some age qualification as such. Yet to test the power to establish an age qualification by the "compelling interest" standard is really to deny a State any choice at all, because no State could demonstrate a "compelling interest" in drawing the line with respect to age at one point rather than another. * * * [14]

Morgan does not hold that Congress has the power to determine what are and what are not "compelling state interests" for equal protection purposes. [*Morgan*] upheld the statute on two grounds: that Congress could conclude that enhancing the political power of the Puerto Rican community by conferring the right to vote was an appropriate means of remedying discriminatory treatment in public services; and that Congress could conclude that the New York statute was tainted by the impermissible purpose of denying the right to vote to Puerto Ricans, an undoubted invidious discrimination under the Equal Protection Clause. Both of these decisional grounds were far-reaching. The Court's opinion made clear that Congress could impose on the States a remedy for the denial of equal protection which elaborated upon the direct command of the Constitution, and that it could override state laws on the ground that they were in fact used as instruments of invidious discrimination even though a court in an individual lawsuit might not have reached that factual conclusion. Cf. *Swain v. Alabama* [p. 837 supra].

But it is necessary to go much further to sustain § 302. The state laws which it invalidates do not invidiously discriminate against any discrete and insular minority. Unlike the statute considered in *Morgan*, § 302 is valid only if Congress has the power not only to provide the means of eradicating situations which amount to a violation of the Equal Protection Clause, but also to determine as a matter of substantive constitutional law what situations fall within the ambit of the clause, and what state interests are "compelling." * * *

Notes and Questions

1. *Mitchell's "interpretation" of Morgan.* (a) To what extent do the opinions in *Mitchell* clarify (or cloud) the scope of Congress' power delineated in *Morgan*? Do either Brennan or Harlan, JJ., do more in *Mitchell* than restate their *Morgan* analyses? Do Black and Stewart, JJ., accurately "read" *Morgan*? Consider Cox, *The Role of Congress in Constitutional Determinations,* 40 U.Cin.L. Rev. 199, 237 (1971): "Justice Stewart's summary of *Morgan* [is] historically inaccurate: the New York literacy statute antedates by decades the arrival of numerous Puerto Ricans. Second, [the] *Morgan* opinion barely hints that Congress was concerned to ascribe a racist purpose to the New York lawmakers. [Finally], even by Justice Stewart's own account, the *Morgan* case sustained a congressional finding of substantive unconstitutionality and thus belies his later assertion that Congress lacks power to make a substantive determination of constitutional law." Do you agree? If Congress believed that "prejudice played a prominent role in the enactment" of the state literacy law in *Morgan*, is it

---

14. [S]o long as a State does not set the voting age higher than 21, the reasonableness of its choice is confirmed by the very Four- teenth Amendment upon which the Government relies [see § 2].

important against which minority group the prejudice was directed? If this was the basis of Congress' "constitutional determination" in *Morgan,* is it the same kind of "substantive determination of constitutional law" by Congress that Brennan, J. sought to uphold in *Mitchell*?

(b) In any event, does Stewart, J.'s "reading" of *Morgan*—that Congress may "override state laws on the ground that they were in fact used as instruments of invidious discrimination"—mean that Congress may outlaw all "de facto" discriminations against "any discrete and insular minority"? Consider 85 Harv.L. Rev. 162–63 (1971): "Congress might be able to revamp a host of state benefit programs that impose particular disabilities on the poor on the rational basis that, in fact, a large fraction of the poor were blacks or members of ethnic minorities. [T]he literacy test analogy seems instructive: the class of citizens to whom the device was a serious obstacle was surely wider than merely blacks, yet Congress' conclusion that a large number of blacks were seriously disadvantaged [was] sufficient to uphold abolishing the practice under Congress' enforcement powers. [On] the other hand, Justice Stewart did not expressly indicate that congressional power to protect such minorities could be stretched this far, since at no point did he indicate what fraction of a group burdened by a given state classification must be blacks or other 'discrete and insular minorities' to justify section five intervention. If Justice Stewart, Justice Blackmun, and Chief Justice Burger are unwilling to review legislative findings carefully, however, it would appear that Congress, as long as it purported to aid blacks or ethnic minorities, could restructure a wide range of state programs it felt treated the poor unfairly. Congress could do this even though the Court itself might refuse to take similar steps on its own for want of the overwhelming proof usually demanded that the programs operate with the effect of invidious discrimination." Do you agree? Or does Stewart, J.'s "reading" of *Morgan* only comprehend congressional power over state laws it finds "tainted by [an] impermissible purpose"? See note 4 infra. See generally Choper, *Congressional Power to Expand Judicial Definitions of the Substantive Terms of the Civil War Amendments,* 67 Minn.L.Rev. 299, 328–34 (1982).

2. *Present status of Morgan.* Between *Morgan* and *Mitchell,* three members of the seven-justice majority in *Morgan* left the Court (Warren, C.J., and Clark and Fortas, JJ.); they were replaced by Burger, C.J., and Marshall and Blackmun, JJ. Since *Mitchell,* Black, Harlan, Douglas and Stewart, JJ., have been succeeded by Powell, Rehnquist, Stevens and O'Connor, JJ. Of what significance is the fact that Burger, C.J. (and Stewart, J.) joined the opinion of White, J., in *Welsh v. United States,* p. 1123 supra, which invoked *Morgan*? That Blackmun and Powell, JJ., joined the opinion of White, J., in *Trafficante v. Metropolitan Life Ins. Co.,* p. 1200 infra, which invoked both *Morgan and* the opinion of Brennan, J., in *Mitchell*?

In EEOC v. WYOMING, 460 U.S. 226, 103 S.Ct. 1054, 75 L.Ed.2d 18 (1983), BURGER, C.J., joined by Powell, Rehnquist and O'Connor, JJ., dissenting—after pointing out that the Court had rejected equal protection challenges to mandatory retirement schemes (p. 934 supra)—denied that Congress had power under § 5 to apply the Age Discrimination in Employment Act to state hiring: "Allowing Congress [to] define rights wholly independently of our case law * * * fundamentally alters our scheme of government. Although the *South Carolina v. Katzenbach* line of cases may be read to allow Congress a degree of flexibility in deciding what the Fourteenth Amendment safeguards, I have always read *Mitchell* as finally imposing a limitation on the extent to which Congress may substitute its own judgment for that of the states and assume this Court's 'role of final arbiter,' (Harlan, J., dissenting)." [d]

3. *Alternative rationale.* Consider Engdahl, *Constitutionality of the Voting Age Statute,* 39 Geo.Wash.L.Rev. 1, 38–39 (1970): "A *state* classification which denies to a significant 'stake-holder' the right to vote in a *national* election cannot be justified unless the citizen's exclusion from the national election sufficiently promotes some sufficient *state* interest. Since no *state,* as such, has a legitimate interest in protecting the integrity of *national* elections, it is difficult to imagine any state interest sufficient to justify, under the equal protection clause, any *state* exclusion of a significant 'stake-holder' in *national* elections. The significant stake which 18, 19 and 20-year-olds hold in federal elections, with their impact upon war and peace, is shown by their peculiar susceptibility to conscription for military service. Under section five of the fourteenth amendment, Congress may act to eliminate any state impediments which prevent these young citizens from participating in the *national* elections in which they have such a substantial stake. * * *

"In view of the fact that [federal elections] ordinarily occur at the same time and even on the same ballot as elections not only for state legislators, but also for other state and local officials as well, the coexistence of different age qualifications for voting for these various officials would produce a good deal of confusion. In its discretion, Congress may therefore determine that to make removal of an unconstitutional impediment to voting in federal elections fully effective, it is necessary to adjust the minimum age for voting in *all* elections— federal, state and local."

Even if § 5 does *not* empower Congress to lower the voting age in *federal* or *state* elections, if Art. I, § 4 *does* empower Congress to lower the voting age in *federal* elections, does the latter part of this analysis justify Congress' also lowering the voting age in *state* elections? [e]

4. *De facto discrimination.* (a) ROME v. UNITED STATES (1980), supra, involved the Attorney General's refusal to approve, under § 5 of the Voting Rights Act, various changes in the city's electoral system and a number of city annexations. A federal court found that the city had not employed any discriminatory barriers to black voting or black candidacy in the past 17 years and that the city had proved that the electoral changes and annexations were not discriminatorily motivated, but that they were prohibited by the Act because they had a discriminatory effect. The Court, per MARSHALL, J., affirmed: "[T]he Act's ban on electoral changes that are discriminatory in effect is an appropriate method of promoting the purposes of the Fifteenth Amendment, even if it is assumed that § 1 of the Amendment prohibits only intentional discrimination in voting. [See *Mobile v. Bolden,* p. 847 supra.] Congress could rationally have concluded that, because electoral changes by jurisdictions with a demonstrable history of intentional racial discrimination in voting create the risk of purposeful discrimination, it was proper to prohibit changes that have a discriminatory impact. See *South Carolina v. Katzenbach.*" [f]

---

d. For the view that "the scope of the definitional power" granted Congress in *Morgan,* "although by no means insignificant, may nonetheless be quite limited," see Choper, note 1(b) supra.

e. For an historical view that, pursuant to Art. I, §§ 2 and 4 and Art. IV, § 4 (the guaranty clause), Congress has "ultimate supervisory authority over voter qualifications in both state and national elections," see Greene, *Congressional Power Over the Elective Franchise: The Unconstitutional Phases of Oregon v. Mitchell,* 52 B.U.L.Rev. 505 (1972).

f. On congressional power to prohibit action that has only a discriminatory impact but which perpetuates the effects of past purposeful discrimination, see *Fullilove v. Klutznick,* p. 921 supra (opinion of Burger, C.J.).

REHNQUIST, J., joined by Stewart, J., dissented: "[Prior] decisions indicate that congressional prohibition of some conduct which may not itself violate the Constitution is 'appropriate' legislation 'to enforce' the Civil War Amendments if that prohibition is necessary to remedy prior constitutional violations by the governmental unit, or if necessary to effectively prevent purposeful discrimination by a governmental unit. [The] Court today identifies the constitutional wrong which was the object of this congressional exercise of power as purposeful discrimination by local governments in structuring their political processes in an effort to reduce black voting strength. [What] the Court explicitly ignores is that in this case the city has proven that these changes are not discriminatory in purpose. * * *

"Congress had before it evidence that various governments were enacting electoral changes and annexing territory to prevent the participation of blacks in local government by measures other than outright denial of the franchise. [G]iven the difficulties of proving that an electoral change or annexation has been undertaken for the purpose of discriminating against blacks, Congress could properly conclude that as a remedial matter it was necessary to place the burden of proving lack of discriminatory purpose on the localities. See *South Carolina v. Katzenbach.* But all of this does not support the conclusion that Congress is acting remedially when it continues the presumption of purposeful discrimination even after the locality has disproved that presumption. Absent other circumstances, it would be a topsy-turvy judicial system which held that electoral changes which have been affirmatively proven to be permissible under the Constitution nonetheless violate the Constitution. [Thus,] the result of the Court's holding is that Congress effectively has the power to determine for itself that this conduct violates the Constitution. This result violates previously well-established distinctions between the Judicial Branch and the Legislative or Executive Branches of the Federal Government." Powell, J., dissented on narrower grounds, see this Sec., supra.

(b) Do you agree that *Rome* empowers Congress "to determine for itself [what] conduct violates the Constitution"? Consider Choper, note 1(b) supra, at 331–32: "[*Rome's*] rationale permits Congress to create a 'conclusive presumption' of racial motivation with respect to specified state or local practices that Congress finds have been widely or consistently employed for the purpose of disadvantaging racial minorities—and thus effectively authorizes a congressional conclusion that such practices violate the substance of the fourteenth amendment. But this is a much narrower license than empowering Congress to declare that all state or local rules with a racially disproportionate impact violate equal protection for that reason alone. [A] variety of factors make it extremely difficult for plaintiffs to prove that a state legislative or administrative body has acted with discriminatory intent and make it much more appropriate for Congress than for the judiciary to combat the problem of illicit motivation. Thus, there are powerful reasons for Congress to choose not to rely upon district judges for the highly sensitive task of ascertaining racially discriminatory intent on a case by case basis in respect to state of local schemes whose real purpose Congress has grounds to suspect. [*Rome*] did no more than recognize this reality when is [used] what is principally a remedial or prophylactic rationale."

(c) At the time of *Mobile* and *Rogers v. Lodge,* pp. 1002, 1009 supra, § 2 of the Voting Rights Act simply provided that "no voting qualification or prerequisite to voting or standard, practice, or procedure shall be imposed or applied by any State or political subdivision *to deny or abridge* the right of any citizen of the United States to vote on account of race or color." [Emphasis added.] *Mobile* interpreted § 2 as "intended to have an effect no different from that of the Fifteenth Amendment itself." In 1982, Congress substituted the words "in a manner which results in a denial or abridgement of" for those words in § 2 italicized above. The Voting Rights Act Amendment of 1982 added: "The extent to which members of a protected class have been elected to office in the State or political subdivision is one circumstance which may be considered: Provided, That nothing in this section establishes a right to have members of a protected class elected in numbers equal to their proportion in the population."

JONES v. ALFRED H. MAYER CO.

392 U.S. 409, 88 S.Ct. 2186, 20 L.Ed.2d 1189 (1968).

MR. JUSTICE STEWART delivered the opinion of the Court.

In this case we are called upon to determine the scope and the constitutionality [of] 42 U.S.C. § 1982 [Sec. 1, I supra].

[P]etitioners filed a complaint [that] respondents had refused to sell them a home [for] the sole reason that petitioner [is] a Negro. Relying in part upon § 1982, the petitioners sought injunctive and other relief.[1] The [courts below] sustained the respondents' motion to dismiss [concluding] that § 1982 applies only to state action ∗ ∗ ∗.[5]

[I]t is important to make clear precisely what this case does *not* involve. Whatever else it may be, § 1982 is not a comprehensive open housing law. In sharp contrast to the Fair Housing Title (Title VIII) of the Civil Rights Act of 1968, the statute in this case deals only with racial discrimination and does not address itself to discrimination on grounds of religion or national origin. It does not deal specifically with discrimination in the provision of services or facilities in connection with the sale or rental of a dwelling. It does not prohibit advertising or other representations that indicate discriminatory preferences. It does not refer explicitly to discrimination in financing arrangements or in the provision of brokerage services.[10] It does not empower a federal administrative agency to assist aggrieved parties. It makes no provision for intervention by the Attorney General. And, although it can be enforced by injunction,[13] it contains no provision expressly authorizing a federal court to order the payment of damages.

Thus, although § 1982 contains none of the exemptions that Congress included in the Civil Rights Act of 1968, it would be a serious mistake to suppose that § 1982 in any way diminishes the significance of the law recently enacted by Congress. ∗ ∗ ∗

1. To vindicate their rights under § 1982, the petitioners invoked the jurisdiction of the District Court to award "damages [or] equitable or other relief under any Act of Congress providing for the protection of civil rights ∗ ∗ ∗." 28 U.S.C. § 1343(4). ∗ ∗ ∗

5. Because we have concluded that the discrimination alleged in the petitioners' complaint violated a federal statute that Congress had the power to enact under the Thirteenth Amendment, we find it unnecessary to decide whether that discrimination also violated [equal protection].

10. In noting that § 1982 differs from the Civil Rights Act of 1968 [we] intimate no view upon the question whether ancillary services or facilities of this sort might in some situations constitute "property" as that term is employed in § 1982. ∗ ∗ ∗

13. [T]hat § 1982 is couched in declaratory terms and provides no explicit method of enforcement does not, of course, prevent a federal court from fashioning an effective equitable remedy.

[See generally Smedley, *A Comparative Analysis of Title VIII and Section 1982*, 22 Vand.L.Rev. 459 (1969); Denno, *The New Fair Housing Law: 1866*, 18 Am.U.L.Rev. 491 (1969).]

[It] is true that a dictum in [*Hurd v. Hodge,* 334 U.S. 24, 68 S.Ct. 847, 92 L.Ed. 1187 (1948)] said that § 1982 was directed only toward "governmental action," but neither *Hurd* nor any other case before or since has presented that precise issue for adjudication in this Court.[25] * * *

On its [face] § 1982 appears to prohibit *all* discrimination against Negroes in the sale or rental of property—discrimination by private owners as well as discrimination by public authorities. * * * Stressing what they consider to be the revolutionary implications of so literal a reading of § 1982, the respondents argue that Congress cannot possibly have intended any such result. Our examination of the relevant history, however, persuades us that Congress meant exactly what it said.

In its original form, § 1982 was part [of] the Civil Rights Act of 1866. [The Court then extensively examined antecedent statutes and studies and debate in the Congress, contemporaneous with the proposal and ratification of the thirteenth amendment, in support of its conclusion respecting § 1982.]

Nor was the scope of the 1866 Act altered when it was re-enacted in 1870, some two years after the ratification of the Fourteenth Amendment. It is quite true that some members of Congress supported the Fourteenth Amendment "in order to eliminate doubt as to the constitutional validity of the Civil Rights Act as applied to the States." *Hurd.* But it certainly does not follow that the adoption of the Fourteenth Amendment or the subsequent readoption of the Civil Rights Act were meant somehow to *limit* its application to state action. The legislative history furnishes not the slightest factual basis for any such speculation, and the conditions prevailing in 1870 make it highly implausible. * * *

The remaining question is whether Congress has power under the Constitution to do what § 1982 purports to [do]. Our starting point is the Thirteenth Amendment, for it was pursuant to that constitutional provision that Congress originally enacted what is now § 1982. [It] has never been [doubted] "that the power vested in Congress to enforce the article by appropriate legislation," [*Civil Rights Cases,*] includes the power to enact laws "direct and primary, operating upon the acts of individuals, whether sanctioned by State legislation or not." Id.

[The] constitutional question in this case, therefore, comes to this: Does the authority of Congress to enforce the Thirteenth Amendment "by appropriate legislation" include the power to eliminate all racial barriers to the acquisition of real and personal property? We think the answer to that question is plainly yes.

"By its own unaided force and effect," the Thirteenth Amendment "abolished slavery, and established universal freedom." *Civil Rights Cases.* Whether or not the Amendment *itself* did any more than that—a question not involved in this case—it is at least clear that the Enabling Clause of that Amendment empowered Congress to do much more.[a] For that clause clothed "Congress with power to pass *all laws necessary and proper for abolishing all badges and incidents of slavery in the United States."* Ibid. (Emphasis added.)

Those who opposed passage of the Civil Rights Act of 1866 argued in effect that the Thirteenth Amendment merely authorized Congress to dissolve the

---

25. Two of this Court's early opinions contain dicta to the general effect that § 1982 is limited to state action. *Virginia v. Rives,* 100 U.S. 313, 317–318, 25 L.Ed. 667; *Civil Rights Cases.* * * *

a. For discussion of the use of judicial power under § 1 of the amendment, see fn. b, p. 1078 supra.

legal bond by which the Negro slave was held to his master. Yet [the] majority leaders in Congress—who were, after all, the authors of the Thirteenth Amendment—had no doubt that its Enabling Clause contemplated the sort of positive legislation that was embodied in the 1866 Civil Rights Act. Their chief spokesman, Senator Trumbull of Illinois, the Chairman of the Judiciary Committee, [argued] that, if the narrower construction of the Enabling Clause were correct, then "the trumpet of freedom that we have been blowing throughout the land has given an 'uncertain sound,' and the promised freedom is a delusion. [I] have no doubt that under this provision [we] may destroy all these discriminations in civil rights against [blacks]. Who is to decide what that appropriate legislation is to be? The Congress * * *."

Surely Senator Trumbull was right. Surely Congress has the power under the Thirteenth Amendment rationally to determine what are the badges and the incidents of slavery, and the authority to translate that determination into effective legislation. Nor can we say that the determination Congress has made is an irrational one. For this Court recognized long ago that, whatever else they may have encompassed, the badges and incidents of slavery—its "burdens and disabilities"—included restraints upon "those fundamental rights which are the essence of civil freedom, namely the same right [to] inherit, purchase, lease, sell and convey property, as is enjoyed by white citizens." *Civil Rights Cases*. Just as the Black Codes, enacted after the Civil War to restrict the free exercise of those rights, were substitutes for the slave system, so the exclusion of Negroes from white communities became a substitute for the Black Codes. And when racial discrimination herds men into ghettos and makes their ability to buy property turn on the color of their skin, then it too is a relic of slavery.

[At] the very least, the freedom that Congress is empowered to secure under the Thirteenth Amendment includes the freedom to buy whatever a white man can buy, the right to live wherever a white man can live. If Congress cannot say that being a free man means at least this much, then the Thirteenth Amendment made a promise the Nation cannot keep. * * *

Reversed.

MR. JUSTICE HARLAN, whom MR. JUSTICE WHITE joins, dissenting.

[I] believe that the Court's construction of § 1982 as applying to purely private action is almost surely wrong, and at the least is open to serious doubt. The issue of the constitutionality of § 1982, as construed by the Court, and of liability under the Fourteenth Amendment alone, also present formidable difficulties. Moreover, the political processes of our own era [have] given birth to a civil rights statute embodying "fair housing" provisions which would at the end of this year make available to others [the] type of relief which the petitioners now seek. It seems to me that this latter factor so diminishes the public importance of this case that by far the wisest course would be [to] dismiss the writ as improvidently granted.

[In a lengthy opinion, Harlan, J., relied on statements in prior Supreme Court opinions, the use of the word "right" in § 1982, the legislative history and debates of the Civil Rights Act of 1866 and of companion legislation, and on the ethics of the times to demonstrate that the Court's construction of § 1982 was "open to the most serious doubt" if not "wholly untenable."] [b]

---

b. The concurring opinion of Douglas, J., is omitted. For conflicting views as to § 1982's legislative history, compare Fairman, *Recon-* *struction and Reunion: 1864–1888, Part One* (1971) with Levinson, *Book Review*, 26 Stan.L. Rev. 461 (1974); Kohl, *The Civil Rights Act of*

SULLIVAN v. LITTLE HUNTING PARK, INC., 396 U.S. 229, 90 S.Ct. 400, 24 L.Ed.2d 386 (1969), involved a "nonstock corporation organized to operate a community park [for] the benefit of residents in an area" of Virginia. Sullivan, owner of a membership share, rented his home and assigned his share to Freeman. The corporation board "refused to approve the assignment because Freeman was a Negro." When Sullivan protested, he was expelled. Sullivan and Freeman sued in state court under § 1982 for injunctions and damages. Relief was denied. The Court, per DOUGLAS, J., reversed, stating that Little Hunting Park was not a "private social club," being "open to every white person within the geographic area." The "effective equitable remedy" that *Mayer* found could be fashioned by a federal court is "available in the state court, if that court is empowered to grant injunctive relief generally, as is the Virginia court." As to damages, the Court pointed to 28 U.S.C.A. § 1343(4), fn. 1 in *Mayer*: "The existence of a statutory right implies the existence of all necessary and appropriate remedies."

Harlan, J., joined by Burger, C.J., and White, J., "would dismiss the writ [as] improvidently granted," for reasons stated in *Mayer* and to avoid "the complexities involved in (1) giving Sullivan relief and (2) engrafting a damage remedy onto § 1982 in a case arising from a state court."

RUNYON v. McCRARY, 427 U.S. 160, 96 S.Ct. 2586, 49 L.Ed.2d 415 (1976), per STEWART, J., relying on *Mayer's* interpretation of § 1982, held that § 1981 Sec. 1, I supra, prohibits private schools—that were operated commercially and open to the public in that they engaged in general advertising to attract students—from refusing to accept blacks. POWELL, J., joined the opinion, but added that "choices, including those involved in entering into a contract, that are 'private' in the sense that they are not part of a commercial relationship offered generally or widely, and that reflect the selectivity exercised by an individual entering into a personal relationship, certainly were never intended to be restricted by" § 1981. Stevens, J., joined the Court's opinion, feeling bound by, but disagreeing with, the statutory interpretation in *Mayer*. White, J., joined by Rehnquist, J., dissented on grounds of statutory interpretation.

Notes and Questions

1. *Scope of §§ 1982 and 1981.* (a) What other discriminations against blacks are presently prohibited by these provisions? Consider Henkin, *On Drawing Lines,* 82 Harv.L.Rev. 63, 85–86 (1968): "Will no bequest stand up which includes a racial discrimination since that would deprive Negroes of 'the same right [to] inherit'? Has there been an easier answer to [Senator Bacon's] will all this time while the Court struggled with theories of state action to find escape from his discrimination [see *Evans v. Newton* and *Evans v. Abney,* pp. 1082, 1100 supra.]? Indeed, does not the Court's reading render superfluous the Civil Rights Act of 1964? Title II of that Act provides that certain places of public accommodations may not discriminate on the basis of race in selling goods and services; the Court's construction of § 1982, when applied to personal property, renders the title (and its limitations) superfluous. Moreover, by the Court's technique of construction, the right 'to make and enforce contracts' guaranteed by [§ 1981] should prevent a restaurant or hotel management from refusing on grounds of race to 'make a contract' for service with a Negro.

1866, Its Hour Come Round at Last, 55 Va.L. Rev. 272 (1969) with Casper, *Jones v. Mayer:*   *Clio, Bemused and Confused Muse,* 1968 Sup. Ct.Rev. 89.

Indeed, that construction should prevent any employer from refusing 'to make a contract' of employment with a Negro; and the fair employment provisions of the 1964 Act likewise become superfluous, as does the entire struggle, since the days of the New Deal, to enact adequate fair employment legislation."

See also Larson, *The New Law of Race Relations,* 1969 Wis.L.Rev. 470, 502–03: "[Sec. 1981] could properly be applied to any [private] club or association when it can be said that the essence of the arrangement is that the club or association supplies certain services or facilities in exchange for the payment of dues. * * * Tested by the standards suggested, a country club falls within the category of organizations supplying valuable services, such as the availability of a golf course, dining rooms, and club rooms, for the payment of a sum of money." c

(b) *Constitutionality.* Are the above racial discriminations "badges and incidents of slavery"? What of the practice by sellers of certain goods or services of charging blacks higher prices? See Note, *Discriminatory Housing Markets, Racial Unconscionability, and Section 1988,* 80 Yale L.J. 516 (1971). Is the initial question inaccurately stated? Do these instances "run the slavery argument into the ground" (*Civil Rights Cases*)?

Does the thirteenth amendment empower Congress to prohibit action that has a racially disproportionate impact, regardless of its purpose? Do §§ 1981–82 do so? See Note, *Section 1981: Discriminatory Purpose or Disproportionate Impact?* 80 Colum.L.Rev. 137 (1980); *Memphis v. Greene,* p. 848 supra.

2. *Scope of § 1985.* GRIFFIN v. BRECKENRIDGE, 403 U.S. 88, 91 S.Ct. 1790, 29 L.Ed.2d 338 (1971), was a damage action under § 1985. Allegedly, respondents had wilfully conspired to assault and terrorize petitioners—who "were travelling upon the federal, state and local highways"—in order to prevent petitioners "and other Negro-Americans [from] seeking the equal protection of the laws and from enjoying the equal rights, privileges and immunities of citizens under the laws"—including rights to free speech, association, petition for redress of grievances, "their rights not to be enslaved nor deprived of life, liberty or property other than by due process of law, and their rights to travel the public highways without restraint in the same terms as white citizens." The Court, per STEWART, J., held "that all indicators—text, companion provisions, and legislative history—point unwaveringly to § 1985's coverage of private conspiracies." And the "constitutional shoals that would lie in the path of interpreting § 1985 as a general federal tort law can be avoided" because the "language requiring intent to deprive of *equal* protection, or *equal* privileges and immunities, means that there must be some racial, or perhaps otherwise class-based, invidiously discriminatory animus behind the conspirators' action.[9]"

The Court then found *at least* two sources of "congressional power to reach the private conspiracy alleged." First, under § 2 of the thirteenth amendment, "the varieties of private conduct which [Congress] may make criminally punishable or civilly remediable extend far beyond the actual imposition of slavery [*Mayer*]." Thus, Congress was "wholly within its powers [in] creating a statutory cause of action for Negro citizens who have been the victims of conspiratorial, racially discriminatory private action aimed at depriving them of the basic

---

c. Does § 1981 make the result in *Moose Lodge v. Irvis,* p. 1112 supra, incorrect? Or do other constitutional provisions (values) justify the decision?

9. We need not decide, given the facts of this case, whether conspiracy motivated by invidiously discriminatory intent other than racial bias would be actionable under the portion of § 1985 before us. [See *Carpenters, Local 610 v. Scott,* infra, holding that § 1985 does not "reach conspiracies motivated by economic or commercial animus."]

rights that the law secures to all free men." Second, "the right of interstate travel is constitutionally protected [against] private as well as governmental interference." Since "it is open to the petitioners to prove at trial that they had been engaging in interstate travel or intended to do so, that [the] conspirators intended to drive out-of-state civil rights workers from the State, or that they meant to deter the petitioners from associating with such persons," this "could make it clear that the petitioners had suffered from conduct which Congress may reach under its power to protect the right of interstate travel." [d]

3. *Beyond racial discrimination.* (a) CARPENTERS, LOCAL 610 v. SCOTT, 463 U.S. 825, 103 S.Ct. 3352, 77 L.Ed.2d 1049 (1983), per White, J., held "that an alleged conspiracy to infringe First Amendment rights is not a violation of § 1985 unless it is proved that the state is involved in the conspiracy or that the aim of the conspiracy is to influence the activity of the state": "*Griffin* did not hold that even when the alleged conspiracy is aimed at a right [such as in the first amendment] that is by definition a right only against state interference the plaintiff in a § 1985 suit nevertheless need not prove that the conspiracy contemplated state involvement of some sort. The complaint in *Griffin* alleged, among other things, a deprivation of First Amendment rights but we did not sustain the action on the basis of that allegation and paid it scant attention. Instead, we upheld the application of § 1985 to private conspiracies aimed at interfering with rights [such as the freedom from slavery and the right to travel] constitutionally protected against private, as well as official, encroachment." Blackmun, J., joined by Brennan, Marshall and O'Connor, JJ., dissented. Does § 1985 provide a cause of action to whites who suffer injury because of their espousal of the rights of blacks?

(b) To what extent does *Jones* empower Congress to define the terms of the Civil War amendments? For example, pursuant to § 2 of the thirteenth amendment, may Congress "rationally determine" that discriminations against groups other than blacks are "badges and incidents of slavery"? See *McDonald v. Santa Fe Trail Trans. Co.* (1976), fn. c. in *United Steelworkers v. Weber*, p. 1247 supra ("Congress is authorized under [§ 2] to legislate in regard to 'every race and individual' "). Consider Note, *Jones v. Mayer: The Thirteenth Amendment and the Federal Anti-Discrimination Laws*, 69 Colum.L.Rev. 1019, 1025–26 (1969): "[T]he Court's conclusion that housing discrimination *today* is a badge or incident of slavery is itself a recognition that the 'slavery' referred to in the thirteenth amendment now encompasses the second class citizenship imposed on members of disparate minority groups. By doing so, the Court has implicitly interpreted 'slavery' as the word has come to mean. [A] victim's people need not have been enslaved in order to invoke its protection. He need only be suffering today under conditions that could reasonably be called symptoms of a slave society, inability to raise a family with dignity caused by unemployment, poor schools and housing, and lack of a place in the body politic. By removing the time element from badges and incidents of slavery, an aggrieved party need not show a continuous link between his plight and actual slavery in order to benefit from the guarantees of the thirteenth amendment." [e] Compare Note, *The "New" Thirteenth Amendment: A Preliminary Analysis*, 82 Harv.L.Rev. 1294

---

d. Harlan, J., joined the Court's opinion but found it unnecessary to rely on the "right of interstate travel."

e. For the view that *McDonald* strongly supports this approach, see Calhoun, *The Thirteenth and Fourteenth Amendments: Con-*

stitutional Authority for Federal Legislation Against Private Sex Discrimination, 61 Minn. L.Rev. 313 (1977). For criticism of *McDonald*, see Note, *The Thirteenth Amendment and Private Affirmative Action*, 89 Yale L.J. 399 (1979).

(1969). Consider Choper, note 1(b) after *Morgan* at 313–14: "*Jones* need not be interpreted as conferring any *definitional* authority on Congress. Rather, it can be persuasively argued on either of two theories that the Court upheld the Civil Rights Act of 1866 as only a *remedial* exercise of Congress's enforcement power under the thirteenth amendment. First, 'slavery' may be regarded as a status to be defined by the Court, [and] the 'badges and incidents of slavery' may be regarded, not as elements of that definition, but as stigmas and disabilities related to slavery. [Thus] to say that Congress may rationally determine the badges and incidents of slavery is nothing more than to say that Congress may prohibit certain practices, although those practices themselves do not constitute slavery, when Congress rationally finds that their prohibition will help to *prevent* slavery.[83] Alternatively, since Congress's power under *Morgan*'s remedial branch encompasses eradicating the *effects* of constitutional violations as well as preventing future ones, the congressional prohibition in *Jones* may be readily sustained as an effort to eliminate the persistent legacies of the past condition of slavery."

4. *Self-executing force of thirteenth amendment.* Apart from federal legislation pursuant to § 2, are any (all) of the discriminations referred to above made unconstitutional by § 1 of "the Amendment *itself*"? If so, by what means should (can) the Court enforce § 1?

---

83. Engdahl, *Constitutional Power: Federal and State in a Nutshell* 247–48 (1974) (emphasis added).

Chapter 9

LIMITATIONS ON JUDICIAL POWER AND REVIEW

SECTION 1. CASE OR CONTROVERSY

I. ADVISORY OPINIONS

MUSKRAT v. UNITED STATES, 219 U.S. 346, 31 S.Ct. 250, 55 L.Ed. 246 (1911): In 1902, Congress made a "final" allotment of lands to certain Cherokee Indians. Subsequent legislation increased the number of allottees. Congress then enacted a statute authorizing four named allottees under the 1902 act to bring suits against the United States in the court of claims with appeal to the Supreme Court, "on their own behalf and on behalf of all other Cherokee citizens" who were allottees under the 1902 act, "to determine the validity of any acts of Congress passed since the said act." For "the speedy disposition of the questions involved" such suits were to be given preference by the courts, and attorneys' fees were to be paid out of tribal funds held by the government if the subsequent legislation were held invalid. Suits were instituted and the court of claims sustained the validity of the subsequent legislation.

The Court, per DAY, J., held that "the jurisdiction conferred" was not "within the power of Congress, having in view the limitations of the judicial power, as established by the Constitution" because "the judicial power is limited to 'cases' and 'controversies.'" Art. III "does not extend the judicial power to every violation of the Constitution which may possibly take place." "By cases and controversies are intended the claims of litigants brought before the courts for determination by such regular proceedings as are established by law or custom for the protection or enforcement of rights, or the prevention, redress, or punishment of wrongs. [The] term implies the existence of present or possible adverse parties, whose contentions are submitted to the court for adjudication."

The Court pointed out that "as early as 1792, an act of Congress" authorized federal courts to decide certain pension claims against the government, subject to revision by the Secretary of War. *Hayburn's Case*, 2 Dall. 409, held that such duties were beyond the judicial power; "by the Constitution, neither the Secretary at War, nor any other executive officer, nor even the legislature, are authorized to sit as a court of errors on the judicial acts or opinions of this court." [a] In 1793, the Court, in response to a request by President Washington

---

a. Consider Currie, *Federal Courts* 9 (3d ed. 1982): "[Such cases are] most easily under- stood in terms of the independence of the courts. The Constitution protects the judges

1187

and Secretary of State Jefferson, declined to offer its advice on "the construction of treaties, laws of nations and laws of the land, which the Secretary said were often presented under circumstances which *'do not give a cognizance of them to the tribunals of the country.'*"

The act in *Muskrat* was found to be nothing more "than an attempt to provide for a judicial determination, final in this court, of the constitutional validity of an act of Congress. [It] is true the United States is made a defendant to this action, but it has no interest adverse to the claimants. The object is not to assert a property right as against the government, or to demand compensation for alleged wrongs because of action upon its part. [The] judgment will not conclude private parties, when actual litigation brings to the court the question of the constitutionality of such legislation. In a legal sense the judgment [amounts] to no more than an expression of opinion upon the validity of the" 1902 act. "If such actions as are here attempted [are] sustained, the result will be that this court, instead of keeping within the limits of judicial power, and deciding cases or controversies arising between opposing parties, [will] be required to give opinions in the nature of advice concerning legislative action,—a function never conferred upon it by the Constitution."

Notes and Questions

1. *Pro's and con's of advisory opinions.* (a) Do you agree with the established principle that bars the Court from advising Congress on the constitutionality of legislation? Consider Note, *Advisory Opinions on the Constitutionality of Statutes,* 69 Harv.L.Rev. 1302, 1305 (1956): "Before it is successfully challenged, an unconstitutional statute may discourage legitimate activity; or, conversely, it may encourage reliance which, when the statute is invalidated, will [cause] injury to those who have based action upon it. Further [there] is frequently an unnecessary expenditure of time and money when the state enacts a statute, invalidates it in lengthy judicial proceedings, and subsequently must enact new legislation; this waste would seem particularly great when the government sets up elaborate machinery to implement a statute later held unconstitutional." See also Note, *The Case for an Advisory Function in the Federal Judiciary,* 50 Geo.L.J. 785, 799 (1962).

(b) Consider Comment, *The Advisory Opinion and the United States Supreme Court,* 5 Ford.L.Rev. 94, 108 (1936): "The advisory opinion, it is said [by Frankfurter, *A Note on Advisory Opinions,* 37 Harv.L.Rev. 1002 (1924)], would distort the entire focus of the judicial function in that it would require the Court to express its judgment on abortive issues without the benefit of all the relevant facts which, in crucial constitutional questions, are the very heart of the case. In addition, the operation of the device would debilitate the creative responsibility of the legislature in that it would tend to induce reliance upon the judiciary, depriving the former of submitting its convictions to the test of trial and error

from indirect pressures on their decisions by guaranteeing them tenure during good behavior at an irreducible salary; to subject their decisions to executive review is a much more direct interference." But, "how far should this principle be carried? Congress, after all, can defeat any money judgment against the United States by failing to vote money to pay it; should the courts therefore refuse to entertain money actions against the Government? Since the President can refuse to enforce judgments against state officers or private litigants, should the courts decline to act at all?" Id. Should the Court refuse to interpret acts of Congress because the Court's decision may be negated by congressional revision? Decline to enforce the terms of executive regulations against executive officers because they may choose to amend or revoke the regulations?

and of accumulating new facts for the vindication of its judgment which, a priori, may run counter to settled legal principles."

(i) As to the "facts" argument, might this be cured by having Congress present the Court with a specific set of facts, real or assumed? Or by having the Court confine its opinion to the statute's application to what it considers the most common set of facts intended to be covered?

(ii) As to the "responsibility of the legislature" argument, might this be cured by limiting the advisory opinion to statutes fully considered and already passed by Congress? [d] Is there *any* answer to the point that the cumulative experience of a statute's operation may shed great light on its constitutionality? If not, is this sufficient to sustain the present advisory opinion practice?

(c) Is the opposition to advisory opinions justified by the necessity for "actual antagonistic assertion of rights by one individual against another"? Consider Note, 69 Harv.L.Rev. 1302, 1309–10 (1956): "Argument in advisory proceedings might in some situations provide more assistance to the court than would argument in a normal adversary proceeding. Representation of diversified interests might provide the justices with a more realistic perspective on the statute than representation of only two parties; and, unlike ordinary litigation where the prosecutor or plaintiff [may] be able to select an opponent with little interest in the proceeding or one who is peculiarly culpable, the parties seeking to appear will generally be strong antagonists."

(d) Consider Note, *Judicial Determinations in Nonadversary Proceedings,* 72 Harv.L.Rev. 723, 724 (1959): "The requirement that a specific injury have been suffered or that the danger of such injury be substantial [probably] has its basis, at least partially, in the belief that the respect in which the courts are held varies with the restraint exercised in deciding only the most critical questions." Is this "belief" founded on the premise that the Court's ability to preserve constitutional values is limited and should be reserved for situations in which it is absolutely necessary? If so, may occasions for some advisory opinions present such a necessity? Or should the enactments of popularly elected representatives be invalidated by a Court of lifetime appointees only when injury is imminent? Even when the popularly elected representatives request the Court's advice? Even when they believe that the withholding of such advice may produce very grave injuries?

2. *Mootness.* (a) Is the principle that "moot cases [are] beyond the judicial power" simply an application of the bar against advisory opinions? That "there is no case or controversy once the matter has been resolved"? Wright, *Federal Courts* 55 (4th ed. 1983). Or is the doctrine merely a judicially created rule for judicial economy? Of what significance is the point in litigation at which a case becomes moot? Consider Note, *Cases Moot on Appeal: A Limit on the Judicial Power,* 103 U.Pa.L.Rev. 772, 774 (1955): "[M]oot cases do not present all the dangers of advisory opinions. The 'impact of actuality' may well be lacking if [the] decrees cannot affect the rights of the parties. But there is a record to which the court may look for facts; there is probably as much experience under the statute as might be had in a case which is not moot; and there are advocates before the court who are prepared to argue the issues."

d. The Voting Rights Act Amendments of 1970, some of which were not to take effect until elections held in 1971, became law on June 22, 1970. Motions for leave to file suits within the Court's original jurisdiction, involv- ing four states challenging the act's constitutionality, were granted on Oct. 6, 1970. The cases were argued on Oct. 19 and decided on Dec. 21, 1970. See *Oregon v. Mitchell,* p. 1166 supra.

(b) In DE FUNIS v. ODEGAARD, p. 889 supra, petitioner was admitted to the University of Washington Law School after a state trial court had sustained his claim that the school's special admissions policy violated equal protection. The Washington supreme court reversed but its judgment was stayed. By the time the case was argued in the Supreme Court, petitioner had registered for the final term of his third year. Although the school stated that if its admissions policy were upheld, petitioner would be subject to it if he had to register for any additional terms, his present registration "would not be cancelled [regardless] of the outcome of this litigation." The Court, per curiam, held the case moot: "There is a line of decisions in this Court standing for the proposition that the 'voluntary cessation of allegedly illegal conduct does not deprive the tribunal of power to hear and determine the case, i.e., does not make the case moot,'" because "otherwise, 'the defendant is free to return to his old ways' * * *. But mootness in the present case depends not at all upon a 'voluntary cessation' of the admissions practices that were the subject of this litigation. It depends, instead, upon the simple fact that DeFunis is now in the final quarter of the final year of his course of study, and the settled and unchallenged policy of the Law School to permit him to complete the term for which he is now enrolled."

BRENNAN, J., joined by Douglas, White and Marshall, JJ., dissented: "Any number of unexpected events—illness, economic necessity, even academic failure—might prevent his graduation at the end of the term. Were that misfortune to befall, and were petitioner required to register for yet another term, the prospect that he would again face the hurdle of the admissions policy is real * * *.[e] Few constitutional questions in recent history have stirred as much debate, and they will not disappear. [Because] avoidance of repetitious litigation serves the public interest, that inevitability counsels against mootness determinations, as here, not compelled by the record."[f]

3. *Collusiveness.* The Court "will not hear collusive cases.[15] Though the rule is not in terms so confined, it is principally applied in constitutional cases, on the notion that 'it never was the thought that by means of a friendly suit, a party beaten in the legislature could transfer to the courts an inquiry as to the constitutionality of the legislative act.'[16] Even here application of the rule has not always been rigid—some of the most famous constitutional decisions have come in what now seem to have been collusive cases.[17]" Wright, supra, at 56.

II. STANDING AND RIPENESS

INTRODUCTORY NOTE

The doctrines of "standing" and "ripeness" both go to determining whether there is a dispute capable of and suitable for judicial resolution. These two

---

e. In response to this point, the Court said: "But such speculative contingencies afford no basis for our passing on the substantive issues" in the absence of "evidence that this is a prospect of 'immediacy and reality.'"

f. "In rare instances the power to refrain from deciding moot cases has been used by the Court to avoid decision of an otherwise difficult matter. In [*Atherton Mills v. Johnston*, 259 U.S. 13, 42 S.Ct. 422, 66 L.Ed. 814 (1922), a law was challenged] regulating the labor of youths between the ages of 14 and 16. The Court held the case for two and a half years after argument, and then decided that since

the plaintiff was by that time over 16, and no longer affected by the statute, the case was moot." Wright, *Federal Courts* 36 (2d ed. 1970).

15. *Lord v. Veazie*, 1850, 8 How. 251, 12 L.Ed. 1067.

16. *Chicago & G.T. Ry. Co. v. Wellman.* See also *U.S. v. Johnson*, 1943, 63 S.Ct. 1075, 319 U.S. 302, 87 L.Ed. 1413.

17. E.g., *Fletcher v. Peck*, [p. 60 supra]; *Dred Scott v. Sandford*, [discussed in *Plessy v. Ferguson*, p. 821 supra.

issues frequently overlap, but may roughly be described as concerning (1) *who* may assert certain contentions (the claimant or someone else)—"standing," and (2) *when* (if ever) may these claims be asserted (now or at some subsequent time after other events have occurred)—"ripeness."

Both doctrines relate to whether there is a "case or controversy" under Art. III. But they also implicate "prudential" principles of "judicial self-restraint," some perspective on which may be found in the following statement of the Court, per RUTLEDGE, J., in RESCUE ARMY v. MUNICIPAL COURT, 331 U.S. 549, 67 S.Ct. 1409, 91 L.Ed. 1666 (1947):

"[T]his Court has followed a policy of strict necessity in disposing of constitutional issues [which] has not been limited to jurisdictional determinations. For, in addition, 'the Court [has] developed, for its own governance in the cases confessedly within its jurisdiction, a series of rules under which it has avoided passing upon a large part of all the constitutional questions pressed upon it for decision.'[31] [Thus], constitutional issues affecting legislation will not be determined in friendly, non-adversary proceedings; in advance of the necessity of deciding them; in broader terms than are required by the precise facts to which the ruling is to be applied; if the record presents some other ground upon which the case may be disposed of; at the instance of one who fails to show that he is injured by the statute's operation, or who has availed himself of its benefits * * *.[a]

"[E]very application has been an instance of reluctance, indeed of refusal, to undertake the most important and the most delicate of the Court's [functions].

"Indeed in origin and in practical effects, though not in technical function, it is a corollary offshoot of the case and controversy rule. And often the line between applying the policy or the rule is very thin.[37] * * *

"The policy's ultimate foundations, some if not all of which also sustain the jurisdictional limitation, [are] found in the delicacy of that function, particularly in view of possible consequences for others stemming also from constitutional roots; the comparative finality of those consequences; the consideration due to the judgment of other repositories of constitutional power concerning the scope of their authority; the necessity, if government is to function constitutionally, for each to keep within its power, including the courts; the inherent limitations of the judicial process, arising especially from its largely negative character and limited resources of enforcement; withal in the paramount importance of constitutional adjudication in our system.

"[Its] execution has involved a continuous choice between the obvious advantages it produces [and] the very real disadvantages, for the assurance of rights, which deferring decision very often entails.[b] On the other hand it is not

---

31. Brandeis, J., with whom Stone, Roberts and Cardozo, JJ., concurred in *Ashwander v. TVA*, 297 U.S. 288, concurring opinion at 346, 56 S.Ct. 466, 482, 80 L.Ed. 688.

a. One of the rules set forth by Brandeis, J., in *Ashwander* was that "when the validity of an act of the Congress is drawn in question, and even if a serious doubt of constitutionality is raised, it is a cardinal principle that this Court will first ascertain whether a construction of the statute is fairly possible by which the question may be avoided." For illustrations of this technique, see *Yates v. United States*, p. 330 supra; *Jones v. Alfred H. Mayer Co.*, p. 1180 supra. But compare *Marbury v.*

Madison, p. 1 supra; *United States v. Robel*, p. 636 supra.

37. Indeed more than once the policy has been applied in order to avoid the necessity of deciding the "case or controversy" jurisdictional question, when constitutional issues were at stake on the merits * * *.

b. "Whether 'justiciability' exists, therefore, has most often turned on evaluating both the appropriateness of the issues for decision by courts and the hardship of denying judicial relief." Frankfurter, J., concurring in *Joint Anti-Fascist Refugee Comm. v. McGrath*, 341 U.S. 123, 71 S.Ct. 624, 95 L.Ed. 817 (1951).

altogether speculative that a contrary policy of accelerated decision, might do equal or greater harm for the security of private rights * * *. For premature and relatively abstract decision, which such a policy would be most likely to promote, have their part too in rendering rights uncertain and insecure.

"* * * Time and experience [have] verified for both that the choice was wisely made. Any other indeed might have put an end to or seriously impaired the distinctively American institution of judicial review.[38]"

A. INJURY REQUIRED FOR STANDING: SUITS BY TAXPAYERS AND CITIZENS

MASSACHUSETTS v. MELLON and FROTHINGHAM v. MELLON, 262 U.S. 447, 43 S.Ct. 597, 67 L.Ed. 1078 (1923), involved a challenge to a federal statute providing funds to states undertaking programs to reduce maternal and infant mortality. The Court, per SUTHERLAND, J., dismissed both cases "for want of jurisdiction."

Massachusetts contended that the act invaded "the power of local self-government, reserved to the states" by the tenth amendment; that a state had an "unconstitutional option either to yield to the federal government a part of their reserved rights or lose their share of the moneys." The Court reasoned that the "powers of the state are not invaded, since the statute imposes no obligation but simply extends an option which the state is free to accept or reject. But we do not rest here." The Court's power under Art. III extends only to proceedings "of a justiciable character * * *. In the last analysis, the complaint of the plaintiff state is brought to the naked contention that Congress has usurped the reserved powers of the several states by the mere enactment of the statute, though nothing has been done and nothing is to be done without their consent; and it is plain that that question, as it is thus presented, is political, and not judicial in character, and therefore is not a matter which admits of the exercise of the judicial power. [W]e are called upon to adjudicate, not rights of person or property, not rights of dominion over physical domain, not quasi sovereign rights actually invaded or threatened, but abstract questions of political power, of sovereignty, of government."

Because "citizens of Massachusetts are also citizens of the United States," neither could the state sue as parens patriae "as the representative of its citizens" "to protect citizens of the United States from the operation of the statutes thereof. [I]t is the United States, and not the state which represents them as parens patriae [and] to the former, and not to the latter, they must look for such protective measures as flow from that status."

Frothingham, a federal taxpayer, also contended that the Maternity Act exceeded Congress' power and "that the effect of the appropriations complained of will be to increase the burden of future taxation and thereby take her property without due process of law." The Court distinguished suits by municipal taxpayers: "The interest of a taxpayer of a municipality in the application of its moneys is direct and immediate and the remedy by injunction to prevent their misuse is not inappropriate." But a federal taxpayer's "interest in the moneys of the treasury [is] shared with millions of others, is comparatively minute and indeterminable, and the effect upon future taxation, of any payment

---

38. It is not without significance for the policy's validity that the periods when the power has been exercised most readily and broadly have been the ones in which this Court and the institution of judicial review have had their stormiest experiences. See e.g., Brant, *Storm Over the Constitution* (1936).

out of the funds, so remote, fluctuating and uncertain, that no basis is afforded for an appeal to the preventive powers of a court of equity." To permit such suits might result in attacks on "every other appropriation act and statute whose administration requires the outlay of public money * * *. The bare suggestion of such a result, with its attendant inconveniences, goes far to sustain the conclusion which we have reached, that a suit of this character cannot be maintained." A person asking the Court to hold a federal act unconstitutional "must be able to show, not only that the statute is invalid, but that he has sustained or is immediately in danger of sustaining some direct injury as the result of its enforcement, and not merely that he suffers in some indefinite way in common with people generally." Here, the complaint "is merely that [federal officials] will execute an act of Congress asserted to be unconstitutional; and this we are asked to prevent. To do so would be, not to decide a judicial controversy, but to assume a position of authority over the governmental acts of another and coequal department, an authority which plainly we do not possess."

In DOREMUS v. BOARD OF EDUC., 342 U.S. 429, 72 S.Ct. 394, 96 L.Ed. 475 (1952), a state court had held that Bible-reading in public schools was not an establishment of religion. Appellants had sued as "citizens" and "taxpayers"; one had a child in the schools who had graduated by the time the case came to the Supreme Court. The Court, per JACKSON, J., dismissed the appeal: As to the graduated student, the matter was held to be moot. Although municipal taxpayers have standing to enjoin "a measurable appropriation or disbursement of [municipal] funds occasioned solely by the activities complained of," there "is no allegation that this activity is supported by any separate tax or paid for from any particular appropriation or that it adds any sum whatever to the cost of conducting the school." Although state courts may render advisory opinions on federal constitutional questions, "because our own jurisdiction is cast in terms of 'case or controversy,' we cannot * * *. The taxpayer's action can meet this test, but only when it is a good-faith pocketbook action." [c]

DOUGLAS, J., joined by Reed and Burton, JJ. dissented: "There is no group more interested in [the] public schools than the taxpayers who support them and the parents whose children attend them. [W]here the clash of interests is as real and as strong as it is here, it is odd indeed to hold there is no case or controversy within the meaning of art. III."

c. Consider Freund in *Supreme Court & Supreme Law* 35 (Cahn ed. 1954): "I think it is a needed change to make standing to raise a federal constitutional question, itself a federal question, so that it will be decided uniformly throughout the country. I disagree with *Doremus* in so far as it lets the state judgment stand and merely declines review. [T]he Court should have [held that] the petition should stand dismissed in the state court and the decree vacated so that it would not be a precedent even in the state court." Does *Doremus* "let the state judgment stand and merely decline review"? What action would

the Court have taken if the New Jersey court had found the statute violative of the first amendment? See Tribe, *American Constitutional Law* 15 n. 56 (Supp.1979). What action should the Court take if a state court refuses to entertain a taxpayer's suit, involving "pocketbook" injury, challenging the constitutionality of a state statute?

See generally Murphy, *Supreme Court Review of Abstract State Court Decisions on Federal Law: A Justiciability Analysis,* 25 St.L.U. L.J. 473 (1981).

FLAST v. COHEN

392 U.S. 83, 88 S.Ct. 1942, 20 L.Ed.2d 947 (1968).

MR. CHIEF JUSTICE WARREN delivered the opinion of the Court.

[As federal taxpayers, appellants sought to enjoin federal expenditures for parochial schools, alleging violation of the religion clauses of the first amendment. A three-judge federal court held that under *Frothingham* appellants lacked standing.]

The jurisdiction of federal courts is defined and limited by [Art. III]. Embodied in the words "cases" and "controversies" are two complementary but somewhat different limitations. In part those words limit the business of federal courts to questions presented in an adversary context and in a form historically viewed as capable of resolution through the judicial process. And in part those words define the role assigned to the judiciary in a tripartite allocation of power to assure that the federal courts will not intrude into areas committed to the other branches of government. Justiciability is the term of art employed to give expression to this dual limitation * * *.

[T]he Government's position is that the constitutional scheme of separation of powers, and the deference owed by the federal judiciary to the other two branches of government within that scheme, presents an absolute bar to taxpayer suits challenging the validity of federal spending programs.[17]

Standing is an aspect of justiciability [and] there are at work in the standing doctrine the many subtle pressures which tend to cause policy considerations to blend into constitutional limitations. [The] fundamental aspect of standing is that it focuses on the party seeking to get his complaint before a federal court and not on the issues he wishes to have adjudicated. The "gist of the question of standing" is whether the party seeking relief has "alleged such a personal stake in the outcome of the controversy as to assure that concrete adverseness which sharpens the presentation of issues upon which the court so largely depends for illumination of difficult constitutional questions." *Baker v. Carr,* [p. 30 supra]. In other words, when standing is placed in issue in a case, the question is whether the person whose standing is challenged is a proper party to request an adjudication of a particular issue and not whether the issue itself is justiciable. Thus, a party may have standing in a particular case, but the federal court may nevertheless decline to pass on the merits of the case because, for example, it presents a political question. [The] question whether a particular person is a proper party to maintain the action does not, by its own force, raise separation of powers problems related to improper judicial interference in areas committed to other branches of the Federal Government. Such problems arise, if at all, only from the substantive issues the individual seeks to have adjudicated. Thus, in terms of Article III limitations on federal court jurisdiction, the question of standing is related only to whether the dispute sought to be adjudicated will be presented in an adversary context and in a form historically viewed as capable of

---

17. The logic of the Government's argument would compel it to concede that a taxpayer would lack standing even if Congress engaged in such palpably unconstitutional conduct as providing funds for the construction of churches for particular sects. The Government [contends] there might be individuals in society other than taxpayers who could invoke federal judicial power to challenge such unconstitutional appropriations. However, if as we conclude there are circumstances under which a taxpayer will be a proper and appropriate party to seek judicial review of federal statutes, the taxpayer's access to federal courts should not be barred because there might be at large in society a hypothetical plaintiff who might possibly bring such a suit.

judicial resolution. [A] taxpayer may or may not have the requisite personal stake in the outcome, depending upon the circumstances of the particular case. [I]n ruling on standing, it is both appropriate and necessary to look to the substantive issues [to] determine whether there is a logical nexus between the status asserted and the claim sought to be adjudicated [to] assure that [the litigant] is a proper and appropriate party to invoke federal judicial power [so as] to satisfy Article III requirements.

The nexus demanded of federal taxpayers has two aspects to it. First, the taxpayer must establish a logical link between that status and the type of legislative enactment attacked. Thus, a taxpayer will be a proper party to allege the unconstitutionality only of exercises of congressional power under the taxing and spending clause of Art. I, § 8, of the Constitution. It will not be sufficient to allege an incidental expenditure of tax funds in the administration of an essentially regulatory statute. This requirement is consistent with the limitation imposed upon state taxpayer standing in federal courts in *Doremus*. Secondly, the taxpayer must establish a nexus between that status and the precise nature of the constitutional infringement alleged. Under this requirement, the taxpayer must show that the challenged enactment exceeds specific constitutional limitations imposed upon the exercise of the congressional taxing and spending power and not simply that the enactment is generally beyond the powers delegated to Congress by Art. I, § 8. * * *

The taxpayer-appellants in this case have satisfied both nexuses * * *. Their constitutional challenge is made to an exercise by Congress of its power under Art. I, § 8, to spend for the general welfare, and the challenged program involves a substantial expenditure of federal tax funds. In addition, appellants have alleged that the challenged expenditures violate the Establishment and Free Exercise Clauses of the First Amendment. Our history vividly illustrates that one of the specific evils feared by those who drafted the Establishment Clause [was] that the taxing and spending power would be used to favor one religion over another or to support religion in general [and] that religious liberty ultimately would be the victim * * *. [T]hat clause of the First Amendment operates as a specific constitutional limitation upon the exercise by Congress of the taxing and spending power conferred by Art. I, § 8.

[The] taxpayer in *Frothingham* attacked a federal spending program and she, therefore, established the first nexus required. However, [she] alleged essentially that Congress, by enacting the challenged statute, had exceeded the general powers delegated to it by Art. I, § 8, and that Congress had thereby invaded the legislative province reserved to the States by the Tenth Amendment. To be sure, Mrs. Frothingham made the additional allegation that her tax liability would be increased as a result of the allegedly unconstitutional enactment, and she framed that allegation in terms of a deprivation of property without due process of law. However, the Due Process Clause of the Fifth Amendment does not protect taxpayers against increases in tax liability * * *. In essence, Mrs. Frothingham was attempting to assert the States' interest in their legislative prerogatives and not a federal taxpayer's interest in being free of taxing and spending in contravention of specific constitutional limitations imposed upon Congress' taxing and spending power.

We have noted that the Establishment Clause of the First Amendment does specifically limit the taxing and spending power conferred by Art. I, § 8. Whether the Constitution contains other specific limitations can be determined only in the context of future cases. [Under] such circumstances, we feel confident that the questions will be framed with the necessary specificity, that the issues will be contested with the necessary adverseness and that the litigation will be pursued with the necessary vigor to assure that the constitutional challenge will be made in a form traditionally thought to be capable of judicial resolution. We lack that confidence in cases such as *Frothingham* where a taxpayer seeks to employ a federal court as a forum in which to air his generalized grievances about the conduct of government or the allocation of power in the Federal System. ＊ ＊ ＊

Reversed.

MR. JUSTICE DOUGLAS [who joined the Court's opinion], concurring. ＊ ＊ ＊

There has long been a school of thought here that the less the judiciary does, the better. It is often said that judicial intrusion should be infrequent [but the] judiciary is an indispensable part of the operation of our federal system. With the growing complexities of government it is often the one and only place where effective relief can be obtained [and] where wrongs to individuals are done by violation of specific guarantees, it is abdication for courts to close their [doors].

MR. JUSTICE STEWART [who joined the Court's opinion], concurring.

[Because the Establishment Clause plainly prohibits taxing and spending in aid of religion, every taxpayer can claim a personal constitutional right not to be taxed for the support of a religious institution. The present case is thus readily distinguishable from *Frothingham* ＊ ＊ ＊.ª

MR. JUSTICE HARLAN, dissenting.

[F]ederal taxpayers may, as taxpayers, contest the constitutionality of tax obligations imposed severally upon them by federal statute. Such a challenge may be made by way of defense to an action by the United States to recover the amount of a challenged tax debt, or to a prosecution for willful failure to pay [the tax].

The lawsuits here and in *Frothingham* are fundamentally different. They present the question whether federal taxpayers qua taxpayers may, in suits in which they do not contest the validity of their previous or existing tax obligations, challenge the constitutionality of the uses for which Congress has authorized the expenditure of public funds. [An] action brought to contest the validity of tax liabilities assessed to the plaintiff is designed to vindicate interests that are personal and proprietary ＊ ＊ ＊. The relief [here] consists entirely of the vindication of rights held in common by all citizens. ＊ ＊ ＊

Surely it is plain that the rights and interests of taxpayers who contest the constitutionality of public expenditures are markedly different from those of "Hohfeldian" plaintiffs,[5] including those taxpayer-plaintiffs who challenge the validity of their own tax liabilities. We must recognize that these non-Hohfeldian plaintiffs complain [not] as taxpayers, but as "private attorneys-general." [These are] "public actions" brought to vindicate public rights.[7]

It does not, however, follow that suits brought by non-Hohfeldian plaintiffs are excluded by the "case or controversy" clause of [Art. III]. This and other federal courts have repeatedly held that individual litigants, acting as private attorneys-general, may have standing as "representatives of the public interest."

---

a. The concurring opinion of Fortas, J., is omitted.

5. The phrase is Professor Jaffe's, adopted, of course, from W. Hohfeld, *Fundamental Legal Conceptions* (1923). I have here employed the phrases "Hohfeldian" and "non-Hohfeldian" plaintiffs to mark the distinction between the personal and proprietary interests of the traditional plaintiff, and the representative and public interests of the plaintiff in a public action. ＊ ＊ ＊

7. Jaffe, *Judicial Control of Administrative Action* 483 (1965).

Scripps-Howard Radio v. FCC, 316 U.S. 4, 15, 62 S.Ct. 875, 882, 86 L.Ed. 1229. See also *Associated Industries v. Ickes,* 134 F.2d 694 * * *.[b]

The Court's analysis consists principally of the observation that the requirements of standing are met if a taxpayer has the "requisite personal stake in the outcome" of his suit. [The] Court implements this standard with the declaration that taxpayers will be "deemed" to have the necessary personal interest if their suits satisfy two [criteria]. The difficulties with these criteria [are] that they are not in any sense a measurement of any plaintiff's interest in the outcome of any [suit.]

It is surely clear that a plaintiff's interest in the outcome of a suit in which he challenges the constitutionality of a federal expenditure is not made greater or smaller by the unconnected fact that the expenditure is, or is not, "incidental" to an "essentially regulatory program." * * * Presumably the Court does not believe that regulatory programs are necessarily less destructive of First Amendment rights, or that regulatory programs are necessarily less prodigal of public funds than are grants-in-aid, for both these general propositions are demonstrably false. * * *

The Court's second criterion is similarly unrelated to its standard for the determination of standing. The intensity of a plaintiff's interest in a suit is not measured, even obliquely, by the fact that the constitutional provision under which he claims is, or is not, a "specific limitation" upon Congress' spending powers. * * *

Although the Court does not altogether explain its position, the essence of its reasoning is evidently that a taxpayer's claim under the Establishment Clause is "not merely one of ultra vires," but instead asserts "an abridgment of individual religious liberty" * * *. Choper, *The Establishment Clause and Aid to Parochial Schools,* 56 Calif.L.Rev. 260, 276. [But] the Court has not adduced, historical evidence that properly permits the Court to distinguish, as it has here, among the Establishment Clause, the Tenth Amendment and the Due Process Clause of the Fifth Amendment as limitations upon Congress' taxing and spending powers. * * *[18]

b. *Scripps-Howard* held that the Communications Act conferred standing on a radio station, as a "person aggrieved," to contest the FCC's grant of a license to an additional station: "The purpose of the Act was to protect the public interest in communications. [T]hese private litigants have standing [as] representatives of the public interest." Consider Jaffe, *Standing to Secure Judicial Review: Public Actions,* 74 Harv.L.Rev. 1265, 1314 (1961): "It might be argued that whatever the purported rationale [of] *Scripps-Howard,* a decision upholding the justiciability of a suit brought by a person of a very limited class which is in fact adversely affected is not a precedent for permitting actions by the unlimited class of citizen or taxpayer. But in *Associated Industries,* Judge Frank, following what he believed to be the rationale of [*Scripps-Howard*], did apply it to a consumer, a member of a class which is coterminous with the entire human population [and] characterized the appellant as a 'private Attorney General.' " Nonetheless, argues Davis, *Standing: Taxpayers and Others,* 35 U.Chi.L.Rev. 601,

616 (1968), "I think it entirely clear that the Court has always required 'economic and other personal interests' as the basis for standing, without exception." See his discussion of the cases, id. at 613–17. For the view that "the notion that the constitution demands injury to a personal interest as a prerequisite to attacks on allegedly unconstitutional action is historically unfounded," see Berger, *Standing to Sue in the Public Actions: Is it a Constitutional Requirement?* 78 Yale L.J. 816 (1969).

The issue of congressionally authorized standing is considered in this Part infra.

18. I have equal difficulty with the argument that the religious clauses of the First Amendment create a "personal constitutional right," held by all *citizens,* such that any *citizen* may, under those clauses, contest the constitutionality of federal expenditures. The essence of the argument would presumably be that freedom from establishment is a right that inheres in every citizen * * *. The Establishment Clause is, after all, only one of many provisions of the Constitution that

[This] Court has previously held that individual litigants have standing to represent the public interest, despite their lack of economic or other personal interests, if Congress has appropriately authorized such suits.[c] I would adhere to that principle. Any hazards to the proper allocation of authority among the three branches of the Government would be substantially diminished if public actions had been pertinently authorized by Congress and the President. * * *

Notes and Questions

1. *The first nexus.* (a) After *Flast,* may a federal taxpayer challenge the issuance of a "commemorative Christmas postage stamp" as violating the establishment clause? Assuming the issuance "involves a substantial expenditure of federal tax funds," does it concern an "exercise of congressional power under the taxing and spending clause" or is it merely an "incidental expenditure of tax funds in the administration of an essentially regulatory" program? *Should* this question be relevant to the taxpayer's standing? Consider 82 Harv.L.Rev. 230 (1968): "If a governmental regulation does violate the establishment clause, a taxpayer would sustain a special injury to conscience by the expenditure of any revenues under the regulatory scheme. Therefore, taxpayers could be designated as properly adverse article III parties to sue to vindicate the public interest. But governmental regulatory action will usually encroach on the legally protected interests of a significant portion of the citizenry as well. Thus there is no justification for concluding that the establishment clause itself should be said to designate a special injury class of litigants as proper parties to challenge this category of governmental conduct." See also Hennigan, *The Essence of Standing: The Basis of a Constitutional Right to be Heard,* 10 Ariz.L.Rev. 438 (1968). Is this analysis consistent with *Flast's* fn. 17?

(b) *The "pocketbook" injury requirement.* On the likely assumption that if this particular stamp is not issued some other one will be, does this activity—like that in *Doremus*—not "add any sum whatever to the cost of conducting" the postal system? If so, is the establishment clause evil nonetheless present because the stamp issuance "involves a substantial expenditure of tax funds" allegedly "to favor one religion over another"? If the school authorities in *Doremus* had annually expended $100 ($10) for the purchase of Bibles, would "appellants [have] established the requisite special injury necessary to a taxpayer's case or controversy"? See Davis, *Standing: Taxpayers and Others,* 35 U.Chi. L.Rev. 601 (1968). Or may it be said that the Bible-reading resulted in the public school being "used to favor one religion over another or to support religion in general" and thus the "substantial expenditure of tax funds" for general operation of the schools was allegedly violative of the establishment clause? See Stuart, *Standing to Contest Federal Appropriations,* 22 Sw.L.J. 612 (1968). Should there be taxpayer standing in both cases? Do the above queries lead to the conclusion that in all these cases taxpayers are "non-Hohfeldian plaintiffs [suing] to vindicate public rights"?

2. *The second nexus.* Does *Flast* find *Frothingham* distinguishable because the different "substantive issues" involved make Mrs. Flast but not Mrs. Frothingham an "appropriate party [as a taxpayer] to invoke federal judicial power," i.e., "Mrs. Frothingham was attempting to assert the States' interest in their

might be characterized in this fashion. [I]t might even be urged that the Ninth and Tenth Amendments, since they are largely confirmatory of rights created elsewhere in the Constitution, were intended to declare the standing of individual citizens to contest the validity of governmental activities. * * *

c. See fn. b supra.

legislative prerogatives" whereas (as phrased by Stewart, J.) Mrs. Flast was asserting "a personal constitutional right not to be taxed for the support of a religious institution"? That Mrs. Flast did—but Mrs. Frothingham did *not*— allegedly suffer a constitutionally prohibited injury?

Does Harlan, J., effectively refute the position that federal taxpayers hold a "personal constitutional right" under the establishment clause? If this "right" is *not to have money collected from the individual by taxation expended for religion by government,* is its existence denied by the fact that a suit to enjoin expenditures does not allege "that the contested expenditures will in any fashion affect the amount of the taxpayers' own existing or foreseeable tax obligations"?

Do all of these analyses speak to the merits rather than standing?

CONGRESSIONAL POWER TO CREATE STANDING

SIERRA CLUB v. MORTON, 405 U.S. 727, 92 S.Ct. 1361, 31 L.Ed.2d 636 (1972): A membership corporation with "a special interest in the conservation and sound maintenance of the national parks," relied on Administrative Procedure Act § 10 (authorizing judicial review by persons "suffering legal wrong" or "adversely affected or aggrieved") as permitting it, as a "representative of the public," to challenge construction of a recreation area in a national forest as violative of federal statutes for preservation of national parks, etc. The Court, per STEWART, J., denied standing: "[Where] Congress has authorized public officials to perform certain functions according to law, and has provided by statute for judicial review of those actions under certain circumstances, the inquiry as to standing must begin with a determination of whether the statute in question authorizes review at the behest of the plaintiff.[3] * * *

"The trend of cases arising under the APA and other statutes authorizing judicial review of federal agency action has been towards recognizing that injuries other than economic harm are sufficient to bring a person within the meaning of the statutory language, and towards discarding the notion that an injury that is widely shared is ipso facto not an injury sufficient to provide the basis for judicial review. We noted this development with approval in [*Association of Data Processing Service Organizations, Inc. v. Camp,* 397 U.S. 150, 90 S.Ct. 827, 25 L.Ed.2d 184 (1970)] in saying that the interest alleged to have been injured 'may reflect "aesthetic, conservational, and recreational" as well as economic values.' But broadening the categories of injury that may be alleged in support of standing is a different matter from abandoning the requirement that the party seeking review must have himself suffered an injury." Here, "the Sierra Club failed to allege that it or its members [use the site in the national forest] for any purpose, much less that they use it in any way that would be significantly affected by the proposed" construction.[a]

---

3. [W]here a dispute is otherwise justiciable, the question whether the litigant is a "proper party to request an adjudication of a particular issue," is one within the power of Congress to determine.

a. Douglas, J., dissented, contending for standing "in the name of the inanimate object about to be despoiled, defaced or invaded by roads and bulldozers and where injury is the subject of public outrage." (See Stone, *Should Trees Have Standing?—Toward Legal Rights for Natural Objects,* 45 So.Cal.L.Rev. 450

(1972)). Blackmun, J. dissented, calling (with Brennan, J.) for "an imaginative expansion of our traditional concepts of standing in order to enable an organization such as the Sierra Club, possessed, as it is, of pertinent, bona-fide and well-recognized attributes and purposes in the area of environment, to litigate environmental issues." (See Sedler, *Standing, Justiciability and All That: A Behavioral Analysis,* 25 Vand.L.Rev. 479 (1973)). Powell and Rehnquist, JJ., did not participate.

TRAFFICANTE v. METROPOLITAN LIFE INS. CO., 409 U.S. 205, 93 S.Ct. 364, 34 L.Ed.2d 415 (1972), per DOUGLAS, J., held that tenants of an apartment complex had standing to complain that the owner racially discriminated in renting in violation of the Civil Rights Act of 1968. The Act gave "persons aggrieved" the right to sue—defined as "any person who claims to have been injured by a discriminatory housing practice." The tenants "claimed they had been injured in that (1) they had lost the social benefits of living in an integrated community; (2) they had missed business and professional advantages which would have accrued if they had lived with members of minority groups; (3) they had suffered embarrassment and economic damage in social, business, and professional activities from being 'stigmatized' as residents of a 'white ghetto.' "

Observing that "the role of 'private attorneys general' is not uncommon in modern legislative programs," the Court found that "the language of the Act is broad and inclusive" and "concluded that the words used showed 'a congressional intention to define standing as broadly as is permitted by [Art. III].' Individual injury or injury in fact to petitioners, the ingredient found missing in *Sierra Club*, is alleged here." [b]

UNITED STATES v. SCRAP, 412 U.S. 669, 93 S.Ct. 2405, 37 L.Ed.2d 254 (1973), per STEWART, J., held that appellee environmental groups, who challenged the ICC's failure to suspend a surcharge on railroad freight rates as violative of the ICC's statutory duties, had standing as persons "adversely affected or aggrieved" under the APA. Appellees alleged "that their members used the forests, streams, mountains, and other resources in the Washington metropolitan area for camping, hiking, fishing, and sightseeing." The Court was willing to follow an "attenuated line of causation to the eventual injury of which the appellees complained—a general rate increase would allegedly cause increased use of nonrecyclable commodities as compared to recyclable goods, thus resulting in the need to use more natural resources to produce such goods, some of which resources might be taken from the Washington area, and resulting in more refuse that might be discarded in national parks in the Washington area." [c]

WHITE, J., joined by Burger, C.J. and Rehnquist, J., dissented: "The allegations here do not satisfy the threshold requirement of injury in fact [for] a justiciable case or controversy. [T]he alleged injuries are so remote, speculative, and insubstantial" as to "no more qualify these appellees to litigate than allegations of a taxpayer that governmental expenditures will increase his taxes and have an impact on his pocketbook, or allegations that governmental decisions are offensive to reason or morals. [If] they are sufficient here, we are well on our way to permitting citizens at large to litigate any decisions of the Government which fall in an area of interest to them and with which they disagree."

The Sierra Club subsequently amended its complaint and obtained standing by alleging its members' use of the national forest.

b. White, J., joined by Blackmun and Powell, JJ., concurred: "Absent the Civil Rights Act of 1968, I would have great difficulty in concluding that petitioners' complaint in this case presented a case or controversy [under] Art. III. But [cf.] *Katzenbach v. Morgan; Ore-*

gon v. Mitchell [opinion of Brennan, J.]"—Ch. 12, Sec. 2.

See also *Gladstone Realtors v. Bellwood*, 441 U.S. 91, 99 S.Ct. 1601, 60 L.Ed.2d 66 (1979) (standing under Fair Housing Act).

c. Blackmun, J., joined by Brennan, J. (and with whom Douglas, J., agreed) concurred, following their view in *Sierra Club* that "injury in fact" need not be required.

Notes and Questions

1. *The cases' rationale.* Do *Sierra Club, Trafficante* and *SCRAP* establish that a litigant must have suffered "injury in fact" to satisfy the case-or-controversy requirement? Or does the Court's definition of "individual injury" in these cases in reality permit "citizens at large to litigate"? Consider Albert, *Standing to Challenge Administrative Action: An Inadequate Surrogate Claim for Relief,* 83 Yale L.J. 425, 489 (1974): "The interests of consumers and environmentalists, while held in common with many, are plainly not equivalent to a citizen's interest in good government. To the contrary, such interests, going to matters that affect the quality of life, leisure, and health, are as tangible and palpable as the typical fare for adjudication. People are injured in real and recognizable ways when action despoiling parks and woodlands is authorized, when a licensee with a poor or discriminatory broadcasting record is renewed, or when an agency fails to act upon unsafe regulated products. [If] litigants presenting these claims, as in *Sierra Club,* do not show injury to themselves from government action, Article III is a barrier. But there is nothing inherent in the nature of the interests or their shared character that raises problems under Article III."

2. *Congressional power and Art. III.* After *Frothingham,* could Congress authorize suit by *any* taxpayer to test the constitutionality of the Maternity Act? *Any* citizen?[d] What was the view of Harlan, J., in *Flast*? Would "such individuals demonstrate the necessary stake in the outcome to satisfy Article III requirements"? How could they if *Frothingham* did not present a "judicial controversy"? Do they suffer greater "injury in fact" than a federal officer who brings a criminal prosecution, or a civil action to enforce regulatory prohibitions, against a private individual? See Sedler, *Standing and the Burger Court: An Analysis and Some Proposals for Legislative Reform,* 30 Rutg.L.Rev. 863, 881–85 (1977). Consider Jaffe, *The Citizen as Litigant in Public Actions: The Non-Hohfeldian or Ideological Plaintiff,* 116 U.Pa.L.Rev. 1033, 1037–38 (1968): "[T]he very fact of [an "ideological plaintiff"] investing money in a lawsuit from which one is to acquire no further monetary profit argues, to my mind, a quite exceptional kind of interest, and one peculiarly indicative of a desire to say all that can be said in the support of one's contention. From this I would conclude that, insofar as the argument for a traditional plaintiff runs in terms of the need for effective advocacy, the argument is not persuasive." See also Tushnet, *The Sociology of Article III,* 93 Harv.L.Rev. 1698, 1711 (1980): "In a legal system based on precedent, a successful litigant benefits from those in the future who can invoke the earlier decision, [yet] the present litigant cannot capture those potential benefits. Thus, as a general proposition, it seems that rational Hohfeldian litigants should underinvest in their litigation. [On the other hand, studies] from the perspective of economics [and] sociology have demonstrated that ["ideological"] litigants who have a continuing interest in the substantive outcomes of litigation, and who have a continuing interest in the development of legal rules favorable to their position, are more likely to invest adequate resources and therefore to succeed in their litigation."

If the "ideological plaintiff" satisfies the case-or-controversy requirement, is there any lawsuit in which plaintiff is not "a proper party to request an adjudication of a particular issue"? Does restriction of standing to "traditional

---

d. The Endangered Species Act, 16 U.S.C. § 1540(g), authorizes "any person" to enjoin   violations. See *TVA v. Hill,* 437 U.S. 153, 98 S.Ct. 2279, 57 L.Ed.2d 117 (1978).

plaintiffs" serve other significant constitutional ends? Should there be standing for "public actions" irrespective of congressional authorization? See note 2 after *Allen v. Wright*, infra.

UNITED STATES v. RICHARDSON, 418 U.S. 166, 94 S.Ct. 2940, 41 L.Ed.2d 678 (1974), per BURGER, C.J., held that a federal taxpayer had no standing to contend that the Central Intelligence Agency Act, which provides that CIA appropriations and expenditures not be made public, violates Art. I, § 9, cl. 7— "a regular Statement of Account of the Receipts and Expenditures of all public money shall be published from time to time": Respondent "makes no claim that appropriated funds are being spent in violation of a 'specific constitutional limitation upon [the] taxing and spending power * * *.' Rather, he asks the courts to compel the Government to give him information on precisely how the CIA spends its funds [without which] he cannot intelligently follow the actions of Congress or the Executive, nor can he properly fulfill his obligations as a member of the electorate in voting for candidates seeking national office.

"This is surely the kind of a generalized grievance described in both *Frothingham* and *Flast* since the impact on him is plainly undifferentiated and 'common to all members of the public.' *Ex parte Levitt*, 302 U.S. 633, 58 S.Ct. 1, 82 L.Ed. 493 (1983).[a] While we can hardly dispute that this respondent has a genuine interest in the use of funds and that his interest may be prompted by his status as a taxpayer, he has not alleged that, as a taxpayer, he is in danger of suffering any particular concrete injury as a result of the operation of this statute. * * *[11]

"[T]he absence of any particular individual or class to litigate these claims gives support to the argument that the subject matter is committed to the surveillance of Congress, and ultimately to the political process. [T]hat the Constitution does not afford a judicial remedy does not, of course, completely disable the citizen * * *. Slow, cumbersome and unresponsive though the traditional electoral process may be thought at times, our system provides for changing members of the political branches when dissatisfied citizens convince a sufficient number of their fellow electors that elected representatives are delinquent in performing duties committed to them."

POWELL, J., who joined the Court's opinion, concurred: "[T]here can be little doubt about respondent's fervor in pursuing his case [and the] intensity of his interest appears to bear no relationship to the fact that, literally speaking, he is not challenging directly a congressional exercise of the taxing and spending power. On the other hand, [it] requires no great leap in reasoning to conclude that the Statement and Account Clause [is] inextricably linked to that power. And that clause might well be seen as a 'specific' limitation on congressional spending. Indeed, it could be viewed as the most democratic of limitations.

a. *Levitt* held that a private individual had no standing to challenge the appointment of a Supreme Court justice as violative of Art. I, § 6, cl. 2.

11. Although we need not reach or decide precisely what is meant by "a regular Statement of Account," it [is] open to serious question whether the Framers of the Constitution ever imagined that general directives to the Congress or the Executive would be subject to enforcement by an individual citizen.

[H]istorical analysis of the genesis of cl. 7 suggests that it was intended to permit some degree of secrecy of governmental operations. The ultimate weapon of enforcement available to the Congress would, of course, be the "power of the purse." Independent of the statute here challenged by respondent, Congress could grant standing to taxpayers or citizens, or both, limited, of course, by the "Cases" and "Controversies" provisions of Art. III. * * *

Thus, although the Court's application of *Flast* to the instant case is probably literally correct, adherence to the *Flast* test in this instance suggests, as does *Flast* itself, that the test is not a sound or logical limitation on standing. [D]espite the diminution of standing requirements in the last decade, the Court has not broken with the traditional requirement that, in the absence of a specific statutory grant of the right of review, a plaintiff must allege some particularized injury that sets him apart from the man on the street. * * * [17]"

STEWART, J., joined by Marshall, J., dissented: "[Respondent] contends that the Statement and Account Clause gives him a right to receive the information and burdens the Government with a correlative duty to supply it. [When] a party is seeking a judicial determination that a defendant owes him an affirmative duty, it seems clear to me that he has standing to litigate the issue of the existence vel non of this duty once he shows that the defendant has declined to honor his claim. [Thus,] there is no necessity to resort to any extended analysis, such as the *Flast* nexus tests [which "were no more than a response to the problem of taxpayer standing to challenge federal legislation enacted in the exercise of the taxing and spending power."] Certainly, after *SCRAP*, it does not matter that those to whom the duty is owed may be many."

BRENNAN, J., dissented, relying on his dissent in *Reservists,* this Sec. infra: "Richardson plainly alleged injury in fact [in] respect of his right as a citizen to know how Congress was spending the public fisc [and] as a voter to receive information to aid his decision how and for whom to vote. These claims may ultimately fail on the merits, but Richardson has 'standing' to assert them." [b]

SCHLESINGER v. RESERVISTS COMM. TO STOP THE WAR, 418 U.S. 208, 94 S.Ct. 2925, 41 L.Ed.2d 706 (1974), per BURGER, C.J., held that respondents lacked standing as citizens to contend that the Secretary of Defense's permitting Members of Congress to be in the Armed Forces Reserve violated the Incompatibility Clause of Art. I, § 6, cl. 2—"No person holding any office under the United States shall be a Member of either House during his continuance in office." Respondents alleged injury because "nonobservance of [the] Clause deprives citizens of the faithful discharge of the legislative duties of Reservist members of Congress" since they would "be subject to the possibility of undue influence by the Executive Branch [and] possible inconsistent obligations." The Court responded:

"[T]hat claimed nonobservance, standing alone, would adversely affect only the generalized interest of all citizens in constitutional governance, and that is an abstract injury. [T]he requirement of concrete injury [serves] the function of insuring that [constitutional] adjudication does not take place unnecessarily. [T]he discrete factual context within which the concrete injury occurred or is threatened insures the framing of relief no more broad than required by the precise facts to which the court's ruling would be applied. This is especially important when the relief sought produces a confrontation with one of the coordinate branches of the government. [T]he fact that the adverse parties sharply conflicted in their interests and views and were supported by able briefs and arguments [is] not a substitute for the actual injury needed [to] focus

---

17. *Baker v. Carr* may have a special claim to sui generis status. It was perhaps a necessary response to the manifest distortion of democratic principles practiced by malapportioned legislatures * * *. *Flast* may also have been a reaction to what appeared at the time as an immutable political logjam that included unsuccessful efforts to confer specific statutory grants of standing.

b. Douglas, J. also dissented.

litigation efforts and judicial decision-making. Moreover, [a] logical corollary to this approach would be the manifestly untenable view that the inadequacy of the presentation on the merits would be an appropriate basis for denying standing.[a] [Our] system of government leaves many crucial decisions to the political processes. The assumption that if respondents have no standing to sue, no one would have standing, is not a reason to find standing. See *Richardson*." [b]

STEWART, J., who joined the Court's opinion, concurred: "[U]nlike *Richardson*, the respondents do not allege that the petitioners have refused to perform an affirmative duty imposed upon them by the Constitution. * * * Standing is not today found wanting because an injury has been suffered by many, but rather because *none* of the respondents has alleged the sort of direct, palpable injury required for standing under [Art. III]."

MARSHALL, J., dissented: Respondents' "specific interest"—"to have the Congress take all the steps necessary to terminate American involvement in Vietnam"—"is certainly not a 'general interest common to all members of the public.' [It] is a sad commentary on our priorities that a litigant who contends that a violation of a federal stature has interfered with his aesthetic appreciation of natural resources can have a claim heard by a federal court, see *SCRAP*, while one who contends that a violation of a specific provision of [the] Constitution has interfered with the effectiveness of expression protected by the First Amendment is turned away." Douglas, J., also dissented.

Notes and Questions

Nature of constitutional provision. (a) Did the claimants in *Reservists* and *Richardson* allege "concrete injury" or only "the generalized interest of all citizens in constitutional governance"? Consider Albert, *Justiciability and Theories of Judicial Review: A Remote Relationship,* 50 So.Cal.L.Rev. 1139, 1153 (1977): "[*Reservists* and *Richardson*] illustrate that the article III concept of 'injury in fact' [involves] a subtle judicial judgment founded upon a construction of the substantive constitutional mandate in issue. [In the Court's view, the Incompatibility Clause and the Statement and Account Clause] gave rise to no definable legal interest, and therefore there was no immediacy or actuality to the alleged harms. But there is no objective calculus for saying that these harms are less immediate or real than injury to schoolchildren from unequal educational financing or to voters from unequal districting. What differs is the source of the judgment, the law on which the claim is founded. Hence, it was a choice between competing views of the unconstrued constitutional provisions in *Richardson* and *Reservists* that determined whether there was 'injury in fact.' "

a. See Davis, *Administrative Law Text* 427–28 (3d ed. 1972): "Standing should not depend upon the probable manner in which a party will present a case; it should depend only upon the question whether the plaintiff should be entitled to judicial assistance in order that justice may be done. Two simple illustrations, one at each pole, should suffice to show this: (1) The best law firm in the country, no matter how skillful its presentation to the court may be, *obviously* lacks standing to get an adjudication of an abstract question of law when neither it nor its client has any interest at stake. (2) An illiterate pauper who refuses legal assistance *obviously* has standing to challenge a $10 fine imposed on him, no matter how badly he may present his case."

b. The Court also denied respondents standing as taxpayers because they "did not challenge an enactment under Art. I, § 8, but rather the action of the Executive Branch." Douglas, J., dissented on this point because "Acts of Congress make various appropriations for the services of reservists" and the Incompatibility Clause " 'was designed as a specific bulwark against such potential abuses [and] operates as a specific constitutional limitation upon' such expenditures." Brennan, J., dissenting, also "would find the injury-in-fact requirement met by the respondents' taxpayer allegation."

(b) Were *Reservists* and *Richardson* based on the judgment that enforcement of the Incompatibility Clause and the Statement and Account Clause should be left "to the political process"? That—as with the states' rights issue in *Frothingham* and unlike the establishment clause issue in *Flast*—no one has "standing to sue"? Consider Davis, *Administrative Law of the Seventies* 522–23 (1976): "The way to protect against too much government by judges is to limit *what* the judges decide, not to limit *who* can raise a question for a court to decide. [The Court] can better accomplish [its] purpose if [it] focuses on the *what,* not on the *who.* [The] law of 'political question' is a much better judicial tool than the law of standing for deciding *what* the courts should decide." Compare Bogen, *Standing Up for Flast: Taxpayer and Citizen Standing to Raise Constitutional Issues,* 67 Ky.L.J. 147, 162 (1978–79): "If the constitutional provision in question is intended to protect a particular right from the majoritarian political process, the Court should not remand the plaintiff to those same processes. The critical question should center on the nature of the constitutional provision in question and whether the particular provision would be more effective if enforced by citizen suits. This issue has not been addressed by the Court."

VALLEY FORGE CHRISTIAN COLLEGE v. AMERICANS UNITED FOR SEPARATION OF CHURCH AND STATE, INC., 454 U.S. 464, 102 S.Ct. 752, 70 L.Ed.2d 700 (1982), per REHNQUIST, J., held that respondents lacked standing as taxpayers or citizens to challenge, as violative of the establishment clause, the giving of surplus federal property to a church college that trained students "for Christian services as either ministers or laymen": "While the [power of judicial review] is a formidable means of vindicating individual rights, when employed unwisely or unnecessarily it is also the ultimate threat to the continued effectiveness of the federal courts in performing that role. '[R]epeated and essentially head-on confrontations between the life-tenured branch and the representative branches of government will not, in the long run, be beneficial to either. The public confidence essential to the former and the vitality critical to the latter may well erode if we do not exercise self-restraint in the utilization of our power to negative the actions of the other branches.' *Richardson* (Powell, J., concurring).[a] Proper regard for the complex nature of our constitutional structure requires neither that the judicial branch shrink from a confrontation with the other two coequal branches of the federal government, nor that it hospitably accept for adjudication claims of constitutional violation by other branches of government where the claimant has not suffered cognizable injury. * * * Art. III, which is every bit as important in its circumscription of the judicial power of the United States as in its granting of that power, is not merely a troublesome hurdle to be overcome if possible so as to reach the 'merits' of a lawsuit * * *.

"[R]espondents fail the first prong of the [*Flast*] test for taxpayer standing [in] two respects. First, the source of their complaint is not a congressional action, but a decision by HEW to transfer a parcel of federal property. *Flast* limited taxpayer standing to challenges directed 'only [at] exercises of congressional power.' Second, [the] property transfer [was] not an exercise of authority conferred by the taxing and spending clause of Art. I, § 8. The authorizing legislation [was] an evident exercise of Congress' power under the Property Clause, Art. IV, § 3, cl. 2.

---

a. See generally Brilmayer, *The Jurisprudence of Article III: Perspectives on the "Case or Controversy" Requirement,* 93 Harv.L.Rev. 297 (1979).

"[The Court of Appeals] decided that respondents' claim differed from those in *Reservists* and *Richardson* [because] 'it is at the very least arguable that the Establishment Clause creates in each citizen a "personal constitutional right" to a government that does not establish religion.' [These cases cannot] be distinguished on the ground that the Incompatibility and Accounts Clauses are in some way less 'fundamental' than the Establishment Clause. Each establishes a norm of conduct which the federal government is bound to honor—to no greater or lesser extent than any other inscribed in the Constitution. To the extent the Court of Appeals relied on a view of standing under which the Art. III burdens diminish as the 'importance' of the claim on the merits increases, we reject that notion. The requirement of standing 'focuses on the party seeking to get his complaint before a federal court and not on the issues he wishes to have adjudicated.' *Flast.* Moreover, we know of no principled basis on which to create a hierarchy of constitutional values or a complementary 'sliding scale' of standing which might permit respondents to invoke the judicial power of the United States. 'The proposition that all constitutional provisions are enforceable by any citizen simply because citizens are the ultimate beneficiaries of those provisions has no boundaries.' *Reservists.*

"The complaint in this case shares a common deficiency with those in *Reservists* and *Richardson*. Although they claim that the Constitution has been violated, [they] fail to identify any personal injury suffered by the plaintiffs *as a consequence* of the alleged constitutional error, other than the psychological consequence presumably produced by observation of conduct with which one disagrees. That is not an injury sufficient to confer standing under Art. III, even though the disagreement is phrased in constitutional terms. It is evident that respondents are firmly committed to the constitutional principle of separation of church and State, but standing is not measured by the intensity of the litigant's interest or the fervor of his advocacy. * * *

"In reaching this conclusion, we do not retreat from our earlier holdings that standing may be predicated on noneconomic injury. See, e.g., *SCRAP, Data Processing Service.* We simply cannot see that respondents have alleged an *injury* of *any* kind, economic or otherwise, sufficient to confer standing.[22] [Their] claim that the government has violated the Establishment Clause does not provide a special license to roam the country in search of governmental wrongdoing and to reveal their discoveries in federal court. [Their] claim of standing implicitly rests on the presumption that violations of the Establishment Clause typically will not cause injury sufficient to confer standing under the 'traditional' view of Art. III. But '[t]he assumption that if respondents have no standing to sue, no one would have standing, is not a reason to find standing.' *Reservists.* This view would convert standing into a requirement that must be observed only when satisfied. Moreover, we are unwilling to assume that injured parties are nonexistent simply because they have not joined respondents in their suit. The law of averages is not a substitute for standing.

22. [The] plaintiffs in *Schempp* [p. 704 supra] had standing, not because their complaint rested on the Establishment Clause—for as *Doremus* demonstrated, that is insufficient—but because impressionable schoolchildren were subjected to unwelcome religious exercises or were forced to assume special burdens to avoid them. Respondents have alleged no comparable injury. [See generally Black, *Religion, "Standing," and the Supreme Court's Role*, 13 J.Pub.L. 459 (1964); Brown, *Quis Custodiet Ipsos Custodes?—The School Prayer Cases*, 1963 Sup.Ct.Rev. 1; Choper, *Religion in the Public Schools: A Proposed Constitutional Standard*, 47 Minn.L.Rev. 329, 366–67 (1963); Dixon, *Religion, Schools, and the Open Society: A Socio-Constitutional Issue*, 13 J.Pub.L. 267 (1964).]

"Were we to accept respondents' claim of standing in this case, there would be no principled basis for confining our exception to litigants relying on the Establishment Clause. Ultimately, that exception derives from the idea that the judicial power requires nothing more for its invocation than important issues and able litigants.[26] [W]e are unwilling to countenance such a departure from the limits on judicial power contained in Art. III * * *."

BRENNAN, J., joined by Marshall and Blackmun, JJ.,[b] dissented: "The Court makes a fundamental mistake when it determines that a plaintiff has failed to satisfy [the] 'injury-in-fact' test, or indeed any other test of 'standing,' without first determining whether the Constitution [defines] injury, and creates a cause of action for redress of that injury, in precisely the circumstance presented to the Court.[5] [One] of the primary purposes of the Establishment Clause was to prevent the use of tax monies for religious purposes. *The taxpayer was the direct and intended beneficiary of the prohibition on financial aid to religion.* [It] may be that Congress can tax for *almost* any reason, or for no reason at all. There is, so far as I have been able to discern, but one constitutionally imposed limit on that authority. Congress cannot use tax money to support a church, or to encourage religion. [T]he history of the Establishment Clause [makes] this clear. History also makes it clear that the federal taxpayer is a singularly 'proper and appropriate party to invoke a federal court's jurisdiction' to challenge a federal bestowal of largesse as a violation of the Establishment Clause. Each, and indeed every, federal taxpayer suffers precisely the injury that the Establishment Clause guards against when the Federal Government directs that funds be taken from the pocketbooks of the citizenry and placed into the coffers of the ministry. * * *

"Blind to history, the Court attempts to distinguish this case from *Flast* by wrenching snippets of language from our opinions, and by perfunctorily applying that language under color of the first prong of *Flast's* two-part nexus test." As for the fact that HEW transferred the property, "to be sure, the First Amendment is phrased as a restriction on Congress' legislative authority; this is only natural since the Constitution assigns the authority to legislate and appropriate only to the Congress. But it is difficult to conceive of an expenditure for which the last governmental actor, either implementing directly the legislative will, or acting within the scope of legislatively delegated authority, is not an Executive Branch official. The First Amendment binds the Government as a whole, regardless of which branch is at work in a particular instance.

"The Court's second purported distinction between this case and *Flast* is equally unavailing. [It] can make no constitutional difference [whether] the donation to the defendant here was in the form of a cash grant to build a facility, see *Tilton v. Richardson,* [p. 728 supra], or in the nature of a gift of property

---

26. Were we to recognize standing premised on an "injury" consisting solely of an alleged violation of a " 'personal constitutional right' to a government that does not establish religion," a principled consistency would dictate recognition of respondents' standing to challenge execution of every capital sentence on the basis of a personal right to a government that does not impose cruel and unusual punishment, or standing to challenge every affirmative action program on the basis of a personal right to a government that does not deny equal protection of the laws, to choose

but two among as many possible examples as there are commands in the Constitution.

b. Stevens, J., dissented separately, agreeing with Brennan, J.

5. When the Constitution makes it clear that a particular person is to be protected from a particular form of government action, then that person has a "right" to be free of that action; when that right is infringed, then there is injury, and a personal stake, within the meaning of Article III.

including a facility already [built.] [19]   Whether undertaken pursuant to the Property Clause or the Spending Clause, the breach of the Establishment Clause, and the relationship of the taxpayer to that breach, is precisely the same."

Notes and Questions

1. *Other "injured parties."*   After *Valley Forge,* would a neighboring college, that alleges competitive disadvantage because of the federal grant of property to Valley Forge Christian, have "an injury sufficient to confer standing"?   If Mrs. Frothingham had refused to pay part of her federal income taxes and was prosecuted for income tax evasion, could she defend on the ground that the Maternity Act expenditures were beyond congressional power?

2. *Other constitutional provisions.*   Apart from the establishment clause, are there any other "specific limitations on the taxing and spending power" that *taxpayers* have standing to enforce?   Suppose Congress appropriated funds for racially segregated facilities?   See McCoy & Nevins, *Standing and Adverseness in Challenges of Tax Exemptions for Discriminatory Private Schools,* 52 Ford.L. Rev. 441, 453–56 (1984).   For polygraphs to be used on all criminal defendants? For a federal censorship office?   For subsidies to some newspapers?   For the administration of general loyalty oaths to all public employees?   Assuming that all of these activities are unconstitutional, whose "rights" do they violate? Taxpayers' "rights"?   How about an appropriation of "$50 to every member of the Republican Party"?

3. *State suits.*   Are the Court's strictures on federal taxpayer and citizen standing also applicable to Supreme Court review of state taxpayer and citizen suits?   Consider Scharpf, *Judicial Review and the Political Question: A Functional Analysis,* 75 Yale L.J. 517, 521 n. 12 (1966): "In *Frothingham,* the Court based its narrow interpretation of [the 'case and controversy'] requirement upon an understanding of the *federal* allocation of functions to the three departments of government: the Court's only legitimate function *within that framework* is to decide 'normal' cases and controversies, and any expansion of that concept would change this balance.   [However, the] Constitution would seem to leave the states free to divide their functions of government differently, and to define the 'judicial power' of their own courts somewhat more broadly than [Art. III]. Thus, if a state permits its own courts to decide taxpayers' suits, and if a federal question should be determined by a state court in such a suit, it seems that the 'separation-of-powers' rationale should carry little or no weight for the Supreme Court's definition of what is a proper 'case and controversy' for purposes of appellate jurisdiction.   In this situation 'case and controversy' might well have a more permissive content, protecting only the functional requisites for the correctness of the Court's constitutional decision: a well developed case, litigated by the best possible parties."

WARTH v. SELDIN
422 U.S. 490, 95 S.Ct. 2197, 45 L.Ed.2d 343 (1975).

Mr. Justice Powell delivered the opinion of the Court.

Petitioners, various organizations and individuals resident in the Rochester, New York, metropolitan area, brought this action [against] the Town of Penfield,

---

19. [By] failing to require any payment from the defendant college, the Secretary apparently determined that the benefit to the United States exceeded the fair market value. But it is entirely clear from *Tilton* that if the facility is and was used for sectarian purposes, the government was required to obtain full market value at the time such use commences.

an incorporated municipality adjacent to Rochester, and against members of Penfield's Zoning, Planning, and Town Boards. Petitioners claimed that the town's zoning [ordinance] effectively excluded persons of low and moderate income from living in the town, in contravention of petitioners' First, Ninth, and Fourteenth Amendment rights and in violation of 42 U.S.C. §§ 1981, 1982, and 1983. The [federal courts below held] that none of the plaintiffs [had standing].

In its constitutional dimension, standing imports justiciability: whether the plaintiff has made out a "case or controversy" between himself and the defendant within the meaning of Art. III. * * *

Apart from this minimum constitutional mandate, this Court has recognized other ["prudential"] limits on the class of persons who may invoke the courts' decisional and remedial powers. First, the Court has held that when the asserted harm is a "generalized grievance" shared in substantially equal measure by all or a large class of citizens, that harm alone normally does not warrant exercise of jurisdiction. E.g., *Reservists.* Second, even when the plaintiff has alleged injury sufficient to meet the "case or controversy" requirement, this Court has held that the plaintiff generally must assert his own legal rights and interests, and cannot rest his claim to relief on the legal rights or interests of third parties.[a] Without such limitations—closely related to Art. III concerns but essentially matters of judicial self-governance—the courts would be called upon to decide abstract questions of wide public significance even though other governmental institutions may be more competent to address the questions and even though judicial intervention may be unnecessary to protect individual rights.

Although standing in no way depends on the merits of the plaintiff's contention that particular conduct is illegal, e.g., *Flast,* it often turns on the nature and source of the claim asserted. The actual or threatened injury required by Art. III may exist solely by virtue of "statutes creating legal rights, the invasion of which creates standing * * *." See *Sierra Club.* Moreover, the source of the plaintiff's claim to relief assumes critical importance with respect to the prudential rules of standing * * *. Essentially, the standing question in such cases is whether the constitutional or statutory provision on which the claim rests properly can be understood as granting persons in the plaintiff's position a right to judicial relief.[12] In some circumstances, countervailing considerations may outweigh the concerns underlying the usual reluctance to exert judicial power when the plaintiff's claim to relief rests on the legal rights of third parties. In such instances, the Court has found, in effect, that the constitutional or statutory provision in question implies a right of action in the plaintiff. Moreover, Congress may grant an express right of action to persons who otherwise would be barred by prudential standing rules. Of course, Art. III's requirement remains: the plaintiff still must allege a distinct and palpable injury to himself, even if it is an injury shared by a large class of other possible litigants. E.g., *SCRAP.* But so long as this requirement is satisfied, persons to whom Congress has granted a right of action, either expressly or by clear implication, may have standing to seek relief on the basis of the legal rights and

---

a. This topic is considered in Part B infra.

12. A similar standing issue arises when the litigant asserts the rights of third parties defensively, as a bar to judgment against him. E.g., *Barrows v. Jackson; McGowan v. Maryland* [Part B infra]. In such circumstances, there is no Art. III standing problem; but the prudential question is governed by considerations closely related to the question whether a person in the litigant's position would have a right of action on the claim.

interests of others, and, indeed, may invoke the general public interest in support of their claim. E.g., *Sierra Club.* * * *

III. With these general considerations in mind, we turn first to the claims of petitioners Ortiz, Reyes, Sinkler, and Broadnax, each of whom asserts standing as a person of low or moderate income and, coincidentally, as a member of a minority racial or ethnic group. We must assume, taking the allegations of the complaint as true, that Penfield's zoning ordinance and the pattern of enforcement [have] the purpose and effect of excluding [such persons]. We also assume, for purposes here, that such intentional exclusionary practices, if proved in a proper case, would be adjudged violative of the constitutional and statutory rights of the persons excluded.

But the fact that these petitioners share attributes common to persons who may have been excluded from residence in the town is an insufficient predicate for the conclusion that petitioners themselves have been excluded, or that the respondents' assertedly illegal actions have violated their rights. Petitioners must allege and show that they personally have been injured * * *.

In their complaint, petitioners Ortiz, Reyes, Sinkler, and Broadnax alleged in conclusory terms that they are among the persons excluded by respondents' actions. None of them has ever resided in Penfield; each claims at least implicitly that he desires, or has desired, to do so. Each asserts, moreover, that he made some effort, at some time, to locate housing in Penfield that was at once within his means and adequate for his family's needs. Each claims that his efforts proved fruitless. We may assume, as petitioners alleged, that respondents' actions have contributed, perhaps substantially, to the cost of housing in Penfield. But there remains the question whether petitioners' inability to locate suitable housing in Penfield reasonably can be said to have resulted, in any concretely demonstrable way, from respondents' alleged constitutional and statutory infractions. Petitioners must allege facts from which it reasonably could be inferred that, absent the respondents' restrictive zoning practices, there is a substantial probability that they would have been able to purchase or lease in Penfield and that, if the court affords the relief requested, the asserted inability of petitioners will be removed.

We find the record devoid of the necessary allegations. [N]one of these petitioners has a present interest in any Penfield property; none is himself subject to the ordinance's strictures; and none has ever been denied a variance or permit by respondent officials. Instead, petitioners claim that respondents' enforcement of the ordinance against third parties—developers, builders, and the like—has had the consequence of precluding the construction of housing suitable to their needs at prices they might be able to afford. The fact that the harm to petitioners may have resulted indirectly does not in itself preclude standing. When a governmental prohibition or restriction imposed on one party causes specific harm to a third party, harm that a constitutional provision or statute was intended to prevent, the indirectness of the injury does not necessarily deprive the person harmed of standing to vindicate his rights. But it may make it substantially more difficult to meet the minimum requirement of Art. III: to establish that, in fact, the asserted injury was the consequence of the defendants' actions, or that prospective relief will remove the harm.

Here, by their own admission, realization of petitioners' desire to live in Penfield always has depended on the efforts and willingness of third parties to build low- and moderate-cost housing. The record specifically refers to only two such efforts: that of Penfield Better Homes Corporation, in late 1969, to obtain the rezoning of certain land in Penfield to allow the construction of subsidized cooperative townhouses that could be purchased by persons of moderate income; and a similar effort by O'Brien Homes, Inc., in late 1971.[15] But the record is devoid of any indication that these projects or other like projects, would have satisfied petitioners needs at prices they could afford, or that, were the court to remove the obstructions attributable to respondents, such relief would benefit petitioners. Indeed, petitioners' descriptions of their individual financial situations and housing needs suggest precisely the contrary—that their inability to reside in Penfield is the consequence of the economics of the area housing market, rather than of respondents' assertedly illegal acts.[16] In short, the facts alleged fail to support an actionable causal relationship between Penfield's zoning practices and petitioners' asserted injury.[18] * * *

V. We turn next to the standing problems presented by the petitioner associations * * *.

A. Petitioner Metro-Act [claims] that, as a result of the persistent pattern of exclusionary zoning [its] members who are Penfield residents are deprived of the benefits of living in a racially and ethnically integrated community. * * *

15. Penfield Better Homes contemplated a series of one to three bedroom units and hoped to sell them—at that time—to persons who earned from $5,000 to $8,000 per year. * * * O'Brien Homes, Inc., projected 51 buildings, each containing four family units, designed for single people and small families, and capable of being purchased by persons "of low income and accumulated funds" * * *.

16. Ortiz states in his affidavit that he [is] concerned with finding a house or apartment large enough for himself, his wife and seven children, but states that he can afford to spend a maximum of $120 per month for housing. Broadnax seeks a four-bedroom house or apartment for herself and six children, and can spend a maximum of about $120 per month for housing. Sinkler also states that she can spend $120 per month for housing for herself and two children. Thus, at least in the cases of Ortiz and Broadnax, it is doubtful that their stated needs could have been satisfied by the small housing units contemplated in the only moderate cost projects specifically described in the record. Moreover, there is no indication that any of the plaintiffs had the resources necessary to acquire the housing available in the projects. The matter is left entirely obscure. The income and housing budget figures supplied in petitioners' affidavits are presumably for the year 1972. The vague description of the proposed O'Brien development strongly suggests that the units, even if adequate to their needs, would have been beyond the means at least of Sinkler and Broadnax. See n. 15, supra. The Penfield Better Homes projected price figures were for 1969, and must be assumed—even if subsidies might still be available—to have increased substantially by 1972, when the complaint was filed. Petitioner Reyes presents a special case: she states that her family has an income of over $14,000 per year, that she can

afford $231 per month for housing, and that, in the past and apparently now, she wants to purchase a residence. [T]he term "low and moderate income" is nowhere defined in the complaint; but Penfield Better Homes defined the term as between $5,000 and $8,000 per year. See n. 15, supra. Since that project was to be subsidized, presumably petitioner Reyes would have been ineligible. There is no indication that in nonsubsidized projects, removal of the challenged zoning restrictions—in 1972—would have reduced the price on new single-family residences to a level that petitioner Reyes thought she could afford.

18. [We] also note that zoning laws and their provisions, long considered essential to effective urban planning, are peculiarly within the province of state and local legislative authorities. They are, of course, subject to judicial review in a proper case. But citizens dissatisfied with provisions of such laws need not overlook the availability of the normal democratic process.

[For a case in which a potential home buyer demonstrated a "substantial probability" that he would have been able to purchase if rezoning were granted and thus "adequately averred an 'actionable causal relationship' between the zoning practice and his asserted injury," see *Arlington Heights v. Metropolitan Housing Dev. Corp.*, 429 U.S. 252, 97 S.Ct. 555, 50 L.Ed.2d 450 (1977). See also *Duke Power Co. v. Carolina Environmental Study Group, Inc.*, Part C infra, finding a "substantial likelihood" of "a 'but for' causal connection" between the injuries alleged and the challenged government action. For a lenient application of this doctrine, upholding standing to raise a nonconstitutional claim, see *Bryant v. Yellen*, 447 U.S. 352, 100 S.Ct. 2232, 65 L.Ed.2d 184 (1980)].

Metro-Act does not assert on behalf of its members any right of action under the 1968 Civil Rights [Act]. In this, we think, lies the critical distinction between *Trafficante* and the situation here. * * *

B. Petitioner Home Builders [asserted] standing to represent its member firms engaged in the development and construction of residential housing in the Rochester area, including Penfield. Home Builders alleged that the Penfield zoning restrictions [had] deprived some of its members of "substantial business opportunities and profits." * * *

Home Builders [can] have standing as the representative of its members only if it has alleged facts sufficient to make out a case or controversy had the members themselves brought suit. No such allegations were made. The complaint refers to no specific project of any of its members that is currently precluded either by the ordinance or by respondents' action in enforcing it. * * *

A like problem is presented with respect to petitioner Housing Council [which] includes in its membership "at least seventeen" groups that have been, are, or will be involved in the development of low- and moderate-cost housing. But, with one exception, the complaint does not suggest that any of these groups has focused its efforts on Penfield or has any specific plan to do so. [The] exception is the Penfield Better Homes Corporation. As we have observed above, it applied to respondents in late 1969 for a zoning variance to allow construction of a housing project designed for persons of moderate income. [It] is therefore possible that in 1969, or within a reasonable time thereafter, Better Homes itself and possibly Housing Council as its representative would have had standing to seek review of respondents' action. The complaint, however, does not allege that the Penfield Better Homes project remained viable in 1972 when this complaint was filed, or that respondents' actions continued to block a then current construction project.[23] In short, neither the complaint nor the record supplies any basis from which to infer that the controversy between respondents and Better Homes, however vigorous it may once have been, remained a live, concrete dispute when this complaint was filed. * * *

Affirmed.

MR. JUSTICE BRENNAN, with whom MR. JUSTICE WHITE and MR. JUSTICE MARSHALL join, dissenting.

[T]he opinion, which tosses out of court almost every conceivable kind of plaintiff who could be injured by the activity claimed to be unconstitutional, can be explained only by an indefensible hostility to the claim on the merits. [I]t is quite clear, when the record is viewed with dispassion, that at least three of the groups of plaintiffs have made allegations, and supported them with affidavits and documentary evidence, sufficient to survive a motion to dismiss for lack of standing.

[O]ne glaring defect of the Court's opinion is that it views each set of plaintiffs as if it were prosecuting a separate lawsuit, refusing to recognize that the interests are intertwined * * *. For example, the Court says that the low-income-minority plaintiffs have not alleged facts sufficient to show that but for the exclusionary practices claimed, they would be able to reside in Penfield. The Court then intimates that such a causal relationship could be shown only if "the

---

23. If it had been averred that the zoning ordinance or respondents were unlawfully blocking a pending construction project, there would be a further question as to whether Penfield Better Homes had employed available administrative remedies, and whether it should be required to do so before a federal court can intervene.

initial focus [is] on a particular project." Later, the Court objects to the ability of the Housing Council to prosecute the suit on behalf of its member, Penfield Better Homes Corporation, *despite* the fact that Better Homes *had* displayed an interest in a particular project, because that project was no longer live. Thus, we must suppose that even if the low-income plaintiffs had alleged a desire to live in the Better Homes project, that allegation would be insufficient because it appears that particular project might never be built. The rights of low-income-minority plaintiffs who desire to live in a locality, then, seem to turn on the willingness of a third party to litigate the legality of preclusion of a particular project, despite the fact that the third party may have no economic incentive to incur the costs of litigation with regard to one project, and despite the fact that the low-income-minority plaintiff's interest is *not* to live in a particular project but to live somewhere in the town in a dwelling they can afford.

[In] effect, the Court tells the low-income-minority and building company plaintiffs they will not be permitted to prove what they have alleged—that they could and would build and live in the town if changes were made in the zoning ordinance and its application—because they have not succeeded in breaching, before the suit was filed, the very barriers which are the subject of the suit.[c]

Low-Income and Minority Plaintiffs. [P]laintiffs Ortiz, Broadnax, Reyes, and Sinkler alleged that "as a result" of respondents' exclusionary practices, they were unable, despite attempts, to find the housing they desired in Penfield, and consequently have incurred high commuting expenses, received poorer municipal services, and, in some instances, been relegated to live in substandard [housing.]

Here, the very fact that, as the Court stresses, these petitioners' claim rests in part upon proving the intentions and capabilities of third parties to build in Penfield suitable housing which they can afford, coupled with the exclusionary character of the claim on the merits, makes it particularly inappropriate to assume that these petitioners' lack of specificity reflects a fatal weakness in their theory of causation.[7] Obviously they cannot be expected, prior to discovery and trial, to know the future plans of building companies, the precise details of

---

c. See also Tribe, *American Constitutional Law* 95 (1978): "[The] Court has not generally required identification of the specific transaction or project that would proceed unhindered but for a challenged rule or practice. Any contrary rule would confront excluded groups with a kind of Catch 22: the more severely and successfully exclusionary a challenged scheme is, the more difficult it would be to find insiders or developers willing to incur the inconvenience and expense of joining outsiders in designing a project or transaction that could meet any judicial test of specific identification."

7. The Court, glancing at the projects mentioned in the record which might have been built but for the exclusionary practices alleged, concludes that petitioners Ortiz and Broadnax earned too little to afford suitable housing in them, and that petitioner Reyes earned too much. As the Court implicitly acknowledges, petitioner Sinkler at least may well have been able to live in the Better Homes Project. Further, there appears in the record as it stands a Report of the Penfield

Housing Task Force [which] defines "moderate income families as families having incomes between $5,500 and $11,000 per year, depending on the size of the family," and moderate-income housing as housing "priced below $20,000 or [carrying] a retail price of less than $150 a month." [The] petitioners here under discussion fell within the Board's own definition of moderate-income families, except for petitioner Reyes * * *. And the Task Force Report *does* set out changes in the zoning ordinance and its application which could result in housing which moderate-income people could afford, even to the extent of setting out a budget provided by a builder for a house costing $18,900. The causation theory which the Court finds improbable, then, was adopted by a Task Force of the Town Board itself. Of course, we do not know at this stage whether the particular named plaintiffs would *certainly* have benefited from the changes recommended by the Task Force, but at least there is a good chance that, after discovery and trial, they could show they would.

the housing market in Penfield, or everything which has transpired in 15 years of application of the Penfield zoning ordinance, including every housing plan suggested and refused. To require them to allege such facts is to require them to prove their case on paper in order to get into court at all, reverting to the form of fact-pleading long abjured in the federal courts. * * *[d]

SIMON v. EASTERN KY. WELFARE RIGHTS ORG., 426 U.S. 26, 96 S.Ct. 1917, 48 L.Ed.2d 450 (1976), per POWELL, J., held that respondents—including persons who had been denied hospital services because of their indigency—had no standing to sue the Secretary of the Treasury under APA § 10 on the ground that a new Revenue Ruling, which granted favorable tax treatment to hospitals despite their refusal to give full service to indigents, was contrary to the Internal Revenue Code: "[T]he constitutional standing requirement under [APA § 10 requires] allegations which, if true, would establish that the plaintiff had been injured in fact by the action he sought to have reviewed. [The] necessity that the plaintiff who seeks to invoke judicial power stand to profit in some personal interest remains an Art. III requirement." Relying on *Warth*, the Court reasoned that "Art. III still requires that a federal court act only to redress injury that fairly can be traced to the challenged action of the defendant, and not injury that results from the independent action of some third party not before the court.[b]

"The complaint here alleged only that petitioners, by the adoption of Revenue Ruling 69–545, had 'encouraged' hospitals to deny service to indigents. The implicit corollary of this allegation is that a grant of respondents' requested relief, resulting in a requirement that all hospitals serve indigents as a condition to favorable tax treatment, would 'discourage' hospitals from denying their services to respondents. But it [is] purely speculative whether the denials of service specified in the complaint fairly can be traced to petitioners' 'encouragement' or instead result from decisions made by the hospitals without regard to the tax implications.

"It is equally speculative whether the desired exercise of the court's remedial powers in this suit would result in the availability to respondents of such services. So far as the complaint sheds light, it is just as plausible that the hospitals to which respondents may apply for service would elect to forego favorable tax treatment to avoid the undetermined financial drain of an increase in the level of uncompensated services." Accordingly, the complaint should be dismissed.[c]

d. The dissenting opinion of Douglas, J., is omitted.

b. The Court recognized "Congress' power to create new interests the invasion of which will confer standing. See *Trafficante*. [But when] Congress has so acted, the requirements of Art. III remain: 'the plaintiff still must allege a distinct and palpable injury to himself, even if it is an injury shared by a large class of other possible litigants.' *Warth*. See also *SCRAP*; cf. *Sierra Club*."

Must the "distinct and palpable injury" alleged by plaintiff at the time suit is filed continue throughout the litigation? See *United States Parole Comm'n v. Geraghty*, fn. g, Part I, supra.

c. Stewart, J., joined the Court's opinion, adding "that I cannot now imagine a case, at least outside the First Amendment area, where a person whose own tax liability was not affected ever could have standing to litigate the federal tax liability of someone else."

See also *Los Angeles v. Lyons*, 461 U.S. 95, 103 S.Ct. 1660, 75 L.Ed.2d 675 (1983) (although person who was subject to allegedly unconstitutional "chokehold" by police after being stopped for traffic violation has standing to sue for damages, that does not constitute sufficiently real and immediate threat of future injury to justify federal injunctive relief). Marshall, J., joined by Brennan, Blackmun and Stevens, JJ., dissented. For criticism of

BRENNAN, J., joined by Marshall, J., dissented from the Court's reasoning: "Any prudential, nonconstitutional considerations that underlay the Court's disposition of the injury in fact standing requirement in cases such as *Linda R.S.* and *Warth* are simply inapposite when review is sought under a congressionally enacted statute conferring standing and providing for judicial review. In such a case considerations respecting 'the allocation of power at the national level [and] a shift away from a democratic form of government,' *Richardson* (Powell, J., concurring), are largely ameliorated. * * *

"Our previous decisions concerning standing to sue under the Administrative Procedure Act conclusively show that the injury in fact demanded is the constitutional minimum identified in *Baker v. Carr*—the allegation of such a 'personal stake in the outcome of the controversy as to ensure' concrete adverseness. *Sierra Club.* True, the Court has required that the person seeking review allege that he personally has suffered or will suffer the injury sought to be avoided, *Sierra Club.* But there can be no doubt that respondents here, by demonstrating a connection between the disputed ruling and the hospitals affecting them, could have adequately served the policy implicated by the pleading requirement of *Sierra Club*—putting 'the decision as to whether review will be sought in the hands of those who have a direct stake in the outcome.' In such a case respondents would not be attempting merely to 'vindicate their own value preferences through the judicial process.' * * *

"Furthermore, our decisions regarding standing to sue in actions brought under the Administrative Procedure Act make plain that standing is not to be denied merely because [the] administrative action ultimately affects the complaining party only through responses to incentives by third parties * * *. *SCRAP.* And the ultimate harm to respondents threatened here is obviously much more 'direct and perceptible' and the 'line of causation' less 'attenuated' than that found sufficient for standing in *SCRAP.* * * *

"Of course the most disturbing aspect of today's opinion is the Court's insistence on resting its decision regarding standing squarely on the irreducible Art. III minimum of injury in fact, thereby effectively placing its holding beyond congressional power to rectify. Thus, any time Congress chooses to legislate in favor of certain interests by setting up a scheme of incentives for third parties, judicial review of administrative action that allegedly frustrates the congressionally intended objective will be denied, because any complainant will be required to make an almost impossible showing."

In ALLEN v. WRIGHT, 468 U.S. 737, 104 S.Ct. 3315, 82 L.Ed.2d 556 (1984), parents of black public school children in districts in the process of desegregating brought a "nationwide class action" seeking (1) a declaratory judgment that IRS guidelines and procedures were inadequate "to fulfill its obligation to deny tax-exempt status to racially discriminatory private schools," and (2) an injunction requiring the IRS to deny tax exemptions to a greater number of private schools. The Court, per O'CONNOR, J., held that respondents had no standing.

First, as for their "claim of stigmatic injury, or denigration, suffered by all members of a racial group when the Government discriminates on the basis of race," respondents "do not allege a stigmatic injury suffered as a direct result of having personally been denied equal treatment. [If] the abstract stigmatic injury were cognizable, standing would extend nationwide to all members of the

Lyons, see Fallon, *Of Justiciability, Remedies, and Public Law Litigation: Notes on the Ju-* risprudence of *Lyons*, 59 N.Y.U.L.Rev. 1 (1984); Tribe, *Constitutional Choices* 99 (1985).

particular racial groups against which the Government was alleged to be discriminating by its grant of tax exemption to a racially discriminatory school, regardless of the location of that school. * * * Constitutional limits on the role of federal courts preclude [this]."

Second, as for their claim "that the federal tax exemptions to racially discriminatory private schools in their communities impair their ability to have their public schools desegregated," under *Eastern Ky.,* the "injury alleged is not fairly traceable to the Government conduct respondents challenge": "The diminished ability of respondent's children to receive a desegregated education would be fairly traceable to unlawful IRS grants of tax exemptions only if there were enough racially discriminatory private schools receiving tax exemptions in respondents' communities for withdrawal of those exemptions to make an appreciable difference in public-school integration. Respondents have made no such allegation. It is, first, uncertain how many racially discriminatory private schools are in fact receiving tax exemptions. Moreover, it is entirely speculative [whether] withdrawal of a tax exemption from any particular school would lead the school to change its policies. It is just as speculative whether any given parent of a child attending such a private school would decide to transfer the child to public school as a result of any changes in educational or financial policy made by the private school once it was threatened with loss of tax-exempt status. It is also pure speculation whether, in a particular community, a large enough number of the numerous relevant school officials and parents would reach decisions that collectively would have a significant impact on the racial composition of the public schools.

"[R]espondents' complaint, which aims at nationwide relief and does not challenge particular identified unlawful IRS actions, alleges no connection between the asserted desegregation injury and the challenged IRS conduct direct enough to overcome the substantial separation-of-powers barriers to a suit seeking an injunction to reform administrative procedures."

BRENNAN, J., dissented: "Viewed in light of the injuries they claim, the respondents have alleged a direct causal relationship between the government action they challenge and the injury they suffer: their inability to receive an education in a racially integrated school is directly and adversely affected by the tax-exempt status granted by the IRS to racially discriminatory schools in their respective school districts. Commonsense alone would recognize that the elimination of tax-exempt status for racially discriminatory private schools would serve to lessen the impact that those institutions have in defeating efforts to desegregate the public schools. [With] all due respect, the Court has either misread the complaint or is improperly requiring the respondents to prove their case on the merits in order to defeat a motion to dismiss. For example, the respondents specifically refer by name to at least 32 private schools that discriminate on the basis of race and yet continue to benefit illegally from tax-exempt status. Eighteen of those schools [are] located in [Memphis] which has been the subject of several court orders to desegregate. * * *[6]

"[By] interposing its own version of pleading formalities between the respondents and the federal courts, the Court not only has denied access to litigants who properly seek vindication of their constitutional rights, but has also ignored

---

6. Even if the Court were correct in its conclusion that there is an insufficient factual basis alleged in the complaint, the proper dis- position would be to remand in order to afford the respondents an opportunity to amend their complaint.

the important historical role that the courts have played in the Nation's efforts to eliminate racial discrimination from our schools."

STEVENS, J., joined by Blackmun, J., agreeing with Brennan, J.'s general analysis, also dissented: "If racially discriminatory private schools lose the 'cash grants' that flow from the operation of the statutes, the education they provide will become more expensive and hence less of their services will be purchased [, thus] reducing their competitiveness for parents seeking 'a racially segregated alternative' to public schools, which is what respondents have alleged many white parents in desegregating school districts seek. [Thus], the laws of economics * * * compel the conclusion that the injury respondents have alleged—the increased segregation of their children's schools because of the ready availability of private schools that admit whites only—will be redressed if these schools' operations are inhibited through the denial of preferential tax treatment.[6]"[a]

Marshall, J., did not participate.

Notes and Questions

1. *"Causation."* How broad are the consequences for the law of standing of the "causation" requirement imposed by *Warth, Eastern Ky.* and *Allen?* Consider 90 Harv.L.Rev. 210 (1976): "As a practical matter, the [requirement] will be largely insignificant in most cases in which private parties seek review of government actions. Where the plaintiff sues the government for an injury inflicted directly by an agency, it is axiomatic that any causation requirement is satisfied and that a court order to the government will affect the alleged harm. Indeed, only in those cases in which a plaintiff sues the government to complain of an injury suffered as a result of the impact of government action on third parties not before the court will the causation/relief issue arise."

2. *Congressional power and Art. III.* (a) Given *Trafficante* and *SCRAP*, to what extent does *Eastern Ky.* limit congressional power to grant standing? For example, suppose Congress authorized "any citizen" to challenge the constitutionality of armed forces reserve status for members of Congress (*Reservists*), or the constitutionality of the secrecy provisions of the CIA Act (*Richardson*)? Any citizen who alleges that such policies diminish his "ability to persuade a member of Congress to vote in a particular way"? Would such litigants allege "concrete harm" (*Reservists*)? A "distinct and palpable injury" (*Eastern Ky.*, fn. b)? What is the significance of *Warth's* categorizing the "generalized grievance" obstacle to standing as "prudential" rather than "constitutional"? See Bice, *Congress' Power to Confer Standing in the Federal Courts,* in Constitutional Government in America 291 (Collins ed. 1980); Nichol, *Standing on the Constitution: The Supreme Court and Valley Forge,* 61 N.C.L.Rev. 798 (1983).

---

6. [W]hile here the source of the causal nexus is the price that white parents must pay to obtain a segregated education, which is inextricably intertwined with the school's tax status, in *Eastern Ky.* the plaintiffs were seeking free care, which hospitals could decide not to provide for any number of reasons unrelated to their tax status. Moreover, in *Eastern Ky.*, the hospitals had to spend money in order to obtain charitable status. Therefore, they had an economic incentive to forego preferential treatment. [Here] the financial incentives run in only one direction.

a. Stevens, J. "doubt[ed] that a nationwide class would be appropriate, but at this stage respondents' allegations of injury must be taken as true, and hence we must assume that respondents can prove the existence of a nationwide policy and its alleged effects."

Is such proof provided by "commonsense alone" (Brennan, J.) or by "the laws of economics" (Stevens, J.)?

(b) What result in *Eastern Ky.* if respondents had sued under a statute specifically conferring standing on such persons instead of under APA § 10 which authorizes judicial review only for persons "adversely affected or aggrieved by agency action"? What result after *Allen* if Congress authorizes "any member of a minority racial group" to challenge "any government discrimination against that group"? If Congress believes that the case-or-controversy requirement is satisfied, should (must) the Court defer (at least to some degree) to the legislative determination? See fn. b in *Trafficante;* cf. *Marbury v. Madison.* Even if the Court agrees that a congressionally authorized suit satisfies Art. III, must the Court decide it despite its own reservations based on "prudential" principles of "self-restraint"? See Monaghan, *Constitutional Adjudication: The Who and When,* 82 Yale L.J. 1363 (1973).

(c) Of what significance is the fact that the question presented—with or without congressional authorization—is constitutional (as in *Richardson* and *Reservists*) rather than one only of statutory interpretation (as in *Trafficante* and *SCRAP*)? That the Court "is asked to undertake constitutional adjudication, the most important and delicate of its responsibilities" (*Reservists*)? That the Court "has followed a policy of strict necessity in disposing of constitutional issues" (*Ashwander*)? Compare Scott, *Standing in the Supreme Court—A Functional Analysis,* 86 Harv.L.Rev. 645 (1973) with Broderick, *The Warth Optional Standing Doctrine: Return to Judicial Supremacy?* 25 Cath.U.L.Rev. 467 (1976). See note 4 after *Poe v. Ullman,* Part C infra.

B. ASSERTION OF THIRD PARTY RIGHTS

BARROWS v. JACKSON, 346 U.S. 249, 73 S.Ct. 1031, 97 L.Ed. 1586 (1953): A homeowner who had agreed with other homeowners in the neighborhood, by signing a restrictive covenant, not to sell her home to a Negro, broke the covenant and was sued for damages for breach by a co-covenantor. Earlier, *Shelley v. Kraemer,* p. 1094 supra, had held "that racial restrictive covenants could not be enforced [by injunction] against Negro purchasers because such enforcement would constitute state action denying equal protection of the laws to the Negroes."

The Court, per MINTON, J., first held that "if a state court awards damages for breach of a restrictive covenant, a prospective seller of restricted land will either refuse to sell to non-Caucasians or else will require non-Caucasions to pay a higher price," thus violating the equal protection rights of non-Caucasions. But "no non-Caucasion is before the Court," only the Caucasian signatories to the covenant.

"Ordinarily, one may not claim standing in this Court to vindicate the constitutional rights of some third party [even] though [the person before the Court] will suffer a direct substantial injury." "But in the instant case, we are faced with a unique situation in which it is the action of the state *court* which might result in a denial of constitutional rights and in which it would be difficult if not impossible for the persons whose rights are asserted to present their grievance before any court. Under the peculiar circumstances of this case, we believe the reasons which underlie our rule denying standing to raise another's rights, which is only a rule of practice, are outweighed by the need to protect the fundamental rights which would be denied by permitting the damages action to be maintained."

The Court observed that restrictive covenants are "widely condemned by the courts" and that the selling homeowner "is the only effective adversary of the unworthy covenant in its last stand." [a]

GRISWOLD v. CONNECTICUT, p. 126 supra, held that birth control clinic officials convicted of abetting married persons in violating the same statute barring use of contraceptives, had standing to assert the constitutional rights of the married persons: "Certainly the accessory should have standing to assert that the offense which he is charged with assisting is not, or cannot constitutionally be a crime. [The] rights of husband and wife, pressed here, are likely to be diluted or adversely affected unless those rights are considered in a suit involving those who have this kind of confidential relation to them."

EISENSTADT v. BAIRD, p. 138 supra, held that a person, convicted for violating a statute forbidding distribution of contraceptive materials to unmarried persons, had standing to assert the constitutional rights of the unmarried persons: "Enforcement of the Massachusetts statute will materially impair the ability of single persons to obtain contraceptives."

Consider Hart & Wechsler's *The Federal Courts and the Federal System* 190 (2d ed. 1973): "Isn't the real question whether the constitutional right of unmarried persons to have contraceptives—if it exists—substantively implies constitutional protection against conviction for supplying contraceptives to such persons? [I]f the state cannot constitutionally prohibit unmarried persons from possessing and using contraceptives, the question whether it can nevertheless prohibit distribution to them depends, does it not, on the substantive scope and purpose of the constitutional policy involved? And doesn't the formulation of the issue in terms of whether a defendant has standing to raise the rights of recipients obscure the true nature of the issue?"

In SINGLETON v. WULFF, 428 U.S. 106, 96 S.Ct. 2868, 49 L.Ed.2d 826 (1976), BLACKMUN, J., joined by Brennan, White and Marshall, JJ., ruled that doctors—who alleged that they "provided, and anticipate providing abortions to welfare patients who are eligible for Medicaid"—had standing to challenge a statute denying Medicaid benefits for abortions:

"A. [The] physicians suffer concrete injury from the operation of the challenged statute. [The] relationship between the parties is classically adverse, and there clearly exists [a] case or controversy in the constitutional sense.

"B. [T]he Court of Appeals also accorded the doctors standing to assert [the] rights of their patients. * * *

"[T]he Court has looked primarily to two factual elements to determine whether the [general rule against assertion of third party rights] should apply in a particular case. The first is the relationship of the litigant to the person whose right he seeks to assert. If the enjoyment of the right is inextricably bound up with the activity the litigant wishes to pursue, the court at least can be sure that its construction of the right is not unnecessary in the sense that the right's enjoyment will be unaffected by the outcome of the suit. Furthermore, the relationship between the litigant and the third party may be such that the former is fully, or very nearly, as effective a proponent of the right as the latter. [See *Griswold; Eisenstadt; Barrows.*] [a]

"The other factual element to which the Court has looked is the ability of the third party to assert his own right. Even where the relationship is close, the reasons for requiring persons to assert their own rights will generally still apply. If there is some genuine obstacle to such assertion, however, the third party's absence from court loses its tendency to suggest that his right is not truly at stake, or truly important to him, and the party who is in court becomes by the default the right's best available proponent. [See *Eisenstadt; Barrows.*][6]

"Application of these principles to the present case quickly yields its proper result. The closeness of the relationship is patent. [A] woman cannot safely secure an abortion without the aid of a physician, and an impecunious woman cannot easily secure an abortion without the physician's being paid by the State.

* * *

"As to the woman's assertion of her own rights, there are several obstacles. For one thing she may be chilled from such assertion by a desire to protect the very privacy of her decision from the publicity of a court suit. A second obstacle is [that in only] a few months, at the most, after the maturing of the decision to undergo an abortion, her right thereto will have been irrevocably lost, assuming, as it seems fair to assume, that unless the impecunious woman can establish Medicaid eligibility she must forgo abortion. It is true that these obstacles are not insurmountable. Suit may be brought under a pseudonym, as so frequently has been done. A woman who is no longer pregnant may nonetheless retain the right to litigate the point because it is 'capable of repetition yet evading review.' *Roe v. Wade.* And it may be that a class could be assembled, whose fluid membership always included some women with live claims. But if the assertion of the right is to be 'representative' to such an extent anyway, there seems little loss in terms of effective advocacy from allowing its assertion by a physician."[b]

POWELL, J., joined by Burger, C.J., and Stewart and Rehnquist, JJ., agreed with Part A but dissented as to Part B because "of whether it is prudent to proceed to decision on particular issues even at the instance of a party whose Art. III standing is clear. * * * [T]he litigation of third-party rights cannot be justified in this case. [T]he 'obstacles' identified by the plurality as justifying departure from the general rule simply are not significant."

seeking declaratory and injunctive relief, see *Craig v. Boren*, p. 956 supra (seller of beer has standing to assert males' equal protection claim against law prohibiting sale of beer to males under age 21 and females under age 18) and *Carey v. Population Services Int'l*, p. 139 supra (seller of contraceptives has standing to assert potential purchasers' right of privacy claims against law regulating distribution of contraceptives). These cases reasoned that if the sellers could not challenge the laws they would be deterred from selling the products and that this "would result indirectly in the violation of third parties' rights."

6. Mr. Justice Powell objects [that] our prior cases allow assertion of third party rights only when such assertion by the third parties themselves would be "in all practicable terms impossible." Carefully analyzed, our cases do not go that far. The Negro real-estate pur-

chaser in *Barrows*, if he could prove that the racial covenant alone stood in the way of his purchase (as presumably he could easily have done, given the amicable posture of the seller in that case), could surely have sought a declaration of its invalidity or an injunction against its enforcement. [The] recipients of contraceptives in *Eisenstadt* (or their counterparts in *Griswold* and *Doe*, for that matter) could have sought similar relief as necessary to the enjoyment of their constitutional rights. The point is not that these were easy alternatives, but that they differed only in the degree of difficulty, if they differed at all, from the alternative in this case of the women themselves seeking a declaration or injunction that would force the State to pay the doctors for their abortions.

b. Stevens, J., concurred in the result but not all of the reasoning in Part B.

C. TIMING OF ADJUDICATION

UNITED PUBLIC WORKERS v. MITCHELL, 330 U.S. 75, 67 S.Ct. 556, 91 L.Ed.2d 754 (1947): Appellants, federal civil service employees, sought a federal declaratory judgment that the Hatch Act's prohibition against taking "any active part in political management or in political campaigns" violated their first amendment rights. They also requested injunctive relief. Only one appellant (Poole) had actually violated the Act. The others alleged that they desired to do so by, inter alia, serving as party officials, writing articles and circulating petitions to support candidates, acting as poll watchers, transporting voters to the polls.[a] The Court, per REED, J., held that "these appellants seem clearly to seek advisory opinions" and that "the facts of their personal interest in their civil rights, of the general threat of possible interference with those rights by the Civil Service Commission under its rules, if specified things are done by appellants, does not make a justiciable case or controversy. * * * We can only speculate as to the kinds of political activity the appellants desire to engage in or as to the contents of their proposed public statements or the circumstances of their publication. [Such] generality of objection is really an attack on the political expediency of the Hatch Act, not the presentation of legal issues. It is beyond the competence of courts to render such a decision. [No] threat of interference by the Commission with rights of these appellants appears beyond that implied by the existence of the law and the regulations [and a] hypothetical threat is not enough."

Poole, however, "has been charged by the Commission with political activity and a proposed order for his removal from his position adopted subject to his right under Commission procedure to reply * * *. Since Poole admits that he violated the rule against political activity and that removal from office is therefore mandatory under the [act], we see no reason why a declaratory judgment action, even though constitutional issues are involved, does not lie." The Court then rejected Poole's challenge on the merits.

DOUGLAS, J., filed the principal dissent: "What these appellants propose to do is plain enough. If they do what they propose to do, it is clear that they will be discharged * * *. The threat against them is real not fanciful, immediate not remote. The case is therefore an actual not a hypothetical one. [T]o require these employees first to suffer the hardship of a discharge is not only to make them incur a penalty; it makes inadequate, if not wholly illusory, any legal remedy which they may have. Men who must sacrifice their means of livelihood in order to test their rights to their jobs must either pursue prolonged and expensive litigation as unemployed persons or pull up their roots, change their life careers, and seek employment in other fields. At least to the average person in the lower income groups the burden of taking that course is irreparable injury [4] * * *." [b]

---

a. One did allege that, at the last congressional election, he wanted to be a poll watcher but was informed by a Civil Service Commission official "that if I used my watcher's certificate, the Civil Service Commission would see that I was dismissed from my job." This matter, the Court found, "had long been moot when this complaint was filed."

4. If the prayer for declaratory relief be considered separately from the prayer for an injunction, as it may be, allegations of irreparable injury threatened are not required.

b. Black, J., agreed with Douglas, J. "that all the petitioners' complaints state a case or controversy" and further that "the challenged provision is unconstitutional on its face." Rutledge, J., agreed with Black, J., as to Poole; as to the others, however, the controversy "is not yet appropriate for the discretionary exercise of declaratory judgment jurisdiction."

Notes and Questions

1. *The Court's rationale.* Specifically, what more could appellants have done? Does the majority accept the proposition that "what these appellants propose to do is plain enough [and] if they do what they propose to do, it is clear that they will be discharged"? If not, should appellants have written their proposed speeches and letters and submitted them to the Court? Or should they have first submitted them to the Commission? Suppose the Commission took the position that it would not give "advisory opinions"? Or is the Court's requirement that all cases must be as "ripe" as Poole's in order to be adjudicated?

2. ADLER v. BOARD OF EDUC., (1952), p. 459 supra, upheld a state law disqualifying from employment in public schools any persons who advocate overthrow of the government by force, or who belong to an organization which so advocates, or who utter any treasonable or seditious words, or do any treasonable or seditious acts. Appellants seeking a declaratory judgment in state court were taxpayers, parents of attending school children, and teachers. The Court discussed only the merits despite FRANKFURTER, J.'s dissent that the case should be dismissed for want of "standing of the parties and ripeness of the constitutional question." In addition to arguing that both the scope of the statutory provisions and the definition of key terms were unclear, he stated: "The allegations in the present action fall short of those found insufficient in [*Mitchell*]. These teachers do not allege that they have engaged in proscribed conduct or that they have any intention to do so. They do not suggest that they have been, or are, deterred from supporting causes or from joining organizations for fear of the [statute's] interdict, except to say generally that the system complained of will have this effect on teachers as a group. They do not assert that they are threatened with action under the law, or that steps are imminent whereby they would incur the hazard of punishment for conduct innocent at the time."

Was *Mitchell* "overruled"? [c] Consider Scharpf, *Judicial Review and the Political Question: A Functional Analysis*, 75 Yale L.J. 517, 528–32 (1966): "[T]he public interest in responsible and realistic constitutional decision is much too serious to be left unprotected against the accidents of ordinary litigation. If this protection cannot be afforded by an enlargement of the Court's jurisdiction to permit the most competent parties to sue, or by an enlargement of the Court's procedural powers to conduct an independent investigation of facts and issues, then it seems reasonable to expect that this protection will be provided by restrictive techniques which will permit the Court to screen the cases in order to select those which provide an adequate basis for the responsible performance of the reviewing function. In order to qualify for the exercise of judicial review, the factual situation of the case would have to illuminate in a concrete fashion the practical implications of the constitutional issue, and the litigants themselves would have to be vitally and antagonistically interested, not only in the outcome of their lawsuit, but in the determination of the constitutional issue as such. I submit that it is this screening function which is being served by the Court's use of the nonconstitutional rules of standing, ripeness and adversariness. [In *Mitchell*] the Court may well have regarded the constitutional balance

Frankfurter, J., concurred in the Court's opinion. Murphy and Jackson, JJ., took no part.

c. Note the 1973 description of *Mitchell* in *United States Civil Service Comm'n v. National Ass'n of Letter Carriers*, p. 637 supra (again upholding the Hatch Act): "[*Mitchell*] determined that with respect to all but one of the plaintiffs there was no case or controversy present within the meaning of Art. III."

between the political rights of civil servants and the legitimate public interest in a neutral civil service as an extremely close one, depending very much upon the actual scope of enforcement and upon the concrete nature of the activities against which sanctions were to be applied. In [*Adler*], the *Mitchell* rule should have applied a fortiori. [But, for the Court majority,] the statute was clearly constitutional * * *. Justices Black and Douglas, dissenting, also saw no reason to worry about standing or ripeness. For them the statute was clearly unconstitutional * * *.[d] The conclusion seems inevitable that Justice Frankfurter alone advocated avoidance because he alone defined the substantive issues in terms of a close balance between the equally legitimate interests of society in its self-preservation and of the teachers in their freedom of thought, inquiry and expression. Thus, in order to strike this balance in the particular case, Frankfurter would have had to know much more about the actual practices of enforcement and the degree of surveillance to which the teachers would be subjected than the bare text of an unenforced statute permitted him to know." See also Albert, note 1 after *Reservists,* at 1158–60.

3. *The discretionary exercise of declaratory judgment jurisdiction.* Should this be influenced by the fact that a constitutional question is involved? See Goldberg-Ambrose, *Access to the Federal Courts in Constitutional Cases,* in Constitutional Government in America 311 (Collins ed. 1980). That the case arises in a state court (*Adler*) rather than a federal court (*Mitchell*)? That the case concerns a state statute rather than a federal statute? Is the *difficulty* of the constitutional question a relevant inquiry? The matter of how *many* people, other than the litigants, will be affected by decision? See *Golden v. Zwickler,* 394 U.S. 103, 89 S.Ct. 956, 22 L.Ed.2d 113 (1969). The nature of the asserted constitutional right? The fact that Congress wishes a determination of constitutionality as quickly as possible? See *Buckley v. Valeo,* 424 U.S. 1, 113–18, 96 S.Ct. 612, 680–82, 46 L.Ed.2d 659 (1976). Whether the Court is inclined to hold the statute valid or invalid? Do some (all) of these questions go beyond the "principled" discretion of the Court? See note 4 after *Poe v. Ullman,* infra. See generally Varat, supra.

LAIRD v. TATUM
408 U.S. 1, 92 S.Ct. 2318, 33 L.Ed.2d 154 (1972).

Mr. Chief Justice Burger delivered the opinion of the Court.

Respondents brought this class action in the District Court seeking declaratory and injunctive relief on their claim that their rights were being invaded by the Army's alleged "surveillance of lawful civilian political activity." * * *

The system put into operation as a result of the Army's 1967 experience [with civil disorders] consisted essentially of the collection of information about public activities that were thought to have at least some potential for civil disorder, the reporting of that information to Army Intelligence headquarters at Fort Holabird, Maryland, the dissemination of these reports from headquarters to major Army posts around the country, and the storage of the reported information in a computer data bank located at Fort Holabird. [T]he principal sources of information were the news media and publications in general circulation. Some of the information came from Army Intelligence agents who attended meetings that were open to the public and who wrote field reports describing the meetings, giving such data as the name of the sponsoring organization, the

---

d. For detailed consideration of the question of whether laws allegedly violative of the first amendment should be held "void on their face," see p. 405 supra.

identity of speakers, the approximate number of persons in attendance, and an indication of whether any disorder occurred. And still other information was provided to the Army by civilian law enforcement agencies. * * *

By early 1970 [the] Army, in the course of a review of the system, ordered a significant reduction in its scope[:] "[R]eports [will] be limited [to] outbreaks of violence or incidents with a high potential for violence beyond the capability of state and local police and the National Guard to control. These reports [will] not be placed in a computer [and] are destroyed 60 days after publication or 60 days after the end of the disturbance. This limited reporting system will ensure that the Army is prepared to respond to whatever directions the President may issue in civil disturbance situations and without watching lawful activities of civilians." * * *[5]

In reversing, the Court of Appeals noted that [respondents] "freely admit that they complain of no specific action of the Army against them. [There] is no evidence of illegal or unlawful surveillance activities. [So] far as is yet shown, the information gathered is nothing more than a good newspaper reporter would be able to gather by attendance at public meetings and the clipping of articles from publications available on any newsstand."

[T]he Court of Appeals [also] had this to say: "[While respondents] do indeed argue that in the future it is possible that information relating to matters far beyond the responsibilities of the military may be misused by the military to the detriment of these [respondents], yet [respondents] do not attempt to establish this as a definitely foreseeable event, or to base their complaint on this ground. Rather, [respondents] contend that the *present existence of this system* of gathering and distributing information, allegedly far beyond the mission requirements of the Army, constitutes an impermissible burden on [respondents] and other persons similarly situated which exercises a *present inhibiting effect* on their full expression and utilization of their First Amendment rights." * * *

In recent years this Court has found in a number of cases that constitutional violations may arise from the deterrent, or "chilling," effect of governmental regulations that fall short of a direct prohibition against the exercise of First Amendment rights. E.g., *Keyishian v. Board of Regents,* [p. 636 supra]. In none of these cases, however, did the chilling effect arise merely from the individual's knowledge that a governmental agency was engaged in certain activities or from the individual's concomitant fear that, armed with the fruits of those activities, the agency might in the future take some *other* and additional action detrimental to that individual. Rather, in each of these cases, the challenged exercise of governmental power was regulatory, proscriptive, or compulsory in nature, and the complainant was either presently or prospectively subject to the regulations, proscriptions, or compulsions * * *.

[T]hese decisions have in no way eroded the "established principle that to entitle a private individual to invoke the judicial power to determine the validity of executive or legislative action he must show that he has sustained or is immediately in danger of sustaining a direct injury as the result of that action."

---

5. In the course of the oral argument, the District Judge [asked] what exactly it was in the Army's activities that tended to chill respondents and others in the exercise of their constitutional rights. Counsel responded that it was "precisely the threat in this case that *in some future civil disorder* of some kind, the Army is going to come in with its list of trouble-makers [and] go rounding up people and putting them in military prisons somewhere." (Emphasis added.) To this the court responded that "we still sit here with the writ of habeas corpus." At another point, counsel for respondents took a somewhat different approach in arguing that "*we're not quite sure exactly what they have in mind* and that is precisely what causes [the] chilling effect." (Emphasis added.)

The respondents do not meet this test; [their] alleged "chilling" effect may perhaps be seen as arising from respondents' very perception of the system as inappropriate to the Army's role under our form of government, or as arising from respondents' beliefs that it is inherently dangerous for the military to be concerned with activities in the civilian sector, or as arising from respondents' less generalized yet speculative apprehensiveness that the Army may at some future date misuse the information in some way that would cause direct harm to respondents.[7] Allegations of a subjective "chill" are not an adequate substitute for a claim of specific present objective harm or a threat of specific future harm; "the federal courts established pursuant to Article III of the Constitution do not render advisory opinions." *Mitchell.*

Stripped to its essentials, what respondents appear to be seeking is a broad scale investigation, conducted by themselves as private parties armed with the subpoena power of a federal district court and the power of cross-examination, to probe into the Army's intelligence-gathering activities, with the district court determining at the conclusion of that investigation the extent to which those activities may or may not be appropriate to the Army's mission. * * *

Carried to its logical end, this approach would have the federal courts as virtually continuing monitors of the wisdom and soundness of Executive action; such a role is appropriate for the Congress [not for] the judiciary, absent actual present or immediately threatened injury resulting from unlawful governmental action.

[O]n this record the respondents have not presented a case for resolution by the courts. * * *

Reversed.

MR. JUSTICE DOUGLAS, with whom MR. JUSTICE MARSHALL concurs, dissenting.

[When] refusal of the Court to pass on the constitutionality of an Act under the normal consideration of forbearance "would itself have an inhibitory effect on freedom of speech" then the Court will act. * * *

One need not wait to sue until he loses his job or until his reputation is defamed. To withhold standing to sue until that time arrives would in practical effect immunize from judicial scrutiny all surveillance activities regardless of their misuse and their deterrent effect. * * *

The present controversy is not a remote, imaginary conflict. Respondents were targets of the Army's surveillance. First, the surveillance was not casual but massive and comprehensive. Second, the intelligence reports were regularly and widely circulated and were exchanged with reports of the FBI, state and municipal police departments, and the CIA. Third, the Army's surveillance was not collecting material in public records but staking-out teams of agents, infiltrating undercover agents, creating command posts inside meetings, posing as

---

7. Not only have respondents left somewhat unclear the precise connection between the mere existence of the challenged system and their own alleged chill, but they have also cast considerable doubt on whether they themselves are in fact suffering from any such chill. [At] the oral argument before the District Court, counsel for respondents admitted that his clients were "not people, obviously, who are cowed and chilled"; indeed, they were quite willing "to open themselves up to public investigation and public scrutiny."

But, counsel argued, these respondents must "represent millions of Americans not nearly as forward [and] courageous" as themselves. [Even] assuming a justiciable controversy, if respondents themselves are not chilled, but seek only to represent those "millions" whom they believe are so chilled, respondents clearly lack that "personal stake in the outcome of the controversy" essential to standing. [A] litigant "has standing to seek redress for injuries done to him, but may not seek redress for injuries done to others."

press photographers and newsmen, posing as TV newsmen, posing as students, shadowing public figures.

Finally, [reports] of the Army have been "taken from the Intelligence Command's highly inaccurate civil disturbance teletype and filed in Army dossiers on persons who have held, or were being considered for, security clearances, thus contaminating what are supposed to be investigative reports with unverified gossip and rumor. This practice directly jeopardized the employment and employment opportunities of persons seeking sensitive positions with the federal government or defense industry."

[The] fact that since this litigation started the Army's surveillance may have been cut back is not an end of the matter. Whether there has been an actual cutback or whether the announcements are merely a ruse can be determined only after a hearing in the District Court. * * *[a]

Notes and Questions

1. *Consistency with prior decisions.* Does *Tatum* confirm the continued vitality of *Mitchell*? Could it be argued in *Tatum* (as Douglas, J., argued in *Mitchell*) that what respondents "propose to do is plain enough" and if they do so "it is clear that they will be discharged from their positions"? Consider 86 Harv.L.Rev. 134 (1972): "Granted, misuse in the *Tatum* situation is conjectural even after the protected activity is pursued, whereas injury for violation of a regulatory or prohibitive statute is clear and immediate. But the temptation to avoid the protected activity which risks unfavorable consequences may be no less when those consequences are undefined; indeed, it will be all the greater if the lack of definition implies the absence of an upward limit on injury."

To what extent did *Tatum* turn on the fact that respondents sought to speak not simply for themselves but for "millions of Americans not nearly as courageous"? Consider id. at 135: "Any decision on the merits would have required a court to weigh in some fashion the first amendment injury against the sufficiency of the Government's interest in military surveillance. Such an undertaking would have necessitated a determination of the relevance of the information gathered to the alleged governmental interest in the suppression of domestic insurrection without the application of blind force. Since the plaintiffs were bringing a class action seeking an injunction of all military surveillance activity and the destruction of all files unrelated to the Army's legitimate mission, this determination would have required consideration of an enormous bulk of information." Is this factor relevant to the discretionary exercise of declaratory judgment jurisdiction? Does it distinguish *Tatum* from *Mitchell*? From *Adler*? Or does this factor go to the substance of the first amendment's scope? Reconsider Scharpf, note 2 after *Mitchell*.

2. *Remote or hypothetical threat of injury.* (a) In O'SHEA v. LITTLETON, 414 U.S. 488, 94 S.Ct. 669, 38 L.Ed.2d 674 (1974), black and white residents who had protested racial discrimination in Cairo, Illinois obtained a federal injunction against state judicial officers, alleging a deliberate pattern of illegal bail, sentencing and jury fee practices against them due to their race and exercise of first amendment rights. Although some respondents "had actually been defendants in proceedings before petitioners and had suffered from the alleged unconstitutional practices," the Court, per WHITE, J., reversed: "Of course, past wrongs are evidence bearing on whether there is a real and immediate threat of

---

a. Brennan, J., joined by Stewart and Marshall, JJ., also dissented, agreeing with the Court of Appeals that the case was justiciable and respondents had standing.

repeated injury. [But] respondents here have not pointed to any imminent prosecutions contemplated against any of their number and they naturally do not suggest that any one of them expects to violate valid criminal laws. [Thus], the threat of injury from the alleged course of conduct they attack is simply too remote to satisfy the 'case or controversy' requirement and permit adjudication by a federal court." [b]

Even if there were "an existing case or controversy," however, "a proper balance in the concurrent operation of federal and state courts" precludes federal equitable relief. The decision below "would contemplate interruption of state proceedings to adjudicate assertions of noncompliance by petitioners. This seems to us nothing less than an ongoing federal audit of state criminal proceedings [that] is antipathetic to established principles of comity.[c] [Respondents] have failed, moreover, to establish the basic requisites of the issuance of equitable relief in these circumstances—the likelihood of substantial and immediate irreparable injury, and the inadequacy of remedies at law. [I]f any of the respondents are ever prosecuted and face trial, or if they are illegally sentenced, there are available state and federal procedures which could provide relief from the wrongful conduct alleged"—e.g., direct review, collateral relief, and federal criminal prosecution of petitioners.[d]

(b) In DOE v. BOLTON, p. 150 supra, physicians with pregnant patients sought a federal declaratory judgment that a state criminal abortion statute deterred them from practicing their profession in violation of their constitutional rights. The Court, per BLACKMUN, J., held that they "present a justiciable controversy and do have standing despite the fact that the record does not disclose that any one of them has been prosecuted, or threatened with prosecution * * *. The physician is the one against whom these criminal statutes directly operate in the event he procures an abortion that does not meet the statutory exceptions and conditions. [They], therefore, assert a sufficiently direct threat of personal detriment. They should not be required to await and undergo a criminal prosecution as the sole means of seeking relief."

Is *Doe* consistent with *Tatum? O'Shea?*

POE v. ULLMAN

367 U.S. 497, 81 S.Ct. 1752, 6 L.Ed.2d 989 (1961).

MR. JUSTICE FRANKFURTER announced the judgment of the Court and an opinion in which THE CHIEF JUSTICE, MR. JUSTICE CLARK and MR. JUSTICE WHITTAKER join.

These appeals challenge the constitutionality [of] Connecticut statutes [which] prohibit the use of contraceptive devices and the giving of medical advice in the use of such devices. In proceedings seeking declarations of law [brought by married couples and their doctor, the state] court has ruled that these statutes would be applicable in the case of married couples and even under claim

b. For similar analysis, see *Rizzo v. Goode,* 423 U.S. 362, 96 S.Ct. 598, 46 L.Ed.2d 561 (1976).

c. Compare *Allee v. Medrano,* 416 U.S. 802, 94 S.Ct. 2191, 40 L.Ed.2d 566 (1974), upholding a federal injunction against state police disruption of unionization efforts. For fuller consideration of the delicacy of federal interference with state criminal proceedings, see Sec. 2, II infra. See also *Rizzo v. Goode,* fn. b,

discussed at 90 Harv.L.Rev. 238 (1976), holding that "principles of equity, comity, and federalism" also restrict federal court supervision of state executive or administrative agencies—in this case, the disciplinary practices of a city police department.

d. Blackmun, J., concurred in the first part of the Court's opinion. Douglas, J., joined by Brennan and Marshall, JJ., dissented.

that conception would constitute a serious threat to the health or life of the female spouse. * * *

Appellants' complaints [do] not clearly, and certainly do not in terms, allege that appellee Ullman threatens to prosecute [them]. The allegations are merely that, in the course of his public duty, he intends to prosecute any offenses against Connecticut law, and that he claims that use of and advice concerning contraceptives would constitute offenses. The lack of immediacy of the threat described by these allegations might alone raise serious questions of non-justiciability of appellants' claims. See *Mitchell.* But even were we to read the allegations to convey a clear threat of imminent prosecutions, we are not bound to accept as true all that is alleged on the face of the complaint and admitted, technically, by demurrer, any more than the Court is bound by stipulation of the parties. Formal agreement between parties that collides with plausibility is too fragile a foundation for indulging in constitutional adjudication.

The Connecticut law prohibiting the use of contraceptives has been on the State's books since 1879. During the more than three-quarters of a century since its enactment, a prosecution for its violation seems never to have been initiated, save in *State v. Nelson,* 126 Conn. 412, 11 A.2d 856. The circumstances of that case, decided in 1940, only prove the abstract character of what is before us. There, a test case was brought to determine the constitutionality of the Act as applied against two doctors and a nurse who had allegedly disseminated contraceptive information. After the Supreme Court of Errors sustained the legislation on appeal from a demurrer to the information, the State moved to dismiss the information. * * * We were advised by counsel for appellants that contraceptives are commonly and notoriously sold in Connecticut drug stores. Yet no prosecutions are recorded; and certainly such ubiquitous, open, public sales would more quickly invite the attention of enforcement officials than the conduct in which the present appellants wish to engage—the giving of private medical advice by a doctor to his individual patients, and their private use of the devices prescribed. The undeviating policy of nullification by Connecticut of its anticontraceptive laws throughout all the long years that they have been on the statute books bespeaks more than prosecutorial paralysis. What was said in another context is relevant here. "Deeply embedded traditional ways of carrying out state policy * * *"—or not carrying it out—"are often tougher and truer law than the dead words of the written text."

The restriction of our jurisdiction to cases and controversies within the meaning of Article III of the Constitution is not the sole limitation on the exercise of our appellate powers, especially in cases raising constitutional questions. The policy reflected in numerous cases and over a long period was thus summarized in the oft-quoted statement of Mr. Justice Brandeis: "The Court [has] developed, for its own governance in the cases confessedly within its jurisdiction, a series of rules under which it has avoided passing upon a large part of all the constitutional questions pressed upon it for decision." In part the rules summarized in the *Ashwander* opinion have derived from the historically defined, limited nature and function of courts and from the recognition that, within the framework of our adversary system, the adjudicatory process is most securely founded when it is exercised under the impact of a lively conflict between antagonistic demands, actively pressed, which make resolution of the controverted issue a practical necessity. * * *

These considerations press with special urgency in cases challenging legislative action or state judicial action as repugnant to the Constitution. [The] various doctrines of "standing," "ripeness," and "mootness," [are] but several manifestations—each having its own "varied application"—of the primary conception that federal judicial power is to be exercised to strike down legislation, whether state or federal, only at the instance of one who is himself immediately harmed, or immediately threatened with harm, by the challenged action. [It] was with respect to a state-originating declaratory judgment proceeding that we said [that] "the discretionary element characteristic of declaratory jurisdiction [offers] a convenient instrument for making * * * effective" the policy against premature constitutional decision. *Rescue Army v. Municipal Court*, [Part II supra, "Introductory Note"].

[If] the prosecutor expressly agrees not to prosecute, a suit against him for declaratory and injunctive relief is not such an adversary case as will be reviewed here. Eighty years of Connecticut history demonstrate a similar, albeit tacit agreement.

[W]e cannot accept, as the basis of constitutional adjudication, other than as chimerical the fear of enforcement of provisions that have during so many years gone uniformly and without exception unenforced.

Justiciability is of course not a legal concept with a fixed content or susceptible of scientific verification. Its utilization is the resultant of many subtle pressures, including the appropriateness of the issues for decision by this Court and the actual hardship to the litigants of denying them the relief sought. Both these factors justify withholding adjudication of the constitutional issue raised under the circumstances and in the manner in which they are now before the Court.

Dismissed.

MR. JUSTICE BLACK dissents because he believes that the constitutional questions should be reached and decided.

MR. JUSTICE BRENNAN, concurring in the judgment.

[The] true controversy in this case is over the opening of birth-control clinics on a large scale; it is that which the State has prevented in the [past]. It will be time enough to decide the constitutional questions urged upon us when, if ever, that real controversy flares up again. * * *

MR. JUSTICE DOUGLAS, dissenting.

[The] Court [goes] outside the record to conclude that there exists a "tacit agreement" that these statutes will not be enforced. No lawyer, I think, would advise his clients to rely on that "tacit agreement." No police official, I think, would feel himself bound by that "tacit agreement." After our national experience during the prohibition era, it would be absurd to pretend that all criminal statutes are adequately enforced. But that does not mean that bootlegging was the less a crime. * * *

When the Court goes outside the record to determine that Connecticut has adopted "The undeviating policy of nullification [of] its anti-contraceptive laws," it selects a particularly poor case in which to exercise such a novel power. This is not a law which is a dead letter. Twice since 1940, Connecticut has reenacted these laws as part of general statutory revisions. Consistently, bills to remove the statutes from the books have been rejected by the legislature. In short, the statutes—far from being the accidental left-overs of another era—are the center of a continuing controversy * * *.

[O]n oral argument, counsel for the appellee stated on his own knowledge that several proprietors had been prosecuted in the "minor police courts of Connecticut" after they had been "picked up" for selling contraceptives. The enforcement of criminal laws in minor courts has just as much impact as in those cases where appellate courts are resorted to. * * *

What are these people—doctor and patients—to do? Flout the law and go to prison? Violate the law surreptitiously and hope they will not get caught? By today's decision we leave them no other alternatives. It is not the choice they need have under the regime of the declaratory judgment * * *.

[On the merits, Douglas J., and Harlan, J., in his opinion that follows, argued that the statute was unconstitutional.]

Mr. Justice Harlan, dissenting.

[There] is no lack of "ripeness" [since] appellants have stated in their pleadings fully and unequivocally what it is that they intend to do; no clarifying or resolving contingency stands in their way before they may embark on that conduct. Thus there is no circumstance besides that of detection or prosecution to make remote the particular controversy. And it is clear beyond cavil that the mere fact that a controversy such as this is rendered still more unavoidable by an actual prosecution, is not *alone* sufficient to make the case too remote * * *.

[This] is not a feigned, hypothetical, friendly or colorable suit such as discloses "a want of a truly adversary contest." * * * I think both the plurality and concurring opinions confuse [the] predictive likelihood that, had [appellants] not brought themselves to appellee's attention, he would not enforce the statute against them, with some entirely suppositious "tacit agreement" not to prosecute, thereby ignoring the prosecutor's claim, asserted in these very proceedings, of a right, at his unbounded prosecutorial discretion, to enforce the statute. * * *

We are brought, then, to the precise failing in these proceedings which is said to justify refusal to exercise our mandatory appellate jurisdiction: that there has been but one recorded Connecticut case dealing with a *prosecution* under the statute. * * * I think it is pure conjecture, and indeed conjecture which to me seems contrary to realities, that an open violation of the statute by a doctor (or more obviously still by a birth-control clinic) would not result in a substantial threat of prosecution. Crucial to the opposite conclusion is the description of the 1940 prosecution instituted in *State v. Nelson* as a "test case" * * *. [T]he respect in which *Nelson* was a test case is only that it was brought for the purpose of making entirely clear the State's power and willingness to enforce against "*any* person, whether a physician or layman" (emphasis supplied), the statute and to eliminate from future cases the very doubt about the existence of these elements which had resulted in eight open birth-control clinics, and which would have made unfair the conviction of Nelson.

* * * I fear that the Court has indulged in a bit of sleight of hand to be rid of this case. It has treated the significance of the absence of prosecutions during the twenty years since *Nelson* as identical with that of the absence of prosecutions during the years before *Nelson*. It has ignored the fact that the very purpose of the *Nelson* prosecution was to change defiance into compliance. It has ignored the very possibility that this purpose may have been successful. * * *

The Court's disposition assumes that to decide the case now, in the absence of any consummated prosecutions, is unwise because it forces a difficult decision in advance of any exigent necessity therefor. [D]espite speculation as to a "tacit agreement" that this law will not be enforced, there is, of course, no suggestion of an estoppel against the State if it should attempt to prosecute appellants.

Neither the plurality nor the concurring opinion suggests that appellants have some legally cognizable right not to be prosecuted if the statute is Constitutional. What is meant is simply that the appellants are more or less free to act without fear of prosecution because the prosecuting authorities of the State, in their discretion and at their whim, are, as a matter of prediction, unlikely to decide to prosecute.

Here is the core of my disagreement with the present disposition. [T]he most substantial claim which these married persons press is their right to enjoy the privacy of their marital relations free of the enquiry of the criminal law, whether it be in a prosecution of them or of a doctor whom they have consulted. And I cannot agree that their enjoyment of this privacy is not substantially impinged upon, when they are told that if they use contraceptives, indeed whether they do so or not, the only thing which stands between them and being forced to render criminal account of their marital privacy is the whim of the prosecutor. [Indeed] it appears that whereas appellants would surely have been entitled to review were this a new statute [the] State here is enabled to maintain at least some substantial measure of compliance with this statute and still obviate any review in this Court, by the device of purely discretionary prosecutorial inactivity. It seems to me to destroy the whole purpose of anticipatory relief to consider the prosecutor's discretion, once all legal and administrative channels have been cleared, as in any way analogous to those other contingencies which make remote a controversy presenting Constitutional claims. * * *

MR. JUSTICE STEWART, dissenting.

For the reasons so convincingly advanced by both Mr. Justice Douglas and Mr. Justice Harlan, I join them in dissenting from the dismissal of these appeals. * * *[a]

Notes and Questions

1. *The Court's rationale.* (a) Does *Poe* undermine the idea that law—good or bad—is to be obeyed? Or does it take the position that the Connecticut statutes were not really "*law*"? Does *Poe* ignore the fact that some (many?) people wish to (will?) obey the law simply because it is "the law," whether or not it will ever be enforced?

(b) Was the law not "a dead letter [because] consistently, bills to remove the statutes from the books have been rejected by the legislature"? Consider Bickel, *The Passive Virtues,* 75 Harv.L.Rev. 40, 63 (1961): "[G]reater strength must be mobilized to repeal a statute than to resist its enactment. When the law is consistently not enforced, the chance of mustering opposition sufficient to move the legislature is reduced to the vanishing point. For consistent failure to enforce is itself a political concession to the opposition, and will satisfy at least some portions of it. [The] unenforced statute is not, in the normal way, a continuing reflection of the balance of political pressures."

2. Is *Poe* distinguishable from *Epperson v. Arkansas,* p. 717 supra, where there was no record of enforcement of a forty year old statute making the teaching of evolution unlawful and, after her school adopted a textbook teaching evolution, a biology teacher sought a declaration that the statute was unconstitutional and an injunction against her dismissal?

3. *"Discretionary" dismissal of appeals.* Was the disposition in *Poe* inconsistent with the fact that the case came to the Court on appeal, thus within the

a. For a further constitutional test, see *Griswold v. Connecticut,* p. 126 supra.

"obligatory jurisdiction" (Ch. 1, Sec. 4)? Consider Comment, *Threat of Enforce-ment—Prerequisite of a Judicial Controversy,* 62 Colum.L.Rev. 106, 126 (1962): "When an appeal is taken from a federal court decision, the Supreme Court, as the ultimate interpreter of federal law may derive its discretionary authority to deny adjudication from the nature of the injunction and declaratory judgment remedies. [B]ut it would seem that state construction of state remedies should be conclusively binding on the Supreme Court in the absence of article III objections. To justify discretion as an inherent power of the Court is equally unsatisfactory in view of the obligatory character of the appeal jurisdiction." Does this distinguish *Mitchell* from *Adler?*

Was the Court's refusal to decide *Poe* justified as commendable restraint in avoiding possibly unnecessary constitutional decision? Consider Note, *The Dis-cretionary Power of the Supreme Court to Dismiss Appeals from State Courts,* 63 Colum.L.Rev. 688, 707 (1963): "[T]he assertion of discretion to refuse the jurisdic-tion that is given [by Congress] is inimical to fundamental postulates of princi-pled judicial restraint; the declaration by the Court of such discretion itself violates the separation of powers philosophy upon which the Court has consis-tently relied. For by asserting power to make exceptions to its jurisdiction, the Court has assumed a power expressly delegated by the Constitution to Congress." See generally Gunther, *The Subtle Vices of the "Passive Virtues"—A Comment on Principle and Expediency in Judicial Review,* 64 Colum.L.Rev. 1 (1964). Does this argument draw an unrealistic dichotomy between (1) what Congress intend-ed in conferring appeal jurisdiction and (2) the Court's rules of "self-limitation" from decision on the merits? See *Molinaro v. New Jersey,* 396 U.S. 365, 90 S.Ct. 498, 24 L.Ed.2d 586 (1970) (appeal dismissed because appellant was fugitive from justice); cf. *Ohio v. Wyandotte Chemicals Corp.,* 401 U.S. 493, 91 S.Ct. 1005, 28 L.Ed.2d 256 (1971) (declining to exercise statutorily granted original jurisdiction). Does it make an unwarranted assumption as to the clarity of the Constitution's allocation of power?

Consider Choper, *Judicial Review and the National Political Process* 406–09, 414 (1980): "[T]he Court should be hesitant to attribute an intention to the political branches that requires [it] to engage in the delicate process of constitu-tional adjudication despite the Justices' belief that it would be inappropriate or wasteful for the Court to do so. [This] suggested ground for nondecision would, of course, be unavailable if a clearly articulated legislative intent forbade a limiting construction of the jurisdictional statute. [In these circumstances, to] justify its deliberate refusal to decide some constitutional questions [the Court] should hold that political edicts to the contrary infringe 'the judicial Power of the United States.' Like all other constitutionally enumerated powers [this] clause implies those accessory powers necessary to its effective discharge, and final interpretation of its meaning belongs to the Supreme Court. [I]t is highly important to recognize the peculiar quality of the judicial assumption of power at issue. Viewed realistically, it is a judicial authority not to enhance the Court's power but rather to confine it, a course not of self-arrogation but rather one of self-denial—a capacity of the judiciary to refrain from exerting influence not wholly dissimilar (though the analogy is far from perfect) to whatever discretion the executive has to decline to enforce laws * * *."

SECTION 2. ELEVENTH AMENDMENT

CHARLES ALAN WRIGHT—FEDERAL COURTS

287–92 (4th ed. 1983).

[In EX PARTE YOUNG, 209 U.S. 123, 28 S.Ct. 441, 52 L.Ed. 714 (1908), railroads sued in federal court to enjoin Young, the Attorney General of Minnesota, from enforcing a state law reducing railroad rates. The railroads alleged that the rates were confiscatory, depriving them of their property without due process. Relief] was given over Young's objection that the suit was in fact a suit against the state, to which the state had not consented, and thus barred by the Eleventh Amendment.   *   *   *

The Supreme Court did not write on a clean slate in deciding Young's case. In 1793, in the unpopular decision of *Chisholm v. Georgia*,[4] it had held that the Constitution permitted a citizen of one state to sue another state in federal court, though the state had not consented to such suit. The Eleventh Amendment was ratified five years later to take away the judicial power of the federal courts in such cases, and though in terms it does not so provide, it was construed as barring suits against a state without its consent even where, as in Young's case, the suit was brought by a citizen of the state and the basis of the jurisdiction was a claim under federal law.[6] [T]he Court held that the injunction against Young was proper. Justice PECKHAM, for the Court, announced the rule which has since been repeatedly followed: "The [use] of the name of the state to enforce an unconstitutional act to the injury of the complainants is a proceeding without the authority of, and one which does not affect, the state in its sovereign or governmental capacity. It is simply an illegal act upon the part of a state official *   *   *. If the act which the state Attorney General seeks to enforce be a violation of the federal Constitution, the officer in proceeding under such enactment comes into conflict with the superior authority of that Constitution, and he is in that case stripped of his official or representative character and is subject in his person to the consequences of his individual conduct."

Only the first Justice HARLAN dissented [:] "The suit was, as to the defendant Young, one against him as, and only because he was, Attorney General of Minnesota. No relief was sought against him individually but only in his capacity as Attorney General. And the manifest—indeed, the avowed and admitted—object of seeking such relief was to tie the hands of the [state]. It would therefore seem clear that within the true meaning of the Eleventh Amendment suit brought in the federal court was one, in legal effect, against the state."

There is no doubt that the reality is as Justice Harlan stated [it]. The fiction has its own illogic. The Fourteenth Amendment runs only to the states;

---

4. 1793, 2 Dall. 419, 1 L.Ed. 440. [See generally Goebel, *Antecedents and Beginnings to 1801*, 726–41 (1971).]

6. *Hans v. Louisiana*, 1890, 10 S.Ct. 504, 134 U.S. 1, 33 L.Ed. 842. [Compare *Parden v. Terminal Ry.*, 377 U.S. 184, 84 S.Ct. 1207, 12 L.Ed.2d 233 (1964) (state, that began operation of interstate railroad after enactment of Federal Employers' Liability Act, "necessarily consented" to federal court suits provided by the Act) with *Employees of Dep't of Public Health v. Dep't of Public Health*, 411 U.S. 279,

93 S.Ct. 1614, 36 L.Ed.2d 251 (1973) (congressional extension of Fair Labor Standards Act to state hospitals and schools did not intend to authorize federal court suits for enforcement by employees). See generally Cullison, *Interpretation of the Eleventh Amendment*, 5 Hous. L.Rev. 1 (1967).

[But neither the eleventh amendment, nor any other provision of the Constitution, affords a state immunity from being sued in the courts of another state. *Nevada v. Hall*, 440 U.S. 410, 99 S.Ct. 1182, 59 L.Ed.2d 416 (1979).]

in order to have a right to relief under the amendment the plaintiff must be able to show that state action is involved in the denial of his rights. [The Court] created the anomaly that enforcement of the Minnesota statute is state action for purposes of the Fourteenth Amendment but merely the individual wrong of Edward T. Young for purposes of the Eleventh Amendment.

What if the action of the state officer is beyond his authority as a matter of state law? [I]t was settled five years after *Young* that action by a state officer claiming to act under authority of the state can be enjoined, even if the state has not authorized such action.[20]

The effect of *Young* is to bring within the scope of federal judicial review actions that might otherwise escape such review * * *. If *Young* had been decided the other way, there would have been no practicable means for the railroads to obtain a court determination of the new rates Minnesota wanted them to charge. The state could, of course, consent to suit, either in its own courts or in federal court, simply as a matter of grace, but even today most states have not done so. The railroads could have refused to obey the new law, and asserted its unconstitutionality as a defense to an action against them for its enforcement, but the state might have chosen to enforce the law by the criminal sanctions it supplied, and these were so severe that the railroads could not risk the possibility that they might lose and have to pay crushing fines. In some situations, as where a state has failed to desegregate its schools, affirmative action is required of the state to fulfill its constitutional obligations, and there would not be even the possibility of raising the constitutional issue defensively.

* * *

The decision [was] greeted with harsh criticism [for] years thereafter. For half a century Congress and the Court have vied in placing restrictions on the doctrine there announced.[a]

Notes and Questions

Scope of congressional power. (a) In EDELMAN v. JORDAN, 415 U.S. 651, 94 S.Ct. 1347, 39 L.Ed.2d 662 (1974), the federal courts below found that Illinois had violated federal regulations under the federal-state funded Aid to the Aged, Blind and Disabled program, and ordered retroactive payment by state officials of the benefits wrongfully withheld. The Court, per REHNQUIST, J., reversed: "[A] suit by private parties seeking to impose a liability which must be paid from public funds in the state treasury is barred by the Eleventh Amendment.[11]

20. *Home Tel. & Tel. Co. v. Los Angeles,* 1913, 33 S.Ct. 312, 227 U.S. 278, 57 L.Ed. 510. [But *Cory v. White,* 457 U.S. 85, 102 S.Ct. 2325, 72 L.Ed.2d 694 (1982), reaffirmed that the eleventh amendment *does* bar federal suits against state officers who are not alleged either "to be acting contrary to federal law or against the authority of state law." And *Pennhurst State Sch. & Hosp. v. Halderman,* 465 U.S. 89, 104 S.Ct. 900, 79 L.Ed.2d 67 (1984), held (5–4) that the eleventh amendment also bars federal suits against state officers for alleged violations of *state* law, reasoning that, unlike the situation in *Young,* federal jurisdiction is not needed "to promote the supremacy of federal law."]

a. Various restrictions—including the congressional provision in 1910 (virtually eliminated in 1976) that no federal injunction re-

straining a state officer from enforcing a state law on grounds of unconstitutionality shall be issued except by a court of three judges (with direct appeal to the Supreme Court)—are discussed in Wright, supra, at 292–302.

11. It may be true, as stated by our Brother Douglas in dissent, that "[m]ost welfare decisions by the federal courts have a financial impact on the States." But we cannot agree [with him] that "[w]hether the decree is prospective only or requires payments for the weeks or months wrongfully skipped over by state officials, the nature of the impact on the state treasury is precisely the same." This argument neglects the fact that where the State has a definable allocation to be used in the payment of public aid benefits, and pursues a certain course of action such as the processing of applications within certain time

"As in most areas of the law, the difference between the type of relief barred by the Eleventh Amendment and that permitted under *Young* will not in many instances be that between day and night. The injunction issued in *Young* was not totally without effect on the State's revenues, since the state law which the Attorney General was enjoined from enforcing provided substantial monetary penalties against railroads which did not conform to its provisions. Later cases from this Court have authorized equitable relief which has probably had greater impact on state treasuries than did that awarded in *Young*. In *Graham v. Richardson,* [p. 938 supra] Arizona and Pennsylvania welfare officials were prohibited from denying welfare benefits to otherwise qualified recipients who were aliens. [But] the fiscal consequences to state treasuries in these cases were the necessary result of compliance with decrees which by their terms were prospective in nature.[b] While the Court of Appeals described this retroactive award of monetary relief as a form of 'equitable restitution,' it is in practical effect indistinguishable in many aspects from an award of damages against the State. It will to a virtual certainty be paid from state funds, and not from the pocket of the individual state official who was the defendant in the action [—and thus is contrary to *Ford Motor Co. v. Department of Treas.,* 323 U.S. 459, 65 S.Ct. 347, 89 L.Ed. 389 (1945)]. There a taxpayer, who had, under protest, paid taxes to the State of Indiana, sought a refund of those taxes from the Indiana state officials who were charged with their collection. The taxpayer claimed that the tax had been imposed in violation of the United States Constitution. [Yet] this Court had no hesitation in holding that the taxpayer's action was a suit against the State, and barred by the Eleventh Amendment. * * *

"The Court of Appeals held in the alternative that even if the Eleventh Amendment be deemed a bar to the retroactive [relief,] Illinois had waived [its] immunity and consented to the bringing of such a suit by participating in the federal AABD program.[c] [But] we will find waiver only where stated 'by the most express language or [by] other overwhelming implications from the [text],' " a condition satisfied here neither by the relevant federal welfare statutes nor by 42 U.S.C.A. § 1983,[d] nor by any action on the part of the state.

(b) FITZPATRICK v. BITZER, 427 U.S. 445, 96 S.Ct. 2666, 49 L.Ed.2d 614 (1976), per REHNQUIST, J., held that the eleventh amendment did not prevent a federal court from awarding retroactive money damages against the state treasury, for the state's having discriminated against plaintiff-employees on the basis of sex in violation of the Title VII of the Civil Rights Act of 1964 (enacted by Congress under § 5 of the fourteenth amendment): "[T]he Eleventh Amendment, and the principle of state sovereignty which it embodies, are necessarily limited by the enforcement provisions of § 5 of the Fourteenth Amendment. [When] Congress acts pursuant to § 5, [it] is exercising that authority under one section of a constitutional Amendment whose other sections by their own terms

periods as did Illinois here, the subsequent ordering by a federal court of retroactive payments to correct delays in such processing will invariably mean there is less money available for payments for the continuing obligations of the public aid system. * * *

b. For the view that "the history of the eleventh amendment supports the Court's distinction between retroactive and prospective relief," see 88 Harv.L.Rev. 243 (1974).

For further reliance on this distinction in awarding relief with "substantial impact on

the state treasury," see *Milliken v. Bradley,* 433 U.S. 267, 97 S.Ct. 2749, 53 L.Ed.2d 745 (1977), discussed in Frug, *The Judicial Power of the Purse,* 126 U.Pa.L.Rev. 715, 750–57 (1978).

c. Douglas, J.—and Marshall, J., joined by Blackmun, J.—dissented on this theory. Brennan, J., also dissented.

d. The conclusion as to § 1983 was reaffirmed in *Quern v. Jordan,* 440 U.S. 332, 99 S.Ct. 1139, 59 L.Ed.2d 358 (1979).

embody limitations on state authority. We think that Congress may, in determining what is 'appropriate legislation' for the purpose of enforcing the provisions of the Fourteenth Amendment, provide for private suits against States or state officials which are constitutionally impermissible in other contexts.[11] See *Edelman; Ford Motor.*" [e]

11. Apart from their claim that the Eleventh Amendment bars enforcement of the remedy established by Title VII in this case, respondents do not contend that the substantive provisions of Title VII as applied here are not a proper exercise of congressional authority under § 5 of the Fourteenth Amendment.

e. Brennan and Stevens, JJ., concurred in the result.

For the view that Congress has authority, pursuant to any of its delegated powers, to authorize federal court suits for damages against the states, see Nowak, *The Scope of Congressional Power to Create Causes of Action Against State Governments and the History of the Eleventh and Fourteenth Amendments,* 75 Colum.L.Rev. 1413 (1975); Tribe, *Intergovernmental Immunities in Litigation, Taxation, and Regulation: Separation of Powers Issues in Controversies About Federalism,* 89 Harv.L.Rev. 682–99 (1976).

For the view that the eleventh amendment does not bar suits against states when another jurisdictional basis—such as federal question or admiralty—exists, see Fletcher, *A Historical Interpretation of the Eleventh Amendment: A Narrow Construction of an Affirmative Grant of Jurisdiction Rather than a Prohibition Against Jurisdiction,* 35 Stan.L.Rev. 1033 (1983); Gibbons, *The Eleventh Amendment and State Sovereign Immunity: A Reinterpretation,* 83 Colum.L.Rev. 1889 (1983). This position has been adopted by Brennan, J., joined by Marshall, Blackmun and Stevens, JJ., dissenting in *Atascadero State Hosp. v. Scanlon,* ___ U.S. ___, 105 S.Ct. 3142, 87 L.Ed.2d 171 (1985).

For the view that state sovereign immunity from suit is only a "common law requirement" and "has no constitutional sanction," see Field, *The Eleventh Amendment and Other Sovereign Immunity Doctrines: Part One,* 126 U.Pa.L.Rev. 515 (1977).

Appendix A

THE JUSTICES OF THE SUPREME COURT

Prepared by JOHN J. COUND

Professor of Law, University of Minnesota

The data which follow, summarizing the prior public careers of the ninety-nine individuals who have served upon the Supreme Court of the United States, are not presented with any notion that they did presage or now explain their judicial performance or constitutional philosophy. The experience which the justices have at any one time brought to bear upon the issues before the Court, however, seem worthy of interest, and may serve as a consideration in assessing charges that the Court has in particular cases rendered "ivory tower" decisions, unaware or heedless of "the realities."

Two conclusions are manifest. First, the diversity of distinguished experience which the bench of the Court has at all times reflected, always among its members and frequently in a single justice, is startling. William Howard Taft is unique, but surely few Americans have lived lives of diversified public service so rich as John Jay, Levi Woodbury, Lucius Q.C. Lamar, Charles Evans Hughes and Fred M. Vinson. Second, a broad background in public service has not assured prominence upon the Court, nor has its absence precluded it. Gabriel Duvall, with prior executive, legislative and judicial experience, was forgotten in the first edition of the *Dictionary of American Biography*. Samuel F. Miller and Joseph P. Bradley, with no prior public offices, surely stand among the front rank of the justices. (The interested student will find stimulation in Frankfurter, *The Supreme Court in the Mirror of Justice*, 105 U.Pa.L.Rev. 781 (1957), which treats particularly of the relevance of prior judicial office).

In the data, the first dates in parentheses are those of birth and death; these are followed by the name of the appointing President, and the dates of service on the Court. The state in which the justice was residing when appointed and his political affiliation at that time are then given. In detailing prior careers, I have followed chronological order, with two exceptions: I have listed first that a justice was a signer of the Declaration of Independence or the Federal Constitution, and I have indicated state legislative experience only once for each justice. I have not distinguished between different bodies in the state legislature, and I have omitted service in the Continental Congresses. Private practice, except where deemed especially signficant, and law teaching have been omitted, except where the justice was primarily engaged therein upon his appointment. (Blackmun, Burger, Douglas, Fortas, Holmes, Hughes, L.Q.C. Lamar, Lurton, McReynolds, Murphy, Roberts, W. Rutledge, Stevens, Stone and Van Devanter in addition to Taft and Frankfurter, had all taught before going on the Court; Story, Strong and Wilson taught while on the court or after leaving it). The activity in which a justice was engaged upon appointment has been italicized. Figures in parentheses indicate years of service in the position. In only a few cases, a justice's extra-Court or post-Court activity has been indicated, or some other note made. An asterisk designates the Chief Justices.

For detailed information on the individuals who have served as members of the Supreme Court, see L. Friedman & F. Israel, eds., *The Justices of the United States Supreme Court 1789–1969: Their Lives and Major Opinions* (Chelsea House, 1969), and the bibliographical references collected therein.

The accompanying Table of Justices on pages [3] and [4] has been planned so that the composition of the Court at any time can be readily ascertained.

(This material has been compiled from a great number of sources, but special acknowledgment must be made to the *Dictionary of American Biography* (Charles Scribner's Sons), the A.N. Marquis Company works, and Ewing, *The Judges of the Supreme Court, 1789–1937* (University of Minnesota Press, 1938).)

BALDWIN, HENRY (1780–1844; Jackson 1830–1844). Pa.Dem.—U.S., House of Representatives (5). *Private practice.*

BARBOUR, PHILIP P. (1783–1841; Jackson, 1836–1841). Va.Dem.—Va., Legislature (2). U.S., House of Representatives (14). Va., Judge, General Court (2); President, State Constitutional Convention, 1829–30, *U.S., Judge, District Court (5).*

BLACK, HUGO L. (1886–1971; F.D. Roosevelt, 1937–1971). Ala.Dem.— Captain, Field Artillery, World War I. Ala., Judge, Police Court (1); County Solicitor (2). *U.S., Senate (10).*

BLACKMUN, HARRY A. (1908–____; Nixon, 1970–____). Minn.Rep.—Resident Counsel, Mayo Clinic, (10). *U.S., Judge, Court of Appeals (11).*

BLAIR, JOHN (1732–1800; Washington, 1789–1796). Va.Fed.—Signer, U.S. Constitution, 1787. Va., Legislature (9); Judge and Chief Justice, General Court (2), *Court of Appeals (9).* His opinion in *Commonwealth v. Caton,* 4 Call 5, 20 (Va.1782), is one of the earliest expressions of the doctrine of judicial review.

BLATCHFORD, SAMUEL (1820–1893; Arthur, 1882–1893). N.Y.Rep.— U.S., Judge, District Court (5); *Circuit Court (10).*

BRADLEY, JOSEPH P. (1803–1892; Grant, 1870–1892). N.J.Rep.—Actuary. *Private practice.*

BRANDEIS, LOUIS D. (1856–1941; Wilson, 1916–1939). Mass.Dem.—*Private practice.* Counsel, variously for the government, for industry, and "for the people", in numerous administrative and judicial proceedings, both state and federal.

BRENNAN, WILLIAM J. (1906–____; Eisenhower, 1956–____). N.J.Dem.— U.S. Army, World War II. N.J., Judge, Superior Court (1); Appellate Division (2); *Supreme Court (4).*

BREWER, DAVID J. (1837–1910; B. Harrison, 1889–1910). Kans.Rep.— Kans., Judge, County Criminal and Probate Court (1), District Court (4); County Attorney (1); Judge, Supreme Court (14), *U.S., Judge, Circuit Court (5).*

BROWN, HENRY, B. (1836–1913; B. Harrison, 1890–1906). Mich.Rep.— U.S., Assistant U.S. Attorney (5). Mich., Judge, Circuit Court (1). *U.S., Judge, District Court (15).*

1789 1790 1791 1793 1795 1796 1798 1799 1801 1804 1806 1807 1811 1823 1826 1829 1830 1835 1836 1837 1841 1845 1846 1851 1853 1858 1862 1863 1864 1865 1867 1870 1872 1874 1877 1880 1881 1882 1888 1889

Field

McKinley
Campbell
Davis

Catron

Harlan

Todd
Trimble
McLean

Swayne

Matthews
Brewer

Iredell

Moore
Johnson, W.

Wayne

*
Bradley

Blair

Chase, Samuel

Duval

Barbour
Daniel

Miller

Wilson

Washington

Baldwin

Grier

Strong

Woods

Lamar, L.

Cushing

Story

Woodbury
Curtis
Clifford

Gray

Jay

Rutledge, J.
Johnson, T.
Paterson

Rutledge, J.
Ellsworth

Marshall, J.

Livingston

Thompson

Taney

Nelson

Chase, Salmon

Hunt

Waite

Blatchford

Fuller

1789 1790 1791 1793 1795 1796 1798 1799 1801 1804 1806 1807 1811 1823 1826 1829 1830 1835 1836 1837 1841 1845 1846 1851 1853 1858 1862 1863 1864 1865 1867 1870 1872 1874 1877 1880 1881 1882 1888 1889

* Catron died in 1865, Wayne in 1867; their positions were abolished by Congress to prevent their being filled by President Johnson; a new position was created in 1869, which traditionally has been regarded as a re-creation of Wayne's seat.

1890 1892 1893 1894 1895 1898 1902 1903 1906 1909 1910 1912 1914 1916 1921 1922 1923 1925 1930 1932 1937 1938 1939 1940 1941 1943 1945 1946 1949 1953 1955 1956 1957 1958 1962 1965 1966 1967 1968 1969 1970 1972 **1975** **1981**

McKenna — Jackson, R. ✮✮ — Rehnquist

Pitney — Sanford — Roberts — Burton — Stewart — O'Connor

Hughes — Clarke — Sutherland — Reed — Whittaker — White, B.

Shiras — Day — Butler — Murphy — Clark — Marshall, T.

Brown — Moody — Lamar, J. — Brandeis — Douglas — **Stevens**

Jackson, H. — Peckham — Lurton — McReynolds — Byrnes — Rutledge — Minton — Brennan

Holmes — Cardozo — Frankfurter — Goldberg — Fortas — Blackmun

White, E. — Van Devanter ** — Black — Powell

White, E. — **Taft** — **Hughes** — **Stone** — **Vinson** — **Warren** — **Burger**

** Fuller died in 1910, and White was named Chief Justice. Hughes resigned in 1941, and Stone was named Chief Justice.

1890 1892 1893 1894 1895 1898 1902 1903 1906 1909 1910 1912 1914 1916 1921 1922 1923 1925 1930 1932 1937 1938 1939 1940 1941 1943 1945 1946 1949 1953 1955 1956 1957 1958 1962 1965 1966 1967 1968 1969 1970 1972 **1975** **1981**

*BURGER, WARREN E. (1907–____; Nixon, 1969–1986). Va.Rep.—U.S., Assistant Attorney General, Civil Division (3), *Judge, Court of Appeals (13).*

BURTON, HAROLD H. (1888–1964; Truman, 1945–1958). Ohio Rep.— Capt., U.S.A., World War I. Ohio, Legislature (2). Mayor, Cleveland, O. (5). *U.S., Senate (4).*

BUTLER, PIERCE (1866–1939; Harding, 1922–1939). Minn.Dem.—Minn., County Attorney (4). *Private practice.*

BYRNES, JAMES F. (1879–1972; F.D. Roosevelt, 1941–1942). S.C.Dem.— S.C., Solicitor, Circuit Court (2). U.S., House of Representatives (14); *Senate (12).* Resigned from the Court to become U.S. Director of Economic Stabilization.

CAMPBELL, JOHN A. (1811–1889; Pierce, 1853–1861). Ala.Dem.—*Private practice.* After his resignation, he became Assistant Secretary of War, C.S.A.

CARDOZO, BENJAMIN N. (1870–1938; Hoover, 1932–1938). N.Y.Dem.— N.Y., Judge, Supreme Court (6 weeks); Associate Judge and *Chief Judge, Court of Appeals (18).*

CATRON, JOHN (1778–1865; Van Buren, 1837–1865). Tenn.Dem.—Tenn., Judge and Chief Justice, Supreme Court of Errors and Appeals (10). *Private practice.*

*CHASE, SALMON P. (1808–1873; Lincoln 1864–1873). Ohio Rep.—U.S., Senate (6). Ohio, Governor (4). *U.S., Secretary of the Treasury (3).*

CHASE, SAMUEL (1741–1811; Washington, 1796–1811). Md.Fed.—Signer, U.S., Declaration of Independence, 1776. Md., Legislature (20); Chief Judge, Court of Oyer and Terminer (2), *General Court (5).* Impeached and acquitted, 1804–05.

CLARK, TOM C. (1899–1977; Truman, 1949–1967). Tex.Dem.—U.S. Army, World War I. Tex., Civil District Attorney (5). U.S., Assistant Attorney General (2), *Attorney General (4).*

CLARKE, JOHN H. (1857–1945; Wilson, 1916–1922). Ohio Dem.—*U.S. Judge, District Court (2).*

CLIFFORD, NATHAN (1803–1881; Buchanan, 1858–1881). Me.Dem.—Me., Legislature (4); Attorney General (4). U.S., House of Representatives (4); Attorney General (2); Minister Plenipotentiary to Mexico, 1848. *Private practice.*

CURTIS, BENJAMIN R. (1809–1874; Fillmore, 1851–1857). Mass.Whig.— Mass., Legislature (1). *Private practice.*

CUSHING, WILLIAM (1732–1810; Washington, 1789–1810). Mass.Fed.— Mass., Judge, Superior Court (3); Justice and *Chief Justice, Supreme Judicial Court (14).*

DANIEL, PETER V. (1784–1860; Van Buren, 1841–1860). Va.Dem.—Va., Legislature (3); Member, Privy Council (23). *U.S., Judge, District Court (5).*

DAVIS, DAVID (1815–1886; Lincoln, 1862–1877). Ill.Rep.—Ill., Legislature (2); *Judge, Circuit Court (14).* His resignation to become U.S. Senator upset the agreed-upon composition of the Hayes-Tilden Electoral Commission.

DAY, WILLIAM R. (1849–1923; T. Roosevelt, 1903–1922). Ohio Rep.—Ohio, Judge, Court of Common Pleas (4). U.S., Assistant Secretary of State (1), Secretary of State (½); Chairman, U.S. Peace Commissioners, 1898; *Judge, Circuit Court of Appeals (4).*

DOUGLAS, WILLIAM O. (1898–1980; F.D. Roosevelt, 1939–1975). Conn. Dem.—Pvt., U.S. Army, World War I. *U.S., Chairman, Securities and Exchange Commission (3).*

DUVAL(L), GABRIEL (1752–1844; Madison, 1811–1935). Md.Rep.—Declined to serve as delegate, U.S. Constitutional Convention, 1787. Md., State Council (3). U.S., House of Representatives (2). Md., Judge, General Court (6). *U.S., Comptroller of the Treasury (9)*.

*ELLSWORTH, OLIVER (1745–1807; Washington, 1796–1800). Conn. Fed.—Delegate, U.S. Constitutional Convention, 1787. Conn., Legislature (2); Member, Governor's Council (4); Judge, Superior Court (5). *U.S., Senate (7)*.

FIELD, STEPHEN J. (1816–1899; Lincoln, 1863–1897). Calif.Dem.—*Calif., Justice, and Chief Justice, Supreme Court (6)*. His was the longest tenure in the history of the Court.

FORTAS, ABE (1910–1982; L.B. Johnson, 1965–1969). Tenn.Dem.—U.S. Government attorney and consultant (A.A.A., S.E.C., P.W.A., Dep't of Interior (9); Undersecretary of Interior (4). *Private practice in Washington, D.C.* Nominated as Chief Justice; nomination withdrawn, 1968. Resigned.

FRANKFURTER, FELIX (1882–1965; F.D. Roosevelt, 1939–1962). Mass. Independent.—U.S., Assistant U.S. Attorney (4); Law Officer, War Department, Bureau of Insular Affairs (3); Assistant to Secretary of War (1). *Professor of Law (25)*.

*FULLER, MELVILLE W. (1833–1910; Cleveland, 1888–1910). Ill.Dem.— Ill., Legislature (2). *Private practice*.

GOLDBERG, ARTHUR J. (1908–___; Kennedy, 1962–1965). Ill.Dem.— Major, U.S.A., World War II. General Counsel, USW–AFL–CIO (13). *U.S., Secretary of Labor (1)*. Resigned to become Ambassador to U.N.

GRAY, HORACE (1828–1902; Arthur, 1881–1902). Mass.Rep.—*Mass., Associate Justice and Chief Justice, Supreme Judicial Court (18)*.

GRIER, ROBERT O. (1794–1870; Polk, 1846–1870). Pa.Dem.—*Pa., Presiding Judge, District Court (13)*.

HARLAN, JOHN M. (1833–1911; Hayes, 1877–1911). Ky.Rep.—Ky., Judge, County Court (1). Col., Union Army, 1861–63. Ky., Attorney General (4). U.S., Member, President's Louisiana Commission, 1877. *Private practice*. Grandfather of:

HARLAN, JOHN M. (1899–1971; Eisenhower, 1955–1971). N.Y.Rep.—Col., U.S.A.A.F., World War II. N.Y. Chief Counsel, State Crime Commission (2). *U.S., Judge, Court of Appeals (1)*.

HOLMES, OLIVER W., JR. (1841–1935; T. Roosevelt, 1902–1932). Mass. Rep.—Lt. Col., Mass. Volunteers, Civil War. *Mass., Associate Justice, and Chief Justice, Supreme Judicial Court (20)*.

*HUGHES, CHARLES E. (1862–1948; Taft, 1910–1916, and Hoover, 1930–1941). N.Y.Rep.—N.Y., Counsel, legislative committees investigating gas and insurance industries, 1905–06. U.S., Special Assistant to Attorney General for Coal Investigation, 1906. *N.Y., Governor (3)*. [Between appointments to the Supreme Court: Presidential Nominee, Republican Party, 1916. U.S., Secretary of State (4). *Member, Permanent Court of Arbitration, The Hague (4). Judge, Permanent Court of International Justice (2)*.] Chief Justice on second appointment.

HUNT, WARD (1810–1886; Grant, 1872–1882). N.Y.Rep.—N.Y., Legislature (2). Mayor of Utica, N.Y. (1). N.Y. Associate Judge, and Chief Judge, Court of Appeals (4); *Commissioner of Appeals (4)*. He did not sit from 1879 to his retirement in 1882.

IREDELL, JAMES (1750–1799; Washington, 1790–1799). N.C.Fed.—Comptroller of Customs (6), Collector of Port (2), Edenton, N.C., N.C., Judge, Superior Court (½); Attorney General (2); Member, Council of State, 1787; *Reviser of Statutes (3).*

JACKSON, HOWELL E. (1832–1895; B. Harrison, 1893–1895). Tenn. Dem.—Tenn., Judge, Court of Arbitration (4); Legislature (1). U.S. Senate (5); *Judge, Circuit Court of Appeals (7).*

JACKSON, ROBERT H. (1892–1954; F.D. Roosevelt, 1941–1954). N.Y. Dem.—U.S., General Counsel, Bureau of Internal Revenue (2); Assistant Attorney General (2); Solicitor General (2); *Attorney General (1).*

*JAY, JOHN (1745–1829; Washington, 1789–1795). N.Y.Fed.—N.Y., Chief Justice, Supreme Court (2). U.S., Envoy to Spain (2); Commissioner, Treaty of Paris, 1782–83; Secretary for Foreign Affairs (6). Co-author, The Federalist.

JOHNSON, THOMAS (1732–1819; Washington, 1791–1793). Md.Fed.—Md., Brigadier-General, Militia (1); Legislature (5); Governor (2); *Chief Judge, General Court (1).*

JOHNSON, WILLIAM (1771–1834; Jefferson, 1804–1834). S.C.Rep.—S.C., Legislature (4); *Judge, Court of Common Pleas (6).*

LAMAR, JOSEPH R. (1857–1916; Taft, 1910–1916). Ga.Dem.—Ga., Legislature (3); Commissioner to Codify Laws (3); Associate Justice, Supreme Court (4). *Private practice.*

LAMAR, LUCIUS Q.C. (1825–1893; Cleveland, 1888–1893). Miss.Dem.—Ga., Legislature (2). U.S., House of Representatives (4). Draftsman, Mississippi Ordinance of Secession, 1861. C.S.A., Lt. Col. (1); Commissioner to Russia (1); Judge-Advocate, III Corps. Army of No. Va. (1). U.S., House of Representatives (4); Senate (8); *Secretary of the Interior (3).*

LIVINGSTON, (HENRY) BROCKHOLST (1757–1823; Jefferson, 1806–1823). N.Y.Rep.—Lt. Col., Continental Army. *N.Y., Judge, Supreme Court (4).*

LURTON, HORACE H. (1844–1914; Taft, 1909–1914). Tenn.Dem.—Sgt. Major, C.S.A. Tenn., Chancellor (3); Associate Justice and Chief Justice, Supreme Court (7). *U.S., Judge, Circuit Court of Appeals (16).*

McKENNA, JOSEPH (1843–1926; McKinley, 1898–1925). Calif.Rep.—Calif., District Attorney (2); Legislature (2). U.S., House of Representatives (7); *Judge, Circuit Court of Appeals (5); Attorney General (1).*

McKINLEY, JOHN (1780–1852; Van Buren, 1837–1852). Ala.Dem.—Legislature (4). U.S., Senate (5); House of Representatives (2); *re-elected to Senate,* but appointed to Court before taking seat.

McLEAN, JOHN (1785–1861; Jackson, 1829–1861). Ohio Dem.—U.S., House of Representatives (4). Ohio, Judge, Supreme Court (6). U.S., Commissioner, General Land Office (1); *Postmaster-General (6).*

McREYNOLDS, JAMES C. (1862–1946; Wilson, 1914–1941). Tenn.Dem.—U.S., Assistant Attorney General (4); *Attorney General (1).*

*MARSHALL, JOHN (1755–1835; J. Adams, 1801–1835). Va.Fed.—Va., Legislature (7); U.S., Envoy to France (1); House of Representatives (1); *Secretary of State (1).*

MARSHALL, THURGOOD (1908–____; L.B. Johnson, 1967–____). N.Y. Dem.—Counsel, Legal Defense and Educational Fund, NAACP (21). U.S., Judge, Court of Appeals (4); *Solicitor General (2).*

MATTHEWS, STANLEY (1824–1889; Garfield, 1881–1889). Ohio Rep.—Ohio, Judge, Court of Common Pleas (2); Legislature (3). U.S., District Attorney (3). Col., Ohio Volunteers. Ohio, Judge, Superior Court (2). Counsel before Hayes-Tilden Electoral Commission, 1877. U.S., Senate (2). *Private practice.* His first appointment to the Court by Hayes in 1881 was not acted upon by the Senate.

MILLER, SAMUEL F. (1816–1890; Lincoln, 1862–1890). Iowa Rep.—Physician. *Private practice.*

MINTON, SHERMAN (1890–1965; Truman, 1949–1956). Ind.Dem.—Capt., Inf., World War I. U.S., Senate (6); *Judge, Court of Appeals (8).*

MOODY, WILLIAM H. (1853–1917; T. Roosevelt, 1906–1910). Mass.Rep.—U.S., District Attorney (5), House of Representatives (7); Secretary of the Navy (2); *Attorney General (2).*

MOORE, ALFRED (1755–1810; J. Adams, 1799–1804). N.C.Fed.—N.C., Col. of Militia; Legislature (2); Attorney General (9). U.S. Commissioner, Treaty with Cherokee Nation (1); *N.C., Judge, Superior Court (1).*

MURPHY, FRANK (1893–1949; F.D. Roosevelt, 1940–1949). Mich.Dem.—Capt., Inf., World War I. U.S., Assistant U.S. Attorney (1). Mich., Judge, Recorder's Court (7). Mayor, Detroit, Mich. (3). U.S., Governor-General, and High Commissioner, P.I. (3). Mich., Governor (2). *U.S., Attorney General (1).*

NELSON, SAMUEL (1792–1873; Tyler, 1845–1872). N.Y.Dem.—N.Y., Judge, Circuit Court (8); Associate Justice, and *Chief Justice, Supreme Court (14).*

O'CONNOR, SANDRA DAY (1930–____; Reagan, 1981–____). Ariz.Rep.—Ariz., Assistant Attorney General (4); Legislature (6). Ariz., Judge, Superior Court (4); *Court of Appeals (2).*

PATERSON, WILLIAM (1745–1806; Washington, 1793–1806). N.J.Fed.—Signer, U.S. Constitution, 1787. N.J., Legislature (2); Attorney General (7). U.S., Senate (1). *N.J., Governor (3).* Reviser of English Pre-Revolutionary Statutes in Force in N.J.

PECKHAM, RUFUS W. (1838–1909; Cleveland, 1895–1909). N.Y.Dem.—N.Y., District Attorney (1); Justice, Supreme Court (3); *Associate Judge, Court of Appeals (9).*

PITNEY, MAHLON (1858–1924; Taft, 1912–1922). N.J.Rep.—U.S., House of Representatives (4). N.J., Legislature (2); Associate Justice, Supreme Court (7); Chancellor (4).

POWELL, LEWIS F. (1907–____; Nixon, 1972–____). Va.Dem.—Col., U.S. A.A.F., World War II. *Private practice.*

REED, STANLEY F. (1884–1980; F.D. Roosevelt, 1938–1957). Ky.Dem.—Ky., Legislature (4). 1st Lt., U.S.A., World War I. U.S., General Counsel, Federal Farm Board (3); General Counsel, Reconstruction Finance Corporation (3); *Solicitor General (3).*

REHNQUIST, WILLIAM H. (1924–____; Nixon, 1972–____). Ariz.Rep.—U.S.A.F., World War II. Law Clerk, Justice Jackson, 1952–53. *U.S., Assistant Attorney General (3).*

ROBERTS, OWEN J. (1875–1955; Hoover, 1930–1945). Pa.Rep.—Pa., Assistant District Attorney (3). U.S., Special Deputy Attorney General in Espionage Act Cases, World War I; Special Prosecutor, Oil Cases, 1924. *Private practice.*

*RUTLEDGE, JOHN (1739–1800; Washington, 1789–1791, and Washington, 1795). S.C.Fed.—Signer, U.S. Constitution, 1787. S.C., Legislature (18); Attorney General (1); President and Governor (6); *Chancellor (7).* [Between appointments to the Supreme Court: *S.C., Chief Justice, Court of Common Pleas and Sessions (4).*] He did not sit under his first appointment; he sat with a recess appointment as Chief Justice, but his regular appointment was rejected by the Senate.

RUTLEDGE, WILEY B. (1894–1949; F.D. Roosevelt, 1943–1949). Iowa Dem.—Mo., then Iowa, Member, National Conference of Commissioners on Uniform State Laws (10). *U.S., Judge, Court of Appeals (4).*

SANFORD, EDWARD T. (1865–1930; Harding, 1923–1930). Tenn.Rep.— U.S., Assistant Attorney General (1); *Judge, District Court (15).*

SHIRAS, GEORGE (1832–1924; B. Harrison, 1892–1903). Pa.Rep. *Private practice.*

STEVENS, JOHN PAUL (1920–____; Ford, 1975–____). Ill.Independent.— U.S.N.R., World War II. Law Clerk, Justice Wiley Rutledge, 1947–48. *Judge, Court of Appeals (5).*

STEWART, POTTER (1915–1985; Eisenhower, 1958–1981). Ohio Rep.—Lt., U.S.N.R., World War II. *U.S., Judge, Court of Appeals (4).*

*STONE, HARLAN F. (1872–1946; Coolidge, later F.D. Roosevelt, 1925–1946). N.Y.Rep.—*U.S., Attorney General (1).* Chief Justice, 1941–1946.

STORY, JOSEPH (1779–1845; Madison, 1811–1845). Mass.Rep.—Mass., Legislature (5). U.S., House of Representatives (2). *Private practice.*

STRONG, WILLIAM (1808–1895; Grant, 1870–1880). Pa.Rep.—U.S., House of Representatives (4). Pa., Justice, Supreme Court (11). *Private practice.*

SUTHERLAND, GEORGE (1862–1942; Harding, 1922–1938). Utah Rep.— Utah, Legislature (4). U.S., House of Representatives (2); Senate (12). *Private practice.*

SWAYNE, NOAH H. (1804–1884; Lincoln, 1862–1881). Ohio Rep.—Ohio, County Attorney (4); Legislature (2). U.S., District Attorney (9). *Private practice.*

*TAFT, WILLIAM H. (1857–1930; Harding, 1921–1930). Conn.Rep.—U.S., Collector of Internal Revenue (1). Ohio, Judge, Superior Court (3). U.S., Solicitor General (2); Judge, Circuit Court of Appeals (8); Governor-General, P.I. (3); Secretary of War (4); President (4). *Professor of Law.*

*TANEY, ROGER B. (1777–1864; Jackson, 1836–1864). Md.Dem.—Md., Legislature (7); Attorney General (2). U.S., Attorney General (2), Secretary of the Treasury (³/₄; rejected by the Senate). *Private practice.*

THOMPSON, SMITH (1768–1843; Monroe, 1823–1843). N.Y.Rep.—N.Y., Legislature (2); Associate Justice, and Chief Justice, Supreme Court (16). *U.S., Secretary of the Navy (4).*

TODD, THOMAS (1765–1826; Jefferson, 1807–1826). Ky.Rep.—*Ky., Judge, and Chief Justice, Court of Appeals (6).*

TRIMBLE, ROBERT (1777–1828; J.Q. Adams, 1826–1828). Ky.Rep.—Ky., Legislature (2). Judge, Court of Appeals (2). U.S., District Attorney (4); *Judge, District Court (9).*

VAN DEVANTER, WILLIS (1859–1941; Taft, 1910–1937). Wyo.Rep.—Wyo., Legislature (2); Chief Justice, Supreme Court (1). U.S., Assistant Attorney General (Interior Department) (6); *Judge, Circuit Court of Appeals (7).*

*VINSON, FRED M. (1890–1953; Truman, 1946–1953). Ky.Dem.—Ky., Commonwealth Attorney (3). U.S., House of Representatives (14); Judge, Court of Appeals (5); Director, Office of Economic Stabilization (2); Federal Loan

Administrator (1 mo.); Director, Office of War Mobilization and Reconversion (3 mo.); *Secretary of the Treasury (1).*

*WAITE, MORRISON R. (1816–1888; Grant, 1874–1888). Ohio Rep.—Ohio, Legislature (2). Counsel for United States, U.S.—Gr. Brit. Arbitration ("Alabama" Claims), 1871–72. *Private practice.*

*WARREN, EARL (1891–1974; Eisenhower, 1953–1969). Calif.Rep.—1st Lt., Inf., World War I. Deputy City Attorney (1); Deputy District Attorney (5); District Attorney (14); Attorney General (4); *Governor (10).*

WASHINGTON, BUSHROD (1762–1829; J. Adams, 1798–1829). Pa.Fed.—Va., Legislature (1). *Private practice.*

WAYNE, JAMES M. (1790–1867; Jackson, 1835–1867). Ga.Dem.—Ga., Officer, Hussars, War of 1812; Legislature (2). Mayor of Savannah, Ga. (2). Ga., Judge, Superior Court (5). *U.S., House of Representatives (6).*

WHITE, BYRON R. (1917–____; Kennedy, 1962–____). Colo.Dem.—U.S. N.R., World War II. Law Clerk, Chief Justice Vinson, 1946–47. *U.S., Deputy Attorney General (1).*

*WHITE, EDWARD D. (1845–1921; Cleveland, later Taft, 1894–1921). La. Dem.—La., Legislature (4); Justice, Supreme Court (2). *U.S., Senate (3).* Chief Justice, 1910–1921.

WHITTAKER, CHARLES E. (1901–1973; Eisenhower, 1957–1962). Mo. Rep.—U.S., Judge, District Court (2); *Court of Appeals (1).*

WILSON, JAMES (1724–1798; Washington, 1789–1798). Pa.Fed.—Signer, U.S. Declaration of Independence, 1776, and U.S. Constitution, 1787. Although he was strongly interested in western-land development companies for several years prior to his appointment, his primary activity in the period immediately preceding his appointment was in obtaining ratification of the Federal and Pennsylvania Constitutions.

WOODBURY, LEVI (1789–1851; Polk, 1845–1851). N.H. Dem.—N.H., Associate Justice, Superior Court (6); Governor (2); Legislature (1). U.S., Senate (6); Secretary of the Navy (3); Secretary of the Treasury (7); *Senate (4).*

WOODS, WILLIAM B. (1824–1887; Hayes, 1880–1887). Ga.Rep.—Mayor, Newark, O. (1). Ohio, Legislature (4). Brevet Major General, U.S. Vol., Civil War. Ala., Chancellor (1). *U.S., Judge, Circuit Court (11).*

Appendix B

THE CONSTITUTION OF THE UNITED STATES

PREAMBLE

We the People of the United States, in Order to form a more perfect Union, establish Justice, insure domestic Tranquility, provide for the common defence, promote the general Welfare, and secure the Blessings of Liberty to ourselves and our Posterity, do ordain and establish this Constitution for the United States of America.

ARTICLE I

Section 1. All legislative Powers herein granted shall be vested in a Congress of the United States, which shall consist of a Senate and House of Representatives.

Section 2. [1] The House of Representatives shall be composed of Members chosen every second Year by the People of the several States, and the Electors in each State shall have the Qualifications requisite for Electors of the most numerous Branch of the State Legislature.

[2] No Person shall be a Representative who shall not have attained to the Age of twenty five Years, and been seven Years a Citizen of the United States, and who shall not, when elected, be an Inhabitant of that State in which he shall be chosen.

[3] Representatives and direct Taxes shall be apportioned among the several States which may be included within this Union, according to their respective Numbers, which shall be determined by adding to the whole Number of free Persons, including those bound to Service for a Term of Years, and excluding Indians not taxed, three fifths of all other Persons. The actual Enumeration shall be made within three Years after the first Meeting of the Congress of the United States, and within every subsequent Term of ten Years, in such Manner as they shall by Law direct. The Number of Representatives shall not exceed one for every thirty Thousand, but each State shall have at Least one Representative; and until such enumeration shall be made, the State of New Hampshire shall be entitled to chuse three, Massachusetts eight, Rhode Island and Providence Plantations one, Connecticut five, New York six, New Jersey four, Pennsylvania eight, Delaware one, Maryland six, Virginia ten, North Carolina five, South Carolina five, and Georgia three.

[4] When vacancies happen in the Representation from any State, the Executive Authority thereof shall issue Writs of Election to fill such Vacancies.

[5] The House of Representatives shall chuse their Speaker and other Officers; and shall have the sole Power of Impeachment.

Section 3. [1] The Senate of the United States shall be composed of two Senators from each State, chosen by the Legislature thereof, for six Years; and each Senator shall have one Vote.

[2] Immediately after they shall be assembled in Consequence of the first Election, they shall be divided as equally as may be into three Classes. The Seats of the Senators of the first Class shall be vacated at the Expiration of the Second Year, of the second Class at the Expiration of the fourth Year, and of the third Class at the Expiration of the sixth Year, so that one third may be chosen every second Year; and if Vacancies happen by Resignation, or otherwise, during the Recess of the Legislature of any State, the Executive thereof may make temporary Appointments until the next Meeting of the Legislature, which shall then fill such Vacancies.

[3] No Person shall be a Senator who shall not have attained to the Age of thirty Years, and been nine Years a Citizen of the United States, and who shall not, when elected, by an Inhabitant of that State for which he shall be chosen.

[4] The Vice President of the United States shall be President of the Senate, but shall have no Vote, unless they be equally divided.

[5] The Senate shall chuse their other Officers, and also a President pro tempore, in the Absence of the Vice President, or when he shall exercise the Office of President of the United States.

[6] The Senate shall have the sole Power to try all Impeachments. When sitting for that Purpose, they shall be on Oath or Affirmation. When the President of the United States is tried, the Chief Justice shall preside: And no Person shall be convicted without the Concurrence of two thirds of the Members present.

[7] Judgment in Cases of Impeachment shall not extend further than to removal from Office, and disqualification to hold and enjoy any Office of honor, Trust, or Profit under the United States: but the Party convicted shall nevertheless be liable and subject to Indictment, Trial, Judgment, and Punishment, according to Law.

Section 4. [1] The Times, Places and Manner of holding Elections for Senators and Representatives, shall be prescribed in each State by the Legislature thereof; but the Congress may at any time by Law make or alter such Regulations, except as to the Places of chusing Senators.

[2] The Congress shall assemble at least once in every Year, and such Meeting shall be on the first Monday in December, unless they shall by Law appoint a different Day.

Section 5. [1] Each House shall be the Judge of the Elections, Returns, and Qualifications of its own Members, and a Majority of each shall constitute a Quorum to do Business; but a smaller Number may adjourn from day to day, and may be authorized to compel the Attendance of absent Members, in such Manner, and under such Penalties as each House may provide.

[2] Each House may determine the Rules of its Proceedings, punish its Members for disorderly Behavior, and, with the Concurrence of two thirds, expel a Member.

[3] Each House shall keep a Journal of its Proceedings, and from time to time publish the same, excepting such Parts as may in their Judgment require

Secrecy; and the Yeas and Nays of the Members of either House on any question shall, at the Desire of one fifth of those Present, be entered on the Journal.

[4] Neither House, during the Session of Congress, shall without the Consent of the other, adjourn for more than three days, nor to any other Place than that in which the two Houses shall be sitting.

Section 6. [1] The Senators and Representatives shall receive a Compensation for their Services, to be ascertained by Law, and paid out of the Treasury of the United States. They shall in all Cases, except Treason, Felony and Breach of the Peace, be privileged from Arrest during their Attendance at the Session of their respective Houses, and in going to and returning from the same; and for any Speech or Debate in either House, they shall not be questioned in any other Place.

[2] No Senator or Representative shall, during the Time for which he was elected, be appointed to any civil Office under the Authority of the United States, which shall have been created, or the Emoluments whereof shall have been increased during such time; and no Person holding any Office under the United States, shall be a Member of either House during his Continuance in Office.

Section 7. [1] All Bills for raising Revenue shall originate in the House of Representatives; but the Senate may propose or concur with Amendments as on other Bills.

[2] Every Bill which shall have passed the House of Representatives and the Senate, shall, before it become a Law, be presented to the President of the United States; If he approve he shall sign it, but if not he shall return it, with his Objections to the House in which it shall have originated, who shall enter the Objections at large on their Journal, and proceed to reconsider it. If after such Reconsideration two thirds of that House shall agree to pass the Bill, it shall be sent together with the Objections, to the other House, by which it shall likewise be reconsidered, and if approved by two thirds of that House, it shall become a Law. But in all such Cases the Votes of both Houses shall be determined by yeas and Nays, and the Names of the Persons voting for and against the Bill shall be entered on the Journal of each House respectively. If any Bill shall not be returned by the President within ten Days (Sundays excepted) after it shall have been presented to him, the Same shall be a Law, in like Manner as if he had signed it, unless the Congress by their Adjournment prevent its Return in which Case it shall not be a Law.

[3] Every Order, Resolution, or Vote, to Which the Concurrence of the Senate and House of Representatives may be necessary (except on a question of Adjournment) shall be presented to the President of the United States; and before the Same shall take Effect, shall be approved by him, or being disapproved by him, shall be repassed by two thirds of the Senate and House of Representatives, according to the Rules and Limitations prescribed in the Case of a Bill.

Section 8. [1] The Congress shall have Power To lay and collect Taxes, Duties, Imposts and Excises, to pay the Debts and provide for the common Defence and general Welfare of the United States; but all Duties, Imposts and Excises shall be uniform throughout the United States;

[2] To borrow money on the credit of the United States;

[3] To regulate Commerce with foreign Nations, and among the several States, and with the Indian Tribes;

[4] To establish an uniform Rule of Naturalization, and uniform Laws on the subject of Bankruptcies throughout the United States;

[5] To coin Money, regulate the Value thereof, and of foreign Coin, and fix the Standard of Weights and Measures;

[6] To provide for the Punishment of counterfeiting the Securities and current Coin of the United States;

[7] To Establish Post Offices and Post Roads;

[8] To promote the Progress of Science and useful Arts, by securing for limited Times to Authors and Inventors the exclusive Right to their respective Writings and Discoveries;

[9] To constitute Tribunals inferior to the supreme Court;

[10] To define and punish Piracies and Felonies committed on the high Seas, and Offenses against the Law of Nations;

[11] To declare War, grant Letters of Marque and Reprisal, and make Rules concerning Captures on Land and Water;

[12] To raise and support Armies, but no Appropriation of Money to that Use shall be for a longer Term than two Years;

[13] To provide and maintain a Navy;

[14] To make Rules for the Government and Regulation of the land and naval Forces;

[15] To provide for calling forth the Militia to execute the Laws of the Union, suppress Insurrections and repel Invasions;

[16] To provide for organizing, arming, and disciplining, the Militia, and for governing such Part of them as may be employed in the Service of the United States, reserving to the States respectively, the Appointment of the Officers, and the Authority of training the Militia according to the discipline prescribed by Congress;

[17] To exercise exclusive Legislation in all Cases whatsoever, over such District (not exceeding ten Miles square) as may, by Cession of particular States, and the Acceptance of Congress, become the Seat of the Government of the United States, and to exercise like Authority over all Places purchased by the Consent of the Legislature of the State in which the Same shall be, for the Erection of Forts, Magazines, Arsenals, dock-Yards, and other needful Buildings;—And

[18] To make all Laws which shall be necessary and proper for carrying into Execution the foregoing Powers, and all other Powers vested by this Constitution in the Government of the United States, or in any Department or Officer thereof.

Section 9. [1] The Migration or Importation of Such Persons as any of the States now existing shall think proper to admit, shall not be prohibited by the Congress prior to the Year one thousand eight hundred and eight, but a Tax or duty may be imposed on such Importation, not exceeding ten dollars for each Person.

[2] The privilege of the Writ of Habeas Corpus shall not be suspended, unless when in Cases of Rebellion or Invasion the public Safety may require it.

[3] No Bill of Attainder or ex post facto Law shall be passed.

[4] No Capitation, or other direct, Tax shall be laid, unless in Proportion to the Census or Enumeration herein before directed to be taken.

[5] No Tax or Duty shall be laid on Articles exported from any State.

[6] No Preference shall be given by any Regulation of Commerce or Revenue to the Ports of one State over those of another: nor shall Vessels bound to, or from, one State be obliged to enter, clear, or pay Duties in another.

[7] No money shall be drawn from the Treasury, but in Consequence of Appropriations made by Law; and a regular Statement and Account of the Receipts and Expenditures of all public Money shall be published from time to time.

[8] No Title of Nobility shall be granted by the United States: And no Person holding any Office of Profit or Trust under them, shall, without the Consent of the Congress, accept of any present, Emolument, Office, or Title, of any kind whatever, from any King, Prince, or foreign State.

Section 10. [1] No State shall enter into any Treaty, Alliance, or Confederation; grant Letters of Marque and Reprisal; coin Money; emit Bills of Credit; make any Thing but gold and silver Coin a Tender in Payment of Debts; pass any Bill of Attainder, ex post facto Law, or Law impairing the Obligation of Contracts, or grant any Title of Nobility.

[2] No State shall, without the Consent of the Congress, lay any Imposts or Duties on Imports or Exports, except what may be absolutely necessary for executing it's inspection Laws: and the net Produce of all Duties and Imposts, laid by any State on Imports or Exports, shall be for the Use of the Treasury of the United States; and all such Laws shall be subject to the Revision and Controul of the Congress.

[3] No State shall, without the Consent of Congress, lay any Duty of Tonnage, keep Troops, or Ships of War in time of Peace, enter into any Agreement or Compact with another State, or with a foreign Power, or engage in War, unless actually invaded, or in such imminent Danger as will not admit of delay.

ARTICLE II

Section 1. [1] The executive Power shall be vested in a President of the United States of America. He shall hold his Office during the Term of four Years, and, together with the Vice President, chosen for the same Term, be elected, as follows:

[2] Each State shall appoint, in such Manner as the Legislature thereof may direct, a Number of Electors, equal to the whole Number of Senators and Representatives to which the State may be entitled in the Congress; but no Senator or Representative, or Person holding an Office of Trust or Profit under the United States, shall be appointed an Elector.

[3] The Electors shall meet in their respective States, and vote by Ballot for two Persons, of whom one at least shall not be an Inhabitant of the same State with themselves. And they shall make a List of all the Persons voted for, and of the Number of Votes for each; which List they shall sign and certify, and transmit sealed to the Seat of the Government of the United States, directed to the President of the Senate. The President of the Senate shall, in the Presence of the Senate and House of Representatives, open all the Certificates, and the Votes shall then be counted. The Person having the greatest Number of Votes shall be the President, if such Number be a Majority of the whole Number of Electors appointed; and if there be more than one who have such Majority, and have an equal Number of Votes, then the House of Representatives shall immediately chuse by Ballot one of them for President; and if no Person have a Majority, then from the five highest on the List the said House shall in like

Manner chuse the President. But in chusing the President, the Votes shall be taken by States the Representation from each State having one Vote; A quorum for this Purpose shall consist of a Member or Members from two thirds of the States, and a Majority of all the States shall be necessary to a Choice. In every Case, after the Choice of the President, the Person having the greater Number of Votes of the Electors shall be the Vice President. But if there should remain two or more who have equal Votes, the Senate shall chuse from them by Ballot the Vice President.

[4] The Congress may determine the Time of chusing the Electors, and the Day on which they shall give their Votes; which Day shall be the same throughout the United States.

[5] No person except a natural born Citizen, or a Citizen of the United States, at the time of the Adoption of this Constitution, shall be eligible to the Office of President; neither shall any Person be eligible to that Office who shall not have attained to the Age of thirty five Years, and been fourteen Years a Resident within the United States.

[6] In case of the removal of the President from Office, or of his Death, Resignation or Inability to discharge the Powers and Duties of the said Office, the Same shall devolve on the Vice President, and the Congress may by Law provide for the Case of Removal, Death, Resignation or Inability, both of the President and Vice President, declaring what Officer shall then act as President, and such Officer shall act accordingly, until the Disability be removed, or a President shall be elected.

[7] The President shall, at stated Times, receive for his Services, a Compensation, which shall neither be increased nor diminished during the Period for which he shall have been elected, and he shall not receive within that Period any other Emolument from the United States, or any of them.

[8] Before he enter on the Execution of his Office, he shall take the following Oath or Affirmation: "I do solemnly swear (or affirm) that I will faithfully execute the Office of President of the United States, and will to the best of my Ability, preserve, protect and defend the Constitution of the United States."

Section 2. [1] The President shall be Commander in Chief of the Army and Navy of the United States, and of the militia of the several States, when called into the actual Service of the United States; he may require the Opinion, in writing, of the principal Officer in each of the Executive Departments, upon any Subject relating to the Duties of their respective Offices, and he shall have Power to grant Reprieves and Pardons for Offenses against the United States, except in Cases of Impeachment.

[2] He shall have Power, by and with the Advice and Consent of the Senate to make Treaties, provided two thirds of the Senators present concur; and he shall nominate, and by and with the Advice and Consent of the Senate, shall appoint Ambassadors, other public Ministers and Consuls, Judges of the supreme Court, and all other Officers of the United States, whose Appointments are not herein otherwise provided for, and which shall be established by Law; but the Congress may by Law vest the Appointment of such inferior Officers, as they think proper, in the President alone, in the Courts of Law, or in the Heads of Departments.

[3] The President shall have Power to fill up all Vacancies that may happen during the Recess of the Senate, by granting Commissions which shall expire at the End of their next Session.

Section 3.   He shall from time to time give to the Congress Information of the State of the Union, and recommend to their Consideration such Measures as he shall judge necessary and expedient; he may, on extraordinary Occasions, convene both Houses, or either of them, and in Case of Disagreement between them, with Respect to the Time of Adjournment, he may adjourn them to such Time as he shall think proper; he shall receive Ambassadors and other public Ministers; he shall take Care that the Laws be faithfully executed, and shall Commission all the Officers of the United States.

Section 4.   The President, Vice President and all civil Officers of the United States, shall be removed from Office on Impeachment for, and Conviction of, Treason, Bribery, or other high Crimes and Misdemeanors.

ARTICLE III

Section 1.   The judicial Power of the United States, shall be vested in one supreme Court, and in such inferior Courts as the Congress may from time to time ordain and establish.   The Judges, both of the supreme and inferior Courts, shall hold their Offices during good Behaviour, and shall, at stated Times, receive for their Services a Compensation, which shall not be diminished during their Continuance in Office.

Section 2.   [1] The judicial Power shall extend to all Cases, in Law and Equity, arising under this Constitution, the Laws of the United States, and Treaties made, or which shall be made, under their Authority;—to all Cases affecting Ambassadors, other public Ministers and Consuls;—to all Cases of admiralty and maritime Jurisdiction;—to Controversies to which the United States shall be a Party;—to Controversies between two or more States;—between a State and Citizens of another State;—between Citizens of different States;—between Citizens of the same State claiming Lands under the Grants of different States, and between a State, or the Citizens thereof, and foreign States, Citizens or Subjects.

[2]   In all Cases affecting Ambassadors, other public Ministers and Consuls, and those in which a State shall be a Party, the supreme Court shall have original Jurisdiction.   In all the other Cases before mentioned, the supreme Court shall have appellate Jurisdiction, both as to Law and Fact, with such Exceptions, and under such Regulations as the Congress shall make.

[3]   The trial of all Crimes, except in Cases of Impeachment, shall be by Jury; and such Trial shall be held in the State where the said Crimes shall have been committed; but when not committed within any State, the Trial shall be at such Place or Places as the Congress may by Law have directed.

Section 3.   [1] Treason against the United States, shall consist only in levying War against them, or, in adhering to their Enemies, giving them Aid and Comfort.   No Person shall be convicted of Treason unless on the Testimony of two Witnesses to the same overt Act, or on Confession in open Court.

[2]   The Congress shall have Power to declare the Punishment of Treason, but no Attainder of Treason shall work Corruption of Blood, or Forfeiture except during the Life of the Person attainted.

ARTICLE IV

Section 1.   Full Faith and Credit shall be given in each State to the public Acts, Records, and judicial Proceedings of every other State.   And the Congress may by general Laws prescribe the Manner in which such Acts, Records and Proceedings shall be proved, and the Effect thereof.

Section 2. [1] The Citizens of each State shall be entitled to all Privileges and Immunities of Citizens in the several States.

[2] A Person charged in any State with Treason, Felony, or other Crime, who shall flee from Justice, and be found in another State, shall on demand of the executive Authority of the State from which he fled, be delivered up, to be removed to the State having Jurisdiction of the Crime.

[3] No Person held to Service or Labour in one State, under the Laws thereof, escaping into another, shall, in Consequence of any Law or Regulation therein, be discharged from such Service or Labour, but shall be delivered up on Claim of the Party to whom such Service or Labour may be due.

Section 3. [1] New States may be admitted by the Congress into this Union; but no new State shall be formed or erected within the Jurisdiction of any other State; nor any State be formed by the Junction of two or more States, or Parts of States, without the Consent of the Legislatures of the States concerned as well as of the Congress.

[2] The Congress shall have Power to dispose of and make all needful Rules and Regulations respecting the Territory or other Property belonging to the United States; and nothing in this Constitution shall be so construed as to Prejudice any Claims of the United States, or of any particular State.

Section 4. The United States shall guarantee to every State in this Union a Republican Form of Government, and shall protect each of them against Invasion; and on Application of the Legislature, or of the Executive (when the Legislature cannot be convened) against domestic Violence.

ARTICLE V

The Congress, whenever two thirds of both Houses shall deem it necessary, shall propose Amendments to this Constitution, or, on the Application of the Legislatures of two thirds of the several States, shall call a Convention for proposing Amendments, which, in either Case, shall be valid to all Intents and Purposes, as part of this Constitution, when ratified by the Legislatures of three fourths of the several States, or by Conventions in three fourths thereof, as the one or the other Mode of Ratification may be proposed by the Congress; Provided that no Amendment which may be made prior to the Year One thousand eight hundred and eight shall in any Manner affect the first and fourth Clauses in the Ninth Section of the first Article; and that no State, without its Consent, shall be deprived of its equal Suffrage in the Senate.

ARTICLE VI

[1] All Debts contracted and Engagements entered into, before the Adoption of this Constitution shall be as valid against the United States under this Constitution, as under the Confederation.

[2] This Constitution, and the Laws of the United States which shall be made in Pursuance thereof; and all Treaties made, or which shall be made, under the Authority of the United States, shall be the supreme Law of the Land; and the Judges in every State shall be bound thereby, any Thing in the Constitution or Laws of any State to the Contrary notwithstanding.

[3] The Senators and Representatives before mentioned, and the Members of the several State Legislatures, and all executive and judicial Officers, both of the United States and of the several States, shall be bound by Oath or Affirmation, to support this Constitution; but no religious Test shall ever be required as a Qualification to any Office or public Trust under the United States.

ARTICLE VII

The Ratification of the Conventions of nine States shall be sufficient for the Establishment of this Constitution between the States so ratifying the Same.

ARTICLES IN ADDITION TO, AND AMENDMENT OF, THE CONSTITUTION OF THE UNITED STATES OF AMERICA, PROPOSED BY CONGRESS, AND RATIFIED BY THE LEGISLATURES OF THE SEVERAL STATES PURSUANT TO THE FIFTH ARTICLE OF THE ORIGINAL CONSTITUTION.

AMENDMENT I [1791]

Congress shall make no law respecting an establishment of religion, or prohibiting the free exercise thereof; or abridging the freedom of speech, or of the press; or the right of the people peaceably to assemble, and to petition the Government for a redress of grievances.

AMENDMENT II [1791]

A well regulated Militia, being necessary to the security of a free State, the right of the people to keep and bear Arms, shall not be infringed.

AMENDMENT III [1791]

No Soldier shall, in time of peace be quartered in any house, without the consent of the Owner, nor in time of war, but in a manner to be prescribed by law.

AMENDMENT IV [1791]

The right of the people to be secure in their persons, houses, papers, and effects, against unreasonable searches and seizures, shall not be violated, and no Warrants shall issue, but upon probable cause, supported by Oath or affirmation and particularly describing the place to be searched, and the persons or things to be seized.

AMENDMENT V [1791]

No person shall be held to answer for a capital, or otherwise infamous crime, unless on a presentment or indictment of a Grand Jury, except in cases arising in the land or naval forces, or in the Militia, when in actual service in time of War or public danger; nor shall any person be subject for the same offence to be twice put in jeopardy of life or limb; nor shall be compelled in any criminal case to be a witness against himself, nor be deprived of life, liberty, or property, without due process of law; nor shall private property be taken for public use, without just compensation.

AMENDMENT VI [1791]

In all criminal prosecutions, the accused shall enjoy the right to a speedy and public trial, by an impartial jury of the State and district wherein the crime shall have been committed, which district shall have been previously ascertained by law, and to be informed of the nature and cause of the accusation; to be confronted with the witnesses against him; to have compulsory process for obtaining witnesses in his favor, and to have the Assistance of Counsel for his defence.

AMENDMENT VII [1791]

In Suits at common law, where the value in controversy shall exceed twenty dollars, the right of trial by jury shall be preserved, and no fact tried by jury, shall be otherwise re-examined in any Court of the United States, than according to the rules of the common law.

AMENDMENT VIII [1791]

Excessive bail shall not be required, nor excessive fines imposed, nor cruel and unusual punishments inflicted.

AMENDMENT IX [1791]

The enumeration in the Constitution, of certain rights, shall not be construed to deny or disparage others retained by the people.

AMENDMENT X [1791]

The powers not delegated to the United States by the Constitution, nor prohibited by it to the States, are reserved to the States respectively, or to the people.

AMENDMENT XI [1798]

The Judicial power of the United States shall not be construed to extend to any suit in law or equity, commenced or prosecuted against one of the United States by Citizens of another State, or by Citizens or Subjects of any Foreign State.

AMENDMENT XII [1804]

The Electors shall meet in their respective states and vote by ballot for President and Vice-President, one of whom, at least, shall not be an inhabitant of the same state with themselves; they shall name in their ballots the person voted for as President, and in distinct ballots the person voted for as Vice-President, and they shall make distinct lists of all persons voted for as President, and of all persons voted for as Vice-President, and of the number of votes for each, which lists they shall sign and certify, and transmit sealed to the seat of the government of the United States, directed to the President of the Senate;— The President of the Senate shall, in the presence of the Senate and House of Representatives, open all the certificates and the votes shall then be counted;— The person having the greatest number of votes for President, shall be the President, if such number be a majority of the whole number of Electors appointed; and if no person have such majority, then from the persons having the highest numbers not exceeding three on the list of those voted for as President, the House of Representatives shall choose immediately, by ballot, the President. But in choosing the President, the votes shall be taken by states, the representation from each state having one vote; a quorum for this purpose shall consist of a member or members from two-thirds of the states, and a majority of all the states shall be necessary to a choice. And if the House of Representatives shall not choose a President whenever the right of choice shall devolve upon them before the fourth day of March next following, then the Vice-President shall act as President, as in the case of the death or other constitutional disability of the President.—The person having the greatest number of votes as Vice-President, shall be the Vice-President, if such number be a majority of the whole number of Electors appointed, and if no person have a majority, then from the two highest numbers on the list, the Senate shall choose the Vice-President; a quorum for the purpose shall consist of two-thirds of the whole number of Senators, and a majority of the whole number shall be necessary to a choice. But no person constitutionally ineligible to the office of President shall be eligible to that of Vice-President of the United States.

Amendment XIII [1865]

Section 1. Neither slavery nor involuntary servitude, except as a punishment for crime whereof the party shall have been duly convicted, shall exist within the United States, or any place subject to their jurisdiction.

Section 2. Congress shall have power to enforce this article by appropriate legislation.

Amendment XIV [1868]

Section 1. All persons born or naturalized in the United States, and subject to the jurisdiction thereof, are citizens of the United States and of the State wherein they reside. No State shall make or enforce any law which shall abridge the privileges or immunities of citizens of the United States; nor shall any State deprive any person of life, liberty, or property, without due process of law; nor deny to any person within its jurisdiction the equal protection of the laws.

Section 2. Representatives shall be apportioned among the several States according to their respective numbers, counting the whole number of persons in each State, excluding Indians not taxed. But when the right to vote at any election for the choice of electors for President and Vice President of the United States, Representatives in Congress, the Executive and Judicial officers of a State, or the members of the Legislature thereof, is denied to any of the male inhabitants of such State, being twenty-one years of age, and citizens of the United States, or in any way abridged, except for participation in rebellion, or other crime, the basis of representation therein shall be reduced in the proportion which the number of such male citizens shall bear to the whole number of male citizens twenty-one years of age in such State.

Section 3. No person shall be a Senator or Representative in Congress, or elector of President and Vice President, or hold any office, civil or military, under the United States, or under any State, who having previously taken an oath, as a member of Congress, or as an officer of the United States, or as a member of any State legislature, or as an executive or judicial officer of any State, to support the Constitution of the United States, shall have engaged in insurrection or rebellion against the same, or given aid or comfort to the enemies thereof. But Congress may by a vote of two-thirds of each House, remove such disability.

Section 4. The validity of the public debt of the United States, authorized by law, including debts incurred for payment of pensions and bounties for services in suppressing insurrection or rebellion, shall not be questioned. But neither the United States nor any State shall assume or pay any debt or obligation incurred in aid of insurrection or rebellion against the United States, or any claim for the loss or emancipation of any slave; but all such debts, obligations and claims shall be held illegal and void.

Section 5. The Congress shall have power to enforce, by appropriate legislation, the provisions of this article.

Amendment XV [1870]

Section 1. The right of citizens of the United States to vote shall not be denied or abridged by the United States or by any State on account of race, color, or previous condition of servitude.

Section 2. The Congress shall have power to enforce this article by appropriate legislation.

AMENDMENT XVI [1913]

The Congress shall have power to lay and collect taxes on incomes, from whatever source derived, without apportionment among the several States, and without regard to any census or enumeration.

AMENDMENT XVII [1913]

[1]   The Senate of the United States shall be composed of two Senators from each State, elected by the people thereof, for six years; and each Senator shall have one vote.   The electors in each State shall have the qualifications requisite for electors of the most numerous branch of the State legislatures.

[2]   When vacancies happen in the representation of any State in the Senate, the executive authority of such State shall issue writs of election to fill such vacancies: *Provided,* That the legislature of any State may empower the executive thereof to make temporary appointments until the people fill the vacancies by election as the legislature may direct.

[3]   This amendment shall not be so construed as to affect the election or term of any Senator chosen before it becomes valid as part of the Constitution.

AMENDMENT XVIII [1919]

Section 1.   After one year from the ratification of this article the manufacture, sale, or transportation of intoxicating liquors within, the importation thereof into, or the exportation thereof from the United States and all territory subject to the jurisdiction thereof for beverage purposes is hereby prohibited.

Section 2.   The Congress and the several States shall have concurrent power to enforce this article by appropriate legislation.

Section 3.   This article shall be inoperative unless it shall have been ratified as an amendment to the Constitution by the legislatures of the several States, as provided in the Constitution, within seven years from the date of the submission hereof to the States by the Congress.

AMENDMENT XIX [1920]

[1]   The right of citizens of the United States to vote shall not be denied or abridged by the United States or by any State on account of sex.

[2]   Congress shall have power to enforce this article by appropriate legislation

AMENDMENT XX [1933]

Section 1.   The terms of the President and Vice President shall end at noon on the 20th day of January, and the terms of Senators and Representatives at noon on the 3d day of January, of the years in which such terms would have ended if this article had not been ratified; and the terms of their successors shall then begin.

Section 2.   The Congress shall assemble at least once in every year, and such meeting shall begin at noon on the 3d day of January, unless they shall by law appoint a different day.

Section 3.   If, at the time fixed for the beginning of the term of the President, the President elect shall have died, the Vice President elect shall become President.   If the President shall not have been chosen before the time fixed for the beginning of his term, or if the President elect shall have failed to qualify, then the Vice President elect shall act as President until a President shall have qualified; and the Congress may by law provide for the case wherein neither a President elect nor a Vice President elect shall have qualified, declaring who shall then act as President, or the manner in which one who is to act shall be selected, and such person shall act accordingly until a President or Vice President shall have qualified.

Section 4.   The Congress may by law provide for the case of the death of any of the persons from whom the House of Representatives may choose a President whenever the right of choice shall have devolved upon them, and for the case of the death of any of the persons from whom the Senate may choose a Vice President whenever the right of choice shall have devolved upon them.

Section 5.   Sections 1 and 2 shall take effect on the 15th day of October following the ratification of this article.

Section 6.   This article shall be inoperative unless it shall have been ratified as an amendment to the Constitution by the legislatures of three-fourths of the several States within seven years from the date of its submission.

AMENDMENT XXI [1933]

Section 1.   The eighteenth article of amendment to the Constitution of the United States is hereby repealed.

Section 2.   The transportation or importation into any State, Territory, or possession of the United States for delivery or use therein of intoxicating liquors, in violation of the laws thereof, is hereby prohibited.

Section 3.   This article shall be inoperative unless it shall have been ratified as an amendment to the Constitution by conventions in the several States, as provided in the Constitution, within seven years from the date of the submission hereof to the States by the Congress.

AMENDMENT XXII [1951]

Section 1.   No person shall be elected to the office of the President more than twice, and no person who has held the office of President, or acted as President, for more than two years of a term to which some other person was elected President shall be elected to the office of President more than once.   But this Article shall not apply to any person holding the office of President when this Article was proposed by the Congress, and shall not prevent any person who may be holding the office of President, or acting as President, during the term within which this Article becomes operative from holding the office of President or acting as President during the remainder of such term.

Section 2.   This article shall be inoperative unless it shall have been ratified as an amendment to the Constitution by the legislatures of three-fourths of the several States within seven years from the date of its submission to the States by the Congress.

AMENDMENT XXIII [1961]

Section 1.   The District constituting the seat of Government of the United States shall appoint in such manner as the Congress may direct:

A number of electors of President and Vice President equal to the whole number of Senators and Representatives in Congress to which the District would be entitled if it were a State, but in no event more than the least populous state; they shall be in addition to those appointed by the states, but they shall be considered, for the purposes of the election of President and Vice President, to be electors appointed by a state; and they shall meet in the District and perform such duties as provided by the twelfth article of amendment.

Section 2.   The Congress shall have power to enforce this article by appropriate legislation.

AMENDMENT XXIV [1964]

Section 1. The right of citizens of the United States to vote in any primary or other election for President or Vice President, for electors for President or Vice President, or for Senator or Representative in Congress, shall not be denied or abridged by the United States or any State by reason of failure to pay any poll tax or other tax.

Section 2. The Congress shall have power to enforce this article by appropriate legislation.

AMENDMENT XXV [1967]

Section 1. In case of the removal of the President from office or of his death or resignation, the Vice President shall become President.

Section 2. Whenever there is a vacancy in the office of the Vice President, the President shall nominate a Vice President who shall take office upon confirmation by a majority vote of both Houses of Congress.

Section 3. Whenever the President transmits to the President pro tempore of the Senate and the Speaker of the House of Representatives his written declaration that he is unable to discharge the powers and duties of his office, and until he transmits to them a written declaration to the contrary, such powers and duties shall be discharged by the Vice President as Acting President.

Section 4. Whenever the Vice President and a majority of either the principal officers of the executive departments or of such other body as Congress may by law provide, transmit to the President pro tempore of the Senate and the Speaker of the House of Representatives their written declaration that the President is unable to discharge the powers and duties of his office, the Vice President shall immediately assume the powers and duties of the office as Acting President.

Thereafter, when the President transmits to the President pro tempore of the Senate and the Speaker of the House of Representatives his written declaration that no inability exists, he shall resume the powers and duties of his office unless the Vice President and a majority of either the principal officers of the executive department or of such other body as Congress may by law provide, transmit within four days to the President pro tempore of the Senate and the Speaker of the House of Representatives their written declaration that the President is unable to discharge the powers and duties of his office. Thereupon Congress shall decide the issue, assembling within forty-eight hours for that purpose if not in session. If the Congress, within twenty-one days after receipt of the latter written declaration, or, if Congress is not in session, within twenty-one days after Congress is required to assemble, determines by two-thirds vote of both Houses that the President is unable to discharge the powers and duties of his office, the Vice President shall continue to discharge the same as Acting President; otherwise, the President shall resume the powers and duties of his office.

AMENDMENT XXVI [1971]

Section 1. The right of citizens of the United States, who are eighteen years of age or older, to vote shall not be denied or abridged by the United States or by any State on account of age.

Section 2. The Congress shall have power to enforce this article by appropriate legislation.

Index

Ref.
342.73085
C766
1986

123228